WORLD Chamber of Commerce DIRECTORY

2011

Published Annually in January

Loveland, Colorado • www.WorldChamberDirectoryOnline.com

World Chamber of Commerce Directory

2011 edition

P.O. Box 1029
Loveland, CO 80539 U.S.A.
(970) 663-3231
Fax (970) 663-6187
Email info@WorldChamberDirectoryOnline.com

ISBN-13: 978-0-943581-24-8
ISBN-10: 0-943581-24-9
ISSN: 1048-2849

Contents
Directory Listings

United States Chamber of Commerce	9
State Chambers of Commerce	11
United States Chambers of Commerce	15
State Boards of Tourism	257
Convention and Visitors Bureaus	259
Economic Development Councils	297
Canadian Chambers of Commerce	363
American Chambers of Commerce Abroad	383
Foreign & Ethnic Chambers of Commerce in the United States	389
Foreign Chambers of Commerce	393

U.S. Government Information

The One-Hundred and Twelfth Congress—First Session Senate and House of Representatives	407
Foreign Embassies in the United States	413
United States Embassies	423

Yellow Pages Directory

Sample Listing

1   Name of City

2   Name of Organization

3   County

4   Population of the Area Served

5   Membership of Organization

6   Ambassador Program

Loveland · *Loveland C/C* · Brian Willms; Pres./CEO; 5400 Stone Creek Circle; 80538; Larimer; P 68,000; M 700; (970) 667-6311; Fax (970) 667-5211; info@loveland.org; www.loveland.org *

LOVELAND VALENTINE RE-MAILING PROGRAM AND SWEETHEART CITY ACTIVITIES, FEBRUARY 1-14; BUSINESS EXPO & TRADE SHOW, APRIL; OLD FASHIONED CORN ROAST FESTIVAL, AUGUST; SCULPTURE IN THE PARK, 2ND WEEKEND IN AUGUST—LARGEST SCULPTURE SHOW WEST OF THE MISSISSIPPI.

Legend

C/C   Chamber of Commerce

P   Population of the Area Served

M   Membership

*   Ambassador Program

Note: Every effort has been made to enter the e-mail and internet addresses as they were provided to us. There is an assumed "http://" at the beginning of each internet (web site) address. If you have problems with a particular e-mail or internet address, please contact the appropriate chamber. Also note that many area codes are changing. If you experience difficulty reaching a number, please check with Directory Assistance.

Directory Listings

U.S. C/C United States Chamber of Commerce

1615 H Street, N.W. • Washington, D.C. • 20062-2000 • (202) 659-6000 • www.uschamber.com

Chairman of the Board		**Vice Chairman of the Board**	
Thomas D. Bell Jr.	(202) 955-1157	John Ruan III	(202) 955-1157

Executive Staff

President & CEO		**Membership Development**	
Thomas J. Donohue	(202) 463-5300	Agnes Warfield	(202) 463-5702
Exec. V.P. & COO		**CFO & CIO**	
David Chavern	(202) 463-5363	Stan Harrell	(202) 463-5590
Exec. V.P. Government Affairs			
R. Bruce Josten	(202) 463-5310		

Department Heads

Communications & Strategy		**Human Resources**	
Thomas Collamore	(202) 463-5939	Shannon DiBari	(202) 463-5391
Center for Capital Markets		**Institute for 21st Energy**	
Amanda S. Engstrom	(202) 463-5430	Karen Alderman Harbert	(202) 463-5606
Congressional & Public Affairs		**Institute for Legal Reform**	
Rolf Lundberg	(202) 463-5600	Lisa Rickard	(202) 463-5819
Economic Policy		**International Affairs**	
Dr. Martin A. Regalia	(202) 463-5620	Myron Brilliant	(202) 463-5460
Environment, Energy & Food Policy		**Labor Relations Policy**	
William L. Kovacs	(202) 463-5457	Randel Johnson	(202) 463-5448
General Counsel		**Political Affairs & Federation Relations**	
Lily Fu Claffee	(202) 463-3124	William C. Miller Jr.	(202) 463-5532

State Chambers of Commerce

Alabama

Bus. Cncl. of Alabama · William J. Canary; Pres./CEO; 2 N. Jackson, 5th Flr.; P.O. Box 76; Montgomery; 36101; Montgomery; P 4,600,000; M 4,500; (334) 834-6000; (800) 665-9647; Fax (334) 241-5984; info@bcatoday.org; www.bcatoday.org

Alaska

Alaska State C of C · Wayne A. Stevens; Pres.; 217 2nd St., Ste. 201; Juneau; 99801; Juneau; P 686,293; M 550; (907) 586-2323; Fax (907) 463-5515; info@alaskachamber.com; www.alaska chamber.com

Arizona

Arizona C of C & Ind. · Glenn Hamer; Pres./CEO; 1850 N. Central Ave., Ste. 1433; Phoenix; 85004; Maricopa; P 6,500,000; M 500; (602) 248-9172; Fax (602) 265-1262; info@azchamber.com; www. azchamber.com

Arkansas

Arkansas State C of C · Randy Zook; Pres./CEO; 1200 W. Capitol; Little Rock; 72201; Pulaski; P 2,800,000; M 1,200; (501) 372-2222; Fax (501) 372-2722; jthatcher@arkansasstate chamber.com; www.arkansasstatechamber.com

California

California C of C · Allan Zaremberg; Pres./CEO; 1215 K St., Ste. 1400; P.O. Box 1736; Sacramento; 95812; Sacramento; P 36,800,000; M 14,000; (916) 444-6670; Fax (916) 325-1272; information@calchamber.com; www.calchamber.com

Colorado

Colorado Assn. of Comm. & Ind. · Chuck Berry; Pres.; 1600 Broadway, Ste. 1000; Denver; 80202; Denver; P 5,900,000; M 500; (303) 831-7411; Fax (303) 860-1439; info@cochamber.com; www. cochamber.com

Connecticut

Connecticut Bus. & Ind. Assn. · John Rathgeber; Pres./CEO; 350 Church St.; Hartford; 06103; Hartford; P 3,500,000; M 10,000; (860) 244-1900; Fax (860) 278-8562; john.rathgeber@cbia.com; www.cbia.com

Delaware

Delaware State C of C · James A. Wolfe; Pres./CEO; 1201 N. Orange St., Ste. 200; P.O. Box 671; Wilmington; 19899; New Castle; P 873,092; M 2,800; (302) 655-7221; (800) 292-9507; Fax (302) 654-0691; info@dscc.com; www.dscc.com

District of Columbia

No State Chamber

Florida

Florida C of C · Mark Wilson; Pres.; 136 S. Bronough St.; P.O. Box 11309; Tallahassee; 32302; Leon; P 18,300,000; M 7,000; (850) 521-1200; Fax (850) 521-1219; info@flchamber.com; www. flchamber.com

Georgia

Georgia C of C · Chris Clark; Pres./CEO; 233 Peachtree St. N.E., Ste. 2000; Atlanta; 30303; Fulton; P 9,700,000; M 4,000; (404) 223-2264; Fax (404) 223-2290; communications@gachamber. com; www.gachamber.com

Hawaii

C of C of Hawaii · James Tollefson; Pres./CEO; 1132 Bishop St., Ste. 402; Honolulu; 96813; Honolulu; P 1,400,000; M 1,100; (808) 545-4300; Fax (808) 545-4369; khouston-sur@cochawaii.org; www.cochawaii.org

Idaho

Idaho Chamber Alliance · Kent Just; Dir.; P.O. Box 2368; Attn: Kent Just; Boise; 83701; Ada; P 1,500,000; (208) 284-2988; (208) 472-5200; Fax contact@idahochamberalliance.com; www. idahochamberalliance.com

Illinois

Illinois C of C · Douglas L. Whitley; Pres./CEO; 300 S. Wacker Dr., Ste. 1600; Chicago; 60606; Cook; P 12,901,563; M 4,000; (312) 983-7100; Fax (312) 983-7101; info@ilchamber.org; www.ilchamber.org

Indiana

Indiana C of C · Kevin Brinegar; Pres.; 115 W. Washington St., Ste. 850S; Indianapolis; 46204; Marion; P 6,300,000; M 4,800; (317) 264-3110; Fax (317) 264-6855; inchamber@indiana chamber.com; www.indianachamber.com

Iowa

Iowa Assn. of Bus. & Ind. · Michael Ralston; Pres.; 904 Walnut St., Ste. 100; Des Moines; 50309; Polk & Warren; P 3,000,000; M 1,200; (515) 280-8000; (800) 383-4224; Fax (515) 282-8085; abi@iowaabi.org; www.iowaabi.org

Kansas

Kansas C of C · Amy Blankenbiller; Pres./CEO; 835 S.W. Topeka Blvd.; Topeka; 66612; Shawnee; P 2,800,000; M 10,000; (785) 357-6321; Fax (785) 357-4732; info@kansaschamber.org; www. kansaschamber.org

Kentucky

Kentucky C of C · David Adkisson; Pres./CEO; 464 Chenault Rd.; Frankfort; 40601; Franklin; P 4,200,000; M 2,400; (502) 695-4700; Fax (502) 695-5051; kcc@kychamber.com; www.kychamber.com

Louisiana

Louisiana Assn. of Bus. & Ind. · Daniel Juneau; Pres.; 3113 Valley Creek Dr.; P.O. Box 80258; Baton Rouge; 70898; East Baton Rouge; P 4,400,000; M 3,000; (225) 928-5388; Fax (225) 929-6054; labi@labi.org; www.labi.org

Maine

Maine State C of C · Dana F. Connors; Pres.; 125 Community Dr., Ste. 101; Augusta; 04330; Kennebec; P 1,300,000; M 1,200; (207) 623-4568; Fax (207) 622-7723; melanieb@maine chamber.org; www.mainechamber.org

Maryland

Maryland C of C · Kathleen T. Snyder CCE; Pres./CEO; 60 West St., Ste. 100; Annapolis; 21401; Anne Arundel; P 5,600,000; M 850; (410) 269-0642; (301) 261-2858; Fax (410) 269-5247; mcc@ mdchamber.org; www.mdchamber.org

Massachusetts

No State Chamber

Michigan

Michigan C of C · Rich Studley; Pres./CEO; 600 S. Walnut St.; Lansing; 48933; Ingham; P 10,003,422; M 7,000; (517) 371-2100; (800) 748-0266; Fax (517) 371-7224; info@michamber.com; www. michamber.com

Minnesota

Minnesota C of C · David Olson; Pres.; 400 Roberts St. N., Ste. 1500; Saint Paul; 55101; Ramsey; P 5,200,000; M 2,600; (651) 292-4650; (800) 821-2230; Fax (651) 292-4656; mbethke@ mnchamber.com; www.mnchamber.com

Mississippi

Mississippi Eco.Cncl. · Blake Wilson; Pres.; P.O. Box 23276; Jackson; 39225; Hinds; P 2,900,000; M 8,000; (601) 969-0022; Fax (601) 353-0247; smaxwell@mec.ms; www.mec.ms

Missouri

Missouri C of C & Ind. · Daniel P. Mehan; Pres./CEO; 428 E. Capitol Ave.; P.O. Box 149; Jefferson City; 65102; Cole; P 6,000,000; M 2,864; (573) 634-3511; Fax (573) 634-8855; dmehan@ mochamber.com; www.mochamber.com

Montana

Montana C of C · Webb Brown; Pres./CEO; P.O. Box 1730; Helena; 59624; Lewis & Clark; P 967,400; M 1,500; (406) 442-2405; Fax (406) 442-2409; leah@montanachamber.com; www.montana chamber.com

Nebraska

Nebraska C of C & Ind. · Barry L. Kennedy CAE IOM; Pres.; P.O. Box 95128; Lincoln; 68509; Lancaster; P 1,800,000; M 2,000; (402) 474-4422; Fax (402) 474-5681; nechamber@nechamber.com; www.nechamber.com

Nevada

Nevada State C of C · Jody Hosterman; Admin. Asst.; One E. First St., 16th Flr.; Reno; 89501; Washoe; P 2,600,000; M 1,500; (775) 337-3030; Fax (775) 337-3038; info@renosparks chamber.org; www.renosparkschamber.org

New Hampshire

Bus. & Ind. Assn. of N.H. · Jim Roche; Pres.; 122 N. Main; Concord; 03301; Merrimack; P 1,300,000; M 400; (603) 224-5388; Fax (603) 224-2872; mail@nhbia.org; www.nhbia.org

New Jersey

New Jersey C of C · Jason McDonald; Mgr., Process & Ofc. Svcs.; 216 W. State St.; Trenton; 08608; Mercer; P 8,500,000; M 1,600; (609) 989-7888; Fax (609) 989-9696; jason.mcdonald@njchamber. com; www.njchamber.com

New Mexico

Assn. of Commerce & Ind. of New Mexico · Dr. Beverlee McClure; Pres./CEO; P.O. Box 9706; Albuquerque; 87119; Bernalillo; P 1,900,000; M 1,300; (505) 842-0644; Fax (505) 842-0734; info@aci-nm.org; www.aci-nm.org

New York

No State Chamber

North Carolina

North Carolina Chamber · S. Lewis Ebert; Pres./CEO; 701 Corporate Center Dr., Ste. 400; Raleigh; 27607; Wake; P 9,222,414; M 1,900; (919) 836-1400; Fax (919) 836-1425; info@ncchamber. net; www.ncchamber.net

North Dakota

North Dakota C of C · Andy Peterson; Pres.; 2000 Schafer St.; P.O. Box 2639; Bismarck; 58502; Burleigh; P 641,481; M 1,100; (701) 222-0929; (800) 382-1405; Fax (701) 222-1611; ndchamber@ ndchamber.com; www.ndchamber.com

Ohio

Ohio C of C · Andrew E. Doehrel; Pres.; 230 E. Town; P.O. Box 15159; Columbus; 43215; Franklin; P 11,485,910; M 4,000; (614) 228-4201; (800) 622-1893; Fax (614) 228-6403; occ@ohio chamber.com; www.ohiochamber.com

Oklahoma

The State Chamber of Oklahoma · Fred S. Morgan; Pres./CEO; 330 N.E. 10th St.; Oklahoma City; 73104; Oklahoma; P 3,600,000; M 3,000; (405) 235-3669; Fax (405) 235-3670; fmorgan@okstate chamber.com; www.okstatechamber.com

Oregon

Oregon State C of C · Dave Hauser; Admin.; P.O. Box 1107; Eugene; 97440; Lane; P 3,800,000; M 33,000; (541) 484-1314; Fax (541) 484-4942; susanm@eugenechamber.com; www.oregonstatechamber.org

Pennsylvania

The Pennsylvania Chamber of Bus. & Ind. · Gene Barr; V.P.; 417 Walnut St.; Harrisburg; 17101; Cumberland, Dauphin & Perry; P 12,448,279; M 9,000; (717) 255-3252; (800) 225-7224; Fax (717) 255 3298; info@pachamber.org; www.pachamber.org

Puerto Rico

Puerto Rico C of C · Edgardo Bigas; Exec. V.P.; P.O. Box 9024033; San Juan; 00902; P 3,900,000; M 2,000; (787) 721-6060; Fax (787) 723-1891; camarapr@camarapr.net; www.camarapr.org

Rhode Island

No State Chamber

South Carolina

South Carolina C of C · Otis Rawl; Pres./CEO; 1201 Main St., Ste. 1700; Columbia; 29201; Richland; P 4,500,000; M 2,000; (803) 799-4601; Fax (803) 779-6043; chamber@scchamber.net; www.scchamber.net

South Dakota

South Dakota C of C & Ind. · David Owen; Pres.; P.O. Box 190; Pierre; 57501; Hughes; P 765,000; M 450; (605) 224-6161; Fax (605) 224-7198; contactus@sdchamber.biz; www.sdchamber.biz

Tennessee

Tennessee C of C & Ind. · Deborah Woolley; Pres.; 611 Commerce St., Ste. 3030; Nashville; 37203; Davidscon; P 6,200,000; M 600; (615) 256-5141; Fax (615) 256-6726; info@tnchamber.org; www.tnchamber.org

Texas

Texas Assn. of Bus. · Bill Hammond; Pres./CEO; 1209 Nueces St.; Austin; 78701; Travis; P 24,300,000; M 5,000; (512) 477-6721; Fax (512) 477-0836; info@txbiz.org; www.txbiz.org

Utah

Utah State C of C · Ryan Evans; Exec. Secy.; 175 E. 400 S., Ste. 600; Salt Lake City; 84111; Salt Lake; P 2,758,000; M 15,500; (801) 328-5090; Fax (801) 328-5098; admin@utahstatechamber.org; www.utahstatechamber.org

Vermont

Vermont C of C · Betsy Bishop; Pres.; P.O. Box 37; Montpelier; 05601; Washington; P 639,000; M 1,500; (802) 223-3443; Fax (802) 223-4257; info@vtchamber.com; www.vtchamber.com

Virginia

Virginia C of C · Barry E. DuVal; Pres./CEO; 9 S. Fifth St.; Richmond; 23219; Richmond City; P 7,883,000; M 1,000; (804) 644-1607; Fax (804) 783-6112; b.duval@vachamber.com; www.vachamber.com

Washington

Assn. of Washington Business · Don Brunell; Pres.; 1414 Cherry St. S.E.; P.O. Box 658; Olympia; 98507; Thurston; P 6,600,000; M 7,100; (360) 943-1600; (800) 521-9325; Fax (360) 943-5811; members@awb.org; www.awb.org

West Virginia

West Virginia C of C · Stephen Roberts; Pres.; 1624 Kanawha Blvd. E.; P.O. Box 2789; Charleston; 25330; Kanawha; P 1,818,470; M 1,800; (304) 342-1115; Fax (304) 342-1130; forjobs@wv chamber.com; www.wvchamber.com.

Wisconsin

Wisconsin Manufacturers & Commerce · James S. Haney; Pres.; 501 E. Washington Ave.; P.O. Box 352; Madison; 53701; Dane; P 5,600,000; M 3,500; (608) 258-3400; Fax (608) 258-3413; wmc@wmc.org; www.wmc.org

Wyoming

No State Chamber

Notes

United States Chambers of Commerce

Alabama

Bus. Cncl. of Alabama · William J. Canary; Pres./CEO; 2 N. Jackson, 5th Flr.; P.O. Box 76; Montgomery; 36101; Montgomery; P 4,600,000; M 4,500; (334) 834-6000; (800) 665-9647; Fax (334) 241-5984; info@bcatoday.org; www.bcatoday.org

Chamber of Commerce Assn. of Alabama · L. Ralph Stacy CAE; Pres./CEO; 2 N. Jackson St.; Montgomery; 36104; Montgomery; P 4,500,000; M 60,000; (334) 264-2112; Fax (334) 264-2113; lrstacy@alaweb.com; www.alabamachambers.org

Abbeville · *Abbeville C/C* · Ronnie Marshall; Pres.; 300 Kirkland St.; P.O. Box 202; 36310; Henry; P 3,000; M 119; (334) 585-2273; Fax (334) 585-2273; abbevillechamber@centurytel.net; www.abbevillecoc.com

Alabaster · *see Pelham*

Albertville · *Albertville C/C* · Jennifer Palmer; Pres.; 316 E. Sand Mountain Dr.; P.O. Box 1457; 35950; Marshall; P 24,156; M 502; (256) 878-3821; (800) 878-3821; Fax (256) 878-3822; albertville chamber@charter.net; www.albertvillechamberofcommerce.com*

Alexander City · *Alexander City C/C* · Marvin Wagoner; Pres./CEO; 120 Tallapoosa St.; P.O. Box 926; 35011; Tallapoosa; P 15,000; M 400; (256) 234-3461; Fax (256) 234-0094; mwagoner@ alexandercitychamber.com; alexandercitychamber.com.*

Aliceville · *Aliceville Area C/C* · Debbie Fason; Mgr.; 419 Memorial Pkwy. N.E., Ste. A; P.O. Drawer A; 35442; Pickens; P 3,009; M 200; (205) 373-2820; Fax (205) 373-8692; acc@ nctv.com; www.cityofaliceville.com

Andalusia · *Andalusia Area C/C* · Janna McGlamory; Pres.; 1208 W. Bypass; P.O. Box 667; 36420; Covington; P 10,000; M 387; (334) 222-2030; Fax (334) 222-7844; ashley@andalusiachamber.com; www.andalusiachamber.com

Anniston · *Calhoun County C/C* · Sherri Sumners CCE; Pres.; 1330 Quintard Ave.; P.O. Box 1087; 36202; Calhoun; P 117,000; M 1,200; (256) 237-3536; (800) 487-1087; Fax (256) 237-0126; info@calhounchamber.com; www.calhounchamber.com*

Arab · *Arab C/C* · Deneille Dunn; Pres.; P.O. Box 626; 35016; Marshall; P 7,600; M 320; (256) 586-3138; (888) 403-2722; Fax (256) 586-0233; info@arab-chamber.org; www.arab-chamber.org*

Ardmore · *see Ardmore, TN*

Ashford · *Ashford Area C/C* · James Ethridge; Pres.; P.O. Box 463; 36312; Houston; P 2,700; M 75; (334) 899-4769; Fax (334) 899-3033; aacc@graceba.net

Athens · *Greater Limestone County C/C* · Hugh Ball; Pres.; 101 S. Beaty St.; 35611; Limestone; P 70,757; M 511; (256) 232-2600; Fax (256) 232-2609; info@tourathens.com; www.tourathens.com*

Atmore · *Atmore Area C/C* · Sheryl Vickery; Exec. Dir.; 501 S. Pensacola Ave.; 36502; Escambia; P 8,000; M 295; (251) 368-3305; Fax (251) 368-0800; atmoreal@frontiernet.net; www.atmorechamber.com*

Auburn · *Auburn C/C* · Lolly Steiner; Pres.; 714 E. Glenn Ave.; P.O. Box 1370; 36831; Lee; P 51,906; M 850; (334) 887-7011; Fax (334) 821-5500; lolly@auburnchamber.com; www.auburnchamber.com*

Bay Minette · *North Baldwin C/C* · Margo Allen; Exec. Dir.; 301 McMeans Ave.; P.O. Box 310; 36507; Baldwin; P 20,000; M 265; (251) 937-5665; Fax (251) 937-5670; assist@northbaldwin chamber.com; www.northbaldwinchamber.com*

Bayou La Batre · *Bayou La Batre Area C/C* · Harold Hodges; Pres.; P.O. Box 486; 36509; Mobile; P 6,000; M 88; (251) 824-4088; Fax (251) 824-4088; info@bayoulabatrechamber.com; www. bayoulabatrechamber.com

Bessemer · *Bessemer Area C/C* · Ronald W. Acker; Pres.; 321 18th St. N.; 35020; Jefferson; P 100,000; M 500; (205) 425-3253; Fax (205) 425-4979; mmilan1@bellsouth.net; www.bessemer chamber.com*

Birmingham · *Birmingham Reg. C/C* · Barry B. Copeland; Interim Pres.; 505 20th St. N., Ste. 200; 35203; Jefferson; P 1,100,000; M 4,200; (205) 324-2100; Fax (205) 324-2560; nbaldwin@birminghambusinessalliance.com; www.birmingham businessalliance.com

Boaz · *Boaz Area C/C* · Keyesta Sherman; Pres.; 100 E. Bartlett Ave.; P.O. Box 563; 35957; Marshall; P 8,000; M 400; (256) 593-8154; Fax (256) 593-1233; boazchamber@charter.net; www.boazchamberofcommerce.com*

Brewton · *Greater Brewton Area C/C* · Judy Crane; Exec. Dir.; 1010-B Douglas Ave.; 36426; Escambia; P 10,000; M 225; (251) 867-3224; jcrane@brewtonchamber.com; www.brewtonchamber.com

Butler · *Choctaw County C/C & Comm. Dev. Found.* · Virginia Loftis; Exec. Dir.; P.O. Box 180; 36904; Choctaw; P 16,000; M 170; (205) 459-3459; (205) 459-3795

Camden · *Wilcox Area C/C* · Camden Floyd Harris; Chrmn.; 1001 Earl Hilliard Rd.; 36726; Wilcox; P 4,000; M 100; (334) 682-4929; wilcoxdev@pinebelt.net; www.wilcoxareachamber.org

Centre · *Cherokee County C/C* · Thereasa Hulgan; Exec. Dir.; 801 Cedar Bluff Rd., Bldg. A; 35960; Cherokee; P 25,000; M 300; (256) 927-8455; Fax (256) 927-2768; cccoc@tds.net; www.cherokee-chamber.org

Centreville · *Bibb County C/C* · Tracey Mitchell; Exec. Dir.; 835 Walnut St.; P.O. Box 25; 35042; Bibb; P 21,000; M 100; (205) 926-5222; director@bibbchamber.org; www.bibbchamber.org*

Chelsea · *see Columbiana*

Chickasaw · *Chickasaw C/C* · Tom Hayward; Pres.; P.O. Box 11307; 36671; Mobile; P 6,364; M 78; (251) 452-8623; (251) 457-2707; www.chickasawchamber.com

Childersburg · *Childersburg C/C* · Peter Storey; Pres./CEO; 805 Third St. S.W.; P.O. Box 527; 35044; Shelby & Talladega; P 6,000; M 225; (256) 378-5482; (256) 510-0027; Fax (256) 378-5833; pbstorey@childersburg.com; www.childersburg.com*

Citronelle · *North Mobile C/C* · Willie Gray; Dir.; 19135 Main St.; P.O. Box 394; 36522; Mobile; P 6,000; M 200; (251) 866-7733; Fax (251) 866-7767; williegray@thecallnews.com; www.cityof citronelle.com

Clanton · *Chilton County C/C* · Mike Robertson; Exec. Dir.; 500 5th Ave. N.; P.O. Box 66; 35046; Chilton; P 43,000; M 300; (205) 755-2400; Fax (205) 755-8444; chiltonchamber@bellsouth.net; www.chiltoncountychamber.com

Clay · *Clay-Pinson C/C* · Becky Johnson; Pres.; P.O. Box 26; 35048; Jefferson; P 5,000; M 100; (205) 680-6445; Fax (205) 680-2757; webmaster@sbmsystems.com; www.claycoc.com

Columbiana · *South Shelby C/C* · Stacy Walkup; Exec. Dir.; 208 E. College St.; P.O. Box 396; 35051; Shelby; P 30,000; M 400; (205) 669-9075; soshelby@bellsouth.net; www.southshelbychamber.com

Cullman · *Cullman Area C/C* · Kirk Mancer IOM CCE; Pres.; 301 2nd Ave. S.W.; P.O. Box 1104; 35056; Cullman; P 81,000; M 1,200; (256) 734-0454; Fax (256) 737-7443; info@cullmanchamber.org; www.cullmanchamber.org*

Dadeville · *Dadeville Area C/C* · Carla Berry; Exec. Secy.; 185 S. Tallassee St., Ste. 103; 36853; Tallapoosa; P 4,000; M 165; (256) 825-4019; Fax (256) 825-0547; chamber@dadeville.com; www.dadeville.com

Daleville · *Daleville C/C* · Pam Souders; Exec. Dir.; 750 S. Daleville Ave.; P.O. Box 688; 36322; Dale; P 4,000; M 100; (334) 598-6331; Fax (334) 598-2333; chamber@dalevilleal.com; www.dalevilleal.com

Daphne · *Eastern Shore C/C* · Darrelyn J. Bender; Pres.; 29750 Larry Dee Cawyer Dr.; P.O. Drawer 310; 36526; Baldwin; P 65,000; M 900; (251) 621-8222; Fax (251) 621-8001; office@eschamber.com; www.eschamber.com*

Dauphin Island · *Dauphin Island C/C* · Gene Fox; Pres.; P.O. Box 5; 36528; Mobile; P 1,400; M 100; (251) 861-5524; Fax (251) 861-0055; www.dauphinislandcoc.com

Decatur · *Decatur-Morgan County C/C* · John Seymour; Pres./CEO; 515 Sixth Ave. N.E.; P.O. Box 2003; 35602; Morgan; P 112,000; M 850; (256) 353-5312; Fax (256) 353-2384; judy@dcc.org; www.dcc.org.*

Demopolis · *Demopolis Area C/C* · Patricia Brady; Ofc. Mgr.; 102 E. Washington St.; P.O. Box 667; 36732; Marengo; P 25,000; M 175; (334) 289-0270; (334) 289-0216; Fax (334) 289-1382; dacc@westal.net; www.demopolischamber.com.

Dora · *see Sumiton*

Dothan · *Dothan Area C/C* · Matt Parker; Pres.; 102 Jamestown Blvd.; P.O. Box 638; 36302; Houston; P 100,000; M 1,000; (334) 792-5138; (800) 221-1027; Fax (334) 794-4796; chamber@dothan.com; www.dothan.com*

Elba · *Elba C/C* · Kaye Whitworth; Exec. Dir.; 329 Putnam St.; 36323; Coffee; P 4,185; M 130; (334) 897-3125; Fax (334) 897-1762; echamber329@troycable.net; www.elbaalabama.net

Enterprise · *Enterprise C/C* · Phil Thomas; Pres.; 553 Glover Ave.; P.O. Box 310577; 36331; Coffee & Dale; P 29,903; M 640; (334) 347-0581; (800) 235-4730; Fax (334) 393-8204; chamberpresident@centurytel.net; www.enterprisealabama.com.*

Eufaula · *Eufaula-Barbour County C/C* · Jim Bradley; Exec. Dir.; 333 E. Broad St.; 36027; Barbour; P 29,000; M 400; (334) 687-6664; (800) 524-7529; Fax (334) 687-5240; info@eufaulachamber.com; www.eufaulachamber.com*

Eutaw · *Eutaw Area C/C* · Sue Vance; 111 Main St.; P.O. Box 31; 35462; Greene; P 11,000; M 40; (205) 372-9002; Fax (205) 372-1393; eutawchamber@bellsouth.net; www.eutawchamber.com

Evergreen · *Evergreen/Conecuh County Area C/C* · Clinton Hyde; Pres.; 100 Depot Sq.; 36401; Conecuh; P 14,000; M 100; (251) 578-1707; Fax (251) 578-5660; emma0916@bellsouth.net; www.evergreenchamberofcommerce.org

Fairfield · *Fairfield C/C* · Betty Smith; Pres.; P.O. Box 528; 35064; Jefferson; P 13,000; M 65; (205) 786-2829; (205) 788-2492; ronjefferson@bellsouth.net

Fairhope · *see Daphne*

Fayette · *Fayette Area C/C* · Anne Hamner; Exec. Dir.; P.O. Box 247; 35555; Fayette; P 4,600; M 165; (205) 932-4587; Fax (205) 932-8788; info@fayetteareachamber.org; www.fayetteareachamber.org

Flomaton · *Flomaton C/C* · Wanda Vanlandingham; Pres.; P.O. Box 693; 36441; Escambia; P 2,000; M 60; (251) 296-1110

Florala · *Tri-Cities C/C* · Jimmy Waldrop; Pres.; 1135 4th St.; 36442; Covington; P 2,000; M 70; (334) 858-6252; floralatricity@yahoo.com; www.tricitieschamberofcommerce.com*

Florence · *Shoals C/C* · Stephen B. Holt; Pres.; 20 Hightower Pl.; P.O. Box 1331; 35631; Lauderdale; P 135,000; M 835; (256) 764-4661; Fax (256) 766-9017; shoals@shoalschamber.com; www.shoalschamber.com.*

Foley · *South Baldwin C/C* · Donna Watts; Pres./CEO; 104 N. McKenzie St.; P.O. Box 1117; 36536; Baldwin; P 50,300; M 715; (251) 943-3291; (877) 461-3712; Fax (251) 943-6810; infodesk@southbaldwinchamber.com; www.southbaldwinchamber.com.*

Fort Deposit · *Fort Deposit C/C* · Barbara Payne; Pres.; P.O. Box 162; 36032; Lowndes; P 1,519; M 30; (334) 227-4411; www.fortdeposit.info

Fort Payne · *Fort Payne C/C* · Carol Beddingfield; Exec. Dir.; 300 Gault Ave. N.; P.O. Box 680125; 35968; DeKalb; P 12,938; M 310; (256) 845-2741; Fax (256) 845-5849; info@fortpaynechamber.com; www.fortpaynechamber.com*

Gadsden · *The Chamber, Gadsden/Etowah County* · Tom Quinn; Pres.; One Commerce Sq.; P.O. Box 185; 35902; Etowah; P 103,000; M 1,200; (256) 543-3472; Fax (256) 543-9887; info@gadsdenchamber.com; www.gadsdenchamber.com.*

Gardendale · *Gardendale C/C* · Kris Marshall; Exec. Dir.; 2109 Moncrief Rd., Ste. 115; P.O. Box 26; 35071; Jefferson; P 13,000; M 280; (205) 631-9195; Fax (205) 631-9034; info@gardendale-chamber.com; www.gardendalechamber.com*

Geneva · *Greater Geneva Area C/C* · Alice Faye Smith; Exec. V.P.; 406 S. Commerce St.; 36340; Geneva; P 5,000; M 95; (334) 684-6582; genevacountychamber@centurylink.net; www.genevaareachamber.com

Gordo · *Gordo Area C/C* · Robin Patterson; Pres.; P.O. Box 33; 35466; Pickens; P 4,537; M 75; (205) 364-7870; Fax (205) 364-7870; info@gordochamber.com; www.gordochamber.com

Grant · *Grant C/C* · Joe Powell; P.O. Box 221; 35747; Marshall; P 665; M 80; (256) 728-8800; grant@nehp.net; www.grantchamberofcommerce.com

Greenville · *Greenville Area C/C* · Francine Wasden; Exec. Dir.; One Depot Sq.; 36037; Butler; P 25,000; M 330; (334) 382-3251; Fax (334) 382-3181; chamber@greenville-alabama.com; www.greenvillealchamber.com

Grove Hill · *Grove Hill Area C/C* · Cheryl Horton; Exec. Dir.; 104 N. Jackson St.; P.O. Box 567; 36451; Clarke; P 1,500; M 70; (251) 275-4188; Fax (251) 275-2278; grovehillcoc@tds.net; www.grovehillal.com

Gulf Shores · *Alabama Gulf Coast C/C* · 3150 Gulf Shores Pkwy.; P.O. Drawer 3869; 36547; Baldwin; P 10,000; M 1,000; (251) 968-6904; Fax (251) 968-5332; info@alagulfcoastchamber.com; www.alagulfcoastchamber.com

Guntersville · *Lake Guntersville C/C* · Morri Yancy; Pres.; 200 Gunter Ave.; P.O. Box 577; 35976; Marshall; P 8,700; M 600; (256) 582-3612; (800) 869-LAKE; Fax (256) 582-3682; gcc@lakeguntersville.org; www.lakeguntersville.org

Haleyville · *Haleyville C/C* · 1200 21st St.; P.O. Box 634; 35565; Winston; P 4,200; M 75; (205) 486-4611; info@haleyvillechamber.org; www.haleyvillechamber.org

Hamilton · *Hamilton Area C/C* · David Hall; Pres.; 422 2nd St. S.W.; P.O. Box 1168; 35570; Marion; P 7,000; M 175; (205) 921-7786; Fax (205) 921-2220; chamber@cityofhamilton.org; www.cityofhamilton.org

Harpersville · *see Columbiana*

Hartselle • *Hartselle Area C/C* • Susan Hines; Pres.; 110 Railroad St. S.W.; P.O. Box 817; 35640; Morgan; P 13,500; M 400; (256) 773-4370; (800) 294-0692; Fax (256) 773-4379; hartsell@hiwaay. net; www.hartsellechamber.com*

Headland • *Headland C/C* • Charles A. Lueck; Pres.; 105 Cleveland St.; 36345; Henry; P 5,000; M 125; (334) 693-3303; Fax (334) 693-3303; headlandchamber@centurytel.net; www. headlandal.com

Heflin • *Cleburne County C/C* • Beverly Casey; Dir.; P.O. Box 413; 36264; Cleburne; P 15,000; M 100; (256) 463-2222; Fax (256) 463-4668; chamber@cleburnecountychamber.com; www. cleburnecountychamber.com

Homewood • *Homewood C/C* • Tricia Ford; Exec. Dir.; 1721 Oxmoor Rd.; P.O. Box 59494; 35259; Jefferson; P 24,000; M 460; (205) 871-5631; Fax (205) 871-5632; director@homewood chamber.org; www.homewoodchamber.org

Hoover • *Hoover Area C/C* • Bill Powell; Exec. Dir.; 1694 Montgomery Hwy., Ste. 108; P.O. Box 36005; 35236; Jefferson; P 70,000; M 1,200; (205) 988-5672; Fax (205) 988-8383; bill@ hooverchamber.org; www.hooverchamber.org

Hueytown • *Hueytown Area C/C* • Rebecca Williams; Exec. Secy.; 2058-A High School Rd.; P.O. Box 3356; 35023; Jefferson; P 19,000; M 221; (205) 491-8039; Fax (205) 491-7961; hueyoed@ bellsouth.net; www.hueytownchamber.com*

Huntsville • *C of C of Huntsville/Madison County* • Brian Hilson; Pres./CEO; 225 Church St.; 35801; Madison; P 168,000; M 2,000; (256) 535-2000; Fax (256) 535-2015; info@hsvchamber. org; www.huntsvillealabamausa.com

Huntsville • *Huntsville Info Center* • David Royalston; Exec. Dir.; 10 America Holly Cir. S.W., Ste. 1; 35824; P 168,000; hunts villeinfo@gmail.com

Irondale • *Greater Irondale C/C* • 1912 1st Ave. S.; 35210; Jefferson; P 11,000; M 100; (205) 956-3104; Fax (205) 956-5964; caboose500@aol.com; www.greaterirondalechamber.com*

Jackson • *Jackson C/C* • LaShaunda Holly; Exec. Dir.; 500 Commerce St.; 36545; Clarke; P 5,600; M 150; (251) 246-3251; Fax (251) 246-3213; jacksonchamber@bellsouth.net; www. jacksonalabama.org

Jasper • *C/C of Walker County* • Linda Lewis; Pres.; 204 19th St. E., Ste. 101; P.O. Box 972; 35502; Walker; P 70,000; M 400; (205) 384-4571; Fax (205) 384-4901; linda@walkerchamber.us; www. walkerchamber.us*

Lafayette • *see Lanett*

Lanett • *Greater Valley Area C/C* • Elinor Crowder; Exec. Dir.; 2102 S. Broad Ave.; P.O. Box 205; 36863; Chambers; P 40,000; M 300; (334) 642-1411; Fax (334) 642-1410; info@greater valleyarea.com; www.greatervalleyarea.com*

Leeds • *Leeds Area C/C* • Sandra McGuire; Exec. Dir.; 7901 Parkway Dr.; P.O. Box 900; 35094; Jefferson; P 11,000; M 200; (205) 699-5001; Fax (205) 699-5001; leedschamber@wind stream.net; www.leedsareachamber.com

Lincoln • *Greater Talladega Area C/C* • Mack Ferguson; Exec. Dir.; 176 Magnolia St.; 35096; Talladega; P 5,000; M ; (205) 763-1535; info@talladegachamber.com; www.talladegachamber.com

Lineville • *Clay County C/C* • Mary Patchunka-Smith; Exec. Dir.; 86838 Hwy. 9; P.O. Box 85; 36266; Clay; P 13,000; M 130; (256) 396-2828; Fax (256) 396-5532; claychamber@centurytel.net; www.claycochamber.com

Lockhart • *see Florala*

Luverne • *Crenshaw County C/C & EIDA* • Martha Dickey; Pres.; P.O. Box 4; 36049; Crenshaw; P 13,514; M 100; (334) 335-4468; Fax (334) 335-4469; robyn@crenshawcounty.net; www.crenshaw county.net

Madison • *Madison C/C* • Tim Knox; Interim Dir.; 190 Lime Quarry Rd., Ste. 105; 35758; Madison; P 40,000; M 600; (256) 325-8317; director@madisonalchamber.com; www.madisonalchamber.com*

Marion • *Perry County C/C* • John L. Martin; Exec. Dir.; 1200 Washington St.; 36756; Perry; P 10,961; M 78; (334) 683-9622; Fax (334) 683-4561; perrycountychamb@bellsouth.net; www. perrycountyalabamachamber.com

Millbrook • *Millbrook Area C/C* • Jonathon Dow; Exec. Dir.; 3540 Main St.; P.O. Box 353; 36054; Elmore; P 18,000; M 305; (334) 285-0085; Fax (334) 285-9854; info@millbrookareachamber.com; www.millbrookareachamber.com

Millport • *South Lamar Area C/C* • Edna Cole; Pres.; P.O. Box 205; 35576; Lamar; P 1,600; M 25; (205) 662-5936

Mobile • *Mobile Area C/C* • Winthrop M. Hallett III; Pres.; 451 Government St.; P.O. Box 2187; 36652; Mobile; P 404,111; M 2,400; (251) 433-6951; Fax (251) 432-1143; info@mobile chamber.com; www.mobilechamber.com.*

Monroeville • *Monroeville/Monroe County C/C* • Sandy C. Smith; Exec. Dir.; 86 N. Alabama Ave.; P.O. Box 214; 36461; Monroe; P 25,000; M 225; (251) 743-2879; (251) 743-2880; Fax (251) 743-2189; info@monroecountyal.com; www.monroe countyal.com

Montevallo • *Montevallo C/C* • Mary Lou Williams; Pres.; 720 Oak St.; 35115; Shelby; P 6,000; M 100; (205) 665-1519; Fax (205) 665-0759; montevallocc@bellsouth.net; www.montevallocc.org

Montgomery • *Montgomery Area C/C* • Randall L. George CEcD; Pres.; 41 Commerce St.; P.O. Box 79; 36101; Montgomery; P 335,000; M 1,858; (334) 834-5200; Fax (334) 265-4745; macc@ montgomerychamber.com; www.montgomerychamber.com*

Montrose • *see Daphne*

Moody • *Moody Area C/C* • Andrea Machen; Exec. Dir.; 670 Park Ave.; 35004; St. Clair; P 13,859; M 140; (205) 640-6262; Fax (205) 640-2996; chamber@moodyalabama.gov; www.moodyalchamber.com*

Moulton • *Lawrence County C/C* • Kim Hood; Pres.; 12467 Alabama Hwy. 157; 35650; Lawrence; P 35,000; M 320; (256) 974-1658; Fax (256) 974-2400; kimhood@lawrencealabama.com; lawrencealabama.com

Mountain Brook • *Mountain Brook C/C* • Suzan Doidge; Exec. Dir.; 32 Vine St.; 35213; Jefferson; P 21,000; M 300; (205) 871-3779; Fax (205) 871-6678; mtnbrookchamber@bellsouth.net; www.mtnbrookchamber.com

Mt. Laurel • *see Columbiana*

Munford • *see Talladega*

Oneonta • *Blount County-Oneonta C/C* • Charles Carr; Exec. Dir.; 225 2nd Ave. E.; P.O. Box 1487; 35121; Blount; P 58,000; M 375; (205) 274-2153; Fax (205) 274-2099; info@blount oneontachamber.org; www.blountoneontachamber.org

Opelika • *Opelika C/C* • Wendi Routhier; Pres.; 601 Ave. A; P.O. Box 2366; 36803; Lee; P 26,000; M 750; (334) 745-4861; Fax (334) 749-4740; coc@opelika.com; www.opelika.com*

Opp • *Opp & Covington County Area C/C* • James Kelsoe; Exec. Dir.; 101 E. Ida Ave.; P.O. Box 148; 36467; Covington; P 7,000; M 250; (334) 493-3070; (800) 239-8054; Fax (334) 493-1060; chamber@oppcatv.com; www.oppchamber.com

Oxford • *see Anniston*

Ozark · *Ozark Area C/C* · Jeanette Reeves; Exec. Dir.; 294 Painter Ave.; 36360; Dale; P 15,000; M 350; (334) 774-9321; (800) 582-8497; Fax (334) 774-8736; info@ozarkalchamber.com; www.ozarkalchamber.com*

Pelham · *Greater Shelby County C/C* · Jennifer Trammell; Pres.; 1301 County Services Dr.; 35124; Shelby; P 143,000; M 1,650; (205) 663-4542; Fax (205) 663-4524; info@shelbychamber.org; www.shelbychamber.org

Pell City · *Greater Pell City C/C* · Lynn Batemon; Exec. Dir.; 1618 Cogswell Ave.; 35125; St. Clair; P 13,000; M 360; (205) 338-3377; (205) 338-1913; Fax (205) 338-1913; pellcitychamber@centurytel.net; www.pellcitychamber.com

Phenix City · *Phenix City-Russell County C/C* · Victor W. Cross; Pres./CEO; 1107 Broad St.; P.O. Box 1326; 36868; Russell; P 53,000; M 435; (334) 298-3639; (800) 892-2248; Fax (334) 298-3846; pcrccham@ldl.net; pc-rcchamber.com*

Point Clear · *see Daphne*

Prattville · *Prattville Area C/C* · Jeremy L. Arthur; Exec. V.P.; 131 N. Court St.; 36067; Autauga; P 35,000; M 875; (334) 365-7392; (800) 588-2796; Fax (334) 361-1314; jarthur@prattville chamber.com; www.prattvillechamber.com*

Prichard · *Prichard Area C/C* · Cederick McMillan; Pres.; 117 E. Clark Ave.; P.O. Box 10266; 36610; Mobile; P 28,000; M 40; (251) 452-2760; chamber@prichardchamber.com; www.prichard chamber.com

Rainsville · *Rainsville C/C* · Tim Eberhart; Exec. Dir.; P.O. Box 396; 35986; DeKalb; P 5,000; M 110; (256) 638-7800; www.rainsvillealabama.com

Reform · *Reform Area C/C* · Amy Richardson; Mgr.; City Hall; P.O. Box 891; 35481; Pickens; P 1,979; M 34; (205) 375-2233; (205) 375-6363

Roanoke · *Randolph County C/C* · Dorothy B. Tidwell; Exec. Dir.; 3355 Hwy. 431, Ste. 11; P.O. Box 431; 36274; Randolph; P 23,253; M 175; (334) 863-6612; (800) 863-6612; Fax (334) 863-7280; rancococ@teleclipse.net; www.randolphcountyal.com

Robertsdale · *Central Baldwin C/C* · Jamie Mangion; Dir. of Op.; 23150 Hwy. 59; P.O. Box 587; 36567; Baldwin; P 4,000; M 300; (251) 947-2626; Fax (251) 947-4809; jmangion@centralbaldwin.com; www.centralbaldwin.com*

Russellville · *Franklin County C/C* · Nina McNatt; Exec. Dir.; 103 N. Jackson Ave.; P.O. Box 44; 35653; Franklin; P 29,000; M 200; (256) 332-1760; Fax (256) 332-1740; franklincountyhelp@charterinternet.com; www.franklincountychamber.org

Saraland · *Saraland Area C/C* · Pamela Burnham; Exec. Dir.; 939 Hwy. 43 S.; 36571; Mobile; P 15,000; M 200; (251) 675-4444; Fax (251) 675-2307; info@saralandcoc.com; www.saralandcoc.com*

Scottsboro · *Greater Jackson County C/C* · Rick Roden; Pres./CEO; 407 E. Willow St.; P.O. Box 973; 35768; Jackson; P 55,000; M 450; (256) 259-5500; (800) 259-5508; Fax (256) 259-4447; chamber@scottsboro.org; www.jacksoncountychamber.com.*

Selma · *Selma-Dallas County C/C* · Sheryl Smedley; Exec. Dir.; 912 Selma Ave.; 36701; Dallas; P 43,000; M 350; (334) 875-7241; Fax (334) 875-7142; info@SelmaAlabama.com; www.SelmaAlabama.com*

Spanish Fort · *see Daphne*

Springville · *Springville Area C/C* · Tina Barron; Pres.; 6496 U.S. Hwy. 11; 35146; St. Clair; P 5,000; M 60; (205) 467-2339; info@springvillealabama.org; www.springvillealabama.org

Sumiton · *East Walker County C/C* · Chee-Vee Whitfield; Dir.; P.O. Box 188; 35148; Walker; P 12,000; M 60; (205) 255-0202; Fax (205) 255-0202; chee-vee@eastwalkerchamber.com; www.eastwalkerchamber.com

Sylacauga · *Sylacauga C/C* · Carol A. Emlich-Bates; Exec. Dir.; 17 W. Fort Williams St.; P.O. Box 185; 35150; Talladega; P 14,000; M 442; (256) 249-0308; Fax (256) 249-0315; agwathney@sylacauga.net; www.sylacaugachamber.com*

Talladega · *Greater Talladega Area C/C* · Mack Ferguson; Exec. Dir.; 210 East St. S.; P.O. Drawer A; 35160; Talladega; P 13,299; M 276; (256) 362-9075; Fax (256) 362-9093; info@talladega chamber.com; www.talladegachamber.com*

Tallassee · *Tallassee C/C* · Ann Christian; Pres.; 650 Gilmer Ave.; 36078; Elmore; P 5,000; M 250; (334) 283-5151; (334) 850-2056; Fax (334) 252-0774; chamber@elmore.rr.com; www.tallassee.al.us

Thomasville · *Southwest Alabama C/C* · Marlo Anderson; Dir.; 138 Wilson Ave.; P.O. Box 44; 36784; Clarke; P 6,000; M 180; (334) 636-1542; Fax (334) 636-2243; coc@southwestalabamachamber.com; www.southwestalabamachamber.com

Tillman's Corner · *Tillman's Corner C/C* · Larry Kent; Dir.; 5055 Carol Plantation Rd.; 36619; Mobile; P 17,000; M 200; (251) 666-2846; Fax (251) 666-2813; tillmanscornerco@bellsouth.net; www.tillmanscornerchamber.com

Troy · *Pike County C/C* · Leigh Anne Windham; Pres.; 100 Industrial Blvd.; P.O. Box 249; 36081; Pike; P 15,000; M 450; (334) 566-2294; Fax (334) 566-2298; pikecoc@troycable.net; www.pikecountychamber.net

Trussville · *Trussville Area C/C* · Diane Poole; Exec. Dir.; 225 Parkway Dr.; 35173; Jefferson; P 18,500; M 350; (205) 655-7535; (800) 494-8222; Fax (205) 655-3705; info@trussvillechamber.com; www.trussvillechamber.com

Tuscaloosa · *C/C of West Alabama* · Terry Waters; Exec. Dir.; 2200 University Blvd.; P.O. Box 020410; 35402; Tuscaloosa; P 250,000; M 1,200; (205) 758-7588; Fax (205) 391-0565; chamber@dbtech.net; www.tuscaloosachamber.com*

Tuskegee · *Tuskegee Area C/C* · Henrietta Anderson; Ofc. Mgr.; 121 S. Main St.; 36083; Macon; P 24,000; M 225; (334) 727-6619; Fax (334) 725-1801; info@tuskegeeareachamber.org; www.tuskegeeareachamber.org

Union Springs · *Union Springs-Bullock County C/C* · Evelyn Smart; Pres.; 212 N. Prairie, Rm. 111; P.O. Box 5006; 36089; Bullock; P 11,714; M 58; (334) 738-2424; info@usacoc.com; www.usacoc.com

Valley · *see Lanett*

Vernon · *Vernon C/C* · Don Dollar; Pres.; P.O. Box 336; 35592; Lamar; P 3,000; M 65; (205) 695-7029; Fax (205) 695-9501

Vestavia Hills · *Vestavia Hills C/C* · Karen Odle; Exec. Dir.; 1975 Merryvale Rd.; 35216; Jefferson; P 32,000; M 950; (205) 823-5011; Fax (205) 823-8974; chamber@vestaviahills.org; www.vestaviahills.org*

Vincent · *see Columbiana*

Westover · *see Columbiana*

Wetumpka · *Wetumpka Area C/C* · Jan Wood; Exec. Dir.; 110 E. Bridge St.; P.O. Box 785; 36092; Elmore; P 16,000; M 250; (334) 567-4811; Fax (334) 567-1811; wacc@bellsouth.net; www.wetumpkachamber.com*

Wilsonville · *see Columbiana*

Winfield · *Winfield C/C* · Chele Bussey; Pres.; P.O. Box 916; 35594; Fayette; P 5,000; M 85; (205) 487-8841; Fax (205) 487-8841; winfield@dlis.net; www.winfieldcity.org

Alaska

Alaska State C of C · Wayne A. Stevens; Pres.; 217 2nd St., Ste. 201; Juneau; 99801; Juneau; P 686,293; M 550; (907) 586-2323; Fax (907) 463-5515; info@alaskachamber.com; www.alaska chamber.com

Anchor Point · *Anchor Point C/C* · Jesse Clutts; Pres.; P.O. Box 610; 99556; Kenai Peninsula; P 2,500; M 150; (907) 235-2600; Fax (907) 235-2600; info@anchorpointchamber.org; www.anchor pointchamber.org

Anchorage · *Anchorage C/C* · Sami Glascott; Pres.; 1016 W. 6th Ave., Ste. 303; 99501; Anchorage; P 279,243; M 1,200; (907) 272-2401; Fax (907) 272-4117; info@anchoragechamber.org; www. anchoragechamber.org*

Barrow · *City of Barrow* · Jane Nelson; City Clerk; P.O. Box 629; 99723; North Slope; P 4,600; (907) 852-5211; Fax (907) 852-5871; jane.nelson@cityofbarrow.org; www.cityofbarrow.org

Bethel · *Bethel C/C* · Jerry Drake; Pres.; 192 Alex Hately; P.O. Box 329; 99559; Bethel; P 6,000; M 75; (907) 543-2911; Fax (907) 543-2255; bethelchamber1@alaska.com; www.bethelakchamber.org

Big Lake · *Big Lake C/C* · Donna Love; P.O. Box 520067; 99652; Matanuska-Susitna; P 3,500; M 115; (907) 892-6109; Fax (907) 892-6120; info@biglakechamber.org; www.biglakechamber.org

Chugiak · *see Eagle River*

Cooper Landing · *Cooper Landing C/C* · Gary Galbraith; Pres.; P.O. Box 809; 99572; Kenai Peninsula; P 300; M 60; (907) 595-8888; info@cooperlandingchamber.com; www.cooper landingchamber.com

Cordova · *Cordova C/C* · Jennifer Gibbins; Pres.; 404 1st St.; P.O. Box 99; 99574; Valdez Cordova; P 2,000; M 150; (907) 424-7260; Fax (907) 424-7259; visitcordova@ak.net; www.cordovachamber.com

Delta Junction · *Delta C/C & Visitor Center* · Brenda Peterson; Exec. Dir.; 2855 Alaska Hwy., Ste. 1B; P.O. Box 987; 99737; SE Fairbanks; P 5,700; M 200; (907) 895-5068; Fax (907) 895-5141; deltacc@deltachamber.org; www.deltachamber.org

Dillingham · *Dillingham C/C* · Casey DelaCruz; P.O. Box 348; 99576; Dillingham; P 2,400; M 70; (907) 842-5115; (907) 842-5148; dlgchmbr@nushtel.com; www.dillinghamak.com

Eagle River · *Chugiak-Eagle River C/C* · Susan Gorski; Exec. Dir.; 11401 Old Glenn Hwy., Ste. 105; P.O. Box 770353; 99577; Anchorage; P 35,000; M 400; (907) 694-4702; Fax (907) 694-1205; info@cer.org; www.cer.org.*

Fairbanks · *Greater Fairbanks C/C* · Lisa Herbert; Exec. Dir.; 100 Cushman St., Ste. 102; 99701; Fairbanks North Star; P 97,970; M 750; (907) 452-1105; Fax (907) 456-6968; info@fairbanks-chamber.org; www.fairbankschamber.org*

Glennallen · *Copper Valley C/C* · Warren Ulrich; P.O. Box 469; 99588; Valdez Cordova; P 3,500; M 185; (907) 822-5555; Fax (907) 822-5559; chamber@cvinternet.net; www.coppervalleychamber.com

Haines · *Haines C/C* · Joan M. Carlson; Ofc. Mgr.; 219 Main St., Ste. 14; P.O. Box 1449; 99827; Haines; P 2,000; M 146; (907) 766-2202; Fax (907) 766-2271; chamber@haineschamber.org; www. haineschamber.org

Healy · *Greater Healy-Denali C/C & Visitors Center* · Connie MacMaster; Admin. Asst.; Healy Spur Rd.; P.O. Box 437; 99743; Denali; P 1,848; M 95; (907) 683-4636; denali.chamber@gmail. com; www.denalichamber.com

Homer · *Homer C/C* · Paul Dauphinais; Exec. Dir.; 201 Sterling Hwy.; 99603; Kenai Peninsula; P 12,000; M 463; (907) 235-7740; Fax (907) 235-8766; info@homeralaska.org; www.homeralaska.org

Houston · *Houston C/C* · Nancy Sult; Pres.; P.O. Box 940356; 99694; Matanuska-Susitna; P 2,100; M 50; (907) 892-6812; houstonakchamber@hotmail.com; houstonakchamber.tripod.com

Hyder · *Stewart-Hyder Intl. C/C* · Gwen McKay; Mgr.; P.O. Box 149; 99923; Prince of Wales-Hyder; P 100; M 85; (250) 636-9224; Fax (250) 636-9224; info@stewart-hyder.com; www.stewart-hyder.com

Juneau · *Juneau C/C* · Cathie Roemmich; CEO; 3100 Channel Dr., Ste. 300; 99801; Juneau; P 32,000; M 450; (907) 463-3488; Fax (907) 463-3489; juneauchamber@gci.net; www.juneauchamber.com

Kenai · *Kenai C/C* · Carol Bannock; Exec. Dir.; 402 Overland; 99611; Kenai; P 8,000; M 371; (907) 283-7989; Fax (907) 283-7183; info@kenaichamber.org; www.kenaichamber.org

Ketchikan · *Greater Ketchikan C/C* · Blaine Ashcraft; Exec. Dir.; P.O. Box 5957; 99901; Gateway; P 14,000; M 400; (907) 225-3184; Fax (907) 225-3187; info@ketchikanchamber.com; www. ketchikanchamber.com

Klawock · *Prince of Wales C/C* · Jan Bush; Pres.; 6488 Klawock Hollis Hwy. Ste. 7; P.O. Box 490; 99925; Prince of Wales-Hyder; P 4,000; M 180; (907) 755-2626; Fax (907) 755-2627; powcc@ aptalaska.net; www.princeofwalescoc.org

Kodiak · *Kodiak C/C* · Trevor Brown; Exec. Dir.; 100 E. Marine Way, Ste. 300; 99615; Kodiak; P 14,000; M 350; (907) 486-5557; Fax (907) 486-7605; chamber@kodiak.org; www.kodiak.org

Kotzebue · *City of Kotzebue* · D. Eugene Smith; Mayor; 258A 3rd Ave.; P.O. Box 46; 99752; NW Arctic; P 3,104; (907) 442-3401; Fax (907) 442-3742; esmith@maniilaq.org; www.cityofkotzebue.com

Nenana · *Nenana Valley C/C* · Miles Martin; Chrmn.; P.O. Box 363; 99760; Yukon-Koyukuk; P 550; M 30; (907) 832-5442; miles@milesofalaska.net; www.nenanahomepage.com

Ninilchik · *Ninilchik C/C* · Charlene McClean; P.O. Box 39164; 99639; Kenai Peninsula; P 1,000; M 50; (907) 567-3571; info@ ninilchikchamber.com; www.ninilchikchamber.com

Nome · *Nome C/C* · Mitch Erickson; Exec. Dir.; P.O. Box 250; 99762; Nome; P 3,500; M 60; (907) 443-3879; Fax (907) 443-3892; www.nomealaska.org

North Pole · *North Pole Comm. C/C & Visitor Center* · Tammy Randolph; P.O. Box 55071; 99705; Fairbanks North Star; P 35,000; M 100; (907) 488-2242; (907) 488-2281; Fax (907) 488-3002; info@northpolechamber.us; www.northpolechamber.us

Palmer · *Greater Palmer C/C* · Jillyan Webb; Exec. Dir.; 550 S. Alaska St., Ste. 101; P.O. Box 45; 99645; Matanuska-Susitna; P 4,800; M 320; (907) 745-2880; Fax (907) 746-4164; info@ palmerchamber.org; www.palmerchamber.org

Petersburg · *Petersburg C/C* · Sally Dwyer; Exec. Dir.; 19 Fram St.; P.O. Box 649; 99833; Petersburg; P 3,000; M 140; (907) 772-3646; (907) 772-4636; Fax (907) 772-2453; pcoc@alaska.com; www.petersburg.org

Seldovia · *Seldovia C/C* · Ila Dillon; Pres.; P.O. Drawer F; 99663; Kenai Peninsula; P 300; M 60; (907) 234-7612; president@ seldoviachamber.org; www.seldoviachamber.org

Seward · *Seward C of C, Conf. & Visitors Bur.* · Cindy Clock; Interim Exec. Dir.; 2001 Seward Hwy.; P.O. Box 749; 99664; Kenai Peninsula; P 3,200; M 400; (907) 224-8051; Fax (907) 224-5353; chamber@seward.net; www.seward.com

Sitka · *Greater Sitka C/C* · Sheila Finkenbinder; Exec. Dir.; 329 Harbor Dr., Ste. 212; P.O. Box 638; 99835; Sitka; P 8,700; M 165; (907) 747-8604; Fax (907) 747-7413; chamber@ptialaska.net; www.sitkacoc.com

Skagway · *Skagway C/C* · Karla Ray; Pres.; P.O. Box 194; 99840; Skagway; P 800; M 160; (907) 983-1898; Fax (907) 983-2031; chamber@aptalaska.net; www.skagwaychamber.org

Soldotna · *Funny River C/C* · Ray Price; Pres.; 35850 Pioneer Access Rd.; 99669; Kenai Peninsula; P 1,000; M 150; (907) 262-0879; (907) 262-6161

Soldotna · *Greater Soldotna C/C & Visitors Info. Center* · Michelle Glaves; Exec. Dir.; 44790 Sterling Hwy.; 99669; Kenai Peninsula; P 5,000; M 650; (907) 262-9814; (907) 262-1337; Fax (907) 262-3566; director@soldotnachamber.com; www.soldotnachamber.com*

Talkeetna · *Talkeetna C/C* · Trisha Costello; Pres.; P.O. Box 334; 99676; Matanuska-Susitna; P 850; M 80; (907) 733-2330; info@talkeetnachamber.org; www.talkeetnachamber.org

Tok · *Tok C/C* · P.O. Box 389; 99780; S.E. Fairbanks; P 1,400; M 43; (907) 883-5775; info@tokalaskainfo.com; www.tokalaskainfo.com

Wasilla · *Greater Wasilla C/C* · Lyn Carden; Exec. Dir.; 415 E. Railroad Ave.; 99654; Matanuska-Susitna; P 7,100; M 702; (907) 376-1299; Fax (907) 373-2560; contact@wasillachamber.org; www.wasillachamber.org*

Whittier · *Greater Whittier C/C* · Kelly Bender; V.P.; P.O. Box 607; 99693; Valdez-Cordova; P 175; M 65; (907) 529-0235; info@whittieralaskachamber.org; www.whittieralaskachamber.org

Willow · *Willow C/C* · Jim Houston; Pres.; P.O. Box 183; 99688; Matanuska-Susitna; P 3,000; M 50; (907) 495-6800; Fax (907) 495-6800; mail@willowchamber.org; www.willowchamber.org

Wrangell · *Wrangell C/C* · Haley Waddington; Ofc. Mgr.; 224 Front St.; P.O. Box 49; 99929; Wrangell; P 2,000; M 113; (907) 874-3901; Fax (907) 874-3905; wrangellchamber@gmail.com; www.wrangellchamber.org

Arizona

Arizona C of C & Ind. · Glenn Hamer; Pres./CEO; 1850 N. Central Ave., Ste. 1433; Phoenix; 85004; Maricopa; P 6,500,000; M 500; (602) 248-9172; Fax (602) 265-1262; info@azchamber.com; www.azchamber.com

Ajo · *Ajo Dist. C/C* · Silvia Howard; Exec. Dir.; 400 Taladro St.; 85321; Pima; P 4,000; M 94; (520) 387-7742; Fax (520) 387-3641; ajocofc@tabletoptelephone.com; www.ajochamber.com

Alpine · *Alpine Area C/C* · Anne MacGregor; Pres.; P.O. Box 410; 85920; Apache; P 600; M 65; (928) 339-4330; thechamber@alpinearizona.com; www.alpinearizona.com

Apache Junction · *Apache Junction C/C* · Larry Johnson; Pres./CEO; 567 W. Apache Trl.; P.O. Box 1747; 85117; Maricopa & Pinal; P 42,000; M 525; (480) 982-3141; (800) 252-3141; Fax (480) 982-3234; ajchamber@qwestoffice.net; www.apachejunctioncoc.com.*

Arizona City · *Arizona City C/C* · Jacque Zeigler; Exec. Dir.; 13640 S. Sunland Gin Rd., Ste. 106; P.O. Box 5; 85223; Pinal; P 6,000; M 125; (520) 466-5141; azchamber@cgmailbox.com; www.azcchamber.com

Avondale · *see Goodyear*

Benson · *Benson-San Pedro Valley C/C* · Robert Mucci; Exec. Dir.; 249 E. 4th St.; P.O. Box 2255; 85602; Cochise; P 4,700; M 160; (520) 586-2842; info@bensonchamberaz.com; www.bensonchamberaz.com

Bisbee · *Bisbee C/C* · Nancy Jacobsen; Dir.; 1 Main St.; P.O. Box BA; 85603; Cochise; P 6,000; M 239; (520) 432-5421; chamber@bisbeearizona.com; www.bisbeearizona.com

Black Canyon City · *Black Canyon City C/C* · Lori Martinez; Pres.; P.O. Box 1919; 85324; Yavapai; P 4,800; M 64; (623) 374-9797; Fax (623) 374-5651; bccadmin@blackcanyoncity.org; www.blackcanyoncity.org

Bouse · *Bouse C/C* · Norm Simpson; Pres.; P.O. Box 817; 85325; La Paz; P 850; M 45; (928) 851-2509; bousechamber@rraz.net; www.bousechamberofcommerce.com

Bowie · *Bowie C/C* · Nancy-Jean Welker; Pres.; P.O. Box 287; 85605; Cochise; P 700; M 50; (520) 253-0930; b2caz@vtc.net; www.bowiechamber.com

Buckeye · *Buckeye Valley C/C* · Deanna K. Kupcik; Pres./CEO; 508 E. Monroe Ave.; 85326; Maricopa; P 50,000; M 350; (623) 386-2727; deanna@buckeyevalleychamber.org; www.buckeyevalleychamber.org*

Bullhead City · *Bullhead Area C/C* · Michael Conner; Pres.; 1251 Hwy. 95; 86429; Mohave; P 45,000; M 730; (928) 754-4121; Fax (928) 754-5514; info@bullheadchamber.com; www.bullheadchamber.com

Camp Verde · *Camp Verde C/C* · Tracie Schimikowsky; Exec. Dir.; 385 S. Main St.; 86322; Yavapai; P 11,500; M 175; (928) 567-9294; Fax (928) 567-4793; info@campverde.org; www.visitcampverde.com.

Carefree · *Carefree Cave Creek C/C* · Patty Villeneuve; Dir. of Op; 748 Easy St., Ste. 2; P.O. Box 734; 85377; Maricopa; P 8,000; M 300; (480) 488-3381; chamber@carefreecavecreek.org; www.carefreecavecreek.org*

Casa Grande · *Greater Casa Grande C/C* · Helen Neuharth; Pres./CEO; 575 N. Marshall St.; 85122; Pinal; P 80,000; M 592; (520) 836-2125; Fax (520) 836-6233; chamber@cgmailbox.com; www.casagrandechamber.org*

Chandler · *Chandler C/C* · Dave Warkentin; Pres./CEO; 25 S. Arizona Pl., Ste. 201; 85225; Maricopa; P 259,936; M 1,400; (480) 963-4571; (800) 963-4571; Fax (480) 963-0188; dave@chandlerchamber.com; www.chandlerchamber.com*

Chino Valley · *Chino Valley Area C/C* · Ab Jackson; CEO; 448 N. Hwy. 89; P.O. Box 419; 86323; Yavapai; P 15,000; M 400; (928) 636-2493; chamber@chinovalley.org; www.chinovalley.org*

Chloride · *Chloride C/C* · Donna Meyer; P.O. Box 268; 86431; Mohave; P 350; M 22; (928) 565-2204; chloride_az@yahoo.com; www.chloridearizona.com

Clarkdale · *Clarkdale C/C* · Becky O'Banion; Pres.; P.O. Box 161; 86324; Yavapai; P 3,600; M 100; (928) 634-9438; (928) 634-8700; Fax (928) 634-9438; cccinfo@clarkdalechamber.com; www.clarkdalechamber.com

Coolidge · *Coolidge C/C* · Lynn Parsons; Exec. Dir.; 320 W. Central Ave.; 85128; Pinal; P 12,800; M 180; (520) 723-3009; Fax (520) 723-9410; info@coolidgechamber.org; www.coolidgechamber.org

Cottonwood · *Cottonwood C/C* · Lana Tolleson; Pres./CEO; 1010 S. Main St.; 86326; Yavapai; P 30,000; M 400; (928) 634-7593; Fax (928) 634-7594; info@cottonwoodchamberaz.org; www.cottonwoodchamberaz.org

Dolan Springs · *Dolan Springs C/C* · Lee MacWilliam; Pres.; P.O. Box 274; 86441; Mohave; P 2,000; M 170; (928) 767-4473; president@dolanspringschamberofcommerce.com; www.dolanspringschamberofcommerce.com

Douglas · *Greater Douglas C/C* · Vicky Merritt; Secy.; 345 16th St.; 85607; Cochise; P 18,000; M 50; (520) 364-2477; Fax (520) 364-6304; vickym@douglasazchamber.org; www.douglasazchamber.org

Eagar · *see Springerville*

El Mirage · *see Surprise*

Eloy · *Eloy C/C* · Belinda Akes; Exec. Dir.; 305 Stuart Blvd.; 85131; Pinal; P 11,000; M 100; (520) 466-3411; Fax (520) 466-4698; info@eloychamber.com; www.eloychamber.com

Flagstaff · *Flagstaff C/C* · Julie Pastrick; Pres./CEO; 101 W. Rte. 66; 86001; Coconino; P 68,000; M 1,200; (928) 774-4505; Fax (928) 779-1209; info@flagstaffchamber.com; www.flagstaff chamber.com*

Florence · *Greater Florence C/C* · Lina Austin; Exec. Dir.; 208 N. Main St.; P.O. Box 929; 85132; Pinal; P 6,200; M 200; (520) 868-9433; (800) 437-9433; Fax (520) 868-5797; info@florenceaz.org; www.florenceaz.org

Fort Mohave · *see Mohave Valley*

Fountain Hills · *Fountain Hills C/C* · Frank S. Ferrara; Pres./CEO; 16837 E. Palisades Blvd.; P.O. Box 17598; 85269; Maricopa; P 25,000; M 550; (480) 837-1654; Fax (480) 837-3077; diane@ fountainhillschamber.com; www.fountainhillschamber.com*

Fredonia · *Fredonia C/C* · Jan Judd; Pres.; P.O. Box 1162; 86022; Coconino; P 1,036; M 20; (928) 643-7241; www.go-arizona.com/ fredonia

Gila Bend · *Gila Bend C/C* · Clyde Kreger; Pres.; P.O. Box CC; 85337; Maricopa; P 1,900; M 30; gilabendchamber@yahoo.com; www.gilabendchamber.com

Gilbert · *Gilbert C/C* · Kathy Tilque; Pres./CEO; 119 N. Gilbert Rd., Ste. 101; P.O. Box 527; 85299; Maricopa; P 250,000; M 600; (480) 892-0056; Fax (480) 892-1980; info@gilbertchamber.com; www. gilbertaz.com*

Glendale · *Glendale C/C* · Don Rinehart; Pres.; 7105 N. 59th Ave.; P.O. Box 249; 85311; Maricopa; P 250,000; M 900; (623) 937-4754; (800) 437-8669; Fax (623) 937-3333; info@glendale azchamber.org; www.glendaleazchamber.org.

Globe · *Globe-Miami Reg. C/C & Eco. Dev. Corp.* · Ellen Kretsch; Dir.; 1360 N. Broad St.; 85501; Gila; P 23,000; M 400; (928) 425-4495; (800) 804-5623; Fax (928) 425-3410; visitorinfo@ globemiamichamber.com; www.globemiamichamber.com

Golden Valley · *Golden Valley C/C* · Bobbi Case; Pres./CEO; 3395 N. Verde Rd.; 86413; Mohave; P 17,000; M 200; (928) 565-3311; Fax (928) 565-3133; chamber@goldenvalleychamber.com; www.goldenvalleychamber.com

Goodyear · *Southwest Valley C/C* · Sharolyn Hohman; Pres./ CEO; 289 N. Litchfield Rd.; 85338; Maricopa; P 110,000; M 1,000; (623) 932-2260; Fax (623) 932-9057; info@southwestvalley chamber.org; www.southwestvalleychamber.org.*

Grand Canyon · *Grand Canyon C/C & Visitors Bur.* · Craig Andresen; Exec. Dir.; P.O. Box 3007; 86023; Coconino; P 1,500; M 115; (928) 638-2901; (888) 472-2696; Fax (928) 638-4095; info@ grandcanyonvisitorbureau.com; www.grandcanyonchamber.com

Green Valley · *Green Valley Sahuarita C/C & Visitor Center* · Jim DiGiacomo; Exec. Dir.; 275 W. Continental Rd., Ste. 123; P.O. Box 566; 85622; Pima; P 75,000; M 600; (520) 625-7575; (800) 858-5872; Fax (520) 648-6154; gvchamber@qwestoffice.net; www.greenvalleychamber.com.

Hayden · *see Kearny*

Heber · *see Overgaard*

Holbrook · *Holbrook C/C* · Yvonne Larson; Exec. Dir.; 100 E. Arizona St.; 86025; Navajo; P 5,544; M 130; (928) 524-6558; (800) 524-2459; Fax (928) 524-1719; holbrook@gotouraz.com; www. holbrookchamberofcommerce.com

Jerome · *Jerome C/C* · P.O. Box K; 86331; Yavapai; P 450; M 125; (928) 634-2900; jcc@jeromechamber.com; www.jeromechamber.com

Kayenta · *Kayenta Chamber & Film Ofc.* · Bill Crawley; P.O. Box 187; 86033; Navajo; P 12,000; M 4; (928) 697-3463; (928) 221-4813; Fax (928) 697-3734; crawleytours@citlink.net; www. crawleytours.com.

Kearny · *Copper Basin C/C* · Myra Warren; Dir.; 355 Alden Rd.; P.O. Box 206; 85137; Pinal; P 5,000; M 65; (520) 363-7607; myra@ copperbasinaz.com; www.copperbasinaz.com

Kingman · *Kingman Area C/C* · Pamela Wilkinson; Pres./CEO; 120 W. Andy Devine Ave.; P.O. Box 1150; 86402; Mohave; P 44,000; M 600; (928) 753-6253; Fax (928) 753-1049; kgmncofc@ctaz.com; www.kingmanchamber.org*

Lake Havasu City · *Lake Havasu Area C/C* · Lisa Krueger; Pres./ CEO; 314 London Bridge Rd.; 86403; Mohave; P 57,000; M 800; (928) 855-4115; Fax (928) 680-0010; lisak@havasuchamber.com; www.havasuchamber.com

Lake Mead City · *see Meadview*

Lakeside · *see Pinetop*

Litchfield Park · *see Goodyear*

Mammoth · *see San Manuel-SMOR C/C*

Marana · *Marana C/C* · Ed Stolmaker; Pres./CEO; 13881 N. Casa Grande Hwy.; 85653; Pima; P 35,000; M 500; (520) 682-4314; Fax (520) 682-2303; info@maranachamber.com; www.marana chamber.com

Maricopa · *Maricopa C/C* · Terri Kingery; Pres./CEO; P.O. Box 1203; 85139; Pinal; P 35,000; M 300; (520) 568-9573; info@ maricopachamber.com; www.maricopachamber.com

Mayer · *Arizona Highway 69 C/C* · 11255 S. Hwy. 69; 86333; Yavapai; P 6,700; M 50; (928) 632-4355; Fax (928) 632-4355; Hwy69chamber@commspeed.net; www.arizonahighway69 chamber.org*

Meadview · *Meadview Area C/C* · Bob Sequera; Pres.; 330 Meadview Blvd.; P.O. Box 26; 86444; Mohave; P 3,000; M 20; (928) 564-2425; www.meadviewazchamber.com

Mesa · *Mesa C/C* · Charles Deaton; Pres./CEO; 120 N. Center St.; 85201; Maricopa; P 460,000; M 1,000; (480) 969-1307; Fax (480) 827-0727; info@mesachamber.org; www.mesachamber.org*

Miami · *see Globe*

Mohave Valley · *Mohave Valley C/C* · Judy Gaston; Admin.; 8045 Hwy. 95, Ste. C; P.O. Box 5439; 86446; Mohave; P 16,000; M 230; (928) 768-2777; Fax (928) 768-6610; info@mohaveval-leychamber.com; www.mohavevalleychamber.com

Nogales · *Nogales-Santa Cruz County C/C* · Olivia Ainza-Kramer; Pres.; 123 W. Kino Park Pl.; 85621; Santa Cruz; P 32,000; M 200; (520) 287-3685; Fax (520) 287-3687; info@thenogales chamber.com; www.thenogaleschamber.com

Oatman · *Oatman-Goldroad C/C* · Linda Woodard; P.O. Box 423; 86433; Mohave; P 150; M 12; (928) 768-6222; oatman@ oatmangoldroad.org; www.oatmangoldroad.org

Oracle · *see San Manuel–SMOR C/C*

Overgaard · *Heber-Overgaard C/C* · Jerry Call; Pres.; P.O. Box 1926; 85933; Navajo; P 4,800; M 160; (928) 535-5777; Fax (928) 535-3254; heberovergaard.coc@hotmail.com; www.heber overgaard.org

Page · *Page-Lake Powell C/C* · Cecilia Cobb; Exec. Dir.; 34 S. Lake Powell Blvd.; P.O. Box 727; 86040; Coconino; P 8,000; M 260; (928) 645-2741; Fax (928) 645-3181; chamber@pagechamber.com; www.pagechamber.com

Parker • *Parker Area C/C* • Randy Hartless; Exec. Dir.; 1217 California Ave.; 85344; La Paz; P 21,529; M 325; (928) 669-2174; Fax (928) 669-6304; parker.chamber@redrivernet.com; www.parkeraz.org*

Payson • *Rim Country Reg. C/C* • John P. Stanton; Mgr.; 100 W. Main St.; P.O. Box 1380; 85547; Gila; P 22,000; M 425; (928) 474-4515; (800) 6-PAYSON; Fax (928) 474-8812; jstanton@npgcable.com; www.rimcountrychamber.com.*

Pearce • *Pearce-Sunsites C/C* • Murray McClelland; Pres.; 225 N. Frontage Rd.; P.O. Box 536; 85625; Cochise; P 2,200; M 75; (520) 826-3535; info@pearcesunsiteschamber.org; www.pearce sunsiteschamber.org

Peoria • *Peoria C/C* • Diana Bedient; Exec. Dir.; 8765 W. Kelton Ln., Bldg. C1; 85382; Maricopa & Yavapai; P 148,000; M 729; (623) 979-3601; (800) 580-2645; Fax (623) 486-4729; info1@peoriachamber.com; www.peoriachamber.com*

Phoenix Area

Ahwatukee Foothills C/C • 10235 S. 51st St., Ste. 185; 85044; Maricopa; P 90,000; M 550; (480) 753-7676; Fax (480) 753-3898; info@ahwatukeechamber.com; www.ahwatukeechamber.com*

Arizona Asian C/C • Madeline Ong-Sakata; Exec. Dir.; c/o 7217 N. 6 Way; 85020; Maricopa; M 410; (602) 222-2009; Fax (602) 870-7562; asiansun@aol.com; www.asianchamber.org

Arizona Hispanic C/C • Armando A. Contreras; Pres./CEO; 255 E. Osborn Rd., Ste. 201; 85012; Maricopa; M 425; (602) 279-1800; Fax (602) 279-8900; info@azhcc.com; www.azhcc.com

Greater Phoenix Black C/C • Ron Busby; Pres./CEO; 201 E. Washington St., Ste. 350; 85004; Maricopa; M 350; (602) 307-5200; Fax (602) 307-5204; heather@phoenixblackchamber.com; www.phoenixblackchamber.com

Greater Phoenix C/C • Todd Sanders; Pres./CEO; 201 N. Central Ave., Ste. 2700; 85004; Maricopa; P 4,023,331; M 3,100; (602) 254-5521; Fax (602) 495-8913; info@phoenixchamber.com; www.phoenixchamber.com*

North Phoenix C/C • Jean Lukens; Exec. Dir.; 12601 N. Cave Creek Rd., Ste. 104; 85022; Maricopa; P 500,000; M 200; (602) 482-3344; (602) 882-8484; Fax (602) 482-3344; jean@north phoenixchamber.com; www.northphoenixchamber.com*

Pinnacle Peak C/C • Kelly Wilson; Exec. Admin.; 2415 E. Camelback Rd., Ste. 700; 85016; Maricopa; (602) 910-3035; info@pinnaclepeakchamber.com; www.pinnaclepeakchamber.com

Pine • *see Payson*

Pinetop • *Pinetop-Lakeside C/C* • Beverly Stepp; Dir.; P.O. Box 4220; 85935; Navajo; P 4,700; M 488; (928) 367-4290; (800) 573-4031; Fax (928) 367-1247; info@pinetoplakesidechamber.com; www.pinetoplakesidechamber.com*

Prescott • *Prescott C/C & Visitors Info. Center* • David Maurer; CEO; 117 W. Goodwin; P.O. Box 1147; 86302; Yavapai; P 43,280; M 1,150; (928) 445-2000; (800) 266-7534; Fax (928) 445-0068; chamber@prescott.org; www.prescott.org*

Prescott Valley • *Prescott Valley C/C* • Marnie Uhl; Pres./CEO; 3001 N. Main St., Ste. 2A; 86314; Yavapai; P 38,000; M 700; (928) 772-8857; Fax (928) 772-4267; info@pvchamber.org; www.pvchamber.org*

Quartzsite • *Quartzsite Business C/C* • Cee Carnevale; Pres.; P.O. Box 2566; 85346; La Paz; P 3,000; M 200; (928) 927-9321; quartz sitebusinesscoc@tds.net; www.quartzsitebusinesschamber.com*

Queen Creek • *Queen Creek C/C* • Rustyn Sherer; Pres.; P.O. Box 505; 85142; Pinal & Maricopa; P 25,000; M 233; (480) 888-1709; info@queencreekchamber.org; www.queencreekchamber.org

Safford • *Graham County C/C* • Marie Freestone; Pres./CEO; 1111 Thatcher Blvd.; 85546; Graham; P 37,338; M 400; (928) 428-2511; (888) 837-1841; Fax (928) 428-0744; info@graham-chamber.com; www.graham-chamber.com.

Saint Johns • *Saint Johns Reg. C/C* • James Pierson; Exec. Dir.; 180 W. Cleveland; P.O. Box 929; 85936; Apache; P 3,900; M 135; (928) 337-2000; Fax (928) 337-2020; info@stjohnschamber.com; www.stjohnschamber.com

Salome • *McMullen Valley C/C* • P.O. Box 700; 85348; La Paz; P 4,000; M 120; (928) 859-3846; Fax (928) 859-4399; mcmullen coc@tds.net; www.azoutback.com*

San Manuel • *SMOR Tri-Community C/C* • Genevieve Schwandt; Dir.; P.O. Box 416; 85631; Pinal; P 4,500; M 60; (520) 385-9322; Fax (520) 385-9322; smor_1992@netzero.net; www.smorchamber.org

Scottsdale • *Scottsdale Area C/C* • Rick Kidder; Pres./CEO; 4725 N. Scottsdale Rd., Ste. 210; 85251; Maricopa; P 225,000; M 1,500; (480) 355-2700; Fax (480) 355-2710; lnyquist@scottsdalechamber.com; www.scottsdalechamber.com*

Sedona • *Sedona C/C* • Jennifer Wesselhoff; Pres./CEO; P.O. Box 478; 86339; Coconino & Yavapai; P 18,000; M 1,020; (928) 204-1123; (928) 282-7722; Fax (928) 204-1064; info@sedonachamber.com; www.visitsedona.com*

Show Low • *Show Low C/C & Tourist Info. Center* • Gordon Kearl; Exec. Dir.; 81 E. Deuce of Clubs; 85901; Navajo; P 12,500; M 500; (928) 537-2326; (888) SHOW-LOW; Fax (928) 532-7610; info@showlowchamberofcommerce.com; www.showlow chamberofcommerce.com*

Sierra Vista • *Greater Sierra Vista Area C/C* • Susan Tegmeyer; Pres./CEO; 21 E. Wilcox Dr.; 85635; Cochise; P 43,000; M 771; (520) 458-6940; Fax (520) 452-0878; info@sierravistachamber.org; www.sierravistachamber.org*

Snowflake • *Snowflake-Taylor C/C* • Greg Hudson; Exec. Dir.; 113 N. Main St., Ste. A; 85937; Navajo; P 10,000; M 350; (928) 536-4331; Fax (928) 536-5656; info@snowflaketaylorchamber.org; www.snowflaketaylorchamber.org*

Sonoita • *Sonoita-Elgin C/C* • Tom Rogos; Pres.; P.O. Box 607; 85637; Santa Cruz; P 3,000; M 100; (520) 455-5498; www.sonoitaelginchamber.org

Springerville • *Springerville-Eagar Reg. C/C* • Becki Christensen; Dir.; 418 E. Main St.; P.O. Box 31; 85938; Apache; P 8,000; M 275; (928) 333-2123; (866) 733-2123; Fax (928) 333-5690; info@springerville-eager.com; www.springerville-eagarchamber.com

Strawberry • *see Payson*

Sun City • *see Surprise*

Sun City West • *see Surprise*

Superior • *Superior C/C* • Pete Casillas; Pres.; 230 Main St.; P.O. Box 95; 85173; Pinal; P 3,200; M 59; (520) 689-0200; Fax (520) 689-0200; support@superiorarizonachamber.org; www.superiorarizonachamber.org

Surprise • *Surprise Reg. C/C* • David Moss; Pres./CEO; 16126 N. Civic Center Plaza; 85374; Maricopa; P 109,000; M 750; (623) 583-0692; Fax (623) 583-0694; chamber@surpriseregionalchamber.com; www.surpriseregionalchamber.com*

Taylor • *see Snowflake*

Tempe • *Tempe C/C* • Mary Ann Miller; Pres./CEO; 909 E. Apache Blvd.; P.O. Box 28500; 85285; Maricopa; P 165,000; M 1,000; (480) 967-7891; Fax (480) 966-5365; info@tempechamber.org; www.tempechamber.org

Tolleson • *see Goodyear*

Tombstone · *Tombstone C/C* · Patrick Greene; Exec. Dir.; P.O. Box 995; 85638; Cochise; P 1,700; M 100; (520) 457-9317; (888) 457-3929; Fax (520) 457-2458; info@tombstonechamber.com; www.tombstonechamber.com

Tonto Basin · *Tonto Basin C/C* · Kathy Meyer; Pres.; 45675 N. Hwy. 188; P.O. Box 687; 85553; Gila; P 2,000; M 45; (928) 479-2839; (800) 404-8923; kathy.meyer56@gmail.com; www.tontobasinchamber.org

Tubac · *Tubac C/C* · Kim Etherington; Exec. Dir.; P.O. Box 1866; 85646; Santa Cruz; P 1,100; M 120; (520) 398-2704; Fax (520) 398-1704; assistance@tubacaz.com; www.tubacaz.com

Tucson Area

Northern Pima County C/C · Ramon A. Gaanderse; Pres./CEO; 200 W. Magee Rd., Ste. 120; 85704; Pima; P 210,000; M 600; (520) 297-2191; Fax (520) 742-7960; president@the-chamber.com; www.the-chamber.com*

Tucson Hispanic C/C · Lea Marquez Peterson; Pres./CEO; 4420 E. Speedway Blvd., Ste. 101; 85712; Pima; P 1,000,000; M 600; (520) 620-0005; office@tucsonhispanicchamber.org; www.tucsonhispanicchamber.org*

Tucson Metropolitan C/C · John Camper CCE; Pres./CEO; 465 W. St. Mary's Rd.; P.O. Box 991; 85702; Pima; P 1,000,000; M 2,000; (520) 792-1212; (520) 792-2250; Fax (520) 882-5704; jcamper@tucsonchamber.org; www.tucsonchamber.org

Wickenburg · *Wickenburg C/C* · Julia Brooks; Exec. Dir.; 216 N. Frontier St.; 85390; Maricopa; P 10,000; M 579; (928) 684-5479; (928) 684-0977; Fax (928) 684-5470; info@wickenburgchamber.com; www.wickenburgchamber.com*

Willcox · *Willcox C/C & Ag.* · Kathy Smith; Exec. Dir.; 1500 N. Circle I Rd.; 85643; Cochise; P 3,900; M 135; (520) 384-2272; (800) 200-2272; Fax (520) 384-0293; willcoxchamber@vtc.net; www.willcoxchamber.com

Williams · *Williams-Grand Canyon C/C* · Rhonda Damjanovich; Pres./CEO; 200 W. Railroad Ave.; 86046; Coconino; P 3,000; M 225; (928) 635-1418; Fax (928) 635-1417; info@williamschamber.com; www.williamschamber.com*

Winkelman · *see Kearny*

Winslow · *Winslow C/C & Visitors Center* · Bob Hall; Exec. Dir.; 523 W. 2nd St.; P.O. Box 460; 86047; Navajo; P 10,500; M 230; (928) 289-2434; Fax (928) 289-5660; winslowchamber@cableone.net; www.winslowarizona.org

Yarnell · *Yarnell-Peeples Valley C/C* · Vicki Velasquez; Pres.; P.O. Box 275; 85362; Yavapai; P 1,500; M 85; (928) 427-6582; (928) 427-6262; visitus@y-pvchamber.com; www.y-pvchamber.com

Youngtown · *see Surprise*

Yuma · *Yuma County C/C* · Ken Rosevear; Exec. Dir.; 180 W. First St., Ste. A; 85364; Yuma; P 200,000; M 1,000; (928) 782-2567; Fax (928) 343-0038; info@yumachamber.org; www.yumachamber.org

Arkansas

Arkansas State C of C · Randy Zook; Pres./CEO; 1200 W. Capitol; Little Rock; 72201; Pulaski; P 2,800,000; M 1,200; (501) 372-2222; Fax (501) 372-2722; jthatcher@arkansasstatechamber.com; www.arkansasstatechamber.com

Altus · *Altus C/C* · Tom Sexton; Pres.; 125 W. Main; P.O. Box 404; 72821; Franklin; P 817; M 20; (479) 468-4684; Fax (479) 468-4684

Arkadelphia · *Arkadelphia Area C/C* · Connie D. Nelson; Exec. Dir.; 2401 Pine St., Ste. B; P.O. Box 38; 71923; Clark; P 10,900; M 257; (870) 246-5542; Fax (870) 246-1462; cnelson@arkadelphiaalliance.com; www.arkadelphia.org*

Arkansas City · *Arkansas City C/C* · Carolyn Blissett; Pres.; P.O. Box 369; 71630; Desha; P 560; M 40; (870) 877-2306; Fax (870) 877-2306

Ash Flat · *see Highland*

Ashdown · *Little River C/C* · Jill Turner; Dir.; P.O. Box 160; 71822; Little River; P 14,000; M 130; (870) 898-2758; Fax (870) 898-6699; lrcoc0436@sbcglobal.net; www.littlerivercounty.org

Augusta · *Augusta Area C/C* · Regina Burkett; Pres.; 115 S. 2nd St.; 72006; Woodruff; P 2,700; M 30; (870) 347-1802

Bald Knob · *Bald Knob Area C/C* · Bertie Yates; Ofc. Mgr.; 411 S. Elm; P.O. Box 338; 72010; White; P 3,500; M 125; (501) 724-3140; Fax (501) 724-3140; baldknobchamber@centurytel.net; www.baldknobchamber.com

Batesville · *Batesville Area C/C* · Crystal Johnson; Pres./CEO; 409 Vine St.; 72501; Independence; P 10,000; M 600; (870) 793-2378; Fax (870) 793-3061; info@mybatesville.org; www.mybatesville.org*

Beebe · *Beebe C/C* · Dr. Ruth Couch; Dir.; 321 N. Elm; 72012; White; P 6,921; M 105; (501) 882-8135; Fax (501) 882-8140; chamber@beebeark.org; www.beebeark.org

Benton · *Benton Area C/C* · Eddie Black; Exec. Dir.; 607 N. Market St., 72015; Saline, P 27,712, M 625, (501) 315-8272, Fax (501) 315-8290; reception@bentonchamber.com; www.bentonchamber.com*

Bentonville · *Bentonville/Bella Vista C/C* · Ed Clifford; Pres./CEO; 200 E. Central; P.O. Box 330; 72712; Benton; P 30,000; M 934; (479) 273-2841; Fax (479) 273-2180; esanders@bbvchamber.com; www.bbvchamber.com.*

Berryville · *Berryville C/C* · Ginger Oaks; Dir.; P.O. Box 402; 72616; Carroll; P 4,600; M 160; (870) 423-3704; chamber@hbeark.com; www.berryvillear.com

Blytheville · *Greater Blytheville Area C/C* · Elizabeth Smith; Exec. Dir.; 300 W. Walnut; P.O. Box 485; 72316; Mississippi; P 22,000; M 300; (870) 762-2012; Fax (870) 762-0551; info@blythevillegosnell.com; www.greaterblytheville.com

Booneville · *South Logan County C/C* · 210 E. Main St.; P.O. Box 55; 72927; Logan; P 4,300; M 135; (479) 675-2666; Fax (479) 675-5158; information1@booneville.com; www.booneville.com

Bradley · *Bradley C/C* · Joe Middlebrooks; Pres.; P.O. Box 662; 71826; Lafayette; P 575; M 85; (870) 894-3554; Fax (870) 894-3554; deloisdm@yahoo.com

Brinkley · *Brinkley C/C* · Lynda Roche; Exec. Asst.; 217 W. Cypress; 72021; Monroe; P 3,000; M 93; (870) 734-2262; Fax (870) 589-2020; brinkleychamber@sbcglobal.net; www.brinkleychamber.com

Bryant · *Bryant C/C* · Rae Ann Fields; Exec. Dir.; P.O. Box 261; 72089; Saline; P 17,174; M 407; (501) 847-4702; Fax (501) 847-7576; bryantcofc@aristotle.net; www.bryant-ar.com*

Bull Shoals · *Bull Shoals Lake-White River C/C* · P.O. Box 354; 72619; Marion; P 2,000; M 150; (870) 445-4443; (800) 447-1290; havefun@bullshoals.org; www.bullshoals.org

Cabot · *Cabot C/C* · Billye Everett; Exec. Dir.; 110 S. First St.; 72023; Lonoke; P 25,000; M 400; (501) 843-2136; chamber@cabotcc.org; www.cabotcc.org*

Calico Rock · *Calico Rock-Pineville Trade Area C/C* · Rebecca Greenwood; Pres.; 102 Main St.; 72519; Izard; P 992; M 50; (870) 297-4129; www.calicorock.us

Camden • *Camden Area C/C* • Beth Osteen; Exec. Dir.; 314 Adams S.W.; P.O. Box 99; 71711; Ouachita; P 13,154; M 300; (870) 836-6426; Fax (870) 836-6400; info@camdenareachamberofcommerce.org; www.teamcamden.com*

Cave City • *Cave City C/C* • Ed Kegley; Pres.; P.O. Box 274; 72521; Independence & Sharp; P 1,900; M 40; (870) 283-7040; www.cavecityarkansas.info

Charleston • *Charleston C/C* • Alice Wood; Pres.; P.O. Box 456; 72933; Franklin; P 2,965; M 55; (479) 965-2201; Fax (479) 965-2205; www.aboutcharleston.com

Cherokee Village • *see Highland*

Clarendon • *Clarendon C/C* • Susan Caplener; Secy.; P.O. Box 153; 72029; Monroe; P 1,960; M 38; (870) 747-5414; (870) 747-3802; www.clarendon-ar.com

Clarksville • *Clarksville-Johnson County C/C* • Vicki Lyons; Exec. Dir.; 101 N. Johnson; 72830; Johnson; P 8,000; M 200; (479) 754-2340; Fax (479) 754-4923; cjccofc@centurytel.net; www.clarksvillearchamber.com*

Clinton • *Clinton Area C/C* • Kathy Sherwood; Dir.; 214 Griggs St.; P.O. Box 52; 72031; Van Buren; P 24,000; M 200; (501) 745-6500; cltchamber@artelco.com; www.clintonchamber.com

Conway • *Conway Area C/C* • Brad Lacy; Pres./CEO; 900 Oak St.; 72032; Faulkner; P 60,000; M 1,500; (501) 327-7788; Fax (501) 327-7790; getsmart@conwayarkansas.org; www.conwayarkansas.org*

Corning • *Corning Area C/C* • Barry Sellers; Dir.; 1621 W. Main St.; P.O. Box 93; 72422; Clay; P 3,600; M 100; (870) 857-3874; Fax (870) 857-3874; corning72422@hotmail.com; www.corningarchamber.org

Cotter • *Cotter Area C/C* • Gary Flippin; P.O. Box 489; 72626; Baxter; P 1,000; M 120; (870) 321-1243; chamber@cotterarkansas.com; www.cotterarkansas.com

Crossett • *Crossett Area C/C* • Pam Ferguson; Exec. Dir.; 101 W. First Ave.; 71635; Ashley; P 13,000; M 170; (870) 364-6591; Fax (870) 364-7488; pam_ferguson@windstream.net; www.crossettchamber.org

Danville • *Danville Area C/C* • Sheila Thomas; Pres./CEO; P.O. Box 1140; 72833; Yell; P 2,500; M 70; (479) 495-3419; Fax (479) 495-3347; danark@danark.com; www.danark.com

Dardanelle • *Dardanelle C/C* • Vicki Sutton; Exec. Dir.; 2011 State Hwy. 22 W.; P.O. Box 208; 72834; Yell; P 4,228; M 125; (479) 229-3328; Fax (479) 229-5086; vsdardchamber@hotmail.com; www.dardanellechamber.com

Decatur • *Decatur C/C* • Royce Johnson; Pres.; 18032 Bethlehem Rd.; 72722; Benton; P 1,350; M 30; (479) 752-8460

DeQueen • *DeQueen/Sevier County C/C* • Patty Sharp; Pres.; 315 W. Stillwell; P.O. Box 67; 71832; Sevier; P 18,000; M 155; (870) 584-3225; Fax (870) 642-7959; dqscoc@ipa.net; www.dequeenchamberofcommerce.com

Dermott • *Dermott Area C/C* • Frank Henry Jr.; Exec. Dir.; P.O. Box 147; 71638; Chicot; P 4,000; M 100; (870) 538-5656; Fax (870) 538-5493; email@dermottchamber.com; www.dermottchamber.com

Des Arc • *Des Arc C/C* • Paul Dickson; P.O. Box 845; 72040; Prairie; P 2,000; M 30; (870) 256-3600; www.desarcchamber.com

DeWitt • *DeWitt C/C* • David Horton; Pres.; P.O. Box 366; 72042; Arkansas; P 3,500; M 125; (870) 946-4666; david.horton.b2wn@statefarm.com; www.dewittchamberofcommerce.com

Diamond City • *Diamond City Area C/C* • Katie deSilva; Pres.; P.O. Box 1161; 72630; Boone; P 730; M 54; (870) 422-7575; dchamber@diamondcity.net; www.diamondcitychamber.com

Dierks • *Dierks C/C* • Wes Howard; Pres.; P.O. Box 292; 71833; Howard; P 1,263; M 40; (870) 286-2019; dierkschamberofcommerce.com

Dover • *Dover C/C* • Sandra Drittler; Bd. Member; P.O. Box 731; 72837; Pope; P 1,500; M 130; (479) 967-2838; Fax (479) 331-4151; drittler3@hotmail.com

Dumas • *Dumas C/C* • Sammye Owen; Exec. Dir.; 165 S. Main St.; P.O. Box 431; 71639; Desha; P 5,000; M 120; (870) 382-5447; Fax (870) 382-3031; dumaschamber@centurytel.net; www.dumasar.net

El Dorado • *El Dorado C/C* • Don Wales; Pres./CEO; 111 W. Main; 71730; Union; P 21,530; M 800; (870) 863-6113; Fax (870) 863-6115; info@goeldorado.com; www.goeldorado.com

Eudora • *Eudora C/C* • Barbara Knapp; 185 S. Main; P.O. Box 325; 71640; Chicot; P 2,900; M 40; (870) 355-8443; Fax (870) 355-8443; eudoracofc@sbcglobal.net

Eureka Springs • *Greater Eureka Springs C/C* • Jess Feldman; Pres.; 516 Village Cir.; P.O. Box 551; 72632; Carroll; P 2,278; M 500; (479) 253-8737; (800) 6-EUREKA; Fax (479) 253-5037; info@eurekaspringschamber.com; www.eurekaspringschamber.com

Fairfield Bay • *Fairfield Bay Area C/C* • Robbie Ingle; Exec. Dir.; 383 Dave Creek Pkwy., Ste. C; P.O. Box 1159; 72088; Cleburne & Van Buren; P 2,600; M 255; (501) 884-3324; Fax (501) 884-6250; ffb@ffbchamber.org; www.ffbchamber.org

Farmington • *Farmington C/C* • Joe Bailey; Pres.; P.O. Box 1152; 72730; Washington; P 4,814; M 100; (479) 267-2368; contact@farmingtonchamberofcommerce.com; www.farmingtonchamberofcommerce.com

Fayetteville • *Fayetteville C/C* • Steve Clark; Pres./CEO; 123 W. Mountain St.; P.O. Box 4216; 72702; Washington; P 60,018; M 1,500; (479) 521-1710; Fax (479) 521-1791; sclark@fayettevillear.com; www.fayettevillear.com*

Flippin • *Flippin C/C* • Claudia Hicks; P.O. Box 118; 72634; Marion; P 1,400; M 75; (870) 453-8480; chicks@tlcbank.net; www.flippinchamber.com

Fordyce • *Fordyce C/C* • Barbara Finley; Exec. Dir.; 119 W. 3rd St.; P.O. Box 588; 71742; Dallas; P 4,799; M 150; (870) 352-3520; Fax (870) 352-8090; fordyce@ipa.net

Forrest City • *Forrest City Area C/C* • David Dunn; Exec. Dir.; 203 N. Izard; 72335; St. Francis; P 14,700; M 200; (870) 633-1651; Fax (870) 633-9500; info@forrestcitychamber.com; www.forrestcitychamber.com

Fort Smith • *Fort Smith Reg. C/C* • Paul Harvel; Pres./CEO; 612 Garrison Ave.; 72901; Crawford, Franklin & Sebastian; P 290,000; M 1,100; (479) 783-3111; Fax (479) 783-6110; info@fortsmithchamber.com; www.fortsmithchamber.com*

Gentry • *Gentry C/C–MainStreet* • Bev Saunders; Dir.; P.O. Box 642; 72734; Benton; P 2,200; M 70; (479) 736-2358; Fax (479) 736-2877; info@gentrychamber.com; www.gentrychamber.com

Glenwood • *Glenwood Reg. C/C* • Verna Cantrell; Pres.; 73 Hwy. 70 E.; P.O. Box 2006; 71943; Pike; P 10,000; M 120; (870) 356-5266; (870) 223-3402; Fax (870) 356-5266; glenwoodchamber@yahoo.com; www.glenwoodarkansaschamber.com

Gravette • *Greater Gravette C/C* • Patrick Hall; Exec. Dir.; P.O. Box 112; 72736; Benton; P 2,500; M 68; (479) 790-7296; www.gravettearkansas.com

Green Forest • *Green Forest C/C* • Tammy Goins; Pres.; P.O. Box 376; 72638; Carroll; P 2,600; M 100; (870) 438-5866; www.greenforestchamber.com

Greenbrier • *Greenbrier C/C* • Jon Patrom; P.O. Box 418; 72058; Faulkner; P 3,200; M 120; (501) 679-4009; info@greenbrier chamber.org; www.greenbrierchamber.org

Greenwood • *Greenwood C/C* • P.O. Box 511; 72936; Sebastian; P 7,000; M 200; (479) 996-6357; Fax (479) 996-1162; info@ greenwoodchamber.net; www.greenwoodarkansas.com

Greers Ferry • *Greers Ferry Area C/C* • Jody Corpier; Pres.; P.O. Box 1354; 72067; Cleburne; P 2,000; M 145; (501) 825-7188; (888) 825-7199; Fax (501) 825-6782; info@greersferry.com; www.greersferry.com

Gurdon • *Gurdon C/C* • David Williams; Pres.; P.O. Box 187; 71743; Clark; P 2,300; M 35; (870) 353-2661; www.gurdon chamberofcommerce.com

Hamburg • *Hamburg Area C/C* • Jennifer Foote; Exec. Dir.; 200 E. Lincoln St.; P.O. Box 460; 71646; Ashley; P 3,098; M 100; (870) 853-8345; Fax (870) 853-8345; hamburgchamber@sbcglobal.net; www.hamburgark.com

Hardy • *see Highland*

Harrisburg • *Harrisburg Area C/C* • Mildred Traynom; Secy./ Treas.; P.O. Box 265; 72432; Poinsett; P 5,500; M 60; (870) 578-5461; Fax (870) 578-4113; www.harrisburgchamber.com

Harrison • *Harrison Reg. C/C* • Patty Methvin; Pres./CEO; 621 E. Rush Ave.; 72601; Boone; P 37,000; M 475; (870) 741-2659; (800) 880-6265; Fax (870) 741-9059; cocinfo@harrison-chamber.com; www.harrison-chamber.com*

Hazen • *Hazen C/C* • Bob Juola; Pres.; P.O. Box 907; 72064; Prairie; P 1,800; M 35; (870) 255-3352

Heber Springs • *Heber Springs Area C/C* • Melisa Gardner; Comm. Rel. Dir.; 1001 W. Main St.; 72543; Cleburne; P 20,000; M 400; (501) 362-2444; chamber@heber-springs.com; www. heber-springs.com*

Helena • *Phillips County C/C* • Dustin Loseke; Pres.; 111 Hickory Hill Dr.; P.O. Box 447; 72342; Phillips; P 24,309; M 210; (870) 338-8327; Fax (870) 338-8882; info@phillipscountychamber.org; www. phillipscountychamber.org*

Highland • *Spring River Area C/C* • Beth McEntire-Bess; Pres.; 2852D Hwy. 62/412; 72542; Sharp; P 6,000; M 130; (870) 856-3210; (870) 994-7324; Fax (870) 856-3320; sracc@centurytel.net; www.sracc.com*

Hope • *Hope-Hempstead County C/C* • Mark Keith; Dir.; 101 W. 2nd; P.O. Box 250; 71802; Hempstead; P 23,587; M 275; (870) 777-3640; Fax (870) 722-6154; hopeark@arkansas.net; www. hopemelonfest.com*

Horseshoe Bend • *Horseshoe Bend Area C/C* • 811 2nd St., Ste. 18; P.O. Box 4083; 72512; Fulton, Izard & Sharp; P 2,278; M 110; (870) 670-5433; info@horseshoebendar.info; www.horseshoe bendarcc.com

Hot Springs • *Greater Hot Springs C/C* • Dave Byerly; Pres.; 659 Ouachita; P.O. Box 6090; 71902; Garland; P 96,000; M 1,122; (501) 321-1700; Fax (501) 321-3551; info@hotspringschamber.com; www.hotspringschamber.com*

Hot Springs Village • *Hot Springs Village Area C/C* • Lee Ann Branch; Exec. Dir.; 4585 Hwy. 7 N., Ste. 9; P.O. Box 8575; 71910; Garland & Saline; P 14,500; M 267; (501) 915-9940; (877) 915-9940; Fax (501) 984-9961; hsvchamber@suddenlinkmail.com; www.hotspringsvillagechamber.com*

Huntsville • *Huntsville Area C/C* • David Pemberton; Exec. Dir.; 113 E. Main; P.O. Box 950; 72740; Madison; P 2,000; M 60; (479) 738-6000; Fax (479) 738-6000; chamber@madisoncounty.net; www.huntsvillearchamber.com

Jacksonville • *Jacksonville C/C* • Amy Mattison; CEO; 200 Dupree Dr.; 72076; Pulaski; P 30,900; M 400; (501) 982-1511; Fax (501) 982-1464; chamber@jacksonville-arkansas.com; www. jacksonville-arkansas.com

Jasper • *Jasper/Newton County C/C* • Nancy Atkinson; Pres.; 204 N. Spring St.; P.O. Box 250; 72641; Newton; P 8,800; M 165; (870) 446-2455; (800) 670-7792; Fax (870) 446-2477; chamber@ ritternet.com; www.theozarkmountains.com

Jonesboro • *Jonesboro Reg. C/C* • Mark Young; Pres./CEO; 1709 E. Nettleton Ave.; P.O. Box 789; 72403; Craighead; P 66,194; M 1,251; (870) 932-6691; Fax (870) 933-5758; donnah@jones borochamber.com; www.jonesborochamber.com*

Lake Village • *Lake Village C/C* • Brianne Connelly; Exec. Dir.; 111 Main St.; P.O. Box 752; 71653; Chicot; P 4,000; M 100; (870) 265-5997; Fax (870) 265-5254; lvccdirector@sbcglobal.net; www.lakevillagechamber.com

Lincoln • *Lincoln Area C/C* • Earl Hunton; Pres.; P.O. Box 942; 72744; Washington; P 1,804; M 52; lincolnareacofc.com

Little Rock • *Little Rock Reg. C/C* • Jay Chesshir CCE; Pres.; 1 Chamber Plaza; 72201; Faulkner, Pulaski & Saline; P 652,834; M 1,710; (501) 374-2001; Fax (501) 374-6018; chamber@ littlerockchamber.com; www.littlerockchamber.com

Lonoke • *Lonoke Area C/C* • John Garner; Mgr.; 102 1/2 N.W. Front St.; P.O. Box 294; 72086; Lonoke; P 4,800; M 151; (501) 676-4399; Fax (501) 676-4399; jgarner@lonokeidc.com; www.lonoke.com

Lowell • *see Rogers*

Magnolia • *Magnolia-Columbia County C/C* • Cammie Hambrice; Dir.; 529 E. Main; P.O. Box 866; 71754; Columbia; P 30,000; M 350; (870) 234-4352; Fax (870) 234-9291; ea@ ccalliance.us; www.magnoliachamber.com

Malvern • *Malvern & Hot Spring County C/C* • Nikki Cranford Thornton; Exec. Dir.; 213 W. 3rd St.; P.O. Box 266; 72104; Hot Spring; P 30,000; M 300; (501) 332-2721; Fax (501) 332-8558; president@malvernchamber.com; www.malvernchamber.com

Mammoth Spring • *Mammoth Spring C/C* • Steve Russell; Pres.; P.O. Box 185; 72554; Fulton; P 1,147; M 43; (870) 625-3518; mammothspring@arkansas.gov; www.mammothspringar.com

Mansfield • *Mansfield-Huntington Area C/C* • P.O. Box 307; 72944; Sebastian; P 1,800; M 90; (479) 928-5552; www.mansfield arkansas.com

Marianna • *Marianna-Lee County C/C* • Steve Gabbie; Pres.; 67 W. Main St.; P.O. Box 584; 72360; Lee; P 5,181; M 150; (870) 295-2469; Fax (870) 295-6207; www.mariannaarkansas.org

Marked Tree • *Marked Tree C/C* • 1 Elm St.; 72365; Poinsett; P 2,800; M 100; (870) 358-3000; Fax (870) 358-7867; www. markedtreearkansas.org

Marshall • *Greater Searcy County C/C* • Jack Treat; Dir.; P.O. Box 1385; 72650; Searcy; P 7,800; M 130; (870) 448-2557; Fax (870) 448-4858; webmaster@searcycountyarkansas.org; www. searcycountyarkansas.org

Maumelle • *Maumelle Area C/C* • Pam Rantisi; Exec. Dir.; 115 Audubon Dr., Ste. 14; P.O. Box 13099; 72113; Pulaski; P 15,200; M 356; (501) 851-9700; Fax (501) 851-6690; execdir@maumelle chamber.com; www.maumellechamber.com*

McGehee • *McGehee C/C* • Paula Mote; Secy.; 901 Holly St.; P.O. Box 521; 71654; Desha; P 4,750; M 130; (870) 222-4451; Fax (870) 222-5729; admin@mcgeheechamber.com; www.mcgeheechamber.com

Mena • *Mena/Polk County Area C/C* • Joey Cathey; Pres.; 524 Sherwood Ave.; 71953; Polk; P 22,000; M 260; (479) 394-2912; chamberofcommerce2@sbcglobal.net; menapolkchamber.com

Monticello • *Monticello/Drew County C/C* • Glenda Nichols; Exec. Dir.; 335 E. Gaines; 71655; Drew; P 18,723; M 200; (870) 367-6741; Fax (870) 367-0050; monticellochamber@sbcglobal. net; www.montdrewchamber.com

Morrilton • *Morrilton Area C/C* • John Gibson; Pres.; 120 N. Division St.; P.O. Box 589; 72110; Conway; P 6,550; M 325; (501) 354-2393; Fax (501) 354-8642; johngibson@suddenlinkmail.com; www.morrilton.com.*

Mount Ida • *Mount Ida Area C/C* • Maureen Walther; Exec. Dir.; 241 Hwy. 270 W.; P.O. Box 6; 71957; Montgomery; P 10,000; M 175; (870) 867-2723; Fax (870) 867-2723; director@mtida chamber.com; www.mtidachamber.com

Mountain Home • *Mountain Home C/C* • Eddie Majeste; Exec. Dir.; 1023 Hwy. 62 E.; P.O. Box 488; 72654; Baxter; P 30,000; M 750; (870) 425-5111; (800) 822-3536; Fax (870) 425-4446; salms@ EnjoyMountainHome.com; www.EnjoyMountainHome.com*

Mountain View • *Mountain View Area C/C* • Michalle Coon; Exec. Dir.; 107 N. Peabody Ave.; P.O. Box 133; 72560; Stone; P 2,900; M 190; (870) 269-8068; (888) 679-2859; Fax (870) 269-8748; mvchamber@mvtel.net; www.yourplaceinthemountains.com

Murfreesboro • *Murfreesboro C/C* • Doug Shuckers; P.O. Box 166; 71958; Pike; P 2,000; M 80; (870) 285-3131; Fax (870) 285-3131; murfreesboro.chamber@yahoo.com; www.murfreesboroark.com

Nashville • *Nashville C/C* • 107 S. Main St.; P.O. Box 1506; 71852; Howard; P 5,000; M 140; (870) 845-1262; Fax (870) 845-1262; nashvillecc@sbcglobal.net; www.nashvillear.com

Newark • *Newark Area C/C* • Brian Pruett; Secy.; 212 E. 4th St.; P.O. Box 222; 72562; Independence; P 1,250; M 50; (870) 799-8888; Fax (870) 799-8493

Newport • *Newport Area C/C* • Julie Allen; Exec. Dir.; 201 Hazel St.; 72112; Jackson; P 7,811; M 250; (870) 523-3618; director@ newportarchamber.org; www.newportarchamber.org*

North Little Rock • *North Little Rock C/C* • Terry C. Hartwick; Pres./CEO; 100 Main St.; P.O. Box 5288; 72119; Pulaski; P 60,000; M 1,200; (501) 372-5959; Fax (501) 372-5955; nlrchamber@ nlrchamber.org; www.nlrchamber.org.*

Osceola • *Osceola-South Mississippi County C/C* • Eric Golde; Exec. Dir.; 116 N. Maple; P.O. Box 174; 72370; Mississppi; P 50,000; M 200; (870) 563-2281; Fax (870) 563-5385; osceolachamber@ sbcglobal.net; www.osceolachamber.net

Ozark • *Ozark Area C/C* • Fred Romo; Dir.; 300 W. Commercial St.; 72949; Franklin; P 3,700; M 200; (479) 667-2525; (800) 951-2525; Fax (479) 667-5750; ozarkareacoc@centurytel.net; www. ozarkareacoc.org

Paragould • *Paragould Reg. C/C* • Sue McGowan; CEO; 300 W. Court St.; P.O. Box 124; 72450; Greene; P 24,000; M 778; (870) 236-7684; Fax (870) 236-7142; smcgowan@paragould.org; www.paragould.org*

Paris • *Paris Area C/C* • Linda Hixson; Exec. Dir.; 301 W. Walnut; 72855; Logan; P 3,707; M 175; (479) 963-2244; Fax (479) 963-8321; pariscoc@gmail.com; www.parisaronline.com

Piggott • *Piggott C/C* • Lynette Cale; Secy.; 100 W. Main St.; P.O. Box 96; 72454; Clay; P 3,980; M 80; (870) 598-3167; Fax (870) 598-3955; pchamber@piggott.net; www.piggottchamber.org

Pine Bluff • *Greater Pine Bluff C/C* • Lou Ann Nisbett; Pres./ CEO; 510 Main St.; P.O. Box 5069; 71611; Jefferson; P 50,000; M 700; (870) 535-0110; Fax (870) 535-1643; nisbett@pinebluff chamber.com; www.pinebluffchamber.com*

Pocahontas • *Randolph County C/C* • Tim Scott; Exec. Dir.; 107 E. Everett; P.O. Box 466; 72455; Randolph; P 18,195; M 200; (870) 892-3956; Fax (870) 892-5399; chamber010@centurytel.net; www.randolphchamber.com*

Prairie Grove • *Prairie Grove C/C* • Natalie Bartholomew; Pres.; P.O. Box 23; 72753; Washington; P 2,800; M 40; (479) 846-2197; info@pgchamber.com; www.pgchamber.com

Prescott • *Prescott-Nevada County C/C* • Brandy Jones; Dir.; 116 E. 2nd S.; P.O. Box 307; 71857; Nevada; P 10,000; M 120; (870) 887-2101; Fax (870) 887-5317; bjones@pnpartnership.org; www. pnpartnership.org

Rector • *Rector Area C/C* • Ron Kemp; Pres.; P.O. Box 307; 72461; Clay; P 2,107; M 60; (870) 595-3035; Fax (870) 595-3611; rector communitydevelopment@centurytel.net; www.rectorarkansas.com

Rogers • *Rogers-Lowell Area C/C* • Raymond M. Burns CCE; Pres./CEO; 317 W. Walnut; 72756; Benton; P 55,000; M 2,100; (479) 636-1240; Fax (479) 636-5485; info@rogerslowell.com; www.rogerslowell.com*

Russellville • *Russellville Area C/C* • Jeff Pipkin; Pres./CEO; 708 W. Main St.; 72801; Pope; P 85,000; M 1,055; (479) 968-2530; Fax (479) 968-5894; chamber@russellville.org; www.russell villechamber.org*

Salem • *Salem C/C* • Holly Pate; Pres.; P.O. Box 649; 72576; Fulton; P 1,574; M 90; (870) 895-5565; chamber@salemar.com; www.salemar.com

Searcy • *Searcy Reg. C/C* • Buck C. Layne Jr. CEcD; Pres.; 2323 S. Main St.; 72143; White; P 50,000; M 800; (501) 268-2458; Fax (501) 268-9530; scc@searcychamber.com; www.searcychamber.com*

Sheridan • *Grant County C/C* • Becky Nichols; Exec. Secy.; 202 N. Oak St.; 72150; Grant; P 16,000; M 151; (870) 942-3021; Fax (870) 942-3378; gccc@windstream.net; www.grantcountychamber.com*

Sherwood • *Sherwood C/C* • Katelyn Rash; Exec. Dir.; 2303 E. Lee St.; P.O. Box 6082; 72124; Pulaski; P 30,000; M 250; (501) 835-7600; Fax (501) 835-2326; shwdchamber@att.net; www. sherwoodchamber.net*

Siloam Springs • *Siloam Springs C/C* • Wayne Mays; Pres./CEO; 108 E. University; P.O. Box 476; 72761; Benton; P 14,000; M 395; (479) 524-6466; Fax (479) 549-3032; info@siloamchamber.com; www.siloamchamber.com*

Smackover • *Smackover C/C* • Tommie Sue Fleming; Mgr.; 710 Pershing Hwy.; P.O. Box 275; 71762; Union; P 2,500; M 84; (870) 725-3521; (870) 944-0221; Fax (870) 725-3521; smkovrcofc@ sbcglobal.net; www.smackoverar.com

Springdale • *Springdale C/C* • Perry Webb; Pres./CEO; 202 W. Emma St.; P.O. Box 166; 72765; Benton & Washington; P 65,000; M 955; (479) 872-2222; (800) 972-7261; Fax (479) 751-4699; info@chamber.springdale.com; www.springdale.com*

Stamps • *Stamps C/C* • Rose Wiegand; Secy.; P.O. Box 274; 71860; Lafayette; P 2,200; M 40; (870) 533-4771; Fax (870) 533-4788

Star City • *Star City C/C* • P.O. Box 88; 71667; Lincoln; P 2,500; M 100; (870) 628-3100; Fax (870) 628-9943; starcitychamber@ yahoo.com; www.stardazefestival.com

Stephens • *Stephens C/C* • Margie L. Wagnon; Secy./Mgr.; 105 N. First St.; P.O. Box 572; 71764; Ouachita; P 1,300; M 34; (870) 786-5221; Fax (870) 786-5749

Stuttgart • *Stuttgart C/C* • Stephen Bell; Exec. V.P.; 507 S. Main; P.O. Box 1500; 72160; Arkansas; P 10,000; M 305; (870) 673-1602; Fax (870) 673-1604; stuttgartchamber@centurytel.net; www. stuttgartarkansas.org

Sulphur Springs · *Sulphur Springs Comm. C/C* · P.O. Box 115; 72768; Benton; P 670; M 15; (479) 298-3218

Texarkana · *see Texarkana, TX*

Trumann · *Trumann Area C/C* · Jackie Ross; Exec. Dir.; 225 Hwy. 463; P.O. Box 215; 72472; Poinsett; P 7,600; M 95; (870) 483-5424; Fax (870) 483-6660; tchamber@centurytel.net; www.trumann chamber.com

Tuckerman · *Tuckerman C/C* · Steve Roley; Pres.; Main St., City Hall; P.O. Box 287; 72473; Jackson; P 1,800; M 40; (870) 349-5313; cityoftuckerman@yahoo.com

Van Buren · *Van Buren C/C* · Jackie Krutsch; Exec. Dir.; 510 Main St.; 72956; Crawford; P 18,986; M 335; (479) 474-2761; Fax (479) 474-6259; www.vanburenchamber.org*

Waldron · *Waldron Area C/C* · Jeff Brewer; Pres.; 323 Washington St.; P.O. Box 1985; 72958; Scott; P 10,628; M 125; (479) 637-2775; www.waldronareachamberofcommerce.com

Walnut Ridge · *Lawrence County C/C* · Kathy Bradley; Exec. Secy.; 109 S.W. Front; P.O. Box 842; 72476; Lawrence; P 17,587; M 204; (870) 886-3232; Fax (870) 886-1736; lawrencecofc@ suddenlinkmail.com; www.lawcochamber.org

Ward · *Ward C/C* · 80 S. 2nd St.; P.O. Box 106; 72176; Lonoke; P 2,500; M 90; (501) 843-6533; (501) 843-8348; www.bestof ward.com

Warren · *Bradley County C/C* · David King; Exec. Dir.; 104 N. Myrtle St.; 71671; Bradley; P 12,600; M 240; (870) 226-5225; Fax (870) 226-6285; bcc.warren@sbcglobal.net; www.bradleychamber.com

Watson · *Watson C/C* · Kalvin Fuller; P.O. Box 16; 71674; Desha; P 288; M 48; (870) 866-7666

West Memphis · *West Memphis Area C/C* · Holmes Hammett; Exec. Dir.; 108 W. Broadway; P.O. Box 594; 72303; Crittenden; P 30,000; M 508; (870) 735-1134; Fax (870) 735-6283; wmcoc@ wmcoc.com; www.wmcoc.com*

White Hall · *White Hall C/C* · Janice Acosta; Pres.; P.O. Box 20429; 71612; Jefferson; P 6,000; M 185; (870) 247-5502; white hallarchamber.com

Wynne · *Cross County C/C* · 1790 N. Falls Blvd., Ste. 2; P.O. Box 234; 72396; Cross; P 20,000; M 220; (870) 238-2601; Fax (870) 238-7844; info@crosscountrychamber.com; www.crosscounty chamber.com

Yellville · *Yellville Area C/C* · Carolyn Vigna; P.O. Box 369; 72687; Marion; P 2,000; M 125; (870) 449-4676; chamber@yellville.com; www.yellville.com

California

California C of C · Allan Zaremberg; Pres./CEO; 1215 K St., Ste. 1400; P.O. Box 1736; Sacramento; 95812; Sacramento; P 36,800,000; M 14,000; (916) 444-6670; Fax (916) 325-1272; information@calchamber.com; www.calchamber.com

Acton · *Acton C/C* · Stan Main; Pres.; P.O. Box 81; 93510; Los Angeles; P 12,000; M 200; (661) 478-9604; Fax (661) 269-4121; info@actoncoc.org; www.actoncoc.org

Adelanto · *Adelanto C/C* · Eric Jensen; P.O. Box 712; 92301; San Bernardino; P 28,000; M 200; (760) 246-5711; Fax (760) 246-4019; office@adelantochamber.com; www.adelantochamber.com

Agoura Hills · *Agoura-Oak Park-Conejo Valley-Calabasas C/C* · Mr. Alex Soteras; Dir.; 30101 Agoura Court, Ste. 207; 91301; Los Angeles; P 23,000; M 1,500; (818) 889-3150; Fax (818) 889-3366; info@agourachamber.org; www.agourachamber.org*

Agua Dulce · *see Santa Clarita*

Alameda · *Alameda C/C* · Barbara Marchand; Pres.; 2210-D South Shore Center; 94501; Alameda; P 78,000; M 400; (510) 522-0414; Fax (510) 522-7677; connect@alamedachamber.com; www.alamedachamber.com*

Alamo · *see Danville*

Albany · *Albany C/C* · Joey Luera; Pres.; 1108 Solano Ave.; 94706; Alameda; P 17,311; M 150; (510) 525-1771; Fax (510) 525-1771; albanychamber@albanychamber.org; www.albanychamber.org

Alhambra · *Alhambra C/C* · Owen Guenthard; Exec. Dir.; 104 S. First St.; 91801; Los Angeles; P 90,000; M 530; (626) 282-8481; Fax (626) 282-5596; alhambrachamber@yahoo.com; www.alhambrachamber.org.*

Aliso Viejo · *see Laguna Hills*

Alpine · *Alpine & Mountain Empire C/C* · Patricia Cannon; Pres.; 2157 Alpine Blvd.; 91901; San Diego; P 18,000; M 400; (619) 445-2722; Fax (619) 445-2871; info@alpinechamber.com; www.alpinechamber.com*

Altadena · *Altadena C/C* · C. Jake; Ofc. Mgr.; 730 E. Altadena Dr.; 91001; Los Angeles; P 42,000; M 225; (626) 794-3988; Fax (626) 794-6015; altadenachamber@yahoo.com; abacus-es.com/altadena

Alturas · *Alturas C/C* · Rose Boulade; Pres.; 600 S. Main St.; 96101; Modoc; P 3,000; M 150; (530) 233-4434; Fax (530) 233-5099; contactus@alturaschamber.org; www.alturaschamber.org

Amador County · *see Jackson*

American Canyon · *American Canyon C/C* · Susan Lane; Pres./CEO; 3419 Broadway, Ste. H11; P.O. Box 10114; 94503; Napa; P 16,000; M 325; (707) 552-3650; Fax (707) 552-9724; chamber@ amcanchamber.org; www.amcanchamber.org*

Anaheim · *Anaheim C/C* · Todd Ament; Pres./CEO; 201 E. Center St.; 92805; Orange; P 350,000; M 800; (714) 758-0222; Fax (714) 758-0468; info@anaheimchamber.org; www.anaheimchamber.org*

Anderson · *Anderson C/C* · Debe Hopkins; Mgr.; 2375 North St.; P.O. Box 1144; 96007; Shasta; P 10,000; M 300; (530) 365-8095; Fax (530) 365-4561; info@andersonchamber.net; www.anderson chamber.info*

Angels Camp · *Calaveras County C/C* · Diane Gray; Exec. Dir.; P.O. Box 1145; 95222; Calaveras; P 41,000; M 486; (209) 736-2580; Fax (209) 736-2576; chamber@calaveras.org; www.calaveras.org*

Angwin · *Angwin Comm. Cncl.* · Dennis Watson; Pres.; P.O. Box 747; 94508; Napa; P 3,000; M 400; (707) 965-2867; president@ angwincouncil.org; www.angwincouncil.org

Antelope · *see North Highlands*

Antioch · *Antioch C/C* · Devi Lanphere; Pres./CEO; 101 H St., Ste. 4; 94509; Contra Costa; P 100,000; M 550; (925) 757-1800; Fax (925) 757-5286; info@antiochchamber.com; www.antiochchamber.com*

Anza · *Anza Valley C/C* · Robyn Garrison; Pres.; P.O. Box 391460; 92539; Riverside; P 9,500; M 90; (951) 763-0141; www.anza valleychamber.com

Apple Valley · *Apple Valley C/C* · Janice Moore; Pres./CEO; 16010 Apple Valley Rd.; 92307; San Bernardino; P 75,000; M 450; (760) 242-2753; Fax (760) 242-0303; info@avchamber.org; www.avchamber.org

Aptos · *Aptos C/C* · Karen Hibble; Dir.; 7605-A Old Dominion Ct.; 95003; Santa Cruz; P 32,000; M 675; (831) 688-1467; Fax (831) 688-6961; info@aptoschamber.com; www.aptoschamber.com

Arcadia · *Arcadia C/C* · Beth Costanza; Exec. Dir.; 388 W. Huntington Dr.; 91007; Los Angeles; P 56,000; M 700; (626) 447-2159; Fax (626) 445-0273; info@arcadiacachamber.org; www.arcadiacachamber.org

Arcata · *Arcata C/C* · Brenda Bishop; Exec. Dir./CEO; 1635 Heindon Rd.; 95521; Humboldt; P 22,000; M 400; (707) 822-3619; Fax (707) 822-3515; arcata@arcatachamber.com; www.arcata chamber.com*

Arroyo Grande · *Arroyo Grande Valley C/C* · Judith Bean; Pres./CEO; 800-A West Branch St.; 93420; San Luis Obispo; P 17,000; M 400; (805) 489-1488; Fax (805) 489-2239; info@agchamber. com; www.agchamber.com*

Arvin · *Arvin C/C* · P.O. Box 645; 93203; Kern; P 16,000; M 60; (661) 854-2265; Fax (661) 854-2265; arvinchamberofcommerce@ yahoo.com; www.arvinchamberofcommerce.com

Atascadero · *Atascadero C/C* · Joanne Main; Pres./CEO; 6904 El Camino Real; 93422; San Luis Obispo; P 28,000; M 600; (805) 466-2044; Fax (805) 466-9218; jmain@atascaderochamber.org; atascaderochamber.org*

Atwater · *also see Los Angeles-Atwater Village C/C*

Atwater · *Atwater C/C* · Kayla Moon; Dir. of Finance; 1181 Third St.; 95301; Merced; P 30,000; M 200; (209) 358-4251; Fax (209) 358-0934; chamber@atwaterchamberofcommerce.org; www. atwaterchamberofcommerce.org*

Auburn · *Auburn C/C* · Bruce L. Cosgrove; CEO; 601 Lincoln Way; 95603; Placer; P 65,000; M 630; (530) 885-5616; (800) 971-1888; Fax (530) 885-5854; info@auburnchamber.net; www.auburn chamber.net.*

Avalon · *Catalina Island C/C & Visitors Bur.* · Wayne Griffin; Pres./CEO; #1 Green Pier; P.O. Box 217; 90704; Los Angeles; P 3,500; M 261; (310) 510-1520; Fax (310) 510-7606; info@ catalinachamber.com; www.catalinachamber.com

Azusa · *Azusa C/C* · Irene Villapania; CEO; 240 W. Foothill Blvd.; 91702; Los Angeles; P 45,200; M 200; (626) 334-1507; Fax (626) 334-5217; info@azusachamber.org; www.azusachamber.org*

Badger · *see Miramonte*

Bakersfield Area

Greater Bakersfield C/C · Debra Moreno; Pres./CEO; 1725 Eye St.; P.O. Box 1947; 93303; Kern; P 338,952; M 1,400; (661) 327-4421; Fax (661) 327-8751; info@bakersfieldchamber.org; www. bakersfieldchamber.org.*

Kern County Bd. of Trade · Rick Davis; Exec. Dir.; 2101 Oak St.; 93301; Kern; P 661,000; (661) 868-5376; Fax (661) 861-2017; kerninfo@co.kern.ca.us; www.visitkern.com

North of the River C/C · Stan Shires; Exec. Dir.; P.O. Box 5551; 93388; Kern; P 100,000; M 125; (661) 871-4555; norchamber@ bak.rr.com; www.norchamber.org

Banning · *Banning C/C* · Jim Smith; P.O. Box 665; 92220; Riverside; P 28,000; M 400; (951) 849-4695; Fax (951) 849-9395; info@banningchamber.net; www.banningchamber.net*

Barstow · *Barstow Area C/C* · Jeri Justus; Exec. Dir.; 681 N. First Ave.; P.O. Box 698; 92312; San Bernardino; P 23,056; M 411; (760) 256-8617; Fax (760) 256-7675; bacc@barstowchamber.com; www. barstowchamber.com

Bass Lake · *Bass Lake C/C* · P.O. Box 126; 93604; Madera; P 2,500; M 27; (559) 642-3676; chamber@basslakechamber.com; www.basslakechamber.com

Bay Point · *see California Delta*

Baywood Park · *see Los Osos*

Beaumont · *Beaumont C/C* · Kathy Munyas; Exec. Dir.; 726 Beaumont Ave.; 92223; Riverside; P 32,403; M 370; (951) 845-9541; Fax (951) 769-9080; info@beaumontcachamber.com; www. beaumontcachamber.com*

Bell · *Bell C/C* · Julie Gonzalez; Gen. Mgr.; 4401 E. Gage Ave.; P.O. Box 294; 90201-0294; Los Angeles; P 42,600; M 125; (323) 560-8755; Fax (323) 560-2060; bellchamber@sbcglobal.net

Bell Gardens · *Bell Gardens C/C* · Dennis Grizzle; Exec. Dir.; 7535 Perry Rd.; 90201-0294; Los Angeles; P 45,000; M 150; (562) 806-2355; Fax (562) 806-1585; bellgardenschamber@hotmail. com; www.bellgardenschamber.org

Bellflower · *Bellflower C/C* · Michele Moore; Chamber Mgr.; 16730 Bellflower Blvd., Ste. A; 90706; Los Angeles; P 75,000; M 275; (562) 867-1744; Fax (562) 866-7545; bellflowercoc@juno. com; www.bellflowerchamber.com

Belmont · *Belmont C/C* · Lenore Griffin; Pres.; 1059A Alameda de las Pulgas; 94002; San Mateo; P 27,000; M 220; (650) 595-8696; Fax (650) 595-8731; execdirector@belmontchamber.org; www.belmontchamber.org

Benicia · *Benicia C/C* · Stephanie L. Christiansen; Pres./CEO; 601 First St., Ste. 100; 94510; Solano; P 28,000; M 500; (707) 745-2120; Fax (707) 745-2275; beniciachamber@aol.com; www. beniciachamber.com*

Berkeley · *Berkeley C/C* · Tammy Cortez; Exec. Asst.; 1834 University Ave.; 94703; Alameda; P 103,000; M 375; (510) 549-7000; Fax (510) 549-1789; tammy@berkeleychamber.com; www. berkeleychamber.com*

Bethel Island · *Bethel Island C/C* · Mark Whitlock; P.O. Box 263; 94511; Contra Costa; P 2,300; M 150; (925) 684-3220; Fax (925) 684-9025; www.bethelisland-chamber.com; www.bethelisland-chamber.com

Beverly Hills · *Beverly Hills C of C & Civic Assoc.* · Dan Walsh; CEO; 239 S. Beverly Dr.; 90212; Los Angeles; P 36,000; M 800; (310) 248-1000; Fax (310) 248-1020; info@beverlyhillschamber. com; www.beverlyhillschamber.com

Big Bear Lake · *Big Bear C/C* · Sara Russ; Exec. Dir.; 630 Bartlett Rd.; P.O. Box 2860; 92315; San Bernardino; P 21,000; M 500; (909) 866-4607; (877) 866-5253; Fax (909) 866-5412; info@bigbear chamber.com; www.bigbearchamber.com

Big Bend · *see Burney*

Bird's Landing · *see California Delta*

Bishop · *Bishop Area C/C & Visitors Bur.* · Tawni Tomson; Exec. Dir.; 690 N. Main St.; 93514; Inyo; P 14,000; M 300; (760) 873-8405; (888) 395-3952; Fax (760) 873-6999; info@bishopvisitor. com; www.bishopvisitor.com

Black Hawk · *see Danville*

Blue Lake · *Blue Lake C/C* · Karen Barnes; Pres.; P.O. Box 476; 95525; Humboldt; P 1,200; M 50; (707) 668-5655; www.bluelake. ci.ca.gov

Blythe · *Blythe Area C/C* · Jim Shipley; COO; 201 S. Broadway; 92225; Riverside; P 13,500; M 350; (760) 922-8166; Fax (760) 922-4010; blythecoc@yahoo.com; www.blytheareachamberof commerce.com

Bolinas · *see Stinson Beach*

Boonville · *Anderson Valley C/C* · Dawn Emery Ballantine; P.O. Box 275; 95415; Mendocino; P 2,000; M 50; (707) 895-2379; info@ andersonvalleychamber.com; www.andersonvalleychamber.com

Boron · *Boron C/C* · James Welling; Pres.; 26962-20 Mule Team Rd.; 93516; Kern; P 3,500; M 50; (760) 762-5810; Fax (760) 762-0012; chamber@boronchamber.com; www.boronchamber.com

Borrego Springs · *Borrego Springs C/C* · 786 Palm Canyon Dr.; P.O. Box 420; 92004; San Diego; P 3,500; M 200; (760) 767-5555; (800) 559-5524; Fax (760) 767-5976; info@borregosprings chamber.com; www.borregospringschamber.com

Brawley · *Brawley C/C* · Ron Hull; Exec. Dir.; 204 S. Imperial Ave.; P.O. Box 218; 92227; Imperial; P 25,000; M 405; (760) 344-3160; Fax (760) 344-7611; chamber@brawleychamber.com; www.brawleychamber.com*

Brea · *Brea C/C* · Sharon Wegner; CEO; One Civic Center Cir.; 92821; Orange; P 38,000; M 950; (714) 529-4938; Fax (714) 529-6103; sharon@breachamber.com; www.breachamber.com*

Brentwood · *Brentwood C/C* · Harry York; CEO; 8440 Brentwood Blvd., Ste. C; 94513; Contra Costa; P 52,000; M 400; (925) 634-3344; Fax (925) 634-3731; info@brentwoodchamber.com; www.brentwoodchamber.com*

Bridgeport · *Bridgeport C/C* · P.O. Box 541; 93517; Mono; P 800; M 65; (760) 932-7500; Fax (760) 932-7500; bridgeportcalifornia@bridgeportcalifornia.com; www.bridgeportcalifornia.com

Brisbane · *Brisbane C/C* · Mitch Bull; Pres./CEO; 50 Park Pl.; 94005; San Mateo; P 3,700; M 228; (415) 467-7283; Fax (415) 467-5421; mitch.bull@brisbanechamber.com; www.brisbane chamber.com

Buellton · *Buellton C/C* · Kathy Vreeland; Exec. Dir.; 597 Ave. of Flags, Ste. 101; P.O. Box 231; 93427; Santa Barbara; P 4,500; M 165; (805) 688-7829; (800) 324-3800; Fax (805) 688-5399; info@buellton.org; www.buellton.org.

Buena Park · *Buena Park Area C/C* · Gail S. Dixon; Pres./CEO; 6601 Beach Blvd.; 90621; Orange; P 82,000; M 300; (714) 521-0261; Fax (714) 521-1851; info@buenaparkchamber.org; www.buenaparkchamber.org

Burbank · *Burbank C/C* · Gary Olson; Pres./CEO; 200 W. Magnolia Blvd.; 91502; Los Angeles; P 105,000; M 1,000; (818) 846-3111; Fax (818) 846-0109; info@burbankchamber.org; www.burbankchamber.org

Burlingame · *Burlingame C/C* · Georgette Naylor; Pres./CEO; 290 California Dr.; 94010; San Mateo; P 29,000; M 450; (650) 344-1735; Fax (650) 344-1763; info@burlingamechamber.org; www.burlingamechamber.org

Burney · *Burney C/C* · Windy Smith; Mgr.; 36879 Main St.; P.O. Box 36; 96013; Shasta; P 3,500; M 120; (530) 335-2111; Fax (530) 335-2122; burneychamber@frontiernet.net; www.burney chamber.com

Buttonwillow · *Buttonwillow C/C & Ag.* · 104 W. 2nd St.; P.O. Box 251; 93206; Kern; P 1,266; M 112; (661) 764-5406; Fax (661) 764-5406; buttonwillowchamber@bak.rr.com; www.button willowchamber.com

Byron · *see California Delta*

Calabasas · *Calabasas C/C* · Carol Washburn; CEO; 23564 Calabasas Rd., Ste. 101; 91302; Los Angeles; P 25,000; M 400; (818) 222-5680; Fax (818) 222-5690; info@calabasaschamber.com; www.calabasaschamber.com*

Calaveras County · *see Angels Camp*

Calexico · *Calexico C/C* · Hildy Carrillo; Exec. Dir.; 1100 Imperial Ave.; P.O. Box 948; 92231; Imperial; P 38,000; M 400; (760) 357-1166; Fax (760) 357-9043; calexicochamber@hotmail.com; www.calexicochamber.net

California City · *California City C/C* · Karen Sanders; Pres.; 8001 California City Blvd.; P.O. Box 2008; 93504; Kern; P 13,500; M 150; (760) 373-8676; Fax (760) 373-1414; californiacitychamber@yahoo.com; www.californiacitychamber.com

California Delta · *California Delta C of C & Visitors Bur.* · Bill Wells; Exec. Dir.; 169 W. Brannan Island Rd.; Isleton; 95641; Sacramento & San Joaquin; P 500,000; M 300; (916) 777-4041; Fax (916) 777-4042; info@californiadelta.org; www.californiadelta.org

Calimesa · *Calimesa C/C* · Stephen A. Carlson; Exec. Dir.; 1007 Calimesa Blvd., Ste. D; 92320; Riverside; P 8,000; M 125; (909) 795-7612; Fax (909) 795-2822; calimesachamber@cybertime.net; www.calimesachamber.org

Calistoga · *Calistoga C/C* · Chris Canning; Exec. Dir./CEO; 1133 Washington St.; 94515; Napa; P 5,200; M 330; (707) 942-6333; (866) 306-5588; Fax (707) 942-9287; office@calistogachamber.net; www.calistogavisitors.com*

Camarillo · *Camarillo C/C* · Thomas P. Kelley; Pres./CEO; 2400 E. Ventura Blvd.; 93010; Ventura; P 66,000; M 700; (805) 484-4383; Fax (805) 484-1395; info@camarillochamber.org; camarillo chamber.org*

Cambria · *Cambria C/C* · Mary Ann Carson; Exec. Dir.; 767 Main St.; 93428; San Luis Obispo; P 6,624; M 385; (805) 927-3624; Fax (805) 927-9426; info@cambriachamber.org; www.cambria chamber.org

Cameron Park · *see Shingle Springs*

Campbell · *Campbell C/C* · Neil V. Collins; Exec. Dir.; 1628 W. Campbell Ave.; 95008; Santa Clara; P 41,000; M 700; (408) 378-6252; Fax (408) 378-0192; ccoc@pacbell.net; www.campbell chamber.com*

Canoga Park · *Canoga Park/West Hills C/C* · Nora Ross; Exec. Dir.; 7248 Owensmouth Ave.; 91303; Los Angeles; P 75,000; M 275; (818) 884-4222; Fax (818) 884-4604; info@cpwhchamber.org; www.cpwhchamber.org

Canyon Country · *see Santa Clarita*

Canyon Lake · *Canyon Lake C/C* · Lee Clark; Exec. Dir.; 31566 Railroad Canyon Rd.; 92587; Riverside; P 13,356; M 194; (951) 244-6124; Fax (951) 244-0831; nanciet@verizon.net; www.canyonlakechamber.net

Capitola · *Capitola-Soquel C/C* · Ms. Toni Castro; CEO; 716-G Capitola Ave.; 95010; Santa Cruz; P 9,500; M 450; (831) 475-6522; (800) 474-6522; Fax (831) 475-6530; capcham@capitolachamber.com; www.capitolasoquelchamber.com

Cardiff-By-The-Sea · *Cardiff 101 Main Street* · Tess Radmill; Program Mgr.; 124 Aberdeen Dr.; P.O. Box 552; 92007; San Diego; P 18,000; M 300; (760) 436-0431; Fax (760) 753-0144; cardiff101mainstreet@gmail.com; www.cardiff101.com

Carlsbad · *Carlsbad C/C* · Ted Owen; Pres./CEO; 5934 Priestly Dr.; 92008; San Diego; P 105,000; M 1,600; (760) 931-8400; Fax (760) 931-9153; carlsbadchamber@carlsbad.org; www.carlsbad.org*

Carmel · *Carmel C/C* · Monta Potter; CEO; P.O. Box 4444; 93921; Monterey; P 4,000; M 550; (831) 624-2522; (800) 550-4333; Fax (831) 624-1329; info@carmelcalifornia.org; www.carmel california.org

Carmel Mountain Ranch · *see San Diego–San Diego North C/C*

Carmel Valley · *Carmel Valley C/C* · Elizabeth Suro; Managing Dir.; P.O. Box 288; 93924; Monterey; P 15,000; M 250; (831) 659-4000; Fax (831) 644-9476; elizabeth@carmelvalleychamber.com; www.carmelvalleychamber.com

Carmichael · *Carmichael C/C* · Linda Melody; Admin. Consultant; 6825 Fair Oaks Blvd., Ste. 100; 95608; Sacramento; P 72,000; M 250; (916) 481-1002; Fax (916) 481-1003; admin@carmichaelchamber.com; www.carmichaelchamber.com*

Carpinteria · *Carpinteria Valley C/C* · Lynda Lang; CEO; 1056B Eugenia Pl.; P.O. Box 956; 93014; Santa Barbara; P 14,600; M 380; (805) 684-5479; Fax (805) 684-3477; info@carpinteriachamber. org; www.carpinteriachamber.org*

Carson · *Carson C/C* · John Wogan; Pres.; 530 E. Del Amo Blvd.; 90746; Los Angeles; P 100,000; M 600; (310) 217-4590; Fax (310) 217-4591; wogan@carsonchamber.com; www.carsonchamber.com

Cassel · *see Burney*

Castaic · *see Santa Clarita*

Castro Valley · *Castro Valley/Eden Area C/C* · Roberta Rivet; Exec. Dir.; 3467 Castro Valley Blvd.; 94546; Alameda; P 60,000; M 400; (510) 537-5300; Fax (510) 537-5335; info@castrovalley chamber.com; www.castrovalleychamber.com*

Castroville · *North Monterey County C/C* · Gary DeAmaral; Pres.; 10700 Merritt St.; P.O. Box 744; 95012; Monterey; P 13,000; M 200; (831) 633-2465; Fax (831) 633-0485; info@northmonterey countychamber.org; www.northmontereycountychamber.org

Catalina Island · *see Avalon*

Cathedral City · *Cathedral City C/C* · Steven Morris; Pres./CEO; 68-950 Hwy. 111, Ste. 106; 92234; Riverside; P 57,000; M 300; (760) 328-1213; Fax (760) 321-0659; info@cathedralcitycc.com; www.cathedralcitycc.com*

Cayucos · *Cayucos C/C* · Bill Shea; Pres.; P.O. Box 346; 93430; San Luis Obispo; P 3,500; M 90; (805) 995-1200; cayucoschamber@ charter.net; www.cayucoschamber.com

Cedarville · *Surprise Valley C/C* · Sarah Armstrong; P.O. Box 518; 96104; Modoc; P 1,500; M 60; (530) 279-2001; Fax (530) 279-2012; contactsvc@surprisevalleychamber.com; www. surprisevalleychamber.com

Century City · *see Los Angeles-Century City C/C*

Ceres · *Ceres C/C* · Pres.; 2908 E. Whitmore Ave., Ste. H-213; 95307; Stanislaus; P 40,000; M 235; (209) 537-2601; Fax (209) 537-2699; chamber@cereschamber.org; www.cereschamber.org

Cerritos · *Cerritos Reg. C/C* · Catherine Gaughen; Exec. Dir.; 13259 E. South St.; 90703; Los Angeles; P 51,488; M 475; (562) 467-0800; Fax (562) 467-0840; chamber@cerritos.org; www.cerritos.org

Chatsworth · *Chatsworth/Porter Ranch C/C* · Rana Ghadban; Exec. Dir.; 10038 Old Depot Plaza Rd.; 91311; Los Angeles; P 90,000; M 300; (818) 341-2428; Fax (818) 341-4930; info@ chatsworthchamber.com; www.chatsworthchamber.com

Chester · *Chester-Lake Almanor C/C* · Susan Bryner; Exec. Dir.; 529 Main St.; P.O. Box 1198; 96020; Plumas; P 5,000; M 302; (530) 258-2426; (800) 350-4838; Fax (530) 258-2760; info@ lakealmanorarea.com; www.lakealmanorarea.com*

Chico · *Chico C/C* · Jolene Francis; Pres./CEO; 300 Salem St.; 95928; Butte; P 105,000; M 800; (530) 891-5556; (800) 852-8570; Fax (530) 891-3613; info@chicochamber.com; www.chicochamber.com*

Chino · *Chino Valley C/C* · Andy Ronquillo; Pres./CEO; 13150 Seventh St.; 91710; San Bernardino; P 150,000; M 650; (909) 627-6177; Fax (909) 627-4180; info@chinovalleychamber.com; www. chinovalleychamber.com.*

Chowchilla · *Chowchilla Dist. C/C* · Jacki Flanagan; Mgr.; 145 W. Robertson Blvd.; P.O. Box 638; 93610; Madera; P 18,780; M 200; (559) 665-5603; Fax (559) 665-0896; chamberofcommerce@ ci.chowchilla.ca.us; www.ci.chowchilla.ca.us

Chula Vista · *Chula Vista C/C* · Lisa Cohen; CEO; 233 Fourth Ave.; 91910; San Diego; P 230,000; M 950; (619) 420-6602; Fax (619) 420-1269; lisa@chulavistachamber.org; www.chulavista chamber.org

Citrus Heights · *Citrus Heights Reg. C/C* · Bettie Cosby; CEO; 7115A Greenback Ln.; P.O. Box 191; 95611; Sacramento; P 87,000; M 525; (916) 722-4545; Fax (916) 722-4543; chamber@ch chamber.com; www.chchamber.com*

City of Industry · *Industry Manufacturers Cncl.* · Donald Sachs; Exec. Dir.; 15651 Stafford St.; 91744; Los Angeles; P 800; M 600; (626) 968-3737; Fax (626) 330-5060; dsachs@cityof industry.org; www.cityofindustry.org*

Clairemont Mesa · *see Del Mar–LaJolla Golden Triangle C/C*

Claremont · *Claremont C/C* · Maureen Aldridge; CEO; 205 Yale Ave.; 91711; Los Angeles; P 35,500; M 550; (909) 624-1681; Fax (909) 624-6629; contact@claremontchamber.org; www. claremontchamber.org*

Clarksburg · *see California Delta*

Clearlake · *Clearlake C/C* · Lori Peters; Dir.; 3245 Bowers Rd.; P.O. Box 5330; 95422; Lake; P 14,000; M 215; (707) 994-3600; Fax (707) 994-3603; clearlakechamber@yahoo.com; www. clearlakechamber.com

Cloverdale · *Cloverdale C/C* · Carla Howell; CEO; 105 N. Cloverdale Blvd.; 95425; Sonoma; P 8,400; M 200; (707) 894-4470; Fax (707) 894-9568; chamberinfo@cloverdale.com; www. cloverdale.net*

Clovis · *Clovis C/C* · Mark Blackney; Pres./CEO; 325 Pollasky Ave.; 93612; Fresno; P 100,000; M 1,100; (559) 299-7363; Fax (559) 299-2969; mark@clovischamber.com; www.clovischamber.com*

Coachella · *Coachella C/C* · Cynthia Tinoco; CEO; 1258 Sixth St.; 92236; Riverside; P 40,000; M 200; (760) 398-8089; Fax (760) 398-8589; contact@coachellachamber.com; www.coachella chamber.com*

Coalinga · *Coalinga Area C/C* · Katie Delano; Exec. Dir.; 380 Coalinga Plz.; 93210; Fresno; P 18,061; M 125; (559) 935-2948; exec@coalingachamber.com; www.coalingachamber.org

Coleville · *see Topaz*

Colfax · *Colfax Area C/C* · Jenny Duncan; Exec. Dir.; P.O. Box 86; 95713; Placer; P 15,000; M 173; (530) 346-8888; Fax (530) 346-6788; contact@colfaxarea.com; www.colfaxarea.com*

Collinsville · *see California Delta*

Colma · *see Daly City*

Colton · *Colton C/C* · Laura Morales; Exec. Dir.; 655 N. La Cadena Dr.; 92324; San Bernardino; P 52,400; M 275; (909) 825-2222; Fax (909) 824-1650; colton@coltonchamber.org; www.coltonchamber.org

Columbia · *Columbia C/C* · Gary Neubert; Pres.; P.O. Box 1824; 95310; Tuolumne; P 2,500; M 46; (209) 536-1672; info@columbia california.com; www.columbiacalifornia.com

Colusa · *Colusa County C/C* · Ben Felt; Pres.; 2963 Davison Ct.; 95932; Colusa; P 22,000; M 240; (530) 458-5525; Fax (530) 458-8180; bfelt@colusachamber.org; www.colusachamber.org*

Commerce · *Commerce Ind. Cncl.-Chamber of Commerce* · Eddie Tafoya; Exec. Dir.; 6055 E. Washington Blvd., Ste. 120; 90040; Los Angeles; P 13,400; M 340; (323) 728-7222; Fax (323) 728-7565; eddie@industrialcouncil.org; www.industrialcouncil.org

Compton · *Compton C/C* · Lestean M. Johnson; Pres.; 700 N. Bullis Rd., Ste. 6A; 90221; Los Angeles; P 130,000; M 300; (310) 631-8611; Fax (310) 631-2066; CptChamber@aol.com; www. comptonchamberofcommerce.com*

Concord · *Greater Concord C/C* · Marilyn Fowler; COO; 2280 Diamond Blvd., Ste. 200; 94520; Contra Costa; P 127,600; M 600; (925) 685-1181; Fax (925) 685-5623; info@concordchamber.com; www.concordchamber.com*

Corcoran · *Corcoran C/C* · Exec. Dir.; 1099 Otis Ave.; P.O. Box 459; 93212; Kings; P 14,000; M 160; (559) 992-4514; Fax (559) 992-2341; lisa@corcoranchamber.com; www.corcoranchamber.com

Corning · *Corning Dist. C/C* · Valanne Cardenas; Mgr.; 1110 Solano St.; P.O. Box 871; 96021; Tehama; P 7,400; M 290; (530) 824-5550; Fax (530) 824-9499; corningchamber@sbcglobal.net; www.corningchamber.org

Corona · *Greater Corona Valley C/C* · Bobby Spiegel; Pres./CEO; 904 E. Sixth St.; 92879; Riverside; P 150,000; M 1,000; (951) 737-3350; Fax (951) 737-3531; info@mychamber.org; www.mychamber.org

Corona del Mar · *Corona del Mar C/C* · Linda Leonhard; Pres./CEO; 2855 E. Coast Hwy., Ste. 101; 92625; Orange; P 14,500; M 400; (949) 673-4050; Fax (949) 673-3940; info@cdmchamber.com; www.cdmchamber.com

Coronado · *Coronado C/C* · Karen Finch; Pres./CEO; 875 Orange Ave., Ste. 102; 92118; San Diego; P 26,000; M 400; (619) 435-9260; Fax (619) 522-6577; info@coronadochamber.com; www.coronadochamber.com*

Corte Madera · *Corte Madera C/C* · Julie Kritzberger; Exec. Dir.; 129 Corte Madera Town Center; 94925; Marin; P 9,700; M 214; (415) 924-0441; Fax (415) 924-1839; chamber@cortemadera.org; www.cortemadera.org*

Costa Mesa · *Costa Mesa C/C* · Ed Fawcett; Pres./CEO; 1700 Adams Ave., Ste. 101; 92626; Orange; P 106,000; M 410; (714) 885-9090; Fax (714) 885-9094; efawcett@costamesachamber. com; www.costamesachamber.com*

Cotati · *Cotati C/C* · Suzanne Whipple; Exec. Dir.; 216 E. School St.; P.O. Box 592; 94931; Sonoma; P 8,000; M 160; (707) 795-5508; Fax (707) 795-5868; chamber@cotati.org; www.cotati.org

Cottonwood · *Cottonwood C/C* · Cheri Skudlarek; P.O. Box 584; 96022; Shasta; P 13,000; M 90; (530) 347-6800; Fax (530) 347-6800; cskudlarek@novb.com; www.cottonwoodcofc.org

Coulterville · *see Mariposa*

Courtland · *see California Delta*

Covelo · *Round Valley C/C* · Pia McIsaac; Pres.; P.O. Box 458; 95428; Mendocino; P 3,000; M 150; rvcc@roundvalley.org; www.roundvalley.org

Covina · *Covina C/C* · Dawn Nelson; Pres./CEO; 935 W. Badillo, Ste. 100; 91722; Los Angeles; P 48,000; M 630; (626) 967-4191; Fax (626) 966-9660; chamber@covina.org; www.covina.org

Crenshaw · *see Los Angeles—Los Angeles Area C/C*

Crescent City · *Crescent City-Del Norte County C/C* · Gina Zottola; Exec. Dir.; 1001 Front St.; 95531; Del Norte; P 29,420; M 350; (707) 464-3174; (800) 343-8300; Fax (707) 464-9676; chamber@delnorte.org; www.delnorte.org*

Crestline · *Crestline/Lake Gregory C/C* · Bob Yeomans; Pres.; 24385 Lake Dr.; P.O. Box 926; 92325; San Bernardino; P 16,000; M 115; (909) 338-2706; info@crestlinechamber.net; www.crestlinechamber.net

Crockett · *Crockett C/C* · Aimee Lohr; Pres.; 1214 A Pomona; P.O. Box 191; 94525; Contra Costa; P 3,300; M 110; (510) 787-1155; Fax (510) 787-1155; crockettchamber@aol.com; www.crockett-ca-chamber.org

Cuddy Valley · *see Frazier Park*

Culver City · *Culver City C/C* · Steven J. Rose; Pres./CEO; 4249 Overland Ave.; 90230; Los Angeles; P 40,000; M 700; (310) 287-3850; Fax (310) 287-1350; ssssteve@culvercitychamber.com; www.culvercitychamber.com

Cupertino · *Cupertino C/C* · Lynn Ching; Pres.; 20455 Silverado Ave.; 95014; Santa Clara; P 55,000; M 300; (408) 252-7054; Fax (408) 252-0638; info@cupertino-chamber.org; www.cupertino-chamber.org*

Cypress · *Cypress C/C* · Ed Munson; Pres./CEO; 5550 Cerritos Ave., Ste. D; 90630; Orange; P 49,647; M 260; (714) 827-2430; Fax (714) 827-1229; ed.munson@cypresschamber.org; www.cypresschamber.org

Daggett · *Daggett C/C* · Chris Santiago; Pres.; P.O. Box 327; 92327; San Bernardino; P 1,000; M 18; (760) 252-8130; tricris39@verizon.net

Daly City · *Daly City-Colma C/C* · Georgette Sarles; Pres./CEO; 355 Gellert Blvd., Ste. 138; 94015; San Mateo; P 101,000; M 535; (650) 755-3900; Fax (650) 755-5160; staff@dalycity-colmachamber.org; www.dalycity-colmachamber.org

Dana Point · *Dana Point C/C* · Nichole Chambers; Pres./CEO; 24681 La Plaza, Ste. 115; 92629; Orange; P 38,000; M 350; (949) 496-1555; (800) 290-DANA; Fax (949) 496-5321; chamber@danapointchamber.com; www.danapointchamber.com*

Danville · *Danville Area C/C* · Melony Newman; Pres./CEO; 117 Town & Country, Ste. E; 94526; Contra Costa; P 53,000; M 610; (925) 837-4400; Fax (925) 837-5709; office@danvilleareachamber. com; www.danvilleareachamber.com*

Davis · *Davis C/C* · Christi Skibbins; Exec. Dir.; 604 3rd St.; 95616; Yolo; P 64,000; M 700; (530) 756-5160; Fax (530) 756-5190; director@davischamber.com; www.davischamber.com*

Death Valley · *see Shoshone*

Del Mar · *LaJolla Golden Triangle C/C* · George Schmall; Pres.; 1011 Camino Del Mar, Ste. 256; 92014; San Diego; P 200,000; M 100; (858) 350-1253; www.ljgtcc.com*

Del Mar · *San Diego Coastal C/C* · Nancy Wasko; Pres./CEO; 1104 Camino Del Mar, Ste. 1; 92014; San Diego; P 43,500; M 425; (858) 755-4844; Fax (858) 793-5293; info@sandiegocoastalchamber. com; www.sandiegocoastalchamber.com*

Del Paso Heights · *see Sacramento—North Sacramento C/C*

Delano · *Delano C/C* · Carla Lapadula; Exec. Dir.; 931 High St.; 93215; Kern; P 50,000; M 216; (661) 725-2518; Fax (661) 725-4743; chamberofdelano@sbcglobal.net; www.chamberofdelano.com.*

Desert Hot Springs · *Desert Hot Springs C/C* · Russ Augustine; Pres.; 11999 Palm Dr.; 92240; Riverside; P 22,000; M 300; (760) 329-6403; (800) 346-3347; Fax (760) 329-2833; info2@deserthotsprings.com; www.dhschamber.org*

Diablo · *see Danville*

Dinuba · *Dinuba C/C* · Sandy Sills; Exec. Dir.; 210 North L St.; 93618; Tulare; P 21,087; M 162; (559) 591-2707; (559) 591-7000; Fax (559) 591-2712; dinubachamber@sbcglobal.net; www.dinubachamber.com*

Discovery Bay · *Discovery Bay C/C* · Greg Spivak; Pres./CEO; P.O. Box 1332; 94505; Contra Costa; P 16,000; M 140; (925) 240-6600; (888) 832-3291; info@discoverybaychamber.com; www.discoverybaychamber.com*

Dixon · *Dixon Dist. C/C* · Carol Pruett; Ofc. Mgr.; 220 N. Jefferson St.; P.O. Box 159; 95620; Solano; P 18,000; M 240; (707) 678-2650; Fax (707) 678-3654; info@dixonchamber.org; www.dixonchamber.org*

Dorris · *Butte Valley C/C* · Gene Lane; Pres.; P.O. Box 541; 96023; Siskiyou; P 2,000; M 85; (530) 398-4631; buttevalleychamber@yahoo.com; www.buttevalleychamber.com

Downey • *Downey C/C* • Susan Nordin; Exec. Dir.; 11131 Brookshire Ave.; 90241; Los Angeles; P 114,000; M 450; (562) 923-2191; Fax (562) 869-0461; info@downeychamber.com; www.downeychamber.com*

Duarte • *Duarte C/C* • Jim Kirchner; Pres./CEO; 1105 Oak Ave.; P.O. Box 1438; 91009; Los Angeles; P 22,000; M 300; (626) 357-3333; Fax (626) 357-3645; jim@duartechamber.com; www.duarte chamber.com*

Dublin • *Dublin C/C* • Nancy Feeley; Pres./CEO; 7080 Donlon Way, Ste. 110; 94568; Alameda; P 45,000; M 350; (925) 828-6200; Fax (925) 828-4247; nancy@dublinchamberofcommerce.org; www. dublinchamberofcommerce.org*

Dunlap • *see Miramonte*

Dunsmuir • *Dunsmuir C of C & Visitors Center* • Denise Bailey; Ofc. Mgr.; 5915 Dunsmuir Ave., Ste. 100; 96025; Siskiyou; P 1,800; M 100; (530) 235-2177; (800) DUNSMUIR; Fax (530) 235-0911; chamber@dunsmuir.com; www.dunsmuir.com

Eagle Rock • *Eagle Rock C/C* • Michael A. Nogueira; Pres.; P.O. Box 41354; 90041; Los Angeles; P 39,000; M 120; (323) 257-2197; Fax (323) 257-4245; erccwebguy@aol.com; www.eaglerock chamberofcommerce.com

Eagleville • *see Cedarville*

East Los Angeles • *see Los Angeles–East Los Angeles C/C*

El Cajon • *San Diego East County C/C* • Cliff Diamond; Interim Pres./CEO; 201 S. Magnolia Ave.; 92020; San Diego; P 151,000; M 800; (619) 440-6161; Fax (619) 440-6164; ceo@eastcounty chamber.org; www.eastcountychamber.org*

El Centro • *El Centro C/C & Visitors Bur.* • Cathy Kennerson; CEO; 1095 S. 4th St.; P.O. Box 3006; 92244; Imperial; P 43,316; M 560; (760) 352-3681; Fax (760) 352-3246; info@elcentrochamber.com; www.elcentrochamber.com*

El Cerrito • *El Cerrito C/C* • Mark L. Scott; Mgr.; 406 Colusa Ave.; P.O. Box 538; 94530; Contra Costa; P 23,200; M 220; (510) 705-1202; Fax (510) 705-1206; info@elcerritochamber.org; www. elcerritochamber.org

El Dorado Hills • *El Dorado Hills C/C* • Debbie Manning; Pres./ CEO; 2085 Vine St., Ste. 105; P.O. Box 5055; 95762; El Dorado; P 43,000; M 550; (916) 933-1335; Fax (916) 933-5908; chamber@ eldoradohillschamber.org; www.eldoradohillschamber.org*

El Monte • *El Monte/South El Monte C/C* • Richard Nichols; Exec. Dir.; 10505 Valley Blvd., Ste. 312; P.O. Box 5866; 91734; Los Angeles; P 135,000; M 500; (626) 443-0180; Fax (626) 443-0463; chamber@emsem.com; www.emsem.com*

El Segundo • *El Segundo C/C* • Marsha Hansen; Exec. Dir.; 427 Main St.; 90245; Los Angeles; P 16,000; M 380; (310) 322-1220; Fax (310) 322-6880; info@elsegundochamber.org; www.el segundochamber.org

El Sobrante • *El Sobrante C/C* • Michael Frith; Pres.; 3769 San Pablo Dam Rd., Ste. B; 94803; Contra Costa; P 40,000; M 100; (510) 223-0757; mariecofces@sbcglobal.net; www.elsobrante chamber.com

Elk Grove • *Elk Grove C/C* • Angela Perry; Exec. Dir.; 9370 Studio Ct., Ste. 110; 95758; Sacramento; P 143,885; M 600; (916) 691-3760; Fax (916) 691-3810; chamber@elkgroveca.com; www. elkgroveca.com*

Emeryville • *Emeryville C/C* • Bob Canter; Pres./CEO; 3980 Harlan St.; 94608; Alameda; P 11,000; M 285; (510) 652-5223; Fax (510) 652-4223; info@emeryvillechamber.com; www.emeryville chamber.com*

Encinitas • *Encinitas C/C* • Stephanie Edwards; Interim Exec. Dir.; 527 Encinitas Blvd., Ste. 106; 92024; San Diego; P 62,000; M 450; (760) 753-6041; Fax (760) 753-6270; info@encinitas chamber.com; www.encinitaschamber.org

Encino • *Encino C/C* • Diana Donovan; CEO; 4933 Balboa Blvd.; 91316; Los Angeles; P 44,000; M 400; (818) 789-4711; Fax (818) 789-2485; info@encinochamber.org; www.encinochamber.org

Escalon • *Escalon C/C* • Pat Brown; Pres.; P.O. Box 222; 95320; San Joaquin; P 8,000; M 50; (209) 838-2793; escaloncofc@gmail. com; www.escalonchambersite.org

Escondido • *Escondido C/C* • Harvey Mitchell; CEO; 720 N. Broadway; 92025; San Diego; P 141,000; M 845; (760) 745-2125; Fax (760) 745-1183; info@escondidochamber.org; www. escondidochamber.org

Esparto • *Esparto Reg. C/C* • Linda Pillard; Pres.; P.O. Box 194; 95627; Yolo; P 3,500; M 87; (530) 787-3242; Fax (530) 787-3373; info@espartoregionalchamber.org; www.espartoregional chamber.org

Etna • *Scott Valley C/C* • Marilyn Seward; Treas.; P.O. Box 374; 96027; Siskiyou; P 5,000; M 30; (530) 467-3355; mwseward@ sisqtel.net; www.scottvalley.org

Eureka • *Greater Eureka C/C* • J. Warren Hockaday; Pres./ CEO; 2112 Broadway; 95501; Humboldt; P 45,000; M 650; (707) 442-3738; (800) 356-6381; Fax (707) 442-0079; chamber@ eurekachamber.com; www.eurekachamber.com*

Exeter • *Exeter C/C* • Sandy Blankenship; Exec. Dir.; 101 W. Pine St.; 93221; Tulare; P 10,700; M 335; (559) 592-2919; Fax (559) 592-3720; chamber@exeterchamber.com; www.exeterchamber.com*

Fair Oaks • *Fair Oaks C/C* • Jan Bass Otto; Exec. Dir.; 10224 Fair Oaks Blvd.; P.O. Box 352; 95628; Sacramento; P 50,000; M 350; (916) 967-2903; Fax (916) 967-8536; info@fairoakschamber.com; www.fairoakschamber.com.*

Fairfax • *Fairfax C/C* • Wendy Baker; Exec. Dir.; P.O. Box 1111; 94978; Marin; P 7,500; M 80; (415) 453-5928; www.fairfaxcoc.com

Fairfield • *Fairfield-Suisun C/C* • G. Leslie Fay; Pres./CEO; 1111 Webster St.; 94533; Solano; P 150,000; M 650; (707) 425-4625; Fax (707) 425-0826; reception@ffsc-chamber.com; www.ffsc-chamber.com*

Fall River Mills • *Fall River Valley C/C* • Ed Siegel; Pres.; P.O. Box 475; 96028; Shasta; P 4,000; M 80; (530) 336-5840; gemsjaz@ gmail.com; www.fallrivervalleycc.org

Fallbrook • *Greater Fallbrook Area C/C* • Richard Kennedy; CEO; 233 E. Mission Rd.; 92028; San Diego; P 55,000; M 450; (760) 728-5845; Fax (760) 728-4031; richard.kennedy@fallbrookchamber ofcommerce.com; www.fallbrookchamberofcommerce.com*

Farmersville • *Farmersville C/C* • Don Mason; Pres.; 1376 N. Farmersville Blvd.; 93223; Tulare; P 9,700; M 30; (559) 747-0223

Ferndale • *Ferndale C/C* • Karen Pingitore; P.O. Box 325; 95536; Humboldt; P 1,400; M 132; (707) 786-4477; Fax (707) 786-4477; info@victorianferndale.com; www.victorianferndale.com

Fillmore • *Fillmore C/C* • David Crockett; Pres.; 557 Ventura St.; P.O. Box 815; 93016; Ventura; P 15,000; M 75; (805) 524-0351; Fax (805) 524-2551; info@fillmorechamber.com; www.fillmorechamber.com

Folsom • *Folsom C/C* • Joseph P. Gagliardi; CEO; 200 Wool St.; 95630; Sacramento; P 73,000; M 1,050; (916) 985-2698; (916) 985-5555; Fax (916) 985-4117; cthompson@folsomchamber.com; www.folsomchamber.com*

Fontana · *Fontana C/C* · Elsie Hernandez; Ofc. Mgr.; 8491 Sierra Ave.; 92335; San Bernardino; P 190,000; M 400; (909) 822-4433; Fax (909) 822-6238; info@fontanachamber.com; www.fontana chamber.org*

Foothill Farms · *see North Highlands*

Foresthill · *Foresthill-Divide C/C* · Sean Salveson; Pres.; 24600 Main St., Ste. A; P.O. Box 346; 95631; Placer; P 6,000; M 150; (530) 367-2474; Fax (530) 367-2474; foresthillchamber@ftcnet.net; www.foresthillchamber.org

Forestville · *Forestville C/C* · Earl Stevens; P.O. Box 546; 95436; Sonoma; P 8,000; M 75; Fax (707) 887-0106; www.forestville chamber.org

Fort Bragg · *Mendocino Coast C/C* · Debra De Graw; CEO; 217 S. Main St.; P.O. Box 1141; 95437; Mendocino; P 20,000; M 497; (707) 961-6300; Fax (707) 964-2056; chamber@mcn.org; www. mendocinocoast.com*

Fortuna · *Fortuna C/C* · Erin Dunn; CEO; 735 14th St.; P.O. Box 797; 95540; Humboldt; P 11,350; M 455; (707) 725-3959; Fax (707) 725-4766; chamber@sunnyfortuna.com; www.sunny fortuna.com*

Foster City · *Foster City C/C* · Chris Messina; Pres./CEO; 1031 E. Hillsdale Blvd., Ste. F; 94404; San Mateo; P 30,359; M 290; (650) 573-7600; Fax (650) 573-5201; info@fostercitychamber.com; www.fostercitychamber.com*

Fountain Valley · *Fountain Valley C/C* · Beverly White; Exec. Dir.; 8840 Warner Ave., Ste. 207; 92708; Orange; P 58,000; M 300; (714) 841-3822; Fax (714) 841-3877; bwhite@fvchamber.com; www.fvchamber.com*

Fowler · *Fowler C/C* · Craig J. Mellon; Pres.; 420 E. Merced St., Ste. 100; 93625; Fresno; P 5,500; M 105; (559) 834-3869; Fax (559) 834-5318; craigmellon@fowlerchamber.com; www. fowlerchamber.com.

Frazier Park · *Mountain Comm. C/C* · Stacey Havener; Pres.; P.O. Box 552; 93225; Kern; P 10,000; M 80; (661) 245-1212; 1mccoc@gmail.com; www.frazierparkinfo.com

Freeport · *see California Delta*

Fremont · *Fremont C/C* · Cindy Bonior; Pres./CEO; 39488 Stevenson Pl., Ste. 100; 94539; Alameda; P 213,000; M 1,000; (510) 795-2244; Fax (510) 795-2240; fmtcc@fremontbusiness. com; www.fremontbusiness.com*

French Camp · *see California Delta*

Fresno · *Central Calif. Hispanic C/C* · John Hernandez; Exec. Dir.; 2331 Fresno St.; 93721; Fresno; P 1,200,000; M 600; (559) 495-4817; Fax (559) 495-4811; info@cchcc.net; www.cchcc.net

Fresno · *Greater Fresno Area C/C* · Al Smith; Pres./CEO; 2331 Fresno St.; 93721; Fresno; P 917,517; M 2,000; (559) 495-4800; Fax (559) 495-4811; info@fresnochamber.com; www.fresnochamber.com*

Friant · *Millerton Lake Area C/C* · P.O. Box 430; 93626; Fresno; P 520; (559) 822-7450; www.millertonlakeca.com

Fruitvale · *see Bakersfield–North of the River C/C*

Fullerton · *Fullerton C/C* · Theresa Harvey; Exec. Dir.; 444 N. Harbor Blvd., Ste. 200; P.O. Box 529; 92836-0529; Orange; P 132,721; M 700; (714) 871-3100; questions@fullertonchamber. com; www.fullertonchamber.com*

Galt · *Galt Dist. C/C* · Rose LaVine; Exec. Dir.; 431 S. Lincoln Way; P.O. Box 1446; 95632; Sacramento; P 22,000; M 300; (209) 745-2529; Fax (209) 745-0840; info@galtchamber.com; www. galtchamber.com*

Garberville · *Garberville-Redway Area C/C* · Dee Way; Exec. Dir.; 782 Redwood Dr.; P.O. Box 445; 95542; Humboldt; P 15,000; M 220; (707) 923-2613; (800) 923-2613; Fax (707) 923-4789; chamber@garberville.org; www.garberville.org

Garden Grove · *Garden Grove C/C* · Connie Margolin IOM; Pres./ CEO; 12866 Main St., Ste. 102; 92840; Orange; P 173,000; M 360; (714) 638-7950; Fax (714) 636-6672; connie.margolin@garden grovechamber.org; www.gardengrovechamber.org*

Garden Grove · *Vietnamese American C/C* · Dr. Tam Nguyen; Pres.; 14331 Euclid St., Ste. 103; 92843; Orange; P 400,000; M 10,000; (714) 390-9312; Fax (714) 265-5588; info@vacoc.com; www.vacoc.com

Gardena · *Gardena Valley C/C* · Wanda Love; Pres.; 1204 W. Gardena Blvd., Ste. E; 90247; Los Angeles; P 69,000; M 435; (310) 532-9905; Fax (310) 329-7307; gardenacc@sbcglobal.net; www. gardenachamber.org

Geyserville · *Geyserville C/C* · Shirley Buchignani; Pres.; P.O. Box 276; 95441; Sonoma; P 1,425; M 286; (707) 857-3745; moreinfo@geyservillecc.com; www.geyservillecc.com

Gilroy · *Gilroy C/C* · Susan Valenta; Pres./CEO; 7471 Monterey St.; 95020; Santa Clara; P 55,000; M 700; (408) 842-6437; svalenta@ gilroy.org; www.gilroy.org*

Glendale · *Glendale C/C* · Judee Kendall; Exec. V.P.; 200 S. Louise St.; 91205; Los Angeles; P 207,000; M 1,100; (818) 240-7870; Fax (818) 240-2872; info@glendalechamber.com; www.glendale chamber.com

Glendale · *Montrose-Verdugo City C/C* · Ted Ayala; Exec. Dir.; 3516 N. Verdugo Rd.; 91208; Los Angeles; P 6,528; M 350; (818) 249-7171; Fax (818) 249-8919; mvcc@montrosechamber.org; www.montrosechamber.org

Glendora · *Glendora C/C* · Kathy Hodge; Dir. of Op.; 131 E. Foothill Blvd.; 91741; Los Angeles; P 52,770; M 300; (626) 963-4128; Fax (626) 914-4822; info@glendora-chamber.org; www. glendora-chamber.org

Goleta · *Goleta Valley C/C* · Kristen Amyx; Pres./CEO; P.O. Box 781; 93116; Santa Barbara; P 86,000; M 550; (805) 967-2500; info@goletavalley.com; www.goletavalleychamber.com

Gonzales · *Gonzales C/C* · Julia Rocha; Pres.; P.O. Box 216; 93926; Monterey; P 7,800; M 55; (831) 675-9019; gonzales chamber@sbcglobal.net; www.gonzaleschamber.org

Gorman · *see Frazier Park*

Graeagle · *Eastern Plumas C/C* · Audrey Ellis; Exec. Dir.; 8989 Hwy. 89; P.O. Box 1043; 96103; Plumas; P 8,000; M 235; (530) 836-6811; Fax (530) 836-6809; epluchmb@psln.com; www. easternplumaschamber.com

Granada Hills · *Granada Hills C/C* · Alison Robinson; Pres.; 17723 Chatsworth St.; 91344; Los Angeles; P 57,000; M 300; (818) 368-3235; Fax (818) 366-7425; email@granadachamber.com; www.granadachamber.com

Grand Terrace · *Grand Terrace Area C/C* · Sally McGuire; Pres.; 22365 Barton Rd., Ste. 101; 92313; San Bernardino; P 15,600; M 150; (909) 783-3581; Fax (909) 370-2906; office@gtchamber. com; www.gtchamber.com

Granite Bay · *see Roseville*

Grass Valley · *Grass Valley/Nevada County C/C* · Mary Ann Mueller; Pres./CEO; 248 Mill St.; 95945; Nevada; P 13,000; M 600; (530) 273-4667; (800) 655-4667; Fax (530) 272-5440; info@ grassvalleychamber.com; www.grassvalleychamber.com.*

Greenville · *Indian Valley C/C* · Lillian Bashan; 408 Main St.; P.O. Box 516; 95947; Plumas; P 2,750; M 90; (530) 284-6633; Fax (530) 284-6907; indianvalleychamber@frontiernet.net; www.indianvalley.net

Gridley · *Gridley Area C/C* · Christine Cunningham; Secy./Mgr.; 613 Kentucky St.; 95948; Butte; P 6,000; M 100; (530) 846-3142; Fax (530) 846-3142; gridleychamber@hotmail.com; gridley areachamber.com

Griffith Park · *see Los Angeles–Atwater Village C/C*

Groveland · *Yosemite C/C* · Jackie Sample; Admin. Asst.; P.O. Box 1263; 95321; Tuolumne; P 5,000; M 140; (209) 962-0429; (800) 449-9120; info@groveland.org; www.groveland.org

Grover Beach · *Grover Beach C/C* · Linda Garcia; CEO; 180 Hwy. 1; 93433; San Luis Obispo; P 15,000; M 240; (805) 489-9091; Fax (805) 489-4147; info@groverbeachchamber.com; www.grover beachchamber.com

Gualala · *Redwood Coast C/C* · Sue Bohlin; Pres.; P.O. Box 199; 95445; Mendocino & Sonoma; P 6,000; M 125; (707) 884-1080; (800) 778-5252; info@redwoodcoastchamber.com; www.red woodcoastchamber.com

Guerneville · *Russian River C/C & Visitor Center* · Margaret Kennett; Pres.; 16209 First St.; P.O. Box 331; 95446; Sonoma; P 7,000; M 250; (707) 869-9000; Fax (707) 869-9009; news@ russianriver.com; www.russianriver.com

Gustine · *Gustine C/C* · Glen Beard; Pres.; 375 5th St.; P.O. Box 306; 95322; Merced; P 5,200; M 150; (209) 854-6975; Fax (209) 854-3511; gustinechamber@att.net; www.gustinechamber ofcommerce.com

Half Moon Bay · *Half Moon Bay Coastside C/C & Visitors Bur.* · Charise McHugh; Pres./CEO; 235 Main St.; 94019; San Mateo; P 28,000; M 720; (650) 726-8380; Fax (650) 726-8389; info@hmbchamber.com; www.hmbchamber.com*

Hanford · *Hanford C/C* · Mike Bertaina; Interim CEO; 109 W. 7th St.; 93230; Kings; P 50,000; M 750; (559) 582-0483; Fax (559) 582-0960; hanfordchamber@comcast.net; www.hanfordchamber.com.*

Happy Camp · *Happy Camp C/C* · Dinah Sulipeck; Pres.; P.O. Box 1188; 96039; Siskiyou; P 3,000; M 50; (530) 493-2900; info@ happycampchamber.com; www.happycampchamber.com

Harbor City · *Harbor City/Harbor Gateway C/C* · Joeann Valle; Pres./CEO; 1400 W. 240th St.; 90710; Los Angeles; P 55,000; M 200; (310) 534-3143; Fax (310) 534-3178; hchgchamber@ sbcglobal.net; www.hchgchamber.com*

Hat Creek · *see Burney*

Hawthorne · *Hawthorne C/C* · Sherice Fernandez; Ofc. Mgr.; 12629 Crenshaw Blvd.; 90250; Los Angeles; P 87,000; M 230; (310) 676-1163; Fax (310) 676-7661; info@hawthorne-chamber.com; www.hawthorne-chamber.com

Hayfork · *see Trinity County*

Hayward · *Hayward C/C* · Kim Huggett; Pres./CEO; 22561 Main St.; 94541; Alameda; P 153,000; M 750; (510) 537-2424; Fax (510) 247-2043; info@hayward.org; www.hayward.org*

Healdsburg · *Healdsburg C/C* · Maureen McElroy; Pres.; 217 Healdsburg Ave.; 95448; Sonoma; P 11,000; M 650; (707) 433-6935; Fax (707) 433-7562; info@healdsburg.com; www. healdsburg.com*

Helendale · *Helendale C/C* · Julia Garland; Pres.; P.O. Box 1449; 92342; San Bernardino; P 7,000; M 172; (760) 952-2231; Fax (760) 245-9908; www.helendalechamberofcommerce.com

Hemet · *Hemet/San Jacinto Valley C/C* · Patti Drusky; Pres./ CEO; 615 N. San Jacinto; 92543; Riverside; P 150,000; M 800; (951) 658-3211; Fax (951) 766-5013; info@hemetsanjacintochamber. com; www.hemetsanjacintochamber.com*

Hercules · *Hercules C/C* · Sylvia Villa-Serrano; Exec. Dir.; P.O. Box 5283; 94547; Contra Costa; P 25,000; M 170; (510) 741-7945; Fax (510) 741-8965; sylvia@herculeschamber.com; www.hercules chamber.com*

Hermosa Beach · *Hermosa Beach C/C* · Carla Merrimen; Exec. Dir.; 1007 Hermosa Ave.; 90254; Los Angeles; P 18,585; M 350; (310) 376-0951; Fax (310) 798-2594; info@hbchamber.net; www. hbchamber.net

Hesperia · *Hesperia C/C* · Yvonne Woytovich; Pres./CEO; 16816 Main St., Ste. D; 92345; San Bernardino; P 91,000; M 500; (760) 244-2135; Fax (760) 244-1333; chamber@hesperiacc.com; www. hesperiacc.com*

Highland · *Highland C/C* · Nanette Peykani; Exec. Dir.; 27255 Messina St.; P.O. Box 455; 92346; San Bernardino; P 53,000; M 295; (909) 864-4073; Fax (909) 864-4583; hcoc@highland chamber.org; www.highlandchamber.org

Hilmar · *Hilmar C/C* · Rob Mitchell; Pres.; P.O. Box 385; 95324; Merced; P 5,000; M 110; (209) 632-2028; info@hilmarchamber. com; www.hilmarchamber.com

Hollister · *San Benito County C/C* · Jessica French; Pres./CEO; 650 San Benito St., Ste. 130; 95023; San Benito; P 63,000; M 450; (831) 637-5315; Fax (831) 637-1008; info1@sanbenitocounty chamber.com; www.sanbenitocountychamber.com*

Hollywood · *Hollywood C/C* · Leron Gubler; Pres./CEO; 7018 Hollywood Blvd.; 90028; Los Angeles; P 300,000; M 1,075; (323) 469-8311; Fax (323) 469-2805; leron@hollywoodchamber.net; www.hollywoodchamber.net

Holtville · *Holtville C/C* · Laura Goodsell; Pres.; 101 W. 5th St.; 92250; Imperial; P 6,000; M 180; (760) 356-2923; Fax (760) 356-2925; info@holtvillechamber.org; www.holtvillechamber.org

Hood · *see California Delta*

Hopland · *see Ukiah*

Huntington Beach · *Huntington Beach C/C* · Perry Cain; Pres./ CEO; 19891 Beach Blvd., Ste. 139; 92648; Orange; P 200,000; M 1,020; (714) 536-8888; Fax (714) 960-7654; hbchamber@hbcoc. com; www.hbchamber.com*

Huntington Park · *Greater Huntington Park Area C/C* · Dante D'Eramo; Exec. Dir./CEO; 6330 Pacific Blvd., Ste. 208; 90255; Los Angeles; P 60,000; M 250; (323) 585-1155; Fax (323) 585-2176; info@hpchamber1.com; www.hpchamber1.com

Idyllwild · *Idyllwild C/C* · P.O. Box 304; 92549; Riverside; P 3,500; M 132; (951) 659-3259; (888) 659-3259; Fax (951) 659-6216; info@idyllwildchamber.com; www.idyllwildchamber.com

Imperial · *Imperial C/C* · Sharon Ryan; CEO; 1101 Airport Rd., Ste. I; 92251; Imperial; P 15,000; M 300; (760) 355-1609; Fax (760) 355-3920; ceo@imperialchamber.org; www.imperialchamber.org*

Imperial Beach · *Imperial Beach C/C & Visitors Bur.* · Patricia Hutchins; Pres.; 700 Seacoast Dr., Ste. 103; 91932; San Diego; P 27,800; M 153; (619) 424-3151; Fax (619) 424-3008; info@ ib-chamber.com; www.ib-chamber.com

Independence · *Independence C/C* · Sharon Avey; Pres.; P.O. Box 397; 93526; Inyo; P 600; M 70; (760) 878-0084; info@ independence-ca.com; www.independence-ca.com

Indian Wells · *Indian Wells C/C* · Ruth Finholt; Exec. Dir./CEO; 74-900 Hwy. 111, Ste. 125; 92210; Riverside; P 4,800; M 300; (760) 346-7095; Fax (760) 346-7605; info@indianwellschamber.com; www.indianwellschamber.com

Indio · *Indio C/C* · Joyce Donaldson; CEO; 82-921 Indio Blvd.; 92201; Riverside; P 83,000; M 650; (760) 347-0676; (800) 775-8440; Fax (760) 347-6069; info@indiochamber.org; www.indiochamber.org.

Inglewood · *Inglewood/Airport Area C/C* · Shannon R. Howe; Exec. V.P.; 330 E. Queen St.; 90301; Los Angeles; P 120,000; M 750; (310) 677-1121; (310) 677-1122; Fax (310) 677-1001; inglewoodchamber@sbcglobal.net; www.inglewoodchamber.org*

Irvine · *Irvine C/C* · Tallia Hart; Pres./CEO; 2485 McCabe Way, Ste. 150; 92614; Orange; P 202,000; M 800; (949) 660-9112; Fax (949) 660-0829; icc@irvinechamber.com; www.irvinechamber.com*

Irvine · *Orange County Bus. Cncl.* · Lucy Dunn; Pres./CEO; 2 Park Plaza, Ste. 100; 92614; Orange; P 3,000,000; M 250; (949) 476-2242; Fax (949) 476-9240; bmoulthrop@ocbc.org; www.ocbc.org

Irwindale · *Irwindale C/C* · Lisa Bailey; Pres./CEO; 16102 Arrow Hwy.; P.O. Box 2307; 91706; Los Angeles; P 1,446; M 306; (626) 960-6606; Fax (626) 960-3868; info@irwindalechamber.org; www.irwindalechamber.org

Isleton · *see California Delta*

Jackson · *Amador County C/C & Visitors Bur.* · Mark Borchin; Pres.; 571 S. Hwy. 49; P.O. Box 596; 95642; Amador; P 37,000; M 653; (209) 223-0350; (800) 649-4988; Fax (209) 223-4425; gold49@amadorcountychamber.com; www.amadorcountychamber.com*

Johnson Park · *see Burney*

Joshua Tree · *Joshua Tree C/C* · Linda Harmon; Ofc. Mgr.; 6448 Hallee Rd., Ste. 9; P.O. Box 600; 92252; San Bernardino; P 10,000; M 205; (760) 366-3723; Fax (760) 366-2573; info@joshuatreechamber.org; www.joshuatreechamber.org

Julian · *Julian C/C* · Michael Menghini; Pres.; 2129 Main St.; P.O. Box 1866; 92036; San Diego; P 4,000; M 280; (760) 765-1857; Fax (760) 765-2544; chamber@julianca.com; www.julianca.com

June Lake · *June Lake Loop C/C* · P.O. Box 2; 93529; Mono; P 630; M 48; www.junelakeloop.org

Kearny Mesa · *see Del Mar–LaJolla Golden Triangle C/C*

Kerman · *Kerman C/C* · Linda Geringer; Exec. Dir.; 783 S. Madera Ave.; 93630; Fresno; P 14,200; M 117; (559) 846-6343; Fax (559) 846-6344; info@kermanchamber.org; www.kermanchamber.org

Kernville · *Kernville C/C* · Jill Thurman; Pres.; 11447 Kernville Rd.; P.O. Box 397; 93238; Kern; P 10,000; M 146; (760) 376-2629; Fax (760) 379-4371; office@kernvillechamber.org; www.kernvillechamber.org

King City · *King City & Southern Monterey County C/C & Ag.* · Cindi B. Mora; Ofc. Mgr.; 200 Broadway, Ste. 40; 93930; Monterey; P 16,000; M 200; (831) 385-3814; Fax (831) 386-9462; kingcitychamber@sbcglobal.net; www.kingcitychamber.com

Kingsburg · *Kingsburg Dist. C/C* · Jess Chambers; Exec. Dir.; 1475 Draper St.; 93631; Fresno; P 11,000; M 230; (559) 897-1111; Fax (559) 897-4621; jessatkingsburg@aol.com; www.kingsburgchamberofcommerce.com

Klamath · *Klamath C/C* · Jan Crandall; Treas.; P.O. Box 476; 95548; Del Norte; P 1,200; M 70; (707) 482-7165; (800) 200-2335; janchinook@hughes.net; www.klamathcc.org

Knightsen · *see California Delta*

La Canada Flintridge · *La Canada Flintridge C/C* · Patricia A. Anderson; Pres./CEO; 4529 Angeles Crest Hwy., Ste. 102; 91011; Los Angeles; P 20,000; M 620; (818) 790-4289; Fax (818) 790-8930; exec@lacanadaflintridge.com; www.lacanadaflintridge.com

La Crescenta · *Crescenta Valley C/C* · Julia Rabago; Exec. Dir.; 3131 Foothill Blvd., Ste. D; 91214; Los Angeles; P 30,000; M 350; (818) 248-4957; Fax (818) 248-9625; cvcoc@aol.com; www.crescentavalleychamber.org

La Habra · *La Habra Area C/C* · Mark Sturdevant; Exec. Dir.; 321 E. La Habra Blvd.; 90631; Orange; P 60,000; M 400; (562) 697-1704; Fax (562) 697-8359; mark@lahabrachamber.com; www.lahabrachamber.com

La Jolla · *also see Del Mar–LaJolla Golden Triangle C/C*

La Jolla · *La Jolla Town Cncl.* · 7734 Herschel Ave., Ste. F; P.O. Box 1101; 92038; San Diego; P 42,000; M 500; (858) 454-1444; Fax (858) 454-1848; lajollatowncncl@san.rr.com; www.lajollatowncouncil.org

La Mesa · *see El Cajon*

La Mirada · *La Mirada C/C* · 15651 E. Imperial Hwy., Ste. 202A; 90638; Los Angeles; P 50,000; M 250; (562) 902-1970; director@lmchamber.org; www.lmchamber.org

La Palma · *La Palma C/C* · Esther De Leon Hernandez; Exec. Dir.; 7872 Walker St., Ste. 107; 90623; Orange; P 15,400; M 120; (714) 228-1214; Fax (714) 228-1218; staff@lapalmachamberofcommerce.com; www.lapalmachamberofcommerce.com

La Quinta · *La Quinta C/C* · David Archer; Pres./CEO; 78-275 Calle Tampico, Ste. B; 92253; Riverside; P 41,000; M 700; (760) 564-3199; Fax (760) 564-3111; contactus@lqchamber.com; www.lqchamber.com

La Verne · *La Verne C/C* · Brian McNerney; Pres./CEO; 2078 Bonita Ave.; 91750; Los Angeles; P 33,000; M 345; (909) 593-5265; (909) 751-6980; Fax (909) 596-0579; ceo@lavernechamber.org; www.lavernechamber.org*

Ladera Ranch · *see Laguna Hills*

Lafayette · *Lafayette C/C* · Jay Lifson; CEO; 100 Lafayette Cir., Ste. 103; 94549; Contra Costa; P 24,000; M 625; (925) 284-7404; Fax (925) 284-3109; info@lafayettechamber.org; www.lafayettechamber.org*

Laguna Beach · *Laguna Beach C/C* · Rose Hancock; Exec. Dir.; 357 Glenneyre; 92651; Orange; P 25,000; M 650; (949) 494-1018; Fax (949) 376-8916; info@lagunabeachchamber.org; www.lagunabeachchamber.org

Laguna Hills · *South Orange County Reg. Chamber of Commerce* · Barbara J. Thomas; Mgmt. Consultant; 24031 El Toro Rd., Ste. 300; 92653; Orange; P 305,000; M 1,000; (949) 600-5470; Fax (949) 600-5474; khume@socchambers.com; www.socchambers.com*

Laguna Niguel · *Laguna Niguel C/C* · Debbie Newman ACE; Pres./CEO; 28062 Forbes Rd., Ste. C; 92677; Orange; P 66,000; M 400; (949) 363-0136; Fax (949) 363-9026; lncc@lnchamber.com; www.lnchamber.com*

Laguna Woods · *see Laguna Hills*

Lake Almanor · *see Chester*

Lake Arrowhead · *Lake Arrowhead Comm. C/C* · Lewis Murray; Pres./CEO; P.O. Box 219; 92352; San Bernardino; P 14,900; M 500; (909) 337-3715; Fax (909) 336-1548; info@lakearrowhead.net; www.lakearrowhead.net

Lake City · *see Cedarville*

Lake County · *see Lakeport*

Lake Elsinore · *Lake Elsinore Valley C/C* · Kim Joseph Cousins; Pres./CEO; 132 W. Graham Ave.; 92530; Riverside; P 52,000; M 400; (951) 245-8848; Fax (951) 245-9127; kim@lakeelsinore chamber.com; www.lakeelsinorechamber.com.*

Lake Forest · *see Laguna Hills*

Lake Isabella · *Kern River Valley C/C* · Rex Emerson; Pres.; 6404 Lake Isabella Blvd., Ste. B; P.O. Box 567; 93240; Kern; P 13,000; M 175; (760) 379-5236; (866) 578-4386; Fax (760) 379-5457; office@kernrivervalley.com; www.kernrivervalley.com

Lake Los Angeles · *Lake Los Angeles C/C* · Mark Jojola; Pres.; P.O. Box 500071; 93591; Los Angeles; P 13,500; M 40; (661) 264-2786; risingclouds@sbcglobal.net; www.lakelachamber.org

Lake View Terrace · *see Tujunga*

Lakeport · *Lake County C/C* · Melissa Fulton; CEO; 875 Lakeport Blvd.; P.O. Box 295; 95453; Lake; P 60,000; M 600; (707) 263-5092; (866) 525-3767; Fax (707) 263-5104; info@lakecochamber. com; www.lakecochamber.com*

Lakeside · *Lakeside C/C* · Kathy Kassel; Exec. Dir.; 9924 Vine St.; 92040; San Diego; P 57,000; M 170; (619) 561-1031; Fax (619) 561-7951; chamber@lakesideca.com; www.lakesideca.com

Lakewood · *Greater Lakewood C/C* · John Kelsall; Pres./CEO; 24 Lakewood Center Mall; P.O. Box 160; 90714; Los Angeles; P 80,000; M 265; (562) 531-9733; Fax (562) 531-9737; info@ lakewoodchamber.com; www.lakewoodchamber.com

Lamont · *Greater Lamont C/C* · Miguel Sanchez; Pres.; P.O. Box 593; 93241; Kern; P 15,500; M 40; (661) 845-1992

Lancaster · *Antelope Valley Bd. of Trade* · Vicki Medina; Exec. Dir.; 548 W. Lancaster Blvd., Ste. 103; 93534; Los Angeles; P 400,000; M 204; (661) 942-9581; Fax (661) 723-9279; vicki@ avbot.org; www.avbot.org

Lancaster · *Antelope Valley Chambers of Commerce-Lancaster* · Ramon Ortega; Pres./CEO; 554 W. Lancaster Blvd.; 93534; Los Angeles; P 135,000; M 730; (661) 948-4518; Fax (661) 949-1212; avcoc@avchambers.com; www.avchambers.com.*

Larkspur · *see Corte Madera*

Lathrop · *Lathrop C/C* · Mary Kennedy-Bracken; Pres./CEO; 15040 Harlan Rd.; P.O. Box 313; 95330; San Joaquin; P 18,000; M 200; (209) 858-4486; (209) 740-6503; Fax (209) 858-9516; lathropchamber@verizon.net; www.lathropchamber.org*

Lawndale · *Lawndale C/C* · Dyan Davis; Exec. Dir.; 14717 A Hawthorne Blvd.; 90260; Los Angeles; P 35,000; M 125; (310) 679-3306; (310) 738-8678; Fax (310) 679-3306; lawndale chamber@sbcglobal.net; www.lawndalechamber.org

Lebec · *see Frazier Park*

Lee Vining · *Lee Vining C/C* · P.O. Box 130; 93541; Mono; P 398; M 23; (760) 647-6629; Fax (760) 647-6377; info@leevining.com; www.leevining.com

Leggett · *Leggett Valley C/C* · Helen Ochoa; Pres.; P.O. Box 105; 95585; Mendocino; P 380; M 15; (707) 925-6385

Lemon Grove · *see El Cajon*

Lemoore · *Lemoore Dist. C/C* · Maureen Azevedo; CEO; 300 E St.; 93245; Kings; P 21,900; M 270; (559) 924-6401; Fax (559) 924-4520; ceo@lemoorechamberofcommerce.com; www.lemoore chamberofcommerce.com

Leucadia · *see Encinitas*

Lewiston · *see Trinity County*

Lincoln · *Lincoln Area C/C* · Bob Romness; CEO; 540 F St.; P.O. Box 608; 95648; Placer; P 40,000; M 360; (916) 645-2035; Fax (916) 645-9455; info@lincolnchamber.com; www.lincolnchamber.com*

Linda · *see Marysville*

Linden · *Linden-Peters C/C* · P.O. Box 557; 95236; San Joaquin; P 2,000; M 145; (209) 547-3046; www.lindenchamber.net

Lindsay · *Lindsay C/C* · Exec. Dir.; 133 W. Honolulu, Ste. E; P.O. Box 989; 93247; Tulare; P 10,000; M 300; (559) 562-4929; Fax (559) 562-5219; lindsaychamber@lindsay.ca.us; www.the lindsaychamber.com*

Littlerock · *Littlerock C/C* · Ronni Di Giovanni; Pres.; P.O. Box 326; 93543; Los Angeles; P 15,000; M 40; (661) 944-6990; s8f230@gmail.com; www.littlerock-ca.us

Live Oak · *Live Oak Dist. C/C* · Annette Bertolini; Pres.; P.O. Box 391; 95953; Sutter; P 6,200; M 85; (530) 695-1519; liveoak chamber@syix.com; www.liveoakchamber.org

Livermore · *Livermore C/C* · Mrs. Dale Kaye; Pres./CEO; 2157 First St.; 94550; Alameda; P 83,000; M 850; (925) 447-1606; Fax (925) 447-1641; lccinfo@livermorechamber.org; www.livermore chamber.org*

Lockeford · *Clements-Lockeford C/C* · Cynthia Haynes; Pres./ CEO; P.O. Box 971; 95237; San Joaquin; P 3,000; M 90; (209) 727-3142; Fax (209) 727-3365; clchamber@sbcglobal.net; www. clementslockefordchamber.org

Lodi · *Lodi Dist. C/C* · Pat Patrick; CEO; 35 S. School St.; 95240; San Joaquin; P 60,000; M 800; (209) 367-7840; Fax (209) 369-9344; info@lodichamber.com; www.lodichamber.com*

Loleta · *Loleta Comm. C/C* · Cindy Davy; Secy.; P.O. Box 327; 95551; Humboldt; P 800; M 50; (707) 498-0450; cindy@lole-tacheese.com; pages.suddenlink.net/loletaperfecta/chamber.html

Loma Linda · *Loma Linda C/C* · Phil Carlisle; CEO; 25541 Barton Rd., Ste. 4; P.O. Box 343; 92354; San Bernardino; P 20,000; M 280; (909) 799-2828; Fax (909) 799-2825; info@lomalindachamber. com; www.lomalindachamber.com

Lomita · *Lomita C/C* · Chuck Taylor; Exec. Dir.; 25332 Narbonne Ave., Ste. 250; P.O. Box 425; 90717; Los Angeles; P 20,065; M 250; (310) 326-6378; Fax (310) 326-2904; info@lomitacoc.com; www. lomitacoc.com

Lompoc · *Lompoc Valley C/C & Visitor Bur.* · C. Dennis Anderson; Pres./CEO; 111 S. I St.; P.O. Box 626; 93438; Santa Barbara; P 58,301; M 500; (805) 736-4567; (800) 240-0999; Fax (805) 737-0453; chamber@lompoc.com; www.lompoc.com.*

Lone Pine · *Lone Pine C/C* · Kathleen New; Pres./CEO; 120 S. Main St.; P.O. Box 749; 93545; Inyo; P 1,665; M 257; (760) 876-4444; info@lonepinechamber.org; www.lonepinechamber.org*

Long Beach · *Long Beach Area C/C* · Randy Gordon; Pres./ CEO; One World Trade Center, Ste. 206; 90831-0206; Los Angeles; P 500,000; M 1,500; (562) 436-1251; Fax (562) 436-7099; info@ lbchamber.com; www.lbchamber.com

Long Beach · *Reg. Hispanic C/C* · Sandy Cajas; CEO; One World Trade Center; P.O. Box 32474; 90832; Los Angeles; P 500,000; M 450; (562) 590-7302; Fax (562) 685-0542; info@regional hispanicc.org; www.regionalhispanicc.org

Loomis · *Loomis Basin C/C* · Jennifer Knisley; Exec. Dir.; 6090 Horseshoe Bar Rd.; 95650; Placer; P 6,300; M 310; (916) 652-7252; Fax (916) 652-7211; manager@loomischamber.com; www. loomischamber.com*

Los Alamitos · *Los Alamitos Area C/C* · Johnnie Strohmyer; CEO; 3231 Katella Ave.; 90720; Orange; P 30,000; M 300; (562) 598-6659; Fax (562) 598-7035; info@losalchamber.org; www. losalchamber.org

Los Altos · *Los Altos C/C* · Julie Rose; Pres.; 321 University Ave.; 94022; Santa Clara; P 36,000; M 500; (650) 948-1455; Fax (650) 948-6238; info@losaltoschamber.org; www.losaltoschamber.org*

Los Angeles Area

Atwater Village C/C · Andy Hasroun; Pres.; P.O. Box 39754; 90039; Los Angeles; P 39,000; M 70; (323) 251-5967; board@ atwaterchamber.org; www.atwaterchamber.org

Black Business Assn. · Earl "Skip" Cooper II; Pres./CEO; P.O. Box 43159; 90043; Los Angeles; P 3,830,000; M 1,200; (323) 857-4600; Fax (323) 857-4610; mail@bbala.org; www.bbala.org

Boyle Heights C/C · Ralph Carmona; Coord.; 5271 E. Beverly Blvd.; 2822 E. Olympic Blvd.; 90023; Los Angeles; P 93,000; M 100; (323) 888-2685; Fax (323) 721-9794; info@boyleheightschamber. com; www.boyleheightschamber.com

Century City C/C · Susan Bursk; Pres./CEO; 2029 Century Park East; Concourse Level; 90067; Los Angeles; P 50,000; M 300; (310) 553-2222; Fax (310) 553-4623; contact@centurycitycc.com; www. centurycitycc.com

Crenshaw C/C · Michael Jones; Pres./CEO; P.O. Box 8193; 90008; Los Angeles; P 135,000; M 230; (323) 293-2900; crenshaw chamber@sbcglobal.net; www.crenshawchamber.com

East Los Angeles C/C · Joe Sandoval; Pres.; P.O. Box 63220; 90063; Los Angeles; P 128,000; M 121; (323) 722-2005; Fax (323) 722-2405; elacoc@pacbell.net; www.elacoc.com

Japanese C/C of Southern Calif. · Toshio Handa; Pres.; 244 S. San Pedro, Ste. 504; 90012; Los Angeles; M 266; (213) 626-3067; Fax (213) 626-3070; office@jccsc.com; www.jccsc.com

Lincoln Heights C/C · Steve Kasten; Pres.; 2716 N. Broadway, Ste. 210; 90031; Los Angeles; P 50,000; M 120; (323) 221-6571; Fax (323) 221-1513; lhcc_info@sbcglobal.net

Los Angeles Area C/C · Gary Toebben; Pres./CEO; 350 S. Bixel St., Ste. 201; 90017; Los Angeles; P 9,128,200; M 1,600; (213) 580-7500; Fax (213) 580-7510; eramseyer@lachamber.com; www.lachamber.com

Silverlake C/C · Steve Melendrez; Pres.; 3531 W. Sunset Blvd.; 90026; Los Angeles; M 300; (323) 908-4086; Fax (323) 908-4086; secretary@silverlakechamber.com; www.silverlakechamber.com

West Los Angeles C/C · Ron Adams; Pres.; P.O. Box 64512; 90064; Los Angeles; P 282,000; M 1,000; (310) 441-2900; Fax (310) 441-2904; info@westlachamber.org; www.westlachamber.org

Los Banos · *Los Banos C/C* · John Whala; Exec. Dir.; 503 J St.; 93635; Merced; P 35,000; M 365; (209) 826-2495; Fax (209) 826-9689; lbcofc@pacbell.net; www.losbanos.com.*

Los Gatos · *Town of Los Gatos C/C* · Ronee Nassi; Exec. Dir.; 349 N. Santa Cruz Ave.; 95030; Santa Clara; P 29,000; M 440; (408) 354-9300; Fax (408) 399-1594; chamber@losgatoschamber.com; www.losgatoschamber.com*

Los Molinos · *Los Molinos C/C* · Betty Joe Morales; Pres.; P.O. Box 334; 96055; Tehama; P 3,000; M 75; (530) 384-2251; Fax (530) 384-2284; lmchamber@att.net; www.losmochamber.com

Los Osos · *Los Osos/Baywood Park C/C* · Julie Downey; Exec. Dir.; 781 Los Osos Valley Rd.; P.O. Box 6282; 93412; San Luis Obispo; P 15,000; M 240; (805) 528-4884; Fax (805) 528-8401; info@lobpchamber.org; www.lobpchamber.org

Lucerne Valley · *Lucerne Valley C/C* · Lorane Abercrombie; Pres.; 32750 Old Woman Springs Rd.; P.O. Box 491; 92356; San Bernardino; P 9,000; M 100; (760) 248-7215; Fax (760) 248-2024; chamber@lucernevalley.net; www.lvcal.org/chamber

Lynwood · *Lynwood C/C* · Maria Garcia; Pres./CEO; 10840 S. Atlantic Ave.; 90262; Los Angeles; P 85,000; M 350; (424) 757-7850; lynwoodchamber@gmail.com; www.lynwoodchamber.org

Madera · *Golden Valley C/C* · Travis Hart; Pres.; 37167 Ave. 12, Ste. 5C; 93636; Madera; P 12,000; M 115; (559) 645-4001; golden valleychamber@theranchos.com

Madera · *Madera C/C* · Debi Bray; Pres./CEO; 120 North E St.; 93638; Madera; P 58,243; M 370; (559) 673-3563; Fax (559) 673-5009; dbray@maderachamber.com; www.maderachamber.com

Malibu · *Malibu C/C* · Rebekah Evans; CEO; 23805 Stuart Ranch Rd., Ste. 210; 90265; Los Angeles; P 15,000; M 600; (310) 456-9025; Fax (310) 456-0195; info@malibu.org; www.malibu.org

Mammoth Lakes · *Mammoth Lakes C/C* · Annette Scholl; Admin.; P.O. Box 3268; 93546; Mono; P 7,500; M 200; (760) 934-6717; Fax (760) 934-7066; info@mammothlakeschamber.org; www.mammothlakeschamber.org.*

Manhattan Beach · *Manhattan Beach C/C* · Helen Duncan; Pres./CEO; 425 15th St.; P.O. Box 3007; 90266; Los Angeles; P 34,000; M 750; (310) 545-5313; Fax (310) 545-7203; info@man hattanbeachchamber.net; www.manhattanbeachchamber.net*

Manteca · *Manteca C/C* · Debby Moorehead; Exec. Dir.; 821 W. Yosemite Ave.; 95337; San Joaquin; P 70,000; M 380; (209) 823-6121; Fax (209) 239-6131; chamber@manteca.org; www.manteca.org*

Marina · *Marina C/C* · Joe Sweeney; Pres.; P.O. Box 425; 93933; Monterey; P 25,000; M 200; (831) 594-1061; info@marina chamber.com; www.marinachamber.com

Marina del Rey · *see Westchester*

Mariposa · *Mariposa County C/C* · Peter Schimmelfennig; Exec. Dir.; 5158 Hwy. 140; P.O. Box 425; 95338; Mariposa; P 17,200; M 300; (209) 966-2456; Fax (209) 966-4193; mariposachamber@ sti.net; www.mariposachamber.org*

Mark West · *see Santa Rosa-Mark West Area C/C*

Markleeville · *Alpine County C/C* · Teresa Burkhauser; Exec. Dir.; P.O. Box 265; 96120; Alpine; P 1,208; M 93; (530) 694-2475; Fax (530) 694-2478; info@alpinecounty.com; www.alpinecounty.com

Martinez · *Martinez C/C* · Cynthia Murdough; CEO; 603 Marina Vista; 94553; Contra Costa; P 36,000; M 300; (925) 228-2345; Fax (925) 228-2356; info@martinezchamber.com; www.martinez chamber.com*

Marysville · *Yuba-Sutter C/C* · Laura Nicholson; Exec. Dir./CEO; 429 10th St.; P.O. Box 1429; 95901; Yuba; P 154,000; M 650; (530) 743-6501; Fax (530) 741-8645; chamber@yubasutterchamber. com; www.yubasutterchamber.com.*

McClellan Park · *see North Highlands*

McCloud · *McCloud C/C* · Claudia Ellis; Pres.; P.O. Box 372; 96057; Siskiyou; P 1,000; M 70; (530) 964-3113; contact@mccloudcham ber.com; www.mccloudchamber.com

McKinleyville · *McKinleyville C/C* · Shonnie Bradbury; V.P.; 1640 Central Ave.; P.O. Box 2144; 95519; Humboldt; P 14,000; M 250; (707) 839-2449; executivedirector@mckinleyvillechamber. com; www.mckinleyvillechamber.com

Menifee · *Menifee Valley C/C* · Dorothy Wolons; Pres./CEO; 29683 New Hub Dr., Ste. C; 92586; Riverside; P 66,000; M 400; (951) 672-1991; Fax (951) 672-4022; ceo@menifeevalleychamber. com; www.menifeevalleychamber.com

Menlo Park · *Menlo Park C/C* · Fran Dehn; Pres./CEO; 1100 Merrill St.; 94025; San Mateo; P 30,648; M 360; (650) 325-2818; Fax (650) 325-0920; info@menloparkchamber.com; www.menlo parkchamber.com*

Merced · *Greater Merced C/C* · Jennifer Krumm; COO; 1640 N St., Ste. 120; 95340; Merced; P 85,000; M 650; (209) 384-7092; Fax (209) 384-8472; info@merced-chamber.com; www.merced-chamber.com*

Merced · *Merced County C/C* · Julius Pekar; CEO; 860 W. 18th St.; 95341; Merced; P 275,000; M 700; (209) 722-3864; Fax (209) 722-2406; julius@mercedcountychamber.com; www.merced countychamber.com*

Mill Valley · *Mill Valley C/C* · Kathy Severson; CEO; 85 Throckmorton Ave.; 94941; Marin; P 13,000; M 400; (415) 388-9700; Fax (415) 388-9770; info@millvalley.org; www.millvalley.org*

Millbrae · *Millbrae C/C* · John Ford; Pres./CEO; 50 Victoria Ave., Ste. 103; 94030; San Mateo; P 22,000; M 200; (650) 697-7324; Fax (650) 259-7918; chamber@millbrae.com; www.millbrae.com

Milpitas · *Milpitas C/C* · Charlene Brooks; Exec. Dir.; 828 N. Hillview Dr.; 95035; Santa Clara; P 70,817; M 700; (408) 262-2613; Fax (408) 262-2823; info@milpitaschamber.com; www.milpitaschamber.com*

Mira Mesa · *see San Diego–San Diego North C/C*

Miramar · *see San Diego–San Diego North C/C*

Miramonte · *Central Sierra C/C* · Dottie Woolum; Pres.; P.O. Box 65; 93641; Fresno; P 2,500; M 100; (559) 336-9076; (559) 336-9886; sulfiati@gmail.com; www.centralsierrachamber.org

Mission Viejo · *see Laguna Hills*

Modesto · *Modesto C/C* · Joy Madison; Pres./CEO; 1114 J St.; P.O. Box 844; 95353; Stanislaus; P 210,000; M 1,100; (209) 577-5757; Fax (209) 577-2673; info@modchamber.org; www.modchamber.org.*

Monrovia · *Monrovia C/C* · Karin Crehan; Exec. Dir.; 620 S. Myrtle Ave.; 91016; Los Angeles; P 40,000; M 450; (626) 358-1159; Fax (626) 357-6036; chamber@monroviacc.com; www.monroviacc.com*

Montclair · *Montclair C/C* · Darleen Curley; Pres./CEO; 5222 Benito St.; 91763; San Bernardino; P 38,000; M 200; (909) 624-4569; Fax (909) 625-2009; info@montclairchamber.com; www.montclairchamber.com*

Montebello · *Montebello C/C* · Andrea Wagg; Pres.; 109 N. 19th St.; 90640; Los Angeles; P 75,000; M 500; (323) 721-1153; Fax (323) 721-7946; andrea@montebellochamber.org; www.montebellochamber.org

Monterey · *Monterey Peninsula C/C* · Jody Hansen; Pres./CEO; 30 Ragsdale Dr., Ste. 200; 93940; Monterey; P 150,000; M 1,000; (831) 648-5360; Fax (831) 649-3502; info@mpcc.com; www.mpcc.com*

Monterey Park · *Monterey Park C/C* · Mr. Vincent Chang; Pres.; 700 El Mercado Ave.; P.O. Box 387; 91754; Los Angeles; P 70,000; M 200; (626) 570-9429; Fax (626) 570-9491; mpccusa@yahoo.com

Montgomery Creek · *see Burney*

Montrose · *see Glendale–Montrose-Verdugo City C/C*

Moorpark · *Moorpark C/C* · Patrick Ellis; Pres./CEO; 18 E. High St.; 93021; Ventura; P 37,086; M 250; (805) 529-0322; Fax (805) 529-5304; patrick@moorparkchamber.com; www.moorparkchamber.com

Moraga · *Moraga C/C* · Edy Schwartz; Pres.; 1480 Moraga Rd., Ste. I #254; 94556; Contra Costa; P 17,500; M 135; (925) 376-3779; info@moragachamber.org; www.moragachamber.org

Moreno Valley · *Moreno Valley C/C* · Oscar Valdepena; Pres./CEO; 12625 Frederick St., Ste. E3; 92553; Riverside; P 180,000; M 300; (951) 697-4404; Fax (951) 697-0995; office@moval chamber.org; www.movalchamber.org

Morgan Hill · *Morgan Hill C/C & Visitors Center* · Christine Giusiana; Pres./CEO; P.O. Box 786; 95037; Santa Clara; P 37,000; M 550; (408) 779-9444; Fax (408) 779-5405; mhcc@morganhill.org; www.morganhill.org*

Morro Bay · *Morro Bay C/C* · Peter Candela; CEO; 845 Embarcadero, Ste. D; 93442; San Luis Obispo; P 10,500; M 500; (805) 772-4467; (800) 231-0592; Fax (805) 772-6038; brownpelican@morrobay.org; www.morrobay.org*

Moss Landing · *Moss Landing C/C* · P.O. Box 41; 95039; Monterey; P 1,000; M 85; (831) 633-4501; Fax (831) 633-4501; www.mosslandingchamber.com

Mount Shasta · *Mount Shasta C/C* · Marie Wells; Exec. Dir.; 300 Pine St.; 96067; Siskiyou; P 3,700; M 360; (530) 926-3696; (800) 926-4865; Fax (530) 926-0976; info@mtshastachamber.com; www.mtshastachamber.com

Mountain View · *Mountain View C/C* · Oscar Garcia; Pres./CEO; 580 Castro St.; 94041; Santa Clara; P 75,000; M 600; (650) 968-8378; Fax (650) 968-5668; info@chambermv.org; www.chambermv.org*

Muir Beach · *see Stinson Beach*

Murrieta · *Murrieta C/C* · Rex Oliver IOM ACE; Pres./CEO; 24801 Monroe Ave.; 92562; Riverside; P 100,700; M 700; (951) 677-7916; Fax (951) 677-9976; roliver@murrietachamber.org; www.murrietachamber.org*

Napa · *Napa C/C* · Lisa Batto ACE; Pres./CEO; 1556 First St.; P.O. Box 636; 94559; Napa; P 79,000; M 1,150; (707) 226-7455; Fax (707) 226-1171; info@napachamber.com; www.napachamber.com

National City · *National City C/C* · Jacqueline L. Reynoso; Pres./CEO; 901 National City Blvd.; 91950; San Diego; P 57,000; M 600; (619) 477-9339; Fax (619) 477-5018; thechamber@national citychamber.org; www.nationalcitychamber.org*

Needles · *Needles C/C* · Sue Godnick; Exec. Dir.; 100 G St.; P.O. Box 705; 92363; San Bernardino; P 5,630; M 185; (760) 326-2050; Fax (760) 326-2194; needleschamber@frontier.com; www.needleschamber.com.

Nevada City · *Nevada City C/C* · Cathy Whittlesey; Exec. Mgr.; 132 Main St.; 95959; Nevada; P 3,000; M 375; (530) 265-2692; (800) 655-NJOY; Fax (530) 265-3892; info@nevadacitychamber.com; www.nevadacitychamber.com.*

Newark · *Newark C/C* · Linda Ashley; Pres./CEO; 37101 Newark Blvd.; 94560; Alameda; P 44,000; M 335; (510) 744-1000; Fax (510) 744-1003; info@newark-chamber.com; www.newark-chamber.com*

Newberry Springs · *Newberry Springs C/C* · Sandra Brittian; Pres.; P.O. Box 116; 92365; San Bernardino; P 4,000; M 30; (760) 257-1072; Fax (760) 257-1072; newberryspringscoc@gmail.com; www.newberryspringscoc.com

Newbury Park · *see Westlake Village*

Newhall · *see Santa Clarita*

Newman · *Newman C/C* · Vicki Lucas; P.O. Box 753; 95360; Stanislaus; P 10,400; M 80; (209) 862-1000; (209) 862-1177; Fax (209) 862-4133; www.cityofnewman.com

Newport Beach · *Newport Beach C/C* · Richard Luehrs; Pres./CEO; 1470 Jamboree Rd.; 92660; Orange; P 86,000; M 1,000; (949) 729-4400; Fax (949) 729-4417; info@newportbeach.com; www.newportbeach.com*

Niland · *Niland C/C* · Maria Nava-Froelich; Pres.; P.O. Box 97; 92257; Imperial; P 1,200; M 150; (760) 359-0870; ; mnava-froelich@nilandchamber.org; www.nilandchamber.org

Nipomo • *Nipomo C/C* • Steve Schumann; Pres.; 671 W. Tefft St., Ste. 2; 93444; San Luis Obispo; P 14,000; M 220; (805) 929-1583; Fax (805) 929-5835; info@nipomochamber.org; www.nipomochamber.org*

Norco • *Norco C/C* • Tommy Vaughan; Pres.; 1204 6th St.; 92860; Riverside; P 24,182; M 200; (951) 737-2531; Fax (951) 737-2574; staff@norcochamber.com; www.norcochamber.com*

North Fork • *North Fork C/C* • Jack McGowan; Pres.; P.O. Box 426; 93643; Madera; P 3,500; M 40; (559) 877-2410; Fax (559) 877-2332; info@north-fork-chamber.com; www.north-fork-chamber.com

North Highlands • *Antelope Highlands C/C* • Keith Weber; Pres.; P.O. Box 20; 95660; Sacramento; P 47,000; M 150; (916) 725-5652; www.antelopehighlandschamber.com

North Hollywood • *Universal City North Hollywood C/C* • Patti Lippel; Ofc. Mgr.; 6369 Bellingham Ave.; 91606; Los Angeles; P 144,188; M 250; (818) 508-5155; Fax (818) 508-5156; info@noho.org; www.noho.org*

North Sacramento • *see Sacramento–North Sacramento C/C*

Northridge • *North Valley Reg. C/C* • Wayne Adelstein; Pres./CEO; 9401 Reseda Blvd., Ste. 100; 91324; Los Angeles; P 277,915; M 350; (818) 349-5676; Fax (818) 349-4343; info@nvrcc.com; www.nvrcc.com

Norwalk • *Norwalk C/C* • Vivian Hansen; Exec. Dir.; 12040 Foster Rd.; 90650; Los Angeles; P 105,000; M 260; (562) 864-7785; Fax (562) 864-8539; ceo@norwalkchamber.com; www.norwalkchamber.com*

Novato • *Novato C/C* • Coy Smith; CEO; 807 DeLong Ave.; 94945; Marin; P 52,000; M 600; (415) 897-1164; Fax (415) 898-9097; info@novatochamber.com; www.novatochamber.com*

Oakdale • *Oakdale Dist. C/C & Visitors Bur.* • Mary Guardiola; CEO; 590 N. Yosemite Ave.; 95361; Stanislaus; P 19,200; M 380; (209) 847-2244; Fax (209) 847-0826; info@oakdalechamber.com; www.oakdalechamber.com.*

Oakhurst • *Oakhurst Area C/C* • Kathy McCorry; Exec. Dir.; 49074 Civic Circle; 93644; Madera; P 13,000; M 380; (559) 683-7766; Fax (559) 683-0784; chamber@oakhurstchamber.com; www.oakhurstchamber.com*

Oakland Area

Oakland African-American C/C • Wil Hardee; Pres./CEO; 449 15th St., Ste. 410; 94612; Alameda; P 500,000; M 480; (510) 268-1600; Fax (510) 268-1602; info@oaacc.org; www.oaacc.org

Oakland Chinatown C/C • Jennie Ong; Exec. Dir.; 388 9th St., Ste. 258; 94607; Alameda; M 400; (510) 893-8979; Fax (510) 893-8988; oaklandctchamber@aol.com; www.oaklandchinatownchamber.org

Oakland Metro C/C • Joseph Haraburda; Pres./CEO; 475 14th St.; 94612; Alameda; P 400,000; M 1,600; (510) 874-4800; Fax (510) 839-8817; lana@oaklandchamber.com; www.oaklandchamber.com*

Oakley • *Oakley C/C* • Noelle Young; CEO; 3510 Main St.; P.O. Box 1340; 94561; Contra Costa; P 26,000; M 100; (925) 625-1035; Fax (925) 625-4051; oakleychamber@sbcglobal.net; www.oakleychamber.com

Oceanside • *Oceanside C/C* • David L. Nydegger; Exec. Dir.; 928 N. Coast Hwy.; 92054; San Diego; P 180,000; M 750; (760) 722-1534; Fax (760) 722-8336; info@oceansidechamber.com; www.oceansidechamber.com.*

Oildale • *see Bakersfield–North of the River C/C*

Ojai • *Ojai Valley C/C* • Scott Eicher; CEO; 201 S. Signal St.; P.O. Box 1134; 93024; Ventura; P 28,000; M 300; (805) 646-8126; Fax (805) 646-9762; info@ojaichamber.org; www.ojaichamber.org

Old Station • *see Burney*

Olive Drive • *see Bakersfield–North of the River C/C*

Ontario • *Ontario C/C* • Charla Lenarth; Dir. of Op.; 500 E. E St., Ste. 200; 91764; San Bernardino; P 175,000; M 450; (909) 984-2458; Fax (909) 984-6439; info@ontario.org; www.ontario.org

Orange • *Orange C/C* • Heidi Larkin-Reed; Pres./CEO; 307 E. Chapman Ave.; 92866; Orange; P 136,000; M 650; (714) 538-3581; Fax (714) 532-1675; info@orangechamber.com; www.orangechamber.com*

Orangevale • *Orangevale C/C* • Maggie Worthington; Ofc. Mgr.; 9267 Greenback Ln., Ste. B91; 95662; Sacramento; P 26,705; M 142; (916) 988-0175; Fax (916) 988-1049; ovchamber@sbcglobal.net; www.orangevalechamber.com*

Orick • *Orick C/C* • John Sutter; Pres.; P.O. Box 234; 95555; Humboldt; P 400; M 30; (707) 488-2885; (707) 488-2602; Fax (707) 488-5295; www.orick.net

Orinda • *Orinda C/C* • Candy Kattenburg; Exec. Dir.; 26 Orinda Way; P.O. Box 2271; 94563; Contra Costa; P 17,500; M 200; (925) 254-3909; Fax (925) 254-8312; info@orindachamber.org; www.orindachamber.org

Orland • *Orland Area C/C* • Candice Anderson; Mgr.; 401 Walker St.; 95963; Glenn; P 7,200; M 200; (530) 865-2311; Fax (530) 865-8171; orlandchamber@sbcglobal.net, www.orland-chamber.com*

Oroville • *Oroville Area C/C* • Claudia Knaus; Exec. Dir.; 1789 Montgomery St.; 95965; Butte; P 55,000; M 450; (530) 538-2542; (800) 655-GOLD; Fax (530) 538-2546; info@orovillechamber.net; www.orovillechamber.net*

Oxnard • *Oxnard C/C* • Nancy Lindholm; Pres./CEO; 400 E. Esplanade Dr., Ste. 302; 93036; Ventura; P 200,000; M 750; (805) 983-6118; Fax (805) 604-7331; info@oxnardchamber.org; www.oxnardchamber.org*

Pacific Beach • *see Del Mar–La Jolla Golden Triangle C/C*

Pacific Grove • *Pacific Grove C/C* • Mr. Moe Ammar; Pres.; 584 Central Ave.; P.O. Box 167; 93950; Monterey; P 15,500; M 500; (831) 373-3304; Fax (831) 373-3317; chamber@pacificgrove.org; www.pacificgrove.org*

Pacific Palisades • *Pacific Palisades C/C* • Arnie Wishnick; Exec. Dir.; 15330 Antioch St.; 90272; Los Angeles; P 27,000; M 450; (310) 459-7963; Fax (310) 459-9534; info@palisadeschamber.com; www.palisadeschamber.com.

Pacifica • *Pacifica C/C* • 225 Rockaway Beach, Ste. 1; 94044; San Mateo; P 39,000; M 250; (650) 355-4122; Fax (650) 355-6949; debbie@pacificachamber.com; www.pacificachamber.com

Palm Desert • *Palm Desert C/C* • Barbara deBoom; Pres./CEO; 72559 Hwy. 111; 92260; Riverside; P 49,000; M 1,400; (760) 346-6111; Fax (760) 346-3263; info@pdcc.org; www.pdcc.org*

Palm Springs • *Palm Springs C/C* • Nona Watson; CEO; 190 W. Amado Rd.; 92262; Riverside; P 47,601; M 950; (760) 325-1577; Fax (760) 325-8549; info@pschamber.org; www.pschamber.org*

Palmdale • *Palmdale C/C* • Stacia Nemeth; Interim CEO; 817 E. Ave. Q-9; 93550; Los Angeles; P 151,346; M 800; (661) 273-3232; Fax (661) 273-8508; chamberstaff@palmdalechamber.org; www.palmdalechamber.org*

Palo Alto • *Palo Alto C/C* • Paula Sandas; Pres./CEO; 122 Hamilton Ave.; 94301; Santa Clara; P 61,200; M 675; (650) 324-3121; Fax (650) 324-1215; info@paloaltochamber.com; www.paloaltochamber.com*

Panorama City · *see Van Nuys*

Paradise · *Paradise Ridge C/C* · 5550 Skyway, Ste. 1; 95969; Butte; P 26,300; M 400; (530) 877-9356; (888) 845-2769; Fax (530) 877-1865; info@paradisechamber.com; www.paradise chamber.com*

Paramount · *Paramount C/C* · Peggy Lemons; Exec. Dir.; 15357 Paramount Blvd.; 90723; Los Angeles; P 60,000; M 350; (562) 634-3980; Fax (562) 634-0891; plemons@paramountchamber.com; www.paramountchamber.com.

Parlier · *Parlier C/C* · Francine Vindiola; Secy.; P.O. Box 453; 93648; Fresno; P 12,000; M 10; (559) 646-9628; Fax (559) 646-9627; info@pcoc.org; www.parlierchamber.org

Pasadena · *Pasadena C/C & Civic Assn.* · Paul Little; Pres./CEO; 844 E. Green St., Ste. 208; 91101; Los Angeles; P 143,080; M 1,300; (626) 795-3355; Fax (626) 795-5603; info@pasadena-chamber.org; www.pasadena-chamber.org*

Paso Robles · *Paso Robles C/C* · Mike Gibson; Pres./CEO; 1225 Park St.; 93446; San Luis Obispo; P 30,000; M 1,100; (805) 238-0506; Fax (805) 238-0527; info@pasorobleschamber.com; www.pasorobleschamber.com.*

Patterson · *Patterson-Westley C/C* · George Macmaster; Pres.; P.O. Box 365; 95363; Stanislaus; P 11,000; M 175; (209) 895-8094; mac@gvni.com; www.patterson-westleychamber.com

Pearblossom · *Pearblossom C/C* · Duane Carles; Pres.; P.O. Box 0591; 93553; Los Angeles; P 3,000; M 75; (661) 944-2564; pear blossom.chamber@gmail.com; www.pearblossomchamber.com

Penn Valley · *Penn Valley Area C/C* · Ed James; Pres.; 11336 Pleasant Valley Rd.; P.O. Box 202; 95946; Nevada; P 14,000; M 140; (530) 432-1802; Fax (530) 432-7762; info@pennvalleycoc.org; www.pennvalleycoc.org

Perris · *Perris Valley C/C* · Vince Agnifili; Pres.; 227 N. D St., Ste. A; 92570; San Luis Obispo; P 50,000; M 136; (951) 657-3555; Fax (951) 657-3085; perrischamberofcommerce@yahoo.com; www.perrischamber.org*

Petaluma · *Petaluma Area C/C* · Onita Pellegrini; CEO; 6 Petaluma Blvd. N., Ste. A-2; 94952; Sonoma; P 58,000; M 800; (707) 762-2785; Fax (707) 762-4721; pacc@petalumachamber.com; www.petalumachamber.com*

Phelan · *Phelan C/C* · Tamie Jennings; Ofc. Mgr.; P.O. Box 290010; 92329; San Bernardino; P 17,000; M 90; (760) 868-3291; Fax (760) 868-3291; phelanchamber@verizon.net; phelanchamber.org

Pico Rivera · *Pico Rivera C/C* · Melanie Coward; Exec. Dir.; 5016 Passons Blvd.; 90660; Los Angeles; P 62,600; M 300; (562) 949-2473; Fax (562) 949-8320; melanie@picoriverachamber.org; www.picoriverachamber.com*

Pine Mountain Club · *see Frazier Park*

Pinehurst · *see Miramonte*

Pinion Pines · *see Frazier Park*

Pinole · *Pinole C/C* · Deanna Million; Exec. Dir.; 2200 San Pablo Ave., Ste. 201; P.O. Box 1; 94564; Contra Costa; P 30,000; M 130; (510) 724-4484; Fax (510) 724-4408; pinolechamber@yahoo.com; www.pinolechamber.org*

Pinon Hills · *Pinon Hills C/C* · Jane Rowan; Pres.; P.O. Box 720095; 92372; San Bernardino; P 7,000; M 75; (760) 868-5801; Fax (760) 868-5801; pinonhillschamber@verizon.net; www.pinonhillschamber.com

Pismo Beach · *Pismo Beach C of C & Visitors Info. Center* · Peter Candela; CEO; 581 Dolliver St.; 93449; San Luis Obispo; P 9,000; M 466; (805) 773-4382; (800) 443-7778; Fax (805) 773-6772; info@pismochamber.com; www.pismochamber.com

Pittsburg · *Pittsburg C/C* · Meredith Ladich; CEO; 985 Railroad Ave.; 94565; Contra Costa; P 78,800; M 500; (925) 432-7301; Fax (925) 427-5555; chamber@pittsburgchamber.org; www.pittsburgchamber.org

Placentia · *Placentia C/C* · 201 E. Yorba Linda Blvd., Ste. C; 92870; Orange; P 50,516; M 225; (714) 528-1873; Fax (714) 528-1879; info@placentiachamber.com; www.placentiachamber.com.*

Placerville · *El Dorado County C/C* · Laurel Brent-Bumb; CEO; 542 Main St.; 95667; El Dorado; P 170,000; M 900; (530) 621-5885; (800) 457-6279; Fax (530) 642-1624; psi@eldoradocounty.org; www.eldoradocounty.org*

Pleasant Hill · *Pleasant Hill C/C* · Charley Daley; Exec. Dir.; 91 Gregory Ln., Ste. 11; 94523; Contra Costa; P 32,500; M 400; (925) 687-0700; Fax (925) 676-7422; info@pleasanthillchamber.com; www.pleasanthillchamber.com*

Pleasanton · *Pleasanton C/C* · Scott Raty; Pres./CEO; 777 Peters Ave.; 94566; Alameda; P 67,000; M 800; (925) 846-5858; Fax (925) 846-9697; scott@pleasanton.org; www.pleasanton.org*

Plumas Lake · *see Marysville*

Point Reyes Station · *West Marin C/C* · Frank Borodic; Pres.; P.O. Box 1045; 94956; Marin; P 8,000; M 100; (415) 663-9232; Fax (415) 663-9203; info@pointreyes.org; www.pointreyes.org

Pomona · *Pomona C/C* · Frank Garcia; Exec. Dir.; 101 W. Mission Blvd., Ste 222A; P.O. Box 1457; 91769; Los Angeles; P 175,000; M 450; (909) 622-1256; Fax (909) 620-5986; info@pomona chamber.org; www.pomonachamber.org

Port Hueneme · *Port Hueneme C/C* · Kathleen Misewitch; Pres./CEO; 220 N. Market St.; 93041; Ventura; P 22,621; M 175; (805) 488-2023; Fax (805) 488-6993; phc@huenemechamber.com; www.huenemechamber.com

Porterville · *Porterville C/C* · Donnette Silva Carter IOM; Pres./CEO; 93 N. Main St., Ste. A; 93257; Tulare; P 52,960; M 630; (559) 784-7502; Fax (559) 784-0770; info@portervillechamber.org; www.portervillechamber.org*

Portola · *see Graeagle*

Poway · *Poway C/C* · Luanne Hulsizer; Pres./CEO; 13381 Poway Rd.; P.O. Box 868; 92074; San Diego; P 90,000; M 550; (858) 748-0016; chamber@poway.com; www.poway.com

Prunedale · *see Castroville*

Quartz Hill · *Quartz Hill C/C* · Lee Barron; Pres.; 42043 50th St. W.; 93536; Los Angeles; P 18,000; M 200; (661) 722-4811; Fax (661) 722-3235; info@qhchamber.org; www.qhchamber.org

Quincy · *Quincy C/C* · Sarah Metzler; Exec. Dir.; 464 Main St.; 95971; Plumas; P 6,849; M 187; (530) 283-0188; (877) 283-0188; Fax (530) 283-5864; office@quincychamber.com; www.quincychamber.com

Ramona · *Ramona C/C* · Thad Clendenen; Pres.; 960 Main St.; 92065; San Diego; P 48,000; M 350; (760) 789-1311; Fax (760) 789-1317; info@ramonachamber.com; www.ramonachamber.com

Rancho Bernardo · *see San Diego—San Diego North C/C*

Rancho Cordova · *Rancho Cordova C/C* · Jane Daly; CEO; 2729 Prospect Park Dr., Ste. 117; 95670; Sacramento; P 58,000; M 750; (916) 273-5688; Fax (916) 273-5727; admin@ranchocordova.org; www.ranchocordova.org*

Rancho Cucamonga · *Rancho Cucamonga C/C* · Michelle Alonzo; Pres./CEO; 7945 Vineyard Ave., Ste. D-5; 91730; San Bernardino; P 172,000; M 1,200; (909) 987-1012; Fax (909) 987-5917; info@ranchochamber.org; www.ranchochamber.org

Rancho Mirage · *Rancho Mirage C/C* · Stuart W. Ackley; Pres./CEO; 42520 Bob Hope Dr., Ste. B; 92270; Riverside; P 17,900; M 400; (760) 568-9351; Fax (760) 779-9684; info@ranchomirage.org; www.ranchomirage.org*

Rancho Penasquitos · *see San Diego–San Diego North C/C*

Rancho Santa Fe · *see Del Mar–San Diego Coastal C/C*

Rancho Santa Margarita · *see Laguna Hills*

Red Bluff · *Red Bluff-Tehama County C/C* · Dave Gowan; CEO; 100 S. Main St.; P.O. Box 850; 96080; Tehama; P 14,500; M 400; (530) 527-6220; (800) 655-6225; Fax (530) 527-2908; info@redbluffchamber.com; www.redbluffchamber.com.

Redding · *Greater Redding C/C* · Frank Strazzarino Jr.; Pres./CEO; 747 Auditorium Dr.; 96001; Shasta; P 90,000; M 1,100; (530) 225-4433; Fax (530) 225-4398; info@reddingchamber.com; www.reddingchamber.com.*

Redlands · *Redlands C/C* · Kathie Thurston; Exec. Dir.; 1 E. Redlands Blvd.; 92373; San Bernardino; P 72,000; M 810; (909) 793-2546; Fax (909) 335-6388; info@redlandschamber.org; www.redlandschamber.org*

Redondo Beach · *Redondo Beach C/C & Visitors Bur.* · Marna Smeltzer; Pres./CEO; 200 N. Pacific Coast Hwy.; 90277; Los Angeles; P 65,000; M 600; (310) 376-6911; Fax (310) 374-7373; info@redondochamber.org; www.redondochamber.org

Redwood City · *Redwood City-San Mateo County C/C* · Laurence Buckmaster; Pres./CEO; 1450 Veterans Blvd., Ste. 125; 94063; San Mateo; P 80,000; M 1,100; (650) 364-1722, Fax (650) 364-1729; info@redwoodcitychamber.com; www.redwoodcitychamber.com*

Reedley · *Greater Reedley C/C* · Valerie Pieroni; Exec. Dir.; 1633 11th St.; 93654; Fresno; P 25,723; M 325; (559) 638-3548; Fax (559) 638-8479; valerie@reedleychamberofcommerce.com; www.reedleychamberofcommerce.com

Rialto · *Rialto C/C* · Midge Zupanic; Interim Exec. Dir.; 120 N. Riverside Ave.; 92376; San Bernardino; P 97,400; M 300; (909) 875-5364; Fax (909) 875-6790; lisa@rialtochamber.com; www.rialtochamber.com*

Richmond · *Richmond C/C* · Judith Morgan; Pres./CEO; 3925 Macdonald Ave.; 94805; Contra Costa; P 103,000; M 500; (510) 234-3512; Fax (510) 234-3540; staff@rcoc.com; www.rcoc.com.*

Ridgecrest · *Ridgecrest C/C* · Nathan Ahle; CEO; 128 E. California Ave., Ste. B; 93555; Kern; P 28,000; M 390; (760) 375-8331; Fax (760) 375-0365; chamber@ridgecrestchamber.com; www.ridgecrestchamber.com.*

Rio Dell · *Rio Dell-Scotia C/C* · Susan Davis; 715B Wildwood Ave.; 95562; Humboldt; P 3,250; M 80; (707) 764-3436; Fax (707) 764-3436; rdscoc@aol.com; www.riodellscotiachamber.org

Rio Linda · *Rio Linda-Elverta C/C* · Kathryn Santos-Reed; Ofc. Mgr.; P.O. Box 75; 95673; Sacramento; P 30,000; M 100; (916) 991-9344; Fax (916) 991-9344; rlechamberofcommerce@sbcglobal.net; www.rlechamber.org

Rio Vista · *Rio Vista C/C* · Mary Peinado; Exec. Dir.; 6 N. Front St.; 94571; Solano; P 10,000; M 150; (707) 374-2700; Fax (707) 374-2424; mary.peinado@riovista.org; www.riovista.org*

Ripon · *Ripon C/C* · Dorothy Booth; Dir.; 929 W. Main St.; P.O. Box 327; 95366; San Joaquin; P 15,000; M 219; (209) 599-7519; Fax (888) 556-4944; execassist@riponchamber.org; www.riponchamber.org*

Riverbank · *Riverbank C/C* · Millicent Sanders & Jerry Van Houten; Co-Chairs; P.O. Box 340; 95367; Stanislaus; P 22,000; M 100; (209) 869-4541; info@riverbankchamber.org; www.riverbankchamber.org

Riverside · *Greater Riverside Chambers of Commerce* · Cindy Roth; Pres./CEO; 3985 University Ave.; 92501; Riverside; P 300,430; M 1,411; (951) 683-7100; Fax (951) 683-2670; rchamber@riverside-chamber.com; www.riverside-chamber.com*

Riverside · *Jurupa Valley C/C* · Diana Leja; Pres.; 5754 Tilton Ave.; PMB AV13; 92509; Riverside; P 92,000; M 250; (951) 681-9242; jurupachamber@aol.com; www.jurupachamber.org

Robla · *see Sacramento-North Sacramento C/C*

Rocklin · *Rocklin Area C/C* · Robin Trimble; CEO; 3700 Rocklin Rd.; 95677; Placer; P 50,000; M 650; (916) 624-2548; Fax (916) 624-5743; info@rocklinchamber.com; www.rocklinchamber.com*

Rodeo · *Rodeo C/C* · Mark Hughes; Pres.; P.O. Box 548; 94572; Contra Costa; P 12,000; M 60; (510) 245-4070; (510) 245-4400; rcoc@rodeoca.org; www.rodeoca.org

Rohnert Park · *Rohnert Park C/C* · Lisa Bagwell; Mgr. of Op.; 101 Golf Course Dr., Ste. C-7; 94928; Sonoma; P 43,000; M 250; (707) 584-1415; Fax (707) 584-2945; info@rohnertparkchamber.org; www.rohnertparkchamber.org.*

Rolling Hills Estate · *Palos Verdes Peninsula C/C* · Kay Finer; Pres./CEO; 707 Silver Spur Rd., Ste. 100; 90274; Los Angeles; P 75,000; M 430; (310) 377-8111; Fax (310) 377-0614; office@palosverdeschamber.com; www.palosverdeschamber.com

Rosamond · *Antelope Valley Chambers of Commerce-Rosamond* · Ramon Ortega; Pres./CEO; 2861 Diamond St.; P.O. Box 365; 93560; Kern; P 20,000; M 750; (661) 256-3248; Fax (661) 256-3249; avcoc@avchambers.com; www.avchambers.com*

Rosedale · *see Bakersfield-North of the River C/C*

Rosemead · *Rosemead C/C* · Min Hsien Wang; Exec. Dir.; 3953 Muscatel Ave.; 91770; Los Angeles; P 60,000; M 250; (626) 288-0811; Fax (626) 288-2514; office@rosemeadchamber.org; www.rosemeadchamber.org*

Roseville · *Roseville C/C* · Wendy Gerig; CEO; 650 Douglas Blvd.; 95678; Placer; P 120,000; M 1,450; (916) 783-8136; Fax (916) 783-5261; admin@rosevillechamber.com; www.rosevillechamber.com*

Rough and Ready · *Rough and Ready C/C* · Charles Creciluis; Pres.; P.O. Box 801; 95975; Nevada; P 2,500; M 120; (530) 272-4320; www.roughandreadychamber.com

Round Mountain · *see Burney*

Rubidoux · *see Riverside–Jurupa Valley C/C*

Running Springs · *Running Springs Area C/C* · Kevin Somes; Pres.; P.O. Box 96; 92382; San Bernardino; P 6,000; M 155; (909) 867-2411; Fax (909) 867-2411; info@runningspringschamber.com; www.runningspringschamber.com

Sabre Springs · *see San Diego–San Diego North C/C*

Sacramento Area

North Sacramento C/C · P.O. Box 15468; 95815; Sacramento; P 50,000; M 102; (916) 925-6773; leadershipteam@northsacramentochamber.org; www.northsacramentochamber.org

Sacramento Hispanic C/C · Steve Gandola; CEO; 1491 River Park Dr., Ste. 101; 95815; Sacramento; P 2,000,000; M 800; (916) 486-7700; Fax (916) 486-7728; info@sachcc.org; www.sachcc.org*

Sacramento Metro Chamber · Matt Mahood; Pres./CEO; One Capitol Mall, Ste. 300; 95814; Sacramento; P 2,000,000; M 2,200; (916) 552-6800; Fax (916) 443-2672; chamber@metrochamber.org; www.metrochamber.org*

Saint Helena · *Saint Helena C/C* · Nancy Levenberg; Pres./CEO; 1010 Main St., Ste. A; 94574; Napa; P 143,000; M 500; (707) 963-4456; Fax (707) 963-5396; nancy@sthelena.com; www.sthelenachamber.com*

Salinas · *Salinas Valley C/C* · Tom Carvey; Pres./CEO; 119 E. Alisal St.; 93901; Monterey; P 152,000; M 800; (831) 751-7725; Fax (831) 424-8639; info@salinaschamber.com; www.salinaschamber.com.*

Salton City · *West Shores C/C of the Salton Sea* · Sherrie Imari Kariotis; Secy.; 2114 Haven Dr.; P.O. Box 5185; 92275; Imperial; P 6,200; M 263; (760) 394-4112; Fax (760) 394-4303; wscc@westshoreschamber.org; www.westshoreschamber.org

San Andreas · *see Angels Camp*

San Anselmo · *San Anselmo C/C* · Connie Rodgers; Pres./CEO; P.O. Box 2844; 94979; Marin; P 13,000; M 250; (415) 454-2510; Fax (415) 258-9458; info@sananselmochamber.org; www.sananselmochamber.org*

San Bernardino · *San Bernardino Area C/C* · Judi Penman; Pres./CEO; 546 W. Sixth St.; P.O. Box 658; 92402; San Bernardino; P 202,000; M 1,000; (909) 885-7515; Fax (909) 384-9979; sba.chamber@verizon.net; www.sbachamber.org

San Bruno · *San Bruno C/C* · Laura Baughman; Exec. Dir.; 618 San Mateo Ave.; 94066; San Mateo; P 41,000; M 200; (650) 588-0180; Fax (650) 588-6473; office@sanbrunochamber.com; www.sanbrunochamber.com

San Carlos · *San Carlos C/C* · David Bouchard; CEO; 1500 Laurel St., Ste. B; 94070; San Mateo; P 28,000; M 750; (650) 593-1068; Fax (650) 593-9108; staff@sancarloschamber.org; www.sancarloschamber.org*

San Clemente · *San Clemente C/C* · Lynn Wood; Pres./CEO; 1100 N. El Camino Real; 92672; Orange; P 66,000; M 500; (949) 492-1131; Fax (949) 492-3764; info@scchamber.com; www.scchamber.com*

San Diego Area

Old Town San Diego C/C · Richard Stegner; Exec. Dir.; 2415 San Diego Ave.; 92110; San Diego; P 1,200,000; M 485; (619) 291-4903; Fax (619) 291-9383; otsd@aol.com; www.oldtownsandiego.org

Otay Mesa C/C · Alejandra Mier y Teran; Exec. Dir.; 9163 Siempre Viva Rd., Ste. I-2; 92154; San Diego; P 14,000; M 370; (619) 661-6111; Fax (619) 661-6178; amieryteran@otaymesa.org; www.otaymesa.org

San Diego County Hispanic C/C · Ivett Chavez; P.O. Box 131548; 92170; San Diego; M 500; (858) 268-0790; Fax (877) 840-6474; info@sdchcc.com; www.sdchcc.com

San Diego North C/C · Debra Rosen; Pres./CEO; 11650 Iberia Pl., Ste. 220; 92128; San Diego; P 240,000; M 900; (858) 487-1767; Fax (858) 487-8051; drosen@sdncc.com; www.sdncc.com

San Diego Reg. C/C · Ruben Barrales; Pres./CEO; 402 W. Broadway, Ste. 1000; 92101; San Diego; P 2,900,000; M 2,800; (619) 544-1300; webinfo@sdchamber.org; www.sdchamber.org

San Dimas · *San Dimas C/C* · Ted Powl; Pres./CEO; 246 E. Bonita Ave.; P.O. Box 175; 91773; Los Angeles; P 35,756; M 415; (909) 592-3818; Fax (909) 592-8178; info@sandimaschamber.com; www.sandimaschamber.com.*

San Francisco Area

Calif. Asia Business Cncl. · Jeremy Potash; Exec. Dir.; 525 Market St., 25th Flr.; 94105; San Francisco; M 100; (415) 986-8808; Fax (415) 957-0108; info@calasia.org; www.calasia.org

San Francisco Area, *continued*

San Francisco C/C · Steven Falk; Pres./CEO; 235 Montgomery St., 12th Flr.; 94104; San Francisco; P 789,000; M 1,900; (415) 392-4520; Fax (415) 392-0485; info@sfchamber.com; www.sfchamber.com.*

San Francisco Chinese C/C · Kenny Pse; Pres.; 730 Sacramento St.; 94108; San Francisco; M 400; (415) 982-3000; Fax (415) 982-4720; chinesechambersf@yahoo.com

San Gabriel · *San Gabriel C/C* · Albert Hernandez; Pres.; 620 W. Santa Anita St.; 91776; Los Angeles; P 49,000; M 300; (626) 576-2525; Fax (626) 289-2901; rosco_sandy@yahoo.com; www.sangabrielchamber.org

San Jacinto · *see Hemet*

San Jose · *San Jose Silicon Valley C/C* · Pat Dando; Pres./CEO; 101 W. Santa Clara St.; 95113; Santa Clara; P 1,001,000; M 2,200; (408) 291-5250; Fax (408) 286-5019; info@sjchamber.com; www.sjchamber.com*

San Juan Capistrano · *San Juan Capistrano C/C* · Mark Bodenhamer; Exec. Dir.; 31421 La Matanza St.; P.O. Box 1878; 92675; Orange; P 35,000; M 350; (949) 493-4700; Fax (949) 489-2695; info@sanjuanchamber.com; www.sanjuanchamber.com.*

San Leandro · *San Leandro C/C* · David P. Johnson; Pres./CEO; 15555 E. 14th St., Ste. 100; 94578; Alameda; P 85,000; M 525; (510) 317-1400; Fax (510) 317-1404; info@sanleandrochamber.com; www.sanleandrochamber.com*

San Luis Obispo · *San Luis Obispo C/C* · David E. Garth; Pres./CEO; 1039 Chorro St.; 93401; San Luis Obispo; P 44,000; M 1,500; (805) 781-2777; Fax (805) 543-1255; slochamber@slochamber.org; www.slochamber.org*

San Marcos · *San Marcos C/C* · Joan Priest; Pres./CEO; 939 Grand Ave.; 92078; San Diego; P 77,000; M 625; (760) 744-1270; Fax (760) 744-5230; janice@sanmarcoschamber.com; www.sanmarcoschamber.com*

San Marino · *San Marino C/C* · Sandra Troup; Pres.; 2304 Huntington Dr., Ste. 202; 91108; Los Angeles; P 13,000; M 250; (626) 286-1022; Fax (626) 286-7765; sanmarinochamber@att.net; www.sanmarinochamber.com

San Mateo County · *see Redwood City*

San Pablo · *San Pablo C/C* · William Erwin; Pres.; 13925 San Pablo Ave., Ste. 205; P.O. Box 6204; 94806; Contra Costa; P 32,000; M 100; (510) 234-2067; Fax (510) 234-0604; spchamber39@yahoo.com; sanpablochamber.org

San Pedro · *San Pedro C/C* · Camilla Townsend; Pres./CEO; 390 W. 7th St.; 90731; Los Angeles; P 81,000; M 470; (310) 832-7272; Fax (310) 832-0685; info@sanpedrochamber.com; www.sanpedrochamber.com

San Rafael · *Hispanic C/C of Marin* · Cecilia Zamora; Pres.; P.O. Box 4423; 94913; Marin; P 265,000; M 185; (415) 721-9686; (415) 454-0102; info@hccmarin.com; www.hccmarin.com

San Rafael · *San Rafael C/C* · Rick Wells; Pres./CEO; 817 Mission Ave.; 94901; Marin; P 56,000; M 650; (415) 454-4163; (800) 454-4163; Fax (415) 454-7039; frontdesk@srchamber.com; www.srchamber.com*

San Ramon · *San Ramon C/C Inc.* · Stewart L. Bambino; Pres./CEO; 2410 Camino Ramon, Ste. 125; 94583; Contra Costa; P 60,000; M 540; (925) 242-0600; Fax (925) 242-0603; info@sanramon.org; www.sanramon.org*

San Simeon · *San Simeon C/C* · Michael Hanchett; Pres.; 250 San Simeon Ave., Ste. 3A; 93452; San Luis Obispo; P 6,000; M 50; (805) 927-3500; Fax (805) 927-6453; sansimeonchamber@yahoo.com; www.sansimeonchamber.com

San Ysidro · *San Ysidro C of C & Visitor Info. Center* · Jason M-B Wells; Exec. Dir.; 663 E. San Ysidro Blvd.; 92173; San Diego; P 40,000; M 200; (619) 428-1281; Fax (619) 428-1294; info@ sanysidrochamber.org; www.sanysidrochamber.org

Sanger · *Sanger Dist. C/C & Visitors Center* · Cheryl Ing; Admin. Asst.; 1789 Jensen Ave., Ste. B; 93657; Fresno; P 25,385; M 275; (559) 875-4575; Fax (559) 875-0745; sanger@psnw.com; www. sanger.org.*

Santa Ana · *Greater Santa Ana Bus. Alliance* · Curt Carson; Interim CEO; 2020 N. Broadway, Ste. 200; 92706; Orange; P 351,000; M 749; (714) 541-5353; Fax (714) 541-2238; info@ santaanachamber.com; www.santaanachamber.com*

Santa Ana · *Orange County Hispanic C/C* · Javier Mier; Chrmn.; 2130 E. 4th St., Ste. 160; 92705; Orange; M 715; (714) 953-4289; Fax (714) 953-0273; mail@hcoc.org; www.hcoc.org*

Santa Barbara · *Hispanic C/C of Santa Barbara* · Sergio Villa; Pres./CEO; P.O. Box 6592; 93160; Santa Barbara; P 86,400; M 350; (805) 637-3680; Fax (805) 681-1260; info@sbhispanicchamber. org; www.sbhispanicchamber.org

Santa Barbara · *Santa Barbara Region C/C* · Steve Cushman; Pres.; 924 Anacapa St., Ste. 1; P.O. Box 299; 93101; Santa Barbara; P 89,000; M 1,500; (805) 965-3023; Fax (805) 966-5954; info@ sbchamber.org; www.sbchamber.org

Santa Clara · *Santa Clara C/C* · Steve Van Dorn; Pres./CEO; 1850 Warburton Ave.; 95050; Santa Clara; P 120,000; M 550; (408) 244-8244; Fax (408) 244-7830; denise.harris@santaclara.orq; www. santaclarachamber.com*

Santa Clarita · *Santa Clarita Valley C/C* · Charles Gill; Interim Exec. Dir.; 27451 Tourney Rd., Ste. 160; 91355; Los Angeles; P 213,178; M 1,200; (661) 702-6977; Fax (661) 702-6980; info@ scvchamber.com; www.scvchamber.com

Santa Cruz · *Santa Cruz C/C* · William Tysseling; Exec. Dir.; 611 Ocean St., Ste. 1; 95060; Santa Cruz; P 58,000; M 750; (831) 457-3713; Fax (831) 423-1847; info@santacruzchamber.org; www.santacruzchamber.org

Santa Fe Springs · *Santa Fe Springs C/C* · Kathie Fink; CEO; 12016 E. Telegraph Rd., Ste. 100; 90670; Los Angeles; P 17,483; M 790; (562) 944-1616; Fax (562) 946-3976; mail@sfschamber. com; www.sfschamber.com*

Santa Maria · *Santa Maria Valley C/C* · Robert Hatch; Pres./ CEO; 614 S. Broadway; 93454; Santa Barbara; P 144,000; M 1,100; (805) 925-2403; (800) 331-3779; Fax (805) 928-7559; info@ santamaria.com; www.santamaria.com.*

Santa Monica · *Santa Monica C/C* · Laurel Rosen; Pres./CEO; 1234 6th St., Ste. 100; 90401; Los Angeles; P 94,000; M 900; (310) 393-9825; Fax (310) 394-1868; info@smchamber.com; www. smchamber.com

Santa Paula · *Santa Paula C/C* · Nan Drake; Chair; 200 N. Tenth St.; P.O. Box 1; 93061; Ventura; P 29,000; M 260; (805) 525-5561; Fax (805) 525-8950; info@santapaulachamber.com; www.santa paulachamber.com

Santa Rosa Area

Hispanic C/C of Sonoma County · Juan M. Hernandez; Pres.; 3033 Cleveland Ave., Ste. 306; P.O. Box 11392; 95406; Sonoma; P 490,000; M 260; (707) 575-3648; Fax (707) 575-3693; hcc admin@hcc-sc.org; www.hcc-sc.org*

Mark West Area C/C & Visitors Center · Will Brodt; Pres.; 4787 Old Redwood Hwy., Ste. 101; 95403; Sonoma; P 25,000; M 175; (707) 578-7975; Fax (707) 578-0397; office@markwest.org; www. markwest.org*

Santa Rosa Area, *continued*

Santa Rosa C/C · Jonathan Coe; Pres./CEO; 637 First St.; 95404; Sonoma; P 160,000; M 1,000; (707) 545-1414; Fax (707) 545-6914; chamber@santarosachamber.com; www.santarosachamber.com

Santee · *Santee C/C* · Warren H. Savage Jr.; Exec. Dir.; 10315 Mission Gorge Rd.; 92071; San Diego; P 58,000; M 267; (619) 449-6572; Fax (619) 562-7906; info@santee-chamber.org; www.santee-chamber.org*

Saratoga · *Saratoga C/C* · Vicki Seelig; Pres.; 14460 Big Basin Way; 95070; Santa Clara; P 31,000; M 325; (408) 867-0753; Fax (408) 867-5213; info@saratogachamber.org; www.saratoga chamber.org*

Saugus · *see Santa Clarita*

Sausalito · *Sausalito C/C* · Oonagh Kavanagh; CEO; 10 Liberty Ship Way, Bay 2, Ste. 250; 94965; Marin; P 7,500; M 400; (415) 331-7262; Fax (415) 332-0323; chamber@sausalito.org; www. sausalito.org*

Scotts Valley · *Scotts Valley C/C* · Sharollynn Ullestad; Exec. Dir.; 360 Kings Village Rd.; 95066; Santa Cruz; P 12,000; M 300; (831) 438-1010; Fax (831) 438-6544; info@scottsvalleychamber. com; www.scottsvalleychamber.com*

Scripps Ranch · *see San Diego–San Diego North C/C*

Seal Beach · *Seal Beach C/C* · Gina Phillips; Dir. of Op.; 201 8th St., Ste. 120; 90740; Orange; P 24,000; M 250; (562) 799-0179; Fax (562) 795-5637; info@sealbeachchamber.org; www.seal beachchamber.org

Seaside · *Seaside-Sand City C/C* · Patrick Orosco; Pres.; 505 Broadway Ave.; 93955; Monterey; P 36,000; M 400; (831) 394-6501; Fax (831) 393-0645; info@sea-sand.com; www.sea-sand.com

Sebastopol · *Sebastopol Area C/C* · Teresa Ramondo; Exec. Dir./ CEO; 265 S. Main St.; P.O. Box 178; 95473; Sonoma; P 35,000; M 350; (707) 823-3032; Fax (707) 823-8439; chamber@ sebastopol.org; www.sebastopol.org*

Selma · *Selma District C/C* · Cindy L. Howell; Exec. Dir.; 1821 Tucker St.; 93662; Fresno; P 24,000; M 350; (559) 891-2235; Fax (559) 896-7075; cindyh@cityofselma.com; www.cityofselma. com/chamber*

Sepulveda · *see Van Nuys*

Shadow Hills · *see Tujunga*

Shafter · *Shafter C/C* · Debbe Haley; Pres.; 336 Pacific Ave.; 93263; Kern; P 15,609; M 90; (661) 746-2600; Fax (661) 746-0607; shafterchamber@shafter.com; www.shafter.com

Shasta Dam · *see Redding*

Shaver Lake · *Shaver Lake C/C* · 41758 Tollhouse Rd.; P.O. Box 58; 93664; Fresno; P 2,200; M 300; (559) 841-3350; (866) 500-3350; Fax (559) 841-8645; info@shaverlakechamber.com; www. shaverlakechamber.com

Sherman Oaks · *Greater Sherman Oaks C/C* · Lisa Clayden; Exec. Dir.; 14827 Ventura Blvd., Ste. 207; 91403; Los Angeles; P 60,000; M 300; (818) 906-1951; Fax (818) 783-3100; chamber@ shermanoakschamber.org; www.shermanoakschamber.org*

Sherman Oaks · *United Chambers of Commerce* · John Parker; Chrmn.; 5121 Van Nuys Blvd., Ste. 208; 91403; Los Angeles; (818) 981-4491; Fax (818) 981-4256; marian@unitedchambers.org; www.unitedchambers.org

Shingle Springs · *Shingle Springs/Cameron Park C/C* · Rebecca Bellas; Pres.; 3300 Coach Lane, Ste. B7; P.O. Box 341; 95682; El Dorado; P 18,000; M 315; (530) 677-8000; Fax (530) 676-8313; info@sscpchamber.org; www.sscpchamber.org*

Sierra City · *Sierra County C/C* · P.O. Box 436; 96125; Sierra; P 3,557; M 71; (800) 200-4949; info@sierracountychamber.com; www.sierracountychamber.com

Sierra Madre · *Sierra Madre C/C* · Bill Coburn; Exec. Dir.; 37 N. Auburn Ave., Ste. 1; 91024; Los Angeles; P 10,700; M 200; (626) 355-5111; Fax (626) 306-1150; info@sierramadrechamber.com; www.sierramadrechamber.com

Signal Hill · *Signal Hill C/C* · Shari Blackwell; Pres.; 2201 E. Willow, Ste. D; PMB 138; 90755; Los Angeles; P 11,500; M 65; (562) 424-6489; info@signalhillchamber.com; www.signalhillchamber.com*

Simi Valley · *Simi Valley C/C* · Leigh Nixon; Pres./CEO; 40 W. Cochran St., Ste. 100; 93065; Ventura; P 126,166; M 830; (805) 526-3900; Fax (805) 526-6234; info@simichamber.org; www.simichamber.org*

Slide Ranch · *see Stinson Beach*

Solana Beach · *Solana Beach C/C* · Frieda Silveira; Exec. Dir.; 210 W. Plaza St.; P.O. Box 623; 92075; San Diego; P 14,000; M 325; (858) 755-4775; Fax (858) 755-4889; info@solanabeachchamber.com; www.solanabeachchamber.com*

Soledad · *Soledad Mission C/C* · Vanesa Caldera; Pres.; 641 Front St.; 93960; Monterey; P 23,200; M 100; (831) 678-3941; Fax (831) 678-3941; soledadmissionchamber@yahoo.com; www.soledadchamber.com

Solvang · *Solvang C/C* · Linda Jackson; Exec. Dir.; 1693 Mission Dr., Ste. 201C; P.O. Box 465; 93464; Santa Barbara; P 5,500; M 300; (805) 688-0701; linda@solvangcc.org; www.solvangusa.com

Sonoma · *Sonoma Valley C/C* · Jennifer Yankovich; Exec. Dir.; 651-A Broadway; 95476; Sonoma; P 10,000; M 720; (707) 996-1033; Fax (707) 996-9402; info@sonomachamber.com; www.sonomachamber.com*

Sonora · *Tuolumne County C/C* · George Segarini; Pres./CEO; 222 S. Shepherd St.; 95370; Tuolumne; P 58,504; M 400; (209) 532-4212; (877) 532-4212; Fax (209) 532-8068; info@tcchamber.com; www.tcchamber.com*

Soquel · *see Capitola*

Sorrento Mesa · *see San Diego–San Diego North C/C*

Sorrento Valley · *see Del Mar–LaJolla Golden Triangle C/C*

South Gate · *South Gate C/C* · Jaime Garcia; Exec. Dir.; 3350 Tweedy Blvd.; 90280; Los Angeles; P 98,000; M 182; (323) 567-1203; Fax (323) 567-1204; jgarcia@sgchamber.org; www.sgchamber.org

South Lake Tahoe · *see Stateline, NV*

South San Francisco · *South San Francisco C/C* · Maria Martinucci; CEO; 213 Linden Ave.; 94080; San Mateo; P 68,500; M 600; (650) 588-1911; Fax (650) 588-2534; info@ssfchamber.com; www.ssfchamber.com*

Spring Valley · *Spring Valley C/C* · Tina Carlson; Exec. Dir.; 3322 Sweetwater Springs Blvd., Ste. 202; P.O. Box 1211; 91979; San Diego; P 100,000; M 300; (619) 670-9902; info@springvalleychamber.org; www.springvalleychamber.org

Springville · *Springville C/C* · Rick Mitchell; Pres.; 35680 Hwy. 190; P.O. Box 104; 93265; Tulare; P 6,500; M 125; (559) 539-0100; chamber@springville.ca.us; www.springville.ca.us

Squaw Valley · *see Miramonte*

Stanton · *Stanton C/C* · Billie Turner; Exec. Dir.; 8381 Katella Ave., Ste. H; P.O. Box 353; 90680; Orange; P 39,000; M 140; (714) 995-1485; Fax (714) 995-1184; service@stantonchamber.org; www.stantonchamber.org.*

Stinson Beach · *Stinson Beach Comm. Center* · Mary Greenwood; P.O. Box 158; 94970; Marin; P 500; (415) 868-1444; Fax (415) 868-1904; info@stinsonbeachcommunitycenter.org; www.stinsonbeachcommunitycenter.org

Stockton · *Greater Stockton C/C* · Douglass W. Wilhoit Jr.; CEO; 445 W. Weber Ave., Ste. 220; 95203; San Joaquin; P 263,000; M 1,600; (209) 547-2770; Fax (209) 466-5271; schamber@stocktonchamber.org; www.stocktonchamber.org*

Studio City · *Studio City C/C* · Esther Walker; Exec. Dir.; 4024 Radford Ave., Ed. 2, Ste. F; 91604; Los Angeles; P 42,000; M 300; (818) 655-5916; Fax (818) 655-8392; admin@studiocitychamber.com; www.studiocitychamber.com

Suisun · *see Fairfield*

Sun Valley · *Sun Valley Area C/C* · Theodore Bradpiece; Pres.; P.O. Box 308; 91353; Los Angeles; P 73,000; M 200; (818) 768-2014; Fax (818) 771-9793; info@svacc.com; www.svacc.com

Sunland · *see Tujunga*

Sunnyvale · *Sunnyvale C/C* · Don Eagleston; Pres./CEO; 260 S. Sunnyvale Ave., Ste. 4; 94086; Santa Clara; P 140,000; M 500; (408) 736-4971; Fax (408) 736-1919; info@svcoc.org; www.svcoc.org*

Susanville · *Lassen County C/C* · Patricia Hagata; Exec. Dir.; 75 N. Weatherlow St.; P.O. Box 338; 96130; Lassen; P 34,109; M 400; (530) 257-4323; Fax (530) 251-2561; director@lassencountychamber.org; www.lassencountychamber.org

Sutter County · *see Marysville*

Taft · *Taft District C/C* · Fred Schell; Exec. Dir.; 400 Kern St.; 93268; Kern; P 22,000; M 250; (661) 765-2165; Fax (661) 765-6639; taftchamber@bak.rr.com; www.taftchamber.com

Tahoe City · *North Lake Tahoe C/C* · Kym Fabel; Mgr.; 380 N. Lake Blvd.; P.O. Box 884; 96145; Placer; P 10,000; M 650; (530) 581-6900; Fax (530) 581-6904; kym@puretahoenorth.com; www.northlaketahoechamber.com

Tarzana · *see Woodland Hills*

Tecopa · *Death Valley C/C* · Jennifer Viereck; Admin. Asst.; P.O. Box 25; 92389; Inyo; P 500; M 30; (760) 852-4420; (760) 852-4524; deathvalleychamber@gmail.com; www.deathvalleychamber.org

Tehachapi · *Greater Tehachapi C/C* · Ida Perkins; Pres.; 209 E. Tehachapi Blvd.; P.O. Box 401; 93581; Kern; P 38,000; M 500; (661) 822-4180; Fax (661) 822-9036; chamber@tehachapi.com; www.tehachapi.com*

Temecula · *Temecula Valley C/C* · Alice Sullivan; Pres./CEO; 26790 Ynez Ct., Ste. A; 92591; Riverside; P 105,000; M 1,200; (951) 676-5090; Fax (951) 694-0201; info@temecula.org; www.temecula.org

Temple City · *Temple City C/C* · Linda Payne; Pres./CEO; 9050 Las Tunas Dr.; 91780; Los Angeles; P 37,000; M 400; (626) 286-3101; Fax (626) 286-2590; info@templecitychamber.org; www.templecitychamber.org

Templeton · *Templeton C/C* · Carrie Van Beurden; Pres.; P.O. Box 701; 93465; San Luis Obispo; P 7,000; M 185; (805) 434-2099; info@templetonchamber.com; www.templetonchamber.com*

Terminous · *see California Delta*

Thermal · *Thermal C/C* · Mike Castaneda; Pres.; P.O. Box 284; 92274; Riverside; P 8,000; M 100; (760) 399-5007

Thornton · *Thornton C/C* · Marlene Corbitt; Secy.; P.O. Box 37; 95686; San Joaquin; P 2,000; M 31; (209) 794-2255; Fax (209) 794-2355; mlcorbitt@att.net

Thousand Oaks · *see Westlake Village*

Thousand Palms · *Thousand Palms C/C* · 72-715 La Canada Way; P.O. Box 365; 92276; Riverside; P 6,000; M 100; (760) 343-1988; tp4business@gmail.com; www.thousandpalmscc.com

Three Rivers · *Sequoia Foothills C/C* · Tony Moreno; Pres.; 42268 Sierra Drive; P.O. Box 818; 93271; Tulare; P 3,000; M 119; (559) 561-3300; (800) 530-3300; merchant@threerivers.com; www.threerivers.com

Tiburon · *Belvedere/Tiburon C/C* · Georgia Kirchmaier; Exec. Mgr.; 96-B Main St.; P.O. Box 563; 94920; Marin; P 9,000; M 225; (415) 435-5633; Fax (415) 435-1132; tibcc@sbcglobal.net; www.tiburonchamber.org

Toluca Lake · *Toluca Lake C/C* · Shirley Duenckel; Pres.; P.O. Box 2312; 91610; Los Angeles; P 15,000; M 125; (818) 761-6594; info@tolucalakechamber.com; www.tolucalakechamber.com

Topanga · *Topanga C/C* · Bruce Royer; Pres.; P.O. Box 185; 90290; Los Angeles; P 14,500; M 200; (310) 455-0790; inquiries@topangachamber.org; www.topangachamber.org

Topaz · *Northern Mono C/C* · 115281 U.S. Hwy. 395; 96133; Mono; P 1,000; M 65; (530) 208-6078; info@northernmono chamber.com; www.northernmonochamber.com

Torrance · *Torrance Area C/C* · Donna Duperron; Pres./CEO; 3400 Torrance Blvd., Ste. 100; 90503; Los Angeles; P 147,400; M 1,000; (310) 540-5858; Fax (310) 540-7662; donna@torrance chamber.com; www.torrancechamber.com

Torrey Highlands · *see San Diego-San Diego North C/C*

Tracy · *Tracy C/C* · Sofia Valenzuela; Op. Mgr.; 223 E. 10th St.; 95376; San Joaquin; P 82,000; M 710; (209) 835-2131; Fax (209) 833-9526; info@tracychamber.org; www.tracychamber.org*

Trinidad · *Greater Trinidad C/C* · Dawne Davis; Pres.; P.O. Box 356; 95570; Humboldt; P 311; M 125; (707) 677-1610; shout@discovertrinidadca.com; www.discovertrinidadca.com

Trinity County · *Trinity County C/C* · Patricia Zugg; Pres.; P.O. Box 517, Weaverville; 96093; Trinity; P 14,000; M 200; (530) 623-6101; (800) 4TRINITY; Fax (530) 623-3753; trinitycoc@yahoo.com; www.trinitycounty.com

Truckee · *Truckee/Donner C/C* · Lynn Saunders; Pres./CEO; 10065 Donner Pass Rd.; 96161; Nevada; P 15,800; M 600; (530) 587-2757; Fax (530) 587-2439; info@truckee.com; www.truckee.com*

Tujunga · *Sunland-Tujunga C/C* · Fran Loiselle; Exec. Dir.; 8250 Foothill Blvd., Ste. A; P.O. Box 571; 91043; Los Angeles; P 43,000; M 145; (818) 352-4433; Fax (818) 353-7551; stchamber91040@gmail.com; www.stchamber.com

Tulare · *Tulare C/C* · Nina Akin; Pres./CEO; 220 E. Tulare Ave.; P.O. Box 1435; 93275; Tulare; P 57,000; M 650; (559) 686-1547; Fax (559) 686-4915; info@tularechamber.org; www.tularechamber.org.*

Tulelake · *Tulelake C/C* · Dave Misso; Pres.; P.O. Box 1152; 96134; Siskiyou; P 1,000; M 30; (530) 667-3276; (530) 667-5522; Fax (530) 667-5351; cityoftulelake@cot.net; www.visittulelakecalifornia.com

Tuolumne County · *see Sonora*

Turlock · *Turlock Chamber/CVB* · Sharon Silva; Pres./CEO; 115 S. Golden State Blvd.; 95380; Stanislaus; P 71,000; M 430; (209) 632-2221; Fax (209) 632-5289; info@turlockchamber.com; www.turlockchamber.com*

Tustin · *Tustin C/C* · Penny Maynard IOM; Interim CEO; 700 W. First St., Ste. 7; 92780; Orange; P 70,000; M 300; (714) 544-5341; Fax (714) 544-2083; info@tustinchamber.org; www.tustinchamber.org*

Twain Harte · *Twain Harte Area C/C* · Brad Menary; Pres.; 23000 Meadow Ln.; P.O. Box 404; 95383; Tuolumne; P 2,500; M 200; (209) 586-4482; Fax (209) 586-0360; info@twainhartecc.com; www.twainhartecc.com

Twentynine Palms · *Twentynine Palms C/C* · Rob Fleck; Exec. Dir.; 73484 Twentynine Palms Hwy.; 92277; San Bernardino; P 30,000; M 249; (760) 367-3445; Fax (760) 367-3366; 29chamber@29chamber.com; www.29chamber.org

Ukiah · *Greater Ukiah C/C* · 200 S. School St.; 95482; Mendocino; P 36,000; M 500; (707) 462-4705; Fax (707) 462-2088; ukiahchamber@gmail.com; www.ukiahchamber.com

Union City · *Union City C/C* · Dana Hernandez; 3939 Smith St.; 94587; Alameda; P 74,000; M 283; (510) 952-9637; Fax (510) 952-9647; dana@unioncitychamber.com; www.unioncity chamber.com*

Universal City · *see North Hollywood*

University City · *see Del Mar–La Jolla Golden Triangle C/C*

Upland · *Upland C/C* · Sonnie Faires; Pres./CEO; 215 N. 2nd Ave., Ste. D; 91786; San Bernardino; P 74,000; M 500; (909) 204-4465; Fax (909) 204-4464; realpeople@uplandchamber.org; www.uplandchamber.org

Vacaville · *Vacaville C/C* · Mark Creffield; Pres./CEO; 300 Main St., Ste. A; 95688; Solano; P 98,000; M 600; (707) 448-6424; Fax (707) 448-0424; mark@vacavillechamber.com; www.vacaville chamber.com.*

Val Verde · *see Santa Clarita*

Valencia · *see Santa Clarita*

Vallejo · *Vallejo C/C* · Anita Hawkes; Pres./CEO; 427 York St.; 94590; Solano; P 119,000; M 500; (707) 644-5551; Fax (707) 644-5590; info@vallejochamber.com; www.vallejochamber.com*

Valley Center · *Valley Center C/C* · Jim Quisquis; Pres.; 27301 Valley Center Rd.; P.O. Box 8; 92082; San Diego; P 19,000; M 150; (760) 749-8472; Fax (760) 749-8483; info@vcchamber.com; www.vcchamber.com

Van Nuys · *Greater San Fernando Valley C/C* · Nancy Hoffman Vanyek; CEO; 7120 Hayvenhurst, Ste. 114; 91406; Los Angeles; P 1,760,000; M 400; (818) 989-0300; Fax (818) 989-3836; info@sanfernandovalleychamber.com; www.sanfernandovalley chamber.com

Venice · *Venice C/C* · Sandy Moring; Admin. Coord.; P.O. Box 202; 90294; Los Angeles; P 52,000; M 170; (310) 822-5425; Fax (310) 314-7641; info@venicechamber.net; www.venicechamber.net

Ventura · *Ventura C/C* · 801 S. Victoria Ave., Ste. 200; 93003; Ventura; P 105,800; M 800; (805) 676-7500; Fax (805) 650-1414; info@ventura-chamber.org; www.venturachamber.com*

Verdugo City · *see Glendale–Montrose-Verdugo City C/C*

Vernon · *Vernon C/C* · Marisa Olguin; Pres./CEO; 3801 Santa Fe Ave.; 90058; Los Angeles; P 90; M 300; (323) 583-3313; Fax (323) 583-0704; www.vernonchamber.org

Victorville · *Victorville C/C* · Michele Spears; Pres./CEO; 14174 Green Tree Blvd.; 92395; San Bernardino; P 110,000; M 600; (760) 245-6506; Fax (760) 245-6505; vvchamber@vvchamber.com; vvchamber.com*

Visalia · *Visalia C/C* · Glenn Morris; Pres./CEO; 220 N. Santa Fe St.; 93292; Tulare; P 128,000; M 800; (559) 734-5876; Fax (559) 734-7479; info@visaliachamber.org; www.visaliachamber.org.*

Vista · *Vista C/C* · Bret Schanzenbach; CEO; 201 Washington St.; 92084; San Diego; P 94,500; M 550; (760) 726-1122; Fax (760) 726-8654; info@vistachamber.org; www.vistachamber.org

Walnut · *Reg. Chamber of Commerce-San Gabriel Valley* · Heidi L Gallegos; CEO; 19720 E. Walnut Dr. S., Ste. 201; 91789; Los Angeles; P 165,000; M 365; (909) 869-0701; Fax (909) 869-0761; info@regionalchambersgv.com; www.regionalchambersgv.org*

Walnut Creek • *Walnut Creek C/C & Visitors Bur.* • Jay Hoyer; Pres./CEO; 1777 Botelho Dr., Ste. 103; 94596; Contra Costa; P 80,000; M 700; (925) 934-2007; Fax (925) 934-2404; chamber@walnut-creek.com; www.walnut-creek.com.*

Wasco • *Wasco C/C* • Vickie Hight; Mgr.; 700 G St.; P.O. Box 783; 93280; Kern; P 26,400; M 130; (661) 758-2746; Fax (661) 758-2900; vhight@ci.wasco.ca.us; www.ci.wasco.ca.us

Watsonville • *Pajaro Valley C/C & Ag.* • Dan Carrillo; Chrmn.; 449 Union St.; P.O. Box 1748; 95077; Santa Cruz; P 50,000; M 450; (831) 724-3900; Fax (831) 728-5300; info@pajarovalleychamber.com; www.pajarovalleychamber.com*

Weaverville • *see Trinity County*

Weed • *Weed C/C & Visitor Center* • Brenda Woods; Pres.; 34 Main St.; 96094; Siskiyou; P 3,000; M 117; (530) 938-4624; (877) 938-4624; Fax (530) 938-1658; weedchamber@ncen.org; www.weedchamber.com

West Covina • *West Covina C/C* • 811 S. Sunset Ave.; 91790; Los Angeles; P 110,000; M 200; (626) 338-8496; Fax (626) 960-0511; gloria@westcovinachamber.com; www.westcovinachamber.com

West Hollywood • *West Hollywood C/C* • Genevieve Morrill; Pres./CEO; 8272 Santa Monica Blvd.; 90046; Los Angeles; P 39,500; M 472; (323) 650-2688; Fax (323) 650-2689; info@wehochamber.com; www.wehochamber.com

West Sacramento • *West Sacramento C/C* • Denice Seals; CEO; 1414 Merkley Ave., Ste. 1; 95691; Yolo; P 42,000; M 450; (916) 371-7042; Fax (916) 371-7007; info@westsacramentochamber.com; www.westsacramentochamber.com*

Westchester • *LAX Coastal Area C/C* • Christina Davis; Pres./CEO; 9100 S. Sepulveda, Ste. 210; 90045; Los Angeles; P 50,000; M 650; (310) 645-5151; Fax (310) 645-0130; christina@laxcoastal.com; www.laxcoastal.com

Westlake Village • *Greater Conejo Valley C/C* • Jill Lederer; Pres./CEO; 600 Hampshire Rd., Ste. 200; 91361; Los Angeles; P 135,905; M 1,300; (805) 370-0035; Fax (805) 370-1083; jlederer@conejochamber.org; www.conejochamber.org*

Westley • *see Patterson*

Westwood • *Westwood Area C/C* • Regina Dickson; Exec. Secy.; 462-885 Third St.; P.O. Box 1247; 96137; Lassen; P 2,200; M 50; (530) 256-2456; wacc1@citlink.net; www.westwoodchamber.org

Wheatland • *see Marysville*

Whittier • *Whittier Area C/C* • Lyn Carty & Carol Crosby; Interim Exec Dirs.; 8158 Painter Ave.; 90602; Los Angeles; P 89,000; M 700; (562) 698-9554; Fax (562) 693-2700; carol@whittierchamber.com; www.whittierchamber.com*

Wildomar • *Wildomar C/C* • Michele Thomas; Exec. Dir.; 33751 Mission Trl.; P.O. Box 885; 92595; Riverside; P 15,000; M 220; (951) 245-0437; Fax (951) 245-0437; info@wildomarchamber.org; www.wildomarchamber.org*

Willits • *Willits C/C* • Lynn R. Kennelly; Exec. Dir.; 299 E. Commercial St.; 95490; Mendocino; P 15,000; M 200; (707) 459-7910; Fax (707) 459-7914; info@willits.org; www.willits.org.

Willow Creek • *Willow Creek C/C* • Tangie Markle; Pres.; P.O. Box 704; 95573; Humboldt; P 1,500; M 85; (530) 629-2693; (800) 628-5156; Fax (530) 629-4051; info@willowcreekchamber.com; www.willowcreekchamber.com

Willows • *Willows C/C* • Rose Marie Thrailkill; Ofc. Mgr.; 118 W. Sycamore; 95988; Glenn; P 6,400; M 152; (530) 934-8150; willowschamber@sbcglobal.net; www.willowschamber.com*

Wilmington • *Wilmington C/C* • Daniel Hoffman; Exec. Dir.; 544 N. Avalon Blvd., Ste. 104; P.O. Box 90; 90748; Los Angeles; P 65,000; M 220; (310) 834-8586; Fax (310) 834-8887; info@wilmington-chamber.com; www.wilmington-chamber.com

Windsor • *Windsor C of C & Visitors Center* • Gary Quackenbush; Pres.; 9001 Windsor Rd.; P.O. Box 367; 95492; Sonoma; P 27,000; M 250; (707) 838-7285; Fax (707) 838-2778; info@windsorchamber.com; www.windsorchamber.com*

Winnetka • *Winnetka C/C* • Gene Giegoldt; Pres.; 20122 Vanowen St.; 91306; Los Angeles; P 19,200; M 75; (818) 340-2282; Fax (818) 340-2282

Winters • *Winters Dist. C/C* • Al Aldrete; Exec. Dir.; 11 Main St.; 95694; Yolo; P 6,900; M 120; (530) 795-2329; Fax (530) 795-3202; chamberwinters@yahoo.com; www.winterschamber.com*

Woodland • *Woodland Area C/C* • Kristy Wright; CEO; 307 1st St.; 95695; Yolo; P 56,000; M 600; (530) 662-7327; Fax (530) 662-4086; kristyw@woodlandchamber.org; www.woodlandchamber.org*

Woodland Hills • *Woodland Hills-Tarzana C/C* • Diana Williams; Exec. Dir.; 20121 Ventura Blvd., Ste. 204; 91364; Los Angeles; P 75,000; M 780; (818) 347-4737; Fax (818) 347-3321; diana@woodlandhillscc.net; www.woodlandhillscc.net

Wrightwood • *Wrightwood C/C* • Clark Fleeup; Pres.; P.O. Box 416; 92397; San Bernardino; P 4,100; M 93; (760) 249-4320; Fax (760) 249-6822; wwchamber@dslextreme.com; www.wrightwoodchamber.org

Yorba Linda • *Yorba Linda C/C* • Phyllis A. Coleman; Exec. Dir.; 17670 Yorba Linda Blvd.; 92886; Orange; P 70,000; M 350; (714) 993-9537; Fax (714) 993-7764; yorbalindachamber@sbcglobal.net; www.yorbalindachamber.org*

Yountville • *Yountville C/C* • Cindy Sauserman; Exec. Dir.; P.O. Box 2064; 94599; Napa; P 3,200; M 270; (707) 944-0904; Fax (707) 944-4465; info@yountville.com; www.yountville.com*

Yreka • *Yreka C/C* • Joan Smith-Freeman; Exec. Dir.; 117 W. Miner St.; 96097; Siskiyou; P 7,300; M 350; (530) 842-1649; Fax (530) 842-2670; info@yrekachamber.com; www.yrekachamber.com.*

Yuba City • *see Marysville*

Yucaipa • *Yucaipa Valley C/C* • Pamela Emenger; Exec. Dir.; 35139 Yucaipa Blvd.; P.O. Box 45; 92399; San Bernardino; P 52,000; M 350; (909) 790-1841; Fax (909) 363-7373; info@yucaipachamber.org; www.yucaipachamber.org

Yucca Valley • *Yucca Valley C/C* • Cheryl Nankervis; Exec. Dir.; 56711 29 Palms Hwy.; 92284; San Bernardino; P 20,000; M 364; (760) 365-6323; Fax (760) 365-0763; chamber@yuccavalley.org; www.yuccavalley.org*

Colorado

Colorado Assn. of Comm. & Ind. • Chuck Berry; Pres.; 1600 Broadway, Ste. 1000; Denver; 80202; Denver; P 5,900,000; M 500; (303) 831-7411; Fax (303) 860-1439; info@cochamber.com; www.cochamber.com

Akron • *Akron C/C* • Annette Bowin; Pres.; P.O. Box 233; 80720; Washington; P 1,800; M 50; (970) 345-2624; akrontown@centurytel.net; www.co.washington.co.us

Alamosa • *Alamosa County C/C* • John Eland; Exec. Dir.; 610 State Ave.; 81101; Alamosa; P 10,000; M 243; (719) 589-3681; (719) 589-6382; Fax (719) 589-6854; office@alamosachamber.com; www.alamosa.org

Alma • *see Fairplay*

Antonito • *Antonito C/C* • Cliff Aragon; Pres.; 220 Main St.; P.O. Box 427; 81120; Conejos; P 1,200; M 65; (719) 376-2277; Fax (719) 376-2277; antonitocofc@surfbest.net; www.colorado directory.com/antonitochamber

Arrowhead • *see Vail*

Arvada • *Arvada C/C* • Dot Wright; Pres.; 7305 Grandview Ave.; 80002; Adams & Jefferson; P 107,000; M 650; (303) 424-0313; Fax (303) 424-5370; dot@arvadachamber.org; www.arvada chamber.org*

Aspen • *Aspen Chamber Resort Assn.* • Debbie Braun; Pres./ CEO; 425 Rio Grande Pl.; 81611; Pitkin; P 6,000; M 860; (970) 925-1940; (800) 670-0792; Fax (970) 920-1173; info@aspenchamber. org; www.aspenchamber.org

Aurora • *Aurora C/C* • Kevin Hougen; Pres./CEO; 14305 E. Alameda Ave., Ste. 300; 80012; Adams, Arapahoe & Douglas; P 315,000; M 1,200; (303) 344-1500; Fax (303) 344-1564; info@ aurorachamber.org; www.aurorachamber.org.*

Bailey • *Platte Canyon Area C/C* • Bill Kulenburg; Pres.; P.O. Box 477; 80421; Park; P 10,000; M 150; (303) 838-9080; info@bailey-colorado.org; www.bailey-colorado.org

Basalt • *Basalt C/C* • Heather Smith; Exec. Dir.; Two Rivers Rd. & Midland Ave.; P.O. Box 514; 81621; Eagle; P 4,000; M 450; (970) 927-4031; Fax (970) 927-2833; info@basaltchamber.com; www. basaltchamber.com

Bayfield • *Bayfield Area C/C & Visitor Info. Center* • 41746 U.S. 160; P.O. Box 7; 81122; La Plata; P 1,800; M 100; (970) 884-7372; (866) 984-7372; Fax (970) 884-7372; pam@bayfieldchamber.org; www.bayfieldchamber.org

Bayfield • *Vallecito Lake C/C* • 17252 County Rd. 501; 81122; La Plata; P 300; M 45; (970) 247-1573; info@vallecitolakechamber. com; www.vallecitolakechamber.com

Beaver Creek • *see Vail*

Bennett • *I-70 Corridor C/C* • John Knight; Pres.; 401 S. First St.; 80102; Adams; P 8,296; M 131; (303) 644-4607; Fax (303) 644-6271; admin@i70ccoc.com; www.i70ccoc.com

Berthoud • *Berthoud Area C/C & Visitors Center* • Don Dana; Exec. Dir.; 344 Mountain Ave.; P.O. Box 1709; 80513; Larimer; P 15,000; M 186; (970) 532-4200; (970) 290-5314; Fax (970) 532-7690; info@berthoudcolorado.com; www.berthoudcolorado.com*

Boulder • *Boulder C/C* • Susan Graf; Pres.; 2440 Pearl St.; P.O. Box 73; 80306; Boulder; P 101,000; M 1,600; (303) 442-1044; Fax (303) 938-8837; frontdesk@boulderchamber.com; www. boulderchamber.com*

Breckenridge • *also see Summit County*

Breckenridge • *Breckenridge Resort C/C* • John McMahon; Pres.; 111 Ski Hill Rd.; P.O. Box 1909; 80424; Summit; P 3,406; M 430; (970) 453-2913; (970) 453-6018; Fax (970) 453-7238; gobreck@gobreck.com; www.gobreck.com

Brighton • *Greater Brighton Area C/C* • Kami Welch; Dir. of Comm. & Events; 1850 E. Egbert, Ste. 140; 80601; Adams; P 35,000; M 330; (303) 659-0223; Fax (303) 655-2153; info@ brightonchamber.com; www.brightonchamber.com*

Broomfield • *Broomfield C/C* • Jennifer Kerr; Pres./CEO; 2095 W. 6th Ave., Ste. 109; 80020; Broomfield; P 55,000; M 500; (303) 466-1775; Fax (303) 466-4481; info@broomfieldchamber.com; www.broomfieldchamber.com

Brush • *Brush Area C/C* • Dr. Ronald Prascher; Exec. Dir.; 218 Clayton St.; 80723; Morgan; P 5,300; M 160; (970) 842-2666; (800) 354-8659; Fax (970) 842-3828; brush@brushchamber.org; www.brushchamber.org.*

Buena Vista • *Buena Vista Area C/C* • Judy Hassell; Exec. Dir.; 343 Hwy. 24 S.; P.O. Box 2021; 81211; Chaffee; P 6,000; M 360; (719) 395-6612; (719) 395-8035; Fax (719) 395-8035; chamber@ buenavistacolorado.org; www.buenavistacolorado.org*

Burlington • *Burlington C/C* • Jenna Zimbelman; Pres.; 420 S. 14th St.; P.O. Box 62; 80807; Kit Carson; P 3,500; M 100; (719) 346-8070; Fax (719) 346-7169; www.burlingtoncolo.com

Byers • *see Bennett*

Canon City • *Canon City C/C* • Doug Shane; Exec. Dir.; 403 Royal Gorge Blvd.; 81212; Fremont; P 49,000; M 372; (719) 275-2331; (800) 876-7922; Fax (719) 275-2332; chamber@canoncity.com; www.canoncitychamber.com.*

Carbondale • *Carbondale Comm. C/C* • Sherri Harrison; Exec. Dir.; 981 Cowen Dr., Ste. C; P.O. Box 1645; 81623; Garfield; P 6,088; M 520; (970) 963-1890; Fax (970) 963-4719; chamber@carbon dale.com; www.carbondale.com*

Castle Rock • *Castle Rock C/C & Visitors Center* • Pam Ridler; Pres.; 420 Jerry St.; P.O. Box 282; 80104; Douglas; P 47,000; M 602; (303) 688-4597; (866) 441-8508; Fax (303) 688-2688; info@castlerock.org; www.visitcastlerock.org.*

Cedaredge • *Cedaredge Area C/C* • Carol Peterson; Admin.; 245 W. Main St.; P.O. Box 278; 81413; Delta; P 6,000; M 150; (970) 856-6961; Fax (970) 856-7292; info@cedaredgechamber.com; www.cedaredgechamber.com

Centennial • *South Metro Denver C/C* • John Brackney; Pres./ CEO; 6840 S. University Blvd.; 80122; Arapahoe; P 2,500,000; M 1,500; (303) 795-0142; info@bestchamber.com; www.best chamber.com

Cherry Creek • *Cherry Creek C/C* • Christine Des Enfants; Exec. Dir.; P.O. Box 6449; Denver; 80206; Denver; P 156,378; M 240; (303) 388-6022; Fax (303) 957-2327; staff@cherrycreekchamber. org; www.cherrycreekchamber.org

Collbran • *Plateau Valley C/C* • Matt Poulton; Pres.; P.O. Box 143; 81624; Mesa; P 3,500; M 20; (970) 314-4999; collbranprojects@ yahoo.com; www.plateauvalleychamber.com

Colorado City • *Greenhorn Valley C/C* • Sara Blackhurst; Exec. Dir.; P.O. Box 19429; 81019; Pueblo; P 5,000; M 90; (719) 676-3000; office@greenhornchamber.org; www.greenhornchamber.org

Colorado Springs • *Greater Colorado Springs C/C* • Dave Csintyan; CEO; 6 S. Tejon St., Ste. 700; 80903; El Paso; P 578,151; M 1,800; (719) 635-1551; Fax (719) 635-1571; info@cscc.org; www.coloradospringschamber.org.*

Colorado Springs • *Southern Colorado Women's C/C* • Beth Kelly; Pres.; P.O. Box 49218; 80949; Pueblo; P 400,000; M 150; (719) 442-2007; board@scwcc.com; www.scwcc.com

Commerce City • *see Westminster*

Como • *see Fairplay*

Conifer • *Conifer Area C/C* • Dawn Smith; Exec. Dir.; P.O. Box 127; 80433; Jefferson; P 22,000; M 270; (303) 838-5711; Fax (303) 838-5712; director@goconifer.com; www.goconifer.com*

Copper Mountain • *see Summit County*

Cordillera • *see Vail*

Cortez • *Cortez Area C/C* • Dena Guttridge; Exec. Dir.; 928 E. Main St.; P.O. Box 968; 81321; Montezuma; P 25,000; M 416; (970) 565-3414; cortezchamber@cityofcortez.com; www.cortezchamber.com*

Cowdrey • *see Walden*

Craig • *Craig C/C* • Christina Oxley; Exec. Dir.; 360 E. Victory Way; 81625; Moffat; P 11,900; M 375; (970) 824-5689; (800) 864-4405; Fax (970) 824-0231; info@craig-chamber.com; www.craig-chamber.com*

Crawford · *Crawford Area C/C* · P.O. Box 22; 81415; Delta; P 1,500; M 75; (970) 921-4000; info@crawfordcountry.org; www.crawfordcountry.org

Creede · *Creede-Mineral County C/C* · Martha K. Owens; Dir.; 904 S. Main St.; P.O. Box 580; 81130; Mineral; P 850; M 100; (719) 658-2374; (800) 327-2102; Fax (719) 658-2717; chamber@creede.com; www.creede.com

Crested Butte · *Crested Butte/Mt. Crested Butte C/C* · Richard Bond; Exec. Dir.; 601 Elk Ave.; P.O. Box 1288; 81224; Gunnison; P 2,500; M 350; (970) 349-6438; Fax (970) 349-1023; cbinfo@cbchamber.com; www.cbchamber.com

Cripple Creek · *Cripple Creek C/C* · Wes Kime; Pres.; P.O. Box 650; 80813; Teller; P 1,000; (719) 689-2223; www.cripple-creek.co.us

Dacono · *see Westminster*

Deer Trail · *see Bennett*

Delta · *Delta Area C/C* · Linda Sanchez; Exec. Dir.; 301 Main St.; 81416; Delta; P 10,000; M 300; (970) 874-8616; Fax (970) 874-8618; director@deltacolorado.org; www.deltacolorado.org.*

Denver Area

Colorado Black C/C · Dr. Eric Lee; Pres.; 410 17th St., Ste. 1110; 80202; Denver; M 800; (303) 831-0720; Fax (303) 831-0755; staff@coloradoblackchamber.org; www.coloradoblackchamber.org

Denver Hispanic C/C · Jeffrey Campos; Pres./CEO; 924 W. Colfax Ave., Ste. 201; 80204; Denver; M 1,800; (303) 534-7783; Fax (303) 595-8977; jcampos@dhcc.com; www.dhcc.com

Denver Metro C/C · Mrs. Kelly Brough; Pres./CEO; 1445 Market St., 4th Flr.; 80202; Denver; P 2,800,000; M 3,000; (303) 534-8500; Fax (303) 534-3200; info@denverchamber.org; www.denverchamber.org.*

Dillon · *see Summit County*

Divide · *Divide C/C* · Lisa Lee; Pres.; P.O. Box 101; 80814; Teller; P 5,000; M 50; (719) 686-7605; chamber@dividechamber.org; www.dividechamber.org

Dolores · *Dolores C/C* · Stewart Hanold; Dir.; 201 Railroad Ave.; P.O. Box 602; 81323; Montezuma; P 1,000; M 147; (970) 882-4018; doloreschamber@centurytel.net; www.doloreschamber.com

Downieville · *see Idaho Springs*

Dumont · *see Idaho Springs*

Durango · *Durango C/C* · Jack Llewellyn; Exec. Dir.; 111 S. Camino del Rio; P.O. Box 2587; 81302; La Plata; P 50,000; M 820; (970) 247-0312; Fax (970) 385-7884; chamber@durangobusiness.org; www.durangobusiness.org*

Eads · *Eads C/C* · Dennis Pearson; Pres.; P.O. Box 163; 81036; Kiowa; P 747; M 30; (719) 438-5590; dennis.pearson@state.co.us; www.kiowacountycolo.com

Eagle · *Eagle Valley C/C* · Michelle Morgan; Pres.; 100 Fairgrounds Rd.; P.O. Box 964; 81631; Eagle; P 5,000; M 435; (970) 328-6464; Fax (970) 328-1120; evcc@centurytel.net; www.eaglevalley.org

Eagle-Vail · *see Vail*

Edwards · *see Vail*

Elizabeth · *Elizabeth Area C/C* · Beverly Durant; Exec. Dir.; 166 Main St.; P.O. Box 595; 80107; Elbert; P 1,700; M 165; (303) 646-4287; Fax (303) 646-2509; director@elizabethchamber.org; www.elizabethchamber.org*

Empire · *see Idaho Springs*

Englewood · *also see Centennial*

Englewood · *Greater Englewood C/C* · Colleen Mello; Exec. Dir.; 3501 S. Broadway, 2nd Flr.; 80113; Arapahoe; P 33,000; M 200; (303) 789-4473; Fax (303) 789-0098; info@myenglewoodchamber.com; www.myenglewoodchamber.com

Erie · *Erie C/C* · Elle Cabbage; Exec. Dir.; 235 Wells St.; P.O. Box 97; 80516; Boulder; P 18,000; M 250; (303) 828-3440; Fax (303) 828-3330; erie@eriechamber.org; www.eriechamber.org

Evans · *Evans Area C/C* · Michele Jones; Exec. Dir.; 3700 Golden St.; 80620; Weld; P 18,500; M 300; (970) 330-4204; Fax (970) 506-2726; ecc@evanschamber.org; www.evanschamber.org*

Evergreen · *Evergreen Area C/C* · Melanie Nuchols; Pres.; 28065 Hwy. 74, Ste. 201; 80439; Jefferson; P 44,000; M 710; (303) 674-3412; Fax (303) 674-8463; admin@evergreenchamber.org; www.evergreenchamber.org

Fairplay · *South Park C/C* · P.O. Box 312; 80440; Park; P 4,000; M 95; (719) 836-3410; info@southparkchamber.com; www.southparkchamber.com

Federal Heights · *see Westminster*

Firestone · *see Frederick*

Firestone · *see Westminster*

Florence · *Florence C/C* · Esther Mauter; Ofc. Mgr.; 117 S. Pikes Peak Ave.; P.O. Box 145; 81226; Fremont; P 5,000; M 125; (719) 784-3544; flochamber@cohsi.net; www.florencecolorado.net

Fort Collins · *Fort Collins Area C/C* · David May; Pres./CEO; 225 S. Meldrum St.; P.O. Drawer D; 80521; Larimer; P 136,665; M 1,050; (970) 482-3746; Fax (970) 482-3774; general@fcchamber.org; www.fortcollinschamber.org

Fort Lupton · *Fort Lupton C/C* · Dawn Massey; Admin.; 321 Denver Ave.; 80621; Weld; P 7,700; M 105; (303) 857-4474; flchamber@frii.com; www.fortluptonchamber.org

Fort Morgan · *Fort Morgan Area C/C* · 300 Main St.; 80701; Morgan; P 27,000; M 280; (970) 867-6702; (800) 354-8660; Fax (970) 867-6121; fortmorganchamber@flci.net; www.fortmorganchamber.org

Fountain · *Fountain Valley C/C* · Linda Puckett; Pres.; 114 N. Main St.; P.O. Box 201; 80817; El Paso; P 25,000; M 140; (719) 382-3190; Fax (719) 322-9395; fvcc@qwest.net; www.fountainchamberofcommerce.com

Fowler · *Fowler C/C* · Shawn Pagnotta; Secy.; P.O. Box 172; 81039; Otero; P 1,200; M 45; (719) 263-4461; www.fowlerchamberofcommerce.com

Fraser Valley · *see Winter Park*

Frederick · *also see Westminster*

Frederick · *Carbon Valley C/C* · Stephanie M. Martin; Exec. Dir.; 8308 Colorado Blvd., Ste. 203; P.O. Box 800; 80530; Weld; P 15,000; M 231; (303) 833-5933; Fax (303) 833-0335; stephanie@carbonvalleychamber.com; www.carbonvalleychamber.com

Frisco · *see Summit County*

Fruita · *Fruita Area C/C* · Mary Lou Wilson; Dir.; 432 E. Aspen Ave.; 81521; Mesa; P 11,000; M 430; (970) 858-3894; Fax (970) 858-3121; info@fruitachamber.org; www.fruitachamber.org*

Georgetown · *see Idaho Springs*

Gilcrest · *see Platteville*

Glendale · *Greater Glendale C/C* · Larry Harte; Exec. Dir.; 950 S. Birch St.; 80246; Arapahoe; P 5,000; M 250; (303) 584-4180; larry@ggchamber.com; www.ggchamber.com

Glenwood Springs · *Glenwood Springs Chamber Resort Assn.* · Marianne Virgili CCE; Exec. Dir.; 1102 Grand Ave.; 81601; Garfield; P 8,500; M 650; (970) 945-6589; Fax (970) 945-1531; info@glenwoodchamber.com; www.glenwoodchamber.com*

Golden · *Greater Golden C/C & Visitors Center* · Gary L. Wink; Pres./CEO; 1010 Washington Ave.; 80401; Jefferson; P 18,000; M 520; (303) 279-3113; (800) 590-3113; Fax (303) 279-0332; info@goldencochamber.org; www.goldencochamber.org

Gould · *see Walden*

Granby · *Greater Granby Area C/C* · Sharon Brenner; Pres./CEO; 365 E. Agate Ave., Ste. B; P.O. Box 35; 80446; Grand; P 1,800; M 185; (970) 887-2311; (800) 325-1661; Fax (970) 887-3895; grcoc@rkymtnhi.com; www.granbychamber.com

Grand Junction · *Grand Junction Area C/C* · Diane Schwenke; Pres.; 360 Grand Ave.; 81501; Mesa; P 150,000; M 1,000; (970) 242-3214; Fax (970) 242-3694; info@gjchamber.org; www.gjchamber.org.*

Grand Lake · *Grand Lake Area C/C* · Lisa Jenkins; Exec. Dir.; P.O. Box 429; 80447; Grand; P 12,000; M 160; (970) 627-3402; (800) 531-1019; Fax (970) 627-8007; glinfo@grandlakechamber.com; www.grandlakechamber.com

Greeley · *Greeley C/C* · Sarah MacQuiddy; Pres.; 902 7th Ave.; 80631; Weld; P 100,000; M 740; (970) 352-3566; Fax (970) 352-3572; info@greeleychamber.com; www.greeleychamber.com*

Greenwood Village · *see Centennial*

Guffey · *see Fairplay*

Gunnison · *Gunnison Country C/C* · Tammy Scott; Exec. Dir.; 500 E. Tomichi; P.O. Box 36; 81230; Gunnison; P 10,000; M 368; (970) 641-1501; (800) 274-7580; info@gunnisonchamber.com; www.gunnisonchamber.com*

Hartsel · *see Fairplay*

Haxtun · *Haxtun C/C* · Barb Shafer; 145 S. Colorado; P.O. Box 535; 80731; Phillips; P 982; M 48; (970) 774-6104; Fax (970) 774-5875; haxtunco@pctelcom.coop; www.haxtunchamber.com

Heeny · *see Summit County*

Highlands Ranch · *C/C of Highlands Ranch* · Steve Dyer; Pres.; 300 W. Plaza Dr., Ste. 225; 80129; Douglas; P 95,000; M 275; (303) 791-3500; Fax (303) 791-3522; steve@highlandsranchchamber.org; www.highlandsranchchamber.org*

Holyoke · *Holyoke C/C* · Mary Tomky; Dir.; 212 S. Interocean; P.O. Box 134; 80734; Phillips; P 2,200; M 100; (970) 854-3517; Fax (970) 854-3514; holyokec@pctelcom.coop; www.holyokechamber.org

Hotchkiss · *Hotchkiss Comm. C/C* · Nathan Sponseller; P.O. Box 158; 81419; Delta; P 1,000; M 80; (970) 872-3226; Fax (970) 872-4050; www.hotchkisschamber.com

Idaho Springs · *Greater Idaho Springs C/C* · Belita Nelson; Exec. Dir.; PO Box 1774; 80452; Clear Creek; P 9,000; M 42; (720) 212-1118; (303) 567-4382; broncolady8707@gmail.com; www.idahospringschamberofcommerce.org

Jefferson County · *see Lakewood*

Johnstown · *Johnstown-Milliken C/C* · Jim & Pam Lutey; Co-Dirs.; P.O. Box 501; 80534; Weld; P 11,500; M 180; (970) 587-7042; Fax (970) 587-8703; info@johnstownmillikenchamber.com; www.johnstownmillikenchamber.com

Julesburg · *Sedgwick County C/C* · Patricia Stever; Exec. Dir.; 100 W. 2nd St.; 80737; Sedgwick; P 2,700; M 50; (970) 474-3504; Fax (970) 474-4008; sced@kci.net; www.sedgwickcountyco.com

Keenesburg · *Keenesburg Area C/C* · Patricia Cooke; Pres.; P.O. Box 44; 80643; Weld; P 1,100; M 40; (303) 732-4009; (303) 732-0131; Fax (303) 732-0137; webmaster@keenesburgco.org; www.keenesburgco.org

Kersey · *Kersey Area C/C* · Sandie Cantrell; Pres.; P.O. Box 397; 80644; Weld; P 1,200; M 35; (970) 304-6171; www.kerseycolorado.com

Keystone · *see Summit County*

Kremmling · *Kremmling Area C/C* · Kacey Beres; Exec. Dir.; P.O. Box 471; 80459; Grand; P 3,000; M 200; (970) 724-3472; (877) 573-6654; Fax (970) 724-0397; kacey@kremmling.net; www.kremmlingchamber.com

La Junta · *La Junta C/C* · 110 Santa Fe Ave.; 81050; Otero; P 7,400; M 186; (719) 384-7411; Fax (719) 384-2217; info@lajuntachamber.com; www.lajuntachamber.com

La Veta · *La Veta/Cuchara C/C* · Bob Baker; Pres.; P.O. Box 32; 81055; Huerfano; P 1,024; M 115; (719) 742-3676; (866) 615-3676; email@lavetacucharachamber.com; www.lavetacucharachamber.com

Lafayette · *Lafayette C/C* · Vicki Trumbo; Exec. Dir.; P.O. Box 1018; 80026; Boulder; P 29,000; M 370; (303) 666-9555; Fax (303) 666-4392; info@lafayettecolorado.com; www.lafayettecolorado.com

Lake City · *Lake City/Hinsdale County C/C* · Jud Hollingsworth; Pres.; 800 N. Gunnison Ave.; P.O. Box 430; 81235; Hinsdale; P 400; M 200; (970) 944 2527; (800) 569 1874; Fax (970) 944 2720; chamber@lakecity.com; www.lakecity.com

Lake County · *see Leadville*

Lakewood · *West C/C Serving Jefferson County* · Amy Sherman; Pres./CEO; 1667 Cole Blvd., Ste. 400; 80401; Jefferson; P 530,000; M 900; (303) 233-5555; Fax (303) 237-7633; info@westchamber.org; www.westchamber.org

Lamar · *Lamar C/C* · Chana Reed; Ofc. Mgr.; 109A E. Beech St.; 81052; Prowers; P 14,000; M 220; (719) 336-4379; Fax (719) 336-4370; lamarchamber@bresnan.net; www.lamarchamber.com*

Las Animas · *Las Animas-Bent County C/C* · Russell Smith; Exec. V.P.; 332 Amb. Thompson Blvd.; 81054; Bent; P 6,500; M 135; (719) 456-0453; Fax (719) 456-0455; russellatchamber@lycos.com; www.bentcounty.org

LaSalle · *see Platteville*

Lawson · *see Idaho Springs*

Leadville · *Leadville/Lake County C/C* · Heather Scanlon; Exec. Dir.; 809 Harrison Ave.; P.O. Box 861; 80461; Lake; P 8,800; M 120; (719) 486-3900; (888) 532-3845; Fax (719) 486-8478; leadville@leadvilleusa.com; www.leadvilleusa.com

Limon · *Limon C/C* · Tim Andersen; Chair; P.O. Box 101; 80828; Lincoln; P 2,315; M 90; (719) 775-9418; Fax (719) 775-8808; limonchamber@yahoo.com; www.limonchamber.com.

Littleton · *see Centennial*

Logan County · *see Sterling*

Longmont · *Longmont Area C/C* · Kathy Weber-Harding; Pres./CEO; 528 Main St.; 80501; Boulder; P 87,000; M 700; (303) 776-5295; staff@longmontchamber.org; www.longmontchamber.org.*

Louisville · *Louisville C/C* · Shelley Angell; Exec. Dir.; 901 Main St.; 80027; Boulder; P 19,500; M 385; (303) 666-5747; Fax (303) 666-4285; info@louisvillechamber.com; www.louisvillechamber.com.

Loveland · *Loveland C/C* · Brian Willms; Pres./CEO; 5400 Stone Creek Circle; 80538; Larimer; P 68,000; M 700; (970) 667-6311; Fax (970) 667-5211; info@loveland.org; www.loveland.org *

LOVELAND VALENTINE RE-MAILING PROGRAM AND SWEETHEART CITY ACTIVITIES, FEBRUARY 1-14; BUSINESS EXPO & TRADE SHOW, APRIL; OLD FASHIONED CORN ROAST FESTIVAL, AUGUST; SCULPTURE IN THE PARK, 2ND WEEKEND IN AUGUST—LARGEST SCULPTURE SHOW WEST OF THE MISSISSIPPI.

Lyons · *Lyons Area C/C* · P.O. Box 426; 80540; Boulder; P 1,600; M 165; (303) 823-5215; (877) LYONS-CO; admin@lyons-colorado.com; www.lyons-colorado.com

Mancos · *Mancos Valley C/C* · Betsy Harrison; 101 E. Bauer Ave.; P.O. Box 494; 81328; Montezuma; P 1,100; M 120; (970) 533-7434; chamber@mancosvalley.com; www.mancosvalley.com

Manitou Springs · *Manitou Springs C/C* · Leslie Lewis; Exec. Dir.; 354 Manitou Ave.; 80829; El Paso; P 5,000; M 280; (719) 685-5089; (800) 642-2567; Fax (719) 685-0355; manitou@pikes-peak.com; www.manitousprings.org.

Meeker · *Meeker C/C* · P.O. Box 869; 81641; Rio Blanco; P 2,500; M 220; (970) 878-5510; Fax (970) 878-0271; info@meeker chamber.com; www.meekerchamber.com*

Mesa · *see Collbran*

Minturn · *see Vail*

Molina · *see Collbran*

Monte Vista · *Monte Vista C/C* · Linda Archuleta; Dir.; 947 1st Ave.; 81144; Rio Grande; P 12,400; M 200; (719) 852-2731; Fax (719) 852-2731; chamber@monte-vista.org; www.monte-vista.org

Montezuma · *see Summit County*

Montrose · *Montrose Assoc. of Commerce & Tourism* · Ken Brengle; Pres./CEO; 1519 E. Main St.; 81401; Montrose; P 41,000; M 630; (970) 249-5000; (800) 923-5515; Fax (970) 249-2907; information@montroseact.com; www.montroseact.com.*

Monument · *Tri-Lakes C/C & Visitor Center* · David Van Ness; Exec. Dir.; 300 Hwy. 105; P.O. Box 147; 80132; El Paso; P 35,000; M 315; (719) 481-3282; Fax (719) 481-1638; director@trilakes chamber.com; www.trilakeschamber.com

Naturita · *Nucla-Naturita Area C/C* · Paula Brown; Pres.; P.O. Box 425; 81422; Montrose; P 1,400; M 50; (970) 865-2350; Fax (970) 865-2350; csbterri@fone.net; www.nucla-naturita.com

Nederland · *Nederland Area C/C* · Susan Tate; Admin.; P.O. Box 85; 80466; Boulder; P 1,500; M 130; (303) 258-3936; info@ nederlandchamber.org; www.nederlandchamber.org

New Castle · *New Castle Area C/C* · Susan Alexander; Admin. Asst.; 386 W. Main St., Ste. 101; P.O. Box 983; 81647; Garfield; P 3,000; M 100; (970) 984-2897; newcastlecc@sopris.net; www.newcastlechamber.org

Northglenn · *see Westminster*

Norwood · *Norwood C/C* · Terry Esch; Pres.; P.O. Box 116; 81423; San Miguel; P 1,300; M 96; (970) 327-4982; (800) 282-5988; Fax (970) 327-4709; info@norwoodcolorado.com; www.norwoodcolorado.com

Nucla · *see Naturita*

Ordway · *Crowley County C/C* · Betty Bruch; P.O. Box 332; 81063; Crowley; P 4,300; M 65; (719) 267-3845

Ouray · *Ouray Chamber Resort Assn.* · Jennifer Loshaw; Exec. Dir.; 1230 Main St.; P.O. Box 145; 81427; Ouray; P 830; M 230; (970) 325-4746; (800) 228-1876; Fax (970) 325-4868; ouray@ ouraycolorado.com; www.ouraycolorado.com

Pagosa Springs · *Pagosa Springs Area C/C* · Mary Jo Coulehan; Exec. Dir.; 402 San Juan St.; P.O. Box 787; 81147; Archuleta; P 13,000; M 600; (970) 264-2360; (800) 252-2204; Fax (970) 264-4625; admin@pagosachamber.com; www.pagosaspringschamber.com.*

Palisade · *Palisade C/C* · Bayley Rogers; Exec. Dir.; 319 S. Main St.; P.O. Box 729; 81526; Mesa; P 2,579; M 225; (970) 464-7458; Fax (970) 464-4757; info@palisadecoc.com; palisadecoc.com

Paonia · *Paonia C/C* · Ed Marston; Pres.; P.O. Box 366; 81428; Delta; P 1,600; M 100; (970) 527-3886; naturally@paoniachamber.com; www.paoniachamber.com

Parker · *Parker C/C* · Joe Sandoval; Chrmn. of the Bd.; 19751 E. Mainstreet, Ste. R-17; 80138; Douglas; P 45,000; M 360; (303) 841-4268; Fax (303) 841-8061; reception@parkerchamber.com; www.parkerchamber.com*

Penrose · *Penrose C/C* · Bill McGuire; Exec. Dir.; P.O. Box 379; 81240; Fremont; P 6,500; M 100; (719) 372-3994; Fax (719) 372-3994; info@penrosechamber.com; www.penrosechamber.com

Plateau City · *see Collbran*

Platteville · *South Central Weld C/C* · Corina Johnson; Coord.; P.O. Box 606; 80651; Weld; P 3,500; M 45; (970) 324-3111; info@south centralweldchamber.com; www.southcentralweldchamber.com

Pueblo · *Greater Pueblo C/C* · Rod Slyhoff; Pres./CEO; 302 N. Santa Fe Ave.; 81003; Pueblo; P 160,000; M 1,200; (719) 542-1704; (800) 233-3446; Fax (719) 542-1624; info@pueblochamber.net; www.pueblochamber.org.*

Rand · *see Walden*

Rangely · *Rangely Area C/C* · Vanessa Popham; Chamber Asst.; 209 E. Main St.; 81648; Rio Blanco; P 2,500; M 150; (970) 675-5290; info@rangelygovt.com; www.rangelychamber.com

Ridgway · *Ridgway Area C/C* · Caitlin Switzer; Exec. Dir.; 150 Racecourse Rd.; 81432; Ouray; P 1,000; M 150; (970) 626-5181; (800) 220-4959; Fax (970) 626-9708; racc@ridgwaycolorado.com; www.ridgwaycolorado.com

Rifle · *Rifle Area C/C* · Annick Pruett; Pres./CEO; 200 Lions Park Cir.; 81650; Garfield; P 8,000; M 330; (970) 625-2085; (800) 842-2085; Fax (970) 625-4757; mail@riflechamber.com; www.riflechamber.com*

Rocky Ford · *Rocky Ford C/C* · Deborah Graffis; Pres.; 105 N. Main St.; 81067; Otero; P 4,300; M 85; (719) 254-7483; Fax (719) 254-7483; rockyfordchamber@secom.net; www.rockyford chamber.info

Salida · *Heart of the Rockies C/C* · Lori Roberts-Pope; Admin.; 406 W. Hwy. 50; 81201; Chaffee; P 5,800; M 480; (719) 539-2068; (877) 772-5432; Fax (719) 539-7844; info@salidachamber.org; www.salidachamber.org.*

Sheridan · *see Centennial*

Silt · *Silt Area C/C* · Ramona Jaeger; Chair; P.O. Box 921; 81652; Garfield; P 2,200; M 75; (970) 876-5020; Fax (970) 876-0307; sacc@siltchamber.org; www.siltchamber.org*

Silver Plume · *see Idaho Springs*

Silverthorne · *see Summit County*

Silverton · *Silverton Area C/C* · Rose Raab; Mgr.; 414 Greene St.; P.O. Box 565; 81433; San Juan; P 531; M 125; (970) 387-5654; (800) 752-4494; Fax (970) 387-0282; info@silvertoncolorado.com; www.silvertoncolorado.com

South Fork · *South Fork C/C* · Traci Gillespie; Ofc. Mgr.; 30359 Hwy. 160; 81154; Rio Grande; P 750; M 80; (719) 588-2901; (800) 571-0881; info@southforkcoloradochamber.com; www.southforkcolorado.org

South Jeffco · *see Lakewood*

Springfield · *Springfield C/C* · Jodi Ricker; Pres.; P.O. Box 12; 81073; Baca; P 1,500; M 55; (719) 523-4061; springfieldcolorado chamber@springfieldco.info; www.springfieldco.info

Sterling · *Logan County C/C* · Kimberly Sellers; Exec. Dir.; 109 N. Front St.; P.O. Box 1683; 80751; Logan; P 21,000; M 352; (970) 522-5070; (866) 522-5070; Fax (970) 522-4082; execdir@logan countychamber.com; www.logancountychamber.com*

Strasburg · *see Bennett*

Summit County · *Summit C/C* · P.O. Box 5450, Frisco; 80443; Summit; P 25,000; M 500; (970) 668-2051; info@summitchamber. org; www.summitchamber.org

Superior · *Superior C/C* · Heather Cracraft; Exec. Dir.; 124 E. Coal Creek Dr.; 80027; Boulder & Jefferson; P 12,000; M 150; (303) 554-0789; Fax (303) 499-1340; info@superiorchamber.com; www.superiorchamber.com

Trinidad · *Trinidad & Las Animas County C/C* · Kim Schultz; Exec. Dir./CEO; 136 W. Main St.; 81082; Las Animas; P 15,000; M 350; (719) 846-9285; (866) 480-4750; Fax (719) 846-3545; kimschultz1@comcast.net; www.trinidadchamber.com.*

Trinidad · *Trinidad-Las Animas County Hispanic C/C* · Jennie Garduno; Pres.; P.O. Box 17; 81082; Las Animas; P 15,000; M 150; (719) 846-8234; jnegarduno@yahoo.com

Vail · *Vail Chamber & Bus. Assn.* · Rich Tenbraak; Exec. Dir.; 241 S. Frontage Rd. E., Ste. 2; 81657; Eagle; P 4,531; M 200; (970) 477-0075; (877) 477-0075; Fax (970) 477-0079; info@vailchamber.org; www.vailchamber.org

Vail · *Vail Valley Partnership* · Chris Romer; Exec. Dir.; P.O. Box 1130; 81658; Eagle; P 48,000; M 700; (970) 476-1000; (800) 525-3875; Fax (970) 476-6008; info@visitvailvalley.com; www. visitvailvalley.com

Walden · *North Park C/C* · Rae Redman; Exec. Dir.; 416 4th St.; P.O. Box 68; 80480; Jackson; P 1,400; M 40; (970) 723-4600; Fax (970) 723-4600; northparkchamber@centurytel.net; www. northparkchamber.com

Walsenburg · *Huerfano County C/C* · Nancy Lave; Pres.; 400 Main St.; 81089; Huerfano; P 4,200; M 56; (719) 738-1065; hcochamber@gmail.com; www.huerfanochamber.com

Watkins · *see Bennett*

Wellington · *Wellington Area C/C* · Mary McCaffrey; Pres.; P.O. Box 1500; 80549; Larimer; P 2,672; M 77; (970) 568-4133; info@ wellingtoncoloradochamber.com; wellingtoncoloradochamber.net

Westcliffe · *Custer County Merchants & C/C* · Donna Hood; Pres.; 110 Rosita Ave., All Aboard Westcliffe Bldg.; P.O. Box 81; 81252; Custer; P 4,200; M 220; (719) 783-9163; (877) 793-3170; Fax (719) 783-2724; info@custercountyco.com; www.custercountyco.com*

Westminster · *Metro North C/C* · Deborah Obermeyer; Pres./ CEO; 2921 W. 120th Ave., Ste. 210; 80234; Adams; P 513,363; M 1,100; (303) 288-1000; Fax (303) 227-1050; amber@met-ronorthchamber.com; www.metronorthchamber.com*

Wheat Ridge · *see Lakewood*

Windsor · *Windsor C/C* · Michal Connors; Exec. Dir.; 421 Main St.; 80550; Weld; P 19,001; M 400; (970) 686-7189; Fax (970) 686-0352; information@windsorchamber.net; www.windsorchamber.net.*

Winter Park · *Winter Park-Fraser Valley C/C* · Catherine Ross; Exec. Dir.; 78841 U.S. Hwy. 40; P.O. Box 3236; 80482; Grand; P 1,500; M 400; (970) 726-4118; (800) 903-7275; Fax (970) 726-9449; visitorcenter@playwinterpark.com; www.playwinterpark.com

Wolcott · *see Vail*

Woodland Park · *Greater Woodland Park C/C* · Debbie Miller; Pres.; Ute Pass Cultural Center, 210 E. Midland; P.O. Box 9022; 80866; Teller; P 25,000; M 450; (719) 687-9885; (800) 551-7886; Fax (719) 687-8216; info@gwpcc.biz; www.woodlandparkchamber.com*

Wray · *Wray C/C* · Kyle R. Hansen; Exec. Dir.; 110 E. 3rd St.; P.O. Box 101; 80758; Yuma; P 2,300; M 115; (970) 332-3484; (970) 630-4563; Fax (970) 332-3486; director@wraychamber.net; www.wraychamber.net

Yuma · *West Yuma County C/C* · Darlene Carpio; Dir.; 14 W. Second Ave.; 80759; Yuma; P 3,500; M 145; (970) 848-2704; director@westyumachamber.com; www.westyumachamber.com

Connecticut

Connecticut Bus. & Ind. Assn. · John Rathgeber; Pres./CEO; 350 Church St.; Hartford; 06103; Hartford; P 3,500,000; M 10,000; (860) 244-1900; Fax (860) 278-8562; john.rathgeber@cbia.com; www.cbia.com

Amesville · *see Lakeville*

Andover · *see Vernon*

Ansonia · *see Shelton*

Avon · *Avon C/C* · Lisa Bohman; Exec. Dir.; 412 W. Avon Rd.; 06001; Hartford; P 17,000; M 310; (860) 675-4832; Fax (860) 675-0469; avonchamber@sbcglobal.net; www.avonchamber.com

Barkhamsted · *see Torrington*

Beacon Falls · *see Shelton*

Berlin · *Berlin C/C* · Katherine Fuechsel; Exec. Dir.; 40 Chamberlin Hwy.; 06037; Hartford; P 18,831; M 230; (860) 829-1033; Fax (860) 829-1243; director@berlinctchamber.org; www. berlinctchamber.org*

Bethel · *Bethel C/C* · Violet Mattone; Exec. Dir.; 16 P.T. Barnum Sq.; 06801; Fairfield; P 18,500; M 400; (203) 743-6500; Fax (203) 744-5265; bethelchamber@aol.com; www.bethelchamber.com*

Bloomfield · *Bloomfield C/C* · Vera Smith-Winfree; Exec. Dir.; 330 Park Ave., 2nd Flr.; P.O. Box 938; 06002; Hartford; P 20,000; M 200; (860) 242-3710; Fax (860) 242-6129; webmail@bloom fieldchamber.org; www.bloomfieldchamber.org

Bolton · *see Vernon*

Branford · *Branford C/C* · Edward Lazarus; Pres.; 239 N. Main St.; 06405; New Haven; P 30,000; M 340; (203) 488-5500; Fax (203) 488-5046; info@branfordct.com; www.branfordct.com*

Bridgeport · *Bridgeport Reg. Bus. Cncl.* · Paul S. Timpanelli; Pres./CEO; 10 Middle St., 14th Flr.; P.O. Box 999; 06601; Fairfield; P 250,000; M 1,000; (203) 335-3800; Fax (203) 366-0105; info@ brbc.org; www.brbc.org

Bristol · *Central Conn. Chambers of Commerce* · Michael Nicastro; Pres./CEO; 200 Main St.; 06010; Hartford; P 150,000; M 1,600; (860) 584-4718; Fax (860) 584-4722; info@central ctchambers.org; www.centralctchambers.org

Brooklyn · *see Danielson*

Burlington · *see Bristol*

Canaan · *see Torrington*

Canton · *Canton C/C* · Phil Worley; Exec. Dir.; 101 River Rd.; P.O. Box 704; 06019; Hartford; P 9,500; M 285; (860) 693-0405; Fax (860) 693-9105; info@cantonchamberofcommerce.com; www. cantonchamberofcommerce.com

Cheshire · *Cheshire C/C* · Sheldon Dill; Pres.; 195 S. Main St.; 06410; New Haven; P 28,000; M 325; (203) 272-2345; Fax (203) 271-3044; info@cheshirechamber.com; www.cheshirechamber.com

Clinton • *Clinton C/C* • Ellen Cavanagh; Exec. Dir.; 50 E. Main St.; P.O. Box 334; 06413; Middlesex; P 13,000; M 350; (860) 669-3889; Fax (860) 669-3889; chamber@clintonct.com; clintonct.com

Colebrook • *see Torrington*

Columbia • *see Vernon*

Cornwall • *see Torrington*

Coventry • *see Vernon*

Danbury • *Greater Danbury C/C* • Stephen Bull; Pres.; 39 West St.; 06810; Fairfield; P 190,000; M 1,000; (203) 743-5565; Fax (203) 794-1439; info@danburychamber.com; www.danburychamber.com

Danielson • *Northeastern Connecticut C/C* • Elizabeth Kuszaj; Exec. Dir.; 3 Central St., Ste. 3; 06239; Windham; P 80,000; M 600; (860) 774-8001; Fax (860) 774-4299; info@nectchamber.com; www.nectchamber.com*

Darien • *Darien C/C* • Carol Wilder-Tamme; Pres./CEO; 10 Corbin Dr.; 06820; Fairfield; P 20,000; M 325; (203) 655-3600; darien chamber@optonline.net; www.darienchamberonline.com*

Derby • *see Shelton*

East Berlin • *see Berlin*

East Granby • *East Granby C/C* • Tami Zawistowski; Pres.; P.O. Box 1335; 06026; Hartford; P 5,000; M 110; (860) 653-3833; Fax (860) 653-3855; admin@eastgranbycoc.org; www.eastgranbycoc.org*

East Hartford • *East Hartford C/C* • Ronald Pugliese; Pres.; 1137 Main St.; 06108; Hartford; P 50,000; M 400; (860) 289-0239; Fax (860) 289-0230; ehchamber@sbcglobal.net; www.ehcoc.com

East Haven • *East Haven C/C* • Mary W. Cacace; Exec. Dir.; 200 Kimberly Ave.; P.O. Box 120055; 06512; New Haven; P 28,000; M 135; (203) 467-4305; Fax (203) 469-2299; generalinfo@ easthavenchamber.com; www.easthavenchamber.com

East Windsor • *see Enfield*

Ellington • *see Vernon*

Enfield • *North Central Connecticut C/C* • Larry Tracey; Exec. Dir.; 73 Hazard Ave.; P.O. Box 294; 06083; Hartford; P 75,726; M 400; (860) 741-3838; Fax (860) 741-3512; chamber@ncccc.org; www.ncccc.org*

Fairfield • *Fairfield C/C* • Patricia L. Ritchie; Pres./CEO; 1597 Post Rd.; 06824; Fairfield; P 58,000; M 400; (203) 255-1011; Fax (203) 256-9990; info@fairfieldctchamber.com; www.fairfield ctchamber.com.*

Falls Village • *see Torrington*

Farmington • *Farmington C/C* • Lisa Whitney; Pres.; 827 Farmington Ave.; 06032; Hartford; P 24,658; M 310; (860) 676-8490; Fax (860) 677-8332; marketing@farmingtonchamber.com; www.farmingtonchamber.com

Glastonbury • *Glastonbury C/C* • Mary Ellen Dombrowski; Pres.; 2400 Main St., Ste. 2; 06033; Hartford; P 33,000; M 550; (860) 659-3587; Fax (860) 659-0102; maryellen@glastonburychamber. com; www.glastonburychamber.com*

Goshen • *see Torrington*

Granby • *Granby C/C* • Roger Voyer; Admin.; P.O. Box 211; 06035; Hartford; P 14,000; M 250; (860) 653-5085; Fax (860) 844-8692; gcoc@granbycoc.org; www.granbycoc.org*

Greenwich • *Greenwich C/C* • Mary Ann Morrison; Pres./CEO; 45 E. Putnam Ave., Ste. 121; 06830; Fairfield; P 65,000; M 700; (203) 869-3500; Fax (203) 869-3502; info@greenwichchamber.com; www.greenwichchamber.com

Guilford • *Guilford C/C* • Pamela Kelly; Exec. Dir.; 1300 Boston Post Rd.; 06437; New Haven; P 20,000; M 300; (203) 453-9677; Fax (203) 453-6022; chamber@guilfordct.com; www.guilfordct.com

Hamden • *Hamden C/C* • Nancy Dudchik; Pres.; 2969 Whitney Ave.; 06518; New Haven; P 58,000; M 400; (203) 288-6431; Fax (203) 288-4499; hcc@hamdenchamber.com; www.hamdenchamber.com

Hartford • *Metro Hartford Alliance* • Karen Routhier; Admin. Coord.; 31 Pratt St., 5th Flr.; 06103; Hartford; P 910,000; M 1,000; (860) 525-4451; Fax (860) 293-2592; info@metrohartford.com; www.metrohartford.com

Harwinton • *see Torrington*

Hebron • *see Vernon*

Kensington • *see Berlin*

Kent • *also see Torrington*

Kent • *Kent C/C* • Elissa Potts; Pres.; P.O. Box 124; 06757; Litchfield; P 3,000; M 150; (860) 927-1463; president@kentct. com; www.kentct.com

Killingly • *see Danielson*

Lakeville • *Tri-State C/C* • Susan Dickinson; Pres.; 326 Main St.; P.O. Box 386; 06039; Litchfield; P 4,500; M 200; (860) 435-0740; info@tristatechamber.com; www.tristatechamber.com

Lime Rock • *see Lakeville*

Litchfield • *see Torrington*

Lyme • *see Old Lyme*

Madison • *Madison C/C* • Eileen Banisch; Exec. Dir.; P.O. Box 706; 06443; New Haven; P 18,000; M 350; (203) 245-7394; Fax (203) 245-4279; chamber@madisonct.com; www.madisonct.com

Manchester • *Greater Manchester C/C* • Sue O'Connor; Pres.; 20 Hartford Rd.; 06040; Hartford; P 55,000; M 550; (860) 646-2223; Fax (860) 646-5871; staffgmcc@manchesterchamber.com; www. manchesterchamber.com*

Mansfield • *see Vernon*

Meriden • *Greater Meriden C/C* • Sean W. Moore; Pres.; 3 Colony St., Ste. 301; 06451; New Haven; P 59,000; M 670; (203) 235-7901; Fax (203) 686-0172; info@meridenchamber.com; www.meridenchamber.com*

Middlebury • *see Southbury*

Middletown • *Middlesex County C/C* • Larry McHugh; Pres.; 393 Main St.; 06457; Middlesex; P 154,241; M 2,400; (860) 347-6924; Fax (860) 346-1043; info@middlesexchamber.com; www. middlesexchamber.com

Milford • *Milford C/C* • Kathleen Alagno; Pres./CEO; 5 Broad St.; P.O. Box 389; 06460; New Haven; P 54,000; M 775; (203) 878-0681; Fax (203) 876-8517; chamber@milfordct.com; www.milfordct.com*

Monroe • *Monroe C/C* • Jo-Ellen Stipak; Exec. Dir.; 641 Main St.; 06468; Fairfield; P 20,000; M 200; (203) 268-6518; info@monroe ctchamber.com; www.monroectchamber.com

Morris • *see Torrington*

Mystic • *Greater Mystic C/C* • Tricia Cunningham; Pres.; 2 Roosevelt Ave.; P.O. Box 143; 06355; New London; P 12,000; M 750; (860) 572-9578; (866) 572-9578; Fax (860) 572-9273; info@mysticchamber.org; www.mysticchamber.org*

Naugatuck • *Naugatuck C/C* • Lynn Ward; Dir.; 195 Water St.; 06770; New Haven; P 30,860; M 200; (203) 729-4511; Fax (203) 729-4512; cligi@waterburychamber.com; www.naugatuck chamber.com*

New Britain · *New Britain C/C* · William Millerick; Pres.; One Court St.; 06051; Hartford; P 70,000; M 450; (860) 229-1665; Fax (860) 223-8341; bill@newbritainchamber.com; www.newbritain chamber.com*

New Canaan · *New Canaan C/C* · Tucker Murphy; Exec. Dir.; 91 Elm St., 2nd Flr.; 06840; Fairfield; P 19,612; M 400; (203) 966-2004; Fax (203) 966-3810; tucker@newcanaanchamber.com; www.newcanaanchamber.com

New Haven · *Greater New Haven C/C* · Anthony P. Rescigno; Pres.; 900 Chapel St., 10th Flr.; 06510; New Haven; P 500,000; M 1,400; (203) 787-6735; Fax (203) 782-4329; info@gnhcc.com; www.newhavenchamber.com

New London · *see Waterford*

New Milford · *Greater New Milford C/C & Visitor Center* · Denise Del Mastro; Exec. Dir.; 11 Railroad St.; 06776; Litchfield; P 30,000; M 350; (860) 354-6080; Fax (860) 354-8526; nmcc@ newmilford-chamber.com; www.newmilford-chamber.com

Newington · *Newington C/C* · Gail Whitney; Exec. Dir.; 1046 Main St.; 06111; Hartford; P 30,000; M 320; (860) 666-2089; Fax (860) 665-7551; office@newingtonchamber.com; www. newingtonchamber.com*

Newtown · *C/C of Newtown Inc.* · Ann Marie Deweese; Pres.; 45 Main St.; P.O. Box 314; 06470; Fairfield; P 26,000; M 200; (203) 426-2695; Fax (203) 426-2695; chamber@newtown-ct.com; www.newtown-ct.com

Norfolk · *see Torrington*

North Branford · *North Branford C/C* · 1599 Foxon Rd.; 06471; New Haven; P 13,000; M 110; (203) 483-6803; www.townof northbranfordct.com

North Canaan · *see Torrington*

North Haven · *see Wallingford*

Norwalk · *Greater Norwalk C/C* · Edward Musante; Pres.; 101 East Ave.; P.O. Box 668; 06852; Fairfield; P 85,000; M 1,000; (203) 866-2521; Fax (203) 852-0583; info@norwalkchamberof commerce.com; www.norwalkchamberofcommerce.com*

Norwich · *see Waterford*

Oakville · *see Waterbury*

Old Lyme · *Lyme & Old Lyme C/C* · Robert Chapman; Pres.; P.O. Box 4152; 06371; New London; P 7,000; M 190; (888) 302-9246; email@lolcc.com; www.lolcc.com

Old Saybrook · *Old Saybrook C/C* · Judy Sullivan; Exec. Dir.; One Main St.; P.O. Box 625; 06475; Middlesex; P 12,000; M 450; (860) 388-3266; Fax (860) 388-9433; info@oldsaybrookchamber.com; www.oldsaybrookchamber.com*

Orange · *Orange C/C* · Janice Lettick; Exec. Dir.; 605A Orange Center Rd.; 06477; New Haven; P 13,500; M 270; (203) 795-3328; Fax (203) 795-5926; info@orangectchamber.com; www.orangectchamber.com

Oxford · *see Shelton*

Plainfield · *see Danielson*

Plainville · *Plainville C/C* · Maureen Saverick; Ofc. Mgr.; 58 W. Main St.; P.O. Box C; 06062; Hartford; P 17,000; M 250; (860) 747-6867; Fax (860) 793-1832; plvchamber@snet.net; www. plainvillechamber.com*

Plymouth · *see Bristol*

Portland · *see Middletown*

Prospect · *see Naugatuck*

Putnam · *see Danielson*

Ridgefield · *Ridgefield C/C* · Marion Roth; Pres./CEO; 9 Bailey Ave.; 06877; Fairfield; P 24,000; M 380; (203) 438-5992; Fax (203) 438-9175; officemanager@ridgefieldchamber.org; www. ridgefieldchamber.org*

Rockville · *see Vernon*

Rocky Hill · *Rocky Hill C/C* · Claudia Baio; Pres.; 2264 Silas Deane Hwy.; 06067; Hartford; P 16,700; M 181; (860) 258-7633; Fax (860) 258-7637; execdir@rhchamber.org; www.rhchamber.org

Salisbury · *see Lakeville*

Seymour · *see Shelton*

Sharon · *see Torrington*

Shelton · *Greater Valley C/C* · William Purcell CAE CCE; Pres.; 900 Bridgeport Ave., 2nd Flr.; 06484; Fairfield; P 100,000; M 650; (203) 925-4981; info@greatervalleychamber.com; www.greater valleychamber.com*

Simsbury · *Simsbury C/C* · Charity P. Folk; Exec. Dir.; 749 Hopmeadow St.; P.O. Box 224; 06070; Hartford; P 23,000; M 475; (860) 651-7307; Fax (860) 651-1933; info@simsburycoc.org; www.simsburycoc.org

Somers · *see Enfield*

Somers · *see Vernon*

South Windsor · *South Windsor C/C* · Cate Evans; Exec. Dir.; 22 Morgan Farms Dr.; 06074; Hartford; P 24,000; M 500; (860) 644-9442; Fax (860) 648-1911; dawn@southwindsorchamber.org; www.southwindsorchamber.org

Southbury · *Tribury C/C* · Margot Melaas; P.O. Box 807; 06488; New Haven; P 35,000; M 160; (203) 267-4466; info@tribury chamber.org; www.triburychamber.org

Southington · *Greater Southington C/C* · Art Secondo; Pres./ CEO; 1 Factory Sq., Ste. 201; 06489; Hartford; P 42,500; M 550; (860) 628-8036; Fax (860) 276-9696; info@southingtoncoc.com; www.southingtoncoc.com*

Stafford · *see Vernon*

Stamford · *Bus. Cncl. of Fairfield County* · Christopher Bruhl; Pres./CEO; One Landmark Sq., Ste. 300; 06901; Fairfield; P 900,440; M 430; (203) 359-3220; Fax (203) 967-8294; info@ businessfairfield.com; www.businessfairfield.com

Stamford · *Stamford C/C* · John P. Condlin; Pres./CEO; 733 Summer St., Ste. 104; 06901; Fairfield; P 121,073; M 2,600; (203) 359-4761; Fax (203) 363-5069; stamfordchamber@stamford chamber.com; www.stamfordchamber.com

Stratford · *see Bridgeport*

Suffield · *Suffield C/C* · Krystal Holmes; Secy.; P.O. Box 741; 06078; Hartford; P 11,370; M 150; (860) 668-4848; Fax (860) 668-4848; info@suffieldchamber.com; www.suffieldchamber.com

Suthington · *see Bristol*

Taconic · *see Lakeville*

Tolland · *see Vernon*

Torrington · *C/C of Northwest Connecticut* · JoAnn Ryan; Pres./ CEO; 333 Kennedy Dr., Ste. R101; P.O. Box 59; 06790; Litchfield; P 190,000; M 750; (860) 482-6586; Fax (860) 489-8851; joann@ nwctchamberofcommerce.org; www.nwctchamberofcommerce.org*

Trumbull · *see Bridgeport*

Union · *see Vernon*

Vernon · *Tolland County C/C* · Candice Corcione; Exec. Dir.; 30 Lafayette Sq.; 06066; Tolland; P 130,705; M 400; (860) 872-0587; Fax (860) 872-0588; tccc@tollandcountychamber.org; www. tollandcountychamber.org*

Wallingford · *Quinnipiac C/C* · Robin Wilson; Pres./CEO; 100 S. Turnpike Rd.; 06492; New Haven; P 64,000; M 750; (203) 269-9891; Fax (203) 269-1358; cindy@quinncham.com; www.quinncham.com*

Warren · *see Torrington*

Washington · *see Torrington*

Waterbury · *Waterbury Reg. C/C* · Lynn G. Ward; Pres./CEO; 83 Bank St.; P.O. Box 1469; 06721; New Haven; P 106,000; M 1,000; (203) 757-0701; Fax (203) 756-3507; info@waterburychamber.com; www.waterburychamber.com*

Waterford · *C/C of Eastern Connecticut* · Tony Sheridan; Pres./CEO; 914 Hartford Tpk.; 06385; New London; P 293,000; M 1,700; (860) 701-9113; Fax (860) 701-9902; info@chamberect.com; www.chamberect.com.*

Watertown · *see Waterbury*

West Hartford · *West Hartford C/C* · Marjorie Luke; Pres.; 948 Farmington Ave.; 06107; Hartford; P 61,045; M 650; (860) 521-2300; Fax (860) 521-1996; info@WHChamber.com; www.WHChamber.com*

West Haven · *West Haven C/C* · Glen Gitterman; Pres.; 140 Captain Thomas Pkwy.; 06516; New Haven; P 55,000; M 450; (203) 933-1500; Fax (203) 931-1940; info@westhavenchamber.com; www.westhavenchamber.com*

Weston · *see Westport*

Westport · *Westport-Weston C/C* · Lisa Thygerson; Pres./CEO; 215 Main St.; 06880; Fairfield; P 33,000; M 400; (203) 227-9234; Fax (203) 454-4019; info@westportwestonchamber.com; www.westportwestonchamber.com.*

Wethersfield · *Wethersfield C/C* · John O'Brien; Pres./CEO; 200 Main St.; P.O. Box 290186; 06129; Hartford; P 27,000; M 205; (860) 721-6200; Fax (860) 721-8703; wethersfield@sbcglobal.net; www.wethersfieldchamber.com

Willimantic · *The Chamber of Commerce Inc. [Windham Region]* · Roger A. Adams; Exec. Dir.; 1010 Main St.; P.O. Box 43; 06226; Windham; P 78,000; M 350; (860) 423-6389; Fax (860) 423-8235; roger@windhamchamber.com; www.windhamchamber.com.*

Willington · *see Vernon*

Wilton · *Wilton C/C* · Stephanie R. Barksdale; Exec. Dir.; 120 Old Ridgefield Rd.; P.O. Box 7094; 06897; Fairfield; P 19,000; M 350; (203) 762-0567; wiltoncoc@snet.net; www.wiltonchamber.com*

Winchester · *see Torrington*

Windsor · *Windsor C/C* · Jane M. Garibay; Exec. Dir.; 261 Broad St.; P.O. Box 9; 06095; Hartford; P 28,400; M 320; (860) 688-5165; Fax (860) 688-0809; jane@windsorcc.org; www.windsorcc.org*

Windsor Locks · *Windsor Locks C/C* · Jared Carillo; Pres.; P.O. Box 257; 06096; Hartford; P 12,190; M 100; (860) 623-9319; Fax (860) 831-1036; info@windsorlockschamber.org; www.windsorlockschamber.org*

Winsted · *see Torrington*

Wolcott · *see Bristol*

Woodbury · *see Southbury*

Delaware

Delaware State C of C · James A. Wolfe; Pres./CEO; 1201 N. Orange St., Ste. 200; P.O. Box 671; Wilmington; 19899; New Castle; P 873,092; M 2,800; (302) 655-7221; (800) 292-9507; Fax (302) 654-0691; info@dscc.com; www.dscc.com*

Bethany Beach · *see Fenwick Island*

Delmar · *Greater Delmar C/C* · John Johnson; Pres.; P.O. Box 416; 19940; Sussex; P 3,500; M 84; (302) 846-3336; www.delmar-chamberofcommerce.com

Dewey Beach · *see Rehoboth Beach*

Dover · *Central Delaware C/C* · Judith Diogo; Pres.; 435 N. DuPont Hwy.; 19901; Kent; P 146,000; M 870; (302) 734-7513; Fax (302) 678-0189; info@cdcc.net; www.cdcc.net

Fenwick Island · *Bethany-Fenwick Area C/C* · Carrie Subity; Exec. Dir.; 36913 Coastal Hwy.; 19944; Sussex; P 20,000; M 800; (302) 539-2100; (800) 962-SURF; Fax (302) 539-9434; info@bethany-fenwick.org; www.bethany-fenwick.org*

Georgetown · *Greater Georgetown C/C* · Ray Hopkins; Pres.; 140 Layton Ave.; P.O. Box 1; 19947; Sussex; P 10,555; M 455; (302) 856-1544; Fax (302) 856-1577; info@georgetowncoc.com; www.georgetowncoc.com*

Laurel · *Laurel C/C* · Pres.; P.O. Box 696; 19956; Sussex; P 17,000; M 126; (302) 875-9319; Fax (302) 875-5908; info@laurelchamber.com; www.laurelchamber.com

Lewes · *Lewes C/C* · Betsy Reamer; Exec. Dir.; 120 Kings Hwy.; P.O. Box 1; 19958; Sussex; P 3,100; M 450; (302) 645-8073; (877) 465-3937; Fax (302) 645-8412; inquiry@leweschamber.com; www.leweschamber.com

Middletown · *Middletown Area C/C* · Margaret Ryan; Admin. Asst.; 216 N. Broad St.; P.O. Box 1; 19709; New Castle; P 10,000; M 325; (302) 378-7545; Fax (302) 378-6260; info@middletownareachamber.com; www.middletownareachamber.com*

Milford · *C/C for Greater Milford Inc.* · Jo Schmeiser; Exec. Dir.; 5 S. Washington St.; 19963; Kent & Sussex; P 16,000; M 300; (302) 422-3344; Fax (302) 422-7503; milford@milfordchamber.com; www.milfordchamber.com*

Millsboro · *Millsboro C/C* · Fran Bruce; Exec. Dir.; 322 Wilson Hwy.; P.O. Box 187; 19966; Sussex; P 4,000; M 290; (302) 934-6777; Fax (302) 934-6065; millsboro@intercom.net; www.millsborochamber.com

Milton · *Milton C/C* · Georgia P. Dalzell; Exec. Dir.; 707 Chestnut St.; P.O. Box 61; 19968; Sussex; P 3,000; M 115; (302) 684-1101; chamber@historicmilton.com; www.historicmilton.com

New Castle · *New Castle County C/C* · Mark Kleinschmidt; Pres.; 12 Penns Way; 19720; New Castle; P 520,000; M 1,700; (302) 737-4343; Fax (302) 322-3593; info@ncccc.com; www.ncccc.com*

Rehoboth Beach · *Rehoboth Beach-Dewey Beach C/C* · Carol Everhart; Pres./CEO; 501 Rehoboth Ave.; P.O. Box 216; 19971; Sussex; P 168,000; M 1,304; (302) 227-2233; (800) 441-1329; Fax (302) 227-8351; rehoboth@beach-fun.com; www.beach-fun.com*

Seaford · *Greater Seaford C/C* · Paula K. Gunson; Exec. Dir.; P.O. Box 26; 19973; Sussex; P 24,000; M 350; (302) 629-9690; Fax (302) 629-0281; admin@seafordchamber.com; www.seafordchamber.com*

District of Columbia

Washington · *Dist. of Columbia C/C* · Barbara B. Lang; Pres./CEO; 506 9th St. N.W.; 20004; District of Columbia; P 550,000; M 2,057; (202) 347-7201; Fax (202) 638-6762; landerson@dcchamber.org; www.dcchamber.org

Washington · *United States C/C* · Thomas J. Donohue; Pres./CEO; 1615 H St. N.W.; 20062; District of Columbia; P 300,000,000; (202) 659-6000; (800) 638-6582; custsvc@uschamber.com; www.uschamber.com

Washington · *United States Hispanic C/C* · Javier Palomarez; Pres./CEO; 1424 K St. N.W., Ste. 401; 20005; District of Columbia; M 200; (202) 842-1212; (800) USHCC86; Fax (202) 842-3221; palomarez@ushcc.com; www.ushcc.com

Florida

Florida C of C · Mark Wilson; Pres.; 136 S. Bronough St.; P.O. Box 11309; Tallahassee; 32302; Leon; P 18,300,000; M 7,000; (850) 521-1200; Fax (850) 521-1219; info@flchamber.com; www.flchamber.com*

Alachua · *Alachua C/C* · Robert Page; Pres.; P.O. Box 387; 32616; Alachua; P 8,000; M 151; (386) 462-3333; Fax (386) 462-3333; info@alachua.com; www.alachua.com

Altamonte Springs · *see Heathrow*

Amelia Island · *Amelia Island-Fernandina Beach-Yulee C/C* · Regina Duncan; Pres.; 961687 Gateway Blvd., Ste. 101G; 32034; Nassau; P 60,000; M 850; (904) 261-3248; Fax (904) 261-6997; regina@aifby.com; www.islandchamber.com

Anna Maria Island · *see Holmes Beach*

Apalachicola · *Apalachicola Bay C/C* · Anita Gregory Grove; Exec. Dir.; 122 Commerce St.; 32320; Franklin; P 3,000; M 400; (850) 653-9419; Fax (850) 653-8219; info@apalachicolabay.org; www.apalachicolabay.org

Apollo Beach · *Apollo Beach C/C* · Joanne C. Gadek; Exec. Dir.; 137 Harbor Village Ln.; 33572; Hillsborough; P 13,000; M 240; (813) 645-1366; Fax (813) 641-2612; abeachchamber@tampabay.rr.com; www.apollobeachchamber.com*

Apopka · *Apopka Area C/C* · Paul Seago; Pres.; 180 E. Main St.; 32703; Orange; P 45,000; M 600; (407) 886-1441; Fax (407) 886-1131; pauls@apopkachamber.org; www.apopkachamber.org.*

Arcadia · *DeSoto County C/C* · Mary Kay Burns; Pres.; 16 S. Volusia Ave.; 34266; DeSoto; P 33,000; M 300; (863) 494-4033; desotochamber@embarqmail.com

Astor · *Astor Area C/C* · Linda Hill; Pres.; 23835 River Rd., Ste. A; P.O. Box 329; 32102; Lake & Volusia; P 4,000; M 76; (352) 759-2679; Fax (352) 759-2679; info@astorchamber.com; www.astorchamber.com

Auburndale · *Auburndale C/C* · Joy Pruitt; Exec. Dir.; 109 Main St.; 33823; Polk; P 15,000; M 300; (863) 967-3400; Fax (863) 967-0880; auburndalechamber@live.com; myauburndalechamber.com

Avon Park · *Avon Park C/C* · David Greenslade; Exec. Dir.; 28 E. Main St.; 33825; Highlands; P 19,500; M 350; (863) 453-3350; Fax (863) 453-0973; apcc@apfla.com; www.apfla.com

Bartow · *Greater Bartow C/C* · Jeff Clark; Exec. Dir.; 510 N. Broadway Ave.; 33830; Polk; P 16,043; M 700; (863) 533-7125; Fax (863) 533-3793; discoverbartow@bartowchamber.com; www.bartowchamber.com*

Bay Harbor Islands · *Florida Gold Coast C/C* · Peter Cohn; Pres.; 9550 Bay Harbor Terrace, Ste. 210; 33154; Miami-Dade; P 45,000; M 200; (305) 866-6020; Fax (305) 866-0635; www.bayharborislands.org

Bayonet Point · *see New Port Richey*

Belle Glade · *Belle Glade C/C* · Brenda Bunting; Exec. Dir.; 540 S. Main St.; 33430; Palm Beach; P 20,000; M 285; (561) 996-2745; Fax (561) 996-2252; bgchamber@aol.com; www.belleglade chamber.com

Belleair Beach · *see Saint Pete Beach*

Belleair Bluffs · *see Saint Pete Beach*

Belleair Shores · *see Saint Pete Beach*

Belleview · *Belleview-South Marion C/C* · Mariah Chaffin; Exec. Dir.; 5301 S.E. Abshier Blvd.; 34420; Marion; P 4,500; M 200; (352) 245-2178; Fax (352) 245-2178; belleviewchamber@gmail.com; www.bsmcc.org

Beverly Beach · *see Palm Coast*

Big Pine Key · *Lower Keys C/C* · Carole Stevens; Exec. Dir.; 31020 Overseas Hwy.; P.O. Box 430511; 33043; Monroe; P 16,000; M 225; (305) 872-2411; (800) 872-3722; Fax (305) 872-0752; lkchamber@aol.com; www.lowerkeyschamber.com

Blountstown · *Calhoun County C/C* · Kristy Terry; Exec. Dir.; 20816 Central Ave. E., Ste. 2; 32424; Calhoun; P 13,000; M 150; (850) 674-4519; Fax (850) 674-4962; chamber@calhounco.org; www.calhounco.org

Boca Grande · *Boca Grande Area C/C* · Lynda Landcaster; Exec. Dir.; 480 E. Railroad Ave.; P.O. Box 704; 33921; Lee; P 1,000; M 275; (941) 964-0568; Fax (941) 964-0620; info@bocagrande chamber.com; www.bocagrandechamber.com

Boca Raton · *Greater Boca Raton C/C* · Troy M. McLellan; Pres./CEO; 1800 N. Dixie Hwy.; 33432; Palm Beach; P 225,000; M 1,500; (561) 395-4433; Fax (561) 392-3780; info@bocaratonchamber.com; www.bocaratonchamber.com*

Bonifay · *Holmes County C/C* · Julia Bullington; Mktg. Coord.; 106 E. Byrd Ave.; 32425; Holmes; P 19,545; M 129; (850) 547-4682; Fax (850) 547-4206; hcflcofc@gmail.com; www.holmes countyonline.com

Bonita Springs · *Bonita Springs Area C/C* · Christine A. Ross; Pres./CEO; 25071 Chamber of Commerce Dr.; 34135; Lee; P 45,000; M 900; (239) 992-2943; Fax (239) 992-5011; info@bonitasprings chamber.com; www.bonitaspringschamber.com*

Boynton Beach · *Greater Boynton Beach C/C* · Glenn P. Jergensen; Pres./CEO; 1880 N. Congress Ave., Ste. 106; 33426; Palm Beach; P 155,000; M 750; (561) 732-9501; Fax (561) 734-4304; chamber@boyntonbeach.org; www.boyntonbeach.org*

Bradenton · *Manatee C/C* · Robert P. Bartz; Pres.; 222 10th St. W.; 4215 Concept Ct., Lakewood Ranch, 34211; 34205; Manatee; P 325,000; M 2,400; (941) 748-3411; Fax (941) 745-1877; info@manateechamber.com; www.manateechamber.com.

Brandon · *Greater Brandon C/C* · Tammy C. Bracewell; Pres./CEO; 330 Pauls Dr., Ste. 100; 33511; Hillsborough; P 255,000; M 1,800; (813) 689-1221; Fax (813) 689-9440; info@brandon chamber.com; www.brandonchamber.com.*

Bristol · *Liberty County C/C* · Michael Wright; Pres.; P.O. Box 523; 32321; Liberty; P 8,000; M 50; (850) 643-2359; Fax (850) 643-3334; info01@libertycountyflorida.com; www.libertycountyflorida.com

Brooksville · *Greater Hernando County C/C* · Pat Crowley; Pres./CEO; 15588 Aviation Loop Dr.; 34604; Hernando; P 166,086; M 1,000; (352) 796-0697; Fax (352) 796-3704; pat@hernando chamber.com; www.hernandochamber.com.*

Bunnell · *see Palm Coast*

Bushnell · *see Lake Panasoffkee*

Callahan · *Greater Nassau County C/C* · David Cobb; Pres.; P.O. Box 98; 32011; Nassau; P 56,843; M 200; (904) 879-1441; Fax (904) 879-4033; info@greaternassaucounty.com; www.greater nassaucounty.com*

Cape Canaveral · *see Cocoa Beach*

Cape Coral · *Cape Coral C/C* · Michael Quaintance; Pres.; 2051 Cape Coral Pkwy. E.; P.O. Box 100747; 33910; Lee; P 169,000; M 800; (239) 549-6900; (800) 226-9609; Fax (239) 549-9609; info@capecoralchamber.com; www.capecoralchamber.com.*

Cape Haze · *see Englewood*

Captiva Islands · *see Sanibel*

Carrabelle · *Carrabelle Area C/C* · Suzanne Zimmerman; Exec. Dir.; 105 St. James Ave.; P.O. Drawer DD; 32322; Franklin; P 1,300; M 175; (850) 697-2585; Fax (850) 697-4206; chamber@nettally. com; www.carrabellechamber.org

Casselberry · *Casselberry C/C* · Colleen Hufford; Pres.; P.O. Box 180731; 32718; Seminole; P 27,000; M 132; (407) 831-1231; Fax (407) 830-1781; casselberrychamber@gmail.com; www. casselberrychamber.org*

Cedar Key · *Cedar Key Area C/C* · Kellie Parkin; Bus. Dev. Dir.; 450 2nd St.; P.O. Box 610; 32625; Levy; P 900; M 130; (352) 543-5600; info@cedarkey.org; www.cedarkey.org

Center Hill · *see Lake Panasoffkee*

Century · *Century C/C* · Benny Barnes; Pres.; P.O. Box 857; 32535; Escambia; P 1,800; M 54; (850) 256-3155; Fax (850) 256-3155; centuryc@erec.net

Chiefland · *Greater Chiefland Area C/C* · Michele Bell; Exec. Dir.; 23 S.E. 2nd Ave.; P.O. Box 1397; 32644; Levy; P 32,500; M 180; (352) 493-1849; Fax (352) 493-0282; info@chieflandchamber. com; www.chieflandchamber.com*

Chipley · *Washington County C/C* · Ted Everett; Exec. Dir.; 672 5th St.; P.O. Box 457; 32428; Washington; P 24,000; M 350; (850) 638-4157; Fax (850) 638-8770; wcchamber@wfeca.net; www. washcomall.com.*

Chokoloskee · *see Everglades City*

Clay County · *see Orange Park*

Clearwater · *Clearwater Reg. C/C* · Bob Clifford; Pres./CEO; 401 Cleveland St.; 33755; Pinellas; P 108,000; M 1,100; (727) 461-0011; Fax (727) 449-2889; info@clearwaterflorida.org; www.clearwaterflorida.org*

Clearwater Beach · *Clearwater Beach C/C* · Darlene Kole; Pres./CEO; 333C S. Gulfview Blvd.; P.O. Box 3573; 33767; Pinellas; P 50,000; M 200; (727) 447-7600; (888) 799-3199; Fax (727) 443-7812; office@beachchamber.com; www.beachchamber.com*

Clermont · *South Lake C/C* · Ray San Fratello; Pres.; 691 W. Montrose St.; 34711; Lake; P 140,000; M 850; (352) 394-4191; Fax (352) 394-5799; office@southlakechamber-fl.com; www. southlakechamber-fl.com*

Clewiston · *Clewiston C/C* · Cathy Garrels; Exec. Dir.; 109 Central Ave.; 33440; Hendry; P 8,000; M 400; (863) 983-7979; Fax (863) 983-7108; clewistonchamber@embarqmail.com; www.clewiston.org

Cocoa Beach · *Cocoa Beach Area C/C* · Melissa Stains; Pres./ CEO; 400 Fortenberry Rd.; Merritt Island; 32952; Brevard; P 250,000; M 1,311; (321) 459-2200; Fax (321) 459-2232; info@ cocoabeachchamber.com; www.cocoabeachchamber.com*

Coconut Grove · *Coconut Grove C/C* · David Guzikowski; Exec. Dir.; 2820 McFarlane Rd.; 33133; Miami-Dade; P 20,000; M 175; (305) 444-7270; Fax (305) 444-2498; info@coconutgrove.com; www.coconutgrovechamber.com

Coleman · *see Lake Panasoffkee*

Cooper City · *see Davie*

Coral Gables · *Coral Gables C/C* · Mark Trowbridge; Pres./CEO; 224 Catalonia Ave.; 33134; Miami-Dade; P 43,000; M 1,500; (305) 446-1657; Fax (305) 446-9900; info@coralgableschamber.org; www.coralgableschamber.org*

Coral Springs · *Coral Springs C/C* · Cindy Brief; Pres.; 11805 Heron Bay Blvd.; 33076; Broward; P 126,500; M 500; (954) 752-4242; info@cschamber.com; www.cschamber.com*

Crawfordville · *Wakulla County C/C* · Petra Shuff; Ofc. Admin.; 23 High Dr.; 32327; Wakulla; P 28,000; M 285; (850) 926-1848; Fax (850) 926-2050; info@wakullacountychamber.com; www. wakullacountychamber.com

Crescent City · *see Palatka*

Crestview · *Crestview Area C/C* · Wayne Harris; Exec. Dir.; 1447 Commerce Dr.; 32539; Okaloosa; P 75,000; M 600; (850) 682-3212; Fax (850) 682-7413; info@crestviewchamber.com; www. crestviewchamber.com*

Cross City · *Dixie County C/C* · Angie Bush; Secy.; P.O. Box 547; 32628; Dixie; P 18,000; M 108; (352) 498-5454; Fax (352) 498-7549; dixiechamber@usa.net; www.dixiechamber.com

Crystal River · *Citrus County C/C* · Josh Wooten; Pres./CEO; 28 N.W. Hwy. 19; 34428; Citrus; P 140,000; M 1,100; (352) 795-3149; (352) 795-2187; Fax (352) 795-1921; cira@citruscountychamber. com; www.citruscountychamber.com*

Dade City · *Greater Dade City C/C* · Joey Wubbena; Pres.; 14112 8th St.; 33525; Pasco; P 17,500; M 400; (352) 567-3769; Fax (352) 567-3770; info@dadecitychamber.org; www.dadecitychamber.org*

Dania Beach · *Greater Dania Beach C/C* · Victoria Payne; Exec. Dir.; 102 W. Dania Beach Blvd.; P.O. Box 1017; 33004; Broward; P 28,000; M 325; (954) 926-2323; Fax (954) 926-2384; info@ greaterdania.org; www.greaterdania.org*

Davenport · *Greater Davenport C/C* · Christine Ulrich; Pres.; P.O. Box 994; 33836; Polk; P 2,800; M 50; (863) 421-2105; secretary@ davenportchamber.com; www.davenportchamber.com

Davie · *Davie-Cooper City C/C* · Alice Harrington; Pres.; 4185 Davie Rd.; 33314; Broward; P 90,000; M 500; (954) 581-0790; Fax (954) 581-9684; dcch@davie-coopercity.org; www.davie-coopercity.org*

Daytona Beach · *Daytona Reg. C/C* · Larry McKinney; Pres./ CEO; 126 E. Orange Ave.; P.O. Box 2676; 32115; Volusia; P 68,000; M 1,200; (386) 255-0981; (800) 854-1234; Fax (386) 258-5104; info@daytonachamber.com; www.daytonachamber.com*

Daytona Beach Shores · *see Port Orange*

DeBary · *see DeLand*

Deerfield Beach · *Greater Deerfield Beach C/C* · Exec. Dir.; 1601 E. Hillsboro Blvd.; 33441; Broward; P 78,000; M 550; (954) 427-1050; Fax (954) 427-1056; info@deerfieldchamber.com; www.deerfieldchamber.com*

DeLand · *DeLand Area C/C* · Exec. Dir.; 336 N. Woodland Blvd.; 32720; Volusia; P 200,000; M 900; (386) 734-4331; Fax (386) 734-4333; office@delandchamber.org; www.delandchamber.org*

Delray Beach · *Greater Delray Beach C/C* · Michael Malone; Pres.; 64-A S.E. 5th Ave.; 33483; Palm Beach; P 40,000; M 950; (561) 278-0424; Fax (561) 278-0555; mike@delraybeach.com; www.delraybeach.com.*

Deltona · *see DeLand*

Destin · *Destin Area C/C* · Shane Moody; Pres./CEO; 4484 Legendary Dr., Ste. A; 32541; Okaloosa; P 12,350; M 950; (850) 837-6241; Fax (850) 654-5612; mail@destinchamber.com; www.destinchamber.com*

Dover · *see Seffner*

Dundee · *Dundee Area C/C* · Lisa-Marie Brewer; Exec. Dir.; 310 Main St.; P.O. Box 241; 33838; Polk; P 3,300; M 200; (863) 439-3261; dundeechamber@hotmail.com; www.dundeechamber.com

Dunedin · *Dunedin C/C* · Lynn Wargo; Pres./CEO; 301 Main St.; 34698; Pinellas; P 37,000; M 430; (727) 733-3197; Fax (727) 734-8942; chamber@dunedin-fl.com; www.dunedin-fl.com*

Dunnellon • *Dunnellon Area C/C* • Beverly Leisure; Exec. Dir.; 20500 E. Pennsylvania Ave.; 34432; Marion; P 65,000; M 250; (352) 489-2320; Fax (352) 489-6846; dunnellonchamber@ bellsouth.net; www.dunnellonchamber.org*

Edgewater • *see New Smyrna Beach*

Englewood • *Englewood-Cape Haze Area C/C* • Jon Bednerik CAE; Exec. Dir.; 1160 S. McCall Rd., Ste. 1B; 34223; Charlotte; P 36,000; M 550; (941) 474-5511; (800) 603-7198; Fax (941) 475-9257; business@englewoodchamber.com; www.englewood chamber.com*

Estero • *Estero C/C* • Grace Fortuna; Exec. Dir.; P.O. Box 588; 33929; Lee; P 30,000; M 250; (239) 948-7990; Fax (239) 948-5072; info@esterochamber.com; www.esterochamber.com; www.estero.org

Eustis • *Lake Eustis Area C/C* • Nancy Muenzmay; Exec. Dir.; 1 W. Orange Ave.; 32726; Lake; P 19,000; M 371; (352) 357-3434; Fax (352) 357-1392; info@eustischamber.org; www.eustischamber.org*

Everglades City • *Everglades Area C/C* • P.O. Box 130; 34139; Collier; P 525; M 147; (239) 695-3172; (800) 914-6355; Fax (239) 695-3171; info@evergladeschamber.com; www.everglades chamber.com

Fernandina Beach • *see Amelia Island*

Flagler Beach • *see Palm Coast*

Florida City • *see Homestead*

Fort Lauderdale • *America C/C* • Jack Miller; Pres./CEO; 1290 Weston Rd., Ste. 312; 33326; Broward; P 1,900,000; M 863; (702) 260-9425; jack@americachamber.com; www.americachamber.com.*

THE CHAMBER THAT MEANS BUSINESS® WAS CREATED TO PROMOTE AND SERVE THE LOCAL, REGIONAL, NATIONAL & INTERNATIONAL NEEDS OF ITS MEMBERS FOR BUSINESS TO BUSINESS & BUSINESS TO CONSUMER.

Fort Lauderdale • *Greater Fort Lauderdale C/C* • Dan Lindblade CAE; Pres./CEO; 512 N.E. Third Ave.; 33301; Broward; P 173,000; M 1,400; (954) 462-6000; Fax (954) 527-8766; info@ ftlchamber.com; www.ftlchamber.com.*

Fort Meade • *Fort Meade C/C* • Priscilla Perry; Coord.; 214 W. Broadway, Ste. B; P.O. Box 91; 33841; Polk; P 5,800; M 100; (863) 285-8253; Fax (863) 285-6968; ftmeadechamber@aol.com; www.fortmeadechamber.com*

Fort Myers Area

Chamber of Southwest Florida • Stephen Tirey; Pres.; 5237 Summerlin Commons Blvd., Ste. 114; 33907; Lee; P 500,000; M 200; (239) 275-2102; Fax (239) 275-2103; chamberswf@gmail.com; www.chamber-swflorida.com*

Greater Fort Myers C/C • Marietta B. Mudgett; Exec. Dir.; 2310 Edwards Dr.; P.O. Box 9289; 33902; Lee; P 550,000; M 1,100; (239) 332-3624; (800) 366-3622; Fax (239) 332-7276; fortmyers@ fortmyers.org; www.fortmyers.org*

Southwest Florida Hispanic C/C • Veronica Culbertson; Pres./CEO; 10051 McGregor Blvd., Ste. 204; 33919; Collier &Lee; P 579,453; M 400; (239) 418-1441; Fax (239) 418-1475; info@ hispanicchamberflorida.org; www.hispanicchamberflorida.org*

Fort Myers Beach • *Fort Myers Beach C/C* • John E. Albion; Pres.; 17200 San Carlos Blvd.; 33931; Lee; P 523,121; M 500; (239) 454-7500; Fax (239) 454-7910; info@fmbchamber.com; www.fortmyersbeach.org*

Fort Walton Beach • *Greater Fort Walton Beach C/C* • Ted Corcoran; Pres./CEO; 34 Miracle Strip Pkwy. S.E.; P.O. Box 640; 32549; Okaloosa; P 125,000; M 1,503; (850) 244-8191; Fax (850) 244-1935; info@fwbchamber.org; www.fwbchamber.com*

Frostproof • *Frostproof Area C/C* • 15 E. Wall St.; P.O. Box 968; 33843; Polk; P 3,000; M 140; (863) 635-9112; Fax (863) 635-7222; info@frostproofchamber.com; www.frostproofchamber.com

Gainesville • *Gainesville Area C/C* • Sonia P. Douglas; V.P./COO; 300 E. University Ave., Ste. 100; P.O. Box 1187; 32602; Alachua; P 253,000; M 1,266; (352) 334-7100; Fax (352) 334-7141; info@ gainesvillechamber.com; www.gainesvillechamber.com.*

Goldenrod • *Goldenrod Area C/C* • Darlene Dangel; Exec. Dir.; 4755 Palmetto Ave.; P.O. Box 61; 32733; Orange; P 100,000; M 250; (407) 677-5980; Fax (407) 677-4928; director@goldenrodchamber.com; www.goldenrodchamber.com*

Green Cove Springs • *see Orange Park*

Groveland • *see Clermont*

Gulf Breeze • *Gulf Breeze Area C/C* • Meg Peltier; Pres./CEO; 409 Gulf Breeze Pkwy.; 32561; Santa Rosa; P 30,000; M 420; (850) 932-7888; Fax (850) 934-4601; info@gulfbreezechamber.com; www.gulfbreezechamber.com*

Haines City • *Haines City-NE Polk County Reg. C/C* • Jane Patton; Pres.; 35610 Hwy. 27; P.O. Box 986; 33845; Polk; P 18,000; M 350; (863) 422-3751; Fax (863) 422-4704; info@hainescity.com; www.hainescity.com

Hallandale Beach • *Hallandale Beach C/C* • Patricia Genetti; Exec. Dir.; 400 S. Federal Hwy., Ste. 192; 33009; Broward; P 38,000; M 250; (954) 454-0541; Fax (954) 454-0930; info@hallandale beachchamber.com; www.hallandalebeachchamber.com.*

Harmony • *see Saint Cloud*

Hawthorne • *Hawthorne Area C/C* • Chris Carson; Pres.; P.O. Box 125; 32640; Alachua; P 2,500; M 55; (352) 481-2411; chamber@ hawthorneflorida.org; www.hawthorneflorida.org

Heathrow • *Seminole County Reg. C/C* • Frank Hale; Pres.; 1055 AAA Dr., Ste. 153; 32746; Seminole; P 375,000; M 3,000; (407) 333-4748; Fax (407) 708-4615; info@seminolebusiness.org; www.seminolebusiness.org*

Hernando County • *see Brooksville*

Hialeah • *Hialeah C of C & Ind. [Latin C/C]* • Daniel Hernandez; Pres.; 240 E. 1st Ave., Ste. 217; 33010; Miami-Dade; P 300,000; M 450; (305) 888-7780; Fax (305) 888-7804; edelcastillo@hialeah chamber.org; www.hialeahchamber.org

High Springs • *High Springs C/C* • Wanda Kemp; Ofc. Coord.; P.O. Box 863; 32655; Alachua; P 4,300; M 130; (386) 454-3120; Fax (386) 454-5848; chamber@highsprings.com; www.highsprings.com

Hobe Sound • *Hobe Sound C/C* • Jennifer Ferrari; Exec. Dir.; 11954 Dixie Hwy.; P.O. Box 1507; 33475; Martin; P 18,000; M 500; (772) 546-4724; Fax (772) 546-9969; info@hobesound.org; www.hobesound.org*

Holiday • *see New Port Richey*

Holly Hill • *Holly Hill C/C* • Rose Schuhmacher; Exec. Dir.; 1056 Ridgewood Ave.; 32117; Volusia; P 15,000; M 300; (386) 255-7311; Fax (386) 267-0485; office@hollyhillchamber.com; www.hollyhillchamber.com*

Hollywood • *Greater Hollywood C/C* • Anne Hotte; Exec. Dir.; 330 N. Federal Hwy.; 33020; Broward; P 139,357; M 800; (954) 923-4000; (800) 231-5562; Fax (954) 923-8737; information@ hollywoodchamber.org; www.hollywoodchamber.org*

Holmes Beach · *Anna Maria Island C/C* · Mary Ann Brockman; Pres.; 5313 Gulf Dr. N.; 34217; Manatee; P 8,500; M 600; (941) 778-1541; (800) 392-9975; Fax (941) 778-9679; info@anna mariaislandchamber.org; www.amichamber.org

Homestead · *Greater Homestead-Florida City C/C* · Mary Finlan; Exec. Dir.; 455 N. Flagler Ave.; P.O. Box 901544; 33090; Miami-Dade; P 59,000; M 500; (305) 247-2332; (888) 352-4891; Fax (305) 224-9101; info@chamberinaction.com; www.chamber inaction.com

Homosassa Springs · *Citrus County C/C* · Josh Wooten; Pres./ CEO; 3495 S. Suncoast Blvd.; 34447; Citrus; P 140,000; M 1,100; (352) 628-2666; Fax (352) 621-0920; renee@citruscountychamber. com; www.citruscountychamber.com*

Hudson · *see New Port Richey*

Immokalee · *Eastern Collier C/C* · Mike Ellis; Pres.; 1300 N. 15th St.. Ste. 2; 34142; Collier; P 30,000; M 200; (239) 657-3237; Fax (239) 657-5450; ecoc@comcast.net; www.easterncollier chamber.com.

Indialantic · *see Melbourne*

Indian Harbour Beach · *see Melbourne*

Indian Rocks Beach · *see Saint Pete Beach*

Indian Shores · *see Saint Pete Beach*

Indiantown · *Indiantown-Western Martin County C/C* · Allon R. Fish; Pres./CEO; 15935 S.W. Warfield Blvd.; P.O. Box 602; 34956; Martin; P 10,000; M 185; (772) 597-2184; Fax (772) 597-6063; itowncc@onearrow.net; www.indiantownfl.org.

Inglis · *Withlacoochee Gulf Area C/C* · Sally Price; Interim Pres.; 167 Hwy. 40 W.; P.O. Box 427; 34449; Levy; P 2,100; M 45; (352) 447-3383; info@gmail.com; www.inglisyankeetown.org*

Inverness · *Citrus County C/C* · Josh Wooten; Pres./CEO; 401 Tompkins St.; 34450; Citrus; P 140,000; M 1,100; (352) 726-2801; Fax (352) 637-6498; suzanne@citruscountychamber.com; www. citruscountychamber.com*

Islamorada · *Islamorada C/C* · Judy Hull; Exec. Dir.; 83224 Overseas Hwy.; P.O. Box 915; 33036; Monroe; P 8,000; M 100; (305) 664-4503; (800) 322-5397; Fax (305) 664-4289; director@ islamoradachamber.com; www.islamoradachamber.com*

Jacksonville · *Jacksonville Reg. C/C* · Walter M. Lee III; Pres.; 3 Independent Dr.; 32202; Duval; P 1,321,013; M 3,300; (904) 366-6600; Fax (904) 632-0617; info@jacksonvillechamber.org; www. opportunityjacksonville.com*

Jacksonville Beach · *Jacksonville Reg. C/C-Beaches Div.* · John Bryan; Dir. of Beaches Div.; 1300 Marsh Landing Pkwy., Ste. 108; 32250; Duval; P 71,000; M 525; (904) 273-5366; Fax (904) 273-9361; beaches@myjaxchamber.com; www.myjaxchamber.com*

Jasper · *Hamilton County C/C* · Joy Howell; Exec. Dir.; 1153 U.S. Hwy 41 N.W., Ste. 9; P.O. Box 366; 32052; Hamilton; P 14,800; M 107; (386) 792-1300; Fax (386) 792-1300; hamcoc@wind stream.net; www.hamiltoncountycoc.com

Jensen Beach · *Jensen Beach C/C* · Ronald Rose; Exec. Dir.; 1900 Ricou Terrace; P.O. Box 1536; 34958; Martin; P 12,000; M 460; (772) 334-3444; Fax (772) 334-0817; info@jensenbeachchamber. biz; www.jensenbeachchamber.biz*

Juno Beach · *see Jupiter*

Jupiter · *Florida State Hispanic C/C* · Arlen Castillo; Exec. Admin.; 800 N. U.S. Hwy. 1; 33477; Palm Beach; P 18,300,000; (561) 748-3951; Fax (561) 748-3951; arlen@fshcc.com; www. fshcc.com

Jupiter · *Northern Palm Beach County C/C* · Ed Chase; Pres./ CEO; 800 N. U.S. Hwy. 1; 33477; Palm Beach; P 140,000; M 1,500; (561) 746-7111; Fax (561) 745-7519; info@npbchamber.com; www.npbchamber.com.*

Keaton Beach · *see Perry*

Kendall · *see South Miami*

Kennedy Space Center · *see Cocoa Beach*

Key Biscayne · *Key Biscayne C of C & Visitors Center* · Kathye Susnjer; Exec. Dir.; 88 W. McIntyre St., Ste. 100; 33149; Miami-Dade; P 13,000; M 350; (305) 361-5207; Fax (305) 361-9411; info@keybiscaynechamber.org; www.keybiscaynechamber.org

Key Colony Beach · *Key Colony Beach Comm. Assn.* · Ms. Lyn Paterson; Pres.; P.O. Box 510884; 33051; Monroe; P 2,500; M 500; (305) 289-1212; lynkcb@yahoo.com; www.keycolonybeach.net

Key Largo · *Key Largo C/C* · Jackie Harder; Pres.; 106000 Overseas Hwy.; 33037; Monroe; P 18,000; M 380; (305) 451-1414; (800) 822-1088; Fax (305) 451-4726; info@keylargochamber.org; www.keylargochamber.org

Key West · *Key West C/C* · Virginia A. Panico; Exec. V.P.; 510 Greene St., 1st Flr.; 33040; Monroe; P 22,364; M 535; (305) 294-2587; (800) LAST-KEY; Fax (305) 294-7806; info@keywestchamber. org; www.keywestchamber.org

Keystone Heights · *see Starke*

Kissimmee · *Kissimmee/Osceola County C/C* · Michael Horner; Pres.; 1425 E. Vine St.; 34744; Osceola; P 267,529; M 1,200; (407) 847-3174; Fax (407) 870-8607; info@kissimmeechamber.com; www.kissimmeechamber.com.*

LaBelle · *Greater LaBelle C/C* · Maureen Jordan; Pres.; 125 E. Hickpochee Ave.; P.O. Box 456; 33975; Hendry; P 12,000; M 250; (863) 675-0125; Fax (863) 675-6160; lchamberofcomm@embarq mail.com; www.labellechamber.com

Lady Lake · *Lady Lake Area C/C* · Peggy Hayes; Exec. Dir.; 106 S. U.S. Hwy. 441/27; P.O. Box 1430; 32158; Lake; P 13,000; M 238; (352) 753-6029; Fax (352) 753-8029; www.ladylakechamber.com*

Lake Alfred · *Lake Alfred C/C* · Fran Beach; Exec. Dir.; 210 N. Seminole Ave.; P.O. Box 956; 33850; Polk; P 4,000; M 181; (863) 291-5380; Fax (863) 291-5380; lachamber@lake-alfred.com; www.lake-alfred.com

Lake Butler · *see Starke*

Lake City · *Lake City-Columbia County C/C* · Dennille Roberts Folsom; Exec. Dir.; 162 S. Marion Ave.; 32025; Columbia; P 69,182; M 678; (386) 752-3690; Fax (386) 755-7744; dennille@lakecity chamber.com; www.lakecitychamber.com*

Lake Mary · *see Heathrow*

Lake Panasoffkee · *Sumter County C/C* · Dawn Cary; Pres.; 102 N. Hwy. 470; P.O. Box 100, Sumterville, 33585; 33538; Sumter; P 78,000; M 420; (352) 793-3099; Fax (352) 793-2120; sumter-coc@sumterchamber.org; www.sumterchamber.org*

Lake Park · *see Jupiter*

Lake Placid · *Greater Lake Placid C/C* · Eileen May; CEO/ Pres. of Op.; 18 N. Oak Ave.; 33852; Highlands; P 25,000; M 500; (863) 465-4331; Fax (863) 465-2588; chamber@lpfla.com; www. visitlakeplacidflorida.com.*

Lake Wales · *Lake Wales Area C/C* · Betty Wojcik; Exec. Dir.; 340 W. Central Ave.; P.O. Box 191; 33859; Polk; P 40,000; M 400; (863) 676-3445; Fax (863) 676-3446; info@lakewaleschamber.com; www.lakewaleschamber.com*

Lake Worth · *Greater Lake Worth C/C* · Beth Johnston; Exec. Dir.; 501 Lake Ave.; 33460; Palm Beach; P 41,000; M 475; (561) 582-4401; Fax (561) 547-8300; lwchamber@lwchamber.com; www.lwchamber.com*

Lakeland · *Lakeland Area C/C* · Kathleen L. Munson; Pres.; 35 Lake Morton Dr.; P.O. Box 3607; 33802; Polk; P 237,000; M 1,800; (863) 688-8551; Fax (863) 683-7454; info@lakelandchamber.com; www.lakelandchamber.com

Land O'Lakes · *Central Pasco C/C* · Kathy Dunkley; Exec. Dir.; 2810 Land O'Lakes Blvd. (US 41); P.O. Box 98; 34639; Pasco; P 40,000; M 620; (813) 909-2722; Fax (813) 909-0827; office@centralpascochamber.com; www.centralpascochamber.com*

Lantana · *Greater Lantana C/C* · Ron Washam; Pres.; 212 Iris Ave.; 33462; Palm Beach; P 9,500; M 200; (561) 585-8664; Fax (561) 585-0644; lantanachamber@bellsouth.net; www.lantanachamber.com*

Largo · *Largo/Mid-Pinellas C/C* · Tom Morrissette; Pres.; 151 3rd St. N.W.; 33770; Pinellas; P 75,000; M 600; (727) 584-2321; Fax (727) 586-3112; info@largochamber.org; www.largochamber.org*

Lauderdale By The Sea · *Lauderdale By The Sea C/C* · Judy Swaggerty; Exec. Dir.; 4201 Ocean Dr.; 33308; Broward; P 7,000; M 220; (954) 776-1000; Fax (954) 769-1560; info@lbts.com; www.lbts.com.

Leesburg · *Leesburg Area C/C* · Jan Zacharchuk; Exec. Dir.; 103 S. 6th St.; P.O. Box 490309; 34749; Lake; P 20,000; M 750; (352) 787-2131; Fax (352) 787-3985; admin@leesburgchamber.com; www.leesburgchamber.com.*

Lehigh Acres · *Lehigh Acres C/C* · Joseph Whalen; Pres./CEO; P.O. Box 757; 33970; Lee; P 68,000; M 400; (239) 369-3322; Fax (239) 368-0500; www.lehighacreschamber.org*

Live Oak · *Suwannee County C/C* · Dennis Cason; Pres.; 816 S. Ohio Ave.; P.O. Drawer C; 32064; Suwannee; P 40,000; M 400; (386) 362-3071; Fax (386) 362-4758; staff@suwanneechamber.com; www.suwanneechamber.com

Longboat Key · *Longboat Key C/C* · Tom Aposporos; Pres.; 5570 Gulf of Mexico Dr.; 34228; Manatee; P 8,000; M 425; (941) 383-2466; Fax (941) 383-8217; info@longboatkeychamber.com; www.longboatkeychamber.com*

Loxahatchee · *Palms West C/C* · Jaene Miranda; CEO; 13901 Southern Blvd.; P.O. Box 1062; 33470; Palm Beach; P 175,000; M 800; (561) 790-6200; Fax (561) 791-2069; info@palmswest.com; www.palmswest.com*

Macclenny · *Baker County C/C* · Darryl Register; Exec. Dir.; 20 E. Macclenny Ave.; 32063; Baker; P 27,000; M 250; (904) 259-6433; Fax (904) 259-2737; dregister@bakerchamberfl.com; www.bakerchamberfl.com

Madeira Beach · *see Saint Pete Beach*

Madison · *Madison County C/C & Tourism* · P.O. Box 817; 32341; Madison; P 19,850; M 204; (850) 973-2788; Fax (850) 973-8864; chamber@madisonfl.org; www.madisonfl.org

Maitland · *Maitland Area C/C* · Mary Hodge; Exec. Dir.; 110 N. Maitland Ave.; 32751; Orange; P 17,600; M 300; (407) 644-0741; Fax (407) 539-2529; mhodge@maitlandchamber.com; www.maitlandchamber.com.

Malabar · *see Palm Bay*

Mango · *see Seffner*

Mangonia Park · *see Jupiter*

Marathon · *Greater Marathon C/C* · Daniel Samess; CEO; 12222 Overseas Hwy.; 33050; Monroe; P 30,000; M 400; (305) 743-5417; (800) 262-7284; Fax (305) 289-0183; info@floridakeysmarathon.com; www.floridakeysmarathon.com*

Marco Island · *Marco Island Area C/C* · Sandi Riedemann; Exec. Dir.; 1102 N. Collier Blvd.; 34145; Collier; P 16,000; M 700; (239) 394-7549; (800) 788-6272; Fax (239) 394-3061; donna@marcoislandchamber.org; www.marcoislandchamber.org*

Marianna · *Jackson County C/C* · Art Kimbrough; Pres./CEO; 4318 Lafayette St.; P.O. Box 130; 32447; Jackson; P 50,000; M 400; (850) 482-8060; Fax (850) 482-8002; info@jacksoncounty.com; www.jacksoncounty.com*

Marineland · *see Palm Coast*

Marion Oaks · *see Belleview*

Mascotte · *see Clermont*

Matlacha · *Greater Pine Island C/C* · Lisa Benton; Exec. Dir.; 3640 S.W. Pine Island Rd.; P.O. Box 525; 33993; Lee; P 15,000; M 275; (239) 283-0888; Fax (239) 283-0336; info@pineislandchamber.org; www.pineislandchamber.org*

Mayo · *Lafayette County C/C* · P.O. Box 416; 32066; Lafayette; P 7,000; M 50; (386) 294-2705; Fax (386) 294-3073; lafayettecnty@aol.com; www.lafayettecountychamber.com

Melbourne · *Melbourne Reg. Chamber of East Central Florida Inc.* · Christine Michaels; Pres./CEO; 1005 E. Strawbridge Ave.; 32901; Brevard; P 300,000; M 1,150; (321) 724-5400; Fax (321) 725-2093; christine@melbourneregionalchamber.com; www.melbourneregionalchamber.com*

Melbourne Beach · *see Melbourne*

Melbourne Village · *see Melbourne*

Merritt Island · *see Cocoa Beach*

Miami · *Greater Miami C/C* · Barry E. Johnson; Pres./CEO; 1601 Biscayne Blvd.; Ballroom Level; 33132; Miami-Dade; P 2,600,000; M 5,500; (305) 350-7700; Fax (305) 374-6902; info@miamichamber.com; www.miamichamber.com

Miami · *Miami-Dade C/C* · Bill Diggs; Pres./CEO; 11380 N.W. 27th Ave.; Bldg. I, Ste. 1328; 33167; Miami-Dade; P 2,000,000; M 500; (305) 751-8648; Fax (305) 758-3839; mdcc@m-dcc.org; www.m-dcc.org

Miami Beach · *Miami Beach C/C* · Jerry Libbin; Pres./CEO; 1920 Meridian Ave.; 33139; Miami-Dade; P 95,000; M 1,200; (305) 674-1300; Fax (305) 538-4336; visitorinfo@miamibeachchamber.com; www.miamibeachchamber.com

Miami Gardens · *North Dade Reg. C/C* · Joel Ransford; Chrmn.; 1300 N.W. 167th St., Ste. 2; 33169; Dade; P 2,300,000; M 2,223; (305) 690-9123; Fax (305) 690-9124; thechamber@thechamber.cc; www.thechamber.cc

Miami Shores · *Greater Miami Shores C/C* · Lew Soli; Exec. Dir.; 9701 N.E. 2nd Ave.; 33138; Miami-Dade; P 10,000; M 275; (305) 754-5466; Fax (305) 759-8872; shoreschamber@bellsouth.net; www.miamishores.com

Middleburg · *see Orange Park*

Milton · *Santa Rosa County C/C* · Donna Tucker; Exec. Dir.; 5247 Stewart St.; 32570; Santa Rosa; P 148,000; M 602; (850) 623-2339; Fax (850) 623-4413; membership@srcchamber.com; www.srcchamber.com*

Minneola · *see Clermont*

Miramar · *see Pembroke Pines*

Monticello · *Monticello-Jefferson County C/C* · Gordon Dean; Pres.; 420 W. Washington St.; 32344; Jefferson; P 14,500; M 260; (850) 997-5552; Fax (850) 997-1020; info@monticellojeffersonfl. com; www.monticellojeffersonfl.com

Montverde · *see Clermont*

Mount Dora · *Mount Dora Area C/C* · Cathy Hoechst; Pres.; 341 Alexander St.; P.O. Box 196; 32756; Lake; P 11,290; M 600; (352) 383-2165; Fax (352) 383-1668; chamber@mountdora.com; www. mountdora.com*

Mulberry · *Greater Mulberry C/C* · Sharron Jones; Exec. Dir.; 400 N. Church Ave.; P.O. Box 254; 33860; Polk; P 3,500; M 180; (863) 425-4414; Fax (863) 425-3837; sharron@mulberrychamber. org; www.mulberrychamber.org

Naples · *Greater Naples C/C* · Michael Reagen; Pres./CEO; 2390 Tamiami Trl. N., Ste. 210; 34103; Collier; P 341,000; M 2,178; (239) 262-6376; Fax (239) 262-8374; lori@napleschamber.org; www. napleschamber.org*

Navarre · *Navarre Beach Area C/C* · Bill Arnett; Pres./CEO; P.O. Drawer 5430; 32566; Santa Rosa; P 35,000; M 634; (850) 939-3267; Fax (850) 939-0085; exec@navarrechamber.com; www.navarrechamber.com*

New Port Richey · *West Pasco C/C* · Joe Alpine; Pres.; 5443 Main St.; 34652; Pasco; P 471,709; M 965; (727) 842-7651; Fax (727) 848-0202; chamber@westpasco.com; www.westpasco.com.*

New Smyrna Beach · *Southeast Volusia C/C* · Samantha Bishop; Exec. V.P.; 115 Canal St.; 32168; Volusia; P 35,000; M 700; (386) 428-2449; Fax (386) 423-3512; sbishop@sevchamber.com; www.sevchamber.com*

Newberry · *Newberry-Jonesville C/C* · Joy Glanzer; Pres.; P.O. Box 495; 32669; Alachua; P 5,000; M 110; (352) 472-6611; info@ newberrychamber.com; www.newberrychamber.com*

Niceville · *Niceville Valparaiso C/C* · Tricia Brunson; Pres./CEO; 1055 E. John Sims Pkwy.; 32578; Okaloosa; P 35,000; M 650; (850) 678-2323; Fax (850) 678-2602; info@nicevillechamber.com; www. nicevillechamber.com*

North Fort Myers · *North Fort Myers C/C* · 2787 N. Tamiami Trl., Ste. 10; 33903; Lee; P 43,000; M 200; (239) 997-9111; Fax (239) 997-4026; info@nfmchamber.org; www.nfmchamber.org

North Miami · *Greater North Miami C/C* · Ron E. Welsandt; Exec. Dir.; 13100 W. Dixie Hwy.; 33161; Miami-Dade; P 60,000; M 420; (305) 891-7811; Fax (305) 893-8522; gnmcc@bellsouth. net; www.northmiamichamber.com.*

North Miami Beach · *Greater North Miami Beach C/C* · Daniel Santamaria; Managing Dir.; 1870 N.E. 171st St.; 33162; Miami-Dade; P 35,000; M 500; (305) 944-8500; chamber@nmbchamber. com; www.nmbchamber.com*

North Palm Beach County · *see Jupiter*

North Port · *North Port Area C/C* · William Gunnin; Exec. Dir.; 15141 Tamiami Trl.; 34287; Sarasota; P 55,000; M 520; (941) 423-5040; Fax (941) 423-5042; info@northportareachamber.com; www.northportareachamber.com

North Redington Beach · *see Saint Pete Beach*

Oak Hill · *see New Smyrna Beach*

Oakland · *see Winter Garden*

Ocala · *Ocala-Marion County C/C* · Ms. Jaye Baillie APR IOM; Pres./CEO; 310 S. E. 3rd St.; 34471; Marion; P 337,962; M 1,687; (352) 629-8051; Fax (352) 629-7651; ourguest@ocalacc.com; www.ocalacc.com*

Ochopee · *see Everglades City*

Ocoee · *see Winter Garden*

Oklawaha · *Lake Weir C/C* · Richard Lillie; Pres.; 13125 S.E. Hwy. C-25; 32179; Marion; P 13,000; M 130; (352) 288-3751; Fax (352) 288-3980; lakeweirchamcom@juno.com; www.searchmelake weir.com

Oldsmar · *Upper Tampa Bay Reg. C/C* · Jerry Custin; Pres./CEO; 163 State Rd. 580 W.; 34677; Hillsborough & Pinellas; P 14,000; M 500; (813) 855-4233; Fax (813) 854-1237; jcustin@utbchamber. com; www.utbchamber.com*

Opa Locka · *see Miami Gardens*

Orange City · *see DeLand*

Orange Park · *Clay County C/C* · Kellie Jo Kilberg; Pres./CEO; 1734 Kingsley Ave.; 32073; Clay; P 190,000; M 800; (904) 264-2651; Fax (904) 264-0070; larassler@claychamber.com; www. claychamber.com*

Orlando · *East Orlando C/C* · David Maloney; Mktg/Comm. Mgr.; 2860 S. Alafaya Trl., Ste. 130; 32828; Orange; P 230,000; M 900; (407) 277-5951; Fax (407) 381-1720; david@eocc.org; www.eocc.org*

Orlando · *Orlando Reg. C/C* · Leslie J. Hielema; Pres.; 75 S. Ivanhoe Blvd.; P.O. Box 1234; 32802; Orange; P 1,851,872; M 6,000; (407) 425-1234; Fax (407) 835-2500; info@orlando.org; www.orlando.org*

Ormond Beach · *Ormond Beach C/C* · Tony Capozzi; Exec. Dir.; 165 W. Granada Blvd.; 32174; Volusia; P 39,000; M 700; (386) 677-3454; Fax (386) 677-3454; obccinfo@ormondchamber.com; www. ormondchamber.com*

Oviedo · *Oviedo-Winter Springs Reg. C/C* · Cory Skeates; Exec. Dir.; 1511 E. State Rd. 434, Ste. 2001; P.O. Box 621236; 32762; Seminole; P 75,000; M 625; (407) 365-6500; Fax (407) 650-2712; staff@oviedowintersprings.org; www.oviedowintersprings.org*

Pahokee · *Pahokee C/C* · Lewis Pope III; Pres.; 115 E. Main St.; 33476; Palm Beach; P 7,000; M 200; (561) 924-5579; Fax (561) 924-8116; pahokeechamber@aol.com; www.pahokee.com

Palatka · *Putnam County C/C* · Dana Jones; Pres.; 1100 Reid St.; 32177; Putnam; P 72,000; M 600; (386) 328-1503; Fax (386) 328-7076; chamber@pcccfl.org; www.putnamcountychamber.com.

Palm Bay · *Greater Palm Bay C/C* · Victoria Northrup; Pres./CEO; 4100 Dixie Hwy. N.E.; 32905; Brevard; P 100,000; M 1,000; (321) 951-9998; (800) 276-9130; Fax (321) 951-0012; info@greater-palmbaychamber.com; www.greaterpalmbaychamber.com*

Palm Beach · *Palm Beach C/C* · Laurel Baker; Exec. Dir.; 400 Royal Palm Way, Ste. 106; 33480; Palm Beach; P 10,500; M 615; (561) 655-3282; Fax (561) 655-7191; info@palmbeachchamber. com; www.palmbeachchamber.com

Palm Beach Gardens · *see Jupiter*

Palm Beach Shores · *see Jupiter*

Palm City · *Palm City C/C* · Carolyn Davi; Exec. Dir.; 880 S.W. Martin Downs Blvd.; 34990; Martin; P 24,000; M 435; (772) 286-8121; Fax (772) 286-3331; info@palmcitychamber.com; www.palmcitychamber.com*

Palm Coast · *Flagler County C/C* · Doug Baxter; Pres.; 20 Airport Rd.; 32164; Flagler; P 91,000; M 950; (386) 437-0106; (800) 881-1022; Fax (386) 437-5700; info@flaglerchamber.org; www.flaglerchamber.org*

Palm Harbor · *Greater Palm Harbor Area C/C* · Connie Davis; Pres./CEO; 1151 Nebraska Ave.; 34683; Pinellas; P 65,000; M 400; (727) 784-4287; Fax (727) 786-2336; phcc@palmharborcc.org; www.palmharborcc.org*

Palm Shores · *see Melbourne*

Panama City · *Bay County C/C* · Carol A. Roberts; Pres./CEO; 235 W. 5th St.; P.O. Box 1850; 32402; Bay; P 169,562; M 968; (850) 785-5206; Fax (850) 763-6229; reception2@baychamberfl.com; www.panamacity.org.*

Panama City Beach · *Panama City Beach C/C* · Beth Oltman; Pres./CEO; 309 Richard Jackson Blvd., Ste. 101; 32407; Bay; P 105,000; M 875; (850) 235-1159; Fax (850) 235-2301; chamber@pcbeach.org; www.pcbeach.org*

Patrick Air Force Base · *see Melbourne and Cocoa Beach*

Paxton · *see Florala, AL*

Pembroke Pines · *Miramar-Pembroke Pines Reg. C/C* · Stella Tokar; Pres.; 10100 Pines Blvd., 4th Flr.; 33026; Broward; P 247,000; M 500; (954) 432-9808; Fax (954) 432-9193; info@miramarpembrokepines.org; www.miramarpembrokepines.org

Pensacola · *Pensacola Bay Area C/C* · James Hizer; Pres./CEO; 117 W. Garden St.; P.O. Box 550; 32591; Escambia; P 311,000; M 1,300; (850) 438-4081; Fax (850) 438-6369; www.pensacolachamber.com*

Pensacola Beach · *Pensacola Beach C of C & Visitor Info. Center* · Maureen Lamar; Exec. Dir.; 735 Pensacola Beach Blvd.; 32561; Escambia; P 3,500; M 121; (850) 932-1500; (800) 635-4803; Fax (850) 932-1551; beachchamber@visitpensacolabeach.com; www.pensacolabeachchamber.com

Perdido Key · *Perdido Key Area C/C* · Tina Morrison; Dir.; 15500 Perdido Key Dr.; Pensacola; 32507; Escambia; P 50,000; M 300; (850) 492-4660; (850) 485-5624; Fax (850) 492-2932; chamber@perdidochamber.com; www.perdidochamber.com*

Perrine · *Perrine Office of the Chamber South* · Mary Scott Russell; Pres.; 900 Perrine Ave.; Miami; 33157; Miami-Dade; P 300,000; M 1,500; (305) 238-7192; Fax (305) 254-0805; msrussell@chambersouth.com; www.chambersouth.com

Perry · *Perry-Taylor County C/C* · Dawn Taylor; Pres./Exec. Dir.; 428 N. Jefferson St.; P.O. Box 892; 32348; Taylor; P 19,422; M 365; (850) 584-5366; (800) 257-8881; Fax (850) 584-8030; taylorchamber@fairpoint.net; www.taylorcountychamber.com.

CHAMBER SERVING THE TAYLOR COUNTY AREA WHICH INCLUDES STEINHATCHEE, KEATON BEACH, SALEM AND SHADY GROVE.

Pinellas Park · *Pinellas Park/Gateway C/C* · Paul Ziegler; Chrmn. of Bd.; 5851 Park Blvd.; 33781; Pinellas; P 62,000; M 600; (727) 544-4777; Fax (727) 209-0837; info@pinellasparkchamber.com; www.pinellasparkchamber.com*

Plant City · *Greater Plant City C/C* · Marion Smith; Pres.; 106 N. Evers St.; P.O. Box CC; 33564; Hillsborough; P 37,000; M 680; (813) 754-3707; (800) 760-2315; Fax (813) 752-8793; info@plantcity.org; www.plantcity.org.*

Plantation · *Greater Plantation C/C* · Siobhan Edwards; Pres.; 7401 N.W. 4th St.; 33317; Broward; P 89,000; M 500; (954) 587-1410; Fax (954) 587-1886; info@plantationchamber.org; www.plantationchamber.org*

Pompano Beach · *Greater Pompano Beach C/C* · Ric Green; Pres./CEO; 2200 E. Atlantic Blvd.; 33062; Broward; P 101,457; M 650; (954) 941-2940; Fax (954) 785-8358; info@pompanobeachchamber.com; www.pompanobeachchamber.com*

Ponte Vedra Beach · *Ponte Vedra Beach C/C* · Ginger Peace; Exec. Dir.; 50 A1A N., Ste. 102; 32082; St. Johns; P 33,000; M 300; (904) 285-2004; Fax (904) 285-8488; info@pontevedrachamber.org; www.pontevedrachamber.org*

Port Charlotte · *Charlotte County C/C* · Julie Mathis; Exec. Dir.; 2702 Tamiami Trl.; 33952; Charlotte; P 150,060; M 1,100; (941) 627-2222; Fax (941) 627-9730; askus@charlottecountychamber.org; www.charlottecountychamber.org*

Port Orange · *Port Orange-South Daytona C/C* · Debbie Connors; Exec. Dir.; 3431 Ridgewood Ave.; 32129; Volusia; P 62,000; M 650; (386) 761-1601; Fax (386) 788-9165; info@pschamber.com; www.pschamber.com*

Port Richey · *see New Port Richey*

Port Saint Joe · *Gulf County C/C* · Sandra Chafin; Exec. Dir.; 150 Captain Fred's Place; P.O. Box 964; 32456; Gulf; P 15,500; M 300; (850) 227-1223; (800) 239-9553; Fax (850) 229-2458; info@gulfchamber.org; www.gulfchamber.org

Port St. Lucie · *St. Lucie County C/C* · Linda Cox; Pres.; 1850 S.W. Fountainview Blvd., Ste. 201; 34986; St. Lucie; P 265,000; M 1,200; (772) 340-1333; Fax (772) 785-7021; info@stluciechamber.org; www.stluciechamber.org.*

Punta Gorda · *Charlotte County C/C* · Julie Mathis; Exec. Dir.; 311 W. Retta Esplanade; 33950; Charlotte; P 150,060; M 1,100; (941) 639-2222; Fax (941) 639-6330; askus@charlottecountychamber.org; www.charlottecountychamber.org*

Quincy · *Gadsden County C/C* · David Gardner; Exec. Dir.; 208 N. Adams St.; P.O. Box 389; 32353; Gadsden; P 50,000; M 400; (850) 627-9231; Fax (850) 875-3299; gadsdencc@tds.net; www.gadsdenfla.com

Redington Beach · *see Saint Pete Beach*

Redington Shores · *see Saint Pete Beach*

Ridge Manor · *see Brooksville*

Riverview · *Greater Riverview C/C* · Tanya Doran; Dir.; 10011 Water Works Ln.; 33578; Hillsborough; P 50,000; M 400; (813) 234-5944; Fax (813) 234-5945; info@riverviewchamber.com; www.riverviewchamber.com*

Riviera Beach · *see Jupiter*

Rockledge · *see Cocoa Beach*

Royal Palm Beach · *see Loxahatchee*

Ruskin · *Ruskin South Shore C/C* · Melanie Morrison; Exec. Dir.; 315 S. Tamiami Trl.; 33570; Hillsborough; P 83,000; M 326; (813) 645-3808; Fax (813) 645-2099; ruskinchamber@earthlink.net; www.ruskinchamber.org*

Safety Harbor · *Safety Harbor C/C* · Darlene Trieste; Chrmn.; 200 Main St.; 34695; Pinellas; P 18,000; M 250; (727) 726-2890; Fax (727) 726-2733; info@safetyharborchamber.com; www.safetyharborchamber.com*

Saint Augustine · *St. Johns County C/C* · Kirk Wendland; Pres.; 1 Riberia St.; 32084; St. Johns; P 175,000; M 1,000; (904) 829-5681; Fax (904) 829-6477; kirk.wendland@sjcchamber.com; www.sjcchamber.com*

Saint Cloud · *St. Cloud/Greater Osceola C/C* · David Lane; Pres./CEO; 1200 New York Ave.; 34769; Osceola; P 30,000; M 615; (407) 892-3671; Fax (407) 892-5289; info@stcloudflchamber.com; www.stcloudflchamber.com*

Saint Pete Beach · *Tampa Bay Beaches C/C* · Robin Grabowski; Pres./CEO; 6990 Gulf Blvd.; 33706; Pinellas; P 40,000; M 500; (727) 360-6957; Fax (727) 360-2233; info@tampabaybeaches.com; www.tampabaybeaches.com*

Saint Petersburg · *St. Petersburg Area C/C* · Mary Lallucci; Interim Pres./CEO; 100 Second Ave. N., Ste. 150; 33701; Pinellas; P 250,000; M 2,400; (727) 821-4069; Fax (727) 895-6326; info@stpete.com; www.stpete.com*

Sand Key · *see Saint Pete Beach*

Sanford · *Sanford Reg. C/C* · Pam Czopp; Exec. Dir.; 400 E. First St.; 32771; Seminole; P 51,000; M 450; (407) 322-2212; Fax (407) 322-8160; info@sanfordchamber.com; www.sanfordchamber.com*

Sanibel · *Sanibel-Captiva Islands C/C* · Ric Base; Pres.; 1159 Causeway Rd.; 33957; Lee; P 6,500; M 608; (239) 472-1080; Fax (239) 472-1070; island@sanibel-captiva.org; www.sanibel-captiva.org*

Santa Rosa Beach · *Walton Area C/C* · Kitty Whitney; Pres./CEO; 63 S. Centre Trl.; 32459; Walton; P 46,000; M 1,251; (850) 267-0683; Fax (850) 267-0603; info@waltonareachamber.com; www.waltonareachamber.com*

Santa Rosa Beach · *Walton County C/C* · Kitty Whitney; Pres./CEO; 63 S. Centre Trl.; 32459; Walton; P 46,000; M 1,251; (850) 267-0683; Fax (850) 267-0603; kitty@waltonareachamber.com; www.waltonareachamber.com*

Santa Rosa County · *see Milton*

Sarasota · *Greater Sarasota C/C* · Stephen Queior; Pres.; 1945 Fruitville Rd.; 34236; Sarasota; P 500,000; M 1,800; (941) 955-8187; Fax (941) 366-5621; info@sarasotachamber.com; www.sarasotachamber.com.*

Satellite Beach · *see Melbourne*

Sebastian · *Sebastian River Area C/C* · Beth Mitchell; Exec. Dir.; 700 Main St.; 32958; Indian River; P 23,000; M 450; (772) 589-5969; Fax (772) 589-5993; info@sebastianchamber.com; www.sebastianchamber.com*

Sebring · *Greater Sebring C/C* · Greg Harris; Pres./CEO; 227 U.S. Hwy. 27 N.; 33870; Highlands; P 100,000; M 675; (863) 385-8448; Fax (863) 385-8810; information@sebring.org; www.sebring.org.*

Seffner · *Greater Seffner Area C/C* · P.O. Box 1920; 33583; Hillsborough; P 75,000; M 158; (813) 627-8686; info@seffner chamber.com; www.seffnerchamber.com*

Seminole · *Greater Seminole Area C/C* · Jimmy Johnson; Exec. Dir.; 8400 113th St. N.; 33772; Pinellas; P 20,000; M 450; (727) 392-3245; Fax (727) 397-7753; jimmyj@myseminolechamber.com; www.seminolechamber.net

Seminole County · *see Heathrow*

Siesta Key · *Siesta Key C/C* · Jim Haberman; Exec. Dir.; 5118 Ocean Blvd.; 34242; Sarasota; P 25,000; M 500; (941) 349-3800; Fax (941) 349-9699; info@siestakeychamber.com; www.siestakeychamber.com*

Sorrento · *East Lake County C/C* · Catherine Hanson; P.O. Box 774; 32776; Lake; P 19,000; M 187; (352) 383-8801; Fax (352) 383-9343; chamber@elcchamber.com; www.elcchamber.com

South Daytona · *see Port Orange*

South Miami · *Chamber South* · Mary Scott Russell; Pres./CEO; 6410 S.W. 80th St.; 33143; Miami-Dade; P 300,000; M 1,500; (305) 661-1621; (305) CHAMBER; Fax (305) 666-0508; vconterio@chambersouth.com; www.chambersouth.com

Spring Hill · *see Brooksville*

Starke · *North Florida Reg. C/C* · Pam Whittle; Pres./CEO; 100 E. Call St.; 32091; Bradford; P 48,000; M 300; (904) 964-5278; Fax (904) 964-2863; pam@northfloridachamber.com; www.northfloridachamber.com

Steinhatchee · *see Perry*

Stuart · *Stuart-Martin County C/C* · Joseph A. Catrambone; Pres./CEO; 1650 S. Kanner Hwy.; 34994; Martin; P 163,503; M 1,500; (772) 287-1088; Fax (772) 220-3437; jcat@stuartmartin chamber.org; www.stuartmartinchamber.org*

Sumterville · *see Lake Panasoffkee*

Sun City Center · *Sun City Center Area C/C* · Dana Dittmar; Exec. Dir.; 1651 Sun City Center Plaza; P.O. Box 5623; 33573; Hillsborough; P 20,000; M 350; (813) 634-5111; Fax (813) 634-8438; sccchamber@aol.com; www.suncitycenterchamber.org*

Sunrise · *Greater Sunrise C/C* · Kitty McGowan; Exec. Dir.; 12717 W. Sunrise Blvd., Ste. 318; 33323; Broward; P 90,000; M 200; (954) 835-2428; Fax (954) 523-0607; suncc@sunrisechamber.org; www.sunrisechamber.org*

Suntree · *see Melbourne and Cocoa Beach*

Tallahassee · *Tallahassee C/C* · Sue Dick; Pres.; P.O. Box 1639; 32302; Leon; P 265,714; M 1,600; (850) 224-8116; Fax (850) 561-3860; info@talchamber.com; www.talchamber.com*

Tamarac · *Tamarac C/C* · Vicki Reid; Exec. Dir.; 7525 Pine Island Rd.; 33321; Broward; P 60,000; M 200; (954) 722-1520; Fax (954) 721-2725; vicki@tamaracchamber.org; www.tamaracchamber.org*

Tampa Area

Greater Tampa C/C · Bob Rohrlack CEcD; Pres./CEO; 201 N. Franklin St., Ste. 201; P.O. Box 420; 33601; Hillsborough; P 1,118,988; M 2,000; (813) 228-7777; (800) 298-2672; Fax (813) 223-7899; info@tampachamber.com; www.tampachamber.com

North Tampa C/C · Carol Rehfelt; Exec. Dir.; P.O. Box 82043; 33682; Hillsborough; P 450,000; M 150; (813) 961-2420; Fax (813) 961-2903; info@northtampachamber.com; www.northtampa chamber.com*

South Tampa C/C · Judy Gay; Exec. Dir.; 2113 S. Dale Mabry Hwy.; 33629; Hillsborough; P 100,000; M 500; (813) 637-0156; executivedirector@southtampachamber.org; www.southtampa chamber.org*

Ybor City C/C · Tom Keating; Pres./CEO; 1800 E. 9th Ave.; 33605; Hillsborough; P 3,600; M 409; (813) 248-3712; Fax (813) 247-1764; tkeating@ybor.org; www.ybor.org

Tarpon Springs · *Tarpon Springs C/C* · Sue Thomas; Pres.; 11 E. Orange St.; 34689; Pinellas; P 22,000; M 380; (727) 937-6109; Fax (727) 937-2879; chamber@tarponspringschamber.org; www.tarponspringschamber.com

Tavares · *Tavares C/C* · Colleen McGinley; Exec. Dir.; 912 N. Sinclair Ave.; 32778; Lake; P 12,552; M 300; (352) 343-2531; Fax (352) 343-7565; info@tavareschamber.com; www.tavareschamber.com*

Taylor County · *see Perry*

Temple Terrace · *Greater Temple Terrace C/C* · Barbara Sparks-McGlinchy; Exec. Dir.; 9385 N. 56th St.; 33617; Hillsborough; P 28,000; M 560; (813) 989-7004; Fax (813) 989-7005; bsparks@templeterracechamber.com; www.templeterracechamber.com*

Tequesta · *see Jupiter*

Titusville · *Titusville Area C/C* · Marcia Gaedcke; 2000 S. Washington Ave.; 32780; Brevard; P 70,000; M 750; (321) 267-3036; Fax (321) 264-0127; wilson@titusville.org; www.titusville.org*

Treasure Island · *see Saint Pete Beach*

Trenton · *Gilchrist County C/C* · Kyle Stone; Exec. Dir.; 220 S. Main St.; 32693; Gilchrist; P 17,106; M 279; (352) 463-3467; Fax (352) 463-3469; chamber@GilchristCounty.com; www.GilchristCounty.com

Umatilla · *Umatilla C/C* · Shananne Cain; Pres.; 23 S. Central Ave.; P.O. Box 300; 32784; Lake; P 2,800; M 200; (352) 669-3511; Fax (352) 669-8900; umatilla@umatillachamber.org; www.umatillachamber.org*

Valparaiso · *see Niceville*

Valrico • *see Seffner*

Venice • *Venice Area C/C* • John G. Ryan; Pres./CEO; 597 Tamiami Trl. S.; 34285; Sarasota; P 30,000; M 1,100; (941) 488-2236; Fax (941) 484-5903; vchamber@venicechamber.com; www.venice chamber.com*

Vero Beach • *Indian River County C/C* • Penny S. Chandler; Exec. Dir.; 1216 21st St.; P.O. Box 2947; 32961; Indian River; P 141,667; M 900; (772) 567-3491; Fax (772) 778-3181; chamber@indian riverchamber.com; www.indianriverchamber.com.*

Viera • *see Melbourne*

Village of North Palm • *see Jupiter*

Wakulla County • *see Crawfordville*

Wauchula • *Hardee County C/C* • Casey Dickson; Exec. Dir.; 107 E. Main St.; P.O. Box 683; 33873; Hardee; P 28,000; M 200; (863) 773-6967; Fax (863) 773-4915; casey@hardeecc.com; www. hardeecc.com

Webster • *see Lake Panasoffkee*

Weeki Wachee • *see Brooksville*

Wellington • *Wellington C/C* • Michela Perillo-Green; Exec. Dir.; 12230 Forest Hill Blvd., Ste. 187; 33414; Palm Beach; P 60,000; M 468; (561) 792-6525; Fax (561) 792-6200; michela@wellington chamber.com; www.wellingtonchamber.com

Wesley Chapel • *Greater Wesley Chapel C/C* • David B. West; Exec. Dir.; 29142 Chapel Park Dr.; 33543; Pasco; P 100,000; M 500; (813) 994-8534; Fax (813) 994-8154; office@wesleychapel chamber.com; www.wesleychapelchamber.com*

West Melbourne • *see Melbourne*

West Palm Beach • *C/C of the Palm Beaches* • Dennis Grady; Pres./CEO; 401 N. Flagler Dr.; 33401; Palm Beach; P 1,200,000; M 1,200; (561) 833-3711; Fax (561) 833-5582; chamber@palm beaches.org; www.palmbeaches.org*

Weston • *Weston Area C/C* • Jack Miller; Pres./CEO; 1290 Weston Rd., Ste. 312; Fort Lauderdale; 33326; Broward; P 2,100,000; M 863; (954) 389-0600; (702) 260-9425; Fax (954) 384-6133; jack@westonchamber.com; www.westonchamber.com.*

THE CHAMBER THAT MEANS BUSINESS® WAS CREATED TO PROMOTE AND SERVE THE LOCAL, REGIONAL, NATIONAL & INTERNATIONAL NEEDS OF ITS MEMBERS FOR BUSINESS TO BUSINESS & BUSINESS TO CONSUMER.

Wildwood • *see Lake Panasoffkee*

Williston • *Williston Area C/C* • Mary Kline; Exec. Dir.; P.O. Box 369; 32696; Levy; P 2,400; M 160; (352) 528-5552; Fax (352) 528-4342; wcoc@willistonfl.com; www.willistonfl.com

Windermere • *see Winter Garden*

Winter Garden • *West Orange C/C* • Stina D'Uva; Pres.; 12184 W. Colonial Dr.; 34787; Orange; P 240,000; M 1,000; (407) 656-1304; Fax (407) 656-0221; info@wochamber.com; www.wochamber.com*

Winter Haven • *Greater Winter Haven C/C* • Bob Gernert Jr.; Exec. Dir.; 401 Ave. B N.W.; P.O. Box 1420; 33882; Polk; P 35,000; M 700; (863) 293-2138; Fax (863) 297-5818; chamber1@winter havenfl.com; www.winterhavenfl.com*

Winter Park • *Winter Park C/C* • Patrick Chapin; Pres./CEO; 151 W. Lyman Ave.; P.O. Box 280; 32790; Orange; P 28,000; M 1,800; (407) 644-8281; Fax (407) 644-7826; wpcc@winterpark.org; www. winterpark.org*

Winter Springs • *see Oviedo*

Ybor City • *see Tampa–Ybor City C/C*

Yulee • *see Amelia Island*

Zephyrhills • *Zephyrhills C/C* • Vonnie Mikkelsen; Exec. Dir.; 38550 Fifth Ave.; 33542; Pasco; P 53,000; M 471; (813) 782-1913; Fax (813) 783-6060; info@zephyrhillschamber.org; www.zephyr hillschamber.org*

Georgia

Georgia C of C • Chris Clark; Pres./CEO; 233 Peachtree St. N.E., Ste. 2000; Atlanta; 30303; Fulton; P 9,700,000; M 4,000; (404) 223-2264; Fax (404) 223-2290; communications@gachamber. com; www.gachamber.com

Adel • *Adel-Cook County C/C* • Susie Abbott; Admin. Asst.; 100 S. Hutchinson Ave.; 31620; Cook; P 16,000; M 240; (229) 896-2281; Fax (229) 896-8201; cookcochamber@windstream.net; www. adelcookchamber.org*

Alamo • *Wheeler County C/C & Dev. Auth.* • Janie Dixon; Pres.; 6 W. Railroad Ave.; P.O. Box 654; 30411; Wheeler; P 5,000; M 59; (912) 568-7808; wchamber1@windstream.net; www.wheelercounty.org

Albany • *Albany Area C/C* • Catherine Glover; Pres./CEO; 225 W. Broad Ave.; 31701; Dougherty; P 170,000; M 1,200; (229) 434-8700; Fax (229) 434-8716; chamber@albanyga.com; www. albanyga.com*

Alma • *Alma-Bacon County C/C* • Cherry Rewis; Exec. Asst.; 1120 W. 12th St.; P.O. Box 450; 31510; Bacon; P 10,000; M 40; (912) 632-5859; Fax (912) 632-7710; abcchamber@accessatc.net; www.almaone.com

Alpharetta • *Greater North Fulton C/C* • Brandon Beach; Pres./ CEO; 11605 Haynes Bridge Rd., Ste. 100; 30009; Fulton; P 500,000; M 1,800; (770) 993-8806; Fax (770) 594-1059; info@gnfcc.com; www.gnfcc.com*

Americus • *Americus-Sumter County C/C* • Angela H. Westra; Pres.; 409 Elm Ave., Ste. A; P.O. Box 724; 31709; Sumter; P 33,000; M 400; (229) 924-2646; Fax (229) 924-8784; info@americus-sumterchamber.com; www.americus-sumterchamber.com*

Ashburn • *Ashburn-Turner County C/C* • Shelley Zorn; Pres./ Eco. Dev.; 238 E. College Ave.; 31714; Turner; P 10,000; M 238; (229) 567-9696; (800) 471-9696; Fax (229) 567-2541; szorn@ windstream.net; www.turnerchamber.com.

Athens • *Athens Area C/C* • Doc Eldridge; Pres.; 246 W. Hancock Ave.; 30601; Clarke; P 103,691; M 1,100; (706) 549-6800; Fax (706) 549-5636; info@athensga.com; www.athensga.com*

Atlanta • *Airport Area C/C* • Neil Harris; Exec. Dir.; Regions Bank Bldg., Ste. 100; 600 S. Central Ave.; 30354; Clayton & Fulton; P 30,000; M 250; (404) 209-0910; Fax (404) 389-0271; info@ airportchamber.com; www.airportchamber.com

Atlanta • *Metro Atlanta C/C* • Sam A. Williams; Pres.; 235 Andrew Young Intl. Blvd. N.W.; 30303; Fulton; P 5,700,000; M 4,000; (404) 880-9000; Fax (404) 586-8416; tdunne@macoc. com; www.metroatlantachamber.com

Atlanta • *South Fulton C/C* • Y. Dyan Matthews; Pres./CEO; 5155 Westpark Dr. S.W.; 30336; South Fulton; P 178,000; M 450; (770) 964-1984; Fax (404) 346-7393; dyan.matthews@southfulton chamber.org; www.sfcoc.org*

Augusta • *Augusta Metro C/C* • Sue Parr; Pres./CEO; 701 Greene St.; 30901; Augusta-Richmond; P 500,000; M 995; (706) 821-1300; (888) 639-8188; Fax (706) 821-1330; info@augustagausa. com; www.augustagausa.com*

Bainbridge • *Bainbridge-Decatur County C/C* • Diane Strickland; Pres.; 100 Boat Basin Cir.; P.O. Box 755; 39818; Decatur; P 28,700; M 420; (229) 246-4774; Fax (229) 243-7633; info@ bainbridgegachamber.com; www.bainbridgegachamber.com*

Barnesville · *Barnesville-Lamar County C/C* · Amanda Rose; Pres./CEO; 100 Commerce Pl.; P.O. Box 506; 30204; Lamar; P 16,000; M 250; (770) 358-5884; Fax (770) 358-5886; lchamber5884@charterinternet.com; www.barnesville.org

Baxley · *Baxley-Appling County C/C* · Karen Glenn; Exec. Dir.; 305 W. Parker St.; P.O. Box 413; 31515; Appling; P 17,500; M 250; (912) 367-7731; Fax (912) 367-2073; baxleychamber@bellsouth.net; www.baxley.org

Blackshear · *Pierce County C/C* · Debra Lee; Exec. Dir.; 200 S. Central Ave.; P.O. Box 47; 31516; Pierce; P 17,000; M 275; (912) 449-7044; Fax (912) 449-7045; pierceco@accessatc.net; www.pierceco.org.

Blairsville · *Blairsville-Union County C/C* · Cindy Williams; Pres.; 78 Blue Ridge Hwy.; P.O. Box 789; 30514; Union; P 22,000; M 550; (706) 745-5789; (877) 745-5789; admin@blairsvillechamber.com; www.visitblairsvillega.com

Blakely · *Blakely-Early County C/C* · Pres.; 214 Court Sq.; P.O. Box 189; 39823; Early; P 12,500; M 145; (229) 723-3741; Fax (229) 723-6876; earlycoc@windstream.net; www.blakelyearlycountychamber.com

Blue Ridge · *Fannin County C/C* · Jan Hackett; Pres.; 152 Orvin Lance Dr.; P.O. Box 1689; 30513; Fannin; P 22,900; M 800; (706) 632-5680; (800) 899-MTNS; Fax (706) 632-2241; fanninchamber@tds.net; www.blueridgemountains.com.*

Brunswick · *Brunswick-Golden Isles C/C* · M.H. 'Woody' Woodside; Pres.; 4 Glynn Ave.; 31520; Glynn; P 75,000; M 1,350; (912) 265-0620; Fax (912) 265-0629; info@brunswickgoldenisleschamber.com; www.brunswickgoldenisleschamber.com.*

Buena Vista · *Buena Vista-Marion County C/C* · Libby Wells; P.O. Box 471; 31803; Marion; P 5,500; M 40; (229) 649-2842; (800) 647-2842; Fax (229) 649-2429; bvmccoc@windstream.net; www.bvmccoc.com

Bulloch County · *see Statesboro*

Butler · *Taylor County C/C* · Patty Jane Bentley; Dir.; 7 Ivy St.; P.O. Box 2220; 31006; Taylor; P 9,000; M 50; (478) 862-6022; Fax (478) 862-2871; pattyjbentley@gmail.com; www.taylorcountycofc.com

Byromville · *see Vienna*

Cairo · *Cairo-Grady County C/C* · Exec. Dir.; 961 N. Broad St.; P.O. Box 387; 39828; Grady; P 25,100; M 300; (229) 377-3663; Fax (229) 377-3901; cairochamber@syrupcity.net; www.cairogachamber.com*

Calhoun · *Gordon County C/C* · Jimmy Phillips; Pres.; 300 S. Wall St.; 30701; Gordon; P 52,044; M 427; (706) 625-3200; (800) 887-3811; Fax (706) 625-5062; jp@gordonchamber.org; www.gordonchamber.org.*

Camden County · *Camden County C/C* · Christine M. Daniel; Pres./CEO; 2603 Osborne Rd., Ste. R; St. Marys; 31558; Camden; P 50,000; M 440; (912) 729-5840; Fax (912) 576-7924; info@camdenchamber.com; www.camdenchamber.com*

Camilla · *Camilla C/C* · 212 E. Broad St.; P.O. Box 226; 31730; Mitchell; P 6,200; M 300; (229) 336-5255; Fax (229) 336-5256; info@camillageorgia.com; www.camillageorgia.com*

Canton · *Cherokee County C/C* · Pamela W. Carnes; Pres./CEO; 3605 Marietta Hwy.; P.O. Box 4998; 30114; Cherokee; P 215,000; M 1,100; (770) 345-0400; Fax (770) 345-0030; info@CherokeeChamber.com; www.CherokeeChamber.com.*

Carnesville · *Franklin County C/C* · 165 Athens St.; P.O. Box 151; 30521; Franklin; P 22,000; M 200; (706) 384-4659; Fax (706) 384-3204; chamber@franklin-county.com; www.franklin-county.com

Carrollton · *Carroll County C/C* · Daniel Jackson; Pres./CEO; 200 Northside Dr.; 30117; Carroll; P 115,143; M 700; (770) 832-2446; Fax (770) 832-1300; daniel@carroll-ga.org; www.carroll-ga.org.*

Cartersville · *Cartersville-Bartow County C/C* · Kay Read; Pres./CEO; 122 W. Main St.; P.O. Box 307; 30120; Bartow; P 98,000; M 850; (770) 382-1466; Fax (770) 382-2704; kay@cartersvillechamber.com; www.cartersvillechamber.com*

Cedartown · *Polk County C/C in Cedartown* · Eric McDonald; Pres.; 609 S. Main St.; 30125; Polk; P 40,000; M 270; (770) 684-8760; Fax (770) 825-9002; emcdonald@polkgeorgia.com; www.polkgeorgia.com

Chatsworth · *Chatsworth-Murray County C/C* · Dinah Rowe; Pres./CEO; 126 N. 3rd Ave.; 30705; Murray; P 42,000; M 220; (706) 695-6060; (800) 969-9490; Fax (706) 517-0198; murraychamber@windstream.net; www.murraycountychamber.org*

Clarkesville · *see Cornelia*

Claxton · *Claxton-Evans County C/C* · Tammi Hall; Exec. Dir.; 4 N. Duval St.; 30417; Evans; P 11,000; M 225; (912) 739-1391; Fax (912) 739-3827; info@claxtonevanschamber.com; www.claxtonevanschamber.com*

Clayton · *Rabun County C/C* · Sean Brady; Exec. Dir.; 232 Hwy. 441 N.; P.O. Box 750; 30525; Rabun; P 16,514; M 430; (706) 782-4812; Fax (706) 782-4810; sean@gamountains.com; www.gamountains.com*

Cleveland · *White County C/C* · Judy Walker; Pres.; 122 N. Main St.; 30528; White; P 26,432; M 500; (706) 865-5356; (800) 392-8279; Fax (706) 865-0758; whitecountychamber@whitecountychamber.org; www.whitecountychamber.org.*

Cochran · *Cochran-Bleckley C/C* · Kathrine Fisher; Pres./CEO; 102 N. Second St., Ste. A; P.O. Box 305; 31014; Bleckley; P 12,448; M 109; (478) 934-2965; (478) 934-1766; Fax (478) 934-0353; cbchamber@comsouth.net; www.cochran-bleckleychamber.org

College Park · *see Jonesboro*

Colquitt · *Colquitt-Miller County C/C* · Veryl Garland-Cockey; Pres.; 302 E. College St.; 39837; Miller; P 8,300; M 185; (229) 758-2400; Fax (229) 758-8140; cmccoc@bellsouth.net; www.colquitt-georgia.com

Columbus · *Greater Columbus C/C* · Mike Gaymon; Pres./CEO; 1200 6th Ave.; P.O. Box 1200; 31902; Muscogee; P 280,000; M 1,500; (706) 327-1566; Fax (706) 327-7512; mgaymon@columbusgachamber.com; www.columbusgachamber.com*

Commerce · *see Jefferson*

Concord · *see Zebulon*

Conyers · *Conyers-Rockdale C/C* · Fred Boscarino; Pres.; 1186 Scott St.; P.O. Box 483; 30012; Rockdale; P 80,000; M 638; (770) 483-7049; Fax (770) 922-8415; katy@conyers-rockdale.com; www.conyers-rockdale.com*

Cordele · *Cordele-Crisp C/C* · Monica G. Simmons; Pres.; 502 2nd St. S.; P.O. Box 158; 31010; Dooly; P 22,000; M 460; (229) 273-1668; Fax (229) 273-5132; info@cordele-crisp-chamber.com; www.cordelecrispga.com.*

Cornelia · *Habersham County C/C* · Judy Taylor, PhD; Pres.; 668 Hwy. 441; P.O. Box 366; 30531; Habersham; P 43,000; M 725; (706) 778-4654; (800) 835-2559; Fax (706) 776-1416; taylorjudy@windstream.net; www.habershamchamber.com

Covington · *Covington/Newton County C/C* · Hunter Hall; Pres.; 2100 Washington St.; P.O. Box 168; 30015; Newton; P 98,000; M 610; (770) 786-7510; Fax (770) 786-1294; info@newtonchamber.com; www.newtonchamber.com*

Crawford · *Oglethorpe County C/C* · 1158 Athens Rd.; P.O. Box 56; 30630; Oglethorpe; P 14,000; M 140; (706) 743-3113; office@oglethorpecofc.org; www.countycommerce.org

Cumming · *Cumming-Forsyth County C/C* · James McCoy; Pres./CEO; 212 Kelly Mill Rd.; 30040; Forsyth; P 170,000; M 950; (770) 887-6461; cfccoc@cummingforsythchamber.org; www.cummingforsythchamber.org

Cuthbert · *Randolph County C/C* · Patricia Goodman; Exec. Dir.; P.O. Box 31; 39840; Randolph; P 10,000; M 150; (229) 732-2683; Fax (229) 732-6590; ppgoodman@hotmail.com

Dahlonega · *Dahlonega-Lumpkin County C/C & CVB* · Amy Booker; Pres./CEO; 13 Park St. S.; 30533; Lumpkin; P 32,000; M 580; (706) 864-3711; (800) 231-5543; Fax (706) 864-0139; info@dahlonega.org; www.dahlonega.org

Dallas · *Paulding County C/C* · Carolyn S. Delamont; Pres./CEO; 455 Jimmy Campbell Pkwy.; 30132; Paulding; P 127,000; M 800; (770) 445-6016; Fax (770) 445-3050; sbohannon@pauldingchamber.org; www.pauldingchamber.org

Dalton · *Dalton-Whitfield C/C* · Brian Anderson; Pres./CEO; 890 College Dr.; 30720; Whitfield; P 93,835; M 900; (706) 278-7373; Fax (706) 226-8739; info@daltonchamber.org; www.daltonchamber.org.*

Danielsville · *Madison County C/C & Ind. Auth.* · Brian Kirk; Chair; 101 Courthouse Sq., Ste. 1; P.O. Box 381; 30633; Madison; P 26,000; M 300; (706) 795-3473; Fax (706) 795-3262; mccc@madisoncountyga.org; www.madisoncountyga.org

Darien · *Darien-McIntosh County C/C & Visitor Center* · Wally Orrel; Pres.; 103 Fort King George Rd.; P.O. Box 1497; 31305; McIntosh; P 17,000; M 303; (912) 437-6684; Fax (912) 437-3505; mandy@mcintoshchamber.com; www.visitdarien.com

Dawson · *Terrell County C/C* · Gina Webb; Exec. Dir.; 211 W. Lee St.; P.O. Box 405; 39842; Terrell; P 11,000; M 110; (229) 995-2011; Fax (229) 995-3971; tccc@windstream.net; www.terrellcountygeorgia.org

Dawsonville · *Dawson County C/C* · Linda Williams; Pres.; 292 Hwy. 400 N.; P.O. Box 299; 30534; Dawson; P 20,000; M 500; (706) 265-6278; Fax (706) 265-6279; info@dawson.org; www.dawson.org

Decatur · *see Tucker*

Dillard · *see Clayton*

Donalsonville · *Donalsonville-Seminole County C/C* · Brenda Broome; Pres.; 122 E. Second St.; P.O. Box 713; 39845; Seminole; P 9,000; M 150; (229) 524-2588; Fax (229) 524-8406; dosemcc@windstream.net; www.donalsonvillega.com.

Douglas · *Douglas-Coffee County C/C* · JoAnne Lewis; Pres.; 211 S. Gaskin Ave.; 31533; Coffee; P 41,000; M 500; (912) 384-1873; Fax (912) 383-6304; jlewis@douglasga.org; www.douglasga.org.*

Douglasville · *Douglas County C/C* · Kali Boatright; Pres.; 6658 Church St.; 30134; Douglas; P 126,000; M 650; (770) 942-5022; Fax (770) 942-5876; info@douglascountygeorgia.com; www.douglascountygeorgia.com

Dublin · *Dublin-Laurens County C/C* · Ms. Willie Paulk; Pres.; 1200 Bellevue Ave.; P.O. Box 818; 31040; Laurens; P 47,000; M 566; (478) 272-5546; (478) 272-5547; Fax (478) 275-0811; chamber@dublin-georgia.com; www.dublin-georgia.com.*

Duluth · *Gwinnett C/C* · James Maran; Pres./CEO; 6500 Sugarloaf Pkwy.; 30097; Gwinnett; P 726,500; M 2,700; (770) 232-3000; Fax (770) 232-8807; info@gwinnettchamber.org; www.gwinnettchamber.org*

Dunwoody · *see Alpharetta*

Eastman · *Eastman/Dodge County C/C* · Judy Madden; Pres./CEO; 1646 College St.; P.O. Box 550; 31023; Dodge; P 19,501; M 250; (478) 374-4723; Fax (478) 374-4626; info@eastman-georgia.com; www.eastman-georgia.com

Eatonton · *Eatonton-Putnam C/C* · Roddie-Anne Blackwell; Pres.; 305 N. Madison Ave.; P.O. Box 4088; 31024; Putnam; P 22,000; M 450; (706) 485-7701; Fax (706) 485-3277; epchamber@eatonton.com; www.eatonton.com*

Elberton · *Elbert County C/C* · Phyllis Brooks; Pres.; 104 Heard St.; P.O. Box 537; 30635; Elbert; P 22,000; M 450; (706) 283-5651; Fax (706) 283-5722; chamber@elbertga.com; www.elbertga.com.

Ellaville · *Ellaville-Schley County C/C* · John T. Greene; P.O. Box 4; 31806; Schley; P 4,200; M 131; (229) 937-2262; Fax (229) 937-2262; chamberofcommerce@ellavillega.com; www.ellavillega.com/chamber_of_commerce

Ellijay · *Gilmer County C/C* · Paige Green; Pres.; 368 Craig St.; P.O. Box 505; 30540; Gilmer; P 35,000; M 600; (706) 635-7400; Fax (706) 635-7410; chamber@ellijay.com; www.gilmerchamber.com.*

Evans · *Columbia County C/C* · Tammy Shepherd; Pres./CEO; 4424 Evans to Locks Rd.; 30809; Columbia; P 102,278; M 700; (706) 651-0018; Fax (706) 651-0023; info@columbiacountychamber.com; www.columbiacountychamber.com

Fannin County · *see Blue Ridge*

Fayetteville · *Fayette County C/C* · Virginia Gibbs; Pres.; 200 Courthouse Sq.; 30214; Fayette; P 111,000; M 800; (770) 461-9983; Fax (770) 461-9622; info@FayetteChamber.org; www.FayetteChamber.org*

Fitzgerald · *Fitzgerald-Ben Hill County C/C* · Betsy Giddens; Exec. Dir.; 805 S. Grant St.; P.O. Box 218; 31750; Ben Hill; P 20,000; M 325; (229) 423-9357; (800) 225-7899; Fax (229) 423-1052; bgiddens@mchsi.com; www.fitzgeraldchamber.org.

Folkston · *Okefenokee C/C* · Dawn Malin; Exec. Dir.; 3795 Main St.; 31537; Charlton; P 12,000; M 100; (912) 496-2536; (912) 496-7755; Fax (912) 496-4601; director@folkston.com; www.folkston.com.*

Forsyth · *Forsyth-Monroe County C/C* · Tiffany G. Andrews; Pres./CEO; 68 N. Lee St.; 31029; Monroe; P 25,000; M 300; (478) 994-9239; (888) 642-4628; Fax (478) 994-9240; tiffany@forsyth-monroechamber.com; www.forsyth-monroechamber.com*

Fort Gaines · *see Cuthbert*

Fort Oglethorpe · *see Ringgold*

Fort Valley · *Peach County C/C* · Perry Swanson; Pres.; 201 Oakland Hts. Pkwy.; P.O. Box 1238; 31030; Peach; P 25,000; M 267; (478) 825-3733; Fax (478) 825-2501; chamber@peachchamber.com; www.peachchamber.com

Franklin · *Heard County C/C* · Kathy Knowles; Pres.; 121 S. Court Sq.; P.O. Box 368; 30217; Heard; P 12,000; M 130; (706) 675-0560; (888) 331-0560; Fax (706) 675-2129; info@heardchamber.com; www.heardchamber.com

Franklin Springs · *see Carnesville*

Gainesville · *Greater Hall C/C* · Kit Dunlap; Pres./CEO; 230 E.E. Butler Pkwy.; P.O. Box 374; 30503; Hall; P 175,000; M 2,800; (770) 532-6206; Fax (770) 535-8419; kit@ghcc.com; www.greaterhallchamber.com

Gray · *Jones County/Gray C/C* · Doug Redmond; Exec. Dir.; 161 W. Clinton St.; P.O. Box 686; 31032; Jones; P 27,000; M 250; (478) 986-1123; Fax (478) 986-1022; info@jonescounty.org; www.jonescounty.org*

Greensboro • *Greene County C/C* • Becky Cronic; Pres.; 111 N. Main St.; P.O. Box 741; 30642; Greene; P 16,396; M 400; (706) 453-7592; Fax (706) 453-1430; chamber@greeneccoc.org; www.greeneccoc.org*

Griffin • *Griffin-Spalding C/C* • Bonnie Pfrogner; Exec. Dir.; 143 N. Hill St.; P.O. Box 73; 30224; Spalding; P 63,913; M 800; (770) 228-8200; Fax (770) 228-8031; griffinchamber@cityofgriffin.com; www.griffinchamber.com*

Gwinnett • *see Duluth*

Habersham County • *see Cornelia*

Hamilton • *Harris County C/C* • Lynda Dawson; Pres.; 143 S. College St.; P.O. Box 426; 31811; Harris; P 30,000; M 324; (706) 628-0010; (888) 478-0010; Fax (706) 628-4429; info@harriscountychamber.org; www.harriscountychamber.org

Hartwell • *Hart County C/C* • Michele Dipert; Pres.; 31 E. Howell St.; P.O. Box 793; 30643; Hart; P 24,000; M 250; (706) 376-8590; hartchamber@hartcom.net; www.hart-chamber.org

Hawkinsville • *Hawkinsville-Pulaski County C/C* • Kim Brown; Exec. Dir.; 46 N. Lumpkin St.; P.O. Box 300; 31036; Pulaski; P 10,000; M 140; (478) 783-1717; Fax (478) 783-1700; hawkinsville@cstel.net; www.hawkinsville.org

Hazlehurst • *Hazlehurst-Jeff Davis County C/C* • Bonnie Hulett; Exec. Dir.; 95 E. Jarman St.; P.O. Box 546; 31539; Jeff Davis; P 13,000; M 200; (912) 375-4543; Fax (912) 375-7948; bhulett@jeffdavisga.com; www.hazlehurst-jeffdavis.com

Helen • *Greater Helen Area C/C* • Jane Simms; P.O. Box 192; 30545; White; P 420; M 130; (706) 878-1908; Fax (706) 878-3064; office@helenchamber.com; www.helenchamber.com

Hiawassee • *Towns County C/C & Tourism Assn.* • 1411 Jack Dayton Cir.; Young Harris; 30582; Towns; P 10,203; M 375; (706) 896-4966; (800) 984-1543; Fax (706) 896-5441; info@mountaintopga.com; www.mountaintopga.com

Hinesville • *Liberty County C/C* • Leah Poole; Interim Exec. Dir.; 425 W. Oglethorpe Hwy.; 31313; Liberty; P 64,000; M 400; (912) 368-4445; Fax (912) 368-4677; director@libertycounty.org; www.libertycounty.org

Hogansville • *see La Grange*

Homer • *Banks County C/C* • Tara Fulcher; Exec. Dir.; P.O. Box 57; 30547; Banks; P 16,000; M 150; (706) 677-2108; (800) 638-5004; Fax (706) 677-2109; bankscountychamber@windstream.net; www.bankscountychamber.com

Homerville • *Homerville-Clinch County C/C* • Phil Martin; Exec. V.P.; 23 W. Plant Ave.; 31634; Clinch; P 6,900; M 120; (912) 487-2360; Fax (912) 487-2384; clinchcountychamberofcommerce@windstream.net; www.clinchcountychamber.org

Jackson • *Butts County C/C* • Melinda Atha; Exec. Dir.; 625 W. Third, Ste. 6; P.O. Box 147; 30233; Butts; P 25,000; M 350; (770) 775-4839; Fax (770) 775-4868; matha2@bellsouth.net; www.chamberbuttscounty.com

Jasper • *Pickens County C/C* • Denise M. Duncan; Pres.; 500 Stegall Dr.; 30143; Pickens; P 30,000; M 600; (706) 692-5600; Fax (706) 692-9453; info@pickenschamber.com; www.pickenschamber.com

Jefferson • *Jackson County Area C/C* • Shane Short; Pres./CEO; 270 Athens St.; P.O. Box 629; 30549; Jackson; P 60,000; M 580; (706) 387-0300; Fax (706) 387-0304; info@jacksoncountyga.com; www.jacksoncountyga.com

Jesup • *Jesup/Wayne County C/C* • John Riddle; Pres./CEO; 124 N.W. Broad St.; 31545; Wayne; P 29,000; M 430; (912) 427-2028; (888) 224-5983; Fax (912) 427-2778; chamberoffice@waynechamber.com; www.waynechamber.com*

Jonesboro • *Clayton County C/C* • Yulonda Beauford; Pres./CEO; 2270 Mt. Zion Rd.; 30236; Clayton; P 236,517; M 675; (678) 610-4021; Fax (678) 610-4025; info@claytonchamber.org; www.claytonchamber.org

Kingsland • *see Camden County*

La Grange • *LaGrange-Troup County C/C* • Page Estes; Pres.; 111 Bull St.; P.O. Box 636; 30241; Troup; P 60,000; M 850; (706) 884-8671; Fax (706) 882-8012; pestes@lagrangechamber.com; www.lagrangechamber.com*

LaFayette • *see Rock Spring*

Lake City • *see Jonesboro*

Lake Park • *Lake Park Area C/C & Visitors Center* • Exec. Dir.; 5227 Millstore Rd.; P.O. Box 278; 31636; Lowndes; P 18,000; M 160; (229) 559-5302; Fax (229) 559-0828; lpacocv@bellsouth.net; www.lakeparkga.com

Lakeland • *Lakeland-Lanier County C/C* • Ruth May; Exec. Dir.; P.O. Box 215; 31635; Lanier; P 8,000; M 125; (229) 482-9755; Fax (229) 482-9501; llcoc@windstream.net; www.lakelandlanierchamber.com

Lavonia • *Lavonia C/C* • Vivian Young; Secy.; 1269 E. Main; 30553; Franklin; P 2,200; M 250; (706) 356-8202; info@lavonia-ga.com; www.lavonia-ga.com

Lawrenceville • *see Duluth*

Leesburg • *Lee County C/C* • Winston A. Oxford; Exec. Dir.; 100 B. Starksville Ave. N.; 31763; Lee; P 35,000; M 400; (229) 759-2422; Fax (229) 759-9224; ldavis@lee.ga.us; www.leechamber.net*

Lilly • *see Vienna*

Lincolnton • *Lincolnton-Lincoln County C/C* • Susan Banks; Exec. Dir.; 112 N. Washington St.; P.O. Box 490; 30817; Lincoln; P 10,000; M 175; (706) 359-7970; Fax (706) 359-5477; sbanks@lincolncountyga.com; lincolncountyga.com

Lithonia • *Greater Lithonia C/C* • Angela Garrett; Pres.; P.O. Box 57; 30058; DeKalb; P 3,000; M 50; (770) 482-1808; angelagarrett57@aol.com; www.lithoniachamber.com

Louisville • *Jefferson County C/C* • Lillian Easterlin; Exec. Dir.; 302 E. Broad St.; P.O. Box 630; 30434; Jefferson; P 17,266; M 100; (478) 625-8134; (866) 527-2642; Fax (478) 625-9060; leasterlin@jeffersoncounty.org; www.jeffersoncounty.org

Lovejoy • *see Jonesboro*

Ludowici • *Long County C/C* • Kerry Hunt; Pres.; P.O. Box 400; 31316; Long; P 11,452; M 75; www.longcountychamber.com

Lyons • *see Vidalia*

Macon • *Greater Macon C/C* • Chip Cherry; Pres.; 305 Coliseum Dr.; P.O. Box 169; 31202; Bibb; P 150,000; M 980; (478) 621-2000; Fax (478) 621-2021; info@maconchamber.com; www.maconchamber.com*

Madison • *Madison-Morgan County C/C & CVB* • Marguerite Copeland; Pres.; 115 E. Jefferson St.; P.O. Box 826; 30650; Morgan; P 17,000; M 370; (706) 342-4454; (800) 709-7406; Fax (706) 342-4455; marguerite@madisonga.org; www.madisonga.org

Marietta • *Cobb C/C* • David Connell; Pres./CEO; 240 Interstate N. Pkwy.; P.O. Box 671868; 30006; Cobb; P 671,868; M 2,500; (770) 980-2000; Fax (770) 980-9510; info@cobbchamber.org; www.cobbchamber.org.*

McDonough • *Henry County C/C* • Kay Pippin; Pres.; 1709 Highway 20 W.; Westridge Business Center; 30253; Henry; P 198,000; M 700; (770) 957-5786; Fax (770) 957-8030; member services@henrycounty.com; www.henrycounty.com.*

McRae • *Telfair County C/C* • Paula Rogers; Pres.; 9 E. Oak St.; 31055; Telfair; P 13,205; M 130; (229) 868-6365; Fax (229) 868-7970; rogers@telfairco.org; www.telfairco.org

Meansville • *see Zebulon*

Metter • *Metter-Candler C/C* • Sue Holland; Exec. Dir.; 1210 S. Lewis St.; P.O. Box 497; 30439; Candler; P 10,500; M 160; (912) 685-2159; Fax (912) 685-2108; ebim@pineland.net; www.metter-candlercounty.com

Milledgeville • *Milledgeville-Baldwin County C/C* • Tara Peters; Pres./CEO; 130 S. Jefferson St.; P.O. Box 751; 31059; Baldwin; P 45,000; M 500; (478) 453-9311; Fax (478) 453-0051; mbcchamber@windstream.net; www.milledgevillega.com*

Millen • *Jenkins County C/C & Dev. Auth.* • Paula Herrington; Exec. Dir.; 548 Cotton Ave.; 30442; Jenkins; P 8,700; M 135; (478) 982-5595; Fax (478) 982-5512; pauladepot@bellsouth.net; www.jenkinscountyga.com

Molena • *see Zebulon*

Monroe • *Walton County C/C* • Teri H. Wommack; Pres.; 132 E. Spring St.; P.O. Box 89; 30655; Walton; P 89,665; M 831; (770) 267-6594; Fax (770) 267-0961; staff@waltonchamber.org; www.waltonchamber.org*

Monroe County • *see Forsyth*

Montezuma • *Macon County C/C & Dev. Auth.* • Jimmy Davis; Pres.; 109 N. Dooly St.; 31063; Macon; P 14,594; M 125; (478) 472-2391; Fax (478) 472-5186; jcdavisjr@windstream.net; maconcountyga.org

Monticello • *Monticello-Jasper County C/C* • Pres.; 119 W. Washington St.; P.O. Box 133; 31064; Jasper; P 15,000; M 150; (706) 468-8994; Fax (706) 468-8043; jasperchamber@historicmonticello.com; www.historicmonticello.com; www.monticelloga.org

Morrow • *see Jonesboro*

Moultrie • *Moultrie-Colquitt County C/C* • Darrell Moore; Pres.; 116 First Ave. S.E.; P.O. Box 487; 31776; Colquitt; P 46,000; M 560; (229) 985-2131; (888) 40-VISIT; Fax (229) 890-2638; contact@moultriechamber.com; www.moultriechamber.com*

Mountain City • *see Clayton*

Mountain Park • *see Alpharetta*

Nahunta • *Brantley County C/C* • P.O. Drawer B; 31553; Brantley; P 15,750; M 85; (912) 462-6282; info@brantleycountychamber.org; www.brantleycountychamber.org

Nashville • *Nashville-Berrien C/C* • Crissy Staley; Exec. Dir.; 101 N. Davis St.; P.O. Box 217; 31639; Berrien; P 17,000; M 300; (229) 686-5123; Fax (229) 686-1905; berrienchamber@windstream.net; www.berrienchamber.com

Newnan • *Newnan-Coweta C/C* • Candace LaForge; Pres.; 23 Bullsboro Dr.; 30263; Coweta; P 123,000; M 650; (770) 253-2270; Fax (770) 253-2271; info@newnancowetachamber.org; www.newnancowetachamber.org

Ocilla • *Ocilla-Irwin C/C* • Hazel McCranie; Pres.; P.O. Box 104; 31774; Irwin; P 11,000; M 165; (229) 468-9114; Fax (229) 468-4452; irwinchamber@windstream.net; www.ocillachamber.net*

Peach County • *see Fort Valley*

Peachtree City • *see Fayetteville*

Pelham • *Pelham C/C* • Deborah Laufenburger; Exec. Dir.; 128 W. Railroad St.; P.O. Box 151; 31779; Mitchell; P 5,200; M 220; (229) 294-4924; Fax (229) 294-1583; pelhamchamber@pelhamga.org; www.pelhamchamber.org*

Pembroke • *North Bryan C/C Inc.* • Mary Warnell; Pres.; 18 E. Bacon St.; P.O. Box 916; 31321; Bryan; P 3,000; M 65; (912) 653-5655; (912) 653-4040; Fax (912) 653-5655; www.bryancounty.org

Perry • *Perry Area C/C* • Megan Smith; Pres./CEO; 101 General Courtney Hodges Blvd., Ste. B; 31069; Houston; P 11,000; M 400; (478) 987-1234; Fax (478) 988-1234; mail@perrygachamber.com; www.perrygachamber.com.*

Pine Mountain • *Pine Mountain C/C* • Judy Adams; Pres.; P.O. Box 483; 31822; Harris & Meriwether; P 1,100; M 65; (706) 663-8850; www.pinemountainchamber.com

Pinehurst • *see Vienna*

Port Wentworth • *Port Wentworth C/C & Visitors Center* • Trisha Growe; Exec. Dir.; P.O. Box 4186; 31407; Chatham; P 4,883; M 100; (912) 965-1999; Fax (912) 966-1157; tgrowe@visitportwentworth.com; www.visitportwentworth.com.

Quitman • *Quitman-Brooks County C/C* • John Cox; Pres.; 900 E. Screven St.; 31643; Brooks; P 16,800; M 190; (229) 263-4841; Fax (229) 263-4822; chamber@quitmangeorgia.org; www.quitmangeorgia.org

Rabun County • *see Clayton*

Reidsville • *Greater Tattnall C/C & Dev. Auth.* • David Avery; Exec. Dir.; P.O. Box 759; 30453; Tattnall; P 23,000; M 240; (912) 557-6323; Fax (912) 557-3046; davidavery61@yahoo.com; www.tattnall.com

Richmond Hill • *Richmond Hill-Bryan County C/C* • Kittie Franklin; Exec. Dir.; 2591 Hwy. 17, Ste. 100; 31324; Bryan; P 28,000; M 295; (912) 756-3444; (800) 834-3960; Fax (912) 756-4236; kfranklin@coastalnow.net; www.rhbcchamber.org*

Ringgold • *Catoosa County C/C* • Martha Eaker; Pres./CEO; 264 Catoosa Cir.; 30736; Catoosa; P 65,000; M 499; (706) 965-5201; (877) 965-5201; meaker@catoosachamberofcommerce.com; www.catoosachamberofcommerce.com*

Riverdale • *see Jonesboro*

Roberta • *Roberta-Crawford County C/C* • 38 Wright Ave.; P.O. Box 417; 31078; Crawford; P 14,000; M 78; (478) 836-3825; Fax (478) 836-3825; rcccoc@pstel.net; www.robertacrawfordchamber.org

Rock Spring • *Walker County C/C* • Stacey Mauer; Pres.; 10052 Hwy. 27 N.; P.O. Box 430; 30739; Walker; P 61,000; M 340; (706) 375-7702; Fax (706) 375-7797; info@walkercochamber.com; www.walkercochamber.com

Rockmart • *Polk County C/C & Dev. Auth.* • Eric McDonald; Pres./CEO; 604 Goodyear St.; 30153; Polk; P 43,000; M 273; (770) 684-8760; Fax (770) 825-9002; info@polkgeorgia.com; www.polkgeorgia.com*

Rome • *Greater Rome C/C* • Al Hodge; Pres./CEO; 1 Riverside Pkwy.; 30161; Floyd; P 100,000; M 1,200; (706) 291-ROME; Fax (706) 232-5755; grcc@romega.com; www.romega.com*

Roswell • *see Alpharetta*

Royston • *see Carnesville*

Saint Simons Island • *see Brunswick*

Sandersville • *Washington County C/C* • Ree Garrett; Pres.; 131 W. Haynes St., Ste. B; P.O. Box 582; 31082; Washington; P 20,000; M 300; (478) 552-3288; Fax (478) 552-1449; wacocofc@sandersville.net; www.washingtoncountyga.com

Sandy Springs • *see Alpharetta*

Savannah · *Savannah Area C/C* · William W. Hubbard; Pres./CEO; 101 E. Bay St.; P.O. Box 1628; 31402; Chatham; P 304,000; M 2,300; (912) 644-6400; Fax (912) 644-6499; info@savannah chamber.com; www.savannahchamber.com.*

Sky Valley · *see Clayton*

Smyrna · *see Marietta*

Soperton · *Soperton-Treutlen C/C* · Tammi Walraven; Secy.; 488 Second St.; P.O. Box 296; 30457; Treutlen; P 6,000; M 56; (912) 529-6868; Fax (912) 529-4385; agt_soperton@hotmail.com; www.soperton.org.

Springfield · *Effingham County C/C & Dev. Auth.* · John A. Henry; Exec. Dir./CEO of Dev. Auth.; 520 W. Third St.; P.O. Box 1078; 31329; Effingham; P 56,000; M 408; (912) 754-3301; Fax (912) 754-1236; welcomehome@effinghamcounty.com; www. effinghamcounty.com.*

St. Marys · *see Camden County*

Statesboro · *Statesboro-Bulloch C/C* · Peggy Chapman; Pres.; 102 S. Main St.; P.O. Box 303; 30459; Bulloch; P 68,521; M 800; (912) 764-6111; Fax (912) 489-3108; peggychapman@statesboro-chamber.org; www.statesboro-chamber.org*

Summerville · *Chattooga County C/C* · David Tidmore; Pres.; 44 Hwy. 48; P.O. Box 217; 30747; Chattooga; P 25,474; M 156; (706) 857-4033; Fax (706) 857-6963; info@chattoogachamber. org; www.chattoogachamber.org

Swainsboro · *Swainsboro-Emanuel County C/C* · Bill Rogers Jr.; Exec. Dir.; 102 S. Main St.; 30401; Emanuel; P 22,600; M 294; (478) 237-6426; Fax (478) 237-7460; swainsborochambr@ bellsouth.net; www.emanuelchamber.org

Sylvania · *Screven County C/C* · Heidi Jeffers; Exec. Dir.; 101 S. Main St.; 30467; Screven; P 15,374; M 370; (912) 564-7878; Fax (912) 564-7245; hjeffers@planters.net; www.screvencounty.com.

Sylvester · *Sylvester-Worth County C/C* · 301 E. Franklin St.; P.O. Box 768; 31791; Worth; P 20,000; M 250; (229) 776-7718; Fax (229) 776-7719; worthchamber@bellsouth.net; www.sylvester worthcochamber.com

Talbotton · *Talbot County C/C* · Pam Jordon; Exec. Dir.; P.O. Box 98; 31827; Talbot; P 6,500; M 100; (706) 665-8079; Fax (706) 665-8660; info@talbotcountychamber.org; www.talbotcountychamber.org

Tallulah Falls · *see Clayton*

Thomaston · *Thomaston-Upson C/C* · Lori Showalter-Smith; Pres.; 110 W. Main St.; P.O. Box 827; 30286; Upson; P 27,000; M 320; (706) 647-9686; Fax (706) 647-1703; lorishowalter@ windstream.net; www.thomastonchamber.com.*

Thomasville · *Thomasville-Thomas County C/C* · Donald P. Sims; Pres.; 401 S. Broad St.; P.O. Box 560; 31799; Thomas; P 45,000; M 650; (229) 226-9600; (229) 225-1422; Fax (229) 226-9603; chamber@rose.net; www.thomasvillechamber.com*

Thomson · *Thomson-McDuffie C/C* · Carolyn Gilbert; Exec. Dir.; 111 Railroad St.; 30824; McDuffie; P 24,000; M 300; (706) 597-1000; Fax (706) 595-2143; cgilbert@thomson-mcduffie.net; www.thomson-mcduffie.com.*

Tifton · *Tifton-Tift County C/C* · Brian Marlowe; Pres./CEO; 100 Central Ave.; P.O. Box 165; 31793; Tift; P 40,000; M 600; (229) 382-6200; (800) 550-TIFT; Fax (229) 386-2232; bmarlowe@ tiftonchamber.org; www.tiftonchamber.org.*

Tiger · *see Clayton*

Toccoa · *Toccoa-Stephens County C/C* · Wendi Bailey; Pres.; 160 N. Alexander St.; P.O. Box 577; 30577; Stephens; P 28,000; M 400; (706) 886-2132; Fax (706) 886-2133; wendi@taccoagachamber. com; www.toccoagachamber.com*

Towns County · *see Hiawassee*

Trenton · *Dade County C/C* · Debbie Tinker; Exec. Dir.; 111 Railway Ln.; P.O. Box 1014; 30752; Dade; P 15,500; M 130; (706) 657-4488; Fax (706) 657-7513; dcoc@tvn.net; www.dadechamber.com

Tucker · *DeKalb C/C* · Leonardo McClarty; Pres.; 100 Crescent Centre Pkwy., Ste. 680; 30084; DeKalb; P 700,000; M 600; (404) 378-8000; Fax (404) 378-3397; info@dekalbchamber.org; www. dekalbchamber.org

Tyrone · *see Fayetteville*

Unadilla · *see Vienna*

Valdosta · *Valdosta-Lowndes County C/C* · Myrna Ballard; Pres.; 416 N. Ashley St.; P.O. Box 790; 31603; Lowndes; P 106,000; M 1,525; (229) 247-8100; Fax (229) 245-0071; chamber@valdosta chamber.com; www.valdostachamber.com.*

Vidalia · *Toombs-Montgomery C/C* · Bill Mitchell; Pres.; 2805 E. First St.; 30474; Toombs & Montgomery; P 34,337; M 500; (912) 537-4466; Fax (912) 537-1805; information@toombschamber. com; www.toombsmontgomerychamber.com.

Vienna · *Dooly County C/C* · Rhonda Lamb-Heath; Exec. Dir.; 117 E. Union St.; P.O. Box 308; 31092; Dooly; P 11,525; M 150; (229) 268-8275; Fax (229) 268-8200; dccofc@sowega.net; www. doolychamber.com

Waco · *Haralson County C/C* · Jennie English; Pres.; 70 Murphy Campus Blvd.; 30182; Haralson; P 29,000; M 375; (770) 537-5594; Fax (770) 537-5873; jenglish@haralson.org; www.haralson.org

Wadley · *see Louisville*

Ware County · *see Waycross*

Warm Springs · *Meriwether County C/C* · Carolyn McKinley; Exec. Dir.; 91 Broad St.; P.O. Box 9; 31830; Meriwether; P 22,534; M 214; (706) 655-2558; Fax (706) 655-2812; meriwetherchamber@ windstream.net; www.meriwethercountychamberofcommerce.com

Warner Robins · *Robins Reg. C/C* · Ed Rodriguez; Pres./CEO; 1228 Watson Blvd.; 31093; Houston; P 125,000; M 1,291; (478) 922-8585; Fax (478) 328-7745; info@warner-robins.com; www. warner-robins.com.*

Warrenton · *Warren County C/C* · O.B. McCorkle; Pres.; 45 Court Sq.; P.O. Box 27; 30828; Warren; P 6,000; M 50; (706) 465-9604; Fax (706) 465-1789; chamber@warrencountyga.com; www. warrencountyga.com

Washington · *Washington-Wilkes C/C* · Judy Anderson; Exec. Dir.; 29 West Sq.; P.O. Box 661; 30673; Wilkes; P 10,671; M 200; (706) 678-2013; (706) 678-5111; Fax (706) 678-3033; tourism@ washingtonwilkes.org; www.washingtonwilkes.org

Watkinsville · *Oconee County C/C* · JR Whitfield; Pres.; 55 Nancy Dr.; P.O. Box 348; 30677; Oconee; P 30,000; M 346; (706) 769-7947; Fax (706) 769-7948; jrwhitfield@oconeechamber.org; www.oconeechamber.org

Waycross · *Waycross-Ware County C/C* · Jan Sanchez; Dir.; 315 Plant Ave., Ste. B; 31501; Ware; P 35,503; M 400; (912) 283-3742; Fax (912) 283-0121; wwcocjsanchez@atc.cc; www.waycrosschamber.org.

Waynesboro · *Burke County C/C* · Ashley Roberts; Exec. Dir.; 241 E. Sixth St.; 30830; Burke; P 20,579; M 200; (706) 554-5451; Fax (706) 554-7091; burkechamber@roelco.net; www.burkechamber.org

West Point · *see Lanett, AL*

Williamson · *see Zebulon*

Winder · *Barrow County C/C* · Tommy Jennings; Pres.; 6 Porter St.; P.O. Box 456; 30680; Barrow; P 70,000; M 500; (770) 867-9444; Fax (770) 867-6366; mmilner@barrowchamber.com; www.barrowchamber.com*

Woodbine · *see Camden County*

Wrens · *see Louisville*

Wrightsville · *Wrightsville-Johnson County C/C* · Lynn Lamb; Admin.; 6745 E. College St.; P.O. Box 94; 31096; Johnson; P 8,600; M 95; (478) 864-7200; Fax (478) 864-7200; commerce@ wrightsville-johnsoncounty.com; www.wrightsville-johnson county.com

Young Harris · *see Hiawassee*

Zebulon · *Pike County C/C & Dev. Auth.* · Karen S. Brown; Pres.; 416 Thomaston St.; P.O. Box 1147; 30295; Pike; P 18,000; M 320; (770) 567-2029; (770) 567-7291; Fax (770) 567-7290; pikeida@ pikecountygachamber.com; www.pikecountygachamber.com*

Guam

Hagatna · *Guam C of C* · David P. Leddy; Pres.; 173 Aspinall Ave., Ste. 101; Ada Plaza Center Bldg.; 96910; P 175,877; M 380; (671) 472-6311; (671) 472-8001; Fax (671) 472-6202; gchamber@ guamchamber.com.gu; www.guamchamber.com.gu

Hawaii

C of C of Hawaii · James Tollefson; Pres./CEO; 1132 Bishop St., Ste. 402; Honolulu; 96813; Honolulu; P 1,400,000; M 1,100; (808) 545-4300; Fax (808) 545-4369; khouston-sur@cochawaii.org; www.cochawaii.org*

Haleiwa · *North Shore C/C* · Antya Miller; Exec. Dir.; 66-434 Kamehameha Hwy.; P.O. Box 878; 96712; Honolulu; P 18,300; M 160; (808) 637-4558; Fax (808) 637-4556; info@gonorthshore. org; www.gonorthshore.org

Hilo · *Hawaii Island C/C* · Mary Begier; Pres.; 106 Kamehameha Ave.; 96720; Hawaii; P 138,000; M 700; (808) 935-7178; Fax (808) 961-4435; exec@hicc.biz; www.hicc.biz

Honolulu · *Chinese C/C of Hawaii* · Wen Chung Lin; Exec. V.P.; 8 S. King St., Ste. 201; 96813; Honolulu; M 350; (808) 533-3181; info@chinesechamber.com; www.chinesechamber.com

Honolulu · *Filipino C/C* · Rosemarie Mendoza; Pres.; 1125 N. King St., Ste. 302; 96817; Honolulu; P 800,000; M 400; (808) 843-8838; info@filipinochamber.org; www.filipinochamber.org

Kailua · *Kailua (Oahu) C/C* · Puna Nam; Pres.; 600 Kailua Rd., Ste. 107; P.O. Box 1496; 96734; Honolulu; P 50,000; M 200; (808) 261-7997; (888) 261-7997; kcoc@kailuachamber.com; www. kailuachamber.com

Kailua-Kona · *Kona-Kohala C/C* · Vivian Landrum; Pres./CEO; 75-5737 Kuakini Hwy., Ste. 208; 96740; Hawaii; P 50,000; M 675; (808) 329-1758; Fax (808) 329-8564; info@kona-kohala.com; www.kona-kohala.com

Kaunakakai · *Moloka'i C/C* · Robert Stephenson; Pres.; P.O. Box 515; 96748; Maui; P 7,000; M 108; (808) 553-4482; Fax (808) 553-4482; molokaichamber@hawaiiantel.biz; www.molokaichamber.org

Lihue · *Kauai C/C* · Randall Francisco; Pres.; 4268 Rice St., Ste. H; P.O. Box 1969; 96766; Kauai; P 58,303; M 450; (808) 245-7363; Fax (808) 245-8815; info@kauaichamber.org; www.kauaichamber.org

Ocean View · *Ka'u C/C* · Starina Leilani; Secy.; P.O. Box 6710; 96737; Hawaii; P 6,000; M 160; (808) 939-8449; (808) 937-2750; info@kauchamber.com; www.kauchamber.com

Wailuku · *Maui C/C* · Pamela Tumpap; Pres.; 270 Hookahi St., Ste. 212; 96793; Maui; P 144,000; M 920; (808) 244-0081; Fax (808) 244-0083; pamela@mauichamber.com; www.mauichamber.com

Idaho

Idaho Chamber Alliance · Kent Just; Dir.; P.O. Box 2368; Attn: Kent Just; Boise; 83701; Ada; P 1,500,000; (208) 284-2988; (208) 472-5200; contact@idahochamberalliance.com; www.idaho chamberalliance.com

American Falls · *American Falls C/C* · P.O. Box 207; 83211; Power; P 4,100; M 50; (208) 226-7214; info@americanfalls chamber.org; www.americanfallschamber.org

Arco · *Butte County C/C* · Jory Twitchell; Pres.; P.O. Box 837; 83213; Butte; P 3,000; M 48; (208) 527-8977; Fax (208) 527-3036; buttecountychamber@atcnet.net; www.cityarco.com

Ashton · *Ashton C/C* · 714 Main St.; P.O. Box 351; 83420; Fremont; P 2,000; M 75; (208) 652-3355; Fax (208) 652-3567; info@ashtonidaho.com; www.ashtonidaho.com

Bayview · *Bayview C/C* · Jeanne Bjergo; Treas.; P.O. Box 121; 83803; Kootenai; P 400; M 80; (208) 683-9290; www.bayview idaho.org

Blackfoot · *Blackfoot C/C* · Rebecca Price; Exec. Dir.; 130 N.W. Main St.; P.O. Box 801; 83221; Bingham; P 10,000; M 250; (208) 785-0510; Fax (208) 785-7974; chamber@blackfootchamber.org; www.blackfootchamber.org

Boise · *Boise Metro C/C* · Yvette Will; Op. Mgr.; 250 S. 5th St., Ste. 300; P.O. Box 2368; 83701; Ada; P 600,000; M 1,800; (208) 472-5200; Fax (208) 472-5201; ywill@boisechamber.org; www. boisechamber.org.*

Bonners Ferry · *Greater Bonners Ferry C/C* · Mike Sloan; Pres.; P.O. Box X; 83805; Boundary; P 10,000; M 110; (208) 267-5922; Fax (208) 267-5922; info@bonnersferrychamber.com; www. bonnersferrychamber.com

Buhl · *Buhl C/C* · Michelle Olsen; Admin.; 716 Hwy. 30 E.; 83316; Twin Falls; P 4,000; M 152; (208) 543-6682; Fax (208) 543-2185; michelle@buhlchamber.org; www.buhlchamber.org*

Burley · *see Heyburn*

Caldwell · *Caldwell C/C* · Theresa Hardin; Exec. Dir.; 704 Blaine St.; 83606; Canyon; P 45,000; M 380; (208) 459-7493; (866) 206-6944; Fax (208) 454-1284; info@caldwellchamber.org; www.caldwellchamber.org.*

Cascade · *Cascade C/C* · Kathy Hull; P.O. Box 571; 83611; Valley; P 1,000; M 100; (208) 382-3833; info@cascadechamber.com; www.cascadechamber.com

Challis · *Challis Area C/C* · Melissa Perkins Fitzgerald; Exec. Dir.; 632 E. Main St.; P.O. Box 1130; 83226; Custer; P 900; M 75; (208) 879-2771; Fax (208) 879-5836; challischamber@custertel.net; www.challischamber.com

Coeur d'Alene · *Coeur d'Alene Area C/C* · Todd Christensen; Pres./CEO; 105 N. 1st St., Ste. 100; 83814; Kootenai; P 45,000; M 1,300; (208) 664-3194; Fax (208) 667-9338; info@cdachamber. com; www.cdachamber.com

Coolin · *Priest Lake C/C* · P.O. Box 174; 83821; Bonner; P 3,000; M 120; (208) 443-3191; (888) 774-3785; Fax (208) 443-3191; info@priestlake.org; www.priestlake.org

Cottonwood · *Cottonwood C/C* · Cheri Holthaus; Pres.; P.O. Box 15; 83522; Idaho; P 944; M ; (208) 962-3231; www.cottonwood idaho.org

Council · *Council C/C* · Ken Bell; Pres.; P.O. Box 527; 83612; Adams; P 815; M 100; (208) 253-6830; Fax (208) 253-6830; council chamber@ctcweb.net; www.councilchamberofcommerce.com

Craigmont · *Greater Craigmont C/C* · Virginia Frazier; P.O. Box 365; 83523; Lewis; P 562; M 25; (208) 924-0050; (208) 924-5432; cm_frazier@wildblue.net; www.craigmontareachamber.com

Darlington · *see Arco*

Dixie · *see Elk City*

Donnelly · *Donnelly Area C/C* · Cheryl Teed; P.O. Box 83; 83615; Valley; P 140; M 58; (208) 325-3978; info@donnellychamber.org; www.donnellychamber.org

Downey · *Downey C/C* · Rex Anderson; Pres.; P.O. Box 353; 83234; Bannock; P 650; M 28; (208) 897-5342; Fax (208) 897-5677; www.downeyidaho.com

Driggs · *Teton Valley C/C* · C. Reid Rogers; Pres.; 255 S. Main; P.O. Box 250; 83422; Teton; P 9,000; M 250; (208) 354-2500; Fax (208) 354-2517; tvcc@tetonvalleychamber.com; www.teton valleychamber.com

Eagle · *Eagle C/C* · Teri Bath; Pres.; 597 E. State St.; P.O. Box 1300; 83616; Ada; P 20,000; M 400; (208) 939-4222; Fax (208) 327-2139; teri@eaglechamber.com; www.eaglechamber.com

Elk City · *Elk City Area Alliance* · Earl Sherrer; Pres.; P.O. Box 402; 83525; Idaho; P 275; M 60; (208) 842-2597; Fax (208) 842-2597; earlsherrer@wildblue.net

Emmett · *Gem County C/C* · Dian Streeby; Exec. Dir.; 127 E. Main St.; P.O. Box 592; 83617; Gem; P 17,000; M 280; (208) 365-3485; Fax (208) 365-3220; chamber@emmettidaho.com; emmettidaho.com

Fruitland · *Fruitland C/C* · P.O. Box 408; 83619; Payette; P 6,000; M 210; (208) 452-4350; Fax (208) 452-5028; chamber@ fmtc.com; www.fruitlandchamber.org

Garden Valley · *Greater Garden Valley Area C/C* · Greg Simione; Pres.; P.O. Box 10; 83622; Boise; P 3,000; M 115; (208) 462-5003; info@gvchamber.org; www.gvchamber.org

Glenns Ferry · *Glenns Ferry C/C & Visitors Center* · P.O. Box 317; 83623; Elmore; P 1,500; M 90; (208) 366-7345; Fax (208) 366-2238; www.glennsferryidaho.org

Grace · *Grace C/C* · P.O. Box 214; 83241; Caribou; P 1,000; M 150; (208) 425-3912; Fax (208) 425-3912; info@graceidaho.com; www. graceidaho.com

Grangeville · *Grangeville C/C* · Melinda Hall; Pres.; Pine & Hwy. 95 N.; P.O. Box 212; 83530; Idaho; P 3,300; M 135; (208) 983-0460; www.grangevilleidaho.com

Hagerman · *Hagerman Valley C/C* · P.O. Box 599; 83332; Gooding; P 850; M 50; (208) 837-9131; info@hagermanchamber. com; www.hagermanchamber.com

Hailey · *Hailey C/C* · 309 S. Main; P.O. Box 100; 83333; Blaine; P 9,500; M 300; (208) 788-3484; Fax (208) 578-1595; info@ haileyidaho.com; www.haileyidaho.com

Hayden · *Hayden C/C* · Nancy Lowery; Pres.; P.O. Box 1210; 83835; Kootenai; P 14,000; M 184; (208) 762-1185; info@hayden chamber.org; www.haydenchamber.org

Heyburn · *Mini-Cassia C/C* · Kae Cameron; Dir.; 1177 7th St.; P.O. Box 640; 83336; Cassia & Minidoka; P 18,000; M 400; (208) 679-4793; Fax (208) 679-4794; visitorinfo@pmt.org; www.minicassia chamber.com*

Homedale · *Homedale C/C* · Gavin Parker; Pres.; P.O. Box 845; 83628; Owyhee; P 2,500; M 30; (208) 337-3271; Fax (208) 337-3272; www.cityofhomedale.com

Horseshoe Bend · *Horseshoe Bend Area C/C* · Shawn Surgeon; P.O. Box 216; 83629; Boise; P 770; M 50; (208) 484-6070; www. horseshoebendchamber.com

Howe · *see Arco*

Idaho City · *Idaho City C/C* · P.O. Box 507; 83631; Boise; P 458; M 40; (208) 392-4159; www.idahocitychamber.com

Idaho Falls · *Greater Idaho Falls C/C* · Robb Chiles; Pres./CEO; 630 W. Broadway; P.O. Box 50498; 83405; Bonneville; P 52,000; M 830; (208) 523-1010; Fax (208) 523-2255; info@idahofalls chamber.com; www.idahofallschamber.com*

Island Park · *Island Park Area C/C* · Connie Funkhouser; Pres.; P.O. Box 83; 83429; Fremont; P 1,500; M 150; (208) 558-7755; ipchamber@yahoo.com; www.islandparkchamber.org

Jerome · *Jerome C/C* · Jon Melone; Exec. Dir.; 104 W. Main St.; P.O. Box 835; 83338; Jerome; P 10,000; M 225; (208) 324-2711; Fax (208) 324-6881; jeromechamber@visitjeromeidaho.com; www.visitjeromeidaho.com.*

Kamiah · *Kamiah C/C* · Robert Simmons; Pres.; 518 Main St.; P.O. Box 1124; 83536; Lewis; P 1,200; M 80; (208) 935-2290; info@ kamiahchamber.com; www.kamiahchamber.com

Kellogg · *Historic Silver Valley C/C* · 10 Station Ave.; 83837; Shoshone; P 2,500; M 280; (208) 784-0821; Fax (208) 783-4343; svchamber@usamedia.tv; www.historicsilvervalleychamberof commerce.com

Ketchum · *see Sun Valley*

Kooskia · *Kooskia C/C* · Lara Smith; Pres.; P.O. Box 310; 83539; Idaho; P 652; M 30; (208) 926-4362; (208) 926-4109; Fax (208) 926-4362; kooskiachamber@qrowireless.com; www.kooskia.com

Kuna · *Kuna C/C* · 123 Swan Falls Rd.; 83634; Ada; P 14,000; M 100; (208) 922-9254; information@kunachamber.com; www. kunachamber.com

Lava Hot Springs · *Greater Lava Hot Springs C/C* · Vicky Lyon; Pres.; P.O. Box 238; 83246; Bannock; P 527; M 66; (208) 776-5500; findout@lavahotsprings.org; www.lavahotsprings.org

Leslie · *see Arco*

Lewiston · *Lewis Clark Valley C/C* · Kristin Kemak; Pres./CEO; 502 Bridge St.; Clarkston, WA 99403; 83501; Nez Perce; P 60,000; M 900; (509) 758-7712; Fax (509) 751-8767 *

Mackay · *see Arco*

McCall · *McCall Area C/C* · Tim Cochrane; Dir.; 802 N. 3rd St.; P.O. Box 350; 83638; Valley; P 3,000; M 260; (208) 634-7631; Fax (208) 634-7752; info@mccallchamber.org; www.mccallchamber.org

Meridian · *Meridian C/C* · Teri Sackman; Pres./CEO; 215 E. Franklin Rd.; P.O. Box 7; 83680; Ada; P 70,000; M 650; (208) 888-2817; Fax (208) 888-2682; info@meridianchamber.org; www.meridianchamber.org

Middleton · *Middleton C/C* · Rick Fried; Pres.; P.O. Box 434; 83644; Canyon; P 5,000; (208) 713-5662; info@middleton chamber.org; www.middletonchamber.org

Moore · *see Arco*

Moscow · *Moscow C/C* · Steven Hacker; Exec. Dir.; 411 S. Main St.; P.O. Box 8936; 83843; Latah; P 21,000; M 650; (208) 882-1800; (800) 380-1801; Fax (208) 882-6186; info@moscowchamber.com; www.moscowchamber.com

Mountain Home · *Mountain Home C/C* · Lori Posey; Exec. Dir.; 205 N. 3rd E.; 83647; Elmore; P 10,000; M 200; (208) 587-4334; Fax (208) 587-0042; chamber@mountainhomechamber.com; www.mountainhomechamber.com

Nampa · *Nampa C/C* · Georgia Bowman; Pres./CEO; 312 13th Ave. S.; 83651; Canyon; P 81,000; M 580; (208) 466-4641; (877) 20-NAMPA; Fax (208) 466-4677; info@nampa.com; www.nampa. com*

New Meadows • *Meadows Valley C/C* • P.O. Box 328; 83654; Adams; P 800; M 70; (208) 347-4636; (208) 347-4636; Fax (208) 347-4637

New Plymouth • *New Plymouth C/C* • Janet Warnke; Bd. Member; P.O. Box 26; 83655; Payette; P 1,430; M 100; (208) 278-3696; www.npidaho.com

Orofino • *Orofino C/C* • Heather Burnham; Exec. Dir.; P.O. Box 2346; 83544; Clearwater; P 3,500; M 100; (208) 476-4335; director@orofino.com; www.orofino.com

Orogrande • *see Elk City*

Payette • *Payette C/C* • Jody Clements; Pres.; 695 2nd Ave. S.; 83661; Payette; P 7,400; M 136; (208) 642-2362; info@payette chamber.com; www.payettechamber.com

Pierce • *see Weippe*

Pocatello • *Greater Pocatello C/C* • Matthew J. Hunter; Exec. Dir.; 324 S. Main; P.O. Box 626; 83204; Bannock; P 62,000; M 831; (208) 233-1525; Fax (208) 233-1527; amiles@pocatelloidaho.com; www.pocatelloidaho.com*

Post Falls • *Post Falls C/C* • Pamela Houser; Pres./CEO; 201 E. 4th Ave.; 83854; Kootenai; P 25,000; M 475; (208) 773-5016; (800) 292-2553; Fax (208) 773-3843; info@postfallschamber.com; www.postfallschamber.com*

Preston • *Greater Preston Bus. Assoc.* • Paul Judd; 47 N. State St.; P.O. Box 552; 83263; Franklin; P 14,000; M 200; (208) 240-8296; pauljudd@mstar.net; www.prestonidaho.org

Priest River • *Priest River C/C* • Nadine Parker; Pres.; P.O. Box 929; 83856; Bonner; P 1,877; M 160; (208) 448-2721; Fax (208) 448-2721; prchamber@conceptcable.com; www.priestriver chamber.com

Rathdrum • *Rathdrum Area C/C* • Marge Huddleston; Ofc. Mgr.; 8184 W. Main St.; 83858; Kootenai; P 6,000; M 130; (208) 687-2866; Fax (208) 687-2866; office@rathdrumchamberofcommerce. com; rathdrumchamberofcommerce.com

Red River • *see Elk City*

Reubens • *see Craigmont*

Rexburg • *Rexburg Area C/C* • Donna Benfield; Exec. Dir.; 127 E. Main St.; 83440; Madison; P 27,000; M 390; (208) 356-5700; donna@rexcc.com; www.rexcc.com.

Riggins • *Salmon River C/C* • Carolyn Friend; P.O. Box 289; 83549; Idaho; P 438; M 100; (866) 221-3901; cfriend@frontiernet. net; www.rigginsidaho.com

Rupert • *see Heyburn*

Saint Anthony • *Greater Saint Anthony C/C* • Cathy Koon; Pres.; 420 N. Bridge St., Ste. C; 83445; Fremont; P 3,400; M 100; (208) 624-4870; sachamber@fretel.com; www.stanthonychamber.com

Saint Maries • *Saint Maries C/C* • Shirley Ackerman; Pres.; 906 Main Ave.; P.O. Box 162; 83861; Benewah; P 2,900; M 150; (208) 245-3563; manager@stmarieschamber.org; www.stmarieschamber.org

Salmon • *Salmon Valley C/C* • Debbie Ellis; Admin.; 200 Main St.; 83467; Lemhi; P 5,702; M 190; (208) 756-2100; (800) 727-2540; Fax (208) 756-4935; info@salmonchamber.com; www. salmonchamber.com

Sandpoint • *Greater Sandpoint C/C* • Amy Little; Exec. Dir.; 231 N. 3rd Ave.; P.O. Box 928; 83864; Bonner; P 8,000; M 550; (208) 263-0887; (800) 800-2106; Fax (208) 265-5289; info@sandpoint chamber.com; www.sandpointchamber.com

Soda Springs • *Soda Springs C/C* • April Johnson; Exec. Dir.; 9 W. 2nd S.; P.O. Box 697; 83276; Caribou; P 3,000; M 130; (208) 547-4964; (888) 399-0888; Fax (208) 547-2601; sodacoc@soda chamber.com; www.sodachamber.com

Spirit Lake • *Spirit Lake C/C* • Tom Russell; Pres.; 32173 N. 5th; P.O. Box 772; 83869; Kootenai; P 1,600; M 94; (208) 623-3411; idbikerckc@verizon.net; www.spiritlakechamber.com

Stanley • *Stanley-Sawtooth C/C* • Greg Edson; Exec. Dir.; Hwy. 21, Community Bldg.; P.O. Box 8; 83278; Custer; P 100; M 110; (208) 774-3411; (800) 878-7950; info@stanleycc.org; www. stanleycc.org

Sun Valley • *Sun Valley-Ketchum C/C & CVB* • Carol Waller; Exec. Dir.; P.O. Box 2420; 83353; Blaine; P 4,547; M 550; (208) 726-3423; (866) 226-8817; Fax (208) 726-4533; info@visitsun valley.com; www.visitsunvalley.com*

Tetonia • *see Driggs*

Twin Falls • *Twin Falls Area C/C* • Shawn Barigar; Pres./CEO; 858 Blue Lakes Blvd. N.; 83301; Twin Falls; P 67,000; M 750; (208) 733-3974; Fax (208) 733-9216; info@twinfallschamber.com; www. twinfallschamber.com*

Victor • *see Driggs*

Wallace • *Historic Wallace C/C* • Bill Dire Jr.; Pres.; 10 River St., Exit 61; 83873; Shoshone; P 1,000; M 185; (208) 753-7151; Fax (208) 753-7151; director@wallaceidahochamber.com; www. wallaceidahochamber.com

Weippe • *Pierce-Weippe C/C* • Joe Douglas; Secy.; P.O. Box 378; 83553; Clearwater; P 1,000; M 42; (208) 435-4406; info@pierce-weippechamber.com; www.pierce-weippechamber.com

Weiser • *Weiser Area C/C* • Laurel Adams; Exec. Dir.; 309 State St.; 83672; Washington; P 5,374; M 200; (208) 414-0452; Fax (208) 414-0451; info@weiserchamber.com; www.weiserchamber.com

Wilder • *Wilder C/C* • Tamara Patrick; Pres.; 20441 Patrick Ln.; 83676; Canyon; P 1,700; M 20; (208) 697-3571; tap@speedyquick. net; www.cityofwilder.org

Winchester • *see Craigmont*

Illinois

Illinois C of C • Douglas L. Whitley; Pres./CEO; 300 S. Wacker Dr., Ste. 1600; Chicago; 60606; Cook; P 12,901,563; M 4,000; (312) 983-7100; Fax (312) 983-7101; info@ilchamber.org; www. ilchamber.org

Abingdon • *Abingdon C/C* • Bunny Dalton; Pres.; 106 N. Monroe; 61410; Knox; P 3,600; M 54; (309) 462-2629; (309) 462-3182; palmerh1@gallatinriver.net; www.abingdonillinois.com

Addison • *Addison C/C & Ind.* • Bernadette LaRocca; Exec. Dir.; 777 W. Army Trl. Rd., Ste. D; 60101; DuPage; P 32,000; M 287; (630) 543-4300; Fax (630) 543-4355; addisonchamber@sbcglobal. net; www.addisonchamber.org

Albion • *Albion Area C/C* • P.O. Box 82; 62806; Edwards; P 2,000; M 80; (618) 445-2303; Fax (618) 445-2911; marche@shawneelink. net; www.albionchamber.com

Aledo • *Aledo Area C/C* • Diane Sharp; Exec. Asst.; 201 W. Main St.; P.O. Box 261; 61231; Mercer; P 17,000; M 120; (309) 582-5373; Fax (309) 582-5373; aledochamber@frontiernet.net; www. aledochamber.org

Algonquin • *see Lake in the Hills*

Alsip · *Alsip C/C* · Mary Schmidt; Exec. Dir.; 12159 S. Pulaski Rd.; 60803; Cook; P 20,000; M 300; (708) 597-2668; (800) IN-ALSIP; Fax (708) 597-5962; alsipccedc@aol.com; www.alsipchamber.org

Altamont · *Altamont C/C* · Terri Beal; Pres.; P.O. Box 141; 62411; Effingham; P 2,283; M 70; (618) 483-5714; info@altamontchamber.com; www.altamontchamber.com

Alton · *see Godfrey*

Amboy · *Amboy Area C/C* · Deanne Hoy; Pres.; P.O. Box 163; 61310; Lee; P 2,561; M 100; (815) 857-3625; (815) 857-3814; amboychamber@gmail.com; www.amboychamber.com

Anna · *Union County C/C* · Jeannie Landis; Exec. Dir.; 330 S. Main St.; 62906; Union; P 18,000; M 185; (618) 833-6311; Fax (618) 833-1903; uccc@ajinternet.net; www.shawneeheartland.com

Antioch · *Antioch C/C & Ind.* · Barbara Porch; Exec. Dir.; 882 Main St.; 60002; Lake; P 13,750; M 350; (847) 395-2233; Fax (847) 395-8954; info@antiochchamber.org; www.antiochchamber.org*

Aptakisic · *see Lincolnshire*

Arcola · *Arcola C/C* · Rachael Crane; Exec. Dir.; P.O. Box 274; 61910; Douglas; P 2,700; M 90; (217) 268-4530; (800) 336-5456; Fax (217) 268-3690; staff@arcolachamber.com; www.arcolachamber.com

Arlington Heights · *Arlington Heights C/C* · Jon S. Ridler; Exec. Dir.; 311 S. Arlington Heights Rd., Ste. 20; 60005; Cook & Lake; P 80,000; M 530; (847) 253-1703; Fax (847) 253-9133; mb@arlingtonhtschamber.com; www.arlingtonhtschamber.com

Arthur · *Arthur Area Assn. of Commerce* · Rod Randall; Pres.; P.O. Box 42; 61911; Douglas & Moultrie; P 2,300; M 100; (217) 543-2999; randall@arthur.k12.il.us; www.arthurchamber.com

Aurora · *Aurora Reg. C/C* · Joseph Henning; Pres./CEO; 43 W. Galena Blvd.; 60506; DuPage, Kane, Kendall & Will; P 182,000; M 1,100; (630) 256-3180; Fax (630) 256-3189; jhenning@aurorachamber.com; www.aurorachamber.com

Bannockburn · *see Deerfield*

Barrington · *Barrington Area C/C* · Janet Meyer; Pres./CEO; 325 N. Hough St., 3rd Flr.; 60010; Cook; P 44,000; M 850; (847) 381-2525; Fax (847) 381-2540; email@barringtonchamber.com; www.barringtonchamber.com*

Bartlett · *Bartlett C/C* · Diane Hubberts; Pres./CEO; 138 S. Oak Ave.; 60103; Cook; P 41,000; M 350; (630) 830-0324; Fax (630) 830-9724; info@BartlettChamber.com; www.BartlettChamber.com

Bartonville · *Limestone Area C/C* · Alan Getz; P.O. Box 4043; 61607; Kankakee; P 20,000; M 110; email@limestonechamber.com; www.limestonechamber.com

Batavia · *Batavia C/C* · Roger Breisch; Exec. Dir.; 106 W. Wilson St.; 60510; Kane; P 27,000; M 340; (630) 879-7134; Fax (630) 879-7215; info@bataviachamber.org; www.bataviachamber.org.*

Beach Park · *see Gurnee*

Beardstown · *Beardstown C/C* · Janice Jamison; Exec. Dir.; 101 W. 3rd St.; 62618; Cass; P 6,000; M 100; (217) 323-3271; info@beardstownil.org; www.beardstownil.org

Beecher · *Beecher C/C* · Patty Meyer; Exec. Dir.; P.O. Box 292; 60401; Will; P 3,000; M 100; (708) 946-6803; info@beecherchamber.com; www.beecherchamber.com

Belleville · *Greater Belleville C/C* · John Lengerman; Exec. Dir.; 216 E. A St.; 62220; St. Clair; P 41,000; M 750; (618) 233-2015; Fax (618) 233-2077; info@bellevillechamber.org; www.bellevillechamber.org*

Bellwood · *Bellwood C/C & Ind.* · P.O. Box 86; 60104; Cook; P 20,241; M 100; (708) 547-5030; Fax (708) 547-5030; www.vil.bellwood.il.us

Belvidere · *Belvidere Area C/C* · Thomas Lassandro; Exec. Dir.; 130 S. State St., Ste. 300; 61008; Boone; P 46,000; M 400; (815) 544-4357; Fax (815) 547-7654; tlassandro@belviderechamber.com; www.belviderechamber.com*

Benld · *see Gillespie*

Bensenville · *Bensenville C/C* · Peter Gallagher; Dir.; 161 N. Church Rd.; P.O. Box 905; 60106; DuPage; P 20,500; M 105; (630) 860-3800; Fax (630) 860-3814; board@bensenvillechamber.com; www.bensenvillechamber.com

Benton · *Benton-West City Area C/C* · Steve Browning; Pres.; 211 N. Main St.; P.O. Box 574; 62812; Franklin; P 8,000; M 200; (618) 438-2121; (866) 536-8423; Fax (618) 438-8011; chamber@bentonwestcity.com; www.bentonwestcity.com

Bethalto · *see Godfrey*

Bloomingdale · *Bloomingdale C/C* · Jane Hove; Exec. Dir.; 108 W. Lake St.; 60108; DuPage; P 24,000; M 270; (630) 980-9082; Fax (630) 980-9092; marianne@bloomingdalechamber.com; www.bloomingdalechamber.com

Bloomington · *McLean County C/C* · Charlie Moore; CEO; 210 S. East St.; P.O. Box 1586; 61702; McLean; P 168,611; M 1,050; (309) 829-6344; Fax (309) 827-3940; info@mcleancochamber.org; www.mcleancochamber.org*

Blue Island · *Blue Island Area C/C & Ind.* · Greg Lochow; Exec. Dir.; 2434 Vermont St.; 60406; Cook; P 22,000; M 150; (708) 388-1000; blueislandchamber@sbcglobal.net; www.blueislandchamber.org

Bolingbrook · *Bolingbrook Area C/C* · Michael Evans; Exec. Dir.; 201-B Canterbury Ln.; 60440; DuPage; P 70,000; M 590; (630) 226-8420; Fax (630) 226-8426; executivedirector@bolingbrookchamber.org; www.bolingbrookchamber.org

Bourbonnais · *Bradley-Bourbonnais C/C* · Jaclyn Dugan-Roof; CEO; 1690 Newtowne Dr.; 60914; Kankakee; P 35,000; M 500; (815) 932-2222; Fax (815) 932-3294; bbcc@bbchamber.com; www.bbchamber.com

Bourbonnais · *Kankakee Reg. C/C* · David Hinderliter; Pres./CEO; 1137 E. 5000 N. Rd.; 60914; Kankakee; P 109,000; M 600; (815) 933-7721; Fax (815) 933-7675; david@kankakee.org; www.kankakee.org*

Breese · *Breese C/C* · Brandon Wade; Pres.; P.O. Box 132; 62230; Clinton; P 4,000; M 100; (618) 526-7731; www.breesechamber.org

Bridgeview · *Bridgeview C/C & Ind.* · Jerry Gresik; Pres.; 7300 W. 87th St.; Bridgeview Bank Bldg.; 60455; Cook; P 15,200; M 280; (708) 598-1700; Fax (708) 598-1709; info@bridgeviewchamber.com; www.bridgeviewchamber.com

Bridgeview · *The Hills C/C* · Phyllis Majka; Pres.; P.O. Box 1164; 60455; Cook; P 32,000; M 175; (708) 364-7739; Fax (708) 364-7735; info@thehillschamber.com; www.thehillschamber.com

Brookfield · *Brookfield C/C* · Betty LeClere; Pres.; P.O. Box 38; 60513; Cook; P 19,323; M 90; (708) 268-8080; info@brookfieldchamber.net; www.brookfieldchamber.net

Bucktown · *see Chicago-Wicker Park and Bucktown C/C*

Buffalo Grove · *Buffalo Grove Area C/C* · Lynne Schneider; Exec. Dir.; 50 1/2 Raupp Blvd.; P.O. Box 7124; 60089; Cook & Lake; P 44,000; M 425; (847) 541-7799; Fax (847) 541-7819; info@bgacc.org; www.buffalogrovechamber.org

Burbank · *Burbank C/C* · Sandra Coleman; Exec. Secy.; 5501 W. 79th St.; 60459; Cook; P 28,100; M 120; (708) 425-4668; Fax (708) 424-9492; burbankchamber@att.net; www.burbankilchamber.com

Burr Ridge • *Willowbrook/Burr Ridge C/C & Ind.* • Cheryl Collins; Exec. Dir.; 8300 S. Madison; 60527; DuPage; P 7,000; M 250; (630) 654-0909; Fax (630) 654-0922; info@wbbrchamber.org; www.wbbrchamber.org

Bushnell • *Bushnell C/C* • Don Swartzbaugh; Pres.; P.O. Box 111; 61422; McDonough; P 3,400; M 50; (309) 772-2171; www.bushnell.illinois.gov/chamber

Byron • *Byron Area C/C* • Caryn Huber; Exec. Dir.; 418 W. Blackhawk Dr., Ste. 101; P.O. Box 405; 61010; Ogle; P 12,000; M 178; (815) 234-5500; Fax (815) 234-7114; byronchamber@byronil.net; www.byronchamber.org

Cahokia • *Cahokia Area C/C* • Debbie Craig; Pres.; 103 Main St.; 62206; St. Clair; P 19,000; M 65; (618) 332-4258; Fax (618) 332-6690; www.cahokiachamber.com

Cairo • *Cairo C/C* • Monica Smith; Pres.; 220 8th St.; 62914; Alexander; P 3,632; M 60; (618) 734-2737; cairochamber@lazernetwireless.net

Calumet City • *Calumet City C/C* • Yolanda Lott; Pres.; 80 River Oaks Center; 60409; Cook; P 40,000; M 100; (708) 891-5888; Fax (708) 891-8877; info@calumetcitychamber.com; www.calumetcitychamber.com

Canton • *Canton Area C/C* • Missy Towery; Dir.; 45 Eastside Sq., Ste. 303; 61520; Fulton; P 15,000; M 247; (309) 647-2677; Fax (309) 647-2712; mtowery@cantonillinois.org; www.cantonillinois.org*

Carbondale • *Carbondale C/C* • Kristin Gregory; Exec. Dir.; 131 S. Illinois Ave.; P.O. Box 877; 62903; Jackson; P 30,000; M 450; (618) 549-2146; Fax (618) 529-5063; carbondalechamberofcommerce@gmail.com; www.carbondalechamber.com

Carlinville • *Carlinville Comm. C/C* • Jessie Johnson; Exec. Dir.; 112 North Side Sq.; 62626; Macoupin; P 5,685; M 150; (217) 854-2141; Fax (217) 854-8548; carlinvillechamber@hotmail.com; www.carlinvillechamber.com

Carmi • *Carmi C/C* • David Port; Exec. Dir.; 225 E. Main St.; 62821; White; P 5,400; M 140; (618) 382-7606; Fax (618) 382-3458; ccc@cityofcarmi.com; www.cityofcarmi.com

Carol Stream • *Carol Stream C/C* • Luanne Triolo Newman; Exec. Dir.; 150 S. Gary Ave.; 60188; DuPage; P 42,000; M 375; (630) 665-3325; info@carolstreamchamber.com; carolstreamchamber.com

Carpentersville • *Northern Kane County C/C* • Melissa Hernandez; Exec. Dir.; 2429 Randall Rd., Ste. B; 60110; Kane; P 70,000; M 260; (847) 426-8565; Fax (847) 426-1098; melissa@nkcchamber.com; www.nkcchamber.com

Carriers Mills • *see Harrisburg*

Carrollton • *Carrollton C/C* • Marty Gross; Pres.; P.O. Box 69; 62016; Greene; P 2,000; M 35; (217) 942-3187; fieldsteve@hotmail.com

Carterville • *Carterville C/C* • Andrea Frailey; Exec. Dir.; 120 N. Greenbriar; P.O. Box 262; 62918; Williamson; P 6,000; M 167; (618) 985-6942; Fax (618) 985-6942; chamber@cartervillechamber.com; www.cartervillechamber.com*

Carthage • *Carthage Area C/C* • April Gavillet; Secy./Treas.; 8 S. Madison St.; P.O. Box 247; 62321; Hancock; P 3,000; M 120; (217) 357-3024; Fax (217) 357-3024; chamber@carthage-il.com; www.carthage-il.com

Cary • *Cary Grove Area C/C* • Suzanne Corr; Exec. Dir.; 27 E. Main St.; 60013; McHenry; P 27,000; M 500; (847) 639-2800; Fax (847) 639-2168; info@carygrovechamber.com; www.carygrovechamber.com*

Casey • *Casey C/C* • P.O. Box 343; 62420; Clark & Cumberland; P 3,000; M 50; (217) 232-3430; www.cityofcaseyil.org

Caseyville • *Caseyville C/C* • Cherie Mandeville; Pres.; 909 S. Main St.; P.O. Box 470; 62232; St. Clair; P 4,500; M 60; (618) 344-1234; www.caseyville.org

Centralia • *Greater Centralia C/C & Tourism Ofc.* • Bob Kelsheimer; Exec. Dir.; 130 S. Locust St.; 62801; Marion; P 20,000; M 375; (618) 532-6789; (888) 533-2600; Fax (618) 533-7305; gccoc@centraliail.com; www.centraliail.com*

Champaign • *Champaign County C/C* • Laura Weis IOM ACE; Pres./CEO; 1817 S. Neil St., Ste. 201; 61820; Champaign; P 180,000; M 1,300; (217) 359-1791; Fax (217) 359-1809; info@champaigncounty.org; www.ccchamber.org*

Channahon • *see Minooka*

Charleston • *Charleston Area C/C* • Cynthia White; Exec. Dir.; 501 Jackson Ave.; P.O. Box 77; 61920; Coles; P 31,528; M 290; (217) 345-7041; Fax (217) 345-7042; cacc@charlestonchamber.com; www.charlestonchamber.com*

Chatham • *Chatham Area C/C* • Jane Hay; Pres.; 320 N. Main; 62629; Sangamon; P 15,000; M 145; (217) 483-6450; Fax (217) 483-6450; info@chatham-il-chamber.com; www.chatham-il-chamber.com*

Chester • *Chester C/C* • Linda Sympson; Exec. Dir.; 10 Chester By-Pass Rd.; P.O. Box 585; 62233; Randolph; P 8,400; M 135; (618) 826-2721; (618) 826-2721; chesterc@egyptian.net; www.chesterill.com

Chicago Area

Albany Park C/C • Liz Griffiths; Exec. Dir.; 3403 W. Lawrence Ave., Ste. 201; 60625; Cook; P 100,000; M 150; (773) 478-0202; Fax (773) 478-0282; lgriffiths@northrivercommission.org; www.albanyparkchamber.org

Bronzeville C/C • Johnnie Blair; Pres.; 4601 S. Cottage Grove; P.O. Box 53-634; 60653; Cook; P 125,000; M 275; (773) 268-1800; Fax (773) 442-0852; brvlchamber@aol.com; www.bronzevillechamber.com*

Chicagoland C/C • Gerald Roper; Pres./CEO; 200 E. Randolph, Ste. 2200; 60601; Cook; P 8,065,633; M 2,600; (312) 494-6700; Fax (312) 861-0660; jroper@chicagolandchamber.org; www.chicagolandchamber.org

Cosmopolitan C/C • Carnice Carey; Exec. Dir.; 203 N. Wabash, Ste. 518; 60601; Cook; P 3,000,000; M 300; (312) 499-0611; Fax (312) 701-0095; chambers203@sbcglobal.net; www.cosmococ.org

East Side C/C • Jackie Herod; Exec. Dir.; 3501 E. 106th, Ste. 200; 60617; Cook; P 26,000; M 100; (773) 721-7948; Fax (773) 721-7446; eastsidechamber@sbcglobal.net

Edgebrook-Sauganash C/C • Bob Madiar; Exec. Dir.; 6440 N. Central Ave.; 60646; Cook; P 17,000; M 140; (773) 775-0378; Fax (773) 775-0371; edgebrookchamber@sbcglobal.net; www.edgebrookchamber.com

Hyde Park C/C • Lenora Austin; Exec. Dir.; 5501 S. Everett; 60637; Cook; P 50,000; M 230; (773) 288-0124; Fax (773) 288-0464; contact@hydeparkchamberchicago.org; www.hydeparkchamberchicago.org

Jefferson Park C/C • Carol Gawron; Exec. Dir.; 4849 N. Milwaukee Ave., Ste. 305; 60630; Cook; P 153,000; M 135; (773) 736-6697; Fax (773) 685-3316; carol@jeffersonpark.net; www.jeffersonpark.net

Lake View East C/C • Maureen Martino; Exec. Dir.; 3138 N. Broadway; 60657; Cook; P 81,000; M 335; (773) 348-8608; Fax (773) 348-7409; info@lakevieweast.com; www.lakevieweast.com

Chicago Area, *continued*

Lincoln Park C/C · Kim Schilf; Pres./CEO; 1925 N. Clybourn, Ste. 301; 60614; Cook; P 64,000; M 550; (773) 880-5200; Fax (773) 880-0266; info@lincolnparkchamber.com; www.lincolnparkchamber.com*

Mount Greenwood C/C · Darlene Myers; Exec. Dir.; 3052 W. 111 St.; 60655; Cook; P 12,000; M 260; (773) 238-6103; Fax (773) 238-6103; dtmyers@ameritech.net; www.mgcofc.org

Portage Park C/C · 5758 W. Irving Park Rd.; 60634; Cook; P 200,000; M 150; (773) 777-2020; Fax (773) 777-0202; info@portageparkchamber.org; www.portageparkchamber.org

Uptown C/C · Mr. Paul Collurafici; Pres.; 4753 N. Broadway, Ste. 822; 60640; Cook; P 64,000; M 150; (773) 878-1184; Fax (773) 878-3678; info@uptownbusinesspartners.com; www.uptownbusinesspartners.com

Wicker Park & Bucktown C/C · Jamie Simon; Prog. Mgr.; 1414 N. Ashland Ave.; 60622; Cook; P 53,000; M 275; (773) 384-2672; Fax (773) 384-7525; info@wickerparkbucktown.com; www.wickerparkbucktown.com

Chicago Ridge · *see Worth*

Chillicothe · *Chillicothe C/C* · Gus Krantz; Pres.; 1028 N. 2nd St.; 61523; Peoria; P 6,000; M 100; (309) 274-4556; info@chillicothechamber.com; www.chillicothechamber.com*

Christopher · *Christopher Area C/C* · Susan Williams; Pres.; P.O. Box 111; 62822; Franklin; P 2,900; M 29; (618) 724-9416

Cicero · *Cicero C/C & Ind.* · Mary Esther Hernandez; Exec. Dir.; 5801 W. Cermak Rd., 2nd Flr.; 60804; Cook; P 95,000; M 230; (708) 863-6000; Fax (708) 863-8981; cicerochamber@att.net; www.cicerochamber.org

Clinton · *Clinton Area C/C* · Marian Brisard; Exec. Dir.; 100 S. Center St., Ste. 101; 61727; Clinton; P 7,485; M 185; (217) 935-3364; Fax (217) 935-0064; chamber@clintonilchamber.com; www.clintonilchamber.com.

Coal City · *see Morris*

Collinsville · *Collinsville C/C* · Wendi Valenti; Exec. Dir.; 221 W. Main St.; 62234; Madison; P 25,200; M 376; (618) 344-2884; Fax (618) 344-7499; info@discovercollinsville.com; www.discovercollinsville.com

Cook County · *Cook County C/C* · Gerald L. Murphy; Pres.; One Westbrook Corporate Center, Ste. 300; Westchester; 60154; Cook; P 5,200,000; M 25; (708) 531-1117; Fax (708) 449-7701; cookbusiness@att.net.

Countryside · *see LaGrange*

Crete · *Crete Area C/C* · Patricia C. Herbert; Exec. Dir.; 1182 Main St.; P.O. Box 263; 60417; Will; P 37,000; M 60; (708) 672-9216; Fax (708) 672-7640; cretechamber@sbcglobal.net; www.cretechamber.com

Crystal Lake · *Crystal Lake C/C* · Gary Reece; Pres.; 427 W. Virginia St.; 60014; McHenry; P 45,349; M 930; (815) 459-1300; Fax (815) 459-0243; info@clchamber.com; www.clchamber.com*

Danville · *Vermilion Advantage-Chamber of Commerce Div.* · Vicki Haugen; Pres./CEO; 28 W. North St.; 61832; Vermilion; P 85,000; M 415; (217) 442-6201; Fax (217) 442-6228; contact@vermilionadvantage.com; www.vermilionadvantage.com

Darien · *Darien C/C* · Angelo Imbrogno; Pres.; 1702 Plainfield Rd.; 60561; DuPage; P 23,000; M 200; (630) 968-0004; Fax (630) 968-2474; www.darienchamber.com

Decatur · *Greater Decatur C/C* · 111 E. Main St., Ste. 110; 62523; Macon; P 118,000; M 875; (217) 422-2200; Fax (217) 422-4576; assistant@decaturchamber.com; www.decaturchamber.com*

Deerfield · *Deerfield Bannockburn Riverwoods C/C* · Victoria Case; Exec. Dir.; 601 Deerfield Rd., Ste. 200; 60015; Lake; P 24,000; M 460; (847) 945-4660; Fax (847) 940-0381; info@dbrchamber.com; www.dbrchamber.com

DeKalb · *DeKalb C/C* · James E. Allen; Exec. Dir.; 164 E. Lincoln Hwy.; 60115; DeKalb; P 45,000; M 500; (815) 756-6306; Fax (815) 756-5164; chamber@dekalb.org; www.dekalb.org

Des Plaines · *Des Plaines C/C & Ind.* · Herman Zelk; Pres.; 1401 E. Oakton St.; 60018; Cook; P 58,700; M 600; (847) 824-4200; Fax (847) 824-7932; info@dpchamber.com; www.dpchamber.com*

Dixon · *Dixon Area C/C & Ind.* · John R. Thompson; Pres./CEO; 101 W. Second St., Ste. 301; 61021; Lee; P 16,000; M 400; (815) 284-3361; Fax (815) 284-3675; dchamber@essex1.com; www.dixonillinoischamber.com*

Dolton · *Dolton C/C* · Larceeda Jefferson; Admin. Asst.; P.O. Box 823; 60419; Cook; P 25,000; M 60; (708) 849-4000; www.vodolton.org

Dorchester · *see Gillespie*

Downers Grove · *Downers Grove Area C/C* · Laura Crawford; Pres./CEO; 2001 Butterfield Rd., Ste. 105; 60515; DuPage; P 50,000; M 700; (630) 968-4050; Fax (630) 968-8368; chamber@downersgrove.org; www.downersgrove.org

Du Quoin · *Du Quoin C/C* · Fred Huff; Pres.; 20 N. Chestnut; P.O. Box 57; 62832; Perry; P 6,448; M 125; (618) 542-9570; Fax (618) 542-8778; dqchamber@comcast.net; www.duquoin.org

Dwight · *Dwight Area C/C* · Dawn Bunting; Admin. Asst.; 119 W. Main St.; 60420; Livingston; P 4,800; M 143; (815) 584-2091; Fax (815) 584-2091; admin@dwightchamber.net; www.dwightchamber.net

Eagarville · *see Gillespie*

East Alton · *see Godfrey*

East Dundee · *see Carpentersville*

East Gillespie · *see Gillespie*

East Moline · *see Moline*

East Peoria · *East Peoria C/C* · Rick Swan; Exec. Dir.; 111 W. Washington St., Ste. 290; 61611; Peoria; P 23,000; M 475; (309) 699-6212; Fax (309) 699-6220; epcc@epcc.org; www.epcc.org*

Edwardsville · *Edwardsville/Glen Carbon C/C* · Carol Foreman; Exec. Dir.; 200 University Park Dr., Ste. 260; 62025; Madison; P 34,000; M 565; (618) 656-7600; Fax (618) 656-7611; cforeman@edglenchamber.com; www.edglenchamber.com*

Effingham · *Greater Effingham C/C & Ind.* · Norma Lansing; Pres.; 903 N. Keller Dr.; P.O. Box 643; 62401; Effingham; P 13,000; M 484; (217) 342-4147; Fax (217) 342-4228; chamber@effinghamchamber.org; www.effinghamchamber.org*

El Paso · *El Paso C/C* · Lisa Barhum; Secy.; P.O. Box 196; 61738; Woodford; P 2,700; M 80; (309) 527-4400; lbarhum@hbtbank.com; www.elpasoil.org/chamber/

Eldorado · *see Harrisburg*

Elgin · *Elgin Area C/C* · Leo Nelson; Pres.; 31 S. Grove Ave.; P.O. Box 648; 60121; Cook & Kane; P 100,000; M 750; (847) 741-5660; Fax (847) 741-5677; info@elginchamber.com; www.elginchamber.com*

Elizabeth · *Elizabeth C/C* · Joe Orourke; Pres.; P.O. Box 371; 61028; Jo Daviess; P 700; M 85; (815) 858-3600; Fax (815) 858-3881; info@elizabeth-il.com; www.elizabeth-il.com

Elk Grove Village · *Greater O`Hare Assn. of Ind. & Comm.* · Shirlanne Lemm; Pres.; P.O. Box 1516; 60009; Cook; P 4,000,000; M 800; (630) 773-2944; Fax (630) 773-2945; info@greater-ohare.com; www.greaterohare.com*

Elmhurst • *Elmhurst C of C & Ind.* • John Quigley; Pres./CEO; 242 N. York St., Ste. 102; P.O. Box 752; 60126; DuPage; P 42,762; M 607; (630) 834-6060; Fax (630) 834-6002; info@elmhurst chamber.org; www.elmhurstchamber.org*

Elmwood Park • *Mont Clare-Elmwood Park C/C* • Barbara Melnyk; Exec. Dir.; 11 Conti Pkwy.; 60707; Cook; P 28,000; M 233; (708) 456-8000; Fax (708) 456-8680; mcepcoc@aol.com; www.mcepchamber.org

Elsah • *see Godfrey*

Evanston • *Evanston C/C* • Jonathan D. Perman; Exec. Dir.; 1840 Oak Ave., Ste. LM 110; 60201; Cook; P 76,000; M 650; (847) 328-1500; Fax (847) 328-1510; info@evchamber.com; www.evchamber.com*

Evergreen Park • *Evergreen Park C/C* • Glenn Pniewski; Exec. Dir.; 3960 W. 95th St., 3rd Flr.; 60805; Cook; P 23,000; M 150; (708) 423-1118; Fax (708) 423-1859; epchamber@sbcglobal.net; www.evergreenparkchamber.org

Fairbury • *Fairbury C/C* • Becky Whitfill; Exec. Secy.; 101 E. Locust; P.O. Box 86; 61739; Livingston; P 3,900; M 130; (815) 692-3899; Fax (815) 692-4273; fcc@fairburyil.org; www.fairburyil.org

Fairfield • *Greater Fairfield Area C/C* • Flo Simpson; Exec. Secy.; 121 E. Main St.; 62837; Wayne; P 5,421; M 130; (618) 842-6116; Fax (618) 842-5654; chamber@fairfieldwireless.net; www.fairfieldillinoischamber.com

Fairview Heights • *Fairview Heights C/C* • Scott A. Leas; Exec. Dir.; 10003 Bunkum Rd.; 62208; St. Clair; P 50,000; M 200; (618) 397-3127; Fax (618) 397-5563; office@fairviewheightschamber.org; www.fairviewheightschamber.org*

Flora • *Flora C/C* • Heather Lucas; Exec. Asst.; 223 W. Railroad St.; 62839; Clay; P 5,100; M 138; (618) 662-5646; Fax (618) 662-5646; commerce@wabash.net; www.florachamber.com

Forest Park • *Forest Park C/C & Dev.* • Laurie Kokenes; Exec. Dir.; 7344 W. Madison St.; 60130; Cook; P 16,000; M 200; (708) 366-2543; Fax (708) 366-3373; laurie@exploreforestpark.com; www.exploreforestpark.com

Fox Lake • *Fox Lake Area C/C & Ind.* • Linnea Pioro; Exec. Dir.; 71 N. Nippersink Blvd.; P.O. Box 203; 60020; Lake; P 10,000; M 230; (847) 587-7474; Fax (847) 587-1725; foxlakechamber@yahoo.com; www.discoverfoxlake.com

Fox River Grove • *see Cary*

Frankfort • *Frankfort C/C* • Karen Blake; Exec. Dir.; 123 Kansas St.; 60423; Will; P 16,000; M 620; (815) 469-3356; (877) 469-3356; Fax (815) 469-4352; karen@frankfortchamber.com; www.frankfortchamber.com

Franklin Park • *Franklin Park/Schiller Park C/C* • Kenneth Kollar; Pres.; P.O. Box 186; 60131; Cook; P 32,000; M 100; (708) 865-9510; info@chamberbyohare.org; www.chamberbyohare.org

Freeburg • *Freeburg C/C* • Allen Watters; Pres.; P.O. Box 179; 62243; St. Clair; P 5,000; M 150; (618) 539-5613; Fax (618) 539-5613; secretary@freeburgchamberofcommerce.com; www.freeburgchamberofcommerce.com

Freeport • *Freeport Area C/C* • Mr. Kim Grimes; Pres./CEO; 27 W. Stephenson St.; 61032; Stephenson; P 26,000; M 500; (815) 233-1350; Fax (815) 233-3226; kim.grimes@aeroinc.net; www.freeportilchamber.com

Fulton • *Fulton C/C* • Heather Bennett; Exec. Dir.; 415 11th Ave.; 61252; Whiteside; P 3,900; M 115; (815) 589-4545; Fax (815) 589-4421; chamber@cityoffulton.us; www.cityoffulton.us

Galatia • *see Harrisburg*

Galena • *Galena Area C/C* • Ed Schmit; Exec. Dir.; 101 Bouthillier St.; 61036; Jo Daviess; P 3,600; M 325; (815) 777-9050; Fax (815) 777-8465; office@galenachamber.com; www.galenachamber.com*

Galesburg • *Galesburg Area C/C* • Robert C. Maus; Pres.; 185 S. Kellogg St.; P.O. Box 749; 61401; Knox; P 33,000; M 401; (309) 343-1194; Fax (309) 343-1195; chamber@galesburg.org; www.galesburg.org*

Galva • *Galva C/C* • Ralph Haga; Pres.; P.O. Box 112; 61434; Henry; P 2,700; M 65; (309) 932-2131; (309) 932-2555; www.galva.com

Geneseo • *Geneseo C/C* • Rhonda Ludwig; Exec. Dir.; 100 W. Main; 61254; Henry; P 6,500; M 180; (309) 944-2686; Fax (309) 944-2647; geneseo@geneseo.net; www.geneseo.org

Geneva • *Geneva C/C* • Jean Gaines; Pres.; 8 S. Third St., 2nd Flr.; P.O. Box 481; 60134; Kane; P 23,000; M 507; (630) 232-6060; (866) 4-GENEVA; Fax (630) 232-6083; chamberinfo@genevachamber.com; www.genevachamber.com

Genoa • *Genoa C/C* • Bonnie Hanson; Exec. Dir.; 327 W. Main St., Upper Level; 60135; DeKalb; P 3,890; M 100; (815) 784-2212; Fax (815) 784-2212; genoachamb@tbcnet.com; www.genoa-il-chamberofcommerce.com*

Gibson City • *Gibson Area C/C* • Pam Bradbury; Secy.; 126 N. Sangamon Ave.; P.O. Box 294; 60936; Ford; P 3,600; M 140; (217) 784-5217; (217) 784-4636; Fax (217) 784-4119; chamber@gibsoncityillinois.com; www.gibsoncityillinois.com

Gilberts • *see Carpentersville*

Gillespie • *Coal Country C/C* • Mickey Robinson; Exec. Dir.; 213 S. Macoupin; P.O. Box 57; 62033; Macoupin; P 10,000; M 110; (217) 839-4888; mrer@madisontelco.com; www.coalcountrychamber.com

Gilman • *Gilman Area C/C* • Rita Silles; Secy./Treas.; P.O. Box 13; 60938; Gilman; P 1,800; M 62; (815) 265-4818; Fax (815) 265-4961; www.gilmanil.com

Girard • *Girard C/C* • Debra Burnett; Secy.; P.O. Box 92; 62640; Macoupin; P 2,300; M 60; (217) 627-3512; Fax (217) 627-3656; cityclerk@royell.org; www.girardilusa.com*

Glen Carbon • *see Edwardsville*

Glen Ellyn • *Glen Ellyn C/C* • Georgia Koch & Mike Formento; Exec. Dirs.; 800 Roosevelt Rd., Ste. D108; 60137; DuPage; P 30,000; M 400; (630) 469-0907; formail@glenellynchamber.com; www.glenellynchamber.com*

Glencoe • *Glencoe C/C* • Sally Sprowl; Exec. Dir.; P.O. Box 575; 60022; Cook; P 8,762; M 90; (847) 835-3333; glencoechamber@yahoo.com; www.glencoechamber.org

Glendale Heights • *Glendale Heights C/C* • Sharon Mennemeier; Prog. Coord.; 440 Gregory Ave.; P.O. Box 5054; 60139; DuPage; P 39,000; M 120; (630) 545-1099; Fax (630) 858-4418; questions@glendaleheightschamber.com; www.glendaleheightschamber.com

Glenview • *Glenview C/C* • Kathleen Miles; Pres.; 2320 Glenview Rd.; 60025; Cook; P 47,000; M 490; (847) 724-0900; Fax (847) 724-0202; gcstaff@glenviewchamber.com; www.glenviewchamber.com*

Godfrey • *River Bend Growth Assn.* • Monica Bristow; Pres.; 5800 Godfrey Rd.; Alden Hall; 62035; Madison; P 100,000; M 650; (618) 467-2280; Fax (618) 466-8289; info@growthassociation.com; www.growthassociation.com*

Golconda • *Golconda/Pope County C/C* • William Altman; Pres.; P.O. Box 688; 62938; Pope; P 4,500; M 25; (618) 683-9702

Grafton • *see Godfrey*

Granite City · *Chamber of Commerce of Southwestern Madison County* · Rosemarie Brown; Exec. Dir.; 3600 Nameoki Rd., Ste. 202; P.O. Box 370; 62040; Madison; P 55,000; M 300; (618) 876-6400; Fax (618) 876-6448; chamber@chambersw madisoncounty.com; www.chamberswmadisoncounty.com*

Grant Park · *Grant Park C/C* · Mike Nicholson; Pres.; P.O. Box 473; 60940; Kankakee; P 1,500; (815) 466-0604; Fax (815) 465-6611; president@grantparkchamber.org; www.grantparkchamber.org

Grayslake · *Grayslake Area C/C & Ind.* · Karen Christian-Smith IOM; Exec. Dir.; 10 S. Seymour St.; P.O. Box 167; 60030; Lake; P 25,000; M 250; (847) 223-6888; Fax (847) 223-6895; business@ grayslakechamber.com; www.grayslakechamber.com

Grayville · *Grayville C/C* · Rick Conner; Dir.; P.O. Box 117; 62844; Edwards & White; P 1,800; M 50; (618) 375-7518; www.cityofgrayville.com

Greenville · *Greenville C/C* · Julia Jenner; Exec. Dir.; P.O. Box 283; 62246; Bond; P 6,300; M 180; (618) 664-9272; (888) 862-8201; greenville@newwavecomm.net; www.Greenvilleusa.org

Grundy County · *see Morris*

Gurnee · *Lake County C/C* · Martha Appelhans; Member Rel. Coord.; 5221 W. Grand Ave.; 60031; Lake; P 582,983; M 400; (847) 249-3800; Fax (847) 249-3892; info@lakecountychamber.com; www.lakecountychamber.com*

Half Day · *see Lincolnshire*

Hampshire · *Hampshire Area C/C* · Katie Mathson; Pres.; 153 S. State St.; P.O. Box 157; 60140; Kane; P 4,000; M 175; (847) 683-1122; Fax (847) 683-1146; hampshirecc@fvi.net; www. hampshirechamber.org

Hanover Park · *Hanover Park C/C & Ind.* · Andrea Fox; Chamber Liaison; 1981 E. Devon Ave.; 60133; Cook & DuPage; P 40,000; M 65; (630) 372-2009; Fax (630) 372-2052; staff@ hanoverparkchamber.com; www.hanoverparkchamber.com

Harrisburg · *Saline County C/C* · Lori Cox; Exec. Dir.; 2 E. Locust, Ste. 200; 62946; Saline; P 27,000; M 150; (618) 252-4192; Fax (618) 252-0210; chamber@salinecountychamber.org; www. salinecountychamber.org

Hartford · *see Godfrey*

Harvard · *Harvard C/C & Ind.* · Crystal Musgrove; Exec. Dir.; 62 N. Ayer, Ste. B; 60033; McHenry; P 9,800; M 200; (815) 943-4404; Fax (815) 943-4410; info@harvcc.net; www.harvcc.net

Havana · *Havana Area C/C* · Melanie Bleem; P.O. Box 116; 62644; Mason; P 3,600; M 115; (309) 543-3528; (888) 236-8406; havana@scenichavana.com; www.scenichavana.com

Henry · *Henry Area C/C* · Chris Laible; Pres.; P.O. Box 211; 61537; Marshall; P 3,000; M 90; (309) 364-3261; Fax (309) 364-3261; henrychamber@henrychamber.org; www.henrychamber.org

Herrin · *Herrin C/C* · Liz Lively; Exec. Dir.; 3 S. Park Ave.; 62948; Williamson; P 11,000; M 390; (618) 942-5163; (888) 942-5163; Fax (618) 942-3301; herrincc@herrinillinois.com; www.herrinillinois.com

Herscher · *Herscher C/C* · Adam Wagner; Pres.; P.O. Box 437; 60941; Kankakee; P 1,600; M 100; (815) 426-2348; www.herscher.net

Hickory Hills · *see Bridgeview-Hills C/C*

Highland · *Highland C/C* · Jami Jansen; Exec. Dir.; 907 Main St.; 62249; Madison; P 10,000; M 300; (618) 654-3721; Fax (618) 654-8966; info@highlandillinois.com; www.highlandillinois.com

Highland Park · *Highland Park C/C* · Virginia Anzelmo Glasner; Exec. Dir.; 508 Central Ave., Ste. 206; 60035; Lake; P 32,000; M 410; (847) 432-0284; Fax (847) 432-2802; chamber@ehigh landpark.com; www.chamberhp.com*

Highwood · *Highwood C/C* · Dominick Ugolini; Pres.; P.O. Box 305; 60040; Lake; P 5,500; M 100; (847) 433-2100; Fax (847) 433-7959; info@highwoodchamberofcommerce.com; www. highwoodchamberofcommerce.com

Hillsboro · *Hillsboro C/C* · Lesley Pollard; Exec. Dir.; 447 S. Main St.; 62049; Montgomery; P 7,000; M 84; (217) 532-3711; Fax (217) 532-5567; info@hillsborochamber.net; www.hillsboro chamber.net

Hillside · *Hillside C/C & Ind.* · Sue Hutsebaut; Secy.; P.O. Box 601; 60162; Cook; P 8,000; M 98; (708) 449-2449; Fax (708) 449-2442; hcochq@sbcglobal.net; www.hillsidechamberofcommerce.com

Hinsdale · *Hinsdale C/C* · Janet Anderson; Exec. Dir.; 22 E. First St.; 60521; DuPage; P 18,000; M 275; (630) 323-3952; Fax (630) 323-3953; info@hinsdalechamber.com; www.hinsdalechamber.com

Hodgkins · *see LaGrange*

Hoffman Estates · *Hoffman Estates C/C* · Cheri Sisson; Exec. Dir.; 2200 W. Higgins Rd., Ste. 201; 60169; Cook; P 50,500; M 350; (847) 781-9100; Fax (847) 781-9172; info@hechamber.com; www. hechamber.com

Homer Glen · *Homer Twp. C/C* · Rosella Trotter; Exec. Dir.; 15801 S. Bell Rd., Ste. 220; 60491; Will; P 25,000; M 300; (708) 301-8111; Fax (708) 301-2751; office@homerchamber.com; www.homerchamber.com*

Homewood · *Chicago Southland C/C* · Patrice Brooks; Exec. V.P.; 920 W. 175th St., Ste. 3; 60430; Cook; P 1,300,000; M 900; (708) 957-6950; Fax (708) 957-6968; info@chicagosouthland.com; www.chicagosouthland.com

Homewood · *Homewood Area C/C* · Kathy Nussbaum; Exec. Dir.; 2023 Ridge Rd.; 60430; Cook; P 22,000; M 190; (708) 206-3384; Fax (708) 206-3605; kathy@homewoodareachamber.com; www.homewoodareachamber.com

Hoopeston · *Hoopeston C/C* · Gloria Bush; Ofc. Mgr.; 301 W. Main St.; P.O. Box 346; 60942; Vermilion; P 5,800; M 200; (217) 283-7873; Fax (217) 283-7873; hoopestonchamber@yahoo.com; www.cityofhoopeston.org

Huntley · *Huntley Area C/C & Ind.* · Rita Slawek; Pres./ CEO; 11419 S. Rte. 47; 60142; McHenry; P 15,000; M 345; (847) 669-0166; Fax (847) 669-0170; info@huntleychamber.org; www. huntleychamber.org*

Indian Creek · *see Lincolnshire*

Indian Head Park · *see LaGrange*

Jacksonville · *Jacksonville Area C/C* · Ginny Fanning; Pres.; 155 W. Morton; 62650; Morgan; P 33,000; M 600; (217) 245-2174; Fax (217) 245-0661; chamber@jacksonvilleareachamber.org; www. jacksonvilleareachamber.org*

Jerseyville · *Jersey County Bus. Assn.* · Alan Gilmore; CEO; 209 N. State St.; 62052; Jersey; P 23,000; M 230; (618) 639-5222; Fax (618) 498-3871; agilmore@jcba-il.us; www.jcba-il.us*

Johnsburg · *see McHenry*

Joliet · *Joliet Region C/C & Ind.* · Russ Slinkard; Pres./CEO; 63 N. Chicago St.; P.O. Box 752; 60434; Will; P 170,000; M 1,500; (815) 727-5371; Fax (815) 727-5374; info@jolietchamber.com; www. jolietchamber.com.*

Kewanee · *Kewanee C/C* · Mark Mikenas; Exec. V.P.; 113 E. Second; 61443; Henry; P 13,000; M 225; (309) 852-2175; Fax (309) 852-2176; chamber@kewanee-il.com; www.kewanee-il.com*

La Salle · *Illinois Valley Area C/C & Eco. Dev.* · Marci Duro; Exec. Dir./CEO; 300 Bucklin St.; 61301; Bureau, LaSalle & Putnam; P 50,000; M 400; (815) 223-0227; Fax (815) 223-4827; ivaced@ ivaced.org; www.ivaced.org*

LaGrange · *West Suburban C/C* · Robert E. Ware; Exec. Dir.; P.O. Box 187; 60525; Cook; P 70,000; M 400; (708) 387-7550; Fax (708) 387-7556; info@westsuburbanchamber.org; www.westsuburban chamber.org

LaGrange Park · *see LaGrange*

Lake Bluff · *see Lake Forest*

Lake Forest · *Lake Forest/Lake Bluff C/C* · Joanna Rolek; Exec. Dir.; 695 N. Western Ave.; 60045; Lake; P 25,000; M 460; (847) 234-4282; Fax (847) 234-4297; info@LFLBchamber.com; www. LFLBchamber.com

Lake in the Hills · *Algonquin-Lake in the Hills C/C* · Sandy Oslance; Exec. Dir.; 2114 W. Algonquin Rd.; 60156; Kane & McHenry; P 61,000; M 400; (847) 658-5300; Fax (847) 658-6546; info@algonquin-lith-chamber.com; www.algonquin-lith-chamber.com

Lake Zurich · *Lake Zurich Area C/C* · Dale Perrin; Exec. Dir.; 1st Bank Plaza, Ste. 308; 60047; Lake; P 33,000; M 500; (847) 438-5572; Fax (847) 438-5574; info@lzacc.com; www.lzacc.com*

Lansing · *Lansing C/C* · Kari Ann Legg; Exec. Dir.; 3404 Lake St.; 60438; Cook; P 30,000; M 300; (708) 474-4170; Fax (708) 474-7393; lansingchamber@yahoo.com; www.chamberoflansing.com

Lawrenceville · *Lawrence County C/C* · Lori Waggoner; Exec. Dir.; 619 12th St.; 62439; Lawrence; P 15,929; M 160; (618) 943-3516; Fax (618) 943-4748; lccc2@frontier.com; lawrencecounty illinois.com/chamber.html

Lebanon · *Lebanon C/C* · Joe Zimmerlee; Pres.; 221 W. St. Louis St.; 62254; St. Clair; P 4,000; M 93; (618) 537-8420; Fax (618) 537-8420; lebanonchamber@gmail.com; www.lebanonil.org

Lemont · *Lemont Area C/C* · Joanna Kmiec; Exec. Dir.; 101 Main St.; 60439; Cook; P 14,000; M 250; (630) 257-5997; Fax (630) 257-3238; info@lemontchamber.com; www.lemontchamber.com

Lewistown · *Lewistown C/C* · Becky Humphrey; 119 S. Adams St.; 61542; Fulton; P 2,531; M 40; (309) 547-2501; (309) 547-4300

Libertyville · *Green Oaks/Libertyville/Mundelein/Vernon Hills C/C* · Carol Levine; Public Relations; 1123 S. Milwaukee Ave.; 60048; Lake; P 83,000; M 700; (847) 680-0750; Fax (847) 680-0760; info@glmvchamber.org; www.glmvchamber.org*

Lincoln · *Lincoln/Logan County C/C* · Andi Hake; Exec. Dir.; 1555 5th St.; 62656; Logan; P 31,000; M 300; (217) 735-2385; Fax (217) 735-9205; chamber@lincolnillinois.com; www.lincoln illinois.com*

Lincoln Park · *see Chicago—Lincoln Park C/C*

Lincolnshire · *Greater Lincolnshire C/C* · Judy Scalzitti; Chamber Liaison; 175 Olde Half Day Rd., Ste. 125; 60069; Lake; P 6,800; M 250; (847) 793-2409; Fax (847) 793-2405; glcc@ lincolnshirechamber.org; www.lincolnshirechamber.org*

Lincolnwood · *Lincolnwood C/C & Ind.* · Diana Lass; Exec. Dir.; 7001 N. Lawndale Ave.; 60712; Cook; P 12,280; M 172; (847) 679-5760; Fax (847) 679-5790; dlass@lincolnwoodchamber.org; www. lincolnwoodchamber.org

Lindenhurst · *Lindenhurst-Lake Villa C/C* · Connie Meadie; Exec. Dir.; 500 E. Grand Ave., P.O. Box 6075, 60046; Lake; P 20,000; M 340; (847) 356-8446; Fax (847) 356-8561; llvchamber@ sbcglobal.net; www.llvchamber.com

Lisle · *Lisle Area C/C* · Tom Althoff; Pres./CEO; 4733 Main St.; 60532; DuPage; P 23,000; M 400; (630) 964-0052; Fax (630) 964-2726; info@lislechamber.com; www.lislechamber.com

Litchfield · *Litchfield C/C* · Rhea Weaver; Exec. Dir.; 311 N. Madison; P.O. Box 334; 62056; Montgomery; P 7,000; M 190; (217) 324-2533; Fax (217) 324-3559; info@litchfieldchamber.com; www.litchfieldchamber.com

Lockport · *Lockport C/C* · Mary Kay Campbell; Exec. Dir.; 921 S. State St.; 60441; Will; P 19,000; M 270; (815) 838-3357; Fax (815) 838-2653; office@lockportchamber.com; www.lockportchamber.com

Lombard · *Lombard Area C/C & Ind.* · Yvonne Invergo; Exec. Dir.; 10 Lilac Ln.; 60148; DuPage; P 42,322; M 250; (630) 627-5040; Fax (630) 627-5519; info@lombardchamber.com; www. lombardchamber.com

Long Grove · *see Lincolnshire*

Loves Park · *Parks C/C* · Diana Johnson; Exec. Dir.; 100 Heart Blvd.; 61111; Winnebago; P 45,000; M 225; (815) 633-3999; Fax (815) 633-4057; info@parkschamber.com; www.parkschamber.com

Lynwood · *Lynwood C/C* · Joseph Levy; Pres.; 21460 Lincoln Hwy.; 60411; Cook; P 9,000; M 65; (708) 474-2272; Fax (708) 474-2207; lynwoodchamber@yahoo.com; www.lynwoodchamber-lcc.com

Machesney Park · *see Loves Park*

Macomb · *Macomb Area C/C & Downtown Dev. Corp.* · Penny Lawyer; Pres.; 214 N. Lafayette St.; P.O. Box 274; 61455; McDonough; P 21,000; M 372; (309) 837-4855; Fax (309) 837-4857; chamber@macomb.com; www.macombareachamber.com*

Madison · *see Granite City*

Mahomet · *Mahomet Area C/C* · Mark Kesler; Pres.; 116 S. Lombard St.; P.O. Box 1031; 61853; Champaign; P 7,000; M 105; (217) 586-3165; Fax (217) 586-3774; office@mahometchamber ofcommerce.com; www.mahometchamberofcommerce.com

Manhattan · *Manhattan C/C* · Glenna Johnston; Exec. Dir.; P.O. Box 357; 60442; Will; P 3,700; M 120; (815) 478-3811; Fax (815) 478-7761; chamber@manhattan-il.com; www.manhattan-il.com

Manito · *Manito Area C/C* · Curt Jibben; Pres.; P.O. Box 143; 61546; Mason; P 1,800; M 62; (309) 968-7200; www.manitoil.com

Manteno · *Manteno C/C* · Warren Brown; Exec. Dir.; P.O. Box 574; 60950; Kankakee; P 8,000; M 175; (815) 468-6226; wbmtwain@aol.com; www.mantenochamber.com

Marengo · *Marengo-Union C/C* · Marlene Slavin; Pres./CEO; 116 S. State St.; 60152; McHenry; P 7,200; M 200; (815) 568-6680; Fax (815) 568-6879; info@marengo-union.com; www.marengo-union.com*

Marion · *Marion Area C/C* · George R. Trammell IOM ACE; Pres./ CEO; 2305 W. Main St.; P.O. Box 307; 62959; Williamson; P 65,000; M 650; (618) 997-6311; (800) 699-1760; Fax (618) 997-4665; marionchamber@marionillinois.com; www.marionillinois.com

Marseilles · *Illinois River Area C/C* · Julie Alaimo; Exec. Dir.; 135 Washington St.; 61341; LaSalle; P 8,000; M 130; (815) 795-2323; Fax (815) 795-4546; iracc@mtco.com; www.iracc.org*

Marshall · *Marshall Area C/C* · George Dalmier; Pres.; 708 Archer Ave.; 62441; Clark; P 3,900; M 55; (217) 826-2034; Fax (217) 826-2034; marshall.chamber@frontier.com; www.marshallilchamber.com

Martinsville · *Martinsville C/C* · Sheila Cribelar; Pres.; P.O. Box 429; 62442; Clark; P 1,300; M 50; (217) 382-4323; www. martinsvilleil.com

Maryville · *see Troy*

Mascoutah · *Mascoutah C/C* · Jack Weyant; Pres.; 200 E. Main St., Ste. 101; 62258; St. Clair; P 5,700; M 129; (618) 566-7355; Fax (618) 566-7355; chamber@mascoutahchamber.com; www. mascoutah.com

Matteson · *Matteson Business Assn.* · Laverne Murphy; Exec. Dir.; 4900 Village Commons Dr.; 60443; Cook; P 60,000; M 20; (708) 283-4765; Fax (708) 283-4951; www.mattesonbusiness.com

Mattoon · *Mattoon C/C* · Mary E. Wetzel; Exec. Dir.; 500 Broadway Ave.; 61938; Coles; P 23,000; M 335; (217) 235-5661; Fax (217) 234-6544; matchamber@consolidated.net; mattoonchamber.com.*

Maywood · *Maywood C/C* · Edwin H. Walker IV; Pres./CEO; P.O. Box 172; 60153; Cook; P 28,000; M 150; (708) 345-7077; Fax (708) 345-9455; info@maywoodchamber.com; www.maywoodchamber.com

McHenry · *McHenry Area C/C* · Kay Rial-Bates; Pres.; 1257 N. Green St.; 60050; McHenry; P 34,000; M 720; (815) 385-4300; Fax (815) 385-9142; info@mchenrychamber.com; www.mchenrychamber.com

McLeansboro · *Hamilton County C/C & EDC* · Mark Epperson; Pres.; P.O. Box 456; 62859; Hamilton; P 9,000; M 100; www.mcleansboro.com

Melrose Park · *Melrose Park C/C* · Cathy Stenberg; Exec. Dir.; 900 N. 25th Ave.; 60160; Cook; P 21,000; M 300; (708) 338-1007; Fax (708) 338-9924; info@melroseparkchamber.org; www.melroseparkchamber.org

Mendota · *Mendota Area C/C* · Alison Wasmer; Exec. Dir.; 800 Washington St.; P.O. Box 620; 61342; LaSalle; P 7,300; M 250; (815) 539-6507; Fax (815) 539-6025; mendotachamber@yahoo.com; www.mendotachamber.com.*

Metropolis · *Metropolis Area C/C, Tourism & Eco. Dev.* · Randy Rushing; Pres.; 607 Market St.; P.O. Box 188; 62960; Massac; P 7,200; M 225; (618) 524-2714; (800) 949-5740; Fax (618) 524-4780; metrochamber@frontier.com; www.metropolischamber.com

Mettawa · *see Lincolnshire*

Midlothian · *Midlothian Area C/C* · Len Feil; Exec. Dir.; P.O. Box 909; 60445; Cook; P 15,000; M 160; (708) 389-0020; Fax (708) 371-5981; midlochamber@yahoo.com; www.midlochamber.com

Milan · *see Moline*

Minooka · *Greater Channahon-Minooka Area C/C* · Mary Edmondson; Exec. Dir.; 500 Bob Blair Rd.; 60447; Grundy; P 22,000; M 200; (815) 521-9999; Fax (815) 521-0903; cmchamber@att.net; www.cmchamber.org

Mitchell · *see Granite City*

Mokena · *Mokena C/C* · Melissa Fedora; Exec. Dir.; 19820A Wolf Rd.; 60448; Will; P 16,000; M 375; (708) 479-2468; Fax (708) 479-7144; chamber@mokena.com; www.mokena.com

Moline · *Quad Cities C/C* · Tara Barney; CEO; 622 19th St.; 61265; Scott County, IA; Henry, Mercer & Rock Island, IL; P 375,000; M 2,000; (309) 757-5416; Fax (309) 757-5435; news@quadcitieschamber.com; www.quadcitieschamber.com*

Momence · *Momence C/C* · Jennifer Workman; Pres.; P.O. Box 34; 60954; Kankakee; P 7,800; M 100; (815) 472-4620; Fax (815) 472-6453; membership@momence.net; www.momence.net

Monee · *Monee Area C/C* · Mike Haller; Pres.; P.O. Box 177; 60449; Will; P 3,500; M 75; (708) 212-4133; Fax (708) 534-5320; info@moneechamber.org; www.moneechamber.org

Monmouth · *Monmouth Area C/C* · Angie McElwee; Exec. Dir.; 90 Public Sq.; P.O. Box 857; 61462; Warren; P 9,800; M 230; (309) 734-3181; Fax (309) 734-6595; macc@maplecity.com; www.monmouthilchamber.com*

Mont Clare · *see Elmwood Park*

Montgomery · *Greater Montgomery Area C/C* · Pat Nagel; Exec. Admin.; 200 Webster St.; 60538; Kane & Kendall; P 14,500; M 144; (630) 897-8137; Fax (630) 897-6747; gmacc@montgomery-illinois.org; www.chamberofmontgomeryil.org

Monticello · *Monticello C/C* · Sue Gortner; Exec. Dir.; P.O. Box 313; 61856; Piatt; P 5,150; M 180; (217) 762-7921; (800) 952-3396; info@monticellochamber.org; www.monticellochamber.org

Morris · *Grundy County C/C & Ind.* · Caroline Portlock; Exec. Dir.; 909 N. Liberty St.; 60450; Grundy; P 40,000; M 400; (815) 942-0113; Fax (815) 942-0117; info@grundychamber.com; www.grundychamber.com

Morrison · *Morrison C/C* · Admin.; 221 W. Main St.; P.O. Box 8; 61270; Whiteside; P 4,500; M 85; (815) 772-3757; Fax (815) 772-3757; morrisonchamber@frontiernet.net; www.morrisonchamber.com

Morton · *Morton C/C* · Jennifer Daly; Exec. Dir.; 415 W. Jefferson St.; 61550; Tazewell; P 16,000; M 320; (309) 263-2491; (888) 765-6588; Fax (309) 263-2401; jdaly@mortonillinois.org; www.mortonchamber.org*

Morton Grove · *Morton Grove C/C & Ind.* · Kathy Hancock; Exec. Dir.; 6101 Capulina Ave., Lower Level; 60053; Cook; P 23,000; M 255; (847) 965-0330; Fax (847) 965-0349; contact@mgcci.org; www.mgcci.org*

Mount Carmel · *Wabash County C/C* · Tanja Bingham; Exec. Dir.; 219 Market St., Ste. 1A; 62863; Wabash; P 12,570; M 140; (618) 262-5116; Fax (618) 262-7702; info@wabashcountychamber.com; www.wabashcountychamber.com.

Mount Carroll · *Mount Carroll C/C* · Nancy Tobin; P.O. Box 94; 61053; Carroll; P 1,800; M 90; (800) 244-9594; info@mtcarrollil.org; www.mtcarrollil.org

Mount Clare · *see Gillespie*

Mount Prospect · *Mount Prospect C/C* · James Uszler; Pres./CEO; 107 S. Main St.; 60056; Cook; P 58,000; M 300; (847) 398-6616; Fax (847) 398-6780; staff@mountprospect.com; www.mountprospectchamber.org*

Mount Vernon · *Jefferson County C/C* · Brandon Bullard; Exec. Dir.; 200 Potomac Blvd.; P.O. Box 1047; 62864; Jefferson; P 40,000; M 600; (618) 242-5725; Fax (618) 242-5130; chamberexec@mvn.net; www.southernillinois.com*

Mount Zion · *Mount Zion C/C* · Judy Kaiser; Admin.; P.O. Box 84; 62549; Macon; P 8,000; M 185; (217) 864-2526; Fax (217) 864-6115; AskJudy4@aol.com; www.mtzionchamber.org

Mundelein · *see Libertyville*

Murphysboro · *Murphysboro C/C* · Christopher Walls; Exec. Dir.; 203 S. 13th St.; P.O. Box 606; 62966; Jackson; P 60,000; M 300; (618) 684-6421; Fax (618) 684-2010; chamber@murphysboro.com; www.murphysboro.com

Naperville · *Naperville Area C/C* · John Schmitt; Pres./CEO; 55 S. Main St., Ste. 351; 60540; DuPage; P 150,000; M 2,000; (630) 355-4141; Fax (630) 355-8335; chamber@naperville.net; www.naperville.net

Nashville · *Nashville C/C* · Kerri Huge; Asst. Dir.; 138 N.E. Court St.; 62263; Washington; P 3,000; M 120; (618) 327-3700; Fax (618) 327-3700; nashvillechamber@sbcglobal.net; www.nashville-il.cc

Nauvoo · *Nauvoo C/C* · Durrel Nelson; Pres.; P.O. Box 41; 62354; Hancock; P 1,071; M 75; (217) 453-6648; info@nauvoochamber.org; www.nauvoochamber.org*

New Baden • *New Baden C/C* • Larry Wankel; Pres.; P.O. Box 22; 62265; Clinton; P 3,000; M 60; (618) 588-3813; www.newbaden chamber.com

New Lenox • *New Lenox C/C* • Debbera Hypke; CEO; 1 Veterans Pkwy., Ste. 104; P.O. Box 42; 60451; Will; P 28,000; M 400; (815) 485-4241; Fax (815) 485-5001; deb@newlenoxchamber.com; www.newlenoxchamber.com*

Newton • *Jasper County C/C* • Milissa Weber; Exec. Dir.; 207 1/2 E. Jourdan St.; P.O. Box 21; 62448; Jasper; P 10,000; M 200; (618) 783-3399; Fax (618) 783-4556; jasperchamber@psbnewton.com; www.newtonillinois.com.

Niles • *Niles C of C & Ind.* • Katie Schneider; Exec. Dir.; 8060 W. Oakton; 60714; Cook; P 30,000; M 478; (847) 268-8180; Fax (847) 268-8186; katie@nileschamber.com; www.nileschamber.com*

Normal • *see Bloomington*

North Aurora • *see Aurora*

North Chicago • *North Chicago C/C* • Marvin Bembry; Pres.; P.O. Box 554; 60064; Lake; P 40,000; M 100; (847) 785-1912; Fax (847) 785-0109; info@northchicagochamber.org; www.northchicago chamber.org

Northbrook • *Northbrook C/C & Ind.* • Tensley Garris; Pres.; 2002 Walters Ave.; 60062; Cook; P 34,400; M 675; (847) 498-5555; Fax (847) 498-5510; info@northbrookchamber.org; www.north brookchamber.org*

Northlake • *Northlake C/C* • Kevin McConkey; P.O. Box 2067; 60164; Cook, P 17,000; M 80; (708) 562-3110; www.northlakecity.com

Oak Brook • *Greater Oak Brook C/C* • Tracy Mulqueen; Pres./ CEO; 619 Enterprise Dr., Ste. 100; 60523; Cook & DuPage; P 8,700; M 400; (630) 472-9377; Fax (630) 954-1327; info@obchamber. com; www.obchamber.com

Oak Forest • *Oak Forest C/C* • Tamara Kostecki; Exec. Dir.; 15440 S. Central Ave.; 60452; Cook; P 31,000; M 200; (708) 687-4600; Fax (708) 687-7878; info@oakforestchamber.org; www.oakforest chamber.org

Oak Lawn • *Oak Lawn C/C* • Rita Olsen; Pres.; 5314 W. 95th St.; 60453; Cook; P 56,000; M 350; (708) 424-8300; Fax (708) 229-2236; office@oaklawnchamber.com; www.oaklawnchamber.com

Oak Park • *Oak Park-River Forest C/C* • Jim Doss; Exec. Dir.; 1110 North Blvd.; 60301; Cook; P 52,500; M 500; (708) 848-8151; Fax (708) 848-8182; info@oprfchamber.org; www.oprfchamber.org

Oakland • *Oakland C/C* • Lynn Mcqueen; Pres.; P.O. Box 283; 61943; Coles; P 1,000; M 40; (217) 346-2125; kpardi1@yahoo.com

Oblong • *Oblong C/C* • P.O. Box 122; 62449; Crawford; P 1,600; M 100; (618) 592-4355; Fax (618) 592-4224; info@theonlyoblong. com; www.theonlyoblong.com

O'Fallon • *O'Fallon-Shiloh C/C* • Debbie Arell-Martinez; Exec. Dir.; 116 E. First St.; P.O. Box 371; 62269; St. Clair; P 27,000; M 400; (618) 632-3377; Fax (618) 632-8162; chamber@ofallonchamber. com; www.ofallonchamber.com*

Okawville • *Okawville C/C* • Jackie Bening; P.O. Box 345; 62271; Washington; P 1,300; M 50; (618) 243-5694; tourokaw@htc.net; www.okawvillecc.com

Olney • *Olney & the Greater Richland County C/C* • Jessica Buckels; Exec. Dir.; 201 E. Chestnut; P.O. Box 575; 62450; Richland; P 16,000; M 200; (618) 392-2241; (888) 393-2241; Fax (618) 392-4179; info@olneychamber.com; www.olneychamber.com.

Oregon • *Oregon Area C/C* • Marcia Heuer; Exec. Dir.; 303 W. Washington; P.O. Box 69; 61061; Ogle; P 10,000; M 350; (815) 732-2100; (815) 631-0080; Fax (815) 732-2177; ococ@comcast. net; www.oregonil.com.*

Orland Park • *Orland Park Area C/C* • Keloryn Putnam IOM; Exec. Dir.; 8799 W. 151st St.; 60462; Cook; P 60,000; M 625; (708) 349-2972; Fax (708) 349-7454; info@orlandparkchamber.org; www.orlandparkchamber.org

Oswego • *Oswego C/C* • Steve Hatcher; Pres./CEO; 22 W. Van Buren St.; 60543; Kendall; P 32,000; M 392; (630) 554-3505; Fax (630) 554-0050; info@oswegochamber.org; www.oswegochamber.org*

Ottawa • *Ottawa Area C/C & Ind.* • Boyd Palmer; Exec. Dir.; 633 E. LaSalle St., Ste. 401; 61350; LaSalle; P 24,000; M 391; (815) 433-0084; Fax (815) 433-2405; info@ottawachamberillinois.com; www.ottawachamberillinois.com

Palatine • *Palatine Area C/C & Ind.* • Mindy Phillips; Dir.; 579 First Bank Dr., Ste. 205; 60067; Cook; P 70,000; M 450; (847) 359-7200; Fax (847) 359-7246; info@palatinechamber.com; www.palatinechamber.com*

Palestine • *Palestine C/C* • Ann Dickerson; Ofc. Mgr.; 103 S. Main St.; P.O. Box 155; 62451; Crawford; P 1,200; M 50; (618) 586-2222; Fax (618) 586-9477; palestinecofc@frontier.com; www.pioneercity.com

Palos Heights • *Palos Heights C/C* • Rob Tymm; Pres.; P.O. Box 138; 60463; Cook; P 21,000; M 200; (708) 923-2300; Fax (708) 361-9711; info@paloschamber.org; www.paloschamber.org

Palos Hills • *see Bridgeview-Hills C/C*

Pana • *Pana C/C* • Jim Deere; Secy./Treas.; 120 E. 3rd St.; 62557; Christian; P 7,100; M 130; (217) 562-4240; Fax (217) 562-3823; panail@consolidated.net; www.panachamber.com*

Paris • *Paris Area C/C & Tourism* • Brenda Buckley; Exec. Dir.; 105 N. Central Ave.; 61944; Edgar; P 9,000; M 370; (217) 465-4179; Fax (217) 465-4170; info@parisilchamber.com; www. parisilchamber.com.

Park Ridge • *Park Ridge C/C* • Gail Haller; Exec. Dir.; 720 Garden St.; 60068; Cook; P 38,000; M 425; (847) 825-3121; Fax (847) 825-3122; info@parkridgechamber.org; www.parkridgechamber.org*

Paxton • *Paxton Area C/C* • P.O. Box 75; 60957; Ford; P 4,600; M 145; (217) 379-4655

Pekin • *Pekin Area C/C* • Bill Fleming; Exec. Dir.; 402 Court St.; 61554; Tazewell; P 35,000; M 400; (309) 346-2106; Fax (309) 346-2104; chamber@pekin.net; www.pekin.net

Peoria • *Peoria Area C/C* • Roberta M. Parks; Pres.; 100 S.W. Water St.; 61602; Peoria; P 110,000; M 1,300; (309) 676-0755; Fax (309) 676-7534; chamber@mail.h-p.org; www.peoriachamber.org. *

Peoria Heights • *Peoria Heights C/C* • Mary Beth Nebel; Pres.; 1203 E. Kingman Ave.; P.O. Box 9783; 61612; Peoria; P 6,700; M 82; (309) 685-4812; Fax (309) 685-4812; office@peoriaheights chamber.com; www.peoriaheightschamber.com

Peotone • *Peotone C/C* • Bob Rademacher; Pres.; P.O. Box 877; 60468; Will; P 3,500; M 60; (708) 258-9450; peotone.chamber@ hotmail.com; www.peotonechamber.com

Petersburg • *Petersburg C/C* • Josh Gronewold; Pres.; 125 S. 7th St.; P.O. Box 452; 62675; Menard; P 2,300; M 80; (217) 632-7363; Fax (217) 632-7363; petersburgchamber@sbcglobal.net; www. petersburgilchamber.com

Pinckneyville • *Pinckneyville C/C* • Jill Fox; Exec. Dir.; 4 S. Walnut St.; P.O. Box 183; 62274; Perry; P 3,300; M 113; (618) 357-3243; Fax (618) 357-2688; pvillechamber.execdirector@ gmail.com; www.pinckneyville.com*

Pittsfield • *Pike County C/C* • Kaye Iftner; Exec. Dir.; 224 W. Washington; P.O. Box 283; 62363; Pike; P 18,000; M 200; (217) 285-2971; Fax (217) 285-5251; info@pikeil.org; www.pikeil.org.*

Plainfield · *Plainfield Area C/C* · Liz Collins; Pres./CEO; 24047 W. Lockport St., Ste. 109; 60544; Will; P 40,000; M 550; (815) 436-4431; Fax (815) 436-0520; pacc@plainfieldchamber.com; www.plainfieldchamber.com

Plano · *Plano Area C/C* · Rich Healy; Pres./CEO; 7050 Burroughs Ave.; 60545; Kendall; P 10,000; M 147; (630) 552-7272; Fax (630) 552-0165; director@planocommerce.org; www.planocommerce.org.*

Polo · *Polo C/C* · Chris Phelps; Pres.; 115 S. Franklin Ave.; 61064; Ogle; P 2,477; M 126; (815) 946-3131; Fax (815) 946-2004; estessecretarialservice@yahoo.com; www.poloil.org

Pontiac · *Pontiac Area C/C* · Cheri Lambert; Pres./CEO; 210 N. Plum St.; P.O. Box 534; 61764; P 12,000; M 250; (815) 844-5131; Fax (815) 844-2600; clambert@pontiacchamber.org; www.pontiacchamber.org.*

Pontoon Beach · *see Granite City*

Prairie View · *see Lincolnshire*

Princeton · *Princeton Area C/C & Main Street* · Kim Frey; Exec. Dir.; 435 S. Main St.; 61356; Bureau; P 8,000; M 300; (815) 875-2616; (877) 730-4306; Fax (815) 875-1156; kfrey@princeton-il.com; www.visitprinceton-il.com*

Quincy · *Quincy Area C/C* · Amy Looten; Exec. Dir.; 300 Civic Center Plz., Ste. 245; 62301; Adams; P 40,366; M 600; (217) 222-7980; Fax (217) 222-3033; qacc@quincychamber.org; www.quincychamber.org*

Rantoul · *Rantoul Area C/C* · Chris Kaler; Exec. Dir.; 601 S. Century Blvd., Ste. 1408; 61866; Champaign; P 15,000; M 360; (217) 893-3323; Fax (217) 893-3325; dir@rantoulchamber.com; www.rantoulchamber.com*

Red Bud · *Red Bud C/C* · P.O. Box 66; 62278; Randolph; P 3,500; M 218; (618) 282-3505; redbudchamber@gmail.com; www.redbudchamber.com

Richmond · *Richmond/Spring Grove C/C* · Loretta Podeszwa IOM; Exec. Dir.; 10906 Main St.; P.O. Box 475; 60071; McHenry; P 6,000; M 260; (815) 678-7742; Fax (815) 678-2070; info@rsgchamber.com; www.rsgchamber.com*

River Forest · *see Oak Park*

Riverdale · *Riverdale C/C* · John Strauss; Pres.; 208 W. 144th St.; 60827; Cook; P 15,055; M 85; (708) 841-3311; Fax (708) 841-1805; rdpl2@earthlink.net; www.district148.net/rcoc

Riverside · *Riverside C/C* · David Moravecek; Pres.; P.O. Box 7; 60546; Cook; P 15,000; M 75; (708) 447-8510; Business@RiversideChamberofCommerce.com; www.riversidechamberofcommerce.com

Riverwoods · *see Deerfield*

Robinson · *Robinson C/C* · Mary Kindt; Admin.; 113 S. Court St.; P.O. Box 737; 62454; Crawford; P 8,000; M 150; (618) 546-1557; Fax (618) 546-0182; robinsonchamber@hotmail.com; www.robinsonchamber.org

Rochelle · *Rochelle Area C/C & Bus. Dev.* · Peggy Friday; Exec. Dir.; 1221 Currency Ct., Ste. A; P.O. Box 220; 61068; Ogle; P 10,000; M 250; (815) 562-4189; Fax (815) 562-4180; swhitmer@hub-city.net; www.rochellechamber.org*

Rock Falls · *Rock Falls C/C* · Doug Wiersema; Pres./CEO; 601 W. 10th St.; 61071; Whiteside; P 9,600; M 400; (815) 625-4500; Fax (815) 625-4558; doug@rockfallschamber.com; www.rockfallschamber.com.*

Rock Island · *see Moline*

Rockford · *Rockford C/C* · Einar K. Forsman; Pres./CEO; 308 W. State St., Ste. 190; 61101; Winnebago; P 371,236; M 1,300; (815) 987-8100; Fax (815) 987-8122; info@rockfordchamber.com; www.rockfordchamber.com*

Rockton · *Rockton C/C* · 330 E. Main St., Ste. 700; 61072; Winnebago; P 7,440; M 130; (815) 624-7625; Fax (815) 624-7385; info@rocktonchamber.com; www.rocktonchamber.com

Rolling Meadows · *Rolling Meadows C/C* · Linda Liles Ballantine; Exec. Dir.; 60008; Cook; P 25,500; M 225; (847) 398-3730; Fax (847) 398-3745; office@rmchamber.org; www.rmchamber.org*

Romeoville · *Romeoville Area C/C* · Bridget Domberg; Exec. Dir.; 10 Montrose Dr.; 60446; Will; P 34,000; M 200; (815) 886-2076; Fax (815) 886-2096; info@romeovillechamber.org; www.romeovillechamber.org

Roscoe · *Roscoe Area C/C* · Cindy Ogden; Exec. Dir.; 5310 Williams Dr.; 61073; Winnebago; P 17,000; M 280; (815) 623-9065; Fax (815) 623-1755; info@roscoechamber.com; roscoechamber.com*

Roselle · *Roselle C/C & Ind.* · Gail Croson; Exec. Dir.; 1350 W. Lake St., Ste. A; 60172; DuPage; P 23,000; M 200; (630) 894-3010; Fax (630) 894-3042; executivedirector@rosellechamber.com; www.rosellechamber.com

Rosemont · *Rosemont C/C* · Pam Hogan; Exec. Dir.; 9501 W. Devon Ave., Ste. 700; 60018; Cook; P 4,200; M 226; (847) 698-1190; Fax (847) 698-1195; info@rosemontchamber.com; www.rosemontchamber.com

Roseville · *Roseville Area C/C* · Ethel Logue; Pres.; P.O. Box 54; 61473; Warren; P 1,100; M 60; (309) 426-2193

Round Lake Beach · *Round Lake Area C/C & Ind.* · Shanna Coakley; Exec. Dir.; 2007 Civic Center Way; 60073; Lake; P 42,000; M 200; (847) 546-2002; Fax (847) 546-2254; info@rlchamber.org; www.rlchamber.org

Roxanna · *see Godfrey*

Rushville · *Rushville Area C/C* · Carolyn Wright; P.O. Box 171; 62681; Schuyler; P 3,300; M 70; (217) 322-3689; www.schuylercountyillinois.com

Saint Charles · *St. Charles C/C* · Lori Hewitt; Pres./CEO; 3755 E. Main St., Ste. 140; 60174; DuPage & Kane; P 45,000; M 750; (630) 584-8384; Fax (630) 584-6065; info@stcharleschamber.com; www.stcharleschamber.com*

Salem · *Greater Salem C/C* · Art Carnahan; Exec. Dir.; 615 W. Main St.; 62881; Marion; P 7,800; M 280; (618) 548-3010; Fax (618) 548-3014; visitus@salemilchamber.com; www.salemilchamber.com

Sandwich · *Sandwich C/C* · John Lux; Exec. Dir.; 128 E. Railroad St.; P.O. Box 214; 60548; DeKalb; P 6,600; M 145; (815) 786-9075; Fax (815) 786-2505; info@sandwich-il.org; www.sandwich-il.org*

Savanna · *Savanna C/C* · Pam Brown; Exec. Dir.; 313 Main St.; P.O. Box 315; 61074; Carroll; P 3,300; M 100; (815) 273-2722; Fax (815) 273-2754; savchamber@grics.net; www.savanna-il.com

Sawyerville · *see Gillespie*

Schaumburg · *Schaumburg Bus. Assn.* · Laurie Stone; Pres.; 1501 E. Woodfield Rd., Ste. 115N; 60173; Cook; P 73,000; M 700; (847) 413-1010; Fax (847) 413-1414; lgoldberg@schaumburgbusiness.com; www.schaumburgbusiness.com

Schiller Park · *see Franklin Park*

Seneca · *see Marseilles*

Sesser · *Sesser Area C/C* · P.O. Box 367; 62884; Franklin; P 2,400; M 35; (618) 625-5566; Fax (618) 625-6291; sesser@dtnspeed.net; www.sesser.org

Shelbyville · *Greater Shelbyville C/C* · Angela Binnion; Ofc. Mgr.; 124 N. Morgan; 62565; Shelby; P 5,000; M 150; (217) 774-2221; Fax (217) 774-2243; chamber01@consolidated.net; www.shelbyvillechamberofcommerce.com

Shorewood · *Shorewood Area C/C* · Jennifer Dylik; Pres.; One Towne Center Blvd., Ste. 103; 60404; Will; P 15,000; M 205; (815) 725-2900; Fax (815) 725-3573; sacc@shorewoodchamber.com; www.shorewoodchamber.com*

Silvis · *see Moline*

Skokie · *Skokie C/C* · Howard Meyer; Exec. Dir.; 5002 Oakton St.; P.O. Box 106; 60077; Cook; P 66,000; M 600; (847) 673-0240; Fax (847) 673-0249; info@skokiechamber.org; www.skokiechamber.org*

Sleepy Hollow · *see Carpentersville*

South Holland · *South Holland Business Assn.* · Blevian Moore; Exec. Dir.; P.O. Box 334; 60473; Cook; P 24,000; M 320; (708) 596-0065; Fax (708) 596-6696; info@shba.org; www.shba.org

South Roxanna · *see Godfrey*

Sparta · *Sparta Area C/C* · Michael Hayes; Pres.; 132 W. Broadway; P.O. Box 93; 62286; Randolph; P 5,000; M 100; (618) 317-7222; spartacc@spartailchamber.com; www.spartailchamber.com

Spring Grove · *see Richmond*

Springfield · *Greater Springfield C/C* · Gary Plummer; Pres./CEO; 1011 S. 2nd St.; 62704; Sangamon; P 194,925; M 1,610; (217) 525-1173; Fax (217) 525-8768; info@gscc.org; www.gscc.org*

Springfield · *Illinois Assn. of C/C Execs.* · Michael Ayers; Pres.; 215 E. Adams St.; 62701; Sangamon; P 11,500,000; M 200; (217) 522-5512; Fax (217) 522-5518; mayers@ilchamber.org; www.iacce.org

Staunton · *Staunton C/C* · P.O. Box 248; 62088; Macoupin; P 5,100; M 55; (618) 635-8356; Fax (618) 635-3644; chamber@stauntonil.com; www.stauntonil.com

Steeleville · *Steeleville C/C* · P.O. Box 177; 62288; Randolph; P 2,077; M 50; (618) 965-3134; www.steeleville.org

Sterling · *Sauk Valley Area C/C* · Kimberly Ewoldsen; Exec. Dir.; 211 Locust St.; 61081; Whiteside; P 16,000; M 400; (815) 625-2400; Fax (815) 625-9361; chamber@essex1.com; www.saukvalleyareachamber.com*

Stockton · *Stockton C/C* · Amy Laskye; Secy.; P.O. Box 3; 61085; Jo Daviess; P 2,000; M 145; (815) 947-2878; Fax (815) 947-2878; info@stocktonil.com; www.stocktonil.com

Streamwood · *Streamwood C/C* · Ann Townsend; Exec. Secy.; 22 W. Streamwood Blvd.; 60107; Cook; P 39,217; M 130; (630) 837-5200; Fax (630) 837-5251; staff@streamwoodchamber.com; www.streamwoodchamber.com

Streator · *Streator Area C/C* · Jack Dzuris; Exec. Dir.; 320 E. Main; P.O. Box 360; 61364; LaSalle; P 25,000; M 250; (815) 672-2921; Fax (815) 672-1768; sacci@mchsi.com; www.streatorchamber.com

Sugar Grove · *Sugar Grove C/C & Ind.* · Shari Baum; Exec. Dir.; 330 Division Dr., Ste. A; P.O. Box 765; 60554; Kane; P 9,000; M 152; (630) 466-7895; Fax (630) 466-7825; www.sugargrovechamber.org

Sullivan · *Sullivan C/C & EDC* · Stepheny McMahon; Exec. Dir.; 112 W. Harrison St.; 61951; Moultrie; P 4,600; M 225; (217) 728-4223; Fax (217) 728-4064; info@sullivanchamber.com; www.sullivanchamber.com

Swansea · *Swansea C/C* · Tom Tyler; Exec. Dir.; 1400 N. Illinois St.; 62226; St. Clair; P 11,341; M 175; (618) 233-3938; Fax (618) 234-0222; swansea@swanseachamber.org; www.swanseachamber.org*

Sycamore · *Sycamore C/C* · Rosemarie M. Treml; Exec. Dir.; 407 W. State St., Ste. 10; 60178; DeKalb; P 14,000; M 450; (815) 895-3456; Fax (815) 895-0125; info@sycamorechamber.com; www.sycamorechamber.com

Taylorville · *Greater Taylorville C/C* · Fred Ronnow; Pres./CEO; 108 W. Market St., 2nd Flr.; 62568; Christian; P 35,372; M 296; (217) 824-4919; Fax (217) 824-6689; fredgtcc@consolidated.net; www.taylorvillechamber.com*

Tinley Park · *Tinley Park C/C* · Kim Scalise; Pres.; 17316 S. Oak Park Ave.; 60477; Cook; P 56,000; M 500; (708) 532-5700; Fax (708) 532-1475; info@tinleychamber.org; www.tinleychamber.org

Trenton · *Trenton C/C* · James Rakers; Pres.; P.O. Box 37; 62293; Clinton; P 2,610; M 86; (618) 224-9329; www.trenton-ilchamber.com

Troy · *Troy/Maryville/St. Jacob Area C/C* · Dawn Mushill; Exec. Dir.; 647 E. U.S. Hwy. 40; 62294; Madison; P 10,000; M 400; (618) 667-8769; (888) 667-8769; Fax (618) 667-8759; info@troymaryvillecoc.com; www.troymaryvillecoc.com*

Tuscola · *Tuscola C/C* · Kara Kinney; Pres.; P.O. Box 434; 61953; Douglas; P 6,000; M 150; (217) 253-5013; www.tuscola.org

Vandalia · *Vandalia C/C* · Kay Wasser; Admin. Secy.; 1408 N. 5th St.; P.O. Box 238; 62471; Fayette; P 6,975; M 140; (618) 283-2728; Fax (618) 283-4439; www.vandaliachamber.org*

Venice · *see Granite City*

Vernon Hills · *see Libertyville*

Vienna · *Johnson County C/C* · Lonnie Hinton; Pres.; 298 E. Vine St.; 62995; Johnson; P 17,000; M 130; (618) 658-2063; Fax (618) 658-2063; jo.co.chamber@juno.com

Villa Park · *Villa Park C/C* · Alesia Bailey; Exec. Dir.; 10 W. Park Blvd.; 60181; DuPage; P 22,500; M 205; (630) 941-9133; Fax (630) 941-9134; info@villaparkchamber.org; www.villaparkchamber.org

Viola · *Viola C/C* · Jim Morrison; Pres.; P.O. Box 403; 61486; Mercer; P 950; M 21; (309) 596-2434; www.villageofviola.org

Virden · *Virden Area Assn. of Comm.* · P.O. Box 252; 62690; Wabash; P 3,400; M 45; (217) 965-5805

Walnut · *Walnut C/C* · 105 N. Main St.; P.O. Box 56; 61376; Bureau; P 1,500; M 140; (815) 379-2141; Fax (815) 379-9375; director@villageofwalnut.com; www.villageofwalnut.com

Warrenville · *Warrenville C/C* · Patricia Haskins; Pres./CEO; 3 S. 240 Warren Ave.; P.O. Box 432; 60555; DuPage; P 14,000; M 170; (630) 393-9080; Fax (630) 393-9171; info@warrenvillechamber.com; www.warrenvillechamber.com

Washington · *Washington C/C* · Carol Hamilton; Dir.; 114 Washington Sq.; 61571; Tazewell; P 13,500; M 270; (309) 444-9921; Fax (309) 444-9225; wcoc@mtco.com; www.washingtoncoc.com

Waterloo · *Waterloo C/C* · Debbie Ruggeri; Exec. Dir.; 118 E. 3rd St.; P.O. Box 1; 62298; Monroe; P 13,000; M 250; (618) 939-5300; Fax (618) 939-1805; chamber@htc.net; www.enjoywaterloo.com

Watseka · *Watseka Area C/C* · Kendra Martin; Exec. Dir.; 110 S. 3rd St.; 60970; Iroquois; P 5,500; M 150; (815) 432-2416; Fax (815) 432-2762; wacc@att.net; www.watsekachamber.org.

Wauconda · *Wauconda Area C/C* · Sandy Hartogh; Exec. Dir.; 100 N. Main St.; 60084; Lake; P 13,000; M 330; (847) 526-5580; Fax (847) 526-3059; info@waucondachamber.org; www.waucondaareachamber.org

Waukegan · *see Gurnee*

West Chicago · *West Chicago C/C & Ind.* · David Sabathne; Pres./CEO; 306 Main St.; 60185; DuPage; P 25,000; M 300; (630) 231-3003; Fax (630) 231-3009; info@westchicagochamber.com; www.westchicagochamber.com

West Dundee · *see Carpentersville*

West Frankfort · *West Frankfort C/C* · Larry Wall; Pres.; 201 E. Nolen St.; 62896; West Frankfort; P 8,526; M 150; (618) 932-2181; Fax (618) 932-6330; wfchamber@frontier.com; www.westfrankfort-il.com

Westchester · *Westchester C/C* · Marianne Bero; Pres.; P.O. Box 7309; 60154; Cook; P 17,301; M 140; (708) 240-8400; Fax (708) 240-8400; mame1234@comcast.net; www.westchesterchamber.org

Western Springs · *see LaGrange*

Westmont · *Westmont C/C & Tourism Bur.* · Larry Forssberg; Exec. Dir.; 1 S. Cass Ave., Ste. 101; 60559; DuPage; P 25,000; M 300; (630) 960-5553; Fax (630) 960-5554; wcctb@westmontchamber.com; www.westmontchamber.com

Wheaton · *Wheaton C/C* · Kerry O'Brien; Member Rel. Mgr.; 108 E. Wesley St.; 60187; DuPage; P 55,000; M 425; (630) 668-6464; Fax (630) 668-2744; info@wheatonchamber.com; www.wheatonchamber.com

Wheeling · *Wheeling-Prospect Heights Area C/C & Ind.* · Catherine Powers; Exec. Dir.; 2 Community Blvd., Ste. 203; 60090; Cook; P 45,000; M 300; (847) 541-0170; Fax (847) 541-0296; info@wphchamber.com; wphchamber.com

Wicker Park · *see Chicago-Wicker Park and Bucktown C/C*

Willow Springs · *see LaGrange*

Willowbrook · *see Burr Ridge*

Wilmette · *Wilmette C/C* · Nada Becker; Exec. Dir.; 1150 Wilmette Ave., Ste. A; 60091; Cook; P 28,000; M 430; (847) 251-3800; Fax (847) 251-6321; info@wilmettechamber.org; www.wilmettechamber.org

Wilmington · *Wilmington C/C* · Eric Fisher; Pres.; 111 S. Water St.; P.O. Box 724; 60481; Will; P 5,100; M 80; (815) 476-5991; (815) 476-7966; Fax (815) 476-7002; www.wilmingtonchamberofcommerce.org

Wilsonville · *see Gillespie*

Winchester · *Winchester C/C* · Andy Moss; Pres.; P.O. Box 201; 62694; Scott; P 1,700; M 83; (217) 742-3219

Winfield · *Winfield C/C* · Rich Bysina; Exec. Dir.; 125 S. Church St.; 60190; DuPage; P 9,000; M 180; (630) 682-3712; (630) 408-3712; Fax (630) 682-3726; winfieldchamber@sbcglobal.net; www.winfieldchamber.biz

Winnetka · *Winnetka C/C* · Teresa Dason; Exec. Dir.; 841 Spruce St., Ste. 204; 60093; Cook; P 12,500; M 250; (847) 446-4451; Fax (847) 446-4452; wcc@winnetkachamber.com; www.winnetkachamber.com

Winthrop Harbor · *Winthrop Harbor C/C* · Sherry Reffell; Pres.; 830 Sheridan Rd.; P.O. Box 347; 60096; Lake; P 10,000; M 37; www.cocwh.com

Wonder Lake · *Wonder Lake C/C* · Donna Sullivan; Exec. Dir.; 7602 Hancock Dr.; 60097; McHenry; P 15,000; M 120; (815) 728-0682; Fax (815) 653-6762; chamber@wonderlake.org; www.wonderlake.org

Wood Dale · *also see Elk Grove Village*

Wood Dale · *Wood Dale C/C* · George Ellefsen; Pres.; P.O. Box 353; 60191; DuPage; P 14,000; M 150; (630) 595-0505; Fax (630) 595-0677; info@wooddalechamber.com; www.wooddalechamber.com

Wood River · *see Godfrey*

Woodridge · *Woodridge Area C/C* · Amy Melinder; Pres./CEO; 6440 Main St., Ste. 330; 60517; Cook, DuPage & Will; P 35,000; M 250; (630) 960-7080; Fax (630) 852-2316; chamber@woodridgechamber.org; www.woodridgechamber.org*

Woodstock · *Woodstock C/C & Ind.* · Shari Gray; Interim Exec. Dir.; 136 Cass St.; 60098; McHenry; P 22,500; M 300; (815) 338-2436; chamber@woodstockilchamber.com; www.woodstockilchamber.com

Worth · *Chicago Ridge-Worth C/C* · Bill Ritter; P.O. Box 356; 60482; Cook; P 25,000; M 50; (708) 923-2050; (708) 448-1181; Fax (708) 930-0090; crwc@crwchamber.com; www.crwchamber.com

Wyoming · *Wyoming C/C* · Dan Shockey; Pres.; P.O. Box 157; 61491; Stark; P 1,424; M 40; (309) 695-2900; Fax (309) 286-5555

Yorkville · *Yorkville Area C/C* · Sherri Farley; Exec. Dir.; 26 W. Countryside Pkwy.; 60560; Kendall; P 11,600; M 300; (630) 553-6853; Fax (630) 553-0702; sherri@yorkvillechamber.org; www.yorkvillechamber.org*

Zion · *Zion Area C/C* · Renee Hill; Ofc. Admin.; 2730 Sheridan Rd., Ste. 1; 60099; Lake; P 22,000; M 160; (847) 872-5405; Fax (847) 872-9309; info@zionchamber.com; www.zionchamber.com

Indiana

Indiana C of C · Kevin Brinegar; Pres.; 115 W. Washington St., Ste. 850S; Indianapolis; 46204; Marion; P 6,300,000; M 4,800; (317) 264-3110; Fax (317) 264-6855; inchamber@indianachamber.com; www.indianachamber.com.

Akron · *Akron C/C* · Royce Wright; Pres.; P.O. Box 248; 46910; Fulton; P 1,100; M 35; (574) 505-0881; Fax (574) 893-7339; www.akronin.com

Albion · *Albion C/C* · Phyllis Herendeen; Pres.; P.O. Box 63; 46701; Noble; P 2,284; M 120; (260) 636-2748; chamber@albionin.org; www.albionin.org

Alexandria · *Alexandria-Monroe C/C* · John Dockrey; Exec. Dir.; 125 N. Wayne St.; 46001; Madison; P 6,000; M 130; (765) 724-3144; Fax (765) 683-3504; info@alexandriachamber.com; www.alexandriachamber.com

Anderson · *Madison County C/C* · Kyle L. Morey; Pres./CEO; 2701 Enterprise Dr., Ste. 109; 46013; Madison; P 59,000; M 600; (765) 642-0264; (765) 642-0265; Fax (765) 642-0266; kyle@getlinkedmadison.com; www.getlinkedmadison.com*

Angola · *Angola Area C/C* · Jack Bercaw; Exec. Dir.; 211 E. Maumee, Ste. B; 46703; Steuben; P 7,500; M 409; (260) 665-3512; Fax (260) 665-7418; info@angolachamber.org; www.angolachamber.org*

Arcadia · *see Cicero*

Ashley · *Ashley-Hudson Area C/C* · Sherri Hoffman; P.O. Box 99; 46705; DeKalb & Steuben; P 1,500; M 60; (260) 587-3300

Atlanta · *see Cicero*

Auburn · *Dekalb Chamber Partnership* · Kelly Knox; Exec. Dir.; 208 S. Jackson St.; P.O. Box 168; 46706; DeKalb; P 46,000; M 325; (260) 925-2100; Fax (260) 925-2199; info@chamberinauburn.com; www.chamberinauburn.com.*

Aurora · *see Lawrenceburg*

Avon · *Greater Avon C/C* · Tom Downard; Exec. Dir.; 8244 E. Hwy. 36, Ste. 140; 46123; Hendricks; P 12,000; M 220; (317) 272-4333; Fax (317) 272-7217; info@avonchamber.org; www.avonchamber.org

Batesville • *Batesville Area C/C* • Melissa Tucker; Exec. Dir.; 16 E. George St.; 47006; Ripley; P 28,324; M 280; (812) 934-3101; Fax (812) 932-0202; chamberexec@batesvillein.com; www.batesvillein.com

Bedford • *Bedford Area C/C* • Adele Bowden-Purlee; Pres.; 1116 16th St.; 47421; Lawrence; P 15,000; M 500; (812) 275-4493; Fax (812) 279-5998; bedford@bedfordchamber.com; www.bedford chamber.com

Berne • *Berne C/C* • Sheree Barkley; Exec. Dir.; 205 E. Main St.; 46711; Adams; P 4,500; M 225; (260) 589-8080; Fax (260) 589-8384; chamber@bernein.com; www.bernein.com

Beverly Shores • *see Chesterton*

Bloomfield • *Bloomfield C/C* • Matt Miller; Pres.; P.O. Box 144; 47424; Greene; P 2,300; M 110; (812) 384-8995; www.bloom fieldcoc.com

Bloomington • *Greater Bloomington C/C* • Christy Gillenwater; Pres./CEO; 400 W. 7th St., Ste. 102; P.O. Box 1302; 47402; Monroe; P 183,000; M 1,000; (812) 336-6381; Fax (812) 336-0651; info@ chamberbloomington.org; www.chamberbloomington.org.*

Bluffton • *Wells County C/C* • Suzanne Huffman; Dir.; 211 W. Water St.; 46714; Wells; P 26,800; M 251; (260) 824-0510; Fax (260) 824-5871; shuffman@wellscoc.com; www.wellscoc.com*

Boonville • *Warrick County C/C* • Shari Sherman; Exec. Dir.; 224 W. Main St., Ste. 203; P.O. Box 377; 47601; Warrick; P 56,000; M 250; (812) 897-2340; Fax (812) 897-2360; ssherman@warrick county.us; www.warrickcounty.us*

Brazil • *Clay County C/C* • Tiffany Cook; Secy.; 535 E. National Ave.; P.O. Box 23; 47834; Clay; P 26,492; M 125; (812) 448-8457; Fax (812) 448-9957; info@claycountychamber.org; www.clay countychamber.org

Bremen • *Bremen C/C* • Larry Balsley; Coord.; 104 W. Plymouth St.; P.O. Box 125; 46506; Marshall; P 5,000; M 100; (574) 546-2044; Fax (574) 546-5487; info@bremenchamberofcommerce. com; www.bremenchamberofcommerce.com

Brookville • *Brookville/Franklin County C/C* • Lois Clark; Exec. Dir.; 444 Main St.; P.O. Box 211; 47012; Franklin; P 20,000; M 250; (765) 647-3177; Fax (765) 647-4150; lois@fcchamber.net; www. fcchamber.net

Brownsburg • *Greater Brownsburg C/C* • Brian Rose; Exec. Dir.; 61 N. Green; P.O. Box 82; 46112; Hendricks; P 20,000; M 310; (317) 852-7885; Fax (317) 852-8688; chamber@brownsburg.com; www. brownsburg.com

Brownstown • *Brownstown C/C* • Janet Peters; Secy./Ofc. Mgr.; 119 W. Walnut St.; P.O. Box 334; 47220; Jackson; P 4,000; M 100; (812) 358-2930; Fax (812) 358-9321; secretary@brownstown chamber.org; www.brownstownchamber.org

Burns Harbor • *see Chesterton*

Butler • *see Auburn*

Carmel • *Carmel C/C* • Maureen Merhoff; Pres.; 37 E. Main, Ste. 300; 46032; Hamilton; P 68,000; M 700; (317) 846-1049; Fax (317) 844-6843; chamberinfo@carmelchamber.com; www.carmel chamber.com*

Cedar Lake • *Cedar Lake C/C* • Diane Jostes; Exec. Dir.; 7925 Lake Shore Dr.; P.O. Box 101; 46303; Lake; P 12,500; M 145; (219) 374-6157; Fax (219) 374-6157; cl-chamber@sbcglobal.net; www.cedarlakechamber.com*

Chesterton • *Chesterton/Duneland C/C* • Heather Ennis; Exec. Dir.; 220 Broadway; 46304; Porter; P 25,000; M 365; (219) 926-5513; Fax (219) 926-7593; hennis@chestertonchamber.org; www. chestertonchamber.org*

Chrisney • *see Rockport*

Churubusco • *Churubusco C/C* • Dee Dee McCoy; Dir.; P.O. Box 83; 46723; Whitley; P 2,200; M 70; (260) 693-9810; Fax (260) 693-3536; www.churubuscochamber.org

Cicero • *Hamilton North C/C* • Jane Hunter; Exec. Dir.; 70 N. Byron St.; P.O. Box 466; 46034; Hamilton; P 4,700; M 160; (317) 984-4079; Fax (317) 984-4079; jane@hamiltonnorthchamber. com; www.hamiltonnorthchamber.com

Clay County • *see Brazil*

Clinton • *Greater Clinton C/C* • P.O. Box 7; 47842; Vermillion; P 16,893; M 131; (765) 832-3844; vermillionchamber@sbcglobal. net; www.greaterclintonchamber.org

Columbia City • *Whitley County C/C* • Sara Lochner-Goff; Pres.; 201 N. Line St.; P.O. Box 166; 46725; Whitley; P 30,000; M 255; (260) 248-8131; Fax (260) 248-8162; office@whitleychamber. com; www.whitleychamber.com*

Columbus • *Columbus Area C/C* • Jack Hess; Pres.; 500 Franklin St.; 47201; Bartholomew; P 69,000; M 700; (812) 379-4457; Fax (812) 378-7308; info@columbusareachamber.com; www. columbusareachamber.com

Connersville • *Connersville/Fayette County C/C* • Katrina Griffin; Exec. Dir.; 504 Central Ave.; 47331; Fayette; P 25,500; M 250; (765) 825-2561; Fax (765) 825-4613; katrina@conners villechamber.com; www.connersvillechamber.com*

Corydon • *C/C of Harrison County* • Lisa M. Long; Pres.; 310 N. Elm St.; 47112; Harrison; P 37,000; M 400; (812) 738-2137; Fax (812) 738-6438; llong@harrisonchamber.org; www.harrison chamber.org.*

Crawfordsville • *Crawfordsville-Montgomery County C/C* • S. David Long; Exec. V.P.; 309 N. Green St.; 47933; Montgomery; P 37,000; M 300; (765) 362-6800; Fax (765) 362-6900; candy. chamber@comcast.net; www.crawfordsvillechamber.com.*

Crown Point • *Crossroads Reg. C/C* • Sue Reed; Exec. Dir.; Old Court House Sq., Ste. 206; P.O. Box 343; 46308; Lake; P 24,000; M 700; (219) 663-1800; Fax (219) 663-1989; geninq@crossroads chamber.org; www.crossroadschamber.org*

Culver • *Culver C/C* • Bobbie Ruhnow; Exec. Secy.; P.O. Box 129; 46511; Marshall; P 1,583; M 91; (574) 842-5253; (888) 252-5253; Fax (574) 842-5253; rruhnow@marshallremc.coop; www.culver chamber.com

Dale • *see Rockport*

Danville • *Greater Danville C/C* • Dorothy Hurst; Admin. Asst.; 49 N. Wayne St.; P.O. Box 273; 46122; Hendricks; P 7,500; M 150; (317) 745-0670; Fax (317) 745-0682; dorothy@danville-chamber. org; www.danville-chamber.org

Decatur • *Decatur C/C* • 125 E. Monroe St.; 46733; Decatur; P 10,000; M 240; (260) 724-2604; Fax (260) 724-3104; info@ decaturchamber.org; www.decaturchamber.org.

Delphi • *Delphi C/C* • Randy Myers; Pres.; P.O. Box 178; 46923; Carroll; P 4,300; M 71; (765) 564-3034; info@delphichamber.org; www.delphichamber.org

DeMotte • *DeMotte C/C* • Bob Jonkman; Pres.; P.O. Box 721; 46310; Jasper; P 4,200; M 155; (219) 987-5800; Fax (219) 987-5800; info@demottechamber.org; www.demottechamber.org

Dillsboro • *see Lawrenceburg*

Dune Acres • *see Chesterton*

Dunkirk • *see Portland*

Dyer • *Dyer C/C* • Judy Hein; Pres.; P.O. Box 84; 46311; Lake; P 15,000; M 125; (219) 865-1045; Fax (219) 865-4233; chamber@ dyerchamberofcommerce.com; www.dyerchamberofcommerce.com

East Chicago · *see Hammond*

Edinburgh · *Edinburgh C/C* · Brad Peter; Chrmn.; P.O. Box 65; 46124; Bartholomew, Johnson & Shelby; P 5,000; M 67; (812) 526-3513; Fax (812) 526-3542; www.edinburgh.in.us

Elkhart · *Greater Elkhart C/C* · Philip Penn; Pres./CEO; 418 S. Main St.; P.O. Box 428; 46515; Elkhart; P 150,000; M 1,200; (574) 293-1531; Fax (574) 294-1859; info@elkhart.org; www.elkhart.org*

Elwood · *Elwood C/C* · Sherry Eubanks; Exec. Dir.; 108 S. Anderson St.; 46036; Madison & Tipton; P 9,000; M 150; (765) 552-0180; Fax (765) 552-1277; elwoodchamber@sbcglobal.net; www.elwoodchamber.org

Evansville · *C of C of Southwest Indiana* · Matt Meadors; Pres./CEO; 318 Main St., Ste. 401; 47708; Vanderburgh; P 300,000; M 1,800; (812) 425-8147; Fax (812) 421-5883; chamberinfo@ccswin.com; www.ccswin.com*

Ferdinand · *Ferdinand C/C* · Pat Miller; Pres.; P.O. Box 101; 47532; Dubois; P 2,500; M 200; (812) 367-0550; Fax (812) 367-1303; www.ferdinandindiana.org

Fishers · *Fishers C/C* · Dan Canan; Pres.; 11601 Municipal Dr.; P.O. Box 353; 46038; Hamilton; P 70,000; M 730; (317) 578-0700; Fax (317) 578-1097; info@fisherschamber.com; www.fishers chamber.com*

Fort Wayne · *Greater Fort Wayne C/C* · Mike Landram; Pres./CEO; 826 Ewing St.; 46802; Allen; P 360,000; M 1,650; (260) 424-1435; Fax (260) 426-7232; mcallicoat@fwchamber.org; www.fwchamber.org.*

Fowler · *Fowler C/C* · Mike Brewer; Pres.; P.O. Box 293; 47944; Benton; P 2,600; M 70; www.townoffowler.com

Francesville · *see Winamac*

Frankfort · *Clinton County C/C* · Kevin Smith; CEO; 259 E. Walnut St.; 46041; Clinton; P 36,000; M 300; (765) 654-5507; Fax (765) 654-9592; shan@ccinchamber.org; www.ccinchamber.org*

Franklin · *Franklin C/C* · Tricia E. Bechman; Exec. Dir.; 370 E. Jefferson St.; 46131; Johnson; P 22,500; M 380; (317) 736-6334; Fax (317) 736-9553; franklincoc@franklincoc.org; www.franklin coc.org*

Fremont · *Fremont Area C/C* · Linda Fulton; Pres.; P.O. Box 462; 46737; Steuben; P 1,700; M 65; (260) 495-9010; www.fremont chamber.org

French Lick · *French Lick-West Baden C/C* · Alan Barnett; Exec. Secy.; 1 Monon St.; P.O. Box 347; 47432; Orange; P 3,000; M 100; (812) 936-2405; Fax (812) 936-2904; flwbchamber@psci.net; www.flwbcc.com

Garrett · *Garrett C/C* · Amy Demske; Exec. Dir.; 111 W. Keyser St.; 46738; Dekalb; P 5,800; M 135; (260) 357-4600; Fax (260) 357-4600; garrettcoc@gmail.com; .

Gary · *Gary C/C* · Charles Hughes; Exec. Dir.; 839 Broadway, Ste. S103; 46402; Lake; P 102,000; M 400; (219) 885-7407; Fax (219) 885-7408; info@garychamber.com; www.garychamber.com*

Gas City · *Gas City Area C/C* · Dawn Brown; Pres.; 316 E. Main St.; 46933; Grant; P 6,296; M 255; (765) 674-7545; Fax (765) 674-1152; gascitychamber@indy.rr.com; www.gascity.com*

Gentryville · *see Rockport*

Goshen · *Goshen C/C* · David B. Daugherty; Pres.; 232 S. Main St.; 46526; Elkhart; P 31,000; M 577; (574) 533-2102; (800) 307-4204; Fax (574) 533-2103; goshenchamber@goshen.org; www.goshen.org*

Grabill · *Grabill C/C* · Susie Witt; 13717 First St.; Grabill Town Hall; 46741; Allen; P 1,113; M 62; (260) 627-5227; Fax (260) 627-0550; wittgrabill@yahoo.com; www.grabillchamberof commerce.org

Grandview · *see Rockport*

Greencastle · *Greater Greencastle C/C* · Tammy Amor; Exec. Dir.; 16 S. Jackson St.; 46135; Putnam; P 36,000; M 310; (765) 653-4517; Fax (765) 848-1015; gchamber@gogreencastle.com; www.gogreencastle.com

Greendale · *see Lawrenceburg*

Greenfield · *Greenfield Area C/C* · Retta Livengood; Pres.; One Courthouse Plaza; 46140; Hancock; P 18,000; M 380; (317) 477-4188; Fax (317) 477-4189; info@greenfieldcc.org; www.greenfieldcc.org*

Greensburg · *Greensburg/Decatur County C/C* · Jeff Emsweller; Exec. Dir.; 125 N. Broadway; 47240; Decatur; P 26,000; M 400; (812) 663-2832; Fax (812) 663-4275; info@greensburg chamber.com; www.greensburgchamber.com

Greenwood · *Greater Greenwood C/C* · Christian Maslowski; Exec. Dir.; 65 Airport Pkwy., Ste. 140; 46143; Johnson; P 200,000; M 650; (317) 888-4856; Fax (317) 865-2609; karen@greenwood-chamber.com; www.greenwood-chamber.com*

Griffith · *Griffith C/C* · Kathleen Reed; Pres.; P.O. Box 204; 46319; Lake; P 17,914; M 75; (219) 838-2661; Fax (219) 838-2401; griffithchamber1@hotmail.com; www.griffithchamberofcom merce.com

Hamilton · *Hamilton C/C* · Mary Vail; Pres.; P.O. Box 66; 46742; Steuben; P 1,600; M 115; (260) 488-3607; www.hamiltonindiana.org

Hammond · *Lakeshore C/C* · Dave Ryan; Exec. Dir.; 5246 Hohman Ave.. Ste. 100; 46320; Lake; P 103,000; M 470; (219) 931-1000; Fax (219) 937-8778; info@lakeshorechamber.com; www.lakeshorechamber.com*

Harrison County · *see Corydon*

Hartford City · *Hartford City C/C* · Susan Gerard; Exec. Asst.; 121 N. High St.; P.O. Box 286; 47348; Blackford; P 6,000; M 100; (765) 348-1905; Fax (765) 348-4945; sgerard@blackfordcoedc.org; www.blackfordcounty.org

Hebron · *Hebron C/C* · Donna Paulk; Pres.; P.O. Box 672; 46341; Porter; P 3,610; M 40; (219) 996-5678; info@visithebron.org; www.visithebron.org

Highland · *Highland C/C* · Mary Luptak; Exec. Dir.; 8536 Kennedy Ave.; 46322; Lake; P 23,696; M 220; (219) 923-3666; Fax (219) 923-3704; mary@highlandchamber.com; www.highland chamber.com

Hobart · *Hobart C/C* · Mike Adams; Exec. Dir.; 1001 Lillian St.; 46342; Lake; P 25,363; M 420; (219) 942-5774; Fax (219) 942-4928; info@hobartchamber.com; www.hobartchamber.com*

Hope · *Hope Area C/C* · Gary Bailey; P.O. Box 131; 47246; Bartholomew; P 2,200; M 20; (812) 546-4673; www.hope chamber.com

Huntingburg · *Huntingburg C/C* · Nick Stevens; Exec. Dir.; 309 N. Geiger St.; 47542; Dubois; P 6,200; M 150; (812) 683-5699; (866) 586-8494; chambersec@psci.net; www.huntingburg chamber.org

Huntington · *Huntington County C/C* · Steve Kimmel; Exec. Dir.; 305 Warren St.; 46750; Huntington; P 38,000; M 350; (260) 356-5300; Fax (260) 356-5434; info@huntington-chamber.com; www.huntington-chamber.com*

Indianapolis · *Greater Indianapolis C/C* · Roland Dorson; Pres.; 111 Monument Cir., Ste. 1950; 46204; Marion; P 1,503,368; M 3,000; (317) 464-2222; (317) 639-4153; Fax (317) 464-2217; rdorson@indylink.com; www.indychamber.com

Jasonville · *Shakamak C/C* · P.O. Box 101; 47438; Greene; P 2,490; M 65; (812) 665-3622

Jasper · *Jasper C/C* · Nancy K. Eckerle; Exec. Dir.; 302 W. 6th St.; P.O. Box 307; 47547; Dubois; P 14,000; M 400; (812) 482-6866; (812) 482-7716; Fax (812) 848-2015; chamber@jasperin.org; www.jasperin.org.*

Jeffersonville · *see New Albany*

Jonesboro · *see Gas City*

Kendallville · *Kendallville Area C/C* · Michael Walton; Exec. Dir.; 122 S. Main St.; 46755; Noble; P 11,000; M 300; (260) 347-1554; Fax (260) 347-1575; mwalton@kendallvillechamber.com; www.kendallvillechamber.com

Kentland · *Kentland Area C/C* · Mel Ward; Pres.; P.O. Box 273; 47951; Newton; P 2,000; M 60; (219) 474-5444; (219) 474-6050; Fax (219) 474-6097; novotnyreins@sugardog.com

Knightstown · *Knightstown C/C* · Amy Blackwell; Pres.; P.O. Box 44; 46148; Henry; P 2,500; M 75; (765) 345-5290; (800) 668-1895; www.knightstownchamber.org

Knox · *Starke County C/C* · Deborah Mix; Exec. Dir.; P.O. Box 5; 46534; Starke; P 25,000; M 160; (574) 772-5548; Fax (574) 772-0867; info@starkecountychamber.com; www.starkecountychamber.com

Kokomo · *Greater Kokomo/Howard County C/C* · Jeb A. Conrad; Pres./CEO; 325 N. Main St.; 46901; Howard; P 85,000; M 486; (765) 457-5301; Fax (765) 452-4564; cweidler@greater kokomo.com; www.greaterkokomo.com*

Kouts · *Kouts C/C* · Julie Jones; Exec. Dir.; P.O. Box 330; 46347; Porter; P 1,698; M 80; (219) 246-0934; koutschamber@verizon.net; www.kouts.info

Lafayette · *The Lafayette-West Lafayette C/C* · Joseph Seaman; Pres./CEO; 337 Columbia St.; P.O. Box 348; 47902; Tippecanoe; P 156,169; M 1,000; (765) 742-4041; Fax (765) 742-6276; information@lafayettechamber.com; www.greater lafayettecommerce.com*

LaGrange · *LaGrange County C/C* · Beth Sherman; Exec. Dir.; 901 S. Detroit St., Ste. A; 46761; LaGrange; P 39,000; M 331; (260) 463-2443; (877) 735-0340; Fax (260) 463-2683; info@lagrange chamber.org; www.lagrangechamber.org*

Lake Station · *Lake Station C/C* · Bill Eaton; P.O. Box 5191; 46405; Lake; P 15,000; M 45; (219) 962-1987; Fax (219) 962-1987; masterphotog@hotmail.com; www.lakestationchamber.org*

Lake Township · *see Roselawn*

Lake Village · *see Roselawn*

Lamar · *see Rockport*

LaPorte · *Greater LaPorte C/C* · Michael B. Seitz; Pres.; 803 Washington St.; P.O. Box 486; 46352; LaPorte; P 22,260; M 310; (219) 362-3178; Fax (219) 324-7349; info@lpchamber.com; www.lpchamber.com*

Lawrence · *Greater Lawrence C/C* · Exec. Dir.; 9120 Otis Ave., Ste. 100; 46216; Marion; P 103,000; M 258; (317) 541-9876; Fax (317) 541-9875; info@lawrencechamberofcommerce.org; www.lawrencechamberofcommerce.org*

Lawrenceburg · *Dearborn County C/C* · Mike Rozow; Pres./COO; 320 Walnut St.; 47025; Dearborn; P 50,000; M 422; (812) 537-0814; (800) 322-8198; Fax (812) 537-0845; mrozow@dear borncountychamber.org; www.dearborncountychamber.org.

Leavenworth · *Crawford County C/C* · Gary Wiseman; Pres.; 6225 E. Industrial Ln., Ste. C; 47137; Crawford; P 11,076; M 75; (812) 739-2246; (812) 739-2248; Fax (812) 739-4180; www.crawfordcountychamber.com

Lebanon · *Boone County C/C* · Michelle Wiltermood; Exec. Dir.; 221 N. Lebanon St.; 46052; Boone; P 50,847; M 280; (765) 482-1320; Fax (765) 482-3114; michelle@boonechamber.org; www.boonechamber.org

Liberty · *Liberty-Union County C/C* · Annie Hofer; Exec. Dir.; 5 W. High St.; 47353; Union; P 7,300; M 87; (765) 458-5976; Fax (765) 458-5976; ucdc@dslmyway.com; www.ucdc.us

Ligonier · *Ligonier C/C* · Suzanne Kistler; V.P.; P.O. Box 121; 46767; Noble; P 4,357; M 67; (260) 894-9909; Fax (260) 894-9913; www.ligonierindianachamber.org

Lincoln Township · *see Roselawn*

Linton · *Linton-Stockton C/C* · Cheryl Hamilton; Exec. Dir.; 159 1st St. N.W.; P.O. Box 208; 47441; Greene; P 6,000; M 226; (812) 847-4846; Fax (812) 847-0246; info@lintonchamber.org; www.lintonchamber.org

Logansport · *Logansport/Cass County C/C* · Brian Shafer; Pres.; 300 E. Broadway, Ste. 103; 46947; Cass; P 40,930; M 400; (574) 753-6388; (800) 425-2071; Fax (574) 735-0909; info@logan-casschamber.com; www.logan-casschamber.com*

Loogootee · *Martin County C/C* · James Stoughton; Treas.; 210 N. Line St.; P.O. Box 257; 47553; Martin; P 11,000; M 100; (812) 295-4093; mccc@martincountyindianachamberofcommerce.org; www.martincountyindianachamberofcommerce.org

Lowell · *Lowell C/C* · Carrie Austgen; Pres.; 428 E. Commercial Ave.; 46356; Lake; P 8,400; M 115; (219) 696-0231; info@lowell inchamber.com; lowellinchamber.com

Madison · *Madison Area C/C* · Lynda Knoebel; 301 E. Main St.; 47250; Jefferson; P 33,000; M 400; (812) 265-3135; Fax (812) 265-9784; info@madisonchamber.org; www.madisonchamber.org*

Marion · *Marion-Grant County C/C* · Michelle Bunker; Bus. Dev. Dir.; 217 S. Adams St.; 46952; Grant; P 75,000; M 450; (765) 664-5107; Fax (765) 668-5443; michelle@marionchamber.org; www.marionchamber.org*

Markle · *see Bluffton*

Martinsville · *Greater Martinsville C/C* · Jamie Thompson; Exec. Dir.; 109 E. Morgan St.; P.O. Box 1378; 46151; Morgan; P 12,000; M 200; (765) 342-8110; Fax (765) 342-5713; info@martinsvillechamber.com; www.martinsvillechamber.com

Medaryville · *see Winamac*

Mentone · *Mentone C/C* · Rita Simpson; Pres.; P.O. Box 366; 46539; Kosciusko; P 900; M 40; (574) 353-7417; www.mentone eggcity.com

Merrillville · *Crossroads Reg. C/C* · Sue Reed; Exec. Dir.; 255 W. 80th Pl.; 46410; Lake; P 35,000; M 700; (219) 769-8180; Fax (219) 736-6223; geninq@crossroadschamber.org; www.crossroads chamber.org*

Michigan City · *Michigan City Area C/C* · Ann Dahm; Pres.; 200 E. Michigan Blvd., 46360, LaPorte; P 34,000; M 350; (219) 874-6221; info@mcachamber.com; www.michigancitychamber.com.*

Middlebury · *Middlebury C/C* · Sam Pohl; Exec. Dir.; P.O. Box 243; 46540; Elkhart; P 3,010; M 175; (574) 825-4300; Fax (574) 825-7541; info@middleburycoc.com; www.middleburycoc.com

Mishawaka · *see South Bend*

Mitchell · *Greater Mitchell C/C* · 533 W. Main St.; P.O. Box 216; 47446; Lawrence; P 5,000; M 115; (812) 849-4441; Fax (812) 849-6669; mitchellchamber@frontier.com; www.mitchell chamberofcommerce.org

Monon · *Monon C/C* · Alicia Cox; Pres.; P.O. Box 777; 47959; White; P 1,750; M 45; (219) 253-6441

Monterey · *see Winamac*

Monticello · *Greater Monticello C/C & Visitors Bur.* · Janet Dold; Exec. Dir.; 116 N. Main St.; P.O. Box 657; 47960; White; P 25,000; M 300; (574) 583-7220; Fax (574) 583-3399; monti cellochamber@sugardog.com; www.monticelloin.com.

Moores Hill · *see Lawrenceburg*

Mooresville · *Mooresville C/C* · Mindy Taylor; Exec. Dir.; 4 E. Harrison St.; P.O. Box 62; 46158; Morgan; P 13,000; M 320; (317) 831-6509; Fax (317) 831-9557; mindy@mooresvillechamber.com; www.mooresvillechamber.com

Morocco · *see Roselawn*

Morristown · *Morristown Area C/C* · Bill White; Pres.; P.O. Box 476; 46161; Shelby; P 1,200; M 119; (765) 763-6012; (765) 745-0138; www.morristownchamber.com

Mount Ayr · *see Roselawn*

Mount Vernon · *C of C of Southwest Indiana* · Tiffani Weatherford; Admin. Dir.; 915 E. Fourth St.; P.O. Box 633; 47620; Posey; P 300,000; M 1,800; (812) 838-3639; Fax (812) 838-6358; tweatherford@ccswin.com; www.ccswin.com*

Muncie · *Muncie-Delaware County C/C* · Jay Julian; Pres./CEO; 401 S. High St.; P.O. Box 842; 47308; Delaware; P 115,000; M 700; (765) 288-6681; (765) 751-9101; Fax (765) 751-9151; eailstock@ muncie.com; www.muncie.com*

Munster · *Munster C/C* · Wendy Mis; Exec. Dir.; 1040 Ridge Rd.; 46321; Lake; P 23,000; M 252; (219) 836-5549; Fax (219) 836-5551; info@chambermunster.org; www.chambermunster.org*

Nashville · *Brown County C/C* · Kim Tiner; Exec. Dir.; 105 Willow St.; P.O. Box 164; 47448; Brown; P 15,000; M 180; (812) 988-0234; Fax (812) 988-1547; commerce@browncounty.org; www.browncounty.org

New Albany · *One Southern Indiana* · Michael Dalby; Pres./CEO; 4100 Charlestown Rd.; 47150; Floyd; P 180,000; M 1,600; (812) 945-0266; Fax (812) 948-4664; info@1si.org; www.1si.org*

New Castle · *New Castle-Henry County C/C* · Missy Modesitt; Exec. Dir.; 100 S. Main St., Ste. 108; 47362; Henry; P 50,000; M 300; (765) 529-5210; Fax (765) 521-7408; info@nchcchamber. com; www.nchcchamber.com*

New Haven · *New Haven C/C* · Vince Buchanan; Pres./CEO; 435 Ann St.; 46774; Allen; P 13,500; M 316; (260) 749-4484; Fax (260) 749-7900; info@newhavenindiana.org; www.newhavenindiana.org*

New Palestine · *New Palestine Area C/C* · Caralee Griffith; Ofc. Coord.; 42 E. Main St.; P.O. Box 541; 46163; Hancock; P 1,000; M 140; (317) 861-2345; newpalchamber@att.net; www.new palestinechamber.com

New Paris · *New Paris C/C* · Dave Parsons; Pres.; P.O. Box 402; 46553; Elkhart; P 1,000; M 50; (574) 831-3600

Newtonville · *see Rockport*

Noblesville · *Noblesville C/C* · Sharon McMahon; Pres.; 601 E. Conner St.; 46060; Hamilton; P 55,000; M 550; (317) 773-0086; Fax (317) 773-1966; info@noblesvillechamber.com; www.nobles villechamber.com*

North Manchester · *North Manchester C/C* · Tim McLaughlin; Exec. Dir.; 109 N. Market St.; 46962; Wabash; P 6,500; M 171; (260) 982-7644; Fax (260) 982-8718; nmcc@northmanchester chamber.com; www.northmanchesterchamber.com.

North Vernon · *Jennings County C/C* · 524 N. State St., Ste. B; P.O. Box 340; 47265; Jennings; P 28,000; M 310; (812) 346-2339; Fax (812) 346-3805; jjames@jenningscountychamber.com; www. jenningscountychamber.com*

North Webster · *North Webster-Tippecanoe Twp. C/C* · Tonya Bowser; Pres.; P.O. Box 19; 46555; Kosciusko; P 1,100; M 120; (574) 834-1600; Fax (574) 834-2168; nwttchamber@gmail.com; www.northwebster.com

Orleans · *Orleans C/C* · Robert Henderson; Exec. Dir.; P.O. Box 9; 47452; Orleans; P 2,273; M 90; (812) 865-9930; Fax (812) 865-3413; historicorleans@netsurfusa.net; www.historicorleans.com

Ossian · *see Bluffton*

Paoli · *Paoli C/C* · Tom Motsinger; Pres.; P.O. Box 22; 47454; Orange; P 4,200; M 100; (812) 723-4769; Fax (812) 723-4307; info@paolichamber.com; www.paolichamber.com

Pendleton · *see Anderson*

Peru · *Miami County C/C* · Sandy Chittum; Pres.; 13 E. Main St.; 46970; Miami; P 27,000; M 365; (765) 472-1923; Fax (765) 472-7099; info@miamicochamber.com; www.miamicochamber.com.*

Petersburg · *Pike County C/C* · Alycia Church; Exec. Dir.; 714 E. Main St.; P.O. Box 291; 47567; Pike; P 12,500; M 100; (812) 354-8155; Fax (812) 354-2335; chamber@frontier.com; www. pikecountyin.org.

Plainfield · *Greater Plainfield C/C* · Kent McPhail; Dir.; 210 W. Main St.; 46168; Hendricks; P 25,000; M 340; (317) 839-3800; (877) 597-4763; Fax (317) 839-9670; chamber@town.plainfield. in.us; www.plainfield-in.com

Plymouth · *Plymouth Area C/C* · 120 N. Michigan St.; 46563; Marshall; P 10,000; M 400; (574) 936-2323; Fax (574) 936-6584; plychamber@plychamber.org; www.plychamber.org*

Poneto · *see Bluffton*

Portage · *Greater Portage C/C* · Terry Hufford; Exec. Dir.; 2642 Eleanor St.; 46368; Porter; P 50,000; M 410; (219) 762-3300; Fax (219) 763-2450; info@portageinchamber.com; www.portage inchamber.com

Porter · *see Chesterton*

Portland · *Jay County C/C* · Vicki Tague; Exec. Dir.; 118 S. Meridian St., Ste. A; 47371; Jay; P 21,500; M 280; (260) 726-4481; Fax (260) 726-3372; vickitague@jaycountychamber.com; www. jaycountychamber.com.

Princeton · *Gibson County C/C* · Karen Thompson; Exec. Dir.; 202 E. Broadway; 47670; Gibson; P 33,000; M 300; (812) 385-2134; office@gibsoncountychamber.org; www.gibson countychamber.org*

Rensselaer · *Greater Rensselaer C/C* · Linda Comingore; Mgr.; 224 W. Washington St.; 47978; Jasper; P 7,000; M 164; (219) 866-8223; Fax (219) 866-0005; info@rensselaerchamber.com; www. rensselaerchamber.com

Richmond · *Wayne County Area C/C* · Suzanne Derengowski; Interim Pres./CEO; 33 S. 7th St., Ste. 2; 47374; Wayne; P 72,000; M 600; (765) 962-1511; Fax (765) 966-0882; chamber. of.commerce@wcareachamber.org; www.wcareachamber.org

Roanoke · *Roanoke C/C* · Lucas Klingenberger; Pres.; P. O. Box 434; 46783; Huntington; P 1,594; M 82; (260) 672-2265; www. discoverroanoke.org

Rochester • *Rochester & Lake Manitou C/C* • Alison Heyde; Exec. Dir.; 822 Main St.; 46975; Fulton; P 7,000; M 250; (574) 224-2666; Fax (574) 224-2329; chamber@rtcol.com; www.contactrochester.org

Rockport • *Spencer County Reg. C/C* • Debbie Barrett; Exec. Dir.; 2792 N. U.S. Hwy. 231, Ste. 100; 47635; Spencer; P 20,000; M 160; (812) 649-2186; (800) 799-2186; scrcc@psci.net; www.spencercoin.org

Rockville • *Parke County C/C* • Sandy Skelton; Exec. Dir.; 105 N. Market St., Ste. A; 47872; Parke; P 17,000; M 160; (765) 569-5565; Fax (765) 569-4271; info@parkecountychamber.com; www.parkecountychamber.com*

Rome City • *Rome City C/C* • Roberta Stone; Pres.; P.O. Box 22; 46784; Noble; P 1,650; M 25; (260) 854-2412; romecitychamber.com

Roselawn • *North Newton Area C/C* • Ronald Gann; Pres.; P.O. Box 266; 46372; Jasper & Newton; P 4,200; M 48; (219) 345-2525; mail@northnewtonchamber.org; www.northnewtonchamber.org

Rushville • *Rush County C/C* • Lorraine Edwards; Mgr.; 315 N. Main St.; 46173; Rush; P 18,500; M 279; (765) 932-2880; Fax (765) 932-4191; pamleisure@rushcounty.com; www.rushcounty.com/chamber

Saint John • *Saint John C/C* • Judi Douma; 9495 Keilman, Ste. 10; 46373; Lake; P 11,000; M 175; (219) 365-4686; Fax (219) 365-4602; office@stjohnchamber.com; www.stjohnchamber.com

Saint Leon • *see Lawrenceburg*

Salem • *Washington County C/C* • Anita Bush; Exec. Secy.; 201 E. Market St., Ste. 104; 47167; Washington; P 27,223; M 215; (812) 883-4303; Fax (812) 883-1467; info@washingtoncountychamber.org; www.washingtoncountychamber.org

Santa Claus • *see Rockport*

Schererville • *Schererville C/C* • Mark Hill; Pres.; 13 W. Joliet St.; 46375; Lake; P 28,900; M 320; (219) 322-5412; Fax (219) 322-0598; info@46375.org; www.46375.org

Scottsburg • *Greater Scott County C/C* • Keith Colbert; Exec. Dir.; 90 N. Main St., Ste. B; 47170; Scott; P 24,000; M 310; (812) 752-4080; Fax (812) 752-4307; scottcom@c3bb.com; www.scottchamber.org*

Seymour • *Greater Seymour C/C* • Bill Bailey; Pres.; 105 S. Chestnut St.; 47274; Jackson; P 20,000; M 475; (812) 522-3681; Fax (812) 524-1800; info@seymourchamber.org; www.seymourchamber.org.

Shelbyville • *Shelby County C/C* • Julie Metz; Exec. Dir.; 501 N. Harrison St.; 46176; Shelby; P 44,300; M 420; (317) 398-6647; (800) 318-4083; Fax (317) 392-3901; chamberinfo@shelbychamber.net; www.shelbychamber.net.

Shipshewana • *see LaGrange*

South Bend • *C/C of St. Joseph County* • Jeff Rea; Pres./CEO; 401 E. Colfax Ave., Ste. 310; P.O. Box 1677; 46634; St. Joseph; P 265,000; M 1,300; (574) 234-0051; Fax (574) 289-0358; info@sjchamber.org; www.sjchamber.org.*

Spencer • *Owen County C/C & Eco. Dev. Corp.* • Denise Shaw; Exec. Dir.; 205 E. Morgan St., Ste. D; P.O. Box 87; 47460; Owen; P 21,000; M 100; (812) 829-3245; Fax (812) 829-0936; info@owencountyindiana.org; www.owencountyindiana.org

Sullivan • *Sullivan County C/C* • Judy K. Harris; Pres.; 31 W. Jackson; P.O. Box 325; 47882; Sullivan; P 21,000; M 154; (812) 268-2897; Fax (812) 268-2898; sullivanchamber@hotmail.com

Syracuse • *Syracuse-Wawasee C/C* • Tammy Cotton; Exec. Dir.; P.O. Box 398; 46567; Kosciusko; P 3,200; M 185; (574) 457-5637; Fax (574) 528-6040; info@swchamber.com; www.swchamber.com

Tell City • *Perry County C/C* • Cheri Taylor; Exec. Dir.; 601 Main St., Ste. A; P.O. Box 82; 47586; Perry; P 18,899; M 305; (812) 547-2385; Fax (812) 547-8378; perrychamber@psci.net; www.perrycountychamber.com

Terre Haute • *Terre Haute C/C* • G. Roderick Henry CCE IOM; Pres./CEO; 630 Wabash Ave., Ste. 105; 47807; Vigo; P 150,000; M 920; (812) 232-2391; Fax (812) 232-2905; bedwards@terrehautechamber.com; www.terrehautechamber.com*

Thayer • *see Roselawn*

Tipton • *Tipton County C/C* • Jennifer Richey; Exec. Dir.; 136 E. Jefferson St.; 46072; Tipton; P 16,000; M 185; (765) 675-7533; jrichey@tiptonchamber.com; www.tiptonchamber.com

Union City • *Union City C/C* • Darlene Wymer; Exec. Dir.; 826 N. State Line; 101 E. Elm St.; 47390; Randolph, IN & Darke, OH; P 5,000; M 140; (765) 964-5409; (937) 968-3141; Fax (765) 964-5409; chamberinfo@myunioncity.com; www.myunioncity.com.

Uniondale • *see Bluffton*

Upland • *Upland C/C* • Patty Hart; Pres.; P.O. Box 157; 46989; Grant; P 4,000; M 70; (765) 998-7439; (765) 998-6012

Valparaiso • *Greater Valparaiso C/C* • Rex Richards; Pres.; 162 W. Lincolnway; 46383; Porter; P 40,000; M 700; (219) 462-1105; Fax (219) 462-5710; gvcc@valparaisochamber.org; www.valparaisochamber.org.*

Vera Cruz • *see Bluffton*

Versailles • *Ripley County C/C* • Amy Thomas; Dir.; 102 N. Main St.; P.O. Box 576; 47042; Ripley; P 27,550; M 155; (812) 689-6654; Fax (812) 689-3934; ripleycc@ripleycountychamber.org; www.ripleycountychamber.org

Vevay • *Switzerland County C/C* • P.O. Box 149; 47043; Switzerland; P 9,500; M 75; (800) 435-5688; Fax (812) 427-2184; visitsc@vevayin.com; www.vevayin.com

Vincennes • *Knox County C/C* • Marc A. McNeece; Pres./CEO; 316 Main St.; P.O. Box 553; 47591; Knox; P 40,000; M 375; (812) 882-6440; Fax (812) 882-6441; marc@knoxcountychamber.com; www.knoxcountychamber.com

Wabash • *Wabash County C/C* • Kimberly Pinkerton; Pres.; 210 S. Wabash St.; 46992; Wabash; P 25,000; M 330; (260) 563-1168; Fax (260) 563-6920; info@wabashchamber.org; www.wabashchamber.org.

Wakarusa • *Wakarusa C/C* • Deb Shively; Exec. Secy.; 100 W. Waterford St.; P.O. Box 291; 46573; Elkhart; P 1,700; M 100; (574) 862-4344; Fax (574) 862-2245; chamber@wakarusachamber.com; www.wakarusachamber.com

Walkerton • *Walkerton Area C/C* • Flora Tibbets; Pres.; 612 Roosevelt Rd.; 46574; St. Joseph; P 2,274; M 100; (574) 586-3100; Fax (574) 586-3469; chamber@walkerton.org; www.walkerton.org

Warren • *Warren Area C/C* • P.O. Box 40; 46792; Huntington; P 2,000; M 50; (260) 375-3175; www.warrenindiana.com

Warrick County • *see Boonville*

Warsaw • *Warsaw/Kosciusko County C/C* • Michelle Goble; Exec. Asst.; 313 S. Buffalo St., Ste. A; 46580; Kosciusko; P 76,000; M 555; (574) 267-6311; Fax (574) 267-7762; info@wkchamber.com; www.wkchamber.com*

Washington • *Daviess County C/C* • Charles Selby; Exec. Dir.; One Train Depot St.; P.O. Box 430; 47501; Daviess; P 32,000; M 319; (812) 254-5262; (800) 449-5262; Fax (812) 254-4003; chamber@dmrtc.net; www.daviesscountychamber.com*

Waterloo · *Waterloo C/C* · Ken Surber; Pres.; P.O. Box 551; 46793; DeKalb; P 2,300; M 27; (260) 837-5323; (260) 837-7428; www.waterlooinchamber.com

West Baden · *see French Lick*

West Harrison · *see Lawrenceburg*

West Lafayette · *see Lafayette*

Westfield · *Westfield C/C* · Julie Sole; Exec. Dir.; 130 Penn St.; 46074; Hamilton; P 30,000; M 400; (317) 804-3030; Fax (317) 804-3035; info@westfield-chamber.org; www.westfield-chamber.org

Westville · *Westville Area C/C* · Sarah Sparks; Admin. Asst.; P.O. Box 215; 46391; LaPorte; P 2,500; M 50; (219) 379-7918; westvillechamber@csinet.net; www.westville.us

Whiting · *Whiting-Robertsdale C/C* · Laurie Brown; Interim Exec. Dir.; 1417 119th St.; 46394; Lake; P 11,000; M 170; (219) 659-0292; Fax (219) 659-5851; turtlemamma@att.net; www.whitingindiana.com

Winamac · *Pulaski County C/C* · Angela Anspach; Coord.; 200 W. Main St.; P.O. Box 113; 46996; Pulaski; P 14,000; M 200; (574) 946-7600; Fax (574) 946-7617; chamber@pulaskionline.org; www.pulaskionline.org

Winchester · *Winchester Area C/C* · Sandie Rowe; Exec. Dir.; 112 W. Washington St.; 47394; Randolph; P 27,066; M 175; (765) 584-3731; Fax (765) 584-5544; chamber@globalsite.net; www.winchesterareachamber.org

Zionsville · *Zionsville C/C* · Ray Cortopassi; Exec. Dir.; 135 S. Elm St.; P.O. Box 148; 46077; Boone; P 20,000; M 350; (317) 873-3836; Fax (317) 873-3836; info@zionsvillechamber.org; www.zionsvillechamber.org

Iowa

Iowa Assn. of Bus. & Ind. · Michael Ralston; Pres.; 904 Walnut St., Ste. 100; Des Moines; 50309; Polk & Warren; P 3,000,000; M 1,200; (515) 280-8000; (800) 383-4224; Fax (515) 282-8085; abi@iowaabi.org; www.iowaabi.org

Ackley · *Ackley C/C* · Korin King; Pres.; P.O. Box 82; 50601; Franklin & Hardin; P 1,800; M 67; (641) 847-3332; www.ackleyiowa.net

Adel · *Adel Partners Main Street C/C* · W.W. Van Buren & Linda Boettcher; Co-Dirs.; 301 S. 10th St.; P.O. Box 73; 50003; Dallas; P 4,500; M 200; (515) 993-5472; Fax (515) 993-3384; chamber@adelpartners.org; www.adelpartners.org

Albia · *Albia Area C/C* · Deborah Morgan; Exec. Dir.; 18 S. Main St.; 52531; Monroe; P 3,706; M 180; (641) 932-5108; Fax (641) 932-3326; albiachamber@albiachamber.org; www.albiachamber.org*

Algona · *Algona Area C/C* · Vicki Mallory; Exec. Dir.; 123 E. State St.; 50511; Kossuth; P 16,000; M 275; (515) 295-7201; Fax (515) 295-5920; vmallory@algona.org; www.algona.org*

Allerton · *see Corydon*

Alta · *Alta C/C* · Carrie Turnquist; Co-Pres.; P.O. Box 34; 51002; Buena Vista; P 2,000; (712) 213-8607; www.altaiowa.com

Altoona · *Altoona Area C/C* · 119 2nd St.; 50009; Polk; P 14,000; M 360; (515) 967-3366; Fax (515) 967-3346; altoona@netins.net; www.altoonachamber.org

Ames · *Ames C/C* · Dan Culhane; Pres./CEO; 1601 Golden Aspen Dr., Ste. 110; 50010; Story; P 52,300; M 675; (515) 232-2310; Fax (515) 232-6716; eve@ameschamber.com; www.ameschamber.com

Anamosa · *Anamosa C/C* · Carla Burge; Admin.; 124 E. Main St.; 52205; Jones; P 5,000; M 120; (319) 462-4879; director@anamosachamber.org; www.anamosachamber.org*

Ankeny · *Ankeny Area C/C* · Julie Cooper; Exec. Dir.; 210 S. Ankeny Blvd.; 50023; Polk; P 44,000; M 800; (515) 964-0685; Fax (515) 964-0487; info@ankeny.org; www.ankeny.org*

Arnolds Park · *Iowa Great Lakes Area C/C* · Tom Kuhlman; Exec. V.P.; 243 W. Broadway; P.O. Box 9; 51331; Dickinson; P 16,424; M 400; (712) 332-2107; (800) 839-9987; Fax (712) 332-7714; tom@okobojichamber.com; www.vacationokoboji.com.

Atlantic · *Atlantic Area C/C* · Ann McCurdy; Exec. Dir.; 102 Chestnut St.; 50022; Cass; P 7,300; M 217; (712) 243-3017; Fax (712) 243-4404; chamber@atlanticiowa.com; www.atlanticiowa.com*

Audubon · *Audubon C/C* · Barbara Smith; Secy.; 800 Market St.; P.O. Box 66; 50025; Audubon; P 2,382; M 153; (712) 563-3780; Fax (712) 563-3780; audchmbr@iowatelecom.net; www.auduboniowa.org

Bedford · *Bedford Area Dev. Center* · Deann Hensley; Exec. Dir.; 601 Madison; 50833; Taylor; P 1,600; M 85; (712) 523-3637; Fax (712) 523-3384; bedfordareadc@frontiernet.net; www.bedford-iowa.com

Bellevue · *Bellevue Area C/C* · Colleen Myers; Exec. Dir.; 210 N. Riverview St.; 52031; Jackson; P 2,350; M 150; (563) 872-5830; Fax (563) 872-3611; chamber@bellevueia.com; www.bellevueia.com

Belmond · *Belmond Area C/C & Ind. Dev.* · Brad Bloemke; Pres.; 235 E. Main St.; 50421; Wright; P 2,600; M 100; (641) 444-3937; Fax (641) 444-3944; www.belmond.com

Bettendorf · *see Davenport*

Bloomfield · *Bloomfield Area C/C* · Shannon Harry; Ofc. Asst.; P.O. Box 159; 52537; Davis; P 9,500; M 80; (641) 664-1726; shannon@daviscounty.org; www.daviscounty.org

Boone · *Boone Area C/C* · Richard Baker; Exec. Dir.; 903 Story St.; 50036; Boone; P 12,813; M 325; (515) 432-3342; (800) 266-6312; Fax (515) 432-3343; boonechamber@iowatelecom.net; www.booneiowa.us

Britt · *Britt C/C* · Sue Miller Taylor; Exec. Dir.; P.O. Box 63; 50423; Hancock; P 2,200; M 82; (641) 843-3867; brittcoc@wctatel.net; www.brittiowa.com

Brooklyn · *Brooklyn Eco. Dev. Group* · 138 Jackson St.; P.O. Box 187; 52211; Poweshiek; P 1,400; (641) 522-5300; Fax (641) 522-5584; brkchmbr@netins.net; www.brooklyniowa.com

Burlington · *Burlington/West Burlington Area C/C* · Dennis Hinkle; Pres./CEO; 610 N. 4th St., Ste. 200; 52601; Des Moines; P 30,000; M 600; (319) 752-6365; (800) 82-RIVER; Fax (319) 752-6454; info@growburlington.com; www.growburlington.com*

Carroll · *Carroll C/C* · Jim Gossett; Exec. Dir.; 407 W. 5th St.; P.O. Box 307; 51401; Carroll; P 10,106; M 425; (712) 792-4383; Fax (712) 792-4384; chamber@carrolliowa.com; www.carrolliowa.com*

Cedar Falls · *Greater Cedar Valley C/C* · Bob Justis; Pres./CEO; 10 Main St.; 50613; Black Hawk; P 38,000; M 850; (319) 266-3593; Fax (319) 277-4325; kassey@greatercedarvalleychamber.com; www.greatercedarvalleychamber.com*

Cedar Rapids · *Cedar Rapids Area C/C* · Shannon Meyer; Pres./CEO; 424 First Ave. N.E.; 52401; Linn; P 135,000; M 1,500; (319) 398-5317; Fax (319) 398-5228; chamber@cedarrapids.org; www.cedarrapids.org*

Centerville · *Centerville-Rathbun Area C/C* · Joyce Bieber; Exec. Dir.; 128 N. 12th St.; 52544; Appanoose; P 14,000; M 250; (641) 437-4102; (800) 611-3800; Fax (641) 437-0527; chamber@centervilleia.com; www.centervilleia.com*

Chariton • *Chariton C/C* • Debra Storm; Exec. Dir.; 104 N. Grand St.; P.O. Box 735; 50049; Lucas; P 5,000; M 200; (641) 774-4059; Fax (641) 774-2801; ccdc@iowatelecom.net; www.chariton chamber.com

Charles City • *Charles City Area C/C* • Veronica Litterer; Dir.; 401 N. Main St.; 50616; Floyd; P 7,800; M 300; (641) 228-4234; Fax (641) 228-4744; info@charlescitychamber.com; www.charles citychamber.com.*

Cherokee • *Cherokee C/C* • Julie Hering-Kent; Exec. Dir.; 416 W. Main St.; 51012; Cherokee; P 5,600; M 210; (712) 225-6414; Fax (712) 225-2803; info@cherokeeiowachamber.com; www. cherokeeiowachamber.com

Clarinda • *Clarinda C/C* • Elaine Farwell; Exec. Dir.; 115 E. Main St.; 51632; Page; P 5,700; M 160; (712) 542-2166; Fax (712) 542-4113; chamber@clarinda.org; www.clarinda.org

Clarion • *Clarion Partnership for Growth* • Jill Harrington; Exec. Dir.; 302 S. Main; P.O. Box 6; 50525; Wright; P 2,950; M 225; (515) 532-2256; clchamb@goldfieldaccess.net; www.clarion-iowa.com

Clear Lake • *Clear Lake Area C/C* • Gary Bright; Exec. Dir.; 205 Main Ave.; P.O. Box 188; 50428; Cerro Gordo; P 8,200; M 430; (641) 357-2159; (800) 285-5338; Fax (641) 357-8141; info@ clearlakeiowa.com; www.clearlakeiowa.com

Clinton • *Clinton Area C/C* • Julie A. Allesee; Pres.; 721 S. 2nd St.; P.O. Box 1024; 52733; Clinton; P 54,000; M 600; (563) 242-5702; Fax (563) 242-5803; chamber@clintonia.com; www.clintonia.com*

Clive • *see Des Moines*

Colfax • *Colfax C/C* • P.O. Box 62; 50054; Jasper; P 2,500; M 40; (515) 674-4033; info@colfaxiowachamber.com; www.colfax iowachamber.com

Conrad • *Conrad Chamber-Main Street Inc.* • Darla Ubben; Dir.; 204 E. Center St.; P.O. Box 414; 50621; Grundy; P 1,055; (641) 366-2108; Fax (641) 366-2109; cmspd@heartofiowa.net; www. conrad.govoffice.com

Corning • *Adams Comm. C/C* • Stacie Hull; Exec. Dir.; 710 Davis Ave.; 50841; Adams; P 4,300; M 140; (641) 322-3243; Fax (641) 322-4387; adamschamber@frontiernet.net; adamscountyiowa.com

Corydon • *Chamber of Commerce Corydon & Allerton* • P.O. Box 435; 50060; Wayne; P 1,500; M 75; (641) 872-1338

Council Bluffs • *Council Bluffs Area C/C* • Bob L. Mundt; Pres./CEO; 149 W. Broadway; P.O. Box 1565; 51502; Pottawattamie; P 59,744; M 768; (712) 325-1000; Fax (712) 322-5698; info@ councilbluffsiowa.com; www.councilbluffsiowa.com*

Cresco • *Cresco Area C/C* • Randy Mashek; Exec. Dir.; 101 Second Ave. S.W.; P.O. Box 403; 52136; Howard; P 9,932; M 200; (563) 547-3434; Fax (563) 547-2056; crescochamber@yahoo.com; www.crescochamber.com

Creston • *Creston C/C* • Ellen Gerharz; Exec. Dir.; 208 W. Taylor St.; P.O. Box 471; 50801; Union; P 8,100; M 250; (641) 782-7021; Fax (641) 782-9927; chamber@crestoniowachamber.com; www. crestoniowachamber.com

Dakota City • *see Humboldt*

Davenport • *Quad Cities C/C* • Tara Barney; CEO; 130 W. 2nd St.; 52801; Scott County, IA; Henry, Mercer & Rock Island, IL; P 375,000; M 2,000; (563) 322-1706; Fax (563) 322-7804; news@ quadcitieschamber.com; www.quadcitieschamber.com*

Decorah • *Decorah Area C/C* • Nikki Brevig; Exec. Dir.; 507 W. Water St.; 52101; Winneshiek; P 8,700; M 406; (563) 382-3990; (800) 463-4692; Fax (563) 382-5515; director@decorah-iowa. com; www.decoraharea.com*

Denison • *Chamber & Dev. Cncl. of Crawford County* • Donald R. Luensmann; Exec. Dir.; 18 S. Main St.; 51442; Crawford; P 16,500; M 200; (712) 263-5621; (712) 263-6622; Fax (712) 263-4789; info@cdcia.org; www.cdcia.org*

Des Moines • *Greater Des Moines Partnership* • Martha Willits; Pres./CEO; 700 Locust St., Ste. 100; 50309; Polk & Warren; P 534,399; M 4,000; (515) 286-4950; (800) 376-9059; Fax (515) 286-4974; info@desmoinesmetro.com; www.desmoinesmetro.com

DeWitt • *DeWitt C/C* • JoElla O'Connell; Exec. Dir.; 1010 6th Ave.; 52742; Clinton; P 5,200; M 245; (563) 659-8500; Fax (563) 659-2410; info@dewitt.org; www.dewitt.org.*

Dubuque • *Dubuque Area C/C* • Molly Grover; Pres./CEO; 300 Main St., Ste. 200; 52001; Dubuque; P 92,000; M 1,450; (563) 557-9200; (800) 798-4748; Fax (563) 557-1591; office@dubuque chamber.com; www.dubuquechamber.com.*

Durant • *Durant C/C* • Dr. Carla Courtney; Pres.; P.O. Box 1111; 52747; Cedar, Muscatine & Scott; P 2,000; M 100; (563) 343-3680; www.durantchamber.com

Dyersville • *Dyersville Area C/C* • Karla Thompson; Exec. Dir.; 1100 16th Ave. Ct. S.E.; 52040; Delaware & Dubuque; P 4,035; M 290; (563) 875-2311; (866) 393-7784; Fax (563) 875-8391; dyersvillechamber@dyersville.org; www.dyersville.org*

Eagle Grove • *Eagle Grove Area C/C* • Rachel Kingery; Exec. Dir.; 120 N. Lucas Ave.; P.O. Box 2; 50533; Wright; P 3,500; M 200; (515) 448-4821; Fax (515) 448-4821; chamber@eaglegrove.com; www. eaglegrove.com*

Eldora • *Greater Eldora C/C Inc.* • P.O. Box 303; 50627; Hardin; P 3,038; M 57; President@eldorachamber.com; www.eldora chamber.com

Eldridge • *Eldridge-North Scott C/C* • Carolyn Scheibe; Exec. Dir.; 220 W. Davenport St.; 52748; Scott; P 9,000; M 190; (563) 285-9965; Fax (563) 285-9964; info@northscottchamber.com; www.northscottchamber.com

Elkader • *Elkader Area C/C* • Mary Harstad; Exec. Secy.; 207 N. Main St.; P.O. Box 599; 52043; Clayton; P 1,500; M 80; (563) 245-2857; elkader@alpinecom.net; www.elkader-iowa.com

Emmetsburg • *Emmetsburg C/C* • Katie Kahler; Exec. Dir.; 1121 Broadway; 50536; Palo Alto; P 4,000; M 150; (712) 852-2283; Fax (712) 852-2156; information@emmetsburg.com; www. emmetsburg.com

Essex • *Essex C/C-Comm. Club* • Dana Wensterand; Exec. Dir.; P.O. Box 334; 51638; Page; P 884; M 175; (712) 586-4541

Estherville • *Estherville Area C/C* • Mrs. Dustin Embree; Exec. Dir.; 620 First Ave. S.; 51334; Emmet; P 6,656; M 170; (712) 362-3541; Fax (712) 362-7742; echamber@ncn.net; www.estherville.org

Fairfield • *Fairfield Area C/C* • Brent Willett; Exec. Dir.; 204 W. Broadway; 52556; Jefferson; P 15,500; M 360; (641) 472-2111; Fax (641) 472-6510; chamber@fairfieldiowa.com; www.fairfield iowa.com

Fayette • *Fayette Chamber Betterment Found.* • Delores Fagle; 708 W. Water; 52142; Fayette; P 1,351; M 20; (563) 425-4410; delores@iowatelecom.net; www.fayetteia.com

Forest City • *Forest City C/C* • Kathy Rollefson; Exec. Dir.; 145 East K St.; 50436; Hancock & Winnebago; P 4,300; M 165; (641) 585-2092; (877) 585-2092; Fax (641) 585-2687; chamber1@ wctatel.net; www.forestcityia.com*

Fort Dodge • *Fort Dodge Area C/C* • Amy Bruno; Exec. Dir.; 1406 Central Ave.; 50501; Webster; P 26,309; M 575; (515) 955-5500; Fax (515) 955-3245; info@fortdodgechamber.com; www. fortdodgechamber.com

Fort Madison · *Fort Madison Area C/C* · Dr. Kristin Maus; Pres.; 614 9th St.; P.O. Box 277; 52627; Lee; P 11,500; M 284; (319) 372-5471; Fax (319) 372-6404; scantrella@fortmadison.com; www.fortmadison.com

Garner · *Garner C/C* · Lisa Formanek; Exec. Dir.; 211 State St.; 50438; Hancock; P 3,000; M 140; (641) 923-3993; Fax (641) 923-3993; chamber@qwestoffice.net; www.garneriachamber.com

George · *George C/C* · Arlyce Elias; Secy.; 105 S. Main; 51237; Lyon; P 1,100; M 65; (712) 475-2870; (712) 475-3612; www.georgeiowa.com

Glenwood · *Glenwood Area C/C & Glenwood/Mills County Eco. Dev. Found.* · Linda Washburn; Exec. Dir.; 32 1/2 N. Walnut St.; 51534; Mills; P 15,500; M 165; (712) 527-3298; Fax (712) 527-4349; glenwoodia@qwestoffice.net; www.glenwoodia.com

Greenfield · *Greenfield Chamber/Main Street* · Ginny Kuhfus; Exec. Dir.; 201 S. First St.; P.O. Box 61; 50849; Adair; P 2,100; M 135; (641) 743-8444; Fax (641) 743-8205; grfld_cc_ms_dev@iowatelecom.net; www.greenfieldiowa.com

Grimes · *Grimes Chamber & Eco. Dev.* · Brian Buethe; Exec. Dir.; 101 N.E. Harvey St.; 50111; Dallas & Polk; P 8,415; M 150; (515) 986-5770; Fax (515) 986-5776; brianb@ci.grimes.ia.us; www.grimesiowa.com

Grinnell · *Grinnell Area C/C* · Angela Harrington; Exec. Dir.; 833 4th Ave.; P.O. Box 538; 50112; Poweshiek; P 9,300; M 300; (641) 236-6555; Fax (641) 236-3499; exec@grinnellchamber.org; www.grinnellchamber.org

Griswold · *Griswold C/C* · Ryan Askeland; Pres.; P.O. Box 376; 51535; Cass; P 1,200; M 80; (712) 778-2615; griswoldchamber@netins.net; www.griswoldia.com

Grundy Center · *Grundy Center Chamber & Dev.* · Kelly Riskedahl; Dir.; 705 F Ave.; 50638; Grundy; P 2,700; M 150; (319) 825-3838; Fax (319) 825-6471; chamber@gcmuni.net; www.grundycenter.com

Guthrie · *Guthrie Center C/C* · Kari Carroll; Secy./Treas.; P.O. Box 193; 50115; Guthrie; P 1,713; M 85; (641) 332-2218; Fax (641) 332-2693; kcarroll@gosbook.com; www.guthriecenter.com

Guttenberg · *Guttenberg Dev. & Tourism* · 323 S. River Park Dr.; P.O. Box 536; 52052; Clayton; P 2,000; M 75; (563) 252-2323; (877) 252-2323; Fax (563) 252-2378; guttenberg@alpinecom.net; www.guttenbergiowa.net

Hampton · *Hampton Area C/C* · Brook S. Boehmler; Exec. Dir.; 5 1st St. S.W.; 50441; Franklin; P 10,000; M 300; (641) 456-5668; brook@hamptoniowa.org; www.hamptoniowa.org*

Harlan · *Shelby County C/C* · Dawn Cundiff; Dir.; 1101 7th St.; 51537; Shelby; P 13,000; M 195; (712) 755-2114; (888) 876-1774; Fax (712) 755-2115; info@exploreshelbycounty.com; www.exploreshelbycounty.com

Hartley · *Hartley C/C* · Cindy Hennings; Pres.; 56 2nd St. S.E.; P.O. Box 146; 51346; O'Brien; P 1,733; M 75; (712) 928-4278; hartleychamber@tcaexpress.net; www.hartleyiowa.com

Hawarden · *Hawarden Chamber & Eco. Dev. Inc.* · Cathie Brown; Dir.; 1150 Central Ave.; 51023; Sioux; P 2,500; M 100; (712) 551-4433; Fax (712) 551-4439; chamber@cityofhawarden.com; www.happ-online.com

Holstein · *Holstein C/C* · 119 S. Main St.; 51025; Ida; P 1,500; M 35; (712) 368-4898; holstein@netllc.net; www.holsteinchamber.com

Hudson · *Hudson C/C* · Tom Finnegan; Pres.; P.O. Box 493; 50643; Black Hawk; P 2,117; M 53; (319) 988-4217; admin@hudsoniachamber.org; www.hudsoniachamber.org

Humboldt · *Humboldt-Dakota City C/C* · Jeff Goodell; Pres.; 29 5th St. S.; P.O. Box 247; 50548; Humboldt; P 5,000; M 126; (515) 332-1481; Fax (515) 332-1496; chamber@goldfieldaccess.net; www.ci.humboldt.ia.us

Ida Grove · *Ida Grove C/C* · Dianne Perry; Pres.; 218 Main St.; P.O. Box 252; 51445; Ida; P 2,500; M 100; (712) 364-3404; Fax (712) 364-2945; idagrovechamber@frontiernet.net; www.idagrovechamber.com

Independence · *Independence Area C/C* · Tammy Rasmussen; Exec. Dir.; 112 1st St. E.; P.O. Box 104; 50644; Buchanan; P 6,014; M 220; (319) 334-7178; (319) 334-0241; Fax (319) 334-7394; indycommerce@indytel.com; www.indycommerce.com*

Indianola · *Indianola C/C* · Denise Day; Exec. Dir.; 515 N. Jefferson, Ste. D; 50125; Warren; P 15,000; M 300; (515) 961-6269; (866) 961-6269; Fax (515) 961-9753; chamber@indianolachamber.com; www.indianolachamber.com.*

Iowa City · *Iowa City Area C/C* · Nancy Quellhorst; Pres.; 325 E. Washington St., Ste. 100; 52240; Johnson; P 114,000; M 1,000; (319) 337-9637; Fax (319) 338-9958; info@iowacityarea.com; www.iowacityarea.com

Iowa Falls · *Iowa Falls C of C/Main Street* · Diana Thies; Exec. Dir.; 520 Rocksylvania; 50126; Hardin; P 5,200; M 170; (641) 648-5549; Fax (641) 648-3702; chamber@iafalls.com; www.iowafallschamber.com

Jefferson · *Jefferson Area C/C* · 220 N. Chestnut St.; 50129; Greene; P 4,626; M 175; (515) 386-2155; Fax (515) 386-2156; chamber@jeffersoniowa.com; gojacc.com

Jesup · *Jesup C/C* · Todd Rohlfsen; Pres.; P.O. Box 592; 50648; Black Hawk & Buchanan; P 2,300; M 62; (319) 827-3100; (319) 827-1522; Fax (319) 827-3510; www.jesupiowa.com

Johnston · *Johnston C/C* · Heather Wilcox; Admin.; P.O. Box 61; 50131; Polk; P 15,000; M 250; (515) 276-9064; Fax (515) 309-0144; heather@growjohnston.com; www.johnstonchamber.com

Kalona · *Kalona Area C/C* · Norma Yoder; Ofc. & Events Coord.; 514 B Ave.; P.O. Box 615; 52247; Washington; P 4,000; M 85; (319) 656-2660; chamber@kctc.net; www.kalonachamber.com

Keokuk · *Keokuk Area C/C* · Katie O'Brien; Exec. Dir.; 329 Main St.; 52632; Lee; P 11,747; M 270; (319) 524-5055; Fax (319) 524-5016; www.keokukchamber.com

Knoxville · *Discover Knoxville Growth Alliance C/C* · Jessie Wilson; Exec. Ofc. Coord.; 309 E. Main St.; 50138; Marion; P 8,270; M 275; (641) 828-7555; Fax (641) 828-7978; jwilson@discoverknoxville.com; www.discoverknoxville.com

La Motte · *see Bellevue*

La Porte City · *La Porte City C/C* · P.O. Box 82; 50651; Black Hawk; P 2,321; M 35; (319) 342-3396; www.laportecityia.com

Lake City · *Lake City Betterment Assoc.* · Anne Reiter; Coord.; P.O. Box 72; 51449; Calhoun; P 1,700; M 41; (712) 464-7611; lakecitybett@iowatelecom.net; www.lakecityiowa.com

Lake Mills · *Lake Mills Chamber Dev. Corp.* · Marilyn Hoffman; Exec. Dir.; 203 N. 1st Ave. W.; P.O. Box 182; 50450; Winnebago; P 2,140; M 120; (641) 592-5253; Fax (641) 592-5252; lmcdc@wctatel.net; www.lakemillsiowa.com

Laurens · *Laurens C/C* · Connie Dallenbach; Secy.; P.O. Box 33; 50554; Pocahontas; P 1,500; M 50; (712) 845-2620; Fax (712) 841-5555; www.laurensiachamber.com

Le Claire · *Le Claire C/C* · Jackie Stepaniak; Secy.; P.O. Box 35; 52753; Scott; P 3,000; M 135; (563) 289-9970; info@leclairechamber.com; www.leclairechamber.com

LeMars • *LeMars Area C/C* • Neal Adler; Exec. Dir.; 50 Central Ave. S.E.; 51031; Plymouth; P 9,500; M 258; (712) 546-8821; Fax (712) 546-7218; lemarschamber@frontiernet.net; www.lemarsiowa.com*

Lenox • *Lenox C/C* • Michelle Tullberg; Coord.; 200 1/2 S. Main St.; 50851; Adams & Taylor; P 1,400; M 85; (641) 333-4272; lenoxchamber@lenoxia.com; www.lenoxia.com

Leon • *Leon C/C* • Marcia Stephens; Pres.; c/o Leon City Hall; 50144; Decatur; P 2,000; M 60; (641) 446-6221

Lisbon • *see Mount Vernon*

Logan • *Logan C/C* • Nikki Allen; P.O. Box 113; 51546; Harrison; P 1,500; M 50; (712) 644-3073; Fax (712) 644-3124; www.loganiowa.com

Manchester • *Manchester Area C/C* • Jack Klaus; Exec. Dir.; 200 E. Main St.; 52057; Delaware; P 5,300; M 200; (563) 927-4141; Fax (563) 927-2958; macc@manchesteriowa.org; www.manchester iowa.org

Manning • *Manning C/C* • Kirk Huehn; Pres.; P.O. Box 345; 51455; Carroll; P 1,500; M 58; (712) 655-3541; Fax (712) 655-2478; chamber@mmctsu.com; www.manningia.com

Manson • *Manson Eco. Dev. Corp. & C/C* • Josh Sturgis; Pres.; P.O. Box 561; 50563; Calhoun; P 2,000; M 35; (712) 469-3311; Fax (712) 469-3311; www.mansoniowa.org

Maquoketa • *Maquoketa Area C/C* • Stacy Driscoll; Exec. Dir.; 117 S. Main St.; 52060; Jackson; P 6,100; M 187; (563) 652-4602; (800) 989-4602; Fax (563) 652-3020; maqchamberassist@qwest office.net; www.maquoketachamber.com*

Marengo • *Marengo C/C* • Tony Hocamp; Pres.; P.O. Box 251; 52301; Iowa; P 2,500; M 35; (319) 642-5506; www.marengochamber.com

Marion • *Marion C/C* • Jill Ackerman; Pres.; 1225 6th Ave., Ste. 100; 52302; Iowa; P 32,000; M 250; (319) 377-6316; Fax (319) 377-1576; jill@marioncc.org; www.marioncc.org

Marquette • *see McGregor*

Marshalltown • *Marshalltown Area C/C* • Ken Anderson; Pres.; 709 S. Center St.; P.O. Box 1000; 50158; Marshall; P 39,311; M 469; (641) 753-6645; Fax (641) 752-8373; kanderson@marshalltown. org; www.marshalltown.org*

Mason City • *Mason City Area C/C* • Robin Anderson; Exec. Dir.; 25 W. State, Ste. B; 50401; Cerro Gordo; P 30,000; M 655; (641) 423-5724; Fax (641) 423-5725; chamber@masoncityia.com; www. masoncityia.com

Massena • *Massena C/C* • Don Henkenius; 100 Main St.; 50853; Cass; P 414; (712) 779-2295

McGregor • *McGregor-Marquette C/C* • Rachel Smith; Exec. Dir.; 146 Main St.; P.O. Box 105; 52157; Clayton; P 1,000; M 125; (563) 873-2186; mac-marq@alpinecom.net; www.mcgreg-marq.org*

Milford • *see Arnolds Park*

Missouri Valley • *Missouri Valley C/C* • Jeff Snyder; Exec. Dir.; 100 S. 4th St.; P.O. Box 130; 51555; Harrison; P 3,000; M 132; (712) 642-2553; Fax (712) 642-3771; chamberofcommerce1@juno.com; www.missourivalleychamber.com

Monona • *Monona C/C & Eco. Dev. Inc.* • 113 N. Page St.; P.O. Box 191; 52159; Clayton; P 1,550; M 10; (563) 539-8340; monona chamber@neitel.net; www.mononachamber.com

Monticello • *Monticello Area C/C* • Kris Kosar; Dir.; 204 E. 1st St.; 52310; Jones; P 3,600; M 152; (319) 465-5626; Fax (319) 465-3527; chamber@macc-ia.us; www.macc-ia.us*

Mount Ayr • *Mount Ayr C/C* • Sheila Shafer; Secy.; 117 S. Fillmore; P.O. Box 445; 50854; Ringgold; P 1,700; M 100; (641) 464-3704; rshafer@iowatelecom.net; www.mountayriowa.org

Mount Pleasant • *Mount Pleasant Area Chamber Alliance* • Kiley Miller; Exec. V.P.; 124 S. Main St.; 52641; Henry; P 9,000; M 319; (319) 385-3101; (877) 385-3103; Fax (319) 385-3012; mpaca@mountpleasantiowa.org; www.mountpleasantiowa.org

Mount Vernon • *Mount Vernon-Lisbon Comm. Dev. Group* • Dir.; P.O. Box 31; 52314; Linn; P 6,000; M 135; (319) 895-8214; info@visitmvl.com; www.visitmvl.com

Muscatine • *Greater Muscatine C/C & Ind.* • Bill Phelan; Pres./ CEO; 102 Walnut St.; 52761; Muscatine; P 23,000; M 400; (563) 263-8895; (800) 257-3275; Fax (563) 263-7662; chamber@ muscatine.com; www.muscatine.com*

Nevada • *Nevada C/C* • Sara Clausen; Exec. Dir.; 1015 6th St.; 50201; Story; P 6,658; M 180; (515) 382-6538; (800) 558-2288; Fax (515) 382-3803; chamber@midiowa.net; www.nevadaiowa.org

New Hampton • *New Horizons Chamber-MainStreet* • Jeannine Burgart CMSM; Exec. Dir.; 15 W. Main; 50659; Chickasaw; P 3,800; M 250; (641) 394-2021; nhc@iowatelecom.net; www. newhamptonia.com

New London • *New London C/C* • 213 W. Main St.; 52645; Henry; P 1,937; M 50; (319) 367-2573

Newton • *Greater Newton Area C/C* • Darrell Sarmento; Exec. Dir.; 113 First Ave. W.; 50208; Jasper; P 15,000; M 200; (641) 792-5545; Fax (641) 791-0879; info@experiencenewton.com; www. experiencenewton.com*

Northwood • *Northwood Area C/C* • P.O. Box 71; 50459; Worth; P 2,000; M 85; (641) 324-1420; info@northwoodchamber.org; www.northwoodchamber.org*

Norwalk • *Norwalk Area C/C* • Deb Mineart; Exec. Dir.; P.O. Box 173; 50211; Polk & Warren; P 8,300; M 125; (515) 981-0619; Fax (515) 981-1890; norwalkchamber@msn.com; www.norwalk chamber.org

Oelwein • *Oelwein Chamber & Area Dev.* • Sally Falb; Exec. Dir.; 25 W. Charles St.; 50662; Fayette; P 6,722; M 250; (319) 283-1105; Fax (319) 283-2890; ocad@oelwein.com; www.oelwein.com

Okoboji • *see Arnolds Park*

Onawa • *Onawa C/C* • Ann Crawford; Dir.; 707 Iowa Ave.; 51040; Monona; P 3,100; M 100; (712) 423-1801; Fax (712) 433-4622; chamber@onawa.com; www.onawa.com*

Orange City • *Orange City C/C* • Mike Hofman; Exec. Dir.; 509 8th St. S.E.; P.O. Box 36; 51041; Sioux; P 6,200; M 260; (712) 707-4510; Fax (712) 707-4523; occhamberexec@orangecitycomm.net; www.orangecityiowa.com

Osage • *Osage C/C* • Wendy Heuton; Exec. Dir.; 808 Main St.; 50461; Mitchell; P 3,500; M 120; (641) 732-3163; Fax (641) 732-3163; chamber@osage.net; www.osage.net/~chamber/

Osceola • *Osceola C/C* • Lacey Nish; Dir.; 115 E. Washington; P.O. Box 425; 50213; Clarke; P 4,700; M 155; (641) 342-4200; Fax (641) 342-6353; ocms@iowatelecom.net; osceolachamber.com

Oskaloosa • *Oskaloosa Area Chamber & Dev. Group* • Jon Sullivan; Dir.; 124 N. Market St.; 52577; Mahaska; P 23,000; M 310; (641) 672-2591; Fax (641) 672-2047; oskycofc@oacdg.org; www.oskaloosachamber.org*

Ottumwa • *Ottumwa Area C/C* • Terry McNitt; Exec. Dir.; 217 E. Main St.; P.O. Box 308; 52501; Wapello; P 35,000; M 400; (641) 682-3465; Fax (641) 682-3466; info@ottumwaiowa.com; www. ottumwaiowa.com

Panora • *Panora C/C* • Michelle Bassett; Pres.; P.O. Box 73; 50216; Guthrie; P 1,200; M 120; (641) 755-3300; train@netins. net; www.panora.org/chamber.html

Parkersburg • *Parkersburg C/C* • Becky Thorne; Treas.; P.O. Box 340; 50665; Butler; P 1,900; M 60; (319) 346-1461; www.parkersburgiowa.info

Pella • *Pella C/C* • Karen Eischen IOM; Exec. Dir.; 818 Washington; 50219; Marion; P 10,000; M 300; (641) 628-2626; (888) 746-3882; Fax (641) 628-9697; pellacoc@pella.org; www.pella.org*

Perry • *Perry Area C/C* • Wendy Goodale; Exec. Dir.; 1102 Willis Ave.; 50220; Dallas; P 8,000; M 178; (515) 465-4601; (515) 465-4602; Fax (515) 465-2256; perrychamber@perryia.org; www.perryia.org*

Pleasant Hill • *Pleasant Hill C/C* • Cathy Jensen; Exec. Dir.; 5160 Maple Dr., Ste. C; 50327; Polk; P 7,000; M 200; (515) 261-0466; Fax (515) 261-0467; phillchamber@qwestoffice.net; www.pleasanthillchamber.org*

Pleasantville • *Pleasantville C/C* • Betty Greenlee; Dir.; 104 E. Monroe St.; P.O. Box 672; 50225; Marion; P 1,600; M 50; (515) 848-3903; pleasantcc@iowatelecom.net; www.therealpleasantville.com

Pocahontas • *Pocahontas C/C* • Pres.; P.O. Box 124; 50574; Pocahontas; P 1,970; M 100; (712) 335-3695; pocahontaschamber@gmail.com; www.pocahontaschamber.com

Postville • *Postville C/C* • P.O. Box 875; 52162; Allamakee & Clayton; P 2,500; M 50; (563) 864-7247

Rathbun • *see Centerville*

Red Oak • *Red Oak Chamber & Ind. Assoc.* • Darrel Steven Carlyle; Exec. Dir.; 307 E. Reed St.; 51566; Montgomery; P 6,000; M 235; (712) 623-4821; (712) 623-4822; Fax (712) 623-4822; execdir@redoakiowa.com; www.redoakiowa.com*

Remsen • *Remsen C/C* • Karen Harnack; Secy./Treas.; P.O. Box 225; 51050; Plymouth; P 1,700; M 100; (712) 786-2416; (712) 786-2136; chamber@remseniowa.net; www.remseniowa.net

Rock Rapids • *Rock Rapids Comm. Affairs Corp.* • Angie Jager; Exec. Dir.; 206 1st Ave.; P.O. Box 403; 51246; Lyon; P 2,600; M 150; (712) 472-3456; Fax (712) 472-2764; chamber@rockrapids.com; www.rockrapids.com

Rock Valley • *Rock Valley C/C* • Curt Strouth; Exec. Dir.; P.O. Box 89; 51247; Sioux; P 3,000; M 94; (712) 476-9300; Fax (712) 476-9116; www.rockvalleychamber.com

Rockwell • *Rockwell C/C* • P.O. Box 156; 50469; Cerro Gordo; P 1,000; M 35; (641) 822-4906; www.rockwell-ia.org

Rockwell City • *Rockwell City Chamber & Dev.* • Leigh Anne Oswald; Coord.; 605 Richmond St.; 50579; Calhoun; P 2,626; M 81; (712) 297-8874; rcdev@iowatelecom.net; www.rockwellcity.com

Sac City • *Chamber-Main Street Sac City* • Laura Zimmerman; Prog. Dir.; 615 W. Main St.; 50583; Sac; P 2,516; M 150; (712) 662-7316; saccitymainstreet@prairieinet.net; www.saccity.org

Saint Ansgar • *Saint Ansgar C/C* • P.O. Box 133; 50472; Mitchell; P 1,100; M 60; (641) 736-4444; www.stansgar.org

Saint Donatus • *see Bellevue*

Schaller • *Schaller C/C* • Theresa Bailey; Secy./Treas.; 1635 250th St.; 51053; Sac; P 850; M 55; (712) 275-4251

Sheldon • *Sheldon Chamber & Dev. Corp.* • Mark Gaul; Exec. Dir.; 416 9th St.; P.O. Box 276; 51201; O'Brien & Sioux; P 5,000; M 208; (712) 324-2813; Fax (712) 324-4602; mgaul@sheldoniowa.com; www.sheldoniowa.com

Shenandoah • *Shenandoah Chamber & Ind. Org.* • Gregg Connell; Exec. Dir.; 100 Maple St.; 51601; Page; P 6,000; M 300; (712) 246-3455; Fax (712) 246-3456; chamber@shenandoahiowa.net; www.shenandoahiowa.net

Sibley • *Sibley C/C* • Amy Smith; Exec. Dir.; 310 9th St.; 51249; Osceola; P 2,600; M 120; (712) 754-3212; Fax (712) 754-3212; chamber@hickorytech.net; www.sibleyiowa.net

Sidney • *Sidney Iowa C/C* • Brian Whipple; Pres.; P.O. Box 401; 51652; Fremont; P 8,000; M 60; (712) 374-3339; Fax (712) 374-3339; info@sidneyiowachamber.com; www.sidneyiowachamber.com

Sioux Center • *Sioux Center C/C* • Ardith Lein; Exec. Dir.; 303 N. Main Ave.; 51250; Sioux; P 6,800; M 205; (712) 722-3457; Fax (712) 722-3465; scchambr@mtcnet.net; www.siouxcenterchamber.com

Sioux City • *Siouxland C/C* • Debi Durham; Pres.; 101 Pierce St.; 51101; Plymouth & Woodbury; P 143,000; M 1,000; (712) 255-7903; Fax (712) 258-7578; chamber@siouxlandchamber.com; www.siouxlandchamber.com.

Spencer • *Spencer C/C* • Robert Rose; Exec. Dir.; 122 W. 5th St.; P.O. Box 7937; 51301; Clay; P 11,317; M 500; (712) 262-5680; Fax (712) 262-5747; spencerchamber@smunet.net; spenceriowachamber.org.*

HOME OF "DEWEY"–THE SMALL TOWN CAT THAT TOUCHED THE WORLD—CLAY COUNTY FAIR HELD EACH SEPTEMBER AND ANNUAL FLAGFEST CELEBRATION EACH JUNE.

Spirit Lake • *Spirit Lake Mainsail C/C* • Blain Andera; Dir.; 1710 Lincoln Ave.; P.O. Box 155; 51360; Dickinson; P 5,000; M 160; (712) 336-4978; Fax (712) 336-4978; mainsail@mchsi.com; www.slmainsail.com

Storm Lake • *Storm Lake United* • Gary Lalone; Exec. Dir.; 119 W. 6th St.; P.O. Box 584; 50588; Buena Vista; P 10,000; M 275; (712) 732-3780; (888) 572-4692; Fax (712) 732-1511; info@stormlakeunited.com; www.visitstormlake.com*

Story City • *Story City Greater Chamber Connection* • Carolyn Honeycutt; Exec. Dir.; 602 Broad St.; 50248; Story; P 3,300; (515) 733-4214; Fax (515) 733-4504; chamber@storycity.net; www.storycity.net

Strawberry Point • *Strawberry Point C/C* • McKenzie Johnson; Eco. Dev. Dir.; P.O. Box 404; 52076; Clayton; P 1,368; M 80; (563) 933-4417; chamber@strawberrypt.com; www.strawberrypt.com

Stuart • *Stuart C/C* • Cory Hansen; Pres.; 119 E. Front St.; P.O. Box 560; 50250; Adair; P 1,800; M 52; (515) 523-1455; stuartchamber@aol.com; www.stuartia.com

Sumner • *Sumner Commercial Club* • P.O. Box 262; 50674; Bremer; P 2,200; M 80; (563) 578-5470

Tama • *see Toledo*

Tipton • *Tipton C/C* • John Todd; Comm. Dev. Dir.; P.O. Box 5; 52772; Cedar; P 3,200; M 100; (563) 886-6350; cddirector@iowatelecom.net; www.tiptoniowa.us

Toledo • *Tama-Toledo Area C/C* • Carolyn Dolezal; Coord.; 103 S. Church St.; P.O. Box 367; 52342; Tama; P 5,000; M 134; (641) 484-6661; tama.toledochamber@yahoo.com; chamber.tamatoledo.org

Traer • *Traer C/C* • Kirstie Seda; Pres.; P.O. Box 431; 50675; Tama; P 1,700; M 40; (319) 478-2346; (319) 429-6667; traerchamber@hotmail.com; www.traer.com

Tripoli • *Tripoli Comm. Club* • Jay Ranard; Pres.; P.O. Box 76; 50676; Bremer; P 1,310; M 40; (319) 882-3002; n.ranard@butler-bremer.com; tripoliiowa.com

Urbandale • *Urbandale C/C* • Tiffany Menke IOM; Exec. Dir.; 2900 Justin Dr., Ste. L; 50322; Dallas & Polk; P 35,904; M 650; (515) 331-6855; Fax (515) 331-2987; info@urbandalechamber.com; www.uniquelyurbandale.com

Villisca · *Villisca C/C* · Mr. Gayle Heard; Treas.; 601 S. 3rd Ave.; 50864; Montgomery; P 1,332; M 32; (712) 826-5222

Vinton · *Vinton Unlimited* · 310 A Ave.; P.O. Box 387; 52349; Benton; P 5,500; M 220; (319) 472-3955; Fax (319) 472-4456; info@vintonia.org; www.vintonia.org*

Washington · *Washington C/C* · Tim Coffey; Exec. Dir.; 205 W. Main St.; 52353; Washington; P 7,200; M 235; (319) 653-3272; Fax (319) 653-5805; washcofc@iowatelecom.net; www.washingtoniowachamber.com*

Waterloo · *Greater Cedar Valley C/C* · Bob Justis; Pres./CEO; 10 W. 4th St., Ste. 310; 50701; Black Hawk; P 68,747; M 850; (319) 233-8431; Fax (319) 233-4580; bob@greatercedarvalleychamber.com; www.greatercedarvalleychamber.com

Waukee · *Waukee Area C/C* · Chad Airhart; Exec. Dir.; 230 W. Hickman Rd.; P.O. Box 23; 50263; Dallas; P 9,500; M 200; (515) 978-7115; Fax (515) 987-1845; info@waukeechamber.com; www.waukeechamber.com

Waukon · *Waukon C/C* · Danny Schlitter; Exec. Dir.; 101 W. Main St.; 52172; Allamakee; P 4,200; M 165; (563) 568-4110; Fax (563) 568-6990; waukoncc@mchsi.com; www.waukon.org

Waverly · *Waverly C/C* · Kelly Engelken; Exec. Dir.; 118 E. Bremer Ave.; 50677; Bremer; P 9,000; M 200; (319) 352-4526; (319) 352-5861; Fax (319) 352-0136; waverly@waverlychamber.com; www.waverlyia.com*

Webster City · *Webster City Area Dev.* · Carrie Fitzgerald; Chamber Dir.; 628 2nd St.; P.O. Box 310; 50595; Hamilton; P 8,100; M 147; (515) 832-2564; Fax (515) 832-5130; info@webstercity-iowa.com; www.webstercity-iowa.com

West Bend · *West Bend C/C* · Tina Banwart; Secy.; P.O. Box 366; 50597; Kossuth & Palo Alto; P 834; M 45; (515) 887-2181; chamber@westbendiowa.com; www.westbendiowa.com

West Des Moines · *West Des Moines C/C* · Linda Hulleman; Exec. Dir.; 4200 Mills Civic Pkwy.; P.O. Box 65320; 50265; Dallas, Polk & Warren; P 53,000; M 650; (515) 225-6009; Fax (515) 225-7129; info@wdmchamber.org; www.wdmchamber.org

West Liberty · *West Liberty C/C* · Letha Ottaway; COO; 405 N. Elm St.; 52776; Muscatine; P 3,500; M 125; (319) 627-4876; Fax (319) 627-3087; wlchambr@lcom.net; westlibertyiowa.com

West Union · *West Union C/C* · Robin Bostrom; Exec. Dir.; 101 N. Vine St.; 52175; Fayette; P 2,500; M 100; (563) 422-3070; Fax (563) 422-6322; wuchamber@alpinecom.net; www.westunion.com

Williamsburg · *Williamsburg C/C* · Barb Hopp; Exec. Asst.; 208 W. State St.; P.O. Box 982; 52361; Iowa; P 2,700; M 100; (319) 668-1500; Fax (319) 668-9112; www.williamsburgiowa.org

Wilton · *Wilton C/C* · Eva Belitz; Dir.; 118 W. 4th St.; P.O. Box 280; 52778; Cedar & Muscatine; P 3,000; M 120; (563) 732-2330; Fax (563) 732-2332; wiltoncc@netwtc.net; www.wiltoniowa.org

Winfield · *Winfield C/C* · Klay Edwards; Pres.; P.O. Box H; 52659; Henry; P 1,131; M 30; (319) 257-3305; www.winfieldiowa.com

Winterset · *Madison County C/C* · 73 Jefferson St.; 50273; Madison; P 20,000; M 160; (515) 462-1185; (800) 298-6119; Fax (515) 462-1393; chamber@madisoncounty.com; www.madisoncounty.com

Woodbine · *Woodbine Main Street C/C* · Patty Reisz; Program Dir.; P.O. Box 264; 51579; Harrison; P 1,800; M ; (712) 647-3434; woodbinechamber@iowatelecom.net

Kansas

Kansas C of C · Amy Blankenbiller; Pres./CEO; 835 S.W. Topeka Blvd.; Topeka; 66612; Shawnee; P 2,800,000; M 10,000; (785) 357-6321; Fax (785) 357-4732; info@kansaschamber.org; www.kansaschamber.org

Abilene · *Abilene Area C/C* · Cindy Issitt; Pres.; 500 N. Buckeye; 67410; Dickinson; P 6,800; M 275; (785) 263-1770; Fax (785) 263-1536; visitus1@sbcglobal.net; www.abileneks.com

Alma · *Alma C/C* · Trish Ringel; Secy.; P.O. Box 234; 66401; Wabaunsee; P 900; M 45; (785) 765-3327; Fax (785) 765-3384

Alta Vista · *Alta Vista C/C* · Brier Kormanik; V.P.; P.O. Box 115; 66834; Wabaunsee; P 500; M 20; (785) 499-5588

Andover · *Andover Area C/C* · Scott Wilson; Pres.; 1607 E. Central; P.O. Box 339; 67002; Butler; P 9,500; M 150; (316) 733-0648; Fax (316) 733-8808; info@andoverchamber.com; www.andoverchamber.com

Anthony · *Anthony C/C* · Gwen Warner; Exec. Dir.; 227 W. Main; P.O. Box 354; 67003; Harper; P 2,400; M 160; (620) 842-5456; Fax (620) 842-3929; info@anthonychamber.com; www.anthonychamber.com

Arkansas City · *Arkansas City Area C/C* · Janet Siebert IOM; Pres./CEO; 106 S. Summit; P.O. Box 795; 67005; Cowley; P 12,000; M 500; (620) 442-0230; Fax (620) 441-0048; ac-ceo@arkcitychamber.org; www.arkcity.org*

Ashland · *Ashland C/C* · P.O. Box 37; 67831; Clark; P 1,032; M 50; (620) 635-0427; (620) 635-2531; aac@ashlandks.com; www.ashlandks.com

Atchison · *Atchison Area C/C* · Jacque Pregont; Pres.; 200 S. 10th St.; P.O. Box 126; 66002; Atchison; P 20,000; M 340; (913) 367-2427; (800) 234-1854; Fax (913) 367-2485; tours@atchisonkansas.net; www.atchisonkansas.net*

Atwood · *Atwood C/C* · Sarah Maaske; Exec. Dir.; 303 Main St.; P.O. Box 152; 67730; Rawlins; P 1,554; M 82; (785) 626-9630; atwoodchamber@rawlinscounty.info; www.atwoodkansas.com

Augusta · *Augusta C/C* · Sharon Sudduth; Exec. Dir.; 112 E. 6th Ave.; 67010; Butler; P 8,700; M 255; (316) 775-6339; Fax (316) 775-1307; augustacoc@sbcglobal.net; www.chamberofaugusta.org*

Baldwin City · *Baldwin City C/C* · Pres.; 720 High St.; P.O. Box 501; 66006; Douglas; P 4,200; M 170; (785) 594-3200; info@baldwincitychamber.com; www.baldwincitychamber.com

Basehor · *Basehor C/C* · Aladdin Ashkar; Pres.; P.O. Box 35; 66007; Leavenworth; P 2,700; (913) 724-9000; info@basehorchamber.org; www.basehorchamber.org

Baxter Springs · *Baxter Springs C/C* · 1004 Military Ave.; 66713; Cherokee; P 5,000; M 110; (620) 856-3131; Fax (620) 856-3185; chamberdirector@baxtersprings.us; www.baxtersprings.us

Belle Plaine · *Belle Plaine Area C/C* · P.O. Box 721; 67013; Sumner; P 1,800; M 36; (620) 488-2604; Fax (620) 488-3517; www.belleplainechamber.com

Belleville · *Belleville Area C/C* · Melinda Pierson; Dir.; 1309 18th St.; P.O. Box 280; 66935; Republic; P 2,239; M 100; (785) 527-5524; Fax (785) 527-5524; bellevcham@nckcn.com; www.bellevilleks.org

Beloit · *Beloit Area C/C* · 123 N. Mill; P.O. Box 582; 67420; Mitchell; P 4,100; M 162; (785) 738-2717; beloitchamber@nckcn.com; www.beloitchamberofcommerce.com

Bird City · *Bird City Comm. Club* · Jane Brubaker; P.O. Box 219; 67731; Cheyenne; P 500; M 30; (785) 734-2616; www.birdcity.com

Blue Rapids • *Blue Rapids C/C* • P.O. Box 253; 66411; Marshall; P 1,135; M 65; (785) 363-7991; bluerapidschamberofcommerce@yahoo.com; skyways.lib.ks.us/towns/BlueRapids

Bonner Springs • *Bonner Springs-Edwardsville Area C/C* • Charlene A. Biles; Exec. V.P./Exec. Secy.; 129 N. Nettleton; P.O. Box 403; 66012; Wyandotte; P 15,000; M 125; (913) 422-5044; Fax (913) 441-1366; bsedscofc@att.net; www.lifeisbetter.org

Burlingame • *Burlingame Area C/C* • Kathy Kraus; Secy.; P.O. Box 102; 66413; Osage; P 1,003; M 20; (785) 654-3322; www.burlingameks.gov

Burlington • *Coffey County C/C* • Jennifer R. Anderson; Exec. Dir.; 110 N. 4th St.; 66839; Coffey; P 9,000; M 135; (620) 364-2002; (877) 364-2002; Fax (620) 364-3048; info@coffeycountychamber.com; www.coffeycountychamber.com

Caldwell • *Caldwell Area C/C* • LuAnn Jamison; Secy.; P.O. Box 42; 67022; Sumner; P 1,300; M 54; (620) 845-6666; (620) 845-2444; www.caldwellkansas.com

Caney • *Caney C/C* • Jackie Freisberg; Pres.; 312 W. Fourth Ave.; P.O. Box 211; 67333; Montgomery; P 2,300; M 85; (620) 879-5131; www.caney.com

Canton • *Canton C/C* • Bernard Rundstrum; Pres.; 104 W. Allen; P.O. Box 275; 67428; McPherson; P 800; M 25; (620) 628-4916; skyways.lib.ks.us/towns/Canton

Cedar Vale • *Cedar Vale C/C* • Priscilla Melton; P.O. Box 112; 67024; Chautauqua; P 740; M 30; (620) 758-2244; (620) 758-2465

Chanute • *Chanute Area C/C & Ofc. of Tourism* • Jane Brophy; Exec. Dir.; 21 N. Lincoln Ave.; P.O. Box 747; 66720; Neosho; P 9,000; M 182; (620) 431-3350; Fax (620) 431-7770; information@chanutechamber.com; www.chanutechamber.com*

Cheney • *Cheney C/C* • P.O. Box 716; 67025; Sedgwick; P 2,200; M 45; (316) 542-3142; (888) 522-7221; www.cheneychamber.com

Cherryvale • *Cherryvale C/C* • Tina Cunningham; Pres.; P.O. Box 112; 67335; Montgomery; P 2,400; M 50; (620) 891-0072; cherryvalechamber@hotmail.com; www.cherryvaleusa.com/chamber

Chetopa • *Chetopa C/C* • Mary Jane Houston; Secy.; 917 Locust St.; 67336; Labette; P 1,300; M 45; (620) 236-7371; (620) 236-7511; Fax (620) 236-7476; www.chetopacity.org

Cimarron • *Cimarron Area C/C* • TruDee Little; Secy./Treas.; 119 S. Main; P.O. Box 602; 67835; Gray; P 2,000; M 50; (620) 855-2507; (620) 855-2215; www.cimarronkansas.net

Clay Center • *Clay Center Area C/C* • Andy Contreras; Pres./CEO; 517 Court St.; 67432; Clay; P 8,500; M 120; (785) 632-5674; Fax (785) 632-5674; visitclay@claycenterkschamber.org; www.claycenterkschamber.org.

Clearwater • *Clearwater C/C* • Jennifer Arnold; Exec. Dir.; 130 E. Ross, Ste. 104; P.O. Box 627; 67026; Sedgwick; P 2,300; M 90; (620) 584-3366; Fax (620) 584-2268; chamber@sktc.net; www.clearwaterkschamber.org

Clyde • *Clyde Comm. C/C* • Jamie Kegle; Pres.; P.O. Box 5; 66938; Cloud; P 750; M 45; (785) 446-2291; www.clydekansas.org

Coffeyville • *Coffeyville Area C/C* • Angela Wilson; Exec. Dir.; 807 Walnut; P.O. Box 457; 67337; Montgomery; P 10,000; M 300; (620) 251-2550; Fax (620) 251-5448; chamber@coffeyville.com; www.coffeyvillechamber.org*

Colby • *Colby/Thomas County C/C* • Holly Whitaker; Exec. Dir.; 350 S. Range Ave., Ste. 10; 67701; Thomas; P 8,000; M 220; (785) 460-3401; Fax (785) 460-4509; colbychamber@thomascounty.com; www.oasisontheplains.com*

Coldwater • *Coldwater C/C* • Johnita Stalcup; Treas.; P.O. Box 333; 67029; Comanche; P 700; M 30; (620) 582-2859; www.coldwaterkansas.com

Columbus • *Columbus C/C* • Jean Pritchett; Dir.; 320 E. Maple; 66725; Cherokee; P 3,500; M 190; (620) 429-1492; Fax (620) 429-1492; columbuschamber@columbus-ks.com; www.columbus-kansas.com/chamber*

Concordia • *Concordia Area C/C* • Roberta Lowrey; Pres.; 606 Washington; 66901; Cloud; P 6,000; M 170; (785) 243-4290; Fax (785) 243-2014; chamber@concordiakansas.org; www.concordiakansas.org

Conway Springs • *Conway Springs C/C* • Jon Ott; Pres.; 208 W. Spring; P.O. Box 392; 67031; Sumner; P 1,350; M 30; (620) 456-2252; jo@statebankcs.com; www.chamberconway.com

Cottonwood Falls • *Chase County C/C* • Debbie Adcock; Admin. Dir.; 318 Broadway; P.O. Box 362; 66845; Chase; P 3,000; M 80; (620) 273-8469; (800) 431-6344; chasechamber@sbcglobal.net; www.chasecountychamber.org

Council Grove • *Council Grove/Morris County Chamber & Tourism* • Genevieve Nichols; Exec. Dir.; 207 W. Main; 66846; Morris; P 2,300; M 141; (620) 767-5413; (800) 732-9211; Fax (620) 767-5553; chamber@councilgrove.com; www.councilgrove.com

Derby • *Derby C/C* • Rhonda Cott; Pres.; 330 E. Madison, Ste. 150; P.O. Box 544; 67037; Sedgwick; P 22,000; M 375; (316) 788-3421; Fax (316) 788-6861; info@derbychamber.com; www.derbychamber.com*

Desoto • *Desoto C/C* • Sara Ritter; Exec. Dir.; P.O. Box 70; 66018; Johnson; P 5,400; M 190; (913) 583-1585; (877) 585-1821; sritter@desotoks.org; www.desotoks.org

Dighton • *Lane County Area C/C* • Chelle Anderson; Secy.; 147 E. Long; P.O. Box 942; 67839; Lane; P 1,261; M 71; (620) 397-2211; Fax (620) 397-2416; info@dightonks.com; www.dightonkansas.com

Dodge City • *Dodge City Area C/C* • Cindy Malek; Pres.; 311 W. Spruce; P.O. Box 939; 67801; Ford; P 31,000; M 525; (620) 227-3119; Fax (620) 227-2957; info@dodgechamber.com; www.dodgechamber.com*

Downs • *Downs C/C* • Majean Scheider; Pres.; 801 Morgan; P.O. Box 172; 67437; Osborne; P 1,150; M 45; (785) 454-3416; www.downschamber.com

El Dorado • *El Dorado C/C* • Shirley Patton; Exec. Dir.; 201 E. Central; 67042; Butler; P 12,600; M 277; (316) 321-3150; Fax (316) 321-5419; info@eldoradochamber.com; www.360eldorado.com*

Elkhart • *Elkhart Area C/C* • Tim Hardy; Pres.; 546 Morton; P.O. Box 696; 67950; Morton; P 2,500; M 125; (620) 697-4600; www.ci.elkhart.ks.us

Ellinwood • *Ellinwood C/C* • 110 1/2 N. Main St.; P.O. Box 482; 67526; Barton; P 2,200; M 155; (620) 564-3300; (620) 566-7353; ellinwoodchamber@hotmail.com; www.ellinwoodchamber.com

Ellis • *Ellis C/C* • Dena Patee; Dir.; 820 Washington; 67637; Ellis; P 2,100; M 90; (785) 726-2660; Fax (785) 726-2661; ellischamber@eaglecom.net; www.ellischamberofcommerce.com

Ellsworth • *Ellsworth-Kanopolis Area C/C* • Nick Slechta; Dir.; 114 1/2 N. Douglas; P.O. Box 315; 67439; Ellsworth; P 2,600; M 120; (785) 472-4071; Fax (785) 472-5668; ecofc@eaglecom.net; www.ellsworthkschamber.net

Emporia • *Emporia Area C/C* • Jeanine McKenna; Pres./CEO; 719 Commercial St.; 66801; Lyon; P 35,600; M 600; (620) 342-1600; chamber@emporiakschamber.org; www.emporiakschamber.org*

Eskridge • *Eskridge C/C* • P.O. Box 313; 66423; Wabaunsee; P 600; M 45; (785) 449-7215

Eudora • *Eudora C/C* • P.O. Box 725; 66025; Douglas; P 6,300; M 62; (785) 542-1212; Fax (785) 542-1235; contactus@eudora chamber.com; www.eudorachamber.com

Eureka • *Eureka Area C/C* • Anita Bjorling; Coord.; Memorial Hall Bldg.; P.O. Box 563; 67045; Greenwood; P 2,974; M 50; (620) 583-5452; Fax (620) 583-5452; www.eurekakansas.com

Everest • *Everest C/C* • Michael Wilburn; P.O. Box 6; 66424; Brown; P 300; M 30; (785) 548-7521

Fairway • *see Mission*

Florence • *Florence C/C* • Mary Jane Grimmett; Pres.; 511 Main; 66851; Marion; P 670; M 30; (620) 878-4296; www.florenceks.com

Fort Scott • *Fort Scott Area C/C* • Vicki Pritchett; Pres./CEO; 231 E. Wall St.; 66701; Bourbon; P 8,500; M 300; (620) 223-3566; (800) 245-FORT; Fax (620) 223-3574; fschamber@fortscott.com; www.fortscott.com

Fredonia • *Fredonia C/C* • Yvonne Hull; Exec. Dir.; 402 N. 7th; P.O. Box 449; 66736; Wilson; P 2,500; M 173; (620) 378-3221; Fax (620) 378-4833; fredoniakschamber@twinmounds.com; www.fredoniachamber.com

Galena • *Galena C/C* • Kathleen Anderson; Pres.; P.O. Box 465; 66739; Cherokee; P 4,500; M 80; (620) 783-1395

Garden City • *Garden City Area C/C* • D. Paul Joseph CCE; Pres.; 1511 E. Fulton Terrace; 67846; Finney; P 40,000; M 450; (620) 276-3264; Fax (620) 276-3290; dpjoseph@gcnet.com; www.gardencitychamber.net*

Gardner • *Gardner Area C/C* • Peter Solie; Pres.; 109 E. Main; P.O. Box 402; 66030; Johnson; P 18,000; M 260; (913) 856-6464; Fax (913) 856-5274; president@gardnerchamber.com; www.gardnerchamber.com

Garnett • *Garnett Area C/C* • Chris Maynard; Pres.; 419 S. Oak; 66032; Anderson; P 3,200; M 90; (785) 448-6767; Fax (785) 448-6767; www.garnettchamber.org

Girard • *Girard Area C/C* • Dr. Harold Bryan; Exec. Dir.; 118 N. Ozark; P.O. Box 41; 66743; Crawford; P 2,800; M 85; (620) 724-4715; girardchamber@ckt.net

Glasco • *Glasco Chamber Pride* • Mrs. Joan Northern; Secy.; 405 E. Spaulding Ave.; P.O. Box 572; 67445; Cloud; P 550; M 20; (785) 568-0120; jnothern334@usd334.org; www.glascokansas.org

Glen Elder • *Glen Elder Community Club* • Megan Duskie; Pres.; 105 S. Hobart; 67446; Mitchell; P 440; M 50; (785) 545-3180; megan_duskie@yahoo.com; www.glenelder.com

Goodland • *Goodland Area C/C* • Jordie Mann; Interim Exec. Dir.; 104 E. 10th; 67735; Sherman; P 6,000; M 180; (785) 899-7130; gdlchmbr@eaglecom.net; www.goodlandchamber.com*

JOIN US FOR OUR ANNUAL EVENTS: FREEDOM FEST-JULY, SHERMAN COUNTY FREE FAIR-AUG, PRO BULL RIDERS/ THUNDER ON THE PLAINS-AUG 4, FLATLANDERS FALL FEST-SEPT. HUNTERS ALWAYS WELCOME!

Great Bend • *Great Bend C/C* • Jan Peters; Pres.; 1125 Williams St.; 67530; Barton; P 16,000; M 930; (620) 792-2401; Fax (620) 792-2404; gbcc@greatbend.org; www.greatbend.org*

Greensburg • *Kiowa County C/C* • Kim Alderfer; Pres.; 101 S. Main; 67054; Kiowa; P 2,200; M 70; (620) 723-2400; tourism@bigwell.org; www.bigwell.org

Halstead • *Halstead C/C* • Mary Lee McDonald; Secy./Treas.; P.O. Box 328; 67056; Harvey; P 1,902; M 72; (316) 217-4996; chamber@discoverhalstead.com; www.discoverhalstead.com

Hanover • *Hanover C/C* • Russ Behrends; 109 W. North; P.O. Box 283; 66945; Washington; P 652; M 45; (785) 337-2598

Harper • *Harper C/C* • 201 W. Main; P.O. Box 337; 67058; Harper; P 1,550; M 30; (620) 896-2511

Havensville • *see Onaga*

Hays • *Hays Area C/C* • 2700 Vine St.; 67601; Ellis; P 20,000; M 600; (785) 628-8201; (785) 628-8206; Fax (785) 628-1471; hayscc@discoverhays.com; www.discoverhays.com*

Haysville • *Haysville C/C* • Forrest Hummel; Pres.; 150 Stewart; P.O. Box 372; 67060; Sedgwick; P 10,000; M 150; (316) 529-2461; Fax (316) 554-2342; haysvillechamber@gmail.com; www.haysvillechamber.com

Herington • *Tri-County Area C/C* • Phyllis Smith; Exec. Dir.; 106 N. Broadway; 67449; Dickinson; P 2,600; M 130; (785) 258-2115; Fax (785) 258-2799; hrngtnch@tctelco.net; www.tricountycofc.com

Herndon • *Herndon C/C* • Jayne Niermeier; Treas.; P.O. Box 217; 67739; Rawlins; P 200; M 100; (785) 322-5619; Fax (785) 322-2020; skyways.lib.ks.us/towns/Herndon

Hesston • *Hesston C/C* • Janet Thrasher; Exec. Dir.; 115 E. Smith; 67062; Harvey; P 3,800; M 125; (620) 327-4102; (800) 442-1563; Fax (620) 327-4595; chamber@hesstonks.org; www.hesstonks.org

Hiawatha • *Hiawatha C of C/CVB* • Beth Spicer; Admin.; 1711 Oregon St.; 66434; Brown; P 3,600; M 140; (785) 742-7136; Fax (785) 742-3966; hiawathachamber@rainbowtel.net; www.hiawathachamber.com

Hill City • *Hill City C/C* • Carolyn Popp; Secy./Mgr.; 801 W. Main St.; P.O. Box 155; 67642; Graham; P 1,660; M 90; (785) 421-5621; hcchamber@ruraltel.net; www.discoverhillcity.com

Hillsboro • *Hillsboro C/C* • Renee Gilkey; Exec. Dir.; 109 S. Main; 67063; Marion; P 3,400; M 133; (620) 947-3506; Fax (620) 947-2585; hillsborochamber@hillsboro-kansas.com; www.hillsboro-kansas.com

Hoisington • *Hoisington C/C* • Stacey Bressler; Exec. V.P; 123 N. Main St.; 67544; Barton; P 3,000; M 110; (620) 653-4311; Fax (620) 653-4311; hoisingtoncofc@embarqmail.com; www.hoisingtonkansas.com*

Holton • *Holton/Jackson County C/C* • Lynne Wagner; Exec. Dir.; 105 W. 4th St.; 66436; Jackson; P 12,000; M 168; (785) 364-3963; Fax (785) 364-3963; chamber@holtonks.net; www.holtonks.net/chamber

Horton • *Horton C/C* • Rita Higley; P.O. Box 105; 66439; Brown; P 2,000; M 70; (785) 486-3321; Fax (785) 486-3321; hortonchamber@rainbowtel.net; www.hortonkansas.org

Howard • *Howard C/C* • Nadine Baumgartel; Treas.; P.O. Box 545; 67349; Elk; P 850; M 75; (620) 374-2172

Hugoton • *Hugoton Area C/C* • Kristin Farnum; Dir.; 630 S. Main St.; 67951; Stevens; P 5,463; M 80; (620) 544-4305; (620) 544-8531; Fax (620) 544-4610; hchamber@pld.com; www.hugotonchamber.com

Humboldt • *Humboldt C/C* • Don Copley; 105 S. 9th St.; P.O. Box 133; 66748; Allen; P 2,000; M 45; (620) 473-3011; www.humboldtks.net

Hutchinson • *Hutchinson/Reno County C/C* • Dave Kerr; Pres.; 117 N. Walnut; P.O. Box 519; 67504; Reno; P 65,000; M 1,400; (620) 662-3391; Fax (620) 662-2168; info@hutchchamber.com; www.hutchchamber.com.*

Independence • *Independence C/C* • Gwen Wilburn; Pres.; 322 N. Penn Ave.; P.O. Box 386; 67301; Montgomery; P 9,200; M 279; (620) 331-1890; Fax (620) 331-1899; chamber@indkschamber.org; www.indkschamber.org*

Inman • *Inman C/C* • P.O. Box 511; 67546; McPherson; P 1,200; M 65; (620) 585-2063; city@inmanks.net; www.inmanks.net

Iola • *Iola Area C/C* • Jana Taylor; Exec. Dir.; 208 W. Madison; 66749; Allen; P 5,700; M 170; (620) 365-5252; Fax (620) 365-8078; director@iolachamber.org; www.iolachamber.org

Jewell • *Jewell C/C* • Becky Loomis; Pres.; P.O. Box 235; 66949; Jewell; P 450; M 50; (785) 428-3600; Fax (785) 428-3600

Johnson • *Stanton County C/C* • Karla Dimmitt; Exec. Dir.; 206 S. Main St.; P.O. Box 9; 67855; Stanton; P 2,200; M 150; (620) 492-6606; stchamb@pld.com

Junction City • *Junction City Area C/C* • 701 N. Jefferson; P.O. Box 26; 66441; Geary; P 20,000; M 366; (785) 762-2632; Fax (785) 762-3353; jcchamber@junctionchamber.org; www.junctioncity chamber.org*

Kanopolis • *see Ellsworth*

Kansas City • *Kansas City Kansas Area C/C* • Cindy Cash; Pres./CEO; 727 Minnesota Ave.; P.O. Box 171337; 66117; Wyandotte; P 160,000; M 840; (913) 371-3070; Fax (913) 371-3732; cham ber@kckchamber.com; www.kckchamber.com*

Kansas City • *Women's C/C* • Therese Bysel; Pres.; 727 Minnesota Ave.; P.O. Box 171337; 66117; Wyandotte; P 160,000; M 120; (913) 371-3165; Fax (913) 371-3732; www.womens chamberkck.org

Kingman • *Kingman Area C/C* • Greg Graffman; Pres.; 322 N. Main; 67068; Kingman; P 3,387; M 107; (620) 532-1853; info@ kingmancc.com; www.kingmancc.com

Kinsley • *Edwards County C/C* • Carlene Engler; Pres.; 200 E. 6th; P.O. Box 161; 67547; Edwards; P 3,500; M 50; (620) 659-2711; Fax (620) 659-2711; ecedcweb@sbcglobal.net; www.edwards countyks.org

Kiowa • *Kiowa C/C* • Kelly Stewart; Pres.; 204 N. 5th St.; 67070; Barber; P 1,160; M 80; (620) 825-4825

LaCrosse • *Rush County C/C* • Leslie Morgan; Secy.; P.O. Box 716; 67548; Rush; P 3,200; M 60; (785) 222-2639; Fax (785) 222-2639; chamber67548@yahoo.com; www.rushcounty.org

Lansing • *see Leavenworth*

Larned • *Larned Area C/C* • Courtland Holman; Exec. Dir.; 502 Broadway; 67550; Pawnee; P 10,000; M 176; (620) 285-6916; (800) 747-6919; Fax (620) 285-6917; larnedcofc@gbta.net; www. larnedks.org*

Lawrence • *Lawrence C/C* • Tom Kern; Pres./CEO; 734 Vermont St., Ste. 101; P.O. Box 586; 66044; Douglas; P 90,000; M 900; (785) 865-4411; Fax (785) 865-4400; tkern@lawrencechamber.com; www.lawrencechamber.com

Leavenworth • *Leavenworth-Lansing Area C/C* • Tim Holverson; Exec. V.P.; 518 Shawnee St.; P.O. Box 44; 66048; Leavenworth; P 43,000; M 500; (913) 682-4112; Fax (913) 682-8170; info@llchamber.com; www.llchamber.com*

Leawood • *Leawood C/C* • Kevin Jeffries; Pres./CEO; 4707 W. 135th St., Ste. 270; 66224; Johnson; P 31,000; M 435; (913) 498-1514; Fax (913) 491-0134; chamber@leawoodchamber.org; www.leawoodchamber.org

Lebanon • *Lebanon Hub Club* • Lori Ladow; Pres.; P.O. Box 125; 66952; Smith; P 230; M 16; (785) 389-3261; (785) 389-1141

Lenexa • *Lenexa C/C* • Blake Schreck CED; Pres.; 11180 Lackman Rd.; 66219; Johnson; P 48,000; M 750; (913) 888-1414; Fax (913) 888-3770; staff@lenexa.org; www.lenexa.org*

Lenora • *Lenora C/C* • Box 331; 67645; Norton; P 306; M 20; (785) 567-4860; skyways.lib.ks.us/towns/Lenora

Liberal • *Liberal C/C* • Rozelle Webb; Exec. Dir.; 4 Rock Island Rd.; P.O. Box 676; 67905; Seward; P 22,000; M 450; (620) 624-3855; Fax (620) 624-8851; info@liberalkschamber.com; www.liberalks chamber.com.*

Lincoln • *Lincoln Area C/C* • Tammy Voeltz; Exec. Dir.; 144 E. Lincoln Ave.; 67455; Lincoln; P 2,600; M 100; (785) 524-4934; Fax (785) 524-4934; lcoc137@sbcglobal.net; www.lincoln kansaschamber.com

Lindsborg • *Lindsborg C/C* • Denise Schwantes; Managing Dir.; 125 N. Main; P.O. Box 3; 67456; McPherson; P 3,000; M 125; (785) 227-3706; lindsborgcofc@sbcglobal.net; www.lindsborg.org

Louisburg • *Louisburg C/C* • Patsy Bortner; Exec. Dir.; P.O. Box 245; 66053; Miami; P 3,700; M 110; (913) 837-2826; chamber@ louisburgkansas.com; www.louisburgkansas.com

Lucas • *Lucas Area C/C* • Connie Dougherty; 201 S. Main; P.O. Box 186; 67648; Russell; P 436; M 45; (785) 525-6288; lucascoc@ wtciweb.com; www.lucaskansas.com

Lyons • *Lyons C/C* • Shannon Young; Mgr.; 116 E. Ave. S.; P.O. Box 127; 67554; Rice; P 3,500; M 100; (620) 257-2842; (866) 257-2842; Fax (620) 257-3426; lyonscc@lyons-chamber.com; www. lyons-chamber.com

Madison • *Madison Area C/C* • P.O. Box 58; 66860; Greenwood; P 800; M 55; (620) 437-3463; www.madisonkschamber.org

Manhattan • *Manhattan Area C/C* • Lyle A. Butler III; Pres./CEO; 501 Poyntz Ave.; 66502; Riley; P 67,000; M 835; (785) 776-8829; Fax (785) 776-0679; chamber@manhattan.org; www.manhattan.org.*

Mankato • *Mankato C/C* • Susan Abel-Diehl; Pres.; 741 N. High St.; 66956; Jewell; P 976; M 50; (785) 378-3141; Fax (785) 378-3478; susan@nckcn.com; skyways.lib.ks.us/towns/Mankato

Marion • *Marion C/C* • Margo Yates; Exec. Secy.; 203 N. 3rd; 66861; Marion; P 2,110; M 125; (620) 382-3425; Fax (620) 382-3993; chinga@eaglecom.net; www.marionks.com

Marysville • *Marysville C/C* • Brenda Staggenborg; Exec. Secy.; 101 N. 10th St.; P.O. Box 16; 66508; Marshall; P 3,200; M 180; (785) 562-3101; (800) 752-3965; Fax (785) 562-3101; info@marysville kansaschamber.org; www.marysvillekansaschamber.org*

McPherson • *McPherson C/C* • Jennifer Burch; Exec. Dir.; 306 N. Main St.; P.O. Box 616; 67460; McPherson; P 14,000; M 380; (620) 241-3303; (620) 241-3304; Fax (620) 241-8708; chamber@ mcphersonks.org; www.mcphersonchamber.org.*

Meade • *Meade C/C* • Louis Podrebarac; Secy.; P.O. Box 576; 67864; Meade; P 1,526; M 34; (620) 873-2979; www.meadechamber.com

Medicine Lodge • *Medicine Lodge Area C/C* • Jessica Rausch; Dir.; 215 S. Iliff; P.O. Box 274; 67104; Barber; P 2,200; M 76; (620) 886-3417; mlchamber@sctelcom.net; www.medicinelodge chamber.com

Merriam • *see Mission*

Miltonvale • *Miltonvale C/C* • Carl Kennedy; 102 S.W. 6th; P.O. Box 98; 67466; Cloud; P 500; M 25; (785) 427-3372; www. miltonvaleks.com

Minneapolis • *Minneapolis Area C/C* • Sandra Clanton; Exec. Dir.; 200 W. 2nd St.; 67467; Ottawa; P 2,000; M 100; (785) 392-3068; mplschamber@sbcglobal.net; www.minneapolischamber.org

Mission • *Northeast Johnson County C/C* • Rob Johnson; Pres.; 5800 Foxridge Dr., Ste. 100; 66202; Johnson; P 77,000; M 350; (913) 262-2141; Fax (913) 262-2146; www.nejcchamber.com

Mission Hills • *see Mission*

Mission Woods • *see Mission*

Moline • *Moline C/C* • Stephanie Bogdahn; Pres.; P.O. Box 253; 67353; Elk; P 470; M 28; (620) 647-3665; Fax (620) 647-8152; molinecity@sktc.net; www.molinekansas.com

Mound City • *Mound City C/C* • P.O. Box A; 66056; Linn; P 800; M 67; (913) 757-4551

Moundridge • *Moundridge Area C/C* • Lisa Teter; Dir.; Box 312; 67107; McPherson; P 1,740; M 50; (620) 345-6300; www.moundridge.com

Mulvane • *Mulvane C/C* • Kent Hixson; Pres.; P.O. Box 67; 67110; Sedgwick; P 5,400; M 68; (316) 777-4850; (316) 737-0534; evans3071@wheatstate.com; www.mulvanechamber.com

Neodesha • *Neodesha C/C* • Karen Porter; Exec. Dir.; First & Main; P.O. Box 266; 66757; Wilson; P 3,000; M 110; (620) 325-2055; karen@neodeshachamber.com; www.neodeshachamber.com

Ness City • *Ness County C/C* • Yvette Schlegel; Exec. Dir.; 102 W. Main St.; P.O. Box 262; 67560; Ness; P 2,500; M 85; (785) 798-2413; nccofc@gbta.net; www.nesscountychamber.com

Newton • *Newton Area C/C* • Jim Schwarzenberger; Exec. Dir.; 500 N. Main, Ste. 101; 67114; Harvey; P 20,000; M 385; (316) 283-2560; (800) 868-2560; Fax (316) 283-8732; billijo@thenewton chamber.org; www.thenewtonchamber.org*

Nickerson • *Nickerson C/C* • Teresa Teufel; Pres.; 15 N. Nickerson St.; P.O. Box 3; 67561; Reno; P 1,135; M 37; (620) 422-3611; www.nickersonks.us

North Overland Park • *see Mission*

Norton • *Norton Area C/C* • Karla Reed; Exec. Dir.; 104 S. State St.; P.O. Box 97; 67654; Norton; P 5,000; M 150; (785) 877-2501; Fax (785) 877-3300; nortoncc@ruraltel.net; www.discovernorton.com*

Oakley • *Oakley Area C/C* • Carinda McConnell; Exec. V.P.; 216 Center Ave.; 67748; Logan; P 2,000; M 85; (785) 672-4862; oakleycc@st-tel.net; www.discoveroakley.com*

Oberlin • *Decatur County Area C/C* • Carol Hackney; Mgr.; 104 S. Penn Ave.; 67749; Decatur; P 4,000; M 75; (785) 475-3441; (785) 475-4035; dcacc@eaglecom.net; www.oberlinks.com

Olathe • *Olathe C/C* • L. Franklin Taylor; Pres.; 18001 W. 106th St., Ste. 160; P.O. Box 98; 66051; Johnson; P 125,000; M 1,200; (913) 764-1050; Fax (913) 782-4636; chamber@olathe.org; www.olathe.org*

Onaga • *Onaga Area C/C* • Diane Roggenkamp; Pres.; P.O. Box 278; 66521; Pottawatomie; P 1,200; M 35; (785) 889-4211; www.onagakansas.org

Osage City • *Osage City C/C* • Robyn Williams; Pres.; P.O. Box 56; 66523; Osage; P 3,050; M 83; (785) 528-8177; (785) 528-4090; chamber@osagecity.com; www.osagecity.com

Osawatomie • *Osawatomie C/C* • Jessica Shaddox; Exec. Dir.; 628 Main St.; P.O. Box 63; 66064; Miami; P 4,600; M 60; (913) 755-4114; Fax (913) 755-4114; osachamber@hotmail.com; www.osawatomiechamber.org

Osborne • *Osborne Area C/C* • Heather Poore; Dir.; 130 N. First St.; 67473; Osborne; P 1,607; M 60; (785) 346-2670; (866) 346-2670; Fax (785) 346-2522; osborneed@ruraltel.net; www.discoverosborne.com

Oswego • *Oswego C/C* • Kevin Sheddrick; Pres.; P.O. Box 8; 67356; Labette; P 2,100; M 120; (620) 795-2600; city@oswegokansas.com; www.oswegokansas.com

Ottawa • *Ottawa Area C/C* • Thomas R. Weigand; Pres./CEO; 109 E. 2nd St.; P.O. Box 580; 66067; Franklin; P 27,000; M 360; (785) 242-1000; (913) 980-3007; Fax (785) 242-4792; chamber@ottawakansas.org; www.ottawakansas.org.*

Overland Park • *Overland Park C/C* • Tracey Osborne CCE; Pres.; 9001 W. 110th St., Ste. 150; 66210; Johnson; P 500,000; M 900; (913) 491-3600; Fax (913) 491-0393; tfielder@opchamber.org; www.opchamber.org

Oxford • *Oxford C/C* • Dr. Deborah Hamm; Pres.; 115 S. Sumner St.; P.O. Box 337; 67119; Sumner; P 1,200; M 29; (620) 455-2223; cityofoxford@sutv.com; www.oxfordks.org

Paola • *Paola C/C* • Carol Everhart; Exec. Dir.; 3 W. Wea St.; 66071; Miami; P 5,338; M 227; (913) 294-4335; mgr@paola chamber.org; www.paolachamber.org*

Park City • *Park City C/C* • Rachel Fenske; 6110 N. Hydraulic St.; 67219; Sedgwick; P 7,000; M 120; (316) 744-2026; www.parkcityks.com

Parsons • *Parsons C/C* • Rikki Hess; Exec. V.P.; 1715 Corning; 67357; Labette; P 11,500; M 250; (620) 421-6500; (800) 280-6401; Fax (620) 421-6501; chamber@parsonschamber.org; www.parsonschamber.org

Phillipsburg • *Phillipsburg Area C/C* • Jackie Swatzell; Dir.; 270 State St.; P.O. Box 326; 67661; Phillips; P 2,800; M 105; (785) 543-2321; Fax (785) 543-0038; cvbcham@ruraltel.net; www.phillipsburgks.us

Pittsburg • *Pittsburg Area C/C* • Blake Benson; Pres.; 117 W. 4th St.; P.O. Box 1115; 66762; Crawford; P 25,000; M 600; (620) 231-1000; Fax (620) 231-3178; bbenson@pittsburgareachamber.com; www.pittsburgareachamber.com*

Pleasanton • *Pleasanton C/C* • Jackie Taylor; Pres.; P.O. Box 478; 66075; Linn; P 1,250; M 45; (913) 352-8257; www.linncountyks.com

Prairie Village • *see Mission*

Pratt • *Pratt Area C/C* • Brian Hoffman; Exec. Dir.; 114 N. Main St.; 67124; Pratt; P 9,700; M 300; (620) 672-5501; (888) 886-1164; Fax (620) 672-5502; info@prattkan.com; www.prattkan.com

Quinter • *Quinter C/C* • Carolyn Tuttle; Secy.; P.O. Box 35; 67752; Gove; P 900; M 50; (785) 754-3538; www.discoverquinter.com

Richmond • *Richmond C/C* • Sandi Ferguson; Pres.; P.O. Box 267; 66080; Franklin; P 400; M 6; (785) 835-6125

Roeland Park • *see Mission*

Rose Hill • *Rose Hill C/C* • Jason Jones; Pres.; P.O. Box 375; 67133; Butler; P 3,950; M 50; (316) 776-2712

Russell • *Russell County Area C/C* • Vicki Frohling; Exec. Dir.; 507 N. Main St.; P.O. Box 58; 67665; Russell; P 8,000; M 200; (785) 483-6960; Fax (785) 483-4535; vicki@russellchamber.com; www.russellks.org

Sabetha • *Sabetha C/C* • Judith Elliott; Secy.; 805 Main; 66534; Nemaha; P 2,600; M 110; (785) 284-2158; sabethachamber@gmail.com; www.sabetha.com

Saint Francis • *St. Francis Area C/C* • Gloria Bracelin; Dir.; 212 E. Washington; P.O. Box 793; 67756; Cheyenne; P 1,500; M 65; (785) 332-2961; Fax (785) 332-8825; coc@cityofstfrancis.net; www.stfranciskansas.com

Saint Marys • *Saint Marys C/C* • Helen Pauly; Exec. Dir.; 702 W. Bertrand; P.O. Box 3; 66536; Pottawatomie; P 2,500; M 120; (785) 437-2077; chamber@saintmarys.com; www.saintmarys.com

Salina • *Salina Area C/C* • Dennis Lauver; Pres./CEO; 120 W. Ash St.; P.O. Box 586; 67402; Saline; P 47,000; M 1,200; (785) 827-9301; Fax (785) 827-9758; dlauver@salinakansas.org; www.salinakansas.org.*

Satanta • *Satanta C/C* • Brent Howie; P.O. Box 98; 67870; Haskell; P 1,300; M 100; chamber@satanta.org; www.satanta.org

Scott City • *Scott City Area C/C & EDC* • Katie Eisenhour; Exec. Dir.; 113 E. 5th; 67871; Scott; P 5,000; M 190; (620) 872-3525; Fax (620) 872-2242; sccc@wbsnet.org; www.scottcitycofc.com

Sedan • *Sedan Area C/C* • Jeannie Walker; Ofc. Mgr.; 108 Sherman; 67361; Chautauqua; P 1,300; M 73; (620) 725-4033; sedanchamber@ksok.biz

Seneca • *Seneca C/C* • Harry Leem; Exec. Dir.; 523 Main St.; 66538; Nemaha; P 2,354; M 110; (785) 336-2294; seneca_chamber@yahoo.com; www.seneca-kansas.us/chamber

Shawnee • *Shawnee C/C* • Linda Leeper; Pres./CEO; 15100 W. 67th St., Ste. 202; 66217; Johnson; P 61,110; M 650; (913) 631-6545; Fax (913) 631-9628; info@shawneekschamber.com; www.shawneekschamber.com*

Smith Center • *Smith Center C/C* • Coleen Kirkendall; Dir.; 219 S. Main; 66967; Smith; P 1,773; M 103; (785) 282-3895; Fax (785) 686-4116; ckirkendall@smithcenter.net; www.smithcenterks.com

Spring Hill • *Spring Hill C/C* • Ann Jensen; Exec. Dir.; P.O. Box 15; 66083; Johnson; P 5,000; M 160; (913) 592-3893; Fax (913) 592-3876; chamber@springhillks.org; www.springhillks.org

Stafford • *Stafford Area C/C* • Carolyn Claypool; Secy.; 130 S. Main St.; P.O. Box 24; 67578; Stafford; P 1,350; M 50; (620) 234-5614; (620) 234-5011; www.cityofstafford.net

Sterling • *Sterling C/C* • Cheryl Buckman; Secy./Treas.; 112 S. Broadway Ave.; P.O. Box 56; 67579; Rice; P 2,200; M 72; (620) 278-3360; lcbuckman@cm.kscoxmail.com; www.sterling-kansas.org

Stockton • *Stockton C/C* • 115 S. Walnut; P.O. Box 1; 67669; Rooks; P 1,407; M 55; (785) 425-6162; Fax (785) 425-6424; stocktoncofc@ruraltel.net; www.stocktonkansas.net

Syracuse • *Syracuse-Hamilton County C/C* • Denise Finlay; Dir.; 118 N. Main; P.O. Box 678; 67878; Hamilton; P 2,666; M 110; (620) 384-5459; schamber@pld.com; www.syracusekschamber.com

Tonganoxie • *Tonganoxie C/C* • Cheryl Hanback; Exec. Dir.; P.O. Box 838; 66086; Leavenworth; P 5,500; M 95; (913) 845-9244; info@tonganoxichamber.org; www.tonganoxiechamber.org

Topeka • *Greater Topeka C/C* • Douglas Kinsinger; Pres./CEO; 120 S.E. 6th, Ste. 110; 66603; Shawnee; P 172,000; M 1,600; (785) 234-2644; Fax (785) 234-8656; topekainfo@topekachamber.org; www.topekachamber.org*

Troy • *Doniphan County C/C* • Lawrence Mays; Exec. Dir.; 120 E. Chestnut; P.O. Box 250; 66087; Doniphan; P 8,000; M 120; (785) 985-2235; Fax (785) 985-2215; lmaysdoniphancounty@yahoo.com; www.dpcountyks.com

Ulysses • *Grant County C/C* • Marieta Hauser; Dir.; 113B S. Main St.; 67880; Grant; P 6,000; M 200; (620) 356-4700; Fax (620) 424-2437; gcccdir@pld.com; www.ulysseschamber.org*

Valley Center • *Valley Center C/C* • Dawn Lechner; Exec. Dir.; 214 W. Main St.; P.O. Box 382; 67147; Sedgwick; P 6,000; M 120; (316) 755-7340; Fax (316) 755-7341; vccc67147@yahoo.com; www.vckschamber.com

Valley Falls • *Valley Falls C/C* • P.O. Box 162; 66088; Jefferson; P 1,250; M 52; (785) 945-3245; Fax (785) 945-6269

WaKeeney • *WaKeeney C/C* • Suzie Bollig; Pres.; P.O. Box 295; 67672; Trego; P 2,600; M 63; (785) 743-2077; Fax (785) 743-5513; wakeeneychamber@yahoo.com; www.wakeeney.org

Wamego • *Wamego Area C/C & Main Street Inc.* • Kourtney Brase; Exec. Dir.; 529 Lincoln Ave.; 66547; Pottawatomie; P 5,500; M 174; (785) 456-7849; Fax (785) 456-7427; wchamber@wamego.net; www.wamegochamber.com

Waterville • *Waterville C/C* • Barb Terry; Pres.; P.O. Box 5; 66548; Marshall; P 680; M 85; (785) 363-2629

Wellington • *Wellington Area C/C & CVB* • Shelley Hansel-Williams; Exec. Dir.; 207 S. Washington; 67152; Sumner; P 8,000; M 372; (620) 326-7466; Fax (620) 326-7467; wellingtoncofc@sutv.com; www.wellingtonks.org*

Wellsville • *Wellsville C/C* • Kristin Adams; Pres.; P.O. Box 472; 66092; Leavenworth; P 1,700; M 80; (785) 883-2296; www.wellsvillechamber.com

Westwood • *see Mission*

Westwood Hills • *see Mission*

Wheaton • *see Onaga*

Wichita • *Wichita Metro C/C* • Bryan S. Derreberry; Pres./CEO; 350 W. Douglas Ave.; 67202; Sedgwick; P 350,000; M 1,600; (316) 265-7771; Fax (316) 265-7502; info@wichitachamber.org; www.wichitachamber.org.*

Wilson • *Wilson C/C* • 2407 Ave. E; P.O. Box 328; 67490; Ellsworth; P 850; M 50; (785) 658-2211; www.wilsonkansas.com

Winfield • *Winfield Area C/C* • Cheryl Lyn Higgins; Pres./CEO; 123 E. 9th Ave.; P.O. Box 640; 67156; Cowley; P 12,000; M 290; (620) 221-2420; Fax (620) 221-2958; win@winfieldchamber.org; www.winfieldks.org*

Winona • *Winona C/C* • P.O. Box 54; 67764; Logan; P 250; M 20; (785) 846-7702

Yates Center • *Woodson County C/C* • Carey Spoon; Exec. Dir.; 108 S. Main; P.O. Box 233; 66783; Woodson; P 4,000; M 75; (620) 625-3235; Fax (620) 625-2416; chamber@wccc.kscoxmail.com; www.woodsoncountychamber.com

Kentucky

Kentucky C/C • David Adkisson; Pres./CEO; 464 Chenault Rd.; Frankfort; 40601; Franklin; P 4,200,000; M 2,400; (502) 695-4700; Fax (502) 695-5051; kcc@kychamber.com; www.kychamber.com

Adairville • *Adairville-South Logan C/C* • Sarah Shoulders; Secy./Treas.; P.O. Box 266; 42202; Logan; P 2,500; M 75; (270) 539-2080; www.visitlogancounty.net

Ashland • *Ashland Alliance* • Jim Purgerson CEcD; Pres.; 1733 Winchester Ave.; P.O. Box 830; 41105; Boyd & Greenup; P 85,000; M 600; (606) 324-5111; Fax (606) 325-4607; bhammond@inicity.net; www.ashlandalliance.com*

Augusta • *Augusta C/C* • Doug Padgett; Dir.; P.O. Box 85; 41002; Bracken; P 1,200; M 60; (606) 756-2183; Fax (606) 756-2185; dpadgett@augustaky.com; www.augustaky.com

Barbourville • *Knox County C/C* • Janet Jones; Ofc. Mgr./Secy.; 196 Daniel Boone Dr., Ste. 205; 40906; Knox; P 33,000; M 110; (606) 546-4300; Fax (606) 546-4300; chamber@barbourville.com; www.knoxcochamber.com

Bardstown • *Bardstown-Nelson County C/C* • Dorothy White; Exec. Dir.; One Court Square; 40004; Nelson; P 40,000; M 550; (502) 348-9545; Fax (502) 348-6478; chamber@bardstown.com; www.bardstownchamber.com*

Barren County • *see Glasgow*

Beattyville • *Beattyville/Lee County C/C* • Carole Kincaid; Pres.; P.O. Box 676; 41311; Lee; P 7,500; M 70; (606) 464-1221; (606) 464-3607; www.beattyville.org

Benton • *Marshall County C/C* • Debbie Buchanan; Exec. Dir.; 17 U.S. Hwy. 68 W.; 42025; Clinton & Marshall; P 30,250; M 280; (270) 527-7665; Fax (270) 527-9193; chamber@marshallcounty.net; www.marshallcounty.net

Berea · *Berea C/C* · David Rowlette; Exec. Dir.; 204 N. Broadway, Ste. 1; 40403; Madison; P 15,000; M 300; (859) 986-9760; Fax (859) 986-2501; chamber@bereachamber.com; www.bereachamber.com.*

Boone County · *see Fort Mitchell*

Bowling Green · *Bowling Green Area C/C* · Pres.; 710 College St.; P.O. Box 51; 42102; Wood; P 141,818; M 1,300; (270) 781-3200; Fax (270) 843-0458; info@bgchamber.com; www.bgchamber.com*

Brandenburg · *Meade County Area C/C* · Russ Powell; Exec. Dir.; P.O. Box 483; 40108; Meade; P 28,500; M 125; (270) 422-3626; Fax (270) 422-1389; info@meadekychamber.org; www.meadekychamber.org

Brooksville · *Bracken County C/C* · Perry Poe; Pres.; P.O. Box 7; 41004; Bracken; P 8,750; M 65; (606) 735-3474; Fax (606) 735-3103; ppoe@windstream.net; www.augustaky.com

Buechel · *see Louisville–Fern Creek Comm. Assn. & C/C*

Burkesville · *Burkesville-Cumberland County C/C* · Stephen Poindexter; Pres.; P.O. Box 312; 42717; Cumberland; P 7,500; M 200; (270) 864-5890; chamber@burkesville.com; www.burkesville.com/chamber

Cadiz · *Cadiz-Trigg County C/C* · Ricky Turner; Pres.; 5748 Hopkinsville Rd.; P.O. Box 647; 42211; Trigg; P 15,000; M 165; (270) 522-3892; Fax (270) 522-6343; info@cadizchamber.com; www.cadizchamber.com

Calhoun · *McLean County C/C* · 297 Main St.; P.O. Box 303; 42327; McLean; P 10,000; M 90; (270) 273-9760; Fax (270) 273-5916; mcleancountychamber@connectgradd.com; www.trailsrus.com/mcleancounty

Campbell County · *see Fort Mitchell*

Campbellsville · *Campbellsville-Taylor County C/C* · Judy Cox; Exec. Dir.; 107 W. Broadway; P.O. Box 116; 42719; Taylor; P 23,000; M 345; (270) 465-8601; Fax (270) 465-0607; chamber@teamtaylorcounty.com; www.campbellsvillechamber.com*

Carrollton · *Carroll County C/C* · Bret Calhoun; Admin. Asst.; 511 Highland Ave.; 41008; Carroll; P 10,000; M 120; (502) 732-7034; (502) 732-7035; Fax (502) 732-7028; chamber@carrollcountyky.com; www.carrollcountyky.com

Cave City · *Cave City C/C & Welcome Center* · Carol Degroft; Exec. Secy.; 418 Mammoth Cave St.; P.O. Box 460; 42127; Barren; P 2,000; M 100; (270) 773-5159; Fax (270) 773-7446; ccchamber@scrtc.com; www.cavecity.com

Central City · *Greater Muhlenberg C/C* · Judy Soderling; Exec. Secy.; 214 N. 1st St.; P.O. Box 671; 42330; Muhlenberg; P 32,000; M 200; (270) 754-2360; Fax (270) 754-2365; js.chamber@muhlon.com; www.muhlenbergchamber.org

Clinton · *Hickman County C/C* · Marla Pruitt; Pres.; P.O. Box 298; 42031; Hickman; P 5,300; M 60; (270) 653-4001; (270) 653-4369; marla.pruitt@clintonbankky.com

Columbia · *Columbia-Adair County C/C* · Sue C. Stivers; Exec. Dir.; 201 Burkesville St.; P.O. Box 116; 42728; Adair; P 18,300; M 247; (270) 384-6020; Fax (270) 384-2056; coladair@duo-county.com; www.columbia-adaircounty.com

Corbin · *Southern Kentucky C/C* · Bruce Carpenter; Exec. Dir.; 101 N. Depot St.; 40701; Knox & Whitley; P 50,000; M 260; (606) 528-6390; Fax (606) 523-6538; info@southernkychamber.org; www.southernkychamber.org*

Covington · *see Fort Mitchell*

Cumberland · *Tri-City C/C & Cumberland Tourist & Conv. Comm.* · W. Bruce Ayers; Exec. Dir.; 506 W. Main St.; 40823; Harlan; P 4,000; M 70; (606) 589-5812; Fax (606) 589-5812; tricitychamber@windstrean.net; www.harlancountytourism.com

Cynthiana · *Cynthiana-Harrison County C/C* · Patricia Grenier; Exec. Dir.; 201 S. Main St.; 41031; Harrison; P 18,000; M 200; (859) 234-5236; Fax (859) 234-6647; cynchamber@setel.com; www.cynthianaky.com

Danville · *Danville-Boyle County C/C* · Paula Fowler; Exec. Dir.; 304 S. Fourth St.; 40422; Boyle; P 28,000; M 400; (859) 236-2361; Fax (859) 236-3197; info@danvilleboylechamber.com; www.danvilleboylechamber.com*

Dawson Springs · *Dawson Springs C/C* · Jenny Sewell; Pres.; 301 W. Arcadia Ave; P.O. Box 107; 42408; Hopkins; P 2,980; M 50; (270) 797-2781; Fax (270) 797-2221; dawsonspringsmains@att.net; www.dawsonspringsky.com

Eddyville · *see Kuttawa*

Edmonton · *Edmonton-Metcalfe County C/C* · Gaye Shaw; Exec. Dir.; P.O. Box 42; 42129; Metcalfe; P 10,037; M 353; (270) 432-3222; Fax (270) 432-3224; metchamb@scrtc.com; www.metcalfechamber.com

Elizabethtown · *Elizabethtown-Hardin County C/C* · 111 W. Dixie Ave.; 42701; Hardin; P 100,000; M 850; (270) 765-4334; (270) 769-2391; Fax (270) 737-0690; president@etownchamber.org; www.etownchamber.org.*

Falmouth · *Pendleton County C/C* · Susan Bishop; Ofc. Supervisor; 230 Main St.; P.O. Box 213; 41040; Pendleton; P 14,000; M 160; (859) 654-4189; Fax (859) 654-4189; pccoc@fuse.net; www.pendletoncountychamber.org

Flatwoods · *see Ashland*

Flemingsburg · *Fleming County C/C* · Crystal L. Ruark; Exec. Dir.; 165 W. Water St.; P.O. Box 24; 41041; Fleming; P 14,000; M 250; (606) 845-1223; Fax (606) 845-1213; crystal@flemingkychamber.com; www.flemingkychamber.com

Fort Mitchell · *Northern Kentucky C/C* · Steve Stevens CCE; Pres.; 300 Buttermilk Pike, Ste. 330; P.O. Box 17416; 41017; Kenton; P 355,000; M 1,900; (859) 578-8800; Fax (859) 578-8802; info@nkychamber.com; www.nkychamber.com*

Frankfort · *Frankfort Area C/C* · Carmen Inman; Exec. Dir.; 100 Capital Ave., 2nd Flr.; 40601; Franklin; P 47,000; M 800; (502) 223-8261; Fax (502) 223-5942; chamber@frankfortky.info; www.frankfortky.info*

Franklin · *Franklin-Simpson C/C* · Teresa Perkins; Pres.; 201 S. Main St.; P.O. Box 513; 42135; Simpson; P 18,000; M 375; (270) 586-7609; Fax (270) 586-5438; cfreese@f-schamber.com; www.f-schamber.com

Frenchburg · *Frenchburg/Menifee County C/C & Tourism* · Lola Thomas; Exec. Dir.; 46 Back St.; P.O. Box 333; 40322; Menifee; P 6,500; M 97; (606) 768-9000; Fax (606) 768-9000; fchamber@mrtc.com; www.frenchburgmenifee.org

Fulton · *see South Fulton, TN*

Georgetown · *Georgetown-Scott County C/C* · John Conner; Exec. Dir.; 160 E. Main St.; 40324; Scott; P 45,431; M 601; (502) 863-5424; Fax (502) 863-5756; info@gtown.org; www.gtown.org*

Glasgow · *Glasgow-Barren County C/C* · Ernie Myers; Exec. V.P.; 118 E. Public Sq.; 42141; Barren; P 39,200; M 471; (270) 651-3161; (800) 264-3161; Fax (270) 651-3122; chamber@glasgow-ky.com; www.glasgowbarrenchamber.com*

Grand Rivers · *Grand Rivers C of C & Tourism Comm.* · P.O. Box 181; 42045; Livingston; P 350; M 65; (270) 362-0152; (888) 493-0152; info@grandrivers.com; www.grandrivers.org

Grayson · *Grayson Area C/C* · Michelle Wilhoit; Pres.; 302 E. Main St.; P.O. Box 612; 41143; Carter; P 5,000; M 102; (606) 474-4401; graysonchamber41143@windstream.net; www.grayson chamber.org

Greensburg · *Greensburg-Green County C/C* · Joel Bennett; Pres.; 110 W. Court St.; 42743; Green; P 11,000; M 80; (270) 932-4298; Fax (270) 932-7778; director@greensburgonline.com; www. greensburgonline.com

Greenville · *Greater Muhlenberg C/C* · Dorothy Walker; Exec. Secy.; 100 E. Main Cross; P.O. Box 313; 42345; Muhlenberg; P 32,000; M 200; (270) 338-5422; Fax (270) 338-5440; dw.chamber@muhlon.com; www.muhlenbergchamber.org*

Hardinsburg · *Breckinridge County C/C* · Sherry D. Stith; Exec. Dir.; 224 S. Main St.; P.O. Box 725; 40143; Breckinridge; P 20,000; M 158; (270) 756-0268; Fax (270) 580-4783; chamber@breckinridgecounty chamberky.com; www.breckinridgecountychamberky.com

Harlan · *Harlan County C/C* · Suzie Mazinidis; Interim Exec. Dir.; 115 N. Cumberland Ave.; P.O. Box 268; 40831; Harlan; P 36,375; M 80; (606) 573-4717; Fax (606) 573-4717; chamber@harlan online.com; www.harlancountychamber.com

Harrison County · *see Cynthiana*

Harrodsburg · *Mercer C/C* · Jill Cutler; Exec. Dir.; 488 Price Ave., Ste. 3; 40330; Mercer; P 22,000; M 170; (859) 734-2365; info@ mercerchamber.com; www.mercerchamber.com

Hartford · *Ohio County C/C* · Laurie Jurgens; Exec. Ofc. Admin.; P.O. Box 3; 42347; Ohio; P 23,000; M 200; (270) 298-3551; Fax (270) 298-3331; chamber@ohiocounty.com; www.ohiocounty.com

Hawesville · *Hancock County C/C* · Edna Rice; Exec. Dir.; P.O. Box 404; 42348; Hancock; P 8,700; M 160; (270) 927-8223; Fax (270) 927-8223; erice@hancockky.us; www.hancockky.us

Hazard · *Hazard-Perry County C/C* · Betsy Clemons; Exec. Dir.; 601 Main St., Ste. 3; 41701; Perry; P 32,000; M 140; (606) 439-2659; Fax (606) 436-6074; hazardcoc1@microtec.com; www.hazardperrychamber.com

Henderson · *Henderson-Henderson County C/C* · Brad Schneider; Pres.; 230 2nd St., Ste. 320; 42420; Henderson; P 45,000; M 450; (270) 826-9531; Fax (270) 827-4461; info@ hendersonchamber.org; www.hendersonky.com*

Hickman · *Hickman C/C* · P.O. Box 166; 42050; Fulton; P 2,700; M 75; (270) 236-2902; hickmanchamber@att.net; www.hickman kychamber.org

Highview · *see Louisville–Fern Creek Comm. Assn. & C/C*

Hodgenville · *LaRue County C/C* · Jessica Davis; Exec. Dir.; 60 Lincoln Sq.; P.O. Box 176; 42748; LaRue; P 13,150; M 150; (270) 358-3411; Fax (270) 358-3411; info@laruecountychamber.org; www.laruecountychamber.org

Hopkinsville · *Hopkinsville-Christian County C/C* · Carter Hendricks; Pres./CEO; 2800 Fort Campbell Blvd.; 42240; Christian; P 73,000; M 850; (270) 885-9096; (800) 842-9959; Fax (270) 886-2059; chamber@hopkinsvillechamber.com; www.hopkins villechamber.com*

Irvine · *Estill Dev. Alliance* · Joe Crawford; Exec. Dir.; P.O. Box 421; 40336; Estill; P 16,000; M 58; (606) 723-2450; info@estill countyky.net; www.estillcountyky.net

Jeffersontown · *The Chamber Jeffersontown* · Carolyn Pfister; Mem. Dev. Dir.; 10434 Watterson Trl.; 40299; Jefferson; P 26,000; M 900; (502) 267-1674; Fax (502) 267-2070; info@jtownchamber. com; www.jtownchamber.com

Kenton County · *see Fort Mitchell*

Kuttawa · *Lyon County C/C* · Rick Fullard; Pres.; 82 Days Inn Dr.; 42055; Lyon; P 9,200; M 160; (270) 388-4769; info@lyoncounty. com; www.lyoncounty.com

La Center · *Ballard County C/C* · Beth Ann Hunt; Exec. Dir.; 547 W. Kentucky Dr.; P.O. Box 322; 42056; Ballard; P 8,900; M 127; (270) 665-8277; bcchamberinfo@brtc.net

LaGrange · *Oldham County C/C* · Deana Epperly Karem; Exec. Dir.; 412 E. Main St.; 40031; Oldham; P 58,000; M 420; (502) 222-1635; Fax (502) 222-3159; dekarem@oldhamcountychamber.com; www.oldhamcountychamber.com*

Lancaster · *Garrard County C/C* · Amy Cloud; Admin. Asst.; P.O. Box 462; 40444; Garrard; P 7,000; M 100; (859) 792-2282; Fax (859) 792-2282; garrardchamber@gmail.com; www.garrard county.ky.gov

Lawrenceburg · *Anderson County C/C* · Catherine Myers; Exec. Dir.; 100 N. Main St., Ste. 213; 40342; Anderson; P 21,000; M 160; (502) 839-5564; Fax (859) 400-0480; accoc@andersonchamberky. org; www.andersonchamberky.org

Lebanon · *Marion County C/C* · Brad Mattingly; Pres.; 239 N. Spalding Ave., Ste. 201; 40033; Marion; P 18,000; M 227; (270) 692-9594; Fax (270) 692-2661; info@marioncountykychamber. com; www.marioncountykychamber.com*

Leitchfield · *Grayson County C/C* · Caryn Lewis; Exec. Dir.; 425 S. Main St.; 42754; Grayson; P 26,000; M 260; (270) 259-5587; (800) 667-5934; Fax (270) 259-9278; info@graysoncountychamber.com; www.graysoncountychamber.com

Lexington · *Commerce Lexington Inc.* · Robert L. Quick; Pres./CEO; 330 E. Main St., Ste. 100; 40507; Fayette; P 325,000; M 1,900; (859) 254-4447; Fax (859) 233-3304; bquick@commercelexington. com; www.commercelexington.com*

Liberty · *Liberty-Casey County C/C* · Judy Emerson; Pres.; 518 Middleburg St.; P.O. Box 278; 42539; Casey; P 16,500; M 80; (606) 787-6463; Fax (606) 787-7992; chamber@libertykentucky.org; www.libertykentucky.org/chamber.html

London · *London/Laurel County C/C* · Randy L. Smith; Exec. Dir.; 409 S. Main St.; 40741; Laurel; P 60,000; M 500; (606) 864-4789; Fax (606) 864-7300; info@londonlaurelchamber.com; www.londonlaurelchamber.com*

Louisville · *Fern Creek Comm. Assn. & C/C* · Jean Henle; Coord.; P.O. Box 91564; 40291; Jefferson; P 30,000; M 170; (502) 239-7550; Fax (502) 239-7650; info@ferncreek.org; www.ferncreek.org

Louisville · *Greater Louisville Inc./The Metro Chamber* · Joe Reagan; Pres./CEO; 614 W. Main St., Ste. 6000; 40202; Jefferson; P 1,200,000; M 2,900; (502) 625-0000; Fax (502) 625-0010; info@ greaterlouisville.com; www.greaterlouisville.com.*

Madisonville · *Madisonville-Hopkins County C/C* · Harriett Whitaker; Pres.; 15 E. Center St.; 42431; Hopkins; P 47,000; M 434; (270) 821-3435; Fax (270) 821-9190; c.commerce@newwave comm.net; www.hopkinschamber.com*

Manchester · *Manchester/Clay County C/C* · Joann Abner; Interim Dir.; 277 White St.; P.O. Box 411; 40962; Clay; P 25,000; M 110; (606) 598-1754; Fax (606) 598-1545; info@kyclay countychamber.org; www.kyclaycountychamber.org

Marion · *Crittenden County C/C* · Susan Alexander; Exec. Dir.; 213 S. Main St.; P.O. Box 164; 42064; Crittenden; P 9,400; M 138; (270) 965-5015; (800) 755-0361; Fax (270) 965-0058; susan@ crittendenchamber.org; www.crittendenchamber.org

Mayfield · *Mayfield & Graves County C/C* · Wendy Hunter; Exec. Dir.; 201 E. College St.; 42066; Graves; P 47,000; M 310; (270) 247-6101; Fax (270) 247-6110; chamber@mayfieldchamber.com; www.mayfieldchamber.com.*

Maysville · *Maysville-Mason County Area C/C* · Vicki Steigleder; Exec. Dir.; 201 E. Third St.; 41056; Mason; P 17,303; M 250; (606) 564-5534; Fax (606) 564-5535; chamber@ maysvilleky.net; www.maysvillekentucky.com.

Middlesboro · *Bell County C/C* · Rob Lincks; Exec. Dir.; 189 N. 20th St.; P.O. Box 788; 40965; Bell; P 30,060; M 230; (606) 248-1075; Fax (606) 248-8851; chamber@bellcountychamber.com; www.bellcountychamber.com

Middletown · *Louisville East-Middletown C/C* · David Eggleston; Program Dir.; 12906 Shelbyville Rd., Ste. 250; 40243; Jefferson; P 8,500; M 200; (502) 244-8086; Fax (502) 244-0185; dave@middletownchamber.com; www.middletownchamber.com

Monticello · *Monticello-Wayne County C/C* · Eulah Johnson; Pres.; 120 S. Main St., Ste. 3, City Hall; P.O. Box 566; 42633; Wayne; P 19,923; M 156; (606) 348-3064; (866) 348-3064; Fax (606) 348-3064; info@monticellokychamber.com; www. monticellokychamber.com

Morehead · *Morehead-Rowan County C/C* · Tracy Williams; Exec. Dir.; 150 E. 1st St.; 40351; Rowan; P 26,000; M 380; (606) 784-6221; Fax (606) 783-1373; tcwilliams@moreheadchamber. com; www.moreheadchamber.com

Morganfield · *Morganfield C/C* · Becky Greenwell; Admin. Asst.; 1295 U.S. Hwy. 60 W.; P.O. Box 66; 42437; Union; P 3,000; M 70; (270) 389-9777; Fax (270) 389-4877; mfieldchamber@ bellsouth.net; www.morganfieldchamber.org

Morgantown · *Morgantown-Butler County C/C* · Amanda Hatcher; Exec. Dir.; 112 S. Main; P.O. Box 408; 42261; Butler; P 13,010; M 135; (270) 526-6827; Fax (270) 526-6830; bc chamber07@bellsouth.net; www.morgantown-ky.com

Mount Sterling · *Mt. Sterling-Montgomery County C/C* · Sandy Romenesko; Exec. Dir.; 126 W. Main St.; 40353; Montgomery; P 26,500; M 400; (859) 498-5343; Fax (859) 498-3947; sandy@ mtsterlingchamber.com; www.mtsterlingchamber.com

Munfordville · *Hart County C/C* · Virginia Davis; Exec. Dir.; 119 E. Union St.; P.O. Box 688; 42765; Hart; P 18,887; M 260; (270) 524-2892; Fax (270) 524-1127; hart_co@scrtc.com; www.hartcountyky.org*

Murray · *Murray-Calloway County C/C* · Lance Allison; Pres./ CEO; 805 N. 12th St.; P.O. Box 190; 42071; Calloway; P 36,000; M 692; (270) 753-5171; (800) 900-5171; Fax (270) 753-0948; chamber@mymurray.com; www.mymurray.com.*

New Castle · *Henry County C/C* · Pat Wallace; Exec. Dir.; 11 N. Main; P.O. Box 355; 40050; Henry; P 16,000; M 178; (502) 845-0806; Fax (502) 845-5313; henrychamber@insightbb.com; chamber.henrycountyky.com

Nicholasville · *Jessamine County C/C* · Nancy Stone; Exec. Dir.; 508 N. Main St., Ste. A; 40356; Jessamine; P 44,000; M 500; (859) 887-4351; Fax (859) 887-1211; jessaminechamber@windstream. net; www.jessaminechamber.com.*

Olive Hill · *Olive Hill Area C/C* · Jonathan Lewis; Secy./Treas.; P.O. Box 1570; 41164; Carter; P 2,500; M 197; (606) 286-6115; (606) 286-5533; ohcoc@atcc.net; www.atcc.net/chamber

Owensboro · *Greater Owensboro C/C* · Jody Wassmer; Pres.; 200 E. 3rd St., Ste. 101; P.O. Box 825; 42302; Daviess; P 92,000; M 900; (270) 926-1860; Fax (270) 926-3364; chamber@owens boro.com; www.owensboro.com.*

Owingsville · *Owingsville-Bath County C/C* · Jackie Watson; P.O. Box 360; 40360; Bath; P 11,000; M 60; (606) 674-8830; www. bathcounty.ky.gov

Paducah · *Paducah Area C/C* · Elaine Spalding; Pres.; 401 Kentucky Ave.; P.O. Box 810; 42002-0810; McCracken; P 65,000; M 1,125; (270) 443-1746; Fax (270) 442-9152; info@paducah chamber.org; www.paducahchamber.org.*

Paintsville · *Paintsville-Johnson County C/C* · Fran Jarrell; Exec. Dir.; 124 Main St.; P.O. Box 629; 41240; Johnson; P 24,000; M 120; (606) 422-8204; franjarrell@pjcchamber.com; www. pjcchamber.com

Paris · *Paris-Bourbon County C/C* · Lucy Cooper; Exec. Dir.; 720 High St.; 40361; Bourbon; P 20,000; M 200; (859) 987-3205; Fax (859) 987-4640; lcooper@parisky.com; www.parisky.org

Pikeville · *Pike County C/C* · Brad Hall; Pres./CEO; 787 Hambley Blvd.; 41501; Pike; P 74,000; M 450; (606) 432-5504; Fax (606) 432-7295; info@pikecountychamber.org; www.pikecountychamber.org*

Prestonsburg · *Floyd County C/C* · Mandy Stumbo; Exec. Dir.; 113 S. Central Ave.; P.O. Box 1508; 41653; Floyd; P 42,094; M 278; (606) 886-0364; Fax (606) 886-0422; floydchamber@setel.com; www.floydcountykentucky.com*

Princeton · *Princeton Caldwell County C/C* · Kate Prince; 110 W. Washington St.; 42445; Caldwell; P 13,000; M 200; (270) 365-5393; chamberofcommerce@pepb.net; www.princetonky.org

Radcliff · *Radcliff-Hardin County C/C* · Jo Emary; Exec. Dir.; 306 N. Wilson Rd.; 40160; Hardin; P 90,000; M 350; (270) 351-4450; Fax (270) 352-4449; jo@radcliffchamber.org; www.radcliffchamber.org*

Richmond · *Richmond C/C* · Mendi Goble; Exec. Dir.; 201 E. Main St.; 40475; Madison; P 30,000; M 650; (859) 623-1720; Fax (859) 623-0839; rchamber@richmondchamber.com; www. richmondchamber.com*

Russell Springs · *Russell County C/C* · Debbie Conner; Admin. Asst.; 650 S. Hwy. 127; P.O. Box 64; 42642; Russell; P 17,500; M 240; (270) 866-4333; (888) 833-4220; Fax (270) 866-4304; info@russellcountyky.com; www.russellcountyky.com.

Russellville · *Logan County C/C* · Lisa Browning; Exec. Dir.; 116 S. Main St.; 42276; Logan; P 26,000; M 300; (270) 726-2206; Fax (270) 726-2237; lisa@loganchamber.com; www.logan chamber.com.*

Scottsville · *Scottsville-Allen County C/C* · Sue Shaver; Exec. Dir.; 110 S. Court St.; P.O. Box 416; 42164; Allen; P 19,500; M 255; (270) 237-4782; Fax (270) 237-5498; chamber@scottsvilleky.info; www.scottsvilleky.info.*

Sebree · *Sebree C/C* · Bruce Wiggins; P.O. Box 326; 42455; Webster; P 1,900; M 48; (270) 835-0330

Shelbyville · *Shelby County C/C* · Shelley Goodwin; Exec. Dir.; 316 Main St.; P.O. Box 335; 40066; Shelby; P 37,219; M 385; (502) 633-1636; Fax (502) 633-7501; info@shelbycountykychamber. com; www.shelbycountykychamber.com*

Shepherdsville · *Bullitt County C/C* · Freida J. Howe; Exec. Dir.; 279 S. Buckman St.; P.O. Box 1656; 40165; Bullitt; P 65,000; M 400; (502) 955-9641; Fax (502) 543-1765; info@bullittchamber. org; www.bullittchamber.org.

Somerset · *Somerset-Pulaski County C/C* · Exec. Dir.; 445 S. Hwy. 27, Ste. 101; 42501; Pulaski; P 60,000; M 650; (606) 679-7323; Fax (606) 679-1744; info@spcchamber.com; www.spcchamber.com*

Springfield · *Springfield/Washington County C/C* · Ralph Blandford; Pres.; 124 W. Main St., Ste. 3; 40069; Washington; P 10,900; M 150; (859) 336-3810; Fax (859) 336-9410; swc chamber@bellsouth.net; www.springfieldkychamber.com

Stanford · *Lincoln County C/C* · Andrea Miller; Exec. Dir.; 201 E. Main St., Ste. 5; 40484; Lincoln; P 23,000; M 200; (606) 365-4118; Fax (606) 365-4118; director@lincolncountychamber.com; www. lincolncountychamber.com*

Stanton · *Red River C/C* · James Combs; Pres.; P.O. Box 1804; 40380; Powell; P 13,500; M 50; (606) 663-6631; Fax (606) 663-2267; james@wbfcam.com; www.kyredriverchamber.com

Sturgis · *Sturgis C/C* · Lisa Jones; Ofc. Mgr.; 513 N. Main St.; P.O. Box 125; 42459; Union; P 2,184; M 65; (270) 333-9316; Fax (270) 333-9319; sturgisc@sturgischamberofcommerce.com; www.sturgischamberofcommerce.com

Taylorsville · *Spencer County-Taylorsville C/C* · Cara Lewis; 19 E. Main St.; P.O. Box 555; 40071; Spencer; P 15,800; M 85; (502) 477-8369; president@spencercountykychamber.com; www.spencercountykychamber.com

Tompkinsville · *Tompkinsville/Monroe County C/C & Eco. Dev.* · Thomas Dodson; Pres.; 202 N. Magnolia St.; 42167; Monroe; P 11,000; M 100; (270) 487-1314; Fax (270) 487-0975; monroe countyedc@live.com; www.monroeky.com

Versailles · *Woodford County C/C* · Tami Vater; Exec. Dir.; 190 N. Main St.; 40383; Woodford; P 25,000; M 267; (859) 873-5122; Fax (877) 817-6585; info@woodfordcountyinfo.com; www. woodfordcountyinfo.com

Warsaw · *Gallatin County C/C* · Steve Henderson; Pres.; P.O. Box 1029; 41095; Gallatin; P 8,000; M 40; (859) 567-7900

West Liberty · *Morgan County C/C* · Hank Allen; Pres.; 565 Main St.; 41472; Morgan; P 18,000; M 50; (606) 743-2300; Fax (606) 743-2202; wliberty@mrtc.com; www.cityofwestliberty.com

West Point · *West Point C/C* · Roszelle Moore; Pres.; 1006 Main St.; 40177; Hardin; P 1,170; M 50; (502) 922-4505; roszelleh@ hotmail.com; www.westpointky.org

Whitesburg · *Letcher County C/C* · Joe DePriest; Pres.; P.O. Box 127; 41858; Letcher; P 24,000; M 60; (606) 832-4020; jbdep@ yahoo.com; www.letchercountychamber.com

Whitley City · *McCreary County C/C* · Greg Burdine; Pres.; P.O. Box 548; 42653; McCreary; P 17,200; M 110; (606) 376-5004; Fax (606) 376-9060; chamber7@highland.net; www.mccreary chamber.com

Williamstown · *Grant County C/C & Eco. Dev.* · Wade Gutman; Dir.; P.O. Box 365; 41097; Grant; P 26,000; M 250; (859) 824-3322; (800) 824-2858; Fax (859) 824-7082; wgutman@grantcommerce. com; www.grantcommerce.com

Winchester · *Winchester-Clark County C/C* · Karen Haley; Pres./CEO; 2 S. Maple St.; 40391; Clark; P 35,000; M 386; (859) 744-6420; Fax (859) 744-9229; todd@winchesterindustry.com; www.winchesterkychamber.com*

Louisiana

Louisiana Assn. of Bus. & Ind. · Daniel Juneau; Pres.; 3113 Valley Creek Dr.; P.O. Box 80258; Baton Rouge; 70898; East Baton Rouge; P 4,400,000; M 3,000; (225) 928-5388; Fax (225) 929-6054; labi@labi.org; www.labi.org

Abbeville · *Greater Abbeville-Vermilion C/C* · Lynn Guillory; Exec. Dir.; 1907 Veterans Memorial Dr.; 70510; Vermilion; P 52,000; M 240; (337) 893-2491; Fax (337) 893-1807; abbeville chamber@abbevillechamber.com; www.abbevillechamber.com

Abita Springs · *see Covington*

Addis · *West Baton Rouge C/C* · Tammi Fabre; Mbrshp. Dir.; 7520 Hwy. 1 S.; P.O. Box 448; 70710; West Baton Rouge; P 23,000; M 315; (225) 383-3140; Fax (225) 685-1044; info@wbrchamber. org; www.wbrchamber.org

Alexandria · *Central Louisiana C/C* · Elton Pody; Pres.; 1118 Third St.; P.O. Box 992; 71309; Rapides; P 400,000; M 822; (318) 442-6671; Fax (318) 442-6734; info@cenlachamber.org; www. cenlachamber.org*

Amite · *Amite C/C* · Clifford Brooke; Pres.; 101 S.E. Central Ave.; 70422; Tangipahoa; P 4,800; M 115; (985) 748-5537; Fax (985) 748-5537; amitecoc@l-55.com; www.amitechamberofcommerce.org

Arcadia · *Arcadia/Bienville Parish C/C* · Virginia Becker; Ofc. Mgr.; 2440 Hazel St.; P.O. Box 587; 71001; Bienville; P 14,000; M 174; (318) 263-9897; Fax (318) 263-9897; arcadiachamber@ bellsouth.net

Arnaudville · *Arnaudville C/C* · Lorna Mills; Pres.; 292 Front St.; P.O. Box 125; 70512; Saint Landry; P 1,400; M 100; (337) 754-5316; Fax (337) 754-5316; arnaudvilleacc@aol.com; www.arnaud villechamber.com

Ascension · *Ascension C/C* · Sherrie Despino; Pres./CEO; 1006 W. Hwy. 30; P.O. Box 1204, Gonzales; 70707; Ascension; P 100,000; M 500; (225) 647-7487; Fax (225) 647-5124; info@ascension chamber.com; www.ascensionchamber.com*

Baker · *Baker C/C* · Monteal Carson-Margolis; Mktg. Dir.; 3439 Groom Rd.; 70714; East Baton Rouge; P 15,000; M 160; (225) 775-3547; Fax (225) 775-8060; bakercoc@bellsouth.net

Bastrop · *Bastrop-Morehouse Parish C/C* · Dorothy Ford; Exec. Dir.; 110 N. Franklin St.; P.O. Box 1175; 71221; Morehouse; P 28,602; M 325; (318) 281-3794; Fax (318) 281-3781; director@ bastroplacoc.org; www.bastroplacoc.org

Baton Rouge · *Baton Rouge Area C/C* · Adam Knapp; Pres./CEO; 564 Laurel St.; 70801; East Baton Rouge; P 780,000; M 1,500; (225) 381-7125; Fax (225) 336-4306; info@brac.org; www.brac.org*

Bogalusa · *Bogalusa C/C* · Marilyn Bateman; Exec. Dir.; 608 Willis Ave.; 70427; Washington; P 16,000; M 200; (985) 735-5731; bogalusachamber@bellsouth.net; www.bogalusachamber.cc

Bossier City · *Bossier C/C* · Lisa Johnson; Pres.; 710 Benton Rd.; 71111; Bossier; P 113,000; M 857; (318) 746-0252; Fax (318) 746-0357; info@bossierchamber.com; www.bossierchamber.com*

Breaux Bridge · *Breaux Bridge Area C/C* · Tina Begnaud; Exec. Dir.; 314 E. Bridge St.; P.O. Box 88; 70517; Saint Martin; P 8,000; M 230; (337) 332-5406; Fax (337) 332-5424; info@breauxbridge live.com; www.gov.breauxbridgelive.com

Bunkie · *Bunkie C/C* · Phyllis O'Quin; Secy.; 110 N.W. Main St.; P.O. Box 70; 71322; Avoyelles; P 5,000; M 110; (318) 346-2575; Fax (318) 346-2576; bunkiechamber@bellsouth.net; www.bunkie.org

Central · *City of Central C/C* · Ron Erickson; Pres.; 13013 Hooper Rd.; P.O. Box 78107; 70837; East Baton Rouge; P 28,000; M 240; (225) 261-5818; Fax (225) 261-5122; chamber@cityofcentral chamber.com; www.cityofcentralchamber.com

Claiborne · *see Homer*

Colfax · *Grant Parish C/C* · Britton Carroll; Pres.; 277 Mead Rd.; P.O. Box 32; 71417; Grant; P 20,000; M 100; (318) 627-2211; info@ grantcoc.org; www.grantcoc.org

Columbia • *Caldwell Parish C/C* • Beth Hefner; Pres.; P.O. Box 726; 71418; Caldwell; P 10,200; M 85; (318) 649-0726; Fax (318) 649-0509; cpchamber60@yahoo.com; www.caldwellparish chamberofcommerce.com

Coushatta • *Red River C/C* • Martha Gates; Exec. Asst.; 620 Rush St.; P.O. Box 333; 71019; Red River; P 9,622; M 126; (318) 932-3289; Fax (318) 932-6919; redriverchamber@bellsouth.net; coushattaredriverchamberofcommerce.com

Covington • *St. Tammany West C/C* • Lacey O. Toledano; Pres.; 610 Hollycrest Blvd.; 70433; Saint Tammany; P 220,000; M 1,050; (985) 892-3216; Fax (985) 893-4244; info@sttammanychamber.org; www.sttammanychamber.org*

Crowley • *Crowley C/C* • Kayla Link; Pres./CEO; 11 N. Parkerson Ave.; P.O. Box 2125; 70527; Acadia; P 14,613; M 300; (337) 788-0177; Fax (337) 783-9507; kayla@crowleychamber.com; www.crowleychamber.com

Cut Off • *see Larose*

Denham Springs • *Livingston Parish C/C* • Jack Stewart; Exec. Dir.; 133 N. Hummell St.; P.O. Box 591; 70727; Livingston; P 102,000; M 385; (225) 665-8155; Fax (225) 665-2411; staff@lpconline.org; www.lpconline.org*

DeQuincy • *DeQuincy C/C* • 218 E. 4th St.; P.O. Box 625; 70633; Calcasieu; P 3,600; M 87; (337) 786-6451; Fax (337) 786-2173; karrlillian@yahoo.com

DeRidder • *Greater Beauregard C/C* • Avon Knowlton IOM; Exec. V.P./Dir.; 111 N. Washington St.; 70634; Beauregard; P 35,500; M 400; (337) 463-5533; Fax (337) 463-2244; deridder@bellsouth.net; www.beauparish.org

Donaldsonville • *Donaldsonville Area C/C* • Becky Katz; Exec. Dir.; 714 Railroad Ave.; 70346; Ascension; P 8,300; M 140; (225) 473-4814; Fax (225) 473-4817; dvillecoc@bellsouth.net; www.donaldsonville.org

Dutchtown • *see Ascension*

Eunice • *Eunice C/C* • Robin McGee; Exec. Dir.; 200 S. C.C. Duson St.; P.O. Box 508; 70535; Saint Landry; P 12,000; M 200; (337) 457-2565; Fax (337) 546-0278; eunicecc@charterinternet.com; www.eunicechamber.com

Farmerville • *Union Parish C/C* • Jean Jones; Pres.; 303 E. Water St.; P.O. Box 67; 71241; Union; P 24,000; M 135; (318) 368-3947; Fax (318) 368-3945; upcoc@bayou.com; www.unionparishchamber.org

Ferriday • *see Vidalia*

Folsom • *see Covington*

Franklin • *St. Mary C/C* • Donna Meyer; Pres.; 600 Main St.; 70538; Saint Mary; P 60,000; M 650; (985) 384-3830; Fax (337) 828-5606; info@stmarychamberofcommerce.com; www.stmarychamberofcommerce.com

Franklinton • *Franklinton C/C* • Linda E. Crain; Exec. Dir.; 1051 Main St.; 70438; Washington; P 3,718; M 145; (985) 839-5822; franklintonchamber@franklinton.net; www.franklintonlouisiana.org

Geismar • *see Ascension*

Gonzales • *see Ascension*

Grambling • *Grambling C/C* • 2035 Martin Luther King Jr. Ave.; P.O. Box 703; 71245; Lincoln; P 5,000; M 35; (318) 247-6120

Gueydan • *Gueydan C/C* • Jamie Gayle; Pres.; P.O. Box 562; 70542; Vermilion; P 1,700; M 120; www.gueydan.org

Hammond • *Hammond C/C* • Charlotte Banks; Exec. Dir.; 400 N.W. Railroad Ave.; P.O. Box 1458; 70404; Tangipahoa; P 25,000; M 650; (985) 345-4457; Fax (985) 345-4749; director@hammondchamber.org; www.hammondchamber.org*

Homer • *Claiborne C/C* • John Watson; Exec. Dir.; 519 S. Main St.; 71040; Claiborne; P 17,000; M 160; (318) 927-3271; Fax (318) 927-3271; jdwatson_ccoc@bellsouth.net; www.claiborneone.org

Houma • *Houma-Terrebonne C/C* • Drake Pothier; Pres./CEO; 6133 Hwy. 311; 70360; Terrebonne; P 109,256; M 905; (985) 876-5600; Fax (985) 876-5611; info@houmachamber.com; www.houmachamber.com*

Jackson • *East Feliciana C/C* • Audrey Faciana; Exec. Dir.; 1752 High St.; P.O. Box 667; 70748; East Feliciana; P 22,000; M 90; (225) 634-7155; Fax (225) 634-7155; tourism1@bellsouth.net; www.felicianatourism.org

Jeanerette • *Jeanerette C/C* • Louis Lancon; Pres.; 803 Hubertville Rd.; P.O. Box 31; 70544; Iberia; P 9,000; M 75; (337) 276-4293; sugarcity70544@att.net; www.jeanerettechamber.org

Jennings • *Jeff Davis Bus. Alliance* • Cynthia Hoffpauir; Pres./CEO; 246 N. Main St.; P.O. Box 1209; 70546; Tangipahoa; P 32,000; M 456; (337) 824-0933; Fax (337) 824-0934; cynthia@jdbusinessalliance.com; www.jdbusinessalliance.com

Jonesboro • *Jackson Parish C/C* • Wilda Smith; Dir.; 102 Fourth St.; 71251; Jackson; P 15,000; M 171; (318) 259-4693; Fax (318) 395-8539; jacksonparishcoc@aol.com; www.jacksonparishchamber.org

Kaplan • *Kaplan Area C/C* • Linda Romero; Event Planner/Secy.; 701 N. Cushing; 70548; Vermilion; P 5,000; M 118; (337) 643-2400; Fax (337) 643-2400; kchamber@kaplantel.net; www.kaplanchamber.com

Kinder • *Kinder C/C* • Pat Paxton; Secy.; P.O. Box 853; 70648; Allen; P 2,800; M 150; (337) 738-5945; kindercc@centurytel.net; www.kinderchamber.com

Lacombe • *Lacombe C/C* • Patti Young; P.O. Box 889; 70445; Saint Tammany; P 9,000; M 120; (985) 882-7442

Lafayette • *Greater Lafayette C/C* • Robert M. Guidry; Pres./CEO; 804 E. St. Mary Blvd.; P.O. Drawer 51307; 70505; Lafayette; P 202,569; M 1,400; (337) 233-2705; Fax (337) 234-8671; rob@lafchamber.org; www.lafchamber.org*

Lake Charles • *The Chamber/Southwest Louisiana* • George Swift; Pres./CEO; 120 W. Pujo St.; P.O. Box 3110; 70602; Calcasieu; P 287,001; M 1,050; (337) 433-3632; Fax (337) 436-3727; gswift@allianceswla.org; www.allianceswla.org*

Larose • *C/C of Lafourche & the Bayou Region* • Lin Kiger; Pres./CEO; 107 W. 26th St.; P.O. Box 1462; 70373; Lafourche; P 90,000; M 400; (985) 693-6700; Fax (985) 693-6702; admin@lafourchechamber.com; www.lafourchechamber.com.*

Leesville • *Vernon C/C* • Eddie Wise; Pres.; 9261 Shreveport Hwy.; P.O. Box 1228; 71496; Vernon; P 60,000; M 300; (337) 238-0349; (877) 234-0349; Fax (337) 238-0340; chambervernonparish@hotmail.com; www.chambervernonparish.com

Logansport • *Logansport C/C* • 606 Main St.; P.O. Box 320; 71049; DeSoto; P 1,700; M 35; (318) 697-0076; (318) 697-5359

Madisonville • *Greater Madisonville Area C/C* • Michelle Vanderbrook; Pres.; P.O. Box 746; 70447; Saint Tammany; P 4,000; M 100; (985) 845-9824; bill@xlinc.net; www.madisonvillechamber.org

Mandeville • *see Covington*

Mansfield • *DeSoto Parish C/C* • Kathi Wells; Exec. Dir.; 115 N. Washington Ave.; 71052; DeSoto; P 26,000; M 200; (318) 872-1310; Fax (318) 871-1875; chamber75@bellsouth.net; www.desotoparishchamber.net

Mansura • *Mansura C/C* • Mr. Nicky Bordelon; Pres.; P.O. Box 536; 71350; Avoyelles; P 4,000; M 150; (318) 964-2887; (318) 964-2931; chamber@cochondelait.com; www.cochondelait.com

Many • *Sabine Parish C/C* • Garland Anthony; Exec. Dir.; 1125 W. Mississippi Ave., Ste. F; 71449; Sabine; P 24,000; M 300; (318) 256-3523; Fax (318) 256-4137; spchamber@cp-tel.net; www.sabineparishchamber.com

Marksville • *Marksville C/C* • Eleanor Gremillion; Secy.; P.O. Box 767; 71351; Avoyelles; P 7,000; M 300; (318) 253-0284; (318) 253-9222; Fax (318) 253-0457; www.marksvillechamberofcommerce.com

Metairie • *Jefferson C/C* • Glenn Hayes; Pres./CEO; 3421 N. Causeway Blvd., Ste. 203; 70002; Jefferson; P 450,000; M 1,000; (504) 835-3880; Fax (504) 835-3828; glenn@jeffersonchamber.org; www.jeffersonchamber.org*

Minden • *Minden-South Webster Parish C/C* • Mike Toland; Chrmn.; 110 Sibley Rd.; 71055; Webster; P 42,000; M 300; (318) 377-4240; Fax (318) 377-4215; info@mindenchamber.com; www.mindenchamber.com

Monroe • *Monroe C/C* • Sue Nicholson; Pres./CEO; 212 Walnut St., Ste. 100; 71201; Ouachita; P 250,000; M 900; (318) 323-3461; (888) 531-9535; Fax (318) 322-7594; sdaniel@monroe.org; www.monroe.org.*

Morgan City • *St. Mary Parish C/C* • Donna Meyer; Pres.; P.O. Box 2606; 70381; Saint Mary; P 53,000; M 600; (985) 384-3830; Fax (985) 384-0771; info@stmarychamber.com; www.stmarychamber.com.*

Napoleonville • *Assumption Area C/C* • Ella Metrejean; Exec. Dir.; 123 Jefferson St.; P.O. Box 718; 70390; Assumption; P 24,000; M 180; (985) 369-2816; Fax (985) 369-2811; assumption@bellsouth.net; www.assumptionchamber.org

Natchitoches • *Natchitoches Area C/C* • Tony Davis; Pres./CEO; 560 Second St.; P.O. Box 3; 71457; Natchitoches; P 39,777; M 371; (318) 352-6894; Fax (318) 352-5385; chamber@natchitoches.net; www.natchitocheschamber.com*

New Iberia • *Greater Iberia C/C* • Janet Faulk; Pres./CEO; 111 W. Main St.; 70560; Iberia; P 75,000; M 700; (337) 364-1836; Fax (337) 367-7405; info@iberiachamber.org; www.iberiachamber.org

New Orleans • *New Orleans C/C* • Ben Johnson; Managing Dir.; 1515 Poydras St., Ste. 1010; 70112; Orleans; P 300,000; M 663; (504) 799-4260; Fax (504) 799-4259; bjohnson@neworleanschamber.org; www.neworleanschamber.org

New Roads • *Greater Pointe Coupee C/C* • Amy Davis; Pres.; P.O. Box 555; 70760; Pointe Coupee; P 23,000; M 150; (225) 638-3500; Fax (225) 638-9858; pointecoupeechamber@yahoo.com; www.pcchamber.org

Oak Grove • *West Carroll C/C* • Doug Ainsworth; Pres.; 302 E. Main St.; P.O. Box 1336; 71263; West Carroll; P 15,000; M 86; (318) 428-8289; Fax (318) 428-4421; wcchamber@bellsouth.net

Oakdale • *Oakdale Area C/C* • John Stigall; Pres.; 107 S. 12th St.; P.O. Box 1138; 71463; Allen; P 8,137; M 153; (318) 335-1729; Fax (318) 215-1729; oakdaleareachamber@bellsouth.net; www.oakdalela.org

Opelousas • *Opelousas-Saint Landry C/C* • Ms. Frankie Bertrand; Pres./CEO; 109 W. Vine St.; 70570; St. Landry; P 120,000; M 490; (337) 942-2683; Fax (337) 942-2684; opelousaschamber@charter.net; www.opelousaschamber.org

Plaquemine • *Iberville C/C* • Hank Grace; Exec. Dir.; 23675 Church St.; P.O. Box 248; 70765; Iberville; P 33,400; M 260; (225) 687-3560; Fax (225) 687-3575; hgrace@ibervillechamber.com; www.ibervillechamber.com

Ponchatoula • *Ponchatoula C/C* • Jamene Dahmer; V.P.; 109 W. Pine; P.O. Box 306; 70454; Tangipahoa; P 9,000; M 300; (985) 386-2533; (985) 386-2536; Fax (985) 386-2533; chamber@ponchatoulachamber.com; www.ponchatoulachamber.com

Prairieville • *see Ascension*

Raceland • *see Larose*

Rayne • *Rayne C/C* • 107 Oak St.; P.O. Box 383; 70578; Acadia; P 8,552; M 125; (337) 334-2332; Fax (337) 334-8341; raynechamber1@bellsouth.net; www.rayne.org/chamber.html

Ruston • *Ruston-Lincoln C/C* • Scott C. Terry PCED IOM; Pres./CEO; 2111 N. Trenton St.; P.O. Box 1383; 71273; Lincoln; P 45,000; M 488; (318) 255-2031; (318) 232-7981; Fax (318) 255-3481; info@rustonlincoln.org; www.rustonlincoln.org

Sabine Parish • *see Many*

Saint Amant • *see Ascension*

Saint Francisville • *Greater St. Francisville C/C* • Linda Osterberger; Dir.; 11936 Ferdinand St.; P.O. Box 545; 70775; West Feliciana; P 15,111; M 200; (225) 635-6717; Fax (225) 635-6717; sfchamber@bellsouth.net; www.stfrancisvillechamber.com

Saint Landry • *see Opelousas*

Saint Martinville • *Saint Martinville C/C* • Marian Melancon; Exec. Dir.; 120 New Market St.; P.O. Box 436; 70582; Saint Martin; P 8,000; M 120; (337) 394-7578; Fax (337) 394-4497; mbmtax@cox.net; www.stmartinvillechamber.com

Shreveport • *Greater Shreveport C/C* • Richard H. Bremer; Pres.; 400 Edwards St.; 71101; Caddo; P 400,000; M 1,920; (318) 677-2500; (800) 448-5432; Fax (318) 677-2541; info@shreveportchamber.org; www.shreveportchamber.org

Slidell • *East St. Tammany C/C* • Dawn Sharpe Brackett; CEO; 118 W. Hall Ave.; 70460; Saint Tammany; P 100,000; M 860; (985) 643-5678; (800) 471-3758; Fax (985) 649-2460; info@estchamber.com; www.estchamber.com*

Sorrento • *see Ascension*

South Webster Parish • *see Minden*

Springhill • *Springhill-North Webster C/C* • Janet Reeves; Mgr.; 400 N. Giles St.; 71075; Webster; P 8,200; M 186; (318) 539-4717; Fax (318) 539-2500; chamberc@cmaaccess.com; www.springhilllouisiana.net

Sulphur • *West Calcasieu Assn. of Commerce* • Janice Ackley; Exec. Dir.; 1906 Maplewood Dr.; 70663; Calcasieu; P 21,103; M 190; (337) 533-1040; associationw@bellsouth.net; www.westcal.org

Tallulah • *Madison Parish C/C* • Terry Murphy; Pres.; P.O. Box 311; 71284; Madison; P 14,000; M 50; (318) 574-2990; Fax (318) 574-9147; www.tallulah-la.gov

Thibodaux • *Thibodaux C/C* • Kathy Benoit; Pres./CEO; 318 E. Bayou Rd.; P.O. Box 467; 70302; Lafourche; P 25,000; M 650; (985) 446-1187; Fax (985) 446-1191; info@thibodauxchamber.com; www.thibodauxchamber.com.*

Vernon • *see Leesville*

Vidalia • *Concordia Parish C/C* • Jamie Burley; Exec. Dir.; 1401 Carter St.; P.O. Box 322; 71373; Concordia; P 19,058; M 300; (318) 336-8223; jamieburley@att.net; www.vidaliala.com

Ville Platte · *Ville Platte C/C* · Camille L. Fontenot; Exec. Dir.; 306 W. Main St.; P.O. Box 331; 70586; Evangeline; P 9,000; M 154; (337) 363-1878; villep001@centurytel.net; www.vpla.com

Vinton · *see Sulphur*

Vivian · *Vivian C/C* · Betty Matthews; Pres.; 100 Front St.; P.O. Box 182; 71082; Caddo; P 4,031; M 40; (318) 375-5300; Fax (318) 375-5300; chamberofcom@centurytel.net; www.vivian.la.us

Welsh · *Welsh C/C* · 201S. Elms St.; P.O. Box 786; 70591; Jefferson Davis; P 3,500; M 50; (337) 734-4772; (337) 734-2231; welshla@centurytel.net; www.townofwelsh.com

West Baton Rouge · *see Addis*

West Monroe · *West Monroe-West Ouachita C/C* · Mary Ann Newton; Pres.; 112 Professional Dr.; 71291; Ouachita; P 15,000; M 661; (318) 325-1961; Fax (318) 325-4296; info@westmonroe chamber.org; westmonroechamber.org*

Westlake · *see Sulphur*

Winnfield · *Winn C/C* · June Melton; Secy.; 499 E. Main St.; P.O. Box 565; 71483; Winn; P 17,714; M 150; (318) 628-4461; Fax (318) 628-2551; winnchamber@bellsouth.net; www.winn chamberofcommerce.com

Winnsboro · *Winnsboro-Franklin Parish C/C* · Howard Dee Smith; Pres.; 3830 Front St.; P.O. Box 1574; 71295; Franklin; P 23,000; M 160; (318) 435-4488; Fax (318) 435-5398; winnsboro chamber@bellsouth.net; www.winnsborochamber.com

Zachary · *Zachary C/C* · Teresa J. Steele; Mbrshp. Dir.; 4633 Main St.; 70791; East Baton Rouge; P 18,250; M 275; (225) 654-6777; Fax (225) 654-3957; tsteele@zacharyla.com; www.zacharyla.com

Maine

Maine State C of C · Dana F. Connors; Pres.; 125 Community Dr., Ste. 101; Augusta; 04330; Kennebec; P 1,300,000; M 1,200; (207) 623-4568; Fax (207) 622-7723; melanieb@mainechamber.org; www.mainechamber.org

Appleton · *see Union*

Auburn · *see Lewiston*

Augusta · *Kennebec Valley C/C* · Peter G. Thompson; Pres.; 21 University Dr.; P.O. Box 676; 04332; Kennebec; P 70,000; M 650; (207) 623-4559; Fax (207) 626-9342; info@augustamaine.com; www.augustamaine.com

Bangor · *Bangor Reg. C/C* · John Porter; Pres.; 519 Main St.; 04401; Penobscot; P 120,000; M 1,000; (207) 947-0307; Fax (207) 990-1427; admin@bangorregion.com; www.bangorregion.com

Bar Harbor · *Bar Harbor C/C* · Mr. Chris Fogg; CEO; P.O. Box 158; 04609; Hancock; P 4,500; M 450; (207) 664-2940; (800) 288-5103; Fax (207) 667-9080; visitors@barharborinfo.com; www.barharborinfo.com*

Bath · *see Topsham*

Belfast · *Belfast Area C/C* · Rob Constantine; Pres.; P.O. Box 58; 04915; Waldo; P 7,000; M 310; (207) 338-5900; Fax (207) 338-5823; info@belfastmaine.org; www.belfastmaine.org

Benedicta · *see Island Falls*

Bethel · *Bethel Area C/C* · Robin Zinchuk; Exec. Dir.; 8 Station Pl.; P.O. Box 1247; 04217; Oxford; P 6,000; M 257; (207) 824-2282; (800) 442-5826; Fax (207) 824-7123; info@bethelmaine.com; www.bethelmaine.com

Biddeford · *see Saco*

Bingham · *Upper Kennebec Valley C/C* · Cyndee Gagnon; Pres.; 356 Main St.; P.O. Box 491; 04920; Somerset; P 5,000; M 85; (207) 672-4100; ukvcofc@yahoo.com; upperkennebecvalleychamber.me

Blue Hill · *Blue Hill Peninsula C/C* · Kurt Stoll; Interim Exec. Dir.; 107 Main St.; P.O. Box 520; 04614; Hancock; P 8,000; M 255; (207) 374-3242; chamber@bluehillpeninsula.org; www.bluehill peninsula.org

Boothbay · *Boothbay C/C & Info. Center* · P.O. Box 187; 04537; Lincoln; P 5,000; M 190; (207) 633-4743; info@boothbay.org; www.boothbay.org

Boothbay Harbor · *Boothbay Harbor Reg. C/C* · Jaimie K. Logan; Exec. Dir.; 192 Townsend Ave.; P.O. Box 356; 04538; Lincoln; P 7,500; M 340; (207) 633-2353; Fax (207) 633-7448; seamaine@ boothbayharbor.com; www.boothbayharbor.com

Bowdoinham · *see Topsham*

Bridgton · *Greater Bridgton Lakes Reg. C/C* · Jim Mains; Exec. Dir.; 101 Portland Rd.; P.O. Box 236; 04009; Cumberland; P 28,000; M 300; (207) 647-3472; Fax (207) 647-8372; info@mainelakes chamber.com; www.mainelakeschamber.com

Brighton · *see Bingham*

Brooklin · *see Blue Hill*

Brooksville · *see Blue Hill*

Brunswick · *see Topsham*

Bucksport · *Bucksport Bay Area C/C* · Exec. Dir.; P.O. Box 1676; 04416; Hancock; P 5,000; M 225; (207) 469-6818; Fax (207) 469-2078; director@bucksportbaychamber.com; www.bucksportbay chamber.com

Burlington · *see Lincoln*

Calais · *St. Croix Valley C/C* · Neil Lane; Exec. Dir.; 39 Union St.; 04619; Washington; P 4,000; M 100; (207) 454-2308; (888) 422-3112; Fax (207) 454-7979; visitstcroixvalley@myfairpoint.net; www.visitstcroixvalley.com

Camden · *Camden-Rockport-Lincolnville C/C* · Dan Bookham; Exec. Dir.; 2 Public Landing; P.O. Box 919; 04843; Knox; P 12,000; M 700; (207) 236-4404; (800) 223-5459; Fax (207) 236-4315; chamber@camdenme.org; www.visitcamden.com

Caratunk · *see Bingham*

Caribou · *Caribou C of C & Ind.* · Wendy Landes; Exec. Dir.; 24 Sweden St., Ste. 101; 04736; Aroostook; P 8,500; M 244; (207) 498-6156; (800) 722-7648; Fax (207) 492-1362; ccci@caribou maine.net; www.cariboumaine.net

Carroll · *see Lincoln*

Casco · *see Windham*

Castine · *see Blue Hill*

Chester · *see Lincoln*

Corinna · *see Newport*

Crystal/Golden Ridge · *see Island Falls*

Damariscotta · *Damariscotta Region C/C* · Carisa Carney Holmes; Dir.; 15 Courtyard St., Ste. 2; P.O. Box 13; 04543; Lincoln; P 2,000; M 300; (207) 563-8340; Fax (207) 563-8348; info@ damariscottaregion.com; www.damariscottaregion.com

Danforth · *Greater East Grand Lake C/C* · Heather Zakupowsky; Chrmn.; P.O. Box 159; 04424; Washington; P 600; M 50; info@ eastgrandlake.net; www.eastgrandlake.net

Deer Isle · *Deer Isle-Stonington C/C* · Christina Shipps; Pres.; P.O. Box 490; 04627; Hancock; P 3,000; M 130; (207) 348-6124; deerisle@deerisle.com; www.deerislemaine.com

Detroit · *see Newport*

Dexter · *see Newport*

Dover-Foxcroft · *Piscataquis C/C* · Debra Boyd; Exec. Dir.; 1033 South St.; P.O. Box 376; 04426; Piscataquis; P 4,300; M 180; (207) 564-7533; Fax (207) 564-7533; exdir@piscataquischamber.com; www.piscataquischamber.com

Durham · *see Lewiston*

Dyer Brook · *see Island Falls*

East Boothbay · *see Boothbay Harbor*

East Millinocket · *see Millinocket*

East Wilson · *see Farmington*

Eastport · *Eastport Area C/C* · Meg Keay; Pres.; 64 Walter St.; P.O. Box 254; 04631; Washington; P 1,650; M 65; (207) 853-4644; Fax (207) 853-4644; info@eastportchamber.net; www.eastport chamber.net

Edgecomb · *see Boothbay Harbor*

Eliot · *see York*

Ellsworth · *Ellsworth Area C/C* · Margaret Sumpter; Exec. Dir.; 163 High St.; P.O. Box 267; 04605; Hancock; P 7,000; M 670; (207) 667-5584; Fax (207) 667-2617; info@ellsworthchamber.org; www.ellsworthchamber.org

Enfield · *see Lincoln*

Etna · *see Newport*

Exeter · *see Newport*

Farmington · *Franklin County C/C* · Lorna Dee Nichols; Exec. Dir.; 248 Wilton Rd.; 04938; Franklin; P 30,000; M 300; (207) 778-4215; Fax (207) 778-2438; info@franklincountymaine.org; www.franklincountymaine.org

Farmington Falls · *see Farmington*

Fort Fairfield · *Fort Fairfield C/C* · 18 Community Center Dr.; 04742; Aroostook; P 4,000; M 75; (207) 472-3802; Fax (207) 472-3810; chamber@fortfairfield.org; www.fortcc.org

Fort Kent · *Greater Fort Kent Area C/C* · Kay Paradis; Pres.; 291 W. Main St.; P.O. Box 430; 04743; Aroostook; P 5,000; M 189; (207) 834-5354; info@fortkentchamber.com; www.fortkent chamber.com

Franklin · *see Winter Harbor*

Freeport · *Freeport Merchants Assn.* · Myra Hopkins; Exec. Dir.; 23 Depot St.; P.O. Box 452; 04032; Cumberland; P 8,200; M 170; (207) 865-1212; (800) 865-1994; Fax (207) 865-0881; info@ freeportusa.com; www.freeportusa.com*

Gouldsboro · *see Winter Harbor*

Gray · *see Windham*

Greene · *see Lewiston*

Greenville · *Moosehead Lake Region C/C* · Bob Hamer; Exec. Dir.; 156 Moosehead Lake Rd.; P.O. Box 581; 04441; Piscataquis; P 1,623; M 130; (207) 695-2702; (888) 876-2778; info@moose headlake.org; www.mooseheadlake.org

Hallowell · *Hallowell Area Bd. of Trade* · P.O. Box 246; 04347; Kennebec; P 2,532; M 90; (207) 620-7477; info@hallowell.org; www.hallowell.org

Harpswell · *see Topsham*

Harrison · *see South Paris*

Hartland · *see Newport*

Hebron · *see South Paris*

Hersey · *see Island Falls*

Hope · *see Union*

Houlton · *Greater Houlton C/C* · Lori Weston; Exec. Dir.; 109 Main St.; 04730; Aroostook; P 8,000; M 236; (207) 532-4216; Fax (207) 532-4961; assistant@greaterhoulton.com; www.greater houlton.com

Howland · *see Lincoln*

Industry · *see Farmington*

Island Falls · *Northern Katahdin Valley Reg. C/C* · Linda Depew; Exec. Dir.; P.O. Box 374; 04747; Aroostook; P 5,621; M 91; (207) 463-4634; Fax (207) 463-4634; nkvrcc1@myfairpoint.net; www.northernmainechamber.com

Jackman · *Jackman-Moose River Region C/C* · P.O. Box 368; 04945; Somerset; P 900; M 45; (207) 668-4171; (888) 622-5225; mooserus@jackmanmaine.org; www.jackmanmaine.org

Kennebunk · *Kennebunk-Kennebunkport C/C* · Exec. Dir.; 17 Western Ave.; P.O. Box 740; 04043; York; P 18,500; M 450; (207) 967-0857; Fax (207) 967-2867; info@visitthekennebunks.com; www.visitthekennebunks.com

Kittery · *see York*

Lakeville · *see Lincoln*

Lee · *see Lincoln*

Leeds · *see Lewiston*

Lewiston · *Androscoggin County C/C* · Charles A. Morrison; Pres.; 415 Lisbon St.; P.O. Box 59; 04243; Androscoggin; P 107,000; M 1,300; (207) 783-2249; Fax (207) 783-4481; cmorrison@ androscoggincounty.com; www.androscoggincounty.com*

Limestone · *Limestone C/C* · Scott Caldwell; Pres.; 93 Main St.; 04750; Aroostook; P 2,400; M 45; (207) 325-4025; Fax (207) 325-3330; chamber@limestonemaine.org; www.limestonemaine.org

Lincoln · *Lincoln Lakes Region C/C* · Cheri Archer; Ofc. Mgr.; 256 W. Broadway; 04457; Penobscot; P 5,800; M 115; (207) 794-8065; Fax (207) 794-8065; llrcc@myfairpoint.net; www.lincolnmechamber.org

Lincolnville · *see Camden*

Lisbon · *see Lewiston*

Livermore · *see Lewiston*

Livermore Falls · *see Lewiston*

Machias · *Machias Bay Area C/C* · Kathleen Shannon; Exec. Dir.; 85 Main St., Ste. 2; P.O. Box 606; 04654; Washington; P 2,800; M 208; (207) 255-4402; Fax (207) 255-4402; info@machias chamber.org; www.machiaschamber.org

Madawaska · *Greater Madawaska C/C* · Chad Carter; Exec. Dir.; 356 Main St.; P.O. Box 144; 04756; Aroostook; P 4,900; M 200; (207) 728-7000; Fax (207) 728-4696; valleyvisit@pwless.net; www.greatermadawaskachamber.com

Magalloway · *see Errol, NH*

Mattamiscontis · *see Lincoln*

Mattawamkeag · *see Lincoln*

Mayfield · *see Bingham*

Mechanic Falls · *see Lewiston*

Medway · *see Millinocket*

Merrill · *see Island Falls*

Millinocket · *Katahdin Area C/C* · Jean Boddy; Ofc. Coord.; 1029 Central St.; 04462; Penobscot; P 5,300; M 140; (207) 723-4443; info@katahdinmaine.com; www.katahdinmaine.com

Minot · *see Lewiston*

Monada/Silver Ridge · *see Island Falls*

Moro Plantation · *see Island Falls*

Moscow • *see Bingham*

Mount Chase/Shin Pond • *see Island Falls*

Naples • *see Windham*

New Sharon • *see Farmington*

New Vineyard • *see Farmington*

Newport • *Sebasticook Valley C/C* • Brenda Seekins; Exec. Dir.; P.O. Box 464; 04953; Somerset; P 25,000; M 250; (207) 368-4698; Fax (207) 368-5312; svcc@midmaine.com; www.ourchamber.org*

Norridgewock • *Norridgewock Area C/C* • Bob Gilcott; Pres.; P.O. Box 184; 04957; Somerset; P 3,990; M 125; (207) 431-5188; www.norridgewockareachamber.com

Northeast Harbor • *Mount Desert C/C* • John Lawrence; Exec. Dir.; 18 Harbor Dr.; P.O. Box 675; 04662; Hancock; P 2,000; M 110; (207) 276-5040; info@mountdesertchamber.org; www.mountdesertchamber.org

Norway • *see South Paris*

Oakfield • *see Island Falls*

Ogunquit • *Ogunquit C/C* • Karen Marie Arel; Pres.; 36 Main St.; P.O. Box 2289; 03907; York; P 1,500; M 425; (207) 646-2939; Fax (207) 641-0856; info@ogunquit.org; www.ogunquit.org*

Old Orchard Beach • *Old Orchard Beach C/C* • 11 First St.; 04064; York; P 9,000; M 250; (207) 934-2500; Fax (207) 934-4994; info@oldorchardbeachmaine.com; www.oldorchardbeachmaine.com

Orland • *see Bucksport*

Otisfield • *see South Paris*

Oxbow • *see Island Falls*

Oxford • *see South Paris*

Palmyra • *see Newport*

Paris • *see South Paris*

Passadumkeag • *see Lincoln*

Patten • *see Island Falls*

Penobscot • *see Blue Hill*

Pittsfield • *see Newport*

Plymouth • *see Newport*

Poland • *see Lewiston*

Portland • *Portland Reg. C/C* • W. Godfrey Wood; CEO; 60 Pearl St.; 04101; Cumberland; P 250,000; M 1,350; (207) 772-2811; Fax (207) 772-1179; chamber@portlandregion.com; www.portlandregion.com*

Prentis • *see Lincoln*

Presque Isle • *Presque Isle Area C/C* • Theresa Fowler; Exec. Dir.; 3 Houlton Rd.; 04769; Aroostook; P 20,400; M 325; (207) 764-6561; Fax (207) 764-1583; info@pichamber.com; www.pichamber.com

Rangeley • *Rangeley Lakes Region C/C* • Rebecca Schinas; Exec. Dir.; 6 Park Rd.; P.O. Box 317; 04970; Franklin; P 1,600; M 230; (207) 864-5571; (800) 685-2537; Fax (207) 864-5366; info@rangeleymaine.com; www.rangeleymaine.com

Raymond • *see Windham*

Rockland • *Penobscot Bay Reg. C/C* • Shari Closter; Interim Exec. Dir.; One Park Dr.; P.O. Box 508; 04841; Knox; P 22,300; M 785; (207) 596-0376; (800) 562-2529; Fax (207) 596-6549; info@therealmaine.com; www.therealmaine.com*

Rockport • *see Camden*

Rumford • *River Valley C/C* • Laurieann Milligan; Admin.; 10 Bridge St.; 04276; Oxford; P 17,000; M 200; (207) 364-3241; info@rivervalleychamber.com; www.rivervalleychamber.com

Sabattus • *see Lewiston*

Saco • *Biddeford-Saco C/C & Ind.* • 138 Main St., Ste. 101; 04072; York; P 45,000; M 500; (207) 282-1567; Fax (207) 282-3149; info@biddefordsacochamber.org; www.biddefordsacochamber.org

Saint Albans • *see Newport*

Saint Francis • *Saint Francis C/C* • P.O. Box 13; 04774; Aroostook; P 550; M 12; (207) 398-3358; jouelet@roadrunner.com

Saint John • *see Saint Francis*

Sanford • *Sanford-Springvale C/C & Eco. Dev.* • Richard L. Stanley; Pres.; 917 Main St., Ste. B; 04073; York; P 55,000; M 360; (207) 324-4280; (207) 324-4281; Fax (207) 324-8290; sancoc@metrocast.net; www.sanfordchamber.org*

Sebago Lake • *see Windham*

Seboeis • *see Lincoln*

Sedgwick • *see Blue Hill*

Sherman Mills • *see Island Falls*

Skowhegan • *Skowhegan Area C/C* • 23 Commercial St.; 04976; Somerset; P 10,000; M 265; (207) 474-3621; Fax (207) 474-3306; exdir@skowheganchamber.com; www.skowheganchamber.com

Smyrna Mills • *see Island Falls*

Solon • *see Bingham*

Sorrento • *see Winter Harbor*

South Berwick • *see York*

South Paris • *Oxford Hills C/C* • Mindy Stewart; Mktg. Dir.; 4 Western Ave.; 04281; Oxford; P 22,000; M 390; (207) 743-2281; Fax (207) 743-0687; info@oxfordhillsmaine.com; www.oxfordhillsmaine.com*

Southport • *see Boothbay Harbor*

Southwest Harbor • *Southwest Harbor-Tremont C/C* • 20 Village Green Way; P.O. Box 1143; 04679; Hancock; P 2,500; M 154; (207) 244-9264; Fax (207) 244-4185; quietside@acadiachamber.com; www.acadiachamber.com

Springvale • *see Sanford*

Stacyville • *see Island Falls*

Standish • *see Windham*

Stetson • *see Newport*

Stonington • *see Deer Isle*

Sullivan • *see Winter Harbor*

Thomaston • *see Rockland*

Topsfield • *see Lincoln*

Topsham • *Southern Midcoast Maine C/C* • Steven Wallace; Pres.; Border Trust Bus. Center Svcs.; 2 Main St.; 04086; Cumberland, Lincoln & Sagadahoc; P 70,222; M 625; (207) 725-8797; (877) 725-8797; Fax (207) 725-9787; chamber@midcoastmaine.com; www.midcoastmaine.com*

Trenton • *see Ellsworth*

Turner • *see Lewiston*

Union • *Union Area C/C* • Erica Morton; Pres.; P.O. Box 603; 04862; Knox; P 12,000; M 90; (207) 785-3300; uacoc@tidewater.net; www.unionareachamber.org

Upton • *see Errol, NH*

Van Buren • *Greater Van Buren C/C* • Ralph Anderson; Prog. Dir.; 51 Main St., Ste. 101; 04785; Aroostook; P 2,500; M 80; (207) 868-5059; vbchamber@gmail.com; www.vanburenmaine.com

Verona • *see Bucksport*

Wales · *see Lewiston*

Warren · *see Rockland*

Washington · *see Union*

Waterford · *see South Paris*

Waterville · *Mid-Maine C/C* · Kimberly N. Lindlof; Pres./CEO; One Post Office Sq.; 04901; Kennebec; P 60,000; M 535; (207) 873-3315; Fax (207) 877-0087; info@midmainechamber.com; www.midmainechamber.com*

Webster Plantation · *see Lincoln*

Weeks Mills · *China Area C/C* · Marlene Reed; 128 Weeks Mills Rd.; 04358; Kennebec; P 4,500; M ; (207) 445-3183

Wellington · *see Bingham*

Wells · *Wells C/C* · Eleanor Vadenais; Exec. Dir.; 136 Post Rd.; P.O. Box 356; 04090; York; P 10,000; M 330; (207) 646-2451; Fax (207) 646-8104; wellschamber@wellschamber.org; www.wellschamber.org

West Enfield · *see Lincoln*

West Forks · *The Forks Area C/C* · Pam Christopher; Exec. Dir.; P.O. Box 1; 04985; Somerset; P 2,150; M 40; (207) 663-2121; Fax (207) 663-2122; info@forksarea.com; www.forksarea.com

West Paris · *see South Paris*

Whiting · *Cobscook Bay Area C/C* · P.O. Box 42; 04691; Washington; P 8,000; M 80; (207) 733-2201; info@cobscookbay.com; www.cobscookbay.com

Wilsons Mills · *see Errol, NH*

Wilton · *see Farmington*

Windham · *Sebago Lakes Region C/C* · Barbara Clark; Exec. Dir.; 747 Roosevelt Trl.-Rte. 302; P.O. Box 1015; 04062; Cumberland; P 55,000; M 370; (207) 892-8265; Fax (207) 893-0110; info@sebagolakeschamber.com; www.sebagolakeschamber.com*

Winn · *see Lincoln*

Winter Harbor · *Schoodic Area C/C* · Linda Elliot; Pres.; P.O. Box 381; 04693; Hancock; P 3,000; M 85; (207) 546-2960; info@acadia-schoodic.org; www.acadia-schoodic.org

Winthrop · *Winthrop Area C/C* · Jeffrey Seguin; Pres.; P.O. Box 51; 04364; Kennebec; P 6,300; M 100; (207) 377-8020; Fax (207) 377-2767; info@winthropchamber.org; www.winthropchamber.org

Yarmouth · *Yarmouth C/C* · Carolyn Schuster; Mgr. Dir.; 162 Main St.; 04096; Cumberland; P 8,600; M 210; (207) 846-3984; Fax (207) 846-5419; info@yarmouthmaine.org; www.yarmouthmaine.org*

York · *Greater York Region C/C* · Catherine R. Goodwin; Pres./CEO; 1 Stonewall Ln.; 03909; York; P 37,000; M 800; (207) 363-4422; Fax (207) 363-7320; info@yorkme.org; www.gatewaytomaine.org*

Maryland

Maryland C of C · Kathleen T. Snyder CCE; Pres./CEO; 60 West St., Ste. 100; Annapolis; 21401; Anne Arundel; P 5,600,000; M 850; (410) 269-0642; (301) 261-2858; Fax (410) 269-5247; mcc@mdchamber.org; www.mdchamber.org*

Aberdeen · *Aberdeen C/C* · Janet Fisher; Dir.; 117 S. Philadelphia Blvd. Rte. 40; 21001; Harford; P 15,000; M 300; (410) 272-2580; aberdeenchamber@verizon.net; www.aberdeencc.com

Annapolis · *Annapolis & Anne Arundel County C/C* · Robert Burdon; Pres./CEO; P.O. Box 346; 21401; Anne Arundel; P 489,656; M 1,100; (410) 266-3960; Fax (410) 266-8270; lmarshall@aaaccc.org; www.annapolischamber.com

Annapolis Junction · *see Laurel*

Anne Arundel County · *see Annapolis and Laurel*

Baltimore · *Baltimore City C/C* · Charles Owens; Pres.; P.O. Box 4483; 21223; Baltimore; P 670,000; M 400; (410) 837-7101; Fax (410) 837-7104; charlieo@baltimorecitychamber.org; www.baltimorecitychamber.org*

Baltimore · *Chesapeake Gateway C/C* · Janelle Gwynn; Admin. Dir.; 405 Williams Ct., Ste. 108; 21220; Baltimore; P 95,000; M 300; (443) 317-8763; Fax (443) 317-8772; info@emrchamber.org; www.emrchamber.org.

Baltimore County · *Baltimore County C/C* · Keith Scott; Pres./CEO; 102 W. Pennsylvania Ave., Ste. 101; Towson; 21204; Baltimore; P 800,000; M 650; (410) 825-6200; Fax (410) 821-9901; kscott@baltcountychamber.com; www.baltcountycc.com

Bel Air · *Harford County C/C* · William Seccurro; Pres./CEO; 108 S. Bond St.; 21014; Harford; P 248,322; M 1,200; (410) 838-2020; (800) 682-8536; Fax (410) 893-4715; ceo@harfordchamber.org; www.harfordchamber.org

Beltsville · *see Laurel*

Berlin · *Berlin C/C* · Olive Mawyer; Coord.; P.O. Box 212; 21811; Worcester; P 3,500; M 200; (410) 641-4775; Fax (410) 641-3118; chamberinfo@berlinmdcc.org; www.berlinmdcc.org

Berwyn Heights · *see Lanham*

Bethesda · *Greater Bethesda-Chevy Chase C/C* · Ginanne M. Italiano; Pres.; 7910 Woodmont Ave., Ste. 1204; 20814; Montgomery; P 1,000,000; M 750; (301) 652-4900; Fax (301) 657-1973; staff@bccchamber.org; www.bccchamber.org*

Bladensburg · *see Lanham*

Bowie · *also see Lanham*

Bowie · *Greater Bowie C/C* · Kelly Pierce; Exec. Dir.; 1525 Pointer Ridge Place, Ste. 302; 20716; Prince George's; P 58,000; M 300; (301) 262-0920; Fax (301) 262-0921; kelly@bowiechamber.org; www.bowiechamber.org*

Brentwood · *see Lanham*

Burtonsville · *see Laurel*

BWI Airport · *see Laurel*

California · *St. Mary's County C/C* · William E. Scarafia; Pres./CEO; 44200 Airport Rd.; 20619; St. Mary's; P 100,000; M 600; (301) 737-3001; Fax (301) 737-0089; info@smcchamber.com; www.smcchamber.com*

Cambridge · *Dorchester County C/C* · Allen Nelson; Exec. Dir.; 528 Poplar St.; 21613; Dorchester; P 30,000; M 540; (410) 228-3575; chamber@dorchesterchamber.org; www.dorchesterchamber.org*

Capitol Heights · *see Lanham*

Catonsville · *Greater Catonsville C/C* · Teal Cary; Exec. Dir.; 924 Frederick Rd.; 21228; Baltimore; P 40,000; M 375; (410) 719-9609; Fax (410) 744-6127; chamber@catonsville.org; www.catonsville.org

Chester · *Queen Anne's County C/C* · Linda Friday; Pres.; 1561 Postal Rd.; P.O. Box 511; 21619; Queen Anne's; P 45,000; M 625; (410) 643-8530; Fax (410) 643-8477; business@qacchamber.com; www.qacchamber.com

Chestertown · *Kent County C/C* · Loretta M. Lodge; Exec. Dir.; 122 N. Cross St.; P.O. Box 146; 21620; Kent; P 19,200; M 305; (410) 810-2968; Fax (410) 778-1406; info@kentchamber.org; www.kentchamber.org

Cheverly · *see Lanham*

Chevy Chase · *see Bethesda*

Churchton · *Southern Anne Arundel C/C* · Carla Catterton; Exec. Dir.; 5503 Muddy Creek Rd.; 20764; Anne Arundel; P 32,000; M 320; (410) 867-3129; Fax (410) 867-3556; southcounty@toad. net; www.southcounty.org

College Park · *see Lanham and Laurel*

Colmar Manor · *see Lanham*

Columbia · *also see Laurel*

Columbia · *Howard County C/C* · Pamela J. Klahr CCE; Pres./ CEO; 5560 Sterrett Pl., Ste. 105; 21044; Howard; P 284,000; M 720; (410) 730-4111; Fax (410) 730-4584; pklahr@howardchamber. com; www.howardchamber.com*

Cottage City · *see Lanham*

Crisfield · *Crisfield Area C/C* · Valerie Howard; Exec. Dir.; 906 W. Main St.; P.O. Box 292; 21817; Somerset; P 2,800; M 135; (410) 968-2500; (800) 782-3913; Fax (410) 968-0524; info@crisfield chamber.com; www.crisfieldchamber.com

Crofton · *Greater Crofton C/C* · Judy Wilson; Exec. Dir.; P.O. Box 4146; 21114; Anne Arundel; P 27,500; M 185; (410) 721-9131; Fax (410) 721-0785; bob@tlcincorporated.com; www.crofton chamber.com

Cumberland · *Allegany County C/C* · Stuart Czapski; Exec. Dir.; Bell Tower Bldg.; 24 Frederick St.; 21502; Allegany; P 72,532; M 425; (301) 722-2820; Fax (301) 722-5995; info@allegany countychamber.com; www.alleganycountychamber.com.*

Delmar · *see Delmar, DE*

District Heights · *see Lanham*

Dundalk · *see Baltimore County*

Eagle Harbor · *see Lanham*

East Baltimore · *see Baltimore County*

Easton · *Talbot County C/C* · Alan I. Silverstein IOM; Pres./CEO; 101 Marlboro Ave., Ste. 53; P.O. Box 1366; 21601; Talbot; P 36,000; M 800; (410) 822-4653; Fax (410) 822-7922; info@talbotchamber. org; www.talbotchamber.org*

Edgemere · *see Baltimore County*

Edmonston · *see Lanham*

Elkridge · *see Laurel*

Elkton · *Cecil County C/C* · Laura Mayse; Exec. Dir.; 233 E. Main St.; 21921; Cecil; P 100,000; M 640; (410) 392-3833; Fax (410) 392-6225; info@cecilchamber.com; www.cecilchamber.com*

Elkton · *Elkton Chamber & Alliance* · Mary Jo Jablonski; Exec. Dir.; 101 E. Main St.; 21921; Cecil; P 18,000; M 105; (410) 398-5076; Fax (410) 398-4971; maryjo@elktonalliance.org; www.elktonalliance.org

Essex · *see Baltimore*

Fairmont Heights · *see Lanham*

Forest Heights · *see Lanham*

Fort Meade · *see Laurel*

Frederick · *Frederick County C/C* · M. Richard Adams; Pres./ CEO; 8420-B Gas House Pike; 21701; Frederick; P 60,000; M 820; (301) 662-4164; Fax (301) 846-4427; info@frederickchamber.org; www.frederickchamber.org*

Gaithersburg · *Gaithersburg-Germantown C/C* · Marilyn Balcombe; Pres.; 4 Professional Dr., Ste. 132; 20879; Montgomery; P 150,000; M 500; (301) 840-1400; Fax (301) 963-3918; mbalcombe@ ggchamber.org; www.ggchamber.org*

Germantown · *Maryland Hispanic C/C* · Maria Welch; Chair; P.O. Box 2392; 20875; Montgomery; P 150,000; (240) 686-0450; customerservice@mdhcc.org; www.mdhcc.org*

Germantown · *see Gaithersburg*

Glen Burnie · *Northern Anne Arundel County C/C* · Frances Schmidt; Exec. Dir.; 7477 Baltimore-Annapolis Blvd., Ste. 204; 21061; Anne Arundel; P 500,000; M 400; (410) 766-8282; Fax (410) 766-5722; info@naaccc.com; www.naaccc.com*

Glenarden · *see Lanham*

Glyndon · *see Reisterstown*

Greenbelt · *see Lanham and Laurel*

Hagerstown · *Hagerstown-Washington County C/C* · Brien Poffenberger; Pres.; 28 W. Washington St., Ste. 200; 21740; Washington; P 131,923; M 611; (301) 739-2015; Fax (301) 739-1278; chamber@hagerstown.org; www.hagerstown.org

Hancock · *Hancock C/C* · Louis Close; Treas.; 126 W. High St.; 21750; Washington; P 1,725; M 82; (301) 678-5900; info@ hancockmd.com; www.hancockmd.com

Hanover · *see Laurel*

Harford County · *see Bel Air*

Havre de Grace · *Havre de Grace C/C* · Cathy Vincenti; Exec. Dir.; 450 Pennington Ave.; 21078; Harford; P 18,000; M 270; (410) 939-3303; (800) 851-7756; Fax (410) 939-3490; hdegchamber1@ comcast.net; www.hdgchamber.com

Howard County · *see Columbia and Laurel*

Hyattsville · *see Lanham*

Jessup · *see Laurel*

Kingsville · *see Baltimore County*

Landover Hills · *see Lanham*

Lanham · *Prince George's C/C* · Rhonda Slade; Pres./CEO; 4640 Forbes Blvd., Ste. 130; 20706; Prince George's; P 865,000; M 927; (301) 731-5000; Fax (301) 731-5011; info@pgcoc.org; www. pgcoc.org

LaPlata · *Charles County C/C* · Ken Gould; Exec. Dir.; 101 Centennial, Ste. A; 20646; Charles; P 124,000; M 800; (301) 932-6500; (301) 870-3089; Fax (301) 932-3945; info@charlescounty chamber.org; www.charlescountychamber.org

Laurel · *also see Lanham*

Laurel · *Baltimore Washington Corridor Chamber* · H. Walter Townshend III; Pres./CEO; 312 Marshall Ave., Ste. 104; 20707; Anne Arundel, Howard, Montgomery & Prince George; P 2,200,000; M 550; (301) 725-4000; (410) 792-9714; Fax (301) 725-0776; bwcc@bwcc.org; www.bwcc.org*

Maryland City · *see Laurel*

McHenry · *Garrett County C/C & Visitors Center* · Nicole Christian; Pres./CEO; 15 Visitors Center Dr.; 21541; Garrett; P 30,000; M 750; (301) 387-4386; (301) 387-6171; Fax (301) 387-2080; info@garrettchamber.com; www.garrettchamber.com

Montgomery County · *see Rockville and Laurel*

Morningside · *see Lanham*

Mount Airy · *Greater Mount Airy C/C* · Kerry Turner; P.O. Box 741; 21771; Carroll & Frederick; P 30,000; M 300; (301) 829-5426; inquiries@mtairybusiness.com; www.mtairybusiness.com

Mount Rainier · *see Lanham*

North East · *North East C/C* · Carolyn Crouch; Pres.; 20 Merganser Ct.; 21901; Cecil; P 20,000; M 120; (410) 287-5252; (800) CECIL-95; info@northeastchamber.org; www.northeastchamber.org

Oakland · *see McHenry*

Ocean City · *Greater Ocean City C/C* · Melanie Pursel; Exec. Dir.; 12320 Ocean Gateway; 21842; Worcester; P 8,400; M 850; (410) 213-0552; Fax (410) 213-7521; info@oceancity.org; www.oceancity.org*

Ocean Pines · *Ocean Pines Area C/C* · Elizabeth Kain-Bolen; Exec. Dir.; 10514 Racetrack Rd., Ste G; 21811; Worcester; P 20,000; M 300; (410) 641-5306; Fax (410) 641-6176; info@oceanpines chamber.org; www.oceanpineschamber.org*

Odenton · *West Anne Arundel County C/C* · Claire Louder; Pres./CEO; 8373 Piney Orchard Pkwy., Ste. 200; 21113; Anne Arundel; P 100,000; M 350; (410) 672-3422; Fax (410) 672-3475; info@westcountychamber.org; www.waaccc.org*

Olney · *Olney C/C* · Pamela Spears; Bd. Chrmn.; 3460 Olney-Laytonsville Rd.. Ste. 211; P.O. Box 550; 20830; Montgomery; P 37,000; M 215; (301) 774-7117; Fax (301) 774-4944; chamber@olneymd.org; www.olneymd.org

Owings Mills · *see Reisterstown*

Oxford · *see Easton*

Parkville · *see Baltimore County*

Perry Hall · *see Baltimore County*

Pikesville · *Pikesville C/C* · Sherrie Becker; Exec. Dir.; 7 Church Ln., Ste. 14; 21208; Baltimore; P 33,090; M 300; (410) 484-2337; Fax (410) 484-4151; info@pikesvillechamber.org; www.pikesville chamber.org

Pocomoke City · *Pocomoke City C/C* · Denise Wagner; Exec. Dir.; 6 Market St.; P.O. Box 356; 21851; Worcester; P 4,500; M 150; (410) 957-1919; Fax (410) 957-4784; pocomokechamber@gmail.com; www.pocomoke.com

Poolesville · *Poolesville Area C/C* · Maggie Nightingale; Exec. Secy.; P.O. Box 256; 20837; Montgomery; P 5,000; M 140; (301) 349-5753; (301) 972-8896; www.poolesvillechamber.com

Potomac · *Potomac C/C* · Adam Greenberg; Pres.; P.O. Box 59160; 20859; Montgomery; P 50,000; M 80; (301) 299-2170; Fax (301) 299-4650; adam@potomacpizza.com; www.potomac chamber.org

Prince Frederick · *Calvert County C/C* · Carolyn McHugh; Pres./CEO; 120 Dares Beach Rd.; P.O. Box 9; 20678; Calvert; P 75,000; M 500; (410) 535-2577; (301) 855-1930; Fax (443) 295-7213; calvertchamber@calvertchamber.org; www.calvertchamber.org*

Prince George County · *see Lanham and Laurel*

Princess Anne · *Princess Anne C/C* · Dennis Williams; Pres.; 11840 Somerset; P.O. Box 642; 21853; Somerset; P 2,313; M 50; (410) 651-2961; Fax (410) 651-3836; www.townofprincessanne.com

Queen Anne's County · *see Chester*

Reisterstown · *Reisterstown-Owings Mills-Glyndon C/C* · Brian Ditto; Exec. Dir.; 100 Owings Ct., Ste. 9; 21136; Baltimore; P 80,000; M 350; (410) 702-7073; Fax (410) 702-7075; romg@romgchamber.com; www.romgchamber.com*

Rockville · *Montgomery County C/C* · Georgette Godwin; Pres./CEO; 51 Monroe St., Ste. 1800; 20850; Montgomery; P 757,000; M 600; (301) 738-0015; Fax (301) 738-8792; ggodwin@mcccmd.com; www.mcccmd.com

Rockville · *Rockville C/C* · Andrea Jolly; Exec. Dir.; 1 Research Ct., Ste. 450; 20850; Montgomery; P 47,000; M 125; (301) 424-9300; Fax (301) 762-7599; rockville@rockvillechamber.org; www.rockvillechamber.org

Rosedale · *see Baltimore County*

Rossville · *see Baltimore County*

Saint Michaels · *see Easton*

Salisbury · *Salisbury Area C/C* · Brad Bellacicco; Exec. Dir.; 144 E. Main St.; 21801; Wicomico; P 100,000; M 877; (410) 749-0144; Fax (410) 860-9925; chamber@salisburyarea.com; www.salisburyarea.com*

Sandy Spring · *see Laurel*

Savage · *see Laurel*

Severna Park · *Greater Severna Park C/C* · Linda Zahn; Exec. Dir.; 1 Holly Ave.; 21146; Anne Arundel; P 40,000; M 650; (410) 647-3900; Fax (410) 647-3999; info@severnaparkchamber.com; www.severnaparkchamber.com*

Silver Spring · *Greater Silver Spring C/C* · Jane Redicker; Pres.; 8601 Georgia Ave., Ste. 203; 20910; Montgomery; P 235,000; M 750; (301) 565-3777; Fax (301) 565-3377; info@gsscc.org; www.gsscc.org*

Snow Hill · *Snow Hill C/C* · Lee Chisholm; Pres.; P.O. Box 176; 21863; Worcester; P 3,200; M 55; (410) 632-0809; (410) 632-1700; blaws@taylorbank.com; www.snowhillmd.com

Talbot County · *see Easton*

Taneytown · *Taneytown C/C* · Donna Sako; Exec. Dir.; 24 E. Baltimore St.; P.O. Box 18; 21787; Carroll; P 25,000; M 144; (410) 756-4234; Fax same; dlsako@verizon.net; www.taneytown chamber.org

Tilghman Island · *see Easton*

Towson · *see Baltimore County*

Upper Marlboro · *see Lanham*

Westminster · *Carroll County C/C* · Richard Haddad; Pres.; 700 Corporate Center Ct., Ste. L; P.O. Box 871; 21158; Carroll; P 170,000; M 500; (410) 848-9050; (410) 876-7212; Fax (410) 876-1023; info@carrollcountychamber.org; www.carroll countychamber.org*

Wheaton · *Wheaton-Kensington C/C* · Kathleen Guinan; Pres.; 2401 Blueridge Ave., Ste. 101; 20902; Montgomery; P 153,000; M 150; (301) 949-0080; Fax (301) 949-0081; contactus@wk chamber.org; www.wkchamber.org

White Marsh · *see Baltimore*

Massachusetts

No State Chamber

Abington · *see Brockton*

Acton · *Middlesex West C/C* · Sarah Fletcher; Exec. Dir.; 77 Great Rd., Ste. 214; 01720; Middlesex; P 92,000; M 400; (978) 263-0010; Fax (978) 264-0303; info@mwcoc.com; www.mwcoc.com*

Adams · *see North Adams*

Agawam · *see Springfield*

Alford · *see Great Barrington*

Amesbury · *Amesbury C/C & Ind. Found. Inc.* · Norma Jean Fowler; Exec. Asst.; 5 Market Sq.; 01913; Essex; P 18,000; M 300; (978) 388-3178; Fax (978) 388-4952; chamber@amesbury chamber.com; www.amesburychamber.com

Amherst · *Amherst Area C/C* · Tony Maroulis; Exec. Dir.; 28 Amity St.; 01002; Hampshire; P 35,000; M 600; (413) 253-0700; Fax (413) 256-0771; info@amherstarea.com; www.amherstarea.com*

Arlington · *Arlington C/C* · Lorraine Kilby; Ofc. Mgr.; One Whittemore Park; 02474; Middlesex; P 42,389; M 310; (781) 643-4600; Fax (781) 646-5581; info@arlcc.org; www.arlcc.org

Ashburnham · *see North Central Mass.*

Ashby · *see North Central Mass.*

Ashland · *see Framingham*

Ashley Falls · *see Great Barrington*

Ashley Falls · *see Lakeville, CT*

Athol · *North Quabbin C/C* · Steve Raymond; Exec. Dir.; 507 Main St.; P.O. Box 157; 01331; Worcester; P 28,000; M 216; (978) 249-3849; Fax (978) 249-7151; nqcc1@verizon.net; www.northquabbinchamber.com*

Attleborough · *United Reg. C/C* · Jack Lank; Pres.; 42 Union St.; 02703; Bristol; M 1,050; (508) 222-0801; Fax (508) 222-1498; jack@unitedregionalchamber.com; www.unitedregionalchamber.com*

Avon · *see Brockton*

Ayer · *see Devens*

Barnstable · *see Hyannis*

Barre · *see Gardner*

Becket · *see Great Barrington*

Bedford · *Bedford C/C* · Maureen Sullivan; Exec. Dir.; 12 Mudgeway; 01730; Middlesex; P 13,000; M 200; (781) 275-8503; bcoc@bedfordchamber.org; www.bedfordchamber.org*

Bellingham · *see Milford*

Belmont · *see Watertown*

Berkley · *see Taunton*

Berlin · *see Clinton and Hudson*

Beverly · *Beverly C/C* · Ilia Stacy; Exec. Dir.; 28 Cabot St.; 01915; Essex; P 40,000; M 400; (978) 232-9559; Fax (978) 232-9372; director@beverlychamber.com; www.beverlychamber.com

Billerica · *Billerica Comm. Alliance* · Pat Zapert; Exec. Dir.; 12 Andover Rd., Ste. 1; 01821; Middlesex; P 40,000; M 120; (978) 667-4174; Fax (978) 670-2797; info@billerica-alliance.org; www.billerica-alliance.org

Blackstone · *see Franklin*

Bolton · *see Clinton and Hudson*

Boston · *Greater Boston C/C* · Paul Guzzi; Pres./CEO; 265 Franklin St., 12th Flr.; 02110; Suffolk; P 6,016,425; M 1,700; (617) 227-4500; Fax (617) 227-7505; info@bostonchamber.com; www.bostonchamber.com

Boston · *Mass. Chamber of Bus. & Ind.* · Debra A. Boronski-Burack; Pres./CEO; 60 State St., Ste. 700; 01028; Suffolk; P 6,500,000; M 1,300; (617) 512-9667; Fax (413) 525-1184; president@masscbi.com; www.masscbi.com

Bourne · *see Cape Cod Canal*

Boylston · *see Clinton*

Brewster · *Brewster C/C* · Kyle Hinkle; Exec. Dir.; P.O. Box 1241; 02631; Barnstable; P 10,519; M 200; (508) 896-3500; info@brewstercapecod.org; www.brewstercapecod.org

Bridgewater · *see Brockton and Middleborough*

Brimfield · *see Sturbridge*

Brockton · *Metro South C/C* · Christopher Cooney; CEO; Sixty School St.; 02301; Plymouth; P 285,000; M 927; (508) 586-0500; Fax (508) 587-1340; chris@metrosouthchamber.com; www.metrosouthchamber.com.*

HOME OF THE NORTHERN LEAGUE BASEBALL TEAM BROCKTON ROX, WORLD CHAMPION BOXERS MARVELOUS MARVIN HAGLER AND ROCKY MARCIANO. KNOWN AS THE CITY OF CHAMPIONS.

Brookline · *Brookline C/C* · Harry Robinson; Exec. Dir.; 251 Harvard St., Ste. 1; 02446; Norfolk; P 57,107; M 230; (617) 739-1330; Fax (617) 739-1200; info@brooklinechamber.com; www.brooklinechamber.com

Cambridge · *Cambridge C/C* · Kelly Thompson Clark; Pres./CEO; 859 Massachusetts Ave.; 02139; Middlesex; P 110,000; M 1,550; (617) 876-4100; Fax (617) 354-9874; ccinfo@cambridgechamber.org; www.cambridgechamber.org*

Canton · *see Brockton and Norwood*

Cape Cod · *Cape Cod C of C & CVB* · Wendy Northcross; CEO; 5 ShootFlying Hill Rd.; Centerville; 02632; Barnstable; P 228,000; M 1,376; (508) 362-3225; (888) 33-CAPECOD; Fax (508) 362-3698; info@capecodchamber.org; www.capecodchamber.org*

Cape Cod Canal · *Cape Cod Canal Region C/C* · Marie Oliva; Pres./CEO; 70 Main St.; Buzzards Bay; 02532; Barnstable; P 19,000; M 650; (508) 759-6000; Fax (508) 759-6965; info@capecodcanalchamber.org; www.capecodcanalchamber.org*

Carver · *see Middleborough*

Charlton · *see Sturbridge*

Chatham · *Chatham C/C* · Lisa Franz; Exec. Dir.; P.O. Box 793; 02633; Barnstable; P 6,800; M 400; (508) 945-5199; (800) 715-5567; Fax (508) 430-7919; chamber@chathaminfo.com; www.chathaminfo.com

Chathamport · *see Chatham*

Chelmsford · *see Lowell*

Chelsea · *Chelsea C/C* · Donald Harney; Exec. Dir.; 308 Broadway; 02150; Suffolk; P 37,000; M 200; (617) 884-4877; Fax (617) 884-4878; dharney@chelseachamber.org; www.chelseachamber.org

Chicopee · *Chicopee C/C* · Gail A. Sherman; Pres.; 264 Exchange St.; 01013; Hampden; P 54,000; M 405; (413) 594-2101; Fax (413) 594-2103; gailsherman@chicopeechamber.org; www.chicopeechamber.org*

Clinton · *Wachusett C/C* · Maegen McCaffrey; Exec. Dir.; 167 Church St.; P.O. Box 703; 01510; Worcester; P 54,000; M 500; (978) 368-7687; Fax (978) 368-7689; maegen@wachusettchamber.com; www.wachusettchamber.com.*

Cohasset · *Cohasset C/C* · Darilynn Evans; Pres.; P.O. Box 336; 02025; Norfolk; P 7,500; M 100; (781) 383-1010; Fax (781) 383-1141; info@cohassetchamber.org; www.cohassetchamber.org

Concord · *Concord C/C* · Stephanie Stillman; Exec. Dir.; 15 Walden St., Ste. 7; 01742; Middlesex; P 16,000; M 300; (978) 369-3120; Fax (978) 369-1515; info@concordchamberofcommerce.org; www.concordchamberofcommerce.org*

Cotuit · *see Hyannis*

Danvers · *North Shore C/C* · Robert G. Bradford; Pres.; 5 Cherry Hill Dr., Ste. 100; 01923; Essex; P 300,000; M 1,500; (978) 774-8565; Fax (978) 774-3418; info@northshorechamber.org; www.northshorechamber.org

Dedham · *see Norwood*

Deerfield · *see Greenfield*

Devens · *Nashoba Valley C/C* · Melissa Fetterhoff; Exec. Dir.; 100 Sherman Ave., Ste. 3; 01434; Middlesex & Worcester; P 3,600; M 400; (978) 772-6976; Fax (978) 772-3503; director@nvcoc.com; www.nvcoc.com

Dighton · *see Taunton*

Dracut · *see Lowell*

Dudley · *see Worcester*

East Boston · *C/C of East Boston* · Ms. Eden Smith; 175 McClellan Hwy., Ste. 1; 02128; Suffolk; P 32,000; M 300; (617) 569-5000; Fax (617) 569-1945; john@eastbostonchamber.com; www.eastbostonchamber.com

East Bridgewater · *see Brockton*

East Longmeadow · *see Springfield*

Eastham · *Eastham C/C* · Jack Dowman; P.O. Box 1329; 02642; Barnstable; P 5,000; M 175; (508) 240-7211; Fax (508) 240-7211; info@easthamchamber.com; www.easthamchamber.com

Easthampton · *Greater Easthampton C/C* · Eric Snyder; Exec. Dir.; 33 Union St.; 01027; Hampshire; P 23,000; M 340; (413) 527-9414; Fax (413) 527-1445; info@easthamptonchamber.org; www.easthamptonchamber.org*

Easton · *see Brockton*

Everett · *Everett C/C* · Robert H. Laquidara; Exec. Dir.; 467 Broadway; 02149; Middlesex; P 35,701; M 300; (617) 387-9100; Fax (617) 389-6655; ecocoffice@aol.com; www.everettma chamber.com

Fall River · *Fall River Area C/C & Ind.* · Robert Mellion; Pres./CEO; 200 Pocasset St.; 02721; Bristol; P 91,000; M 700; (508) 676-8226; Fax (508) 675-5932; info@fallriverchamber.com; www.fallriverchamber.com

Falmouth · *Falmouth C/C* · Jay Zavala; Pres.; 20 Academy Ln.; 02540; Barnstable; P 32,000; M 800; (508) 548-8500; (800) 526-8532; Fax (508) 548-8521; info@falmouthchamber.com; www.falmouthchamber.com*

Fitchburg · *see North Central Mass.*

Foxborough · *see Mansfield*

Framingham · *MetroWest C/C* · A. Theodore Welte CCE; Pres.; 1671 Worcester Rd., Ste. 201; 01701; Middlesex; P 220,000; M 875; (508) 879-5600; Fax (508) 875-9325; chamber@metrowest.org; www.metrowest.org*

Franklin · *United Reg. C/C* · Jack Lank; Pres./CEO; 620 Old West Central St., Ste. 202; 02038; Norfolk; P 150,000; M 1,050; (508) 528-2800; Fax (508) 520-7864; jack@unitedregionalchamber.com; www.unitedregionalchamber.com*

Gardner · *Greater Gardner C/C* · James Bellina; Pres./CEO; 210 Main St.; 01440; Worcester; P 50,000; M 450; (978) 632-1780; Fax (978) 630-1767; ggcc@gardnerma.com; www.gardnerma.com*

Gloucester · *Cape Ann C/C* · Bob Hastings; Exec. Dir.; 33 Commercial St.; 01930; Essex; P 45,000; M 1,000; (978) 283-1601; Fax (978) 283-4740; info@capeannchamber.com; www.cape annvacations.com*

Granby · *see South Hadley*

Great Barrington · *Southern Berkshire C/C* · Christine B. Ludwiszewski; Exec. Dir.; 40 Railroad St., Ste. 2; P.O. Box 810; 01230; Berkshire; P 16,027; M 500; (413) 528-4284; Fax (413) 528-2200; info@southernberkshirechamber.com; www.southern berkshirechamber.com

Greenfield · *Franklin County C/C* · Ann L. Hamilton; Pres.; 395 Main St.; P.O. Box 898; 01302; Franklin; P 78,000; M 550; (413) 773-5463; Fax (413) 773-7008; fccc@crocker.com; www.franklin cc.org

Groton · *see North Central Mass.*

Halifax · *see Brockton and Middleborough*

Hamilton · *see Danvers*

Hampden · *see Springfield*

Hanover · *Hanover C/C* · Francie Donohue; Exec. Secy.; P.O. Box 68; 02339; Plymouth; P 15,000; M 185; (781) 826-8865; Fax (781) 826-7721; chamber@hanovermachamber.com; www.hanover machamber.com

Hanson · *see Brockton*

Harvard · *see Clinton and North Central Mass.*

Harwich Port · *Harwich C/C* · Sandra Davidson; Exec. Dir.; Rte. 28; One Schoolhouse Rd.; 02646; Barnstable; P 14,000; M 325; (508) 430-1165; (800) 4-HARWICH; Fax (508) 430-2105; info@ harwichcc.com; www.harwichcc.com*

Haverhill · *Greater Haverhill C/C* · James P. Jajuga; Pres.; 80 Merrimack St., 2nd Flr.; 01830; Essex; P 65,000; M 700; (978) 373-5663; Fax (978) 373-8060; info@haverhillchamber.com; www.haverhillchamber.com*

Holbrook · *see Brockton*

Holden · *Holden Area C/C* · Jennifer Stanovich; Exec. Dir.; 1174 Main St.; 01520; Worcester; P 30,000; M 170; (508) 829-9220; Fax (508) 829-9220; info@holdenareachamber.org; www.holden areachamber.org

Holland · *see Sturbridge*

Holliston · *see Framingham and Milford*

Holyoke · *Greater Holyoke C/C* · Doris Ransford; Pres.; 177 High St.; 01040; Hampden; P 50,000; M 500; (413) 534-3376; Fax (413) 534-3385; info@holycham.com; www.holyokechamber.com*

Hopedale · *see Milford*

Hopkinton · *see Framingham and Milford*

Housatonic · *see Great Barrington*

Hubbardston · *see Gardner*

Hudson · *Assabet Valley C/C* · Sarah B. Cressy; Pres./CEO; 18 Church St.; P.O. Box 578; 01749; Middlesex; P 34,000; M 460; (978) 568-0360; Fax (978) 562-4118; info@assabetvalleychamber.org; www.assabetvalleychamber.org

Hull · *Hull/Nantasket Beach C/C* · Larry Kellem; Admin.; P.O. Box 140; 02045; Plymouth; P 12,000; M 125; (339) 236-1264; info@hullchamber.com; www.hullchamber.com

Hyannis · *Hyannis Area C/C* · Deborah Converse; Pres./CEO; 397 Main St.; P.O. Box 100; 02601; Barnstable; P 48,000; M 650; (508) 775-7778; Fax (508) 775-7131; deborah@hyannis.com; www.hyannis.com

Ipswich · *Ipswich C/C* · Bob McNeil; Pres.; P.O. Box 94; 01938; Essex; P 13,500; M 260; (978) 356-9055; info@ipswichchamber.org; www.ipswichma.com

Lakeville · *see Middleborough*

Lancaster · *see Clinton and North Central Mass.*

Lawrence · *Merrimack Valley C/C* · Joseph J. Bevilacqua; Pres./CEO; 264 Essex St.; 01840; Essex; P 200,000; M 1,000; (978) 686-0900; Fax (978) 794-9953; thechamber@merrimackvalleychamber.com; www.merrimackvalleychamber.com*

Lee · *Lee C/C* · Danielle Mullen; Exec. Dir.; 3 Park Pl.; P.O. Box 345; 01238; Berkshire; P 9,000; M 152; (413) 243-0852; info@ leechamber.org; www.leechamber.org

Lenox · *Lenox C/C* · Ralph Petillo; Dir.; 12 Housatonic St.; P.O. Box 646; 01240; Berkshire; P 5,800; M 200; (413) 637-3646; Fax (413) 637-3626; info@lenox.org; www.lenox.org

Leominster · *see North Central Mass.*

Lexington · *Lexington C/C* · Mary Jo Bohart; Exec. Dir.; 1875 Massachusetts Ave.; 02420; Middlesex; P 31,000; M 300; (781) 862-2480; Fax (781) 862-5995; jterhune@lexingtonchamber.org; www.lexingtonchamber.org

Lincoln · *see Waltham*

Lowell · *Greater Lowell C/C* · Jeanne Osborn; Pres./CEO; 131 Merrimack St.; 01852; Middlesex; P 200,000; M 1,000; (978) 459-8154; Fax (978) 452-4145; info@greaterlowellchamber.org; www.glcc.biz*

Ludlow · *see Springfield*

Lunenburg · *see North Central Mass.*

Lynn · *Lynn Area C/C* · Leslie Gould; Exec. Dir.; 100 Oxford St.; 01901; Essex; P 89,050; M 450; (781) 592-2900; Fax (781) 592-2903; info@lynnareachamber.com; www.lynnareachamber.com*

Lynnfield · *see Danvers and Lynn*

Malden · *Malden C/C* · Edward Coates; Exec. Dir.; Malden Government Center; 200 Pleasant St., Ste. 416; 02148; Middlesex; P 56,000; M 500; (781) 322-4500; Fax (781) 322-4866; info@maldenchamber.org; www.maldenchamber.org

Mansfield · *Tri-Town C/C* · Kara J. Griffin; Exec. Dir.; 280 School St., Ste. L100; Mansfield Crossing; 02048; Bristol; P 50,000; M 300; (508) 339-5655; Fax (508) 339-8333; office@tri-townchamber.org; www.tri-townchamber.org.*

SERVING FOXBOROUGH, MANSFIELD AND NORTON. HOME TO GILLETTE STADIUM, PATRIOT PLACE, TPC BOSTON, DEUTSCHE BANK CHAMPIONSHIP, COMCAST CENTER. STRIVING TO IMPROVE THE ECONOMIC DEVELOPMENT IN ALL OUR COMMUNITIES.

Marblehead · *Marblehead C/C* · Ann Marie Casey; Exec. Dir.; 62 Pleasant St.; 01945; Essex; P 20,000; M 450; (781) 631-2868; Fax (781) 639-8582; info@marbleheadchamber.org; www.marbleheadchamber.org

Marlborough · *Marlborough Reg. C/C* · Susanne Morreale-Leeber CCE IOM; Pres./CEO; 11 Florence St.; 01752; Middlesex; P 40,000; M 685; (508) 485-7746; Fax (508) 481-1819; marlcham@marlboroughchamber.org; www.marlboroughchamber.org.*

Marshfield · *Marshfield C/C* · Laurel Egan Kenny; Pres.; 2021 Ocean St.; 02050; Plymouth; P 25,000; M 155; (781) 834-8911; office@marshfieldchamberofcommerce.com; www.marshfieldchamberofcommerce.com

Marstons Mills · *see Hyannis*

Martha's Vineyard · *see Vineyard Haven*

Mashpee · *Mashpee C/C* · Mary Lou Palumbo; Exec. Dir.; 520 Main St.; P.O. Box 1245; 02649; Barnstable; P 15,000; M 250; (508) 477-0792; Fax (508) 477-5541; info@mashpeechamber.com; www.mashpeechamber.com*

Maynard · *see Hudson*

Medfield · *see Norwood*

Medford · *Medford C/C* · Cheryl White; Exec. Dir.; 1 Shipyard Way, Ste. 302; 02155; Middlesex; P 70,000; M 400; (781) 396-1277; Fax (781) 396-1278; director@medfordchamberma.com; www.medfordchamberma.com

Medway · *see Milford*

Melrose · *Melrose C/C* · Joan Mongeau; Exec. Dir.; One W. Foster St.; 02176; Middlesex; P 27,000; M 300; (781) 665-3033; Fax (781) 665-5595; info@melrosechamber.org; www.melrosechamber.org

Mendon · *see Milford*

Middleborough · *Cranberry Country C/C* · Mary Ann Marvel; Exec. Admin.; 40 N. Main St., Ste. F-1; 02346; Plymouth; P 125,000; M 300; (508) 947-1499; Fax (508) 947-1446; info@cranberrycountry.org; www.cranberrycountry.org

Milford · *Milford Area C/C* · Barry Feingold; Pres./CEO; 258 Main St., Ste. 306; P.O. Box 621; 01757; Middlesex; P 135,000; M 750; (508) 473-6700; Fax (508) 473-8467; chamber@milfordchamber.org; www.milfordchamber.org

Millis · *see Milford*

Monterey · *see Great Barrington*

Mount Washington · *see Great Barrington*

Nahunt · *see Lynn*

Nantucket · *Nantucket Island C/C* · P.J. Smith; Exec. Dir.; Zero Main St., 2nd Flr.; 02554; Nantucket; P 12,000; M 680; (508) 228-3643; Fax (508) 325-4925; info@nantucketchamber.org; www.nantucketchamber.org

Natick · *see Framingham*

Needham · *see Newton*

New Bedford · *New Bedford Area C/C* · Roy M. Nascimento IOM; Pres./CEO; 794 Purchase St.; P.O. Box 8827; 02742; Bristol & Plymouth; P 250,000; M 1,000; (508) 999-5231; Fax (508) 999-5237; info@newbedfordchamber.com; www.newbedfordchamber.com.*

Newburyport · *Greater Newburyport C/C* · Ann Ormond; Pres.; 38 R Merrimac St.; 01950; Essex; P 17,000; M 800; (978) 462-6680; Fax (978) 465 4145; info@newburyportchamber.org; www.newburyportchamber.org

Newton · *Newton-Needham C/C* · Thomas O'Rourke; Pres.; 281 Needham St.; Upper Level; 02464; Middlesex; P 112,000; M 700; (617) 244-5300; Fax (617) 244-5302; info@nnchamber.com; www.nnchamber.com*

Norfolk · *see Franklin*

North Adams · *Berkshire C/C* · Michael Supranowicz; Pres./CEO; 6 W. Main St.; 01247; Berkshire; P 135,150; M 1,100; (413) 499-4000; Fax (413) 447-9641; info@berkshirechamber.com; www.berkshirechamber.com

North Attleborough · *United Reg. C/C* · Jack Lank; Pres./CEO; 31 N. Washington St., Ste. 5; 02760; Bristol; M 1,050; (508) 695-6011; Fax (508) 695-6096; jack@unitedregionalchamber.com; www.unitedregionalchamber.com*

North Central Mass. · *North Central Mass. C/C* · David L. McKeehan CCE; Pres.; 860 South St.; Fitchburg; 01420; Worcester; P 200,000; M 1,500; (978) 353-7600; Fax (978) 353-4896; chamber@massweb.org; northcentralmass.com

North Chatham · *see Chatham*

North Easton · *see Brockton*

North Egremont · *see Great Barrington*

North Reading · *see Reading*

North Truro · *Truro C/C* · Jane Peters; Secy./Treas.; P.O. Box 26; 02652; Barnstable; P 2,087; (508) 487-1288; info@trurochamberofcommerce.com; www.trurochamberofcommerce.com

Northampton · *Greater Northampton C/C* · Suzanne Beck; Exec. Dir.; 99 Pleasant St.; 01060; Hampshire; P 30,000; M 750; (413) 584-1900; Fax (413) 584-1934; info@explorenorthampton.com; www.explorenorthampton.com

Northborough · *see Westborough*

Northfield · *see Greenfield*

Norton · *see Mansfield*

Norwell · *Norwell C/C* · Tom Malames; P.O. Box 322; 02061; Plymouth; P 10,000; M 100; info@norwellchamberofcommerce. com; www.norwellchamberofcommerce.com

Norwood · *Neponset Valley C/C* · Sue McQuaid; Pres./CEO; 190 Vanderbilt Ave.; 02062; Norfolk; P 180,000; M 1,000; (781) 769-1126; Fax (781) 769-0808; sue@nvcc.com; www.nvcc.com*

Orleans · *Orleans C/C* · Mary J. Corr; Exec. Dir.; 44 Main St.; P.O. Box 153; 02653; Barnstable; P 6,800; M 285; (508) 255-1386; Fax (508) 255-2774; info@orleanscapecod.org; www.orleanscapecod.org

Osterville · *see Hyannis*

Otis · *see Great Barrington*

Oxbury · *see Worcester*

Palmer · *Quaboag Hills C/C* · Lenny Weake; Pres.; 3 Converse St., Ste. 103; 01069; Hampden; P 85,000; M 330; (413) 283-2418; Fax (413) 289-1355; info@qhcc.biz; www.qhcc.biz

Peabody · *Peabody C/C* · Deanne Healey; Exec. Dir.; 24 Main St.; 01960; Essex; P 49,000; M 400; (978) 531-0384; Fax (978) 532-7227; pcc@peabodychamber.com; www.peabodychamber.com

Pepperell · *see North Central Mass.*

Pittsfield · *Berkshire C/C–Pittsfield Ofc.* · Michael Supranowicz; Pres./CEO; 75 North St., Ste. 360; 01201; Berkshire; P 135,150; M 1,200; (413) 499-4000; Fax (413) 447-9641; info@ berkshirechamber.com; www.berkshirechamber.com*

Plainville · *see North Attleborough*

Plymouth · *Plymouth Area C/C* · Denis Hanks; Exec. Dir.; 134 Court St.; 02360; Plymouth; P 580,000; M 800; (508) 830-1620; Fax (508) 830-1621; info@plymouthchamber.com; www.plymouth chamber.com*

Plympton · *see Middleborough*

Princeton · *see North Central Mass.*

Provincetown · *Provincetown C/C* · Candice Collins-Boden; Exec. Dir.; 307 Commerical St.; P.O. Box 1017; 02657; Barnstable; P 3,800; M 300; (508) 487-3424; Fax (508) 487-8966; info@ ptownchamber.com; www.ptownchamber.com

Quincy · *South Shore C/C* · Peter Forman; Pres./CEO; 36 Miller Stile Rd.; P.O. Box 690625; 02169; Norfolk; P 220,000; M 2,000; (617) 479-1111; Fax (617) 479-9274; info@southshorechamber. org; www.southshorechamber.org*

Randolph · *Randolph C/C* · Alexandra Alexopoulos; Pres.; 1 Credit Union Way, Ste. 210; P.O. Box 941; 02368; Norfolk; P 31,000; M 200; (781) 963-6862; Fax (781) 963-5252; info@randolphcham berofcommerce.org; www.randolphchamberofcommerce.org*

Raynham · *see Taunton*

Reading · *Reading-North Reading C/C* · Irene Collins; Exec. Dir.; P.O. Box 771; 01867; Middlesex; P 37,000; M 265; (781) 944-8824; (978) 664-5060; Fax (781) 944-6125; rnrchambercom@aol. com; www.readingnreadingchamber.org

Rehoboth · *see Taunton*

Revere · *Revere C/C* · Laura Leone; Exec. Dir.; 270 Broadway, Ste. 10; 02151; Suffolk; P 60,000; M 175; (781) 289-8009; Fax (781) 289-2166; info@reverechamber.org; www.reverechamber.org

Rochester · *see Middleborough*

Rockland · *Rockland C/C* · Thomas Banks; Pres.; P.O. Box 45; 02370; Plymouth; P 18,000; M 70; (781) 982-6497; thomas banks@rocklandchamberofcommerce.com; www.rockland chamberofcommerce.com

Rockport · *Rockport C/C* · Peter Webber; Mgr.; 170 Main St.; P.O. Box 67; 01966; Essex; P 7,931; M 230; (978) 546-6575; Fax (978) 283-4740; info@rockportusa.com; www.rockportusa.com*

Salem · *Salem C/C* · Rinus Oosthoek; Exec. Dir.; 265 Essex St.; 01970; Essex; P 42,000; M 650; (978) 744-0004; Fax (978) 745-3855; info@salem-chamber.org; www.salem-chamber.org*

Salisbury · *Salisbury 'By the Sea' C/C* · Maria Miles; P.O. Box 1000; 01952; Essex; P 8,000; M 250; (978) 465-3581; Fax (978) 465-3581; salisburychamber@aol.com; www.salisburychamber.com

Sandisfield · *see Great Barrington*

Sandwich · *see Cape Cod Canal*

Saugus · *Saugus C/C* · Anthony Speziale; 394 Lincoln Ave.; 01906; Essex; P 30,000; M 300; (781) 233-8407; Fax (781) 231-1145; sauguschamber@verizon.net; www.sauguschamber.org

Scituate · *Scituate C/C* · Marie Flaherty; P.O. Box 401; 02066; Plymouth; P 18,779; M 125; (781) 545-4000; info@scituate chamber.org; www.scituatechamber.org

Sheffield · *see Great Barrington*

Sheffield · *see Lakeville, CT*

Shelburne · *see Greenfield*

Sherborn · *see Framingham*

Shirley · *see North Central Mass.*

Shrewsbury · *see Westborough*

Somerville · *Somerville C/C* · Stephen V. Mackey; Pres./CEO; 2 Alpine St.; P.O. Box 440343; 02144; Middlesex; P 78,000; M 325; (617) 776-4100; smackey@somervillechamber.org; www.somer villechamber.org

South Chatham · *see Chatham*

South Egremont · *see Great Barrington*

South Hadley · *South Hadley & Granby C/C* · Susan Stockman; Exec. Dir.; 116 Main St., Ste. 4; 01075; Hampshire; P 20,000; M 125; (413) 532-6451; mail@shchamber.com; www.south hadleygranbychamber.com

South Yarmouth · *Yarmouth Area C/C* · Robert E. DuBois; Exec. Dir.; P.O. Box 479; 02664; Barnstable; P 24,700; M 400; (508) 778-1008; (800) 732-1008; Fax (508) 778-5114; yarmouth@capecod. net; www.yarmouthcapecod.com

Southborough · *see Framingham and Westborough*

Southbridge · *see Sturbridge*

Spencer · *see Sturbridge*

Springfield · *Affiliated Chambers of Commerce of Greater Springfield Inc.* · Russell F. Denver; Pres.; 1441 Main St., Ste. 136, 1st Flr.; 01103; Hampden; P 157,000; M 1,800; (413) 787-1555; Fax (413) 731-8530; denver@myonlinechamber.com; www. myonlinechamber.com*

Sterling · *see Clinton and North Central Mass.*

Stockbridge · *Stockbridge C/C* · Barbara Zanetti; Exec. Dir.; 50 Main St.; P.O. Box 224; 01262; Berkshire; P 2,500; M 100; (413) 298-5200; Fax (413) 931-3128; info@stockbridgechamber.org; www.stockbridgechamber.org

Stoneham · *Stoneham C/C* · Sharon Iovanni; Exec. Dir.; 271 Main St., Ste. L-02; 02180; Middlesex; P 24,000; M 275; (781) 438-0001; Fax (781) 438-0007; info@stonehamchamber.org; www. stonehamchamber.org

Stoughton · *Stoughton C/C* · Terry Schneider; Exec. Dir.; P.O. Box 41; 02072; Norfolk; P 30,000; M 175; (781) 297-7450; chamber@ stoughtonma.com; www.stoughtonma.com

Stow • *see Hudson*

Sturbridge • *Central Mass. South C/C* • Alexandra McNitt; Exec. Dir.; 380 Main St.; 01566; Worcester; P 60,000; M 420; (508) 347-2761; (800) 628-8379; Fax (508) 347-5218; info@sturbridge townships.org; www.cmschamber.org

Sudbury • *see Framingham*

Swampscott • *see Lynn*

Taunton • *Taunton Area C/C* • Kerrie Babin; Pres./CEO; 12 Taunton Green, Ste. 201; 02780; Bristol; P 70,000; M 500; (508) 824-4068; Fax (508) 884-8222; info@tauntonareachamber.org; www.tauntonareachamber.org*

Templeton • *see Gardner*

Tewksbury • *see Lowell*

Three Rivers • *Three Rivers C/C* • Mr. Kszepka; P.O. Box 233; 01080; Hampden; P 3,500; M 60; (413) 283-6425; www.america towns.com/ma/threerivers

Townsend • *see North Central Mass.*

Truro • *see North Truro*

Tyngsboro • *see Lowell*

Upton • *see Milford*

Vineyard Haven • *Martha's Vineyard C/C* • Nancy Gardella; Exec. Dir.; Beach Rd.; P.O. Box 1698; 02568; Dukes; P 15,000; M 1,050; (508) 693-0085; (800) 505-4815; Fax (508) 693-7589; info@mvy.com; www.mvy.com

Wakefield • *Wakefield C/C* • Nancy Bertrand; Exec. Dir.; 465 Main St.; P.O. Box 585; 01880; Middlesex; P 25,000; M 300; (781) 245-0741; chamber@wakefieldma.org; www.wakefieldma.org

Wales • *see Sturbridge*

Walpole • *Walpole C/C* • Mike Flaherty; Pres.; P.O. Box 361; 02081; Norfolk; P 23,000; M 200; (508) 668-0081; office@ walpolechamber.com; www.walpolechamber.com

Waltham • *Waltham West Suburban C/C* • John Peacock; Exec. Dir.; 84 South St.; 02453; Middlesex; P 60,000; M 600; (781) 894-4700; Fax (781) 894-1708; jpeacock@walthamchamber.com; www.walthamchamber.com.

Wareham • *see Cape Cod Canal and Middleborough*

Watertown • *Watertown-Belmont C/C* • Brenda Fanara; Exec. Dir.; 182 Main St.; P.O. Box 45; 02471; Middlesex; P 52,000; M 450; (617) 926-1017; Fax (617) 926-2322; info@wbcc.org; www.wbcc.org*

Wayland • *see Framingham*

Webster • *see Worcester*

Wellesley • *Wellesley C/C* • Maura O'Brien; Pres./CEO; One Hollis St., Ste. 232; 02482; Norfolk; P 26,615; M 250; (781) 235-2446; Fax (781) 235-7326; cmcgrath@wellesleychamber.org; www. wellesleychamber.org

Wellfleet • *Wellfleet C/C* • Marcia Sexton; Exec. Secy.; Off Rte. 6; P.O. Box 571; 02667; Barnstable; P 3,000; M 230; (508) 349-2510; Fax (508) 349-3740; info@wellfleetchamber.com; www.well fleetchamber.com

Wenham • *see Danvers*

West Barnstable • *see Hyannis*

West Boylston • *see Clinton*

West Bridgewater • *see Brockton*

West Chatham • *see Chatham*

West Dennis • *Dennis C/C* • Spyro Mitrokostas; Exec. Dir.; 238 Swan River Rd.; P.O. Box 1001; 02670; Barnstable; P 16,000; M 400; (508) 398-3568; Fax (508) 760-5212; info@dennischamber. com; www.dennischamber.com

West Springfield • *see Springfield*

West Stockbridge • *see Great Barrington*

West Yarmouth • *see South Yarmouth*

Westborough • *also see Framingham*

Westborough • *Corridor Nine Area C/C* • Barbara Clifford; Pres.; 30 Lyman St., Ste. 6; P.O. Box 1555; 01581; Worcester; P 73,000; M 800; (508) 836-4444; Fax (508) 836-2652; events@corridornine. org; www.corridornine.org*

Westfield • *see Springfield*

Westford • *see Lowell*

Westminster • *see North Central Mass.*

Weston • *see Waltham*

Westwood • *see Norwood*

Whitinsville • *Blackstone Valley C/C* • Jeannie Hebert; Pres./ CEO; 110 Church St.; 01588; Worcester; P 95,000; M 500; (508) 234-9090; Fax (508) 234-5152; administrator@blackstonevalley. org; www.blackstonevalley.org*

Whitman • *see Brockton*

Wilbraham • *see Springfield*

Williamstown • *Williamstown C/C* • Judy Giamborino; Exec. Dir.; P.O. Box 357; 01267; Berkshire; P 8,300; M 200; (413) 458-9077; Fax (413) 458-2666; info@williamstownchamber.com; www.williamstownchamber.com

Wilmington • *Wilmington C/C* • Nancy Vallee; Exec. Dir.; 226 Lowell St.; P.O. Box 463; 01887; Middlesex; P 21,000; M 150; (978) 657-7211; Fax (978) 657-0139; wilmingtonchamber@verizon.net; www.wilmingtonbusiness.com

Winchendon • *see Gardner*

Winchester • *Winchester C/C* • Catherine S. Alexander; Exec. Dir.; 25 Waterfield Rd.; 01890; Middlesex; P 21,000; M 210; (781) 729-8870; Fax (781) 729-8884; info@winchesterchamber.com; www.winchesterchamber.com

Winthrop • *Winthrop C/C* • Eric Gaynor; Exec. Dir.; 207 Hagman Rd.; 02152; Suffolk; P 18,000; M 425; (617) 846-9898; Fax (617) 846-9922; info@winthropchamber.com; www.winthropchamber.com*

Woburn • *North Suburban C/C* • Maureen A. Rogers; Pres.; 76R Winn St., Ste. 3-D; 01801; Middlesex; P 100,000; M 427; (781) 933-3499; Fax (781) 933-1071; info@northsuburbanchamber. com; www.northsuburbanchamber.com

Worcester • *Worcester Reg. C/C* • Richard Kennedy; Pres./CEO; 446 Main St., Ste. 200; 01608; Worcester; P 174,000; M 3,000; (508) 753-2924; Fax (508) 754-8560; rkennedy@worcester chamber.org; www.worcesterchamber.org*

Wrentham • *see Franklin*

Yarmouth • *see South Yarmouth*

Michigan

Michigan C of C • Rich Studley; Pres./CEO; 600 S. Walnut St.; Lansing; 48933; Ingham; P 10,003,422; M 7,000; (517) 371-2100; (800) 748-0266; Fax (517) 371-7224; info@michamber.com; www.michamber.com

Adrian · *Adrian Area C/C* · Ann Hughes; Pres./CEO; 136 E. Maumee St., Ste. 15; 49221; Lenawee; P 22,000; M 450; (517) 265-2320; Fax (517) 265-2432; info@adrianareachamber.com; www.adrianareachamber.com*

Albion · *Greater Albion C/C* · Carlen Kernish; Pres.; 203 S. Superior St.; P.O. Box 238; 49224; Calhoun; P 10,000; M 220; (517) 629-5533; Fax (517) 629-4284; carlen@greateralbionchamber.org; www.greateralbionchamber.org*

Algonac · *Greater Algonac C/C* · 1396 St. Clair River Dr.; P.O. Box 375; 48001; St. Clair; P 4,500; M 106; (810) 794-5511; Fax (866) 643-0023; execdirector@algonacchamber.com; www.algonacchamber.com

Allegan · *Allegan Area C/C* · Jeff Clearwater; Pres.; 221 Trowbridge St., Ste. B; 49010; Allegan; P 10,000; M 153; (269) 673-2479; Fax (269) 673-7190; mail@alleganchamber.com; www.alleganchamber.com

Allen Park · *Allen Park C/C* · Gerri Stewart-Conway; Exec. Dir.; 6543 Allen Rd.; 48101; Wayne; P 27,000; M 176; (313) 382-7303; Fax (313) 382-4409; allenparkchamber@wowway.biz; www.allenparkchamber.org.*

Allendale · *Allendale Area C/C* · Amy Millard; Dir.; 6181 Lake Michigan Dr.; PMB #167; 49401; Ottawa; P 15,000; M 225; (616) 892-2632; Fax (616) 895-2600; aacc@allendalechamber.org; www.allendalechamber.org

Alma · *Gratiot Area C/C* · Patricia Nelson; Exec. Dir.; 110 W. Superior St.; P.O. Box 516; 48801; Gratiot; P 39,000; M 450; (989) 463-5525; Fax (989) 463-6588; chamber@gratiot.org; www.gratiot.org

Alpena · *Alpena Area C/C* · Jaclynn A. Krawczak; Exec. Dir.; 235 W. Chisholm St.; 49707; Alpena; P 30,000; M 400; (989) 354-4181; (800) 4-ALPENA; Fax (989) 356-3999; info@alpenachamber.com; www.alpenachamber.com.*

Ann Arbor · *Ann Arbor/Ypsilanti Reg. C/C* · Diane Keller; Pres./CEO; 115 W. Huron St., 3rd Flr.; 48104; Washtenaw; P 114,000; M 1,500; (734) 665-4433; Fax (734) 665-4191; diane@a2ychamber.org; www.a2ychamber.org*

Armada · *see Romeo*

Ashley · *see Alma*

Atlanta · *Atlanta C/C* · Phil LaMore; Pres.; P.O. Box 410; 49709; Montmorency; P 2,500; M 200; (989) 785-3400; Fax (989) 785-3400; info@atlantamichigan.com; www.atlantamichigan.com

Au Gres · *Au Gres Area C/C* · J.R. Stoltz; Pres.; P.O. Box 455; 48703; Arenac; P 1,000; M 73; (989) 876-6688; staff@augreschamber.com; www.augreschamber.com

Au Sable · *see Oscoda*

Auburn · *Auburn Area C/C* · Sam Carlin Jr.; Pres.; P.O. Box 215; 48611; Bay; P 4,000; M 65; (989) 662-4001; Fax (989) 662-3333; contact@auburnchambermi.org; www.auburnchambermi.org

Auburn Hills · *Auburn Hills C/C* · Denise Asker; Exec. Dir.; P.O. Box 214083; 48321; Oakland; P 20,000; M 300; (248) 853-7862; Fax (248) 853-0763; info@auburnhillschamber.com; www.auburnhillschamber.com*

Bad Axe · *Bad Axe C/C* · Josh Rogenbuck; Pres.; P.O. Box 87; 48413; Huron; P 3,642; M 120; (989) 269-6936; Fax (989) 269-2611; chamberinfo@badaxemich.com; www.badaxemich.com

Baldwin · *Lake County C/C & Tourist Center* · 911 Michigan Ave.; P.O. Box 130; 49304; Lake; P 10,000; M 200; (231) 745-4331; (800) 245-3240; info@lakecountymichigan.com; www.lakecountymichigan.com

Bannister · *see Alma*

Battle Creek · *Battle Creek Area C/C* · Jeff Roller; Interim Dir./CFO; 77 E. Michigan Ave., Ste. 80; Commerce Pointe Bldg.; 49017; Calhoun; P 134,000; M 600; (269) 962-4076; Fax (269) 962-6309; dbaker@battlecreek.org; www.battlecreek.org*

Bay City · *Bay Area C/C* · Michael Seward; Pres./CEO; 901 Saginaw St.; 48708; Bay; P 110,000; M 800; (989) 893-4567; Fax (989) 895-5594; chamber@baycityarea.com; www.baycityarea.com.*

Beaver Island · *Beaver Island C/C* · Steve West; Exec. Dir.; P.O. Box 5; 49782; Charlevoix; P 2,000; M 120; (231) 448-2505; chamber@beaverisland.org; www.beaverisland.org

Belding · *Belding Area C/C* · 120 Covered Village Mall; 48809; Ionia; P 6,000; M 80; (616) 794-9890; info@beldingchamber.org; www.beldingchamber.org

Bellaire · *Bellaire Area C/C* · Patricia Savant; Exec. Dir.; 308 E. Cayuga; P.O. Box 205; 49615; Antrim; P 1,250; M 160; (231) 533-6023; Fax (231) 533-8764; info@bellairechamber.org; www.bellairechamber.org

Belleville · *Belleville Area C/C* · Candace Connon; Exec. Dir.; 248 Main St.; 48111; Wayne; P 44,000; M 230; (734) 697-7151; info@bellevilleareachamber.org; www.bellevilleareachamber.org

Benton Harbor · *Cornerstone C/C* · Pat Moody; Exec. V.P.; 38 W. Wall St.; 49022; Berrien; P 160,000; M 625; (269) 925-6100; Fax (269) 925-4471; rciaravino@cornerstonechamber.com; www.cornerstonechamber.com.*

Benzonia · *Benzie County C/C* · Mary Carroll; Pres.; 826 Michigan Ave.; P.O. Box 204; 49616; Benzie; P 17,000; M 450; (231) 882-5801; Fax (231) 882-9249; director@benzie.org; www.benzie.org.

Bergland · *Lake Gogebic Area C/C* · Mary Lou Driesenga; Secy.; P.O. Box 114; 49910; Gogebic & Ontonagon; P 600; M 81; (906) 827-3842; (888) 464-3242; info@lakegogebicarea.com; www.lakegogebicarea.com

Berkley · *Berkley Area C/C* · Julie Melrose; Exec. Dir.; P.O. Box 72-1253; 48072; Oakland; P 15,500; M 115; (248) 414-9157; Fax (248) 246-6290; julie@berkleychamber.com; www.berkleychamber.com

Berrien Springs · *Berrien Springs-Eau Claire C/C* · Scott Bormann; Pres.; P.O. Box 177; 49103; Berrien; P 11,000; M 100; (269) 471-2484; www.bsechamber.org

Bessemer · *Bessemer C/C* · Candice Snyder; Secy.; P.O. Box 243; 49911; Gogebic; P 2,148; M 110; (906) 663-0026; bessemerchamber@hotmail.com; www.bessemerchamber.org

Big Rapids · *Mecosta County Area C/C* · Anja J. Wing; Exec. Dir.; 246 N. State St.; 49307; Mecosta; P 40,000; M 500; (231) 796-7649; Fax (231) 796-1625; info@mecostacounty.com; www.mecostacounty.com*

Birch Run · *Birch Run Area C/C & CVB* · Jessica Standen; Exec. Dir.; 11600 N. Beyer Rd., Ste. 100; 48415; Saginaw; P 10,815; M 160; (989) 624-9193; (888) 624-9193; Fax (989) 624-5337; info@birchrunchamber.com; www.birchrunchamber.com

Birmingham · *Birmingham-Bloomfield C/C* · Joe Bauman; Pres.; 725 S. Adams Rd., Ste. 130; 48009; Oakland; P 75,000; M 650; (248) 644-1700; Fax (248) 644-0286; thechamber@bbcc.com; www.bbcc.com*

Boyne City · *Boyne Area C/C* · Jim Baumann; Exec. Dir.; 28 S. Lake St.; 49712; Charlevoix; P 3,500; M 300; (231) 582-6222; Fax (231) 582-6963; info@boynechamber.com; www.boynechamber.com

Breckenridge · *see Alma*

Bridgeport • *Bridgeport Area C/C* • Jan Crane; Exec. Secy.; P.O. Box 564; 48722; Saginaw; P 11,000; M 107; (989) 777-1801; Fax (989) 777-2223; execsecbridgeportcoc@yahoo.com; bridgeport chambermi.org

Brighton • *Greater Brighton Area C/C* • Pamela McConeghy; Pres./CEO; 131 Hyne St.; 48116; Livingston; P 85,000; M 1,200; (810) 227-5086; Fax (810) 227-5940; info@brightoncoc.org; www.brightoncoc.org*

Bronson • *see Coldwater*

Brooklyn • *Brooklyn-Irish Hills C/C* • Cindy Hubbell; Exec. Dir.; 131 N. Main St.; P.O. Box 805; 49230; Jackson; P 25,000; M 245; (517) 592-8907; Fax same; info@brooklynmi.com; www. brooklynmi.com.*

Bruce Township • *see Romeo*

Buchanan • *Buchanan Area C/C* • Monroe Lemay; Exec. Dir.; P.O. Box 127; 49107; Berrien; P 5,000; M 110; (269) 695-3291; Fax (269) 695-3813; bacc@buchanan.mi.us; www.buchanan.mi.us

Burr Oak • *see Sturgis*

Cadillac • *Cadillac Area C/C* • Bill Tencza; Pres.; 222 Lake St.; 49601; Wexford; P 35,000; M 420; (231) 775-9776; Fax (231) 775-1440; info@cadillac.org; www.cadillac.org*

Canton • *Canton C/C* • Dianne Cojei; Pres.; 45525 Hanford Rd.; 48187; Wayne; P 85,000; M 670; (734) 453-4040; Fax (734) 453-4503; info@cantonchamber.com; www.cantonchamber.com*

Capac • *Capac Area C/C* • Lara Laakso; Pres.; P.O. Box 386; 48014; St. Clair; P 1,600; M 50; (810) 395-8350; info@capacchamber.org; www.capacchamber.org

Caro • *Caro C/C* • Brenda Caruthers; Exec. Dir.; 157 N. State St.; 48723; Tuscola; P 4,200; M 194; (989) 673-5211; Fax (989) 673-2517; executivedirector@carochamber.org; www.carochamber.org

Caseville • *Caseville Area C/C* • Debbie Fulgham; Coord.; P.O. Box 122; 48725; Huron; P 2,700; M 170; (989) 856-3818; (800) 606-1347; Fax (989) 856-2596; ccofc@avci.net; www.caseville chamber.com

Cass City • *Cass City C/C* • Dee Mulligan; Admin.; 6506 Main St.; 48726; Tuscola; P 5,000; M 120; (989) 872-4618; (989) 551-7274; Fax (989) 872-4855; ccc@casscitychamber.com; www.casscity chamber.com

Cedarville • *Les Cheneaux Islands C/C* • Amy Polk; Coord.; P.O. Box 10; 49719; Mackinac; P 2,200; M 117; (906) 484-3935; (888) 364-7526; Fax (906) 484-9941; lcichamber@lescheneaux.net; www.lescheneaux.net

Center Line • *see Mount Clemens*

Central Lake • *Central Lake Area C/C* • Jackie White; 2587 N. M-88 Hwy.; P.O. Box 428; 49622; Antrim; P 1,000; M 90; (231) 544-3322; (231) 350-1112; clcc@torchlake.com; www.central-lake.com

Charlevoix • *Charlevoix Area C/C* • Erin Bemis; Exec. Dir.; 109 Mason St.; 49720; Charlevoix; P 26,000; M 500; (231) 547-2101; Fax (231) 547-6633; info@charlevoix.org; www.charlevoix.org

Charlotte • *Charlotte C/C* • Ann M. Garvey; Dir.; 126 N. Bostwick; P.O. Box 356; 48813; Eaton; P 10,500; M 320; (517) 543-0400; Fax (517) 748-5013; www.charlottechamber-mi.org*

Cheboygan • *Cheboygan Area C/C* • Kimberlee Pappas; Mgr.; 124 N. Main St.; 49721; Cheboygan; P 29,000; M 312; (231) 627-7183; (800) 968-3302; Fax (231) 627-2770; kpappas@cheboygan. com; www.cheboygan.com*

Chelsea • *Chelsea Area C/C* • Bob Pierce; Exec. Dir.; 310 N. Main St., Ste. 120; 48118; Washtenaw; P 8,000; M 300; (734) 475-1145; Fax (734) 475-6102; bpierce@chelseamichamber.org; www. chelseamichamber.org*

Chesaning • *Chesaning C/C* • Christopher Wood; Pres.; 218 N. Front St.; P.O. Box 83; 48616; Saginaw; P 4,200; M 155; (989) 845-3055; Fax (989) 845-6006; info@chesaningchamber.org; www. chesaningchamber.org

Chesterfield Twp • *see Mount Clemens and New Baltimore*

Clare • *Clare Area C/C* • Jennifer Heinzman; Ofc. Mgr.; 429 N. McEwan; 48617; Clare & Isabella; P 3,050; M 270; (989) 386-2442; (888)AT-CLARE; Fax (989) 386-3173; manager@claremichigan. com; www.claremichigan.com

Clarkston • *Clarkston Area C/C* • Penny Shanks; Exec. Dir.; 5856 S. Main St.; 48346; Oakland; P 32,000; M 600; (248) 625-8055; Fax (248) 625-8041; info@clarkston.org; www.clarkston.org*

Clarksville • *see Lake Odessa*

Clawson • *Clawson C/C* • Sheryl Geralds; Exec. Dir.; P.O. Box 217; 48017; Oakland; P 13,000; M 140; (248) 435-6500; Fax (248) 435-6868; sheryl@clawsonchamberofcommerce.com; www. clawsonchamber.com

Clinton Twp • *see Mount Clemens*

Clio • *Clio Area C/C* • 192 W. Vienna St.; P.O. Box 543; 48420; Genesee; P 30,000; M 260; (810) 686-4480; chamber@cliomi.org; www.cliomi.org

Coldwater • *Branch County Area C/C* • Pres.; 20 Division St.; 49036; Branch; P 45,000; M 600; (517) 278-5985; Fax (517) 278-8369; info@ branchareachamber.com; www.branchareachamber.com

Coloma • *Coloma-Watervliet Area C/C* • Chana Kniebes; Coord.; P.O. Box 418; 49038; Berrien; P 15,000; M 140; (269) 468-9160; Fax (269) 468-7088; info@coloma-watervliet.org; www.coloma-watervliet.org

Commerce Twp. • *see Walled Lake*

Coopersville • *Coopersville Area C/C* • Cynthia Timmerman; Exec. Dir.; 289 Danforth St.; 49404; Ottawa; P 4,000; M 250; (616) 997-5164; Fax (616) 997-6679; ctimmerman@cityofcoopersville. com; www.coopersville.com*

Corunna • *see Owosso*

Curtis • *Curtis Area C/C* • John Townley; Pres.; N9687 H33; P.O. Box 477; 49820; Mackinac; P 1,100; M 150; (906) 586-3700; curtiscofc@sbcglobal.net; www.curtischamber.com

Davison • *Davison Area C/C* • LaDawn Hastings; Exec. Dir.; 709 S. State Rd., Ste. A; 48423; Genesee; P 32,000; M 250; (810) 653-6266; Fax (810) 653-0669; contact@davisonchamberofcommerce. com; www.davisonchamberofcommerce.com*

Dearborn • *Dearborn C/C* • Jennifer Giering; Pres.; 22100 Michigan Ave.; 48124; Wayne; P 100,000; M 600; (313) 584-6100; Fax (313) 584-9818; jgiering@dearbornchamber.org; www. dearbornchamber.org

Dearborn Heights • *Dearborn Heights C/C* • Wendy Fichter; Exec Dir.; 24951 W. Warren Ave.; 48127; Wayne; P 58,000; M 120; (313) 274-7480; Fax (313) 724-0757; info@dearbornheights chamber.com; www.dearbornheightschamber.com

Decatur • *Greater Decatur C/C* • David Moormann; Pres.; P.O. Box 211; 49045; Van Buren; P 1,900; M 60; (269) 423-2411; Fax (269) 423-2411; info@decaturmi.org; www.decaturmi.org

Delton • *see Hastings*

Detroit • *Detroit Reg. Chamber* • Sandy K. Baruah; Pres./CEO; One Woodward Ave., Ste. 1900; P.O. Box 33840; 48232; Wayne; P 5,200,000; M 20,000; (313) 964-4000; Fax (313) 964-0183; tcarnrik@detroitchamber.com; www.detroitchamber.com*

Dexter • *Dexter Area C/C* • Abby Erickson; Exec. Dir.; 3074 Baker Rd.; 48130; Washtenaw; P 3,700; M 215; (734) 426-0887; Fax (734) 426-5069; info@dexterchamber.org; www.dexterchamber.org

Dowagiac • *Greater Dowagiac C/C* • Vickie Phillipson; Prog. Dir.; 200 Depot Dr.; 49047; Cass; P 6,400; M 150; (269) 782-8212; vphillipson@dowagiac.org; www.dowagiacchamber.com

Durand • *Greater Durand Area C/C* • Vicki Fuja; Exec. Dir.; 109 N. Saginaw St.; 48429; Shiawassee; P 5,000; M 116; (989) 288-3715; Fax (989) 288-5177; office@durandchamber.com; www.durandchamber.com*

East Jordan • *East Jordan Area C/C* • Mary H. Faculak; Pres.; 100 Main St., Ste. B; P.O. Box 137; 49727; Charlevoix; P 3,500; M 290; (231) 536-7351; Fax (231) 536-0966; info@ejchamber.org; www.ejchamber.org*

Eastpointe • *Eastpointe-Roseville C/C* • Catherine Green; Exec. Dir.; 24840 Gratiot Ave., Ste. B; 48021; Macomb; P 36,000; M 225; (586) 776-5520; Fax (586) 776-7808; director@epchamber.com; www.epchamber.com

Eaton Rapids • *Eaton Rapids Area C/C* • Donald Wyckoff; Exec. Dir.; 228 S. Main St.; P.O. Box 420; 48827; Eaton; P 5,330; M 85; (517) 663-6480; info@eatonrapidschamber.com; www.eatonrapidschamber.com

Eau Claire • *see Berrien Springs*

Edmore • *Edmore Area C/C* • Kristin Callow; Pres.; P.O. Box 102; 48829; Montcalm; P 1,300; M 60; (989) 289-2428; kristin@edmore.com

Edwardsburg • *Edwardsburg Area C/C* • Karen Sinkiewicz; Admin.; 26225 U.S. 12; P.O. Box 575; 49112; Cass; P 5,200; M 85; (574) 343-3721; (269) 663-2244; Fax (269) 663-0072; administration@edwardsburg.biz; www.edwardsburg.biz

Elk Rapids • *Elk Rapids Area C/C* • Sheila Marker; Exec. Dir.; 305 U.S.−31 N.; 49629; Antrim; P 2,500; M 260; (231) 264-8202; (800) 626-7328; Fax (231) 264-6591; info@elkrapidschamber.org; www.elkrapidschamber.org

Elwell • *see Alma*

Escanaba • *Delta County Area C/C* • Vickie Micheau; Dir.; 230 Ludington St.; 49829; Delta; P 37,780; M 700; (906) 786-2192; (888) DELTA-MI; Fax (906) 786-8830; info@deltami.org; www.deltami.org*

Evart • *Evart Area C/C* • Jan Booher; Secy.; P.O. Box 688; 49631; Osceola; P 1,745; M 75; (231) 734-9799; Fax (231) 734-9799; jabooher102@yahoo.com; www.evart.org

Fair Haven • *see Algonac*

Farmington Hills • *Greater Farmington Area C/C* • Mary L. Engelman; Exec. Dir.; 33425 Grand River Ave., Ste. 101; 48335; Oakland; P 100,000; M 650; (248) 919-6917; Fax (248) 919-6921; info@gfachamber.com; www.gfachamber.com*

Farwell • *Farwell Area C/C* • Mike Fetzer; Chair; 221 W. Main; P.O. Box 771; 48622; Clare; P 31,000; M 95; (989) 588-0580; Fax (989) 588-0580; facc@farwellareachamber.com; www.farwellareachamber.com

Fennville • *Greater Fennville C/C* • Paul Hix; Pres.; P.O. Box 484; 49408; Allegan; P 1,500; M 91; (269) 639-9533; treasurer@greaterfennville.com; www.greaterfennville.com

Fenton • *Fenton Reg. C/C* • Shelly Day; Pres.; 114 N. Leroy St.; 48430; Genesee; P 33,000; M 450; (810) 629-5447; Fax (810) 629-6608; info@fentonchamber.com; www.fentonchamber.com*

Ferndale • *Ferndale Area C/C* • Jennifer Roosenberg; Exec. Dir.; 407 E. Nine Mile Rd.; 48220; Oakland; P 21,000; M 275; (248) 542-2160; Fax (248) 542-8979; info@ferndalechamber.com; www.ferndalechamber.com*

Ferrysburg • *see Grand Haven*

Fife Lake • *Fife Lake C/C* • Merri Nixon; Pres.; P.O. Box 59; 49633; Grand Traverse; P 468; M 40; (231) 879-4154; president@fifelakechamber.com; www.fifelakechamber.com

Flint • *Genesee Reg. C/C* • Tim Herman; CEO; 519 S. Saginaw St., Ste. 200; 48502; Genesee; P 430,459; M 850; (810) 600-1404; Fax (810) 600-1461; info@thegrcc.org; www.thegrcc.org.*

Flushing • *Flushing Area C/C* • Susan Little; Ofc. Admin.; 133 E. Main St.; P.O. Box 44; 48433; Genesee; P 16,000; M 200; (810) 659-4141; Fax (810) 659-6964; flushingchamber@sbcglobal.net; www.flushingchamber.com*

Frankenmuth • *Frankenmuth C/C* • Jamie Furbush; Pres./CEO; 635 S. Main St.; 48734; Saginaw; P 4,832; M 500; (989) 652-6106; (989) 652-6107; Fax (989) 652-3841; chamber@frankenmuth.org; www.frankenmuth.org

Frankfort • *Frankfort-Elberta Area C/C* • Joanne Bartley; Exec. Dir.; 517 Main St.; P.O. Box 566; 49635; Benzie; P 1,703; M 185; (231) 352-7251; Fax (231) 352-6750; fcofc@frankfort-elberta.com; www.frankfort-elberta.com

Fraser • *see Saint Clair Shores*

Freeport • *see Hastings & Lake Odessa*

Fremont • *Fremont Area C/C* • Ron Vliem; Exec. Dir.; 7 E. Main St.; 49412; Newaygo; P 12,000; M 300; (231) 924-0770; Fax (231) 924-9248; info@fremontcommerce.com; www.fremontcommerce.com.

Garden City • *Garden City C/C* • Amelia Oliverio; Exec. Dir.; 30120 Ford Rd., Ste. D; 48135; Wayne; P 32,000; M 210; (734) 422-4448; Fax (734) 422-1601; www.gardencity.org

Gaylord • *Gaylord Area C/C* • Paul Beachnau; Exec. Dir.; 101 W. Main St.; P.O. Box 513; 49734; Otsego; P 26,000; M 500; (989) 732-6333; Fax (989) 732-7990; info@gaylordchamber.com; www.gaylordchamber.com.*

Gladwin • *Gladwin County C/C* • Tom Tucholski; Pres.; 608 W. Cedar Ave.; 48624; Gladwin; P 25,700; M 180; (989) 426-5451; Fax (989) 426-1074; chamber@ejourney.com; www.gladwincountychamber.com

Glen Arbor • *Glen Lake C/C* • David Marshall; Pres.; P.O. Box 217; 49636; Leelanau; P 1,200; M 130; (231) 334-3238; Fax (231) 334-3238; katywiesen@gmail.com; www.visitglenarbor.com

Grand Beach • *see New Buffalo*

Grand Blanc • *Grand Blanc C/C* • Jet Kilmer; Pres.; 512 E. Grand Blanc Rd.; 48439; Genesee; P 45,000; M 525; (810) 695-4222; Fax (810) 695-0053; www.grandblancchamber.com*

Grand Haven • *The Chamber-Grand Haven, Spring Lake, Ferrysburg* • Joy A. Gaasch; Pres.; One S. Harbor Dr.; P.O. Box 509; 49417; Ottawa; P 49,000; M 700; (616) 842-4910; Fax (616) 842-0379; areainfo@grandhavenchamber.org; www.grandhavenchamber.org*

Grand Ledge • *Grand Ledge Area C/C* • Susan Sasse; Secy./Treas.; 222 S. Bridge St.; 48837; Eaton; P 7,000; M 125; (517) 627-2383; Fax (517) 627-9213; glaccgl@gmail.com; www.grandledgemi.com

Grand Marais • *Grand Marais C/C* • Aleta Hubbard; Pres.; P.O. Box 139; 49839; Elger; P 400; M 36; (906) 494-2447; president@ grandmaraismichigan.com; www.grandmaraismichigan.com

Grand Rapids • *Grand Rapids Area C/C* • Jeanne Englehart; Pres./CEO; 111 Pearl St. N.W.; 49503; Kent; P 547,000; M 2,800; (616) 771-0300; Fax (616) 771-0318; info@grandrapids.org; www.grandrapids.org*

Grandville • *Grandville-Jenison C/C* • Sandy LeBlanc; Exec. Dir.; 2905 Wilson, Ste. 202-A; 49418; Kent & Ottawa; P 63,000; M 500; (616) 531-8890; Fax (616) 531-8896; sandy@grandjen.com; www. grandvillejenisonchamber.com*

Grayling • *Grayling Reg. C/C* • Traci Cook; Exec. Dir./Ofc. Mgr.; 213 N. James St.; P.O. Box 406; 49738; Crawford; P 17,000; M 215; (989) 348-2921; Fax (989) 348-7315; officemanager@grayling chamber.com; www.graylingchamber.com*

Greenbush • *Greenbush C/C* • Nebbie Kushmaul; Pres.; 4115 S. U.S. 23; 48738; Alcona; P 1,373; M 200; (989) 739-7635

Greenville • *Greenville Area C/C* • Candy Kerschen; Dir.; 108 N. Lafayette, Ste. A; 48838; Montcalm; P 12,000; M 300; (616) 754-5697; Fax (616) 754-4710; info@greenvillemi.org; www.greenvillemi.org.

Grosse Pointes • *see Saint Clair Shores*

Gwinn • *Gwinn-Sawyer Area C/C* • Jeanette Maki; Pres.; 248 Wellington Dr.; 49841; Marquette; P 8,000; M 165; (906) 346-9666; (888) 346-4946; Fax (906) 346-9695; gccdir@gwinnmi.com; www.gwinnmi.com

Hamburg • *see Brighton*

Harbert • *see New Buffalo*

Harbor Beach • *Harbor Beach C/C* • Bob Montana; Pres.; P.O. Box 113; 48441; Huron; P 2,089; M 100; (989) 479-6477; (800) HB-MICH-5; Fax (989) 479-6477; visitor@harborbeachchamber. com; www.harborbeachchamber.com

Harbor Springs • *Harbor Springs Area C/C* • Scott A. Herceg; Exec. Dir.; 368 E. Main St.; 49740; Emmet; P 1,100; M 380; (231) 526-7999; Fax (231) 526-5593; info@harborspringschamber.com; www.harborspringschamber.com*

Harper Woods • *see Saint Clair Shores*

Harrison • *Harrison Area C/C* • Liz Crafton; Ofc. Mgr.; 809 N. First St.; P.O. Box 682; 48625; Clare; P 2,213; M 187; (989) 539-6011; Fax (989) 539-6099; harrisonchamber@sbcglobal.net; www. harrisonchamber.com

Harrison Twp • *see Mount Clemens*

Harrisville • *Huron Shores C/C* • 410 E. Main; 48740; Alcona; P 10,000; M 130; (989) 724-5107; (800) 432-2823; Fax (989) 724-6656; huronshorescc.com

Harsens Island • *see Algonac*

Hart • *Hart-Silver Lake-Mears C/C & Visitor Bur.* • 2388 N. Comfort Dr.; 49420; Oceana; P 28,200; M 210; (231) 873-2247; (800) 870-9786; Fax (231) 873-1683; director@thinkdunes.com; www.thinkdunes.com*

Hartland • *Hartland Area C/C* • Jana Warford; Dir.; 3508 Avon St.; P.O. Box 427; 48353; Livingston; P 15,194; M 136; (810) 632-9130; info@hartlandchamber.org; www.hartlandchamber.org*

Hastings • *Barry County C/C* • Valerie Byrnes; Pres.; 221 W. State St.; 49058; Barry; P 58,774; M 323; (269) 945-2454; Fax (269) 945-3839; valerie@barrychamber.com; www.mibarry.com*

Hazel Park • *see Madison Heights*

Hesperia • *Hesperia Area C/C* • Rick Roberson; Pres.; P.O. Box 32; 49421; Oceana; P 900; M 70; (231) 854-3695; www.hesperia chamberofcommerce.org

Hessel • *see Cedarville*

Highland • *see Milford*

Hillman • *Hillman Area C/C* • Marsha Marqardt; Pres.; P.O. Box 506; 49746; Alpena & Montmorency; P 10,000; M 120; (989) 742-3739; Fax (989) 742-4757; www.hillmanchamber.com

Hillsdale • *Hillsdale County C/C* • Karri Doty IOM; Pres./Exec. Dir.; 22 N. Manning; 49242; Hillsdale; P 45,000; M 400; (517) 437-6401; Fax (517) 437-6408; info@hillsdalecountychamber.com; www.hillsdalecountychamber.com*

Holland • *Holland Area C/C* • Jane Clark; Pres.; 272 E. 8th St.; 49423; Ottawa; P 100,000; M 1,200; (616) 392-2389; Fax (616) 392-7379; info@hollandchamber.org; www.hollandchamber.org*

Holly • *Holly Area C/C* • Sandra Kleven; Pres.; 202 S. Saginaw St., 2nd Flr.; P.O. Box 214; 48442; Oakland; P 35,000; M 150; (248) 215-7099; Fax (248) 215-7106; staffhollychamber@yahoo.com; www.hollychamber.com*

Houghton • *Keweenaw Peninsula C/C* • Dallas Bond; Exec. Dir.; 902 College Ave.; P.O. Box 336; 49931; Houghton; P 38,000; M 600; (906) 482-5240; (866) 304-5722; Fax (906) 482-5241; info@ keweenaw.org; www.keweenaw.org.*

Houghton Lake • *Houghton Lake C/C* • Linda Tuck; Ofc. Mgr.; 1625 W. Houghton Lake Dr.; 48629; Roscommon; P 25,000; M 350; (989) 366-5644; (800) 248-5253; Fax (989) 366-9472; hlcc@ houghtonlakechamber.org; www.houghtonlakechamber.org

Howard City • *Montcalm County Panhandle Area C/C* • Marianne VanBennekom; Exec. Dir.; P.O. Box 474; 49329; Montcalm; P 10,000; M 110; (231) 937-5681; panhandle chamber@hotmail.com; www.panhandlechamber.com

Howell • *Howell Area C/C* • Pat Convery; Pres.; 123 E. Washington St.; 48843; Livingston; P 40,000; M 719; (517) 546-3920; Fax (517) 546-4115; chamber@howell.org; www.howell.org*

Hudson • *Hudson Area C/C* • Dave Sheely; Pres.; P.O. Box 45; 49247; Lenawee; P 2,000; M 40; (517) 448-8983; Fax (517) 448-5303; www.hudsonmich.com

Hudsonville • *Hudsonville Area C/C* • Laurie Van Haitsma; Exec. Dir.; 5340 Plaza Ave., Ste. A; P.O. Box 216; 49426; Ottawa; P 8,000; M 160; (616) 662-0900; Fax (616) 662-4557; hudchamber@att. net; www.hudsonvillechamber.com

Imlay City • *Imlay City Area C/C* • Kim Marrone; Exec. Dir.; 150 N. Main St.; 48444; Lapeer; P 4,000; M 150; (810) 724-1361; info@ imlaycitymich.com; www.imlaycitymich.com

Indian River • *Indian River Resort Reg. C/C* • Dawn Bodnar; Exec. Dir.; 3435 S. Straits Hwy.; P.O. Box 57; 49749; Cheboygan; P 4,500; M 280; (231) 238-9325; (800) EXIT-310; Fax (231) 238-0949; info@irchamber.com; www.irchamber.com*

Interlochen • *Interlochen Area C/C* • Tom Ingold; Pres.; 2110 M-137 S.; P.O. Box 13; 49643; Grand Traverse; P 3,800; M 99; (231) 276-7141; interlochenchamber@juno.com; www.interlochen chamber.org

Ionia • *Ionia Area C/C* • Tina Conner Wellman; Exec. Dir.; 439 W. Main St.; 48846; Ionia; P 10,500; M 252; (616) 527-2560; Fax (616) 527-0894; info@ioniachamber.net; www.ioniachamber.org*

Ira Twp • *see New Baltimore*

Iron Mountain • *Dickinson Area Partnership* • Lynda Zanon; Exec. Dir.; 600 S. Stephenson Ave.; 49801; Dickinson; P 26,868; M 468; (906) 774-2002; Fax (906) 774-2004; lzanon@dickinson chamber.com; www.dickinsonchamber.com.*

Iron River • *Iron County C/C* • William Leonoff; Exec. Dir.; 50 E. Genesee St.; 49935; Iron; P 13,138; M 308; (906) 265-3822; (888) TRY-IRON; Fax (906) 265-5605; info@iron.org; www.iron.org

Ironwood · *Ironwood Area C/C* · Donna Scorse; Exec. Dir.; 150 N. Lowell St.; P.O. Box 45; 49938; Gogebic; P 18,000; M 180; (906) 932-1122; Fax (906) 932-2756; chamber@ironwoodmi.org; www. ironwoodmi.org*

Ishpeming · *Ishpeming Ofc. of Lake Superior Comm. Partnership* · Amy Clickner; CEO; 215 W. Hematite Drive; 49849; Marquette; P 64,616; M 900; (906) 486-4841; (888) 57-UNITY; Fax (906) 486-4850; lscp@marquette.org; www.marquette.org*

Ithaca · *see Alma*

Jackson · *Jackson County C/C* · Mindy Bradish-Orta; Pres./Exec. Dir.; 141 S. Jackson St.; 49201; Jackson; P 162,400; M 725; (517) 782-8221; Fax (517) 780-3688; mindy@jacksonchamber.org; www.jacksonchamber.org*

Jenison · *see Grandville*

Kalamazoo · *Kalamazoo Reg. C/C* · Steward Sandstrom; Pres./CEO; 346 W. Michigan Ave.; 49007; Kalamazoo; P 241,000; M 1,800; (269) 381-4000; Fax (269) 343-0430; info@kazoo chamber.com; www.kazoochamber.com*

Kalkaska · *Kalkaska Area C/C* · April Smith; Admin. Asst.; 353 S. Cedar St.; P.O. Box 291; 49646; Grand Traverse; P 16,571; M 150; (231) 258-9103; (800) 487-6880; Fax (231) 258-6155; kalkaska@ tcchamber.org; www.kalkaskami.com*

Kentwood · *see Wyoming*

Lake City · *Lake City Area C/C* · Kim Mosher; Admin. Asst.; 107 S. Main St.; P.O. Box H; 49651; Missaukee; P 15,000; M 205; (231) 839-4969; Fax (231) 839-5991; lcacc@centurytel.net; www. lakecitymich.com*

Lake Odessa · *Lakewood Area C/C* · Marnie Thomas; Exec. Dir.; Page Memorial Bldg.; 839 4th Ave.; 48849; Berry, Eaton & Ionia; P 1,800; M 60; (616) 374-0766; director@lakewoodareacoc.org; www.lakewoodareacoc.org

Lake Orion · *Orion Area C/C* · Alaina Campbell; Exec. Dir.; P.O. Box 484; 48361; Oakland; P 30,000; M 250; (248) 693-6300; Fax (248) 693-9227; info@lakeorionchamber.com; www.lakeorion chamber.com

Lakeland · *see Brighton*

Lakeside · *see New Buffalo*

Lakeview · *Lakeview Area C/C* · Brian Brasser; P.O. Box 57; 48850; Montcalm; P 1,200; M 50; info@lakeviewmichigan.com; www.lakeviewmichigan.com

L'Anse · *Baraga County C/C* · Karen DeKleyn; Secy./Treas.; P.O. Box 122; 49946; Baraga; P 3,300; M 87; (906) 353-8808; baraga chamber@baragacountycc.org; www.baragacountycc.org

Lansing · *Lansing Reg. C/C* · Tim Daman; Pres./CEO; 500 E. Michigan Ave., Ste. 200; 48912; Clinton, Eaton & Ingham; P 447,728; M 1,275; (517) 487-6340; Fax (517) 484-6910; tdaman@lansingchamber.org; www.lansingchamber.org.*

Lapeer · *Lapeer Area C/C* · Neda Payne; Exec. Dir.; 108 W. Park St.; 48446; Lapeer; P 90,000; M 400; (810) 664-6641; Fax (810) 664-4349; staff@lapeerareachamber.org; www.lapeerarea chamber.org*

Leelanau Peninsula · *see Suttons Bay*

Lenox Twp · *see New Baltimore*

LeRoy · *LeRoy Area C/C* · Carey Johnson; Pres.; 98 Underwood Ave.; P.O. Box 28; 49655; Osceola; P 3,500; M 35; (231) 768-4489; info@leroymichigan.org; www.leroymichigan.org

Les Cheneaux · *see Cedarville*

Leslie · *Leslie Area C/C* · Bruce Crockett; Pres.; P.O. Box 214; 49251; Ingham; P 4,371; M 125; (517) 589-8236; www.leslie chamber.com

Lewiston · *Lewiston Area C/C* · Elaine Dixon; Chrmn. of the Bd.; 2946 Kneeland St.; P.O. Box 656; 49756; Montmorency; P 4,000; M 180; (989) 786-2293; Fax (989) 786-4515; lewistonchamber@ i2k.com; www.lewistonchamber.com

Lexington · *Greater Croswell-Lexington C/C* · Marcy Bartniczak; Pres.; P.O. Box 142; 48450; Sanilac; P 6,500; M 170; (810) 359-2262; croslex@greatlakes.net; www.cros-lex-chamber.com

Lincoln Park · *Lincoln Park C/C* · Karen Maniaci; Exec. Dir.; 1335 Southfield Rd.; P.O. Box 382; 48146; Wayne; P 43,000; M 100; (313) 386-0140; Fax (313) 386-0140; info@lpchamber.org; www. lpchamber.org

Linden · *see Fenton*

Linwood · *see Pinconning*

Litchfield · *Litchfield C/C* · P.O. Box 236; 49252; Hillsdale; P 1,483; M 50; (517) 542-2921; Fax (517) 542-2491; clerk@ cityoflitchfield.org; www.cityoflitchfield.org

Livonia · *Livonia C/C* · Dan West; Pres.; 33233 Five Mile Rd.; 48154; Wayne; P 100,000; M 770; (734) 427-2122; Fax (734) 427-6055; dwest@livonia.org; www.livonia.org.*

Lowell · *Lowell Area C/C* · Liz Baker; Exec. Dir.; 113 Riverwalk Plaza; P.O. Box 224; 49331; Kent; P 4,000; M 300; (616) 897-9161; Fax (616) 897-9101; info@lowellchamber.org; www.discover lowell.org.*

Ludington · *Ludington & Scottville C/C* · Kathryn Maclean; Pres./CEO; 5300 W. U.S. 10; 49431; Mason; P 25,000; M 442; (231) 845-0324; Fax (231) 845-6857; chamberinfo@ludington.org; www.ludington.org.*

Mackinaw City · *Mackinaw City C/C* · Dawn Edwards; Exec. Dir.; 300 E. Central Ave., Ste. D; P.O. Box 856; 49701; Cheboygan & Emmet; P 850; M 233; (231) 436-5574; (888) 455-8100; info@ mackinawchamber.com; www.mackinawchamber.com*

Macomb Twp · *see Mount Clemens*

Madison Heights · *Madison Heights-Hazel Park C/C* · Rickey Busler; Exec. Dir.; 724 W. 11 Mile Rd.; 48071; Oakland; P 52,000; M 400; (248) 542-5010; Fax (248) 542-6821; rickey@mhhp chamber.org; www.madisonheightschamber.com.*

Mancelona · *Mancelona Area C/C* · P.O. Box 558; 49659; Antrim; P 1,400; M 100; (231) 587-5500; www.mancelonachamber.org

Manchester · *Manchester Area C/C* · Ray Berg; Pres.; P.O. Box 521; 48158; Washtenaw; P 2,000; M 105; (734) 476-4565; president@manchestermi.org; www.48158.com

Manistee · *Manistee Area C/C* · Melissa Reed; Exec. Dir.; 11 Cypress St.; 49660; Manistee; P 23,330; M 408; (231) 723-2575; (800) 288-2286; Fax (231) 723-1515; www.manisteechamber.com*

Manistique · *Schoolcraft County C/C* · Connie Diller; Exec. Dir.; 1000 W. Lakeshore Dr.; 49854; Schoolcraft; P 8,576; M 230; (906) 341-5010; (888) 819-7420; Fax (906) 341-1549; chamber@reiters. net; www.schoolcraftcountychamber.com.*

Manton · *Manton C/C* · Stacey Altman; Pres.; P.O. Box 313; 49663; Wexford; P 1,300; M 115; (231) 824-4158; Fax (231) 824-3664; info@mantonmichigan.org; www.mantonmichigan.org

Maple Valley · *see Howard City*

Marine City · *Marine City C/C* · Georgia Phelan; Pres.; 218 S. Water St.; 48039; St. Clair; P 4,500; M 110; (810) 765-4501; Fax (810) 765-3077; chamberoffice@marinecitychamber.net; www. marinecitychamber.net*

Marion • *Marion Area C/C* • Anndrea McCrimmon; Pres.; P.O. Box 294; 49665; Osceola; P 816; M 40; (231) 743-2461; Fax (231) 743-2461

Marlette • *Marlette Area C/C* • Virginia Labelle; Pres.; P.O. Box 222; 48453; Sanilac; P 2,104; M 100; (989) 635-7448; cityof marlette.com

Marquette • *Marquette Area C/C-Lake Superior Comm. Partnership* • Amy Clickner; CEO; 501 S. Front St.; 49855; Marquette; P 64,616; M 900; (906) 226-6591; (888) 57-UNITY; Fax (906) 226-2099; info@marquette.org; www.marquette.org

Marshall • *Marshall Area C/C* • Monica Anderson; Pres./CEO; 424 E. Michigan Ave.; 49068; Calhoun; P 15,000; M 350; (269) 781-5163; (800) 877-5163; Fax (269) 781-6570; info@marshallmi. org; www.marshallmi.org*

Marysville • *see Port Huron*

Mason • *Mason Area C/C* • Douglas J. Klein; Exec. Dir.; 148 E. Ash St.; 48854; Ingham; P 15,000; M 280; (517) 676-1046; (517) 676-4816; Fax (517) 676-8504; masonchamber@masonchamber. org; www.masonchamber.org.*

Mears • *see Hart*

Memphis • *Memphis C/C* • Judy Weaver; Pres.; P.O. Box 41006; 48041; Macomb & St. Clair; P 1,200; M 20; (810) 392-5065; (810) 392-2385

Menominee • *see Marinette, WI*

Metamora • *Metamora C/C* • Wes Wickham; Pres.; P.O. Box 16; 48455; Lapeer; M 90; (810) 678-6222; Fax (810) 678-3312; info@ metamorachamber.org; www.metamorachamber.org

Michiana • *see New Buffalo*

Middleton • *see Alma*

Middleville • *see Hastings*

Midland • *Midland Area C/C* • Sid Allen; Pres./CEO; 300 Rodd St., Ste. 101; 48640; Midland; P 80,000; M 1,000; (989) 839-9901; Fax (989) 835-3701; chamber@macc.org; www.macc.org*

Milan • *Milan Area C/C* • Christine Mann; 153 E. Main; P.O. Box 164; 48160; Monroe & Washtenaw; P 5,500; M 122; (734) 439-7932; Fax (734) 241-3520; info@milanchamber.org; www. milanchamber.org

Milford • *Huron Valley C/C* • Joell Beether; Exec. Dir.; 317 Union St., Ste. F; 48381; Oakland; P 60,000; M 415; (248) 685-7129; Fax (248) 685-9047; info@huronvcc.com; www.huronvcc.com*

Mio • *C/C for Oscoda County* • Kendle Nichols; Pres.; P.O. Box 670; 48647; Oscoda; P 10,000; M 160; (989) 826-3331; (800) 800-6133; Fax (989) 826-6679; info@oscodacountymi.org; www. oscodacountymi.org

Monroe • *Monroe County C/C* • Michelle S. Dugan; Exec. Dir.; 1645 N. Dixie Hwy., Ste. 2; 48162; Monroe; P 160,000; M 450; (734) 384-3366; Fax (734) 384-3367; chamber@monroecounty chamber.com; www.monroecountychamber.com

Montague • *see Whitehall*

Montrose • *Montrose Area C/C* • Jerry Whitney; Pres.; P.O. Box 628; 48457; Genesee; P 8,000; M 50; (810) 639-4357; www. cityofmontrose.us

Morrice • *see Perry*

Mount Clemens • *Macomb County Chamber* • Grace M. Shore; CEO/COO; 28 First St., Ste. B; 48043; Macomb; P 850,000; M 1,000; (586) 493-7600; Fax (586) 493-7602; grace@macombcounty chamber.com; www.macombcountychamber.com*

Mount Pleasant • *Mt. Pleasant Area C/C* • Lisa Hadden; Pres./CEO; 200 E. Broadway St.; 48858; Isabella; P 64,663; M 716; (989) 772-2396; Fax (989) 773-2656; lhadden@mt-pleasant.net; www. mt-pleasant.net.*

Munising • *Alger County C/C* • Joni Flynn; Chrmn.; 129 E. Munising Ave.; P.O. Box 405; 49862; Alger; P 9,612; M 150; (906) 387-2138; Fax (906) 387-1858; info@algercounty.org; www. algercounty.org

Muskegon • *Muskegon Area C/C* • Cindy Larsen; Pres.; 380 W. Western Ave., Ste. 202; 49440; Muskegon; P 140,000; M 1,200; (231) 722-3751; Fax (231) 728-7251; macc@muskegon.org; www.muskegon.org*

Napoleon • *Napoleon C/C* • Paula Jester; Co-Pres.; P.O. Box 224; 49261; Jackson; P 9,000; M 38; (517) 536-0547

Nashville • *see Hastings*

Negaunee • *see Ishpeming*

New Baltimore • *also see Mount Clemens*

New Baltimore • *Anchor Bay C/C* • Lisa M. Edwards; Pres.; 36341 Front St., Ste. 2; 48047; Macomb; P 58,436; M 230; (586) 725-5148; Fax (866) 643-0023; info@anchorbaychamber.com; www.anchorbaychamber.com*

New Boston • *Huron Charter Township C/C* • Teresa Trosin; Exec. Ofc. Secy.; P.O. Box 247; 48164; Wayne; P 15,000; M 50; (734) 753-4220; Fax (734) 753-4602; hurontwpchmbrcomm@yahoo.com; www.members.tripod.com/htcc48164

New Buffalo • *Harbor Country C/C* • 530 S. Whittaker, Ste. F; 49117; Berrien; P 8,000; M 502; (269) 469-5409; (800) 362-7251; Fax (269) 469-2257; chamber@harborcountry.org; www.harbor country.org*

New Haven • *see New Baltimore*

New Haven Center • *see Alma*

Newaygo • *Newaygo Area C/C* • Don Henning; Exec. Dir.; 28 State St.; P.O. Box 181; 49337; Newaygo; P 16,500; M 115; (231) 652-3068; Fax (231) 652-9489; info@newaygonaturally.com; www.newaygonaturally.com

Newberry • *Newberry Area C/C* • Angela Harris; Pres.; 4947 E. County Rd. 460; P.O. Box 308; 49868; Luce; P 8,000; M 117; (906) 293-5562; (800) 831-7292; Fax (906) 293-5739; newberry@ lighthouse.net; www.newberrychamber.net*

Niles • *Four Flags Area C/C* • Ronald Sather; Pres./CEO; 321 E. Main St.; P.O. Box 10; 49120; Berrien; P 12,000; M 700; (269) 683-3720; Fax (269) 683-3722; chamber@nilesmi.com; www. nilesmi.com*

Northstar • *see Alma*

Northville • *Northville Comm. C/C* • Jody Humphries; Exec. Dir.; 195 S. Main St.; 48167; Oakland & Wayne; P 28,000; M 450; (248) 349-7640; Fax (248) 349-8730; chamber@northville.org; www. northville.org*

Novi • *Novi C/C* • Linda Daly; Exec. Dir.; 41875 W. 11 Mile Rd., Ste. 201; 48375; Oakland; P 50,000; M 550; (248) 349-3743; Fax (248) 349-9719; info@novichamber.com; www.novichamber.com*

Oakland County • *see Detroit*

Onaway • *Onaway Area C/C* • Beverly Brougham; 20774 State St.; P.O. Box 274; 49765; Presque Isle; P 990; M 100; (989) 733-2874; (800) 711-3685; Fax (989) 733-2874; info@onawaychamber. com; www.onawaychamber.com

Ontonagon • *Ontonagon County C/C* • Vikki James; Pres.; P.O. Box 266; 49953; Ontonagon; P 7,918; M 100; (906) 884-4735; ontcofc@up.net; www.ontonagonmi.org

Ortonville • *Greater Ortonville Area C/C* • Joe Carrier; Pres.; P.O. Box 152; 48462; Oakland; P 12,000; M 84; (248) 627-8079; Fax (248) 627-8079; president@ortonvillechamber.com; www.ortonvillechamber.com

Oscoda • *Oscoda-Au Sable C/C* • Leisa Sutton; Exec. Dir.; 4440 N. U.S. 23; 48750; Iosco; P 9,000; M 234; (989) 739-7322; (800) 235-4625; Fax (989) 739-9195; events@oscodachamber.com; www.oscodachamber.com

Otsego • *Otsego C/C* • Lynn Higgs; Exec. Dir.; 135 E. Allegan St.; 49078; Allegan; P 1,200; M 110; (269) 694-6880; director@otsegochamber.org; otsegochamber.org

Owosso • *Shiawassee Reg. C/C* • Renita Mikolajczyk; Pres.; 215 N. Water St.; 48867; Shiawassee; P 71,000; M 600; (989) 723-5149; Fax (989) 723-8353; customerservice@shiawasseechamber.org; www.shiawasseechamber.org*

Oxford • *Oxford Area C/C* • Holly Bills; Exec. Dir.; P.O. Box 142; 48371; Oakland; P 13,500; M 250; (248) 628-0410; Fax (248) 628-0430; info@oxfordchamberofcommerce.com; www.oxfordchamberofcommerce.com

Paradise • *Paradise C/C* • P.O. Box 82; 49768; Chippewa; P 1,000; M 50; (906) 492-3219; paradisecoc@jamadots.com; www.paradisemichigan.org

Paw Paw • *Greater Paw Paw Area C/C* • Mary E. H. Springer; Exec. Dir.; 129 S. Kalamazoo St.; 49079; Van Buren; P 7,174; M 245; (269) 657-5395; Fax (269) 655-8755; ppccdda@btc-bci.com; www.pawpawchamber.com*

Pearl Beach • *see Algonac*

Pentwater • *Pentwater C/C* • Deanna Helmlinger; Exec. Dir.; 324 S. Hancock St.; P.O. Box 614; 49449; Oceana; P 1,000; M 175; (231) 869-4150; Fax (231) 869-5286; travelinfo@pentwater.org; www.pentwater.org*

Perrinton • *see Alma*

Perry • *Perry/Morrice Area C/C* • Dory Bortman; P.O. Box 803; 48872; Shiawassee; P 5,600; M 40; (517) 625-8122; www.perry.mi.us

Petoskey • *Petoskey Reg. C/C* • Carlin Smith; Pres.; 401 E. Mitchell St.; 49770; Emmet; P 30,000; M 740; (231) 347-4150; Fax (231) 348-1810; chamber@petoskey.com; www.petoskey.com.

Pierson • *see Howard City*

Pigeon • *Pigeon C/C* • June Schweitzer; Pres.; P.O. Box 618; 48755; Huron; P 1,200; M 100; (989) 453-7400; pgncofc@avci.net; www.pigeonchamber.com

Pinckney • *see Brighton*

Pinconning • *Pinconning & Linwood Area C/C* • Lorie Czyperski; P.O. Box 856; 48650; Bay; P 7,000; M 85; (989) 879-2816; (989) 879-2360; chamber@pinconninglinwood.com; www.pinconninglinwood.com

Plainwell • *Plainwell C/C* • Chris Haas; Event Coord.; 798 E. Bridge St., Ste. A; 49080; Allegan; P 4,000; M 100; (269) 685-8877; Fax (269) 685-1844; info@plainwellchamber.com; www.plainwellchamber.com

Plymouth • *Plymouth Comm. C/C* • G. Wesley Graff; Exec. Dir.; 850 W. Ann Arbor Trl.; 48170; Wayne; P 38,000; M 600; (734) 453-1540; Fax (734) 453-1724; chamber@plymouthmich.org; www.plymouthmich.org*

Pontiac • *Pontiac Reg. Chamber* • Dawnaree Demrose; Pres.; 402 N. Telegraph; 48341; Oakland; P 71,000; M 400; (248) 335-9600; Fax (248) 335-9601; info@pontiacchamber.com; www.pontiacchamber.com

Port Austin • *Greater Port Austin Area C/C* • Joyce Stanek; Exec. Dir.; 2 W. Spring St.; P.O. Box 274; 48467; Huron; P 1,747; M 110; (989) 738-7600; pacofc@airadvantage.net; www.portaustinarea.com

Port Huron • *Blue Water Area C/C* • Vickie Ledsworth; Pres./CEO; 512 McMorran Blvd.; 48060; St. Clair; P 162,000; M 400; (810) 985-7101; (800) 361-0526; Fax (810) 985-7311; info@bluewaterchamber.com; www.bluewaterchamber.com*

Portland • *Portland Area C/C* • Kory Blastic; Pres.; 1126 E. Grand River Ave.; P.O. Box 303; 48875; Ionia; P 3,000; M 100; (517) 647-2100; Fax (517) 647-2100; pacc@power-net.net; www.portlandareachamber.com*

Potterville • *Potterville Area Chamber of Businesses* • P.O. Box 76; 48876; Eaton; P 2,300; M 40; (517) 645-2313; Fax (517) 645-7889; info@gizzardfest.com; www.pottervillechamber.org; www.gizzardfest.com

Prescott • *see Skidway Lake*

Quincy • *Quincy C/C* • P.O. Box 132; 49082; Branch; P 4,411; M 65; (517) 639-8369; info@branchareachamber.com; www.branchareachamber.com

Ravenna • *Ravenna C/C* • Larry D. Gardiner; Pres.; P.O. Box 332; 49451; Muskegon; P 1,200; M 50; (231) 853-2360; www.ravennami.com

Ray Township • *see Romeo*

Redford • *Redford Twp. C/C* • Mary Jo Mullen; Exec. Dir.; 26050 Five Mile; 48239; Wayne; P 51,622; M 350; (313) 535-0960; (313) 535-0976; Fax (313) 535-6356; rtcc@wanemail.com; redfordchamber.org.*

Reed City • *Reed City Area C/C* • Suzie Williams; Exec. Dir.; 200 N. Chestnut; P.O. Box 27; 49677; Osceola; P 2,400; M 250; (231) 832-5431; (877) 832-7332; Fax (231) 832-5431; suzie@reedcitycrossroads.com; www.reedcitycrossroads.com*

Reese • *Reese Area C/C* • Kay Bierlein; Dir.; P.O. Box 113; 48757; Tuscola; P 1,500; M 65; (989) 868-4291; kabierlein@gmail.com; www.villageofreese.net

Reynolds • *see Howard City*

Richmond • *Richmond Area C/C* • Kim Galante; Exec. Dir.; 68371 Oak St.; 48062; Macomb; P 25,000; M 150; (586) 727-3266; Fax (586) 727-3635; info@robn.org; www.robn.org

Riverdale • *see Alma*

Rochester • *Rochester Reg. C/C* • Sheri L. Heiney; Exec. Dir.; 71 Walnut, Ste. 110; 48307; Oakland; P 80,000; M 1,200; (248) 651-6700; Fax (248) 651-5270; info@rrc-mi.com; www.rrc-mi.com.*

Rockford • *Rockford C/C* • Brenda Davis; Exec. Dir.; 598 Byrne Industrial Dr.; P.O. Box 520; 49341; Kent; P 30,000; M 290; (616) 866-2000; Fax (616) 866-2141; info@rockfordmichamber.com; www.rockfordmichamber.com*

Rogers City • *Rogers City Area C/C* • Ray Spain; Exec. Dir.; 292 S. Bradley Hwy.; 49779; Presque Isle; P 3,300; M 201; (989) 734-2535; (800) 622-4148; Fax (989) 734-7767; rcchamber1@charterinternet.com; www.rogerscity.com

Romeo • *Greater Romeo-Washington C/C* • Kelley Stephens; Exec. Dir.; 228 N. Main, Ste. D; P.O. Box 175; 48065; Macomb; P 38,850; M 375; (586) 752-4436; Fax (586) 752-2835; contact@rwchamber.com; www.rwchamber.com*

Romulus • *Greater Romulus C/C* • Karen LaBelle; Exec. Dir.; 11189 Shook St., Ste. 200; 48174; Wayne; P 23,000; M 180; (734) 893-0694; Fax (734) 893-0696; info@romuluschamber.com; www.romuluschamber.org

Roscommon · *Higgins Lake-Roscommon C/C* · Connie Allen; Ofc. Coord.; 709 Lake St.; P.O. Box 486; 48653; Roscommon; P 25,469; M 197; (989) 275-8760; Fax (989) 275-2029; info@hlrcc.com; www.hlrcc.com

Rose City · *Rose City-Lupton Area C/C* · Mike Dunn; Pres.; P.O. Box 100; 48654; Ogemaw; P 1,200; M 80; (989) 685-2936; info@rosecityluptonchamber.com; www.rosecityluptonchamber.com

Roseville · *see Saint Clair Shores*

Royal Oak · *Greater Royal Oak C/C* · Shelly Kemp; Interim Exec. Dir.; 200 S. Washington Ave.; 48067; Oakland; P 60,000; M 700; (248) 547-4000; Fax (248) 547-0504; shellyk@royaloakchamber.com; www.royaloakchamber.com

Saginaw · *Saginaw County C/C* · Bob Van Deventer; Pres.; 515 N. Washington Ave., 2nd Flr.; 48607; Saginaw; P 210,039; M 900; (989) 752-7161; Fax (989) 752-9055; info@saginawchamber.org; www.saginawchamber.org*

Saint Charles · *Saint Charles Area C/C* · P.O. Box 26; 48655; Saginaw; P 2,215; M 75; (989) 865-8289; Fax (989) 865-6480; www.stcmi.com

Saint Clair Shores · *Metro East C/C* · Heather Lynn; Admin.; 27601 Jefferson; 48081; Macomb; P 250,000; M 450; (586) 777-2741; Fax (586) 777-4811; info@metroeastchamber.org; www.metroeastchamber.org*

Saint Helen · *Saint Helen C/C* · Jan Waltz; P.O. Box 642; 48656; Roscommon; P 3,500; M 100; (989) 389-3725; sainthelen_chamber@yahoo.com; www.sainthelenchamber.net

Saint Johns · *Clinton County C/C* · Brenda Terpening; Exec. Dir.; 1013 S. U.S. 27; P.O. Box 61; 48879; Clinton; P 68,000; M 300; (989) 224-7248; Fax (989) 224-7667; ccchamber@power-net.net; www.clintoncountychamber.org*

Saline · *Saline Area C/C* · Larry Osterling; Exec. Dir.; 141 E. Michigan Ave.; P.O. Box 198; 48176; Washtenaw; P 55,000; M 500; (734) 429-4494; Fax (734) 944-6835; office@salinechamber.org; www.salinechamber.org*

Sandusky · *Sandusky C/C* · 26 W. Speaker St.; 48471; Sanilac; P 2,800; M 135; (810) 648-4445; Fax (810) 648-3959; quieann78@yahoo.com; www.ci.sandusky.mi.us

Sanford · *Sanford Area C/C* · Mr. Pat Wortley; Pres.; P.O. Box 98; 48657; Midland; P 1,000; M 21; (989) 687-2800; (989) 687-5000; info@sanfordmi.com; sanfordmi.com/chamber

Sault Sainte Marie · *Sault Sainte Marie C/C* · Leisa Mansfield; Exec. Dir.; 2581 I-75 Business Spur; 49783; Chippewa; P 38,000; M 360; (906) 632-3301; Fax (906) 632-2331; info@saultstemarie.org; www.saultstemarie.org*

Sawyer · *see Gwinn*

Scottville · *see Ludington*

Sebewaing · *Sebewaing C/C* · Jeff Sigmund; Pres.; P.O. Box 622; 48759; Huron; P 2,000; M 60; (989) 883-2150; Fax (989) 883-9367; www.sebewaingchamber.com

Shelby Township · *see Sterling Heights*

Shepherd · *Shepherd Area C/C* · P.O. Box 111; 48883; Isabella; P 1,500; M 45; (989) 828-6442; (989) 828-5175

Silver Lake · *see Hart*

Skidway Lake · *Skidway Lake Area C/C* · Mary Cline; Mgr.; P.O. Box 4041; 48756; Ogemaw; P 5,000; M 70; (989) 873-4150

South Haven · *Greater South Haven Area C/C* · Rachel Vochaska; Exec. Dir.; 606 Phillips St.; 49090; Van Buren; P 20,000; M 400; (269) 637-5171; Fax (269) 639-1570; cofc@southhavenmi.com; www.southhavenmi.com*

South Lyon · *C/C for the South Lyon Area* · Laura Hogan; Ofc. Mgr.; 125 N. Lafayette; 48178; Oakland; P 60,000; M 350; (248) 437-3257; Fax (248) 437-4116; laura@southlyonchamber.com; www.southlyonchamber.com*

Southfield · *Southfield Area C/C* · Ed Powers; Pres.; 17515 W. 9 Mile Rd., Ste. 190; 48075; Oakland; P 78,000; M 350; (248) 557-6661; Fax (248) 557-3931; southfieldchamber@yahoo.com; www.southfieldchamber.com*

Sparta · *Sparta C/C* · Elizabeth Gorski; Exec.Dir.; 156 E. Division St.; P.O. Box 142; 49345; Kent; P 8,000; M 135; (616) 887-2454; ddadirector@spartami.org; www.spartachamber.com

Spring Lake · *see Grand Haven*

St. Clair · *St. Clair C/C* · Jodi Skonieczny; Exec. V.P.; 201 N. Riverside Ave.; P.O. Box 121; 48079; St. Clair; P 5,800; M 248; (810) 329-2962; Fax (810) 329-2422; info@stclairchamber.com; www.stclairchamber.com

St. Ignace · *St. Ignace C/C* · Janet Peterson; Exec. Dir.; 560 N. State St.; 49781; Mackinac; P 3,000; M 210; (906) 643-8717; Fax (906) 643-9380; sichamber@lighthouse.net; www.saintignace.org.*

St. Joseph · *see Benton Harbor*

St. Louis · *see Alma*

Standish · *Standish Area C/C* · Andrew Radatz; Pres.; 108 E. Cedar St.; P.O. Box 458; 48658; Arenac; P 3,300; M 100; (989) 846-7867; www.standishchamber.com

Sterling Heights · *also see Mount Clemens*

Sterling Heights · *Sterling Heights Reg. C/C & Ind.* · Wayne Oehmke; Pres.; 12900 Hall Rd., Ste. 100; 48313; Macomb; P 230,000; M 1,600; (586) 731-5400; Fax (586) 731-3521; WOehmke@shrcci.com; www.shrcci.com.*

Stevensville · *Lakeshore C/C* · Griffin Ott; Pres.; 4290 Red Arrow Hwy.; P.O. Box 93; 49127; Berrien; P 15,465; M 165; (269) 429-1170; Fax (269) 429-8882; information@lakeshorechamber.org; www.lakeshorechamber.org

Sturgis · *Sturgis Area C/C* · Cathi Garn Abbs; Exec. Dir.; 200 W. Main St.; P.O. Box 189; 49091; St. Joseph; P 12,000; M 380; (269) 651-5758; Fax (269) 651-4124; info@sturgischamber.com; www.sturgischamber.com*

Sumner · *see Alma*

Sumpter Township · *see Belleville*

Sunfield · *see Lake Odessa*

Suttons Bay · *Leelanau Peninsula C/C* · Sally Guzowski; Exec. Dir.; 5046 S. West Bayshore Dr., Ste. G; 49682; Leelanau; P 20,000; M 475; (231) 271-9895; (800) 980-9895; Fax (231) 271-9896; info@leelanauchamber.com; www.leelanauchamber.com

Suttons Bay · *Suttons Bay C/C* · Amy Peterson; Pres.; P.O. Box 46; 49682; Leelanau; P 1,000; M 125; (231) 271-5077; www.suttonsbayarea.com

Swartz Creek · *see Flint*

Tawas City · *Tawas Area C/C* · Mark Hitchcock; Dir.; 402 E. Lake St.; P.O. Box 608; 48764; Iosco; P 6,000; M 260; (989) 362-8643; (800) 55-TAWAS; Fax (989) 362-7880; info@tawas.com; www.tawas.com

Taylor · *Southern Wayne County Reg. C/C* · Saundra Mull; Pres.; 20904 Northline Rd.; 48180; Wayne; P 450,000; M 900; (734) 284-6000; Fax (734) 284-0198; sandy@swcrc.com; www.swcrc.com.*

Tecumseh · *Tecumseh Area C/C* · Vicki Philo; Exec. Dir.; 132 W. Chicago Blvd.; 49286; Lenawee; P 10,000; M 175; (517) 423-3740; (888) 261-3367; Fax (517) 423-5748; chamber@tecumsehchamber.org; www.tecumsehchamber.org*

Tekoncha · *see Coldwater*

Three Oaks · *see New Buffalo*

Three Rivers · *Three Rivers Area C/C* · 57 N. Main St.; 49093; St. Joseph; P 21,000; M 300; (269) 278-8193; Fax (269) 273-1751; info@trchamber.com; www.trchamber.com*

Traverse City · *Traverse City Area C/C* · Douglas Luciani; Pres./CEO; 202 E. Grandview Pkwy.; 49684; Grand Traverse; P 84,952; M 2,100; (231) 947-5075; Fax (231) 946-2565; info@tcchamber.org; www.tcchamber.org*

Troy · *Multicultural C/C* · Dr. Shakil A. Khan; Pres.; 1787 W. Big Beaver Rd.; 48084; Oakland; P ; M 50; (248) 614-5200; Fax (248) 636-4111; info@multiculturalcouncil.org; www.multicultural council.org.

Troy · *Troy C/C* · Michele Hodges; Pres.; 4555 Investment Dr., Ste. 300; 48098; Oakland; P 82,000; M 720; (248) 641-8151; Fax (248) 641-0545; theteam@troychamber.com; www.troychamber.com*

Trufant · *Trufant Area C/C* · Ralph Krantz; Pres.; P.O. Box 129; 49347; Montcalm; P 500; M 87; (616) 984-2555; (616) 984-2396; Fax (616) 984-6311

Union Pier · *see New Buffalo*

Utica · *see Sterling Heights*

VanBuren Township · *see Belleville*

Vassar · *Vassar C/C* · P.O. Box 126; 48768; Tuscola; P 2,823; M 38; (989) 823-2601; (989) 823-8517; vassarchamber@att.net; www.vassarchamberofcommerce.net

Wakefield · *Wakefield C/C* · Suzanne Backman; Pres.; P.O. Box 93; 49968; Gogebic; P 2,100; M 65; (906) 224-2222; www.visitwakefield.com

Walled Lake · *Lakes Area C of C* · Jo Alley; Exec. Dir.; 305 N. Pontiac Trl., Ste. A; 48390; Oakland; P 126,356; M 500; (248) 624-2826; Fax (248) 624-2892; info@lakesareachamber.com; www.lakesareachamber.com

Warren · *see Mount Clemens*

Washington Township · *see Romeo*

Waterford · *Waterford C/C* · Marie Hauswirth; Exec. Dir.; 2309 Airport Rd.; 48327; Oakland; P 74,000; M 515; (248) 666-8600; Fax (248) 666-3325; info@waterfordchamber.org; www.waterfordchamber.org*

Waterford Twp. · *see Walled Lake*

Wayland · *Wayland Area C/C* · Denise Behm; Exec. Dir.; 117 S. Main St., Ste. 6; 49348; Allegan; P 4,000; M 200; (269) 792-9246; Fax (269) 509-4512; info@waylandchamber.org; www.waylandchamber.org*

Wayne · *Wayne C/C* · Jill Dauget; Exec. Dir.; 34844 W. Michigan Ave.; 48184; Wayne; P 19,899; M 170; (734) 721-0100; Fax (734) 721-3070; www.waynechamber.net*

West Bloomfield · *West Bloomfield C/C* · Ann Corwell; Exec. Dir.; 6668 Orchard Lake Rd., Ste. 207; 48322; Oakland; P 64,862; M 250; (248) 626-3636; Fax (248) 626-4218; wbcc@sbcglobal.net; www.westbloomfieldchamber.com*

West Branch · *West Branch Area C/C* · Christie Blackford; Pres.; 422 W. Houghton Ave.; 48661; Ogemaw; P 30,000; M 250; (989) 345-2821; (800) 755-9091; Fax (989) 345-9075; chamber@westbranch.com; www.wbacc.com.

Westland · *Westland C/C* · Brookellen Swope; Pres./CEO; 36900 Ford Rd.; 48185; Wayne; P 85,000; M 400; (734) 326-7222; Fax (734) 326-6040; info@westlandchamber.com; www.westlandchamber.com*

Wheeler · *see Alma*

White Cloud · *White Cloud Area C/C* · Jim Maike; Chrmn.; 12 N. Charles St.; 49349; Newaygo; P 10,000; M 120; (231) 689-6607; kb8ife@ncats.net; www.whitecloudchamber.org

White Lake Twp. · *see Walled Lake*

Whitehall · *White Lake Area C/C* · Amy VanLoon; Exec. Dir.; 124 W. Hanson St.; 49461; Muskegon; P 18,000; M 334; (231) 893-4585; (800) 879-9702; Fax (231) 893-0914; info@whitelake.org; www.whitelake.org.*

Whitmore Lake · *see Brighton*

Whittemore · *Whittemore Area C/C* · Paula Engle; Secy.; P.O. Box 178; 48770; Losco; P 2,000; M 18; (989) 756-5231; (989) 756-3011

Williamston · *Williamston Area C/C* · Barbara Burke; Exec. Dir.; 369 W. Grand River Ave.; P.O. Box 53; 48895; Ingham; P 5,000; M 170; (517) 655-1549; Fax (517) 655-8859; info@williamston.org; www.williamston.org*

Winfield · *see Howard City*

Wixom · *see Walled Lake*

Wolverine Village · *see Walled Lake*

Woodland · *see Hastings & Lake Odessa*

Wyoming · *Wyoming-Kentwood Area C/C* · Ken Malik; Pres./CEO; 590 32nd St. S.E.; 49548; Kent; P 118,000; M 450; (616) 531-5990; Fax (616) 531-0252; ken@southkent.org; www.southkent.org*

Yale · *Yale C/C* · Barb Stasik; Pres.; P.O. Box 59; 48097; St. Clair; P 3,000; M 100; (810) 387-9253; yale@yalechamber.com; www.yalechamber.com

Ypsilanti · *Ann Arbor/Ypsilanti Reg. C/C* · Diane Keller; Pres./CEO; 301 W. Michigan Ave., Ste. 101; 48197; Washtenaw; P 114,000; M 1,500; (734) 665-4433; Fax (734) 665-4191; diane@a2ychamber.org; www.a2ychamber.org*

Zeeland · *Zeeland C/C* · James Schoettle; Pres.; 149 Main Pl.; 49464; Ottawa; P 23,000; M 400; (616) 772-2494; Fax (616) 772-0065; zchamber@zeelandchamber.org; www.zeelandchamber.org.*

Minnesota

Minnesota C of C · David Olson; Pres.; 400 Roberts St. N., Ste. 1500; Saint Paul; 55101; Ramsey; P 5,200,000; M 2,600; (651) 292-4650; (800) 821-2230; Fax (651) 292-4656; mbethke@mnchamber.com; www.mnchamber.com

Ada · *Ada C/C* · Lee Ann Hall; Secy./Treas.; P.O. Box 1; 56510; Norman; P 1,700; M 73; (218) 784-3542; Fax (218) 784-3890; leeannko@loretel.net; www.ci.ada.mn.us

Aitkin · *Aitkin Area C/C* · 114 Minnesota Ave. N.; P.O. Box 127; 56431; Aitkin; P 2,000; M 288; (218) 927-2316; (800) 526-8342; Fax (218) 927-4494; upnorth@aitkin.com; www.aitkin.com

Albany · *Albany C/C* · Kim Fish; Exec. Secy.; P.O. Box 634; 56307; Stearns; P 23,000; M 115; (320) 845-7777; Fax (320) 845-2346; albanycc@albanytel.com; www.albanymnchamber.com

Albert Lea · *Albert Lea-Freeborn County C/C* · Randy Kehr; Dir.; 2580 Bridge Ave.; Northbridge Mall; 56007; Freeborn; P 30,927; M 500; (507) 373-3938; Fax (507) 373-0344; alfccoc@albertlea.org; www.albertlea.org.*

Albertville · *see Rogers*

Aldrich · *see Staples*

Alexandria · *Alexandria Lakes Area C/C* · Coni McKay; Exec. Dir.; 206 Broadway; 56308; Douglas; P 35,000; M 610; (320) 763-3161; (800) 245-ALEX; Fax (320) 763-6857; cmckay@alexandriamn.org; www.alexandriamn.org.*

Andover · *see Anoka*

Angle Inlet · *see Baudette*

Annandale · *Annandale Area C/C* · Keith Jerpseth; P.O. Box 417; 55302; Wright; P 2,700; M 180; (320) 274-2474; www.annandale chamber.org

Anoka · *Anoka Area C/C* · Peter Turok; Pres.; 12 Bridge Sq.; 55303; Anoka; P 100,000; M 650; (763) 421-7130; Fax (763) 421-0577; mail@anokaareachamber.com; www.anokaareachamber.com*

Apple Valley · *Apple Valley C/C & CVB* · Edward Kearney; Pres.; 14800 Galaxie Ave., Ste. 101; 55124; Dakota; P 51,300; M 350; (952) 432-8422; (800) 301-9435; Fax (952) 432-7964; info@ applevalleychamber.com; www.applevalleychamber.com

Appleton · *Appleton Area C/C* · Shala Korstjens; Dir.; 127 W. Sorenson; P.O. Box 98; 56208; Swift; P 2,800; M 60; (320) 289-1527; appletonmn@mchsi.com; www.appletonmn.com

Arden Hills · *see Saint Paul*

Arlington · *Arlington Area C/C* · Dr. Lyle Rud; Pres.; P.O. Box 543; 55307; Sibley; P 2,048; M 60; (507) 964-5177; www. arlingtonmn.com

Atwater · *Atwater C/C* · Goldie Smith; P.O. Box 59; 56209; Kandiyohi; P 1,079; M 50; (320) 974-8760; Fax (320) 974-8760; atwaterchamber@yahoo.com; www.atwaterchamber.com

Austin · *Austin Area C/C* · Sandy Forstner; Exec. Dir.; 329 N. Main St., Ste. 102; 55912; Mower; P 23,300; M 380; (507) 437-4561; (888) 319-5655; Fax (507) 437-4869; execdir@austincoc. com; www.austincoc.com.*

Avon · *Avon Area C/C* · Janine Kutter; Pres.; P.O. Box 293; 56310; Stearns; P 1,400; M 75; (320) 356-4115; info@avonmnchamber. com; www.avonmnchamber.com

Barnesville · *Barnesville Main Street Program* · Ryan Tonsfeldt; Pres.; 202 Front St. N.; P.O. Box 550; 56514; Clay; P 2,200; M 152; (218) 354-2479; mainstreet@bvillemn.net; www.barnesvillemn.com

Baudette · *Baudette-Lake of the Woods Area C/C* · 930 W. Main; P.O. Box 659; 56623; Lake of the Woods; P 4,000; M 100; (218) 634-1174; (800) 382-3474; Fax (218) 634-2915; info@ lakeofthewoodsmn.com; www.lakeofthewoodsmn.com

Bay Lake · *see Crosby*

Becker · *Becker Area C/C* · Julie Brand; Pres.; P.O. Box 313; 55308; Sherburne; P 5,000; M 134; (763) 262-2420; Fax (763) 262-2150; info@beckerchamber.org; www.beckerchamber.org*

Belle Plaine · *Belle Plaine C/C* · 204 N. Meridian St.; 56011; Scott; P 5,200; M 90; (952) 873-4295; Fax (952) 873-4142; bellepln@frontiernet.net; www.belleplainemn.com*

Bemidji · *Bemidji Area C/C* · Lori Paris; Pres.; 300 Bemidji Ave.; P.O. Box 850; 56619; Beltrami; P 25,000; M 500; (218) 444-3541; (800) 458-2223; Fax (218) 444-4276; info@bemidji.org; www. bemidji.org*

Benson · *Benson Area C/C* · 1228 Atlantic Ave.; 56215; Swift; P 3,500; M 135; (320) 843-3618; Fax (320) 843-3618; benson-chamber@embarqmail.com; www.bensonareachamber.com*

Bethel · *see Blaine*

Big Lake · *Big Lake C/C* · Tricia Skodje; Pres.; 160 N. Lake St.; P.O. Box 241; 55309; Sherburne; P 20,000; M 150; (763) 263-7800; (877) 363-0549; Fax (763) 263-7668; blchamber@sherbtel.net; www.biglakechamber.com

Birchdale · *see Baudette*

Birchwood Village · *see White Bear Lake*

Blaine · *MetroNorth C/C* · Lori Higgins; Exec. Dir.; 9380 Central Ave., Ste. 320; 55434; Anoka; P 350,000; M 800; (763) 783-3553; Fax (763) 783-3557; chamber@metronorthchamber.org; www. metronorthchamber.org*

Blooming Prairie · *Blooming Prairie C/C* · Becky Noble; Exec. Dir.; 138 Hwy. 218 S.; P.O. Box 805; 55917; Steele; P 1,900; M 100; (507) 583-4472; Fax (507) 583-4520; bpcofc@frontiernet.net; www.bloomingprairie.com

Bloomington · *Bloomington C/C* · Maureen Scallen Failor; Exec. Dir.; 9633 Lyndale Ave. S., Ste. 200; 55420; Hennepin; P 88,700; M 1,000; (952) 888-8818; Fax (952) 888-0508; mscallenfailor@ bloomingtonchamber.org; www.minneapolischamber.org*

Blue Earth · *Blue Earth Area C/C* · Shelly Greimann; Exec. Dir.; 113 S. Nicollet; 56013; Faribault; P 4,000; M 200; (507) 526-2916; Fax (507) 526-2244; chamber@bevcomm.net; www.blueearth chamber.com*

Brainerd · *Brainerd Lakes C/C* · 124 N. 6th St.; 56401; Crow Wing; P 22,000; M 1,200; (218) 829-2838; (800) 450-2838; Fax (218) 829-8199; info@explorebrainerdlakes.com; www.explore brainerdlakes.com*

Breckenridge · *see Wahpeton, ND*

Breezy Point · *see Pequot Lakes*

Brooklyn Center · *see Plymouth–TwinWest C/C*

Brooklyn Park · *see Osseo*

Buffalo · *Buffalo Area C/C* · Sally Custer; Pres.; 205 Central Ave.; 55313; Wright; P 14,000; M 280; (763) 682-4902; Fax (763) 682-5677; sally@buffalochamber.org; www.buffalochamber.org

Burnsville · *Burnsville C/C* · Daron Van Helden; Pres.; 101 W. Burnsville Pkwy., Ste. 150; 55337; Dakota; P 60,220; M 650; (952) 435-6000; Fax (952) 435-6972; chamber@burnsvillechamber.com; www.burnsvillechamber.com

Caledonia · *Caledonia Area C/C & Tourism Center* · Karen Ness; Pres.; 214 E. Main St.; 55921; Houston; P 2,965; M 69; (507) 725-5477; (877) 439-4893; caledoniacc@acegroup.cc; www. caledoniamn.gov

Cambridge · *Cambridge Area C/C* · Nicki Klanderud; Pres.; 140 N. Buchanan St., Ste. 174; P.O. Box 343; 55008; Isanti; P 36,000; M 250; (763) 689-2505; Fax (763) 552-2505; info@cambridge-chamber.com; www.cambridge-chamber.com

Canby · *Canby Area C/C* · Joyce Baer; Coord.; 123 First St. E.; 56220; Yellow Medicine; P 1,903; M 175; (507) 223-7775; www. canbychamber.com

Cannon Falls · *Cannon Falls Area C/C* · Patricia A. Anderson; Pres.; 103 N. 4th St.; P.O. Box 2; 55009; Goodhue; P 4,000; M 190; (507) 263-2289; tourism@cannonfalls.org; www.cannonfalls.org

Carver · *see Chaska*

Cass Lake · *Cass Lake C/C* · P.O. Box 548; 56633; Cass; P 800; M 110; (218) 335-2250; (800) 356-8615; info@casslake.com; www.casslake.com

Center City · *see Lindstrom*

Centerville · *see Circle Pines*

Champlin · *see Anoka*

Chanhassen · *see Chaska*

Chaska · *SouthWest Metro C/C* · Deb McMillan; Pres.; 564 Bavaria Ln., Ste. 100; 55318; Carver; P 58,000; M 450; (952) 448-5000; Fax (952) 448-4261; info@swmetrochamber.com; www.swmetrochamber.com*

Chatfield • *Chatfield Commerical Club* • 21 2nd St. S.E.; 55923; Fillmore & Olmsted; P 2,800; M 75; (507) 867-3810; www.ci.chatfield.mn.us

Chisago City • *see Lindstrom*

Chisholm • *Chisholm Area C/C* • Shannon Kishel-Roche; Exec. Dir.; 223 W. Lake St.; 55719; St. Louis; P 5,000; M 140; (218) 254-7930; (800) 422-0806; Fax (218) 254-7932; info@chisholm chamber.com; www.chisholmchamber.com*

Circle Pines • *Quad Area C/C* • P.O. Box 430; 55014; Anoka; P 40,000; M 50; (651) 815-2750; annamwicks@msn.com; www. quadchamber.org

Claremont • *Claremont Area C/C* • Dean Schuette; Pres./CEO; P.O. Box 236; 55924; Dodge; P 670; M 40; (507) 456-3899; Fax (507) 528-2126; schuette@myclearwave.net; www.claremontmn.com

Clarissa • *Clarissa Commercial Club* • Jason Polavick; P.O. Box 188; 56440; Todd; P 600; M 25; (218) 756-2131

Clementson • *see Baudette*

Cloquet • *Cloquet Area C/C & Tourism* • 225 Sunnyside Dr.; 55720; Carlton; P 12,000; M 285; (218) 879-1551; (800) 554-4350; Fax (218) 878-0223; chamber@cloquet.com; www.cloquet.com*

Cokato • *Cokato C/C* • Louann Worden; Secy.; 255 Broadway Ave. S.; P.O. Box 819; 55321; Wright; P 2,700; M 85; (320) 286-5505; Fax (320) 286-5876; depclerk@cokato.mn.us; www.cokato.mn.us

Cold Spring • *Cold Spring Area C/C* • 20 Red River Ave. S., Ste. 110; 56320; Stearns; P 3,000; M 108; (320) 685-4186; Fax (320) 685-4186; info@coldspringmn.com; www.coldspringmn.com*

Columbia Heights • *see New Brighton*

Cook • *Cook Area C/C* • P.O. Box 296; 55723; St. Louis; P 800; M 75; (218) 666-5850; (800) 648-5897; Fax (218) 666-6073; chamber@cookminnesota.com; www.cookminnesota.com

Coon Rapids • *see Blaine*

Corcoran • *see Rogers*

Cottage Grove • *Cottage Grove Area C/C* • Bill Simoni; Pres.; 7064 W. Point Douglas Rd. S.; P.O. Box 16; 55016; Washington; P 35,000; M 140; (651) 458-8334; Fax (651) 458-8383; office@ cottagegrovechamber.org; www.cottagegrovechamber.org

Crookston • *Crookston Area C/C* • Lori Wagner; Pres./CEO; 107 W. 2nd St.; P.O. Box 115; 56716; Polk; P 8,198; M 220; (218) 281-4320; (800) 809-5997; Fax (218) 281-4349; chamber@ visitcrookston.com; www.visitcrookston.com*

Crosby • *Cuyuna Lakes C/C* • Johnna Johnson; Dir.; P.O. Box 23; 56441; Crow Wing; P 1,200; M 192; (218) 546-8131; Fax (218) 546-2618; info@cuyunacountry.net; www.cuyunacountry.net*

Crosslake • *Crosslake Ofc. of Brainerd Lakes C/C* • P.O. Box 315; 56442; Crow Wing; P 5,000; M 1,200; (218) 692-1828; (800) 450-2838; info@explorebrainerdlakes.com; www.explore brainerdlakes.com

Crystal • *see Plymouth–TwinWest C/C*

Cuyuna • *see Crosby*

Dakota County • *Dakota County Reg. C/C* • Ruthe Batulis; Pres.; 1121 Town Centre Dr., Ste. 102; Eagan; 55123; Dakota; P 150,000; M 600; (651) 452-9872; Fax (651) 452-8978; info@ dcrchamber.com; www.dcrchamber.com*

Dawson • *Dawson Area C/C* • Kim Miller; Pres.; P.O. Box 382; 56232; Lac qui Parle; P 1,700; M 100; (320) 769-2981; dawson chamber@frontiernet.net; www.dawsonchamber.com

Dayton • *see Anoka and Rogers*

Deer River • *Deer River C/C* • P.O. Box 505; 56636; Itasca; P 903; M 125; (218) 246-8055; (888) 701-2226; drchamb@deerriver.org; www.deerriver.org

Deerwood • *see Crosby*

Delano • *Delano Area C/C* • J. Kopp; Exec. Dir.; 265 N. River St., Ste. 109; P.O. Box 27; 55328; Wright; P 5,100; M 145; (763) 972-6756; Fax (763) 972-9326; info@delanochamber.com; www. delanochamber.com

Dellwood • *see White Bear Lake*

Detroit Lakes • *Detroit Lakes Reg. C/C* • Carrie Johnston; Pres.; 700 Summit Ave.; P.O. Box 348; 56502; Becker; P 10,000; M 480; (218) 847-9202; (800) 542-3992; Fax (218) 847-9082; dlcham-ber@visitdetroitlakes.com; www.VisitDetroitLakes.com.*

Duluth • *Duluth Area C/C* • David Ross; Pres./CEO; 5 W. First St., Ste. 101; 55802; St. Louis; P 84,167; M 1,150; (218) 722-5501; Fax (218) 722-3223; inquiry@duluthchamber.com; www.duluth chamber.com*

Eagan • *see Dakota County*

East Bethel • *see Blaine*

East Grand Forks • *The Chamber Grand Forks–East Grand Forks* • Barry Wilfahrt; Pres./CEO; P.O. Box 315; 56721; Grand Forks; P 65,000; M 920; (701) 772-7271; Fax (701) 772-9238; info@gochamber.org; www.gochamber.org*

Eden Prairie • *Eden Prairie C/C* • Pat MulQueeny; Pres.; 11455 Viking Dr., Ste. 270; 55344; Hennepin; P 58,000; M 510; (952) 944-2830; Fax (952) 944-0229; adminj@epchamber.org; www. epchamber.org*

Eden Valley • *Eden Valley C/C* • Randy Hanson; Pres.; P.O. Box 557; 55329; Meeker; P 866; M 47; (320) 453-2368; www.eden valleychamber.com

Edina • *Edina C/C* • Ms. Arrie Larsen Manti; Pres.; 3300 Edinborough Way, Ste. 150; 55435; Hennepin; P 47,000; M 400; (952) 806-9060; Fax (952) 806-9065; chamber@edina.org; www. edinachamber.com*

Elbow Lake • *Elbow Lake C/C* • Edie Johnson; Managing Dir.; P.O. Box 1083; 56531; Grant; P 1,275; M 120; (218) 685-5380; chamber@runestone.net; www.elbowlakechamber.com

Elk River • *Elk River Area C/C* • Debbi Rydberg; Pres.; 509 Hwy. 10; 55330; Sherburne; P 24,000; M 400; (763) 441-3110; Fax (763) 441-3409; eracc@elkriverchamber.org; www.elkriverchamber.org*

Ely • *Ely C/C* • Linda Fryer; Admin. Dir.; 1600 E. Sheridan St.; 55731; St. Louis; P 3,700; M 300; (218) 365-6123; (800) 777-7281; Fax (218) 365-5929; fun@ely.org; www.ely.org

Elysian • *Elysian Area C/C* • Ron Greenwald; Pres.; P.O. Box 95; 56028; Le Sueur; P 600; M 80; (507) 267-4708; (507) 267-4040; Fax (507) 267-4750; www.elysianmn.com

Eveleth • *see Virginia*

Excelsior • *South Lake/Excelsior C/C* • Linda Murrell; Exec. Dir.; 202 Water St., Ste. 209; P.O. Box 32; 55331; Hennepin; P 16,000; M 165; (952) 474-6461; Fax (952) 474-3139; eacc@isd.net; www. southlake-excelsiorchamber.com

Fairfax • *Fairfax Civic & Commerce* • Craig Buboltz; Pres.; P.O. Box 114; 55332; Renville; P 1,275; M 60; fairfax.govoffice.com

Fairmont • *Fairmont Area C/C* • Bob Wallace; Pres.; 323 E. Blue Earth Ave.; P.O. Box 826; 56031; Martin; P 11,000; M 277; (507) 235-5547; Fax (507) 235-8411; info@fairmontchamber.org; www. fairmontchamber.org*

Falcon Heights • *see Saint Paul*

Faribault • *Faribault Area C/C* • Kymn Anderson; Pres.; 530 Wilson Ave.; P.O. Box 434; 55021; Rice; P 28,000; M 490; (507) 334-4381; (800) 658-2354; Fax (507) 334-1003; chamber@ faribaultmn.org; www.faribaultmn.org

Farmington • *see Dakota County*

Fergus Falls • *Fergus Falls Area C/C* • Lisa Workman; Exec. Dir.; 202 S. Court St.; 56537; Otter Tail; P 14,000; M 300; (218) 736-6951; chamber@prtel.com; www.fergusfalls.com*

Flag Island • *see Baudette*

Floodwood • *Floodwood Bus./Comm. Partnership* • Deb Arro; Pres.; P.O. Box 337; 55736; St. Louis; P 500; M 45; (218) 476-3210; fbcp55736@yahoo.com; www.floodwoodbusinesses.com

Forest Lake • *Forest Lake Area C/C* • Colleen Eddy; Pres.; 56 E. Broadway Ave., Ste. 204; P.O. Box 474; 55025; Washington; P 45,000; M 275; (651) 464-3200; Fax (651) 464-3201; chamber@ flacc.org; www.flacc.org*

Frankfort Twp. • *see Rogers*

Fridley • *see New Brighton*

Gaylord • *Gaylord C/C* • Avery Grochow; Pres.; 332 Main Ave.; P.O. Box 7; 55334; Sibley; P 2,300; M 50; (507) 237-5869; Fax (507) 237-5121; gaylordchamber@exploregaylord.org; www. exploregaylord.org

Gem Lake • *see White Bear Lake*

Gilbert • *see Virginia*

Glencoe • *Glencoe Area C/C* • Dan Ehrke; Pres.; 630 10th St.; 55336; McLeod; P 5,700; M 150; (320) 864-3650; Fax (320) 864-6405; chamber@glencoemn.org; www.glencoemn.org

Glenwood • *Glenwood Lakes Area C/C* • Cody Rogahn; Dir.; 2 E. Minnesota Ave., Ste. 100; 56334; Pope; P 11,236; M 225; (320) 634-3636; (866) 634-3636; Fax (320) 634-3637; chamber@ glenwoodlakesarea.info; www.glenwoodlakesarea.org*

Golden Valley • *see Plymouth–TwinWest C/C*

Grand Marais • *Greater Grand Marais C/C* • Bev Wolke; Exec. Dir.; P.O. Box 805; 55604; Cook; P 2,200; M 100; gmcc@boreal.org; www.grandmaraismn.com

Grand Rapids • *Grand Rapids Area C/C* • Bud Stone; Pres./CEO; One N.W. Third St.; 55744; Itasca; P 40,000; M 600; (218) 326-6619; (800) 472-6366; Fax (218) 326-4825; info@grandmn.com; www.grandmn.com*

Granite Falls • *Granite Falls Area C/C* • Nicole Zempel; Exec. Dir.; 646 Prentice St.; 56241; Yellow Medicine; P 3,451; M 125; (320) 564-4039; Fax (320) 564-3843; gfchamber@mvtvwireless. com; www.granitefallschamber.com

Greenfield • *see Rogers*

Hackensack • *Hackensack C/C* • Jean Dawson; Coord.; 100 Fleisher Ave. S.; P.O. Box 373; 56452; Cass; P 275; M 100; (218) 675-6135; (800) 279-6932; Fax (218) 675-6135; chamber@ hackensackchamber.com; www.hackensackchamber.com

Ham Lake • *Ham Lake C/C* • Kim Hogdal; Exec. Dir.; 1207 Constance Blvd. N.E.; 55304; Anoka; P 50,000; M 100; (763) 434-3011; Fax (763) 434-6668; info@hamlakecc.org; www.hamlakecc.org

Hamel • *see Rogers*

Hanover • *see Rogers*

Hassan Twp. • *see Rogers*

Hastings • *Hastings Area C/C & Tourism Bur.* • Michelle Jacobs; Pres.; 111 E. Third St.; 55033; Dakota; P 22,000; M 300; (651) 437-6775; (888) 612-6122; Fax (651) 437-2697; info@hastingsmn.org; www.hastingsmn.org

Hayfield • *Hayfield C/C* • Tom Monahan; Pres.; P.O. Box 1113; 55940; Dodge; P 1,325; M 90; (507) 477-2000; (507) 477-3492; www.hayfieldchamber.com*

Hermantown • *Hermantown Area C/C* • Michael Lundstrom; Exec. Dir.; 4940 Lightning Dr.; 55811; St. Louis; P 9,760; M 310; (218) 729-6843; Fax (218) 729-7132; www.hermantownchamber.com*

Hibbing • *Hibbing Area C/C* • Lory Fedo; Pres./CEO; 211 E. Howard St.; P.O. Box 727; 55746; St. Louis; P 17,000; M 400; (218) 262-3895; (800) 4-HIBBING; Fax (218) 262-3897; hibbcofc@ hibbing.org; www.hibbing.org*

Hilltop • *see Blaine*

Hinckley • *Hinckley Area C/C* • Betty Miller; Dir.; 108 Main St. E.; P.O. Box 189; 55037; Pine; P 1,400; M 80; (320) 384-7837; info@ hinckleychamber.com; www.hinckleychamber.com

Hopkins • *see Plymouth–TwinWest C/C*

Houston • *Houston Area C/C* • Karla Kinstler; Secy.; 215 W. Plum St.; P.O. Box 3; 55943; Houston; P 3,000; M 50; (507) 896-4668; nature@acegroup.cc; www.houstonmnchamber.com

Hoyt Lakes • *Hoyt Lakes C/C* • Robert Bartholomew; Pres.; P.O. Box 429; 55750; St. Louis; P 2,700; M 100; (218) 225-2787; www. hoytlakes.com

Hugo • *see White Bear Lake*

Hutchinson • *Hutchinson Area C/C* • Bill Corby; Pres.; 2 Main St. S.; 55350; McLeod; P 13,977; M 350; (320) 587-5252; Fax (320) 587-4752; info@explorehutchinson.com; www.explorehutchinson.com*

International Falls • *International Falls Area C/C* • Faye Whitbeck; Pres.; 301 2nd Ave.; 56649; Koochiching; P 14,000; M 210; (218) 283-9400; Fax (218) 283-3572; chamber@intlfalls. org; www.ifallschamber.com.*

Inver Grove Heights • *River Heights C/C* • Jennifer Gale; Pres.; 5782 Blackshire Path; 55076; Dakota; P 53,470; M 350; (651) 451-2266; Fax (651) 451-0846; info@riverheights.com; www. riverheights.com*

Ironton • *see Crosby*

Isanti • *Isanti Area C/C* • Jan Peterson; Exec. Dir.; 121 W. Main St.; P.O. Box 203; 55040; Isanti; P 6,000; M 165; (763) 444-8515; admin@isantichamber.com; www.isantichamber.com

Jackson • *Jackson Area C/C* • Marilyn Reese; Exec. Dir.; 82 W. Ashley St.; 56143; Jackson; P 3,501; M 130; (507) 847-3867; Fax (507) 847-3869; chamber@jacksonmn.com; www.jacksonmn.com

Janesville • *Janesville C/C* • Paul Pfenning; Pres.; P.O. Box 0; 56048; Waseca; P 2,200; M 40; (507) 234-5110; Fax (507) 234-5236; janesville.govoffice.com

Jordan • *Jordan Area C/C* • 212 Second St. E., Ste. 104; 55352; Scott; P 5,000; M 140; (952) 492-2355; Fax (952) 492-3739; info@ jordanchamber.org; www.jordanchamber.org

Kasson • *Kasson C/C* • Cathy Pletta; P.O. Box 326; 55944; Dodge; P 5,200; M 100; (507) 634-7618; kassonchamber@kmtel.com; www.kassonchamber.org

Kimball • *Kimball Area C/C* • Leo Wirth; Pres.; P.O. Box 214; 55353; Stearns; P 650; M 55; (320) 398-8211; www.kimball areachamber.com

La Crescent • *La Crescent C/C* • Eileen Krenz; Exec. Secy.; 109 S. Walnut, Ste. 2; P.O. Box 132; 55947; Houston; P 5,000; M 130; (507) 895-2800; (800) 926-9480; Fax (507) 895-2619; lacrescent. chamber@acegroup.cc; www.lacrescentmn.com

Lake Benton • *Lake Benton Area C/C & CVB* • 110 S. Center St.; P.O. Box 205; 56149; Lincoln; P 700; M 55; (507) 368-9577; lbenton@itctel.com; www.lakebentonminnesota.com

Lake City · *Lake City Area C/C* · Mary Huselid; Exec. Dir.; 101 W. Center St.; 55041; Wabasha; P 5,000; M 220; (651) 345-4123; (800) 369-4123; Fax (651) 345-4195; lcchamber@lakecity.org; www.lakecity.org

Lake Crystal · *Lake Crystal Area C/C* · Julie Reed; Coord.; 129 S. Main; P.O. Box 27; 56055; Blue Earth; P 2,500; M 100; (507) 726-6088; lcchambr@hickorytech.net; www.lakecrystalchamber.com

Lake Lillian · *Lake Lillian Civic & Commerce* · Wendy Lund; Pres.; P.O. Box 205; 56253; Kandiyohi; P 200; M 20; (320) 664-4111; www.lakelillian.govoffice.com

Lakeville · *Lakeville Area C/C* · Todd J. Bornhauser; Exec. Dir.; 19950 Dodd Blvd., Ste. 101; 55044; Dakota; P 55,000; M 450; (952) 469-2020; Fax (952) 469-2028; info@lakevillechambercvb.org; www.lakevillechambercvb.org

Lamberton · *Lamberton Comm. Club* · Barb Lagrue; Secy.; P.O. Box 356; 56152; Redwood; P 800; M 55; (507) 752-7808; www.rrcnet.org/~lambrton/

Lanesboro · *Lanesboro Area C/C* · Julie Kiehne; Dir.; 100 Milwaukee Rd.; P.O. Box 348; 55949; Fillmore; P 788; M 135; (507) 467-2696; (800) 944-2670; Fax (507) 467-3060; info@lanesboro.com; www.lanesboro.com*

Lauderdale · *see Saint Paul*

Le Center · *Le Center Area C/C* · Don Hayden; Exec. Dir.; 10 W. Tyrone St.; P.O. Box 54; 56057; Le Sueur; P 2,200; M 100; (507) 357-6737; Fax (507) 357-6888; donlc@frontiernet.net; www.cityoflecenter.com

Le Sueur · *Le Sueur Area C/C* · Julie Boyland; Exec. Dir.; 500 N. Main St.; 56058; Le Sueur; P 4,300; M 185; (507) 665-2501; Fax (507) 665-4372; julieb@lesueurchamber.org; www.lesueurchamber.org*

Lewiston · *Lewiston C/C* · Craig Porter; Pres.; P.O. Box 423; 55952; Winona; P 1,800; M 70; (507) 523-2300; www.lewistonmn.org

Lexington · *see Circle Pines*

Lilydale · *see Dakota County*

Lindstrom · *Chisago Lakes Area C/C* · Tangi Schaapveld; Exec. Dir.; 30525 Linden St.; P.O. Box 283; 55045; Chisago; P 15,000; M 200; (651) 257-1177; Fax (651) 257-1770; clacc@frontiernet.net; www.chisagolakeschamber.com

Lino Lakes · *see Circle Pines*

Litchfield · *Litchfield C/C* · Dee Schutte; Exec. Dir.; 219 Sibley Ave. N.; 55355; Meeker; P 6,500; M 300; (320) 693-8184; Fax (320) 593-8184; litch@litch.com; www.litch.com*

Little Canada · *see Saint Paul*

Little Falls · *Little Falls Area C/C* · Debora Boelz; Pres./CEO; 200 N.W. First St.; 56345; Morrison; P 32,900; M 350; (320) 632-5155; Fax (320) 632-2122; assistance@littlefallsmnchamber.com; www.littlefallsmnchamber.com*

Littlefork · *Littlefork Area C/C* · 313 Main St.; P.O. Box 131; 56653; Koochiching; P 700; M 40; (218) 278-6617; www.lakesnwoods.org

Long Lake · *Long Lake C/C* · Matt Stahl; Pres.; P.O. Box 662; 55356; Hennepin; P 2,200; M 100; www.longlake-orono.org*

Long Prairie · *Long Prairie Area C/C* · Lyle Danielson; Mgr.; 42 N. 3rd St.; 56347; Todd; P 3,040; M 115; (320) 732-2514; info@longprairie.org; www.longprairie.org

Longville · *Longville C/C* · Phyllis Eck; Pres.; P.O. Box 33; 56655; Cass; P 300; M 90; (218) 363-2630; (800) 756-7583; chamber@longville.com; www.longville.com

Lonsdale · *Lonsdale Area C/C* · Andrea Nelson; Pres.; 102 Main St. N.; P.O. Box 37; 55046; Rice; P 2,900; M 90; (507) 744-4962; lacc@means.net; www.lonsdalechamber.net

Loretto · *see Rogers*

Luverne · *Luverne Area C/C* · Jane Wildung Lanphere; Exec. Dir.; 213 E. Luverne St.; Rock County Veterans Mem. Bldg.; 56156; Rock; P 4,600; M 180; (507) 283-4061; Fax (507) 283-4061; luverne-chamber@co.rock.mn.us; www.luvernechamber.com

Madelia · *Madelia Area C/C* · Lisa Visher; Pres.; 127 W. Main St.; P.O. Box 171; 56062; Watonwan; P 2,400; M 100; (507) 642-8822; (888) 941-7283; Fax (507) 642-8832; chamber@madeliamn.com; www.visitmadelia.com

Madison · *Madison Area C/C* · Maynard R. Meyer; Coord.; 623 W. 3rd St.; P.O. Box 70; 56256; Lac qui Parle; P 2,000; M 100; (320) 598-7301; Fax (320) 598-7955; klqpfm@farmerstel.net; www.madisonmn.info

Mahnomen · *Mahnomen County C/C* · Tom Ryan; Pres.; P.O. Box 36; 56557; Mahnomen; P 5,250; M 65; (218) 935-2573; www.mahnomen.govoffice.com

Mahtomedi · *see White Bear Lake*

Mankato · *Greater Mankato Growth Inc.* · Jonathan Zierdt; Pres./CEO; 1961 Premier Dr., Ste. 100; 56001; Blue Earth; P 50,000; M 770; (507) 385-6640; (800) 697-0652; Fax (507) 345-4451; info@greatermankato.com; www.greatermankato.com*

Maple Grove · *see Osseo*

Maple Plain · *West Hennepin C/C* · P.O. Box 363; 55359; Hennepin; P 25,000; M 130; (763) 479-1988; Fax (952) 472-8828; info@whcc-mn.org; www.whcc-mn.org

Mapleton · *Mapleton Area C/C* · Melissa Anne; Coord.; P.O. Box 288; 56065; Blue Earth; P 2,400; M 75; (507) 524-4756; coordinator@mapletonchamber.com; www.mapletonchamber.com

Maplewood · *see Saint Paul*

Marshall · *Marshall Area C/C* · Dir.; 317 W. Main St.; 56258; Lyon; P 13,000; M 320; (507) 532-4484; Fax (507) 532-4485; chamber@marshall-mn.org; www.marshall-mn.org*

McGregor · *McGregor Area C/C* · Kathy Larson; P.O. Box 68; 55760; Aitkin; P 500; M 100; (218) 768-3692; chamber@mcgregormn.com; www.mcgregormn.com

Medicine Lake · *see Plymouth—TwinWest C/C*

Medina · *see Rogers*

Melrose · *Melrose Area C/C* · 223 E. Main St.; 56352; Stearns; P 3,293; M 110; (320) 256-7174; Fax (320) 256-7177; chamber@meltel.net; www.melrosemn.org*

Mendota Heights · *see Dakota County*

Milaca · *Milaca Area C/C* · Becky Bergstrom; Coord.; 255 1st St. E.; P.O. Box 155; 56353; Mille Lacs; P 2,800; M 100; (320) 983-3140; Fax (320) 983-3142; info@milacachamber.com; www.milacachamber.com

Minneapolis · *Minneapolis Reg.C/C* · Todd Klingel; Pres./CEO; 81 S. 9th St., Ste. 200; 55402; Hennepin; P 2,968,806; M 1,000; (612) 370-9100; Fax (612) 370-9195; info@minneapolischamber.org; www.minneapolischamber.org.*

Minneapolis · *Northeast Minneapolis C/C* · Christine Levens; Exec. Dir.; 2329 Central Ave. N.E.; 55418; Hennepin; M 1,000; (612) 378-0050; Fax (612) 378-8870; info@minneapolischamber.org; www.minneapolischamber.org*

Minneota · *Minneota Area C/C* · Rick Konold; P.O. Box 413; 56264; Lyon; P 1,500; M 75; (507) 872-6144; www.minneotamn.com

Minnetonka · *see Plymouth—TwinWest C/C*

Montevideo · *Montevideo Area C/C* · 301 N. 1st St., Ste. 100; 56265; Chippewa; P 5,500; M 250; (320) 269-5527; (800) 269-5527; Fax (320) 269-5696; generalinfo@montechamber.com; www.montechamber.com*

Monticello · *Monticello C/C* · Sandy Suchy; Dir.; 205 Pine St.; P.O. Box 192; 55362; Wright; P 12,000; M 285; (763) 295-2700; Fax (763) 295-2705; info@monticellocci.com; www.monticellocci.com*

Montrose · *Montrose-Waverly C/C* · Jim Tourville; P.O. Box 421; 55363; Wright; P 2,700; (612) 508-6474; jamest55363@msn.com; www.montrosewaverlychamber.com*

Moorhead · *Fargo Moorhead C/C* · Craig Whitney; Pres./CEO; 202 1st Ave. N.; 56560; Clay, MN & Cass, ND; P 175,000; M 1,960; (218) 233-1100; Fax (218) 233-1200; info@fmchamber.com; www.fmchamber.com*

Moose Lake · *Moose Lake Area C/C* · Lisa Cekalla; Exec. Dir.; 4524 Arrowhead Ln.; P.O. Box 110; 55767; Carlton; P 4,000; M 140; (218) 485-4145; (800) 635-3680; mlchamber@moose-tec.com; www.mooselake-mn.com

Mora · *Mora Area C/C* · Karen Onan Amundson; Exec. Dir.; 111 S. Union St., Ste. 2; 55051; Kanabec; P 15,000; M 125; (320) 679-5792; (800) 291-5792; Fax (320) 679-3279; karen@moramn.com; www.moramn.com*

Morris · *Morris Area C/C* · Karen Arnold; Exec. Dir.; 507 Atlantic Ave.; 56267; Stevens; P 5,000; M 200; (320) 589-1242; Fax (320) 585-4814; mchamber@fedtel.net; www.morrismnchamber.org*

Morton · *Morton Area C/C & Tourism Bur.* · Shirley Dove; P.O. Box 0127; 56270; Renville; P 448; M 30; (507) 697-6912; mortoncityhall@mchsi.com; www.mortonmnchamber.com

Motley · *see Staples*

Mounds View · *see New Brighton*

Mountain Iron · *see Virginia*

Mountain Lake · *Mountain Lake C/C* · Rob Anderson; Dir.; 930 Third Ave.; P.O. Drawer C; 56159; Cottonwood; P 2,100; M 70; (507) 427-2999; Fax (507) 427-3327; eda@mountainlake.govoffice.com; www.mountainlakemn.com

Nashwauk · *Nashwauk Area C/C* · Mike Olson; Pres.; P.O. Box 156; 55769; Itasca; P 1,000; M 70; (218) 969-3538; (218) 969-1234; www.nashwaukchamber.com

New Brighton · *Twin Cities North C/C* · Tim Roche; Pres./CEO; 525 Main St., Ste. 200; 55112; Ramsey; P 87,000; M 700; (763) 571-9781; Fax (763) 572-7950; info@twincitiesnorth.org; www.twincitiesnorth.org

New Hope · *see Plymouth–TwinWest C/C*

New London · *see Willmar*

New Prague · *New Prague C/C* · Kristy Mach; Exec. Dir.; 101 E. Main St.; P.O. Box 191; 56071; Le Sueur & Scott; P 6,200; M 185; (952) 758-4360; Fax (952) 758-5396; info@newprague.com; www.newprague.com

New Ulm · *New Ulm Area C/C* · Sharon Weinkauf; Pres./CEO; 1 N. Minnesota St.; P.O. Box 384; 56073; Brown; P 14,000; M 370; (507) 233-4300; (888) 4NEWULM; Fax (507) 354-1504; nuchamber@newulmtel.net; www.newulm.com*

New York Mills · *New York Mills Civic & Commerce Assn.* · Lindsey Tibbets; Pres.; P.O. Box 176; 56567; Otter Tail; P 1,200; M 60; (218) 385-3339; info@explorenewyorkmills.com; www.explorenewyorkmills.com

Nisswa · *Nisswa C/C* · Molly Gerber; Exec. Dir.; 25532 Main St.; P.O. Box 185; 56468; Crow Wing; P 2,000; M 300; (218) 963-2620; (800) 950-9610; info@nisswa.com; www.nisswa.com

North Branch · *North Branch Area C/C* · Kathy Lindo; Exec. Dir.; 6063 Main St.; P.O. Box 577; 55056; Chisago; P 10,000; M 300; (651) 674-4077; Fax (651) 674-2600; nbachamber@izoom.net; northbranchchamber.com

North Maplewood · *see White Bear Lake*

North Oaks · *see Saint Paul and White Bear Lake*

North Saint Paul · *see Saint Paul*

Northfield · *Northfield Area C/C* · Kathy Feldbrugge; Exec. Dir.; 205 Third St. W., Ste A; P.O. Box 198; 55057; Rice; P 19,000; M 245; (507) 645-5604; (800) 658-2548; Fax (507) 663-7782; info@northfieldchamber.com; www.northfieldchamber.com.*

Norwood Young America · *Norwood Young America C/C* · Jeff Hebeisen; Pres.; P.O. Box 292; 55368; Carver; P 7,000; M 80; (952) 467-4003; info@nyachamber.org; www.nyachamber.org

Oak Grove · *see Blaine*

Oak Island · *Northwest Angle & Island C/C* · Debra Kellerman; P.O. Box 11; 56741; Lake of the Woods; P 150; M 200; (218) 223-4611; www.lakeofthewoodsresorts.com

Oakdale · *see Saint Paul*

Olivia · *Olivia Area C/C* · Nancy Standfuss; Exec. Dir.; 909 W. DePue Ave.; P.O. Box 37; 56277; Renville; P 2,600; M 100; (320) 523-1350; (888) 265-CORN; Fax (320) 523-1514; oliviachamber@tds.net; www.oliviachamber.org

Orr · *Orr C/C* · P.O. Box 64; 55771; St. Louis; P 300; M 30; (218) 757-3288; info@orrchamber.com; www.orrchamber.com

Ortonville · *Big Stone Lake Area C/C* · Katie Weber; Dir.; 987 U.S. Hwy. 12; 56278; Big Stone; P 2,100; M 180; (320) 839-3284; Fax (320) 839-2621; chamber@bigstonelake.com; www.bigstonelake.com

Osakis · *Osakis C/C & Info. Center* · Laura Backes; Pres.; P.O. Box 399; 56360; Douglas & Todd; P 1,615; M 80; (320) 859-3777; cityhall@cityofosakis.com; www.visitosakis.com

Osseo · *North Hennepin Area C/C* · Jill Johnson; Exec. Dir.; 229 1st Ave. N.E.; 55369; Hennepin; P 120,000; M 450; (763) 424-6744; bonny@nhachamber.com; www.nhachamber.com*

Otsego · *see Rogers*

Owatonna · *Owatonna Area C/C & Tourism* · Brad Meier; Pres./CEO; 320 Hoffman Dr.; 55060; Steele; P 26,000; M 600; (507) 451-7970; (800) 423-6466; Fax (507) 451-7972; oacct@owatonna.org; www.owatonna.org*

Park Rapids · *Park Rapids Lakes Area C/C & CVB* · Katharine B. Magozzi; Exec. Dir.; 1204 Park Ave. S.; P.O. Box 249; 56470; Hubbard; P 30,000; M 400; (218) 732-4111; (800) 247-0054; Fax (218) 732-4112; chamber@parkrapids.com; www.parkrapids.com*

Paynesville · *Paynesville Area C/C* · Linda Musel; Ofc. Mgr.; P.O. Box 4; 56362; Stearns; P 2,267; M 125; (320) 243-3233; (800) 547-9034; chamber@lakedalelink.net; www.paynesvillechamber.org

Pelican Rapids · *Pelican Rapids Area C/C* · Angela M. Harvala-Asleson; Exec. Dir.; 25 N. Broadway; P.O. Box 206; 56572; Otter Tail; P 3,700; M 120; (218) 863-1221; Fax (218) 863-4606; tourism@loretel.net; www.pelicanrapidschamber.com*

Pequot Lakes · *Pequot Lakes Ofc. of Brainerd Lakes C/C* · P.O. Box 208; 56472; Crow Wing; P 1,802; M 1,200; (218) 568-8911; (800) 950-0291; Fax (218) 568-8910; info@explorebrainerdlakes.com; www.explorebrainerdlakes.com*

Perham · *Perham Area C/C* · Don Schroeder; Exec. Dir.; 185 E. Main St.; 56573; Otter Tail; P 12,000; M 262; (218) 346-7710; (800) 634-6112; Fax (218) 346-7712; chamber@perham.com; www.perham.com*

Pillager · *see Staples*

Pine City · *Pine City Area C/C* · Rick Herzog; Pres.; 315 Main St. S., Ste. 155; 55063; Pine; P 3,400; M 150; (320) 322-4040; info@pinecitychamber.com; www.pinecitychamber.com

Pine River · *Pine River C/C* · John Wetrosky; Dir.; P.O. Box 131; 56474; Cass; P 4,000; M 125; (218) 587-4000; (800) 728-6926; Fax (218) 587-4096; prcofc@uslink.net; www.pinerivermn.com*

Pipestone · *Pipestone Area C/C* · Mick Myers; Exec. Dir.; 117 8th Ave. S.E.; P.O. Box 8; 56164; Pipestone; P 4,280; M 130; (507) 825-3316; Fax (507) 825-3317; pipecham@pipestoneminnesota.com; www.pipestoneminnesota.com*

Plymouth · *also see Rogers*

Plymouth · *TwinWest C/C* · Bruce Nustad; Pres.; 10700 Old County Rd. 15, Ste. 170; 55441; Hennepin; P 250,000; M 1,000; (763) 450-2220; Fax (763) 450-2221; bruce@twinwest.com; www.twinwest.com*

Princeton · *Princeton Area C/C* · Mary Chapman; Admin. Asst.; 705 2nd St. N.; 55371; Mille-Lacs; P 4,600; M 148; (763) 389-1764; Fax (763) 631-1764; pacc@sherbtel.net; www.princetonmnchamber.org*

Prior Lake · *Prior Lake Area C/C* · Sandi Fleck; Exec. Dir.; 4785 Dakota St.; P.O. Box 114; 55372; Scott; P 21,000; M 250; (952) 440-1000; Fax (952) 440-1611; sandi@priorlakechamber.com; www.priorlakechamber.com*

Proctor · *Proctor Area C/C* · Rich Borg; P.O. Box 1016; 55810; St. Louis; P 2,900; M 100; (218) 624-4136; info@proctorchamber.com; www.proctorchamber.com*

Ramsey · *see Anoka*

Raymond · *Raymond Civic & Commerce* · Larry Macht; P.O. Box 353; 56282; Kandiyohi; P 800; M 60; (320) 967-4439; Fax (320) 967-4439; raymondminnesota@yahoo.com; www.raymondminnesota.com

Red Wing · *Red Wing Area C/C* · Patty Brown; Pres.; 439 Main St.; 55066; Goodhue; P 16,000; M 300; (651) 388-4719; frontdesk@redwingchamber.com; www.redwingchamber.com*

Redwood Falls · *Redwood Area Chamber & Tourism* · Jean Hallberg; Exec. Dir.; 200 S. Mill St.; 56283; Redwood; P 5,400; M 160; (507) 637-2828; Fax (507) 637-5202; chamber@redwoodfalls.org; www.redwoodfalls.org*

Remer · *Remer Area C/C* · Bob Stoekel; Pres.; P.O. Box 101; 56672; Cass; P 342; M 70; (218) 566-1680; (800) 831-5262; info@remerchamber.com; www.remerchamber.com

Rice · *Rice C/C* · Barb Johnson; P.O. Box 179; 56367; Benton; P 1,346; M 65; (320) 393-2280; chamber@riceminnesota.com; www.riceminnesota.com

Richfield · *Richfield C/C* · Steven O. Lindgren; Pres.; 6601 Lyndale Ave. S., Ste. 106; 55423; Hennepin; P 35,000; M 200; (612) 866-5100; richcofc@aol.com; www.richfieldchambercvb.org*

Richmond · *Richmond Civic & Commerce* · Randy Rothstein; Pres.; P.O. Box 355; 56368; Stearns; P 1,200; M 75; (320) 597-5300; richmondmn@hotmail.com; www.richmondmn.com

Riverton · *see Crosby*

Robbinsdale · *Robbinsdale C/C* · Dave Kiser; P.O. Box 22646; 55422; Hennepin; P 14,500; M 68; (763) 531-1279; dkiser@twelve.tv; www.robbinsdalemn.com/chamber.htm

Rochester · *Rochester Area C/C* · John Wade; Pres.; 220 S. Broadway, Ste. 100; 55904; Olmsted; P 120,000; M 1,260; (507) 288-1122; chamber@rochestermnchamber.com; www.rochestermnchamber.com*

Rockford · *see Rogers*

Rogers · *I-94 West C/C* · Kathleen Poate; Pres.; 21370 John Milless Dr.; P.O. Box 95; 55374; Hennepin & Wright; P 35,000; M 650; (763) 428-2921; Fax (763) 428-9068; requests@i94westchamber.org; www.i94westchamber.org*

Roosevelt · *see Baudette*

Roseau · *Roseau Civic & Commerce* · Lyle Grindy; P.O. Box 304; 56751; Roseau; P 4,000; M 128; (218) 463-0009; (800) 815-1824; Fax (218) 463-1252; roseaupromotions@mncable.net; www.city.roseau.mn.us

Rosemount · *see Dakota County*

Roseville · *see Saint Paul*

Rush City · *Rush City Area C/C* · JoAnn Belau; Exec. Dir.; 325 S. 5th St.; P.O. Box 713; 55069; Goodhue; P 3,000; M 80; (320) 358-4639; Fax (320) 358-4639; director@rushcitychamber.com; www.rushcitychamber.com

Rushford · *Rushford Area C/C* · T.L. Benson; Exec. Coord.; P.O. Box 338; 55971; Fillmore; P 1,679; M 90; (507) 864-3338; chamber@rushfordchamber.com; www.rushfordchamber.com

Saint Anthony · *Saint Anthony C/C* · 3301 Silver Lake Rd.; 55418; Hennepin; P 8,000; M 76; (612) 782-3301; info@saintanthonychamber.org; www.saintanthonychamber.org

Saint Cloud · *Saint Cloud Area C/C* · Teresa Bohnen; Pres.; 110 S. 6th Ave.; P.O. Box 487; 56302; Stearns; P 85,000; M 1,010; (320) 251-2940; Fax (320) 251-0081; information@stcloudareachamber.com; www.stcloudareachamber.com*

Saint Francis · *see Anoka*

Saint James · *Saint James Area C/C* · Lori Nusbaum; Exec. Dir.; 516 1st Ave. S.; P.O. Box 346; 56081; Watonwan; P 4,900; M 125; (507) 375-3333; (866) 375-3334; chamber@stjamesmn.org; www.stjameschamberofcommerce.com

Saint Joseph · *Saint Joseph C/C* · Jean Dotzler; Pres.; P.O. Box 696; 56374; Stearns; P 5,100; M 80; (320) 267-8609; www.stjosephchamber.com

Saint Louis Park · *see Plymouth–TwinWest C/C*

Saint Michael · *see Rogers*

Saint Paul · *Saint Paul Area C/C* · Matt Kramer; Pres.; 401 Robert St. N., Ste. 150; 55101; Ramsey; P 600,000; M 2,000; (651) 223-5000; Fax (651) 223-5119; info@saintpaulchamber.com; www.saintpaulchamber.com*

Saint Peter · *Saint Peter Area C/C* · Anderns Ringdahl-Mayland; Pres./CEO; 101 S. Front St.; 56082; Nicollet; P 11,000; M 240; (507) 934-3400; Fax (507) 934-8960; spchamb@hickorytech.net; www.stpeterchamber.org*

Sandstone · *Sandstone Area C/C* · 402 N. Main; P.O. Box 23; 55072; Pine; P 2,200; M 58; (320) 245-2271; info@sandstonechamber.com; www.sandstonechamber.com

Sartell · *Sartell Area C/C* · Cathy Vande Vrede; Admin. Asst.; P.O. Box 82; 56377; Stearns; P 10,500; M 150; (320) 258-6061; info@sartellchamber.com; www.sartellchamber.com*

Sauk Centre · *Sauk Centre Area C/C* · Cindy Uhlenkamp; Exec. Dir.; 1220 S. Main St.; P.O. Box 222; 56378; Stearns; P 5,000; M 150; (320) 352-5201; Fax (320) 352-5202; chamber@saukcentrechamber.com; www.saukcentrechamber.com

Savage · *Savage C/C* · Lori Anderson; Exec. Dir.; 6050 McColl Dr.; 55378; Scott; P 25,000; M 225; (952) 894-8876; Fax (952) 894-9906; mail@savagechamber.com; www.savagechamber.com*

Shafer · *see Lindstrom*

Shakopee • *Shakopee Area C/C* • Angela Whitcomb; Pres.; 1801 E. Cty. Rd. 101; 55379; Scott; P 35,000; M 225; (952) 445-1660; Fax (952) 445-1669; chamber@shakopee.org; www.shakopee.org*

Sherburn • *Sherburn Area Civic & Commerce Org.* • Dorothy Behne; Pres.; P.O. Box 108; 56171; Martin; P 1,082; M 40; (507) 764-3151; www.sherburnmn.net

Shoreview • *see Saint Paul*

Silver Bay • *see Two Harbors*

Slayton • *Slayton Area C/C* • Karen Onken; 2635 Broadway Ave.; 56172; Murray; P 2,100; M 95; (507) 836-6902; Fax (507) 836-6650

Sleepy Eye • *Sleepy Eye Area C/C* • Julie Schmitt; Exec. Dir.; 115 2nd Ave. N.E.; 56085; Brown; P 3,600; M 125; (507) 794-4731; (800) 290-0588; Fax (507) 794-4732; secofc@sleepyeyetel.net; www.sleepyeyechamber.com*

Soudan • *see Tower*

South Saint Paul • *see Inver Grove Heights*

Spring Lake Park • *see New Brighton*

Spring Valley • *Spring Valley Area C/C* • Jayson Smith; Pres.; P.O. Box 13; 55975; Fillmore; P 2,600; M 42; (507) 346-1015; (507) 346-7367; springvalley.govoffice.com

Springfield • *Springfield Area C/C & CVB* • Marlys Vanderwerf; Exec. Secy.; 33 S. Cass; P.O. Box 134; 56087; Brown; P 2,178; M 134; (507) 723-3508; Fax (507) 723-5213; spfdchamber@newulmtel.net; www.springfieldmnchamber.org

Staples • *Staples-Motley Area C/C* • P.O. Box 133; 56479; Todd; P 4,000; M 120; (218) 894-3974; info@staples-motleyarea.com; www.staples-motleyarea.com

Starbuck • *Starbuck C/C* • Lori Vaadeland; Dir.; P.O. Box 234; 56381; Pope; P 1,300; M 125; (320) 239-4220; Fax (320) 239-4250; starbuckchamber@hcinet.net; www.starbuckmn.org*

Stewartville • *Stewartville Area C/C* • Kami Rogers; Admin.; 417 S. Main St.; P.O. Box 52; 55976; Olmsted; P 6,000; M 87; (507) 533-6006; stewchamber@charterinternet.com; www.stewartvillechamber.com*

Stillwater • *Greater Stillwater C/C* • Jennifer Severson; Exec. Dir.; 1950 N. Western Ave. S., Ste. 101; 55082; Washington; P 19,000; M 450; (651) 439-4001; Fax (651) 439-4035; info@ilovestillwater.com; www.ilovestillwater.com

Sunfish Lake • *see Dakota County*

Thief River Falls • *Thief River Falls C/C* • Ben Anderson; Exec. Dir.; 2017 Hwy. 59 S.E.; 56701; Hennepin; P 8,334; M 250; (218) 681-3720; (800) 827-1629; Fax (218) 681-3739; info@trfchamber.com; www.trfchamber.com

Tower • *Lake Vermilion Area C/C* • Troy Swanson; Exec. Dir.; 401 N. 3rd St.; P.O. Box 776; 55790; St. Louis; P 3,500; M 63; (218) 753-8909; troy@lakevermilioncommerce.com; www.lakevermilioncommerce.com

Tracy • *Tracy Area C/C* • Val Roskens Lubben; Dir.; 372 Morgan St.; 56175; Lyon; P 2,268; M 97; (507) 629-4021; Fax (507) 629-5530; tracychamber@iw.net; www.tracymnchamber.com

Trimont • *Trimont Area C/C* • Mary Ebeling; Exec. Secy.; P.O. Box 278; 56176; Martin; P 750; M 50; (507) 639-3082; trimontchamber@hotmail.com

Trommald • *see Crosby*

Two Harbors • *Two Harbors Area C/C* • Gordy Anderson; Pres./CEO; 1330 Hwy. 61; 55616; Lake; P 3,630; M 260; (218) 834-2600; Fax (218) 834-2600; thchamber@twoharborschamber.com; www.twoharborschamber.com

Tyler • *Tyler Area Commercial Club* • P.O. Box 445; 56178; Lincoln; P 1,253; M 50

Vadnais Heights • *see Saint Paul and White Bear Lake*

Victoria • *see Chaska*

Virginia • *Laurentian C/C* • Jim Currie; Pres./CEO; 403 1st St. North; 55792; St. Louis; P 15,000; M 290; (218) 741-2717; Fax (218) 749-4913; jcurrie@laurentianchamber.org; www.laurentianchamber.org*

Wabasha • *Wabasha-Kellogg Chamber/CVB* • Chris Fancher; Director; 137 W. Main St.; P.O. Box 105; 55981; Wabasha; P 3,200; M 120; (651) 565-4158; (800) 565-4158; Fax (651) 565-2808; info@wabashamn.org; www.wabashamn.org*

Waconia • *Waconia Area C/C* • Kellie Sites; Pres.; 209 S. Vine St.; 55387; Carver; P 10,000; M 200; (952) 442-5812; Fax (952) 856-4476; ksites@destinationwaconia.org; www.destinationwaconia.org*

Wadena • *Wadena Area C/C* • Shirley Uselman; Dir.; 5 Aldrich Ave. S.E.; P.O. Box 107; 56482; Wadena; P 4,292; M 150; (218) 632-7704; (877) 631-7704; Fax (218) 632-7705; wadenachamberofcommerce@charterinternet.com; www.wadena.org*

Walker • *Leech Lake Area C/C* • Jamie Tatge; Pres.; 205 Minnesota Ave.; P.O. Box 1089; 56484; Cass; P 1,100; M 250; (218) 547-1313; (800) 833-1118; Fax (218) 547-1338; walker@eot.com; www.leech-lake.com*

Warren • *Warren C/C* • Mike Williams; 120 E. Bridge Ave.; 56762; Marshall; P 1,675; M 65; (218) 745-4321; Fax (218) 745-5344, www.warrenminnesota.com

Warroad • *Warroad Area C/C & CVB* • Donna LaDuke; Exec. Dir.; P.O. Box 551; 56763; Roseau; P 2,300; M 115; (218) 386-3543; (800) 328-4455; Fax (218) 386-3454; wcoc@wiktel.com; www.warroad.org

Waseca • *Waseca Area C/C* • Kim Foels; Pres.; 111 N. State St.; 56093; Waseca; P 9,827; M 240; (507) 835-3260; (888) 9-WASECA; Fax (507) 835-3267; info@wasecachamber.com; www.wasecachamber.com*

Watertown • *Watertown Area C/C* • Evonne Dennis; Exec. Dir.; P.O. Box 994; 55388; Carver; P 4,000; M 68; (952) 955-5175; secretary@watertown-chamber.com; www.watertown-chamber.com

Waterville • *Waterville Area C/C* • Marlys Meskan; Exec. Secy.; 213 Blowers; 56096; Le Sueur; P 1,800; M 55; (507) 362-4968; (507) 362-4609; lmesk@frontiernet.net; www.watervillemn.com

Waverly • *see Montrose*

Wayzata • *Greater Wayzata Area C/C* • Peggy Douglas; Pres.; 402 E. Lake St.; 55391; Hennepin; P 4,100; M 380; (952) 473-9595; Fax (952) 473-6266; info@wayzatachamber.com; www.wayzatachamber.com*

Wells • *Wells Area C/C* • Jim Heckman; Pres.; 28 S. Broadway; P.O. Box 134; 56097; Faribault; P 2,494; M 80; (507) 553-6450; (866) 553-6450; Fax (507) 553-6451; wellscc@bevcomm.net; www.cityofwells.net*

West Saint Paul • *see Dakota County*

Wheaton • *Wheaton Area C/C* • P.O. Box 493; 56296; Traverse; P 1,619; M 60; (320) 563-4460; www.cityofwheaton.com

White Bear Lake • *White Bear Area C/C* • Jay Geisbauer; Exec. Dir.; 4801 Hwy. 61, Ste. 305; 55110; Ramsey; P 86,000; M 300; (651) 429-8593; Fax (651) 429-8592; info@whitebearchamber.com; www.whitebearchamber.com

White Bear Lake Township • *see White Bear Lake*

Willernie • *see White Bear Lake*

Williams · *see Baudette*

Willmar · *Willmar Lakes Area C/C* · Ken Warner; Pres.; 2104 Hwy. 12 E.; 56201; Kandiyohi; P 20,000; M 510; (320) 235-0300; Fax (320) 231-1948; chamber@willmarareachamber.com; www.willmarareachamber.com*

Windom · *Windom Area C/C & CVB* · Cheryl Hanson; Pres.; 303 9th St.; 56101; Cottonwood; P 5,000; M 175; (507) 831-2752; Fax (507) 831-2755; windomchamber@windomnet.com; www.winwacc.com*

Winnebago · *Winnebago C/C* · Scott Robertson; Pres.; P.O. Box 516; 56098; Faribault; P 1,500; M 40; (507) 893-4600; www.winnebago.govoffice.com

Winona · *Winona Area C/C* · Della Schmidt; Pres.; 67 Main St.; P.O. Box 870; 55987; Winona; P 27,069; M 560; (507) 452-2272; Fax (507) 454-8814; info@winonachamber.com; www.winonachamber.com*

Winsted · *Winsted Area C/C* · Tom Ollig; Pres.; P.O. Box 352; 55395; McLeod; P 2,400; M 75; (320) 485-2351; info@winstedchamber.com; www.winstedchamber.com*

Winthrop · *Winthrop Area C/C* · Doug Hanson; Exec. Secy.; P.O. Box 594; 55396; Sibley; P 1,300; M 85; (507) 647-2627; (800) 647-9461; winthropchamber@hotmail.com

Woodbury · *Woodbury C/C* · Nancy Kennedy; Ofc. Mgr.; 7650 Currell Blvd., Ste. 360; 55125; Washington; P 60,000; M 260; (651) 578-0722; Fax (651) 578-7276; chamber@woodburychamber.org; www.woodburychamber.org*

Worthington · *Worthington Area C/C* · Darlene Macklin; Exec. Dir.; 1121 Third Ave.; 56187; Nobles; P 11,230; M 310; (507) 372-2919; (800) 279-2919; Fax (507) 372-2827; wcofc@frontiernet.net; www.worthingtonmnchamber.com

Zimmerman · *Greater Zimmerman Area C/C* · Deb Kazle; Admin.; 12980 Fremont Ave., Ste. C; 55398; Sherburne; P 10,734; M 106; (763) 856-4404; zimmchamber@izoom.net; www.zimmermanchamber.org*

Mississippi

Mississippi Eco.Cncl. · Blake Wilson; Pres.; P.O. Box 23276; Jackson; 39225; Hinds; P 2,900,000; M 8,000; (601) 969-0022; Fax (601) 353-0247; smaxwell@mec.ms; www.mec.ms

Aberdeen · *Monroe County C/C* · Tony Green; Exec. Dir.; 124 W. Commerce St.; P.O. Box 727; 39730; Monroe; P 38,014; M 300; (662) 369-6488; Fax (662) 369-6489; chamber@gomonroe.org; www.gomonroe.org*

Amory · *Monroe County C/C* · Tony Green; Exec. Dir.; 1619 Hwy. 25 N.; 38821; Monroe; P 38,014; M 300; (662) 256-7194; Fax (662) 256-9671; tony@gomonroe.org; www.gomonroe.org*

Baldwyn · *Baldwyn Mainstreet Chamber* · Lori Tucker; Exec. Dir.; P.O. Box 40; 38824; Prentiss; P 3,600; M 85; (662) 365-1050; Fax (662) 365-3969; www.baldwyn.ms

Batesville · *Panola Partnership Inc.* · Sonny Simmons; CEO; 150A Public Sq.; 38606; Panola; P 34,250; M 300; (662) 563-3126; (888) 872-6652; Fax (662) 563-0704; sonnysimmons@cableone.net; www.panolacounty.com*

Bay Saint Louis · *Hancock County C/C* · Tish Williams; Dir.; 412 Hwy. 90, Ste. 6; 39520; Hancock; P 42,000; M 690; (228) 467-9048; Fax (228) 467-6033; www.hancockchamber.org

Belzoni · *Belzoni-Humphreys Dev. Found.* · Steve Anderson; Exec. Dir.; P.O. Box 145; 39038; Humphreys; P 11,000; M 60; (662) 247-4838; Fax (662) 247-4805; catfish@belzonicable.com; www.belzonims.com

Biloxi · *Biloxi Bay C/C* · Tina Ross-Seamans; Exec. Dir.; P.O. Box 889; 39533; Harrison; P 60,000; M 1,200; (228) 435-6149; info@biloxibaychamber.org; www.biloxibaychamber.org

Bolivar County · *see Cleveland*

Booneville · *Booneville Area C/C* · Rhonda Greening; Exec. Dir.; 100 W. Church St.; P.O. Box 927; 38829; Prentiss; P 9,000; M 200; (662) 728-4130; (800) 300-9302; Fax (662) 728-4134; chamber@boonevillemississippi.com; www.boonevillemississippi.com

Brandon · *Rankin County C/C* · Gale Martin; Exec. Dir.; 101 Service Dr.; P.O. Box 428; 39043; Rankin; P 118,000; M 1,000; (601) 825-2268; Fax (601) 825-1977; information@rankinchamber.com; www.rankinchamber.com*

Brookhaven · *Brookhaven-Lincoln County C/C* · Cliff Brumfield; Exec. V.P.; 230 S. Whitworth Ave.; P.O. Box 978; 39602; Lincoln; P 33,000; M 600; (601) 833-1411; Fax (601) 833-1412; info@brookhavenchamber.com; www.brookhavenchamber.com

Bruce · *Bruce C/C* · #102 Public Sq.; P.O. Box 1013; 38915; Calhoun; P 2,200; M 49; (662) 983-2222; Fax (662) 983-7300; chamber@brucetelephone.com

Burnsville · *Burnsville C/C* · Kim Grisson; Pres.; P.O. Box 211; 38833; Tishomingo; P 1,000; M 40; (662) 427-9526

Byhalia · *Byhalia Area C/C* · Sarah Sawyer; Exec. Dir.; 2452 Church St.; P.O. Box 910; 38611; Marshall; P 36,000; M 300; (662) 838-8127; Fax (662) 838-8128; info@gobyhalia.com; www.gobyhalia.com

Calhoun City · *Calhoun City C/C* · James Franklin; 102 S. Monroe St.; P.O. Box 161; 38916; Calhoun; P 2,000; M 75; (662) 628-6990; Fax (662) 628-8931; www.calhouncity.net

Canton · *Canton C/C Main St. Assoc.* · Lise Foy; Exec. Dir.; 100 Depot Dr.; 39046; Madison; P 12,000; M 200; (601) 859-5816; ccoc@canton-mississippi.com; www.canton-mississippi.com*

Carthage · *Leake County C/C* · Renodda Dorman; Exec. Dir.; 103 N. Pearl St.; P.O. Box 209; 39051; Leake; P 20,940; M 200; (601) 267-9231; Fax (601) 267-8123; director@leakems.com; www.leakems.com

Clarksdale · *Clarksdale-Coahoma County C/C & Ind. Found.* · Ronald E. Hudson; Exec. Dir.; P.O. Box 160; 38614; Coahoma; P 20,000; M 300; (662) 627-7337; Fax (662) 627-1313; chamberofcommerce@clarksdale-ms.com; www.clarksdale-ms.com*

Cleveland · *Cleveland-Bolivar County C/C* · Judson Thigpen III; Exec. Dir.; 600 Third St.; P.O. Box 490; 38732; Bolivar; P 42,000; M 400; (662) 843-2712; Fax (662) 843-2718; judson@clevelandmschamber.com; www.clevelandmschamber.com*

Clinton · *Clinton C/C* · 100 E. Leake; P.O. Box 143; 39060; Hinds; P 25,000; M 570; (601) 924-5912; (800) 611-9980; Fax (601) 925-4009; public-relations@clintonchamber.org; www.clintonchamber.org*

Coffeeville · *Coffeeville Area C/C* · Beverly Freer; Treas.; P.O. Box 184; 38922; Yalobusha; P 1,000; M 20; (662) 675-8385; www.coffeevillems.com

Collins · *Covington County C/C* · Marie Shoemake; Exec. Dir.; 500 Komo St.; P.O. Box 1595; 39428; Covington; P 19,600; M 200; (601) 765-6012; Fax (601) 765-1740; ms@covingtonchamber.com; www.covingtonchamber.com

Columbia · *Marion County Dev. Partnership* · Carolyn Burton; V.P. of Chamber; 412 Courthouse Sq.; P.O. Box 272; 39429; Marion; P 27,000; M 350; (601) 736-6385; Fax (601) 736-6392; info@mcdp.info; www.mcdp.info*

Columbus • *Columbus-Lowndes Dev. Link* • Joe Max Higgins Jr.; CEO; 1102 Main St.; P.O. Box 1328; 39703; Lowndes; P 63,000; M 680; (662) 328-8369; (800) 748-8882; Fax (662) 327-3417; info@cldlink.org; www.cldlink.org.*

Como • *see Batesville*

Corinth • *The Alliance* • Gary Chandler; Pres.; 810 Tate St.; P.O. Box 1089; 38835; Alcorn; P 35,692; M 378; (662) 287-5269; (800) 347-0545; Fax (662) 287-5260; info@corinthalliance.com; www.corinth.ms*

Courtland • *see Batesville*

Crenshaw • *see Batesville*

Crystal Springs • *Crystal Springs C/C* • Donna Y. Wells; Exec. Dir.; 286 E. Railroad Ave.; P.O. Box 519; 39059; Copiah; P 6,005; M 145; (601) 892-2711; Fax (601) 892-4870; crystalsprings chamber@gmail.com

Decatur • *Greater Decatur C/C* • Brenda Harper; Pres.; P.O. Box 474; 39327; Newton; P 1,420; M 60; (601) 635-2761

DeKalb • *Kemper County C/C* • Juanice Evans; Exec. Dir.; 14064 Industrial Park Dr.; P.O. Box 518; 39328; Kemper; P 10,000; M 300; (601) 743-2754; Fax (601) 743-2760; www.kempercounty.com

D'Iberville • *D'Iberville-St. Martin Area C/C* • Sharon Seymour; Exec. Dir.; P.O. Box 6054; 39540; Harrison; P 10,000; M 265; (228) 392-2293; Fax (228) 396-3216; dsmchmbr@datasync.com; www.dsmchamber.com

Drew • *Drew C/C* • 129 Shaw Ave.; 38737; Sunflower; P 2,500; M 90; (662) 745-8975; www.drew-ms.netfirms.com

Flora • *see Ridgeland-Madison County C/C*

Forest • *Forest Area C/C* • Mandi Arinder; Exec. Dir.; 120 S. Davis St.; P.O. Box 266; 39074; Scott; P 6,000; M 200; (601) 469-4332; Fax (601) 469-3224; chamberguide@bellsouth.net; www.forest mschamber.com

Fulton • *Itawamba County Dev. Cncl.* • Greg Deakle; Exec. Dir.; 107 W. Wiygul St.; P.O. Box 577; 38843; Itawamba; P 22,000; M 320; (662) 862-4571; (800) 371-8642; Fax (662) 862-5637; icdc@itawamba.com; www.itawamba.com

Greenville • *Delta Eco. Dev. Center* • Sheree Hobart; Exec. Dir.; 342 Washington Ave., Ste. 101; P.O. Box 933; 38702; Washington; P 72,000; M 600; (662) 378-3141; Fax (662) 378-3143; general info@deltaedc.com; www.greenvilleareachamber.com

Greenwood • *Greenwood-Leflore County C/C* • Beth Stevens; Exec. Dir.; 402 Hwy. 82 W.; P.O. Box 848; 38935; Leflore; P 19,000; M 700; (662) 453-4152; Fax (662) 453-8003; info@greenwoodms.com; www.greenwoodms.com*

Grenada • *Grenada County C/C* • Phillip Heard; Exec. Dir.; P.O. Box 628; 38902; Grenada; P 23,263; M 400; (662) 226-2571; (800) 373-2571; Fax (662) 226-9745; www.grenadamississippi.com

Gulfport • *Mississippi Gulf Coast C/C* • Kimberly Nastasi; Exec. V.P./CEO; 11975 Seaway Rd., Ste. B-120; 39503; Harrison; P 141,000; M 1,100; (228) 604-0014; Fax (228) 604-0105; info@mscoastchamber.com; www.mscoastchamber.com

Hattiesburg • *Area Dev. Partnership* • Angie Godwin; Pres.; One Convention Center Plaza; 39401; Lamar; P 138,932; M 1,500; (601) 296-7500; (800) 238-HATT; Fax (601) 296-7505; adp@theadp.com; www.theadp.com

Hazlehurst • *Hazlehurst Area C/C* • Randall Day; Exec. Dir.; P.O. Box 446; 39083; Copiah; P 4,500; M 100; (601) 894-3752; Fax (601) 894-3752; hazlechamber@bellsouth.net

Hernando • *Hernando Main Street Chamber of Commerce* • Angie Hick; Exec. Dir.; 2440 Hwy. 51 S.; 38632; DeSoto; P 15,000; M 400; (662) 429-9055; Fax (662) 429-2909; chamber@hernando ms.org; www.hernandoms.org*

Holly Springs • *Holly Springs C/C* • Amy S. Heaton; Exec. Dir.; 148 E. College Ave.; 38635; Marshall; P 8,000; M 200; (662) 252-2943; Fax (662) 252-2934; director@hschamber.org; www.hschamber.org

Horn Lake • *Horn Lake C/C* • Larry Witherspoon; Exec. Dir.; 3010 Goodman Rd. W., Ste. B; 38637; DeSoto; P 25,000; M 310; (662) 393-9897; Fax (662) 393-2942; info@hornlakechamber.com; www.hornlakechamber.com

Houston • *Chickasaw Dev. Found.* • Joyce East; Exec. Dir.; 635 Starkville Rd.; 38851; Chickasaw; P 19,000; M 160; (662) 456-2321

Indianola • *Indianola C/C* • Jennifer P. Carithers; Exec. Dir.; 112 S. MLK Dr.; P.O. Box 151; 38751; Sunflower; P 13,500; M 250; (662) 887-4454; Fax (662) 887-4454; icoc@tecinfo.com; www.indianolams.org

Inverness • *Inverness C/C* • Beth Evans; P.O. Box 13; 38753; Sunflower; P 1,153; M 105; (662) 265-6060; (662) 265-5741; bethevans@in-ms.org; www.in-ms.org

Jackson • *Greater Jackson Chamber Partnership* • Duane O'Neill; Pres./CEO; 201 S. President St.; P.O. Box 22548; 39225; Hinds; P 512,000; M 2,200; (601) 948-7575; Fax (601) 352-5539; doneill@greaterjacksonpartnership.com; www.greaterjackson partnership.com*

Laurel • *Jones County C/C* • Larkin Simpson; Dir.; P.O. Box 527; 39441; Jones; P 64,958; M 450; (601) 649-3031; Fax (601) 428-2047; info@edajones.com; www.jonescounty.com; www.jonescounty.com.*

Leland • *Leland C/C* • Robert Neill; Exec. Dir.; 206 Broad St.; P.O. Box 67; 38756; Washington; P 5,000; M 100; (662) 686-2687; Fax (662) 686-2689; lcoc@tecinfo.com; www.lelandms.org

Lexington • *Holmes County C/C* • Jean Carson; Exec. Dir.; 104 W. China St., Ste. A; 39095; Holmes; P 21,609; M 75; (662) 834-3372; Fax (662) 834-4544

Liberty • *Liberty Area C/C* • Cheryl Blalock; Secy./Treas.; P.O. Box 18; 39645; Amite; P 700; M 50; (601) 657-8051

Long Beach • *see Gulfport*

Louisville • *Louisville-Winston County C/C* • Linda Skelton; Dir.; 311 W. Park St.; P.O. Box 551; 39339; Winston; P 20,160; M 200; (662) 773-3921; Fax (662) 773-8909; linda@winstoncounty.com; www.winstoncounty.com*

Lucedale • *George County Eco. Dev. Found. & C/C* • Mike Smith; Pres.; 116 Beaver Dam Rd.; P.O. Box 441; 39452; George; P 23,000; M 105; (601) 947-2755; Fax (601) 947-2650; georgecountyedf@bellsouth.net

Lyman • *see Gulfport*

Macon • *Noxubee County C/C & Eco. Dev. Ofc.* • Jim Robbins; 503 S. Washington St.; P.O. Box 308; 39341; Noxubee; P 12,548; M 100; (662) 726-4456; (800) 487-0165; Fax (662) 726-1041; noxubeecountychamber@yahoo.com

Madison • *Madison C/C* • Rosie Vassallo; Exec. Dir.; 2023 Main St.; P.O. Box 544; 39130; Madison; P 27,000; M 800; (601) 856-7060; Fax (601) 856-4852; info@madisonthecitychamber.com; www.madisonthecitychamber.com*

Magee • *Magee C/C* • Beulah Stephens; Dir.; 117 N.W. 1st Ave.; 39111; Simpson; P 5,000; M 200; (601) 849-2517; Fax (601) 849-2517; commercechamber@bellsouth.net

Magnolia • *South Pike Area C/C* • Sherri O'Brian; Secy.; 180 S. Cherry; 39652; Pike; P 2,071; M 45; (601) 783-5267; (601) 783-0550

McComb • *Pike County C/C & Eco. Dev. Dist.* • J. Britt Herrin; Exec. Dir.; 112 N. Railroad Blvd.; P.O. Box 83; 39648; Pike; P 38,000; M 450; (601) 684-2291; Fax (601) 684-4899; pcedd@ pikeinfo.com; www.pikeinfo.com

Meadville • *Franklin C/C* • Brad Jones; Pres.; 36 Main St.; P.O. Box 400; 39653; Franklin; P 9,000; M 200; (601) 384-2305; www.franklincountyms.com

Mendenhall • *Mendenhall Area C/C* • Marsha Bratcher; Secy.; P.O. Box 635; 39114; Simpson; P 2,555; M 125; (601) 847-1725

Meridian • *East Mississippi Bus. Dev. Corp.* • Wade Jones; Pres.; 1901 Front St., Ste. A; P.O. Box 790; 39302; Lauderdale; P 78,000; M 700; (601) 693-1306; Fax (601) 693-5638; info@embdc.org; www.embdc.org

Monticello • *Lawrence County C/C* • Bob Smira; Pres./CEO; 517 Broad St. E.; P.O. Box 996; 39654; Lawrence; P 13,000; M 80; (601) 587-3007; Fax (601) 587-0765; bsmira@lccda.org; www.lccda.org

Moorhead • *Moorhead C/C* • Byron Wright; V.P.; P.O. Box 177; 38761; Sunflower; P 3,500; M 22; (662) 207-0084; bryonsr@ hotmail.com

Morton • *Morton C/C* • Brenda M. McCaughn; Exec. Dir.; P.O. Box 530; 39117; Scott; P 3,500; M 100; (601) 732-6135; Fax (601) 732-7188; www.cityofmorton.com

Natchez • *Natchez-Adams County C/C* • Debbie Hudson; Pres./CEO; 211 Main St., Ste. A; P.O. Box 1403; 39121; Adams; P 35,000; M 350; (601) 445-4611; Fax (601) 445-9361; natchezchamber@ natchezchamber.com; www.natchezchamber.com

Newton • *Newton C/C* • Kay Crenshaw; Pres.; P.O. Box 301; 39345; Newton; P 4,000; M 150; (601) 683-2201; Fax (601) 683-2201; chambernewton@bellsouth.net; www.newtonmschamber.com

Ocean Springs • *Ocean Springs C/C* • Margaret Miller; Exec. Dir.; 1000 Washington Ave.; 39564; Jackson; P 18,000; M 600; (228) 875-4424; Fax (228) 875-0332; mail@oceanspringschamber.com; www.oceanspringschamber.com

Okolona • *Okolona Area C/C-Main Street Program* • Linda M. Carnathan; Dir.; 219 Main St.; P.O. Box 446; 38860; Chickasaw; P 3,056; M 150; (662) 447-5913; Fax (662) 447-0254; linda@ okolona.org; www.okolonams.org

Olive Branch • *Olive Branch C/C* • Vickie DuPree; Exec. Dir.; 9123 Pigeon Roost; P.O. Box 608; 38654; DeSoto; P 34,000; M 500; (662) 895-2600; Fax (662) 895-2625; vickie.dupree@olivebranchms. com; www.olivebranchms.com.*

Orange Grove • *see Gulfport*

Oxford • *Oxford-Lafayette County C/C* • Max D. Hipp CEcD; Pres./CEO; P.O. Box 147; 38655; Lafayette; P 50,000; M 500; (662) 234-4651; Fax (662) 234-4655; frontdesk@oxfordms.com; www. oxfordms.com

Pascagoula • *Jackson County C/C* • Carla Todd IOM; Pres./CEO; 720 Krebs Ave.; P.O. Box 480; 39568; Jackson; P 137,200; M 850; (228) 762-3391; Fax (228) 769-1726; chamber@jcchamber.com; www.jcchamber.com.*

Pass Christian • *see Gulfport*

Pearl • *Pearl C/C* • Kathy Deer; Exec. Dir.; 110 George Wallace Dr.; P.O. Box 54125; 39288; Rankin; P 27,000; M 350; (601) 939-3338; Fax (601) 936-5717; kathy@pearlms.org; www.pearlms.org

Petal • *Petal Area C/C* • Deborah Reynolds; Pres.; 712 S. Main St., Ste. B; P.O. Box 421; 39465; Forrest; P 10,000; M 250; (601) 583-3306; Fax (601) 583-3312; dacofc@aol.com; www.petalchamber.com

Philadelphia • *Community Dev. Partnership* • David Vowell; Pres.; 256 W. Beacon St.; P.O. Box 330; 39350; Neshoba; P 30,000; M 220; (601) 656-1000; (877) 752-2643; Fax (601) 656-1066; info@neshoba.org; www.neshoba.org

Picayune • *Greater Picayune Area C/C* • Pres.; 201 Hwy. 11 N.; P.O. Box 448; 39466; Pearl River; P 15,000; M 465; (601) 798-3122; Fax (601) 798-6984; chambercommerce1@bellsouth.net; www. picayunechamber.org

Pontotoc • *Pontotoc County C/C* • Cecilia Derrington; Exec. Dir.; 109 N. Main; P.O. Box 530; 38863; Pontotoc; P 28,581; M 200; (662) 489-5042; Fax (662) 489-5263; chamber@pontotocchamber. com; www.pontotocchamber.com

Pope • *see Batesville*

Poplarville • *Poplarville C/C* • Peggy Smith; Secy./Treas.; P.O. Box 367; 39470; Pearl River; P 3,000; M 100; (601) 795-0578; Fax (601) 795-0578; poplarvillechamber@gmail.com; www. poplarville.org

Port Gibson • *Port Gibson-Claiborne County C/C* • Judith Scruggs; Exec. Dir.; 1601 Church St.; P.O. Box 491; 39150; Claiborne; P 11,831; M 60; (601) 437-4351; portgibson_cofc@ bellsouth.net; www.portgibsononthemississippi.com

Prentiss • *Jefferson Davis County C/C* • Missy Chain; Secy.; P.O. Box 1797; 39474; Jefferson Davis; P 1,400; M 100; (601) 792-5142; Fax (601) 792-5190

Quitman • *Clarke County C/C* • 100 S. Railroad Ave.; P.O. Box 172; 39355; Clarke; P 17,900; M 75; (601) 776-5701; Fax (601) 776-5745; clarkechamber@att.net; www.clarkecountychamber.com

Raymond • *Raymond C/C* • John Barber; Exec. Dir.; P.O. Box 1162; 39154; Hinds; P 4,000; M 75; (601) 857-8942; www. raymondchamber.com

Ridgeland • *City of Ridgeland C/C* • Linda T. Bynum; Exec. Dir.; 754 S. Pear Orchard Rd.; P.O. Box 194; 39158; Madison; P 26,000; M 950; (601) 991-9996; Fax (601) 991-9997; admin@ridgeland chamber.com; www.ridgelandchamber.com*

Ridgeland • *Madison County C/C* • Dianne Dyar; Exec. Dir.; 618 Crescent Blvd., Ste. 101; 39157; Madison; P 72,000; M 450; (601) 605-2554; Fax (601) 605-2260; info@madisoncountychamber. com; www.madisoncountychamber.com

Ruleville • *Ruleville C/C* • Thelma Johnson; Pres.; 200 N. Front Ave.; P.O. Box 552; 38771; Sunflower; P 3,500; M 75; (662) 402-0727; (662) 756-2249; Fax (662) 756-0187; jofroth@cableone.net

Sardis • *Sardis-Sardis Lake C/C* • Patty Carter; Exec. Secy.; P.O. Box 377; 38666; Panola; P 2,250; M 75; (662) 487-3451; Fax (662) 487-3389; www.sardislake.com

Senatobia • *Tate County C/C, Eco. Dev. Found. & Main Street* • J.E. Mortimer; Exec. Dir.; 135 N. Front St.; 38668; Tate; P 27,000; M 260; (662) 562-8715; Fax (662) 562-5786; jemortimer@cityof senatobia.com; www.cityofsenatobia.com; www.tate-county.com

Southaven • *Southaven C/C* • Ginger Adams; Exec. Dir.; 8700 Northwest Dr.; P.O. Box 211; 38671; DeSoto; P 40,000; M 600; (662) 342-6114; (800) 272-6551; Fax (662) 342-6365; info@ southavenchamber.com; www.southavenchamber.com

Starkville • *Greater Starkville Dev. Partnership/Chamber* • Allison Matthews; V.P. of Mbrshp. Dev.; 200 E. Main St.; 39759; Oktibbeha; P 38,375; M 387; (662) 323-3322; Fax (662) 323-5815; info@starkville.org; www.starkville.org*

Tunica • *Tunica County C/C* • Lyn Arnold; Pres./CEO; 1301 Main St.; P.O. Box 1888; 38676; Tunica; P 10,930; M 323; (662) 363-2865; Fax (662) 357-0378; larnold@tunicachamber.com; www. tunicachamber.com

Tupelo • *Comm. Dev. Found.* • David Rumbarger; Pres./CEO; 300 W. Main St.; P.O. Box A; 38802; Lee; P 40,000; M 1,400; (662) 842-4521; Fax (662) 841-0693; info@cdfms.org; www.cdfms.org

Tylertown • *Walthall County C/C* • Jewel Magee; Pres.; P.O. Box 227; 39667; Walthall; P 15,380; M 172; (601) 876-2680; Fax (601) 876-2680; walthallchamber@bellsouth.net; www.walthall countychamber.org

Union • *Union C/C* • John C. Knoop; Exec. Dir.; P.O. Box 90; 39365; Newton; P 2,193; M 143; (601) 774-9586; (601) 575-5190; Fax (601) 774-9586; unioncommerce@bellsouth.net; www.union chamberofcommerce.net

Vicksburg • *Vicksburg-Warren County C/C* • Christi Kilroy; Exec. Dir.; 2020 Mission 66; 39180; Warren; P 50,000; M 400; (601) 636-1012; Fax (601) 636-4422; info@vicksburgchamber.org; www. vicksburgchamber.org

Water Valley • *Water Valley Area C/C* • Bonnie Cox; Ofc. Mgr.; P.O. Box 726; 38965; Yalobusha; P 3,500; M 75; (662) 473-9443; Fax (662) 473-1477; wvchamber@bellsouth.net; www.water valleychamber.info*

Waynesboro • *Wayne County C/C* • Shirley Yates; Pres.; 707-A Azalea Dr.; P.O. Box 864; 39367; Wayne; P 20,000; M 100; (601) 735-3311; sassy56@starband.net; www.waynesboroinfo.com

Wesson • *Wesson C/C* • Clara Crow; V.P.; P.O. Box 557; 39191; Copiah; P 1,693; M 75; (601) 643-5000; Fax (601) 643-5000

Winston County • *see Louisville*

Yazoo City • *Yazoo County C/C* • Henry Cote; Exec. Dir.; 212 E. Broadway; P.O. Box 172; 39194; Yazoo; P 28,000; M 175; (662) 746-1273; Fax (662) 746-7238; ccyazoo@bellsouth.net; www. yazoochamber.org

Missouri

Missouri C of C & Ind. • Daniel P. Mehan; Pres./CEO; 428 E. Capitol Ave.; P.O. Box 149; Jefferson City; 65102; Cole; P 6,000,000; M 2,864; (573) 634-3511; Fax (573) 634-8855; dmehan@ mochamber.com; www.mochamber.com.

Affton • *Affton C/C* • Joan Edleson; Exec. Dir.; 10203 Gravois Rd.; 63123; St. Louis; P 40,000; M 320; (314) 849-6499; info@ afftonchamber.com; www.afftonchamber.com*

Albany • *Albany C/C* • Connie Worden; Pres.; 106 E. Clay St.; 64402; Gentry; P 2,000; M 55; (660) 726-3935; ecodev@albanymo. net; www.albanymo.net*

Anderson • *see Pineville*

Arnold • *Arnold C/C* • Troy Hardin; Pres.; 1838 Old Lemay Ferry Rd.; 63010; Jefferson; P 20,000; M 320; (636) 296-1910; kelly@ arnoldchamber.org; www.arnoldchamber.org*

Augusta • *Greater Augusta C/C* • Robin White; Pres.; P.O. Box 31; 63332; St. Charles; P 216; M 55; (636) 228-4005; Fax (636) 228-0000; anchormillinn@msn.com; www.augusta-chamber.org

Aurora • *Aurora C/C* • Shannon Walker; Exec. Dir.; 121 E. Olive; P.O. Box 257; 65605; Lawrence; P 7,400; M 185; (417) 678-4150; Fax (417) 678-1387; auroracoc@mo-net.com; www.aurora mochamber.com

Ava • *Ava Area C/C* • Judy Shields; Exec. Dir.; 810 S.W. 13th Ave.; P.O. Box 1103; 65608; Douglas; P 13,500; M 144; (417) 683-4594; Fax (417) 683-9464; director@avachamber.org; www.avachamber.org

Ballwin • *see Ellisville*

Belton • *Belton C/C* • Kay Stanbarger; Coord.; 323 Main St.; P.O. Box 350; 64012; Cass; P 25,000; M 300; (816) 331-2420; Fax (816) 331-8736; chamber@beltonmochamber.com; www.beltonmo chamber.com

Bethany • *Bethany Area C/C* • Jeff Nichols; Pres.; 116 N. 16th St.; 64424; Harrison; P 5,000; M 82; (660) 425-6358; bchamber@ grm.net; www.bethanyareachamber.com

Blue Springs • *Blue Springs C/C* • Lara Vermillion; Pres.; 1000 W. Main St.; 64015; Jackson; P 55,000; M 400; (816) 229-8558; Fax (816) 229-1244; info@bluespringschamber.com; www. bluespringschamber.com.*

Bolivar • *Bolivar Area C/C* • Diana Leslie; Exec. Dir.; 454 S. Springfield Ave.; P.O. Box 202; 65613; Polk; P 10,700; M 215; (417) 326-4118; Fax (417) 777-9080; bolchamb@windstream.net; www. bolivarchamber.com

Bonne Terre • *Bonne Terre C/C* • Nancy Dill; Exec. Dir.; 522 Benham St.; P.O. Box 175; 63628; St. Francois; P 5,000; M 200; (573) 358-4000; Fax (573) 358-0071; btchamberofcommerce@ yahoo.com; www.bonneterrechamber.com

Boonville • *Boonville Area C/C* • Kim Krajicek-Alberts; Exec. Dir.; 320 First St., Ste. A; 65233; Cooper; P 8,202; M 300; (660) 882-2721; Fax (660) 882-5660; cc.director@yahoo.com; www. boonvillemochamber.com

Bowling Green • *Bowling Green C/C* • Christine Rutherford; Pres.; 16A W. Church St.; P.O. Box 401; 63334; Pike; P 3,500; M 75; (573) 324-3733; bgmocc@att.net; www.bgchamber.org

Branson • *Branson/Lakes Area C/C* • Ross Summers; Pres./ CEO; 269 State Hwy. 248; P.O. Box 1897; 65615; Taney; P 35,000; M 1,000; (417) 334-4084; (800) 214-3661; Fax (417) 334-4139; info@bransoncvb.com; www.explorebranson.com*

Braymer • *Braymer C/C* • MaryLou Tuck; Secy./Treas.; 2nd & Main St.; 64624; Caldwell; P 900; M 50; (660) 645-2802

Breckenridge Hills • *see Bridgeton*

Brentwood • *Brentwood C/C* • Christine Albrecht; Secy.; 8754 Rosalie Ave.; 63144; St. Louis; P 7,400; M 150; (314) 963-9007; chamber@brentwoodmo.org; www.brentwoodmochamber.com

Bridgeton • *Northwest C/C* • Larry Perney; Exec. Dir.; 11965 St. Charles Rock Rd., Ste. 203; 63044; St. Louis; P 90,000; M 300; (314) 291-2131; Fax (314) 291-2153; tina@northwestchamber. com; www.northwestchamber.com*

Brookfield • *Brookfield Area C/C* • Fran Graff; Dir.; 101 S. Main St.; 64628; Linn; P 4,888; M 160; (660) 258-7255; Fax (660) 258-7255; chamber@brookfieldmochamber.com; www.brookfield mochamber.com

Brunswick • *Brunswick Area C/C* • Colleen Johnson; Secy.; P.O. Box 104; 65236; Chariton; P 925; M 54; (660) 548-3171; (660) 548-3028; info@brunswickmo.com; www.brunswickmo.com

Buckner • *Buckner C/C* • Patrick Farrell; Pres.; P.O. Box 325; 64016; Jackson; P 2,725; M 50; (816) 650-5535; sibleyorchards@ hotmail.com

Buffalo • *Buffalo Area C/C* • Kathy Kesler; Exec. Dir.; 101 N. Maple; P.O. Box 258; 65622; Dallas; P 2,781; M 100; (417) 345-2852; Fax (417) 345-2852; chamber@buffalococ.com; www.buffalococ.com

Butler • *Butler C/C* • Kelli Schapeler; Bd. Pres.; 7 W. Dakota; 64730; Bates; P 5,000; M 176; (660) 679-3380; (660) 679-3155; office@butlermochamber.org; www.butlermochamber.org

Cabool • *Cabool Area C/C* • Debbi Lemon; Dir.; P.O. Box 285; 65689; Texas; P 2,006; M 82; (417) 962-3002; Fax (417) 962-3002; chamber@caboolchamber.com; www.caboolchamber.com

California · *California Area C/C* · Ruth Ellis; Exec. Secy.; P.O. Box 85; 65018; Moniteau; P 4,200; M 120; (573) 796-3040; Fax (573) 796-8309; office@calmo.com; www.calmo.com

Camdenton · *Camdenton Area C/C* · Bruce Mitchell; Exec. Dir.; 739 W. U.S. Hwy. 54; P.O. Box 1375; 65020; Camden; P 15,000; M 460; (573) 346-2227; (800) 769-1004; Fax (573) 346-3496; info@camdentonchamber.com; www.camdentonchamber.com

Cameron · *Cameron Area C/C* · Michelle Fagerstone; Exec. Dir.; 205 N. Main St.; 64429; Clinton & DeKalb; P 9,788; M 170; (816) 632-2005; Fax (816) 632-2005; office@cameronmochamber.com; www.cameronmochamber.com*

Canton · *Canton C/C* · Mark Fryer; Pres.; P.O. Box 141; 63435; Lewis; P 2,600; M 75; (573) 288-8300

Cape Fair · *Cape Fair C/C* · Chuck Mills; P.O. Box 104; 65624; Stone; P 600; M 45; (417) 538-2222; info@capefairchamber.com; www.capefairchamber.com

Cape Girardeau · *Cape Girardeau Area C/C* · John E. Mehner; Pres./CEO; 1267 N. Mount Auburn Rd.; 63701; Cape Girardeau; P 75,000; M 1,300; (573) 335-3312; Fax (573) 335-4686; info@capechamber.com; www.capechamber.com*

Carl Junction · *Carl Junction Area C/C* · Gary Stubblefield; Pres.; P.O. Box 301; 64834; Jasper; P 6,200; M 60; (417) 385-7645; cjacc@carljunctioncc.com; www.carljunctioncc.com

Carrollton · *Carrollton C/C* · Sharon Metz; Exec. Dir.; 111 N. Mason; 64633; Carroll; P 4,100; M 150; (660) 542-0922; Fax (660) 542-3489; director@carrolltonareachamber.org; www.carrolltonareachamber.org

Carthage · *Carthage C/C* · Sabrina Drackert; Pres./Dir. of Eco. Dev.; 402 S. Garrison Ave.; 64836; Jasper; P 13,800; M 365; (417) 358-2373; Fax (417) 358-7479; sdrackert@carthagechamber.com; www.carthagechamber.com*

Caruthersville · *Caruthersville C/C* · Bobby Culler; Pres.; 200 W. 3rd; P.O. Box 806; 63830; Pemiscot; P 6,760; M 200; (573) 333-1222; Fax (573) 333-4586; chamber@caruthersvillecity.com; www.caruthersvillecity.com

Cassville · *Cassville Area C/C* · Mindi Artherton; Exec. Dir.; 504 Main St.; 65625; Barry; P 3,000; M 210; (417) 847-2814; chamber@cassville.com; www.cassville.com*

Centralia · *Centralia C/C* · Ginny Zoellers; Exec. Dir.; 101 W. Singleton; P.O. Box 235; 65240; Boone; P 3,800; M 91; (573) 682-2272; Fax (573) 682-1111; ginny@midamerica.net; www.centraliamochamber.com

Chaffee · *Chaffee C/C* · Jennifer Lynn; Pres.; P.O. Box 35; 63740; Scott; P 3,500; M 60; (573) 887-3558; information@chaffeechamber.com; www.chaffeechamber.spicecat.com

Charlack · *see Bridgeton*

Charleston · *Charleston C/C* · Claudia Arington; Exec. Dir.; 110 E. Commercial St.; P.O. Box 407; 63834; Mississippi; P 4,600; M 190; (573) 683-6509; Fax (573) 683-6799; chamber@charlestonmo.org; www.charlestonmo.org

Chesterfield · *Chesterfield C/C* · Joan Schmelig; Pres.; 101 Chesterfield Business Pkwy.; 63005; St. Louis; P 48,602; M 925; (636) 532-3399; (888) 242-4262; Fax (636) 532-7446; joan@chesterfieldmochamber.com; www.chesterfieldmochamber.com.*

Chillicothe · *Chillicothe Area C/C* · Lindy Chapman; Exec. Dir.; 514 Washington St.; P.O. Box 407; 64601; Livingston; P 10,000; M 300; (660) 646-4050; (877) 224-4554; Fax (660) 646-3309; chamber@chillicothemo.com; www.chillicothemo.com*

Clarksville · *Clarksville C/C* · Shirley Underwood; Pres.; 111 Howard St.; 63336; Pike; P 490; M 25; (573) 242-3336; (573) 242-3994; Fax (573) 242-3450; www.clarksvillemo.us

Clayton · *Clayton C/C* · Ellen Gale; Exec. Dir.; 225 S. Meramec Ave., Ste. 300; 63105; St. Louis; P 13,000; M 450; (314) 726-3033; Fax (314) 726-0637; ccc@claytoncommerce.com; www.claytoncommerce.com*

Clinton · *Clinton Area C/C* · Debby VanWinkle; Dir.; 200 S. Main St.; 64735; Henry; P 9,500; M 375; (660) 885-8166; (800) 222-5251; Fax (660) 885-8168; debby@clintonmo.com; www.clintonmo.com.*

Cole Camp · *Cole Camp C/C* · Storm Walker; Pres.; P.O. Box 94; 65325; Benton; P 1,100; M 90; (660) 668-2295; chamber@colecampmo.com; www.colecampmo.com

Columbia · *Columbia C/C* · Donald M. Laird; Pres.; 300 S. Providence Rd.; P.O. Box 1016; 65205; Boone; P 150,000; M 1,300; (573) 874-1132; Fax (573) 443-3986; dlaird@columbiamochamber.com; www.columbiamochamber.com.*

Concord · *see South County*

Concordia · *Concordia Area C/C* · Cara Harris; Exec. Dir.; 802 S. Gordon; P.O. Box 143; 64020; Lafayette; P 2,360; M 100; (660) 463-2454; Fax (660) 463-2845; concordiachamber@centurytel.net; www.concordiamo.com

Crane · *Crane C/C* · Terry Burpo; P.O. Box 287; 65633; Stone; P 1,250; M 40; (417) 723-0031; cranechamber@aol.com; www.cranemo.com

Crestwood · *Crestwood-Sunset Hills Area C/C* · Mary Ann McWilliams; Exec. Dir.; 9058-A Watson; 63126; St. Louis; P 20,000; M 240; (314) 843-8545; Fax (314) 843-8526; info@ourchamber.com; www.ourchamber.com*

Creve Coeur · *Creve Coeur-Olivette C/C* · Nancy M. Gray; Exec. V.P.; 10950 Olive Blvd., Ste. 101; 63141; St. Louis; P 20,000; M 300; (314) 569-3536; Fax (314) 569-3073; info@ccochamber.com; www.ccochamber.com

Crocker · *Crocker Comm. C/C* · Dot Gilstrap; Pres.; P.O. Box 833; 65452; Pulaski; P 1,077; M 35; (573) 736-5922; Fax (573) 736-5922

Crystal City · *see Festus*

Cuba · *Cuba Area C/C & Visitor Center* · Norma Bretz; Secy.; 71 Hwy. P; P.O. Box 405; 65453; Crawford; P 3,500; M 195; (573) 885-2531; (877) 212-8429; Fax (573) 885-0988; cuba@misn.com; www.cubamochamber.com

Dardenne Prairie · *Lake Saint Louis-Dardenne Prairie Area C/C* · Gena Breyne; Pres./CEO; 2032 Hanley Rd., Ste. 113; 63368; St. Charles; P 19,884; M 210; (636) 755-5335; info@lsldpchamber.com; www.lsldpchamber.com*

De Soto · *De Soto C/C* · Julie Craig; Ofc. Coord.; 412 S. Main St.; 63020; Jefferson; P 6,700; M 125; (636) 586-5591; Fax (636) 586-5591; chamber@desotomo.com; chamber.desotomo.com

Des Peres · *see Kirkwood*

Desloge · *Desloge C/C* · Betty Coale; Pres.; 200 N. Lincoln; 63601; St. Francois; P 4,802; M 50; (573) 431-3006; deslogechamber@sbcglobal.net; www.deslogechamberofcommerce.com*

Dexter · *Dexter C/C* · Janet Coleman; Exec. Dir.; 515 W. Market; P.O. Box 21; 63841; Stoddard; P 13,000; M 285; (573) 624-7458; (800) 332-8857; Fax (573) 624-7459; info@dexterchamber.com; www.dexterchamber.com

Doniphan · *Ripley County C/C* · Jason Seter; Pres.; 209 W. Hwy. St.; P.O. Box 718; 63935; Ripley; P 13,781; M 138; (573) 996-2212; Fax (573) 351-1441; rcchamber@windstream.net; www.ripleycountymissouri.org*

Earth City • *see Bridgeton*

East Prairie • *East Prairie C/C* • Bryan Mainord; Pres.; 106 S. Washington; 63845; Mississippi; P 3,713; M 100; (573) 649-5243; Fax (573) 649-2024; mc_rsvp@yahoo.com; www.eastprairiemo.net

Edgerton • *Edgerton C/C* • Staley Snook; Treas.; 503 Aller Ave.; P.O. Box 62; 64444; Platte; P 544; M 32; (816) 790-3325

Edina • *Edina C/C* • Amy Miller; P.O. Box 124; 63537; Knox; P 1,200; M 35; www.knoxcountychamber.org

Edmundson • *see Bridgeton*

El Dorado Springs • *El Dorado Springs C/C* • Tiffany McGuirk; Exec. Dir.; 1303 S. Hwy. 32; 64744; Cedar; P 4,000; M 125; (417) 876-4154; Fax (417) 876-4154; info@eldomo-cofc.org; www.eldomo-cofc.org

Eldon • *Eldon Area C/C* • 203 E. First St.; P.O. Box 209; 65026; Miller; P 5,000; M 250; (573) 392-3752; Fax (573) 392-0634; www.eldonchamber.com*

Ellington • *Ellington C/C* • David Burns; Pres.; P.O. Box 515; 63638; Reynolds; P 1,000; M 55; (573) 663-7997; chamber@ellingtonmo.com; www.ellingtonmo.com

Ellisville • *West St. Louis County C/C* • Lori Kelling; Exec. Dir.; 15965 Manchester Rd., Ste. 102; 63011; St. Louis; P 200,000; M 384; (636) 230-9900; Fax (636) 230-9912; info@westcountychamber.com; www.westcountychamber.com*

Elsberry • *Elsberry C/C* • Rita Eggers; Pres.; P.O. Box 32; 63343; Lincoln; P 2,400; M 40; (573) 898-9124; secretary@elsberrycofc.org; www.elsberrycofc.org

Elvins • *see Park Hills*

Eminence • *Eminence Area C/C* • Carol Chrisco; P.O. Box 415; 65466; Shannon; P 600; M 135; (573) 226-3318; chamber@eminencemo.com; www.eminencemo.com

Esther • *see Park Hills*

Eureka • *Eureka C/C* • Tracie Bibb; Pres.; 22 Dreyer Ave.; 63025; St. Louis; P 9,500; M 360; (636) 938-6062; Fax (636) 938-5202; execdirector@eurekachamber.us; www.eurekachamber.org*

Excelsior Springs • *Excelsior Springs Area C/C* • Terry Smelcer; Exec. Dir.; 461 S. Thompson Ave.; P.O. Box 632; 64024; Clay; P 20,000; M 230; (816) 630-6161; (816) 630-7500; Fax (816) 630-7500; escoc@sbcglobal.net; www.exspgschamber.com

Fair Grove • *Fair Grove Area C/C* • Renee Bradford; Pres.; P.O. Box 91; 65648; Greene; P 1,107; M 62; (417) 759-2807; info@fairgrove.org; www.fairgrove.org

Farmington • *Farmington C/C* • Douglas McDermott; Exec. Dir.; 302 N. Washington St.; P.O. Box 191; 63640; St. Francois; P 16,000; M 300; (573) 756-3615; Fax (573) 756-1003; chamber@farmingtonmo.org; www.farmingtonmo.org*

Fayette • *Fayette Area C/C* • Kurt Himmelmann; Pres.; P.O. Box 414; 65248; Howard; P 4,000; M 50; (660) 248-2235; info@fayettemochamber.com; www.fayettemochamber.org

Fenton • *Fenton Area C/C* • Jeannie Braun; Exec. Dir.; 964 S. Hwy. Dr., Ste. 103; 63026; St. Louis; P 64,000; M 450; (636) 717-0200; Fax (636) 717-0214; exdir@fentonmochamber.com; www.fentonmochamber.com*

Festus • *Twin City Area C/C* • Claudia Kirn; Admin.; 114 E. Main St.; 63028; Jefferson; P 20,000; M 360; (636) 931-7697; (636) 931-7697; Fax (636) 937-0925; twincity.chamber@sbcglobal.net; www.twincity.org.*

Flat River • *see Park Hills*

Florissant • *Greater North County C/C* • Diana Weidinger; Pres.; 420 W. Washington St.; 63031; St. Louis; P 140,000; M 500; (314) 831-3500; Fax (314) 831-9682; info@greaternorthcountychamber.com; www.greaternorthcountychamber.com.*

Forsyth • *Forsyth C/C* • Donna Bassett; Exec. Dir.; 16075 U.S. Hwy. 160; P.O. Box 777; 65653; Taney; P 1,600; M 135; (417) 546-2741; Fax (417) 546-4192; forsyth.chamber@yahoo.com; www.forsythmissouri.org*

Fredericktown • *Madison County C/C* • Sandy Francis; Exec. Dir.; 120 W. Main; 63645; Madison; P 15,728; M 100; (573) 783-2604; Fax (573) 783-2645; chamberdirector@fredericktownmissouri.net; www.fredericktownmissouri.net*

Frontenac • *see Town & Country*

Fulton • *Kingdom of Callaway C/C* • Nancy Lewis; Exec. Dir.; 409 Court St.; 65251; Callaway; P 42,086; M 325; (573) 642-3055; (800) 257-3554; Fax (573) 642-5182; cocommerce@sbcglobal.net; www.callawaychamber.com.

Gainesville • *Ozark County C/C* • Lynn Bentele; Pres.; P.O. Box 605; 65655; Ozark; P 10,000; M 95; (417) 679-4913; ozcocofc@yahoo.com; www.ozarkcounty.net

Gerald • *Gerald Area C/C* • Pat Holland; P.O. Box 274; 63037; Franklin; P 1,300; M 105; (573) 764-4627; geraldcc@fidnet.com; www.fidnet.com/~geraldcc

Gladstone • *Gladstone Area C/C* • Amy Harlin; Pres.; 6913 N. Cherry St.; 64118; Clay; P 28,000; M 420; (816) 436-4523; Fax (816) 436-4352; info@gladstonechamber.com; www.gladstonechamber.com*

Glasgow • *Glasgow C/C* • Dr. Steve Jones; Pres.; P.O. Box 192; 65254; Howard; P 1,300; M 50; (660) 338-2300; www.glasgowmo.com

Grain Valley • *Grain Valley C/C* • Jen Morgan; Chamber Admin.; 513 Main St.; P.O. Box 195; 64029; Jackson; P 15,000; M 130; (816) 847-2627; Fax (816) 847-2555; gvc@grainvalleychamber.org; www.grainvalleychamber.org*

Grandview • *Grandview Area C/C* • Kim Curtis; Pres.; 12500 S. 71 Hwy., Ste. 100; 64030; Jackson; P 25,500; M 280; (816) 761-6505; Fax (816) 763-8460; ksc@grandview.org; www.grandview.org*

Grant City • *Grant City C/C* • Amber Monticue; Secy./Treas.; P.O. Box 134; 64456; Worth; P 1,000; M 25; (660) 564-4000

Green City • *Green City C/C* • Doug Kelly; Pres.; 17643 Hwy. YY; 63545; Sullivan; P 700; M 20; (660) 874-5048

Greenfield • *Greenfield C/C* • Perry Lewis; Pres.; P.O. Box 63; 65661; Dade; P 1,500; M 80; (417) 637-2040; mamalowe@hotmail.com; www.greenfieldmochamber.com

Hannibal • *Hannibal Area C/C* • Terry R. Sampson; Exec. Dir.; 623 Broadway; P.O. Box 230; 63401; Marion & Ralls; P 17,757; M 400; (573) 221-1101; Fax (573) 221-3389; info@hannibalchamber.org; www.hannibalchamber.org*

Harrisonville • *Harrisonville Area C/C* • Cherry Mickelson; Exec. Dir.; 2819 Cantrell Rd.; 64701; Cass; P 8,900; M 215; (816) 380-5271; (866) 380-5271; Fax (816) 884-4291; info@harrisonvillechamber.com; www.harrisonvillechamber.com*

Hazelwood • *see Bridgeton*

Hermann • *Hermann Area C/C* • June Diebal; Mgr.; 312 Market St.; 65041; Gasconade; P 2,700; M 199; (573) 486-2313; Fax (573) 486-3066; hermannchamber@centurytel.net; www.visithermann.com

Higginsville · *Higginsville C/C* · Teri Ray; Exec. Dir.; 1813 N. Main St.; P.O. Box 164; 64037; Lafayette; P 4,682; M 200; (660) 584-3030; Fax (660) 584-3033; chamber@ctcis.net; www.higginsvillechamber.org*

High Ridge · *Northwest Jefferson County C/C* · Susan Tuggle; Pres.; P.O. Box 371; 63049; Jefferson; P 50,000; M 130; (636) 671-8010; nwjcounty@sbcglobal.net; www.nwchamberweb.org

Hillsboro · *Greater Hillsboro C/C* · Mandy Alley; Admin.; P.O. Box 225; 63050; Jefferson; P 2,000; M 75; (636) 789-4920; Fax (636) 789-4920; chamberoffice@sbcglobal.net; www.hillsboromo.org

Holden · *Holden C/C* · Linda Frazier; Pres.; 100 E. 2nd; 64040; Johnson; P 2,500; M 67; (816) 732-6844; info@holdenchamber.org; www.holdenchamber.com

Hollister · *Hollister Area C/C* · P.O. Box 674; 65673; Taney; P 3,867; M 190; (417) 334-3050; Fax (417) 334-5501; info@hollisterchamber.net; www.hollisterchamber.net*

Houston · *Houston Area C/C* · Sharon Horbyk; Dir.; 501 E. Walnut; P.O. Box 374; 65483; Texas; P 4,636; M 185; (417) 967-2220; (417) 967-2178; Fax (417) 967-2178; chamberdirector@centurytel.net; www.houstonmochamber.com

Humansville · *Humansville C/C* · Mike Strowls; Pres.; P.O. Box 195; 65674; Polk; P 1,000; M 60; (417) 754-2501; www.humansville.net

Independence · *Independence C/C* · Rick Hemmingsen; Pres.; 210 W. Truman Rd.; P.O. Box 1077; 64051; Jackson; P 113,000; M 700; (816) 252-4745; Fax (816) 252-4917; rhemmingsen@independencechamber.org; www.independencechamber.org*

Ironton · *Arcadia Valley C/C* · Judy Schaaf-Wheeler; Pres.; 630-21 Hwy.; P.O. Box 343; 63650; Iron; P 3,500; M 100; (573) 546-7117; Fax (573) 546-7019; www.arcadiavalley.biz

Jackson · *Jackson C/C* · Brian Gerau; Exec. Dir.; 125 E. Main; P.O. Box 352; 63755; Cape Girardeau; P 11,947; M 450; (573) 243-8131; (888) 501-8827; Fax (573) 243-0725; director@jacksonmochamber.org; www.jacksonmochamber.org*

Jamesport · *Jamesport Comm. Assn.* · Joe Burkholder; P.O. Box 215; 64648; Daviess; P 505; M 50; (660) 684-6146; (660) 684-6704; jamesportmo@yahoo.com; www.jamesportmissouri.org

Jefferson City · *Jefferson City Area C/C* · Randall Allen; Pres./CEO; 213 Adams St.; P.O. Box 776; 65102-0776; Cole; P 50,000; M 960; (573) 634-3616; Fax (573) 634-3805; info@jcchamber.org; www.jeffersoncitychamber.org.*

Joplin · *Joplin Area C/C* · Rob O'Brian CEcD; Pres.; 320 E. 4th St.; 64801; Jasper; P 50,000; M 11,001,050; (417) 624-4150; Fax (417) 624-4303; info@joplincc.com; www.joplincc.com*

Kahoka · *Kahoka/Clark County C/C* · Beverly Laffoon; Pres.; 250 N. Morgan St.; 63445; Clark; P 8,000; M 76; (660) 727-3143; Fax (660) 727-3750

Kansas City Area

Black C/C of Greater Kansas City Inc. · Chuck Bert; Pres.; 1501 E. 18th St.; 64108; Jackson; P 640,000; M 540; (816) 474-9901; Fax (816) 842-1748; info@bcckc.org; www.bcckc.org

Greater Kansas City C/C · Dick Gibson; CAO; 911 Main St., Ste. 2600; 64105; Jackson; P 1,800,000; M 8,000; (816) 221-2424; Fax (816) 221-7440; chamber@kcchamber.com; www.kcchamber.com

Northeast Kansas City C/C · Rebecca Koop; Exec. Dir.; 6400 Independence Ave.; P.O. Box 240392; 64124; Jackson; P 40,000; M 107; (816) 231-3312; Fax (816) 231-2101; nekcchamber@aol.com; www.nekcchamber.com

Northland Reg. C/C · Sheila Tracy; Pres.; 634 N.W. Englewood Rd.; 64118; Clay & Platte; P 296,000; M 800; (816) 455-9911; Fax (816) 455-9933; northland@northlandchamber.com; www.northlandchamber.com*

South Kansas City C/C · Vickie Wolgast; Pres.; 406 E. Bannister Rd., Ste. F; 64131; Jackson; P 80,000; M 250; (816) 761-7660; Fax (816) 761-7340; vwolgast@southkcchamber.com; www.southkcchamber.com*

Kearney · *Kearney C/C* · Siouxsan Eisen; Exec. Dir.; P.O. Box 242; 64060; Clay; P 8,700; M 240; (816) 628-4229; Fax (816) 902-1234; info@kearneychamber.org; Z*

Kennett · *Kennett C/C* · Jan McElwrath; Exec. Dir.; 1601 First St.; P.O. Box 61; 63857; Dunklin; P 12,000; M 400; (573) 888-5828; (866) 848-5828; Fax (573) 888-9802; info@kennettmo.com; www.kennettmo.com

Kimberling City · *Table Rock Lake Area C/C* · Kim Steed; Interim Pres.; 14226 Hwy. 13; P.O. Box 495; 65686; Stone; P 20,000; M 320; (417) 739-2564; www.visittablerocklake.com*

Kirksville · *Kirksville Area C/C* · Sandra Williams; Exec. Dir.; 304 S. Franklin; P.O. Box 251; 63501; Adair; P 17,304; M 355; (660) 665-3766; Fax (660) 665-3767; kvacoc@cableone.net; www.kirksvillechamber.com*

Kirkwood · *Kirkwood-Des Peres Area C/C* · Jim Wright; Pres./CEO; 108 W. Adams; 63122; St. Louis; P 50,000; M 670; (314) 821-4161; Fax (314) 821-5229; info@thechamber.us; www.kirkwooddesperes.com.*

LaGrange · *LaGrange C/C* · Ken Schuetz; Pres.; P.O. Box 67; 63448; Lewis; P 1,000; M 70; (573) 655-2297; www.cityoflagrangemo.gov

Lake Ozark · *Lake Area C/C* · Trisha Creach; Exec. Dir.; 1 Willmore Ln.; P.O. Box 1570; 65049; Miller; P 5,300; M 950; (573) 964-1008; (800) 451-4117; Fax (573) 964-1010; info@lakeareachamber.com; www.lakeareachamber.com

Lamar · *Barton County C/C* · Nancy Curless; Exec. Dir.; 102 W. 10th St.; P.O. Box 577; 64759; Barton; P 12,600; M 200; (417) 682-3595; Fax (417) 682-9566; nancy@bartoncounty.com; www.bartoncounty.com*

Lebanon · *Lebanon Area C/C* · Debbie Wikowsky; Exec. Dir.; 186 N. Adams; P.O. Box 505; 65536; Laclede; P 14,000; M 431; (417) 588-3256; (888) 588-5710; Fax (417) 588-3251; stephanie@lebanonmissouri.com; www.lebanonmissouri.com*

Lee's Summit · *Lee's Summit C/C* · Nancy K. Bruns; Pres.; 220 S.E. Main; 64063; Jackson; P 92,000; M 950; (816) 524-2424; Fax (816) 524-5246; lscoc@lschamber.com; www.lschamber.com*

Lexington · *Lexington Area C/C* · Harrison Hook; 1029 Franklin Ave.; 64067; Lafayette; P 5,000; M 200; (660) 259-3082; Fax (660) 259-7776; chamberdirector@historiclexington.com; www.historiclexington.com

Liberty · *Liberty Area C/C* · Gayle Potter; Pres.; 9 S. Leonard St.; 64068; Clay; P 30,000; M 410; (816) 781-5200; Fax (816) 781-4901; info@libertychamber.com; www.libertychamber.com.*

Licking · *Licking C/C* · Kyle Smith; Pres.; P.O. Box 89; 65542; Texas; P 3,000; M 50; (573) 674-2510; Fax (573) 674-2914

Lincoln · *Lincoln C/C* · Janice Swearngin; V.P.; P.O. Box 246; 65338; Benton; P 1,100; M 40; (660) 547-2718; (877) 947-9954; www.lincolnmissouri.com

Louisiana · *Louisiana C/C* · 202 S. 3rd, Ste. 120; 63353; Pike; P 4,000; M 112; (573) 754-5921; Fax (573) 754-5921; lamochamber@sbcglobal.net; www.louisiana-mo.com

Macon • *Macon Area C/C* • Sharon Scott; Exec. Dir.; 119 N. Rollins St.; 63552; Macon; P 2,900; M 220; (660) 385-2811; Fax (660) 385-6543; director@maconmochamber.com; www.maconmo chamber.com.

Malden • *Malden C/C* • Denton Kooyman; Pres.; 607 N. Douglass; 63863; Dunklin; P 4,782; M 105; (573) 276-4519; Fax (573) 276-4925; info@maldenchamber.com; www.maldenchamber.com

Manchester • *see Ellisville*

Mansfield • *Mansfield Area C/C* • Sheri Alsup; Pres.; P.O. Box 322; 65704; Wright; P 2,500; M 70; (417) 924-3525; mansfield cofc@gmail.com; www.mansfieldchamber.com

Maplewood • *Maplewood C/C* • Jeannine Beck; Exec. Dir.; 2915 Sutton Blvd.; 63143; St. Louis; P 10,000; M 140; (314) 781-8588; Fax (314) 781-5397; info@maplewood-chamber.com; www.maplewood-chamber.com*

Marceline • *Marceline C/C* • Darrell Gardner; Pres.; P.O. Box 93; 64658; Chariton & Linn; P 2,500; M 50; (660) 376-2332; www.marceline.com

Marshall • *Marshall C/C* • Ken Yowell; Exec. Dir.; 214 N. Lafayette; 65340; Saline; P 14,000; M 202; (660) 886-3324; Fax (660) 831-0349; ken@marshallchamber.com; www.marshall chamber.com*

Marshfield • *Marshfield Area C/C & Tourist Info. Center* • Pam Cook; Exec. Secy.; 1350 Spur Dr., Ste. 190; 65706; Webster; P 7,200; M 165; (417) 859-3925; Fax (417) 468-3944; mfldcoc@fidnet.com; www.marshfieldmochamberofcommerce.com

Marthasville • *Marthasville Area C/C* • Larry Shroth; Pres.; P.O. Box 95; 63357; Warren; P 2,000; M 90; (636) 433-5242; rrichard son@marthasvillecoc.net; www.marthasvillemo.net

Maryland Heights • *Maryland Heights C/C* • Kim Braddy; Dir.; 547 West Port Plaza; St. Louis; 63146; St. Louis; P 26,000; M 450; (314) 576-6603; Fax (314) 576-6855; www.mhcc.com*

Maryville • *Greater Maryville C/C* • Luke Reven; Exec. Dir.; 423 N. Market; 64468; Nodaway; P 22,099; M 250; (660) 582-8643; (660) 582-8850; chamber@asde.net; www.maryvillechamber.com*

Maysville • *Maysville C/C* • 701 E. Main St.; P.O. Box 521; 64469; DeKalb; P 1,200; M 40; (816) 449-2062

Mehlville • *see South County*

Mexico • *Mexico Area C/C* • Dana Keller; Exec. Dir.; 100 W. Jackson St.; 65265; Audrain; P 12,500; M 400; (573) 581-2765; (800) 581-2765; Fax (573) 581-6226; dkeller@mexico-chamber.org; www.mexico-chamber.org.*

Moberly • *Moberly Area C/C* • Deborah Dean-Miller; Exec. Dir.; 211 W. Reed St.; 65270; Randolph; P 27,000; M 245; (660) 263-6070; Fax (660) 263-9443; chamber@moberly.com; www.moberlychamber.com

Monett • *Monett C/C* • Suzy McElmurry; Exec. Dir.; 200 E. Broadway; P.O. Box 47; 65708; Barry & Lawrence; P 8,000; M 250; (417) 235-7919; Fax (417) 235-4076; chamber@monett-mo.com; www.monett-mo.com

Monroe City • *Mark Twain Lake C/C* • Doug Smith; Pres.; P.O. Box 182; 63456; Monroe & Ralls; P 20,000; M 35; (573) 565-2228; mtlcoc@socket.net; www.visitmarktwainlake.org

Monroe City • *Monroe City Area C/C* • Mandy Shortridge; Pres.; 314 S. Main St.; P.O. Box 22; 63456; Marion, Monroe & Ralls; P 2,588; M 90; (573) 735-4391; mcchamber@centurytel.net; www.monroecitymo.com

Montgomery City • *Montgomery City Area C/C* • Steven Deves; City Admin.; P.O. Box 31; 63361; Montgomery; P 2,400; M 100; (573) 564-2712; Fax (573) 564-3802; mcchamber1@yahoo.com; www.montgomerycitymo.org

Mount Vernon • *Mount Vernon C/C* • Doris McBride; Exec. Secy.; 425 E. Mt. Vernon Blvd.; P.O. Box 373; 65712; Lawrence; P 5,020; M 220; (417) 466-7654; Fax (417) 466-7654; mtvchamber@mchsi.com; www.mtvernonchamber.com

Mountain Grove • *Mountain Grove C/C* • Mary Armstrong; Exec. Dir.; 205 W. 3rd, Ste. 8; P.O. Box 434; 65711; Wright; P 4,500; M 200; (417) 926-4135; Fax (417) 926-5440; chamber@mountain grovechamber.com; www.mountaingrovechamber.com

Mountain View • *Mountain View C/C* • Daniel Conklin; Exec. Dir.; P.O. Box 24; 65548; Howell; P 2,400; M 218; (417) 934-2794; Fax (417) 934-2882; mvcoc@centurytel.net; www.mountain viewmo.com

Neosho • *Neosho Area C/C* • Shana Griffin; Exec. Dir.; 216 W. Spring; P.O. Box 605; 64850; Newton; P 10,505; M 400; (417) 451-1925; Fax (417) 451-8097; director@neoshocc.com; www.neoshocc.com

Nevada • *Nevada-Vernon County C/C & Tourism Dept.* • Cat McGrath-Farmer; Exec. Dir.; 225 W. Austin, Ste. 200; 64772; Vernon; P 20,000; M 260; (417) 667-5300; Fax (417) 667-3492; chamber1@nevada-mo.com; www.nevada-mo.com*

New Haven • *New Haven Area C/C* • Linda Faretta; P.O. Box 201; 63068; Franklin; P 2,000; M 100; (573) 237-3830; info@newhavenmo.com; www.newhavenmo.com

New Madrid • *New Madrid C/C* • Christina McWaters; Dir.; 537 Mott St.; P.O. Box 96; 63869; New Madrid; P 3,340; M 120; (573) 748-5300; (877) 748-5300; Fax (573) 748-5402; chambernm@yahoo.com; www.new-madrid.mo.us

New Melle • *New Melle C/C* • Harry Kishpaugh; Pres.; P.O. Box 212; 63365; St. Charles; P 300; M 100; (636) 828-5600; www.newmelle.org

Nixa • *Nixa Area C/C* • Sharon Whitehill Gray; Pres./CEO; 105 Sherman Way, Ste. 108-110; 65714; Christian; P 18,000; M 464; (417) 725-1545; Fax (417) 725-4532; info@nixachamber.com; www.nixachamber.com*

Oak Grove • *Oak Grove C/C* • Donna Minnick; Exec. Dir.; 1212 Broadway, Ste. B; P.O. Box 586; 64075; Jackson; P 6,000; M 70; (816) 690-4147; Fax (816) 690-4147; oakgrovechamber@yahoo.com; oakgrovechamber.biz

Oakland • *see Kirkwood*

Oakville • *see South County*

Odessa • *Odessa C/C* • Kate Gosoroski; Exec. Dir.; 309A Park Ln.; 64076; Lafayette; P 5,000; M 78; (816) 633-4044; Fax (816) 633-4044; odessacoc@embarqmail.com; www.odessamochamber.com

O'Fallon • *O'Fallon C/C* • Erin Williams; Pres./CEO; 1299 Bryan Rd.; 63366; St. Charles; P 70,000; M 485; (636) 240-1818; info@ofallonchamber.org; www.ofallonchamber.org*

Olivette • *see Creve Coeur*

Oran • *Oran C/C* • Ed Evans; P.O. Box 49; 63771; Scott; P 1,284; M 17; (573) 262-3942

Osceola • *Osceola Comm. C/C* • Ron Hogan; Pres.; P.O. Box 422; 64776; St. Clair; P 834; M 50; (417) 646-2727; rhogan@osceola mochamber.com; www.osceolamochamber.com

Overland • *see Bridgeton*

Owensville · *Owensville C/C* · Bob Neibruegge; Exec. Dir.; P.O. Box 77; 65066; Gasconade; P 2,500; M 125; (573) 437-4270; Fax (573) 437-4270; chamber1@fidnet.com; www.owensvillemissouri.com

Ozark · *Ozark Area C/C* · Dori Grinder; Exec. Dir.; 191 N. 18th St.; P.O. Box 1450; 65721; Christian; P 10,200; M 260; (417) 581-6139; Fax (417) 581-0639; info@ozarkmissouri.com; www.ozark chamber.com*

Pacific · *Pacific C/C* · Bill McLaren; Pres.; 333 Chamber Dr.; 63069; Franklin; P 7,500; M 190; (636) 271-6639; Fax (636) 257-2109; exdir@pacificchamber.com; www.pacificchamber.com*

Palmyra · *Palmyra C/C* · Ginny Kuntemeyer; Pres.; 411 S. Main; P.O. Box 446; 63461; Marion; P 3,500; M 75; (573) 769-0777; palmyrachamber@centurytel.net; www.showmepalmyra.com

Paris · *Paris Area C/C* · Vanessa Forrest; Exec. Dir.; 208 N. Main St.; 65275; Monroe; P 1,500; M 67; (660) 327-4450; Fax (660) 327-1376; chamber@parismo.net; www.parismo.net

Park Hills · *Park Hills-Leadington C/C* · Tamara Burns; Exec. Dir.; #5 Municipal Dr.; 63601; St. Francois; P 9,000; M 150; (573) 431-1051; Fax (573) 431-2327; phlcoc@sbcglobal.net; www. phlcoc.net

Peculiar · *Peculiar Area C/C* · Kim Duey; Pres.; P.O. Box 669; 64078; Cass; P 6,000; M 72; (816) 758-6900; peculiarchamber@ gmail.com; www.peculiarchamber.com

Perryville · *Perryville Area C/C* · Melissa Hemmann; Exec. Dir.; 2 W. Ste. Maries St.; 63775; Perry; P 7,667; M 420; (573) 547-6062; Fax (573) 547-6071; perryvillemo@sbcglobal.net; www. perryvillemo.com.

Piedmont · *Piedmont Area C/C* · Robert Gayle; Pres.; 215 S. Main St.; P.O. Box 101; 63957; Wayne; P 3,000; M 120; (573) 223-4046; Fax (573) 223-4046; contact@piedmontchamber.com; www.piedmontchamber.com

Pineville · *McDonald County C/C* · Colleen Epperson-Hollman; Exec. Dir.; P.O. Box 593; 64856; McDonald; P 27,000; M 250; (417) 223-8888; Fax (417) 223-8889; info@mcdonaldcountychamber. org; www.mcdonaldcountychamber.org

Platte City · *Platte City Area C/C & Eco. Dev. Cncl.* · Karen Wagoner; Exec. Dir.; 620 3rd St.; P.O. Box 650; 64079; Platte; P 9,000; M 259; (816) 858-5270; chamber@plattecitymo.com; www.plattecitymo.com*

Plattsburg · *Plattsburg C/C* · Wade Wilken Jr.; Pres.; P.O. Box 134; 64477; Clinton; P 2,500; M 80; (816) 539-2649; (816) 539-2148; Fax (816) 539-3530; chamber@plattsburgmo.com; www. plattsburgmo.com

Poplar Bluff · *Greater Poplar Bluff Area C/C* · Steve Halter; Pres.; 1111 W. Pine St.; 63901; Butler; P 17,000; M 720; (573) 785-7761; Fax (573) 785-1901; info@poplarbluffchamber.org; www. poplarbluffchamber.org*

Portageville · *Portageville C/C* · Sandy Stewart; Pres.; 301 E. Main; P.O. Box 409; 63873; New Madrid & Pemiscot; P 3,295; M 130; (573) 379-5789; Fax (573) 379-3080; pvillechall@ sbcglobal.net

Potosi · *Washington County & Potosi C/C* · Kris Richards; Pres.; 501 E. High St.; P.O. Box 404; 63664; Washington; P 2,700; M 75; (573) 438-4517; Fax (573) 438-3676; www.potosichamber.com

Raymore · *Raymore C/C* · Cherie Turney; Ofc. Mgr.; 1000 W. Foxwood Dr.; P.O. Box 885; 64083; Cass; P 20,000; M 175; (816) 322-0599; Fax (816) 322-7127; info@raymorechamber.com; www.raymorechamber.com*

Raytown · *Raytown Area C/C* · Vicki Turnbow; Pres.; 5909 Raytown Trafficway; 64133; Jackson; P 31,000; M 300; (816) 353-8500; Fax (816) 353-8525; staff@raytownchamber.com; www. raytownchamber.com

Republic · *Republic Area C/C* · Julie Messick; Exec. Dir.; 113 W. Hwy. 174; 65738; Greene; P 14,000; M 200; (417) 732-5200; Fax (417) 732-2851; director@republicchamber.com; www.republic chamber.com*

Rich Hill · *Rich Hill C/C* · Randy Bell; Pres.; P.O. Box 165; 64779; Bates; P 1,461; M 40; (417) 395-2275; www.richhillmo.com

Richmond · *Richmond C/C* · Ellen Franklin; Exec. Dir.; 104 W. North Main; 64085; Ray; P 6,116; M 192; (816) 776-6916; Fax (816) 776-6917; cofcommerce@mchsi.com; www.richmondchamber.org*

Richmond Heights · *Richmond Heights C/C* · Tino DiFranco; Pres.; 7960 Clayton Rd.; 63117; St. Louis; P 10,000; M 50; (314) 781-0282; ytrop@aol.com; www.richmondheights.org

Rivermines · *see Park Hills*

Riverside · *Riverside Area C/C* · Cynthia Rice; Exec. Dir.; P.O. Box 9074; 64168; Platte; P 3,000; M 170; (816) 746-1577; riverside chamber@msn.com; www.riversidemochamber.com

Rock Port · *Rock Port C/C* · P.O. Box 134; 64482; Atchison; P 1,300; M 45; (660) 744-6562

Rogersville · *Rogersville Area C/C* · Gwen Mackey; Ofc. Admin.; 107 E. Center St.; P.O. Box 77; 65742; Christian, Greene & Webster; P 40,000; M 130; (417) 753-7538; Fax (417) 753-2606; rogersville coc@sbcglobal.net; www.rogersvillechamber.com

Rolla · *Rolla Area C/C* · Stevie Kearse; Exec. Dir.; 1311 Kingshighway; 65401; Phelps; P 18,000; M 500; (573) 364-3577; Fax (573) 364-5222; stevie@rollachamber.org; www.rollachamber.org*

Saint Ann · *see Bridgeton*

Saint Charles · *Saint Charles C/C* · Scott Tate; Pres./CEO; 2201 First Capitol Dr.; 63301; Saint Charles; P 66,000; M 600; (636) 946-0633; Fax (636) 946-0301; info@stcharleschamber.org; www.stcharleschamber.org.*

Saint Clair · *St. Clair Area C/C* · 920 Plaza Dr., Suite F; 63077; Frankin; P 15,000; M 125; (636) 629-1889; Fax (636) 629-5510; chamber@stclairmo.com; www.stclairmo.com*

Saint James · *Saint James C/C* · Dan Cavender; Pres.; 111 S. Jefferson; P.O. Box 358; 65559; Phelps; P 3,900; M 178; (573) 265-6649; Fax (573) 265-6650; info@stjameschamber.net; www. stjameschamber.net

Saint Johns · *see Bridgeton*

Saint Joseph · *St. Joseph Area C/C* · Ted Allison; Pres./CEO; 3003 Frederick Ave.; 64506; Buchanan; P 76,107; M 975; (816) 232-4461; Fax (816) 364-4873; chamber@saintjoseph.com; www.saintjoseph.com.*

Saint Louis · *Lemay C/C* · Barbara Hehmeyer; Exec. Dir.; P.O. Box 6642; 63125; St. Louis; P 20,000; M 250; (314) 631-2796; Fax (314) 638-9500; lemaychamber@sbcglobal.net; www. lemaychamber.com*

Saint Louis · *St. Louis Reg. Chamber & Growth Assn.* · Richard C.D. Fleming; Pres./CEO; One Metropolitan Square, Ste. 1300; 63102; P 2,803,000; M 4,000; (314) 231-5555; Fax (314) 444-1122; inforcga@stlrcga.org; www.stlrcga.org.

Saint Mary · *Saint Mary C/C* · Bob Bartels; Pres.; P.O. Box 38; 63673; St. Genevieve; P 377; M 16; (573) 543-2230

Saint Peters • *Saint Peters C/C* • Ed Weeks; Pres./CEO; 1236 Jungermann Rd., Ste. C; 63376; St. Charles; P 57,000; M 600; (636) 447-3336; Fax (636) 447-9575; info@stpeterschamber.com; www.stpeterschamber.com*

Salem • *Salem Area C/C* • Genie Zakrzewski; Dir.; 200 S. Main St.; 65560; Dent; P 5,000; M 200; (573) 729-6900; Fax (573) 729-6741; chamber@salemmo.com; www.salemmo.com

Salisbury • *Salisbury Area C/C* • Judy Fehling; Pres.; P.O. Box 5; 65281; Chariton; P 1,800; M 52; (660) 388-6116; salisburymo@yahoo.com; www.c-magic.com/salisbury

Sarcoxie • *Sarcoxie Area C/C* • Johnny Hankins; Pres.; P.O. Box 171; 64862; Jasper; P 1,400; M 97; (417) 548-6130; (417) 548-6390; j_hankins@mo-net.com; www.sarcoxiemo.com

Savannah • *Savannah Area C/C* • Christy Sipes; Coord.; P.O. Box 101; 64485; Andrew; P 5,100; M 135; (816) 324-3976; Fax (816) 324-5728; sacc@gmail.com; www.savannahmochamber.com

Scott City • *Scott City Area C/C* • Chodra Mason; Secy./Treas.; 215 Chester Ave.; 63780; Scott; P 4,600; M 40; (573) 264-2157; scottcitymo.org

Sedalia • *Sedalia Area C/C & Conv. & Visitors Bur.* • 600 E. Third St.; 65301; Pettis; P 22,000; M 300; (660) 826-2222; Fax (660) 826-2223; chamber@sedaliamo.org; www.sedaliachamber.com*

Seligman • *Seligman Greater Area C/C* • David VanPetty; Pres.; P.O. Box 250; 65745; Barry; P 10,000; M 48; (417) 662-3611; info@seligmanchamber.com; www.seligmanchamber.com

Seneca • *Seneca C/C* • Josh Dodson; Pres.; P.O. Box 332; 64865, Newton; P 2,300; M 90; (417) 776-2100; chamberpresident@senecamochamber.com; www.senecamochamber.com

Seymour • *Greater Seymour Area C/C* • Heather Johns; Pres.; P.O. Box 700; 65746; Webster; P 2,200; M 35; (417) 935-9300; april@seymourmochamber.com; www.seymourmochamber.com

Shelbina • *Shelbina C/C* • Thad Requet; Pres.; P.O. Box 646; 63468; Shelby; P 2,000; M 75; (573) 588-1506; thadweekly@centurytel.net; www.cityofshelbina.com

Shell Knob • *Shell Knob C/C* • Sheila House; Exec. Dir.; 25364 State Hwy. 39; P.O. Box 193; 65747; Barry; P 8,000; M 190; (417) 858-3300; Fax (417) 858-9428; info@shellknob.com; www.shellknob.com*

Sikeston • *Sikeston Area C/C* • Missy Marshall; Exec. Dir.; One Industrial Dr.; 63801; New Madrid & Scott; P 30,000; M 500; (573) 471-2498; Fax (573) 471-2499; chamber@sikeston.net; www.sikeston.net

Slater • *Slater C/C* • Cathie Jeffries; Pres.; P.O. Box 24; 65349; Saline; P 2,100; M 50; (660) 529-2271; Fax (660) 529-2593; info@cityofslater.com; www.cityofslater.com

Smithville • *Smithville Area C/C* • Kim Palmer; Exec. Dir.; 105 W. Main; 64089; Clay; P 6,000; M 215; (816) 532-0946; Fax (816) 532-3513; smithvillechamber@sbcglobal.net; www.smithvillechamber.org

South County • *South County C/C* • Donna Abernathy; Exec. Dir.; 6921 S. Lindbergh; St. Louis; 63125; St. Louis; P 140,000; M 380; (314) 894-6800; Fax (314) 894-6888; dascounty@sbcglobal.net; www.southcountychamber.net*

Springfield • *Springfield Area C/C* • James B. Anderson; Pres.; 202 S. John Q. Hammons Pkwy.; P.O. Box 1687; 65801; Greene; P 430,900; M 1,800; (417) 862-5567; Fax (417) 862-1611; info@springfieldchamber.com; www.springfieldchamber.com.*

St. Robert • *Waynesville-St. Robert Area C/C* • Cecilia Murray; Exec. Dir.; 137 St. Robert Blvd., Ste. B; 65584; Pulaski; P 9,087; M 424; (573) 336-5121; Fax (573) 336-5472; info@wsrchamber.com; www.waynesville-strobertchamber.com*

Ste. Genevieve • *Ste. Genevieve C/C* • Dena Kreitler; Exec. Dir.; 251 Market St.; 63670; Ste. Genevieve; P 17,500; M 318; (573) 883-3686; Fax (573) 883-7092; stegenchamber@sbcglobal.net; www.stegenchamber.org

Steele • *Steele C/C* • Debra Adair; Pres.; 101 S. Walnut St.; 63877; Pemiscot; P 2,200; M 50; (573) 695-3690; (573) 695-4732; www.cityofsteele.org

Steelville • *Steelville C/C* • Peggy Cardoni; Pres.; P.O. Box 956; 65565; Crawford; P 1,500; M 87; (573) 775-5533; Fax (573) 775-5521; chamber@misn.com; www.steelville.com

Stockton • *Stockton Area C/C* • Charlotte Haden; Exec. Dir.; P.O. Box 410; 65785; Cedar; P 2,000; M 135; (417) 276-5213; stocktonchamber@windstream.net; www.stocktonmochamber.com

Stover • *Stover C/C* • P.O. Box 370; 65078; Morgan; P 968; M 48; (573) 377-4510; Fax (573) 377-2521

Strafford • *Strafford Area C/C* • Debbie Phillips; Pres.; P.O. Box 21; 65757; Greene; P 3,000; M 60; (417) 759-1175; straffordmissouri@yahoo.com; www.straffordmissouri.org

Sullivan • *Sullivan Area C/C* • Deborah Campbell; Exec. Dir.; 2 W. Springfield Rd.; 63080; Franklin; P 7,000; M 276; (573) 468-3314; Fax (573) 860-2313; chamber@fidnet.com; www.sullivanmochamber.com.*

Summersville • *Summersville C/C* • Jessi Berry; Pres.; P.O. Box 251; 65571; Shannon & Texas; P 544; M 20; (417) 932-5373; Fax (417) 932-4791; catron@hotmail.com; www.summersvillemo.com

Sunrise Beach • *Lake of the Ozarks West C/C* • Mike Kenagy; Exec. Dir.; P.O. Box 340; 65079; Camden & Morgan; P 16,000; M 455; (573) 374-5500; (877) 227-4086; Fax (573) 374-8576; info@lakewestchamber.com; www.lakewestchamber.com*

Sweet Springs • *Sweet Springs C/C* • Tara Brewer; Pres.; P.O. Box 255; 65351; Saline; P 1,700; M 50; (660) 335-6321; Fax (660) 335-4592

Table Rock Lake • *see Kimberling City*

Tarkio • *Tarkio C/C* • Lori Seymour; Pres.; P.O. Box 222; 64491; Atchison; P 1,935; M 75; (660) 736-5772; www.tarkiomo.com

Thayer • *Thayer C/C* • LaRee Rees; Secy.; P.O. Box 14; 65791; Oregon; P 2,300; M 88; (417) 264-7324; www.thayerchamber.com

Theodosia • *Theodosia Area C/C* • Vikki Cook; Pres.; P.O. Box 11; 65761; Ozark & Taney; P 8,000; M 100; (417) 273-4245; theodosiachamber@yahoo.com; www.theodosiaareachamber.com

Tipton • *Tipton C/C* • Dave Bixler; Pres.; P.O. Box 307; 65081; Moniteau; P 3,500; M 85; (660) 433-6377; chamber@tiptonmo.com; www.tiptonmo.com

Town & Country • *Town & Country/Frontenac C/C* • Tammy Wildman Baldanza; Exec. Dir.; 13443 Clayton Rd., Ste. 2; 63131; St. Louis; P 11,000; M 130; (314) 469-3335; tcfchamber@charter.net; www.tcfchamber.com

Trenton • *Trenton Area C/C* • Jordan Ferguson; Pres.; 617 Main St.; 64683; Grundy; P 6,500; M 200; (660) 359-4324; Fax (660) 359-4606; trentonchamber@grundyec.net; www.trentonmochamber.com*

Union • *Union C/C* • Tammy Stowe; Exec. Dir.; 103 S. Oak St.; P.O. Box 168; 63084; Franklin; P 9,000; M 360; (636) 583-8979; Fax (636) 583-4001; director@unionmochamber.org; www.unionmochamber.org

Van Buren • *Van Buren Area C/C* • Wanda Cumins; Pres.; P.O. Box 693; 63965; Carter; P 6,000; M 110; (573) 323-0800; chamber@seevanburen.com; www.seevanburen.com

Vandalia • *Vandalia Area C/C* • Karen Shaw; City Clerk; 200 E. Park St.; 63382; Audrain & Ralls; P 3,963; M 70; (573) 594-6186

Versailles • *Versailles Area C/C* • Mary Henderson; Secy.; 109 N. Monroe; P.O. Box 256; 65084; Morgan; P 2,500; M 125; (573) 378-4401; Fax (573) 378-2499; info@versailleschamber.com; www.versailleschamber.com

Vinita Park • *see Bridgeton*

Warrensburg • *Greater Warrensburg Area C/C & Visitors Center* • Tammy Long; Exec. Dir.; 100 S. Holden St.; 64093; Johnson; P 18,500; M 436; (660) 747-3168; Fax (660) 429-5490; chamber@warrensburg.org; www.warrensburg.org*

Warrenton • *Warrenton Area C/C* • Scott Costello; Pres.; 1000 Outlet Center Dr., Box 32; 63383; Warren; P 6,500; M 200; (636) 456-2542; Fax (636) 456-2329; info@warrentoncoc.com; www.warrentoncoc.com*

Warsaw • *Warsaw Area C/C* • Adrienne Fisher; Exec. V.P.; 818 E. Main St.; P.O. Box 264; 65355; Benton; P 2,000; M 200; (660) 438-5922; Fax (660) 438-3493; info@warsawmo.org; www.warsawmo.org

Warson Woods • *see Kirkwood*

Washington • *Washington Area C/C* • Mark Wessels; Pres./CEO; 323 W. Main St.; 63090; Franklin; P 15,000; M 595; (636) 239-2715; Fax (636) 239-1381; mwessels@washmo.org; www.washmo.org.*

Waynesville • *see St. Robert*

Webb City • *Webb City Area C/C* • Dixie Meredith; Exec. Dir.; 66 W. Broadway; P.O. Box 287; 64870; Jasper; P 12,000; M 215; (417) 673-1154; info@webbcitychamber.com; www.webbcitychamber.com*

Webster Groves • *Webster Groves/Shrewsbury Area C/C* • Diane Lamboley; Pres./CEO; 353 Marshall Ave., Ste. A; 63119; St. Louis; P 30,000; M 300; (314) 962-4142; Fax (314) 962-9398; chamber-info@go-webster.com; www.webstershrewsburychamber.com*

Wentzville • *Wentzville C/C* • Tony Mathews; Pres./Ceo; P.O. Box 11; 63385; St. Charles; P 27,000; M 400; (636) 327-6914; Fax (636) 634-2760; info@wentzvillechamber.com; www.wentzvillechamber.com*

West Plains • *Greater West Plains Area C/C* • Joanne Wix; Exec. Dir.; 401 Jefferson Ave.; 65775; Howell; P 11,000; M 504; (417) 256-4433; Fax (417) 256-8711; info@wpchamber.com; www.wpchamber.com.*

Weston • *Weston C/C* • Bonnie Stewart; Secy. of the Bd.; 526 Main St.; 64098; Platte; P 1,631; M 100; (816) 640-2909; Fax (816) 640-2909; westonmo@kc.rr.com; www.westonmo.com

Westport • *see Maryland Heights*

Wildwood • *see Ellisville*

Willard • *Willard Area C/C* • Jeff Staley; Pres.; P.O. Box 384; 65781; Greene; P 4,500; M 95; (417) 742-2442; willardchamber@yahoo.com; www.willardmochamber.org

Willow Springs • *Willow Springs Area C/C* • Kristin Allen; Exec. Dir.; 112 E. Main St.; 65793; Howell; P 2,400; M 95; (417) 469-5519; Fax (417) 469-3192; wschamber@centurytel.net; www.willowspringsmo.com

Winchester • *see Ellisville*

Windsor • *Windsor Area C/C* • Teresa Pennock; Pres.; 102 N. Main; 65360; Henry; P 3,087; M 115; (660) 647-2318; windsorm@iland.net; www.windsormo.org

Woodson Terrace • *see Bridgeton*

Wright City • *Wright City Area C/C* • Pam Beckham; Pres.; P.O. Box 444; 63390; Warren; P 8,000; M 100; (636) 745-7855; wcchamber@wrightcitychamber.com; www.wrightcitychamber.com

Montana

Montana C of C • Webb Brown; Pres./CEO; P.O. Box 1730; Helena; 59624; Lewis & Clark; P 967,400; M 1,500; (406) 442-2405; Fax (406) 442-2409; leah@montanachamber.com; www.montanachamber.com

Alder • *see Twin Bridges*

Anaconda • *Anaconda C/C* • Edith Fransen; Exec. Dir.; 306 E. Park St.; 59711; Deer Lodge; P 9,400; M 195; (406) 563-2400; Fax (406) 563-2400; anacondachamber@rfwave.net; www.anacondamt.org

Baker • *Baker C of C & Ag.* • Karol Zachmann; Pres.; P.O. Box 849; 59313; Fallon; P 1,850; M 88; (866) 862-2537; (406) 778-3382; www.bakermt.com

Belgrade • *Belgrade C/C* • Debra K. Youngberg; Exec. Dir.; 10 E. Main; 59714; Gallatin; P 16,000; M 335; (406) 388-1616; Fax (406) 388-2090; info@belgradechamber.org; www.belgradechamber.org.*

Big Sandy • *Big Sandy C/C* • Conrad Heimbigner; Pres.; P.O. Box 411; 59520; Chouteau; P 700; M 40; (406) 378-2418; www.bigsandymt.org

Big Sky • *Big Sky C/C* • Marne Hayes; Exec. Dir.; 3091 Pine Dr.; P.O. Box 160100; 59716; Gallatin; P 2,200; M 450; (406) 995-3000; (800) 943-4111; Fax (406) 995-3054; info@bigskychamber.com; www.bigskychamber.com

Big Timber • *Sweet Grass County C/C & Visitor Info. Center* • 1350 Hwy. 10 W.; P.O. Box 1012; 59011; Sweet Grass; P 3,500; M 80; (406) 932-5131; info@bigtimber.com; www.bigtimber.com

Bigfork • *Bigfork Area C/C* • Diane Kautzman; Pres.; 8155 MT Hwy. 35; P.O. Box 237; 59911; Flathead; P 2,000; M 335; (406) 837-5888; Fax (406) 837-5808; chamber@bigfork.org; www.bigfork.org

Billings • *Billings Area C/C* • John Brewer; Pres./CEO; 815 S. 27th St.; P.O. Box 31177; 59107; Yellowstone; P 130,000; M 1,100; (406) 245-4111; Fax (406) 245-7333; info@billingschamber.com; www.billingschamber.com*

Birney • *see Lame Deer*

Bozeman • *Bozeman Area C/C* • Daryl Schliem; Pres./CEO; 2000 Commerce Way; 59715; Gallatin; P 40,000; M 900; (406) 586-5421; info@bozemanchamber.com; www.bozemanchamber.com.

Broadus • *Powder River C/C* • Alice Hinck; P.O. Box 484; 59317; Powder River; P 500; M 54; (406) 436-2778; powderriverchamber@rangeweb.net; www.powderriverchamber.org

Browning • *Browning Area C/C* • Joe Bremner; Chair; P.O. Box 469; 59417; Glacier; P 1,200; M ; (406) 338-2344; (406) 338-4015; info@browningchamber.com; www.browningmontana.com

Busby • *see Lame Deer*

Butte • *Butte-Silver Bow C/C* • Marko Lucich; Exec. Dir.; 1000 George St.; 59701; Silver Bow; P 35,000; M 700; (406) 723-3177; (800) 735-6814; Fax (406) 723-1215; chamber@buttechamber.org; www.buttechamber.org*

Checkerboard • *see White Sulpher Springs*

Chester • *Liberty County C/C* • Lynda Vande Sandt; Coord.; 30 Main St.; P.O. Box 632; 59522; Liberty; P 2,100; M 105; (406) 759-4848; Fax (406) 759-5523; lynda@libertycountycc.com; www.libertycountycc.com

Chinook • *Chinook C/C* • Larry Surber; Pres.; P.O. Box 744; 59523; Blaine; P 1,350; M 90; (406) 357-3459; info@chinookmontana. com; www.chinookmontana.com

Choteau • *Choteau C/C* • Gabrielle Rasmussen & Jennifer French; 815 Main Ave. N.; P.O. Box 897; 59422; Teton; P 1,500; M 100; (406) 466-5316; choteauchamber@choteaumontana.com; www.choteaumontana.com

Circle • *Circle C of C & Ag.* • Julie Howard; Treas.; P.O. Box 321; 59215; McCone; P 2,000; M 60; (406) 485-2741; chamber@ midrivers.com; www.circle-montana.com

Colstrip • *Colstrip C/C* • Cathy Franks; Pres.; P.O. Box 1100; 59323; Rosebud; P 2,000; M 50; www.colstripchamber.com

Columbia Falls • *Columbia Falls Area C/C* • Carol Pike; Exec. Dir.; 233 13th St. E.; P.O. Box 312; 59912; Flathead; P 4,200; M 200; (406) 892-2072; info@columbiafallschamber.org; www.columbiafallschamber.org

Columbus • *Stillwater County C/C* • Charles Sangmeister; Pres.; P.O. Box 783; 59019; Stillwater; P 8,500; M 100; (406) 322-4505; admin@stillwatercountychamber.com; www.stillwatercounty chamber.com

Conrad • *Conrad Area C/C* • Molly Bock; Exec. Secy.; 7 Sixth Ave. S.W.; 59425; Pondera; P 3,500; M 200; (406) 271-7791; Fax (406) 271-2924; chamber@3rivers.net; www.conradmt.com

Cooke City • *Colter Pass, Cooke City, Silver Gate C/C* • Bev Chatelain; Pres.; 109 W. Main; P.O. Box 1071; 59020; Park; P 100; M 45; (406) 838-2495; Fax (406) 838-2495; info@cookecity chamber.org; www.cookecitychamber.org

Culbertson • *Culbertson C/C* • W. Bruce Houle; Pres.; P.O. Box 639; 59218; Roosevelt; P 720; M 40; (406) 787-6643; culbertson mt@hotmail.com; www.culbertsonmt.com

Cut Bank • *Cut Bank Area C/C* • Jeff Billman; P.O. Box 1243; 59427; Glacier; P 3,400; M 120; (406) 873-4041; info@cutbank chamber.com; www.cutbankchamber.com

Deer Lodge • *Powell County C/C* • David Williams; Exec. Dir.; 1109 Main St.; 59722; Powell; P 7,200; M 80; (406) 846-2094; Fax (406) 846-2094; chamber@powellcountymontana.com; www. powellcountymontana.com

Dillon • *Beaverhead C/C* • Melissa Hannah; Exec. Dir.; 10 W. Reeder; P.O. Box 425; 59725; Beaverhead; P 5,000; M 265; (406) 683-5511; Fax (406) 683-9233; info@beaverheadchamber.org; www.beaverheadchamber.org

Drummond • *Drummond C/C* • Mary Ellen McGowan; Pres.; P.O. Box 364; 59832; Granite; P 348; M 20; (406) 288-3297; www.drummondmontana.com

East Glacier Park • *East Glacier C/C* • Terry Sherburne; Pres.; Hwy. 49 N.; P.O. Box 260; 59434; Glacier; P 396; M 20; (406) 226-4403; Fax (406) 226-4403; mtnpine@3rivers.net; www. eastglacierpark.info

Ekalaka • *Carter County C/C* • Rhonda Knapp; Pres.; P.O. Box 108; 59324; Carter; P 1,500; M 30; (406) 775-6886; www.carter countychamberofcommerce.com

Ennis • *Ennis Area C/C* • Pamela Kimmey; Exec. Dir.; P.O. Box 291; 59729; Madison; P 1,000; M 225; (406) 682-4388; Fax (406) 682-4328; info@ennischamber.com; www.ennischamber.com

Eureka • *Eureka Area C/C* • Randy McIntyre; Exec. Dir.; P.O. Box 186; 59917; Lincoln; P 4,000; M 152; (406) 889-4636; randy@ welcome2eureka.com; www.welcome2eureka.com; www. eurekaevents.com

Fairfield • *Fairfield C/C* • Marci Shaw; Pres.; P.O. Box 776; 59436; Teton; P 700; M 76; (406) 467-2493; (406) 590-1042; ffchamber@ hotmail.com

Fairview • *Fairview C/C* • Ray Trumpower; Pres.; P.O. Box 374; 59221; Richland; P 800; M 60; (406) 742-5259; Fax (406) 742-5259; trumpwer@midrivers.com; www.midrivers.com/~fairview

Forsyth • *Forsyth Area C/C & Ag.* • Stephanie Nielson; Pres.; P.O. Box 448; 59327; Rosebud; (406) 347-5656; Fax (406) 346-2492; forsythmontana.org

Fort Benton • *Fort Benton C/C & Info. Center* • Stella Scott; Pres.; P.O. Box 12; 59442; Chouteau; P 1,400; M 60; (406) 622-3864; info@fortbenton.com; www.fortbenton.com

Gardiner • *Gardiner C/C* • Keren Walters; Exec. Dir.; 222 Park St.; P.O. Box 81; 59030; Park; P 851; M 130; (406) 848-7971; Fax (406) 848-2446; info@gardinerchamber.com; www.gardinerchamber.com

Glasgow • *Glasgow Area C/C & Ag.* • Diane Brandt; Exec. Dir.; 23 E. Hwy. 2; P.O. Box 832; 59230; Valley; P 3,500; M 200; (406) 228-2222; Fax (406) 228-2244; chamber@glasgowmt.net; www. glasgowmt.net

Glendive • *Glendive C of C & Ag.* • Kim Trangmoe; Exec. Dir.; 808 N. Merrill; 59330; Dawson; P 5,000; M 265; (406) 377-5601; (800) 859-0824; Fax (406) 377-5602; chamber@midrivers.com; www. glendivechamber.com

Great Falls • *Great Falls Area C/C* • Percy "Steve" Malicott; Pres./ CEO; 100 1st Ave. N.; 59401; Cascade; P 75,000; M 675; (406) 761-4434; Fax (406) 761-6129; Info@greatfallschamber.org; www.greatfallschamber.org*

Hamilton • *Bitterroot Valley C/C* • Rick O'Brien; Exec. Dir.; 105 E. Main St.; 59840; Ravalli; P 40,500; M 600; (406) 363-2400; Fax (406) 363-2402; localinfo@bvchamber.com; www.bitterroot valleychamber.com*

Hardin • *Hardin Area C/C & Ag.* • Dorothy Stenerson; Secy.; 10 E. Railway; P.O. Box 446; 59034; Big Horn; P 5,000; M 80; (406) 665-1672; (406) 665-3577; Fax (406) 665-3577; hardinchamber@ bhwi.net; www.hardinmtchamber.com

Harlowton • *Harlowton Area C/C & Ag.* • Kim Guesanduru; Exec. Dir.; P.O. Box 694; 59036; Wheatland; P 1,000; M 80; (406) 632-4694; chamber@harlowtonchamber.com; www.harlowton chamber.com

Havre • *Havre Area C/C* • Debbie Vandeberg; Exec. Dir.; 130 5th Ave.; P.O. Box 308; 59501; Hill; P 10,000; M 270; (406) 265-4383; Fax (406) 265-7748; chamber@havremt.net; www.havremt.com.*

Helena • *Helena Area C/C* • Cathy Burwell; Pres./CEO; 225 Cruse Ave., Ste. A; 59601; Lewis & Clark; P 45,000; M 850; (406) 442-4120; (800) 743-5362; Fax (406) 447-1532; lhegstad@ helenachamber.com; www.helenachamber.com

Hot Springs • *Hot Springs C/C* • Sandra Prongua; Secy.; P.O. Box 580; 59845; Sanders; P 530; M 60; (406) 741-2662; hscofc@ hotspringsmt.net; www.hotspringsmtchamber.org

Hysham • *Hysham C/C* • Cora Marks; Secy.; P.O. Box 63; 59038; Treasure; P 800; M 25; (406) 342-5457; www.hysham.org

Jordan • *Garfield County C/C & Ag.* • Rocky Nelson; Pres.; 434 Main St.; P.O. Box 370; 59337; Garfield; P 1,600; M 125; (406) 557-6158; Fax same; chamber@garfieldcounty.com; www. garfieldcounty.com

Kalispell • *Kalispell Area C/C* • Joe Unterreiner; Pres./CEO; 15 Depot Park; 59901; Flathead; P 87,000; M 700; (406) 758-2800; Fax (406) 758-2805; info@kalispellchamber.com; www.kalispell chamber.com*

Lakeside • *Lakeside-Somers C/C* • Dave Christensen; Pres.; P.O. Box 177; 59922; Flathead; P 3,500; M 150; (406) 844-3715; info@lakesidesomers.org; www.lakesidesomers.org

Lame Deer • *Lame Deer C/C* • Suzanne Trusler; Pres.; P.O. Box 991; 59043; Rosebud; P 3,000; M 15; (406) 477-8844

Laurel • *Laurel C/C* • Joanne Flynn; Exec. Secy.; 108 E. Main; 59044; Yellowstone; P 7,000; M 131; (406) 628-8105; lchamber@rbbmt.org; www.laurelmontana.org

Laurin • *see Twin Bridges*

Lennep • *see White Sulpher Springs*

Lewistown • *Lewistown Area C/C* • Connie L. Fry; Exec. Dir.; 408 N.E. Main; 59457; Fergus; P 7,000; M 300; (406) 535-5436; (866) 912-3980; Fax (406) 535-5437; lewchamb@midrivers.com; www.lewistownchamber.com

Libby • *Libby Area C/C* • Dusti Thompson; Exec. Dir.; 905 W. 9th St.; P.O. Box 704; 59923; Lincoln; P 10,000; M 275; (406) 293-4167; Fax (406) 293-2197; libbyacc@libbychamber.org; www.libbychamber.org

Lincoln • *Lincoln Valley C/C* • Ron Erickson; Pres.; P.O. Box 985; 59639; Powell; P 1,500; M 62; (406) 362-4949; lincolnmontana@linctel.net; www.lincolnmontana.com

Livingston • *Livingston Area C/C* • LouAnn Nelson; Ofc. Mgr.; 303 E. Park St.; 59047; Musselshell; P 7,500; M 450; (406) 222-0850; Fax (406) 222-0852; info@livingston-chamber.com; www.livingston-chamber.com

Malta • *Malta Area C/C* • Krista Fahlgren; Secy.; 10 1/2 S. 4 E.; P.O. Box 1420; 59538; Phillips; P 4,900; M 125; (406) 654-1776; Fax (406) 654-1776; malta@mtintouch.net; www.maltachamber.com

Manhattan • *Manhattan Area C/C* • Susan Douma; Exec. Secy.; 106 S. Broadway; P.O. Box 606; 59741; Gallatin; P 3,000; M 150; (406) 284-4162; manhattanmontana@yahoo.com; www.manhattanareachamber.com

Martinsdale • *see White Sulpher Springs*

Miles City • *Miles City Area C/C* • John Laney; Exec. Dir.; 511 Pleasant St.; 59301; Custer; P 8,700; M 306; (406) 234-2890; Fax (406) 234-6914; mcchamber@mcchamber.com; www.visitmilescitymt.com

Missoula • *Missoula Area C/C* • Kim Latrielle; CEO; 825 E. Front; P.O. Box 7577; 59807; Missoula; P 100,086; M 1,000; (406) 543-6623; Fax (406) 543-6625; info@missoulachamber.com; www.missoulachamber.com

Philipsburg • *Philipsburg C/C* • P.O. Box 661; 59858; Granite; P 915; M 30; (406) 859-3388; chamber@philipsburgmt.com; www.philipsburgmt.com

Plains • *Plains-Paradise C/C* • P.O. Box 1531; 59859; Sanders; P 1,500; M 90; (406) 826-4700; www.wildhorseplainschamber.com

Plentywood • *Sheridan County C/C & Ag.* • Richard Rice; Pres.; 108 N. Main St.; P.O. Box 104; 59254; Sheridan; P 4,000; M 100; (406) 765-1733; chamber@mygreeter.com; www.sheridancountychamber.org

Polson • *Polson C/C* • 418 Main St.; P.O. Box 667; 59860; Lake; P 4,600; M 222; (406) 883-5969; Fax (406) 883-1716; chamber@polsonchamber.com; www.polsonchamber.com

Red Lodge • *Red Lodge Area C/C* • Patty Davis; Exec. Dir.; 601 N. Broadway; P.O. Box 988; 59068; Carbon; P 8,000; M 190; (406) 446-1718; redlodgechamber@qwestoffice.net; www.redlodgechamber.org

Ringling • *see White Sulpher Springs*

Ronan • *Ronan C/C* • P.O. Box 254; 59864; Lake; P 1,800; M 100; (406) 676-8300; info@ronanchamber.com; www.ronanchamber.com

Roundup • *Roundup C/C* • Meryl Hunt; Pres.; P.O. Box 751; 59072; Musselshell; P 2,049; M 69; (406) 323-1966; Fax (406) 323-1966; roundupc@midrivers.com; www.roundupchamber.net

Saco • *Saco C/C* • Joy Linn; Pres.; P.O. Box 75; 59261; Phillips; P 200; M 10; (406) 527-3434

Saint Ignatius • *Saint Ignatius C/C* • Amy Miller; 333 Mountain View; P.O. Box 566; 59865; Lake; P 700; M 40; (406) 745-3900; Fax (406) 745-5038; stignatiusinfo@stignatius.net; www.stignatiusmontana.com

Scobey • *Daniels County C/C & Ag.* • 120 Main St.; P.O. Box 91; 59263; Daniels; P 1,082; M 43; (406) 487-2061; scobey@nemontel.net; www.scobeymt.com

Seeley Lake • *Seeley Lake Area C/C* • Cheryl Thompson; Exec. Dir.; 2920 Hwy. 83 N.; P.O. Box 516; 59868; Missoula; P 2,500; M 95; (406) 677-2880; Fax (406) 677-2880; slchamber@blackfoot.net; www.seeleylakechamber.com

Shelby • *Shelby Area C/C* • Audie Bancroft; Exec. Dir.; 100 Montana Ave.; P.O. Box 865; 59474; Toole; P 3,500; M 100; (406) 434-7184; Fax (406) 424-7234; shelbycoc@3rivers.net; www.shelbymtchamber.org

Sheridan • *see Twin Bridges*

Sidney • *Sidney Area C/C & Ag.* • Wade J. VanEvery; Exec. Dir.; 909 S. Central Ave.; 59270; Richland; P 7,500; M 250; (406) 433-1916; Fax (406) 433-1127; schamber@midrivers.com; www.sidneymt.com*

Silver Gate • *see Cooke City*

Silver Star • *see Twin Bridges*

St. Regis • *see Superior*

Stanford • *Judith Basin C/C* • P.O. Box 5; 59479; Judith Basin; P 2,000; M 50

Superior • *Mineral County C/C* • Jim Hollenbeck; Pres.; P.O. Box 483; 59872; Mineral; P 4,000; M 50; (406) 649-6400; mccoc@blackfoot.net; www.montanarockies.org

Swan Lake • *Swan Lake C/C* • Diane Kautzman; Pres.; P.O. Box 5096; 59911; Flathead; P 300; M 110; (406) 886-2303

Terry • *Prairie County C/C* • Glenda Ueland; Pres.; P.O. Box 667; 59349; Prairie; P 1,200; M 50; (406) 635-5513; (406) 635-2126; Fax (406) 635-5513; www.terrytribune.com

Thompson Falls • *Thompson Falls C/C* • Melissa Wilson; Mgr.; P.O. Box 493; 59873; Sanders; P 1,800; M 110; (406) 827-4930; tfchamber@thompsonfallschamber.com; www.thompsonfallschamber.com

Three Forks • *Three Forks C/C & Visitor Center* • Barbara Frost; Pres.; P.O. Box 1103; 59752; Gallatin; P 1,800; M 113; (406) 285-4753; (406) 285-3011; phillips@holcim.com; www.threeforksmontana.com

Townsend • *Townsend Area C/C* • M.A. Upton; Secy.; P.O. Box 947; 59644; Broadwater; P 4,000; M 90; (406) 266-4101; (877) 266-4101; Fax (406) 266-4042; townsendchamber@mt.net

Troy • *Troy C/C* • Melody Condron; P.O. Box 3005; 59935; Lincoln; P 1,000; M 51; (406) 295-1064; secretary@troymtchamber.org; www.troymtchamber.org

Twin Bridges • *Greater Ruby Valley C/C* • Karen W. Town; Pres.; P.O. Box 134; 59754; Madison; P 1,500; M 160; (406) 684-5678; info@rubyvalleychamber.com; www.rubyvalleychamber.com

Virginia City · *Virginia City Area C/C* · P.O. Box 218; 59755; Madison; P 140; M 70; (406) 843-5555; (800) 829-2969; info@virginiacity.com; www.virginiacity.com

West Yellowstone · *West Yellowstone C/C & Visitors Center* · 30 Yellowstone Ave.; P.O. Box 458; 59758; Gallatin; P 1,020; M 224; (406) 646-7701; Fax (406) 646-9691; visitorservices@westyellowstonechamber.com; www.westyellowstonechamber.com

White Sulphur Springs · *Meagher County C/C* · Kelly Huffield; Pres.; P.O. Box 356; 59645; Meagher; P 1,000; M 60; (406) 547-2250; info@meagherchamber.com; www.meagherchamber.com

Whitefish · *Whitefish C/C* · Kevin Gartland; Exec. Dir.; 520 E. 2nd St.; P.O. Box 1120; 59937; Flathead; P 8,300; M 540; (406) 863-2400; Fax (406) 862-9494; visitus@whitefishchamber.org; www.whitefishchamber.org

Whitehall · *Whitehall C/C* · P.O. Box 72; 59759; Jefferson; P 2,000; M 50; (406) 287-2260; www.whitehallmt.com

Wibaux · *Wibaux County C/C* · Renee Nelson; Pres.; P.O. Box 159; 59353; Wibaux; P 900; M 20; (406) 796-2412

Wolf Point · *Wolf Point C of C & Ag.* · Kt Northington; Exec. Dir.; 218 3rd Ave. S., Ste. B; 59201; Roosevelt; P 3,200; M 125; (406) 653-2012; wpchmber@nemont.net; www.wolfpointchamber.org

Nebraska

Nebraska C of C & Ind. · Barry L. Kennedy CAE IOM; Pres.; P.O. Box 95128; Lincoln; 68509; Lancaster; P 1,800,000; M 2,000; (402) 474-4422; Fax (402) 474-5681; nechamber@nechamber.com; www.nechamber.com.

Ainsworth · *Ainsworth Area C/C & North Central Dev. Center* · Lesley Holmes; Exec. Secy.; 335 N. Main St.; 69210; Brown; P 3,000; M 150; (402) 387-2740; chamber@threeriver.net; www.ainsworthchamber.com

Albion · *Albion C/C* · Shirley Petsche; Pres; 420 W. Market; 68620; Boone; P 1,700; M 115; (402) 395-6012; ccalbn@hotmail.com; www.cityofalbion-ne.com

Alliance · *Alliance Area C/C* · Dixie Nelson; Exec. Dir.; 111 W. 3rd; P.O. Box 392; 69301; Box Butte; P 9,000; M 230; (308) 762-1520; Fax (308) 762-4919; director@bbc.net; www.alliancechamber.com.

Alma · *Alma C/C* · Bonnie Nurnberg; Pres.; P.O. Box 52; 68920; Harlan; P 1,200; M 60; (308) 928-2992; Fax (308) 928-2683; hctour@megavision.com; www.ci.alma.ne.us

Arapahoe · *Arapahoe C/C* · Tammie Middagh; Secy.; P.O. Box 624; 68922; Furnas; P 1,028; M 65; (308) 962-7777; chamber@arapahoe-ne.com; www.arapahoe-ne.com

Arnold · *Arnold C/C* · Becky Dailey; Pres.; P.O. Box 166; 69120; Custer; P 680; M 79; (308) 848-2522; www.arnoldne.org

Arthur · *Arthur C/C* · Ron Jageler; Pres.; 103 N. Hwy. 61; 69121; Arthur; P 120; M 4; (308) 764-2367

Ashland · *Ashland C/C* · Nancy Maack; Pres.; P.O. Box 5; 68003; Saunders; P 2,500; M 85; (402) 944-2050; www.historicashland.com

Atkinson · *Atkinson C/C* · Pam Winer; Pres.; P.O. Box 871; 68713; Holt; P 1,200; M 70; (402) 925-5313; bonnielech@morcomm.net; www.atkinsonne.com

Auburn · *Auburn C/C* · Ben Hall; Pres.; 1211 J St.; 68305; Nemaha; P 3,500; M 200; (402) 274-3521; Fax (402) 274-4020; auburnchamberofcommerce@gmail.com; www.auburnneb.com

Aurora · *Aurora Area Chamber & Dev. Corp.* · Christian Evans; Exec. Dir.; 1604 L St.; P.O. Box 146; 68818; Hamilton; P 4,400; M 275; (402) 694-6911; Fax (402) 694-5766; christian.evans@auroranebraska.com; www.auroranebraska.com

Axtell · *Axtell C/C* · Jim Messer; P.O. Box 26; 68924; Kearney; P 696; M 75; (308) 743-2437; www.axtellne.com

Bassett · *Bassett/Rock County C/C* · Bill Sanger; P.O. Box 537; 68714; Rock; P 1,700; M 73; (402) 684-3935; www.bassettnebr.com

Beatrice · *Beatrice Area C/C* · Lori Warner; Pres./CEO; 205 N. 4th St.; 68310; Gage; P 12,894; M 430; (402) 223-2338; (800) 755-7745; Fax (402) 223-2339; info@beatricechamber.com; www.beatricechamber.com*

Beaver City · *Beaver City C/C* · Linda Tomlinson; Coord.; P.O. Box 303; 68926; Furnas; P 680; M 40; (308) 268-9966; steveandlinda@frontiernet.net

Beaver Crossing · *Beaver Crossing C/C* · Kathy Fisher; 413 Martin Ave.; 68313; Seward; P 475; M 30; (402) 532-3875; chamber@beavercrossingne.com; www.beavercrossingne.com

Bellevue · *Bellevue C/C* · Megan Lucas; Pres./CEO; 1102 Galvin Rd. S.; 68005; Sarpy; P 80,000; M 520; (402) 898-3000; Fax (402) 291-8729; bellevue@bellevuenebraska.com; www.bellevuenebraska.com*

Benkelman · *Benkelman C/C* · P.O. Box 661; 69021; Dundy; P 1,000; M 36; (308) 423-5210; benkchamber@bwtelcom.net

Bennington · *see Elkhorn*

Big Springs · *Big Springs C/C* · Ron Hendrickson; P.O. Box 436; 69122; Deuel; P 400; M 20; (308) 889-3681; www.ci.big-springs.ne.us

Blair · *Blair Area C/C* · Harriet Waite; Exec. Dir.; 1646 Washington St.; 68008; Washington; P 7,800; M 240; (402) 533-4455; Fax (402) 533-4456; mail@blairchamber.org; www.blairchamber.org

Bloomfield · *Bloomfield C/C* · P.O. Box 292; 68718; Knox; P 1,126; M 60; (402) 373-4396; Fax (402) 373-4597; www.ci.bloomfield.ne.us

Blue Hill · *Blue Hill Comm. Club* · P.O. Box 63; 68930; Webster; P 867; M 25; (402) 756-2056; www.bluehillne.com

Bridgeport · *Prairie Winds C/C* · Bill Boyer; P.O. Box 640; 69336; Morrill; P 1,600; M 100; (308) 262-1623; www.bridgeport-ne.com

Broken Bow · *Broken Bow C/C* · Denise Russell; Exec. Dir.; 444 S. 8th Ave.; 68822; Custer; P 3,400; M 215; (308) 872-5691; Fax (308) 872-6137; info@brokenbow-ne.com; www.brokenbow-ne.com

Burwell · *Burwell C/C* · David Sawyer; Dir.; P.O. Box 131; 68823; Garfield; P 1,300; M 150; (308) 346-5210; Fax (308) 346-5121; burwellecondev@nctc.net; www.visitburwell.org

Callaway · *Callaway C/C* · Shirley Trout; Pres.; P.O. Box 272; 68825; Custer; P 700; M 70; (308) 836-2245; (402) 310-9070; strout@inebraska.com; www.callaway-ne.com

Cambridge · *Cambridge C/C* · Amy Shaner; P.O. Box 8; 69022; Furnas; P 1,100; M 50; (308) 697-3305; www.swnebr.net

Campbell · *Campbell Area C/C* · William Pearson; P.O. Box 219; 68932; Franklin; P 440; M 66; (402) 756-8851; www.campbellnebraska.org

Central City · *Central City Area C/C* · Kendra Jefferson; Exec. Dir.; 1532 17th Ave.; 68826; Merrick; P 3,000; M 200; (308) 946-3897; cchamber@cablene.com; www.centralcitychamber.com

Chadron · *Chadron C/C* · Collette Fernandez; Exec. Dir.; 706 W. 3rd; P.O. Box 646; 69337; Dawes; P 5,588; M 200; (308) 432-4401; (800) 603-2937; Fax (308) 432-4757; chamber@chadron.com; www.chadron.com

Chappell · *Chappell C/C* · P.O. Box 121; 69129; Deuel; P 980; M 50; (308) 874-9912; Fax (308) 874-2929; chamber69129@yahoo.com; www.chappellchamber.com

Clearwater · *Clearwater C/C* · Curt Thiele; Pres.; 85314 516th Ave.; 68726; Antelope; P 380; M 100; (402) 640-5734; (402) 485-2365; curtthiele@hotmail.com; www.clearwaterne.com

Columbus · *Columbus Area C/C* · K.C. Belitz; Pres.; 764 33rd Ave.; P.O. Box 515; 68602; Platte; P 22,000; M 750; (402) 564-2769; Fax (402) 564-2026; chamber@megavision.com; www.thecolumbuspage.com *

Cozad · *Cozad Area C/C* · Lydia Loewenstein; Dir.; 135 W. 8th St.; 69130; Dawson; P 5,000; M 250; (308) 784-3930; Fax (308) 784-3026; chamber@cozadnebraska.net; www.cozadnebraska.net *

Crawford · *Crawford C/C* · Jessica Espinoza; Pres.; P.O. Box 145; 69339; Dawes; P 1,107; M 65; (308) 665-1817; (866) 665-1817; crawfordchamber@yahoo.com; www.crawfordnebraska.biz

Creighton · *Creighton Area C/C* · Steve Morrill; P.O. Box 7; 68729; Knox; P 1,200; M 90; (402) 360-4148; creightonchamber@gpcom.net; www.creighton.org

Crete · *Crete C/C* · P.O. Box 465; 68333; Saline; P 6,500; M 100; (402) 826-2136; Fax (402) 826-2136; cretechamber@neb.rr.com; www.cretechamber.org

Crofton · *Crofton Comm. Club* · Doyle & Joyce Stevens; P.O. Box 81; 68730; Knox; P 800; M 45; (402) 388-4583; ccclub@gpcom.net; www.crofton-nebraska.com

Curtis · *Medicine Creek C/C* · P.O. Box 463; 69025; Frontier; P 800; M 30; (308) 367-4122; medcreekchamber@curtis-ne.com; www.curtis-ne.com/chamber.html

David City · *Butler County C/C* · Stephanie Dubbs; Exec. Dir.; 457 D St.; 68632; Butler; P 8,500; M 120; (402) 367-4238; dcchamber@windstream.net; www.davidcityne.com*

Deshler · *Deshler C/C* · P.O. Box 449; 68340; Thayer; P 892; M 50; (402) 365-4260; Fax (402) 365-4415; www.deshlernebraska.com

Elgin · *Elgin C/C* · Greg Tharnish; Pres.; P.O. Box 277; 68636; Antelope; P 700; M 50; (402) 843-2411; www.elginne.com

Elkhorn · *Western Douglas County C/C* · Jim Tomanek; Pres.; 20801 Elkhorn Dr.; P.O. Box 202; 68022; Douglas; P 10,000; M 250; (402) 289-9560; Fax (402) 289-9560; wdccc@wdccc.org; www.wdccc.org

Elm Creek · *Elm Creek C/C* · Jan Hinrichsen; Pres.; P.O. Box 103; 68836; Buffalo; P 950; M 40; (308) 856-4913; www.elmcreekne.com

Elwood · *Elwood C/C* · Jenna Reed; Dir.; P.O. Box 92; 68937; Gosper; P 700; M 56; (308) 785-2280; jenna.reed@pinnbank.com; www.elwoodnebraska.com

Eustis · *Eustis C/C* · Sharon Larsen; P.O. Box 372; 69028; Frontier; P 450; M 50; (308) 486-5515; www.eustisnebraska.com

Fairbury · *Fairbury C/C* · Sharon Priefert; Exec. Dir.; 518 E St.; P.O. Box 274; 68352; Jefferson; P 4,000; M 230; (402) 729-3000; Fax (402) 729-3076; fairburychamber@diodecom.net; www.fairburychamber.org

Falls City · *Falls City Area C/C* · 1705 Stone St.; 68355; Richardson; P 4,600; M 155; (402) 245-4228; Fax (402) 245-4228; fcchamber@sentco.net; www.fallscityonline.com

Fremont · *Fremont Area C/C* · Allan Hale; Pres.; 605 N. Broad St.; P.O. Box 182; 68026; Dodge; P 25,184; M 675; (402) 721-2641; Fax (402) 721-9359; info@fremontne.org; www.fremontne.org*

Friend · *Friend C/C* · Vickie Himmelberg; 201 Maple St.; 68359; Saline; P 1,200; M 52; (402) 947-2711; www.ci.friend.ne.us

Geneva · *Geneva C/C* · Lori Loontjer; Exec. Dir.; 145 N. 9th St.; P.O. Box 85; 68361; Fillmore; P 2,200; M 85; (402) 759-1155; Fax (402) 759-3629; revitalizegeneva@cityofgeneva.org; www.cityofgeneva.org/chamber/

Genoa · *Genoa C/C* · Tony Mathis; Pres.; P.O. Box 331; 68640; Platte; P 982; M 20; (402) 993-2330; www.ci.genoa.ne.us

Gering · *see Scottsbluff*

Gibbon · *Gibbon C/C* · Tom Baxter; Pres.; P.O. Box 56; 68840; Buffalo; P 1,759; M 60; (308) 468-6118; gibbonchamber@nctc.net; www.gibbonchamber.org

Gordon · *Gordon Area C/C* · Fred Hlava; Exec. Dir.; 311 N. Oak St.; P.O. Box 160; 69343; Sheridan; P 1,800; M 106; (308) 282-0730; gcc@gordonchamber.com; www.gordonchamber.com

Gothenburg · *Gothenburg Area C/C* · Anne Anderson; Exec. Dir.; 1021 Lake Ave.; P.O. Box 263; 69138; Dawson; P 4,513; M 200; (308) 537-3505; (800) 482-5520; Fax (308) 537-2541; chamber@gothenburgdelivers.com; www.gothenburgdelivers.com*

Grand Island · *Grand Island Area C/C* · Cindy Johnson; Pres.; 309 W. 2nd St.; P.O. Box 1486; 68802; Hall; P 43,000; M 735; (308) 382-9210; Fax (308) 382-1154; info@gichamber.com; www.gichamber.com

Grant · *Perkins County C/C* · 118 Central Ave.; P.O. Box 767; 69140; Perkins; P 3,000; M 80; chamber@gpcom.net; www.perkinscountychamber.com

Greeley · *Greeley C/C* · P.O. Box 306; 68842; Greeley; P 585; M 15; (308) 428-3925; www.cnbgreeley.com

Gretna · *Gretna Area C/C* · P.O. Box 431; 68028; Sarpy; P 5,000; M 174; (402) 332-3535; info@gretnachamber.com; www.gretnachamber.com

Hartington · *Hartington C/C* · Stephanie Skoggan; Pres.; P.O. Box 742; 68739; Cedar; P 1,640; M 120; (402) 254-6357; Fax (402) 254-6391; www.ci.hartington.ne.us

Hastings · *Hastings Area C/C* · Tom Hastings; Pres.; 301 S. Burlington Ave.; P.O. Box 1104; 68902; Adams; P 25,000; M 715; (402) 461-8400; Fax (402) 461-4400; info@hastingschamber.com; www.hastingschamber.com.*

Hay Springs · *Hay Springs C/C* · Nicole Toos; Treas.; P.O. Box 264; 69347; Sheridan; P 650; M 60; (308) 638-4487

Hebron · *Hebron C/C* · Tina Reed; Exec. Dir.; 216 Lincoln Ave.; P.O. Box 172; 68370; Thayer; P 1,565; M 80; (402) 768-7156; Fax (402) 768-6176; hebronchamber@yahoo.com; www.hebronnebraska.us

Hemingford · *Hemingford C/C* · Amy Raben; Pres.; P.O. Box 51; 69348; Box Butte; P 993; M 40; (308) 487-5578; www.bbc.net/chamber

Henderson · *Henderson C/C* · Kelsey Bergen; Dir.; P.O. Box 225; 68371; York; P 1,000; M 90; (402) 723-4228; Fax (402) 723-5785; hchamber@mainstaycomm.net; www.cityofhenderson.org

Hickman · *Hickman C/C* · 830 E. 9th St.; 68372; Lancaster; P 1,400; M 12; (402) 792-2212; www.hickman-ne.com

Holdrege · *Holdrege Area C/C* · Michele Ehresman; Dir.; 316 East Ave.; P.O. Box 200; 68949; Phelps; P 5,650; M 225; (308) 995-4444; Fax (308) 995-4445; chamber@justtheplacenebraska.com; www.justtheplacenebraska.com

Humboldt · *Humboldt C/C* · Kathy Kanel; Secy.; P.O. Box 125; 68376; Richardson; P 941; M 70; (402) 862-2821; www.ci.humboldt.ne.us

Hyannis · *Sandhills C/C* · 313 Morton St.; P.O. Box; 69350; Grant; P 500; M 8; (308) 458-2716

Imperial • *Imperial C/C* • Sue Moore; P.O. Box 87; 69033; Chase; P 2,000; M 100; (308) 882-5444; Fax (308) 882-4319; www.imperialchamber.com

Kearney • *Kearney Area C/C* • Jan Rodehorst; Exec. Dir.; 1007 2nd Ave.; P.O. Box 607; 68848; Buffalo; P 46,000; M 900; (308) 237-3101; (800) 227-8340; Fax (308) 237-3103; jrodehorst@kearneycoc.org; www.kearneycoc.org.*

Kimball • *Kimball-Banner County C/C* • Rod Horton; Exec. Dir.; 122 S. Chestnut St.; 69145; Kimball; P 3,500; M 202; (308) 235-3782; Fax (308) 235-3825; kbccc@megavision.com; www.kimballbannercountychamber.com

LaVista • *LaVista Area C/C* • Kim Madrigal; Exec. Dir.; 9647 Giles Rd.; 68128; Sarpy; P 15,000; M 300; (402) 339-2078; Fax (402) 339-2026; info@lavistachamber.org; www.lavistachamber.org

Lexington • *Lexington Area C/C* • Susan Bennett; Exec. Dir.; 302 E. 6th St., Ste. 2; P.O. Box 97; 68850; Dawson; P 10,000; M 230; (308) 324-5504; Fax (308) 324-5505; susan@lexcoc.com; www.visitlexington.org*

Lincoln • *Lincoln C/C* • Wendy Birdsall; Pres.; 1135 M St.; P.O. Box 83006; 68501; Lancaster; P 250,000; M 1,450; (402) 436-2350; Fax (402) 436-2360; info@lcoc.com; www.lcoc.com*

Long Pine • *Long Pine C/C* • P.O. Box 234; 69217; Brown; P 346; M 22; (402) 273-4395; www.cityoflongpine.org

Loup City • *Loup City Area C/C* • Eric Kowalski; Pres.; P.O. Box 24; 68853; Sherman; P 1,600; M 40; (308) 745-0430; lcchamber@cornhusker.net; www.loupcity.com

Madison • *Madison Area C/C* • Linda Haack; Exec. Dir.; P.O. Box 287; 68748; Madison; P 2,400; M 75; (402) 454-2251; Fax (402) 454-2262; madisonchamber@telebeep.com; www.ci.madison.ne.us

McCook • *McCook Area C/C* • Pamela Harsh; Exec. Dir.; 402 Norris Ave., Ste. 203; P.O. Box 337; 69001; Red Willow; P 8,000; M 230; (308) 345-3200; Fax (308) 345-3201; info@aboutmccook.com; www.aboutmccook.com

Milford • *Milford C/C* • Roger Wittrock; P.O. Box 174; 68405; Seward; P 2,000; M 75; (402) 761-3247; chamber@milford-ne.com; www.milfordnechamber.com

Minden • *Minden C/C* • Judy Hansen; Ofc. Mgr.; 325 N. Colorado Ave.; P.O. Box 375; 68959; Kearney; P 3,000; M 180; (308) 832-1811; Fax (308) 832-1811; mindenchamber@gtmc.net; www.mindenne.org

Mitchell • *Mitchell C/C* • Carol Bernard; P.O. Box 72; 69357; Scotts Bluff; P 1,800; M 31; (308) 623-1523; www.mitchellcity.net

Nebraska City • *Nebraska City Tourism & Commerce Inc.* • Rebecca Turner; Exec. Dir.; 806 1st Ave.; 68410; Otoe; P 7,400; M 250; (402) 873-6654; (800) 514-9113; Fax (402) 873-6701; roser@nebraskacity.com; www.nebraskacity.com *

Neligh • *Neligh C/C* • Walter Storey; Pres.; 110 E. 4th; 68756; Antelope; P 1,700; M 100; (402) 887-4447; Fax (402) 887-4399; www.neligh.net

Norfolk • *Norfolk Area C/C* • Dennis Houston; Pres./CEO; 405 W. Madison Ave.; P.O. Box 386; 68702; Madison; P 25,000; M 625; (402) 371-4862; Fax (402) 371-0182; dhouston@norfolkareachamber.com; www.norfolkareachamber.com.

North Bend • *North Bend C/C* • Nathan Arneal; Pres.; P.O. Box 361; 68649; Dodge; P 1,200; M 65; (402) 652-8312; www.northbendne.org

North Platte • *North Platte Chamber & Dev. Corp.* • Dan S. Mauk IOM; Pres./CEO; 502 S. Dewey St.; 69101; Lincoln; P 30,000; M 620; (308) 532-4966; Fax (308) 532-4827; dan@nparea.com; www.nparea.com.*

Oakland • *Oakland C/C* • Andy Rennerfeldt; Pres.; 212 N. Oakland Ave.; 68045; Burt; P 1,300; M 150; (402) 685-6282

Ogallala • *Ogallala/Keith County C/C* • Brenda Ketcham; Exec. Dir.; 418 N. Spruce St., Ste. A; P.O. Box 628; 69153; Keith; P 8,877; M 395; (308) 284-4066; (800) 658-4390; Fax (308) 284-3126; info@visitogallala.com; www.visitogallala.com.

Omaha • *Greater Omaha C/C* • David G. Brown; Pres./CEO; 1301 Harney St.; 68102; Douglas; P 838,855; M 3,500; (402) 346-5000; Fax (402) 346-7050; info@omahachamber.org; www.omahachamber.org

O'Neill • *O'Neill Area C/C* • Pat Fritz; Exec. Dir.; 125 S. 4th St.; 68763; Holt; P 15,000; M 230; (402) 336-2355; Fax (402) 336-4563; oneill@telebeep.com; www.oneillchamber.org*

Ord • *Ord Area C/C* • Caleb Pollard; Exec. Dir.; 1514 K St.; 68862; Valley; P 2,100; M 200; (308) 728-7875; (877) 728-7875; Fax (308) 728-7691; ordnebraska@frontier.com; www.ordnebraska.com

Oshkosh • *Garden County C/C* • Buddy Paulsen; P.O. Box 256; 69154; Garden; P 1,900; M 70; (308) 772-4468; buddypaulsen@yahoo.com; www.gardencone.com

Papillion • *Sarpy County C/C* • Jane Nielsen; Pres.; 7775 Olson Dr., Ste. 207; 68046; Sarpy; P 147,000; M 575; (402) 339-3050; Fax (402) 339-9968; chamber@sarpychamber.org; www.sarpychamber.org *

Pawnee City • *Pawnee City C/C* • Steve Glen; P.O. Box 6; 68420; Pawnee; P 1,000; (402) 852-2444; www.pawneecity.com

Pender • *Pender Thurston C/C* • Connie Wichman, P.O. Box 250; 68047; Thurston; P 1,500; M 69; (402) 385-3200; www.penderthurston.com

Peru • *Peru C/C* • Ruth Hazwood; Pres.; P.O. Box 246; 68421; Nemaha; P 922; M 20; growchamberofcommerce@windstream.com; www.ci.peru.ne.us

Pierce • *Pierce C/C* • Cindy Warnecke; Pres.; P.O. Box 82; 68767; Pierce; P 1,800; M 50; (402) 329-6879; www.piercenebraska.com

Plainview • *Plainview C/C* • 306 W. Park Ave.; P.O. Box 474; 68769; Pierce; P 1,400; M 65; (402) 582-7800

Plattsmouth • *Plattsmouth C/C* • Max Kathol; Exec. Dir.; 918 Washington Ave.; 68048; Cass; P 7,500; M 230; (402) 296-6021; Fax (402) 296-6974; mrkathol@plattsmouthchamber.com; www.plattsmouthchamber.com

Ralston • *Ralston Area C/C* • Marlene Hansen; Pres.; 5505 Miller Ave.; 68127; Douglas; P 6,200; M 275; (402) 339-7737; Fax (402) 339-7954; chamber@cityofralston.com; www.ralstonareachamber.org *

Ravenna • *Ravenna C/C* • Margaret Treffer; Exec. Dir.; P.O. Box 56; 68869; Buffalo; P 1,347; M 77; (402) 910-4231; (308) 452-3225; Fax (308) 452-3296; ravchamber@towncountrybank.net; www.ci.ravenna.ne.us

Red Cloud • *Red Cloud C/C* • Ken Van Wey; Co-Pres.; P.O. Box 327; 68970; Webster; P 1,131; M 40; (402) 746-3238; redcloudchamber@hotmail.com; www.redcloudguiderock.com

Saint Paul • *Saint Paul Area C/C* • MaryAnn Fredrick; Exec. Dir.; 619 Howard Ave.; 68873; Howard; P 2,200; M 130; (308) 754-5558; Fax (308) 754-5558; stpaulcham@qwestoffice.net; www.stpaulnebraska.com

Schuyler • *Schuyler Area C/C* • Exec. Dir.; 1107 B St.; 68661; Colfax; P 5,100; M 182; (402) 352-5472; Fax (402) 352-2754; www.ci.schuyler.ne.us/chamber.asp

Scottsbluff • *Scottsbluff/Gering United C/C* • Karen Anderson; Exec. Dir.; 1517 Broadway, Ste. 104; 69361; Scotts Bluff; P 24,000; M 475; (308) 632-2133; (800) 788-9475; Fax (308) 632-7128; chamber@scottsbluffgering.net; www.scottsbluffgering.net.*

Scribner · *Scribner C/C* · P.O. Box 25; 68057; Dodge; P 970; M 65; (402) 664-2450; www.scribnernebraska.com

Seward · *Seward Area C/C* · Ms. Pat Coldiron; Exec. Dir.; 616 Bradford St.; 68434; Seward; P 8,000; M 200; (402) 643-4189; Fax (402) 643-4713; sewcham@sewardne.com; www.sewardne.com*

Shelby · *Shelby C/C* · P.O. Box 27; 68662; Polk; P 690; M 60; (402) 527-5198; www.ci.shelby.ne.us

Sidney · *Cheyenne County C/C* · Megan McGown; Exec. Dir.; 740 Illinois St.; 69162; Cheyenne; P 10,000; M 230; (308) 254-5851; (800) 421-4769; Fax (308) 254-3081; info@cheyennecounty chamber.com; www.cheyennecountychamber.com*

South Sioux City · *South Sioux City Area C/C* · Pat Anderson; Pres.; 3900 Dakota Ave., Ste. 11; 68776; Dakota; P 12,500; M 360; (402) 494-1626; Fax (402) 494-5010; patmanderson@cableone. net; www.southsiouxchamber.org.*

Stamford · *Stamford C/C* · Rolena T. Novak; Secy.; P.O. Box 34; 68977; Harlan; P 202; (308) 868-2401

Stratton · *Stratton Area C/C* · P.O. Box 264; 69043; Hitchcock; P 396; M 24; (308) 276-2184; chamber@stratton-ne.org; www. stratton-ne.org

Superior · *Superior Area C/C* · Sherry Kniep; Admin.; 354 N. Commercial Ave.; 68978; Nuckolls; P 2,000; M 150; (402) 879-3419; superiorcc@windstream.net; www.ci.superior.ne.us*

Sutherland · *Sutherland C/C* · Phillip Charleton; P.O. Box 81; 69165; Lincoln; P 1,200; M 36; (308) 386-4345; (308) 386-4721; www.ci.sutherland.ne.us

Syracuse · *Syracuse C/C* · Carolyn Gigstad; Exec. Dir.; P.O. Box J; 68446; Otoe; P 1,800; M 75; (402) 269-3242; chamber@ syracusene.com; www.syracusene.com

Table Rock · *Table Rock Comm. Club* · 712 State; 68447; Pawnee; P 250; (402) 839-2180

Tecumseh · *Tecumseh C/C* · Eloise Bartels; Secy.; 136 N. 5th St.; P.O. Box 126; 68450; Johnson; P 1,720; M 64; (402) 335-3400; Fax (402) 335-3235; tecumsehchamber@windstream.net; www. tecumsehne.com

Tekamah · *Tekamah C/C* · Harriet Shafer; Secy.; P.O. Box 231; 68061; Burt; P 1,900; M 110; (402) 374-2020; Fax (402) 374-1392; www.tekamahchamberofcommerce.com

Valentine · *Valentine C/C* · Dean Jacobs; Exec. Dir.; 239 S. Main St.; P.O. Box 201; 69201; Cherry; P 3,000; M 200; (402) 376-2969; (800) 658-4024; Fax (402) 376-2688; valentinecc@qwestoffice. net; www.visitvalentine.com

Valley · *see Elkhorn*

Wahoo · *Wahoo C/C* · Doug Watts; Exec. Dir.; 640 N. Broadway St.; 68066; Saunders; P 4,225; M 350; (402) 443-4001; Fax (402) 443-3077; watts@wahoo.ne.us; www.wahoo.ne.us

Waterloo · *see Elkhorn*

Waverly · *Waverly C/C* · Alex Hill; Secy.; P.O. Box 331; 68462; Lancaster; P 2,500; M 50; (402) 786-5111; www.waverlyne.org

Wayne · *Wayne Area C/C & Eco. Dev.* · Wes Blecke; Asst. Dir.; 108 W. 3rd St.; P.O. Box 275; 68787; Wayne; P 6,000; M 200; (402) 375-2240; (877) 929-6363; Fax (402) 375-2246; ifletcher@ wayneworks.org; www.wayneworks.org

Weeping Water · *Weeping Water C/C* · Kay Gerdes; P.O. Box 329; 68463; Cass; P 1,107; M 50; (402) 267-5152; www.weeping waternebraska.com

West Point · *West Point C/C* · Tina Welding; Exec. Dir.; P.O. Box 125; 68788; Cuming; P 3,660; M 125; (402) 372-2981; Fax (402) 372-1105; info@westpointchamber.com; www.westpointchamber.com

Wilber · *Wilber Area C/C* · Tim Linscott; Pres.; P.O. Box 1164; 68465; Saline; P 1,700; M 40; (402) 821-2732; Fax (402) 821-2691; www.ci.wilber.ne.us

Winnetoon · *see Creighton*

York · *Greater York Area C/C* · Todd Kirshenbaum; Exec. Dir.; 603 N. Lincoln Ave.; 68467; York; P 14,000; M 300; (402) 362-5531; Fax (402) 362-5953; yorkcc@yorkchamber.net; www.yorkchamber.org*

Nevada

Nevada State C of C · Jody Hosterman; Admin. Asst.; One E. First St., 16th Flr.; Reno; 89501; Washoe; P 2,600,000; M 1,500; (775) 337-3030; Fax (775) 337-3038; info@renosparkschamber. org; www.renosparkschamber.org

Women's Chamber of Commerce of Nevada · June Beland; Pres./CEO; 2300 W. Sahara Ave., Ste. 800; Las Vegas; 89102; Clark; P 2,400,000; M 401; (702) 733-3955; Fax (702) 926-9270; info@ womenschamberofnevada.org; www.womenschamberofnevada.org.*

Amargosa Valley · *Amargosa Valley C/C* · Jon Delee; Pres.; P.O. Box 2; 89020; Nye; P 1,400; M 30; (775) 372-5459; (702) 544-2570; Fax (775) 372-5362; amargosachamber.com

Austin · *Greater Austin C/C* · Phillip Williams; Pres.; 122 Main St.; P.O. Box 212; 89310; Lander; P 350; M 37; (775) 964-2200; Fax (775) 964-2200; austinnvchamber@yahoo.com; www.austin nevada.com

Battle Mountain · *Battle Mountain C/C* · Sarah Burkhart; Exec. Dir.; P.O. Box 333; 89820; Lander; P 5,500; M 127; (775) 635-8245; Fax (775) 635-8064; bmcommerce@yahoo.com; www.shopbattle mountain.com

Beatty · *Beatty C/C* · P.O. Box 956; 89003; Nye; P 1,100; M 50; (775) 553-2424; Fax (775) 553-2424; beattychamber@sbcglobal. net; www.beattynevada.org

Boulder City · *Boulder City C/C* · Jill Rowland-Lagan; CEO; 465 Nevada Way; 89005; Clark; P 16,000; M 420; (702) 293-2034; Fax (702) 293-0574; info@bouldercitychamber.com; www.boulder citychamber.com.*

Carson City · *Carson City Area C/C* · Ronni Hannaman; Exec. Dir.; 1900 S. Carson St., Ste. 200; 89701; Carson City; P 57,600; M 516; (775) 882-1565; Fax (775) 882-4179; service@carson citychamber.com; www.carsoncitychamber.com

Crystal Bay · *see Tahoe City, CA*

Dayton · *Dayton Area C/C* · Jojo Myers; Pres.; P.O. Box 2408; 89403; Lyon; P 17,000; M 200; (775) 246-7909; Fax (775) 246-5838; info@daytonnvchamber.org; www.daytonnvchamber.org*

Elko · *Elko Area C/C* · Jennifer Sprout; CEO; 1405 Idaho St.; 89801; Elko; P 38,000; M 550; (775) 738-7135; (800) 428-7143; Fax (775) 738-7136; chamber@elkonevada.com; www.elkonevada.com*

Ely · *White Pine C/C* · Wayne Cameron; 636 Aultman St.; 89301; White Pine; P 9,000; M 175; (775) 289-8877; Fax (775) 289-6144; elycc@whitepinechamber.com; www.whitepinechamber.com

Fallon · *Fallon C/C* · Rick Dentino; Exec. Dir.; 85 N. Taylor; 89406; Churchill; P 30,030; M 240; (775) 423-2544; Fax (775) 423-0540; info@fallonchamber.com; www.fallonchamber.com

Fernley · *Fernley C/C* · Sandy Jenner; Exec. Dir.; 70 N. West St.; 89408; Lyon; P 20,000; M 330; (775) 575-4459; Fax (775) 575-2626; fernleychamber@sbcglobal.net; www.fernleychamber.org*

Gardnerville · *Carson Valley C/C & Visitors Auth.* · Bill Chernock; Exec. Dir.; 1477 Hwy. 395, Ste. A; 89410; Douglas; P 52,000; M 450; (775) 782-8144; (800) 727-7677; Fax (775) 782-1025; info@carsonvalleynv.org; www.carsonvalleynv.org*

Goldfield · *Goldfield C/C* · Carol Miguez; Pres.; 165 E. Crook Ave.; P.O. Box 204; 89013; Esmeralda; P 950; M 35; (775) 485-3560; Fax (775) 485-3560; gfnvchamber@aol.com; goldfield nevada.org

Hawthorne · *Mineral County C/C* · Roy Colbert; Exec. Dir.; 822 5th St.; P.O. Box 2250; 89415; Mineral; P 3,500; M 60; (775) 945-2507; info@mineralcountychamber.com; www.mineral countychamber.com

Henderson · *Henderson C/C* · Alice Martz; Pres./CEO; 590 S. Boulder Hwy.; 89015; Clark; P 280,000; M 1,500; (702) 565-8951; Fax (702) 565-3115; info@hendersonchamber.com; www.hender sonchamber.com

Incline Village · *see Tahoe City, CA*

Lake Tahoe · *see Stateline*

Las Vegas · *Las Vegas C/C* · Matt Crosson; Pres./CEO; 6671 Las Vegas Blvd. S., Ste. 300; 89119; Clark; P 2,000,000; M 6,500; (702) 641-5822; Fax (702) 735-2273; info@lvchamber.com; www.lvchamber.com*

Las Vegas · *Latin C/C* · Otto Merida; Pres./CEO; 300 N. 13th St.; 89101; Clark; M 1,400; (702) 385-7367; Fax (702) 385-2614; otto@lvlcc.com; www.lvlcc.com

Laughlin · *Laughlin C/C* · Janet Barela; Exec. Dir.; 1585 Casino Dr.; 89029; Clark; P 8,500; M 425; (702) 298-2214; (800) 227-5245; Fax (702) 298-5708; director@laughlinchamber.com; www.laughlinchamber.com

Lovelock · *Greater Pershing Partnership* · 350 Main St.; P.O. Box 821; 89419; Pershing; P 5,000; M 152; (775) 273-7213; Fax (775) 273-1732; info@pershingcountynevada.com; www. pershingcountynevada.com

Mesquite · *Mesquite Area C/C* · Anna Miranda; Exec. Dir.; 12 W. Mesquite Blvd., Ste. 107; 89027; Clark; P 21,253; M 331; (702) 346-2902; Fax (702) 346-6138; info@mesquite-chamber.com; www.mesquite-chamber.com*

North Las Vegas · *North Las Vegas C/C* · Michael C. Varney; Pres./CEO; 3365 W. Craig Rd., Ste. 25; 89032; Clark; P 2,000,000; M 600; (702) 642-9595; Fax (702) 642-0439; contact@nlvchamber. org; www.northlasvegaschamber.com*

Overton · *Moapa Valley C/C* · Vernon Robison; P.O. Box 361; 89040; Clark; P 10,000; M 78; (702) 398-7160; chamber@moapa valley.com; www.moapavalley.com

Pahrump · *Pahrump Valley C/C* · Michael Selbach; Exec. Dir.; 1301 S. Hwy. 160, 2nd Flr.; P.O. Box 42; 89041; Nye; P 37,000; M 500; (775) 727-5800; (866) 722-5800; Fax (775) 727-3909; info@pahrumpchamber.com; www.pahrumpvalleychamber.com.*

Pioche · *Pioche C/C* · Barbara Constantine; Pres.; P.O. Box 127; 89043; Lincoln; P 750; M 40; (775) 962-5544; (775) 962-5271; info@piochenevada.com; www.piochenevada.com

Reno · *Reno Sparks C/C* · Doug Kurkul; CEO; One E. First St., 16th Flr.; P.O. Box 3499; 89505; Washoe; P 374,000; M 15,000; (775) 337-3030; Fax (775) 337-3038; info@renosparkschamber.org; www.renosparkschamber.org*

Silver Springs · *Silver Springs Area C/C* · Stephanie Newness; 1050 Hwy. 50 E.; P.O. Box 617; 89429; Lyon; P 11,500; M 60; (775) 577-4336; Fax (775) 577-4399; ssnvchamber@gmail.com; *

Sparks · *Northern Nevada C/C* · Len Stevens; Exec. Dir.; 1420 Scheels Dr., Ste. 108; P.O. Box 1776; 89432; Washoe; P 91,237; M 1,500; (775) 358-1976; Fax (775) 358-1992; info@northern nevadachamber.org; www.northernnevadachamber.org.*

Stateline · *TahoeChamber.org* · Betty Gorman; Pres.; 169 Hwy. 50, 3rd Flr.; P.O. Box 7139; 89449; Douglas; P 40,000; M 775; (775) 588-1728; Fax (775) 588-1941; info@tahoechamber.org; www. tahoechamber.org*

Tonopah · *Tonopah C/C* · Randy Alexander; Prog. Coord.; 200 S. Main St.; P.O. Box 82; 89049; Nye; P 3,200; M 60; (775) 482-3859; Fax (775) 482-9846; tdcoffice@yahoo.com; www.tonopahcham berofcommerce.com

Wells · *Wells C/C* · Thad Ballard; Pres.; P.O. Box 615; 89835; Elko; P 1,450; M 75; (775) 752-3540; www.wellsnevada.com

Winnemucca · *Humboldt County C/C* · Debbie Stone; Exec. Dir.; 30 W. Winnemucca Blvd.; 89445; Humboldt; P 17,000; M 250; (775) 623-2225; Fax (775) 623-6478; chamber@winnemucca.net; www.humboldtcountychamber.com

Yerington · *Yerington-Mason Valley C/C* · Pres.; 227 S. Main St.; 89447; Lyon; P 4,500; M 145; (775) 463-2245; Fax (775) 463-0030; info@masonvalleychamber.org; www.masonvalleychamber.org

New Hampshire

Bus. & Ind. Assn. of N.H. · Jim Roche; Pres.; 122 N. Main; Concord; 03301; Merrimack; P 1,300,000; M 400; (603) 224-5388; Fax (603) 224-2872; mail@nhbia.org; www.nhbia.org

Acworth · *see Bellows Falls, VT*

Amherst · *Souhegan Valley C/C* · May Balsama; Exec. Dir.; 69 Rte. 101A; 03031; Hillsborough; P 60,000; M 300, (603) 673-4360; Fax (603) 673-5018; may@souhegan.net; www.souhegan.net*

Berlin · *Androscoggin Valley C/C* · 961 Main St.; 03570; Coos; P 17,000; M 200; (603) 752-6060; (800) 992-7480; Fax (603) 752-1002; info@androscogginvalleychamber.com; www.androscoggin valleychamber.com

Bethlehem · *Bethlehem C/C* · Victor Hoffman; Treas.; 2182 Main St.; P.O. Box 748; 03574; Grafton; P 2,200; M 67; (603) 869-3409; info@bethlehemwhitemtns.com; www.bethlehem whitemtns.com

Brentwood · *see Exeter*

Bretton Woods · *see Twin Mountain*

Bristol · *Newfound Region C/C* · Leslie Sturgeon; Exec. Dir.; P.O. Box 454; 03222; Grafton; P 3,300; M 92; (603) 744-2150; newfoundchamber@metrocast.net; www.newfoundchamber.com

Brookline · *see Amherst*

Cambridge · *see Errol*

Campton · *Waterville Valley Region C/C* · Joe Collie; Exec. Dir.; 12 Vintinner Rd.; 03223; Grafton; P 15,000; M 230; (603) 726-3804; Fax (603) 726-4058; info@watervillevalleyregion.com; www.watervillevalleyregion.com

Center Harbor · *see Meredith*

Center Ossipee · *Greater Ossipee Area C/C* · Jamison Killeen; Pres.; P.O. Box 323; 03814; Carroll; P 12,000; M 175; (603) 539-6201; (866) 683-6295; Fax (603) 941-0133; info@ossipeevalley. org; www.ossipeevalley.org

Charlestown · *see Claremont*

Claremont · *Greater Claremont C/C* · Shelly Hudson; Exec. Dir.; 24 Opera House Sq., Ste. 100; 03743; Sullivan; P 13,902; M 250; (603) 543-1296; Fax (603) 542-1469; executive@claremontnh chamber.org; www.claremontnhchamber.org

Colebrook · *North Country C/C* · P.O. Box 1; 03576; Coos; P 5,000; M 200; (603) 237-8939; (800) 698-8939; Fax (603) 237-4573; nccoc@ncia.net; www.northcountrychamber.org

Concord · *Greater Concord C/C* · Timothy G. Sink; Pres.; 40 Commercial St.; 03301; Merrrimack; P 43,000; M 900; (603) 224-2508; Fax (603) 224-8128; info@concordnhchamber.com; www.concordnhchamber.com*

Conway · *Conway C/C* · Laura Gorman; Pres.; P.O. Box 1019; 03818; Carroll; P 5,000; M 130; (603) 447-2639; info@conwaychamber.com; www.conwaychamber.com

Cornish · *see Windsor, VT*

Derry · *Greater Derry Londonderry C/C* · Gina Gulino-Payne; Exec. Dir.; 29 W. Broadway; 03038; Rockingham; P 35,000; M 250; (603) 432-8205; Fax (603) 432-7938; derrychamber@earthlink.net; www.derry-chamber.org*

Dover · *Greater Dover C/C* · Kirt Schuman; Exec. Dir.; 550 Central Ave.; 03820; Strafford; P 30,000; M 525; (603) 742-2218; info@dovernh.org; www.dovernh.org*

Dummer · *see Berlin*

East Kingston · *see Exeter*

Easton · *see Franconia*

Effingham · *see Center Ossipee*

Epping · *see Exeter*

Errol · *Umbagog Area C/C* · Christina Cote; P.O. Box 113; 03579; Coos; P 300; M 30; info@umbagogchambercommerce.com; www.umbagogchambercommerce.com

Exeter · *Exeter Area C/C* · Michael Schidlovsky; Pres.; 24 Front St., Ste. 101; P.O. Box 278; 03833; Rockingham; P 51,000; M 500; (603) 772-2411; Fax (603) 772-9965; info@exeterarea.org; www.exeterarea.org*

Franconia · *Franconia Notch C/C* · Frank Grima; Pres.; 421 Main St.; P.O. Box 780; 03580; Grafton; P 2,500; M 165; (603) 823-5661; info@franconianotch.org; www.franconianotch.org

Freedom · *see Center Ossipee*

Gorham · *see Berlin*

Greenfield · *see Amherst*

Greenville · *see Amherst*

Hampton · *Hampton Area C/C* · B.J. Noel; Pres.; 1 Lafayette Rd.; P.O. Box 790; 03843; Rockingham; P 36,000; M 425; (603) 926-8718; Fax (603) 926-9977; info@hamptonchamber.com; www.hamptonchamber.com*

Hanover · *Hanover Area C/C* · Janet Rebman; Exec. Dir.; 216 Nugget Bldg.; P.O. Box 5105; 03755; Grafton; P 11,000; M 370; (603) 643-3115; Fax (603) 643-5606; hacc@hanoverchamber.org; www.hanoverchamber.org*

Hillsborough · *Hillsborough C/C* · Babette Haley; Exec. Asst.; 25 School St.; P.O. Box 541; 03244; Hillsborough; P 8,000; M 140; (603) 464-5858; hcofc@conknet.com; www.hillsboroughnhchamber.com*

Hollis · *see Amherst*

Hudson · *Hudson C/C* · Brenda Collins; Exec. Dir.; 71 Lowell Rd.; 03051; Hillsborough; P 22,000; M 140; (603) 889-4731; Fax (603) 889-7939; info@hudsonchamber.com; www.hudsonchamber.com*

Jackson · *Jackson Area C/C* · Kathleen Driscoll; Exec. Dir.; P.O. Box 304; 03846; Carroll; P 900; M 100; (603) 383-9356; (800) 866-3334; Fax (603) 383-0931; info@jacksonnh.com; www.jacksonnh.com

Jaffrey · *Jaffrey C/C* · Lee Bruder; Pres.; P.O. Box 2; 03452; Cheshire; P 5,700; M 210; (603) 532-4549; Fax (603) 532-8823; info@jaffreychamber.com; www.jaffreychamber.com*

Jefferson · *see Berlin*

Keene · *Greater Keene C/C* · Tom Dowling; Pres.; 48 Central Sq.; 03431; Cheshire; P 21,000; M 443; (603) 352-1303; Fax (603) 358-5341; info@keenechamber.com; www.keenechamber.com*

Kensington · *see Exeter*

Kinston · *see Exeter*

Laconia · *Lakes Region C/C* · Sandy Marshall; Chrmn.; 383 S. Main St.; 03246; Belknap; P 18,000; M 550; (603) 524-5531; Fax (603) 524-5534; info@laconia-weirs.org; www.laconia-weirs.org*

Lake Sunapee · *see New London*

Lancaster · *Northern Gateway C/C* · Denise Boynton; Dir.; P.O. Box 537; 03584; Coos; P 13,000; M 125; (603) 788-2530; (877) 788-2530; info@northerngatewaychamber.org; www.northerngatewaychamber.org

Lebanon · *Lebanon Area C/C* · Paul Boucher; Pres./CEO; P.O. Box 97; 03766; Grafton; P 12,500; M 330; (603) 448-1203; Fax (603) 448-6489; lebanonchamber@lebanonchamber.com; www.lebanonchamber.com.

Lincoln · *Lincoln-Woodstock C/C* · Mark LaClair; Exec. Dir.; Rte. 112; P.O. Box 1017; 03251; Grafton; P 3,000; M 240; (603) 745-6621; Fax (603) 745-4908; info@lincolnwoodstock.com; www.lincolnwoodstock.com

Littleton · *Littleton Area C/C* · Chad Stearns; Exec. Dir.; P.O. Box 105; 03561; Grafton; P 6,200; M 325; (603) 444-6561; Fax (603) 444-2427; cstearns@littletonareachamber.com; www.littletonareachamber.com

Londonderry · *see Manchester*

Lyndeborough · *see Amherst*

Madison · *see Center Ossipee*

Manchester · *Greater Manchester C/C* · Robin Comstock; Pres./CEO; 54 Hanover St.; 03101; Hillsborough; P 108,000; M 1,000; (603) 666-6600; Fax (603) 626-0910; info@Manchester-Chamber.org; www.Manchester-Chamber.org*

Mason · *see Amherst*

Meredith · *Meredith Area C/C* · Susan Cerutti; Exec. Dir.; P.O. Box 732; 03253; Belknap; P 20,000; M 340; (603) 279-6121; Fax (603) 279-4525; meredith@lr.net; www.meredithcc.org

Merrimack · *Merrimack C/C* · Deb Courtemanche; Exec. Dir.; 246 Daniel Webster Hwy.; 03054; Hillsborough; P 28,000; M 200; (603) 424-3669; Fax (603) 429-4325; info@merrimackchamber.org; www.merrimackchamber.org

Milan · *see Berlin*

Milford · *see Amherst*

Millsfield · *see Errol*

Mont Vernon · *see Amherst*

Moultonboro · *see Meredith*

Nashua · *Greater Nashua C/C* · Chris Williams; Pres.; 142 Main St., 5th Flr.; 03060; Hillsborough; P 188,000; M 750; (603) 881-8333; Fax (603) 881-7323; chamber@nashuachamber.com; www.nashuachamber.com*

New Ipswich · *see Amherst*

New London · *Lake Sunapee Region C/C* · Rob Bryant; Exec. Dir.; 328 Main St.; P.O. Box 532; 03257; Merrimack & Sullivan; P 15,000; M 175; (603) 526-6575; (877) 526-6575; chamberinfo@tds.net; www.lakesunapeenh.org

Newfields · *see Exeter*

Newmarket · *see Exeter*

Newport • *Newport Area C/C* • Ella M. Casey; Exec. Dir.; 2 N. Main St.; 03773; Sullivan; P 6,200; M 120; (603) 863-1510; Fax (603) 863-9486; chamber@newportnhchamber.org; www. newportnhchamber.org

North Conway • *Mount Washington Valley C/C & Visitors Bur.* • Janice Crawford; Exec. Dir.; P.O. Box 2300; 03860; Carroll; P 15,000; M 800; (603) 356-5701; (800) 367-3364; Fax (603) 356-7069; info@ mtwashingtonvalley.org; www.mtwashingtonvalley.org

North Walpole • *see Bellows Falls, VT*

Ossipee • *see Center Ossipee*

Peterborough • *Greater Peterborough C/C* • Jack Burnett; Exec. Dir.; P.O. Box 401; 03458; Cheshire; P 6,200; M 350; (603) 924-7234; Fax (603) 924-7235; info@peterboroughchamber.com; www.peterboroughchamber.com*

Plainfield • *see Windsor, VT*

Plymouth • *Plymouth C/C* • Scott Stephens; Exec. Dir.; P.O. Box 65; 03264; Grafton; P 6,000; M 240; (603) 536-1001; (800) 386-3678; Fax (603) 536-4017; info@plymouthnh.org; www. plymouthnh.org*

Portsmouth • *Greater Portsmouth C/C* • Douglas Bates; Pres.; 500 Market St.; P.O. Box 239; 03802; Rockingham; P 125,000; M 1,025; (603) 436-3988; Fax (603) 436-5118; info@portsmouth chamber.org; www.portsmouthchamber.org*

Randolph • *see Berlin*

Raymond • *see Exeter*

Rindge • *Rindge C/C* • Carlotta Pini; Pres.; P.O. Box 911; 03461; Cheshire; P 5,615; M 72; (603) 899-5051; info@rindgechamber. org; www.rindgechamber.org

Rochester • *Greater Rochester C/C* • Laura A. Ring; Pres./CEO; 18 S. Main St.; 03867; Strafford; P 80,000; M 450; (603) 332-5080; Fax (603) 332-5216; info@rochesternh.org; www.rochesternh.org*

Salem • *Greater Salem C/C* • Donna Morris; Exec. Dir.; 224 N. Broadway; 03079; Rockingham; P 70,000; M 350; (603) 893-3177; Fax (603) 894-5158; donna@gschamber.com; www.gschamber.com*

Sandwich • *see Center Ossipee*

Shelburne • *see Berlin*

Somersworth • *Greater Somersworth C/C* • Jennifer Soldati; Exec. Dir.; 58 High St.; P.O. Box 615; 03878; Strafford; P 11,500; M 200; (603) 692-7175; Fax (603) 692-4501; info@somersworth chamber.com; www.somersworthchamber.com*

Stratham • *see Exeter*

Sugar Hill • *see Franconia*

Sunapee • *see New London*

Tamworth • *see Center Ossipee*

Temple • *see Amherst*

Twin Mountain • *Twin Mountain-Bretton Woods C/C* • P.O. Box 194; 03595; Coos; P 800; M 50; (800) 245-TWIN; info@ twinmountain.org; www.twinmountain.org

Wakefield • *Greater Wakefield C/C* • Chris Racine; Pres.; P.O. Box 111; 03872; Carroll; P 4,569; M 95; (603) 522-6106; post master@wakefieldnh.org; www.wakefieldnh.org

Walpole • *see Bellows Falls, VT*

Waterville Valley • *see Campton*

Weirs Beach • *see Laconia*

West Ossipee • *see Center Ossipee*

Westmoreland • *see Bellows Falls, VT*

Wilton • *see Amherst*

Wolfeboro • *Wolfeboro Area C/C* • Mary DeVries; Exec. Dir.; P.O. Box 547; 03894; Carroll; P 6,000; M 300; (603) 569-2200; (800) 516-5324; Fax (603) 569-2275; wolfeborochamber@conknet.com; www.wolfeboroonline.com

New Jersey

New Jersey C of C • Jason McDonald; Mgr., Process & Ofc. Svcs.; 216 W. State St.; Trenton; 08608; Mercer; P 8,500,000; M 1,600; (609) 989-7888; Fax (609) 989-9696; jason.mcdonald@njchamber. com; www.njchamber.com

Aberdeen • *see Matawan*

Allumuchy • *see Washington*

Alpha • *see Washington*

Asbury Park • *Asbury Park C/C* • Cindi D'Onofrio; Exec. Dir.; 308 Main St.; P.O. Box 649; 07712; Monmouth; P 20,000; M 300; (732) 775-7676; Fax (732) 775-7675; cindi@asburyparkchamber.com; www.asburyparkchamber.com

Atlantic City • *Greater Atlantic City C/C* • Joseph Kelly; Pres.; 12 S. Virginia Ave.; 08401; Atlantic; P 252,552; M 700; (609) 345-4524; Fax (609) 345-1666; acchamber@aol.com; www.acchamber.com*

Atlantic Highlands • *see Hazlet*

Avalon • *Avalon C/C* • John Allison; Pres.; 30th & Ocean Dr.; P.O. Box 22; 08202; Cape May; P 2,162; M 250; (609) 967-3936; Fax (609) 967-1815; chamber@avalonbeach.com; www.avalonbeach.com

Basking Ridge • *Bernards Twp. Reg. C/C* • Albert LiCata; Exec. Dir.; P.O. Box 11; 07920; Somerset; P 28,000; M 210; (908) 766-6755; Ren1co@aol.com; www.bernardstwpregionalchamber.org

Bay Head • *see Point Pleasant Beach*

Bayonne • *Bayonne C/C* • Gen. Mgr.; 621 Ave. C; P.O. Box 266; 07002; Hudson; P 64,000; M 120; (201) 436-4333; info@bayonne chamber.org; www.bayonnenj.org

Bayville • *see Toms River*

Belford • *see Hazlet*

Belmar • *Belmar C/C* • Tracy Keller; Exec. Dir.; 1005 1/2 Main St.; 07719; Monmouth; P 7,340; M 125; (732) 681-2900; Fax (732) 681-8471; admin@belmarchamber.com; www.belmarchamber.com

Belvidere • *see Washington*

Bergen • *see Hasbrouck Heights*

Berkeley Heights • *see Summit*

Bernardsville • *Bernardsville C/C* • Caesar Mistretta Sr.; Pres./ Exec. Dir.; P.O. Box 672; 07924; Somerset; P 7,400; M 160; (908) 766-9900; Fax (908) 766-3833; nancymclurebcc@gmail.com; bvillechamber.com

Blairstown • *see Washington*

Bloomfield • *Suburban Essex C/C* • Donna Pietroiacovo; Exec. Admin.; 256 Broad St., Rm. 2F; 07003; Essex; P 48,000; M 250; (973) 748-2000; Fax (973) 748-2450; admin@suburbanessex chamber.com; www.suburbanessexchamber.com

Bloomingdale • *Tri-Boro Area C/C* • Gerald Vinci; Pres.; P.O. Box 100; 07403; Passaic; P 30,922; M 80; (973) 838-5678; Fax (973) 838-5229; triborochamber@aol.com; www.triborochamber.org

Bogota • *C/C of Bogota* • Louis Knaube; Pres.; P.O. Box 81; 07603; Bergen; P 8,000; M 48; (201) 487-8983; info@bogota chamber.org; www.bogotachamber.org

Boonton • *Tri-Town C/C* • Gina Ramich; Exec. Dir.; P.O. Box 496; 07005; Morris; P 16,300; M 170; (973) 334-4117; Fax (973) 263-4164; info@tritownchamber.org; www.tritownchamber.org

Bordentown · *Northern Burlington Reg. C/C* · Diane DiSpaldo; Exec. Secy.; P.O. Box 65; 08505; Burlington; P 8,000; M 80; (609) 298-7774; Fax (609) 291-5008; information@nbrchamber.org; www.nbrchamber.org

Bound Brook · *Bound Brook Area C/C* · Deanne Confalone; Pres.; P.O. Box 227; 08805; Somerset; P 15,000; M 50; (732) 356-7273; bbacoc@gmail.com; www.bbareachamber.com

Brick · *Brick Twp. C/C* · Michele Eventoff; Exec. Dir.; 270 Chambers Bridge Rd.; 08723; Ocean; P 85,000; M 600; (732) 477-4949; Fax (732) 477-5788; info@brickchamber.com; www.brickchamber.com*

Bridgeton · *Bridgeton Area C/C* · Anthony Stanzione; Exec. Dir.; 76 Magnolia Ave.; P.O. Box 1063; 08302; Cumberland; P 38,000; M 190; (856) 455-1312; Fax (856) 453-9795; bacc@baccnj.com; www.baccnj.com

Bridgewater · *Somerset County Bus. Partnership* · Michael Kerwin; Pres./CEO; 360 Grove St. at Rte. 22 E.; P.O. Box 833; 08876; Somerset; P 315,000; M 650; (908) 218-4300; Fax (908) 722-7823; info@scbp.org; www.scbp.org*

Brielle · *Brielle C/C* · Joe Higgins; Pres.; P.O. Box 162; 08730; Monmouth; P 4,900; M 100; (732) 528-0377; info@briellechamber.com; www.briellechamber.com

Brigantine Beach · *Brigantine Beach C/C* · Emmett Turner; Pres.; P.O. Box 484; 08203; Atlantic; P 12,000; M 115; (609) 266-3437; info@brigantinechamber.com; www.brigantinechamber.com

Broadway · *see Washington*

Budd Lake · *Mt. Olive Area C/C* · Jeff Stadelman; Pres.; P.O. Box 192; 07828; Morris; P 26,000; M 130; (973) 691-0109; info@mtolivechambernj.com; www.mtolivechambernj.com

Burlington · *Greater Burlington C/C* · Sue Woolman; Secy.; P.O. Box 67; 08016; Burlington; P 35,000; M 55; (609) 387-4528; swoolman@cornerstonebank.net; www.greaterburlingtoncoc.com

Burlington County · *see Mount Laurel*

Butler · *see Bloomingdale and Wayne*

Caldwell · *see West Caldwell*

Camden · *see Cherry Hill*

Cape May · *C/C of Greater Cape May* · John Cooke; Pres.; P.O. Box 556; 08204; Cape May; P 5,000; M 300; (609) 884-5508; Fax (609) 884-2054; request@capemaychamber.com; www.capemaychamber.com

Cape May County · *Cape May County C/C* · Vicki Clark IOM; Pres.; P.O. Box 74; Cape May Court House; 08210; Cape May; P 98,000; M 965; (609) 465-7181; Fax (609) 465-5017; info@cmcchamber.com; www.capemaycountychamber.com*

Cape May Court House · *Middle Township C/C* · Barbara Peltzer; Pres.; P.O. Box 6; 08210; Cape May; P 15,000; M 125; (609) 463-1655; middletownshipchamberofcom@middletownshipchamberofcommerce.org; www.middletownshipchamberofcommerce.org

Carneys Point · *Salem County C/C* · Jennifer A. Jones; Exec. Dir.; 91A S. Virginia Ave.; 08069; Salem; P 65,000; M 400; (856) 299-6699; Fax (856) 299-0299; sccoc@verizon.net; www.salemnjchamber.homestead.com*

Cedar Grove · *see West Caldwell*

Cedar Knolls · *see Florham Park*

Chatham · *Chatham Area C/C* · Carolyn Cherry; Exec. Dir.; P.O. Box 231; 07928; Morris; P 40,000; M 200; (973) 635-2444; Fax (973) 635-2953; chathamchamber@gmail.com; www.chathamchambernj.org

Cherry Hill · *Cherry Hill Reg. C/C* · Arthur Campbell; Pres.; 1060 Kings Hwy. N. , Ste. 200; 08034; Camden; P 70,000; M 950; (856) 667-1600; Fax (856) 667-1464; info@cherryhillregional.com; www.cherryhillregional.com

Cliffside Park · *Cliffside Park C/C* · Lynne Nesbihal; Exec. Dir.; 645 Anderson Ave.; 07010; Bergen; P 24,000; M 350; (201) 941-9505; Fax (201) 941-8499; info@cliffsideparkchamber.org; www.cliffsideparkonline.com/chamber

Clifton · *North Jersey Reg. C/C* · Gloria Martini; Pres.; 1033 Rte. 46 E., Ste. A103; 07013; Passaic; P 150,000; M 600; (973) 470-9300; Fax (973) 470-9245; staff@njrcc.org; www.njrcc.org

Clinton · *see Flemington*

Colts Neck · *see Freehold*

Columbia · *see Washington*

Cranford · *Cranford C/C* · J. Robert Hoeffler; Exec. Dir.; 8 Springfield Ave.; P.O. Box 165; 07016; Union; P 25,000; M 175; (908) 272-6114; Fax (908) 272-3742; cranfordchamber@comcast.net; www.cranford.com/chamber

Dennis Township · *see Ocean View*

Denville · *Denville C/C* · Kristin Pamperin; Pres.; P.O. Box 333; 07834; Morris; P 14,000; M 155; (973) 625-1171; president@denville-nj.com; www.denville-nj.com

Dover · *Dover Area C/C* · P.O. Box 506; 07802; Ocean; P 16,000; M 100; (973) 676-8725; Fax (973) 673-5828; email@doverareachamber.com; www.doverareachamber.com

Dumont · *Dumont C/C* · P.O. Box 10; 07628; Bergen; P 18,000; M 60; (201) 280-4441; michaelbrown@brownfineproperties.com

Dunellen · *see Piscataway*

East Brunswick · *East Brunswick Reg. C/C* · P.O. Box 56; 08816; Middlesex; P 100,000; M 190; (732) 257-3009; Fax (732) 257-0949; office@ebchamber.org; www.ebchamber.org

East Hanover · *see Florham Park*

East Millstone · *see Franklin Twp.*

East Newark · *see Jersey City*

East Orange · *East Orange C/C* · Amir Hashemi; Pres.; P.O. Box 2418; 07019; Essex; P 80,000; M 50; (973) 674-0900; Fax (973) 673-5027; info@eastorangechamber.biz; www.eastorangechamber.biz

East Windsor · *see Mercerville*

Eatontown · *see Red Bank*

Edison · *Edison C/C* · Barbara C. Roos; Pres./CEO; 336 Raritan Center Pkwy.; Campus Plaza 6; 08837; Middlesex; P 103,000; M 300; (732) 738-9482; Fax (732) 738-9485; president@edisonchamber.com; www.edisonchamber.com*

Egg Harbor City · *Egg Harbor City C/C* · Miles Lederer; Pres.; P.O. Box 129; 08215; Atlantic; P 4,545; M 50; (856) 237-6630; (609) 965-0081; venicegrill@verizon.net; www.eggharborcity.org

Elizabeth · *Gateway Reg. C/C* · James R. Coyle; Pres.; 135 Jefferson Ave.; P.O. Box 300; 07207; Union; P 504,000; M 1,800; (908) 352-0900; Fax (908) 352-0865; jamescoyle@gatewaychamber.com; www.gatewaychamber.com

Elizabeth · *Greater Elizabeth C/C* · Gordon F. Haas; Pres./CEO; 456 N. Broad St., 2nd Flr.; 07208; Union; P 127,000; M 450; (908) 355-7600; Fax (908) 436-2054; gecc@juno.com; elizabethchamber.com.*

Englewood · *Englewood C/C* · Karen Rawl; Exec. Dir.; 2-10 N. Van Brunt St.; 07631; Bergen; P 27,500; M 175; (201) 567-2381; Fax (201) 871-4549; englewoodchamber@gmail.com; www.englewood-chamber.com

Englewood Cliffs • *Englewood Cliffs C/C* • Shari DePalma; Pres.; P.O. Box 954; 07632; Bergen; P 6,500; M 55; (201) 567-9344; Fax (201) 227-5029; www.englewoodcliffschamber.com

Englishtown • *see Freehold*

Essex County • *see Wayne and West Caldwell*

Essex Fells • *see West Caldwell*

Ewing • *see Mercerville*

Fair Haven • *see Red Bank*

Fair Lawn • *Fair Lawn C/C* • Debbie Berowitz; Exec. Dir.; 18-00 Fair Lawn Ave.; 07410; Bergen; P 33,000; M 250; (201) 796-7050; Fax (201) 475-0619; info@fairlawnchamber.org; www.fairlawn chamber.org

Fairfield • *see Wayne and West Caldwell*

Farmingdale • *Farmingdale C/C* • John Doyle; Pres.; 11 Asbury Ave.; 07727; Monmouth; P 1,587; M 60; (732) 921-9160; (732) 938-4077; Fax (732) 938-2023

Flemington • *Hunterdon County C/C* • Christopher J. Phelan; Pres./CEO; 1 Church St., Ste. 73; 08822; Hunterdon; P 121,000; M 550; (908) 782-7115; Fax (908) 782-7283; info@hunterdon-chamber.org; www.hunterdon-chamber.org*

Florham Park • *Hanover Area C/C* • Steven F. Miller; Pres.; P.O. Box 168; 07932; Morris; P 25,000; (973) 884-3278; info@hanoverareachamber.org; www.hanoverareachamber.org

Florham Park • *Morris County C/C* • Paul Boudreau; Pres.; 325 Columbia Tpk., Ste. 101; 07932; Morris; P 421,361; M 784; (973) 539-3882; Fax (973) 377-0859; laura@morrischamber.org; www.morrischamber.org.*

Fort Lee • *The Greater Fort Lee C/C* • Liz Crawford; Admin. Asst.; 210 Whiteman St.; 07024; Bergen; P 36,000; M 200; (201) 944-7575; Fax (201) 944-5168; assistant@fortleechamber.com; www.fortleechamber.com

Franklin Lakes • *Franklin Lakes C/C* • Lorianne Brunsch; Exec. Asst.; P.O. Box 81; 07417; Bergen; P 9,200; M 50; (973) 209-1714; info@flcoc.org; www.flcoc.org

Franklin Twp. • *Franklin Twp. C/C* • Mary L. Smith; Exec. Dir.; 675 Franklin Blvd.; Somerset; 08873; Somerset; P 51,000; M 200; (732) 545-7044; Fax (732) 745-7043; director@franklinchamber.com; www.franklinchamber.com

Freehold • *Greater Monmouth C/C* • Loretta Kuhnert; Pres.; 17 Broad St.; 07728; Monmouth; P 183,096; M 450; (732) 462-3030; Fax (732) 462-2123; info@greatermonmouthchamber.com; www.greatermonmouthchamber.com

Garfield • *C/C of Garfield* • Judy Messineo; V.P./Secy.; P.O. Box 525; 07026; Bergen; P 27,000; M 201; (973) 773-7500; Fax (973) 340-3941; info@chamberofgarfield.com; www.chamberofgarfield.com

Gibbstown • *see Cherry Hill*

Glassboro • *Greater Glassboro C/C* • Karal Corradetti; Pres.; P.O. Box 651; 08028; Gloucester; P 19,870; M 90; (609) 221-0983; Fax (856) 881-7755; info@glassborochamber.com; www.glassboro chamber.com

Glen Brook • *see Piscataway*

Glen Rock • *Glen Rock C/C* • Pam Wolak; Pres.; 199 Rock Rd.; 07452; Bergen; P 11,600; M 65; (201) 447-3434; Fax (201) 447-2973; glenrockchamber@yahoo.com; www.glenrocknj.net

Gloucester County • *see Cherry Hill*

Great Meadows • *see Washington*

Griggstown • *see Franklin Twp.*

Guttenberg • *see Jersey City*

Hackensack • *Hackensack Reg. C/C* • Darlene Damstrom; Exec. Dir.; 5 University Plaza Dr.; 07601; Bergen; P 42,000; M 225; (201) 489-3700; Fax (201) 489-1741; chamberhacknj@aol.com; www.hackensackchamber.org*

Hackettstown • *see Washington*

Haddonfield • *see Voorhees*

Haledon • *see Wayne*

Hammonton • *Greater Hammonton C/C* • Michele Samanic; Exec. Dir.; 10 S. Egg Harbor Rd.; P.O. Box 554; 08037; Atlantic; P 13,500; M 125; (609) 561-9080; Fax (609) 561-9411; info@hammontonnj.us; www.hammontonnj.us

Hanover Twp. • *see Florham Park*

Hardwick • *see Washington*

Harrison • *see Jersey City*

Hasbrouck Heights • *Hasbrouck Heights C/C* • Ray Vorisek; Pres.; P.O. Box 1; 07604; Bergen; P 12,000; M 100; (201) 288-5464; heightsflowershoppe@verizon.net; www.hasbrouck-heights.org

Hawthorne • *Hawthorne C/C* • Joann Ciampa; Exec. Secy.; 471 Lafayette Ave.; P.O. Box 331; 07507; Passaic; P 17,000; M 230; (973) 427-5078; Fax (973) 427-6066; hawcofc@aol.com; www.hawthornecofc.com

Hazlet • *Northern Monmouth C/C* • Paul Morris; Exec. Dir.; 1340 Hwy. 36, Ste. 22; P.O. Box 5007; 07730; Monmouth; P 90,000; M 350; (732) 203-0340; Fax (732) 203-0341; director@northern monmouthchamber.com; www.northernmonmouthchamber.com

Highlands • *see Hazlet*

Hightstown • *see Mercerville*

Hillside • *Hillside C/C* • John Kruse; Pres.; P.O. Box 965; 07205; Union; P 65,000; M 100; (908) 964-6659; Fax (908) 964-3781; jwayjohn@aol.com; www.hillsidechamber.com

Hoboken • *Hoboken C/C* • Brian Battaglia; Pres.; P.O. Box 349; 07030; Hudson; P 38,000; M 160; (201) 222-1100; Fax (201) 222-9120; info@hobokenchamber.biz; www.hobokenchamber.com

Hohokus • *Ho-Ho-kus C/C* • Stephen E. Eiman; Pres.; P.O. Box 115; 07423; Bergen; P 4,000; M 20; (201) 444-6664; (201) 670-5743; Fax (201) 444-6292; www.ho-ho-kusboro.com

Holmdel • *see Hazlet*

Hope • *Hope Area C/C* • Chris Maier; Pres.; P.O. Box 2; 07844; Warren; P 7,000; M 45; (908) 475-8322; chamberhope@yahoo.com; www.hopeareachamber.com

Hopewell Township • *see Mercerville*

Howell • *Howell C/C* • Susan Dominguez; Exec. Dir.; 103 W. 2nd St., Ste. 2; P.O. Box 196; 07731; Monmouth; P 50,000; M 246; (732) 363-4114; Fax (732) 363-8747; info@howellchamber.com; www.howellchamber.com

Irvington • *Irvington C/C* • Luz Carde; Exec. Dir.; P.O. Box 323; 07111; Essex; P 65,000; M 150; (973) 676-8725; Fax (973) 673-5828; email@irvington-nj.com; www.irvington-nj.com

Iselin • *see Woodbridge*

Jackson • *Jackson C/C* • Clara Glory; Pres.; 1021 W. Commodore Blvd.; 08527; Ocean; P 51,870; M 245; (732) 833-0005; Fax (732) 833-7033; jcinfo@jacksonchamber.com; www.jacksonchamber.com

Jersey City • *Hudson County C/C* • Brian Dunlap; Pres.; 857 Bergen Ave., 3rd Flr.; 07306; Hudson; P 600,000; M 500; (201) 386-0699; Fax (201) 386-8480; info@hudsonchamber.org; www.hudsonchamber.org

Johnsonburg • *see Washington*

Keansburg • *see Hazlet*

Kearny · *see Jersey City*

Kingston · *see Franklin Twp.*

Kinnelon · *see Bloomingdale and Wayne*

Lake Hiawatha · *Parsippany Area C/C* · Robert Peluso; Pres.; 12-14 N. Beverwyck Rd.; 07034; Morris; P 55,000; M 300; (973) 402-6400; craig@parsippanychamber.org; www.parsippany chamber.org

Lake Hopatcong · *Jefferson Twp. C/C* · Jack Devore; Pres.; 604 Central Ave.; P.O. Box 64; 07849; Sussex; P 19,000; M 70; (973) 663-2240; jefftwpcc@gmail.com; www.jeffersontownshipchamber.org

Lakewood · *Lakewood C/C* · Maureen Stankowitz; Exec. Dir.; 395 Rte. 70 W., Ste. 125; 08701; Ocean; P 71,359; M 490; (732) 363-0012; Fax (732) 367-4453; maureen@mylakewoodchamber. com; www.mylakewoodchamber.com.

Lambertville · *Lambertville Area C/C* · Ellen Pineno; Ofc. Mgr.; 59 N. Union St., Unit B; 08530; Hunterdon; P 4,300; M 200; (609) 397-0055; info@lambertville.org; www.lambertville.org

Landing · *see Ledgewood*

Lavallette · *see Toms River*

Lawrenceville · *see Mercerville*

Lebanon · *see Flemington*

Ledgewood · *Roxbury Area C/C* · Elaine Honig; Secy.; P.O. Box 436; 07852; Morris; P 22,000; M 120; (973) 770-0740; elaine@ roxburynjchamber.org; www.roxburynjchamber.org

Leonardo · *see Hazlet*

Lincoln Park · *see Wayne*

Little Falls · *see Clifton, Wayne & West Caldwell*

Little Silver · *see Red Bank*

Livingston · *Livingston Area C/C* · Beth Lippman; Exec. Dir./ Admin.; 25 S. Livingston Ave.; 2nd Flr., Ste. E; 07039; Essex; P 27,000; M 160; (973) 992-4343; Fax (973) 992-8024; info@ livingstonchambernj.com; www.livingstonchambernj.com

Long Branch · *Greater Long Branch C/C* · Nancy Kleiberg; Exec. Dir.; 228 Broadway; P.O. Box 628; 07740; Monmouth; P 40,000; M 280; (732) 222-0400; Fax (732) 571-3385; longbranchchamber@ verizon.net; www.longbranchchamber.org.

Madison · *Madison C/C* · Karen Meyer; Exec. Dir.; P.O. Box 152; 07940; Morris; P 17,000; M 200; (973) 377-7830; Fax (973) 822-0451; info@madisonnjchamber.org; www.madisonnjchamber.org

Mahwah · *Mahwah Reg. C/C* · Sharon Rounds; Exec. Dir.; 65 Ramapo Valley Rd., Ste. 211; 07430; Bergen; P 26,000; M 520; (201) 529-5566; Fax (201) 529-8122; sharon@mahwah.com; www.mahwah.com

Manahawkin · *see Ship Bottom*

Manalapan · *see Freehold*

Manasquan · *Manasquan C/C* · John Newman; Pres.; 107 Main St.; 08736; Monmouth; P 6,000; M 150; (732) 223-8303; info@ manasquanchamber.org; www.manasquanchamber.org

Manville · *see Franklin Twp.*

Maplewood · *Maplewood C/C* · Rene Conlon; Exec. Secy.; P.O. Box 423; 07040; Essex; P 24,000; M 150; (973) 761-4333; Fax (973) 762-9105; contact11@mindspring.com; www.maplewood chamber.org

Marlboro · *see Freehold*

Marlton · *see Mount Laurel*

Matawan · *Matawan-Aberdeen C/C* · Mike Moyers; Pres.; P.O. Box 522; 07747; Monmouth; P 30,000; M 130; (732) 290-1125; Fax (732) 290-1125; macocnj@macocnj.com; www.macocnj.com

Maywood · *Maywood C/C* · Dr. Timothy Eustace; Pres.; 140 W. Pleasant Ave.; 07607; Bergen; P 9,536; M 75; (201) 843-3111; teustace@aol.com; www.maywoodboro.org

Meadowlands · *see Rutherford-Meadowlands Reg. C/C*

Medford · *see Burlington*

Mercerville · *Mercer Reg. C/C* · Robert D. Prunetti; Pres./CEO; 1A Quakerbridge Plaza Dr., Ste. 2; 08619; Mercer; P 366,222; M 1,300; (609) 689-9960; Fax (609) 586-9989; info@mercer chamber.org; www.mercerchamber.org

Metuchen · *Metuchen Area C/C* · Caroline Woodruff; Ofc. Admin.; 323 Main St., Ste. B; 08840; Middlesex; P 13,000; M 300; (732) 548-2964; Fax (732) 548-4094; metuchen.chamber@verizon. net; www.metuchenchamber.com

Middlesex · *see Piscataway*

Middlesex County · *see New Brunswick*

Middletown · *see Hazlet*

Midland Park · *Midland Park C/C* · Mr. Chris Rossi; Pres.; P.O. Box 267; 07432; Bergen; P 8,000; M 75; (201) 445-0100; www. mpnj.com

Millburn · *Millburn-Short Hills C/C* · Karol McNulty; Exec. Dir.; 343 Millburn Ave., Ste. 303; P.O. Box 651; 07041; Essex; P 18,600; M 250; (973) 379-1198; Fax (973) 376-5678; info@millburnshort hillschamber.com; www.millburnchamber.com

Millstone · *see Freehold*

Millville · *Greater Millville C/C* · Earl Sherrick; Exec. Dir.; 4 City Park Dr.; P.O. Box 831; 08332; Cumberland; P 26,000; M 200; (856) 825-2600; Fax (856) 825-5333; chamber@millville-nj.com; www. millville-nj.com

Monmouth Beach · *see Red Bank*

Montclair · *see West Caldwell*

Montville · *Montville Twp. C/C* · Margaret Miller-Sanders; Pres.; 195 Changebridge Rd.; 07045; Morris; P 20,863; M 190; (973) 263-3310; Fax (973) 263-3453; info@montvillechamber.com; www. montvillechamber.com

Moorestown · *see Mount Laurel*

Mooresville · *see Mount Laurel*

Mount Freedom · *Randolph Area C/C* · Bill Burke; Pres.; P.O. Box 391; 07970; Morris; P 26,000; M 80; (973) 361-3462; Fax (973) 895-3297; www.randolphchamber.org

Mount Laurel · *Burlington County C/C* · Kristi Howell-Ikeda; Pres.; 100 Technology Way, Ste. 110; 08054; Burlington; P 396,000; M 425; (856) 439-2520; Fax (856) 439-2523; bccoc@ bccoc.com; www.bccoc.com*

Mount Olive · *see Budd Lake*

Mountain Lakes · *see Boonton*

Mountainside · *see Elizabeth*

Navesink · *see Hazlet*

New Brunswick · *Middlesex County Reg. C/C* · Alex Hollywood; Op. Mgr.; 109 Church St.; 08901; Middlesex; P 750,162; M 750; (732) 745-8090; Fax (732) 745-8098; info@mcrcc.org; www.mcrcc. org; www.gocentraljersey.com

New Providence · *see Summit*

Newark • *Newark Reg. Bus. Partnership* • Chip Hallock; Pres./CEO; National Newark Bldg.; 744 Broad St., 26th Flr.; 07102; Essex; P 280,000; M 500; (973) 522-0099; Fax (973) 824-6587; ndrake@newarkrbp.org; www.newarkrbp.org

Newark • *Statewide Hispanic C/C of NJ* • Dr. Daniel H. Jara; Pres./CEO; 1 Gateway Center, Ste. 615; 07102; Essex; P 500,000; M 2,800; (201) 451-9512; Fax (866) 226-1828; chamber@shccnj.org; www.shccnj.org

Newton • *Sussex County C/C* • Tammie Horsfield; Pres.; 120 Hampton House Rd.; 07860; Sussex; P 135,000; M 700; (973) 579-1811; Fax (973) 579-3031; mail@sussexcountychamber.org; www.sussexcountychamber.org*

North Bergen • *see Jersey City*

North Caldwell • *see West Caldwell*

Northfield • *see Atlantic City*

Nutley • *Nutley C/C* • Richard Spector; Ofc. Mgr.; 172 Chestnut St.; 07110; Essex; P 28,000; M 150; (973) 667-5300; Fax (973) 667-5300; chamber@nutleychamber.com; www.nutleychamber.com

Oakhurst • *Greater Ocean Twp. C/C* • Kim Horn-Blanda; Interim Bus. Mgr.; 2002 Bellmore St.; P.O. Box 656; 07755; Monmouth; P 30,000; M 250; (732) 660-1888; Fax (732) 660-1688; info@gotcc.org; gotcc.org

Ocean City • *Ocean City C/C* • Michele Gillian; Exec. Dir.; 16 E. 9th St.; 08226; Cape May; P 15,000; M 500; (609) 399-1412; (800) BEACH-NJ; Fax (609) 398-3932; info@oceancitychamber.com; www.oceancityvacation.com

Ocean County • *see Toms River*

Ocean Grove • *Ocean Grove Area C/C* • Lois Hetfield; Admin.; 45 Pilgrim Pathway; P.O. Box 415; 07756; Monmouth; P 7,500; M 122; (732) 774-1391; (800) 388-4768; Fax (732) 774-3799; info@oceangrovenj.com; www.oceangrovenj.com

Ocean Twp. • *see Oakhurst*

Ocean View • *Dennis Twp. C/C* • Thomas Giansante; Pres.; P.O. Box 85; 08230; Cape May; P 7,000; M 85; (609) 408-4119; info@dennistwpchamber.com; www.dennistwpchamber.com

Oceanport • *see Red Bank*

Old Bridge • *The C/C serving Old Bridge, Sayreville & South Amboy* • Reggie Butler; Pres.; P.O. Box 5241; 08857; Middlesex; P 150,000; M 145; (732) 607-6340; Fax (732) 607-6341; info@obssachamber.org; www.obssachamber.org

Oradell • *see River Edge*

Ortley Beach • *see Toms River*

Oxford • *see Washington*

Paramus • *Greater Paramus C/C* • Fred Rohdieck; Pres./CEO; 58 E. Midland Ave.; P.O. Box 325; 07652; Bergen; P 45,000; M 426; (201) 261-3344; Fax (201) 261-3346; office2005@paramuschamber.com; www.paramuschamber.com.*

Parsippany • *see Lake Hiawatha*

Passaic • *see Clifton*

Passaic County • *see Wayne*

Paterson • *Greater Paterson C/C* • James Dykes II; Pres.; 100 Hamilton Plz., Ste. 1201; 07505; Passaic; P 170,000; M 650; (973) 881-7300; Fax (973) 881-8233; gpcc@greaterpatersoncc.org; www.greaterpatersoncc.org

Paulsboro • *Greater Paulsboro C/C* • Tony Salvatore; Pres.; P.O. Box 181; 08066; Gloucester; P 6,000; M 50; (856) 423-7600; president@paulsborochamber.com; www.paulsborochamber.com

Pennington • *see Mercerville*

Pequannock • *see Bloomingdale and Wayne*

Perth Amboy • *Perth Amboy C/C* • Miguel Chavez; Admin. Asst.; P.O. Box 1910; 08862; Middlesex; P 35,000; M 160; (732) 442-7400; Fax (908) 755-9303; pachamberofcommerce@verizon.net; www.perthamboychamber.com

Phillipsburg • *Phillipsburg Area C/C* • J. Michael Dowd; V.P.; 314 S. Main St.; 08865; Warren; P 35,000; M 250; (908) 859-5161; (610) 739-1521; Fax (908) 859-6861; miked@lehighvalleychamber.org; www.lehighvalleychamber.org*

Pine Beach • *see Toms River*

Piscataway • *Piscataway/Middlesex/South Plainfield C/C* • Linda Griggs; Exec. Dir.; 377 Hoes Ln., Ste. 105; 08854; Middlesex; P 70,000; M 110; (732) 394-0220; Fax (732) 560-1198; chamber@pmspcoc.org; www.pmspcoc.org

Plainfield • *Plainfield C/C* • 320 Park Ave.; 07060; Union; P 48,600; M 200; (908) 753-2296; Fax (908) 753-6609; chamber@positivelyplainfield.org; www.positivelyplainfield.org

Point Pleasant Beach • *Point Pleasant Beach C/C* • Carol Vaccaro; Exec. Dir.; 517A Arnold Ave.; 08742; Ocean; P 6,000; M 310; (732) 899-2424; (888) PPBFUN2; Fax (732) 899-0103; info@pointpleasantbeachnj.com; www.pointpleasantbeachnj.org

Pompton Lakes • *Pompton Lakes C/C* • Art Kaffka; Pres.; P.O. Box 129; 07442; Passaic; P 11,000; M 95; (973) 839-0187; Fax (973) 839-0187; info@pomptonchamber.com; www.pomptonlakeschamber.com

Port Murray • *see Washington*

Princeton • *Princeton Reg. C/C* • Peter Crowley; Pres./CEO; 9 Vandeventer Ave.; 08542; Mercer; P 150,000; M 745; (609) 924-1776; Fax (609) 924-5776; info@princetonchamber.org; www.princetonchamber.org

Princeton Junction • *see Princeton*

Randolph • *see Mount Freedom*

Readington • *see Flemington*

Red Bank • *Eastern Monmouth Area C/C* • Lynda Rose; Pres./COO; 47 Reckless Pl., Ste. A; 07701; Monmouth; P 100,000; M 650; (732) 741-0055; Fax (732) 741-6778; info@emacc.org; www.emacc.org

Ridgewood • *Ridgewood C/C* • Joan Groome; Exec. Dir.; 27 Chestnut St., Ste. 1B; 07450; Bergen; P 25,000; M 250; (201) 445-2600; Fax (201) 251-1958; info@ridgewoodchamber.com; www.ridgewoodchamber.com

Ringwood • *Ringwood C/C* • Edward W. Martin; Pres.; P.O. Box 62; 07456; Passaic; P 13,000; M 200; president@ringwoodchamber.com; www.ringwoodchamber.com

River Edge • *River Edge C/C* • Jonathan Rochlin; Pres.; P.O. Box 15; 07661; Bergen; P 11,000; M 75; (201) 576-9400; jonathan.rochlin@ml.com; www.riveredgechamber.org

Riverdale • *see Bloomingdale and Wayne*

Rochelle Park • *see Paramus*

Roseland • *see West Caldwell*

Roxbury • *see Ledgewood*

Rumson • *see Red Bank*

Rutherford • *Meadowlands Reg. Chamber* • James Kirkos; Pres./CEO; 201 Route 17 N., 2nd Flr.; 07070; Bergen; P 1,000,000; M 800; (201) 939-0707; Fax (201) 939-0522; office@meadowlands.org; www.meadowlands.org*

Rutherford • *Rutherford C/C* • Alice Allen; Exec. Secy.; P.O. Box 216; 07070; Bergen; P 19,000; M 75; (201) 933-3633; Fax (201) 507-7077; info@rutherfordchamber.com; www.rutherfordchamber.com

Saddle Brook · *see Hackensack*

Salem · *see Carneys Point*

Sandy Hook · *see Hazlet*

Sayreville · *see Old Bridge*

Scotch Plains · *see Westfield*

Sea Bright · *see Red Bank*

Sea Girt · *see Wall*

Sea Isle City · *Greater Sea Isle City C/C* · Christopher Glancey; Pres.; P.O. Box 635; 08243; Cape May; P 3,000; M 85; (609) 263-9090; Fax (609) 263-9090; www.seaislechamber.com

Seaside Heights · *see Toms River*

Seaside Park · *see Toms River*

Secaucus · *see Jersey City*

Ship Bottom · *Southern Ocean County C/C* · Rick Reynolds; Exec. Dir.; 265 W. 9th St.; 08008; Ocean; P 50,000; M 700; (609) 494-7211; (800) 292-6372; Fax (609) 494-5807; info@discover southernocean.com; www.discoversouthernocean.com

Short Hills · *see Millburn*

Shrewsbury · *see Red Bank*

Somerset · *see Franklin Twp.*

Somerville · *see Bridgewater*

South Amboy · *see Old Bridge*

South Orange · *South Orange C/C* · Allen Noel; Pres.; P.O. Box 621; 07079; Essex; P 17,000; M 60; (973) 763-8601; Fax (973) 762-6221; director@southorangechamber.com; www.south orangechamber.com

South Plainfield · *see Piscataway*

Spring Lake · *Greater Spring Lake C/C* · 302 Washington Ave.; P.O. Box 694; 07762; Monmouth; P 25,000; M 140; (732) 449-0577; www.springlake.org

Stewartsville · *see Washington*

Stone Harbor · *Stone Harbor C/C* · Bill Barbar; Pres.; P.O. Box 422; 08247; Cape May; P 1,100; M 200; (609) 368-6101; Fax (609) 368-6102; www.stoneharborbeach.com

Summit · *Suburban C/C* · Maureen Kelly; Pres.; 71 Summit Ave.; 07901; Union; P 75,000; M 300; (908) 522-1700; Fax (908) 522-9252; mkelly@suburbanchambers.org; www.suburbanchambers.org

Sussex County · *see Newton*

Teaneck · *Teaneck C/C* · Larry Bauer; Pres.; 802 Cedar Ln.; 07666; Bergen; P 39,255; M 100; (201) 801-0012; info@teaneck chamber.org; www.teaneckchamber.org

Tenafly · *Tenafly C/C* · Bob Kutik; Pres.; 100 Riveredge Rd.; P.O. Box 163; 07670; Bergen; P 13,852; M 100; (201) 568-8857; (201) 568-6100; www.tenaflychamberofcommerce.com

Tinton Falls · *see Red Bank*

Toms River · *Toms River-Ocean County C/C* · Jean Hryniw; Interim Pres.; 1200 Hooper Ave.; 08753; Ocean; P 135,000; M 800; (732) 349-0220; Fax (732) 349-1252; info@oc-chamber.com; www.oc-chamber.com.*

Totowa · *see Clifton and Wayne*

Turnersville · *Washington Twp. C/C* · Wendy Bartlett; Pres.; 5001 Rte. 42, Ste. C; P.O. Box 734; 08012; Gloucester; P 49,000; M 175; (856) 227-1776; Fax (856) 227-1225; www.washington townshipchamber.org

Union · *Union Twp. C/C* · Meera Rao; Exec. Dir.; 355 Chestnut St., 2nd Flr.; 07083; Union; P 54,500; M 300; (908) 688-2777; Fax (908) 688-0338; info@unionchamber.com; www.unionchamber.com

Union Beach · *see Hazlet*

Union City · *see Jersey City*

Vernon · *Vernon C/C* · P.O. Box 308; 07462; Sussex; P 25,000; (973) 764-0764; info@vernonchamber.com; www.vernonchamber.com

Verona · *see West Caldwell*

Vineland · *Greater Vineland C/C* · Dawn Hunter; Exec. Dir.; 2115 S. Delsea Dr.; 08360; Cumberland; P 60,000; M 500; (856) 691-7400; Fax (856) 691-2113; info@vinelandchamber.org; www.vinelandchamber.org

Voorhees · *Chamber of Commerce Southern NJ* · Debra DiLorenzo; Pres./CEO; Piazza 6014 at Main St.; 08043; Camden; P 2,500,000; M 2,000; (856) 424-7776; Fax (856) 424-8180; info@ chambersnj.com; www.chambersnj.com

Wall · *Southern Monmouth C/C* · Evelyn Mars; Exec. Dir.; P.O. Box 1305; 07719; Monmouth; P 90,000; M 350; (732) 280-8800; Fax (732) 280-8505; info@smcconline.org; www.smcconline.org*

Wanaque · *Wanaque C/C* · Michael Ryan; Pres.; P.O. Box 93; 07465; Passaic; P 11,000; M 55; (973) 835-1906; info@afamily town.org; www.afamilytown.org

Washington · *Warren County Reg. C/C* · Robert Goltz; Pres./ CEO; 10 Brass Castle Rd.; 07882; Warren; P 105,765; M 396; (908) 835-9200; Fax (908) 835-9296; info@warrencountychamber.org; www.warrencountychamber.org*

Washington Township · *see Turnersville*

Wayne · *Tri-County C/C* · Caryn Luberto; Pres.; P.O. Box 2420; 07474; Passaic; P 120,000; M 350; (862) 210-8328; Fax (973) 882-0464; caryn@tricounty.org; www.tricounty.org*

Weehawken · *see Jersey City*

West Caldwell · *North Essex C/C* · 3 Fairfield Ave.; 07006; Essex; P 52,000; M 650; (973) 226-5500; Fax (973) 403-9335; email@ northessexchamber.com; www.northessexchamber.com

West Milford · *West Milford C/C* · Nancy Hunt; Pres.; P.O. Box 234; 07480; Passaic; P 25,000; M 100; (973) 728-3150; www. westmilford.com

West New York · *West New York C/C* · Michael Parkes; Pres.; 425 60th St.; 07093; Hudson; P 47,500; M 210; (201) 295-5065; www.westnewyorknj.org

West Orange · *West Orange C/C* · Micky Wagner; Exec. Dir.; P.O. Box 83; 07052; Essex; P 45,000; M 190; (973) 731-0360; Fax (973) 736-3156; mail@westorangechamber.com; www.westorange chamber.com

West Patterson · *see Clifton and Wayne*

West Windsor · *see Mercerville*

Westfield · *Westfield Area C/C* · Neil Pinkman; Exec. Dir.; 173 Elm St., 3rd Flr.; 07090; Union; P 28,870; M 350; (908) 233-3021; Fax (908) 654-8183; info@westfieldareachamber.com; www. westfieldareachamber.com

Whippany · *see Florham Park*

Wildwood · *Greater Wildwood C/C* · Tracey DuFault; Exec. Dir.; 3306 Pacific Ave.; 08260; Cape May; P 12,000; M 600; (609) 729-4000; Fax (609) 729-4003; info@gwcoc.org; www.gwcoc.com

Willingboro · *see Mount Laurel*

Woodbridge · *Woodbridge Metro C/C* · Carol S. Hila; Pres.; 52 Main St.; 07095; Middlesex; P 100,000; M 450; (732) 636-4040; Fax (732) 636-3492; woodbridgechamber@comcast.net; www. woodbridgechamber.com.

Woodbury · *Greater Woodbury C/C* · Shirley Bierbrunner; Exec. Dir.; P.O. Box 363; 08096; Gloucester; P 10,500; M 300; (856) 845-4056; Fax (856) 848-4445; www.greaterwoodburychamber.com

Wyckoff · *Wyckoff C/C* · Diane Kuiken; Bus. Admin.; P.O. Box 2; 07481; Bergen; P 20,000; M 130; (201) 891-3616; info@wyckoff chamber.com; www.wyckoffchamber.com

Zarepath · *see Franklin Twp.*

New Mexico

Assn. of Commerce & Ind. of New Mexico · Dr. Beverlee McClure; Pres./CEO; P.O. Box 9706; Albuquerque; 87119; Bernalillo; P 1,900,000; M 1,300; (505) 842-0644; Fax (505) 842-0734; info@aci-nm.org; www.aci-nm.org

Alamogordo · *Alamogordo C/C* · Mike Espiritu; Exec. Dir.; 1301 N. White Sands Blvd.; 88310; Otero; P 38,582; M 887; (575) 437-6120; (800) 826-0294; Fax (575) 437-6334; chamber@ alamogordo.com; www.alamogordo.com*

Albuquerque Area

Albuquerque Hispano C/C · Alex O. Romero; Pres./CEO; 1309 4th St. S.W.; 87102; Bernalillo; P 600,000; M 1,500; (505) 842-9003; (888) 451-7824; Fax (505) 764-9664; alex@ahcnm.org; www.ahcnm.org

American Indian C/C of New Mexico · Theodore M. Pedro; Exec. Dir.; 2401 12th St. NW, Ste. 5-S; 87104; Bernalillo; P 1,900,000; M 375; (505) 766-9545; Fax (505) 766-9499; americanindianch@qwestoffice.net; www.aiccnm.com

Greater Albuquerque C/C · Mrs. Terri L. Cole CCE; Pres./ CEO; 115 Gold Ave. S.W., Ste. 201; 87102; Bernalillo; P 850,000; M 5,600; (505) 764-3700; Fax (505) 764-3714; infospec@ abqchamber.com; www.abqchamber.com

Algodones · *see Rio Rancho*

Angel Fire · *Angel Fire C/C* · Katherine McDermott; Pres.; 3407 Mountain View Blvd., Centro Plaza; P.O. Box 547; 87710; Colfax; P 1,600; M 215; (575) 377-6661; (800) 446-8117; Fax (575) 377-3034; askus@angelfirechamber.org; www.angelfirechamber.org

Anthony · *Anthony C/C* · Theresa Olguin Fisher; Pres.; P.O. Box 1086; 88021; Dona Ana; P 12,000; M 30; (915) 471-5115; tfisher@ tapscorp.com

Artesia · *Greater Artesia C/C & Visitors Center* · Hayley Klein; Exec. Dir.; 107 N. First St.; 88210; Eddy; P 16,000; M 400; (575) 746-2744; (800) 658-6251; Fax (575) 746-2745; chamber@ artesiachamber.com; www.artesiachamber.com*

Aztec · *Aztec C of C & Visitor Center* · Dir.; 110 N. Ash; 87410; San Juan; P 6,378; M 250; (505) 334-9551; (888) 868-9551; Fax (505) 334-7648; director@aztecchamber.com; www.aztec chamber.com

Belen · *Greater Belen C/C* · Leeanáe Griego; Ofc. Mgr.; 712 Dalies Ave.; 87002; Valencia; P 7,000; M 300; (505) 864-8091; Fax (505) 864-7461; belenchamber@belenchamber.org; www.belenchamber.org*

Bernalillo · *see Rio Rancho*

Bloomfield · *Bloomfield C/C* · Bernadette Smith; Exec. Dir.; 224 W. Broadway; 87413; San Juan; P 7,500; M 170; (505) 632-0880; (800) 461-1245; Fax (505) 634-1431; askus@bloomfieldchamber. info; www.bloomfieldchamber.info*

Bosque Farms · *see Los Lunas*

Capitan · *Capitan C/C & Visitors Center* · Peter Renich; 433 Smokey Bear Blvd.; P.O. Box 441; 88316; Lincoln; P 1,500; M 40; (575) 354-2273; Fax (575) 354-3666; chamber@villageofcapitan. com; www.villageofcapitan.com

Carlsbad · *Carlsbad C/C* · Robert P. Defer; CEO; 302 S. Canal St.; P.O. Box 910; 88220; Eddy; P 25,000; M 515; (575) 887-6516; Fax (575) 885-1455; director@carlsbadchamber.com; www.carlsbad chamber.com*

Carrizozo · *Carrizozo C/C* · Pres.; P.O. Box 567; 88301; Lincoln; P 950; M 70; (575) 648-2732; zozoccc@tularosa.net; www. carrizozochamber.org

Chama · *Chama Valley C/C* · Rose Martinez; Exec. Dir.; P.O. Box 306-RB; 87520; Rio Arriba; P 1,400; M 182; (575) 756-2306; (800) 477-0149; Fax (575) 756-2892; info@chamavalley.com; www. chamavalley.com

Cimarron · *Cimarron C/C* · Carol Baker; Exec. Secy.; 104 N. Lincoln Ave.; P.O. Box 604; 87714; Colfax; P 900; M 55; (575) 376-2417; cimarronnm@gmail.com; www.cimarronnm.com

Clayton · *Clayton-Union County C/C* · Rose Ramirez; Exec. Dir.; 1103 S. 1st St.; P.O. Box 476; 88415; Union; P 2,524; M 100; (575) 374-9253; (800) 390-7858; Fax (575) 374-9250; cuchamber@ plateautel.net; www.claytonnewmexico.org

Cloudcroft · *Cloudcroft C/C* · Jason Baldwin; Dir.; P.O. Box 1290; 88317; Otero; P 768; M 185; (575) 682-2733; (866) 874-4447; Fax (575) 682-6028; cloudcroft@cloudcroft.net; www.cloudcroft.net

Clovis · *Clovis/Curry County C/C* · Mrs. Ernie Kos; Exec. Dir.; 105 E. Grand Ave.; 88101; Curry; P 45,000; M 800; (575) 763-3435; Fax (575) 763-7266; ernie@clovisnm.org; www.clovisnm.org.*

Cuba · *Cuba Area C/C* · Dan Delgado; Dir.; P.O. Box 1000; 87013; Sandoval; P 8,000; M 75; (575) 289-3514; (575) 289-0302; info@ cubanewmexico.com; www.cubanewmexico.com

Deming · *Deming-Luna County C/C* · Cyndi Longoria; Exec. Dir.; 800 E. Pine; P.O. Box 8; 88031; Luna; P 26,000; M 230; (575) 546-2674; (800) 848-4955; Fax (575) 546-9569; info@demingchamber. com; www.demingchamber.com*

Eagle Nest · *Eagle Nest C/C* · P.O. Box 322; 87718; Colfax; P 360; M 60; (575) 377-2420; Fax (575) 377-2697; info@eaglenest chamber.org; www.eaglenestchamber.org

Edgewood · *Edgewood C/C* · Robin Foshee; Exec. Dir.; P.O. Box 457; 87015; Santa Fe; P 2,000; M 110; (505) 286-2577; info@ edgewoodchambernm.com; www.edgewoodchambernm.com

Elephant Butte · *Elephant Butte C/C* · Susan LaFont; Chrmn. of the Bd.; 608 Hwy. 195; P.O. Box 1355; 87935; Sierra; P 2,200; M 110; (575) 744-4708; (877) 744-4900; Fax (575) 744-0044; info@elephantbuttechamberofcommerce.com; www.elephant buttechamberofcommerce.com

Espanola · *Espanola Valley C/C* · Deborah Torres; Exec. Dir.; 1 Calle de las Espanolas, Ste. F & G; P.O. Box 190; 87532; Rio Arriba; P 50,000; M 280; (505) 753-2831; Fax (505) 753-1252; info@ espanolanmchamber.com; www.espanolanmchamber.com

Eunice · *Eunice C/C* · Kenny Reed; Pres.; 1021 Main; P.O. Box 838; 88231; Lea; P 3,000; M 170; (575) 394-2755; Fax (575) 394-3937; eunicechamberofcommerce@gmail.com; www.cityofeunice.org

Farmington · *Farmington C/C* · Dorothy Nobis; Pres./CEO; 100 W. Broadway; 87401; San Juan; P 47,000; M 750; (505) 325-0279; (888) 325-0279; Fax (505) 327-7556; chamber@gofarmington. com; www.gofarmington.com*

Fort Sumner • *Fort Sumner/DeBaca County C/C* • Sandy Paul; Exec. Dir.; P.O. Box 28; 88119; DeBaca; P 2,300; M 121; (575) 355-7705; Fax (575) 355-2850; ftsumnercoc@plateautel.net; www.ftsumnerchamber.com

Gallup • *Gallup-McKinley County C/C* • Bill Lee; Exec. Dir.; 106 W. Hwy. 66; 87301; McKinley; P 20,000; M 320; (505) 722-2228; (800) 380-4989; Fax (505) 863-2280; bill@thegallupchamber.com; www.thegallupchamber.com

Grants • *Grants/Cibola County C/C* • Star Gonzales; Exec. Dir.; 100 N. Iron Ave.; P.O. Box 297; 87020; Cibola; P 26,000; M 200; (505) 287-4802; Fax (505) 287-8224; discover@grants.org; www.grants.org*

Hatch • *Hatch Valley C/C* • Marcia Nordyke; Pres.; 110 W. Hall, Ste. F; P.O. Box 38; 87937; Dona Ana; P 1,600; M 60; (575) 267-5050; mnordyke@zianet.com; www.hatchchilefest.com

Hobbs • *Hobbs C/C* • Ray Battaglini; Pres./CEO; 400 N. Marland Blvd.; 88240; Lea; P 32,000; M 805; (575) 397-3202; (800) 658-6291; Fax (575) 397-1689; hobbschamber@leaconet.com; www.hobbschamber.org*

Jal • *Jal C/C* • Amelia Trevino; P.O. Box 1205; 88252; Lea; P 2,000; M 125; (575) 395-2620; Fax (575) 395-2620; jalchamber@leaco.net; www.jalnm.com

Las Cruces • *Greater Las Cruces C/C* • Jim Berry; Pres./CEO; 760 W. Picacho Ave.; P.O. Drawer 519; 88004; Dona Ana; P 100,000; M 996; (575) 524-1968; Fax (575) 527-5546; jberry@lascruces.org; www.lascruces.org

Las Cruces • *Hispano C/C de Las Cruces* • Amanda Olivarez Cruz; Exec. Dir.; 3530 Foothills Rd., Ste. E; P.O. Box 1964; 88004; Dona Ana; P 80,000; M 350; (575) 532-9255; Fax (575) 532-9258; hispanochamberlc@qwestoffice.net; www.hispanochamberdelascruces.org

Las Vegas • *Las Vegas-San Miguel C/C* • Diane Ortiz; Exec. Dir.; 503 6th St.; P.O. Box 128; 87701; San Miguel; P 28,323; M 150; (505) 425-8631; (505) 425-9294; Fax (505) 425-3057; lvexec@qwestoffice.net; www.lasvegasnewmexico.com

Logan • *Logan/Ute Lake C/C* • Cindee Whitaker; Secy.; P.O. Box 277; 88426; Quay; P 1,000; M 40; (575) 487-5723; ctjwes@yahoo.com; www.utelakeloganchamber.com

Lordsburg • *Lordsburg-Hidalgo County C/C* • Cecilia Gomez; Mgr.; 206 Main St.; 88045; Hidalgo; P 5,000; M 60; (575) 542-9864; (575) 542-3052; Fax (575) 542-9059; lordsburgcoc@aznex.net; www.lordsburghidalgocounty.net

Los Alamos • *Los Alamos C/C* • Katy Korkos; Member Svcs. Coord.; 109 Central Park Sq.; P.O. Box 460; 87544; Los Alamos; P 18,000; M 300; (505) 662-8105; Fax (505) 662-8399; chamber@losalamos.com; www.losalamoschamber.com

Los Lunas • *Valencia County C/C* • Jacqueline Calixto; Exec. Dir.; 3445 Lambros; P.O. Box 13; 87031; Valencia; P 14,000; M 300; (505) 352-3596; Fax (505) 352-3589; bcchamber@loslunasnm.gov; www.loslunasnm.gov/chamber

Lovington • *Lovington C/C* • Ky Atwood; Exec. Dir.; 201 S. Main; 88260; Lea; P 9,600; M 180; (575) 396-5311; Fax (575) 396-2823; lovingtonchamber@hotmail.com; www.lovingtonchamber.org*

Magdalena • *Magdalena C/C* • P.O. Box 281; 87825; Socorro; P 970; M 60; (866) 854-3217; info@magdalena-nm.com; www.magdalena-nm.com

Melrose • *Melrose C/C* • Pres.; P.O. Box 235; 88124; Curry; P 750; M 100; (575) 253-4274

Mora • *Mora Valley C/C* • Merl Witt; Pres.; P.O. Box 800; 87732; Mora; P 5,500; M 60; (575) 387-6072; moranews@moranm.net; www.morachamber.com

Moriarty • *Moriarty C/C* • Debbie Ortiz; Exec. Dir.; P.O. Box 96; 87035; Torrance; P 1,900; M 125; (505) 832-4087; Fax (505) 832-5436; info@moriartychamber.com; www.moriartychamber.com

Mountainair • *Mountainair C/C* • Scott Remmich; Pres.; P.O. Box 595; 87036; Torrance; P 1,200; M 40; (505) 847-2795; mcc@mountainairchamber.com; www.mountainairchamber.com

Placitas • *see Rio Rancho*

Portales • *Roosevelt County/Portales C/C* • Sharon King; Exec. Dir.; 100 S. Ave. A; 88130; Roosevelt; P 20,000; M 300; (575) 356-8541; (800) 635-8036; Fax (575) 356-8542; chamber@portales.com; www.portales.com

Raton • *Raton C/C* • Scott Weese; Pres.; 100 Clayton Rd.; P.O. Box 1211; 87740; Colfax; P 7,282; M 143; (575) 445-3689; (800) 638-6161; ratonchamber@bacavalley.com; www.raton.info

Red River • *Red River C/C* • Carrie Venezia; Dir. of Chamber Svcs.; P.O. Box 870; 87558; Taos; P 500; M 176; (575) 754-2366; (800) 348-6444; Fax (575) 754-3104; rrinfo@redrivernewmex.com; www.redrivernewmex.com

Rio Rancho • *Rio Rancho Reg. C/C* • Debbi Moore; Pres./CEO; 4001 Southern Blvd. S.E., Ste. B; 87124; Sandoval; P 80,000; M 500; (505) 892-1533; Fax (505) 892-6157; info@rrrcc.org; www.rrrcc.org*

Roswell • *Roswell C/C* • Dorrie Faubus-McCarty; Exec. Dir.; 131 W. Second St.; 88201; Chaves; P 53,000; M 550; (575) 623-5695; (877) 849-7679; Fax (575) 624-6870; information@roswellnm.org; www.roswellnm.org

Ruidoso • *Ruidoso Valley C/C & Visitors Center* • Sandi Aguilar; Dir.; 720 Sudderth Dr.; 88345; Lincoln; P 9,000; M 600; (575) 257-7395; (877) 784-3676; Fax (575) 257-4693; info@ruidosonow.com; www.ruidosonow.com

San Miguel • *see Las Vegas*

Sandia Pueblo • *see Rio Rancho*

Santa Ana Pueblo • *see Rio Rancho*

Santa Fe • *Santa Fe C/C* • Simon Brackley; Pres./CEO; 8380 Cerrillos Rd., Ste. 302; P.O. Box 1928; 87504; Santa Fe; P 139,000; M 1,250; (505) 988-3279; Fax (505) 984-2205; info@santafechamber.com; www.santafechamber.com

Silver City • *Silver City-Grant County C/C* • Lola Polley; Exec. Dir.; 201 N. Hudson St.; 88061; Grant; P 31,000; M 550; (575) 538-3785; (800) 548-9378; Fax (575) 538-3786; info@silvercity.org; www.silvercity.org

Socorro • *Socorro County C/C* • 101 Plaza; P.O. Box 743; 87801; Socorro; P 19,000; M 270; (575) 835-0424; Fax (575) 835-9744; chamber@socorro-nm.com; www.socorro-nm.com

Taos • *Taos County C/C* • Steve Fuhlendorf; CEO; 108 F Kit Carson Rd.; 87571; Taos; P 32,152; M 550; (575) 751-8800; (800) 732-8267; Fax (575) 758-8801; info@taoschamber.com; www.taoschamber.com

Tatum • *Tatum C/C* • Marilyn Burns; Pres.; P.O. Box 814; 88267; Lea; P 800; M 30; (575) 398-5455; Fax (575) 398-5455; mburns@leaco.net; www.tatumschool.org

Tijeras • *East Mountain C/C* • Jeff Burdette; P.O. Box 2436; 87059; Bernalillo; P 1,060; M 80; (505) 281-1999; info@eastmountainchamber.com; www.eastmountainchamber.com

Truth or Consequences • *Truth or Consequences & Sierra County C/C* • Jessica Mackenzie; Pres.; 207 S. Foch St.; 87901; Sierra; P 10,000; M 87; (575) 894-3536; contact@truthorconsequenceschamberofcommerce.com; www.truthorconsequencesnm.net

Tucumcari · *Tucumcari-Quay County C/C* · Exec. Dir.; 404 W. Rte. 66; P.O. Drawer E; 88401; Quay; P 5,500; M 140; (575) 461-1694; Fax (575) 461-3884; chamber@tucumcarinm.com; www.tucumcarinm.com

White's City · *see Carlsbad*

New York

No State Chamber

Adams · *South Jefferson C/C* · Crystal Cobb; Pres.; 14 E. Church; P.O. Box 167; 13605; Jefferson; P 10,634; M 204; (315) 232-4215; Fax (315) 232-3967; chamrep@northnet.org; www.southjeffersonchamber.com

Adirondack Region · *see Glens Falls*

Albany · *Albany-Colonie Reg. C/C* · Mark Eagan; Pres./CEO; Five Computer Dr. S.; 12205; Albany; P 294,281; M 3,000; (518) 431-1400; Fax (518) 431-1402; info@acchamber.org; www.acchamber.org*

Albion · *Orleans County C/C* · Kevin Lake; Exec. Dir.; 102 N. Main St.; 14411; Orleans; P 43,735; M 450; (585) 798-4287; Fax (585) 798-4371; klake@orleanschamber.com; www.orleanschamber.com*

Alden · *Alden C/C* · Barbara Hoskyns; Exec. Secy.; P.O. Box 149; 14004; Erie; P 12,000; M 300; (716) 937-6177; secretary@aldenny.org; www.aldenny.org

Alexandria Bay · *Alexandria Bay C/C* · Susan Boyer; Exec. Dir.; 7 Market St.; 13607; Jefferson; P 10,000; M 250; (315) 482-9531; (800) 541-2110; Fax (315) 482-5434; info@alexbay.org; www.alexbay.org

Amenia · *see Lakeville, CT*

Amherst · *Amherst C/C* · Colleen DiPirro; Pres./CEO; 350 Essjay Rd., Ste. 200; Williamsville; 14221; Erie; P 116,000; M 2,300; (716) 632-6905; Fax (716) 632-0548; www.amherst.org

Amityville · *Amityville C/C* · Janice Soares; Exec. Dir.; P.O. Box 885; 11701; Suffolk; P 15,000; M 170; (631) 598-0695; chamber@amityvillechamber.org; www.amityvillechamber.org

Amsterdam · *Montgomery County C/C* · Deborah Auspelmyer; Pres.; 1166 Riverfront Center; 12010; Montgomery; P 49,708; M 485; (518) 842-8200; Fax (518) 684-0111; chamber@montgomerycountyny.com; www.montgomerycountyny.com*

Angola · *Evans-Brant C/C* · John Latimore; Pres.; 70 N. Main St.; 14006; Erie; P 25,000; M 50; (716) 549-3221; Fax (716) 549-3475; chamber@ebccny.org; www.ebccny.org

Arcade · *Arcade Area C/C* · Dorie Clinch; Exec. Secy.; 684 W. Main St.; 14009; Wyoming; P 3,800; M 400; (585) 492-2114; Fax (585) 492-5103; www.arcadechamber.org

Athens · *see Coxsackie*

Auburn · *Cayuga County C/C* · 36 South St.; 13021; Cayuga; P 81,400; M 600; (315) 252-7291; Fax (315) 255-3077; www.cayugacountychamber.com*

Avoca · *see Bath*

Avon · *Avon C/C* · Tom Vonglis; Pres.; 74 Genesee St.; 14414; Livingston; P 6,600; M 150; (585) 226-8080; www.avonny.org

Baldwin · *Baldwin C/C* · Ralph Rose & Erik Mahler; Co-Pres.; P.O. Box 804; 11510; Nassau; P 31,000; M 100; (516) 223-8080; info@baldwinchamber.com; www.baldwinchamber.com

Baldwinsville · *Greater Baldwinsville C/C* · Lee Wilder; Exec. Dir.; 3 Marble St.; 13027; Onondaga; P 35,000; M 300; (315) 638-0550; bchamber07@verizon.net; www.baldwinsvillechamber.com

Ballston Lake · *see Clifton Park*

Ballston Spa · *see Clifton Park*

Batavia · *Genesee County C/C* · L N Freeman; Pres.; 210 E. Main St.; 14020; Genesee; P 61,000; M 1,000; (585) 343-7440; Fax (585) 343-7487; chamber@geneseeny.com; www.geneseeny.com

Bath · *Greater Bath Area C/C* · Bill Caudill; Pres.; 10 Pulteney Sq. W.; 14810; Steuben; P 30,250; M 250; (607) 776-7122; Fax (607) 776-7122; email@bathnychamber.com; www.bathnychamber.com

Bay Shore · *C/C of Greater Bay Shore* · Donna Periconi; Pres.; 77 E. Main St.; P.O. Box 5110; 11706; Suffolk; P 30,000; M 300; (631) 665-7003; Fax (631) 665-5204; www.bayshorecommerce.com

Beacon · *see Wappingers Falls*

Bedford Hills · *Bedford Hills C/C* · Gregory J. Riley; P.O. Box 162; 10507; Westchester; P 6,500; M 100; (914) 381-3356; Fax (914) 241-8719; www.bedfordhills.org

Bellmore · *C/C of the Bellmores* · Joni Caputo; Exec. Dir.; 1514 Bellmore Ave.; 11710; Hempstead; P 25,000; M 350; (516) 679-1875; Fax (516) 409-0544; bellmorecc@aol.com; www.bellmorechamber.com

Bellmore · *Nassau Cncl. of Chambers of Commerce* · E. Christopher Murray; Pres.; P.O. Box 365; 11710; Nassau; P 3,200,000; M 6,000; (516) 248-1112; Fax (516) 663-6715; www.ncchambers.org

Bellport · *Bellport C/C* · Ron Trotta; Pres.; P.O. Box 246; 11713; Suffolk; P 2,400; M 105; (631) 776-9268; email@bellportchamber.com; www.bellportchamber.com

Belmont · *Greater Allegany County C/C* · Sherry Grugel; Exec. Dir.; 6087 State Rte. 19N, Ste. 120; 14813; Allegany; P 49,000; M 125; (585) 268-5500; Fax (585) 268-7473; contact@alleganychamber.org; www.alleganychamber.org*

Bethlehem · *see Delmar*

Bethpage · *Bethpage C/C* · Gary Bretton; Pres.; P.O. Box 636; 11714; Nassau; P 8,000; M 120; (516) 433-0010; info@pobcoc.com; www.bethpagecommunity.com/chamber

Binghamton · *Greater Binghamton C/C* · Lou Santoni; Pres./CEO; Metrocenter, 49 Court St.; P.O. Box 995; 13902; Broome; P 200,536; M 900; (607) 772-8860; (800) 836-6740; Fax (607) 722-4513; lsantoni@greaterbinghamtonchamber.com; www.greaterbinghamtonchamber.com

Blue Mountain Lake · *see Indian Lake*

Bolton Landing · *Bolton Landing C/C* · Joe DiNapoli; Pres.; 4928 Lakeshore Dr.; P.O. Box 368; 12814; Warren; P 2,117; M 150; (518) 644-3831; Fax (518) 644-5951; www.boltonchamber.com

Boonville · *Boonville Area C/C* · Kim Lynch; Pres.; 122 Main St.; P.O. Box 163; 13309; Oneida; P 4,400; M 180; (315) 942-5112; Fax (315) 942-6823; info@boonvillechamber.com; www.boonvillechamber.com

Bradford · *see Bath*

Brant · *see Angola*

Brewerton · *Fort Brewerton/Greater Oneida Lake C/C* · Pearl Wilson; Exec. Secy.; P.O. Box 655; 13029; Oneida, Onondaga & Oswego; P 15,000; M 125; (315) 668-3408; www.oneidalakechamber.com

Brewster · *Brewster C/C* · Beth Murtha; Exec. Dir.; 16 Mount Ebo Rd. S., Ste. 12A; 10509; Putnam; P 19,000; M 200; (845) 279-2477; Fax (845) 278-8349; info@brewsterchamber.com; www.brewsterchamber.com

Brockport · *Greater Brockport C/C* · Elaine Bader; Pres.; P.O. Box 119; 14420; Monroe; P 13,716; M 90; (585) 234-1512; (585) 637-5997; www.brockportchamber.org

Bronx · *Bronx C/C* · Lenny Caro; Pres./CEO; 1200 Waters Pl., Ste. 106; 10461; New York; P 1,500,000; M 600; (718) 828-3900; Fax (718) 409-3748; lenny@bronxchamber.org; www.bronxchamber.org*

Bronxville · *Bronxville C/C* · Ruth Wood; Exec. Dir.; 81 Pondfield Rd., Ste. 7; 10708; Westchester; P 6,200; M 250; (914) 337-6040; Fax (914) 337-6040; info@bronxvillechamber.com; www.bronx villechamber.com

Brooklyn · *Brooklyn C/C* · Carl Hum; Pres./CEO; 25 Elm Pl., Ste. 200; 11201; Kings; P 2,500,000; M 1,200; (718) 875-1000; Fax (718) 237-4274; info@brooklynchamber.com; www.ibrooklyn.com

Broome County · *see Binghamton*

Buffalo · *Buffalo Niagara Partnership* · Andrew J. Rudnick; Pres./CEO; 665 Main St., Ste. 200; 14203; Erie; P 1,292,000; M 2,500; (716) 852-7100; (800) 241-0474; Fax (716) 852-2761; www.thepartnership.org

Burnt Hills · *see Clifton Park*

Cambria · *see Sanborn*

Camden · *Camden Area C/C* · Diane Miller; Pres.; P.O. Box 134; 13316; Oneida; P 6,200; M 130; (315) 245-5000; www.camden nychamber.com

Camillus · *Greater Camillus C/C* · Kathy Kitt; Secy.; P.O. Box 415; 13031; Onondaga; P 25,000; M 200; (315) 247-5992; kathykitt@ gmail.com; www.camilluschamber.com

Campbell · *see Bath*

Canajoharie · *see Amsterdam*

Canandaigua · *Canandaigua Area C/C* · Alison Grems; Pres./CEO; 113 S. Main St.; 14424; Ontario; P 11,197; M 696; (585) 394-4400; Fax (585) 394-4546; chamber@canandaiguachamber.com; www.canandaiguachamber.com*

Canastota · *Canastota C/C* · Rick Stevens; Pres.; 222 S. Peterboro St.; P.O. Box 206; 13032; Madison; P 5,000; M 80; (315) 697-3677; www.canastota.org

Candor · *Candor C/C* · Butch Crowe; Pres.; P.O. Box 802; 13743; Tioga; P 5,000; M 90; (607) 659-7450; www.candorny.org

Canton · *Canton C/C* · Sally Hill; Exec. Dir.; P.O. Box 369; 13617; St. Lawrence; P 11,600; M 200; (315) 386-8255; Fax (315) 386-8255; cantoncc@northnet.org; www.cantonnychamber.org

Canton · *St. Lawrence County C/C* · Patricia McKeown; Exec. Dir.; 101 Main St., 1st Flr.; 13617; St. Lawrence; P 111,000; M 800; (315) 386-4000; (877) 228-7810; Fax (315) 379-0134; info@ stlawrencecountychamber.org; www.northcountryguide.com

Cape Vincent · *Cape Vincent C/C* · Shelley Higgins; Exec. Dir.; 175 N. James St.; P.O. Box 482; 13618; Jefferson; P 1,200; M 250; (315) 654-2481; Fax (315) 654-4141; thecape@tds.net; www. capevincent.org

Carmel · *Carmel-Kent C/C* · Bill Nulk; Treas.; P.O. Box 447; 10512; Putnam; P 20,000; M 150; (845) 278-3004; Fax (845) 225-7835; www.ci.carmel.ny.us

Carthage · *Carthage Area C/C* · Edie Roggie; Dir.; 120 S. Mechanic St.; 13619; Jefferson; P 10,000; M 230; (315) 493-3590; Fax (315) 493-3590; carthagechamber@centralny.twcbc.com; www.carthageny.com

Catskill · *Greene County C/C* · Tracy McNally; Exec. Dir.; 1 Bridge St., 2nd Flr.; 12414; Greene; P 49,000; M 370; (518) 943-4222; Fax (518) 943-1700; tmcnally@greenecounty-chamber.com; www. greenecounty-chamber.com

Catskill · *Heart of Catskill Assn.–Catskill C/C* · 327 Main St.; P.O. Box 248; 12414; Greene; P 12,000; M 450; (518) 943-0989; catskillchamber@mhcable.com; www.catskillny.org

Cayuga County · *see Auburn*

Cazenovia · *Greater Cazenovia Area C/C* · 59 Albany St.; 13035; Madison; P 6,500; M 350; (315) 655-9243; (888) 218-6305; cazchamber@windstream.net; www.cazenovia.com

Center Moriches · *Moriches C/C* · Dr. Judith Savino-Burd; Pres.; P.O. Box 686; 11934; Suffolk; P 15,000; M 140; (631) 874-3849; info@surpassyourdreams.com; www.moricheschamber.org

Centereach · *The Greater Middle Country C/C* · Jeff Freund; Pres.; P.O. Box 65; 11720; Suffolk; P 65,000; M 150; (631) 681-8708; suggestions@middlecountrychamber.com; www. middlecountrychamber.com

Chaumont · *see Three Mile Bay*

Chautauqua · *see Mayville*

Cheektowaga · *Cheektowaga C/C* · Debra Liegl; Pres./CEO; 2875 Union Rd., Ste. 50; 14227; Erie; P 99,314; M 900; (716) 684-5838; Fax (716) 684-5571; chamber@cheektowaga.org; www.cheektowaga.org

Chemung County · *see Elmira*

Cherry Valley · *Greater Cherry Valley C/C* · Jackie Hall; Pres.; P.O. Box 37; 13320; Otsego; P 1,600; M 90; (607) 264-3100; Fax (607) 264-3447; www.cherryvalleychamber.org

Cicero · *Greater Cicero C/C* · Darlene Pettersen; Admin. Secy.; P.O. Box 1269; 13039; Onondaga; P 32,000; (315) 699-1358; www.cicerochamber.com

Cicero · *Plank Road C/C* · Angela Tucciarone; Exec. Dir.; 5885 E. Circle Dr., Ste. 225; 13039; Onondaga; M 125; (315) 458-4181; info@plankroadchamber.com; www.plankroadchamber.com

Clarence · *Clarence C/C* · David Hartzel; Pres.; 8975 Main St.; 14031; Erie; P 28,500; M 600; (716) 631-3888; Fax (716) 631-3946; info@clarence.org; www.clarence.org*

Clarkson · *see Brockport*

Clayton · *1000 Islands-Clayton Area C/C* · Karen Goetz; Exec. Dir.; 517 Riverside Dr.; 13624; Jefferson; P 4,500; M 275; (315) 686-3771; (800) 252-9806; Fax (315) 686-5564; info@1000islands-clayton.com; www.1000islands-clayton.com

Clifton Park · *The Chamber of Southern Saratoga County* · Peter L. Aust; Pres./CEO; 15 Park Ave., Ste. 7; 12065; Saratoga; P 104,300; M 950; (518) 371-7748; Fax (518) 371-5025; info@ southernsaratoga.org; www.southernsaratoga.org*

Clifton Springs · *Clifton Springs Area C/C* · Brian Morris; Pres.; 2 E. Main St.; P.O. Box 86; 14432; Ontario; P 2,300; M 70; (315) 462-8200; info@cliftonspringschamber.com; www.clifton springschamber.com

Clinton · *Clinton C/C* · Ferris Betrus Jr.; Exec. V.P.; P.O. Box 142; 13323; Oneida; P 10,000; M 270; (315) 853-1735; Fax (315) 853-1735; info@clintonnychamber.org; www.clintonnychamber.org

Clyde · *Clyde C/C* · Rudolph DeLisio; Pres.; P.O. Box 69; 14433; Wayne; P 2,400; M 75; (315) 923-9862; Fax (315) 923-9862; www.clydeontheerie.com

Cohoes · *see Albany*

Cold Spring · *Cold Spring Area C/C* · P.O. Box 36; 10516; Putnam; P 10,000; M 180; (845) 265-3200; chamberdirector@ gmail.com; www.coldspringchamber.com*

Colonie · *see Albany*

Columbia County · *Columbia County C/C* · David B. Colby; Pres./CEO; 507 Warren St.; Hudson; 12534; Columbia; P 62,000; M 850; (518) 828-4417; Fax (518) 822-9539; dcolby@columbia chamber-ny.com; www.columbiachamber-ny.com*

Conklin · *see Binghamton*

Cooperstown • *Cooperstown C/C* • Susan O'Handley; Exec. Dir.; 31 Chestnut St.; 13326; Otsego; P 2,160; M 600; (607) 547-9983; Fax (607) 547-6006; info1@cooperstownchamber.org; www.cooperstownchamber.org

Copiague • *Copiague C/C* • Sharon Fattoruso; Pres.; 1285 Montauk Hwy.; P.O. Box 8; 11726; Suffolk; P 26,000; M 121; (631) 226-2956; www.copiaguechamber.org

Corning • *Corning Area C/C* • Denise Ackley; Pres.; 1 W. Market St., Ste. 302; 14830; Steuben; P 30,000; M 325; (607) 936-4686; Fax (607) 936-4685; info@corningny.com; www.corningny.com*

Cortland • *Cortland County C/C* • Bob Haight; Exec. Dir.; 37 Church St.; 13045; Cortland; P 49,000; M 440; (607) 756-2814; Fax (607) 756-4698; info@cortlandchamber.com; www.cortlandchamber.com

Coxsackie • *Coxsackie Area C/C* • Renee Mathes; Exec. Dir.; P.O. Box 251; 12051; Greene; P 14,000; M 130; (518) 731-7300; info@coxsackieareachamber.com; www.coxsackieareachamber.com

Crompond • *see Yorktown Heights*

Croton-on-Hudson • *see Peekskill*

Cutchogue • *see Southold*

Dansville • *Dansville Area C/C* • William Bacon; Pres.; 126 Main St.; P.O. Box 105; 14437; Livingston; P 5,000; M 400; (585) 335-6920; (800) 949-0174; dansvillechamber@hotmail.com; www.dansvilleny.net

Delhi • *Delaware County C/C* • Mary Beth Silano; Exec. Dir.; 5 1/2 Main St.; 13753; Delaware; P 47,000; M 720; (607) 746-2281; Fax (607) 746-3571; info@delawarecounty.org; www.delawarecounty.org

Delmar • *Bethlehem C/C* • Marty DeLaney; Pres.; 318 Delaware Ave., Ste. 11; 12054; Albany; P 33,000; M 650; (518) 439-0512; (888) 439-0512; Fax (518) 475-0910; info@bethlehemchamber.com; www.bethlehemchamber.com

Depew • *see Lancaster*

Deposit • *Deposit on the Delaware C/C* • Nick Barone; Pres.; P.O. Box 222; 13754; Delaware; P 2,000; M 60; (607) 467-4161; www.depositchamber.com

Dunkirk • *Chautauqua County C/C* • 10785 Bennett Rd.; 14048; Chautauqua; P 139,000; M 1,350; (716) 366-6200; Fax (716) 366-4276; cccc@chautauquachamber.org; www.chautauquachamber.org

East Amherst • *see Amherst*

East Aurora • *Greater East Aurora C/C* • Gary D. Grote; Exec. Dir.; 652 Main St.; 14052; Erie; P 13,500; M 600; (716) 652-8444; Fax (716) 652-8384; eanycc@verizon.net; www.eanycc.com

East Fishkill • *see Wappingers Falls*

East Hampton • *East Hampton C/C* • Marina Van; Exec. Dir.; 42 Gingerbread Ln.; 11937; Suffolk; P 22,000; M 315; (631) 324-0362; Fax (631) 329-1642; info@easthamptonchamber.com; www.easthamptonchamber.com

East Islip • *East Islip Comm. Chamber* • Mike Visgauss; Pres.; P.O. Box 225; 11730; Suffolk; P 13,000; M 35; (631) 581-1200; catdennehy@optonline.com; www.eastislipcc.com

East Meadow • *see Garden City*

East Moriches • *see Center Moriches*

East Quogue • *see Southampton*

East Setauket • *Three Village C/C* • Kathryn Farren; Admin. Dir.; P.O. Box 6; 11733; Suffolk; (631) 689-8838; Fax (631) 246-9037; threevillagechamberofcommerce@yahoo.com; www.threevillagechamber.com

East Williston • *see Williston Park*

East Yaphank • *East Yaphank C/C* • Michael Giacomaro; Pres.; 524 Birch Hollow Dr.; 11967; Suffolk; P 5,000; M 132; (631) 345-0805; Fax (631) 924-8193

Eastport • *Eastport C/C* • Andrea Milano; Pres.; P.O. Box 458; 11941; Suffolk; P 10,000; M 110; (631) 325-5911

Eden • *Eden C/C* • Patrick O'Brien; Pres.; 8584 S. Main St.; 14057; Erie; P 8,074; M 200; (716) 992-4799; Fax (716) 992-4751; edenchamber@yahoo.com; www.edenny.org

Ellenville • *Ellenville-Wawarsing C/C* • Janet McDonnell; Ofc. Secy.; 124 Canal St.; P.O. Box 227; 12428; Ulster; P 16,000; M 130; (845) 647-4620; info@ewcoc.com; www.ewcoc.com

Ellicottville • *Ellicottville C/C* • Brian McFadden; 9 W. Washington St.; P.O. Box 456; 14731; Cattaraugus; P 1,700; M 350; (716) 699-5046; Fax (716) 699-5636; info@ellicottvilleny.com; www.ellicottvilleny.com

Elma • *see Lancaster*

Elmira • *Chemung County C/C* • Kevin D. Keeley; Pres./CEO; 400 E. Church St.; 14901; Chemung; P 96,000; M 800; (607) 734-5137; Fax (607) 734-4490; info@chemungchamber.org; www.chemungchamber.org*

Evans • *see Angola*

Fair Haven • *Fair Haven Area C/C* • Alan Avrich; Pres.; P.O. Box 13; 13064; Cayuga; P 6,000; M 55; (315) 947-6037; info@fairhavenny.com; www.fairhavenny.com

Farmington • *Farmington C/C* • Cal Cobb; Pres.; P.O. Box 25001; 14425; Ontario; P 11,000; M 200; (585) 398-2861; cl5827@aol.com; www.farmingtoncofc.com

Farnham • *see Angola*

Fayetteville • *Fayetteville C/C* • Scott Schaal; Pres.; P.O. Box 712; 13066; Onondaga; P 4,200; M 85; (315) 637-5544; fayettevillechamber@twcny.rr.com; www.fayettevillechamber.org

Fire Island Pines • *Greater Fire Island Pines C/C* • PJ Mcateer; Pres.; P.O. Box 695; Sayville; 11782; Suffolk; P 3,000; M 51; (631) 597-3058; info@pineschamber.com; www.pineschamber.com

Fishkill • *see Wappingers Falls*

Fleischmanns • *Fleischmanns C/C* • P.O. Box 126; 12430; Delaware; P 300; M 20; (845) 254-4884; www.fleischmannsny.com

Floral Park • *Floral Park C/C* • Sal Bonagura; Pres.; P.O. Box 20093; 11002; Nassau; P 16,000; M 177; (516) 641-1200; Fax (516) 488-5107; www.floralparkchamber.org

Flushing • *see Queens*

Fonda • *see Amsterdam*

Forest Hills • *Forest Hills C/C* • Leslie Brown; Pres.; P.O. Box 751123; 11375; Queens; P 320,000; M 150; (718) 268-6565; www.foresthillschamber.org

Fort Edward • *Fort Edward C/C* • Larry P. Moffitt; Pres.; P.O. Box 267; 12828; Washington; P 6,000; M 80; (518) 747-3000; fechamberpres@live.com; www.fortedwardchamber.com

Fort Plain • *see Amsterdam*

Franklin • *Greater Franklin C/C* • Marc Burgin; Pres.; P.O. Box 814; 13775; Delaware; P 2,700; M 72; (607) 829-8500; franklinnychamber@yahoo.com; www.franklinny.org

Fredonia • *see Dunkirk*

Freeport • *Freeport C/C* • Jerri Quibell; Pres.; 300 Woodcleft Ave.; 11520; Nassau; P 43,000; M 213; (516) 223-8840; Fax (516) 223-1211; freeportchamber@juno.com; www.freeportchamberofcommerce.com

Fulton • *see Oswego*

Fulton County · *see Gloversville*

Fultonville · *see Amsterdam*

Garden City · *Garden City C/C* · Althea Robinson; Exec. Dir.; 230 Seventh St.; 11530; Nassau; P 21,000; M 370; (516) 746-7724; Fax (516) 746-7725; gcchamber@verizon.net; www.gardencity chamber.org

Genesee County · *see Batavia*

Geneseo · *Livingston County C/C* · Cynthia Oswald; Pres.; 4635 Millennium Dr.; 14454; Livingston; P 67,000; M 1,200; (585) 243-2222; Fax (585) 243-4824; coswald@frontiernet.net; www. livingstoncountychamber.com

Geneva · *Geneva Area C/C* · Rob Gladden; Pres.; 35 Lakefront Dr.; P.O. Box 587; 14456; Ontario; P 18,000; M 500; (315) 789-1776; Fax (315) 789-3993; info@genevany.com; www.genevany.com*

Getzville · *see Amherst*

Glen Cove · *Glen Cove C/C* · Phyllis Gorham; Exec. Dir.; 19 Village Sq.; 11542; Nassau; P 25,000; M 255; (516) 676-6666; Fax (516) 676-5490; info@glencovechamber.org; www.glencovechamber.org

Glens Falls · *Adirondack Reg. C/C* · Peter Aust; Pres./CEO; 136 Glen St., Ste. 3; 12801; Warren; P 145,600; M 1,000; (518) 798-1761; Fax (518) 792-4147; paust@adirondackchamber.org; www. adirondackchamber.org.*

Gloversville · *Fulton County Reg. C/C & Ind.* · Wally Hart; Pres.; 2 N. Main St.; 12078; Fulton; P 55,500; M 942; (518) 725-0641; (800) 676-3858; Fax (518) 725-0643; info@fultoncountyny.org; www.fultoncountyny.org*

Goshen · *Goshen C/C* · Lynn Cione; Exec. Dir.; 223 Main St.; P.O. Box 506; 10924; Orange; P 13,500; M 200; (845) 294-7741; Fax (845) 294-7746; info@goshennychamber.com; www.goshen nychamber.com

Gouverneur · *Gouverneur C/C* · Donna M. Lawrence; Exec. Dir.; 214 E. Main St.; Lawrence Manor Bldg.; 13642; St. Lawrence; P 8,000; M 130; (315) 287-0331; Fax (315) 287-3694; www. gouverneurchamber.net

Gowanda · *Gowanda Area C/C* · Jennine Sauriol; Pres.; 49 W. Main St.; P.O. Box 45; 14070; Cattaraugus; P 19,000; M 150; (716) 532-2834; Fax (716) 532-2834; GowandaUSA@yahoo.com; www. gowanda-chamber.com

Grand Island · *Grand Island C/C* · John Bonora; Pres.; 2257 Grand Island Blvd.; 14072; Erie; P 20,000; M 300; (716) 773-3651; Fax (716) 773-3316; info@gichamber.org; www.gichamber.org

Granville · *Granville Area C/C* · 1 Main St.; P.O. Box 13; 12832; Washington; P 5,000; M 125; (518) 642-2815; jcpeterson@ roadrunner.com; www.granvillechamber.com

Great Neck · *Great Neck C/C* · Valerie Link; Pres.; P.O. Box 220432; 11022; Nassau; P 60,000; M 300; (516) 487-2000; great neckinfo@gmail.com; www.greatneckchamber.org

Greece · *Greece C/C* · Jodie A. Perry IOM; Pres./CEO; 2496 W. Ridge Rd., Ste. 201; 14626; Monroe; P 95,000; M 750; (585) 227-7272; Fax (585) 227-7275; info@greecechamber.org; www.greecechamber.org*

Greene · *Greater Greene C/C* · Stephanie Hartman; Exec. Dir.; P.O. Box 441; 13778; Chenango; P 6,000; (607) 656-8225; info@ greenenys.com; www.greenenys.com

Greenport · *see Southold*

Greenvale · *Greenvale C/C* · M. T. Lucarelli; Secy.; P.O. Box 123; 11548; Nassau; P 2,500; M 60; (516) 621-2110; www.greenvale chamber.com.

Greenwich · *Greater Greenwich C/C* · Kathy Nichols-Tomkins; Secy.; 6 Academy St.; 12834; Washington; P 10,000; M 245; (518) 692-7979; Fax (518) 692-7979; info@greenwichchamber.org; www.greenwichchamber.org

Greenwich Village · *see New York–Greenwich Village-Chelsea C/C*

Guilderland · *Guilderland C/C* · Kathy Burbank; Exec. Dir.; 2050 Western Ave., Ste. 109; 12084; Albany; P 37,000; M 600; (518) 456-6611; Fax (518) 456-6690; info@guilderlandchamber.com; www.guilderlandchamber.com*

Hague · *Hague-on-Lake George C/C* · P.O. Box 615; 12836; Warren; P 850; (518) 543-6353; chamber@hagueticonderoga. com; www.visithague.com

Halfmoon · *see Clifton Park*

Hamburg · *Hamburg C/C* · Betty Newell; Pres./CEO; 6122 S. Park Ave.; P.O. Box 848; 14075; Erie; P 57,000; M 700; (716) 649-7917; (877) 322-6890; Fax (716) 649-6362; hccmail@hamburg-chamber. org; www.hamburg-chamber.org.

Hammond · *Black Lake C/C* · P.O. Box 12; 13646; St. Lawrence; P 1,300; M 60; (315) 375-8640; info@blacklakeny.com; www. blacklakeny.com

Hammondsport · *Hammondsport C/C* · John Jensen; Pres.; 47 Shethar St.; P.O. Box 539; 14840; Steuben; P 8,000; M 165; (607) 569-2989; Fax (607) 569-2989; info@hammondsport.org; www. hammondsport.org

Hampton Bays · *Hampton Bays C/C* · Stan Glinka; Pres.; 140 W. Main St., Ste. 1; 11946; Suffolk; P 13,092; M 115; (631) 728-2211; Fax (631) 728-0308; hamptonbayschamber@verizon.net; www. hamptonbayschamber.com

Hancock · *Hancock Area C/C* · 158 E. Front St.; P.O. Box 525; 13783; Delaware; P 1,400; M 45; hancockchamber@hancock.net; www.hancockareachamber.com

Harlem · *see New York–Greater Harlem C/C*

Harrison · *Harrison C/C* · Ada B. Angarano; Pres./CEO; 1 Heineman Pl.; 10528; Westchester; P 27,000; M 140; (914) 282-7895; harrisoncc04@yahoo.com; www.theharrisoncofc.org

Hartland · *see Sanborn*

Hastings-On-Hudson · *Hastings-On-Hudson C/C* · Carl Carvalho; Pres.; 578 Warburton Ave.; 10706; Westchester; P 8,000; M 34; (914) 445-1767; (914) 478-3400; Fax (866) 251-8392; carl@ hohchamber.com; www.hohchamber.com

Haverstraw · *Greater Haverstraw C/C* · Maria Rodd; Exec. Dir.; 4 Broadway; P.O. Box 159; 10927; Rockland; P 10,000; M 150; (845) 947-5646; info@haverstrawchamber.org; www.haverstraw chamber.org

Hempstead · *Hempstead C/C* · Leo Fernandez; Pres.; 1776 Denton Green Park; P.O. Box 4264; 11550; Nassau; P 50,000; M 125; president@hempsteadchamber.com; www.hempstead chamber.com

Henderson Harbor · *Henderson Harbor C/C* · P.O. Box 468; 13651; Jefferson; P 1,300; M 160; (315) 938-5568; (888) 938-5568; thechambertreasurer@gmail.com; www.hendersonharborny.com

Hicksville · *Hicksville C/C* · Lionel J. Chitty; Pres.; 10 W. Marie St.; 11801; Nassau; P 51,000; M 274; (516) 931-7170; Fax (516) 931-8546; info@hicksvillechamber.com; www.hicksvillechamber.com

Highland · *Southern Ulster County C/C* · Barbara Brouillard; Pres.; 20 Milton Ave., Ste. 3; 12528; Ulster; P 40,000; M 110; (845) 691-6070; Fax (845) 691-9194; info@southernulsterchamber.org; www.southernulsterchamber.org

Hinsdale · *see Cicero–Plank Road C/C*

Holbrook · *Holbrook C/C* · Rick Ammirati; Pres.; P.O. Box 585; 11741; Suffolk; P 25,000; M 250; (631) 471-2725; Fax (631) 343-4816; info@holbrookchamber.com; www.holbrookchamber.com

Holtsville · *Farmingville/Holtsville C/C* · Wayne Carrington; Pres.; P.O. Box 66; 11742; Suffolk; P 35,000; M 60; (631) 926-8259

Honeoye · *Honeoye Lake C/C* · Tina Ketchum; Secy.; P.O. Box 305; 14471; Ontario; P 20,000; M 500; (585) 229-4226; info@honeoyelakechanber.org; www.honeoyelakechamber.org

Hopewell Junction · *see Wappingers Falls*

Hornell · *Hornell Area C/C* · James W. Griffin; Pres.; 40 Main St.; 14843; Steuben; P 11,000; M 450; (607) 324-0310; Fax (607) 324-3776; griff@hornellny.com; www.hornellny.com

Hudson · *see Columbia County*

Hunter · *Town of Hunter C/C* · P.O. Box 177; 12442; Greene; P 2,100; M 124; (518) 263-4900; Fax (518) 589-0117; chamber info@hunterchamber.org; www.hunterchamber.org

Huntington · *Huntington Twp. C/C* · Ellen O'Brien; Exec. Dir.; 164 Main St.; 11743; Suffolk; P 197,000; M 700; (631) 423-6100; Fax (631) 351-8276; ellen@huntingtonchamber.com; www.huntingtonchamber.com*

Hyde Park · *Hyde Park C/C* · John Coppola; Pres.; P.O. Box 17; 12538; Dutchess; P 21,000; M 200; (845) 229-8612; Fax (845) 229-8638; info@hydeparkchamber.org; www.hydeparkchamber.org

Indian Lake · *Indian Lake C/C* · 5 Main St.; P.O. Box 724; 12842; Hamilton; P 4,900; M 50; (518) 648-5112; www.indian-lake.com

Inlet · *Inlet Info. Ofc.* · Adele Burnett; Tourism Dir.; 160 Rte. 28; P.O. Box 266; 13360; Hamilton; P 485; M 106; (315) 357-5501; (866) GO-INLET; Fax (315) 357-3570; info@inletny.com; www.inletny.com

Islip · *Islip C/C* · Liz Mayott; Secy.; P.O. Box 112; 11751; Suffolk; P 16,000; M 200; (631) 581-2720; Fax (631) 581-2720; info@islipchamberofcommerce.com; www.islipchamberofcommerce.com

Ithaca · *Tompkins County C/C* · Jean McPheeters; Pres.; 904 E. Shore Dr.; 14850; Tompkins; P 106,000; M 691; (607) 273-7080; Fax (607) 272-7617; jean@tompkinschamber.org; tompkinschamber.org*

Jamaica · *Jamaica C/C* · Robert M. Richards; Pres.; 157-11 Rockaway Blvd.; 11434; Queens; P 500,000; M 500; (718) 657-4800; Fax (718) 413-2325; jamaicachamber@aol.com; www.jamaicachambernyc.com.

Jamestown · *Chautauqua County C/C* · Todd Tranum; Exec. Dir.; 512 Falconer St.; 14701; Chautauqua; P 139,000; M 1,600; (716) 484-1101; Fax (716) 487-0785; cccc@chautauquachamber.org; www.chautauquachamber.org

Jefferson Valley · *see Yorktown Heights*

Jeffersonville · *Jeffersonville Area C/C* · P.O. Box 463; 12748; Sullivan; P 300; (845) 482-5688; info@jeffersonvilleny.com; www.jeffersonvilleny.com

Kanona · *see Bath*

Katonah · *Katonah C/C* · Jennifer Cook & Sara Zipp; Co-Pres.; P.O. Box 389; 10536; Westchester; P 5,000; M 135; (914) 232-2668; info@katonahchamber.org; www.katonahchamber.org

Kenmore · *Kenmore-Town of Tonawanda C/C* · Tracey M. Lukasik; Exec. Dir.; 3411 Delaware Ave.; 14217; Erie; P 82,414; M 650; (716) 874-1202; Fax (716) 874-3151; info@ken-ton.org; www.ken-ton.org

Kings Park · *Kings Park C/C* · Charles Gardner; Pres.; P.O. Box 322; 11754; Suffolk; P 25,000; M 140; (631) 269-7678; info@kingsparkli.com; www.kingsparkli.com

Kingston · *C of C of Ulster County* · Ward Todd; Pres.; 55 Albany Ave.; 12401; Ulster; P 178,000; M 1,300; (845) 338-5100; Fax (845) 338-0968; info@ulsterchamber.org; www.ulsterchamber.org*

Lackawanna · *Lackawanna Area C/C* · Michael Sobaszek; Exec. Dir.; 638 Ridge Rd.; 14218; Erie; P 20,000; M 350; (716) 823-8841; Fax (716) 823-8848; info@lackawannachamber.com; www.lackawannachamber.com

Lake George · *Lake George Reg. C/C & CVB* · Janice Fox; Pres.; 2176 State Rte. 9; P.O. Box 272; 12845; Warren; P 3,900; M 400; (518) 668-5755; (800) 705-0059; Fax (518) 668-4286; info@lakegeorgechamber.com; www.lakegeorgechamber.com

Lake Placid · *Lake Placid C/C* · James McKenna; Pres./CEO; 49 Parkside Dr.; 12946; Essex; P 8,000; M 600; (800) 447-5224; (518) 523-2445; Fax (518) 523-2605; info@lakeplacid.com; www.lakeplacid.com

Lake Pleasant · *see Speculator*

Lakewood · *see Jamestown*

Lancaster · *Lancaster Area C/C* · Megan Burns-Moran; Exec. Dir.; 41 Central Ave.; P.O. Box 284; 14086; Erie; P 50,000; M 500; (716) 681-9755; Fax (716) 684-3385; director@laccny.org; www.laccny.org*

Latham · *Colonie C/C* · Tom Nolte; Exec. Dir.; 950 New Loudon Rd.; 12110; Albany; P 78,000; M 550; (518) 785-6995; Fax (518) 785-7173; info@coloniechamber.org; www.coloniechamber.org

Levittown · *Levittown C/C* · P.O. Box 207; 11756; Nassau; P 50,000; M 150; (516) 520-8000; Fax (516) 520-8000; info@levittownchamber.com; www.levittownchamber.com

Liberty · *see Monticello*

Liverpool · *Greater Liverpool C/C* · Lucretia Hudzinski; Exec. Dir.; 314 2nd St.; 13088; Onondaga; P 55,000; M 400; (315) 457-3895; Fax (315) 234-3226; chamber@liverpoolchamber.com; www.liverpoolchamber.com

Lockport · *see Sanborn*

Long Beach · *Long Beach C/C* · Michael J. Kerr; Pres.; 350 National Blvd.; 11561; Nassau; P 35,000; M 300; (516) 432-6000; Fax (516) 432-0273; www.longbeachnychamber.com

Long Island City · *see Queens*

Long Island City · *Sunnyside C/C* · Luke Adams; Consultant; c/o LaGuardia Comm. College; 3110 Thomson Ave., Ste. M222; 11101; Queens; M 110; (718) 482-6053; luke@sunnysidechamber.org; www.sunnysidechamber.org

Lowville · *Lewis County C/C* · Anne L. Merrill; Exec. Dir.; 7559 S. State St.; 13367; Lewis; P 27,167; M 460; (315) 376-2213; (800) 724-0242; Fax (315) 376-0326; anne@lewiscountychamber.org; www.lewiscountychamber.org

Lyme · *see Three Mile Bay*

Lynbrook · *Lynbrook C/C* · Bill Gaylor; Pres.; 11 Atlantic Ave.; 11563; Nassau; P 19,000; M 210; (516) 599-3436; info@lynbrookusa.com; www.lynbrookusa.com

Lyons · *Lyons C/C* · P.O. Box 39; 14489; Wayne; P 5,000; M 60; (315) 946-6691; www.lyonsny.com

Mahopac · *Greater Mahopac-Carmel C/C* · Eileen Martinelli; Ofc. Admin.; P.O. Box 160; 10541; Putnam; P 31,886; M 460; (845) 628-5553; info@mahopaccarmelchamber.com; www.mahopaccarmelchamber.com

Malone · *Malone C/C* · Hugh Hill; Exec. Dir.; 497 E. Main St.; 12953; Franklin; P 14,000; M 254; (518) 483-3760; (877) 625-6631; Fax (518) 483-3172; director@visitmalone.com; www.visitmalone.com

Malta · *see Clifton Park*

Mamaroneck · *Mamaroneck C/C* · Jennifer M. Graziano; Pres.; 430 Center Ave.; 10543; Westchester; P 19,000; M 150; (914) 698-4400; chamber10543@optonline.net; www.mamaroneck chamberofcommerce.org

Manhattan · *see New York–Manhattan C/C*

Manorville · *Manorville C/C* · Karen Lee Dunne; Pres.; P.O. Box 232; 11949; Suffolk; P 11,819; M 75; info@manorvillechamber. org; www.manorvillechamber.org

Marcy · *Marcy C/C* · Everett Smith; Treas.; P.O. Box 429; 13403; Oneida; P 10,000; M 140; (315) 865-6144; Fax (315) 865-6144; www.marcychamber.com

Margaretville · *Central Catskills C/C* · Carol O'Beirne; Exec. Dir.; P.O. Box 605; 12455; Delaware & Ulster; P 3,000; M 160; (845) 586-3300; chamber@centralcatskills.com; www.centralcatskills.com

Massapequa · *C/C of the Massapequas* · Phyllis Doria; Pres.; 674 Broadway; 11758; Nassau; P 77,590; M 325; (516) 541-1443; masscoc@aol.com; www.massapequachamber.com

Massena · *Greater Massena C/C* · Michael Gleason; Exec. Dir.; 50 Main St.; 13662; St. Lawrence; P 14,000; M 365; (315) 769-3525; Fax (315) 769-5295; chamber@massenachamber.com; www.massenaworks.com/chamber*

Mastic · *Mastics-Shirley C/C* · Mark Smothergill; Pres.; P.O. Box 4; 11950; Suffolk; P 53,000; M 145; (631) 399-2228; admin@ masticshirleychamber.com; www.masticshirleychamber.com

Mattituck · *Mattituck C/C* · Terry McShane; Pres.; P.O. Box 1056; 11952; Suffolk; P 5,400; M 170; (631) 298-5230; (631) 298-5757; info@mattituckchamber.org; www.mattituckchamber.org

Mattydale · *see Cicero–Plank Road C/C*

Mayville · *Mayville/Chautauqua Area C/C* · Deborah Marsala; P.O. Box 22; 14757; Chautauqua; P 4,666; M 80; (716) 753-3113; Fax (716) 753-3113; info@mayvillechautauquachamber.org; www.mayvillechautauquachamber.org

Mechanicville · *Mechanicville Area C/C* · Barbara Corsale; 312 N. 3rd Ave.; 12118; Saratoga; P 5,500; M 180; (518) 664-7791; Fax (518) 664-0826; mechanicvillechamber@verizon.net

Medford · *Medford C/C* · Michael Gorton Jr.; Pres.; P.O. Box 926; 11763; Suffolk; P 20,000; M 65; (631) 475-3374; medfordchamber ofcommerce@gmail.com; www.medfordchamberny.org

Melville · *Long Island Assn.* · Kevin S. Law; Pres.; 300 Broadhollow Rd., Ste. 110W; 11747; Suffolk; P 2,754,718; M 3,000; (631) 493-3000; info@liaonline.org; www.liaonline.org*

Mexico · *Greater Mexico C/C* · Brian Roach; Pres.; P.O. Box 158; 13114; Oswego; P 7,500; M 60; (315) 963-1042; www.mexicony.net

Middleburgh · *Schoharie County C/C* · 335 Main St.; P.O. Box 966; 12122; Schoharie; P 33,000; M 375; (518) 827-3900; (800) 41-VISIT; Fax (518) 827-7453; info@schohariechamber.com; www. schohariechamber.com

Miller Place · *CDM C/C–Council of Dedicated Merchants* · Dr. Thomas J. Ianniello; Pres.; P.O. Box 512; 11764; Suffolk; P 35,000; M 290; (631) 821-1313; Fax (631) 331-0027; info@cdmlongisland. com; www.cdmlongisland.com

Millerton · *see Lakeville, CT*

Mineola · *Mineola C/C* · Ray Sikorski; Pres.; P.O. Box 62; 11501; Nassau; P 25,000; M 225; (516) 746-2262; www.mineolachamber. com

Mohawk · *Herkimer County C/C* · John Scarano; Exec. Dir.; 28 W. Main St.; P.O. Box 129; 13407; Herkimer; P 64,400; M 450; (315) 866-7820; (877) 984-4636; Fax (315) 866-7833; hcccomm@ ntcnet.com; www.herkimercountychamber.com

Mohegan Lake · *see Yorktown Heights*

Montauk · *Montauk C/C* · Laraine Creegan; Exec. Dir.; 742 Montauk Hwy.; 11954; Suffolk; P 5,500; M 380; (631) 668-2428; Fax (631) 668-9363; www.montaukchamber.com

Montgomery · *Orange County C/C* · Dr. John A. D'Ambrosio; Pres.; 30 Scotts Corner Dr.; 12549; Orange; P 300,000; M 1,800; (845) 457-9700; Fax (845) 457-8799; rudyh@orangeny.com; www.orangeny.com.*

Montgomery · *Town of Montgomery C/C* · Ray Lustig; Pres.; P.O. Box 662; 12549; Orange; P 18,500; M 150; (845) 778-0514; (845) 457-2660; Fax (845) 457-9981; www.townofmontgomery chamber.com

Monticello · *Sullivan County C/C* · Terri Ward; Pres./CEO; 457 Broadway, Ste. 1; 12701; Sullivan; P 80,000; M 600; (845) 791-4200; Fax (845) 791-4220; chamber@catskills.com; www.catskills.com

Morehouse · *see Speculator*

Moriches · *see Center Moriches*

Mount Kisco · *Mount Kisco C/C* · Vincent Lemma; Pres.; 3 N. Moger Ave.; 10549; Westchester; P 10,000; M 200; (914) 666-7525; Fax (914) 666-7663; mtkiscochamber@aol.com; www.mtkiscochamber.com*

Mount Sinai · *see Miller Place*

Mount Vernon · *African American C/C* · Robin Douglas; Pres.; P.O. Box 3730; 10553; Rockland & Westchester; M 250; (914) 699-9050; Fax (914) 699-6279; robinlisadouglas@cs.com; www. aaccnys.org

Mount Vernon · *Mount Vernon C/C* · Frank T. Fraley; Pres.; P.O. Box 351; 10604; Westchester; P 68,000; M 210; (914) 667-7500; Fax (914) 699-0139; mtvcoc@hotmail.com; www.mtvernon chamber.org

Narrowsburg · *Narrowsburg C/C* · Jane Luchsinger; Pres.; P.O. Box 300; 12764; Sullivan; P 1,400; M 45; (845) 252-7234; www. narrowsburgchamber.org

New Baltimore · *see Coxsackie*

New City · *New City C/C* · Michael Di Bella; Pres.; 65 N. Main St., 2nd Flr.; 10956; Rockland; P 36,000; M 120; Fax (845) 638-4636; www.newcitychamber.com

New Hartford · *New Hartford C/C* · Mark Turnbull; Pres.; P.O. Box 372; 13413; Oneida; P 23,000; M 150; (315) 735-1974; Fax (315) 266-1231; info@newhartfordchamber.com; www.new hartfordchamber.com

New Hyde Park · *Greater New Hyde Park C/C* · P.O. Box 247; 11040; Nassau; P 25,000; M 225; (516) 647-5496; Fax (516) 358-7770; info@nhpchamber.com; www.nhpchamber.com

New Paltz · *New Paltz Reg. C/C* · Joyce M. Minard; Pres.; 257 Main St.; 12561; Ulster; P 12,830; M 800; (845) 255-0243; Fax (845) 255-5189; info@newpaltzchamber.org; www.newpaltz chamber.org*

New Rochelle · *C/C of New Rochelle* · Eli Gordon; Exec. Dir.; 459 Main St.; 10801; Westchester; P 69,500; M 250; (914) 632-5700; Fax (914) 632-0708; rmonreal@newrochellechamber.org; www. newrochellechamber.org

New Suffolk • *see Southold*

New York Area

Greater Harlem C/C • Lloyd Williams; Pres./CEO; 200A W. 136th St.; 10030; New York; P 500,000; M 1,900; (212) 862-7200; Fax (212) 862-8745; www.harlemdiscover.com

Greater New York C/C • Mark S. Jaffe; Pres./CEO; 20 W. 44th St., 4th Flr.; 10036; Manhattan; P 15,000,000; M 2,000; (212) 686-7220; Fax (212) 686-7232; info@chamber.com; www.ny-chamber.com

Greenwich Village-Chelsea C/C • Lauren Danziger; Exec. Dir.; 154 Christopher St., Ste. 3A; 10014; New York; M 200; (212) 337-5923; lauren@villagechelsea.com; www.villagechelsea.com

Manhattan C/C • Nancy Ploeger; Pres.; 1375 Broadway, 3rd Flr.; 10018; New York; P 8,000,000; M 1,500; (212) 479-7772; Fax (212) 473-8074; info@manhattancc.org; www.manhattan cc.org*

West Manhattan C/C • Andrew Albert; Exec. Dir.; P.O. Box 1028; Planetarium Station; 10024; New York; P 250,000; M 400; (212) 787-1112; Fax (212) 787-1115; mail@westmanhattanchamber. org; www.westmanhattanchamber.org

Newark • *Greater Newark C/C* • John Tickner; Pres.; 199 Van Buren St.; 14513; Wayne; P 15,000; M 225; (315) 331-2705; Fax (315) 331-2705; newarkchamber@rochester.rr.com; www. newarknychamber.org

Newburgh • *see Montgomery*

Newfane • *see Sanborn*

Niagara Falls • *see Sanborn*

North Creek • *Gore Mountain Reg./North Creek C/C* • Dave Bulmer; Pres.; P.O. Box 84; 12853; Warren; P 2,450; M 145; (518) 251-2612; info@gorechamber.com; www.gorechamber.com

North Tonawanda • *C/C of the Tonawandas* • Joyce M. Santiago; Exec. Dir.; 15 Webster St.; 14120; Erie & Niagara; P 49,398; M 650; (716) 692-5120; Fax (716) 692-1867; chamber@ the-tonawandas.com; www.the-tonawandas.com

Northport • *Northport C/C* • Jane Fontane; Pres.; P.O. Box 33; 11768; Suffolk; P 7,800; M 200; (631) 754-3905; chamber@ northportny.com; www.northportny.com

Norwich • *Commerce Chenango* • Maureen Carpenter; Pres./ CEO; 19 Eaton Ave.; 13815; Chenango; P 52,000; M 500; (607) 334-1400; (877) CHENANGO; Fax (607) 336-6963; info@chenangony. org; www.chenangony.org*

Nyack • *C/C of the Nyacks* • Carol Fleischmann; Pres.; P.O. Box 677; 10960; Rockland; P 7,500; M 195; (845) 353-2221; Fax (845) 353-4204; info@nyackchamber.com; www.nyackchamber.com

Oceanside • *Oceanside C/C* • Gail Carlin; Pres.; P.O. Box 1; 11572; Nassau; P 36,000; M 175; (516) 763-9177; (516) 620-8006; info@ oceansidechamber.org; www.oceansidechamber.org

Ogdensburg • *Greater Ogdensburg C/C* • Sandra Porter; Exec. Dir.; 330 Ford St.; 13669; St. Lawrence; P 12,364; M 280; (315) 393-3620; Fax (315) 393-1380; chamber@gisco.net; www.ogdensburgny.com

Old Field • *see East Setauket*

Olean • *C/C of Olean & Vicinity* • Margaret A. Kenney; Exec. Dir.; 319 N. Union St.; 14760; Cattaraugus; P 14,000; M 350; (716) 373-4230; Fax (716) 372-1204; margek9061@aol.com; www. oleanny.org

Olean • *Greater Olean Area C/C* • Meme Krahe Yanetsko; COO; 120 N. Union St.; 14760; Cattaraugus; P 35,000; M 712; (716) 372-4433; Fax (716) 372-7912; info@oleanny.com; www.oleanny.com.*

HOME AND GARDEN SHOW, ART IN THE PARK, SANTA CLAUS LANE, RALLY IN THE VALLEY, TASTE OF OLEAN, REC/SPORT SHOW, AND MORE.

Oneida • *Greater Oneida C/C* • John Reinhardt; Exec. Dir.; 136 Lenox Ave.; 13421; Madison; P 11,000; M 130; (315) 363-4300; Fax (315) 361-4558; oneidachamber@cnymail.com; www. oneidachamber.com.

Oneonta • *The Otsego County Chamber* • Rob Robinson; Pres./ CEO; 189 Main St., Ste. 201; 13820; Otsego; P 61,676; M 600; (607) 432-4500; Fax (607) 432-4506; tocc@otsegocountychamber. com; www.otsegocountychamber.com

Ontario • *Ontario C/C* • Donna Burolla; Dir.; P.O. Box 100; 14519; Wayne; P 10,000; M 159; (315) 524-5886; Fax (315) 524-7465; burolla@ontariotown.org; www.ontariotown.org

Orange County • *see Montgomery*

Orchard Park • *Orchard Park C/C* • Nancy L. Conley; Exec. Dir.; 4211 N. Buffalo St., Ste. 14; 14127; Erie; P 30,000; M 600; (716) 662-3366; Fax (716) 662-5946; opcc@orchardparkchamber.com; www.orchardparkchamber.com

Ossining • *Greater Ossining C/C* • Jerry Gershner; Pres.; 2 Church St.; 10562; Westchester; P 35,000; M 150; (914) 941-0009; info@ ossiningchamber.org; www.ossiningchamber.org

Oswego • *Greater Oswego-Fulton C/C* • Beth Hilton; Exec. Dir.; 44 E. Bridge St.; 13126; Oswego; P 20,000; M 700; (315) 343-7681; Fax (315) 342-0831; gofcc@oswegofultonchamber.com; www.oswegofultonchamber.com*

Owego • *Tioga County C/C* • Martha Sauerbrey; Pres./CEO; 80 North Ave.; 13827; Tioga; P 50,000; M 300; (607) 687-2020; Fax (607) 687-9028; business@tiogachamber.com; www.tiogachamber.com

Oxford • *Promote Oxford Now* • Bill Troxell & David Emerson; Co-Dirs.; P.O. Box 11; 13830; Chenango; P 4,500; M 100; (607) 843-8722; (607) 843-9538; www.oxfordny.com

Oyster Bay • *Oyster Bay C/C* • Michele Browner; Pres.; P.O. Box 21; 11771; Nassau; P 12,000; M 100; (516) 922-6464; oben chamber@gmail.com; www.visitoysterbay.com

Painted Post • *Painted Post Area Bd. of Trade* • Thomas Magnusen; Pres.; P.O. Box 128; 14870; Steuben; P 2,000; M 100; info@paintedpostny.com; www.paintedpostny.com

Palatine Bridge • *see Amsterdam*

Patchogue • *Greater Patchogue C/C* • Gail Hoag; Exec. Dir.; 15 N. Ocean Ave.; 11772; Suffolk; P 20,000; M 400; (631) 207-1000; Fax (631) 475-1599; info@patchoguechamber.com; www.patchogue chamber.com

Patterson • *Patterson C/C* • Vince Murphy; Interim Pres.; P.O. Box 316; 12563; Putnam; P 11,500; M 75; (845) 363-6304; info@ pcofc.org; www.pcofc.org

Pawling • *Pawling C/C* • Peter Cris; Pres.; P.O. Box 19; 12564; Dutchess; P 5,000; M 200; (845) 855-0500; www.pawling chamber.org

Pearl River • *Pearl River C/C* • P.O. Box 829; 10965; Rockland; P 17,000; secretary@pearlriverny.org; www.pearlriverny.org

Peekskill • *Hudson Valley Gateway C/C* • Debbie Milone; Exec. Dir.; One S. Division St.; 10566; Westchester; P 57,000; M 550; (914) 737-3600; Fax (914) 737-0541; info@hvgatewaychamber. com; www.hvgatewaychamber.com*

Pelham · *Pelham C/C* · John DeCicco; Pres.; P.O. Box 8465; 10803; Westchester; P 13,000; M 110; (914) 738-7380; Fax (914) 712-3682; www.pelhamchamberofcommerce.com

Pendleton · *see Sanborn*

Penn Yan · *Yates County C/C* · Michael Linehan; Pres./CEO; 2375 Route 14A; 14527; Yates; P 24,500; M 425; (315) 536-3111; (800) 868-9283; Fax (315) 536-3791; info@yatesny.com; www.yatesny.com

Perry · *Perry Area C/C* · Joseph Dally; Pres.; P.O. Box 35; 14530; Wyoming; P 4,000; M 87; (585) 237-5040; joinus@perrychamber.com; www.perrychamber.com

Perry · *Wyoming County C/C* · Laura Lane; Pres./CEO; 6470 Route 20A, Ste. 6; 14530; Wyoming; P 45,000; M 503; (585) 237-0230; Fax (585) 237-0231; info@wycochamber.org; www.wycochamber.org

Phelps · *Phelps C/C* · Chuck Molloy; Pres.; P.O. Box 1; 14532; Ontario; P 2,000; M 100; (315) 548-5481; chamber@phelpsny.com; www.phelpsny.com

Phoenix · *see Fulton*

Piseco · *see Speculator*

Plainview · *Plainview-Old Bethpage C/C* · Gary Epstein; Pres.; P.O. Box 577; 11803; Nassau; P 37,000; (516) 937-5646; chamber@pobcoc.com; www.pobcoc.com

Plattsburgh · *Plattsburgh-North Country C/C* · Garry Douglas; Pres./CEO; 7061 Rte. 9; P.O. Box 310; 12901; Clinton; P 200,000; M 3,500; (518) 563-1000; Fax (518) 563-1028; chamber@westelcom.com; www.northcountrychamber.com.*

Pleasantville · *Pleasantville C/C* · William Flooks, Jr.; Pres.; P.O. Box 94; 10570; Westchester; P 7,000; M 165; (914) 747-6419; Fax (914) 769-0037; info@pleasantville.com; www.pleasantville.com

Poquott · *see East Setauket*

Port Chester · *see Rye Brook*

Port Jefferson · *Greater Port Jefferson C/C* · Suzanne Velazquez; Interim Pres.; 118 W. Broadway; 11777; Suffolk; P 7,850; M 270; (631) 473-1414; Fax (631) 474-4540; info@portjeffchamber.com; www.portjeffchamber.com

Port Jervis · *Tri-State C/C* · Charlene Trotter; Exec. Dir.; P.O. Box 121; 12771; Orange; P 9,800; M 325; (845) 856-6694; Fax (845) 856-6695; info@tristatechamber.org; www.tristatechamber.net

Port Washington · *Port Washington C/C* · Roberta Polay; Exec. Dir.; P.O. Box 121; 11050; Nassau; P 32,000; M 300; (516) 883-6566; Fax (516) 883-6591; pwcoc@optonline.net; www.pwguide.com

Potsdam · *Potsdam C/C* · Marylee Ballou; Exec. Dir.; One Market St.; P.O. Box 717; 13676; St. Lawrence; P 17,000; M 300; (315) 274-9000; Fax (315) 274-9222; potsdam@slic.com; www.potsdamchamber.com

Poughkeepsie · *Dutchess County Reg. C/C* · Charles North; Pres./CEO; 1 Civic Center Plaza, Ste. 400; 12601; Dutchess; P 275,000; M 1,800; (845) 454-1700; Fax (845) 454-1702; office@dcrcoc.org; www.dcrcoc.org*

Prattsburg · *see Bath*

Pulaski · *Pulaski/Eastern Shore C/C* · Margaret Clerkin; Pres.; 3044 State Rte. 13; P.O. Box 34; 13142; Oswego; P 3,000; M 69; (315) 298-2213; info@pulaskieasternshorechamber.com; www.pulaskieasternshorechamber.com*

Queens · *C/C of the Borough of Queens* · Jack Friedman; Exec. Dir.; 75-20 Astoria Blvd., Ste. 140; Jackson Heights; 11370; Queens; P 2,000,000; M 1,700; (718) 898-8500; Fax (718) 898-8599; info@queenschamber.org; www.queenschamber.org*

Red Hook · *Red Hook Area C/C* · Ed Pruitt; Pres.; P.O. Box 254; 12571; Dutchess; P 10,000; M 220; (845) 758-0824; info@redhookchamber.org; www.redhookchamber.org

Rensselaer County · *see Troy*

Rhinebeck · *Rhinebeck Area C/C* · Nancy Amy; Exec. Dir.; 23F E. Market St.; P.O. Box 42; 12572; Dutchess; P 45,000; M 400; (845) 876-5904; Fax (845) 876-8624; info@rhinebeckchamber.com; www.rhinebeckchamber.com*

Richfield Springs · *Richfield Area C/C* · Carmela Chiado; Pres.; P.O. Box 909; 13439; Otsego; P 1,800; M 50; (315) 858-7028; richfieldchamber@stny.rr.com; www.richfieldspringschamber.net

Riverhead · *Riverhead C/C* · 542 E. Main St., Ste. 2; 11901; Suffolk; P 27,000; M 350; (631) 727-7600; Fax (631) 727-7946; info@riverheadchamber.com; www.riverheadchamber.com

Rochester · *Rochester Business Alliance* · Sandra Parker; CEO; 150 State St.; 14614; Monroe; P 1,062,420; M 2,400; (585) 244-1800; Fax (585) 244-4864; www.rochesterbusinessalliance.com

Rockville Centre · *Rockville Centre C/C* · Lawrence Siegel; Pres.; P.O. Box 226; 11571; Nassau; P 24,568; M 175; (516) 766-0666; Fax (516) 706-1550; mailbox@rvcchamber.org; www.rvcchamber.com

Rocky Point · *see Miller Place*

Rome · *Rome Area C/C* · William K. Guglielmo; Pres.; 139 W. Dominick St.; 13440; Oneida; P 35,000; M 600; (315) 337-1700; Fax (315) 337-1715; info@romechamber.com; www.romechamber.com.*

Ronkonkoma · *Ronkonkoma C/C* · Steve Browne; Pres.; P.O. Box 2546; 11779; Suffolk; P 15,400; M 195; info@ronkonkomachamber.com; www.ronkonkomachamber.com

Roscoe · *Roscoe-Rockland C/C* · Elaine Fettig; Pres.; P.O. Box 443; 12776; Sullivan; P 1,800; M 75; (607) 498-5765; info@roscoeny.com; www.roscoeny.com

Round Lake · *see Clifton Park*

Royalton · *see Sanborn*

Rye · *Rye C/C* · Lisa Summa-Guarino; Pres.; 57 Purchase St.; P.O. Box 72; 10580; Westchester; P 15,000; M 130; (914) 925-6701; lisa.summa-guarino@capitalonebank.com; www.ryechamberofcommerce.com

Rye Brook · *Port Chester-Rye Brook-Rye Town C/C* · Ken Manning; Exec. Dir.; 122 N. Ridge St.; 10573; Westchester; P 35,000; M 400; (914) 939-1900; Fax (914) 437-7779; pcrbchamber@gmail.com; www.pcrbchamber.com

Sabael · *see Indian Lake*

Sackets Harbor · *Sackets Harbor C/C* · Tim Scee; Pres.; 301 W. Main; P.O. Box 17; 13685; Jefferson; P 1,500; M 75; (315) 646-1700; shvisit@gisco.net; www.sacketsharborchamberofcommerce.com

Sag Harbor · *Sag Harbor C/C* · Bob Evjen; Pres.; The Windmill; P.O. Box 2810; 11963; Suffolk; P 2,500; M 200; (631) 725-0011; Fax (631) 919-1662; info@sagharborchamber.com; www.sagharborchamber.com

Saint James · *Saint James C/C* · Lawrence Glazer; Pres.; P.O. Box 286; 11780; Suffolk; P 15,000; M 125; (631) 584-8510; Fax (631) 862-9839; info@stjameschamber.org; www.stjameschamber.org

Salamanca · *Salamanca Area C/C* · Jayne Fenton; Pres.; 26 Main St.; 14779; Cattaraugus; P 6,800; M 125; (716) 945-2034; Fax (716) 945-9143; sal.cofc@verizon.net; www.salamancachamber.com

Sanborn · *Niagara USA Chamber* · Deanna Alterio Brennen; Pres./CEO; 6311 Inducon Corporate Dr.; 14132; Niagara; P 220,000; M 1,000; (716) 285-9141; Fax (716) 285-0941; mcardamone@niagarachamber.org; www.niagarachamber.org

Saranac Lake • *Saranac Lake Area C/C* • Sylvie D. Nelson; Exec. Dir.; 193 River St.; 12983; Essex & Franklin; P 5,000; M 490; (518) 891-1990; (800) 347-1992; Fax (518) 891-7042; info@saranaclake.com; www.saranaclake.com

Saratoga Springs • *Saratoga County C/C* • Joseph W. Dalton Jr. CCE; Pres.; 28 Clinton St.; 12866; Saratoga; P 230,000; M 2,800; (518) 584-3255; Fax (518) 587-0318; info@saratoga.org; www.saratoga.org*

Savona • *see Bath*

Sayville • *Greater Sayville C/C* • Richard Trpicovsky; Pres.; Lincoln Ave. & Montauk Hwy.; P.O. Box 235; 11782; Suffolk; P 17,000; M 200; (631) 567-5257; Fax (631) 218-0881; info@sayvillechamber.com; www.sayvillechamber.com

Scarsdale • *Scarsdale C/C* • Jen Flores; Secy.; P.O. Box 635; 10583; Westchester; P 18,000; info@scarsdalechamber.org; www.scarsdalechamber.org

Schenectady • *The Chamber of Schenectady County C/C* • Charles Steiner; Pres.; 306 State St.; 12305; Schenectady; P 150,000; M 1,500; (518) 372-5656; (800) 962-8007; Fax (518) 370-3217; info@schenectadychamber.org; www.schenectadychamber.org*

Schroon Lake • *Schroon Lake Area C/C* • Laura Donaldson; Pres.; 1075 U.S. Rte. 9; P.O. Box 726; 12870; Essex; P 2,000; M 100; (518) 532-7675; Fax (518) 532-7675; schroon@capital.net; www.schroonlakechamber.com

Schuylerville • *Schuylerville Area C/C* • Dave Roberts; Pres.; 43 Spring St.; 12871; Saratoga; P 25,000; M 100; (518) 424-9673; info@schuylervillechamber.org; www.schuylervillechamber.org

Seneca Falls • *Seneca County C/C* • Jeff Shipley; Exec. Dir.; 2020 Rtes. 5 & 20 W.; P.O. Box 70; 13148; Seneca; P 33,486; M 500; (315) 568-2906; Fax (315) 568-1730; info@senecachamber.org; www.senecachamber.org*

Setauket • *see East Setauket*

Shelter Island • *Shelter Island C/C* • P.O. Box 598; 11964; Suffolk; P 1,234; (631) 749-0399; www.shelterislandchamber.com

Shirley • *see Mastic*

Shoreham • *see Wading River*

Shrub Oak • *see Yorktown Heights*

Sidney • *Sidney C/C* • John Marano; Pres.; 24 River St.; P.O. Box 2295; 13838; Delaware; P 4,000; M 130; (607) 561-2642; Fax (607) 561-2644; office@sidneychamber.org; www.sidneychamber.org

Skaneateles • *Skaneateles C/C* • Susan Dove; Exec. Dir.; 22 Jordan St.; P.O. Box 199; 13152; Onondaga; P 8,000; M 400; (315) 685-0552; Fax (315) 685-0552; info@skaneateles.com; www.skaneateles.com

Sleepy Hollow • *see Tarrytown*

Smithtown • *Smithtown C/C* • Barbara Franco; Exec. Dir.; P.O. Box 1216; 11787; Suffolk; P 14,000; M 375; (631) 979-8069; Fax (631) 979-2206; bfranco@smithtownchamber.com; www.smithtownchamber.com*

Snyder • *see Amherst*

Sodus • *Sodus C/C* • Mary Jane Mumby; Pres.; P.O. Box 187; 14551; Wayne; P 10,000; M 90; (315) 576-3818; chamber14551@yahoo.com; sodusny.org

Somers • *Somers C/C* • Corinne Stanton-Procopis; Pres.; P.O. Box 602; 10589; Westchester; P 20,000; M 150; (914) 276-3904; president@somerschamber.com; www.somerschamber.com

Somerset • *see Sanborn*

Sound Beach • *see Miller Place*

South Setauket • *see East Setauket*

Southampton • *Southampton C/C* • Karen Connolly & Linda Euell; Co-Exec. Dirs.; 76 Main St.; 11968; Suffolk; P 50,000; M 475; (631) 283-0402; Fax (631) 283-8707; info@southamptonchamber.com; www.southamptonchamber.com

Southern Dutchess • *see Wappingers Falls*

Southold • *North Fork C/C* • Joseph Corso; Pres.; P.O. Box 1415; 11971; Suffolk; P 22,000; M 300; (631) 765-3161; (631) 477-1383; Fax (631) 765-3161; info@northforkchamber.org; www.northforkchamberofcommerce.org*

Speculator • *Adirondacks Speculator Region C/C* • Lisa Turner; Dir. of Tourism; Rtes. 30 & 8; P.O. Box 184; 12164; Hamilton; P 5,000; M 200; (518) 548-4521; Fax (518) 548-4905; info@speculatorchamber.com; www.speculatorchamber.com

Sprakers • *see Amsterdam*

Springville • *Springville Area C/C* • Katherine Moody; Exec. Dir.; 23 N. Buffalo St., Ste. 23; P.O. Box 310; 14141; Erie; P 12,000; M 175; (716) 592-4746; information@springvillechamber.com; www.springvillechamber.com

St. Johnsville • *see Amsterdam*

Staten Island • *Staten Island C/C* • Linda M. Baran; Pres./CEO; 130 Bay St.; 10301; Richmond; P 500,000; M 900; (718) 727-1900; Fax (718) 727-2295; info@sichamber.com; www.sichamber.com

Stillwater • *see Clifton Park*

Stony Brook • *see East Setauket*

Suffern • *Suffern C/C* • Aury Licata; Pres.; 71 Lafayette Ave.; P.O. Box 291; 10901; Rockland; P 10,000; M 125; (845) 357-8424; suffernchamberofcommerce@yahoo.com; www.suffernchamberofcommerce.org

Sugarloaf • *SugarLoaf C/C* • Kiki Rosner; Pres.; P.O. Box 125; 10981; Orange; P 12,000; M 40; (845) 469-9181; info@sugarloafnewyork.com; www.sugarloafnewyork.com

Sweden • *see Brockport*

Syracuse • *Greater Syracuse C/C* • Darlene Kerr; Pres.; 572 S. Salina St.; 13202; Onondaga; P 458,336; M 2,200; (315) 470-1800; Fax (315) 471-8545; info@syracusechamber.com; www.syracusechamber.com*

Tarrytown • *Sleepy Hollow Tarrytown C/C* • John Sardy; Exec. Dir.; 1 Neperan Rd.; 10591; Westchester; P 19,000; M 250; (914) 631-1705; info@sleepyhollowchamber.com; www.sleepyhollowtarrytownchamber.com

Terryville • *see Port Jefferson*

Three Mile Bay • *Chaumont-Three Mile Bay C/C* • P.O. Box 24; 13693; Jefferson; P 2,500; (315) 649-3404; chaumontchamber@yahoo.com; www.chaumontchamber.com

Ticonderoga • *Ticonderoga Area C/C* • Barbara Brassard; Exec. Dir.; 94 Montcalm St., Ste. 1; 12883; Essex; P 5,167; M 160; (518) 585-6619; Fax (518) 585-9184; chamberinfo@ticonderogany.com; www.ticonderogany.com*

Tioga County • *see Owego*

Tonawanda • *see North Tonawanda*

Troy • *Rensselaer County Reg. C/C* • Linda Hillman; Pres.; 255 River St.; 12180; Rensselaer; P 192,000; M 1,125; (518) 274-7020; Fax (518) 272-7729; info@renscochamber.com; www.renscochamber.com*

Trumansburg • *Trumansburg Area C/C* • Heidi Sherwood; Secy.; P.O. Box 478; 14886; Tompkins; P 2,000; M 60; (607) 387-9254; info@trumansburgchamber.com; www.trumansburgchamber.com

Tuckahoe • *Eastchester-Tuckahoe C/C* • Sandra Albanese & Maria Macchia; Co-Pres.; Village Hall; 65 Main St., Ste. 202; 10707; Westchester; P 24,000; M 120; (914) 779-7344; cetcoc@aol.com; www.eastchestertuckahoechamberofcommerce.com

Tupper Lake • *Tupper Lake C/C* • Marti Mozdzier; Exec. Dir.; 121 Park St.; P.O. Box 987; 12986; Franklin; P 6,000; M 242; (518) 359-3328; Fax (518) 359-2434; chamber@tupper-lake.com; tupper-lake.com

Ulster County • *see Kingston*

Unadilla • *Unadilla C/C* • Chris Wilson; Treas.; P.O. Box 275; 13849; Otsego; P 10,000; M 150; (607) 563-8600; www.unadillachamber.org*

Utica • *Mohawk Valley C/C* • Frank Elias; Pres.; 200 Genesee St.; Radisson Hotel Ste. 1; 13502; Herkimer, Madison & Oneida; P 228,000; M 900; (315) 724-3151; Fax (315) 724-3177; info@mvchamber.org; www.mvchamber.org*

Valley Stream • *Valley Stream C/C* • Debbie Gyulay; Pres.; P.O. Box 1016; 11582; Nassau; P 35,000; M 200; (516) 825-1741; Fax (516) 825-1741; valleystreamcc@gmail.com; www.valleystreamchamber.org

Victor • *Victor C/C* • Mitch Donovan; Pres.; 37 E. Main St.; 14564; Ontario; P 10,000; M 350; (585) 742-1476; Fax (866) 857-6338; info@victorchamber.com; www.victorchamber.com*

Victory • *see Schuylerville*

Waddington • *Waddington Area C/C* • Alicia Murphy; Pres.; 38 Main St.; P.O. Box 291; 13694; St. Lawrence; P 2,000; M 67; (315) 388-4079; waddingtonchamber@gmail.com; www.waddingtonny.com

Wading River • *Wading River-Shoreham C/C* • Mike Roth; Pres.; P.O. Box 348; 11792; Suffolk; M 60; (631) 929-8201; info@wrschamber.org; www.wrschamber.org

Walden • *see Montgomery*

Walton • *Walton C/C* • Maureen Wacha; Pres.; 129 North St.; 13856; Delaware; P 8,500; M 125; (607) 865-6656; walton_chamber@yahoo.com; www.waltonchamber.com

Wantagh • *Wantagh C/C* • Marc Nadelman; Exec. Dir.; P.O. Box 660; 11793; Nassau; P 19,000; M 215; (516) 679-0100; www.wantaghchamber.com

Wappingers Falls • *Greater Southern Dutchess C/C* • Ann Meagher; Pres.; 2582 South Ave.; 12590; Dutchess; P 260,000; M 1,100; (845) 296-0001; Fax (845) 296-0006; info@gsdcc.org; www.gsdcc.org*

Warrensburg • *Warrensburg C/C* • Lynn Smith; Pres.; 3847 Main St.; 12885; Warren; P 4,000; M 120; (518) 623-2161; Fax (518) 623-2184; info@warrensburgchamber.com; www.warrensburgchamber.com

Warsaw • *Greater Warsaw C/C* • Becky Ryan; Pres.; P.O. Box 221; 14569; Wyoming; P 5,000; M 200; (585) 786-3730; (585) 786-3080; info@warsawchamber.com; www.warsawchamber.com

Warwick • *Warwick Valley C/C* • Michael A. Johndrow; Exec. Dir.; South St., 'Caboose'; P.O. Box 202; 10990; Orange; P 32,000; M 475; (845) 986-2720; Fax (845) 986-6982; info@warwickcc.org; www.warwickcc.org

Washingtonville • *Blooming Grove/Washingtonville C/C* • P.O. Box 454; 10992; Rockland; P 20,000; M 100; (845) 497-7717

Waterford • *see Clifton Park*

Watertown • *Greater Watertown-North Country C/C* • Peter J. Whitmore; Pres./CEO; 1241 Coffeen St.; 13601; Jefferson; P 118,000; M 918; (315) 788-4400; Fax (315) 788-3369; chamber@watertowny.com; www.watertowny.com*

Watkins Glen • *Watkins Glen Area C/C* • Rebekah LaMoreaux; Pres.; 100 N. Franklin St.; 14891; Schuyler; P 18,888; M 340; (607) 535-4300; (800) 607-4552; Fax (607) 535-6243; info@watkinsglenchamber.com; www.watkinsglenchamber.com

Waverly • *see Sayre, PA*

Webster • *Webster C/C* • Elizabeth Bernard; Admin.; 1110 Crosspointe Ln., Ste. C; 14580; Monroe; P 45,000; M 600; (585) 265-3960; Fax (585) 265-3702; bbernard@websterchamber.com; www.websterchamber.com*

Wells • *see Speculator*

Wellsville • *Wellsville Area C/C* • Steve Havey; Exec. Dir.; 114 N. Main St.; 14895; Allegheny; P 49,500; M 280; (585) 593-5080; Fax (585) 593-5088; info@wellsvilleareachamber.com; www.wellsvilleareachamber.com

West Amherst • *see Amherst*

West Islip • *West Islip C/C* • Kevin Crumlish; P.O. Box 58; 11795; Suffolk; P 30,000; M 400; (631) 661-3838; www.westislip.org

West Seneca • *West Seneca C/C* • Carrie A. Smith; Exec. Dir.; 950A Union Rd., Ste. 5; 14224; Erie; P 50,000; M 400; (716) 674-4900; Fax (716) 674-5846; carrie@westseneca.org; www.westseneca.org

Westbury • *Westbury-Carle Place C/C* • Steven Levy; Pres.; P.O. Box 474; 11590; Nassau; P 16,000; M 150; (516) 997-3966; info@wcpchamber.com; www.wcpchamber.com

Westchester County • *Bus. Cncl. of Westchester* • Marsha Gordon; Pres./CEO; 108 Corporate Park Dr., Ste. 101; White Plains; 10604; Westchester; P 923,000; M 1,000; (914) 948-2110; Fax (914) 948-0122; info@westchesterny.org; www.westchesterny.org*

Westfield • *Westfield Barcelona C/C* • P.O. Box 125; 14787; Chautauqua; P 5,200; M 100; (716) 326-4000; www.westfieldny.com

Westhampton Beach • *Greater Westhampton C/C* • 7 Glover's Ln.; P.O. Box 1228; 11978; Suffolk; P 3,300; M 180; (631) 288-3337; Fax (631) 288-3322; info@whbcc.org; www.whbcc.org

Westport • *Westport C/C* • P.O. Box 394; 12993; Essex; P 1,200; M 100; (518) 962-8383; Chamber@WestportNY.com; www.westportny.com

White Plains • *see Westchester County*

Whitehall • *Whitehall C/C* • Scott Ray; P.O. Box 97; 12887; Washington; P 3,800; M 80; (518) 499-0033; Fax (518) 499-0033; scott.whitehall-chamber@live.com; www.whitehall-chamber.org

Williamson • *Williamson C/C* • Lorraine Mason; Pres.; P.O. Box 907; 14589; Wayne; P 7,000; M 80; (315) 589-2857; williamsoncofc@aol.com; www.williamsonchamberofcommerce.org

Williamsville • *see Amherst*

Williston Park • *C/C of the Willistons* • Lucille Walters; Exec. Dir.; P.O. Box 207; 11596; Nassau; P 7,500; M 100; (516) 739-1943; Fax (516) 294-1444; www.chamberofthewillistons.org

Wilson • *see Sanborn*

Windham • *Windham C/C* • Jane Pierson; Chair; P.O. Box 613; 12496; Greene; P 1,660; M 115; (518) 734-3852; windhamchamber2@aol.com; www.windhamchamber.org

Woodstock • *Woodstock C/C* • Joyce Beymer; Pres.; P.O. Box 36; 12498; Ulster; P 6,290; M 260; (845) 679-6234; info@woodstockchamber.com; www.woodstockchamber.com

Yonkers • *Yonkers C/C* • Kevin T. Cacace; Pres.; 55 Main St., 2nd Flr.; 10701; Westchester; P 195,000; M 500; (914) 963-0332; Fax (914) 963-0455; info@yonkerschamber.com; www.yonkerschamber.com.

Yorktown Heights • *Yorktown C/C* • Arlette Rossignol; Dir. of Ops.; P.O. Box 632; 10598; Westchester; P 38,000; M 400; (914) 245-4599; Fax (914) 734-7171; info@yorktownchamber.org; www.yorktownchamber.org*

North Carolina

North Carolina Chamber • S. Lewis Ebert; Pres./CEO; 701 Corporate Center Dr., Ste. 400; Raleigh; 27607; Wake; P 9,222,414; M 1,900; (919) 836-1400; Fax (919) 836-1425; info@ncchamber.net; www.ncchamber.net

Ahoskie • *Ahoskie C/C* • Jerry W. Castelloe; Exec. V.P.; 310 S. Catherine Creek Rd.; P.O. Box 7; 27910; Hertford; P 25,000; M 200; (252) 332-2042; Fax (252) 332-8617; ahoskiechamber@ahoskie.net; www.ahoskiechamber.com

Albemarle • *Stanly County C/C* • Tom Ramseur; Pres./CEO; 116 E. North St.; P.O. Box 909; 28002; Stanly; P 60,000; M 500; (704) 982-8116; Fax (704) 983-5000; info@stanlychamber.org; www.stanlychamber.org*

Andrews • *Andrews C/C* • Tom Nash; Dir. of Tourism; 345 Locust St.; P.O. Box 800; 28901; Cherokee; P 1,900; M 135; (828) 321-3584; (877) 558-0005; Fax (828) 321-3584; info@andrewschamber.com; www.andrewschambercommerce.com

Angier • *Angier C/C* • Jamie Strickland; Exec. Dir.; 24 E.Depot St.; P.O. Box 47; 27501; Harnett; P 4,000; M 250; (919) 639-2500; Fax (919) 639-8826; angiercc@angierchamber.org; www.angierchamber.org

Apex • *Apex C/C* • Brenda Steen; Exec. Dir.; 220 N. Salem St.; 27502; Wake; P 34,000; M 543; (919) 362-6456; (800) 345-4504; Fax (919) 362-9050; info@apexchamber.com; www.apexchamber.com

Archdale • *Archdale-Trinity C/C* • Beverly M. Nelson; Pres.; 213 Balfour Dr.; P.O. Box 4634; 27263; Randolph; P 25,000; M 265; (336) 434-2073; Fax (336) 431-5845; info@archdaletrinitychamber.com; www.archdaletrinitychamber.com

Asheboro • *Asheboro/Randolph C/C* • George Gusler Jr.; Pres.; 317 E. Dixie Dr.; 27203; Randolph; P 139,218; M 665; (336) 626-2626; Fax (336) 626-7077; chamber@asheboro.com; chamber.asheboro.com*

Asheville • *Asheville Area C/C* • Richard J. Lutovsky; Pres./CEO; 36 Montford Ave.; P.O. Box 1010; 28802; Buncombe; P 235,123; M 2,100; (828) 258-6101; Fax (828) 251-0926; asheville@ashevillechamber.org; www.ashevillechamber.org*

Aurora • *Aurora Richland Twp. C/C* • Christy Carpenter; Exec. Dir.; P.O. Box 326; 27806; Beaufort; P 4,700; M 68; (252) 322-4405; aurorachamber@embarqmail.com; www.aurorarichlandchamber.com

Ayden • *Ayden C/C* • Stacy B. Gaskins; Exec. Dir.; P.O. Box 31; 28513; Pitt; P 4,622; M 85; (252) 746-2266; Fax (252) 746-2266; chamber@ayden.com; www.aydenchamber.com

Banner Elk • *Avery County C/C* • Susan Freeman; Exec. Dir.; 4501 Tynecastle Hwy., Ste. 2; 28604; Avery; P 19,980; M 315; (828) 898-5605; (800) 972-2183; Fax (828) 898-8287; chamber@averycounty.com; www.averycounty.com

Bat Cave • *see Lake Lure*

Beech Mountain • *Beech Mountain Area C/C* • Peggy Koscia; Ofc. Mgr.; 403A Beech Mountain Pkwy.; 28604; Avery; P 380; M 100; (828) 387-9283; (800) 468-5506; Fax (828) 387-3572; chamber@beechmtn.com; www.beechmtn.com

Belhaven • *Belhaven Comm. C/C* • Gary Dean; Exec. Dir.; 125 W. Main St.; P.O. Box 147; 27810; Beaufort; P 1,900; M 75; (252) 943-3770; Fax (252) 943-3769; belhaveninfo@gotricounty.com; www.belhavenchamber.com

Belmont • *Belmont C/C* • Ted Hall; Pres.; 32 N. Main St.; P.O. Box 368; 28012; Gaston; P 9,000; M 240; (704) 825-5307; Fax (704) 825-5550; info@belmontchamber.com; www.belmontchamber.com

Benson • *Benson Area C/C* • Loretta Byrd; Exec. Dir.; 303 E. Church St.; P.O. Box 246; 27504; Johnston; P 3,500; M 350; (919) 894-3825; Fax (919) 894-1052; info@benson-chamber.com; www.benson-chamber.com

Bessemer City • *Bessemer City Area C/C* • Joan Bolen; Exec. Dir.; 201 W. Washington Ave.; P.O. Box 1342; 28016; Gaston; P 5,500; M 75; (704) 629-3900; bsmrctychamber@bellsouth.net; www.bessemercity.com

Black Mountain • *Black Mountain-Swannanoa C/C* • Bob McMurray; Exec. Dir.; 201 E. State St.; 28711; Buncombe; P 9,511; M 400; (828) 669-2300; (800) 669-2301; Fax (828) 669-1407; BMChamber@juno.com; www.exploreblackmountain.com*

Blowing Rock • *Blowing Rock C/C* • Charles Hardin; Exec. Dir.; 7738 Valley Blvd.; P.O. Box 406; 28605; Watauga; P 1,600; M 520; (828) 295-7851; (800) 295-7851; Fax (828) 295-4643; info@blowingrock.com; www.blowingrock.com

Bolivia • *see Southport*

Boone • *Boone Area C/C* • Dan Meyer; Pres./CEO; 208 Howard St.; 28607; Watauga; P 43,000; M 897; (828) 264-2225; Fax (828) 264-6644; info@boonechamber.com; www.boonechamber.com

Boonville • *see Yadkinville*

Brevard • *Brevard-Transylvania C/C* • Libby Freeman; Exec. Dir.; 175 E. Main St.; 28712; Transylvania; P 30,500; M 510; (828) 883-3700; Fax (828) 883-8550; libby@brevardncchamber.org; www.brevardncchamber.org

Bryson City • *Swain County C/C* • Karen Wilmot; Exec. Dir.; 210 Main St.; P.O. Box 509; 28713; Swain; P 13,000; M 360; (828) 488-3681; (800) 867-9246; Fax (828) 488-6858; chamber@greatsmokies.com; www.greatsmokies.com

Burgaw • *Burgaw Area C/C* • Donna Best-Klingel; Exec. Dir.; 203 S. Dickerson St.; P.O. Box 1096; 28425; Pender; P 5,000; M 175; (910) 259-9817; info@burgawchamber.com; www.burgawchamber.com

Burlington • *Alamance County Area C/C* • Mac Williams; Pres.; 610 S. Lexington Ave.; P.O. Box 450; 27216; Alamance; P 138,000; M 800; (336) 228-1338; Fax (336) 228-1330; info@alamancechamber.com; www.thecarolinacorridor.com

Burnsville • *Yancey County/Burnsville C/C* • Ashley Grindstaff; Exec. Dir.; 106 W. Main St.; 28714; Yancey; P 17,000; M 410; (828) 682-7413; (800) 948-1632; Fax (828) 682-6599; info@yanceychamber.com; www.yanceychamber.com

Cabarrus County • *see Kannapolis*

Canton • *see Waynesville*

Carolina Beach • *Pleasure Island C/C* • Gail McCloskey; Exec. Dir.; 1121 N. Lake Park Blvd.; 28428; New Hanover; P 10,000; M 387; (910) 458-8434; Fax (910) 458-7969; visitor@pleasureislandnc.org; www.pleasureislandnc.org

Carrboro • *see Chapel Hill*

Carteret County • *see Morehead City*

Cary • *Cary C/C* • Howard S. Johnson; Pres.; 307 N. Academy St.; P.O. Box 4351; 27519; Wake; P 135,000; M 1,300; (919) 467-1016; (800) 919-2279; Fax (919) 469-2375; hjohnson@carychamber.com; www.carychamber.com

Cashiers · *Cashiers Area C/C* · Sue Bumgarner; Exec. Dir.; P.O. Box 238; 28717; Jackson; P 2,500; M 450; (828) 743-5191; Fax (828) 743-9446; cashcham@dnet.net; www.cashiers-nc.com

Catawba County · *see Hickory*

Chadbourn · *Greater Chadbourn C/C* · Denzel Worthington; P.O. Box 200; 28431; Columbus; P 2,200; M 60; (910) 654-3445; (910) 654-3518; www.townofchadbournnc.gov

Chapel Hill · *Chapel Hill-Carrboro C/C* · Aaron Nelson; Pres./CEO; 104 S. Estes Dr.; P.O. Box 2897; 27515; Orange; P 60,000; M 900; (919) 967-7075; Fax (919) 968-6874; info@carolina chamber.org; www.carolinachamber.org.*

Charlotte · *Charlotte C/C* · Bob Morgan; Pres.; 330 S. Tryon St.; P.O. Box 32785; 28232; Mecklenburg; P 935,304; M 3,800; (704) 378-1300; Fax (704) 374-1903; awilliams@charlottechamber.com; www.charlottechamber.com

Cherokee · *Cherokee C/C* · Darlene Waycaster; Exec. Dir.; 1148 Tsali Blvd.; P.O. Box 1838; 28719; Swain; P 13,500; M 400; (828) 497-9195; (877) 433-6700; www.cherokeesmokies.com

Cherryville · *Cherryville C of C* · Richard Randall; Pres.; 220 E. Main St.; P.O. Box 305; 28021; Gaston; P 5,700; M 130; (704) 435-3451; Fax (704) 435-4200; cherryvillechamber@bellsouth. net; www.cherryvillechamber.com

Chimney Rock · *also see Lake Lure*

Chimney Rock · *Hickory Nut Gorge C/C* · Cheryl Sondak; Mbrshp. Mgr.; P.O. Box 32; 28720; Rutherford; P 2,800; M 250; (828) 625-2725; (877) 625-2725; Fax (828) 625-9601; director@ hickorynut.org; www.hickorynut.org*

Clayton · *Clayton C/C* · Jim Godfrey; Exec. Dir.; 301 E. Main St.; P.O. Box 246; 27528; Johnston; P 15,500; M 400; (919) 553-6352; Fax (919) 553-1758; jim@claytonchamber.com; www.clayton chamber.com*

Clinton · *Clinton-Sampson C/C* · Amber Cava; Exec. Dir.; 414 Warsaw Rd.; P.O. Box 467; 28329; Sampson; P 60,000; M 430; (910) 592-6177; Fax (910) 592-5770; info@clintonsampson chamber.org; www.clintonsampsonchamber.org

Coats · *Coats Area C/C* · Carolyn Spears; Exec. Dir.; 127 S. McKinley St.; P.O. Box 667; 27521; Harnett; P 2,580; M 200; (910) 897-6213; Fax (910) 897-4672; chamber@coatschamber.com; www.coatschamber.com

Columbus · *see Tryon*

Concord · *see Kannapolis*

Cornelius · *Lake Norman C/C* · W.E. 'Bill' Russell; Pres.; 19900 W. Catawba Ave., Ste. 102; P.O. Box 760; 28031; Mecklenburg; P 65,000; M 1,100; (704) 892-1922; Fax (704) 892-5313; chamber@ lakenorman.org; www.lakenormanchamber.org

Currituck County · *see Kill Devil Hills*

Dare County · *see Kill Devil Hills*

Davidson · *see Cornelius*

Davie County · *see Mocksville*

Denton · *Denton Area C/C* · 27 E. Salisbury St.; P.O. Box 1268; 27239; Davidson; P 1,650; M 100; (336) 859-5922; Fax (336) 859-5922; tdenton@triad.rr.com; www.dentonnorthcarolina.com

Dunn · *Dunn Area C/C* · Tammy Williams; Exec. V.P.; 209 W. Divine St.; P.O. Box 548; 28335; Harnett; P 10,000; M 460; (910) 892-4113; Fax (910) 892-4071; tammy@dunnchamber.com; www.dunnchamber.com*

Durham · *Greater Durham C/C* · Casey Steinbacher; Pres./CEO; 300 W. Morgan St., Ste. 1400; P.O. Box 3829; 27702; Durham; P 265,290; M 900; (919) 328-8700; Fax (919) 688-8351; info@ durhamchamber.org; www.durhamchamber.org

Eden · *Eden C/C* · Jean Ann Wood; Pres.; 678 S. Van Buren Rd.; 27288; Rockingham; P 16,500; M 400; (336) 623-3336; (336) 623-8800; Fax (336) 623-8800; info@edenchamber.com; www. edenchamber.com*

Edenton · *Edenton-Chowan C/C* · Richard Bunch; Exec. Dir.; 116 E. King St.; P.O. Box 245; 27932; Chowan; P 16,000; M 300; (252) 482-3400; Fax (252) 482-7093; www.visitedenton.com

Elizabeth City · *Elizabeth City Area C/C* · Jennifer Palestrant; Pres.; 502 E. Ehringhaus St.; P.O. Box 426; 27907; Pasquotank; P 39,000; M 600; (252) 335-4365; Fax (252) 335-5732; informa tion@elizabethcitychamber.org; www.elizabethcitychamber.org

Elizabethtown · *Elizabethtown-White Lake Area C/C* · Lisa Fisher; Mbrshp. Dir.; 805 W. Broad St.; P.O. Box 306; 28337; Bladen; P 15,000; M 185; (910) 862-4368; Fax (910) 862-2425; chamber 28337@embarqmail.com; www.elizabethtownwhitelake.com

Elkin · *Yadkin Valley C/C* · Pres./CEO; 116 E. Market St.; P.O. Box 496; 28621; Surry; P 4,111; M 354; (336) 526-1111; Fax (336) 526-1879; mmatthews@yadkinvalley.org; www.yadkinvalley.org*

Erwin · *Erwin Area C/C* · Pamela S. Addison; Dir.; 100 West F St.; P.O. Box 459; 28339; Harnett; P 4,864; M 133; (910) 897-7300; Fax (910) 897-5543; contact@erwinchamber.org; www.erwin-nc.org*

Fair Bluff · *Fair Bluff C/C* · Karen Grainger; Pres.; P.O. Box 648; 28439; Columbus; P 1,100; M 30; (910) 649-7202; riverbendout fitters@weblnk.net; www.fairbluff.com

Farmville · *Farmville C/C* · P.O. Box 150; 27828; Pitt; P 4,500; M 77; (252) 753-4670; Fax (252) 753-7313; chamber@farmville-nc.com; www.farmville-nc.com

Fayetteville · *Fayetteville-Cumberland County C/C* · Douglas Peters; Pres./CEO; 1019 Hay St.; P.O. Box 9; 28302; Cumberland; P 306,518; M 1,400; (910) 483-8133; Fax (910) 483-0263; chamberreceptionist@fayettevillencchamber.org; www.fayette villencchamber.org*

Franklin · *Franklin Area C/C* · Linda Harbuck; Exec. Dir.; 425 Porter St.; 28734; Macon; P 35,000; M 560; (828) 524-3161; (800) 336-7829; Fax (828) 369-7516; facc@franklin-chamber.com; www.franklin-chamber.com

Franklin County · *Franklin County C/C* · Brenda Fuller; Dir.; 112 E. Nash St.; P.O. Box 62, Louisburg; 27549; Franklin; P 55,000; M 200; (919) 496-3056; Fax (919) 496-0422; bfuller@franklin-chamber.org; www.franklin-chamber.org

Fuquay-Varina · *Fuquay-Varina Area C/C* · Ron Tropcich; Exec. Dir.; 121 N. Main St.; 27526; Wake; P 16,000; M 450; (919) 552-4947; Fax (919) 552-1029; director@fuquay-varina.com; www. fuquay-varina.com

Garner · *Garner C/C* · Neal Padgett; Pres.; 401 Circle Dr.; 27529; Wake; P 24,400; M 580; (919) 772-6440; Fax (919) 772-6443; info@garnerchamber.com; www.garnerchamber.com

Gastonia · *Gaston Reg. C/C* · Elyse Cochran; Pres./CEO; 601 W. Franklin Blvd.; P.O. Box 2168; 28053; Gaston; P 190,000; M 970; (704) 864-2621; Fax (704) 854-8723; edsmith@gastonchamber. com; www.gastonchamber.com

Goldsboro · *C/C of Wayne County* · Steve Hicks; Pres.; 308 N. William St.; P.O. Box 1107; 27533; Wayne; P 140,000; M 786; (919) 734-2241; Fax (919) 734-2247; steveh@waynecountychamber. com; www.waynecountychamber.com*

Grantsboro · *Pamlico County C/C* · Joyce Swimm; Exec. Dir.; 10642 NC Hwy. 55; P.O. Box 92; 28529; Pamlico; P 13,000; M 150; (252) 745-3008; Fax (252) 745-3090; pamlicochamber@embarq mail.com; www.pamlicochamber.com

Greensboro · *Greensboro C/C* · 342 N. Elm St.; P.O. Box 3246; 27402; Guilford; P 240,000; M 1,900; (336) 387-8300; Fax (336) 275-9299; info@greensboro.org; www.greensborochamber.com.

Greenville · *Greenville-Pitt County C/C* · Susanne D. Sartelle CCE; Pres.; 302 S. Greene St.; 27834; Pitt; P 165,000; M 1,000; (252) 752-4101; Fax (252) 752-5934; chamber@greenvillenc.org; www.greenvillenc.org.*

Grifton · *Grifton C/C* · Jennifer Rice; Secy.; P.O. Box 133; 28530; Pitt; P 2,374; M 25; (252) 524-5169; Fax (252) 524-5826; grifton 4u2@embarqmail.com; www.grifton.com

Hampstead · *Greater Hampstead C/C* · Liz Schoenleber; Exec. Dir.; P.O. Box 211; 28443; Pender; P 8,000; M 235; (910) 270-9642; (800) 833-2483; Fax (910) 270-4000; hampsteadcoc1@bellsouth. net; www.hampsteadchamber.com

Havelock · *Havelock C/C* · George Cook; Chrmn.; 201 Tourist Center Dr.; P.O. Box 21; 28532; Craven; P 23,000; M 250; (252) 447-1101; Fax (252) 447-0241; info1@havelockchamber.org; www. havelockchamber.org*

Hayesville · *Clay County C/C* · Marcile Smith; Exec. Dir.; 388 Bus. Hwy. 64; 28904; Clay; P 10,500; M 325; (828) 389-3704; Fax (828) 389-1033; info@ncmtnchamber.com; www.ncmtnchamber.com

Henderson · *Henderson-Vance County C/C* · Bill Edwards; Pres.; 414 S. Garnett St.; P.O. Box 1302; 27536; Vance; P 44,700; M 467; (252) 438-8414; Fax (252) 492-8989; chamber@henderson vance.org; www.hendersonvance.org

Hendersonville · *Henderson County C/C* · Bob Williford; Pres.; 204 Kanuga Rd.; 28739; Henderson; P 104,293; M 1,000; (828) 692-1413; Fax (828) 693-8802; chamber@hendersoncounty chamber.org; www.hendersoncountychamber.org*

Hertford · *Perquimans County C/C* · Sid Eley; Dir.; 118 W. Market St.; 27944; Perquimans; P 12,000; M 285; (252) 426-5657; Fax (252) 426-7542; chamber@perquimans.com; www.visit perquimans.com

Hickory · *Catawba County C/C* · G. Daniel Hearn CCE; Pres./CEO; 1055 Southgate Corp. Park S.W.; P.O. Box 1828; 28603; Catawba; P 153,000; M 900; (828) 328-6111; Fax (828) 328-1175; info@ catawbachamber.org; www.catawbachamber.org.

High Point · *High Point C/C* · Thomas W. Dayvault; Pres./ CEO; 1634 N. Main St.; P.O. Box 5025; 27262; Guilford; P 98,490; M 1,100; (336) 882-5000; Fax (336) 889-9499; tom@highpoint chamber.org; www.highpointchamber.org

Highlands · *Highlands Area C/C* · Bob Kieltyka; Exec. Dir.; 269 Oak St.; P.O. Box 62; 28741; Macon; P 3,000; M 240; (828) 526-5841; Fax (828) 526-5803; visitor@highlandschamber.org; www. highlandschamber.org

Hillsborough · *Hillsborough/Orange County C/C* · Margaret Cannell; Exec. Dir.; 102 N. Churton St.; 27278; Orange; P 125,000; M 325; (919) 732-8156; Fax (919) 732-4566; info@hillsborough chamber.com; www.hillsboroughchamber.com

Holly Springs · *Holly Springs C/C* · Chris Scoop Green; Exec. Dir.; 344 Raleigh St., Ste. 100; P.O. Box 695; 27540; Wake; P 22,646; M 311; (919) 567-1796; Fax (919) 567-1380; director@ hollyspringschamber.org; hollyspringschamber.org

Hope Mills · *Hope Mills Area C/C* · Jan Spell; Pres.; 5546 Trade St.; P.O. Box 451; 28348; Cumberland; P 13,000; M 180; (910) 423-4314; Fax (910) 423-6796; hmacc@hopemillschamber.com; www. hopemillschamber.com

Hot Springs · *see Mars Hill*

Huntersville · *see Cornelius*

Jackson · *Northampton County C/C* · Judy Collier; Exec. Dir.; 102 E. Jefferson St.; P.O. Box 1035; 27845; Northampton; P 23,000; M 125; (252) 534-1383; Fax (252) 534-1739; jcolliernhcoc@ embarqmail.com; www.northamptonchamber.org

Jacksonville · *Jacksonville Onslow C/C* · Mona Padrick; Pres.; 1099 Gum Branch Rd.; 28540; Onslow; P 167,000; M 800; (910) 347-3141; Fax (910) 347-4705; info@jacksonvilleonline.org; www.jacksonvilleonline.org*

Jonesville · *see Elkin*

Kannapolis · *Cabarrus Reg. C/C* · John S. Cox; CEO; 3003 Dale Earnhardt Blvd.; 28083; Cabarrus; P 160,000; M 1,000; (704) 782-4000; Fax (704) 782-4050; jcox@cabarrus.biz; www.cabarrus.biz

Kenansville · *Kenansville Area C/C* · Cristal Jenkins; Secy./Treas.; 141 Routledge St.; 28349; Duplin; P 1,215; M 60; (910) 296-0369; crjenkins@embarqmail.com; www.kenansvillechamber.com

Kenly · *Kenly Area C/C* · P.O. Box 190; 27542; Johnston; P 1,700; M 150; (919) 284-5510; Fax (919) 284-1179; kacc@embarqmail. com; www.kenlynorthcarolina.com

Kernersville · *Kernersville C/C* · Bruce Boyer; Pres./CEO; 136 E. Mountain St.; 27284; Forsyth; P 22,300; M 450; (336) 993-4521; Fax (336) 993-3756; kchamber@kernersvillenc.com; www. kernersvillenc.com*

Kill Devil Hills · *Outer Banks C/C* · John Bone; Pres./CEO; 101 Town Hall Dr.; P.O. Box 1757; 27948; Dare; P 51,000; M 1,100; (252) 441-8144; Fax (252) 441-0338; chamber@outer-banks.com; www.outerbankschamber.com*

King · *King C/C* · Deanne Moore; Exec. Dir.; 124 S. Main St.; P.O. Box 863; 27021; Stokes; P 40,000; M 200; (336) 983-9308; Fax (336) 983-9526; kcoc@windstream.net; www.kingnc.com

Kings Mountain · *Kings Mountain-Branch of Cleveland County C/C* · Shirley Brutko; Dir.; 150 W. Mountain St.; P.O. Box 794; 28086; Cleveland; P 12,000; M 145; (704) 739-4755; Fax (704) 739-8149; shirley@clevelandchamber.org; www.clevelandchamber.org

Kinston · *Kinston-Lenoir County C/C* · Laura Lee Sylvester; Pres.; 301 N. Queen St.; P.O. Box 157; 28502; Lenoir; P 60,000; M 650; (252) 527-1131; Fax (252) 527-1914; info@kinston chamber.com; www.kinstonchamber.com*

Kitty Hawk · *see Kill Devil Hills*

Knightdale · *Knightdale C/C* · Jennifer Bryan; Exec. Dir.; 207 Main St.; 27545; Wake; P 11,000; M 400; (919) 266-4603; (919) 266-8170; Fax (919) 266-8010; knightdalechamber@knightdale chamber.org; www.knightdalechamber.org*

LaGrange · *see Kinston*

Lake Gaston · *see Littleton*

Lake Lure · *also see Chimney Rock*

Lake Lure · *Hickory Nut Gorge C/C* · Cheryl Sondak; Mbrshp. Mgr.; 2926 Memorial Hwy.; 28746; Rutherford; P 2,800; M 250; (828) 625-2725; (877) 625-2725; Fax (828) 625-9601; director@ hickorynut.org; www.hickorynut.org*

Laurinburg · *Laurinburg/Scotland County Area C/C* · Theresa Lamson; Pres.; 606 Atkinson St.; P.O. Box 1025; 28353; Scotland; P 35,050; M 465; (910) 276-7420; Fax (910) 277-8785; tlamson@ laurinburgchamber.com; www.laurinburgchamber.com

Leland · *North Brunswick C/C* · Terry Grillo; Exec. Dir.; 151 Poole Rd., Ste. 3; 28451; Brunswick; P 15,000; M 300; (910) 383-0553; (888) 383-0553; Fax (910) 383-1992; nbchamber@nbchamber. net; www.nbchamberofcommerce.com

Lenoir · *Caldwell County C/C* · Deborah Ashley; Pres./CEO; 1909 Hickory Blvd. S.E.; 28645; Caldwell; P 80,000; M 500; (828) 726-0616; (828) 726-0323; Fax (828) 726-0385; visitors@caldwell cochamber.org; www.caldwellcochamber.org

Lexington · *Lexington Area C/C* · Burr Sullivan; Pres./CEO; 16 E. Center St.; P.O. Box C; 27293; Davidson; P 21,000; M 450; (336) 248-5929; Fax (336) 248-2161; chamber@lexingtonchamber.net; www.lexingtonchamber.net*

Liberty · *Liberty C/C* · A. Pike Johnson; Exec. Dir.; 112 S. Greensboro; P.O. Box 986; 27298; Randolph; P 3,000; M 100; (336) 622-4937; libertychamber@rtelco.net

Lillington · *Lillington Area C/C* · Aneta Brewer; Exec. Dir.; 24 W. Front St.; P.O. Box 967; 27546; Harnett; P 3,600; M 190; (910) 893-3751; Fax (910) 893-3751; contact@lillingtonchamber.org; www.lillingtonchamber.org

Lincolnton · *Lincolnton-Lincoln County C/C* · Ken Kindley; Pres.; 101 E. Main St.; P.O. Box 1617; 28093; Lincoln; P 80,000; M 700; (704) 735-3096; Fax (704) 735-5449; lincolnchambernc@ bellsouth.net; www.lincolnchambernc.org*

Littleton · *Lake Gaston C/C & Visitors Center Inc.* · Almira Papierniak; Exec. Dir.; 2475 Eaton Ferry Rd.; 27850; Halifax; P 8,500; M 280; (252) 586-5711; Fax (252) 586-3152; lgcc@ earthlink.net; www.lakegastonchamber.com

Louisburg · *see Franklin County*

Lumberton · *Lumberton Area C/C* · Cindy S. Kern; Exec. Dir.; 800 N. Chestnut St.; P.O. Box 1008; 28359; Robeson; P 28,885; M 550; (910) 739-4750; Fax (910) 671-9722; lumberton chamber@bellsouth.net; www.lumbertonchamber.com*

Madison · *Western Rockingham C/C* · Gary Corns; Exec. Dir.; 112 W. Murphy St.; 27025; Rockingham; P 10,000; M 300; (336) 548-6248; Fax (336) 548-4466; info@mywrcc.com; www.my wrcc.com

Maggie Valley · *Maggie Valley Area C/C & CVB* · Teresa Smith; Pres.; 2511 Soco Rd.; P.O. Box 279; 28751; Haywood; P 647; M 225; (828) 926-1686; (800) 624-4431; Fax (828) 926-9398; cmaggie@ maggievalley.org; www.maggievalley.org

Manteo · *see Kill Devil Hills*

Marion · *McDowell C/C* · Rod Birdsong; Exec. Dir.; 1170 W. Tate St.; 28752; McDowell; P 45,000; M 425; (828) 652-4240; Fax (828) 659-9620; mountains@mcdowellchamber.com; www.mcdowell chamber.com*

Mars Hill · *Madison County C/C* · Maxine Brown; Pres.; 635-4 Carl Eller Rd.; P.O. Box 1527; 28754; Madison; P 20,000; M 250; (828) 689-9351; (877) 2-MADISON; madisonchamber@main. nc.us; www.madisoncounty-nc.com

Marshall · *see Mars Hill*

Marshville · *Marshville C/C* · Robert Palmer; 201 W. Main; P.O. Box 337; 28103; Union; P 2,893; M 65; (704) 624-3183; www. marshvillenc.govoffice2.com

Matthews · *Matthews C/C* · Tina Whitley; Exec. Dir.; 210 Matthews Stations St.; P.O. Box 601; 28106; Mecklenburg; P 24,000; M 480; (704) 847-3649; Fax (704) 847-3364; tbwhitley@matthews chamber.com; www.matthewschamber.com

Mayodan · *see Madison*

Mocksville · *Davie County C/C* · Carolyn McManamy; Pres.; 135 S. Salisbury St.; 27028; Davie; P 40,971; M 385; (336) 751-3304; Fax (336) 751-5697; chamber@daviecounty.com; www. daviechamber.com

Monroe · *Union County C/C* · James G. Carpenter CCE; Pres.; 903 Skyway Dr.; P.O. Box 1789; 28111; Union; P 193,000; M 650; (704) 289-4567; Fax (704) 282-0122; jim@unioncountycoc.com; www. unioncountycoc.com*

Montgomery County · *see Troy*

Mooresville · *Mooresville-South Iredell C/C* · Karen Shore; Pres./CEO; 149 E. Iredell Ave.; P.O. Box 628; 28115; Iredell; P 65,000; M 1,000; (704) 664-3898; Fax (704) 664-2549; info@ mooresvillenc.org; www.mooresvillenc.org*

Morehead City · *Carteret County C/C* · Mike Wagoner; Pres.; 801 Arendell St., Ste. 1; 28557; Carteret; P 63,800; M 950; (252) 726-6350; (800) 622-6278; Fax (252) 726-3505; cart.coc@nccoast chamber.com; www.nccoastchamber.com*

Morganton · *Burke County C/C* · Michael McNally; Pres./ CEO; 110 E. Meeting St.; 28655; Burke; P 89,361; M 500; (828) 437-3021; Fax (828) 437-1613; info@burkecounty.org; www. burkecounty.org*

Morrisville · *Morrisville C/C* · Sharon Rosche; Pres.; 260 Town Hall Dr., Ste. A; 27560; Wake; P 13,827; M 500; (919) 463-7150; Fax (919) 380-9021; chamber@morrisvillenc.com; www.morrisville nc.com

Mount Airy · *Greater Mount Airy C/C* · Betty Ann Collins; Pres.; 200 N. Main St.; P.O. Box 913; 27030; Surry; P 11,179; M 500; (336) 786-6116; Fax (336) 786-1488; president1@mtairyncchamber.org; www.mtairyncchamber.org*

Mount Olive · *Mount Olive Area C/C* · Tyler Barwick; Pres.; 123 N. Center St.; 28365; Wayne; P 4,800; M 200; (919) 658-3113; Fax (919) 658-3125; moacc@bellsouth.net; www.moachamber.com

Murfreesboro · *Murfreesboro C/C* · Judy Hachey; Exec. Dir.; 116 E. Main St.; P.O. Box 393; 27855; Hertford; P 23,000; M 60; (252) 398-4886; Fax (252) 398-5871; murfreesborochamber@ gmail.com; www.townofmurfreesboro.com

Murphy · *Cherokee County C/C* · Phylis J. Blackmon; Exec. Dir.; 805 W. U.S. 64; 28906; Cherokee; P 27,000; M 450; (828) 837-2242; Fax (828) 837-6012; info@cherokeecountychamber.com; www.cherokeecountychamber.com*

Nags Head · *see Kill Devil Hills*

Nashville · *Nashville C/C* · Meredith Holland; Pres.; P.O. Box 1003; 27856; Nash; P 5,000; M 100; (252) 459-4050; m_holland@ embarqmail.com; www.townofnashville.com

New Bern · *New Bern Area C/C* · Kevin Roberts; Pres.; 316 S. Front St.; P.O. Drawer C; 28563; Craven; P 91,599; M 910; (252) 637-3111; Fax (252) 637-7541; nbchamber@newbernchamber. com; www.newbernchamber.com

North Wilkesboro · *Wilkes C/C* · Linda S. Cheek; Pres.; 717 Main St.; P.O. Box 727; 28659; Wilkes; P 67,310; M 702; (336) 838-8662; Fax (336) 838-3728; info@wilkesnc.org; www.wilkesnc.org

Oak Island · *see Southport*

Ocracoke Island · *see Kill Devil Hills*

Old Fort · *Old Fort C/C* · 25 W. Main St.; P.O. Box 1447; 28762; McDowell; P 5,000; M 50; (828) 668-7223; chamber@oldfort chamber.com; www.oldfortchamber.com

Outer Banks · *see Kill Devil Hills*

Oxford · *Granville County C/C* · Ginnie D. Currin; Exec. Dir.; 124 Hillsboro St.; P.O. Box 820; 27565; Granville; P 50,000; M 480; (919) 693-6125; Fax (919) 693-6126; granvillechamber@embarq mail.com; www.granville-chamber.com

Pembroke • *Pembroke Area C/C* • Denise Fuller; P.O. Box 1978; 28372; Robeson; P 3,000; M 50; (910) 522-2162; Fax (910) 521-3122; pembrokechamber@aol.com; www.pembrokechamber.com

Pinehurst • *see Southern Pines*

Pittsboro • *see Siler City*

Plymouth • *Washington County C/C* • Shaylee Wright; Exec. Dir.; 701 Washington St.; 27962; Washington; P 14,000; M 180; (252) 793-4804; Fax (252) 793-2143; chamber@washconc.org; www.washconc.org

Raeford • *Raeford-Hoke C/C* • Jackie Lynch; Bus. Admin.; 101 N. Main St.; 28376; Hoke; P 37,000; M 200; (910) 875-5929; Fax (910) 875-1010; rae-hokchamber@embarqmail.com; www.raefordhokechamber.com

Raleigh • *Greater Raleigh C/C* • Harvey A. Schmitt; Pres./CEO; 800 S. Salisbury St.; P.O. Box 2978; 27602; Wake; P 782,283; M 2,800; (919) 664-7000; Fax (919) 664-7097; info@raleighchamber.org; www.raleighchamber.org

Randleman • *Randleman C/C* • David Caughron; Exec. Dir.; 102 W. Naomi St.; P.O. Box 207; 27317; Randolph; P 5,000; M 130; (336) 495-1100; Fax (336) 495-1133; www.randlemanchamber.com

Red Springs • *Red Springs C/C* • Fran Ray; Exec. Dir.; 225 S. Main; 28377; Robeson; P 4,000; M 160; (910) 843-5441; Fax (910) 843-2975; franrschamber@aol.com

Reidsville • *Reidsville C/C* • Beth Simmons; Pres./CEO; 513 S. Main St.; P.O. Box 1020; 27323; Rockingham; P 15,300; M 335; (336) 349-8481; Fax (336) 349-8495; info@reidsvillechamber.org; www.reidsvillechamber.org*

Roanoke Rapids • *Roanoke Valley C/C* • Allen Purser; Pres.; 260 Premier Blvd.; P.O. Box 519; 27870; Halifax; P 75,000; M 709; (252) 537-3513; Fax (252) 535-5767; apurser@rvchamber.com; www.rvchamber.com

Robeson County • *see Lumberton*

Rockingham • *Richmond County C/C* • Emily Tucker; Pres.; 101 W. Broad Ave.; P.O. Box 86; 28380; Richmond; P 44,518; M 400; (910) 895-9058; (800) 858-1688; Fax (910) 895-9056; info@richmondcountychamber.com; www.richmondcountychamber.com.*

Rocky Mount • *Rocky Mount Area C/C* • Edward J. Baysden; CEO; 100 Coast Line St., 2nd Flr.; P.O. Box 392; 27802; Nash; P 145,000; M 700; (252) 446-0323; Fax (252) 446-5103; rmacc@rockymountchamber.org; www.rockymountchamber.org*

Roxboro • *Roxboro Area C/C* • Marcia A. O'Neil; Pres./CEO; 211 N. Main St.; 27573; Person; P 39,000; M 350; (336) 599-8333; Fax (336) 599-8334; chamber@roxboronc.com; www.roxboronc.com.

Rutherfordton • *Rutherford County C/C* • Bill Hall; Exec. Dir.; 162 N. Main St.; 28139; Rutherford; P 64,000; M 500; (828) 287-3090; Fax (828) 287-0799; info@rutherfordcoc.com; www.rutherfordcoc.com

Saint Pauls • *Saint Pauls C/C* • Paul Terry; Exec. Dir.; P.O. Box 243; 28384; Robeson; P 2,137; M 80; (910) 865-3890; spnccofc@aol.com

Salisbury • *Rowan County C/C* • Robert H. Wright; Pres.; 204 E. Innes St., Ste. 110; P.O. Box 559; 28145; Rowan; P 130,000; M 950; (704) 633-4221; Fax (704) 639-1200; info@rowanchamber.com; www.rowanchamber.com

Sanford • *Sanford Area C/C* • Bob Joyce; Pres.; 143 Charlotte Ave.; P.O. Box 519; 27331; Lee; P 55,000; M 650; (919) 775-7341; Fax (919) 776-6244; info@sanford-nc.com; www.sanford-nc.com

Selma • *see Smithfield*

Shallotte • *Brunswick County C/C* • Cathy Altman; Pres./CEO; 4948 Main St.; P.O. Box 1185; 28459; Brunswick; P 106,000; M 650; (910) 754-6644; (800) 426-6644; Fax (910) 754-6539; info@brunswickcountychamber.org; www.brunswickcountychamber.org*

Shelby • *Cleveland County C/C* • Michael Chrisawn; Pres.; 200 S. Lafayette St.; P.O. Box 879; 28151; Cleveland; P 96,287; M 725; (704) 487-8521; Fax (704) 487-7458; info@clevelandchamber.org; www.clevelandchamber.org.*

Siler City • *Chatham C/C* • Cindy Poindexter; Dir.; 1609 E. Eleventh St.; 27344; Chartham; P 66,000; M 300; (919) 742-3333; Fax (919) 742-1333; info@ccucc.net; www.ccucc.net

Smithfield • *Greater Smithfield-Selma Area C/C* • Richard W. Childrey; Pres.; 1115 Industrial Park Dr.; P.O. Box 467; 27577; Johnston; P 25,000; M 550; (919) 934-9166; Fax (919) 934-1337; rchildrey@smithfieldselma.com; www.smithfieldselma.com*

Snow Hill • *Greene County C/C* • Angie Turnage; Dir.; P.O. Box 364; 28580; Greene; P 19,000; M 90; (252) 747-8090; Fax 527478090; gcdirector@greenechamber.com; www.greenechamber.com

Southern Pines • *Moore County C/C* • Patrick J. Coughlin CCE; Pres./CEO; 10677 Hwy. 15-501; 28387; Moore; P 84,000; M 900; (910) 692-3926; Fax (910) 692-0619; info@moorecountychamber.com; www.moorecountychamber.com*

Southern Shores • *see Kill Devil Hills*

Southport • *Southport-Oak Island Area C/C* • Karen Sphar; Exec. V.P.; 1 Airport Rd. S.E.; 28461; Brunswick; P 20,000; M 560; (910) 457-6964; (800) 457-6964; Fax (910) 457-0598; info@southport-oakisland.com; www.southport-oakisland.com.*

Sparta • *Alleghany County C/C* • Bob Bamberg; Exec. Dir.; 58 S. Main St.; P.O. Box 1237; 28675; Alleghany; P 10,875; M 350; (336) 372-5473; (800) 372-5473; Fax (336) 372-8251; info@sparta-nc.com; www.sparta-nc.com

Spindale • *see Rutherfordton*

Spring Hope • *Spring Hope Area C/C* • P.O. Box 255; 27882; Nash; P 1,400; M 60; (252) 478-1919; swissmilen@aol.com; www.springhopechamber.com

Spring Lake • *Greater Spring Lake C/C* • Becky Horton; Exec. Dir.; 300 Ruth St.; P.O. Box 333; 28390; Cumberland; P 40,000; M 130; (910) 497-8821; Fax (910) 497-1897; contactus@springlakechamber.com; www.springlakechamber.com

Spruce Pine • *Mitchell County C/C* • Shirley Hise; Dir.; 79 Parkway Maintenance Rd.; P.O. Box 858; 28777; Mitchell; P 15,900; M 450; (828) 765-9483; (800) 227-3912; Fax (828) 765-0202; getinfo@mitchell-county.com; www.mitchell-county.com

Statesville • *Greater Statesville C/C* • David Bradley; Pres.; 115 E. Front St.; 28677; Iredell; P 68,000; M 900; (704) 873-2892; Fax (704) 871-1552; smclaughlin@statesvillechamber.org; www.statesvillechamber.org*

Stoneville • *see Madison*

Surf City • *Greater Topsail Area C/C & Tourism* • P.O. Box 2486; 28445; Onslow; P 5,808; M 333; (910) 329-4446; (800) 626-2780; Fax (910) 329-4432; info@topsailcoc.com; www.topsailcoc.com

Swan Quarter • *Greater Hyde County C/C* • 20646 U.S. Hwy. 264; 27885; Hyde; P 5,826; M 220; (252) 926-9171; (888) 493-3826; Fax (252) 926-9041; hydecocc@embarqmail.com; www.hydecountychamber.org

Sylva • *Jackson County C/C* • Julie Spiro; Exec. Dir.; 773 W. Main St.; 28779; Jackson; P 36,000; M 475; (828) 586-2155; (800) 962-1911; Fax (828) 586-4887; jctta@nc-mountains.com; www.mountainlovers.com

Tabor City · *Greater Tabor City C/C* · Cynthia Nelson; Exec. V.P.; P.O. Box 446; 28463; Columbus; P 4,000; M 125; (910) 653-2031; Fax (910) 653-2031; tccofc@earthlink.net; www.taborcitync.org

Tarboro · *Tarboro Edgecombe C/C* · JoBeth Cobb; Ofc. Mgr.; 509 Trade St.; P.O. Drawer F; 27886; Edgecombe; P 30,000; M 230; (252) 823-7241; Fax (252) 823-1499; jbcobb@tarborochamber.com; www.tarborochamber.com

Taylorsville · *Alexander County C/C* · Jodi Smith; Admin.; 16 W. Main Ave.; 28681; Alexander; P 35,000; M 205; (828) 632-8141; Fax (828) 632-1096; news@alexandercountychamber.com; www.alexandercountychamber.com

Thomasville · *Thomasville Area C/C* · Doug Croft; Pres.; 6 W. Main St.; P.O. Box 1400; 27361; Davidson; P 26,917; M 300; (336) 475-6134; Fax (336) 475-4802; tvillecoc@northstate.net; www.thomasvillechamber.net

Troy · *Montgomery County C/C* · Judy Stevens; Dir.; 444 N. Main St.; P.O. Box 637; 27371; Montgomery; P 26,822; M 200; (910) 572-4300; Fax (910) 572-5193; chamber@montgomery-county.com; www.montgomery-county.com

Tryon · *Carolina Foothills C/C* · Janet W. Sciacca; Exec. Dir.; 2753 Lynn Rd., Ste. A; 28782; Polk, NC & Spartanburg, SC; P 23,000; M 400; (828) 859-6236; Fax (828) 859-2301; janet@carolinafoothillschamber.com; www.carolinafoothillschamber.com*

Wadesboro · *Anson County C/C* · Lynn Edwards; Exec. Dir.; 107-A E. Wade St.; P.O. Box 305; 28170; Anson; P 25,275; M 279; (704) 694-4181; Fax (704) 694-3830; ansonchamber@windstream.net; www.ansoncounty.org

Wake Forest · *Wake Forest Area C/C* · Jodi LaFreniere; Exec. Dir.; 350 S. White St.; 27587; Wake; P 28,000; M 700; (919) 556-1519; Fax (919) 556-8570; info@wakeforestchamber.org; www.wakeforestchamber.org

Wallace · *Wallace C/C* · Lou Powell; Dir.; P.O. Box 427; 28466; Duplin; P 3,800; M 165; (910) 285-4044; lou@wallacechamber.com; www.wallacechamber.com

Warrenton · *C/C of Warren County* · 130 N. Main St.; P.O. Box 826; 27589; Warren; P 20,000; M 165; (252) 257-2657; Fax (252) 257-2657; info@warren-chamber.org; www.warren-chamber.org

Warsaw · *Warsaw C/C* · Linda F. Kitchin; Exec. Dir.; 121 S. Front St.; P.O. Box 585; 28398; Duplin; P 2,687; M 96; (910) 293-7804; Fax (910) 293-6773; warsawchamber@embarqmail.com; townofwarsawnc.com

Washington · *Washington-Beaufort County C/C* · Catherine Glover; Exec. Dir.; 102 Stewart Pkwy.; P.O. Box 665; 27889; Beaufort; P 45,000; M 380; (252) 946-9168; Fax (252) 946-9169; cglover@wbcchamber.com; www.wbcchamber.com*

Waynesville · *Haywood County C/C* · CeCe Hipps IOM; Dir.; 28 Walnut St.; P.O. Box 600; 28786; Haywood; P 60,000; M 600; (828) 456-3021; info@haywood-nc.com; www.haywood-nc.com

Wendell · *Wendell C/C* · Ula Mae Life; Exec. Dir.; 115 N. Pine St.; P.O. Box 562; 27591; Wake; P 4,700; M 225; (919) 365-6318; Fax (919) 366-2010; wendellcc@ncrrbiz.com; www.wendellchamber.com

West Jefferson · *Ashe County C/C & Visitors Center* · Cabot Hamilton; Exec. Dir.; 1 N. Jefferson Ave., Ste. C; P.O. Box 31; 28694; Ashe; P 25,000; M 460; (336) 846-9550; Fax (336) 846-8671; director@ashechamber.com; www.ashechamber.com*

Whiteville · *Greater Whiteville C/C* · Janice Young; Exec. V.P.; 601 S. Madison St.; 28472; Columbus; P 5,400; M 385; (910) 642-3171; (888) 533-7196; Fax (910) 642-6047; whitevillechamber@centurylink.net; www.whitevillechamber.org.

Wilkesboro · *see North Wilkesboro*

Williamston · *Martin County C/C* · Ashley Smith; Exec. Dir.; 419 E. Blvd.; 27892; Martin; P 26,000; M 299; (252) 792-4131; (252) 792-0755; Fax (252) 792-1013; info@martincountync.com; www.MartinCountyNC.com

Wilmington · *Greater Wilmington C/C* · Connie Majure-Rhett CCE; Pres./CEO; 1-Estell Lee Pl.; 28401; New Hanover; P 190,000; M 1,500; (910) 762-2611; Fax (910) 762-9765; info@wilmingtonchamber.org; www.wilmingtonchamber.org.*

Wilson · *Wilson C/C* · Bruce Beasley; Pres.; 200 West Nash St.; P.O. Box 1146; 27894; Wilson; P 78,000; M 630; (252) 237-0165; Fax (252) 243-7931; bbeasley@wilsonncchamber.com; www.wilsonncchamber.com

Windsor · *Windsor/Bertie County C/C* · Collins Cooper; Exec. Dir.; 102 N. York St.; P.O. Box 572; 27983; Bertie; P 25,000; M 172; (252) 794-4277; Fax (252) 794-5070; windsorchamber@embarqmail.com; www.windsorbertie.com

Winston-Salem · *Greater Winston-Salem C/C* · Gayle Anderson; Pres.; 601 W. Fourth St., Ste. 101; 27101; Forsyth; P 338,774; M 1,800; (336) 728-9200; Fax (336) 721-2209; info@winstonsalem.com; www.winstonsalem.com*

Yadkinville · *Yadkin County C/C* · Bobby Todd; Exec. Dir.; 205 S. Jackson St.; P.O. Box 1840; 27055; Yadkin; P 38,500; M 205; (336) 679-2200; Fax (336) 679-3034; jamie@yadkinchamber.org; www.yadkinchamber.org

Yanceyville · *Caswell County C/C* · Sharon Sexton; Dir.; 142 Main St.; P.O. Box 29; 27379; Caswell; P 23,000; M 140; (336) 694-6106; Fax (336) 694-6106; sharon@caswellchamber.com; www.caswellchamber.com*

Zebulon · *Zebulon C/C* · Tammy Russo; Exec. Dir.; 815 N. Arendell Ave.; P.O. Box 546; 27597; Wake; P 4,700; M 275; (919) 269-6320; Fax (919) 269-6350; zebcoc@bellsouth.net; www.zebulonchamber.org

North Dakota

North Dakota C of C · Andy Peterson; Pres.; 2000 Schafer St.; P.O. Box 2639; Bismarck; 58502; Burleigh; P 641,481; M 1,100; (701) 222-0929; (800) 382-1405; Fax (701) 222-1611; ndchamber@ndchamber.com; www.ndchamber.com

Ashley · *Ashley C/C* · Karen Mosset; Pres.; 706 W. Main St.; 58413; McIntosh; P 1,000; M 37; (701) 288-3286; Fax (701) 288-3596; 4horse@drtel.net; www.ashley-nd.com

Beach · *Beach Area C/C* · Cory McCaskey; Pres.; P.O. Box 757; 58621; Golden Valley; P 1,200; M 75; (701) 872-3121; beachchamber@yahoo.com; www.beachnd.com

Belfield · *Belfield Area C/C* · Terry Johnson; 515 6th St. N.E.; P.O. Box 959; 58622; Stark; P 800; M 30; (701) 575-8135; www.belfieldnd.com

Beulah · *Beulah C/C* · Steffanie Boeckel; Exec. Dir.; 120 Central Ave. N.; P.O. Box 730; 58523; Mercer; P 3,200; M 125; (701) 873-4585; (800) 441-2649; Fax (701) 873-5361; chamber@westriv.com; www.beulahnd.org

Bismarck · *Bismarck-Mandan Area C/C* · Kelvin Hullet; Pres.; 1640 Burnt Boat Dr.; P.O. Box 1675; 58502; Burleigh; P 106,286; M 1,200; (701) 223-5660; Fax (701) 255-6125; info@bismarckmandan.com; www.bismarckmandan.com.*

Bottineau · *Greater Bottineau Area C/C & CVB* · Clint Reinoehl; Exec. Dir.; 519 Main St.; 58318; Bottineau; P 2,400; M 175; (701) 228-3849; (800) 735-6932; Fax (701) 228-5130; bcc@utma.com; www.bottineau.org

Bowman • *Bowman Area C/C* • Jeanine Clendenen; Pres.; P.O. Box 1143; 58623; Bowman; P 1,800; M 160; (701) 523-5880; Fax (701) 523-3322; chamber@bowmannd.com; www.bowmannd.com

Cando • *Cando Area C/C* • Jamie Halverson; Pres.; 1310 4th Ave.; 58324; Towner; P 1,150; M 46; (701) 968-4535; (701) 968-3632; www.candond.com

Carrington • *Carrington Area C/C* • Laurie Dietz; Exec. Dir.; 871 Main St.; P.O. Box 439; 58421; Foster; P 2,300; M 130; (701) 652-2524; (800) 641-9668; Fax (701) 652-2391; chambergal@daktel.com; www.cgtn-nd.com

Cavalier • *Cavalier Area C/C* • Shari Hanson; Exec. Dir.; 206 Division Ave. S.; P.O. Box 271; 58220; Pembina; P 1,540; M 110; (701) 265-8188; Fax (701) 265-8720; cacc@polarcomm.com; www.caviernd.com

Crosby • *Crosby C/C* • Sandra Simonson; Pres.; P.O. Box 635; 58730; Divide; P 1,200; M 50; (701) 965-6352; www.crosby nd.com

Devils Lake • *Devils Lake Area C/C* • John Campbell; Pres.; 208 Hwy. 2 W.; P.O. Box 879; 58301; Ramsey; P 8,000; M 300; (701) 662-4903; (800) 233-8048; Fax (701) 662-2147; chamber@gondtc.com; www.devilslakend.com

Dickinson • *Dickinson Area C/C* • Lexi Sebastian; Exec. Dir.; 314 3rd Ave. W.; P.O. Box C; 58602; Stark; P 18,000; M 470; (701) 225-5115; Fax (701) 225-5116; team@dickinsonchamber.org; www.dickinsonchamber.org*

Drayton • *Drayton Comm. C/C* • Larry Ritzo; P.O. Box 265; 58225; Pembina; P 1,000; M 53; (701) 454-3474; chamber@draytonnd.com; www.draytonnd.com

Fargo • *C/C of Fargo Moorhead* • Craig Whitney; Pres./CEO; P.O. Box 2443; 58108; Cass, ND & Clay, MN; P 175,000; M 1,960; (218) 233-1100; Fax (218) 233-1200; info@fmchamber.com; www.fmchamber.com.*

Garrison • *Garrison C/C* • Diane Affeldt; P.O. Box 459; 58540; McLean; P 1,318; M 80; (701) 463-2600; Fax (701) 463-7400; garrisonchamber@rtc.coop; garrisonnd.com

Grafton • *Grafton Area C/C* • Tabatha Widner; Exec. V.P./Events Coord.; 432 Hill Ave.; 58237; Walsh; P 4,500; M 150; (701) 352-0781; gracha@polarcomm.com; www.graftonchamber.com*

Grand Forks • *The Chamber Grand Forks-East Grand Forks* • Barry Wilfahrt; Pres./CEO; 202 N. Third St.; 58203; Grand Forks; P 65,000; M 920; (701) 772-7271; Fax (701) 772-9238; info@ gochamber.org; www.gochamber.org.*

Harvey • *Harvey Area C/C* • Todd Lewis; Exec. Dir.; 120 W. 8th St., Ste. 3; 58341; Wells; P 1,998; M 145; (701) 324-2604; Fax (701) 324-2674; chamber@harveynd.com; www.harveynd.com

Hazen • *Hazen C/C* • Exec. Dir.; 146 E. Main; P.O. Box 423; 58545; Mercer; P 2,600; M 115; (701) 748-6848; Fax (701) 748-2559; hazenchamber@westriv.com; www.hazennd.org

Hettinger • *Hettinger Area C/C* • Earleen Friez; Admin. Secy.; 120 S. Main St.; P.O. Box 1031; 58639; Adams; P 1,300; M 110; (701) 567-2531; adamschmbr@ndsupernet.com; www.hettingernd.com

Jamestown • *Jamestown Area C/C* • JoDee Rasmusson; Exec. Dir.; 120 2nd St. S.E.; P.O. Box 1530; 58402; Stutsman; P 22,000; M 355; (701) 252-4830; Fax (701) 952-4837; info@jamestown chamber.com; www.jamestownchamber.com

Kenmare • *Kenmare Assn. of Commerce* • Jamie Livingston; Pres.; P.O. Box 324; 58746; Ward; P 1,200; M 90; (701) 385-4287; news@kenmarend.com; www.kenmarend.com

Langdon • *Langdon C/C* • Barb Mehlhoff; Exec. Dir.; 324 8th Ave.; P.O. Box 348; 58249; Cavalier; P 2,300; M 100; (701) 256-3079; Fax (701) 256-2156; langdonchamber@cityoflangdon.com; www.cityoflangdon.com

Lisbon • *Lisbon Civic & Comm.* • Sherri Geyer; Secy./Treas.; P.O. Box 812; 58054; Ransom; P 2,300; M 120; (701) 683-5680; Fax (701) 683-5680; lisboncivccommerce@yahoo.com; www.lisbonnd.com

Mandan • *see Bismarck*

Medora • *Medora C/C* • Jennifer Ondracek; Pres.; P.O. Box 186; 58645; Billings; P 100; M 40; (701) 623-4910; medorachamber@ midstate.net; www.medorandchamber.com

Minot • *Minot Area C/C* • L. John MacMartin CCE; Pres.; 1020 20th Ave. S.W.; P.O. Box 940; 58702; Ward; P 36,567; M 650; (701) 852-6000; Fax (701) 838-2488; chamber@minotchamber.org; www.minotchamber.org.*

New England • *New England Commercial Club* • Butch Frank; Pres.; P.O. Box 151; 58647; Hettinger; P 555; M 40; (701) 579-8001; Fax (701) 579-8033; DJThomps@goesp.com; www.newenglandcommercialclub.com

New Rockford • *New Rockford Area C/C* • Jeanette Perleberg; Chair; P.O. Box 67; 58356; Eddy; P 1,500; M 42; (701) 947-2211; www.newrockford-nd.com

New Town • *New Town C/C* • Brad Reese; Pres.; P.O. Box 422; 58763; Mountrail; P 1,500; M 91; (701) 627-4812; (701) 627-3500; Fax (701) 627-4316; ntchamb@rtc.coop; www.newtown chamber.com

Oakes • *Oakes Area C/C* • Audrey O'Brien; Ofc. Mgr.; 412 Main; 58474; Dickey; P 2,000; M 165; (701) 742-3508; (888) 259-6448; Fax (701) 742-3139; oakesnd@drtel.net; www.oakesnd.com

Ray • *Ray C/C* • John Halseth; Pres.; P.O. Box 153; 58849; Williams; P 580; M 23; (701) 568-3343; rfdchief@ncray.net; www.raynd.com

Rolla • *Rolla C/C* • Todd Mears; P.O. Box 712; 58367; Rolette; P 1,471; M 84; (701) 477-3891; chamber@utma.com; rolla.nd.utma.com

Rugby • *Geographical Center of North America C/C* • Dondi Sobolik; Exec. Dir.; 224 Hwy 2 S.; 58368; Pierce; P 3,000; M 135; (701) 776-5846; Fax (701) 776-6390; rugbychamber@gondtc.com; www.rugbynorthdakota.com*

Stanley • *Stanley Commercial Club* • Box 974; 58784; Mountrail; P 1,277; M 67; (701) 628-2225; Fax (701) 628-2232; www.stanleynd.com

Tioga • *Tioga C/C* • Harlan Germundson; Pres.; P.O. Box 52; 58852; Williams; P 1,200; M 60; (701) 664-2807; Fax (701) 664-2543; tiogand.net

Valley City • *Valley City Area C/C & CVB* • Exec. V.P.; 250 Main St. W.; P.O. Box 724; 58072; Barnes; P 7,100; M 250; (701) 845-1891; (888) 288-1891; Fax (701) 845-1892; chamber@hellovalley.com; www.hellovalley.com*

Velva • *Velva Assn. of Commerce* • Mr. Cory Schmaltz; Pres.; P.O. Box 334; 58790; McHenry; P 1,200; M 44; (701) 338-2816; www.velva.net

Wahpeton • *Wahpeton Breckenridge Area C/C* • Jim Oliver; Exec. V.P.; 118 6th St. N.; 58075; Richland; P 12,127; M 285; (701) 642-8744; (800) 892-6673; Fax (701) 642-8745; info@wahpetonbreck-enridgechamber.com; www.wahpetonbreckenridgechamber.com.*

Walhalla • *Walhalla Area C/C* • Liann Zeller; Exec. Dir.; P.O. Box 34; 58282; Pembina; P 1,131; M 100; (701) 549-3939; Fax (701) 549-2410; walcity@utma.com; www.walhalland.org

Watford City · *Watford City Area C/C* · Mary Gumke; P.O. Box 458; 58854; McKenzie; P 1,500; M 90; (701) 580-1493; wcchamber@ ruggedwest.com; www.4eyes.net

West Fargo · *West Fargo Area C/C* · Kent P. Campbell IOM; Exec. Dir.; 109 3rd St. E.; P.O. Box 753; 58078; Cass; P 24,000; M 460; (701) 282-4444; Fax (701) 282-3665; chamber@westfargo chamber.com; www.westfargochamber.com

Williston · *Williston Area C/C* · Diane Hagen; Exec. Dir.; 10 Main St.; P.O. Box G; 58802; Williams; P 25,000; M 450; (701) 577-6000; Fax (701) 577-8591; wchamber@nemont.net; www.williston chamber.net*

Ohio

Ohio C of C · Andrew E. Doehrel; Pres.; 230 E. Town; P.O. Box 15159; Columbus; 43215; Franklin; P 11,485,910; M 4,000; (614) 228-4201; (800) 622-1893; Fax (614) 228-6403; occ@ohio chamber.com; www.ohiochamber.com

Ada · *Ada Area C/C* · Jo Nell Hanratty; Secy./Treas.; P.O. Box 225; 45810; Hardin; P 3,500; M 59; (419) 634-0199; www.adafirst.com

Akron · *Greater Akron C/C* · Daniel C. Colantone; Pres./CEO; One Cascade Plaza, 17th Flr.; 44308; Summit; P 833,000; M 1,600; (330) 376-5550; (800) 621-8001; Fax (330) 379-3164; info@ greaterakronchamber.org; www.greaterakronchamber.org*

Alliance · *Alliance Area C/C* · R. Mark Locke; Pres.; 210 E. Main St.; 44601; Stark; P 50,000; M 450; (330) 823-6260; Fax (330) 823-4434; info@allianceohiochamber.org; www.allianceohiochamber.org.

Andover · *Andover Area C/C* · Michael Creed; Pres.; P.O. Box 503; 44003; Ashtabula; P 2,400; M 75; (440) 293-5895; Fax (440) 293-7374; www.andoverohio.com

Antwerp · *Antwerp C/C* · Cheryl Lichty; Secy.; P.O. Box 1111; 45813; Paulding; P 1,741; M 65; (419) 258-1722; www.antwerpohio.com

Archbold · *Archbold Area C/C* · Marsha Dowdy; Dir.; 300 N. Defiance St.; P.O. Box 102; 43502; Fulton; P 4,600; M 200; (419) 445-2222; Fax (419) 445-0205; aacc@rtecexpress.net; www. archboldchamber.com

Ashland · *Ashland Area C/C* · Barbara A. Lange; Pres.; 211 Claremont Ave.; 44805; Ashland; P 60,000; M 400; (419) 281-4584; Fax (419) 281-4585; chamber@ashlandoh.com; www. ashlandohio.com*

Ashtabula · *Ashtabula Area C/C* · James Timonere; Pres./CEO; 4536 Main Ave.; 44004; Ashtabula; P 101,000; M 375; (440) 998-6998; Fax (440) 812-0109; jim@ashtabulachamber.net; www.ashtabulachamber.net

Athens · *Athens Area C/C* · Wendy W. Jakmas; Pres.; 449 E. State St.; 45701; Athens; P 64,000; M 500; (740) 594-2251; wendy@ athenschamber.com; www.athenschamber.com*

Aurora · *Aurora Area C/C* · Mary Sullivan; Exec. Dir.; 9 E. Garfield Rd., Ste. 101; 44202; Portage; P 15,000; M 200; (330) 562-3355; Fax (330) 995-9052; mary@allaboutaurora.com; www.allaboutaurora.com

Avon · *see Avon Lake*

Avon Lake · *North Coast C/C* · John Sobolewski; Exec. Dir.; P.O. Box 275; 44012; Lorain; P 40,000; M 300; (440) 933-9311; contact@northcoastchamber.com; www.northcoastchamber.com

Baltimore · *Baltimore Area C/C* · Bob Badgeley; Pres.; P.O. Box 193; 43105; Fairfield; P 5,000; M 85; (740) 438-0837; president@ baltimoreareachamber.com; www.baltimoreareachamber.com

Barberton · *Barberton-South Summit C/C* · Joe Fazek; CEO; 503 W. Park Ave.; 44203; Summit; P 48,800; M 315; (330) 745-3141; Fax (330) 777-0597; southsummitcc@att.net; www. southsummitchamber.org

Barnesville · *Barnesville Area C/C* · Barbara Roby; Ofc. Mgr.; 130 W. Main St.; 43713; Belmont; P 4,326; M 115; (740) 425-4300; Fax (740) 425-1048; bacc@sbcglobal.net; www.barnesvilleohio.com

Beachwood · *Beachwood C/C* · Wayne Lawrence; Exec. Dir.; 25550 Chagrin Blvd., Ste. 201; 44122; Cuyahoga; P 15,000; M 550; (216) 831-0003; Fax (216) 831-1209; chamber@beachwood.org; www.beachwood.org

Beavercreek · *Beavercreek C/C* · Clete Buddelmeyer; Exec. Dir.; 3299 Kemp Rd.; 45431; Greene; P 60,000; M 650; (937) 426-2202; Fax (937) 426-2204; clete@beavercreekchamber.org; www. beavercreekchamber.org*

Bedford · *Bedford C/C* · Gina Pieragostine; Ofc. Mgr.; 33 S. Park St.; 44146; Cuyahoga; P 15,000; M 130; (440) 232-0115; Fax (440) 232-0521; bedfordchamberoh@sbcglobal.net; www.bedford chamberoh.org

Bedford Heights · *Bedford Heights C/C* · 24816 Aurora Rd., Ste. C; 44146; Cuyahoga; P 12,000; M 100; (440) 232-3369; Fax (440) 232-4862; bedfordhtscofc@aol.com; www.bedfordheights chamber.com

Belden · *see Jackson Twp.*

Bellaire · *Bellaire Area C/C* · Colleen DeBlasis; Pres.; P.O. Box 428; 43906; Belmont; P 4,898; M 70; (740) 676-9723; Fax (740) 676-9723; belleairechamber@yahoo.com; www.bellairechamber.com

Bellbrook · *Bellbrook-Sugarcreek Area C/C* · Chris Ewing; Exec. Dir.; 64 W. Franklin St.; 45305; Greene; P 14,000; M 195; (937) 848-4930; Fax (937) 848-4930; info@bellbrooksugarcreek chamber.com; www.bellbrooksugarcreekchamber.com

Bellefontaine · *Logan County C/C* · Fred Burkhardt; Pres./ CEO; 100 S. Main St.; 43311; Logan; P 46,000; M 380; (937) 599-5121; Fax (937) 599-2411; info@logancountyohio.com; www.logancountyohio.com*

Bellevue · *Bellevue Area C/C* · Mick Dwyer; Pres.; 110 W. Main St.; 44811; Sandusky; P 8,900; M 175; (419) 483-2182; Fax (419) 483-4259; chamber@cros.net; www.bellevuechamberof commerce.org*

Bellville · *Clear Fork Valley C/C* · Joan Jones; Pres.; P.O. Box 336; 44813; Richland; P 2,000; M 35; (419) 886-2245; Fax (419) 886-2297; joanljones@msn.com; www.bellvilleohio.net

Belpre · *Belpre Area C/C* · Erica Bennekamper; Exec. Dir.; 713 Park Dr.; P.O. Box 8; 45714; Washington; P 10,000; M 300; (740) 423-8934; Fax (740) 423-6616; info@belprechamber.com; belprechamber.com

Berea · *Berea C/C* · Judy Groty; Exec. Dir.; 173 Front St.; P.O. Box 232; 44017; Cuyahoga; P 18,970; M 225; (440) 243-8415; Fax (440) 243-8470; bereachamber@sbcglobal.net; www.bereaohio. com/business

Beverly · *Beverly-Waterford Area C/C* · Jessica Dixon; Pres.; P.O. Box 908; 45715; Washington; P 3,000; M 85; jdixon@chrco.com; www.bwchamber.net

Beverly · *Muskingum Valley Area C/C* · Glen Miller; Chrmn.; P.O. Box 837; 45715; Washington; P 60,000; M 150; (740) 984-8259; www.mvacc.com

Bexley · *Bexley Area C/C* · Mary Greenman; Pres.; 2770 E. Main St., Ste. 5; 43209; Franklin; P 13,203; M 150; (614) 236-4500; info@bexleyareachamber.org; www.bexleyareachamber.org

Blanchester · *Blanchester Area C/C* · Peggy Scott; P.O. Box 274; 45107; Clinton; P 5,000; M 60; (937) 783-2433; blanchester chamber@hotmail.com; www.blanchesterohio.com

Bluffton · *Bluffton Area C/C* · Fred Steiner; CEO; P.O. Box 142; 45817; Allen & Hancock; P 3,900; M 140; (419) 358-5675; bluff tonchamber@gmail.com; www.explorebluffton.com

Bowling Green · *Bowling Green C/C* · Earlene Kilpatrick; Exec. Dir.; 163 N. Main St.; P.O. Box 31; 43402; Wood; P 29,636; M 510; (419) 353-7945; Fax (419) 353-3693; chamber@bgchamber.net; www.bgchamber.net*

Brecksville · *Brecksville C/C* · Jeri Vespoli; Pres.; 49 Public Sq.; 44141; Cuyahoga; P 13,000; M 175; (440) 526-7350; Fax (440) 526-7889; brecksvillecoc@sbcglobal.net; www.brecksvillechamber.com

Bremen · *Bremen C/C* · Connie Moyer; Pres.; P.O. Box 45; 43107; Fairfield; P 1,400; M 50; (740) 569-9150; (740) 569-4121; bremen-coc@frontier.com; www.bremenvillage.com

Bridgeport · *Bridgeport Area C/C* · Ann Gallagher; Secy.; 410 Bennett St.; P.O. Box 86; 43912; Belmont; P 5,000; M 104; (740) 635-3377

Brimfield · *see Kent-Brimfield Area C/C*

Broadview Heights · *Broadview Heights C/C* · Cheryle Costa; Pres.; P.O. Box 470211; 44147; Cuyahoga; P 19,000; M 140; (440) 838-4510; office@broadviewhts.org; www.broadviewhts.org*

Brook Park · *Brook Park C/C* · Sharon Zimmer; Exec. Dir.; 5855 Smith Rd., Ste. 5; 44142; Cuyahoga; P 22,500; M 95; (216) 898-9755; Fax (216) 898 9755; bpchamber@sbcglobal.net; www.bpcoc.com

Brooklyn Heights · *see Independence*

Brookville · *Brookville C/C* · Carla Beatty; Pres.; 245 Sycamore St.; P.O. Box 84; 45309; Montgomery; P 5,900; M 110; (937) 833-2375; Fax (937) 833-2375; brookvillechamber@frontier.com; www.brookvilleohio.com

Brunswick · *Brunswick Area C/C* · Melissa Krebs; Pres./CEO; 1434 Towne Center Blvd., Ste. C50; 44212; Medina; P 38,000; M 270; (330) 225-8411; Fax (330) 273-8172; office@brunswick areachamber.org; www.brunswickareachamber.org*

Bryan · *Bryan Area C/C* · Daniel S. Yahraus; Exec. Dir.; 138 S. Lynn St.; 43506; Williams; P 9,000; M 350; (419) 636-2247; Fax (419) 636-5556; bryancc@cityofbryan.net; www.bryanchamber.org.

Buckeye Lake · *Greater Buckeye Lake C/C* · Jessica Bradley; Pres.; P.O. Box 5; 43008; Fairfield, Licking & Perry; P 3,049; M 142; (740) 928-2048; info@buckeyelakecc.com; www.buckeyelakecc.com

Bucyrus · *Bucyrus Area C/C* · Deb Pinion IOM; Exec. Dir.; 122 W. Rensselaer St.; 44820; Crawford; P 13,500; M 300; (419) 562-4811; Fax (419) 562-9966; bacc@bucyrusohio.com; www.bucyrusohio.com.

Burton · *Burton C/C* · Brian Brockway; Pres.; 14590 E. Park St.; P.O. Box 537; 44021; Geauga; P 4,500; M 200; (440) 834-4204; info@burtonchamberofcommerce.org; www.burtonchamber ofcommerce.org

Butler · *see Vandalia*

Cadiz · *Harrison Reg. C/C* · Anita Coultrap; V.P.; 37840 Cadiz-Dennison Rd.; 43907; Harrison; P 16,000; M 90; (740) 942-3350; Fax (740) 942-0009; hrcctour@eohio.net; pages.eohio.net/ harrisonchamber

Calcutta · *St. Clair Twp. Area C/C* · Lori Kline; Exec. Dir.; 15442 Pugh Rd., Ste. 2A; 43920; Columbiana; P 8,000; M 110; (330) 386-6060; Fax (330) 386-6060; calcuttaareachamber@stclairtwp.com; www.calcuttaohiochamber.com

Caldwell · *Noble County C/C* · Herman Gray Jr.; Pres.; P.O. Box 41; 43724; Noble; P 14,058; M 100; (740) 732-5288; www.noble countychamber.com

Cambridge · *Cambridge Area C/C* · Joanne Sexton; Pres.; 607 Wheeling Ave.; 43725; Guernsey; P 40,000; M 320; (740) 439-6688; Fax (740) 439-6689; info@cambridgeohiochamber.com; www.cambridgesupersite.com

Camden · *Camden Area C/C* · Karen Feix; V.P.; P.O. Box 90; 45311; Preble; P 3,600; M 54; (937) 452-1684; paintedfeather@ embarqmail.com

Canal Fulton · *Canal Fulton Area C/C* · Donna Lemmon; Ofc. Mgr.; P.O. Box 636; 44614; Stark; P 20,000; M 50; (330) 854-9095; Fax (330) 854-9095; cfcc@sssnet.com; www.discovercanalfulton.com

Canal Winchester · *Canal Winchester Area C/C* · Kim Rankin; Pres.; 20 N. High St.; 43110; Fairfield & Franklin; P 9,700; M 300; (614) 837-1556; Fax (614) 837-9901; chamber@canalwinchester. com; www.canalwinchester.com

Canton · *Canton Reg. C/C* · Dennis P. Saunier; Pres.; 222 Market Ave. N.W.; 44702; Stark; P 379,000; M 1,580; (330) 456-7253; (800) 533-4302; Fax (330) 452-7786; dennys@cantonchamber. org; www.cantonchamber.org.

Carey · *Carey Area C/C* · Angela Tackett; Exec. Dir.; P.O. Box 94; 43316; Wyandot; P 4,000; M 107; (419) 396-7856; (419) 250-1295; Fax (419) 396-7856; careychamber@udata.com; www.careychamber.com

Carlisle · *Carlisle Area C/C* · Tammy Trees; Pres.; 516 E. Central Ave.; 45005; Montgomery & Warren; P 5,121; M 75; www. carlisleareachamber.org

Carrollton · *Carroll County C/C & Eco. Dev.* · Wayne Chunat; Exec. Dir.; 61 N. Lisbon St.; P.O. Box 277; 44615; Carroll; P 29,500; M 180; (330) 627-4811; (800) 956-4684; Fax (330) 627-3647; carrollchamber@eohio.net; www.carrollohchamber.com.

Celina · *Celina-Mercer County C/C* · Pam Buschur; Exec. Dir.; 226 N. Main St.; 45822; Mercer; P 40,471; M 390; (419) 586-2219; Fax (419) 586-8645; info@celinamercer.com; www.celinamercer.com*

Chagrin Falls · *Chagrin Valley C/C* · Darci Spilman; Exec. Dir.; 88 N. Main St.; 44022; Cuyahoga; P 4,000; M 445; (440) 247-6607; darci@cvcc.org; www.cvcc.org

Chardon · *Chardon Area C/C* · Erna Leagan-Mabel; Exec. Secy.; 111 South St.; 44024; Geauga; P 14,000; M 200; (440) 285-9050; Fax (440) 286-8964; emabel@chardonchamber.com; www. chardonchamber.com

Chesterland · *Chesterland C/C* · Kelly Monaco; Sales/Mktg. Mgr.; 8228 Mayfield Rd., Ste. 4B; 44026; Geauga; P 13,000; M 225; (440) 729-7297; Fax (440) 729-2690; kelly@chesterlandchamber. com; www.chesterlandchamber.com

Chillicothe · *Chillicothe Ross C/C* · Marvin E. Jones; Pres./CEO; 45 E. Main; 45601; Ross; P 74,500; M 611; (740) 702-2722; Fax (740) 702-2727; mjones@chillicotheohio.com; www.chillicothe ohio.com*

Cincinnati Area

African American C/C–Greater Cincinnati & Northern KY · Sean Rugless; Pres./CEO; 2945 Gilbert Ave.; 45206; Hamilton; M 350; (513) 751-9900; Fax (513) 751-9100; info@african-americanchamber.com; african-americanchamber.com

Anderson Area C/C · Eric Miller; Exec. Dir.; 7850 Five Mile Rd.; 45230; Hamilton; P 42,000; M 500; (513) 474-4802; Fax (513) 474-4857; info@andersonareachamber.org; www.anderson areachamber.org

Cincinnati Area, *continued*

Cincinnati USA Reg. Chamber · Ellen van der Horst; Pres./CEO; 300 Carew Tower; 441 Vine St.; 45202; Hamilton; P 1,900,000; M 6,000; (513) 579-3100; Fax (513) 579-3101; info@cincinnati chamber.com; www.cincinnatichamber.com*

Clermont C/C · Matthew Van Sant; Pres./CEO; 4355 Ferguson Dr., Ste. 150; 45245; Hamilton; P 175,000; M 1,100; (513) 576-5000; Fax (513) 576-5001; clermontchamber@clermontchamber.com; www.clermontchamber.com*

Hamilton County C/C · J. Gruber; Exec. Dir.; P.O. Drawer 42250; 45242; Hamilton; P 1,700,000; M 1,200; (513) 984-6555; Fax (513) 793-1063; hccc@fuse.net; .

Over-the-Rhine C/C · Cheryl Curtis; V.P.; 111 E. 13th St.; 45202; Hamilton; P 9,000; M 500; (513) 241-2690; Fax (513) 241-6770; ccurtis@otrchamber.com; www.otrchamber.com

Circleville · *Pickaway County C/C* · Amy Elsea; Pres./CEO; 325 W. Main St.; 43113; Pickaway; P 52,000; M 350; (740) 474-4923; Fax (740) 477-6800; aelsea@pickaway.com; www.pickaway.com*

Clermont County · *see Cincinnati—Clermont C/C*

Cleveland · *Greater Cleveland African American C/C* · Shirley A. Stevens; Pres./Exec. Dir.; 3775 E. 131st St., Unit 3; 44120; Cuyahoga; P 2,900,000; M 500; (216) 624-5119; estevensii@aol.com; www.gcaaccs.com

Cleveland · *Greater Cleveland Partnership* · Joe Roman; Pres./CEO; 100 Public Sq., Ste. 210; 44113; Cuyahoga; P 2,945,831; M 17,000; (216) 621-3300; (888) 304-GROW; Fax (216) 621-6013; customerservice@gcpartnership.com; www.gcpartnership.com

Cleveland Heights · *Heights-Hillcrest Reg. C/C* · Angie Pohlman; Exec. Dir.; 3109 Mayfield Rd., Ste. 202; 44118; Cuyahoga; P 155,000; M 350; (216) 397-7322; Fax (216) 397-7353; info@hrcc.org; www.hrcc.org

Coldwater · *Coldwater Area C/C* · Greg Homan; Pres.; P.O. Box 57; 45828; Mercer; P 4,482; M 150; (419) 678-4882; info@coldwaterchamberofcommerce.com; www.coldwaterchamberofcommerce.com

Columbiana · *Columbiana Area C/C* · Terry McCoy; Pres.; 328 N. Main St.; 44408; Columbiana; P 6,900; M 199; (330) 482-3822; Fax (330) 482-3960; info@columbianachamber.com; www.columbianachamber.com

Columbus · *Clintonville Area C/C* · Jenny Smith; Pres.; 4219 N. High St.; 43214; Franklin; P 30,000; M 400; (614) 262-2790; Fax (614) 262-2791; jenny@clintonvillechamber.com; www.clintonvillechamber.com*

Columbus · *Greater Columbus C/C* · 150 S. Front St., Ste. 200; 43215; Franklin; P 1,200,000; M 2,300; (614) 221-1321; Fax (614) 221-1408; membership@columbus.org; www.columbus.org*

Columbus Grove · *Columbus Grove Area C/C* · Ed Cassidy; Pres.; P.O. Box 3; 45830; Putnam; P 2,600; M 60; (419) 659-2366; (419) 659-2365; www.columbusgrove.org

Conneaut · *Conneaut Area C/C* · Wendy DuBey; Exec. Dir.; 235 Main St.; 44030; Ashtabula; P 10,000; M 200; (440) 593-2402; Fax (440) 599-1514; conneautchamber@suite224.net; www.conneautchamber.org

Coshocton · *Coshocton County C/C* · Carol Remington; Exec. Dir.; 401 Main St.; 43812; Coshocton; P 36,131; M 300; (740) 622-5411; Fax (740) 622-9902; info@coshocton.com; www.visitcoshocton.com

Covington · *Covington Area C/C* · Dustina Monnier; Pres.; P.O. Box 183; 45318; Miami; P 2,567; M 90; covingtonchamber secretary@gmail.com; www.covingtonohiochamber.com*

Crestline · *Crestline Area C/C* · P.O. Box 355; 44827; Crawford; P 5,000; M 75; (419) 683-3818; Fax (419) 683-0175; crestline advocate@twcbc.com; www.crestlineoh.com

Cuyahoga Falls · *Cuyahoga Falls C/C* · Laura A. Petrella; CEO; 151 Portage Trl., Ste. 1; 44221; P 50,000; M 300; (330) 929-6756; Fax (330) 929-4278; info@cfchamber.com; www.cfchamber.com

Dalton · *Dalton Area C/C* · Kerry Pickett; Pres.; P.O. Box 168; 44618; Wayne; P 1,800; M 80; (330) 828-2323; Fax (330) 828-2326; kerry@daltonohchamber.com; www.daltonohchamber.com

Dayton · *Dayton Area C/C* · Phillip L. Parker; Pres./CEO; One Chamber Plaza; 45402; Montgomery; P 970,000; M 3,000; (937) 226-1444; Fax (937) 226-8254; info@dacc.org; www.dayton chamber.org*

Deerfield · *Deerfield C/C* · Sandie Welch; Pres.; P.O. Box 193; 44411; Warren; P 2,263; M 14; (330) 584-8440; sandie.welch@yahoo.com

Defiance · *Defiance Area C/C* · Isaac Lee; Pres.; 615 W. Third St.; 43512; Defiance; P 39,350; M 750; (419) 782-7946; Fax (419) 782-0111; isaaclee@defiancechamber.com; www.defiancechamber.com

Delaware · *Delaware Area C/C* · Holly Quaine; Pres.; 35 S. Sandusky St.; 43015; Delaware; P 110,000; M 475; (740) 369-6221; Fax (740) 369-4817; dachamber@delawareohiochamber.com; www.delawareohiochamber.com

Delphos · *Delphos Area C/C* · Jennifer Moenter; Exec. Dir.; 310 N. Main St.; 45833; Allen; P 7,000; M 255; (419) 695-1771; Fax (419) 692-1751; info@delphoschamber.com; www.delphos chamber.com.

Delta · *Delta C/C* · Marcy LeFevre; Pres.; 401 Main St.; P.O. Box 96; 43515; Fulton; P 3,000; M 60; (419) 822-3089; Fax (419) 822-3089

Dennison · *see Uhrichsville*

Deshler · *Deshler C/C* · Jackie Arps; Secy./Treas.; P.O. Box 123; 43516; Henry; P 2,000; M 55; (419) 278-8129; www.deshler ohiochamber.com

Dublin · *Dublin C/C* · Margery S. Amorose; Exec. Dir.; 129 S. High St.; 43017; Franklin; P 40,000; M 1,200; (614) 889-2001; Fax (614) 889-2888; info@dublinchamber.org; www.dublinchamber.org

East Liverpool · *East Liverpool Area C/C* · Pamela Y. Hoppel; CEO; 529 Market St.; P.O. Box 94; 43920; Columbiana; P 15,000; M 200; (330) 385-0845; Fax (330) 385-0581; office@elchamber.com; www.elchamber.com

East Palestine · *East Palestine Area C/C* · Donald Elzer; Pres.; 15 S. Market St.; P.O. Box 329; 44413; Columbiana; P 9,000; M 61; (330) 426-2128; contact@eastpalestinechamber.com; www.eastpalestinechamber.com

East Toledo · *see Oregon*

Eastlake · *see Wickliffe*

Eaton · *Preble County C/C* · Matt Appenzeller; Exec. Dir.; 122 W. Decatur St.; P.O. Box 303; 45320; Preble; P 43,000; M 200; (937) 456-4949; Fax (937) 456-4949; chamberoffices@preblecountyohio.com; www.preblecountyohio.com

Edgerton · *Edgerton C/C* · Roger Strup; Secy.; P.O. Box 399; 43517; Williams; P 2,300; M 75; (419) 298-2335

Edon · *Edon Area C/C* · Nikki Poorman; Pres.; P.O. Box 153; 43518; Williams; P 1,000; M 50; (419) 272-2219; www.edon-ohio.com

Elyria · *Lorain County C/C* · Frank DeTillio; Pres.; 226 Middle Ave., 5th Flr.; 44035; Lorain; P 282,465; M 500; (440) 328-2550; Fax (440) 328-2557; fdetillio@loraincountychamber.com; www.loraincountychamber.com

Englewood • *Northmont Area C/C* • Cathy Hutton; CEO; P.O. Box 62; 45322; Montgomery; P 33,700; M 300; (937) 836-2550; Fax (937) 836-2485; cathy.hutton@northmont-area-coc.org; www.northmont-area-coc.org.

Euclid • *Euclid C/C* • David L. Carlson; Chrmn.; 22639 Euclid Ave.; 44117; Cuyahoga; P 45,000; M 200; (216) 731-9322; Fax (216) 731-8354; info@euclidchamber.com; www.euclidchamber.com

Fairborn • *Fairborn Area C/C* • Paul Newman; Exec. Dir.; 12 N. Central Ave.; 45324; Greene; P 33,000; M 450; (937) 878-3191; Fax (937) 878-3197; chamber@fairborn.com; www.fairborn.com*

Fairfield • *Fairfield C/C* • Kert Radel; Pres./CEO; 670 Wessel Dr.; 45014; Butler; P 44,000; M 480; (513) 881-5500; Fax (513) 881-5503; president@fairfieldchamber.com; www.fairfieldchamber.com*

Fairlawn • *Fairlawn Area C/C* • Polly Riffle; Exec. Dir.; P.O. Box 13388; 44334; Summit; P 7,302; M 350; (330) 777-0032; Fax (330) 777-0032; info@fairlawnareachamber.org; www.fairlawnareachamber.org

Fayette • *Fayette Area C/C* • Lowell Beaverson; Exec. Secy.; P.O. Box 8; 43521; Fulton; P 1,300; M 45; (419) 237-2036; Fax (419) 237-9043; www.villageoffayette.com

Findlay • *Findlay-Hancock County C/C-Greater Findlay Inc.* • Dionne Neubauer; Exec. V.P.; 123 E. Main Cross St.; 45840; Hancock; P 72,000; M 850; (419) 422-3313; Fax (419) 422-9508; info@greaterfindlayinc.com; www.greaterfindlayinc.com*

Fort Recovery • *Fort Recovery C/C* • Bob Walters; Pres.; P.O. Box 671; 45846; Mercer; P 1,300; M 75; (419) 375-2530; Fax (419) 375-4709; www.fortrecovery.org

Fostoria • *Fostoria Area C/C* • 121 N. Main St.; 44830; Seneca; P 14,000; M 245; (419) 435-0486; Fax (419) 435-0936; chamberfost@aol.com; www.fostoriachamber.com

Franklin • *Franklin Area C/C* • Peggy Darragh-Jeromos; Exec. Dir.; 340 S. Main St.; P.O. Box 721; 45005; Warren; P 30,000; M 165; (937) 746-8457; chamber45005@gmail.com; www.chamber45005.org

Fremont • *C/C of Sandusky County* • Holly Stacy; CEO; 101 S. Front St.; 43420; Sandusky; P 61,000; M 500; (419) 332-1591; Fax (419) 332-8666; communications@scchamber.org; www.scchamber.org*

Gahanna • *Gahanna Area C/C* • Leslee Blake; Pres.; 1000 Creekside Plz.; 43230; Franklin; P 35,000; M 430; (614) 471-0451; Fax (614) 471-5122; info@gahannaareachamber.com; www.gahannaareachamber.com*

Galion • *Galion Area C/C* • Joe Kleinknecht; Pres./CEO; 106 Harding Way E.; 44833; Crawford; P 11,341; M 300; (419) 468-7737; Fax (419) 462-5487; galionchamber@galionchamber.org; www.galionchamber.org.*

Gallipolis • *Gallia County C/C* • Lorie Neal; Exec. Dir.; 16 State St.; P.O. Box 465; 45631; Gallia; P 30,912; M 200; (740) 446-0596; Fax (740) 446-7031; lneal@galliacounty.org; www.galliacounty.org.*

Garfield Heights • *Garfield Heights C/C* • Mary Stamler; Exec. Dir.; 5706 Turney Rd.; 44125; Cuyahoga; P 31,000; M 211; (216) 475-7775; Fax (216) 475-2237; mstamler@garfieldchamber.com; www.garfieldchamber.com

Garrettsville • *Garrettsville Area C/C* • Hallie Higgins; P.O. Box 1; 44231; Portage; P 3,000; M 132; (330) 527-2411; patricks@apk.net; www.garrettsvillearea.com

Geneva • *Geneva Area C/C* • Sue Ellen Foote; Exec. Dir.; 866 E. Main St.; P.O. Box 84; 44041; Ashtabula; P 26,000; M 325; (440) 466-8694; Fax (440) 466-0823; info@genevachamber.org; www.genevachamber.org

Geneva-on-the-Lake • *Geneva-on-the-Lake C/ C & CVB* • Tony Zala; Pres. of Bd.; 5536 Lake Rd.; 44041; Ashtabula; P 1,600; M 100; (440) 466-8600; (800) 862-9948; Fax (440) 466-8911; golvb@windstream.net; www.visitgenevaonthelake.com

Genoa • *Genoa Area C/C* • Timothy A. Davies; Pres.; P.O. Box 141; 43430; Ottawa; P 6,000; M 175; (419) 707-5774; gaccinfo2010@yahoo.com; www.genoachamber.com

Georgetown • *Brown County C/C* • Ray Becraft; Exec. Dir.; 110 E. State St.; 45121; Brown; P 45,000; M 312; (937) 378-4784; (888) 276-9664; Fax (937) 378-1634; brchcom@yahoo.com; www.browncountyohiochamber.com

Germantown • *Germantown C/C* • Jeff Fannin; Pres.; P.O. Box 212; 45327; Montgomery; P 8,000; M 55; (937) 855-3471; www.germantown.oh.us

Girard • *Greater Girard Area C/C* • Jeff Kay; Pres.; 16 W. Liberty; 44420; Trumble; P 15,000; M 75; (330) 545-8108; www.girardchamber.org

Grand Rapids • *Grand Rapids Area C/C* • P.O. Box 391; 43522; Wood; P 1,200; M 50; (419) 832-1106; Fax (419) 832-1106; information@grandrapidsohio.com; www.grandrapidsohio.com

Grandview Heights • *Grandview Area Chamber* • Michelle Wilson; Exec. Dir.; 1258-B Grandview Ave.; 43212; Franklin; P 7,000; M 225; (614) 486-0196; mwilson@grandviewchamber.org; www.grandviewchamber.org*

Granville • *Granville Area C/C* • Maggie Barno; Dir.; P.O. Box 603; 43023; Licking; P 5,000; M 180; (740) 587-4490; info@granvilleoh.com; www.granvilleoh.com

Greentown • *see Hartville*

Greenville • *Darke County C/C* • Sharon Deschambeau; Pres.; 622 S. Broadway; 45331; Darke; P 53,309; M 361; (937) 548-2102; Fax (937) 548-5608; info@darkecountyohio.com; www.darkecountyohio.com.*

Greenwich • *see Willard*

Grove City • *Grove City Area C/C* • William H. Diehl; Exec. Dir.; 4069 Broadway; 43123; Franklin; P 35,000; M 550; (614) 875-9762; (877) 870-5393; Fax (614) 875-1510; e.dir@gcchamber.org; www.gcchamber.org*

Groveport • *Southeastern Franklin County C/C* • Susan Brobst; Exec. Dir.; 5151 Berger Rd.; 43125; Franklin; P 5,000; M 200; (614) 836-1138; Fax (614) 836-1138; chambersefc@aol.com; www.chambersefc.com

Hamilton • *Greater Hamilton C/C* • Kenny Craig; Pres./CEO; 201 Dayton St.; 45011; Butler; P 62,000; M 600; (513) 844-1500; Fax (513) 844-1999; info@hamilton-ohio.com; www.hamilton-ohio.com*

Hartville • *Lake Township C/C* • Christa Kozy; Pres./CEO; P.O. Box 1207; 44632; Stark; P 25,892; M 175; (330) 877-5500; Fax (330) 877-2149; president@lakechamber.com; www.lakechamber.com

Hicksville • *Hicksville C/C* • Shannon Villena; Dir.; P.O. Box 244; 43526; Defiance; P 4,000; M 94; (419) 542-7173; chamber@hicksvillechamber.org; www.hicksvillechamber.org

Highland Hills • *see Warrensville Heights*

Hilliard • *Hilliard Area C/C* • Libby Gierach; Pres./CEO; 4081 Main St.; 43026; Franklin; P 25,000; M 400; (614) 876-7666; Fax (614) 876-3113; info@hilliardchamber.org; www.hilliardchamber.org

Hillsboro · *Highland County C/C* · Katy Farber; Pres.; 1575 N. High St., Ste. 400; 45133; Highland; P 41,000; M 350; (937) 393-1111; Fax (937) 393-9604; hccoc@cinci.rr.com; www.highland countychamber.com*

Hinckley · *Hinckley C/C* · Amanda M. Phahl; Pres.; P.O. Box 354; 44233; Medina; P 7,100; M 35; (330) 278-2066; Fax (330) 225-0239; www.hinckleytwp.org

Holland · *Holland/Springfield C/C* · Pat Hicks; Exec. Dir.; 940 Clarion St.; P.O. Box 986; 43528; Lucas; P 23,000; M 280; (419) 865-2110; Fax (419) 865-3740; info@hollandspringfieldcoc.org; www.hollandspringfieldcoc.org

Hubbard · *Hubbard Area C/C* · Deborah Shields; Exec. Dir.; 105B N. Main St.; P.O. Box 177; 44425; Trumbull; P 17,000; M 70; (330) 534-5120; Fax (330) 534-5120; hacc44425@yahoo.com; www. hubbardchamber.org

Huber Heights · *Huber Heights C/C* · Anita Brock; Exec. Dir.; 4756 Fishburg Rd.; 45424; Greene, Miami & Montgomery; P 40,000; M 300; (937) 233-5700; Fax (937) 233-5769; anita. brock@hubercc.com; www.huberheightschamber.com*

Hudson · *Hudson Area C/C* · Carolyn Konefal; Pres.; 245 N. Main St., Ste. 100; 44236; Summit; P 24,000; M 300; (330) 650-0621; Fax (330) 656-1646; info@hudsoncoc.org; www.explorehudson.com

Huron · *Huron C/C* · Sheila Ehrhardt; Dir.; 509 Huron St.; P.O. Box 43; 44839; Erie; P 10,000; M 285; (419) 433-5700; Fax same; chamber@huron.net; www.huron.net*

Independence · *Cuyahoga Valley C/C* · Eileen Hawkins; Exec. Dir.; P.O. Box 31326; 44131; Cuyahoga; P 9,000; M 250; (216) 573-2707; Fax (216) 328-9812; cvcc@cuyahogavalleychamber.org; www.cuyahogavalleychamber.org

Ironton · *see South Point*

Jackson · *Jackson Area C/C* · Randy Heath; Exec. Dir.; 234 Broadway St.; 45640; Jackson; P 6,500; M 275; (740) 286-2722; Fax (740) 286-8443; rheath@zoomnet.net; www.jacksonohio.org

Jackson Twp. · *Jackson-Belden C/C* · Ruthanne Wilkof; Pres./CEO; 5735 Wales Ave. N.W.; 44646; Stark; P 42,500; M 775; (330) 833-4400; Fax (330) 833-4456; info@jbcc.org; www.jbcc.org.*

Jamestown · *Jamestown C/C* · Ann Laughhunn; P.O. Box 66; 45335; Greene; P 4,000; M 60; (937) 675-2700; ann@abstractor services.com; www.jtchamber.com

Jefferson · *Jefferson Area C/C* · Pat Bradek; Pres.; P.O. Box 100; 44047; Ashtabula; P 3,600; M 120; (440) 576-0133; Fax (440) 576-4352; chamber@jeffersonchamber.com; www.jeffersonchamber.com

Jerusalem · *see Oregon*

Kelleys Island · *Kelleys Island C/C* · Deb Herwick; Dir.; P.O. Box 783-F; 43438; Erie; P 300; M 65; (419) 746-2360; Fax (419) 746-2360; staff@kelleysislandchamber.com; www.kelleysisland chamber.com

Kent · *Brimfield Area C/C* · Scott Mikula; P.O. Box 3414; 44240; Portage; P 9,500; M 67; (330) 677-6439; (330) 678-5885; smikula@ homesavingsbnk.com; www.brimfieldchamber.com

Kent · *Kent Area C/C & Info. Center* · Lori Wemhoff; Exec. Dir.; 138 E. Main St., Ste. 102; 44240; Portage; P 27,906; M 245; (330) 673-9855; Fax (330) 673-9860; lwemhoff@kentbiz.com; www. kentbiz.com

Kenton · *Hardin County Chamber & Bus. Alliance* · Jannette Jacobs; V.P. of Chamber & Tourism; 225 S. Detroit St.; 43326; Hardin; P 31,945; M 280; (419) 673-4131; Fax (419) 674-4876; alliance@hardinohio.org; www.hardinohio.org*

Kettering · *Kettering-Moraine-Oakwood C/C* · Ann-Lisa Rucker; Exec. Dir.; 2977 Far Hills Ave.; 45419; Greene & Montgomery; P 80,000; M 875; (937) 299-3852; Fax (937) 299-3851; info@kmo-coc.org; www.kmo-coc.org

Lakewood · *Lakewood C/C* · Patricia L. Ryan; Pres./CEO; 16017 Detroit Ave.; 44107; Cuyahoga; P 56,000; M 350; (216) 226-2900; Fax (216) 226-1340; pryan@lakewoodchamber.org; www.lake woodchamber.org

Lancaster · *Lancaster-Fairfield County C/C* · Travis Markwood; Pres.; 109 N. Broad St., Ste. 100; P.O. Box 2450; 43130; Fairfield; P 136,000; M 625; (740) 653-8251; Fax (740) 653-7074; alicia@ lancoc.org; www.lancoc.org*

Lawrence County · *see South Point*

Lebanon · *Lebanon Area C/C* · Sara Arseneau; Exec. Dir.; 20 N. Broadway; 45036; Warren; P 24,000; M 400; (513) 932-1100; Fax (513) 932-9050; info@lebanonchamber.org; www.lebanon chamber.org*

Leipsic · *Leipsic Area C/C* · Cammie Flores; Pres.; 142 E. Main St.; 45856; Putnam; P 2,300; M 60; (419) 943-2009; www.leipsic.net

Lewisburg · *Lewisburg Area C/C* · P.O. Box 436; 45338; P 2,000; M 25; (937) 962-2377; www.lewisburg.net

Lexington · *see Mansfield*

Lima · *Lima/Allen County C/C* · Jed E. Metzger; Pres./CEO; 144 S. Main St., Ste. 100; 45801; Allen; P 109,000; M 1,100; (419) 222-6045; Fax (419) 229-0266; chamber@limachamber.com; www. limachamber.com.*

Lisbon · *Lisbon Area C/C* · Marilyn McCullough; Exec. Dir.; 120 N. Market St.; 44432; Columbiana; P 3,082; M 86; (330) 424-1803; Fax (330) 424-9003; lacoc2@sbcglobal.net; www.lisbonareachamber.com

Lodi · *Lodi Area C/C* · Kate Heil; Admin.; P.O. Box 6; 44254; Medina; P 3,000; M 95; (330) 948-8047; info@lodiohiochamber. com; www.lodiohiochamber.com

Logan · *Logan-Hocking C/C* · Bill Rienhart; Exec. Dir.; 4 E. Hunter St.; P.O. Box 838; 43138; Hocking; P 28,700; M 250; (740) 385-6836; (800) 414-6731; Fax (740) 385-7259; lo-hock chamber@hocking.net; www.logan-hockingchamber.com

Logan County · *see Bellefontaine*

London · *Madison County C/C* · Sean Hughes; Exec. Dir.; 730 Keny Blvd.; 43140; Madison; P 47,000; M 300; (740) 852-2250; Fax (740) 852-5133; sean@madisoncountychamber.org; www. madisoncountychamber.org*

Lorain · *see Elyria*

Loudonville · *Loudonville-Mohican C/C* · Jeanne Leckrone; Ofc. Mgr.; 131 W. Main St.; 44842; Ashland; P 2,900; M 160; (419) 994-4789; Fax (419) 994-5950; info@loudonville-mohican.com; www.loudonville-mohican.com

Louisville · *Louisville Area C/C* · Kelly Chaney; Chrmn.; P.O. Box 67; 44641; Stark; P 8,900; M 55; (330) 875-7371; Fax (330) 875-3839; louisvilleareachamber@gmail.com; www.louisville ohchamber.com

Loveland · *Loveland Area C/C* · Jodi K. Inabnitt; Pres./CEO; 442 W. Loveland Ave.; 45140; Clermont, Hamilton & Warren; P 20,000; M 350; (513) 683-1544; Fax (513) 683-5449; info@loveland chamber.org; www.lovelandchamber.org*

Lyndhurst · *see Beachwood*

Madison · *Madison-Perry Area C/C* · Cynthia Girdler IOM CCEO-AP; Pres.; 5965 N. Ridge Rd.; P.O. Box 4; 44057; Lake; P 25,000; M 305; (440) 428-3760; Fax (440) 428-6668; exec@ mpacc.org; www.mpacc.org

Mansfield · *Mansfield-Richland Area C/C* · Kevin Nestor; Pres.; 55 N. Mulberry St.; 44902; Richland; P 129,000; M 860; (419) 522-3211; Fax (419) 526-6853; info@mrachamber.com; www.mrachamber.com.*

Marblehead · *Marblehead Peninsula C/C* · Judy Balsom; Exec. Asst.; 5681 E. Harbor Rd.; 43440; Ottawa; P 4,000; M 188; (419) 734-9777; Fax (419) 734-9777; info@marbleheadpeninsula.com; www.marbleheadpeninsula.com

Marietta · *Marietta Area C/C* · Charlotte Keim; Pres.; 100 Front St., Ste. 200; 45750; Washington; P 62,000; M 558; (740) 373-5176; Fax (740) 373-7808; info@mariettachamber.com; www.mariettachamber.com*

Marion · *Marion Area C/C* · Pamela S. Hall; Pres.; 205 W. Center St., Ste. 100; 43302; Marion; P 66,217; M 600; (740) 382-2181; Fax (740) 387-7722; phall@marionareachamber.org; www.marionareachamber.org*

Martins Ferry · *Martins Ferry Area C/C* · Dorothy Powell; Exec. Dir.; 108 S. Zane Hwy.; 43935; Belmont; P 7,226; M 100; (740) 633-2565; Fax (740) 633-2641; m.chamber@att.net; www.martinsferrychamber.com

Marysville · *Union County C/C* · Eric S. Phillips; CEO/Dir.; 227 E. Fifth St.; 43040; Union; P 23,216; M 530; (937) 642-6279; (800) 642-0087; Fax (937) 644-0422; chamber@unioncounty.org; www.wheteprideresides.org.*

Mason · *NE Cincinnati C/C* · John Harris; Pres.; 316 W. Main St.; 45040; Warren; P 48,000; M 600; (513) 398-2188; (513) 336-0125; Fax (513) 398-6371; jharris@necchamber.org; www.necchamber.org*

Massillon · *Massillon Area C/C* · Robert A. Sanderson; Pres.; 137 Lincoln Way E.; 44646; Stark; P 32,000; M 375; (330) 833-3146; Fax (330) 833-8944; info@massillonohchamber.com; www.massillonohchamber.com.

Maumee · *Maumee C/C* · Brenda Clixby; Exec. Dir.; 605 Conant St.; 43537; Lucas; P 15,752; M 450; (419) 893-5805; Fax (419) 893-8699; info@maumeechamber.com; www.maumeechamber.com*

Mayfield Heights · *Mayfield Area C/C* · 1280 SOM Ctr. Rd., Ste. 308; 44124; Cuyahoga; P 55,000; M 175; (216) 556-4598; jasspring@aol.com; www.mayfieldareachamber.org

McArthur · *Vinton County C/C* · Brandi Betts; Mktg. Dir.; 104 W. Main St.; P.O. Box 307; 45651; Vinton; P 13,429; M 130; (740) 596-5033; Fax (740) 596-9262; info@vintoncounty.com; www.vintoncounty.com

McConnelsville · *Morgan County C/C* · Amy Grove; Bd. Member; 155 E. Main St.; P.O. Box 508; 43756; Morgan; P 14,000; M 130; (740) 962-3200; (740) 962-4854; Fax (740) 962-6508; info@morgancounty.org; www.morgancounty.org

Medina · *Greater Medina C/C* · Debra Lynn-Schmitz; Pres.; 145 N. Court St.; 44256; Medina; P 30,000; M 520; (330) 723-8773; Fax (330) 722-6844; info@medinaohchamber.com; www.medinaohchamber.com*

Mentor · *Mentor Area C/C* · Marie S. Pucak; Exec. Dir.; 6972 Spinach Dr.; 44060; Lake; P 52,000; M 650; (440) 255-1616; Fax (440) 255-1717; info@mentorchamber.org; www.mentorchamber.org.

Miami Twp. · *see Milford*

Middleburg Heights · *Middleburg Heights C/C* · Doris J. Wroble; Exec. Dir.; 16000 Bagley Rd.; P.O. Box 30161; 44130; Cuyahoga; P 15,790; M 210; (440) 243-5599; Fax (440) 243-8660; info@middleburgheightschamber.com; www.middleburgheightschamber.com

Middlefield · *Middlefield C/C* · Lynnette Bramley; Exec. Secy.; P.O. Box 801; 44062; Geauga; P 2,500; M 100; (440) 632-5705; Fax (440) 632-5705; mccinfo@middlefieldcc.com; www.middlefieldcc.com

Middletown · *The C/C serving Middletown, Monroe & Trenton* · Bill Triick; Pres./CEO; 1500 Central Ave.; 45044; Butler & Warren; P 125,000; M 500; (513) 422-4551; Fax (513) 422-6831; info@thechamberofcommerce.org; www.thechamberofcommerce.org.*

Milan · *Milan C/C* · Anne Basilone-Jones; Secy.; P.O. Box 544; 44846; Erie; P 1,500; M 200; (419) 499-4909; Fax (419) 499-9004; secretary@milanohio.com; www.milanohio.com

Milford · *Milford-Miami Twp. C/C* · Karen Huff; CEO; 983 Lila Ave.; 45150; Clermont & Hamilton; P 43,000; M 320; (513) 831-2411; Fax (513) 831-3547; director@milfordmiamitownship.com; www.milfordmiamitownship.com

Millersburg · *Holmes County C/C & Tourism Bur.* · Shasta Mast; Exec. Dir.; 35 N. Monroe St.; 44654; Holmes; P 42,000; M 400; (330) 674-3975; Fax (330) 674-3976; info@holmescountychamber.com; www.holmescountychamber.com

Minerva · *Minerva Area C/C* · Jim Arrasmith; Exec. Dir.; 203 N. Market St.; 44657; Carroll & Stark; P 12,000; M 100; (330) 868-7979; www.minervachamber.org

Minster · *see New Bremen*

Monroe · *see Middletown*

Montpelier · *Montpelier Area C/C* · Ms. Terry L. Buntain; Exec. Dir.; 410 W. Main St.; 43543; Williams; P 4,200; M 155; (419) 485-4410; Fax (419) 485-4416; macofc@frontier.com; www.montpelierchamber.com

Moraine · *see Kettering*

Morrow · *Little Miami Area C/C* · Norma Rayl; Secy./Treas.; P.O. Box 164; 45152; Warren; P 4,282; M 76; (513) 899-4466; (513) 932-3299; Fax (513) 932-3299; info@lmachamber.com; www.lmachamber.com

Mount Gilead · *Morrow County C/C & Visitors Bur.* · Rosemary Levings; CEO; 17 1/2 W. High St.; P.O. Box 174; 43338; Morrow; P 34,000; M 186; (419) 946-2821; Fax (419) 946-3861; chamuway@bright.net; www.morrowchamber.org*

Mount Vernon · *Mount Vernon-Knox County C/C* · Carol Grubaugh; Exec. Dir.; 400 S. Gay St.; 43050; Knox; P 58,561; M 379; (740) 393-1111; Fax (740) 393-1590; chamber@knox-chamber.com; www.knoxchamber.com*

Munroe Falls · *see Stow*

Napoleon · *Napoleon/Henry County C/C* · Joel Miller; Pres.; 611 N. Perry St.; 43545; Henry; P 29,893; M 291; (419) 592-1786; Fax (419) 592-4945; hcncoc@ohiohenrycounty.com; www.naphcchamber.com

Nelsonville · *Nelsonville Area C/C* · Pres.; P.O. Box 276; 45764; Athens; P 5,444; M 122; (740) 753-4346; info@nelsonvillechamber.com; www.nelsonvillechamber.com

New Albany · *New Albany C/C* · Eileen Leuby; Pres.; 220 Market St., Ste. 204; P.O. Box 202; 43054; Franklin; P 25,000; M 500; (614) 855-4400; Fax (614) 855-4446; director@newalbanychamber.com; www.newalbanychamber.com

New Bremen · *Southwestern Auglaize County C/C* · Scott M. Frey; Exec. Dir.; 22 S. Water St.; P.O. Box 3; 45869; Auglaize; P 8,000; M 300; (419) 629-0313; Fax (419) 629-0411; info@auglaize.org; www.auglaize.org

New Carlisle · *New Carlisle Area C/C* · Linda Campbell; P.O. Box 483; 45344; Clark; P 5,735; M 35; (937) 845-3911; www.newcarlisleareachamberofcommerce.com

New Concord • *New Concord Area Bd. of Trade* • Janice Hutcheson; Dir.; 1 W. Main; 43762; Muskingum; P 4,000; M 150; (740) 826-7676; Fax (740) 826-4500; renee.coll@collmaterials.com; www.ncboardoftrade.com

New Lexington • *Perry County C/C* • John Ulmer; Exec. Dir.; 121 S. Main St.; 43764; Perry; P 33,000; M 170; (740) 342-3547; Fax (740) 342-9124; pcccofc@yahoo.com; www.perrycountyohiocofc.com

New Paris • *New Paris Area C/C* • Dale Hall; Pres.; P.O. Box 101; 45347; Preble; P 1,600; M 65; (937) 437-2511; www.newparisoh.com

New Philadelphia • *Tuscarawas County C/C* • Jill R. McCartney IOM; Pres.; 1323 Fourth St. N.W.; 44663; Tuscarawas; P 90,000; M 600; (330) 343-4474; Fax (330) 343-6526; info@tuschamber.com; www.tuschamber.com*

Newark • *Licking County C/C* • Cheri Hottinger; Pres.; 50 W. Locust St.; P.O. Box 702; 43058; Licking; P 154,000; M 700; (740) 345-9757; Fax (740) 345-5141; chottinger@lickingcountychamber.com; www.lickingcountychamber.com

Newcomerstown • *Newcomerstown C/C* • Gary Chaney; Treas.; P.O. Box 456; 43832; Tuscarawas; P 8,000; M 100; (740) 498-7244; Fax (740) 498-6310; gjc@sota-oh.com

Niles • *see Youngstown*

North Baltimore • *North Baltimore Area C/C* • Kathy Healy; Pres.; P.O. Box 284; 45872; Wood; P 3,300; M 50; (419) 257-5050; (419) 257-3514; info@nbacc.org; www.nbacc.org

North Canton • *North Canton Area C/C* • Doug Lane; Pres.; 121 S. Main St.; 44720; Stark; P 17,000; M 400; (330) 499-5100; Fax (330) 499-7181; info@northcantonchamber.org; www.northcantonchamber.org*

North Olmsted • *North Olmsted C/C* • John Sobolewski; Exec. Dir.; 28938 Lorain Rd., Ste. 204; 44070; Cuyahoga; P 34,204; M 250; (440) 777-3368; Fax (440) 777-9361; nocc@nolmstedchamber.org; www.nolmstedchamber.org

North Randall • *see Warrensville Heights*

North Ridgeville • *North Ridgeville C/C* • Ms. Dayle Noll; Pres./CEO; 34845 Lorain Rd.; 44039; Lorain; P 30,000; M 200; (440) 327-3737; nrcoc@nrchamber.com; www.nrchamber.com*

North Royalton • *North Royalton C/C* • Kevin Lynch; Pres.; 13737 State Rd.; P.O. Box 33122; 44133; Cuyahoga; P 32,500; M 220; (440) 237-6180; Fax (440) 237-6181; rrnews@aol.com; www.nroyaltonchamber.com

Northfield • *Nordonia Hills C/C* • Laura Sparano; Exec. Dir.; P.O. Box 34; 44067; Summit; P 22,000; M 310; (330) 467-8956; Fax (330) 468-4901; laura@nordoniahillschamber.org; www.nordoniahillschamber.org*

Northwood • *see Oregon*

Norwalk • *Huron County C/C* • Melissa James; Exec. Dir.; 10 W. Main St.; 44857; Huron; P 60,000; M 480; (419) 668-4155; Fax (419) 663-6173; chamber@accnorwalk.com; www.huroncountychamber.com.

Norwood • *Norwood C/C* • Kathy Walters; Exec. Dir.; P.O. Box 12144; 45212; Hamilton; P 21,000; M ; (513) 956-7935; Fax (513) 741-8778; kathy@norwoodchamber.org; www.norwoodchamber.org

Oak Harbor • *Oak Harbor Area C/C* • Valerie Winterfield; Exec. Dir.; 161 W. Water St., Ste. A; 43449; Ottawa; P 5,000; M 150; (419) 898-0479; Fax (419) 898-2429; chamber@oakharborohio.net; www.oakharborohio.net

Oak Hill • *Oak Hill Area C/C* • Kurtis Strickland; Pres.; P.O. Box 354; 45656; Jackson; P 1,700; M 100; (740) 682-8414; www.oakhillchamber.org

Oakwood • *see Kettering*

Oberlin • *Oberlin Area C/C* • Annie Cunningham; Exec. Dir.; 13 S. Main St., 2nd Flr.; 44074; Lorain; P 8,200; M 130; (440) 774-6262; Fax (440) 775-2423; oberlinchamber@oberlin.net; www.oberlinchamber.org

Olmsted Falls • *Olmsted C/C* • Todd Hoadley; Pres.; P.O. Box 38043; 44138; Cuyahoga; P 23,000; M 70; (440) 235-0032; www.olmstedchamber.org

Oregon • *Eastern Maumee Bay C/C* • Sarah Beavers; Exec. Dir.; 2460 Navarre Ave., Ste. 4; 43616; Lucas; P 25,000; M 200; (419) 693-5580; Fax (419) 693-9990; director@embchamber.org; www.embchamber.org

Orrville • *Orrville Area C/C* • Jennifer Reusser; Pres.; 132 S. Main St.; 44667; Wayne; P 8,900; M 260; (330) 682-8881; Fax (330) 682-8383; chamberoffice@orrvillechamber.com; www.orrvillechamber.com

Orwell • *Orwell-Grand Valley Area C/C* • Diane Giel; P.O. Box 261; 44076; Ashtabula; P 1,600; M 53; (440) 437-5782; orwellgv@fairpoint.net; www.orwellgvchamber.org

Ottawa • *Ottawa Area C/C* • Mary Jo Bockrath; Exec. Dir.; 129 Court St.; P.O. Box 68; 45875; Putnam; P 4,367; M 270; (419) 523-3141; Fax (419) 523-5860; ottawachamber@earthlink.net; ottawachamber.org

Ottoville • *Ottoville Area C/C* • P.O. Box 275; 45876; Putnam; P 1,000; M 69; (419) 453-2426; www.villageofottoville.org

Oxford • *Oxford C/C* • JoNell Rowan; Pres.; 30 W. Park Pl., 2nd Flr.; 45056; Butler; P 26,000; M 250; (513) 523-5200; Fax (513) 523-2308; jonell@oxfordchamber.org; www.oxfordchamber.org.

Painesville • *Painesville Area C/C* • Linda Reed; Exec. Dir.; One Victoria Pl., Ste. 265A; 44077; Lake; P 50,000; M 420; (440) 357-7572; Fax (440) 357-8752; exec@painesvilleohchamber.org; www.painesvilleohchamber.org

Pandora • *Pandora Area C/C* • Stan Schneck; Village Admin.; P.O. Box 333; 45877; Putnam; P 1,188; M 10; (419) 384-3112; Fax (419) 384-3110; villageadministrator@bright.net; www.pandoraoh.com

Parkman • *Parkman C/C* • Faith Kumber; Pres.; P.O. Box 525; 44080; Geauga; P 3,200; M 26; (440) 476-4337; (440) 548-5213; parkmanohio@gmail.com; www.parkmanohio.com

Parma • *Parma Area C/C* • Lisa Masotti-Zaremba; Exec. Dir.; 7908 Day Dr.; Parmatown Mall; 44129; Cuyahoga; P 125,000; M 620; (440) 886-1700; Fax (440) 886-1770; chamber@parmaareachamber.org; www.parmaareachamber.org

Parma Heights • *see Parma*

Pataskala • *Pataskala Area C/C* • Bart Weiler; Pres.; P.O. Box 132; 43062; Licking; P 15,000; M 180; (740) 964-6100; PACC132@embarqmail.com; www.pataskalachamber.com

Paulding • *Paulding C/C* • Conrad Clippinger; Exec. Dir.; Corner Main & Caroline St.; P.O. Box 237; 45879; Paulding; P 3,650; M 210; (419) 399-5215; Fax (419) 399-2047; pcoc@paulding-net.com; www.pauldingchamber.com

Perrysburg • *Perrysburg Area C/C* • Sandy Latchem; Exec. Dir.; 105 W. Indiana Ave.; 43551; Wood; P 28,000; M 300; (419) 874-9147; Fax (419) 872-9347; director@perrysburgchamber.com; www.perrysburgchamber.com

Picaway County • *see Circleville*

Pickerington • *Pickerington Area C/C* • Helen Mayle; Pres.; 13 W. Columbus St.; 43147; Fairfield; P 38,000; M 425; (614) 837-1958; Fax (614) 837-6420; president@pickeringtonchamber.com; www.pickeringtonchamber.com*

Pioneer • *Pioneer Area C/C* • Jim Fee; Pres.; P.O. Box 633; 43554; Williams; P 1,500; M 80; (419) 737-2614; Fax (419) 737-2066; www.pioneerchamber.com

Piqua • *Piqua Area C/C* • Lisa Whitaker; Pres.; 326 N. Main; P.O. Box 1142; 45356; Miami; P 22,000; M 400; (937) 773-2765; Fax (937) 773-8553; lisa.whitaker@piquaareachamber.com; www.piquaareachamber.com*

Plymouth • *see Willard*

Pomeroy • *Meigs County C/C* • Michelle R. Donovan; Exec. Dir.; 238 W. Main St.; 45769; Megis; P 24,000; M 160; (740) 992-5005; Fax (740) 992-7942; michelle@meigscountychamber.com; www.meigscountychamber.com

Port Clinton • *Port Clinton Area C/C* • Laura Schlachter; Pres./CEO; 110 Madison St.; 43452; Ottawa; P 6,300; M 464; (419) 734-5503; Fax (419) 734-4768; info@portclintonchamber.com; www.portclintonchamber.com*

Portsmouth • *Portsmouth Area C/C* • Robert Huff; Pres./CEO; 342 2nd St.; P.O. Box 509; 45662; Scioto; P 20,909; M 700; (740) 353-7647; (800) 648-2574; Fax (740) 353-5824; rhuff@portsmouth.org; www.portsmouth.org

Powell • *Greater Powell Area C/C* • Paul Melcher; Pres.; 50 S. Liberty St., Ste. 170; 43065; Delaware; P 20,000; M 250; (614) 888-1090; Fax (614) 888-4803; admin@powellchamber.com; www.powellchamber.com

Put-In-Bay • *Put-In-Bay C/C & Visitors Bur.* • Maggie Beckford; Exec. Dir.; 148 Delaware Ave.; P.O. Box 250; 43456; Ottawa; P 550; M 185; (419) 285-2832; maggie@visitputinbay.com; visitputinbay.com

Ravenna • *Ravenna Area C/C* • Jack Ferguson; Exec. Dir.; 135 E. Main St.; 44266; Portage; P 22,000; M 153; (330) 296-3886; Fax (330) 296-6986; ravennachamber@att.net; www.ravennaareachamber.com

Reading • *Reading C/C* • Kathy Walters; Admin. Dir.; P.O. Box 15164; 45215; Hamilton; P 12,000; M 100; (513) 741-7951; (513) 786-7274; Fax (513) 741-8778; mkwalters@cinci.rr.com; www.readingohiochamber.org

Reynoldsburg • *Reynoldsburg Area C/C* • Jan Hills; Pres./CEO; 1580 Brice Rd.; 43068; Fairfield, Franklin & Licking; P 35,000; M 335; (614) 866-4753; Fax (614) 866-7313; jan@reynoldsburgchamber.com; www.reynoldsburgchamber.com*

Richland • *see Mansfield*

Richmond Heights • *see Beachwood*

Rittman • *Rittman Area C/C* • Mindi Vance; Exec. Dir.; 12 N. Main St., Ste. 2; 44270; Wayne; P 6,500; M 95; (330) 925-4828; Fax (330) 925-4828; rittmanchamber@ohio.net; www.rittmanchamber.com

Riverside • *Riverside Area C/C* • Brett Domescik; Chrmn.; 5100 Springfield Pk., Ste. 105; 45431; Montgomery; P 35,000; M 50; (937) 253-5674; Fax (937) 253-7693; chairman@riversidechamber.com; www.riversidechamber.com

Rockford • *Rockford C/C* • Terra Henkle; P.O. Box 175; 45882; Mercer; P 1,200; M 90; (419) 305-8563; www.rockfordalive.com

Rocky River • *Rocky River C/C* • Liz Manning; Exec. Dir.; 19543 Center Ridge Rd.; 44116; Cuyahoga; P 20,500; M 350; (440) 331-1140; Fax (440) 331-3485; info@rockyriverchamber.com; www.rockyriverchamber.com

Rootstown • *Rootstown Area C/C* • Joe Paulus; Pres.; P.O. Box 254; 44272; Portage; P 7,300; M 68; www.rootstownchamber.org

Russells Point • *Indian Lake Area C/C* • Pam Miller; Exec. Dir.; 8200 State Rte. 366, Ste. D; P.O. Box 717; 43348; Logan; P 14,500; M 425; (937) 843-5392; Fax (937) 843-9051; office@indianlakechamber.org; www.indianlakechamber.org

Saint Bernard • *Saint Bernard C/C* • Bob Sawtell; Pres.; 110 Washington Ave.; 45217; Hamilton; P 5,000; M 65; (513) 242-7770; Fax (513) 641-1840; www.cityofstbernard.org

Saint Clairsville • *Saint Clairsville Area C/C* • Amy Aspenwall; Exec. Dir.; 130 W. Main St.; 43950; Belmont; P 12,000; M 310; (740) 695-9623; info@stcchamber.com; www.stcchamber.com

Saint Marys • *Saint Marys Area C/C* • Kelly Kill; Exec. Dir.; 301 E. Spring St.; 45885; Auglaize; P 8,500; M 250; (419) 300-4611; Fax (419) 300-6202; amy@stmarysohio.org; www.stmarysohio.org

Salem • *Salem Area C/C* • Audrey C. Null; Exec. Dir.; 713 E. State St.; 44460; Columbiana; P 16,000; M 340; (330) 337-3473; Fax (330) 337-3474; info@salemohiochamber.org; www.salemohiochamber.org*

Sandusky • *Erie County C/C* • John Moldovan; Pres.; 225 W. Washington Row; 44870; Erie; P 80,000; M 465; (419) 625-6421; Fax (419) 625-7914; director@eriecountyohiocofc.com; www.eriecountyohiocofc.com*

Sebring • *Sebring Area C/C* • Gayle Agnew; Pres.; 135 E. Ohio Ave.; 44672; Mahoning; P 4,912; M 70; (330) 938-1243; www.sebringchamber.org

Seven Hills • *see Parma*

Seville • *Seville Area C/C* • Velvet Eby; Pres.; P.O. Box 471; 44273; Medina; P 1,900; M 70; (330) 769-1522; sevilleareaohiochamber@gmail.com; www.sevilleareachamberofcommerce.com

Shadyside • *Shadyside Area C/C* • Pat Heller; Pres.; P.O. Box 115; 43947; Belmont; P 3,700; M 50; (740) 676-3202

Shaker Heights • *see Beachwood*

Sharonville • *Sharonville C/C* • Richard Arnold; Pres.; 4015 Executive Park Dr., Ste. 302; 45241; Butler & Hamilton; P 36,800; M 230; (513) 554-1722; Fax (513) 554-1307; info@sharonvillechamber.com; www.sharonvillechamber.com*

Sheffield Lake • *see Avon Lake*

Sheffield Village • *see Avon Lake*

Shelby • *Shelby C/C* • Pres.; 142 N. Gamble, Ste. A; 44875; Richland; P 9,600; M 165; (419) 342-2426; (888) 245-2426; Fax (419) 342-2189; carol.knapp@shelbyoh.com; www.shelbyoh.com

Sidney • *Sidney-Shelby County C/C* • Jeff Raible; Pres.; 101 S. Ohio Ave., Flr. 2; 45365; Shelby; P 48,000; M 506; (937) 492-9122; Fax (937) 498-2472; office@sidneyshelbychamber.com; www.sidneyshelbychamber.com

Solon • *Solon C/C* • Nancy S. Traum; Pres./CEO; 33595 Bainbridge Rd., Ste. 101; 44139; Cuyahoga; P 25,000; M 550; (440) 248-5080; Fax (440) 248-9121; staff@solonchamber.com; www.solonchamber.com

South Euclid • *see Beachwood*

South Point • *Greater Lawrence County Area C/C* • Bill Dingus; Exec. Dir.; 216 Collins Ave.; P.O. Box 488; 45680; Lawrence; P 65,000; M 300; (740) 377-4550; cofcagency@zoominternet.net; www.lawrencecountyohio.org*

Spencerville • *Spencerville C/C* • Doris Proctor; 108 S. Broadway; 45887; Allen; P 2,300; (419) 647-2020; spencervillechamber@yahoo.com; www.spencervilleoh.com

Spring Valley • *Spring Valley Area C/C* • Judy Madden; Pres.; P.O. Box 396; 45370; Greene; P 2,800; M 80; (937) 862-4110; www.springvalleyoh.com

Springboro · *Springboro Area C/C* · Carol Hughes; Exec. Dir.; 325 S. Main St.; 45066; Warren; P 28,000; M 440; (937) 748-0074; Fax (937) 748-0525; chamber@springboroohio.org; www.spring boroohio.org*

Springfield · *Greater Springfield C/C* · Michael McDorman; Pres.; 20 S. Limestone St., Ste. 100; 45502; Clark; P 168,000; M 820; (937) 325-7621; (800) 803-1553; Fax (937) 325-8765; mmcdorman@ greaterspringfield.com; www.greaterspringfield.com*

Steubenville · *Jefferson County C/C* · Susan L. Hershey; Pres.; 630 Market St.; 43952; Jefferson; P 73,894; M 450; (740) 282-6226; Fax (740) 282-6285; info@jeffersoncountychamber.com; www.jeffersoncountychamber.com*

Stow · *Stow-Munroe Falls C/C* · Doris Stewart; Exec. Dir.; 4381 Hudson Dr., Ste. K-2; 44224; Summit; P 44,000; M 360; (330) 688-1579; Fax (330) 688-6234; smfcc@smfcc.com; www.smfcc.com

Streetsboro · *Streetsboro Area C/C* · Meghan Urbon; Exec. Dir.; 9205 State Rte. 43, Ste. 202; 44241; Portage; P 15,000; M 180; (330) 626-4769; Fax (330) 422-1118; sacc@streetsborochamber. org; www.streetsborochamber.org

Strongsville · *Strongsville C/C* · Jim Mocho; Pres.; 18829 Royalton Rd.; 44136; Cuyahoga; P 49,000; M 600; (440) 238-3366; Fax (440) 238-7010; info@strongsvillechamber.com; www. strongsvillechamber.com

Stryker · *Stryker C/C* · Mike Short; Pres.; P.O. Box 58; 43557; Williams; P 1,500; M 100; (419) 682-4231; (419) 682-1108; web@ strykerchamber.org; www.villageofstryker.com

Sunbury · *Sunbury/Big Walnut Area C/C* · Cindy Hall; Exec. Dir.; 45. S. Columbus St.; P.O. Box 451; 43074; Delaware; P 11,000; M 250; (740) 965-2860; Fax (740) 965-2860; chall@sunburybig walnutchamber.com; www.sunburybigwalnutchamber.com

Swanton · *Swanton Area C/C* · Neil Toeppe; Exec. Dir./Secy.; 100 Broadway St.; 43558; Fulton & Lucas; P 16,000; M 120; (419) 826-1941; Fax (419) 826-3242; swantoncc@aol.com; www. swantonareacoc.com

Sylvania · *Sylvania Area C/C* · Ms. Pat Nowak; Exec. Dir.; 5632 N. Main St.; 43560; Lucas; P 50,000; M 550; (419) 882-2135; Fax (419) 885-7740; info@sylvaniachamber.org; www.sylvaniachamber.org

Tallmadge · *Tallmadge C/C* · Mary Cea; Exec. Dir.; 80 Community Rd.; 44278; Portage & Summit; P 18,000; M 200; (330) 633-5417; Fax (330) 633-5415; tallmadgechamber@onecommail.com; www. tallmadge-chamber.com

Tiffin · *Tiffin Area C/C* · John Detwiler; Pres./CEO; 62 S. Washington St.; 44883; Seneca; P 25,000; M 328; (419) 447-4141; Fax (419) 447-5141; info@tiffinchamber.com; www.tiffinchamber.com*

Tipp City · *Tipp City Area C/C* · Matt Owen; Pres./CEO; 12 S. Third St.; 45371; Miami; P 16,200; M 212; (937) 667-8300; Fax (937) 667-8862; mowen@tippcitychamber.com; www. tippcitychamber.org

Toledo · *Toledo Reg. C/C* · Mark A. V'Soske CAE; Pres.; 300 Madison Ave.; Enterprise Ste. 200; 43604; Lucas; P 658,000; M 2,850; (419) 243-8191; (419) CHAMBER; Fax (419) 241-8302; joinus@toledochamber.com; www.toledochamber.com.*

Toronto · *Toronto Ohio C/C* · P.O. Box 158; 43964; Jefferson; P 6,000; M 79; (740) 537-4355; Fax (740) 537-4355; info@ torontoohiochamber.com; www.torontoohiochamber.com

Trenton · *see Middletown*

Trotwood · *Trotwood C/C* · Marie Battle CPS; Exec. Dir.; 4444 Lake Center Dr.; 5790 Denlinger Rd., Door 15; 45426; Montgomery; P 27,000; M 100; (937) 837-1484; Fax (937) 837-1508; trotwood chamber@earthlink.net; www.trotwoodchamber.org

Troy · *Troy Area C/C* · J.C. Wallace; Pres.; 405 S.W. Public Sq., Ste. 330; 45373; Miami; P 30,000; M 420; (937) 339-8769; (937) 339-1716; Fax (937) 339-4944; tacc@troyohiochamber.com; www.troyohiochamber.com*

Twinsburg · *Twinsburg C/C* · Douglas H. Johnson; Exec. Dir.; 2250 E. Enterprise Pkwy.; 44087; Summit; P 18,000; M 285; (330) 963-6249; Fax (330) 963-6995; djohnson@twinsburgchamber. com; www.twinsburgchamber.com

Uhrichsville · *Twin City C/C* · Teri Edwards; Exec. Dir.; P.O. Box 49; 44683; Tuscarawas; P 11,000; M 250; (740) 922-5623; Fax (740) 922-1371; twincitychamber@sbcglobal.net; www.twin citychamber.org

Union City · *see Union City, IN*

Uniontown · *see Hartville*

University Heights · *see Beachwood*

Upper Arlington · *Upper Arlington Area C/C* · Becky Hajost; Pres.; 2152 Tremont Center; 43221; Franklin; P 33,000; M 584; (614) 481-5710; Fax (614) 481-5711; admin@uachamber.org; www.uachamber.org*

Upper Sandusky · *Upper Sandusky Area C/C* · Aaron Korte; Exec. Dir.; 108 E. Wyandot Ave.; P.O. Box 223; 43351; Wyandot; P 22,800; M 250; (419) 294-3349; Fax (419) 294-3531; upper chamber@udata.com; www.uppersanduskychamber.com

Urbana · *Champaign County C/C & Visitors Bur.* · Tina Knotts; Exec. Dir.; 113 Miami St.; 43078; Champaign; P 38,900; M 280; (937) 653-5764; (877) 873-5764; Fax (937) 652-1599; info@ champaignohio.com; www.champaignohio.com

Valley City · *Valley City C/C* · Cindy Kintop; Pres.; P.O. Box 304; 44280; Medina; P 4,500; M 109; (330) 483-1111; chamberof commerce@valleycity.org; www.valleycity.org

Valley View · *see Independence*

Van Wert · *Van Wert Area C/C* · Kate Gribble; Pres./CEO; 1199 Professional Dr.; 45891; Van Wert; P 30,000; M 335; (419) 238-4390; Fax (419) 238-4589; chamber@vanwertchamber.com; www.vanwertchamber.com*

Vandalia · *Vandalia-Butler C/C* · Will Roberts; Exec. Dir.; 544 W. National Rd.; P.O. Box 224; 45377; Montgomery; P 25,000; M 400; (937) 898-5351; Fax (937) 898-5491; info@vandaliabutler chamber.org; www.vandaliabutlerchamber.org

Vermilion · *Vermilion C/C* · Pam Cooper; Pres.; 5495 Liberty Ave.; 44089; Erie; P 11,000; M 350; (440) 967-4477; Fax (440) 967-2877; vermilionchamber@centurytel.net; www.vermilionohio.com

Wadsworth · *Wadsworth C/C* · Michelle Masica; CEO; 123 Broad St., Ste. C; 44281; Medina; P 19,000; M 329; (330) 336-6150; Fax (330) 336-2672; business@wadsworthchamber.com; www. wadsworthchamber.com*

Walbridge · *see Oregon*

Walton Hills · *see Independence*

Wapakoneta · *Wapakoneta Area C/C* · Dan Graf; Exec. Dir.; 30 E. Auglaize St.; P.O. Box 208; 45895; Auglaize; P 15,000; M 285; (419) 738-2911; Fax (419) 738-2977; chamber@wapakoneta.com; www.wapakoneta.com

Warren · *see Youngstown*

Warrensville Heights · *Tri-City C/C* · Steve Petti; Pres./ CEO; P.O. Box 22098; 44122; Cuyahoga; P 45,000; M 135; (216) 454-0199; Fax (216) 378-7371; steve@tricitychamber.com; www. tricitychamber.com

Washington Court House · *Fayette County C/C* · Roger Blackburn; Pres.; 101 E. East St.; 43160; Fayette; P 32,000; M 320; (740) 335-0761; (800) 479-7797; Fax (740) 335-0762; fayette chamber@yahoo.com; www.fayettecountyohio.com*

Waterville · *Waterville Area C/C* · Corina Pfleghaar; Exec. Dir.; 122 Farnsworth Rd.; P.O. Box 74; 43566; Lucas; P 5,000; M 115; (419) 878-5188; Fax (419) 878-5199; admin@watervillechamber. com; www.watervillechamber.com.

Wauseon · *Wauseon C/C* · Debbie Nelson; Exec. Dir.; 115 N. Fulton St.; P.O. Box 217; 43567; Fulton; P 7,400; M 180; (419) 335-9966; Fax (419) 335-7693; debbie@wauseonchamber.com; www. wauseonchamber.com

Waverly · *Pike County C/C* · 12455 St. Rte. 104; P.O. Box 107; 45690; Pike; P 27,695; M 250; (740) 947-7715; Fax (740) 947-7716; pikechamber@yahoo.com; www.pikechamber.org.

Waynesburg · *Waynesburg Area Bus. Assn.* · Steve Chandler; Pres.; P.O. Box 394; 44688; Stark; P 1,000; M 61; (330) 866-3435; Fax (330) 866-3488; stevechandler40@aol.com

Waynesville · *Waynesville Area C/C* · Dawn Schroeder; Exec. Dir.; P.O. Box 281; 45068; Warren; P 2,800; M 282; (513) 897-8855; Fax (513) 897-9833; waynsville@aol.com; www.waynesvilleohio.com.

Wellington · *Wellington Area C/C* · Virginia Haynes; Pres.; P.O. Box 42; 44090-0042; Lorain; P 4,500; M 70; (440) 647-2222; www.villageofwellington.com

Wellston · *Wellston Area C/C* · J. Edgar Evans; Pres.; 203 E. Broadway St.; 45692; Jackson; P 6,500; M 135; (740) 384-3051; Fax (740) 384-3357; www.jacksonohio.org

Wellsville · *Wellsville Area C/C* · Randy Allmon; Pres.; 1200 Main St.; P.O. Box 636; 43968; Columbiana; P 4,000; M 85; (330) 843-3475; rallmon@hotmail.com; www.wellsvilleohiochamber.com

West Chester · *West Chester Chamber Alliance* · Joseph A. Hinson; Pres./CEO; 7617 Voice of America Centre Dr.; 45069; Butler; P 100,000; M 900; (513) 777-3600; Fax (513) 777-0188; www.westchesterchamberalliance.com*

West Lafayette · *West Lafayette C/C* · Christie Maurer; Pres.; P.O. Box 113; 43845; Coshocton; P 2,300; M 61; (740) 545-9370; www.westlafayettevillage.com

West Union · *Adams County C/C* · Deana Swayne; Exec. Dir.; 509 E. Main St.; P.O. Box 398; 45693; Adams; P 27,000; M 230; (937) 544-5454; Fax (937) 544-6957; deana@adamscounty chamber.org; www.adamscountychamber.org

West Unity · *West Unity Area C/C* · Martha Heer; Secy./Treas.; P.O. Box 263; 43570; Williams; P 1,200; M 49; (419) 924-2952; cofc@williams-net.com; www.westunity.org

Westerville · *Westerville Area C/C* · Janet Tressler-Davis; Pres./ CEO; 99 Commerce Park Dr.; 43082; Franklin & Delaware; P 40,000; M 640; (614) 882-8917; Fax (614) 882-2085; info@westerville chamber.com; www.westervillechamber.com*

Westlake · *West Shore C/C* · John Sobolewski; Exec. Dir.; West Lake Holiday Inn; 1100 Crocker Rd.; 44145; Cuyahoga; P 32,000; M 375; (440) 835-8787; Fax (440) 835-8798; sandy@westshore chamber.org; www.westshorechamber.org

Whitehall · *Whitehall Area C/C* · Tim Hill; Pres.; P.O. Box 13607; 43213; Franklin; P 25,000; M 125; (614) 237-7792; info@white hallchamber.org; www.whitehallchamber.org

Whitehouse · *Whitehouse C/C* · Josh Torres; Pres./CEO; 6726 Providence St., Ste. D; P.O. Box 2451; 43571; Lucas; P 4,000; M 225; (419) 877-2747; jtorres@whitehouseohchamber.com; www.whitehouseohiochamber.com*

Wickliffe · *Western Lake County C/C* · Karen W. Tercek; Pres.; The Provo House; 28855 Euclid Ave.; 44092; Lake; P 50,000; M 210; (440) 943-1134; Fax (440) 943-1114; president@westernlake countychamber.org; www.westernlakecountychamber.org

Willard · *Willard Area C/C* · Ricky Branham; Exec. Dir.; 16 S. Myrtle Ave.; P.O. Box 73; 44890; Huron; P 6,800; M 135; (419) 935-1888; willardareachamber@yahoo.com; www.willardchamber.com

Willoughby · *Willoughby Area C/C* · Nikki Matala; Exec. Dir.; 28 Public Sq.; 44094; Lake; P 38,000; M 414; (440) 942-1632; Fax (440) 942-0586; nikki@willoughbyareachamber.com; www.willoughbyareachamber.com

Willowick · *see Wickliffe*

Wilmington · *Wilmington Clinton County C/C* · Kimberly Danker; Dir.; 40 N. South St.; 45177; Clinton; P 40,000; M 250; (937) 382-2737; wccadmast@wccchamber.com; www.wccchamber.com

Woodsfield · *Monroe County C/C* · Rusty Atkinson; Pres.; 117 N. Main St.; P.O. Box 643; 43793; Monroe; P 15,500; M 165; (740) 472-5499; Fax same; monroechamber@gmn4u.com; www.monroecountyohio.net

Wooster · *Wooster Area C/C* · Jeff Griffin; Pres.; 377 W. Liberty St.; 44691; Wayne; P 28,000; M 780; (330) 262-5735; Fax (330) 262-5745; jgriffin@woosterchamber.com; www.woosterchamber.com*

Worthington · *Worthington Area C/C* · Kathryn Paugh; Exec. Dir.; 25 W. New England Ave., Ste. 100; 43085; Franklin; P 62,000; M 720; (614) 888-3040; Fax (614) 841-4842; connect@worthing tonchamber.org; www.worthingtonchamber.org*

Xenia · *Xenia Area C/C* · Alan D. Liming; Pres./CEO; 334 W. Market St.; 45385; Greene; P 27,000; M 475; (937) 372-3591; Fax (937) 372-2192; xacc@xacc.com; www.xacc.com*

Yellow Springs · *Yellow Springs C/C* · Karen Wintrow; Exec. Dir.; 101 Dayton St.; 45387; Greene; P 4,000; M 269; (937) 767-2686; Fax (937) 767-7876; info@yellowspringsohio.org; www.yellow springsohio.org

Youngstown · *Youngstown Warren Reg. C/C* · Thomas M. Humphries; Pres./CEO; 11 Central Sq., Ste. 1600; 44503; Mahoning; P 796,905; M 2,974; (330) 744-2131; Fax (330) 746-0330; amanda@regionalchamber.com; www.regionalchamber.com*

Zanesville · *Zanesville-Muskingum County C/C* · Thomas C. Poorman; Pres.; 205 N. Fifth St.; 43701; Muskingum; P 83,388; M 835; (740) 455-8282; Fax (740) 454-2963; tpoorman@zm chamber.com; www.zmchamber.com

Oklahoma

The State Chamber of Oklahoma · Fred S. Morgan; Pres./CEO; 330 N.E. 10th St.; Oklahoma City; 73104; Oklahoma; P 3,600,000; M 3,000; (405) 235-3669; Fax (405) 235-3670; fmorgan@okstate chamber.com; www.okstatechamber.com.

Ada · *Ada Area C/C* · Jeff Warmuth; Pres./CEO; 209 W. Main; P.O. Box 248; 74821; Pontotoc; P 35,000; M 400; (580) 332-2506; Fax (580) 332-3265; adachamber@adachamber.com; www.adachamber.com*

Adair · *Adair Area C/C* · Mary Steiner; Secy./Treas.; P.O. Box 377; 74330; Mayes; P 850; M 50; (918) 785-4242; adairchamber@ upperspace.net; www.adairok.com

Aline · *Aline C/C* · Carolyn Rexroat; 33 Heritage Rd.; 73716; Alfalfa; P 300; M 25; (580) 463-2563; www.1aj.org

Allen · *Allen C/C* · Dianna Brannan; Pres.; P.O. Box 396; 74825; Hughes & Pontotoc; P 1,000; M 40; (580) 857-2687; www.allenoklahoma.com

Altus · *Altus C/C* · Holley Urbanski; Pres.; 301 W. Commerce St.; P.O. Box 518; 73522; Jackson; P 26,000; M 300; (580) 482-0210; Fax (580) 482-0223; altuschamber@altuschamber.com; www.altuschamber.com

Alva · *Alva Area C/C* · Alexandra Mantz; Eco. & Comm. Dev. Specialist; 502 Oklahoma Blvd.; 73717; Woods; P 5,500; M 170; (580) 327-1647; Fax (580) 327-1647; chamber@alvaok.net; www.alvaok.net

Anadarko · *Anadarko C/C* · Carla Hall; Exec. Dir.; 516 W. Kentucky; P.O. Box 366; 73005; Caddo; P 6,500; M 145; (405) 247-6651; Fax (405) 247-6652; coc@anadarko.org; www.anadarko.org*

Antlers · *Pushmataha County C/C* · Jo Ann Matthews; Pres.; P.O. Box 25; 74523; Pushmataha; P 5,500; M 30; (580) 298-2488; Fax (580) 298-5566; pushmatahachamber@gmail.com; www.pushchamber.com*

Apache · *Apache C/C* · Ronnie Orf; Pres.; P.O. Box 461; 73006; Caddo; P 1,600; M 100; (580) 588-3440; www.apache-ok.com

Ardmore · *Ardmore C/C* · D. Weston Stucky; Pres./CEO; 410 W. Main; 73401; Carter; P 50,000; M 780; (580) 223-7765; Fax (580) 223-7825; mbates@ardmore.org; www.ardmore.org*

Atoka · *Atoka County C/C* · Jewell Darst; Secy.; 415 E. Court; P.O. Box 778; 74525; Atoka; P 4,200; M 189; (580) 889-2410; Fax (580) 889-2410; chamber1atoka@sbcglobal.net; www.atokachamber.com

Barnsdall · *Barnsdall C/C* · Mitzi Whinery; Pres.; P.O. Box 443; 74002; Osage; P 2,000; M 50; (918) 847-2202; (918) 638-7608; Fax (918) 847-2164; barnsdallchamber@yahoo.com

Bartlesville · *Bartlesville Reg. C/C* · Shane Frye; Pres.; 201 S.W. Keeler; P.O. Box 2366; 74005; Osage & Washington; P 50,000; M 700; (918) 336-8708; Fax (918) 337-0216; reception@bartlesville.com; www.bartlesville.com*

Beaver · *Beaver County C/C* · Charlene Marshall; Secy./Mgr.; 33 W. 2nd St.; P.O. Box 878; 73932; Beaver; P 2,000; M 83; (580) 625-4726; Fax (580) 625-4726; bvrchamber@ptsi.net; www.beavercountychamberofcommerce.com

Beggs · *Beggs C/C* · Crystal Simmons; Pres.; P.O. Box 270; 74421; Okmulgee; P 1,500; M 35; (918) 267-4935; (918) 267-5240; information@beggschamber.org; www.beggschamber.org

Bethany · *Northwest C/C* · Jill McCartney; Pres./CEO; 7440 N.W. 39th Expy.; P.O. Box 144; 73008; Oklahoma; P 22,000; M 300; (405) 789-1256; Fax (405) 789-2478; info@nwokc.com; www.nwokc.com*

Billings · *Billings Comm. C/C* · Rick Hartz; Pres.; P.O. Box 264; 74630; Noble; P 500; M 22; (580) 725-3242

Bixby · *Bixby C/C* · Lisa Navrkal; Pres.; P.O. Box 158; 74008; Tulsa & Wagoner; P 19,000; M 400; (918) 366-9445; Fax (918) 366-9443; chamber@bixbychamber.com; www.bixbychamber.com*

Blackwell · *Blackwell Area C/C* · Jeff Seymour; Exec. Dir.; 120 S. Main; P.O. Box 230; 74631; Kay; P 7,600; M 200; (580) 363-4195; Fax (580) 363-1704; info@blackwellareachamber.com; www.blackwellchamber.org.*

Blanchard · *Blanchard C/C* · Laura Callaham; Exec. Dir.; 113 W. Broadway; P.O. Box 1190; 73010; Grady & McClain; P 8,000; M 125; (405) 485-8787; Fax (405) 485-8707; office@blanchardchamber.com; www.blanchardchamber.com

Boise City · *Cimarron County C/C* · John Smith; Pres.; 6 N.E. Square; P.O. Box 1027; 73933; Cimarron; P 3,000; M 50; (580) 544-3344; cccc@ptsi.net; www.ccccok.org

Boley · *Boley C/C* · Dr. Francis Shelton; Pres.; P.O. Box 31; 74829; Okfuskee; P 1,100; M 200; (918) 667-3477; www.boley-ok.com

Bristow · *Bristow C/C* · One Railroad Pl.; P.O. Box 127; 74010; Creek; P 4,500; M 165; (918) 367-5151; www.visitbristowok.com/chambers

Broken Arrow · *Broken Arrow Area C/C & EDC* · Mickey Thompson CEcD; Pres./CEO; 123 N. Main; 74012; Tulsa & Wagoner; P 100,000; M 830; (918) 251-1518; Fax (918) 251-1777; info@brokenarrowchamber.com; www.brokenarrowchamber.com*

Broken Bow · *Broken Bow C/C* · Charity O'Donnell; Exec. Dir.; 113 W. Martin Luther King Dr.; 74728; McCurtain; P 3,800; M 295; (580) 584-3393; (800) 528-7337; Fax (580) 584-7698; bchamber@pine-net.com; www.brokenbowchamber.com

Buffalo · *Buffalo C/C* · James Leonard; P.O. Box 521; 73834; Harper; P 1,200; M 40; (580) 735-2521; buffalo@pldi.net; www.buffalooklahoma.com

Canton · *Canton C/C* · Troy Everett; Pres.; P.O. Box 128; 73724; Blaine; P 650; M 50; (580) 886-2212; www.cantonlakeoklahoma.com

Carnegie · *Carnegie C/C* · Orval Williams; Pres.; P.O. Box 615; 73015; Caddo; P 1,637; M 60; (580) 654-2121

Catoosa · *Catoosa C/C* · Jonnie Mott; Mgr.; 650 S. Cherokee, Ste. C; P.O. Box 297; 74015; Rogers & Wagoner; P 6,000; M 134; (918) 266-6042; Fax (918) 266-6314; catoosachamber@gmail.com; www.catoosachamber.org*

Chandler · *Chandler C/C* · Marilyn Emde; Exec. Dir.; 400 E. Rte. 66; 74834; Lincoln; P 3,000; M 110; (405) 258-0673; Fax (405) 258-0008; chandlerchamber@sbcglobal.net; www.chandlerok.com

Checotah · *Checotah C/C* · Lloyd Jernigan; Exec. Dir.; 201 N. Broadway; 74426; McIntosh; P 20,600; M 120; (918) 473-2070; Fax (918) 473-1453; checotahchamber@windstream.net; www.checotah.com*

Chelsea · *Chelsea Area C/C* · Rick Johnson; Pres.; 618 Pine; 74016; Rogers; P 2,100; M 60; (918) 789-2220; Fax (918) 789-5899; chelseaokchamber@earthlink.net; www.chelseachamber.com

Cherokee · *Cherokee Mainstreet C/C* · Susie Koontz; Prog. Mgr.; 121 E. Main St.; 73728; Alfalfa; P 1,505; M 120; (580) 596-3575; (580) 596-6111; Fax (580) 596-2464; mainstreet@akslc.net

Cheyenne · *Cheyenne-Roger Mills C/C & Tourism* · Rhonda Robertson; Pres.; 101 S. LL Males Ave.; P.O. Box 57; 73628; Roger Mills; P 1,369; M 57; (580) 497-3318; Fax (580) 497-3318; cheyennecoc@yahoo.com; www.cheyenneokcoc.com

Chickasha · *Chickasha C/C* · Bud Andrus; Pres.; 221 Chickasha Ave.; P.O. Box 1717; 73023; Grady; P 17,000; M 420; (405) 224-0787; Fax (405) 222-3730; info@chickashachamber.com; www.chickashachamber.com*

Choctaw · *Choctaw C/C* · Tracy Mosley; Pres./CEO; 2437 Main St.; P.O. Box 1000; 73020; Oklahoma; P 11,500; M 268; (405) 390-3303; Fax (405) 390-3330; chocchamber@tds.net; www.choctawchamber.com

Chouteau · *Chouteau C/C* · Neil Patel; Pres.; P.O. Box 332; 74337; Mayes; P 1,000; M 60; (918) 476-8222; www.chouteauok.net

Claremore · *Claremore Area C/C* · Dell Davis; CEO; 419 W. Will Rogers Blvd.; 74017; Rogers; P 17,008; M 450; (918) 341-2818; Fax (918) 342-0663; chamber@claremore.org; www.claremore.org*

Cleveland · *Cleveland Area C/C* · Diana Tilley-Esparza; Exec. Dir.; 113 N. Broadway St.; P.O. Box 240; 74020; Pawnee; P 3,282; M 93; (918) 358-2131; Fax (918) 358-5710; info@chamberofcleveland.com; www.chamberofcleveland.com*

Clinton · *Clinton C/C* · Julie Menge; Pres.; 101 S. 4th St.; 73601; Custer & Washita; P 10,000; M 350; (580) 323-2222; Fax (580) 323-2931; office@clintonok.org; www.clintonok.org*

Coalgate · *Coal County C/C* · Clint Hardison; Pres.; P.O. Box 323; 74538; Coal; P 6,000; M 80; (580) 927-2119; mos274@yahoo.com; www.coalcounty.blogspot.com

Colcord · *Colcord Area C/C* · Tiffany Whorton; Pres.; P.O. Box 265; 74338; Delaware; P 1,000; M 25; (918) 326-4563; (918) 326-1033

Collinsville · *Collinsville C/C* · Ernie Davis; Pres.; 1126 W. Main St.; P.O. Box 245; 74021; Rogers & Tulsa; P 5,000; M 150; (918) 371-4703; Fax (918) 371-4703; cvillechamber3477@sbcglobal. net; www.collinsvillechamber.net

Cordell · *Cordell C/C* · Debbie Fuselier; Admin.; 116 S. College; 73632; Washita; P 2,867; M 125; (580) 832-3538; (888) CORDELL; Fax (580) 832-5432; chamberoffice@att.net; cordellchamber.org

Coweta · *Coweta C/C* · Heather Davis; Exec. Dir.; 107 S. Broadway; P.O. Box 70; 74429; Wagoner; P 10,000; M 172; (918) 486-2513; Fax (918) 279-0829; cowetachamber1@windstream. net; www.cowetachamber.com*

Crescent · *Crescent C/C* · John V. Anderson; Treas.; P.O. Box 333; 73028; Logan; P 1,651; M 60; (405) 969-2814

Cushing · *Cushing C of C & Ind.* · Brent Thompson; Exec. Dir.; 1301 E. Main; 74023; Payne; P 10,000; M 200; (918) 225-2400; Fax (918) 225-2903; manager@cushingchamber.org; www. cushingchamber.org*

Davenport · *Davenport C/C* · Steve Guest; Secy.; P.O. Box 66; 74026; Lincoln; P 1,000; M 125; (918) 377-2241; Fax (918) 377-2506; davenportcoc@brightok.net; www.davenportok.org

Davis · *Davis C/C* · Julie Hefley; Exec. Dir.; 100 E. Main St ; P.O. Box 5; /3030; Murray; P 2,800; M 190; (580) 369-2402; Fax (580) 369-3719; davischamber@sbcglobal.net; www.davisok.org

Del City · *Del City C/C* · Kay Bibens; Exec. Dir.; 4505 S.E. 15th St.; P.O. Box 15643; 73155; Oklahoma; P 25,000; M 109; (405) 677-1910; Fax (405) 672-5285; delcitychamber@sbcglobal.net; www.delcitychamber.com*

Drumright · *Drumright C/C* · Cleo Ramsey; Pres.; 103 E. Broadway; P.O. Box 828; 74030; Creek & Payne; P 3,000; M 110; (918) 352-2204; Fax (918) 352-2065; drumrightchamber@aol. com; www.drumright.com; drumright.net/chamber.htm

Duncan · *Duncan C of C & Ind.* · Debra Burch; Pres./CEO; 911 Walnut Ave.; P.O. Box 699; 73534; Stephens; P 24,000; M 393; (580) 255-3644; Fax (580) 255-6482; dccadmin@duncanchamber. com; www.duncanchamber.com*

Durant · *Durant Area C/C* · Janet Reed; Exec. Dir.; 215 N. 4th Ave.; 74701; Bryan; P 16,500; M 500; (580) 924-0848; (580) 924-0849; Fax (580) 924-0348; volunteerinfo@durantchamber.org; www.durantchamber.org*

Edmond · *Edmond Area C/C* · Ken Moore; Pres.; 825 E. 2nd, Ste. 100; 73034; Oklahoma; P 83,259; M 1,100; (405) 341-2808; Fax (405) 340-5512; info@edmondchamber.com; www.edmondchamber.com*

El Reno · *El Reno C/C* · Prog. Dir.; 206 N. Bickford Ave.; 73036; Canadian; P 16,000; M 200; (405) 262-1188; Fax (405) 262-1189; elrenochamber@swbell.net; www.elrenochamber.com*

Elgin · *Elgin C/C* · Leslie Durham; Secy.; P.O. Box 362; 73538; Comanche; P 2,000; M 78; (580) 492-5290; info@elginchamber. net; www.elginchamber.net

Elk City · *Elk City C/C* · Susie Cupp; Exec. Dir.; P.O. Box 972; 73648; Beckham; P 13,000; M 340; (580) 225-0207; Fax (580) 225-1008; elkcitychamber@itlnet.net; www.visitelkcity.com.*

Enid · *Greater Enid C/C* · Jon Blankenship; Pres./CEO; 210 Kenwood Blvd.; P.O. Box 907; 73702; Garfield; P 70,000; M 550; (580) 237-2494; Fax (580) 237-2497; joan@enidchamber.com; www.enidchamber.com.*

Erick · *Erick C/C* · Paula Harris; Pres.; P.O. Box 1232; 73645; Beckham; P 1,100; M 40; (580) 526-3332; erickchamber@yahoo. com; www.erickchamber.com

Eufaula · *Eufaula Area C/C* · Ms. Jimmie Phelan; Exec. Dir.; 321 N. Main St.; P.O. Box 738; 74432; McIntosh; P 3,500; M 180; (918) 689-2791; Fax (918) 689-7746; chamber@eufaulachamberof commerce.com; www.eufaulachamberofcommerce.com

Fairfax · *Fairfax C/C* · Jamie Sears; Pres.; 242 N. Main St.; P.O. Box 35; 74637; Osage; P 1,700; M 20; (918) 642-1271; (918) 642-5266; bob_stephens@msn.com; www.fairfaxchamber.com

Fairview · *Fairview C/C* · Jeannie Marlin; Exec. Dir.; 624 N. Main; P.O. Box 180; 73737; Major; P 2,700; M 145; (580) 227-2527; Fax (580) 227-2258; fairviewchamber@att.net; www.fairviewok chamber.com*

Fort Gibson · *Fort Gibson C/C* · Gary Perkins; Exec. Dir.; 112 N. Lee St.; P.O. Box 730; 74434; Cherokee & Muskogee; P 4,300; M 120; (918) 478-4780; Fax (918) 478-4780; fortgibson@ sbcglobal.net; www.fortgibson.com

Fort Sill · *see Lawton*

Frederick · *Frederick C/C & Ind.* · Sharon Bennett; Exec. Dir.; 100 S. Main St.; 73542; Tillman; P 4,000; M 150; (580) 335-2126; Fax (580) 335-3767; frederickcc@pldi.net; www.frederickok chamber.org*

Freedom · *Freedom C/C* · Mark Nixon; Secy./Treas.; P.O. Box 125; 73842; Woods; P 300; M 120; (580) 621-3276; Fax (580) 621-3275; www.freedomokla.com

Gage · *Gage C/C* · Tim Puclik; Pres.; P.O. Box 328; 73843; Ellis; P 400; M 15; (580) 923-7727

Garber · *Garber Comm. Improvement Assn.* · P.O. Box 574; 73738; Garfield; P 700; M 30; (580) 863-2279

Geary · *Geary C/C* · Kay Hagerman; Pres.; P.O. Box 273; 73040; Blaine; P 1,350; M 30; (405) 884-2765

Glenpool · *Glenpool C/C* · Diane Bileck; Exec. Dir.; 494 E. 141st St.; P.O. Box 767; 74033; Tulsa; P 10,000; M 155; (918) 322-3505; Fax (918) 322-3505; director@glenpoolchamber.org; www. glenpoolchamber.org*

Gore · *Gore C/C* · Linda Bighorse; Secy.; P.O. Box 943; 74435; Sequoyah; P 900; M 70; goreokchamber@yahoo.com; www. goreok.net

Grove · *Grove Area C/C* · Lisa Friden; Pres.; 9630 Hwy 59N, Ste. A; 74344; Delaware; P 16,640; M 400; (918) 786-9079; Fax (918) 786-2909; grovecc@sbcglobal.net; www.groveok.org*

Guthrie · *Guthrie C/C* · Mary Coffin; Pres.; 212 W. Oklahoma Ave.; P.O. Box 995; 73044; Logan; P 13,000; M 358; (405) 282-1947; (800) 299-1889; Fax (405) 282-0061; info@guthrieok.com; www.guthrieok.com*

Guymon · *Guymon C/C* · Ronni Malone; Exec. Dir.; 711 S.E. Hwy. 3; Rte. 5, Box 120; 73942; Texas; P 22,000; M 220; (580) 338-3376; Fax (580) 338-0014; guycofc@ptsi.net; www.guymoncofc.org*

Harrah · *Harrah C/C* · Gordon Jeney; Pres.; P.O. Box 907; 73045; Oklahoma; P 4,800; M 125; (405) 454-2190; Jeneycoinc@yahoo. com; www.harrahchamberofcommerce.com

Hartshorne · *Hartshorne C/C* · Jerry Earp; Pres.; P.O. Box 343; 74547; Pittsburg; P 2,200; M 55; (918) 297-2055; (918) 297-3651; www.cityofhartshorneok.com

Haskell · *Haskell Area C/C* · Shawn Danielson; P.O. Box 252; 74436; Muskogee; P 6,000; M 63; (918) 482-1245; Fax (918) 482-5619; info@haskellchamber.com; www.haskellchamber.com

Healdton · *Healdton C/C* · Renee Miller; Pres.; 315 E. Main; 73438; Carter; P 2,700; M 100; (580) 229-0900; Fax (580) 229-0900; healdtonchamber@suddenlinkmail.com; www.healdton chamber.com

Heavener · *Heavener C/C* · 501 W. 1st St.; 74937; Le Flore; P 3,600; M 100; (918) 653-4303; Fax (918) 653-2438

Henryetta · *Henryetta C/C* · Roy Madden; Exec. Dir.; 115 S. 4th; 74437; Okmulgee; P 6,000; M 120; (918) 652-3331; Fax (918) 652-3332; chamber@henryetta.org; www.henryetta.org

Hinton · *Hinton C/C* · Jason Garner; Pres.; P.O. Box 48; 73047; Caddo; P 2,000; M 70; (405) 542-6428; www.hintonok.com

Hobart · *Hobart C/C* · Nancy Ledford; Exec. Dir.; 106 W. 4th St.; 73651; Kiowa; P 3,500; M 110; (580) 726-2553; Fax (580) 726-2553; hobartchamber@cableone.net; www.hobartok.com*

Holdenville · *Holdenville C/C* · Diane Hamilton; Exec. Dir.; 105 S. Hinckley; P.O. Box 70; 74848; Hughes; P 10,000; M 84; (405) 592-4221; Fax (405) 379-6968; chamber@holdenville.org; www.holdenville.org

Hominy · *Hominy C/C* · Jerry Stumpff; Pres.; P.O. Box 99; 74035; Osage; P 3,200; M 50; (918) 885-4939; Fax (918) 885-4049; hominychamberofcommerce@windstream.net; www.hominychamber.com

Hooker · *Hooker C/C* · Linda Martin; Pres.; P.O. Box 989; 73945; Texas; P 1,788; M 80; (580) 652-2809

Hugo · *Hugo Area C/C* · Judy Wilson; Exec. Dir.; 200 S. Broadway; 74743; Choctaw; P 5,700; M 135; (580) 326-7511; Fax (580) 326-7512; hugo-chamber@sbcglobal.net; www.hugochamber.org*

Idabel · *Idabel C of C & Ag.* · Betty L. Johnson; Exec. Dir.; 7 S.W. Texas St.; 74745; McCurtain; P 7,000; M 214; (580) 286-3305; Fax (580) 286-6708; idabelchamber@yahoo.com; www.idabel chamberofcommerce.com*

Jay · *Jay C/C* · Jackie Coatney; P.O. Box 806; 74346; Delaware; P 2,482; M 62; (918) 253-4148; delcohsmuseum@grandsavings bank.com; www.jayokchamber.com

Jenks · *Jenks C/C* · Annette Bowles; Pres.; 224 E. A St.; P.O. Box 902; 74037; Tulsa; P 17,000; M 350; (918) 299-5005; Fax (918) 299-5799; info@jenkschamber.com; www.jenkschamber.com*

Kaw City · *Kaw City Area C/C* · Rosie Kirk; Pres.; 300 Washunga Dr.; P.O. Box 241; 74641; Kay; P 300; M 50; kawcitychamber@kawcityok.net; www.kawcitychamber.org

Kingfisher · *Kingfisher C/C* · Judy Whipple; Mgr.; 123 W. Miles; 73750; Kingfisher; P 5,000; M 95; (405) 375-4445; Fax (405) 375-5304; chamber@pldi.net; www.kingfisher.org

Kingston · *see Madill*

Konawa · *Konawa C/C* · P.O. Box 112; 74849; Seminole; P 1,500; M 65; (580) 925-3220

Langley · *Grand Lake Area C/C* · Jim Sellers; Exec. Dir.; P.O. Box 215; 74350; Mayes; P 25,000; M 350; (918) 782-3214; Fax (918) 782-3215; jksellers@grandlakechamber.org; www.grandlake chamber.org

Laverne · *Laverne Area C/C* · Terri Wheeler; Exec. Dir.; 108 W. Jane Jayroe Blvd.; P.O. Box 634; 73848; Harper; P 1,097; M 30; (580) 921-3612; lvrnokcc@ptsi.net; www.laverneok.com

Lawton · *Lawton Fort Sill C/C & Ind.* · Shelia O. Lee IOM CCE; Pres./CEO; 629 S.W. C Ave.; P.O. Box 1376; 73501; Comanche; P 114,000; M 900; (580) 355-3541; (800) 872-4540; Fax (580) 357-3642; frontdesk@lawtonfortsillchamber.com; www.lawton fortsillchamber.com.*

Lindsay · *Lindsay C/C* · Paula Barker; Mgr.; 107 N. Main St.; P.O. Box 504; 73052; Garvin; P 3,000; M 123; (405) 756-4312; Fax (405) 756-8657; lchamber@oriok.net; www.lindsayokchamber ofcommerce.com

Locust Grove · *Locust Grove Area C/C* · P.O. Box 525; 74352; Mayes; P 1,400; M 60; (918) 479-6336; locustgroveokchamber@hotmail.com; www.lgchamber.com

Madill · *Marshall County C/C* · Jeff Hudson; Exec. Dir.; 1 County Courthouse St., Ste. 106; P.O. Box 542; 73446; Marshall; P 20,000; M 220; (580) 795-2431; Fax (580) 795-5870; info@mccoconline.org; www.mccoconline.org

Mangum · *Greer County C/C* · Wayne Vaughn; Exec. Dir.; 222 W. Jefferson; 73554; Greer; P 6,095; M 165; (580) 782-2444; Fax (580) 782-2444; info@greercountychamber.com; www.greer countychamber.com*

Mannford · *Mannford Area C/C* · Rita Bougher; Pres.; P.O. Box 487; 74044; Creek, Pawnee & Tulsa; P 5,000; M 100; (918) 865-2000; Fax (918) 865-3187; info@mannfordchamberofcommerce.com; www.mannfordchamberofcommerce.com

Marietta · *Love County C/C* · Gwen Wyatt; Secy.; P.O. Box 422; 73448; Love; P 3,000; M 100; (580) 276-3102; lovecounty chamber@yahoo.com; www.lovecountyokla.org

Marlow · *Marlow C/C* · Debbe Ridley; Exec. Dir.; 223 W. Main; 73055; Stephens; P 4,592; M 230; (580) 658-2212; marlow chamber@cableone.net; www.marlowchamber.org

Maysville · *Maysville C/C* · Johnny Bob Williams; Pres.; P.O. Box 313; 73057; Garvin; P 1,240; M 40; (405) 867-4485; (405) 867-5850

McAlester · *McAlester Area C/C & Ag.* · Karen Stephens; Exec. Dir.; 345 E. Adams; P.O. Box 759; 74501; Pittsburg; P 20,000; M 400; (918) 423-2550; Fax (918) 423-1345; info@mcalester.org; www.mcalester.org*

McLoud · *McLoud C/C* · Jayne Sconyers; Exec. Dir.; P.O. Box 254; 74851; Pottawatomie; P 3,548; M 70; (405) 964-6566; Fax (405) 964-6566; jayne@mcloudchamber.com; www.mcloudchamber.com

Miami · *Miami C/C* · Cindy Morris; Pres.; 103 E. Central Ave., Ste. 100; 74354; Ottawa; P 14,800; M 300; (918) 542-4481; Fax (918) 540-1260; info@miamiokchamber.com; www.miamiokchamber.com*

Midwest City · *Midwest City C/C* · Bonnie Cheatwood; Exec. Dir.; 5905 Trosper Rd.; P.O. Box 10980; 73140; Oklahoma; P 56,123; M 560; (405) 733-3801; Fax (405) 733-5633; information@midwestcityok.com; www.midwestcityok.com*

Minco · *Minco C/C* · John Hacker; Pres.; P.O. Box 451; 73059; Grady; P 1,579; M 26; (405) 352-4382

Moore · *Moore C/C* · Brenda Roberts; Exec. Dir.; 305 W. Main; P.O. Box 6305; 73153; Cleveland; P 55,000; M 637; (405) 794-3400; Fax (405) 794-8555; brendar@moorechamber.com; www.moorechamber.com*

Muldrow · *Muldrow C/C* · Katherine Jones; Mayor; 100 S. Main; P.O. Box 429; 74948; Sequoyah; P 4,000; (918) 427-7668

Muskogee · *Greater Muskogee Area C/C & Tourism* · Sue Harris; Pres.; 310 W. Broadway; P.O. Box 797; 74402; Muskogee; P 40,000; M 800; (918) 682-2401; (866) 381-6543; Fax (918) 682-2403; info@muskogeechamber.org; www.muskogeechamber.org*

Mustang · *Mustang C/C* · Becky Julian; Exec. Dir.; 1201 N. Mustang Rd.; P.O. Box 213; 73064; Canadian; P 17,000; M 291; (405) 376-2758; Fax (405) 376-4764; mustangc@icon.net; www.mustangchamber.com*

Newcastle • *Newcastle C/C* • Kim Brown; Exec. Dir.; P.O. Box 1006; 73065; McClain; P 7,200; M 160; (405) 387-3232; Fax (405) 387-3885; www.newcastleok.org

Newkirk • *Newkirk C/C* • Chris Tiger; Pres.; 114 S. Main St.; 74647; Kay; P 3,800; M 115; (580) 362-2155; Fax (580) 362-3774; ncof104@sbcglobal.net; www.newkirkchamber.com*

Noble • *Noble C/C* • Christine Frank; Exec. Dir.; 114 S. Main; P.O. Box 678; 73068; Cleveland; P 5,000; M 100; (405) 872-5535; Fax (405) 872-2020; info@nobleok.org; www.nobleok.org

Norman • *Norman C/C* • Anna-Mary Suggs; Exec. Dir.; 115 E. Gray St.; P.O. Box 982; 73070; Cleveland; P 108,000; M 1,350; (405) 321-7260; Fax (405) 360-4679; normanchamber@norman chamber.com; www.normanchamber.com*

Nowata • *Nowata Area C/C* • Billie L. Roane; Exec. Dir.; 126 S. Maple; P.O. Box 202; 74048; Nowata; P 5,000; M 150; (918) 273-2301; nowatachamber@sbcglobal.net; www.nowatachamber.net

Oilton • *Oilton C/C* • Kay Lewis; Pres.; P.O. Box 624; 74052; Creek; P 1,600; M 35; (918) 862-3202

Okeene • *Okeene C/C* • Sherri Feely; Exec. Dir.; 116 W. E St.; P.O. Box 704; 73763; Blaine; P 1,200; M 75; (580) 822-3005; okchamber@pldi.net; www.okeene.com

Okemah • *Okemah C/C* • Ronald Gott; Exec. Dir.; 407 W. Broadway; P.O. Box 508; 74859; Okfuskee; P 3,600; M 225; (918) 623-2440; okemahchamber@okemah.org; www.okemahok.org

Oklahoma City • *Greater Oklahoma City C/C* • Roy H. Williams; Pres./CEO, 123 Park Ave.; 73102; Oklahoma; P 1,172,300; M 4,200; (405) 297-8900; Fax (405) 297-8916; tepps@okcchamber.com; www.okcchamber.com*

Oklahoma City • *South Oklahoma City C/C* • Elaine Lyons; Pres.; 701 S.W. 74th St.; 73139; Oklahoma; P 140,246; M 750; (405) 634-1436; Fax (405) 634-1462; info@southokc.com; www.southokc.com*

Okmulgee • *Okmulgee C/C* • Nolan Crowley; Exec. Dir.; 112 N. Morton Ave.; 74447; Okmulgee; P 13,000; M 200; (918) 756-6172; Fax (918) 756-6441; okmulgeeinfo@okmulgeechamber.org; www.okmulgeeonline.com*

Oologah • *Oologah Area C/C* • Amos Berry; Pres.; P.O. Box 109; 74053; Rogers; P 1,500; M 110; (918) 443-2790; Fax (918) 443-2790; chamber@oologah.org; www.oologah.org

Owasso • *Owasso C/C* • Gary Akin; Pres.; 315 S. Cedar; 74055; Rogers & Tulsa; P 45,000; M 500; (918) 272-2141; Fax (918) 272-8564; info@owassochamber.com; www.owassochamber.com*

Pauls Valley • *Pauls Valley C/C* • Della Wilson; Exec. Dir.; 112 E. Paul; P.O. Box 638; 73075; Garvin; P 6,900; M 270; (405) 238-6491; Fax (405) 238-2335; pvchamber@sbcglobal.net; www.paulsvalley.com*

Pawhuska • *Pawhuska C/C* • Michael McCartney; Exec. Dir.; 210 W. Main; P.O. Box 5; 74056; Osage; P 3,825; M 150; (918) 287-1208; Fax (918) 287-3159; pawhuskachamber@sbcglobal.net; www.pawhuskachamber.com

Pawnee • *Pawnee C/C* • Bill Gosnell; Mgr.; 613 Harrison St.; 74058; Pawnee; P 2,200; M 105; (918) 762-2108; pawnee chamber@cowboy.net; www.cityofpawnee.com

Perkins • *Perkins C/C* • David Massey; Pres.; P.O. Box 502; 74059; Payne; P 2,500; M 88; (405) 747-6809; www.cityofperkins.net

Perry • *Perry C/C* • Brett Powers; Exec. Dir.; 327 N. 7th St.; P.O. Box 426; 73077; Noble; P 5,200; M 250; (580) 336-4684; Fax (580) 336-3522; information@perrychamber.net; www.perryokchamber.com

Piedmont • *Piedmont C/C* • Cindy Teakwood; Pres.; P.O. Box 501; 73078; Canadian & Kingfisher; P 5,000; M 132; (405) 373-2234; piedmontokchamber@att.net; www.piedmontokchamber.org

Ponca City • *Ponca City Area C/C* • Rich Cantillon; Pres./CEO; 420 E. Grand Ave.; P.O. Box 1109; 74602; Kay & Osage; P 26,000; M 600; (580) 765-4400; Fax (580) 765-2798; rich@poncacity chamber.com; www.poncacitychamber.com*

Poteau • *Poteau C/C* • Karen Wages; Pres./CEO; 201 S. Broadway; 74953; LeFlore; P 9,000; M 386; (918) 647-9178; Fax (918) 647-4099; poteauchamber@windstream.net; www.poteauchamber.com*

Prague • *Prague C/C* • 820 Jim Thorpe Blvd.; P.O. Box 111; 74864; Lincoln; P 2,300; M 80; (405) 567-2616; Fax (405) 567-2616; praguecoc@windstream.net; www.pragueok.org

Pryor • *Pryor Area C/C* • Barbara Hawkins; Pres.; 100 E. Graham Ave.; P.O. Box 367; 74362; Mayes; P 9,500; M 310; (918) 825-0157; Fax (918) 825-0158; info@pryorchamber.com; www.pryorchamber.com

Purcell • *Heart of Oklahoma C/C* • Mark Alfonso; Exec. Dir.; 302 W. Main St., Ste. 104; 73080; McClain; P 5,500; M 200; (405) 527-3093; Fax (405) 527-4351; purcellchamber@cebridge.net; www.theheartofoklahomachamber.com

Roff • *Roff C/C* • Nelda Burrows; Pres.; P.O. Box 303; 74865; Pontotoc; P 720; M 20; (580) 456-7774; hjcrawford@cableone.net

Roland • *Roland C/C* • Keith Wasson; Pres.; P.O. Box 492; 74954; Sequoyah; P 4,000; M 45; (479) 651-0321; info@rolandchamber.com; www.rolandchamber.com

Salina • *Salina Area C/C* • Smokey Tennison; Pres.; P.O. Box 971; 74365; Mayes; P 1,500; M 15; (918) 434-8223; suetennison@yahoo.com

Sallisaw • *Sallisaw C/C* • Judy Martens; Exec. Dir.; 301 E. Cherokee; P.O. Box 251; 74955; Sequoyah; P 8,500; M 200; (918) 775-2558; Fax (918) 775-4021; sallisawchamber@yahoo.com; www.sallisawchamber.com

Sand Springs • *Sand Springs Area C/C* • Mr. J.C. Kinder; Pres.; 121 N. Main; 74063; Osage & Tulsa; P 18,000; M 300; (918) 245-3221; Fax (918) 245-2530; info@sandspringschamber.com; www.sandspringschamber.com*

Sapulpa • *Sapulpa C/C* • Suzanne Shirey; Pres.; 101 E. Dewey; 74066; Creek & Tulsa; P 20,000; M 331; (918) 224-0170; Fax (918) 224-0172; suzanne@sapulpachamber.com; www.sapulpachamber.com.*

Sayre • *Sayre C/C* • Niki Callahan; Dir.; 117 N. 4th; P.O. Box 474; 73662; Beckham; P 3,500; M 115; (580) 928-3386; Fax (580) 928-8976; sayrechamber@att.net; www.sayrechamber.com

Seiling • *Seiling C/C* • Todd Kourt; Pres.; P.O. Box 794; 73663; Dewey; P 900; M 30; www.seilingchamber.com

Seminole • *Seminole C/C* • Amy Britt; Exec. Dir.; 326 E. Evans; P.O. Box 1190; 74818; Seminole; P 7,500; M 250; (405) 382-3640; Fax (405) 382-3529; info@seminoleokchamber.org; www.seminoleokchamber.org.*

Sentinel • *Sentinel C/C* • Fran Babek; Pres.; P.O. Box 131; 73664; Washita; P 850; M 60; (580) 393-2171

Shattuck • *Shattuck C/C* • David W. Romine; Exec. Dir.; 115 S. Main St.; P.O. Box 400; 73858; Ellis; P 3,000; M 110; (580) 938-2818; (580) 938-1425; Fax (580) 938-2852; shattuckcc@pldi.net; www.shattuckchamber.org

Shawnee • *Greater Shawnee Area C/C* • Nancy Keith; Pres./CEO; 131 N. Bell; P.O. Box 1613; 74802; Pottawatomie; P 32,000; M 520; (405) 273-6092; Fax (405) 275-9851; nkeith@shawneechamber.com; www.shawneechamber.com*

Shidler · *Shidler C/C* · Molly Bivin; P.O. Box 281; 74652; Osage; P 500; M 56; (918) 793-4171; www.shidleroklahoma.com

Skiatook · *Skiatook C/C* · Stephanie Upton; Exec. Dir.; 304 E. Rogers Blvd.; 74070; Osage & Tulsa; P 8,500; M 130; (918) 396-3702; Fax (918) 396-3577; info@skiatookchamber.com; www.skiatookchamber.com

Spencer · *Spencer C/C* · Tony Wangler; Exec. Dir.; 8606 Main St.; P.O. Box 53; 73084; Oklahoma; P 3,550; M 87; (405) 771-9933

Spiro · *Spiro Area C/C* · Marcia Day; Exec. Dir.; 210 S. Main St.; P.O. Box 401; 74959; Le Flore; P 2,300; M 100; (918) 962-3816; Fax (918) 962-3816; info@myspiro.com; www.myspiro.com

Stigler · *Stigler/Haskell County C/C* · Janice Williams; Exec. Dir.; 204 E. Main St.; 74462; Haskell; P 12,000; M 70; (918) 967-8681; Fax (918) 967-4319; chamber@tulsaconnect.com

Stillwater · *Stillwater C/C* · Larry Brown; Pres./CEO; 409 S. Main; P.O. Box 1687; 74076; Payne; P 46,976; M 650; (405) 372-5573; Fax (405) 372-4316; info@stillwaterchamber.org; www.stillwaterchamber.org*

Stilwell · *Stilwell Area C/C* · Betty Barker; Secy.; P.O. Box 845; 74960; Adair; P 3,000; M 100; (918) 696-7845; www.strawberry capital.com

Stratford · *Stratford C/C* · Jay Johnson; Pres.; P.O. Box 491; 74872; Garvin; P 1,600; M 35; (580) 759-3300; www.stratford chamber.biz

Stroud · *Stroud C/C* · Tommy Smith; Pres.; 216 W. Main; 74079; Creek & Lincoln; P 2,700; M 145; (918) 968-3321; Fax (918) 968-4113; stroudch@brightok.net; www.stroudok.com

Sulphur · *Sulphur C/C* · Shelly Sawatzky; Exec. Dir.; 717 W. Broadway; 73086; Murray; P 5,000; M 230; (580) 622-2824; Fax (580) 622-4217; sulphur@brightok.net; www.sulphurokla.com

Tahlequah · *Tahlequah Area C/C* · David Moore; Exec. Dir.; 123 E. Delaware St.; 74464; Cherokee; P 46,000; M 500; (918) 456-3742; (800) 456-4860; Fax (918) 456-3751; tahlequahchamber@swbell.net; www.tahlequahchamber.com*

Talihina · *Talihina C/C* · Vera Nelson; Dir.; 900 2nd St., Ste. 12; 74571; Le Flore; P 1,297; M 65; (918) 567-3434; Fax (918) 567-3388; chamber@talihinacc.com; www.talihinacc.com

Tecumseh · *Tecumseh C/C* · Autumn Brown; Exec. Dir.; 114 N. Broadway St.; 74873; Pottawatomie; P 6,200; M 95; (405) 598-8666; Fax (405) 598-6760; chambertecumseh@windstream.net; www.tecumsehchamber.com

Temple · *Temple C/C* · Lana Spake; Pres.; P.O. Box 58; 73568; Cotton; P 1,200; M 67; (580) 342-6908

Thomas · *Thomas Area C/C* · Vicki Litsch; Exec. V.P.; 122 W. Broadway; P.O. Box 250; 73669; Custer; P 1,238; M 130; (580) 661-3685; (580) 661-3687; Fax (580) 661-3689; thomascoc@pldi.net

Tipton · *Tipton C/C* · Linton Deskins; Pres.; P.O. Box 403; 73570; Tillman; P 1,200; M 130; (580) 305-8549

Tishomingo · *Johnston County C/C* · Janis Stewart; Exec. Dir.; 106 W. Main; 73460; Johnston; P 11,000; M 150; (580) 371-2175; Fax (580) 371-2175; chamber@johnstoncountyok.org; www.johnstoncountyok.org*

Tonkawa · *Tonkawa C/C* · Dianne Smith; Pres.; 102 E. Grand Ave.; 74653; Kay; P 3,299; M 160; (580) 628-2220; Fax (580) 628-2221; info@tonkawachamber.org; www.tonkawachamber.org

Tulsa · *American Indian C/C of Oklahoma* · Cathy Wilkins; State Exec. Dir.; 5103 S. Sheridan Rd., Ste. 695; 74145; Osage, Rogers, Tulsa & Wagoner; (918) 665-7087; (800) 652-4226; Fax (918) 343-3578; chamber@aicco.org; www.aicco.org

Tulsa · *Tulsa Metro C/C* · Mike Neal; Pres./CEO; Two W. Second St., Ste. 150; 74103; Osage, Rogers, Tulsa & Wagoner; P 916,079; M 2,900; (918) 585-1201; Fax (918) 599-6122; webmaster@tulsachamber.com; www.tulsachamber.com

Tuttle · *Tuttle Area C/C* · Lara Hughes Douglas; Mgr.; 2422 E. Hwy. 37; P.O. Box 673; 73089; Grady; P 6,000; M 150; (405) 381-4600; Fax (405) 381-4600; lara@tuttlechamber.org; www.tuttlechamber.org

Vici · *Vici C/C* · Molly Randall; Secy.; 107 E. Broadway; P.O. Box 2; 73859; Dewey; P 750; M 40; (580) 995-3425; Fax (580) 995-4987; vicichamber@vicihorizon.com; www.viciok.com

Vinita · *Vinita Area C/C* · B.J. Mooney; Exec. Dir.; 125 S. Scraper St.; P.O. Box 882; 74301; Craig; P 7,000; M 237; (918) 256-7133; Fax (918) 256-8261; chamber@vinita.com; www.vinita.com*

Wagoner · *Wagoner Area C/C* · Meredith Zehr; Exec. Dir.; 301 S. Grant; 74467; Wagoner; P 30,000; M 275; (918) 485-3414; Fax (918) 485-2523; chamber@thecityofwagoner.org; www.thecityofwagoner.org*

Walters · *Walters C/C* · Mike Schmidt; Pres.; 116 N. Broadway; P.O. Box 352; 73572; Cotton; P 2,657; M 75; (580) 875-3335; Fax (580) 875-3652; www.waltersok.us

Warner · *Warner C/C* · Roger Thomason; Pres.; P.O. Box 170; 74469; Muskogee; P 1,600; M 30; (918) 463-2696; www.warnerok.com

Watonga · *Watonga C/C* · Todd Lafferty; Pres.; P.O. Box 537; 73772; Blaine; P 3,500; M 175; (580) 623-5452; Fax (580) 623-5428; cwatonga@pldi.net; www.watongachamber.com

Waurika · *Waurika C/C* · Brad Scott; Pres.; P.O. Box 366; 73573; Jefferson; P 1,900; M 75; (580) 228-2041; www.jeffcoinfo.org

Waynoka · *Waynoka C/C* · Wayne LaMunyon; Pres.; P.O. Box 173; 73860; Woods; P 1,000; M 100; (580) 824-4741; (580) 824-2261; waynokachamber@gmail.com; www.waynokachamber.com

Weatherford · *Weatherford Area C/C* · Debbie Pearcy; Exec. Dir.; 522 W. Rainey; P.O. Box 857; 73096; Custer; P 14,000; M 307; (580) 772-7744; (800) 725-7744; Fax (580) 772-7751; director@weatherfordchamber.com; www.weatherfordchamber.com*

Wellston · *Wellston C/C* · Marcia Balleweg; Pres.; P.O. Box 188; 74881; Lincoln; P 925; M 35; (405) 356-2471

Westville · *Westville C/C* · Patsy Winn; Comm. Bldg.; P.O. Box 1020; 74965; Adair; P 1,600; M 25; (918) 723-3243; Fax (918) 723-4936; pswinn58@hotmail.com

Wetumka · *Wetumka C/C* · Vernon Stout; 202 N. Main; 74883; Hughes; P 1,700; M 50; (405) 452-3237; wetumkacoc@hotmail.com

Wewoka · *Wewoka C/C* · Tara Morgan; Exec. Dir./Secy.; 101 W. Park; P.O. Box 719; 74884; Seminole; P 4,000; M 200; (405) 257-5485; Fax (405) 257-2662; wewokachamber@sbcglobal.net; www.wewokachamber.samsbiz.com

Wilburton · *Wilburton C/C* · 302 W. Main; 74578; Latimer; P 3,500; M 88; (918) 465-2759; Fax (918) 465-2759; wilburton chamber@sbcglobal.net; www.wilburtonchamber.com

Woodward · *Woodward C/C* · CJ Montgomery; Pres.; 1006 Oklahoma Ave.; P.O. Box 1026; 73802; Woodward; P 15,000; M 400; (580) 256-7411; (800) 364-5352; Fax (580) 254-3585; wwchamber@sbcglobal.net; www.woodwardchamber.com.

Wynnewood · *Wynnewood C/C* · Sandy Garrett; Pres.; P.O. Box 616; 73098; Garvin; P 2,400; M 50; (405) 665-4466; wynnewood okla@sbcglobal.net; www.wynnewoodokla.com

Yale · *Yale C/C* · Cindy White; Pres.; P.O. Box 132; 74085; Payne; P 1,342; M 30; (918) 387-2406; (918) 387-2444; cwhite@ahb-ok.com

Yukon • *Yukon C/C* • Sandy Meier; Dir.; 510 Elm; 73099; Canadian; P 25,000; M 400; (405) 354-3567; Fax (405) 350-0724; chamber@yukoncc.com; www.yukoncc.com*

Oregon

Oregon State C of C • Dave Hauser; Admin.; P.O. Box 1107; Eugene; 97440; Lane; P 3,800,000; M 33,000; (541) 484-1314; Fax (541) 484-4942; susanm@eugenechamber.com; www.oregonstatechamber.org

Albany • *Albany Area C/C* • Janet Steele; Pres./CEO; 435 W. First Ave.; P.O. Box 548; 97321; Benton & Linn; P 48,000; M 625; (541) 926-1517; Fax (541) 926-7064; info@albanychamber.com; www.albanychamber.com.*

Ashland • *Ashland C/C* • Sandra Slattery; Exec. Dir.; 110 E. Main St.; P.O. Box 1360; 97520; Jackson; P 20,000; M 805; (541) 482-3486; Fax (541) 482-2350; katharine@ashlandchamber.com; www.ashlandchamber.com.*

Astoria • *Astoria-Warrenton Area C/C* • Skip Hauke; Exec. Dir.; 111 W. Marine Dr.; P.O. Box 176; 97103; Clatsop; P 16,000; M 550; (503) 325-6311; (800) 875-6807; Fax (503) 325-9767; info@oldoregon.com; www.oldoregon.com*

Baker City • *Baker County Chamber & Visitor Bur.* • Debi Bainter; Exec. Dir.; 490 Campbell St.; 97814; Baker; P 10,000; M 420; (541) 523-5855; (800) 523-1235; Fax (541) 523-9187; info@visitbaker.com; www.visitbaker.com

Bandon • *Bandon C/C* • Julie Miller; Exec. Dir.; 300 S.E. Second; P.O. Box 1515; 97411; Coos; P 3,000; M 369; (541) 347-9616; Fax (541) 347-7006; bandoncc@mycomspan.com; www.bandon.com*

Banks • *Banks C/C* • Ray Deeth; Admin.; P.O. Box 206; 97106; Washington; P 1,400; M 50; (503) 324-1081; www.oregonbankschamber.com

Beaver • *see Cloverdale*

Beaverton • *Beaverton Area C/C* • Lorraine Clarno; Pres.; 12655 S.W. Center St., Ste. 140; 97005; Washington; P 88,000; M 690; (503) 644-0123; Fax (503) 526-0349; info@beaverton.org; www.beaverton.org.*

Bend • *Bend C/C* • Tim Casey; Exec. Dir.; 777 N.W. Wall St., Ste. 200; 97701; Deschutes; P 82,000; M 1,400; (541) 382-3221; (800) 905-BEND; Fax (541) 385-9929; info@bendchamber.org; www.bendchamber.org*

Blaine • *see Cloverdale*

Boardman • *Boardman C/C* • Diane Wolfe; Exec. Dir.; 206 N. Main St.; P.O. Box 1; 97818; Morrow; P 3,310; M 180; (541) 481-3014; Fax (541) 481-2733; boardmanchamber@centurytel.net; www.boardmanchamber.org*

Boring • *see Milwaukie*

Brookings • *Brookings-Harbor C/C* • Les Cohen; Pres./CEO; 16330 Lower Harbor Rd.; P.O. Box 940; 97415; Curry; P 14,000; M 370; (541) 469-3181; (800) 535-9469; Fax (541) 469-4094; www.brookingsor.com*

Brownsville • *Brownsville Comm. C/C* • Mandy Cole; Pres.; P.O. Box 161; 97327; Linn; P 1,700; M 55; (541) 466-5709; events@historicbrownsville.com; www.historicbrownsville.com

Burns • *Harney County C/C* • Julia Olson; Exec. Dir.; 484 N. Broadway; 97720; Harney; P 7,300; M 200; (541) 573-2636; Fax (541) 573-3408; info@harneycounty.com; www.harneycounty.com

Canby • *Canby Area C/C* • Bev Doolittle; Exec. Dir.; 191 S.E. 2nd Ave.; P.O. Box 35; 97013; Clackamas; P 15,000; M 300; (503) 266-4600; Fax (503) 266-4338; chamber@canby.com; www.canbyareachamber.org

Cannon Beach • *Cannon Beach C/C & Info. Center* • Jeff Jewel; Exec. Dir.; 207 N. Spruce St.; P.O. Box 64; 97110; Clatsop; P 1,600; M 265; (503) 436-2623; Fax (503) 436-0910; chamber@cannonbeach.org; www.cannonbeach.org

Canyonville • *Canyonville C/C* • Jake Young; Pres.; P.O. Box 1028; 97417; Douglas; P 1,649; M 50; (541) 839-4291; www.canyonvillechamber.org

Cave Junction • *Illinois Valley C/C* • Dulcie Moore; Ofc. Mgr.; 201 Caves Hwy.; P.O. Box 312; 97523; Josephine; P 18,000; M 120; (541) 592-3326; ivchamberofcommerce@cavenet.com; www.cavejunctionoregon.com.*

Central Point • *Central Point C/C & Visitors Center* • Cindy Hudson; Admin.; 150 Manzanita St.; 97502; Jackson; P 19,500; M 180; (541) 664-5301; Fax (541) 664-3667; cpchamber@qwestoffice.net; www.centralpointchamber.org*

Christmas Valley • *Christmas Valley C/C* • Willy Weaver; Pres.; P.O. Box 65; 97641; Lake; P 3,000; M 110; (541) 576-3838; Fax (541) 576-2387; info@christmasvalleychamber.org; www.christmasvalleychamber.org

Clackamas • *African American C/C of Oregon* • Roy Jay; Pres./CEO; P.O. Box 2979; 97015; Clackamas; P 1,000,000; M 950; (503) 244-5794; Fax (503) 293-2094; roy@africanamericanchamberofcommerce.com; www.blackchamber.info

Clackamas • *see Milwaukie*

Clatskanie • *Clatskanie C/C* • John Moore; Pres.; 155 W. Columbia River Hwy.; P.O. Box 635; 97016; Columbia; P 1,800; M 60; (503) 728-2502; Fax (503) 728-2135; www.clatskanie.com/chamber

Cloverdale • *Pacific City-Nestucca Valley C/C* • Bill Goodman; Pres.; P.O. Box 75; 97112; Tillamook; P 1,027; M 150; (503) 392-4340; Fax (503) 965-6579; manager@pcnvchamber.org; www.pacificcity.com

Columbia City • *see St. Helens*

Condon • *Condon C/C* • Nichole Schott; Pres.; 116 S. Main St.; P.O. Box 315; 97823; Gilliam; P 785; M 62; (541) 384-7777; info@condonchamber.org; www.condonchamber.org

Coos Bay • *Bay Area C/C & Visitors Center* • Timm Slater; Exec. Dir.; 145 Central Ave.; 97420; Coos; P 26,000; M 570; (541) 266-0868; (800) 824-8486; Fax (541) 267-6704; timmslater@oregonsbayarea.org; www.oregonsbayarea.org.*

Coquille • *Coquille C of C & Visitor Info. Center* • Doris Hutchinson; Dir.; 119 N. Birch St.; 97423; Coos; P 4,300; M 100; (541) 396-3414; Fax (541) 824-0138; coquillechamber@mycomspan.com; www.coquillechamber.net

Cornelius • *Cornelius C/C* • Joel Peterson; Exec. Dir.; 120 N. 13th Ave.; P.O. Box 681; 97113; Washington; P 10,785; M 70; (503) 359-4037; Fax (503) 992-1997; corneliuschamber@verizon.net; www.corneliuschamber.org

Corvallis • *Corvallis Benton Chamber Coalition* • Marcy Eastham; Pres.; 420 N.W. 2nd St.; 97330; Benton; P 54,890; M 700; (541) 757-1505; Fax (541) 766-2996; info@cbchambercoalition.com; www.cbchambercoalition.com*

Cottage Grove • *Cottage Grove Area C/C* • James E. Gilroy; Exec. Dir.; 700 E. Gibbs, Ste. C; 97424; Lane; P 9,100; M 271; (541) 942-2411; Fax (541) 767-0783; info@cgchamber.com; www.cgchamber.com*

Creswell • *Creswell C/C* • Arlene Macauley; Ofc. Admin.; 99 S. 1st St.; P.O. Box 577; 97426; Lane; P 5,000; M 80; (541) 895-5161; Fax (541) 895-5161; creswell-cc@centurytel.net; www.creswellchamber.com

Crooked River Ranch • *Crooked River Ranch–Terrebonne C/C* • Hope Johnson; Exec. Dir.; P.O. Box 1502; 97760; Jefferson; P 4,500; M 150; (541) 923-2679; info@crrchamber.com; www.crrchamber.com

Dallas • *Dallas Area C/C & Visitors Center* • Chelsea Pope; Exec. Dir.; 119 S.W. Court St.; P.O. Box 377; 97338; Polk; P 73,000; M 315; (503) 623-2564; Fax (503) 623-8936; chamber@dallasoregon.org; www.dallasoregon.org

Damascus • *see Milwaukie*

Deer Island • *see St. Helens*

Depoe Bay • *Depoe Bay C/C* • Carole Barkhurst; Mgr.; 223 S.W. Hwy. 101, Ste. B; P.O. Box 21; 97341; Lincoln; P 1,500; M 160; (541) 765-2889; Fax (541) 765-2836; info@depoebaychamber.org; www.depoebaychamber.org.

WHALE WATCHING CAPITOL OF OREGON. APRIL–WOODEN BOAT SHOW. SEPTEMBER–INDIAN SALMON BAKE. YEAR-ROUND STORMS AND SUNSETS.

Drain • *Drain C/C* • Janon Rogers; Pres.; P.O. Box 885; 97435; Douglas; P 1,100; M 60; (541) 787-7562; (541) 836-2867; www.354.com/drain

Eagle Point • *Eagle Point Upper Rogue C/C* • Bob Pinnel; Pres.; P.O. Box 1539; 97524; Jackson; P 8,700; M 97; (541) 826-6945; info@eaglepointchamber.org; www.eaglepointchamber.org*

Elgin • *Elgin C/C* • Christy Piercey; Pres.; P.O. Box 1001; 97827; Union; P 1,700; M 40; (541) 910-0880; (541) 786-1770; contact@elginoregonchamber.com; www.elginoregonchamber.com

Enterprise • *Wallowa County C/C* • Vicki Searles; Exec. Dir.; 115 Tejaka Ln.; P.O. Box 427; 97828; Wallowa; P 7,000; M 375; (541) 426-4622; (800) 585-4121; Fax (541) 426-2032; info@wallowacounty.org; www.wallowacountychamber.com

Estacada • *Estacada C/C* • Jordan Winthrop; Pres.; 475 S.E. Main; P.O. Box 298; 97023; Clackamas; P 2,855; M 164; (503) 630-3483; estacadachamber@cascadeaccess.com; www.estacadachamber.org

Eugene • *Eugene Area C/C* • David Hauser CCE; Pres.; 1401 Willamette St.; P.O. Box 1107; 97440; Lane; P 157,100; M 1,120; (541) 484-1314; Fax (541) 484-4942; info@eugenechamber.com; www.eugenechamber.com*

Florence • *Florence Area C/C* • Kady Sneddon; Dir.; 290 Hwy. 101; 97439; Lane; P 17,000; M 200; (541) 997-3128; Fax (541) 997-4101; florence@oregonfast.net; www.florencechamber.com*

Forest Grove • *Forest Grove C/C* • Teri Koerner; Exec. Dir.; 2417 Pacific Ave.; 97116; Washington; P 20,000; M 215; (503) 357-3006; Fax (503) 357-2367; info@fgchamber.org; www.fgchamber.org

Gladstone • *see Milwaukie*

Gold Beach • *Gold Beach C/C* • Sandy Vieira; Exec. Dir.; 29692 Ellensburg Ave., Ste. 7; P.O. Box 489; 97444; Curry; P 2,500; M 285; (541) 247-0923; Fax (541) 247-4394; info@goldbeachchamber.com; www.goldbeachchamber.com

Grants Pass • *Grants Pass/Josephine County C/C* • Jon Jordan; Pres./CEO; 1995 N.W. Vine St.; P.O. Box 970; 97528; Josephine; P 83,290; M 650; (541) 476-7717; Fax (541) 476-9574; gpcoc@grantspasschamber.org; www.grantspasschamber.org*

Gresham • *Gresham Area C/C* • CEO; 701 N.E. Hood Ave.; P.O. Box 1768; 97030; Multnomah; P 100,000; M 850; (503) 665-1131; Fax (503) 666-1041; gacc@greshamchamber.org; www.greshamchamber.org*

Happy Valley • *see Milwaukie*

Harney County • *see Burns*

Harrisburg • *see Junction City*

Hebo • *see Cloverdale*

Hemlock • *see Cloverdale*

Heppner • *Heppner C/C* • Sheryll Bates; Exec. Dir.; 123 N.W. May St.; P.O. Box 1232; 97836; Morrow; P 1,200; M 114; (541) 676-5536; Fax (541) 676-9650; heppnerchamber@centurytel.net; www.heppnerchamber.com

Hermiston • *Greater Hermiston C/C* • Debbie Pedro; Exec. Dir.; 415 S. Hwy. 395; P.O. Box 185; 97838; Umatilla; P 16,000; M 450; (541) 567-6151; Fax (541) 564-9109; info@hermistonchamber.com; www.hermistonchamber.com*

Hillsboro • *Hillsboro C/C* • Deanna Palm; Pres.; 5193 N.E. Elam Young Pkwy., Ste. A; 97124; Washington; P 91,000; M 775; (503) 648-1102; Fax (503) 681-0535; info@hillchamber.org; www.hillchamber.org*

Hood River • *Hood River County C/C* • Kerry Cobb; Exec. Dir.; 720 E. Port Marina Dr.; 97031; Hood River; P 21,000; M 450; (541) 386-2000; (800) 366-3530; Fax (541) 386-2057; info@hoodriver.org; www.hoodriver.org*

Huntington • *Huntington C/C* • Steve Stacy; P.O. Box 280; 97907; Baker; P 500; M 7; (541) 869-2529

Illinois Valley • *see Cave Junction*

Independence • *see Monmouth*

Jacksonville • *Jacksonville C of C & Visitors Info.* • Sandi Torrey; Dir. of Visitor Center; 185 N. Oregon St.; P.O. Box 33; 97530; Jackson; P 2,800; M 130; (541) 899-8118; Fax (541) 899-4462; chamber@jacksonvilleoregon.org; www.jacksonvilleoregon.org

John Day • *Grant County C/C & Visitors Center* • Sharon Mogg; Exec. Dir.; 301 W. Main St.; 97845; Grant; P 7,500; M 160; (541) 575-0547; (800) 769-5664; Fax (541) 575-1932; gcadmin@gcoregonlive.com; www.gcoregonlive.com

Johnson City • *see Milwaukie*

Joseph • *Joseph C/C* • Debbie Short; Ofc. Mgr.; 102 E. 1st St.; P.O. Box 13; 97846; Wallowa; P 1,150; M 110; (541) 432-1015; cjdays@eoni.com; www.chiefjosephdays.com

Junction City • *Junction City-Harrisburg C/C* • Rick Kissock; Exec. Dir.; 585 Greenwood St.; 97448; Lane; P 9,500; M 230; (541) 998-6154; Fax (541) 998-1037; info@jch-chamber.org; www.jch-chamber.org.*

Keizer • *Keizer C/C* • Christine Dieker; Exec. Dir.; 980 Chemawa Rd. N.E.; 97303; Marion; P 36,000; M 380; (503) 393-9111; Fax (503) 393-1003; christine@keizerchamber.com; www.keizerchamber.com.*

Klamath Falls • *Klamath County C/C* • Charles Massie; Exec. Dir.; 205 Riverside Dr., Ste. A; 97601; Klamath; P 69,000; M 610; (541) 884-5193; (877) KLAMATH; Fax (541) 884-5195; inquiry@klamath.org; www.klamath.org*

La Grande • *Union County C/C* • Judy Hector; Exec. Dir.; 102 Elm St.; 97850; Union; P 26,000; M 400; (541) 963-8588; (800) 848-9969; Fax (541) 963-3936; director@unioncountychamber.org; www.unioncountychamber.org*

La Pine • *La Pine C of C & Visitor Center* • Dan Varcoe; Exec. Dir.; 51425 Hwy. 97, Ste. A; P.O. Box 616; 97739; Deschutes; P 16,600; M 250; (541) 536-9771; Fax (541) 536-8410; director@lapine.org; www.lapine.org*

Lake Oswego · *Lake Oswego C/C* · Jerry L. Wheeler Sr.; CEO; 242 B Ave.; P.O. Box 368; 97034; Clackamas & Multnomah; P 39,000; M 600; (503) 636-3634; (866) 341-5253; Fax (503) 636-7427; info@lake-oswego.com; www.lake-oswego.com*

Lakeside · *Lakeside C/C* · Mrs. Jonie Reeder; Pres.; P.O. Box 333; 97449; Coos; P 1,200; M 50; (541) 759-3981; lkchamber@presys.com; www.lakesideoregonchambers.com

Lakeview · *Lake County C/C* · Caro Johnson; Exec. Dir.; 126 North E St.; 97630; Lake; P 3,500; M 225; (541) 947-6040; (877) 947-6040; Fax (541) 947-4892; information@lakecountychamber.org; www.lakecountychamber.org

Lebanon · *Lebanon Area C/C* · Shelley Garrett; Exec. Dir.; 1040 Park St.; 97355; Linn; P 15,400; M 346; (541) 258-7164; (877) 447-8873; Fax (541) 258-7166; shelley@lebanon-chamber.org; www.lebanon-chamber.org*

Lincoln City · *Lincoln City C/C* · Linda Roy; Exec. Dir.; 4039 N.W. Logan Rd. & Hwy. 101; 97367; Lincoln; P 9,000; M 370; (541) 994-3070; Fax (541) 994-8339; info@lcchamber.com; www.lcchamber.com*

Madras · *Madras-Jefferson County C/C* · Holli VanWert; Exec. Dir.; 274 S.W. 4th St.; P.O. Box 770; 97741; Jefferson; P 22,450; M 350; (541) 475-2350; (800) 967-3564; Fax (541) 475-4341; office@madraschamber.com; www.madraschamber.com.*

Manzanita · *see Wheeler*

McMinnville · *McMinnville C/C* · Phil Hutchinson; Pres./CEO; 41/ N.W. Adams St.; 97128; Yamhlll; P 32,000; M 460, (503) 472-6196; Fax (503) 472-6198; chamberinfo@mcminnville.org; www.mcminnville.org

Medford · *The Chamber of Medford/Jackson County* · Brad S. Hicks; Pres./CEO; 101 E. 8th St.; 97501; Jackson; P 202,310; M 1,330; (541) 779-4847; Fax (541) 776-4808; business@medfordchamber.com; www.medfordchamber.com.*

Mill City · *North Santiam C/C* · Nicole Miller; Exec. Dir.; P.O. Box 222; 97360; Linn & Marion; P 7,500; M 325; (503) 897-5000; director@nschamber.org; www.nschamber.org

Milton-Freewater · *Milton-Freewater Area C/C* · Cheryl York; Exec. Dir.; 157 S. Columbia; 97862; Umatilla; P 6,500; M 158; (541) 938-5563; Fax (541) 938-5564; mfmdfrog@charterinternet.com; www.mfchamber.com*

Milwaukie · *North Clackamas County C/C* · Wilda Parks ACE; Pres./CEO; 7740 S.E. Harmony Rd.; 97222; Clackamas; P 170,000; M 700; (503) 654-7777; Fax (503) 653-9515; info@yourchamber.com; www.yourchamber.com.*

Molalla · *Molalla Area C/C* · Sheri Kelly; Exec. Dir.; 105 E. Main St., Ste. 3; P.O. Box 578; 97038; Clackamas; P 13,000; M 200; (503) 829-6941; Fax (503) 829-7949; macc@molalla.net; www.molallachamber.com

Monmouth · *Monmouth-Independence C/C* · Marilyn Morton; Mgr.; 309 N. Pacific Ave.; 97361; Polk; P 16,500; M 175; (503) 838-4268; Fax (503) 838-6658; micc@micc-or.org; www.mitownchamber.org

Mount Angel · *Mount Angel C/C* · Mary Grant; Pres.; P.O. Box 221; 97362; Marion; P 3,700; M 120; (503) 845-9440; Fax (503) 845-6190; maureen@mtangeltel.net; www.mtangelchamber.org

Mount Hood · *see Welches*

Myrtle Creek · *Myrtle Creek–Tri City Area C/C* · Ted Romas; Pres.; P.O. Box 31; 97457; Douglas; P 8,000; M 100; (541) 863-3037; president@myrtlecreekchamber.com; www.myrtlecreekchamber.com

Nehalem · *see Wheeler*

Neskowin · *see Cloverdale*

Newberg · *Chehalem Valley C/C* · Sheryl Kelsh; Exec. Dir.; 415 E. Sheridan St.; 97132; Yamhill; P 20,500; M 460; (503) 538-2014; Fax (503) 538-2463; info@chehalemvalley.org; www.chehalemvalley.org*

Newport · *Greater Newport C/C* · Lorna Davis; Exec. Dir.; 555 S.W. Coast Hwy.; 97365; Lincoln; P 10,300; M 626; (541) 265-8801; (800) 262-7844; Fax (541) 265-5589; info@newportchamber.org; www.newportchamber.org*

North Bend · *see Coos Bay*

North Plains · *North Plains C/C* · Patti Burns; P.O. Box 152; 97133; Washington; P 1,700; M 51; (503) 647-2207; Fax (503) 647-5349; lochlolly1@aol.com; www.northplainschamberofcommerce.org

Nyssa · *Nyssa C/C & Ag.* · Susan Barton; Secy.; 105 Main St.; 97913; Malheur; P 3,200; M 85; (541) 372-3091; Fax (541) 372-3091; nyssachamber@nyssachamber.com; www.nyssachamber.com

Oakridge · *Oakridge-Westfir Area C/C* · Randy Dreiling; Exec. Dir.; P.O. Box 217; 97463; Lane; P 5,000; M 75; (541) 782-4146; Fax (541) 782-1081; info@oakridgechamber.com; www.oakridgechamber.com

Ontario · *Ontario C/C* · John Breidenbach; Pres./CEO; 876 S.W. 4th Ave.; 97914; Malheur; P 11,400; M 340; (541) 889-8012; Fax (541) 889-8331; ceo@ontariochamber.com; www.ontariochamber.com.*

Oregon City · *Oregon City C/C* · Amber Holveck; Exec. Dir.; 1201 Washington St.; P.O. Box 226; 97045; Clackamas; P 30,000; M 300, (503) 656-1619; Fax (503) 656-2274; chamberinfo@oregoncity.org; www.oregoncity.org*

Pacific City · *see Cloverdale*

Pendleton · *Pendleton C/C* · Leslie Carnes; Exec. Dir.; 501 S. Main St.; 97801; Umatilla; P 17,000; M 470; (541) 276-7411; (800) 547-8911; Fax (541) 276-8849; info@pendletonchamber.com; www.pendletonchamber.com*

Philomath · *Philomath Area C/C* · Nancy Elwer; Dir.; P.O. Box 606; 97370; Benton; P 4,400; M 100; (541) 929-2454; director@philomathchamber.org; www.philomathchamber.org*

Phoenix · *Phoenix C of C & Info. Center* · 205 Fern Valley Rd., Ste. M-1; P.O. Box 998; 97535; Jackson; P 4,740; M 120; (541) 535-6956; Fax (541) 535-5210; info@phoenixoregonchamber.org; www.phoenixoregonchamber.org

Port Orford · *Port Orford/North Curry County C/C* · David Smith; Pres.; P.O. Box 637; 97465; North Curry; P 2,000; M 60; (541) 332-8055; Fax (541) 332-8055; chamber@portorfordchamber.com; www.portorfordchamber.com

Portland · *African American C/C of Oregon* · Roy Jay; Exec. Dir.; 4300 N.E. Fremont St., Ste. 220; 97213; Clackamas, Multnomah & Washington; P 1,000,000; M 950; (503) 244-5794; Fax (503) 293-2094; roy@africanamericanchamberofcommerce.com; www.blackchamber.info

Portland · *Portland Bus. Alliance-Greater Portland's C/C* · Sandra McDonough; Pres./CEO; 200 S.W. Market St., Ste. 150; 97201; Multnomah; P 2,121,910; M 1,400; (503) 224-8684; Fax (503) 323-9186; info@portlandalliance.com; www.portlandalliance.com*

Prineville · *Prineville-Crook County C/C & Visitors Center* · 102 N.W. 2nd St.; 97754; Crook; P 26,000; M 350; (541) 447-6304; Fax (541) 447-6537; info@visitprineville.com; www.visitprineville.com.*

Ranier · *Ranier C/C* · Judith Taylor; Pres.; P.O. Box 1085; 97048; Columbia; P 1,750; M 50; (503) 556-7212; Fax (503) 556-1855

Redmond · *Redmond Chamber & CVB* · Eric Sande; Exec. Dir.; 446 S.W. 7th St.; 97756; Deschutes; P 25,000; M 718; (541) 923-5191; Fax (541) 923-6442; info@visitredmondoregon.com; www.visitredmondoregon.com*

Reedsport · *Reedsport/Winchester Bay C/C* · Robin Dollar; Mgr.; 855 Hwy. Ave.; P.O. Box 11; 97467; Douglas; P 5,000; M 150; (541) 271-3495; (800) 247-2155; Fax (541) 271-3496; info@reedsportcc.org; www.reedsportcc.org.*

Rockaway Beach · *Rockaway Beach C/C* · Dave Farr; Pres.; 103 S. 1st St.; P.O. Box 198; 97136; Tillamook; P 1,200; M 100; (503) 355-8108; answers@rockawaybeach.net; www.rockawaybeach.net

Rogue River · *Rogue River Area C/C* · Dean Stirm; Pres.; 8898 Rogue River Hwy.; P.O. Box 457; 97537; Jackson; P 2,085; M 100; (541) 582-0242; info@rrchamber.cc; www.rrchamber.cc

Roseburg · *Roseburg Area C/C* · Debbie Fromdahl; Pres./CEO; 410 S.E. Spruce St.; P.O. Box 1026; 97470; Douglas; P 40,000; M 660; (541) 672-2648; (800) 444-9584; Fax (541) 673-7868; debbie@roseburgareachamber.org; www.roseburgareachamber.org.

Salem · *Salem Area C/C* · Michael T. McLaran; CEO; 1110 Commercial St. N.E.; 97301; Marion; P 165,000; M 1,270; (503) 581-1466; Fax (503) 581-0972; info@salemchamber.org; www.salemchamber.org*

Sandlake · *see Cloverdale*

Sandy · *Sandy Area C/C* · Hollis MacLean-Wenzel; Exec. Dir.; 38963 Pioneer Blvd.; P.O. Box 536; 97055; Clackamas; P 8,200; M 275; (503) 668-4006; Fax (503) 668-3459; chamber@sandyoregonchamber.org; www.sandyoregonchamber.org*

Scappoose · *see St. Helens*

Seaside · *Seaside C/C* · Al Smiles; Exec. Dir.; 7 N. Roosevelt; P.O. Box 7; 97138; Clatsop; P 6,300; M 370; (503) 738-6391; (800) 444-6740; Fax (503) 738-5732; info@seasidechamber.com; www.seasidechamber.com

Sherwood · *Sherwood C/C* · Nancy Bruton; Exec. Dir.; 16065 S.W. Railroad St.; P.O. Box 805; 97140; Washington; P 16,700; M 380; (503) 625-7800; Fax (503) 625-7550; chamber@sherwoodchamber.org; www.sherwoodchamber.org*

Silverton · *Silverton Area C/C* · Stacy Palmer; Exec. Dir.; 426 S. Water St.; P.O. Box 257; 97381; Marion; P 9,600; M 290; (503) 873-5615; Fax (503) 873-7144; info@silvertonchamber.org; www.silvertonchamber.org*

Sisters · *Sisters Area C/C* · Erin Borla; Exec. Dir.; 291 E. Main Ave.; P.O. Box 430; 97759; Deschutes; P 9,000; M 400; (541) 549-0251; Fax (541) 549-4253; info@sisterscountry.com; www.sisterscountry.com

Springfield · *Springfield Area C/C* · Dan Egan; Exec. Dir.; 101 South A St.; P.O. Box 155; 97477; Lane; P 58,000; M 1,000; (541) 746-1651; Fax (541) 726-4727; info@springfield-chamber.org; www.springfield-chamber.org*

St. Helens · *South Columbia County C/C* · Tina Kammerzelt; Ofc. Mgr.; 2194 Columbia Blvd.; 97051; Columbia; P 25,000; M 250; (503) 397-0685; Fax (503) 397-7196; mgr@sccchamber.org; www.sccchamber.org*

Stayton · *Stayton-Sublimity C/C* · Kelly Schreiber; Exec. Dir.; 175 E. High St.; P.O. Box 121; 97383; Marion; P 10,000; M 320; (503) 769-3464; Fax (503) 769-3463; sscoc@wvi.com; www.staytonsublimitychamber.org

Sunriver · *Sunriver Area C/C* · P.O. Box 3246; 97707; Deschutes; P 9,000; M 250; (541) 593-8149; Fax (541) 593-3581; info@sunriverchamber.com; www.sunriverchamber.com

Sutherlin · *Sutherlin Area C/C* · Ann Laycock; Pres.; 100 E. Central; P.O. Box 1404; 97479; P 7,300; M 120; (541) 459-3280; www.sutherlinchamber.com

Sweet Home · *Sweet Home C/C* · Andrea Culy; Exec. Mgr.; 1575 Main St.; 97386; Linn; P 8,300; M 150; (541) 367-6186; Fax (541) 367-6150; info@sweethomechamber.org; www.sweethomechamber.org*

The Dalles · *The Dalles Area C/C* · Dana Schmidling; Exec. Dir.; 404 W. 2nd St.; 97058; Wasco; P 13,500; M 504; (541) 296-2231; (800) 255-3385; Fax (541) 296-1688; info@thedalleschamber.com; www.thedalleschamber.com*

Tierra del Mar · *see Cloverdale*

Tigard · *Tigard Area C/C* · Debi Mollahan; CEO; 12345 S.W. Main St.; 97223; Washington; P 49,500; M 430; (503) 639-1656; Fax (503) 639-6302; info@tigardchamber.org; www.tigardchamber.org

Tillamook · *Tillamook Area C/C* · Andy Neal; Exec. Dir.; 3705 Hwy. 101 N.; 97141; Tillamook; P 4,600; M 300; (503) 842-7525; Fax (503) 842-7526; tillchamber@oregoncoast.com; www.gotillamook.com

Toledo · *Toledo C/C* · Don Amberg; Dir.; P.O. Box 249; 97391; Lincoln; P 3,580; M 100; (541) 336-3183; info@visittoledooregon.com; www.visittoledooregon.com

Troutdale · *West Columbia Gorge C/C* · John Leamy; Op. Dir.; 226 W. Historic Columbia River Hwy.; P.O. Box 245; 97060; Multnomah; P 15,000; M 225; (503) 669-7473; Fax (503) 492-3613; jleamy@westcolumbiagorgechamber.com; www.westcolumbiagorgechamber.com*

Tualatin · *Tualatin C/C* · Linda Moholt; CEO; 18791 S.W. Martinazzi Ave.; P.O. Box 701; 97062; Clackamas & Washington; P 28,000; M 325; (503) 692-0780; Fax (503) 692-6955; chamber@tualatinchamber.com; www.tualatinchamber.com*

Umatilla · *Umatilla C/C* · Karen Hutchinson-Talaski; Exec. Dir.; 100 Cline Ave.; P.O. Box 67; 97882; Umatilla; P 6,500; M 71; (541) 922-4825; Fax (541) 922-4825; karen@umatillachamber.net; www.umatillaoregonchamber.org

Vale · *Vale C/C* · Logan Hamilton; Pres.; 255 A St. W.; P.O. Box 661; 97918; Malheur; P 2,010; M 92; (541) 473-3800; Fax (541) 473-3800; info@valechamber.com; www.valechamber.com.

Veneta · *Fern Ridge C/C* · Gina Haley-Morrell; Pres.; 24949 Hwy. 126; P.O. Box 335; 97487; Lane; P 4,700; M 140; (541) 935-8443; Fax (541) 935-1164; staff@fernridgechamber.com; www.fernridgechamber.com

Vernonia · *Vernonia Area C/C* · Donna Webb; Pres.; 1001 Bridge St.; 97064; Columbia; P 2,300; M 75; (503) 429-6081; Fax (503) 429-4232; info@vernoniachamber.org; www.vernoniachamber.org

Waldport · *Waldport C/C & Visitor Center* · Ron Remund; Pres.; 620 N.W. Spring St.; P.O. Box 669; 97394; Lincoln; P 2,500; M 100; (541) 563-2133; Fax (541) 563-6326; chamber@peak.org; www.waldport-chamber.com

Warren · *see St. Helens*

Wedderburn · *see Gold Beach*

Welches · *Mount Hood Area C/C* · Coni Scott; Pres.; P.O. Box 819; 97067; Clackamas; P 8,000; M 138; (503) 622-3017; Fax (503) 622-4881; chamber@mthood.org; www.mthood.org

West Linn · *West Linn C/C* · Linda Neace; Pres.; 5695 Hood St.; 97068; Clackamas; P 24,482; M 220; (503) 655-6744; chamberinfo@westlinnchamber.com; www.westlinnchamber.com

Westfir · *see Oakridge*

Wheeler · *Nehalem Bay Area C/C & Visitor Center* · Deanna Hendricks; Dir.; P.O. Box 601; 97147; Tillamook; P 1,200; M 70; (503) 368-5100; (877) 368-5100; Fax (503) 368-4641; nehalem@nehalemtel.net; www.nehalembaychamber.com

Willamina · *Willamina Coastal Hills C/C* · Dennis Ulrich; V.P.; P.O. Box 411; 97396; Polk & Yamhill; P 1,850; M 35; (503) 876-4222; Fax (503) 876-6132; www.willamina.org

Wilsonville · *Wilsonville C/C* · Steve Gilmore; CEO; 29600 S.W. Park Pl.; P.O. Box 3737; 97070; Clackamas & Washington; P 20,000; M 375; (503) 682-0411; (800) 647-3843; Fax (503) 682-4189; info@wilsonvillechamber.com; www.wilsonvillechamber.com*

Winchester Bay · *see Reedsport*

Winston · *Winston-Dillard Area C/C & Visitors Info. Center* · Tamara Lee; Pres.; 30 N.W. Glenhart; P.O. Box 68; 97496; Douglas; P 10,000; M 100; (541) 679-0118; Fax (541) 679-4270; winston vic@charter.net; www.winstonoregon.net

Woodburn · *Woodburn Area C/C* · Don Judson; Exec. Dir.; 124 W. Lincoln St.; P.O. Box 194; 97071; Marion; P 22,000; M 260; (503) 982-8221; Fax (503) 982-8410; welcome@woodburnchamber.org; www.woodburnchamber.org

Woods · *see Cloverdale*

Yachats · *Yachats Area C/C & Visitors Center* · Beverly Wilson; Exec. Dir.; P.O. Box 728; 97498; Lincoln; P 650; M 205; (541) 547-3530; (800) 929-0477; info@yachats.org; www.yachats.org

Pennsylvania

The Pennsylvania Chamber of Bus. & Ind. · Gene Barr; V.P.; 417 Walnut St.; Harrisburg; 17101; Cumberland, Dauphin & Perry; P 12,448,279; M 9,000; (717) 255-3252; (800) 225-7224; Fax (717) 255-3298; info@pachamber.org; www.pachamber.org.

Adams County · *see Gettysburg*

Allegheny · *see Pittsburgh*

Allentown · *Greater Lehigh Valley C/C* · Tony Iannelli; Pres./CEO; 840 Hamilton St., Ste. 205; 18101; Lehigh; P 579,156; M 5,000; (610) 841-4582; (610) 841-5800; Fax (610) 437-4907; info@lehighvalleychamber.org; www.lehighvalleychamber.org*

Altoona · *Blair County C/C* · Joseph D. Hurd; Pres./CEO; 3900 Industrial Park Dr., Ste. 12; 16602; Blair; P 135,000; M 1,000; (814) 943-8151; Fax (814) 943-5239; chamber@blairchamber.com; www.blairchamber.com*

Ambridge · *Ambridge Area C/C* · 562 Merchant St.; 15003; Beaver; P 8,000; M 160; (724) 266-3040; www.ambridge chamberofcommerce.com

Antrim · *see Greencastle*

Apollo · *see Kittanning*

Archbald · *see Carbondale*

Aspinwall · *Aspinwall C/C* · Harold Sankey; Pres.; 217 Commercial Ave.; 15215; Allegheny; P 2,960; M 125; (412) 781-0213; www.aspinwallpa.com

Athens · *see Sayre*

Audubon · *see Eagleville*

Baldwin · *see Pittsburgh–Brentwood Baldwin Whitehall C/C*

Bangor · *see Pen Argyl*

Beaver · *Beaver County C/C* · Pres.; 300 S. Walnut Ln., Ste. 202; 15009; Beaver; P 185,000; M 600; (724) 775-3944; Fax (724) 728-9737; info@bcchamber.com; www.bcchamber.com*

Bedford · *Bedford County C/C* · Kellie Goodman Shaffer; Exec. Dir.; 137 E. Pitt St.; 15522; Bedford; P 50,000; M 550; (814) 623-2233; Fax (814) 623-6089; linda@bedfordcountychamber.org; www.bedfordcountychamber.org.

Bellefonte · *Bellefonte Intervalley Area C/C* · Gary V. Hoover; Exec. Dir.; 320 W. High St.; Train Station; 16823; Centre; P 120,000; M 200; (814) 355-2917; Fax (814) 355-2761; bellefontecoc@aol.com; www.bellefontechamber.org

Bellevue · *North Suburban C/C* · Connie Rankin; 547 Lincoln Ave.; 15202; Allegheny; P 30,000; M 60; (412) 761-2113; www.northsuburbancoc.org

Bensalem · *see Fairless Hills*

Berlin · *see Somerset*

Berwick · *see Bloomsburg*

Bethlehem · *see Allentown*

Birdsboro · *see Pottstown*

Bloomsburg · *Columbia Montour C/C* · Fred Gaffney; Pres.; 238 Market St.; 17815; Columbia; P 82,500; M 400; (570) 784-2522; Fax (570) 784-2661; chamber@columbiamontourchamber.com; www.columbiamontourchamber.com.*

Boyertown · *see Pottstown*

Brackenridge · *Allegheny Valley C/C* · Mary Bowlin; Pres.; 1030 Broadview Blvd., Ste. 1; 15014; Allegheny; P 50,000; M 400; (724) 224-3400; Fax (724) 224-3442; staff@alleghenyvalley chamber.com; www.alleghenyvalleychamber.com

Bradford · *Bradford Area C/C* · Ron Orris; Exec. Dir.; 121 Main St.; 16701; McKean; P 19,435; M 340; (814) 368-7115; Fax (814) 368-6233; info@bradfordchamber.com; www.bradfordchamber.com

Brentwood · *see Pittsburgh–Brentwood Baldwin Whitehall C/C*

Bridgeport · *see Eagleville*

Bridgeville · *see Pittsburgh–South West Comm. C/C*

Brockway · *see DuBois*

Brookville · *Brookville Area C/C* · 100 Main St., Ste. A; 15825; Jefferson; P 4,200; M 285; (814) 849-8448; Fax (814) 849-8455; brookvillechamber@windstream.net; www.brookvillechamber.com

Brownsville · *Greater Brownsville Area C/C* · 325 Market St.; 15417; Fayette; P 6,000; M 70; (724) 785-4160; Fax (724) 785-5631

Butler · *Butler County C/C* · Stan Kosciuszko; Pres.; 101 E. Diamond St., Ste. 116; P.O. Box 1082; 16003; Butler; P 184,000; M 650; (724) 283-2222; Fax (724) 283-0224; www.butlercounty chamber.com

California · *California Area C/C* · Mark Koehler; Pres.; P.O. Box 311; 15419; Washington; P 5,207; M 20; (724) 938-3470

Camp Hill · *West Shore C/C* · Kathleen Mangan; Pres./CEO; 4211 Trindle Rd.; 17011; Cumberland; P 172,000; M 900; (717) 761-0702; Fax (717) 761-4315; wschamber@wschamber.org; www.wschamber.org

Canonsburg · *Greater Canonsburg C/C* · Consuelo Fossum; Admin. Secy.; 169 E. Pike St.; 15317; Washington; P 12,000; M 200; (724) 745-1812; Fax (724) 745-5211; info@canonchamber.com; www.canonchamber.com

Canton · *Canton Area C/C* · Jodi Wesneski; Pres.; P.O. Box 153; 17724; Bradford; P 2,000; M 55; (570) 364-2600; cantonarea chamberofcommerce@yahoo.com; www.cantonareachamberof commerce.com

Carbondale · *Greater Carbondale C/C* · Steve Ursich; Pres.; 27 N. Main St.; 18407; Lackawanna; P 11,000; M 400; (570) 282-1690; Fax (570) 282-1206; info@carbondale-pa-coc.com; www.carbondale-pa-coc.com

Carlisle · *Greater Carlisle Area C/C* · Michelle Crowley; Pres.; 212 N. Hanover St.; P.O. Box 572; 17013; Cumberland; P 72,000; M 670; (717) 243-4515; Fax (717) 243-4446; info@carlisle chamber.org; www.carlislechamber.org*

Cecil · *see Canonsburg*

Chambersburg · *Greater Chambersburg C/C* · David G. Sciamanna; Pres.; 100 Lincoln Way East, Ste. A; 17201; Franklin; P 50,000; M 1,000; (717) 264-7101; Fax (717) 267-0399; chamber@chambersburg.org; www.chambersburg.org*

Champion · *see Donegal*

Charleroi · *Mon Valley Reg. C/C* · Debra Keefer; Exec. Dir.; One Chamber Plaza; 15022; Washington; P 50,000; M 275; (724) 483-3507; Fax (724) 489-1045; info@mvrchamber.org; www.mvrchamber.org

Chester County · *see Malvern*

Childs · *see Carbondale*

Clairton · *see McKeesport*

Clarion · *Clarion Area Chamber of Bus. & Ind.* · Tracy J. Becker CFEE; Exec. Dir.; 21 N. 6th Ave.; 16214; Clarion; P 39,990; M 294; (814) 226-9161; (814) 226-9632; Fax (814) 226-4903; tracy@clarionpa.com; www.clarionpa.com

Clearfield · *Clearfield C/C* · Amy Potter; Exec. Dir.; 125 E. Market St.; 16830; Clearfield; P 18,000; M 380; (814) 765-7567; Fax (814) 765-6948; info@clearfieldchamber.com; www.clearfieldchamber.com

Clifford · *see Carbondale*

Clinton County · *see Lock Haven*

Coatesville · *Western Chester County C/C* · Donna Siter; Exec. Dir.; 50 S. First Ave.; 19320; Chester; P 12,000; M 275; (610) 384-9550; Fax (610) 384-9550; info@westernchestercounty.com; www.westernchestercounty.com

Collegeville · *Perkiomen Valley C/C* · Renee Blomstrom; Dir. of PR; 351 E. Main St.; 19426; Montgomery; P 65,000; M 500; (610) 489-6660; Fax (610) 454-1270; info@pvchamber.net; www.pvchamber.net*

Collier Twp. · *see Pittsburgh—South West Comm. C/C*

Columbia · *Susquehanna Valley C/C & Visitors Center* · Kathleen L. Hohenadel; Exec. Dir.; 445 Linden St.; P.O. Box 510; 17512; Lancaster & York; P 15,000; M 250; (717) 684-5249; Fax (717) 684-5142; svcc@parivertowns.com; www.parivertowns.com

Confluence · *see Somerset*

Connellsville · *Greater Connellsville C/C* · June Newill; Ofc. Mgr.; 923 W. Crawford Ave.; 15425; Fayette; P 30,000; M 215; (724) 628-5500; Fax (724) 628-5676; info@greaterconnellsville.org; www.greaterconnellsville.org

Coraopolis · *see Pittsburgh-Pittsburgh Airport Area C/C*

Corry · *Corry Area C/C* · Lori Trisket; Exec. Dir.; 221 N. Center St.; 16407; Crawford, Erie & Warren; P 10,000; M 110; (814) 665-9925; Fax (814) 665-9925; cacc@velocity.net; www.corrychamber.org

Coudersport · *Coudersport Area C/C* · Stan Swank; Pres.; 6 E. 2nd St.; P.O. Box 261; 16915; Potter; P 5,500; M 115; (814) 274-8165; Fax (814) 274-8165; cacoc@zitomedia.net; www.coudersport.org

Cranberry Township · *THE CHAMBER of Commerce Inc.* · Susan H. Balla; Exec. Dir.; 2525 Rochester Rd., Ste. 200; 16066; Allegheny; P 25,000; M 1,100; (724) 776-4949; Fax (724) 776-5344; naccc@naccc.com; www.naccc.com*

Crescent Twp. · *see Pittsburgh—Pittsburgh Airport Area C/C*

Cresson · *Borough of Cresson C/C* · Veronica Harkins; Secy.; P.O. Box 113; 16630; Cambria; P 5,000; M 65; (814) 886-8100; info@cressonarea.com; www.cressonarea.com

Cressona · *see Pottsville*

Danville · *see Bloomsburg*

Delmont · *see Greensburg*

Donegal · *Mountain Laurel C/C* · Sarah Harkam; Pres.; P.O. Box 154; 15628; Westmoreland; P 15,000; M 180; (724) 593-8900; (888) 455-8900; Fax (724) 593-8900; mlcc@lhtot.com; www.mountainlaurelchamber.com

Donora · *Donora C/C* · 638 McKean Ave.; 15033; Washington; P 6,500; M 100; (724) 379-5929

Dormont · *see Pittsburgh—South Hills C/C*

Downingtown · *Downingtown Area C/C* · Alane Butler; Exec. Dir.; 38 W. Lancaster Ave.; 19335; Chester; P 9,000; M 300; (610) 269-1523; Fax (610) 269-8713; info@downingtownchamber.org; www.downingtownchamber.org

Doylestown · *Central Bucks C/C* · Dr. Vail P. Garvin; Exec. Dir.; Bailiwick, Ste. 23; 252 W. Swamp Rd.; 18901; Bucks; P 44,984; M 2,600; (215) 348-3913; (215) 345-7051; Fax (215) 348-7154; info@centralbuckschamber.com; www.centralbuckschamber.com

Dravosburg · *Borough of Dravosburg* · Brenda Honick; 226 Maple Ave.; 15034; Allegheny; P 2,000; M 6; (412) 466-5200; Fax (412) 466-6027

DuBois · *Greater DuBois C/C* · Nancy Micks; Pres./CEO; 3 S. Brady St., Ste. 205; 15801; Clearfield & Jefferson; P 38,000; M 462; (814) 371-5010; Fax (814) 371-5005; dacc@duboispachamber.com; www.duboispachamber.com

Duquesne · *see McKeesport*

Eagleville · *Montgomery County C/C* · Albert Paschall; Managing Dir.; The Historic King of Prussia Inn; P.O. Box 200; 19408; Montgomery; P 600,000; M 1,550; (610) 265-1776; Fax (610) 265-0473; info@montgomerycountychamber.org; www.montgomerycountychamber.org*

East Bangor · *see Pen Argyl*

East Greenville · *Upper Perkiomen Valley C/C* · Luanne Stauffer; Exec. Dir.; 300 Main St.; 18041; Montgomery; P 18,638; M 300; (215) 679-3336; Fax (215) 679-2624; info@upvchamber.org; www.upvchamber.org*

Easton · *see Allentown*

Elizabethtown · *Elizabethtown C/C* · Beth Wood Bergman; Exec. Dir.; 29 S. Market St., Ste. 101; 17022; Lancaster; P 30,000; M 220; (717) 361-7188; Fax (717) 361-7666; info@elizabethtowncoc.com; www.elizabethtowncoc.com

Elizabethville · *Northern Dauphin Reg. C/C* · Mandy Carl; Secy.; P. O. Box 218; 17023; Dauphin; P 15,000; M 70; (717) 362-1280; ndrcc@ndrcc.org; www.ndrcc.org

Ellwood City · *Ellwood City Area C/C* · Thomas Stachura; Exec. Dir.; 314 Fifth St.; 16117; Beaver & Lawrence; P 8,800; M 175; (724) 758-5501; Fax (724) 758-2143; info@ellwoodchamber.org; www.ellwoodchamber.org

Emmaus · *see Allentown*

Emporium • *Cameron County C/C* • Tina Lorson; Exec. Dir.; 34 E. Fourth St.; 15834; Cameron; P 5,913; M 92; (814) 486-4314; cameroncountychamber@windstream.net; www.cameron countychamber.org

Ephrata • *Ephrata Area C/C* • Michelle Stout; Pres.; 16 E. Main St., Ste. 1; 17522; Lancaster; P 125,000; M 232; (717) 738-9010; Fax (717) 738-9012; info@ephrata-area.org; www.ephrata-area.org

Erie • *Erie Reg. Chamber & Growth Partnership* • Jim Dible; Pres./CEO; 208 E. Bayfront Pkwy., Ste. 100; 16507; Erie; P 105,000; M 850; (814) 454-7191; Fax (814) 459-0241; jdible@eriepa.com; www.eriepa.com*

Export • *see Greensburg*

Exton • *Exton Region C/C* • Robert Johnston; Pres./CEO; 967 E. Swedesford Rd., Ste. 409; 19341; Chester; P 50,000; M 650; (610) 644-4985; Fax (610) 644-2370; chamber@ercc.net; www.ercc.net

Eynon • *see Carbondale*

Fairless Hills • *Lower Bucks County C/C* • Clark L. Shuster; Pres./CEO; 409 Hood Blvd.; 19030; Bucks; P 600,000; M 1,600; (215) 943-7400; Fax (215) 943-7404; info@lbccc.org; www.lbccc.org*

Falls Creek • *see DuBois*

Findlay Twp. • *see Pittsburgh–Pittsburgh Airport Area C/C*

Forest City • *see Carbondale*

Forest Hills • *see McKeesport*

Franklin • *Franklin Area C/C* • Lynn Cochran; Exec. Dir.; 1259 LIberty St.; 16323; Venango; P 7,200; M 578; (814) 432-5823; Fax (814) 437-2453; administrator@franklinareachamber.org; www.franklinareachamber.org.

Frazer • *see Malvern-Great Valley Reg. C/C*

Freeland • *Freeland C/C* • Charles Reczkowski; Pres.; P.O. Box 31; 18224; Luzerne; P 4,200; M 55; (570) 636-0670; www.freeland chamber.org

Galeton • *Galeton Area C/C* • Janet Dimon; Pres.; P.O. Box 154; 16922; Potter; P 3,000; M 60; (814) 435-8737; visitgaleton@yahoo.com; www.visitgaleton.com

Gettysburg • *Gettysburg Adams C/C* • Carrie Stuart; Pres.; 18 Carlisle St., Ste. 203; 17325; Adams; P 100,779; M 610; (717) 334-8151; Fax (717) 334-3368; info@gettysburg-chamber.org; www.gettysburg-chamber.org

Gibsonia • *Twp. of Richland* • Herbert C. Dankmyer; Chrmn.; 4019 Dickey Rd.; 15044; Allegheny; P 9,231; (724) 443-5921; Fax (724) 443-8860; www.richland.pa.us

Girard • *Girard-Lake City C/C* • 522 Main St.; 16417; Erie; P 6,000; M 50; (814) 774-3535; chamberbiz@msn.com; www.girard-lakecity.com

Glenside • *Greater Glenside C/C* • Barbara Nye; Pres.; 452 N. Easton Rd.; 19038; Montgomery; P 44,000; M 370; (215) 887-3110; info@glensidechamber.org; www.glensidechamber.org

Gratz • *see Elizabethville*

Greencastle • *Greencastle-Antrim C/C* • Joel Fridgen; Exec. Dir.; 217 E. Baltimore St.; P.O. Box 175; 17225; Franklin; P 17,500; M 350; (717) 597-4610; Fax (717) 597-0709; info@greencastle pachamber.org; www.greencastlepachamber.org

Greensburg • *Westmoreland C/C* • Thomas L. Sochacki; Pres.; 241 Tollgate Hill Rd.; 15601; Westmoreland; P 250,000; M 1,000; (724) 834-2900; Fax (724) 837-7635; info@westmoreland chamber.com; www.westmorelandchamber.com*

Greentown • *see Hamlin*

Greenville • *Greenville Area C/C* • Frederick Kiser; Comm. Liaison; 182 Main St.; P.O. Box 350; 16125; Mercer; P 15,000; M 280; (724) 588-7150; Fax (724) 588-2013; info@greenville chamber-pa.com; www.greenvillechamber-pa.com

Grove City • *Grove City Area C/C* • Beth Black; Exec. Dir.; 119 S. Broad St.; 16127; Mercer; P 15,000; M 250; (724) 458-6410; Fax (724) 458-6841; gcchamber@shopgrovecity.com; www.shopgrovecity.com

Halifax • *see Elizabethville*

Hamlin • *Southern Wayne Reg. C/C* • Patty Blaum; Exec. Dir.; P.O. Box 296; 18427; Wayne; P 15,000; M 225; (570) 689-4199; Fax (570) 689-4391; swrchamber@swrchamber.org; www.swrchamber.org

Hanover • *Hanover Area C/C* • Gary Laird; Pres.; 146 Carlisle St.; 17331; York; P 55,000; M 650; (717) 637-6130; Fax (717) 637-9127; office@hanoverchamber.com; www.hanoverchamber.com*

Harmony • *see Zelienople*

Harrisburg • *Harrisburg Reg. C/C & CREDC* • David E. Black; Pres./CEO; 3211 N. Front St., Ste. 201; 17110; Dauphin; P 550,000; M 1,500; (717) 232-4099; (877) 883-8339; Fax (717) 232-5184; info@hbgrc.org; www.HarrisburgRegionalChamber.org.*

Hatboro • *Greater Hatboro C/C* • Christ Dubil; Pres.; 220 S. York Rd.; 19040; Montgomery; P 7,300; M 600; (215) 956-9540; Fax (215) 956-9635; office@hatborochamber.org; hatborochamber.org

Hatfield • *Hatfield C/C* • Larry Stevens; Exec. Dir.; P.O. Box 445; 19440; Montgomery; P 20,000; M 500; (215) 855-3335; Fax (215) 855-3335; admin@hatfieldchamber.com; www.hatfieldchamber.com

Hawley • *Pocono Lake Region C/C* • Debbie Gillette; Exec. Dir.; 2512 Rte. 6, Ste. 2; 18428; Pike & Wayne; P 30,000; M 260; (570) 226-3191; Fax (570) 226-9387; visit@lakeregioncc.com; www.lakeregioncc.com

Hazleton • *Greater Hazleton C/C* • Donna Palermo; Pres.; 20 W. Broad St.; 18201; Luzerne; P 80,000; M 750; (570) 455-1509; Fax (570) 450-2013; dpalermo@hazletonchamber.org; www.hazletonchamber.org.*

Hershey • *see Harrisburg*

Homestead • *see Steel Valley*

Honesdale • *Wayne County C/C* • Donna LaBar; Exec. Dir.; 32 Commercial St.; 18431; Wayne; P 48,000; M 500; (570) 253-1960; (800) 433-9008; Fax (570) 253-1517; exec@waynecountycc.com; www.waynecountycc.com

Horsham • *see Lansdale*

Houston • *see Canonsburg*

Hummelswharf • *see Milton*

Huntingdon • *Huntingdon County C/C* • Yvonne Martin; Exec. Dir.; 500 Allegheny St.; 16652; Huntingdon; P 46,000; M 370; (814) 643-1110; Fax (814) 643-1115; mail@huntingdonchamber.com; www.huntingdonchamber.com

Indiana • *Indiana County C/C* • Dana P. Henry; Pres.; 1019 Philadelphia St.; 15701; Indiana; P 90,000; M 800; (724) 465-2511; Fax (724) 465-3706; dphenry@wpia.net; www.indianapa.com/chamber*

Irwin • *Norwin C/C* • Rosanne Barry Novotnak; Pres.; 321 Main St.; 15642; Westmoreland; P 34,000; M 350; (724) 863-0888; Fax (724) 863-5133; info@norwinchamber.com; www.norwinchamber.com*

Jeannette • *see Greensburg*

Jefferson Borough • *see McKeesport*

Jenkintown · *Eastern Montgomery County C/C* · Wendy Klinghoffer; Exec. Dir.; 436 Old York Rd.; 19046; Montgomery; P 100,000; M 700; (215) 887-5122; info@emccc.org; www.emccc.org*

Jermyn · *see Carbondale*

Jim Thorpe · *see Lehighton*

Johnsonburg · *Johnsonburg C/C* · Ron King; Exec. Dir.; 186 East Ave.; 15845; Elk; P 3,583; M 95; (814) 965-2039; Fax (814) 965-3215

Johnstown · *Greater Johnstown/Cambria County C/C Inc.* · Robert F. Layo; Pres./CEO; 245 Market St., Ste. 100; 15901; Cambria; P 145,000; M 712; (814) 536-5107; (800) 790-4522; Fax (814) 539-5800; chamber@johnstownchamber.com; www.johnstownchamber.com.*

Jones Mills · *see Donegal*

Kane · *Kane C/C* · 54 Fraley St.; 16735; McKean; P 4,100; M 135; (814) 837-6565; Fax (814) 837-8257; kanepa.chamber@verizon.net; www.kanepa.com

Kennett Square · *Southern Chester County C/C* · Roxane Ferguson; Exec. Dir.; 217 W. State St.; P.O. Box 395; 19348; Chester; P 38,000; M 600; (610) 444-0774; Fax (610) 444-5105; info@scccc.com; www.scccc.com*

Kittanning · *Armstrong County C/C* · Lynda Pozzuto; Exec. Dir.; 124 Market St.; 16201; Armstrong; P 72,514; M 305; (724) 543-1305; Fax (724) 548-2951; accc1@alltel.net; www.armstrongchamber.org

Kutztown · *Northeast Berks C/C* · Liz P. Weiss; Exec. Dir.; 110 W. Main St.; P.O. Box 209; 19530; Berks; P 30,000; M 265; (610) 683-8860; Fax (610) 683-8544; nbcc@ptd.net; www.northeastberkschamber.com*

Lake Ariel · *see Hamlin*

Lake Wallenpaupack · *see Hawley*

Lancaster · *The Lancaster C/C & Ind.* · Thomas T. Baldrige; Pres.; 100 S. Queen St.; P.O. Box 1558; 17608; Lancaster; P 482,000; M 2,700; (717) 397-3531; Fax (717) 293-3159; info@lcci.com; www.lancasterchamber.com*

Lansdale · *Penn Suburban C/C* · R. Michael Owens; Pres./CEO; 229 S. Broad St.; 19446; Montgomery; P 125,000; M 1,200; (215) 362-9200; Fax (215) 362-0393; info@pennsuburban.org; www.pennsuburban.org

Lansford · *see Lehighton*

Laporte · *see Muncy Valley*

Latrobe · *Latrobe Area C/C* · Andrew M. Stofan; Pres.; 326 McKinley Ave., Ste. 102; 15650; Westmoreland; P 50,000; M 400; (724) 537-2671; Fax (724) 537-2690; info@latrobearea.com; www.latrobearea.com*

Lebanon · *Lebanon Valley C/C* · Larry A. Bowman CCE; Pres./CEO; 728 Walnut St.; P.O. Box 899; 17042; Lebanon; P 128,000; M 805; (717) 273-3727; Fax (717) 273-7940; info@lvchamber.org; www.lvchamber.org.*

Lehighton · *Carbon County C/C* · David Althouse; Chrmn.; 110 N. 3rd St., Ste. 216; 18235; Carbon; P 63,500; M 332; (610) 379-5000; mail@carboncountychamber.org; www.carboncountychamber.org

Lewisburg · *see Shamokin Dam*

Lewistown · *Juniata Valley Area C/C* · Jim Tunall; Pres.; Historic Courthouse; One W. Market St., Ste. 119; 17044; Mifflin; P 68,463; M 505; (717) 248-6713; Fax (717) 248-6714; info@juniatarivervalley.org; www.juniatarivervalley.org

Ligonier · *Ligonier Valley C/C* · Carrie Blough; Exec. Dir.; 120 E. Main St.; 15658; Westmoreland; P 7,000; M 350; (724) 238-4200; thechamber@ligonier.com; www.ligonier.com

Linesville · *Linesville Area C/C* · Virginia Headley; Pres.; P.O. Box 651; 16424; Crawford; P 1,155; M 25; (814) 683-1006; www.linesville.org

Littlestown · *Littlestown Area C/C* · Ivan Cornwell; Exec. Dir.; 1A S. Queen St.; P.O. Box 384; 17340; Adams; P 4,500; M 60; (717) 359-7006; Fax (717) 334-3368; office@littlestownchamber.org; www.littlestownchamber.org

Lock Haven · *Clinton County Eco. Partnership* · Peter Lopes; Chamber/Tourism Dir.; 212 N. Jay St.; P.O. Box 506; 17745; Clinton; P 37,000; M 350; (570) 748-5782; Fax (570) 893-0433; tourism@kcnet.org; www.clintoncountyinfo.com

Lower Mount Bethel · *see Pen Argyl*

Malvern · *Chester County Chamber of Bus. & Ind.* · Nancy Keefer CCE; Pres./CEO; 1600 Paoli Pike; 19355; Chester; P 442,815; M 1,000; (610) 725-9100; Fax (610) 725-8479; info@cccbi.org; www.cccbi.org

Malvern · *Great Valley Reg. C/C* · Mary Ann Severance; Pres.; 7 Great Valley Pkwy.; 19355; Chester; P 30,000; M 270; (610) 889-2069; Fax (610) 889-2063; greatchamber@gvrcc.org; www.greatvalleyonline.com

Manheim · *Manheim Area C/C* · Teresa Shelly; Exec. Dir.; 13 E. High St.; 17545; Lancaster; P 18,000; M 140; (717) 665-6330; Fax (717) 665-7656; info@manheimchamber.com; www.manheimchamber.com*

Mansfield · *Greater Mansfield Area C/C* · Irene Morgan; Pres.; 51-B S. Main St.; 16933; Tioga; P 10,000; M 125; (570) 662-3442; info@mansfield.org; www.mansfield.org

Marietta · *see Columbia*

Mayfield · *see Carbondale*

McConnellsburg · *Fulton County C/C* · Brenda Gordon; Exec. Dir.; 201 Lincolnway W., Ste. 101; P.O. Box 141; 17233; Fulton; P 14,900; M 183; (717) 485-4064; info@fultoncountypa.com; www.fultoncountypa.com

McDonald · *see Canonsburg*

McKeesport · *Reg. Chamber Alliance* · Exec. Dir.; 201 Lysle Blvd.; 15132; Allegheny; P 180,000; M 500; (412) 678-2450; Fax (412) 678-2451; director@rca-pa.com; www.rca-pa.com

McMurray · *Peters Twp. C/C* · Carol A. Foley; Exec. Dir.; 3909 Washington Rd., Ste. 321; P.O. Box 991; 15317; Washington; P 21,430; M 420; (724) 941-6345; Fax (724) 942-2345; info@peterstownshipchamber.com; www.peterstownshipchamber.com

Meadowlands · *see Canonsburg*

Meadville · *Meadville-Western Crawford County C/C* · Kathleen Bishop; Pres./CEO; 908 Diamond Park; 16335; Crawford; P 13,900; M 525; (814) 337-8030; Fax (814) 337-8022; info@meadvillechamber.com; www.meadvillechamber.com

Mechanicsburg · *Mechanicsburg C/C* · Jeff Palm; Exec. Dir.; 6 W. Strawberry Ave.; 17055; Cumberland; P 60,000; M 400; (717) 796-0811; Fax (717) 796-1977; info@mechanicsburgchamber.org; www.mechanicsburgchamber.org*

Media · *Delaware County C/C* · Michael Brady; Pres.; 602 E. Baltimore Pike, 2nd Flr.; 19063; Delaware; P 547,641; M 2,300; (610) 565-3677; Fax (610) 565-1606; info@delcochamber.org; www.delcochamber.org*

Mercer · *Mercer Area C/C* · Deborah Plant; Exec. Dir.; 143 N. Diamond St.; 16137; Mercer; P 2,500; M 219; (724) 662-4185; Fax (724) 662-0211; mercerchamber@zoominternet.net; www.mercerareachamber.com*

Mercersburg • *Tuscarora Area C/C* • Mary-Anne Gordon; Exec. Dir.; 19 N. Main St.; 17236; Franklin; P 1,817; M 172; (717) 328-5827; Fax (717) 328-4814; info@mercersburg.org; www.mercersburg.org

Meyersdale • *see Somerset*

Middleburg • *see Milton*

Middletown • *see Harrisburg*

Mifflinburg • *see Shamokin Dam*

Milford • *Pike County C/C* • Danielle Jordan; CEO; 209 E. Harford St.; 18337; Pike; P 54,000; M 550; (570) 296-8700; Fax (570) 296-3921; info@pikechamber.com; www.pikechamber.com*

Millersburg • *see Elizabethville*

Milton • *Central Pennsylvania C/C* • Maria Culp; Pres./CEO; 30 Lawton Ln.; 17847; Northumberland; P 9,056; M 300; (570) 742-7341; Fax (570) 742-2008; info@centralpachamber.com; www.centralpachamber.com

Monessen • *Greater Monessen C/C* • Gary W. Boatman; Pres.; Ste. 154, Eastgate 11; 15062; Westmoreland; P 9,500; M 100; (724) 684-3200; Fax (724) 684-8470; info@monessenchamberofcommerce.com; www.monessenchamberofcommerce.com

Monongahela • *Monongahela Area C/C* • Judy Loughman; Dir.; 211 1/2 2nd St.; 15063; Washington; P 13,310; M 130; (724) 258-5919; Fax (724) 258-5919; www.cityofmonongahela-pa.gov

Monroeville • *Monroeville Area C/C* • Chad M. Amond; Pres.; 2790 Mosside Blvd., Ste. 715; 15146; Allegheny; P 50,000; M 710; (412) 856-0622; Fax (412) 856-1030; macc@monroevillechamber.com; www.monroevillechamber.com*

Montrose • *Montrose Area C/C* • Marilyn Morgan; Pres.; P.O. Box 423; 18801; Susquehanna; P 1,700; (570) 278-1174; www.montrosearea.com

Moon Twp. • *see Pittsburgh–Pittsburgh Airport Area C/C*

Mount Carmel • *see Shamokin*

Mount Joy • *Mount Joy C/C* • Delores Showalter; Exec. Dir.; 62 E. Main, Ste. 1; 17552; Lancaster; P 7,000; M 230; (717) 653-0773; Fax (717) 653-0773; info@mountjoychamber.com; www.mountjoychamber.com

Mount Lebanon • *see Pittsburgh-South Hills C/C*

Mount Pleasant • *Laurel Highlands C/C* • 10 S. Church St.; 15666; Westmoreland; P 30,000; M 380; (724) 547-7521; marjorie@laurelhighlandschamber.com; www.laurelhighlandschamber.com

Mount Union • *Mount Union Area C/C* • Jonathan Shapiro; P.O. Box 12; 17066; Huntingdon; P 2,500; M 60; (814) 542-9413; muchamber@verizon.net; www.muacoc.com

Muncy Valley • *Sullivan County C/C* • Florence Suarez; Admin. Dir.; 1240 Rte. 220, Ste. 3; P.O. Box 134; 17758; Sullivan; P 6,500; M 145; (570) 482-4088; Fax (570) 482-4089; sulchamc@epix.net; www.sullivanpachamber.com

Munhall • *see Steel Valley*

Murrysville • *see Greensburg*

Nanticoke • *South Valley C/C* • Mill House; 495 E. Main St.; 18634; Luzerne; P 11,000; M 100; (570) 735-6990; Fax (570) 735-6951; svcc495@verizon.net; www.southvalleycofc.com*

Natrona Heights • *see Brackenridge*

Nazareth • *Nazareth Area C/C* • Tina Smith; Pres.; 201 N. Main St.; 18064; Northampton; P 25,000; M 400; (610) 759-9188; Fax (610) 759-5262; bsmith@nazarethchamber.com; www.nazarethchamber.com

Nesquehoning • *see Lehighton*

Neville Island • *see Pittsburgh–Pittsburgh Airport Area C/C*

New Bethlehem • *Red Bank Valley C/C* • 309 Broad St., Ste. 2; 16242; Clarion; P 10,000; M 96; (814) 275-3929; nbchamber@windstream.net; www.newbethlehemarea.com

New Castle • *Lawrence County C/C* • Robert McCracken; Exec. V.P.; Shenango Street Station; 138 W. Washington St.; 16101; Lawrence; P 94,643; M 900; (724) 654-5593; Fax (724) 654-3330; info@lawrencecountychamber.org; www.lawrencecountychamber.org

New Hope • *Greater New Hope C/C* • Stephanie Nagy; Admin.; 8 Stockton Ave.; 18938; Bucks; P 3,000; M 200; (215) 862-9990; info@newhopechamber.com; www.newhopechamber.com

New Kensington • *New Kensington Area C/C* • Thomas P. Ansani; Pres.; 858 4th Ave.; 15068; Westmoreland; P 14,300; M 160; (724) 339-6616; Fax (724) 339-3346; admin@nkchamber.org; www.nkchamber.org*

New Oxford • *New Oxford Area C/C* • P.O. Box 152; 17350; Adams & York; P 1,700; M 200; (717) 624-2800; info@newoxford.org; www.newoxford.org

New Stanton • *see Greensburg*

Newfoundland • *see Hamlin*

Norristown • *see Eagleville*

North East • *North East Area C/C* • Sue Spacht; Comm. Coord.; 17 E. Main St.; 16428; Erie; P 11,000; M 302; (814) 725-4262; Fax (814) 725-3994; info@nechamber.org; www.nechamber.org.

North Fayette Twp. • *see Pittsburgh–Pittsburgh Airport Area C/C*

North Huntingdon • *see Irwin*

Northampton • *see Allentown*

Northern Allegheny County • *see Wexford*

Ohiopyle • *see Donegal*

Oil City • *Venango Area C/C* • Susan Williams; Exec. Dir.; 41 Main St.; P.O. Box 376; 16301; Venango; P 51,000; M 484; (814) 676-8521; Fax (814) 676-8185; chamber@venangochamber.org; www.venangochamber.org*

Oxford • *Oxford Area C/C* • Eleanor Roper; Exec. Secy.; P.O. Box 4; 19363; Chester; P 20,364; M 215; (610) 932-0740; Fax (610) 932-0827; oxfordchamber@zoominternet.net; www.oxfordpa.org

Palmerton • *Palmerton Area C/C* • Peter Kern; 410 Delaware Ave.; P.O. Box 214; 18071; Carbon; P 14,000; M 160; (610) 824-6954; www.palmertonpa.com/chamber

Paoli • *see Malvern-Great Valley Reg. C/C*

Pen Argyl • *Slate Belt C/C* • Laura McLain; Ofc. Mgr.; 856 W. Pennsylvania Ave.; P.O. Box 5; 18072; Northampton; P 34,250; M 270; (610) 863-0315; Fax (610) 863-0315; sbcc@frontiernet.net; www.slatebeltchamber.org

Penfield • *see DuBois*

Penn Twp. • *see Greensburg*

Perkasie • *Pennridge C/C* • Elizabeth Graver; Exec. Dir.; 538 W. Market St.; 18944; Bucks; P 42,000; M 350; (215) 257-5390; Fax (267) 354-6924; pennridgecc@pennridge.com; www.pennridge.com*

Peters Twp. • *see McMurray*

Philadelphia Area

African American C/C of PA, NJ & DE • Nicole R. Giles; Exec. Dir.; 30 S. 15th St.; Ground Floor; 19106; Philadelphia; M 400; (215) 751-9501; Fax (215) 751-9509; info@aachamber.org; www.aachamber.org

Philadelphia Area, *continued*

Greater Northeast Philadelphia C/C · Al Taubenberger; Pres.; 8601 Roosevelt Blvd.; 19152; Philadelphia; P 550,000; M 900; (215) 332-3400; Fax (215) 332-6050; gnpccoffice@aol.com; www.gnpcc.org.*

Greater Philadelphia C/C · Rob Wonderling; Pres./CEO; 200 S. Broad St., Ste. 700; 19102; Philadelphia; P 6,000,000; M 5,000; (215) 545-1234; Fax (215) 790-3600; www.greaterphilachamber.com*

Philipsburg · *Moshannon Valley Eco. Dev. Partnership* · Stanley LaFuria; Exec. Dir.; 200 Shady Ln.; 16866; Centre; P 34,000; M 170; (814) 342-2260; Fax (814) 342-2878; slafuria@mvedp.org; www.mvedp.org

Phoenixville · *Phoenixville Reg. C/C* · Kim Cooley; Exec. Dir.; 171 E. Bridge St.; 19460; Chester; P 20,000; M 500; (610) 933-3070; Fax (610) 917-0503; info@phoenixvillechamber.org; www.phoenixvillechamber.org

Pitcairn · *see McKeesport*

Pittsburgh Area

Brentwood Baldwin Whitehall C/C · Mary Dilla; Secy.; 3501 Brownsville Rd.; 15227; Allegheny; P 15,000; M 174; (412) 884-1233; secretary@bbwchamber.com; www.bbwchamber.com

East Liberty Quarter C/C · Paul G. Brecht; Exec. Dir.; 5907 Penn Ave., Ste. 305; 15206; Allegheny; P 65,000; M 90; (412) 661-9660; Fax (412) 661-9661; pbrecht@eastlibertychamber.org; www.eastlibertychamber.org

Greater Pittsburgh C/C · Barbara McNees; Pres.; 425 Sixth Ave., Ste. 1100; 15219; Allegheny; P 2,394,800; M 1,200; (412) 392-4500; Fax (412) 392-4520; info@pittsburghchamber.com; www.pittsburghchamber.com

Northside Northshore C/C · Robin Rosemary Miller; Exec. Dir.; 809 Middle St.; 15212; Allegheny; P 54,600; M 215; (412) 231-6500; Fax (412) 321-6760; nsccrobin@hotmail.com; www.northsidechamberofcommerce.com*

Penn Hills C/C · 12013 Frankstown Rd.; 15235; Allegheny; P 47,000; M 220; (412) 795-8741; Fax (412) 795-7993; s.werner@pennhillschamber.org; www.pennhillschamber.org

Pittsburgh Airport Area C/C · Sally Haas; Pres.; 850 Beaver Grade Rd.; Moon Twp.; 15108; Allegheny; P 170,000; M 1,000; (412) 264-6270; Fax (412) 264-1575; info@paacc.com; www.paacc.com

South Hills C/C · Angie Kazmeraski; Exec. Dir.; 1910 Cochran Rd.; Manor Oak One, Ste. 140; 15220; Allegheny; P 225,000; M 574; (412) 306-8090; Fax (412) 306-8093; office@shchamber.org; www.shchamber.org

South Side C/C · Nancy Eshelman; Pres.; 1505 E. Carson St.; P.O. Box 42380; 15203; Allegheny; P 15,000; M 150; (412) 431-3360; Fax (412) 481-2624; office@southsidechamber.aol; www.southsidechamber.org

South West Communities C/C · Emerald VanBuskirk; Exec. Dir.; 990 Washington Pike; Bridgeville; 15017; Allegheny; P 20,615; M 437; (412) 221-4100; Fax (412) 257-1210; info@swccoc.org; www.swccoc.org.*

Wilkinsburg C/C · Vicki Cherney; Pres.; 1001 Wood St.; 15221; Allegheny; P 20,680; M 100; (412) 242-0234; info@wilkinsburgchamber.com; www.wilkinsburgchamber.com

Pittston · *Greater Pittston C/C* · Rosemary Dessoye; Exec. V.P.; 104 Kennedy Blvd.; P.O. Box 704; 18640; Luzerne; P 49,672; M 400; (570) 655-1424; Fax (570) 655-0336; info@pittstonchamber.org; www.pittstonchamber.org.

Plainfield · *see Pen Argyl*

Pleasant Hills · *see McKeesport*

Plum Borough · *see Greensburg*

Pocono Mountains · *see Stroudsburg*

Portland · *see Pen Argyl*

Pottstown · *TriCounty Area C/C* · Eileen Dautrich; Pres.; 152 High St., Ste. 360; 19464; Montgomery; P 175,000; M 550; (610) 326-2900; Fax (610) 970-9705; eileen@tricountyareachamber.com; www.tricountyareachamber.com*

Pottsville · *Schuylkill C/C* · Bob Carl; Exec. Dir.; 91 S. Progress Ave.; 17901; Schuylkill; P 150,336; M 800; (570) 622-1942; (800) 755-1942; Fax (570) 622-1638; info@schuylkillchamber.com; www.schuylkillchamber.com

Punxsutawney · *Punxsutawney Area C/C* · Marlene Lellock; Exec. Dir.; 102 W. Mahoning St.; 15767; Jefferson; P 6,800; M 300; (814) 938-7700; (800) 752-PHIL; Fax (814) 938-4303; chamber@punxsutawney.com; www.punxsutawney.com

Quakertown · *Upper Bucks C/C* · Tara King; Exec. Dir.; 2170 Portzer Rd.; 18951; Bucks; P 50,000; M 700; (215) 536-3211; Fax (215) 536-7767; info@ubcc.org; www.ubcc.org

Quarryville · *Southern Lancaster County C/C* · Callie Rineer; Exec. Secy.; P.O. Box 24; 17566; Lancaster; P 2,500; M 110; (717) 786-1911; (717) 786-8361; info@southernlancasterchamber.com; www.southernlancasterchamber.com

Reading · *Greater Reading C/C & Ind.* · Ellen T. Horan; Pres./CEO; 201 Penn St., Ste. 501; 19601; Berks; P 373,638; M 1,800; (610) 376-6766; Fax (610) 376-4135; info@greaterreadingchamber.org; www.greaterreadingchamber.org*

Richmondale · *see Carbondale*

Ridgway · *Ridgway-Elk County C/C* · 300 Main St.; 15853; Elk; P 5,000; M 170; (814) 776-1424; Fax (814) 772-2118; ridgwaychamber@ncentral.com; www.ridgwaychamber.com

Robinson Twp. · *see Pittsburgh-Pittsburgh Airport Area C/C*

Rochester · *Rochester C/C* · 350 Adams St., Ste. 4C; 15074; Beaver; P 4,000; M 169; (724) 728-4998; rochesterpachamber@yahoo.com; www.thenostalgialeague.com/rochester

Rockwood · *see Somerset*

Roseto · *see Pen Argyl*

Royersford · *Spring-Ford C/C* · Beth Haveron; Exec. Dir.; P.O. Box 26; 19468; Montgomery; P 6,000; M 235; (610) 948-1771; Fax (610) 948-1783; beth@springfordchamber.com; www.springfordchamber.com

Saint Marys · *St. Marys Area C/C* · Sally J. Wilson; Exec. Dir.; 53 S. St. Marys Street; 15857; Elk; P 14,000; M 280; (814) 781-3804; Fax (814) 781-7302; swilson@stmaryschamber.org; www.stmaryschamber.org

Saltlick · *see Donegal*

Saxton · *Broad Top C/C* · John Husick; Pres.; P.O. Box 121; 16678; Bedford; P 10,000; M 50; (814) 635-0597; www.saxtonbroad.chamber.com

Sayre · *Greater Valley C/C* · Greg Joseph; Pres.; 703 S. Elmer Ave.; 18840; Bradford, PA & Tioga, NY; P 40,000; M 235; (570) 888-2217; Fax (570) 888-6558; gvcc@cqservices.com; www.greatervalleychamberofcommerce.com

Scottdale · *Scottdale Area C/C* · Joan Brown; Pres.; 318 Pittsburgh St.; 15683; Westmoreland; P 5,000; M 75; (724) 887-3611; scottdalechamber@gmail.com; www.scottdale.com

Scranton · *Greater Northeast C/C* · John Gleason; Chrmn.; P.O. Box 3893; 18505; Lackawanna; M 200; (570) 457-1130; Fax (570) 300-1645; office@gnecc.com; www.gnecc.com

Scranton · *Greater Scranton C/C* · Austin J. Burke; Pres.; 222 Mulberry St.; P.O. Box 431; 18501; Lackawanna; P 213,295; M 2,200; (570) 342-7711; Fax (570) 347-6262; info@scranton chamber.com; www.scrantonchamber.com.*

Selinsgrove · *see Shamokin Dam*

Sellersville · *see Doylestown*

Shamokin · *Brush Valley Reg. C/C* · Sandy Winhofer; Dir.; 2 E. Arch St., Ste. 313A; 17872; Northumberland; P 45,000; M 235; (570) 648-4675; Fax (570) 648-0679; swinhofer@censop.com; www.brushvalleychamber.com*

Shamokin Dam · *Greater Susquehanna Valley C/C* · Charlie Ross; Pres./CEO; 2859 N. Susquehanna Trl.; P.O. Box 10; 17876; Snyder; P 130,000; M 720; (570) 743-4100; Fax (570) 743-1221; info@gsvcc.org; www.gsvcc.org*

Shanksville · *see Somerset*

Sharon · *Shenango Valley C/C* · Deanne Koch; Mktg. & Mbrshp. Coord.; 41 Chestnut Ave.; 16146; Mercer; P 52,000; M 450; (724) 981-5880; Fax (724) 981-5480; deanne@svchamber.com; www. svchamber.com.*

Shenandoah · *see Schuylkill*

Shippensburg · *Shippensburg Area C/C* · Tim Ebersole; Interim Exec. Dir.; 53 W. King St.; 17257; Cumberland & Franklin; P 30,000; M 300; (717) 532-5509; Fax (717) 532-7501; chamber@shippensburg. org; www.shippensburg.org

Simpson · *see Carbondale*

Smethport · *Smethport C/C* · Nathan Muller; P.O. Box 84; 16749; McKean; P 1,700; M 60; (814) 887-4134; njmuller@smethport chamber.com; www.smethportchamber.com

Somerset · *Somerset County C/C* · Ron Aldom; Exec. Dir.; 601 N. Center Ave.; 15501; Somerset; P 80,000; M 735; (814) 445-6431; Fax (814) 443-4313; info@somersetcountychamber.com; www. somersetcountychamber.com.*

Souderton · *Indian Valley C/C* · Sharon Minninger; Exec. Dir.; 100 Penn Ave.; P.O. Box 64077; 18964; Montgomery; P 60,000; M 400; (215) 723-9472; Fax (215) 723-2490; ivchamber@indian valleychamber.com; www.indianvalleychamber.com*

South Fayette Twp. · *see Pittsburgh–South West Comm. C/C*

South Sterling · *see Hamlin*

South Waverly · *see Sayre*

Spring City · *see Pottstown*

Stahlstown · *see Donegal*

State College · *Chamber of Bus. & Ind. of Centre County* · Pres./CEO; 200 Innovation Blvd., Ste. 150; 16803; Centre; P 124,000; M 1,086; (814) 234-1829; Fax (814) 234-5869; cbicc@ cbicc.org; www.cbicc.org*

Steel Valley · *Steel Valley C/C* · John J. Karafa Jr.; Pres.; 3910 Main St.; Munhall; 15120; Lawrence & Mercer; P 44,892; M 125; (412) 461-4141; Fax (412) 461-9804; svchamber@hotmail.com; www.steelvalleychamber.com

Sterling · *see Hamlin*

Stroudsburg · *Greater Pocono C/C* · Robert Phillips IOM; Pres./ CEO; 556 Main St.; 18360; Monroe; P 200,000; M 1,400; (570) 421- 4433; Fax (570) 424-7281; rphillips@greaterpoconochamber.com; www.greaterpoconochamber.com*

Summit Hill · *see Lehighton*

Sunbury · *see Shamokin Dam*

Tamaqua · *Tamaqua Area C/C* · Linda Yulanavage; Exec. Dir.; 114 W. Broad St.; 18252; Schuylkill; P 7,000; M 170; (570) 668- 1880; Fax (570) 668-0826; tamaquachamber@verizon.net; www. tamaqua.net.

Telford · *see Souderton*

Titusville · *Titusville Area C/C* · Christa Battin; Exec. Dir.; 202 W. Central Ave.; 16354; Crawford; P 6,000; M 300; (814) 827-2941; Fax (814) 827-2914; christab@titusvillechamber.com; www. titusvillechamber.com

Towanda · *Central Bradford County C/C* · Sharon M. Kaminsky; Admin.; 421 Main St.; P.O. Box 146; 18848; Bradford; P 10,000; M 116; (570) 268-2787; Fax (570) 265-4558; sharon@bcrac.org; www.cbradchamber.org

Trafford · *see McKeesport*

Trooper · *see Eagleville*

Tunkhannock · *Wyoming County C/C* · Maureen E. Dispenza; Exec. Dir.; 81B Warren St.; P.O. Box 568; 18657; Wyoming; P 12,000; M 440; (570) 836-7755; (570) 875-8325; Fax (570) 836-6049; maureen@wyccc.com; www.wyccc.com

Turtle Creek · *see McKeesport*

Tyrone · *Tyrone Area C/C* · Rose Black; Exec. Dir.; 1004 Logan Ave.; 16686; Blair; P 5,400; M 200; (814) 684-0736; Fax (814) 684- 6070; rose@tyronechamber.com; www.tyronechamber.com

Uniontown · *Fayette C/C* · Muriel J. Nuttall; Exec. Dir.; 65 W. Main St.; 15401; Fayette; P 55,000; M 560; (724) 437-4571; (800) 916-9365; Fax (724) 438-3304; info@fayettechamber.com; www. fayettechamber.com

Upper Mount Bethel · *see Pen Argyl*

Upper St. Clair · *Upper St. Clair C/C* · Rosemary Siddall; Exec. Dir.; P.O. Box 12619; 15241; Allegheny; P 20,000; M 100; (412) 833-9111; www.uscchamber.org

Valley Forge · *see Eagleville*

Vandergrift · *StrongLand C/C* · A. Allan Walzak; Pres.; 1129 Industrial Park Rd.; Box 10, Ste. 108; 15690; Armstrong; P 65,000; M 350; (724) 845-5426; Fax (724) 845-5428; strongland@wind stream.net; www.strongland.org

Vandling · *see Carbondale*

Warminster · *The Greater BucksMont C/C* · Bruce Mandes; Ofc. Mgr.; 228 York Rd., Ste. C; 18974; Bucks; P 36,000; M 350; (215) 672-6633; Fax (215) 672-7637; admin@bucksmontchamber.com; www.bucksmontchamber.com

Warren · *Warren County Chamber of Bus. & Ind.* · James Decker; Pres./CEO; 308 Market St.; 16365; Warren; P 42,000; M 285; (814) 723-3050; Fax (814) 723-6024; info@wccbi.org; www.wccbi.org

Washington · *Washington County C/C* · Jeff M. Kotula; Pres.; 20 E. Beau St.; 15301; Washington; P 203,000; M 900; (724) 225-3010; Fax (724) 228-7337; info@washcochamber.com; www. washcochamber.com

Watsontown · *see Milton*

Wayne · *Main Line C/C* · Eileen Connolly-Robbins; Exec. V.P. & COO; 175 Strafford Ave., Ste. 130; 19087; Delaware; P 265,000; M 1,800; (610) 687-6232; Fax (610) 687-8085; info@mlcc.org; www.mlcc.org*

Waynesboro · *Greater Waynesboro C/C* · Carlene Willhide; Exec. Dir.; 5 Roadside Ave.; 17268; Franklin; P 40,000; M 420; (717) 762-7123; Fax (717) 762-7124; carlene@waynesboro.org; www.waynesboro.org

Waynesburg • *Waynesburg C/C* • Melody Longstreth; Exec. Dir.; 143 E. High St.; 15370; Greene; P 15,000; M 300; (724) 627-5926; Fax (724) 627-8017; waynesburgchamber@windstream.net; www.waynesburgchamber.com

Wellsboro • *Wellsboro Area C/C* • Julie VanNess; Exec. Dir.; 114 Main St.; P.O. Box 733; 16901; Tioga; P 3,500; M 300; (570) 724-1926; Fax (570) 724-5084; info@wellsboropa.com; www.wellsboropa.com

West Chester • *C/C of Greater West Chester Inc.* • Katie Walker; Pres.; 119 N. High St.; 19380; Chester; P 81,000; M 800; (610) 696-4046; Fax (610) 696-9110; info@gwcc.org; www.greaterwestchester.com*

West Elizabeth • *see McKeesport*

West Homestead • *see Steel Valley*

West Mifflin • *see McKeesport and Steel Valley*

Westfield • *see Galeton*

Westinghouse Valley • *see McKeesport*

Wexford • *THE CHAMBER of Commerce Inc.* • Susan H. Balla; Exec. Dir.; 5000 Brooktree Rd., Ste. 100; 15090; Allegheny; P 25,000; M 1,100; (724) 934-9700; Fax (724) 934-9710; info@thechamberinc.com; www.thechamberinc.com*

Whitaker • *see Steel Valley*

White Oak • *see McKeesport*

Wilkes-Barre • *Greater Wilkes-Barre Chamber of Bus. & Ind.* • Todd Vonderheid; Pres./CEO; Two Public Square; P.O. Box 5340; 18710; Luzerne; P 353,000; M 1,150; (570) 823-2101; Fax (570) 822-5951; wbcofc@wilkes-barre.org; www.wilkes-barre.org.*

Williamsport • *Williamsport/Lycoming C/C* • Vincent J. Matteo; Pres./CEO; 100 W. Third St.; 17701; Lycoming; P 130,000; M 875; (570) 326-1971; Fax (570) 321-1208; chamber@williamsport.org; www.williamsport.org.

Willow Grove • *see Lansdale*

Wind Gap • *see Pen Argyl*

Windber • *see Somerset*

Wrightsville • *see Columbia*

Wyalusing • *Greater Wyalusing C/C & IDC* • Carol Goodman; Pres.; 20 Main St.; P.O. Box 55; 18853; Bradford; P 5,000; M 150; (570) 746-4922; Fax (570) 746-0235; wchamber@epix.net; www.wyalusing.net

Wysox • *Wysox Comm. C/C* • Evan Barnes; Pres.; P.O. Box 63; 18854; Bradford; P 1,800; M 80; (570) 265-7511; info@wysoxpacc.com; www.wysoxchamber.com

York • *York County C/C* • Thomas E. Donley; Pres.; 96 S. George, Ste. 300; 17401; York; P 401,613; M 2,000; (717) 848-4000; Fax (717) 843-6737; info@YorkChamber.com; www.YorkChamber.com*

Zelienople • *Zelienople-Harmony Area C/C* • Meg M. Kessler; Exec. Dir.; 111 W. New Castle St.; P.O. Box 464; 16063; Butler; P 8,000; M 200; (724) 452-5232; Fax (724) 452-5712; meg@zhchamber.com; www.zhchamber.com*

Puerto Rico

Puerto Rico C of C • Edgardo Bigas; Exec. V.P.; P.O. Box 9024033; San Juan; 00902; P 3,900,000; M 2,000; (787) 721-6060; Fax (787) 723-1891; camarapr@camarapr.net; www.camarapr.org

Mayaguez • *C/C of the West of Puerto Rico* • Elisamuel Rivera; Pres.; P.O. Box 9; 00681-0009; P 2,000,000; M 250; (787) 832-3749; Fax (787) 832-4287; info@ccopr.org; www.ccopr.org

Ponce • *Southern Puerto Rico C/C* • Hector E. Lopez; Exec. Dir.; P.O. Box 7455; 00732-7455; P 200,000; M 500; (787) 844-4400; Fax (787) 844-4705; camarasur@camarasur.org; www.camarasur.org.

Rhode Island

No State Chamber

Barrington • *see Warren*

Block Island • *Block Island C/C* • Kathleen Szabo; Exec. Dir.; P.O. Box D; 02807; Washington; P 950; M 250; (401) 466-2982; bichamber@yahoo.com; www.blockislandchamber.com

Bristol • *see Warren*

Burrillville • *see Lincoln*

Central Falls • *see Lincoln*

Centredale • *see Johnston*

Charlestown • *Charlestown C/C* • Heather Paliopta; Exec. Dir.; 4945 Old Post Rd.; P.O. Box 633; 02813; Washington; P 8,000; M 300; (401) 364-3878; Fax (401) 364-8794; charlestowncoc@earthlink.net; www.charlestownrichamber.com

Cranston • *Cranston C/C* • Susan Pagnozzi; Pres.; 875 Oaklawn Ave.; 02920; Providence; P 79,000; M 500; (401) 785-3780; Fax (401) 785-3782; susan@cranstonchamber.com; www.cranstonchamber.com*

Cumberland • *see Lincoln*

East Greenwich • *East Greenwich C/C* • Jerry Meyer; Exec. Dir.; 580 Main St.; P.O. Box 514; 02818; Kent; P 12,948; M 400; (401) 885-0020; Fax (401) 885-0048; info@eastgreenwichchamber.com; www.eastgreenwichchamber.com*

East Providence • *East Providence Area C/C* • Laura A. McNamara; Exec. Dir.; 1011 Waterman Ave.; 02914; Providence; P 48,000; M 250; (401) 438-1212; Fax (401) 435-4581; office@eastprovchamber.com; www.eastprovchamber.com

Foster • *see Johnston*

Glocester • *see Johnston*

Jamestown • *Jamestown C/C* • Arlene Petit; Exec. Dir.; P.O. Box 35; 02835; Newport; P 6,200; M 135; (401) 423-3650; info@jamestownrichamber.com; www.jamestownrichamber.com

Johnston • *North Central C/C* • Deborah Ramos; Pres.; 255 Greenville Ave.; 02919; Providence; P 150,000; M 250; (401) 349-4674; Fax (401) 349-4676; chamber@ncrichamber.com; www.ncrichamber.com*

Lincoln • *Northern Rhode Island C/C* • John C. Gregory; Pres./CEO; 6 Blackstone Valley Pl., Ste. 301; 02865; Providence; P 250,000; M 900; (401) 334-1000; Fax (401) 334-1009; jgregory@nrichamber.com; www.nrichamber.com*

Middletown • *Newport County C/C* • Jody Sullivan; Exec. Dir.; 35 Valley Rd.; 02842; Newport; P 100,000; M 1,300; (401) 847-1600; Fax (401) 849-5848; info@newportchamber.com; www.newportchamber.com*

Narragansett • *Narragansett C/C* • Deborah Kelso; Exec. Dir.; P.O. Box 742; 02882; Washington; P 16,000; M 400; (401) 783-7121; (401) 788-0684; Fax (401) 789-0220; dkelso@narragansettri.com; www.narragansettri.com/chamber

Newport • *see Middletown*

North Kingstown • *North Kingstown C/C* • Karla P. Driscoll; Exec. Dir.; 8045 Post Rd.; 02852; Washington; P 26,000; M 500; (401) 295-5566; Fax (401) 295-5582; info@northkingstown.com; www.northkingstown.com*

North Providence · *see Johnston*

North Smithfield · *see Lincoln*

Pawcatuck · *see Westerly*

Pawtucket · *see Lincoln*

Providence · *Greater Providence C/C* · Laurie L. White; Pres.; 30 Exchange Terrace; 02903; Providence; P 180,000; M 2,300; (401) 521-5000; Fax (401) 621-6109; chamber@provchamber. com; www.providencechamber.com*

Scituate · *see Johnston*

Smithfield · *see Johnston and Lincoln*

South Kingstown · *see Wakefield*

Wakefield · *South Kingstown C/C* · Joe Iacoi; Exec. Dir.; 230 Old Tower Hill Rd.; 02879; Washington; P 35,000; M 655; (401) 783-2801; Fax (401) 789-3120; info@skchamber.com; www. skchamber.com

Warren · *East Bay C/C* · Betty J. Pleacher; Pres.; 16 Cutler St., Ste. 102; 02885; Bristol; P 50,000; M 500; (401) 245-0750; Fax (401) 245-0110; info@eastbaychamberri.org; www.eastbaychamberri.org

Warwick · *Central Rhode Island C/C* · Lauren Slocum; Pres./CEO; 3288 Post Rd.; 02886; Kent; P 150,000; M 1,200; (401) 732-1100; Fax (401) 732-1107; business@centralrichamber.com; www.centralrichamber.com*

West Warwick · *Pawtuxet Valley C/C* · Lauren Young; Exec. Dir.; 1192 Main St.; 02893; Kent; P 75,000; M 280; (401) 823-3349; Fax (401) 823 8162; lauren@pawtuxetvalleychamber.org; www. pvccommerce.org

Westerly · *Greater Westerly-Pawcatuck Area C/C* · Lisa Konicki; Exec. Dir.; 1 Chamber Way; 02891; Washington; P 23,000; M 880; (401) 596-7761; (800) 732-7636; Fax (401) 596-2190; lkonicki@westerlychamber.org; www.westerlychamber.org.*

Woonsocket · *see Lincoln*

South Carolina

South Carolina C of C · Otis Rawl; Pres./CEO; 1201 Main St., Ste. 1700; Columbia; 29201; Richland; P 4,500,000; M 2,000; (803) 799-4601; Fax (803) 779-6043; chamber@scchamber.net; www. scchamber.net

Abbeville · *Greater Abbeville C/C* · Kacy Pearman; Exec. Dir.; 107 Court Sq.; 29620; Abbeville; P 26,000; M 177; (864) 366-4600; Fax (864) 366-4068; abvchamber@wctel.net; www.visitabbevillesc.com

Aiken · *Greater Aiken C/C* · David Jameson; Pres./CEO; 121 Richland Ave. E.; P.O. Box 892; 29802; Aiken; P 165,000; M 950; (803) 641-1111; Fax (803) 641-4174; chamber@aikenchamber. net; www.aikenchamber.net*

Anderson · *Anderson Area C/C* · Lee R. Luff; Pres.; 907 N. Main St., Ste. 200; 29621; Anderson; P 181,098; M 850; (864) 226-3454; Fax (864) 226-3300; info@andersonscchamber.com; www.anderson scchamber.com*

Andrews · *see Georgetown*

Aynor · *Aynor C/C* · Bobby Page; Chair; P.O. Box 175; 29511; Horry; P 500; M 75; (843) 358-4808; info@aynorscchamber.org; www.aynorscchamber.org

Bamberg · *Bamberg County C/C* · Demmie Raysor; Interim Dir.; 604 Airport Rd.; 29003; Bamberg; P 16,991; M 94; (803) 245-4427; Fax (803) 245-4428; info@bambergcountychamber.org; www.bambergcountychamber.org

Barnwell · *Barnwell County C/C* · Ms. Carolyne S. Williams; Chair; 367 Fuldner Rd.; P.O. Box 898; 29812; Barnwell; P 23,478; M 200; (803) 259-7446; Fax (803) 259-0030; executivedirector@ barnwellcountychamber.org; www.barnwellcountychamber.org

Batesburg-Leesville · *Greater Batesburg-Leesville C/C & Visitors Center* · Monica Motes; Pres./CEO; 350 E. Columbia Ave.; P.O. Box 2178; 29070; Lexington; P 6,500; M 340; (803) 532-4339; Fax (803) 532-3978; monica@batesburg-leesvillechamber.org; www.batesburg-leesvillechamber.org*

Beaufort · *Beaufort Reg. C/C & Visitors Center* · Carlotta Ungaro; Pres.; 1106 Carteret St.; P.O. Box 910; 29901; Beaufort; P 147,000; M 900; (843) 525-8500; Fax (843) 986-5405; carlotta@ beaufortsc.org; www.beaufortsc.org

Bennettsville · *Bennettsville C/C* · Rhonda Frazier; Dir.; 304 W. Main St.; P.O. Box 1036; 29512; Marlboro; P 30,000; M 200; (843) 479-3941; Fax (843) 479-4859; info@visitbennettsville.com; www. visitbennettsville.com

Bishopville · *Lee County C/C* · Pam Kelley; Exec. Dir.; 219 N. Main St.; P.O. Box 187; 29010; Lee; P 22,000; M 190; (803) 484-5145; Fax (803) 484-4270; kingcotton@ftc-i.net; www. leecountychambersc.com

Bluffton · *Hilton Head Island-Bluffton C/C* · William G. Miles; Pres./CEO; 9 Oak Forest Rd., Ste. 202; 29910; Beaufort; P 42,000; M 1,700; (843) 757-1624; Fax (843) 757-6021; bluffton@hilton headisland.org; www.hiltonheadisland.org

Bowman · *see Saint George*

Branchville · *see Saint George*

Camden · *Kershaw County C/C & Visitors Center* · Liz Horton; Exec. Dir.; 607 S. Broad St.; P.O. Box 605; 29021; Kershaw; P 58,000; M 500; (803) 432-2525; (800) 968-4037; Fax (803) 432-4181; lhorton@camden-sc.org; www.kershawcountychamber.org*

Cayce · *West Metro C/C & Visitors Center* · Gregg Pinner; Pres./CEO; 1006 12th St.; 29033; Lexington; P 35,000; M 380; (803) 794-6504; (866) 720-5400; Fax (803) 794-6505; info@westmetro chamber.com; www.westmetrochamber.com

Central · *see Clemson*

Chapin · *Greater Chapin C/C* · Laura G. Howell; Pres./CEO; 302 Columbia Ave.; P.O. Box 577; 29036; Lexington; P 50,000; M 315; (803) 345-1100; info@chapinchamber.com; www.chapinchamber.com*

Charleston · *Charleston Metro C/C* · Charles H Van Rysselberge CCE; CEO; 4500 Leeds Ave., Ste. 100; P.O. Box 975; 29402; Charleston; P 530,000; M 2,400; (843) 577-2510; Fax (843) 723-4853; mail@charlestonchamber.org; www.charlestonchamber.net*

Cheraw · *Greater Cheraw C/C* · Patsy J. Hendley; Pres.; 221 Market St.; 29520; Chesterfield; P 9,999; M 400; (843) 537-7681; Fax (843) 537-5886; cherawchamber@bellsouth.net; www. cherawchamber.com

Chester · *Chester County C/C* · Christi Buffington; Admin. Asst.; 109 Gadsden St.; P.O. Box 489; 29706; Chester; P 34,000; M 300; (803) 581-4142; (800) 377-3137; Fax (803) 581-2431; pres chamber@truvista.net; www.chesterchamber.com*

Chesterfield · *Greater Chesterfield C/C* · Donna Curtis; Exec. Dir.; 100 Main St.; P.O. Box 230; 29709; Chesterfield; P 1,404; M 200; (843) 623-2343; Fax (843) 623-2424; info@chesterfield scchamber.com; www.chesterfieldscchamber.com

Clemson · *Clemson Area C/C* · Chris Hardy; Pres.; 1105 Tiger Blvd.; P.O. Box 1622; 29633; Pickens; P 40,000; M 500; (864) 654-1200; (800) 542-0746; Fax (864) 654-5096; chris@clemson chamber.org; www.clemsonchamber.org*

Clover · *Greater Clover C/C* · 118 Bethel St.; P.O. Box 162; 29710; York; P 4,500; M 145; (803) 222-3312; Fax (803) 222-3312; scclo-verchamber@aol.com; www.cloverchamber.org

Columbia · *Greater Columbia C/C* · Ike McLeese; Pres./CEO; 930 Richland St.; 29201; Richland; P 650,000; M 2,000; (803) 733-1110; Fax (803) 733-1149; mbostic@columbiachamber.com; www.columbiachamber.com

Conway · *Conway Area C/C* · Bridgette Johnson; Exec. Dir.; 203 Main St.; P.O. Box 831; 29526; Horry; P 13,700; M 550; (843) 248-2273; Fax (843) 248-0003; info@conwayscchamber.com; www.conwayscchamber.com*

Cross · *see Saint George*

Darlington · *Greater Darlington C/C* · Mrs. Pat Godbold; Chair; 38 Public Sq.; 29532; Darlington; P 66,000; M 300; (843) 393-2641; Fax (843) 393-8059; info@darlingtonchamber.net; www.darlingtonchamber.net

Dillon · *Dillon County C/C* · Johnnie P. Luehrs; Pres./CEO; 100 N. MacArthur Ave.; P.O. Box 1304; 29536; Dillon; P 31,000; M 200; (843) 774-8551; Fax (843) 774-0114; dillonchamber@bellsouth.net; www.dilloncitysc.com*

Dorchester · *see Saint George*

Easley · *Greater Easley C/C* · Kent Dykes; Pres.; 2001 E. Main St.; P.O. Box 241; 29641; Pickens; P 60,000; M 450; (864) 859-2693; Fax (864) 859-1941; ecc@easleychamber.org; www.easleychamber.org*

Edisto Island · *Edisto C/C* · Dan Carter; Exec. Dir.; P.O. Box 206; 29438; Colleton; P 3,500; M 180; (843) 869-3867; (888) 333-2781; eichamber@aol.com; www.edistochamber.com

Elloree · *see Orangeburg*

Eutawville · *see Saint George*

Florence · *Greater Florence C/C* · Tom Marschel; Pres.; 610 W. Palmetto St.; 29501; Florence; P 130,000; M 842; (843) 665-0515; Fax (843) 662-2010; info@flochamber.com; www.flochamber.com*

Fort Mill · *see Rock Hill*

Fountain Inn · *Fountain Inn C/C* · John R. Hastings Sr.; Pres./CEO; 102 Depot St.; 29644; Greenville; P 8,650; M 241; (864) 862-2586; Fax (864) 862-1086; info@fountaininnchamber.org; www.fountaininnchamber.org

Gaffney · *Cherokee County C/C* · Kayla Robbs; Exec. Dir.; 225 S. Limestone St.; 29340; Cherokee; P 53,000; M 500; (864) 489-5721; Fax (864) 487-3399; comcher@bellsouth.net; www.cherokeechamber.org

Garden City · *see Georgetown*

Georgetown · *Georgetown County C/C* · Annette Fisher; Pres.; 531 Front St.; 29440; Georgetown; P 65,000; M 800; (843) 546-8436; Fax (843) 520-4876; info@visitgeorge.com; www.georgetownchamber.com

Greeleyville · *see Kingstree*

Greenville · *Greenville C/C* · Ben Haskew; Pres./CEO; 24 Cleveland St.; 29601; Greenville; P 424,000; M 2,400; (864) 242-1050; (866) 485-5262; Fax (864) 282-8509; info@greenvillechamber.org; www.greenvillechamber.org.*

Greenwood · *Greenwood Area C/C* · Angelle LaBorde; Pres.; 110 Phoenix St.; P.O. Box 980; 29648; Greenwood; P 68,000; M 725; (864) 223-8431; Fax (864) 229-9785; info@greenwoodscchamber.org; www.greenwoodscchamber.org*

Greer · *Greater Greer C/C* · Allen Smith; Pres./CEO; 111 Trade St.; 29651; Greenville; P 50,000; M 580; (864) 877-3131; Fax (864) 877-0961; info@greerchamber.com; www.greerchamber.com*

Grover · *see Saint George*

Hampton · *Hampton County C/C* · P.O. Box 122; 29924; Hampton; P 21,386; M 120; (803) 943-3784; Fax (803) 943-7538; jlamprecht@hamptoncountysc.org

Hardeeville · *Greater Hardeeville C/C* · Paul Bathe; Pres.; P.O. Box 307; 29927; Jasper; P 21,000; M 103; (843) 784-3606; Fax (843) 784-2781; info@hardeevillechamber.com; www.hardeevillechamber.com

Harleyville · *see Saint George*

Hartsville · *Greater Hartsville C/C* · Sharman Poplava; Pres.; P.O. Box 578; 29551; Darlington; P 31,472; M 337; (843) 332-6401; Fax (843) 332-8017; president@hartsvillechamber.org; www.hartsvillechamber.org

Hemingway · *see Kingstree*

Hilton Head Island · *Hilton Head Island-Bluffton C/C* · William G. Miles; Pres./CEO; 1 Chamber of Commerce Dr.; P.O. Box 5647; 29938; Beaufort; P 42,000; M 1,700; (843) 785-3673; (800) 523-3373; Fax (843) 785-7110; info@hiltonheadisland.org; www.hiltonheadisland.org.*

Holly Hill · *Tri-County Reg. C/C* · Teresa Mizzell Hatchell; Exec. Dir.; 8603 Old State Rd.; P.O. Box 1012; 29059; Orangeburg; P 88,000; M 315; (803) 496-3831; (888) 568-5646; Fax (803) 496-3831; tcrcc@bellsouth.net; www.tri-crcc.com*

Inman · *Greater Inman Area C/C* · Bessie Fisher; Pres.; P.O. Box 227; 29349; Spartanburg; P 2,500; M 115; (864) 472-3654; inmanchamber1@gmail.com; www.inmanscchamber.org

Irmo · *Greater Irmo C/C* · Meredith Allan; Pres./CEO; 1248 Lake Murray Blvd.; 29063; Lexington; P 90,000; M 790; (803) 749-9355; Fax (803) 732-7986; info@greaterirmochamber.com; www.greaterirmochamber.com

Jasper County · *see Ridgeland*

Johnston · *Edgefield County C/C* · Donna C. Livingston; Admin.; 416 Calhoun St.; 29832; Edgefield; P 24,000; M 175; (803) 275-0010; Fax (803) 275-0010; info@edgefieldcountychamber.org; www.edgefieldcountychamber.org

Kingstree · *Williamsburg HomeTown C/C* · Leslee Spivey; Exec. Dir.; 130 E. Main St.; P.O. Box 696; 29556; Williamsburg; P 35,000; M 250; (843) 355-6431; Fax (843) 355-3343; whtc@FTC-i.net; www.williamsburgsc.org

Lake City · *Greater Lake City C/C* · Penny Hill; Exec. Dir.; 144 S. Acline Ave.; P.O. Box 669; 29560; Florence; P 7,500; M 225; (843) 374-8611; Fax (843) 374-7938; lccoc1@ftc-i.net; www.lakecitysc.org

Lake Wylie · *Lake Wylie C/C* · Susan Bromfield; Pres.; P.O. Box 5233; 29710; York; P 25,000; M 400; (803) 831-2827; Fax (803) 831-2460; info@lakewyliesc.com; www.lakewyliesc.com

Lancaster · *Lancaster County C/C* · Dean Faile IOM; Pres.; 453 Colonial Ave.; P.O. Box 430; 29721; Lancaster; P 77,000; M 450; (803) 283-4105; Fax (803) 286-4360; info@lancasterchambersc.com; www.lancasterchambersc.org*

Lane · *see Kingstree*

Laurens · *Laurens County C/C* · Greg Alexander; Pres./CEO; P.O. Box 248; 29360; Laurens; P 72,000; M 500; (864) 833-2716; Fax (864) 833-6935; mail@laurenscounty.org; www.laurenscounty.org*

Leesville · *see Batesburg-Leesville*

Lexington · *Greater Lexington Chamber & Visitors Center* · Randy Halfacre; Pres./CEO; 321 S. Lake Dr.; P.O. Box 44; 29071; Lexington; P 65,000; M 800; (803) 359-6113; Fax (803) 359-0634; info@lexingtonsc.org; www.lexingtonsc.org.*

Liberty • *Liberty C/C* • P.O. Box 123; 29657; Pickens; P 3,500; M 30; (864) 843-3021; info@libertychamberofcommerce.com; www.libertychamberofcommerce.com

Litchfield Beach • *see Georgetown*

Little River • *Little River C/C* • Jennifer Walters; Exec. Dir.; 1180 Hwy. 17 N., Ste. 1; P.O. Box 400; 29566; Horry; P 8,000; M 400; (843) 249-6604; (866) 817-8082; Fax (843) 249-9788; jennifer@littleriverchamber.org; www.littleriverchamber.org*

Loris • *Loris Chamber and Visitors & Conv. Bur.* • Samantha Norris; Exec. Asst.; 4242 Main St.; P.O. Box 356; 29569; Horry; P 4,300; M 180; (843) 756-6030; Fax (843) 756-5661; info@lorischambersc.com; www.lorischambersc.com

Manning • *Clarendon County C/C* • Dawn Griffith; Exec. Dir.; 19 N. Brooks St.; 29102; Clarendon; P 32,000; M 320; (803) 435-4405; (800) 731-LAKE; Fax (803) 435-4406; chamber@clarendoncounty.com; www.clarendoncounty.com

Marion • *Marion C/C* • Judy J. Johnson; Exec. V.P.; 209 E. Bobby Gerald Pkwy.; P.O. Box 35; 29571; Marion; P 8,000; M 300; (843) 423-3561; Fax (843) 423-0963; marionsc@bellsouth.net; www.marionscchamber.com

Mauldin • *Greater Mauldin C/C* • Pat Pomeroy; Exec. Dir.; 101 E. Butler Rd.; P.O. Box 881; 29662; Greenville; P 22,000; M 390; (864) 297-1323; Fax (864) 297-5645; info@mauldinchamber.org; www.mauldinchamber.org*

McCormick • *McCormick County C/C* • Shaaron Kohl; Pres.; 100 S. Main St.; P.O. Box 938; 29835; McCormick; P 10,410; M 175; (864) 852-2835; Fax (864) 852-2382; abarron@mccormickscchamber.org; www.mccormickscchamber.org*

Moncks Corner • *Berkeley County C/C* • Bill McCall; Pres.; 1004 Old Hwy. 52; P.O. Box 968; 29461; Berkeley; P 146,000; M 650; (843) 761-8238; (800) 882-0337; Fax (843) 899-6491; info@berkeleysc.org; www.berkeleysc.org

Mullins • *Greater Mullins C/C* • Cindy Lesieur; Exec. Dir.; 1 N. Main St.; P.O. Box 595; 29574; Marion; P 5,500; M 250; (843) 464-6651; Fax (843) 464-7138; mullinschamber@bellsouth.net; www.mullinschamber.com*

Murrells Inlet • *see Georgetown*

Myrtle Beach • *Myrtle Beach Area C/C* • Dana Lilly; Dir. of Sales; 1200 N. Oak St.; P.O. Box 2115; 29578; Horry; P 150,000; M 2,400; (843) 626-7444; (800) 356-3016; Fax (843) 448-3010; info@visitmyrtlebeach.com; www.visitmyrtlebeach.com*

Newberry • *Newberry County C/C* • Ted Smith; Exec. Dir.; 1109 Main St.; P.O. Box 396; 29108; Newberry; P 38,326; M 300; (803) 276-4274; Fax (803) 276-4373; chamber@newberrycounty.org; www.newberrycounty.org.

Ninety Six • *Ninety Six C/C* • Diane Quinn; Secy.; P.O. Box 8; 29666; Greenwood; P 1,935; M 115; (864) 543-2047; Fax (864) 543-4304; 96chamber@gmail.com; www.96chamber.web.officelive.com

North Augusta • *North Augusta C/C* • Brian Tucker; Pres.; 406 West Ave.; P.O. Box 6246; 29861; Aiken; P 25,000; M 380; (803) 279-2323; Fax (803) 279-0003; info@northaugustachamber.org; www.northaugustachamber.org*

North Myrtle Beach • *North Myrtle Beach C/C* • Marc Jordan; Pres./CEO; 270 Hwy. 17 N.; 29582; Horry; P 15,000; M 1,200; (843) 281-2662; (877) 332-2662; Fax (843) 280-2930; info@north-myrtlebeachchamber.com; www.northmyrtlebeachchamber.com.*

Orangeburg • *Orangeburg County C/C* • David L. Coleman; Pres.; 155 Riverside Dr.; P.O. Box 328; 29116; Orangeburg; P 91,000; M 550; (803) 534-6821; (800) 545-6153; Fax (803) 531-9435; chamber@orangeburgsc.net; www.orangeburgchamber.com.

Pageland • *Pageland C/C* • Sondra Price; 128 N. Pearl St.; P.O. Box 56; 29728; Chesterfield; P 3,000; M 100; (843) 672-6400; Fax (843) 672-6401; pagelandcham@shtc.net; www.pagelandchamber.com

Pawleys Island • *see Georgetown*

Pickens • *Greater Pickens C/C* • Mike Parrott; Exec. Dir.; 222 W. Main St.; P.O. Box 153; 29671; Pickens; P 18,049; M 214; (864) 878-3258; Fax (864) 878-7317; info@pickenschamber.net; www.pickenschamber.org

Pine Ridge • *see Cayce*

Providence • *see Saint George*

Reevesville • *see Saint George*

Ridgeland • *Jasper County C/C* • Kendall Malphrus; Exec. Dir.; 403 Russell St.; P.O. Box 1267; 29936; Jasper; P 21,953; M 275; (843) 726-8126; Fax (843) 726-6290; jasperchamber@jaspersc.org; www.jaspercountychamber.com

Ridgeville • *see Saint George*

Rock Hill • *York County Reg. C/C* • Rob Youngblood; Pres.; 116 E. Main St.; P.O. Box 590; 29731; York; P 200,000; M 1,050; (803) 324-7500; Fax (803) 324-1889; info@yorkcountychamber.com; www.yorkcountychamber.com*

Saint George • *Tri-County Reg. C/C* • Teresa Mizzell Hatchell; Exec. Dir.; 225 Parler Ave.; 29477; Dorchester; P 365,000; M 330; (843) 563-9091; (800) 788-5646; Fax (843) 563-9091; tcrcc@bellsouth.net; www.tri-crcc.com.*

Saint Matthews • *Calhoun County C/C* • Jane Dyches; Exec. Dir.; Courthouse Annex, Rm. 114; 29135; Calhoun; P 15,185; M 100; (803) 655-5650; Fax (803) 655-6110; jdyches@calhouncounty.sc.gov; www.calhouncountychamber.org

Saluda • *Saluda County C/C* • Don Hancock; P.O. Box 246; 29138; Saluda; P 19,000; M 100; (864) 445-4100; saludacountychamber@embarqmail.com; www.saludacountychamber.com

Santee • *see Orangeburg and Saint George*

Santee • *see Orangeburg and Saint George*

Seneca • *Oconee County C/C* • Pamela Ramey; Interim Exec. Dir.; 105A Ram Cat Alley; P.O. Box 855; 29679; Oconee; P 77,000; M 300; (864) 882-2097; Fax (864) 882-2881; info@oconeechambersc.com; www.oconeechambersc.com*

Simpsonville • *Simpsonville Area C/C* • Kelly Wilkins; Pres.; 211 N. Main St.; P.O. Box 605; 29681; Greenville; P 19,000; M 400; (864) 963-3781; Fax (864) 228-0003; kwilkins@simpsonvillechamber.com; www.simpsonvillechamber.com*

South Congaree • *see Cayce*

Spartanburg • *Spartanburg Area C/C* • David Cordeau; Pres./CEO; 105 N. Pine St.; P.O. Box 1636; 29304; Spartanburg; P 280,738; M 1,200; (864) 594-5000; Fax (864) 594-5055; spartanburgchamber@spartanburgchamber.com; www.spartanburgchamber.com.*

Springdale • *see Cayce*

Summerville • *Greater Summerville/Dorchester County C/C* • Rita Berry; Pres./CEO; 402 N. Main St.; P.O. Box 670; 29484; Dorchester; P 113,000; M 575; (843) 873-2931; Fax (843) 875-4464; jbrooks@greatersummerville.org; www.greatersummerville.org.*

Sumter • *Greater Sumter C/C* • Grier U. Blackwelder; Pres.; 32 E. Calhoun St.; 29150; Sumter; P 108,000; M 1,200; (803) 775-1231; Fax (803) 775-0915; info@sumterchamber.com; www.sumterchamber.com.*

Tega Cay • *see Rock Hill*

Union · *Union County C/C* · Torance Inman; Exec. Dir.; 135 W. Main St.; 29379; Union; P 29,000; M 210; (864) 427-9039; (877) 202-8755; Fax (864) 427-9030; torance@unionsc.com; www.unionsc.com

Vance · *see Saint George*

Walhalla · *Walhalla C/C* · Barbara Justus; Exec. Dir.; 214 E. Main St.; 29691; Oconee; P 5,000; M 135; (864) 638-2727; Fax (864) 638-2727; walhallacoc@bellsouth.net; www.walhallachamber.com*

Walterboro · *Walterboro-Colleton C/C* · David M. Smalls; Pres./CEO; 109 Benson St.; P.O. Box 426; 29488; Colleton; P 40,000; M 325; (843) 549-9595; Fax (843) 549-5775; info@walterboro.org; www.walterboro.org.

Warrenville · *Midland Valley Area C/C* · Al McKay; Chrmn.; 1805 Jefferson Davis Hwy.; 29851; Aiken; P 15,000; M 200; (803) 593-3030; Fax (803) 593-0085; www.midlandvalleyarea.com

West Columbia · *see Cayce*

Westminster · *Westminster C/C* · Sandra Powell; Dir.; 135 E. Main St.; P.O. Box 155; 29693; Oconee; P 3,000; M 125; (864) 647-5316; Fax (864) 647-5013; wcoc@nuvox.net; www.westminstersc.com

Winnsboro · *Fairfield County C/C* · Terry N. Vickers; Pres.; 100 Congress St.; P.O. Box 297; 29180; Fairfield; P 25,000; M 200; (803) 635-4242; (803) 635-7955; Fax (803) 712-2996; fchamber@truvista.net; www.fairfieldchambersc.com*

Woodruff · *see Spartanburg*

York · *Greater York C/C* · Paul Boger; Exec. Dir.; 23 E. Liberty St.; P.O. Box 97; 29745; York; P 25,000; M 310; (803) 684-2590; (877) 684-2590; Fax (803) 684-2575; info@greateryorkchamber.com; www.greateryorkchamber.com

South Dakota

South Dakota C of C & Ind. · David Owen; Pres.; P.O. Box 190; Pierre; 57501; Hughes; P 765,000; M 450; (605) 224-6161; Fax (605) 224-7198; contactus@sdchamber.biz; www.sdchamber.biz

Aberdeen · *Aberdeen Area C/C* · Gail Ochs; Pres.; 516 S. Main St.; P.O. Box 1179; 57402; Brown; P 25,000; M 650; (605) 225-2860; (800) 874-9038; Fax (605) 225-2437; info@aberdeen-chamber.com; www.aberdeen-chamber.com.*

Badlands · *see Wall*

Belle Fourche · *Belle Fourche C/C* · Teresa Schanzenbach; Exec. Dir.; 415 5th Ave.; 57717; Butte; P 4,900; M 310; (605) 892-2676; Fax (605) 892-4633; events@bellefourchechamber.org; www.bellefourchechamber.org

Beresford · *Beresford C/C* · Sara Bovill; P.O. Box 167; 57004; Lincoln & Union; P 2,000; M 75; (605) 763-2021; Fax (605) 763-2021; chamber@bmtc.net; www.bmtc.net

Brandon · *Brandon Valley Area C/C* · Kim Cerwick; Exec. Dir.; 109 N. Pipestone Ave.; P.O. Box 182; 57005; Minnehaha; P 8,000; M 285; (605) 582-7400; Fax (605) 582-8941; brancofc@alliance com.net; www.brandonvalleychamber.com*

Britton · *Britton Area C/C* · Julie Zuehlke; Secy./Treas.; P.O. Box 96; 57430; Marshall; P 1,500; M 80; (605) 448-5323; britton chamber@venturecomm.net; www.brittonsouthdakota.com

Brookings · *Brookings Area C/C* · Al Heuton; Exec. Dir.; 414 Main Ave.; P.O. Box 431; 57006; Brookings; P 25,000; M 435; (605) 692-6125; Fax (605) 697-8109; chamber@brookings.net; www.brookingssd.com*

Buffalo · *Harding County C/C* · Diane Haivala; P.O. Box 113; 57720; Harding; P 1,000; M 25; (605) 375-3844; (605) 375-3130; Fax (605) 375-3119

Canton · *Canton C/C* · Lisa Alden; Coord.; P.O. Box 34; 57013; Lincoln; P 3,110; M 100; (605) 764-7864; Fax (605) 764-7865; lisa.canton@iw.net; www.cantonsouthdakota.org

Centerville · *Centerville C/C* · Doug Voss; Pres.; P.O. Box 266; 57014; Turner; P 920; M 60; (605) 563-2291; Fax (605) 563-2615; doug.voss@k12.sd.us; www.centervillesd.org

Chamberlain · *Chamberlain-Oacoma Area C/C & CVB* · April Reis; Dir.; 115 W. Lawler; 57325; Brule; P 2,900; M 162; (605) 234-4416; Fax (605) 234-4418; chamber@chamberlainsd.org; www.chamberlainsd.org

Custer · *Custer Area C/C* · David Ressler; Exec. Dir.; 615 Washington St.; P.O. Box 5018; 57730; Custer; P 1,860; M 310; (605) 673-2244; (800) 992-9818; Fax (605) 673-3726; info@custersd.com; www.custersd.com

Deadwood · *Deadwood C/C & Visitors Bur.* · George Milos; Exec. Dir.; 767 Main St.; 57732; Lawrence; P 1,300; M 400; (605) 578-1876; (800) 999-1876; Fax (605) 578-2429; visit@deadwood.org; www.deadwood.org

Dell Rapids · *Dell Rapids C/C* · Kelly Krogstad; Pres.; P.O. Box 81; 57022; Minnehaha; P 3,100; M 75; (605) 428-4167; Fax (605) 428-4167; chamber@dellrapids.org; www.dellrapids.org

DeSmet · *DeSmet C/C* · Connie Halverson; P.O. Box 105; 57231; Kingsbury; P 1,300; M 72; (605) 854-3652; www.desmetsd.com

Edgemont · *Edgemont C/C* · Lisa Scheinost; Ofc. Mgr.; P.O. Box 797; 57735; Custer; P 799; M 70; (605) 662-5900; edgemont chamber@gwtc.net; www.edgemont-sd.com

Eureka · *Eureka C/C* · Jim Schumacher; Pres.; P.O. Box 272; 57437; McPherson; P 1,101; M 50; (605) 577-6294; (605) 284-2441; www.eurekasd.com

Flandreau · *Flandreau Civic & Commerce Assn.* · P.O. Box 343; 57028; Moody; P 2,400; M 65; (605) 997-2492; Fax (605) 997-2915; chuck@cityofflandreau.com; www.cityofflandreau.com

Fort Pierre · *Fort Pierre C/C* · Pat Sutley; 310 Casey Tibbs St.; P.O. Box 426; 57532; Stanley; P 2,000; (605) 223-2178; www.fortpierre.com

Freeman · *Freeman Chamber/Comm. Dev.* · Shane Vetch; Pres.; P.O. Box 43; 57029; Hutchinson; P 1,300; M 100; (605) 925-4444; Fax (605) 925-7920; dennis@cityoffreeman.org; www.freemansd.com

Garretson · *Garretson Commercial Club* · P.O. Box 349; 57030; Minnehaha; P 1,165; M 60; (605) 594-6721; kvegas@alliancecom.net; www.garretsonsd.com

Gettysburg · *Gettysburg C/C* · Molly McRoberts; 110 S. Exene St.; P.O. Box 33; 57442; Potter; P 1,300; M 60; (605) 765-2528; gburgchamber@venturecomm.net; www.gettysburgsd.net

Gregory · *Gregory Commercial Club* · Guyla Husman; Secy.; 1313 Main St.; 57533; Gregory; P 1,350; M 90; (605) 835-8229; Fax (605) 835-9023; guylahusman@hotmail.com; www.cityofgregory.com

Hill City · *Hill City Area C/C* · Lori Nonnast; Pres.; 23935 Hwy. 385; P.O. Box 253; 57745; Pennington; P 900; M 139; (605) 574-2368; (800) 888-1798; Fax (605) 574-2055; officemanager@hillcitysd.com; www.hillcitysd.com

Hot Springs · *Hot Springs Area C/C* · George Kotti; Exec. Dir.; 801 S. 6th St.; P.O. Box 342; 57747; Fall River; P 4,300; M 250; (605) 745-4140; (800) 325-6991; Fax (605) 745-5849; hschamber@gwtc.net; www.hotsprings-sd.com*

Huron · *Huron Area Chamber & Visitor Bur.* · Peggy Woolridge; Exec. Dir.; 1725 Dakota Ave. S.; 57350; Beadle; P 11,500; M 400; (605) 352-0000; (800) 487-6673; Fax (605) 352-8321; cvb@huronsd.com; www.huronsd.com*

Keystone • *Keystone C/C* • Bonnetta Eich; Exec. Dir.; P.O. Box 653; 57751; Pennington; P 311; M 92; (605) 666-4896; (800) 456-3345; Fax (605) 666-4896; info@keystonechamber.com; www.keystonechamber.com

Kimball • *Kimball C/C* • Corinne Overweg; Secy.; P.O. Box 2; 57355; Jerauld; P 750; M 100; (605) 680-1794; kimballsd@midstatesd.net; www.kimballsd.org

Lead • *Lead Area C/C* • Melissa Johnson; Exec. Dir.; 160 W. Main; 57754; Lawrence; P 3,800; M 250; (605) 584-1100; Fax (605) 584-2209; leadcoc@knology.net; www.leadmethere.org

Lemmon • *Lemmon Area C/C* • Stacy Dailey; COO; 100 3rd St. W.; 57638; Perkins; P 1,350; M 120; (605) 374-5716; Fax (605) 374-5789; lchamber@sdplains.com; www.lemmonsd.com

Lennox • *Lennox Commercial Club* • Mike Fjerstad; Pres.; P.O. Box 181; 57039; Lincoln; P 2,700; M 25; (605) 647-2284; Fax (605) 647-2218; www.cityoflennoxsd.com

Madison • *Madison Area C/C* • Julie Gross; Exec. Dir.; 315 S. Egan Ave.; P.O. Box 467; 57042; Lake; P 6,540; M 280; (605) 256-2454; Fax (605) 256-9606; director@chamberofmadisonsd.com; www.chamberofmadisonsd.com

Milbank • *Milbank Area C/C* • Laura Foss; Exec. Dir.; 1001 E. 4th Ave., Ste. 101; 57252; Grant; P 3,500; M 198; (605) 432-6656; (800) 675-6656; Fax (605) 432-6507; chamber@milbanksd.com; www.milbanksd.com

Miller • *Miller Civic & Commerce Assn.* • Greg Palmer; Pres.; 103 W. 3rd St.; 57362; Hand; P 1,500; M 100; (605) 853-3098; Fax (605) 853-3276; amy@millersd.org; millersd.net

Mitchell • *Mitchell Area C/C* • Bryan Hisel; Exec. Dir.; 601 N. Main St.; P.O. Box 1026; 57301; Davison; P 32,000; M 500; (605) 996-5567; (605) 996-1140; Fax (605) 996-8273; info@mitchellchamber.com; www.mitchellchamber.com*

Mobridge • *Mobridge C/C* • Cindy Melcher; Exec. Dir.; 103 N. Main St.; 57601; Walworth; P 3,500; M 200; (605) 845-2387; (888) 614-3474; Fax (605) 845-3223; info@mobridge.org; www.mobridge.org*

Murdo • *Murdo C/C* • Sherry Dykema; P.O. Box 242; 57559; Jones; P 600; M 80; (605) 669-3333; murdoinfo@murdosd.com; www.murdosd.com

Oacoma • *see Chamberlain*

Philip • *Philip C/C* • Kent Olson; P.O. Box 378; 57567; Haakon; P 800; M 100; (605) 859-2175; Fax (605) 859-2622; info@philipsouthdakota.com; www.philipsouthdakota.com

Pierre • *Pierre Area C/C* • Laura Schoen Carbonneau; CEO; 800 W. Dakota Ave.; P.O. Box 548; 57501; Hughes; P 16,000; M 500; (605) 224-7361; (800) 962-2034; Fax (605) 224-6485; contactchamber@pierre.org; www.pierre.org*

Platte • *Platte Area C/C* • Laura VandenBerg; Exec. Dir.; P.O. Box 393; 57369; Charles Mix; P 1,367; M 130; (605) 337-2275; (888) 297-8175; Fax (605) 337-3988; plattechamber@midstatesd.net; www.plattesd.org

Presho • *Presho Area C/C* • P.O. Box 415; 57568; Lyman; P 600; M 50; (605) 895-9445; preshochamber@kennebectelephone.com; www.presho.net

Rapid City • *Rapid City Area C/C* • Linda Rabe IOM CCE; Pres./CEO; 444 Mt. Rushmore Rd. N.; P.O. Box 747; 57709; Pennington; P 89,000; M 1,400; (605) 343-1744; Fax (605) 343-6550; info@rapidcitychamber.com; www.rapidcitychamber.com.*

Redfield • *Redfield Area C/C* • Cathy Fink; Coord.; 626 Main St.; 57469; Spink; P 2,800; M 100; (605) 472-0965; Fax (605) 472-4553; redfieldchamber@redfield-sd.com; www.redfield-sd.com

Sioux Falls • *Sioux Falls Area C/C* • Evan C. Nolte; Pres./CEO; 200 N. Phillips Ave., Ste. 102; P.O. Box 1425; 57101; Minnehaha; P 220,000; M 2,250; (605) 336-1620; Fax (605) 336-6499; sfacc@siouxfalls.com; www.siouxfalls.com*

Sisseton • *Sisseton Area C/C & Visitors Bur.* • Sandi Jaspers; Exec. Dir.; 1608 SD Hwy. 10, Ste. A; 57262; Roberts; P 2,500; M 80; (605) 698-7261; (888) 512-1966; sissetonchamber@venturecomm.net; www.sisseton.com

Spearfish • *Spearfish Area C/C* • Lisa Langer IOM; Exec. Dir.; 106 W. Kansas St.; P.O. Box 550; 57783; Lawrence; P 14,500; M 596; (605) 642-2626; (800) 626-8013; Fax (605) 642-7310; info@spearfishchamber.org; www.spearfishchamber.org.*

Sturgis • *Sturgis Area C/C & VB* • Michele Loobey-Gertsch; Exec. Dir.; 2040 Junction Ave.; P.O. Box 504; 57785; Meade; P 6,500; M 350; (605) 347-2556; Fax (605) 347-6682; info@sturgis-sd.org; sturgis-sd.org

Vermillion • *Vermillion Area C/C & Dev. Co.* • Steve Howe; Exec. Dir.; 116 Market St.; 57069; Clay; P 13,000; M 300; (605) 624-5571; (800) 809-2071; Fax (605) 624-0094; vcdc@vermillionchamber.com; www.vermillionchamber.com*

Wagner • *Wagner C/C* • Matt Cerny; Pres.; 60 Main Ave. S.E.; P.O. Box 40; 57380; Charles Mix; P 1,558; M 65; (605) 384-3741; Fax (605) 384-5644; developwagner@hcinet.net; www.cityofwagner.org

Wall • *Wall Badlands Area C/C* • Lindsey Hildebrand; Exec. Dir.; 501 Main St.; P.O. Box 527; 57790; Pennington; P 1,000; M 70; (605) 279-2665; Fax (605) 279-2067; wallchamber@gwtc.net; www.wall-badlands.com

Watertown • *Watertown Area C/C* • Megan Olson; Pres./CEO; 20 S. Maple; P.O. Box 1113; 57201; Codington; P 21,000; M 715; (605) 886-5814; Fax (605) 886-5957; coc@watertownsd.com; www.watertownsd.com

Webster • *Webster Area C/C* • Marcia Lefman; Secy./Treas.; P.O. Box 123; 57274; Day; P 1,661; M 175; (605) 345-4668; (888) 571-7582; wchamber@itctel.com; www.webstersd.com. www.proudanglers.com

Wessington Springs • *Wessington Springs Area C/C* • Matthew Orstad; Pres.; P.O. Box 513; 57382; Jerauld; P 1,011; M 45; (605) 539-1929; wsprings@venturecomm.net; www.wessingtonsprings.com

White River • *Mellette County C/C* • Rose West; Treas.; 502 N. Main St.; P.O. Box 223; 57579; Mellette; P 2,083; M 41; (605) 259-3651; melettecounty@yahoo.com

Winner • *Winner C/C* • Amy Moe; Exec. Dir.; 201 S. Monroe St.; P.O. Box 268; 57580; Tripp; P 3,200; M 150; (605) 842-1533; thechamber@gwtc.net; www.winnersd.org

Yankton • *Yankton Area C/C* • Carmen Schramm; Dir. of Chamber Svcs.; 803 E. Fourth St.; P.O. Box 588; 57078; Yankton; P 14,000; M 400; (800) 888-1460; Fax (605) 665-7501; chamber@yanktonsd.com; www.yanktonsd.com*

Tennessee

Tennessee C of C & Ind. • Deborah Woolley; Pres.; 611 Commerce St., Ste. 3030; Nashville; 37203; Davidscon; P 6,200,000; M 600; (615) 256-5141; Fax (615) 256-6726; info@tnchamber.org; www.tnchamber.org

Alamo • *Crockett County C/C* • Melissa Cox; Exec. Dir.; 29 N. Bells St.; 38001; Crockett; P 14,000; M 162; (731) 696-5120; Fax (731) 696-4855; contact@crockettchamber.com; www.crockettchamber.com

Ardmore · *Ardmore C/C* · 29910 Ardmore Ave.; P.O. Box 845; 38449; Giles; P 2,224; M 124; (256) 423-7588; Fax (256) 423-8950

Arlington · *Arlington C/C* · Glen Bascom II; Pres.; 6220 Greenlee St., Ste. 3B; P.O. Box 545; 38002; Shelby; P 10,000; M 145; (901) 867-0545; Fax (901) 867-4066; info@arlingtontnchamber.com; arlingtontnchamber.com

Ashland City · *Cheatham County C/C* · Chris Neese; Exec. Dir.; 108 N. Main St.; P.O. Box 354; 37015; Cheatham; P 39,000; M 400; (615) 792-6722; (615) 792-1335; Fax (615) 792-5001; info@cheathamchamber.org; www.cheathamchamber.org

Athens · *Athens Area C/C* · Rob Preston; Pres./CEO; 13 N. Jackson St.; 37303; McMinn; P 15,000; M 600; (423) 745-0334; Fax (423) 745-0335; info@athenschamber.org; www.athenschamber.org

Bartlett · *Bartlett Area C/C* · John P. Threadgill; Pres./CEO; 2969 Elmore Park Rd.; 38134; Shelby; P 48,000; M 615; (901) 372-9457; Fax (901) 372-9488; info@bartlettchamber.org; www.bartlettchamber.org.*

Bellevue · *Bellevue C/C* · Cindy Tremblay; Exec. Dir.; 177-A Belle Forest Circle; 37221; Davidson; P 35,000; M 290; (615) 662-2737; (877) 660-2737; Fax (615) 662-0197; info@thebellevuechamber.com; www.thebellevuechamber.com

Benton · *Polk County C/C* · P.O. Box 560; 37307; Polk; P 18,000; M 200; (423) 338-5040; (800) 633-7655; Fax (423) 338-0056; westoffice@ocoeecountry.com; www.ocoeecountry.com

Big Sandy · *see Paris*

Bolivar · *Hardeman County C/C* · Anne Crighton; Pres.; 500 W. Market St.; P.O. Box 313; 38008; Hardeman; P 28,105; M 180; (731) 658-6554; Fax (731) 658-6874; info@hardemancountychamber.org; www.hardemancountychamber.org

Brentwood · *Brentwood Cool Springs C/C* · Cindi Parmenter; Pres./Dir.; 5211 Maryland Way, Ste. 1080; 37027; Williamson; P 150,000; M 1,000; (615) 373-1595; Fax (615) 373-8810; info@brentwoodcoolsprings.org; www.brentwoodcoolsprings.org

Bristol · *Bristol C/C* · Lisa Meadows CTTP; Pres./CEO; 20 Volunteer Pkwy.; P.O. Box 519; 37620; Sullivan; P 45,000; M 750; (423) 989-4850; (423) 989-4848; Fax (423) 989-4867; frontdesk@bristolchamber.org; www.bristolchamber.org*

Brownsville · *Brownsville-Haywood County C/C* · Joe Ing; Exec. Dir.; 121 W. Main; 38012; Haywood; P 20,000; M 320; (731) 772-2193; Fax (731) 772-2195; brownsvillechamber@newwavecomm.net; www.haywoodcountybrownsville.com

Bybee · *see Newport*

Byrdstown · *Byrdstown-Pickett County C/C* · Lana Baker Rossi; Pres.; 109 W. Main St.; P.O. Box 447; 38549; Pickett; P 5,000; M 140; (931) 864-7195; (888) 406-4704; Fax (931) 864-6845; pickettinfo@twlakes.net; www.dalehollow.com

Camden · *Benton County/Camden C/C* · Bill Kee; Exec. Dir.; 266 Hwy. 641 N.; 38320; Benton; P 16,328; M 209; (731) 584-8395; Fax (731) 584-5544; chamber1@usit.net; www.bentoncountycamden.com.*

Carthage · *Smith County C/C* · Regina Brooks; Admin. Dir.; 939 Upper Ferry Rd.; P.O. Box 70; 37030; Smith; P 17,712; M 171; (615) 735-2093; Fax (615) 735-2093; info@smithcountychamber.org; www.smithcountychamber.org

Celina · *Clay County C/C* · Ray Norris; Exec. Dir.; 424 Brown St.; 38551; Clay; P 8,000; M 100; (931) 243-3338; Fax (931) 243-6809; claychamber@twlakes.net; www.dalehollowlake.net

Centerville · *Hickman County C/C* · Nancy S. Roland; Exec. Dir.; 405 W. Public Sq.; P.O. Box 126; 37033; Hickman; P 25,000; M 150; (931) 729-5774; Fax (931) 729-0874; hickmancountycha@bellsouth.net; www.hickmanco.org

Chattanooga · *Chattanooga Area C/C* · Tom Edd Wilson; Pres./CEO; 811 Broad St.; 37402; Hamilton; P 332,000; M 1,600; (423) 756-2121; Fax (423) 267-7242; info@chattanoogachamber.com; www.chattanoogachamber.com.*

Chester County · *see Henderson*

Church Hill · *East Hawkins County C/C* · Steve Loller; P.O. Box 1314; 37642; Hawkins; P 20,000; M 30; (423) 357-6365; (423) 357-2943

Clarksville · *Clarksville Area C/C* · James Chavez; Pres./CEO; 25 Jefferson St., Ste. 300; P.O. Box 883; 37040; Montgomery; P 122,000; M 1,000; (931) 647-2331; Fax (931) 645-1574; cacc@clarksville.tn.us; www.clarksvillechamber.com

Cleveland · *Cleveland/Bradley C/C* · Gary Farlow; Pres./CEO; 225 Keith St. S.W.; P.O. Box 2275; 37320; Bradley; P 95,443; M 700; (423) 472-6587; Fax (423) 472-2019; info@clevelandchamber.com; www.clevelandchamber.com.*

Clinton · *Anderson County C/C* · Jackie L. Nichols; Pres.; 245 N. Main St., Ste. 200; 37716; Anderson; P 75,000; M 400; (865) 457-2559; (865) 457-2977; Fax (865) 463-7480; accc@andersoncountychamber.org; www.andersoncountychamber.org*

Collierville · *Collierville C/C* · Fran Persechini; Pres.; 485 Halle Park Dr.; 38017; Shelby; P 43,000; M 683; (901) 853-1949; Fax (901) 853-2399; info@colliervillechamber.com; www.colliervillechamber.com*

Collinwood · *Wayne County C/C* · Rena' Purdy; Exec. Dir.; 219 E. Broadway; 38450; Wayne; P 18,000; M 125; (931) 724-4337; Fax (931) 724-4347; chamber@netease.net; www.waynecountychamber.org

Columbia · *Maury County C/C & Eco. Dev. Alliance* · Brandom Gengelbach; Pres.; 106 W. 6th St.; P.O. Box 1076; 38402; Maury; P 80,000; M 500; (931) 388-2155; Fax (931) 380-0335; scobb@mauryalliance.com; www.mauryalliance.com.*

Cookeville · *Putnam County C/C* · George Halford; Pres./CEO; 1 W. First St.; 38501; Putnam; P 70,000; M 900; (931) 526-2211; (800) 264-5541; Fax (931) 526-4023; info@cookevillechamber.com; www.cookevillechamber.com*

Cool Springs · *see Brentwood*

Copperhill · *Polk County C/C* · P.O. Box 960; 37317; Polk; P 16,050; M 200; (423) 496-9000; (877) 790-2157; Fax (423) 496-5415; eastoffice@ocoeecountry.com; www.ocoeecountry.com

Cosby · *see Newport*

Covington · *Covington-Tipton County C/C* · Lee Johnston; Exec. Dir.; 106 W. Liberty; P.O. Box 683; 38019; Tipton; P 56,000; M 340; (901) 476-9727; Fax (901) 476-0056; tiptoncounty_covingto@comcast.net; www.covington-tiptoncochamber.com

Crossville · *Crossville-Cumberland County C/C* · Beth Alexander; Pres./CEO; 34 S. Main St.; 38555; Cumberland; P 54,000; M 550; (931) 484-8444; (877) 465-3861; Fax (931) 484-7511; thechamber@crossville-chamber.com; www.crossville-chamber.com.*

Dandridge · *Jefferson County C/C* · Don Cason; Pres./CEO; P.O. Box 890; 37725; Jefferson; P 55,000; M 430; (865) 397-9642; Fax (865) 397-0164; info@jeffersoncountytennessee.com; www.jeffersoncountytennessee.com

Dayton · *Dayton C/C* · Cynthia Rodriguez; Admin. Asst.; 107 Main St.; 37321; Rhea; P 30,000; M 240; (423) 775-0361; Fax (423) 570-0105; chamber@volstate.net; www.rheacountyetc.com*

Del Rio • *see Newport*

Dickson • *Dickson County C/C* • David Hamilton; Pres./CEO; 119 Hwy. 70 E.; 37055; Dickson; P 52,500; M 450; (615) 446-2349; Fax (615) 441-3112; contactus@dicksoncountychamber.com; www.dicksoncountychamber.com*

Donelson • *see Nashville–Donelson-Hermitage*

Dover • *Stewart County C/C* • Tana Sheets; Pres.; 117 Visitors Center Ln.; P.O. Box 147; 37058; Stewart; P 15,000; M 85; (931) 232-8290; Fax (931) 232-4973; stewartcountycha@bellsouth.net; www.stewartcountychamberofcommerce.com.

Dresden • *Weakley County C/C* • Barbara Virgin; Exec. Dir.; 114 W. Maple St.; P.O. Box 67; 38225; Weakley; P 34,000; M 400; (731) 364-3787; Fax (731) 364-2099; wccc@crunet.com; www.weakleycountychamber.com.

Dunlap • *Sequatchie County-Dunlap C/C* • Howard Hatcher; Exec. Dir.; 15643 Rankin Ave.; P.O. Box 1653; 37327; Sequatchie; P 5,000; M 250; (423) 949-7608; Fax (423) 949-8052; sequatchie@bledsoe.net; www.sequatchie.com

Dyersburg • *Dyersburg/Dyer County C/C* • Allen Hester CCE; Pres./CEO; 2000 Commerce Ave.; 38024; Dyer; P 40,000; M 620; (731) 285-3433; Fax (731) 286-4926; ellenc@dyerchamber.com; www.dyerchamber.com

Elizabethton • *Elizabethton/Carter County C/C* • Candy Craig; Exec. Dir.; 500 Veterans Memorial Pkwy.; P.O. Box 190; 37644; Carter; P 59,000; M 320; (423) 547-3850; Fax (423) 547-3854; executive@elizabethtonchamber.com; www.elizabethtonchamber.com*

Erin • *Houston County C/C* • Betsy Ligon; Pres.; P.O. Box 603; 37061; Houston; P 8,000; M 110; (931) 289-5100; Fax (931) 289-5600; irish@peoplestel.net; www.houstoncochamber.com

Erwin • *Unicoi County C/C* • Amanda Bennett; Exec. Dir.; 100 S. Main Ave.; P.O. Box 713; 37650; Unicoi; P 18,000; M 200; (423) 743-3000; Fax (423) 743-0942; amanda@unicoicounty.org; www.unicoicounty.org

Etowah • *Etowah Area C/C* • Durant Tullock; Exec. Dir.; L & N Depot; P.O. Box 458; 37331; McMinn; P 40,000; M 200; (423) 263-2228; Fax (423) 263-1670; info@etowahcoc.org; www.etowahcoc.org

Fairview • *Fairview Area C/C* • Mitzi Mangrum; Ofc. Mgr.; 7200 City Center Cirle; P.O. Box 711; 37062; Williamson; P 12,000; M 145; (615) 799-9290; Fax (615) 799-9290; fairviewchamber@bellsouth.net; www.fairviewchamber.org

Fayetteville • *Fayetteville-Lincoln County C/C* • Carolyn Denton; Exec. Dir.; 208 Elk Ave. S.; P.O. Box 515; 37334; P 37,000; M 360; (931) 433-1234; (888) 433-1238; Fax (931) 433-9087; flcchamber@fpunet.com; www.fayettevillelincolncountychamber.com

Franklin • *Williamson County-Franklin C/C* • Nancy P. Conway; Pres./CEO; 134 2nd Ave. N.; P.O. Box 156; 37065; Williamson; P 157,000; M 1,550; (615) 794-1225; (800) 356-3445; Fax (615) 790-5337; info@wcfchamber.com; www.williamson-franklinchamber.com*

Gainesboro • *Jackson County C/C* • Carla Khouri; Pres.; P.O. Box 827; 38562; Jackson; P 10,000; M 80; (931) 268-0971; Fax (931) 268-3540; www.gainesboro-jcchamber.com

Gallatin • *Gallatin C/C* • Paige Brown Strong; Dir.; 118 W. Main St.; P.O. Box 26; 37066; Sumner; P 28,000; M 500; (615) 452-4000; (800) 452-5286; Fax (615) 452-4021; info@gallatintn.org; www.gallatintn.org

Gatlinburg • *Gatlinburg C/C* • Victoria Simms; Exec. Dir.; 811 East Pkwy.; P.O. Box 527; 37738; Sevier; P 3,550; M 620; (865) 436-4178; (800) 568-4748; Fax (865) 430-3876; info@gatlinburg.com; www.gatlinburg.com*

Germantown • *Germantown Area C/C* • Pat Scroggs; Exec. Dir.; 2195 S. Germantown Rd., Ste. 100; 38138; Shelby; P 40,000; M 700; (901) 755-1200; Fax (901) 755-9168; info@germantownchamber.com; www.germantownchamber.com

Gleason • *see Dresden*

Goodlettsville • *Goodlettsville Area C/C* • David Wilson; Exec. Dir.; 117 N. Main St.; 37072; Davidson; P 13,800; M 500; (615) 859-7979; Fax (615) 859-1480; david@goodlettsvillechamber.com; www.goodlettsvillechamber.com*

Greeneville • *Greene County Partnership* • Randy Harrell; Pres./CEO; 115 Academy St.; 37743; Greene; P 65,945; M 500; (423) 638-4111; Fax (423) 638-5345; gcp@greenecop.com; www.GreeneCountyPartnership.com*

Greenfield • *see Dresden*

Gruetli • *see Monteagle*

Hartford • *see Newport*

Hartsville • *Hartsville-Trousdale County C/C* • Seth H. Thurman; Exec. Dir.; 240 Broadway; 37074; Trousdale; P 7,500; M 250; (615) 374-9243; Fax (615) 374-0068; sthurman@hartsvilletrousdale.com; www.hartsvilletrousdale.com

Helenwood • *Scott County C/C* • Stacey Kidd; Dir.; 12025 Scott Hwy.; P.O. Box 766; 37755; Scott; P 23,000; M 158; (423) 663-6900; (800) 645-6905; Fax (423) 663-6906; scchamber@highland.net; www.scottcountychamber.com

Henderson • *Chester County-City of Henderson C/C* • Kristen Hicks; Exec. Dir.; 130 E. Main St.; P.O. Box 1976; 38340; Chester; P 16,000; M 200; (731) 989-5222; Fax (731) 983-5518; khester@chestercountychamber.com; www.chestercountychamber.com

Hendersonville • *Hendersonville Area C/C* • Brenda Payne; Pres.; 100 Country Club Dr., Ste. 104; 37075; Sumner; P 47,614; M 780; (615) 824-2818; Fax (615) 250-3637; brenda@hendersonvillechamber.com; www.hendersonvillechamber.com*

Hohenwald • *Hohenwald-Lewis County C/C* • Mark Graves; Pres.; 106 N. Court St.; 38462; Lewis; P 12,000; M 145; (931) 796-4084; Fax (931) 796-6020; director@hohenwaldlewischamber.com; www.hohenwaldlewischamber.com

Humboldt • *Humboldt C/C* • Gil Fletcher; Dir.; 1200 Main St.; 38343; Gibson; P 9,500; M 267; (731) 784-1842; Fax (731) 784-1573; gil@humboldttnchamber.org; www.humboldttnchamber.org

Huntingdon • *Carroll County C/C* • Brad Hurley; Pres.; 20740 E. Main St.; P.O. Box 726; 38344; Carroll; P 29,322; M 320; (731) 986-4664; Fax (731) 986-2029; cchamber@earthlink.net; www.carrollcounty-tn-chamber.com

Jacksboro • *Campbell County C/C* • E.L. Morton; Exec. Dir.; 1016 Main St.; P.O. Box 305; 37757; Campbell; P 39,854; M 230; (423) 566-0329; Fax (423) 566-4896; chamber@campbellcountygov.com; co.campbell.tn.us

Jackson • *Jackson Area C/C* • Kyle Spurgeon; Pres./CEO; 197 Auditorium St.; P.O. Box 1904; 38302; Madison; P 100,000; M 1,300; (731) 423-2200; Fax (731) 424-4860; chamber@jacksontn.com; www.jacksontn.com.*

Jamestown • *Fentress County C/C* • Walt Page CTTP; Exec. Dir.; 114 Central Ave. W.; P.O. Box 1294; 38556; Fentress; P 17,500; M 200; (931) 879-9948; Fax (931) 879-6767; wpage@jamestowntn.org; www.jamestowntn.org*

Jasper • *Marion County C/C* • Alinda Richards; Pres.; 302 Betsy Pack Dr.; 37347; Marion; P 27,942; M 146; (423) 942-5103; Fax (423) 942-0098; marioncoc@bellsouth.net; www.marioncountychamber.com

Jefferson City • *see Dandridge*

Johnson City · *The Chamber of Commerce* · Gary Mabrey; Pres./CEO; 603 E. Market St.; P.O. Box 180; 37605; Washington; P 120,000; M 640; (423) 461-8000; Fax (423) 461-8047; frontdesk@johnson citytnchamber.com; www.johnsoncitytnchamber.com*

Jonesborough · *see Johnson City*

Kingsport · *Kingsport Area C/C* · Miles Burdine; Pres./CEO; 151 E. Main St.; 37660; Sullivan; P 50,000; M 700; (423) 392-8800; Fax (423) 246-7234; info@kingsportchamber.org; www.kingsport chamber.org*

Kingston · *Roane Alliance* · Leslie Henderson; Pres./CEO; 1209 N. Kentucky; 37763; Roane; P 52,000; M 400; (865) 376-5572; Fax (865) 376-4978; info@roanealliance.org; www.roanealliance.org

Knoxville · *Knoxville Area Chamber Partnership* · Mike Edwards; Pres./CEO; 17 Market Sq., Ste. 201; 37902; Knox; P 430,019; M 2,000; (865) 637-4550; Fax (865) 523-2071; medwards@knoxvillechamber. com; www.knoxvillechamber.com.*

La Vergne · *Rutherford County C/C* · Paul Latture IOM; Pres.; 5093 Murfreesboro Rd.; 37086; Rutherford; P 223,000; M 2,200; (615) 793-5444; Fax (615) 793-6025; chamber@lavergne.org; www.rutherfordchamber.org*

Lafayette · *Macon County C/C* · Lona Vinson; Exec. Secy.; 685 Hwy. 52 Bypass W.; 37083; Macon; P 22,800; M 178; (615) 666-5885; Fax (615) 666-6969; mchamber@nctc.com; www. maconcountytn.com

Lake City · *Lake City C/C* · Janet Phillips; Pres./CEO; 506 S. Main St.; P.O. Box 1054; 37769; Anderson; P 2,000; M 100; (865) 426-9595; lcchambe@bellsouth.net

Lawrenceburg · *Lawrence County C/C* · Chad Chancellor; Exec. Dir.; 1609 N. Locust Ave.; P.O. Box 86; 38464; Lawrence; P 40,000; M 350; (931) 762-4911; (877) 388-4911; Fax (931) 762-3153; info@selectlawrence.com; www.selectlawrence.com

Lebanon · *Lebanon-Wilson County C/C* · Sue Vanatta; Pres./CEO; 149 Public Sq.; 37087; Wilson; P 104,000; M 800; (615) 444-5503; (615) 444-7132; Fax (615) 443-0596; lebanonchamber@ charterinternet.com; www.lebanonwilsontnchamber.org*

Lenoir City · *see Loudon*

Lewisburg · *Marshall County C/C* · Ritaanne Weaver; Exec. Dir.; 227 Second Ave. N.; 37091; Marshall; P 30,000; M 280; (931) 359-3863; Fax (931) 359-8411; director@marshallchamber.org; www. marshallchamber.org

Lexington · *Henderson County C/C* · Vicki Bunch; Exec. Dir.; 149 Eastern Shores Dr.; 38351; Henderson; P 27,000; M 300; (731) 968-2126; Fax (731) 968-7006; vickibunch@hctn.org; www.hctn.org

Livingston · *Livingston-Overton County C/C* · Gregg McDonald; Exec. Dir.; 222 E. Main St.; P.O. Box 354; 38570; Overton; P 22,218; M 244; (931) 823-6421; Fax (931) 823-6422; chamber@twlakes.net; www.overtonco.com

Loudon · *Loudon County C/C* · Michael Bobo; Pres.; 318 Angel Row; P.O. Box 87; 37774; Loudon; P 45,000; M 450; (865) 458-2067; Fax (865) 458-1206; michael@loudoncountychamber.com; www.loudoncountychamber.com

Lynchburg · *Lynchburg-Moore County C/C* · Dr. Becker; Pres.; P.O. Box 421; 37352; Moore; P 7,500; M 80; (931) 759-4111; info@ lynchburgtn.com; www.lynchburgtn.com

Madison · *Madison-Rivergate Area C/C* · Debbie Pace; Exec. Dir.; P.O. Box 97; 37116; Davidson; P 36,000; M 350; (615) 865-5400; Fax (615) 865-0448; president@madisonrivergatechamber. com; www.madisonrivergatechamber.com

Madisonville · *Monroe County C/C* · William Wells III; Pres./CEO; 520 Cook St., Ste. A; 37354; Monroe; P 45,000; M 340; (423) 442-4588; Fax (423) 442-9016; info@monroecountychamber.org; www.monroecountychamber.org*

Manchester · *Manchester Area C/C* · Susie McEacharn; Exec. Dir.; 110 E. Main St.; 37355; Coffee; P 55,000; M 325; (931) 728-7635; Fax (931) 723-0736; manchestercoc@macoc.org; www.macoc.org*

Martin · *see Dresden*

Maryville · *Blount County C/C* · Bryan Daniels CEcD CCE IOM; Pres./CEO; 201 S. Washington St.; 37804; Blount; P 120,000; M 1,360; (865) 983-2241; Fax (865) 984-1386; info@blount chamber.com; www.blountchamber.com.*

Maynardville · *Union County C/C* · Julie Graham; Exec. Dir.; P.O. Box 848; 37807; Union; P 25,000; M 115; (865) 992-2811; Fax (865) 992-9812; info@comeherecomehome.com; www. comeherecomehome.com

McEwen · *see Waverly*

McMinnville · *McMinnville-Warren County C/C* · Alicea Weddington; Pres.; 110 S. Court Sq.; P.O. Box 574; 37111; Warren; P 38,000; M 325; (931) 473-6611; (931) 473-6612; Fax (931) 473-4741; aweddington@warrentn.com; www.warrentn.com.

Memphis · *Greater Memphis C/C* · John W. Moore; Pres./CEO; 22 N. Front St., Ste. 200; P.O. Box 224; 38101; Shelby; P 1,280,000; M 2,300; (901) 543-3500; (901) 543-5333; Fax (901) 543-3510; info@memphischamber.com; www.memphischamber.com

Milan · *Milan C/C* · Julie Allen Burke; Dir./Exec. V.P.; 1061 S. Main St.; 38358; Gibson; P 7,600; M 180; (731) 686-7494; Fax (731) 686-7495; chamber@cityofmilantn.com; www.cityofmilantn.com

Millington · *Millington Area C/C* · Cary Vaughn; Pres./CEO; 7743 Church St.; 38053; Shelby; P 10,500; M 346; (901) 872-1486; Fax (901) 872-0727; info@millingtonchamber.com; www.millington chamber.com

Monteagle · *Monteagle Mountain C/C* · Maxine Wade; Exec. Dir.; P.O. Box 353; 37356; Marion; P 5,000; M 200; (931) 924-5353; Fax (931) 924-2264; info@monteaglechamber.com; www. monteaglechamber.com

Morristown · *Morristown Area C/C* · C. Thomas Robinson CCE CEcD; Pres./CEO; 825 W. First N. St.; P.O. Box 9; 37815; Hamblen; P 63,000; M 726; (423) 586-6382; Fax (423) 586-6576; macc@ morristownchamber.com; www.morristownchamber.com.*

Mount Carmel · *see Rogersville*

Mount Juliet · *Mount Juliet/West Wilson County C/C* · Mark Hinesley; Pres./CEO; 46 W. Caldwell St.; 37122; Wilson; P 25,000; M 475; (615) 758-3478; Fax (615) 754-8595; mtjuliet@tds.net; www.mtjulietchamber.com*

Mount Pleasant · *see Columbia*

Mountain City · *Johnson County C/C* · David Sexton; Pres.; P.O. Box 66; 37683; Johnson; P 18,000; M 250; (423) 727-5800; Fax (423) 727-4943; info@johnsoncountychamber.org; www. johnsoncountychamber.org

Munford · *South Tipton County C/C* · Rosemary Bridges; Pres.; P.O. Box 1198; 38058; Tipton; P 57,000; M 340; (901) 837-4600; Fax (901) 837-4602; chamber@southtipton.com; www.southtipton.com

Murfreesboro · *Rutherford County C/C* · Paul Latture IOM; Pres.; 501 Memorial Blvd.; P.O. Box 864; 37133; Rutherford; P 241,355; M 2,200; (615) 893-6565; (800) 716-7560; Fax (615) 890-7600; info@rutherfordchamber.org; www.rutherfordchamber.org*

Nashville · *Donelson-Hermitage C/C* · Lori K. Weir; Exec. Dir.; 125 Donelson Pike; P.O. Box 140200; 37214; Davidson; P 70,000; M 450; (615) 883-7896; Fax (615) 391-4880; info@d-hchamber.com; www.d-hchamber.com*

Nashville · *Nashville Area C/C* · 211 Commerce St., Ste. 100; 37201; Davidson; P 580,450; M 2,500; (615) 743-3000; Fax (615) 256-3074; info@nashvillechamber.com; www.nashvillechamber.com

New Johnsonville · *see Waverly*

Newport · *Cocke County Partnership C/C* · Valerie Stepp; Dir.; 433-B Prospect Ave.; 37821; Cocke; P 35,000; M 300; (423) 623-7201; (423) 623-7216; Fax (423) 625-1846; ccpchamber@bellsouth.net; www.cockecounty.org

Norris · *see Clinton*

Oak Ridge · *Oak Ridge C/C* · Parker Hardy CCE; Pres./CEO; 1400 Oak Ridge Tpk.; 37830; Anderson; P 28,000; M 700; (865) 483-1321; Fax (865) 483-1678; lchristman@orcc.org; www.orcc.org

Oliver Springs · *see Clinton*

Oneida · *see Helenwood*

Paris · *Paris-Henry County C/C* · Jennifer Wheatley; Exec. Dir.; 2508 E. Wood St.; 38242; Henry; P 31,115; M 400; (731) 642-3431; Fax (731) 642-3454; pariscoc@paristnchamber.com; www.paristnchamber.com*

Parrottsville · *see Newport*

Parsons · *Decatur County C/C* · Bridgette Scallion; Exec. Dir.; 139 Tenn. Ave. N.; P.O. Box 245; 38363; Decatur; P 11,000; M 207; (731) 847-4202; Fax (731) 847-4222; dccc@netease.net; www.decaturcountytennessee.org

Pigeon Forge · *City of Pigeon Forge Dept. of Tourism* · 2450 Pkwy.; P.O. Box 1390-I; 37868; Sevier; P 5,784; M 976; (865) 453-8574; (800) 251-9100; Fax (865) 429-7362; inquire@MyPigeonForge.com; www.mypigeonforge.com

Pigeon Forge · *Pigeon Forge C/C* · Cathy Sizemore; Exec. Dir.; 3171 Pkwy., Ste. A; 37863; Sevier; P 5,083; M 150; (865) 453-5700; (800) 221-9858; Fax (865) 492-9040; pifchamber@kmsfia.com; www.pigeonforgechamber.com

Pikeville · *Pikeville-Bledsoe County C/C* · Hank Williams; P.O. Box 205; 37367; Bledsoe; P 14,000; M 85; (423) 447-2791; directors@pikeville-bledsoe.com; www.pikeville-bledsoe.com

Portland · *Portland C/C* · Amy Wald; Exec. Dir.; 106 Main St.; P.O. Box 387; 37148; Sumner; P 12,000; M 200; (615) 325-9032; Fax (615) 325-8399; portcofc@bellsouth.net; www.portlandcofc.com

Pulaski · *Giles County C/C* · Donna Baker; Exec. Dir.; 110 N. Second St.; 38478; Giles; P 29,447; M 300; (931) 363-3789; Fax (931) 363-7279; secretary@gilescountychamber.com; www.gilescountychamber.com*

Ridgely · *Ridgely C/C* · 140 N. Main; 38080; Lake; P 1,700; M 35; (731) 264-0330

Ripley · *Lauderdale Chamber/ECD* · Lisa Hankins; Exec. Dir.; 123 S. Jefferson St.; 38063; Lauderdale; P 27,101; M 275; (731) 635-9541; (731) 635-8463; Fax (731) 635-9064; mail@lauderdalecountytn.org; www.lauderdalecountytn.org*

Rogersville · *Rogersville/Hawkins County C/C* · Nancy Barker; Exec. Dir.; 107 E. Main St., Ste. 100; 37857; Hawkins; P 57,148; M 300; (423) 272-2186; Fax (423) 272-2186; hawkinschamber@chartertn.net; www.rogersvillechamber.us.*

Savannah · *Hardin County C/C* · Beth Pippin; Exec. Dir.; 320 Main St.; P.O. Box 996; 38372; Hardin; P 27,000; M 300; (731) 925-2363; Fax (731) 925-8069; info@hardincountychamber.com; www.hardincountychamber.com

Selmer · *McNairy County C/C & EDC* · Matthew Ernst; Exec. Dir.; 144 Cypress Ave.; P.O. Box 7; 38375; McNairy; P 26,000; M 375; (731) 645-6360; Fax (731) 645-7663; mcnairy@charterinternet.com; www.mcnairy.com

Sevierville · *Sevierville C/C* · Brenda McCroskey; Exec. Dir.; 110 Gary Wade Blvd.; 37862; Sevier; P 17,500; M 585; (865) 453-6411; Fax (865) 453-9649; info@seviervillechamber.com; www.visitsevierville.com*

Sewanee · *see Monteagle*

Sharon · *see Dresden*

Shelbyville · *Shelbyville-Bedford County C/C* · Walter W. Wood CEcD; CEO; 100 N. Cannon Blvd.; 37160; Bedford; P 40,253; M 520; (931) 684-3482; (888) 662-2525; Fax (931) 684-3483; bedfordchamber@bellsouth.net; www.shelbyvilletn.com

Smithville · *Smithville-DeKalb County C/C* · Suzanne Williams; Exec. Dir.; 301 N. Public Sq.; P.O. Box 64; 37166; DeKalb; P 17,500; M 200; (615) 597-4163; Fax (615) 597-4164; chamber@dekalbtn.com; www.smithvilletn.com

Smyrna · *Rutherford County C/C* · Paul Latture IOM; Pres.; 315 S. Lowry St.; 37167; Rutherford; P 223,000; M 2,200; (615) 355-6565; Fax (615) 355-5715; chamber@townofsmyrna.org; www.rutherfordchamber.org*

Somerville · *Fayette County C/C* · Julie Perrine; Exec. Dir.; 13145 N. Main St.; P.O. Box 411; 38068; Fayette; P 38,402; M 342; (901) 465-8690; Fax (901) 465-6497; fcc@fayettecountychamber.net; www.fayettecountychamber.com

South Fulton · *Twin Cities C/C* · Thea Vowell; Exec. Dir.; 700 Milton Counce Dr.; P.O. Box 5077; 38257; Obion; P 5,000; M 125; (731) 479-7029; Fax (731) 479-7029; twincitieschamber@bellsouth.net; www.fultonsouthfultonchamber.com

Sparta · *Sparta-White County C/C* · Wallace G. Austin; Pres.; 16 W. Bockman Way; 38583; White; P 26,000; M 250; (931) 836-3552; Fax (931) 836-2216; sparta-chamber@sparta-chamber.net; www.sparta-chamber.net

Spencer · *Greater Van Buren County/Spencer C/C* · Ann McCormick; Pres.; 90 Sparta St.; P.O. Box 814; 38585; Van Buren; P 5,500; M 60; (931) 946-7033; vbchamber@blomand.net; www.vanburenchamber.com

Spring City · *Spring City C/C* · Nancy Miller; Bus. Mgr.; 390 Front St.; P.O. Box 355; 37381; Rhea; P 3,500; M 140; (423) 365-5210; Fax (423) 365-9790; scchamber@bellsouth.net; www.springcitychamberofcommerce.com

Spring Hill · *Spring Hill C/C* · Stacy Neisler; Chair; P.O. Box 1815; 37174; Maury; P 23,000; M 200; (931) 486-0625; info@springhillchamber.net; www.springhillchamber.net

Springfield · *Robertson County C/C* · Margot Fosnes; Exec. Dir.; 503 W. Court Sq.; 37172; Robertson; P 59,380; M 400; (615) 384-3800; Fax (615) 384-1260; mfosnes@robertsonchamber.org; www.robertsonchamber.org

Tazewell · *Claiborne County C/C* · Dennis Shipley; Exec. Dir./V.P.; 1732 Main St., Ste. 1; P.O. Box 649; 37879; Claiborne; P 32,000; M 220; (423) 626-4149; Fax (423) 626-1611; chamber@claibornecounty.com; www.claibornecounty.com

Tiptonville · *Reelfoot Area C/C* · Marcia Mills; Exec. Dir.; 130 S. Court St.; 38079; Lake; P 7,954; M 45; (731) 253-8144; Fax (731) 253-9923; info@reelfootareachamber.com; www.reelfootareachamber.com

Townsend · *see Maryville*

Tracy City · *see Monteagle*

Trenton · *Greater Gibson County Area C/C* · Tara Bradford; Exec. Dir.; 200 E. Eaton St.; P.O. Box 464; 38382; Gibson; P 48,152; M 275; (731) 855-0973; Fax (731) 855-0979; info@gibsoncounty tn.com; www.gibsoncountytn.com

Tullahoma · *Tullahoma Area C/C* · Diane Bryant; Exec. Dir.; 135 W. Lincoln St.; P.O. Box 1205; 37388; Coffee & Franklin; P 25,332; M 425; (931) 455-5497; tullahomachamber@tullahoma.org; www.tullahoma.org.*

Union City · *Obion County C/C* · Jim Cooper; Exec. Dir.; 214 E. Church St.; 38261; Obion; P 31,000; M 337; (731) 885-0211; Fax (731) 885-7155; jcooper@obioncounty.org; www.obioncounty.org

Wartburg · *Morgan County C/C* · P.O. Box 539; 37887; Morgan; P 20,000; M 65; (423) 346-5740; Fax (423) 346-9707; www. morgancountychamber.com

Wartrace · *Wartrace C/C* · Pearl Change; Secy.; P.O. Box 543; 37183; Bedford; P 575; M 29; (931) 389-9999; www.wartracechamber.org

Washington County · *see Johnson City*

Watertown · *Watertown-East Wilson County C/C* · Jerry Lee; Pres.; P.O. Box 5; 37184; Wilson; P 1,400; M 140; (615) 237-0270; info@watertowntn.com; www.watertowntn.com

Waverly · *Humphreys County Area C/C* · Wendy Lee; Dir.; 124 E. Main St.; P.O. Box 733; 37185; Humphreys; P 17,192; M 213; (931) 296-4865; Fax (931) 296-2285; hcchamber@bellsouth.net; waverly.net/hcchamber

Waynesboro · *see Collinwood*

Westmoreland · *Westmoreland C/C* · David Harrison; Pres.; P.O. Box 536; 37186; Sumner; P 2,132; M 75; (615) 644-6397; www. westmorelandtn.com

White House · *White House Area C/C* · Julie Bolton; Exec. Dir.; 414 Hwy. 76; P.O. Box 521; 37188; Robertson; P 9,895; M 245; (615) 672-3937; Fax (615) 672-2828; whcoc@bellsouth.net; www. whitehousechamber.org*

Winchester · *Franklin County C/C* · Judy DeWeese Taylor; Exec. Dir.; 44 Chamber Way; P.O. Box 280; 37398; Franklin; P 43,000; M 400; (931) 967-6788; Fax (931) 967-9418; judy@franklincounty chamber.com; www.franklincountychamber.com.*

Woodbury · *Historic Cannon County C/C* · Carolyn Motley; Svcs. Coord.; 313 Main St.; P.O. Box 140; 37190; Cannon; P 13,500; M 101; (615) 563-2222; cannontn@dtccom.net; www.cannoncounty.info

Texas

Texas Assn. of Bus. · Bill Hammond; Pres./CEO; 1209 Nueces St.; Austin; 78701; Travis; P 24,300,000; M 5,000; (512) 477-6721; Fax (512) 477-0836; info@txbiz.org; www.txbiz.org.

Abilene · *Abilene C/C* · Mike McMahan; Pres.; 174 Cypress, Ste. 200; P.O. Box 2281; 79604; Taylor; P 117,000; M 1,200; (325) 677-7241; Fax (325) 677-0622; info@abilenechamber.com; www. abilenechamber.com*

Addison · *Metrocrest C/C* · Greg Vaughn; Pres.; 5100 Beltline Rd., Ste. 430; 75001; Dallas; P 158,000; M 650; (972) 416-6600; Fax (972) 416-7874; greg@metrocrestchamber.com; www.metrocrest chamber.com

Alamo · *Alamo C/C* · Carrol Moering; Ofc. Mgr.; 130 S. 8th St.; 78516; Hidalgo; P 20,000; M 90; (956) 787-2117; alamo.chamber@ yahoo.com; www.alamochamber.com

Alamo Heights · *Alamo Heights C/C* · Mike Clements; Pres.; P.O. Box 6141; 78209; Bexar; P 10,000; M 150; (210) 822-7027; admin@ alamoheightschamber.org; www.alamoheightschamber.org

Albany · *Albany C/C* · Chuck Senter; Exec. Dir.; #2 Railroad; P.O. Box 2047; 76430; Shackelford; P 1,921; M 200; (325) 762-2525; Fax (325) 762-3125; chamberc@bitstreet.com; www.albanytexas.com

Aldine · *see Houston—Houston Intercontinental C/C*

Aledo · *see Willow Park*

Alice · *Alice C/C* · Juan Navejar Jr.; Exec. V.P.; 612 E. Main St.; P.O. Box 1609; 78333; Jim Wells; P 19,000; M 411; (361) 664-3454; Fax (361) 664-2291; jnavejar@alicetxchamber.org; www.alicetx.org*

Allen · *Allen-Fairview C/C* · Sharon Mayer; Pres./CEO; 210 W. McDermott; 75013; Collin; P 85,000; M 563; (972) 727-5585; (972) 656-4237; Fax (972) 727-9000; info@allenchamber.com; www.allenchamber.com*

Alpine · *Alpine C/C* · Mark Hannan; Pres.; 106 N. 3rd St.; 79830; Brewster; P 6,300; M 300; (432) 837-2326; (800) 561-3712; Fax (432) 837-1259; info@alpinetexas.com; www.alpinetexas.com

Alvarado · *Alvarado Area C/C* · Jacob Wheat; Pres.; P.O. Box 712; 76009; Johnson; P 3,800; M 90; (817) 783-2233; www. alvaradococ.com

Alvin · *Alvin-Manvel Area C/C* · Connie Elies; Pres.; 105 W. Willis; 77511; Brazoria; P 33,000; M 450; (281) 331-3944; (800) 331-4063; Fax (281) 585-8662; chamber@amacc.org; www. alvinmanvelchamber.org*

Amarillo · *Amarillo C/C* · Gary Molberg; Pres./CEO; 1000 S. Polk St.; P.O. Box 9480; 79105; Porter & Randall; P 190,000; M 1,780; (806) 373-7800; Fax (806) 373-3909; chamber@amarillo-chamber. org; www.amarillo-chamber.org.*

Anahuac · *Anahuac Area C/C* · Robbie King; Exec. Dir.; 603 Miller St.; P.O. Box R; 77514; Chambers; P 2,500; M 125; (409) 267-4190; Fax (409) 267-3907; anahuacchamber@windstream. net; www.anahuacchamber.com*

Andrews · *Andrews C/C & CVB* · Julia Wallace; Exec. Dir.; 700 W. Broadway; 79714; Andrews; P 13,000; M 250; (432) 523-2695; Fax (432) 523-2375; achamber@andrewstx.com; www.andrewstx.com*

Angleton · *Greater Angleton C/C* · Beth Journeay; Pres./CEO; 445 E. Mulberry; 77515; Brazoria; P 20,000; M 550; (979) 849-6443; Fax (979) 849-4520; beth@angletonchamber.org; www. angletonchamber.org*

Annetta · *see Willow Park*

Anson · *Anson C/C* · Marsha Bailey; Mgr.; 1132 W. Court Plz.; P.O. Box 351; 79501; Jones; P 2,500; M 150; (325) 823-3259; Fax (325) 823-4326; ansoncofc@att.net

Anthony · *see Anthony, NM*

Aransas Pass · *Aransas Pass C/C* · Rosemary Vega; CEO; 130 W. Goodnight; 78336; San Patricio; P 8,136; M 270; (361) 758-2750; (800) 633-3028; Fax (361) 758-8320; chamberasst@cableone.net; www.aransaspass.org.

Argyle · *Argyle C/C* · Kim Hinnrichs; Exec. Dir.; P.O. Box 245; 76226; Denton; P 3,300; M 150; (940) 464-9990; Fax (940) 294-2525; chamber@argylechamber.org; www.argylechamber.org

Arlington · *Arlington C/C* · Wes Jurey; Pres./CEO; 505 E. Border; 76010; Tarrant; P 375,000; M 1,200; (817) 275-2613; Fax (817) 261-7389; cwyatt@arlingtontx.com; www.arlingtontx.com

Arp · *Arp Area C/C* · Jan Gibson; Pres.; P.O. Box 146; 75750; Smith; P 1,000; M 70; (903) 859-6131; (903) 859-2055; www. arptexaschamber.com

Aspermont · *Aspermont C/C & Eco. Dev. Corp.* · Martha McDowell; Exec. Dir.; 612 Washington; P.O. Box 556; 79502; Stonewall; P 1,693; M 49; (940) 989-3197; Fax (940) 989-2517; marthaedc@srcaccess.net; www.aspermonttexas.com

Athens • *Athens C/C* • Sarah Hueber; Pres.; 1206 S. Palestine; P.O. Box 2600; 75751; Henderson; P 12,000; M 419; (903) 675-5181; (800) 755-7878; Fax (903) 675-5183; info@athenscc.org; www.athenscc.org*

Atlanta • *Atlanta Area C/C* • Beverly Johnson; Ofc. Mgr.; 101 N. East St.; P.O. Box 29; 75551; Cass; P 5,745; M 165; (903) 796-3296; Fax (903) 796-5711; atlantaareacoc@sbcglobal.net; www.atlantatexas.net

Aubrey • *Aubrey Area C/C* • Pat Brockett; Ofc. Mgr.; 903 S. Hwy. 377; 76227; Denton; P 4,000; M 365; (940) 365-9781; Fax (940) 365-9781; chamber@aubreycoc.org; www.aubreycoc.org

Aurora • *South Wise County C/C* • 303 Derting Rd.; 76078; Wise; P 20,000; M 280; (817) 636-2783; cityofaurora@hotmail.com; www.southwisechamber.com

Austin Area

Greater Austin C/C • Michael W. Rollins CCE; Pres./CEO; 210 Barton Springs Rd., Ste. 400; 78704; Travis; P 1,400,000; M 2,600; (512) 478-9383; Fax (512) 478-8819; info@austinchamber.com; www.austinchamber.com*

Greater Austin Hispanic C/C • Andrew Martinez; Pres.; 2800 S. IH-35, Ste. 260; 78704; Travis; M 650; (512) 476-7502; Fax (512) 476-6417; amartinez@gahcc.org; www.gahcc.org*

Lake Travis C/C • Laura Mitchell; Pres.; 1415 RR 620 S., Ste. 202; P.O. Box 340034; 78734; Travis; P 20,000; M 410; (512) 263-5833; (877) 263-0073; Fax (512) 263-1355; info@laketravischamber.com; www.laketravischamber.com*

Women's C/C of Texas • Rose Batson; Pres.; P.O. Box 26051; 78755; Travis; M 500; (512) 338-0839; austin@womenschambertexas.com; www.womenschambertexas.com

Avinger • *Avinger C/C* • W.J. Salmon Jr.; Pres.; c/o P.O. Box 218; 75630; Cass; P 420; M 25; (903) 562-1000; (903) 562-1325; avingertxchamber.com

Azle • *Azle Area C/C* • Kim Ware; Pres.; 252 W. Main St., Ste. A; 76020; Parker & Tarrant; P 30,000; M 312; (817) 444-1112; Fax (817) 444-1143; info@azlechamber.com; www.azlechamber.com

Bacliff • *see Dickinson*

Baird • *Baird C/C* • 328 Market St.; 79504; Callahan; P 1,651; M 75; (325) 854-2003; Fax (325) 854-2003; chamber@bairdtexas.com; www.bairdtexas.com

Balch Springs • *Balch Springs C/C* • Sandra Wood; Pres.; 4000 Pioneer Rd., Ste. 201A; P.O. Box 800095; 75180; Dallas; P 22,000; M 132; (972) 557-0988; info@balchspringschamber.org; www.balchspringschamber.org

Ballinger • *Ballinger C/C* • Tammie Virden; Exec. V.P.; 700 Railroad Ave.; P.O. Box 577; 76821; Runnels; P 4,200; M 160; (325) 365-2333; Fax (325) 365-3445; coc@ballingertx.org; www.ballingertx.org

Bandera • *Bandera County C/C* • Cerise Ripps; Exec. Admin.; P.O. Box 2445; 78003; Bandera; P 22,000; M 325; (830) 796-3280; Fax (830) 796-3970; cowboy@banderatex.com; www.banderatex.com

Bartlett • *Bartlett Area C/C* • Barbara Sandobal; Pres.; P.O. Box 103; 76511; Bell & Williamson; P 1,675; M 50; (254) 527-0196; tina@steglich.net; www.bartletttexas.net

Bastrop • *Bastrop C/C* • Susan Weems Wendel IOM; Pres./CEO; 927 Main St.; 78602; Bastrop; P 8,300; M 605; (512) 303-0558; Fax (512) 303-0305; info@bastropchamber.com; www.bastropchamber.com

Bay City • *Bay City C/C & Ag.* • Mitch Thames; Pres.; 201 Seventh St.; P.O. Box 768; 77404; Matagorda; P 20,000; M 700; (979) 245-8333; (800) 806-8333; Fax (979) 245-1622; mitchthames@visitbaycity.org; www.baycitychamber.org.

Baytown • *Baytown C/C* • Tracey S. Wheeler; Pres./CEO; 1300 Rollingbrook, Ste. 400; 77521; Harris; P 70,000; M 1,400; (281) 422-8359; Fax (281) 428-1758; info@baytownchamber.com; www.baytownchamber.com.*

Baytown • *The Hispanic Chamber of Commerce of Greater Baytown* • Ruben F. de Hoyos; Pres.; 1300 Rollingbrook, Ste. 502; P.O. Box 815; 77522; Harris; P 80,000; M 115; (281) 422-6908; (281) 728-4221; Fax (281) 427-8988; hccgb@verizon.net; www.hccgb.org*

Bayview • *see Dickinson*

Beaumont • *Greater Beaumont C/C* • Jim Rich; Pres.; 1110 Park St.; P.O. Box 3150; 77704; Jefferson; P 115,000; M 1,500; (409) 838-6581; Fax (409) 833-6718; chamber@bmtcoc.org; www.bmtcoc.org.*

Bedford • *Hurst-Euless-Bedford C/C* • Mary Martin Frazior; Pres./CEO; 2109 Martin Dr.; P.O. Box 969; 76095; Tarrant; P 135,000; M 1,000; (817) 283-1521; Fax (817) 267-5111; chamber@heb.org; www.heb.org*

Beeville • *Bee County C/C* • Lisa Del Bosque; Pres./CEO; 1705 N. St. Marys St.; 78102; Bee; P 32,300; M 333; (361) 358-3267; Fax (361) 358-3966; info@beecountychamber.org; www.beecountychamber.org

Bellaire • *Greater Southwest Houston C/C* • Toni Franklin; Pres./CEO; 6900 S. Rice Ave.; 77401; Harris; P 350,000; M 400; (713) 666-1521; Fax (713) 666-1523; info@gswhcc.org; www.gswhcc.org*

Bellmead • *Bellmead C/C* • Vivian Nowlin; 3400 Bellmead Dr.; P.O. Box 154615; 76715; McLennan; P 10,500; M 200; (254) 799-1552; Fax (254) 799-9370; contactus@bellmeadchamber.com; www.bellmeadchamber.com

Bellville • *Bellville C/C* • Tammy Hall; Exec. Dir.; 10 S. Holland St.; 77418; Austin; P 4,500; M 250; (979) 865-3407; bellvillechamber@sbcglobal.net; www.bellville.com*

Belton • *Belton Area C/C* • Stephanie O'Banion; Pres./CEO; 412 E. Central Ave.; P.O. Box 659; 76513; Bell; P 19,000; M 500; (254) 939-3551; Fax (254) 939-1061; info@beltonchamber.com; www.beltonchamber.com*

Benbrook • *Benbrook Area C/C* • Jamie Presley; Ofc. Mgr.; 8507 Benbrook Blvd.; P.O. Box 26745; 76126; Tarrant; P 27,000; M 278; (817) 249-4451; Fax (817) 249-3307; chamberinfo@benbrookchamber.org; www.benbrookchamber.org*

Bertram • *Bertram C/C* • P.O. Box 508; 78605; Burnet; P 1,200; M 40; (512) 355-2197; www.bertramtx.org

Big Lake • *Big Lake C/C* • Nita Schubert; Dir./Mgr.; 120 N. Main St.; P.O. Box 905; 76932; Reagan; P 2,600; M 15; (325) 884-2980; Fax (325) 884-1416; blcoc@verizon.net; www.biglaketx.com*

Big Sandy • *Big Sandy C/C* • Travis Brewer; 100 N. Tyler St.; P.O. Box 175; 75755; Upshur; P 1,200; M 25; (903) 636-2238; info@bigsandytx.com; bigsandytx.net

Big Spring • *Big Spring Area C/C* • Debbye ValVerde IOM; Exec. Dir.; 215 W. 3rd St.; P.O. Box 1391; 79721; Howard; P 30,000; M 390; (432) 263-7641; (800) 734-7641; Fax (432) 264-9111; info@bigspringchamber.com; www.bigspringchamber.com*

Bishop • *Bishop C/C* • Judy Gonzalez; Exec. Dir.; 213 E. Main; P.O. Box 426; 78343; Nueces; P 3,200; M 75; (361) 584-2214; Fax (361) 584-2214; bishopcc@intcomm.net; www.bishoptx.org

Blanco • *Blanco C/C* • Penny Thomas; Dir.; P.O. Box 626; 78606; Blanco; P 1,500; M 200; (830) 833-5101; Fax (830) 469-4455; info@blancochamber.com; www.blancochamber.com

Boerne · *Greater Boerne C/C* · Terri Politi; Pres.; 126 Rosewood Ave.; P.O. Box 2328; 78006; Kendall; P 14,000; M 830; (830) 249-8000; Fax (830) 249-9639; boerne@gvtc.com; www.boerne.org*

Bonham · *Bonham Area C/C* · Bill Jones; Exec. Dir.; 119 E. 5th St.; 75418; Fannin; P 13,092; M 300; (903) 583-4811; Fax (903) 583-7972; bonhamchamber@cableone.net; www.bonhamchamber.com*

Booker · *Booker C/C* · Jackie Reeves; Pres.; P.O. Box 22; 79005; Lipscomb & Ochiltree; P 1,300; M 50; (806) 658-4545

Borger · *Borger C/C* · Beverly Benton; Pres.; 613 N. Main St.; P.O. Box 490; 79008; Hutchinson; P 15,000; M 300; (806) 274-2211; Fax (806) 273-3488; borgerchamber@amaonline.com; www.borgerchamber.org*

Bovina · *Bovina C/C* · Mindy Neal-Widner; Pres.; P.O. Box 607; 79009; Parmer; P 1,800; M 65; (806) 251-1116; (806) 251-1300; Fax (806) 251-1805; www.cityofbovina.net

Bowie · *Bowie-Montague County C/C* · Bonnie Julius Hamilton; Exec. V.P.; 309 N. Smythe St.; 76230; Montague; P 5,700; M 259; (940) 872-1173; (866) 872-1173; Fax (940) 872-3291; info@bowietxchamber.org; www.bowietxchamber.org

Brackettville · *Kinney County C/C* · Hattie Berleth; Pres.; P.O. Box 1737; 78832; Kinney; P 3,119; M 140; (830) 563-2466; kcchamber@sbcglobal.net; *

Brady · *Brady/McCulloch County C/C* · Kathi Masonheimer; Dir.; 101 E. 1st St.; 76825; McCulloch; P 8,000; M 192; (325) 597-3491; (888) 577-5657; Fax (325) 792-9181; info@bradytx.com; www.bradytx.com*

Brazoria · *Brazoria C/C* · Erica Beaver; Exec. Dir.; 202 W. Smith St.; P.O. Box 992; 77422; Brazoria; P 2,932; M 175; (979) 798-6100; Fax (979) 798-6101; brazoriachamber@brazoriainet.com; www.brazoriachamber.net

Brazosport · *Brazosport Area C/C* · Sandra Shaw; Pres./CEO; 300 Abner Jackson Pkwy.; 77566; Brazoria; P 75,000; M 710; (979) 285-2501; (888) 477-2505; Fax (979) 285-2505; chamber2@sbcglobal.net; www.brazosport.org.*

Breckenridge · *Breckenridge C/C* · Mary Ann Olson; Exec. Dir.; 100 E. Elm St.; P.O. Box 1466; 76424; Stephens; P 5,868; M 300; (254) 559-2301; (254) 559-2803; Fax (254) 559-7104; chamber@breckenridgetexas.com; www.breckenridgetexas.com*

Bremond · *Bremond C/C* · Jeanne Wierzbicki; Pres.; P.O. Box 487; 76629; Roberston; P 900; M 40; (254) 746-7636; bremondchamber@yahoo.com; www.bremondtexas.org

Brenham · *Washington County C/C* · Page Michel; Pres./CEO; 314 S. Austin St.; 77833; Washington; P 31,000; M 770; (979) 836-3695; (888) BRENHAM; Fax (979) 836-2540; info@brenhamtexas.com; www.brenhamtexas.com*

Bridge City · *Bridge City C/C* · Angela Beck; Exec. V.P.; 150 W. Roundbunch; 77611; Orange; P 8,651; M 193; (409) 735-5671; Fax (409) 735-7017; bcchamber@sbcglobal.net; *

Bridgeport · *Bridgeport Area C/C* · Teri Bland; Exec. Dir.; 812 A Halsell St.; P.O. Box 1104; 76426; Wise; P 5,800; M 320; (940) 683-2076; Fax (940) 683-3969; www.bridgeportchamber.org.*

Bridgeport · *Greater Runaway Bay Alliance* · Clay Dent; Chrmn.; 51 Runaway Bay Dr.; P.O. Box 291; 76426; Wise; P 1,200; M 100; (940) 575-4745; www.greaterrunawaybayalliance.com

Brookshire · *see Pattison*

Brownfield · *Brownfield C/C & Visitor Info. Center* · Lorena Valencia; Exec. Dir.; 211 Lubbock Rd.; P.O. Box 152; 79316; Terry; P 9,488; M 185; (806) 637-2564; Fax (806) 637-2565; helpdesk@brownfieldchamber.com; www.brownfieldchamber.com.*

Brownsboro · *see Chandler*

Brownsville · *Brownsville C/C* · Angela R. Burton; Pres./CEO; 1600 University Blvd.; 78520; Cameron; P 180,000; M 1,192; (956) 542-4341; Fax (956) 504-3348; info@brownsvillechamber.com; www.brownsvillechamber.com

Brownwood · *Brownwood Area C/C* · Laura Terhune; Exec. V.P.; 600 Depot St.; P.O. Box 880; 76804; Brown; P 40,000; M 530; (325) 646-9535; Fax (325) 643-6686; information@brownwoodchamber.org; www.brownwoodchamber.org.*

Bryan · *Bryan-College Station C/C* · Royce Hickman; Pres./CEO; 4001 E. 29th St., Ste. 175; P.O. Box 3579; 77805; Brazos; P 159,830; M 1,500; (979) 260-5200; Fax (979) 260-5208; receptionist@bcschamber.org; www.bcschamber.org*

Buchanan Dam · *Lake Buchanan-Inks Lake C/C & Tourist Center* · Ray McCasland; Pres.; 17816 Hwy. 29 at Buchanan Dam; P.O. Box 282; 78609; Llano; P 3,500; M 250; (512) 793-2803; Fax (512) 793-2112; buchanan@zeecon.com; www.buchanan-inks.org

Buda · *Buda Area C/C* · Richard W. (Dick) Schneider; Pres.; 203 N. Railroad St., Ste. 1C; P.O. Box 904; 78610; Hays; P 6,000; M 300; (512) 295-9999; Fax (512) 295-3569; bacc@austin.rr.com; www.budachamber.com*

Buffalo · *Buffalo C/C* · JoAnn Cockerell; Secy.; 941 N. Hill St.; P.O. Box 207; 75831; Leon; P 2,982; M 120; (903) 322-5810; chamber@buffalotxchamberofcommerce.org; www.buffalotxchamberofcommerce.org

Bullard · *Bullard Area C/C* · Bryan Capps; Pres.; 114 S. Phillips; P.O. Box 945; 75757; Cherokee & Smith; P 3,500; M 80; (903) 894-4238; Fax (903) 894-9308; contact@bullardtexaschamber.com; www.bullardtexaschamber.com

Bulverde · *see Spring Branch*

Buna · *Buna C/C* · Kathy Griffis; Ofc. Mgr.; 480 State Hwy. 62; P.O. Box 1782; 77612; Jasper; P 3,000; M 74; (409) 994-5586; Fax (409) 994-3855; bunatexas@att.net; www.bunatexas.net

Burkburnett · *Burkburnett C/C* · Dick Vallon; Dir.; 104 W. Third; 76354; Wichita; P 11,000; M 150; (940) 569-3304; Fax (940) 569-3306; dvallon@burkburnett.org; www.yourehomenow.org

Burleson · *Burleson Area C/C* · Dan-O Strong; Pres.; 1044 S.W. Wilshire; P.O. Box 9; 76097; Johnson & Tarrant; P 35,000; M 800; (817) 295-6121; Fax (817) 295-6192; dstrong@burleson.org; www.burlesonareachamber.com*

Burnet · *Burnet C/C* · Kim Winkler; Mgr.; 229 S. Pierce; 78611; Burnet; P 5,000; M 450; (512) 756-4297; Fax (512) 756-2548; info@burnetchamber.org; www.burnetchamber.org*

Caldwell · *Burleson County C/C-Caldwell Office* · Angie Cruz; Ofc. Mgr.; 301 N. Main; 77836; Burleson; P 18,000; M 289; (979) 567-0000; Fax (979) 567-0818; info@burlesoncountytx.com; www.burlesoncountytx.com*

Calvert · *Calvert C/C* · 300 Main St.; P.O. Box 132; 77837; Robertson; P 1,400; M 50; (979) 364-2559; www.calverttx.com

Cameron · *Cameron Area C/C* · Ginger Watkins; Dir.; 102 E. 1st St.; P.O. Drawer 432; 76520; Milam; P 5,629; M 204; (254) 697-4979; Fax (254) 697-2345; chamber@cameron-tx.com; www.cameron-tx.com

Camp Wood · *Nueces Canyon C/C* · Ben Cox; Pres.; P.O. Box 369; 78833; Real; P 1,300; M 49; (830) 597-6241; n3ctexas@gmail.com; www.mycampwood.com

Canadian · *Canadian-Hemphill County C/C* · Tamera Julian; Dir.; 119 N. 2nd St.; 79014; Hemphill; P 2,500; M 130; (806) 323-6234; Fax (806) 323-9243; canadiantx@sbcglobal.net; www.canadiantx.org.

Canton • *Canton C/C* • Pete Davis; Chrmn.; 720 N. Hwy. 19, Ste. 2; 75103; Van Zandt; P 5,126; M 412; (903) 567-2991; Fax (903) 567-5708; info@chambercantontx.com; www.cantontexas chamberofcommerce.com*

Canyon • *Canyon C/C* • Cheryl Malcolm; Exec. Dir.; 1518 5th Ave.; 79015; Randall; P 13,000; M 350; (806) 655-7815; (800) 999-9481; Fax (806) 655-4608; info@canyonchamber.org; www.canyonchamber.org*

Canyon Lake • *Canyon Lake Area C/C & Visitor Center* • Kim Morris; Pres.; 3934 FM 2673; 78133; Comal; P 40,000; M 525; (830) 964-2223; (800) 528-2104; Fax (830) 964-3209; admin@canyonlakechamber.com; www.canyonlakechamber.com*

Carrizo Springs • *Dimmit County C/C* • Paula Seydel; Mgr.; P.O. Box 699; 78834; Dimmit; P 10,248; M 90; (830) 876-5205; Fax (830) 876-5206; chambermanager@dimmitcountytx.com; www.dimmitcountytx.com

Carthage • *Panola County C of C/Carthage CVB* • Ms. Tommie Ritter Smith; Pres.; 300 W. Panola St.; 75633; Panola; P 25,000; M 300; (903) 693-6634; Fax (903) 693-8578; chamber@carthage texas.com; www.carthagetexas.com*

Castroville • *Castroville Area C/C* • Ashlee Bates; Mgr.; 100 Karm St.; P.O. Box 572; 78009; Medina; P 3,000; M 285; (830) 538-3142; (800) 778-6775; Fax (830) 538-3295; chamber@castroville.com; www.castroville.com*

Cedar Creek Lake • *see Mabank*

Cedar Hill • *Cedar Hill C/C* • Amanda Skinner; Pres.; 300 Houston St.; 75104; Dallas; P 43,000; M 450; (972) 291-7817; Fax (972) 291-8101; info@cedarhillchamber.org; www.cedarhillchamber.org*

Cedar Park • *Cedar Park C/C* • Harold Dean; Pres.; 1460 E. Whitestone Blvd., Ste. 180; P.O. Box 805; 78630; Williamson; P 60,000; M 670; (512) 260-7800; Fax (512) 260-9269; info@cedarparkchamber.org; www.cedarparkchamber.org*

Celina • *Greater Celina C/C* • Jeran Akers; Pres.; 201 S. Preston Rd., Ste. 109; P.O. Box 1476; 75009; Collin & Denton; P 6,100; M 100; (972) 382-3300; Fax (972) 382-3304; info@celinachamber.org; www.celinachamber.org

Center • *Shelby County C/C* • Pam Phelps; Exec. Dir.; 100 Courthouse Sq., Ste. A-101; 75935; Shelby; P 25,000; M 335; (936) 598-3682; Fax (936) 598-8163; info@shelbycountychamber.com; www.shelbycountychamber.com*

Centerville • *Centerville C/C* • Bobby Walters; Pres.; P.O. Box 422; 75833; Leon; P 1,000; M 100; (903) 536-7261; centerville75833@yahoo.com; www.centervilletexas.com

Chandler • *Chandler/Brownsboro Area C/C* • Bertha Pritchard; Admin. Asst.; 811 Hwy. 31 E.; P.O. Box 1500; 75758; Henderson; P 30,000; M 97; (903) 849-5930; cbacc2@embarqmail.com; www.cbacc.net

Channelview • *see Houston–North Channel Area C/C*

Childress • *Childress C/C* • Susan J. Leary; Exec. Dir.; 237 Commerce St.; P.O. Box 35; 79201; Childress; P 7,200; M 175; (940) 937-2567; Fax (940) 937-8836; c_chamber@att.net; www.childresschamber.com.

Cibolo • *see Selma*

Cisco • *Cisco C/C* • James Ramsay; Exec. Dir.; 309 Conrad Hilton Blvd.; 76437; Eastland; P 3,851; M 195; (254) 442-2537; Fax (254) 442-2553; ciscoinfo@ciscotx.com; www.ciscochamber.com

Clarendon • *Clarendon-Donley County C/C* • Judith P. Burlin; Exec. Dir.; 318 S. Kearney; P.O. Box 730; 79226; Donley; P 3,828; M 103; (806) 874-2421; (800) 579-4023; Fax (806) 874-2911; judith@windstream.net; www.donleytx.com

Clarksville • *Historic Red River County C/C* • W.F. Higgins; Pres.; 101 N. Locust; 75426; Red River; P 3,879; M 165; (903) 427-2645; Fax (903) 427-5454; redrivercc@windstream.net; www.red-river.net*

Clear Lake City • *see Houston–Clear Lake Area C/C*

Clear Lake Shores • *also see Houston–Clear Lake Area C/C*

Clear Lake Shores • *see Dickinson*

Cleburne • *Cleburne C/C* • Cathy Marchel; Pres.; 1511 W. Henderson St.; P.O. Box 701; 76033; Johnson; P 30,000; M 947; (817) 645-2455; Fax (817) 641-3069; info@cleburnechamber.com; www.cleburnechamber.com.*

Cleveland • *Greater Cleveland C/C* • Tracey Walters; CEO; 210 Peach Ave., Ste. B; 77327; Liberty; P 7,605; M 400; (281) 592-8786; Fax (281) 592-6949; info@clevelandtxchamber.com; www.clevelandtxchamber.com*

Clifton • *Clifton C/C* • Paige Key; Exec. Dir.; 115 N. Ave. D; 76634; Bosque; P 3,800; M 325; (254) 675-3720; Fax (254) 675-4630; info@cliftontexas.org; www.cliftontexas.org*

Clyde • *Clyde C/C* • Glenn Campbell; Pres.; 614 N. 1st St.; P.O. Box 257; 79510; Callahan; P 3,500; M 100; (325) 893-4221; Fax (325) 893-2778; clydecoc@camalott.com

Coldspring • *Coldspring-San Jacinto County C/C* • Barbara Brock; Pres.; 31 N. Butler; P.O. Box 980; 77331; San Jacinto; P 22,500; M 145; (936) 653-2184; Fax (936) 653-2184; ccc@coldspringtexas.org; www.coldspringtexas.org

Coleman • *Coleman County C/C, Ag. & Tourist Bur.* • Mary Griffis; Exec. Dir.; 218 Commercial; P.O. Box 796; 76834; Coleman; P 8,798; M 215; (325) 625-2163; Fax (325) 625-2164; chamber@colemantexas.org; www.colemantexas.org

College Station • *see Bryan*

Colleyville • *Colleyville Area C/C* • Mary Smith; Pres.; 6700 Colleyville Blvd.; 76034; Tarrant; P 24,000; M 750; (817) 488-7148; Fax (817) 488-4242; info@colleyvillechamber.org; www.colleyvillechamber.org*

Colorado City • *Colorado City Area C/C* • Amanda Ritchey; Dir.; 157 W. 2nd St.; P.O. Box 242; 79512; Mitchell; P 3,500; M 86; (325) 728-3403; Fax (325) 728-2911; ccitychamber@sbcglobal.net; www.coloradocitychamberofcommerce.com*

Columbus • *Columbus Area C/C* • Kim Dyer; Exec. Dir.; 425 Spring St.; 78934; Colorado; P 4,000; M 225; (979) 732-8385; Fax (979) 732-5881; kim@columbustexas.org; www.columbustexas.org

Comanche • *Comanche C/C & Ag.* • Christine Perkins; Exec. Dir.; 100 Indian Creek Dr.; P.O. Box 65; 76442; Comanche; P 4,823; M 227; (325) 356-3233; Fax (325) 356-2940; comanchechamber@verizon.net; www.comanchechamber.org

Comfort • *Comfort C/C* • Regina Alexander; Ofc. Mgr.; 630 Hwy. 27; P.O. Box 777; 78013; Kendall; P 2,500; M 225; (830) 995-3131; Fax (830) 995-5252; info@comfort-texas.com; www.comfortchamberofcommerce.com

Commerce • *Commerce C/C* • Trey Boyles; Mgr.; 1114 Main St.; P.O. Box 290; 75429; Hunt; P 8,136; M 300; (903) 886-3950; Fax (903) 886-8012; commercechamber@embarqmail.com; www.commerce-chamber.com*

Conroe • *Greater Conroe/Lake Conroe Area C/C* • E.S. "Stew" Darsey; Pres.; 505 W. Davis; 77301; Montgomery; P 43,000; M 1,300; (936) 756-6644; Fax (936) 756-6462; rsvp@conroe.org; www.conroe.org*

Converse • *see Selma*

  U.S. Chambers of Commerce

Cooper · *Delta County C/C* · Gracie Young; Ofc. Mgr.; 41 W. Side Sq.; P.O. Box 457; 75432; Delta; P 5,500; M 150; (903) 395-4314; Fax (903) 395-4318; deltacounty@neto.com; www.deltacounty.org

Coppell · *Coppell C/C* · Beverly Widner; Pres.; 509 W. Bethel Rd., Ste. 200; P.O. Box 452; 75019; Dallas; P 39,000; M 420; (972) 393-2829; Fax (972) 393-0659; info@coppellchamber.org; www.coppellchamber.org*

Copperas Cove · *Copperas Cove C/C* · Martha Smith; Pres.; 204 E. Robertson Ave.; 76522; Coryell; P 30,000; M 430; (254) 547-7571; Fax (254) 547-5015; chamber@copperascove.com; www.copperascove.com*

Corpus Christi · *Corpus Christi C/C* · Foster Edwards; Pres./CEO; 1201 N. Shoreline Blvd.; 78401; Nueces; P 308,000; M 1,350; (361) 881-1800; Fax (361) 882-4256; foster@theccchamber.org; www.corpuschristichamber.org*

Corpus Christi · *Corpus Christi Hispanic C/C* · Exec. Dir.; 615 N. Upper Broadway, Ste. 410; P.O. Box 5523; 78465; Nueces; P 387,500; M 750; (361) 887-7408; Fax (361) 888-9473; aelizondo@cchispanicchamber.org; www.cchispanicchamber.org*

Corsicana · *Corsicana/Navarro County C/C* · Paul Hooper; Exec. Pres.; 120 N. 12th St.; 75110; Navarro; P 50,000; M 400; (903) 874-4731; (877) 376-7477; Fax (903) 874-4187; chamber@corsicana.org; www.corsicana.org*

Cotulla · *Cotulla-La Salle County C/C* · Mariane Hall; Mgr.; 290 N. IH-35 Access Rd.; 78014; La Salle; P 5,100; M 125; (830) 879-2326; (800) 256-2326; Fax (830) 879-2326; cotcoc@att.net; www.cotulla-chamber.com

Crandall · *Greater Crandall C/C* · Ken Godey; Pres.; P.O. Box 669; 75114; Kaufman; P 3,800; M 60; (972) 472-8663; coordinator@crandallchamber.net; www.crandallchamber.net

Crane · *Crane County C/C* · Micah Lozano; Secy.; 409 S. Gaston St.; 79731; Crane; P 3,311; M 50; (432) 558-2311; Fax (432) 558-2311; craneccc@sbcglobal.net; www.cranechamber.net

Crockett · *Crockett Area C/C* · Jeana Culp; Exec. Dir.; 1100 Edmiston Dr.; P.O. Box 307; 75835; Houston; P 23,000; M 360; (936) 544-2359; (888) 269-2359; Fax (936) 544-4355; sheila@crockettareachamber.org; www.crockettareachamber.org*

Crosby · *Crosby-Huffman C/C* · Judy Richard & Dayna Rankin; Co-Coord.; 5611 S. Main St.; P.O. Box 452; 77532; Harris; P 34,000; M 200; (281) 328-6984; Fax (281) 328-7296; chamber@crosbyhuffmancc.org; www.crosbyhuffmancc.org*

Crosbyton · *Crosbyton C/C* · Jacque James; Dir.; 124 S. Berkshire; P.O. Box 202; 79322; Crosby; P 1,894; M 60; (806) 675-2261; Fax (806) 675-7012; jjames@crosbyton.com

Cross Plains · *Cross Plains C/C* · Karen Lenz; Pres.; 209 N.W. Main; P.O. Box 233; 76443; Callahan; P 1,068; M 50; (254) 725-7251; Fax (254) 725-6747; cpchamber@windstream.net; www.crossplainschamberofcommerce.com

Crowell · *Crowell C/C* · JoAnna Mills; Pres.; 107 N. Main; P.O. Box 164; 79227; Foard; P 1,600; M 100; (940) 684-1310; www.crowelltex.com

Crowley · *Crowley Area C/C* · Eileen Yarborough; Pres.; 201 N. Hampton Rd.; 76036; Johnson & Tarrant; P 11,000; M 364; (817) 297-4211; Fax (817) 297-7334; info@crowleyareachamber.org; www.crowleyareachamber.org

Crystal Beach · *Bolivar Peninsula C/C* · Anne Willis; Pres.; 1750 Hwy. 87; P.O. Box 1170; 77650; Galveston; P 4,500; M 125; (409) 684-5940; info@bolivarchamber.org; www.bolivarchamber.org

Cuero · *Cuero C of C & Ag. & Visitors Center* · Kay Lapp; Exec. Dir.; 124 E. Church St.; 77954; DeWitt; P 7,000; M 350; (361) 275-2112; Fax (361) 275-6351; cuerocc@cuero.org; www.cuero.org.*

Cypress · *Cy-Fair Houston C/C* · Mary Evans; Pres.; 11734 Barker Cypress, Ste. 105; 77433; Harris; P 800,000; M 680; (281) 373-1390; Fax (281) 373-1394; staff@cyfairchamber.com; www.cyfairchamber.com*

Daingerfield · *Daingerfield C/C* · Sherry Ray; Ofc. Mgr.; 102 Coffey St.; 75638; Morris; P 2,500; M 100; (903) 645-2646; Fax (903) 645-2646; daingerfieldchamberofcommerce@cebridge.net; www.daingerfieldtx.net

Dalhart · *Dalhart Area C/C* · Kristine Olsen; Pres.; 102 E. 7th St.; P.O. Box 967; 79022; Dallam & Hartley; P 12,000; M 265; (806) 244-5646; (806) 249-5646; Fax (806) 244-4945; chamber@dalhart.org; www.dalhart.org*

Dallas Area

Dallas Black C/C · Charles O' Neal; Pres.; 2838 MLK Jr. Blvd.; 75215; Dallas; M 1,800; (214) 421-5200; Fax (214) 421-5510; cro@dbcc.org; www.dbcc.org

Dallas Reg. C/C · James C. Oberwetter; Pres.; 700 N. Pearl St., Ste. 1200; 75201; Dallas; P 3,000,000; M 3,000; (214) 746-6600; Fax (214) 746-6799; information@dallaschamber.org; www.dallaschamber.org.*

Greater East Dallas C/C · Mary Poss; Chrmn.; 9543 Losa Dr., Ste. 118; 75218; Dallas; P 250,000; M 350; (214) 328-4100; Fax (214) 328-4124; president@eastdallaschamber.com; www.eastdallaschamber.com*

North Dallas C/C · Stephen E. Taylor; Pres.; 10707 Preston Rd.; 75230; Dallas; P 500,000; M 900; (214) 368-6485; Fax (214) 368-6695; mailbox@ndcc.org; www.ndcc.org*

Oak Cliff C/C · Bob Stimson; Pres.; 400 S. Zang Blvd., Ste. 110; 75208; Dallas; P 330,000; M 650; (214) 943-4567; Fax (214) 943-4582; occ@oakliffchamber.org; www.oakliffchamber.org*

Southeast Dallas C/C · Carl Raines; Chrmn.; P.O. Box 170132; 75217; Dallas; P 100,000; M 300; (214) 398-9590; Fax (214) 398-9591; info@sedcc.org; www.sedcc.org

Dayton · *also see Liberty*

Dayton · *Dayton C/C* · Tammy Pratka; Exec. Dir.; 801 S. Cleveland; 77535; Liberty; P 30,000; M 270; (936) 257-2393; Fax (936) 257-2394; tpratka@daytontxchamber.com; www.daytontxchamber.com*

Decatur · *Decatur C/C* · Misty Hudson; Exec. Dir.; 308 W. Main; P.O. Box 474; 76234; Wise; P 6,250; M 340; (940) 627-3107; Fax (940) 627-3771; misty.hudson@netcommander.com; www.decaturtx.com

Deer Park · *Deer Park C/C* · Tim Culp; Pres./CEO; 110 Center St.; 77536; Harris; P 28,520; M 600; (281) 479-1559; Fax (281) 476-4041; info@deerpark.org; www.deerpark.org*

DeKalb · *DeKalb C/C* · Judd Johns; Pres.; P.O. Box 219; 75559; Bowie; P 3,000; M 150; (903) 667-4949; (903) 667-7904; info@dekalbtexas.org; www.dekalbtexas.org

Del Rio · *Del Rio C/C* · Al Arreola Jr.; Exec. Dir.; 1915 Veterans Blvd.; 78840; Val Verde; P 45,000; M 500; (830) 775-3551; (800) 889-8149; Fax (830) 774-1813; info@drchamber.com; www.drchamber.com.*

DeLeon · *DeLeon C/C & Ag.* · Linda Levens; Exec. Dir.; 109 S. Texas St.; 76444; Comanche; P 2,500; M 143; (254) 893-2083; Fax (254) 893-7028; chamber@cctc.net; www.deleontexas.com

Dell City · *Dell Valley C/C* · Mary Ann Clute; Pres.; P.O. Box 225; 79837; Hudspeth; P 400; M 40; (915) 964-2312

Denison · *Denison Area C/C* · Anna H. McKinney; Pres./CEO; 313 W. Woodard; P.O. Box 325; 75020; Grayson; P 24,000; M 546; (903) 465-1551; Fax (903) 465-8443; information@denisontexas.us; www.denisontexas.us*

Denton · *Denton C/C* · C.W. Carpenter; Pres.; 414 Parkway St.; 76201; Denton; P 120,000; M 878; (940) 382-9693; (940) 382-7895; Fax (940) 382-0040; info@denton-chamber.org; www.denton-chamber.org*

Denver City · *Denver City C of C & CVB* · Daun McLeroy; Exec. V.P.; 120 N. Main St.; 79323; Yoakum; P 5,000; M 134; (806) 592-5424; Fax (806) 592-7613; denvercitycofc@valornet.com; www.denvercitychamber.com*

DeSoto · *DeSoto C/C* · Cammy Jackson; Pres.; 2010 N. Hampton, Ste. 200; 75115; Dallas; P 47,250; M 390; (972) 224-3565; Fax (972) 354-1022; admin@desotochamber.org; www.desoto chamber.org*

Devine · *Greater Devine C/C* · James Caldwell; Pres.; 200 E. Hondo Ave.; P.O. Box 443; 78016; Medina; P 5,000; M 90; (830) 663-2739; Fax (830) 663-2739; chamber@devinechamber.com; www.devinechamber.com

Dickinson · *North Galveston County C/C* · Theresa Graham; Pres.; 218 FM 517 W.; 77539; Galveston; P 98,000; M 300; (281) 534-4380; Fax (281) 534-4389; ngccc@ci.dickinson.tx.us; www. northgalvestoncountychamber.com.*

Dimmitt · *Dimmitt C/C* · Lourdes Chavez; Exec. Dir.; 115 W. Bedford; 79027; Castro; P 4,375; M 170; (806) 647-2524; Fax (806) 647-2469; dimmitchamber@gmail.com; www.dimmittchamber.com

Dripping Springs · *Dripping Springs C/C* · Kim Johnson; Exec. Dir.; 600 Hwy. 290 E.; P.O. Box 206; 78620; Hays; P 2,000; M 380; (512) 858-4740; Fax (512) 858-4144; dschamber@verizon.net; www.drippingspringstx.org*

Dublin · *Dublin C/C* · Karen Wright; Exec. Dir.; 111 S. Patrick; P.O. Box 309; 76446; Erath; P 3,800; M 120; (254) 445-3422; Fax (254) 445-0394; dublintxchamber@embarqmail.com; www.dublintx chamber.com

Dumas · *Dumas/Moore County C/C & Visitor Center* · Sam Cartwright; Pres./CEO; 1901 S. Dumas Ave.; P.O. Box 735; 79029; Moore; P 23,000; M 320; (806) 935-2123; (888) 840-8911; Fax (806) 935-2124; sam@dumaschamber.com; www.dumas chamber.com.*

Duncanville · *Duncanville C/C* · Steve Martin; Pres.; 300 E. Wheatland Rd.; 75116; Dallas; P 36,500; M 400; (972) 780-4990; Fax (972) 298-9370; info@duncanvillechamber.org; www.duncan villechamber.org

Eagle Lake · *Eagle Lake C/C* · Laura Myres; Pres.; 303 E. Main; 77434; Colorado; P 3,664; M 120; (979) 234-2780; Fax (979) 234-2780; info@visiteaglelake.com; www.visiteaglelake.com*

Eagle Pass · *Eagle Pass C/C* · Sandra Martinez; Exec. Dir.; 400 Garrison St.; P.O. Box 1188; 78853; Maverick; P 53,000; M 300; (830) 773-3224; (888) 355-3224; Fax (830) 773-8844; chamber@ eaglepasstexas.com; www.eaglepasstexas.com

Early · *Early C/C* · Wanda Furgason; Exec. Dir.; 104 E. Industrial Dr.; 76802; Brown; P 2,600; M 227; (325) 649-9300; (325) 649-9317; Fax (325) 643-4746; wanda@earlytx.com; www.early chamber.com*

East Bernard · *East Bernard C/C* · Ray Kerlick; Pres.; P.O. Box 567; 77435; Wharton; P 2,300; M 100; (979) 335-9900; rkerlick@ wadleperches.com; www.ebchamber.com

East Tawakoni · *see Quinlan*

Eastland · *Eastland C/C* · Cristal Rose; Mgr.; 209 W. Main St., Ste. A; 76448; Eastland; P 4,000; M 200; (254) 629-2332; (877) 2-OLDRIP; Fax (254) 629-1629; ecofc@eastland.net; www.eastlandchamber.com

Eden · *Eden C/C* · Dwain Psencik; Pres.; P.O. Box 367; 76837; Concho; P 1,700; M 50; (325) 869-3336; edenchamber@verizon. net; www.edentexas.com

Edinburg · *Edinburg C/C* · Letty Gonzalez; Pres.; 602 W. University Dr.; P.O. Box 85; 78540; Hidalgo; P 72,424; M 400; (956) 383-4974; (800) 800-7214; Fax (956) 383-6942; chamber@ edinburg.com; www.edinburg.com*

Edna · *Jackson County C/C & Ag.* · Clinton Tegeler; Exec. Dir.; 317 W. Main St.; P.O. Box 788; 77957; Jackson; P 14,500; M 300; (361) 782-7146; Fax (361) 782-2811; j.chamber@att.net; www. cityofedna.com*

El Campo · *El Campo C/C & Ag.* · Rebecca Munos; Exec. Dir.; 201 E. Jackson; P.O. Box 1400; 77437; Wharton; P 10,945; M 620; (979) 543-2713; Fax (979) 543-5495; ecc@elcampochamber.com; www. elcampochamber.com.*

El Lago · *see Houston—Clear Lake Area C/C*

El Paso · *El Paso Hispanic C/C* · Cindy Ramos-Davidson; Pres./ CEO; 2401 E. Missouri St.; 79903; El Paso; P 875,000; M 1,137; (915) 566-4066; Fax (915) 566-9714; jmontemayor@ephcc.org; www.ephcc.org*

El Paso · *Greater El Paso C/C* · Richard E. Dayoub; Pres./CEO; 10 Civic Center Plaza; 79901; El Paso; P 734,600; M 1,700; (915) 534-0500; (800) 651-8065; Fax (915) 534-0510; info@elpaso.org; www.elpaso.org.

Elbert · *see Throckmorton*

Electra · *Electra C/C* · Sherry Strange & Mary Ann Stockton; 112 W. Cleveland; 76360; Wichita; P 3,100; M 40; (940) 495-3577; Fax (940) 495-3022; electracoc@electratel.net; www.electratexas.org

Elgin · *Greater Elgin C/C* · Gena Carter; Pres.; 114 Central Ave.; P.O. Box 408; 78621; Bastrop & Travis; P 7,200; M 205; (512) 285-4515; Fax (512) 281-3393; info@elgintxchamber.com; www. elgintxchamber.com

Emory · *Rains County C/C* · Nan Satterwhite; Pres.; 410 W. Tawakoni Dr.; 75440; Rains; P 11,500; M 120; (903) 473-3913; Fax (903) 473-3913; info@rainschamber.com; www.rainschamber.com

Ennis · *Ennis Area C/C* · Jeannette J. Patak; Pres.; 108 Chamber of Commerce Dr.; P.O. Box 1177; 75120; Ellis; P 20,000; M 450; (972) 878-2625; Fax (972) 875-1473; manager@ennis-chamber. com; www.ennis-chamber.com.*

Euless · *see Bedford*

Eustace · *see Mabank*

Everman · *see Forest Hill*

Fairfield · *Fairfield C/C* · Cheryl Cockerell; Exec. Admin.; 900 W. Commerce; P.O. Box 899; 75840; Freestone; P 3,306; M 165; (903) 389-5792; (903) 389-6122; Fax (903) 389-8382; chamber@ fairfieldtx.com; www.fairfieldtexaschamber.com

Falfurrias · *Falfurrias C/C* · Gus Barrera; Exec. Dir.; 124 N. St. Mary St.; P.O. Box 476; 78355; Brooks; P 8,300; M 140; (361) 325-3333; Fax (361) 325-2956; c_of_commerce@yahoo.com.

Falls City · *Falls City C/C* · Arlene Jurgajtis; Pres.; P.O. Box 298; 78113; Karnes; P 591; M 50; (830) 745-2154

Farmers Branch · *Farmers Branch C/C* · Anne Acuna; Dir. of Chamber Relations; One Medical Pkwy., Ste. 104; 75234; Dallas; P 28,000; M 280; (972) 243-8966; aacuna@fbchamber.com; www.fbchamber.com*

Farmersville · *Farmersville C/C & Visitors Center* · Cynthia Craddock-Clark; Ofc. Mgr.; 201 S. Main; 75442; Collin; P 3,319; M 100; (972) 782-6533; Fax (972) 782-6603; chamber@ci.farmersvilletx.us; www.farmersvilletx.com

Farwell · *Farwell C/C* · Rob Pomper; Pres.; P.O. Box 1005; 79325; Parmer; P 1,400; M 50; (806) 481-3620

Fayetteville · *Fayetteville C/C* · P.O. Box 217; 78940; Fayette; P 270; M 60; (888) 575-4553; info@fayettevilletx.com; www.fayettevilletx.com

Flatonia · *Flatonia C/C* · Beverly Ponder; Exec. Dir.; 208 E. N. Main; P.O. Box 610; 78941; Fayette; P 1,300; M 125; (361) 865-3920; Fax (361) 865-2451; flatoniacofc@sbcglobal.net; www.flatoniachamber.com*

Florence · *Florence C/C* · Robert Chambers; Pres.; 210 Patterson; P.O. Box 201; 76527; Williamson; P 2,000; M 42; (254) 793-4300; robertchambers@aol.com; www.florencechamberofcommerce.org

Floresville · *Floresville C/C* · Paul W. Sack; Pres.; 910 10th St.; 78114; Wilson; P 7,500; M 160; (830) 393-0074; Fax (830) 393-9224; info@floresvillecoc.com; www.floresvillecoc.com

Flower Mound · *Flower Mound C/C* · Cindi Howard; V.P.; 700 Parker Sq., Ste. 100; 75028; Denton; P 63,000; M 800; (972) 539-0500; Fax (972) 539-4307; c.howard@flowermoundchamber.com; www.flowermoundchamber.com

Floydada · *Floydada C/C & Ag.* · Gina Adams; P.O. Box 147; 79235; Floyd; P 3,676; M 115; (806) 983-3434; gina@assiter.biz; www.floydadachamber.com

Forest Hill · *South Tarrant County C/C* · Sam Shafeeq CCM CCE; Chrmn.; P.O. Box 1338; 76140; Tarrant; P 30,000; M 150; (817) 478-6185; Fax (817) 568-3049; st.chamber@yahoo.com

Forney · *Forney C/C* · Laurie Barkham; Pres.; 100 U.S. Hwy. 80; P.O. Box 570; 75126; Kaufman; P 18,000; M 250; (972) 564-2233; Fax (972) 564-3677; lauriebarkham@sbcglobal.net; www.forneychamber.com

Fort Davis · *Fort Davis C/C* · Lisa Nugent; Exec. Dir.; P.O. Box 378; 79734; Jeff Davis; P 2,100; M 120; (432) 426-3015; (800) 524-3015; Fax (432) 426-3978; info@fortdavis.com; www.fortdavis.com

Fort Hood · *see Killeen*

Fort Stockton · *Fort Stockton C/C* · Arna McCorkle; Exec. V.P.; 1000 Railroad Ave.; 79735; Pecos; P 8,000; M 220; (432) 336-2264; (800) 336-2166; Fax (432) 336-6114; director@fortstockton.org; www.fortstockton.org*

Fort Worth · *Fort Worth C/C* · Bill Thornton; Pres./CEO; 777 Taylor, Ste. 900; 76102; Tarrant; P 618,600; M 3,500; (817) 336-2491; Fax (817) 877-4034; bthornton@fortworthchamber.com; www.fortworthchamber.com

Fort Worth · *Fort Worth Hispanic C/C* · Rosa Navejar; Pres.; 1327 N. Main St.; 76164; Tarrant; P 450,000; M 1,100; (817) 625-5411; Fax (817) 625-1405; rosa.navejar@fwhcc.org; www.fwhcc.org*

Franklin · *Franklin C/C* · Peggy Baxter; Exec. Dir.; 351 Cooks Ln.; P.O. Box 126; 77856; Robertson; P 1,800; M 300; (979) 828-3276; Fax (979) 828-1816; franklincc@valornet.com; www.franklintexas.com

Frankston · *Lake Palestine C/C* · Larry Paxton; Pres.; P.O. Box 1002; 75763; Anderson; P 1,850; M 44; (903) 876-5310; info@lakepalestinechamber.com; www.lakepalestinechamber.com

Fredericksburg · *Fredericksburg C/C* · Frances Rushing; Pres.; 302 E. Austin; 78624; Gillespie; P 10,432; M 800; (830) 997-6523; Fax (830) 997-8588; president@fbgtxchamber.org; www.fredericksburg-texas.com*

Freer · *Freer C/C* · Margaret Despain; Exec. Mgr.; P.O. Box 717; 78357; Duval; P 3,271; M 150; (361) 394-6891; Fax (361) 394-6891; freercofc@yahoo.com

Friendswood · *Friendswood C/C* · Carol Jones; Pres.; 1100 S. Friendswood Dr.; P.O. Box 11; 77546; Galveston; P 35,000; M 550; (281) 482-3329; Fax (281) 482-3911; fwdchmbr@swbell.net; www.friendswood-chamber.com*

Friona · *Friona C/C & Ag.* · Chris Alexander; Exec. V.P.; 621 Main St.; 79035; Parmer; P 3,800; M 200; (806) 250-3491; Fax (806) 250-2348; fedc@wtrt.net; www.frionachamber.com

Frisco · *Frisco C/C* · Tony Felker; Pres./CEO; 6843 Main St.; 75034; Collin & Denton; P 110,000; M 1,100; (972) 335-9522; Fax (972) 335-6654; info@friscochamber.com; www.friscochamber.com.

Fulshear · *see Pattison*

Gainesville · *Gainesville Area C/C* · Kristi Rigsby; Exec. Dir.; 311 S. Weaver St.; P.O. Box 518; 76241; Cooke; P 16,000; M 500; (940) 665-2831; (940) 665-2832; Fax (940) 665-2833; kristi@gainesvillecofc.com; www.gogainesville.net*

Galena Park · *see Houston–North Channel Area C/C*

Galveston · *Galveston C/C* · Gina Spagnola; Pres.; 519 25th St.; 77550; Galveston; P 57,247; M 850; (409) 763-5326; Fax (409) 763-8271; GSpagnola@galvestonchamber.com; www.galvestonchamber.com*

Garden Oaks · *see Houston–Houston Intercontinental C/C*

Garden Ridge · *see Selma*

Garland · *Garland C/C* · Paul Mayer; CEO; 520 N. Glenbrook Dr.; 75040; Dallas; P 240,876; M 453; (972) 272-7551; (469) 326-7444; Fax (972) 276-9261; paul.mayer@garlandchamber.com; www.garlandchamber.com

Gatesville · *Gatesville Area C/C & Agribusiness* · Susie Gunnels; Exec. Dir.; 2307 Hwy. 36 S.; 76528; Coryell; P 10,000; M 200; (254) 865-2617; Fax (254) 865-5581; chamber@gatesvilletx.info; www.gatesvilletx.info

George West · *George West C/C* · Becky Allen; Exec. Dir.; 400 N. Nueces; P.O. Box 359; 78022; Live Oak; P 12,000; M 110; (361) 449-2033; Fax (361) 449-2481; chamber@georgewest.org; www.georgewest.org

Georgetown · *Georgetown C/C* · Mel Pendland; Pres.; 100 Stadium Dr.; P.O. Box 346; 78627; Williamson; P 48,000; M 1,133; (512) 930-3535; Fax (512) 930-3587; info@georgetownchamber.org; www.georgetownchamber.org*

Giddings · *Giddings Area C/C* · Denice Harlan; Exec. Dir.; 171 E. Hempstead; 78942; Lee; P 5,500; M 270; (979) 542-3455; Fax (979) 542-7060; giddingscofc@verizon.net; www.giddingstx.com

Gilmer · *Gilmer Area C/C* · Joan Small; Exec. Dir.; 106 Buffalo St.; P.O. Box 854; 75644; Upshur; P 36,000; M 300; (903) 843-2413; Fax (903) 843-3759; upchamber@aol.com; www.gilmerareachamber.com

Gladewater · *Gladewater C/C* · Marsha Valdetero; Mgr.; 215 N. Main St.; P.O. Box 1409; 75647; Gregg & Upshur; P 6,078; M 230; (903) 845-5501; (800) 627-0315; Fax (903) 845-6326; gladewatercoc@suddenlinkmail.com; www.gladewaterchamber.com

Glen Rose · *Glen Rose-Somervell County C/C* · Darrell Best; Chrmn.; 112 Walnut St.; P.O. Box 605; 76043; Somervell; P 7,500; M 300; (254) 897-2286; grcc@glenrosechamber.com; www.glenrosechamber.com

Goldthwaite · *Mills County-Goldthwaite C/C* · Becca Miles; Exec. Dir.; 1001 Fisher St.; P.O. Box 308; 76844; Mills; P 5,000; M 148; (325) 648-3619; gcc@centex.net; www.goldthwaite.biz

Goliad · *Goliad C/C* · Mona Foust; Exec. Mgr.; 231 S. Market St.; P.O. Box 606; 77963; Goliad; P 9,200; M 100; (361) 645-3563; (800) 848-8674; Fax (361) 645-3579; goliadcc@goliad.net; www.goliadcc.org

Gonzales · *Gonzales C/C* · Barbara Hand; Mgr.; 414 St. Lawrence St.; 78629; Gonzales; P 7,202; M 290; (830) 672-6532; Fax (830) 672-6533; info@gonzalestexas.com; www.gonzalestexas.com.

Gorman · *Gorman C/C* · Terry Treadway; Secy./Mgr.; P.O. Box 266; 76454; Eastland; P 1,500; M 40; (254) 639-2317; terry@cctc.net; www.gormantx.com

Graford · *Possum Kingdom Lake C/C* · Gayla Chambers; Exec. Dir.; 362 N. FM 2353; 76449; Palo Pinto; P 2,500; M 350; (940) 779-2424; pkchamber@possumkingdomlake.com; www.possum kingdomlake.com

Graham · *Graham C/C* · DeAnna Bullock Armstrong; Pres.; 608 Elm St.; P.O. Box 299; 76450; Young; P 8,716; M 350; (940) 549-3355; (800) 256-4844; Fax (940) 549-6391; info@grahamtx chamber.com; www.grahamtxchamber.com*

Granbury · *Granbury C/C* · Mike Scott; CEO; 3408 E. Hwy. 377; 76049; Hood; P 54,900; M 900; (817) 573-1622; Fax (817) 573-0805; info@granburychamber.com; www.granburychamber.com*

Grand Prairie · *Grand Prairie C/C* · Lynn McGinley; Pres.; 900 Conover Dr.; 75051; Dallas; P 170,000; M 600; (972) 264-1558; Fax (972) 264-3419; info@grandprairiechamber.org; www.grandprairiechamber.org*

Grand Saline · *Grand Saline C/C* · Lisa Morrison; Secy.; 203 N.E. Pacific; 75140; Van Zandt; P 3,200; M 125; (903) 962-7147; chamber@grandsaline.com; www.grandsaline.com

Grandfalls · *Grandfalls-Royalty C/C* · Jim Crawford; Pres.; P.O. Box 269; 79742; Ward; P 300; M 20; (432) 547-2383; (432) 547-2331

Grandview · *Greater Grandview C/C* · Chris Gabel; Pres.; P.O. Box 276; 76050; Johnson; P 5,100; M 50; (817) 866-4881; info@grandviewchamber.net; www.grandviewchamber.net

Grapevine · *Grapevine C/C* · RaDonna Hessel; Pres./CEO; 200 E. Vine St.; 76051; Tarrant; P 49,797; M 880; (817) 481-1522; Fax (817) 424-5208; info@grapevinechamber.org; www.grapevine chamber.org.*

Greenspoint · *see Houston–Houston Intercontinental C/C*

Greenville · *Greenville Area C/C & CVB* · Sally A. Bird; Pres./CEO; 2713 Stonewall St.; P.O. Box 1055; 75403; Hunt; P 30,000; M 555; (903) 455-1510; Fax (903) 455-1736; chamber@green villechamber.com; www.greenvillechamber.com.*

Groesbeck · *Groesbeck C/C* · Thomas Hawkins; Pres.; 115 N. Ellis St.; P.O. Box 326; 76642; Limestone; P 4,200; M 120; (254) 729-3894; (254) 729-5103; Fax (254) 729-8310; www.groesbeck texas.org

Groves · *Groves C/C & Tourist Bur.* · Ronnie Boneau; Exec. Mgr.; 4399 Main Ave.; 77619; Jefferson; P 16,000; M 148; (409) 962-3631; (800) 876-3631; Fax (409) 963-0745; gchamberofcommer@ gt.rr.com; www.grovescofc.com*

Groveton · *Trinity County C/C* · Paul E. Snyder; Exec. Dir.; 135 S. Main St.; P.O. Box 366; 75845; Trinity; P 6,000; M 65; (936) 642-1715; (936) 635-7583; Fax (936) 642-2144; tccoc@valornet.com; www.trinitycountychamber.org

Gruver · *Gruver C/C* · Steve McKay; Mgr.; 201 E. Broadway; P.O. Box 947; 79040; Hansford; P 1,162; M 40; (806) 733-5114; Fax (806) 733-5038; www.gruvertexas.com

Gun Barrel City · *see Mabank*

Gunter · *Gunter Area C/C* · Michael Elliot; Pres.; P.O. Box 830; 75058; Grayson; P 1,300; M 75; (214) 551-1383; chamberadmin@ guntertxchamber.com; ww.guntertxchamber.com

Hale Center · *Hale Center C/C* · Jimmy Cameron; Pres.; 703 Main St.; P.O. Box 487; 79041; Hale; P 2,200; M 106; (806) 839-2642; Fax (806) 839-2642; halecentercoc@hotmail.com; halecenterchamber.mine.nu.*

Hallettsville · *Hallettsville C/C* · Lori Popp; 1614 N. Texana; P.O. Box 313; 77964; Lavaca; P 2,531; M 200; (361) 798-2662; Fax (361) 798-1553; visit@hallettsville.com; www.hallettsville.com

Hallsville · *Hallsville Area C/C* · P.O. Box 899; 75650; Harrison; P 2,700; M 80; (903) 668-2313; www.cityofhallsville.org

Haltom City · *Northeast Tarrant C/C* · Robert Hamilton; Pres./CEO; 5001 Denton Hwy.; 76117; Tarrant; P 135,000; M 1,000; (817) 281-9376; Fax (817) 281-9379; ngibson@netarrant.org; www.netarrant.org*

Hamilton · *Hamilton C/C* · Steve Almquist; Mgr.; 204 E. Main St.; P.O. Box 429; 76531; Hamilton; P 3,000; M 144; (254) 386-3216; Fax (254) 386-3563; cofc@htcomp.net; www.hamilton texas.com

Hamlin · *Hamlin C/C* · Lonnie Powell; Pres.; P.O. Box 402; 79520; Jones; P 2,000; M 100; (325) 576-3501

Harker Heights · *Harker Heights C/C* · Bill Kozlik; Pres.; 552 E. FM 2410, Ste. B; 76548; Bell; P 29,000; M 900; (254) 699-4999; Fax (254) 699-5194; bill@hhchamber.com; www.hhchamber.com*

Harlingen · *Harlingen Area C/C & Visitor Bur.* · Crisanne Zamponi; Exec. Dir.; 311 E. Tyler St.; 78550; Cameron; P 84,832; M 850; (956) 423-5440; (800) 531-7346; Fax (956) 425-3870; czamponi@harlingen.com; www.harlingen.com*

Harlingen · *Harlingen Hispanic C/C* · Sergio Contreras; Chrmn.; 2309 N. Ed Carey Dr.; P.O. Box 530967; 78553; Cameron; P 65,000; M 300; (956) 421-2400; Fax (956) 364-1879; hhcoc@harlingen chamber.com; www.harlingenchamber.com*

Haskell · *Haskell C/C & Visitors Bur.* · Sally Rueffer; Gen. Mgr.; 510 S. 2nd St.; 79521; Haskell; P 3,200; M 90; (940) 864-2477; haskellcc@srcaccess.net; www.haskelltxchamber.com

Haslet · *see Roanoke*

Hawk Cove · *see Quinlan*

Hawkins · *Hawkins Area C/C* · Larry Huston; Pres.; 205 N. Beaulah St.; P.O. Box 345; 75765; Wood; P 1,500; M 59; (903) 769-4482; hawkinsareachamberofcommerce@juno.com; www.hawkinschamberofcommerce.com

Hemphill · *Sabine County C/C* · Marc Griffin; Pres.; 717 Sabine St.; P.O. Box 717; 75948; Sabine; P 11,000; M 225; (409) 787-2732; Fax (409) 787-2158; sabinecounty1@windstream.net; www.sabinecountytexas.com*

Hempstead · *Hempstead C/C* · John Stanley; Pres.; P.O. Box 517; 77445; Waller; P 7,500; M 220; (979) 826-8217; Fax (979) 826-2566; info@hempsteadtxchamber.com; www.hempstead txchamber.com

Henderson · *Henderson Area C/C* · Judy Sewell; Exec. Dir.; 201 N. Main St.; 75652; Rusk; P 47,255; M 350; (903) 657-5528; Fax (903) 657-9454; info@hendersontx.com; www.hendersontx.com*

Henrietta · *Henrietta/Clay County C/C* · Deborah Clark; Pres.; 202 W. Omega St.; P.O. Box 75; 76365; Clay; P 3,800; M 100; (940) 538-5261; claycountychamber@sbcglobal.net; www.hccchamber.org

Hereford · *Deaf Smith County C/C* · Sid C. Shaw; Exec. V.P.; 701 N. Main; P.O. Box 192; 79045; Deaf Smith; P 20,000; M 325; (806) 364-3333; Fax (806) 364-3342; deafs@wtrt.net; www.herefordtx.org

Hewitt · *Greater Hewitt C/C* · Diane Frank; Exec. Dir.; 101 Third St.; P.O. Box 661; 76643; McLennan; P 13,500; M 315; (254) 666-1200; Fax (254) 666-3181; greaterhewitt@grandecom.net; www.hewitt-texas.com*

Hico · *Hico C/C* · 76457; Hamilton; P 1,341; M 40; (254) 796-4620; mike.james@homesteadhico.com; www.hico-tx.com

Hidalgo · *Hidalgo C/C* · Joe Vera; Pres.; 611 E. Coma Ave.; 78557; Hidalgo; P 13,000; M 570; (956) 843-2734; Fax (956) 843-2722; chamber@hidalgotexas.com; www.hidalgotexas.com

Highlands · *Greater Highlands & Lynchburg C/C* · Jessica Woods; Exec. Admin.; 127 San Jacinto St.; 77562; Harris; P 12,500; M 100; (281) 426-7227; Fax (281) 426-7227; info@allabouthighlands.org; www.allabouthighlands.com

Hillje · *see Louise*

Hillsboro · *Hillsboro Area C/C & CVB* · Greg Solomon; Exec. Dir.; 115 N. Covington St.; P.O. Box 358; 76645; Hill; P 8,500; M 360; (254) 582-2481; (800) 445-5726; Fax (254) 582-0465; info@hillsborochamber.org; www.hillsborochamber.org*

Hitchcock · *Hitchcock C/C* · Teresa Weishuhn; Exec. Dir.; 8300 Hwy. 6, Ste. A; P.O. Box 389; 77563; Galveston; P 6,386; M 200; (409) 986-9224; Fax (409) 986-6317; hcofc662@verizon.net; www.hitchcocktexaschamber.com

Hondo · *Hondo Area C/C* · Wade Smith; Exec. Dir.; 1607 Ave. K; 78861; Medina; P 9,000; M 250; (830) 426-3037; Fax (830) 426-5357; info@hondochamber.com; www.hondochamber.com*

Honey Grove · *Honey Grove C/C* · Patti Hicks; Pres.; P.O. Box 92; 75446; Fannin; P 1,800; M 74; (903) 378-7211; info@honeygrovechamber.com; www.honeygrovechamber.com

Houston Area

Clear Lake Area C/C · Cindy Harreld; Pres./CEO; 1201 NASA Pkwy.; 77058; Harris; P 250,000; M 1,800; (281) 488-7676; Fax (281) 488-8981; chamber@clearlakearea.com; www.clearlakearea.com*

Galleria C/C · Don Sweat; Pres.; 5005 Woodway, Ste. 215; 77056; Harris; P 210,000; M 765; (713) 629-5555; Fax (713) 629-6403; info@galleriachamber.com; www.galleriachamber.com*

Greater Heights Area C/C · Kenneth E. Stallman; Pres./CEO; 545 W. 19th St.; 77008; Harris; P 350,000; M 400; (713) 861-6735; Fax (713) 861-9310; president@heightschamber.com; www.heightschamber.com*

Greater Houston Partnership · Bojan Vukovic; Mgr. of Intl. Bus. Programs; 1200 Smith St., Ste. 700; 77002; Harris; P 5,867,489; M 2,000; (713) 844-3636; Fax (713) 844-0236; bvukovic@houston.org; www.houston.org*

Houston East End C/C · Frances Castaneda Dyess; Pres.; 550 Gulfgate Center; 77087; Harris; P 110,000; M 500; (713) 926-3305; Fax (713) 926-0960; monica@eecoc.org; www.eecoc.org*

Houston Intercontinental C/C · Reggie Gray; Pres.; 250 N. Sam Houston Pkwy. E., Ste. 200; 77060; Harris; P 900,000; M 500; (281) 260-3163; Fax (281) 260-3161; rgray@houstonicc.org; www.houstonicc.org

Houston Area, *continued*

Houston Northwest C/C · Barbara Thomason; Pres.; 3920 FM 1960 W., Ste. 120; 77068; Harris; P 865,000; M 700; (281) 440-4160; Fax (281) 440-5302; chamberinfo@houstonnwchamber.org; www.houstonnwchamber.org*

Houston West C/C · Jeannie Bollinger; Pres./CEO; 10370 Richmond Ave., Ste. 125; 77042; Harris; P 1,000,000; M 615; (713) 785-4922; Fax (713) 785-4944; info@hwcoc.org; www.hwcoc.org*

North Channel Area C/C · Wayne R. Oquin; Pres./CEO; 13301 I-10 E. Frwy., Ste. 100; P.O. Box 9759; 77213; Harris; P 210,000; M 700; (713) 450-3600; Fax (713) 450-0700; wayneoq@flash.net; www.northchannelarea.com*

South Belt-Ellington C/C · Sally Mitchell; Exec. Dir.; 10500 Scarsdale Blvd.; 77089; Harris; P 81,000; M 400; (281) 481-5516; Fax (281) 922-7045; info@southbeltchamber.com; www.southbeltchamber.com*

Hubbard · *City of Hubbard C/C* · Margo Foster; V.P.; P.O. Box 221; 76648; Hill; P 1,600; M 100; (254) 576-2521; Fax (254) 576-2688; mfoster396@aol.com; www.hubbardchamber.com

Hudson Oaks · *see Willow Park*

Huffman · *see Crosby*

Hughes Springs · *Hughes Springs C/C* · Judi Howell; Exec. Dir.; 603 E. 1st St.; P.O. Box 218; 75656; Cass; P 5,000; M 100; (903) 639-2351; Fax (903) 639-3769; hughesspringscofc@hotmail.com; www.hughesspringscofc.com

Humble · *Lake Houston Area C/C* · Charlie Dromgoole; Pres.; 110 W. Main St.; P.O. Box 3337; 77347; Harris; P 253,336; M 1,200; (281) 446-2128; Fax (281) 446-7483; cdromgoole@lakehouston.org; www.lakehoustonareachamber.org*

Huntsville · *Huntsville-Walker County C/C* · Carol Smith; Pres.; 1327 11th St.; P.O. Box 538; 77342; Walker; P 62,000; M 500; (936) 295-8113; (877) 646-8068; Fax (936) 295-0571; chamber@chamber.huntsville.tx.us; www.chamber.huntsville.tx.us.*

Hurst · *see Bedford*

Hutto · *Hutto C/C* · Tom Britton; Pres.; 122 East St.; P.O. Box 99; 78634; Williamson; P 17,200; M 296; (512) 759-4400; Fax (512) 846-1618; info@hutto.org; www.hutto.org*

Ingleside · *Ingleside C/C* · Jan Hart; Pres./CEO; 2867 Ave. J; P.O. Box 686; 78362; San Patricio; P 9,338; M 200; (361) 776-2906; (888) 899-2906; ingchamber1@cableone.net; www.inglesidetxchamber.org*

Ingram · *West Kerr County C/C* · Jo Anne Gray; Exec. Dir.; 3186 Junction Hwy.; P.O. Box 1006; 78025; Kerr; P 10,000; M 158; (830) 367-4322; wkccc1@ktc.com; www.wkcc.com

Iowa Park · *Iowa Park C/C* · David Owen; Dir. of Eco. Dev.; 102 N. Wall St.; 76367; Wichita; P 6,500; M 125; (940) 592-5441; dowen@iowapark.com; www.iowapark.com

Iraan · *Iraan-Sheffield C/C* · Dana St. Clair; Ofc. Mgr.; 501 W. 6th; P.O. Box 153; 79744; Pecos; P 1,250; M 60; (432) 639-2232; Fax (432) 639-2125; iraanchamber@yahoo.com; www.iraantx.com

Iredell · *Iredell C/C* · LaMona Boyd; P.O. Box 111; 76649; Bosque; P 360; M 12; (254) 364-2436; (254) 364-2450

Irving · *Greater Irving-Las Colinas C/C* · Chris Wallace; Pres.; 5201 N. O'Connor Blvd., Ste. 100; 75039; Dallas; P 200,000; M 1,400; (214) 217-8484; Fax (214) 389-2513; cwallace@irvingchamber.com; www.irvingchamber.com*

Jacksboro · *Jacksboro C/C* · Brenda Tarpley; Ofc. Mgr.; 302 S. Main St.; 76458; Jack; P 4,500; M 130; (940) 567-2602; Fax (940) 567-3161; office@jacksborochamber.com; www.jacksborochamber.com

Jacksonville · *Jacksonville C/C* · Peggy Renfro; Pres.; 526 E. Commerce; P.O. Box 1231; 75766; Cherokee; P 14,203; M 435; (903) 586-2217; Fax (903) 586-6944; chamber@jacksonvilletexas.com; www.jacksonvilletexas.com*

Jasper · *Jasper-Lake Sam Rayburn Area C/C* · Liz Street; Exec. Dir.; 246 E. Milam St.; 75951; Jasper; P 8,500; M 395; (409) 384-2762; jaspercc@jaspercoc.org; www.jaspercoc.org

Jefferson · *Marion County C/C* · Charlie Chitwood; Bd. Pres.; 101 N. Polk St.; 75657; Marion; P 2,100; M 224; (903) 665-2672; (888) 467-3529; Fax (903) 665-8233; jeffersonchamber@sbcglobal.net; www.jefferson-texas.com

Jewett · *Jewett Area C/C* · Scott Serafin; Pres.; 111 N. Robinson Rd.; P.O. Box 220; 75846; Leon; P 1,250; M 95; (903) 626-4202; Fax (903) 626-6599; contactus@jewetttexas.org; www.jewetttexas.org

Johnson City · *Johnson City Chamber & Visitors Center* · Dale Hardy; Pres.; 100 E. Main; P.O. Box 485; 78636; Blanco; P 1,350; M 140; (830) 868-7684; Fax (830) 868-5700; info@johnsoncitytexaschamber.com; www.johnsoncity-texas.com

Joshua · *Joshua Area C/C* · Tana Howell; Pres.; 104 N. Main St.; P.O. Box 1781; 76058; Johnson; P 8,200; M 187; (817) 558-2821; Fax (817) 645-7824; joshchamber@att.net; www.joshuachamber.org

Jourdanton · *Jourdanton C/C* · Rhonda Lem; Pres.; 1101 Campbell Ave.; P.O. Box 747; 78026; Atascosa; P 3,700; M 50; (830) 769-2866; (830) 769-3087; Fax (830) 769-4082; jourdlib@texun.net; www.jourdanton.net

Junction · *Kimble County C/C & Junction Tourism* · Constance E. Booth; Exec. Dir.; 402 Main St.; 76849; Kimble; P 5,000; M 275; (325) 446-3190; (800) KIMBLE4; Fax (325) 446-2871; junctiontx@cebridge.net; www.junctiontexas.net

Karnack · *Caddo Lake Area C/C & Tourism* · Sara Smith; Pres.; 984 TJ Taylor Ave.; P.O. Box 228; 75661; Harrison; P 700; M 58; info@caddolake.org; www.caddolake.org

Karnes City · *Karnes City Comm. C/C* · Mary Ada Blackmon; Ofc. Dir.; 210 E. Calvert St.; 78118; Karnes; P 3,578; M 110; (830) 780-3112; Fax (830) 780-3112; office@karnescitychamber.net; www.karnescitychamber.net

Kashmere · *see Houston—Houston Intercontinental C/C*

Katy · *Katy Area C/C* · Ann Hodge; Pres./CEO; 23501 Cinco Ranch Blvd., Ste. B206; 77494; Fort Bend, Harris & Waller; P 219,348; M 800; (281) 391-5289; Fax (281) 391-7423; info@katychamber.com; www.katychamber.com*

Kaufman · *Greater Kaufman C/C* · Anne Glasscock; Pres./CEO; 2100 S. Washington; P.O. Box 146; 75142; Kaufman; P 7,120; M 240; (972) 932-3118; Fax (972) 932-8373; info@kaufmanchamber.com; www.kaufmantx.com

Keene · *Keene C/C* · Gwen Beeson; Pres.; P.O. Box 817; 76059; Johnson; P 6,258; M 125; (817) 556-2995; info@keenechamber.org; www.keenechamber.org

Keller · *Greater Keller C/C* · Susanne Johnson; Pres./CEO; 420 Johnson Rd., Ste. 301; 76248; Tarrant; P 36,000; M 700; (817) 431-2169; Fax (817) 431-3789; info@kellerchamber.com; www.kellerchamber.com*

Kemah · *also see Houston—Clear Lake Area C/C*

Kemah · *see Dickinson*

Kemp · *see Mabank*

Kenedy · *Kenedy C/C* · Carolyn McDonald; Exec. Dir.; 205 S. 2nd St.; 78119; Karnes; P 3,400; M 135; (830) 583-3223; (830) 583-5929; Fax (830) 583-3223; kenedycc@sbcglobal.net; www.kenedychamber.org

Kennedale · *Kennedale C/C* · Pat Doescher; Chrmn.; P.O. Box 1552; 76060; Tarrant; P 7,200; M 185; (817) 985-2109; Fax (817) 985-2119; kennedalechamber@yahoo.com; www.kennedalechamber.com*

Kerens · *Kerens C/C* · Rita West; Secy.; 101 S. Colket; P.O. Box 117; 75144; Navarro; P 1,600; M 100; (903) 396-2391; Fax (903) 396-2391; kerenschamber@txun.net; www.ci.kerens.tx.us

Kermit · *Kermit C/C* · Stefanie Haley; Pres.; 112 N. Poplar St.; 79745; Winkler; P 6,000; M 100; (432) 586-2507; (432) 586-2508; Fax (432) 586-2508; kermitchamber@cebridge.net; *

Kerrville · *Kerrville Area C/C* · Brian J. Bondy IOM; Pres./CEO; 1700 Sidney Baker St., Ste. 100; 78028; Kerr; P 44,000; M 1,222; (830) 896-1155; Fax (830) 896-1175; president@kerrvilletx.com; www.kerrvilletx.com*

Kilgore · *Kilgore C/C* · Michael Coston; Pres.; 813 N. Kilgore St.; P.O. Box 1582; 75663; Gregg; P 11,990; M 550; (903) 984-5022; (866) 984-0400; Fax (903) 984-4975; info@kilgorechamber.com; www.kilgorechamber.com*

Killeen · *Greater Killeen C/C* · John Crutchfield III; Pres./CEO; One Santa Fe Plaza; P.O. Box 548; 76540; Bell; P 116,000; M 1,295; (254) 526-9551; (866) 790-4769; Fax (254) 526-6090; info@gkcc.com; www.gkcc.com.*

Kingsland · *Kingsland/Lake LBJ C/C* · Letha Garrett; Ofc. Mgr.; 2743 W. RR 1431; P.O. Box 465; 78639; Burnet & Llano; P 12,500; M 250; (325) 388-6211; Fax (325) 388-5391; kchamber@zeecon.com; www.kingslandchamber.org

Kingsville · *Kingsville C/C* · Alice L. Byers; Exec. Dir.; 635 E. King Ave.; 78363; Kleberg; P 26,000; M 340; (361) 592-6438; chamber@kingsville.org; www.kingsville.org*

Kirby · *see Selma*

Kirbyville · *Kirbyville C/C* · Angie Brown; Secy.; 105 S. Elizabeth; 75956; Jasper; P 2,000; M 60; (409) 423-5827; Fax (409) 423-3353; abrownkcc@yahoo.com; www.digitalkirbyville.com

Knox City · *Knox City C/C* · Sunnie Gail Turner; Mgr.; 123 N. Central Ave.; P.O. Box 91; 79529; Knox; P 1,000; M 50; (940) 658-3442; kcchamber@srcaccess.net; www.knoxcitychamberofcommerce.com

Kountze · *Kountze C/C* · Ann Boyett; Pres.; P.O. Box 878; 77625; Hardin; P 2,153; M 88; (409) 246-3413; (866) 4-KOUNTZ; Fax (409) 246-4659; contact@kountzechamber.com; www.kountzechamber.com

Kyle · *Kyle Area C/C & Visitors Bur.* · Ray Hernandez; Exec. Dir.; 100 N. Front St.; P.O. Box 900; 78640; Hays; P 30,000; M 320; (512) 268-4220; Fax (800) 903-1564; ray@kylechamber.org; www.kylechamber.org*

La Grange · *La Grange Area C/C* · Dan Gilmore; Pres./CEO; 171 S. Main; 78945; Fayette; P 22,698; M 325; (979) 968-5756; (800) LA-GRANGE; Fax (979) 968-8000; chamber@lagrangetx.org; www.lagrangetx.org

La Porte · *La Porte-Bayshore C/C* · Colleen Hicks; Pres.; 712 W. Fairmont Pkwy.; P.O. Box 996; 77572; Harris; P 38,000; M 450; (281) 471-1123; Fax (281) 471-1710; info-lpcc@laportechamber.org; www.laportechamber.org*

La Vernia · *Greater La Vernia C/C* · Lynn Kotzur; P.O. Box 1055; 78121; Wilson; P 1,000; M 100; (830) 534-8558; lynnkotzur@aol.com; www.lavernia.org

Ladonia · *Ladonia C/C* · Lavonne Duncan; Pres.; P.O. Box 44; 75449; Fannin; P 667; M 30; (903) 367-7011; chamber@cityofladonia.com; www.cityofladonia.com

Lago Vista • *Lago Vista & Jonestown Area C/C & CVB* • Sandra E. Boatright; Exec. Dir.; P.O. Box 4946; 78645; Travis; P 5,800; M 231; (512) 267-7952; (888) 328-LAGO; Fax (512) 267-2338; info@lagovista.org; www.lagovista.org*

Lake Conroe • *see Conroe*

Lake Dallas • *Lake Cities C/C* • Holly Deitrick; Exec. Dir.; 104 Swisher Rd., Ste. 105; P.O. Box 1028; 75065; Denton; P 130,566; M 310; (940) 497-3097; Fax (972) 534-1375; lccc@lakecities chamber.com; www.lakecitieschamber.com

Lake Tawakoni • *see Quinlan*

Lake Worth • *Northwest Tarrant C/C* • Brendon Payne; Exec. Dir.; 3918 Telephone Rd., Ste. 200; 76135; Tarrant; P 35,000; M 160; (817) 237-0060; Fax (817) 237-2365; chamber@nwtcc.org; www.nwtcc.org*

Lakewood • *see Houston–Houston Intercontinental C/C*

Lamesa • *Lamesa Area C/C* • Sandra Adams; Exec. V.P.; 123 Main St.; P.O. Box 880; 79331; Dawson; P 15,000; M 240; (806) 872-2181; Fax (806) 872-5700; lamesaareacoc@growlamesa.com; www.growlamesa.com

Lampasas • *Lampasas County C/C* • Jill Carroll; Dir.; 205 S. U.S. Hwy. 281; P.O. Box 627; 76550; Lampasas; P 18,500; M 310; (512) 556-5172; Fax (512) 556-2195; info@lampasaschamber.org; www. lampasaschamber.org*

Lancaster • *Lancaster C/C* • Mr. Joe Johnson IOM; Pres./CEO; 103 N. Dallas Ave.; P.O. Box 1100; 75146; Dallas; P 38,000; M 350; (972) 227-2579; Fax (972) 227-9555; chamber@lancastertx.org; www.lancastertx.org*

Laredo • *Laredo-Webb County C/C* • Miguel Conchas; Pres./CEO; 2310 San Bernardo Ave.; P.O. Box 790; 78042; Webb; P 259,000; M 780; (956) 722-9895; Fax (956) 791-4503; chamber@laredo chamber.com; www.laredochamber.com*

League City • *also see Houston–Clear Lake Area C/C*

League City • *League City C/C* • Jason E. Ebey; Pres./CEO; 1101 W. Main, Ste. R; 77573; Galveston; P 62,000; M 700; (281) 338-7339; Fax (281) 554-8103; lcchamber@leaguecitychamber.com; www.leaguecitychamber.com*

Leakey • *Frio Canyon C/C* • P.O. Box 743; 78873; Real; P 399; M 90; (830) 232-5222; friochamber@hctc.net; www.friocanyon chamber.com

Leander • *Greater Leander C/C* • Mary E. Bradshaw; Pres.; 100 N. Brushy St.; P.O. Box 556; 78646; Travis & Williamson; P 30,000; M 330; (512) 259-1907; (512) 560-4252; Fax (512) 259-9114; contactus@leandercc.org; www.leandercc.org*

Leonard • *Leonard C/C* • Angela Sadler; Pres.; P.O. Box 117; 75452; Fannin; P 1,846; M 75; (903) 587-0174; Fax (903) 587-2580

Levelland • *Levelland Area C/C* • Mary Siders; Pres.; 1101 Ave. H; 79336; Hockley; P 14,000; M 274; (806) 894-3157; msiders@ levelland.com; www.levelland.com*

Lewisville • *Lewisville C/C* • Matt McCormick; Pres.; 551 N. Valley Pkwy.; 75067; Denton; P 100,000; M 750; (972) 436-9571; Fax (972) 436-5949; info@lewisvillechamber.org; www.lewis villechamber.org.*

Liberty • *Liberty-Dayton Area C/C* • Mary Anne Campbell; Pres.; 1801 Trinity St.; P.O. Box 1270; 77575; Liberty; P 50,000; M 450; (936) 336-5736; Fax (936) 336-1159; chamber@imsday.com; www.libertydaytonchamber.com

Liberty Hill • *Liberty Hill C/C* • Rich Tulp; Chrmn.; P.O. Box 586; 78642; Williamson; P 1,400; M 90; (512) 548-6343; membership@ mylibertyhill.net; www.mylibertyhill.net

Lindale • *Lindale Area C/C* • Shelbie Glover; Exec. Dir.; 110 E. Hubbard; P.O. Box 670; 75771; Smith; P 4,900; M 450; (903) 882-7181; Fax (903) 882-1790; info@lindalechamber.org; www. lindalechamber.org

Linden • *Linden Area C/C* • Carla Surratt; Pres.; 201 N. Main St.; P.O. Box 993; 75563; Cass; P 2,256; M 50; (903) 756-3106; Fax (903) 756-7842; www.lindentexas.org

Littlefield • *Littlefield C/C* • Gini Coffman; Exec. V.P.; 4th & LFD Dr.; P.O. Box 507; 79339; Lamb; P 6,500; M 130; (806) 385-5331; Fax (806) 385-0108; chamber@littlefieldchamber.org

Live Oak • *see Selma*

Livingston • *Polk County C/C* • Sydney Murphy; Exec. Dir.; U.S. Hwy. 59 Loop N.; P.O. Box 600; 77351; Polk; P 48,000; M 470; (936) 327-4929; (800) 918-1305; Fax (936) 327-2660; chamberadmin@ livingston.net; www.polkchamber.com.*

Llano • *Llano C/C & Visitor Center* • Doris Messer; Exec. Dir.; 100 Train Station Dr.; 78643; Llano; P 3,500; M 300; (325) 247-5354; (866) 539-5535; Fax (325) 248-6917; info@llanochamber.org; www.llanochamber.org

Lockhart • *Lockhart C/C* • Wayne Bock; Pres./CEO; 631 S. Colorado St.; P.O. Box 840; 78644; Caldwell; P 13,500; M 300; (512) 398-2818; Fax (512) 376-2632; staff@lockhartchamber.com; www.lockhartchamber.com.*

Lockney • *Lockney C/C* • Archie Jones; Pres.; P.O. Box 477; 79241; Floyd; P 2,200; M 150

Lone Oak • *see Quinlan*

Lone Star • *Lone Star C/C* • Robert Rodden; Pres.; P.O. Box 0505; 75668; Morris; P 1,615; M 47; (903) 656-2595

Longview • *Longview C/C* • Kelly Hall; Pres.; 410 N. Center St.; 75601; Gregg & Harrison; P 78,000; M 1,300; (903) 237-4000; Fax (903) 237-4049; info1@longviewtx.com; www.longviewtx.com.*

Los Fresnos • *Los Fresnos Area C/C* • Michael Garza; Exec. Dir.; 203 N. Arroyo Blvd., Ste. A; 78566; Cameron; P 6,000; M 150; (956) 233-4488; (956) 350-3000; losfresnoschamber@yahoo.com; www. losfresnoschamber.com

Louise • *Louise-Hillje C/C* • Debbie Townsend; P.O. Box 156; 77455; Wharton; P 1,000; M 75; (979) 648-2108; Fax (979) 648-2598; shellyfritz@yahoo.com; www.louisehilljechamber.org

Lubbock • *Lubbock C/C* • Eddie McBride; Pres.; 1500 Broadway, Ste. 101; 79401; Lubbock; P 267,269; M 2,160; (806) 761-7000; (800) 321-5822; Fax (806) 761-7013; info@lubbockbiz.org; www. lubbockchamber.com*

Lufkin • *Lufkin/Angelina County C/C* • Jerry Huffman; Pres./ CEO; 1615 S. Chestnut; P.O. Box 1606; 75901; Angelina; P 85,000; M 1,400; (936) 634-6644; Fax (936) 634-8726; chamber@lufkin texas.org; www.lufkintexas.org.*

Luling • *Luling Area C/C & Visitor Center* • Ada Potts; Pres.; 421 E. Davis St.; P.O. Box 710; 78648; Caldwell; P 5,500; M 200; (830) 875-3214; Fax (830) 875-2082; info@lulingcc.org; www.lulingcc.org

Lumberton • *Lumberton C/C* • Tammy Melvin; Exec. Dir.; 826 N. Main; P.O. Box 8574; 77657; Hardin; P 20,000; M 200; (409) 755-0554; Fax (409) 755-2516; lcoc@lumbertoncoc.com; www. lumbertoncoc.com*

Lytle • *Greater Lytle C/C* • Brad Boyd; Pres.; P.O. Box 2131; 78052; Atascosa, Bexar & Medina; P 3,000; M 50; (830) 709-4304; brushcountry@brushcountry.com; www.lytlechamber.com

Mabank • *Cedar Creek Lake Area C/C* • JoAnn Hanstrom; Pres.; 604 S. Third St., Ste. E; P.O. Box 581; 75147; Henderson & Kaufman; P 51,065; M 450; (903) 887-3152; Fax (903) 887-3695; info@cedar creeklakechamber.com; www.cedarcreeklakechamber.com*

Madisonville • *Madison County C/C* • Christi Campbell; Exec. Dir.; 113 W. Trinity; 77864; Madison; P 4,400; M 200; (936) 348-3591; Fax (936) 348-2212; info@madisoncountytxchamber.com; www.madisoncountytxchamber.com*

Magnolia • *Magnolia Area C/C* • Barbara Gardner; Chair; 18935 FM 1488; P.O. Box 399; 77353; Montgomery; P 51,000; M 450; (281) 356-1488; Fax (281) 356-2552; info@magnoliatexas.org; www.magnoliatexas.org*

Malakoff • *Malakoff Area C/C* • Kathy Roland; Pres.; P.O. Box 1042; 75148; Henderson; P 2,100; M 70; (903) 489-1518; Fax same; malakoffcofc@embarqmail.com; www.malakoffchamber.com

Mansfield • *Mansfield Area C/C* • Lucretia G. Mills; Pres.; 114 N. Main St.; 76063; Ellis, Johnson & Tarrant; P 60,000; M 620; (817) 473-0507; Fax (817) 473-8687; lucretia@mansfieldchamber.org; www.mansfieldchamber.org*

Marathon • *Marathon C/C* • Patsy Ruth Cavness; Exec. Dir.; 105 Hwy. 90 W.; P.O. Box 163; 79842; Brewster; P 500; M 50; (432) 386-4516; sconemaker@hotmail.com; www.marathontexas.com

Marble Falls • *Marble Falls/Lake LBJ C/C* • Christian Fletcher; Exec. Dir.; 916 Second St.; 78654; Burnet; P 30,000; M 800; (830) 693-2815; (800) 759-8178; Fax (830) 693-1620; info@marblefalls.org; www.marblefalls.org

Marfa • *Marfa C/C* • Burt Compton; Pres.; 207 N. Highland; P.O. Box 635; 79843; Presidio; P 2,424; M 134; (432) 729-4942; (800) 650-9696; Fax (432) 729-4956; info@marfacc.com; www.marfacc.com

Marion • *see Selma*

Marlin • *Marlin C/C* • Cynthia Dees; Gen. Mgr.; 245 Coleman St.; P.O. Box 369; 76661; Falls; P 17,000; M 125; (254) 803-3301; Fax (254) 883-2171; marlintxchamber@att.net; www.marlintexas.com

Marquez • *Marquez Area C/C* • Jimmy Hill; Pres.; 150 Pearl St.; P.O. Box 751; 77865; Leon; P 220; M 35; (903) 529-1419; (979) 324-8868

Marshall • *Marshall C/C* • Connie Ware; Pres./CEO; 213 W. Austin St.; P.O. Box 520; 75670; Harrison; P 24,000; M 700; (903) 935-7868; (800) 953-7868; Fax (903) 935-9982; www.marshalltxchamber.com*

Mason • *Mason County C/C* • Dakota Wawrzyniak; Exec. Dir.; 108 Ft. McKavitt; P.O. Box 156; 76856; Mason; P 2,250; M 220; (325) 347-5758; masontexas@hctc.net; www.masontxcoc.com

McAllen • *McAllen C/C* • Steve Ahlenius; Pres./CEO; 1200 Ash Ave.; P.O. Box 790; 78501; Hidalgo; P 130,000; M 1,950; (956) 682-2871; Fax (956) 687-2917; steve@mcallenchamber.com; www.mcallenchamber.com.*

McCamey • *McCamey C/C* • Velma Beasley; Sec./Mgr.; 201 E. 6th St.; P.O. Box 906; 79752; Upton; P 1,805; M 83; (432) 652-8202; Fax (432) 652-8202; mccameychamber@sbcglobal.net; www.mccameychamber.com

McGregor • *McGregor C/C* • Meghan Mullens; Exec. V.P.; 303 S. Main St.; 76657; Coryell & McLennan; P 5,000; M 125; (254) 840-2806; Fax (254) 840-2950; mcgregorchamber@mcgregor-texas.com; www.mcgregor-texas.com

McKinney • *McKinney C/C* • Jodi Ann LaFreniere CCE; Pres.; 2150 S. Central Expy., Ste. 150; 75070; Collin; P 125,000; M 1,200; (972) 542-0163; Fax (972) 548-0876; info@mckinneychamber.com; www.mckinneychamber.com*

Melissa • *Melissa Area C/C* • Carrie Wells; Chair; 1501 W. Harrison St.; P.O. Box 121; 75454; Collin; P 5,000; M 140; (972) 837-4277; Fax (972) 837-4277; melissaareachamber@gmail.com; www.melissatx.org*

Memphis • *Memphis C/C* • Judy Stewart; Pres.; 515 W. Main; 79245; Hall; P 2,500; M 75; (806) 259-3144; Fax (806) 259-3144; memphistexaschamber@valornet.com

Menard • *Menard County C/C* • Tina Hodge; Ofc. Mgr.; 100 E. San Saba Ave.; P.O. Box 64; 76859; Menard; P 2,400; M 150; (325) 396-2365; Fax (325) 396-4545; info@menardchamber.com; www.menardchamber.com

Mercedes • *Mercedes Area C/C* • Donna Jackson; Ofc. Mgr.; 417 S. Ohio; P.O. Box 37; 78570; Hidalgo; P 14,000; M 140; (956) 565-2221; Fax same; donna@mercedeschamber.com; www.mercedeschamber.com*

Meridian • *Meridian C/C* • Dan Markman; Pres.; P.O. Box 758; 76665; Bosque; P 1,539; M 135; (254) 435-2966; meridian-chamber@sbcglobal.net; www.meridian-chamber.com

Merkel • *Merkel C/C & Eco. Dev. Corp.* • Roger Todd Moore; Dir.; P.O. Box 536; 79536; Taylor; P 2,715; M 50; (325) 928-5722; Fax (325) 928-5722; rmandm@gmail.com; www.merkeltexas.com

Mesquite • *Mesquite C of C & CVB* • Terry McCullar; Pres.; 617 N. Ebrite; 75149; Dallas; P 134,000; M 650; (972) 285-0211; (800) 541-2355; Fax (972) 285-3535; info@mesquitechamber.com; www.mesquitechamber.com.*

Mexia • *Mexia Area C/C* • Linda Archibald; Exec. Dir.; 405 E. Milam, Ste. 2; 76667; Limestone; P 10,000; M 175; (254) 562-5569; (888) 535-5476; Fax (254) 562-7138; linda@mexiachamber.com; www.mexiachamber.com

Miami • *Miami/Roberts County C/C* • Rusty Early; Pres.; P.O. Box 355; 79059; Roberts; P 600; M 75; (806) 868-4791; info@miamitexas.org; www.miamitexas.org

Midland • *Midland C/C* • Rob Cunningham; Pres./CEO; 109 N. Main St.; 79701; Midland; P 119,500; M 1,367; (432) 683-3381; (800) 624-6435; Fax (432) 686-3556; info@midlandtxchamber.com; www.midlandtxchamber.com.*

Midlothian • *Midlothian C/C* • Sara Garcia; Interim Pres./CEO; 310 N. 9th St.; 76065; Ellis; P 16,000; M 425; (972) 723-8600; Fax (972) 723-9300; info@midlothianchamber.org; www.midlothianchamber.org.*

Mineola • *Mineola Area C/C* • Shirley Chadwick; Exec. Dir.; 101 E. Broad St.; P.O. Box 68; 75773; Wood; P 5,611; M 270; (903) 569-2087; Fax (903) 569-5510; chamber@mineola.com; www.mineolachamber.org

Mineral Wells • *Mineral Wells Area C/C* • Beth Watson; Exec. Dir.; 511 E. Hubbard; P.O. Box 1408; 76068; Palo Pinto; P 27,960; M 430; (940) 325-2557; (800) 252-6989; Fax (940) 328-0850; info@mineralwellstx.com; www.mineralwellstx.com*

Mission • *Greater Mission C/C* • Matt Z. Ruszczak; Pres./CEO; 202 W. Tom Landry; 78572; Hidalgo; P 75,000; M 830; (956) 585-2727; (800) 580-2700; Fax (956) 585-3044; scastillo@missionchamber.com; www.missionchamber.com*

Monahans • *Monahans C/C* • Teresa Burnett; Exec. Dir.; 401 S. Dwight Ave.; 79756; Ward; P 7,000; M 280; (432) 943-2187; Fax (432) 943-6868; chamber@monahans.org; www.monahans.org.*

Mont Belvieu • *West Chambers County C/C* • M.G. Malechek; Pres.; 11340 Eagle Dr., Ste. 4; P.O. Box 750; 77580; Chambers; P 3,000; M 350; (281) 576-5440; Fax (281) 576-2135; missy@thewcccc.com; www.westchamberscoc.com*

Morton • *Morton Area C/C* • Bryant Sears; Pres.; 201 E. Wilson; 79346; Cochran; P 2,000; M 30; (806) 266-5200

Moulton • *Moulton C/C* • P.O. Box 482; 77975; Lavaca; P 1,000; M 150; (361) 596-7205; Fax (361) 596-4384; chamber@moultontexas.com; www.moultontexas.com

Mount Pleasant • *Mount Pleasant-Titus County C/C & CVB* • Faustine Curry; Exec. Dir.; 1604 N. Jefferson; 75455; Titus; P 14,000; M 385; (903) 572-8567; Fax (903) 572-0613; info@mtpleasanttx.com; www.mtpleasanttx.com.*

Mount Vernon • *Franklin County C/C* • Patricia Oertel; Mgr.; 109 S. Kaufman St.; P.O. Box 554; 75457; Franklin; P 12,000; M 170; (903) 537-4365; Fax (903) 537-4160; chamber@mt-vernon.com; www.franklincountytx.com*

Muenster • *Muenster C/C* • John Broyles; Exec. Dir.; 1000 E. Division St., Ste. D; P.O. Box 714; 76252; Cook; P 2,000; M 135; (940) 759-2227; Fax (940) 759-2228; chamber@ntin.net; www.muensterchamber.com

Muleshoe • *Muleshoe C/C & Ag.* • Becky Hoksbergen; Exec. Asst.; 115 E. American Blvd.; P.O. Box 356; 79347; Bailey; P 4,530; M 100; (806) 272-4248; Fax (806) 272-4614; chamber@fivearea.com; www.muleshoechamber.com

Munday • *Munday C/C and Ag.* • Rita Carney; Dir.; 121 E. B St.; P.O. Drawer L; 76371; Knox; P 1,525; M 150; (940) 422-4540; Fax (940) 421-3288; mundaychamber@gmail.com; www.munday texas.com

Nacogdoches • *Nacogdoches County C/C* • Bruce R. Partain; Pres.; 2516 North St.; 75965; Nacogdoches; P 60,000; M 860; (936) 560-5533; Fax (936) 560-3920; chamber@nactx.com; www.nacogdoches.org.*

THE MOST DELICIOUS FESTIVAL IN TEXAS! FRESH BLUEBERRIES, BLUEBERRY PANCAKES, BLUEBERRY PIE/COBBLER, LIVE ENTERTAINMENT, KIDS AREA. FUN FOR EVERYONE!

Naples • *Naples C/C* • Johnny Strong; Pres.; 101 WL Doc Dodson E.; 75568; Morris; P 1,700; M 25; (903) 897-2041

Nassau Bay • *see Houston—Clear Lake Area C/C*

Navasota • *Navasota/Grimes County C/C* • Shanna Mayhall; Exec. Dir.; 117 S. LaSalle; P.O. Box 530; 77868; Grimes; P 25,895; M 300; (936) 825-6600; Fax (936) 825-3699; assistant@navasota grimeschamber.com; www.navasotagrimeschamber.com*

Nederland • *Nederland C/C* • Stephanie Shimek; Interim Exec. Dir.; 1515 Boston Ave.; P.O. Box 891; 77627; Jefferson; P 17,400; M 350; (409) 722-0279; Fax (409) 722-0615; nedcofc@nederland tx.com; www.nederlandtx.com.*

Needville • *Needville Area C/C* • Glenn Schmidt; Pres.; 8903 Line St.; P.O. Box 1200; 77461; Fort Bend; P 2,600; M 250; (979) 793-5700; www.needville.org

New Boston • *New Boston C/C* • Deborah Cook IOM; Exec. Dir.; 100 N. Center St.; 75570; Bowie; P 4,808; M 202; (903) 628-2581; Fax (903) 628-6340; chamber@newbostontx.org; www.new bostontx.org.*

New Braunfels • *Greater New Braunfels C/C Inc.* • Michael Meek; Pres.; 390 S. Seguin Ave.; P.O. Box 311417; 78131; Comal; P 102,000; M 1,570; (830) 625-2385; Fax (830) 625-7918; nbcc@nbcham.org; www.nbcham.org*

New Caney • *Comm. C/C of East Montgomery County* • Andy Dill; Pres.; 21575 U.S. Hwy. 59 N., Ste. 100; 77357; Montgomery; P 74,000; M 440; (281) 354-0051; Fax (281) 354-0091; info@community chamberemc.com; www.communitychamberemc.com*

Newton • *Newton County C/C* • Susan Karpel; Secy.; 313 Rusk St.; P.O. Box 66; 75966; Newton; P 18,500; M 100; (409) 379-5527; chamber@newton-texas.com; www.newton-texas.com

Nocona • *Nocona Area C/C* • Wanda Wood; Exec. Dir.; 1522 E. Hwy. 82; P.O. Box 27; 76255; Montague; P 3,198; M 100; (940) 825-3526; Fax (940) 825-5389; noconachamber@nocona.org; www.nocona.org*

Normangee • *Normangee Area C/C* • Becki Willis; Pres.; P.O. Box 436; 77871; Leon; P 704; M 30; (936) 396-5001; www.normangeechamber.com

North Richland Hills • *see Haltom City*

Northlake • *see Roanoke*

Northline • *see Houston—Houston Intercontinental C/C*

Odessa • *Odessa C/C* • Mike George; Pres./CEO; 700 N. Grant, Ste. 200; P.O. Box 3626; 79760; Ector; P 96,948; M 1,900; (432) 332-9111; (800) 780-4678; Fax (432) 333-7858; info@odessachamber.com; www.odessachamber.com.*

Olney • *Olney C/C* • Malinda Morrow; Coord.; 108 E. Main St.; 76374; Young; P 3,000; M 56; (940) 564-5445; Fax (940) 564-3610; chamber@brazosnet.com; www.olneychamberofcommerce.com

Olton • *Olton C/C & Ag.* • Teresa Perez; Mgr.; 518 8th St.; P.O. Box 487; 79064; Lamb; P 2,288; M 49; (806) 285-2292; occa@oltonchamber.org; www.oltonchamber.org

Omaha • *Omaha C/C* • Cheryl Durrett; Pres.; P.O. Box 816; 75571; Morris; P 999; M 50; (903) 946-2229; (903) 884-3600; Fax (903) 884-3649

Onalaska • *Onalaska C/C* • Greg Smith; P.O. Box 1300; 77360; Polk; P 4,500; M 42; (936) 646-5000; lewvail@suddenlink.net; www.cityofonalaska.us

Orange • *Greater Orange Area C/C* • Ida Schossow; Pres./CEO; 1012 Green Ave.; 77630; Orange; P 52,000; M 482; (409) 883-3536; Fax (409) 886-3247; thechamber@orangetexaschamber.org; www.orangetexaschamber.org*

Overton • *Overton-New London Area C/C* • Charlie Stanley; Pres.; 121 E. Henderson St.; P.O. Box 6; 75684; Rusk & Smith; P 2,105; M 95; (903) 834-3542; Fax (903) 834-3063; onlchamber@embarqmail.com; www.onlchamber.com

Ozona • *Ozona C/C & Visitor Center* • Shanon Biggerstaff; Exec. Dir.; 505 15th St.; P.O. Box 1135; 76943; Crockett; P 3,800; M 160; (325) 392-3737; Fax (325) 392-3485; oztxcoc@aol.com; www.ozona.com

Paducah • *Paducah C/C* • Ronnie Manley; Pres.; P.O. Box 863; 79248; Cottle; P 1,400; M 57; (806) 492-2044; (806) 492-2167; info@paducahtx.com; www.paducahtx.com

Palacios • *Palacios C/C* • Patsy Gibson; Exec. Dir.; 420 Main St.; 77465; Matagorda; P 5,000; M 130; (361) 972-2615; (800) 611-4567; Fax (361) 972-9980; palcoc@tisd.net; www.palacios chamber.com

Palestine • *Palestine Area C/C* • Meghan Hill; Exec. Dir.; 401 W. Main St.; P.O. Box 1177; 75802; Anderson; P 55,000; M 476; (903) 729-6066; Fax (903) 729-2083; info@palestinechamber.org; www.palestinechamber.org*

Pampa • *Greater Pampa Area C/C* • Joe Weaver; Exec. Dir.; 200 N. Ballard; P.O. Box 1942; 79066; Gray; P 18,000; M 350; (806) 669-3241; Fax (806) 669-3244; harvest@pampachamber.com; www.pampachamber.com

Panhandle • *Panhandle C/C* • Mary Smith; Pres.; P.O. Box 1021; 79068; Carson; P 2,600; M 74; (806) 537-4325; chamber@pan handletx.com; www.panhandletx.govoffice2.com

Paris • *Lamar County C/C* • Mindy Moree; Pres.; 8 W. Plaza; 75460; Lamar; P 46,000; M 600; (903) 784-2501; Fax (903) 784-2503; chamber@paristexas.com; www.paristexas.com*

Pasadena • *also see Houston-Clear Lake Area C/C*

Pasadena • *Pasadena C/C* • Sherry Trainer; Pres./CEO; 4334 Fairmont Pkwy.; 77504; Harris; P 150,000; M 750; (281) 487-7871; Fax (281) 487-5530; info@pasadenachamber.org; www.pasadena chamber.org.*

Pattison • *West I-10 C/C* • Greg Turner; Pres.; 907 Bains St.; P.O. Box 100; 77466; Waller; P 5,000; M 100; (281) 375-8100; Fax (281) 934-2012; chamber@westi10chamber.org; www.westi10chamber.org*

Pearland • *Pearland C/C* • Carol Artz-Bucek CCE; Pres./CEO; 6117 Broadway; 77581; Brazoria; P 100,000; M 725; (281) 485-3634; Fax (281) 485-2420; commerceinformation@pearlandtexas chamber.us; www.pearlandtexaschamber.us. *

Pearsall • *Pearsall C/C* • Janie Elizondo; 317 S. Oak St.; 78061; Frio; P 7,864; M 51; (830) 334-9414; info@pearsalltexas.com; www.pearsalltexas.com

Pecos • *Pecos Area C/C* • Linda Gholson; Exec. Dir.; 111 S. Cedar; P.O. Box 27; 79772; Reeves; P 9,501; M 120; (432) 445-2406; Fax (432) 445-2407; pcoc@cebridge.net; www.pecostx.com.

Perryton • *Perryton-Ochiltree C/C* • Marilyn Reiswig; Pres.; 2000 S. Main; P.O. Drawer 789; 79070; Ochiltree; P 10,000; M 400; (806) 435-6575; Fax (806) 435-9821; pococ@ptsi.net; www.perryton.org*

Pflugerville • *Pflugerville C/C* • Patricia Gervan-Brown IOM; Pres./CEO; 101 S. 3rd St.; P.O. Box 483; 78691; Travis; P 50,000; M 400; (512) 251-7799; Fax (512) 251-7802; gpcc2@sbcglobal.net; www.pfchamber.com*

Pharr • *Pharr C/C* • Luis A. Bazan; Pres./CEO; 308 W. Park Ave.; P.O. Box 1715; 78577; Hidalgo; P 728,000; M 700; (956) 787-1481; Fax (956) 787-7972; lbazan@pharrchamber.com; www.pharr chamber.com*

Pilot Point • *Pilot Point C/C* • Karen Walterscheid; Exec. Dir.; 300 S. Washington; P.O. Box 497; 76258; Denton; P 5,100; M 150; (940) 686-5385; Fax (940) 686-9392; ppchamberofcommerce@ suddenlinkmail.com; www.pilotpoint.org

Pittsburg • *Pittsburg/Camp County C/C* • Lynda Stringer; Exec Dir.; 202 Jefferson St.; 75686; Camp; P 15,000; M 200; (903) 856-3442; Fax (903) 856-3570; info@pittsburgchamber.com; www.pittsburgchamber.com*

Plains • *Plains C/C* • Terry Howard; Pres.; P.O. Box 364; 79355; Yoakum; P 1,450; M 20; (806) 456-2288; chamber@plainschamber.org; www.plainschamber.org

Plainview • *Plainview C/C* • Dee Blevins; Exec. Dir.; 1906 W. 5th St.; 79072; Hale; P 21,000; M 350; (806) 296-7431; (800) 658-2685; Fax (806) 296-0819; info@plainviewtexaschamber.com; www.plainviewtexaschamber.com

Plano • *Plano C/C* • Jamee Jolly; Pres.; 1200 E. 15th St.; 75074; Collin; P 262,000; M 1,100; (972) 424-7547; Fax (972) 422-5182; info@planochamber.org; www.planochamber.org*

Pleasanton • *Pleasanton C/C* • Jessie Schievelbein; Mgr.; 605 Second St.; P.O. Box 153; 78064; Atascosa; P 9,500; M 180; (830) 569-2163; Fax (830) 569-8539; pleasantoncofc@yahoo.com; www.pleasantoncofc.com

Point • *see Quinlan*

Port Aransas • *Port Aransas C/C* • Ann B. Vaughan; Exec. Dir.; 403 W. Cotter; 78373; Nueces; P 3,370; M 379; (361) 749-5919; Fax (361) 749-4672; info@portaransas.org; www.portaransas.org

Port Arthur • *Greater Port Arthur C/C* • Mary Ann Reid; Pres.; 4749 Twin City Hwy., Ste. 300; 77642; Jefferson; P 57,755; M 720; (409) 963-1107; portarthurchamber@portarthurtexas.com; www.portarthurtexas.com*

Port Isabel • *Port Isabel C/C* • Betty Wells; Pres.; 421 E. Queen Isabella Blvd.; 78578; Cameron; P 5,100; M 237; (956) 943-2262; (800) 527-6102; Fax (956) 943-4001; director@portisabel.org; www.portisabel.org*

Port Lavaca • *Port Lavaca C/C* • Lacey Ekberg; Exec. Dir.; 2300 Hwy. 35 N.; 77979; Calhoun; P 20,000; M 250; (361) 552-2959; (361) 552-1234; Fax (361) 552-1288; information@portlavacatx.org; www.portlavacatx.org*

Port Mansfield • *Port Mansfield C/C* • Terry Neal Sr.; Pres.; 101 E. Port Dr.; P.O. Box 75; 78598; Willacy; P 400; M 100; (956) 944-2354; Fax (956) 944-2515; pmft@granderiver.net; www.portmansfieldchamber.org

Port Neches • *Port Neches C/C* • Debbie Plaia; Exec. Dir.; 1110 Port Neches Ave.; P.O. Box 445; 77651; Jefferson; P 15,000; M 240; (409) 722-9154; Fax (409) 722-7380; pncoc@swbell.net; www.portnecheschamber.com*

Port O'Connor • *Port O'Connor C/C* • Linda Butler; Pres.; 207 Trevor St.; P.O. Box 701; 77982; Calhoun; P 1,200; M 150; (361) 983-2898; Fax (361) 983-2898; poccc@tisd.net; www.port oconnorchamber.org

Portland • *Portland C/C* • Stacy Stork; Exec. Dir.; 904-B Memorial Pkwy.; P.O. Box 388; 78374; Nueces & San Patricio; P 19,000; M 300; (361) 643-2475; Fax (361) 643-7377; director@ portlandtx.org; www.portlandtx.org*

Post • *Post Area C/C* • Janice Plummer; Mgr.; 131 E. Main; P.O. Box 610; 79356; Garza; P 6,000; M 108; (806) 495-3461; Fax (806) 495-0414; chamberofcommerce@postcitytexas.com; www.postcitytexas.com

Poteet • *Poteet C/C* • Carol Rivera; P.O. Box 577; 78065; Atascosa; P 3,100; M 40; (830) 742-8144; (888) 742-8144; Fax (830) 742-3608; www.strawberryfestival.com

Pottsboro • *Pottsboro Area C/C* • Rosemary Hall; Mgr.; 615 Hwy. 120 E.; P.O. Box 995; 75076; Grayson; P 10,000; M 300; (903) 786-6371; Fax (903) 786-4965; info@pottsborochamber.com; pottsborochamber.com*

Prairie View • *Prairie View C/C* • George Higgs; Pres.; P.O. Box 847; 77446; Waller; P 4,410; M 55; (936) 857-5817; (936) 857-3226; Fax (936) 857-5806; prairieviewtexas.gov.

Premont • *Premont C/C* • Epi Vargas; Pres.; P.O. Box 1107; 78375; Jim Wells; P 3,000; M 45; (361) 348-3933

Presidio • *Presidio C/C* • Nora Arias; Pres.; 202 E. O'Reilly St.; P.O. Box 2497; 79845; Presidio; P 7,500; M 90; (432) 229-3199; presidiococ@yahoo.com

Princeton • *Princeton Area C/C* • Virginia Gathright; Pres.; 275 W. Princeton Dr., Ste. 105; 75407; Collin; P 6,500; M 85; (972) 736-6462; Fax (972) 734-5276; info@princetontxchamber.com; www.princetontxchamber.com

Prosper • *Prosper C/C* • Susan Lane; Dir.; 100 N. Preston Rd.; P.O. Box 432; 75078; Collin & Denton; P 9,000; M 150; (972) 508-4200; prosperchamber@grandecom.net; www.prosperchamberonline.com

Quanah • *Quanah C/C* • Bertha Woods; Dir.; 220 S. Main; P.O. Box 158; 79252; Hardeman; P 3,114; M 125; (940) 663-2222; Fax (940) 663-2222; quanahcoc@cebridge.net; www.quanah.net.*

Quinlan • *Lake Tawakoni Reg. C/C* • Kym French; Exec. Dir.; 100 Hwy. 276 W.; P.O. Box 1149; 75474; Hunt; P 20,000; M 150; (903) 447-3020; Fax (903) 447-3820; laketawakonichamber@yahoo.com; www.laketawakonichamber.org

Quitaque • *Quitaque C/C* • Jack Johnson; Pres.; P.O. Box 487; 79255; Briscoe; P 432; M 30; (806) 455-1225; Fax (806) 455-1225; chamber@quitaque.org; www.quitaque.org

Quitman · *Greater Quitman Area C/C* · Toni Cole; Exec. Dir.; 100 Gov. Hogg Pkwy.; P.O. Box 426; 75783; Wood; P 2,261; M 140; (903) 763-4411; qtmncoc@peoplescom.net; www.quitman.com

Ralls · *Ralls C/C & Ag.* · Terrie Acker; Mgr.; 808 Ave. I; 79357; Crosby; P 2,500; M 50; (806) 253-2342; rallscofc@esc17.net; www.cityofralls.org

Raymondville · *Raymondville C/C* · Elma Chavez; Mgr.; 700 FM 3168; P.O. Box 746; 78580; Willacy; P 20,000; M 180; (956) 689-1864; (888) 603-6994; Fax (956) 689-1863; chamber@granderiver.net; www.raymondvillechamber.com.*

Red Oak · *Red Oak Area C/C* · Shelley Oglesby; Pres.; P.O. Box 2098; 75154; Ellis; P 20,000; M 200; (972) 617-0906; Fax (972) 576-3737; admin@redoakareachamber.org; www.redoakarea chamber.org*

Refugio · *Refugio County C/C* · Lenny Anzaldua; Pres.; 301 N. Alamo; 78377; Refugio; P 8,000; M 100; (361) 526-2835; Fax (361) 526-1289; refugiochamber@sbcglobal.net; www.refugiocountytx.org

Richardson · *Richardson C/C* · Bill Sproull; Pres./CEO; 411 Belle Grove Dr.; 75080; Dallas; P 103,380; M 1,200; (972) 792-2800; Fax (972) 792-2825; bill@richardsonchamber.com; www.richardson chamber.com*

Richland Hills · *see Haltom City*

Richmond · *see Rosenberg*

River Oaks · *Tri-City Area C/C* · Sherrie Dast; Pres.; P.O. Box 10005; 76114; Tarrant; P 11,100; M 115; (817) 377-4227; mayor jack@aol.com; www.tricityareachamber.org

Roanoke · *Northwest Metroport C/C* · Sally Michalak; Pres.; 600 E. Byron Nelson Blvd., Ste. 500; P.O. Box 74; 76262; Denton; P 18,000; M 300; (817) 491-1222; Fax (817) 430-5822; sally@nwmetroportchamber.org; www.nwmetroportchamber.org*

Robstown · *Robstown Area Dev. Comm.* · 1150 E. Main Ave.; P.O. Box 111; 78380; Nueces; P 14,000; M 100; (361) 387-3933; Fax (361) 387-7280; radc@verizon.net; www.robstownadc.com

Rockdale · *Rockdale C/C* · Denice Doss; Pres.; 1203 W. Cameron Ave.; 76567; Milam; P 6,000; M 290; (512) 446-2030; Fax (512) 446-5969; info@rockdalechamber.com; www.rockdalechamber.com

Rockport · *Rockport-Fulton C/C* · Diane Probst; Pres./CEO; 404 Broadway; 78382; P 24,000; M 700; (361) 729-6445; (800) 242-0071; Fax (361) 729-7681; president@lrockport.org; www.rockport-fulton.org.*

Rocksprings · *Edwards County C/C* · Paige Hendley; P.O. Box 267; 78880; Edwards; P 2,295; M 100; (830) 683-6466; Fax (830) 683-3182; info@rockspringstexas.net; www.rockspringstexas.net

Rockwall · *Rockwall Area County C/C* · Margie Hooper; Pres.; 697 E. I-30; 2850 Shoreline Trl., Ste. 63; 75032; Rockwall; P 50,000; M 900; (972) 771-5733; Fax (972) 772-3642; info@rockwallchamber.org; www.rockwallchamber.org*

Rosebud · *Rosebud C/C & Ag.* · Royce Spivey; Pres.; 402 W. Main; P.O. Box 369; 76570; Falls; P 1,493; M 100; (254) 583-7979; Fax (254) 583-2157; shaunfield@aol.com; www.rosebudtx.org

Rosenberg · *Central Fort Bend Chamber Alliance* · Gail Parker; Pres./CEO; 4120 Ave. H; 77471; Fort Bend; P 200,000; M 800; (281) 342-5464; Fax (281) 342-2990; reservations@cfbca.org; www.cfbca.org*

Round Rock · *Round Rock C/C* · Joe Vining; Interim Pres./CEO; 212 E. Main St.; 78664; Travis & Williamson; P 150,000; M 1,250; (512) 255-5805; Fax (512) 255-3345; info@roundrockchamber.org; www.roundrockchamber.org*

Round Top · *Round Top C/C* · Laurie Fisbeck; Dir.; 102 E. Mill St.; P.O. Box 216; 78954; Fayette; P 77; M 250; (979) 249-4042; Fax (979) 249-2085; info@roundtop.org; www.roundtop.org

Rowlett · *Rowlett C/C* · Lisa Ferrell; Pres.; 3910 Main St.; P.O. Box 610; 75030; Dallas & Rockwall; P 55,000; M 400; (972) 475-3200; Fax (972) 463-1699; lisaferrell@rowlettchamber.com; www.rowlettchamber.com*

Royse City · *Royse City C/C* · Julia Bryant; Exec. Dir.; 216 N. Arch St., Ste. A; P.O. Box 547; 75189; Rockwall; P 10,000; M 225; (972) 636-5000; Fax (972) 636-0051; info@roysecitychamber.com; www.roysecitychamber.com

Rule · *Rule C/C* · Orheana Greeson; Secy.; 701 Union Ave.; P.O. Box 58; 79547; Haskell; P 576; M 15; (940) 997-2141

Rusk · *Rusk C/C* · Bob Goldsberry; Exec. Dir.; 184 S. Main St.; P.O. Box 67; 75785; Cherokee; P 5,325; M 200; (903) 683-4242; (800) 933-2381; Fax (903) 683-1054; cbrown@ruskchamber.com; www.ruskchamber.com

Sabinal · *Sabinal C/C* · P.O. Box 55; 78881; Uvalde; P 1,800; M 20; (830) 988-2010; sab@sabinalchamber.com; www.sabinal chamber.com

Sachse · *Sachse C/C* · Amy Berry; Events Coord.; 2924 5th St.; 75048; Dallas; P 18,000; M 290; (972) 496-1212; info@sachse chamber.com; www.sachsechamber.com*

Saginaw · *Saginaw Area C/C* · Tracy Sutton & Lindsay Juetten; Chamber Execs.; 301 S. Saginaw Blvd.; 76179; Tarrant; P 100,000; M 400; (817) 232-0500; Fax (817) 232-2311; chamber@saginaw txchamber.org; www.saginawtxchamber.org*

Saint Jo · *Saint Jo C/C* · Howard Davies; Pres.; 108 S. Broad; P.O. Box 130; 76265; Montague; P 1,000; M 40; (940) 995-2188; stjo@saintjochamber.com; www.saintjochamber.com

Salado · *Salado C/C* · Nicole Stairs; Pres.; 601 N. Main St.; P.O. Box 849; 76571; Bell; P 3,500; M 230; (254) 947-5040; Fax (254) 947-3126; chamber@salado.com; www.salado.com*

San Angelo · *San Angelo C/C & Visitor Center* · Phil Neighbors; Pres.; 418 W. Ave. B; 76903; Tom Green; P 90,483; M 1,400; (325) 655-4136; Fax (325) 658-1110; chamber@sanangelo.org; www.sanangelo.org.*

San Antonio Area

Alamo City Black C/C · Theodore Guidry III; Chrmn.; 600 Hemisfair Plaza Way; Bldg. 204-10; 78205; Bexar; P 1,750,000; M 250; (210) 226-9055; Fax (210) 226-0524; info@alamocity chamber.org; www.alamocitychamber.org.

Greater San Antonio C/C · Richard Perez; Pres.; 602 E. Commerce; 78205; Bexar; P 1,349,000; M 1,800; (210) 229-2100; Fax (210) 229-1600; info@sachamber.org; www.sachamber.org*

North San Antonio C/C · E. Duane Wilson; Pres./CEO; 12930 Country Pkwy.; 78216; Bexar; P 1,500,000; M 1,350; (210) 344-4848; Fax (210) 525-8207; mwhite@northsachamber.com; www.northsachamber.com*

San Antonio Hispanic C/C · Ramiro A. Cavazos; Pres./CEO; 200 E. Grayson, Ste. 203; 78212; Bexar; M 1,600; (210) 225-0462; Fax (210) 225-2485; jessicac@.sahcc.org; www.sahcc.org*

South San Antonio C/C · Cindy Taylor; Pres.; 7902 Challenger Dr.; 78235; Bexar; P 500,000; M 700; (210) 533-1600; Fax (210) 533-1611; southsachamber@southsachamber.org; www.southsachamber.org

San Augustine · *San Augustine County C/C* · Exec. Dir.; 611 W. Columbia St.; 75972; San Augustine; P 9,000; M 225; (936) 275-3610; Fax (936) 288-0380; info@sanaugustinetx.com; www.sanaugustinetx.com*

San Benito · *San Benito C/C* · Zeke Padilla; Pres.; 400 N. Travis; 78586; Cameron; P 28,600; M 200; (956) 361-3800; Fax (956) 361-3810; zpadilla@cityofsanbenito.com; www.cityofsanbenito.com*

San Juan · *San Juan C/C* · Edgar Ruiz Jr.; Pres.; 709 S. Nebraska; 78589; Hidalgo; P 35,000; M 42; (956) 223-2358; (956) 783-3448; Fax (956) 702-6445; chamber@cityofsanjuantexas.com; www.cityofsanjuan.com*

San Leon · *see Dickinson*

San Marcos · *San Marcos Area C/C* · Pres.; 202 N. CM Allen Pkwy.; P.O. Box 2310; 78667; Hays; P 60,000; M 930; (512) 393-5900; Fax (512) 393-5912; chamber@sanmarcostexas.com; www.sanmarcostexas.com.*

San Saba · *San Saba County C/C* · Fern Reed; Exec. Dir.; 302 E. Wallace St.; 76877; San Saba; P 2,700; M 142; (325) 372-5141; Fax (325) 372-5141; executive.director@sansabachamber.com; www.sansabachamber.com

Sanderson · *Sanderson C/C* · Jim Street; Pres.; P.O. Box 734; 79848; Terrell; P 900; M 25; (432) 345-2509; (432) 345-2676; Fax (432) 345-2678; bhawn2@hughes.net; www.sanderson chamberofcommerce.info

Sanger · *Sanger Area C/C* · Lynn McCaughan; Dir./Admin.; 300 Bolivar St.; P.O. Box 537; 76266; Denton, P 6,500; M 170; (940) 458-7702; Fax (940) 458-7823; chamber@sangertexas.com; www.sangertexas.com

Sansom Park · *see River Oaks*

Santa Anna · *Santa Anna C/C* · 303 S. Houston; 76878; Coleman; P 1,249; M 35; (325) 348-3535; www.santaannatex.org

Santa Fe · *Santa Fe C/C* · Fay Picard; Pres./CEO; 12408 Hwy. 6; 77510; Galveston; P 10,000; M 200; (409) 925-8558; Fax (409) 925-8551; sfchamber@comcast.net; www.santafetexaschamber.com*

Schertz · *see Selma*

Schulenburg · *Greater Schulenburg C/C* · Mike Stroup; Exec. Dir.; 618 N. Main; P.O. Box 65; 78956; Fayette; P 2,700; M 200; (979) 743-4514; (866) 504-5294; Fax (979) 743-9155; info@ schulenburgchamber.org; www.schulenburgchamber.org

Sea Brook · *see Houston—Clear Lake Area C/C*

Seadrift · *Seadrift C/C* · Jason Jones; Pres.; P.O. Box 3; 77983; Calhoun; P 1,352; M 60; (361) 785-5321; Fax (361) 785-2162; jjones@fnbportlavaca.com; www.seadriftchamber.com

Seagoville · *Seagoville C/C* · Phil Greenawalt; Exec. Dir.; 107 Hall Rd.; 75159; Dallas; P 11,400; M 195; (972) 287-5184; Fax (972) 287-5815; seagovillechamber@sbcglobal.net; www.seagovillecoc.org

Seagraves · *Seagraves Area C/C* · Lisa Webb; Exec. Dir.; 401 Main; P.O. Box 1257; 79359; Gaines; P 2,600; M 75; (806) 387-2609; seagraveschamber@yahoo.com

Sealy · *Sealy C/C* · Lou Cox; Pres.; 309 Main St.; P.O. Box 586; 77474; Austin; P 6,000; M 300; (979) 885-3222; Fax (979) 885-7184; sealycoc@sbcglobal.net; www.sealychamber.com*

Seguin · *Seguin Area C/C* · Shanta Kuhl; Pres.; 116 N. Camp St.; P.O. Box 710; 78156; Guadalupe; P 112,000; M 800; (830) 379-6382; (800) 580-7322; Fax (830) 379-6971; cofc@seguinchamber.com; www.seguinchamber.com*

Selma · *Randolph Metrocom C/C* · Cassandra Miller; Exec. Dir.; 9374 Valhalla; 78154; Bexar; P 200,000; M 475; (210) 658-8322; Fax (210) 658-1817; executive_director@metrocomchamber.org; www.metrocomchamber.org

Seminole · *Seminole Area C/C* · Shelby Concotelli; Pres./CEO; 119 S.E. Ave. B; P.O. Box 1198; 79360; Gaines; P 6,500; M 270; (432) 758-2352; Fax (432) 758-6698; seminolechamber@warp driveonline.com; www.seminoletxchamber.org*

Seven Points · *see Mabank*

Seymour · *Seymour C/C* · Myra Busby; Exec. Dir.; 400 N. Main St.; P.O. Box 1379; 76380; Baylor; P 2,900; M 80; (940) 889-2921; Fax (940) 889-8882; scoc@nts-online.net; www.seymourtxchamber.org

Shamrock · *Shamrock C/C* · David Rushing; Dir.; 105 E. 12th St.; 79079; Wheeler; P 2,000; M 65; (806) 256-2501; Fax (806) 256-2224; irishedb@hotmail.com; www.shamrocktx.net

Sheffield · *see Iraan*

Shepherd · *Greater Shepherd C/C* · Darlene Moore; Exec. Dir.; W. Hwy. 150; P.O. Box 520; 77371; San Jacinto; P 3,000; M 45; (936) 628-3890; Fax (936) 628-3890

Sherman · *Sherman C/C* · Traci Carlson; Pres.; 307 W. Washington St., Ste. 100; P.O. Box 1029; 75091; Grayson; P 40,000; M 850; (903) 893-1184; Fax (903) 893-4266; info@shermanchamber.us; www.shermanchamber.us*

Shiner · *Shiner C/C* · Marilyn Parker; Pres.; P.O. Box 221; 77984; Lavaca; P 2,000; M 200; (361) 594-4180; shinercc@shinertx.com; www.shinertx.com

Silsbee · *Silsbee C/C* · Jessie Andersen; Pres.; 545 N. 5th St.; 77656; Hardin; P 15,000; M 400; (409) 385-5562; Fax (409) 385-5695; jim@silsbeechamber.com; www.silsbeechamber.com

Sinton · *Sinton C/C* · Dir.; 218 W. Sinton St.; 78387; San Patricio; P 6,000; M 125; (361) 364-2307; Fax (361) 364-3538; sinton chamber@sbcglobal.net; www.sintontexas.org

Slaton · *Slaton C/C* · Leslie Robinson; Mgr.; 200 W. Garza; P.O. Box 400; 79364; Lubbock; P 6,100; M 85; (806) 828-6238; Fax (806) 828-5115; slatoncoc@sbcglobal.net; www.slatonchamber ofcommerce.org

Smithville · *Smithville Area C/C* · Adena Lewis; Pres.; 100 N.W. First St.; P.O. Box 716; 78957; Bastrop; P 5,000; M 360; (512) 237-2313; Fax (512) 237-2605; chamber@smithvilletx.org; www.smithvilletx.org

Snyder · *Snyder C/C* · Melissa Elam; Exec. Dir.; 2302 Ave. R; P.O. Box 840; 79550; Scurry; P 12,000; M 245; (325) 573-3558; Fax (325) 573-9721; director@snydertex.com; www.snyderchamber.org*

Somerville · *Burleson County C/C-Somerville Office* · Barbara Bray; Ofc. Mgr.; 131 7th St.; P.O. Box 596; 77879; Burleson; P 18,000; M 250; (979) 596-2383; Fax (979) 596-2140; somer villetx@hotmail.com; www.burlesoncountytx.com.*

Sonora · *Sonora C/C* · Donna Garrett; Exec. Dir.; 205 Hwy. 277 N., Ste. B; P.O. Box 1172; 76950; Sutton; P 4,000; M 250; (325) 387-2880; (888) 387-2880; Fax (325) 387-5357; soncoc@sonoratx.net; www.sonoratx-chamber.com

South Houston · *South Houston C/C* · JoAnn Parish; Pres.; 58 Spencer Hwy.; 77587; Harris; P 15,000; M 200; (713) 943-0244; Fax (713) 943-3978; sohochamber@sbcglobal.net; www.south houstonchamber.org.

South Padre Island · *South Padre Island C/C* · Roxanne Guenzel; Pres.; 600 Padre Blvd.; 78597; Cameron; P 5,000; M 500; (956) 761-4412; Fax (956) 761-2739; info@spichamber.com; www.spichamber.com*

Southlake • *Southlake C/C* • Dana D. Davis; Pres./CEO; 1501 Corporate Circle, Ste. 100; 76092; Denton & Tarrant; P 28,000; M 600; (817) 481-8200; Fax (817) 749-8202; info@southlake chamber.com; www.southlakechamber.com*

Spearman • *Spearman C/C & Eco. Dev.* • Keith Hight; Exec. V.P.; 211 Main St.; P.O. Box 161; 79081; Hansford; P 3,197; M 150; (806) 659-5555; spearcc@hotmail.com; www.spearman.org

Spring Branch • *Bulverde-Spring Branch Area C/C* • Sylvia Beatty; Admin. Asst.; P.O. Box 1132; 78070; Comal; P 20,000; M 380; (830) 438-4285; (866) 285-8373; Fax (830) 438-8572; bsbacoc@gvtc.com; www.bulverdespringbranchchamber.com*

Springtown • *Springtown Area C/C* • Oleta Parker; Exec. Dir.; 112 S. Main St.; P.O. Box 296; 76082; Parker; P 2,700; M 350; (817) 220-7828; (817) 220-7820; Fax (817) 523-3268; director@ springtownchamber.org; www.springtownchamber.org*

Spur • *Spur Area C/C* • Joan Day; Secy.; P.O. Box 103; 79370; Dickens; P 1,088; M 48; (806) 271-3363; info@spurchamber.com; www.spurchamber.com

Stamford • *Stamford C/C* • Rick DeFoore; Pres.; 107 E. McHarg St.; 79553; Jones; P 10,000; M 70; (325) 773-2411; Fax (325) 773-2411; chamber@stamfordcoc.org; www.stamfordcoc.org

Stanton • *Martin County C/C* • Kim Baker; Exec. Dir.; 209 N. St. Peter; P.O. Box 615; 79782; Martin; P 4,735; M 100; (432) 756-3386; martincountychamber@msn.com; www.stantontex.com

Stephenville • *Stephenville C/C* • July Danley; Pres./CEO; 187 W. Washington St.; P.O. Box 306; 76401; Erath; P 16,100; M 600; (254) 965-5313; Fax (254) 965-3814; info@stephenvilletexas.org; www.stephenvilletexas.org*

Stockdale • *Stockdale C/C* • P.O. Box 578; 78160; Wilson; P 1,300; (830) 996-3128; www.stockdaletx.org

Stonewall • *Stonewall C/C* • Shane Meier; Pres.; 250 Peach St.; P.O. Box 1; 78671; Gillespie; P 300; M 200; (830) 644-2735; Fax (830) 644-2165; chamber@stonewalltexas.com; www.stonewalltexas.com

Stratford • *Stratford C/C* • Beverlyn Lasley; Pres.; P.O. Box 570; 79084; Sherman; P 2,000; M 167; (806) 366-2260; stxcc79084@xit. net; www.stratfordtxchamber.org

Sugar Land • *Fort Bend C/C* • Keri Schmidt; Pres./CEO; 445 Commerce Green Blvd.; 77478; Fort Bend; P 510,000; M 1,300; (281) 491-0800; Fax (281) 491-0112; keri@fortbendcc.org; www. fortbendchamber.com

Sulphur Springs • *Hopkins County C/C* • Meredith Caddell; Pres./CEO; 300 Connally St.; P.O. Box 347; 75483; Hopkins; P 32,000; M 600; (903) 885-6515; Fax (903) 885-6516; meredith caddell@suddenlinkmail.com; www.sulphursprings-tx.com.*

Sweeny • *Sweeny C/C* • Kim Wallace; Exec. Dir.; 111 W. 3rd St.; 77480; Brazoria; P 3,500; M 120; (979) 548-3249; Fax (979) 548-3251; sweenychamber@windstream.net; www.sweeny chamberofcommerce.org

Sweetwater • *Sweetwater C/C* • Jacque McCoy; Exec. Dir.; 810 E. Broadway Ave.; P.O. Box 1148; 79556; Nolan; P 12,000; M 270; (325) 235-5488; (800) 658-6757; Fax (325) 235-1026; jacque@ sweetwatertexas.org; www.sweetwatertexas.org*

Taft • *Taft C/C* • Mary Griffin; Secy.; 501 Green Ave.; P.O. Box 123; 78390; San Patricio; P 5,117; M 51; (361) 528-3230; Fax (361) 528-3515; mgriffin@cityoftaft.net; *

Taylor • *Taylor C/C & Visitor Info. Center* • Thomas E. Martinez; Pres.; 1519 N. Main St.; 76574; Williamson; P 30,000; M 350; (512) 352-6364; (512) 365-8485; Fax (512) 352-6366; info@ taylorchamber.org; www.taylorchamber.org*

Taylor Lake Village • *see Houston–Clear Lake Area C/C*

Teague • *Teague C/C* • Marilyn Michaud; 316 Main St.; P.O. Box 484; 75860; Freestone; P 4,000; M 85; (254) 739-2061; Fax (254) 739-2061; www.cityofteaguetx.com

Temple • *Temple C/C* • Bourdon Wooten; Pres.; 2 N. 5th St.; P.O. Box 158; 76503; Bell; P 100,000; M 1,200; (254) 773-2105; Fax (254) 773-0661; temple@templetx.org; www.templetx.org.*

Terrell • *Terrell C/C & CVB* • Danny R. Booth; Pres./CEO; 1314 W. Moore Ave.; P.O. Box 97; 75160; Kaufman; P 19,000; M 580; (972) 563-5703; (877) TERRELL; Fax (972) 563-2363; danny@ terrelltexas.com; www.terrelltexas.com.*

Texarkana • *Texarkana C/C* • Jeff Sandford; Pres.; 819 State Line Ave.; P.O. Box 1468; 75504; Bowie; P 62,000; M 1,400; (903) 792-7191; Fax (903) 793-4304; chamber@texarkana.org; www. texarkana.org*

Texas City • *Texas City-La Marque C/C* • Jimmy Hayley; Pres.; 9702 Emmett F. Lowry Expy.; P.O. Box 1717; 77592; Galveston; P 57,000; M 850; (409) 935-1408; Fax (409) 316-0901; dedra@ texascitychamber.com; www.texascitychamber.com.*

The Colony • *The Colony C/C* • P.O. Box 560006; 75056; Denton; P 42,000; M 300; (972) 625-8027; Fax (972) 625-8027; info@ thecolonychamber.org; www.thecolonychamber.com*

The Woodlands • *South Montgomery County Woodlands C/C* • Karen Hoylman; Pres./CEO; 1400 Woodloch Forest Dr., Ste. 300; 77380; Montgomery; P 394,517; M 2,000; (281) 367-5777; Fax (281) 292-1655; lobby@woodlandschamber.org; www. woodlandschamber.org

Thorndale • *Thorndale Area C/C* • Brian Morton; Pres.; P.O. Box 668; 76577; Milam & Williamson; P 1,278; M 90; (512) 898-2121; (512) 898-2523; admin@txchamber.org; www.thorndaletx.com

Three Rivers • *Three Rivers C/C* • Mike Pierson; Exec. Dir.; P.O. Box 1648; 78071; Live Oak; P 2,000; M 100; (361) 786-4330; trchamber@threeriverstx.org; www.threeriverstx.org

Throckmorton • *Throckmorton County C/C & Ag.* • Russell Walker; Pres.; P.O. Box 711; 76483; Throckmorton; P 1,800; M 40; (940) 849-0222; Fax (940) 849-0222; throckchamber@yahoo.com; www.throckmortonchamberofcommerce.com

Timpson • *Timpson C/C* • Mike Thrift; Pres.; 191 Bremond St.; P.O. Box 987; 75975; Shelby; P 1,100; M 70; (936) 254-3500; timpsgen@sbcglobal.net

Tomball • *Greater Tomball Area C/C* • Bruce E. Hillegeist; Pres.; 29201 Quinn Rd., Ste. B; P.O. Box 516; 77377; Harris; P 700,000; M 900; (281) 351-7222; (866) 670-7222; Fax (281) 351-7223; admin@tomballchamber.org; www.tomballchamber.org*

Tool • *see Mabank*

Trinity • *Trinity Peninsula C/C* • Liz Drake; Pres.; 702 S. Robb; P.O. Box 549; 75862; Trinity; P 15,000; M 105; (936) 594-3856; Fax (936) 594-0558; info@trinitychamber.org; www.trinitychamber.org

Trophy Club • *see Roanoke*

Troup • *Troup C/C* • Gene Whitsell; Exec. V.P.; P.O. Box 336; 75789; Cherokee & Smith; P 1,949; M 50; (903) 842-4113; gwhitsell@ embarqmail.com; www.trouptexas.org

Tulia • *Tulia C/C* • Shelly Borchardt; Dir.; 127 S.W. 2nd; P.O. Box 267; 79088; Swisher; P 5,117; M 200; (806) 995-2296; Fax (806) 995-4426; exec@tuliachamber.com; www.tuliachamber.com

Tyler • *Tyler Area C/C* • Henry M. Bell; COO; 315 N. Broadway; P.O. Box 390; 75710; Smith; P 102,000; M 2,000; (903) 592-1661; Fax (903) 593-2746; hbell@tylertexas.com; www.tylertexas.com*

Tyler • *Tyler Metro Black C/C* • Darryl Bowdre; Pres./COO; 2000 W. Gentry Pkwy.; 75702; Smith; P 90,000; M 100; (903) 593-6026; Fax (903) 593-6995; dbowdre@tylermetrochamber.org; www.tylermetrochamber.org

Union Valley • *see Quinlan*

Universal City • *see Selma*

Uvalde • *Uvalde C/C* • Wendy Speer; Exec. Dir.; 311 N. Getty; 78801; Uvalde; P 18,500; M 350; (830) 278-3361; Fax (830) 278-3363; director@uvalde.org; www.uvalde.org*

Van • *Van Area C/C* • Lynn Ward; P.O. Box 55; 75790; Van Zandt; P 2,362; M 130; (903) 963-5051; Fax (903) 963-8883; van chamber@vantexas.com; www.vantexas.com

Van Alstyne • *Van Alstyne Area C/C* • Brenda McDonald; Pres.; 228 E. Marshall; P.O. Box 698; 75495; Collin & Grayson; P 3,800; M 125; (903) 482-6066; Fax (903) 712-0966; info@vanalstyne chamber.org; www.vanalstynechamber.org

Van Horn • *Van Horn C/C* • Marie "Sooky" Borrego; Pres.; P.O. Box 762; 79855; Culberson; P 2,400; M 20; (432) 283-2043; (866) 424-6939; info@vanhorntexas.org; www.vanhornchamber.com

Vega • *Oldham County C/C* • Linda Drake; Mgr.; P.O. Box 538; 79092; Oldham; P 2,200; M 170; (806) 267-2828; Fax (806) 267-2645; oldhamco@arn.net; www.oldhamcofc.org

Vernon • *Vernon C/C* • Carrie Hawkins; Exec. Dir.; 1614 Main St.; P.O. Box 1538; 76385; Wilbarger; P 11,660; M 217; (940) 552-2564; (800) 687-3137; Fax (940) 552-0654; vernonchamber@sbcglobal.net; www.vernontexas.net

Victoria • *Victoria C/C* • Randy Vivian; Pres./CEO; 3404 N. Ben Wilson; P.O. Box 2465; 77902; Victoria; P 86,916; M 1,132; (361) 573-5277; Fax (361) 573-5911; info@victoriachamber.org; www.victoriachamber.org*

Vidor • *Vidor C/C* • Jane Carter; Exec. Secy.; 945 N. Main St.; 77662; Orange; P 20,000; M 275; (409) 769-6339; Fax (409) 769-0227; vidorchamber@sbcglobal.net; www.vidorchamber.com

Waco • *CenTex Hispanic C/C* • Joe Rodriguez; Exec. Dir.; 915 LaSalle Ave.; 76706; McLennan; P 112,000; M 220; (254) 754-7111; Fax (254) 754-3456; joe@wacohispanicchamber.com; www.wacohispanicchamber.com

Waco • *Greater Waco C/C* • James G. Vaughan Jr.; Pres./CEO; 101 S. 3rd St.; P.O. Box 1220; 76703; McLennan; P 226,189; M 1,508; (254) 752-6551; Fax (254) 752-6618; info@wacochamber.com; www.wacochamber.com*

Waller • *Waller Area C/C* • Trey Duhon; Pres.; 2313 Main St.; P.O. Box 53; 77484; Waller; P 15,000; M 167; (936) 372-5300; info@wallerchamber.com; www.wallerchamber.com

Watauga • *see Haltom City*

Waxahachie • *Waxahachie C/C* • Debra Wakeland; Pres./CEO; 102 YMCA Dr.; 75165; Ellis; P 30,000; M 800; (972) 937-2390; (972) 938-9617; Fax (972) 938-9827; dwakeland@waxahachie chamber.com; www.waxahachiechamber.com.*

Weatherford • *Weatherford C/C* • Timmy Gazzola; Pres.; 401 Ft. Worth Hwy.; P.O. Box 310; 76086; Parker; P 35,000; M 900; (817) 594-3801; (888) 594-3801; Fax (817) 613-9216; info@weatherford-chamber.com; www.weatherford-chamber.com.*

Webster • *see Houston-Clear Lake Area C/C*

Weimar • *Weimar Area C/C* • Sandra Michna; Exec. Dir.; 109 E. Main; P.O. Box 90; 78962; Colorado; P 1,981; M 128; (979) 725-9511; Fax (979) 725-6890; weimarcc@cvctx.com; www.weimartx.org

Wellington • *Collingsworth County C/C* • P.O. Box 267; 79095; Collingsworth; P 2,800; M 100; (806) 447-5848; chamberof commerce@wellingtontexas.net; www.wellingtontexas.net

Weslaco • *Rio Grande Valley Partnership C/C* • Veronica Villegas; V.P.; 322 S. Missouri; P.O. Box 1499; 78599; Hidalgo; P 1,100,000; M 850; (956) 968-3141; Fax (956) 968-0210; mail@valleychamber.com; www.valleychamber.com

Weslaco • *Weslaco Area C/C* • Martha Noell; Pres./CEO; 301 W. Railroad St.; P.O. Box 8398; 78599; Hidalgo; P 32,000; M 550; (956) 968-2102; Fax (956) 968-6451; chamber@weslaco.com; www.weslaco.com*

West • *West C/C* • Toni Kaska; Pres.; 308 N. Washington St.; P.O. Box 123; 76691; McLennan; P 2,800; M 110; (254) 826-3188; Fax (254) 826-3188; westchamber@sbcglobal.net; www.westtx chamber.com

West Columbia • *West Columbia C/C* • 202 E. Brazos Ave.; P.O. Box 837; 77486; Brazoria; P 4,400; M 225; (979) 345-3921; Fax (979) 345-6526; chamber@westcolumbiachamber.org; www.westcolumbiachamber.com*

West Tawakoni • *see Quinlan*

Westlake • *see Roanoke*

Westworth Village • *see River Oaks*

Wharton • *Wharton C/C* • Rebecca Klima; Bd. Chair; 225 N. Richmond Rd.; 77488; Wharton; P 10,200; M 350; (979) 532-1862; Fax (979) 532-0102; admin@whartonchamber.com; www.whartontexas.com*

Wheeler • *Wheeler C/C & Eco. Dev.* • Chad Helton; Pres.; 505 Alan L. Bean Blvd.; P.O. Box 221; 79096; Wheeler; P 1,391; M 50; (806) 826-3408; Fax (806) 826-5601; kristi@wildlifetexas.com; www.wheelertexas.org

White Settlement • *White Settlement Area C/C* • Roger Chambers; Chamber Mgr.; 8224 White Settlement Rd., Ste. 100; P.O. Box 150578; 76108; Tarrant; P 16,400; M 105; (817) 246-1121; Fax (817) 246-1121; wsacc@whitesettlement-tx.com; www.whitesettlement-tx.com

Whitehouse • *Whitehouse Area C/C* • Phil Rogers; Pres.; P.O. Box 1041; 75791; Smith; P 7,000; M 147; (903) 839-8200; info@whitehousetx.com; www.whitehousetx.com

Whitesboro • *Whitesboro Area C/C* • Juanita Kirby; Pres.; 2535 Hwy. 82 E., Ste. C; P.O. Box 522; 76273; Grayson; P 4,400; M 300; (903) 564-3331; Fax (903) 564-3397; chamber@whitesborotx.com; www.whitesborotx.com

Whitewright • *Whitewright Area C/C* • Brett Christoffel; Pres.; 113 W. Grand; P.O. Box 189; 75491; Grayson; P 1,760; M 94; (903) 364-2000; Fax (903) 364-1079; chamber@whitewright.org; www.whitewright.org

Whitney • *Lake Whitney C/C* • Diana Reed; Secy.; 102 W. Railroad Ave.; P.O. Box 604; 76692; Hill; P 20,000; M 205; (254) 694-2540; Fax (254) 694-3005; bluewater@lakewhitneychamber.com; www.lakewhitneychamber.com

Wichita Falls • *Wichita Falls Chamber of Comm. & Ind.* • Tim Chase; Pres./CEO; 900 8th St., Ste. 218; P.O. Box 1860; 76307; Wichita; P 104,000; M 1,200; (940) 723-2741; Fax (940) 723-8773; chamber@wf.net; www.wichitafallscommerce.com.*

Willow Park • *East Parker County C/C* • Lisa Flowers; Pres.; 100 Chuck Wagon Trl.; 76087; Parker; P 30,000; M 400; (817) 441-7844; Fax (817) 441-1544; info@eastparkerchamber.com; www.eastparkerchamber.com*

Wills Point · *Wills Point C/C* · Jennifer Ross; Pres.; 307 N. 4th St.; 75169; Van Zandt; P 5,000; M 200; (903) 873-3111; (800) WP-BLUBIRD; Fax (903) 873-3111; willspointtx@sbcglobal.net; www.willspointchamber.com

Wilmer · *Wilmer C/C* · 128 N. Dallas Ave.; 75172; Dallas; P 3,600; M 20; (972) 441-3222

Wimberley · *Wimberley Chamber & Visitor Center* · Jenelle Flocke; Chrmn.; P.O. Box 12; 78676; Hays; P 9,000; M 425; (512) 847-2201; Fax (512) 847-3189; info@wimberley.org; www.wimberley.org*

Windcrest · *see Selma*

Wink · *Wink C/C* · Bill Beckham; Pres.; P.O. Box 401; 79789; Winkler; P 919; M 8; (432) 527-3365; Fax (432) 527-3949

Winnie · *Winnie Area C/C* · Gloria Roemer; Exec. Mgr.; 327 E. LeBlanc Rd.; P.O. Box 1715; 77665; Chambers; P 5,275; M 125; (409) 296-2231; Fax (409) 296-4213; winnie@winnietexas.com; www.winnietexas.com

Winnsboro · *Winnsboro Area C/C* · Larry Merchant; Pres.; 100 E. Broadway; 75494; Wood; P 4,000; M 270; (903) 342-3666; Fax (903) 342-3666; info@winnsboro.com; www.winnsboro.com

Winters · *Winters Area C/C* · Amanda Collom; Mgr.; 100 W. Dale St.; P.O. Box 662; 79567; Runnels; P 3,000; M 125; (325) 754-5210; wacc@wtxs.net; www.winters-texas.us

Wolfforth · *Wolfforth Area C/C & Ag.* · Cindy Stephens; Pres.; P.O. Box 35; 79382; Lubbock; P 4,000; M 60; (806) 535-3748; wolfforthchamber@gmail.com; www.wolfforthtx.us

Woodson · *see Throckmorton*

Woodville · *Tyler County C/C* · Kathy Fetner; Pres.; 717 W. Bluff St.; 75979; Tyler; P 20,000; M 210; (409) 283-2632; Fax (409) 283-6884; tylerctychamber@sbcglobal.net; www.tylercountychamber.com

Wylie · *Wylie C/C* · Mike Agnew; Pres.; 108-A W. Marble; 75098; Collin; P 41,000; M 392; (972) 442-2804; Fax (972) 429-0139; info@wyliechamber.org; www.wyliechamber.org*

Yoakum · *Yoakum Area C/C* · Bill Lopez; 105 Huck St.; P.O. Box 591; 77995; DeWitt & Lavaca; P 5,700; M 150; (361) 293-2309; Fax (361) 293-3507; info@yoakumareachamber.com; www.yoakumareachamber.com.

Yorktown · *Yorktown C/C* · Melissa Armstrong; Exec. Dir.; 141 S. Riedel St.; P.O. Box 488; 78164; DeWitt; P 2,271; M 150; (361) 564-2661; Fax (361) 564-2518; 4yorktowntx@sbcglobal.net; www.yorktowntx.com

Zapata · *Zapata County C/C* · Paco Mendoza Jr.; Pres./CEO; 601 N. Hwy. 83 S.; P.O. Box 1028; 78076; Zapata; P 16,000; M 209; (956) 765-4871; (800) 292-LAKE; Fax (956) 765-5434; customercare@zapatachamber.com; www.zapatausa.com.

Utah

Utah State C of C · Ryan Evans; Exec. Secy.; 175 E. 400 S., Ste. 600; Salt Lake City; 84111; Salt Lake; P 2,758,000; M 15,500; (801) 328-5090; Fax (801) 328-5098; admin@utahstatechamber.org; www.utahstatechamber.org

American Fork · *American Fork C/C* · Debby Lauret; Exec. Dir.; 51 E. Main St.; 84003; Utah; P 60,000; M 240; (801) 756-5110; chamber@afcity.net; www.afchamber.org

Beaver · *Beaver Valley C/C* · Ursula Carstensen; Pres.; P.O. Box 760; 84713; Beaver; P 2,500; M 50; (435) 438-5081; (888) 848-5081; chamber@beaverutchamber.com; www.beaverutchamber.com

Blanding · *Blanding C/C* · Harold Lyman; Pres.; 12 N. Grayson Pkwy.; 84511; San Juan; P 4,500; M 50; (435) 678-2791; (435) 678-3338

Bluffdale · *see Riverton*

Bountiful · *see Kaysville*

Brian Head · *Brian Head C/C* · Angie Haderlie; Exec. Dir.; 56 N. Hwy. 143; P.O. Box 190325; 84719; Iron; P 80; M 50; (888) 677-2810; Fax (435) 677-2154; angie@brianheadchamber.com; www.brianheadchamber.com

Brigham City · *Brigham City Area C/C* · Monica Holdaway; Exec. Dir.; 6 N. Main; P.O. Box 458; 84302; Box Elder; P 18,000; M 335; (435) 723-3931; Fax (435) 723-5761; chamber@brighamchamber.com; www.brighamchamber.com

Cedar City · *Cedar City Area C/C* · Scott Jolley; Exec. Dir.; 77 N. Main St.; 84720; Iron; P 27,000; M 435; (435) 586-4484; Fax (435) 586-4022; director@infowest.com; www.chambercedarcity.org

Centerville · *see Kaysville*

Clearfield · *see Kaysville*

Clinton · *see Kaysville*

Cottonwood Heights · *see Salt Lake City–Chamber East*

Delta · *Delta Area C/C* · Lorie L. Skeem; Ofc. Mgr.; 80 N. 200 W.; 84624; Millard; P 8,000; M 105; (435) 864-4316; Fax (435) 864-4313; chamber@deltautah.com; www.chamber.deltautah.com

Draper · *Draper Area C/C* · William E. Rappleye; Pres./CEO; 1160 E. Pioneer Rd.; P.O. Box 1002; 84020; Salt Lake & Utah; P 1,500,000; M 200; (801) 553-0928; Fax (801) 816-0478; wrappleye@integraonline.com; www.draperchamber.com*

Farmington · *see Kaysville*

Fillmore · *Fillmore Area C/C* · Michael King; Pres.; P.O. Box 164; 84631; Millard; P 2,300; M 30; (435) 743-7803; (435) 743-6816; www.fillmoreutahchamber.com

Fruit Heights · *see Kaysville*

Garden City · *Bear Lake Rendezvous C/C* · Angie McPhie; Pres.; P.O. Box 55; 84028; Rich; P 450; M 60; (800) 448-2327; (435) 946-2197; info@bearlakechamber.com; www.bearlakechamber.com

Green River · *Green River C/C* · Keith Brady; Chrmn.; P.O. Box 250; 84525; Emery; P 997; M 30; (435) 564-3490; (877) 564-3490; chamber@etv.net; www.greenriverchamber.org

Heber City · *Heber Valley C/C* · 475 N. Main St.; 84032; Wasatch; P 25,000; M 300; (435) 654-3666; Fax (435) 654-3667; info@gohebervalley.com; www.gohebervalley.com

Herriman · *see Riverton*

Hurricane · *Hurricane Valley C/C* · Jeff Harding; Pres.; 1155 W. State St., 2nd Flr.; 84737; Washington; P 15,000; M 79; (435) 635-3402; Fax (435) 635-3402; kbeardall@hvchamber.com; www.hvchamber.com

Kanab · *Kanab Area C/C* · Kelly Stowell; Pres.; 78 S. 100 E.; 84741; Kane; P 6,500; M 125; (435) 644-5033; (800) 733-5263; Fax (435) 644-5923; info@kanabchamber.com; www.kanabchamber.com

Kaysville · *Davis C/C* · Jim Smith; Pres./CEO; 450 S. Simmons Way, Ste. 220; 84037; Davis; P 265,000; M 900; (801) 593-2200; Fax (801) 593-2212; daviscc@davischamberofcommerce.com; www.davischamberofcommerce.com

Kearns · *see West Valley City*

Layton · *see Kaysville*

Lehi · *Lehi Area C/C* · Donna Milakovic; Pres.; 235 E. State St.; P.O. Box 154; 84043; Utah; P 80,000; M 100; (801) 766-9657; Fax (801) 766-8599; lehichamber@gmail.com; www.lehiareachamber.org

Logan • *Cache Valley C/C* • Sandra Emile; Pres.; 160 N. Main St.; 84321; Cache; P 105,000; M 630; (435) 752-2161; Fax (435) 753-5825; semile@cachechamber.com; www.cachechamber.com*

Manila • *Flaming Gorge Area C/C* • Tina Benington; Pres.; P.O. Box 122; 84046; Daggett; P 920; M 50; (435) 784-3184; www.daggettcounty.org

Midvale • *see Salt Lake City–Chamber East*

Millcreek • *see Salt Lake City–Chamber East*

Moab • *Moab Area C/C* • Kammy Wells; Exec. Dir.; 217 E. Center St., Ste. 250; 84532; Grand; P 9,000; M 250; (435) 259-7814; Fax (435) 259-8519; moabchamber@live.com; www.moabchamber.com

Monticello • *Monticello C/C* • Michael Martin; Pres.; P.O. Box 217; 84535; San Juan; P 2,000; M 50; (435) 587-2992; info@monticelloutahchamber.com; www.monticelloutahchamber.com

Mount Pleasant • *Mount Pleasant Main Street Comm.* • Monte Bona; Dir.; 115 W. Main St.; City Hall; 84647; Sanpete; P 2,800; M 55; (435) 462-2456; Fax (435) 462-2581; www.mtpleasantcity.com

Murray • *Murray Area C/C* • Scott Baker; Pres./CEO; 5250 S. Commerce Dr., Ste. 180; 84107; Salt Lake; P 48,000; M 400; (801) 263-2632; Fax (801) 263-8262; scott@murraychamber.net; www.murraychamber.org

Nephi • *Nephi City C/C* • Jamie John; Pres.; P.O. Box 219; 84648; Juab; P 8,000; M 60; (435) 623-1992; nephichamberofcommerce.com

North Salt Lake • *see Kaysville*

Ogden • *Ogden-Weber C/C* • Dave Hardman; Pres./CEO; 2484 Washington Blvd., Ste. 400; 84401; Weber; P 230,000; M 900; (801) 621-8300; Fax (801) 392-7609; dave@ogdenweberchamber.com; www.ogdenweberchamber.com.

Orem • *see Provo*

Park City • *Park City C/C* • Bill Malone; Pres./CEO; 1910 Prospector Ave., Ste. 103; P.O. Box 1630; 84060; Summit & Wasatch; P 24,500; M 1,075; (435) 649-6100; Fax (435) 649-4132; info@parkcityinfo.com; www.parkcityinfo.com*

Payson • *Payson C/C* • Carolyn Bowman; Exec. Dir.; 20 S. Main; P.O. Box 176; 84651; Utah; P 17,500; M 100; (801) 465-2634; paysonchamber@yahoo.com; www.paysoncitychamber.org

Pleasant Grove • *Pleasant Grove Bus. Alliance* • Jennifer Wright; Dir.; 70 S. 100 E.; 84062; Utah; P 31,000; M 600; (801) 380-3179; (801) 785-5045; Fax (801) 785-8925; info@pgbaut.com; www.pgbaut.com

Price • *Carbon County C/C* • Ann Evans; Coord.; 81 N. 200 E., Ste. 3; 84501; Carbon; P 22,000; M 300; (435) 637-2788; Fax (435) 637-7010; cccc@carboncountychamber.net; www.carboncountychamber.net

Provo • *Utah Valley C/C* • Steven T. Densley; Pres.; 51 S. University Ave., Ste. 215; 84601; Utah; P 200,000; M 820; (801) 851-2555; Fax (801) 851-2557; info@thechamber.org; www.thechamber.org*

Richfield • *Richfield Area C/C* • Lorraine Gregerson; Exec. Dir.; 250 N. Main, Ste. B42; 84701; Sevier; P 7,200; M 145; (435) 896-4241; Fax (435) 896-4313; lorraine@richfieldareachamber.com; www.richfieldareachamber.com

Riverdale • *see Ogden*

Riverton • *Southwest Valley C/C* • Susan Schilling; Exec. Officer; 4168 W. 12600 S.; P.O. Box 330; 84065; Salt Lake; P 60,000; M 140; (801) 280-0595; susan@swvchamber.org; www.swvchamber.org

Roosevelt • *Duchesne County Area C/C* • Irene Hansen; Exec. Dir.; 50 E. 200 S.; P.O. Box 1417; 84066; Duchesne; P 18,000; M 280; (435) 722-4598; Fax (435) 722-4579; dcac@ubtanet.com; www.duchesne.net

Roy • *see Ogden*

Salem • *see Spanish Fork*

Salt Lake City • *Chamber East* • Marie Marshall; Pres./CEO; 3335 S. 900 E., Ste. 220; 84106; Salt Lake; P 150,000; M 400; (801) 561-3880; info@chambereast.com; www.chambereast.com

Salt Lake City • *Salt Lake C/C* • Lane Beattie; Pres./CEO; 175 E. University Blvd. (400 S.), Ste. 600; 84111; Salt Lake; P 978,701; M 4,200; (801) 364-3631; Fax (801) 328-5098; info@slchamber.com; www.slchamber.com.*

Sandy • *Sandy Area C/C* • Nancy Workman; Pres./CEO; 8807 S. 700 E.; 84070; Salt Lake; P 100,000; M 870; (801) 566-0344; Fax (801) 566-0346; nancy.workman@sandychamber.com; www.sandychamber.com

Smithfield • *Greater Smithfield C/C* • Gary Fox; Pres.; P.O. Box 31; 84335; Cache; P 7,000; M 40; (435) 232-7342; Stacey@SmithfieldChamber.com; www.smithfieldchamber.com

South Jordan • *South Jordan C/C* • Yvonne Margis; Admin.; 1665 W. 10600 S., Ste. 2; 84095; Salt Lake; P 53,000; M 200; (801) 253-5200; Fax (801) 253-5201; info@southjordanchamber.org; www.southjordanchamber.org*

South Salt Lake City • *South Salt Lake C/C* • Stacey Liddiard; Pres./CEO; P.O. Box 65001; 84165; Salt Lake; P 23,000; M 230; (801) 466-3377; Fax (801) 467-3322; info@sslchamber.com; www.sslchamber.com*

South Weber • *see Kaysville*

Spanish Fork • *Spanish Fork/Salem Area C/C* • Ms. Cary Hanks; Exec. Dir.; 40 S. Main, Ste. 10; 84660; Utah; P 30,000; M 225; (801) 798-8352; office@spanishforkchamber.com; www.spanishforkchamber.com

Springville • *Springville Area C/C* • Robert Shearer; Exec Dir.; 224 S. Main, Ste. 440; 84663; Utah; P 25,000; M 97; (801) 489-4681; (801) 368-5672; Fax (801) 489-4681; springvillechamber@qwestoffice.net; www.springvilleareachamber.com

St. George • *St. George Area C/C* • Russell G. Behrmann; Pres.; 97 E. St. George Blvd.; 84770; Washington; P 140,000; M 800; (435) 628-1650; Fax (435) 673-1587; hotspot@stgeorgechamber.com; www.stgeorgechamber.com*

Sugar House • *see Salt Lake City–Chamber East*

Sunset • *see Kaysville*

Syracuse • *see Kaysville*

Taylorsville • *see West Valley City*

Tooele • *Tooele County C/C* • Debbie Winn; Exec. Dir.; 86 S. Main; P.O. Box 460; 84074; Tooele; P 64,342; M 360; (435) 882-0690; (800) 378-0690; Fax (435) 833-0946; chamber@tooelechamber.com; www.tooelechamber.com

Tremonton • *Bear River Valley C/C* • Micah Capener; Pres.; 12 W. 100 N.; P.O. Box 311; 84337; Box Elder; P 20,000; M 150; (435) 257-7587; bearriverchamber@gmail.com; www.brvcc.com*

Vernal • *Vernal Area C/C* • Adam Massey; Exec. Dir.; 134 W. Main; 84078; Uintah; P 27,000; M 250; (435) 789-1352; Fax (435) 789-1355; vchambermgr@easilink.com; www.vernalchamber.com*

West Bountiful • *see Kaysville*

West Jordan · *West Jordan C/C* · N. Craig Dearing; Pres./CEO; 8000 S. Redwood Rd.; 84088; Salt Lake; P 100,000; M 350; (801) 569-5151; Fax (801) 569-5153; info@westjordanchamber.com; www.westjordanchamber.com

West Point · *see Kaysville*

West Valley City · *ChamberWest* · Alan Anderson; Pres./CEO; 1241 Village Main Dr., Ste. B; 84119; Salt Lake; P 200,000; M 420; (801) 977-8755; Fax (801) 977-8329; chamber@chamberwest.org; www.chamberwest.org*

Woods Cross · *see Kaysville*

Vermont

Vermont C of C · Betsy Bishop; Pres.; P.O. Box 37; Montpelier; 05601; Washington; P 639,000; M 1,500; (802) 223-3443; Fax (802) 223-4257; info@vtchamber.com; www.vtchamber.com

Andover · *see Ludlow*

Arlington · *see Manchester Center*

Ascutney · *see Windsor*

Athens · *see Bellows Falls*

Barre · *Central Vermont C/C* · George Malek; Exec. V.P.; P.O. Box 336; 05641; Washington; P 60,000; M 450; (802) 229-5711; Fax (802) 229-5713; cvchamber@aol.com; www.central-vt.com.

Barton · *Barton Area C/C* · Nancy Rodgers; Pres.; P.O. Box 776; 05822; Orleans; P 5,000; M 130; (802) 239-4147; info@centerof thekingdom.com; www.centerofthekingdom.com

Bellows Falls · *Great Falls Reg. C/C* · Roger Riccio; Exec. Dir.; 17 Depot St.; 05101; Windham; P 12,000; M 290; (802) 463-4280; Fax (802) 463-4280; info@gfrcc.org; www.gfrcc.org*

Bennington · *Bennington Area C/C* · Joann Erenhouse; Dir.; 100 Veterans Memorial Dr.; 05201; Bennington; P 15,000; M 500; (802) 447-3311; (800) 229-0252; Fax (802) 447-1163; chamber@ bennington.com; www.bennington.com*

Berlin · *see Barre*

Bethel · *see Randolph*

Bradford · *see Wells River*

Braintree · *see Randolph*

Brandon · *Brandon Area C/C* · Janet Mondlak; Exec. Dir.; P.O. Box 267; 05733; Rutland; P 4,000; M 175; (802) 247-6401; info@ brandon.org; www.brandon.org

Brattleboro · *Brattleboro Area C/C* · Jerry Goldberg; Exec. Dir.; 180 Main St.; 05301; Windham; P 35,000; M 610; (802) 254-4565; (877) 254-4565; Fax (802) 254-5675; info@brattleborochamber. org; www.brattleborochamber.org

Bristol · *see Middlebury*

Brookfield · *see Randolph*

Burke Hollow · *see East Burke*

Burlington · *Lake Champlain Reg. C/C* · Tom Torti; Pres.; 60 Main St., Ste. 100; 05401; Chittenden; P 149,286; M 2,500; (802) 863-3489; (877) 686-5253; Fax (802) 863-1538; vermont@ vermont.org; www.vermont.org*

Cavendish · *see Ludlow*

Chelsea · *see Randolph*

Chester · *see Ludlow*

Dorset · *Dorset C/C* · P.O. Box 121; 05251; Bennington; P 2,000; M 65; chamber@dorsetvt.com; www.dorsetvt.com

East Burke · *Burke Area C/C* · Hannah Collins; P.O. Box 347; 05832; Caledonia; P 2,000; M 50; (802) 626-4124; burke chamber@burkevermont.com; www.burkevermont.com

Fair Haven · *Vermont Lakes Region C/C* · Kathleen Mongeur; Pres.; P.O. Box 206; 05743; Rutland; P 8,000; M 60; (802) 265-8600; contact@fairhavenchambervt.com; www.fairhaven chambervt.com

Grafton · *see Bellows Falls*

Hancock · *see Randolph*

Hardwick · *Heart of Vermont* · Maria Roosevelt; Pres.; P.O. Box 111; 05843; Caledonia; P 7,000; M 125; (802) 472-5906; chamber@heartofvt.com; www.heartofvt.com

Hartland · *see Windsor*

Island Pond · *Island Pond C/C* · P.O. Box 255; 05846; Essex; P 2,000; M 20; (802) 723-9889; info@islandpondchamber.org; www.islandpondchamber.org

Jeffersonville · *Smugglers Notch Area C/C* · Ray Saloomey; Pres.; P.O. Box 364; 05464; Lamoille; P 3,000; M 98; (802) 644-8232; info@smugnotch.com; www.smugnotch.com

Killington · *Killington C/C* · Phil Black; Pres.; P.O. Box 114; 05751; Rutland; P 1,000; M 200; (802) 773-4181; (800) 337-1928; Fax (802) 775-7070; info@killingtonchamber.com; www. killingtonchamber.com

Lake Champlain Islands · *see North Hero*

Lincoln · *see Middlebury*

Londonderry · *Londonderry Area C/C* · James J. Lind; Exec. Dir.; P.O. Box 58; 05148; Windham; P 1,700; M 106; (802) 824-8178; londcham@aol.com

Ludlow · *Okemo Valley Reg. C/C* · Marji Graf; Exec. Dir.; 57 Pond St., Clock Tower; P.O. Box 333; 05149; Rutland, Windham & Windsor; P 3,000; M 350; (802) 228-5830; Fax (802) 228-7642; mgraf@yourplaceinvermont.com; www.yourplaceinvermont.com*

Lyndonville · *Lyndon Area C/C* · Steve Nichols; Pres.; P.O. Box 886; 05851; Caledonia; P 9,000; M 100; (802) 626-9696; Fax (802) 626-1167; info@lyndonvermont.com; www.lyndonvermont.com

Manchester Center · *Manchester & The Mountains Reg. C/C* · Berta Maginniss; Exec. Dir.; 5046 Main St.; 05255; Bennington; P 3,800; M 730; (802) 362-2100; (800) 362-4144; Fax (802) 362-3451; visitor@manchesterchamber.net; www.manchestervermont.net

Middlebury · *Addison County C/C* · Andrew Mayer; Pres.; 93 Court St.; 05753; Addison; P 37,000; M 700; (802) 388-7951; (800) 733-8376; Fax (802) 388-8066; info@addisoncounty.com; www. addisoncounty.com

Monkton · *see Middlebury*

Montpelier · *see Barre*

Morrisville · *Lamoille Region C/C* · Cindy Locke; Exec. Dir.; 34 Pleasant St., Ste. 1; 05661; Lamoille; P 21,225; M 390; (802) 888-7607; (800) 849-9985; Fax (802) 888-5006; info@lamoillechamber. com; www.lamoillechamber.com*

Mount Holly · *see Ludlow*

New Haven · *see Middlebury*

Newbury · *see Wells River*

Newport · *Vermont's North Country C/C* · Donna Higgins; Exec. Dir.; 246 The Causeway; 05855; Caledonia, Essex & Orleans; P 30,000; M 184; (802) 334-7782; chamber@vtnorthcountry.org; www.vtnorthcountry.org

North Hero • *Lake Champlain Islands C/C* • Ruth Wallman; Exec. Dir.; P.O. Box 213; 05474; Grand Isle; P 7,000; M 200; (802) 372-8400; (800) 262-5226; Fax (802) 372-5107; info@champlain islands.com; www.champlainislands.com

Northfield • *see Barre*

Plymouth • *see Ludlow*

Poultney • *Poultney Area C/C* • Nina Corbin; Admin. Asst.; 66 Beaman St.; P.O. Box 151; 05764; Rutland; P 3,500; M 140; (802) 287-2010; poultneyvt@yahoo.com; www.poultneyvt.com

Putney • *see Bellows Falls*

Randolph • *Randolph Area C/C* • Deb Jones; Exec. Dir.; 31 VT Rte. 66; P.O. Box 9; 05060; Orange; P 30,000; M 188; (802) 728-9027; Fax (802) 728-4705; contact@randolph-chamber.com; www. randolph-chamber.com

Reading • *see Windsor*

Rochester • *see Randolph*

Rockingham • *see Bellows Falls*

Royalton • *see Randolph*

Rutland • *Rutland Region C/C* • Thomas L. Donahue; Exec. V.P.; 50 Merchants Row; 05701; Rutland; P 18,230; M 600; (802) 773-2747; (800) 756-8880; Fax (802) 773-2772; rrccvt@aol.com; www. rutlandvermont.com

Saint Albans • *Franklin County Reg. C/C* • Jim Walsh; Exec. Dir.; 2 N. Main St., Ste. 101; 05478; Franklin; P 45,000; M 600; (802) 524-2444, (877) 524-2445; info@fcrccvt.com; www.fcrccvt.com

Saint Johnsbury • *Northeast Kingdom C/C* • Darcie McCann; Exec. Dir.; 51 Depot Sq., Ste. 3; 05819; Caledonia; P 63,612; M 400; (802) 748-3678; (800) 639-6379; Fax (802) 748-0731; nekinfo@ nekchamber.com; www.nekchamber.com

Saxton's River • *see Bellows Falls*

Sharon • *see Randolph*

Smugglers Notch • *see Jeffersonville*

Springfield • *Springfield Reg. C/C* • Patricia Chaffee; Exec. V.P.; 56 Main St., Ste. 2; 05156; Windsor; P 9,550; M 330; (802) 885-2779; Fax (802) 885-6826; chamber@springfieldvt.com; www. springfieldvt.com

Starksboro • *see Middlebury*

Stockbridge • *see Randolph*

Stowe • *Stowe Area Assn.* • Ed Stahl; Exec. Dir.; 51 Main St.; P.O. Box 1320; 05672; Lamoille; P 4,300; M 315; (802) 253-7321; (877) GO-STOWE; Fax (802) 253-6628; askus@gostowe.com; www. gostowe.com

Swanton • *Swanton C/C* • Adam Paxman; Pres.; P.O. Box 237; 05488; Franklin; P 6,000; M 62; (802) 868-7200; chamberoffice@ swantonchamber.com; www.swantonchamber.com

Tunbridge • *see Randolph*

Vergennes • *see Middlebury*

Waitsfield • *Mad River Valley C/C* • Susan Klein; Dir.; P.O. Box 173; 05673; Washington; P 4,000; M 240; (802) 496-3409; (800) 828-4748; Fax (802) 496-5420; info@madrivervalley.com; www. madrivervalley.com

Waterbury • *see Barre*

Wells River • *Lower Cohase Reg. C/C* • Mark Nielsen; Exec. Dir.; P.O. Box 35; 05081; Orange; P 9,000; M 210; (802) 757-2549; info@cohase.org; www.cohase.org

West Burke • *see East Burke*

West Windsor • *see Windsor*

Westminster • *see Bellows Falls*

Weston • *see Ludlow*

White River Junction • *Hartford Area C/C* • 100 Railroad Row; 05001; Windsor; P 11,000; M 400; (802) 295-7900; (800) 295-5451; Fax (802) 296-8280; info@hartfordvtchamber.com; www. hartfordvtchamber.com

White River Junction • *Upper Valley Bi-State Reg. C/C* • Geoffrey Ross; Chair; P.O. Box 697; 05001; Windsor; P 10,000; M 250; (802) 295-6200; Fax (802) 295-3779; director@upper valleychamber.com; www.uppervalleychamber.com

Wilmington • *Mt. Snow Valley C/C* • Laura Sibilia; Exec. Dir.; 21 West Main St.; P.O. Box 3; 05363; Windham; P 3,500; M 350; (802) 464-8092; (877) 887-6884; Fax (802) 464-0287; info@ visitvermont.com; www.visitvermont.com

Windsor • *Windsor-Mount Ascutney Region C/C* • Jeannie Surrell; Exec. Dir.; 3 Railroad Ave.; P.O. Box 41; 05089; Windsor; P 15,000; M 156; (802) 674-5910; Fax (802) 674-5910; chamber@ windsorvermont.net; www.windsorvermont.net

Woodstock • *Woodstock Area C/C* • Elizabeth Finlayson; Dir.; 59 Central St.; P.O. Box 486; 05091; Windsor; P 3,232; M 305; (802) 457-3555; (888) 496-6378; Fax (802) 457-1601; info@ woodstockvt.com; www.woodstockvt.com

Virgin Islands

St. Croix • *St. Croix C/C* • Michael Dembeck; Exec. Dir.; 3009 Orange Grove Suite 12; Christiansted; 00820; P 55,000; M 325; (340) 773-1435; Fax (340) 773-8172; info@stxchamber.org; www.stxchamber.org

St. Thomas • *St. Thomas-St. John C/C* • Joe S. Aubain; Exec. Dir.; P.O. Box 324; 00804; P 57,514; M 600; (340) 776-0100; Fax (340) 776-0588; chamber.vi@gmail.com; www.usvichamber.com

Virginia

Virginia C of C • Barry E. DuVal; Pres./CEO; 9 S. Fifth St.; Richmond; 23219; Richmond City; P 7,883,000; M 1,000; (804) 644-1607; Fax (804) 783-6112; b.duval@vachamber.com; www. vachamber.com

Abingdon • *Washington County C/C* • Suzanne Lay; Exec. Dir.; 179 E. Main St.; 24210; Washington; P 53,000; M 560; (276) 628-8141; Fax (276) 628-3984; chamber@eva.org; www.washington vachamber.org.

Alexandria • *Alexandria C/C* • Tina Leone; Pres./CEO; 801 N. Fairfax St., Ste. 402; 22314; Alexandria City; P 132,000; M 850; (703) 549-1000; Fax (703) 739-3805; info@alexchamber.com; www.alexchamber.com

Altavista • *Altavista Area C/C* • Patty Eller; Pres.; 414 Washington St.; P.O. Box 606; 24517; Campbell; P 4,200; M 200; (434) 369-6665; Fax (434) 369-4202; pattyeller@altavista chamber.com; www.altavistachamber.com.

Amherst • *Amherst County C/C* • Pres.; 154 S. Main St.; P.O. Box 560; 24521; Amherst; P 32,000; M 200; (434) 946-0990; Fax (434) 946-0879; information@amherstvachamber.com; www.amherstvachamber.com

Annandale • *also see Vienna–Fairfax County C/C*

Annandale • *Annandale C/C* • Vicki Burman; Exec. Dir.; 7263 Maple Pl., Ste. 207; 22003; Fairfax; P 130,000; M 240; (703) 256-7232; Fax (703) 256-7233; info@annandalechamber.com; www. annandalechamber.com

Appomattox • *Appomattox County C/C* • Spencer Coleman; Pres.; 276 Court St.; P.O. Box 704; 24522; Appomattox; P 15,000; M 165; (434) 352-2621; Fax (434) 352-0294; chamber@appomattox chamber.org; www.appomattoxchamber.org

Arlington • *Arlington C/C* • Richard V. Doud Jr.; Pres.; 2009 N. 14th St., Ste. 111; 22201; Arlington; P 210,000; M 720; (703) 525-2400; Fax (703) 522-5273; chamber@arlingtonchamber.org; www.arlingtonchamber.org.*

Ashland • *Hanover Assn. of Businesses & C/C* • Jennifer Y. Scott; Exec. Dir.; P.O. Box 16; 23005; Hanover; P 100,000; M 400; (804) 798-8130; Fax (804) 798-0014; habcc@habcc.com; www.habcc.com

Augusta County • *see Fishersville*

Baileys Crossroads • *see Vienna–Fairfax County*

Bedford • *Bedford Area C/C* • Susan Martin; Pres.; 305 E. Main St.; 24523; Bedford City; P 66,000; M 630; (540) 586-9401; Fax (540) 587-6650; info@bedfordareachamber.com; www.bedford areachamber.com*

Berryville • *see Winchester*

Blacksburg • *Montgomery County C/C* • Catherine Gambill Sutton CAE; Exec. Dir.; 103 Professional Park Dr.; 24060; Montgomery; P 180,000; M 1,100; (540) 552-2636; (540) 552-2637; Fax (540) 552-2639; chamber@montgomerycc.org; www.montgomerycc.org*

Blackstone • *Blackstone C/C* • Jane Barnes; Exec. Dir.; 121 N. Main St., Ste. A; P.O. Box 295; 23824; Nottoway; P 4,000; M 130; (434) 292-1677; Fax (434) 292-1588; chamber@blackstoneva.com; www.blackstoneva.com*

Blairs • *Danville-Pittsylvania County C/C* • Laurie S. Moran CCE; Pres.; 8653 U.S. Hwy. 29; P.O. Box 99; 24527; Pittsylvania; P 110,000; M 725; (434) 836-6990; Fax (434) 836-6955; chamber@dpchamber.org; www.dpchamber.org*

Bland County • *see Wytheville*

Botetourt County • *see Fincastle*

Bristol • *Bristol C/C* • Lisa Meadows CTTP; Pres./CEO; 20 Volunteer Pkwy.; P.O. Box 519; 24201; Bristol; P 45,000; M 780; (423) 989-4850; (423) 989-4848; Fax (423) 989-4867; frontdesk@bristolchamber.org; www.bristolchamber.org.*

Broadway • *see Timberville*

Brookneal • *Brookneal Area C/C* • Lori Shepherd; P.O. Box 387; 24528; Campbell; P 1,300; M 43; (434) 376-3124; brookneal chamberofcommerce@gmail.com; www.redhillwinefestival.com

Buckingham County • *see Dillwyn*

Burke • *see Vienna–Fairfax County*

Burkeville • *see Crewe*

Callao • *Northumberland County C/C* • Ann Lekander; Exec. Dir.; 129 Northumberland Hwy.; P.O. Box 149; 22435; Northumberland; P 12,500; M 160; (804) 529-5031; Fax (804) 529-5031; northumber landcoc@verizon.net; www.northumberlandcoc.org

Cape Charles • *see Eastville*

Centreville • *see Vienna–Fairfax County*

Chantilly • *Dulles Reg. C/C* • Eileen Curtis; Pres./CEO; 3901 Centerview Dr., Ste. S; 20151; Fairfax; P 50,000; M 930; (571) 323-5300; Fax (703) 787-8859; info@dullesregionalchamber.org; www.dullesregionalchamber.org*

Charlottesville • *Charlottesville Reg. C/C* • Timothy Hulbert; Pres.; Fifth & E. Market St.; P.O. Box 1564; 22902; Charlottesville City; P 120,000; M 1,200; (434) 295-3141; Fax (434) 295-3144; desk@cvillechamber.com; www.cvillechamber.com*

Chase City • *Chase City C/C* • Exec. Dir.; 316 N. Main St.; 23924; Mecklenburg; P 2,460; M 100; (434) 372-0379; Fax (434) 372-4699; chasecityva@verizon.net; www.chasecitychamberofcomm.com

Chatham • *see Blairs*

Cheriton • *see Eastville*

Chesapeake • *see Hampton Roads*

Chesterfield • *Chesterfield County C/C* • Lenita Gilreath; Pres.; 9330 Iron Bridge Rd., Ste. B; 23832; Chesterfield; P 304,000; M 600; (804) 748-6364; Fax (804) 425-5669; admin@chesterfield chamber.com; www.chesterfieldchamber.com*

Chincoteague • *Chincoteague C/C* • Suzanne Taylor; Exec. Dir.; 6733 Maddox Blvd.; P.O. Box 258; 23336; Accomack; P 4,000; M 300; (757) 336-6161; Fax (757) 336-1242; chincochamber@verizon.net; www.chincoteaguechamber.com

Christiansburg • *see Blacksburg*

Clarksville • *Clarksville Lake Country C/C* • Linda Williams; Exec. Dir.; 105 2nd St.; P.O. Box 1017; 23927; Mecklenburg; P 6,000; M 207; (434) 374-2436; Fax (434) 374-8174; clarksville@kerrlake.com; www.clarksvilleva.com

Clifton • *see Vienna–Fairfax County*

Clifton Forge • *see Covington*

Clintwood • *Dickenson County C/C* • Rita Surratt; Pres./CEO; 194 Main St.; P.O. Box 1990; 24228; Dickenson; P 16,400; M 350; (276) 926-6074; chamber@dcwin.org; www.dickensonchamber.net

Colonial Beach • *Colonial Beach C/C* • Carey Geddes; Pres.; 106 Hawthorn St.; P.O. Box 475; 22443; Westmoreland; P 3,300; M 132; (804) 224-8145; Fax (804) 224-8145; info@colonialbeach.org; www.colonialbeach.org

Colonial Heights • *Colonial Heights C/C* • Roger M. Green; Exec. Dir.; 201 Temple Ave., Ste. E; 23834; Colonial Heights City; P 18,000; M 400; (804) 526-5872; Fax (804) 526-9637; chchamber@colonialheights.cc; www.colonial-heights.com/ChamberofCommerce.htm

Covington • *Alleghany Highlands C/C* • Teresa A. Hammond; Exec. Dir.; 241 W. Main St.; 24426; Covington City; P 23,025; M 260; (540) 962-2178; (888) 430-5786; Fax (540) 962-2179; info@ahchamber.com; www.ahchamber.com

Crewe • *Crewe-Burkeville C/C* • Eddie Higgins; Pres.; P.O. Box 305; 23930; Nottoway; P 2,300; M 60; (434) 645-8509; Fax (434) 645-7232; chamber@creweburkeville.org; www.creweburkeville.org

Culpeper • *Culpeper County C/C & Visitor Center* • Jim Charapich; Pres./CEO; 109 S. Commerce St.; 22701; Culpeper; P 46,287; M 600; (540) 825-8628; (888) 285-7373; Fax (540) 825-1449; info@culpepervachamber.com; www.culpepervachamber.com*

Dahlgren • *King George County C/C* • Stan Calizoda; Pres.; P.O. Box 1073; 22448; King George; P 20,000; M 95; kinggeorge chamber@gmail.com; www.kinggeorgechamber.com

Danville • *see Blairs*

Dillwyn • *Buckingham County C/C* • Janet Miller; Pres.; P.O. Box 951; 23936; Buckingham; P 17,000; M 165; (434) 983-2372; info@buckinghamchamber.org; www.buckinghamchamber.org

Dublin • *Pulaski County C/C* • Peggy White; Exec. Dir.; 4440 Cleburne Blvd., Ste. B; 24084; Pulaski; P 35,000; M 500; (540) 674-1991; Fax (540) 674-4163; pcchamber@swva.net; www.pulaskichamber.info*

Eastville • *Northampton County C/C* • Exec. Dir.; 16429A Courthouse Rd.; P.O. Box 475; 23347; Northampton; P 14,000; M 300; (757) 678-0010; chamber@northamptoncountychamber.com; www.northamptoncountychamber.com

Edinburg • *Edinburg Area C/C* • Steve Wood; Pres.; P.O. Box 511; 22824; Shenandoah; P 860; M 30; (540) 984-8318; chamcom@ shentel.net; www.edinburgchamber.com

Emporia • *Emporia-Greensville C/C* • Bill Hodge; Exec. Dir.; Emporia Train Depot; 400 Halifax St.; 23847; Emporia City; P 18,000; M 385; (434) 634-9441; Fax (434) 634-3485; ontrack@ telpage.net; www.emporia-greensvillechamber.com

Exmore • *see Eastville*

Fairfax • *Central Fairfax C/C* • Curt Hoffman; Bd. Member; 11166 Fairfax Blvd., Ste. 407; 22030; Fairfax; P 200,000; M 900; (703) 591-2450; info@cfcc.org; www.cfcc.org

Falls Church • *also see Fairfax County C/C*

Falls Church • *Greater Falls Church C/C* • Sally Cole; Exec. Dir.; 417 W. Broad St., Ste. 205; 22046; Falls Church City; P 10,000; M 250; (703) 532-1050; Fax (703) 237-7904; info@fallschurch chamber.org; www.fallschurchchamber.org*

Farmville • *Farmville Area C/C* • Wanda Whitus; Pres.; 405 D E. Third St.; P.O. Box 361; 23901; Prince Edward; P 17,500; M 240; (434) 392-3939; Fax (434) 392-3818; wwhitus@farmvillearea chamber.org; www.farmvilleareachamber.org

Fincastle • *Botetourt County C/C* • Dan Naff; Exec. Dir.; 13 W. Main St.; P.O. Box 81; 24090; Botetourt; P 32,000; M 350; (540) 473-8280; Fax (540) 473-8365; bccoc@rbnet.com; www.bot-co-chamber.com

Fishersville • *Greater Augusta Reg. C/C* • Pres./CEO; 30 Ladd Rd.; P.O. Box 1107; 22939; Augusta; P 104,000; M 1,104; (540) 324-1133; (540) 949-8203; Fax (540) 324-1136; chamber@ntelos. net; www.augustachamber.org.*

Floyd • *Floyd County C/C* • John McEnhill; Pres.; 201 E. Main St.; 24091; Floyd; P 14,000; M 200; (540) 745-4407; chamber@swva. net; www.visitfloyd.org

Forest • *Bedford Area C/C-Forest Satellite Ofc.* • Susan Martin; Pres.; 14805 Forest Rd., Ste. 107; 24551; Bedford; P 66,000; M 680; (434) 525-7860; Fax (434) 525-7862; chamberinfo@ bedfordareachamber.com; www.bedfordareachamber.com

Franklin • *Franklin-Southampton Area C/C* • Teresa Beale; Exec. Dir.; 108 W. Third Ave.; P.O. Box 531; 23851; Franklin City; P 25,500; M 250; (757) 562-4900; Fax (757) 562-6138; join@ fsachamber.com; www.fsachamber.com*

Franklin County • *see Rocky Mount*

Frederick County • *see Winchester*

Fredericksburg • *Fredericksburg Reg. C/C* • Susan Spears; CEO; 2300 Fall Hill Ave., Ste. 240; P.O. Box 7476; 22404; Fredericksburg City; P 290,600; M 1,100; (540) 373-9400; Fax (540) 373-9570; susan@ fredericksburgchamber.org; www.fredericksburgchamber.org*

Front Royal • *Front Royal-Warren County C/C* • Niki Foster; Pres.; 104 E. Main St.; 22630; Warren; P 34,000; M 605; (540) 635-3185; Fax (540) 635-9758; info@frontroyalchamber.com; www. frontroyalchamber.com*

Gainesville • *see Manassas*

Galax • *Twin County Reg. C/C* • Judy Brannock; Exec. Dir.; 405 N. Main St.; 24333; Galax City; P 53,900; M 320; (276) 236-2184; Fax (276) 236-1338; info@twincountychamber.com; www. twincountychamber.com.*

Gate City • *Scott County C/C* • Penny Horton; Exec. Secy.; 180 W. Jackson St.; P.O. Box 609; 24251; Scott; P 23,403; M 110; (276) 386-6665; Fax (276) 386-6158; chamber@scottcountyva.com; www.scottcountyva.org

Giles County • *Giles County C/C* • Barbara M. Stafford; Exec. Dir.; 101 S. Main St.; Pearisburg; 24134; Giles; P 17,000; M 150; (540) 921-5000; Fax (540) 921-3892; gcc@i-plus.net; www.gilescounty.org

Gloucester • *Gloucester County C/C* • Makalia Records; Exec. Dir.; 3558 George Washington Memorial Hwy.; 6699 Fox Centre Pkwy., Ste. 609; 23061; Gloucester; P 35,000; M 300; (804) 693-2425; Fax (804) 693-7193; chamberexec@glocochamber.org; www.gloucestervachamber.org*

Goochland • *Goochland County C/C* • Bonnie Creasy; Exec. Dir.; 2941 River Rd. W.; P.O. Box 123; 23063; Goochland; P 18,500; M 300; (804) 556-3811; Fax (804) 556-2131; director@goochland chamber.org; www.goochlandchamber.org*

Gretna • *see Blairs*

Grundy • *Buchanan County C/C* • Mary M. Belcher; Exec. Dir.; 20786A Riverside Dr.; P.O. Box 2818; 24614; Buchanan; P 27,000; M 129; (276) 935-4147; bcchamber1@verizon.net

Hampton • *Virginia Peninsula C/C* • Mike Kuhns; Pres./CEO; 21 Enterprise Pkwy., Ste. 100; 23666; Hampton City; P 529,680; M 1,000; (757) 262-2000; (800) 556-1822; Fax (757) 262-2009; info@vpcc.org; www.vpcc.org*

Hampton Roads • *Hampton Roads C/C-Headquarters* • John A. Hornbeck Jr. CCE; Pres./CEO; 500 E. Main St., Ste. 700; P.O. Box 327, Norfolk; 23501; Norfolk City; P 1,316,300; M 2,500; (757) 622-2312; Fax (757) 622-5563; info@hrccva.com; www.hampton roadschamber.com.*

Harrisonburg • *Harrisonburg-Rockingham C/C* • Frank M. Tamberrino; Pres.; 800 Country Club Rd.; 22802; Harrisonburg City; P 120,500; M 800; (540) 434-3862; Fax (540) 434-4508; information@hrchamber.org; www.hrchamber.org*

Herndon • *see Chantilly*

Hillsville • *Carroll County-Hillsville C/C* • P.O. Box 1184; 24343; Carroll; P 29,000; M 100; (276) 728-5397; Fax (276) 728-7825; info@carrollvachamber.com; www.carrollvachamber.com

Hopewell • *Hopewell-Prince George C/C* • Becky McDonough; Exec. V.P.; 210 N. 2nd Ave.; P.O. Box 1297; 23860; Hopewell City; P 100,000; M 400; (804) 458-5536; (804) 458-9498; Fax (804) 458-0041; admin@hpgchamber.org; www.hpgchamber.org*

Hot Springs • *Bath County C/C* • Melinda Nichols; Exec. Dir.; 2696 Main St., Ste. 6; P.O. Box 718; 24445; Bath; P 4,800; M 186; (540) 839-5409; (800) 628-8092; Fax (540) 839-5409; info@ discoverbath.com; www.discoverbath.com

Huntington • *see Vienna–Fairfax County*

Hurt • *see Blairs*

Irvington • *Irvington Improvement Assn. & C/C* • Larry Worth; Pres.; P.O. Box 282; 22480; Lancaster; P 600; M 75; (804) 438-9371; lworth878@verizon.net; www.townofirvington.com

Isle of Wight • *see Smithfield*

James City County • *see Williamsburg and Hampton*

Kenbridge • *see Lunenburg*

Kilmarnock • *Lancaster by the Bay C/C* • Edie Jett; Exec. Dir.; 506 N. Main St.; P.O. Box 1868; 22482; Lancaster & Northumberland; P 12,000; M 300; (804) 435-6092; Fax (804) 435-3092; info@lancasterva.com; www.lancasterva.com*

Ladysmith • *Caroline County C/C* • Betty Frizzell; Exec. Dir.; 18067 Jefferson Davis Hwy.; P.O. Box 250; 22501; Caroline; P 28,000; M 200; (804) 448-5264; Fax (804) 448-0844; chamber@ bealenet.com; www.carolinechamber.com

Lawrenceville • *Brunswick C/C* • Wendy Wright; Exec. Dir.; 400 N. Main St.; 23868; Brunswick; P 18,000; M 103; (434) 848-3154; Fax (434) 848-9356; brunschamber@lawrencevilleweb.com; www.brunswickchamber.com

Lebanon • *Russell County C/C & Tourism* • Linda Tate; Exec. Dir.; 131 Highland Dr.; P.O. Box 926; 24266; Russell; P 30,000; M 200; (276) 889-8041; Fax (276) 889-8002; lindatate@bvunet.net; www.russellcountyva.org

Leesburg • *Loudoun County C/C* • Tony Howard; Pres.; P.O. Box 1298; 20177; Loudoun; P 275,000; M 1,200; (703) 777-2176; Fax (703) 777-1392; info@loudounchamber.org; www.loudounchamber.org*

Lexington • *The C/C serving Lexington, Buena Vista & Rockbridge County* • James Samuel Moore; Dir.; 100 E. Washington St.; 24450; Lexington City; P 35,000; M 550; (540) 463-5375; Fax (540) 463-3567; chamber@lexrockchamber.com; www.lexrockchamber.com

Loudoun County • *see Leesburg*

Louisa • *Louisa County C/C* • Deana Meredith; Exec. Dir.; 214 Fredericksburg Ave.; P.O. Box 955; 23093; Louisa; P 29,500; M 160; (540) 967-0944; info@louisachamber.org; www.louisachamber.org

Lunenburg • *Lunenburg County C/C* • General Delivery; 23952; Lunenburg; P 13,194; M 100; (434) 696-2282; info@lunenburgva.org; www.lunenburgva.org*

Luray • *Luray-Page County C/C* • 18 Campbell St.; 22835; Page; P 20,000; M 450; (540) 743-3915; (888) 743-3915; Fax (540) 743-3944; info@luraypage.com; www.luraypage.com*

Lynchburg • *Lynchburg Reg. C/C* • Rex Hammond; Pres.; 2015 Memorial Ave.; 24501; Lynchburg City; P 242,000; M 900; (434) 845-5966; Fax (434) 522-9592; info@lynchburgchamber.org; www.lynchburgchamber.org.*

Madison • *Madison C/C & Visitor Center* • Tracey Gardner; Exec. Dir.; 110A N. Main; P.O. Box 373; 22727; Madison; P 13,000; M 210; (540) 948-4455; Fax (540) 948-3174; chamber@madison-va.com; www.madison-va.com

Manassas • *Prince William C/C* • Robert H. Clapper II; Pres./CEO; 9720 Capitol Ct., Stes. 203-204; 20110; Manassas City; P 400,000; M 1,800; (703) 368-6600; Fax (703) 368-4733; rclapper@pwchamber.org; www.pwchamber.org*

Marion • *C/C of Smyth County* • Kristin Untiedt-Barnett; Exec. Dir.; 214 W. Main St.; P.O. Box 924; 24354; Smyth; P 33,081; M 400; (276) 783-3161; Fax (276) 783-8003; info@smythchamber.org; www.smythchamber.org

Martinsville • *Martinsville-Henry County C/C* • Amanda Witt; Pres.; 115 Broad St.; P.O. Box 709; 24114; Martinsville City; P 72,000; M 638; (276) 632-6401; (866) 632-3378; Fax (276) 632-5059; mhccoc@mhcchamber.com; www.martinsville.com.*

Massaponax • *see Eastville*

Mathews • *Mathews County C/C* • Brenda Moore; V.P.; P.O. Box 1126; 23109; Mathews; P 9,100; M 107; (804) 725-9000; postmaster@mathewschamber.org; www.mathewschamber.org

McLean • *Greater McLean C/C* • Marcia Twomey; Pres.; 1437 Balls Hill Rd.; 22101; Fairfax; P 66,000; M 400; (703) 356-5424; Fax (703) 356-9244; info@mcleanchamber.org; www.mcleanchamber.org

Melfa • *Eastern Shore of Virginia C/C* • Jeff Davis; Pres.; 19056 Parkway; P.O. Box 460; 23410; Accomack; P 53,000; M 550; (757) 787-2460; Fax (757) 787-8687; info@esvachamber.org; www.esvachamber.org

Merrifield • *see Vienna–Fairfax County*

Moneta • *Smith Mountain Lake Reg. C/C* • Vicki Gardner; Exec. Dir.; 16430 Booker T. Washington Hwy., Ste. 2; 24121; Bedford; P 25,000; M 800; (540) 721-1203; (800) 676-8203; Fax (540) 721-7796; vgardner@visitsmithmountainlake.com; www.visitsmithmountainlake.com*

Monterey • *Highland County C/C* • Tim O'Roark; Exec. Dir.; 61 Highland Center Dr., Ste. 1; P.O. Box 223; 24465; Highland; P 2,635; M 196; (540) 468-2550; Fax (540) 468-2551; info@highlandcounty.org; www.highlandcounty.org

Mount Jackson • *Mount Jackson Area C/C* • Lora Loving; Pres.; P.O. Box 111; 22842; Shenandoah; P 1,800; M 69; (540) 477-3275; mjcc@shentel.net; www.mountjacksonva.org

Mount Vernon-Lee • *Mount Vernon-Lee C/C* • Holly Hicks Dougherty; Exec. Dir.; 6911 Richmond Hwy., Ste. 320; Alexandria; 22306; Fairfax; P 250,000; M 400; (703) 360-6925; Fax (703) 360-6928; info@MtVernon-LeeChamber.org; www.MtVernon-LeeChamber.org*

New Kent • *New Kent C/C* • William Story; Pres.; 7324 Vineyard Pkwy.; 23124; New Kent; P 15,000; M 120; (804) 966-8581; president@newkentchamber.org; www.newkentchamber.org

New Market • *New Market Area C/C* • Lisa Hirsh; 100 W. Lee St.; P.O. Box 57; 22844; Shenandoah; P 1,800; M 106; (540) 740-3212; (877) 740-3212; Fax (540) 740-4234; nmchambr@shentel.net; www.newmarketcoc.net

Newington • *see Vienna–Fairfax County*

Newport News • *see Hampton*

Norfolk • *see Hampton Roads*

Norton • *Wise County/City of Norton C/C* • Joyce M. Payne; Exec. V.P.; 765 Park Ave.; P.O. Box 226; 24273; Norton City; P 44,000; M 540; (276) 679-0961; Fax (276) 679-2655; wisecountycoc@verizon.net; www.wisecountychamber.org*

Oakton • *see Vienna*

Orange • *Orange County C/C* • Barbara Bannar; Exec. Dir.; 103 N. Madison Rd.; P.O. Box 146; 22960; Orange; P 36,000; M 285; (540) 672-5216; Fax (540) 672-2304; barbara@orangevachamber.com; www.orangevachamber.com.

Palmyra • *Fluvanna County C/C* • Cheryl Martino; Pres.; 177 Main St.; P.O. Box 93; 22963; Fluvanna; P 30,000; M 180; (434) 589-3262; Fax (434) 589-6212; fluvannacountycoc@embarqmail.com; www.fluvannachamber.org*

Pennington Gap • *Lee County Area C/C* • Rita McCann; Pres.; P.O. Box 417; 24277; Lee; P 25,000; M 100; (276) 546-2233; director@leecountyvachamber.org; www.leecountyvachamber.org

Petersburg • *Petersburg C/C* • Cynthia Raitt Devereaux; Pres./CEO; 325 E. Washington St.; P.O. Box 928; 23804; Petersburg City; P 33,000; M 500; (804) 733-8131; Fax (804) 733-9891; info@petersburgvachamber.com; www.petersburgvachamber.com*

Poquoson • *see Hampton*

Portsmouth • *see Hampton Roads*

Powhatan • *Powhatan C/C* • Tina Bustos; Exec. Dir.; 3887 Old Buckingham Rd.; 23139; Powhatan; P 28,000; M 240; (804) 598-2636; Fax (804) 598-0023; info@powhatanchamber.org; www.powhatanchamber.org*

Prince William • *see Manassas*

Pulaski • *see Dublin*

Radford • *Radford C/C* • 200 3rd Ave., Ste. C; 24141; Radford City; P 16,000; M 300; (540) 639-2202; Fax (540) 639-2228; info@radfordchamber.com; www.radfordchamber.com

Reston • *also see Vienna–Fairfax County C/C*

Reston • *Greater Reston C/C, Bus. & Visitors Center* • 1763 Fountain Dr.; 20190; Fairfax; P 67,910; M 1,000; (703) 707-9045; Fax (703) 707-9049; restonbiz@restonchamber.org; www.restonchamber.org*

Richlands • *Richlands Area/Tazewell County C/C* • Ginger H. Branton; Exec. Dir.; 1413 Front St.; 24641; Tazewell; P 20,000; M 300; (276) 963-3385; Fax (276) 963-4278; richlandschamber@roadrunner.com; richlandschamber.com*

Richmond • *Greater Richmond C/C* • Kim Scheeler; Pres./CEO; 600 E. Main St., Ste. 700; P.O. Box 1598; 23218; Richmond City; P 1,000,000; M 2,000; (804) 648-1234; Fax (804) 783-9366; denise.feys@grcc.com; www.grcc.com*

Roanoke • *Roanoke Reg. C/C* • Joyce Waugh; Pres.; 210 S. Jefferson St.; 24011; Roanoke City; P 298,108; M 1,200; (540) 983-0700; Fax (540) 983-0723; business@roanokechamber.org; www.roanokechamber.org.*

Rocky Mount • *Franklin County C/C* • Janie Hopkins; Exec. Dir.; 52 Franklin St.; P.O. Box 158; 24151; Franklin; P 52,841; M 350; (540) 483-9542; Fax (540) 483-0653; info@franklincounty.org; www.franklincounty.org*

Salem • *Salem-Roanoke County C/C* • Debbie Kavitz; Exec. Dir.; 611 E. Main St.; P.O. Box 832; 24153; Salem; P 110,773; M 500; (540) 387-0267; Fax (540) 387-4110; chamber@s-rcchamber.org; www.s-rcchamber.org*

Scottsville • *Scottsville Comm. C/C* • Brian LaFontaine; Pres.; P.O. Box 11; 24590; Albemarle; P 560; M 110; (434) 286-6000; Fax (434) 286-9102; sccc@bnsi.net; www.scottsvilleva.com

Seven Corners • *see Vienna–Fairfax County*

Smithfield • *Isle of Wight-Smithfield-Windsor C/C* • Constance Rhodes; Pres.; 100 Main St.; P.O. Box 38; 23431; Isle of Wight; P 35,000; M 450; (757) 357-3502; (888) 284-3475; Fax (757) 357-6884; chamber@theisle.org; www.theisle.org

South Boston • *Halifax County C/C* • Nancy Pool; Pres.; 515 Broad St.; P.O. Box 399; 24592; Halifax; P 37,500; M 415; (434) 572-3085; Fax (434) 572-1733; info@halifaxchamber.net; www.halifaxchamber.net

South Hill • *South Hill C/C* • Frank Malone; Exec. Dir.; 201 S. Mecklenburg Ave.; 23970; Chesapeake; P 5,000; M 300; (434) 447-4547; Fax (434) 447-4461; frank@southhillchamber.com; www.southhillchamber.com

Spotsylvania • *see Fredericksburg*

Springfield • *Greater Springfield C/C* • Nancy-jo Manney; Exec. Dir.; 6434 Brandon Ave., Ste. 3A; 22150; Fairfax; P 90,000; M 300; (703) 866-3500; Fax (703) 866-3501; admin@springfieldchamber.org; www.springfieldchamber.org*

Stafford • *see Fredericksburg*

Staunton • *see Fishersville*

Strasburg • *Strasburg C/C* • Jackie C. Thompson; Admin. Asst.; 157 N. Holliday St.; P.O. Box 42; 22657; Shenandoah; P 6,000; M 150; (540) 465-3187; Fax (540) 465-2812; schamber@shentel.net; www.strasburgvachamber.com

Stuart • *Patrick County C/C* • Tom Bishop; Exec. Dir.; 20475 Jeb Stuart Hwy.; P.O. Box 577; 24171; Patrick; P 19,407; M 300; (276) 694-6012; Fax (276) 694-3582; patcchamber@embarqmail.com; www.patrickchamber.com

Suffolk • *see Hampton Roads*

Surry • *Surry County C/C* • Jason Wiedel; Pres.; 57 Colonial Trl. E.; P.O. Box 353; 23883; Surry; P 7,128; M 47; (757) 294-0066; mail@surrychamber.org; www.surrychamber.org

Sussex • *Sussex County C/C* • P.O. Box 1371; 23884; Sussex; P 10,000; M 40; (434) 246-4503; Fax (434) 246-4503; info@sussexvachamber.org; www.sussexvachamber.org

Tappahannock • *Tappahannock-Essex County C/C* • Ronnie Gill; Exec. Secy.; P.O. Box 481; 22560; Essex; P 10,000; M 200; (804) 443-5241; Fax (804) 443-4157; www.essex-virginia.org

Tazewell • *Tazewell Area C/C* • Rebecca Duncan; Dir.; Tazewell Mall; Box 6; 24651; Tazewell; P 47,070; M 250; (276) 988-5091; Fax (276) 988-5093; info@tazewellchamber.org; www.tazewellchamber.com

Timberville • *Broadway-Timberville C/C* • Crystal Collins; Secy.; 233 McCauley Dr.; 22853; Rockingham; P 4,000; M 100; (540) 896-7413; Fax (540) 896-2825; secretary@btchamber.org; www.btchamber.org

Tysons Corner • *see Vienna*

Victoria • *see Lunenburg*

Vienna • *Fairfax County C/C* • Jim Corcoran; Pres./CEO; 8230 Old Courthouse Rd., Ste. 350; 22182; Fairfax; P 1,041,200; M 1,800; (703) 749-0400; Fax (703) 749-9075; cthoren@fairfaxchamber.org; fairfaxchamber.org

Vienna • *ViennaTysons Reg. C/C* • Diane Poldy; Pres.; 513 Maple Ave. W., 2nd Flr.; 22180; Fairfax; P 1,000,000; M 446; (703) 281-1333; Fax (703) 242-1482; info@vtrcc.org; www.vtrcc.org*

Vinton • *Vinton Area C/C* • Angie Chewning Lewis; Exec. Dir.; 116 S. Poplar St., Ste. 1A; 24179; Roanoke; P 8,000; M 208; (540) 343-1364; info@vintonchamber.com; www.vintonchamber.com

Virginia Beach • *see Hampton Roads*

Warren County • *see Front Royal*

Warrenton • *Fauquier County C/C* • Karen Henderson; Pres.; 205-1 Keith St.; P.O. Box 127; 20188; Fauquier; P 57,000; M 500; (540) 347-4414; Fax (540) 347-7510; mailbox@fauquierchamber.org; www.fauquierchamber.org.*

Warsaw • *Warsaw-Richmond County C/C* • Adriane Rouse; Secy.; P.O. Box 1141; 22572; Richmond; P 8,000; M 80; (804) 313-2252; warsawrcchamber@gmail.com; www.warsaw-rcchamber.com

Waynesboro • *see Fishersville*

West Point • *West Point/Tri-Rivers C/C* • Sandra Willis; Pres.; 621 Main St.; P.O. Box 1035; 23181; King William; P 3,000; M 60; (804) 843-4620; Fax (804) 843-2434; wptrcc@oasisonline.com; www.westpointvachamber.com

Williamsburg • *Greater Williamsburg C/C & Tourism Alliance* • Richard Schreiber; Pres./CEO; 421 N. Boundary St.; P.O. Box 3495; 23187; Williamsburg City; P 200,000; M 967; (757) 229-6511; (800) 368-6511; Fax (757) 229-2047; wacc@williamsburgcc.com; www.williamsburgcc.com*

Winchester • *Top of Virginia Reg. Chamber* • Randy Collins IOM; Pres./CEO; 407 S. Loudoun St.; 22601; Winchester City; P 142,462; M 900; (540) 662-4118; Fax (540) 722-6365; cocinfo@regionalchamber.biz; www.regionalchamber.biz*

Windsor • *see Smithfield*

Wise County • *see Norton*

Woodbridge • *see Manassas*

Woodstock • *Woodstock C/C* • Jean Ellis-Copp; Exec. Secy.; 103 S. Main St.; P.O. Box 605; 22664; Shenandoah; P 5,000; M 196; (540) 459-2542; Fax (540) 459-2513; www.woodstockvachamber.com

Wythe County • *see Wytheville*

Wytheville · *Wytheville-Wythe-Bland C/C* · Jennifer W. Atwell; Exec. Dir.; 150 E. Monroe St.; P.O. Box 563; 24382; Wythe; P 31,000; M 400; (276) 223-3365; Fax (276) 223-3412; chamber@wytheville.org; www.wwbchamber.com

York County · *see Hampton and Williamsburg*

Yorktown · *York County C/C* · Chuck Jarrett; Pres.; P.O. Box 1103; 23692; York; P 40,000; M 180; (757) 877-5920; ycccadmin@yorkcountycc.org; www.yorkcountycc.org

Washington

Assn. of Washington Business · Don Brunell; Pres.; 1414 Cherry St. S.E.; P.O. Box 658; Olympia; 98507; Thurston; P 6,600,000; M 7,100; (360) 943-1600; (800) 521-9325; Fax (360) 943-5811; members@awb.org; www.awb.org

Washington C of C Execs. · Robert Green; Pres./CEO; P.O. Box 1349; Enumclaw; 98022; King; M 125; (360) 802-4595; Fax (877) 381-8834; information@wcce.org; www.wcce.org

Aberdeen · *Grays Harbor C/C* · LeRoy Tipton; Pres.; 506 Duffy St.; 98520; Grays Harbor; P 68,400; M 500; (360) 532-1924; (800) 321-1924; Fax (360) 533-7945; info@graysharbor.org; www.graysharbor.org.*

Airway Heights · *see Spokane–West Plains C/C*

Allyn · *see Belfair*

Amboy · *see La Center*

Anacortes · *Anacortes C/C* · Mitch Everton; Exec. Dir.; 819 Commercial Ave., Ste. F; 98221; Skagit; P 16,000; M 470; (360) 293-7911; (360) 293-3832; Fax (360) 293-1595; info@anacortes.org; www.anacortes.org*

Arlington · *Arlington-Smokey Point C/C* · Michael Prihoda; Exec. Dir.; 3710–168th St. N.E., Ste. C101; 98223; Snohomish; P 17,000; M 200; (360) 659-5453; Fax (360) 657-1002; excutive@arlington-smokeypointchamber.com; www.arlington-smokeypointchamber.com*

Asotin · *Asotin C/C* · Wes Vaughn; Pres.; P.O. Box 574; 99402; Asotin; P 1,200; M 20; (509) 243-4242; Fax (509) 243-4243; asotin@cableone.net; www.cityofasotin.org

Auburn · *Auburn Area C/C* · Nancy E. Wyatt; Pres./CEO; 108 S. Division, Ste. B; 98001; King; P 67,000; M 575; (253) 833-0700; Fax (253) 735-4091; auburncc@auburnareawa.org; www.auburnareawa.org.*

Bainbridge Island · *Bainbridge Island C/C* · Kevin Dwyer; Exec. Dir.; 395 Winslow Way E.; 98110; Kitsap; P 23,000; M 1,000; (206) 842-3700; Fax (206) 842-3713; info@bainbridgechamber.com; www.bainbridgechamber.com

Ballard · *see Seattle–Ballard C/C*

Battle Ground · *Battle Ground C/C* · Julie Bocanegra; Chair; 1419 W. Main St., Ste. 110; 98604; Clark; P 16,000; M 374; (360) 687-1510; Fax (360) 687-4505; info@battlegroundchamber.org; www.battlegroundchamber.org*

Belfair · *North Mason C/C* · Mark W. Costa; Pres./CEO; 23910 N.E. State Rte. 3; P.O. Box 416; 98528; Mason; P 22,000; M 450; (360) 275-6258; Fax (360) 275-0853; communications@northmasonchamber.com; www.northmasonchamber.com

Bellevue · *Bellevue C/C* · Betty Nokes; Pres./CEO; 302 Bellevue Sq.; 98004; King; P 120,000; M 1,100; (425) 454-2464; Fax (425) 462-4660; staffteam@bellevuechamber.org; www.bellevuechamber.org*

Bellingham · *Bellingham/Whatcom C/C & Ind.* · Ken Oplinger; Pres./CEO; 119 N. Commercial Street, Ste. 110; P.O. Box 958; 98227; Whatcom; P 140,000; M 700; (360) 734-1330; Fax (360) 734-1332; chamber@bellingham.com; www.bellingham.com.*

Benton City · *Benton City C/C* · Rom Castilleja; Pres.; P.O. Box 401; 99320; Benton; P 2,800; M 60; (509) 588-4984; info@bentoncitychamber.org; www.bentoncitychamber.org

Bingen · *see White Salmon*

Blaine · *Birch Bay C/C & Visitors Info. Center* · 7900 Birch Bay Dr.; 98230; Whatcom; P 6,800; M 90; (360) 371-5004; Fax (360) 371-5004; info@birchbaychamber.com; www.birchbaychamber.com

Blaine · *Blaine C/C* · Carroll Solomon; Exec. Dir.; 728 Peace Portal Dr.; 98230; Whatcom; P 4,800; M 70; (360) 332-6484; (360) 332-4544; info@blainechamber.com; www.blainechamber.com

Bonney Lake · *Bonney Lake C/C* · Lora Butterfield; Exec. Dir.; P.O. Box 7171; 98391; Pierce; P 16,200; M 125; (253) 222-5945; lora@bonneylake.com; www.bonneylake.com*

Bothell · *Greater Bothell C/C* · Lori Cadwell; Exec. Dir.; P.O. Box 1203; 98041; King & Snohomish; P 30,000; M 275; (425) 485-4353; Fax (425) 368-0396; info@bothellchamber.com; www.bothellchamber.com*

Bremerton · *Bremerton Area C/C* · Frank Gentile; Op. Mgr.; 286 Fourth St.; 98337; Kitsap; P 250,000; M 400; (360) 479-3580; (360) 479-3579; Fax (360) 479-1033; chamber@bremertonchamber.org; www.bremertonchamber.org*

Brewster · *Brewster C/C* · Coleen Couch; Pres.; P.O. Box 1087; 98812; Okanogan; P 2,195; M 66; (509) 689-3464; info@brewsterchamber.org; www.brewsterchamber.org

Bridgeport · *Bridgeport Area C/C* · David Lorz; Pres.; P.O. Box 395; 98813; Douglas; P 2,150; M 25; (509) 449-5089; Fax (509) 686-3901; www.bridgeportchamber.net

Brier · *see Lynnwood*

Brinnon · *see Quilcene*

Buckley · *Buckley C/C* · Ron Callis; Pres.; 769 Main St.; P.O. Box 168; 98321; Pierce; P 4,000; M 60; (360) 829-0975; Fax (360) 829-9201; information@buckleychamber.org; www.buckleychamber.org

Burien · *see Seattle–Southwest King County C/C*

Burlington · *Burlington C/C* · Linda Fergusson; Pres.; 111 S. Cherry St.; P.O. Box 1087; 98233; Skagit; P 8,421; M 380; (360) 757-0994; Fax (360) 757-0821; info@burlington-chamber.com; www.burlington-chamber.com*

Camano Island · *Camano Island C/C* · Karen Daum; Dir. of Tourism & Op.; 370 N. East Camano Dr., Ste. 5-80; 98282; Island; P 18,000; M 130; (360) 629-7136; Fax (360) 629-7136; chamber@camanoisland.org; www.camanoisland.org

Camas · *Camas-Washougal C/C* · Brent Erickson; Exec. Dir.; 422 N.E. 4th Ave.; P.O. Box 919; 98607; Clark; P 37,000; M 260; (360) 834-2472; info@cwchamber.com; www.cwchamber.com.*

Carnation · *Carnation C/C* · Collienne Becker; P.O. Box 603; 98014; King; P 1,900; M 50; (425) 333-5556; (425) 333-5556; info@carnationchamber.com; www.carnationchamber.com

Cashmere · *Cashmere C/C* · Jill FitzSimmons; Mgr.; 101 Cottage Ave.; P.O. Box 834; 98815; Chelan; P 2,900; M 125; (509) 782-7404; Fax (509) 782-1265; info@cashmerechamber.com; www.cashmerechamber.com

Cathlamet · *Wahkiakum C/C* · Lynda Gerlach; Chamber Coord.; 102 Main St., Ste. 205; P.O. Box 52; 98612; Wahkiakum; P 4,000; M 180; (360) 795-9996; Fax (360) 795-3944; wchamber@cni.net; www.wahkiakumchamber.com

Centralia • *see Chehalis*

Chehalis • *Centralia-Chehalis C/C* • Jim Valley; Exec. Dir.; 500 N.W. Chamber of Commerce Way; 98532; Lewis; P 72,500; M 575; (360) 748-8885; Fax (360) 748-8763; thechamber@chamberway. com; www.chamberway.com*

Chelan • *Lake Chelan C/C* • Mike Steele; Exec. Dir.; 102 E. Johnson Ave.; P.O. Box 216; 98816; Chelan; P 10,000; M 500; (509) 682-3503; (800) 4-CHELAN; Fax (509) 682-3538; info@lakechelan. com; www.lakechelan.com

Chewelah • *Chewelah C/C* • Jeanne Nixon; Mgr.; 214 E. Main St.; P.O. Box 94; 99109; Stevens; P 2,500; M 120; (509) 935-8595; Fax (509) 935-8520; info@chewelah.org; www.chewelah.org*

Chimacum • *see Port Townsend*

Clallam Bay • *Clallam Bay-Sekiu C/C & Visitor Center* • Patti Adler; Pres.; 16753 Hwy. 112; P.O. Box 355; 98326; Clallam; P 1,000; M 70; (360) 963-2339; (877) 694-9433; chamber@ clallambay.com; www.clallambay.com

Clarkston • *Lewis Clark Valley C/C* • Kristin Kemak; Pres./CEO; 502 Bridge St.; 99403; Asotin; P 60,000; M 900; (509) 758-7712; (800) 933-2128; Fax (509) 751-8767; *

Cle Elum • *Cle Elum–Roslyn C/C* • Judy Tokarsyck; Exec. Dir.; 401 W. 1st; P.O. Box 43; 98922; Kittitas; P 3,200; M 157; (509) 674-5958; Fax (509) 674-1674; cle_elum@cleelum.com; www. cleelumroslyn.org

Colfax • *Colfax C/C* • Judy Liddle; Secy.; 109 E. Wall; 99111; Whitman; P 3,000; M 134; (509) 397-3712; Fax (509) 397-4458; colfaxchamber@gmail.com; www.visitcolfax.com

Colville • *Colville C/C* • Debbie Garringer; Mgr.; 121 E. Astor; 99114; Stevens; P 5,000; M 250; (509) 684-5973; Fax (509) 684-1344; colvillecoc@colville.com; www.colville.com

Conconully • *Town of Conconully C/C* • Tom Gibson; Pres.; P.O. Box 309; 98819; Okanogan; P 210; M 58; (509) 826-9050; (877) 826-9050; conconullychamber@yahoo.com; www.conconully.com

Concrete • *Concrete C/C* • Valerie Stafford; Pres.; 45770 Main St.; P.O. Box 743; 98237; Skagit; P 4,500; M 45; (360) 853-8767; chamber@concrete-wa.com; www.concrete-wa.com

Connell • *Greater Connell Area C/C* • Monica Pruett; Admin.; 600 S. Columbia; P.O. Box 401; 99326; Franklin; P 3,100; M 70; (509) 234-8731; Fax (509) 234-8722; www.cityofconnell.com

Cosmopolis • *see Aberdeen*

Coulee City • *Coulee City C/C* • Terri Zapone; Secy./Treas.; P.O. Box 896; 99115; Grant; P 550; M 50; (509) 632-5331; (509) 632-5043; www.couleecity.com

Coupeville • *Central Whidbey C/C & Visitors Info. Center* • Lynda Eccles; Exec. Dir.; 23 N.W. Front St., Ste. 8A; P.O. Box 152; 98239; Island; P 2,000; M 198; (360) 678-5434; (360) 678-5664; Fax (360) 678-5564; director@centralwhidbeychamber.com; www.centralwhidbeychamber.com

Crescent Bar • *see Quincy*

Dallesport • *see White Salmon*

Davenport • *Davenport C/C* • Danita Hammond; Pres.; P.O. Box 869; 99122; Lincoln; P 1,780; M 90; (509) 725-6711; (509) 721-1459; danita_hammond@davenportwa.org; www.davenport wa.org

Dayton • *Dayton C of C & Visitor Center* • Lisa Ronnberg; Exec. Dir.; 166 E. Main; 99328; Columbia; P 4,100; M 196; (509) 382-4825; (800) 882-6299; Fax (509) 382-1969; chamber@ historicdayton.com; www.historicdayton.com

Deer Park • *Deer Park C/C* • Rose Whapeles; Ofc. Mgr.; 316 E. Crawford, Upper Level; 99006; Spokane; P 3,150; M 140; (509) 276-5900; Fax (509) 276-5900; info@deerparkchamber.com; www.deerparkchamber.com

Dungeness Valley • *see Sequim*

Duvall • *Duvall C/C* • Aaron Keating; Pres.; 15321 Main St. N.E., Ste. 320B; P.O. Box 581; 98019; King; P 5,600; M 180; (425) 788-9182; (425) 788-8384; info@duvallchamberofcommerce.com; www.duvallchamberofcommerce.com

East Wenatchee • *see Wenatchee*

Eastsound • *Orcas Island C/C* • Lance Evans; Exec. Dir.; 65 N. Beach Rd.; P.O. Box 252; 98245; San Juan; P 5,000; M 315; (360) 376-2273; Fax (360) 376-8889; info@orcasislandchamber.com; www.orcasislandchamber.com

Eatonville • *Greater Eatonville C/C* • Dawn Newkirk; Pres.; P.O. Box 845; 98328; Pierce; P 2,100; M 97; (360) 832-4000; eatonville. wa.chamber@gmail.com; www.eatonvillechamber.com

Edmonds • *Greater Edmonds C/C* • Jan Vance; Exec. Dir.; 121 5th Ave. N.; P.O. Box 146; 98020; Snohomish; P 40,000; M 420; (425) 670-1496; Fax (425) 712-1808; admin@edmondswa.com; www. edmondswa.com

Ellensburg • *Kittitas County C/C & EDC* • Bob Hansen; Interim Exec. Dir.; 609 N. Main St.; 98926; Kittitas; P 18,000; M 500; (509) 925-2002; (888) 925-2204; Fax (509) 962-6148; info@ellensburg-chamber.com; www.ellensburg-chamber.com.*

Elma • *Elma C/C* • Suzi Haley; Pres.; P.O. Box 798; 98541; Grays Harbor; P 3,400; M 100; (360) 482-3055; info@elmachamber.org; www.elmachamber.org

Enumclaw • *Enumclaw Area C/C* • Tracey McCallum; Exec. Dir.; 1421 Cole St.; 98022; King; P 11,400; M 250; (360) 825-7666; Fax (360) 825-8369; info@enumclawchamber.com; www.enumclaw chamber.com.*

Ephrata • *Ephrata C/C* • Tia Tracy; Dir.; 1 Basin St. S.W.; P.O. Box 275; 98823; Grant; P 7,101; M 200; (509) 754-4656; Fax (509) 754-5788; info@ephratawachamber.com; www.ephratawa chamber.com

Everett • *Everett Area C/C* • Louise Stanton-Masten; Pres./CEO; 2000 Hewitt Ave., Ste. 205; 98201; Snohomish; P 101,000; M 600; (425) 257-3222; Fax (425) 257-2074; info@everettchamber.com; www.everettchamber.com*

Everson • *Everson Nooksack C/C* • Richard May; Pres.; 103 W. Main St.; P.O. Box 234; 98247; Whatcom; P 3,000; M 90; (360) 966-3407; info@eversonnooksackchamber.org; www.everson nooksackchamber.org

Fairfield • *Hangman Creek C/C* • Ken Fuchs; Pres.; P.O. Box 345; 99012; Spokane; P 1,719; M 43; (509) 892-4412; vplank@banner bank.com; www.hangmancreekchamber.com

Fall City • *see North Bend*

Federal Way • *Federal Way C/C* • Tom Pierson; Pres./CEO; 31919 1st Ave. S., Ste. 202; P.O. Box 3440; 98003; King; P 85,000; M 600; (253) 838-2605; Fax (253) 661-9050; federalway@federalway chamber.com; www.federalwaychamber.com*

Ferndale • *Ferndale C/C* • Guy Occhiogrosso; Dir.; 5683 2nd Ave.; P.O. Box 1264; 98248; Whatcom; P 11,100; M 185; (360) 384-3042; Fax (360) 384-3009; info@ferndale-chamber.com; www.ferndale-chamber.com

Fife • *Fife Milton Edgewood C/C* • Aaron Williams; Exec. Dir.; 2026 54th Ave. E; 98424; Pierce; P 15,000; M 300; (253) 922-9320; Fax (253) 922-1638; awilliams@fifechamber.org; www. fifechamber.org*

Forks · *Forks C/C* · Marcia Bingham; Dir.; 1411 S. Forks Ave.; P.O. Box 1249; 98331; Clallam; P 5,500; M 300; (360) 374-2531; (800) 44-FORKS; Fax (360) 374-9253; info@forkswa.com; www.forkswa.com

Frederickson · *see Puyallup*

Freeland · *Greater Freeland C/C* · Chet Ross; Pres.; 1664 Main St.; P.O. Box 361; 98249; Island; P 1,700; M 160; (360) 331-1980; Fax (360) 331-1980; freeland@whidbey.com; www.freeland-wa.org

Friday Harbor · *San Juan Island C/C* · 135 Spring St.; P.O. Box 98; 98250; San Juan; P 7,300; M 300; (360) 378-5240; Fax (360) 370-5289; chamberinfo@sanjuanisland.org; www.sanjuanisland.org

George · *see Quincy*

Gig Harbor · *Gig Harbor Peninsula Area C/C* · Warren Zimmerman; Exec. Dir.; 3311 Harborview Dr., Ste. 101; P.O. Box 102; 98335; Pierce; P 66,000; M 500; (253) 851-6865; (800) 359-8804; Fax (253) 851-6881; executivedirector@gigharborchamber.com; www.gigharborchamber.com

Glenwood · *see White Salmon*

Goldendale · *Greater Goldendale Area C/C* · Rachel Olp; Exec. Dir.; 903 E. Broadway; 98620; Klickitat; P 6,000; M 187; (509) 773-3400; Fax (509) 773-3411; info@goldendalechamber.org; www.goldendalechamber.org

Graham · *see Puyallup*

Grand Coulee · *Grand Coulee Dam Area C/C* · Susan Miller; Exec. Dir.; 306 Midway; P.O. Box 760; 99133; Grant; P 4,000; M 100; (509) 633-3074; (800) 268-5332; Fax (509) 633-2366; chamber@grandcouleedam.org; www.grandcouleedam.org

Grandview · *Grandview C/C* · Brad Smith; Pres.; 133 W. 2nd St.; 98930; Yakima; P 9,150; M 350; (509) 882-2100; Fax (509) 882-5014; info@visitgrandview.org; www.visitgrandview.org

Granger · *Granger C/C* · Gabriel Martinez; Pres.; P.O. Box 250; 98932; Yakima; P 3,000; M 45; (509) 854-7304; grangerchamber@gmail.com; www.grangerchamber.org

Grapeview · *see Belfair*

Grayland · *Cranberry Coast C/C* · Beverly Ripley; P.O. Box 305; 98547; Grays Harbor; P 3,000; M 60; (360) 267-2003; (800) 473-6018; Fax (360) 267-2003; info@2thebeach.org; www.cranberrycoastcoc.com

Grays Harbor · *see Aberdeen*

Grays River · *see Cathlamet*

Greenbank · *see Coupeville*

Hockinson · *see La Center*

Hoquiam · *see Aberdeen*

Husum · *see White Salmon*

Irondale · *see Port Townsend*

Issaquah · *Issaquah C/C* · Matthew Bott; CEO; 155 N.W. Gilman Blvd.; 98027; King; P 26,320; M 455; (425) 392-7024; Fax (425) 392-8101; info@issaquahchamber.com; www.issaquahchamber.com*

Kalama · *Kalama C/C* · Brad Whittaker; Pres.; P.O. Box 824; 98625; Cowlitz; P 3,000; M 80; (360) 673-6299; info@kalamachamber.com; www.kalamachamber.com

Kelso · *see Longview*

Kenmore · *see Bothell*

Kennewick · *Tri City Reg. C/C* · Lori Mattson; Pres./CEO; 7130 W. Grandridge Blvd., Ste. C; 99336; Benton; P 275,000; M 1,350; (509) 736-0510; Fax (509) 783-1733; info@tricityregionalchamber.com; www.tricityregionalchamber.com*

Kent · *Kent C/C* · Andrea Keikkala; Exec. Dir.; 524 W. Meeker St., Ste. 1; P.O. Box 128; 98035; King; P 86,660; M 500; (253) 854-1770; Fax (253) 854-8567; info@kentchamber.com; www.kentchamber.com*

Kettle Falls · *Kettle Falls Area C/C* · Cheryl Largent; Pres.; P.O. Box 119; 99141; Stevens; P 1,611; M 80; (509) 738-2300; kettlefallscoc@dashwireless.com; www.kettlefalls.com

Kingston · *Greater Kingston Comm. C/C* · Linda Fyfe; Exec. Dir.; 11201 Hwy. 104 N.E.; P.O. Box 78; 98346; Kitsap; P 10,000; M 250; (360) 297-3813; exec@kingstonchamber.com; www.kingstonchamber.com*

Kirkland · *Greater Kirkland C/C* · Bill Vadino; Exec. Dir.; 401 Parkplace, Ste. 102; 98033; King; P 50,000; M 400; (425) 822-7066; Fax (425) 827-4878; info@kirklandchamber.org; www.kirklandchamber.org*

Klickitat · *see White Salmon*

La Center · *La Center North Clark County C/C* · Linda Tracy; Pres.; P.O. Box 83; 98629; Clark; P 6,000; M 50; (360) 263-4636; info@lacenternorthclarkcountychamber.com; www.lacenternorthclarkcountychamber.com

La Conner · *La Conner C/C* · Marci Plank; Exec. Dir.; 606 Morris St.; P.O. Box 1610; 98257; Skagit; P 900; M 160; (360) 466-4778; (888) 642-9284; Fax (360) 466-0204; info@laconnerchamber.com; www.laconnerchamber.com

Lacey · *Lacey C/C* · Mike Beehler; Exec. Dir.; 8300 Quinault Dr. N.E., Ste. A; 98516; Thurston; P 38,000; M 380; (360) 491-4141; Fax (360) 491-9403; info@laceychamber.com; www.laceychamber.com*

Lake Stevens · *Greater Lake Stevens C/C* · Donna Foster; Ofc. Mgr.; 9327 4th St. N.E., Ste. 7; P.O. Box 439; 98258; Snohomish; P 36,000; M 200; (425) 334-0433; info@lakestevenschamber.com; www.lakestevenschamber.com*

Lakewood · *Lakewood C/C* · Linda K. Smith; Pres./CEO; 4650 Steilacoom Blvd. S.W.; Bldg. 19, Ste. 109; 98499; Pierce; P 60,000; M 500; (253) 582-9400; Fax (253) 581-5241; chamber@lakewood-wa.com; www.lakewood-chamber.com*

Langley · *Langley C/C & Visitor Info. Center* · Sherry Jennings; Exec. Dir.; 208 Anthes Ave.; P.O. Box 403; 98260; Island; P 15,700; M 205; (360) 221-6765; Fax (360) 221-2979; langley@whidbey.com; www.visitlangley.com

Latah · *see Fairfield*

Leavenworth · *Leavenworth C/C* · Nancy Smith; Exec. Dir.; 940 Hwy. 2, Ste. B; P.O. Box 327; 98826; Chelan; P 2,700; M 575; (509) 548-5807; Fax (509) 548-1014; info@leavenworth.org; www.leavenworth.org*

Liberty Lake · *see Spokane Valley*

Lind · *Lind C/C* · Connie Field; Secy.; P.O. Box 561; 99341; Adams; P 500; M 20; (509) 677-3655; lchamber@lindwa.com; www.lindwa.com

Longview · *Kelso Longview C/C* · Rick Winsman; Pres./CEO; 1563 Olympia Way; 98632; Cowlitz; P 46,000; M 785; (360) 423-8400; Fax (360) 423-0432; info@kelsolongviewchamber.org; www.kelsolongviewchamber.org*

Lopez Island · *Lopez Island C/C* · Becky Smith; Pres.; 265 Lopez Rd., Ste. F; P.O. Box 102; 98261; San Juan; P 2,200; M 187; (360) 468-4664; lopezchamber@lopezisland.com; www.lopezisland.com

Lyle · *see White Salmon*

Lynden · *Lynden C/C* · Gary Vis; Dir.; 518 Front St.; 98264; Whatcom; P 12,000; M 340; (360) 354-5995; Fax (360) 354-0401; lynden@lynden.org; www.lynden.org

Lynnwood · *South Snohomish County C/C* · Jean Hales; Pres./CEO; 3815 196th St. S.W., Ste. 136; 98036; Snohomish; P 150,000; M 500; (425) 774-0507; Fax (425) 774-4636; info@s2c3.com; www.s2c3.com*

Maple Valley · *Greater Maple Valley-Black Diamond C/C* · Susie Davies; Ofc. Mgr.; 23745 225th Way S.E., Ste. 205; 98038; King; P 35,000; M 250; (425) 432-0222; Fax (888) 778-6823; info@maplevalleychamber.org; www.blackdiamondchamber.org*

Marblemount · *North Cascades C/C* · Tim O'Mara; Exec. Dir.; 59831 State Rte. 20; P.O. Box 175; 98267; Skagit; P 1,000; M 25; (360) 873-4150; chamber@marblemount.com; www.marblemount.com

Marcus · *see Kettle Falls*

Marysville · *Greater Marysville Tulalip C/C* · Caldie Rogers IOM; Pres./CEO; 8825 34th Ave. N.E., Ste. C; P 60,000; M 400; (360) 659-7700; Fax (360) 653-7539; caldie@marysvilletulalipchamber.com; www.marysvilletulalipchamber.com

Maury Island · *see Vashon*

McCleary · *McCleary Comm. C/C* · Pauline Martin; Pres.; P.O. Box 53; 98557; Grays Harbor; P 1,600; M 30; (360) 495-3667; (360) 495-3344; mcclearychamber.com

McKenna · *see Yelm*

Medical Lake · *see Spokane–West Plains C/C*

Mercer Island · *Mercer Island C/C* · Terry Moreman; Exec. Dir.; 7605 S.E. 27th, Ste. 109; P.O. Box 108; 98040; King; P 23,000; M 225; (206) 232-3404; Fax (206) 232-8903; mi_chamber@msn.com; www.mercerislandchamber.com*

Metaline Falls · *Metalines C/C* · Jeanie Law; Pres.; P.O. Box 388; 99153; Pend Oreille; P 350; M 40; (509) 446-1721; www.experiencewa.com

Mica · *see Fairfield*

Mill Creek · *see Bothell*

Millwood · *see Spokane Valley*

Milton · *see Puyallup*

Monroe · *Monroe C of C & Visitor Info. Center* · Kim Probst; Mgr.; 111 W. Main St.; 98272; Snohomish; P 16,700; M 350; (360) 794-5488; Fax (360) 794-2044; info@chamber-monroe.org; www.monroewachamber.com*

Montesano · *Montesano C/C & Visitor Info. Center* · P.O. Box 688; 98563; Grays Harbor; P 3,300; M 100; (360) 249-5522; info@montesanochamber.org; www.montesanochamber.org

Morton · *Morton C/C* · 1391 Main St.; P.O. Box 10; 98356; Lewis; P 1,200; M 50; (360) 496-6086; Fax (360) 496-6210; chamber@lewiscounty.com; mortonchamber.lewiscounty.com

Moses Lake · *Moses Lake Area C/C* · Debbie Doran-Martinez; Exec. Dir.; 324 S. Pioneer Way; 98837; Grant; P 40,000; M 440; (509) 765-7888; (800) 992-6234; Fax (509) 765-7891; information@moseslake.com; www.moseslake.com*

Mount St. Helens · *see Toutle*

Mount Vernon · *Mount Vernon C/C* · Kristen Whitener IOM; Pres./CEO; 105 E. Kincaid St., Ste. 101; P.O. Box 1007; 98273; Skagit; P 32,000; M 450; (360) 428-8547; Fax (360) 424-6237; info@mountvernonchamber.com; www.mountvernonchamber.com*

Mountlake Terrace · *see Lynnwood*

Mukilteo · *see Lynnwood*

Naselle · *see Cathlamet*

Newhalem · *see Marblemount*

Newport · *Greater Newport Area C/C* · Luanne Ryman; Exec. Dir.; 325 W. 4th St.; 99156; Pend Oreille; P 2,500; M 125; (509) 447-5812; (877) 818-1008; Fax (509) 447-5812; chamber@conceptcable.com; www.newportoldtownchamber.org

Nooksack · *see Everson*

Normandy Park · *see Seattle–Southwest King County C/C*

North Bend · *Snoqualmie Valley C/C* · Fritz Ribary; Exec. Dir.; P.O. Box 357; 98045; King; P 39,000; M 350; (425) 888-6362; Fax (425) 888-4665; info@snovalley.org; www.snovalley.org*

North Creek Area · *see Bothell*

Oak Harbor · *Greater Oak Harbor C/C & Visitor Info. Center* · Jill Johnson; Exec. Dir.; 32630 S.R. 20; P.O. Box 883; 98277; Island; P 42,000; M 480; (360) 675-3755; (360) 675-3755; Fax (360) 679-1624; info@oakharborchamber.com; www.oakharborchamber.com*

Oakville · *Oakville C/C* · Bill Scholl; Pres.; P.O. Box 331; 98568; Grays Harbor; P 700; M 30; (360) 273-2702; info@oakville-wa.org; www.oakville-wa.org

Ocean City · *Washington Coast C/C* · Patricia Cox; Publ. Rel.; 2616-A State Rte. 109; 98569; Grays Harbor; P 4,000; M 50; (360) 289-4552; Fax (360) 289-4552; wacoast@techline.com; www.washingtoncoastchamber.com

Ocean Park · *Ocean Park Area C/C* · P.O. Box 403; 98640; Pacific; P 1,400; M 75; (360) 665-4448; (888) 751-9354; opchamber@opwa.com; www.opwa.com

Ocean Shores · *Ocean Shores/North Beach C/C* · Mark & Holly Plackett; Co-Dirs.; 873 Pt. Brown Ave. N.W., Ste. 1; P.O. Box 382; 98569; Grays Harbor; P 4,800; M 270; (360) 289-2451; (888) 48-BEACH; Fax (360) 289-5005; chamber@oceanshores.org; www.oceanshores.org

Odessa · *Odessa C/C* · Marlon Schafer; Pres.; P.O. Box 355; 99159; Lincoln; P 970; M 73; (509) 982-0049; www.odessachamber.net

Okanogan · *Okanogan C/C* · Judy Kawahana; Pres.; P.O. Box 1125; 98840; Okanogan; P 2,415; M 36; (509) 422-1135; (888) 782-1134; Fax (509) 422-1541; okchamber@communitynet.org

Olympia · *Thurston County C/C* · David Schaffert; Pres./CEO; 809 Legion Way; P.O. Box 1427; 98507; Thurston; P 238,000; M 1,450; (360) 357-3362; Fax (360) 357-3376; info@thurstonchamber.com; www.thurstonchamber.com*

Omak · *Omak C/C* · Corina Radford; Pres.; 401 Omak Ave.; P.O. Box 3100; 98841; Okanogan; P 5,000; M 105; (509) 826-1880; (800) 225-6625; omakchamber@northcascades.net; www.omakchamber.com

Orcas Island · *see Eastsound*

Oroville · *Oroville C/C* · Gary DeVon; Pres.; P.O. Box 2140; 98844; Okanogan; P 3,000; M 68; (509) 476-3602; orovillewashington@gmail.com; www.orovillewashington.com*

Orting · *see Puyallup*

Othello · *Greater Othello C/C* · Grace Shelby; Mgr.; 33 E. Larch St.; P.O. Box 2813; 99344; Adams; P 10,000; M 150; (509) 488-2683; manager@othellochamber.com; www.othellochamber.com

Palouse · *Palouse C/C* · Bev Pearce; Pres.; P.O. Box 174; 99161; Whitman; P 1,000; M 50; (509) 878-1811; palousechamber@visitpalouse.com; www.visitpalouse.com

Pasco · *Pasco C/C* · Nikki Gerds; Exec. Dir.; 1925 N. 20th Ave.; 99301; Franklin; P 76,000; M 376; (509) 547-9755; Fax (509) 547-9756; info@pascochamber.org; www.pascochamber.org

Pateros · *Pateros C/C* · Joni Parks; Pres.; P.O. Box 613; 98846; Okanogan; P 625; M 30; (509) 923-2571; info@pateros.com; www.pateros.com

Point Roberts · *Point Roberts C/C* · Heather McPhee; Secy.; P.O. Box 128; 98281; Whatcom; P 1,340; M 57; (360) 945-2313; info@pointrobertschamberofcommerce.com; www.pointrobertschamberofcommerce.com

Pomeroy · *Pomeroy C/C* · Stephanie Newberg; Exec. Dir.; P.O. Box 916; 99347; Garfield; P 1,515; M 65; (509) 843-5110; info@pomeroychamberofcommerce.com; www.pomeroychamberofcommerce.com

Port Angeles · *Port Angeles Reg. C/C & Visitor Center* · Russell Veenema; Exec. Dir.; 121 E. Railroad Ave.; 98362; Clallam; P 20,000; M 550; (360) 452-2363; Fax (360) 457-5380; russ@portangeles.org; www.portangeles.org*

Port Hadlock · *see Port Townsend*

Port Ludlow · *see Port Townsend*

Port Orchard · *Port Orchard C/C* · Coreen Haydock Johnson; Exec. Dir.; 1014 Bay St., Ste. 8; 98366; Kitsap; P 10,400; M 340; (360) 876-3505; Fax (360) 895-1920; office@portorchard.com; www.portorchard.com*

Port Townsend · *The Jefferson County C/C* · Jennifer Wells; Exec. Dir.; 440 12th St.; 98368; Jefferson; P 25,000; M 425; (360) 385-7869; Fax (360) 379-8204; director@jeffcountychamber.org; jeffcountychamber.org*

Poulsbo · *Greater Poulsbo C/C* · Adele T. Heinrich; Exec. Dir.; 19351 8th Ave., Ste. 108; P.O. Box 1063; 98370; Kitsap; P 7,500; M 450; (360) 779-4848; (877) 768-5726; Fax (360) 779-3115; info@poulsbochamber.com; www.poulsbochamber.com.*

Prosser · *Prosser C/C & Visitor Info. Center* · Jim Milne; Exec. Dir.; 1230 Bennett Ave.; 99350; Benton; P 5,600; M 250; (509) 786-3177; (800) 408-1517; Fax (509) 786-4545; info@prosserchamber.org; www.tourprosser.com.

Pullman · *Pullman C/C* · Tammy Lewis; Exec. Dir.; 415 N. Grand Ave.; 99163; Whitman; P 28,000; M 460; (509) 334-3565; (800) 365-6948; Fax (509) 332-3232; chamber@pullmanchamber.com; www.pullmanchamber.com*

Puyallup · *Puyallup/Sumner C/C* · Shelly Schlumpf; Exec. Dir.; 323 N. Meridian, Ste. A; P.O. Box 1298; 98371; Pierce; P 175,000; M 650; (253) 845-6755; Fax (253) 848-6164; info@puyallupsumnerchamber.com; www.puyallupsumnerchamber.com*

Quilcene · *North Hood Canal C/C* · Mike McFadden; Pres.; P.O. Box 774; 98376; Jefferson; P 1,200; M 90; (360) 765-4999; visitorscenter@embarqmail.com; www.emeraldtowns.com

Quincy · *Quincy Valley C/C* · Karen Vizena; Exec. Dir.; 119 F St. S.E.; P.O. Box 668; 98848; Grant; P 10,000; M 270; (509) 787-2140; Fax (509) 787-4500; qvcc@quincyvalley.org; www.quincyvalley.org

Rainier · *see Yelm*

Raymond · *Willapa Harbor C/C & Visitor Info.* · Laurie Hatfield; Dir.; 415 Commercial St.; P.O. Box 1249, South Bend; 98586; Pacific; P 3,500; M 200; (360) 942-5419; info@willapaharbor.org; www.willapaharbor.org

Redmond · *Greater Redmond C/C* · Christine Hoffmann; Pres./CEO; 16210 N.E. 80th St.; 98052; King; P 53,680; M 550; (425) 885-4014; Fax (425) 882-0996; daniellel@redmondchamber.org; www.redmondchamber.org*

Renton · *Renton C/C* · Bill Taylor; Pres.; 300 Rainier Ave. N.; 98057; King; P 82,548; M 600; (425) 226-4560; Fax (425) 226-4287; info@gorenton.com; www.gorenton.com.*

Republic · *Republic Area C/C* · Dave Blanck; P.O. Box 502; 99166; Ferry; P 9,000; M 100; (509) 775-2704; info@republicchamber.org; www.republicchamber.org

Richfield · *see La Center*

Richland · *see Kennewick*

Ritzville · *Ritzville Area C/C & Visitor Bur.* · Al Seaton; V.P.; 111 W. Main; P.O. Box 122; 99169; Adams; P 1,800; M 115; (509) 659-1936; Fax (509) 659-0142; chamber@ritzville.com; www.ritzvillechamber.org

Rockford · *see Fairfield*

Rockport · *see Marblemount*

Rosalia · *Rosalia C/C* · Pat Voge; Pres.; P.O. Box 132; 99170; Whitman; P 642; M 55; (509) 523-5962; staff@rosaliachamber.com; www.rosaliachamber.com

Rosburg · *see Cathlamet*

Roslyn · *see Cle Elum*

Roy · *see Yelm*

Salmon Creek · *see La Center*

Sammamish · *Sammamish C/C* · Deborah Sogge; Exec. Dir.; 704 228th Ave. N.E., Ste. 123; 98074; King; P 44,000; M 268; (425) 681-4910; info@sammamishchamber.org; www.sammamishchamber.org*

San Juan Island · *see Friday Harbor*

Sauk Valley · *see Marblemount*

Sea Tac · *see Seattle–Southwest King County C/C*

Seattle Area

Ballard C/C · Beth Williamson Miller; Exec. Dir.; 2208 N.W. Market St., Ste. 100; 98107; King; P 70,000; M 350; (206) 784-9705; Fax (206) 783-8154; info@ballardchamber.com; www.ballardchamber.com

Fremont C/C · Jessica Vets; Exec. Dir.; 908 N. 34th St.; P.O. Box 31139; 98103; King; P 35,000; M 206; (206) 632-1500; Fax (206) 632-7156; director@fremont.com; www.fremont.com

Greater Lake City C/C · Diane Haugen; Exec. Dir.; 12345 30th Ave. N.E., Ste. F-G; 98125; King; P 40,000; M 200; (206) 363-3287; Fax (206) 363-6456; chamber@lakecitychamber.org; www.lakecitychamber.org*

Greater Queen Anne C/C · Dave Peterson; Pres.; P.O. Box 19386; 98109; King; P 80,000; M 300; (206) 282-4539; (206) 283-6876; contact@qachamber.org; www.qachamber.org*

Greater Seattle C/C · Phil Bussey; Pres./CEO; 1301 5th Ave., Ste. 2500; 98101; King; P 500,000; M 2,400; (206) 389-7200; Fax (206) 389-7288; info@seattlechamber.com; www.seattlechamber.com*

Greater University C/C · Teresa Lord Hugel; Exec. Dir.; 4710 University Way N.E., Ste. 114; 98105; King; P 70,000; M 170; (206) 547-4417; Fax (206) 547-5266; director@udistrictchamber.org; www.udistrictchamber.org

Magnolia C/C · Nathan Walker; Pres.; 3214 W. McGraw St., Ste. 301B; 98199; King; P 21,500; M 150; (206) 284-5836; Fax (206) 352-7494; info@magnoliachamber.org; www.magnoliachamber.org

Northgate C/C · Tatyana Sineeva; Admin.; 9594 First Ave. N.E., Ste. 296; 98115; King; P 500,000; M 100; (206) 733-0115; info@northgatechamber.com; www.northgatechamber.com*

Southwest King County C/C · Nancy Hinthorne; Pres./CEO; 14220 Interurban Ave. S., Ste. 134, Tukwila; P.O. Box 58591; 98138; King; P 105,000; M 375; (206) 575-1633; (800) 638-8613; Fax (206) 575-2007; staff@swkcc.org; www.swkcc.org*

Wallingford C/C · Pres.; 2100 N. 45th St.; 98103; King; P 20,000; M 110; (206) 632-0645; Fax (206) 632-4759; info@wallingfordchamber.org; www.wallingfordchamber.org

Seattle Area, *continued*

Washington State Hispanic C/C • Cristobal Guillén; Pres./CEO; 1100 Dexter Ave N., Ste. 100; 98109; King; M 1,000; (206) 551-5534; info@awshcc.com; www.awshcc.com

West Seattle C/C • Patricia Mullen; Pres./CEO; 3614A California Ave. S.W.; 98116; King; P 125,000; M 286; (206) 932-5685; Fax (206) 938-7437; info@wschamber.com; www.wschamber.com

White Center C/C • Mark Ufkes; Pres.; 1327 S.W. 102nd St.; P.O. Box 108; 98146; King; P 30,000; M 125; (206) 763-4196; Fax (206) 763-1042; wcchamber@hotmail.com; www.whitecenterchamber.org

Sedro-Woolley • *Sedro-Woolley C/C* • Pola Kelley; Exec. Dir.; 714B Metcalf St.; 98284; Skagit; P 16,000; M 238; (360) 855-1841; Fax (360) 855-1582; swchamber@sedro-woolley.com; www.sedro-woolley.com*

Selah • *Selah C/C* • Shirley M. Wasilewski; Admin. Asst.; 216 S. 1st St.; P.O. Box 415; 98942; Yakima; P 8,000; M 120; (509) 698-7303; Fax (509) 698-7309; selahchamber@fairpoint.net; www.selahchamber.org

Sequim • *Sequim-Dungeness Valley C/C & Visitor Info. Center* • Vickie Maples; Exec. Dir.; 1192 E. Washington; P.O. Box 907; 98382; Clallam; P 25,000; M 450; (360) 683-6197; Fax (360) 683-6349; info@sequimchamber.com; www.sequimchamber.com*

Shelton • *Shelton-Mason County C/C* • Terri Jeffreys; Exec. Dir.; 215 W. Railroad Ave.; P.O. Box 2389; 98584; Mason; P 56,000; M 350; (360) 426-2021; (800) 576-2021; Fax (360) 426-8678; info@sheltonchamber.org; www.sheltonchamber.org*

Shoreline • *Shoreline C/C* • Sharon Knight; Mgr.; 18560 1st Ave. N.E.; 98155; King; P 58,000; M 205; (206) 361-2260; Fax (206) 361-2268; info@shorelinechamber.com; www.shorelinechamber.com*

Silverdale • *Silverdale C/C & Visitors Info. Center* • Exec. Dir.; 3100 Buckland Hill, Ste. 107; P.O. Box 1218; 98383; Kitsap; P 16,000; M 450; (360) 692-6800; Fax (360) 692-1379; info@silverdalechamber.com; www.silverdalechamber.com*

Skamokawa • *see Cathlamet*

Smokey Point • *see Arlington*

Snohomish • *Snohomish C/C* • Pam Osborne; Mgr.; 127 Ave. A; P.O. Box 135; 98291; Snohomish; P 9,800; M 200; (360) 568-2526; Fax (360) 568-3869; manager@cityofsnohomish.com; www.cityofsnohomish.com*

Snoqualmie • *see North Bend*

Snoqualmie Pass • *see North Bend*

Soap Lake • *Soap Lake C/C* • Denise Keegan; P.O. Box 433; 98851; Grant; P 1,733; M 52; (509) 246-1821; slcoc@soaplakecoc.org; www.soaplakecoc.org

South Bend • *see Raymond*

South Hill • *see Puyallup*

Spangle • *see Fairfield*

Spokane • *Greater Spokane Inc.* • Richard Hadley; Pres./CEO; 801 W. Riverside Ave., Ste. 100; 99201; Spokane; P 510,000; M 1,500; (509) 624-1393; Fax (509) 747-0077; info@greaterspokane.org; www.greaterspokane.org.*

Spokane • *West Plains C/C* • Kathleen Zinke; Mgr.; 8727 W. Hwy. 2, 2nd Flr.; 99224; Spokane; P 60,000; M 200; (509) 747-8480; chamberoffice@westplainschamber.org; www.westplainschamber.org.

Spokane Valley • *Greater Spokane Valley C/C* • Eldonna Shaw; Pres./CEO; 9507 E. Sprague Ave.; 99206; Spokane; P 104,000; M 950; (509) 924-4994; (866) 475-1436; Fax (509) 924-4992; info@spokanevalleychamber.org; www.spokanevalleychamber.org.*

Sprague • *Sprague C/C* • Sylvia Fox; Pres.; P.O. Box 17; 99032; Lincoln; P 500; M 30; (509) 979-3539; president@spraguechamber.org

Springdale • *Springdale Area C/C* • Janet Buche; Pres.; 204 N. Second St.; P.O. Box 275; 99173; Stevens; P 300; M 15; (509) 258-4548; (509) 258-7805; springdalecommunitynews@hotmail.com; www.higherelevations.com/springdale_chamber.htm

Stanwood • *Stanwood C/C* • Stacy Johnson; Exec. Dir.; 8725 271st St. N.W.; P.O. Box 641; 98292; Snohomish; P 28,000; M 150; (360) 629-0562; info@stanwoodchamber.org; www.stanwoodchamber.org

Steilacoom • *Steilacoom C/C* • Cynthia L. McKitrick; Pres.; P.O. Box 88584; 98388; Pierce; P 6,500; M 125; (253) 353-6982; steilacoomchamberofcommerce@comcast.net; www.steilacoom.org*

Stevenson • *Skamania County C/C* • Casey Roeder; Exec. Dir.; 167 N.W. Second St.; P.O. Box 1037; 98648; Skamania; P 12,000; M 280; (509) 427-8911; (800) 989-9178; Fax (509) 427-5122; info@skamania.org; www.skamania.org

Sultan • *Sky Valley C/C & Visitor Info. Center* • Debbie Copple; Dir.; 320 Main St.; P.O. Box 46; 98294; Snohomish; P 9,000; M 90; (360) 793-0983; Fax (360) 793-3241; debbie@skyvalleyvic.net; www.skyvalleychamber.com

Sumas • *Sumas C/C* • Tony Kelley; Pres.; P.O. Box 268; 98295; Whatcom; P 1,200; M 30; (360) 988-2028; tony@kelleyinsurance.com; www.sumaschamber.com

Summit • *see Puyallup*

Sumner • *see Puyallup*

Sunland Estates • *see Quincy*

Sunnyside • *Sunnyside C/C* • Pam Turner; Exec. Dir.; 230 E. Edison; P.O. Box 360; 98944; Yakima; P 15,000; M 250; (509) 837-5939; (800) 457-8089; Fax (509) 837-8015; info@sunnysidechamber.com; www.sunnysidechamber.com

Tacoma • *Tacoma-Pierce County C/C* • Michael Hansch; Pres./CEO; 950 Pacific Ave., Ste. 300; P.O. Box 1933; 98401; Pierce; P 790,500; M 1,000; (253) 627-2175; Fax (253) 597-7305; info@tacomachamber.org; www.tacomachamber.org*

Tahuya • *see Belfair*

Tenino • *Tenino C/C* • P.O. Box 506; 98589; Thurston; P 1,600; M 60; (360) 264-4116; Fax (360) 264-4436; www.teninochamberofcommerce.com

Toledo • *South Lewis County C/C* • Rachel Phillipps; Chair; 408 Silver St.; P.O. Box 607; 98591; Lewis; P 5,000; M 90; (360) 864-8844; Fax (360) 864-8846; slccc@toledotel.com; www.thelewiscountychamber.com

Tonasket • *Tonasket C/C* • Kari Alexander; Pres.; P.O. Box 523; 98855; Okanogan; P 1,010; M 85; (509) 486-4543; (866) 440-8828; Fax (509) 486-4543; info@tonasketchamber.com; www.tonasketchamber.com; www.ci.tonasket.wa.us

Toppenish • *Toppenish C/C & Visitor Info. Center* • Stephanie Carpenter; Dir.; 504 S. Elm St.; P.O. Box 28; 98948; Yakima; P 9,000; M 100; (509) 865-3262; (800) 863-6375; Fax (509) 865-3549; chamber@toppenish.net; www.toppenish.net

Toutle • *Mount St. Helens C/C* • Greg Drew; Pres.; 5304 Spirit Lake Hwy.; 98649; Cowlitz; P 2,500; M ; (360) 274-8920

Trout Lake • *see White Salmon*

Tukwila • *see Seattle–Southwest King County C/C*

Tulalip · *Greater Marysville Tulalip C/C* · Caldie Rogers IOM; Pres./CEO; 8825 34th Ave. N.E., Ste. C; 98271; Snohomish; P 100,000; M 400; (360) 659-7700; Fax (360) 653-7539; caldie@marysville tulalipchamber.com; www.marysvilletulalipchamber.com*

Tumwater · *Tumwater Area C/C* · 5304 Littlerock Rd. S.W.; 98512; Thurston; P 60,000; M 350; (360) 357-5153; Fax (360) 786-1685; director@tumwaterchamber.com; www.tumwaterchamber.com

Twisp · *Twisp C/C* · Wanda Iverson; Secy.; P.O. Box 686; 98856; Okanogan; P 1,000; M 85; (509) 997-2020; info@twispinfo.com; www.twispinfo.com

Valleyford · *see Fairfield*

Vancouver · *Greater Vancouver C/C* · Kelly Parker; Pres./CEO; 1101 Broadway, Ste. 100; 98660; Clark; P 400,000; M 1,100; (360) 694-2588; Fax (360) 693-8279; info@vancouverusa.com; www. vancouverusa.com*

Vashon · *Vashon-Maury Island C/C* · Lee Ockinga; Exec. Dir.; 17205 Vashon Hwy. S.W., Ste. C-2; P.O. Box 1035; 98070; King; P 10,123; M 225; (206) 463-6217; Fax (206) 463-7590; discover@vashonchamber.com; www.vashonchamber.com

Victor · *see Belfair*

Walla Walla · *Walla Walla Valley C/C* · Susan Hall; V.P. of Op.; 29 E. Sumach; P.O. Box 644; 99362; Walla Walla; P 57,500; M 800; (509) 525-0850; Fax (509) 522-2038; info@wwvchamber.com; www.wwvchamber.com*

Washougal · *see Camas*

Waterville · *Waterville C/C* · Keith Soderstrom; Pres.; P.O. Box 628; 98858; Douglas; P 1,180; M 20; (509) 745-8871; waterville@nwi.net; www.watervillewashington.org

Waverly · *see Fairfield*

Wenatchee · *Northcentral Washington Hispanic C/C* · Claudia De Robles; Pres.; P.O. Box 2001; 98807; Chelan; M 63; (509) 665-9960; Fax (509) 663-2022; www.ncwhcc.org*

Wenatchee · *Wenatchee Valley C/C* · Craig Larsen; Exec. Dir.; 300 S. Columbia St., 3rd Flr.; P.O. Box 850; 98807; Chelan; P 45,000; M 600; (509) 662-2116; Fax (509) 663-2022; info@wenatchee.org; www.wenatchee.org*

West Richland · *West Richland Area C/C* · May Hays; Exec. Dir.; 6102 W. Van Giesen; P.O. Box 4023; 99353; Benton; P 12,000; M 185; (509) 967-0521; Fax (509) 967-2950; wrcc@westrichland chamber.org; www.westrichlandchamber.org

West Seattle · *see Seattle-West Seattle C/C*

West Spokane County · *see Spokane–West Plains C/C*

Westport · *Westport/Grayland C/C* · Leslie Eichner; Exec. Dir.; 2985 S. Montesano St.; P.O. Box 306; 98595; Grays Harbor; P 6,000; M 130; (360) 268-9422; (800) 345-6223; Fax (360) 268-1990; westport@techline.com; www.westportcam.com.*

Whidbey Island · *see Coupeville, Langley and Oak Harbor*

White Salmon · *Mt. Adams C/C* · Marsha Holliston; Ofc. Admin.; P.O. Box 449; 98672; Klickitat; P 7,000; M 223; (509) 493-3630; (866) 493-3630; info@mtadamschamber.com; www.mtadams chamber.com.

Wilbur · *Wilbur C/C* · Mel Novotney; Pres.; P.O. Box 111; 99185; Lincoln; P 950; M 60; (509) 647-5551; Fax (509) 647-5552; www. wilburwachamber.com

Winchester · *see Quincy*

Winthrop · *Winthrop C/C* · 202 Hwy. 20; P.O. Box 39; 98862; Okanogan; P 350; M 140; (509) 996-2125; (888) 463-8469; info@winthropwashington.com; www.winthropwashington.com

Woodinville · *Greater Woodinville C/C* · David H. Witt; Exec. Dir.; 14421 Woodinville-Redmond Rd. N.E.; 98072; King; P 12,000; M 245; (425) 481-8300; Fax (425) 481-9743; info@woodinville chamber.org; www.woodinvillechamber.org*

Woodland · *Woodland C/C* · Bill Raybell; Pres.; 900 Goerig St.; P.O. Box 1012; 98674; Cowlitz; P 5,250; M 205; (360) 225-9552; Fax (360) 225-3490; info@woodlandwachamber.com; www. woodlandwachamber.com

Woodway · *see Lynnwood*

Yakima · *Greater Yakima C/C* · Dan Schenkein; Pres./CEO; 10 N. Ninth St.; P.O. Box 1490; 98907; Yakima; P 250,000; M 900; (509) 248-2021; Fax (509) 248-0601; chamber@yakima.org; www.yakima.org.*

Yelm · *Yelm Area C/C* · Cecelia Jenkins; Exec. Dir.; 701 Prairie Park Lane S.E., Ste. A; P.O. Box 444; 98597; Thurston; P 12,000; M 450; (360) 458-6608; Fax (360) 458-6383; info@yelmchamber. com; www.yelmchamber.com*

Zillah · *Zillah C/C* · Ken Waymire; Pres.; P.O. Box 1294; 98953; Yakima; P 2,720; M 50; (509) 829-5055; zillahchamber@zillah chamber.com; www.zillahchamber.com

West Virginia

West Virginia C of C · Stephen Roberts; Pres.; 1624 Kanawha Blvd. E.; P.O. Box 2789; Charleston; 25330; Kanawha; P 1,818,470; M 1,800; (304) 342-1115; Fax (304) 342-1130; forjobs@wv chamber.com; www.wvchamber.com.

Barrackville · *see Fairmont*

Beckley · *Beckley-Raleigh County C/C* · Ellen M. Taylor; Pres./CEO; 245 N. Kanawha St.; 25801; Raleigh; P 18,000; M 700; (304) 252-7328; Fax (304) 252-7373; ellentaylor@suddenlinkmail.com; www.brccc.com.

Berkeley Springs · *Berkeley Springs-Morgan County C/C* · Andrea Curtin; Exec. Dir.; 127 Fairfax St.; 25411; Morgan; P 16,000; M 193; (304) 258-3738; chamber@berkeleysprings.com; www.berkeleyspringschamber.com

Bluefield · *Greater Bluefield C/C* · Marc Meachum; Pres./CEO; 619 Bland St.; P.O. Box 4098; 24701; Mercer; P 11,000; M 550; (304) 327-7184; Fax (304) 325-3085; info@bluefieldchamber.com; www.bluefieldchamber.com.

Buckhannon · *Buckhannon-Upshur C/C* · Julia Keehner; Pres.; P.O. Box 442; 26201; Upshur; P 23,000; M 160; (304) 472-1722; Fax (304) 472-4938; buckhannon@wvdsl.net; www.buchamber.com

Charles Town · *Jefferson County C/C* · Heather Morgan; Exec. Dir.; 29 Keyes Ferry Rd., Ste. 200; P.O. Box 426; 25414; Jefferson; P 50,000; M 500; (304) 725-2055; (800) 624-0577; Fax (304) 728-8307; chamber@jeffersoncountywvchamber.org; www. jeffersoncountywvchamber.org

Charleston · *Charleston Area Alliance* · Matthew G. Ballard; Pres./CEO; 1116 Smith St.; 25301; Kanawha; P 273,000; M 600; (304) 340-4253; Fax (304) 340-4275; info@charlestonareaalliance. org; www.charlestonareaalliance.org

Chester · *Chester-Newell Area C/C* · 449 Carolina Ave.; P.O. Box 2; 26034; Hancock; P 3,000; M 95; (304) 387-2025; Fax (304) 387-2025

Clarksburg · *Harrison County C/C* · Katherine Wagner PCED IOM; Pres.; 520 W. Main St.; 26301; Harrison; P 79,000; M 550; (304) 624-6331; Fax (304) 624-5190; info@harrisoncountycham ber.com; www.harrisoncountychamber.com*

Davis • *Tucker County C/C* • Bill Smith; Dir.; 410 William Ave. & 4th St.; P.O. Box 565; 26260; Tucker; P 7,800; M 60; (304) 259-5315; Fax (304) 259-4210; tuckerchamber@canaanvalley.org

Delbarton • *see Williamson*

Elkins • *Elkins-Randolph County C/C* • Robbie Morris; Exec. Dir.; 200 Executive Plaza; 26241; Randolph; P 28,000; M 268; (304) 636-2717; Fax (304) 636-8046; chamber@elkinsrandolph countywv.com; erccc.com

Fairmont • *Marion County C/C* • Tina Shaw; Pres.; 110 Adams St.; 26554; Marion; P 57,000; M 500,450; (304) 363-0442; (800) 296-3379; Fax (304) 363-0480; mccc@marionchamber.com; www.marionchamber.com

Fairview • *see Fairmont*

Farmington • *see Fairmont*

Follansbee • *Follansbee C/C* • Tony Paesano; Pres.; 1334 Main St.; 26037; Brooke; P 4,000; M 60; (304) 527-2668; Fax (304) 527-2615; www.follansbeewv.com

Gilbert • *see Williamson*

Grant Town • *see Fairmont*

Harrisville • *Ritchie County C/C* • David Scott; Pres.; 217 W. Main St.; P.O. Box 177; 26362; Ritchie; P 10,500; M 80; (304) 643-2500; Fax (304) 643-2502; ritchiechamber@zoominternet.net; www.ritchiechamber.com

Hinton • *Summers County C/C* • Mary Haley; Pres.; 200 Ballengee St.; 25951; Summers; P 14,204; M 90; (304) 466-5332; Fax (304) 466-5301; info@summerscounty.net; www.hintonwva.com

Huntington • *Huntington Reg. C/C* • Mark Bugher; Pres./CEO; 720 Fourth Ave.; P.O. Box 1509; 25716; Cabell; P 51,000; M 520; (304) 525-5131; Fax (304) 525-5158; katie@huntingtonchamber.org; www.huntingtonchamber.org.*

Hurricane • *see Teays*

Keyser • *Mineral County C/C* • Anne Palmer; Exec. Dir.; 1 Grand Central Park; 26726; Mineral; P 27,234; M 150; (304) 788-2513; Fax (304) 788-3887; office@mineralchamber.com; www.mineral chamber.com

Kingwood • *Preston County C/C* • Sheila Haney; Exec. Dir.; 200 W. Main St.; 26537; Preston; P 30,000; M 225; (304) 329-0576; Fax (304) 329-1407; prestoncoc@labyrinth.net; www.preston chamber.com

Lewisburg • *Greater Greenbrier C/C* • Katie C. Ickes; Exec. Dir.; 200 W. Washington St., Ste. C; 24901; Greenbrier; P 35,000; M 325; (304) 645-2818; Fax (304) 647-3001; info@greenbrierwvchamber.org; www.greenbrierwvchamber.org

Logan • *Logan County C/C* • Debrina J. Williams; Managing Dir.; 214 Stratton St.; 25601; Logan; P 37,710; M 200; (304) 752-1324; Fax (304) 752-5988; logancountychamberofcommerce@verizon.net; www.logancountychamberofcommerce.com

Mannington • *see Fairmont*

Marlinton • *Pocahontas County C/C* • David J. Cain; Treas.; P.O. Box 272; 24954; Pocahontas; P 9,000; M 70; (304) 799-4476; info@pccocwv.com; www.pccocwv.com

Martinsburg • *Martinsburg-Berkeley County C/C* • Tina Combs; Pres./CEO; 198 Viking Way; 25401; Berkeley; P 107,347; M 530; (304) 267-4841; (800) 332-9007; Fax (304) 263-4695; chamber@berkeleycounty.org; www.berkeleycounty.org

Matewan • *see Williamson*

Monongah • *see Fairmont*

Morgantown • *Morgantown Area C/C* • Ken Busz; Pres./CEO; 1029 University Ave, Ste. 101; P.O. Box 658; 26507; Monongalia; P 88,640; M 400; (304) 292-3311; (800) 618-2525; Fax (304) 296-6619; info@morgantownchamber.org; www.morgantown chamber.org.*

Moundsville • *Marshall County C/C* • David W. Knuth; Exec. Dir.; 609 Jefferson Ave.; 26041; Marshall; P 34,800; M 257; (304) 845-2773; Fax (304) 845-2773; dknuth@marshallcountychamber.com; www.marshallcountychamber.com

Mullens • *Mullens Area C/C* • Kay King; Pres.; P.O. Box 235; 25882; Wyoming; P 2,000; M 30; (304) 294-6714; kayking@jetbroadband.com

New Martinsville • *Wetzel County C/C* • Qulia Utt; Ofc. Mgr.; 201 Main St.; P.O. Box 271; 26155; Wetzel; P 16,329; M 175; (304) 455-3825; Fax (304) 455-3637; chamber@wetzelcountychamber.com; www.wetzelcountychamber.com

Oak Hill • *Fayette County C/C* • Sharon P. Cruikshank; Exec. Dir.; 310 Oyler Ave.; 25901; Fayette; P 47,000; M 300; (304) 465-5617; Fax (304) 465-5618; fayette@wvdsl.net; www.fayettecounty.com

Parkersburg • *C/C of the Mid-Ohio Valley* • Jill Parsons; Pres./CEO; 214 8th St.; 26101; Wood; P 135,000; M 400; (304) 422-3588; Fax (304) 422-3580; info@movchamber.org; www.movchamber.org.*

Petersburg • *Grant County C/C* • Tammy Kesner; Pres.; 126 N. Main St.; 26847; Grant; P 11,300; M 129; (304) 257-2722; gowv@gowv.com; www.gowv.com

Philippi • *Barbour County C/C* • Donald A. Smith; Exec. Dir.; 101 College Hill Dr.; Box 2124; 26416; Barbour; P 16,000; M 150; (304) 457-1958; Fax (304) 457-6239; info@barbourchamber.com; www.barbourchamber.com

Pineville • *Pineville Area C/C* • Tim Ellison; Mayor; P.O. Box 116; 24874; Wyoming; P 1,500; M 37; (304) 732-6255; (304) 732-9371; Fax (304) 732-0024; info@pinevillechamber.com; www.pineville chamber.com

Point Pleasant • *Mason County Area C/C* • Hilda Austin; Exec. Dir.; 305 Main St.; 25550; Mason; P 25,178; M 90; (304) 675-1050; Fax (304) 675-1601; mccofc@pointpleasantwv.org; www.mason countychamber.org

Princeton • *Princeton-Mercer County C/C* • Robert Farley; Pres./CEO; 1522 N. Walker St.; 24740; Mercer; P 63,000; M 300; (304) 487-1502; Fax (304) 425-0227; pmccc@frontiernet.net; www.pmccc.com.

Ravenswood • *Greater Ravenswood C/C* • Kathy Meadows; Pres.; P.O. Box 743; 26164; Jackson; P 4,500; M 50; (304) 942-2282; (304) 273-2621; www.ravenswoodwvchamber.com

Reedsville • *see Fairmont*

Richwood • *Richwood Area C/C* • Vikki Mayse; Exec. Secy.; 1 E. Main St.; P.O. Box 267; 26261; Nicholas; P 2,200; M 100; (304) 846-6790; Fax (304) 846-6790; rwdchamber@frontier.com; richwoodchamberofcommerce.org

Romney • *Hampshire County C/C* • Sandra Hunt; Dir.; 91 S. High St.; 26757; Hampshire; P 21,000; M 170; (304) 822-7221; Fax (304) 822-7221; hampshirechamberofcommerce@citlink.net; www.hampshirecountychamber.com

Saint Albans • *St. Albans Area C/C* • Dale Withrow; Pres.; P.O. Box 675; 25177; Kanawha; P 13,000; M 50; (304) 727-7251; Fax (304) 727-7251; sachamber@frontier.com; www.stalbanswv.com

Salem • *Salem Area C/C* • Kevin Fluharty; Pres.; P.O. Box 191; 26426; Harrison; P 2,000; M 50; chamber@salemwv.com; www.salemwv.com

South Charleston • *South Charleston C/C* • Kelly L. Pruett; Exec. Dir.; 401 D St.; P.O. Box 8595; 25303; Kanawha; P 10,000; M 131; (304) 744-0051; Fax (304) 744-1649; soccoc@wvdsl.net; www.southcharlestonchamber.org

Spencer • *Roane County C/C* • Kim Davis; Admin. Asst.; P.O. Box 1; 25276; Roane; P 15,446; M 80; (304) 927-1780; Fax (304) 927-5953; rchamber@commission.state.wv.us; www.roanechamberwv.org

Summersville • *Summersville Area C/C* • Mary Ann Taylor; Exec. Dir.; P.O. Box 567; 26651; Nicholas; P 26,662; M 120; (304) 872-1588; (800) 760-6158; Fax (304) 883-2588; info@summersville chamber.com; www.summersvillechamber.com

Teays • *Putnam County C/C* • Martin S. Chapman; Pres.; 5664 State Rte. 34 N.; P.O. Box 553; 25569; Putnam; P 55,000; M 475; (304) 757-6510; Fax (304) 757-6562; chamber@putnamcounty. org; www.putnamchamber.org*

Weirton • *Weirton Area C/C* • Brenda Mull; Pres.; 3174 Pennsylvania Ave., Ste. 1; 26062; Hancock; P 19,250; M 410; (304) 748-7212; Fax (304) 748-0241; info@weirtonchamber.com; www. weirtonchamber.com.*

Welch • *McDowell C/C* • Mary Lou Odom; Pres.; 92 McDowell St., Ste. 100; 24801; McDowell; P 27,000; M 162; (304) 436-4260; (866) 571-0746; www.mcdowellchamberofcommerce.com

Wellsburg • *Wellsburg C/C* • Barbara Finley; Exec. Dir.; P.O. Box 487; 26070; Brooke; P 3,500; M 100; (304) 479-2115; Fax (304) 737-1660; wellsburgchamber@gmail.com; www.wellsburg chamber.com

Weston • *Lewis County C/C* • Gerhard St. John; Exec. Dir.; 115 E. Second St.; 26452; Lewis; P 17,000; M 149; (304) 269-2608; Fax (304) 517-1608; lcinfo@lcchamber.org; www.lcchamber.org

Wheeling • *Wheeling Area C/C* • Terry A. Sterling; Pres.; 1310 Market St.; 26003; Ohio; P 154,000; M 700; (304) 233-2575; Fax (304) 233-1320; terrysterling@wheelingchamber.com; www. wheelingchamber.com*

White Sulphur Springs • *see Lewisburg*

Williamson • *Tug Valley C/C* • Natalie Young; Exec. Dir.; 75 E. 2nd Ave. & Court St.; P.O. Box 376; 25661; Mingo; P 42,000; M 150; (304) 235-5240; Fax (304) 235-4509; tvcc1@verizon.net; www. tugvalleychamberofcommerce.com

Winfield • *see Teays*

Worthington • *see Fairmont*

Wisconsin

Wisconsin Manufacturers & Commerce • James S. Haney; Pres.; 501 E. Washington Ave.; P.O. Box 352; Madison; 53701; Dane; P 5,600,000; M 3,500; (608) 258-3400; Fax (608) 258-3413; wmc@wmc.org; www.wmc.org

Abbotsford • *Abbotsford-Colby Area C/C* • Todd Schmidt; Pres.; 100 W. Spruce St.; P.O. Box 418; 54405; Clark & Marathon; P 5,000; M 150; (715) 223-3444 x102; www.ci.abbotsford.wi.us

Adams • *see Friendship*

Algoma • *Algoma Area C/C* • Pam Ritchie; Exec. Dir.; 1226 Lake St.; 54201; Kewaunee; P 3,500; M 210; (920) 487-2041; (800) 498-4888; Fax (920) 487-5519; chamber@itol.com; www.algoma.org*

Almena • *Almena Commercial Club* • Jessica Vohs; Pres.; P.O. Box 175; 54805; Barron; P 736; M 30; (715) 357-3592

Antigo • *Antigo/Langlade County C/C* • Deena Grabowsky; Exec. Dir.; 1005 S. Superior St.; 54409; Langlade; P 20,165; M 220; (715) 623-4134; (888) 526-4523; Fax (715) 623-4135; info@ antigochamber.com; www.antigochamber.com*

Appleton • *Fox Cities C/C & Ind.* • William J. Welch; Pres.; 125 N. Superior St.; P.O. Box 1855; 54912; Calumet, Outagamie & Winnebago; P 207,660; M 1,750; (920) 734-7101; Fax (920) 734-7161; informa tion@foxcitieschamber.com; www.foxcitieschamber.com*

Arbor Vitae • *see Minocqua*

Ashland • *Ashland Area C/C* • Mary McPhetridge; Exec. Dir.; 1716 W. Lake Shore Dr.; P.O. Box 746; 54806; Ashland; P 8,700; M 300; (715) 682-2500; (800) 284-9484; Fax (715) 682-9404; ashchamb@centurytel.net; www.visitashland.com*

Baileys Harbor • *Baileys Harbor Comm. Assn.* • P.O. Box 31; 54202; Door; P 1,100; M 100; (920) 839-2366; bhinfo@dcwis.com; www.baileysharbor.com

Baldwin • *Baldwin-Woodville C/C & Visitor Bur.* • Tracy Carlson; Pres.; P.O. Box 142; 54002; St. Croix; P 2,667; M 95; (715) 684-2221; info@baldwin-woodvillechamber.org; www.baldwin-woodvillechamber.org

Bangor • *Bangor Bus. Club* • Chad Wehrs; Pres.; P.O. Box 154; 54614; La Crosse; P 1,571; M 40; (608) 486-4343

Baraboo • *Baraboo Area C/C* • 600 W. Chestnut St.; P.O. Box 442; 53913; Sauk; P 14,500; M 375; (608) 356-8333; Fax (608) 356-8422; visitus@baraboo.com; www.baraboo.com.*

Bayfield • *Bayfield C/C & Visitor Bur.* • Cari Obst; Exec. Dir.; 42 S. Broad St.; P.O. Box 138; 54814; Bayfield; P 615; M 400; (715) 779-3335; (800) 447-4094; Fax (715) 779-5080; chamber@bayfield. org; www.bayfield.org

Beaver Dam • *Beaver Dam Area C/C* • Philip Fritsche; Exec. Dir.; 127 S. Spring St.; 53916; Dodge; P 21,000; M 325; (920) 887-8879; Fax (920) 887-9750; info@beaverdamchamber.com; www.beaver damchamber.com*

Belgium • *Belgium Area C/C* • Joan Gottsacker; Secy.; P.O. Box 215; 53004; Ozaukee; P 2,500; M 58; (262) 285-7887; (262) 285-7931; www.belgiumchamberofcommerce.com

Belleville • *Belleville C/C* • AnnaMaria Bliven; Exec. Dir.; P.O. Box 392; 53508; Dale & Green; P 2,000; M 72; (608) 424-3336; www. belleville-wi.com

Beloit • *Greater Beloit C/C* • Amy Loudenbeck; Interim Pres.; 500 Public Ave.; 53511; Rock; P 65,000; M 325; (608) 365-8835; Fax (608) 365-6850; info@greaterbeloitchamber.com; greaterbeloit chamber.com*

Black River Falls • *Black River Area C/C* • Barbara Brower; Exec. Dir.; 120 N. Water St.; 54615; Jackson; P 5,000; M 320; (715) 284-4658; (800) 404-4008; Fax (715) 284-9476; chamber@ blackrivercountry.net; www.blackrivercountry.net

Blanchardville • *Blanchardville Comm. Pride* • 208 Mason St.; P.O. Box 52; 53516; Iowa & Lafayette; P 800; M 10; (608) 523-2274; Fax (608) 523-4321; bcpi@tds.net; www.blanchardville.com

Bloomer • *Bloomer C/C* • 1731 17th Ave.; P.O. Box 273; 54724; Chippewa; P 3,400; M 145; (715) 568-3339; Fax (715) 568-3346; bchamber@bloomer.net; www.bloomerchamber.com

Boscobel • *Boscobel C/C* • Susie Fralick; Secy./Treas.; 800 Wisconsin Ave.; 53805; Grant; P 3,076; M 84; (608) 375-2672; bchamber@centurytel.net; www.boscobelwisconsin.com

Boulder Junction • *Boulder Junction C/C* • Theresa Smith; Exec. Dir.; P.O. Box 286; 54512; Vilas; P 1,000; M 113; (715) 385-2400; (800) GO-MUSKY; Fax (715) 385-2379; boulderjct@boulderjct.org; www.boulderjct.org

Brillion • *Brillion C/C* • Tammy Fischer; Pres.; P.O. Box 123; 54110; Calumet; P 3,000; M 75; (920) 756-3435; www.brillion chamber.com

Brodhead • *Brodhead C/C* • Nancy Sutherland; Secy.; P.O Box 16; 53520; Green & Rock; P 5,000; M 60; (608) 897-8411; info@brodheadchamber.org; www.brodheadchamber.org

Brookfield • *Greater Brookfield C/C* • Carol White; Pres.; 1305 N. Barker Rd., Ste. 5; 53045; Waukesha; P 35,000; M 450; (262) 786-1886; Fax (262) 786-1959; carol@brookfieldchamber.com; www.brookfieldchamber.com

Brooklyn • *Brooklyn Area C/C* • LaVorn Dvorak; Pres.; 100 E. Main; P.O. Box 33; 53521; Green; P 1,165; M 18; (608) 455-1627; info@brooklynwisconsin.com; www.brooklynwisconsin.com

Bryant • *see Antigo*

Burlington • *Burlington Area C/C* • Janice Ludtke; Exec. Dir.; 113 E. Chestnut St.; P.O. Box 156; 53105; Racine & Walworth; P 16,000; M 490; (262) 763-6044; Fax (262) 763-3631; info@burlingtonchamber.org; www.burlingtonchamber.org*

Butler • *Butler Area C/C* • Linda Ryfinski; Exec. Dir.; 12808 W. Hampton Ave.; 53007; Waukesha; P 1,900; M 100; (262) 781-5195; Fax (262) 781-7870; linda@butlerchamber,org; www.butlerchamber.org

Cable • *Cable Area C/C* • James Bolen; Exec. Dir.; 13380 County Hwy. M; P.O. Box 217; 54821; Bayfield; P 2,000; M 190; (715) 798-3833; (800) 533-7454; Fax (715) 798-4456; info@cable4fun.com; www.cable4fun.com

Cadott • *Cadott Area C/C* • Huntz Geissler; Pres.; P.O. Box 84; 54727; Chippewa; P 1,352; M 100; (715) 289-3338; info@cadottchamber.org; www.cadottchamber.org

Cambridge • *Cambridge C/C* • P.O. Box 572; 53523; Dane & Jefferson; P 1,300; M 70; (608) 423-3780; chamber@smallbytes.net; www.cambridgewi.com

Campbellsport • *Campbellsport C/C* • Julie Roth; Treas.; P.O. Box 535; 53010; Fond du Lac; P 1,800; M 52; (920) 533-8386; campbellsport@care2.com

Cedarburg • *Cedarburg C/C* • Kristine Hage; Exec. Dir.; W61 N480 Washington Ave.; P.O. Box 104; 53012; Ozaukee; P 16,000; M 300; (262) 377-5856; (262) 377-9620; Fax (262) 377-6470; info@cedarburg.org; www.cedarburg.org

Chetek • *Chetek Area C/C* • P.O. Box 747; 54728; Barron; P 3,800; M 109; (715) 924-3200; (800) 317-1720; info@chetekwi.net; www.chetekwi.net

Chilton • *Chilton C/C* • Tammy Pethan; Secy.; P.O. Box 351; 53014; Calumet; P 3,708; M 155; (920) 418-1650; info@chiltonchamber.com; www.chiltonchamber.com

Chippewa Falls • *Chippewa Falls Area C/C* • Mike D. Jordan; Pres.; 10 S. Bridge St.; 54729; Chippewa; P 13,000; M 500; (715) 723-0331; (888) 723-0024; Fax (715) 723-0332; info@chippewachamber.org; www.chippewachamber.org*

Clam Lake • *see Cable*

Clear Lake • *Clear Lake Comm. Club* • TJ Buhr; Pres.; P.O. Box 266; 54005; Polk; P 1,000; M 40; (715) 263-2157; www.clearlakewi.com

Cleveland • *Cleveland C/C* • Tim Schueler; Pres.; c/o Cleveland State Bank; 1250 W. Washington Ave.; 53015; Manitowoc; P 1,600; (920) 693-8256

Clintonville • *Clintonville Area C/C* • Sandy Yaeger; Exec. Dir.; 18 S. Main St.; P.O. Box 56; 54929; Waupaca; P 4,700; M 150; (715) 823-4606; cvlchmbr@frontiernet.net; clintonvillewi.org/chamber

Colby • *see Abbotsford*

Columbus • *Columbus Area C/C* • Jenny Augustine; P.O. Box 362; 53925; Columbia & Dodge; P 4,500; M 90; (920) 623-3699; www.cityofcolumbuswi.com

Combined Locks • *see Kaukauna*

Conover • *Conover C/C* • P.O. Box 32; 54519; Vilas; P 1,265; M 87; (715) 479-4928; (866) 394-4386; Fax (715) 479-4928; conover.org@gmail.com; www.conover.org

Crandon • *Forest County C/C* • Melinda Otto; Exec. Dir.; 116 S. Lake Ave.; 54520; Forest; P 10,000; M 130; (715) 478-3450; info@visitforestcounty.com; www.visitforestcounty.com*

Cross Plains • *Cross Plains Area C/C* • Amy Hansen; Exec. Dir.; P.O. Box 271; 53528; Dane; P 3,500; M 100; (608) 843-3166; cpbaexecdir@yahoo.com; www.crossplainschamber.net

Cuba City • *Cuba City C/C* • Mike Lisle; Pres.; 103 S. Main St.; P.O. Box 706; 53807; Grant & Lafayette; P 2,156; M 70; (608) 744-3761

Cudahy • *Cudahy C/C* • Raymond Glowacki; Pres.; 3569 E. Barnard Ave.; 53110; Milwaukee; P 19,000; M 150; (414) 483-8615; Fax (414) 486-9918; support@cudahywichamber.com; www.cudahywichamber.com

Cumberland • *Cumberland C/C* • P.O. Box 665; 54829; Barron; P 2,000; M 150; (715) 822-3378; bagafest@cumberland-wisconsin.com; www.cumberland-wisconsin.com

Danbury • *Danbury Area C/C* • Jenny Hill; P.O. Box 173; 54830; Burnett; P 400; M 14; (715) 656-3100; Fax (715) 656-3131; discoverdanbury@yahoo.com; www.discoverdanbury.com

Darboy • *see Kaukauna*

Darlington • *Darlington Chamber Main Street* • Suzi Osterday; Exec. Dir.; 447 Main St.; 53530; Lafayette; P 2,400; M 100; (608) 776-3067; Fax (608) 776-3067; mainstprogram@centurytel.net; www.darlingtonwi.org

Deer Park • *see New Richmond*

Deerbrook • *see Antigo*

DeForest • *DeForest Area C/C* • Lisa Beck; Exec. Dir.; 201 DeForest St.; 53532; Dane; P 16,000; M 200; (608) 846-2922; dacc1@centurytel.net; www.deforestarea.com*

Delafield • *Delafield Area C/C & Tourism* • Deborah Smith; Exec. Dir.; P.O. Box 180171; 53018; Waukesha; P 6,996; M 250; (262) 646-8100; (888) 294-1082; Fax (262) 646-8237; info@visitdelafield.org; www.visitdelafield.org

Delavan • *Delavan-Delavan Lake Area C/C* • Jackie Busch; Exec. Dir.; 52 E. Walworth Ave.; 53115; Walworth; P 12,000; M 230; (262) 728-5095; Fax (262) 728-9199; info@delavanwi.org; www.delavanwi.org*

Denmark • *Denmark Comm. Bus. Assn.* • Mark Looker; Pres.; P.O. Box 97; 54208; Brown; P 2,132; M 50; (920) 863-8423; Fax (920) 863-3237; www.dcbawis.com

Dodgeville • *Dodgeville Area C/C* • Bob Berglin; Exec. Dir.; 338 N. Iowa St.; 53533; Iowa; P 4,220; M 200; (608) 935-9200; (877) 863-6343; Fax (608) 930-5324; info@dodgeville.com; www.dodgeville.com

Dousman • *Dousman Area C/C* • Mary Mecikalski; Pres.; P.O. Box 2; 53118; Waukesha; P 1,500; M 100; (262) 965-3764; mary.mecikalski@associatedbank.com; www.dousmanchamber.org*

Drummond • *see Cable*

Dundas • *see Kaukauna*

Eagle River · *Eagle River C/C* · Conrad Heeg; Exec. Dir.; 201 N. Railroad St.; P.O. Box 1917; 54521; Vilas; P 1,500; M 400; (715) 479-6400; (800) 359-6315; Fax (715) 479-1960; info@eagleriver.org; www.eagleriver.org

Eagle River · *Vilas County C/C* · 330 Court St.; 54521; Vilas; P 21,033; M 12; (715) 479-3649; Fax (715) 479-1978

East Troy · *East Troy Area C/C* · Katie Matteson; Exec. Dir.; 2096 Church St., Ste. A; P.O. Box 312; 53120; Walworth; P 9,604; M 188; (262) 642-3770; Fax (262) 642-8769; info@easttroywi.org; www.easttroywi.org

Eau Claire · *Eau Claire Area C/C* · Bob McCoy; Pres./CEO; 101 N. Farwell St., Ste. 101; P.O. Box 1107; 54702; Eau Claire; P 99,000; M 1,160; (715) 834-1204; Fax (715) 834-1956; information@eauclairechamber.org; www.eauclairechamber.org*

Edgerton · *Edgerton Area C/C* · Kathy Citta; Admin.; 20 S. Main St.; P.O. Box 5; 53534; Dane & Rock; P 5,300; M 100; (608) 884-4408; Fax (608) 884-4408; edgertonchamber@verizon.net; www.edgertonchamber.org

Elcho · *see Antigo*

Elkhart Lake · *Elkhart Lake Area C/C* · Lynn Shovan; Pres.; 41 E. Rhine St.; P.O. Box 425; 53020; Sheboygan; P 1,028; M 120; (920) 876-2922; (877) 355-3554; Fax (920) 876-3659; elcoc@verizon.net; www.elkhartlake.com

Elkhorn · *Elkhorn Area C/C & Tourism Center* · Christine Clapper; Exec. Dir.; 203 E. Walworth St.; P.O. Box 41; 53121; Walworth; P 9,000; M 250; (262) 723-5788; Fax (262) 723-5784; info@elkhorn-wi.org; www.elkhornchamber.com.*

Ellsworth · *Ellsworth Area C/C* · Peggy Nelson; Pres.; P.O. Box 927; 54011; Pierce; P 3,418; M 134; (715) 273-6442; info@ellsworthchamber.com; www.ellsworthchamber.com

Elroy · *Elroy Area Advancement Corp.* · Kris Yager; P.O. Box 52; 53929; Juneau; P 1,623; M 50; (608) 462-5316; eaac@centurytel.net; www.elroychamber.com

Elton · *see Antigo*

Evansville · *Evansville Area C/C & Tourism* · Jackie Liebel; Exec. Dir.; 8 W. Main St.; 53536; Rock; P 5,000; M 125; (608) 882-5131; evansvillecoc@litewire.net; www.evansvillechamber.org

Fennimore · *Fennimore Area C/C* · Linda Parrish; Promo. Coord.; 850 Lincoln Ave.; 53809; Grant; P 2,400; M 100; (608) 822-3599; Fax (608) 822-6007; promo@fennimore.com; www.fennimore.com*

Fish Creek · *Fish Creek Civic Assn.* · James DeGroot; Ofc. Mgr.; 4097 Main St.; P.O. Box 74; 54212; Door; P 1,000; M 140; (920) 868-2316; (800) 577-1880; manager@fishcreekinfo.com; www.visitfishcreek.com

Fitchburg · *Fitchburg C/C* · Angela Kinderman; Exec. Dir.; 5540 Research Park Dr.; 53711; Dane; P 22,000; M 315; (608) 288-8284; akinderman@fitchburgchamber.com; www.fitchburgchamber.com

Florence · *Florence County C/C* · Russ Trip; Pres.; P.O. Box 643; 54121; Florence; P 5,200; M 100; (715) 528-5377; (715) 528-4270; www.florencecountychamber.org

Fond du Lac · *Fond du Lac Area Assn. of Commerce* · Joseph R. Reitemeier CCE; Pres./CEO; 207 N. Main St.; 54935; Fond du Lac; P 97,000; M 900; (920) 921-9500; Fax (920) 921-9559; info@fdlac.com; www.fdlac.com.*

Fontana · *Geneva Lake West C/C* · Karen Beckman; Pres.; 175 Valley View Dr.; P.O. Box 118; 53125; Walworth; P 8,000; M 130; (262) 275-5102; chamber@genevalakewest.com; www.genevalakewest.com

Forest Junction · *see Kaukauna*

Fort Atkinson · *Fort Atkinson Area C/C* · Dianne A. Hrobsky; Exec. V.P.; 244 N. Main St.; 53538; Jefferson; P 12,000; M 400; (920) 563-3210; (888) 733-3678; Fax (920) 563-8946; facoc@fortchamber.com; www.fortchamber.com*

Fox Lake · *Fox Lake Area C/C* · Julie Quade; Pres.; P.O. Box 94; 53933; Dodge; P 1,500; M 75; (920) 928-3777; (800) 858-4904; Fax (920) 928-2033; info@foxlakechamber.com; www.foxlakechamber.com

Franklin · *see Oak Creek*

Frederic · *Frederic Area C/C* · Rebecca Harlander; Secy./Treas.; P.O. Box 250; 54837; Polk; P 1,267; M 125; (715) 327-4836; www.frederic-wi.com

Freedom · *see Kaukauna*

Fremont · *Fremont Area C/C* · P.O. Box 114; 54940; Waupaca; P 750; M 81; (920) 446-3838; www.travelfremont.com

Friendship · *Adams County C/C & Tourism* · Heidi Roekle; Exec. Dir.; 500 Main St.; P.O. Box 295; 53934; Adams; P 18,000; M 160; (608) 339-6997; chamber@visitadamscountywi.com; www.visitadamscountywi.com

Friesland · *Friesland C/C* · Don De Young; Pres.; 126 N. Madison St.; P.O. Box 127; 53935; Columbia; P 300; M 11; (920) 348-5267; friesland@centurytel.net

Galesville · *Galesville Area C/C* · Bob Ristow; Pres.; P.O. Box 196; 54630; Trempealeau; P 1,440; M 100; (608) 582-2868; info@galesvillewi.com; www.galesvillewi.com

Germantown · *Germantown Area C/C* · Lynn Grgich; Exec. Dir.; W156 N11251 Pilgrim Rd.; P.O. Box 12; 53022; Washington; P 20,000; M 210; (262) 255-1812; Fax (262) 255-9033; executivedirector@germantownchamber.org; www.germantownchamber.org*

Glendale · *Glendale C/C* · Dale Schmidt; Dir.; P.O. Box 170056; 53217; Milwaukee; P 13,337; M 220; (414) 332-0900; Fax (414) 332-0914; d.schmidt@glendale-chamber.com; www.glendale-chamber.com

Grafton · *Grafton Area C/C* · Nancy Hundt; Exec. Dir.; 1624 Wisconsin Ave.; P.O. Box 132; 53024; Ozaukee; P 11,500; M 280; (262) 377-1650; Fax (262) 375-7087; chamber@grafton-wi.org; www.grafton-wi.org

Grand View · *see Cable*

Grantsburg · *Grantsburg C/C* · Ronda Taber; Pres.; 316 S. Brad St.; P.O. Box 451; 54840; Burnett; P 1,400; M 75; (715) 463-2405; Fax (715) 463-5555; info@grantsburgchamber.com; www.grantsburgchamber.com

Green Bay · *Green Bay Area C/C* · Paul Jadin; Pres.; 300 N. Broadway, Ste. 3A; P.O. Box 1660; 54305; Brown; P 220,000; M 1,400; (920) 437-8704; Fax (920) 437-1024; info@titletown.org; www.titletown.org*

Green Lake · *Green Lake Area C/C* · Ellen Koeppen; Exec. Dir.; 550 Mill St.; P.O. Box 337; 54941; Green Lake; P 1,100; M 200; (920) 294-3231; (800) 253-7354; Fax (920) 294-3415; info@visitgreenlake.com; www.visitgreenlake.com

Greendale · *Greendale C/C* · Gregory Turay; Pres.; P.O. Box 467; 53129; Milwaukee; P 16,861; M 50; (414) 423-3900; info@greendalechamber.com; www.greendalechamber.com

Greenfield · *Greenfield C/C* · Judy Baxter; Pres.; 4818 S. 76th St., Ste. 129; 53220; Milwaukee; P 34,000; M 125; (414) 327-8500; gcc@thegreenfieldchamber.com; www.thegreenfieldchamber.com

Greenleaf · *see Kaukauna*

Greenwood · *Greenwood C/C* · Pat Linder; Pres.; 212 S. Main St.; P.O. Box 87; 54437; Clark; P 1,000; M 60; (715) 267-7221

Hartford • *Hartford Area C/C* • Kim Infalt; Exec. Dir.; 225 N. Main St.; P.O. Box 270305; 53027; Washington; P 12,278; M 250; (262) 673-7002; Fax (262) 673-7057; info@hartfordchamber.org; www.hartfordchamber.org*

Hartland • *Hartland C/C* • Lynn Minturn; Exec. Dir.; 116 W. Capitol Dr.; 53029; Waukesha; P 8,000; M 200; (262) 367-7059; Fax (262) 367-2980; admin@hartland-wi.org; www.hartland-wi.org*

Hayward • *Hayward Area C/C* • Kevin Ruetten; Exec. Dir.; P.O. Box 726; 54843; Sawyer; P 8,000; M 310; (715) 634-8662; (800) 724-2992; Fax (715) 634-8498; info@haywardareachamber.com; www.haywardareachamber.com

Holland • *see Kaukauna*

Holmen • *see Onalaska*

Horicon • *Horicon C/C* • Karen Boersma; Secy./Treas.; 620 Washington St.; P.O. Box 23; 53032; Dodge; P 4,000; M 80; (920) 485-3200; Fax (920) 485-3200; writeus@horiconchamber.com; www.horiconchamber.com

Hudson • *Hudson Area C/C & Tourism Bur.* • Kim Heinemann; Pres.; 502 Second St.; 54016; St. Croix; P 30,000; M 650; (715) 386-8411; (800) 657-6775; Fax (715) 386-8432; info@hudsonwi. org; www.hudsonwi.org

Hurley • *Hurley Area C/C* • Jessica Bolich; Exec. Dir.; 316 Silver St.; 54534; Iron; P 2,000; M 180; (715) 561-4334; Fax (715) 561-3742; info@hurleywi.com; www.hurleywi.com

Iola • *Iola-Scandinavia Area C/C* • Chris Aasen; Pres.; P.O. Box 167; 54945; Waupaca; P 1,289; M 60, (715) 445-4000; Fax (715) 445-4169; aasen@mwwb.net; www.ischamber.org

Iron River • *Iron River Area C/C* • Jesse Loewen; Exec. Dir.; P.O. Box 448; 54847; Bayfield; P 2,000; M 140; (715) 372-8558; Fax (715) 372-8558; info@visitironriver.com; www.visitironriver.com

Janesville • *Forward Janesville Inc.* • John Beckord; Pres.; 14 S. Jackson St.; 53548; Rock; P 62,000; M 500; (608) 757-3160; Fax (608) 757-3170; forward@forwardjanesville.com; www. forwardjanesville.com*

Jefferson • *Jefferson C/C* • Janet M. Werner; Exec. Dir.; 122 W. Garland St.; 53549; Jefferson; P 8,000; M 200; (920) 674-4511; (920) 674-4835; Fax (920) 674-1499; coc@jefnet.com; www. jeffersonchamberwi.com*

Johnson Creek • *Johnson Creek Area C/C* • Connie Oestreich; Exec. Dir.; 417 Union St.; P.O. Box 527; 53038; Jefferson; P 2,012; M 100; (920) 699-4949; creekchamber@tds.net; www.johnson creekchamber.com*

Juneau • *Juneau C/C* • Gretchen Last; Pres.; P.O. Box 4; 53039; Dodge; P 2,500; M 70; (920) 386-3359; juneau@juneauwi.org; www.juneauwi.org

Kaukauna • *Heart of the Valley C/C* • Bobbie Beckman; Exec. Dir.; 101 E. Wisconsin Ave.; 54130; Outagamie; P 50,000; M 600; (920) 766-1616; Fax (920) 766-5504; bbeckman@heartofthe valleychamber.com; www.heartofthevalleychamber.com*

Kempster • *see Antigo*

Kenosha • *Kenosha Area C/C* • Lou Molitor; Exec. Dir.; 600 52nd St., Ste. 130; 53140; Kenosha; P 150,934; M 700; (262) 654-1234; Fax (262) 654-4655; info@kenoshaareachamber.com; www. kenoshaareachamber.com*

Kewaskum • *Kewaskum Area C/C* • Cheryl Peterson; Pres.; P.O. Box 300; 53040; Fond du Lac & Washington; P 3,500; M 70; (262) 626-3336; www.kewaskum.org

Kewaunee • *Kewaunee Area C/C* • Coord.; 308 N. Main; P.O. Box 243; 54216; Kewaunee; P 3,000; M 120; (920) 388-4822; (800) 666-8214; jsperber@kewaunee.org; www.kewaunee.org

Kiel • *Kiel Area Assn. of Commerce* • P.O. Box 44; 53042; Calumet & Manitowoc; P 3,450; M 125; (920) 894-4638; www.kielwi.org

Kimberly • *see Kaukauna*

La Crosse • *La Crosse Area C/C* • Dick Granchalek; Pres.; 712 Main St.; 54601; La Crosse; P 120,000; M 900; (608) 784-4880; (800) 889-0539; Fax (608) 784-4919; lse_chamber@centurytel. net; www.lacrossechamber.com.*

Lac du Flambeau • *Lac du Flambeau C/C* • 602 Peace Pipe Rd.; P.O. Box 456; 54538; Vilas; P 3,400; M 75; (715) 588-3346; (877) 588-3346; Fax (715) 588-9408; info@lacduflambeauchamber. com; www.lacduflambeauchamber.com

Ladysmith • *Greater Ladysmith Area C/C* • Ron Moore; Pres.; 209 W. 5th St. S.; 54848; Rusk; P 4,000; M 150; (715) 532-7328; Fax (715) 532-2649; ladysmithchamber@centurytel.net; www. ladysmithchamber.com

Lake Geneva • *Geneva Lake Area C/C* • George F. Hennerley; Exec. V.P.; 201 Wrigley Dr.; 53147; Walworth; P 7,900; M 377; (262) 248-4416; Fax (262) 248-1000; lgcc@lakegenevawi.com; www.lakegenevawi.com

Lake Mills • *Lake Mills Area C/C* • 200C Water St.; 53551; Jefferson; P 5,000; M 100; (920) 648-3585; Fax (920) 648-6751; chamber@lakemills.org; www.lakemills.org

Lake Nebagamon • *Nebagamon Comm. Assn.* • Swan Dawson; Prog. Chair; P.O. Box 517; 54849; Douglas; P 1,000; M 50; (715) 374-3101, Fax (715) 374-3766; ccoletta@centurytel.net; www. lakenebagamonwi.com

Lakewood • *Lakewood Area C/C* • P.O. Box 87; 54138; Oconto; P 2,300; M 100; (715) 276-6500; info@lakewoodareachamber. com; www.lakewoodareachamber.com

Lancaster • *Lancaster Area C/C* • Angie Day; Exec. Dir.; 206 S. Madison St.; P.O. Box 292; 53813; Grant; P 4,200; M 130; (608) 723-2820; Fax (608) 723-7409; chamber@lancasterwisconsin. com; www.lancasterwisconsin.com

Land O'Lakes • *Land O'Lakes C/C* • Kathy Schuh; Pres.; 6484 Hwy. 45 N.; P.O. Box 599; 54540; Vilas; P 800; M 135; (715) 547-3432; (800) 236-3432; Fax (715) 547-8010; infolandolakes@gmail. com; www.landolakes-wi.org

LaPointe • *Madeline Island C/C* • P.O. Box 274; 54850; Ashland; P 272; M 100; (715) 747-2801; (888) 475-3386; Fax (715) 747-2800; vacation@madelineisland.com; www.madelineisland.com

Lena • *Lena Comm. Dev. Corp.* • Deanna Patnade; Secy./Treas.; 339 W. Main St.; P.O. Box 178; 54139; Oconto; P 600; M 45; (920) 829-5327

Little Chute • *see Kaukauna*

Lodi • *Lake Wisconsin C/C* • Wayne Sadek; Pres.; P.O. Box 98; 53555; Columbia; P 6,500; M 92; (608)333-4060; info@lake wisconsin.org; www.lakewisconsin.org

Lodi • *Lodi C/C* • Dori Bilse; Exec. Asst.; P.O. Box 43; 53555; Columbia; P 3,200; M 100; (608) 592-4412; information@lodi wisconsin.com; www.lodiwisconsin.com

Lomira • *Lomira Area C/C* • Jim Bisek; Pres.; P.O. Box 386; 53048; Dodge; P 2,200; M 100; (920) 269-7229; (920) 269-4112; www. lomira.com

Luxemburg • *Luxemburg C/C* • Jim Lemens; Pres.; P.O. Box 141; 54217; Kewaunee; P 2,200; M 200; (920) 845-1005; Fax (920) 845-1018; www.luxemburgusa.com

Madison · *Greater Madison C/C* · Jennifer Alexander; Pres.; 615 E. Washington Ave., 2nd Flr.; P.O. Box 71; 53701; Dane; P 460,000; M 1,750; (608) 256-8348; Fax (608) 256-0333; info@greater madisonchamber.com; www.greatermadisonchamber.com

Manawa · *Manawa Area C/C* · Ken Groholski; Pres.; P.O. Box 221; 54949; Waupaca; P 1,400; M 45; (920) 596-2495; manawa@ wolfnet.net; www.manawachamber.com

Manitowish Waters · *Manitowish Waters C/C* · Jodi McMahon; Dir.; 4 Airport Rd.; P.O. Box 251; 54545; Vilas; P 700; M 125; (715) 543-8488; (888) 626-9877; Fax (715) 543-2519; funinfo@manitowishwaters.org; www.manitowishwaters.org

Manitowoc · *Chamber of Manitowoc County* · Karen Szyman; Exec. Dir.; 1515 Memorial Dr.; 54220; Manitowoc; P 34,000; M 500; (920) 684-5575; (866) 727-5575; Fax (920) 684-1915; info@chambermanitowoccounty.org; www.chambermanitowoc county.org*

Marinette · *Marinette/Menominee Area C/C* · Mary D. Johns; Exec. Dir.; 601 Marinette Ave.; 54143; Marinette; P 25,000; M 410; (715) 735-6681; Fax (715) 735-6682; infochamber@centurytel. net; www.mandmchamber.com*

Markesan · *Markesan Area C/C* · Clyde Olson; Pres.; P.O. Box 327; 53946; Green Lake; P 1,397; M 45; (920) 398-8023; (888) LT-GREEN; bonnieandclyde@charter.net; www.markesanwi.com

Marshfield · *Marshfield Area C/C & Ind.* · Scott Larson; Exec. Dir.; 700 S. Central Ave.; P.O. Box 868; 54449; Marathon & Wood; P 20,000; M 600; (715) 384-3454; Fax (715) 387-8925; info@ marshfieldchamber.com; www.marshfieldchamber.com.*

Mauston · *Greater Mauston Area C/C* · Virginia Hustad; Ofc. Admin.; 503 State Rd. 82 E.; P.O. Box 171; 53948; Juneau; P 4,143; M 202; (608) 847-4142; chamber@mauston.com; www.mauston. com

Mayville · *Mayville Area C/C* · Linda Turk; 48 N. Main St.; P.O. Box 185; 53050; Dodge; P 5,000; M 100; (920) 387-5776; (800) 256-7670; Fax (920) 387-5776; info@mayvillechamber.com; www.mayvillechamber.com

Mazomanie · *Greater Mazomanie Area C/C* · P.O. Box 84; 53560; Dane; P 1,550; M 25; (608) 795-9824; info@mazomanie chamber.com; www.mazomaniechamber.com

McFarland · *McFarland C/C* · Dawn Corrigan-DeFoer; Exec. Dir.; 4869 Larson Beach Rd., Ste. B; P.O. Box 372; 53558; Dane; P 7,000; M 125; (608) 838-4011; Fax (608) 838-4011; info@mcfarland chamber.com; www.mcfarlandchamber.com

Medford · *Medford Area C/C* · Susan Emmerich; Exec. Dir.; 104 E. Perkins St.; P.O. Box 172; 54451; Taylor; P 4,300; M 325; (715) 748-4729; (888) 682-9567; Fax (715) 748-6899; medfordchamber@tds. net; www.medfordwis.com

Menomonee Falls · *Menomonee Falls Comm. C/C* · Sue Jeskewitz; Exec. Dir.; N88 W16621 Appleton Ave.; 53051; Waukesha; P 100,000; M 340; (262) 251-2430; Fax (262) 251-0969; sue@fallschamber.com; www.fallschamber.com*

Menomonie · *Greater Menomonie Area C/C* · Lisa Montgomery; CEO; 342 E. Main St.; 54751; Dunn; P 15,100; M 500; (715) 235-9087; Fax (715) 235-2824; info@menomoniechamber.org; www. menomoniechamber.org*

Mequon · *see Thiensville*

Mercer · *Mercer C/C* · Tina Brunell; Ofc. Mgr.; 5150 N. Hwy. 51; 54547; Iron; P 1,808; M 125; (715) 476-2389; Fax (715) 476-2389; info@mercercc.com; www.mercercc.com

Merrill · *Merrill Area C/C* · Debbe Kinsey; Exec. Dir.; 705 N. Center Ave.; 54452; Lincoln; P 10,000; M 256; (715) 536-9474; (877) 90-PARKS; Fax (715) 539-2043; info@merrillchamber.org; www.merrillchamber.org*

Middleton · *Middleton C/C* · Van Nutt; Exec. Dir.; 7507 Hubbard Ave.; 53562; Dane; P 17,000; M 550; (608) 827-5797; Fax (608) 831-7765; chamber@middletonchamber.com; www.middleton chamber.com

Milltown · *Milltown Comm. Club* · P.O. Box 402; 54858; Polk; P 900; M 20; (715) 825-2222; (715) 825-3258; info@milltown-wi. com; www.milltown-wi.com

Milton · *Milton Area C/C, Ind. & Tourism* · Christina Slaback; Exec. Dir.; 508 Campus St., Ste. 3; P.O. Box 222; 53563; Rock; P 6,000; M 150; (608) 868-6222; Fax (608) 868-6222; info@maccit. com; www.maccit.com*

Milwaukee · *Metro Milwaukee Assn. of Commerce* · Timothy Sheehy; Pres.; 756 N. Milwaukee St., Ste. 400; 53202; Milwaukee, Washington & Waukesha; P 1,500,000; M 2,000; (414) 287-4100; Fax (414) 271-7753; info@mmac.org; www.mmac.org

Mineral Point · *Mineral Point C/C* · Joy Gieseke; Exec. Dir.; 225 High St.; 53565; Iowa; P 2,617; M 150; (608) 987-3201; (888) POINT-WI; Fax (608) 987-4425; info@mineralpoint.com; www. mineralpoint.com

Minocqua · *Minocqua-Arbor Vitae-Woodruff Area C/C* · Diane Geis Hapka; Exec. Dir.; 8216 Hwy. 51 S.; P.O. Box 1006; 54548; Oneida; P 10,000; M 460; (715) 356-5266; Fax (715) 358-2446; mavwacc@minocqua.org; www.minocqua.org*

Mishicot · *Mishicot Area Growth & Improvement Committee* · P.O. Box 237; 54228; Manitowoc; P 1,400; M 40; (920) 755-3411; magic@tm.net; www.mishicot.org

Mondovi · *Mondovi Business Assn.* · Nan Wolfe; Pres.; P.O. Box 25; 54755; Buffalo; P 2,700; M 40; (715) 926-4858; www. mondovi.com

Monona · *Monona C/C* · Terri Groves; Exec. Dir.; 6320 Monona Dr., Ste. 100; 53716; Dane; P 8,000; M 256; (608) 222-8565; Fax (608) 222-8596; chamber@monona.com; www.monona.com*

Monroe · *Monroe C/C & Ind.* · Pamela L. Christopher; Exec. Dir.; 1505 9th St.; 53566; Green; P 36,000; M 265; (608) 325-7648; Fax (608) 328-2241; thechamber@tds.net; www.monroechamber.org.*

Montello · *Marquette Now* · P.O. Box 219; 53949; Marquette; P 14,000; M 264; (608) 297-7420; (888) 318-0362; accentsby laureen@aol.com; www.marquettenow.com

Mosinee · *Mosinee Area C/C* · Tammy Campo; Exec. Dir.; 224 Main St.; 54455; Marathon; P 5,000; M 128; (715) 693-4330; Fax (715) 693-9555; macoc@mtc.net; www.mosineechamber.org*

Mount Horeb · *Mount Horeb Area C/C* · Melissa Theisen; Exec. Dir.; 300 E. Main St.; 53572; Dane; P 8,000; M 200; (608) 437-5914; (88) TROLLWAY; Fax (608) 437-1427; info@trollway.com; www.trollway.com

Mountain · *see Lakewood*

Mukwonago · *Mukwonago Area C/C & Tourism Center* · April D. Reszka; Exec. Dir.; 801 Main St., Ste. 1; 53149; Waukesha; P 14,600; M 300; (262) 363-7758; Fax (262) 363-7730; director@ mukwonagochamber.org; www.mukwonagochamber.org.*

Muscoda · *Muscoda Chamber & Ind. Dev. Corp.* · Jack Enslow; Pres.; P.O. Box 587; 53573; Grant & Iowa; P 1,500; M 40; (608) 739-9158; plsmuscoda@yahoo.com

Muskego · *Muskego Area C/C* · Kathy Chiaverotti; Exec. Dir.; S. 74 W. 16894 Janesville Rd.; P.O. Box 234; 53150; Waukesha; P 23,000; M 240; (414) 422-1155; Fax (414) 422-1415; info@muskego.org; www.muskego.org

Namakagon · *see Cable*

Necedah · *Necedah C/C* · Roger Herried; Admin.; 101 Center St.; P.O. Box 244; 54646; Juneau; P 888; M 61; (608) 565-2261; necedahadmin@necedah.us; www.necedah.us

Neenah · *see Appleton*

Neillsville · *Neillsville Area C/C* · Cindy Schwanz; Exec. Dir.; 106 W. Division; P.O. Box 52; 54456; Clark; P 2,800; M 171; (715) 743-6444; Fax (715) 743-8262; nacc@tds.net; www.neillsville.org

New Berlin · *New Berlin Chamber & Visitors Bur.* · Bob Bruemmer; Pres.; 2140 S. Calhoun Rd.; 53151; Waukesha; P 39,000; M 185; (262) 786-5280; Fax (262) 786-9165; office@nb-chamber.org; www.nb-chamber.org

New Glarus · *New Glarus C/C* · 418 Railroad St.; 53574; Green; P 2,000; M 125; (608) 527-2095; (800) 527-6838; Fax (608) 527-4991; info@swisstown.com; www.swisstown.com

New Holstein · *New Holstein Area C/C* · Robert Bosma; Pres.; P.O. Box 17; 53061; Calumet; P 3,400; M 91; (920) 898-5771; nhchamber.newholsteinchamber@gmail.com; newholstein.org

New Lisbon · *New Lisbon Area C/C* · Nancy Cowan; Exec. Secy.; 218 E. Bridge St.; P.O. Box 79; 53950; Juneau; P 1,500; M 75; (608) 562-3555; Fax (608) 562-5625; nlchambr@mwt.net; www.newlisbonchamber.com

New London · *New London Area C/C* · Laurie Shaw; Exec. Dir.; 301 E. Beacon Ave.; 54961; Outagamie & Waupaca; P 7,000; M 250; (920) 982-5822; Fax (920) 982-6344; chamber@newlondonwi.org; www.newlondonchamber.com

New Richmond · *New Richmond Area C/C & Visitors Bur.* · Russ Korpela; Exec. Dir.; 245A S. Knowles Ave.; 54017; St. Croix; P 8,000; M 250; (715) 246-2900; (800) 654-6380; Fax (715) 246-7100; nrchamber@pressenter.com; www.newrichmondchamber.com

Oak Creek · *South Suburban C/C* · Barbara Wesener CAE; Exec. Dir.; 8580 S. Howell Ave.; 53154; Milwaukee; P 55,000; M 420; (414) 768-5845; Fax (414) 768-5848; info@southsuburban chamber.com; www.southsuburbanchamber.com

Oconomowoc · *Oconomowoc Area C/C* · Pat Ornberg; Exec. Dir.; 175 E. Wisconsin Ave.; 53066; Waukesha; P 14,000; M 330; (262) 567-2666; Fax (262) 567-3477; chamber@oconomowoc.org; www.oconomowoc.org.*

Oconto · *Oconto Area C/C* · Nancy Rhode; Secy.; 110 Brazeau Ave.; P.O. Box 174; 54153; Oconto; P 4,900; M 120; (920) 834-6254; www.ocontocounty.org

Oconto Falls · *Oconto Falls Area C/C* · Ken O' Dierno; Pres.; P.O. Box 24; 54154; Oconto; P 2,500; M 90; (920) 846-8306; ofchamber@centurytel.net; www.ocontofallschamber.com

Omro · *Omro Area C/C* · Jesse Koonce; Dir.; 130 W. Larrabee St.; 54963; Winnebago; P 3,500; M 125; (920) 685-6960; Fax (920) 685-0384; omrochamber@charterinternet.net; www.omro-wi.com

Onalaska · *Center for Commerce & Tourism* · Jean Lunde; Tourism Dir.; 1101 Main St.; 54650; La Crosse; P 16,800; (608) 781-9570; (800) 873-1901; Fax (608) 781-9572; info@discover onalaska.com; www.discoveronalaska.com

Oostburg · *Oostburg Area C/C* · Dennis Flipse; Pres.; P.O. Box 700433; 53070; Sheboygan; P 3,000; M 50; (920) 564-6500; www.oostburg.org

Oregon · *Oregon Area C/C* · Marechiel Santos-Lang; Exec. Dir.; 733 N. Main St., Lower Level; P.O. Box 123; 53575; Dane; P 8,000; M 206; (608) 835-3697; Fax (608) 835-2475; director@oregonwi.com; www.oregonwi.com

Osceola · *Osceola Area C/C* · Paul Anderson; Pres.; 310 Chieftain St.; P.O. Box 251; 54020; Polk; P 2,700; M 70; (715) 755-3300; (800) 947-0581; Fax (715) 294-2210; osceolachamber@centurytel.net; www.osceolachamber.org

Oshkosh · *Oshkosh C/C* · John A. Casper; Pres./CEO; 120 Jackson St.; 54901; Winnebago; P 64,132; M 1,021; (920) 303-2266; Fax (920) 303-2263; info@oshkoshchamber.com; www.oshkoshchamber.com*

Owen · *Owen-Withee Area C/C* · Sid Borgeson; Pres.; P.O. Box 186; 54460; Clark; P 1,600; M 75; (715) 229-2697; info@owen witheechamber.org; www.owenwitheechamber.org

Palmyra · *Palmyra Area C/C* · Rick Ball; Pres.; P.O. Box 139; 53156; Jefferson; P 1,780; M 45; (262) 495-8316; (414) 531-4357; information@palmyrawi.com; www.palmyrawi.com

Pardeeville · *Pardeeville Area Bus. Assn.* · Bob Becker; Treas.; P.O. Box 337; 53954; Columbia; P 2,100; M 35; (608) 617-9201

Park Falls · *Park Falls Area C/C* · Sue Holm; Exec. Dir.; 400 4th Ave. S.; 54552; Price; P 4,000; M 220; (715) 762-2703; (877) 762-2703; Fax (715) 762-4130; chamber@parkfalls.com; www.parkfalls.com*

Parrish · *see Antigo*

Pearson · *see Antigo*

Pelican Lake · *Pelican Lake C/C* · Chet Haatvedt; Pres.; P.O. Box 45; 54463; Oneida; P 650; M 60; (715) 487-5222; pelicanlakecc@frontiernet.net; www.pelicanlakewi.org

Peshtigo · *Peshtigo C/C* · Cindy Hagert; Secy.; P.O. Box 36; 54157; Marinette; P 4,100; M 100; (715) 582-0327; Fax (715) 582-0327; peshtigochamber@centurytel.net; www.peshtigochamber.com

Pewaukee · *Pewaukee C/C* · Kathy Eckhardt; Exec. Dir.; 214 Oakton Ave.; 53072; Waukesha; P 20,000; M 200; (262) 691-8851; Fax (262) 691-0922; info@pewaukeechamber.org; www.pewaukeechamber.org

Phelps · *Phelps C/C* · P.O. Box 217; 54554; Vilas; P 1,400; M 78; (715) 545-3800; (877) 669-7077; phelpschamber@gmail.com; www.phelpscofc.org

Phillips · *Phillips Area C/C* · Judith Boers; Exec. Dir.; 305 S. Lake Ave.; 54555; Price; P 1,748; M 180; (715) 339-4100; (888) 408-4800; Fax (715) 339-4190; pacc@pctcnet.net; phillipswisconsin.net

Phlox · *see Antigo*

Pickerel · *see Antigo*

Platteville · *Platteville C/C* · Kathy Kopp; Exec. Dir.; 275 Bus. Hwy. 151 W.; P.O. Box 724; 53818; Grant; P 10,007; M 280; (608) 348-8888; Fax (608) 348-8890; chamber@platteville.com; www.platteville.com*

Plover · *see Stevens Point*

Plymouth · *Plymouth C/C* · Lisa Hurley; Exec. Dir.; 647 Walton Dr.; P.O. Box 584; 53073; Sheboygan; P 8,600; M 350; (920) 893-0079; (888) 693-8263; Fax (920) 893-8473; plymouthchamber@excel.net; www.plymouthwisconsin.com

Polar · *see Antigo*

Port Washington · *Port Washington C/C* · Mary Monday; Exec. Dir.; 126 E. Grand Ave.; P.O. Box 514; 53074; Ozaukee; P 10,500; M 200; (262) 284-0900; (800) 719-4881; Fax (262) 284-0591; info@portwashingtonchamber.com; www.portwashingtonchamber.com

Portage · *Portage Area C/C* · Marianne Hanson; Exec. Dir.; 104 W. Cook St., Ste. A; 53901; Columbia; P 14,300; M 340; (608) 742-6242; (800) 474-2525; Fax (608) 742-3799; pacc@portagewi.com; www.portagewi.com*

Potosi · *Potosi-Tennyson Area C/C* · Marilyn Hauth; Pres.; P.O. Box 11; 53820; Grant; P 711; M 40; (608) 763-2261; (608) 763-2539; www.potosiwisconsin.com

Poynette · *Poynette Area C/C* · Brit Schoeneberg; Pres.; P.O. Box 625; 53955; Columbia; P 2,800; M 90; (608) 635-2425; britlivw@aol.com; www.poynettechamber.com

Prairie du Chien · *Prairie du Chien Area C/C* · Robert Moses; Exec. Dir.; 211 S. Main St.; 53821; Crawford; P 10,000; M 350; (608) 326-8555; Fax (608) 326-7744; pdccoc@mhtc.net; www.prairieduchien.org*

Prairie du Sac · *Sauk Prairie Area C/C* · 421 Water St., Ste. 105; 53578; Sauk; P 7,500; M 170; (608) 643-4168; (800) 683-2453; Fax (608) 643-3544; saukprairie@verizon.net; www.saukprairie.com

Prescott · *Prescott Area C/C* · Trisha Huber; Coord.; 237 Broad St. N.; 54021; Pierce; P 4,000; M 115; (715) 262-3284; Fax (715) 262-5943; info@prescottwi.com; www.prescottwi.com

Presque Isle · *Presque Isle C/C* · P.O. Box 135; 54557; Vilas; P 600; M 50; (715) 686-2910; (888) 835-6508; info@presqueisle.com; www.presqueisle.com

Princeton · *Greater Princeton Area C/C* · Ron Calbaum; Pres.; P.O. Box 45; 54968; Green Lake; P 1,500; M 150; (920) 295-3877; Fax (920) 295-4375; info@princetonwi.com; www.princetonwi.com*

Pulaski · *Pulaski Area C/C* · Gloria Morgan; Exec. Dir.; 159 W. Pulaski St.; P.O. Box 401; 54162; Brown, Oconto & Shawano; P 3,600; M 95; (920) 822-4400; Fax (920) 822-4455; pacc@netnet.net; www.pulaskichamber.org

Racine · *Racine Area Mfg. & Commerce* · Roger Caron; Pres.; 300 Fifth St.; 53403; Racine; P 189,000; M 750; (262) 634-1931; Fax (262) 634-7422; rcaron@racinechamber.com; www.racinechamber.com*

Randolph · *Randolph C/C* · Joyce Gorr; Secy./Treas.; P.O. Box 66; 53956; Columbia & Dodge; P 1,800; M 65; (920) 326-4769; Fax (920) 326-5032; www.randolphwi.net

Reedsburg · *Reedsburg Area C/C* · Kristine Koenecke; Exec. Dir.; 142 Railroad St.; P.O. Box 142; 53959; Sauk; P 10,000; M 210; (608) 524-2850; reedsbrg@rucls.net; www.reedsburg.org*

Rhinelander · *Rhinelander Area C/C* · Kim Swisher; Exec. Dir.; 450 W. Kemp St.; P.O. Box 795; 54501; Oneida; P 9,000; M 285; (715) 365-7464; (800) 236-4386; Fax (715) 365-7467; info@rhinelanderchamber.com; www.rhinelanderchamber.com*

Rice Lake · *Rice Lake Area C/C* · Karen Heram; Exec. Dir.; 37 S. Main St.; 54868; Barron; P 10,000; M 300; (715) 234-2126; Fax (715) 234-2085; chamber@rice-lake.com; www.ricelakechamber.org*

Richland Center · *Richland Chamber & Dev. Alliance* · Susan Price; Exec. Dir.; 397 W. Seminary; P.O. Box 128; 53581; Richland; P 17,000; M 150; (608) 647-6205; info@richlandchamber.com; www.richlandchamber.com

Ripon · *Ripon Area C/C* · Paula Price; Exec. Dir.; 127 Jefferson St.; P.O. Box 305; 54971; Fond du Lac; P 8,000; M 300; (920) 748-6764; info@ripon-wi.com; www.ripon-wi.com

River Falls · *River Falls Area C/C & Tourism Bur.* · Rosanne Bump; CEO; 214 N. Main St.; 54022; Pierce & St. Croix; P 13,000; M 275; (715) 425-2533; Fax (715) 425-2305; info@rfchamber.com; www.rfchamber.com

Saint Croix Falls · *Falls C/C* · Cindy Stimmler; Exec. Dir.; 106 S. Washington; P.O. Box 178; 54024; Polk; P 3,000; M 150; (715) 483-3580; (800) 447-4958; Fax (715) 483-3580; director@fallschamber.org; www.fallschamber.org

Saint Germain · *Saint Germain C/C* · William Neider; Dir.; 473 Hwy. 70 E.; P.O. Box 155; 54558; Vilas; P 2,000; M 160; (715) 477-2205; (800) 727-7203; Fax (715) 542-3423; info@st-germain.com; www.st-germain.com

Sauk City · *see Prairie Du Sac*

Saukville · *Saukville C/C* · Stacey Frey; Exec. Dir.; P.O. Box 80238; 53080; Ozaukee; P 4,200; M 110; (262) 268-1970; Fax (262) 268-1970; saukvillechamber@earthlink.net; www.saukvillechamber.org

Sayner · *Sayner-Starlake C/C* · P.O. Box 191; 54560; Vilas; P 550; M 50; (715) 542-3789; saynerstarlake@wildblue.net; www.sayner-starlake.org

Sharon · *Sharon C/C* · Linda DiPiero; Pres.; P.O. Box 383; 53585; Walworth; P 1,552; M 27; (262) 736-1250; info@villageofsharon.com; www.villageofsharon.com/chamber

Shawano · *Shawano Country C/C* · Nancy Smith; Exec. Dir.; 1263 S. Main St.; P.O. Box 38; 54166; Shawano; P 40,000; M 430; (715) 524-2139; (800) 235-8528; Fax (715) 524-3127; chamber@shawano.com; www.shawanocountry.com*

Sheboygan · *Sheboygan County C/C* · 712 Riverfront Dr., Ste. 101; 53081; Sheboygan; P 113,000; M 850; (920) 457-9491; Fax (920) 457-6269; chamber@sheboygan.org; www.sheboygan.org*

Sheboygan Falls · *Sheboygan Falls C/C* · Nancy Verstrate; Exec. Dir.; 504 Broadway St.; 53085; Sheboygan; P 7,000; M 178; (920) 467-6206; Fax (920) 467-9571; chambermnst@sheboyganfalls.org; www.sheboyganfalls.org

Sherwood · *see Kaukauna*

Siren · *Siren Area C/C* · Chris Moeller; Pres.; P.O. Box 57; 54872; Burnett; P 900; M 90; (715) 349-8399; chamber@visitsiren.com; www.visitsiren.com

Slinger · *Slinger Advancement Assn.* · Dr. Don Crego; Pres.; P.O. Box 422; 53086; Washington; P 5,000; M 55; (262) 644-5866; saa@slingersaa.com; www.slingersaa.com

Somerset · *also see New Richmond*

Somerset · *Somerset Area C/C* · Casey Goessl; Pres.; P.O. Box 357; 54025; St. Croix; P 2,400; M 41; (715) 247-3366; schamber@somtel.net; www.somerset-chamber.com

South Milwaukee · *South Milwaukee C/C* · Bryan Lorentzen; Pres.; 2424 15th Ave.; P.O. Box 207; 53172; Milwaukee; P 25,000; M 120; (414) 762-2222; Fax (414) 768-9505; laurac@smaconline.com; www.smaconline.com

Sparta · *Sparta Area C/C* · Sharon Folcey; Exec. Dir.; 111 Milwaukee St.; 54656; Monroe; P 9,160; M 345; (608) 269-4123; (800) 354-2453; Fax (608) 269-3350; spartachamber@centurytel.net; www.spartachamber.org

Spencer · *Spencer Area C/C* · Clint Gosse; Pres.; P.O. Box 52; 54479; Marathon; P 1,941; M 31; (715) 659-5423

Spooner · *Spooner Area C/C* · Ted Schmitz; Pres.; 122 N. River St.; 54801; Washburn; P 2,500; M 100; (715) 635-2168; (800) 367-3306; Fax (715) 635-5170; spoonerareachamber@centurytel.net; www.spoonerchamber.org

Spring Green · *Spring Green Area C/C* · Dawn Eno; Ofc. Mgr.; P.O. Box 3; 53588; Sauk; P 2,500; M 125; (608) 588-2054; sgacc@frontier.com; www.springgreen.com

Spring Valley · *Spring Valley C/C* · P.O. Box 351; 54767; Pierce & St. Croix; P 1,189; M 60; (715) 778-5015; tony@springvalley wisconsin.org; www.springvalleywisconsin.org

Stanley · *Stanley Area C/C* · Dale Johnson; Treas.; 117 N. Broadway St.; P.O. Box 123; 54768; Chippewa & Clark; P 2,000; M 70; (715) 644-3336

Star Prairie · *see New Richmond*

Starlake · *see Sayner*

Stevens Point · *Portage County Bus. Cncl.* · Lori Dehlinger; Exec. Dir.; 5501 Vern Holmes Dr.; 54482; Portage; P 69,000; M 526; (715) 344-1940; Fax (715) 344-4473; info@portagecountybiz. com; www.portagecountybiz.com*

Stone Lake · *Stone Lake C/C* · Susan Walker; Pres.; P.O. Box 75; 54876; Washburn; P 300; M 20; (715) 865-3378; (715) 865-3302; www.stonelakewi.us

Stoughton · *Stoughton C/C* · David B. Phillips; Exec. Dir.; 532 E. Main St.; 53589; Dane; P 13,000; M 250; (608) 873-7912; (888) 873-7912; Fax (608) 873-7743; administrator@stoughtonwi.com; www.stoughtonwi.com

Stratford · *Stratford C/C* · Dan Bergs; Pres.; P.O. Box 312; 54484; Marathon; P 1,600; M 100; (715) 687-4466; www.stratfordwi.com

Summit Lake · *see Antigo*

Sun Prairie · *Sun Prairie C/C* · Ann Smith; Exec. Dir.; 109 E. Main St.; 53590; Dane; P 28,000; M 379; (608) 837-4547; spchamber@ sunprairiechamber.com; www.sunprairiechamber.com*

Superior · *Superior-Douglas County C/C* · David W. Minor; Pres./CEO; 205 Belknap St.; 54880; Douglas; P 44,100; M 415; (715) 394-7716; (800) 942-5313; Fax (715) 394-3810; vacation@ superiorchamber.org; www.superiorchamber.org*

Sussex · *Sussex Area C/C* · Sheri Pellechia; Exec. Dir.; N64 W24050 Main St.; P.O. Box 24; 53089; Waukesha; P 9,812; M 120; (262) 246-4940; Fax (262) 246-7350; info@sussexareachamber. org; www.sussexareachamber.org

Thiensville · *Mequon-Thiensville Area C/C* · Tina Schwantes; Exec. Dir.; 250 S. Main St.; 53092; Ozaukee; P 25,000; M 400; (262) 512-9358; Fax (262) 512-9359; info@mtchamber.org; www.mtchamber.org*

Thorp · *Thorp Area C/C* · Randy Reeg; Pres.; P.O. Box 16; 54771; Clark; P 1,650; M 60; (715) 669-5371; www.cityofthorp.com

Three Lakes · *Three Lakes Area C/C* · Terilyn Fritz; Exec. Dir.; 1704 Superior St.; P.O. Box 268; 54562; Oneida; P 2,400; M 120; (715) 546-3344; (800) 972-6103; vacation@threelakes.com; www.threelakes.com

Tomah · *Greater Tomah Area C/C* · Christopher Hanson; Exec. Dir.; 901 Kilbourn Ave.; P.O. Box 625; 54660; Monroe; P 9,000; M 310; (608) 372-2166; (800) 94-TOMAH; Fax (608) 372-2167; info@tomahwisconsin.com; www.tomahwisconsin.com*

Tomahawk · *Tomahawk Reg. C/C* · Tamra Anderson; Exec. Dir.; 208 N. 4th St.; P.O. Box 412; 54487; Lincoln; P 4,000; M 300; (715) 453-5334; (800) 569-2160; Fax (715) 453-1178; jan@gototoma- hawk.com; www.gototomahawk.com.*

Townsend · *see Lakewood*

Trempealeau · *Trempealeau C/C* · Jean Galasinski; Pres.; 24455 3rd St.; P.O. Box 242; 54661; Trempealeau; P 1,541; M 45; (608) 534-6780; chamber@trempealeau.net; www.trempealeau.net

Twin Lakes · *Twin Lakes Area Chamber & Bus. Assn. Inc.* · Joanne Oreilly; Ofc. Admin.; 349 E. Main St.; P.O. Box 64; 53181; Kenosha; P 5,164; M 125; (262) 877-2220; Fax (262) 877-9437; info@twinlakeschamber.com; www.twinlakeschamber.com

Two Rivers · *see Manitowoc*

Union Grove · *Greater Union Grove Area C/C* · Terri Gray; Exec. Dir.; 925 15th Ave.; P.O. Box 44; 53182; Racine; P 15,000; M 118; (262) 878-4606; Fax (262) 878-9125; ugchamber@att.net; www. uniongrovechamber.org

Verona · *Verona Area C/C* · Karl Curtis; Exec. Dir.; 205 S. Main; P.O. Box 930003; 53593; Dane; P 10,000; M 296; (608) 845-5777; Fax (608) 845-2519; info@veronawi.com; www.veronawi.com

Viroqua · *Viroqua C/C Main St.* · Rebecca Eby; Exec. Dir.; 220 S. Main St.; 54665; Vernon; P 4,335; M 200; (608) 637-2575; infodesk@viroqua-wisconsin.com; www.viroqua-wisconsin.com

Wabeno · *Wabeno C/C* · Ron Drott; P.O. Box 105; 54566; Forest; P 1,500; M 49; (715) 473-5400

Washburn · *Washburn Area C/C* · Bruce Hanson; Exec. Dir.; P.O. Box 74; 54891; Bayfield; P 2,350; M 135; (715) 373-5017; (800) 253-4495; Fax (715) 373-0240; info@washburnchamber.com; www.washburnchamber.com

Washington Island · *Washington Island C/C* · Marianna Gibson; Secy./Treas.; 2206 W. Harbor Rd.; 54246; Door; P 670; M 100; (920) 847-2179; info@washingtonislandchamber.com; www.washingtonisland-wi.com

Waterford · *Waterford Area C/C* · Jennifer Thomas; Exec. Dir.; 102 E. Main St.; P.O. Box 203; 53185; Racine; P 5,000; M 225; (262) 534-5911; Fax (262) 534-6507; chamber@waterford-wi.org; www. waterford-wi.org*

Waterloo · *Waterloo C/C* · 117 E. Madison St.; P.O. Box 1; 53594; Jefferson; P 3,000; M 65; (920) 478-2500; chamber@waterloowi. us; www.waterloowi.us

Watertown · *Watertown Area C/C* · Kim Erdmann; Exec. Dir.; 519 E. Main St.; 53094; Dodge & Jefferson; P 23,200; M 350; (920) 261-6320; info@watertownchamber.com; www.watertownchamber.com

Waukesha · *Waukesha County C/C* · Suzanne Kelley; Pres.; 2717 N. Grandview Blvd., Ste. 204; 53188; Waukesha; P 100,000; M 825; (262) 542-4249; Fax (262) 542-8068; chamber@waukesha. org; www.waukesha.org

Waunakee · *Waunakee/Westport C/C* · Ellen K. Schaaf; Exec. Dir.; 100 E. Main St.; P.O. Box 41; 53597; Dane; P 12,000; M 250; (608) 849-5977; Fax (608) 849-9825; waunakeechamber@tds.net; www.waunakee.com

Waupaca · *Waupaca Area C/C* · Terri Schulz; Pres.; 221 S. Main St.; 54981; Waupaca; P 16,000; M 400; (715) 258-7343; (888) 417-4040; Fax (715) 258-7868; info@waupacaareachamber.com; www. waupacaareachamber.com.*

Waupun · *Waupun Area C/C* · Kristie Buwalda; Exec. Dir.; 324 E. Main St.; 53963; Fond du Lac; P 10,986; M 150; (920) 324-3491; Fax (920) 324-4357; waupunchamber@sbcglobal.net; www. waupunchamber.com

Wausau · *Wausau Region C/C* · Roger A. Luce; Exec. Dir.; 200 Washington St., Ste. 120; P.O. Box 6190; 54402; Marathon; P 127,000; M 1,200; (715) 845-6231; Fax (715) 845-6235; info@wausauchamber.com; www.wausauchamber.com*

Wautoma · *Waushara Area C/C* · Judy Downie; Admin.; 440 W. Main St.; P.O. Box 65; 54982; Waushara; P 24,000; M 240; (920) 787-3488; (877) WAUTOMA; Fax (920) 787-3788; WausharaWI@ live.com; www.wausharachamber.com

Wauwatosa · *Wauwatosa West Suburban Assoc. of Commerce* · Exec. Dir.; 10437 Innovation Dr., Ste. 130; 53226; Milwaukee; P 50,000; M 400; (414) 453-2330; Fax (414) 453-2336; info@tosa.org; www.tosachamber.org

Webster • *Webster Area C/C* • P.O. Box 48; 54893; Burnett; P 681; M 100; websterchamber@yahoo.com; www.webster wisconsin.com

West Allis • *West Allis/West Milwaukee C/C* • Diane Brandt; Exec. Dir.; 7447 W. Greenfield Ave.; 53214; Milwaukee; P 70,000; M 400; (414) 302-9901; Fax (414) 302-9918; contact@wawm chamber.com; www.wawmchamber.com

West Bend • *West Bend Area C/C* • Craig Farrell; Exec. Dir.; 304 S. Main St.; 53095; Washington; P 30,000; M 500; (262) 338-2666; info@wbachamber.org; www.wbachamber.org

West Milwaukee • *see West Allis*

West Salem • *see Onalaska*

Westby • *Westby Area C/C* • Trish Evenstad; Exec. Dir.; P.O. Box 94; 54667; Vernon; P 2,045; M 80; (608) 634-4011; westbycoc@ mwt.net; www.westbywi.com

Westfield • *Westfield C/C* • Roger Peterson; Pres.; P.O. Box 393; 53964; Marquette; P 1,230; M 45; (608) 296-4146; www. westfieldwi.com

Westport • *see Waunakee*

Weyauwega • *Weyauwega Area C/C* • Becca Eckhardt; Pres.; P.O. Box 531; 54983; Waupaca; P 1,806; M 61; (920) 867-2500; info@weyauwegachamber.com; www.weyauwegachamber.com

White Lake • *see Antigo*

Whitehall • *Whitehall Area C/C* • Karen Witte; Treas.; P.O. Box 155; 54773; Trempealeau; P 1,671; M 45; (715) 538-4353; www. whitehall-chamber.com

Whitewater • *Whitewater Area C/C* • Deb Williamson; Exec. Dir.; 171 W. Main St.; P.O. Box 34; 53190; Jefferson & Walworth; P 15,000; M 175; (262) 473-4005; (866) 4-WWTOUR; Fax (262) 753-0067; wacc@idcnet.com; www.whitewaterchamber.com

Williams Bay • *see Fontana*

Wind Lake • *Wind Lake C/C* • Nancy Hoppe; Pres.; 26422 Oakridge Dr.; 53185; Racine; P 7,643; M 50; (262) 895-7566; www.windlake-wi.org

Winneconne • *Winneconne Area C/C* • Scott Rupnow; Pres.; 31 S. 2nd St.; P.O. Box 126; 54986; Winnebago; P 12,000; M 80; (920) 582-4775; chamber@winneconne.org; www.winneconne.org

Winter • *Winter Area C/C* • P.O. Box 245; 54896; Sawyer; P 1,500; M 90; (715) 266-2204; (800) 762-7179; mail@winterwi.com; www.winterwi.com

Wisconsin Rapids • *Heart of Wisconsin Bus. Alliance* • Connie Loden; Exec. Dir.; 1120 Lincoln St.; 54494; Wood; P 40,000; M 490; (715) 423-1830; Fax (715) 423-1865; info@heartofwi.com; www. heartofwi.com*

Wittenberg • *Wittenberg Area C/C* • Anita Kostuch; P.O. Box 284; 54499; Shawano; P 1,150; M 50; (715) 253-3525; chamber@ wittenbergnet.net; www.wittenbergchamber.org

Woodruff • *see Minocqua*

Wrightstown • *see Kaukauna*

Wyoming

No State Chamber

Afton • *Star Valley C/C* • Melanie S. Wilkes; Exec. Dir.; 150 S. Washington; P.O. Box 190; 83110; Lincoln; P 16,000; M 135; (307) 885-2759; (800) 426-8833; Fax (307) 885-2758; info@starvalley chamber.com; www.starvalleychamber.com

Basin • *Basin Area C/C* • Barbara Anne Greene; Pres.; 407 C. St.; P.O. Box 883; 82410; Big Horn; P 1,224; M 60; (307) 568-3055; basincc@tctwest.net; www.basincc.com

Buffalo • *Buffalo C/C* • Angela Jarvis; Exec. Dir.; 55 N. Main St.; 82834; Johnson; P 5,500; M 270; (307) 684-5544; (800) 227-5122; Fax (307) 684-0291; info@buffalowyo.com; www.buffalowyo.com*

Casper • *Casper Area C/C* • Lori Becker; Exec. Dir.; 500 N. Center St.; P.O. Box 399; 82602; Natrona; P 54,000; M 815; (307) 234-5311; (866) 234-5311; Fax (307) 265-2643; chamber@casper wyoming.org; www.casperwyoming.org.*

Cheyenne • *Greater Cheyenne C/C* • Dale G. Steenbergen; Pres./CEO; 121 W. 15th St., Ste. 204; 82001; Laramie; P 90,000; M 780; (307) 638-3388; Fax (307) 778-1407; info@cheyennechamber.org; www.cheyennechamber.org*

Chugwater • *see Wheatland*

Cody • *Cody Country C/C* • Kimberly Jones; Exec. Dir.; 836 Sheridan Ave.; 82414; Park; P 9,000; M 600; (307) 587-2777; Fax (307) 527-6228; info@codychamber.org; www.codychamber.org*

Cokeville • *Cokeville C/C* • Carolyn Reed; P.O. Box 358; 83114; Lincoln; P 506; M 30; (307) 279-3200; Fax (307) 279-3105; cvchamber@allwest.net; www.wyomingtourism.org

Diamondville • *see Kemmerer*

Douglas • *Douglas Area C/C* • Helga Bull; Dir.; 121 Brownfield Rd.; 82633; Converse; P 6,000; M 250; (307) 358-2950; (877) 937-4996; Fax (307) 358-2972; chamber@jackalope.org; www. douglaschamber.com

Dubois • *Dubois C/C* • 616 W. Ramshorn; P.O. Box 632; 82513; Fremont; P 1,000; M 185; (307) 455-2556; duboiscc@dteworld. com; www.duboiswyomingchamber.org

Evanston • *Evanston C/C* • Dawn Darby; Exec. Dir.; 1020 Front St.; P.O. Box 365; 82931; P 12,500; M 220; (307) 783-0370; (800) 328-9708; Fax (307) 789-4807; chamber@etownchamber.com; www.etownchamber.com*

Gillette • *Campbell County C/C* • Julie Simon; Pres.; 314 S. Gillette Ave.; 82716; Campbell; P 40,433; M 594; (307) 682-3673; Fax (307) 682-0538; frontoffice@gillettechamber.com; www. gillettechamber.com*

Glendo • *see Wheatland*

Glenrock • *Glenrock Area C/C* • Mary Kay Kindt; Dir.; 506 W. Birch St.; P.O. Box 411; 82637; Converse; P 2,400; M 123; (307) 436-5652; Fax (307) 436-5477; gacc@sdwinc.com; www.glen rockchamber.com

Green River • *Green River C/C* • Janet Hartford; Exec. Dir.; 1155 W. Flaming Gorge Way; 82935; Sweetwater; P 13,500; M 270; (307) 875-5711; (307) 875-8992; Fax (307) 875-8993; info@ grchamber.com; www.grchamber.com*

Greybull • *Greybull Area C/C* • Julie Owens; Pres.; 521 Greybull Ave.; 82426; Big Horn; P 1,900; M 80; (307) 765-2100; chamber@ greybull.com; www.greybull.com

Guernsey • *see Wheatland*

Hartville • *see Wheatland*

Hulett • *Hulett C/C* • Rose Ann Olson; Pres.; P.O. Box 421; 82720; Crook; P 425; M 45; (307) 467-5747; Fax (307) 467-5765; www. hulett-wyoming.com

Jackson • *Jackson Hole C/C* • Tim O'Donoghue; Exec. Dir.; 980 W. Broadway; P.O. Box 550; 83001; Teton; P 19,000; M 904; (307) 733-3316; Fax (307) 733-5585; info@jacksonholechamber.com; www.jacksonholechamber.com

Kaycee • *Kaycee Area C/C* • Christy Cleveland; Secy.; 100 Park Ave.; P.O. Box 147; 82639; Johnson; P 250; M 80; (307) 738-2444; Fax (307) 738-2444; kayceechamber@rtconnect.net; www.kayceewyoming.org

Kemmerer • *Kemmerer/Diamondville Area C/C* • Teri Picerno; Exec. Dir.; 800 Pine Ave.; Triangle Park; 83101; Lincoln; P 4,000; M 100; (307) 877-9761; (888) 300-3413; Fax (307) 877-9762; chamber@hamsfork.net; www.kemmererchamber.com

Lander • *Lander Area C/C* • Scott Goetz; Exec. Dir.; 160 N. 1st St.; 82520; Fremont; P 7,500; M 328; (307) 332-3892; (800) 433-0662; Fax (307) 332-3893; info@landerchamber.org; www.landerchamber.com

Laramie • *Laramie Area C/C* • 800 S. Third St.; 82070; Albany; P 27,000; M 500; (307) 745-7339; (866) 876-1012; Fax (307) 745-4624; chamberofcommerce@laramie.org; www.laramie.org*

Lovell • *Lovell Area C/C* • Suzanne Winterholler; Secy.; 287 E. Main; 82431; Big Horn; P 2,361; M 90; (307) 548-7552; lovell@tctwest.net; www.lovellchamber.com

Lusk • *Niobrara C/C* • Jackie Bredthauer; Exec. Dir.; 224 S. Main; P.O. Box 457; 82225; Niobrara; P 2,500; M 120; (307) 334-2950; (800) 223-LUSK; Fax (307) 334-2951; luskchamberofcommerce@yahoo.com; www.luskwyoming.com

Lyman • *Greater Bridger Valley C/C* • Chuck James; Exec. Dir.; 100 E. Sage St.; P.O. Box 1506; 82937; Uinta; P 6,000; M 100; (307) 787-6738; bvchamber@bvea.net; www.bridgervalleychamber.com

Marbleton • *see Pinedale*

Moorcroft • *Moorcroft C/C* • Susan Millard; P.O. Box 932; 82721; Crook; P 1,500; M 35; (307) 756-3526

Newcastle • *Newcastle Area C/C* • Norma Shelton; Exec. Dir.; 1323 Washington Blvd.; 82701; Weston; P 6,500; M 160; (307) 746-2739; Fax (307) 746-2739; nacoc@rtconnect.net; www.newcastlewyo.com*

Pine Bluffs • *Pine Bluffs C/C* • Cate Cundall; P.O. Box 429; 82082; Laramie; P 1,163; M 65; (307) 245-3746; Fax (307) 245-3883; pinebluffs@rtconnect.net; www.pinebluffs.org

Pinedale • *Sublette County C/C & Visitor Center* • Terrie Swift; Exec. Dir.; 19 E. Pine; P.O. Box 176; 82941; Sublette; P 9,000; M 230; (307) 367-2242; (888) 285-7282; Fax (307) 367-2248; director@sublettechamber.com; www.sublettechamber.com

Platte County • *see Wheatland*

Powell • *Powell Valley C/C* • Naomi Burns; Exec. Dir.; 111 S. Day St.; P.O. Box 1258; 82435; Park; P 5,300; M 250; (307) 754-3494; (800) 325-4278; Fax (307) 754-3483; info@powellchamber.org; www.powellchamber.org*

Rawlins • *Rawlins-Carbon County C/C* • Exec. Dir.; 519 W. Cedar St.; P.O. Box 1331; 82301; Carbon; P 10,000; M 200; (307) 324-4111; Fax (307) 324-5078; chamberdirector@qwestoffice.net; www.rawlinschamberofcommerce.org*

Riverton • *Riverton C/C* • Jim Davis; Exec. Dir.; 213 W. Main St., Ste.C; 82501; Fremont; P 10,000; M 330; (307) 856-4801; Fax (307) 857-0873; info@rivertonchamber.org; www.rivertonchamber.org.*

Rock Springs • *Rock Springs C/C* • Dave Hanks; CEO; 1897 Dewar Dr.; P.O. Box 398; 82901; Sweetwater; P 28,000; M 600; (307) 362-3771; (800) 46-DUNES; Fax (307) 362-3838; rschamber@sweetwaterhsa.com; www.rockspringschamber.com

Saratoga • *Saratoga/Platte Valley C/C* • Stacy Crimmins; Dir.; 210 W. Elm St.; P.O. Box 1095; 82331; Carbon; P 1,726; M 180; (307) 326-8855; Fax (307) 326-8850; info@saratogachamber.info; www.saratogachamber.info

Sheridan • *Sheridan County C/C* • Janelle Martinsen; Exec. Dir.; P.O. Box 707; 82801; Sheridan; P 28,600; M 525; (307) 672-2485; (800) 453-3650; Fax (307) 672-7321; info@sheridanwyomingchamber.org; www.sheridanwyomingchamber.org*

Shoshoni • *Shoshoni C/C* • Oscar Lawson; Pres.; P.O. Box 324; 82649; Fremont; P 800; M 110; (307) 851-7650; olawson_bmo@hotmail.com; www.windrivercountry.com

Sundance • *Sundance Area C/C* • Jeff Moberg; Pres.; P.O. Box 1004; 82729; Crook; P 1,100; M 40; (307) 283-1000; (800) 477-9340; chamber@sundancewyoming.com; www.sundancewyoming.com

Ten Sleep • *see Worland*

Thayne • *see Afton*

Thermopolis • *Thermopolis-Hot Springs C/C* • Kathy Wallingford; Exec. Dir.; 220 Park St.; P.O. Box 768; 82443; Hot Springs; P 3,300; M 238; (307) 864-3192; (877) 864-3192; Fax (307) 864-3128; thercc@rtconnect.net; www.thermopolis.com*

Torrington • *Goshen County C/C* • Rhonda Schulte; Exec. Dir.; 350 W. 21st Ave.; 82240; Goshen; P 12,538; M 275; (307) 532-3879; Fax (307) 534-2360; goshencountychamber@yahoo.com; www.goshencountychamber.com*

Upton • *Upton C/C* • P.O. Box 756; 82730; Weston; P 872; M 60; (307) 468-2228; www.uptonwyo.com

Wheatland • *Platte County C/C* • Cheryl Deuel; Exec. Dir.; 65 16th St.; 82201; Platte; P 8,800; M 242; (307) 322-2322; Fax (307) 322-3419; info@plattechamber.com; www.plattechamber.com*

Worland • *Worland-Ten Sleep C/C* • Terry Sutherland; Exec. Dir.; 120 N. 10th St.; 82401; Washakie; P 5,250; M 245; (307) 347-3226; Fax (307) 347-3025; wtschamber@rtconnect.net; www.worlandchamber.com.*

Notes

Alabama · *Alabama Tourism Dept.* · Lee Sentell; Dir.; 401 Adams Ave., Ste. 126; P.O. Box 4927; Montgomery; 36103; Montgomery; (334) 242-4169; (800) ALABAMA; Fax (334) 242-4554; info@tourism.alabama.gov; www.alabama.travel

Alaska · *Alaska Travel Industry Assn.* · Ron Peck; Pres./CEO; 2600 Cordova St., Ste. 201; Anchorage; 99503; (907) 929-2200; Fax (907) 561-5727; atia@AlaskaTIA.org; www.travelalaska.com

Arizona · *Arizona Office of Tourism* · Sherry Henry; Exec. Dir.; 1110 W. Washington St., Ste. 155; Phoenix; 85007; Maricopa; (602) 364-3700; (866) 275-5816; Fax (602) 364-3701; mstanton@azot.gov; www.azot.gov

Arkansas · *Arkansas Dept. of Parks & Tourism* · Joe David Rice; Dir. of Tourism; One Capitol Mall; Little Rock; 72201; Pulaski; (501) 682-7777; Fax (501) 682-2523; info@arkansas.com; www.arkansas.com

California · *California Travel & Tourism* · Caroline Beteta; Exec. Dir.; P.O. Box 1499; Sacramento; 95812; Sacramento; (916) 444-4429; (877) 225-4367; Fax (916) 444-0410; aluiz@visitcalifornia.com; www.visitcalifornia.com

Colorado · *Colorado Office of Tourism* · Don Marostica; Exec. Dir.; 1625 Broadway, Ste. 2700; Denver; 80202; Denver; (303) 892-3885; (800) COLORADO; Fax (303) 892-3848; info@colorado.com; www.colorado.com

Connecticut · *Connecticut Commission on Culture & Tourism* · Karen Senich; Exec. Dir.; One Constitution Plaza, 2nd Flr.; Hartford; 06103; Hartford; (860) 256-2800; (888) CT-VISIT; Fax (860) 270-2811; ct.travelinfo@ct.gov; www.ctvisit.com

Delaware · *Delaware Tourism Office* · Linda Parkowski; Dir.; 99 Kings Hwy.; Dover; 19901; Kent; (302) 739-4271; (866) 284-7483; Fax (302) 739-5749; tina.madanat@state.de.us; www.visitdelaware.com

Florida · *Visit Florida* · Chris Thompson; Pres./CEO; 2540 W. Executive Center Cir., Ste. 200; Tallahassee; 32301; Leon; (850) 488-5607; Fax (850) 201-6908; kathy@visitflorida.org; www.visitflorida.org

Georgia · *Georgia Dept. of Eco. Dev.* · Heidi Green; Commissioner; 75 Fifth St. N.W., Ste. 1200; Atlanta; 30308; Fulton; (404) 962-4000; Fax (404) 962-4093; dbelk@georgia.org; www.georgia.org

Hawaii · *Hawaii Tourism Auth.* · Mike McCartney; Pres./CEO; 1801 Kalakaua Ave.; Honolulu; 96815; Honolulu; (808) 973-2255; Fax (808) 973-2253; info@hawaiitourismauthority.org; www.hawaiitourismauthority.org

Idaho · *Idaho Div. of Tourism* · Karen Ballard; Admin.; 700 W. State St., 2nd Flr.; Boise; 83720; Ada; (208) 334-2470; (800) 635-7820; Fax (208) 334-2631; info@tourism.idaho.gov; www.visitidaho.org

Illinois · *Illinois Bur. of Tourism* · Jan Kostner; Dir.; DCEO; 500 E. Monroe; Springfield; 62701; Sangamon; (217) 557-2407; Fax (217) 785-6336; jan.kostner@illinois.gov; www.enjoyillinois.com

Indiana · *Indiana Office of Tourism Dev.* · Amy Vaughan; Dir.; One N. Capitol, Ste. 600; Indianapolis; 46204; Marion; (317) 232-8860; (800) 677-9800; Fax (317) 233-6887; www.in.gov/visitindiana

Iowa · *Iowa Tourism Office* · Shawna Lode; Mgr.; 200 E. Grand Ave.; Des Moines; 50309; Polk; (888) 472-6035; (800) 345-IOWA; Fax (515) 725-3010; shawna.lode@iowa.gov; www.traveliowa.com

Kansas · *Kansas Travel & Tourism* · Becky Blake; Div. Dir.; 1000 S.W. Jackson St., Ste. 100; Topeka; 66612; Shawnee; (785) 296-2009; (800) 2-KANSAS; Fax (785) 296-6988; travtour@kansascommerce.com; www.travelks.com

Kentucky · *Kentucky Dept. of Tourism* · Mike Cooper; Commissioner; Capital Plaza Tower, 22nd Flr.; 500 Mero St.; Frankfort; 40601; Franklin; (502) 564-4930; (800) 225-8747; Fax (502) 564-5695; info@kentuckytourism.com; www.kentuckytourism.com

Louisiana · *Louisiana Office of Tourism* · James L. Hutchinson; Asst. Secy. of Tourism; P.O. Box 94291; Baton Rouge; 70804; E. Baton Rouge; (225) 342-8100; Fax (225) 342-1051; jhutchinson@crt.state.la.us; www.louisianatravel.com

Maine · *Maine Office of Tourism* · Patricia Eltman; Dir.; 59 State House Station; Augusta; 04333; Kennebec; (207) 287-5711; (888) 624-6345; Fax (207) 287-8070; Pat.Eltman@maine.gov; www.visitmaine.com

Maryland · *Maryland Div. of Tourism* · Hannah Lee Byron; Asst. Secy.; 401 E. Pratt St., 14th Flr.; Baltimore; 21202; (410) 767-3400; (866) 639-3526; Fax (410) 333-6643; info@visitmaryland.org; www.visitmaryland.org

Massachusetts · *Massachusetts Office of Travel & Tourism* · Betsy Wall; Exec. Dir.; 10 Park Plaza, Ste. 4510; Boston; 02116; Suffolk; (617) 973-8500; (800) 227-MASS; Fax (617) 973-8525; VacationInfo@state.ma.us; www.massvacation.com

Michigan · *Travel Michigan* · George Zimmermann; V.P.; 300 N. Washington Sq., 2nd Flr.; Lansing; 48913; Ingham; (888) 784-7328; Fax (517) 373-0059; lorenzd@michigan.org; www.michigan.org

Minnesota · *Explore Minnesota Tourism* · John Edman; Dir.; 121 7th Pl. E., Ste. 100; Saint Paul; 55101; Ramsey; (651) 296-5029; (888) 868-7476; Fax (651) 296-7095; explore@state.mn.us; www.exploreminnesota.com

Mississippi · *Mississippi Div. of Tourism* · Mary Beth Wilkerson; Dir.; P.O. Box 849; Jackson; 39205; Hinds; (601) 359-3297; Fax (601) 359-5757; tourdiv@mississippi.org; www.visitmississippi.org

Missouri · *Missouri Div. of Tourism* · Kathleen Steele-Danner; Dir.; P.O. Box 1055; Jefferson City; 65102; Cole; (573) 751-4133; Fax (573) 751-5160; tourism@ded.mo.gov; www.visitmo.com

Montana · *Montana Office of Tourism* · Anna Marie Moe; Interim Travel Dir.; 301 S. Park Ave.; Helena; 59620; Lewis & Clark; (406) 841-2870; (800) 847-4868; Fax (406) 841-2871; www.visitmt.com

Nebraska · *Nebraska Tourism* · Christian Hornbaker; Dir.; P.O. Box 98906; Lincoln; 68509; Lancaster; (402) 471-3796; (877) 632-7275; Fax (402) 471-3026; tourism@visitnebraska.gov; www.visitnebraska.gov

Nevada · *Nevada Commission on Tourism* · Dann Lewis; Dir.; 401 N. Carson St.; Carson City; 89701; (775) 687-4322; (800) 237-0774; Fax (775) 687-6779; ncot@travelnevada.com; www.travelnevada.com

New Hampshire · *New Hampshire Div. of Travel & Tourism Dev.* · Lori Harnois; Dir.; P.O. Box 1856; Concord; 03302; Merrimack; (603) 271-2665; Fax (603) 271-6870; travel@dred.state.nh.us; www.visitnh.gov

New Jersey · *New Jersey Office of Travel & Tourism* · Phyllis Oppenheimer; Tourism Rep.; 225 W. State St. 5th Flr.; P.O. Box 460; Trenton; 08625; Mercer; (609) 599-6540; (800) VISIT-NJ; Fax (609) 633-7418; www.visitnj.org

New Mexico · *New Mexico Tourism Dept.* · Mike Cerletti; Cabinet Secy.; 491 Old Santa Fe Trl.; Santa Fe; 87501; Santa Fe; (505) 827-7400; (800) 545-2070; Fax (505) 827-7402; Mike.Cerletti@state.nm.us; www.newmexico.org

New York · *New York State Div. of Tourism* · Lisa Yarusso; Supervisor; 30 S. Pearl St., 4th Flr.; Albany; 12207; Albany; (518) 474-4116; (800) CALL-NYS; Fax (518) 292-5893; www.iloveny.com

North Carolina · *North Carolina Div. of Tourism, Film & Sports Dev.* · Lynn Minges; Asst. Secy. for Tourism; 301 N. Wilmington St.; Raleigh; 27601; Wake; (919) 733-4171; (800) 847-4862; Fax (919) 733-8582; lminges@nccommerce.com; www.visitnc.com

North Dakota · *North Dakota Tourism Div.* · Sara Otte Coleman; Dir.; 1600 E. Century Ave., Ste. 2; P.O. Box 2057; Bismarck; 58502; Burleigh; (701) 328-2525; (800) 435-5663; Fax (701) 328-4878; tourism@nd.gov; www.ndtourism.com

Ohio · *Ohio Div. of Travel & Tourism* · Pat Barker; Asst. Tourism Dir.; 77 S. High St.; P.O. Box 1001; Columbus; 43216; Delaware, Fairfield & Franklin; (614) 466-8844; (800) BUCKEYE; Fax (614) 466-6744; www.discoverohio.com

Oklahoma · *Oklahoma Tourism & Rec. Dept.* · Hardy Watkins; Exec. Dir.; P.O. Box 52002; Oklahoma City; 73152; Canadian, Cleveland, Oklahoma & Pottawatomie; (405) 230-8400; (800) 652-6552; Fax (405) 230-8600; information@travelok.com; www.travelok.com

Oregon · *Travel Oregon* · Todd Davidson; CEO; 670 Hawthorne Ave. S.E., Ste. 240; Salem; 97301; Marion; (503) 378-8850; (800) 547-7842; Fax (503) 378-4574; todd@traveloregon.com; www.traveloregon.com

Pennsylvania · *Pennsylvania Tourism Office* · Rose Mape; Exec. Dir. of Tourism & Mktg.; Commonwealth Keystone Bldg.; 400 North St., 4th Flr.; Harrisburg; 17120; Dauphin; (717) 787-5453; (800) VISITPA; Fax (717) 787-0687; rmape@state.pa.us; www.visitpa.com

Rhode Island · *Rhode Island Tourism* · Mark Brodeur; Dir.; 315 Iron Horse Way., Ste. 101; Providence; 02908; Providence; (401) 278-9100; (800) 250-7384; Fax (401) 273-8270; mbrodeur@riedc.com; www.visitrhodeisland.com

South Carolina · *South Carolina Dept. of Parks & Rec. & Tourism* · Chad Prosser; Dir.; 1205 Pendleton St.; Columbia; 29201; Richland & Lexington; (803) 734-1700; Fax (803) 734-1409; vlewis@scprt.com; www.discoversouthcarolina.com

South Dakota · *South Dakota Office of Tourism* · Melissa Miller; Dir.; 711 E. Wells Ave.; Pierre; 57501; Hughes; (605) 773-3301; (800) S-DAKOTA; Fax (605) 773-3256; sdinfo@state.sd.us; www.travelsd.com

Tennessee · *Tennessee Dept. of Tourist Dev.* · Susan Whitaker; Commissioner; 312 Rosa L. Parks Ave., 25th Flr.; Nashville; 37243; Davidson; (615) 741-2159; (800) GO2-TENN; Fax (615) 741-9071; tourdev@tn.gov; www.tnvacation.com

Texas · *Office of Gov. Eco. Dev. & Tourism Dev.* · Julie Chase; Dir. of Tourism; P.O. Box 12428; Austin; 78711; Travis; (512) 936-0100; Fax (512) 936-0303; jchase@governor.state.tx.us; www.traveltex.com

Utah · *Utah Office of Tourism* · Leigh Von Der Esch; Dir.; 300 N. State. St.; Salt Lake City; 84114; Salt Lake; (801) 538-1030; (800) 200-1160; Fax (801) 538-1399; travel@utah.gov; www.utah.travel

Vermont · *Vermont Dept. of Tourism & Mktg.* · Bruce Hyde; Commissioner; One National Life Dr., 6th Flr.; Montpelier; 05620; Washington; (802) 828-3237; (800) VERMONT; Fax (802) 828-3233; info@vermontvacation.com; www.vermontvacation.com

Virginia · *Virginia Tourism Corp.* · Alisa Bailey; Pres./CEO; 901 E. Byrd St.; Richmond; 23219; Richmond City; (804) 545-5500; (800) VISIT-VA; Fax (804) 545-5501; VAinfo@helloinc.com; www.virginia.org

Washington · *Washington State Tourism* · Marsha Massey; Dir.; 1011 Plum St. S.E.; P.O. Box 42525; Olympia; 98504; Thurston; (360) 725-4100; (800) 544-1800; Fax (360) 753-4470; tourism@cted.wa.gov; www.experiencewashington.com

West Virginia · *West Virginia Div. of Tourism* · Betty Carver; Commissioner; 90 MacCorkle Ave. S.W.; South Charleston; 25303; Kanawha; (304) 558-2200; (800) 225-5982; Fax (304) 558-2956; betty.b.carver@wv.gov; www.wvtourism.com

Wisconsin · *Wisconsin Dept. of Tourism* · Kelli Trumble; Secy.; P.O. Box 8690; Madison; 53708; Dane; (608) 266-7621; (800) 432-8747; Fax (608) 266-3403; tourinfo@travelwisconsin.com; www.travelwisconsin.com

Wyoming · *Wyoming Travel & Tourism* · Diane Shober; Dir.; 1520 Etchepare Cir.; Cheyenne; 82007; Laramie; (307) 777-7777; (800) 225-5996; Fax (307) 777-2877; info@visitwyo.gov; www.wyomingtourism.org

Alabama

Anniston • *Calhoun County CVB* • Mike Galloway; Dir. of Tourism; 1330 Quintard Ave.; P.O. Box 1087; 36202; Calhoun; P 117,000; (256) 237-3536; (800) 489-1087; Fax (256) 237-0126; info@calhounchamber.com; www.calhounchamber.com

Auburn • *Auburn/Opelika Tourism Bur.* • John Wild; Pres.; 714 E. Glenn Ave.; 36830; Lee; P 118,000; (334) 887-8747; (866) 880-8747; Fax (334) 821-5500; info@aotourism.com; www.aotourism.com

Birmingham • *Greater Birmingham CVB* • James Smither; Pres.; 2200 9th Ave. N.; 35203; Jefferson; P 1,000,000; (205) 458-8000; (800) 458-8085; Fax (205) 458-8086; info@birminghamal.org; www.birminghamal.org

Decatur • *Decatur-Morgan County CVB* • Tami Reist; Pres.; 719 6th Ave. S.E.; P.O. Box 2349; 35602; Morgan; P 55,000; (256) 350-2028; (800) 524-6181; Fax (256) 350-2054; info@decaturcvb.org; www.decaturcvb.org

Dothan • *Dothan Area CVB* • Bob Hendrix; Exec. Dir.; 3311 Ross Clark Circle; P.O. Box 8765; 36304; Houston; P 63,000; (334) 794-6622; (888) 449-0212; Fax (334) 712-2731; dothancvb@ala.net; www.dothanalcvb.com

Eufaula • *Eufaula/Barbour County Tourism Cncl.* • Corey Kirkland; Tourism Dir.; 333 E. Broad St.; 36027; Barbour; P 29,000; (334) 687-7099; (800) 524-7529; Fax (334) 687-5240; info@eufaulachamber.com; www.eufaulachamber.com

Fort Payne • *DeKalb County Tourist Assn.* • John Dersham; Exec. Dir.; P.O. Box 681165; 35968; DeKalb; P 65,000; M 200; (256) 845-3957; (888) 805-4740; Fax (256) 845-3946; info@tourdekalb.com; www.tourdekalb.com

Gulf Shores • *Alabama Gulf Coast CVB* • Herbert Malone Jr.; Pres./CEO; 900 Commerce Loop; 36542; Baldwin; P 11,000; (251) 974-1510; (800) 745-7263; Fax (251) 974-1509; info@gulfshores.com; www.gulfshores.com

Guntersville • *Marshall County CVB* • Lisa Socha; Exec. Dir.; 200 Gunter Ave.; P.O. Box 711; 35976; Marshall; P 85,000; (256) 582-7015; (800) 582-6282; Fax (256) 582-3682; marshallcountycvb@charterinternet.com; www.marshallcountycvb.com

Huntsville • *Huntsville-Madison County CVB* • Judy S. Ryals; Pres./CEO; 500 Church St., Ste 1; 35801; Madison; P 350,000; (256) 551-2230; (800) 772-2348; Fax (256) 551-2324; info@huntsville.org; www.huntsville.org

Mobile • *Mobile Bay CVB* • Leon Maisel; Pres./CEO; 1 S. Water St.; P.O. Box 204; 36601; Mobile; P 400,000; (251) 208-2000; (800) 5-MOBILE; Fax (251) 208-2060; lmaisel@mobilebay.org; www.mobilebay.org

Montgomery • *Montgomery Area CVB* • Dawn Hathcock; V.P.; 300 Water St.; P.O. Box 79; 36101; Montgomery; P 335,000; (334) 261-1100; (800) 240-9452; Fax (334) 261-1111; tourism@montgomerychamber.com; www.visitingmontgomery.com

Orange Beach • *see Gulf Shores*

Scottsboro • *Greater Jackson County CVB* • John R. Parsons; V.P. Destination Mktg.; 407 E. Willow St.; P.O. Box 973; 35768; Jackson; P 55,000; M 450; (256) 259-5500; (800) 259-5508; Fax (256) 259-4447; tourjackson@scottsboro.org; www.jacksoncountychamber.com

Selma • *Selma CVB* • Lauri S. Cothran; Pres.; 912 Selma Ave.; 36701; Dallas; P 46,365; (334) 875-7241; (800) 45-SELMA; Fax (334) 875-7142; info@SelmaAlabama.com; www.SelmaAlabama.com

Tuscaloosa • *Tuscaloosa CVB* • Robert Ratliff; Exec. Dir.; 1305 Greensboro Ave.; P.O. Box 3167; 35403; Tuscaloosa; P 170,000; (205) 391-9200; (800) 538-8696; Fax (205) 759-9002; robert@tcvb.org; www.tcvb.org

Tuscumbia • *Colbert County Tourism CVB* • Susann Hamlin; Exec. Dir.; P.O. Box 740425; 35674; Colbert; P 150,000; (256) 383-0783; (800) 344-0783; Fax (256) 383-2080; colberttourism@comcast.net; www.colbertcountytourism.org

Alaska

Anchorage • *Anchorage CVB* • Julie Saupe; Pres./CEO; 524 W. Fourth Ave.; 99501; Anchorage; P 277,000; M 1,500; (907) 276-4118; (800) 446-5352; Fax (907) 278-5559; info@anchorage.net; www.anchorage.net

Fairbanks • *Fairbanks CVB* • Deb Hickok; Pres./CEO; 101 Dunkel St., Ste. 111; 99701; Fairbanks North Star; P 100,000; M 400; (907) 456-5774; (800) 327-5774; Fax (907) 459-3757; info@explorefairbanks.com; www.explorefairbanks.com

Gustavus • *Gustavus Visitors Assn.* • P.O. Box 167; 99826; Hoonah Angoon; P 420; M 33; (907) 697-2454; info@gustavusak.com; www.gustavusak.com

Haines • *Haines CVB* • Lori Stepansky; Dir.; P.O. Box 530; 99827; Haines; P 2,300; (907) 766-2234; (800) 458-3579; Fax (907) 766-3155; hcvb@haines.ak.us; www.haines.ak.us

Homer • *Homer Visitor Info. Center* • Paul Dauphinais; Exec. Dir.; 201 Sterling Hwy.; 99603; Kenai Peninsula; P 5,400; (907) 235-7740; Fax (907) 235-8766; info@homeralaska.org; www.homeralaska.org

Iliamna • *Iliamna Cncl. Visitor Info.* • P.O. Box 286; 99606; Lak & Peninsula; P 150; (907) 571-1246; Fax (907) 571-1256; ilivc@aol.com

Juneau • *Juneau CVB* • Lorene Palmer; Pres./CEO; One Sealaska Plaza, Ste. 305; 99801; Juneau; P 32,000; M 300; (907) 586-1737; (800) 587-2201; Fax (907) 586-1449; info@traveljuneau.com; www.traveljuneau.com

Kenai • *Kenai CVB* • Natasha Ala; Exec. Dir.; 11471 Kenai Spur Hwy.; 99611; Kenai Peninsula; P 7,000; M 250; (907) 283-1991; Fax (907) 283-2230; info@visitkenai.com; www.visitkenai.com

Ketchikan • *Ketchikan Visitors Bur.* • Patricia Mackey; Exec. Dir.; 131 Front St.; 99901; Ketchikan Gateway; P 14,000; M 287; (907) 225-6166; (800) 770-3300; Fax (907) 225-4250; info@visit-ketchikan.com; www.visit-ketchikan.com

King Salmon • *King Salmon Visitor Center* • King Salmon Airport; P.O. Box 298; 99613; Bristol Bay; P 350; (907) 246-4250; Fax (907) 246-8550

Kodiak • *Kodiak Island CVB* • Janet Buckingham; Exec. Dir.; 100 Marine Way, Ste. 200; 99615; Kodiak Island; P 13,479; M 245; (907) 486-4782; (800) 789-4782; Fax (907) 486-6545; visit@kodiak.org; www.kodiak.org

Nome • *Nome CVB* • Mike Cavin; Dir.; 301 Front St.; P.O. Box 240; 99762; Nome; P 3,500; (907) 443-6555; Fax (907) 443-5832; nomeinfo@gci.net; www.visitnomealaska.com

Palmer · *Mat-Su CVB* · Bonnie Quill; Exec. Dir.; 7744 E. Visitors View Ct.; 99645; Matanuska Susitna; P 82,500; M 260; (907) 746-5000; Fax (907) 746-2688; info@alaskavisit.com; www.alaska visit.com

Petersburg · *Petersburg Visitors Info. Center* · Sally Dwyer; Mgr.; P.O. Box 649; 99833; Petersburg; P 3,200; (907) 772-4636; (866) 484-4700; Fax (907) 772-2453; inforequest@petersburg.org; www.petersburg.org

Sitka · *Sitka CVB* · Sandy Lorrigan; Exec. Dir.; 303 Lincoln St., Ste. 4; P.O. Box 1226; 99835; Sitka; P 8,900; M 200; (907) 747-5940; (800) 55-SITKA; Fax (907) 747-3739; scvb@sitka.org; www.sitka.org

Skagway · *Skagway CVB* · 245 Broadway; P.O. Box 1029; 99840; Skagway; P 862; (907) 983-2854; (888) 762-1898; Fax (907) 983-3854; skagwayinfo@gmail.com; www.skagway.com

Soldotna · *Kenai Peninsula Tourism Marketing Cncl.* · Shanon Hamrick; Exec. Dir.; 35571 Kenai Spur Hwy.; 99669; Kenai Peninsula; P 51,000; M 400; (907) 262-5229; (800) 535-3624; Fax (907) 262-5212; info@kenaipeninsula.org; www.kenaipeninsula.org

Tok · *Tok's 'Alaska Mainstreet' Visitor Center* · P.O. Box 389; 99780; Southeast Fairbanks; P 1,405; M 168; (907) 883-5775; info@TokAlaskaInfo.com; www.TokAlaskaInfo.com

Unalaska · *Unalaska/Port of Dutch Harbor CVB* · Brenda Wallace; CEO; P.O. Box 545; 99685; Aleutians West; P 4,600; M 64; (907) 581-2612; unalaskacvb@gmail.com; www.unalaska.info

Valdez · *Valdez CVB* · David Petersen; Exec. Dir.; 104 Chenega; P.O. Box 1603; 99686; Valdez Cordova; P 4,100; M 135; (907) 835-2984; Fax (907) 835-4845; info@valdezalaska.org; www.valdezalaska.org

White Mountain · *White Mountain Visitor Info. Center* · % City Hall; P.O. Box 130; 99784; Nome; P 215; (907) 638-3411; (907) 638-2230; Fax (907) 638-3421

Wrangell · *Wrangell CVB* · Carol Rushmore; Eco. Dev. Dir.; 296 Campbell Dr.; P.O. Box 1350; 99929; Wrangell; P 2,000; (907) 874-2829; (800) 367-9745; wrangell@wrangell.com; www.wrangellalaska.org

Arizona

Arizona City · *Sunland Visitor Center* · Cynthia Yates; Dir.; P.O. Box 280; 85223; Pinal; P 35,000; (520) 466-3007; (888) 786-3007; Fax (520) 466-3007; snlndvc@localnet.com; www.sunlandvisitorcenter.org

Ash Fork · *Ash Fork Tourism* · Ann McCullough; Dir.; 901 W. Rte. 66; P.O. Box 494; 86320; Yavapai; P 900; (928) 637-0204; (928) 637-2245; Fax (928) 637-2442

Flagstaff · *Flagstaff Visitor Center* · Heather Ainardi; Dir.; 1 E. Rte. 66; 86001; Coconino; P 62,000; (800) 842-7293; (928) 774-9541; Fax (928) 556-1308; visitorcenter@ci.flagstaff.az.us; www.flagstaffarizona.org

Florence · *Pinal County Visitor Center* · Pat Judy; Dir.; 330 E. Butte; P.O. Box 967; 85232; Pinal; P 179,727; (520) 868-4331; (800) 557-4331; Fax (520) 868-1099; visitpinal@pcvc.phxcoxmail.com; www.co.pinal.az.us/visitorcenter

Glendale · *Glendale Ofc. of Tourism & Visitor Center* · Lorraine Pino; Tourism Mgr.; 5800 W. Glenn Dr., Ste. 140; 85301; Maricopa; P 247,987; (623) 930-4500; Fax (623) 463-2337; tourinfo@visitglendale.com; www.visitglendale.com

Lake Havasu City · *Lake Havasu City CVB* · 314 London Bridge Rd.; 86403; Mohave; P 57,000; (928) 453-3444; (800) 242-8278; Fax (928) 453-3344; info@golakehavasu.com; www.golakehavasu.com

Mesa · *Mesa CVB* · Robert W. Brinton; Pres./CEO; 120 N. Center St.; 85201; Maricopa; P 460,000; (480) 827-4700; (800) 283-6372; Fax (480) 827-4704; info@visitmesa.com; www.visitmesa.com.

Phoenix · *Greater Phoenix CVB* · J. Steven Moore; Pres./CEO; 400 E. Van Buren, Ste. 600; 85004; Maricopa; P 3,800,000; (602) 254-6500; (877) 225-5749; Fax (602) 253-4415; www.visitphoenix.com

Scottsdale · *Scottsdale CVB* · Rachel Sacco; Pres./CEO; 4343 Scottsdale Rd., Ste. 170; Galleria Corporate Center; 85251; Maricopa; P 250,000; (480) 421-1004; (800) 782-1117; Fax (480) 421-9733; visitorinformation@scottsdalecvb.com; www.scottsdalecvb.com

Sedona · *Sedona Chamber Tourism Bur.* · Michelle Conway; Dir. of Tourism; P.O. Box 478; 86339; Coconino & Yavapai; P 18,000; (928) 204-1123; (928) 282-7722; Fax (928) 204-1064; info@sedonachamber.com; www.visitsedona.com

Sierra Vista · *Sierra Vista Visitors Center* · Kay Daggett; 1011 N. Coronado Dr.; 85635; Cochise; P 44,000; (520) 417-6960; (800) 288-3861; Fax (520) 417-4890; info@visitsierravista.com; www.visitsierravista.com

Sun City · *Sun City Visitors Center* · Paul Herrmann; Exec. Dir.; 16824 N. 99th Ave.; 85351; Maricopa; P 44,000; (623) 977-5000; (800) 437-8146; Fax (623) 977-4224; scvc@suncityaz.org; www.suncityaz.org

Tempe · *Tempe CVB* · Ginger Dude; Ofc. Mgr.; 51 W. Third St., Ste. 105; 85281; Maricopa; P 165,000; (480) 894-8158; (800) 283-6734; Fax (480) 968-8004; info@tempecvb.com; www.tempecvb.com

Tombstone · *Tombstone Ofc. of Tourism* · Paula Jean Reed; Chrmn.; P.O. Box 248; 85638; Cochise; P 1,500; (520) 457-3421; (800) 457-3423; Fax (520) 457-3189; tombstonebirdcage@gmail.com; www.tombstoneaz.net

Tucson · *Metropolitan Tucson CVB* · Jonathan Walker; Pres.; 100 S. Church Ave.; 85701; Pima; P 1,000,000; M 750; (520) 624-1817; Fax (520) 884-7804; info@visittucson.org; www.visittucson.org

Williams · *Williams-Grand Canyon Visitors Center* · Virginia Docherty; 200 W. Railroad Ave.; 86046; Coconino; P 3,150; (928) 635-1418; Fax (928) 635-1417; info@williamschamber.com; www.williamschamber.com

Yuma · *Yuma Visitors Bur.* · Robert Ingram; Exec. Dir.; 201 N. 4th Ave.; 85364; Yuma; P 120,000; M 300; (928) 783-0071; (800) 293-0071; Fax (928) 783-1897; info@visityuma.com; www.visityuma.com

Arkansas

Bentonville · *Bentonville CVB* · Kalene Griffith; Pres.; 104 E. Central; 72712; Benton; P 33,700; (479) 271-9153; (800) 410-2535; Fax (479) 464-4298; admin@bentonville.org; www.bentonville.org

Fort Smith · *Fort Smith CVB* · Claude Legris; Exec. Dir.; 2 N. B St.; 72901; Crawford, Franklin & Sebastian; P 80,000; (479) 783-8888; (800) 637-1477; Fax (479) 784-2421; tourism@fortsmith.org; www.fortsmith.org

Harrison · *Harrison CVB* · Terry Cook; Exec. Dir.; 122 E. Rush; P.O. Box 940; 72602; Boone; P 13,000; (870) 741-1789; (888) 283-2163; Fax (870) 741-1159; tcook@harrisonarkansas.org; www.harrisonarkansas.org

Hot Springs · *Hot Springs CVB* · Steve Arrison; CEO; 134 Convention Blvd.; P.O. Box 6000; 71902; Garland; P 96,371; (501) 321-2277; (800) 543-2284; Fax (501) 321-2136; hscvb@hotsprings.org; www.hotsprings.org

Little Rock · *Little Rock CVB* · Dan O'Byrne; Exec. Dir./CEO; P.O. Box 3232; 72203; Pulaski; P 184,000; (501) 376-4781; (800) 844-4781; Fax (501) 376-4138; lrcvb@littlerock.com; www.littlerock.com

Pine Bluff · *Pine Bluff CVB* · Bob Purvis; Exec. Dir.; Pine Bluff Conv. Center; One Convention Center Plz.; 71601; Jefferson; P 54,000; (870) 536-7600; (800) 536-7660; Fax (870) 850-2105; pbinfo@pinebluff.com; www.pinebluffcvb.org

Rogers · *Rogers-Lowell CVB* · Tom Galyon; Dir.; 317 W. Walnut; 72756; Benton; P 50,000; (479) 636-1240; Fax (479) 636-5485; info@rogerslowell.com; www.rogerslowell.com

California

Anaheim · *Anaheim/Orange County Visitor & Conv. Bur.* · Charles Ahlers; Pres.; 800 W. Katella Ave.; P.O. Box 4270; 92803; Orange; P 2,280,400; M 750; (714) 765-8888; (888) 598-3200; Fax (714) 765-3672; visitorinfo@anaheimoc.org; www.anaheimoc.org

Bakersfield · *Bakersfield CVB* · Don I. Cohen; 515 Truxtun Ave.; 93301; Kern; P 500,000; (661) 852-7282; (866) 425-7353; Fax (661) 325-7074; cvb@visitbakersfield.com; www.visitbakers field.com

Berkeley · *Berkeley CVB* · Barbara Hillman; Exec. Dir.; 2015 Center St.; 94704; Alameda; P 105,000; (510) 549-7040; (800) 847-4823; Fax (510) 644-2052; berkeleycvb@mindspring.com; www.visitberkeley.com

Beverly Hills · *Beverly Hills Conf. & Visitors Bur.* · Kathy Smits; Dir.; 239 S. Beverly Dr.; 90212; Los Angeles; P 36,000; (310) 248-1015; (800) 345-2210; Fax (310) 248-1020; smits@beverlyhills behere.com; www.lovebeverlyhills.org

Bodega Bay · *Sonoma Coast Visitor Center* · Brad Evans; Dir.; 850 Coast Hwy. 1; P.O. Box 518; 94923; Sonoma; P 1,250; (707) 875-3866; Fax (707) 875-3055; visitorcenter@innatthetides.com; www.bodegabay.com

Burlingame · *San Mateo County/Silicon Valley CVB* · Anne LeClair; Pres./CEO; 111 Anza Blvd., Ste. 410; 94010; San Mateo; P 722,762; M 365; (650) 348-7600; (800) 28-VISIT; Fax (650) 348-7687; info@smccvb.com; www.visitsanmateocounty.com

Carlsbad · *Carlsbad CVB* · Frankie Laney; Public Rel. Dir.; 400 Carlsbad Village Dr.; 92008; San Diego; P 100,000; (760) 434-6093; (800) CARLSBAD; Fax (760) 434-6056; info@visitcarlsbad.com; www.visitcarlsbad.com

Coronado · *Coronado Visitors Center* · Becky Emerson; Mgr.; 1100 Orange Ave.; 92118; San Diego; P 25,000; (619) 437-8788; vcmgr@coronadovisitorcenter.com; www.coronadovisitorcenter.com

Costa Mesa · *Costa Mesa Conf. & Visitor Bur.* · Diane Pritchett; Exec. Dir.; P.O. Box 5071; 92628; Orange; P 123,955; (714) 435-8530; (866) 918-4749; Fax (714) 435-8522; tourism@southcoast metro.com; www.travelcostamesa.com

Davis · *Yolo County Visitors Bur.* · Diane Parro; Exec. Dir.; 604 2nd St.; 95616; Yolo; P 185,000; (530) 297-1900; (877) 713-2847; Fax (530) 297-1901; info@yolocvb.org; www.yolocvb.org

Desert Hot Springs · *Desert Hot Springs Visitors Hospitality Center* · Eric Pontius; Pres.; 67616 Desert View Ave.; 92240; Riverside; P 23,544; (760) 329-7610; (866) 941-7610; info2@deserthotsprings.com; www.deserthotsprings.com

Escondido · *San Diego North CVB* · Cami Mattson; Pres./CEO; 360 N. Escondido Blvd.; 92025; San Diego; (760) 745-4741; (800) 848-3336; Fax (760) 745-4796; info@sandiegonorth.com; www.sandiegonorth.com

Eureka · *Humboldt County CVB* · 1034 Second St.; 95501; Humboldt; P 128,000; M 400; (707) 443-5097; (800) 346-3482; Fax (707) 443-5115; info@redwoods.info; www.redwoods.info

Fresno · *Fresno CVB* · Jeff L. Eben; Pres./CEO; 848 M St., 3rd Flr.; 93721; Fresno; P 500,000; M 365; (559) 445-8300; (800) 788-0836; Fax (559) 445-0122; info@fresnocvb.org; www.fresnocvb.org

Gilroy · *Gilroy Visitors Bur.* · Jane Howard; Exec. Dir.; 7780 Monterey St.; 95020; Santa Clara; P 55,000; (408) 842-6436; Fax (408) 842-6438; info@gilroyvisitor.org; www.gilroyvisitor.org

Hanford · *Hanford Conv. & Visitor Agency* · Dave Jones; Exec. Dir.; 504 W. 7th St,; 93230; Kings; P 48,000; (559) 582-5024; Fax (559) 582-5730; visithanford@att.net; www.visithanford.com

Huntington Beach · *Huntington Beach Mktg. & Visitors Bur.* · Stephen Bone; Pres./CEO; 301 Main St., Ste. 208; 92648; Orange; P 200,000; (714) 969-3492; (800) 729-6232; Fax (714) 969-5592; info@surfcityusa.com; www.surfcityusa.com

Lake Tahoe · *North Lake Tahoe Resort Assn.* · Andy Chapman; Tourism Dir.; P.O. Box 1755, Tahoe City; 96145; Placer; P 13,000; M 600; (800) 824-6348; (530) 581-8709; Fax (530) 581-1686; info@gotahoenorth.com; www.gotahoenorth.com

Lee Vining · *Mono Lake Comm. Info. Center* · Erika Obedzinski; Ofc. Dir.; Hwy. 395 & Third St.; P.O. Box 29; 93541; Mono; P 398; (760) 647-6595; Fax (760) 647-6377; info@monolake.org; www.monolake.org

Lodi · *Lodi Conf. & Visitors Bur.* · Jasmine Savoie; Exec. Asst.; 115 S. School St., Ste. 9; 95240; San Joaquin, P 65,000; (209) 365-1195; (800) 798-1810; Fax (209) 365-1191; info@visitlodi.com; www.visitlodi.com

Long Beach · *Long Beach Area CVB* · Steven Goodling; Pres./CEO; 301 E. Ocean Blvd., Ste. 1900; 90802; Los Angeles; P 470,000; M 450; (562) 436-3645; (800) 452-7829; Fax (562) 435-5653; info@longbeachcvb.org; www.visitlongbeach.com

Los Angeles · *Los Angeles CVB* · Mark Liberman; Pres.; 333 S. Hope St., 18th Flr.; 90071; Los Angeles; P 18,200,000; M 1,000; (213) 624-7300; (800) 366-6116; Fax (213) 624-9746; www.discoverlosangeles.com

Lucerne · *Lake County Visitor Info. Center* · Linda Armstrong; Ofc. Mgr.; 6110 E. Hwy. 20; P.O. Box 1025; 95458; Lake; P 59,000; (707) 274-5652; (800) 525-3743; Fax (707) 274-5664; info@lakecounty.com; www.lakecounty.com

Mammoth Lakes · *Mammoth Lakes Tourism* · Danna Stroud; Dir.; 2520 Main St.; P.O. Box 48; 93546; Mono; P 7,093; (760) 934-2712; (888) GO-MAMMOTH; Fax (760) 934-7066; info@visitmammoth.com; www.visitmammoth.com

Marin County · *see San Rafael*

Marina del Rey · *Marina del Rey CVB* · Tiffani Miller; Op. Mgr.; 4701 Admiralty Way; 90292; Los Angeles; (310) 305-9545; info@VisitMarina.com; www.VisitMarina.com

Mariposa · *Coulterville Visitor Center* · Hwy. J 132; P.O. Box 425; 95338; Mariposa; P 1,800; (209) 878-3074; (209) 966-2456; Fax (209) 966-4193; coultervillevc@mariposachamber.org; www.mariposachamber.org

Mariposa · *Mariposa County Visitors Center* · Diane Hernandez; Ofc. Mgr.; P.O. Box 425; 95338; Mariposa; P 1,400; (209) 966-7081; (800) 425-3663; Fax (209) 966-4193; mari-posavc@sti.net; www.mariposachamber.org

Modesto · *Modesto CVB* · Jennifer Mullen; Dir.; 1150 9th St., Ste. C; 95354; Stanislaus; P 246,000; (209) 526-5588; (888) 640-8467; Fax (209) 526-5586; info@visitmodesto.com; www.visitmodesto.com

Monterey · *Monterey County CVB* · John Reyes; CEO; P.O. Box 1770; 93942; Monterey; P 386,000; (831) 657-6400; (800) 555-6290; Fax (831) 648-5373; info@mccvb.org; www.seemonterey.com.

Morro Bay · *Morro Bay Visitors Center* · Peter Candela; CEO; 845 Embarcadero, Ste. D; 93442; San Luis Obispo; P 10,400; (805) 772-4467; (800) 231-0592; Fax (805) 772-6038; baywatch@morrobay.org; www.morrobay.org

Napa · *Napa Valley Destination Cncl.* · David Turgeon; COO; 1310 Napa Town Center; 94559; Napa; P 133,051; M 4,000; (707) 226-5813; Fax (707) 255-2066; info@legendarynapavalley.com; www.legendarynapavalley.com

Newport Beach · *Newport Beach Conf. & Visitors Bur.* · Loretta Walker; Deputy Dir./Ofc. Mgr.; 1200 Newport Center Dr., Ste. 120; 92660; Orange; P 74,000; (949) 719-6100; (800) 94-COAST; Fax (949) 719-6101; info@visitnewportbeach.com; www.visitnewportbeach.com

Oakhurst · *Yosemite Sierra Visitors Bur.* · Dan Cunning; CEO; 41969 Hwy. 41; 93644; Madera; P 20,000; M 146; (559) 683-4636; Fax (559) 683-5697; ysvb@yosemitethisyear.com; www.yosemitethisyear.com

Oceanside · *California Welcome Center Oceanside* · Leslee Gaul; Dir. of Tourism; 928 N. Coast Hwy.; 92054; San Diego; P 187,000; (760) 721-1101; (800) 350-7873; Fax (760) 722-8336; touristinfo@oceansidechamber.com; www.visitoceanside.org

Ontario · *Ontario CVB* · Bob Brown; Gen. Mgr.; 2000 E. Convention Center Way; 91764; San Bernardino; P 170,000; (909) 937-3000; (800) 455-5755; Fax (909) 937-3080; info@ontariocvb.com; www.ontariocc.com

Oxnard · *Oxnard CVB* · Janet Sederquist; Pres./CEO; 1000 Town Center Dr., Ste. 130; 93036; Ventura; P 200,000; (805) 385-7545; (800) 2-OXNARD; Fax (805) 385-7571; info@visitoxnard.com; www.visitoxnard.com

Palm Desert · *Palm Desert Visitor Center* · Donna Gomez; Mgr.; 72-567 Hwy. 111; 92260; Riverside; P 50,000; (760) 568-1441; (800) 873-2428; Fax (760) 779-5271; vcenter@citypalm-desert.org; www.palm-desert.org

Pasadena · *Pasadena CVB* · Nan Marchand; Exec. Dir.; 300 E. Green St.; 91101; Los Angeles; P 132,000; (626) 795-9311; (800) 307-7977; Fax (626) 795-9656; cvb@pasadenacal.com; www.visitpasadena.com

Pismo Beach · *Pismo Beach Conf. & Visitors Bur.* · Suzen Brasile; Exec. Dir.; 760 Mattie Rd.; 93449; San Luis Obispo; P 8,600; (805) 773-7034; (800) 443-7778; Fax (805) 779-1202; pbcity@pismobeach.org; www.ClassicCalifornia.com

Pleasanton · *Tri-Valley CVB* · Amy Blaschka; Exec. Dir.; 349 Main St., Ste. 203; 94566; Alameda; P 190,000; M 350; (925) 846-8910; (888) 874-9253; Fax (925) 846-9502; info@trivalleycvb.com; www.trivalleycvb.com

Quincy · *Plumas County Visitor Bur.* · Suzi Brakken; Dir.; 550 Crescent St.; 95971; Plumas; P 23,090; (530) 283-6345; (800) 326-2247; Fax (530) 283-5465; pcvb@psln.com; www.plumascounty.org

Rancho Mirage · *Palm Springs-Desert Resort Communities CVA* · Jeff Beckelman; Pres./CEO; 70-100 Hwy. 111; 92270; Riverside; P 300,000; M 900; (760) 770-9000; (800) 967-3767; Fax (760) 770-9001; jbeckelman@palmspringsusa.com; www.palmspringsusa.com

Redding · *Redding CVB* · Chris Gonzalez; Mgr.; 777 Auditorium Dr.; 96001; Shasta; P 90,491; (530) 225-4130; (888) 225-4130; Fax (530) 225-4354; info@visitredding.org; www.visitredding.com

Redondo Beach · *Redondo Beach C/C & Visitors Bur.* · Marna Smeltzer; Pres./CEO; 200 N. Pacific Coast Hwy.; 90277; Los Angeles; P 65,000; (310) 376-6911; (800) 282-0333; Fax (310) 374-7373; info@redondochamber.org; www.redondochamber.org

Ridgecrest · *Ridgecrest Area CVB & Film Commission* · Douglas Lueck; Exec. Dir.; 139 Balsam St., Ste. 1700; 93555; Kern; P 41,000; M 57; (760) 375-8202; (800) 847-4830; Fax (760) 375-9850; racvb@filmdeserts.com; www.visitdeserts.com

Riverside · *Riverside CVB* · Debbie Megna; Exec. Dir.; 3750 University Ave., Ste. 175; 92501; Riverside; P 300,000; (951) 222-4700; (888) 748-7733; Fax (951) 222-4712; dmegna@riversidecvb.com; www.riversidecvb.com

Sacramento · *Sacramento CVB* · Steve Hammond; Pres./CEO; 1608 I St.; 95814; Sacramento; P 450,000; M 600; (916) 808-7777; (800) 292-2334; Fax (916) 808-7788; www.sacramentocvb.org; www.discovergold.org

San Bernardino · *San Bernardino CVB* · Wayne Austin; Pres./CEO; 1955 Hunts Ln., Ste. 102; 92408; San Bernardino; P 210,000; (909) 891-1151; (800) 867-8366; Fax (909) 891-1873; info@san-bernardino.org; www.san-bernardino.org

San Diego · *San Diego CVB* · Joe Terzi; Pres./CEO; 2215 India St.; 92101; San Diego; P 2,911,468; (619) 236-1212; Fax (619) 696-9371; sdinfo@sandiego.org; www.sandiego.org

San Francisco · *San Francisco CVB* · Joe D'Alessandro; Pres./CEO; 201 Third St., Ste. 900; 94103; San Francisco; P 744,230; M 1,800; (415) 974-6900; Fax (415) 227-2602; admin@sanfrancisco.travel; www.onlyinsanfrancisco.com

San Jose · *San Jose CVB* · Daniel Fenton; Pres./CEO; 408 Almaden Blvd.; 95110; Santa Clara; P 1,000,000; (408) 295-9600; (800) SAN-JOSE; Fax (408) 295-3937; dfenton@sanjose.org; www.sanjose.org

San Luis Obispo · *San Luis Obispo County Visitors & Conf. Bur.* · John Solu; Pres.; 811 El Capitan Way, Ste. 200; 93401; San Luis Obispo; P 260,000; (805) 541-8000; (800) 634-1414; Fax (805) 543-9498; info@sanluisobispocounty.com; www.sanluisobispocounty.com

San Rafael · *The Marin CVB* · Mark Essman; Pres.; 1 Mitchell Blvd., Ste. B; 94903; Marin; P 250,000; (415) 925-2060; (866) 925-2060; Fax (415) 925-2063; info@visitmarin.org; www.visitmarin.org

Santa Barbara · *Santa Barbara CVB & Film Commission* · Kathy Janega-Dykes; Pres./CEO; 1601 Anacapa St.; 93101; Santa Barbara; P 400,000; M 175; (805) 966-9222; (800) 676-1266; Fax (805) 966-1728; tourism@santabarbaraca.com; www.santabarbaraca.com

Santa Clara · *Santa Clara CVB* · Steve VanDorn; Pres.; 1850 Warburton Ave.; 95050; Santa Clara; P 106,000; (408) 244-9660; (800) 272-6822; Fax (408) 244-7830; steve.vandorn@santaclara.org; www.santaclara.org

Santa Cruz · *Santa Cruz County Conf. & Visitors Cncl.* · Maggie Ivy; CEO; 1211 Ocean St.; 95060; Santa Cruz; P 255,000; (831) 425-1234; (800) 833-3494; Fax (831) 425-1260; comments@santacruz.org; www.santacruz.org

Santa Maria · *Santa Maria Valley Visitors & Conv. Bur.* · Gina Keough; Mgr.; 614 S. Broadway; 93454; Santa Barbara; P 128,843; (805) 925-2403; (800) 331-3779; Fax (805) 928-7559; info@santamaria.com; www.santamaria.com

Santa Monica · *Santa Monica CVB* · Misti Kerns; Pres./CEO; 1920 Main St., Ste. B; 90405; Los Angeles; P 84,400; (310) 319-6263; Fax (310) 319-6273; info@santamonica.com; www.santamonica.com

Santa Rosa · *Santa Rosa CVB & CA Welcome Center* · Maureen McElroy; Exec. Dir.; 9 Fourth St.; 95401; Sonoma; P 157,000; (707) 577-8674; (800) 404-7673; Fax (707) 571-5949; info@visitsanta rosa.com; www.visitsantarosa.com

Santa Rosa · *Sonoma County Tourism Bur.* · Ken Fischang; Pres.; 420 Aviation Blvd., Ste. 106; 95403; Sonoma; P 450,000; (707) 522-5800; (800) 576-6662; Fax (707) 539-7252; info@ sonomacounty.com; www.sonomacounty.com

Sherman Oaks · *San Fernando Valley CVB* · 5121 Van Nuys Blvd., Ste. 200; 91403; Los Angeles; P 2,000,000; M 1,000; (818) 377-6388; Fax (818) 379-7077; information@valleyofthestars.org; www.visitvalleyofthestars.org

Solvang · *Solvang CVB* · Tracy Farhad; Exec. Dir.; 1511 Mission Dr., Ste. A; P.O. Box 70; 93464; Santa Barbara; P 8,000; (805) 688-6144; (800) 468-6765; Fax (805) 688-8620; info@solvangusa.com; www.solvangusa.com

Sonora · *Tuolumne County Visitors Bur.* · Nanci Sikes; Exec. Dir.; 542 W. Stockton Rd.; P.O. Box 4020; 95370; Tuolumne; P 59,500; M 280; (209) 533-4420; (800) 446-1333; Fax (209) 533-0956; tcvb@mlode.com; www.tcvb.com

South Lake Tahoe · *see Stateline, NV*

Temecula · *Temecula Valley CVB* · Kimberly Adams; Pres./CEO; 26790 Ynez Ct., Ste. B; 92591; Riverside; P 100,000; (951) 491-6085; (888) 363-2852; Fax (951) 491-6089; info@temeculacvb. com; www.temeculacvb.com

Vallejo · *Vallejo CVB* · Mike Browne; Exec. Dir.; 289 Mare Island Way; 94590; Solano; P 120,000; M 210; (707) 642-3653; (800) 482-5535; Fax (707) 644-2206; vjocvb@visitvallejo.com; www. visitvallejo.com

Ventura · *Ventura Visitors & Conv. Bur.* · James Luttjohann; Exec. Dir.; 101 S. California St.; 93001; Ventura; P 106,000; (805) 648-2075; (800) 333-2989; Fax (805) 648-2150; tourism@ ventura-usa.com; www.ventura-usa.com

West Hollywood · *West Hollywood Mktg. & Visitors Bur.* · Bradley Burlingame; Pres.; 8687 Melrose Ave., Ste. M38; 90069; Los Angeles; P 39,000; (310) 289-2525; (800) 368-6020; Fax (310) 289-2529; info@visitwesthollywood.com; www.visitwesthollywood.com

Colorado

Boulder · *Boulder CVB* · Mary Ann Mahoney; Exec. Dir.; 2440 Pearl St.; 80302; Boulder; P 110,000; (303) 442-2911; (800) 444-0447; Fax (303) 938-2098; info@bouldercvb.com; www. bouldercoloradousa.com

Colorado Springs · *Colorado Springs CVB* · Mr. Terry Sullivan; Pres./CEO; 515 S. Cascade Ave.; 80903; El Paso; P 587,000; M 700; (719) 635-7506; (800) 368-4748; Fax (719) 635-4968; info@ visitcos.com; www.visitcos.com

Denver · *VISIT DENVER CVB* · 1555 California St., Ste. 300; 80202; Denver; P 2,600,000; (303) 892-1112; Fax (303) 892-1636; www.visitdenver.com

Empire · *see Idaho Springs*

Estes Park · *Estes Park CVB* · Peggy Campbell; Exec. Dir.; 500 Big Thompson Ave.; P.O. Box 1200; 80517; Larimer; P 6,500; (970) 577-9900; (800) 44-ESTES; Fax (970) 577-1677; cvbinfo@estes. org; www.estesparkcvb.com

Fort Collins · *Fort Collins CVB* · Jim Clark; Pres./CEO; 19 Old Town Sq., Ste. 137; 80524; Larimer; P 140,000; M 225; (970) 232-3840; (800) 274-3678; Fax (970) 232-3841; information@ftcollins. com; www.visitftcollins.com

Grand Junction · *Grand Junction Visitor & Conv. Bur.* · Debbie Kovalik; Exec. Dir.; 740 Horizon Dr.; 81506; Mesa; P 136,000; (970) 244-1480; (800) 962-2547; Fax (970) 243-7393; info@visitgrand junction.com; www.visitgrandjunction.com

Greeley · *Greeley CVB* · Sarah MacQuiddy; Pres.; 902 7th Ave.; 80631; Weld; P 97,000; (970) 352-3567; (800) 449-3866; Fax (970) 352-3572; info@greeleychamber.com; www.greeleychamber.com

Idaho Springs · *Tourism Bur. of Clear Creek County* · 2060 Miner St.; P.O. Box 100; 80452; Clear Creek; P 9,000; (303) 567-4660; (866) 674-9237; Fax (303) 569-6296; info@clearcreekcounty. org; www.clearcreekcounty.org

Loveland · *Loveland Visitor Center* · Vickie Rasmussen; Coord.; 5400 Stone Creek Circle; 80538; Larimer; P 65,000; (970) 667-5728; (800) 258-1278; Fax (970) 667-5211; info@loveland.org; www.loveland.org

Montrose · *Montrose Visitors & Conv. Bur.* · Jenni Sopsic; Dir.; 1519 E. Main St.; 81401; Montrose; P 18,000; (970) 252-0505; (800) 873-0244; Fax (970) 249-2907; jenni@visitmontrose.net; www.visitmontrose.com

Silver Plume · *see Idaho Springs*

South Fork · *South Fork Visitors Center* · Josephine Pierce; Dir.; 28 Silver Thread Ln.; 81154; Rio Grande; P 750; (719) 873-5512; Fax (719) 873-5693; southfrk@amigo.net; www.southfork.org

Steamboat Springs · *Steamboat Springs Chamber Resort Assn./ Visitors Center* · Kyleigh DeMicco; Mgr.; 125 Anglers Dr.; P.O. Box 774408; 80477; Routt; P 11,000; (970) 879-0882; Fax (970) 879-2543; info@steamboatchamber.com; www.steamboatchamber.com

Telluride · *Telluride & Mountain Village CVB* · Scott McQuade; CEO; 630 W. Colorado; P.O. Box 1009; 81435; San Miguel; P 3,000; (970) 728-3041; (888) 355-8743; Fax (970) 728-6475; info@visit-telluride.com; www.visittelluride.com

Vail · *Vail Valley Partnership* · Michael Kurz; Pres./CEO; P.O. Box 1130; 81658; Eagle; P 48,000; (970) 476-1000; (800) 525-3875; Fax (970) 476-6008; info@visitvailvalley.com; www.visitvailvalley.com

Connecticut

Hartford · *Central Reg. Tourism Dist.* · Anne Lee; Exec. Dir.; One Constitution Plaza, 2nd Flr.; 06103; Hartford; P 1,100,000; (860) 787-9640; (800) 793-4480; Fax (860) 256-2811; annel@ visitctriver.com; www.enjoycentralct.com

Hartford · *Greater Hartford CVB* · Scott Phelps; Pres./CEO; 31 Pratt St., 4th Flr.; 06103; Hartford; P 822,260; M 220; (860) 728-6789; (800) 446-7811; Fax (860) 293-2365; ghcvb@hartfordcvb. org; www.enjoyhartford.com

Litchfield · *NW Connecticut CVB* · Janet Sera; Dir.; P.O. Box 968; 06759; Fairfield; P 8,000; (860) 567-4506; Fax (860) 567-5214; lhcvbnwct@aol.com; www.litchfieldhills.com

Mystic · *Mystic Country* · Edward Dombroskas; Exec. Dir.; 27 Coogan Blvd., Bldg. 3A; 06355; New London; P 300,000; (860) 536-8822; Fax (860) 536-8855; info@mysticcountry.com; www. mystic.org

New Haven · *Greater New Haven CVB* · Ginny Kozlowski; Pres./ CEO; 169 Orange St.; 06510; New Haven; P 600,000; (203) 777-8550; (800) 332-STAY; Fax (203) 782-7755; www.visitnewhaven.com

Norwalk · *Fairfield County CVB* · Catherine Sidor; Exec. Dir.; 297 West Ave.; 06850; Fairfield; P 700,000; (203) 853-7770; (800) 866-7925; Fax (203) 853-7775; info@fairfieldcountyctcvb.com; www.visitfairfieldcountyct.com

Delaware

Dover • *Kent County Delaware CVB* • Cynthia S. Small; Exec. Dir.; 435 N. Dupont Hwy.; 19901; Kent; P 150,000; (302) 734-1736; (800) 233-5368; Fax (302) 734-0167; kctc@visitdover.com; www.visitdover.com

Wilmington • *Greater Wilmington CVB* • Sarah Willoughby; Exec. Dir.; 100 W. 10th St., Ste. 20; 19801; New Castle; P 600,000; M 360; (302) 295-2210; (800) 489-6664; Fax (302) 652-4726; info@wilmcvb.org; www.visitwilmingtonde.com

District of Columbia

Washington • *Destination D.C.* • William Hanbury; Pres./CEO; 901 7th St. N.W., 4th Flr.; 20001; District of Columbia; P 6,000,000; M 1,400; (202) 789-7000; (800) 422-8644; Fax (202) 789-7037; www.washington.org

Florida

Bradenton • *Bradenton Area CVB* • Elliot Falcione; Interim Dir.; P.O. Box 1000; 34206; Manatee; P 300,000; (941) 729-9177; (800) 4-MANATEE; Fax (941) 729-1820; info@annamariaisland-longboatkey.com; www.annamariaisland-longboatkey.com

Brooksville • *Hernando County Welcome Center* • Susan Rupe; Dir.; 30305 Cortez Blvd.; 34602; Hernando; P 165,000; (352) 754-4405; (800) 601-4580; Fax (352) 754-4406; WelcomeCtr@hernandocounty.us; www.naturallyhernando.org

Cape Canaveral • *see Cocoa Village*

Clearwater • *St. Petersburg/Clearwater Area CVB* • D.T. Minich; Exec. Dir.; 13805 58th St. N., Ste. 2-200; 33760; Pinellas; P 900,000; (727) 464-7200; (877) 352-3224; Fax (727) 464-7222; dt@visitspc.com; www.visitstpeteclearwater.com

Cocoa Village • *Florida's Space Coast Ofc. of Tourism* • Rob Varley; Exec. Dir.; 430 Brevard Ave., Ste. 150; 32922; Brevard; P 543,050; (321) 433-4470; (877) 572-3224; Fax (321) 433-4476; info@space-coast.com; www.space-coast.com

Davenport • *Central Florida Visitors & Conv. Bur.* • Hank Longo; Mgr.; 101 Adventure Ct.; 33837; Polk; P 500,000; (863) 420-2586; (800) 828-7655; Fax (863) 420-2593; www.visitcentralflorida.org

Daytona Beach • *Daytona Beach Area CVB* • Janet Kersey; Pres./CEO; 126 E. Orange Ave.; 32114; Volusia; P 65,000; (386) 255-0415; (800) 544-0415; Fax (386) 255-5478; info@daytonabeachcvb.org; www.daytonabeach.com

Ecofina • *See Perry*

Fort Lauderdale • *Greater Ft. Lauderdale CVB* • Nicki E. Grossman; Pres.; 100 E. Broward Blvd., Ste. 200; 33301; Broward; P 1,700,000; (954) 765-4466; (800) 22-SUNNY; Fax (954) 765-4467; gflcvb@broward.org; www.sunny.org

Fort Myers • *Lee County Visitors & Conv. Bur.* • Tamara Pigott; Exec. Dir.; 12800 University Dr., Ste. 550; 33907; Lee; P 623,725; (239) 338-3500; (800) 237-6444; Fax (239) 334-1106; vcb@leegov.com; www.fortmyers-sanibel.com

Fort Pierce • *St. Lucie County Tourism Dev. Cncl.* • Charlotte Lombard; Tourism Dev. Mgr.; 2300 Virginia Ave.; 34982; St. Lucie; P 271,000; (772) 462-1539; (800) 344-8443; Fax (772) 462-2131; lombardc@stlucieco.org; www.visitstluciefla.com

Fort Walton Beach • *Emerald Coast CVB Inc.* • Mark Bellinger; Exec. Dir.; 1540 Miracle Strip Pkwy. S.E.; P.O. Box 609; 32549; Okaloosa; P 181,236; (850) 651-7131; (800) 322-3319; Fax (850) 651-7149; emeraldcoast@co.okaloosa.fl.us; www.destin-fwb.com

Gainesville • *Alachua County Visitors & Conv. Bur.* • Roland Loog CDME CMP; Dir.; 30 E. University Ave.; 32601; Alachua; P 216,000; (352) 374-5231; (866) 778-5002; Fax (352) 338-3213; info@visitgainesville.com; www.visitgainesville.com

Groveland • *Lake County CVB* • Greg Mihalic; Dir.; 20763 U.S. Hwy. 27; 34736; Lake; P 300,000; (352) 429-3673; (800) 798-1071; Fax (352) 429-4870; gmihalic@lakecountyfl.gov; www.lakecountyfl.com

Homosassa • *Citrus County Visitors & Conv. Bur.* • Marla Chancey; Dir. of Tourism; 9225 W. Fishbowl Dr.; 34448; Citrus; P 120,000; (352) 628-9305; (800) 587-6667; Fax (352) 628-0703; info@visitcitrus.com; www.visitcitrus.com

Jacksonville • *Visit Jacksonville* • 208 N. Laura St., Ste. 102; 32202; Duval; P 800,000; M 294; (904) 798-9111; (800) 733-2668; Fax (904) 798-9110; visitorinfo@jaxcvb.com; www.visitjacksonville.com

Keaton Beach • *See Perry*

Key Largo • *Florida Keys Visitor Center* • Jackie Harder; Pres.; 106000 Overseas Hwy.; 33037; Monroe; P 12,000; M 369; (800) 822-1088; (305) 451-6266; Fax (305) 451-4726; info@keylargochamber.org; www.keylargo.org; www.fla-keys.com

Key West • *Monroe County Tourist Dev. Cncl.* • Harold Wheeler; Dir.; 1201 White St., Ste. 102; P.O. Box 866; 33040; Monroe; P 78,284; (305) 296-1552; Fax (305) 296-0788; www.fla-keys.com

Kissimmee • *Kissimmee CVB* • Tom Lang; Dir.; 1925 E. Irlo Bronson Mem. Hwy.; 34744; Osceola; P 190,187; (407) 847-5000; (800) 327-9159; Fax (407) 742-8226; meet@floridakiss.com; www.visitkissimmee.com

Melbourne • *The Melbourne Coast CVB* • Christine Michaels; Pres./CEO; 1005 E. Strawbridge Ave.; 32901; Brevard; P 400,000; M 60; (321) 724-5400; (800) 771-9922; Fax (321) 725-2093; chuck@melbourneregionalchamber.com; www.melbourneregionalchamber.com

Miami • *Greater Miami CVB* • William D. Talbert III; Pres./CEO; 701 Brickell Ave., Ste. 2700; 33131; Miami-Dade; P 2,000,000; (305) 539-3000; (800) 933-8448; Fax (305) 539-3125; www.miamiandbeaches.com

Naples • *Naples Area Visitors Center* • Michael Reagen; Pres./CEO; 2390 Tamiami Trail N., Ste. 206; 34103; Collier; P 341,000; (239) 262-6141; Fax (239) 262-8374; info@napleschamber.org; www.napleschamber.org

New Port Richey • *Pasco County Ofc. of Tourism* • Eric Keaton; Pbl. Comm. Mgr.; 7530 Little Rd., Ste. 340; 34654; Pasco; P 407,800; (727) 847-8990; (800) 842-1873; Fax (727) 847-8168; tourism@pascocountyfl.net; www.visitpasco.net

Orlando • *Orlando/Orange County CVB Inc.* • Gary Sain; Pres./CEO; 6700 Forum Dr., Ste. 100; 32821; Orange; P 1,886,934; (407) 363-5872; (800) 972-3304; Fax (407) 370-5000; info@orlandocvb.com; www.orlandoinfo.com

Panama City Beach • *Panama City Beach CVB* • Dan Rowe; Pres./CEO; 17001 Panama City Beach Pkwy.; 32417; Bay; P 25,000; (850) 233-5070; Fax (850) 233-5072; info@visitpanamacitybeach.com; www.visitpanamacitybeach.com.

Pensacola • *Pensacola Bay Area C/C - Conv. & Visitors Info. Center* • Evon Emerson; 1401 E. Gregory St.; 32502; Escambia; P 385,000; (850) 434-1234; (800) 874-1234; Fax (850) 432-8211; www.visitpensacola.com

Perry • *Taylor County Tourism Dev. Cncl.* • Dawn Taylor; Exec. Dir.; 428 N. Jefferson St.; P.O. Box 892; 32348; Taylor; P 19,422; (850) 584-5366; (800) 257-8881; Fax (850) 584-8030; taylorchamber@fairpoint.net; www.taylorcountychamber.com

TOURIST CENTER FOR TAYLOR COUNTY WHICH INCLUDES STEINHATCHEE, PERRY, KEATON BEACH AND ECONFINA.

Port Charlotte • *Charlotte Harbor Visitors Bur.* • Becky Bovell; Dir.; 18501 Murdock Cir., Ste. 502; 33948; (888) 4-PURFLA; Charlotte; P 160,454; (941) 743-1900; Fax (941) 743-2245; www.charlotteharbortravel.com

Saint Augustine • *St. Augustine, Ponte Vedra & The Beaches Visitors & Conv. Bur.* • Richard Goldman; Exec. Dir.; 29 Old Mission Ave.; 32084; St. Johns; P 165,000; (904) 829-1711; (800) 653-2489; Fax (904) 829-6149; rgoldman@getaway4florida.com; www.getaway4florida.com

Saint Petersburg • *see Clearwater*

Santa Rosa Beach • *Walton County Tourist Dev. Cncl.* • Dawn Moliterno; Exec. Dir.; 25777 U.S. 331 S.; P.O. Box 1248; 32459; Walton; P 43,000; (850) 267-1216; (800) 822-6877; Fax (850) 267-3943; florida@beachesofsouthwalton.com; www.beaches ofsouthwalton.com

Sarasota • *Sarasota CVB* • Virginia Haley; Pres.; 766 Hudson Ave., Ste. A; 34236; Sarasota; P 315,000; M 370; (941) 955-0991; (800) 522-9799; Fax (941) 955-1929; info@sarasotafl.org; www.sarasotafl.org

Sebring • *Highlands County Visitor & CB* • John Scherlacher; Tourism Dir.; 501 S. Commerce Ave., Ste. 3; 33870; Highlands; P 99,000; (863) 402-6909; Fax (863) 402-6795; tdc@highlandscvb.com; www.visithighlandscounty.com

Steinhatchee • *See Perry*

Tallahassee • *Tallahassee Area CVB* • Kerri Post; Pres./CEO; 106 E. Jefferson St.; 32301; Leon; P 243,300; M 500; (850) 606-2305; (800) 628-2866; Fax (850) 606-2301; vic@visittallahassee.com; www.visittallahassee.com

Tampa • *Tampa Bay & Co.* • Paul Catoe; Pres./CEO; 401 E. Jackson St., Ste. 2100; 33602; Hillsborough; P 1,140,000; (813) 223-1111; (800) 826-8358; Fax (813) 229-6616; www.visittampabay.com

Tampa • *West Tampa Conv. Center* • 3005 W. Columbus Dr.; 33607; Hillsborough; P 854,000; M 150; (813) 870-0559; (813) 870-3144; Fax (813) 443-2134

Tampa • *Ybor City Visitor Info. Center* • Rose Barbie; Mgr.; 1600 E. 8th Ave., Ste. B104; 33605; Hillsborough; P 800,000; M 450; (813) 241-8838; Fax (813) 242-0398; info@ybor.org; www.ybor.org

West Palm Beach • *Palm Beach County Tourist Dev. Cncl.* • 1555 Palm Beach Lakes Blvd., Ste. 900; 33401; Palm Beach; P 1,200,000; (561) 233-3130; Fax (561) 233-3113; www.palm beachfl.com

Ybor City • *see Tampa—Ybor City Visitor Info. Center*

Georgia

Albany • *Albany CVB* • Lisa Riddle; CVB Dir.; 112 N. Front St.; 31701; Dougherty; P 90,000; M 1,200; (229) 317-4760; (866) 750-0840; Fax (229) 317-4765; lriddle@albanyga.com; www.visitalbanyga.com.

Alpharetta • *Alpharetta CVB* • Janet Rodgers; Pres./CEO; Park Plaza; 178 S. Main St., Ste. 200; 30009; Fulton; P 50,000; (678) 297-2811; (800) 294-0923; Fax (678) 297-9197; info@awesome alpharetta.com; www.awesomealpharetta.com

Athens • *Athens CVB* • Chuck Jones; Dir.; 300 N. Thomas St.; 30601; Athens & Clarke; P 116,000; (706) 357-4430; Fax (706) 546-8040; tourinfo@visitathensga.com; www.visitathensga.com

Atlanta • *Atlanta CVB* • Spurgeon Richardson; Pres./CEO; 233 Peachtree St. N.E., Ste. 1400; 30303; Fulton; P 4,000,000; M 1,300; (404) 521-6600; (800) ATLANTA; Fax (404) 577-3293; info@atlanta.net; www.atlanta.net

Atlanta • *Cobb County CVB* • Joyce Calandra; CEO; One Galleria Pkwy., Ste. 1A2A; 30339; Fulton; P 530,000; M 285; (678) 303-2622; (800) 451-3480; Fax (678) 303-2625; cobb@cobbcvb.com; www.cobbcvb.com

Augusta • *Augusta CVB* • Barry E. White; Exec. Dir.; 1450 Greene St., Ste. 110; P.O. Box 1331; 30903; Richmond; P 200,000; (706) 823-6600; (800) 726-0243; Fax (706) 823-6609; acvb@augustaga.org; www.augustaga.org

Brunswick • *Brunswick-Golden Isles Visitors Bur.* • Bill Tipton; Exec. Dir.; 4 Glynn Ave.; 31520; Glynn; P 74,000; (912) 265-0620; (800) 809-1790; Fax (912) 265-0629; info@comecoastawhile.com; www.bgicvb.com

Calhoun • *Gordon County CVB* • Beth Grubbs; Dir.; 300 S. Wall St.; 30701; Gordon; P 52,044; (706) 625-3200; (800) 887-3811; Fax (706) 625-5062; bgrubbs@gordonchamber.org; www.exploregordoncounty.com

Carrollton • *Carrollton Area CVB* • Jonathan Dorsey; Exec. Dir.; 102 N. Lakeshore Dr.; 30117; Carroll; P 100,000; (770) 214-9746; (800) 292-0871; Fax (770) 830-1765; visit@carrollton-ga.gov; www.visitcarrollton.com

Cartersville • *Cartersville-Bartow County CVB* • Ellen Archer; Exec. Dir.; 1 Friendship Plaza, Ste. 1; P.O. Box 200397; 30120; Bartow; P 90,000; (770) 387-1357; (800) 733-2280; cvb@not atlanta.org; www.notatlanta.org

Clayton • *Rabun County CVB* • Mary Boland; Exec. Dir.; P.O. Box 788; 30525; Rabun; P 17,500; (706) 782-5271; (706) 982 4754; mary@gamountains.com; www.explorerabun.com

Columbus • *Columbus CVB* • Peter Bowden; Pres./CEO; 900 Front Ave.; P.O. Box 2768; 31902; Muscogee; P 225,000; (706) 322-1613; (800) 999-1613; Fax (706) 322-0701; ccvb@columbusga.org; www.visitcolumbusga.com

Covington • *Covington-Newton County CVB* • Clara Deemer; Dir. of Tourism; 2101 Clark St.; P.O. Box 168; 30015; Newton; P 90,000; (770) 787-3868; (800) 616-8626; Fax (770) 786-1294; cdeemer@newtonchamber.com; www.newtonchamber.com

Dalton • *Dalton CVB* • Margaret Thigpen; Exec. Dir.; P.O. Box 6177; 30722; Whitfield; P 87,000; (706) 270-9960; (800) 331-3258; Fax (706) 876-1561; info@visitdaltonga.com; www.daltoncvb.com; www.visitdaltonga.com

Douglas • *Douglas Area Welcome Center* • Dorie Bacon; Tourism Coord.; 211 S. Gaskin Ave.; 31533; Coffee; P 38,000; (912) 384-4555; (888) 426-3334; Fax (912) 383-6304; tourism@cityofdouglas.com; www.cityofdouglas.org

Duluth • *Gwinnett CVB* • Caryn McGarity; Exec. Dir.; 6500 Sugarloaf Pkwy., Ste. 200; 30097; Gwinnett; P 650,000; (770) 623-3600; (888) 494-6638; Fax (770) 623-1667; info@gcvb.org; www.gcvb.org

Fort Gaines • *Clay County Visitors Bur.* • Jean O. Turn; Dir.; P.O. Box 275; 39851; Clay; P 3,200; (229) 768-2248; Fax (229) 768-2248; www.fortgaines.com

Gainesville • *Lake Lanier CVB* • Stacey Dickson; Pres.; P.O. Box 2995; 30503; Hall; P 175,000; (770) 536-5209; (888) 536-0005; Fax (770) 503-1349; info@lakelaniercvb.com; www.lakelaniercvb.com

Hazlehurst • *Hazlehurst-Jeff Davis County Bd. of Tourism* • 95 E. Jarman St.; P.O. Box 546; 31539; Jeff Davis; P 13,100; (912) 375-4543; Fax (912) 375-7948; hjdtour@bellsouth.net; www.hazlehurst-jeffdavis.com

Helen • *Alpine Helen/White County CVB* • 726 Bruckenstrasse; P.O. Box 730; 30545; White; P 15,000; (706) 878-3842; (800) 858-8027; Fax (706) 878-4032; info@helenga.org; www.helenga.org

Jekyll Island · *Jekyll Island CVB* · Eric Garvey; Dir.; 100 James Rd.; 31527; Glynn; P 1,300; (912) 635-4080; (877) 453-5955; Fax (912) 635-4004; egarvey@jekyllisland.com; www.jekyllisland.com

Jonesboro · *Clayton County CVB* · Patrick Duncan; Pres.; 127 N. Main St.; 30236; Clayton; P 225,000; (678) 610-4242; (800) 662-STAY Fax (678) 610-4087; pduncan@visitscarlett.com; www.visitscarlett.com

Kingsland · *Kingsland CVB* · Tonya Rosado; Exec. Dir.; 1190 E. Boone Ave.; P.O. Box 1928; 31548; Camden; P 50,000; (912) 729-5999; (800) 433-0225; Fax (912) 729-7258; info@visitkingsland.com; www.visitkingsland.com

Macon · *Macon-Bibb County CVB* · Janice W. Marshall; Pres./CEO; 450 Martin Luther King Jr. Blvd.; P.O. Box 6354; 31208; Bibb; P 153,887; (478) 743-3401; (800) 768-3401; Fax (478) 745-2022; maconcvb@maconga.org; www.visitmacon.org

Madison · *Madison-Morgan County C/C & CVB* · Marguerite Copelan; Exec. Dir.; 115 E. Jefferson St.; P.O. Box 826; 30650; Morgan; P 17,000; (706) 342-4454; (800) 709-7406; Fax (706) 342-4455; marguerite@madisonga.org; www.madisonga.org

Milledgeville · *Milledgeville-Baldwin County CVB* · Jane Sowell; Dir.; 200 W. Hancock St.; P.O. Box 219; 31059; Baldwin; P 50,000; (478) 452-4687; (800) 653-1804; Fax (478) 453-4440; tourism@windstream.net; www.milledgevillecvb.com

Peachtree City · *Peachtree City Tourism Assn.* · Lauren Yawn; Exec. Dir.; 10 Planterra Way; 30269; Fayette; P 35,000; (678) 216-0282; (877) 782-4250; Fax (770) 631-2575; info@visitpeachtreecity.com; www.visitpeachtreecity.com

Perry · *Perry Area CVB* · Sheila Averett Jones; Exec. Dir.; 101 Gen. Courtney Hodges Blvd.; P.O. Box 1609; 31069; Houston; P 12,000; (478) 988-8000; Fax (478) 988-8005; info@perryga.com; www.perryga.com

Pine Mountain · *Pine Mountain Tourism Assn.* · Hank Arnold; Exec. Dir.; 101 Broad St.; P.O. Box 177; 31822; Harris; P 1,200; (706) 663-4000; (800) 441-3502; Fax (706) 663-4726; tourism@pinemountain.org; www.pinemountain.org

Rome · *Greater Rome CVB* · Lisa Smith; Exec. Dir.; 402 Civic Center Dr.; 30161; Floyd; P 94,800; (706) 295-5576; (800) 444-1834; Fax (706) 236-5029; lisa@romegeorgia.org; www.romegeorgia.org.

Roswell · *Historic Roswell CVB* · Dotty Etris; Exec. Dir.; 617 Atlanta St.; 30075; Fulton; P 85,000; (770) 640-3253; (800) 776-7935; Fax (770) 640-3252; info@cvb.roswell.ga.us; www.visitroswellga.com

Saint Mary's · *St. Mary's CVB Auth.* · Janet Brinko; Dir.; 406 Osborne St.; 31558; Camden; P 48,000; (912) 882-4000; (800) 868-8687; Fax (912) 882-6246; info@stmaryswelcome.com; www.stmaryswelcome.com

Savannah · *Savannah Area CVB* · Joseph Marinelli; Pres.; 101 E. Bay St.; P.O. Box 1628; 31402; Chatham; P 310,704; (912) 644-6401; (877) SAVANNAH; Fax (912) 644-6499; www.savannahvisit.com

Statesboro · *Statesboro CVB* · Jaime Riggs; Exec. Dir.; 332 S. Main St.; P.O. Box 1516; 30459; Bulloch; P 62,000; (912) 489-1869; (800) 568-3301; Fax (912) 489-2688; scvb@frontiernet.net; www.visitstatesboroga.com

Thomasville · *Thomasville CVB* · Katie Brenckle; Tourism Coord.; 144 E. Jackson St.; P.O. Box 3319; 31799; Thomas; P 43,000; (229) 228-7977; (866) 577-3600; Fax (229) 228-4188; visitus@rose.net; www.thomasvillega.com

Thomson · *Thomson-McDuffie Tourism CVB* · Elizabeth Vance; Exec. Dir.; 111 Railroad St.; 30824; McDuffie; P 22,140; (706) 597-1000; evance@thomson-mcduffie.net; www.exploremcduffiecounty.com

Tucker · *DeKalb CVB* · Jon Manns; Pres./CEO; 1957 Lakeside Pkwy., Ste. 510; 30084; DeKalb; P 700,000; (770) 492-5000; Fax (770) 492-5033; gerthah@dcvb.org; www.dcvb.org

Tybee Island · *Tybee Island Visitors Info. Center* · Georgeanne Inglis; Mgr.; 802 1st St.; P.O. Box 491; 31328; Chatham; P 3,500; (912) 786-5444; (800) 868-2322; Fax (912) 786-5895; vc@tybeevisit.com; www.tybeevisit.com

Valdosta · *Valdosta-Lowndes County Conf. Center & Tourism Auth.* · Michael Jetter; Exec. Dir.; P.O. Box 1964; 31603; Lowndes; P 106,000; (229) 245-0513; (800) 569-TOUR; Fax (229) 245-5240; mjetter@valdostatourism.com; www.valdostatourism.com

Vidalia · *Vidalia Area CVB* · Elizabeth Harvill; Exec. Dir.; 100 Vidalia Sweet Onion Dr., Ste. A; 30474; Toombs; P 15,000; (912) 538-8687; Fax (912) 538-1466; vacvb@bellsouth.net; www.vidaliaarea.com

Warner Robins · *Warner Robins CVB* · Marsha Buzzell; Dir.; 99 N. 1st St.; 31093; Houston; P 58,000; (478) 922-5100; Fax (478) 225-2631; cvb@warnerrobinsga.gov; www.warnerrobinsga.gov

Waycross · *Waycross Tourism Bur.* · Vickie Leverette; Dir.; 315-A Plant Ave.; 31501; Ware; P 37,000; (912) 283-3744; Fax (912) 283-0121; waycrosstour@accessatc.net; www.swampgeorgia.com

Hawaii

Honolulu · *Hawaii CVB* · John Monahan; Pres./CEO; 2270 Kalakaua Ave., Ste. 801; 96815; Honolulu; P 1,400,000; (808) 923-1811; (800) 464-2924; Fax (808) 924-0290; info@hvcb.org; www.gohawaii.com

Kaunakakai · *Moloka'I Visitors Assn.* · Julie Bicoy; Dir.; P.O. Box 960; 96748; Maui; P 8,100; M 97; (808) 553-3876; (800) 800-6367; Fax (808) 553-5288; mvajulie@gmail.com; www.molokai-hawaii.com

Idaho

Boise · *Boise CVB* · Roberta Patterson; Exec. Dir.; 312 S. 9th St., Ste. 100; 83702; Ada; P 208,000; (208) 344-7777; (800) 635-5240; Fax (208) 344-6236; receptionist@boisecvb.org; www.boise.org

Coeur d'Alene · *Coeur d'Alene Visitors Bur.* · Jonathan Coe; Pres./Gen. Mgr.; 105 1st St.; 83814; Kootenai; P 43,683; (208) 664-3194; (877) 782-9232; Fax (208) 667-9338; info@coeurdalene.org; www.coeurdalene.org

Idaho Falls · *Idaho Falls CVB* · Bob Everhart; Exec. Dir.; 630 W. Broadway; P.O. Box 50498; 83405; Bonneville; P 52,000; (208) 523-1010; (866) 365-6943; Fax (208) 523-2255; info@visitidahofalls.com; www.visitidahofalls.com

Ketchum · *Sun Valley Ketchum CVB* · Carol Waller; Exec. Dir; 491 Sun Valley Rd.; P.O. Box 2420; 83353; Blaine; P 4,547; (208) 726-3423; (866) 226-8817; info@visitsunvalley.com; www.visitsunvalley.com

McCall · *McCall Area Visitors Bur.* · Tamara Sandmeyer; Exec. Dir.; 102 N. 3rd St.; P.O. Box 350; 83638; Valley; P 3,000; (208) 634-7631; (800) 260-5130; Fax (208) 634-7752; info@mccallchamber.org; www.mccallchamber.org

Pocatello • *Greater Pocatello CVB* • Rebecca Satter; Exec. Dir.; 324 S. Main St., Ste. B; P.O. Box 626; 83204; Bannock; P 60,000; (208) 235-7659; (877) 922-7659; Fax (208) 233-1527; rsatter@pocatelloidaho.com; www.pocatellocvb.com

Illinois

Alton • *Alton Reg.CVB* • Brett Stawar; Pres.; 200 Piasa St.; 62002; Madison; P 100,000; (618) 465-6676; (800) ALTON-IL; Fax (618) 465-6151; info@visitalton.com; www.visitalton.com

Anna • *Southernmost Illinois Tourism Bur.* • Cindy Cain; Dir.; P.O. Box 378; 62906; Union; P 71,500; (618) 833-9928; (800) 248-4373; Fax (618) 833-9924; sitb@ajinternet.net; www.southernmostillinois.com

Arlington Heights • *see Prospect Heights*

Aurora • *Aurora Area CVB* • Sue Vos; Pres./CEO; 43 W. Galena Blvd.; 60506; DuPage, Kane, Kendall & Will; P 289,708; (630) 897-5581; (800) 477-4369; Fax (630) 897-5589; market@enjoyaurora.com; www.enjoyaurora.com

Belleville • *Belleville Illinois Tourism* • Cathleen Lindauer; Dir.; 216 E. A St.; 62220; St. Clair; P 44,000; (618) 233-6769; (800) 677-9255; Fax (618) 233-2077; clindauer@bellevillechamber.org; www.belleville.net

Belvidere • *Northern Illinois Tourism Dev. Ofc.* • Bonnie Heimbach; Exec. Dir.; 200 S. State St.; 61008; Boone; P 3,000,000; (815) 547-3740; Fax (815) 547-3749; nitdo@visitnorthernillinois.com; www.visitnorthernillinois.com

Bloomington • *Bloomington-Normal Area CVB* • Crystal Howard; Dir.; 3201 CIRA Dr., Ste. 201; 61704; McLean; P 145,000; (800) 433-8226; (309) 665-0033; Fax (309) 661-0743; www.bloomingtonnormalcvb.org

Carbondale • *Carbondale Conv. & Tourism Bur.* • Debbie Moore; Exec. Dir.; 1185 E. Main St., Ste. 1046; University Mall; 62901; Jackson; P 49,000; (618) 529-4451; (800) 526-1500; Fax (618) 529-5590; www.cctb.org

Champaign • *Champaign County CVB* • Scott Hockman; Exec. Dir.; 1817 S. Neil St., Ste. 201; 61820; Champaign; P 190,000; (217) 351-4133; (800) 369-6151; Fax (217) 359-1809; scotth@champaigncounty.org; www.visitchampaigncounty.org

Chicago • *Chicago Ofc. of Tourism* • Dorothy Coyle; Dir.; Chicago Cultural Center; 78 E. Washington St., 4th Flr.; 60602; Cook; P 2,731,743; (312) 744-2400; (877) CHICAGO; Fax (312) 744-2359; www.cityofchicago.org/tourism

Collinsville • *Gateway Center* • Lisa Smith; Dir. of Sales; One Gateway Dr.; 62234; Madison; P 24,707; (618) 345-8998; (800) 289-2388; Fax (618) 345-9024; lsmith@gatewaycenter.com; www.gatewaycenter.com

Danville • *Danville Area CVB* • Sue Porritt; Ofc. Mgr.; 100 W. Main St., Ste. 146; 61832; Vermilion; P 33,000; (217) 442-2096; Fax (217) 442-2137; info@danvilleareainfo.com; www.danvilleareainfo.com.

Decatur • *Decatur Area CVB* • Denene Wilmeth; Exec. Dir.; 202 E. North St.; 62523; Macon; P 100,000; (217) 423-7000; (800) 331-4479; Fax (217) 423-7455; denene@decaturcvb.com; www.decaturcvb.com

Du Quoin • *Du Quoin Tourism Comm.* • Judy Smid; Pres.; 20 N. Chestnut St.; P.O. Box 1037; 62832; Perry; P 6,448; (618) 542-8338; (800) 455-9570; Fax (618) 542-2098; duquointourism@yahoo.com; www.duquointourism.org

Elgin • *Elgin Area CVB* • Kimberly Bless; Pres./CEO; 77 Riverside Dr.; 60120; Kane; P 285,000; M 100; (847) 695-7540; (800) 217-5362; Fax (847) 695-7668; elgincvb@northernfoxrivervalley.com; www.northernfoxrivervalley.com

Fairview Heights • *The Tourism Bur. Southwestern Illinois* • jo kathmann; Pres./CEO; 10950 Lincoln Trl; 62208; St. Clair; P 700,000; (618) 397-1488; (800) 442-1488; Fax (618) 397-1945; info@thetourismbureau.org; www.thetourismbureau.org

Freeport • *Freeport/Stephenson County CVB* • Connie Sorn; Exec. Dir.; 4596 U.S. Rte. 20 E.; 61032; Stephenson; P 48,000; (815) 233-1357; (800) 369-2955; Fax (815) 233-1358; stephcvb@aeroinc.net; www.stephenson-county-il.org

Galena • *Galena/Jo Daviess County CVB* • Betsy Eaton; Exec. Dir.; 720 Park Ave.; 61036; Jo Daviess; P 22,289; M 300; (815) 777-3557; (877) 464-2536; Fax (815) 777-3566; director@galena.org; www.galena.org

Galesburg • *Galesburg Area CVB* • Diane Bruening; Exec. Dir.; 2163 E. Main St.; P.O. Box 60; 61402; Knox; P 34,500; (309) 343-2485; (800) 916-3330; Fax (309) 343-2521; visitors@visitgalesburg.com; www.visitgalesburg.com

Gurnee • *Lake County, Illinois CVB* • Maureen Riedy; Pres.; 5465 W. Grand Ave., Ste. 100; 60031; Lake; P 617,975; M 135; (847) 662-2700; (800) LAKE-NOW; Fax (847) 662-2702; tourism@lakecounty.org; www.lakecounty.org

Jacksonville • *Jacksonville Area CVB* • Patricia Anderson; Exec. Dir.; 310 E. State St.; 62650; Morgan; P 24,000; (217) 243-5678; (800) 593-5678; Fax (217) 243-5862; events@jacksonvilleil.org; www.jacksonvilleil.org

Joliet • *Heritage Corridor CVB* • Robert Navarro; CEO; 339 W. Jefferson St.; 60435; Kendall & Will; P 100,000; M 250; (800) 926-2262; Fax (815) 727-2324; info@hccvbil.com; www.heritagecorridorcvb.com

Kankakee • *Kankakee County CVB* • Larry Williams; Exec. Dir.; 1 Dearborn Sq., Ste. 1; 60901; Kankakee; P 105,000; (815) 935-7390; (800) 74-RIVER; Fax (815) 935-5169; larry@visitkankakeecounty.com; www.visitkankakeecounty.com

Lake County • *see Gurnee*

Lansing • *Chicago Southland CVB* • Jim Garrett; Pres./CEO; 2304 173rd St.; 60438; Cook; P 871,138; M 500; (708) 895-8200; (888) 895-8233; Fax (708) 895-8288; info@visitchicagosouthland.com; www.visitchicagosouthland.com

Lincoln • *Abraham Lincoln Tourism Bur. of Logan County* • Geoff Ladd; Exec. Dir.; 1555 5th St.; 62656; Logan; P 35,000; (217) 732-8687; Fax (217) 735-9205; info@abe66.com; www.abe66.com

Lisle • *Lisle CVB* • Priscilla Tomei; Exec. Dir.; 4746 Main St.; 60532; DuPage; P 21,000; (630) 769-1000; (800) 733-9811; Fax (630) 769-1006; lislevisitor@stayinlisle.com; www.stayinlisle.com

Macomb • *Macomb Area CVB* • Katherine Walker; Pres.; 201 S. Lafayette St.; 61455; McDonough; P 20,000; (309) 833-1315; Fax (309) 833-3575; macvb@macomb.com; www.makeitmacomb.com

Macomb • *Western IL Tourism Dev. Ofc.* • Roger Carmack; Exec. Dir.; 581 S. Deere Rd.; 61455; McDonough; (309) 837-7460; Fax (309) 833-4754; witdo@visitwesternillinois.info; www.visitwesternillinois.info

Marion • *Williamson County CVB* • Shannon Johnson; Exec. Dir.; 1602 Sioux Dr.; 62959; Williamson; P 65,000; (618) 997-3690; (800) 433-7399; Fax (618) 997-1874; info@vistisi.com; www.visitsi.com

Moline · *Quad-Cities CVB* · Joe Taylor; Pres./CEO; 1601 River Dr., Ste. 110; 61265; Rock Island & Scott; P 400,000; M 400; (309) 277-0937; (800) 747-7800; Fax (309) 764-9443; cvb@visitquadcities.com; www.visitquadcities.com

Mount Vernon · *Mount Vernon CVB* · Bonnie Jerdon; Dir.; 200 Potomac Blvd.; P.O. Box 1708; 62864; Jefferson; P 17,000; (618) 242-3151; (800) 252-5464; Fax (618) 242-6849; tourism@mvn.net; www.mtvernon.com.

Naperville · *Naperville Dev. Partnership & CVB* · Christine Jeffries; Pres.; 212 S. Webster, Ste. 104; 60540; DuPage & Will; P 140,000; (630) 305-7701; (877) 236-2737; Fax (630) 305-7793; www.visitnaperville.com; www.naper.org

Oak Brook · *DuPage CVB* · JoEllen Strittmatter; Exec. Dir.; 915 Harger Rd., Ste. 240; 60523; Cook & DuPage; P 904,161; M 300; (630) 575-8070; (800) 232-0502; Fax (630) 575-8078; visitor@discoverdupagecvb.com; www.discoverdupage.com

Pekin · *Pekin Visitors Bur.* · Steve Brown; Exec. Dev. Coord.; 111 S. Capitol; 61554; Tazewell; P 33,857; (309) 477-2300; (877) 669-7741; Fax (309) 346-2095; tourism@ci.pekin.il.us; www.pekintourism.com

Peoria · *Peoria Area CVB* · Brent Lonteen; Pres./CEO; 456 Fulton St., Ste. 300; 61602; Peoria; P 344,000; (309) 676-0303; (800) 747-0302; Fax (309) 676-8470; blonteen@peoria.org; www.peoria.org

Polo · *Blackhawk Waterways CVB* · Diane Bausman; Exec. Dir.; 201 N. Franklin Ave.; 61064; Ogle; P 96,000; (815) 946-2108; (800) 678-2108; Fax (815) 946-2277; www.bwcvb.com

Pontiac · *Pontiac Tourism* · Ellie Alexander; Dir.; 115 W. Howard St.; 61764; Livingston; P 12,000; (815) 844-5847; (800) 835-2055; Fax (815) 842-3885; tourism@pontiac.org; www.pontiac.org

Prospect Heights · *Chicago's North Suburbs CVB* · 8 N. Elmhurst Rd., Ste. 100; 60070; Cook; P 17,000; M 40; (847) 577-3666; (800) 955-7259; Fax (847) 577-8306; info@chicagonorthsuburbs.com; www.chicagonorthsuburbs.com

Quincy · *Quincy Area CVB* · Holly Cain; Exec. Dir.; 532 Gardner Expy.; 62301; Adams; P 90,000; (217) 214-3700; (800) 978-4748; Fax (217) 214-2721; hcain@seequincy.com; www.seequincy.com

Rock Island · *see Moline*

Rockford · *Rockford Area CVB* · John Groh; Pres./CEO; 102 N. Main St.; 61101; Winnebago; P 400,000; (815) 963-8111; (800) 521-0849; Fax (815) 963-4298; info@gorockford.com; www.gorockford.com

Rosemont · *Rosemont CVB* · William Anderson; Gen. Mgr.; 9301 W. Bryn Mawr Ave.; 60018; Cook; P 4,500; (847) 823-2100; Fax (847) 696-9700; rcb@rosemont.com; www.rosemont.com

Schaumburg · *Woodfield Chicago Northwest Conv. Bur.* · Fran Bolson; Pres.; 1375 E. Woodfield Rd., Ste. 120; 60173; Cook; P 640,000; M 300; (847) 490-1010; (800) 847-4849; Fax (847) 490-1212; info@chicagonorthwest.com; www.chicagonorthwest.com

Shelbyville · *Lake Shelbyville Area CVB/Shelby County Tourism* · Ms. Freddie Fry; Dir.; 315 E. Main St.; 62565; Shelby; P 20,000; (217) 774-2244; (800) 874-3529; info@lakeshelbyville.com; www.lakeshelbyville.com

Springfield · *Central IL Tourism Dev. Ofc.* · Heather Wilkins; Exec. Dir.; 700 E. Adams St.; 62701; Sangamon; (217) 525-7980; (866) 378-7866; Fax (217) 525-8004; citdo@visitcentralillinois.com; www.visitcentralillinois.com

Springfield · *Springfield CVB* · Tim Farley; Exec. Dir.; 109 N. 7th St.; 62701; Sangamon; P 125,000; (217) 789-2360; (800) 545-7300; Fax (217) 544-8711; www.visit-springfieldillinois.com

St. Charles · *St. Charles CVB* · Amy Bull; Exec. Dir.; 311 N. 2nd St., Ste. 100; 60174; Kane; P 33,000; (630) 377-6161; (800) 777-4373; Fax (630) 513-0566; info@visitstcharles.com; www.visitstcharles.com

Indiana

Anderson · *Anderson/Madison County V & CB* · Ralph Day; Exec. Dir.; 6335 S. Scatterfield Rd.; 46013; Madison; P 135,000; (765) 643-5633; (800) 533-6569; Fax (765) 643-9083; info@heartlandspirit.com; www.heartlandspirit.com.

Angola · *Steuben County Tourism Bur.* · 207 S. Wayne St.; 46703; Steuben; P 33,722; (260) 665-5386; (800) LAKE-101; Fax (260) 665-5461; lakes101@locl.net; www.lakes101.org

Avon · *see Danville*

Bloomington · *Bloomington/Monroe County CVB* · Mike McAfee; Exec. Dir.; 2855 N. Walnut St.; 47404; Monroe; P 110,000; (812) 334-8900; (800) 800-0037; Fax (812) 334-2344; cvb@visitbloomington.com; www.visitbloomington.com

Carmel · *Hamilton County CVB* · Brenda Myers; Exec. Dir.; 37 E. Main St.; 46032; Hamilton; P 261,661; M 195; (317) 848-3181; (800) 776-TOUR; Fax (317) 848-3191; info@hamiltoncountytowns.com; www.hccvb.org

Columbus · *Columbus Area Visitors Center* · Cindy Frey; Assoc. Dir.; 506 5th St.; 47201; Bartholomew; P 39,000; (812) 378-2622; (800) 468-6564; Fax (812) 372-7348; visitcol@sbcglobal.net; www.columbus.in.us

Corydon · *Harrison County CVB* · Jim Epperson; Exec. Dir.; 310 N. Elm St.; 47112; Harrison; P 34,500; (812) 738-2138; (888) 738-2137; Fax (812) 738-3609; info@thisisindiana.org; www.thisisindiana.org

Crawfordsville · *Montgomery County VCB* · Sharon Kenny; Exec. Dir.; 218 E. Pike St.; 47933; Montgomery; P 36,000; (765) 362-5200; (800) 866-3973; Fax (765) 362-5215; info@crawfordsville.org; www.crawfordsville.org

Danville · *Hendricks County CVB* · Emory Lencke; Exec. Dir.; 8 W. Main St.; 46122; Hendricks; P 123,476; (317) 718-8750; (800) 321-9666; Fax (317) 718-9913; info@tourhendrickscounty.com; www.tourhendrickscounty.com

Elkhart · *Elkhart County CVB* · Diana Lawson; Exec. Dir.; 219 Caravan Dr.; 46514; Elkhart; P 195,362; (574) 262-8161; (800) 262-8161; Fax (574) 262-3925; ecconv@amishcountry.org; www.amishcountry.org

Evansville · *Evansville CVB* · Marilee Fowler; Exec. Dir.; 401 S.E. Riverside Dr.; 47713; Vanderburgh; P 170,000; (812) 421-2200; (800) 433-3025; Fax (812) 421-2207; info@evansvillecvb.org; www.evansvillecvb.org

Fort Wayne · *Fort Wayne/Allen County CVB* · Daniel R. O'Connell; Pres./CEO; 927 S. Harrison St., Ste. 101; 46802; Allen; P 300,000; M 240; (260) 424-3700; (800) 767-7752; Fax (260) 424-3914; visitorinfo@visitfortwayne.com; www.visitfortwayne.com

Greencastle · *Putnam County/Covered Bridge Country Visitors Bur.* · Karla Lawless; 12 W. Washington St.; 46135; Putnam; P 45,000; (765) 653-8743; (800) 829-4639; Fax (765) 653-0851; cbc@coveredbridgecountry.com; www.coveredbridgecountry.com

Hammond · *Lake County CVB* · Speros Batistatos; Pres./CEO; 7770 Corinne Dr.; 46323; Lake; P 500,000; (219) 989-7770; (800) ALL-LAKE; Fax (219) 989-7777; www.lakecountycvb.com

Huntington • *Huntington County Visitor & Conv. Bur.* • Rose Meldrum; Exec. Dir.; 407 N. Jefferson St.; P.O. Box 212; 46750; Huntington; P 37,521; (260) 359-8687; (800) 848-4282; Fax (260) 359-9754; info@visithuntington.org; www.visithuntington.org

Indianapolis • *Indianapolis Conv. & Visitors Assn.* • Don Welsh; Pres. & CEO; 37 S. Meridian St., Ste. 410; P.O. Box 7248; 46227; Marion; P 865,000; (317) 639-4282; Fax (317) 639-5273; icva@visitindy.com; www.visitindy.com

Jasper • *Dubois County Visitors Center* • Kristen Ruhe; Exec. Dir.; 2704 Newton St.; 47546; Dubois; P 38,000; (812) 482-9115; (800) 968-4578; Fax (812) 481-2809; info@visitduboiscounty.com; www.visitduboiscounty.com

Jeffersonville • *Clark-Floyd County CVB* • James P. Keith; Exec. Dir.; 315 Southern Indiana Ave.; 47130; Clark; P 200,000; (812) 282-6654; (800) 552-3842; Fax (812) 282-1904; tourism@sunnysideoflouisville.org; www.sunnysideoflouisville.org

Kendallville • *Noble County, Indiana CVB* • Sarah Thomas; Exec. Dir.; 2010 W. North St.; P.O. Box 934; 46755; Noble; P 9,646; (260) 599-0060; (877) 202-5761; Fax (260) 599-0066; info@visitnoblecounty.com; www.visitnoblecounty.com

Knox • *Starke County Tourism Comm.* • Anthony Manning; Coord.; 400 N. Heaton St.; 46534; Starke; P 25,000; (574) 772-0896; (877) 733-2736; Fax (574) 772-0867; travel@explorestarkecounty.com; www.explorestarkecounty.com

Kokomo • *Kokomo/Howard County CVB* • Peggy Hobson; Dir.; 1504 N. Reed Rd.; 46901; Howard; P 82,000; (765) 457-6802; (800) 837-0971; Fax (765) 457-1572; information@visitkokomo.org; www.visitkokomo.org

Lafayette • *Lafayette/West Lafayette CVB* • Joann L. Wade; Pres.; 301 Frontage Rd.; 47905; Tippecanoe; P 153,875; (765) 447-9999; (800) 872-6648; Fax (765) 447-5062; info@homeofpurdue.com; www.homeofpurdue.com

Lawrenceburg • *Dearborn County Conv., Visitor & Tourism Bur.* • Deborah Smith; Dir.; 320 Walnut St.; 47025; Dearborn; P 50,000; (812) 537-0814; (800) 322-8198; Fax (812) 537-0845; dsmith@visitsoutheastindiana.com; www.visitsoutheastindiana.com

Madison • *Madison Area CVB* • Linda Lytle; Dir.; 601 W. 1st St.; 47250; Jefferson; P 29,000; (812) 265-2956; (800) 559-2956; Fax (812) 273-3694; info@visitmadison.org; www.visitmadison.org

Marion • *Grant County CVB* • Karen Niverson; Exec. V.P.; 428 S. Washington, Ste. 261; 46953; Grant; P 75,000; (765) 668-5435; (800) 662-9474; Fax (765) 668-5424; info@showmegrantcounty.com; www.showmegrantcounty.com

Michigan City • *LaPorte County CVB* • Jack Arnedt; Exec. Dir.; 4073 S. Franklin St.; 46360; LaPorte; P 120,000; (800) 634-2650; (219) 872-5055; Fax (219) 872-3660; info@laportecountycvb.com; www.visitlaportecountycvb.com

Mishawaka • *see South Bend*

Muncie • *Muncie Visitors Bur.* • James Mansfield; Exec. Dir.; 425 N. High St., Ste. 5; 47305; Delaware; P 70,000; (765) 284-2700; (800) 568-6862; Fax (765) 284-3002; jim@visitmuncie.org; www.visitmuncie.org

Nashville • *Brown County CVB* • Jane Ellis; Exec. Dir.; 10 N. Van Buren; P.O. Box 840; 47448; Brown; P 14,950; (812) 988-7303; (800) 753-3255; Fax (812) 988-1070; info@browncounty.com; www.browncounty.com

New Castle • *Henry County CVB* • Susie Thompson; Exec. Dir.; 3205 S. Memorial Dr.; 47362; Henry; P 48,000; (765) 593-0764; (888) 676-4302; Fax (765) 593-0766; info@henrycountyin.org; www.henrycountyin.org

Plainfield • *see Danville*

Plymouth • *Marshall County CVB* • Mike Woolfington; Exec. Dir.; 220 N. Center; P.O. Box 669; 46563; Marshall; P 38,000; (574) 936-1882; (800) 626-5353; Fax (574) 936-9845; mcw@marshallcountytourism.org; www.marshallcountytourism.org

Porter • *Porter County Conv., Rec & Visitor Comm.* • Lorelei Weimer; Dir.; 1420 Munson Rd.; 46304; Porter; P 150,000; (219) 926-2255; (800) 283-TOUR; Fax (219) 929-5395; info@indiana-dunes.com; www.indianadunes.com

Portland • *Jay County Visitor & Tourism Bur.* • Gyneth Augsburger; Exec. Dir.; 118 S. Meridian St., Ste. C; 47371; Jay; P 21,500; (260) 726-3366; (877) 726-4481; Fax (260) 726-3372; info@visitjaycounty.com; www.visitjaycounty.com

Richmond • *Richmond/Wayne County Tourism Bur.* • Mary Walker; Exec. Dir.; 5701 National Rd. E.; 47374; Wayne; P 70,000; (765) 935-8687; (800) 828-8414; Fax (765) 935-0440; welcomecenter@visitrichmond.org; www.visitrichmond.org

Rising Sun • *Rising Sun/Ohio County CVB* • Sherry Timms; Exec. Dir.; 120 N. Walnut St.; P.O. Box 112; 47040; Ohio; P 5,200; (812) 438-4933; (888) 776-4786; Fax (812) 438-4932; sherrytourism@gmail.com; www.enjoyrisingsun.com

Rockville • *Parke County Inc.* • Cathy Harkrider; Exec. Secy.; P.O. Box 165; 47872; Parke; P 15,000; M 300; (765) 569-5226; Fax (765) 569-3900; pci@ticz.com; www.coveredbridges.com

Seymour • *Jackson County Visitor Center* • Tina Stark; Exec. Dir.; P.O. Box 607; 47274; Jackson; P 40,000; (888) 524-1914; Fax (812) 524-1915; jacksoncountyin@verizon.net; www.jacksoncountyin.com

South Bend • *South Bend/Mishawaka CVB* • Rob DeCleene CDME; Exec. Dir.; 401 E. Colfax Ave., Ste. 310; P.O. Box 1677; 46634; St. Joseph; P 265,000; (574) 232-0231; (800) 519-0577; Fax (574) 289-0358; info@exploresouthbend.org; www.exploresouthbend.org

Tell City • *Perry County CVB* • Beverly Minto; Exec. Dir.; 601 Main St., Ste. A; P.O. Box 721; 47586; Perry; P 20,100; (812) 547-7933; (888) 343-6262; Fax (812) 547-8378; perrycountycvb@psci.net; www.perrycountyindiana.org

Terre Haute • *Terre Haute CVB of Vigo County* • David A. Patterson; Exec. Dir.; 5353 E. Margaret Dr.; 47803; Vigo; P 106,829; (812) 234-5555; (800) 366-3043; Fax (812) 234-6750; info@terrehaute.com; www.terrehaute.com

Vevay • *Switzerland County Welcome Center* • David Attaway; Exec. Dir.; P.O. Box 149; 47043; Switzerland; P 10,000; (812) 427-3237; (800) 435-5688; Fax (812) 427-2184; visitsc@gmail.com; www.vevayin.com

Vincennes • *Vincennes/Knox County CVB* • Shyla Beam; Exec. Dir.; P.O. Box 602; 47591; Knox; P 40,000; (812) 886-0400; (800) 886-6443; Fax (812) 885-0033; info@vincennescvb.org; www.vincennescvb.org

Wabash • *Wabash County CVB* • Trula Cramer; Exec. Dir.; 36 E. Market St.; P.O. Box 746; 46992; Wabash; P 35,000; (260) 563-7171; (800) 563-1169; Fax (260) 569-1782; tourism@wabashcountycvb.com; www.wabashcountycvb.com

Warsaw • *Kosciusko County CVB* • Mary Kittrell; Dir.; 111 Capital Dr.; 46582; Kosciusko; P 75,667; (574) 269-6090; (800) 800-6090; Fax (574) 269-2405; info@koscvb.org; www.koscvb.org

Washington • *Daviess County CVB* • Charles Selby; Exec. Dir.; One Train Depot St.; P.O. Box 430; 47501; Daviess; P 28,000; (812) 254-5262; (800) 449-5262; Fax (812) 254-4003; cselby@dccham ber.com; www.daviesscounty.net

Winchester · *Randolph County Visitor Info. Center* · Eric Fields; Pres.; 112 W. Washington St.; 47394; Randolph; P 27,066; (765) 584-3731; Fax (765) 584-5544; chamber@globalsite.net; www.winchesterareachamber.org

Iowa

Amana · *Amana Colonies CVB* · Kristie Wetjen; Exec. Dir.; 622 46th Ave.; P.O. Box 310; 52203; Iowa; P 1,500; (319) 622-7622; (800) 579-2294; Fax (319) 622-6395; info@amanacolonies.com; www.amanacolonies.com

Ames · *Ames CVB* · Julie Weeks; Dir.; 1601 Golden Aspen Dr., Ste. 110; 50010; Story; P 52,300; M 210; (515) 232-4032; (800) 288-7470; Fax (515) 232-6716; info@amescvb.com; www.visitames.com

Bettendorf · *see Moline, IL*

Burlington · *Greater Burlington CVB* · Beth Nickel; Exec. Dir.; 610 N. 4th St., Ste. 200; 52601; Des Moines; P 30,000; (319) 752-6365; (800) 82-RIVER; Fax (319) 752-6454; tourism@grow burlington.com; www.visitburlingtoniowa.com

Cedar Falls · *Cedar Falls Tourism & Visitors Bur.* · Kim Burger; Exec. Dir.; 6510 Hudson Rd.; 50613; Black Hawk; P 36,000; (319) 268-4266; (800) 845-1955; Fax (319) 277-9707; visit@cedar fallstourism.org; www.cedarfallstourism.org

Cedar Rapids · *Cedar Rapids Area CVB* · Tim Boyle; Pres./CEO; 119 First Ave. S.E; 52401; Linn; P 200,000; (319) 398-5009; (800) 735-5557; Fax (319) 398-5089; tim@cedar-rapids.com; www. cedar-rapids.com

Clear Lake · *Clear Lake Area CVB* · Tourism Dir.; 205 Main Ave.; P.O. Box 188; 50428; Cerro Gordo; P 8,200; (641) 357-2159; (800) 285-5338; Fax (641) 357-8141; info@clearlakeiowa.com; www. clearlakeiowa.com

Clinton · *Clinton CVB* · Dir.; 721 S. 2nd St.; P.O. Box 1024; 52733; Clinton; P 50,149; (563) 242-5702; Fax (563) 242-5803; cvb@ clintonia.com; www.clintoniowatourism.com

Coralville · *Iowa City/Coralville Area CVB* · Josh Schamberger; Exec. Dir./Pres.; 900 1st Ave.; 52241; Johnson; P 77,000; M 291; (319) 337-6592; (800) 283-6592; Fax (319) 337-9953; guest@ iowacitycoralville.org; www.iowacitycoralville.org

Council Bluffs · *Council Bluffs CVB* · Bob Mundt; Pres./CEO; 7 N. 6th St.; P.O. Box 1565; 51502; Pottawattamie; P 59,744; (712) 325-1000; (800) 228-6878; Fax (712) 322-5698; cvb@council bluffsiowa.com; www.councilbluffsiowa.com

Davenport · *see Moline, IL*

Des Moines · *Greater Des Moines CVB* · Greg Edwards; Pres./ CEO; 400 Locust, Ste. 265; 50309; Polk & Warren; P 500,000; M 425; (515) 286-4960; (800) 451-2625; Fax (515) 244-9757; ngoode@desmoinescvb.com; www.seedesmoines.com

Fairfield · *Fairfield Iowa Conv. & Visitors Center* · Rustin Lippincott; Exec. Dir.; 200 N. Main; 52556; Jefferson; P 10,000; (641) 472-2828; Fax (641) 472-7890; rlippincott@travelfairfield iowa.com; www.travelfairfieldiowa.com

Fort Madison · *Fort Madison Area CVB* · Sandy Brown; Exec. Dir.; 614 9th St.; P.O. Box 425; 52627; Lee; P 10,700; (319) 372-5472; (800) 210-TOUR; tourism@visitfortmadison.com; www. visitfortmadison.com

Keokuk · *Keokuk Area Conv. & Tourism Bur.* · 329 Main St.; 52632; Lee; P 11,531; (319) 524-5599; (800) 383-1219; info@ keokukiowatourism.org; www.keokukiowatourism.org

Marshalltown · *Marshalltown CVB* · Shannon Espenscheid; Dir.; 709 S. Center St.; P.O. Box 1000; 50158; Marshall; P 26,009; (641) 753-6645; (800) 697-3155; Fax (641) 752-8373; cvb@ marshalltown.org; www.visitmarshalltown.com

Mason City · *Mason City CVB* · Sue Armour; Exec. Dir.; 25 W. State, Ste. B; 50401; Cerro Gordo; P 30,000; (641) 422-1663; (800) 423-5724; Fax (641) 423-5725; cvb@visitmasoncityiowa.com; www.visitmasoncityiowa.com

Muscatine · *Muscatine CVB* · Heather Shoppa; Mgr.; 102 Walnut St.; 52761; Muscatine; P 23,000; M (563) 263-8895; (800) 257-3275; Fax (563) 263-7662; meetmuscatine@muscatine.com; www. meetmuscatine.com

Newton · *Newton CVB* · Linda Bacon; Exec. Dir.; 113 First Ave. W.; 50208; Jasper; P 16,000; (641) 792-0299; Fax (641) 791-0879; lindab@pcpartner.net; www.visitnewton.com

Ottumwa · *Ottumwa Area CVB* · Kathy Speas; Dir.; 102 Church St.; P.O. Box 1673; 52501; Wapello; P 25,000; (641) 684-7000; (800) 564-5274; info@ottumwaiowa.com; www.visitottumwa.com

Red Oak · *Western Iowa Tourism Region* · Michele Walker; Exec. Dir.; 103 N. Third St.; 51566; Montgomery; P 461,879; M 155; (712) 623-4232; (888) 623-4232; Fax (712) 623-9814; witr@ traveliowa.org; www.visitwesterniowa.com

Sioux City · *Sioux City Conv. & Tourism Bur.* · Aran Rush; Exec. Dir.; 801 4th St.; P.O. Box 3183; 51102; Woodbury; P 125,000; (712) 279-4800; (800) 593-2228; Fax (712) 279-4900; arush@ sioux-city.org; www.siouxcitytourism.com

Walnut · *Walnut Visitors Center* · Eldon Ranney; Dir.; 607 Highland St.; P.O. Box 265; 51577; Pottawattamie; P 897; (712) 784-2100; www.walnutiowa.net

Waterloo · *Waterloo CVB* · Aaron Buzza; Exec. Dir.; 313 E. 5th St.; 50703; Black Hawk; P 68,000; (319) 233-8350; (800) 728-8431; Fax (319) 233-2733; susan@travelwaterloo.com; www. travelwaterloo.com

Decorah · *Decorah & Winneshiek County CVB* · 507 W. Water St.; 52101; Winneshiek; P 8,700; (563) 382-2023; (800) 463-4692; Fax (563) 382-5515; wctc@alpinecom.net

Kansas

Abilene · *Abilene CVB* · Glenda Purkis; Dir.; 201 N.W. 2nd St.; 67410; Dickinson; P 10,000; (785) 263-2231; (800) 569-5915; Fax (785) 263-4125; tourism@abilenecityhall.com; www.abilenekansas.org

Arkansas City · *Arkansas City CVB* · Connie Kimsey; Dir.; 106 S. Summit; P.O. Box 795; 67005; Cowley; P 12,000; (620) 442-0236; Fax (620) 441-0048; ac-cvb@arkcitychamber.org; www.arkcity.org

Atchison · *Atchison Area Tourism Bur.* · Dane Normile; Tourism Coord.; 200 S. 10th St.; P.O. Box 126; 66002; Atchison; P 20,000; (913) 367-2427; Fax (913) 367-2485; tours@atchisonkansas.net; www.atchisonkansas.net

Augusta · *Augusta CVB* · Sharon Sudduth; Exec. Dir.; 112 E. 6th Ave.; 67010; Butler; P 8,700; (316) 775-6339; Fax (316) 775-1307; augustacoc@sbcglobal.net; www.visitaugustaks.com

Colby · *Colby CVB* · Leilani Thomas; Dir.; 350 S. Range, Ste. 10; 67701; Thomas; P 5,500; (785) 460-7643; (800) 611-8835; Fax (785) 460-4509; cvb@thomascounty.com; www.oasisontheplains.com

Dodge City · *Dodge City CVB* · Jan Stevens; Dir.; 400 W. Wyatt Earp Blvd.; P.O. Box 1474; 67801; Ford; P 27,000; (620) 225-8186; (800) OLD-WEST; Fax (620) 225-8268; cvb@dodgecity.org; www. visitdodgecity.org

Emporia • *Emporia CVB* • Betty Senn; Dir.; 719 Commercial; 66801; Lyon; P 27,000; (620) 342-1803; (800) 279-3730; Fax (620) 342-3223; visitors@emporiakschamber.org; www.emporiaks chamber.org

Garden City • *Finney County Conv. & Tourism Bur.* • Lynn Schoonover; Dir.; 1511 E. Fulton Terrace; 67846; Finney; P 40,000; (620) 276-3264; (800) 879-9803; Fax (620) 276-3290; ctb@gcnet. com; www.gardencitychamber.net/ctb

Goodland • *Sherman County CVB* • Donna Price; Exec. Dir.; P.O. Box 927; 67735; Sherman; P 7,400; (785) 890-3515; (785) 821-4170; Fax (785) 890-6980; cvb@goodlandnet.com; www. goodlandnet.com/cvb

Hays • *Hays CVB* • Jana Jordan; Dir.; 2700 Vine St.; 67601; Ellis; P 20,000; (785) 628-8202; (800) 569-4505; Fax (785) 628-1471; jjordan@haysusa.com; www.haysusa.net

Hutchinson • *Greater Hutchinson CVB* • LeAnn Cox; Dir.; 117 N. Walnut; P.O. Box 519; 67504; Reno; P 65,000; (620) 662-3391; (800) 691-4282; Fax (620) 662-2168; leannc@hutchchamber.com; www.visithutch.com

Independence • *Independence CVB* • Kerrie Manues; Tourism Dir.; 322 N. Penn; P.O. Box 386; 67301; Montgomery; P 10,050; (620) 331-1890; (800) 882-3606; Fax (620) 331-1899; tourism@ indkschamber.org; www.indkschamber.org

Kansas City • *Kansas City Kansas/Wyandotte County CVB* • Bridgette Jobe; Dir.; 727 Minnesota Ave.; P.O. Box 171517; 66117; Wyandotte; P 152,000; (913) 321-5800; (800) 264-1563; Fax (913) 371-3732; info@visitthedot.com; www.visitthedot.com

Lawrence • *Lawrence Visitor Center* • Deborah White; Mgr.; 402 N. 2nd; 66044; Douglas; P 100,000; (785) 865-4499; Fax (785) 865-4488; visinfo@visitlawrence.com; www.visitlawrence.com

Leavenworth • *Leavenworth CVB* • Connie Hachenberg; Dir.; 518 Shawnee St.; P.O. Box 44; 66048; Leavenworth; P 35,000; (913) 682-4113; Fax (913) 682-8170; connie.cvb@visitlvks.com; www.visitleavenworthks.com

Lenexa • *Lenexa CVB* • Julie Steiner; Dir.; 11180 Lackman Rd.; 66219; Johnson; P 48,000; (913) 888-1414; (800) 950-7867; Fax (913) 888-3770; jsteiner@lenexa.org; www.lenexa.org

Lindsborg • *Lindsborg CVB* • Carla Wilson; Dir.; 104 E. Lincoln; P.O. Box 70; 67456; McPherson; P 3,300; M (785) 227-8687; (888) 227-2227; cvbdir@lindsborgcity.org; www.visitlindsborg.com

Manhattan • *Manhattan CVB* • Karen Hibbard; Dir.; 501 Poyntz Ave.; 66502; Riley; P 51,707; (785) 776-8829; (800) 759-0134; Fax (785) 776-0679; cvb@manhattan.org; www.manhattancvb.org

Newton • *Newton CVB* • Jennifer Mueller; Dir.; 500 N. Main, Ste. 101; 67114; Harvey; P 20,000; (316) 283-7555; (800) 899-0455; Fax (316) 283-8732; jennifer@infonewtonks.org; www.thenew tonchamber.org.

Norton • *Norton Travel & Tourism* • Karla Reed; Exec. Dir.; 104 S. State; P.O. Box 132; 67654; Norton; P 2,806; (785) 877-2501; Fax (785) 877-3300; nortoncc@ruraltel.net; www.us36.net/norton kansas; www.discovernorton.com

Oberlin • *Oberlin CVB* • 104 S. Penn; 67749; Decatur; P 2,100; (785) 475-3441; Fax (785) 475-2128; dcacc@eaglecom.net; www. oberlinks.com

Olathe • *Olathe Chamber CVB* • Ashley Holverson; Dir.; 18001 W. 106th St., Ste. 160; P.O. Box 98; 66051; Johnson; P 120,000; (913) 764-1050; (800) 921-5678; Fax (913) 782-4636; cvb@olathe.org; www.olathecvb.org

Ottawa • *Franklin County Conv. & Visitors Bur.* • Kristi Lee; Dir.; 2011 E. Logan; P.O. Box 203; 66067; Franklin; P 25,000; (785) 242-1411; Fax (785) 242-2238; director@visitottawakansas.com; www.visitottawakansas.com

Overland Park • *Overland Park CVB* • Gerald Cook; Pres.; 9001 W. 110th St., Ste. 100; 66210; Johnson; P 170,000; (913) 491-0123; (800) 262-PARK; Fax (913) 491-0015; jlcook@opcvb.org; www.opcvb.org

Parsons • *Labette County CVB* • Jim Zaleski; Tourism Dir.; 1715 Corning; 67357; Labette; P 11,500; (620) 421-6500; (800) 280-6401; Fax (620) 421-6501; tourism@parsonsks.com; www. parsonschamber.org

Phillipsburg • *Phillips County CVB* • Jackie Swatzell; Dir.; 270 State St.; P.O. Box 326; 67661; Phillips; P 2,700; (785) 543-2321; Fax (785) 543-0038; cvbcham@ruraltel.net; www.phillipsburgks.us

Pittsburg • *Crawford County CVB* • Craig Hull; Dir.; 117 W. 4th St.; P.O. Box 1933; 66762; Crawford; P 38,242; (620) 231-1212; (800) 879-1112; Fax (620) 231-3178; chull@pittsburgareacham ber.com; www.visitcrawfordcounty.com

Russell • *Russell County Eco. Dev. & CVB* • Janae Talbott; Dir.; 331 E. Wichita Ave.; 67665; Russell; P 8,000; (785) 483-4000; Fax (785) 483-2827; cvb2@russellks.org; www.russellcoks.org

Sedan • *Yellow Brick Road Visitors Center* • Nita Jones; Dir.; 215 E. Main; 67361; Chautauqua; P 1,300; (620) 725-5797; (620) 725-3663; Fax (620) 725-5707; jonesrealtyusa@yahoo.com; sedankansas.com

Shawnee • *Shawnee CVB* • Linda Leeper; Pres.; 15100 W. 67th St., Ste. 202; 66217; Johnson; P 58,000; (913) 631-6545; Fax (913) 631-9628; info@shawneekscvb.com; www.shawneekscvb.com

Topeka • *Visit Topeka* • Olivia Simmons; Exec. Dir./CEO; 1275 S.W. Topeka Blvd.; 66612; Shawnee; P 125,000; (785) 234-1030; (800) 235-1030; Fax (785) 234-8282; info@visittopeka.org; www. visittopeka.org

Wichita • *Go Wichita CVB* • John Rolfe; Pres./CEO; 515 S. Main St., Ste. 115; 67202; Sedgwick; P 600,000; M 550; (316) 265-2800; Fax (316) 265-0162; info@gowichita.com; www.gowichita.com

Winfield • *Winfield Conv. & Tourism* • Sarah Werner; Comm. Events Coord.; 123 E. 9th Ave.; P.O. Box 640; 67156; Cowley; P 12,500; (620) 221-2421; (877) 729-7440; Fax (620) 221-2958; tourism@winfieldpartners.org; www.wowwinfield.org

Kentucky

Ashland • *Ashland Area CVB* • Sue G. Dowdy; Exec. Dir.; 1509 Winchester Ave.; 41101; Boyd; P 21,000; (606) 329-1007; (800) 377-6249; Fax (606) 329-1056; aacvb@visitashlandky.com; www. visitashlandky.com

Bardstown • *Bardstown-Nelson County Visitors Bur.* • One Court Sq.; P.O. Box 867; 40004; Nelson; P 11,000; (502) 348-4877; (800) 638-4877; Fax (502) 349-0804; info@bardstowntourism. com; www.visitbardstown.com

Benton • *Marshall County Tourist Comm.* • Randy Newcomb; Exec. Dir.; 93 Carroll Rd.; 42025; Marshall; P 30,000; (270) 527-3128; (800) 467-7145; Fax (270) 527-9193; fun@kentuckylake. org; www.kentuckylake.org

Bowling Green • *Bowling Green Area CVB* • Vicki Fitch; Exec. Dir.; 352 Three Springs Rd.; 42104; Warren; P 101,000; (270) 782-0800; (800) 326-7465; Fax (270) 842-2104; info@visitbgky.com; www.visitbgky.com

Campbellsville · *Taylor County Tourist Comm.* · Marilyn Clarke; Exec. Dir.; P.O. Box 4021; 42719; Taylor; P 23,000; (270) 465-3786; (800) 738-4719; Fax (270) 465-3786; taylorcounty tourism@kyol.net; www.campbellsvilleky.com

Cave City · *Cave City Tourist & Conv. Center* · Brian Dale; Dir.; P.O. Box 518; 42127; Barren; P 2,000; (270) 773-3131; (800) 346-8908; Fax (270) 773-8834; cavecity@scrtc.com; www.cavecity.com

Covington · *Northern Kentucky CVB* · Tom Caradonio; Pres./CEO; 50 E. RiverCenter Blvd., Ste. 200; 41011; Carroll; P 300,000; (859) 261-4677; (800) 447-8489; Fax (859) 261-5135; info@nkycvb.com; www.nkycvb.com

Danville · *Danville-Boyle County CVB* · Adam Johnson; Exec. Dir.; 105 E. Walnut St.; 40422; Boyle; P 28,000; (859) 236-7794; (800) 755-0076; Fax (859) 236-9134; info@danvillekentucky.com; www.danvillekentucky.com

Elizabethtown · *Elizabethtown Tourism & Conv. Bur.* · Sherry Murphy; Exec. Dir.; 1030 N. Mulberry St.; 42701; Hardin; P 22,500; (270) 765-2175; (800) 437-0092; Fax (270) 737-6568; www.touretown.com

Frankfort · *Frankfort/Franklin County Tourist & Conv. Comm.* · Joy Jeffries; Exec. Dir.; 100 Capital Ave.; 40601; Franklin; P 47,000; (502) 875-8687; (800) 960-7200; Fax (502) 227-2604; inquire@visitfrankfort.com; www.visitfrankfort.com

Georgetown · *Georgetown-Scott County Tourism Comm.* · John Simpson; Exec. Dir.; 399 Outlet Center Dr.; P.O. Box 825; 40324; Scott; P 42,000; (502) 863-2547; (888) 863-8600; Fax (502) 863-2561; gtown@mis.net; www.georgetownky.com

Harlan · *Harlan Tourist & Conv. Comm.* · Kim Collier; Exec. Dir.; 201 South Main Street; P.O. Box 489; 40831; Harlan; P 35,000; (606) 573-4156; Fax (606) 573-9485; htcc@harlanonline.net; www.harlantourism.com

Harrodsburg · *Harrodsburg/Mercer County Tour Comm.* · Karen Hackett; Exec. Dir.; 488 Price Ave.; P.O. Box 283; 40330; Mercer; P 30,000; (859) 734-2364; Fax (859) 734-9938; tourism@harrodsburgky.com; www.harrodsburgky.com

Henderson · *Henderson Tourist Comm.* · Marcia Eblen; Exec. Dir.; 101 N. Water St., Ste. B; 42420; Henderson; P 42,000; (270) 826-3128; Fax (270) 826-0234; info@hendersonky.org; www.hendersonky.org

Hopkinsville · *Hopkinsville-Christian County CVB* · Cheryl Cook; Exec. Dir.; 2800 Fort Campbell Blvd.; 42240; Christian; P 70,000; (270) 885-9096; (800) 842-9959; Fax (270) 886-2059; tourism@visithopkinsville.com; www.visithopkinsville.com

Jamestown · *see Russell Springs*

Leitchfield · *Grayson County Tourist Comm.* · Ilsa Johnson; Exec. Dir.; 425 S. Main St.; 42754; Grayson; P 25,600; (270) 259-2735; (888) 624-9951; Fax (270) 230-0615; mail@graysoncounty tourism.com; www.graysoncountytourism.com

Lexington · *Lexington CVB* · David Lord; Pres.; 301 E. Vine St.; 40507; Fayette; P 265,000; (859) 233-1221; (800) 845-3959; Fax (859) 254-4555; www.visitlex.com

London · *London/Laurel County Tourist Comm.* · Ken Harvey; Exec. Dir.; 140 Faith Assembly Church Rd.; 40741; Laurel; P 56,000; (606) 878-6900; (800) 348-0095; Fax (606) 877-1689; tourism@lltc.net; www.laurelkytourism.com

Louisville · *Greater Louisville CVB* · Jim Wood; Pres.; 401 W. Main St., Ste 2300; 40202; Jefferson; P 2,000,000; (502) 584-2121; (800) 626-5646; Fax (502) 561-3120; jwood@gotolouisville.com; www.gotolouisville.com

Mayfield · *Mayfield Tourism Comm.* · 201 E. College St.; 42066; Graves; P 37,000; (270) 247-6101; Fax (270) 247-6110; tourism@mayfieldchamber.com; www.mayfieldtourism.com

Maysville · *Maysville-Mason County CVB* · Duff Giffen; Exec. Dir.; 216 Bridge St.; 41056; Mason; P 18,000; (606) 564-9419; Fax (606) 564-9416; chamber@maysvilleky.net; www.cityof maysville.com

Mount Sterling · *Mt. Sterling-Montgomery County Tourism Comm.* · 126 W. Main St.; 40353; Montgomery; P 24,550; (859) 498-8732; (866) 415-7439; Fax (859) 498-3947; mtourism@mis.net; www.mtsterlingtourism.com

Murray · *Murray CVB* · Lindsay Geib; Dir.; 201 S. 4th St.; P.O. Box 321; 42071; Calloway; P 15,000; (270) 759-2199; (800) 651-1603; Fax (270) 761-6793; tourism@murray-ky.net; www.tourmurray.com

Owensboro · *Owensboro-Daviess County CVB* · Karen Miller; Exec. Dir.; 215 E. 2nd St.; 42303; Daviess; P 100,000; (270) 926-1100; (800) 489-1131; Fax (270) 926-1161; info@visitowensboro.com; www.visitowensboro.com

Paducah · *Paducah McCracken County CVB* · Mary Hammond; Exec. Dir.; 128 Broadway; 42001; McCracken; P 64,213; (270) 443-8783; (800) PADUCAH; Fax (270) 443-0122; info@paducah.travel; www.paducah.travel

Paintsville · *Paintsville Tourism & Conv. Center* · Carol Logsdon; Dir.; P.O. Box 809; 41240; Johnson; P 23,000; (606) 297-1469; (800) 542-5790; Fax (606) 297-1470; tourpvil@foothills.net; www.paintsville.org

Radcliff · *Radcliff/Fort Knox Tourism Comm.* · Kelly Barron; Exec. Dir.; 562 A1 N. Dixie; P.O. Box 845; 40159; Hardin; P 22,000; (270) 352-1204; (800) 334-7540; Fax (270) 352-2075; radcliff tourism@bbtel.com; www.radclifftourism.org

Richmond · *Richmond Tourism & Main Street Dept.* · Lori Murphy; Exec. Dir.; 345 Lancaster Ave.; 40475; Madison; P 30,000; (859) 626-8474; (800) 866-3705; Fax (859) 626-8121; tourism@richmond.ky.us; www.richmondkytourism.com

Russell Springs · *Russell County Tourist Comm.* · Renee Bradshaw; Admin. Asst.; 650 S. Hwy. 127; P.O. Box 64; 42642; Russell; P 17,500; (270) 866-4333; (888) 833-4220; Fax (270) 866-4304; lake@duo-county.com; www.lakecumberland vacation.com

Russellville · *Logan County Tourism Ofc.* · Teresa Perkins; Ofc. Mgr.; P.O. Box 1678; 42276; Logan; P 27,100; (270) 726-1678; Fax (270) 726-2705; logancountytour@bellsouth.net; www.visitlogancounty.net

Shelbyville · *Shelbyville/Shelby County Tourist Comm.* · 316 Main St.; P.O. Box 622; 40066; Shelby; P 37,000; (502) 633-6388; (800) 680-6388; Fax (502) 633-7501; tours@shelbyvilleky.com; www.shelbyvilleky.com

Shepherdsville · *Shepherdsville-Bullitt County Tourist & Conv. Comm* · Elaine Wilson; Exec. Dir.; 395 Paroquet Springs Dr.; 40165; Bullitt; P 65,000; (800) 526-2068; (502) 543-TOUR; Fax (502) 543-4889; ewilson@travelbullitt.org; www.travelbullitt.org

Williamsburg · *Williamsburg Tourism & Conv. Comm.* · Alvin Sharpe; Dir. of Tourism; P.O. Box 2; 40769; Whitley; P 5,600; (606) 549-0530; (800) 552-0530; Fax (606) 539-0095; wtour@bellsouth.net; www.williamsburgky.com

Winchester · *Winchester-Clark County Tourism Comm.* · Nancy Turner; Dir. of Tourism; 2 S. Maple St.; 40391; Clark; P 35,056; (859) 744-0556; (800) 298-9105; Fax (859) 744-9229; info@tourwinchester.com; www.tourwinchester.com

Louisiana

Abbeville · *Vermilion Parish Tourist Comm.* · Ali Miller; Dir.; P.O. Box 1106; 70511; Vermilion; P 12,000; (337) 898-6600; Fax (337) 893-1807; director@vermilion.org; www.vermilion.org

Albany · *Livingston Parish CVB* · Eric Edwards; Dir.; P.O. Box 1057; 70711; Livingston; P 111,863; M 10; (225) 567-7899; Fax (225) 567-7840; eric@visitlivingstonparish.com; www.visit livingstonparish.com

Alexandria · *Alexandria/Pineville Area CVB* · Sherry Ellington; Exec. Dir.; 707 Main St.; P.O. Box 1070; 71309; Rapides; P 133,937; (318) 442-9546; (318) 443-7049; Fax (318) 443-1617; inquire@apacvb.org; www.theheartoflouisiana.com.

Baton Rouge · *Baton Rouge Area CVB* · Paul Arrigo; Pres./CEO; 359 Third St.; P.O. Drawer 4149; 70821; East Baton Rouge; P 500,000; (225) 383-1825; (800) LAROUGE; Fax (225) 346-1253; paul@visitbatonrouge.com; www.visitbatonrouge.com

Crowley · *Acadia Parish Tourist, Conv. & Visitors Bur.* · Gwen Hanks; Exec. Dir.; 401 Tower Rd.; P.O. Box 1342; 70527; Acadia; P 56,000; (337) 783-2108; Fax (337) 783-2142; aptc@bellsouth. net; www.acadiatourism.org

Donaldsonville · *see Sorrento*

Grand Isle · *Grand Isle Tourist Comm.* · Josie Cheramie; Tourist Comm.; 2757 LA Hwy. 1; P.O. Box 817; 70358; Jefferson; P 1,500; (985) 787-2997; Fax (985) 787-2997; tourism@grand-isle.com; www.grand-isle.com

Houma · *Houma Area CVB* · Sharon Alford; Exec. Dir.; P.O. Box 2792; 70361; Terrebonne; P 140,000; (985) 868-2732; (800) 688-2732; Fax (985) 868-7170; www.houmatravel.com

Jackson · *East Feliciana Parish Tourist Comm.* · Audrey Faciane; Exec. Dir.; 1752 High St.; P.O. Box 667; 70748; East Feliciana; P 22,000; (225) 634-7155; Fax (225) 634-7155; tourism1@bellsouth.net; www.felicianatourism.org

Lafayette · *Lafayette Conv. & Vistors Comm.* · Gerald P. Breaux; Exec. Dir.; 1400 N.W. Evangeline Thruway; P.O. Box 52066; 70505; Lafayette; P 206,976; M 348; (337) 232-3737; (800) 346-1958; Fax (337) 232-0161; info@lafayettetravel.com; www. lafayette.travel

Lake Charles · *Southwest Louisiana CVB* · Shelley Johnson; Exec. Dir.; 1205 N. Lakeshore Dr.; P.O. Box 1912; 70602; Calcasieu; P 172,200; (337) 436-9588; (800) 456-SWLA; Fax (337) 494-7952; touristinfo@visitlakecharles.org; www.visitlakecharles.org

Mandeville · *Louisiana Northshore* · Donna O'Daniels; Exec. Dir.; St. Tammany Tourist & Conv. Comm.; 68099 Hwy. 59; 70471; Saint Tammany; P 250,000; (985) 892-0520; (800) 634-9443; Fax (985) 892-1441; mail@louisiananorthshore.com; www.louisiana northshore.com

Mansfield · *DeSoto Parish Tourist Bur.* · Edna Thornton; Dir.; 115 N. Washington Ave.; 71052; DeSoto; P 26,000; (318) 872-1177; Fax (318) 871-1875; touristb@bellsouth.net; www. discoverdesoto.com.

Many · *Sabine Parish Tourist Comm.* · Linda Curtis-Sparks; Tourism Dir.; 1601 Texas Hwy.; 71449; Sabine; P 24,000; (318) 256-5880; (800) 358-7802; Fax (318) 256-4137; sptourist@cp-tel.net; www.toledobendlakecountry.com

Minden · *Minden Webster Parish Tourist CVB* · Lynn Warnock-Dorsey; Exec. Dir.; 110 Sibley Rd.; P.O. Box 1528; 71058; Webster; P 42,000; (318) 377-4240; (888) 972-7474; Fax (318) 377-4215; lynn@visitwebster.com; www.visitwebster.com

Morgan City · *Cajun Coast Visitors & Conv. Bur.* · Carrie Stansbury; Exec. Dir.; P.O. Box 2332; 70381; Saint Mary; P 60,000; (985) 395-4905; (800) 256-2931; Fax (985) 395-7041; info@cajuncoast.com; www.cajuncoast.com

Natchitoches · *Natchitoches Parish Tourist Comm.* · Iris Harper; Exec. Dir.; 781 Front St.; 71457; Natchitoches; P 35,000; (318) 352-8072; (800) 259-1714; Fax (318) 352-2415; est1714@natchitoches.net; www.natchitoches.net

New Iberia · *Iberia Parish CVB* · Fran Thibodeaux; Exec. Dir.; 2513 Hwy. 14; 70560; Iberia; P 72,000; (337) 365-1540; (888) 942-3742; Fax (337) 367-3791; info@iberiatravel.com; www. iberiatravel.com

New Orleans · *New Orleans Metropolitan CVB* · J. Stephen Perry; Pres./CEO; 2020 St. Charles Ave.; 70130; Orleans; P 675,000; (504) 566-5011; (800) 672-6124; Fax (504) 566-5046; internet@neworleanscvb.com; www.neworleanscvb.com; www.new orleanscvb.com

Ruston · *Ruston/Lincoln CVB* · Kyle Edmiston; Pres.; 2111 N. Trenton St.; P.O. Box 1383; 71270; Lincoln; P 43,000; (318) 255-2031; (800) 392-9032; Fax (318) 255-3481; kedmiston@rustonlincoln.com; www.rustonlincoln.com

Saint Francisville · *West Feliciana Parish Tourist Comm.* · Kitty Martin; Dir.; P.O. Box 1548; 70775; West Feliciana; P 15,000; (225) 635-6769; (800) 789-4221; Fax (225) 635-4626; tourism@stfrancisville.us; www.stfrancisville.us

Saint Martinville · *St. Martinville Tourist Info. Center* · Brenda Comeau Trahan; Tourism Dir.; 125 S. New Market; P.O. Box 379; 70582; Saint Martin; P 8,000; (337) 394-2233; Fax (337) 394-2260; info@acadianmemorial.org; www.stmartinville.org

Shreveport · *Shreveport-Bossier Conv. & Tourist Bur.* · Stacy Brown; Pres.; 629 Spring; P.O. Box 1761; 71166; Caddo; P 298,000; (318) 222-9391; (800) 551-8682; Fax (318) 222-0067; info2@sbctb.org; www.shreveport-bossier.org

Sorrento · *Ascension Parish Tourism Comm.* · Ramon Gomez; Proj./Events Mgr.; 6967 Hwy. 22; 70778; Ascension; P 120,000; (225) 675-6550; (888) 775-7990; Fax (225) 675-6558; rgomez@eatel.net; www.ascensiontourism.com

West Monroe · *Monroe-West Monroe CVB* · Alana Cooper; Exec. Dir.; 601 Constitution Dr.; P.O. Box 1436; 71294; Ouachita; P 150,000; (318) 387-5691; (800) 843-1872; Fax (318) 324-1752; mwmcvb@monroe-westmonroe.org; www.monroe-westmonroe.org

Maine

Bangor · *Greater Bangor CVB* · Kerrie Tripp; Dir.; 40 Harlow St.; 04401; Penobscot; P 100,000; M 175; (207) 947-5205; (800) 916-6673; Fax (207) 942-3548; kerrie@visitbangormaine.com; www. visitbangormaine.com

Portland · *Greater Portland CVB* · Barbara Whitten; Pres.; 94 Commercial St., Ste. 300; 04101; Cumberland; P 230,000; M 475; (207) 772-4994; (207) 772-5800; Fax (207) 874-9043; info@visitportland.com; www.visitportland.com

Maryland

Baltimore · *Baltimore Area CVB* · Cathy Xanthakos; Dir. of Admin.; 100 Light St., 12th Flr.; 21202; Baltimore; P 786,000; (410) 659-7300; (800) 343-3468; Fax (410) 727-2308; shisamoto@baltimore.org; www.baltimore.org

Chester • *Queen Anne's County Ofc. of Tourism* • Barbara Siegert; Tourism Mgr.; 425 Piney Narrows Rd.; 21619; Queen Anne's; P 45,000; (410) 604-2100; Fax (410) 604-2101; bsiegert@qac.org; www.discoverqueenannes.com

Denton • *Caroline Ofc. of Tourism* • Natalie Chabot; Tourism Dir.; 15 S. Third St.; 21629; Caroline; P 31,300; (410) 479-0655; Fax (410) 479-5563; info@tourcaroline.com; www.tourcaroline.com

Easton • *Talbot County Ofc. of Tourism* • Deborah Dodson; Exec. Dir.; 11 S. Harrison St.; 21601; Talbot; P 35,000; (410) 770-8000; Fax (410) 770-8057; ddodson@talbgov.org; www.tourtalbot.org

Frederick • *Tourism Cncl. of Frederick County Inc.* • John Fieseler; Exec. Dir.; 19 E. Church St.; 21701; Frederick; P 221,850; (301) 600-2888; (800) 999-3613; Fax (301) 600-4044; tourism@fredco-md.net; www.fredericktourism.org

Germantown • *Montgomery County Visitor Info. Center* • Kelly Groff; Exec. Dir.; 12900 Middlebrook Rd., Ste. 1400; 20874; Montgomery; P 873,341; (301) 916-0698; (800) 925-0880; Fax (301) 916-1259; visitmoco@aol.com; www.visitmontgomery.com

Hagerstown • *Hagerstown/Washington County CVB* • Thomas Riford; Pres.; 16 Public Sq.; 21740; Washington; P 140,000; M 185; (301) 791-3246; (888) 257-2600; Fax (301) 791-2601; info@marylandmemories.org; www.marylandmemories.org

Ocean City • *Ocean City CVB* • Michael Noah; Exec. Dir.; 4001 Coastal Hwy.; 21842; Worcester; P 10,000; (410) 289-8181; (800) OC-OCEAN; Fax (410) 723-8655; dabbot@ococean.com; www.ococean.com

Rockville • *Montgomery County Conf. & Visitors Bur. (Admin.)* • Kelly Groff; Exec. Dir.; 111 Rockville Pike, Ste. 800; 20850; Montgomery; P 873,341; (240) 777-2060; (877) 789-6904; Fax (301) 777-2065; office@visitmontgomery.com; www.visitmontgomery.com

Massachusetts

Adams • *Berkshire Visitors Bur.* • Lauri Klefos; Pres./CEO; 3 Hoosac St.; 01220; Berkshire; P 150,000; M 750; (413) 743-4500; (800) 237-5747; Fax (413) 743-4560; info@berkshires.org; www.berkshires.org

Boston • *Greater Boston CVB* • Patrick Moscaritolo; Pres./CEO; Two Copley Pl., Ste. 105; 02116; Suffolk; P 2,000,000; M 1,200; (617) 536-4100; (888) SEE-BOSTON; Fax (617) 424-7664; visitus@bostonusa.com; www.bostonusa.com

New Bedford • *Southeastern Mass. CVB* • Kathleen Nemer; Op. Mgr.; 70 N. Second St.; 02740; Bristol; P 534,678; M 200; (508) 997-1250; (800) 288-6263; Fax (508) 997-9090; explorer@bristol-county.org; www.bristol-county.org

Peabody • *North of Boston CVB* • Julie McConchie; Exec. Dir.; 17 Peabody Sq.; 01960; Essex; P 723,419; M 250; (978) 977-7760; (877) 662-9299; Fax (978) 977-7758; info@northofboston.org; www.northofboston.org

Provincetown • *Provincetown Tourism Ofc.* • Bob Sanborn; Tourism Dir.; 330 Commercial St.; 260 Commercial St.; 02657; Barnstable; P 3,400; (508) 487-3298; Fax (508) 487-7085; bsanborn@provincetown-ma.gov; www.provincetowntourismoffice.org

Salem • *Salem Office of Tourism & Cultural Affairs Inc.* • Kate Fox; Exec. Dir.; P.O. Box 630; 01970; Essex; P 45,000; M 100; (978) 744-3663; (877) SALEM-MA; Fax (978) 741-7539; salem@salem.org; www.salem.org

Somerville • *Somerville CVB* • Stephen V. Mackey; Pres./CEO; 2 Alpine St.; P.O. Box 440343; 02144; Middlesex; P 78,000; (617) 776-4100; info@somervillechamber.org; www.somervillechamber.org

Springfield • *Greater Springfield CVB* • Mary Kay Wydra; Pres.; 1441 Main St.; 01103; Hampden; P 450,000; M 311; (413) 787-1548; (800) 723-1548; Fax (413) 781-4607; marykay@valleyvisitor.com; www.valleyvisitor.com

Worcester • *Central MA CVB* • Donna McCabe; Pres.; 91 Prescott St.; 01609; Worcester; P 700,000; M 250; (508) 755-7400; (866) 755-7439; Fax (508) 754-2703; dmccabe@worcester.org; www.worcester.org

Michigan

Allegan • *Allegan County Parks, Rec. & Tourism* • 3255 122nd Ave., Ste. 102; 49010; Allegan; P 105,000; (269) 686-9088; (888) 4-ALLEGAN; Fax (269) 673-0454; parks@allegancounty.org; www.visitallegancounty.com

Alpena • *Alpena Area CVB* • Deborah Pardike; Dir.; 235 W. Chisholm St.; 49707; Alpena; P 40,000; M 70; (989) 354-4181; (800) 4-ALPENA; Fax (989) 356-3999; info@chartermi.net; www.alpenacvb.com

Ann Arbor • *Ann Arbor CVB* • Mary A. Kerr; Pres.; 120 W. Huron St.; 48104; Washtenaw; P 250,000; M 300; (734) 995-7281; (800) 888-9487; Fax (734) 995-7283; info@annarbor.org; www.visitannarbor.org

Battle Creek • *Battle Creek/Calhoun Co. CVB* • Dwight Butt; Pres.; 77 E. Michigan Ave., Ste. 100; 49017; Calhoun; P 93,000; (269) 962-2240; (800) 397-2240; Fax (269) 962-6917; info@battlecreekvisitors.org; www.battlecreekvisitors.org

Bay City • *Bay City CVB* • Annette Rummel; Pres./CEO; 100 Center Ave.; 48708; Bay; P 111,000; (989) 893-1222; arummel@visitsaginawvalley.com; www.tourbaycitymi.org

Benton Harbor • *Southwestern Michigan Tourist Cncl.* • Millicent Huminsky; Exec. Dir.; 2300 Pipestone Rd.; 49022; Berrien; P 150,000; M 250; (269) 925-6301; Fax (269) 925-7540; info@swmichigan.org; www.swmichigan.org

Benzonia • *Benzie County CVB* • Mary Carroll; Pres.; 826 Michigan Ave.; P.O. Box 204; 49616; Benzie; P 17,000; (231) 882-5801; (800) 882-5801; Fax (231) 882-9249; director@benzie.org; www.visitbenzie.com

Big Rapids • *Mecosta County Area CVB* • Connie Koepke; Exec. Dir.; 246 N. State St.; 49307; Mecosta; P 42,391; (231) 796-7640; Fax (231) 796-0832; events@bigrapids.org; www.bigrapids.org

Cadillac • *Cadillac Area Visitors Bur.* • Robert Gattin; Exec. Dir.; 222 N. Lake St.; 49601; Wexford; P 10,100; (231) 775-0657; (800) 22-LAKES; Fax (231) 775-1440; rgattin@cadillacmichigan.com; www.cadillacmichigan.com

Calumet • *Keweenaw CVB* • 56638 Calumet Ave.; 49913; Calumet; P 37,000; M 210; (906) 337-4579; (800) 338-7982; Fax (906) 337-4285; info@keweenaw.info; www.keweenaw.info

Caro • *Thumb Area Tourism Cncl.* • Kris McArdle; Mktg. Dir.; 1111 W. Caro Rd., Ste. B; 48723; Tuscola; P 57,500; (810) 569-6856; kris@thumbtourism.org; www.thumbtourism.org

Charlevoix • *Charlevoix Area CVB* • 100 Michigan Ave.; 49720; Charlevoix; P 3,500; (800) 367-8557; Fax (231) 547-6633; info@charlevoixlodging.com; www.charlevoixlodging.com

Clare • *Clare County CVB* • P.O. Box 226; 48617; Clare; P 28,000; M 50; (989) 386-6400; (800) 233-1359; www.clarecounty.com

Coldwater • *Branch County Tourism Bur.* • Debra Yee; Exec. Dir.; 28 W. Chicago St., Ste. 1C; 49036; Branch; P 42,000; (517) 278-0241; Fax (517) 278-8369; dyee@discover-michigan.com; www.discover-michigan.com

Detroit · *Detroit Metro CVB* · Larry Alexander; Pres./CEO; 211 W. Fort St., Ste. 1000; 48226; Wayne; P 4,500,000; (313) 202-1800; (800) DETROIT; Fax (313) 202-1808; lalexander@visitdetroit.com; www.visitdetroit.com

Flint · *Flint Area CVB* · Gloria DeHart; V.P. of Sales; 502 Church St.; 48502; Genesee; P 431,000; M 285; (810) 232-8900; (877) 354-6864; Fax (810) 232-1515; info@flint.org; www.visitflint.org

Frankenmuth · *Frankenmuth CVB* · Jamie Furbush; Pres./CEO; 635 S. Main St.; 48734; Saginaw; P 4,800; M 400; (989) 652-6106; (800) 386-8696; Fax (989) 652-3841; chamber@frankenmuth.org; www.frankenmuth.org

Gaylord · *Gaylord Area Conv. & Tourism Bur.* · 101 W. Main St.; 49735; Otsego; P 23,000; (989) 732-4000; (800) 345-8621; Fax (989) 732-7990; info@gaylordmichigan.net; www.gaylord michigan.net

Grand Haven · *Grand Haven Area CVB* · Marci Cisneros; Exec. Dir.; One S. Harbor; 49417; Ottawa; P 187,768; (616) 842-4499; (800) 303-4092; Fax (616) 842-0379; web@visitgrandhaven.com; www.visitgrandhaven.com

Grand Rapids · *Grand Rapids/Kent County CVB* · George Helmstead; Exec. V.P.; 171 Monroe Ave. N.W., Ste. 700; 49503; Kent; P 1,100,000; (616) 459-8287; (800) 678-9859; Fax (616) 459-7291; mailbox@visitgrandrapids.org; www.visitgrandrapids.org

Grand Rapids · *West Michigan Tourist Assn.* · Rick Hert; Exec. Dir.; 741 Kenmoor Ave., Ste. E; 49546; Kent; P 300,000; M 1,000; (616) 245-2217; (800) 442-2084; Fax (616) 954-3924; rick@wmta. org; www.wmta.org

Grayling · *Grayling Visitors Bur.* · Ilene Geiss-Wilson; Exec. Dir.; P.O. Box 217; 49738; Crawford; P 13,000; (989) 348-4945; (800) 937-8837; Fax (989) 348-9168; visitor@grayling-mi.com; www. grayling-mi.com

Holland · *Holland Area CVB* · Sally Laukitis; Exec. Dir.; 76 E. 8th St.; 49423; Ottawa; P 110,000; (616) 394-0000; (800) 506-1299; Fax (616) 394-0122; sally@holland.org; www.holland.org

Howell · *Livingston County CVB* · 123 E. Washington St.; 48843; Livingston; P 105,000; (517) 548-1795; (800) 686-8474; Fax (517) 546-4115; info@lccvb.org; www.lccvb.org

Iron Mountain · *Dickinson Area Partnership* · Lynda Zanon; Dir.; 600 S. Stephenson Ave.; 49801; Dickinson; P 26,868; (906) 774-2002; Fax (906) 774-2004; info@dickinsonchamber.com; www.dickinsonchamber.com

Iron Mountain · *Upper Peninsula Travel & Rec. Assn.* · P.O. Box 400; 49801; Dickinson; P 350,000; M 900; (906) 774-5480; (800) 562-7134; Fax (906) 774-5190; info@uptravel.com; www. uptravel.com

Ironwood · *Western U.P. CVB* · P.O. Box 706; 49938; Gogebic; P 35,000; M 125; (906) 932-4850; (800) 522-5657; Fax (906) 932-3455; bigsnow@westernup.info; www.westernup.info

Kalamazoo · *Kalamazoo County CVB* · Greg Ayers; Pres.; 141 E. Michigan Ave., Ste. 100; 49007; Kalamazoo; P 287,000; (269) 488-9000; (800) 888-0509; jbach@discoverkalamazoo.com; www. discoverkalamazoo.com

L'Anse · *Baraga County CVB* · 755 E. Broad St.; 49946; Baraga; P 8,000; M 100; (906) 524-7444; (800) 743-4908; Fax (906) 524-7454; bctra@up.net; www.baragacountytourism.org

Lansing · *Greater Lansing CVB* · W. Lee Hladki; Pres./CEO; 500 E. Michigan Ave., Ste. 180; 48912; Ingham; P 450,000; (517) 487-0077; (888) 252-6746; Fax (517) 487-5151; lhladki@lansing.org; www.lansing.org

Ludington · *Ludington Area CVB* · Amy Seng; Exec. Dir.; 5300 W. U.S. 10; 49431; Mason; P 25,000; M 100; (231) 845-5430; (800) 542-4600; Fax (231) 845-6857; amys@ludington.org; www. destinationludington.org

Mackinac Island · *Mackinac Island Tourism Bur.* · 7274 Main St.; P.O. Box 451; 49757; Mackinac; P 500; M 240; (906) 847-3783; (800) 454-5227; info@mackinacisland.org; www.mackinacisland.org

Mackinaw City · *Mackinaw Area Visitors Bur.* · Diane Klose; Admin. Asst.; 10800 W. U.S. 23; 49701; Emmet; P 900; M 180; (231) 436-5664; (800) 666-0160; Fax (231) 436-5991; info@ mackinawcity.com; www.mackinawcity.com

Marquette · *Marquette Country CVB* · Pat Black; Exec. Dir.; 337 W. Washington St.; 49855; Marquette; P 61,000; (906) 228-7749; (800) 544-4321; Fax (906) 228-3642; mailroom@marquette country.org; www.marquettecountry.org

Midland · *Midland County CVB* · 300 Rodd St., Ste. 101; 48640; Midland; P 80,670; (989) 839-9522; (888) 464-3526; Fax (989) 835-3701; info@midlandcvb.org; www.midlandcvb.org

Monroe · *Monroe County Conv. & Tourism Bur.* · John Patterson; Pres./CEO; 103 W. Front St.; 48161; Monroe; P 150,000; (734) 457-1030; Fax (734) 457-1097; thebureau@monroeinfo. com; www.monroeinfo.com

Mount Pleasant · *Mount Pleasant Area CVB* · Chris Rowley; Exec. Dir.; 200 E. Broadway; 48858; Isabella; P 60,000; M (989) 772-4433; Fax (989) 772-2909; visitor@mountpleasantwow.com; www.mountpleasantwow.com

Muskegon · *Muskegon County CVB* · Sam Wendling; Dir.; 610 W. Western Ave.; 49440; Muskegon; P 170,200; (231) 724-3100; (800) 250-9283; Fax (231) 724-1398; visitmuskegon@ co.muskegon.mi.us; www.visitmuskegon.org

Newberry · *Newberry Area Tourism Assn.* · P.O. Box 308; 49868; Luce; P 8,000; (906) 293-5562; (800) 831-7292; Fax (906) 293-5739; newberry@lighthouse.net; www.newberry chamber.net

Niles · *Four Flags Area Cncl. on Tourism* · Melinda Michael; Exec. Dir.; P.O. Box 1300; 49120; Berrien; P 52,000; M 100; (269) 684-7444; Fax (269) 683-3722; info@fourflagsarea.org; www. fourflagsarea.org

Oscoda · *Oscoda CVB* · Amy Ridgway; Pres.; P.O. Box 572; 48750; Iosco; P 7,000; (989) 739-0900; (877) 8-OSCODA; Fax (989) 739-0900; staff@oscoda.com; www.oscoda.com

Owosso · *Shiawassee County CVB* · Kimberly Springsdorf; CVB Dir.; 215 N. Water St.; 48867; Shiawassee; P 72,000; (989) 723-1199; Fax (989) 723-8353; cvbshia@shiawassee.org; www. shiawassee.org

Paradise · *Paradise Area Tourism Cncl.* · P.O. Box 64; 49768; Chippewa; P 400; (906) 492-3927; info@paradisemi.org; www. paradisemi.org

Petoskey · *Petoskey Area Visitors Bur.* · Peter Fitzsimons; Exec. Dir.; 401 E. Mitchell St.; 49770; Emmet; P 20,000; (231) 348-2755; (800) 845-2828; Fax (231) 348-1810; info@petoskeyarea.com; www.petoskeyarea.com

Port Huron · *Blue Water Area CVB* · 520 Thomas Edison Pkwy.; 48060; St. Clair; P 165,000; (810) 987-8687; (800) 852-4242; Fax (810) 987-1441; bluewater@bluewater.org; www.bluewater.org

Saginaw · *Saginaw Valley CVB* · Annette Rummel; Pres./CEO; 515 N. Washington Ave., 3rd Flr.; 48607; Saginaw; P 210,039; (989) 752-7164; (800) 444-9979; Fax (989) 752-6642; info@ visitsaginawvalley.com; www.visitsaginawvalley.com

Saugatuck · *Saugatuck/Douglas CVB* · Felicia Fairchild; Exec. Dir.; 2902 Blue Star Hwy.; P.O. Box 28; 49453; Allegan; P 1,000; M 3; (269) 857-1701; ffairchild@saugatuck.com; www.saugatuck.com

Sault Ste. Marie · *Sault Ste. Marie CVB* · Linda Hoath; Exec. Dir.; 536 Ashmun St.; 49783; Chippewa; P 15,000; M 33; (906) 632-3366; (800) MI-SAULT; Fax (906) 632-6161; info@saultste marie.com; www.saultstemarie.com

South Haven · *South Haven Visitors Bur.* · Lisa Shanley; Exec. Dir.; 546 Phoenix St.; 49090; Van Buren; P 6,000; M 43; (269) 637-5252; (800) SO-HAVEN; Fax (269) 637-8710; relax@southhaven.org; www.southhaven.org

St. Ignace · *St. Ignace Visitors Bur.* · 6 Spring St., Ste 100; 49781; Mackinac; P 2,700; (906) 643-6950; (800) 338-6660; Fax (906) 643-8067; info@stignace.com; www.stignace.com

Tawas City · *Tawas Bay Tourist & Conv. Bur.* · Heidi Dewalt; Secy./Treas.; P.O. Box 10; 48764; Iosco; P 6,000; M 57; (989) 876-6018; (877) TO-TAWAS; info@tawas.com; www.tawasbay.com

Three Rivers · *River Country Tourism Cncl.* · P.O. Box 214; 49093; St. Joseph; P 60,000; M 90; (269) 321-0640; (800) 447-2821; rivercountryinfo@gmail.com; www.rivercountry.com

Traverse City · *Traverse City CVB* · Brad VanDommelen; Pres.; 101 W. Grandview Pkwy.; 49684; Grand Traverse; P 18,105; (231) 947-1120; (800) 940-1120; Fax (231) 947-2621; www.visit traversecity.com

West Branch · *West Branch Visitors Bur.* · Christie Blackford; Exec. Dir.; 422 W. Houghton Ave.; 48661; Ogemaw; P 30,000; M 4; (989) 345-2821; (800) 755-9091; Fax (989) 345-9075; info@visitwestbranch.com; www.visitwestbranch.com

Ypsilanti · *Ypsilanti Area CVB* · Debbie Locke-Daniel; Exec. Dir.; 106 W. Michigan Ave.; 48197; Washtenaw; P 71,000; (734) 483-4444; (800) 265-9045; Fax (734) 483-0400; dlocke@ypsilanti.org; www.ypsilanti.org

Minnesota

Albert Lea · *Albert Lea CVB* · Susie Petersen; Exec. Dir.; 2566 N. Bridge Ave.; 56007; Freeborn; P 18,500; (507) 373-2316; (800) 345-8414; Fax (507) 552-1248; cvbdirector@albertlea.org; www.albertleatourism.org

Alexandria · *Alexandria Lakes Area Mktg.* · Coni McKay; Exec. Dir.; 206 Broadway; 56308; Douglas; P 30,000; M 120; (320) 763-3161; (800) 235-9441; Fax (320) 763-6857; info@alexandriamn.org; www.alexandriamn.org

Austin · *Austin CVB* · Cheryl Corey; Exec. Dir.; 104 11th Ave. N.W., Ste. D; 55912; Mower; P 23,000; (507) 437-4563; (800) 444-5713; Fax (507) 433-1052; visitor@austinmn.com; www.austincvb.com

Baudette · *Lake of the Woods Tourism* · Denelle Cauble; Exec. Dir.; 930 W. Main; P.O. Box 518; 56623; Lake of the Woods; P 4,000; (218) 634-1174; (800) 382-3474; Fax (218) 634-2915; lakwoods@wiktel.com; www.lakeofthewoodsmn.com

Bemidji · *Visit Bemidji* · Gayle Quistgard; Exec. Dir.; 300 Bemidji Ave.; P.O. Box 66; 56619; Beltrami; P 12,076; (218) 759-0164; (877) 250-5959; Fax (218) 759-0810; gayle@visitbemidji.com; www.visitbemidji.com

Bloomington · *Bloomington CVB* · 7900 International Dr., Ste. 990; 55425; Hennepin; P 85,000; (952) 858-8500; (800) 346-4289; Fax (952) 858-8854; www.bloomingtonmn.org

Blue Earth · *Blue Earth Area CVB* · Shelly Greimann; Dir.; 113 S. Nicollet St.; 56013; Faribault; P 4,000; (507) 526-2916; Fax (507) 526-2244; chamber@bevcomm.net; www.blueearthchamber.com

Burnsville · *Burnsville CVB* · Amie Burrill; Exec. Dir.; 101 W. Burnsville Pkwy., Ste. 150B; 55337; Dakota; P 62,000; (952) 898-5646; (800) 521-6055; Fax (952) 487-1777; info@burnsvillemn.com; www.burnsvillemn.com

Caledonia · *see Harmony*

Crane Lake · *Crane Lake Visitors & Tourism Bur.* · 7238 Handberg Rd.; 55725; St. Louis; P 150; (218) 993-2901; (800) 362-7405; Fax (218) 993-2902; vacation@visitcranelake.com; www.visitcranelake.com

Detroit Lakes · *Detroit Lakes Tourism Bur.* · Cleone Stewart; Tourism Dir.; 700 Summit Ave.; P.O. Box 348; 56502; Becker; P 8,500; (218) 847-9202; (800) 542-3992; Fax (218) 847-9082; dlchamber@visitdetroitlakes.com; www.visitdetroitlakes.com

Duluth · *Visit Duluth* · Terry Mattson; Pres.; 21 W. Superior St., Ste. 100; 55802; St. Louis; P 90,000; M 450; (218) 722-4011; (800) 4-DULUTH; Fax (218) 722-1322; cvb@visitduluth.com; www.visitduluth.com

Eagan · *Eagan CVB* · Brent Cory; Exec. Dir.; 1501 Central Pkwy., Ste. E; 55121; Dakota; P 64,235; (651) 675-5546; (866) 324-2620; Fax (651) 675-5545; enjoyeagan@eaganmn.com; www.eaganmn.com

Fairmont · *Fairmont CVB* · Stephanie Busiahn; Dir.; 323 E. Blue Earth Ave.; P.O. Box 976; 56031; Martin; P 10,889; (507) 235-8585; (800) 657-3280; Fax (507) 235-8411; director@fairmontcvb.com; www.visitfairmontmn.com

Faribault · *Faribault Area Tourism* · Kymn Anderson; Pres.; 530 Wilson Ave.; P.O. Box 434; 55021; Rice; P 28,000; (507) 334-4381; (800) 658-2354; Fax (507) 334-1003; chamber@faribaultmn.org; www.faribaultmn.org

Grand Rapids · *Visit Grand Rapids* · Cheri M. Zeppelin; Exec. Dir.; 501 S. Pokegama Ave., Ste. 3; 55744; Itasca; P 8,000; (218) 326-9607; (800) 355-9740; Fax (218) 326-8219; cheri@visitgrand rapids.com; www.visitgrandrapids.com

Harmony · *Historic Bluff Country/Southeastern Reg. CVB* · Kris Nolte; Exec. Dir.; P.O. Box 609; 55939; Fillmore; (800) 428-2030; Fax (507) 886-2934; hbc@harmonytel.net; www.bluffcountry.com

Hutchinson · *Hutchinson Area CVB* · Bill Corb; Pres.; 2 Main St. S.; 55350; McLeod; P 14,500; (320) 587-5252; (800) 572-6689; Fax (320) 587-4752; info@explorehutchinson.com; www.explore hutchinson.com

Little Falls · *Little Falls CVB* · Cathy VanRisseghem; Exec. Dir.; 606 S.E. First St.; 56345; Morrison; P 8,500; (320) 616-4959; (800) 325-5916; Fax (320) 616-4961; lfcvb@charter.net; www.littlefallsmn.com

Mankato · *Greater Mankato CVB* · Anna Thill; Pres.; 1 Civic Center Plz., Ste. 200; 56001; Blue Earth, Le Sueur & Nicollet; P 55,000; (507) 385-6660; (800) 657-4733; Fax (507) 345-8376; visitors@greatermankato.com; www.visitgreatermankato.com

Marshall · *Marshall CVB* · Linda Erb; Exec. Dir.; 317 W. Main; 56258; Lyon; P 12,500; (507) 537-1865; Fax (507) 532-4485; info@visitmarshallmn.com; www.visitmarshallmn.com

Minneapolis · *Meet Minneapolis Conv. & Visitors Assn.* · Bill Deef; V.P. Tourism; 250 Marquette Ave. S., Ste. 1300; 55401; Hennepin; P 2,968,000; M 800; (612) 767-8000; (888) 676-6757; Fax (612) 767-8001; www.meetminneapolis.com

Minneapolis · *Visit Minneapolis North* · Dave Looby; Exec. Dir.; 6200 Shingle Creek Pkwy., Ste. 248; 55430; Hennepin; P 400,000; (763) 566-7722; (800) 541-4364; Fax (763) 566-6526; info@visitminneapolisnorth.com; www.visitminneapolisnorth.com

Moorhead · *see Fargo, ND*

Pipestone • *Pipestone CVB* • Mick Myers; Exec. Dir.; 117 8th Ave. S.E.; P.O. Box 8; 56164; Pipestone; P 4,280; (507) 825-3316; (800) 336-6125; Fax (507) 825-3317; pipecham@pipestoneminnesota.com; www.pipestoneminnesota.com

Red Wing • *Red Wing Visitors & Conv. Bur.* • Kathy Silverthorn; Exec. Dir.; 420 Levee St.; 55066; Goodhue; P 17,000; M 70; (651) 385-5934; (800) 498-3444; Fax (651) 388-3900; visitorscenter@redwing.org; www.redwing.org

Redwood Falls • *Redwood Area Tourism* • 200 S. Mill St.; 56283; Redwood; P 5,459; (507) 637-2828; (800) 657-7070; Fax (507) 637-5202; chamber@redwoodfalls.org; www.redwoodfalls.org

Rochester • *Rochester CVB* • Brad Jones; Exec. Dir.; 30 Civic Center Dr. S.E., Ste. 200; 55904; Olmsted; P 100,000; (507) 288-4331; (800) 634-8277; Fax (507) 288-9144; info@rochestercvb.org; www.visitrochestermn.com

Saint Cloud • *Saint Cloud Area CVB* • Julie Lunning; Exec. Dir.; 525 Hwy. 10 S., Ste. 1; 56304; Sherburne; P 150,000; (320) 251-4170; (800) 264-2940; Fax (320) 656-0401; julie@granitecountry.com; www.granitecountry.com

Saint Paul • *Saint Paul Conv. & Visitors Auth.* • Karolyn Kirchgesler; Pres./CEO; 175 W. Kellogg Blvd., Ste. 502; 55102; Ramsey; P 267,000; M 400; (651) 265-4900; (800) 627-6101; Fax (651) 265-4999; info@visitsaintpaul.com; www.visitsaintpaul.com

Sauk Centre • *Sauk Centre CVB* • Cindy Uhlenkamp; Mktg. Mgr.; 1220 S. Main St.; P.O. Box 222; 56378; Stearns; P 5,000; (320) 352-5201; Fax (320) 352-5202; sccvb@mainstreetcom.com; www.visitsaukcentre.com

Shakopee • *Shakopee CVB* • Carol Schultz; Pres.; 1801 E. Cty. Rd. 101; P.O. Box 717; 55379; Scott; P 32,000; (952) 445-1660; (800) 574-2150; Fax (952) 445-1669; cschultz@shakopee.org; www.shakopee.org

Thief River Falls • *Thief River Falls CVB* • Laura Anderson; Dir.; 2042 Hwy. 1 W.; P.O. Box 176; 56701; Pennington; P 8,600; (218) 686-9785; Fax (218) 683-5107; trfcvb@mncable.net; www.visittrf.com

Virginia • *Iron Range Tourism Bur.* • 403 N. 1st St.; 55792; St. Louis; (218) 749-8161; (800) 777-8497; Fax (218) 749-8055; info@ironrange.org; www.ironrange.org

Wadena • *Wadena Area CVB* • Shirley Uselman; Dir.; 5 Aldrich Ave. S.E.; P.O. Box 107; 56482; Wadena; P 4,292; (218) 632-7704; (877) 631-7704; Fax (218) 632-7705; www.wadena.org

Willmar • *Willmar Lakes Area CVB* • Beth Fischer; Exec. Dir.; 2104 E. Hwy. 12; 56201; Kandiyohi; P 20,000; (320) 235-3552; (800) 845-TRIP; Fax (320) 231-1948; info@seeyouinwillmar.com; www.seeyouinwillmar.com

Winona • *Visit Winona* • Pat Mutter; Exec. Dir.; 160 Johnson St.; P.O. Box 1069; 55987; Winona; P 27,069; (507) 452-0735; (800) 657-4972; Fax (507) 454-0006; pmutter@visitwinona.com; www.visitwinona.com

Worthington • *Worthington Area CVB* • Darlene Macklin; Dir.; 1121 Third Ave.; 56187; Nobles; P 11,230; (507) 372-2919; (800) 279-2919; Fax (507) 372-2827; wcofc@frontiernet.net; www.worthingtonmnchamber.com

Mississippi

Aberdeen • *Aberdeen Visitors Bur.* • Deborah Stubblefield; Dir.; 204 E. Commerce St.; P.O. Box 288; 39730; Monroe; P 6,500; (662) 369-9440; (800) 634-3538; Fax (662) 369-3436; info@aberdeenms.org; www.aberdeenms.org

Belzoni • *Catfish Capital Visitors Center* • Steve Anderson; Exec. Dir.; 111 Magnolia St.; P.O. Box 145; 39038; Humphreys; P 11,000; (662) 247-4838; (800) 408-4838; Fax (662) 247-4805; catfish@belzonicable.com; www.catfishcapitalonline.com

Canton • *Canton CVB* • JoAnn Gordon; Exec. Dir.; 147 N. Union St.; P.O. Box 53; 39046; Madison; P 13,500; (601) 859-1307; (800) 844-3369; Fax (601) 859-0346; canton@cantontourism.com; www.cantontourism.com

Columbus • *Columbus CVB* • James Tsismanakis; Exec. Dir.; 318 7th St. N.; P.O. Box 789; 39703; Lowndes; P 64,000; (662) 329-1191; (800) 327-2686; Fax (662) 329-8969; ccvb@columbus-ms.org; www.columbus-ms.org

Corinth • *Corinth Area CVB* • Kristy White; Exec. Dir.; 215 N. Filmore St.; 38834; Alcorn; P 35,000; (662) 287-8300; (800) 748-9048; Fax (662) 286-0102; tourism@corinth.net; www.corinth.net

Greenwood • *Greenwood CVB* • Paige Hunt; Exec. Dir.; 111 E. Market St.; P.O. Drawer 739; 38935; Leflore; P 18,000; (662) 453-9197; (800) 748-9064; Fax (662) 453-5526; info@gcvb.com; www.greenwoodms.org.

Grenada • *Grenada Tourism Comm.* • Walter McCool; Exec. Dir.; 95 S.W. Frontage Rd.; P.O. Box 1824; 38902; Grenada; P 23,263; (662) 226-2571; (800) 373-2571; Fax (662) 226-9745; phillip heard@yahoo.com; www.grenadamississippi.com

Gulfport • *Mississippi Gulf Coast CVB* • Richard Forester; Exec. Dir.; P.O. Box 6128; 39506; Harrison; P 335,450; (228) 896-6699; (888) 467-4853; Fax (228) 896-6788; tourism@gulfcoast.org; www.gulfcoast.org

Hattiesburg • *Hattiesburg CVB* • Richard Taylor; Dir.; 5 Convention Center Plz.; 39401; Lamar; P 65,000; (601) 296-7475; (866) 4-HATTIE; Fax (601) 296-7404; www.visithattie.com

Jackson • *Jackson CVB* • Wanda Collier-Wilson; Exec. Dir.; 111 Capitol St., Ste. 102; P.O. Box 1450; 39215; Hinds; P 200,000; (601) 960-1891; (800) 354-7695; Fax (601) 960-1827; wcwilson@visitjackson.com; www.visitjackson.com

Meridian • *Meridian/Lauderdale County Tourism Bur.* • Suzy Johnson; Exec. Dir.; 212 Constitution Ave.; 39301; Lauderdale; P 75,555; (601) 482-8001; (888) 868-7720; Fax (601) 486-4988; tourism@visitmeridian.com; www.visitmeridian.com

Natchez • *Natchez CVB* • Connie Taunton; Exec. Dir.; 640 S. Canal St.; Box C; 39120; Adams; P 20,000; (601) 446-6345; (800) 647-6724; Fax (601) 442-0814; info@visitnatchez.org; www.visitnatchez.org

Oxford • *Oxford CVB* • Mary Allyn Roulhac; Tourism Coord.; 107 Courthouse Sq.; 38655; Lafayette; P 19,000; (662) 234-4680; Fax (662) 232-8680; tourism@oxfordcvb.com; www.oxfordcvb.com

Ridgeland • *Ridgeland Tourism Comm.* • Doyle Warrington; Exec. Dir.; 1000 Highland Colony Pkwy., Ste. 6006; 39157; Madison; P 22,000; (601) 605-5252; (800) 468-6078; Fax (601) 605-5248; info@visitridgeland.com; www.visitridgeland.com

Starkville • *Starkville CVB* • Jennifer Glaze; V.P. of Tourism; 200 E. Main St.; 39759; Oktibbeha; P 43,000; (662) 323-3322; (800) 649-8687; Fax (662) 323-5815; info@starkville.org; www.starkville.org

Tunica • *Tunica County CVB* • Webster Franklin; Pres./CEO; 13625 Hwy. 61 N.; P.O. Box 2739; 38676; Tunica; P 9,000; (662) 363-3800; (888) 4-TUNICA; Fax (662) 363-1493; tunicams@tunica-travel.com; www.tunicatravel.com

Tupelo • *Tupelo CVB* • Linda Butler Johnson; Exec. Dir.; 399 E. Main St.; P.O. Drawer 47; 38802; Lee; P 36,000; (662) 841-6521; (800) 533-0611; Fax (662) 841-6558; visittupelo@tupelo.net; www.tupelo.net

Vicksburg · *Vicksburg CVB* · Bill Seratt; Exec. Dir.; P.O. Box 110; 39181; Warren; P 50,000; (601) 636-9421; (800) 221-3536; Fax (601) 636-9475; dellis@vicksburgcvb.org; www.visitvicksburg.com

Yazoo City · *Yazoo County CVB* · Tonja Ray-Smith; Exec. Dir.; 332 N. Main St.; P.O. Box 186; 39194; Yazoo; P 28,000; (662) 746-1815; (800) 381-0662; Fax (662) 746-1816; tonja.smith@yazoo.org; www.yazoo.org

Holly Springs · *Holly Spings Tourism & Rec. Bur.* · Stephanie Movre; Exec. Dir.; 148 E. College Ave.; 38635; Marshall; P M; (662) 252-2515; (888) 687-4765; Fax (662) 252-2696; info@visitholly springs.org; www.visithollysprings.org

Missouri

Cape Girardeau · *Cape Girardeau CVB* · Chuck Martin; Exec. Dir.; 400 Broadway, Ste. 100; 63701; Cape Girardeau; P 36,000; (573) 335-1631; (800) 777-0068; Fax (573) 334-6702; info@visitcape.com; www.visitcape.com

Carthage · *Carthage CVB* · Wendi Douglas; Exec. Dir.; 402 S. Garrison Ave.; 64836; Jasper; P 13,000; (417) 359-8181; (866) 357-8687; Fax (417) 359-9119; cvb@ecarthage.com; www.visit-carthage.com

Columbia · *Columbia CVB* · Lorah Steiner; Dir.; 300 S. Providence Rd.; 65203; Boone; P 102,000; (573) 875-1231; (800) 652-0987; Fax (573) 443-3986; info@gocolumbiamo.com; www.visitcolumbiamo.com

Independence · *Independence Tourism Dept.* · Cori Day; Dir.; 111 E. Maple; 64050; Jackson; P 116,000; (816) 325-7111; (800) 748-7323; Fax (816) 325-7932; cday@indepmo.org; www.visitindependence.com

Jefferson City · *Jefferson City CVB* · Steve Picker; Exec. Dir.; 100 E. High St.; P.O. Box 2227; 65102; Cole; P 40,000; (573) 632-2820; Fax (573) 638-4892; info@visitjeffersoncity.com; www.visitjeffersoncity.com

Joplin · *Joplin CVB* · Vince Lindstrom; Dir.; 602 S. Main St.; 64801; Jasper; P 48,000; (417) 625-4789; (800) 657-2534; Fax (417) 624-7948; cvb@joplinmo.org; www.visitjoplinmo.com

Kansas City · *Kansas City Conv. & Vistors Assn.* · Rick Hughes; Pres./CEO; 1100 Main St., Ste. 2200; 64105; Jackson; P 1,900,000; (816) 221-5242; (800) 767-7700; Fax (816) 691-3805; info@visitkc.com; www.visitkc.com

Maryland Heights · *Maryland Heights CVB* · Karen Krispin; Dir.; P.O. Box 2125; 63043; St. Louis; P 26,000; (888) MORE2DO; karen@mhcvb.com; www.more2do.org

Nevada · *Nevada/Vernon County C/C & Tourism* · April Transue; Tourism Coord.; 225 W. Austin Blvd., Ste. 200; 64772; Vernon; P 20,000; (417) 667-5300; Fax (417) 667-3492; visitors@nevada-mo.com; www.visitnevadamo.com

Osage Beach · *Lake of the Ozarks CVB* · Tim Jacobsen; Exec. Dir.; P.O. Box 1498; 65065; Camden; P 7,000; M 650; (573) 348-1599; (800) 386-5253; Fax (573) 348-2293; info@funlake.com; www.funlake.com

Saint Charles · *Greater St. Charles CVB* · David Rosenwasser; Dir./CEO; 230 S. Main St.; 63301; St. Charles; P 70,000; (636) 946-7776; (800) 366-2427; Fax (636) 949-3217; gsccvb@historic stcharles.com; www.historicstcharles.com

Saint Joseph · *St. Joseph CVB* · Marci Bennett; Exec. Dir.; 109 S. 4th; P.O. Box 445; 64502; Buchanan; P 80,000; (816) 233-6688; (800) 785-0360; Fax (816) 233-9120; anull@stjomo.com; www.stjomo.com

Saint Louis · *St. Louis Conv. & Visitors Comm.* · Kathleen Ratcliffe; Pres.; 701 Convention Plz., Ste. 300; 63101; St. Louis; P 2,423,200; (314) 421-1023; (800) 916-0092; Fax (314) 421-0039; kratcliffe@explorestlouis.com; www.explorestlouis.com

Sikeston · *Sikeston CVB* · Lynne Williams; Exec. Dir.; One Industrial Dr.; P.O. Box 1983; 63801; Scott; P 20,000; (573) 471-6362; (888) 309-6591; Fax (573) 471-2499; cvb@visitsikeston.com; www.visitsikeston.com

Springfield · *Springfield CVB* · Mr. Tracy Kimberlin; Pres.; 815 E. St. Louis St.; 65806; Greene; P 175,000; (417) 881-5300; (800) 678-8767; Fax (417) 881-2231; cvb@springfieldmo.org; www.stayinspringfield.com

Washington · *Washington Div. of Tourism* · 323 W. Main; 63090; Franklin; P 14,000; (636) 239-2715; (888) 7-WASH-MO; Fax (636) 239-1381; tourism@washmo.org; www.washmo.org

Montana

Billings · *Billings CVB* · Joan Kronebusch; Dir.; 815 S. 27th St.; P.O. Box 31177; 59107; Yellowstone; P 130,000; (406) 245-4111; Fax (406) 245-7333; info@billingschamber.com; www.visitbillings.com

Nebraska

Beatrice · *Beatrice/Gage County CVB* · 226 S. 6th St.; 68310; Gage; P 23,000; (402) 223-2338; Fax (402) 223-2339; infocvb@visitbeatrice.com; www.visitbeatrice.com

Columbus · *Columbus/Platte County CVB* · Deb Loseke; Dir.; 764 33rd Ave.; P.O. Box 515; 68602; Platte; P 21,000; (402) 564-2769; Fax (402) 564-2026; dloseke@megavision.com; www.visitcolumbusne.com

Fairbury · *Jefferson County Visitors Committee* · Sharon Priefert; Exec. Dir.; 518 E St.; P.O. Box 274; 68352; Jefferson; P 4,262; (402) 729-3000; Fax (402) 729-3076; jcvc@diodecom.net; www.visitoregontrail.org.

Fremont · *Fremont & Dodge County CVB* · Leslie Carter; Exec. Dir.; P.O. Box 182; 68025; Dodge; P 35,000; (402) 753-6414; (800) 727-8323; Fax (402) 721-9359; lcarter@fdcvb.org; www.fdcvb.org

Grand Island · *Grand Island/Hall County CVB* · Renee Seifert; Exec. Dir.; 2424 S. Locust St., Ste. C; 68801; Hall; P 51,000; (308) 382-4400; (800) 658-3178; Fax (308) 382-4908; info@visitgrand island.com; www.visitgrandisland.com

Hastings · *Hastings/Adams County CVB* · Kaleena Fong; Exec. Dir.; 100 North Shore Dr.; P.O. Box 941; 68902; Adams; P 24,000; (402) 461-2370; (800) 967-2189; Fax (402) 461-7273; info@visithastingsnebraska.com; www.visithastingsnebraska.com

Kearney · *Kearney Visitors Bur.* · Roger Jasnoch; Dir.; P.O. Box 607; 68848; Buffalo; P 29,506; (308) 237-3178; (800) 652-9435; Fax (308) 236-9116; rjasnoch@visitkearney.org; www.visitkearney.org

Lincoln · *Lincoln CVB* · Jeff Maul; Exec. Dir.; 1135 M St., Ste. 300; P.O. Box 83737; 68501; Lancaster; P 250,000; (402) 434-5335; (800) 423-8212; Fax (402) 436-2360; info@lincoln.org; www.lincoln.org

McCook · *Red Willow County CVB* · Carol Schlegel; Coord.; 107 Norris Ave.; P.O. Box 337; 69001; Red Willow; P 11,450; (308) 345-3200; (800) 657-2179; Fax (308) 345-3201; bwchief@qwest.net; www.visitmccook.com

Norfolk · *Madison County CVB* · 405 Madison Ave.; P.O. Box 386; 68702; Madison; P 33,000; (402) 371-2932; (888) 371-2932; Fax (402) 371-0182; mcvb@norfolk.ne.us; www.visitnorfolkne.com

North Platte • *North Platte/Lincoln County CVB* • Lisa Burke; Exec. Dir.; 219 S. Dewey; P.O. Box 1207; 69103; Lincoln; P 24,000; (308) 532-4729; (800) 955-4528; Fax (308) 532-5914; info@visitnorthplatte.com; www.visitnorthplatte.com

Ogallala • *Ogallala/Keith County CVB* • Orla Kitt; Tourism & Events Coord.; P.O. Box 628; 69153; Keith; P 8,877; (308) 284-4066; (800) 658-4390; Fax (308) 284-3126; info@visitogallala.com; www.visitogallala.com

Omaha • *Greater Omaha CVB* • Dana Markel; Exec. Dir.; 1001 Farnam; 68102; Douglas; P 813,170; (402) 444-4660; (866) 937-6624; Fax (402) 444-4511; dmarkel@visitomaha.com; www.visitomaha.com

South Sioux City • *South Sioux City CVB* • Brent Clark; Exec. Dir.; 3900 Dakota Ave., Ste. 11; 68776; Dakota; P 12,000; (402) 494-1307; (866) 494-1307; Fax (402) 494-5010; directorcvb@cableone.net; www.visitsouthsiouxcity.com

York • *York County CVB* • Bob Sautter; Exec. Dir.; 601 N. Lincoln Ave.; 68467; York; P 14,500; (402) 362-4575; Fax (402) 362-3344; bobsautter@windstream.net; www.yorkvisitors.org

Nevada

Crystal Bay • *see Incline Village*

Incline Village • *Lake Tahoe-Incline Village Crystal Bay Visitor Bur.* • William Hoffman; Exec. Dir.; 969 Tahoe Blvd.; 89451; Washoe; P 9,143; (775) 832-1606; (800) GO-TAHOE; Fax (775) 832-1605; info@gotahoe.com; www.gotahoenorth.com

Las Vegas • *Las Vegas Conv. & Visitors Auth.* • Rossi Ralenkotter; Pres./CEO; 3150 Paradise Rd.; 89109; Clark; P 1,900,000; (702) 892-0711; (800) 332-5333; Fax (702) 892-2803; www.visitlasvegas.com

Reno • *Reno-Sparks Conv. & Visitors Auth.* • Ellen Oppenheim; Pres./CEO; 4001 S. Virginia St., Ste. G; P.O. Box 837; 89504; Washoe; P 323,670; (775) 827-7600; (800) 443-1482; Fax (775) 827-7666; info@rscva.com; www.visitrenotahoe.com

Stateline • *Lake Tahoe Visitors Auth.* • Patrick Kaler; Exec. Dir.; 169 Hwy. 50; P.O. Box 5878; 89449; Douglas; P 30,000; (775) 588-5900; (800) AT-TAHOE; Fax (775) 588-1941; info@ltva.org; www.bluelaketahoe.com

Tonopah • *Tonopah Conv. Center* • Diane Perchetti; 301 W. Brougher Ave.; P.O. Box 408; 89049; Nye; P 3,000; (775) 482-3558; Fax (775) 482-3932; www.tonopahnevada.com

New Jersey

Atlantic City • *Atlantic City Conv. & Visitors Auth.* • Jeffrey Vasser; Pres.; 2314 Pacific Ave.; 08401; Atlantic; P 380,000; (609) 449-7100; (888) 228-4748; Fax (609) 345-2200; www.atlanticcitynj.com

Bridgewater • *Somerset County Bus. Partnership & Visitor Center* • Kimberly Charne; Tourism Coord.; 360 Grove St.; 08807; Somerset; P 315,000; (908) 218-4300; Fax (908) 722-7823; kcharne@scbp.org; www.scbp.org

Cape May County • *Cape May County Dept. of Tourism* • Diane Wieland; Dir. of Tourism; 4 Moore Rd., DN136; P.O. Box 365, Cape May Court House; 08210; Cape May; P 100,000; (609) 463-6415; (800) 227-2297; Fax (609) 465-4639; tourism@co.cape-may.nj.us; www.thejerseycape.net

Red Bank • *Red Bank Visitors Center* • Margaret Mass; Exec. Dir.; 20 Broad St.; P.O. Box 806; 07701; Monmouth; P 13,000; (732) 741-9211; (888) HIPTOWN; Fax (732) 842-7615; visitors@redbankrivercenter.org; www.visit.redbank.com

Washington • *Warren County CVB* • Robert Goltz; Pres./CEO; 10 Brass Castle Rd.; 07882; Warren; P 105,765; M (908) 835-9200; Fax (908) 835-9296; info@visitwarren.com; www.visitwarren.com

New Mexico

Albuquerque • *Albuquerque CVB* • Dale Lockett; Pres./CEO; 20 First Plz. N.W., Ste. 601; P.O. Box 26866; 87125; Bernalillo; P 700,000; M 1,000; (505) 842-9918; (800) 733-9918; Fax (505) 247-9101; lockett@itsatrip.org; www.itsatrip.org

Farmington • *Farmington CVB* • Debbie Dusenbery; Exec. Dir.; 3041 E. Main St.; 87402; San Juan; P 120,000; M 125; (505) 326-7602; (800) 448-1240; Fax (505) 327-0577; fmncvb@earthlink.net; www.farmingtonnm.org

Gallup • *Gallup Visitor Info. Center* • Alice Perez; 103 W. Hwy. 66; 87301; McKinley; P 22,000; (505) 722-2228; (800) 380-4989; Fax (505) 863-2280; alice@thegallupchamber.com

Las Cruces • *Las Cruces CVB* • Ken Mompellier; Exec. Dir.; 211 N. Water St.; 88001; Dona Ana; P 85,000; (575) 541-2444; Fax (575) 541-2164; cvb@lascrucescvb.org; www.lascrucescvb.org; 800FIESTAS

Rio Rancho • *Rio Rancho CVB* • Matt Geishel; CVB Mgr.; 3200 Civic Center Cr. N.E.; 87144; Sandoval; P 75,000; (505) 891-7258; (888) 746-7262; Fax (505) 892-8328; info@rioranchonm.org; www.rioranchonm.org

Roswell • *Roswell Civic Center* • Ruben Sanchez; Dir. of Civic Ctr.; 912 N. Main; 88201; Chaves; P 50,000; (575) 624-6860; Fax (575) 624-6863; rubens@cableone.net; www.roswellmysteries.com

Roswell • *Roswell Visitors Bur.* • Suzy Wood; Dir.; 912 N. Main; 88201; Chaves; P 50,000; (575) 624-7704; Fax (575) 624-6863; VIS1@cableone.net; www.roswellmysteries.com.

Ruidoso • *Ruidoso Conv. Center* • Gail Bailey; Dir. of Sales; 111 Sierra Blanca Dr.; 88345; Lincoln; P 10,500; (575) 258-5445; Fax (575) 258-5040; www.ruidosoconventioncenter.com

Santa Fe • *Santa Fe CVB* • Keith Toler; Exec. Dir.; P.O. Box 909; 87504; Santa Fe; P 67,000; (505) 955-6200; (800) 777-2489; Fax (505) 955-6222; info@santafe.org; www.santafe.org

Santa Rosa • *Santa Rosa Info & Tourism Center* • Richard Delgado; Tourism Dir.; 244 S. 4th St.; P.O. Box 429; 88435; Guadalupe; P 2,640; (575) 472-3763; rdelgado@srnm.org; www.santarosanm.org; www.srnm.org

Taos • *Taos Visitors Center* • Michelle Hammer; Supt.; 1139 Paseo del Pueblo Sur.; 87571; Taos; P 31,800; (575) 758-3873; (800) 732-8267; Fax (575) 758-3872; information@taosvisitor.com; www.taosvisitor.com

New York

Albany • *Albany County CVB* • Michele Vennard; Pres./CEO; 25 Quackenbush Sq.; 12207; Albany; P 300,000; M 300; (518) 434-1217; (800) 258-3582; Fax (518) 434-0887; accvb@albany.org; www.albany.org

Binghamton • *Greater Binghamton CVB* • Louis R. Santoni; Pres./CEO; 49 Court St.; P.O. Box 995; 13902; Broome; P 45,000; (607) 772-8860; (800) 836-6740; Fax (607) 722-4513; lou@visitbinghamton.org; www.visitbinghamton.org.

Buffalo • *Buffalo/Niagara CVB* • Richard Geiger; Pres./CEO; 617 Main St., Ste. 200; 14203; Erie; P 985,000; (716) 852-0511; (800) BUFFALO; Fax (716) 852-0131; info@buffalocvb.org; www.visitbuffaloniagara.com

Catskill · *Greene County Tourism Promotion* · Daniela Marino; Dir.; Rte. 23B at NYS Thruway, Exit 21; P.O. Box 527; 12414; Greene; P 48,195; (518) 943-3223; (800) 355-CATS; Fax (518) 943-2296; tourism@discovergreene.com; www.greenetourism.com

Chautauqua · *Chautauqua County Visitors Bur.* · Andrew Nixon; Dir.; P.O. Box 1441; 14722; Chautauqua; P 141,000; M 325; (716) 357-4569; (800) 242-4569; Fax (716) 357-2284; info@tourchautauqua.com; www.tourchautauqua.com

Corning · *Steuben County Conference & Visitors Bur.* · Peggy Coleman; Pres.; 1 W. Market St., Ste. 301; 14830; Steuben; P 98,000; (607) 936-6544; (866) 946-3386; Fax (607) 936-6575; sccvb@corningfingerlakes.com; www.corningfingerlakes.com

Goshen · *Orange County Tourism* · Susan H. Cayea; Dir.; 124 Main St.; 10924; Orange; P 375,000; (845) 291-2136; (800) 762-8687; Fax (845) 291-2137; tourism@co.orange.ny.us; www.orangetourism.org

Hauppauge · *Long Island CVB* · R. Moke McGowan; Pres.; 330 Motor Pkwy., Ste. 203; 11788; Suffolk; P 2,300,000; M 475; (631) 951-3900; (800) 441-4601; Fax (631) 951-3439; www.discoverlongisland.com

Ithaca · *Ithaca/Tompkins County CVB* · Fred Bonn; Dir.; 904 E. Shore Dr.; 14850; Tompkins; P 96,000; (607) 272-1313; (800) 284-8422; Fax (607) 272-7617; info@visitithaca.com; www.visitithaca.com

Lake Placid · *Lake Placid-Essex County Visitors Bur.* · James McKenna; Pres./CEO; 49 Parkside Dr.; P.O. Box 1570; 12946; Essex; P 38,000; M 700; (518) 523-2445; (800) 447-5224; Fax (518) 523-2605; info@lakeplacid.com; www.lakeplacid.com

Little Valley · *Cattaraugus County Tourism* · Debra Opserbeck; Tour. Spec.; 303 Court St.; 14755; Cattaraugus; P 83,955; (716) 938-2307; (800) 331-0543; Fax (716) 938-2779; visitor@enchantedmountains.info; www.enchantedmountains.info

Long Island · *see Hauppauge*

New York · *New York City CVB* · George Fertitta; Pres./CEO; 810 7th Ave., 3rd Flr.; Visitors Center; 10019; New York; P 11,685,650; (212) 484-1200; Fax (212) 246-6310; www.nycvisit.com

Plattsburgh · *Adirondack Coast Visitors & Conv. Bur.* · Michele Powers; Dir. of Tourism; 7061 Rte. 9; P.O. Box 310; 12901; Clinton; P 200,000; (518) 563-1000; Fax (518) 563-1028; chamber@westelcom.com; www.northcountrychamber.com

Rochester · *Greater Rochester Visitors Assn.* · Greg Marshall; V.P.; 45 East Ave., Ste. 400; 14604; Monroe; P 1,000,000; M 450; (585) 279-8300; (800) 677-7282; Fax (585) 232-4822; www.visitrochester.com

Saratoga Springs · *Saratoga Conv. & Tourism Bur.* · David Zunker; Pres.; 60 Railroad Pl., Ste. 100; 12866; Saratoga; P 27,000; M 375; (518) 584-1531; Fax (518) 584-2969; mail@discoversaratoga.org; www.discoversaratoga.org

Southampton · *Hamptons Visitors Cncl.* · P.O. Box 908; 11968; Suffolk; www.hamptonsvisitorscouncil.com

Syracuse · *Syracuse CVB* · David Holder; Pres.; 572 S. Salina St.; 13202; Onondaga; P 460,000; (315) 470-1910; (800) 234-4797; Fax (315) 471-8545; info@visitsyracuse.org; www.visitsyracuse.org

Utica · *Oneida County CVB* · Kelly Blazosky; Pres.; NY State Thruway, Exit 31; P.O. Box 551; 13503; Oneida; P 235,000; (315) 724-7221; Fax (315) 724-7335; info@oneidacountytourism.com; www.oneidacountytourism.com

White Plains · *Westchester County Ofc. of Tourism* · Kim Sinistore; Dir.; 222 Mamaroneck Ave.; 10605; Westchester; P 900,000; (914) 995-8500; (800) 833-9282; Fax (914) 995-8505; tourism@westchestergov.com; www.westchestertourism.com

Wilmington · *Whiteface Mountain Reg. Visitors Bur.* · Diane Buckley; Mgr.; 5753 NYS Rte. 86; P.O. Box 277; 12997; Essex; P 3,000; M 100; (518) 946-2255; (888) WHITE-FACE; Fax (518) 946-2683; info@whitefaceregion.com; www.whitefaceregion.com

North Carolina

Albemarle · *Stanly County CVB* · Chris Lambert; Exec. Dir.; 1000 N. 1st St., Ste. 11; P.O. Box 1456; 28001; Stanly; P 59,000; (704) 986-2583; (800) 650-1476; Fax (704) 986-3685; chris@stanlycvb.com; www.visitstanly.com

Alleghany County · *see Boone*

Ashe County · *see Boone*

Asheboro · *Randolph County Tourism Dev. Auth.* · Tammy O'Kelley; Exec. Dir.; 222 Sunset Ave., Ste. 107; 27203; Randolph; P 138,367; (336) 626-0364; (800) 626-2672; Fax (336) 626-0977; www.visitrandolphcounty.com

Asheville · *Asheville CVB* · Mr. Kelly Miller; Exec. Dir./Exec. V.P.; 36 Montford Ave.; 28801; Buncombe; P 391,000; (828) 258-6102; (828) 258-6101; Fax (828) 254-6054; comments@exploreasheville.com; www.exploreasheville.com

Avery County · *see Boone*

Belmont · *Gaston County Dept. of Tourism* · Walter Israel; Exec. Dir.; 620 N. Main St.; 28012; Gaston; P 190,365; (704) 825-4044; (800) 849-9994; Fax (704) 825-4029; walter.israel@co.gaston.nc.us; www.gastontourism.com

Boone · *Boone CVB* · Mac Forehand; Dir.; 208 Howard St.; 28607; Watauga; P 14,200; (828) 262-3516; (800) 852-9506; Fax (828) 264-6644; info@visitboonenc.com; www.visitboonenc.com

Boone · *North Carolina High Country Host* · 1700 Blowing Rock Rd.; 28607; Watauga; P 98,100; M 375; (828) 264-1299; (800) 438-7500; Fax (828) 265-0550; info@highcountryhost.com; www.mountainsofnc.com

Burlington · *Burlington/Alamance County CVB* · Robert Cox; V.P.; 610 S. Lexington Ave.; P.O. Box 519; 27216; Alamance; P 135,453; (336) 570-1444; (800) 637-3804; Fax (336) 228-1330; info@visitalamance.com; www.visitalamance.com

Canton · *see Waynesville*

Chapel Hill · *Chapel Hill/Orange County Visitors Bur.* · Laurie Paolicelli; Exec. Dir.; 501 W. Franklin St.; 27516; Orange; P 123,766; (919) 968-2060; (888) 968-2060; Fax (919) 968-2062; info@visitchapelhill.org; www.visitchapelhill.org

Charlotte · *Visit Charlotte* · Mike Butts; Exec. Dir.; 500 S. College St., Ste. 300; 28202; Mecklenburg; P 664,342; M 670; (704) 334-2282; (800) 722-1994; Fax (704) 342-3972; mike.butts@visitcharlotte.com; www.visitcharlotte.com

Cherokee · *Cherokee Travel & Tourism* · Josie Long; Coord.; 498 Tsali Blvd.; P.O. Box 460; 28719; Swain; P 13,500; (828) 497-9195; (800) 438-1601; Fax (828) 497-8196; travel@nc-cherokee.com; www.cherokee-nc.com

Columbus · *Polk County Travel & Tourism* · Melinda Young; Dir.; 20 E. Mills St.; P.O. Box 308; 28722; Polk; P 19,000; (828) 894-2324; (800) 440-7848; Fax (828) 894-6142; visit@firstpeaknc.com; www.firstpeaknc.com

Cornelius · *Visit Lake Norman* · Sally Ashworth; Exec. Dir.; 19900 W. Catawba Ave., Ste. 102; 28031; Mecklenburg; P 65,000; (704) 987-3300; (800) 305-2508; Fax (704) 892-5313; info@lakenorman.org; www.visitlakenorman.org

Davidson · *see Cornelius*

Dunn · *Dunn Area Tourism Auth.* · Brandy Hall; Mktg. Dir.; 209 W. Divine St.; P.O. Box 310; 28335; Harnett; P 10,000; (910) 892-3282; Fax (910) 892-4071; tourism@dunnchamber.com; www.dunntourism.org; www.visitdunn.com

Durham · *Durham CVB* · Reyn Bowman; Pres./CEO; 101 E. Morgan St.; 27701; Durham; P 208,816; (919) 687-0288; (800) 446-8604; Fax (919) 683-9555; reyn@durham-cvb.com; www.durham-nc.com

Edenton · *Chowan County Tourism Dev. Auth.* · Nancy Nicholls; Tourism Dir.; 116 E. King St.; P.O. Box 245; 27932; Chowan; P 15,500; (252) 482-3400; (800) 775-0111; Fax (252) 482-7093; nancy.nicholls@ncmail.net; www.visitedenton.com

Elizabeth City · *Elizabeth City/Pasquotank County Tourism & Dev. Auth.* · Charlotte Underwood; Dir. of Tourism; 400 S. Water St., Ste. 101; 27909; Pasquotank; P 40,000; (252) 335-5330; (866) 324-8948; Fax (252) 335-1733; info@discoverelizabethcity.com; www.discoverelizabethcity.com

Fayetteville · *Fayetteville Area CVB* · John Meroski; Pres./CEO; 245 Person St.; 28301; Cumberland; P 302,000; (910) 483-5311; (800) 255-8217; Fax (910) 484-6632; facvb@visitfayettevillenc.com; www.visitfayettevillenc.com

Greensboro · *Greensboro Area CVB* · Henri Fourrier; Pres./CEO; 2200 Pinecrost Rd.; 27407; Guilford; P 235,262; (336) 274-2282; (800) 344-2282; Fax (336) 230-1183; hfourrier@visitgreensboronc.com; www.visitgreensboronc.com

Greenville · *Greenville-Pitt County CVB* · Debbie Vargas; Exec. Dir./CEO; 303 S.W. Greenville Blvd.; P.O. Box 8027; 27835; Pitt; P 140,000; (252) 329-4200; (800) 537-5564; Fax (252) 329-4205; info@visitgreenvillenc.com; www.visitgreenvillenc.com

Hendersonville · *Henderson County Travel & Tourism* · Melody Heltman; Exec. Dir.; 201 S. Main St.; 28792; Henderson; P 100,000; (828) 693-9708; (800) 828-4244; Fax (828) 697-4556; viewmtns@hotmail.com; www.historichendersonville.org.

Hickory · *Hickory Metro CVB* · Bebe Leitch; Pres.; 1960-A 13th Ave. Dr. S.E.; 28602; Catawba; P 325,000; (828) 322-1335; (800) 509-2444; Fax (828) 322-8983; bleitch@hickorymetro.com; www.hickorymetro.com

High Point · *High Point CVB* · Charlotte Young; Pres./CEO; 300 S. Main St.; P.O. Box 2273; 27261; Guilford; P 94,739; (336) 884-5255; (800) 720-5255; Fax (336) 884-4352; HPCVB@HighPoint.org; www.HighPoint.org

Highlands · *Highlands Visitor Center* · Jan V. Healey; Dir.; 269 Oak St.; P.O. Box 404; 28741; Macon; P 3,000; (828) 526-2112; Fax (828) 526-5803; visitor@highlandschamber.org; www.highlandschamber.org

Huntersville · *see Cornelius*

Jacksonville · *Onslow County Tourism* · Theresa Carter; Mgr.; 1099 Gum Branch Rd.; 28540; Onslow; P 154,000; (910) 455-1113; (800) 932-2144; Fax (910) 347-4705; tcarter@jacksonvilleonline.org; www.onslowcountytourism.com

Kinston · *Kinston CVB* · Laura Lee Sylvester; Pres.; 301 N. Queen St.; P.O. Box 157; 28502; Lenoir; P 60,000; (252) 523-2500; (800) 869-0032; Fax (252) 527-1914; llsylvester@kinstonchamber.com; www.visitkinston.com

Lake Norman · *see Cornelius*

Maggie Valley · *see Waynesville*

Mitchell County · *see Boone*

Morehead City · *Crystal Coast Tourism Auth.* · Carol Lohr; Exec. Dir.; 3409 Arendell St.; 28557; Carteret; P 69,000; (252) 726-8148; (800) 786-6962; Fax (252) 726-0990; brochure@sunnync.com; www.crystalcoastnc.org

Morganton · *Burke County Travel & Tourism Comm.* · Rosemary Niewold; Exec. Dir.; 102 E. Union St.; Courthouse Sq.; 28655; Burke; P 89,466; (828) 433-6793; (888) 462-2921; Fax (828) 433-6715; rosemary@discoverburkecounty.org; www.discoverburkecounty.org

New Bern · *New Bern/Craven County CVB* · Sandra Chamberlin; Dir.; 203 S. Front St.; P.O. Box 1713; 28563; Craven; P 91,436; (252) 637-9400; (800) 437-5767; Fax (252) 637-0250; info@visitnewbern.com; www.visitnewbern.com

Pinehurst · *see Southern Pines*

Raleigh · *Greater Raleigh CVB* · Dennis Edwards; Pres./CEO; 421 Fayetteville St., Ste. 1505; 27601; Wake; P 385,000; (919) 834-5900; (800) 849-8499; Fax (919) 831-2887; visit@visitraleigh.com; www.visitraleigh.com

Southern Pines · *CVB of Pinehurst, Southern Pines, Aberdeen Area* · Caleb Miles; Pres./CEO; 10677 Hwy. 15-501; 28387; Moore; P 84,000; (910) 692-3330; (800) 346-5362; Fax (910) 692-2493; cvb4golf@ncrrbiz.com; www.homeofgolf.com

Sparta · *Alleghany County Welcome Center* · Bob Bamberg; Exec. Dir.; 58 S. Main St.; P.O. Box 1237; 28675; Alleghany; P 10,900; (336) 372-5473; (800) 372-5473; Fax (336) 372-8251; info@sparta-nc.com; www.sparta-nc.com

Spruce Pine · *Mitchell County Visitor Center* · Patti Jensen; Travel/Tourism Dir.; P.O. Box 858; 28777; Mitchell; P 15,900; (828) 765-9483; (800) 227-3912; Fax (828) 765-9034; getinfo@mitchell-county.com; www.mitchell-county.com

Statesville · *Statesville CVB* · Michael Keith; Exec. Dir.; 1551 E. Broad St.; 28625; Iredell; P 27,000; (704) 878-3480; (877) 531-1819; Fax (704) 878-3489; info@visitstatesville.org; www.visitstatesville.org

Thomasville · *Thomasville Visitors Center* · Mark Scott; Dir.; 44 W. Main St.; P.O. Box 1512; 27361; Davidson; P 25,000; (336) 472-4422; (800) 611-9907; mscott@thomasvilletourism.com; www.thomasvilletourism.com

Watauga County · *see Boone*

Waynesville · *Haywood County Tourism Dev. Auth.* · Lynn Collins; Exec. Dir.; 1233 N. Main St., Ste. 1-40; 28786; Haywood; P 57,000; (828) 452-0152; (800) 334-9036; Fax (828) 452-0153; hctda@smokeymountains.net; www.smokeymountains.net

Williamston · *Martin County Tourism Dev. Auth.* · Sarah Katherine Adams; Exec. Dir.; 100 E. Church St.; P.O. Box 382; 27892; Martin; P 25,500; (252) 792-6605; (800) 776-8566; Fax (252) 792-8710; tourism@visitmartincounty.com; www.visitmartincounty.com

Wilmington · *Wilmington/Cape Fear Coast CVB* · Kim Hufham; Pres./CEO; 24 N. 3rd St.; 28401; New Hanover; P 184,000; (910) 341-4030; (800) 222-4757; Fax (910) 341-4029; visit@capefearcoast.com; www.capefearcoast.com

Wilson · *Wilson Visitors Bur.* · Sandra Homes; 4916 E. Hayes Pl.; P.O. Box 2882; 27894; Wilson; P 75,515; (252) 243-8440; (800) 497-7398; Fax (252) 243-7550; info@wilson-nc.com; www.wilson-nc.com

Winston-Salem • *Visit Winston-Salem* • Robert McCoy; Pres.; 200 Brookstown Ave.; 27101; Forsyth; P 227,727; (336) 728-4200; (866) 728-4200; Fax (336) 721-2202; info@visitwinstonsalem. com; www.visitwinstonsalem.com

North Dakota

Beulah • *Beulah CVB* • Steffanie Boeckel; Exec. Dir.; 120 Central Ave.; P.O. Box 730; 58523; Mercer; P 3,200; (701) 873-4585; (800) 441-2649; Fax (701) 873-5361; chamber@westriv.com; www. beulahnd.org

Bismarck • *Bismarck-Mandan CVB* • Terry Harzinski; Exec. Dir.; 1600 Burnt Boat Dr.; 58503; Burleigh; P 72,403; M 221; (701) 222-4308; (800) 767-3555; Fax (701) 222-0647; visitnd@discover bismarckmandan.com; www.bismarckmandancvb.com

Bottineau • *Bottineau CVB* • Clint Reinoehl; Coord.; 519 Main St.; 58318; Bottineau; P 2,500; (701) 228-3849; (800) 735-6932; Fax (701) 228-5130; bcc@utma.com; www.bottineau.com

Carrington • *Carrington CVB* • Susan Stoddard; Pres.; 871 Main St.; P.O. Box 439; 58421; Foster; P 2,300; (701) 652-2524; (800) 641-9668; Fax (701) 652-2391; chambergal@daktel.com; www. carringtonnd.com

Devils Lake • *Devils Lake Visitors Bur.* • Susan Johnsrud; Tourism Dir.; 208 Hwy. 2 W.; P.O. Box 879; 58301; Ramsey; P 8,000; (701) 662-4903; (800) 233-8048; Fax (701) 662-2147; tourism@ gondtc.com; www.devilslakend.com

Dickinson • *Dickinson CVB* • Terri Thiel; Exec. Dir.; 72 E. Museum Dr.; 58601; Stark; P 17,000; (701) 483-4988; (800) 279-7391; Fax (701) 483-9261; info@visitdickinson.com; www.visitdickinson.com.

Fargo • *Fargo-Moorhead CVB* • Cole Carley; Exec. Dir.; 2001 44th St. S.; 58103; Cass; P 175,000; (701) 282-3653; (800) 235-7654; Fax (701) 282-4366; cole@fargomoorhead.org; www.fargomoorhead.org

Grand Forks • *Greater Grand Forks CVB* • Julie Rygg; Exec. Dir.; 4251 Gateway Dr.; 58203; Grand Forks; P 59,000; M 100; (701) 746-0444; (800) 866-4566; Fax (701) 746-0775; info@visitgrand forks.com; www.visitgrandforks.com

Hettinger • *Dakota Buttes Visitors Cncl.* • Earleen Friez; Admin. Secy.; 120 S. Main St.; P.O. Box 1031; 58639; Adams; P 1,300; (701) 567-2531; adamschmbr@ndsupernet.com; www.hettingernd.com

Jamestown • *Buffalo City Tourism* • Nina Sneider; Dir.; 404 Louis L'Amour Ln.; P.O. Box 917; 58402; Stutsman; P 15,500; (701) 251-9145; (800) 222-4766; guestinfo@tourjamestown.com; www. tourjamestown.com

Jamestown • *Jamestown Civic Center/CVB* • Pamela Fosse; Dir.; 212 3rd Ave. N.E.; 58401; Stutsman; P 15,500; (701) 252-4835; Fax (701) 252-8089; director@jamestownciviccenter.com; www. jamestownciviccenter.com

Minot • *Minot CVB* • Wendy Howe; Exec. Dir.; 1020 S. Broadway; 58701; Ward; P 57,000; M 225; (701) 857-8206; (800) 264-2626; Fax (701) 857-8228; info@visitminot.org; www.visitminot.org

Rugby • *Rugby CVB* • Dondi Sobolik; Exec. Dir.; 224 Hwy. 2 S.W.; 58368; Pierce; P 3,000; (701) 776-5846; Fax (701) 776-6390; rugbychamber@gondtc.com; www.rugbynorthdakota.com

Williston • *Williston CVB* • Amy Krueger; Exec. Dir.; 212 Airport Rd.; 58801; Williams; P 15,000; (701) 774-9041; (800) 615-9041; Fax (701) 774-0411; cvbsales@ci.williston.nd.us; www.visit williston.com

Ohio

Akron • *Akron/Summit CVB* • Susan Hamo; Pres.; 77 E. Mill St.; 44308; Summit; P 515,000; (330) 374-7560; (800) 245-4254; Fax (330) 374-7626; information@visitakron-summit.org; www. visitakron-summit.org

Amherst • *Lorain County Visitors Bur.* • Barb Bickel; Exec. Dir.; 8025 Leavitt Rd.; 44001; Lorain; P 285,000; (440) 984-5282; (800) 334-1673; Fax (440) 984-7363; visitors@visitloraincounty.com; www.visitloraincounty.com

Ashland • *Ashland Area CVB* • Amy Daubenspeck; Exec. Dir.; 211 Claremont Ave.; 44805; Ashland; P 50,000; (419) 281-4584; Fax (419) 281-4585; cvb@ashlandoh.com; www.ashlandohio.com

Austinburg • *Ashtabula County CVB* • Mark Winchell; Exec. Dir.; 1850 Austinburg Rd.; 44010; Ashtabula; P 101,207; (440) 275-3202; (800) 337-6746; Fax (440) 275-3210; visitus@visitashta bulacounty.com; www.visitashtabulacounty.com

Batavia • *Clermont County CVB* • June Creager; Exec. Dir.; 410 E. Main St.; P.O. Box 100; 45103; Clermont; P 200,000; (513) 732-3600; (800) 796-4282; Fax (513) 732-2244; info@visitclermont ohio.com; www.visitclermontohio.com

Beavercreek • *Greene County CVB* • Kathleen Young; Exec. Dir.; 1221 Meadowbridge Dr., Ste. A; 45434; Greene; P 140,000; (937) 429-9100; (800) 733-9109; Fax (937) 429-7726; kyoung@ greenecountyohio.org; www.greenecountyohio.org

Bellefontaine • *Logan County CVB* • Ed Wallace; Pres./CEO; 100 S. Main St.; 43311; Logan; P 46,000; (937) 599-5121; (888) LOGAN-CO; Fax (937) 599-2411; info@logancountyohio.com; www.logancountyohio.com

Bowling Green • *Bowling Green CVB* • Wendy Stram; Exec. Dir.; 119 E. Court St.; 43402; Wood; P 29,636; (419) 353-9445; (800) 866-0046; Fax (419) 353-9446; info@visitbgohio.org; www.visitbgohio.org

Cambridge • *Cambridge/Guernsey County VCB* • Debbie Robinson; Exec. Dir.; 627 Wheeling Ave., Ste. 200; 43725; Guernsey; P 40,792; (740) 432-2022; (800) 933-5480; Fax (740) 432-5976; info@VisitGuernseyCounty.com; www.VisitGuernseyCounty.com

Canton • *Canton/Stark County CVB* • John Kiste; Dir.; 222 Market Ave. N.; 44702; Stark; P 379,000; (330) 454-1439; (800) 533-4302; Fax (330) 456-3600; johnk@cantonstarkcvb.com; www.cantonstarkcvb.com

Chillicothe • *Ross-Chillicothe CVB* • Kyrsten Vogel; Exec. Dir.; 45 E. Main St.; P.O. Box 353; 45601; Ross; P 75,000; (740) 702-7677; (800) 413-4118; Fax (740) 702-2727; kyrsten@visitchillicothe ohio.com; www.visitchillicotheohio.com

Cincinnati • *Cincinnati USA CVB* • Dan Lincoln; Pres./CEO; 525 Vine St., Ste. 1500; 45202; Hamilton; P 1,900,000; (513) 621-2142; (800) 543-2613; Fax (513) 621-5020; dlincoln@cincyusa. com; www.cincyusa.com

Circleville • *Pickaway County Visitors Bur.* • Charlie Jackson; Exec. Dir.; 325 W. Main St.; 43113; Pickaway; P 52,000; (740) 474-3636; (888) 770-PICK; Fax (740) 477-6800; cjackson@pickaway. com; www.pickaway.com

Cleveland • *Positively Cleveland CVB* • Dennis Roche; Pres.; 100 Public Sq., Ste. 100; 44113; Cuyahoga; P 1,866,519; M 700; (216) 621-4110; (800) 321-1001; Fax (216) 621-5967; cvb@positively cleveland.com; www.positivelycleveland.com

Columbus · *Experience Columbus* · Paul Astleford; Pres./CEO; 277 W. Nationwide Blvd., Ste. 125; 43215; Franklin; P 1,600,000; M 909; (614) 221-6623; (800) 354-2657; Fax (614) 221-5618; www.experiencecolumbus.com

Coshocton · *Coshocton County CVB* · Belinda Williamson; Dir.; 401 Main St.; P.O. Box 905; 43812; Coshocton; P 36,131; (740) 622-4877; (800) 338-4724; Fax (740) 622-9902; coshcvb@coshocton.com; www.visitcoshocton.com

Dayton · *Dayton/Montgomery County CVB* · Jacquelyn Powell; Pres./CEO; 1 Chamber Plaza, Ste. A; 45402; Montgomery; P 780,000; (937) 226-8211; (800) 221-8235; Fax (937) 226-8294; jypowell@daytoncvb.net; www.daytoncvb.com

Delaware · *Delaware County CVB* · Debbie Shatzer; Exec. Dir.; 44 E. Winter St.; 43015; Delaware; P 156,000; (740) 368-4748; (888) DEL-OHIO; Fax (740) 369-9277; info@visitdelohio.com; www.visitdelohio.com

Findlay · *Hancock County CVB* · Angela Crist; Exec. Dir./V.P.; 123 E. Main Cross St.; 45840; Hancock; P 72,000; (419) 422-3315; (800) 424-3315; Fax (419) 422-9508; info@visitfindlay.com; www.visitfindlay.com

Fremont · *Fremont/Sandusky County CVB* · Connie Durdel; Exec. Dir.; 712 North St., Ste. 102; 43420; Sandusky; P 62,000; (419) 332-4470; (800) 255-8070; Fax (419) 332-4359; carol@sanduskycounty.org; www.sanduskycounty.org

Hamilton · *Greater Hamilton CVB* · One High St.; 45011; Butler; P 61,000; (513) 844-8080; (800) 311-5353; Fax (513) 844-8090; hamiltonohcvb@fuse.net; www.hamilton-cvb.com

Heath · *Greater Licking County CVB* · Susan Fryer; Exec. Dir.; 455 Hebron Rd.; 43056; Licking; P 135,800; (740) 345-8224; (800) 589-8224; Fax (740) 345-4403; sfryer@lccvb.com; www.lccvb.com

Hillsboro · *Highland County CVB* · Sara Lukens; Dir.; 1575 N. High St., Ste 400; P.O. Box 638; 45133; Highland; P 41,000; (937) 393-4883; Fax (937) 393-2697; highland.county@dragonbbs.com; www.highlandcounty.com

Lima · *Lima/Allen County CVB* · Christine Pleva; Exec. Dir.; 144 S. Main St., Ste. 101; 45801; Allen; P 110,000; (419) 222-6075; (888) 222-6075; Fax (419) 222-0134; info@lima-allencvb.com; www.lima-allencvb.com

Mansfield · *Mansfield/Richland County CVB* · Lee Tasseff; Pres.; 124 N. Main St.; 44902; Richland; P 120,000; (419) 525-1300; (800) 642-8282; Fax (419) 524-7722; visitors@mansfieldtourism.com; www.mansfieldtourism.com

Marietta · *Marietta/Washington County CVB* · 121 Putnam St., Ste. 110; 45750; Washington; P 62,254; (740) 373-5178; (800) 288-2577; Fax (740) 376-2911; info@mariettaohio.org; www.mariettaohio.org

Marion · *Marion Area CVB* · Diane Watson; Exec. Dir.; 1713 Marion Mount Gilead Rd., Ste. 110; 43302; Marion; P 65,000; (740) 389-9770; (800) 371-6688; Fax (740) 725-9295; info@visitmarionohio.com; www.visitmarionohio.com

Marysville · *Union County CVB* · Christy Clark; Dir.; 227 E. Fifth St.; 43040; Union; P 40,909; (937) 642-6279; (800) 642-0087; Fax (937) 644-0422; cvb@unioncounty.org; www.unioncounty.org

McConnelsville · *Morgan County Visitor Center* · 155 E. Main St.; P.O. Box 508; 43756; Morgan; P 14,000; (740) 962-3200; Fax (740) 962-3516; www.morgancounty.org

Medina · *Medina County CVB* · Daniel D. Hostetler III; Exec. Dir.; 32 Public Sq.; 44256; Medina; P 151,000; M 220; (330) 722-5502; (800) 860-2943; Fax (330) 723-4713; info@visitmedinacounty.com; www.visitmedinacounty.com

Mount Vernon · *Knox County CVB* · Mr. Pat Crow; Dir.; 107 S. Main St.; 43050; Knox; P 55,000; (740) 392-6102; (800) 837-5282; Fax (740) 392-7840; info@visitknoxohio.org; www.VisitKnoxOhio.org

North Ridgeville · *North Ridgeville Visitors Bur.* · Ms. Dayle Noll; Pres./CEO; 34845 Lorain Rd.; 44039; Lorain; P 26,000; (440) 327-3737; Fax (440) 327-1474; nrvisbur@nrchamber.com; www.nrchamber.com

Norwalk · *Huron County Visitors Bur.* · Melissa James; Exec. Dir.; 10 W. Main St.; 44857; Huron; P 60,000; (419) 668-4155; (877) 668-4155; chamber@accnorwalk.com; www.VisitHuronCounty.com

Pomeroy · *Meigs County Tourism* · Michelle Donovan; Exec. Dir.; 238 W. Main St.; 45769; Meigs; P 25,000; (740) 992-2239; (877) MEIGS-CO; Fax (740) 992-7942; director@meigscountytourism.com; www.meigscountytourism.com

Port Clinton · *Lake Erie Shores & Islands West* · Larry Fletcher; Exec. Dir.; 770 S.E. Catawba Rd.; 43452; Ottawa; P 40,000; (419) 734-4386; (800) 441-1271; Fax (419) 734-9798; tourism@lake-erie.com; www.shoresandislands.com

Saint Marys · *Auglaize & Mercer Counties CVB* · Donna Grube; Exec. Dir.; 900 Edgewater Dr.; 45885; Auglaize; P 85,000; M 450; (419) 394-1294; (800) 860-4726; Fax (419) 394-1642; seemore@bright.net; www.seemore.org

Sandusky · *Lake Erie Shores & Islands* · Joan VanOfferen; Exec. Dir.; 4424 Milan, Ste. A; 44870; Erie; P 79,000; (419) 625-2984; (800) 255-3743; Fax (419) 625-5009; www.shoresandislands.com

South Point · *Greater Lawrence County Area CVB* · Viviane Vallance; Dir.; 216 Collins Ave.; P.O. Box 488; 45680; Lawrence; P 64,000; (740) 377-4550; (800) 408-1334; Fax (740) 377-2091; vkvallance@zoominternet.net; www.lawrencecountyohio.org

Springfield · *Springfield-Clark County CVB* · Chris Schutte; CVB Mktg.; 20 S. Limestone St., Ste. 100; 45502; Clark; P 168,000; (937) 325-7621; (800) 803-1553; Fax (937) 325-8765; cschutte@greaterspringfield.com; www.greaterspringfield.com

Tiffin · *Seneca County CVB* · Malinda Ruble; Exec. Dir.; 114 S. Washington St.; 44883; Seneca; P 59,000; M 110; (419) 447-5866; visitor@senecacounty.com; www.senecacounty.com

Toledo · *Greater Toledo CVB* · Steve Miller; Gen. Mgr.; 401 Jefferson Ave.; 43604; Lucas; P 300,000; (419) 321-6404; (800) 243-4667; Fax (419) 255-7731; www.dotoledo.org

Upper Sandusky · *Wyandot County Visitors Bur.* · Sara Lou Brown; Exec. Dir.; 108 E. Wyandot Ave., Ste. 2; 43351; Wyandot; P 22,000; M 25; (419) 294-3556; Fax (419) 294-3556; wyandotcovb@udata.com; www.visitwyandotcounty.com

Van Wert · *Van Wert County CVB* · Larry Lee; Exec. Dir.; 136 E. Main St.; 45891; Van Wert; P 30,000; (419) 238-9378; (877) 989-2282; Fax (419) 238-4589; info@visitvanwert.org; www.visitvanwert.org

Washington Court House · *Fayette County Travel & Tourism* · Roger Blackburn; Exec. Dir.; 101 E. East St.; 43160; Fayette; P 32,000; (740) 335-8008; (800) 479-7797; Fax (740) 335-0762; fayettechamber@yahoo.com; www.fayettecountyohio.com

Waverly · *Pike County CVB* · Sharon Manson; Exec. Dir.; 12455 St., Rte. 104; P.O. Box 134; 45690; Pike; P 27,695; (740) 947-9650; Fax (740) 947-7716; piketravel@yahoo.com; www.piketravel.com

West Union · *Adams County Travel & Visitors Bur.* · Tom Cross; Exec. Dir.; 110 N. Manchester St.; 45693; Adams; P 27,000; M 52; (937) 544-5454; (877) 232-6764; Fax (937) 544-6957; info@adamscountytravel.org; www.adamscountytravel.org

Wooster · *Wayne County CVB* · Martha Starkey; Dir.; 428 W. Liberty St.; 44691; Wayne; P 111,564; (330) 264-1800; (800) 362-6474; Fax (330) 264-1141; waynecvb@cs.com; www.waynecounty cvb.org

Zanesville · *Zanesville-Muskingum CVB* · Tom Poorman; Dir.; 205 N. Fifth St.; 43701; Muskingum; P 82,000; (740) 455-8282; (800) 743-2303; Fax (740) 454-2963; kashby@zmchamber.com; www.visitzanesville.com

Oklahoma

Ardmore · *Ardmore Tourism Auth.* · Mita Bates; V.P.; 410 W. Main; 73401; Carter; P 45,000; (580) 223-7765; Fax (580) 223-7825; www.ardmore.org

Bartlesville · *Bartlesville Area CVB* · Maria Swindell Gus; Exec. Dir.; 201 S.W. Keeler Ave.; P.O. Box 2366; 74005; Osage & Washington; P 35,000; (918) 336-8708; (800) 364-8708; Fax (918) 337-0216; msgus@bartlesville.com; www.visitbartlesville.com

Claremore · *Claremore CVB* · Tanya Andrews; Exec. Dir.; 419 W. Will Rogers Blvd.; 74017; Rogers; P 17,500; (918) 341-8688; Fax (918) 342-0663; cvb@claremore.org; www.visitclaremore.org

Duncan · *Duncan CVB* · Loisdawn Jones; Dir.; 800 Chisholm Trail Pkwy.; P.O. Box 981; 73534; Stephens; P 25,000; (580) 252-2900; Fax (580) 252-3799; tourism@simmonscenter.com; www.duncanok.org

Edmond · *Edmond CVB* · Cathy Williams-White; Dir.; 1030 S. Bryant; P.O. Box 2970; 73083; Oklahoma; P 80,000; (405) 341-4344; (405) 216-7781; Fax (405) 216-7783; cwwhite@visitedmondok.com; www.visitedmondok.com

El Reno · *El Reno CVB* · Gene Stroman; Dir.; 110 S. Bickford Ave.; 73036; Canadian; P 16,212; (405) 262-8687; (888) 535-7366; Fax (405) 262-4637; gstroman@elrenotourism.org; www.elrenotourism.org

Guthrie · *Guthrie CVB* · Mary Coffin; Pres./CEO; 212 W. Oklahoma Ave.; P.O. Box 995; 73044; Logan; P 10,500; (405) 282-1948; (800) 299-1889; Fax (405) 282-0061; info@guthrieok.com; www.guthrieok.com

Guymon · *Guymon Conv. & Tourism Dept.* · Vicki Ayres-McCune; Dir.; 802 N.E. 6th St.; 73942; Texas; P 14,000; (580) 338-5838; Fax (580) 338-1854; cddirector@guymonok.org; www.guymonok.org

McAlester · *City of McAlester Tourism Dept.* · Jerry Lynn Wilson; Dir.; P.O. Box 578; 74502; Pittsburg; P 20,000; (918) 420-3976; Fax (918) 423-1092; tourism@cityofmcalester.com; www.cityofmcalester.com

Miami · *Miami CVB* · Amanda Davis; Prog. Exec.; 101 N. Main; P.O. Box 1288; 74355; Ottawa; P 13,704; (918) 542-4435; Fax (918) 542-4546; info@visitmiamiok.com; www.visitmiamiok.com

Muskogee · *Greater Muskogee Area Tourism* · Treasure McKenzie; Tourism Dir.; 310 W. Broadway; P.O. Box 797; 74402; Muskogee; P 39,000; (918) 682-2401; (866) 381-6543; Fax (918) 682-2403; tourism@muskogeechamber.org; www.muskogee chamber.org

Norman · *Norman CVB* · Stephen Koranda; Exec. Dir.; 223 E. Main St.; 73069; Cleveland; P 108,000; (405) 366-8095; (800) 767-7260; Fax (405) 366-8096; info@visitnorman.com; www.visitnorman.com

Oklahoma City · *Oklahoma City CVB* · Mike Carrier; Pres.; Div. of Greater OKC C/C; 189 W. Sheridan Ave.; 73102; Oklahoma; P 1,144,400; (405) 297-8912; (800) 225-5652; Fax (405) 297-8888; okccvb@okccvb.org; www.visitokc.com

Okmulgee · *Okmulgee Tourism* · Nolan Crowley; Dir.; 112 N. Morton; 74447; Okmulgee; P 13,000; (918) 758-1015; Fax (918) 756-6441; okmulgeemainstreet@sbcglobal.net; www.okmulgee online.com

Ponca City · *Ponca City Tourism Bur.* · Kristi Brown; Coord.; 420 E. Grand Ave.; P.O. Box 1109; 74602; Kay & Osage; P 26,000; (580) 763-8092; (866) 763-8092; Fax (580) 765-2798; info@poncacity tourism.com; www.poncacitytourism.com

Shawnee · *Greater Shawnee Area CVB* · Gordona Rowell; Dir.; 131 N. Bell; 74801; Pottawatomie; P 30,562; (405) 275-9780; (888) 404-9633; Fax (405) 275-9851; info@visitshawnee.com; www.visitshawnee.com

Stillwater · *Stillwater CVB* · Cristy Morrison; Exec. Dir.; 409 S. Main; 74074; Payne; P 46,383; (405) 743-3697; (800) 991-6717; Fax (405) 372-0765; cristy@visitstillwater.org; www.visitstill water.org.

Tahlequah · *Tahlequah Area C/C Tourism Cncl.* · Kate Kelly; Tourism Dir.; 123 E. Delaware St.; 74464; Cherokee; P 46,000; M 520; (918) 456-3742; (800) 456-4860; Fax (918) 456-3751; tour@tourtahlequah.com; www.tourtahlequah.com

Tulsa · *Tulsa CVB* · Mike Neal; Pres./CEO; Williams Center Tower II; Two W. Second St., Ste. 150; 74103; Osage, Rogers, Tulsa & Wagoner; P 916,079; (918) 585-1201; Fax (918) 592-6244; www.visittulsa.com

Oregon

Albany · *Albany Visitors Assn.* · Jimmie Lucht; Exec. Dir.; 250 Broadalbin St. S.W., Ste. 110; P.O. Box 965; 97321; Linn; P 47,300; (541) 928-0911; (800) 526-2256; Fax (541) 926-1500; info@albanyvisitors.com; www.albanyvisitors.com

Ashland · *Ashland CVB* · Sandra Slattery; Exec. Dir.; 110 E. Main St.; P.O. Box 1360; 97520; Jackson; P 21,000; (541) 482-3486; Fax (541) 482-2350; www.ashlandchamber.com

Aurora · *Aurora Colony Visitors Assn.* · Barbara Johnson; Treas.; P.O. Box 86; 97002; Marion; P 750; M 40; (503) 939-0312; info@auroracolony.com; www.auroracolony.com

Beaverton · *Washington County Visitors Assn.* · 11000 S.W. Stratus St., Ste. 170; 97008; Washington; P 500,000; M (503) 644-5555; (800) 537-3149; Fax (503) 644-9784; info@wcva.org; www.visitwashingtoncountyoregon.com

Bend · *Visit Bend* · Valerie Warren; Welcome Center Mgr.; 917 N.W. Harriman St., Ste. 101; 97701; Deschutes; P 82,000; (541) 382-8048; (800) 949-6086; Fax (541) 382-8568; info@visitbend.com; www.visitbend.com

Charleston · *Charleston Visitor Center* · P.O. Box 5735; 97420; Coos; P 5,000; (541) 888-2311; (541) 888-4875; www.charlestonoregon-merchants.com

Corvallis · *Visit Corvallis* · Curtis Wright; Pres.; 553 N.W. Harrison Blvd.; 97330; Benton; P 54,000; (541) 757-1544; (800) 334-8118; Fax (541) 753-2664; info@visitcorvallis.com; www.visitcorvallis.com

Eugene · *Travel Lane County* · Kari Westlund; Pres./CEO; 754 Olive St.; P.O. Box 10286; 97440; Lane; P 340,000; M 575; (541) 484-5307; (800) 547-5445; Fax (541) 343-6335; info@travel lanecounty.org; www.travellanecounty.org

Gold Beach · *Gold Beach Visitors Center* · Jeff Fergoson; Dir.; 94080 Shirley Ln.; P.O. Box 375; 97444; Curry; P 2,200; (541) 247-7526; (800) 525-2334; Fax (541) 247-0187; visit@goldbeach.org; www.goldbeach.org

Grants Pass · *Grants Pass VCB* · Kerrie Walters; Mktg. Coord.; 1995 N.W. Vine St.; 97526; Josephine; P 81,618; (541) 476-5510; Fax (541) 476-9574; vcb@visitgrantspass.org; www.visitgrants pass.org

Klamath Falls · *Discover Klamath* · Jim Chadderdon; Exec. Dir.; 205 Riverside Dr., Ste. B; 97601; Klamath; P 45,000; (541) 882-1501; (800) 445-6728; Fax (541) 273-2017; visit@discoverklamath. com; www.discoverklamath.com

La Grande · *Union County Tourism* · Janet Dodson; Exec. Dir.; 102 Elm St.; 97850; Union; P 25,000; (541) 963-8588; (800) 848-9969; Fax (541) 963-3936; visitlg@eoni.com; www.visitlagrande.com

Lincoln City · *Lincoln City Visitor & Conv. Bur.* · Sandy Pfass; Exec. Dir.; 801 S.W. Hwy. 101, Ste. 401; 97367; Lincoln; P 7,500; (541) 996-1274; (800) 452-2151; Fax (541) 994-2408; events@ lincolncity.org; www.oregoncoast.org

Medford · *Medford VCB* · Anne Jenkins; Sr. V.P.; 101 E. 8th St.; 97501; Jackson; P 174,000; (541) 779-4847; Fax (541) 776-4808; vcb@visitmedford.org; www.visitmedford.org

North Bend · *North Bend Visitor Info. Center* · Barbara Dunham; Mgr.; 1380 Sherman Ave. (Hwy. 101); 97459; Coos; P 10,000; (541) 756-4613; (800) 472-9176; Fax (541) 756-8527; bdunham@uci.net; www.northbendcity.org

Ontario · *Ontario Visitors & Conv. Bur.* · John Breidenbach; Pres./CEO; 676 S.W. 4th Ave.; 97914; Malheur; P 12,000; (541) 889-8012; (866) 989-8012; Fax (541) 889-8331; info@ontario chamber.com; www.ontariochamber.com

Portland Area

African American Conv. & Tourism-A.C.T. · Roy Jay; Natl. Pres./CEO; P.O. Box 5488; 97228; Clackamas, Multnomah & Washington; M 2,310; (800) 909-2882; Fax (503) 698-2896; ACT. NOW@USA.NET; www.blackconventions.com

Oregon Conv. & Visitor Svcs. Network · Roy Jay; Pres./CEO; P.O. Box 5488; 97228; Clackamas, Multnomah & Washington; P 1,000,000; M 1,000; (503) 244-5794; Fax (503) 293-2094; www.oregoncvb.com

Travel Portland · Jeff Miller; Pres./CEO; 1000 S.W. Broadway, Ste. 2300; 97205; Clackamas, Multnomah & Washington; P 1,950,000; M 1,100; (503) 275-9750; (800) 962-3700; Fax (503) 275-9284; info@travelportland.com; www.travelportland.com

Roseburg · *Roseburg Visitors & Conv. Bur.* · Jean Kurtz; Exec. Dir.; 410 S.E. Spruce St.; P.O. Box 1262; 97470; Douglas; P 21,500; (541) 672-9731; (800) 444-9584; Fax (541) 673-7868; info@ visitroseburg.com; www.visitroseburg.com.

Salem · *Travel Salem* · Angie Morris; CEO; 181 High St. N.E.; 97301; Marion; P 154,510; (503) 581-4325; (800) 874-7012; Fax (503) 581-4540; information@travelsalem.com; www. travelsalem.com

Seaside · *Seaside Civic & Conv. Center* · Russell Vandenberg; Gen. Mgr.; 415 First Ave.; 97138; Clatsop; P 7,000; (503) 738-8585; (800) 394-3303; Fax (503) 738-0198; sales@seaside convention.com; www.seasideconvention.com

Seaside · *Seaside Visitors Bur.* · Jon Rahl; Dir. of Tourism Mktg.; 7 N. Roosevelt; 989 Broadway; 97138; Clatsop; P 6,500; (503) 738-3097; (888) 306-2326; Fax (503) 717-8299; visit@seaside-oregon. com; www.seasideor.com

Winston · *Winston-Dillard Area Visitors Bur.* · Bernice McClellan; Coord.; 30 N.W. Glenhart; P.O. Box 68; 97496; Douglas; P 10,000; M 125; (541) 679-0118; Fax (541) 679-4270; winston vic@charter.net; www.winstonoregon.net

Pennsylvania

Altoona · *Allegheny Mountains CVB* · Cheryl Ebersole; Exec. Dir.; One Convention Center Dr.; 16602; Blair; P 54,000; (814) 943-4183; (800) 84-ALTOONA; Fax (814) 943-8094; info@amcvb. com; www.allegheny mountains.com

Beaver Falls · *Beaver County Rec. & Tourism Dept.* · Tom King; Dir.; Recreation Facility; 121 Bradys Run Rd.; 15010; Beaver; P 186,000; M 110; (724) 891-7030; (800) 342-8192; Fax (724) 891-7085; bctpa@beavercountypa.gov; www.visitbeavercounty.com

Bedford · *Bedford County Visitors Bur.* · Dennis Tice; Exec. Dir.; 131 S. Juliana St.; 15522; Bedford; P 49,000; M 130; (814) 623-1771; (800) 765-3331; Fax (814) 623-1671; bccvb@bedford.net; www.bedfordcounty.net

Ben Salem · *Bucks County Conf. & Visitors Bur.* · Jerry Lepping; Exec. Dir.; 3207 Street Rd.; 19020; Bucks; P 600,000; M 500; (215) 639-0300; (800) 836-2825; Fax (215) 642-3277; info@buckscounty.travel; www.buckscounty.travel

Bloomsburg · *Columbia-Montour Visitors Bur.* · David Kurecian; Exec. Dir.; 121 Papermill Rd.; 17815; Columbia & Montour; P 82,720; M 201; (570) 784-8279; Fax (570) 784-1166; itour@cmvb.com; www.itourcolumbiamontour.com

Bradford · *Allegheny Natl. Forest Vacation Bur.* · Linda Devlin; Exec. Dir.; 80 E. Corydon St.; P.O. Box 371; 16701; McKean; P 46,500; (800) 473 9370; Fax (814) 368-9370; info@visitanf.com; www.visitanf.com

Brookville · *Northwest Penn. Great Outdoors Visitors Bur.* · David Morris; Exec. Dir.; 175 Main St.; 15825; Jefferson; P 500,000; (814) 849-5197; (800) 348-9393; Fax (814) 849-1969; info@ visitpago.com; www.visitpago.com

Carlisle · *see Harrisburg*

Chadds Ford · *Brandywine Conf. & Visitors Bur.* · Tore Fiore; Exec. Dir.; One Beaver Valley Rd.; 19317; Delaware; P 553,000; (610) 565-3679; (800) 343-3983; Fax (610) 361-0459; tfiore@ brandywinecvb.org; www.brandywinecountry.org

Coudersport · *Potter County Visitors Assn.* · David Brooks; Exec. Dir.; P.O. Box 245; 16915; Potter; P 18,000; (814) 274-3365; (888) POTTER-2; Fax (814) 274-4334; potter@penn.com; www. visitpottercounty.com

Danville · *Columbia-Montour Visitors Bur.* · David Kurecian; Exec. Dir.; 316 Mill St.; 17821; Montour; P 65,000; M 201; (570) 275-8185; Fax (570) 275-1662; itour@cmvb.com; www.itour columbiamontour.com

Erie · *Visit Erie* · John Oliver; Pres.; 208 E. Bayfront Pkwy., Ste. 103; 16507; Erie; P 200,000; (814) 454-1000; (800) 524-ERIE; Fax (814) 459-0241; info@visiterie.com; www.visiterie.com

Gettysburg · *Gettysburg CVB* · Norris Flowers; Pres.; P.O. Box 4117; 17325; Adams; P 91,292; M 210; (717) 334-6274; Fax (717) 334-1166; info@gettysburg.travel; www.gettysburg.travel

Harrisburg · *Hershey-Harrisburg Reg. Visitors Bur.* · Mary Smith; Pres.; 17 S. 2nd St,; 17101; Dauphin; (717) 231-7788; (877) 727-8573; Fax (717) 231-2808; info@hersheyharrisburg. org; www.hersheyharrisburg.org

Hershey · *see Harrisburg*

Hesston · *Raystown Lake Reg. Visitors Bur.* · Matthew Price; Exec. Dir.; 6993 Seven Points Rd., Ste. 2; 16647; Huntingdon; P 44,000; M 250; (814) 658-0060; (888) RAYSTOWN; Fax (814) 658-0068; info@raystown.org; www.raystown.org

Indiana · *Indiana County Tourist Bur.* · Penny Perman; Exec. Dir.; 2334 Oakland Ave.; 15701; Indiana; P 90,000; M 200; (724) 463-7505; (877) 746-3426; Fax (724) 465-3819; info@visitindiana countypa.org; www.visitindianacountypa.org

Johnstown · *Greater Johnstown/Cambria County CVB* · Lisa M. Rager; Exec. Dir.; 416 Main St., Ste. 100; 15901; Cambria; P 144,319; M 275; (814) 536-7993; (800) 237-8590; Fax (814) 539-3370; jstcvb@visitjohnstownpa.com; www.visitjohnstownpa.com

King of Prussia · *Valley Forge CVB* · Paul Decker; Pres.; 1000 1st Ave., Ste. 101; 19406; Montgomery; P 140,000; (610) 834-1550; (800) 441-3549; Fax (610) 834-0202; info@valleyforge.org; www.valleyforge.org

Kittanning · *Armstrong County Tourist Bur.* · Jessica Coil; Dir.; 125 Market St.; 16201; Armstrong; P 8,000; M 225; (724) 543-4003; (888) 265-9954; Fax (724) 545-3119; touristbur@ co.armstrong.pa.us; www.armstrongcounty.com

Lancaster · *Pennsylvania Dutch CVB* · Christopher Barrett; Pres.; 501 Greenfield Rd.; 17601; Lancaster; P 460,000; M 630; (717) 299-8901; (800) PA-DUTCH; Fax (717) 299-0470; info@ padutchcountry.com; www.padutchcountry.com

Lehigh Valley · *Lehigh Valley CVB* · Michael Stershic; Pres.; P.O. Box 20785; 18002; Northampton; P 600,000; M 490; (610) 882-9200; Fax (610) 882-0343; geninfo@lehighvalleypa.org; www.lehighvalleypa.org

Lewisburg · *Susquehanna Valley Visitors Bur.* · Andrew Miller; Exec. Dir.; 81 Hafer Rd.; 17837; Union; P 37,000; M 250; (570) 524-7234; (800) 525-7320; Fax (570) 524-7282; info@visitcentralpa. org; www.visitcentralpa.org

Lewistown · *Juniata River Valley Visitors Bur.* · Jim Tunall; Exec. Dir.; Historic Courthouse; One W. Market St., Ste. 103; 17044; Mifflin; P 68,463; (717) 248-6713; (877) 568-9739; Fax (717) 248-6714; jrvvb@juniatarivervalley.org; www.juniatarivervalley.org

Ligonier · *Laurel Highlands Visitors Bur.* · Annie Urban; Exec. Dir.; 120 E. Main St.; Town Hall; 15658; Westmoreland; P 856,693; M 511; (724) 238-5661; (800) 333-5661; Fax (724) 238-3673; aurban@laurelhighlands.org; www.laurelhighlands.org

Lock Haven · *Clinton County Eco. Partnership* · Peter Lopes; Chamber/Tourism Dir.; 212 N. Jay St.; P.O. Box 506; 17745; Clinton; P 37,914; M 385; (570) 748-5782; (888) 388-6991; Fax (570) 893-0433; tourism@kcnet.org; www.clintoncountyinfo.com

Mayfield · *Lackawanna County CVB* · Tracy Barone; Exec. Dir.; 1300 Old Plank Rd.; 18433; Lackawanna; P 219,000; M 206; (570) 963-6363; (800) 22-WELCOME; Fax (570) 963-6852; info@ visitnepa.org; www.visitnepa.org

Meadville · *Crawford County CVB* · Juanita Hampton; Exec. Dir.; 16709 Conneaut Lake Rd.; 16335; Crawford; P 90,360; (814) 333-1258; (800) 332-2338; Fax (814) 333-9032; welcome@ visitcrawford.org; www.visitcrawford.org

Monroeville · *CVB of Greater Monroeville* · Karrie Burns; Exec. Dir.; 209 Mall Blvd.; 15146; Allegheny; P 30,000; (412) 856-7422; Fax (412) 856-6979; info@visitmonroeville.com; www.visitmonroeville.com

New Castle · *Lawrence County Tourist Promo. Agency* · JoAnn McBride; Exec. Dir.; 229 S. Jefferson St.; 16101; Lawrence; P 95,000; M 170; (724) 654-8408; (888) 284-7599; Fax (724) 654-2044; info@ visitlawrencecounty.com; www.visitlawrencecounty.com

Philadelphia · *Philadelphia CVB* · Thomas O. Muldoon; Pres.; 1700 Market St., Ste. 3000; 19103; Philadelphia; (215) 636-3300; Fax (215) 636-3327; info@philadelphiausa.travel; www.philadelphiausa.travel

Pittsburgh · *VisitPittsburgh* · Joseph McGrath; Pres./CEO; 425 Sixth Ave., 30th Flr.; 15219; Allegheny; P 2,390,000; M 800; (412) 281-0482; (800) 359-0758; Fax (412) 644-5512; info@visitpitts burgh.com; www.visitpittsburgh.com

Plymouth Meeting · *see King of Prussia*

Pottsville · *Schuylkill County Visitors Bur.* · Mark T. Major; Exec. Dir.; 200 E. Arch St.; 17901; Schuylkill; P 150,000; M 184; (570) 622-7700; (800) 765-7282; Fax (570) 622-8035; tourism@ schuylkill.org; www.schuylkill.org

Reading · *Greater Reading CVB* · Crystal Seitz; Pres.; 201 Washington St.; 19602; Berks; P 370,000; (610) 375-4085; (800) 443-6610; Fax (610) 375-9606; info@readingberkspa.com; www. readingberkspa.com

Sharon · *Mercer County CVB* · Peggy Mazyck; Exec. Dir.; 50 N. Water Ave.; 16146; Mercer; P 120,293; M 160; (724) 346-3771; Fax (724) 346-0575; mcpa@visitmercercountypa.com; www. visitmercercountypa.com

State College · *Central PA CVB* · Betsey Howell; Exec. Dir.; 800 E. Park Ave.; 16803; Centre; P 138,000; M 415; (814) 231-1400; (800) 358-5466; Fax (814) 231-8123; info@centralpacvb.org; www.centralpacvb.org

Stroudsburg · *Pocono Mountains Vacation Bur.* · Carl Wilgus; Exec. Dir.; 1004 Main St.; 18360; Monroe; P 172,000; M 500; (570) 421-5791; (800) POCONOS; Fax (570) 421-6927; pocomts@ poconos.org; www.800poconos.com

Tunkhannock · *Endless Mountains Visitors Bur.* · Jean Gasper; Exec. Dir.; 4 Werks Plz.; 18657; Wyoming; P 145,091; M 250; (570) 836-5431; (800) 769-8999; Fax (570) 836-3927; emvb@epix.net; www.endlessmountains.org

Warren · *Warren County Visitors Bur.* · Mike Olewine; Exec. Dir.; 22045 Rte. 6; 16365; Warren; P 43,876; M 125; (814) 726-1222; (800) 624-7802; Fax (814) 726-7266; info@wcvb.net; www.wcvb.net

Washington · *Washington County Tourism Promo. Agency* · J.R. Shaw; Exec. Dir.; 273 S. Main St; 15301; Washington; P 204,584; M 130; (724) 228-5520; (866) WASH-WOW; Fax (724) 228-5514; info@washwow.com; www.visitwashingtoncountypa.com

Waynesburg · *Greene County Tourist Promo. Agency* · Jeanie Patton; Exec. Dir.; 417 E. Roy Furman Hwy.; 15370; Greene; P 41,000; M 250; (724) 627-8687; (724) 627-TOUR; Fax (724) 627-8608; tourism@co.greene.pa.us; www.greenecountytourism.org

Wellsboro · *Tioga County Visitors Bur.* · Sandra L. Spencer; Exec. Dir.; P.O. Box 139; 16901; Tioga; P 40,000; (570) 724-0635; (888) TIOGA-28; Fax (570) 723-1016; sspencer@epix.net; www. visittiogapa.com

West Chester · *Chester County Conf. & Visitors Bur.* · Blair Mahoney; Exec. Dir.; 17 Wilmont Mews, Ste. 400; 19382; Chester; P 475,000; M 460; (610) 719-1730; (800) 566-0109; Fax (610) 719-1736; www.brandywinevalley.com

Williamsport · *Lycoming County Visitors Bur.* · Jason Fink; Dir.; 210 William St.; 17701; Lycoming; P 121,000; (570) 327-7700; (800) 358-9900; Fax (570) 327-7900; visitorinfo@ williamsport.org; www.vacationpa.com

York · *York County CVB* · Anne Druck; Pres.; 155 W. Market St.; 17401; York; P 382,000; (717) 852-9675; (888) 858-9675; Fax (717) 854-5095; info@yorkpa.org; www.yorkpa.org

Zelienople · *Butler County Tourism & Conv. Bur.* · Jack Cohen; Exec. Dir.; 310 E. Grandview Ave.; 16063; Butler; P 182,000; (724) 234-4619; (866) 856-8444; Fax (724) 234-4643; visitors@visit butlercounty.com; www.visitbutlercounty.com

Puerto Rico

San Juan • *Puerto Rico Conv. Bur.* • Ana Maria Viscasillas; Pres./CEO; Edificio Ochoa; 500 Tanca, Ste. 402; 00902; P 4,000,000; M 550; (787) 725-2110; (800) 875-4765; Fax (787) 725-2133; info@meetpuertorico.com; www.meetpuertorico.com

Rhode Island

Newport • *Newport County CVB* • Evan Smith; Pres./CEO; 23 America's Cup Ave.; 02840; Newport; P 25,000; (401) 849-8048; (800) 326-6030; Fax (401) 849-0291; jbailey@gonewport.com; www.gonewport.com

Providence • *Providence Warwick CVB* • Martha Sheridan; Pres./CEO; 144 Westminster, 2nd Flr.; 02903; Providence; P 160,000; M 400; (401) 456-0200; Fax (401) 351-2090; information@pwcvb.com; www.pwcvb.com

Warwick • *City of Warwick Dept. of Tourism & Culture* • Karen Jedson; Dir.; Warwick City Hall; 3275 Post Rd.; 02886; Kent; P 86,000; (800) 492-7942; Fax (401) 732-7662; karen.jedson@warwickri.com; www.visitwarwickri.com

South Carolina

Charleston • *Charleston Area CVB* • Helen T. Hill; Exec. Dir.; 423 King St.; 29403; Charleston; P 583,434; (843) 853-8000; (800) 868-8118; Fax (843) 853 0444; info@charlestoncvb.com; www.charlestoncvb.com

Columbia • *Columbia Metropolitan CVB* • Ric Luber; Pres.; 1101 Lincoln St.; P.O. Box 15; 29202; Richland; P 664,229; (803) 545-0000; (800) 264-4884; Fax (803) 545-0013; www.columbiaconventioncenter.com

Greenville • *Greenville CVB* • Chris Stone; Pres.; P.O. Box 10527; 29603; Greenville; P 400,000; M 250; (864) 421-0000; (800) 351-7180; Fax (864) 421-0005; www.greenvillecvb.com

Greenwood • *Greenwood Reg. Tourism & Visitors Bur.* • Kelly McWhorter; Exec. Dir.; 120 Main St.; P.O. Box 40; 29648; Greenwood; P 150,000; (864) 953-2466; (866) 493-8474; Fax (864) 953-2468; info@visitgreenwoodsc.com; www.visitgreenwoodsc.com

Hilton Head Island • *Hilton Head Island-Bluffton CVB* • William G. Miles; Pres./CEO; One Chamber Dr.; P.O. Box 5647; 29938; Beaufort; P 42,000; (843) 785-3673; Fax (843) 785-7110; info@hiltonheadisland.org; www.hiltonheadisland.org

Myrtle Beach • *Myrtle Beach Area CVB* • Dana Lilly; V.P.; 1200 N. Oak St.; P.O. Box 2115; 29578; Horry; P 217,608; (843) 626-7444; (800) 488-8998; Fax (843) 448-3010; info@visitmyrtlebeach.com; www.visitmyrtlebeach.com

North Myrtle Beach • *North Myrtle Beach CVB* • Marc Jordan; Pres./CEO; 270 Hwy. 17 N.; P.O. Box 349; 29597; Horry; P 12,000; (843) 281-2662; Fax (843) 280-2930; info@northmyrtlebeachchamber.com; www.northmyrtlebeachchamber.com

Rock Hill • *Rock Hill/York County CVB* • Bennish Brown; Exec. Dir.; P.O. Box 11377; 29731; York; P 170,000; M 75; (803) 329-5200; (800) 866-5200; Fax (803) 329-0145; www.visityorkcounty.com

Spartanburg • *Spartanburg CVB* • 298 Magnolia St.; 29306; Spartanburg; P 261,000; (864) 594-5050; (800) 374-8326; Fax (864) 594-5052; lponder@visitspartanburg.com; www.visitspartanburg.com

South Dakota

Aberdeen • *Aberdeen CVB* • Nancy Krumm; Exec. Dir.; 10 Railroad Ave. S.W.; P.O. Box 78; 57402; Brown; P 24,658; (605) 225-2414; (800) 645-3851; Fax (605) 225-3573; info@visitaberdeensd.com; www.visitaberdeensd.com

Brookings • *Brookings Area C/C & CVB* • Al Heuton; Dir.; 414 Main Ave.; P.O. Box 431; 57006; Brookings; P 18,703; M 425; (605) 692-6125; (800) 699-6125; Fax (605) 697-8109; chamber@brookings.net; www.brookingssd.com

Huron • *Huron CVB* • Peggy Woolridge; Exec. Dir.; 1705 Dakota Ave. S.; 57350; Beadle; P 11,500; (605) 352-0000; (800) 487-6673; Fax (605) 352-8321; cvb@huronsd.com; www.huronsd.com

Mitchell • *Corn Palace CVB* • Hannah Walters; Dir.; 601 N. Main St.; P.O. Box 1026; 57301; Davison; P 14,558; (605) 996-6223; Fax (605) 996-8273; cvb@cornpalace.com; www.cornpalace.com

Pierre • *Pierre CVB* • Laura Schoen Carbonneau; CEO; 800 W. Dakota Ave.; P.O. Box 548; 57501; Hughes; P 16,000; (605) 224-7361; (800) 962-2034; Fax (605) 224-6485; contactchamber@pierre.org; www.pierre.org

Rapid City • *Rapid City CVB* • Michelle Lintz; Exec. Dir.; P.O. Box 747; 57709; Pennington; P 68,000; (605) 343-1744; (800) 487-3223; Fax (605) 348-9217; info@visitrapidcity.com; www.visitrapidcity.com

Sioux Falls • *Sioux Falls CVB* • Teri Ellis Schmidt; Exec. Dir.; 200 N. Phillips Ave., Ste. 102; 57104; Minnehaha; P 154,000; (605) 336-1620; (800) 333-2072; Fax (605) 336-6499; sfcvb@siouxfalls.com; www.siouxfallscvb.com

Watertown • *Watertown CVB* • Karen D. Witt; Exec. Dir.; 1200 Mickelson Dr.; P.O. Box 225; 57201; Codington; P 20,000; (605) 753-0282; cvb@visitwatertownsd.com; www.visitwatertownsd.com

Yankton • *Yankton CVB* • Lisa Scheve; Dir.; 803 E. Fourth St.; P.O. Box 588; 57078; Yankton; P 14,000; M (800) 888-1460; Fax (605) 665-7501; visityankton@yanktonsd.com; www.yanktonsd.com

Tennessee

Bristol • *see Bristol, VA*

Chattanooga • *Chattanooga Area CVB* • Bob Doak; Pres./CEO; 2 Broad St.; 37402; Hamilton; P 475,000; M (423) 756-8687; (800) 322-3344; Fax (423) 265-1630; www.chattanoogafun.com

Clarksville • *Clarksville-Montgomery County CVB* • Theresa Harrington; Exec. Dir.; 25 Jefferson St., Ste. 300; P.O. Box 883; 37041; Montgomery; P 144,602; (931) 647-2331; (800) 530-2487; Fax (931) 645-1574; tourdir@clarksville.tn.us; www.clarksville.tn.us

Cleveland • *Cleveland/Bradley CVB* • Melissa Woody; V.P.; 225 Keith St. S.W.; P.O. Box 2275; 37320; Bradley; P 95,443; (423) 472-6587; (800) 472-6588; Fax (423) 472-2019; info@clevelandchamber.com; www.visitclevelandtn.com

Columbia • *Maury County CVB* • Brenda Pierce; Exec. Dir.; 8 Public Sq.; 38401; Maury; P 70,770; (931) 381-7176; (888) 852-1860; Fax (931) 375-4119; maurycvb@maurycounty-tn.gov; www.antebellum.com

Cookeville • *Cookeville-Putnam County CVB* • Laura Canada; CVB Dir.; 1 W. First St.; 38501; Putnam; P 68,000; (931) 526-2211; (800) 264-5541; Fax (931) 526-4023; lcanada@cookevillechamber.com; www.mustseecookeville.com; www.cookevillechamber.com

Crossville · *Crossville-Cumberland County CVB* · Beth Alexander; Pres./CEO; 34 S. Main St.; 38555; Cumberland; P 54,000; (931) 484-8444; (877) 465-3861; Fax (931) 484-7511; thechamber@crossville-chamber.com; www.crossville-chamber.com

Franklin · *Williamson County CVB* · Mark Shore; Exec. Dir.; 108 4th Ave. S., Ste. 203; 37064; Williamson; P 155,000; (615) 791-7554; (866) 253-9207; Fax (615) 550-2707; info@visitwilliamson.com; www.visitwilliamson.com

Gatlinburg · *Gatlinburg Dept. of Tourism & Conv. Center* · Walter Yeldell; Tourism Mgr.; 303 Reagan Dr.; 37738; Sevier; P 3,600; (865) 436-2392; (800) 343-1475; Fax (865) 436-3704; waltery@ci.gatlinburg.tn.us; www.gatlinburg-tn.com

Johnson City · *Johnson City CVB* · Brenda Whitson; Exec. Dir.; 603 E. Market St.; P.O. Box 180; 37605; Washington; P 58,000; (423) 461-8000; Fax (423) 461-8047; whitson@johnsoncitytnchamber.com; www.johnsoncitytnchamber.com

Kingsport · *Kingsport CVB* · Jud Teague; Exec. Dir.; 151 E. Main St.; 37660; Sullivan; P 51,000; (423) 392-8820; (800) 743-5282; Fax (423) 392-8803; kcvb@kcvb.org; www.visitkingsport.com

Knoxville · *Knoxville Tourism & Sports Corp.* · Gloria Ray; Pres./CEO; 301 S. Gay St.; 37902; Knox; P 392,995; (865) 523-7263; (800) 727-8045; Fax (865) 522-3974; www.knoxville.org

La Vergne · *Rutherford County CVB* · Mona Herring; V.P.; 5093 Murfreesboro Rd.; 37086; Rutherford; P 27,255; (615) 893-6565; (800) 716-7560; Fax (615) 890-7600; info@rutherfordchamber.org; www.rutherfordchamber.org

Lenoir City · *Loudon County Visitors Bur.* · Mary Bryant; Dir.; 1075 Hwy. 321 N.; 37771; Loudon; P 43,000; (865) 986-6822; (888) 568-3662; Fax (865) 988-8959; mbryant@visitloudoncounty.com; www.visitloudoncounty.com

Maryville · *Smokey Mountain CVB* · Bryan Daniels CEcD CCE IOM; Pres./CEO; 201 S. Washington St.; 37804; Blount; P 120,000; (865) 983-2241; (865) 448-6134; Fax (865) 984-1386; info@smokeymountains.org; www.smokymountains.org

Memphis · *Memphis CVB* · Kevin Kane; Pres.; 47 Union Ave.; 38103; Shelby; P 1,100,000; (901) 543-5300; (800) 873-6282; Fax (901) 543-5350; kkanemcvb@aol.com; www.memphistravel.com

Murfreesboro · *Rutherford County CVB* · Mona Herring; V.P.; 501 Memorial Blvd.; P.O. Box 864; 37133; Rutherford; P 241,355; (615) 893-6565; (800) 716-7560; Fax (615) 890-7600; info@rutherfordchamber.org; www.rutherfordchamber.org

Nashville · *Nashville CVB* · Butch Spyridon; Pres.; 1 Nashville Pl.; 150 4th Ave. N., Ste. G-250; 37219; Davidson; P 596,000; (615) 259-4730; (800) 657-6910; Fax (615) 259-4717; nashcvb@visitmusiccity.com; www.visitmusiccity.com

Oak Ridge · *Oak Ridge CVB* · Katy Brown; Pres.; 102 Robertsville Rd., Ste. C; 37830; Anderson; P 27,000; (865) 482-7821; (800) 887-3429; Fax (865) 481-3543; info@oakridgevisitor.com; www.oakridgevisitor.com

Paris · *Northwest Tennessee Tourism* · Gary Mason; Dir.; P.O. Box 807; 38242; Henry; P 235,291; M 100; (731) 593-0171; (866) 698-6386; Fax (731) 644-3051; info@kentuckylaketourism.com; www.kentuckylaketourism.com

Pigeon Forge · *City of Pigeon Forge Dept. of Tourism* · Leon Downey; Exec. Dir.; 2450 Pkwy.; P.O. Box 1390; 37868; Sevier; P 5,784; M 976; (865) 453-8574; (800) 251-9100; Fax (865) 429-7362; inquire@MyPigeonForge.com; www.mypigeonforge.com

Pulaski · *Giles County Tourism Found.* · Tim Turner; Coord.; P.O. Box 678; 38478; Giles; P 29,447; (931) 363-3789; Fax (931) 363-7279; gctourism@gilescountytourism.com; www.gilescountytourism.com

Rugby · *Historic Rugby* · Cheryl Cribbet; Exec. Dir.; 5517 Rugby Hwy.; P.O. Box 8; 37733; Morgan; P 85; (423) 628-2441; (888) 214-3400; Fax (423) 628-2266; rugbylegacy@highland.net; www.historicrugby.org

Savannah · *Hardin County CVB* · Rachel Baker; Tourism Dir.; 495 Main St.; 38372; Hardin; P 25,000; (731) 925-2364; (800) 552-FUNN; Fax (731) 925-6987; info@tourhardincounty.org; www.tourhardincounty.org

Smyrna · *Rutherford County CVB* · Mona Herring; V.P.; 315 S. Lowry St.; 37167; Rutherford; P 38,073; (615) 893-6565; (800) 716-7560; Fax (615) 890-7600; info@rutherfordchamber.org; www.rutherfordchamber.org

Townsend · *See Maryville*

Texas

Abilene · *Abilene CVB* · Nanci M. Liles; Exec. Dir.; 1101 N. First; 79601; Taylor; P 120,000; (325) 676-2556; (800) 727-7704; Fax (325) 676-1630; info@abilenevisitors.com; www.abilenevisitors.com

Alvin · *Alvin CVB* · Julie Siggers; Tourism Dir.; 121 E. Willis; 77511; Brazoria; P 48,524; (281) 585-3359; (800) 331-4063; Fax (281) 756-8688; jsiggers@cityhall.cityofalvin.com; www.alvintexas.org

Amarillo · *Amarillo Conv. & Visitor Cncl.* · Jerry Holt; V.P.; 1000 S. Polk St.; 79101; Potter; P 190,000; (806) 374-1497; (800) 692-1338; Fax (806) 373-3909; klynn@visitamarillotx.com; www.visitamarillotx.com

Arlington · *Arlington CVB* · Jay Burress; Pres./CEO; 1905 E. Randol Mill Rd.; 76011; Tarrant; P 370,000; (817) 265-7721; (800) 433-5374; Fax (817) 265-5640; visitinfo@arlington.org; www.arlington.org

Arlington · *Arlington CVB* · Mary German; Sr. Dir. of Bus. Svcs. & Programs; 1905 E. Randol Mill Rd.; 76011; Tarrant; P 370,000; (817) 461-3888; (800) 433-5374; visitinfo@arlington.org; www.arlington.org

Austin · *Austin CVB* · Robert Lander; Pres./CEO; 301 Congress Ave., Ste. 201; 78701; Travis; P 998,543; (512) 474-5171; (800) 926-2282; Fax (512) 583-7282; www.austintexas.org

Bandera · *Bandera CVB* · Patricia Moore; Exec. Dir.; 126 Hwy. 16 S.; P.O. Box 171; 78003; Bandera; P 22,000; (830) 796-3045; (800) 364-3833; Fax (830) 796-4121; cowpoke@banderacowboycapital.com; www.banderacowboycapital.com

Bay City · *Matagorda County CVB* · Mitch Thames; Pres./CEO; 201 Seventh St.; P.O. Box 768; 77404; Matagorda; P 38,000; (979) 245-8333; (800) 806-8333; Fax (979) 245-1622; mitchthames@visitbaycity.org; www.visitmatagorda.com

Beaumont · *Beaumont CVB* · Dean Conwell; Dir.; 505 Willow St.; P.O. Box 3827; 77704; Jefferson; P 115,000; (409) 880-3749; (800) 392-4401; Fax (409) 880-3750; smoye@ci.beaumont.tx.us; www.beaumontcvb.com

Boerne · *Boerne CVB* · Larry Wood; Dir.; 1407 S. Main; 78006; Kendall; P 9,300; (830) 249-7277; (888) 842-8080; Fax (830) 249-9626; www.visitboerne.org

Brady · *Brady Tourist & Conv. Bur.* · Kathi Masonheimer; Comm. Dev. Dir.; 101 E. 1st St.; 76825; McCulloch; P 5,523; (325) 597-3491; (888) 577-5657; Fax (325) 792-9181; info@bradytx.com; www.bradytx.com

Brazosport · *Brazosport Conv. & Visitors Cncl.* · Edith Fischer; Dir. of Tourism; 300 Abner Jackson Pkwy.; 77566; Brazoria; P 75,000; (979) 285-2501; (888) 477-2505; Fax (979) 285-2505; edithfischer@sbcglobal.net; www.visitbrazosport.com

Brenham • *Brenham/Washington County CVB* • Seneca McAdams; Sales/Mktg. Mgr.; 314 S. Austin St.; 77833; Washington; P 31,000; (979) 836-3695; (888) 273-6426; Fax (979) 836-2540; info@brenhamtexas.com; www.brenhamtexas.com

Brownsville • *Brownsville CVB* • Mariano Ayala; Pres./CEO; 650 FM 802; P.O. Box 4697; 78523; Cameron; P 180,000; (956) 546-3721; (800) 626-2639; Fax (956) 546-3972; brownsvilleinfo@brownsville.org; www.brownsville.org

Bryan • *see College Station*

College Station • *Bryan/College Station CVB* • Shannon Overby; Dir.; 715 University Dr. E.; 77840; Brazos; P 126,804; (979) 260-9898; (800) 777-8292; Fax (979) 260-9800; info@visitaggieland.com; www.visitaggieland.com

Conroe • *Conroe CVB* • Harold Hutchison; Dir.; 505 W. Davis St.; 77301; Montgomery; P 53,000; (936) 522-3500; (877) 4-CONROE; Fax (936) 756-6752; cvbinfo@cityofconroe.org; www.conroecvb.net

Corpus Christi • *Corpus Christi CVB* • Keith Arnold; Pres./CEO; 101 N. Shoreline Blvd., Ste. 430; 78401; Nueces; P 281,000; (361) 881-1888; (800) 678-6232; Fax (361) 888-4998; rgposada@visitcorpuschristitx.org; www.visitcorpuschristitx.org

Dallas • *Dallas CVB* • Phillip Jones; Pres./CEO; 325 N. St. Paul, Ste. 700; 75201; Dallas; P 1,189,000; (214) 571-1000; Fax (214) 571-1008; info@dallascvb.com; www.visitdallas.com

Denton • *Denton CVB* • Kim Phillips; V.P.; 414 Pkwy.; 76201; Denton; P 120,000; (940) 382-7895; (888) 381-1818; Fax (940) 382-6287; admin@discoverdenton.com; www.discoverdenton.com

El Paso • *El Paso CVB* • William Blaziek; Gen. Mgr.; #1 Civic Center Plaza; 79901; El Paso; P 755,000; (915) 534-0600; Fax (915) 534-0687; info@elpasocvb.com; www.visitelpaso.com

Fort Stockton • *Fort Stockton CVB* • Doug May; Dir. of Tourism; 1000 Railroad Ave.; 79735; Pecos; P 8,000; (432) 336-2264; (800) 336-2166; Fax (432) 336-6114; edc@fortstockton.org; www.cityfs.net

Fort Worth • *Fort Worth CVB* • David DuBois; Pres./CEO; 111 W. 4th St., Ste. 200; 76102; Tarrant; P 670,000; (817) 336-8791; (800) 433-5747; Fax (817) 336-3282; www.fortworth.com

Fredericksburg • *Fredericksburg CVB* • Ernest Loeffler; Dir.; 302 E. Austin St.; 78624; Gillespie; P 10,432; (830) 997-6523; (888) 997-3600; Fax (830) 997-8588; visitorinfo@fbgtx.org; www.fredtexlodging.com.

Galveston • *Galveston Island Visitors Center* • Stacy Gilbert; Dir.; 2328 Broadway; 77550; Galveston; P 65,000; (409) 763-4311; (888) GALISLE; Fax (409) 744-7873; www.galveston.com

Garland • *Garland CVB* • Lucia Arrant; Mgr.; P.O. Box 469002; 75046; Dallas; P 220,000; (972) 205-2749; (888) 879-0264; Fax (972) 205-3634; larrant@ci.garland.tx.us; www.ci.garland.tx.us

Georgetown • *Georgetown CVB* • Cari Miller; Tourism Mgr.; 101 W. 7th St.; P.O. Box 409; 78627; Williamson; P 36,000; (512) 930-3545; (800) 436-8696; Fax (512) 930-3697; cvb@georgetowntx.org; www.visitgeorgetown.com

Granbury • *Granbury CVB* • Charlie McIlvain CTP; Dir.; 116 W. Bridge; 76048; Hood; P 7,500; (817) 573-5548; (800) 950-2212; Fax (817) 573-5789; cmcilvain@granburytx.com; www.granburytx.com

Grand Prairie • *City of Grand Prairie* • Randy Sisson; Tourism Mgr.; 2170 N. Belt Line Rd.; 75050; Dallas; P 160,641; (972) 263-9588; (800) 288-8386; Fax (972) 642-4350; rsisson@gptx.org; www.gptexas.com

Grapevine • *Grapevine CVB* • Paul W. McCallum; Exec. Dir.; One Liberty Park Plz.; 76051; Tarrant; P 49,600; (817) 410-3185; (800) 457-6338; Fax (817) 410-3038; pmccallum@grapevinetexasusa.com; www.grapevinetexasusa.com

Houston • *Greater Houston CVB* • Ken Middleton; V.P. of Sales; 901 Bagby, Ste. 100; 77002; Harris; P 5,000,000; (713) 437-5200; (800) 4-HOUSTON; Fax (713) 227-6336; www.visithoustontexas.com

Huntsville • *Sam Houston Statue & Huntsville Visitor Bur.* • Kimm Thomas; Mgr.; 7600 Hwy. 75 S.; P.O. Box 1230; 77342; Walker; P 66,000; (936) 291-9726; (800) 289-0389; Fax (936) 291-6636; kthomas@huntsvilletx.gov; www.huntsvilletexas.com

Irving • *Irving CVB* • Maura Gast; CEO; 222 W. Las Colinas Blvd., Ste. 1550; 75039; Dallas; P 200,000; (972) 252-7476; (800) 2-IRVING; Fax (972) 257-3153; info@irvingtexas.com; www.irvingtexas.com

Kemah • *Kemah Visitors Center* • Peggy Taylor; Dir. of Mktg.; 604 Bradford; 77565; Galveston; P 3,000; (281) 334-3181; visitkemah@kemah-tx.com; www.kemah-tx.gov

Kerrville • *Kerrville CVB* • Sudie Burditt; Exec. Dir.; 2108 Sidney Baker; 78028; Kerr; P 24,000; (830) 792-3535; Fax (830) 792-3230; kerrcvb@ktc.com; www.kerrvilletexascvb.com

Killeen • *Killeen CVB* • Connie Kuehl; Dir.; 3601 South W.S. Young Dr.; P.O. Box 1329; 76540; Bell; P 120,000; (254) 501-3888; Fax (254) 554-3219; info@killeen-cvb.com; www.killeen-cvb.com

Kingsville • *Kingsville CVB* • Carol Ann Anderson; Exec. Dir.; 1501 N. Hwy. 77; 78363; Kleberg; P 25,575; (361) 592-8516; (800) 333-5032; Fax (361) 592-3227; cvb@kingsvilletexas.com; www.kingsvilletexas.com

Laredo • *Laredo CVB* • Blasita Lopez; Dir.; 501 San Agustin Ave.; 78040; Webb; P 200,000; (956) 795-2200; (800) 361-3360; Fax (956) 795-2185; lcvb@ci.laredo.tx.us; www.visitlaredo.com

Longview • *Longview CVB* • Paul R. Anderson; Sr. V.P.; 410 N. Center St.; 75601; Gregg & Harrison; P 78,000; (903) 753-3281; Fax (903) 758-4791; lcvb@longviewtx.com; www.visitlongviewtexas.com

Lubbock • *Lubbock CVB* • Wells Fargo Center; 1500 Broadway, 6th Flr.; 79401; Lubbock; P 210,000; (806) 747-5232; (800) 692-4035; Fax (806) 747-1419; abie@visitlubbock.org; www.visitlubbock.org

Lufkin • *Lufkin CVB* • Tara Watson-Watkins; Exec. Dir.; P.O. Box 190; 75902; Angelina; P 35,000; (936) 633-0349; (936) 633-0359; Fax (936) 634-8726; twatkins@cityoflufkin.com; www.visitlufkin.com

Marshall • *Marshall Conv. & Visitor Bur.* • John Arend; Brand Mgr.; 213 W. Austin St.; P.O. Box 1437; 75671; Harrison; P 65,000; (903) 935-7868; Fax (903) 935-9982; cvb@visitmarshalltexas.org; www.visitmarshalltexas.org

McAllen • *McAllen CVB* • Steve Ahlenius; Pres./CEO; 1200 Ash Ave.; P.O. Box 790; 78505; Hidalgo; P 120,000; (956) 682-2871; (877) MCALLEN; Fax (956) 687-2917; steve@mcallenchamber.com; www.mcallenchamber.com

McKinney • *McKinney CVB* • Diann Bayes; Exec. Dir.; 1575 Heritage Dr., Ste. 100; 75069; Collin; P 120,000; (214) 544-1407; (888) 649-8499; Fax (972) 542-6341; info@visitmckinney.com; www.visitmckinney.com

Midland • *Midland CVB* • Gaylia Olivas; Dir.; 109 N. Main; 79701; Midland; P 102,000; (432) 683-3381; (800) 624-6435; Fax (432) 686-3556; info@visitmidlandtexas.com; www.visitmidlandtexas.com

Mineola • *Mineola CVB* • Lynda Rauscher; Comm. Dev. Dir.; 114 N. Pacific; P.O. Box 179; 75773; Wood; P 5,611; (903) 569-6983; (800) MINEOLA; Fax (903) 569-0856; ced@mineola.com; www.mineola.com

Mineral Wells • *Mineral Wells Area C/C* • Beth Watson; Exec. Dir.; 511 E. Hubbard; P.O. Box 1408; 76068; Palo Pinto; P 29,000; M 413; (940) 325-2557; (800) 252-MWTX; Fax (940) 328-0850; info@mineralwellstx.com; www.mineralwellstx.com

Nacogdoches • *Nacogdoches CVB* • Melissa Sanford; Exec. Dir.; 200 E. Main; 75961; Nacogdoches; P 30,000; (936) 564-7351; (888) 653-3788; Fax (936) 462-7688; info@visitnacogdoches.org; www.visitnacogdoches.org

New Braunfels • *New Braunfels CVB* • Judy Young; Dir.; 390 S. Seguin Ave.; P.O. Box 311417; 78131; Comal; P 47,000; (830) 625-2385; (800) 572-2626; Fax (830) 625-7918; nbcc@nbcham.org; www.nbcham.org

Odessa • *Odessa CVB* • Linda Sweatt; Dir.; 700 N. Grant, Ste. 200; 79761; Ector; P 96,948; (432) 333-7871; (800) 780-4678; Fax (432) 333-7858; info@odessacvb.com; www.odessacvb.com

Orange • *Orange CVB* • Darline Zavada; Admin.; 803 W. Green Ave.; P.O. Box 520; 77631; Orange; P 18,643; (409) 883-1011; (800) 528-4906; Fax (409) 988-7321; cvb@orangetx.org; www.orangetexas.org

Palestine • *Palestine CVB* • 825 Spring St.; 75801; Anderson; P 19,000; (903) 723-3014; (800) 659-3484; Fax (903) 729-6067; palestinecvb@flash.net; www.visitpalestine.com

Paris • *Paris Visitor & Conv. Cncl.* • Becky Semple; Tourism Dir.; 8 W. Plaza; 75460; Lamar; P 50,000; (903) 784-2501; (800) 727-4789; Fax (903) 784-2503; visitus@paristexas.com; www.paristexas.com

Plano • *Plano CVB* • Mark Thompson; Dir.; P.O. Box 860358; 75086; Collin; P 250,000; (972) 941-5840; (800) 81-PLANO; Fax (972) 424-0002; www.planocvb.com

Port Aransas • *Port Aransas CVB* • Ann B. Vaughan; Exec. Dir.; 403 W. Cotter; 78373; Nueces; P 3,370; (361) 749-5919; (800) 452-6278; Fax (361) 749-4672; info@portaransas.org; www.portaransas.org

Port Arthur • *Port Arthur CVB* • Tammy Kotzur; Dir.; 3401 Cultural Center Dr.; 77642; Jefferson; P 58,000; (409) 985-7822; (800) 235-7822; Fax (409) 985-5584; tjhenderson@portarthurtexas.com; www.visitportarthurtx.com

Richardson • *Richardson Conv. & Visitors Bur.* • Geoff Wright; Dir.; 411 W. Arapaho Rd., Ste. 105; 75080; Dallas; P 98,000; (972) 744-4034; (972) 744-4036; Fax (972) 744-5834; cvb@cor.gov; www.richardsontexas.org

San Angelo • *San Angelo CVB* • Pamela Miller; V.P. of CVB; 418 W. Avenue B; 76903; Tom Green; P 90,000; (325) 655-4136; Fax (325) 658-1110; chamber@sanangelo.org; www.visitsanangelo.org

San Antonio • *San Antonio CVB* • Scott White; Exec. Dir.; 203 S. St. Mary's, Ste. 200; 78205; Bexar; P 1,800,000; (210) 207-6700; (800) 447-3372; Fax (210) 207-6768; visitsanantonio.com

San Marcos • *San Marcos CVB* • Rebecca Ybarra; Exec. Dir.; 617 IH 35 N.; 78666; Hays; P 53,000; (512) 393-5930; cvb@sanmarcostexas.com; www.toursanmarcos.com

Schulenburg • *Tourist Info. Center* • Mike Stroup; Exec. Dir.; 618 N. Main; P.O. Box 65; 78956; Fayette; P 2,799; (979) 743-4514; (866) 504-5294; Fax (979) 743-9155; info@schulenburgchamber.org; www.schulenburgchamber.org

Seguin • *Seguin Area CVB* • Sherry Nefford; Dir.; P.O. Box 710; 78156; Guadalupe; P 25,090; (830) 379-6382; (800) 580-7322; Fax (830) 379-6971; cvb@seguinchamber.com; www.visitseguin.com

Sherman • *Sherman Dept. of Tourism* • April Patterson; Dir.; 405 N. Rusk, 2nd Flr.; P.O. Box 2312; 75091; Grayson; P 40,000; (903) 957-0310; (888) 893-1188; Fax (903) 870-4045; info@shermantx.org; www.shermantx.org

South Padre Island • *South Padre Island CVB* • Dan Quandt; Exec. Dir.; 600 Padre Blvd.; 78597; Cameron; P 2,800; (956) 761-6433; (800) SOPADRE; Fax (956) 761-9462; www.sopadre.com

Sweetwater • *Sweetwater CVB* • Jacque McCoy; Exec. Dir.; 810 E. Broadway; P.O. Box 1148; 79556; Nolan; P 11,500; (325) 235-5488; (800) 658-6757; Fax (325) 235-1026; chamber@sweetwatertexas.org; www.sweetwatertexas.org

Terrell • *Terrell C/C & CVB* • Raylan Smith; Dir. of Tourism; 1314 W. Moore Ave.; 75160; Kaufman; P 19,000; (972) 563-5703; (877) TERRELL; Fax (972) 563-2363; tourism@terrelltexas.com; www.terrelltexas.com

Tyler • *Tyler CVB* • Henry M. Bell III; COO; 315 N. Broadway; P.O. Box 390; 75710; Smith; P 102,000; (903) 592-1661; Fax (903) 592-1268; hbell@tylertexas.com; www.tylertexas.com

Uvalde • *Uvalde CVB* • Joanne Nelson; Exec. Dir.; 300 E. Main St.; 78801; Uvalde; P 17,817; (830) 278-4115; Fax (830) 278-3994; tourism@visituvalde.com; www.visituvalde.com

Van Horn • *Van Horn CVB* • Brenda Hinojos; Dir.; 1801 W. Broadway; P.O. Box 488; 79855; Culberson; P 2,400; (432) 283-2682; (866) 424-6939; Fax (432) 283-1413; info@vanhorntexas.org; www.vanhorntexas.org

Victoria • *Victoria CVB* • Bridgette Bise; Exec. Dir.; 3404 N. Ben Wilson; P.O. Box 2488; 77902; Victoria; P 86,916; (361) 582-4285; (800) 926-5774; Fax (361) 573-5911; info@visitvictoriatexasinfo.com; www.visitvictoriatexas.com

Waco • *Waco CVB* • Elizabeth Taylor; Exec. Dir.; 100 Washington Ave.; P.O. Box 2570; 76702; McLennan; P 222,439; (254) 750-5810; (800) 321-9226; Fax (254) 750-5801; lizt@ci.waco.tx.us; www.wacocvb.com

Utah

Cedar City • *Cedar City/Brian Head Tourism & Conv. Bur.* • Maria Twitchell; Exec. Dir.; 581 N. Main; 84721; Iron; P 27,784; (435) 586-5124; (800) 354-4849; Fax (435) 586-4022; tourism@netutah.com; www.scenicsouthernutah.com

Layton • *Davis Area CVB* • Barbara Riddle; Pres./CEO; 748 W. Heritage Park Blvd., Ste. 201; 84041; Davis; P 265,000; (801) 774-8200; (888) 777-9771; Fax (801) 774-8335; info@davisareacvb.com; www.davis.travel

Logan • *Cache Valley Visitors Bur.* • Julie Hollist; Dir.; 199 N. Main St.; 84321; Cache; P 47,023; (435) 755-1890; (800) 882-4433; Fax (435) 755-1993; cvinfo@tourcachevalley.com; www.tourcachevalley.com

Moab • *Moab Area Travel Cncl.* • Marian DeLay; Exec. Dir.; P.O. Box 550; 84532; Grand; P 9,000; (435) 259-8825; (800) 635-6622; Fax (435) 259-1376; mdelay@discovermoab.com; www.discovermoab.com

Monticello • *Utah's Canyon Country Visitors Bur.* • Charlie DeLorme; Dir.; P.O. Box 490; 84535; San Juan; P 14,200; (435) 587-3235; (800) 574-4386; Fax (435) 587-2425; www.utahscanyoncountry.com

Nephi • *Juab Travel Cncl.* • Jens Mickelson; Pres.; 4 S. Main St.; P.O. Box 71; 84648; Juab; P 8,000; (435) 623-5203; (800) 748-4361; Fax (435) 623-4609; info@juabtravel.com; www.juabtravel.com

Ogden • *Ogden Weber CVB* • Sara Toliver; Pres.; 2501 Wall Ave., Ste. 201; 84401; Weber; P 86,000; (801) 627-8288; (866) 867-8824; Fax (801) 399-0783; info@ogdencvb.org; www.ogden.travel

Panguitch • *Garfield County Ofc. of Tourism* • K. Bruce Fullmer; Exec. Dir.; P.O. Box 200; 84759; Garfield; P 4,735; (435) 676-1160; (800) 444-6689; Fax (435) 676-8239; travgar@color-country.net; www.brycecanyoncountry.com

Park City • *Park City CVB* • Bill Malone; Exec. Dir.; 1910 Prospector Ave.; P.O. Box 1630; 84060; Summit & Wasatch; P 24,500; (435) 649-6100; (800) 453-1360; Fax (435) 649-4132; info@parkcityinfo.com; www.parkcityinfo.com

Saint George • *Saint George Area CVB* • Pam Hilton; Mktg. Dir.; 1835 Convention Center Dr.; Dixie Center; 84790; Washington; P 125,000; (435) 634-5747; (800) 869-6635; Fax (435) 628-1619; info@utahstgeorge.com; www.utahstgeorge.com

Virgin Islands

Saint Croix • *Virgin Islands Dept. of Tourism* • Beverly Nicholson-Doty; Commissioner; P.O. Box 224538; Christiansted; 00822; P 60,000; (340) 773-0495; Fax (340) 773-5074; www.usvitourism.vi

Saint Croix • *Virgin Islands Dept. of Tourism* • Beverly Nicholson-Doty; Commissioner; 200 Strand St., Custom House; Frederiksted; 00840; P 60,000; (340) 772-0357; Fax (340) 773-5074; www.usvitourism.vi

Saint Thomas • *Virgin Islands Dept. of Tourism* • Beverly Nicholson-Doty; Commissioner; P.O. Box 6400; Charlotte Amalie; 00804; P 60,000; (340) 774-8784; (800) 372-8784; Fax (340) 774-4390; www.usvitourism.vi

Virginia

Abingdon • *Abingdon CVB* • Myra Cook; Dir. of Tourism, 335 Cummings St.; 24210; Washington; P 7,700; (276) 676-2282; (800) 435-3440; Fax (276) 676-3076; acvb@abingdon.com; www.abingdon.com

Alexandria • *Alexandria Conv. & Visitors Assn.* • Stephanie Brown; Pres./CEO; 421 King St., Ste. 300; 22314; Alexandria City; P 135,000; (703) 838-4200; (800) 388-9119; Fax (703) 838-4683; acva@funside.com; www.funside.com

Arlington • *Arlington Conv. & Visitors Svcs.* • Emily Cassell; Mktg. Dir.; 1100 N. Glebe Rd., Ste. 1500; 22201; Arlington; P 189,453; (703) 228-0888; (800) 296-7996; Fax (703) 228-0806; ecassell@arlingtonva.us; www.stayarlington.com

Ashland • *Ashland/Hanover Visitors Center* • Donna Baxter; Mgr.; 112 N. Railroad Ave; 23005; Hanover; P 86,320; (804) 752-6766; (800) 897-1479; Fax (804) 752-2380; donnabahvc1@netscape.com; www.town.ashland.va.us

Bedford • *Bedford Welcome Center* • Sergei Troubetzkoy CTP; 816 Burks Hill Rd.; 24523; Bedford City; P 70,000; (540) 587-5681; Fax (540) 587-5983; sergei@visitbedford.com; www.visitbedford.com

Blacksburg • *Blacksburg/Christiansburg Visitors Center* • Shane Adams; Pres./CEO; 103 Professional Park Dr.; 24060; Montgomery; P 100,000; (540) 552-2636; (877) FOR-GUIDE; Fax (540) 552-2639; info@virginianaturally.com; www.virginianaturally.com

Bluefield • *Tazewell County Visitor Center* • June Brown; Mgr.; 200 Sanders Ln.; 24605; Tazewell; P 45,000; (276) 322-1345; (800) 588-9401; Fax (276) 322-3908; tcvc@4seasonswireless.net; www.tazewellcounty.org

Bristol • *Bristol CVB* • 20 Volunteer Pkwy.; P.O. Box 519; 24203; Bristol; P 43,000; (423) 989-4850; Fax (423) 989-4867; tourism@bristolchamber.org; www.bristolchamber.org

Charlottesville • *Charlottesville-Albemarle CVB* • Kurt Burkhart; Dir.; 610 E. Main St.; P.O. Box 178; 22902; Charlottesville City; P 130,000; (434) 293-6789; (877) 386-1103; Fax (434) 295-2176; visitorscenter@charlottesville.org; www.pursuecharlottesville.com

Chesapeake • *Chesapeake Conventions & Tourism* • Kimberly Murden; Dir.; 3815 Bainbridge Blvd.; 23324; Chesapeake City; (757) 502-4898; (888) 889-5551; Fax (757) 502-4883; www.visitchesapeake.com

Fredericksburg • *Fredericksburg Ofc. of Tourism & Eco. Dev.* • Karen Hedelt; Dir.; 706 Caroline St.; 22401; Spotsylvania; P 21,000; (540) 372-1216; (800) 260-3646; Fax (540) 372-6587; khedelt@fredericksburgva.gov; www.visitfred.com

Fredericksburg • *Spotsylvania County Dept. of Tourism* • 4704 Southpoint Pkwy.; 22407; Spotsylvania; P 106,305; (540) 507-7210; (877) 515-6197; Fax (540) 507-7207; tourism@spotsylvania.va.us; www.spotsylvania.va.us

Gloucester • *Gloucester Parks, Rec. & Tourism* • Jenny Graziano; Tourism Coord.; 6467 Main St.; 23061; Gloucester; P 35,000; (804) 693-0014; (804) 758-4917; jgrazian@gloucesterva.info; www.gloucesterva.info

Hampton • *Hampton CVB* • Sallie Grant-DiVenuti; Exec. Dir.; 1919 Commerce Dr., Ste. 290; 23666; Hampton City; P 138,000; (757) 722-1222; (800) 487-8778; Fax (757) 896-4600; sallie@hamptoncvb.com; www.hamptoncvb.com

Harrisonburg • *Harrisonburg Tourism & Visitor Svcs.* • Brenda Black; Tourism Mgr.; 212 S. Main St.; 22801; Harrisonburg City; P 120,000; M (540) 432-8935; Fax (540) 437-0631; tourism@ci.harrisonburg.va.us; www.harrisonburgtourism.com

Hopewell • *City of Hopewell, Dept. of Tourism* • LuAnn Fortenherry; Dir.; 4100 Oaklawn Blvd.; 23860; Hopewell City; P 23,000; (804) 541-2461; (800) 863-8687; Fax (804) 541-2459; info@hopewellva.gov; www.hopewellva.gov

Leesburg • *Loudon Conv. & Vistors Assn.* • Cheryl Kilday; Pres.; 112 South St. S.E., Ste. G; 20175; Loudon; P 268,817; (703) 771-2170; (800) 752-6118; Fax (703) 771-4973; vchost@visitloudon.org; www.visitloudon.org

Lexington • *Lexington & the Rockbridge Visitor Center* • Jean Clark; Dir.; 106 E. Washington St.; 24450; Lexington City; P 34,000; (540) 463-3777; (877) 453-9822; Fax (540) 463-1105; lexingtontourismdirector@rockbridge.net; www.lexingtonvirginia.com

Lorton • *Fairfax County Visitors Center* • Sue Porter; Dir. of Visitor Svcs.; 8180-A Silverbrook Rd.; 22079; Fairfax; P 1,000,000; (703) 550-2450; (800) 732-4732; Fax (703) 550-9418; fxva@fxva.com; www.fxva.com

Lovingston • *Nelson County Eco. Dev. & Tourism* • Maureen Corum; Dir.; 8519 Thomas Nelson Hwy.; P.O. Box 636; 22949; Nelson; P 15,000; (434) 263-7015; (800) 282-8223; Fax (434) 263-6823; info@nelsoncounty.org; www.nelsoncounty.com

Lynchburg • *Lynchburg Visitor Info. Center* • Alison Chadbourne; Mgr.; 216 12th St.; 24504; Lynchburg City; P 243,000; (434) 847-1811; (800) 732-5821; Fax (434) 455-4320; tourism@lynchburgchamber.org; www.discoverlynchburg.org.

Manassas • *Prince William County/Manassas CVB* • 8609 Sudley Rd., Ste. 105; 20110; Prince William; P 340,000; (703) 396-7130; (800) 432-1792; Fax (703) 396-7160; info@visitpwc.com; www.visitpwc.com

McLean • *Fairfax County Conv. & Visitors Corp.* • 7927 Jones Branch Dr., South Wing 100; 22102; Fairfax; P 1,000,000; (703) 790-0643; Fax (703) 790-5097; fxva@fxva.com; www.fxva.com

Newport News • *Newport News Visitor Center* • Janie Tross; Mgr.; 13560 Jefferson Ave.; 23603; Newport News City; P 185,226; (757) 886-7777; (888) 493-7386; Fax (757) 886-7920; jtross@nngov.com; www.newport-news.org; tourism@nngov.com

Norfolk · *Norfolk CVB* · Donna Allen; V.P. Sales; 232 E. Main St.; 23510; Norfolk City; P 245,000; (757) 664-6620; (800) 368-3097; Fax (757) 622-3663; www.norfolkcvb.com

Northern Neck · *see Warsaw–Northern Neck Tourism Comm.*

Orange · *Orange County Dept. of Tourism* · Joe Ward; Dir.; 122 E. Main St.; P.O. Box 133; 22960; Orange; P 29,000; (540) 672-1653; (877) 222-8072; Fax (540) 672-1746; tourorangeco@firstva.com; www.visitocva.com

Petersburg · *Petersburg Vistors Center* · Frances Lilly; Supervisor; 19 Bollingbrook St.; 23803; Petersburg City; P 36,000; (804) 733-2400; (800) 368-3595; Fax (804) 861-0883; petgtourism@earthlink.net; www.petersburg-va.org

Portsmouth · *Portsmouth Visitor Center* · Caroline Penney; Visitor Svcs. Mgr.; 6 Crawford Pkwy.; 23704; Portsmouth City; P 100,000; (757) 393-5111; (800) 767-8782; penneyc@portsmouthva.gov; www.visitportsva.com

Richmond · *Richmond Metro CVB* · Jack Berry; Pres.; 401 N. 3rd St.; 23219; Richmond City; P 1,000,000; (804) 782-2777; (800) 370-9004; Fax (804) 780-2577; www.visit.richmond.com

Roanoke · *Roanoke Valley CVB* · David Kjolhede; Exec. Dir.; 101 Shenandoah Ave. N.E.; 24016; Roanoke City; P 288,309; M 180; (540) 342-6025; (800) 635-5535; Fax (540) 342-7119; info@visitroanokeva.com; www.visitroanokeva.com

Smithfield · *Smithfield & Isle of Wight CVB* · Judy Winslow; Dir.; 335 Main St.; 23431; Isle of Wight; P 40,000; (757) 357-5182; (800) 365-9339; Fax (757) 365-4360; kchapman@isleofwightus.net; www.smithfield-virginia.com

South Boston · *Halifax County Tourism Dept.* · Linda Sheppard; Dir.; 700 Bruce St.; 24592; Halifax; P 38,000; (434) 572-2543; Fax (434) 517-0021; info@gohalifaxva.com; www.gohalifaxva.com

Staunton · *Staunton CVB* · Sheryl Wagner; Dir. of Tourism; 116 W. Beverly St., 3rd Flr.; P.O. Box 58; 24402; Staunton City; P 24,000; (540) 332-3865; (800) 342-7982; Fax (540) 851-4005; wagnerss@ci.staunton.va.us; www.visitstaunton.com

Suffolk · *Suffolk Div. of Tourism* · Lynette White; Dir. of Tourism; 321 N. Main St.; 23434; Suffolk City; P 85,000; (757) 923-3880; (866) 733-7835; Fax (757) 923-3882; VisitSuffolk@city.suffolk.va.us.; www.suffolk-fun.com

Virginia Beach · *Virginia Beach CVB* · James Ricketts; Dir.; 2101 Parks Ave., Ste. 500; 23451; Virginia Beach City; P 450,000; (757) 385-4700; (800) 700-7702; Fax (757) 437-4747; vbgov@vbgov.com; www.vbfun.com

Warrenton · *Warrenton-Fauquier County Visitor Center* · Becky Crouch; Mgr.; 33 N. Calhoun St.; 20186; Fauquier; P 68,000; (540) 341-0988; (800) 820-1021; visitorcenter@warrentonva.gov; www.visitfauquier.com

Warsaw · *Northern Neck Tourism Comm.* · Lisa Hull; Tourism Dir.; P.O. Box 1707; 22572; Richmond; P 30,000; M 160; (804) 333-1919; (800) 393-6180; Fax (804) 333-5274; nntc@northernneck.org; www.northernneck.org

Warsaw · *Richmond County Museum & Visitors Center* · 5874 Richmond Rd.; P.O. Box 884; 22572; Richmond; P 8,000; (804) 333-3607; Fax (804) 333-3408

Winchester · *Winchester-Frederick Co. CVB* · Sally Coates; Exec. Dir.; 1400 S. Pleasant Valley Rd.; 22601; Frederick; P 100,000; (540) 542-1326; (877) 871-1326; Fax (540) 450-0099; info@visitwinchesterva.com; www.visitwinchesterva.com

Woodstock · *Shenandoah County Tourism Cncl.* · Susie Hill; Dir. of Tourism; 600 N. Main St., Ste. 101; 22664; Shenandoah; P 39,000; (540) 459-6220; (888) 367-3960; Fax (540) 459-6228; tourism@shenandoahcountyva.us; www.shenandoahtravel.org

Wytheville · *Blue Ridge Travel Assn. of VA* · P.O. Box 1395; 24382; Wythe; M 100; (800) 446-9670; info@virginiablueridge.org; www.virginiablueridge.org

Wytheville · *Reg. Visitors Center* · Rosa Lee Jude; Dir.; 975 Tazewell St.; 24382; Wythe; P 28,500; (276) 223-3441; (877) 347-8303; Fax (276) 223-3443; cvb@wytheville.org; www.virginiablueridge.org

Wytheville · *Wytheville CVB* · Rosa Jude; Dir. of Tourism; 975 Tazewell St.; P.O. Box 533; 24382; Wythe; P 28,500; (276) 223-3355; (877) 347-8307; Fax (276) 223-3446; cvb@wytheville.org; www.visitwytheville.com.

Yorktown · *York County Tourism Dev.* · Kristi Olsen; Tourism Dev. Mgr.; P.O. Box 532; 23690; York; (757) 890-3500; (757) 890-3300; Fax (757) 890-3509; www.yorkcounty.gov/tourism

Washington

Clarkston · *Hells Canyon Visitor Bur.* · Michelle Peters; Pres./CEO; 504 Bridge St.; 99403; Asotin; P 60,000; (509) 758-7489; (877) 774-7248; Fax (509) 751-8767; info@hellscanyonvisitor.com; www.hellscanyonvisitor.com

Kelso · *see Longview*

Kennewick · *Tri-Cities VCB* · Kris Watkins; Pres./CEO; 7130 W. Grandridge Blvd., Ste. B; 99336; Benton; P 242,000; M 644; (509) 735-8486; (800) 254-5824; Fax (509) 783-9005; info@VisitTri-Cities.com; www.VisitTri-Cities.com

Long Beach · *Long Beach Peninsula VB* · Una Boyle; Exec. Dir.; P.O. Box 562; 98631; Pacific; P 30,000; M 397; (360) 642-2400; (800) 451-2542; Fax (360) 642-3900; una@funbeach.com; www.funbeach.com

Longview · *Cowlitz Reg. Conf. Center* · Mike Moss; Dir.; 1900 7th Ave.; 98632; Cowlitz; P 99,905; (360) 577-3121; Fax (360) 577-6254; www.thecenterofthenorthwest.com

Packwood · *Destination Packwood Assoc.* · Edie Aydelott; Ofc. Admin.; 12990 U.S. Hwy. 12; P.O. Box 64; 98361; Lewis; P 1,500; M 100; (360) 494-2223; Fax (360) 494-2216; dpa@lewiscounty.com; www.destinationpackwood.com

Port Angeles · *Olympic Peninsula Visitors Bur.* · Diane Schostak; Exec. Dir.; 338 W. 1st St., Ste. 104; P.O. Box 670; 98362; Clallam; P 70,400; (360) 452-8552; (800) 942-4042; info@olympicpeninsula.org; www.olympicpeninsula.org

Seattle · *Seattle CVB* · Tom Norwalk; Pres./CEO; 1 Convention Place; 701 Pike St., Ste. 800; 98101; King; P 563,000; (206) 461-5800; (866) 732-2695; Fax (206) 461-5855; visitorinfo@visitseattle.org; www.visitseattle.org

Seattle · *Seattle Southside Visitor Info.* · Katherine Kertzman; Program Dir.; 3100 S. 176th St.; 98188; King; P 157,830; (206) 575-2489; (877) 885-9452; Fax (206) 575-2529; info@seattlesouthside.com; www.seattlesouthside.com

Spokane · *Spokane Reg. CVB* · 801 W. Riverside, Ste. 301; 99201; Spokane; P 497,000; M 650; (509) 624-1341; (800) 662-0084; Fax (509) 623-1297; conventions@visitspokane.com; www.visitspokane.com

Tacoma · *Tacoma Reg. CVB* · Tammy Blount; Pres./CEO; 1119 Pacific Ave., Ste. 500; P.O. Box 1754; 98401; Pierce; P 713,400; M 300; (253) 627-2836; (800) 272-2662; Fax (253) 627-8783; info@traveltacoma.com; www.traveltacoma.com

Vancouver • *Vancouver USA Reg. Tourism Ofc.* • Jennifer Kirby; Mktg. & Comm. Mgr.; 101 E. 8th St., Ste. 240; 98660; Clark; P 403,000; (360) 750-1553; (877) 600-0800; Fax (360) 750-1933; info@visitvancouverusa.com; www.visitvancouverusa.com

Wenatchee • *Wenatchee Valley Visitor Bur.* • Roger Clute; Exec. Dir.; 5 S. Wenatchee Ave., Ste. 100; 98801; Chelan; P 100,000; (509) 663-3723; (800) 572-7753; Fax (509) 663-3983; info@wenatcheevalley.org; www.wenatcheevalley.org

West Virginia

Beckley • *Southern West Virginia CVB* • Doug Maddy; Exec. Dir./CEO; 1406 Harper Rd.; 25801; Raleigh; P 225,000; M 400; (304) 252-2244; (800) VISIT-WV; Fax (304) 252-2252; travel@visitwv.com; www.visitwv.com

Bluefield • *Mercer County CVB* • Beverly Wellman; Exec. Dir.; 704 Bland St.; P.O. Box 4088; 24701; Tazewell; P 64,980; (304) 325-8438; (800) 221-3206; Fax (304) 324-8483; info@mccvb.com; www.mccvb.com

Bridgeport • *Greater Bridgeport CVB* • Cynthia Hunter; Exec. Dir.; 164 W. Main St.; 26330; Harrison; P 8,000; (304) 842-7272; (800) 368-4324; Fax (304) 842-1941; info@greater-bridgeport.com; www.greater-bridgeport.com

Buckhannon • *Buckhannon CVB* • 22 N. Locust St., Ste. 37; 26201; Upshur; P 23,000; (304) 472-4100; Fax (304) 472-0432; buckhannoncvb2009@gmail.com; www.buckhannoncvb.org

Charleston • *Charleston CVB* • Patricia Bradley-Pitrolo; Pres./CEO; 200 Civic Center Dr.; 25301; Kanawha; P 60,000; (304) 344-5075; (800) 733-5469; Fax (304) 344-1241; info@charlestonwv.com; www.charlestonwv.com

Elkins • *West Virginia Mountain Highlands Visitors Bur.* • Bonnie Branciaroli; Exec. Dir.; P.O. Box 1456; 26241; Randolph; P 10,000; M 130; (304) 636-8400; Fax (304) 637-9900; info@mountainhighlands.com; www.mountainhighlands.com

Hinton • *Summers County CVB* • Londa Justin; Exec. Dir.; 206 Temple St.; 25951; Summers; P 15,000; (304) 466-5420

Huntington • *Cabell-Huntington CVB* • Tyson Compton; Exec. Dir.; P.O. Box 347; 25701; Cabell; P 51,000; M 150; (304) 525-7333; (800) 635-6329; Fax (304) 525-7345; info@wvvisit.org; www.wvvisit.org

Hurricane • *Putnam County CVB* • Linda Bush; Exec. Dir.; #1 Valley Park Dr.; 25526; Putnam; P 53,000; (304) 562-0518; Fax (304) 562-5375; tourism@putnamcounty.org; www.putnamcounty.org/tourism/

Keyser • *Mineral County CVB* • Anne Palmer; Exec. Dir.; One Grand Central Park; 26726; Mineral; P 27,234; (304) 788-2513; Fax (304) 788-3887; www.mineralchamber.com

Lewisburg • *Greenbrier County CVB* • Kara Dense; Exec. Dir.; 540 N. Jefferson St.; Box 17, Ste. N; 24901; Greenbrier; P 34,693; (304) 645-1000; (800) 833-2068; Fax (304) 647-3001; info@greenbrierwv.com; www.greenbrierwv.com

Morgantown • *Greater Morgantown CVB* • Peggy Myers-Smith; Exec. Dir.; 68 Donley St.; 26501; Monongalia; P 75,000; (304) 292-5081; (800) 458-7373; Fax (304) 291-1354; info@tourmorgantown.com; www.tourmorgantown.com

Oak Hill • *New River Gorge CVB* • Sharon Cruikshank; Exec. Dir.; 310 Oyler Ave.; 25901; Fayette; P 48,655; (304) 465-5617; (800) 927-0263; Fax (304) 465-5618; fayette@wvdsl.net; www.newrivergorgecvb.com

Parkersburg • *Greater Parkersburg CVB* • Steven W. Nicely; Pres.; 350 7th St.; 26101; Wood; P 100,000; M 190; (304) 428-1130; (800) 752-4982; Fax (304) 428-8117; info@parkersburgcvb.org; www.greaterparkersburg.com

South Charleston • *South Charleston CVB* • Bob T. Anderson Sr.; Exec. Dir.; 311 D St.; P.O. Box 8599; 25303; Kanawha; P 16,000; (304) 746-5552; (800) 238-9488; Fax (304) 746-2970; sochascvb@yahoo.com; www.southcharlestonwv.org

Summersville • *Summersville CVB* • Keith Spangler; Exec. Dir.; 2 Armory Way; P.O. Box 231; 26651; Nicholas; P 2,500; (304) 872-3722; Fax (304) 872-0901; keith@summersvillecvb.com; www.summersvillecvb.com

Weston • *Lewis County CVB* • Chris Richards; Dir.; 499 U.S. Hwy. 33 E., Ste. 102; 26452; Lewis; P 17,223; (304) 269-7328; (800) 296-7329; Fax (304) 269-3271; tour@stonewallcountry.com; www.stonewallcountry.com

Wheeling • *Wheeling CVB* • Frank O'Brien; Exec. Dir.; 1401 Main St.; 26003; Ohio; P 36,000; (304) 233-7709; (800) 828-3097; Fax (304) 233-1470; fobrien@wheelingcvb.com; www.wheelingcvb.com

White Hall • *CVB of Marion County* • Marianne Moran; Exec. Dir.; 2 Mountain Park Dr.; P.O. Box 58; 26554; Marion; P 57,000; M 107; (304) 368-1123; (800) 834-7365; Fax (304) 333-0155; cvb@marioncvb.com; www.marioncvb.com

Wisconsin

Appleton • *Fox Cities CVB* • Lynn R. Peters; Exec. Dir.; 3433 W. College Ave.; 54914; Calumet, Outagamie & Winnebago; P 227,708; (920) 734-3358; (800) 2DO-MORE; Fax (920) 734-1080; tourism@foxcities.org; www.foxcities.org

Beloit • *Beloit CVB* • Martha Mitchell; Exec. Dir.; 500 Public Ave.; 53511; Rock; P 37,000; (608) 365-4838; (800) 4-BELOIT; Fax (608) 365-6850; info@visitbeloit.com; www.visitbeloit.com

Brookfield • *Brookfield CVB* • Nancy Justman; Exec. Dir.; 17100 W. Bluemound Rd., Ste. 203; 53005; Waukesha; P 46,000; (262) 789-0220; (800) 388-1835; Fax (262) 789-0221; nancy@brookfieldcvb.com; www.visitbrookfield.com

Cedarburg • *Cedarburg Visitors Center* • Kristine Hage; Exec. Dir.; W61 N480 Washington Ave.; P.O. Box 104; 53012; Ozaukee; P 16,000; (262) 377-9620; (800) 237-2874; Fax (262) 377-6470; info@cedarburg.org; www.cedarburg.org

Door County • *see Sturgeon Bay*

Eau Claire • *Eau Claire Area CVB* • Linda John; Exec. Dir.; 4319 Jeffers Rd., Ste. 201; 54703; Eau Claire; P 63,214; M 400; (888) 523-3866; (715) 831-2345; Fax (715) 831-2340; betty@visiteauclaire.com; www.visiteauclaire.com

Fond du Lac • *Fond du Lac Area CVB* • 171 S. Pioneer Rd.; 54935; Fond du Lac; P 42,000; (920) 923-3010; (800) 937-9123; Fax (920) 929-6846; visitor@fdl.com; www.fdl.com

Green Bay • *Greater Green Bay CVB* • Brad Toll; Pres.; 1901 S. Oneida St.; P.O. Box 10596; 54307; Brown; P 256,908; (920) 494-9507; (888) 867-3342; Fax (920) 405-1271; visitorinfo@greenbay.com; www.greenbay.com

Hazelhurst • *Hazelhurst Info. Center* • Ted Cushing; Chrmn.; P.O. Box 67; 54531; Oneida; P 1,369; M 30; (715) 356-5800; info@hazelhurstwi.com; www.hazelhurstwi.com

Holmen • *see Onalaska*

Janesville · *Janesville Area CVB* · Christine Rebout; Exec. Dir.; 20 S. Main St., Ste. 17; 53545; Rock; P 60,000; (608) 757-3171; (800) 48-PARKS; Fax (608) 754-2115; jvlcvb@jvlnet.com; www.janesvillecvb.com

Kenosha · *Kenosha Area CVB* · Dennis DuChene; Pres.; 812 56th St.; 53140; Kenosha; P 150,000; (262) 654-7307; (800) 654-7309; Fax (262) 654-0882; www.kenoshacvb.com

La Crosse · *La Crosse Area CVB* · Dave Clements; Exec. Dir.; 410 Veterans Memorial Dr.; 54601; La Crosse; P 52,000; M 360; (608) 782-2366; (800) 658-9424; Fax (608) 782-4082; info@explore lacrosse.com; www.explorelacrosse.com

Ladysmith · *Rusk County Tourism* · Andy Albarado; Dir.; 205 W. 9th St. S.; 54848; Rusk; P 15,000; (715) 532-2642; (800) 535-RUSK; Fax (715) 532-2649; www.ruskcounty.org

Lake Geneva · *Lake Geneva CVB* · George F. Hennerley; Exec. V.P.; 201 Wrigley Dr.; 53147; Walworth; P 7,400; (262) 248-4416; Fax (262) 248-1000; lgcc@lakegenevawi.com; www.lakegenevawi.com

Madison · *Greater Madison CVB* · Deb Archer; Pres.; 615 E. Washington Ave.; 53703; Dane; P 220,000; M 550; (608) 255-2537; (800) 373-6376; Fax (608) 258-4950; gmcvb@visitmadison.com; www.visitmadison.com

Manitowoc · *Manitowoc Area Visitor & Conv. Bur.* · Kathleen Galas; Pres.; 4221 Calumet Ave.; P.O. Box 966; 54221; Manitowoc; P 35,000; M 150; (920) 686-3070; (800) 627-4896; Fax (920) 683-4876; visitmanitowoc@manitowoc.info; www.manitowoc.info

Marshfield · *Marshfield CVB* · Sharon Kirn; Exec. Dir.; 700 S. Central Ave.; P.O. Box 868; 54449; Marathon & Wood; P 20,000; (715) 384-4314; (800) 422-4541; Fax (715) 387-8925; sharon@ visitmarshfieldwi.com; www.visitmarshfieldwi.com

Mauston · *Juneau County VB/Castle Rock & Petenwell Lakes Assn.* · Barbara Baker; Exec. Dir.; 807 Division St.; 53948; Juneau; P 27,000; (608) 847-1904; Fax (608) 847-1904; juneauctourism@ yahoo.com; www.castlerockpetenwell.com

Menomonee Falls · *Menomonee Falls Visitor Center* · Suzanne Jeskewitz; Exec. Dir.; N88 W16621 Appleton Ave.; P.O. Box 73; 53052; Waukesha; P 34,600; (262) 251-2430; (800) 801-6565; Fax (262) 251-0969; sue@fallschamber.com; www.menomonee fallschamber.com

Milwaukee · *Visit Milwaukee* · Doug Neilson; Pres./CEO; 648 N. Plankinton Ave., Ste, 425; 53203; Milwaukee, Washington & Waukesha; P 597,000; M 740; (414) 273-3950; (800) 231-0903; Fax (414) 273-5596; www.visitmilwaukee.org

Oconomowoc · *Oconomowoc CVB* · 174 E. Wisconsin Ave.; P.O. Box 27; 53066; Sheboygan; P 13,870; (262) 569-2186; (800) 524-3744; Fax (262) 569-3238; info@oconomowocusa.com; www.oconomowocusa.com

Onalaska · *Center for Commerce & Tourism* · Jean Lunde; Tourism Dir.; 1101 Main St.; 54650; La Crosse; P 16,500; (608) 781-9570; (800) 873-1901; Fax (608) 781-9572; info@discover onalaska.com; www.discoveronalaska.com

Oshkosh · *Oshkosh CVB* · Wendy Hielsberg; Exec. Dir.; 2401 W. Waukau Ave.; 54904; Winnebago; P 63,000; (920) 303-9200; (877) 303-9200; Fax (920) 303-9294; wendy@visitoshkosh.com; www.visitoshkosh.com

Pewaukee · *see Waukesha*

Phillips · *Price County Tourism Dept.* · Kathy Reinhard; Dir.; 126 Cherry St., Rm. 9; 54555; Price; P 15,851; (715) 339-4505; (800) 269-4505; Fax (715) 339-3089; tourism@co.price.wi.us; www.pricecountywi.net

Rice Lake · *Rice Lake Tourism Comm.* · 37 S. Main St.; 54868; Barron; P 10,000; (715) 234-8888; (800) 523-6318; info@ricelake tourism.com; www.ricelaketourism.com

Rothschild · *Wausau/Central Wisconsin CVB* · Darien Schaefer; Exec. Dir.; 10204 Park Plz., Ste. B; 54474; Marathon; P 80,000; (715) 355-8788; (888) 948-4748; Fax (715) 359-2306; info@ visitwausau.com; www.visitwausau.com

Stevens Point · *Stevens Point Area CVB* · Sara Brish; Exec. Dir.; 340 Division St. N.; 54481; Portage; P 67,000; (715) 344-2556; Fax (715) 344-5818; info@stevenspointarea.com; www.stevenspoint area.com.

Sturgeon Bay · *Door County Visitor Bur.* · Jack Moneypenny; Pres./CEO; 1015 Green Bay Rd.; P.O. Box 406; 54235; Door; P 29,000; (920) 743-4456; (800) 52-RELAX; Fax (920) 743-7873; info@doorcounty.com; www.doorcounty.com

Sturtevant · *Real Racine* · Dave Blank; Pres./CEO; 14015 Washington Ave.; 53177; Racine; P 195,000; (262) 884-6400; Fax (262) 884-6404; infodesk@racine.org; www.racine.org

Superior · *Superior-Douglas County CVB* · David W. Minor; CEO; 205 Belknap St.; 54880; Douglas; P 45,000; M 450; (715) 394-7716; (800) 942-5313; Fax (715) 394-3810; vacation@ superiorchamber.org; www.superiorchamber.org

Tomah · *Tomah CVB* · Christopher Hanson; Exec. Dir.; 901 Kilbourn Ave.; P.O. Box 625; 54660; Monroe; P 8,000; (608) 372-2166; (800) 94-TOMAH; Fax (608) 372-2167; info@tomahwisconsin.com; www.tomahwisconsin.com

Waukesha · *Waukesha & Pewaukee CVB* · Tammy Tritz; Exec. Dir.; N14 W23755 Stone Ridge Dr., Ste. 225; 53188; Waukesha; P 77,000; (262) 542-0330; (800) 366-8474; Fax (262) 542-2237; info@visitwaukesha.org; www.visitwaukesha.org

West Salem · *see Onalaska*

Wisconsin Dells · *Wisconsin Dells Visitor & Conv. Bur.* · P.O. Box 390; 53965; Columbia; P 3,787; M 650; (608) 254-8088; (800) 223-3557; Fax (608) 254-4293; info@wisdells.com; www.wisdells.com

Wisconsin Rapids · *Heart of Wisconsin Bus. & Eco. Alliance* · Connie Loden; Exec. Dir.; 1120 Lincoln St.; 54494; Wood; P 40,000; M 490; (715) 423-1830; Fax (715) 423-1865; info@heartofwi.com; www.heartofwi.com

Wyoming

Casper · *Casper Area CVB* · Aaron McCreight; CEO; 992 N. Poplar St.; 82601; Natrona; P 69,000; (307) 234-5362; (800) 852-1889; visitors@casperwyoming.info; www.casperwyoming.info

Cheyenne · *Cheyenne Area CVB* · Darren Rudloff; Pres.; One Depot Sq.; 121 W. 15th St., Ste. 202; 82001; Laramie; P 83,000; (307) 778-3133; (800) 426-5009; Fax (307) 778-3190; info@ cheyenne.org; www.cheyenne.org

Cody · *Cody Country Visitors & Conv. Cncl.* · Kimberly Jones; Exec. Dir.; 836 Sheridan Ave.; P.O. Box 2454; 82414; Park; P 25,000; (307) 587-2297; (800) 393-2639; Fax (307) 527-6228; info@ codychamber.org; www.codychamber.org

Evanston · *Bear River Travel Info. Center & State Park* · Wade Henderson; Supt.; 601 Bear River Dr.; 82930; Uinta; P 12,000; (307) 789-6547; (307) 789-6540; Fax (307) 789-2618; www.artsparkshistory.com

Laramie · *Albany County Tourism Bd.* · Fred Ockers; Dir.; 210 Custer; 82070; Albany; P 40,000; (307) 745-4195; (800) 445-5303; Fax (307) 721-2926; director@visitlaramie.org; www.visitlaramie.org

Meeteetse • *Meeteetse Visitor Center* • P.O. Box 238; 82433; Park; P 600; (307) 868-2454; Fax (307) 868-2454; director@ tctwest.net; www.meeteetsewy.com

Rawlins • *Carbon County Visitors Cncl.* • Lisa Howell; Exec. Dir.; 816 W. Spruce St.; P.O. Box 1017; 82301; Carbon; P 14,000; (307) 324-3020; (800) 228-3547; Fax (307) 324-8440; info@wyoming carboncounty.com; www.wyomingcarboncounty.com

Sheridan • *Sheridan Travel & Tourism* • Penny Becker; Exec. Dir.; 117 Wyarno Rd.; P.O. Box 7155; 82801; Sheridan; P 17,000; (307) 673-7120; Fax (307) 672-7321; stt@sheridanwyoming.org; www.sheridanwyoming.org

C&VB

Notes

Economic Development Councils

If the area that interests you is not listed in this section, please refer to the **United States Chambers of Commerce** Section. Many chambers double as the Economic Development Council for their area.

Alabama

Federal

U.S. SBA, Alabama Dist. Ofc. • Tom Todt; Dist. Dir.; 801 Tom Martin Dr., Ste. 201; Birmingham; 35211; Jefferson; P 4,447,100; M 340,000; (205) 290-7101; Fax (205) 290-7404; thomas.todt@sba.gov; www.sba.gov/al

State

Alabama Dev. Ofc. • Linda Swann; Dir.; 401 Adams Ave., 6th Flr.; P.O. Box 304106; Montgomery; 36130; Montgomery; (334) 242-0400; Fax (334) 242-5669; ado.info@ado.alabama.gov; www.ado.alabama.gov

Communities

Alexander City • *Lake Martin Area Eco. Dev. Alliance* • Don McClellan; Dir.; 1675 Cherokee Rd.; P.O. Box 1105; 35011; Tallapoosa; P 40,000; (256) 215-4411; dmcclelland@cacc.cc.al.us; lakemartinalliance.com

Athens • *Limestone County Eco. Dev. Assn.* • Tom Hill; Pres.; 1806 Wilkinson St.; P.O. Box 1346; 35612; Limestone; P 54,164; (256) 232-2386; Fax (256) 233-1034; tomhill@lceda.com; www.lceda.com

Atmore • *Escambia County Ind. Dev. Auth.* • Ms. Marshall Rogers; Exec. Dir.; 406 S. Trammell St.; P.O. Box 1266; 36504; Escambia; P 35,000; (251) 368-5404; Fax (251) 368-1328; ecidamr@frontiernet.net; www.escambiaida.com

Auburn • *Auburn EDC* • T. Phillip Dunlap; Dir.; City Hall; 144 Tichenor Ave., Ste. 2; 36830; Lee; P 47,290; (334) 501-7270; Fax (334) 501-7298; webecondev@auburnalabama.org; www.auburnalabama.org

Bessemer • *City of Bessemer* • Forest Davis; Dir. of Eco. Dev. Dept.; 1800 3rd Ave. N.; 35020; Jefferson; P 30,000; (205) 424-4060; Fax (205) 426-8374; www.bessemeral.org

Birmingham • *Birmingham Bus. Alliance* • Barry B. Copeland; Interim Pres.; 505 20th St. N., Ste. 200; 35203; Jefferson; P 1,100,000; (205) 324-2100; Fax (205) 324-2560; nbaldwin@birminghambusinessalliance.com; www.birminghambusinessalliance.com

Birmingham • *City of Birmingham Ofc. of Eco. Dev.* • Tracey Morant Adams; Dir.; 710 N. 20th St.; 35203; Jefferson; P 265,000; (205) 254-2799; Fax (205) 254-7741; www.birminghamal.gov

Brewton • *Coastal Gateway Eco. Dev. Auth.* • Wiley Blankenship; Pres.; 24300 Hwy. 41; 36426; Escambia; P 77,729; (251) 248-2143; (800) 915-6576; Fax (251) 248-2676; info@cgeda.net; www.cgeda.net

Cullman • *Cullman Comm. & Eco. Dev.* • Peggy Smith; Dir.; 200 First Ave. N.E.; P.O. Box 1009; 35056; Cullman; P 77,000; (256) 739-1891; Fax (256) 739-6721; cullmaneda@cullmaneda.org; www.cullmaneda.org

Decatur • *Morgan County Eco. Dev. Assn.* • Jeremy Nails; Pres./CEO; 300 Market St. N.E., Ste. 2; 35601; Morgan; P 117,000; (256) 353-1213; Fax (256) 353-0407; mceda@mceda.org; www.mceda.org

Decatur • *North Alabama Ind. Dev. Assn.* • Tate Godfrey; Pres./CEO; 410 Johnston St., Ste. A; P.O. Box 1668; 35602; Morgan; P 900,000; (256) 353-9450; Fax (256) 353-5982; tgodfrey@naida.com; www.northalabamausa.com

Double Springs • *Ind. Dev. Auth. of Winston County* • Grady Batchelor; Pres.; 11 Blake Dr., Ste. 3; 35553; Winston; P 25,000; (205) 269-1780; Fax (205) 269-1780; grady@idawinston.org; www.idawinston.org

Enterprise • *Enterprise Coffee Geneva Eco. Dev. Corp.* • Frank Thompson CEcD; Exec. Dir.; P.O. Box 310130; 36331; Coffee; P 50,000; M 70; (334) 393-4769; Fax (334) 393-8127; fthompson@entercomp.com; www.ecgedc.org

Evergreen • *Conecuh County Eco. Dev. Auth.* • Daryl Harper; Dir.; 100 Depot Sq.; 36401; Conecuh; P 14,000; (251) 578-1000; Fax (251) 578-5660

Florence • *Shoals Eco. Dev. Auth.* • Forrest Wright CEcD; Pres.; 20 Hightower Pl., Ste. 1; P.O. Box 580; 35630; Lauderdale; P 143,000; (256) 764-0351; (800) 239-6087; Fax (256) 764-3850; shoalseda@seda-shoals.com; www.seda-shoals.com

Gadsden • *Gadsden-Etowah County Ind. Dev. Auth.* • Michael McCain; Exec. Dir.; P.O. Box 271; 35902; Etowah; P 103,059; (256) 543-9423; Fax (256) 547-2351; info@gadsdenida.org; www.gadsdenida.org

Greenville • *Butler County Comm. for Eco. Dev.* • Richard McLaney; Exec. Dir.; P.O. Box 758; 36037; Butler; P 23,000; (334) 371-8400; (800) 743-1210; Fax (334) 371-8402; rmclaney@bcced.com; www.bcced.com

Huntsville • *Huntsville Trade Dev.* • Bob Albert; Exec. Dir.; 10 America Holly Cir., Ste 1; 35824; Madison; P 168,000; huntsvilleinfo@gmail.com

Huntsville • *Madison County Comm., Intl. Trade Dev. Center* • Anne Burkett; Exec. Dir.; Dept. of Planning & Eco. Dev.; 100 Northside Sq.; 35801; Madison; P 280,000; (256) 532-3505; Fax (256) 532-3704; naita@naita.org; www.naita.org

Lanett • *Chambers County Dev. Auth.* • Valerie G. Gray; Exec. Dir.; 2102 S. Broad Ave.; P.O. Box 269; 36863; Chambers; P 36,000; (334) 642-1412; (334) 642-1415; Fax (334) 642-6548; info@chambersida.com; www.chambersda.com

Madison • *Madison Eco. Dev.* • Amy Bell Furfori; Dir. of Comm. Dev. & Planning; 104 Main St.; 35758; Madison; P 40,000; (256) 509-5028; amy.furfori@madisonal.gov; www.ci.madison.al.us

Mobile • *Mobile Airport Auth.-Brookley Complex* • 1891 9th St.; 36615; Mobile; P 470,000; (251) 438-7334; Fax (251) 694-7667; info@mobairport.com; www.mobairport.com

Montgomery • *Montgomery Area Coop. Dev.* • Randall George; Pres.; 41 Commerce St.; P.O. Box 79; 36101; Montgomery; P 352,000; (334) 834-5200; Fax (334) 265-4745; www.montgomerychamber.com

Moulton • *Lawrence County Ind. Dev. Bd.* • Luke Slaton; Exec. Dir.; 12001 Alabama Hwy. 157; P.O. Box 367; 35650; Lawrence; P 35,000; (256) 974-0100

Opelika • *Opelika EDC* • Alfred F. Cook; Dir.; c/o City Hall; 36803; Lee; P 25,000; (334) 705-5115; Fax (334) 705-5113

Pelham · *Shelby County Eco. & Ind. Dev. Auth.* · James Dedes; Exec. Dir.; 1126 County Services Dr.; 35124; Shelby; P 178,182; (205) 620-6640; info@sceida.org; www.sceida.org

Pell City · *St. Clair-Blount Eco. Dev. Cncl.* · Edwin Gardner Jr.; Exec. Dir.; P.O. Box 1999; 35125; St. Clair; P 128,000; (205) 814-1440; chill@stclairedc.com; www.stclairedc.com

Robertsdale · *Baldwin County Eco. Dev. Alliance* · Robert D. Ingram; Pres./CEO; P.O. Box 1340; 36567; Baldwin; P 175,000; (251) 947-2445; Fax (251) 947-4229; info@baldwineda.com; www.baldwineda.com

Russellville · *Franklin County Dev. Auth.* · Sherri Price; 16109 Hwy. 43, Ste. C; 35653; Franklin; P 32,000; (256) 332-8726; Fax (256) 332-8728; business@franklineda.com; www.franklineda.com

Scottsboro · *Jackson County Eco. Dev. Auth.* · Goodrich A. Rogers; Pres./CEO; 817 S. Broad St.; 35768; Jackson; P 52,000; (256) 574-1331; Fax (256) 259-0873; jceda@scottsboro.org; www.jacksoncountyeda.org

Selma · *Selma & Dallas County Eco. Dev. Auth.* · M. Wayne Vardaman; Exec. Dir.; 912 Selma Ave.; 36701; Dallas; P 40,000; (334) 875-8365; (800) 457-3562; Fax (334) 875-8453; vardaman@selmaeda.com; www.selmaalabama.com

Sylacauga · *Talladega County Eco. Dev. Auth.* · Calvin Miller; Exec. Dir.; P.O. Box 867; 35150; Talladega; P 81,673; (256) 245-8332; Fax (256) 245-8336; millercalv@tceda.com; www.tceda.com

Troy · *Pike County Eco. Dev. Corp.* · Marsha Gaylard; Pres.; 100 Industrial Blvd.; 36081; Pike; P 30,000; (334) 670-2274; Fax (334) 566-2298; mgaylard@troycable.net; www.troy-pike-edc.org

Tuscaloosa · *Tuscaloosa County Ind. Dev. Auth.* · P.O. Box 2667; 35403; Tuscaloosa; P 170,000; (205) 349-1414; Fax (205) 349-1416; info@tcida.com; www.tcida.com

Union Springs · *Bullock County Dev. Auth.* · Dr. Julian Cope; Admin.; 106 E. Conecuh Ave.; P.O. Box 87; 36089; Bullock; P 12,000; (334) 738-5411; Fax (334) 738-5310; bcda@ustconline.net

Wetumpka · *Elmore County Eco. Dev. Auth.* · Eric Basinger; Exec. Dir.; P.O. Box 117; 36092; Elmore; P 127,000; (334) 514-5843; Fax (334) 567-1109; bmask@elmoreco.org; www.elmoreeda.com

Alaska

Federal

Eco. Dev. Admin. · Shirley Kelly; 510 L St., Ste. 444; Anchorage; 99501; (907) 271-2272; Fax (907) 271-2273; skelly@eda.doc.gov; www.eda.gov

U.S. SBA, Alaska Dist. Ofc. · Karen Forsland; Dist. Dir.; 510 L St., Ste. 310; Anchorage; 99501; (907) 271-4022; Fax (907) 271-4545; karen.forsland@sba.gov; www.sba.gov/ak

State

Alaska Bus. Dev. Center Inc. · Gary Selk; Pres.; 840 K St., Ste. 202; Anchorage; 99501; (907) 562-0335; Fax (907) 562-6988; lindsay@abdc.org; www.abdc.org

Communities

Anchorage Area

Alaska Ind. Dev. & Export Auth. · Ted Leonard; Exec. Dir.; 813 W. Northern Lights Blvd.; 99503; Anchorage; P 700,000; (907) 771-3000; Fax (907) 771-3044; www.aidea.org

Alaska Village Initiative · Charles Parker; Pres./CEO; 1577 C St., Ste. 304; 99501; Anchorage; P 50,000; M 170; (907) 274-5400; Fax (907) 263-9971; rweaver@akvillage.com; www.akvillage.com

Anchorage Area, *continued*

Anchorage Eco. Dev. Corp. · Bill Popp; Pres./CEO; 510 L St., Ste. 603; Anchorage; 99501; P 260,000; M 170; (907) 258-3700; Fax (907) 258-6646; info@aedcweb.com; www.aedcweb.com

Southwest Alaska Muni. Conf. · Michael Catsi; Exec. Dir.; 3300 Arctic Blvd., Ste. 203; Anchorage; 99503; Anchorage; P 29,078; (907) 562-7380; Fax (907) 562-0438; info@swamc.org; www.swamc.org

Fairbanks · *Fairbanks Eco. Dev. Corp.* · Jim Dodson; CEO; 301 Cushman, Ste. 301; 99701; Fairbanks North Star; P 89,000; (907) 452-2185; Fax (907) 451-9534; fedc@ak.net; www.investfairbanks.com

Glennallen · *Copper Valley Dev. Assn.* · Barb Challoner; Bus. Mgr.; P.O. Box 9; 99588; Valdez Cordova; P 3,086; (907) 822-5001; Fax (907) 822-5009; cvda@cvinternet.net; www.coppervalley.org

Juneau · *Juneau Eco. Dev. Cncl.* · Brian Holst; Exec. Dir.; 612 W. Willoughby Ave., Ste. A; 99801; Juneau; P 30,000; (907) 523-2300; Fax (907) 463-3929; info@jedc.org; www.jedc.org

Kenai · *Kenai Peninsula Borough Eco. Dev. Dist.* · John Torgerson; Exec. Dir.; 14896 Kenai Spur Hwy., Ste. 103A; 99611; Kenai Peninsula; P 55,000; (907) 283-3335; Fax (907) 283-3913; info@kpedd.org; www.kpedd.org

Kotzebue · *NW Arctic Borough Eco. Dev. Commission* · Jade Hill; Exec. Dir.; P.O. Box 1110; 99752; Northwest Arctic; P 7,200; (907) 442-2500; Fax (907) 442-2930; www.nwabor.org

Palmer · *Matanuska-Susitna Borough Eco. Dev.* · Dave Hanson; Dir.; 350 E. Dahlia; 99645; Matanuska Susitna; P 80,000; (907) 745-9508; Dave.Hanson@matsugov.us; www.matsugov.us/business.cfm

Sitka · *Sitka Eco. Dev. Assn.* · Garry White; Exec. Dir.; 329 Harbor Dr., Ste. 212; 99835; Sitka; P 8,947; (907) 747-2660; Fax (907) 747-7688; inforequest@sitka.net; www.sitka.net

Sitka · *Sitka Eco. Dev. Comm.* · Wells Williams; Planning Dir.; 100 Lincoln St.; 99835; Sitka; P 8,947; (907) 747-1824; Fax (907) 747-6138; www.cityofsitka.com

Skagway · *Skagway Dev. Corp.* · Trish Sims; Dir.; 701 State St.; P.O. Box 1236; 99840; Skagway; P 860; (907) 983-3414; skagdev@aptalaska.net; www.skagwaydevelopment.org

Wrangell · *Wrangell Eco. Dev. Dept.* · Carol Rushmore; Eco. Dev. Dir.; 205 Brueger St.; P.O. Box 531; 99929; Wrangell; P 2,200; (907) 874-2381; ecodev@wrangell.com; www.wrangell.com

Arizona

Federal

U.S. SBA, Arizona Dist. Ofc. · Robert J. Blaney; Dist. Dir.; 2828 N. Central Ave., Ste. 800; Phoenix; 85004; Maricopa; (602) 745-7200; Fax (602) 745-7210; robert.blaney@sba.gov; www.sba.gov/az

State

Arizona Commerce Auth. · Don Cardon; Pres./CEO; 1700 W. Washington, Ste. 600; Phoenix; 85007; Maricopa; (602) 771-1100; Fax (602) 771-1200; commerce@azcommerce.com; www.azcommerce.com

Communities

Apache Junction · *City of Apache Junction Eco. Dev.* · Steve Filipowicz; Eco. Dev. Dir.; 300 E. Superstition Blvd.; 85219; Pinal; P 41,000; (480) 474-5064; Fax (480) 474-5110; www.ajcity.net

Ash Fork • *Ash Fork Dev. Assn.* • Fayrene Hume; Pres.; 518 Louis Ave.; P.O. Box 293; 86320; Yavapai; P 2,000; (928) 637-2774; Fax (928) 637-0394

Avondale • *Avondale Eco. Dev.* • Dina Mathias; Eco. Dev. Specialist; 11465 W. Civic Center Dr., Ste. 210; 85323; Maricopa; P 76,000; (623) 333-1400; Fax (623) 333-0140; dmathias@avondale.org; www.avondale.org

Benson • *Southeast AZ Eco. Dev. Group* • George Scott; Exec. Dir.; P.O. Box 1312; 85602; Cochise; P 126,000; (520) 586-2330; saedg@qwestoffice.net; www.saedg.org

Buckeye • *Town of Buckeye, Eco. Dev. Dept.* • 1101 E. Ash Ave.; 85326; Maricopa; P 33,000; M 37; (623) 349-6150; Fax (623) 349-6099; www.buckeyeaz.gov

Bullhead City • *Bullhead Reg. Eco. Dev. Auth.* • 1848 Hwy. 95, Ste. 104; 86442; Mohave; P 45,000; (928) 704-6374; Fax (928) 704-6376; bceda@frontiernet.net; www.bullheadeconomicdevelopment.com

Casa Grande • *Central Arizona Reg. Eco. Dev. Found.* • Barry Albrecht; Exec. Dir.; 540 N. Camino Mercado, Ste. 2; 85222; Pinal; P 74,250; M 150; (520) 836-6868; Fax (520) 836-4898; ceo@caredf.org; www.caredf.org

Chandler • *Chandler Eco. Dev. Div.* • Christine Mackay; Dir.; P.O. Box 4008; 85224; Maricopa; P 250,000; (480) 782-3030; (888) 663-2489; Fax (480) 782-3040; christine.mackay@chandleraz.gov; www.chandleraz.gov

Coolidge • *Growth Management Dept.* • C. Alton Bruce; Eco. Dev. Dir.; 131 W. Pinkley Ave.; 85228; Pinal; P 11,000; (520) 723-6075; Fax (520) 723-6079; www.coolidgeaz.com

Cottonwood • *Cottonwood Eco. Dev. Cncl.* • Casey Rooney; Dir.; 827 N. Main St.; 86326; Yavapai; P 76,000; (928) 634-5505; Fax (928) 634-0260; crooney@ci.cottonwood.az.us; www.cottonwoodedc.com

Douglas • *Douglas Eco. Cncl.* • Victor Gonzalez; Eco. Dev. Dir.; 425 Tenth St.; 85607; Cochise; P 18,000; (520) 417-7310; Fax (520) 364-7507; www.douglasaz.gov

Eloy • *Eco. Dev. Group of Eloy* • Gene Wilson; Pres.; 628 N. Main St.; 85231; Pinal; P 11,000; (520) 466-1014; (888) 795-3569; Fax (888) 690-2767; info@edgeaz.org; www.edgeaz.org

Flagstaff • *City of Flagstaff Comm. Inv.* • 211 W. Aspen Ave.; 86001; Coconino; P 200,000; (928) 779-7632; Fax (928) 779-7684; ecodev@ci.flagstaff.az.us; www.cityofinnovation.com

Gilbert • *Gilbert Eco. Dev. Advisory Bd.* • Dan Henderson CEcD; Bus. Dev. Mgr.; 90 E. Civic Center Dr.; 85296; Maricopa; P 203,500; (480) 503-6865; Fax (480) 503-6170; dan.henderson@ci.gilbert.az.us; www.ci.gilbert.az.us

Glendale • *City of Glendale Eco. Dev. Dept.* • Brian Friedman; Dir.; Eco. Dev. Dept.; 5850 W. Glendale Ave.; 85301; Maricopa; P 250,000; (623) 930-2983; Fax (623) 931-5730; bfriedman@glendaleaz.com; www.glendaleaz.com

Globe • *Gila County Comm. Dev. Ofc.* • Robert Gould; Dir.; 1400 E. Ash; 85501; Gila; P 51,000; (928) 425-3231; Fax (928) 425-0829; www.gilacountyaz.gov

Goodyear • *Goodyear Eco. Dev. Dept.* • Harry Paxton; Dir.; 190 N. Litchfield Rd.; 85338; Maricopa; P 44,000; (623) 932-3025; Fax (623) 932-3028; gyecdev@goodyearaz.gov; www.goodyearaz.gov

Kingman • *Mohave County Eco. Dev. Div.* • Jonas Peterson; Deputy Dir. of Eco. Dev.; P.O. Box 7000; 86402; Mohave; P 170,000; (928) 753-0723; Fax (928) 753-0776; jonas.peterson@co.mohave.az.us

Lake Havasu City • *Partnership for Eco. Dev.* • Gary Kellogg; Pres.; 314 London Bridge Rd.; 86403; Mohave; P 51,000; (928) 505-7333; www.lakehavasu.org

Maricopa • *Maricopa Eco. Dev. Dept.* • Danielle Casey; Mgr, of Eco. Dev.; 45145 W. Madison Ave.; P.O. Box 610; 85239; Pinal; P 20,000; (520) 316-6812; Fax (520) 568-9120; danielle.casey@maricopa-az.gov; www.maricopamatters.com

Mesa • *City of Mesa* • William J. Jabjiniak; Eco. Dev. Dir.; P.O. Box 1466; 85211; Maricopa; P 456,000; (480) 644-3561; Fax (480) 644-3458; William.Jabjiniak@mesaaz.gov; www.mesaaz.gov

Peoria • *Peoria Eco. Dev. Dept.* • 8401 W. Monroe St., Rm. 190; 85345; Maricopa; P 146,000; (623) 773-7735; Fax (623) 773-7519; www.peoriaaz.gov

Phoenix • *City of Phoenix Comm. & Eco. Dev. Dept.* • Donald Maxwell; Dir.; 200 W. Washington, 20th Flr.; 85003; Maricopa; P 1,400,000; (602) 262-5040; Fax (602) 495-5097; www.phoenix.gov/econdev/

Phoenix • *Greater Phoenix Eco. Cncl.* • Barry G. Broome; Pres./CEO; 2 N. Central Ave., Ste. 2500; 85004; Maricopa; P 3,648,545; (602) 256-7700; (800) 421-4732; Fax (602) 256-7744; info@gpec.org; www.gpec.org

Prescott • *City of Prescott, Eco. Dev.* • Jane Bristol; Eco. Dev. Dir.; P.O. Box 2059; 86302; Yavapai; P 45,000; (928) 777-1100; Fax (928) 777-1255; citystaff@cityofprescott.net; www.prescotted.com

Safford • *Safford Eco. Dev.* • Peter Stasia; Eco. Dev. Dir.; 808 S. 8th Ave.; P.O. Box 272; 85546; Graham; P 10,000; (928) 348-8515; Fax (928) 348-8515; pstasiak@ci.safford.az.us; www.saffordeconomicdevelopment.com

Sahuarita • *Sahuarita Eco. Dev.* • Kathy Ward; Eco. Dev. Mgr.; 375 W. Sahuarita Center Way; 85629; Pima; P 10,000; (520) 822-8815; kward@ci.sahuarita.az.us; www.ci.sahuarita.az.us

Saint Johns • *Eco. Dev. for Apache County* • Dana Overson; Dir.; 395 S. First W.; 85936; Apache; P 69,000; (928) 337-2644; Fax (928) 337-2646; doverson@co.apache.az.us; www.apachecounty.com

Scottsdale • *City of Scottsdale, Scottsdale Eco. Vitality Dept.* • Kathy Montalvo; Admin. Asst.; 4021 N. 75th St., Ste. 102; 85251; Maricopa; P 220,000; (480) 312-7989; Fax (480) 312-2672; kmontalvo@scottsdaleaz.gov; www.scottsdaleaz.gov

Sierra Vista • *Sierra Vista Eco. Dev. Found.* • Bob Shepard; Exec. Dir.; P.O. Box 2380; 85636; Cochise; P 83,000; (520) 458-6948; Fax (520) 458-7453; admin@svedf.org; www.svedf.org

Superior • *Eco. Dev. Advisory Bd.* • Melanie Oliver; Town Mgr.; 734 Main St.; 85273; Pinal; P 3,200; (520) 689-5752; Fax (520) 689-5822; townmanager@superior-arizona.com; www.superior-arizona.com

Tempe • *Tempe C/C Eco. Dev.* • Mary Ann Miller; Pres./CEO; 909 E. Apache Blvd.; P.O. Box 28500; 85285; Maricopa; P 165,000; (480) 967-7891; Fax (480) 966-5365; info@tempechamber.org; www.tempechamber.org

Tolleson • *Tolleson Eco. Dev.* • Paul Magallanez; Eco. Dev. Dir.; 9555 W. Van Buren; 85353; Maricopa; P 5,000; (623) 474-4998; Fax (623) 936-7117; www.tollesonaz.org

Tucson • *Tucson Reg. Eco. Opportunities* • Joe Snell; Pres./CEO; 120 N. Stone Ave., Ste. 200; 85701; Pima; P 800,000; M 300; (520) 243-1900; Fax (520) 243-1910; info@treoaz.org; www.treoaz.org

Wickenburg • *Wickenburg Eco. Dev. Comm* • Gary Edwards; Town Mgr.; 155 N. Tegner St., Ste. A; 85390; Maricopa; P 6,077; (928) 684-5451; Fax (602) 506-1580; managersoffice@ci.wickenburg.az.us; www.ci.wickenburg.az.us

Willcox · *Willcox Eco. Dev.* · Kathy Smith; Exec. Dir.; 1500 N. Circle I Rd.; 85643; Cochise; P 4,000; (520) 384-2272; Fax (520) 384-0293; willcoxchamber@vtc.net; www.willcoxchamber.com

Winslow · *City of Winslow Eco. Dev.* · Jim Ferguson; City Mgr.; 21 Williamson Ave.; 86047; Navajo; P 9,800; (928) 289-2423; Fax (928) 289-3742; www.ci.winslow.az.us

Yuma · *Greater Yuma Eco. Dev. Corp.* · Julie Engel; Pres./CEO; 170 W. 16th St., Ste. 200; 85364; Yuma; P 196,000; (928) 782-7774; Fax (928) 782-7775; info@greateryuma.org; www.greateryuma.org

Arkansas

Federal

U.S. SBA, Arkansas Dist. Ofc. · Linda Nelson; Dist. Dir.; 2120 Riverfront Dr., Ste. 250; Little Rock; 72202; Pulaski; (501) 324-7379; Fax (501) 324-7394; carol.silverstrom@sba.gov; www.sba.gov/ar

State

Arkansas Eco. Dev. Comm. · Maria Haley; Exec. Dir.; 900 W. Capitol Ave.; Little Rock; 72201; Pulaski; (501) 682-7675; Fax (501) 682-7341; info@arkansasedc.com; www.arkansasedc.com

Communities

Arkadelphia · *Arkadelphia Reg. Eco. Dev. Alliance* · Shawnie Carrier; Exec. Dir.; 2401 Pine Street, Ste. B; P.O. Box 400; 71923; Clark; P 11,000; (870) 246-1460; Fax (870) 246-1462; shawnie@arkadelphiaalliance.com; www.arkadelphiaalliance.com

Benton · *City of Benton* · Rick Holland; Mayor; 114 S. East St.; P.O. Box 607; 72018; Saline; P 27,717; (501) 776-5900; Fax (501) 776-5910; www.benton.ar.gov

Bentonville · *Bentonville Ind. Dev. Corp.* · Ed Clifford; Pres./CEO; 200 E. Central Ave.; P.O. Box 330; 72712; Benton; P 60,000; (479) 273-2841; Fax (479) 273-2180; eclifford@bbvchamber.com; www.bbvchamber.com

Booneville · *Booneville Dev. Corp.* · 210 E. Main St.; P.O. Box 55; 72927; Logan; P 4,300; (479) 675-2666; Fax (479) 675-5158; information@booneville.com; www.booneville.com

Camden · *Camden Area Ind. Dev. Corp.* · Alan Dean; Pres.; 314 Adams S.W.; P.O. Box 99; 71711; Ouachita; P 13,000; (870) 836-6426; Fax (870) 836-6400; caidcark@yahoo.com; www.teamcamden.com

Conway · *Conway Dev. Corp.* · Brad Lacy; Dir. of Eco. Dev.; 900 Oak St.; 72032; Faulkner; P 120,000; (501) 329-7788; Fax (501) 327-7790; brad@conwayarkansas.org; www.conwayarkansas.org

Crossett · *Crossett Eco. Dev. Found.* · Mike Smith; Exec. Dir.; 125 Main St.; 71635; Ashley; (870) 364-8745; Fax (870) 364-2358; mike@cityofcrossett.net; www.considercrossett.net

El Dorado · *El Dorado Ind. Dev. Corp.* · Don Wales; Exec. V.P.; 111 W. Main; 71730; Union; P 22,000; M 40; (870) 863-6113; Fax (870) 863-6115; www.goeldorado.com

Fayetteville · *Green Valley Dev.* · Steve Rust; Pres./CEO; One E. Center St., Ste. 275; 72701; Washington; P 40,000; (479) 442-8885; Fax (479) 439-0126; steve@greenvalleydevelopment.com; www.greenvalleydevelopment.com

Heber Springs · *Cleburne County Ofc. of Eco. Dev.* · Jim Jackson; Dir.; 300 W. Main St.; 72543; Cleburne; P 26,000; (501) 362-8402; Fax (501) 362-4605; www.cleburnecountyarkansas.com

Helena · *Phillips County Port Auth.* · Martin Chaffin; Exec. Dir.; 1201 Hwy. 49 W.; P.O. Box 407; 72342; Phillips; P 28,000; (870) 338-6444; Fax (870) 338-6445; director@helenaharbor.com; www.helenaharbor.com

Hope · *Hempstead County Eco. Dev. Corp.* · Wesley Woodard; Pres.; P.O. Box 971; 71802; Hempstead; P 20,000; (870) 777-8485; Fax (870) 777-5266; wesley@hopeusa.com; www.hopeusa.com

Hot Springs · *West Central AR Plan. & Dev. Dist. Inc.* · Dwayne Pratt; Exec. Dir.; 1000 Central Ave.; P.O. Box 21100; 71903; Garland; P 291,449; (501) 525-7577; Fax (501) 525-7677; www.wcapdd.dina.org

Little Rock · *Little Rock Port Auth.* · Paul Latture; Exec. Dir.; 7500 Lindsey Rd.; 72206; Pulaski; P 183,000; (501) 490-1468; Fax (501) 490-1800; platture@comcast.net; lrport.dina.org

Magnolia · *Magnolia Eco. Dev. Corp.* · Mike Lewis; Pres.; 529 E. Main St.; P.O. Box 866; 71754; Columbia; P 25,000; (870) 234-4352; (800) 206-0889; Fax (870) 234-9291; ea@ccalliance.us; www.medc.cc

Marion · *Marion Eco. Dev.* · 13 Military Rd.; 72364; Crittenden; P 10,000; (870) 739-5414; Fax (870) 739-5448; eddirector@marionarkansas.org; www.marionarkansas.org

Monticello · *Monticello Eco. Dev. Comm.* · Truman Hamilton; Exec. Dir.; 211 W. Gaines; P.O. Box 1890; 71657; Drew; P 19,000; (870) 367-3076; (888) 909-8019; director@monticelloedc.org; www.monticelloedc.org

Morrilton · *Conway County Eco. Dev. Corp.* · John Gibson; Pres.; 120 N. Division St.; P.O. Box 589; 72110; Conway; P 20,300; M 325; (501) 354-2393; Fax (501) 354-8642; johngibson@suddenlinkmail.com; www.morrilton.com

Paragould · *Paragould EDC* · Sue McGowan; Dir.; 300 W. Court St.; P.O. Box 124; 72451; Greene; P 24,000; (870) 236-7684; Fax (870) 236-7142; smcgowan@paragould.org; www.paragould.org

Pine Bluff · *The Eco. Dev. Alliance of Jefferson County* · Lou Ann Nisbett; Pres./CEO; 510 Main St.; P.O. Box 5069; 71611; Jefferson; P 55,085; (870) 535-0110; Fax (870) 535-1643; nisbett@pinebluffchamber.com; www.jeffersoncountyalliance.com

Prescott · *Prescott Eco. Dev. Ofc.* · Mary Godwin; Dir.; 116 E. 2nd St.; P.O. Box 307; 71857; Nevada; (870) 887-6208; Fax (870) 887-5317; mgodwin@iocc.com; www.pnpartnership.org

Russellville · *Arkansas Valley Alliance for Eco. Dev.* · Jeff Pipkin CEcD; 708 W. Main St.; 72801; Pope; P 56,000; (479) 858-6555; Fax (479) 858-6496; jpipkin@russellville.org; www.russellville.org

Wynne · *Cross County Eco. Dev. Corp.* · 1790 N. Falls Blvd., Ste. 2; P.O. Box 234; 72396; Cross; P 20,000; (870) 238-9300; Fax (870) 238-7844; info@crosscountychamber.com; www.crosscountychamber.com

California

Federal

U.S. SBA, Fresno Dist. Ofc. · Carlos Mendoza; Dist. Dir.; 2719 N. Air Fresno Dr., Ste. 200; Fresno; 93727; Fresno; (559) 487-5791; Fax (559) 487-5636; melende.ward@sba.gov; www.sba.gov/ca

U.S. SBA, Los Angeles Dist. Ofc. · Alberto Alvarado; Dist. Dir.; 330 N. Brand, Ste. 1200; Glendale; 91203; Los Angeles; (818) 552-3201; Fax (818) 552-3286; christina.stace@sba.gov; www.sba.gov/ca

U.S. SBA, Sacramento Dist. Ofc. • Jim O'Neal; Dist. Dir.; 6501 Sylvan Rd., Ste. 100; Citrus Heights; 95610; Sacramento; (916) 735-1700; Fax (916) 735-1719; kathy.chapman@sba.gov; www.sba.gov/ca

U.S. SBA, San Diego Dist. Ofc. • Ruben Garcia; Dist. Dir.; 550 W. C St., Ste. 550; San Diego; 92101; San Diego; (619) 557-7250; Fax (619) 727-4883; kathleen.moran@sba.gov; www.sba.gov/ca

U.S. SBA, San Francisco Dist. Ofc. • Mark Quinn; Dist. Dir.; 455 Market St., 6th Flr.; San Francisco; 94105; San Francisco; (415) 744-6820; mark.quinn@sba.gov; www.sba.gov/ca

U.S. SBA, Santa Ana Dist. Ofc. • Adalberto Quijada; Dist. Dir.; 200 W. Santa Ana Blvd., Ste. 700; Santa Ana; 92701; Orange; (714) 550-7420; Fax (714) 550-7409; adalberto.quijada@sba.gov; www.sba.gov/ca

State

Calif. Assn. for Local Eco. Dev. Prof. • Wayne Schell; Pres./CEO; 550 Bercut Dr., Ste. G; Sacramento; 95811; Sacramento; (916) 448-8252; Fax (916) 448-3811; wschell@caled.org; www.caled.org

Communities

Anaheim • *City of Anaheim Eco. Dev.* • City Hall East; 200 S. Anaheim Blvd., 1st Flr.; 92805; Orange; P 328,000; (714) 765-4323; economicdevelopment@anaheim.net; www.anaheim.net

Apple Valley • *Apple Valley Eco. Dev.* • Kenneth J. Henderson; Asst. Town Mgr.; 14955 Dale Evans Pkwy.; 92307; San Bernardino; P 75,000; (760) 240-7000; Fax (760) 240-7910; development@applevalley.org; www.applevalley.org

Arcata • *Arcata Eco. Dev. Corp.* • Ross Welch; Exec. Dir.; 100 Ericson Ct., Ste. 100A; 95521; Humboldt; P 370,000; (707) 822-4616; ross@aedc1.org; www.aedc1.org

Auburn • *Placer County Eco. Dev.* • David Snyder; Dir.; 175 Fulweiler Ave.; 95603; Placer; P 317,000; (530) 889-4016; Fax (530) 889-4095; dsnyder@placer.ca.gov; www.placer.ca.gov

Bakersfield • *Kern Eco. Dev. Corp.* • Richard Chapman; Pres./CEO; 2700 M St., Ste. 200; 93301; Kern; (661) 862-5150; Fax (661) 862-5151; chapmanr@kedc.com; www.kedc.com

Belmont • *San Mateo County Eco. Dev. Assn.* • Dan Cruey; Pres./CEO; 1301 Shoreway Rd., Ste. 150; 94002; San Mateo; P 775,000; (650) 413-5600; Fax (650) 413-5909; samceda@samceda.org; www..org

Berkeley • *Berkeley Eco. Dev.* • 2180 Milvia St.; 94704; Alameda; P 103,000; (510) 981-7530; Fax (510) 981-7099; ecodev@cityofberkeley.info; www.ci.berkeley.ca.us

Brawley • *Brawley Eco. Dev. Comm.* • Sheila Riley; 204 S. Imperial Ave.; P.O. Box 218; 92227; Imperial; P 25,000; (760) 344-3160; Fax (760) 344-7611; www.brawleychamber.com

Brea • *Brea Eco. Dev.* • Eric Nicoll; Dir.; 1 Civic Center Circle; Level 2; 92821; Orange; P 38,000; (714) 671-4421; Fax (714) 671-4480; ericn@cityofbrea.net; www.ci.brea.ca.us

Burbank • *Burbank Eco. Dev.* • Scott McGookin; Mgr.; 275 E. Olive Ave.; 91510; Los Angeles; P 105,000; (818) 238-5180; Fax (818) 238-5174; smcgookin@ci.burbank.ca.us; www.burbankca.org

Calexico • *Calexico Redev. Agency* • Ralph Velez; Exec. Dir.; 608 Heber Ave.; 92231; Imperial; P 37,652; (760) 768-2177; Fax (760) 357-3831; www.calexico.ca.gov

California City • *California City Eco. Dev. Corp.* • James Quiggle; Pres.; 8001 California City Blvd.; 93505; Kern; P 13,500; M 56; (760) 373-2007; Fax (760) 373-1414; californiacityedc@verizon.net; www.californiacityedc.org

Camarillo • *Ventura County Eco. Dev. Assn.* • Darlene Ruz; V.P.; 1601 Carmen Dr., Ste. 215; 93010; Ventura; P 700,500; M 300; (805) 388-3457; Fax (805) 388-9972; info@vceda.org; www.vceda.org

Carson • *Carson Eco. Dev.* • Cliff Graves; Mgr.; 701 E. Carson St.; 90745; Los Angeles; P 100,000; (310) 233-4802; (310) 830-7600; cgraves@carson.ca.us; www.ci.carson.ca.us

Ceres • *Ceres Eco. Dev.* • Bryan Briggs; Eco. Dev. Mgr.; 2720 2nd St.; 95307; Stanislaus; (209) 538-5756; Fax (209) 538-5780; bryan.briggs@ci.ceres.ca.us; www.ci.ceres.ca.us

Chico • *Tri County EDC* • Marc Nemanic; Dir.; 3120 Cohasset Rd., Ste. 5; 95973; Butte; P 282,200; (530) 893-8732; Fax (530) 893-0820; www.tricountyedc.org

Chula Vista • *South County Eco. Dev. Cncl.* • Cindy Gompper-Graves; Exec. Dir.; 1111 Bay Blvd., Ste. E; 91911; San Diego; P 700,000; (619) 424-5143; Fax (619) 424-5738; info@sandiegosouth.com; www.sandiegosouth.com

Colton • *Colton Eco. Dev. Cncl.* • Candace Cassel; Dir.; 650 N. La Cadena Dr.; 92324; San Bernardino; P 52,000; (909) 370-5167; Fax (909) 370-5167; rda@ci.colton.ca.us; www.ci.colton.ca.us

Colusa • *Colusa County Eco. Dev. Corp.* • Lynda Reynolds; 2963 Davison Ct.; P.O. Box 1077; 95932; Colusa; P 22,000; (530) 458-3028; lyndareynolds@colusacountyedc.com; www.colusacountyedc.com

Commerce • *Comm. Dev. Dept.* • Robert Zarrilli; Dir.; 2535 Commerce Way; 90040; Los Angeles; P 13,000; (323) 722-4805; Fax (323) 888-6537; www.ci.commerce.ca.us

Concord • *Contra Costa Cncl.* • Linda Best; Exec. Dir.; 1355 Willow Way, Ste. 253; 94520; Contra Costa; P 900,000; (925) 246-1880; Fax (925) 674-1654; info@contracostacouncil.com; www.contracostacouncil.com

Cypress • *City of Cypress Comm. Dev.* • Ted Commerdinger; Comm. Dev. Dir.; 5275 Orange Ave.; P.O. Box 609; 90630; Orange; P 47,000; (714) 229-6720; Fax (714) 229-0154; cdd@ci.cypress.ca.us; www.ci.cypress.ca.us

El Cajon • *San Diego East County Eco. Dev. Cncl.* • Deanna Weeks; Dir.; 1870 Cordell Ct., Ste. 202; 92020; San Diego; P 415,000; (619) 258-3670; Fax (619) 258-3674; www.eastcountyedc.org

El Centro • *Imperial County Planning & Eco. Dev.* • Jurg Heuberger; Dir.; 801 Main St.; 92243; Imperial; P 144,200; (760) 482-4236; Fax (760) 353-8338; www.imperialcounty.net

Escondido • *City of Escondido Eco. Dev. Div.* • Jo Ann Case; Eco. Dev. Mgr.; 201 N. Broadway; 92025; San Diego; P 143,000; (760) 839-4563; Fax (760) 739-7004; www.escondido.org

Eureka • *Redwood Region Eco. Dev. Comm.* • 520 E St.; 95501; Humboldt; P 127,000; (707) 445-9651; Fax (707) 445-9652; www.rredc.com

Fairfield • *Solano EDC* • Mike Ammann; Pres.; 360 Campus Ln., Ste. 102; 94534; Solano; P 500,000; M 175; (707) 864-1855; Fax (707) 864-6621; info@solanoedc.org; www.solanoedc.org

Fontana • *Fontana Eco. Dev.* • Elisa Grey; Mgr.; 8353 Sierra Ave.; 92335; San Bernardino; P 190,000; (909) 350-6741; Fax (909) 350-6616; www.fontanabusiness.org

Fortuna • *Fortuna Bus. Improvement Dist.* • David Reed; Coord.; P.O. Box 1000; 95540; Humboldt; P 11,350; (707) 725-9261; Fax (707) 725-0806; info@fortunabusiness.com; www.fortunabusiness.com

Fountain Valley • *City of Fountain Valley, Planning Dept.* • Andy Perea; Dir.; 10200 Slater Ave.; 92708; Orange; P 57,000; (714) 593-4400; Fax (714) 593-4525; www.fountainvalley.org

Fresno · *Eco. Dev. Corp. serving Fresno County* · Steve Geil; Pres./CEO; 906 N St., Ste. 120; 93716; Fresno; P 917,515; (559) 476-2500; Fax (559) 233-2156; info@fresnoedc.com; www.fresnoedc.com

Fullerton · *City of Fullerton Redev. & Eco. Dev.* · Nicole Coats; Project Mgr.; 303 W. Commonwealth; 92832; Orange; P 133,000; (714) 738-4102; (714) 738-6877; Fax (714) 738-6843; nicolec@ci.fullerton.ca.us; www.cityoffullerton.com

Garden Grove · *Garden Grove Eco. Dev.* · Chet Yoshizaki; Dir.; 11222 Acacia Pkwy.; 92840; Orange; P 166,000; (714) 741-5120; business@ci.garden-grove.ca.us; www.ci.garden-grove.ca.us

Gilroy · *Gilroy Eco. Dev. Corp.* · Richard Vahner; Pres.; 7471 Monterey St.; 95020; Santa Clara; P 52,000; (408) 847-7611; Fax (408) 842-6010; gilroy@gilroyedc.org; www.gilroyedc.org

Glendale · *City of Glendale Comm. Redev. & Housing* · Ken Hitts; Eco. Dev. Mgr.; 633 E. Broadway, Ste. 201; 91206; Los Angeles; P 207,000; (818) 548-3155; Fax (818) 409-7239; khitts@ci.glendale.ca.us; www.thinkglendale.com

Grass Valley · *Nevada County Eco. Resource Cncl.* · Gil Mathew; Pres./CEO; 960 McCourtney Rd., Ste. A; 95949; Nevada; P 95,300; (530) 274-8455; Fax (530) 274-3942; info@ncerc.org; www.ncerc.org

Hanford · *Kings County Eco. Dev. Corp.* · John S. Lehn; Pres./CEO; 120 N. Irwin St.; 93230; Kings; P 155,000; (559) 585-3576; Fax (559) 585-7398; john.lehn@co.kings.ca.us; www.kingsedc.org

Hesperia · *Hesperia Eco. Dev.* · Steve Lantsberger; Dir.; 9700 7th Ave.; 92345; San Bernardino; P 91,000; (760) 947-1906; Fax (760) 947-1000; www.cityofhesperia.us

Hollister · *Eco. Dev. Corp. of San Benito County* · P.O. Box 1265; 95024; San Benito; P 57,000; (831) 636-1882; Fax (831) 636-1359; edcsbc@hollinet.com

Huntington Beach · *Huntington Beach Eco. Dev.* · Stanley Smalewitz; Dir.; 2000 Main St.; 92648; Orange; P 200,000; (714) 536-5582; Fax (714) 375-5087; ssmalewitz@surfcity-hb.org; www.surfcity-hb.org

Irvine · *Orange County Bus. Cncl.* · Lucy Dunn; Pres./CEO; 2 Park Plz., Ste. 100; 92614; Orange; P 3,000,000; (949) 476-2242; Fax (949) 476-9240; www.ocbc.org

Irwindale · *San Gabriel Valley Eco. Partnership* · Cynthia J. Kurtz; Pres./CEO; 4900 Rivergrade Rd., Ste. A310; 91706; Los Angeles; P 2,000,000; M 200; (626) 856-3400; Fax (626) 856-5115; www.valleyconnect.com

Jackson · *Amador Eco. Dev. Corp.* · Ron Mittelbrunn; Exec. Dir.; P.O. Box 1077; 95642; Amador; P 36,000; (209) 223-0351; Fax (209) 223-2261; www.amador-edc.org

Lake Elsinore · *Lake Elsinore Eco. Dev.* · Cathy Barrozo; GIS Analyst; 130 S. Main St.; 92530; Riverside; P 42,000; (951) 674-3124; Fax (951) 674-2392; cbarrozo@lake-elsinore.org; www.lake-elsinore.org

Lancaster · *Greater Antelope Valley Eco. Alliance* · Mel Layne; Pres./CEO; 1028 W. Ave L-12, Ste. 101; 93534; Los Angeles; P 450,000; (661) 945-2741; Fax (661) 945-7711; info@aveconomy.org; www.aveconomy.org

Lemon Grove · *Lemon Grove Redev. Agency* · Graham Mitchell; City Mgr.; 3232 Main St.; 91945; San Diego; P 25,000; (619) 825-3800; Fax (619) 825-3804; www.ci.lemon-grove.ca.us

Lompoc · *Lompoc Eco. Dev. Resources* · Kathleen Griffith; Mgr.; 100 Civic Center Plaza; P.O. Box 8001; 93438; Santa Barbara; P 40,000; (805) 736-1261; Fax (805) 875-8232; www.cityoflompoc.com

Long Beach · *Eco. Dev. & Cultural Affairs Bur.* · Robert Swayze; Mgr.; Bus. Dev. Center; 110 Pine Ave., Ste. 1100; 90802; Los Angeles; P 461,000; (562) 570-3800; Fax (562) 570-3897; www.longbeach.gov

Los Angeles · *LA County Eco. Dev. Corp.* · William C. Allen; Pres./CEO; 444 S. Flower St., 34th Flr.; 90071; Los Angeles; P 10,150,000; (213) 622-4300; Fax (213) 622-7100; bill.allen@laedc.org; www.laedc.org

Lynwood · *Eco. Resources Corp.* · Dutch Ross; Pres.; 2600 Industry Way; 90262; Los Angeles; P 65,000; (310) 537-4610; Fax (310) 762-6211; www.economicresources.org

Madera · *Madera County Eco. Dev. Comm.* · Bobby Kahn; Exec. Dir.; 2425 W. Cleveland Ave., Ste. 101; 93637; Madera; P 135,000; (559) 675-7768; Fax (559) 675-3252; bkahn@maderacountyedc.com; www.maderacountyedc.com

Martinez · *City of Martinez Eco. Dev.* · Philip Vince; Mgr.; 525 Henrietta St.; 94553; Contra Costa; P 36,000; (925) 372-3500; Fax (925) 299-5012; www.cityofmartinez.org

Martinez · *Contra Costa County Comm. Dev. Agency* · James Kennedy; Dir.; 2530 Arnold Dr., Ste. 190; 94553; Contra Costa; P 1,100,000; (925) 335-7200; Fax (925) 335-7201; www.ccreach.org

Merced · *City of Merced Eco. Dev. Ofc.* · Frank Quintero; Dev. Mgr.; 678 W. 18th St.; 95340; Merced; P 76,000; (209) 385-4788; (800) 723-4788; Fax (209) 723-1780; quinterof@cityofmerced.org; www.cityofmerced.org

Merced · *Merced County EDC* · Scott Galbraith; Pres./CEO; 1733 O St.; 95340; Merced; P 210,000; (209) 723-3889; Fax (209) 723-4450; www.mcedco.com

Modesto · *Stanislaus Eco. Dev. & Workforce Alliance* · Bill Bassitt; CEO; P.O. Box 3091; 95353; Stanislaus; P 521,497; (209) 567-4985; Fax (209) 567-4944; bassittb@stanalliance.com; www.stanalliance.com

Montebello · *Dept. of Comm. Dev.* · Mike Huntley; Dir.; 1600 W. Beverly Blvd.; 90640; Los Angeles; P 70,000; (323) 887-1390; Fax (323) 887-1401; www.cityofmontebello.com

Moreno Valley · *Moreno Valley Eco. Dev. Dept.* · Barry Foster; Eco. Dev. Dir.; 14177 Frederick St.; P.O. Box 88005; 92552; Riverside; P 180,000; (951) 413-3460; Fax (951) 413-3478; www.moreno-valley.ca.us

Morgan Hill · *Morgan Hill Eco. Dev.* · Tammy Brownlow; Project Mgr.; 17555 Peak Ave.; 95037; Santa Clara; P 37,000; (408) 776-7373; Fax (408) 778-7869; tammy.brownlow@morgan-hill.ca.gov; www.morgan-hill.ca.gov

Napa · *Napa Valley Eco. Dev. Corp.* · Charles Bogue; P.O. Box 6777; 94581; Napa; P 128,000; (707) 253-3212; nvedcinfo@nvedc.org; www.nvedc.org;

Needles · *City of Needles Eco. & Comm. Dev.* · Cindy Semione; Dev. Asst.; 817 Third St.; 92363; San Bernardino; P 6,000; (760) 326-5740; Fax (760) 326-5008; ndlspldr@citlink.net; cityofneedles.com

Newport Beach · *Newport Beach Eco. Dev. Div.* · Leigh De Santis; Eco. Dev. Administrator; 3300 Newport Blvd.; 92663; Orange; P 86,000; (949) 644-3225; (949) 644-3207; Fax (949) 644-3229; ldesantis@city.newport-beach.ca.us; www.city.newport-beach.ca.us

North Fork · *North Fork Comm. Dev. Cncl.* · Volney Dunavan; Admin.; P.O. Box 1484; 93643; Madera; P 3,500; (559) 877-2244; Fax (559) 877-4267; info@northforkcdc.org; www.northforkcdc.org

Oakland • *City of Oakland Comm. & Eco. Dev. Agency* • Gregory Hunter; Deputy Dir. of Redev.; 250 Frank H. Ogawa Plz., Ste. 5313; 94612; Alameda; P 600,000; (510) 238-3015; Fax (510) 238-3691; www.oaklandnet.com

Oakland • *Eco. Dev. Alliance for Bus.-EDAB* • Bruce Kern; Dir.; 1221 Oak St., Ste. 555; 94612; Alameda; P 1,498,000; M 600; (510) 272-3874; Fax (510) 272-5007; bkern@edab.org; www.edab.org; www.acgov.org

Oceanside • *City of Oceanside Eco. & Comm. Dev.* • Jane McVey; Eco. & Comm. Dev. Dir.; 300 N. Coast Hwy.; 92054; San Diego; P 176,644; (760) 435-3352; Fax (760) 722-1057; jmcvey@ci.oceanside.ca.us; www.ci.oceanside.ca.us

Ontario • *City of Ontario Redev. Agency* • John P. Andrews; Redev. Dir.; 603 N. Euclid; 91762; San Bernardino; P 145,000; (909) 395-2005; Fax (909) 395-2290; www.ci.ontario.ca.us

Oxnard • *Eco. Dev. Corp. of Oxnard* • Steven L. Kinney; Pres.; 400 E. Esplanade Dr., Ste. 301; 93036; Ventura; P 189,000; (805) 385-7444; (800) 422-6332; Fax (805) 385-7452; steve@edco.us; www.edco.us

Palm Desert • *Coachella Valley Eco. Partnership* • Shawnna Trombetta; Dir. of Bus. Dev.; 73-710 Fred Waring Dr., Ste. 106; 92260; Riverside; P 326,000; (760) 340-1575; (888) 318-CVEP; Fax (760) 340-9212; admin@cvep.com; www.cvep.com

Pasadena • *City of Pasadena Planning & Dev.* • Richard Bruckner; Dir. of Planning & Dev.; 175 N. Garfield, 3rd Flr.; 91109; Los Angeles; P 140,000; (626) 744-4660; Fax (626) 744-7041; www.cityofpasadena.net

Pico Rivera • *Pico Rivera Redev. Agency* • Jeff Brauckmann; Admin.; 6615 Passons Blvd.; P.O. Box 1016; 90660; Los Angeles; P 67,000; (562) 801-4379; Fax (562) 801-4765; www.pico-rivera.org

Placerville • *El Dorado County Eco. Dev.* • Samuel Driggers; Dir.; 330 Fair Ln.; 95667; El Dorado; P 177,000; (530) 621-5570; samuel.driggers@edcgov.us; www.edcgov.us

Quincy • *Plumas Corp.* • John Sheehan; Exec. Dir.; 550 Crescent St.; P.O. Box 3880; 95971; Plumas; P 23,090; (530) 283-3739; Fax (530) 283-5465; plumasco@psln.com; www.plumascounty.org

Red Bluff • *Tehama Local Dev. Corp.* • Dexter Wright; Exec. Dir.; 1740 Airport Blvd.; P.O. Box 1224; 96080; Tehama; P 65,000; (530) 529-7100; Fax (530) 529-0453; tldc@tehama.net; www.tldc.com

Redding • *Eco. Dev. of Shasta County* • Greg O'Sullivan; Pres.; 410 Hemsted, Ste. 220; 96002; Shasta; P 180,000; (530) 224-4920; (800) 207-4278; Fax (530) 224-4921; edc@shastaedc.org; www.shastaedc.org

Redding • *Superior Calif. Eco. Dev. Inc.* • Robert Nash; CEO; 499 Hemsted Dr.., Ste. A; 96002; Shasta; P 250,000; (530) 225-2760; Fax (530) 225-2769; www.scedd.org

Rialto • *Rialto Redev. Agency* • Robb Steel; Dir.; 131 S, Riverside Ave.; 92376; San Bernardino; P 97,400; (909) 879-1140; Fax (909) 875-5467; rda@rialtoca.gov; www.ci.rialto.ca.us

Riverside • *Inland Empire Eco. Partnership* • 1201 Research Park Dr., Ste. 100; 92507; Riverside; (951) 779-6700; Fax (951) 779-0675; dgoodrich@ieep.com; www.ieep.com

Riverside • *Riverside County Eco. Dev. Agency* • Robin Zimpser; Asst. CEO; 1325 Spruce St., Ste. 400; P.O. Box 1180; 92502; Riverside; P 1,946,000; (951) 955-8916; Fax (951) 955-6686; mortiz-sosa@rivcoeda.org; www.rivcoeda.org

Sacramento • *Sacramento Area Commerce & Trade Org.* • Barbara A. Hayes; Exec. Dir.; 400 Capitol Mall, Ste. 2500; 95814; Sacramento; (916) 441-2144; Fax (916) 441-2312; www.sacto.org

Sacramento • *Valley Vision* • Bill Mueller; CEO; 2320 Broadway; 95818; Sacramento; P 457,000; (916) 325-1630; Fax (916) 325-1635; mail@valleyvision.org; www.valleyvision.org

San Bernardino • *San Bernardino County Eco. Dev.* • Simone McFarland; Mgr.; 215 N. D St. Ste. 201; 92415; San Bernardino; P 1,970,000; (909) 387-4700; Fax (909) 387-9855

San Diego • *San Diego Reg. Eco. Dev. Corp.* • Julie Meier Wright; Pres./CEO; 530 B St., 7th Flr.; 92101; San Diego; P 3,500,000; (619) 234-8484; Fax (619) 234-1935; www.sandiegobusiness.org

San Francisco • *Mission Eco. Dev. Agency* • Luis Granados; Exec. Dir.; 3505 20th St.; 94110; San Francisco; P 700,000; (415) 282-3334; Fax (415) 282-3320; lgranados@medasf.org; www.medasf.org

San Francisco • *San Francisco Center for Eco. Dev.* • Dennis Conaghan; Exec. Dir.; 235 Montgomery St., Flr. 12; 94104; San Francisco; P 740,000; (415) 217-5187; info@sfced.org; www.sfced.org

San Jose • *City of San Jose Ofc. of Eco. Dev.* • Paul Krutko; Dir.; 200 E. Santa Clara St., 17th Flr.; 95113; Santa Clara; P 1,000,000; (408) 535-8181; Fax (408) 292-6719; www.sjeconomy.com

San Juan Capistrano • *San Juan Capistrano Eco. Dev.* • Douglas Dumhart; Mgr.; 32400 Paseo Adelanto; 92675; Orange; P 35,000; (949) 493-1171; (949) 443-6316; Fax (949) 493-1053; ddumhart@sanjuancapistrano.org; www.sanjuancapistrano.org

San Luis Obispo • *San Luis Obispo Eco. Dev.* • Claire Clark; Mgr.; 990 Palm St.; 93401; San Luis Obispo; P 44,000; (805) 781-7164; Fax (805) 781-7109; cclark@slocity.org; www.ci.san-luis-obispo.ca.us

Santa Ana • *Southland Eco. Dev. Corp.* • James Davis; Pres.; 400 N. Tustin Ave., Ste. 125; 92705; Orange; P 4,000,000; (714) 868-0001; Fax (714) 868-0003; www.southlandedc.com

Santa Cruz • *City of Santa Cruz Dept. of Planning & Comm. Dev.* • Ken Thomas; Future Planning; 809 Center St., Rm. 206; 95060; Santa Cruz; P 54,593; (831) 420-5100; Fax (831) 420-5101; www.ci.santa-cruz.ca.us

Santa Maria • *Santa Maria Valley Eco. Dev. Comm.* • Robert P. Hatch; Pres./CEO; 614 S. Broadway; 93454; Santa Barbara; P 137,000; (805) 925-2403; (888) 768-6274; Fax (805) 928-7559; chmbrchief@aol.com; www.santamariaedc.com

Santa Monica • *Santa Monica Eco. Dev. Div.* • Miriam Mack; Mgr.; 1901 Main St., Ste. E; 90405; Los Angeles; P 94,000; (310) 458-8906; Fax (310) 391-9996; econdevel.mailbox@smgov.net; www.smgov.net

Santa Rosa • *Sonoma County Eco. Dev. Bd.* • Ben Stone; Dir.; 401 College Ave., Ste. D; 95401; Sonoma; (707) 565-7170; Fax (707) 565-7231; bstone@sonoma-county.org; www.sonoma-county.org

Seaside • *City of Seaside Eco. Dev.* • Ray Corpuz; City Mgr.; 440 Harcourt Ave.; 93955; Monterey; P 34,000; (831) 899-6700; Fax (831) 899-6227; www.ci.seaside.ca.us

Shasta Lake • *City of Shasta Lake* • Fred Castagna; Proj. Mgr.; 1650 Stanton Dr.; P.O. Box 777; 96019; Shasta; P 10,000; (530) 275-7400; Fax (530) 275-7414; info@ci.shasta-lake.ca.us; www.ci.shasta-lake.ca.us

Simi Valley • *City of Simi Valley* • Brian Gablar; Dir. of Eco. Dev.; 2929 Tapo Canyon Rd.; 93063; Ventura; P 125,000; (805) 583-6701; Fax (805) 526-2489; bgabler@simivalley.org; www.simivalley.org

Sonora • *Central Sierra Planning Cncl.* • Larry Busby; Exec. Dir.; 53 W. Bradford Ave., Ste. 200; 95370; Tuolumne; (209) 532-8768; Fax (209) 532-7599; cspc@mlode.com

Stockton · *San Joaquin Partnership* · Michael E. Locke; Pres./CEO; 2800 W. March Ln., Ste. 470; 95219; San Joaquin; P 664,000; (209) 956-3380; (800) 570-5627; Fax (209) 956-1520; www.sjpnet.org

Temecula · *Temecula Eco. Dev.* · 43200 Business Park Dr.; P.O. Box 9033; 92589; Riverside; P 101,000; (951) 694-6444; (888) 836-2852; www.cityoftemecula.org

Thousand Oaks · *Thousand Oaks Eco. Dev.* · Gary Wartik; Eco. Dev. Mgr.; 2100 Thousand Oaks Blvd.; 91362; Ventura; P 125,000; (805) 449-2313; (805) 449-2100; www.toaks.org

Tulare · *Tulare County Eco. Dev. Corp.* · Paul Saldana; Pres./CEO; 4500 S. Laspina St.; 93274; Tulare; P 370,000; (559) 688-3388; Fax (559) 688-1406; info@edctulare.com; www.sequoiavalley.com

Twenty-nine Palms · *City of Twenty-nine Palms* · Charles LaClaire; Comm. Dev. Dir.; 6136 Adobe Rd.; 92277; San Bernardino; P 27,337; (760) 367-6799; Fax (760) 367-4890; admin@ci.twentynine-palms.ca.us; www.ci.twentynine-palms.ca.us

Vacaville · *City of Vacaville* · Michael Palombo; Eco. Dev. Mgr.; City Hall; 650 Merchant St.; 95688; Solano; P 98,000; (707) 449-5114; Fax (707) 449-5149; mpalombo@cityofvacaville.com; www.cityofvacaville.com

Vallejo · *City of Vallejo Eco. Dev. Div.* · Susan McCue; Prog. Mgr.; 555 Santa Clara St.; 94590; Solano; P 120,000; (707) 648-4444; Fax (707) 648-4499; econdev@ci.vallejo.ca.us; www.ci.vallejo.ca.us

Van Nuys · *Valley Eco. Dev. Center* · Roberto Barragan; Pres.; 5121 Van Nuys Blvd., 3rd Flr.; 91403; Los Angeles; P 213,000; (818) 907-9977; Fax (818) 907-9720; www.vedc.org

Ventura · *City of Ventura Eco. Dev.* · 501 Poli St., Rm. 218; P.O. Box 99; 93002; Ventura; P 104,000; (805) 677-3935; Fax (805) 677-3949; edr@cityofventura.net; www.cityofventura.net

Victorville · *Victor Valley Eco. Dev. Dept.* · Keith Metzler; Dir.; 14343 Civic Dr.; 92392; San Bernardino; P 104,000; (760) 955-5032; (760) 955-5000; Fax (760) 269-0080; info@victorvalleyca.com; www.victorvalleyca.com

Visalia · *Visalia Eco. Dev. Corp.* · Jim Claybaugh; Exec. Dir.; 220 N. Santa Fe; 93292; Tulare; P 120,000; (559) 773-8332; Fax (559) 734-7479; jim@visaliaedc.com; www.visaliaedc.com

Vista · *City of Vista Eco. Dev. Dept.* · 600 Eucalyptus Ave.; 92084; San Diego; P 94,500; (760) 639-6165; Fax (760) 724-3363; edinfo@cityofvista.com; www.cityofvista.com

Walnut · *City of Walnut Eco. Dev. Dept.* · Robert M. Wishner; City Mgr.; 21201 La Puente Rd.; 91789; Los Angeles; P 32,000; (909) 595-7543; Fax (909) 595-6095; rwishner@ci.walnut.ca.us; www.ci.walnut.ca.us

Watsonville · *Watsonville Eco. Dev.* · Jacqueline Ventura; Admin. Analyst; P.O. Box 50000; 95077; Santa Cruz; (831) 768-3095; Fax (831) 763-4114; jventura@ci.watsonville.ca.us; www.ci.watsonville.ca.us

West Sacramento · *City of West Sacramento/Eco. Dev.* · Diane Richards; Eco. Dev. Coord.; 1110 W. Capital Ave.; 95691; Yolo; P 42,000; (916) 617-4535; Fax (916) 373-5848; dianer@cityofwestsacramento.org; www.westsacrda.org

Westminster · *Westminster Redev. Agency* · Comm. Dev. Dir.; 8200 Westminster Blvd.; 92683; Orange; P 86,000; (714) 898-3311; Fax (714) 373-4684

Woodland · *Yolo County Eco. Dev.* · Wes Ervin; Mgr.; 625 Court St.; 95695; Yolo; P 185,000; (530) 666-8066; Fax (530) 668-4029; wes.ervin@yolocounty.org; www.yolocounty.org

Yreka · *Siskiyou Cty EDC* · Tonya Dowse; Exec. Dir.; 1512 S. Oregon St.; 96097; Siskiyou; P 45,150; (530) 842-1638; Fax (530) 842-2685; scedc@siskiyoucounty.org; www.siskiyoucounty.org

Yuba City · *Yuba-Sutter Eco. Dev. Corp.* · 1227 Bridge St., Ste. C; 95991; Sutter; P 135,200; (530) 751-8555; Fax (530) 751-8515; ysedc@ysedc.org; www.ysedc.org

Colorado

Federal

U.S. SBA, Colorado Dist. Ofc. · Greg Lopez; Dist. Dir.; 721 19th St., Ste. 426; Denver; 80202; Denver; (303) 844-2607; Fax (303) 844-6468; greg.lopez@sba.gov; www.sba.gov/co

State

Colorado Ofc. of Eco. Dev. & Intl. Trade · 1625 Broadway, Ste. 2700; Denver; 80202; Denver; (303) 892-3840; Fax (303) 892-3848; don.marostica@state.co.us; www.advancecolorado.com

Communities

Alamosa · *San Luis Valley Dev. Resources Group* · Michael D. Wisdom; Exec. Dir.; 610 State St.; P.O. Box 300; 81101; Alamosa; P 48,506; (719) 589-6099; Fax (719) 589-6299; www.slvdrg.org

Aurora · *Aurora Eco. Dev. Cncl.* · Dick Hinson Sr.; V.P.; 562 Sable Blvd., Ste. 240; 80011; Arapahoe; P 300,000; M 135; (303) 340-2101; Fax (303) 340-2111; hinson@auroraedc.com; www.auroraedc.com

Boulder · *Boulder Eco. Cncl.* · Frances Draper; Exec. Dir.; 2440 Pearl St.; 80306; Boulder; P 103,000; (303) 786-7567; Fax (303) 938-8837; www.boulderbusiness.org

Brighton · *Brighton Eco. Dev. Corp.* · Raymond H. Gonzales; Pres./CEO; 1850 E. Egbert St. Suite 140; 80601; Adams & Weld; P 36,000; (303) 655-2155; Fax (303) 655-2153; rgonzales@brightonedc.org; www.brightonedc.org

Broomfield · *Broomfield Eco. Dev. Corp.* · Donald G. Dunshee; Pres.; 2655 W. Midway Blvd., Ste. 370; 80020; Broomfield; P 53,000; M 105; (303) 469-7645; Fax (303) 469-9183; admin@broomfieldbusiness.com; www.broomfieldedc.com

Canon City · *Fremont Eco. Dev. Corp.* · Eddie McLish; Eco. Dev. Coord.; 402 Valley Rd.; 81212; Fremont; P 47,000; (719) 275-8601; (800) 426-4794; Fax (719) 275-4400; info@fremontedc.org; fremontedc.org

Castle Rock · *Castle Rock Eco. Dev. Cncl.* · Frank Gray; Pres./CEO; 513 Wilcox St., Ste. 230; 80104; Douglas; P 42,000; M 55; (303) 688-7488; Fax (303) 688-5338; info@credco.org; www.credco.org

Colorado Springs · *Colorado Springs Reg. Eco. Dev. Corp.* · Michael J. Kazmierski; Pres./CEO; 90 S. Cascade Ave., Ste. 1050; 80903; El Paso; P 654,350; M 300; (719) 471-8183; (887) 471-8183; Fax (719) 471-9733; csedc@csedc.org; www.coloradosprings.org

Commerce City · *City of Commerce City Eco. Dev.* · Brittany Morris; Eco. Dev. Dir.; 7887 E. 60th Ave.; 80022; Adams; P 40,000; (303) 289-3620; Fax (303) 289-3688; commercecityed.com

Denver · *Denver Ofc. of Eco. Dev.* · Andre Pettigrew; Exec. Dir.; 201 W. Colfax; Dept. 1005; 80202; Denver; P 554,000; (720) 913-1999; Fax (720) 913-1802; oed@denvergov.org; www.milehigh.com

Denver · *The Downtown Denver Partnership Inc.* · Tamara Door; Pres./CEO; 511 Sixteenth St., Ste. 200; 80202; Denver; P 554,000; (303) 534-6161; Fax (303) 534-2803; info@downtowndenver.com; www.downtowndenver.com

Durango • *La Plata Eco. Dev. Action Partnership* • Jack Llewellyn; Exec. Dir.; P.O. Box 3874; 81302; La Plata; P 47,000; (970) 259-1700; Fax (970) 385-7884; jack@durangobusiness.org; www.laplatacountycolorado.org

Englewood • *City of Englewood* • Alan White; Dir. of Comm. Dev.; 1000 Englewood Pkwy.; 80110; Arapahoe; P 32,000; (303) 762-2300; Fax (303) 783-6895; commdev@englewoodgov.org; www.englewoodgov.org

Englewood • *Southeast Bus. Partnership* • John Lay; Pres./CEO; 304 Inverness Way S., Ste. 315; 80112; Arapahoe; P 1,371,000; (303) 792-9447; Fax (303) 792-9452; jlay@sebp.org; www.sebp.org

Fort Collins • *see Loveland*

Fort Morgan • *Morgan County Eco. Dev. Corp.* • Kari K. Linker; Exec. Dir.; 300 Main St.; 80701; Weld; P 29,308; M 163; (970) 542-3527; (800) 522-4333; Fax (970) 542-3528; mcedc@morgancountyinfo.com; www.morgancountyinfo.com

Georgetown • *Clear Creek Eco. Dev. Corp.* • Peggy Stokstad; Pres./CEO; 502 6th St., 2nd Flr.; P.O. Box 2030; 80444; Clear Creek; P 10,000; (303) 569-2133; Fax (303) 569-3940; info@clearcreekedc.org; www.clearcreekedc.org

Georgetown • *Georgetown Promotion Comm.* • Town Hall; 404 6th St.; P.O. Box 426; 80444; Clear Creek; P 1,000; (303) 569-2555; Fax (303) 569-2705; www.town.georgetown.co.us

Golden • *Jefferson Eco. Cncl.* • Preston Gibson; Pres./CEO; 1667 Cole Blvd., Ste. 400; 80401; Jefferson; P 530,000; M 126; (303) 202-2965; Fax (303) 202-2967; info@jeffco.org; www.jeffco.org

Grand Junction • *Grand Junction Eco. Partnership* • Ann Driggers; Pres./CEO; 122 N. 6th St.; 81501; Mesa; P 138,000; M 220; (970) 245-4332; (800) 621-6683; Fax (970) 245-4346; gjep@gjep.org; www.gjep.org

Greeley • *Upstate Colorado* • Larry Burkhardt; Pres./CEO; 822 7th St., Ste. 550; 80631; Weld; P 228,000; M 100; (970) 356-4565; Fax (970) 352-2436; info@upstatecolorado.org; www.upstatecolorado.org

Holyoke • *Phillips County Eco. Dev. Corp.* • Nici Bishop; Dir.; P.O. Box 424; 80734; Phillips; P 4,680; M 50; (970) 854-4386; Fax (970) 854-4387; pced@pctelcom.coop; www.phillipscountyco.org

Julesburg • *Sedgwick County Eco. Dev. Corp.* • Patricia Stever; Exec. Dir.; 100 W. 2nd St.; 80737; Sedgwick; P 2,700; (970) 474-3504; (800) 226-0069; Fax (970) 474-4008; sced@kci.net; www.sedgwickcountyco.com

La Junta • *La Junta Eco. Dev.* • Ron Davis; Exec. Dir.; 1802 Colorado Ave.; 81050; Otero; P 9,000; (719) 384-6965; (719) 469-1081; Fax (719) 384-6960; ron.davis@ojc.edu; www.lajuntaeconomicdevelopment.net

Lakewood • *City of Lakewood* • Rebecca Clark; Dir. of Comm. Planning & Dev.; 480 S. Allison Pkwy.; Civic Center North; 80226; Jefferson; P 144,000; (303) 987-7730; Fax (303) 987-7090; ed@lakewood.org; www.lakewood-colorado.org

Littleton • *Littleton Bus./Ind. Affairs Dept.* • Christian Gibbons; Dir.; 2255 W. Berry Ave.; 80165; Arapahoe; P 42,000; (303) 795-3760; Fax (303) 795-3856; cgibbons@littletongov.org; www.littletongov.org

Longmont • *Longmont Area Eco. Cncl.* • John Cody; Pres./CEO; 528 Main St.; 80501; Boulder; P 86,000; (303) 651-0128; Fax (303) 682-5446; laec@longmont.org; www.longmont.org

Loveland • *Northern Colorado Eco. Dev. Corp.* • Mike Masciola; COO; 3553 Clydesdale Pkwy., Ste. 230; 80538; Larimer; P 230,000; M 250; (970) 667-0905; Fax (970) 669-4680; info@ncedc.com; www.ncedc.com

Montrose • *Montrose Eco. Dev. Corp.* • Sandy Head; Pres.; 100 Tessitori Ct., Ste. A; 81401; Montrose; P 38,000; M 160; (970) 249-9438; (800) 270-0211; Fax (970) 249-9459; sandyh@montroseedc.org; www.montroseedc.org

Northglenn • *City of Northglenn Eco. Dev.* • Kristin Sullivan; Eco. Dev. Coord.; 11701 Community Center Dr.; P.O. Box 330061; 80233; Adams; P 37,000; (303) 450-8743; Fax (303) 450-8793; www.northglenn.org

Pagosa Springs • *Archuleta County Eco. Dev. Assn.* • Bart Mitchell; Exec. Dir.; P.O. Box 1183; 81147; Archuleta; P 11,000; (970) 731-1443; info@archuletaeconomicdevelopment.org; www.archuletaeconomicdevelopment.org

Parker • *Parker Eco. Dev. Cncl.* • Benjamin Snow; Exec. Dir.; 19751 E. Mainstreet, Ste. R-11; 80138; Douglas; P 42,000; (303) 841-8683; Fax (303) 841-1979; bsnow@parkercolorado.org; www.parkercolorado.org

Pueblo • *Southern Colo. Eco. Dev. Dist.* • Allison Cortner; Exec. Dir.; 1104 N. Main St.; 81003; Pueblo; P 306,000; (719) 545-8680; Fax (719) 545-9908; allison@scedd.com; www.scedd.com

Rifle • *Associated Governments of NW Colorado* • Aron Diaz; Dir.; P.O. Box 351; 81650; Garfield; P 218,000; (970) 625-1723; Fax (970) 625-1147; www.agnc.org

Rocky Ford • *Rocky Ford Growth & Progress Inc.* • Julie Worley; Exec. Dir.; 203 S. Main St.; 81067; Otero; P 4,286; (719) 254-7414; Fax (719) 254-7416; jworley@ci.rocky-ford.co.us

San Luis • *Costilla County Eco. Cncl.* • P.O. Box 9; 81152; Costilla; P 3,500; (719) 672-0999

Silverthorne • *NW Colorado Cncl. of Govt.* • Ashley Wilson; Exec. Dir.; 249 Warren Ave.; P.O. Box 2308; 80498; Summit; (970) 468-0295; (800) 332-3669; Fax (970) 468-1208; www.nwc.cog.co.us

Stratton • *The Prairie Dev. Corp.* • Mrs. Jo Downey; Exec. Dir.; 128 Colorado Ave.; P.O. Box 202; 80836; Kit Carson; P 25,660; (719) 348-5562; (800) 825-0208; Fax (719) 348-5887; www.prairiedevelopment.com

Thornton • *City of Thornton Dev. Dept.* • Jeff Coder; Deputy City Mgr.; 9500 Civic Center Dr.; 80229; Adams; P 117,213; (303) 538-7295; Fax (303) 538-7373; citydevelopment@cityofthornton.net; www.cityofthornton.net

Trinidad • *Trinidad-Las Animas County Eco. Dev. Inc.* • Nancy Lackey; Pres.; 134 W. Main St., Ste. 12; 81082; Las Animas; P 16,302; (719) 846-9412; (800) 748-1970; Fax (719) 846-4550; tlac@tlac.net; www.tlac.net

Wellington • *Wellington Eco. & Bus. Resource Comm.* • P.O. Box 1500; 80549; Larimer; (970) 568-4133; info@wellingtoncoloradochamber.com; www.wellingtoncoloradochamber.com

Westminster • *Adams County Eco. Dev. Inc.* • Bill Becker; Pres./CEO; 12050 Pecos St., Ste. 200; 80234; Adams; P 425,000; (303) 450-5106; Fax (303) 252-8230; www.adamscountyed.com

Westminster • *City of Westminster* • Susan Grafton; Eco. Dev. Mgr.; 4800 W. 92nd Ave.; 80031; Adams; P 108,000; (303) 658-2400; Fax (303) 706-3922; sgrafton@cityofwestminster.us; www.cityofwestminster.us

Wheat Ridge • *City of Wheat Ridge* • Ryan Stachelski; Eco. Dev. Mgr.; 7500 W. 29th Ave.; 80033; Jefferson; P 32,000; (303) 235-2806; Fax (303) 234-5924; rstachelski@ci.wheatridge.co.us; www.ci.wheatridge.co.us

Yuma • *Yuma County Eco. Dev. Corp.* • Pat Duran; Exec. Dir.; P.O. Box 244; 80759; Yuma; P 10,000; (970) 848-3011; Fax (970) 848-3800; ycedc@ConsiderYumaCounty.com; www.ConsiderYumaCounty.com

Connecticut

Federal

U.S. SBA, Connecticut Dist. Ofc. · Bernard Sweeney; Dist. Dir.; 330 Main St., 2nd Flr.; Hartford; 06106; Hartford; (860) 240-4700; Fax (860) 240-4659; bernard.sweeney@sba.gov; www.sba.gov/ct

Communities

Bridgeport · *Ofc. of Planning & Eco. Dev.* · Edward Lavernoich; Deputy Dir.; 999 Broad St.; 06604; Fairfield; P 135,000; (203) 576-7221; (203) 576-7200; Fax (203) 332-5611; www.ci.bridgeport.ct.us

Cheshire · *Town of Cheshire Eco. Dev. Comm.* · Jerry Sitko; Coord.; 84 S. Main St.; 06410; New Haven; P 26,000; (203) 271-6670; Fax (203) 271-6688; jsitko@cheshirect.org; www.cheshire ct.org

Fairfield · *Town of Fairfield Comm. & Eco. Dev.* · Mark Barnhart; Dir.; 611 Old Post Rd.; 06824; Fairfield; P 57,340; (203) 256-3120; Fax (203) 256-3114; www.fairfieldct.org

Hartford · *Metro Hartford Alliance* · John Shemo; V.P. & Dir. of Eco. Dev.; 31 Pratt St., 5th Flr.; 06103; Hartford; P 709,000; (860) 525-4451; Fax (860) 293-2592; dmclane@metrohartford.com; www.metrohartford.com

Monroe · *Monroe Eco. Dev. Comm.* · Vinny Mangiacopra; Eco. Dev. Coord.; 7 Fan Hill Rd.; 06468; Fairfield; P 19,551; (203) 452-2819; (203) 452-5400; Fax (203) 261-6197; monroemeans business@monroect.org; www.monroect.org

New Britain · *New Britain C/C-Eco. Dev.* · Bill Carroll; Bus. Dev. Coord.; One Court St.; 06051; Hartford; P 72,000; (860) 229-1665; Fax (860) 223-8341; www.newbritainchamber.com

Old Saybrook · *Old Saybrook Eco. Dev. Comm.* · Wilma Asch; Exec. Dir.; 302 Main St., Town Hall; 06475; Middlesex; P 10,500; (860) 395-3139; Fax (860) 395-3125; wasch@town.old-saybrook. ct.us; www.oldsaybrookct.org

Waterbury · *Waterbury Dev. Corp.* · Leo Frank; CEO; 24 Leavenworth St.; 06702; New Haven; P 140,000; (203) 346-2607; Fax (203) 346-3910; frank@wdconline.org; www.wdconline.org

Windsor Locks · *Windsor Locks Eco. & Ind. Dev. Comm.* · Patrick McMahon; Coord.; 50 Church St.; 06096; Hartford; P 13,000; (860) 654-8923; (860) 627-1444; Fax (860) 292-1121; wleidc@sbcglobal.net; www.windsorlocksct.org

Delaware

State

Delaware Eco. Dev. Ofc. · Alan Levin; Dir.; 99 Kings Hwy.; Dover; 19901; Kent; (302) 739-4271; Fax (302) 739-5749; bernice.whaley@state.de.us; dedo.delaware.gov

Communities

Dover · *Kent Eco. Partnership* · Dan Wolfensberger; CEO; 435 N. Dupont Hwy.; 19901; Kent; P 146,000; (302) 678-3028; Fax (302) 678-0815; director@cdedc.org; www.cdedc.org

Wilmington · *Wilmington Eco. Dev. Corp.* · William Abernethy; Dir.; 100 W. 10th St., Ste. 706; 19801; New Castle; P 80,000; (302) 571-9088; Fax (302) 652-5679; www.wedco.org

Wilmington · *Wilmington Ofc. of Eco. Dev.* · Joe DePinto; Dir.; 800 N. French St., 3rd Flr.; 19801; New Castle; P 80,000; (302) 576-2120; Fax (302) 571-4326; joedipinto@ci.wilmington.de.us; www.ci.wilmington.de.us

District of Columbia

Federal

Eco. Dev. Admin. · John Fernandez; Asst. Secy. of Commerce; 1401 Constitution Ave. N.W., Ste. 7800; Washington, 20230; District of Columbia; (202) 482-5081; Fax (202) 273-4781; www.eda.gov

Ofc. of Natl. Ombudsman · Esther Vassar; Natl. Ombudsman; 409 3rd St. S.W., MC2120; Washington; 20416; District of Columbia; (888) 734-3247; Fax (202) 481-5719; ombudsman@ sba.gov; www.sba.gov/ombudsman

U.S. SBA, Washington D.C. Dist. Ofc. · Bridget Bean; Dist. Dir.; 740 15th St. N.W., Ste. 300; Washington; 20005; District of Columbia; (202) 272-0345; theodore.holloman@sba.gov; www. sba.gov/dc

State

Deputy Mayor's Ofc. for Planning & Eco. Dev. · Valerie Santos; Deputy Mayor; 1350 Pennsylvania Ave. N.W., Ste. 317; Washington; 20004; District of Columbia; (202) 727-6700; Fax (202) 727-6703; dmped.eom@dc.gov; www.dcbiz.dc.gov

Communities

Washington · *Dept. of Housing & Comm. Dev.* · Leila Finucane Edmonds; Dir.; 1800 Martin Luther King Jr. Ave. S.E.; 20002; District of Columbia; (202) 442-7200; Fax (202) 442-8391; www. dhcd.dc.gov

Washington · *Greater Washington Bd. of Trade* · John Kane; Pres./CEO; 1725 I St. N.W., Ste. 200; 20006; District of Columbia; (202) 857-5900; Fax (202) 223-2648; www.bot.org

Florida

Federal

U.S. SBA, Jacksonville Dist. Ofc. · Wilfredo Gonzalez; Dist. Dir.; 7825 Bay Meadows Way, Ste.100B; Jacksonville; 32256; Duval; (904) 443-1900; Fax (904) 443-1980; wilfredo. gonzalez@sba.gov; www.sba.gov/fl

U.S. SBA, Miami Dist. Ofc. · Francisco Marrero; Dist. Dir.; 100 S. Biscayne Blvd., 7th Flr.; Miami; 33131; Miami-Dade; (305) 536-5521; Fax (305) 536-5058; francisco.marrero@sba.gov; www.sba.gov/fl

State

Enterprise Florida · John Adams Jr.; Pres./CEO; 800 N. Magnolia Ave., Ste. 1100; Orlando; 32803; Orange; (407) 956-5600; Fax (407) 956-5579; rbenash@eflorida.com; www.eflorida.com

Communities

Apopka · *Apopka Area Eco. Dev. Cncl.* · Paul Seago; Pres.; 180 E. Main St.; 32703; Orange; P 40,000; (407) 886-1441; Fax (407) 886-1131; pauls@apopkachamber.org; www.apopkachamber.org

Bartow · *Central Florida Dev. Cncl.* · Tom Patton; Exec. Dir.; 600 N. Broadway Ave., Ste. 300; 33830; Polk; P 567,000; (863) 534-4370; Fax (863) 534-0886; tom@cfdc.org; www.cfdc.org

Bonifay · *Holmes County Dev. Comm.* · Jim Brook; Exec. Dir.; 106 E. Byrd Ave.; 32425; Holmes; P 19,000; (850) 547-4682; Fax (850) 547-4206; hcdc@wfeca.net; www.holmescountyonline.com

Boynton Beach · *City of Boynton Beach Eco. Dev.* · Quintus Greene; Dir. of Dev.; 100 E. Boynton Beach Blvd.; P.O. Box 310; 33425; Palm Beach; P 67,000; (561) 742-6372; Fax (561) 742-6357; www.boynton-beach.org

Bradenton · *Bradenton Downtown Dev. Auth.* · Karen Kyser; Program Admin.; 101 Old Main St.; 34205; Manatee; P 52,000; (941) 932-9440; Fax (941) 932-9552; www.ddabradenton.com

Bradenton · *Eco. Dev. Cncl., Manatee C/C* · Nancy A. Engel; Exec. Dir.; 222 10th St. W.; P.O. Box 321; 34206; Manatee; P 311,000; M 130; (941) 748-3411; Fax (941) 750-6041; info@ManateeEDC.com; www.manateeEDC.com

Brooksville · *Hernando County Ofc. of Bus. Dev.* · Michael McHugh; Dir.; 15800 Flight Path Ave.; 34601; Hernando; P 150,000; (352) 540-6400; Fax (352) 754-5361; www.hernandobusiness.com

Clearwater · *City of Clearwater* · William B. Horne; City Mgr.; 112 S. Osceola Ave.; P.O. Box 4748; 33758; Pinellas; P 110,000; (727) 562-4040; Fax (727) 562-4052; www.myclearwater.com

Crystal River · *Citrus County EDC* · John Siefert; Exec. Dir.; 28 N.W. US Hwy. 19; 34428; Citrus; P 130,000; M 70; (352) 795-2000; Fax (352) 795-0009; info@citrusedc.com; www.citrusedc.com

Daytona Beach · *County of Volusia Eco. Dev. Dept.* · Phil Ehlinger; Dir.; 700 Catalina Dr., Ste. 200; 32114; Volusia; P 507,105; (386) 248-8048; (800) 554-3801; Fax (386) 238-4761; www.floridabusiness.org

Fort Lauderdale · *Broward Alliance* · Joan Goodridge; Exec. V.P.; 110 E. Broward Blvd., Ste. 1900; 33301; Broward; P 1,000,500; M 800; (954) 524-3113; (800) 741-1420; Fax (954) 524-3167; www.browardalliance.org

Fort Myers · *Lee County Ofc. of Eco. Dev.* · James Moore; Exec. Dir.; 12800 University Dr., Ste. 300; 33907; Lee; P 615,741; (239) 338-3161; (800) 330-3161; Fax (239) 338-3227; edo@leegov.com; www.leecountybusiness.com

Fort Walton Beach · *Eco. Dev. Cncl. of Okaloosa Co.* · Larry Sassano; Pres.; P.O. Box 4097; 32549; Okaloosa; P 180,291; M 200; (850) 651-7374; Fax (850) 651-7378; info@florida-edc.org; www.florida-edc.org

Gainesville · *Gainesville Cncl. for Eco. Outreach* · Brent Christensen; Pres./CEO; 300 E. University Ave., Ste. 100; P.O. Box 2342; 32602; Alachua; P 240,000; (352) 378-7300; Fax (352) 378-7703; council@gceo.com; www.gceo.com

Hialeah · *Hialeah-Dade Dev. Inc.* · Mario Arus; Exec. Dir.; 501 Palm Ave.; 33010; Miami-Dade; P 254,000; (305) 884-1219; Fax (305) 884-1740

Hollywood · *South FL Reg. Planning Cncl.* · Carolyn Dekle; Exec. Dir.; 3440 Hollywood Blvd., Ste. 140; 33021; Broward; (954) 985-4416; Fax (954) 985-4417; sfadmin@sfrpc.com; www.sfrpc.com

Jacksonville · *Flagler Dev. Group* · Armando Codina; CEO; 10151 Deerwood Park Blvd.; Bldg. #100, Ste. 330; 32256; Duval; P 1,000,000; (904) 565-4100; Fax (904) 565-4144; www.flaglerdev.com

Jacksonville · *Jacksonville Port Auth.* · Roy Schleicher; CCO; 2831 Talleyrand Ave.; P.O. Box 3005; 32206; Duval; P 266,000; (904) 357-3030; Fax (904) 357-3066; info@jaxport.com; www.jaxport.com

Jacksonville Beach · *Jacksonville Beach Planning & Dev. Dept.* · Steve Lindorff; Dir.; 11 N. 3rd St.; 32250; Duval; P 23,900; (904) 247-6231; Fax (904) 247-6107; planning@jaxbchfl.net; www.jacksonvillebeach.org

Lake City · *Columbia County Ind. Dev. Auth.* · Jim Poole; Exec. Dir.; 164 N.W. Madison St., Ste. 103; 32055; Columbia; P 66,681; (386) 758-1033; Fax (386) 758-1167; jim@ccflida.com; www.columbiacountyfla.com

Lakeland · *Lakeland Downtown Dev. Auth.* · Anne B. Furr; Exec. Dir.; 228 S. Massachusetts Ave.; 33801; Polk; P 85,000; (863) 687-8910; Fax (863) 683-2783; anne.furr@lakelandgov.net; www.ldda.org

Lakeland · *Lakeland Eco. Dev. Cncl.* · Steven J. Scruggs; Exec. Dir.; 210 S. Florida Ave., Ste. 328; 33801; Polk; P 93,428; (863) 687-3788; Fax (863) 688-2941; sscruggs@lakelandedc.com; www.lakelandedc.com

Live Oak · *Comprehensive Comm. Svcs. Corp.* · Bobbie Lake; Exec. Dir.; 511 Goldkist Blvd.; 32064; Suwannee; P 12,000; (386) 362-7143; Fax (386) 362-7058

Live Oak · *Suwannee County Dev. Auth.* · Dennis Cason; Pres.; 816 S. Ohio Ave.; P.O. Drawer C; 32064; Suwannee; P 38,500; (386) 362-3071; Fax (386) 362-4758; dcason@suwanneechamber.com; www.suwanneechamber.com

Lutz · *Pasco Eco. Dev. Cncl.* · Mary Jane Stanley CEcD; Pres./CEO; 16506 Pointe Village Dr., Ste. 101; 33558; Hillsborough; P 424,355; (813) 926-0827; (800) 607-2726; Fax (813) 926-0829; mjstanley@pascoedc.com; www.pascoedc.com

Macclenny · *Baker County Dev. Comm.* · Darryl Register; Exec. Dir.; 20 E. Macclenny Ave.; 32063; Baker; P 25,000; (904) 259-6433; Fax (904) 259-2737; dregister@bakerchamberfl.com; www.bakerchamberfl.com

Mexico Beach · *Mexico Beach Comm. Dev. Cncl.* · Kimberly Shoaf; Dir.; P.O. Box 13382; 32410; Bay; P 1,300; (850) 648-8196; (888) 723-2546; Fax (850) 648-9403; kimberly@mexicobeach.com; www.mexicobeach.com/cdc

Miami Area

Dade County Ind. Dev. Auth. · James Wagner Jr.; Exec. Dir.; 80 S.W. 8th St., Ste. 2801; 33130; Miami-Dade; P 933,700; (305) 579-0070; Fax (305) 579-0225; info@mdcida.org; www.mdcida.org

Dept. of Bus. Dev. · Penelope Townsley; Dir.; 111 N.W. 1st St.; 19th Flr.; 33128; Miami-Dade; (305) 375-3111; Fax (305) 375-3160; www.miamidade.gov

Downtown Dev. Auth. of Miami · Alyce Robertson; Exec. Dir.; 200 S. Biscayne Blvd., Ste. 2929; 33131; Miami-Dade; (305) 579-6675; Fax (305) 371-2423; dda@miamidda.com; www.miamidda.com

Miami Beach · *Miami Beach Comm. Dev. Corp.* · Roberto Datorre; Pres.; 945 Pennsylvania Ave.; 33139; Miami-Dade; P 350,000; (305) 538-0090; Fax (305) 538-2863; www.miamibeachcdc.org

Milton · *City of Milton Planning & Dev. Dept.* · City Hall; P.O. Box 909; 32572; Santa Rosa; P 7,500; (850) 983-5440; Fax (850) 983-5415; www.ci.milton.fl.us

Milton · *Team Santa Rosa Eco. Dev. Cncl.* · Cindy Anderson; Exec. Dir.; 6491 Caroline St., Ste. 4; 32570; Santa Rosa; P 147,000; (850) 623-0174; Fax (850) 623-5932; canderson@teamsantarosa.com; www.teamsantarosa.com

Naples · *Eco. Dev. Cncl. of Collier County* · Tammie Nemecek; Pres./CEO; 3050 N. Horseshoe, Ste. 120; 34104; Collier; P 290,000; M 250; (239) 263-8989; (866) 362-7537; Fax (239) 263-6021; edc@enaplesflorida.com; www.enaplesflorida.com

Ocala · *Ocala-Marion County Eco. Dev. Corp.* · Peter Tesch; Pres./CEO; 3003 S.W. College Rd., Ste. 105; 34474; Marion; P 271,000; (352) 291-4410; Fax (352) 291-4414; marketing@ocalaedc.org; www.ocalaedc.org

Orange Park · *Clay County Dev. Auth.* · Danita Andrews; Dir.; 1734 Kingsley Ave.; 32073; Clay; P 180,000; (904) 264-7373; Fax (904) 269-0363; info@clayedo.com; www.clayedo.com

Orlando · *Metro Orlando Eco. Dev. Comm.* · Mike Bobroff; V.P./ COO; 301 E. Pine St., Ste. 900; 32801; Orange; P 1,800,023; M 450; (407) 422-7159; Fax (407) 425-6428; info@orlandoedc.com; www. orlandoedc.com

Palatka · *Putnam County Dev. Auth.* · Dana Jones; Exec. Dir.; 1100 Reid St.; 32177; Putnam; P 72,000; (386) 328-1503; Fax (386) 328-7076; dana@pcccfl.org; www.putnamcountychamber.org

Palm Coast · *Enterprise Flagler* · Greg Rawls; Deputy Dir.; 20 Airport Rd., Ste. A; 32164; Flagler; P 92,000; M 935; (386) 586-1224; Fax (386) 586-1226; expansion@enterpriseflagler.org; www.enterpriseflagler.org

Panama City · *Bay County Eco. Dev. Alliance* · Janet Watermeier; Exec. Dir.; 235 W. 5th St.; P.O. Box 1850; 32402; Bay; P 169,000; (850) 215-3752; (888) 229-7483; Fax (850) 763-6229; janet@bayeda.com; www.bayeda.com

Pensacola · *Pensacola Area C/C* · Charles Wood; Sr. V.P., Eco. Dev.; 117 W. Garden St.; P.O. Box 550; 32591; Escambia; P 305,000; (850) 438-4081; Fax (850) 438-6369; cwood@pensacolachamber. com; www.pensacolachamber.com

Perry · *Taylor County Dev. Auth.* · Rick Breer; Dir. of Eco. Dev.; 103 E. Ellis St.; P.O. Box 449; 32348; Taylor; P 19,422; (850) 584-5627; Fax (850) 223-0161; tcda@gtcom.net; www.tcda-fl.org

Plant City · *Greater Plant City Eco. Dev. Cncl.* · Marion Smith; Pres.; 106 N. Evers St.; P.O. Box CC; 33564; Hillsborough; P 34,750; (813) 754-1745; (800) 760-2315; Fax (813) 752-8793; info@ plantcity.org; www.plantcity.org

Pompano Beach · *Pompano Eco. Group* · Ric Green; Pres./CEO; 2200 E. Atlantic Blvd.; 33062; Broward; P 101,457; (954) 941-2940; Fax (954) 785-8358; www.pompanobeachchamber.com

Port Charlotte · *Charlotte County Eco. Dev. Ofc.* · Don Root; Dir.; 18501 Murdock Cir., Ste. 502; 33948; Charlotte; P 154,716; (941) 627-3023; (800) 729-5836; Fax (941) 627-6314; florida edo@charlottefl.com; www.floridaedo.com

Riviera Beach · *Riviera Beach Comm. Redev. Agency* · Floyd Johnson; Exec. Dir.; 2001 Broadway, Ste. 300; 33404; Palm Beach; P 35,000; (561) 844-3408; Fax (561) 881-8043; fjohnson@rbcra. org; www.rbcra.org

Rockledge · *Eco. Dev. Comm. of Florida's Space Coast* · Lynda Weatherman; Pres./CEO; 597 Haverty Ct., Ste. 100; 32955; Brevard; P 505,000; (321) 638-2000; (800) 535-0203; Fax (321) 633-4200; info@spacecoastedc.org; www.spacecoastedc.org

Saint Petersburg · *Eco. Dev. Dept., City of St. Petersburg* · Dave Goodwin; Dir. of Eco. Dev.; One 4th St. N., 9th Flr.; P.O. Box 2842; 33731; Pinellas; P 251,151; (727) 893-7100; (800) 874-9026; Fax (727) 892-5465; business@stpete.org; www.stpete.org

Saint Petersburg · *St. Petersburg Downtown Partnership* · Dr. Peter Betzer; Pres./CEO; 244 2nd Ave. N., Ste. 201; 33701; Pinellas; P 250,000; (727) 821-5166; Fax (727) 896-6302; peter@ stpetepartnership.org; www.stpetepartnership.org

Sarasota · *Eco. Dev. Corp. of Sarasota County* · Kathleen D. Baylis CEcD; Pres./CEO; 2601 Cattlemen Rd., Ste. 102; 34232; Sarasota; P 375,000; M 465; (941) 309-1200; Fax (941) 309-1209; kbaylis@edcsarasotacounty.com; www.edcsarasotacounty.org

Sebring · *Highlands County Eco. Dev. Comm.* · Dan P. Murphy; Exec. Dir.; 2113 U.S. 27 S.; 33870; Highlands; P 95,000; M 145; (863) 385-1025; (888) 388-4233; Fax (863) 385-1379; executive@ highlandsedc.com; www.highlandsedc.com

Starke · *Bradford Co. Eco. Dev. Auth.* · Jerome Johns; Chrmn.; 100 E. Call St.; 32091; Bradford; P 28,000; (904) 964-5278; Fax (904) 964-2863; pam@northfloridachamber.com; www.north floridachamber.com

Stuart · *Eco. Cncl. of Martin County* · Tammy Simoneau; Exec. Dir.; 1002 S.E. Monterey Commons Blvd., Ste. 203B; 34996; Martin; P 143,000; (772) 288-1225; www.mceconomy.org

Sunrise · *City of Sunrise, Ofc. of Eco. Dev.* · Lou Sandora; Dir. of Eco. Dev.; 10770 W. Oakland Park Blvd.; 33351; Broward; P 90,000; (954) 746-3430; Fax (954) 746-3439; www.sunrisefl.gov

Tampa Area

Greater Tampa C/C–Eco. Dev. · Bob Rohrlack; Pres./CEO; 615 Channelside Dr., Ste. 108; P.O. Box 420; 33601; Hillsborough; P 1,118,988; (813) 228-7777; Fax (813) 223-7899; info@ tampachamber.com; www.tampachamber.com

Tampa Bay Partnership · Stuart Rogel; Pres./CEO; 4300 W. Cypress St., Ste. 250; 33607; Hillsborough; P 3,700,000; M 200; (813) 878-2208; Fax (813) 872-9356; srogel@tampabay.org; www.tampabay.org

Tampa Port Auth. · Richard Wainio; Dir.; 1101 Channelside Dr.; P.O. Box 2192; 33601; Hillsborough; (813) 905-7678; Fax (813) 905-5109; www.tampaport.com

Titusville · *Space Coast Eco. Dev. Comm.* · Matt Chesnut; Exec. Dir.; 2000 S. Washington Ave., Ste. 2; 32780; Brevard; P 45,000; (321) 269-3221; (800) 749-3224; Fax (321) 567-0051; sedc@ titusville.com; www.Nspacecoastedc.org

West Palm Beach · *Bus. Dev. Bd. of Palm Beach County Inc.* · Kelly Smallridge; Pres.; 310 Evernia St.; 33401; Palm Beach; P 1,268,548; (561) 835-1008; Fax (561) 835-1160; www.bdb.org

West Palm Beach · *West Palm Beach Downtown Dev. Auth.* · Melissa Wohlust; Exec. Dir.; 301 Clematis St., Ste. 200; 33401; Palm Beach; P 90,000; (561) 833-8873; Fax (561) 833-5870; www.westpalmbeachdda.com

Winter Haven · *East Polk Committee of 100* · Jack Barnhart; Exec. Dir.; P.O. Box 1420; 33882; Polk; P 276,000; M 324; (863) 293-2525; Fax (863) 297-5818; contact@epc100.org; www. epc100.org

Georgia

Federal

U.S. SBA, Georgia Dist. Ofc. · Terri Denison; Dist. Dir.; 233 Peachtree St. N.E., Ste. 1900; Atlanta; 30303; Fulton; (404) 331-0100; Fax (404) 331-0101; www.sba.gov/ga

State

Georgia Dept. of Eco. Dev. · Heidi Green; Comm.; 75 Fifth St. N.W., Ste. 1200; Atlanta; 30308; Fulton; (404) 962-4000; Fax (404) 962-4009; business@georgia.org; www.georgia.org

Communities

Albany · *Albany/Dougherty Eco. Dev. Comm.* · 225 W. Broad Ave.; 31701; Dougherty; P 96,000; (229) 434-0044; Fax (229) 434-1310; info@choosealbany.com; www.choosealbany.com

Athens · *East Athens Dev. Corp.* · Winston Heard; Dir.; 410 McKinley Dr.; 30601; Clarke; P 20,000; (706) 208-0048; Fax (706) 208-0015; info@eadcinc.com; www.eadcinc.com

Atlanta · *Atlanta Dev.Auth.* · Peggy McCormick; Pres.; 86 Pryor St. S.W., Ste. 300; 30303; Fulton; P 361,000; (404) 880-4100; Fax (404) 880-0863; www.atlantada.com

Atlanta · *Fulton County Comm. Dev.* · Michelle Anderson; Eco. Dev. Dept.; 141 Pryor St. S.W., Ste. 5001; 30303; Fulton; P 904,801; (404) 612-3917; Fax (404) 730-8112; www.fultonecd.org

Blackshear • *Pierce County Ind. Dev. Auth.* • Jim Waters; Chair; 200 S. Central Ave.; P.O. Box 47; 31516; Pierce; P 17,000; (912) 449-7044; Fax (912) 449-7045; pierceco@accessatc.net; www.pierceco.org

Brunswick • *Brunswick & Glynn County Dev. Auth.* • S. Nathan Sparks; Exec. Dir.; 4 Glynn Ave.; 31520; Glynn; P 78,000; (912) 265-6629; Fax (912) 265-9460; snathansparks@bwkeda.com; www.georgiasgoldenopportunity.com

Camilla • *SW Georgia Reg. Dev. Center* • Dan Bollinger; Dir.; 30 W. Broad St.; P.O. Box 346; 31730; Mitchell; P 322,000; (229) 522-3552; Fax (229) 522-3558; dbollinger@swgrdc.org; www.swgrdc.org

Carnesville • *Franklin County Ind. Bldg. Auth.* • Lyn Allen; Dir. of Eco. Dev.; 165 Athens St.; P.O. Box 151; 30521; Franklin; P 22,365; (706) 384-5112; Fax (706) 384-3204; iba@franklin-county.com; www.franklin-county.com

Carrollton • *Carroll Tomorrow* • Daniel Jackson; CEO; 200 Northside Dr.; 30117; Carroll; P 107,325; (770) 832-2446; Fax (770) 832-1300; daniel@carroll-ga.org; www.carrolltomorrow.com

Claxton • *Claxton-Evans County Ind. Dev. Auth.* • Randy Mayfield; Chrmn.; 4 N. Duval St.; 30417; Evans; P 11,000; (912) 739-1391; Fax (912) 739-3827; info@claxtonevanschamber.com; www.claxtonevanschamber.com

Clayton • *Rabun County Eco. Dev. Auth.* • Sean Brady; Exec. Dir.; 232 Hwy. 441 N.; P.O. Box 761; 30525; Rabun; P 17,500; (706) 782-4812; Fax (706) 782-4810; sean@qamountains.com; www.gamountains.com

Cordele • *Cordele/Crisp Ind. Dev. Cncl.* • Bruce Drennan; Exec. Dir.; 202 S. 7th St.; P.O. Box 38; 31010; Crisp; P 23,000; (229) 273-9570; Fax (229) 273-9571; brucedrennan@crispidc.com; www.crispidc.com.

Cumming • *Forsyth County Dev.* • Jeff Chance; Dir.; 110 E. Main St.; 30040; Forsyth; P 110,000; (770) 781-2115; Fax (770) 781-2199; forsythco.com

Dallas • *Paulding County Ind. Bldg. Auth.* • C.B. Fair; Chrmn.; 455 Jimmy Campbell Pkwy.; 30132; Paulding; P 127,000; (770) 505-7700; Fax (770) 445-3050; www.pauldingcountychamber.org

Dalton • *North Georgia CDC Inc.* • Barry Tarter; Exec. Dir.; 503 W. Waugh St.; 30720; Whitfield; P 209,000; (706) 226-1110; Fax (706) 272-2253; ngcdc@ngcdc.org; www.ngcdc.org

Darien • *McIntosh County Dev. Auth.* • David Lyon; Dir.; 105 Fort King George Dr.; P.O. Box 896; 31305; McIntosh; P 11,500; (912) 437-6659; Fax (912) 437-3505; mcda@darientel.net; www.georgiascoast2success.com

Dublin • *Dublin-Laurens County Dev. Auth.* • M. Willie Paulk; Pres.; 1200 Bellevue Ave.; P.O. Box 818; 31040; Laurens; P 48,000; (478) 272-3118; (478) 272-3128; Fax (478) 275-0811; cwray@dublinlaurensgeorgia.com; www.dublinlaurensgeorgia.com

Eatonton • *Putnam Dev. Auth.* • Charles Haley; Chair; 305 N. Madison Ave.; P.O. Box 4088; 31024; Putnam; P 18,000; (706) 485-7701; Fax (706) 485-3277; epchamber@eatonton.com; www.eatonton.com

Fitzgerald • *Fitzgerald/Ben Hill County Dev. Auth.* • John Flythe; Dir.; P.O. Box 218; 31750; Ben Hill; P 20,000; (229) 423-9357; Fax (229) 423-1052; jflythe@windstream.net; www.fitzgeraldchamber.org

Fort Gaines • *Clay County Eco. Dev. Cncl.* • Ken Penuel; Chrmn.; P.O. Box 825; 39851; Clay; P 3,500; (229) 768-3238; www.fortgaines.com; www.claycountyga.org

Fort Oglethorpe • *see Rock Spring*

Fort Valley • *Dev. Auth. of Peach County* • Charles Sims; Exec. Dir.; 201 Oakland Heights Pkwy.; P.O. Box 935; 31030; Peach; P 24,000; (478) 825-3826; Fax (478) 825-4187; www.peachcounty.net

Hazlehurst • *Joint Dev. Auth. of Jeff Davis County* • Keith Carter; Exec. Dir.; 95 E. Jarman St.; P.O. Box 546; 31539; Jeff Davis; P 12,684; (912) 375-4543; Fax (912) 375-7948; devauthjd@bellsouth.net; www.hazlehurst-jeffdavis.com

Hinesville • *Liberty County Dev. Auth.* • Ronald E. Tolley CEcD; CEO; 425 W. Oglethorpe Hwy.; 31313; Liberty; P 72,000; (912) 368-3356; Fax (912) 368-5585; ron.tolley@lcda.com; www.lcda.com

Jackson • *Butts County Ind. Dev. Auth.* • Allan E. White; Exec. Dir.; 625 W. Third St.; P.O. Box 1085; 30233; Butts; P 26,000; (770) 775-4851; Fax (770) 775-3118; buttscoida@bellsouth.net; www.buttscountyida.com

Jasper • *Pickens-Jasper Eco. Dev.* • Gerald Nechvatal; Dir.; 500 Stegall Dr.; 30143; Pickens; P 30,000; (706) 692-5600; economicdevelopment@pickenschamber.com; pickenscountyga.gov

Jonesboro • *Dev. Auth. of Clayton County* • Grant Wainscott; Dir.; Jonesboro Historical Courthouse; 121 S. McDonough St.; 30236; Clayton; P 266,814; (770) 477-4591; Fax (678) 479-5385; grant.wainscott@co.clayton.ga.us; www.co.clayton.ga.us

Macon • *Middle Georgia Reg. Dev. Center* • Ralph Nix; Exec. Dir.; 175 Emery Hwy., Ste. C; 31217; Bibb; P 440,121; (478) 751-6160; Fax (478) 751-6517; www.mgrdc.org

Madison • *Ind. Dev. Comm.* • 115 E. Jefferson St.; P.O. Box 826; 30650; Morgan; P 17,000; (706) 342-4454; (800) 709-7406; Fax (706) 342-4455; www.madisonga.org

McDonough • *Henry County Dev. Auth.* • Robert C. White; Exec. Dir.; 140 Henry Pkwy.; 30253; Henry; P 175,000; (770) 288-8000; Fax (770) 288-8008; bwhite@hcda.org; www.hcda.org

Moultrie • *Colquitt County Eco. Dev. Corp.* • Darrel Moore; Pres.; 116 First Ave. S.E.; P.O. Box 487; 31776; Colquitt; P 43,500; (229) 985-2131; Fax (229) 890-2638; contact@moultriechamber.com; www.moultriechamber.com

Rabun County • *see Clayton*

Reidsville • *Tattnall County Dev. Auth.* • John Cheney; Exec. Dir.; 138 Brazell; P.O. Box 399; 30453; Tattnall; P 22,305; (912) 557-4119; Fax (912) 557-6318; tattnall@alltel.net; www.tattnall.com

Rock Spring • *NW Georgia Joint Dev. Auth.* • Jeff Mullis; Exec. Dir.; 10052 N. Hwy. 27; P.O. Box 220; 30739; Walker; P 58,000; (706) 375-5793; (800) 966-8092; Fax (706) 375-5795; www.nwgajda.com

Rome • *Coosa Valley Reg. Dev. Center* • William Steiner; Exec. Dir.; 1 Jackson Hill Dr.; P.O. Box 1798; 30162; Floyd; P 556,207; (706) 295-6485; Fax (706) 295-6665; wsteiner@nwgrc.org; www.cvrdc.org

Savannah • *Savannah Eco. Dev. Auth.* • Lynn Pitts; Sr. V.P.; P.O. Box 128; 31402; Chatham; P 308,000; (912) 447-8450; Fax (912) 447-8455; lpitts@seda.org; www.seda.org

Springfield • *Effingham County Ind. Dev. Auth.* • John A. Henry; CEO; 520 W. Third St.; P.O. Box 1078; 31329; Effingham; P 56,000; (912) 754-3301; Fax (912) 754-1236; effingham@effinghamcounty.com; www.effinghamcounty.com

Statesboro • *Dev. Auth. of Bulloch County* • Peggy Chapman; Exec. Dir.; 102 S. Main St.; P.O. Box 303; 30459; Bulloch; P 60,000; (912) 764-6111; Fax (912) 489-3108; peggychapman@statesboro-chamber.org; www.statesboro-chamber.org

Sylvania • *Screven County Ind. Dev. Auth.* • Gayle Boykin; Exec. Dir.; 101 S. Main St.; 30467; Screven; P 15,374; (912) 564-7850; Fax (912) 564-0081; www.screvencounty.com

Sylvester · *Worth County Eco. Dev. Auth.* · Greg Sellars; Exec. Dir.; 122 N. Main St.; 31791; Worth; P 22,000; (229) 776-7599; Fax (229) 776-0233; worthcoeda@bellsouth.net; www.worthcountyeda.com

Thomasville · *Thomasville-Thomas County C/C-Eco. Dev. Div.* · Donald P. Sims; Pres.; 401 S. Broad St.; P.O. Box 560; 31799; Thomas; P 45,000; (229) 225-1422; Fax (229) 226-9603; chamber@rose.net; www.thomasvillechamber.com

Thomson · *McDuffie County Dev. Auth.* · Mike Carrington; Exec. Dir.; 111 Railroad St.; 30824; McDuffie; P 22,000; (706) 597-1000; Fax (706) 595-2143; mcarrington@thomson-mcduffie.net; www.thomson-mcduffie.net

Valdosta · *Valdosta-Lowndes County Ind. Auth.* · Brad Lofton; Exec. Dir.; P.O. Box 1963; 31603; Lowndes; P 98,000; (229) 259-9972; Fax (229) 259-9973; info@industrialauthority.com; www.industrialauthority.com

Vienna · *Dooly County Eco. Dev. Cncl.* · Robert Jeter; Exec. Dir.; 402 Hawkinsville Rd.; 31092; Dooly; P 11,525; (229) 268-4554; Fax (229) 268-4500; bobjeter@sowega.net; www.doolyedc.org

Villa Rica · *Downtown Dev. Auth. of Villa Rica* · Barbara Daniell; Mgr.; 571 W. Bankhead Hwy.; 30180; Carroll; P 10,200; (678) 785-1000; Fax (770) 459-7003; bdaniell@villarica.org; www.villarica.org

Warm Springs · *Meriwether County IDA* · Kip Purvis; Pres.; 91 Broad St.; P.O. Box 9; 31830; Meriwether; P 22,534; (706) 655-2558; Fax (706) 655-2812; www.meriwetherida.com

Warner Robins · *Houston County Dev. Auth.* · Morgan Law; Exec. Dir.; 200 Carl Vinson Pkwy.; 31088; Houston; P 130,000; (478) 923-5470; Fax (478) 923-5472; hcda@houstoncountyga.net; www.houstoncountyga.net

Waynesboro · *Dev. Auth. of Burke County* · Jerry C. Long Sr.; Exec. Dir.; 241 E. Sixth St.; 30830; Burke; P 23,000; (706) 554-2923; Fax (706) 554-7091; jclong@burkecounty-ga.gov; www.burkecounty-ga.gov

Hawaii

Federal

Honolulu · *U.S. SBA, Hawaii Dist. Ofc.* · Jane Sawyer; Dist. Dir.; 500 Ala Moana Blvd., Ste. 1-306; 96813; Honolulu; (808) 541-2990; Fax (808) 541-2976; jane.sawyer@sba.gov; www.sba.gov/hi

State

Honolulu · *State of Hawaii Dept. of Bus., Eco. Dev. & Tourism* · Theodore E. Liu; Dir.; 250 S. Hotel St.; P.O. Box 2359; 96804; Honolulu; (808) 586-2355; Fax (808) 587-2377; library@dbedt.hawaii.gov; www.hawaii.gov/openforbusiness/

Communities

Hilo · *County of Hawaii, Dept. of Research & Dev.* · Randy Kurohara; Dir.; 25 Aupuni St., Rm. 109; 96720; Hawaii; P 162,971; (808) 961-8366; Fax (808) 935-1205; chresdev@co.hawaii.hi.us; www.co.hawaii.hi.us

Hilo · *Hawaii Island Eco. Dev. Bd.* · Jacqui Hoover; Exec. Dir.; 117 Keawe St., Ste. 107; 96720; Hawaii; P 168,000; (808) 935-2180; Fax (808) 935-2187; www.hiedb.org

Honolulu Area

City & County of Honolulu · Mufi Hannemann; Mayor; City Hall; 530 S. King St., Rm. 300; 96813; Honolulu; P 1,000,000; (808) 768-4141; Fax (808) 768-5552; www.honolulu.gov

Eco. Dev. & Tourism of Honolulu · Theodore Liu; Dir.; 250 S. Hotel St.; 96813; Honolulu; P 1,285,498; (808) 586-2423; Fax (808) 586-2377; www.hawaii.gov/dbedt

Honolulu Area, *continued*

Enterprise Honolulu · Pono Shim; Pres./CEO; 735 Bishop St., Ste. 412; 96813; Honolulu; P 1,276,000; (808) 521-3611; Fax (808) 536-2281; info@enterprisehonolulu.com; www.enterprisehonolulu.com

Lihue · *County of Kauai Ofc. of Eco. Dev.* · George Costa; Dir.; 4444 Rice St., Ste. 200; 96766; Kauai; P 62,000; (808) 241-4946; Fax (808) 241-6399; www.kauai.gov

Lihue · *Kauai Eco. Dev. Bd.* · Matilda Yoshioka; Pres.; 4290 Rice St.; 96766; Kauai; P 63,000; (808) 245-6692; Fax (808) 246-1089; www.kedb.com

Maui · *Maui Eco. Dev. Bd.* · Jeanne Skog; Pres./CEO; 1305 N. Holopono St., Ste. 1; Kihei; 96753; Maui; P 120,000; (808) 875-2300; Fax (808) 879-0011; info@medb.org; www.medb.org

Wailuku · *County of Maui* · Deidre Tegarden; Coord.; Ofc. of Eco. Dev.; 2200 Main St., Ste. 305; 96793; Maui; P 130,000; (808) 270-7710; Fax (808) 270-7995; www.mauicounty.gov

Idaho

Federal

U.S. SBA, Idaho Dist. Ofc. · Norm Proctor; Dist. Dir.; 380 E. Parkcenter Blvd., Ste. 330; Boise; 83706; Ada; (208) 334-1696; Fax (208) 334-9353; norman.proctor@sba.gov; www.sba.gov/id

State

Boise · *Idaho Dept. of Comm.* · Don Dietrich; Dir.; 700 W. State St.; P.O. Box 83720; 83720; Ada; (208) 334-2470; Fax (208) 334-2631; don.dietrich@commerce.idaho.gov; www.commerce.idaho.gov

Communities

Boise · *Boise Valley Eco. Partnership* · Paul Hiller; Exec. Dir.; 250 S. 5th St., Ste. 300; P.O. Box 2368; 83701; Ada; P 562,932; (208) 472-5229; Fax (208) 472-5201; rwinston@bvep.org; www.bvep.org

Caldwell · *Caldwell Eco. Dev. Cncl.* · Steve Fultz; Exec. Dir.; P.O. Box 668; 83606; Canyon; P 44,000; (208) 454-0087; Fax (208) 459-8115; sfultz@caldwellonline.org; www.caldwellonline.org

Garden City · *Sage Comm. Resources* · Kathleen Simko; Pres.; 125 E. 50th St.; 83714; Ada; P 415,281; (208) 322-7033; (800) 859-0321; Fax (208) 322-3569; www.sageidaho.com

Heyburn · *Mini-Cassia Dev. Comm.* · 1177 7th St.; P.O. Box 638; 83336; Minidoka; P 50,000; (208) 878-0576; Fax (208) 878-0577;

Idaho Falls · *Grow Idaho Falls Inc.* · Linda K. Martin CEcD; CEO; 151 N. Ridge Ave., Ste. A; 83402; Bonneville; P 140,000; (208) 522-2014; (800) 900-2014; Fax (208) 522-3824; linda@growidahofalls.org; www.growidahofalls.org

Jerome · *Jerome Eco. & Comm. Dev.* · Ben Marchant; Eco. Dev. Spec.; 152 East Ave., Ste. A; 83338; Jerome; P 18,342; (208) 324-8189; Fax (208) 324-8204; www.ci.jerome.id.us

Pocatello · *Bannock Dev. Corp.* · Gynii Gilliam; Exec. Dir.; ISU Research & Bus. Park; 1651 Alvin Ricken Dr.; 83201; Bannock; P 70,000; (208) 233-3500; Fax (208) 233-0268; www.bannockdevelopment.org

Pocatello · *SE Idaho Cncl. of Govts.* · Kathleen Lewis; Exec. Dir.; 214 E. Center; P.O. Box 6079; 83205; Bannock; P 154,000; (208) 233-4032; Fax (208) 233-4841; kathleen@sicog.org; www.sicog.org

Rexburg · *Madison Eco. Dev. Corp.* · Clair D. Boyle; Exec. Dir.; 310 N. 2nd E., Ste. 114; 83440; Madison; P 28,000; (208) 356-5009; clair@madisoneconomicpartners.org; www.idahobusiness.org

Twin Falls · *Region IV Dev. Assn.* · Joe Herring; Exec. Dir.; 315 Falls Ave.; P.O. Box 5079; 83303; Twin Falls; P 180,000; (208) 732-5727; Fax (208) 732-5454; joe@rivda.org; www.rivda.org

Wallace · *Silver Valley Eco. Dev. Corp.* · Vince Rinaldi; Exec. Dir.; 703 Cedar St.; 83873; Shoshone; P 12,827; (208) 752-5511; (800) 523-7889; Fax (208) 556-2351; www.silvervalleyedc.com

Weiser · *Washington County Eco. Dev. Comm.* · 309 State St.; 83672; Washington; P 11,000; (208) 414-0452; info@weiser chamber.com; www.weiserchamber.com

Illinois

State

Illinois Dept. of Comm. & Eco. Opportunity · Warren Ribley; Dir.; 500 E. Monroe; Springfield; 62701; Sangamon; (217) 782-7500; (877) 221-4403; Fax (217) 524-0864; patrick.blair@ commerce.state.il.us; www.commerce.state.il.us

Communities

Aledo · *Mercer Eco. Dev. Partnership* · Jenny Garner; Dir.; 2106 S.E. Third St.; P.O. Box 267; 61231; Mercer; P 16,912; (309) 582-7695; Fax (309) 582-7690; www.aledoil.org

Alexis · *see Monmouth*

Aurora · *Aurora Eco. Dev. Comm.* · Sherman Jenkins; Exec. Dir.; 43 W. Galena Blvd.; 60506; DuPage, Kane, Kendall & Will; P 175,000; (630) 897-5500; Fax (630) 897-0469; aedc@aurora-il. org; www.aurora-il.org/aedc

Berwyn · *Berwyn Dev. Corp.* · Anthony Griffin; Exec. Dir.; 3322 S. Oak Park Ave., 2nd Flr.; 60402; Cook; P 54,017; M 290; (708) 788-8100; Fax (708) 788-0966; info@berwyn.net; www.berwyn.net

Biggsville · *see Monmouth*

Carbondale · *Carbondale Bus. Dev. Corp.* · Kevin Baity; Asst. City Mgr. of EDC; 200 S. Illinois Ave.; P.O. Box 2047; 62901; Jackson; P 27,033; (618) 457-3226; kbaity@ci.carbondale.il.us; www.explorecarbondale.com

Champaign · *Champaign County Eco. Dev.* · 1817 S. Neil St., Ste. 201; 61820; Champaign; P 178,591; (217) 351-4133; Fax (217) 359-1809; www.champaigncountyedc.org

Charleston · *see Mattoon*

Chester · *Randolph County Progress Comm. Inc.* · Edward R. Crow; Exec. Dir.; 1 Taylor St.; P.O. Box 332; 62233; Randolph; P 33,900; (618) 826-5000; Fax (618) 826-3750; rndlfedc@ egyptian.net; www.randolphco.org

Chicago Area

Calumet Area Ind. Comm. · Ted Stalnos; Pres.; 1000 E. 111th St.; 10th Flr.; 60628; Cook; P 250,000; M 130; (773) 928-6000; Fax (773) 928-6016; teds@calumetareaindustrial.com; www. calumetareaindustrial.com

Mount Greenwood Local Redev. Corp. · Mary Kiedrow; Exec. Dir.; 3333 W. 111 St., Ste. B; 60655; Cook; P 18,000; (773) 881-0622; Fax (773) 881-4622; mglrc2000@wowway.com; www.mglrc.com

Planning & Dev. Comm. of the City of Chicago · Chris Raguso; Comm.; 121 N. LaSalle, Ste. 1000; 60602; Cook; P 3,000,000; (312) 744-9476; Fax (312) 742-9899; community development2@cityofchicago.org; www.cityofchicago.org

Cissna Park · *Cissna Park Eco. Dev. Bd.* · %Village Hall; 60924; Iroquois; P 1,000; (815) 457-2905

Clinton · *DeWitt County Dev. Comm.* · Ken Bjelland; Chrmn.; P.O. Box 376; 61727; DeWitt; P 18,000; (217) 935-2126; Fax (217) 935-6840; www.dewittcountyill.com

Danville · *Vermilion Advantage-EDC Div.* · Vicki Haugen; Pres.; 28 W. North St.; 61832; Vermilion; P 85,000; (217) 442-6201; (800) 373-6201; Fax (217) 442-6228; contact@vermilion advantage.com; www.vermilionadvantage.com

Decatur · *Eco. Dev. Corp. of Decatur-Macon County* · Craig Coil; Pres.; 101 S. Main St.; 62523; Macon; P 114,500; (217) 422-9520; Fax (217) 422-9307; ccoil@decaturedc.com; www. decaturedc.com

Des Plaines · *Des Plaines Eco. Dev. Comm.* · Mike Conlan; Deputy Dir. of Comm. & Eco. Dev.; 1420 Miner St.; 60016; Cook; P 57,000; (847) 391-5306; Fax (847) 827-2196; jganser@des plaines.org; www.desplaines.org

Dixon · *Lee County Ind. Dev. Assn.* · John R. Thompson; Pres./ CEO; 101 W. Second St., Ste. 301; 61021; Lee; P 35,000; (815) 284-3361; Fax (815) 284-3675; dchamber@essex1.com; www. dixonillinoischamber.com

Dolton · *Village of Dolton Eco. Dev.* · Bert Herzog; Dir.; 14014 Park Ave.; 60419; Cook; P 25,614; (708) 849-4000; bherzog@ vodolton.org; www.vodolton.org

Fairfield · *Fairfield-Wayne County Area Dev. Comm.* · Susan Murphy; Exec. Dir.; 121 E. Main St.; 62837; Wayne; P 5,421; (618) 842-4802; Fax (618) 842-4802; adc@fairfieldwireless.net; www. fairfield-il.com

Flora · *Flora Ind. Comm.* · Dan Sulsberger; Dir.; 131 E. 2nd; P.O. Box 249; 62839; Clay; P 5,100; (618) 662-7111; Fax (618) 662-7204; www.florail.us

Freeport · *Freeport Area Eco. Dev. Found.* · 27 W. Stephenson St.; 61032; Stephenson; P 26,000; (815) 233-1350; Fax (815) 235-4038; www.freeport-il-econ-dev.com

Gladstone · *see Monmouth*

Godfrey · *River Bend Growth Assn.* · Monica Bristow; Pres.; 5800 Godfrey Rd.; Alden Hall; 62035; Madison; P 100,000; M 650; (618) 467-2280; Fax (618) 466-8289; info@growthassociation. com; www.growthassociation.com

Granite City · *Tri-City Reg. Port Dist.* · Robert Wydra; Exec. Dir.; 1635 W. 1st St.; 62040; Madison; P 60,000; (618) 877-8444; (618) 452-3337; Fax (618) 452-3402; bwydra@tricityport.com; www. tricityport.com

Gulfport · *see Monmouth*

Jacksonville · *Jacksonville Reg. EDC* · Terry Denison; Pres.; 221 E. State St.; 62650; Morgan; P 45,000; M 170; (217) 479-4627; Fax (217) 479-4629; terry@jredc.org; www.jredc.org

Joliet · *Will County Center for Eco. Dev.* · John E. Greuling; Pres./ CEO; 116 N. Chicago St., Ste. 101; 60432; Kendall & Will; P 690,000; (815) 723-1800; Fax (815) 723-6972; info@willcountyced.com; www.willcountyced.com

Kankakee · *Eco. Alliance of Kankakee County* · Michael Van Mill; CEO; 200 E. Ct., Ste. 507; 60901; Kankakee; P 107,000; (815) 935-1177; Fax (815) 935-1181; eda@kankakeecountyed.com; www.kankakeecountyeda.com

Kirkwood · *see Monmouth*

Lawrenceville · *Lawrence County Ind. Dev. Cncl.* · Ann Emken; Exec. Dir.; 718 11th St., Ste. 2; 62439; Lawrence; P 15,545; M 200; (618) 943-5219; Fax (618) 943-5910; lcidc@lawrencecounty illinois.com; www.lawrencecountyillinois.com

Libertyville · *Lake County Partners* · David Young; Pres.; 28055 Ashley Cir., Ste. 212; 60048; Lake; P 617,000; (847) 247-0137; Fax (847) 247-0423; lcp@lakecountypartners.com; www.lakecounty partners.com

Lincoln · *Lincoln & Logan County Dev. Partnership* · Joel Smiley; Exec. Dir.; 1555 5th St.; 62656; Logan; P 31,500; (217) 732-8739; econdev@lincolnlogan.com; www.lincolnlogan.com

Little York · *see Monmouth*

Lockport · *City of Lockport* · Kimberly Jones; Eco. Dev. Coord.; Ofc. of Eco. Dev.; 921 S. State St.; 60441; Will; P 25,000; M 116; (815) 838-9500; Fax (815) 838-1861; www.lockport.org

Lomax · *see Monmouth*

Loves Park · *City of Loves Park EDC* · Dan Jacobson; Dir. of Dev.; 100 Heart Blvd.; City Hall; 61111; Winnebago; P 23,000; (815) 654-5033; Fax (815) 654-5004; www.loves-park.il.us

Macomb · *Macomb Area Eco. Dev. Corp* · Kim Pierce; Exec. Dir.; 510 N. Pearl St., Ste. 300; 61455; McDonough; P 21,000; (309) 837-4684; Fax (309) 837-4688; maedco@wiu.edu; www.maedco.org

Mattoon · *Coles Together* · Angela Griffin; Pres.; 400 Airport Rd.; 61938; Coles; P 52,000; (217) 258-5627; Fax (217) 235-9492; angela@colestogether.com; www.colestogether.com

McHenry · *McHenry County Eco. Dev. Corp.* · Jan Schober; Pres.; 5435 Bull Valley Rd.; 60050; McHenry; P 290,000; M 250; (815) 363-0444; Fax (815) 363-0464; info@mcedc.com; www.mcedc.com

Media · *see Monmouth*

Monmouth · *Western Illinois Eco. Dev. Partnership* · Jolene Willis; Exec. Dir.; 88-A Public Sq., Ste. 2; 61462; Warren; P 19,000; (309) 734-4253; Fax (309) 734-8811; jwillis@wiedp.org; www.wiedp.org

Mount Vernon · *Jefferson County Dev. Corp.* · Mary Ellen Bechtel; Exec. Dir.; 200 Potomac Blvd.; P.O. Box 523; 62864; Jefferson; P 40,523; (618) 244-3554; Fax (618) 244-7533; mbechtel@jeffcodev.org; www.jeffcodev.org

Naperville · *Naperville Dev.Partnership* · Christine Jeffries; Pres.; 212 S. Webster St., Ste, 104; 60540; DuPage & Will; P 140,000; (630) 305-7701; (877) 236-2737; Fax (630) 305-7793; ndp@naper.org; www.visitnaperville.com

Normal · *Eco. Dev. Cncl.of the Bloomington-Normal Area* · Marty Vanags; Exec. Dir.; 200 W. College Ave., Ste. 402; 61761; McLean; P 150,433; (309) 452-8437; mvanags@bnbiz.org; www.bnbiz.org

Oak Forest · *City of Oak Forest* · Adam Dotson; Comm. Dev. Dir.; 15440 S. Central Ave.; City Hall; 60452; Cook; P 28,000; (708) 687-4050; Fax (708) 687-1179; www.oak-forest.org

Oak Lawn · *Village of Oak Lawn* · Chad Weiler; Dir. of Comm. Dev.; 9446 S. Raymond Ave.; 60453; Cook; P 56,000; (708) 636-4400; Fax (708) 499-7823; www.oaklawn-il.gov

Oakland · *see Mattoon*

Olney · *Richland County Dev. Corp.* · Brandi Stennett; Exec. Dir.; 503 E. Main St.; 62450; Richland; P 17,000; (618) 392-2305; Fax (618) 392-2405; bstennett@rcdc.com; www.rcdc.com

Oquawka · *see Monmouth*

Orland Park · *Orland Park Planning/Comm.Dev.* · Robert Sullivan; Dir. of Comm. Dev.; 14700 Ravinia Ave.; 60462; Cook; P 56,876; (708) 403-6115; Fax (708) 403-6215; bsullivan@orland-park.il.us; www.orland-park.il.us

Ottawa · *Ottawa Eco. Dev. Task Force* · Boyd Palmer; Chrmn.; 633 LaSalle St., Ste. 401; 61350; LaSalle; P 19,000; (815) 433-0084; Fax (815) 433-2405; info@ottawachamberillinois.com; www.ottawachamberillinois.com

Pana · *Pana Ind. Dev. Corp.* · Jim Deere; Exec. Dir.; 120 E. 3rd St.; City Hall; 62557; Christian; P 7,100; (217) 562-3109; Fax (217) 562-3823; panail@consolidated.net; www.panaindustrial.com

Park Forest · *Park Forest Eco. Dev. & Planning* · Hildy Kingma; Dir.; 350 Victory Dr.; 60466; Cook; P 15,300; (708) 283-5622; Fax (708) 748-4355; hkingma@vopf.com; www.villageofpark forest.com

Peoria · *Eco. Dev. Cncl. for Central IL* · Vickie Clark; COO; 100 S.W. Water St.; 61602; Peoria; P 370,000; (309) 676-7500; Fax (309) 676-7534; rparks@edc.h-p.org; www.edc.centralillinois.org

Pittsfield · *Pittsfield Eco. Dev. Ofc.* · William W. McCartney; Dir.; 215 N. Monroe; 62363; Pike; P 4,614; (217) 285-4484; Fax (217) 285-4485; pittsed@pittsfieldil.org; www.pittsfieldil.org

Plano · *Plano Eco. Dev. Corp.* · Rich Healy; 7050 Burroughs Ave.; 60545; Kendall; P 10,000; (630) 552-9119; info@planoedc.org; www.planoedc.org

Quincy · *Great River Eco. Dev. Found.* · James Mentesti; Pres.; 300 Civic Center Plz., Ste. 256; 62301; Adams; P 42,202; (217) 223-4313; Fax (217) 231-2030; gredf@gredf.org; www.gredf.org

Raritan · *see Monmouth*

Riverdale · *Village of Riverdale Comm. & Eco. Dev.* · Janice Morrissy; Dir.; 157 W. 144th St.; 60827; Cook; P 16,500; (708) 841-2125; Fax (708) 841-7587; esilas@villageofriverdale.org; www.villageofriverdale.org

Rock Island · *Quad-City Dev. Group* · Nancy Mulcahey; Pres./CEO; 1830 Second Ave., Ste. 200; 61201; Rock Island; P 360,000; (309) 788-7436; Fax (309) 788-4964; etallman@quadcities.org; www.quadcities.org

Rockford · *Rockford Dept. of Comm. & Eco. Dev.* · Reid Montgomery; Dir.; 425 E. State St.; 61104; Winnebago; P 150,115; (815) 987-5600; Fax (815) 967-6933; www.rockfordil.gov

Roseville · *see Monmouth*

Springfield · *Dept. of Comm. & Eco. Opportunity* · Warren Ribley; Dir.; 620 E. Adams; 62701; Sangamon; (217) 785-6276; (800) 226-6632; warren.ribley@illinois.gov; www.enjoyillinois.com

Springfield · *Ofc. of Planning & Eco. Dev.* · Chuck Rose; Sr. Bus. Projects Mgr.; 800 E. Monroe, Ste. 107; 62701; Sangamon; P 111,000; (217) 789-2377; Fax (217) 789-2380; crose@cwlp.com; www.springfield.il.us

Sterling · *Greater Sterling Dev. Corp.* · Heather Sotelo; Exec. Dir.; 1741 Industrial Dr.; 61081; Whiteside; P 16,000; (815) 625-5255; Fax (815) 625-5094; hsotelo@sterlingdevelopment.org; www.sterlingdevelopment.org

Stronghurst · *see Monmouth*

Taylorville · *Christian County EDC* · Mary Renner; Exec. Dir.; 108 W. Market St., 2nd Flr.; 62568; Christian; P 12,000; (217) 287-2580; Fax (217) 824-6689; www.christiancountyedc.com

Washington · *Washington Eco. Dev. Comm.* · Carol Hamilton; Dir.; 114 Washington Sq.; 61571; Tazewell; P 13,500; (309) 444-8909; Fax (309) 444-9225; wcoc@mtco.com; www.washington coc.com

Waukegan · *Waukegan Port Dist.* · Harbor Master; 55 S. Harbor Pl.; P.O. Box 620; 60079; Lake; (847) 244-3133; Fax (847) 244-1348; www.waukeganport.com

Wheaton • *DuPage County Eco. Dev. Dept.* • Tom Cuculich; Dir.; 421 N. County Farm Rd.; 60187; DuPage; P 930,000; (630) 407-6700; Fax (630) 407-6702; www.dupageco.org

Woodridge • *Village of Woodridge Planning & Dev. Dept.* • Michael Mays; Dir.; 5 Plz. Dr.; 60517; Cook, DuPage & Will; P 33,253; (630) 719-4711; Fax (630) 719-4906; mmays@vil.woodridge.il.us; www.vil.woodridge.il.us

Yorkville • *Yorkville Eco. Dev. Corp.* • Lynn Dubajic; Exec. Dir.; 651 Prairie Pointe Dr., Ste. 102; 60560; Kendall; P 14,000; M 200; (630) 553-0843; Fax (630) 553-0889; dubajic@yedconline.org; www.yedconline.org

Zion • *City of Zion Eco. Dev. Corp.* • Delaine Rogers; Eco. Dev. Dir.; 2828 Sheridan Rd.; 60099; Lake; P 22,066; (847) 746-4015; Fax (847) 746-4017; delainer@zion.il.us; www.cityofzion.com

Indiana

Federal

U.S. SBA, Indiana Dist. Ofc. • Gail Gesell; Dist. Dir.; 8500 Keystone Crossing, Ste. 400; Indianapolis; 46240; Marion; (317) 226-7272; Fax (317) 226-7259; g.gesell@sba.gov; www.sba.gov/in

State

Indiana Eco. Dev. Corp. • Mitch Roob; CEO & Secy. of Comm.; One N. Capitol Ave., Ste. 700; Indianapolis; 46204; Marion; (317) 232-8992; Fax (317) 233-5123; mroob@iedc.in.gov; www.iedc.in.gov

Communities

Anderson • *Corp. for Eco. Dev. (CED)* • Rob Sparks; Exec. Dir.; 2701 Enterprise Dr., Ste. 109; 46013; Madison; P 131,501; (765) 642-1860; Fax (765) 642-0266; robsparks@cedanderson.com; www.cedanderson.com

Avon • *Hendricks County Eco. Dev. Partnership* • Cinda Kelley; Exec. Dir.; 5250 E. U.S. Hwy. 36, Ste. 1000-5; 46123; Hendricks; P 104,093; (317) 745-2400; Fax (317) 745-0757; kelley@hcedp.org; www.hcedp.org

Bedford • *Lawrence County Eco. Growth Cncl.* • Gene McCracken; Exec. Dir.; 1116 16th St.; 47421; Lawrence; P 46,413; (812) 275-5123; (812) 275-4493; Fax (812) 279-5998; gene@lawrencecountygrowth.com; www.lawrencecountygrowth.com

Bloomington • *Bloomington Eco. Dev. Corp.* • Ron Walker; Pres.; 400 W. 7th St., Ste. 101; 47404; Monroe; P 123,000; (812) 335-7346; Fax (812) 335-7348; rwalker@bedc.bloomington.in.us; www.comparebloomington.org

Bluffton • *Wells County Eco. Dev.* • Mike Row; Dir.; 211 W. Water St.; 46714; Wells; P 26,800; (260) 824-0510; Fax (260) 824-5871; mrow@wellsedc.com; www.wellsedc.com

Bremen • *Town of Bremen Dept. of Eco. Dev.* • Richard Martin; Dir.; 111 S. Center; 46506; Marshall; P 4,486; (574) 546-2044; Fax (574) 546-5487; townbremenin@mchsi.com; www.bremenin.org

Clinton • *Vermillion County Eco. Dev. Cncl.* • William Laubernds; Exec. Dir.; 259 Vine St.; 47842; Vermillion; P 16,733; (765) 832-3870; (765) 832-1899; Fax (765) 832-3871; susie@vermillioncountyedc.com; www.vermillioncountyedc.com

Columbus • *Columbus Eco. Dev. Bd.* • Corey Carr; Exec. Dir.; 500 Franklin St.; 47201; Bartholomew; P 70,000; M 100; (812) 378-7300; Fax (812) 372-6756; www.columbusin.org

Corydon • *Harrison County Eco. Dev. Corp.* • Darrell Voelker; Dir.; 310 N. Elm St.; 47112; Harrison; P 37,067; (812) 738-2137; Fax (812) 738-6438; dvoelker@hcedcindiana.org; www.hcedcindiana.org

Crawfordsville • *Montgomery County Eco. Dev.* • Bill Henderson; Exec. Dir.; 309 N. Green St.; 47933; Montgomery; P 37,800; (765) 362-6851; Fax (765) 362-6900; info@mcedinc.com; www.mcedinc.com

Decatur • *Adams County Eco. Dev. Corp.* • Larry D. Macklin; Exec. Dir.; 313 W. Jefferson St.; P.O. Box 492; 46733; Adams; P 33,625; (260) 724-2588; lmacklin@adamscountyedc.com; www.adamscountyedc.com

Elkhart • *North Central Indiana Bus. Assistance Center* • Philip Penn; Pres.; 418 S. Main St.; P.O. Box 2586; 46515; Elkhart; P 320,000; M 1,200; (574) 293-3209; Fax (574) 294-1859; info@elkhart.org; www.elkhart.org

Evansville • *Southwest Indiana EDC* • Greg Wathen; Pres./CEO; 100 N.W. 2nd St., Ste. 208; P.O. Box 20127; 47708; Vanderburgh; P 300,000; (812) 423-2020; (800) 401-7683; Fax (812) 423-2080; areafacts@southwestindiana.org; www.southwestindiana.org

Fort Wayne • *Fort Wayne-Allen County Eco. Dev. Alliance* • 111 W. Wayne St.; 46802; Allen; P 502,141; (260) 426-5568; Fax (260) 426-0837; email@theallianceonline.com; www.theallianceonline.com

Fowler • *Benton County Dev. Corp.* • P.O. Box 511; 47944; Benton; P 9,500; (765) 884-1200; Fax (765) 884-3239

Franklin • *Johnson County Dev. Corp.* • Cheryl Morphew; Exec. Dir.; 2797 N. Morton St., Ste. E; 46131; Johnson; P 135,951; (317) 736-4300; Fax (317) 736-7220; cmorphew@jcdc.org; www.jcdc.org

Greencastle • *Greencastle/Putnam County Dev. Center* • William A. Dory Jr.; Exec. Dir.; 2 S. Jackson St.; 46135; Putnam; P 38,000; (765) 653-2474; Fax (765) 653-6385; economic_development@greencastle.com; www.putnamcountyindianaeconomicdevelopment.com

Greenfield • *Hancock Eco. Dev. Cncl.* • Dennis Maloy; Dir.; One Courthouse Plz.; 46140; Hancock; P 57,000; (317) 477-7241; Fax (317) 477-2353; dmaloy@cedhc.org; www.cedhc.org

Greenwood • *see Franklin*

Hartford City • *Blackford County Eco. Dev. Corp.* • Rob Cleveland; Exec. Dir.; 121 N. High St.; P.O. Box 71; 47348; Blackford; P 14,000; (765) 348-4944; Fax (765) 348-4945; rcleveland@blackfordcoedc.org; www.blackfordcoedc.org

Huntington • *Huntington County United Eco. Dev. Corp.* • Mark Whickersham; Exec. Dir.; 8 W. Market St.; 46750; Huntington; P 39,293; (260) 356-5688; (888) 356-6660; Fax (260) 358-5692; helen@hcued.com; www.hcued.com

Indianapolis • *Indy Partnership* • Ron Gifford; Pres./CEO; 111 Monument Cir., Ste. 1800; 46204; Marion; P 1,882,000; (317) 236-6262; Fax (317) 236-6275; www.indypartnership.com

Kendallville • *Eco. Dev. Steering Comm.* • Anita Shepherd; Coord.; 122 S. Main St.; 46755; Noble; P 10,018; (260) 347-1554; (877) 347-1554; Fax (260) 347-1575; info@kendallchamber.com; www.kendallvillechamber.com

Knox • *Starke County Dev. Found.* • Charles Weaver; Exec. Dir.; 4 N. Main St.; 46534; Starke; P 25,000; (574) 772-5627; (800) 359-5627; Fax (574) 772-5912; execdir@starkecounty.com; www.starkecounty.com

Kokomo • *Greater Kokomo Eco. Dev. Alliance* • Jeb Conrad; Pres.; 700 E. Firmin St., Ste, 200; 46902; Howard; P 85,000; (765) 457-2000; Fax (765) 854-0481; jconrad@khdc.org; www.khdc.org

Lafayette · *Greater Lafayette Commerce* · 337 Columbia St.; P.O. Box 348; 47902; Tippecanoe; P 156,169; (765) 742-4044; Fax (765) 742-6276; www.lwldc.org

Leavenworth · *Crawford County Eco. Dev. Comm.* · Don DuBois; Exec. Dir.; 6225 E. Industrial Ln., Ste. B; 47137; Crawford; P 11,076; (812) 739-2248; don@selectcc.com; www.selectcc.com

Lebanon · *Boone County Eco. Dev. Corp.* · Dax Norton; Exec. Dir.; 218 E. Washington St.; 46052; Boone; P 52,000; (765) 482-5761; Fax (765) 482-5782; info@booneedc.org; www.booneedc.org

Liberty · *Union County Dev. Corp.* · Blanche Stelle; Exec. Dir.; 5 W. High St.; 47353; Union; P 7,300; (765) 458-5976; Fax (765) 458-5976; ucdc@dslmyway.com; www.ucdc.us

Linton · *Greene County Eco. Dev. Corp.* · Joan Bethell; Exec. Dir.; P.O. Box 7; 47441; Greene; P 32,573; (812) 847-4500; Fax (812) 847-0936; www.gcedc.us

Logansport · *Logansport-Cass County Eco. Dev. Found.* · Judi Barr; Exec. Asst.; 311 S. 5th; 46947; Cass; P 40,930; M 110; (574) 722-5988; Fax (574) 735-0909; skip@ledf.com; www.ledf.com

Marion · *Grant County Eco. Growth Cncl.* · Timothy K. Eckerle; Exec. Dir.; 301 S. Adams St., Ste. 109; 46952; Grant; P 73,403; (765) 662-0650; (888) 668-3203; Fax (765) 662-8340; www.grantcoindevelopment.com

Merrillville · *Merrillville Chamber Advancement Found.* · 255 W. 80th Pl.; 46410; Lake; P 35,000; (219) 769-8180; Fax (219) 736-6223; www.merrillvillecoc.org;

Middletown · *Middletown Progress Group* · 653 W. Locust St.; 47356; Henry; P 2,600; (765) 354-2268;

Monticello · *White County Eco. Dev.* · Connie Neininger; Exec. Dir.; 110 N. Main St.; P.O. Box 1031; 47960; White; P 25,267; (574) 583-6557; Fax (574) 583-6230; ledo@whitecountyindiana.us; www.whitecountyin.org

Mooresville · *Morgan County Eco. Dev. Corp.* · 4 E. Harrison St.; P.O. Box 606; 46158; Morgan; P 68,656; (317) 831-9544; Fax (317) 831-9548; mcedc@morgancoed.com; www.morgancoed.com

Mount Comfort · *see Greenfield*

New Castle · *New Castle/Henry County Eco. Dev. Corp.* · 100 S. Main St., Ste. 203; 47362; Henry; P 48,000; (765) 521-7402; Fax (765) 521-7404; info@midwestdevelopment.org; www.midwestdevelopment.org

Newburgh · *Warrick County Eco. Dev. Dept.* · Larry Taylor; Exec. Dir.; 7199 Parker Dr.; P.O. Box 875; 47629; Warrick; P 51,609; (812) 858-3555; Fax (812) 858-3558; bizinfo@warrick-edd.org; www.warrick-edd.org

North Vernon · *Jennings County Eco. Dev. Comm.* · Kathy Ertel; Exec. Dir.; P.O. Box 15; 47265; Jennings; P 27,500; (812) 346-2388; Fax (812) 346-7992; kertel@jenningsedc.com; www.jenningsedc.com

Peru · *Miami County Eco. Dev. Auth.* · James Tidd; Exec. Dir.; 1525 W. Hoosier Blvd., Ste. 201; 46970; Miami; P 36,082; (765) 689-0159; (800) 472-0449; Fax (765) 689-0168; info@miamicountyeda.com; www.miamicountyeda.com

Petersburg · *Pike County Eco. Dev. Growth Cncl.* · Paul Lake; Exec. Dir.; 714 1/2 Main St.; P.O. Box 204; 47567; Pike; P 13,000; (812) 354-2271; Fax (812) 354-7196; pikegrowth@verizon.net; www.pikecogrowth.org

Plymouth · *Plymouth Ind. Dev. Corp.* · 120 N. Michigan St.; 46563; Marshall; P 10,000; (574) 936-2323; Fax (574) 936-6584

Portage · *Northwest IN Forum Inc.* · Vincent Galbiati; Pres.; 6100 S. Port Rd.; 46368; Porter; P 787,000; (219) 763-6303; (800) 693-6786; Fax (219) 763-2653; www.nwiforum.org

Portland · *Jay County Dev. Corp.* · Bill Bradley; Exec. Dir.; 118 S. Meridian St., Ste. B; 47371; Jay; P 22,000; (260) 726-9311; Fax (260) 726-4477; bbradley@jaycodev.org; www.jaycountydevelopment.org

Richmond · *EDC of Wayne County* · Tim Rogers; Pres./CEO; 500 S. A St.; P.O. Box 1919; 47375; Wayne; P 72,000; (765) 983-4769; Fax (765) 966-8956; info@edcwc.com; www.edcwc.com; 800410GROW

Rochester · *Fulton Eco. Dev. Corp.* · Shane Blair; Exec. Dir.; 822 Main St.; 46975; Fulton; P 20,600; (574) 223-3326; Fax (574) 224-2329; sblair@fultondevelopment.org; www.fultondevelopment.org

Rockport · *Lincolnland Eco. Dev. Corp.* · Tom Utter; Exec. Dir.; 2792 N. U.S. Hwy. 23; P.O. Box 276; 47635; Spencer; P 21,000; (812) 649-2119; Fax (812) 649-2236; lincoln@psci.net; www.ledc.org

Rushville · *Rush County Eco. & Comm. Dev. Corp.* · Brad Buening; Exec. Dir.; 315 N. Main St.; 46173; Rush; P 18,016; (765) 938-3232; Fax (765) 932-4191; bbuening@rushecdc.org; www.rushcounty.com/ecdc

Salem · *Washington County Eco. Growth Partnership* · Jess Helsel; Pres.; 1707 N. Shelby St., Ste. 109; 47167; Washington; P 28,000; (812) 883-8803; Fax (812) 883-8739; infoi@wcegp.org; www.wcegp.org

Seymour · *Jackson County Ind. Dev. Corp.* · James Plump; Exec. Dir.; 301 N. Chestnut St.; P.O. Box 783; 47274; Jackson; P 41,335; (812) 522-4951; Fax (812) 522-1235; jimplump@jcidc.com; www.jcidc.com

Shelbyville · *Shelby County Dev. Corp.* · Dan Theobald; Exec. Dir.; 16 Public Sq., Ste. A; 46176; Shelby; P 44,300; (317) 398-8903; Fax (317) 398-8915; d.theobald@shelbydevelopment.com; www.shelbydevelopment.com

South Bend · *Project Future* · Patrick M. McMahon; Exec. Dir.; 401 E. Colfax Ave., Ste. 305; P.O. Box 1677; 46634; St. Joseph; P 265,559; (574) 234-6590; (800) 228-8086; Fax (574) 236-1060; www.projectfuture.org

Tell City · *Perry County Dev. Corp.* · 601 Main St. Ste. A; P.O. Box 731; 47586; Perry; P 18,843; (812) 547-8377; Fax (812) 547-8378; www.pickperry.com

Tell City · *Tell City Eco. Dev. Comm.* · Mary Cardinal; Pres.; City Hall Bldg.; P.O. Box 515; 47586; Perry; P 8,000; (812) 547-5511; Fax (812) 547-5111

Terre Haute · *Terre Haute Eco. Dev. Corp.* · 630 Wabash Ave., Ste. 101; 47807; Vigo; P 105,000; (812) 234-2524; Fax (812) 232-6054; info@terrehauteedc.com; www.terrehauteedc.com

Tipton · *Tipton County Eco. Dev. Corp.* · 136 E. Jefferson St.; 46072; Tipton; P 16,577; (765) 675-7417; (800) 461-4907; Fax (765) 675-8917; www.tiptonedc.com

Vincennes · *Knox County Dev. Corp.* · 1101 N. 3rd St.; P.O. Box 701; 47591; Knox; P 41,838; (812) 886-6993; Fax (812) 886-0888; info@kcdc.com; www.kcdc.com

Wabash · *Eco. Dev. Group of Wabash County* · William Konyha; Pres./CEO; 214 S. Wabash St.; 46992; Wabash; P 33,843; M 61; (260) 563-5258; (877) 509-9919; Fax (260) 563-4728; info@edgwc.com; www.edgwc.com;

Walkerton · *Walkerton Area Eco. Dev. Corp.* · Phillip Buckmaster; Exec. Dir.; 612 Roosevelt Rd.; 46574; St. Joseph; P 2,274; (574) 586-7766; Fax (574) 586-2248; waedc@walkerton.org; www.walkerton.org

Warsaw • *Kosciusko Dev. Inc.* • Kim Nance; Coord.; 313 S. Buffalo St.; 46580; Kosciusko; P 76,115; (574) 267-6311; (800) 776-6311; Fax (574) 267-7762; knance@kdi-in.com; www.kdi-in.com

Zanesville • *see Lebanon*

Iowa

Federal

U.S. SBA, Cedar Rapids Dist. Ofc. • Dennis Larkin; Branch Mgr.; 2750 1st Ave. N.E., Ste. 350; Cedar Rapids; 52402; Linn; (319) 362-6405; Fax (319) 362-7861; g.d.larkin@sba.gov; www.sba.gov/ia

U.S. SBA, Des Moines Dist. Ofc. • Joseph Folsom; Dist. Dir.; 210 Walnut St., Rm. 749; Des Moines; 50309; Polk; (515) 284-4422; Fax (515) 284-4572; j.folsom@sba.gov; www.sba.gov/ia

State

Iowa Dept. of Eco. Dev. • Bret Mills; Admin. Dir.; 200 E. Grand Ave.; Des Moines; 50309; Polk; (515) 725-3000; Fax (515) 725-3010; bret.mills@iowa.gov; www.iowalifechanging.com

Communities

Ackley • *Ackley Eco. Dev. Comm.* • Michael Nuss; Eco. Dev. Dir.; City Hall; 208 State St.; 50601; Hardin; P 1,809; (641) 847-2214; Fax (641) 847-3204; ackley@mchsi.com; www.ackleyiowa.net

Albia • *Albia Ind. Dev. Corp.* • Dave Johnson; Pres.; Bates Bldg.; 1 Benton Ave. W.; 52531; Monroe; P 8,016; (641) 932-7233; Fax (641) 932-3044; aidc@iowatelecom.net; www.albiaindustrial.com

Algona • *Kossuth/Palo Alto County EDC* • Maureen Elbert; Exec. Dir.; 106 S. Dodge St., Ste. 210; 50511; Kossuth; P 27,310; (515) 295-7979; Fax (515) 295-8873; kcedc@kossuthia.com; www.paloaltoiowa.com

Altoona • *Eastern Polk Reg. Dev. Inc.* • Don Coates; Exec. Dir.; 119 Second St. S.E., Ste. B; 50009; Polk; P 30,000; (515) 957-0088; Fax (515) 957-0089; eprd@iowa-property.com; www.iowa-property.com

Ames • *Ames Eco. Dev. Comm.* • Dan Culhane; Pres./CEO; 1601 Golden Aspen Dr., Ste. 110; 50010; Story; P 52,300; M 130; (515) 232-2310; Fax (515) 232-6716; dan@ameschamber.com; www.amesedc.com

Ankeny • *Ankeny Eco. Dev. Corp.* • Don Zuck; Exec. Dir.; 210 S. Ankeny Blvd.; P.O. Box 488; 50021; Polk; P 39,000; M 60; (515) 964-0747; Fax (515) 964-0487; www.ankenyedc.com

Arnolds Park • *Iowa Great Lakes Ind. Dev. Bd.* • Tom Kuhlman; Exec. Dir.; 243 W. Broadway; P.O. Box 9; 51331; Dickinson; P 16,424; (712) 332-2107; Fax (712) 332-7714; tom@okobojichamber.com; www.vacationokoboji.com

Atlantic • *Southwest Iowa Planning Cncl.* • M.J. Broomfield; Exec. Dir.; 1501 S.W. 7th St.; 50022; Cass; P 182,531; (712) 243-4196; (866) 279-4720; Fax (712) 243-3458; swipco@swipco.org; www.swipco.org

Audubon • *Audubon County Eco. Dev. Corp.* • 800 Market St.; 50025; Audubon; P 6,870; M 100; (712) 563-2742; Fax (712) 563-2537; aced@iowatelecom.net; www.auduboncounty.com

Avoca • *Western Iowa Dev. Assn.* • Lori Holste; Exec. Dir.; 1911 N. LaVista Height Rd., Ste. 102; P.O. Box 579; 51521; Pottawattamie; P 11,000; (712) 343-6368; Fax (712) 343-2136; lori@wida.org; www.wida.org

Bedford • *Bedford Area Dev. Center* • Deann Hensley; Exec. Dir.; 601 Madison; 50833; Taylor; P 1,600; (712) 523-3637; Fax (712) 523-3384; bedfordareadc@frontiernet.net; www.bedford-iowa.com

Belle Plaine • *Belle Plaine Comm. Dev. Corp.* • Jon Dayton; Exec. Dir.; 826 12th St.; 52208; Benton; P 2,878; M 140; (319) 434-6481; Fax (319) 434-6026; BPCDC@netins.net; www.belleplainecommunitydevelopment.com

Belmond • *BIDCO Ind. Dev.* • Dee Schrodt; Secy.; 327 E. Main St., Ste. 100; 50421; Wright; P 2,600; M 60; (641) 444-3937; Fax (641) 444-3944; bacoc@frontiernet.net; www.belmond.com

Bettendorf • *Bettendorf Dev. Corp.* • Steve VanDyke; Dir.; 1609 State St.; 52722; Scott; P 31,275; M 25; (563) 344-4060; Fax (563) 344-4012; svandyke@bettendorf.org; www.bettendorf.org

Bloomfield • *Davis County Dev. Corp.* • John Schroeder; Exec. Dir.; 111 S. Washington St.; P.O. Box 159; 52537; Davis; P 8,513; (641) 664-2300; www.daviscounty.org

Bondurant • *see Altoona*

Boone • *Boone's Future Inc.* • Robert Fisher; Exec. Dir.; 903 Story St.; 50036; Boone; P 12,805; M 70; (515) 432-7868; Fax (515) 432-3343; boonechamber@iowatelecom.net; www.booneiowa.com

Burlington • *Greater Burlington Partnership* • Dennis Hinkle; Pres.; 610 N. 4th St., Ste. 200; 52601; Des Moines; P 30,000; (319) 752-6365; (800) 827-4837; Fax (319) 752-6454; dhinkle@growburlington.com; www.growburlington.com

Carroll • *Carroll Area Dev. Corp.* • Jim Gossett; Exec. Dir.; 407 W. 5th St.; P.O. Box 307; 51401; Carroll; P 21,421; M 40; (712) 792-4383; Fax (712) 792-4384; chamber@carrolliowa.com; www.carrollareadev.com

Cascade • *Cascade Eco. Dev. Corp.* • Fred Kremer; Pres.; P.O. Box 695; 52033; Dubuque; P 1,958; (563) 852-7214; Fax (563) 852-7554; www.cityofcascade.org

Cedar Falls • *Cedar Falls Dept. of Dev. Svcs.* • Bob Seymour; Comm. Svcs. Mgr.; 220 Clay St.; 50613; Black Hawk; P 36,145; (319) 273-8606; Fax (319) 273-8610; bob.seymour@cedarfalls.com; www.50613.com

Cedar Rapids • *Priority One, Eco. Dev. Cedar Rapids C/C* • Mark Seckman; Pres.; 424 First Ave. N.E.; 52401; Linn; P 195,000; (319) 730-1420; Fax (319) 398-5228; mseckman@cedarrapids.org; www.priority1.com

Centerville • *Appanoose Eco. Dev. Corp.* • Tod Faris; Pres.; 307 N. 13th St.; P.O. Box 370; 52544; Appanoose; P 14,000; M 300; (641) 856-3388; Fax (641) 856-6046; aedcdirector@iowatelecom.net; www.appanoosecounty.org

Chariton • *Lucas County Dev. Corp.* • Ruth Comer; Exec. Dir.; 104 N. Grand; P.O. Box 735; 50049; Lucas; P 10,000; (641) 774-4059; Fax (641) 774-2801; ccdc@iowatelecom.net; www.charitonchamber.com

Charles City • *Charles City Area Dev. Corp.* • Timothy S. Fox CEcD; Exec. Dir.; 401 N. Main St.; 50616; Floyd; P 20,000; M 100; (641) 228-3020; (800) 640-2936; Fax (641) 228-4744; ccadc@charlescityia.com; www.charlescityia.com

Cherokee • *Cherokee Area Eco. Dev. Corp.* • Mark Buschkamp; Exec. Dir.; 418 W. Cedar St., Ste. B; 51012; Cherokee; P 5,035; (712) 225-5739; Fax (712) 225-1991; markcaedc@evertek.net; www.cherokeeia.com

Clinton • *Clinton Reg. Dev. Corp.* • Steven Ames; Pres.; 721 S. 2nd St.; 52732; Clinton; P 110,000; M 150; (563) 242-4536; Fax (563) 242-4554; sames@clintondevelopment.com; www.clintondevelopment.com

Columbus Junction • *Columbus Comm. Club* • Kirsten Shellabarger; Pres.; 232 2nd St.; 52738; Louisa; P 1,900; M 50; (319) 728-7971; Fax (319) 728-7502; www.columbusjunctioniowa.org

Conrad · *Conrad Chamber-Main Street* · Darla Ubben; Prog. Dir.; 204 E. Center St.; P.O. Box 414; 50621; Grundy; P 1,054; (641) 366-2108; Fax (641) 366-2109; cmspd@heartofiowa.net; www.conrad.govoffice.com

Coon Rapids · *Coon Rapids Dev. Group* · Doug Carpenter; Pres.; P.O. Box 226; 50058; Carroll; P 1,310; M 115; (712) 999-2734; (712) 999-2225; crdg@crmu.net; www.coonrapidsiowa.com

Corning · *Adams Comm. Eco. Dev. Corp.* · Beth Waddle; Exec. Dir.; 710 Davis Ave.; 50841; Adams; P 1,800; (641) 322-5229; Fax (641) 322-4387; acedc@frontiernet.net; www.adamscountyiowa.com

Council Bluffs · *City of Council Bluffs Comm. Dev. Dept.* · Donald Gross; Dir.; 209 Pearl St.; 51503; Pottawattamie; P 58,000; (712) 328-4629; Fax (712) 328-4915; community@councilbluffs-ia.gov; www.communitydev.councilbluffs-ia.gov

Cresco · *Howard County Eco. Dev.* · Ken Paxton; Eco. Dev. Dir.; 101 Second Ave. S.W.; P.O. Box 403; 52136; Howard; P 9,932; (563) 547-3434; Fax (563) 547-2056; kpaxton@howard-county.com; www.howard-county.com

Des Moines · *City of Des Moines–Ofc. of Eco. Dev.* · Rick Clark; City Mgr.; City Hall; 400 Robert D. Ray Dr.; 50309; Polk & Warren; P 200,000; (515) 283-4004; Fax (515) 237-1667; www.dmgov.org

Des Moines · *Iowa Area Dev. Group* · Rand M. Fisher; Pres.; 2700 Westown Pkwy., Ste. 425; 50266; Polk & Warren; P 540,000; (515) 223-4817; Fax (515) 223-5719; rfisher@iadg.com; www.iadg.com

DeWitt · *DeWitt Dev. Co.* · Tami Petsche; Exec. Dir.; 1010 6th Ave.; 52742; Clinton; P 5,149; (563) 659-8508; Fax (563) 659-9450; ddc.ceo@dewitt.org; www.dewittdevelopmentcompany.com

Dubuque · *Greater Dubuque Dev. Corp.* · Rick Dickinson; Exec. Dir./COO; 300 Main St., Ste. 120; 52001; Dubuque; P 91,000; (563) 557-9049; Fax (563) 557-1059; www.greaterdubuque.org

Dysart · *Dysart Dev. Corp.* · Dwayne Luze; Pres.; P.O. Box 223; 52224; Tama; P 1,303; (319) 476-2332; www.dysartiowa.com

Eddyville · *Eddyville Bus. Center* · Ron Richards; Pres.; P.O. Box 585; 52553; Wapello; P 1,500; (641) 969-4952; Fax (641) 969-5528

Eldora · *City of Eldora Eco. Dev.* · Deb Crosser; Exec. Dir.; 1442 Washington St.; 50627; Hardin; P 3,035; (641) 939-3241; Fax (641) 939-7555; www.eldoraiowa.com

Elkader · *Main Street Elkader/Eco. Dev.* · Roger Thomas; Dir.; 207 N. Main St.; P.O. Box 125; 52043; Clayton; P 1,500; (563) 245-2770; Fax (563) 245-1033; mse@alpinecom.net; www.elkader-iowa.com

Fairfield · *Fairfield Eco. Dev. Assn.* · Brent M. Willett; Exec. Dir.; 204 W. Broadway; 52556; Jefferson; P 15,500; M 75; (641) 472-3436; Fax (641) 472-6510; bwillett@fairfieldiowa.com; www.fairfieldiowa.com

Forest City · *Forest City Dev. Inc.* · David Kingland; Pres.; 145 E. K St.; 50436; Winnebago; P 4,500; M 45; (641) 585-5560; Fax (641) 585-2687; www.forestcityia.com

Fort Dodge · *The Dev. Corp. of Fort Dodge & Webster County* · John Kramer; Pres.; 822 Central Ave., Ste. 406; 50501; Webster; P 44,000; (515) 955-7788; Fax (515) 955-5421; john@wcfddevelopment.com; www.wcfddevelopment.com

Fredericksburg · *Fredericksburg Comm. Dev. Corp.* · Cindy Lantow; Eco. Dev. Dir.; 151 W. Main; P.O. Box 318; 50630; Chickasaw; P 984; (563) 237-5725; www.fredericksburgiowa.com

Garner · *Garner Area Comm. Betterment Assn.* · Howard Parrott; Secy./Treas.; 265 E. Lyon St.; 50438; Hancock; P 2,922; M 105; (641) 923-2739; hmparrot@ncn.net; www.garneriowa.org

Gladbrook · *Gladbrook Dev. Corp.* · Denny Gienger; Treas.; P.O. Box 309; 50635; Tama; P 1,100; (641) 473-3056; Fax (641) 473-3056

Greenfield · *Greenfield Main Street Dev. Corp.* · Ginny Kuhfus; Dir.; 201 S. First St.; P.O. Box 61; 50849; Adair; P 2,195; (641) 743-8444; Fax (641) 743-8205; grfld_cc_ms_dev@iowatelecom.net; www.greenfieldiowa.com

Grinnell · *Poweshiek Area Dev.* · Bill Menner; Exec. Dir.; 927 4th Ave.; 50112; Poweshiek; P 9,100; (641) 236-1626; Fax (641) 236-2626; bill@powi80.com; www.powi80.com

Hampton · *Franklin County Dev. Assn.* · Karen Mitchell; Eco. Dev. Dir.; 5 First St. S.W.; 50441; Franklin; P 11,800; (641) 456-5668; Fax (641) 456-5660; fcda_director@mchsi.com; www.franklincountyiowa.com

Harlan · *Shelby County DevelopSource* · 1901 Hawkeye Ave., Ste. 101; 51537; Shelby; P 13,000; (712) 755-3569; Fax (712) 733-8921; scds@developsource.com; www.DevelopSource.com

Hartley · *Hartley Eco. Dev. Corp.* · Brian Pals; City Admin.; 11 S. Central Ave.; 51346; O'Brien; P 1,733; (712) 928-2240; Fax (712) 928-2878; www.hartleyiowa.com

Hull · *Hull Ind. Dev. Corp.* · Les VanRoekel; City Admin.; City Hall; P.O. Box 816; 51239; Sioux; P 1,960; (712) 439-1521; Fax (712) 439-2512; www.cityofhull.org

Ida Grove · *Ida Grove Eco. Dev. Corp.* · Clay Miller; Pres.; 501 Second St.; P.O. Box 111; 51445; Ida; P 2,350; (712) 364-3393; Fax (712) 364-3293; www.idagrovechamber.com

Independence · *Buchanan County Eco. Dev. Comm.* · Greg Halverson; Dir.; P.O. Box 109; 50644; Buchanan; P 21,000; (319) 334-7497; Fax (319) 334-5982; director@growbuchanan.com; www.growbuchanan.com

Independence · *Independence Enterprises Inc.* · Steve Ohl; Pres.; 115 First St. E.; 50644; Buchanan; P 6,500; (319) 334-4329; (319) 334-7497; Fax (319) 334-6335; steveohl@indytel.com

Indianola · *Warren County Eco. Dev. Corp.* · Tiffany Coleman; Exec. Dir.; 515 N. Jefferson Way, Ste. C; 50125; Warren; P 43,062; (515) 961-1067; Fax (515) 961-1156; wcedc@mchsi.com; www.wcedc.com

Inwood · *Inwood Dev. Corp.* · Carol VanderKolk; City Clerk; P.O. Box 298; 51240; Lyon; P 875; (712) 753-4833; Fax (712) 753-2538; cityofinwood@hotmail.com; www.inwoodiowa.com

Iowa City · *Iowa City Area Dev. Group* · Joseph Raso; Pres.; 325 E. Washington St., Ste. 101; 52240; Johnson; P 125,000; (319) 354-3939; Fax (319) 338-9958; jraso@iowacityarea.com; www.iowacityareadevelopment.com

Iowa Falls · *Iowa Falls Area Dev. Corp.* · Thomas Deimerly; Exec. Dir.; 520 Rocksylvania Ave.; 50126; Hardin; P 5,200; M 45; (641) 648-5604; Fax (641) 648-3702; ifadc@iafalls.com; www.iowafallsdevelopment.com

Jefferson · *Greene County Dev. Corp.* · Ken Paxton; Exec. Dir.; 220 N. Chestnut St.; 50129; Greene; P 9,800; M 58; (515) 386-8255; (515) 386-2155; Fax (515) 386-2156; tourism@greenecountyiowa.com; www.greenecountyiowadevelopment.org

Johnston · *Iowa Bus. Growth Co.* · Dan Robeson; Exec. V.P.; 5409 N.W. 88th St., Ste. 100; 50131; Polk; (515) 223-4511; Fax (515) 223-5017; www.iowabusinessgrowth.com

Knoxville · *Knoxville C/C Eco. Dev.* · Roxanne Johnson; Exec. Dir.; 309 E. Main St.; 50138; Marion; P 8,270; (641) 828-7555; Fax (641) 828-7978; www.knoxville-iowa.com

Lake Mills • *Winn-Worth BETCO* • Teresa Nicholson; Exec. Dir.; 203A N. 1st Ave. W.; P.O. Box 93; 50450; Winnebago; P 19,000; (641) 592-0800; Fax (641) 592-0801; wwb2@wctatel.net; www.win-worthbetco.com

LeMars • *LeMars Bus. Initiative Corp.* • Neal Adler; Exec. Dir.; 50 Central Ave. S.E.; 51031; Plymouth; P 9,500; (712) 546-8821; Fax (712) 546-7218; neal@lemarschamber.org; www.lemarsiowa.com

Lenox • *Lenox Dev. Corp.* • Gary Zabel; Dir.; P.O. Box 92; 50851; Adams & Taylor; P 1,400; (641) 333-2255; (641) 333-4272; www.lenoxia.com

Logan • *Harrison County Dev. Corp.* • Renea Anderson; Exec. Dir.; 109 N. 4th Ave., Ste. 2; 51546; Harrison; P 15,666; M 100; (712) 644-3081; Fax (712) 644-3107; hcdc@iowatelecom.net; www.hcdconline.com

Lorimor • *Lorimor Comm. Dev. Corp.* • F. Dennis Orwan; Pres.; P.O. Box 63; 50149; Union; P 427; (641) 763-2334; fdorwan@grm.net; www.lorimor.org

Manchester • *Delaware County Eco. Dev. Comm.* • Donna Boss; Exec. Dir.; 200 E. Main St.; 52057; Delaware; P 18,404; (563) 927-3325; Fax (563) 927-2958; dboss@delawarecountyia.com; www.delawarecountyia.com

Mapleton • *Maple Valley Dev. Inc.* • Marsha Craig; Pres.; P.O. Box 164; 51034; Monona; P 1,300; M 84; (712) 881-1351; (712) 882-1343; www.mapleton.com

Marcus • *Marcus for Progress* • Angie Cowan; Dir.; 222 N. Main St.; 51035; Cherokee; P 1,200; (712) 376-2680; marcus@midlands.net; www.marcusiowa.com

Marengo • *Marengo Ind. Dev. Corp.* • Virgil Head; Pres.; P.O. Box 168; 52301; Iowa; P 2,535; (319) 642-5511; Fax (319) 642-1111; marengoiowa.com

Marshalltown • *Marshall Eco. Dev. Impact Comm.* • Joel Akason; Pres.; 709 S. Center St.; P.O. Box 1000; 50158; Marshall; P 39,311; (641) 753-6645; (800) 725-5301; Fax (641) 752-8373; akason@marshalltown.org; www.marshalltownworks.com

Mason City • *North Iowa Corridor Eco. Dev. Corp.* • Gregg Gillman; Exec. Dir.; 25 W. State St., Ste. B; 50401; Cerro Gordo; P 8,200; M 125; (641) 423-0315; (800) 944-1708; info@northiowacorridor.com; www.northiowacorridor.com

Mitchellville • *see Altoona*

Monticello • *Monticello Dev. Corp.* • Bob Goodyear; P.O. Box 191; 52310; Jones; P 3,607; (319) 480-0171; Fax (319) 465-4611; www.ci.monticello.ia.us

Mount Ayr • *Ringgold County Dev. Corp.* • Sandy Lamb; Coord.; 117 S. Fillmore; 50854; Ringgold; P 5,400; (641) 464-3704; Fax (641) 464-3704; rdevco@iowatelecom.net

Nevada • *Nevada Eco. Dev. Cncl.* • LaVon Schiltz; Exec. Dir.; 516 K Ave., Ste. 100; P.O. Box 157; 50201; Story; P 7,000; (515) 382-1430; Fax (515) 382-1460; nedc@iowatelecom.net; www.nevadaec.com

New Hampton • *New Hampton Eco. Dev.* • Bob Soukup; Dir. of Eco. Dev.; 112 E. Spring St.; P.O. Box 435; 50659; Chickasaw; P 4,000; (641) 394-2437; Fax (641) 394-4514; info@newhamptonia.com; www.newhamptonia.com

Oakland • *Golden Hills Resource Conservation & Dev.* • Shirley Frederiksen; Coord.; 712 S. Hwy. 6; P.O. Box 189; 51560; Pottawattamie; P 200,000; (712) 482-3029; Fax (712) 482-5590; www.goldenhillsrcd.org

Osceola • *Clarke County Dev. Corp.* • William Trickey; Exec. Dir.; P.O. Box 426; 50213; Clarke; P 4,659; M 100; (641) 342-2944; Fax (641) 342-6353; info@clarkecountyiowa.com; www.clarkecountyiowa.com

Ottumwa • *Ottumwa Eco. Dev. Corp.* • Roger Jones; Exec. Dir.; 217 E. Main St.; P.O. Box 1288; 52501; Wapello; P 35,000; M 200; (641) 682-3465; (800) 479-0828; Fax (641) 682-3466; inforequest@ottumwadevelopment.org; www.ottumwadevelopment.org

Panora • *Panora Reg. Ind. Dev. Enterprise [PRIDE]* • Orville Terry; Pres.; P.O. Box 187; 50216; Guthrie; P 3,000; (641) 755-3124; panora.org

Pleasant Hill • *see Altoona*

Remsen • *Remsen Dev. Corp.* • Chris Feller; Pres.; P.O. Box 613; 51050; Plymouth; P 1,762; (712) 786-2136; www.remseniowa.net

Rock Valley • *Rock Valley Dev. Corp.* • James Vandervelde; Dev. Dir.; 1507 Main St.; 51247; Sioux; P 3,000; (712) 476-2576; (712) 470-2137; Fax (712) 476-1074; jvv@cityofrockvalley.com; www.cityofrockvalley.com

Rockwell City • *Calhoun County Eco. Dev. Corp.* • Pamela Meeder; Dir.; P.O. Box 47; 50579; Calhoun; P 11,000; (712) 297-5601; Fax (712) 297-5481; ccedc@iowatelecom.net; www.calhoundev.com

Roland • *Roland Dev. Corp.* • Marc Soderstrum; V.P.; P.O. Box 288; 50236; Story; P 1,324; (515) 388-4861; Fax (515) 388-5595; cityhall@cityofroland.org; www.cityofroland.org

Rolfe • *Rolfe Dev. Comm.* • 319 Garfield St.; 50581; Pocahontas; P 675; (712) 848-3124; Fax (712) 848-3128; www.rolfeiowa.com

Sac City • *Sac Eco. & Tourism Dev.* • Shirley Phillips; Exec. Dir.; 615 W. Main St.; 50583; Sac; P 12,324; M 70; (712) 662-7383; shirley@saccountyiowa.com; www.saccountyiowa.com

Saint Ansgar • *St. Ansgar Eco. Dev. Corp.* • Newlin Jensen; Pres.; P.O. Box 244; 50472; Mitchell; P 1,100; (641) 713-4501; (641) 713-4325; www.stansgar.org

Shenandoah • *Shenandoah Chamber & Ind. Org.* • Gregg Connell; Exec. Dir.; 100 Maple St.; 51601; Page; P 6,000; M 300; (712) 246-3455; Fax (712) 246-3456; gconnell@shenandoahiowa.net; www.shenandoahiowa.net

Sigourney • *Sigourney Area Dev. Corp.* • 112 E. Washington; 52591; Keokuk; P 2,200; (641) 622-2288; Fax (641) 622-2396; sadc@sigourney.com; www.sigourney.com

Sioux Center • *Sioux Center Land Dev.* • 335 1st Ave. N.W.; 51250; Sioux; P 6,000; (712) 722-0761; Fax (712) 722-0760; citysc@siouxcenter.org; www.siouxcenter.org

Sioux City • *Siouxland Eco. Dev. Corp.* • Ken Beekley; Dir.; 1106 4th St., Ste. 201; 51102; Woodbury; P 190,000; (712) 279-6430; Fax (712) 224-2510; www.siouxlandedc.com

Sioux City • *The Siouxland Initiative* • Debi Durham; Pres.; 101 Pierce St.; 51101; Plymouth & Woodbury; P 143,000; (712) 255-7903; Fax (712) 258-7578; ddurham@siouxlandchamber.com; www.siouxlandchamber.com

Spencer • *Spencer Industries Found.* • Kathy Everet; Pres.; 122 W. 5th St.; P.O. Box 7937; 51301; Clay; P 18,000; (712) 262-5680; Fax (712) 262-5747; www.spenceriowachamber.org

Story City • *Story City Dev. Corp.* • Mark Jackson; City Admin.; 504 Broad St.; 50248; Story; P 3,228; (515) 733-2121; Fax (515) 733-2460;

Strawberry Point • *Strawberry Point Eco. Dev. Center* • 105 W. Mission; P.O. Box 85; 52076; Clayton; P 1,500; (563) 933-4417; Fax (563) 933-4417; econdev@strawberrypt.com; www.strawberrypt.com

Stuart · *Midwest Partnership Dev. Corp.* · Jason White; Exec. Dir.; 615 S. Division; P.O. Box 537; 50250; Adair; P 30,000; M 157; (515) 523-1262; Fax (515) 523-1397; info@midwestpartnership. com; www.midwestpartnership.com

Stuart · *Stuart Dev. Corp.* · Everett Shepherd; Pres.; 212 S. Division; 50250; Adair; P 2,600; M 110; (515) 523-2102; (515) 523-2721; www.stuartiowa.com

Sumner · *Sumner's Future Inc.* · Bill Nauholz; P.O. Box 207; 50674; Bremer; P 2,300; (563) 578-5470; Fax (563) 578-5853

Tama · *Tama Ind. Dev. Corp.* · Christopher Bearden; Mayor; 305 Siegel St.; 52339; Tama; P 2,800; (641) 484-3822; tamacity@ iowatelecom.net; www.tamacity.govoffice2.com

Tipton · *Cedar County Eco. Dev. Comm.* · Stephen Lacina; Exec. Dir.; 218 W. 5th St.; 52772; Cedar; P 18,187; M 60; (563) 886-3761; (800) 737-5576; info@cedarcountyia.org; www. cedarcountyia.org

Urbandale · *City of Urbandale Comm. Dev.* · Paul Dekker; Dir.; 3600 86th St.; 50322; Dallas & Polk; P 35,732; (515) 278-3935; Fax (515) 278-3927; pdekker@urbandale.org; www.urbandale.org

Victor · *Victor Comm. Dev. Assn.* · Dr. Leonard Seda; Pres.; 617 Main St.; P.O. Box F; 52347; Iowa; P 1,000; (319) 647-3240; Fax (319) 647-2727; lseda@netins.net

Wapello · *Wapello Dev. Corp.* · Roger Huddle; Secy.; P.O. Box 226; 52653; Louisa; P 2,050; (319) 523-4221; Fax (319) 523-5603

Washington · *Washington Eco. Dev. Group* · Ed Raber; Exec. Dir.; 205 W. Main St.; 52353; Washington; P 21,000; M 102; (319) 653-3942; wedg@iowatelecom.net; www.washingtoniowa.org

Waterloo · *Black Hawk Eco. Dev. Inc.* · 304 South St.; P.O. Box 330; 50704; Black Hawk; P 128,012; (319) 235-2960; Fax (319) 235-9171; bhedc@aol.com; www.bhed.org

Waterloo · *Greater Cedar Valley Alliance* · Linda Laylin; Dir. Bus. Svcs.; 10 W. Fourth St., Ste. 310; 50701; Black Hawk; P 164,593; (319) 232-1156; (800) 369-0513; Fax (319) 232-1829; info@cedarvalleyalliance.com; www.cedarvalleyalliance.com

Waukon · *Allamakee County Eco. Dev.* · Mike Kruckenberg; Pres.; 101 W. Main St.; 52172; Allamakee; P 14,000; (563) 568-2624; Fax (563) 568-6990; neiatourism@mchsi.com; www. allamakeecounty.com

Waverly · *Waverly Eco. Dev. Dept.* · Jason Passmore; Econ. Dev. Dir.; 200 1st St. N.E.; P.O. Box 616; 50677; Bremer; P 9,000; (319) 352-9210; Fax (319) 352-5772; Jason@ci.waverly.ia.us; www. waverlyia.com

Webster City · *Webster City Area Assn. of Bus. & Ind.* · Gary Sandholm; EDC Dir.; 628 2nd St.; P.O. Box 310; 50595; Hamilton; P 8,176; M 215; (515) 832-2564; Fax (515) 832-5130; info@ webstercity-iowa.com; www.webstercity-iowa.com

West Des Moines · *West Des Moines Dev. Svcs.* · City of West Des Moines; P.O. Box 65320; 50265; Polk; P 54,459; (515) 222-3620; Fax (515) 273-0602; www.wdm-ia.com

West Union · *Fayette County Eco. Dev. Comm.* · Robin Bostrom; Exec. Dir.; 101 N. Vine St.; 52175; Fayette; P 2,500; (563) 422-5073; Fax (563) 422-6322; fced@alpinecom.net; www.fayettecountyia.com

Wilton · *Wilton Dev. Corp.* · Jackie Barten; P.O. Box 443; 52778; Muscatine; P 2,900; M 40; (563) 732-5002; www.wiltoniowa.org

Woodbine · *Woodbine Betterment Corp.* · Paul Fouts; 501 Normal St.; 51579; Harrison; P 1,800; (712) 647-2221;

Kansas

Federal

U.S. SBA, Kansas Dist. Ofc. · Wayne Bell; District Dir.; 271 W. 3rd St. N., Ste. 2500; Wichita; 67202; Sedgwick; (316) 269-6616; Fax (316) 269-6499; wayne.bell@sba.gov; www.sba.gov/ks

State

Kansas Dept. of Commerce · Steve Kelly; Bus. Dev. Dir.; 1000 S.W. Jackson St., Ste. 100; Topeka; 66612; Shawnee; (785) 296-3481; Fax (785) 296-5055; skelly@kansascommerce.com; www. kansascommerce.com

Communities

Abilene · *Abilene Eco. Dev. Cncl.* · James Holland; Comm. Dev. Dir.; 419 N. Broadway; P.O. Box 519; 67410; Dickinson; P 6,835; (785) 263-2550; Fax (785) 263-2552; citydevelop@abilenecityhall. com; www.abilenecityhall.com

Atchison · *Atchison Eco. Dev. Cncl.* · Christy Isaacs; Comm. Dev. Dir.; 515 Kansas Ave.; 66002; Atchison; P 20,000; (913) 367-5500; Fax (913) 367-3654; christy@growatchison.com; growatchison.com

Burlington · *Coffey County Eco. Dev.* · Jon Hotaling; Dir.; 110 S. 6th St.; 66839; Coffey; P 10,000; (620) 364-8780; Fax (620) 364-2045; www.coffeycountyks.org

Clay Center · *Clay County Eco. Dev. Group* · Jami Williams; Exec. Dir.; 517 Court; 67432; Clay; P 9,200; (785) 632-5974; jami@ claycountykansas.org; www.claycountykansas.org

Colby · *Thomas County Eco. Dev. Alliance* · Rick Patrick; Exec. Dir.; 350 S. Range, Ste. 12; 67701; Thomas; P 8,258; (785) 460-4511; Fax (785) 460-4509; ecodev@thomascounty.com; www. thomascounty.com

Columbus · *Columbus Eco. Dev. Corp.* · Jim Dahmen; Chrmn.; 224 S. Kansas; 66725; Cherokee; P 3,500; (620) 429-3132; (620) 429-1492; Fax (620) 429-1704; coltelco@columbus-ks.com; www. columbus-ks.com

Concordia · *CloudCorp* · Kirk G. Lowell; Exec. Dir.; 606 Washington St.; P.O. Box 456; 66901; Cloud; P 5,714; (785) 243-2010; Fax (785) 243-2014; kirk.lowell@cloudcorp.net

Council Grove · *Greater Morris County Dev. Corp.* · C. Kay Hutchinson; Exec. Secy.; P.O. Box 276; 66846; Morris; P 6,200; M 80; (620) 767-7355; Fax (785) 466-2270; kayhutch@tctelco.net; www.councilgrovedevelopment.com

Derby · *City of Derby* · Kathleen Sexton; City Mgr.; 611 Mulberry Rd., Ste. 300; 67037; Sedgwick; P 22,000; (316) 788-3081; Fax (316) 788-6067; kathysexton@derbyweb.com; www.derbyweb.com

Dodge City · *Dodge City/Ford County Dev. Corp.* · Joann Knight; Exec. Dir.; 311 W. Spruce St.; P.O. Box 818; 67801; Ford; P 35,000; M 60; (620) 227-9501; Fax (620) 338-8734; jknight@ dodgedev.org; www.dodgedev.org

El Dorado · *Butler County Eco. Dev.* · David Alfaro; Dir.; 121 S. Gordy; 67042; Butler; P 62,000; (316) 322-4242; (800) 794-6907; Fax (316) 322-4245; bced@bucoks.com; www.bucoks.com

Emporia · *Reg. Dev. Assn. of East Central Kansas* · Kent Heermann CEcD; Pres.; 719 Commercial St.; P.O. Box 703; 66801; Lyon; P 26,760; (620) 342-1600; Fax (620) 342-3223; kheermann@ emporiarda.org; www.emporiarda.org

Garden City · *Finney County Eco. Dev. Corp.* · Eric Depperschmidt; Pres.; 1509 E. Fulton Terrace; 67846; Finney; P 40,000; (620) 271-0388; Fax (620) 271-0588; fcedc@ficoedc. com; www.ficoedc.com

Goodland · *Sherman County Eco. Dev.* · Helen Norman Dobbs; Ofc. Mgr.; 104 E. 10th St.; P.O. Box 614; 67735; Sherman; P 5,500; (785) 890-3743; Fax (785) 890-3744; shermancoecdev@good landnet.com; www.gogoodlandnet.com

Hays · *Ellis County Coalition for Eco. Dev.* · Mike Michaelis; Exec. Dir.; 2700 Vine St.; 67601; Ellis; P 27,000; (785) 628-3102; Fax (785) 628-1471; mike@haysamerica.net; www.haysamerica.net

Hiawatha · *Hiawatha Found. for Eco. Dev.* · Marianne Schmitt; Treas.; P.O. Box 378; 66434; Brown; P 3,500; M 14; (785) 742-7825; sheila@heartland-realty.com; www.hiawathaecomonicdevelop ment.org

Hill City · *NW Kansas Planning & Dev. Comm.* · Randall Hrabe; Exec. Dir.; 319 N. Pomeroy; P.O. Box 248; 67642; Graham; P 106,625; (785) 421-2151; Fax (785) 421-3496; nwkpdc@ruraltel.net

Hillsboro · *Hillsboro Dev. Corp.* · Clint Seibel; Exec. Dir.; 116 E. Grand; 67063; Marion; P 3,000; (620) 947-3458; Fax (620) 947-2585; cseibel@cityofhillsboro.net

Horton · *Horton Ind. Dev. Corp.* · 205 E. 8th St.; 66439; Brown; P 1,900; (785) 486-2681; cityofhorton@hortonkansas.net

Hugoton · *Stevens County Eco. Dev. Bd.* · Neal R. Gillespie; Dir.; 630 S. Main; 67951; Stevens; P 5,463; (620) 544-4440; Fax (620) 544-4610; ecodevo@pld.com; www.hugotonchamber.com

Hutchinson · *Reno County Eco. Dev. Cncl.* · Dave Kerr; Pres.; 117 N. Walnut; P.O. Box 519; 67504; Reno; P 65,000; (620) 662-3391; Fax (620) 662-2168; davek@hutchchamber.com; www. hutchecodevo.com

Independence · *Montgomery County Action Cncl.* · Brad Eilts; Dir.; P.O. Box 588; 67301; Montgomery; P 40,000; (620) 331-3830; Fax (620) 331-3834; eilts@actioncouncil.com; www. actioncouncil.com

Jewell · *Jewell County Comm. Dev.* · Martha Matthews; Coord.; 606 Broadway St.; 66949; Jewell; P 4,000; (785) 428-3634

Junction City · *Junction City/Geary County EDC* · Jeffrey Black; Dir.; 701 N. Jefferson, Ste. B104; P.O. Box 1876; 66441; Geary; (785) 762-1976; Fax (785) 210-1976; www.jcgced.com

Kansas City · *Dept. of Dev.* · LaVert Murray; Dir.; 701 N. 7th St., Ste. 421; 66101; Wyandotte; P 145,000; (913) 573-5730; Fax (913) 573-5745; www.wycokck.org

Kingman · *Kingman County Eco. Dev.* · Jane Wallace; Exec. Dir.; 324 N. Main; 67068; Kingman; P 8,679; (620) 532-3694; www. kingmanks.com

Kinsley · *Edwards County Eco. Dev. Corp.* · Lynette Miller; Exec. Dir.; 200 E. 6th; P.O. Box 161; 67547; Edwards; P 3,500; (877) 464-3929; Fax (620) 659-3304; ecedc@sbcglobal.net; www.edwardscounty.org

Larned · *Pawnee County Eco. Dev. Comm.* · 502 Broadway; 67550; Pawnee; P 7,600; (620) 285-6916; (800) 747-6919; Fax (620) 285-6917; larnedcofc@gbta.net; www.larnedks.org

Leavenworth · *Leavenworth County Dev. Corp.* · Steve Jack; Exec. Dir.; 1294 Eisenhower Rd.; 66048; Leavenworth; P 74,500; M 85; (913) 727-6111; Fax (913) 727-5515; mail@lvcountyed.org; www.lvcountyed.org

Lenexa · *Lenexa Eco. Dev. Cncl.* · Blake Schreck; Pres.; 11180 Lackman Rd.; 66219; Johnson; P 48,000; M 80; (913) 888-1414; Fax (913) 888-3770; staff@lenexa.org; www.lenexa.org

Liberal · *Liberal/Seward County Joint Eco. Dev. Cncl.* · P.O. Box 2199; 67905; Seward; P 23,000; (620) 626-2255; Fax (620) 626-0589; ecodevo@cityofliberal.com; www.cityofliberal.com

Lincoln · *Lincoln Co. Eco. Dev. Found.* · 216 E. Lincoln Ave.; 67455; Lincoln; P 3,400; (785) 524-8954; Fax (785) 524-5206

McPherson · *McPherson Ind. Dev. Co.* · Marvin Peters; Exec. Dir.; P.O. Box 1008; 67460; McPherson; P 14,000; (620) 245-2521; Fax (620) 245-2529; midc@mcpbpu.com; www.mcphersonks.org

Minneapolis · *Minneapolis Dev. Corp.* · Barry Hodges; City Admin.; 218 N. Rock St.; 67467; Ottawa; P 2,042; M 75; (785) 392-2176; cityminne@nckcn.com; www.minneapolisks.org

Mound City · *Linn County Eco. Dev.* · Dennis Arnold; Dir.; 306 Main St.; P.O. Box 350; 66056; Linn; P 9,800; (913) 795-2274; Fax (913) 795-2016; darnold@linncountyks.com; www.linn countyksed.com

Newton · *Harvey County Eco. Dev. Cncl.* · Mickey Fornaro-Dean; Exec. Dir.; 500 N. Main St., Ste. 109; P.O. Box 82; 67114; Harvey; P 34,000; (316) 283-6033; Fax (316) 283-8732; info@harveycoedc. org; www.harveycoedc.org

Norton · *Norton City/County Eco. Dev.* · Diane Stiles; Exec. Dir.; 113 N. Norton Ave., Ste. B; 67654; Norton; P 5,400; (785) 874-4816; Fax (785) 874-4817; nortoneda@ruraltel.net; www. nortoned.com

Olathe · *Olathe Chamber EDC* · Tim McKee; Exec. V.P.; 18001 W. 106th St., Ste. 160; P.O. Box 98; 66051; Johnson; P 120,000; M 100; (913) 764-1050; (800) 921-5678; Fax (913) 782-4636; edc@olathe. org; www.olathe.org

Osborne · *Osborne Dept. of Eco. Dev.* · 130 N. First St.; 67473; Osborne; P 1,500; (785) 346-2670; (866) 346-2670; Fax (785) 346-2522; osborneed@ruraltel.net; www.discoverosborne.com

Ottawa · *Ottawa/Franklin County Eco. Dev.* · Thomas R. Weigand; Secy./Treas.; 109 E. 2nd; P.O. Box 580; 66067; Franklin; P 27,000; M 72; (785) 242-1000; Fax (785) 242-4792; chambertw@ ottawakansas.org; www.ottawakansas.org

Overland Park · *Overland Park Eco. Dev. Cncl.* · Tracey Osborne CCE; Pres.; 9001 W. 110th St., Ste. 150; 66210; Johnson; P 162,000; M 70; (913) 491-3600; Fax (913) 491-0393; info@ opedc.org; www.opedc.org

Pittsburg · *City of Pittsburg Eco. Dev. Corp.* · Mark Turnbull; Dir.; 201 W. 4th St.; P.O. Box 688; 66762; Crawford; P 19,000; (620) 231-4100; Fax (620) 231-0964; mark.turnbull@pittks.org; www. pittks.org

Russell · *Russell County EDC* · Janae Talbott; Dir.; 445 E. Wichita Ave.; 67665; Russell; P 4,600; (785) 483-4000; (877) 830-3737; Fax (785) 483-2827; rced@russellks.org; www.visitrussellcoks.com

Sabetha · *Sabetha Ind. Dev. Corp.* · Doug Allen; City Admin.; 805 Main St.; P.O. Box 187; 66534; Nemaha; P 2,583; (785) 284-2158; Fax (785) 284-2112; www.skyways.org/towns/sabetha

Shawnee · *Shawnee Eco. Dev. Cncl.* · Jim Martin; Exec. Dir.; 15100 W. 67th St., Ste. 202; 66217; Johnson; P 60,000; M 60; (913) 631-6545; Fax (913) 631-9628; jmartin@shawnee-edc.com; www. shawnee-edc.com

Stockton · *Rooks County Eco. Dev. Comm.* · Roger Hrabe; Dir.; 115 N. Walnut; 67669; Rooks; P 5,300; (785) 425-6881; (800) 496-9930; Fax same; rooksed@ruraltel.net; www.rookscounty.net

Topeka · *City of Topeka Housing & Neighborhood Dev.* · Randy Speaker; Dir.; 620 S.E. Madison, 1st Flr.; 66607; Shawnee; P 123,000; (785) 368-3711; Fax (785) 368-2546; www.topeka.org

Tribune · *Greeley County Comm. Dev.* · Christy Hopkins; Dir.; P.O. Box 656; 67879; Greeley; P 1,350; (620) 376-2548; greeleyc@ fairpoint.net; www.greeleycounty.org

WaKeeney · *Trego County Eco. Dev.* · Charlene Neish; Dir.; 216 N. Main; P.O. Box 355; 67672; Trego; P 3,100; (785) 743-5785; Fax (785) 743-5530; tregocoed@ruraltel.net; www.tregocountyks.com

Wamego • *Pottawatomie County Eco. Dev. Corp.* • Robert L. Cole; Dir.; 1004 Lincoln; P.O. Box 288; 66547; Pottawatomie; P 18,700; (785) 456-9776; Fax (785) 456-9775; bobcole@ecodevo.com; www.ecodevo.com

Wellington • *Sumner County Eco. Dev.* • Janis Hellard; Dir.; P.O. Box 279; 67152; Sumner; P 26,000; (620) 326-8779; Fax (620) 326-6544; scedc@co.sumner.ks.us; www.gosumner.com

Wichita • *South Central KS Eco. Dev. Dist. Inc.* • Bill Bolin; Exec. Dir.; 200 W. Douglas Ave., Ste. 710; 67202; Sedgwick; P 685,000; (316) 262-7035; (800) 326-8353; Fax (316) 262-7062; bill@sckedd.org; www.sckedd.org

Winfield • *Cowley County Eco. Dev. Partnership* • Heidi Hill; Dir.; P.O. Box 832; 67156; Cowley; P 37,000; (620) 221-9951; Fax (620) 221-7782; www.cowleyfirst.com

Kentucky

Federal

U.S. SBA, Kentucky Dist. Ofc. • Steven R. Ayers; Dist. Dir.; 600 M.L. King Jr. Pl., Rm. 188; Louisville; 40202; Jefferson; (502) 582-5971; Fax (502) 582-5819; steven.ayers@sba.gov; www.sba.gov/ky

State

Kentucky Cabinet for Eco. Dev. • Larry Hayes; Secy.; Old Capital Annex; 300 W. Broadway; Frankfort; 40601; Franklin; (502) 564-7140; Fax (502) 564-3256; george.burgess@ky.gov; www.thinkkentucky.com

Communities

Ashland • *City of Ashland Eco. Dev. Dept.* • Chris Pullem; Dir.; P.O. Box 1839; 41105; Boyd; P 22,000; (606) 327-2005; Fax (606) 326-0787; www.ashlandky.org

Calhoun • *McLean County Ind. Found.* • Charles Mann Jr.; Pres.; 297 Main St.; P.O. Box 303; 42327; McLean; P 10,000; M 25; (270) 273-9760; Fax (270) 273-9760; chamfond@owensboro.net

Carrollton • *Carroll County Comm. Dev. Corp.* • Joan Moore; Exec. Dir.; 511 Highland Ave.; P.O. Box 334; 41008; Carroll; P 10,634; (502) 732-7035; Fax (502) 732-7028; development@carrollcountyky.com; www.carrollcountyky.com

Corbin • *Corbin Eco. Dev. Agency* • Bruce Carpenter; Exec. Dir.; 101 N. Depot St.; 40701; Whitley; P 25,000; (606) 528-6390; Fax (606) 523-6538; becarpenter@corbinky.org; www.corbinky.org

Covington • *Northern KY Tri-ED* • Dan Tobergte; Pres.; 300 Buttermilk Pike, Ste. 332; P.O. Box 17246; 41017; Carroll; P 300,000; (859) 344-0040; (888) 874-3365; Fax (859) 344-8130; www.northernkentuckyusa.com

Danville • *Boyle County Ind. Found.* • Jody Lassiter; Pres./CEO; 304 S. 4th St.; 40422; Boyle; P 28,000; (859) 236-0636; Fax (859) 236-3197; info@betterindanville.com; www.betterindanville.com

Edmonton • *Edmonton-Metcalfe County Ind. Dev. Auth.* • Barry Gilley; Chrmn.; P.O. Box 380; 42129; Metcalfe; P 10,000; (270) 432-7190; Fax (270) 432-7199

Florence • *Northern KY Area Dev. Dist.* • John Mays; Exec. Dir.; 22 Spiral Dr.; 41042; Boone; P 370,000; (859) 283-1885; Fax (859) 283-8178; www.nkadd.org

Franklin • *Franklin/Simpson Ind. Auth.* • Dennis Griffin; Dir.; 201 S. Main St.; P.O. Box 876; 42135; Simpson; P 18,000; (270) 586-4477; Fax (270) 586-3685; fsindustry@aol.com; www.f-sindustry.com

Fulton • *Fulton County Eco. Dev. Partnership* • P.O. Box 1413; 42041; Fulton; P 7,500; (270) 472-2125; Fax (270) 472-1944; www.westkyeconomic.com

Greensburg • *Green County Ind. Found.* • Judy Weatherholt; Pres.; 110 W. Court St.; 42743; Green; P 11,400; (270) 932-4298; Fax (270) 932-7778; judyweatherholt@greensburgonline.com; www.greensburgonline.com

Greenville • *Muhlenberg Eco. Enterprises* • Barbara Williams; Dir. Asst.; P.O. Box 636; 42345; Muhlenberg; P 32,000; (270) 338-4102; Fax (270) 338-4106; barbarau.williams@ky.gov

Harrodsburg • *Harrodsburg-Mercer County Ind. Dev. Auth.* • Drew Dennis; Exec. Dir.; 488 Price Ave.; 40330; Mercer; P 22,000; (859) 734-0063; www.mercerkybusiness.com

Hartford • *Ohio County Ind. Found.* • Hayward Spinks; Pres.; P.O. Box 3; 42347; Ohio; P 23,000; (270) 298-3551; Fax (270) 298-3331; industry@ohiocounty.com; www.ohiocountyindustrialfoundation.com

Hazard • *Kentucky River Area Dev. Dist.* • Paul Hall; Exec. Dir.; 917 Perry Park Rd.; 41701; Perry; P 122,000; (606) 436-3158; Fax (606) 436-2144; www.kradd.org

Henderson • *Henderson-Henderson County Ind. Found.* • CB West; Pres.; 201 N. Main; 42420; Henderson; P 46,000; (270) 826-9531; Fax (270) 827-4461; www.hendersonky.com

Henderson • *Northwest Kentucky Forward* • Kevin Sheilley; Pres./CEO; P.O. Box 674; 42419; Henderson; P 46,000; (270) 826-7505; Fax (270) 827-2969; kevin@northwestky.com; www.northwestky.com

Hopkinsville • *Hopkinsville-Christian County Eco. Dev. Cncl.* • Lee Conrad; Dir.; 2800 Fort Campbell Blvd.; 42240; Christian; P 72,300; (270) 885-1499; Fax (270) 886-2059; info@hopkinsvilleindustry.com; www.hopkinsvilleindustry.com

Hopkinsville • *Pennyrile Area Dev. Dist.* • Dan Bozarth; Exec. Dir.; 300 Hammond Dr.; 42240; Christian; P 206,000; (270) 886-9484; (800) 928-7233; Fax (270) 886-3211; www.peadd.org

Irvine • *Estill County Dev. Alliance* • Joe Crawford; Exec. Dir.; P.O. Box 421; 40336; Estill; P 16,000; M 40; (606) 723-2450; info@estillcountyky.net; www.estillcountyky.net

Kevil • *Ballard County Eco. & Ind. Dev.* • Terry Simmons; Pres./CEO; 101 Liberty Dr., Ste. 4; 42053; McCracken; P 9,000; (270) 744-3232; Fax (270) 744-3308; bceidb@brtc.net

Lebanon • *Marion County Eco. Dev.* • Tom Lund; Exec. Dir.; 223 N. Spaulding Ave., Ste. 300; 40033; Marion; P 19,212; (270) 692-6002; (877) 692-6002; Fax (270) 692-0510; tlund@marioncountyky.com; www.marioncountyky.com

Lexington • *Bluegrass Area Dev. Dist.* • Lenny Stoltz II; Exec. Dir.; 699 Perimeter Dr.; 40517; Fayette; P 600,000; (859) 269-8021; Fax (859) 269-7917; lharris@bgadd.org; www.bgadd.org

Lexington • *Lexington-Fayette Urban County Govt.* • Anthony Wright; Dir.; Mayor's Ofc. of Eco. Dev.; 200 E. Main St.; 40507; Fayette; P 268,080; (859) 258-3131; Fax (859) 258-3194; www.lexingtonky.gov

London • *Cumberland Valley Area Dev. Dist.* • Mike Patrick; Exec. Dir.; P.O. Box 1740; 40743; Laurel; P 240,000; (606) 864-7391; Fax (606) 878-7361; mpatrick@cvadd.org; www.cvadd.org

London • *Laurel County Ind. Dev. Auth.* • Charles Pennington; Exec. Dir.; 4598 Old Whitley Rd.; 40744; Laurel; P 56,000; (606) 864-8115; Fax (606) 878-7107; llcida2@windstream.net

Louisville · *Eco. Dev. Dept. of Louisville Metro Gov.* · C. Bruce Taughber; Dir.; 444 S. 5th St., Ste. 600; 40202; Jefferson; P 1,000,000; (502) 574-4140; Fax (502) 574-4143; bruce.taughber@louisvilleky.gov; www.louisvilleky.gov

Louisville · *Louisville & Jefferson County Riverport Auth.* · Larry McFall; Pres.; 6900 Riverport Dr.; P.O. Box 58010; 40268; Jefferson; P 300,000; (502) 935-6024; Fax (502) 935-6050; www.jeffersonriverport.com

Madisonville · *Madisonville/Hopkins County Eco. Dev. Corp.* · 755 Industrial Rd.; 42431; Hopkins; P 60,000; (270) 821-1939; (800) 821-1939; Fax (270) 821-1945; www.kymtec.org

Mayfield · *Graves Growth Alliance* · 201 E. College; 42066; Graves; P 35,300; (270) 247-0626; Fax (270) 247-6781; mgldc@bellsouth.net; www.mayfield-graves.com

Maysville · *Buffalo Trace Area Dev. Dist.* · Amy Kennedy; Exec. Dir.; 201 Govt. St., Ste. 300; P.O. Box 460; 41056; Mason; P 55,229; (606) 564-6894; Fax (606) 564-0955; akennedy@btadd.com; www.btadd.com

Middlesboro · *Bell County Ind. Found.* · Nioma Lawson; Dir.; N. 20th St.; P.O. Box 788; 40965; Bell; P 30,060; (606) 248-1075; Fax (606) 248-8851; chamber@bellcountychamber.com; www.bellcountychamber.com

Morganfield · *Union County First* · Kim Humphrey; Exec. Dir.; P.O. Box 374; 42437; Union; P 16,000; M 123; (270) 389-9600; Fax (270) 389-0944; www.ucfirst.org

Mount Sterling · *Mt. Sterling-Montgomery County Ind. Auth.* · Sandy Romenesko; Exec. Dir.; 126 W. Main St.; 40353; Montgomery; P 26,500; (859) 498-5400; Fax (859) 498-3947; sandy@mtsterlingchamber.com; www.mtsterlingchamber.com

Owensboro · *Greater Owensboro Eco. Dev. Corp.* · 200 E. 3rd St., Ste. 200; P.O. Box 782; 42302; Daviess; P 92,000; (270) 926-4339; Fax (270) 926-2178; www.owensboro.com

Owensboro · *Green River Area Dev. Dist.* · Mr. Jiten Shah; Exec. Dir.; 3860 U.S. Hwy. 60 W.; 42301; Daviess; P 200,000; (270) 926-4433; Fax (270) 684-0714; www.gradd.com

Paducah · *Greater Paducah Eco. Dev. Cncl.* · Wayne Sterling; Pres./CEO; 401 Ky Ave.; P.O. Box 1155; 42002; McCracken; P 65,514; M 125; (270) 575-6633; Fax (270) 575-6648; wsterling@gpedc.com; www.gpedc.com

Prestonsburg · *Big Sandy Area Dev. Dist.* · Sandy Runyon; Exec. Dir.; 110 Resource Ct.; 41653; Floyd; P 160,532; (606) 886-2374; Fax (606) 886-3382; terry.trimble@bigsandy.org; www.bigsandy.org

Richmond · *Richmond Ind. Dev. Corp.* · James H. Howard; Exec. Dir.; 239 W. Main St.; 40476; Madison; P 33,000; (859) 623-1000; Fax (859) 623-7168; ridc@richmond.ky.us; www.richmond-industrial.org

Shelbyville · *Shelby County Ind. & Dev. Found.* · Bobby Hudson; Pres.; 316 Main St.; P.O. Box 335; 40066; Shelby; P 35,000; (502) 633-5068; Fax (502) 633-7501; www.shelbycountyindustrialfoundation.com

Somerset · *Center for Rural Dev.* · Lonnie Lawson; Exec. Dir.; 2292 S. Hwy. 27, Ste. 300; 42501; Pulaski; P 500,000; (606) 677-6000; Fax (606) 677-6010; www.centertech.com

Versailles · *Woodford County Eco. Dev. Auth.* · Michael Duckworth; Pres.; 141 N. Main St.; P.O. Box 1509; 40383; Woodford; P 23,208; (859) 879-5829; (859) 873-5122; Fax (859) 873-4576; woodford@woodfordchamber-ky.com; www.woodfordchamber-ky.com

Williamsburg · *Williamsburg Eco. Dev.* · Alvin Sharpe; Coord.; P.O. Box 2; 40769; Whitley; P 5,033; (606) 549-0530; Fax (606) 539-0095; www.williamsburgky.com

Winchester · *Winchester-Clark County Ind. Dev. Auth.* · Todd Denham; Dir. of Eco. Dev.; 2 S. Maple St.; 40391; Clark; P 35,000; (859) 744-5627; Fax (859) 744-9229; todd@winchesterindustry.com; www.winchesterindustry.com

Louisiana

Federal

U.S. SBA, Louisiana Dist. Ofc. · Michael Ricks; Dist. Dir.; 365 Canal St., Ste. 2820; New Orleans; 70130; Orleans; (504) 589-2853; Fax (504) 589-2339; loretta.poree@sba.gov; www.sba.gov/la

State

Louisiana Dept. of Eco. Dev. · Stephen Moret; Secy.; 1051 N. 3rd St.; Baton Rouge; 70802; East Baton Rouge; (225) 342-3000; Fax (225) 342-9095; lednews@info.ledlouisiana.com; www.opportunitylouisiana.com

Communities

Alexandria · *Kisatchie-Delta Reg. Planning & Dev. Dist.* · Heather Smoak Urena; Exec. Dir.; 3516 Parliament Ct.; 71303; Rapides; P 312,026; (318) 487-5454; Fax (318) 487-5451; kdelta@kricket.net; www.kdelta.org

Bastrop · *Morehouse Eco. Dev. Corp.* · Kay King; Pres./CEO; Capital One Bank Bldg.; 101 Franklin St., Ste. A; 71220; Morehouse; P 30,000; (318) 283-4000; Fax (318) 283-0651; morehouseedc@att.net; www.morehouseedc.org

Baton Rouge · *Capital Region Planning Comm.* · Huey P. Dugas; Exec. Dir.; 333 N. 19th St.; P.O. Box 3355; 70821; East Baton Rouge; (225) 383-5203; Fax (225) 383-3804; hdugas@brgov.com; www.crpc-la.org

Baton Rouge · *Cncl. for a Better Louisiana* · Robert Levy; Chrmn.; P.O. Box 4308; 70821; East Baton Rouge; (225) 344-2225; Fax (225) 338-9470; info@cabl.org; www.cabl.org

Bogalusa · *Washington Eco. Dev. Found. Inc.* · Dr. Dennis LaRavi; Pres.; P.O. Box 668; 70429; Washington; P 45,000; (985) 735-7565; Fax (985) 730-2500; widf@bellsouth.net; www.wedf.com

Hammond · *Tangipahoa Eco. Dev. Found.* · Bob Basford; Exec. Dir.; 1514 Martens Dr.; 70401; Tangipahoa; P 117,000; (985) 549-3170; Fax (985) 549-2127; tedf@i-55.com; www.tedf.org

Jonesboro · *Jackson Eco. Dev. Corp.* · Frank Johnson; P.O. Box 610; 71251; Jackson; P 3,900; (318) 259-2385; Fax (318) 259-4177

Lafayette · *Lafayette Eco. Dev. Auth.* · Gregg Gothreaux; Pres./CEO; 211 E. Devalcourt St.; 70506; Lafayette; P 202,000; (337) 593-1400; Fax (337) 234-3009; pamelal@lafayette.org; www.lafayette.org

Lake Charles · *Southwest Louisiana Eco. Dev. Alliance* · George Swift; Pres./CEO; 120 W. Pujo St.; P.O. Box 3110; 70602; Calcasieu; P 287,001; M 1,028; (337) 433-3632; Fax (337) 436-3727; gswift@allianceswla.org; www.allianceswla.org

Livingston · *Livingston Eco. Dev. Cncl. Inc.* · Stuart Litvin; Pres./CEO; 20355 Government Blvd., Ste. E; P.O. Box 809; 70754; Livingston; P 92,000; (225) 686-3982; Fax (225) 686-3983; stuart@ledc.net; www.ledc.net

Mandeville · *St. Tammany Eco. Dev. Found.* · Brenda Reine Bertus; Exec. Dir.; 21489 Koop Dr., Ste. 7; 70471; St. Tammany; P 234,155; (985) 809-7874; stedfinfo@stedf.org; www.stedf.org

Minden · *South Webster Ind. Dist.* · Mike Moore; Secy.; 110 Sibley Rd.; 71055; Webster; P 28,000; (318) 377-4240; Fax (318) 377-4215; www.mindenchamber.com

Monroe · *North Delta Reg. Planning & Dev. Dist.* · David Creed; Exec. Dir.; 1913 Stubbs Ave.; 71201; Ouachita; (318) 387-2572; Fax (318) 387-9054; david@northdelta.org

Monroe · *North Louisiana Eco. Partnership* · Kurt Foreman; Pres.; 1900 N. 18th St., Ste. 440; 71201; Ouachita; P 120,000; (318) 387-0787; Fax (318) 387-8529; kforeman@nlep.org; www.nlep.org

New Iberia · *Iberia Ind. Dev. Found.* · Mike Tarantino; Exec. Dir.; 101 Burke St.; 70560; Iberia; P 73,000; (337) 367-0834; (888) 879-9669; Fax (337) 367-7421; info@iberiabiz.org; www.iberiabiz.org

New Orleans · *Greater New Orleans Inc.* · Michael Hecht; Pres./CEO; 365 Canal St., Ste. 2300; 70130; Orleans; P 1,151,000; M 150; (504) 527-6900; Fax (504) 527-6970; www.gnoinc.org

New Orleans · *Reg. Planning Comm.* · Walter Brooks; Exec. Dir.; 10 Veterans Memorial Blvd.; 70124; Orleans; (504) 483-8500; Fax (504) 483-8526; rpc@norpc.org; www.norpc.org

Oakdale · *Ind. Dev. Bd. of Elizabeth-Oakdale Inc.* · Andrew Hayes; Mayor; P.O. Box 728; 71463; Allen; P 8,137; (318) 335-1111

Opelousas · *St. Landry Parish Eco. Ind. Dev. Dist.* · Gerard Perron; Exec. Dir.; 5367 I-49 S. Svc. Rd.; 70570; St. Landry; P 87,000; (337) 948-1391; Fax (337) 407-2283; sleidd@bellsouth.net; www.sleidd.com

Ruston · *Ruston-Lincoln Ind. Dev. Corp.* · Scott C. Terry; Exec. Dir.; 2111 N. Trenton St.; P.O. Box 1383; 71272; Lincoln; P 43,000; (318) 232-7984; (800) 392-9032; Fax (318) 255-3481; sterry@rustonlincoln.org; www.rustonlincoln.org

Saint Francisville · *West Feliciana Comm. Dev. Found.* · 5934 Commerce St.; P.O. Box 3044; 70775; West Feliciana; P 15,111; M 200; (225) 635-6767; Fax (225) 635-6885; admin@wfped.com; www.stfrancisville.org

Shreveport · *North Louisiana Eco. Partnership* · Kurt Foreman; Pres.; 400 Edwards St.; 71101; Caddo; P 740,000; (318) 677-2536; (318) 387-0787; Fax (318) 677-2548; edinquiry@nlep.org; www.nlep.org

Shreveport · *The Coord. & Dev. Corp.* · M.D. LeComte; Pres./CEO; 5210 Hollywood Ave.; P.O. Box 37005; 71133; Caddo; P 378,000; (318) 632-2022; Fax (318) 632-2099; info@cdconline.org; www.cdconline.org

Springhill · *North Webster Parish Ind. Park* · Toby Stevens; Mgr.; P.O. Box 176; 71075; Webster; P 12,000; (318) 539-5058; Fax (318) 994-2753; websterboard@centurytel.net; www.nwpid.com

Tallulah · *Madison Eco. Dev. Found.* · Thomas Joe Williams; Pres.; % LA Technical College; P.O. Drawer 1740; 71284; Madison; P 14,000; (318) 493-9010; (800) 215-3905; Fax (318) 574-1868; sccox@ltc.edu

Vidalia · *Vidalia Eco. Dev.* · Hyram Copeland; Mayor; P.O. Box 2010; 71373; Concordia; P 6,500; (318) 336-5206; Fax (318) 336-6253; www.seevidalia.com

Winnsboro · *Franklin Eco. Dev. Found.* · Kayla France-Knight; Exec. Dir.; 3830 Front St.; P.O. Box 69; 71295; Franklin; P 23,000; (318) 435-3781; Fax (318) 435-5398; kaylafrance@bellsouth.net

Maine

Federal

U.S. SBA, Maine Dist. Ofc. · Maurice Dube; Dist. Dir.; 68 Sewall St.; Augusta; 04330; Kennebec; (207) 622-8551; Fax (207) 622-8277; marilyn.geroux@sba.gov; www.sba.gov/me

State

Maine Dept. of Eco. & Comm. Dev. · Thaxter R. Trafton; Comm.; 59 State House Station; Augusta; 04333; Kennebec; (207) 624-9800; Fax (207) 287-2861; biz.growth@maine.gov; www.econdevmaine.com

Communities

Auburn · *Auburn Comm. Eco. Dev.* · Roland Miller; Dir.; 60 Court St.; 04210; Androscoggin; P 23,203; (207) 333-6600; Fax (207) 333-6621; www.auburnmaine.org

Augusta · *Augusta Bd. of Trade* · C. Wayne Mitchell; Exec. Dir.; 330 Civic Center Dr., Ste. 2; P.O. Box 2346; 04338; Kennebec; P 75,000; (207) 622-9100; Fax (207) 622-9111

Bangor · *Eastern Maine Dev. Corp.* · Michael Aube; Pres./CEO; 40 Harlow St.; 04401; Penobscot; P 90,000; (207) 942-6389; (800) 339-6389; Fax (207) 942-3548; info@emdc.org; www.emdc.org

Belfast · *City of Belfast* · Joseph Slocum; City Mgr.; 131 Church St.; City Hall; 04915; Waldo; P 6,500; (207) 338-3370; Fax (207) 338-2419; www.cityofbelfast.org

Berwick · *Town of Berwick* · Keith Trefethen; Town Mgr.; 11 Sullivan Sq.; P.O. Box 696; 03901; York; P 6,500; (207) 698-1101; Fax (207) 698-5181; www.berwickmaine.org

Brewer · *Ofc. of Eco. Dev.* · Darcy Main-Boyington; Dir. of Eco. Dev.; 80 N. Main St.; 04412; Penobscot; P 9,100; (207) 989-7500; Fax (207) 989-8425; www.brewerme.org

Farmington · *Greater Franklin Dev. Corp.* · Alison Hagerstrom; Exec. Dir.; 107 Church St.; P.O. Box 107; 04938; Franklin; P 30,000; (207) 778-5887; Fax (207) 778-3442; info@greaterfranklin.com; www.greaterfranklin.com

Fort Kent · *Ofc. of Planning & Eco. Dev.* · John Bannen; Eco. Dev. Dir.; 416 W. Main St.; 04743; Aroostook; P 4,300; (207) 834-3507; Fax (207) 834-3126; www.fortkent.org

Gardiner · *Gardiner Eco. Dev. Dept.* · Jason Simcock; Dir.; City Hall; 6 Church St.; 04345; Kennebec; P 6,746; (207) 582-6888; Fax (207) 582-6895; econdev@gardinermaine.com; www.gardinermaine.com

Gorham · *Gorham Eco. Dev. Corp.* · Thomas Ellsworth; Pres.; 286 New Portland Rd.; 04038; Cumberland; P 15,000; (207) 854-5077; Fax (207) 856-1300; gedc@gorhammeusa.org; www.gorhammeusa.org

Greenville · *Ofc. of Eco. Dev.-Town of Greenville* · John Simko; Town Mgr.; 7 Minden St.; P.O. Box 1109; 04441; Piscataquis; P 1,800; (207) 695-2421; Fax (207) 695-4611; www.greenvilleme.com

Houlton · *Houlton Comm. Dev.* · Douglas Hazlett; Town Mgr.; 21 Water St.; 04730; Aroostook; P 6,400; (207) 532-7113; Fax (207) 532-1304; www.houlton-maine.com

Jay · *Town of Jay* · Ruth Cushman; Town Mgr.; 340 Main St.; 04239; Franklin; P 4,985; (207) 897-6785; Fax (207) 897-9420; jmanager@jay-maine.org; www.jay-maine.org

Lewiston · *Lewiston-Auburn Eco. Growth Cncl.* · Lucien B. Gosselin; Pres.; 415 Lisbon St.; P.O. Box 1188; 04243; Androscoggin; P 60,000; (207) 784-0161; Fax (207) 786-4412; laegc@economicgrowth.org; www.economicgrowth.org

Limestone · *Limestone Dev. Found. Inc.* · Lisa Anderson; Secy.; 93 Main St.; 04750; Aroostook; P 2,400; (207) 325-4025; Fax (207) 325-3330; chamber@limestonemaine.org; www.limestonemaine.org

Limestone · *Loring Dev. Auth.* · Carl Flora; Pres./CEO; 154 Development Dr., Ste. F; 04750; Aroostook; P 1,458; (207) 328-7005; Fax (207) 328-6811; lda@loring.org; www.loring.org

Lubec · *Lubec Eco. & Comm. Dev. Ofc.* · 40 School St.; 04652; Washington; P 1,650; (207) 733-2342; Fax (207) 733-4737; www.lubecme.govoffice2.com

Old Town · *Old Town Ind. Dev. Comm.* · Dave White; City Mgr.; 256 Main St.; 04468; Penobscot; P 8,100; (207) 827-3965; Fax (207) 827-3966; dwhite@ old-town.org; www.old-town.org

Portland · *Planning & Urban Dev. Dept., City of Portland* · Penny Littell; Dir.; 389 Congress St., 4th Flr.; 04101; Cumberland; P 63,000; (207) 874-8721; www.portlandmaine.gov

Skowhegan · *Town of Skowhegan-Eco./Comm. Dev.* · Jeff Hewett; Dir.; 225 Water St.; 04976; Somerset; P 9,000; (207) 474-6905; (207) 474-6900; Fax (207) 474-9413; skowecon@skowhegan.org; www.skowhegan.org

Waterville · *City of Waterville Eco. Dev.* · City Mgr.; 1 Common St.; 04901; Kennebec; P 15,000; (207) 680-4204; Fax (207) 680-4207; adomini@waterville-me.gov; www.waterville-me.gov

Winslow · *Town of Winslow EDA* · Michael Heavener; Town Mgr.; 114 Benton Ave.; 04901; Kennebec; P 8,000; (207) 872-2776; Fax (207) 872-1999; www.winslowmaine.org

Wiscasset · *Coastal Enterprises Inc.* · Ellen Golden; Sr. V.P.; 36 Water St.; P.O. Box 268; 04578; Lincoln; P 35,200; (207) 882-7552; Fax (207) 882-7308; cei@ceimaine.org; www.ceimaine.org

Maryland

Federal

U.S. SBA, Maryland Dist. Ofc. · Stephen Umberger; Dist. Dir.; City Crescent Bldg., 6th Flr.; 10 S. Howard St.; Baltimore; 21201; Baltimore; (410) 962-6195; Fax (410) 962-1805; rachel.howard@sba.gov; www.sba.gov/md

State

Maryland Dept. of Bus. & Eco. Dev. · Christian S. Johansson; Secy.; 401 E. Pratt St., 9th Flr.; Baltimore; 21202; Baltimore; P 5,633,597; (410) 767-6300; (888) CHOOSE-MD; Fax (410) 333-8628; rwalker@choosemaryland.org; www.choosemaryland.org

Communities

Annapolis · *Anne Arundel Eco. Dev. Corp.* · Robert Hannon; Pres./CEO; 2660 Riva Rd., Ste. 200; 21401; Anne Arundel; P 517,000; (410) 222-7410; Fax (410) 222-7415; www.aaedc.org

Baltimore · *City of Baltimore Dev. Corp.* · M.J. Brodie; Pres.; 36 S. Charles St., Ste. 1600; 21201; Baltimore; P 750,000; (410) 837-9305; Fax (410) 837-6363; www.baltimoredevelopment.com

Baltimore · *Dept. of Bus. & Eco. Dev.* · Christian Johansson; Secy.; 217 E. Redwood St., 23rd Flr.; 21202; Baltimore; (410) 767-6300; Fax (410) 333-8628; cjohansson@choosemaryland.org; www.choosemaryland.org

Bel Air · *Harford County Ofc. of Eco. Dev.* · James Richardson; Dir.; 220 S. Main St.; 21014; Harford; P 257,000; (410) 638-3059; (888) 495-SITE; Fax (410) 879-8043; www.harfordbusiness.work

Cambridge · *Dorchester County Eco. Dev. Ofc.* · 5263 Bucktown Rd.; 21613; Dorchester; P 31,600; (410) 228-0155; Fax (410) 228-9518

Chestertown · *Kent County Eco. Dev.* · Jack Steinmetz; Dir.; 400 High St.; 21620; Kent; P 19,197; (410) 778-7434; Fax (410) 778-0810; jsteinmetz@kentgov.org; www.kentcounty.com

Cumberland · *Allegany County Dept. of Eco. Dev.* · Matthew Diaz; Dir.; 701 Kelly Rd., Ste. 400; 21502; Allegany; P 73,500; (301) 777-5967; (800) 555-4080; Fax (301) 777-2194; www.alleganyworks.org

Federalsburg · *Federalsburg Eco. Dev. Comm.* · Frank M. Adams; Pres.; 319 Bloomingdale Ave.; 21632; Caroline; P 2,800; (410) 754-9945; Fax (410) 754-5341; fmadams@comcast.net

Frederick · *Frederick County Ofc. of Eco. Dev.* · Laurie Boyer; Exec. Dir.; 5340 Spectrum Dr., Ste. A; 21703; Frederick; P 227,000; (301) 600-1058; (800) 248-2296; Fax (301) 600-2340; jwbrown@fredco-md.net; www.discoverfrederickmd.com

Hagerstown · *Hagerstown-Washington County Eco. Dev. Comm.* · Timothy Troxell CEcD; Exec. Dir.; 100 W. Washington St., Rm. 103; 21740; Washington; P 145,113; (240) 313-2280; ttroxell@hagerstownedc.org; www.hagerstownedc.org

Indian Head · *Indian Head Eco. Dev. Comm.* · Randy L. Albright; 4195 Indian Head Hwy.; 20640; Charles; P 3,422; (301) 743-5511; Fax (301) 743-9008; www.townofindianhead.org

Largo · *Prince George's County Eco. Dev. Corp.* · Holman Kwasi; Pres./CEO; 1100 Mercantile Ln.; 20774; Prince George's; P 850,000; (301) 583-4650; Fax (301) 772-8540; www.pgcedc.com

Oakland · *Garrett County Eco. Dev. Dept.* · Jim Hinebaugh; Exec. Dir.; 203 S. Fourth St., Ste. 208; 21550; Garrett; P 30,000; (301) 334-1921; Fax (301) 334-1985; www.gcedonline.com

Prince Frederick · *Calvert County Dept. of Eco. Dev.* · Linda Vassallo; Dir.; 175 Main St.; 20678; Calvert; P 85,000; (410) 535-4583; (800) 331-9771; Fax (410) 535-4585; info@ecalvert.com; www.ecalvert.com

Princess Anne · *Somerset County Eco. Dev. Comm.* · 11916 Somerset Ave., Rm. 202; 21853; Somerset; P 25,000; (410) 651-0500; Fax (410) 651-3836; edc@co.somerset.md.us; www.somersetcountyedc.org

Rockville · *Montgomery County Dept. of Eco. Dev.* · Steve Silverman; Dir.; 111 Rockville Pike, Ste. 800; 20850; Montgomery; P 950,000; (240) 777-2000; Fax (240) 777-2001; www.montgomerycountymd.gov/ded

Salisbury · *Salisbury-Wicomico Eco. Dev. Inc.* · One Plaza East, Ste. 501; P.O. Box 4700; 21803; Wicomico; P 89,000; (410) 749-1251; (800) 521-7933; Fax (410) 749-1252; www.swed.org

Takoma Park · *Takoma Park Housing & Comm. Dev.* · Sara Anne Daines; Dir. of Eco. & Comm. Dev.; 7500 Maple Ave.; 20912; Montgomery; P 18,000; (301) 891-7119; Fax (301) 270-4568; www.takomaparkmd.gov

Towson · *Baltimore County Dept. of Eco. Dev.* · David Iannucci; Exec. Dir.; 400 Washington Ave.; 21204; Baltimore; P 785,600; (410) 887-8000; Fax (410) 887-8017; diannucci@baltimorecountymd.gov; www.baltimorecountymd.gov/business

Westminster · *Carroll County Dept. of Eco. Dev.* · Lawrence Twele; Dir.; 225 N. Center St., Ste. 101; 21157; Carroll; P 175,000; (410) 386-2070; Fax (410) 876-8471; info@carrollbiz.org; www.carrollbiz.org

Massachusetts

Federal

U.S. SBA, Massachusetts Dist. Ofc. · Robert H. Nelson; Dist. Dir.; 10 Causeway St., Rm. 265; Boston; 02222-1093; Essex, Middlesex, Norfolk, Plymouth, Suffolk & Worcester; (617) 565-5590; Fax (617) 565-5598; robert.nelson@sba.gov; www.sba.gov/ma

Communities

Chicopee · *Eco. Dev. Cncl. of Western Mass.* · Allan Blair; Pres.; 255 Padgette St., Ste. 1; 01022; Hampden; P 600,000; (413) 593-6421; Fax (413) 755-1371; www.WesternMassedc.com

Easthampton · *Eco. Dev. Comm.* · Stuart Beckley; City Planner; 50 Payson Ave.; 01027; Hampshire; P 16,000; (413) 529-1406; (413) 529-1460; Fax (413) 529-1433; stuartb@easthampton.org; www.easthampton.org

Fitchburg · *Fitchburg Eco. Dev. Div.* · Lisa Wong; Mayor; 718 Main St.; 01420; Worcester; P 41,000; (978) 345-9550; Fax (978) 345-9553; rmcnutt@ci.fitchburg.ma.us; www.discoverfitchburg.com

Holyoke · *Holyoke Ofc. of Planning & Dev.* · Kathleen Anderson; Dir.; One Court Plaza; 01040; Hampden; P 40,115; (413) 322-5655; Fax (413) 534-2299; www.holyoke.org

Lynn · *Eco. Dev. & Ind. Corp. of Lynn* · James Cowdell; Exec. Dir.; Lynn City Hall, Rm. 307; 01901; Essex; P 90,000; (781) 581-9399; Fax (781) 581-9731; www.ediclynn.org

Orange · *Orange EDIC* · Ann Marie Holmgren; Chair; % Town Hall; 6 Prospect St.; 01364; Franklin; P 7,500; (978) 544-1100; Fax (978) 544-1101; commdev@townoforange.org; www.townoforange.org

Plymouth · *Plymouth Reg. Eco. Dev. Foundation Inc.* · Denis Hanks; Exec. Dir.; 134 Court St.; 02360; Plymouth; P 580,000; (508) 830-1620; dhanks@townhall.plymouth.ma.us; www.plymouthbusiness.org

Springfield · *see Chicopee*

Winchendon · *Winchendon Planning & Dev. Ofc.* · James Kreidler; Town Mgr.; 109 Front St.; 01475; Worcester; P 9,857; (978) 297-0085; (978) 297-3308; Fax (978) 297-5411; www.townofwinchendon.com

Michigan

Federal

U.S. SBA, Michigan Dist. Ofc. · Richard Temkin; Dist. Dir.; 477 Michigan Ave., Rm. 515; Detroit; 48226; Wayne; (313) 226-6075; Fax (313) 226-4769; april.holloway@sba.gov; www.sba.gov/mi

State

Dept. of Energy, Labor & Eco. Growth · Andrew Levin; Interim Dir.; P.O. Box 30004; Lansing; 48909; Ingham; (517) 373-1820; Fax (517) 373-2129; mediainfo@michigan.gov; www.michigan.gov/dleg

Communities

Adrian · *Lenawee Eco. Dev. Corp.* · James Gartin; Pres./CEO; 5285 W. U.S. 223, Ste. A; 49221; Lenawee; P 100,000; M 450; (517) 265-5141; Fax (517) 263-6065; cjackson@theledc.org; www.onelenawee.com

Allendale · *Ottawa County Eco. Dev. Ofc.* · Kenneth J. Rizzio; Exec. Dir.; 6676 Lake Michigan Dr.; P.O. Box 539; 49401; Ottawa; P 238,314; (616) 892-4120; Fax (616) 895-6670; krizzio@altelco.net; www.ocedo.org

Alpena · *Target Alpena Eco. Dev. Corp.* · Lee Shirey; Dir.; 235 W. Chisolm; P.O. Box 65; 49707; Alpena; P 32,700; (989) 354-2666; Fax (989) 356-3999; targetalpena@chartermi.net; www.targetalpena.com

Ann Arbor · *Ann Arbor Spark* · Michael Finney; Pres./CEO; 201 S. Division St., Ste. 430; 48104; Washtenaw; P 313,000; (734) 761-9317; Fax (734) 761-9062; info@annarborusa.org; www.annarborusa.org

Bad Axe · *Huron County EDC* · Carl Osentoski; Exec. Dir.; 250 E. Huron Ave., Rm. 303; 48413; Huron; P 36,000; (989) 269-6431; (800) 35-THUMB; Fax (989) 269-8209; info@huroncounty.com; www.huroncounty.com

Battle Creek · *Battle Creek Unlimited Inc.* · 4950 W. Dickman Rd., Ste. A1; 49037; Calhoun; P 56,000; (269) 962-7526; Fax (269) 962-8096; www.bcunlimited.org

Bay City · *Bay County Growth Alliance* · 721 Washington Ave., Ste. 504; 48708; Bay; P 110,000; (989) 893-5596; Fax (989) 893-8420

Bay City · *Bay Future Inc.* · Frederick Hollister; Pres./CEO; 721 Washington Ave., Ste. 309; 48708; Bay; P 111,000; (989) 892-1400; Fax (989) 892-1402

Big Rapids · *Mecosta County Dev. Corp.* · William Mrdeza; Exec. Dir.; 246 N. State St.; 49307; Mecosta; P 40,000; (231) 592-3403; Fax (231) 592-4085; www.mecostaedc.com

Boyne City · *Northern Lakes Eco. Alliance* · Andy Hayes; Pres.; P.O. Box 8; 49712; Charlevoix; P 70,000; (231) 582-6482; Fax (231) 582-3213; info@northernlakes.net; www.northernlakes.net

Coloma · *North Berrien Comm. Dev.* · Chana Kniebes; Comm. Dev. Coord.; 209 N. Paw Paw St.; P.O. Box 1028; 49038; Berrien; P 15,000; (269) 468-4430; Fax (269) 468-7088; info@coloma-watervliet.org; www.coloma-watervliet.org

Detroit Area

Detroit Eco. Growth Corp. · George Jackson Jr.; Pres.; 500 Griswold, Ste. 2200; 48226; Wayne; P 2,000,000; (313) 963-2940; Fax (313) 963-8839; www.degc.org

Detroit Reg. Eco. Partnership · John Carroll; Sr. V.P.; One Woodward Ave., Ste. 1900; P.O. Box 33840; 48232; Wayne; P 5,200,000; (313) 964-4000; Fax (313) 964-0183; www.detroitchamber.com

Wayne County Eco. Dev. · Turkia Awada Mullin; Dir.; Wayne County Bldg., 3rd Flr.; 600 Randolph St.; 48226; Wayne; P 2,100,000; (313) 224-0410; Fax (313) 224-8458; www.waynecounty.com

Eastpointe · *City of Eastpointe* · Steve Horstman; Dir.; 23200 Gratiot; 48021; Macomb; P 35,000; (586) 445-5016; Fax (586) 445-5191; stevehorstman@hotmail.com; www.ci.eastpointe.mi.us

Escanaba · *Central Upper Peninsula Plan. & Dev. Reg. Comm.* · Lloyd R. Matthes; Exec. Dir.; 2415 14th Ave. S.; 49829; Delta; P 180,000; (906) 786-9234; Fax (906) 786-4442; cuppad@chartermi.net; www.cuppad.org

Flint · *Genesee County Metro Planning Comm.* · Julie Hinterman; Dir.; 1101 Beach St., Rm. 223; 48502; Genesee; P 436,141; (810) 257-3010; Fax (810) 257-3185; gcmpc@co.genesee.mi.us; www.gcmpc.org

Gaylord · *Northeast Michigan Cncl. of Governments* · Diane Rekowski; Exec. Dir.; 121 E. Mitchell; P.O. Box 457; 49734; Otsego; P 141,199; (989) 732-3551; Fax (989) 732-5578; ppapendic@nemcog.org; www.nemcog.org

Grand Rapids Area

Eco. Dev. Found. · Sandra Bloem; Dir.; 1345 Monroe Ave. N.W., Ste. 132; 49505; Kent; P 600,000; (616) 459-4825; Fax (616) 458-5736; info@growmichigan.com; www.growmichigan.com

The Right Place Inc. · Birgit Klohs; Pres.; 161 Ottawa Ave. N.W., Ste. 400; 49503; Kent; P 1,302,000; (616) 771-0325; Fax (616) 771-0555; info@rightplace.org; www.rightplace.org

West MI Reg. Planning Comm. · Dave Bee; Dir.; 820 Monroe N.W., Ste. 214; 49503; Kent; P 1,100,000; (616) 774-8400; Fax (616) 774-0808; dbee@wmrpc.org; www.wmrpc.org

Hillsdale · *Hillsdale County Ind. Dev. Comm.* · Howard Turner; Exec. Dir.; 23 Care Dr.; 49242; Hillsdale; P 48,000; M 200; (517) 437-3200; Fax (517) 437-3735; info@hillsdaleedp.org; www.hillsdaleedp.org

Howell · *Eco. Dev. Cncl. of Livingston County* · Fred Dillingham; Dir.; 1240 Packard Dr., Ste. 101; 48843; Livingston; P 129,080; (517) 546-0822; Fax (517) 546-4084; info@livingstonedc.com; www.livingstonedc.com

Ionia · *Ionia Downtown Dev. Auth.* · Jason Eppler; City Mgr.; 114 N. Kidd; P.O. Box 496; 48846; Ionia; P 10,569; (616) 527-4170; Fax (616) 527-0810; www.ci.ionia.mi.us

Iron Mountain · *Dickinson Area Partnership* · Bruce Orttenburger; Pres./CEO; 600 S. Stephenson Ave.; 49801; Dickinson; P 26,340; M 489; (906) 774-2202; Fax (906) 774-2004; ortennburger@dickinsonchamber.com; www.dickinsonchamber.com

Ironwood · *Downtown Ironwood Dev. Auth.* · Dan Petersen; Dir. of Comm. Dev.; 213 S. Marquette St.; 49938; Gogebic; P 6,300; (906) 932-5050; Fax (906) 932-5745; petersend@cityofironwood.org; www.cityofironwood.org

Ithaca · *Greater Gratiot Dev. Inc.* · Donald C. Schurr; Pres.; 136 S. Main; 48847; Gratiot; P 43,000; (989) 875-2083; Fax (989) 875-2990; donschurr@gratiot.org; www.gratiot.org

Jackson · *Enterprise Group of Jackson Inc.* · Scott Fleming; Pres./CEO; 1 Jackson Sq., Ste. 1100; P.O. Box 80; 49204; Jackson; P 162,000; (517) 788-4455; Fax (517) 782-0061; sfleming@enterprisegroup.org; www.enterprisegroup.org

Kalamazoo · *City of Kalamazoo Eco. Dev. & Bus. Assistance* · Jerome Kisscorni; Dir.; 445 W. Michigan Ave., Ste. 101; 49007; Kalamazoo; P 77,145; (269) 337-8082; Fax (269) 337-8429; cokeconomicdevelopment@kalamazoocity.org; www.kalamazoocity.org

Kalamazoo · *Southwest Michigan First* · Ron Kitchens; CEO; P.O. Box 50827; 49005; Kalamazoo; P 241,000; (269) 553-9588; Fax (269) 553-6897; www.southwestmichiganfirst.com

Kincheloe · *Eco. Dev. Corp. of Chippewa County* · Kathy Noel; Pres.; 5019 W. Airport Dr.; 49788; Chippewa; P 35,000; (906) 495-5631; Fax (906) 495-5714; ccedc@sault.com

Lansing · *Michigan Eco. Dev. Corp.* · 300 N. Washington Sq.; 48913; Ingham; (517) 373-9808; www.michiganadvantage.org

Ludington · *Mason County Growth Alliance* · Julie Van Dyke; Pres./CEO; 5300 W. U.S. 10; 49431; Mason; P 28,000; (231) 845-6646; Fax (231) 845-6857; jvandyke@masoncountygrowth.com; www.masoncountygrowth.com

Marlette · *Thumb Area-Michigan Works* · Marvin Pichla; Exec. Dir.; 3270 Wilson; 48453; Sanilac; P 225,000; (989) 635-3561; Fax (989) 635-2230; www.thumbworks.org

Marquette · *Lake Superior Comm. Partnership-Marquette Area C/C* · Amy Clickner; Exec. Dir.; 501 S. Front St.; 49855; Marquette; P 64,000; (906) 226-9658; (888) 578-6489; Fax (906) 226-2099; lscp@marquette.org; www.marquette.org

Mason · *Ingham County Eco. Dev. Corp.* · Susan Pigg; Eco. Dev. Coord.; 121 E. Maple St.; 48854; Ingham; P 275,000; (517) 676-7285; Fax (517) 676-7358; spigg@ingham.org; www.ingham.org

Midland · *Midland Tomorrow* · 300 Rodd St., Ste. 201; 48640; Midland; P 83,400; (989) 839-0340; Fax (989) 839-7372; info@midlandtomorrow.org; www.midlandtomorrow.org

Monroe · *Monroe County Ind. Dev. Corp.* · William P. Morris; Pres.; 102 E. Front St.; P.O. Box 926; 48161; Monroe; P 136,000; (734) 241-8081; Fax (734) 241-0813; mail@monroecountyidc.com; www.monroecountyidc.com

Mount Clemens · *Macomb County Area Dev. Ofc.* · Robert Tess; Program Mgr.; 1 S. Main, 7th Flr.; 48043; Macomb; P 830,000; (586) 469-5285; Fax (586) 469-6787; planning@macombcountymi.gov; www.macombcountymi.gov

Mount Pleasant · *Middle MI Dev. Corp.* · George Dunn; Pres.; 111 S. University; 48858; Isabella; P 98,000; (989) 772-2858; Fax (989) 773-2115; info@mmdc.org; www.mmdc.org

Muskegon · *Muskegon Area First* · Ed Garner; Pres.; 380 W. Western, Ste. 202; 49440; Muskegon; P 172,000; (231) 722-3751; Fax (231) 728-7251; info@muskegon.org; www.muskegonareafirst.org

Newberry · *Eco. Dev. Corp. of Luce County* · Carmen McLaren; 407 W. Harrie St.; 49868; Luce; P 7,024; (906) 293-5982; Fax (906) 293-2904; mclaren@up.net

Niles · *Southwestern Michigan Eco. Growth Alliance Inc.* · Sharon J. Witt; Exec. Dir.; 1950 Industrial Dr.; 49120; Berrien; P 60,000; M 200; (269) 683-1833; Fax (269) 683-7515; switt@michigan-business.info; www.michigan-business.info

Novi · *Novi Comm. Dev. Dept.* · Barbara McBeth; Deputy Dir.; 45175 W. Ten Mile Rd.; 48375; Oakland; P 53,677; (248) 347-0475; Fax (248) 735-5600; www.cityofnovi.org

Port Huron · *Eco. Dev. Alliance of St. Clair County* · Doug Alexander; Exec. Dir.; 735 Erie St., Ste. 250; 48060; St. Clair; P 164,000; (810) 982-9511; Fax (810) 982-9531; www.edascc.com

Saginaw · *Saginaw Future Inc.* · JoAnn Crary CEcD; Pres.; 515 N. Washington; 3rd Flr.; 48607; Saginaw; P 210,000; (989) 754-8222; Fax (989) 754-1715; info@saginawfuture.com; www.saginawfuture.com

Saline · *Eco. Dev. Corp.* · Lee Bourgoin; Dir.; 100 N. Harris; 48176; Washtenaw; P 27,000; (734) 429-4907; www.cityofsaline.org

Sault Ste. Marie · *Sault Ste. Marie Eco. Dev. Corp.* · James Hendricks; Exec. Dir.; 1301 W. Easterday Ave.; 49783; Chippewa; P 15,000; (906) 635-9131; Fax (906) 635-1999; info@saultedc.com; www.saultedc.com

Southgate · *Downriver Comm. Conf.-Eco. Dev. Dept.* · Paula Boase; Eco. Dev. Dir.; 15100 Northline Rd., Ste. 135; 48195; Wayne; P 500,000; (734) 362-3477; Fax (734) 281-6661; paula.boase@dccwf.org; www.dccwf.org

St. Joseph · *Berrien County Comm. Dev. Dept.* · Dan Fette; Exec. Dir.; 701 Main St.; 49085; Berrien; P 162,453; (269) 983-7111; Fax (269) 982-8611; jarent@berriencounty.org; www.berriencounty.org

Tawas City · *Tawas Area Ind. Dev. Corp.* · 402 E. Lake St.; P.O. Box 608; 48764; Iosco; P 6,000; (989) 362-8643; (800) 55-TAWAS; Fax (989) 362-7880; www.tawas.com

Tecumseh · *City of Tecumseh Eco. Dev. Dept.* · Paula Holtz; Dir.; 112 S. Ottawa St.; 49286; Lenawee; P 8,500; (517) 424-6003; pholtz@tecumseh.mi.us; www.tecumseh.mi.us

Traverse City · *Traverse Bay Eco. Dev. Corp.* · Tino Breithaupt; Sr. V.P.; 202 E. Grandview Pkwy.; 49684; Grand Traverse; P 156,305; (231) 995-7105; Fax (231) 946-2565; tbedc@tcchamber.org; www.tcchamber.org/tbedc

Waterford · *Oakland County Planning & Eco. Dev. Dept.* · Dan Hunter; Mgr.; 2100 Pontiac Lake Rd.; Bldg. 41W; 48328; Oakland; (248) 858-0720; Fax (248) 975-9555; www.oakgov.com/peds

Wayne · *Dept. of Planning & Dev. for the City of Wayne* · Peter McInerney; Comm. Dev. Dir.; 3355 S. Wayne Rd.; 48184; Wayne; P 19,051; (734) 722-2002; Fax (734) 722-5052; commdev@ci.wayne.mi.us; www.ci.wayne.mi.us

West Branch · *Ogemaw County EDC/MSUE* · Kathy Adair; Pres.; 205 S. Eighth St.; 48661; Ogemaw; P 21,645; (989) 345-0692; Fax (989) 345-1284; www.growogemaw.com

Minnesota

Federal

U.S. SBA, Minnesota Dist. Ofc. · Nancy Libersky; Dist. Dir.; 100 N. 6th St., Ste. 210-C; Minneapolis; 55403; Hennepin; (612) 370-2325; Fax (202) 481-0139; sherree.stratton@sba.gov; www.sba.gov/mn

State

Dept. of Employment & Eco. Dev. · Dan McElroy; Comm.; 1st Natl. Bank Bldg.; 332 Minnesota St., Ste. E200; Saint Paul; 55101; Ramsey; (651) 259-7114; Fax (651) 215-3841; deed. customerservice@state.mn.us; www.deed.state.mn.us

Communities

Ada · *Ada Eco. Dev. Auth.* · 404 W. Main; 56510; Norman; P 1,600; (218) 784-5520; Fax (218) 784-2711; www.ci.ada.mn.us

Alexandria · *Alexandria Area Eco. Dev. Comm.* · Jason Murray; Exec. Dir.; 610 Fillmore St., Ste. 1; 56308; Douglas; P 33,368; (320) 763-4545; Fax (320) 763-4457; aaedc@rea-alp.com; www.alexmn.org

Anoka · *Anoka Eco. Dev. Comm.* · Robert Kirchner; Dir.; 2015 1st Ave. N.; 55303; Anoka; P 18,000; (763) 576-2720; Fax (763) 576-2727; www.ci.anoka.mn.us

Austin · *Dev. Corp. of Austin* · John Garry; Exec. Dir.; 329 N. Main St., Ste. 106L; 55912; Mower; P 23,000; (507) 433-9495; (507) 433-9496; Fax (507) 433-9470; austindca@austindca.org; www.spamtownusa.com

Barnum · *Build Barnum Ind. Dev.* · Jim Benson; Chrmn.; 3743 Main St.; 55707; Carlton; P 585; (218) 389-3224; (218) 389-6814; Fax (218) 389-3235; www.buildbarnum.com

Bemidji · *Headwaters Reg. Dev. Comm.* · Cliff Tweedale; Exec. Dir.; P.O. Box 906; 56619; Beltrami; P ; (218) 444-4732; Fax (218) 444-4722; www.hrdc.org

Blue Earth · *Blue Earth EDA* · Kathy Bailey; City Admin.; 125 W. 6th St.; P.O. Box 38; 56013; Faribault; P 3,621; (507) 526-7336; Fax (507) 526-7352; kbailey@becity.org; www.becity.org

Brainerd · *Brainerd Lakes Area Dev. Corp.* · Sheila Haverkamp; Exec. Dir.; 124 N. Sixth St.; 56401; Crow Wing; P 60,000; M 140; (218) 828-0096; Fax (218) 829-8199; info@bladc.org; wwwbladc.org; 88832BLADC

Brooklyn Park · *Eco. Dev. Auth.* · Robert J. Schreier; Exec. Dir.; 5200 85th Ave. N.; 55443; Hennepin; P 73,000; (763) 493-8059; Fax (763) 493-8391; bpedahp@brooklynpark.org; www.brooklyn park.org

Champlin · *City of Champlin Comm. Dev. Dept.* · John Cox; Dev. Dir.; 11955 Champlin Dr.; 55316; Hennepin; P 23,900; (763) 421-8100; Fax (763) 421-5256; www.ci.champlin.mn.us

Chaska · *City of Chaska Comm. Dev. Dept.* · Bart Fischer; Eco. Dev. Coord.; 1 City Hall Plaza; 55318; Carver; P 20,000; (952) 448-2851; Fax (952) 448-9300; www.chaskamn.com

Coon Rapids · *City of Coon Rapids Comm. Dev.* · Marc Nevinski; Comm. Dev. Dir.; 11155 Robinson Dr.; 55433; Anoka; P 63,000; (763) 767-6430; Fax (763) 767-6573; www.coonrapidsmn.gov

Cottage Grove · *Cottage Grove Eco. Dev. Auth.* · Ryan Schroeder; City Admin.; 7516 80th St. S.; 55016; Washington; P 34,000; (651) 458-2822; Fax (651) 458-2897; info@cottage-grove.org; www.cottage-grove.org

Becker County Eco. Dev. · John Thomsen; Dir.; 712 Minnesota Ave.; P.O. Box 1617; 56502; Becker; P 30,000; (218) 846-7330; Fax (218) 846-7329; www.co.becker.mn.us

Becker Lakes Ind. Dev. Corp. · Larry Remmen AICP; Exec. Dir.; 1025 Roosevelt Ave.; 56502; Becker; P 30,000; (218) 847-5658; Fax (218) 847-8969; lremmen@lakesnet.net

Comm. Dev. of Detroit Lakes · Larry Remmen; Dir.; 1025 Roosevelt Ave.; P.O. Box 647; 56502; Becker; P 10,000; (218) 847-5658; Fax (218) 847-8969; lremmen@lakesnet.net; www.ci.detroitlakes.mn.us

Detroit Lakes Dev. Auth. · Larry Remmen AICP; Comm. Dev. Dir.; 1025 Roosevelt Ave.; P.O. Box 647; 56502; Becker; P 8,300; (218) 847-5658; Fax (218) 847-8969; lremmen@lakesnet.net; www.ci.detroit-lakes.mn.us

Midwest Minnesota Comm. Dev. Corp. · Arlen Kangas; Pres.; 119 Graystone Plz., Ste. 100; P.O. Box 623; 56502; Becker; P 7,500; (218) 847-3191; Fax (218) 844-6345; info@mmcdc.com; www.mmcdc.com

Duluth · *Ofc. of Planning & Dev.* · Cindy Petkac; City Hall, Rm. 402; 411 W. 1st St.; 55802; St. Louis; P 87,000; (218) 730-5580; Fax (218) 730-5904

Fairmont · *Fairmont Eco. Dev. Auth.* · Michael Humpal; Asst. City Admin.; 100 Downtown Plz.; P.O. Box 751; 56031; Martin; P 12,000; (507) 238-9461; Fax (507) 238-9469; ecodevo@fairmont.org; www.fairmont.org

Fridley · *City of Fridley Comm. Dev.* · Scott Hickok; Comm. Dev. Dir.; 6431 University Ave. N.E.; 55432; Anoka; P 29,000; (763) 572-3590; Fax (763) 571-1287; www.ci.fridley.mn.us

Grand Marais · *Cook County/Grand Marais Joint Eco. Dev. Auth.* · Matt Geretschlaeger; Dir.; P.O. Box 597; 55604; Cook; P 4,700; (218) 387-3067; Fax (218) 387-3018; edamatt@boreal.org

Grand Rapids · *Itasca EDC* · Diane Weber; Interim Pres.; 12 N.W. 3rd St.; 55744; Itasca; P 43,000; (218) 326-9411; Fax (218) 327-2242; info@itascadv.org; www.itascadv.org

Granite Falls · *Granite Falls Eco. Dev. Auth.* · Dennis VanHoff; Exec. Dir.; 641 Prentice St.; 56241; Yellow Medicine; P 3,081; (320) 564-2255; eda@granitefalls.com; www.granitefalls.com

Hibbing · *Hibbing Bus. Dev. Corp.* · 1515 E. 25th St.; P.O. Box 783; 55746; St. Louis; P 17,050; (218) 262-6703; Fax (218) 262-7399

International Falls · *Koochiching Eco. Dev. Auth.* · Paul Nevanen; Dir.; 405 3rd St.; P.O. Box 138; 56649; Koochiching; P 15,500; (218) 283-8585; Fax (218) 283-4688; keda@northwinds.net; www.businessupnorth.com

Jackson · *Jackson Eco. Dev. Corp.* · 80 W. Ashley St.; 56143; Jackson; P 3,501; (507) 847-4423; edc@cityofjacksonmn.com; www.jacksonmn.com

Lake City · *Lake City Eco. Dev. Auth.* · Erin Sparks; Exec. Dir.; 205 W. Center St.; 55041; Wabasha; P 5,350; (651) 345-6808; Fax (651) 345-3208; esparks@lakecityeda.com; www.lakecityeda.com

Le Center · *Le Center Area Eco. Dev. Auth.* · Don Hayden; Exec. Dir.; 10 W. Tyrone St.; P.O. Box 54; 56057; Le Sueur; P 2,200; (507) 357-6737; Fax (507) 357-6888; donlc@frontiernet.net

Luverne · *Luverne Eco. Dev. Auth.* · Ted LaFrance; Eco. Dev. Dir.; 305 E. Luverne St.; P.O. Box 659; 56156; Rock; P 4,600; (507) 449-5033; Fax (507) 449-5034; tlafrance@cityofluverne.org; www.cityofluverne.org

Mankato • *Greater Mankato Growth* • Jonathan Zierdt; Pres./CEO; 1961 Premier Dr., Ste. 100; 56001; Blue Earth; P 50,000; M 750; (507) 385-6640; (800) 697-0652; Fax (507) 345-4451; info@greatermankato.com; www.greatermankato.com

Minneapolis • *Minneapolis Comm. Planning & Eco. Dev.* • Mike Christenson; Dir.; 105 5th Ave. S., Ste. 1200; Crown Roller Mill; 55401; Hennepin; P 360,000; (612) 673-5095; Fax (612) 673-5100; www.ci.minneapolis.mn.us/cped

Montevideo • *Montevideo Eco. Dev. Auth.* • 103 Canton Ave.; P.O. Box 517; 56265; Chippewa; P 5,482; (320) 269-6575; Fax (320) 269-9340; eda@montevideomn.org; www.montevideomn.net

Monticello • *City of Monticello Eco. Dev.* • 505 Walnut St., Ste. 1; 55362; Wright; P 10,000; (763) 271-3208; Fax (763) 295-4404; www.ci.monticello.mn.us

Morris • *Stevens County Eco. Imp. Comm.* • Michael Haynes; Exec. Dir.; 507 Atlantic Ave.; 56267; Stevens; P 10,634; (320) 585-2609; Fax (320) 585-4814; www.sceic.org

Ortonville • *Ortonville Eco. Dev. Auth.* • Vicki Oakes; Secy.; 315 Madison Ave.; 56278; Big Stone; P 2,000; (320) 839-3428; Fax (320) 839-2613; eda@ortonville.net; www.ortonville.net

Osakis • *Osakis Eco. Dev. Auth.* • Angela Jacobson; Admin.; P.O. Box 486; 56360; Douglas & Todd; P 1,615; (320) 859-2150; Fax (320) 859-3978; cityhall@cityofosakis.com; www.cityofosakis.com

Pipestone • *Pipestone Eco. Dev. Auth.* • Jeff Jones; City Admin.; 119 2nd Ave. S.W.; 56164; Pipestone; P 4,400; (507) 825-3324; Fax (507) 825-5353; dnelson@cityofpipestone.com; www.progressivepipestone.com

Red Lake Falls • *Red Lake Falls Comm. Dev. Corp.* • Allen Bertilrud; Pres.; P.O. Box 207; 56750; Red Lake; P 1,590; (218) 253-2143; Fax (218) 253-2141

Redwood Falls • *Redwood Area Dev. Corp.* • Julie Rath; Eco. Dev. Spec.; 200 S. Mill St.; P.O. Box 481; 56283; Redwood; P 17,000; (507) 637-4004; Fax (507) 637-4082; julie@redwood-falls.org; www.radc.org

Rochester • *Rochester Area Eco. Dev.* • Gary Smith; Pres.; 220 S. Broadway, Ste. 100; 55904; Olmsted; P 100,000; (507) 288-0208; Fax (507) 282-8960; tbernard@raedi.com; www.raedi.com

Saint Charles • *St. Charles Eco. Dev. Auth.* • 830 Whitewater Ave.; 55972; Winona; P 3,600; (507) 932-3020; Fax (507) 932-5301; www.stcharlesmn.org

Saint Cloud • *St. Cloud Area Eco. Dev. Partnership* • Tom Moore; Pres.; P.O. Box 1091; 56302; Stearns; P 150,000; (320) 656-3815; Fax (320) 251-0081; info@scapartnership.com; www.scapartnership.com

Saint Paul • *City of St. Paul* • Dept. of Plan. & Eco. Dev.; 25 W. 4th, 1300 City Hall Annex; 55102; Ramsey; P 272,243; (651) 266-6565; Fax (651) 228-3261

Saint Paul • *Grand Ave. Bus. Assoc.* • Ben Johnson; Pres.; 867 Grand Ave.; 55105; Ramsey; P ; (651) 699-0029; Fax (651) 699-7775; www.grandave.com

Saint Paul • *Saint Paul Port Auth.* • Louis Jambois; Pres.; 345 St. Peter St., Ste. 1900; 55102; Ramsey; (651) 224-5686; (800) 328-8417; Fax (651) 223-5198; info@sppa.com; www.sppa.com

Saint Peter • *Dept. of Comm. Dev.* • Russ Wille; Dir.; 227 S. Front St.; 56082; Nicollet; P 10,401; (507) 934-0661; Fax (507) 934-4917; gettheedge@saintpeteradvantage.com; www.saintpeteradvantage.com

Slayton • *Southwest Reg. Dev. Comm.* • Jay Trusty; Exec. Dir.; 2401 Broadway Ave., Ste. 1; 56172; Murray; P 130,000; (507) 836-8549; (507) 836-8547; Fax (507) 836-8866; execdir@swrdc.org; www.swrdc.org

Spicer • *Spicer Eco. Dev. Auth.* • P.O. Box 431; 56288; Kandiyohi; P 1,183; (320) 796-5562; Fax (320) 796-2044; spicer06@tds.net; www.spicermn.com

Vadnais Heights • *Vadnais Heights Eco. Dev. Corp.* • Keith Warner; Exec. Dir.; 800 E. County Rd. E; 55127; Ramsey; P 13,500; (651) 204-6000; www.cityvadnaisheights.com

Virginia • *Virginia Eco. Dev. Auth.* • John Tourville; Op. Dir.; 327 1st St. S.; City Hall; 55792; St. Louis; P 8,953; (218) 748-7535; Fax (218) 749-3580; veda@virginiamn.us; www.virginia-mn.com

White Bear Lake • *White Bear Lake Area Comm. Dev. Dept.* • Jim Robinson; Comm. Dev. Dir.; 4701 Hwy. 61; 55110; Ramsey; P 25,000; (651) 429-8562; Fax (651) 429-8503; www.whitebearlake.org

Willmar • *Mid-Minnesota Dev. Comm.* • Donn Winckler; Exec. Dir.; 333 6th St. S.W., Ste. 2; 56201; Kandiyohi; P 116,000; (320) 235-8504; Fax (320) 235-4329; mmrdc@mmrdc.org; www.mmrdc.org

Worthington • *Worthington Reg. Eco. Dev. Corp.* • Glen Thuringer; Mgr.; 1121 Third Ave.; 56187; Nobles; P 12,000; (507) 372-5515; Fax (507) 372-7165; wredc@frontiernet.net; www.wgtn.net

Mississippi

Federal

U.S. SBA, Mississippi Dist. Ofc. • Janita R. Stewart; Dist. Dir.; 210 E. Capital St., Ste. 900; Jackson; 39201; Hinds; (601) 965-4378; Fax (601) 965-5629; janita.r.stewart@sba.gov; www.sba.gov/ms

State

Mississippi Dev. Auth. • Gray Swoope; Exec. Dir.; 501 N. West St.; P.O. Box 849; Jackson; 39205; Hinds; (601) 359-3449; Fax (601) 359-2832; mmedley@mississippi.org; www.mississippi.org

Communities

Belzoni • *Belzoni-Humphreys Dev. Found.* • Steve Anderson; Exec. Dir.; 111 Magnolia St.; P.O. Box 145; 39038; Humphreys; P 11,000; M 60; (662) 247-4838; Fax (662) 247-4805; catfish@belzonicable.com; www.belzonims.com

Booneville • *Prentiss County Dev. Assn.* • W. Gerald Williams; Exec. Dir.; 402 W. Parker Dr.; P.O. Box 672; 38829; Prentiss; P 25,556; (662) 728-3505; Fax (662) 728-0086; gwilliams@goprentiss.com; www.goprentiss.com

Brandon • *Rankin First Eco. Dev. Auth.* • Tom Troxler; Exec. Dir.; 101 Service Dr.; P.O. Box 129; 39043; Rankin; P 128,000; (601) 825-2268; Fax (601) 825-1977; ttroxler@rankinfirst.com; www.rankinfirst.com

Brookhaven • *Lincoln County Ind. Dev. Found.* • Cliff Brumfield; Exec. V.P.; 230 S. Whitworth Ave.; P.O. Box 978; 39602; Lincoln; P 33,166; (601) 833-1411; (800) 613-4667; Fax (601) 833-1412; chb@brookhavenchamber.com; www.brookhavenchamber.com

Cleveland • *Cleveland-Bolivar County Ind. Dev. Found.* • Judson Thigpen III; Exec. Dir.; 600 Third St.; P.O. Box 490; 38732; Bolivar; P 42,000; (662) 843-2712; (800) 295-7473; Fax (662) 843-2718; judson@clevelandmschamber.com; www.clevelandmschamber.com

Columbus · *Columbus-Lowndes Dev. Link* · Joe Max Higgins Jr.; CEO; 1102 Main St.; P.O. Box 1328; 39703; Lowndes; P 63,000; (662) 328-8369; (800) 748-8882; Fax (662) 327-3417; info@cldlink.org; www.cldlink.org

Corinth · *The Alliance* · Gary Chandler; Pres./COO; P.O. Box 1089; 38835; Alcorn; P 35,000; M 360; (662) 287-5269; Fax (662) 287-5260; alliance@corinthalliance.com; www.corinthalliance.com

DeKalb · *Kemper County Eco. Dev. Auth.* · Brian Henson; Exec. Dir.; 14062 Hwy. 16 W.; 39328; Kemper; P 12,000; (601) 743-2754; Fax (601) 743-2760; kceda@bellsouth.net; www.kempercounty.com

Fulton · *Itawamba County Dev. Cncl.* · Greg Deakle; Exec. Dir.; 107 W. Wiygul St.; P.O. Box 577; 38843; Itawamba; P 22,000; M 320; (662) 862-4571; (800) 371-8642; Fax (662) 862-5637; icdc@itawamba.com; www.itawamba.com

Greenwood · *Greenwood LeFlore/Carroll Eco. Dev. Found.* · Angela Curry; Exec. Dir.; 402 Hwy. 82 Bypass; P.O. Box 26; 38935; Leflore; P 60,000; M 150; (662) 453-5321; (800) 844-SITE; Fax (662) 453-8003; angcur@bellsouth.net; www.glcedf.com

Gulfport · *Harrison Co. Dev. Comm.* · Larry Barnett; Exec. Dir.; 12281 Intraplex Pkwy.; 39503; Harrison; (228) 896-5020; Fax (228) 896-6020; hcdc@mscoast.org; www.mscoast.org

Gulfport · *Southern Miss. Planning & Dev. Dist.* · Leslie Newcomb; Exec. Dir.; 9229 Hwy. 49; 39503; Harrison; P 731,620; (228) 868-2311; (800) 444-8014; Fax (228) 868-2550; www.smpdd.com

Hattiesburg · *Area Dev. Partnership* · Chad Newell; Pres.; One Convention Center Plaza; 39401; Lamar; P 128,171; M 1,100; (601) 296-7500; Fax (601) 296-7505; adp@theadp.com; www.theadp.com; 800238HATT

Hernando · *DeSoto Cncl.* · Jim Flanagan; Pres./CEO; 316 W. Commerce St.; 38632; DeSoto; P 144,000; M 600; (662) 429-4414; Fax (662) 429-0952; jflanagan@desotocounty.com; www.desotocounty.com

Houston · *Chickasaw Dev. Found.* · Joyce East; Exec. Dir.; 635 Starkville Rd.; P.O. Box 505; 38851; Chickasaw; P 19,000; (662) 456-2321; Fax (662) 456-2595; jeastcdf@bellsouth.net; www.cdfhoustonms.org

Kosciusko · *Kosciusko-Attala Dev. Corp.* · Steve Zea; Pres.; 124 N. Jackson; 39090; Attala; P 20,000; (662) 289-2981; Fax (662) 289-2986; info@kadcorp.org; www.kadcorp.org

Laurel · *Eco. Dev. Auth. of Jones County* · Wm. M. 'Mitch' Stennett; Pres.; 153 Base Dr., Ste. 3; P.O. Box 527; 39441; Jones; P 64,958; M 450; (601) 649-3031; Fax (601) 428-2047; info@edajones.com; www.edajones.com; www.jonescounty.com

Louisville · *Winston County Eco. Dev. Dist.* · Gerald Mills; Dir.; P.O. Box 551; 39339; Winston; P 20,160; (662) 773-8719; Fax (662) 773-8909; gmills@winstoncounty.com; www.winstoncounty.com

McComb · *Pike County Eco. Dev. Dist.* · J. Britt Herrin; Exec. Dir.; 112 N. Railroad Blvd.; P.O. Box 83; 39648; Pike; P 38,000; (601) 684-2291; (800) 399-4404; Fax (601) 684-4899; pcedd@pikeinfo.com; www.pikeinfo.com

Meridian · *East Mississippi Bus. Dev. Corp.* · Wade Jones; Pres.; 1901 Front St., Ste. A; P.O. Box 790; 39302; Lauderdale; P 78,000; M 600; (601) 693-1306; Fax (601) 693-5638; info@embdc.org; www.embdc.org

Monticello · *Lawrence County Comm. Dev. Assn.* · Bob Smira; Pres./CEO; 517 Broad St. E.; P.O. Box 996; 39654; Lawrence; P 13,000; (601) 587-3007; Fax (601) 587-0765; info@lawrencecounty.org; www.lawrencecounty.org

Natchez · *Natchez-Adams County Dev. Auth.* · Jefferson Rowell; Exec. Dir.; 211 Main, Ste. B; P.O. Box 700; 39121; Adams; P 34,350; (601) 445-0288; (800) 7-NATCHEZ; Fax (601) 445-0234; clyles@natchezadams.com; www.natchezadams.com

New Albany · *Union County Dev. Assn.* · Stephen Surles; Exec. Dir.; P.O. Box 125; 38652; Union; P 25,362; M 200; (662) 534-4354; (888) 534-8232; Fax (662) 538-4107; info@ucda-newalbany.com; www.ucda-newalbany.com

Oxford · *Oxford-Lafayette Eco. Dev.* · Max D. Hipp CID; Pres.; 299 W. Jackson Ave. W.; P.O. Box 108; 38655; Lafayette; P 40,000; (662) 234-4651; (800) 880-6967; Fax (662) 234-4655; max@oxfordms.com; www.oxfordms.com

Pascagoula · *Jackson County Eco. Dev. Found.* · George Freeland; Exec. Dir.; 3033 Pascagoula St.; P.O. Drawer 1558; 39568; Jackson; P 133,000; (228) 769-6263; (800) 362-0103; Fax (228) 762-8431; www.jcedf.org

Pascagoula · *Jackson County Port Auth.* · Mark McAndrews; Port Dir.; 3033 Pascagoula St.; P.O. Box 70; 39568; Jackson; P 119,000; (228) 762-4041; Fax (228) 762-7476; www.portofpascagoula.com

Philadelphia · *Ind. Dev. Auth. of Neshoba County* · David Vowell; Exec. Dir.; 256 W. Beacon St.; P.O. Box 330; 39350; Neshoba; P 29,000; (601) 656-1000; (877) 752-2643; Fax (601) 656-1066; dvowell@bellsouth.net; www.neshoba.org

Picayune · *Partners for Pearl River County* · Ron Fine; Dir.; P.O. Box 278; 39466; Pearl River; P 70,000; (601) 749-4919; Fax (601) 749-4250; www.partners.ms

Purvis · *Lamar County Eco. Dev. Dist.* · Lasheba Boren; Ofc. Admin.; P.O. Box 598; 39475; Lamar; P 52,000; (601) 794-1011; Fax (601) 794-1025; information@lamarcounty.com; www.lamarcounty.com

Ridgeland · *Madison County Eco. Dev. Auth.* · Tim Corsey; Exec. Dir.; 623 Highland Colony Pkwy.; 39157; Madison; P 80,000; (601) 605-0368; (800) 896-5087; Fax (601) 605-8662; tim@madisoncountyeda.com; www.madisoncountyeda.com

Ripley · *Tippah County Dev. Found.* · Duane Bullard; Pres./CEO; 212 E. Jefferson St.; 38663; Tippah; P 24,000; M 200; (662) 837-3353; (662) 837-6592; Fax (662) 837-3006; tcdf@dixie-net.com; www.tippahcounty.ripley.ms

Senatobia · *Tate County Eco. Dev. Found.* · J.E. Mortimer; Exec. Dir.; 135 N. Front St.; 38668; Tate; P 27,000; (662) 562-8715; Fax (662) 562-5786; jemortimer@cityofsenatobia.com; www.tate-county.com

Starkville · *Oktibbeha County Eco. Dev. Auth.* · Jon Maynard; Pres./CEO; 200 E. Main St.; 39759; Oktibbeha; P 42,970; (662) 323-3322; Fax (662) 323-5815; www.starkville.org

Tupelo · *Comm. Dev. Found.* · David Rumbarger; Pres./CEO; 300 W. Main St.; P.O. Box A; 38802; Lee; P 34,211; M 1,425; (662) 842-4521; (800) 523-3463; Fax (662) 841-0693; info@cdfms.org; www.cdfms.org

Vicksburg · *Vicksburg-Warren County Eco. Dev. Found.* · Wayne Mansfield; Exec. Dir.; P.O. Box 820363; 39182; Warren; P 50,000; M 160; (601) 631-0555; Fax (601) 631-6953; www.vicksburgedf.org

Waynesboro · *Wayne County EDC* · Larry Harvey; Dir.; 610 Azalea Dr.; 39367; Wayne; P 20,000; (601) 735-6056; Fax (601) 735-6246; www.waynesboroinfo.com

West Point · *North Miss. Ind. Dev. Assn.* · Joseph Geddie; Exec. Dir.; P.O. Box 718; 39773; Clay; (662) 494-4633; Fax (662) 494-3231; www.nmida.com

West Point · *West Point/Clay County Comm. Growth Alliance* · Amber Smith; Comm. Dev. Dir.; 510 E. Broad St.; 39773; Clay; P 21,000; M 100; (662) 494-5121; Fax (662) 494-6396; www.westpointms.org

Winona · *Eco. Dev. Partnership* · Sue Stidham; Exec. Dir.; P.O. Box 248; 38967; Montgomery; P 5,705; M 242; (662) 283-4828; Fax (662) 283-5986; mcedp@duckwood.net; www.mcedp.ms

Yazoo City · *Greater Yazoo Growth & Dev. Found.* · Henry Cote; Pres.; 212 E. Broadway; P.O. Box 172; 39194; Yazoo; P 28,000; (662) 746-1273; Fax (662) 746-7238; ccyazoo@bellsouth.net; www.yazoochamber.org

Missouri

Federal

U.S. SBA, Kansas City Dist. Ofc. · Gary Cook; Dist. Dir.; 1000 Walnut St., Ste. 500; Kansas City; 64106; Jackson; (816) 426-4902; Fax (816) 426-4939; barbara.caldwell@sba.gov; www.sba.gov/mo

U.S. SBA, St. Louis Dist. Ofc. · Dennis Melton; Dist. Dir.; 200 N. Broadway, Ste. 1500; Saint Louis; 63102; (314) 539-6600; Fax (314) 539-3785; sherry.mueller@sba.gov; www.sba.gov/mo

State

State of Missouri Dept. of Eco. Dev. · David Kerr; Dir.; 301 W. High St.; P.O. Box 1157; Jefferson City; 65102; Cole; P 5,900,000; (573) 751-4962; Fax (573) 526-7700; ecodev@ded.mo.gov; www.ded.mo.gov

Communities

Belton · *Belton Corp. for Eco. Dev. [BCED]* · Art Ruiz; Exec. Dir.; 7926 E. 171st, Ste. 104; P.O. Box 525; 64012; Cass; P 25,000; (816) 331-4449; Fax (816) 322-2826; bced@beltonbced.com; www.beltonbced.com

Branson · *City of Branson Eco. Dev.* · Garrett Anderson; Eco. Dev. Dir.; 110 W. Maddux; 65616; Taney; P 6,500; (417) 337-8589; (417) 337-8548; Fax (417) 334-6095; ganderson@bransonmo.gov; www.bransonmo.gov

Cape Girardeau · *Cape Girardeau Area C of C/Eco. Dev.* · John E. Mehner; Pres./CEO; 1267 N. Mount Auburn Rd.; 63701; Cape Girardeau; P 75,000; (573) 335-3312; Fax (573) 335-4686; info@capechamber.com; www.capechamber.com

Chillicothe · *Chillicothe Ind. Dev. Corp.* · Steve Franke; Pres.; 514 Washington; P.O. Box 1022; 64601; Livingston; P 9,500; (660) 646-4071; Fax (660) 646-5571; cdc@chillicothemo.com; www.chillicothemo.com

Clayton · *City of Clayton, Eco. Dev. Div.* · Susan Istenes; Dir. of Planning & Dev.; 10 N. Bemiston; 63105; St. Louis; P 15,926; (314) 290-8453; Fax (314) 863-0296; sistenes@ci.clayton.mo.us; www.ci.clayton.mo.us

Clinton · *City of Clinton Eco. Dev. Dept.* · Christy Maggi; City Admin.; 105 E. Ohio; 64735; Henry; P 10,000; (660) 885-6121; Fax (660) 885-2023; cmaggi@cityofclintonmo.com; www.clintonmo.com

Columbia · *Reg. Eco. Dev. Inc.* · Bernard K. Andrews CEcD; Exec. V.P.; 302 Campusview Dr., Ste. 208; P.O. Box 6015; 65205; Boone; P 146,626; (573) 442-8303; Fax (573) 443-8834; bka@gocolumbia mo.com; www.columbiaredi.com

Ferguson · *City of Ferguson Eco. Dev. Dept.* · Sam Anselm; City Mgr. Asst.; 110 Church St.; 63135; St. Louis; P 22,290; (314) 521-7721; Fax (314) 524-5173; sanselm@fergusoncity.com; www.fergusoncity.com

Fulton · *Fulton Area Dev. Corp.* · Bruce Hackmann; Pres./CEO; 2625 Fairway Dr., Ste. A; 65251; Callaway; P 42,000; (573) 642-4841; (877) 642-5964; Fax (573) 642-5964; hackmann@fadc.org; www.fadc.org

Grandview · *Grandview Area Eco. Dev. Cncl.* · Kim Curtis; Exec. Dir.; 12500 S. 71 Hwy., Ste. 100; 64030; Jackson; P 25,500; M 55; (816) 761-6505; Fax (816) 763-8460; ksc@grandview.org; www.grandview.org

Hannibal · *Northeast Missouri Eco. Dev. Cncl.* · George Walley; Exec. Dir.; 201 N. Third, Ste. 220; 63401; Marion; P 18,000; (573) 221-1033; Fax (573) 221-1033; gwalley@nemodev.org; www.nemodev.org

Harrisonville · *City of Harrisonville Comm. Dev. Dept.* · Rick DeLuca; Comm. Dev. Dir.; 300 E. Pearl St.; P.O. Box 367; 64701; Cass; P 9,400; (816) 380-8900; Fax (816) 380-8910; developdir@ci.harrisonville.mo.us; www.ci.harrisonville.mo.us

Independence · *Independence Cncl. for Eco. Dev.* · Tom Lesnak; Pres.; 201 N. Forest Ave., Ste. 120; 64050; Jackson; P 114,345; (816) 252-5777; Fax (816) 252-5777; tlesnak@independencemo.biz; www.independencemo.biz

Joplin · *Joplin Bus. & Ind. Dev. Corp.* · Rob O'Brian; Pres.; 320 E. 4th St.; 64801; Jasper; P 169,031; (417) 624-4150; Fax (417) 624-4303; info@joplincc.com; www.joplinregionalpartnership.com

Kansas City Area

Clay County Eco. Dev. Cncl. · Jim Hampton; Exec. Dir.; 1251 N.W. Briarcliff Pkwy., Ste. 25; 64116; Clay; P 180,000; M 700; (816) 468-4989; Fax (816) 587-1996; info@clayedc.com; www.clayedc.com

Kansas City Area Dev. Cncl. · Robert J. Marcusse; Pres./CEO; 2600 Commerce Tower; 911 Main St.; 64105; Jackson; P 2,000,000; (816) 221-2121; (888) 99KC-ADC; Fax (816) 842-2865; kcadc@thinkKC.com; www.thinkKC.com

Platte County Eco. Dev. Cncl. Inc. · Burdette Fullerton; Exec. Dir.; 11724 N.W. Plaza Cir., Ste. 400; 64153; Platte; P 85,000; M 650; (816) 270-2119; Fax (816) 270-2135; pfullerton@plattecountyedc.com; www.plattecountyedc.com

Kearney · *Kearney Area Dev. Cncl.* · Jim Eldridge; Secy.; 100 E. Washington; P.O. Box 291; 64060; Clay; P 7,000; (816) 628-3343; jeldridge@ci.kearney.mo.us; www.kearneyadc.com

Lamar · *Barton County Comm. Dev. Corp.* · Robert Harrington; Eco. Dev. Dir.; 128 W. 10th St., Ste. 9; 64759; Barton; P 12,600; (417) 681-2500; Fax (417) 681-2501; rob@bartoncountycdc.org; www.bartoncountycdc.org

Lee's Summit · *Lee's Summit Eco. Dev. Cncl.* · James A. Devine; Pres./CEO; 218 S.E. Main St.; P.O. Box 710; 64063; Jackson; P 90,000; (816) 525-6617; Fax (816) 524-8851; www.leessummit.org

Mexico · *City of Mexico Dept. of Eco. Dev.* · Russell Runge; Dir.; 300 N. Coal; 65265; Audrain; P 11,390; (573) 581-2100; Fax (573) 581-2305; rrunge@mexicomissouri.org; www.mexicomissouri.net

Moberly · *Moberly Area Eco. Dev. Corp.* · Corey J. Mehaffy; Pres.; 115 A N. Williams; P.O. Box 549; 65270; Randolph; P 35,000; M 50; (660) 263-8811; (660) 998-0097; Fax (660) 263-8883; info@moberly-edc.com; www.moberly-edc.com

Nevada · *Eco. Dev. of City of Nevada* · Ron Clow; Dir.; 110 S. Ash; 64772; Vernon; P 20,000; (417) 448-2700; Fax (417) 448-2707; rclow@nevadamo.org; www.nevadamo.org

Perryville · *Perry County Eco. Dev. Auth.* · Larry Tucker CEcD; Exec. Dir.; 112 W. Ste. Maries St.; P.O. Box 109; 63775; Perry; P 18,132; (573) 547-1097; Fax (573) 547-7327; perryida@perrycountymo.org; www.perrycountymo.org

Saint Charles · *St. Charles County Eco. Dev. Center* · Gregory Prestemon; Pres./Exec. Dir.; 5988 Mid Rivers Mall Dr.; 63304; St. Charles; P 311,000; (636) 441-6880; Fax (636) 441-6881; www.edcscc.com

Saint Louis · *St. Louis County Eco. Cncl.* · Denny Coleman; Pres./CEO; 121 S. Meramec, Ste. 900; 63105; St. Louis; P 1,000,000; (314) 615-7663; Fax (314) 615-7666; www.slcec.com

Sikeston · *Sikeston Dept. of Eco. Dev.* · Ed Dust; Dir.; 128 N. New Madrid St.; 63801; New Madrid & Scott; P 17,000; (573) 471-2780; (800) 494-6476; Fax (573) 471-7564; ded@sikeston.org; www.sikeston.org

Springfield · *Dept. of Planning & Dev.* · Ralph Rognstad; Dir.; 840 Boonville Ave.; 65802; Greene; P 156,228; (417) 864-1031; Fax (417) 864-1030; rrognstad@springfieldmo.gov; www.springfieldmo.gov

Springfield · *Springfield Bus. & Dev. Corp.* · Ryan Mooney; Sr. V.P. of Eco. Dev.; 202 S. John Q. Hammons Pkwy.; P.O. Box 1687; 65801; Greene; P 407,092; (417) 862-5567; Fax (417) 862-1611; ryan@springfieldchamber.com; www.business4springfield.com

Washington · *City of Washington Eco. Dev. Dept.* · Richard Oldenburg; Dir.; 405 Jefferson St.; 63090; Franklin; P 15,000; (636) 390-1004; (636) 667-9310; Fax (636) 239-8945; roldenburg@ci.washington.mo.us; www.ci.washington.mo.us

Wright City · *Wright City Eco. Dev. Dept.* · Karen Girondo; Eco. Developer; P.O. Box 436; 63390; Warren; P 3,100; (636) 745-3101; Fax (636) 745-3119; econdevelop@wrightcity.org; www.wrightcity.org

Montana

Federal

U.S. SBA, Montana Dist. Ofc. · Michelle Johnston; Dist. Dir.; 10 W. 15th St., Ste. 1100; Helena; 59626; Lewis & Clark; (406) 441-1081; Fax (406) 441-1090; crystal.baker@sba.gov; www.sba.gov/mt

Communities

Colstrip · *Southeastern Montana Dev. Corp./Small Bus. Dev.* · Jim Atchison; Exec. Dir.; 6200 Main St.; P.O. Box 1935; 59323; Rosebud; P 30,000; (406) 748-2990; Fax (406) 748-2990; www.semdc.org

Havre · *Bear Paw Dev. Corp.* · Paul Tuss; Exec. Dir.; 48 2nd Ave., Ste. 202; P.O. Box 170; 59501; Hill; P 36,411; (406) 265-9226; Fax (406) 265-5602; www.bearpaw.org

Kalispell · *Montana West Eco. Dev.* · Lyle Phillips; CEO; 314 Main St.; 59901; Flathead; P 81,000; (406) 257-7711; (888) 870-5440; Fax (406) 257-7772; info@dobusinessinmontana.com; www.dobusinessinmontana.com

Saint Ignatius · *Mission Valley Old Town Dev. Corp.* · Stuart Morton; Pres.; P.O. Box 400; 59865; Lake; P 2,500; (406) 745-2190

Nebraska

Federal

US SBA, Nebraska Dist. Ofc. · Leon Milobar; Dist. Dir.; 10675 Bedford Ave., Ste. 100; Omaha; 68134; Douglas; (402) 221-4691; Fax (402) 221-3680; leon.milobar@sba.gov; www.sba.gov/ne

State

Nebraska Dept. of Eco. Dev. · Richard Baier; Dir.; 301 Centennial Mall S.; P.O. Box 94666; Lincoln; 68509; Lancaster; (402) 471-3111; Fax (402) 471-3778; richard.baier@nebraska.gov; www.neded.org

Communities

Alliance · *Box Butte Dev. Corp.* · John Olafson; Exec. Dir.; 204 E. 3rd; 69301; Box Butte; P 11,374; M 82; (308) 762-1800; Fax (308) 762-4268; info@boxbuttedevelopment.com; www.boxbuttedevelopment.com

Arnold · *Arnold EDC* · P.O Box 376; 69120; Custer; P 680; (308) 848-2211; Fax (308) 848-2211; aedc@gpcom.net; www.arnoldne.org

Atkinson · *Atkinson Dev. Corp.* · Mike Butterfield; Pres.; P.O. Box 129; 68713; Holt; P 1,244; (402) 925-2801; www.atkinsonne.com

Bassett · *Bassett Area Dev.* · Donald Coash; Pres.; P.O. Box 145; 68714; Rock; P 800; (402) 684-2711; www.bassettnebr.com

Beatrice · *Gage County Eco. Dev.* · Terri Dageford; Dir.; 5109 W. Scott Rd., Ste. 411; 68310; Gage; P 24,000; (402) 223-6650; Fax (402) 223-6651; terri@gced.us; www.gced.us

Bloomfield · *Bloomfield Eco. Dev.* · Jason Hefner; Pres.; P.O. Box 687; 68718; Knox; P 900; (402) 373-2557; (402) 373-2272; www.ci.bloomfield.ne.us

Cambridge · *Cambridge Eco. Dev Bd.* · Andela Taylor; Dir.; 722 Patterson St.; P.O Box Q; 69022; Furnas; P 1,041; (308) 697-3711; Fax (308) 697-3253; edcity@swnebr.net; www.cambridgene.org

Central City · *Merrick County Dev. Corp.* · Clayton Erickson; Mayor; City Hall; P.O. Box 418; 68826; Merrick; P 9,000; (308) 946-3806; Fax (308) 946-3334

Chadron · *Nebraska Northwest Dev. Corp.* · Brenda Johnson; Exec. Dir.; 706 W. 3rd St.; 69337; Dawes; (308) 432-4023; Fax (308) 432-6740; bjnndc@bbc.net; www.nndc.chadron-nebraska.com

Clay Center · *Clay Center Comm. Found.* · Linda Redline; Pres.; 416 W. South St.; P.O. Box 185; 68933; Clay; P 867; (402) 762-3356; www.ci.clay-center.ne.us

Cozad · *Dawson Area Dev.* · Jennifer Wolf; Exec. Dir.; 209 W. 8th St.; P.O. Box 106; 69130; Dawson; P 25,000; (308) 784-3902; Fax (308) 784-3941; jwdad@cozadtel.net

Curtis · *Medicine Valley Eco. Dev. Corp.* · P.O. Box 437; 69025; Frontier; P 800; (308) 367-4122; Fax (308) 367-4125; www.medicinevalleyedc.com

Fairbury · *Jefferson County Eco. Dev. Corp.* · Julie Earhart; Exec. Dir.; 518 E St.; P.O. Box 606; 68352; Jefferson; P 8,333; (402) 729-4061; Fax (402) 729-6472; jcedc@diodecom.net; www.visitjeffersoncounty.com;

Falls City · *Falls City Eco. Dev.* · Becki Cromer; Exec. Dir.; 3424 N. Hwy. 73; P.O. Box 574; 68355; Richardson; P 5,000; (402) 245-2105; Fax (402) 245-2106; info@fallscityedge.com; www.fallscityedge.com

Fremont · *Greater Fremont Dev. Cncl.* · Kevin Wilkins; Exec. Dir.; 400 E. Military Ave.; P.O. Box 182; 68025; Dodge; P 25,174; (402) 753-8126; Fax (402) 727-2667; info@fremontne.org; www.gfdc.net

Geneva · *Fillmore County Dev. Corp.* · Patt Lentfer; Exec. Dir.; 1032 G St.; 68361; Fillmore; P 7,000; M 80; (402) 759-4910; Fax (402) 759-4455; lentfer.fcdc@genevamail.com; www.fillmorecountydevelopment.org

Gothenburg · *Gothenburg Comm. Dev. Ofc.* · Anne Anderson; Exec. Dir.; 1021 Lake Ave.; P.O. Box 263; 69138; Dawson; P 3,619; (308) 537-3505; Fax (308) 537-2541; annea@gothenburgdelivers.com; www.gothenburgdelivers.com

Grand Island · *Grand Island Area Eco. Dev. Corp.* · Marlan Ferguson; Pres.; 308 N. Locust St., Ste. 400; P.O. Box 1151; 68802; Hall; P 53,000; M 270; (308) 381-7500; (800) 658-4283; Fax (308) 398-7205; giaedc@grandisland.org; www.grandisland.org

Hartington · *Hartington Comm. Dev. Corp.* · Carla Becker; Coord.; 107 W. State St.; P.O. Box 427; 68739; Cedar; P 1,640; (402) 254-6353; Fax (402) 254-6391; devcoor@hartel.net; www.ci.hartington.ne.us

Hastings · *Hastings Eco. Dev. Corp.* · Mr. Dee Haussler; Exec. Dir.; 301 S. Burlington; P.O. Box 1104; 68902; Adams; P 25,437; (402) 461-8406; Fax (402) 461-4400; dhaussler@hastingsedc.com; www.hastingsedc.com

Holdrege · *Phelps County Dev. Corp.* · Monica Boyken; Exec. Dir.; 502 E. Ave., Ste. 201; P.O. Box 522; 68949; Phelps; P 9,747; M 50; (308) 995-4148; Fax (308) 995-4158; pcdc@justtheplacenebraska.com; www.justtheplacenebraska.com

Kearney · *Buffalo County Eco. Dev. Cncl.* · Jonathan Krebs; Exec. Dir.; P.O. Box 607; 68848; Buffalo; P 42,000; (308) 237-9346; Fax (308) 234-2764; www.ci.kearney.ne.us

Kimball · *City of Kimball Eco. Dev. Assn.* · Kent Worker; Eco. Dev. Dir.; 223 S. Chestnut; 69145; Kimball; P 4,900; (308) 235-3639; (888) 274-6004; Fax (308) 235-2971; econdev@megavision.com; www.ci.kimball.ne.us

Lincoln · *USDA Rural Dev.* · Maxine Moul; State Dir.; Rm. 308, Fed. Bldg.; 100 Centennial Mall N.; 68508; Lancaster; (402) 437-5551; Fax (402) 437-5408; www.rurdev.usda.gov/ne

McCook · *McCook Eco. Dev.* · Rex Nelson; Exec. Dir.; 301 Norris Ave., Ste. 200; P.O. Box 626; 69001; Red Willow; P 8,000; (308) 345-1200; (800) 658-4213; Fax (308) 345-2152; medc@mccookne.org; www.mccookne.org

Nebraska City · *River Country Eco. Dev. Corp.* · Stephanie Shrader; Exec. Dir.; 1024 Central Ave.; 68410; Otoe; P 7,200; (402) 873-4293; Fax (402) 873-4578; rcedc@windstream.net; www.rivercountryedc.org

Norfolk · *Northeast Nebraska Eco. Dev. Dist.* · Tom Higginbotham; Exec. Dir.; 111 S. 1st; 68701; Madison; P 220,000; (402) 379-1150; Fax (402) 379-9207; thomash@nenedd.org; www.nenedd.org

North Platte · *North Platte Area Chamber & Dev. Corp.* · Dan Mauk IOM; Pres./CEO; 502 S. Dewey St.; 69101; Lincoln; P 30,000; (308) 532-4966; Fax (308) 532-4827; dan@nparea.com; www.nparea.com

Oakland · *Oakland Comm. Dev. Corp.* · Jeff Troupe; Pres.; 218 N. Oakland Ave.; 68045; Burt; P 1,400; (402) 685-5706; Fax (402) 685-5706; www.ci.oakland.ne.us

Ogallala · *Keith County Area Dev.* · Marion Kroeker; Dir.; P.O. Box 418; 69153; Keith; P 8,850; M 60; (308) 284-4066; Fax (308) 284-3126; marion@visitogallala.com; www.kcad.org

Ogallala · *West Central Neb. Dev. Dist.* · 201 E. 2nd St., Ste. C; P.O. Box 599; 69153; Keith; P 103,000; (308) 284-6077; Fax (308) 284-6070; www.west-central-nebraska.com

Omaha · *Greater Omaha Eco. Dev. Partnership* · Rod Moseman; V.P. of Eco. Dev.; 1301 Harney St.; 68102; Douglas; P 804,000; (402) 346-5905; Fax (402) 346-7050; rmoseman@selectgreateromaha.com; www.selectgreateromaha.com

Omaha · *Sarpy County Eco. Dev. Corp.* · Toby Churchill; Exec. Dir.; 1301 Harney St.; 68102; Douglas; P 125,000; M 60; (402) 346-5000; Fax (402) 346-7050; tchurchill@omahachamber.org; www.omahachamber.org

Ord · *Valley County Eco. Dev. Bd.* · Caleb Pollard; Dir.; 1514 K St.; 68862; Valley; P 4,600; (308) 728-7875; Fax (308) 728-7691; valleycountyed@frontiernet.net; www.ordnebraska.com

Plattsmouth · *Plattsmouth Ind. Dev. Corp.* · George Miller; Pres.; 136 N. 5th St.; 68048; Cass; P 6,996; (402) 296-2522; Fax (402) 296-3228; info@plattsmouth.org; www.plattsmouth.org

Randolph · *Randolph Comm. Club* · P.O. Box 624; 68771; Cedar; P 960; M 100; (402) 337-1234; www.ci.randolph.ne.us

Scottsbluff · *Twin Cities Dev. Assn. Inc.* · Rawnda Pierce; Exec. Dir.; 2620 College Park; 69361; Scotts Bluff; P 35,000; M 150; (308) 635-6710; (877) 635-6710; Fax (308) 635-6704; twincitiesdev@wncc.net; www.tcdne.org

Sidney · *Sidney/Cheyenne County Eco. Dev.* · Gary Person; City Mgr.; 1115 13th Ave.; P.O. Box 79; 69162; Cheyenne; P 15,960; (308) 254-4444; Fax (308) 254-3164; garyperson@cityofsidney.org; www.cityofsidney.org

Wahoo · *Wahoo Area Eco. Dev.* · Doug Watts; Exec. Dir.; 640 N. Broadway; 68066; Saunders; P 4,225; M 350; (402) 443-4001; Fax (402) 443-3077; watts@wahoo.ne.us; www.wahoo.ne.us

Wayne · *Wayne Area Chamber & Eco. Dev.* · David Simonsen; Exec. Dir.; 108 W. 3rd St.; 68787; Wayne; P 6,000; (402) 375-2240; (866) 929-6363; Fax (402) 375-2246; dsimonsen@waedi.org; www.wayneworks.org

West Point · *West Point Dev. Corp.* · Glen Prinz; Secy./Treas.; P.O. Box 265; 68788; Cuming; P 3,600; (402) 372-2495; www.ci.westpoint.ne.us

York · *York County Dev. Corp.* · 224 W. 6th; 68467; York; P 14,500; M 125; (402) 362-3333; (888) 733-9675; Fax (402) 362-3344; info@yorkdevco.com; www.comegrowwithyork.org

Nevada

Federal

U.S. SBA, Nevada Dist. Ofc. · Edward Cadena; Dist. Dir.; 400 S. 4th St., Ste. 250; Las Vegas; 89101; Clark; (702) 388-6611; Fax (702) 388-6469; christina.matamoros@sba.gov; www.sba.gov/nv

State

Comm. on Eco. Dev./State of Nevada · Michael E. Skaggs; Exec. Dir.; 808 W. Nye Ln.; Carson City; 89703; P 50,000; (775) 687-9900; Fax (775) 687-9924; mskaggs@diversifynevada.com; www.diversifynevada.com

Nevada Dev. Auth. · A. Somer Hollingsworth; Pres./CEO; 6700 Via Austi Pkwy., Ste. B; Las Vegas; 89119; Clark; (702) 791-0000; (888) 466-8293; Fax (702) 796-6483; info@nevadadevelopment.org; www.nevadadevelopment.org

Communities

Carson City · *Northern Nevada Dev. Auth.* · Robert C. Hooper; Exec. Dir.; 704 W. Nye Ln., Ste. 201; 89703; Carson City; P 150,000; M 400; (775) 883-4413; Fax (775) 883-0494; nnda@nnda.org; www.nnda.org

Elko · *Elko County Eco. Divers. Auth.* · Elaine Barkdull-Spencer; Exec. Dir.; 723 Railroad St.; 89801; Elko; P 46,000; (775) 738-2100; (866) 937-3356; Fax (775) 738-7978; elaine@eceda.com; www.eceda.com

Ely · *White Pine County Eco. Divers. Cncl.* · Karen Rajala; Coord.; 957 Campton; 89301; Clark; P 9,542; (775) 289-3065; Fax (775) 289-8860; wpcedc@mwpower.net; www.elynevada.net

Fallon · *Churchill Eco. Dev. Auth.* · Eric Grimes; Exec. Dir.; 90 N. Main St.; P.O. Box 1236; 89407; Churchill; P 30,000; (775) 423-8587; Fax (775) 423-1759; ceda@ceda-nv.org; www.ceda-nv.org

Henderson · *Henderson Dev. Assoc.* · Alice Martz; CEO; 590 S. Boulder Hwy.; 89015; Clark; P 262,000; (702) 565-8951; Fax (702) 565-3115; info@hendersonchamber.com; www.hendersonchamber.com

Las Vegas · *City of Las Vegas, Ofc. of Bus. Dev.* · Bill Arent; Dir.; 400 Stewart Ave., 2nd Flr.; 89101; Clark; P 2,000,000; (702) 229-6551; Fax (702) 385-3128; www.lasvegasnevada.gov

Las Vegas · *Southern Nevada Certified Dev. Co.* · Thomas Gutherie; Pres./CEO; 2770 S. Maryland Pkwy., Ste. 212; 89109; Clark; P 1,500,000; (702) 732-3998; Fax (702) 738-2705; sncdc@ad.com

North Las Vegas · *City of North Las Vegas Planning & Zoning* · Frank Fiori; Dir.; 2240 Civic Center Dr.; 89030; Clark; P 190,000; (702) 633-1537; Fax (702) 649-6091; www.cityof-northlasvegas.com

Reno · *Eco. Dev. Auth. of Western Nevada* · Chuck Alvey; CEO/Pres.; 201 W. Liberty St., Ste. 200; 89501; Washoe; P 330,000; (775) 829-3700; (800) 256-9761; Fax (775) 829-3710; info@edawn.org; www.edawn.org

New Hampshire

Federal

U.S. SBA, New Hampshire Dist. Ofc. · Witmer Jones; Dist. Dir.; 55 Pleasant St., Ste. 3101; Concord; 03301; Merrimack; (603) 225-1400; Fax (603) 225-1409; alice.zachos@sba.gov; www.sba.gov/nh

State

Bus. Resource Center · Chris Way; Bus. Svcs. Mgr.; 172 Pembroke Rd.; P.O. Box 1856; Concord; 03302; Merrimack; (603) 271-2591; Fax (603) 271-6784; cway@dred.state.nh.us; www.nheconomy.com

Communities

Berlin · *Bus. Enterprise Dev. Corp.* · William J. Andreas; Exec. Dir.; P.O. Box 628; 03570; Coos; P 110,000; (603) 752-3319; Fax (603) 752-4421; www.bedco.org

Concord · *Capital Reg. Dev. Cncl.* · Stephen Heavener; Exec. Dir.; 91 N. State St.; P.O. Box 664; 03302; Merrimack; P 200,000; (603) 228-1872; Fax (603) 226-3588; www.crdc-nh.com

Concord · *City of Concord Bus. Dev. Div.* · Carlos Baia; Deputy City Mgr.; City Hall; 41 Green St.; 03301; Merrimack; P 43,000; (603) 225-8595; Fax (603) 228-2701; cbaia@concordnh.gov; concordnh.gov

Dover · *City of Dover* · Daniel J. Barufaldi; Eco. Dev. Dir.; 288 Central Ave.; 03820; Strafford; P 29,000; (603) 516-6043; Fax (603) 516-6049; d.barufaldi@dover.nh.gov; www.dover.nh.gov

Exeter · *Exeter Dev. Comm.* · Sylvia von Aulock; Town Planner; 10 Front St.; 03833; Rockingham; P 14,500; (603) 778-0591; Fax (603) 772-4709; www.town.exeter.nh.us

Keene · *Monadnock Eco. Dev. Corp.* · John G. Dugan; Pres./CEO; 39 Central Sq., Ste. 201; 03431; Cheshire; P 70,000; (603) 352-4939; Fax (603) 357-4917; info@monadnock-development.org; www.monadnock-development.org

Manchester · *Manchester Eco. Dev. Ofc.* · Jay Minkarah; Dir.; 1 City Hall Plaza; 03101; Hillsborough; P 109,000; (603) 624-6505; Fax (603) 624-6308; econdev@manchesternh.gov; www.yourmanchesternh.com

Peterborough · *see Keene*

Portsmouth · *Granite State Dev. Corp.* · Alan Abraham; Pres.; One Cate St., 3rd Flr.; P.O. Box 1491; 03802; Rockingham; P 1,200,000; (603) 436-0009; Fax (603) 436-5547; www.granitestatedev.com

Rochester · *City of Rochester* · Kenneth Ortmann; Planning & Dev. Dir.; 31 Wakefield St.; 03867; Strafford; P 30,000; (603) 335-1338; Fax (603) 335-7585; kenn.ortmann@rochesternh.net; www.rochesternh.net

Wilton · *Wilton Main Street Assoc.* · Pat Condon; Program Mgr.; P.O. Box 310; 03086; Hillsborough; P 1,250; (603) 654-3020; wmsa@tds.net; www.mainstreet.wilton.nh.us

New Jersey

Federal

U.S. SBA, New Jersey Dist. Ofc. · James A. Kocsi; Dist. Dir.; Two Gateway Center, Ste. 1501; Newark; 07102; Essex; (973) 645-2434; Fax (973) 645-6265; james.kocsi@sba.gov; www.sba.gov/nj

State

New Jersey Eco. Dev. Auth. · Caren S. Franzini; CEO; 36 W. State St.; P.O. Box 990; Trenton; 08625; Mercer; (609) 292-1800; customercare@njeda.com; www.njeda.com

Communities

Absecon · *Eco. Dev. Comm. of City Cncl.* · Lynn Caterson; Council Pres.; 500 Mill Rd.; Absecon Municipal Complex; 08201; Atlantic; P 7,800; (609) 641-0663; Fax (609) 645-5098; www.absecon-newjersey.org

Asbury Park · *Asbury Park Ofc. of Eco. Dev.* · Tom Gilmore; Dir. of Commerce; 1 Municipal Plaza; 07712; Monmouth; P 18,000; (732) 502-5749; Fax (732) 775-1483; www.cityofasburypark.com

Atlantic City · *Atlantic City Div. of Planning* · William Crane; Dir.; City Hall, Rm. 506; 1301 Bacharach Blvd.; 08401; Atlantic; P 40,517; (609) 347-5404; (609) 347-5300; Fax (609) 347-5345; bcrane@cityofatlanticcity.org; www.cityofatlanticcity.org

Atlantic City · *Metropolitan Bus. & Citizens Assoc.* · Mr. Gary Hill; Pres.; 1616 Pacific Ave., 6th Flr.; 08401; Atlantic; P 253,000; (609) 348-1903; Fax (609) 344-5244; comments@acmetbiz.com; www.mbcanj.com

Bayonne · *Bayonne Eco. Dev. Corp.* · Michael O'Connor; Exec. Dir.; 630 Ave. C, Rm. 10; 07002; Hudson; P 65,000; (201) 339-0052; Fax (201) 339-0744; bayonne.edc@verizon.net; www.bayonnenj.org

Bayville · *Berkeley Twp. Ind. Comm.* · Berkeley Municipal Bldg.; P.O. Box B; 08721; Ocean; P 41,946; (732) 244-7400; Fax (732) 244-3428; www.twp.berkeley.nj.us

Bridgeport · *Pureland Ind. Complex* · Charles J. Walters; V.P.; P.O. Box 585; 08014; Gloucester; P 7,000; (856) 467-2333; Fax (856) 467-5552; www.purelandindustrialcomplex.com

Bridgeton Area

City of Bridgeton Dept. of Dev. & Planning · 50 E. Broad St.; 08302; Cumberland; P 19,000; (856) 451-3407; Fax (856) 455-7421; listona@cityofbridgeton.com; www.cityofbridgeton.com

Cumberland County Ofc. of Planning & Eco. Dev. · Robert Brewer; Exec. Dir.; 790 E. Commerce St.; 08302; Cumberland; P 147,000; (856) 453-2177; Fax (856) 453-9138; www.co.cumberland.nj.us

Cumberland Dev. Corp. · Anthony M. Stanzione; Exec. Dir.; P.O. Box 1021; 08302; Cumberland; P 147,000; (856) 451-4200; Fax (856) 453-9795; cdc@cdcnj.com; www.cdcnj.com

Bridgewater • *Somerset County Bus. Partnership* • Thomas Sharpe; Pres./CEO; 360 Grove St. at Rte. 22 E.; 08807; Somerset; P 315,000; M 610; (908) 218-4300; Fax (908) 722-7823; info@somersetbusinesspartnership.com; www.scbp.org

Buena Vista • *Buena Vista Eco. Dev. Advisory Bd.* • Chuck Chiarello; Mayor; 890 Harding Hwy.; 08310; Atlantic; P 7,600; (856) 697-2100; Fax (856) 697-8651; www.buenavistatownship.org

Camden • *Camden Redev. Agency* • Carrie Turner; Exec. Dir.; City Hall; 520 Market St., Ste. 1300; 08101; Camden; P 87,000; (856) 757-7600; Fax (856) 964-2262; CRAInfo@ci.camden.nj.us; www.camdenredevelopment.com

Camden • *South Jersey Port Corp.* • Joseph A. Balzano; Exec. Dir./CEO; 2nd & Beckett St.; 08103; Camden; (856) 757-4969; Fax (856) 757-4903; www.southjerseyport.com

Cape May Court House • *Ofc. of Eco. Resources & Capital Planning* • #4 Moore Rd.; 08210; Cape May; P 102,000; (609) 465-6875; Fax (609) 463-1269; www.capemaycountygov.net

Cherry Hill • *Cherry Hill Twp. Community Dev.* • 820 Mercer St.; 08002; Camden; P 70,000; (856) 665-6500; Fax (856) 488-7893; www.cherryhill-nj.com

Clifton • *Clifton Eco. Dev.* • Harry Swanson; Eco. Dev. Dir.; City Hall; 900 Clifton Ave.; 07013; Passaic; P 81,000; (973) 470-5200; Fax (973) 773-7470; www.cliftonnj.org

Columbia • *Knowlton Twp. Eco. Dev.* • Municipal Bldg.; 628 Rte. 94; 07832; Warren; P 3,000; M 45; (908) 496-4816; Fax (908) 496-8144; deputyclerk@knowlton-nj.com; www.knowlton-nj.com

Deptford • *Deptford Twp. Bus. Advisory Comm.* • Charles Kirschner; Chrmn.; 1011 Cooper St.; 08096; Gloucester; P 27,000; (856) 845-5300; Fax (856) 848-8227; www.deptford-nj.org

East Orange • *East Orange Dept. of Eco. Dev.* • Norma Mackey; Eco. Dev. Mgr.; 44 City Hall Plaza; Lower Level; 07019; Essex; P 78,000; (973) 266-5404; Fax (973) 674-2180; norma@ci.east-orange.nj.us; www.eastorange-nj.org

Edgewater Park • *Edgewater Park Eco. Dev. Comm.* • 400 Delanco Rd.; 08010; Burlington; P 7,800; (609) 877-2050; Fax (609) 877-2308; www.edgewaterpark-nj.com

Edison • *New Jersey Alliance for Action* • Philip K. Beachem; Pres.; P.O. Box 6438; 08818; Middlesex; M 600; (732) 225-1180; Fax (732) 225-4694; www.allianceforaction.com

Egg Harbor City • *Egg Harbor City Ind. Park* • Rick Dovey; Chrmn.; 500 London Ave.; 08215; Atlantic; P 4,500; (609) 965-5264; Fax (609) 965-0715; www.eggharborcity.org

Elizabeth • *Elizabeth Dev. Co.* • Daniel Devanney; Exec. Dir.; 288 N. Broad St.; P.O. Box 512; 07207; Union; P 120,000; (908) 289-0262; Fax (908) 558-1142; www.edcnj.org

Elizabeth • *Planning & Comm. Dev.* • Oscar Ocasio; Dir. of Planning; City Hall; 50 Winfield Scott Plaza; 07201; Union; P 120,000; (908) 820-4160; Fax (908) 820-3776; www.elizabethnj.org

Florence • *Florence Twp. Eco. Dev. Cncl.* • Municipal Complex; 711 Broad St.; 08518; Burlington; P 10,746; (609) 499-2525; Fax (609) 499-1186; www.florence-nj.com

Forked River • *Lacey Twp. Dept. of Comm. Dev.* • John Curtin; Dir.; 818 W. Lacey Rd.; Municipal Bldg.; 08731; Ocean; P 25,346; (609) 693-1100; Fax (609) 693-8466; www.laceytownship.org

Freehold • *Monmouth County Dept. of Eco. Dev. & Tourism* • 31 E. Main St.; 07728; Monmouth; P 645,000; (732) 431-7470; Fax (732) 294-5930; www.visitmonmouth.com

Galloway • *Galloway Twp. Eco. Dev. Advisory Comm.* • 300 E. Jimmy Leeds Rd.; 08205; Atlantic; P 38,207; (609) 652-3700; Fax (609) 652-1967; www.aclink.org/galloway

Hamilton • *Twp. of Hamilton Dept. of Tech. & Eco. Dev.* • Michael Angarone; Dir. of Tech.; 2090 Greenwood Ave.; P.O. Box 00150; 08650; Mercer; P 90,000; (609) 890-3519; Fax (609) 890-3876; mangarone@hamiltonnj.com; www.hamiltonnj.com

Hillsborough • *Hillsborough Twp. Eco. & Bus. Dev. Comm.* • Gene Strupinsky; Bus. Advocate; 379 S. Branch Rd.; 08844; Somerset; P 36,600; (908) 369-4313; Fax (908) 369-6034; ebdc@hillsborough-nj.org; www.hillsborough-nj.org

Jersey City • *Jersey City Eco. Dev. Corp.* • Eugene Nelson; CEO; 30 Montgomery St., Rm. 820; 07302; Hudson; P 240,000; (201) 333-7797; Fax (201) 333-9323; www.jcedc.org

Kearny • *Kearny Enterprise Zone/Dev. Corp.* • Town Hall Annex; 402 Kearny Ave.; 07032; Hudson; P 40,513; (201) 955-7400; Fax (201) 998-5171; www.kearnynjuez.org

Lakewood • *Lakewood Dev. Corp.* • Russell K. Corby; Exec. Dir.; 231 3rd St.; 08701; Ocean; P 60,000; (732) 364-2500; Fax (732) 901-3647; www.twp.lakewood.nj.us

Long Branch • *Long Branch Dept. of Eco. Dev.* • Jacob Jones; Dir.; 344 Broadway; 07740; Monmouth; P 32,350; (732) 923-2043; Fax (732) 263-0218; www.longbranch.org

Manalapan • *Manalapan Twp. Eco. Dev. Comm.* • Tara Lovrich; Admin.; 120 Rte. 522; Municipal Complex; 07726; Monmouth; P 33,000; (732) 446-3200; Fax (732) 446-9615; www.twp.manalapan.nj.us

Mays Landing • *Hamilton Twp. Ind. Comm.* • Robert Ravell; Chrmn.; 6101 13th St.; 08330; Atlantic; P 23,000; (609) 625-0368; Fax (609) 909-1348; www.hamiltonbusinesspark.com

Mickleton • *East Greenwich Twp. Enterprise Comm.* • James Watson; Dir.; 159 Democrat Rd.; 08056; Gloucester; P 5,430; (856) 423-0654; Fax (856) 224-0296; www.eastgreenwichnj.com

Millville • *Millville Eco. Dev.* • Donald Ayres; Dir.; City Hall, 12 S. High St.; P.O. Box 609; 08332; Cumberland; P 26,000; (856) 825-7000; Fax (856) 825-3236; www.millville.nj.gov

Monmouth Junction • *South Brunswick Twp. Ind. & Commerce Comm.* • Dan Frankel; Chrmn.; Planning Dept.; P.O. Box 190; 08852; Middlesex; P 41,000; (732) 329-4000; Fax (732) 274-2084; www.sbtnj.net

Monroe Twp. • *Monroe Twp. Eco. Dev. Comm.* • Michael C. Konowicz; Chrmn.; 1 Municipal Complex; 08831; Middlesex; P 35,000; (732) 521-4400; Fax (732) 521-5659; www.monroetwp.com

Moorestown • *Moorestown Dept. of Comm. Dev.* • Thomas Ford; Dir.; 2 Executive Dr., Ste. 10B; 08057; Burlington; P 19,000; (856) 235-0912; Fax (856) 914-3081; www.moorestown.nj.us

Morristown • *Morris County Eco. Dev. Corp.* • Maggie Peters; Exec. Dir.; 30 Schuyler Pl.; P.O. Box 900; 07963; Morris; P 490,593; (973) 539-8270; Fax (973) 326-9025; mpeters@co.morris.nj.us; www.morriscountyedc.org

Mount Holly • *Burlington County Eco. Dev. & Reg. Planning* • Mark Remsa; Dir.; 50 Rancocas Rd.; P.O. Box 6000; 08060; Burlington; P 423,394; (609) 265-5055; Fax (609) 265-5006; www.co.burlington.nj.us

New Brunswick • *Middlesex County Ofc. of Eco. Dev.* • Carl Spataro; Dir.; JFK Square; P.O. Box 871; 08901; Middlesex; P 786,971; (732) 745-3433; Fax (732) 745-5911; carl.spataro@co.middlesex.nj.us; www.co.middlesex.nj.us

New Brunswick • *New Brunswick Dev. Corp.* • Christopher Paladino; Pres.; 120 Albany St., 7th Flr.; 08901; Middlesex; P 49,000; (732) 249-2220; Fax (732) 249-4671; www.devco.org

Newark · *Eco. Dev. Corp. Essex County* · Deborah Collins; Exec. Dir.; 465 Martin Luther King Blvd., Rm. 49; 07102; Essex; P 798,000; (973) 621-4457; (973) 621-5420; Fax (973) 621-2545

Northfield · *Atlantic County Ofc. of Policy, Planning & Eco. Dev.* · Joseph Maher; Dept. Head; Dolphin Ave. & New Rd.; P.O. Box 719; 08225; Atlantic; P 271,015; (609) 645-5898; Fax (609) 645-5836; www.aclink.org

Old Bridge · *Old Bridge Eco. Dev. Corp.* · 1 Old Bridge Plaza; 08857; Middlesex; P 64,000; (732) 721-5600; Fax (732) 607-7957; www.oldbridge.com

Paramus · *Commerce & Ind. Assn. of N. J.* · John Galandak; Pres.; S. 61 Paramus Rd.; 07652; Bergen; P 1,000,000; M 1,500; (201) 368-2100; Fax (201) 368-3438; info@cianj.org; www.cianj.org

Paterson · *City of Paterson Dept. of Comm. Dev.* · Gary Melchiano; Dir. of Eco. Dev.; 125 Ellison St., 2nd Flr.; 07505; Passaic; P 139,000; (973) 321-1212; Fax (973) 321-1202; www.cityofpaterson.com

Perth Amboy · *Ofc. of Eco. & Comm. Dev.* · 1 Olive St., 2nd Flr.; 08861; Middlesex; P 47,303; (732) 826-1690; Fax (732) 442-9274; www.ci.perthamboy.nj.us

Piscataway · *Piscataway Ind. Adv. Comm.* · Jim Perry; Chrmn.; 455 Hoes Ln.; 08854; Middlesex; P 59,000; (732) 562-2300; Fax (732) 743-2500; www.piscatawaynj.org

Plainfield · *Plainfield Ofc. of Eco. Dev.* · 515 Watchung Ave.; City Hall, 2nd Flr.; 07060; Union; P 48,000; (908) 753-3699; Fax (908) 753-3070; www.plainfield.com

Rahway · *Rahway Center Partnership* · Ray Mikell; Exec. Dir.; 67 Lewis St., 2nd Flr.; P.O. Box 1711; 07065; Union; P 25,000; (732) 396-3545; Fax (732) 396-3693; rmikell9@aol.com

Rutherford · *Rutherford Eco. Dev. Comm.* · 176 Park Ave.; 07070; Bergen; P 18,000; (201) 460-3001; Fax (201) 460-3003; www.rutherford-nj.com

South Orange · *Organization Dev. Network* · Dr. Peter F. Norlin; 71 Valley St., Ste. 301; 07079; Essex; M 4,200; (973) 763-7337; Fax (973) 763-7488; www.odnetworking.org

Totowa · *Passaic County Dept. of Eco. Dev.* · Deborah Hoffman; Dir.; 930 Riverview Dr., Ste. 250; 07512; Passaic; P 499,060; (973) 569-4720; Fax (973) 569-4725; ecodev@passaiccountynj.org; www.passaiccountynj.org

Trenton · *Div. of Eco. Dev.* · City of Trenton; 319 E. State St.; 08608; Mercer; P 85,403; (609) 989-3509; Fax (609) 989-4243; www.trentonnj.org

Trenton · *Mercer County Ofc. of Eco. Opportunity* · Mercer County Admin. Bldg.; 640 S. Broad St.; 08650; Mercer; P 350,000; (609) 989-6555; Fax (609) 695-4943; charlesh@mercercounty.org; www.mercercounty.org

Union · *Union County Eco. Dev. Corp. (UCEDC)* · Thomas Brown; Pres.; Liberty Hall Center; 1085 Morris Ave.; 07083; Union; P 540,000; (908) 527-1166; Fax (908) 527-1207; www.ucedc.com

Union City · *Union City Comm. Dev.* · Kennedy Ng; Dir.; 3715 Palisade Ave.; 07087; Hudson; P 65,000; (201) 348-2764; Fax (201) 348-9069

Vineland · *Vineland Eco. Dev.* · City Hall; 640 E. Wood St., 4th Flr.; 08360; Cumberland; P 59,248; (856) 794-4000; Fax (856) 794-6199; economicdevelopment@vinelandcity.org; www.vinelandbusiness.com

Voorhees · *Voorhees Twp. Eco. Dev.* · Michael Marchitto Jr.; Dir.; 620 Berlin Rd.; 08043; Camden; P 30,000; (856) 216-0473; Fax (856) 428-2514; edc@voorheesnj.com; www.voorheesnj.com

Washington · *Warren County Eco. Dev. Corp.* · Robert Goltz; Pres./CEO; 10 Brass Castle Rd.; 07882; Warren; P 105,765; (908) 835-9200; Fax (908) 835-9296; info@warrencountychamber.org; www.warrencountychamber.org

Wayne · *Wayne Twp. Ind. & Eco. Dev. Comm.* · John Szabo; Exec. Dir.; 475 Valley Rd.; 07470; Passaic; P 54,069; (973) 694-1800; Fax (973) 694-8136; www.waynetownship.com

West Milford · *West Milford Planning Dept.* · 1480 Union Valley Rd.; 07480; Passaic; P 27,000; (973) 728-2796; Fax (973) 728-2843; planning@westmilford.org; www.westmilford.org

West Orange · *Downtown West Orange Alliance* · Denise Esposito; Exec. Dir.; 66 Main St.; 07052; Essex; P 46,000; (973) 325-4109; Fax (973) 325-6359; downtown@westorange.org; www.downtownwestorange.org

Westfield · *Downtown Westfield Corp.* · Shery Cronin; Exec. Dir.; 105 Elm St.; 07090; Union; P 30,000; (908) 789-9444; Fax (908) 789-7550; s.cronin@westfieldtoday.com; www.westfieldtoday.com

Woodbridge · *Woodbridge Eco. Dev. Corp.* · 90 Woodbridge Center Dr., 2nd Flr.; 07095; Middlesex; P 100,000; (732) 602-6029

Woodbury · *Gloucester County Bus. & Eco. Dev.* · Lisa Morina; Dir.; CC Budd Blvd., Rte. 45; 08096; Gloucester; P 260,000; (856) 384-6930; Fax (856) 384-6938; www.co.gloucester.nj.us

New Mexico

State

State of New Mexico Eco. Dev. Dept. · Cabinet Secy.; 1100 St. Francis Dr., Ste. 1060; Santa Fe; 87505; Santa Fe; (505) 827-0300; Fax (505) 827-0328; edd.info@state.nm.us; www.gonm.biz

Communities

Albuquerque · *Albuquerque Eco. Dev. Inc.* · Gary Tonjes; Pres.; 851 University Blvd. S.E., Ste. 203; 87106; Bernalillo; P 801,000; M 411; (505) 246-6200; (800) 451-2933; Fax (505) 246-6219; info@abq.org; www.abq.org

Belen · *Belen Eco. Dev. Corp.* · Claudette Riley; Exec. Dir.; 100 S. Main St.; 87002; Valencia; P 7,100; (505) 459-6159; Fax (505) 864-8408; belenedc@belenedc.org; www.belenedc.org

Carlsbad · *Carlsbad Dept. of Dev.* · 107 W. Mermod; P.O. Box 1090; 88221; Eddy; P 25,600; (575) 887-6562; (800) 658-2709; Fax (575) 885-0818; cdod@developcarlsbad.org; www.developcarlsbad.org

Farmington · *San Juan Eco. Dev. Svc.* · Margaret McDaniel; Dir.; 5101 College Blvd.; 87402; San Juan; P 126,208; (505) 566-3720; (800) 854-5053; Fax (505) 566-3698; sjeds@sanjuaneds.com; www.sanjuaneds.com

Gallup · *NW New Mexico Cncl. of Governments* · Patty Lundstrom; Exec. Dir.; 409 S. 2nd; 87301; McKinley; P 176,000; (505) 722-4327; Fax (505) 722-9211

Grants · *Cibola Communities Eco. Dev. Found.* · Star Gonzales; Exec. Dir.; P.O. Box 277; 87020; Cibola; P 10,000; (505) 287-4802; (800) 748-2142; Fax (505) 287-8224; www.discovergrants.org

Hobbs · *Eco. Dev. Corp. of Lea County* · Bethe Cunningham; Pres./CEO; 200 E. Broadway, Ste. A201; P.O. Box 1376; 88241; Lea; P 55,000; (575) 397-2039; Fax (575) 392-2300; www.edclc.org

Las Cruces · *MVEDA* · Steve Vierck; Pres.; 505 S. Main, Ste. 134; P.O. Box 1299; 88004; P 189,000; (505) 525-2852; (800) 523-6833; Fax (505) 523-5707; info@mveda.com; www.mveda.com

Los Alamos • *Los Alamos Commerce Dev. Corp.* • Kevin Holsapple; Exec. Dir.; 190 Central Park Sq.; P.O. Box 1206; 87544; Los Alamos; P 18,000; (505) 662-0001; Fax (505) 662-0099; lacdc@losalamos.org; www.losalamos.org/lacdc

Portales • *Roosevelt County Comm. Dev.* • Don Thomas; V.P. of Comm. Dev.; 100 S. Ave. A; 88130; Roosevelt; P 18,500; (505) 356-8541; (800) 635-8036; Fax (505) 356-8542; chamber@portales.com; www.portales.com

Raton • *Raton Eco. Dev. Cncl.* • 100 Clayton Rd.; P.O. Box 1211; 87740; Colfax; P 7,282; (505) 445-3689; (800) 638-6161; Fax (505) 445-3680; ratonchamber@bacavalley.com; www.raton.info

Rio Rancho • *AMREP Southwest* • Jimmy Wall Jr.; V.P.; 333 Rio Rancho Blvd. N.E.; 87124; Sandoval; P 62,000; (505) 892-9200; Fax (505) 896-9180; www.amrepsw.com

Rio Rancho • *Rio Rancho Eco. Dev. Corp.* • Noreen Scott; Pres./Exec. Dir.; 1201 Rio Rancho Blvd., Ste. C; 87124; Sandoval; P 70,000; (505) 891-4305; (800) 544-8373; Fax (505) 891-4297; info@rredc.org; www.rredc.org

Roswell • *Chaves County Dev. Found.* • Bob Donnell; Exec. Dir.; 131 W. Second St.; P.O. Box 849; 88202; Chaves; P 61,382; (505) 622-1975; Fax (505) 624-6870; rdonnell@chavescounty.net; www.chavescounty.net

Santa Fe • *Santa Fe Eco. Dev. Inc.* • Catherine Zacher; Pres.; 624 Agua Fria St.; P.O. Box 8184; 87504; Santa Fe; P 130,000; (505) 984-2842; Fax (505) 989-8614; sfedi@sfedi.org; www.sfedi.org

Silver City • *Silver City-Grant County Eco. Dev. Corp.* • John Rossfeld; Pres.; 1203 N. Hudson St.; P.O. Box 2672; 88061; Grant; P 32,000; (505) 534-1045; Fax (505) 538-6391; ralph@silvercitybusiness.com; www.silvercity-business.com

Tucumcari • *Greater Tucumcari Eco. Dev. Corp.* • Patrick Vanderpool; Exec. Dir.; 1500 W. Tucumcari Blvd.; P.O. Box 1392; 88401; Quay; P 6,000; M 48; (575) 461-4079; Fax (575) 461-1838; www.tucumcari.biz

New York

Federal

U.S. SBA, Syracuse Dist. Ofc. • Bernard Paprocki; Dist. Dir.; 224 Harrison St., 5th Flr.; Syracuse; 13202; Onondaga; (315) 471-9393; Fax (315) 471-9288; deborah.miller@sba.gov; www.sba.gov/ny/syracuse

State

Empire State Dev. • Dennis Mullen; Chrmn.; 30 S. Pearl St.; Albany; 12245; Albany; (518) 292-5100; nfisher@empire.state.ny.us; www.empire.state.ny.us

Communities

Albany • *Center for Eco. Growth Inc.* • 63 State St.; 12207; Albany; P 1,157,000; (518) 465-8975; Fax (518) 465-6681; www.ceg.org

Albany • *NYS Eco. Dev. Cncl.* • Brian McMahon; Exec. Dir.; 111 Washington Ave., 6th Flr.; 12210; Albany; P 18,000,000; (518) 426-4058; Fax (518) 426-4059; www.nysedc.org

Amsterdam • *City of Amsterdam IDA* • Frank Valiante; Exec. Dir.; 61 Church St.; 12010; Montgomery; P 19,800; (518) 842-5011; Fax (518) 843-2862; www.amsterdamida.com

Auburn • *City of Auburn Ofc. of Plan. & Eco. Dev.* • Jennifer Haines; Memorial City Hall; 24 South St.; 13021; Cayuga; P 28,574; (315) 255-4115; Fax (315) 253-0282; www.ci.auburn.ny.us

Babylon • *Babylon Ind. Dev. Agency* • Robert Stricoff; CEO; 47 W. Main, Ste. 3; 11702; Suffolk; P 227,000; (631) 587-3679; Fax (631) 587-3675; www.babylonida.org

Batavia • *Genessee County Eco. Dev. Center* • Steven G. Hyde; Pres./CEO; 1 Mill St.; 14020; Genesee; P 59,000; (585) 343-4866; Fax (585) 343-0848; gcedc@gcedc.com; www.gcedc.com

Bath • *Steuben County Ind. Dev. Agency* • James P. Sherron; Exec. Dir.; 7234 Rte. 54; P.O. Box 393; 14810; Steuben; P 100,000; (607) 776-3316; Fax (607) 776-5039; www.steubencountyida.com

Belmont • *Allegany County Ofc. of Dev.* • Crossroad Commerce Conf. Center; 6087 State Rte. 19 N.; 14813; Allegany; P 49,000; (585) 268-7472; Fax (585) 268-7473; development@alleganyco.com; www.alleganyco.com

Belmont • *Friendship Empire Zone* • Wendall E. Brown; Dir.; Crossroads Commerce Center; 6087 State Rte. 19 N., Ste. 170; 14813; Allegany; P 2,500; (585) 268-9095; Fax (585) 268-5085; wbrown@accordcorp.org; www.friendshipempirezone.com

Bethpage • *Greater NY Dev. Co./Long Island Dev. Corp.* • Roslyn D. Goldmacher; Pres./CEO; 45 Seaman Ave.; 11714; Nassau; P 2,700,000; (516) 433-5000; (866) 433-5432; Fax (516) 433-5046; biz-loans@gnydc.org; www.lidc.org

Binghamton Area

Broome County Ind. Dev. Agency • Richard D'Attilio; Exec. Dir.; 44 Hawley St., 5th Flr.; P.O. Box 1510; 13902; Broome; P 201,533; (607) 584-9000; Fax (607) 584-9009; info@bcida.com; www.bcida.com

Empire State Dev.-Southern Tier • Kevin McLaughlin; Reg. Dir.; 44 Hawley St., Ste. 1508; State Office Bldg.; 13901; Broome; (607) 721-8605; Fax (607) 721-8613; www.empire.state.ny.us

NYS Trade Adjust. Asst. Ctr. • Louis G. McKeage; Dir.; 81 State St., Ste. 4; 13901; Broome; (607) 771-0875; Fax (607) 724-2404; www.nystaac.org

Buffalo Area

Buffalo Niagara Enterprise • 665 Main St., Ste. 200; 14203; Erie; P 1,292,000; (716) 842-1330; (800) 916-9073; Fax (716) 842-1724; info@buffaloniagara.org; www.buffaloniagara.org

Empire State Dev.-Western NY Region • Christina Orsi; Reg. Dir.; 95 Perry St., Ste. 500; 14203; Erie; (716) 846-8260; Fax (716) 856-1744; www.empire.state.ny.us

Erie County Ofc. of Eco. Dev. • Edward A. Rath County Ofc. Bldg.; 95 Franklin St., 10th Flr.; 14202; Erie; P 952,000; (716) 858-8390; Fax (716) 858-7248; www.erie.gov

Canandaigua • *Ontario County Eco. Dev.* • Michael J. Manikowski; Exec. Dir.; 20 Ontario St., Ste. 106-B; 14424; Ontario; P 100,000; (585) 396-4460; Fax (585) 396-4594; golfbag@co.ontario.ny.us; www.ontariocountydev.org

Canastota • *Madison County Ind. Dev. Agency* • Kipp Hicks; Exec. Dir.; 3215 Seneca Tpk.; 13032; Madison; P 70,000; (315) 697-9817; Fax (315) 697-8169; director@madisoncountyida.com; www.madisoncountyida.com

Canton • *St. Lawrence County Ofc. of Eco. Dev.* • Raymond H. Fountain; Dir.; 80 State Hwy. 310, Ste. 8; 13617; St. Lawrence; P 111,973; (315) 379-9806; Fax (315) 386-2573; rfountain@co.st-lawrence.ny.us; www.slcida.com

Carmel • *Putnam County Eco. Dev. Corp.* • Kevin Bailey; Pres.; 34 Gleneida Ave.; 10512; Putnam; (845) 228-8066; Fax (845) 225-0311; www.putnamedc.org

Champlain • *Town of Champlain IDA* • Robert Casey; Chrmn.; P.O. Box 3144; 12919; Clinton; P 6,700; (518) 298-8160; Fax (518) 298-8896

Corning • *Three Rivers Dev. Inc.* • John E. Benjamin; Pres.; 114 Pine St., Ste. 201; 14830; Steuben; P 30,000; (607) 962-4693; Fax (607) 936-9132; www.threeriversdevelopment.com

Coxsackie • *Greene County Ind. Dev. Agency* • Alexander Mathes; Exec. Dir.; 270 Mansion St.; 12051; Greene; (518) 731-5500; Fax (518) 731-5520; www.greeneida.com

Dutchess • *see New Windsor*

Elmira • *Chemung County Ind. Dev. Agency* • George Miner; Dir.; 400 E. Church St.; 14901; Chemung; P 90,000; (607) 733-6513; Fax (607) 734-2698; gminer@steg.com; www.steg.com

Endwell • *Local Dev. Corp. for Town of Union* • Joseph Moody; Eco. Dev. Dir.; 3111 E. Main St.; 13760; Broome; P 60,000; (607) 786-2945; Fax (607) 786-2321; jmoody@townofunion.com; www.townofunion.com

Farmingville • *Town of Brookhaven Supv. Ofc./Eco. Dev.* • Rick Kruse; Dir.; 1 Independence Hill; 11738; Suffolk; P 470,000; (631) 451-6563; Fax (631) 451-6925; www.brookhaven.org

Fonda • *Montgomery County Eco. Dev. & Planning* • Kenneth Rose; Dir.; Bus. Dev. Center, 9 Park St.; P.O. Box 1500; 12068; Montgomery; P 51,000; (518) 853-8334; Fax (518) 853-8336; krose@co.montgomery.ny.us; www.co.montgomery.ny.us

Fort Edward • *Washington County Local Dev. Corp.* • County Municipal Center; 383 Broadway; 12828; Washington; P 61,042; (518) 746-2292; Fax (518) 746-2293; info@wcldc.org; www.wcldc.org

Garden City • *Nassau County Ind. Dev. Agency* • Joseph Gioino; Exec. Dir.; 1100 Franklin Ave., Ste. 300; 11530; Nassau; P 1,338,000; (516) 571-4160; Fax (516) 571-4161; www.nassauida.org

Geneseo • *Livingston County Eco. Dev. Dept.* • Patrick J. Rountree; Dir.; 6 Court St., Rm. 306; 14454; Livingston; P 65,000; (585) 243-7124; Fax (585) 243-7126; build-here@co.livingston.ny.us; www.build-here.com

Goshen • *Orange County Partnership* • Maureen Halahan; Pres./CEO; 40 Matthews St., Ste. 108; 10924; Orange; (845) 294-2323; Fax (845) 294-8023; info@ocpartnership.org; www.ocpartnership.org

Hauppauge • *Empire State Dev.-Long Island Reg.* • Andrea Lohneiss; Reg. Dir.; 150 Motor Pkwy., Ste. 311; 11788; Suffolk; (631) 435-0717; Fax (631) 435-3399; alohneiss@empire.state.ny.us; www.nylovesbiz.com

Hauppauge • *Suffolk County Dept. of Eco. Dev.* • 100 Veterans Memorial Hwy.; P.O. Box 6100; 11788; Suffolk; P 1,419,369; (631) 853-4800; Fax (631) 853-4888; www.suffolkcountyny.gov

Hempstead • *Incorporated Village of Hempstead Comm. Dev Agency* • Claude Gooding; Commissioner; 50 Clinton St., Ste. 504; 11550; Nassau; P 50,000; (516) 485-5737; Fax (516) 485-1667; www.hempsteadeda.org

Hempstead • *Planning & Eco. Dev. Agency of Hempstead* • 200 N. Franklin Ave.; 11550; Nassau; P 780,000; (516) 538-7100; Fax (516) 538-4264; www.townofhempstead.org

Herkimer • *Herkimer County Ind. Dev. Agency* • Mark D. Feane; Exec. Dir.; 320 N. Prospect St.; P.O. Box 390; 13350; Herkimer; P 64,000; (315) 867-1373; Fax (315) 867-1515; ida@herkimercounty.org; www.herkimercountyida.com

Hornell • *Hornell Ind. Dev. Agency* • James W. Griffin; Exec. Dir.; 40 Main St.; 14843; Steuben; P 11,000; (607) 324-0310; Fax (607) 324-3776; griff@hornellny.com; www.hornellny.com

Hudson • *Columbia County Planning Dept.* • Timothy Stalker; Chrmn.; 401 State St.; 12534; Columbia; P 63,094; (518) 828-3375; Fax (518) 828-2825; www.columbiacountyny.com

Islip • *Town of Islip Eco. Dev. Div.* • William Mannix; Dir.; 40 Nassau Ave.; 11751; Suffolk; P 300,000; (631) 224-5512; Fax (631) 224-5532; www.isliptown.org

Ithaca • *Tompkins County Area Dev., Inc.* • 200 E. Buffalo St., Ste. 102A; 14850; Tompkins; P 100,000; (607) 273-0005; Fax (607) 273-8964; info@tcad.org; www.tcad.org

Jamestown • *County of Chautauqua Ind. Dev. Agency* • William Daly; Admin. Dir.; 200 Harrison St.; 14701; Chautauqua; P 141,000; (716) 661-8900; Fax (716) 664-4515; ccida@ccida.com; www.chautauquacounty.biz

Johnstown • *Fulton County Eco. Dev. Corp.* • Jeff Bray; Exec. V.P.; 110 Decker Dr., Ste. 110; 12095; Fulton; P 55,073; (518) 773-8700; Fax (518) 773-8701; www.sites4u.org

Johnstown • *Fulton County Ind. Dev. Agency* • James Mraz; Exec. Dir.; Fulton County Planning Dept.; 1 E. Montgomery St.; 12095; Fulton; P 55,073; (518) 736-5660; Fax (518) 762-4597; www.fultoncountyny.gov

Kingston • *Ulster County Dev. Corp.* • 5 Development Ct.; 12401; Ulster; P 178,000; (845) 338-8840; Fax (845) 338-0409; www.ulserny.com

Little Valley • *Cattaraugus County Dept. of Eco. Dev. & Tourism* • Thomas Livak; Dir.; 303 Court St.; 14755; Cattaraugus; P 83,955; (716) 938-2313; (800) 331-0543; Fax (716) 938-2779; jhisaacson@cattco.org; www.cattco.org

Lockport • *Lockport IDA* • Alan Hamilton; Chrmn.; Town Hall; 6560 Dysinger Rd.; 14094; Niagara; P 21,000; (716) 439-9535; Fax (716) 439-9715; town-lkptida@elockport.com; www.lockportida.com

Lyons • *Wayne County Ind. Dev. Agency* • Peg Churchill; Exec. Dir.; 16 William St.; 14489; Wayne; P 95,000; (315) 946-5917; Fax (315) 946-5918; wedcny@co.wayne.ny.us; www.wedcny.org

Malone • *County of Franklin Ind. Dev. Agency* • Brad Jackson; Exec. Dir.; 10 Elm St., Ste. 2; 12953; Franklin; P 51,134; (518) 483-9472; Fax (518) 483-2900; www.franklinida.org

Mohawk • *Mohawk Valley Eco. Dev. Dist.* • Gregory A Eisenhut; Exec. Dir.; 26 W. Main St.; P.O. Box 69; 13407; Herkimer; P 450,000; (315) 866-4671; Fax (315) 866-9862; mvedd@twcny.rr.com

Monticello • *Partnership for Eco. Dev. for Sullivan County* • 198 Bridgeville Rd.; 12701; Sullivan; (845) 794-1110; Fax (845) 794-2324; www.scpartnership.com

New Windsor • *Empire State Dev.-Mid-Hudson Reg. Ofc.* • Susan Jaffe; Dir.; 33 Airport Center Dr., Ste. 201; 12553; Orange; (845) 567-4882; Fax (845) 567-6085; www.empire.state.ny.us

New Windsor • *Hudson Valley Eco. Dev. Corp.* • Anthony Campagiorni; Pres./CEO; 555 Hudson Valley Ave., Ste. 106; 12553; Orange; (845) 220-2244; Fax (845) 220-2247; www.hvedc.com

New York • *Empire State Dev.-NYC* • Marisa Lago; 633 3rd Ave., 37th Flr.; 10017; New York; (212) 803-2200; Fax (212) 803-3715; www.empire.state.ny.us

New York • *New York City Eco. Dev. Corp.* • 110 Williams St., 4th Flr.; 10038; New York; (212) 619-5000; Fax (212) 312-3913; www.nycedc.com

Newburgh • *Hudson Valley Reg. Cncl.* • 1662 Rte. 300; 12550; Orange; P 1,000,000; (845) 564-4075; hvrc@hvi.net; www.hvregionalcouncil.org

Oneonta • *Otsego County Eco. Dev. Dept.* • Carolyn Lewis; Eco. Dev. Dir.; 242 Main St.; 13820; Otsego; P 61,000; (607) 432-8871; Fax (607) 432-5117; lewisc@otsegocounty.com; www.otsegoeconomicdevelopment.com

Ontario • *Town of Onatario Ofc. of Eco. Dev.* • William Riddell; Dir.; 6551 Knickerbocker Rd.; 14519; Wayne; P 10,000; (315) 524-5908; Fax (315) 524-7465; riddell@ontariotown.org; www.ontariotown.org

Orange • *see New Windsor*

Oswego • *Operation Oswego County* • L. Michael Treadwell; Exec. Dir.; 44 W. Bridge St.; 13126; Oswego; P 121,785; (315) 343-1545; Fax (315) 343-1546; ooc@oswegocounty.org; www.oswegocounty.org

Owego • *Tioga County Ind. Dev. Agency* • Aaron Gowan; Chrmn.; 56 Main St.; 13827; Tioga; P 50,000; (607) 687-8255; Fax (607) 687-1435; www.developtioga.com

Pearl River • *Rockland Eco. Dev. Corp.* • Eric Dranoff; Chair; Two Blue Hill Plaza; P.O. Box 1575; 10965; Rockland; P 293,626; (845) 735-0205; Fax (845) 735-5736; www.redc.org

Penn Yan • *Yates County IDA* • Steve Griffin; CEO; One Keuka Business Park; 14527; Yates; P 24,600; (315) 536-7328; Fax (315) 536-2389; info@yatesida.com; www.yatesida.com

Plattsburgh • *The Development Corp.* • Mrs. A. Kurtz; Pres.; 61 Area Development Dr.; 12901; Clinton; P 80,000; (518) 563-3100; (888) 699-6757; Fax (518) 562-2232; www.thedevelopcorp.com

Poughkeepsie • *Dutchess County Eco. Dev. Corp.* • John MacEnroe; Pres./CEO; 3 Neptune Rd.; 12601; Dutchess; P 280,000; (845) 463-5410; Fax (845) 463-5401; dcedc@dcedc.com; www.thinkdutchess.com

Putnam • *see New Windsor*

Rochester • *County of Monroe Ind. Dev. Agency* • Judy Seil; Exec. Dir.; City Place, Ste. 8100; 50 W. Main St.; 14614; Monroe; P 720,000; (585) 753-2000; Fax (585) 753-2028; www.monroecounty.gov

Rochester • *Empire State Dev.-Finger Lakes* • Robert McNary; Reg. Dir.; 400 Andrews St., Ste. 100; 14604; Monroe; (585) 325-1944; Fax (585) 325-6505; www.empire.state.ny.us

Rockland • *see New Windsor*

Rome • *Mohawk Valley Edge* • Steven DiMeo; Pres.; 153 Brooks Rd.; 13441; Oneida; P 300,000; (315) 338-0393; Fax (315) 338-5694; sjdimeo@mvedge.org; www.mvedge.org

Salamanca • *Salamanca Ind. Dev. Agency* • Matt Bull; Proj. Mgr,; 225 Wildwood Ave., Ste. 9; 14779; Cattaraugus; P 6,800; (716) 945-3230; Fax (716) 945-8289; www.salmun.com

Saranac Lake • *Adirondack Eco. Dev. Corp.* • 67 Main St., Ste. 200; P.O. Box 1088; 12983; Essex & Franklin; P 150,000; (518) 891-5523; (888) 243-2332; Fax (518) 891-9820; www.aedconline.com

Saratoga Springs • *Saratoga Eco. Dev. Corp.* • Dennis Brobston; Pres.; 28 Clinton St.; 12866; Saratoga; P 196,200; M 350; (518) 587-0945; Fax (518) 587-5855; dbrobston@saratogaedc.com; saratogaedc.com

Schenectady • *Schenectady Eco. Dev. Corp.* • 301 Nott St.; 12305; Schenectady; P 150,000; (518) 393-7252; Fax (518) 393-8687

Sullivan • *see New Windsor*

Syracuse • *Empire State Dev.* • 620 Erie Blvd. W., Ste. 112; 13204; Onondaga; (315) 425-9110; Fax (315) 425-7156; www.empire.state.ny.us

Syracuse • *Onondaga County IDA* • 421 Montgomery St., 14th Flr.; 13202; Onondaga; P 486,000; (315) 435-3770; (877) 797-8222; Fax (315) 435-3669; www.syracusecentral.com

Ulster • *see New Windsor*

Utica • *Empire State Dev.-Mohawk Valley Reg. Ofc.* • Kenneth M. Tompkins; Reg. Dir.; 207 Genesee St., Rm. 1604; 13501; Herkimer, Madison & Oneida; (315) 793-2366; Fax (315) 793-2705; www.empire.state.ny.us

Watkins Glen • *Schuyler County IDA/Scoped Inc.* • Kevin Murphy; Chrmn.; 2 N. Franklin St.; 14891; Schuyler; P 19,500; (607) 535-4341; Fax (607) 535-7221; info@scoped.biz; www.scoped.biz

West Amherst • *Amherst Ind. Dev. Agency* • James Allen; Exec. Dir.; 4287 Main St.; 14226; Erie; P 115,000; (716) 688-9000; Fax (716) 688-0205; www.amherstida.com

Westchester • *see New Windsor*

White Plains • *Westchester County Ofc. of Eco. Dev.* • Salvatore Carrera; Dir.; 148 Martine Ave., Rm. 903; 10601; Westchester; (914) 995-2926; Fax (914) 995-3044; www.westchestergov.com/economic

Yonkers • *Yonkers Ofc. of Eco. Dev.* • Louis Kirven; Dir.; City Hall; 40 S. Broadway, Ste. 416; 10701; Westchester; P 200,000; (914) 377-6797; Fax (914) 377-6003; Louis.Kirven@YonkersNY.Gov; www.yonkersny.gov

North Carolina

Federal

U.S. SBA, North Carolina Dist. Ofc. • Ms. Lynn Douthett; Dist. Dir.; 6302 Fairview Rd., Ste. 300; Charlotte; 28210; Mecklenburg; (704) 344-6563; Fax (704) 344-6769; charlotte.nc@sba.gov; www.sba.gov/nc

State

North Carolina Dept. of Comm. • Cindy Messer; Reg. Mgr.; 134 Wright Bros. Way; Fletcher; 28732; Henderson; (828) 654-9852; Fax (828) 654-9859; cmesser@nccommerce.com; www.nccommerce.com

North Carolina Dept. of Commerce • Susan Fleetwood; Dir. of Bus. & Ind.; 301 N. Wilmington; 4301 Mail Service Center; Raleigh; 27699; Wake; (919) 733-4151; Fax (919) 733-4563; info@nccommerce.com; www.nccommerce.com

Communities

Albemarle • *Stanly County Econ. Dev. Comm.* • 1000 N. 1st St., Ste. 11; 28001; Stanly; P 60,166; (704) 986-3682; Fax (704) 986-3685; edc@co.stanly.nc.us; www.stanlyedc.org

Asheboro • *Randolph County Eco. Dev. Corp.* • Bonnie Renfro; Pres.; 145 Worth St., Ste. A; P.O. Box 2001; 27204; Randolph; P 135,000; (336) 626-2233; Fax (336) 626-0777; brenfro@rcedc.com; www.rcedc.com

Asheville • *Asheville Area C/C-Eco. Dev. Dept.* • Ray Denny; V.P. Eco. Dev.; 36 Montford Ave.; P.O. Box 1010; 28802; Buncombe; P 224,000; M 2,000; (828) 258-6117; Fax (828) 251-0926; rdenny@ashevillechamber.org; www.ashevillechamber.org

Beech Mountain • *see Boone*

Black Mountain • *see Asheville*

Blowing Rock • *see Boone*

Boone • *North Carolina Dept. of Commerce* • Joe Holbrook; Sr. Eco. Dev.; 206 Southgate Dr.; 28607; Watauga; (828) 262-1345; Fax (828) 262-1495; jholbrook@nccommerce.com; www.investnc.com

Boone • *Watauga County Eco. Dev. Comm.* • Joe Furman; Dir.; P.O. Box 404; 28607; Watauga; P 43,117; (828) 264-3082; Fax (828) 265-8080; www.wataugaedc.org

Brevard · *Transylvania County Eco. Dev.* · Mark Burrows; Dir.; P.O. Box 1578; 28712; Transylvania; P 29,334; (828) 884-3205; Fax (828) 884-3275; mark.burrows@transylvaniacounty.org; econdev.transylvaniacounty.org

Canton · *see Waynesville*

Clyde · *see Waynesville*

Danbury · *Stokes County Eco. Dev.* · Bryan Steen; Dir.; 1014 Main St.; P.O. Box 20; 27016; Stokes; P 47,000; (336) 593-2496; Fax (336) 593-2346; questions@stokescounty.org; www.stokescounty.org

Dobson · *Surry County Eco. Dev. Partnership Inc.* · Jan Critz; V.P.; 118 Hamby Rd., Ste. 146; P.O. Box 1282; 27017; Surry; P 73,028; M 150; (336) 401-9900; Fax (336) 401-9901; surryedp@surry.net; www.surryedp.com

Edenton · *Edenton-Chowan Eco. Dev.* · Richard Bunch; Exec. Dir.; 116 E. King St.; P.O. Box 245; 27932; Chowan; P 16,000; (252) 482-3400; Fax (252) 482-7093; richard.bunch@ncmail.net; www.visitedenton.com

Edenton · *Northeastern NC Reg. Eco. Dev. Comm.* · Vann Rogerson; Pres./CEO; 119 W. Water St.; 27932; Chowan; P 340,000; (252) 482-4333; Fax (252) 482-3366; info@ncnortheast.com; www.ncnortheast.com

Elizabeth City · *Albemarle Eco. Dev. Comm.* · Wayne Harris; Dir.; 405 E. Main St,, Ste. 4; P.O. Box 70; 27907; Pasquotank; P 40,000; (252) 338-0169; Fax (252) 338-0160; info@discoverec.com; www.discoverec.com

Elizabethtown · *Bladen County Eco. Dev. Comm.* · 218A Aviation Pkwy.; 28337; Bladen; P 32,400; (910) 645-2292; Fax (910) 645-2293; edc@bladenco.org; www.bladeninfo.org

Farmville · *Farmville Dev. Partnership* · Jan Greene; Admin. Asst.; P.O. Box 150; 27828; Pitt; P 4,500; (252) 753-4670; Fax (252) 753-7313; www.farmville-nc.com

Forest City · *Rutherford County Eco. Dev. Comm.* · Tom Johnson; Exec. Dir.; 142 E. Main St., Ste. 100; 28043; Rutherford; P 63,570; (828) 248-1716; Fax (828) 248-1771; tjohnson@rutherfordncedc.com; www.rutherfordncedc.com

Gastonia · *Gaston County Eco. Dev. Comm.* · Donny Hicks CEcD; Exec. Dir.; P.O. Box 2339; 28053; Gaston; P 195,000; (704) 825-4046; Fax (704) 825-4066; edc@gaston.org; www.gaston.org

Goldsboro · *Wayne County Dev. Alliance* · Joanna Thompson; Pres.; P.O. Box 1280; 27533; Wayne; P 114,000; (919) 731-7700; Fax (919) 580-9147; www.waynealliance.org

Greensboro · *Greensboro Eco. Dev. Alliance* · Dan Lynch; Pres.; 342 N. Elm St.; 27401; Guilford; P 245,000; (336) 387-8302; Fax (336) 510-0295; greensboroeda@greensboro.org; www.greensboroeda.com

Greenville · *Pitt County Dev. Comm.* · Wanda Yuhas; Exec. Dir.; 111 S. Washington; P.O. Box 837; 27835; Pitt; P 155,000; (252) 758-1989; Fax (252) 758-0128; pittedc@co.pitt.nc.us; www.locateincarolina.com

Hazelwood · *see Waynesville*

Henderson · *Vance County EDC* · 1775 Graham Ave., Ste. 105; P.O. Box 2017; 27536; Vance; P 44,000; (252) 492-2094; Fax (252) 492-4428; www.vancecountyedc.com

Hickory · *Catawba County Eco. Dev. Corp.* · Scott L. Millar; Pres.; 1960 13th Ave. Dr. S.E.; P.O. Box 3388; 28603; Catawba; P 148,913; (828) 267-1564; Fax (828) 267-1884; smillar@catawbacountync.gov; www.catawbaedc.org

High Point · *High Point Eco. Dev. Corp.* · Mr. Loren Hill; Pres.; 211 S. Hamilton St.; P.O. Box 230; 27261; Guilford; P 92,489; (336) 883-3116; Fax (336) 883-3057; loren.hill@highpointnc.gov; www.high-point.net/edc/

Hillsborough · *Orange County Eco. Dev. Comm.* · 110 E. King St.; P.O. Box 1177; 27278; Orange; P 122,000; (919) 245-2325; Fax (919) 644-3008; www.co.orange.nc.us/ecodev

Jacksonville · *Onslow County Eco. Dev.* · Jim Reichardt; Dir. of Eco. Dev.; 1099 Gum Branch Rd.; 28540; Onslow; P 160,000; (910) 347-3141; Fax (910) 347-2842; jreichardt@jacksonvilleline.org; www.onslowedc.com

Jefferson · *Ashe County Eco. Dev. Comm.* · Dr. Patricia Mitchell; Dir.; 150 Government Cir., Ste. 2500; 28640; Ashe; P 25,274; (336) 846-5502; Fax (336) 846-5516; director@ashencedc.com; www.ashencedc.com

Kenansville · *Duplin County EDC* · Cynthia Potter; Admin. Secy.; P.O. Box 929; 28349; Duplin; P 50,000; (910) 296-2180; Fax (910) 296-2184; info@duplinedc.com; www.duplinedc.com

Kinston · *Lenoir County Eco. Dev. Dept.* · D. Mark Pope; Exec. Dir.; 301 N. Queen St.; P.O. Box 897; 28502; Lenoir; P 60,000; (252) 527-1963; Fax (252) 527-1914; mpope@lenoiredc.com; www.lenoiredc.com

Lenoir · *Caldwell County Eco. Dev. Comm.* · Alan Wood; Sr. Dev. Mgr.; 1909 Hickory Blvd.; P.O. Box 2888; 28645; Caldwell; P 77,000; (828) 728-0768; Fax (828) 726-8926; info@caldwelledc.org; www.caldwelledc.org

Lexington · *Davidson County Eco. Dev.* · Steve Googe; Exec. Dir.; P.O. Box 1287; 27293; Davidson; P 164,000; (336) 243-1900; Fax (336) 243-3027; slgooge@davidsoncountyedc.com; www.co.davidson.nc.us/dcedc

Lincolnton · *Lincoln Eco. Dev. Assn.* · Barry Matherly; Exec. Dir.; 502 E. Main St.; 28092; Lincoln; P 70,000; M 150; (704) 732-1511; Fax (704) 736-8451; leda@lincolneda.org; www.lincolneda.org

Marion · *McDowell Eco. Dev. Assn.* · Charles Abernathy; Exec. Dir.; 25 S. Garden St.; P.O. Box 1289; 28752; McDowell; P 43,000; (828) 652-9391; Fax (828) 652-8775; medainc@verizon.net; www.mcdowelleda.org

Mocksville · *Davie County Eco. Dev. Comm.* · Terry Bralley; Pres.; 135 S. Salisbury St.; 27028; Davie; P 36,000; (336) 751-5513; (336) 751-2714; Fax (336) 751-7408; terry.bralley@daviecounty.com; www.daviecounty.com; www.co.davie.nc.us

Monroe · *Union County Partnership for Progress* · Maurice Ewing CEcD; Pres./CEO; P.O. Box 1789; 28111; Union; P 160,000; (704) 283-0640; info@unioncpp.com; www.unioncpp.com

Morehead City · *Carteret County Eco. Dev. Cncl.* · Miles Michael Stempin; Exec. Dir.; 3615 Arendell St.; 28557; Carteret; P 64,000; M 300; (252) 222-6122; (252) 222-6121; Fax (252) 222-6124; edc@carteret.edu; www.carteretedc.com

New Bern · *Craven County EDC* · James T. Davis III; Exec. Dir.; 100 Industrial Dr.; 28562; Craven; P 93,000; (252) 633-5300; Fax (252) 633-3253; cravenedc@cconnect.net; www.cravenedc.com

North Wilkesboro · *Wilkes Eco. Dev. Corp.* · Donald Alexander; Exec. Dir.; 717 Main St.; P.O. Box 727; 28659; Wilkes; P 65,000; (336) 838-1501; Fax (336) 838-1693; dalexander@wilkesedc.com; www.wilkesedc.com

Oxford · *Granville Eco. Dev. Comm.* · Jay Tilley; Exec. Dir.; 310 Williamsboro St.; P.O. Box 26; 27565; Granville; P 55,000; (919) 693-5911; Fax (919) 693-1952; gedcoffice@granvillecounty.com; www.granvillecounty.com

Pinehurst · *Moore County Partners in Progress* · Ray Ogden; Exec. Dir.; P.O. Box 5885; 28374; Moore; P 82,292; M 35; (910) 246-0311; Fax (910) 246-0312; econdev@moorebusiness.org; www.moorebusiness.org

Roanoke Rapids · *Halifax Dev. Comm.* · Cathy A. Scott; Exec. Dir.; P.O. Box 246; 27870; Halifax; P 57,500; (252) 519-2630; Fax (252) 519-2632; cathyscott@halifaxdevelopment.com; www.halifaxdevelopment.com

Rocky Mount · *Carolinas Gateway Partnership* · John Gessaman; Pres./CEO; 427 Falls Rd.; 27804; Nash; P 143,000; (252) 442-0114; Fax (252) 442-7315; cgp@econdev.org; www.econdev.org

Salisbury · *Salisbury-Rowan Eco. Dev. Comm.* · Robert Van Geons; Exec. Dir.; 204 E. Innes St.; 28144; Rowan; P 130,000; (704) 637-5526; Fax (704) 637-0173; robert@rowanedc.com; www.rowanedc.com

Sparta · *Alleghany County Eco. Dev. Corp.* · Don Adams; County Mgr.; 348 S. Main St.; P.O. Box 366; 28675; Alleghany; P 10,874; (336) 372-4179; Fax (336) 372-5969; manageralc@skybest.com; www.alleghanycounty-nc.gov

Spruce Pine · *Mitchell County Eco. Dev. Comm.* · Jack Dobson; Dir.; 167 Locust Ave.; 28777; Mitchell; P 15,900; (828) 766-6009; Fax (828) 765-9655; becky@beckyanderson-consulting.com

Statesville · *Greater Statesville Dev. Corp.* · C. Michael Smith; Dir.; 115 E. Front St.; 28677; Iredell; P 70,000; (704) 871-0062; Fax (704) 871-0223; info@greaterstatesville.org; www.greaterstatesville.org

Troy · *Montgomery Eco. Dev. Corp.* · Judy Stevens; Exec. Dir.; 444 N. Main St.; P.O. Box 637; 27371; Montgomery; P 27,000; (910) 572-2575; Fax (910) 572-5193; judy@montgomery-county.com; www.montgomery-county.com

Wadesboro · *Anson County Eco. Dev. Dept.* · Misty Harris; Dir. of Eco. Dev.; P.O. Box 339; 28170; Anson; P 25,500; (704) 694-9513; Fax (704) 694-3138; mharris@co.anson.nc.us; www.ansonedc.org

Warrenton · *Warren County Eco. Dev. Comm.* · Dir.; 130 N. Main St.; P.O. Box 804; 27589; Warren; P 20,000; (252) 257-3114; Fax (252) 257-2277; edc@warrencountync.org; www.warrencountync.org

Washington · *Beaufort County Eco. Dev. Comm.* · Tom Thompson; Exec. Dir.; 705 Page Rd.; 27889; Beaufort; P 4,550; (252) 946-3970; Fax (252) 946-0849; info@beaufortedc.com; www.beaufortedc.com

Waynesville · *Haywood County Eco. Dev. Comm.* · Mark Clasby; Exec. Dir.; 144 Industrial Park Dr.; 28786; Haywood; P 57,097; (828) 456-3737; Fax (828) 452-1352; mclasby@haywoodnc.net; www.haywoodedc.org

Weaverville · *see Asheville*

Williamston · *Martin County Eco. Dev. Corp.* · James D. Ward; Exec. Dir.; 415 East Blvd.; 27892; Martin; P 25,078; (252) 792-2044; Fax (252) 792-0993; info@martincountyedc.com; www.martincountyedc.com

Wilson · *Wilson Eco. Dev. Cncl.* · Jennifer Lantz; Exec. Dir.; 126 W. Nash St.; P.O. Box 728; 27894; Wilson; P 79,000; (252) 237-1115; (800) 241-4920; Fax (252) 237-1116; jlantz@wilsonedc.com; www.wilsonedc.com

Winston-Salem · *Winston-Salem Bus Inc.* · Robert E. Leak Jr. CID CEcD; Pres.; 1080 W. 4th St.; 27101; Forsyth; P 317,643; (336) 723-8955; Fax (336) 716-1069; rleak@wsbusinessinc.com; www.wsbusinessinc.com

Winton · *Hertford Co. Eco. Dev. Comm.* · William S. Early; Dir.; P.O. Box 429; 27986; Hertford; P 22,601; (252) 358-7801; Fax (252) 358-7806; hertford.county@hertfordcountync.gov; www.hertfordcounty.com

Youngsville · *Franklin County Eco. Dev. Comm.* · Ronnie Goswick; Dir.; 112-D Wheaton Dr.; 27596; Franklin; P 56,000; (919) 554-1863; Fax (919) 554-1781; rgoswick@franklincountync.us; www.franklinedc.com

North Dakota

Federal

U.S. SBA, North Dakota Dist. Ofc. · James Stai; Dist. Dir.; 657 2nd Ave. N., Rm. 218; P.O. Box 3086; Fargo; 58108; Cass; (701) 239-5131; Fax (701) 239-5645; north.dakota@sba.gov; www.sba.gov/nd

State

North Dakota Dept. of Commerce · Shane Goettle; Comm.; 1600 E. Century Ave., Ste. 2; P.O. Box 2057; Bismarck; 58502; Burleigh; P 650,000; (701) 328-5300; Fax (701) 328-5320; commerce@nd.gov; www.ndcommerce.com

Communities

Bismarck · *Bismarck-Mandan Dev. Assn.* · Russell Staiger; Pres./CEO; 400 E. Broadway Ave., Ste. 417; P.O. Box 2615; 58502; Burleigh; P 95,000; (701) 222-5530; (888) 222-5497; Fax (701) 222-3843; rstalger@bmda.org; www.bmda.org

Bottineau · *Bottineau County Eco. Dev. Corp.* · Diane Olson; EDC Dir.; 519 Main St.; 58318; Bottineau; P 2,400; M 100; (701) 228-3922; Fax (701) 228-5130; edc@utma.com; www.bottineau.com

Carrington · *Carrington Comm. Dev. Corp.* · Robin Anderson; Pres.; 871 Main; P.O. Box 439; 58421; Foster; P 2,300; (701) 652-2524; (800) 641-9668; Fax (701) 652-2391; chambergal@daktel.com; www.cgtn-nd.com; www.carringtonnd.com

Colfax · *Colfax Dev. Corp.* · 6635 165th Ave. S.E.; 58018; Richland; P 92; (701) 372-3877;

Cooperstown · *Cooperstown/Griggs County Eco. Dev. Corp.* · Becky Meidinger; Dev. Spec.; P.O. Box 553; 58425; Griggs; P 2,500; (701) 797-3712; Fax (701) 797-3713; cooperedc@invisimax.com; ww.growingcooperstown.com

Devils Lake · *FORWARD Devils Lake Dev. Corp.* · Chris Schilken; Exec. Dir.; P.O. Box 879; 58301; Ramsey; P 7,000; (701) 662-4933; Fax (701) 662-2147; forwarddl@gondtc.com; www.forwarddl.com

Dickinson · *Roosevelt-Custer Cncl. For Dev.* · Rod Landblom; Dir.; 300 13th Ave., Ste. 3; 58601; Stark; P 38,365; (701) 483-1241; Fax (701) 483-1243; info@rooseveltcuster.com

Fargo · *Greater Fargo Moorhead Eco. Dev. Corp.* · Kevin McKinnon; Pres.; 51 Broadway, Ste. 500; 58102; Cass; P 188,000; (701) 364-1900; Fax (701) 293-7819; info@fmedc.com; www.fmedc.com

Fargo · *Lake Agassie Reg. Cncl.* · Irvin Rustad; Exec. Dir.; 417 Main Ave.; 58103; Cass; P 150,000; (701) 239-5373; Fax (701) 235-6706; www.lakeagassie.com

Grand Forks · *Grand Forks Reg. Eco. Dev. Corp.* · Klaus Thiessen; Pres./CEO; 600 Demers Ave., Ste. 501; 58201; Grand Forks; P 100,000; (701) 746-2720; Fax (701) 746-2725; judiths@grandforks.org; www.grandforks.org

Harvey · *Harvey Area Eco. Dev. Inc.* · Kim Moon; Dir.; 120 8th St. W.; 58341; Wells; P 1,998; (701) 324-2000; Fax (701) 324-2674; kim@harveynd.com; www.harveynd.com

Hazen · *Hazen Comm. Dev.* · Duke Rosendahl; Exec. Dir.; 146 Main St. E.; P.O. Box 717; 58545; Mercer; P 2,457; (701) 748-6886; Fax (701) 748-2559; hcd@westriv.com; www.hazennd.org

Hettinger · *Adams County Dev. Corp.* · Ed Gold; Exec. Dir.; 120 S. Main; P.O. Box 1323; 58639; Adams; P 2,554; (701) 567-2531; Fax (701) 567-2690; adamscdc@ndsupernet.com; www.hettingernd.com

Hillsboro · *Hillsboro Eco. Dev. Corp.* · Mike Bitz; P.O. Box 502; 58045; Traill; P 1,700; (701) 636-2338; (701) 636-4620; www.hillsborond.com

Kulm · *Kulm Comm. Dev. Corp.* · Jerry Johnson; Pres.; P.O. Box 223; 58456; Lamoure; P 450; (701) 647-2448

Linton · *Linton Ind. Dev. Corp.* · Sharon Jangula; Coord.; P.O. Box 433; 58552; Emmons; P 1,321; (701) 254-4267; Fax (701) 254-4223; lidcbek@bektel.com; www.lintonnd.org

Mayville · *Traill County Eco. Dev.* · Melissa Hennen; Exec. Dir.; 330 3rd St. N.E., Ste, 1856; 58257; Traill; P 8,700; (701) 788-4746; tcedc@polarcomm.com; www.tcedc.com

Minnewaukan · *Minnewaukan Area Dev. Corp.* · P.O. Box 98; 58351; Benson; P 300; (701) 473-5436

Minot · *Minot Area Dev. Corp.* · 1020 20th Ave. S.W.; 58701; Ward; P 52,000; M 265; (701) 852-1075; Fax (701) 857-8234; madc@minotusa.com; www.minotusa.com

Oakes · *Oakes Enhancement Inc.* · Dale Skjefte; Pres.; P.O. Box 365; 58474; Dickey; P 2,000; (701) 742-3508; oakesnd@drtel.net; www.oakesnd.com

Rugby · *Rugby Eco. Dev. Corp.* · P.O. Box 136; 58368; Pierce; P 3,000; (701) 776-7655; Fax (701) 776-5281; www.rugbynorthdakota.com

Underwood · *Underwood Area Eco. Dev. Corp.* · Becky Bowlen; Exec. Dir.; P.O. Box 368; 58576; McLean; P 1,000; (701) 442-5481; Fax (701) 442-5482; becky@underwoodnd.net; www.underwoodnd.net

Valley City · *Valley City-Barnes County Dev. Corp.* · Jennifer Feist; Dir. of Dev.; 250 W. Main St.; P.O. Box 724; 58072; Barnes; P 6,900; (701) 845-1891; Fax (701) 845-1892; vdg@hellovalley.com; www.hellovalley.com

Wahpeton · *City of Wahpeton Eco. Dev. Dept.* · Jane Priebe CEcD; Dir.; 1900 4th St. N.; 58075; Richland; P 8,567; (701) 642-8559; (888) 850-9544; Fax (701) 642-1428; info@wahpeton.com; www.wahpeton.com

Washburn · *Washburn Area Eco. Dev. Assn.* · P.O. Box 608; 58577; McLean; P 1,389; (701) 462-3801; Fax (701) 462-8598; www.washburnnd.com

Williston · *Tri-County Reg. Dev. Cncl.* · Everette Enno; Exec. Dir.; 22 E. Broadway, 2nd Flr.; P.O. Box 697; 58802; Williams; P 32,863; (701) 577-1358; Fax (701) 577-1363

Williston · *Williston Eco. Dev.* · Thomas Rolfstad; Exec. Dir.; 22 E. Broadway; P.O. Box 1306; 58802; Williams; P 14,000; (701) 577-8110; Fax (701) 577-8880; tomr@ci.williston.nd.us; www.willistonnd.com

Ohio

Federal

U.S. SBA, Cleveland Dist. Ofc. · Gilbert Goldberg; Dist. Dir.; 1350 Euclid Ave., Ste. 211; Cleveland; 44115; Cuyahoga; (216) 522-4180; Fax (216) 522-2038; james.duffy@sba.gov; www.sba.gov/oh

U.S. SBA, Columbus Dist. Ofc. · Thomas Mueller; Dist. Dir.; 401 N. Front St., Ste. 200; Columbus; 43215; Franklin; (614) 469-6860; Fax (614) 469-2391; douglas.sweazy@sba.gov; www.sba.gov/oh

State

Columbus · State of Ohio Dept. of Dev. · Mark Barbash; Dir.; 77 S. High St., 28th Flr.; 43216; Franklin; (614) 466-8737; (800) 848-1300; Fax (614) 644-0745; mark.barbash@development.ohio.gov; www.development.ohio.gov

Communities

Alliance · *Greater Alliance Dev. Corp.* · Thomas Pukys; Mgr.; 2490 W. State St.; 44601; Stark; P 50,000; M 52; (330) 823-0700; Fax (330) 823-2660; aadf@allianceadf.com

Ashland · *Mohican Area Growth Found. Inc.* · Evan Scurti; Dir.; 206 Claremont Ave.; 44805; Ashland; P 2,893; (419) 289-3200; Fax (419) 289-3233; www.mohicanareagrowthfoundation.com

Ashtabula · *see Jefferson*

Athens · *Athens County Eco. Dev. Cncl.* · Todd Shelton; Dir.; 340 W. State St., Ste. 26; 45701; Athens; P 64,000; (740) 597-1420; Fax (740) 597-1548; todd@businessremixed.com; www.businessremixed.com

Bellefontaine · *Logan County Comm. Improvement Corp.* · Ed Wallace; Pres.; 100 S. Main St.; 43311; Logan; P 46,000; (937) 599-5121; Fax (937) 599-2411; ewallace@logancountyohio.com; www.logancountyohio.com

Brook Park · *City of Brook Park Dev. Dept.* · Michelle Boczek; Eco. Dev. Commissioner; 6161 Engle Rd.; 44142; Cuyahoga; P 22,000; (216) 433-1300; Fax (216) 433-1511; www.cityofbrookpark.com

Bryan · *Williams County Eco. Dev. Corp. [WEDCO]* · Diamond Zimmerman; Coord.; 228 S. Main St.; 43506; Williams; P 39,188; M 100; (419) 636-8727; Fax (419) 636-5589; economic@wedco.info; www.wedco.info

Cambridge · *Cambridge-Guernsey County Comm. Improvement Corp.* · Norman Blanchard; Dir.; 806 Cochran Ave.; 43725; Guernsey; P 40,792; (740) 432-1881; Fax (740) 432-1990; cgccic@verizon.net; www.cgccic.org

Cambridge · *Ohio Mid-Eastern Govts. Assn.* · Greg DiDonato; Exec. Dir.; 326 Highland Ave.; P.O. Box 130; 43725; Guernsey; P 592,776; (740) 439-4471; Fax (740) 439-7783; director@omegadistrict.org; www.omegadistrict.org

Canton · *Stark Dev. Bd.* · Stephen L. Paquette; Pres.; 116 Cleveland Ave. N.W., Ste. 600; 44702; Stark; P 360,000; (330) 453-5900; Fax (330) 453-1793; www.starkcoohio.com

Chillicothe · *Eco. Dev. Alliance of Southern Ohio* · Christopher M. Manegold CEcD; CEO; 45 E. Main St.; 45601; Ross; P 75,000; (740) 772-5100; (877) 70-EDASO; cmanegold@edaso.org; www.edaso.org.

Chillicothe · *Ross County Comm. Improvement Corp.* · 45 E. Main St.; 45601; Ross; P 74,000; (740) 702-2720; Fax (740) 702-2727; www.chillicotheohio.com

Cincinnati · *Dept. of Comm. Dev.* · Michael Cervay; Dir.; 805 Central Ave., Ste. 700; 45202; Hamilton; P 400,000; (513) 352-3950; Fax (513) 352-6257; communitydevelopment@cincinnati-oh.gov; www.cincinnati-oh.gov

Cincinnati · *Hamilton County Dev. Co.* · David K. Main; Pres.; 1776 Mentor Ave., Ste. 100; 45212; Hamilton; P 800,000; (513) 631-8292; Fax (513) 631-4887; maind@hcdc.com; www.hcdc.com

Cleveland · *City of Cleveland Dept. of Eco. Dev.* · Tracey A. Nichols; Dir.; 601 Lakeside Ave., Rm. 210; 44114; Cuyahoga; P 500,000; (216) 664-2406; Fax (216) 664-3681; www.city.cleveland.oh.us

Columbus · *Mid-Ohio Reg. Planning Comm.* · 111 Liberty St., Ste. 100; 43215; Franklin; (614) 228-2663; Fax (614) 228-1904; www.morpc.org

Conneaut · *see Jefferson*

Dayton Area

City of Dayton, Ofc. of Eco. Dev. · Shelley Dickstein; Dir.; 101 W. 3rd St., City Mgr. Ofc.; 45402; Montgomery; P 166,000; (937) 333-3600; Fax (937) 333-4298; shelley.dickstein@cityofdayton.org; www.cityofdayton.org

CityWide Dev. Corp. · Steve Budd; Pres.; 8 N. Main St.; 45402; Montgomery; (937) 226-0457; Fax (937) 222-7035; www.citywidedev.com

Dayton Area C/C Eco. Dev. Div. · Chris Kershner; V.P.; One Chamber Plaza; 45402; Montgomery; P 970,000; (937) 226-1444; Fax (937) 226-8254; www.daytonchamber.org

Elyria · *Lorain County Comm. Dev.* · Donald Romancak; Interim Dir.; 226 Middle Ave., 5th Flr.; 44035; Lorain; P 284,664; (440) 328-2322; Fax (440) 328-2349; rajones@loraincounty.us; www.loraincounty.us

Euclid · *Dept. of Comm. Svc. & Eco. Dev.* · Frank Pietravoia; Dir.; 585 E. 222nd St.; 44123; Cuyahoga; P 52,717; (216) 289-8158; Fax (216) 289-8366; www.cityofeuclid.com

Fairfield · *Fairfield Dev. Svcs.* · Timothy Bachman; Dir.; 5350 Pleasant Ave.; 45014; Butler; P 41,000; (513) 867-5345; Fax (513) 867-5324; development@fairfield-city.org; www.fairfield-city.org

Findlay · *Greater Findlay Inc.* · Ray De Winkle; Pres./CEO; 123 E. Main Cross St.; 45840; Hancock; P 72,000; (419) 422-3313; Fax (419) 422-9508; rdewinkle@greaterfindlayinc.com; www.greaterfindlayinc.com

Forest Park · *City of Forest Park Eco. Dev.* · Paul Brehm; Dir.; 1201 W. Kemper Rd.; 45240; Hamilton; P 20,000; (513) 595-5207; Fax (513) 595-5285; www.forestpark.org

Fostoria · *Fostoria Eco. Dev. Corp.* · Joan M. Reinhard; Exec. Dir.; 121 N. Main St.; 44830; Seneca; P 15,000; (419) 435-7789; Fax (419) 435-0936; fostoriaed@aol.com; www.fostoriaed.org

Fremont · *Sandusky County Eco. Dev. Corp.* · Kay E. Reiter; Exec. Dir.; 2511 Countryside Dr.; 43420; Sandusky; P 62,000; (419) 332-2882; Fax (419) 332-3347; director@sanduskycountyedc.org; www.sanduskycountyedc.org

Galion · *Galion Ind. Dev.* · Joe Kleinknecht; Dir.; 106 Harding Way E.; 44833; Crawford; P 11,341; (419) 468-7737

Geneva · *see Jefferson*

Hamilton · *Butler County Dept. of Eco. Dev.* · Michael Juengling; Dir.; 130 High St.; 45011; Butler; P 351,276; (513) 887-3413; Fax (513) 785-5723; www.butlercounty.biz

Jefferson · *Growth Partnership for Ashtabula County* · Joseph Mayernick; Exec. Dir; 17 N. Market St.; 44047; Ashtabula; P 120,000; (440) 576-9126; (800) 487-4769; Fax (440) 576-5003; joe@ashtabulagrowth.com; www.ashtabulagrowth.com

Lima · *Allen Eco. Dev. Group* · Marcel Wagner; Pres./CEO; 144 S. Main, Ste. 200; 45801; Allen; P 108,493; (419) 222-7706; (877) 222-7706; Fax (419) 222-7916; info@aedg.org; www.aedg.org

Lorain · *Comm. Dev. Dept.-City of Lorain* · Sanford A. Prudoff; Dir.; 200 W. Erie Ave., 5th Flr.; 44052; Lorain; P 68,652; (440) 204-2020; Fax (440) 204-2080; www.cityoflorain.org

Mansfield · *City of Mansfield Eco. Dev.* · Tim Bowersock; Dir.; 30 N. Diamond St.; 44902; Richland; P 54,000; (419) 755-9794; Fax (419) 755-9465; tbowersock@ci.mansfield.oh.us; www.ci.mansfield.oh.us

Mansfield · *Richland Eco. Dev. Corp.* · Mike Greene; Pres.; 24 W. Third St., Ste. 204; 44902; Richland; P 130,650; (419) 522-7332; Fax (419) 522-7356; mikeg@redec.org; www.redec.org

Marion · *Marion CAN DO Inc.* · 205 W. Center St.; 43302; Marion; P 66,310; (740) 387-2267; (800) 841-7302; Fax (740) 387-5522; www.marioncando.com

Marysville · *Union County Eco. Dev.* · Eric S. Phillips; CEO/Dir.; 227 E. Fifth St.; 43040; Union; P 40,909; (937) 642-6279; (800) 642-0087; Fax (937) 644-0422; chamber@unioncounty.org; www.whereprideresides.org

Massillon · *Massillon Dev. Found.* · Bob Sanderson; Exec. Dir.; 137 LincolnWay E.; 44646; Stark; P 33,000; M 60; (330) 833-3146; Fax (330) 833-8944; info@massillonohchamber.com; www.massillonohchamber.com

Mentor · *City of Mentor Comm. Dev.* · Ronald Traub; Dir.; 8500 Civic Center Blvd.; 44060; Lake; P 51,000; (440) 974-5740; Fax (440) 205-3605; traub@cityofmentor.com; www.cityofmentor.com

Mount Vernon · *Area Dev. Found.* · Steve Waers; Pres.; 110 E. High St.; 43050; Knox; P 54,500; (740) 393-3806; (888) 411-4233; Fax (740) 397-5762; steve@knoxadf.com; www.knoxadf.com

Napoleon · *Henry County Comm. Improvement Corp.* · Ralph Lanse; Exec. Dir.; 104 E. Washington, Ste. 301; 43545; Henry; P 29,000; (419) 592-4637; Fax (419) 599-9865; cic@bright.net; www.hencoed.com

New London · *New London Comm. Improvement Corp.* · 115 E. Main St.; 44851; Huron; P 3,000; M 65; (419) 929-4091; Fax (419) 929-0738; www.newlondonohio.com

New Philadelphia · *Comm. Improvement Corp. of Tuscarawas County* · Gary D. Little; Exec. Dir.; 330 University Dr. N.E.; 44663; Tuscarawas; P 90,000; (330) 308-7524; Fax (330) 308-7552; garylittle@tusccic.com; www.tusccic.com

Norwood · *City of Norwood Dev. Dept.* · Richard Dettmer; Dir.; 4645 Montgomery Rd.; 45212; Hamilton; P 21,000; (513) 458-4596; www.norwood-ohio.com

Oak Harbor · *Ottawa County Comm. Improvement Corp.* · Jamie Beier Grant; Dir.; 8043 W. State Rte. 163, Ste. 100; 43449; Ottawa; P 40,500; (419) 898-6242; (866) 734-6789; Fax (419) 898-6244; jbgrant@ocic.biz; www.ocic.biz

Orrville · *Orrville Area Dev. Found.* · Jenni Reusser; Pres.; 132 S. Main St.; 44667; Wayne; P 8,500; (330) 682-8881; Fax (330) 682-8383; jenni@orrvillechamber.com; www.orrvillechamber.com

Painesville · *Lake County Port Auth.* · John Loftus; Exec. Dir.; One Victoria Pl., Ste. 265A; 44077; Lake; P 232,892; (440) 357-2290; Fax (440) 357-2296; jloftus@lcedc.org; www.lcedc.org

Piqua · *City of Piqua Eco. Dev.* · 201 W. Water; 45356; Miami; P 21,004; (937) 778-8198; Fax (937) 778-0809; info@piquaoh.org; www.piquaoh.org

Pomeroy · *Meigs County EDC* · Perry Varnadoe; Dev. Dir.; 238 W. Main St.; 45769; Meigs; P 25,000; (740) 992-3034; Fax (740) 992-7942; director@meigscountyohio.com; www.meigscountyohio.com

Portsmouth · *Southern Ohio Growth Partnership* · Robert Huff; Pres./CEO; 342 2nd St.; P.O. Box 509; 45662; Scioto; P 79,195; (740) 353-7647; (800) 648-2574; Fax (740) 353-5824; lcarver@portsmouth.org; www.portsmouth.org

Reno · *Buckeye Hills-Hocking Valley Reg. Dev. Dist.* · Misty Casto; Exec. Dir.; P.O. Box 520; 45773; Washington; P 255,000; (740) 374-9436; Fax (740) 374-8038; info@buckeyehills.org; www.buckeyehills.org

Saint Clairsville · *Dept. of Dev. of Belmont County* · Sue Douglass; Exec. Dev. Dir.; 117 E. Main St.; 43950; Belmont; P 60,000; (740) 695-9678; Fax (740) 695-1536; sue.douglass.belmont county@comcast.net; www.aplacetogrowyourbusiness.com

Saint Mary's · *City of St. Mary's Eco. Dev.* · Todd Fleagle; Mgr. Ind. Dev.; 101 E. Spring St.; 45885; Auglaize; P 8,342; (419) 394-3303; Fax (419) 394-2452; stmarys@cityofstmarys.net; www. cityofstmarys.net

Sandusky · *Erie County Eco. Dev. Corp.* · Peter Zaehringer; Exec. Dir.; 247 Columbus Ave., Ste. 126; 44870; Erie; P 80,000; (419) 627-7791; Fax (419) 627-7595; director@eriecountyedc.org; www. eriecountyedc.org

Sidney · *West Ohio Dev. Cncl.* · Mike Dodds; Dir.; 101 S. Ohio Ave., 2nd Flr.; 45365; Shelby; P 48,000; (937) 498-9554; Fax (937) 498-2472; mdodds@westohiodevelopment.com; www. westohiodevelopment.com

South Point · *Lawrence Eco. Dev. Corp.* · Dr. Bill Dingus; Exec. Dir.; 216 Collins Ave.; P.O. Box 488; 45680; Lawrence; P 64,000; (740) 377-4550; Fax (740) 377-2091; dingus@ohio.edu; www. lawrencecountyohio.org

Springfield · *Comm. Improvement Corp. of Springfied & Clark County* · Michael McDorman; Pres.; 20 S. Limestone St., Ste. 100; 45502; Clark; P 168,000; (937) 325-7621; (800) 803-1553; Fax (937) 325-8765; mmcdorman@greaterspringfield.com; www. greaterspringfield.com

Steubenville · *Progress Alliance* · Ed Looman; Exec. Dir.; 630 Market St.; P.O. Box 187; 43952; Jefferson; P 73,894; M 47; (740) 283-2476; Fax (740) 283-2607; elooman@progressalliance.com; www.progressalliance.com

Struthers · *CASTLO Comm. Improvement Corp.* · William DeCicco; Exec. Dir.; 100 S. Bridge St.; 44471; Mahoning; P 36,513; (330) 750-1363; info@castlo.com; www.castlo.com

Tiffin · *Seneca Ind. & Eco. Dev. Corp.* · Richard Focht Jr.; Pres./ CEO; 62 S. Washington St.; 44883; Seneca; P 55,000; (419) 447-4141; Fax (419) 447-5141; siedc@bpsom.com; www.siedc.com

Toledo · *Reg. Growth Partnership* · Steve Weathers; Pres./CEO; 300 Madison Ave., Ste. 270; 43604; Lucas; P 618,000; (419) 252-2700; Fax (419) 252-2724; www.rgp.org

Troy · *Troy Dev. Cncl.* · Charles Cochran; Pres.; 405 S.W. Public Sq., Ste. 330; 45373; Miami; P 32,000; (937) 339-7809; Fax (937) 339-4944; tdc@troyohiochamber.com; www.troyohiochamber.com

Urbana · *Champaign County Eco. Dev.* · Michael Morris; Eco. Dev. Officer; 113 Miami St.; 43078; Champaign; P 38,900; (937) 653-5764; (877) 873-5764; Fax (937) 652-1599; mmorris@ co.champaign.oh.us; www.champaignohio.biz

Van Wert · *Van Wert County Eco. Dev.* · Nancy Bowen; Dir.; 515 E. Main St.; 45891; Van Wert; P 30,000; (419) 238-2999; Fax (419) 238-1397; www.vanwertcounty-edg.com

Warren · *Youngstown/Warren Reg. C/C* · Walter M. Good; V.P. Eco. Dev.; 197 W. Market St., 7th Flr.; 44481; Trumbull; P 600,000; M 3,000; (330) 392-6140; Fax (330) 746-0330; regionalchamber@ regionalchamber.com; www.regionalchamber.com

Wauseon · *Fulton County Eco. Dev.* · Lisa Arend; Dir.; 604 S. Shoop Ave., Ste. 110; 43567; Fulton; P 42,084; M 22; (419) 337-9215; Fax (419) 337-9285; larend@fultoncountyoh.com; www. fultoncountyoh.com

Xenia · *Xenia Eco. Growth Corp.* · Steve Brodsky; Exec. Dir.; 181 W. Main St.; 45385; Greene; P 27,000; (937) 376-6389; (800) GO-XENIA; Fax (937) 372-3509; sbrodsky@xegc.org; www.xegc.org

Youngstown · *City of Youngstown Eco. Dev.* · T. Sharon Woodberry; Dev. Dir.; 20 W. Federal, Ste. M8; 44503; Mahoning; P 83,000; (330) 744-1708; Fax (330) 744-1951; www.ytown development.com

Youngstown · *Mahoning Valley Eco. Dev. Corp.* · Donald L. French; Exec. Dir.; 4319 Belmont Ave.; 44505; Mahoning; P 600,000; (330) 759-3668; (330) 369-6026; Fax (330) 759-3686; www.mvedc.com

Zanesville · *Zanesville-Muskingum County Port Auth.* · Jerry Nolder; Exec. Dir.; 205 N. 5th St.; 43701; Muskingum; P 83,388; (740) 455-0742; (800) 988-4388; Fax (740) 452-9703; jerry. nolder@zmcport.com; www.zmcport.com

Oklahoma

Federal

U.S. SBA, Oklahoma Dist. Ofc. · Dorothy Overal; Dist. Dir.; 301 N.W. 6th, Ste. 116; Oklahoma City; 73102; Oklahoma; (405) 609-8000; Fax (405) 609-8990; darla.booker@sba.gov; www. sba.gov/ok

State

Oklahoma Dept. of Commerce · Natalie Shirley; Secy. of Commerce; 900 N. Stiles Ave.; Oklahoma City; 73104; Oklahoma; (405) 815-6552; Fax (405) 815-5290; jason_ mccarty@okcommerce.gov; www.okcommerce.gov

Oklahoma Industries Auth. · Gary Bush; Gen. Mgr.; 123 Park Ave.; Oklahoma City; 73102; Oklahoma; (405) 232-9921; Fax (405) 235-5112

Communities

Altus · *Altus/Southwest Area Eco. Dev. Corp.* · 220 E. Commerce; 73521; Jackson; P 23,000; (580) 481-2287; Fax (580) 481-2203; mayor@cityofaltus.org; www.cityofaltus.org

Ardmore · *Ardmore Dev. Auth.* · Brien Thorstenberg; V.P., Dev.; 410 W. Main; P.O. Box 1585; 73402; Carter; P 35,000; (580) 223-6162; Fax (580) 223-7825; bthorstenberg@ardmore.org; www. ardmoredevelopment.com

Atoka · *Atoka County Ind. Auth.* · Don Walker; City Mgr.; 315 E. A St.; P.O. Box 900; 74525; Atoka; P 14,000; (580) 889-3341; Fax (580) 889-7584; www.atokacity.org

Bartlesville · *Bartlesville Dev. Corp.* · David Wood; Pres./CEO; 201 S.W. Keeler Ave.; 74003; Washington; P 35,000; (918) 337-8086; Fax (918) 337-0216; dwood@bdcok.org; www.bdcok.org

Blackwell · *Blackwell Ind. Auth.* · Jeff Seymour; Exec. Dir.; 120 S. Main; P.O. Box 150; 74631; Kay; P 7,500; (580) 363-2934; Fax (580) 363-1704; info.bia@blackwellareachamber.com; www. blackwellindustrialauthority.com

Buffalo · *Buffalo Eco. Dev.* · James Leonard; Dir.; P.O. Box 439; 73834; Harper; P 1,200; (580) 735-2521; buffalo@pldi.net; www.BuffaloOklahoma.com

Claremore · *Claremore Ind. & Eco. Dev. Auth.* · Tim Hight; Exec. Dir; 2000 University Dr., Ste. 2; 74017; Rogers; P 20,000; (918) 341-4755; Fax (918) 343-7532; thight@claremoreusa.com; www. claremoreusa.com

Duncan · *Duncan Area Eco. Dev. Found.* · Lyle Roggow; Pres.; 8100 N. Hwy. 81; 73533; Stephens; P 43,000; (580) 255-9675; (888) 254-9675; Fax (580) 255-2647; cora@ok-duncan.com; www.ok-duncan.com

Durant · *Durant Ind. Auth.* · Tommy Kramer; Exec. Dir.; 215 N. 4th Ave.; 74701; Bryan; P 16,450; (580) 924-4570; Fax (580) 924-0348; tkramer@durant.org; www.ok-durant.org

Grove · *Grove Ind. Dev. Auth.* · 104 W. Third; 74344; Delaware; P 6,000; (918) 786-6107; Fax (918) 786-8939; www.cityofgrove.com

Guthrie · *Logan County Eco. Dev. Cncl.* · Kay Wade; Dir.; 212 W. Oklahoma; P.O. Box 995; 73044; Logan; P 29,000; (405) 282-0060; (405) 282-1947; Fax (405) 282-0061; www.logancountyedc.com

Idabel · *Idabel Ind. Dev. Auth.* · Walt Frey; Chrmn.; 7 S.W. Texas St.; 74745; McCurtain; P 6,900; (580) 286-3305; Fax (580) 286-6708; iida@idabelok.net

Lawton · *Eco. Dev. Div., Lawton Fort Sill C/C* · Ed Cole; V.P.; 629 S.W. C Ave.; 73501; Comanche; P 112,000; (580) 355-3541; (800) 872-4540; Fax (580) 357-3642; ecole@lawtonfortsillchamber.com; www.lawtonfortsillchamber.com

Miami · *Miami Area Eco. Dev. Svc.* · Judee Snodderly; Exec. Dir.; 2 N. Main, Ste. 601; 74354; Ottawa; P 35,000; (918) 542-8405; Fax (918) 542-7751; maeds@miami-ok.org; www.miami-ok.org

Midwest City · *MWC Comm. & Eco. Dev.* · David Burnett CEcD; Dir. of Econ. Dev.; 5905 Trosper Rd.; P.O. Box 10980; 73140; Oklahoma; P 57,000; (405) 733-3801; Fax (405) 733-5633; david.burnett@midwestcityok.com; www.mwcok.com

Muskogee · *Muskogee Dev. Corp.* · Leisha V. Haworth; Exec. Dir.; 216 W. Okmulgee; 74401; Muskogee; P 40,000; (918) 683-2816; (800) 483-2816; Fax (918) 683-2110; gmdc@muskogeedevelopment.orq; www.muskogeedevelopment.org

Norman · *Norman Eco. Dev. Coalition* · Don Wood; Exec. Dir.; 710 Asp Ave., Ste. 100; 73069; Cleveland; P 103,101; (405) 573-1900; Fax (405) 573-1999; nedc@nedcok.com; www.nedcok.com

Oklahoma City · *Oklahoma City Eco. Dev. Found.* · Roy Williams; Pres./CEO; 123 Park Ave.; 73102; Oklahoma; P 538,000; (405) 297-8900; Fax (405) 297-8908; rwilliams@okcchamber.com; www.okcchamber.com

Perry · *Perry Eco. Dev. Auth.* · Jim Davis; City Mgr.; 300 6th St.; P.O. Box 798; 73077; Noble; P 5,200; (580) 336-4241; Fax (580) 336-4065; vicki.hagerman@sbcglobal.net; www.cityofperryok.com

Tulsa · *Eco. Dev. Div., Tulsa Metro C/C* · Jim Fram; Sr. V.P.; Two W. 2nd St., Ste. 150; 74103; Osage, Rogers, Tulsa & Wagoner; P 810,000; (918) 560-0231; (918) 585-1201; Fax (918) 585-8386; jimfram@tulsachamber.com; www.growmetrotulsa.com

Tulsa · *Tulsa Area Partnership* · Angie Moore; Prog. Mgr.; Two W. 2nd St., Ste. 150; 74103; Osage, Rogers, Tulsa & Wagoner; P 1,300,000; (918) 560-0217; Fax (918) 585-8386; angiemoore@tulsachamber.com; www.tulsaareapartnership.com;

Wewoka · *Eco. Dev. City of Wewoka* · Mark Mosley; City Mgr.; P.O. Box 719; 74884; Seminole; P 3,500; (405) 257-5485; Fax (405) 257-2662; wewokachamber@sbcglobal.net

Oregon

Federal

U.S. SBA, Oregon Dist. Ofc. · Harry DeWolf; Dist. Dir.; 601 S.W. 2nd Ave., Ste. 950; Portland; 97204; Multnomah; (503) 326-2682; Fax (503) 326-2808; sylvia.gercke@sba.gov; www.sba.gov/or

State

Business Oregon · Tim McCabe; Dir.; 775 Summer St. N.E., Ste. 200; Salem; 97301; Marion; (503) 986-0123; Fax (503) 581-5115; biz.info@state.or.us; www.oregon4biz.com

Communities

Albany · *Albany-Millersburg Eco. Dev. Corp.* · John Pascone; Pres.; 435 W. First Ave.; P.O. Box 548; 97321; Linn; P 45,000; (541) 926-1519; Fax (541) 926-7064; pasconj@peak.org; www.albany-millersburg.com

Albany · *Cascade West Eco. Dev.* · Cynthia Solie; Dir.; 1400 Queen Ave. S.E., Ste. 205A; 97322; Linn; P 209,400; (541) 967-8551; Fax (541) 967-4651; www.ocwcog.org

Baker City · *Baker City/County Comm. Dev.* · Jennifer Watkins; Dir.; P.O. Box 650; 97814; Baker; P 10,500; (541) 523-6541; Fax (541) 524-2024; www.bakercity.com

Bend · *Eco. Dev. for Central Oregon* · Roger Lee; Exec. Dir.; 109 N.W. Greenwood Ave., Ste. 102; 97701; Deschutes; P 185,230; M 320; (541) 388-3236; Fax (541) 388-6705; info@edcoinfo.com; www.edcoinfo.com

Dallas · *Dallas Eco. Dev. Comm.* · Jerry Wyatt; City Mgr.; 187 S.E. Court St.; 97338; Polk; P 15,000; (503) 623-2338; Fax (503) 623-2339; www.ci.dallas.or.us

Enterprise · *Northeast Oregon Eco. Dev. Dist.* · Lisa Dawson; Exec. Dir.; 101 N.E. First St., Ste. 100; 97828; Wallowa; P 45,000; (541) 426-3598; Fax (541) 426-9058; lisadawson@neoedd.org; www.neoedd.org

Eugene Area

Lane Cncl. of Govts. · Steve Dignam; Eco. Dev. Coord.; 859 Willamette St., Ste. 500; 97401; Lane; P 334,000; (541) 682-4283; Fax (541) 682-4099; susanl.muir@ci.eugene.or.us; www.lcog.org

Lane Metro Partnership · Jack Roberts; Exec. Dir.; 1401 Willamette, 2nd Flr.; P.O. Box 10398; 97440; Lane; P 334,000; (541) 686-2741; Fax (541) 686-2325; business@lanemetro.com; www.lanemetro.com

Planning & Dev. Dept. · Susan Muir; Exec. Dir.; 99 W. 10th Ave.; 97401; Lane; P 145,000; (541) 682-6077; Fax (541) 682-8335; susan.l.muir@ci.eugene.or.us; www.eugene-or.gov

Hillsboro · *Hillsboro Downtown Bus. Assn.* · Kay Mattson; Downtown Bus. Mgr.; 232 N.E. Lincoln St., Ste. J; P.O. Box 611; 97123; Washington; P 88,000; (503) 844-6685; (503) 648-7817; Fax (503) 844-6215; info@hillsborodowntown.org; www.hillsborodowntown.org

Hillsboro · *Washington County Ofc. of Comm. Dev.* · Peggy Linden; Prog. Mgr.; 328 W. Main, Ste. 100; 97123; Washington; P 357,000; (503) 846-8814; Fax (503) 846-2882; www.co.washington.or.us

Jackson County · *Southern Oregon Reg. Eco. Dev. Inc. [SOREDI]* · Colleen Padilla; Bus. Dev. Mgr.; 673 Market St.; Medford; 97504; Jackson; P 280,000; (541) 773-8946; (800) 805-8740; Fax (541) 779-0953; colleen@soredi.org; www.soredi.org

Josephine County · *Southern Oregon Reg. Eco. Dev. Inc. [SOREDI]* · Colleen Padilla; Bus. Dev. Mgr.; 673 Market St.; Medford; 97504; Jackson; P 280,000; (541) 773-8946; (800) 805-8740; Fax (541) 779-0953; colleen@soredi.org; www.soredi.org

Klamath Falls · *Klamath County Eco. Dev. Assn.* · Trey Senn; Exec. Dir.; 706 Main St.; P.O. Box 1777; 97601; P 67,000; (541) 882-9600; Fax (541) 882-7648; www.sobusi.com

Klamath Falls · *Small Bus. Dev. Center* · Jamie Albert; Dir.; OR Inst. of Tech.; 3201 Campus Dr., Boivin Hall 119; 97601; Klamath; P 56,000; (541) 885-1760; Fax (541) 885-1761; sbdc@oit.edu; www.bizcenter.org

La Grande · *Union County Eco. Dev. Corp.* · Mike Sanford; Exec. Dir.; P.O. Box 1208; 97850; Union; P 25,110; M 50; (541) 963-0926; Fax (541) 963-0689; ucedc@eoni.com; www.ucedc.org

McMinnville · *McMinnville Eco. Dev. Partnership* · Jody Christensen; Exec. Dir.; 417 N.W. Adams St.; 97128; Yamhill; P 32,400; (503) 474-0544; Fax (503) 550-8504; info@mcminn villeedp.com; www.mcminnvilleedp.com

McMinnville · *Yamhill County Dept. of Plan. & Dev.* · Michael Brandt; Dir.; 525 N.E. 4th St.; 97128; Yamhill; P 89,200; (503) 434-7516; Fax (503) 434-7544; www.co.yamhill.or.us/plan

Moro · *County Eco. Dev. Ofc.* · Georgia Macnab; Planning Dir.; 110 Main St., Ste. 2; P.O. Box 381; 97039; Sherman; P 1,900; (541) 565-3601; Fax (541) 565-3078; georgiamac@embarqmail.com; www.co.sherman.or.us

North Bend · *Bus. Center* · Debbie Thompson; Secy.; 2455 Maple Leaf; 97459; Coos; P 62,000; (541) 756-6778; Fax (541) 756-5404; bec@portofcoosbay.com; www.portofcoosbay.com

Ontario · *Malheur County Eco. Dev.* · Jim Jensen; Dir.; 316 N.E. Goodfellow St., Ste. 2; 97914; Malheur; P 32,000; (541) 881-0327; Fax (541) 881-0329; ecodev.malheurco.org

Oregon City · *Clackamas County Bus. & Eco. Dev. Team* · Gary Barth; Deputy Dir. Bus. & Comm. Svc.; 150 Beaver Creek Rd.; 97045; Clackamas; P 370,000; (503) 742-4329; Fax (503) 742-4349; garybar@co.clackamas.or.us; www.co.clackamas.or.us/business

Portland · *Portland Dev. Comm.* · Bruce Warner; Exec. Dir.; 222 N.W. 5th Ave.; 97209; Clackamas, Multnomah & Washington; P 2,050,650; (503) 823-3200; Fax (503) 823-3368; www.pdc.us

Redmond · *City of Redmond Comm. Dev.* · Heather Richards; Interim Dir.; 716 S.W. Evergreen Ave.; 97756; Deschutes; P 21,109; (541) 923-7721; Fax (541) 548-0706; www.ci.redmond.or.us

Redmond · *Redmond Eco. Dev. Inc.* · Jon Stark; Mgr.; 446 S.W. 7th St.; 97756; Deschutes; P 25,800; (541) 923-5223; Fax (541) 923-6442; redap@redap.org; www.redap.org

Roseburg · *CCD Bus. Dev.* · Wayne Luzier; Exec. Dir.; 744 S.E. Rose St.; 97470; Douglas; P 200,000; (541) 672-6728; Fax (541) 672-7011; www.ccdbusiness.com

Salem · *Strategic Eco. Dev. Corp.-SEDCOR* · Ray Burstedt; Pres.; 626 High St. N.E., Ste. 200; 97301; Marion; P 388,000; (503) 588-6225; Fax (503) 588-6240; rburstedt@sedcor.com; www.sedcor.com

Springfield · *City of Springfield Eco. Dev. Div.* · John Tamulonis; Comm. Dev. Mgr.; 225 5th St.; 97477; Lane; P 57,500; (541) 726-3656; (541) 726-3700; Fax (541) 726-2363; jtamulonis@ci.springfield.or.us; www.ci.springfield.or.us

Sweet Home · *Sweet Home Eco. Dev. Group* · Ron Moore; Pres.; P.O. Box 430; 97386; Linn; P 8,300; (541) 367-3061; www.sweethomeoregon.org

The Dalles · *Mid-Columbia Eco. Dev. Dist.* · Amanda Remington; Exec. Dir.; 515 E. 2nd St.; 97058; Wasco; P 77,000; (541) 296-2266; Fax (541) 296-3283; mcedd@mcedd.org; www.mcedd.org

Tillamook · *Eco. Dev. Cncl. of Tillamook County* · Marshall Doak; Exec. Dir.; 1906-A 3rd St.; 97141; Tillamook; P 24,800; (503) 842-2236; Fax (503) 842-9368; info@edctc.com; www.edctc.com

Umatilla · *Port of Umatilla* · Mr. Kim Puzey; Gen. Mgr.; P.O. Box 879; 97882; Umatilla; P 62,000; (541) 922-3224; Fax (541) 922-5609; www.portofumatilla.com

Winston · *Winston Area Dev. Comm.* · Anita Cox; Chrmn.; 30 N.W. Glenhart; P.O. Box 68; 97496; Douglas; P 10,000; M 10; (541) 679-0118; Fax (541) 679-4270; winstonvic@charter.net; www.winstonoregon.net

Pennsylvania

Federal

U.S. SBA, Philadelphia Dist. Ofc. · David Dickson; Dist. Dir.; 1150 First Ave., Ste. 1001; King of Prussia; 19406; Philadelphia; (610) 382-3062; miriam.mcmullen@sba.gov; www.sba.gov/pa

U.S. SBA, Pittsburgh Dist. Ofc. · Carl Knoblock; Dist. Dir.; 411 7th Ave., Ste. 1450; Pittsburgh; 15219; Allegheny; (412) 395-6560; Fax (412) 395-6562; barbara.fisher@sba.gov; www.sba.gov/pa

Communities

Altoona · *Altoona Blair County Dev. Corp.* · Martin J. Marasco; Pres./CEO; 3900 Industrial Park Dr.; 16602; Blair; P 137,000; (814) 944-6113; Fax (814) 946-0157; www.abcdcorp.org

Bedford · *Bedford County Dev. Assn.* · Bette Slayton; Pres.; 1 Corporate Dr., Ste. 101; 15522; Bedford; P 49,984; (814) 623-4816; (800) 634-8610; Fax (814) 623-6455; www.bcda.org

Berwick · *Berwick Ind. Dev. Assn.* · Stephen Phillips; Exec. Dir.; 107 S. Market St., Ste. 5; 18603; Columbia; P 12,000; (570) 752-3612; Fax (570) 752-2334; bida@pa.metrocast.net; www.bida.com

Bethlehem · *Lehigh Valley Eco. Dev. Corp.* · Phil Mitman; Pres./CEO; 2158 Ave. C, Ste. 200; 18017; Northampton; P 600,000; (610) 266-6775; Fax (610) 266-7623; lvedc@lehighvalley.org; www.lehighvalley.org

Bethlehem · *Lehigh Valley Ind. Park Inc.* · Kerry Wrobel; Pres.; 1720 Spillman Dr., Ste. 150; 18015; Northampton; P 600,000; (610) 866-4600; Fax (610) 867-9154; www.lvip.org

Bloomsburg · *Columbia Alliance for Eco. Growth/Ind. Dev. Auth.* · Edward G. Edwards; Pres.; 238 Market St.; 17815; Columbia; P 63,000; (570) 784-2522; Fax (570) 784-2661; chamber@columbiamontourchamber.com; www.columbiamontourchamber.com

Brackenridge · *Allegheny Valley Dev. Corp.* · Laurie Singer; Pres.; 1030 Broadview Blvd., Ste. 1; 15014; Allegheny; P 50,000; (724) 224-5858; Fax (724) 224-3442

Brookville · *Jefferson County Dept. of Dev.* · Craig Coon; Dir. of Comm. & Eco. Dev.; Jefferson Pl.; 155 Main St., 2nd Flr.; 15825; Jefferson; P 46,083; (814) 849-1603; Fax (814) 849-5049; www.jeffersoncountypa.com

Butler · *Comm. Dev. Corp. of Butler County* · Diane Mintus Sheets; Exec. Dir.; 112 Woody Dr.; 16001; Butler; P 176,000; (724) 283-1961; (800) 283-0021; Fax (724) 283-3599; commdev@nauticom.net; www.butlercountycdc.com

Carbondale · *Carbondale Comm. Dev.* · Nancy Perri; 10 Enterprise Dr.; 18407; Lackawanna; P 9,804; (570) 282-1255; Fax (570) 282-1426; nperri@echoes.net

Chambersburg · *Franklin County Area Dev. Corp.* · L. Michael Ross; Pres.; 1900 Wayne Rd.; 17202; Franklin; P 133,000; (717) 263-8282; Fax (717) 263-0662; info@fcadc.com; www.fcadc.com

Clearfield · *Clearfield County Eco. Dev. Corp.* · Rob Swales; Exec. Dir.; 511 Spruce St., Ste. 5; 16830; Clearfield; P 82,000; (814) 768-7838; (877) 768-7838; Fax (814) 768-7338; info@clearlyahead.com; www.clearlyahead.com

Donora · *Middle Mononghela Ind. Dev. Assn.* · LueAnn Pawlick; Exec. Dir.; P.O. Box 491; 15033; Washington; P 45,000; (724) 379-5600; Fax (724) 379-9308; lpawlick@mmida.com; mmida.com

Doylestown · *Bucks County Eco. Dev. Corp.* · Dr. Kathleen Dominick; Exec. Dir.; 2 E. Court St.; 18901; Bucks; P 625,000; (215) 348-9031; Fax (215) 348-8829; rfc@bcedc.com; www.bcedc.com

East Norriton · *Montgomery County Ind. Dev. Corp.* · Mr. Carmen Italia Jr.; Pres.; 420 W. Germantown Pike; 19403; Montgomery; P 750,097; (610) 272-5000; Fax (610) 272-6235; www.mcidc.com

Easton · *Easton Redev. Auth.* · 1 S. 3rd St.; 18042; Northampton; P 26,000; (610) 250-6721; Fax (610) 250-6607; www.easton-pa.gov

Erie · *Greater Erie Ind. Dev. Corp.* · K. Smith; Pres./CEO; 5240 Knowledge Pkwy.; 16510; Erie; P 276,000; (814) 899-6022; Fax (814) 899-0250; www.connectforsuccess.org

Exton · *Chester County Eco. Dev. Cncl.* · Gary Smith; Pres./CEO; 737 Constitution Dr.; 19341; Chester; P 376,000; (610) 458-5700; Fax (610) 458-7770; www.cceconomicdevelopment.com

Greensburg · *Eco. Growth Connection of Westmoreland* · John A. Skiavo; CEO; 40 N. Penn Ave., Ste. 510; 15601; Westmoreland; P 375,000; (724) 830-3604; Fax (724) 850-3974; www.economicgrowthconnection.com

Greenville · *Greenville Area Eco. Dev. Corp.* · James Lowry; Dir.; 12 N. Diamond St.; 16125; Mercer; P 18,000; (724) 588-1161; Fax (724) 588-9881; www.gaedc.org

Grove City · *79-80 Interstate Dev. Corp.* · Leann Smith; V.P.; 119 S. Broad St.; 16127; Mercer; P 16,000; M 53; (724) 458-6410; Fax (724) 458-6841; info@79-80idc.com; www.79-80idc.com

Harrisburg Area

Capital Region Eco. Dev. Corp. · David Black; Pres./CEO; 3211 N. Front St., Ste. 201; 17110; Dauphin; P 550,000; (717) 232-4099; Fax (717) 232-5184; www.harrisburgregionalchamber.org

Dauphin County Ofc. of Eco. Dev. · 112 Market, 7th Flr.; P.O. Box 1295; 17108; Dauphin; P 257,000; (717) 780-6250; Fax (717) 257-1513; drobinson@dauphinc.org; www.dauphincounty.org

Pennsylvania Dept. of Comm. & Eco. Dev. · George Cornelius; Secy.; 400 North St., 4th Flr.; 17120; Dauphin; (717) 787-3003; (866) 466-3972; Fax (717) 787-6866; readysetsucceed@newpa.com; www.newpa.com

Hazleton · *CAN DO Inc. [Ind. Dev. Corp.]* · 1 S. Church St., Ste. 200; 18201; Luzerne; P 25,000; (570) 455-1508; Fax (570) 454-7787; cando@hazletoncando.com; www.hazletoncando.com

Huntingdon · *Huntingdon County Bus. & Ind.* · Steve Sliver; Pres.; 419 14th St.; 16652; Huntingdon; P 45,000; M 200; (814) 643-4322; Fax (814) 506-1282; felicen@juniata.edu; www.hcbi.com

Indiana · *Indiana County Center for Eco. Op.* · Dana P. Henry; Pres.; 1019 Philadelphia St.; 15701; Indiana; P 90,000; (724) 465-2662; Fax (724) 465-3706; info@indpacoc.org; www.indianacountyceo.com

Jim Thorpe · *Carbon County Bur. of Eco. Dev.* · Dawn Ferrante; Dir.; P.O. Box 291; 18229; Carbon; P 59,000; (570) 325-2810; Fax (570) 325-8924; www.carbonecon.com

Johnstown · *Johnstown Ind. Dev. Corp.* · Linda Thomson; Pres.; 245 Market St., Ste. 200; 15901; Cambria; P 200,000; (814) 535-8675; Fax (814) 535-8677; www.jari.com

Kittanning · *Armstrong County Dept. of Eco. Dev.* · Michael P. Coonley; Exec. Dir.; Armsdale Admin. Bldg.; 124 Armsdale Rd, Ste 205; 16201; Armstrong; P 72,392; (724) 548-1500; idc@co.armstrong.pa.us; www.armstrongidc.org

Lancaster · *Eco. Dev. Co. of Lancaster County* · David Nikoloff; Pres.; 100 S. Queen St.; P.O. Box 1558; 17608; Lancaster; P 482,000; (717) 397-4046; Fax (717) 293-3159; edc@edclancaster.com; www.edclancaster.com

Lebanon · *Lebanon Valley Eco. Dev. Corp.* · Charles Blankenship; Pres.; 445 Schaeffer Rd.; P.O. Box 52; 17042; Lebanon; P 120,000; (717) 274-3180; Fax (717) 274-1367; cblankenship@lvedc.org; www.lvedc.org

Lewisburg · *Union County Ind. Dev. Corp.* · Michael Adams; Pres.; 155 N. 15th St.; 17837; Union; P 36,176; (570) 524-3852; Fax (570) 524-0261; madams@unionco.org; www.unioncoidc.org

Lewistown · *Mifflin County Ind. Dev. Corp.* · Robert P. Postal; Pres.; 6395 S.R. 103 N.; 17044; Mifflin; P 46,400; (717) 242-0393; Fax (717) 242-1842; www.mcidc.org

Lock Haven · *Clinton County Eco. Partnership* · Michael K. Flanagan; Pres./CEO; 212 N. Jay St.; P.O. Box 506; 17745; Clinton; P 37,000; M 385; (570) 748-5782; Fax (570) 893-0433; flanagan@kcnet.org; www.clintoncountyinfo.com

McKeesport · *McKeesport Ind. Dev.* · Dennis Pittman; Admin.; 502 5th Ave.; 15132; Allegheny; P 24,040; (412) 675-5020; Fax (412) 675-5049

Meadville · *Redev. Auth. of the City of Meadville* · Andy Walker; Exec. Dir.; 984 Water St.; 16335; Crawford; P 13,600; (814) 337-8200; Fax (814) 337-7257; www.redevelopmeadville.com

Media · *Delaware County Eco. Dev. Oversight Bd.* · J. Patrick Killian; Dir.; 200 E. State St., Ste. 205; 19063; Delaware; P 570,000; (610) 566-2225; Fax (610) 566-7337; www.delcopa.org

Mercer · *Penn-Northwest Dev. Corp.* · Larry D. Reichard; Exec. Dir.; 749 Greenville Rd.; 16137; Mercer; P 120,000; M 80; (724) 662-3705; Fax (724) 662-0283; lreichard@penn-northwest.com; www.penn-northwest.com

Milford · *Pike County Ind. Dev. Corp.* · 209 E. Harford St.; 18337; Pike; P 58,000; (570) 296-7332; Fax (570) 296-2852; vp@pidco.com; www.pidco.com

Natrona Heights · *see Brackenridge*

New Castle · *Lawrence County Eco. Dev. Corp.* · 100 E. Reynolds St., Ste. 100; 16101; Lawrence; P 95,000; (724) 658-1488; Fax (724) 658-0313; nitch@lawrencecounty.com; www.lawrencecounty.com

Norristown · *Montgomery County Dept. of Eco. & Workforce Dev.* · Jerry Birkelbach; Exec. Dir.; 1430 Dekalb St., 5th Flr.; P.O. Box 311; 19404; Montgomery; P 706,000; (610) 278-5950; Fax (610) 278-5944; www.montcopa.org

Northern Cambria · *Northern Cambria Comm. Dev. Corp.* · Matthew Barczak; Pres.; 4200 Crawford Ave., Ste. 200; 15714; Cambria; P 40,000; (814) 948-4444; Fax (814) 948-4449

Oil City · *NW Pennsylvania Reg. Planning & Dev. Comm.* · 395 Seneca St.; P.O. Box 1127; 16301; Venango; (814) 677-4800; Fax (814) 677-7663; www.nwcommission.org

Oil City · *Oil Region Alliance of Bus. & Ind.* · 217 Elm St.; 16301; Venango; P 56,000; (814) 677-3152; Fax (814) 677-5206; bsquire@oilregion.org; www.oilregion.org

Philadelphia · *Delaware Valley Reg. Planning Comm.* · Barry Seymour; Exec. Dir.; 190 N. Independence Mall West; 19106; Philadelphia; P 5,000,000; (215) 592-1800; Fax (215) 592-9125; www.dvrpc.org

Philadelphia · *Philadelphia Ind. Dev. Corp.* · 1500 Market St.; 2600 Centre Sq. W.; 19102; Philadelphia; P 1,700,000; (215) 496-8020; Fax (215) 977-9618; www.pidc-pa.org

Philipsburg · *Moshannon Valley Eco. Dev. Partnership* · Jeff Mitchell; Pres.; 200 Shady Ln.; 16866; Centre; P 34,000; M 170; (814) 342-2260; Fax (814) 342-2878; www.mvedp.org

Pittsburgh · *Allegheny County Dept. of Eco. Dev.* · Dennis Davin; Dir.; 425 Sixth Ave., Ste. 800; 15219; Allegheny; P 1,200,000; (412) 350-1000; Fax (412) 642-2217; www.county.allegheny.pa.us

Pittsburgh · *Reg. Ind. Dev. Corp. of Southwestern PA* · Donald F. Smith Jr.; Pres.; 425 6th Ave., Ste. 500; 15219; Allegheny; P 2,100,000; (412) 471-3939; Fax (412) 471-1740; dsmith@ridcswpa.com; www.ridc.org

Pittston · *Northeastern Pennsylvania Alliance* · Jeffrey Box; Pres./CEO; 1151 Oak St.; 18640; Luzerne; (570) 655-5581; Fax (570) 654-5137; www.nepa-alliance.org

Pottsville · *Schuylkill EDC* · Frank J. Zukas; Pres.; 91 S. Progress Ave.; 17901; Schuylkill; P 151,000; (570) 622-1943; Fax (570) 622-2903; www.sed-co.com

Quakertown · *Nockamixon-Bucks Ind. & Comm. Dev. Auth.* · Stephen Shelly; Solicitor; 525 W. Broad St.; 18951; Bucks; P 200,000; (215) 538-1400; Fax (215) 538-9033

Reading · *Greater Berks Dev. Fund* · Debra Millman; Dir. of Bus. Dev.; P.O. Box 8621; 19603; Berks; P 375,000; (610) 376-6739; Fax (610) 478-9553; greaterberks@readingpa.com; www.readingpa.com

Saint Mary's · *St. Mary's Area Eco. Dev. Corp.* · Raymond Klaiber Jr.; Exec. Dir.; 111 Erie Ave.; 15857; Elk; P 14,500; (814) 834-2125; Fax (814) 834-2126; stmarysedc@penn.com

Scranton · *Lackawanna County Ind. Dev. Auth.* · Mary Ellen Clark; Secy.; 200 Adams Ave., 5th Flr.; 18503; Lackawanna; P 212,455; (570) 963-6862; Fax (570) 342-4088

Shamokin · *Shamokin Area Ind. Corp.* · Edward Twiggar; Pres.; 415 E. Sunbury St.; 17872; Northumberland; P 25,000; (570) 648-1541; Fax (570) 988-4436

Shippensburg · *Shippensburg Area Dev. Corp.* · Brad Everly; Pres.; 53 W. King St.; 17257; Cumberland & Franklin; P 30,000; (717) 532-5509; Fax (717) 532-7501; www.shippensburg.org

Somerset · *Somerset County Eco. Dev. Cncl.* · Jeffrey Silka; Exec. Dir.; 125 N. Center Ave.; P.O. Box 48; 15501; Somerset; P 82,000; (814) 445-9655; Fax (814) 443-4610; contact@scedc.net; www.scedc.net

State College · *Chamber of Bus. & Ind. of Centre County* · John F. Coleman Jr.; Pres./CEO; 200 Innovation Blvd., Ste. 150; 16803; Centre; P 124,000; M 1,000; (814) 234-1829; Fax (814) 234-5869; cbicc@cbicc.org; www.cbicc.org

Sunbury · *Northumberland County Ind. Dev. Auth.* · James E. King; Exec. Dir.; 399 S. Fifth St.; 17801; Northumberland; P 100,000; M 150; (570) 988-4279; (570) 988-4100; Fax (570) 988-4436; jking@norrycopa.net; www.centralpachamber.com

Titusville · *Titusville Ind. Fund* · P.O. Box 425; 16354; Crawford; P 6,000; (814) 827-3668; Fax (814) 827-2696; www.tcda.org

Tobyhanna · *Pocono Mountains Eco. Dev.* · Chuck Leonard; Exec. Dir.; 300 Community Dr., Ste. D; 18466; Monroe; P 163,000; (570) 839-1992; (877) 736-7700; Fax (570) 839-6681; cleonard@pmedc.com; www.pmedc.com

Uniontown · *Fay-Penn Eco. Dev. Cncl.* · 2 W. Main St., Ste. 407; 15401; Fayette; P 148,644; (724) 437-7913; Fax (724) 437-7315; www.faypenn.org

Washington · *Redev. Auth. of the County of Washington* · William McGowen; Exec. Dir.; 100 W. Beau St.; 15301; Washington; P 209,000; (724) 228-6875; Fax (724) 228-6829; redevelopment@racw.net; www.racw.net

Waynesburg · *Greene County Ind. Dev. Auth.* · Ms. Robbie Matesic; Exec. Dir.; 49 S. Washington St.; 15370; Greene; P 40,000; (724) 852-5300; Fax (724) 852-2944; rmatesic@co.greene.pa.us; www.co.greene.pa.us

Wilkes-Barre Area

Greater Wilkes-Barre Chamber of Bus. & Ind. · Todd Vonderheid; Pres./CEO; Two Public Square; P.O. Box 5340; 18710; Luzerne; P 353,000; (570) 823-2101; Fax (570) 822-5951; wbcofc@wilkes-barre.org; www.wilkes-barre.org

Greater Wilkes-Barre Dev. Corp. · Todd Vonderheid; Pres./CEO; Two Public Square; P.O. Box 5340; 18710; Luzerne; P 353,000; (570) 823-2101; Fax (570) 822-5951; wbcofc@wilkes-barre.org; www.wilkes-barre.org

Luzerne County Ofc. of Comm. Dev. · Andrew Reilly; Dir.; 54 W. Union St.; 18702; Luzerne; P 328,000; (570) 824-7214; Fax (570) 829-2910; www.luzernecounty.org

York · *York County Eco. Dev. Corp.* · Darrell Auterson; Pres.; 144 Roosevelt Ave., Ste. 100; 17401; York; P 416,322; (717) 846-8879; Fax (717) 843-8837; ycedc@ycedc.org; www.ycedc.org

Puerto Rico

Communities

Hato Rey · *Puerto Rico Ind. Dev. Co.* · Javier Morales; Exec. Dir.; #355 FD Roosevelt Ave., Ste. 404; 00918; P 3,920,000; (787) 758-4747; Fax (787) 764-1415; www.pridco.com

Rhode Island

Federal

U.S. SBA, Rhode Island Dist. Ofc. · Mark S. Hayward; Dist. Dir.; 380 Westminster St., Rm. 511; Providence; 02903; Providence; (401) 528-4561; Fax (401) 528-4539; normand.deragon@sba.gov; www.sba.gov/ri

State

Rhode Island Eco. Dev. Corp. · Keith Stokes; Exec. Dir.; 315 Iron Horse Way, Ste. 101; Providence; 02908; Providence; (401) 278-9100; Fax (401) 273-8270; info@riedc.com; www.riedc.com

Communities

Bristol · *Bristol Eco. Dev. Comm.* · Diane Williamson; Dir. of Comm. Dev.; 10 Court St.; 02809; Bristol; P 24,000; (401) 253-7000; Fax (401) 253-1570; www.onlinebristol.com

Cranston · *City of Cranston-Dept. of Eco. Dev.* · Lawrence DiBoni; Dir.; City Hall; 869 Park Ave.; 02910; Providence; P 81,000; (401) 780-3166; Fax (401) 780-3179; www.cranstonri.com

Cumberland · *Eco. Dev. Found. of Rhode Island* · Scott A. Gibbs; Pres.; 1300 Highland Corp. Dr., Ste. 202; 02864; Providence; P 250,000; (401) 658-1050; Fax (401) 658-1064; sgibbs@edf-ri.com; www.edf-ri.com

Cumberland · *New England Eco. Dev. Svcs. Inc.* · Scott A. Gibbs; Pres.; 1300 Highland Corp. Dr., Ste. 202; 02864; Providence; P 250,000; (401) 658-0665; Fax (401) 658-0630; sgibbs@needsinc.com; www.needsinc.com

East Providence · *East Providence Eco. Dev. Comm.* · Jeanne Boyle; Dir. of Planning; 145 Taunton Ave.; City Hall; 02914; Providence; P 48,600; (401) 435-7500; Fax (401) 435-7611; www.eastprovidenceri.net

Lincoln · *Lincoln Town Planning Dept.* · T. Joseph Almond; Town Admin.; 100 Old River Rd.; P.O. Box 100; 02865; Providence; P 21,000; (401) 333-1100; Fax (401) 333-3648; www.lincolnri.org

Pawtucket · *Dept. of Planning & Redev.–City of Pawtucket* · Michael D. Cassidy; Dir.; 175 Main St., 3rd Flr.; 02860; Providence; P 72,958; (401) 724-5200; Fax (401) 726-6237; www.pawtucket ri.com

Warwick · *Warwick Eco. Dev. Dept.* · Warwick City Hall; 3275 Post Rd.; 02886; Kent; P 86,000; (401) 738-2000; Fax (401) 738-6639; econ.dir@warwickri.com; www.movetowarwickri.com

West Warwick · *West Warwick Planning Bd.* · Fred Presley; Town Planner; 1170 Main St.; 02893; Kent; P 30,000; (401) 827-9026; Fax (401) 822-9252; fpresley@westwarwickri.org; www.westwarwickri.org

Westerly · *Westerly Town* · Marilyn Shellman; Town Planner; 45 Broad St.; 02891; Washington; P 22,695; (401) 348-2549; Fax (401) 348-2513; www.westerly.govoffice.com

South Carolina

State

South Carolina Dept. of Commerce · Joe Taylor Jr.; Secy. of Commerce; 1201 Main St., Ste.1600; Columbia; 29201; Richland; (803) 737-0400; Fax (803) 737-0418; info@sc commerce.com; www.sccommerce.com

Communities

Abbeville · *Abbeville County Dev. Bd.* · Steve Bowles; Dev. Svcs. Dir.; P.O. Box 533; 29620; Abbeville; P 26,000; (864) 366-2181; Fax (864) 366-9266; acdb@wctel.net; www.discoverabbeville.com

Aiken · *Eco. Dev. Partnership* · Fred Humes; Dir.; P.O. Box 1708; 29802; Aiken; P 170,000; (803) 641-3300; Fax (803) 641-3369; fhumes@edpsc.org; www.edpsc.org

Allendale · *Allendale County Dev. Bd.* · Sue Myrick; Cncl. Clerk; P.O. Box 190; 29810; Allendale; P 11,200; (803) 584-4611; Fax (803) 584-7042; www.allendalecounty.com

Anderson · *Anderson County Eco. Dev.* · Heather Jones; Dir.; 126 N. McDuffie St.; 29621; Anderson; P 187,000; (864) 260-4386; Fax (864) 260-4369; hjones@andersoncountysc.org; www.advance2anderson.com

Bamberg · *Bamberg County Dev. Bd.* · Booker Patrick; Finance Dir.; P.O. Box 149; 29003; Bamberg; P 16,991; (803) 245-5191; Fax (803) 245-3027; www.bambergcountydevelopmentboard.com

Barnwell · *Barnwell County Eco. Dev. Comm.* · Marshall Martin; Exec. Dir.; P.O. Box 898; 29812; Barnwell; P 25,000; (803) 259-1263; Fax (803) 259-0030; bcedc1@bellsouth.net; www.discoverbarnwellcounty.com

Beaufort · *Lowcountry Eco. Network* · Kim Statler; Exec. Dir.; 917 Bay St., Ste. 207; 29902; Beaufort; P 120,937; (843) 379-3955; Fax (843) 379-3954; www.lowcountrynet.org

Bennettsville · *Marlboro County Eco. Dev. Partnership* · Butch Mills; Exec. Dir.; 214 E. Market St.; 29512; Marlboro; P 28,813; (843) 479-5626; Fax (843) 479-2663; butchmills@ marlborocountysc.org; www.marlborocountysc.org

Bishopville · *Lee County Eco. Dev. Alliance* · Jeff Burgess; Exec. Dir.; 102 E. Council St.; P.O. Box 481; 29010; Lee; P 20,090; (803) 484-9832; Fax (803) 484-4373; info@leecountysc.com; www.leecountysc.com

Camden · *Kershaw County Eco. Dev. Bd.* · Nelson Lindsey; Exec. Dir.; 700 W. Dekalb St.; P.O. Box 763; 29020; Kershaw; P 52,647; (803) 425-7685; Fax (803) 425-7687; econ.develop@kershaw.sc.gov; www.kershawcountysc.org

Cheraw · *see Chesterfield*

Chesterfield · *Chesterfield County Eco. Dev. Bd.* · Cherry McCoy; Exec. Dir.; P.O. Box 192; 29709; Chesterfield; P 43,000; (843) 623-6500; Fax (843) 623-3167; cherryatcc@shtc.net; www.chesterfieldcountysc.org

Columbia · *Central SC Alliance* · G. Michael Briggs; Pres./CEO; 1201 Main St., Ste. 100; 29201; Richland; P 986,276; (803) 733-1131; (866) 278-9098; Fax (803) 733-1125; info@centralsc.org; www.centralsc.org

Columbia · *Palmetto Eco. Dev. Corp.* · Ralph U. Thomas; Pres.; 1201 Main St., Ste. 1710; 29201; Richland; P 800,000; (803) 254-9211; Fax (803) 771-0233; mail@scpowerteam.com; www.scpowerteam.com

Conway · *Myrtle Beach Reg. Eco. Dev. Corp.* · Hugh Owens; Pres./CEO; 2431 Hwy. 501 E.; 29526; Horry; P 175,000; M 100; (843) 347-4604; Fax (843) 347-2292; info@myrtlebeachdevelop ment.com; www.myrtlebeachdevelopment.com

Dillon · *Dillon County Dev. Bd.* · Dave Bailey; Exec. Dir.; P.O. Drawer 911; 29536; Dillon; P 32,000; (843) 774-1402; Fax (843) 841-3872; dilloncountydb@bellsouth.net; www.dilloncounty.org

Fort Mill · *York County Eco. Dev. Bd.* · Mark Farris; Dir.; 1830 Second Baxter Crossing; 29708; York; P 190,097; (803) 802-4300; Fax (803) 802-4299; mark.farris@yorkcountygov.com; www.ycedb.com

Fountain Inn · *Fountain Inn Eco. Dev.* · Van Broad; Eco. Dev. Dir.; 315 N. Main; 29644; Laurens; P 6,000; (864) 409-1050; van.broad@fountaininn.org; www.fountaininn.org

Gaffney · *Cherokee County Eco. Dev. Bd.* · Jim Cook III; Exec. Dir.; 101 Campus Dr.; 29341; Cherokee; P 53,000; (864) 206-2804; Fax (864) 206-2801; cookj@sccsc.edu; www.cherokeecounty-sc.org

Georgetown · *Georgetown County Eco. Dev.* · Wayne Gregory; Dir. of Eco. Dev.; 716 Prince St.; 29440; Georgetown; P 60,000; (843) 545-3161; Fax (843) 545-3259; info@seegeorgetown.com; www.seegeorgetown.com

Greenwood · *Greenwood Partnership Alliance* · Mark H. Warner; CEO; 109 Court Ave. W.; 29646; Greenwood; P 67,000; (864) 388-1250; Fax (864) 388-1253; mwarner@partnership alliance.com; www.partnershipalliance.com

Hampton · *Hampton County Eco. Dev. Comm.* · Sandy Fowler; Exec. Dir.; P.O. Box 672; 29924; Hampton; P 21,386; (803) 943-7521; Fax (803) 943-7538; www.hamptoncountyedc.com

Kingstree · *Williamsburg County Dev. Bd.* · Frank Hilton McGill Jr.; Exec. Dir.; P.O. Box 1132; 29556; Williamsburg; P 37,217; (843) 382-9393; Fax (843) 382-5353; hmcgill@ftc-i.net; www.williamsburgcountydevelopment.com

Lancaster · *Lancaster County Eco. Dev. Corp.* · Allen Keith Tunnell; Pres.; 210 W. Gay St.; P.O. Box 973; 29721; Lancaster; P 67,000; (803) 285-9471; Fax (803) 285-9472; keith.tunnell@ lancastersc-edc.com; www.lancasterscworks.com

Manning · *Clarendon County Dev. Bd.* · John Truluck; Exec. Dir.; P.O. Box 670; 29102; Clarendon; P 32,000; (803) 435-8813; (800) 729-0973; Fax (803) 435-4925; jtruluck@sc.rr.com; www.clarendoncountyusa.com

Marion · *Marion County Eco. Dev. Comm.* · Rodney Berry; Exec. Dir.; P.O. Box 840; 29571; Marion; P 35,000; (843) 423-8235; Fax (843) 423-8233; rberry@marionsc.org; www.marioncountysc.com

McCall · *see Bennettsville*

McCormick · *McCormick County Dev. Bd.* · George Woodsby; Eco. Dev. Dir.; 362 Airport Rd.; 29835; McCormick; P 10,000; (864) 852-2231; Fax (864) 852-2783; mccormickco@wctel.net; www.mccormickcountysc.gov

Moncks Corner · *Berkeley County Eco. Dev. Dept.* · Gene Butler; Eco. Dev. Dir.; P.O. Box 6122; 29461; Berkeley; P 160,000; (843) 719-4096; Fax (843) 719-4381; gbutler@co.berkeley.sc.us; www.berkeleycountysc.gov

North Charleston · *Charleston Reg. Dev. Alliance* · David Ginn; Pres./CEO; Trident Research Center; 5300 International Blvd., Ste. 103-A; 29418; Charleston; P 550,000; (843) 767-9300; Fax (843) 760-4535; alliance@crda.org; www.crda.org

Orangeburg · *Orangeburg County Dev. Comm.* · C. Gregory Robinson; Exec. Dir.; P.O. Box 1303; 29116; Orangeburg; P 91,582; (803) 536-3333; Fax (803) 534-1165; grobinson@ocdc.com; www.ocdc.com

Pageland · *see Chesterfield*

Pickens · *Eco. Dev. Alliance-Pickens County* · A. Ray Farley II CEcD; Exec. Dir.; P.O. Box 279; 29671; Pickens; P 110,757; (864) 898-1500; Fax (864) 898-1550; rfarley@alliancepickens.com; www.alliancepickens.com

Rock Hill · *Rock Hill Eco. Dev. Corp.* · Rick Norwood; Mktg. Mgr.; 155 Johnston St.; P.O. Box 11706; 29731; York; P 61,200; (803) 329-7090; Fax (803) 329-7007; rnorwood@ci.rock-hill.sc.us; www.rockhillusa.com

Saint Matthews · *Calhoun County Dev. Comm.* · Courthouse Annex, Rm. 114; 29135; Calhoun; P 15,185; (803) 655-5650; Fax (803) 655-6110; calhounchamber@sc.rr.com; www.calhouncountychamber.org

Spartanburg · *Spartanburg Dev. Assn.* · 1004 S. Pine St.; 29302; Spartanburg; P 250,000; (864) 585-1007; Fax (864) 573-6534; info@thesda.org; www.thesda.org

Summerville · *Dorchester County Eco. Dev. Dept.* · Jon Baggett; Dir.; 402 N. Main St., Ste. C; 29483; Dorchester; P 119,000; (843) 875-9109; Fax (843) 821-9994; info@dorchesterforbusiness.com; www.dorchesterforbusiness.com

Sumter · *Sumter Dev. Bd.* · Jay Schwedler; Pres.; 32 E. Calhoun St.; 29150; Sumter; P 112,000; (803) 418-0700; Fax (803) 775-0915; www.sumteredge.com

Union · *Union County Dev. Bd.* · Andrena Powell-Baker; Dir.; 207 S. Herndon St.; 29379; Union; P 30,000; (864) 319-1097; Fax (864) 319-1099; www.unioncountydevelopment.com

Walhalla · *Oconee County Eco. Dev. Comm.* · Jim Alexander; Dir.; 502 E. Main St.; 29691; Oconee; P 70,840; (864) 638-4210; jalexander@oconeesc.com; www.oconeescedc.com

South Dakota

Federal

U.S. SBA, South Dakota Dist. Ofc. · John L. Brown II; Dist. Dir.; 2329 N. Career Ave., Ste. 105; Sioux Falls; 57107; Minnehaha; (605) 330-4243; Fax (605) 330-4215; michele.arends@sba.gov; www.sba.gov/sd

State

Dept. of Tourism & State Dev. · Richard Benda; Cabinet Secy.; 711 E. Wells Ave.; Pierre; 57501; Hughes; (605) 773-3301; (800) 872-6190; Fax (605) 773-3256; mary.leheckanelson@state.sd.us; www.tsd.sd.gov

Communities

Aberdeen · *Aberdeen Dev. Corp.* · James C. Barringer; Exec. V.P.; 416 Production St. N.; 57401; Brown; P 25,000; (605) 229-5335; Fax (605) 229-6839; jimbarringer@midco.net; www.adcsd.com

Aberdeen · *NE Cncl. of Govt.* · Eric Senger; Exec. Dir.; 2201 6th Ave. S.E.; P.O. Box 1985; 57402; Brown; (605) 626-2595; Fax (605) 626-2975

Belle Fourche · *Belle Fourche Dev. Corp.* · Teresa Schanzenbach; Exec. Dir.; 415 5th Ave.; 57717; Butte; P 5,000; M 50; (605) 892-2676; (888) 345-5859; Fax (605) 892-4633; director@bellefourchechamber.org; www.bellefourchechamber.org

Beresford · *Beresford Ind. Dev.* · Jerry Zeimetz; City Mgr.; 101 N. 3rd; 57004; Lincoln & Union; P 2,100; (605) 763-2008

Brandon · *Brandon Dev. Found. Inc.* · Joel Jorgenson; Dir.; 304 Main Ave.; P.O. Box 95; 57005; Minnehaha; P 7,000; (605) 582-6515; Fax (605) 582-6831; www.brandonsd.com

Britton · *Britton Dev. Corp.* · Tom Farber; Pres.; P.O. Box 413; 57430; Marshall; P 4,000; (605) 448-5150; Fax (605) 448-2810; www.brittonchamber.com

Centerville · *Centerville Dev. Corp.* · Bill Hansen; Eco. Dev. Coord.; 2201 State St.; 57014; Turner; P 1,000; (605) 563-2019; www.centervillesd.org

Chamberlain · *Lake Francis Case Dev.* · April Reis; Exec. Dir.; 115 W. Lawler Ave.; 57325; Brule; P 2,432; (605) 234-4419; Fax (605) 234-4418; lfcdc@midstatesd.net; www.dakotadevelopment.com

Dakota Dunes · *Dakota Dunes Dev. Co.* · Dennis Melstad; Pres.; 335 Sioux Point Rd., Ste. 100; 57049; Union; P 2,627; (605) 232-5990; Fax (605) 232-5925; www.dakotadunes.com

Dell Rapids · *Dell Rapids Dev. Corp.* · Lee Burggraff; Pres.; 503 W. 4th; 57022; Minnehaha; P 3,200; (605) 428-3909; www.dellrapids.net

Estelline · *Estelline Area Eco. Dev. Corp.* · Ed Ebbers; Secy.; P.O. Box 278; 57234; Hamlin; P 700; M 130; (605) 873-2241

Faith · *Faith Country Dev. Corp.* · Randy Thomas; Pres.; P.O. Box 341; 57626; Meade; P 500; (605) 967-2242; (605) 967-2001

Gregory · *Gregory Bus. & Ind. Dev.* · Ron Kyburz; Pres.; %City of Gregory; P.O. Box 436; 57533; Gregory; P 1,350; (605) 835-8270; www.cityofgregory.com

Hayti · *Hamlin County Ind. Dev. Comm.* · Dick Wagner; Chrmn.; P.O. Box 237; 57241; Hamlin; P 5,540; (605) 783-3201; Fax (605) 783-3201

Herreid · *Herreid Eco. Dev. Corp.* · Dean Schwartz; Pres.; 110 S. Main; P.O. Box 275; 57632; Campbell; P 500; (605) 437-2294; Fax (605) 437-2278; www.herreidsd.com

Hosmer · *Eco. Dev. Comm.* · John Eisenberisz; Treas.; 33920 127th St.; 57448; Edmunds; P 350; (605) 283-2639;

Howard · *Howard Industries* · Dave Callies; Secy.; P.O. Box 187; 57349; Miner; P 900; (605) 772-4561; Fax (605) 772-5492; www.howardsd.com

Huron · *Greater Huron Dev. Corp.* · Jim Borszich; Exec. Dir.; 1705 Dakota Ave. S.; 57350; Beadle; P 11,987; M 210; (605) 352-0363; (800) 487-6673; Fax (605) 352-8321; ghdc@huronsd.com; www.huronsd.com

Lennox • *Lennox Area Dev. Corp.* • Alan Rops; Pres.; P.O. Box 157; 57039; Lincoln; P 2,700; (605) 647-2286; (605) 647-2603; Fax (605) 647-2281; www.cityoflennox.com

McLaughlin • *McLaughlin Eco. Dev.* • Arnold Schott; Mayor; P.O. Box 169; 57642; Corson; P 775; (605) 823-4428; Fax (605) 823-4429

Mitchell • *Mitchell Area Dev. Corp.* • Bryan Hisel; Exec. Dir.; 601 N. Main; P.O. Box 1087; 57301; Davison; P 18,741; M 210; (605) 996-1140; Fax (605) 996-8273; bhiselmadc@santel.net; www. mitchellsd.org

Pierre • *Pierre Eco. Dev. Corp.* • Jim Protexter; Exec. Dir.; 800 W. Dakota; P.O. Box 548; 57501; Hughes; P 14,000; (605) 224-6610; (800) 962-2034; Fax (605) 224-6485; www.pedco.biz

Rapid City • *Rapid City Area Eco. Dev. Partnership* • 525 University Loop, Ste. 101; 57701; Pennington; P 119,000; (605) 343-1880; Fax (605) 343-1916; info@rapiddevelopment.com; www.rapiddevelopment.com

Redfield • *Redfield Dev. Corp.* • Corwy Baloun; Pres.; 626 Main; 57469; Spink; P 2,800; (605) 472-4551; Fax (605) 472-4553; www. redfield-sd.com

Scotland • *Scot-Del Inc.* • Dick Behl; Treas.; 550 Main; 57059; Bon Homme; P 1,000; (605) 583-2234; Fax (605) 583-4205;

Sioux Falls • *Sioux Falls Dev. Found.* • Slater R. Barr; Pres.; 200 N. Phillips Ave., Ste. 101; P.O. Box 907; 57101; Minnehaha; P 217,500; M 360; (605) 339-0103; Fax (605) 339-0055; slater@ siouxfalls.com; www.siouxfallsdevelopment.com

Spearfish • *Spearfish Eco. Dev. Corp.* • Bryan Walker; Eco. Dev. Dir.; 106 W. Kansas; P.O. Box 550; 57783; Lawrence; P 13,000; (605) 642-3832; spearfishdevelopment@rushmore.com; www. spearfishdevelopment.com

Sturgis • *Black Hills Comm. Eco. Dev. Inc.* • Jim Doolittle; Exec. Dir.; 2885 Dickson Dr.; P.O. Box 218; 57785; Meade; P 100,000; (605) 347-5837; Fax (605) 347-5223

Sturgis • *Sturgis Eco. Dev. Corp.* • Nort Johnson; Pres.; 2885 Dickson Dr.; P.O. Box 218; 57785; Meade; P 6,500; (605) 347-4906; Fax (605) 347-5223

Tripp • *Tripp Dev. Corp.* • Bob Just; Bd. Member; P.O. Box 105; 57376; Hutchinson; P 750; (605) 935-6661

Tyndall • *Tyndall Dev. Co.* • Ron Wagner; Pres.; P.O. Box 454; 57066; Bon Homme; P 1,239; (888) 877-5035; Fax (605) 589-4109

Wakonda • *Wakonda Dev. Corp.* • Ron Peterson; Treas.; 29714 455th Ave.; 57073; Clay; P 400; (605) 263-3526

Watertown • *Focus Watertown* • Craig Atkins; Pres.; P.O. Box 332; 57201; Codington; P 21,000; (605) 884-0340; (888) 898-6767; Fax (605) 882-0199; info@focuswatertown.com; www.focuswatertown.com

Webster • *Webster Area Dev. Corp.* • Jeff Grobe; Eco. Dev. Coord.; P.O. Box 6; 57274; Day; P 1,950; (605) 345-3159; (605) 345-3639; Fax (605) 345-3509; www.webstersd.com

Wessington Springs • *Wessington Springs Area Dev. Corp.* • Laura Kieser; Coord.; 101 Wallace Ave. S.; P.O. Box 132; 57382; Jerauld; P 1,011; M 100; (605) 539-1929; Fax (605) 539-0249; wsprings@venturecomm.net; www.wessingtonsprings.com

Wilmot • *Wilmot Comm. Dev. Corp.* • Jeffrey Jurgens; Pres.; P.O. Box 160; 57279; Roberts; P 550; (605) 938-4661

Winner • *South Central Dev. Corp.* • Brad Schramm; Exec. Dir.; 201 Monroe; P.O. Box 624; 57580; Tripp; P 3,400; (605) 842-1551; develop@winnersd.org; www.winnersd.org

Yankton • *Yankton Ofc. of Eco. Dev.* • Mike Dellinger; Exec. Dir.; 803 E. Fourth St.; P.O. Box 588; 57078; Yankton; P 14,000; (888) 926-5866; Fax (605) 665-7501; ecodev@yanktonsd.com; www. yanktonedc.com

Tennessee

Federal

U.S. SBA, Tennessee Dist. Ofc. • Walter N. Perry III; Dist. Dir.; 50 Vantage Way, Ste. 201; Nashville; 37228; Davidson; (615) 736-5881; Fax (615) 736-7232; walter.perry@sba.gov; www. sba.gov/tn

State

Tennessee Eco. Dev. Dept. • Matt Kisber; Comm.; 312 Rosa L. Parks Ave., 11th Flr.; Nashville; 37243; Davidson; (615) 741-3282; Fax (615) 741-5829; matt.kisber@tn.gov; www.state. tn.us/ecd

Communities

Athens • *McMinn County Eco. Dev. Auth.* • Jack Hammontree; Exec. V.P.; P.O. Box 767; 37371; McMinn; P 50,270; M 110; (423) 745-1506; Fax (423) 745-1507; jack@mcminncoeda.org; www. mcminncoeda.org

Chattanooga • *Chattanooga Area C/C-Eco. Dev. Dept.* • Trevor Hamilton; V.P. Eco. Dev.; 811 Broad St., Ste. 100; 37402; Hamilton; P 492,047; (423) 756-2121; Fax (423) 267-7242; info@chattanooga chamber.com; www.chattanoogachamber.com

Columbia • *Maury County C/C & Eco. Dev. Alliance* • Brandom Gengelbach; Pres.; 106 W. 6th St.; P.O. Box 1076; 38402; Maury; P 80,000; (931) 388-2155; Fax (931) 380-0335; ewest@ mauryalliance.com; www.mauryalliance.com

Dayton • *Rhea Eco. & Tourism Cncl.* • Raymond Walker; Exec. Dir.; 107 Main St.; 37321; Rhea; P 29,400; (423) 775-6171; Fax (423) 570-0105; director@rheacountyetc.com; www.rhea countyetc.com

Gallatin • *City of Gallatin Eco. Dev. Agency* • Clay Walker; Exec. Dir.; 132 W. Main St.; P.O. Box 773; 37066; Sumner; P 25,000; (615) 451-5940; clay.walker@gallatin-tn.gov; www.gallatin tn-eda.com

Hendersonville • *Eco/Community Dev. Comm. of City of Hendersonville* • Don Long; Dir.; 101 Maple Dr. N.; 37075; Sumner; P 42,000; (615) 264-5329; (615) 822-1000; Fax (615) 264-5327; www.gohendersonvilletn.com

Jackson • *West Tennessee Ind. Assn.* • Michael M. Philpot; Exec. Dir.; 26 Conrad Dr.; 38305; Madison; (731) 668-4300; (800) 336-2036; Fax (731) 668-7554; westtn@wtia.org; www.wtia.org

Jasper • *Marion County Partnership for Eco. Dev.* • Howell Moss; Chrmn.; 302 Betsy Pack Dr.; 37347; Marion; P 27,776; (423) 942-5103; Fax (423) 942-0098; marioncoc@bellsouth.net; www. marioncountychamber.com

Johnson City • *Johnson City/Jonesborough/Washington County EDB* • P.C. Snapp; Exec. Dir.; 603 E. Market St., Ste. 200; 37601; Washington; P 110,000; (423) 975-2380; Fax (423) 975-2385; pcsnapp@jcedb.org; www.jcedb.org

La Vergne • *see Murfreesboro*

Lebanon • *Wilson County Joint Eco. & Comm. Dev. Bd.* • G.C. Hixson; Exec. Dir.; 115 Castle Heights Ave. N., Ste. 102; 37087; Wilson; P 104,000; (615) 443-1210; Fax (615) 443-0277; info@ doingbiz.org; www.doingbiz.org

Lewisburg · *Lewisburg Ind. Dev. Bd.* · Terry Wallace; Dir.; P.O. Box 1968; 37091; Marshall; P 10,422; (931) 359-1544; Fax (931) 359-7055; twallace@ctyoflew.com; www.lewisburgtn.com

Loudon · *Loudon County Eco. Dev. Agency* · Doyle Arp; Chrmn.; 274 Blair Bend Dr.; 37774; Loudon; P 37,086; (865) 458-8889; Fax (865) 458-3792; lceda@loudoncountyeda.org; www.loudon countyeda.org

Manchester · *Ind. Bd. of Coffee County* · Ted Hackney; Exec. Dir.; 1329 McArthur, Ste. 4; 37355; Coffee; P 50,869; (931) 723-5120; Fax (931) 723-5121; ib@coffeetn.com; www.coffee tn.com

Maryville · *Eco. Dev. Bd. of Blount County/Alcoa & Maryville* · Bryan Daniels CEcD CCE IOM; Pres./CEO; 201 S. Washington St.; 37804; Blount; P 120,000; (865) 983-7715; Fax (865) 984-1386; info@blountindustry.com; www.blountindustry.com

Memphis · *Mid-South Minority Bus. Cncl.* · Luke Yancy III; Pres./CEO; 158 Madison Ave., Ste. 300; 38103; Shelby; P ; M 500; (901) 525-6512; Fax (901) 525-5204; lyancy@mmbc-memphis.org; www.mmbc-memphis.org

Mount Juliet · *see Lebanon*

Murfreesboro · *Rutherford County C/C* · Holly S. Weber; V.P. of Eco. Dev.; 501 Memorial Blvd.; P.O. Box 864; 37133; Rutherford; P 223,000; (615) 869-0345; Fax (615) 278-2013; info@rutherford chamber.org; www.rutherfordchamber.org

Newport · *Newport/Cocke County Eco. Dev. Comm.* · Eddie Lennon; Exec. Dir.; 433 Prospect Ave.; 37821; Cocke; P 33,565; (423) 623-3008; Fax (423) 625-1846; donhurst@bellsouth.net; www.edcncc.com

Pigeon Forge · *Pigeon Forge Comm. Dev.* · David Taylor; Dir.; 225 Pine Mountain Rd.; P.O. Box 1350; 37868; Sevier; P 5,913; M 704; (865) 429-7474; Fax (865) 429-7322; dtaylor@cityof pigeonforge.com; www.cityofpigeonforge.com

Pulaski · *Pulaski-Giles County Eco. Dev. Comm.* · Dan Speer; Exec. Dir.; 203 S. First St.; 38478; Giles; P 29,269; (931) 363-9138; Fax (931) 424-4460; dan@gilescountyedc.com; www.gilescounty edc.com

Savannah · *Savannah Ind. Dev. Corp.* · Steve Bunnell; CEO; 495 Main St.; 38372; Hardin; P 27,000; (731) 925-8181; Fax (731) 925-6987; info@tourhardincounty.org; www.tourhardincounty.org

Sevierville · *Sevier County Eco. Dev. Cncl.* · Allen Newton; Exec. Dir.; P.O. Box 4066; 37864; Sevier; P 81,000; (865) 428-2212; Fax (865) 453-2312; www.scedc.com

Smyrna · *see Murfreesboro*

Union City · *Obion County Joint EDC* · Jim Cooper; Dir.; 214 E. Church St.; 38261; Obion; P 31,000; (731) 885-0211; Fax (731) 885-7155; jcooper@obioncounty.org; www.obioncounty.org

Vonore · *Tellico Reservoir Dev. Agency* · Ron Hammontree; Exec. Dir.; 59 Excellence Way.; 37885; Monroe; P 15,000; (865) 673-8599; (800) 562-8732; Fax (423) 884-6869; trda@tds.net; www.tellico.com

Watertown · *see Lebanon*

Waverly · *Humphreys County Eco. Dev. Cncl.* · John Hedge; Exec. Dir.; 301 N. Church St.; P.O. Box 218; 37185; Humphreys; P 18,000; (931) 296-5199; Fax (931) 296-2135; humpco_edc@ waverly.net

Texas

Federal

U.S. SBA, Dallas/Fort Worth Dist. Ofc. · Herbert Austin; Dist. Dir.; 4300 Amon Carter Blvd., Ste. 114; Fort Worth; 76155; Tarrant; (817) 684-5500; Fax (817) 684-5516; arlene.brown@ sba.gov; www.sba.gov/tx

U.S. SBA, El Paso Dist. Ofc. · Phillip Silva; Dist. Dir.; 211 N. Florence, Ste. 201; El Paso; 79901; El Paso; (915) 834-4600; Fax (915) 834-4689; anna.rivera@sba.gov; www.sba.gov/tx

U.S. SBA, Houston Dist. Ofc. · Manuel Gonzalez; Dist. Dir.; 8701 S. Gessner Dr., Ste. 1200; Houston; 77074; Harris; (713) 773-6500; Fax (713) 773-6550; myung.moss@sba.gov; www. sba.gov/tx

U.S. SBA, Lower Rio Grande Valley Dist. Ofc. · Sylvia Zamponi; Dist. Dir.; 222 E. Van Buren Ave., Ste. 500; Harlingen; 78550; Cameron; (956) 427-8533; Fax (956) 427-8537; graciela. guillen@sba.gov; www.sba.gov/tx

US SBA, Lubbock Dist. Ofc. · Edward J. Cadena; Interim Dist. Dir.; 1205 Texas Ave., Rm. 408; Lubbock; 79401; Lubbock; (806) 472-7462; Fax (806) 472-7487; josie.salinas@sba.gov; www. sba.gov/tx

U.S. SBA, San Antonio Dist. Ofc. · Pamela Sapia; Dist. Dir.; 17319 San Pedro Ave., Ste. 200; San Antonio; 78232; Bexar, Comal & Medina; (210) 403-5900; Fax (210) 403-5936; linda. olinick@sba.gov; www.sba.gov/tx

Communities

Abilene · *Abilene Ind. Found.* · Bill Ehrie; Pres.; 174 Cypress St., Ste. 300; P.O. Box 2281; 79604; Taylor; P 125,000; (325) 673-7349; Fax (325) 673-9193; www.developabilene.com

Alice · *Alice-Jim Wells County EDC* · Dean Kruckenberg; Dir.; 612 E. Main St.; P.O. Box 1609; 78333; Jim Wells; P 40,017; (361) 664-3454; Fax (361) 664-2291; deank@alicetx.org; www.alicetx.org

Angleton · *Eco. Dev. Alliance for Brazoria County* · Robert M. Worley; Pres./CEO; 4005 Technology Dr., Ste. 1010; 77515; Brazoria; P 320,000; M 120; (800) 759-1822; Fax (979) 848-0403; robertw@eda-bc.com; www.eda-bc.com.

Aransas County · *see Corpus Christi*

Bay City · *Matagorda County Eco. Dev. Corp.* · Owen Bludau; Exec. Dir.; 2200 7th St., Ste. 304; 77414; Matagorda; P 39,000; (979) 245-8913; Fax (979) 245-5661; obludau@co.matagorda. tx.us; www.mcedc.net

Baytown · *Baytown West Chambers County Eco. Dev. Found.* · Michael Shields; Exec. Dir.; 1300 Rollingbrook, Ste. 401; 77521; Harris; P 72,000; (281) 420-2961; Fax (281) 422-7682; baytownedf@bwccedf.com; www.bwccedf.com

Bedford · *Hurst-Euless-Bedford Eco. Dev. Found.* · Mary Martin Frazior; Dir.; 2109 Martin Dr.; P.O. Drawer 969; 76095; Tarrant; P 136,000; (817) 540-1053; Fax (817) 267-5111; chamber@heb.org; www.heb.org

Bee County · *see Corpus Christi*

Bellville · *Bellville EDC* · Mr. Monte Byrd; Pres.; P.O. Box 670; 77418; Austin; P 4,000; (979) 865-3136; Fax (979) 865-9760; bedc@sbcglobal.net; www.bellville.com

Belton · *Belton Eco. Dev. Corp.* · Tommy Baker; Exec. Dir.; P.O. Box 1388; 76513; Bell; P 20,000; (254) 770-2270; Fax (254) 770-2279; www.beltonedc.org

Belton · *Dev. Dist. of Central Texas* · Beth Correa; Reg. Planner; P.O. Box 729; 76513; Bell; (254) 770-2200; Fax (254) 770-2360; ddoctinfo@ddoct.org; www.ddoct.org

Brady · *McCulloch County Ind. Found.* · Mark Magee; Pres.; 101 E. 1st St.; 76825; McCulloch; P 8,000; (325) 597-3491; Fax (325) 792-9181; www.bradytx.com

Brazoria County · *see Angleton*

Breckenridge · *Breckenridge Eco. Dev.* · Virgil Moore; Exec. Dir.; 100 E. Elm St.; P.O. Box 1466; 76424; Stephens; P 10,000; (254) 559-6228; Fax (254) 559-7104; vmoore@breckenridgetexas.com; www.breckenridgetexas.com

Brenham · *Eco. Dev. Found. of Brenham* · Page Michel; Pres./CEO; 314 S. Austin St.; 77833; Washington; P 14,000; (979) 836-8927; Fax (979) 836-3563; edf@brenhamtexas.com; www.brenhamtexas-edf.com

Brownsville · *Brownsville Eco. Dev. Cncl.* · Jason Hilts; Pres.; 301 Mexico Blvd., Ste. F1; 78520; Cameron; P 172,000; M 200; (956) 541-1183; (800) 552-5352; Fax (956) 546-3938; info@bedc.com; www.bedc.com

Bryan · *see College Station*

Buffalo · *Buffalo EDC* · Ken Jones; Exec. Dir.; P.O. Box 1186; 75831; Leon; P 3,000; (903) 388-1881; bedc@buffalotex.com; www.buffalotex.com

Caldwell · *Burleson County Ind. Found.* · Sal Zaccagnino; Pres.; 301 N. Main; 77836; Burleson; P 18,000; (979) 567-7979; Fax (979) 567-0818; www.burlesoncountytx.com

Canadian · *Canadian EDC* · Tamera Julian; Dir.; 119 N. 2nd St.; 79014; Hemphill; P 2,500; (806) 323-6234; Fax (806) 323-9243; canadiantx@sbcglobal.net; www.canadiantx.com

Carrollton · *Carrollton Eco. Dev.* · Brad Mink; Dir.; P.O. Box 110535; 75011; Collin, Dallas & Denton; P 121,000; (972) 466-3391; Fax (972) 466-4882; econdev@cityofcarrollton.com; www.cityofcarrollton.com

Childress · *Childress Eco. Dev. Corp.* · Russell Graves; Exec. Dir.; 1902 Ave. G N.W.; P.O. Box 10; 79201; Childress; P 6,700; (940) 937-8629; Fax (940) 937-2520; info@childresstexas.com; www.childresstexas.com

Clarendon · *Clarendon-Donley County Eco. Dev. Corp.* · Machiel Covey; City Secy.; P.O. Box 1089; 79226; Donley; P 1,974; (806) 874-3438

Cleveland · *Cleveland Eco. Dev. Corp.* · Kelly McDonald; Interim City Mgr.; 907 E. Houston St.; 77327; Liberty; P 7,605; (281) 592-2667; Fax (281) 592-6624; citymanager@citycleveland.net; www.clevelandtexas.com

College Station · *Research Valley Partnership* · Todd McDaniel; Pres./CEO; 1500 Research Pkwy., Ste. 270; 77845; Brazos; P 150,000; (979) 260-1755; (800) 449-4012; Fax (979) 260-5252; tmcdaniel@researchvalley.org; www.researchvalley.org

Comanche · *Comanche Eco. Dev. Corp.* · P.O. Box 144; 76442; Comanche; P 4,638; (325) 356-2032; www.comanchechamber.org

Conroe · *Greater Conroe Eco. Dev. Cncl.* · Tom Stinson CEcD; Dir.; 505 W. Davis St.; P.O. Box 2347; 77305; Montgomery; P 46,110; (936) 538-7118; Fax (936) 756-6162; www.gcedc.org

Coppell · *City of Coppell Planning Dept.* · Gary Sieb; Dir. of Planning; 255 Parkway Blvd.; 75019; Denton; P 39,500; (972) 304-3678; Fax (972) 304-7092; gsieb@coppelltx.gov; www.coppelltx.gov

Corpus Christi · *Coastal Bend Cncl. of Govts.* · John Buckner; Exec. Dir.; 2910 Leopard; P.O. Box 9909; 78469; Nueces; P 323,000; (361) 883-5743; Fax (361) 883-5749; www.cbcog98.org

Corpus Christi · *Corpus Christi Reg. Eco. Dev. Corp.* · Roland Mower; Pres./CEO; 1 Shoreline Plaza; 800 N. Shoreline, Ste. 1300S; 78401; Nueces; P 410,749; (361) 882-7448; Fax (361) 882-9930; rcmower@ccredc.com; www.ccredc.com

Crockett · *Crockett Eco. & Ind. Dev. Corp.* · Thom Lambert; Exec. Dir.; 1100 Edmiston Dr.; P.O. Box 307; 75835; Houston; P 7,100; (936) 546-5636; Fax (936) 544-4355; suzanne@crockett.org; www.crockett.org

Crowell · *Crowell Ind. Dev.* · Stacy Henry; Pres.; P.O. Box 848; 79227; Foard; P 1,200; (940) 684-1531

Crystal City · *Crystal City Eco. Dev.* · 101 E. Dimmit; P.O. Drawer 706; 78839; Zavala; P 9,000; (830) 374-2900; Fax (830) 374-2123

Dallas · *City of Dallas Dept. of Eco. Dev.* · Karl Zavitkovsky; Dir.; City Hall; 1500 Marilla, Rm. 5C South; 75201; Dallas; P 1,300,000; (214) 670-1685; Fax (214) 670-0158; www.dallas-ecodev.org

Dallas · *Dallas Reg. Chamber Eco. Dev. Group* · Mike Rosa; V.P. of Eco. Dev.; 700 N. Pearl, Ste. 1200; 75201; Dallas; P 5,000,000; (214) 746-6735; Fax (214) 746-6669; information@dallaschamber.org; www.dallaschamber.org

Del Rio · *Del Rio Area Dev. Found.* · Frank Larson; Pres.; 1915 Veteran's Blvd.; 78840; Val Verde; P 45,000; (830) 775-3551; Fax (830) 774-1813; al@drchamber.com; www.drchamber.com

DFW Airport · *North Texas Comm.* · Dan S. Petty; Pres.; P.O. Box 610246; 75261; Dallas; P 4,600,000; (972) 621-0400; Fax (972) 929-0916; ntc@ntc-dfw.org; www.ntc-dfw.org

Dumas · *Dumas Eco. Dev. Corp.* · Michael M. Running; Exec. Dir.; 1015 N. Maddox; P.O. Box 595; 79029; Moore; P 16,000; (806) 934-3332; Fax (806) 934-0180; running@dumasedc.org; www.dumasedc.org.

Eagle Pass · *Maverick County Dev. Corp.* · Raul E. Perez; Exec. Dir.; P.O. Box 3693; 78853; Maverick; P 47,297; (830) 773-6166; (800) 970-MCDC; Fax (830) 773-6287; info@eaglepassmcdc.com; www.eaglepassmcdc.com

Early · *Early Eco. Dev. Corp. Small Bus. Incubator* · Wanda Furgason; CDC; 104 E. Industrial Dr.; 76802; Brown; P 2,588; (325) 649-9300; Fax (325) 643-4746; wanda@earlytx.com; www.earlychamber.com

Edinburg · *Cncl. for South Texas Eco. Progress* · 2540 W. Trenton Rd.; 78539; Hidalgo; P 2,700,000; (956) 682-6371; (800) 682-6371; Fax (956) 971-3319; www.costep.org

El Paso · *El Paso Reg. Eco. Dev.* · Bob Cook; Pres.; 201 E. Main St., Ste. 1711; 79901; El Paso; P 2,600,000; (915) 534-0523; Fax (915) 534-0516; bcook@elpasoredco.org; www.elpasoredco.org

Euless · *see Bedford*

Farmers Branch · *Farmers Branch Eco. Dev.* · John Land; Dir.; 13000 William Dodson Pkwy.; 75234; Dallas; P 27,000; (972) 919-2512; fbinfo@farmersbranch.info; www.farmersbranch.info

Flower Mound · *Town of Flower Mound Eco. Dev.* · Melissa Glasgow; Dir. of Eco. Dev.; 2121 Cross Timbers Rd.; 75028; Denton & Tarrant; P 62,884; (972) 874-6044; Fax (972) 874-6451; melissa.glasgow@flower-mound.com; www.flower-mound.com/econdev

Floydada · *Floydada Eco. Dev. Corp.* · Justin Jaworski; Exec. Dir.; 105 S. 5th St.; P.O. Box 15; 79235; Floyd; P 3,676; (806) 983-3318; Fax (806) 983-6017; www.floydadaedc.com

Fort Stockton · *Fort Stockton EDC* · Doug May; Exec. Dir.; 1000 Railroad Ave.; 79735; Pecos; P 8,000; (432) 336-2264; (800) 336-2166; Fax (432) 336-6114; edc@fortstockton.org; www.fortstockton.org

Fredericksburg • *Gillespie County EDC* • Tim Lehmberg; Exec. Dir.; 302 E. Austin; 78624; Gillespie; P 10,432; (830) 997-6523; Fax (830) 997-8588; edc@fbgtx.org; www.fredericksburg-texas.com

Friona • *Friona Eco. Dev. Corp.* • Bill Stovell; Pres.; 621 Main; 79035; Parmer; P 3,800; (806) 250-3491; Fax (806) 250-2348; fedc@wtrt.net; www.frionachamber.com

Garland • *Garland Eco. Dev. Partnership* • Paul Mayer; CEO; 520 N. Glenbrook Dr.; 75040; Dallas; P 240,876; (972) 272-7551; (469) 326-7444; Fax (972) 276-9261; paul.mayer@garlandchamber.com; www.garlandchamber.com

George West • *Live Oak County Comm. Dev. Corp.* • P.O. Box 19; 78022; Live Oak; P 12,309; (361) 786-4330; www.georgewest.org/edc.htm

Georgetown • *City of Georgetown Eco. Dev. Dept.* • Mark Thomas; Dir.; 614 Main St.; P.O. Box 409; 78627; Williamson; P 50,000; (512) 930-8475; Fax (512) 930-8445; ed@georgetowntx.org; www.investgeorgetown.org

Giddings • *Giddings Eco. Dev. Corp.* • Joyce Bise; Dir.; 289 W. Railroad Ave.; 78942; Lee; P 5,400; (979) 542-2067; Fax (979) 540-2183; jmbise@giddings.net; www.giddingsedc.com

Gladewater • *Gladewater Eco. Dev. Corp.* • Lon Welton; Exec. Dir.; P.O. Box 1445; 75647; Gregg & Upshur; P 6,087; (903) 845-5441; Fax (903) 845-1282; gedco@suddenlinkmail.com; www.gladewateredc.com

Gonzales • *Gonzales Area Dev. Corp.* • Ross Hendershot Jr.; Pres.; P.O. Box 904; 78629; Gonzales; P 18,500; (830) 672-6532; Fax (830) 672-6533; www.gonzalestexas.com

Gorman • *Gorman Eco. Dev. Corp.* • Cliffa Vaughn; Dir.; 118 S. Kent; P.O. Box 236; 76454; Eastland; P 1,236; (254) 734-3933; Fax (254) 734-2270; cliffa.gormanedc.vaughn@gmail.com

Graham • *Graham Ind. Assoc.* • Neal Blanton; Exec. Dir.; P.O. Box 1465; 76450; Young; P 9,000; (940) 549-6006; Fax (940) 549-5030; nblanton@grahamtexas.net; www.cityofgrahamtexas.com

Grand Prairie • *Grand Prairie Eco. Dev. Dept.* • Bob O'Neal; Eco. Dev. Dir.; P.O. Box 534045; 75053; Dallas, Ellis & Tarrant; P 160,000; (972) 237-8160; Fax (972) 237-8161; boneal@gptx.org; www.gptx.org

Groesbeck • *Groesbeck Eco. Dev. Corp.* • Martha Stanton; 402 W. Navasota; 76642; Limestone; P 4,300; (254) 729-3293; Fax (254) 729-8155; www.groesbeckedc.com

Hamilton • *Hamilton Eco. Dev. Corp.* • Jane Crouch; Exec. Dir.; 204 E. Main; P.O. Box 224; 76531; Hamilton; P 3,000; (254) 386-5954; Fax (254) 386-3563; hamiltonedc@htcomp.net; www.hamiltontexas.com

Henderson • *Henderson Eco. Dev. Corp.* • Sue Henderson; Gen. Mgr.; 400 W. Main St.; 75652; Rusk; P 12,000; (903) 657-6551; Fax (903) 655-1296; hedco@hendersontx.us; www.hendersontx.us

Houston • *Bay Area Houston Eco. Partnership* • Bob Mitchell; Pres.; P.O. Box 58724; 77258; Harris; P 422,000; (281) 486-5535; Fax (281) 486-5068; barbara@bayareahouston.com; www.bayareahouston.com

Houston • *Greater Houston Partnership* • Maria Velasquez; Mgr. of Intl. Bus. Programs; Eco. Dev. Div.; 1200 Smith St., Ste. 700; 77002; Harris; P 5,087,127; M 2,500; (713) 844-3636; Fax (713) 844-0236; mvelasquez@houston.org; www.houston.org

Huntsville • *Huntsville Eco. Dev. Cncl.* • William Baine; City Mgr.; 1212 Ave. M; 77340; Walker; P 38,500; (936) 291-5400; Fax (936) 291-5409; bbaine@huntsvilletx.gov; www.huntsvilletx.gov

Hurst • *see Bedford*

Jacksonville • *Jacksonville Dev. Corp.* • Darrell Prcin; Pres.; 526 E. Commerce; P.O. Box 1604; 75766; Cherokee; P 15,000; (903) 586-2217; (800) 376-2217; Fax (903) 586-6944; mandy@jacksonvilletexas.com; www.jacksonvilleedc.com

Jasper • *Jasper Eco. Dev. Corp.* • Kari Ellis; Exec. Dir.; 246 E. Milam; 75951; Jasper; P 8,500; (409) 383-6120; Fax (409) 383-6122; info@jasperedc.com; www.jasperedc.com

Jim Wells County • *see Corpus Christi*

Keller • *Eco. Dev., City of Keller* • Lisa Culos; Eco. Dev. Dir.; 1100 Bear Creek Pkwy.; P.O. Box 770; 76244; Tarrant; P 37,000; (817) 743-4020; Fax (817) 743-4190; economicdevelopment@cityofkeller.com; www.cityofkeller.com

Kemah • *Kemah Comm. Dev. Corp.* • Teresa-Vazquez-Evans; Pres.; 1401 Hwy. 146; 77565; Galveston; P 2,330; (281) 334-1611; Fax (281) 334-6583; selam@kemah-tx.com; www.kemah-tx.gov

Kerrville • *Kerr Eco. Dev. Found.* • Guy Overby; Pres.; 1700 Sidney Baker St., Ste. 100; 78028; Kerr; P 50,000; (830) 896-1157; Fax (830) 896-1166; information@kerredf.org; www.kerredf.org

Killeen • *Killeen Eco. Dev.* • John Crutchfield; Pres.; One Santa Fe Plz.; P.O. Box 548; 76540; Bell; P 112,000; (254) 526-9551; Fax (254) 526-6090; jcrutchfield@gkcc.com; www.killeenchamber.com

Kingsville • *Kingsville Eco. Dev. Cncl.* • Dick Messbarger; Exec. Dir.; 635 E. King St.; P.O. Box 5032; 78364; Kleberg; P 26,812; (361) 592-6438; Fax (361) 592-0866; edc@kingsville.org; www.kingsvilleedc.org

Kleberg County • *see Corpus Christi*

Lago Vista • *Lago Vista Eco. Dev. Found.* • Frank Robbins; Asst. City Mgr./Dev.; P.O. Box 4727; 78645; Travis; P 5,800; (512) 934-4134; (512) 267-1155; Fax (512) 267-2338; www.lagovistatexas.org

Laredo • *Laredo Dev. Found.* • Roger Creery; Exec. Dir.; 616 Leal St.; P.O. Box 2682; 78044; Webb; P 236,941; (956) 722-0563; Fax (956) 722-6247; www.ldfonline.org

Live Oak County • *see Corpus Christi*

Longview • *Longview Eco. Dev. Corp.* • Susan Mazarakes-Gill CEcD; Exec. Dir.; 410 N. Center St.; 75601; Gregg & Harrison; P 80,000; (903) 753-7878; (800) 952-2613; Fax (903) 753-3646; susan@longviewusa.com; www.longviewusa.com

Lubbock • *Lubbock Eco. Dev. Alliance* • John Osborne; CEO; 1500 Broadway, 6th Flr.; 79401; Lubbock; P 261,227; (806) 749-4500; Fax (806) 749-4501; john.osborne@lubbockeda.org; www.lubbockeda.org

Madisonville • *Madison County Eco. Dev. Corp.* • 113 W. Trinity St.; P.O. Box 1392; 77864; Madison; P 14,000; (936) 349-0163; mcedc@madisoncountyedc.com; www.madisoncountyedc.com

McAllen • *Lower Rio Grande Valley Dev. Cncl.* • Kenneth N. Jones; Exec. Dir.; 311 N. 15th St.; 78501; Hidalgo; P 1,036,636; (956) 682-3481; Fax (956) 631-4670; www.lrgvdc.org

McAllen • *McAllen Eco. Dev. Corp.* • Keith Patridge; Pres./CEO; 6401 S. 33rd St.; 78503; Hidalgo; P 470,000; (956) 682-2875; Fax (956) 682-3077; info@medc.org; www.medc.org

McKinney • *McKinney Eco. Dev. Corp.* • David Pitstick; Pres./CEO; 321 N. Central Expy., Ste. 200; 75070; Collin; P 120,000; (972) 562-5430; (800) 839-6259; Fax (972) 562-1222; info@mckinneyedc.com; www.mckinneyedc.com

Midland • *Midland Dev. Corp.* • Mike Hatley; Pres.; 109 N. Main St., 2nd Flr.; 79701; Midland; P 121,300; (432) 686-3579; (800) 624-6435; Fax (432) 687-8214; info@midlandtxedc.com; www.midlandtxedc.com

Mineola · *Mineola Dev. Inc.* · Linda Rauscher; Dev. Dir.; 300 Greenville Ave.; P.O. Box 179; 75773; Wood; P 5,611; (903) 569-6983; (800) MINEOLA; Fax (903) 569-0856; lrauscher@mineola.com; www.mineola.com

Monahans · *Monahans Eco. Dev. Corp.* · Morse Haynes; Eco. Dev. Dir.; 303 S. Allen; P.O. Box 61; 79756; Ward; P 7,500; (432) 943-2062; Fax (432) 943-6868; monahansedc@monahans.org; www.monahans.org

Mount Pleasant · *Mount Pleasant Ind. Found.* · Charles L. Smith CEcD; Exec. Dir.; 1604 N. Jefferson; 75455; Titus; P 28,118; (903) 572-6602; Fax (903) 572-0613; charleslsmith@mpcity.org; www.mpedc.org

New Braunfels · *New Braunfels EDC* · Rusty Brockman; Dir. of EDC; 390 S. Seguin Ave.; P.O. Box 311417; 78131; Comal; P 58,000; M 1,700; (830) 625-2385; (866) 927-0905; Fax (830) 625-7918; rusty@nbcham.org; www.nbcham.org

Nueces County · *see Corpus Christi*

Odessa · *Odessa Ind. Dev. Corp.* · Gary Vest; Dir.; 700 N. Grant, Ste. 200; P.O. Box 3626; 79760; Ector; P 96,948; (877) 363-3772; Fax (432) 333-7858; info@odessaecodev.com; www.odessatex.com

Pampa · *Pampa Eco. Dev. Corp.* · Clay Rice; Exec. Dir.; 106 N. Cuyler; P.O. Box 2398; 79065; Gray; P 18,000; (806) 665-0800; pampaedc@sbcglobal.net; www.pampaedc.com

Pearland · *Pearland Eco. Dev. Corp.* · Ed Thompson; Pres.; 3519 Liberty Dr.; 77581; Brazoria, Fort Bend & Harris; P 80,000; (281) 652-1627; (800) 240-3684; Fax (281) 997-0522; jvega@pearlandedc.tx.us; www.pearlandedc.com

Plainview · *Plainview/Hale County Ind. Found.* · Kevin Carter; Exec. Dir.; 1906 W. 5th St.; 79072; Hale; P 32,000; (806) 293-8536; Fax (806) 296-0819; kcarter@phcif.org; www.phcif.org

Plano · *Plano Eco. Dev. Bd.* · Sally Bane; Exec. Dir.; 5601 Granite Pkwy., Ste. 310; 75024; Collin; P 253,000; (972) 208-8300; Fax (972) 208-8305; sallyb@plano.gov; www.planotexas.org

Port Neches · *Port Neches Eco. Dev. Corp.* · Amy Guidroz; Exec. Dir.; 1110 Port Neches Ave.; P.O. Box 445; 77651; Jefferson; P 15,000; (409) 727-6776; director@pnedc.com

Post · *Post Eco. Dev. Corp.* · Giles Dalby; Chrmn. of Bd.; 228 E. Main; 79356; Garza; P 4,200; (806) 495-2818; Fax (806) 495-2376

Quanah · *Quanah Eco. Dev. Corp.* · Eugene Johnson; Exec. Dir.; 305 S. Main St.; 79252; Hardeman; P 2,950; (940) 663-2690; qedc@speednet.com; www.quanahnet.com/quanaheconomicdevelopment

Quitman · *Wood County Ind. Comm.* · Gary McKinley; Exec. Dir.; Wood County Airport Terminal Bldg.; P.O. Box 578; 75783; Wood; P 41,776; (903) 768-2402; (888) 506-3458; Fax (903) 768-2403; woodcic@peoplescom.net; www.woodcountytx.com

Richardson · *Richardson Eco. Dev. Partnership* · John Jacobs; Sr. V.P.; 411 Belle Grove Dr.; 75080; Dallas; P 97,467; (972) 792-2800; Fax (972) 792-2825; john@telecomcorridor.com; www.telecomcorridor.com

Robstown · *Robstown Area Dev. Comm.* · 1150 E. Main Ave.; P.O. Box 111; 78380; Nueces; P 14,000; (361) 387-3933; Fax (361) 387-7280; radc@verizon.net; www.robstownadc.com

Rockwall · *Rockwall Eco. Dev. Corp.* · Sheri Franza; Pres./CEO; 697 E. I-30; P.O. Box 968; 75087; Rockwall; P 30,000; (972) 772-0025; Fax (972) 771-8828; sfranza@rockwalledc.com; www.rockwalledc.com

Rosenberg · *Rosenberg Dev. Corp.* · Matt Fielder; Eco. Dev. Dir.; P.O. Box 32; 77471; Fort Bend; P 28,000; (832) 595-3330; Fax (832) 595-3311; mattf@ci.rosenberg.tx.us; www.rosenbergecodev.com

San Antonio · *San Antonio Eco. Dev. Found.* · Mario Hernandez; Pres.; 602 E. Commerce St.; P.O. Box 1628; 78296; Bexar; P 1,200,000; (210) 226-1394; Fax (210) 223-3386; edf@sanantonioedf.com; www.sanantonioedf.com

San Juan · *Eco. Dev. Corp. of San Juan* · Miki McCarthy; Exec. Dir.; 430 N. Standard Ave.; 78589; Hidalgo; P 35,000; (956) 783-3448; Fax (956) 783-5413; miki@sanjuanedc.com; www.sanjuanedc.com

Seminole · *Seminole Eco. Dev. Corp.* · Donna Johnson; Exec. Dir.; 111 N.E. 3rd St.; P.O. Box 816; 79360; Gaines; P 6,505; (432) 758-8804; Fax (432) 758-2349; director@mywdo.com; www.seminoleedc.org.

South Padre Island · *Eco. Dev. Corp.* · Darla Lapeyre; Exec. V.P.; 6801 Padre Blvd.; 78597; Cameron; P 2,500; (956) 761-4522; Fax (956) 761-4523; spiedc@aol.com; www.townspi.com

Southlake · *City of Southlake Ofc. of Eco. Dev.* · Greg Last; Dir.; 1400 Main St., Ste. 300; 76092; Denton & Tarrant; P 25,700; (817) 748-8039; Fax (817) 748-8040; glast@ci.southlake.tx.us; www.cityofsouthlake.com

Stamford · *Dev. Corp. of Stamford* · Fareed Hassen; Exec. Dir.; P.O. Box 669; 79553; Jones; P 4,000; (325) 773-2495; Fax (325) 773-2851; eddirector@stamfordtx.com; www.stamfordtx.com

Sudan · *Sudan Eco. Dev. Corp.* · Clay Carr; Pres.; P.O. Box 59; 79371; Lamb; P 1,039; (806) 227-2112; sudancityhall@yahoo.com; www.sudantexas.com

Sulphur Springs · *Sulphur Springs/Hopkins County Eco. Dev. Corp.* · Roger Feagley; Exec. Dir.; 1200 Enterprise; 75482; Hopkins; P 35,000; (903) 439-0101; Fax (903) 439-6396; rfeagley@ss-edc.com; www.ss-edc.com

Sweetwater · *Sweetwater Enterprise for Eco. Dev.* · Ken Becker; Exec. Dir.; 810 E. Broadway; P.O. Box 785; 79556; Nolan; P 15,500; (325) 235-0555; (877) 301-SEED; Fax (325) 235-1026; ken@sweetwatertexas.net; www.sweetwatertexas.net

Temple · *Temple Eco. Dev. Corp.* · Lee Peterson; Pres.; 1 S. 1st St.; 76501; Bell; P 60,000; (254) 773-8332; Fax (254) 773-8856; info@choosetemple.com; www.choosetemple.com

Terrell · *Terrell Eco. Dev. Corp.* · Danny Booth; Admin.; P.O. Box 97; 75160; Kaufman; P 18,500; (972) 524-5704; Fax (972) 563-2363; danny@terrelltexas.com; www.terrelltexas.com

Weatherford · *Weatherford Eco. Dev. Auth.* · Dennis Clayton CEcD; Exec. Dir.; 202 W. Oak St.; P.O. Box 255; 76086; Parker; P 27,000; (817) 594-9429; (817) 598-4302; Fax (817) 594-4786; dclayton@weatherfordtx.gov; www.weatherfordtxeda.org

White Settlement · *White Settlement Eco. Dev. Corp.* · Jim Ryan; Eco. Dev. Dir.; Eco. Dev. Dept.; 214 Meadow Park Dr.; 76108; Tarrant; P 16,000; (817) 246-4971; Fax (817) 367-0885; www.wstx.us

Whitesboro · *Whitesboro Eco. Dev. Corp.* · Janis Crawley; Exec. Dir.; 111 W. Main; P.O. Box 340; 76273; Grayson; P 4,200; (903) 564-4000; Fax (903) 564-6105; edc@whitesborotexas.com; www.whitesborotexas.com

Wichita Falls · *Wichita Falls C/C & Ind.* · Kevin Pearson; Exec. V.P.; 900 8th St., Ste. 218; P.O. Box 1860; 76307; Wichita; P 104,000; (940) 723-2741; Fax (940) 723-8773; chamber@wf.net; www.wichitafallscommerce.com

Wills Point · *Wills Point EDC* · Pam Pearson; Exec. Dir.; 36549 Hwy. 64, Ste. 104; P.O. Box 217; 75169; Van Zandt; P 4,000; (903) 873-3381; Fax (903) 873-3081; WPEDC@sbcglobal.net; www.cityofwillspoint.com

EDC

Yoakum · *Yoakum Eco. Dev. Corp.* · Patrick J. Kennedy; Dir.; 808 U.S. Hwy. 77A S.; P.O. Box 738; 77995; DeWitt & Lavaca; P 5,731; (361) 293-6321; Fax (361) 293-3318; ccook@cityofyoakum.org; www.yoakumusa.com

Utah

Federal

U.S. SBA, Utah Dist. Ofc. · Stan Nakano; Dist. Dir.; 125 S. State St., Rm. 2227; Salt Lake City; 84138; Salt Lake; (801) 524-3217; Fax (801) 524-4410; cheryl.richens@sba.gov; www.sba.gov/ut

State

Eco. Dev. Corp. of Utah · Jeffrey Edwards; Pres./CEO; 201 S. Main St., Ste. 2150; Salt Lake City; 84111; Salt Lake; M 200; (801) 328-8824; Fax (801) 531-1460; jedwards@edcutah.org; www.edcutah.org

Labor Comm. of Utah · Sherrie Hayashi; Comm.; 160 E. 300 S., Ste. 300; P.O. Box 146610; Salt Lake City; 84114; Salt Lake; (801) 530-6800; Fax (801) 530-6390; laborcommission@utah.gov; www.laborcommission.utah.gov

Communities

Cedar City · *Cedar City/Iron County Eco. Dev.* · Brennan Wood; Exec. Dir.; 10 N. Main St.; 84720; Iron; P 41,000; (435) 586-2770; Fax (435) 586-2949; www.cedarcity.org

Fillmore · *Fillmore City Redev. Agency* · Marlene Cummings; City Recorder; 75 W. Center St.; 84631; Millard; P 2,300; (435) 743-5233; Fax (435) 743-5195; www.fillmorecity.org

Logan · *Cache Eco. Dev.* · Sandra Emile; Pres.; 160 N. Main St.; 84321; Cache; P 105,000; (435) 752-2161; Fax (435) 753-5825; semile@cachechamber.com; www.cachechamber.com

Moab · *Moab Area Eco. Dev. Ofc.* · Ken Davey; Specialist; 217 E. Center; 84532; Grand; P 8,500; (435) 259-5121; Fax (435) 259-4951; ken@moabcity.org; www.moabcity.org

Nephi · *Juab Comm. Eco. Dev. Agency* · Byron Woodland; Dir.; 160 N. Main; 84648; Juab; P 8,500; (435) 623-3400; Fax (435) 623-4609; byronw@co.juab.ut.us; www.co.juab.ut.us

Ogden Area

Ogden City Comm. & Eco. Dev. · Dave Harmer; Dir.; 2549 Washington Blvd., Ste. 420; 84401; Weber; P 70,000; (801) 629-8910; Fax (801) 629-8993; www.ogdencity.com

Weber County Comm. · Craig Zogmaister; Chrmn.; 2380 Washington Blvd., Ste. 360; 84401; Weber; P 196,533; (801) 399-8401; Fax (801) 399-8305; www.co.weber.ut.us

Weber Eco. Dev. Corp. · Ron Kusina; Exec. Dir.; 2484 Washington Blvd., Ste. 400; 84401; Weber; P 213,000; (801) 621-8300; Fax (801) 392-7609; ronk@echamber.cc; www.webergrowth.com

Orem · *Comm. For Eco. Dev. in Orem* · Brad Whittaker; Exec. Dir.; 777 S. State St.; 84058; Utah; P 91,000; (801) 226-1521; Fax (801) 226-2678; info@cedo.org; www.cedo.org

Panguitch · *Garfield Eco. Dev.* · Justin Fischer; Planner; P.O. Box 77; 84759; Garfield; P 4,600; (435) 676-8826; Fax (435) 676-8239

Price · *Carbon County Eco. Dev.* · Delynn Fielding; Dir.; 120 E. Main St.; 84501; Carbon; P 23,000; (435) 636-3295; Fax (435) 636-3210; www.carbon-county.com

Provo · *also see Orem*

Provo · *Provo City Dept. of Eco. Dev.* · Leland Gamette; Dir.; 86 N. University Ave., Ste. 240; 84601; Utah; P 116,000; (801) 852-6161; Fax (801) 375-1469; dholmes@provo.utah.gov; www.provo.org

Tooele · *Tooele County Eco. Dev.* · Nicole Cline; AICP; 47 S. Main; 84074; Tooele; P 54,375; (435) 843-3160; Fax (435) 843-3427; ncline@co.tooele.ut.us; www.tooeleeconomicdevelopment.com

Vermont

Federal

U.S. SBA, Vermont Dist. Ofc. · Darcy Carter; Dist. Dir.; 87 State St., Rm. 205; P.O. Box 605; Montpelier; 05601; Washington; (802) 828-4422; Fax (802) 828-4485; kathleen.herrington@sba.gov; www.sba.gov/vt

Communities

Bennington · *Bennington County Ind. Corp.* · Peter Odierna; Exec. Dir.; 215 South St.; P.O. Box 923; 05201; Bennington; P 35,000; (802) 442-8975; Fax (802) 447-1101; peter@bcic.org; www.bcic.org

Burlington · *Greater Burlington Industrial Corp. (GBIC)* · Frank Cioffi; Pres.; 60 Main St.; P.O. Box 786; 05402; Chittenden; P 146,000; (802) 862-5726; Fax (802) 860-1899; frank@vermont.org; www.gbicvt.org

Middlebury · *Addison County Eco. Dev. Corp.* · Robin Scheu; Exec. Dir.; 1590 Rte. 7 S., Ste. 8; 05753; Addison; P 30,000; (802) 388-7953; Fax (802) 388-0119; info@addisoncountyedc.org; www.addisoncountyedc.org

Montpelier · *Central Vermont Eco. Dev. Corp.* · Susan Matthews; Exec. V.P.; 1 National Life Dr.; P.O. Box 1439; 05601; Washington; P 62,000; M 120; (802) 223-4654; (888) 769-2957; Fax (802) 223-4655; cvedc@sover.net; www.central-vt.com/cvedc

Morrisville · *Lamoille Eco. Dev. Corp.* · John Mandeville; Exec. Dir.; P.O. Box 455; 05661; Lamoille; P 25,000; (802) 888-5640; Fax (802) 851-1136; john@lamoilleeconomy.org; www.lamoilleeconomy.org

Rutland · *Rutland Eco. Dev. Corp.* · James B. Stewart; Exec. Dir.; 112 Quality Ln.; 05701; Rutland; P 63,014; (802) 773-9147; Fax (802) 773-8009; info@rutlandeconomy.com; www.rutlandeconomy.com

Saint Albans · *Franklin County Ind. Dev. Corp.* · Timothy Smith; Exec. Dir.; 2 N. Main; P.O. Box 1099; 05478; Franklin; P 46,000; (802) 524-2194; Fax (802) 524-6793; info@fcidc.com; www.fcidc.com

Saint Johnsbury · *Northeastern Vermont Dev. Assn.* · Steven Patterson; Exec. Dir.; 36 Eastern Ave.; P.O. Box 630; 05819; Caledonia, Essex & Orleans; P 62,438; (802) 748-5181; Fax (802) 748-1223; spatterson@nvda.net; www.nvda.net

Springfield · *Springfield Reg. Dev. Corp.* · Bob Flint; Exec. Dir.; 14 Clinton St., Ste. 7; 05156; Windsor; P 26,000; (802) 885-3061; Fax (802) 885-3027; info@springfielddevelopment.org; www.springfielddevelopment.org

White River Junction · *Green Mountain Eco. Dev. Corp.* · Joan Goldstein; Exec. Dir.; P.O. Box 246; 05001; Windsor; P 55,000; M 100; (802) 295-3710; Fax (802) 295-3779; jgoldstein@gmedc.com; www.gmedc.com

Windsor · *Connecticut River Dev. Corp.* · Winthrop Townsend; Exec. V.P.; P.O. Box 88; 05089; Windsor; P 45,000; (802) 674-2900; Fax (802) 674-2999; WinTownsend@yahoo.com

Virgin Islands

Communities

St. Croix · *Virgin Islands Eco. Dev. Auth.* · Percival Clouden; CEO; 116 King St. Frederiksted; 00840; P 1,200,000; (340) 773-6499; www.usvieda.org

St. Thomas · *Virgin Islands Eco. Dev. Auth.* · Percival Clouden; CEO; 1050 Norre Gade, Ste. 5; P.O. Box 305038; 00803; P 1,200,000; (340) 714-1700; www.usvieda.org

Virginia

Federal

U.S. SBA, Richmond Dist. Ofc. · Ronald Bew; Dist. Dir.; The Federal Bldg.; 400 N. 8th St., Ste. 1150; Richmond; 23219; Richmond City; (804) 771-2400; Fax (804) 771-2764; richmond. va@sba.gov; www.sba.gov/va

State

Virginia Eco. Dev. Partnership · Jeffrey Anderson; Pres./CEO; 901 E. Byrd St.; P.O. Box 798; Richmond; 23218; Richmond City; (804) 545-5600; Fax (804) 545-5611; info@yesvirginia.org; www.yesvirginia.org

Communities

Alexandria · *Alexandria Eco. Dev. Partnership* · Stuart Litvin CEcD; Pres./CEO; 1729 King St., Ste. 410; 22314; Alexandria City; P 140,000; (703) 739-3820; Fax (703) 739-1384; info@alexecon. org; www.alexecon.org

Arlington · *Arlington County Eco. Dev. Div.* · Terry Holzheimer; Dir.; 1100 N. Glebe Rd., Ste. 1500; 22201; Arlington; P 185,500; (703) 228-0808; Fax (703) 228-0805; www.arlingtonvirginiausa.com

Bland · *ABB Inc.* · Chuck Huhman; Gen. Mgr.; 171 Industry Dr.; P.O. Box 38; 24315; Bland; P 6,700; (276) 688-3325; Fax (276) 688-4588; www.abb.com/us;

Charles City · *Charles City Dept. of Dev.* · Christina Green; Dir.; P.O. Box 66; 23030; Charles City; P 6,926; (804) 652-4707; Fax (804) 829-5819; www.co.charles-city.va.us

Charlottesville · *City of Charlottesville Eco. Dev. Dept.* · Aubrey Watts Jr.; Dir.; P.O. Box 911; 22902; Charlottesville City; P 45,000; (434) 970-3110; Fax (434) 970-3299; www.charlottesville.org

Chatham · *Pittsylvania County Eco. Dev.* · Kenneth Bowman; Dir.; P.O. Box 426; 24531; Pittsylvania; P 61,745; (434) 432-1669; (800) 491-2842; Fax (434) 432-1709; www.pittced.com

Chesapeake · *see Norfolk*

Chesterfield · *Chesterfield County Eco. Dev.* · E. Wilson Davis Jr.; Dir.; 9401 Courthouse Rd., Ste. B; 23832; Chesterfield; P 300,000; (804) 318-8550; Fax (804) 796-3638; www.chesterfieldbusiness.com

Christiansburg · *Montgomery Reg. Eco. Dev. Comm.* · 755 Roanoke St., Ste. 2H; 24073; Montgomery; P 88,454; (540) 382-5732; Fax (540) 381-6888; www.yesmontgomery.va.org

Culpeper · *Culpeper County Eco. Dev. Ofc.* · Carl Sachs; Dir.; 233 E. Davis St.; 22701; Culpeper; P 45,000; (540) 727-3410; (800) 793-0631; Fax (540) 727-3448; csachs@culpepercounty.gov; www. culpepercounty.gov

Culpeper · *Foreign Trade Zone #185* · Jim Charapich; Pres./CEO; 109 S. Commerce St.; 22701; Culpeper; P 45,372; (540) 825-8628; Fax (540) 825-1449; jcharapich@culpepervachamber.com; www. culpepervachamber.com

Danville · *City of Danville, Eco. Dev. Ofc.* · Jeremy Stratton; Dir.; 427 Patton St.; P.O. Box 3300; 24543; Danville City; P 48,411; (434) 793-1753; Fax (434) 797-9606; econdev@discoverdanville. com; www.discoverdanville.com

Emporia · *Emporia-Greensville Ind. Dev. Corp.* · Jack W. Davenport; Exec. Dir.; 425-H S. Main St.; 23847; Emporia City; P 16,000; (434) 634-9400; Fax (434) 634-0511; www.emporia greensvilleidc.com

Fairfax County · *Fairfax County Eco. Dev. Auth.* · Gerald L. Gordon; Pres./CEO; 8300 Boone Blvd., Ste. 450; Vienna; 22182; Fairfax; P 1,606,529; (703) 790-0600; Fax (703) 893-1269; ggordon@fceda.org; www.fairfaxcountyeda.org

Falls Church · *City of Falls Church Ofc. of Eco. Dev.* · Rick Goff; Exec. Dir.; 300 Park Ave.; 22046; Falls Church City; P 10,000; (703) 248-5491; Fax (703) 248-5103; econdev@fallschurchva.gov; www. fallschurchva.gov

Fincastle · *Botetourt County Eco. Dev.* · One W. Main St.; Box 1; 24090; Botetourt; P 32,000; (540) 473-8239; Fax (540) 473-8207; www.botetourt.org

Fredericksburg · *Fredericksburg Ofc. of Tourism & Eco. Dev.* · Karen Hedelt; Dir.; 706 Caroline St.; 22401; Spotsylvania; P 22,000; (540) 372-1216; Fax (540) 372-6587; khedelt@ fredericksburgva.gov; www.visitfred.com

Fredericksburg · *Spotsylvania County Dept. of Eco. Dev.* · Russell Seymour; Dir.; 10304 Spotsylvania Ave., Ste. 440; 22408; Spotsylvania; P 119,000; (540) 507 7210; Fax (540) 507-7207; www.spotsylvania.org

Front Royal · *Eco. Dev. Auth. of Front Royal & Warren County* · Jennifer McDonald; Exec. Dir.; 400 D Kendrick Ln.; P.O. Box 445; 22630; Warren; P 30,000; (540) 635-2182; Fax (540) 635-1853; www.wceda.com

Galax · *City of Galax Eco. Dev.* · Keith Holland; City Mgr.; 111 E. Grayson St.; 24333; Galax City; P 6,837; (276) 236-5773; Fax (276) 236-2889; www.ingalax.net

Gate City · *Scott County Eco. Dev. Auth.* · Penny Horton; Secy.; 180 W. Jackson St.; 24251; Scott; P 23,403; (276) 386-2525; Fax (276) 386-6158; scotteda@mounet.com; www.scottcountyva.org

Gloucester · *Dept. of Eco. Dev.* · Douglas Meredith; Dir.; 6467 Main St.; P.O. Box 915; 23061; Gloucester; P 34,700; (804) 693-1415; Fax (804) 693-6004; dmeredit@gloucesterva.info; www. gloucesterva.info

Henrico · *Eco. Dev. Auth. of Henrico County* · Gary McLaren; Exec. Dir.; 4300 E. Parham Rd.; 23228; Henrico; P 281,000; (804) 501-7654; Fax (804) 501-7890; www.henrico.com

Hopewell · *City of Hopewell Dept. of Dev.* · Tevya Williams; City Planner; 300 N. Main St.; 23860; Hopewell City; P 23,101; (804) 541-2220; Fax (804) 541-2318; twilliams@hopewellva.gov; www.hopewellva.gov

Lawrenceville · *Brunswick County Ind. Dev. Auth.* · Joan Moore; Exec. Dir.; P.O. Box 48; 23868; Brunswick; P 18,000; (434) 848-0248; Fax (434) 848-0202; www.bcida.org

Leesburg · *Loudoun County Dept. of Eco. Dev.* · Larry Rosenstrauch; Dir.; 1 Harrison St. S.E.; MSC #63; 20175; Loudon; P 500,000; (703) 777-0426; Fax (703) 771-5363; good4biz@ loudoun.gov; www.biz.loudoun.gov

Lexington · *The Rockbridge Partnership* · Michael B. Webb; Exec. Dir.; 6 S. Randolph St.; 24450; Lexington City; P 35,000; (540) 463-7346; Fax (540) 463-7348; trp@rockbridge.net; www. rockbridgepartnership.org

Lynchburg • *Lynchburg Ofc. of Eco. Dev.* • Marjette G. Upshur; Dir.; 828 Main St., 10th Flr.; 24504; Lynchburg City; P 70,000; (434) 455-4490; (434) 455-4491; marjette.upshur@lynchburgva.gov; www.lynchburgva.gov

Manassas • *Prince William County Dept. of Eco. Dev.* • Martin Briley; Exec. Dir.; 10530 Linden Lake Plz., Ste. 105; 20109; Prince William; P 320,000; (703) 792-5500; Fax (703) 792-5502; econdev@pwcgov.org; www.pwcecondev.org

Mechanicsville • *Hanover County Dept. of Eco. Dev.* • Marc Weiss; Dir.; 9097 Atlee Station Rd., Ste. 304; 23116; Hanover; P 100,000; (804) 365-6464; (800) 936-6168; Fax (804) 365-6463; www.hanovercounty.biz

Newport News • *Peninsula Cncl. for Workforce Dev.* • Matthew James; Pres./CEO; 11820 Fountain Way; 23606; Newport News City; P 460,000; (757) 826-3327; Fax (757) 826-6706; www.pcfwd.org

Norfolk • *Hampton Roads Eco. Dev. Alliance* • Darryl Gosnell; Pres.; 500 E. Main St., Ste. 1300; 23510; Norfolk City; P 1,670,000; (757) 627-2315; Fax (757) 623-3081; www.hreda.com

Portsmouth • *also see Norfolk*

Portsmouth • *Portsmouth Dept. of Eco. Dev.* • Steven Lynch; Dir.; 200 High St., Ste. 200; 23704; Portsmouth City; P 100,565; (757) 393-8804; (800) 848-5690; Fax (757) 393-8293; www.portsmouthvaed.com

Prince George • *Prince George County* • John Kines; County Admin.; 6602 Courts Dr.; P.O. Box 68; 23875; Prince George; P 36,900; (804) 722-8600; Fax (804) 732-3604; jkines@princegeorgeva.org; www.princegeorgeva.org

Radford • *New River Valley Eco. Dev. Alliance* • Aric Bopp; Exec. Dir.; 6226 University Park Dr., Ste. 2200; 24141; Radford City; P 165,000; (540) 267-0007; Fax (540) 267-0013; info@nrvalliance.org; www.nrvalliance.org

Richmond • *Dept. of Eco. Dev., City of Richmond* • Carthan F. Currin III; Dir.; 501 E. Franklin St., Ste. 800; 23219; Richmond City; P 200,000; (804) 646-5633; Fax (804) 646-6793; econdev@richmondgov.com

Richmond • *Greater Richmond Partnership* • Gregory H. Wingfield; Pres./CEO; 901 E. Byrd St., Ste. 801; West Tower; 23219; Richmond City; P 1,000,000; M 275; (804) 643-3227; (800) 229-6332; Fax (804) 343-7167; ghw@grpva.com; www.grpva.com

Roanoke • *Dept. of Eco. Dev., City of Roanoke* • 117 Church Ave. S.W.; 24011; Roanoke City; P 95,000; (540) 853-2715; Fax (540) 853-1213; www.roanokeva.gov

South Boston • *Ind. Dev. Auth. of Halifax County* • Mike Sexton; Exec. Dir.; 515 Broad St.; P.O. Box 1281; 24592; Halifax; P 38,000; (434) 572-1734; Fax (434) 572-1762; meades@halifaxvirginia.com; www.halifaxvirginia.com

Staunton • *Staunton Dept. of Eco. Dev.* • William Hamilton; Dir.; 116 W. Beverley St.; P.O. Box 58; 24402; Staunton City; P 25,000; (540) 332-3869; Fax (540) 851-4008; www.staunton.va.us

Suffolk • *also see Norfolk*

Suffolk • *City of Suffolk Eco. Dev.* • Cindy Cave; Dir.; 127 E. Washington St., Ste. 200; 23434; Suffolk City; P 76,586; (757) 514-4040; Fax (757) 923-3628; www.suffolk.va.us

Virginia Beach • *Virginia Beach Dept. of Eco. Dev.* • Warren D. Harris; Dir.; 222 Central Park Ave., Ste. 1000; 23462; Virginia Beach City; P 440,000; (757) 385-6464; Fax (757) 499-9894; www.yesvirginiabeach.com

Warm Springs • *Bath County Ind. Dev. Auth.* • Joe Tuning; Chrmn.; P.O. Box 309; 24484; Bath; P 4,826; (540) 839-7221; Fax (540) 839-7222; www.bathcountyva.org

Winchester • *Winchester-Frederick County Eco. Dev. Comm.* • Patrick Barker; Exec. Dir.; 45 E. Boscawen St.; 22601; Winchester City; P 100,000; (540) 665-0973; Fax (540) 722-0604; info@winva.com; www.winva.com

Woodstock • *Shenandoah County Eco. Dev.* • Susie Hill; Dir. of Eco. Dev.; 600 N. Main St., Ste. 101; 22664; Shenandoah; P 39,000; (540) 459-6220; Fax (540) 459-6228; shill@shenandoahcountyva.us; www.shenandoah-ed.org

Wytheville • *Joint Ind. Dev. Auth. of Wythe County* • Alan Hawthorne; Exec. Dir.; 190 S. First St.; P.O. Box 569; 24382; Wythe; P 28,421; (276) 223-3370; Fax (276) 223-3427; jointida@wytheville.org; www.wytheIDA.org

Washington

Federal

U.S. SBA, Washington Dist. Ofc. • Nancy Porzio; Dist. Dir.; 2401 4th Ave., Ste. 450; Seattle; 98121; King; (206) 553-7310; Fax (206) 553-0194; julie.mcfarlane@sba.gov; www.sba.gov/wa

State

State Dept. of Comm. • Rogers Weed; Dir.; 1011 Plum St. S.E.; P.O. Box 42525; Olympia; 98504; Thurston; (360) 725-4000; Fax (360) 586-8440; joe.olson@commerce.wa.gov; www.commerce.wa.gov

Communities

Aberdeen • *Grays Harbor Eco. Dev. Cncl.* • Michael Tracy; Pres.; 506 Duffy St.; 98520; Grays Harbor; P 70,500; (360) 532-7888; Fax (360) 532-7922; www.ghedc.com

Bainbridge Island • *see Bremerton*

Bellingham • *Bellingham Whatcom Eco. Dev. Cncl.* • Nancy Jordan; Exec. Dir.; 115 Unity St., Ste. 101; P.O. Box 2803; 98227; Whatcom; P 170,000; (360) 676-4255; (800) 810-4255; Fax (360) 647-9413; bwedc@bwedc.org; www.bwedc.org

Benton City • *Benton City Eco. Dev. Cncl.* • Randy Rutledge; Coord.; 513 9th St.; P.O. Box 1038; 99320; Benton; P 2,800; (509) 588-6481; (509) 947-7332; Fax (509) 588-6481; bcedc@bentonrea.com; www.bentoncity.org

Bremerton • *Kitsap Eco. Dev. Alliance* • William Stewart; Dir.; 4312 Kitsap Way, Ste. 103; 98312; Kitsap; P 240,000; M 50; (360) 377-9499; (877) 465-4872; Fax (360) 479-4653; info@kitsapeda.org; www.kitsapeda.org

Cathlamet • *Lower Columbia Eco. Dev. Cncl.* • David Goodroe; Exec. Dir.; 102 Main St., Ste. 203; P.O. Box 243; 98612; Wahkiakum; P 4,000; (360) 795-3996; Fax (360) 795-3944; lcedc@cni.net; www.lowercolumbiaedc.org

Chehalis • *Lewis County Eco. Dev. Cncl.* • Dick Larman; Exec. Dir.; 1611 N. National Ave.; P.O. Box 916; 98532; Lewis; P 67,000; (360) 748-0114; Fax (360) 748-1238; lewisedc@localaccess.com; www.lewisedc.com

Clarkston • *Palouse Eco. Dev. Cncl.* • 845 Port Way; 99403; Asotin; P 69,800; (509) 751-9144; Fax (509) 758-1309; www.palouse.org

College Place • *see Walla Walla*

Colville • *Tri-County Eco. Dev. Dist.* • 347 W. 2nd, Ste. A; 99114; Stevens; P 40,700; (509) 684-4571; Fax (509) 684-4788; admin@teddonline.com; www.teddonline.com

Coupeville • *Island County Eco. Dev. Cncl.* • Sharon Hart; Exec. Dir.; 180 N.W. Coveland; P.O. Box 279; 98239; Island; P 77,200; M 120; (360) 678-6889; Fax (360) 678-2976; icedc@whidbey.net; www.islandcountyedc.com

Everett • *Eco. Dev. Cncl. of Snohomish County* • Deborah Knutsen; Pres.; 728 134th St. S.W., Ste. 128; 98204; Snohomish; P 593,500; M 200; (425) 743-4567; Fax (425) 745-5563; www.snoedc.org

Ferry County • *see Colville*

Garfield • *Whitman Rural Dev. Corp.* • Maureen Byrne; Secy.; P.O. Box 454; 99130; Whitman; P 610; M 15; (509) 635-1604

Longview • *Cowlitz Eco. Dev. Cncl.* • Ted Sprague; Pres.; 1452 Hudson, Ste. 208; P.O. Box 1278; 98632; Cowlitz; P 94,000; (360) 423-9921; Fax (360) 423-1923; www.cowlitzedc.com

Moses Lake • *Big Bend Eco. Dev. Cncl.* • Michael Buchanan; Exec. Dir.; 410 W. Third Ave., Ste. E; 98837; Grant; P 95,000; (509) 764-8591; Fax (509) 764-8591; bigbendedc@moseslake-wa.com

Mount Vernon • *Eco. Dev. Assn. of Skagit County* • Don Wick; Exec. Dir.; 204 W. Montgomery; P.O. Box 40; 98273; Skagit; P 122,000; M 560; (360) 336-6114; Fax (360) 336-6116; don@skagit.org; www.skagit.org

Pend Orielle County • *see Colville*

Port Angeles • *Clallam County EDC* • Linda Rotmark; Exec. Dir.; P.O. Box 1085; 98362; Clallam; P 67,000; (360) 457-7793; Fax (360) 452-9618; lrotmark@clallam.org; www.clallam.org

Port Orchard • *see Bremerton*

Poulsbo • *see Bremerton*

Prescott • *see Walla Walla*

Prosser • *Prosser Eco. Dev. Assn.* • Deb Heintz; Exec. Dir.; 1230 Bennett Ave.; 99350; Benton; P 12,000; (509) 786-3600; Fax (509) 786-2399; info@prosser.org; www.prosser.org

Raymond • *Pacific County Eco. Dev. Cncl.* • Cathy Russ; Exec. Dir.; 530 Commercial St.; 98577; Pacific; P 21,800; M 160; (360) 875-9330; Fax (360) 875-9305; www.pacificedc.org

Seattle • *Enterprise Seattle* • Tom Flavin; CEO; 1301 Fifth Ave., Ste. 2500; 98101; King; (206) 389-8650; Fax (206) 389-8651; info@enterpriseseattle.org; www.enterpriseseattle.org

Silverdale • *see Bremerton*

Stevens County • *see Colville*

Stevenson • *Skamania County Eco. Dev. Cncl.* • Peggy Bryan; Exec. Dir.; 167 N.W. Second St.; P.O. Box 436; 98648; Skamania; P 10,800; (509) 427-5110; Fax (509) 427-5122; scedc@skamania-edc.org; www.skamania-edc.org

Tacoma • *Eco. Dev. Bd. for Tacoma-Pierce County* • Bruce Kendall; Pres./CEO; P.O. Box 1555; 98401; Pierce; P 733,700; (253) 383-4726; Fax (253) 383-4676; info@edbtpc.org; www.gopierce.org

Tacoma • *Pierce County Dept. of Comm. Svcs.* • Tom Hilyard; Dir.; 3602 Pacific Ave.; 98418; Pierce; P 725,000; (253) 798-7205; Fax (253) 798-6604; thilyar@co.pierce.wa.us; www.co.pierce.wa.us

Vancouver • *Columbia River Eco. Dev. Cncl.* • 805 Broadway, Ste. 412; 98660; Clark; P 392,000; M 160; (360) 694-5006; Fax (360) 694-9927; info@credc.org; www.credc.org

Waitsburg • *see Walla Walla*

Walla Walla • *Port of Walla Walla* • Paul Gerola; Eco. Dev. Dir.; 310 A St.; 99362; Walla Walla; P 54,000; (509) 525-3100; Fax (509) 525-3101; www.portwallawalla.com

Winslow • *see Bremerton*

Yakima • *Yakima County Dev. Assn.* • David McFadden; Pres./CEO; 10 N. 9th St.; P.O. Box 1387; 98907; Yakima; P 225,000; (509) 575-1140; Fax (509) 575-1508; newvision@ycda.com; www.ycda.com

West Virginia

Federal

U.S. SBA, West Virginia Dist. Ofc. • Judy McCauley; Dist. Dir.; 320 W. Pike St., Ste. 330; Clarksburg; 26301; Harrison; (304) 623-5631; Fax (304) 623-0023; wvinfo@sba.gov; www.sba.gov/wv

State

West Virginia Eco. Dev. Auth. • David Warner; Exec. Dir.; Northgate Bus. Park; 160 Association Dr.; Charleston; 25311; Kanawha; (304) 558-3650; Fax (304) 558-0206; caren.d.wilcher@wv.gov; www.wveda.org

Communities

Beckley • *4-C Eco. Dev. Auth.* • Judy Radford; Exec. Dir.; 116 N. Heber St., Ste. B; 25801; Raleigh; P 188,685; (304) 254-8115; Fax (304) 254-8112; 4ceda@4ceda.org; www.4ceda.org

Berkeley Springs • *Morgan County Eco. Dev. Auth.* • William Clark; Exec. Dir.; 35 N. Mercer; P.O. Box 86; 25411; Morgan; P 14,943; (304) 258-8546; Fax (304) 258-7305; www.morgancounty.com/eda

Bluefield • *Dev. Auth. of Mercer County* • Janet E. Bailey; Exec. Dir.; P.O. Box 4098; 24701; Mercer; P 62,000; (304) 487-2896; (304) 487-8379; Fax (304) 487-5616; mercercounty@citlink.net; www.mercercoeda.com

Bridgeport • *Harrison County Dev. Auth.* • 1215 Johnson Ave.; 26330; Harrison; P 69,088; (304) 326-0213; Fax (304) 326-0215; hcda@westvirginia.com; www.hcdawv.com

Buckhannon • *Upshur County Dev. Auth.* • Stephen Foster; Exec. Dir.; 1 Edmiston Way; P.O. Box 109; 26201; Upshur; P 23,404; (304) 472-1757; Fax (304) 472-4998; info@upshurda.com; www.upshurda.com

Charleston • *West Virginia Dev. Ofc.* • Kelley Goes; Exec. Dir.; State Capitol Complex; Bldg. 6, Rm. 525; 25305; Kanawha; (304) 558-2234; Fax (304) 558-1189; kim.l.harbour@wv.gov; www.wvdo.org

Elkins • *Randolph County Dev. Auth.* • Mark Doak; Pres.; 10 11th St.; 26241; Randolph; P 29,000; (304) 637-0803; Fax (304) 637-4902; www.rcdawv.org

Fairmont • *Marion Reg. Dev. Corp.* • Sharon Shaffer; Exec. Dir.; 112 Adams St., Ste. 201; 26554; Marion; P 57,000; (304) 333-6732; Fax (304) 333-6735; director@marionrdc.com; www.dobizinmarion.com

Grafton • *Taylor County Dev. Auth.* • Bob Gorey; Dir.; 214 W. Main St.; Rm. 100; 26354; Taylor; P 16,089; (304) 265-3938; Fax (304) 265-5450; bobgorey@yahoo.com

Keyser • *Mineral County Dev. Auth.* • Mona Ridder; Exec. Dir.; One Grand Central Bus. Center, Ste. 3011; 26726; Mineral; P 27,700; (304) 788-2233; Fax (304) 788-2998; info@wv-mcda.com; www.wv-mcda.com

Marshall • *see Wheeling*

Martinsburg • *Berkeley County Dev. Auth.* • Stephen L. Christian; Exec. Dir.; 300 Foxcroft Ave., Ste. 201; P.O. Box 2448; 25401; Berkeley; P 89,000; (304) 267-4144; Fax (304) 267-2283; www.developmentauthority.com

Maxwelton • *Greenbrier Valley EDC* • Richard Ellard; Exec. Dir.; P.O. Box 33; 24957; Greenbrier; P 35,000; (304) 497-4300; Fax (304) 497-4330; info@gvedc.com; www.gvedc.com

Moorefield • *Hardy County Rural Dev. Auth.* • Mallie J. Combs; Exec. Dir.; P.O. Box 209; 26836; Hardy; P 13,000; (304) 530-6287; (304) 530-3047; Fax (304) 530-6995; hardyrda@hardynet.com; wvweb.com/www/hardy_county.html

New Martinsville • *Greater New Martinsville Dev. Corp.* • Don Riggenbach; Pres.; P.O. Box 271; 26155; Wetzel; P 18,000; (304) 455-3825; Fax (304) 455-3637; chamber@wetzelcountychamber.com; www.wetzelcountychamber.com

Ohio • *see Wheeling*

Petersburg • *Grant County Dev. Auth.* • Bill Ross; Dir.; 114 N. Grove St.; 26847; Grant; P 12,000; (304) 257-2168; Fax (304) 257-5454; www.grantcowv.com

Point Pleasant • *Mason County Dev. Auth.* • Charles Humphreys; Exec. Dir.; 305 Main St.; 25550; Mason; P 26,000; (304) 675-1497; Fax (304) 675-1601; mcdaadm@masoncounty.org; www.masoncounty.org

Ripley • *Jackson County Dev. Auth.* • Mark Whitley; Exec. Dir.; 104 Miller Dr.; 25271; Jackson; P 38,000; (304) 372-1151; Fax (304) 372-1153; info@jcda.org; www.jcda.org

Spencer • *Roane County Eco. Dev. Auth.* • Mark Whitley; Eco. Dev. Dir.; P.O. Box 1; 25276; Roane; P 15,446; M 80; (304) 927-5189; Fax (304) 927-5953; director@roanecountyeda.org; www.roanecountyeda.org

Summersville • *Nicholas County Comm.* • Spurgeon Hinkle; Pres.; 700 Main St., Ste. 1; 26651; Nicholas; P 26,500; (304) 872-7830; Fax (304) 872-9602; ncc_pattyneff@yahoo.com; www.nicholascountywv.org

Webster Springs • *Webster County Eco. Dev. Auth.* • 139 Baker St.; 26288; Webster; P 10,000; (304) 847-2145; Fax (304) 847-5198; wcda@websterwv.com; www.websterwv.com

Welch • *McDowell County Eco. Dev. Auth.* • Rachael Lester; Dir.; 92 McDowell St., Ste. 100; 24801; McDowell; P 27,000; (304) 436-3833; Fax (866) 571-0746; mcdeda@citlink.net; www.mcdowelleda.com

Wheeling • *Reg. Eco. Dev. Partnership* • Don Rigby; Exec. Dir.; P.O. Box 1029; 26003; Ohio; P 160,000; (304) 232-7722; Fax (304) 232-7727; tmarking@redp.org; www.redp.org

Whitehall • *Region VI Planning & Dev. Cncl.* • James Hall; Exec. Dir.; 34 Mountain Park Dr.; 26554; Marion; P 253,304; (304) 366-5693; Fax (304) 367-0804; regionvi@regionvi.com; www.regionvi.com

Wisconsin

State

Wisconsin Dept. of Commerce • Aaron Olver; Secy. of Commerce; P.O. Box 7970; Madison; 53707; Dane; (608) 266-1018; Fax (608) 266-3447; helen.stewart@wisconsin.gov; www.commerce.wi.gov

Forward Wisconsin • Jan Alf; Dir.; 800 Main St.; Pewaukee; 53072; Waukesha; (262) 691-7873; jalf@execpc.com; www.forwardwi.com

Communities

Algoma • *Community Dev. Comm.* • Bruce Charles; Chrmn.; 416 Fremont St.; 54201; Kewaunee; P 3,370; (920) 487-5203; Fax (920) 487-3499; algoma@algomacity.org; www.algomacity.org

Almena • *Impact Seven Inc.* • William Bay; Pres.; 147 Lake Almena Dr.; 54805; Barron; (715) 357-3334; Fax (715) 357-6233; impact@impactseven.org; www.impactseven.org

Antigo • *Langlade County Comm. Dev. Corp.* • Christine Berry; Dir.; 837 Clermont St.; 54409; Langlade; P 20,000; (715) 627-6384; Fax (715) 627-6385; cberry@co.langlade.wi.us; www.langladecounty.org

Ashland • *Ashland Area Dev. Corp.* • Dale Kupczyk; Exec. Dir.; 422 3rd St. W., Ste. 101; 54806; Ashland; P 16,000; (715) 682-8344; Fax (715) 682-8415; info@ashlandareadevelopment.org; www.ashlandareadevelopment.org

Athens • *Athens Area Dev. Corp.* • Randy Decker; Pres.; P.O. Box A; 54411; Marathon; P 1,102; (715) 257-7531; www.athenswis.com

Baraboo • *Baraboo Eco. Dev. Comm.* • Ed Geick; City Admin.; 135 4th St.; 53913; Sauk; P 11,710; (608) 355-2715; Fax (608) 355-2719; egeick@cityofbaraboo.com; www.cityofbaraboo.com

Baraboo • *Sauk County Dev. Corp.* • Gene Dalhoff; Exec. Dir.; 522 South Blvd.; P.O. Box 33; 53913; Sauk; P 62,000; (608) 355-2084; (608) 393-2953; Fax (608) 355-2083; scdc@baraboo.com; www.scdc.com

Beaver Dam • *Beaver Dam Area Dev. Corp.* • Trent Campbell; Exec. V.P.; 203 Corporate Dr.; P.O. Box 492; 53916; Dodge; P 21,000; (920) 887-4661; bdadc@charter.net

Beloit • *Greater Beloit Eco. Dev. Corp.* • Andrew Janke CPM; Exec. Dir.; 100 State St.; 53511; Rock; P 37,110; (608) 364-6748; (608) 364-6610; Fax (608) 364-6756; jankea@ci.beloit.wi.us; www.greaterbeloitworks.com

Berlin • *Berlin Comm. Dev. Corp.* • 108 N. Capron; P.O. Box 272; 54923; Green Lake; P 5,400; (920) 361-5403; Fax (920) 361-5405; www.1berlin.com

Boscobel • *City of Boscobel Eco. Dev.* • Arlie Harris; City Admin.; 1006 Wisconsin Ave.; 53805; Grant; P 3,308; (608) 375-4400; Fax (608) 375-4750; contact@boscobelwisconsin.com; www.boscobelwisconsin.com

Cashton • *Cashton Dev. Corp.* • Scot Wall; Pres.; 723 Main St.; P.O. Box 70; 54619; Monroe; P 1,000; M 10; (608) 654-5121; Fax (608) 654-5297

Chippewa Falls • *Chippewa County Eco. Dev. Corp.* • Charlie Walker CEcD; Pres./CEO; 770 Scheidler Rd., Ste. 3; 54729; Chippewa; P 65,000; (715) 723-7150; Fax (715) 723-7140; ccedc@chippewa-wi.com; www.chippewa-wi.com

Clear Lake • *Clear Lake Ind. Dev. Corp.* • Al Banink; Clerk/Treas.; 350 4th Ave.; P.O. Box 48; 54005; Polk; P 1,085; (715) 263-2157; Fax (715) 263-2666; vilofcl@cltcomm.net; www.clearlakewi.com

Cottage Grove • *Cottage Grove Eco. Dev. Corp.* • Ken Dahl; Eco. Coord.; 624 Crawford Dr.; 53527; Dane; P 10,000; (608) 575-3879; webmaster@cottagegroveonline.com; www.cottagegroveonline.com

Cuba City • *Cuba City Comm. Dev. Corp.* • Richard Brown; 108 N. Main St.; 53807; Grant & Lafayette; P 2,100; (608) 744-2152; Fax (608) 744-2151; gdroessler@wppienergy.org; www.cubacitywi.com

Delafield • *Delafield Plan Comm.* • Ed McAleer; Chair; City Hall; 500 Genesee St.; 53018; Waukesha; P 6,876; (262) 646-6220; Fax (262) 646-6223; www.cityofdelafield.com

Delavan • *Delavan Dev. Corp.* • Joe Salitros; City Admin.; 123 S. Second St.; P.O. Box 465; 53115; Walworth; P 8,128; (262) 728-5585; Fax (262) 728-4566; www.ci.delavan.wi.us

Dodgeville • *Eco. Dev. Comm.* • James C. McCaulley; Mayor; 100 E. Fountain St.; City Hall; 53533; Iowa; P 4,568; (608) 930-5228; Fax (608) 930-3520; info@dodgeville.com

Eau Claire • *City of Eau Claire Comm. Dev.* • Michael Schatz; Eco. Dev. Dir.; 203 S. Farwell St.; P.O. Box 5148; 54702; Eau Claire; P 63,000; (715) 839-4914; Fax (715) 839-4939; mike.schatz@eauclairewi.gov; www.eauclairedevelopment.com

Eau Claire • *Eau Claire Area Eco. Dev. Corp.* • Brian Doudna; Exec. Dir.; 101 N. Farwell St.; P.O. Box 1108; 54702; Eau Claire; P 100,000; (715) 834-0070; (800) 944-2449; Fax (715) 834-1956; ec.info@eauclaire-wi.com; www.eauclaire-wi.com

Edgerton • *Eco. Dev. Corp. of Edgerton* • Ramona Flanigan; City Admin.; 12 Albion St.; 53534; Dane & Rock; P 5,000; (608) 884-3341; Fax (608) 884-8892; rflanigan@charter.net; www.cityofedgerton.com

Elkhorn • *Elkhorn Dev. Co.* • Sam Tapson; City Admin.; 9 S. Broad St.; P.O. Box 920; 53121; Walworth; P 8,526; (262) 723-2219; Fax (262) 741-5131; www.cityofelkhorn.org

Fennimore • *Fennimore Ind. & Eco. Dev. Corp.* • Linda Parrish; Promo. Coord.; 850 Lincoln Ave.; 53809; Grant; P 2,400; (608) 822-3599; Fax (608) 822-6007; promo@fennimore.com; www.fennimore.com

Fennimore • *Grant County Eco. Dev. Corp.* • Ron Brisbois; Exec. Dir.; 1800 Bronson Blvd.; 53809; Grant; P 49,597; (608) 822-3501; Fax (608) 822-6019; gcedc@grantcounty.org; www.grantcounty.org

Florence • *Florence County Eco. Dev. Comm.* • Wendy Gehlhoff; Dir.; 501 Lake Ave.; P.O. Box 88; 54121; Florence; P 5,200; (715) 528-3294; Fax (715) 528-5071; wgehlhoff@co.florence.wi.us; www.florencewisconsin.com/BusinessAssistance/business_assistance.htm

Fond du Lac • *Fond du Lac County Eco. Dev. Corp.* • Brenda Hicks Sorensen; Pres.; 140 N. Main St.; P.O. Box 1303; 54936; Fond du Lac; P 101,000; (920) 929-2928; Fax (920) 929-7126; info@fcedc.com; www.fcedc.com

Fort Atkinson • *Fort Atkinson Ind. Dev. Corp.* • Sheldon Mielke; Pres.; 244 N. Main St.; 53538; Jefferson; P 12,000; M 40; (920) 563-3210; Fax (920) 563-8946; idc@fortchamber.com; www.fortchamber.com/businessdevelopment

Francis Creek • *Francis Creek Comm. Dev. Corp.* • Joseph W. Debilzen; Treas.; P.O. Box 357; 54214; Manitowoc; P 620; (920) 683-5710; www.franciscreek.org

Friendship • *Adams County Rural & Ind. Dev. Comm.* • P.O. Box 236; 53934; Adams; P 20,000; (608) 339-6945; Fax (608) 339-0052; economicdevelopment@adamscountywi.com; www.adamscountywi.com

Germantown • *Germantown Planning* • Jeff Retzlaff; Planner; P.O. Box 337; 53022; Washington; P 19,400; (262) 250-4735; www.village.germantown.wi.us

Grantsburg • *Grantsburg Ind. Dev. Corp.* • Gary Nelson; Pres.; P.O. Box 365; 54840; Burnett; P 1,400; M 90; (715) 463-2405; info@grantsburgidc.com; www.grantsburgwi.com

Green Bay • *Advance Bus. Dev. Center* • Fred Monique; V.P. Eco. Dev.; 2701 Larsen Rd.; 54303; Brown; P 250,000; M 1,400; (920) 496-9010; Fax (920) 496-6009; monique@titletown.org; www.titletown.org

Hartford • *City of Hartford Eco. Dev. Dept.* • Gary Koppelberger; Coord.; 109 N. Main St.; 53027; Washington; P 13,550; (262) 673-8202; Fax (262) 673-8218; www.ci.hartford.wi.us

Hurley • *Iron County Dev. Zone Cncl.* • Mr. Kelly Klein; Coord.; 100 Cary Rd.; P.O. Box 97; 54534; Iron; P 6,500; (715) 561-2922; Fax (715) 561-3103; jenni@ironcountywi.com; www.ironcountywi.com

Janesville • *City of Janesville Eco. Dev. Agency* • Douglas Venable; Dir.; 18 N. Jackson St.; P.O. Box 5005; 53547; Rock; P 60,000; (608) 755-3181; Fax (608) 755-3196; venabled@ci.janesville.wi.us; www.ci.janesville.wi.us

Janesville • *Forward Janesville Inc.* • John Beckord; Pres.; 14 S. Jackson St.; 53548; Rock; P 60,000; M 600; (608) 757-3160; Fax (608) 757-3170; forward@forwardjanesville.com; www.forwardjanesville.com

Juneau • *Juneau Comm. Dev. Auth.* • Bob Buhr; CDA; 150 Miller St.; P.O. Box 163; 53039; Dodge; P 2,498; (920) 386-4800; Fax (920) 386-4802; bbuhr@cityofjuneau.net; www.juneaueconomicdevelopment.com

Kenosha • *Kenosha Area Bus. Alliance* • Todd Battle; Pres.; 600 52nd St., Ste. 120; 53140; Kenosha; P 156,082; (262) 605-1100; Fax (262) 605-1111; info@kaba.org; www.kaba.org

Kiel • *Kiel Ind. Dev. Corp.* • John Laun; Secy.; 627 Fremont St.; P.O. Box 156; 53042; Calumet & Manitowoc; P 3,500; (920) 894-3488; Fax (920) 894-2150; www.kielwi.org

La Crosse • *La Crosse Area Dev. Corp.* • James P. Hill; Exec. Dir.; 712 Main St.; 54601; La Crosse; P 126,838; M 100; (608) 784-5488; (888) 208-0698; Fax (608) 784-5408; ladco@centurytel.net; www.ladcoweb.org

Ladysmith • *Ladysmith Comm. Ind. Dev. Corp.* • Al Christianson; City Admin.; 120 W. Miner Ave.; P.O. Box 431; 54848; Rusk; P 4,000; (715) 532-2600; Fax (715) 532-2620

Lancaster • *Lancaster Eco. Dev. Comm.* • Scot Simpson; City Admin.; 206 S. Madison St.; 53813; Grant; P 4,100; (608) 723-4246; Fax (608) 723-4789; www.lancasterwisconsin.com

Manitowoc • *EDC of Manitowoc County* • Connie Loden; Exec. Dir.; 202 N. 8th St., Ste. 101; P.O. Box 813; 54221; Manitowoc; P 81,500; (920) 482-0540; (920) 482-0541; Fax (920) 682-6816; cloden@edcmc.org; www.edcmc.org

Manitowoc • *Manitowoc Ind. Dev. Corp.* • David Less; City Planner; 900 Quay St.; 54220; Manitowoc; P 35,000; (920) 686-6930; Fax (920) 686-6939; dless@manitowoc.org; www.manitowoc.org

Marinette • *Marinette Area Eco. Dev. Corp.* • Mary D. Johns; Exec. Dir.; 601 Marinette Ave.; 54143; Marinette; P 21,000; (715) 735-6681; Fax (715) 735-6682; chamber@centurytel.net; www.mandmchamber.com

Marion • *Marion Eco. Dev. Corp.* • Tom Pamperin; Secy./Treas.; c/o Premier Community Bank; 230 Mavis Rd.; 54950; Shawano & Waupaca; P 1,250; (715) 754-2535; tpamperin@premiercommunity.com; www.marion.govoffice2.com

Marshfield • *Marshfield Area C/C & Ind.* • Scott Larson; Exec. Dir.; 700 S. Central Ave.; P.O. Box 868; 54449; Marathon & Wood; P 20,000; (715) 384-3454; Fax (715) 387-8925; info@marshfieldchamber.com; www.marshfieldchamber.com

Mauston • *Greater Mauston Area Dev. Corp.* • Barb Martin; Exec. Dir.; 103 Division St.; 53948; Juneau; P 28,000; (608) 847-7483; Fax (608) 847-5814; gmadc@mwt.net; www.mauston.com

Medford • *Medford Area Dev. Found.* • Mark Hoffman; Pres.; 104 E. Perkins St.; P.O. Box 172; 54451; Taylor; P 4,324; (715) 748-4729; www.medfordwis.com

Menomonie · *Dunn County Eco. Dev. Corp.* · Christopher A. Smith; Dir.; 401 Technology Dr. E., Ste. 400; 54751; Dunn; P 40,315; (715) 232-4009; Fax (715) 232-4034; info@dunnedc.com; www.dunnedc.com

Milwaukee · *Metro Milwaukee Assn. of Commerce* · Timothy Sheehy; Pres.; 756 N. Milwaukee St.; 53202; Milwaukee, Washington & Waukesha; P 1,500,000; M 2,000; (414) 287-4100; Fax (414) 271-7753; www.mmac.org

Milwaukee · *Milwaukee County Eco.& Comm. Dev.* · Robert Dennik; Dir.; 2711 W. Wells St., 5th Flr.; 53208; Milwaukee, Washington & Waukesha; P 970,000; (414) 278-4905; Fax (414) 223-1917; econdevelop@milwcnty.com; www.co.mil.wi.us;

Monticello · *Monticello Ind. Dev. Corp.* · Dennis Thoman; Pres.; P.O. Box 72; 53570; Green; P 1,207; (608) 938-4610; (608) 938-4383; www.monticello-wi.com

Neenah · *Future Neenah Inc.* · 135 W. Wisconsin Ave.; P.O. Box 896; 54957; Winnebago; P 25,000; (920) 722-1920; Fax (920) 722-6585; www.neenah.org

Neillsville · *Neillsville Dept. of Eco. Dev.* · Diane Murphy; Mayor; 118 W. 5th St.; City Hall; 54456; Clark; P 2,731; (715) 743-2105; Fax (715) 743-2727; neills@tds.net; www.neillsville-wi.com

New Glarus · *New Glarus Comm. Dev. Auth.* · Nicholas Owen; Village Admin.; P.O. Box 399; 53574; Green; P 2,107; (608) 527-2510; Fax (608) 527-2062; www.newglarusvillage.com

New Holstein · *New Holstein Ind. Dev. Corp.* · Lee Watson; Dir.; 2110 Washington St.; 53061; Calumet; P 3,335; (920) 898-5766; Fax (920) 898-5879; lwatson@tcei.com; www.ci.new-holstein.wi.us

New London · *New London Eco. Dev.* · Kent Hager; City Admin.; 215 N. Shawano St.; 54961; Outagamie & Waupaca; P 7,187; (920) 982-8500; Fax (920) 982-8665; www.newlondonwi.org

New London · *Waupaca County Eco. Dev. Corp.* · David Thiel; Exec. Dir.; N. 3512 Dawn Dr.; 54961; Outagamie & Waupaca; P 50,000; (920) 982-1582; Fax (920) 982-9047; wcedc@charter.net; www.wcedc.org

New Richmond · *Eco. Dev. Comm.* · Robert Barbian; Eco. Dev. Dir.; 156 E. 1st St.; 54017; St. Croix; P 7,858; (715) 246-4718; Fax (715) 246-7129; bbarbian@newrichmondwi.gov; www.ci.new-richmond.wi.us

Oak Creek · *Oak Creek Dept. of Comm. Dev.* · Doug Seymour; Dir.; 8640 S. Howell Ave.; 53154; Milwaukee; P 32,000; (414) 768-6526; Fax (414) 768-9587; dseymour@oakcreekwi.org; www.oakcreekwi.org

Oconomowoc · *Oconomowoc Bur. of Eco. Dev.* · Robert Duffy; Dir.; 174 E. Wisconsin Ave.; P.O. Box 27; 53066; Sheboygan; P 14,000; (262) 569-2185; (800) 524-3744; Fax (262) 569-3238; info@oconomowocusa.com; www.oconomowocusa.com

Omro · *Omro Area Dev. Corp.* · Steve Volkert; Dir.; 130 W. Larrabee St.; 54963; Winnebago; P 3,500; (920) 685-7005; Fax (920) 685-0384; omromarketing@charterinternet.net; www.omro-wi.com

Park Falls · *Park Falls Area Ind. Dev. Corp.* · 1224 S. 4th Ave.; 54552; Price; P 3,000; (715) 744-4700; pfacdc@pctcnet.net; www.pfacdc.org

Pewaukee · *Waukesha County Eco. Dev. Corp.* · Bill Mitchell; Exec. Dir.; 892 Main St., Ste. D; 53072; Waukesha; P 34,000; (262) 695-7900; Fax (262) 695-7902; www.understandingbusiness.org

Phillips · *Phillips Ind. Dev. Corp.* · Dennis Mathison; V.P.; 174 N. Avon; 54555; Price; P 1,500; (715) 339-2230; Fax (715) 339-4975

Platteville · *Platteville Area Ind. Dev. Corp.* · George Krueger; Exec. Dir.; 52 Means Dr., Ste. 104; 53818; Grant; P 10,000; (608) 348-3050; Fax (608) 348-3426; plattevilleindustry@centurytel.net; www.plattevilleindustry.com

Prairie du Chien · *Prairie du Chien Ind. Dev. Corp.* · Dick Mergen; Pres.; P.O. Box 247; 53821; Crawford; P 20,000; (608) 326-8187; Fax (608) 326-8187; www.prairieduchien.org

Prentice · *Prentice Ind. Dev. Corp.* · Dale Heikkinen; Pres.; 605 Spruce St.; 54556; Price; P 640; M 25; (715) 428-2124; Fax (715) 428-2120; daleh@pctcnet.net; www.vil.prentice.wi.gov

Reedsburg · *Reedsburg Ind. Dev. Comm.* · Don Lichte; Chrmn.; P.O. Box 490; 53959; Sauk; P 9,028; (608) 524-6404; Fax (608) 524-8458; www.reedsburgwi.gov

Rhinelander · *Oneida County Eco. Dev. Corp.* · Jim Kumbera; Exec. Dir.; 3375 Airport Rd.; P.O. Box 682; 54501; Oneida; P 33,853; (715) 369-9110; (715) 356-5590; Fax (715) 369-5758; ocedc@newnorth.net; www.ocedc.org

Rice Lake · *Red Cedar Dev. Corp.* · Bruce Markgren; Pres.; P.O. Box 526; 54868; Barron; P 8,312; (715) 234-7008; www.cityofricelake.com

Richland Center · *Richland County Eco. Dev. Corp.* · Ronda Fostering; Exec. Dir.; 140 Sextonville Rd.; P.O. Box 49; 53581; Richland; P 18,500; (608) 647-4310; Fax (608) 647-6118; RCEDC@mwt.net; www.richlandcounty.com

Shawano · *Shawano County Eco. Progress Inc.* · Stephen Sengstock; Exec. Dir.; 1263 S. Main; P.O. Box 35; 54166; Shawano; P 41,000; (715) 526-5839; Fax (715) 526-2125; scepi@frontiernet.net; www.shawanoecondev.org

Sheboygan · *Sheboygan Dev. Corp.* · 712 Riverfront Dr., Ste. 101; 53081; Sheboygan; P 113,000; (920) 457-9491; Fax (920) 457-6269

Shullsburg · *Shullsburg Comm. Dev. Corp.* · Cheryl Fink; Pres.; P.O. Box 3; 53586; Lafayette; P 1,247; M 25; (608) 965-4579; (608) 965-4424; cdc@mhtc.net; www.shullsburgwisconsin.org

Siren · *Burnett County Dev. Assn.* · Michael Kornmann; Advisor; 7410 County Rd. K, Ste. 129; 54872; Burnett; P 16,000; M 12; (715) 349-2979; www.burnettcounty.com

Soldiers Grove · *Soldiers Grove Comm. Dev.* · Tammy Kepler; Clerk/Treas.; P.O. Box 121; 54655; Crawford; P 640; (608) 624-3264; Fax (608) 624-5209; sgrove@mwt.net; www.soldiersgrove.com

Sparta · *City of Sparta Eco. Dev.* · Ken Witt; City Admin.; 201 W. Oak St.; 54656; Monroe; P 9,000; (608) 269-4340; (608) 269-7212; www.spartawisconsin.org

Sturgeon Bay · *Door County Eco. Dev. Corp.* · William D. Chaudoir; Exec. Dir.; 185 E. Walnut St.; 54235; Door; P 30,000; M 150; (920) 743-3113; Fax (920) 743-3811; bill@doorcounty-business.com; www.doorcountybusiness.com

Sturtevant · *Racine County Eco. Dev. Corp.* · Gordon Kacala; Exec. Dir.; 2320 Renaissance Blvd.; 53177; Racine; P 185,000; (262) 898-7400; gkacala@racinecountyedc.org; www.racinecountyedc.org

Superior · *The Dev. Assn. Inc.* · Andrew Lisak; Exec. Dir.; 1401 Tower Ave., Ste. 302; 54880; Douglas; P 71,400; M 160; (715) 392-4749; Fax (715) 392-6131; lisaka@developmentassociation.com; www.developmentassociation.com

Thorp · *Thorp Area Dev. Corp.* · P.O. Box 175; 54771; Clark; P 1,657; (715) 669-5628; www.cityofthorp.com

Tomah · *Forward Tomah Dev. Inc.* · Christopher Hanson; Exec. Dir.; P.O. Box 625; 54660; Monroe; P 8,100; (608) 372-2166; (800) 94-TOMAH; Fax (608) 372-2167; info@tomahwisconsin.com; www.tomahwisconsin.com

Viroqua · *Viroqua Dev. Assn.* · Jeff Gohlke; Ind. Coord.; 202 N. Main St.; 54665; Vernon; P 4,417; (608) 637-7154; Fax (608) 637-3108; cityadmin@mwt.net; www.viroqua-wisconsin.com

Waupun · *Waupun Ind. Dev. Corp.* · Gary Rogers; City Admin.; 201 E. Main St.; 53963; Fond du Lac; P 11,000; (920) 324-7919; Fax (920) 324-7939; www.cityofwaupun.org

Wausau · *MCDEVCO* · Roger A. Luce; Exec. Dir.; P.O. Box 6190; 54402; Marathon; P 127,280; (715) 845-6231; Fax (715) 845-6235; info@wausauchamber.com; www.wausauchamber.com

Wauwatosa · *Wauwatosa Eco. Dev. Corp.* · Paulette S. Enders; Eco. Dev. Dir.; 7725 W. North Ave.; 53213; Milwaukee; P 47,271; (414) 479-3531; Fax (414) 479-3532; penders@wauwatosa.net; www.wauwatosa.net

West Allis · *City of West Allis Dev. Dept.* · John F. Stibal; Dir. of Dev.; 7525 W. Greenfield Ave.; 53214; Milwaukee; P 60,410; (414) 302-8460; Fax (414) 302-8401; www.ci.west-allis.wi.us

West Bend · *West Bend Eco. Dev. Corp.* · Dan Anhalt; 400 University Dr.; c/o UW-Washington County; 53095; Washington; P 30,000; M 40; (262) 335-5218; Fax (262) 338-1771; info@wbachamber.org; www.wbachamber.org

Winneconne · *Winneconne Dev. Corp.* · Steve McNeil; Village Admin ; 30 S. 1st St.; P.O. Box 488; 54986; Winnebago; P 2,500; (920) 582-4381; Fax (920) 582-0660; smcneil@winneconnewi.gov; www.winneconniewi.gov

Wisconsin Rapids · *Heart of Wisconsin Bus. & Eco. Alliance* · Connie Loden; Exec. Dir.; 1120 Lincoln St.; 54494; Wood; P 40,000; (715) 423-1830; Fax (715) 423-1865; info@heartofwi.com; www.heartofwi.com

Wyoming

Federal

U.S. SBA, Wyoming Dist. Ofc. · Steven Despain; Dist. Dir.; 100 E. B St., Rm. 4001; Casper; 82601; Natrona; (307) 261-6500; Fax (307) 261-6535; robert.auflick@sba.gov; www.sba.gov/wy

Communities

Casper · *Casper Area Eco. Dev. Alliance* · Robert Barnes CEcD; Pres./CEO; 300 S. Wolcott, Ste. 300; 82601; Natrona; P 70,000; (307) 577-7011; (800) 634-5012; Fax (307) 577-7014; info@caeda.net; www.casperworks.biz

Cheyenne · *Cheyenne Leads* · Randy Bruns; CEO; 121 W. 15th St., Ste. 304; 82001; Laramie; P 80,000; (307) 638-6000; Fax (307) 638-7728; leads@cheyenneleads.org; www.cheyenneleads.org

Cody · *Cody Retention, Expansion & Education* · Garrett Growney; Chair; 836 Sheridan Ave.; 82414; Park; P 9,000; (307) 587-2639; Fax (307) 527-6228; admin@codychamber.org; www.codychamber.org

Diamondville · *So. Lincoln County Eco. Dev. Corp.* · Gigi Henkel; Dir.; P.O. Box 495; 83116; Lincoln; P 3,500; M 25; (307) 877-9781; Fax (307) 877-6709; slcedc@gmail.com; www.diamondvillewyo.com

Evanston · *City of Evanston Eco. Dev.* · Jim Davis; Clerk; City Hall; 1200 Main St.; 82930; Uinta; P 13,000; (307) 783-6300; Fax (307) 783-6390; www.evanstonwy.org

Evanston · *Uinta County Eco. Dev. Comm.* · Dell Atkinson; Dir.; 225 9th St.; 82930; Uinta; P 21,000; (307) 783-0378; Fax (307) 783-0379; deatkinson@uintacounty.com; www.uintacounty.com

Gillette · *Campbell County Eco. Dev. Corp.* · Phillipe M. Chino; Exec. Dir.; 201 W. Lakeway Rd., Ste. 1004; P.O. Box 3948; 82717; Campbell; P 36,000; M 85; (307) 686-2603; (800) 376-0848; Fax (307) 686-7268; ccedc@ccedc.net; www.gillettewyoming.com

Gillette · *North East Wyoming Eco. Dev. Coalition* · Linda Harris; Exec. Dir.; 2201 S. Douglas Hwy., Ste. 140; 82717; Campbell; P 53,000; (307) 686-3672; Fax (307) 686-3673; linda@newedc.com; www.newedc.com

Glendo · *Glendo Eco. Dev. Assn.* · Brenda Hagen; Town Clerk; 204 S. Yellowstone; P.O. Box 396; 82213; Platte; P 250; (307) 735-4242; Fax (307) 735-4422; townofglendo@yahoo.com; www.glendowy.govoffice2.com

Laramie · *Laramie Eco. Dev. Corp.* · Gaye Stockman; Pres./CEO; 313 S. 2nd St., Ste. B; P.O. Box 1250; 82073; Albany; P 30,000; (307) 742-2212; (307) 760-9905; Fax (307) 742-8200; ledc@laramiewy.org; www.laramiewy.org

Meeteetse · *Meeteetse Eco. Dev. Alliance* · P.O. Box 238; 82433; Park; P 600; (307) 868-2454; www.meeteetsewy.com;

Rawlins · *Carbon County Eco. Dev. Corp.* · Cindy Wallace; Exec. Dir.; 215 W. Buffalo St., Ste. 304; 82301; Carbon; P 15,720; (307) 324-3836; Fax (307) 324-3820; info@ccwyed.net; www.ccwyed.net

Riverton · *Riverton Mfg. Works* · Phillip Christopherson; 213 W. Main St., Ste. C; 82501; Fremont; P 10,000; (307) 856-0952; www.manufacturing-works.com

Rock Springs · *Sweetwater Eco. Dev. Assn.* · Michelle Hostetler; Dir.; 1400 Dewar Dr., Ste. 205A; 82901; Sweetwater; P 46,150; (307) 352-6874; (307) 371-5420; Fax (307) 371-6876; mhostetler@sweda.net; www.sweda.net

Sheridan · *Forward Sheridan* · John N. Thurow; Op. Mgr.; 203 S. Main St., Ste. 2003; 82801; Sheridan; P 27,111; M 67; (307) 673-8004; Fax (307) 673-8006; info@forwardsheridan.com; www.forwardsheridan.com

Torrington · *Goshen County Eco. Dev. Corp.* · Lisa Johnson; Exec. Dir.; 117 W. 22nd Ave.; P.O. Box 580; 82240; Goshen; P 13,000; M 90; (307) 532-5162; Fax (307) 532-7641; progress@goshenwyo.com; www.goshenwyo.com

Wheatland · *Wheatland Area Dev. Corp.* · 1560 Johnston St,; P.O. Box 988; 82201; Platte; P 3,500; (307) 322-4232; Fax (307) 322-1629; wadco@wyomingwireless.com; www.wadco.org

Worland · *Washakie Dev. Assn.* · LeAnn Baker; Exec. Dir.; 107 S. 7th St.; P.O. Box 228; 82401; Washakie; P 8,500; M 85; (307) 347-8900; wda@rtconnect.net; www.washakiedevelopment.com

Notes

The Canadian Chamber of Commerce

Canadian C/C

Head Office

360 Albert Street, Suite 420 • Ottawa, Ontario K1R 7X7
Telephone: (613) 238-4000 • FAX: (613) 238-7643
Email: info@chamber.ca • Website: www.chamber.ca

Toronto Office

55 University Ave., Suite 901 • Toronto, Ontario M5J 2H7
Telephone: (416) 868-6415 • FAX: (416) 868-0189
Website: www.chamber.ca

Montreal Office

1155 University Street, Suite 709 • Montreal, Quebec H3B 3A7
Telephone: (514) 866-4334 • FAX: (514) 866-7296
Website: www.chamber.ca

Calgary Office

186 Panorama Hills Close N.W. • Calgary, Alberta T3K 5J3
Telephone: (403) 271-0595 • FAX: (403) 226-6930
Website: www.chamber.ca

Senior Officers

Chair of the Board (September 2010–September 2011)
Elyse Allan, Pres./CEO of GE Canada (c/o Head Office)

President & Chief Executive Officer
Honourable Perrin Beatty (c/o Head Office)

Senior Vice President, Policy
Warren Everson (c/o Head Office)

Executive Vice President, Communications and Chamber Relations
Michel Barsalou (c/o Head Office)

Vice President and Chief Financial Officer
Adéle Laronde, CA (c/o Head Office)

Senior Vice President, Corporate Relations
Michael P. Nixon (c/o Toronto Office)

Canadian Chambers of Commerce

Alberta

Alberta Chambers of Commerce • Ken Kobly; Pres./CEO; 10025–102A Ave., Ste. 1808; Edmonton; T5J 2Z2; P 3,000,000; M 22,000; (780) 425-4180; Fax (780) 429-1061; info@ab chamber.ca; www.abchamber.ca

Airdrie • *Airdrie C/C* • Mike Brandrick; Pres.; #106, 120–2nd Ave. N.E.; Box 3661; T4B 2N2; P 39,000; M 435; (403) 948-4412; Fax (403) 948-3141; info@airdriechamber.ab.ca; www.airdriechamber.ab.ca

Alix • *Alix C/C* • Clarence Verveda; P.O. Box 145; T0C 0B0; P 825; M 15; (403) 747-2405; Fax (403) 747-2414

Athabasca • *Athabasca Dist. C/C* • Joan Veenstra; Secy.; P.O. Box 3074; T9S 2B9; P 10,500; M 60; chamber@athabascachamber.ca; www.athabascachamber.ca

Barrhead • *Barrhead & Dist. C/C* • Darren Strawson; Pres.; P.O. Box 4524; T7N 1A4; P 10,000; M 87; (780) 674-4600; info@barr headchamber.ca; www.barrheadchamber.ca

Beaverlodge • *Beaverlodge & Dist. C/C* • Herb Smith; Pres.; P.O. Box 303; T0H 0C0; P 2,900; M 65; (780) 354-8785; Fax (780) 354-2101

Berwyn • *Berwyn & Dist. C/C* • Linda Johnson; Pres.; P.O. Box 250; T0H 0E0; P 606; M 15; (780) 338-3922; vberwyn@wispernet. ca; www.berwyn.govoffice.com

Blairmore • *Crowsnest Pass C/C* • Cathy Mountford; Exec. Dir.; 12707 20th Ave.; P.O. Box 706; T0K 0E0; P 5,500; M 115; (403) 562-7108; cnpchamber@telus.net; www.cnpchamber.ca

Boyle • *Boyle & Dist. C/C* • Gordon Clark; P.O. Box 496; T0A 0M0; P 850; M 25; (780) 689-3636

Breton • *Breton & Dist. C/C* • Glory Tornack; Pres.; P.O. Box 364; T0C 0P0; P 2,000; M 25; (780) 696-2557; Fax (780) 696-2557

Brooks • *Brooks & Dist. C/C* • Tracy Acorn; Mgr.; #6-403 2nd Ave. W.; P.O. Box 400; T1R 1B4; P 25,000; M 300; (403) 362-7641; Fax (403) 362-6893; manager@brookschamber.ab.ca; www.brookschamber.ab.ca

Calgary • *Calgary C/C* • Heather Douglas; Pres./CEO; 100 6th Ave. S.W.; T2P 0P5; P 1,000,000; M 2,000; (403) 750-0400; Fax (403) 266-3413; chinfo@calgarychamber.com; www.calgarychamber.com

Camrose • *Camrose C/C* • Sharon Anderson; Exec. Dir.; 5402–48 Ave.; T4V 0J7; P 40,000; M 386; (780) 672-4217; (780) 679-0064; Fax (780) 672-1059; camcham@telus.net; www.camrosechamber.ca

Canmore • *Tourism Canmore* • John Samms; Exec. Dir.; 907 7th Ave.; P.O. Box 8608; T1W 2V3; P 17,000; M 200; (403) 678-1295; (866) 226-6673; Fax (403) 678-1296; info@tourismcanmore.com; www.tourismcanmore.com

Cardston • *Cardston & Dist. C/C* • Zenith Gaynor; Pres.; P.O. Box 1212; T0K 0K0; P 3,500; M 100; (403) 653-2798; info@cardston chamber.com; www.cardstonchamber.com

Coaldale • *Coaldale & Dist. C/C* • Dixie McCarley; Ofc. Mgr.; 1401 20 Ave.; P.O. Box 1117; T1M 1M9; P 6,000; M 150; (403) 345-2358; Fax (403) 345-2339; info@coaldalechamber.com; www.coaldalechamber.com

Cochrane • *Cochrane & Dist. C/C* • Gerri Polis; Mgr.; #5–205 1st St. E.; T4C 1X6; P 17,000; M 270; (403) 932-0320; Fax (403) 932-6824; c.business@cochranechamber.ca; www.cochranechamber.ca

Cold Lake • *Cold Lake Reg. C/C* • Sherri Bohme; Exec. Dir.; 4910– 50th Ave., Bay 109; P.O. Box 454; T9M 1P1; P 12,540; M 350; (780) 594-4747; Fax (780) 594-3711; clrcc@incentre.net; coldlakechamber.ca

Consort • *Consort & Dist. C/C* • Charlene Robichaud; Pres.; P.O. Box 335; T0C 1B0; P 2,300; M 40; (403) 577-7907; charlene.robichaud@ rbc.com; www.village.consort.ab.ca; psdahl@xplorenet.com

Devon · *Devon & Dist. C/C* · Wade Kosiorek; Ofc. Mgr.; 35 Athabasca Ave.; T9G 1G5; P 6,300; M 65; (780) 987-5177; Fax (780) 987-5135; devoncc@telus.net

Didsbury · *Didsbury & Dist. C/C* · Margo Ward; Pres.; P.O. Box 981; T0M 0W0; P 4,500; M 80; (403) 335-3265; Fax (403) 335-3265; info@didsburychamber.ca; www.didsburychamber.ca

Drayton Valley · *Drayton Valley & Dist. C/C* · Tara Petersen; Admin.; P.O. Box 5318; T7A 1R5; P 6,800; M 150; (780) 542-7578; Fax (780) 542-9211; chambrdv@telusplanet.net; www.dvchamber.com

Drumheller · *Drumheller & Dist. C/C* · Heather Bitz; Gen. Mgr.; 60–1 Ave. W.; Box 999; T0J 0Y0; P 7,800; M 210; (403) 823-8100; Fax (403) 823-4469; info@drumhellerchamber.com; www.drumhellerchamber.com

Edgerton · *Edgerton & Dist. C/C* · Box 192; T0B 1K0; P 403; (780) 755-3933; www.edgerton/oasis.ca;

Edmonton · *Edmonton C of C/World Trade Centre* · Martin D. Salloum; Pres./CEO; World Trade Centre; #700–9990 Jasper Ave.; T5J 1P7; P 1,034,945; M 3,000; (780) 426-4620; Fax (780) 424-7946; info@edmontonchamber.com; www.edmontonchamber.com

Edson · *Edson & Dist. C/C* · Heather Kelly; Mgr.; 5433 3rd Ave.; T7E 1L5; P 8,500; M 320; (780) 723-4918; Fax (780) 723-5545; manager@edsonchamber.com; www.edsonchamber.com

Elk Point · *Elk Point C/C* · Sandy Smith; Pres.; Box 639; T0A 1A0; P 1,500; M 58; (780) 724-2966; (780) 724-3810; www.elkpoint.ca

Evansburg · *Evansburg & Entwistle C/C* · Sarah Leteta; Mgr.; P.O. Box 598; T0E 0T0; P 2,000; M 80; (780) 727-4035; Fax (780) 727-4035; info@partnersonthepembina.com; www.partnersonthepembina.com

Fairview · *Fairview & Dist. C/C* · P.O. Box 1034; T0H 1L0; P 3,500; M 120; (780) 835-5999; Fax (780) 835-5991; fairviewchamber@telus.net; www.fairviewchamber.com

Falher · *Falher C/C* · Greg Radstaak; P.O. Box 814; T0H 1M0; P 5,000; M 60; (780) 837-2364; www.falherchamber.com

Falher · *Smoky River Reg. Eco. Dev. Bd.* · David Kane; Eco. Dev. Officer; P.O. Box 210; T0H 1M0; P 5,000; (780) 837-2364; Fax (780) 837-2453; dkane@mdsmokyriver.com; www.smokyriverregion.com

Foremost · *Foremost & Dist. C/C* · P.O. Box 272; T0K 0X0; P 500; M 50; (403) 867-3077; Fax (403) 867-2700; cofc4mst@la.shockware.com; www.foremostalberta.com

Fort Macleod · *Fort Macleod & Dist. C/C* · Emily McTighe; Pres.; P.O. Box 1959; T0L 0Z0; P 3,200; M 83; (403) 553-3391; (877) 622-5366; Fax (403) 553-2426; www.fortmacleod.com

Fort McMurray · *Fort McMurray C/C* · Diane Slater; CAO; #304–9612 Franklin Ave.; T9H 2J9; P 85,000; M 500; (780) 743-3100; Fax (780) 790-9757; fmcoc@telus.net; www.fortmcmurraychamber.ca

Fort McMurray · *Fort McMurray Tourism Assn.* · Denise Barrow; Ofc. Mgr.; 400 Sakitawaw Trl.; T9H 4Z3; P 80,000; M 150; (780) 791-4336; (800) 565-3947; Fax (780) 790-9509; info@fortmcmurraytourism.com; www.fortmcmurraytourism.com

Fort Saskatchewan · *Fort Saskatchewan C/C* · Conal MacMillan; Exec. Dir.; 10030– 99 Ave.; P.O. Box 3072; T8L 2T1; P 20,000; M 330; (780) 998-4355; Fax (780) 998-1515; chamber@fortsaskchamber.com; www.fortsaskchamber.com

Grande Cache · *Grande Cache C/C* · Richard Thompson; Pres.; P.O. Box 1342; T0E 0Y0; P 4,500; M 60; (780) 827-1217; (888) 827-3790; Fax (780) 827-5351; www.grandecache.ca

Grande Prairie · *Grande Prairie C/C* · Dan Pearcy; CEO; #217-11330 106th St.; T8V 7X9; P 50,000; M 1,100; (780) 532-5340; Fax (780) 532-2926; info@gpchamber.com; www.gpchamber.com

Grimshaw · *Grimshaw & Dist. C/C* · Jason Doris; Pres.; P.O. Box 919; T0H 1W0; P 2,500; M 67; info@grimshawchamber.com; www.grimshawchamber.com

High Level · *High Level & Dist. C/C* · Daina French; Mgr.; 10803 96th St.; T0H 1Z0; P 4,500; M 166; (780) 926-2470; hlchambr@incentre.net; www.highlevelchamber.com

High River · *High River & Dist. C/C* · Lynette McCracken; Mgr.; P.O. Box 5244; T1V 1M4; P 12,000; M 190; (403) 652-3336; Fax (403) 652-7660; hrdcc@telus.net; www.hrchamber.ca

Hinton · *Hinton & Dist. C/C* · Lori Phillips; Exec. Dir.; 309 Gregg Ave.; T7V 2A7; P 10,000; M 140; (780) 865-2777; (877) 446-8666; Fax (780) 865-1062; hintoncc@telus.net; www.hintonchamber.com

Jasper · *Jasper Tourism & Commerce* · Helen Kelleher-Empey; Gen. Mgr.; 409 Patrica St.; P.O. Box 98; T0E 1E0; P 5,000; M 300; (780) 852-3858; Fax (780) 852-4932; info@jaspercanadianrockies.com; www.jaspercanadianrockies.com

Killam · *Killam & Dist. C/C* · Dan Fee; Pres.; P.O. Box 189; T0B 2L0; P 1,100; M 35; (780) 385-3977; (780) 385-3034; www.town.killam.ab.ca

Lacombe · *Lacombe & Dist. C/C* · Anna Boruck; Pres.; 6005-50 Ave.; T4L 1K7; P 11,000; M 275; (403) 782-4300; Fax (403) 782-4302; info@lacombechamber.ca; www.lacombechamber.ca

Leduc · *Leduc & Dist. C/C* · Iris Yanish; Mgr.; 6420-50 St.; T9E 7K9; P 20,000; M 550; (780) 986-5454; Fax (780) 986-8108; info@leduc-chamber.com; www.leduc-chamber.com

Lethbridge · *Lethbridge C/C* · Jody Nilsson; Gen. Mgr.; 529-6th St. S., Ste. 200; T1J 2E1; P 82,000; M 650; (403) 327-1586; Fax (403) 327-1001; office@lethbridgechamber.com; www.lethbridgechamber.com

Lloydminster · *Lloydminster C/C* · Pat Tenney; Exec. Dir.; 4419–52nd Ave.; T9V 0Y8; P 25,000; M 520; (780) 875-9013; Fax (780) 875-0755; lloydminster@lloydminsterchamber.com; www.lloydminsterchamber.com

Marwayne · *Marwayne & Dist. C/C* · Sharon Kneen; Pres.; P.O. Box 183; T0B 2X0; P 569; M 25; (780) 847-3962; marwayne@hmsinet.ca; www.village.marwayne.ab.ca

McLennan · *McLennan C/C* · Jill Moses; Pres.; P.O. Box 90; T0H 2L0; P 900; M 33; (780) 324-3894; www.townofmclennan.com

Medicine Hat · *Medicine Hat & Dist. C/C* · MaryLou Hansen; Pres./CEO; 413-6 Ave. S.E.; T1A 2S7; P 60,000; M 675; (403) 527-5214; Fax (403) 527-5182; info@medicinehatchamber.com; www.medicinehatchamber.com;

Nanton · *Nanton C/C* · Jason Calvert; Interim Dir.; P.O. Box 711; T0L 1R0; P 2,000; M 75; (403) 336-2000; (403) 646-2029; president@nantonchamber.com; www.nantonchamber.com

Okotoks · *Okotoks & Dist. C/C* · Susan Klein; Exec. Asst.; 14 McRae St.; P.O. Box 1053; T1S 1B1; P 20,000; M 320; (403) 938-2848; Fax (403) 938-6649; okotokschamber@telus.net; www.okotokschamber.ca

Onoway · *Onoway & Dist. C/C* · Marinus Landsman; P.O. Box 723; T0E 1V0; P 2,800; M 20; (780) 967-6892; www.onoway.com

Oyen · *Oyen & Dist. C/C* · Kari Kuzmiski; Pres.; P.O. Box 718; T0J 2J0; P 1,500; M 50; (403) 664-0406; oyenecho@telusplanet.net

Peace River · *Peace River C/C* · Don Ames; Gen. Mgr.; 9309 100 St.; P.O. Box 6599; T8S 1S4; P 6,687; M 207; (780) 624-4166; Fax (780) 624-4663; www.peaceriverchamber.com

Picture Butte · *Picture Butte & Dist. C/C* · Andrew Noel; Pres.; 120 4th St. N.; P.O, Box 540; T0K 1V0; P 1,501; M 80; (403) 732-4302; (403) 732-4555; chamber@picturebutte.ca; www.picturebutte.ca

Pincher Creek • *Pincher Creek & Dist. Chamber of Eco. Dev.* • Kim Buckingham; P.O. Box 2287; T0K 1W0; P 7,000; M 150; (403) 627-5199; Fax (403) 627-5850; info@pincher-creek.com; www.pincher-creek.com

Ponoka • *Ponoka & Dist. C/C* • Darren Galan; Pres.; #1 4900 Hwy. 2A; P.O. Box 4188; T4J 1R6; P 10,000; M 190; (403) 783-3888; Fax (403) 783-3888; chamber@ponoka.org; ponokalive.ca

Provost • *Provost & Dist. C/C* • Anne Fraser; Secy./Treas.; P.O. Box 637; T0B 3S0; P 2,045; M 77; (780) 753-6288; Fax (780) 753-6060

Red Deer • *Red Deer C/C* • Tim Creedon; Exec. Dir.; 3017 Gaetz Ave.; T4N 5Y6; P 89,891; M 949; (403) 347-4491; Fax (403) 343-6188; rdchamber@reddeerchamber.com; www.reddeerchamber.com

Redwater • *Redwater & Dist. C/C* • Myron Buryn; Treas.; P.O. Box 322; T0A 2W0; P 2,400; M 40; (780) 942-3635

Rimbey • *Rimbey C/C* • Mary Rose Barr; Pres.; 5025 50th Ave.; Box 87; T0C 2J0; P 2,300; M 80; (403) 843-4000; rimbeychamber@rimbey.com; www.rimbey.com

Rocky Mountain House • *Rocky Mountain House & Dist. C/C* • 5406–48th St.; Box 1374; T4T 1B1; P 7,200; M 355; (403) 845-5450; Fax (403) 845-7764; rmhcofc@rockychamber.org; www.rockychamber.org

Saint Albert • *St. Albert C/C* • Lynda Moffet; Pres./CEO; 71 St. Albert Rd.; T8N 6L5; P 58,000; M 650; (780) 458-2833; Fax (780) 458-6515; chamber@stalbertchamber.com; www.stalbertchamber.com

Saint Paul • *St. Paul & Dist. C/C* • Rhea Labrie; Exec. Dir.; P.O. Box 887; T0A 3A0; P 5,200; M 145; (780) 645-5820; (780) 645-4481; Fax (780) 645-5820; admin@stpaulchamber.ca; www.stpaulchamber.ca

Sedgewick • *Sedgewick C/C* • Sue Freadrich; Secy./Treas.; T0B 4C0; P 891; M 50; (780) 384-2278; (780) 384-3504; www.sedgewickca.com

Sexsmith • *Sexsmith C/C* • Freda King; Pres.; P.O. Box 146; T0H 3C0; P 2,300; M 46; (780) 568-4663; chmbrtos@telusplanet.net; www.sexsmith.ca

Sherwood Park • *Sherwood Park & Dist. C/C* • Todd Banks; Exec. Dir.; 100 Ordze Ave.; T8B 1M6; P 82,000; M 875; (780) 464-0801; (866) 464-0801; Fax (780) 449-3581; exec@sherwoodparkchamber.com; www.sherwoodparkchamber.com

Smoky Lake • *Smoky Lake & Dist. C/C* • Wayne Taylor; Pres.; P.O. Box 635; T0A 3C0; P 4,500; M 50; (780) 656-3842; Fax (780) 451-3321; wayne@ethicaladvisor.com; www.smokylakeregion.ca

Spruce Grove • *Spruce Grove & Dist. C/C* • Brenda Johnson; Exec. Dir.; 99 Campsite Rd.; Box 4210; T7X 3B4; P 23,000; M 550; (780) 962-2561; Fax (780) 962-4417; info@sprucegrovechamber.com; www.sprucegrovechamber.com

Stettler • *Stettler Reg. Bd. of Trade & Comm. Dev.* • Keith Ryder; Exec. Dir.; 6606 50th Ave.; T0C 2L2; P 5,700; M 200; (403) 742-3181; (877) 742-9499; Fax (403) 742-3123; info@stettlerboardoftrade.com; www.stettlerboardoftrade.com

Stony Plain • *Stony Plain & Dist. C/C* • Denise Glubish; Exec. Asst.; 4815–44 Ave.; T7Z 1V5; P 13,500; M 545; (780) 963-4545; Fax (780) 963-4542; office@stonyplainchamber.ca; www.stonyplainchamber.ca

Swan Hills • *Swan Hills C/C* • Rita Krawiec; Pres.; P.O. Box 149; T0G 2C0; P 1,800; M 50; (780) 333-2209; (780) 333-4477; www.townofswanhills.com

Sylvan Lake • *Sylvan Lake C/C* • Laurie Breeze; Exec. Dir.; P.O. Box 9119; T4S 1S6; P 12,500; M 150; (403) 887-3048; Fax (403) 887-3048; info@sylvanlakechamber.com; www.sylvanlakechamber.com

Taber • *Taber & Dist. C/C* • Louie Tams; Pres.; 4702–50 St.; T1G 2B6; P 7,671; M 260; (403) 223-2265; Fax (403) 223-2291; tdcofc@telusplanet.net; www.taberchamber.com

Thorhild • *Thorhild C/C* • Michelle Boychuk; P.O. Box 384; T0A 3J0; P 3,000; M 40; (780) 398-2292; (780) 398-3550; thorhildchamber@telus.net; www.thorhild.com

Vegreville • *Vegreville & Dist. C/C* • Elaine Kucher; Gen. Mgr.; 5009 50th Ave.; P.O. Box 877; T9C 1R9; P 5,800; M 155; (780) 632-2771; Fax (780) 632-6958; vegchamb@telus.net; www.vegrevillechamber.com

Vermilion • *Vermilion & Dist. C/C* • 4606–52nd St.; T9X 0A1; P 4,435; M 110; (780) 853-6593; Fax (780) 853-1740; vermcofc@telusplanet.net; www.vermilionchamber.ca

Vulcan • *Vulcan & Dist. C/C* • Trish Standing; Pres.; P.O. Box 385; T0L 2B0; P 1,850; M 70; (403) 485-4105; www.vulcanchamber.com

Westlock • *Westlock & Dist. C/C* • Lesa Muller-Schmaus; P.O. Box 5917; T7P 2P7; P 5,200; M 78; (780) 349-2903; info@westlock.ca; www.westlock.ca

Wetaskiwin • *Wetaskiwin & Dist. C/C* • Brandi La Bonte; Exec. Dir.; 4910 55-A St.; T9A 2R7; P 12,000; M 232; (780) 352-8003; Fax (780) 352-6226; info@wetaskiwinchamber.ca; www.wetaskiwinchamber.ca

Whitecourt • *Whitecourt & Dist. C/C* • Pat VanderBurg; Mgr.; Box 1011; T7S 1N9; P 9,200; M 250; (780) 778-5363; Fax (780) 778-2351; manager@whitecourtchamber.com; www.whitecourtchamber.com

British Columbia

British Columbia C/C • John Winter; Pres./CEO; 1201-750 W. Pender St.; Vancouver; V6C 2T8; (604) 683-0700; Fax (604) 683-0416; bccc@bcchamber.org; www.bcchamber.org

100 Mile House • *South Cariboo C/C* • Christine Jordaan; Mgr.; #2–385 Birch Ave.; P.O. Box 2312; V0K 2E0; P 20,000; M 150; (250) 395-6124; Fax (250) 395-8974; manager@southcariboochamber.org; www.southcariboochamber.org

Abbotsford • *Abbotsford C/C* • David D. Hull; Exec. Dir.; 32900 S. Fraser Way, Unit 207; V2S 5A1; P 135,000; M 750; (604) 859-9651; Fax (604) 850-6880; acoc@telus.net; www.abbotsfordchamber.com

Armstrong • *Armstrong-Spallumcheen C/C* • Patti Noonan; Mgr.; P.O. Box 118; V0E 1B0; P 9,600; M 201; (250) 546-8155; Fax (250) 546-8868; manager@aschamber.com; www.aschamber.com

Bamfield • *Bamfield C/C* • John Mass; Pres.; General Delivery; V0R 1B0; P 365; M 40; (250) 728-3006; info@bamfieldchamber.com; www.bamfieldchamber.com

Barriere • *Barriere & Dist. C/C* • Lorne Richardson; Mgr.; P.O. Box 1190; V0E 1E0; P 3,500; M 55; (250) 672-9221; info@barrieredistrict.com; www.barrieredistrict.com

Bowen Island • *Bowen Island C/C* • Daniel Heald; Pres.; P.O. Box 199; V0N 1G0; P 3,500; M 125; (604) 947-9024; Fax (604) 947-0633; info@bowenisland.org; www.bowenisland.org

Burnaby • *Burnaby Bd. of Trade* • Darlene Gering; Exec. Dir.; 4555 Kingsway, Unit 201; V5H 4T8; P 150,000; M 850; (604) 412-0100; Fax (604) 412-0102; admin@bbot.ca; www.bbot.ca

Burns Lake • *Burns Lake & Dist. C/C* • Kelly Friesen; Mgr.; P.O. Box 339; V0J 1E0; P 13,000; M 100; (250) 692-3773; Fax (250) 692-3493; bldcoc@telus.net; www.bldchamber.ca

Cache Creek · *Cache Creek C/C* · Gordon Daily; Pres.; P.O. Box 460; V0K 1H0; P 1,100; M 30; (250) 457-9668; (250) 457-7661; Fax (250) 457-7662; benroy@telus.net

Campbell River · *Campbell River & Dist. C/C* · Colleen Evans; Exec. Dir.; 900 Alder St.; P.O. Box 400; V9W 5B6; P 30,000; M 500; (250) 287-8807; Fax (250) 286-6490; chamber@campbellriver chamber.ca; www.campbellriverchamber.ca

Castlegar · *Castlegar & Dist. C/C* · Pam McLeod; Exec. Dir.; 1995 6th Ave.; V1N 4B7; P 18,000; M 250; (250) 365-6313; (877) 365-6313; Fax (250) 365-5778; info@castlegar.com; www.castlegar.com

Celista · *North Shuswap C/C* · Jeff Tarry; Pres.; P.O. Box 101; V0E 1L0; P 3,800; M 100; (250) 955-2113; Fax (250) 955-2113; requests@northshuswapbc.com; www.northshuswapbc.com

Chase · *Chase & Dist. C/C* · Diana Ball; Mgr.; P.O. Box 592; V0E 1M0; P 15,000; M 100; (250) 679-8432; Fax (250) 679-3120; admin@chasechamber.com; www.chasechamber.com

Chemainus · *Chemainus & Dist. C/C & Visitor Center* · Mona Kennedy; Pres.; 9796 Willow St.; P.O. Box 575; V0R 1K0; P 8,000; M 130; (250) 246-3944; Fax (250) 246-3251; ccoc@islandnet.com; www.chemainus.bc.ca

Chetwynd · *Chetwynd & Dist. C/C* · Tonia Richter; Mgr.; 5217 N. Access Rd.; P.O. Box 870; V0C 1J0; P 5,000; M 125; (250) 788-3345; (250) 788-1943; Fax (250) 788-3655; manager@chetwyndchamber. ca; www.chetwyndchamber.ca

Chilliwack · *Chilliwack C/C* · Lisa Caruth; CEO; 46093 Yale Rd., Unit 201; Unit 16; V2P 2M3; P 80,000; M 515; (604) 793-4323; Fax (604) 793-4303; info@chilliwackchamber.com; www.chilli wackchamber.com

Christina Lake · *Christina Lake C/C* · Sheldon Weigel; Pres.; Hwy. 3 & Kimura Rd.; V0H 1E2; P 1,500; M 54; (250) 447-6161; Fax Same; cltourism@live.ca; www.christinalake.com

Clearwater · *Clearwater & Dist. C/C* · Bill Cairns; Mgr.; Box 1988; V0E 1N0; P 5,000; M 100; (250) 674-2646; Fax (250) 674-3693; info@clearwaterbcchamber.com; www.clearwater bcchamber.com

Cloverdale · *Cloverdale Dist. C/C* · Bill Reid; Exec. Dir.; 17685 56A Ave., Unit 201; V3S 1G4; P 40,000; M 300; (604) 574-9802; Fax (604) 574-9122; clovcham@axion.net; www.cloverdale.bc.ca

Coquitlam · *Tri-Cities C/C* · Suzette McFaul; Exec. Dir.; 1209 Pinetree Way; V3B 7Y3; P 200,000; M 830; (604) 464-2716; Fax (604) 464-6796; info@tricitieschamber.com; www.tricitieschamber.com

Courtenay · *Comox Valley C/C & Visitor Center* · Dianne Hawkins; Exec. Dir.; 2040 Cliffe Ave.; V9N 2L3; P 65,000; M 675; (250) 334-3234; Fax (250) 334-4908; admin@comoxvalley chamber.com; www.comoxvalleychamber.com

Cranbrook · *Cranbrook & Dist. C/C* · Karin Penner; Mgr.; 2279 Cranbrook St. N.; P.O. Box 84; V1C 4H6; P 25,000; M 480; (250) 426-5914; Fax (250) 426-3873; info@cranbrookchamber.com; www.cranbrookchamber.com

Crawford Bay · *Kootenay Lake C/C* · Paul Hindson; Pres.; P.O. Box 120; V0B 1E0; P 1,200; M 75; (250) 227-9233; info@kootenay lake.bc.ca; www.kootenaylake.bc.ca

Creston · *Creston C/C* · Mimika Coleman; Mgr.; P.O. Box 268; V0B 1G0; P 15,000; M 200; (250) 428-4342; Fax (250) 428-9411; crestonchamber@kootenay.com; www.crestonchamber.com

Cumberland · *Cumberland C/C & Visitors Center* · Mary Kornelsen; Mgr.; P.O. Box 250; V0R 1S0; P 3,000; M 70; (250) 336-8313; Fax (250) 336-2455; cumbcham@shaw.ca; www.cumberlandbc.org

Dawson Creek · *Dawson Creek & Dist. C/C* · Stefanie Oestreich; Mgr.; 10201 10th St.; V1G 3T5; P 12,500; M 300; (250) 782-4868; Fax (250) 782-2371; info@dawsoncreekchamber.ca; www.dawsoncreekchamber.ca

Dease Lake · *Dease Lake & Dist. C/C* · Amanda Jacobs; Ofc. Mgr.; P.O. Box 338; V0C 1L0; P ; M ; (250) 771-3900; Fax (250) 771-3900; www.stikine.net/community.html

Delta · *Delta C/C* · Peter Roaf; Exec. Dir.; 6201 60th Ave.; V4K 4E2; P 100,000; M 400; (604) 946-4232; Fax (604) 946-5285; execdirector@deltachamber.com; www.deltachamber.com

Duncan · *Duncan-Cowichan C/C* · Cathy Mailhot; Mgr.; 381 Trans-Canada Hwy.; V9L 3R5; P 80,000; M 340; (250) 748-1111; Fax (250) 746-8222; chamber@duncancc.bc.ca; www.duncancc.bc.ca

Elkford · *Elkford C/C* · Melody Anderson; Mgr.; P.O. Box 220; V0B 1H0; P 2,800; M 70; (250) 865-4614; Fax (250) 865-2442; info@ tourismelkford.ca; www.tourismelkford.ca

Enderby · *Enderby & Dist. C/C* · Tate Bengtson; Exec. Dir.; P.O. Box 1000; V0E 1V0; P 7,000; M 125; (250) 838-6727; Fax (250) 838-0123; enderbychamber@sunwave.net; www.enderbychamber.com

Esquimalt · *Esquimalt C/C* · Marilyn Holder; Mgr.; 1153 Esquimalt Rd.; P.O. Box 36019; V9A 7J5; P 16,151; (250) 704-2525; Fax (250) 380-6932; info@esquimaltchamber.com; www.esquimaltchamber.com

Falkland · *Falkland & Dist. C/C* · Pres.; P.O. Box 92; V0E 1W0; P 700; M 10; falklandchamber@yahoo.ca; www.falklandbc.ca

Fernie · *Fernie C/C* · Lynn Flokstra; Mgr.; 102 Commerce Rd.; V0B 1M5; P 4,900; M 310; (250) 423-6868; Fax (250) 423-3811; office@ferniechamber.com; www.ferniechamber.com

Fort Langley · *see Langley*

Fort Nelson · *Fort Nelson & District C/C* · Val Lefebvre; Exec. Dir.; P.O. Box 196; V0C 1R0; P 5,000; M 200; (250) 774-2956; Fax (250) 774-2958; info@fortnelsonchamber.com; www.fort nelsonchamber.com

Fort St. James · *Fort St. James C/C* · Mindy Thompson; Mgr.; P.O. Box 1164; V0J 1P0; P 5,000; M 110; (250) 996-7023; Fax (250) 996-7047; fsjchamb@fsjames.com; www.fortstjameschamber.com

Fort St. John · *Fort St. John & Dist. C/C* · Annette Oake; Mgr.; 9325 100 St., Unit 202; V1J 4N4; P 18,000; M 400; (250) 785-6037; Fax (250) 785-6050; info@fsjchamber.com; www.fsjchamber.com

Fraser Lake · *Fraser Lake & Dist. C/C* · Audrey Fenneme; Pres.; P.O. Box 1059; V0J 1S0; P 1,300; M 32; (250) 699-8667; info@ fraserlakechamber.com;

Gabriola Island · *Gabriola Island C/C* · Carol Ramsay; Mgr.; 377 Berry Point Rd., Unit 5; P.O. Box 249; V0R 1X0; P 5,000; M 110; (250) 247-9332; Fax (250) 247-9332; giccmanager@shaw.ca; www.gabriolaisland.org

Galiano Island · *Galiano Island C/C* · Carolyn Jerome; Pres.; P.O. Box 73; V0N 1P0; (250) 539-2233; info@galianoisland.com; www.galianoisland.com

Gibsons · *Gibsons & Dist. C/C* · Dean Walford; Exec. Dir.; P.O. Box 1190; V0N 1V0; P 25,000; M 240; (604) 886-2325; Fax (604) 886-2379; gibsonsbcchamber@telus.net; www.gibsonsbc.ca/chamber

Gold River · *Gold River C/C* · Gabriella Pentz; Pres.; #1 Hwy. 28; V0P 1G0; P 1,400; M 22; (250) 283-7333; villageofgoldriver@ cablerocket.com; www.goldriver.ca;

Golden · *Kicking Horse Country C/C* · Ruth Kowalski; Mgr.; P.O. Box 1320; V0A 1H0; P 8,800; M 221; (250) 344-7125; Fax (250) 344-6688; info@goldenchamber.bc.ca; www.goldenchamber.bc.ca

Grand Forks • *Grand Forks & Dist. C/C* • Cher Wyers; Mgr.; P.O. Box 1086; V0H 1H0; P 4,235; M 145; (250) 442-2833; Fax (250) 442-5688; manager@grandforkschamber.com; www.grandforkschamber.com

Greenwood • *Greenwood Bd. of Trade* • Al Warren; Pres.; P.O. Box 430; V0H 1J0; P 900; M 30; (250) 445-6323; Fax (250) 445-6166; gbtic@direct.ca; www.greenwoodcity.com

Harrison Hot Springs • *Harrison Agassiz C/C* • Robert Reyerse; Pres.; P.O. Box 429; V0M 1K0; P 7,500; M 70; (604) 796-3664; Fax (604) 796-3694; infoserve@harrison.ca; www.harrison.ca

Hope • *Hope & Dist. C/C* • Karen Scalise; Ofc. Mgr.; P.O. Box 588; V0X 1L0; P 10,000; M 100; (604) 869-3111; Fax (604) 869-8208; info@hopechamber.bc.ca; www.hopechamber.bc.ca

Houston • *Houston & Dist. C/C* • Maureen Czirfusz; Mgr.; P.O. Box 396; V0J 1Z0; P 3,500; M 93; (250) 845-7640; Fax (250) 845-3682; manager@houstonchamber.ca; www.houstonchamber.ca

Inveremere • *Columbia Valley C/C* • Al Miller; Pres.; P.O. Box 1019; V0A 1K0; P 10,000; M 275; (250) 342-2844; Fax (250) 342-3261; info@cvchamber.ca; www.cvchamber.ca

Kamloops • *Greater Kamloops C/C* • Deb McClelland; Exec. Dir.; 1290 W. Trans-Canada Hwy.; V2C 6R3; P 84,000; M 750; (250) 372-7722; (800) 662-1994; Fax (250) 828-9500; mail@kamloopschamber.bc.ca; www.kamloopschamber.bc.ca

Kaslo • *Kaslo & Dist. C/C* • Debra Hamilton; Pres.; P.O. Box 329; V0G 1M0; P 1,036; M 55; (250) 353-7323; rbdlang@netidea.com; www.kaslochamber.com

Kelowna • *Kelowna C/C* • Weldon LeBlanc; CEO; 544 Harvey Ave.; V1Y 6C9; P 100,400; M 1,670; (250) 861-3627; Fax (250) 861-3624; weldon@kelownachamber.org; www.kelownachamber.org

Keremeos • *Similkameen Country Dev. Assoc.* • Gary Yuzik; Pres.; P.O. Box 490; V0X 1N0; P 5,000; M 126; (250) 499-5225; Fax (250) 499-5225; siminfo@nethop.net; www.similkameencountry.org

Kimberley • *Kimberley & Dist. C/C & Visitors Center* • Sioban Staplin; Exec. Dir.; 270 Kimberley Ave.; V1A 3N3; P 7,000; M 200; (250) 427-3666; Fax (250) 427-5378; info@kimberleychamber.ca; www.kimberleychamber.com

Kitimat • *Kitimat C/C* • Trish Parsons; Mgr.; 2109 Forest Ave.; P.O. Box 214; V8C 2G7; P 9,000; M 190; (250) 632-6294; Fax (250) 632-4685; info@visitkitimat.com; www.visitkitimat.com

Ladysmith • *Ladysmith C/C & Visitor Info. Center* • Brian Bancroft; Pres.; 132C Roberts St.; P.O. Box 598; V9G 1A4; P 7,200; M 210; (250) 245-2112; Fax (250) 245-2124; info@ladysmithcofc.com; www.ladysmithcofc.com

Lake Country • *Lake Country C/C & Visitors Center* • Linda Wilson; Mgr.; 9522 Main St., Unit 40; V4V 2L9; P 10,000; M 211; (250) 766-5670; (888) 766-5670; Fax (250) 766-0170; admin@lakecountrychamber.com; www.lakecountrychamber.com

Lake Cowichan • *Cowichan Lake Dist. C/C* • Jim Humphrey; Pres.; 125C S. Shore Rd.; P.O. Box 824; V0R 2G0; P 6,953; M 107; (250) 749-3244; Fax (250) 749-0187; info@cowichanlake.ca; www.cowichanlake.ca

Langley • *Greater Langley C/C* • Lynn Whitehouse; Exec. Dir.; 5761 Glover Rd., Unit 1; V3A 8M8; P 125,000; M 1,100; (604) 530-6656; Fax (604) 530-7066; chamber@langleychamber.com; www.langleychamber.com

Likely • *Likely & Dist. C/C* • P.O. Box 29; V0L 1N0; P 350; M 45; (250) 790-2127; chamber@likely-bc.ca; www.likely-bc.ca

Lillooet • *Lillooet & Dist. C/C* • Scott Hutchinson; Pres.; P.O. Box 650; V0K 1V0; P 10,000; M 50; (250) 256-3578; info@lillooetchamberofcommerce.com; www.lillooetchamberofcommerce.com

Lumby • *Lumby & Dist. C/C* • Stephanie Sexsmith; Mgr.; P.O. Box 534; V0E 2G0; P 5,800; M 100; (250) 547-2300; Fax (250) 547-2390; lumbychamber@shaw.ca; www.monasheetourism.com

Lytton • *Lytton & Dist. C/C* • Peggy Chute; Secy./Treas.; P.O. Box 460; V0K 1Z0; P 3,000; M 70; (250) 455-2523; Fax (250) 455-6669; lyttoncofc@lyttonbc.net; www.lyttonchamber.com

Mackenzie • *Mackenzie C/C* • Kelly McEachnie; Mgr.; 88 Centennial Dr.; P.O. Box 880; V0J 2C0; P 3,000; M 70; (250) 997-5459; Fax (250) 997-6117; office@mackenziechamber.bc.ca; www.mackenziechamber.bc.ca

Madeira Park • *Pender Harbour & Egmont C/C* • Kerry Milligan; Mgr.; 12911 Madeira Park Rd.; P.O. Box 265; V0N 2H0; P 2,900; M 86; (604) 883-2561; (604) 740-2712; Fax (604) 883-2561; info@penderharbour.ca; www.penderharbour.ca

Maple Ridge • *Maple Ridge-Pitt Meadows C/C* • Dean Barbour; Exec. Dir.; 22238 Lougheed Hwy.; V2X 2T2; P 90,000; M 600; (604) 463-3366; Fax (604) 463-3201; admin@ridgemeadowschamber.com; www.ridgemeadowschamber.com

Mayne Island • *Mayne Island Comm. C/C* • Peter Sara; Chrmn.; P.O. Box 2; V0N 2J0; P 900; M 50; (250) 539-5034; info@mayneislandchamber.ca; www.mayneislandchamber.ca

McBride • *McBride & Dist. C/C* • Bill Arnold; Pres.; P.O. Box 2; V0J 2E0; P 2,500; M 65; (250) 569-3366; (866) 569-3366; come2mcbride@telus.net; www.mcbridebc.info

Merritt • *Merritt & Dist. C/C* • Guy Duchaine; Pres.; P.O. Box 1649; V1K 1B8, P , M ; (250) 378-5634; Fax (250) 378-6561; manager@merrittchamber.com; www.merrittchamber.com

Mill Bay • *South Cowichan C/C* • Rosalie Power; Mgr.; 2720 Mill Bay Rd., Unit 368; V0R 2P1; P 15,000; M 155; (250) 743-3566; Fax (250) 743-5332; southcowichanchamber@shaw.ca; www.southcowichanchamber.org

Mission • *Mission Reg. C/C* • Michelle Favero; Mgr.; 34033 Lougheed Hwy.; V2V 5X8; P 37,500; M 390; (604) 826-6914; (877) 826-6914; Fax (604) 826-5916; manager@missionchamber.bc.ca; www.missionchamber.bc.ca

Nakusp • *Nakusp & Dist. C/C & Visitor Center* • Marilyn Rivers; Mgr.; P.O. Box 387; V0G 1R0; P 1,700; M 150; (250) 265-4234; Fax (250) 265-3808; chamber@nakusparrowlakes.com; www.nakusparrowlakes.com

Nanaimo • *Greater Nanaimo C/C* • S.D. (Lee) Mason; Exec. Dir.; 2133 Bowen Rd.; V9S 1H8; P 130,000; M 875; (250) 756-1191; Fax (250) 756-1584; lee@nanaimochamber.bc.ca; www.nanaimochamber.bc.ca

Nelson • *Nelson & Dist. C/C & Visitors Center* • Tom Thomson; Exec. Dir.; 225 Hall St.; V1L 5X4; P 9,700; M 480; (250) 352-3433; (877) 663-5706; Fax (250) 352-6355; info@discovernelson.com; www.discovernelson.com

New Denver • *Slocan Dist. C/C* • P.O. Box 448; V0G 1S0; P 2,000; M 50; (250) 358-2544; Fax (250) 358-7998; chamber@slocanlake.com; www.slocanlake.com

New Westminster • *New Westminster C/C* • David Brennan; Exec. Dir.; 601 Queens Ave.; V3M 1L1; P 58,000; M 340; (604) 521-7781; Fax (604) 521-0057; nwcc@newwestchamber.com; www.newwestchamber.com

North Vancouver • *North Vancouver C/C* • Anne McMullin; Pres./Gen. Mgr.; 102-124 W. 1st St.; V7M 3N3; P 130,000; M 900; (604) 987-4488; Fax (604) 987-8272; wayne@nvchamber.ca; www.nvchamber.ca

Okanagan Falls • *see Oliver*

Oliver · *South Okanagan C/C* · Bonnie Dancey; Mgr.; 34205 99th St.; P.O. Box 460; V0H 1T0; P 35,000; M 345; (250) 498-6321; (205) 498-7030; Fax (250) 498-3156; manager@sochamber.ca; www.sochamber.ca

Osoyoos · *see Oliver*

Parksville · *Parksville & Dist. C/C* · Gary Child; Pres.; P.O. Box 99; V9P 2G3; P 39,000; M 457; (250) 248-3613; Fax (250) 248-5210; info@parksvillechamber.com; www.parksvillechamber.com

Peachland · *Peachland C/C* · Darlene Hartford; Mgr.; 5812 Beach Ave.; V0H 1X7; P 4,880; M 100; (250) 767-2455; Fax (250) 767-2420; peachlandchamber@shawcable.com; www.peachlandchamber.bc.ca

Pemberton · *Pemberton & Dist. C/C* · Shirley Henry; Mgr.; P.O. Box 370; V0N 2L0; P 7,000; M 172; (604) 894-6477; Fax (604) 894-5571; info@pembertonchamber.com; www.pembertonchamber.com

Pender Island · *Pender Island C/C* · Carol Budnyk; Pres.; P.O. Box 123; V0N 2M0; P 2,500; M 100; (250) 629-3988; travel@penderislandchamber.com; www.penderislandchamber.com

Penticton · *Penticton & Wine Country C/C* · Lorraine Renyard; Gen Mgr.; 553 Railway St.; V2A 8S3; P 33,000; M 700; (250) 492-4103; Fax (250) 492-6119; admin@penticton.org; www.penticton.org

Pitt Meadows · *see Maple Ridge*

Port Hardy · *Port Hardy & Dist. C/C* · Yana Hrdy; Gen. Mgr.; 7250 Market St.; P.O. Box 249; V0N 2P0; P 5,000; M 223; (250) 949-7622; Fax (250) 949-6653; phcc@cablerocket.com; www.ph-chamber.bc.ca

Port McNeill · *Port McNeill & Dist. C/C* · C.L. Jorgenson; Exec. Dir.; 1594 Beach Dr.; P.O. Box 129; V0N 2R0; P 2,800; M 115; (250) 956-3131; Fax (250) 956-3132; pmccc@island.net; www.portmcneill.net

Port Renfrew · *Port Renfrew C/C* · Rose Betsworth; Pres.; P.O. Box 39; V0S 1K0; P 300; M 32; (250) 647-0175; rosieb1@telus.net; www.portrenfrewcommunity.com

Powell River · *Powell River C/C* · Kim Miller; Mgr.; 6807 Wharf St.; V8A 1T9; P 12,000; M 300; (604) 485-4051; office@powellriverchamber.com; www.powellriverchamber.com

Prince George · *Prince George C/C* · Jennifer Brandle-McCall; CEO; 890 Vancouver St.; V2L 2P5; P 80,000; M 1,000; (250) 562-2454; Fax (250) 562-6510; chamber@pgchamber.bc.ca; www.pgchamber.bc.ca

Prince Rupert · *Prince Rupert & Dist. C/C* · Lynne Graham; Exec. Dir.; 215 Cow Bay Rd., Unit 100; V8J 1A2; P 13,500; M 245; (250) 624-2296; Fax (250) 624-6105; manager@princerupertchamber.ca; www.princerupertchamber.ca

Princeton · *Princeton & Dist. C/C & Visitors Center* · Lori Thomas; Mgr.; P.O. Box 540; V0X 1W0; P 5,000; M 100; (250) 295-3103; Fax (250) 295-3255; chamber@nethop.net; www.princeton.ca

Qualicum Beach · *Qualicum Beach C/C* · Judi Ainsworth; Gen. Mgr.; 124 W. 2nd Ave.; P.O. Box 159; V9K 1S7; P 8,502; M 275; (250) 752-0960; Fax (250) 752-2923; chamber@qualicum.bc.ca; www.qualicum.bc.ca

Quathiaski Cove · *Discovery Islands C/C* · Rod Burns; Pres.; P.O. Box 790; V0P 1N0; P 3,800; M 93; (866) 285-2724; chamber@discoveryislands.ca; www.discoveryislands.ca/chamber

Quesnel · *Quesnel & Dist. C/C* · Coralee Oakes; Mgr.; 335 E. Vaughan St.; V2J 2T1; P 25,000; M 220; (250) 747-0125; Fax (250) 992-7262; qchamber@quesnelbc.com; www.quesnelchamber.com

Radium · *Radium Hot Springs C/C* · Kent Kebe; Mgr.; P.O. Box 225; V0A 1M0; P 800; M 120; (250) 347-9331; (888) 347-9331; Fax (250) 347-9127; info@radiumhotsprings.com; www.radiumhotsprings.com

Revelstoke · *Revelstoke C/C* · John Dewitt; Exec. Dir.; P.O. Box 490; V0E 2S0; P 8,800; M 254; (250) 837-5345; Fax (250) 837-4223; revelstokeinfo@telus.net; www.revelstokechamber.com

Richmond · *Richmond C/C* · Craig Jones; Exec. Dir.; Ste. 101, South Tower; 5811 Cooney Rd.; V6X 3M1; P 181,203; M 1,200; (604) 278-2822; Fax (604) 278-2972; cjones@richmondchamber.ca; www.richmondchamber.ca

Rossland · *Rossland C/C* · Julie Parker; Mgr.; 2197 Columbia Ave.; P.O. Box 1385; V0G 1Y0; P 3,500; M 190; (250) 362-5666; Fax (250) 362-5399; commerce@rossland.com; www.rossland.com

Saanich Peninsula · *see Sidney*

Salmo · *Salmo & Dist. C/C* · Heather Street; Mgr.; P.O. Box 400; V0G 1Z0; P 3,300; M 30; (250) 357-2596; Fax Same; salmoch@telus.net; www.salmo.net

Salmon Arm · *Salmon Arm & Dist. C/C* · Corryn Garyston; Gen. Mgr.; 20 Hudson Ave. N.E., Unit 101; P.O. Box 999; V1E 4P2; P 17,000; M 395; (250) 832-6247; (877) 725-6667; Fax (250) 832-8382; admin@sachamber.bc.ca; www.sachamber.bc.ca

Salt Spring Island · *Salt Spring Island C/C* · Paul Neale; Gen. Mgr.; 121 Lower Ganges Rd.; V8K 2T1; P 12,000; M 321; (250) 537-4223; Fax (250) 537-4276; chamber@ssisland.com; www.saltspringtourism.com

Sandspit · *Sandspit/North Moresby C/C* · 343 Alliford Bay Rd., Ste. 1; P.O. Box 148; V0T 1T0; P 460; M 45; (250) 637-2466;

Sechelt · *Sechelt & Dist. C/C* · Colleen Clark; Exec. Dir.; 102 5700 Cowrie St.; P.O. Box 360; V0N 3A0; P 10,000; M 240; (604) 885-0662; Fax (604) 885-0691; sdcoc9@telus.net; www.secheltchamber.bc.ca

Seton · *Shalalth Dist. C/C* · Dennis DeYagher; Pres.; P.O. Box 2067; V0N 3B0; P 800; M 20; (250) 259-8268; snor@uniserve.com

Sicamous · *Sicamous & Dist. C/C* · Doreen Favel; Exec. Dir.; 110 Finlayson St.; P.O. Box 346; V0E 2V0; P 3,166; M 200; (250) 836-3313; Fax (250) 836-4368; sicamouschamber@cablelan.net; www.sicamouschamber.bc.ca

Sidney · *Saanich Peninsula C/C* · Eileen Leddy; Exec. Dir.; 201-2453 Beacon Ave.; P.O. Box 2014; V8L 3S3; P 45,000; M 400; (250) 656-3616; Fax (250) 656-7111; info@peninsulachamber.ca; www.peninsulachamber.ca

Smithers · *Smithers Dist. C/C* · Heather Gallagher; Mgr.; P.O. Box 2379; V0J 2N0; P 5,217; M 200; (250) 847-5072; Fax (250) 847-3337; info@smitherschamber.com; www.smitherschamber.com

Sooke · *Sooke Harbour C/C* · John Zaremba; Mgr.; 2070 Phillips Rd.; P.O. Box 18; V9Z 0E4; P 11,000; M 176; (250) 642-6112; info@sookeharbourchamber.com; www.sookeharbourchamber.com

Sorrento · *South Shuswap C/C* · Judy Smith; Pres.; P.O. Box 7; V0E 2W0; P 8,000; M 105; (250) 835-4669; sorrentochamber@telus.net; www.southshuswapchamberofcommerce.org

Sparwood · *Sparwood & Dist. C/C* · Katrina Cohrs; Mgr.; P.O. Box 1448; V0B 2G0; P 4,211; M 110; (250) 425-2423; (877) 485-8185; Fax (250) 425-7130; manager@sparwoodchamber.bc.ca; www.sparwoodchamber.bc.ca

Squamish · *Squamish C/C* · Kenny G. Music; Gen. Mgr.; 38551 Loggers Ln., Ste. 102; V8B 0H2; P 17,000; M 500; (604) 815-4990; (604) 815-4991; admin@squamishchamber.com; www.squamishchamber.com

Stewart • *Stewart-Hyder Intl. C/C* • Gwen McKay; Mgr.; P.O. Box 306; V0T 1W0; P 500; M 60; (250) 636-9224; Fax (250) 636-2199; info@stewart-hyder.com; www.stewart-hyder.com

Summerland • *Summerland Chamber of Eco. Dev. & Tourism* • Lisa Jaager; Mgr.; 15600 Hwy. 97; P.O. Box 130; V0H 1Z0; P 12,000; M 750; (250) 494-2686; Fax (250) 494-4039; summerland chamber@shawbiz.ca; www.summerlandchamber.bc.ca

Surrey • *Surrey Bd. of Trade* • Anita Huberman; Exec. Dir.; 101-14439 104th Ave.; V3R 1M1; P 460,000; M 1,300; (604) 581-7130; Fax (604) 588-7549; info@businessinsurrey.com; www.businessinsurrey.com

Tahsis • *Tahsis C/C* • Darrell Hunter; P.O. Box 278; V0P 1X0; P 600; M 20; (250) 934-6425; Fax (250) 934-6667; info@tahsischamber. com; www.tahsischamber.com

Terrace • *Terrace & Dist. C/C* • Carol Fielding; Exec. Dir.; 4511 Keith Ave.; V8G 1K1; P 20,000; M 350; (250) 635-2063; (250) 638-7117; Fax (250) 635-2573; terracechamber@telus.net; www. terracechamber.com

Tofino • *Tofino-Long Beach C/C* • Michael Tilitzky; Exec. Dir.; P.O. Box 249; V0R 2Z0; P 1,600; M 250; (250) 725-3153; Fax (250) 725-3296; info@tofinochamber.org; tofinochamber.org

Trail • *Trail & Dist. C/C* • Kristan Iorio; Exec. Dir.; 200-1199 Bay Ave.; V1R 4A4; P 19,000; M 240; (250) 368-3144; Fax (250) 368-6427; tcoc2@netidea.com; www.trailchamber.com

Tumbler Ridge • *Tumbler Ridge C/C* • Neel Trasy; Pres.; 340 Front St.; P.O. Box 1780; V0C 2W0; P 4,000; M 99; (250) 242-0015; Fax (250) 242-0025; trcofc@pris.ca; www.tumblerridgechamber.ca

Ucluelet • *Ucluelet C/C* • Marny Saunders; Gen. Mgr.; P.O. Box 428; V0R 3A0; P 1,800; M 140; (250) 726-4641; Fax (250) 726-4611; marny@uclueletinfo.com; www.uclueletinfo.com

Valemount • *Valemount & Area C/C* • Marie Birkeck; Exec. Dir./ Mgr.; P.O. Box 690; V0E 2Z0; P ; M ; (250) 566-0061; Fax (250) 566-0061; chamber@valemount.com

Vananda • *Texada Island C/C* • Elayne Boloten; Secy.; P.O. Box 249; V0N 3K0; P 1,200; M 95; (604) 486-7457; Fax (604) 486-6703; brakes@telus.net; www.texada.org

Vancouver Area

Kitsilano C/C • Terry Clark; Pres.; 2628 Granville St., Unit 207; V6H 4B4; P 75,000; M 395; (604) 731-4454; (877) 312-1898; Fax (604) 681-4545; admin@kitsilanochamber.com; www. kitsilanochamber.com

Tourism Vancouver-Tourist Info. Centre • Rick Antonson; Pres./CEO; Plaza Level; 200 Burrard St.; V6C 3L6; P 2,200,000; M 1,200; (604) 683-2000; Fax (604) 682-6839; info@tourism vancouver.com; www.tourismvancouver.com

Vancouver Bd. of Trade • Darcy Rezac; Mgr. Dir./CEO; 400–999 Canada Pl.; V6C 3E1; P 2,200,000; M 5,500; (604) 681-2111; Fax (604) 681-0437; contactus@boardoftrade.com; www.boardoftrade.com

Vanderhoof • *Vanderhoof & Dist. C/C* • Erin Siemens; Mgr.; P.O. Box 126; V0J 3A0; P 4,500; M 170; (250) 567-2124; Fax (250) 567-3316; manager@vanderhoofchamber.com; www.vanderhoof chamber.com

Vernon • *Greater Vernon C/C* • Val Trevis; Mgr.; 2901 32nd St.; V1T 5M2; P 50,000; M 710; (250) 545-0771; Fax (250) 545-3114; info@vernonchamber.ca; www.vernonchamber.ca

Victoria • *Greater Victoria C/C* • Bruce Carter; CEO; 100-852 Fort St.; V8W 1H8; P 350,000; M 1,550; (250) 383-7191; Fax (250) 385-3552; chamber@gvcc.org; www.victoriachamber.ca

Victoria • *WestShore C/C* • Dan Spinner; CEO; 2830 Aldwynd Rd.; V9B 3S7; P 50,000; M 470; (250) 478-1130; Fax (250) 478-1584; chamber@westshore.bc.ca; www.westshore.bc.ca

Wells • *Wells & Dist. C/C* • Wanda Johnstone; Mgr.; P.O. Box 123; V0K 2R0; P 250; M 50; (250) 994-3223; (877) 451-9355; Fax (250) 994-3223; info@wellsbc.com; www.wellsbc.com

West Vancouver • *West Vancouver C/C* • Leagh Gabriel; Exec. Dir.; 1846 Marine Dr.; V7V 1J6; P 43,000; M 300; (604) 926-6614; Fax (604) 925-7220; admin@westvanchamber.com; www.west vanchamber.com

Westbank • *Westbank & Dist. C/C* • Leah Thordarson; Exec. Dir.; 2375 Pamela Rd., Unit 4; V4T 2H9; P 50,000; M 500; (250) 768-3378; Fax (250) 768-3465; chamber@westbankchamber.com; www.westbankchamber.com

Whistler • *Whistler C/C* • Fiona Famulak; Pres./CEO; 4230 Gateway Dr., Unit 201; V0N 1B4; P 10,000; M 830; (604) 932-5922; Fax (604) 932-3755; chamber@whistlerchamber.com; www. whistlerchamber.com

White Rock • *White Rock & South Surrey C/C* • Doug Hart; Exec. Dir.; 100-15261 Russell Ave.; V4B 2P7; P 100,000; M 700; (604) 536-6844; Fax (604) 536-4994; info@whiterockchamber.com; www.whiterockchamber.com

Williams Lake • *Williams Lake & Dist. C/C* • Claudia Blair; Exec. Dir.; P.O. Box 4878; V2G 2V8; P 12,000; M 300; (250) 392-5025; Fax (250) 392-4214; visitors@telus.net; www.williamslakechamber.com

Zeballos • *Zeballos Bd. of Trade* • P.O. Box 208; V0P 2A0; P 150; (250) 761-4201; (250) 761-4229; www.zeballos.com;

Manitoba

Manitoba C/C • Graham S. Starmer; Pres.; 227 Portage Ave.; Winnipeg; R3B 2A6; P 1,200,000; M 10,000; (204) 948-0100; Fax (204) 948-0110; mbchamber@mbchamber.mb.ca; www. mbchamber.mb.ca

Altona • *Altona & Dist. C/C* • Brad Derksen; Pres.; P.O. Box 329; R0G 0B0; P 3,900; M 150; (204) 324-8793; Fax (204) 324-1314; chamber@shopaltona.com; www.shopaltona.com

Arborg • *Arborg & Dist. C/C* • Lorne Floyd; Pres.; P.O. Box 415; R0C 0A0; P 6,000; M 47; (204) 376-2878; lnlfloyd@mymts.net

Ashern • *Ashern & Dist. C/C* • Clayton Gibson; Pres.; Box 582; R0C 0E0; P 1,500; M 57; president@ashern.ca; www.ashern.ca

Beausejour • *Beausejour & Dist. C/C* • Ken Zirk; Pres.; Box 224; R0E 0C0; P 8,000; M 80; (204) 268-3502; beausejourchamber@ mts.net; www.mybeausejour.com/chamber

Boissevain • *Boissevain & Dist. C/C* • Donna Fraser; Pres.; P.O. Box 734; R0K 0E0; P 2,000; M 50; (204) 534-2010; Fax (204) 534-2015; ffamfarm@explorenet.com; www.boissevain.ca

Brandon • *Brandon C/C* • Nathan Peto; Gen. Mgr.; 1043 Rosser Ave.; R7A 0L5; P 45,000; M 650; (204) 571-5340; Fax (204) 571-5347; gm@brandonchamber.ca; www.brandonchamber.ca

Carberry • *Carberry & Dist. C/C* • Betty Buurma; Pres.; Box 101; R0K 0H0; P 4,000; M 50; (204) 834-2700; Fax (204) 834-2842; carberrysigns@mts.net; www.townofcarberry.ca

Carman • *Carman & Comm. C/C* • Cor Lodder; Pres.; P.O. Box 249; R0G 0J0; P 8,000; M 155; (204) 750-3050; ccchamber@gmail.com; www.carmanchamberofcommerce.com

Churchill • *Churchill C/C* • Rose Preteau; Pres.; Box 176; R0B 0E0; P 900; M 50; (204) 675-2022; (888) 389-2327; Fax (204) 675-2021; churchillchamber@mts.net; www.churchill.ca

Crystal City · *Crystal City & Dist. C/C* · Doug Treble; Box 56; R0K 0N0; P 750; M 36; (204) 873-2427; Fax (204) 873-2656; chamberofcommerce@crystalcitymb.ca; www.crystalcitymb.ca

Cypress River · *Cypress River C/C* · Jim Cassels; Pres.; P.O. Box 261; R0K 0P0; P 200; M 22; (204) 743-2119; Fax (204) 743-2339; cypressmotorinnone@hotmail.com; www.cypressriver.ca

Dauphin · *Dauphin & District C/C* · Lisa Fee; Coord.; 100 Main St. S.; R7N 1K3; P 10,000; M 187; (204) 622-3140; Fax (204) 622-3141; dauphinchamber@mts.net; www.dauphinchamber.ca

Deloraine · *Deloraine & Dist. C/C* · Deb Calverley; Pres.; P.O. Box 748; R0M 0M0; P 1,500; M 50; (204) 747-2842; Fax (204) 747-2856; debcalv@mts.net; www.deloraine.org

Elie · *Elie C/C* · Rick Desilets; Pres.; P.O. Box 175; R0H 0H0; P 1,000; M 58; (204) 353-2892;

Elkhorn · *Elkhorn C/C* · Sharlean Bickerton; Pres.; Box 141; R0M 0N0; P 490; M 20; (204) 845-2388; (204) 845-2161; info@elkhorn.mb.ca; www.elkhorn.mb.ca

Eriksdale · *Eriksdale & Dist. C/C* · Keith Lundale; Pres.; P.O. Box 434; R0C 0W0; P 920; M 20; (204) 739-2606; jcwatson@xplornet.com; www.areyouonline.biz/chamber

Falcon Beach · *Falcon-West Hawk-Caddy Lakes C/C* · Shaun Harbottle; Pres.; Box 187; R0E 0N0; P 400; M 54; (204) 349-2214; Fax (204) 349-3008; info@chamber-southwhiteshell.ca; www.chamber-southwhiteshell.ca

Fisher Branch · *Fisher Branch C/C* · Darcy Plett; Pres.; Box 566; R0C 0Z0; P 500; M 36; (204) 372-6253; Fax (204) 372-8545; testocki@mts.net

Flin Flon · *Flin Flon & Dist. C/C* · Idelite Branedhorst; Secy./Mgr.; 235-35 Main St.; R8A 1J7; P 9,000; M 100; (204) 687-4518; Fax (204) 687-4456; flinflonchamber@mts.net; www.cityofflinflon.com/chamber

Gillam · *Gillam C/C* · John Cullen; Pres.; P.O. Box 366; R0B 0L0; P 1,200; M 27; (204) 652-5135; Fax (204) 652-5155; jcullen@hydro.mb.ca; www.townofgillam.com

Glenboro · *Glenboro Comm. Dev. Corp.* · Christine Tanasichuk; Dev. Officer; Box 296; R0K 0X0; P 1,500; M 200; (204) 827-2575; Fax (204) 827-2575; gcdc@glenboro.com; www.glenboro.com

Grandview · *Grandview & Dist. C/C* · Lisa Boughton; P.O. Box 28; R0L 0Y0; P 1,000; M 35; (204) 546-5250; grandviewchamberofcommerce@hotmail.com; www.grandviewmanitoba.net

Grunthal · *Grunthal & Dist. C/C* · Leonard Hiebert; Pres.; P.O. Box 451; R0A 0R0; P 3,000; M 26; (204) 434-6750; Fax (204) 434-9353; leonard@emergencyvehicles.ca; www.grunthal.ca

Hamiota · *Hamiota C/C* · Wayne Mathison; Pres.; P.O. Box 310; R0M 0T0; P 1,000; M 45; (204) 764-2487; (204) 764-3050; Fax (204) 764-3055; midwestrec@hamiota.com; www.hamiota.com

Hartney · *Hartney & Dist. C/C* · Carol Thomas; Pres.; P.O. Box 224; R0M 0X0; P 450; M 40; (204) 858-2089; Fax (204) 858-2089; slwevans@mts.net

Headingley · *Headingley Reg. C/C* · Jill Ruth; Pres.; 5353 Portage Ave.; R4H 1J9; P ; M ; (204) 889-3132; Fax (204) 831-0816; dwhitermofheadingley@mts.net; www.rmofheadingley.ca

Killarney · *Killarney & Dist. C/C* · Ms. Lee Bartley; Pres.; Box 809; R0K 1G0; P 3,500; M 100; (204) 523-4202; Fax (204) 523-4202; killarneychamberofcommerce@hotmail.com; www.killarneymanitoba.com

La Salle · *La Salle & Dist. C/C* · Donna Bell; Pres.; P.O. Box 608; R0G 1B0; P 3,000; M 39; (204) 736-4555; Fax (204) 736-4363; taketwo@taketwoinc.com

Lac Du Bonnet · *Lac Du Bonnet & Dist. C/C* · Donna Tschetter; Pres.; P.O. Box 598; R0E 1A0; P 3,350; M 125; (204) 345-8194; Fax (204) 345-8194; kimbuhay@mts.net; www.lacdubonnetchamber.com

Landmark · *Landmark & Area C/C* · Brian Ryall; P.O. Box 469; R0A 0X0; P ; M ; (204) 355-4035; office@landmarkonline.ca; www.landmarkonline.ca

Macgregor · *MacGregor & Dist. C/C* · Keith McFall; Pres.; P.O. Box 685; R0H 0R0; P 3,024; M 45; (204) 685-2945; (204) 685-2033; Fax (204) 685-3032; edbraak@mts.net; www.macgregorchamber.com

Melita · *Melita & Dist. C/C* · Murray Cameron; Pres.; P.O. Box 666; R0M 1L0; P 1,200; M 71; (204) 522-3285; Fax (204) 522-3536; gvanbese@mts.net; www.melitamb.ca

Minnedosa · *Minnedosa & Dist. C/C* · Don Farr; Pres.; Box 857; R0J 1E0; P 5,000; M 103; (204) 867-6350; Fax (204) 867-6391; chamber@minnedosachamber.ca; www.minnedosachamber.ca

Morden · *Morden & Dist. C/C* · Pamela Hiebert; Mktg & Promotions Dir.; 311 N. Railway St.; R6M 1S9; P 7,500; M 235; (204) 822-5630; Fax (204) 822-2041; marketing@mordenchamber.com; www.mordenchamber.com

Morris · *Morris & Dist. C/C* · Rick Edel; Pres.; P.O. Box 98; R0G 1K0; P 1,650; M 75; (204) 746-2223; Fax (204) 746-8963; fehrscle@mts.net; www.town.morris.mb.ca

Neepawa · *Neepawa & Dist. C/C* · Amanda Naughton-Gale; Pres.; P.O. Box 726; R0J 1H0; P 3,500; M 140; (204) 476-5292; Fax (204) 476-5231; neepawachamber@mts.net; www.neepawachamber.com

Niverville · *Niverville C/C* · Leighton Reimer; Pres.; P.O. Box 157; R0A 1E0; P 3,500; M 90; (204) 388-4325; chamber@niverville.com; www.niverville.com

Notre Dame · *Notre Dame C/C* · Lise Deleurme; Pres.; P.O. Box 107; R0G 1M0; P 619; M 60; (204) 248-2073; Fax (204) 248-2073; deleurme@mts.net; www.notre-dame-de-lourdes.ca

Oak Lake · *Oak Lake C/C* · Greg Vincent; Pres.; P.O. Box 23; R0M 1P0; P ; M ; (204) 855-3287; Fax (204) 855-3287; gvincent@mts.net

Oakville · *Oakville & Dist. C/C* · Warren Bracken; Pres.; P.O. Box 263; R0H 0Y0; P 600; M 50; (204) 267-2792; (204) 267-2112; Fax (204) 267-7015; bingram@mts.net

Pilot Mound · *Pilot Mound & Dist. C/C* · Carolanne Bayne; Pres.; P.O. Box 356; R0G 1P0; P 1,000; M 50; (204) 825-2432; Fax (204) 825-2438; chamberofcommerce@pilotmound.com

Pinawa · *Pinawa C/C* · Marsha Sheppard; P.O. Box 544; R0E 1L0; P ; M ; (204) 753-2747; Fax (204) 753-8478; chamber@granite.mb.ca; www.pinawachamber.com

Plum Coulee · *Plum Coulee & Dist. C/C* · Moira Porte; Pres.; Box 392; R0G 1R0; P 800; M 32; (204) 829-3615; Fax (204) 325-4132; brewstr@mts.net; www.plumcoulee.com

Portage la Prairie · *Portage la Prairie & Dist. C/C* · Michele Redmond; Exec. Dir.; 11-2nd St. N.E.; R1N 1R8; P 18,000; M 275; (204) 857-7778; Fax (204) 857-4095; info@portagechamber.com; www.portagechamber.com

Rivers · *Rivers & Dist. C/C* · Jean Young; Secy./Treas.; P.O. Box 795; R0K 1X0; P 1,100; M 50; (204) 328-7316; Fax (204) 328-4460; mbeever@mts.net

Riverton · *Riverton & Dist. C/C* · Bernice Danielson; Pres.; P.O. Box 238; R0C 2R0; P 560; M 60; (204) 378-2855; rivertoncoop@mts.net; www.rivertoncanada.com

Roblin • *Roblin & Dist. C/C* • Gerald Stuart; Pres.; P.O. Box 160; R0L 1P0; P 1,800; M 85; (204) 937-3194; (204) 937-2176; Fax (204) 937-3817; rdcoc@mts.net; www.roblinmanitoba.com

Rosenort • *Rosenort & Dist. C/C* • Alvin Rempel; Pres.; P.O. Box 222; R0G 1W0; P ; M ; (204) 746-4217; Fax (204) 746-8878; alvdia@mts.net; www.rosenortchamber.blogspot.com

Rossburn • *Rossburn & Dist. C/C* • Valerie White; Secy.; P.O. Box 579; R0J 1V0; P 500; M 30; (204) 859-2409; (204) 859-3334; Fax (204) 859-2134; wheatland@mts.net; www.town.rossburn.mb.ca

Russell • *Russell & Dist. C/C* • Mark Keating; Pres.; P.O. Box 579; R0J 1W0; P 2,000; M 100; (204) 773-2456; Fax (204) 773-3525; chamber@russellmb.com; www.russellmb.com

Saint-Boniface • *Saint-Boniface C/C* • Michele Lecuyer-Hutton; Pres.; CP 204; R2H 3B4; P 100,000; M 150; (204) 235-1406; Fax (204) 233-1017; info@ccfsb.mb.ca; www.ccfsb.mb.ca

Selkirk • *Selkirk & Dist. C/C* • Beverley Clagg; Ofc. Mgr.; 200 Eaton Ave.; R1A 0W6; P 25,000; M 130; (204) 482-7176; Fax (204) 482-5448; sadcoc@mts.net, info@selkirkanddistrictchamber.ca; www.selkirkanddistrictchamber.ca

Shoal Lake • *Shoal Lake C/C Inc.* • Norm Sims; Pres.; P.O. Box 547; R0J 1Z0; P 1,150; M 70; (204) 759-3343; Fax (204) 759-2740; cyrilp@mts.net; www.shoallake.ca

Souris • *Souris & Glenwood C/C* • Colleen Robbins; Pres.; P.O. Box 939; R0K 2C0; P 1,653; M 85; (204) 483-2070

Sprague • *Piney & Dist. C/C* • Dennis Konchak; Pres.; P.O. Box 50; R0A 1Z0; P ; M ; (204) 437-2259; Fax (204) 437-2561; dwk@wiband.ca

Ste. Rose du Lac • *Ste. Rose & Dist. C/C* • Trefor Gates; Pres.; P.O. Box 688; R0L 1S0; P 1,050; M 50; (204) 447-2196; Fax (204) 447-2692; storestarter@yahoo.ca; www.town.sterosedulac.mb.ca

Steinbach • *Steinbach C/C* • Paul Neustaedter; Pres.; 225 Reimer Ave., Unit B; P.O. Box 1795; R5G 1N4; P 25,000; M 264; (204) 326-9566; Fax (204) 346-3638; stbcofc@mts.net; www.steinbach chamberofcommerce.com

Stonewall • *Stonewall & Dist. C/C* • Deborah Jensen; Pres.; Box 762; R0C 2Z0; P 5,000; M 76; (204) 467-8377; (204) 467-7125; info@stonewallchamber.com; www.stonewallchamber.com

St-Pierre-Jolys • *St. Pierre C/C* • Marcel Mulaire; Box 71; R0A 1V0; P 1,000; M 53; (204) 433-7123; Fax (204) 433-3015; marcel@delowater.ca; www.stpierrejolys.com

Swan River • *Swan Valley C/C* • Colleen Immerkar; Exec. Asst.; P.O. Box 1540; R0L 1Z0; P 4,500; M 165; (204) 734-3102; Fax (204) 734-4342; srcc@svcn.mb.ca

Teulon • *Teulon & Dist. C/C* • Michael Ledarney; Pres.; P.O. Box 235; R0C 1H0; P 5,000; M 40; (204) 886-3662; Fax (204) 886-3232; president@teulonchamber.ca; www.teulon.com

The Pas • *The Pas & Dist. C/C* • Mrs. Shel Hein; Box 996; R9A 1L1; P 12,800; M 170; (204) 623-7256; Fax (204) 623-2589; tpinfo@mts.net; www.thepaschamber.com

Thompson • *Thompson C/C* • Keith MacDonald; Pres.; P.O. Box 363; R8N 1N2; P 15,000; M 185; (204) 677-4155; Fax (204) 677-3434; commerce@mts.net; www.thompsonchamber.mb.ca

Treherne • *Treherne & Dist. C/C* • Keith Sparling; Pres.; P.O. Box 344; R0G 2V0; P ; M ; (204) 723-2774; (204) 723-2665; ksparling@inethome.ca; www.treherne.ca

Virden • *Virden Comm. C/C* • Madison Mossop; Mgr.; Box 899; R0M 2C0; P 3,500; M 110; (204) 851-1551; virdencc@mts.net; www.virden.ca

Waskada • *Waskada & Dist. C/C* • Margie Hannah; Pres.; P.O. Box 239; R0M 2E0; P 150; M 15; (204) 673-2656; (204) 673-2522; Fax (204) 673-2535; waskada@shurgro.com; www.waskada.ca

Winkler • *Winkler & Dist. C/C* • Brenda Storey; Exec. Dir.; 185 Main St.; R6W 1B4; P 9,000; M 280; (204) 325-9758; Fax (204) 325-8290; chamber@winkleronline.com; www.winklerchamber.com

Winnipeg Area

Aboriginal C/C • Darrell Brown; Pres.; 203-350 Portage Ave.; R3C 0C3; P 700,000; M 50; (204) 237-9359; Fax (204) 947-0145; info@aboriginalchamber.ca; www.aboriginalchamber.ca

Assiniboia C/C • Ernest Nairn; Exec. Dir.; 1867 Portage Ave.; Box 42122, RPO Ferry Road; R3J 3X7; P ; M 23; (204) 774-4154; Fax (204) 774-4201; info@assiniboiacc.mb.ca; www.assiniboiacc.mb.ca

Winnipeg C/C • Dave Angus; Pres./CEO; 100–259 Portage Ave.; R3B 2A9; P 700,000; M 1,800; (204) 944-8484; Fax (204) 944-8492; info@winnipeg-chamber.com; www.winnipeg-chamber.com

Zhoda • *Pansy & Dist. C/C* • Michael Narth; P.O. Box 87; R0A 2P0; P 750; M 12; (204) 425-3530; Fax (204) 425-3048

New Brunswick

New Brunswick C/C • Peter Lindfield; Pres.; 1 Canada Rd.; Edmundston; E3V 1T6; (506) 737-1868; Fax (506) 737-1862; info@nbchamber.ca; www.nbchamber.ca

Baie Ste-Anne • *Baie Ste-Anne C/C* • Seraphie Martin; 346 CH Riviere du Portage; E9A 1G8; P 2,000; (506) 228-4837

Bathurst • *Greater Bathurst C/C* • Donna Landry; Gen. Mgr.; 725 College St.; CEI Bldg.; E2A 4B9; P 50,000; M 311; (506) 548-8498; Fax (506) 548-2200; bathcham@nbnet.nb.ca; www.bathurst chamber.ca

Boiestown • *Miramichi Bd. of Trade* • Olga Ross; Secy.; 6506 Rte. 8; E6A 1Z7; P 2,414; M 25; (506) 369-2617;

Bouctouche • *Bouctouche C/C* • Claude LeBlanc; Pres.; 211 Irving Blvd.; P.O. Box 2104; E4S 2J2; P 32,000; M 130; (506) 743-2411; (506) 955-5757; Fax (506) 743-8991; chambouc@nb.aibn.com; www.bouctouche.ca

Campbellton • *Campbellton Reg. C/C* • Greg Davis; Pres.; 18 Water St.; P.O. Box 234; E3N 3G4; P 7,000; M 215; (506) 759-7856; Fax (506) 759-7557; crcc@nbnet.nb.ca; www.campbellton regionalchamber.ca

Caraquet • *La Chambre de Commerce de Caraquet* • Reginald Boudreau; Pres.; 220 boul. St-Pierre W.; P.O. Box 5570; E1W 1B8; P 4,200; M 200; (506) 727-2931; Fax (506) 727-3191; chambre@nb.aira.com; www.chambregrandcaraquet.com

Centreville • *Centreville C/C* • Kathleen Simonson; Secy.; 836 Central St.; E7K 2E7; P 550; M 45; (506) 276-3674; www.villageofcentreville.ca

Edmundston • *Edmundston Reg. C/C* • Mrs. Amelie Jarret; Gen. Mgr.; 1 Canada Rd.; E3V 1T6; P 18,000; M 350; (506) 737-1866; Fax (506) 737-1862; info@ccedmundston.com; www.ccedmundston.com

Florenceville • *Florenceville C/C* • Robert McNutt; P.O. Box 601; E7L 1Y7; P 862; M 43; (506) 392-0900; (506) 392-5249; www.florencevillenb.ca

Fredericton · *Enterprise Fredericton* · Doug Motty; Exec. Dir.; 570 Queen St., Ste. 102; E3B 6Z6; P 125,000; (506) 444-4686; Fax (506) 444-4649; www.enterprisefredericton.ca

Fredericton · *Fredericton C/C* · Anthony Knight; CEO; 270 Rookwood Ave.; P.O. Box 275; E3B 4Y9; P 46,000; M 860; (506) 458-8006; Fax (506) 451-1119; fchamber@frederictonchamber.ca; www.frederictonchamber.ca

Grand Bay–Westfield · *River Valley C/C* · Cindy Price; Mgtg. Mgr.; P.O. Box 3123; E5K 4V4; P 12,000; M 87; (506) 657-6369; Fax (506) 657-6361; www.rvchamberofcommerce.com

Grand' Digue · *Cocagne & Notre Dame C/C* · Mr. Gilles Allain; Pres.; 27 Michel Rd.; E4R 4V9; P 9,000; M 45; (506) 532-8956; Fax (506) 576-6073; gallain@mobility.blackberry.net

Grand Falls · *Grand Falls, Saint-Andre & Drummond C/C* · Klod Binette; Gen. Dir.; 131 rue Pleasant Rd., Ste. 200; E3Z 1G6; P 30,000; M 244; (506) 473-1905; Fax (506) 475-7779; gfcocgs@nbnet.nb.ca; www.grandfalls.com

Grand Manan · *Grand Manan C/C* · Joan Gallant; Secy./Treas.; 101 Green St.; E5G 3B7; P 2,800; M 100; (506) 662-3442; info@grandmanannb.com; www.grandmanannb.com

Hampton · *Hampton Area C/C* · Gail Kilpatrick; Secy.; 27 Centennial Rd., Unit 6; E5N 6N3; P 5,000; M 82; (506) 832-2559; Fax (506) 832-2807; hacc@nbnet.nb.ca; www.hamptonareachamber.org

Miramichi · *Greater Miramichi C/C* · Veronique Arsenault; Exec. Dir.; P.O. Box 342; E1N 3A7; P 18,000; M 200; (506) 622-5522; Fax (506) 622-5959; mirchamber@nb.aibn.com; www.miramichi chamber.com

Moncton · *Greater Moncton C/C* · Valerie Roy; CEO; 910 Main St., Ste. 100; E1C 1G6; P 120,000; M 800; (506) 857-2883; Fax (506) 857-9209; www.gmcc.nb.ca

Oromocto · *Oromocto & Area C/C* · Lloyd Chambers; Pres.; P.O. Box 20124; E2V 2R6; P 25,000; M 100; (506) 446-6043; Fax (506) 446-6925; oromoctochamber@nb.aibn.com; www.oromocto chamber.nb.ca

Richibucto · *Kent-Centre C/C* · Tim Burns; Pres.; 9235 Main St., Ste. 1; E4W 4B4; P 1,300; M 32; (506) 523-7870; kccc@richibucto. org; www.richibucto.org

Riviere du Portage · *Riviere du Portage C/C* · Jean-Robert Godin; Pres.; 5898B Route 11; E9H 1X2; P 2,000; M 15; (506) 393-7977;

Rogersville · *Collette C/C* · Maurice Desroches; Pres.; 60 Rue Des Arbres; E4Y 1G4; P 700; (506) 775-2898;

Rogersville · *Rogersville C/C* · Ivan Bourque; Pres.; 11033 Principal St.; E4Y 2L7; P 3,000; M 84; (506) 775-2728; www.rogersville.info

Sackville · *Greater Sackville C/C* · Kate Bredin; Exec. Dir.; 87 Main St., Unit 8; E4L 4A9; P 5,600; M 120; (506) 364-8911; Fax (506) 364-8082; gscc@eastlink.ca

Saint Andrews · *St. Andrews C/C* · Julie Crichton; Exec. Dir.; 46 Reed Ave.; E5B 1A1; P 1,900; M 110; (506) 529-3555; Fax (506) 529-8095; stachamb@nbnet.nb.ca; www.standrewsbythesea.ca

Saint Francois · *Saint Francois C/C* · Camille Landry; Pres.; P.O. Box 378; E7A 1G4; P 1,575; M 225; (506) 992-6050; Fax (506) 992-6067

Saint John · *Saint John Bd. of Trade* · Imelda Gilman; Pres.; 40 rue King St.; P.O. Box 6037; E2L 4R5; P 120,000; M 650; (506) 634-8111; Fax (506) 632-2008; info@sjboardoftrade.com; www.sjboardoftrade.com

Saint-Simon · *Saint-Simon C/C* · 403 S. le Boutheller St.; E8P 1Z6; P 800; M 30; (506) 727-2467

Shippagan · *Shippagan C/C* · Natasha Landry; Dir.; 227 blvd. J.D. Gauthier; E8S 1N2; P 2,000; M 140; (506) 336-3993; chambre decommercedeshippagan@nb.aibn.com

St. Stephen · *St. Stephen Area C/C* · 73 Milltown Blvd., Ste. 112; E3L 1G5; P 5,000; M 150; (506) 466-7703; Fax (506) 466-7753; info@town.ststephen.nb.ca; www.town.ststephen.nb.ca

Sussex · *Sussex & Dist. C/C* · Phil Sellars; Pres.; 66 Broad St., Unit 2; P.O. Box 5152; E4E 5L2; P 35,000; M 145; (506) 433-1845; Fax (506) 433-1886; sdcc@nb.aibn.com; www.sdccinc.org

Woodstock · *Greater Woodstock C/C* · Lynn Rose; Pres.; 220 King St., Unit 2; E7M 1Z8; P 5,000; M 135; (506) 325-9049; Fax (506) 328-4683; woodstockchamberofcommerce@nb.aibn.com

Newfoundland

Newfoundland & Labrador C/C · Paul Brocklehurst; Mgr.; P.O. Box 352; Gander; A1V 1W7; P 516,900; M 2,700; (709) 651-6522; Fax (709) 256-5808; execdirector@nlchamber.ca; www.nlchamber.ca

Bonavista · *Bonavista Area C/C* · Neal Tucker; Pres.; P.O. Box 280; A0C 1B0; P 6,500; M 55; Fax (709) 468-2495; info@bacc.ca; www.bacc.ca

Carbonear · *Baccalieu Trail Bd. of Trade* · Bob White; College of the North Atlantic; A1Y 1A7; P 9,000; M 174; (709) 596-4555; Fax (709) 596-4565; staff@baccalieutrail.ca; www.baccalieutrail.ca

Clarenville · *Clarenville Area C/C* · Terri-Lynn Davis; Ofc. Mgr.; 292A Memorial Dr.; A5A 1P1; P 5,270; M 122; (709) 466-5800; Fax (709) 466-5803; info@clarenvilleareachamber.net; www. clarenvilleareachamber.net

Corner Brook · *Greater Corner Brook Bd. of Trade* · Mel Woodman; Pres.; P.O. Box 475; A2H 6E6; P 20,000; M 200; (709) 634-5831; Fax (709) 639-9710; sherry@gcbbt.com; www.gcbbt.com

Deer Lake · *Deer Lake C/C* · Tammy Harding; Exec. Dir.; 9A Church St.; A8A 1C9; P 4,900; M 167; (709) 635-3260; Fax (709) 635-5857; info@deerlakechamber.com; www.deerlakechamber.com

Gander · *Gander & Area C/C* · Hazel Bishop; Exec. Dir.; 109 Trans Canada Hwy.; A1V 1P6; P 35,000; M 306; (709) 256-7110; Fax (709) 256-4794; ganderchamber@ganderchamber.nf.ca; www. ganderchamber.nf.ca

Grand Falls-Windsor · *Exploits Reg. C/C* · Sean Cooper; Exec. Dir.; P.O. Box 272; A2A 2J7; P 35,000; M 200; (709) 489-7512; Fax (709) 489-7532; info@exploitschamber.com; www.exploits chamber.com

Happy Valley · *Labrador North C/C* · Sterling Payton; Pres.; P.O. Box 460; A0P 1E0; P 8,500; M 150; (709) 896-8787; Fax (709) 896-8039; admin@chamberlabrador.com; www.chamberlabrador.com

Kelligrews · *Conception Bay Area C/C* · Glenda Noseworthy; Admin.; 702 Conception Bay Hwy., Ste. 3; A1X 3A5; P 25,000; M 200; (709) 834-5670; Fax (709) 834-5760; info@cbachamber. com; www.cbachamber.com

Labrador City · *Labrador West C/C* · Patsy Ralph; Bus. Mgr.; P.O. Box 273; A2V 2K5; P 12,000; M 87; (709) 944-3723; Fax (709) 944-4699; lwc@crrstv.net; www.labradorwestchamber.ca

Lewisporte · *Lewisporte & Area C/C* · Philip Patey; Pres.; P.O. Box 953; A0G 3A0; P 4,000; M 88; (709) 535-2500; Fax (709) 535-2482; lacc@easlewisporte.ca; www.lewisporteareachamber ofcommerce.ca

Mount Pearl • *Mount Pearl C/C* • Barry Furlong; Pres.; 253 Commonwealth Ave.; A1N 4L3; P 26,000; M 190; (709) 364-8513; (709) 364-2130; Fax (709) 364-8500; info@mountpearlchamber.com; www.mountpearlchamber.com

Port-Aux-Basques • *Port-Aux-Basques & Area C/C* • William Bailey; Pres.; P.O. Box 1389; A0M 1C0; P 10,000; M 100; (709) 695-3688; Fax (709) 695-7925; pabchamber@thezone.net; www.pabchamber.com

Saint John's • *St. John's Bd. of Trade* • Bruce Templeton; Chair; P.O. Box 5127; A1C 5V5; P 180,000; M 800; (709) 726-2961; Fax (709) 726-2003; info@bot.nf.ca; www.bot.nf.ca

Springdale • *Springdale C/C* • Glen Seabright; Pres.; P.O. Box 37; A0J 1T0; P 3,100; M 30; (709) 673-3837; Fax (709) 673-3897

St. Anthony • *St. Anthony & Area C/C* • P.O. Box 650; A0K 4S0; P 10,000; M 75; (709) 454-6667; stanthonyandareachamber@yahoo.ca

Stephenville • *Bay St. George C/C* • 35 Carolina Ave.; A2N 3P4; P 8,000; M 100; (709) 643-5854; Fax (709) 643-6398; bsgcoc@wec-center.nl.ca; www.bsgcc.org

Northwest Territories

Northwest Territories C/C • Peter Long; Exec. Dir.; 4802 50th Ave., Unit 13; Yellowknife; X1A 1C4; P 42,000; M 850; (867) 920-9505; Fax (867) 873-4174; admin@nwtchamber.com; www.nwtchamber.com

Fort Simpson • *Fort Simpson C/C* • Kirby Groat; P.O. Box 244; X0E 0N0; P 2,500; M 22; (867) 695-6540; KIRBY@northwestel.net

Fort Smith • *Fort Smith C/C* • Bernie Minute; P.O. Box 121; X0E 0P0; P 2,600; M 65; (867) 872-8400; (867) 872-3473

Hay River • *Hay River C/C* • Brian Lefebvre; Pres.; 10K Gagnier St.; X0E 1G1; P 3,800; M 105; (867) 874-2565; Fax (867) 874-3631; info@hayriverchamber.com; www.hayriverchamber.com

Norman Wells • *Norman Wells & Dist. C/C* • P.O. Box 400; X0E 0V0; P 700; M 50; (867) 587-6609; www.normanwells.com

Yellowknife • *Yellowknife C/C* • Ellie Sasseville; Exec. Dir.; 21-4910-50th Ave., 3rd Flr.; X1A 3S5; P 21,000; M 375; (867) 920-4944; Fax (867) 920-4640; admin@ykchamber.com; www.ykchamber.com

Nova Scotia

Nova Scotia Chambers of Commerce • Tim Tucker; Exec. Dir.; 605 Prince St.; P.O. Box 54; Truro; B2N 5B6; P 934,000; M 50; (902) 895-6329; Fax (902) 897-6641; tim@nschamber.ca; www.nschamber.ca

Annapolis • *Annapolis & Dist. Bd. of Trade* • Tina Halliday; Admin.; P.O. Box 2; B0S 1A0; P 7,000; M 98; (902) 532-5454; (902) 526-0944; info@tradeannapolis.com; www.tradeannapolis.com

Antigonish • *Antigonish C/C* • Phil Hughes; Pres.; 21-B James St. Plz.; B2G 1R6; P 18,836; M 185; (902) 863-6308; Fax (902) 863-2656; contact@antigonishchamber.com; www.antigonishchamber.com

Berwick • *Berwick & Dist. Bd. of Trade* • Terry Gayle; Pres.; P.O. Box 664; B0P 1E0; P 2,500; M 85; (902) 538-8068

Bridgewater • *Bridgewater & Area C/C* • Ann O'Connell; Exec. Dir.; 220 North St.; P.O. Box 100; B4V 2V6; P 20,000; M 170; (902) 543-4263; Fax (902) 543-1156; bacc@eastlink.ca; www.bridgewaterchamber.com

Chester • *Chester Municipal C/C* • Angela Jessome; Exec. Dir.; 4171 Hwy. , RR 2, Ste. 13; B0J 1J0; P 10,000; M 200; (902) 275-4709; Fax (902) 275-4709; admin@chesterareans.com; www.chesterareans.com

Church Point • *Clare C/C* • Marc Robichaud; Pres.; P.O. Box 35; B0W 1M0; P 10,000; M 100; (902) 645-2368; chambrede commerce@hotmail.com; www.commercedeclare.ca;

Dartmouth • *Halifax C/C* • Valerie Payn; Pres./CEO; 656 Windmill Rd., Ste. 200; B3B 1B8; P 300,000; M 2,000; (902) 468-7111; Fax (902) 468-7333; info@halifaxchamber.com; www.halifaxchamber.com

Digby • *Digby & Area Bd. of Trade* • Kristy Herron; Pres.; P.O. Box 641; B0V 1A0; P 10,000; M 50; (902) 245-8879; dabot@tartannet.ns.ca; tartannet.ns.ca/~dabot

Kentville • *Atlantic Provinces C/C* • Bill Denyar; Pres./CEO; 325 Main St.; P.O. Box 832; ; B4N 4H8; P 2,300,000; M 15,000; (902) 678-6284; Fax (902) 678-7420; janice@apcc.ca; www.apcc.ca

Kentville • *Eastern Kings C/C* • Judy Rafuse; Exec. Dir.; 325 Main St.; P.O. Box 314; B4N 3X1; P 27,500; M 400; (902) 678-4634; Fax (902) 678-5448; executivedirector@ekcc.ca; www.ekcc.ca

Lantz • *East Hants & Dist. C/C* • Tanya-Eisnor Whynot; Ofc. Mgr.; P.O. Box 1053; B2S 3G7; P 15,000; M 165; (902) 883-1010; Fax (902) 883-7862; info@ehcc.ca; www.ehcc.ca

Liverpool • *South Queens C/C* • David Noel; Dir.; P.O. Box 1378; B0K 1K0; P 12,500; M 30; (902) 354-4163; Fax (902) 354-2354; secretary@southqueenschamber.com; www.southqueenschamber.com

Lunenburg • *Lunenburg Bd. of Trade* • Andria Wicker; P.O. Box 1300; B0J 2C0; P 2,600; M 200; (902) 634-3170; lbt@ns.aliantzinc.ca; www.lunenburgns.com

New Glasgow • *Pictou County C/C* • Faus Johnson; Exec. Dir.; 980 E. River Rd.; B2H 3S8; P 47,500; M 230; (902) 755-3463; Fax (902) 755-2848; info@pictouchamber.com; www.pictouchamber.com

Parrsboro • *Parrsboro C/C & Bd. of Trade* • Karen Dickinson; Pres.; P.O. Box 297; B0M 1S0; P 1,650; M 75; (902) 546-2342; admin@parrsborodistrictboardoftrade.com; www.parrsboro districtboardoftrade.com

Pictou County • *see New Glasgow*

Port Hawkesbury • *Strait Area C/C* • Shannon MacDougall; Exec. Dir.; 4 MacIntosh Ave., Unit 2; B9A 3K5; P 35,000; M 187; (902) 625-1588; Fax (902) 625-5985; info@straitareachamber.ca; www.straitareachamber.ca

Riverport • *Riverport Dist. Bd. of Trade* • Matt Durnford; Pres.; P.O. Box 28; B0J 2W0; P 1,000; M 30; (902) 766-4104; Fax (902) 766-4104; www.riverport.org

Springhill • *Springhill C/C* • Rev. Frank Likely; Pres.; P.O. Box 1030; B0M 1X0; P 4,000; M 60; (902) 597-8462; (902) 597-3026; amcentre@eastlink.ca

Sydney • *Sydney & Area C/C* • Michael MacSween; Exec. Dir.; P.O. Box 131; B1P 1G9; P 100,000; M 590; (902) 564-6453; Fax (902) 539-7487; info@sydneyareachamber.ca; www.sydneyareachamber.ca

Tatamagouche • *North Shore Comm. Dev. Assn.* • Linda Byers; Chair; 225 Main St.; P.O. Box 152; B0K 1V0; P 1,000; M 15; (902) 657-3811; Fax (902) 657-2619; www.tatamagouchetoday.com

Truro • *Truro & Dist. C/C* • Tim Tucker; Exec. Dir.; 605 Prince St.; P.O. Box 54; B2N 5B6; P 46,000; M 403; (902) 895-6328; Fax (902) 897-6641; tim@trurochamber.com; www.trurochamber.com

Windsor · *West Hants C/C* · Gordon Winston; Pres.; P.O. Box 2188; B0N 2T0; P 19,000; M 70; (902) 798-5106; info@whcc.ca; www.whcc.ca

Yarmouth · *Yarmouth Area C/C* · Jim Greig; Exec. Dir.; P.O. Box 532; B5A 4B4; P 28,000; M 192; (902) 742-3074; Fax (902) 749-1383; info@yarmouthchamberofcommerce.com; www.yarmouthchamberofcommerce.com

Nunavut

Baker Lake · *Baker Lake C/C & EDC* · P.O. Box 149; X0C 0A0; P 1,700; (867) 793-2874; Fax (867) 793-2509

Iqaluit · *Baffin Reg. C/C* · Hal Timer; Exec. Dir.; Box 59, Bldg. 607; X0A 0H0; P 15,000; M 120; (867) 979-4654; (867) 979-4656; Fax (867) 979-2929; execdir@baffinchamber.ca; www.baffinchamber.ca

Rankin Inlet · *Kivalliq C/C* · Ellie Cansfield; Pres.; P.O. Box 146; X0C 0G0; P 7,500; M 150; (867) 645-2817; Fax (867) 645-2483; krmanson@artic.ca

Ontario

Ontario C/C · Len Crispino; Pres./CEO; 180 Dundas St. W., Ste. 505; Toronto; M5G 1Z8; P 10,000,000; M 65,000; (416) 482-5222; Fax (416) 482-5879; info@occ.on.ca; www.occ.on.ca

Alliston · *Alliston & Dist. C/C* · Crystal Kellard; Ofc. Mgr.; 51 Victoria St. E.; P.O. Box 32; L9R 1T9; P 25,000; M 330; (705) 435-7921; Fax (705) 435-0289; info@adcc.ca; www.adcc.ca

Amherstburg · *Amherstburg C/C* · Katie Deslippe; Admin. Asst.; 268 Dalhousie St.; P.O. Box 101; N9V 2Z3; P 21,748; M 190; (519) 736-2001; acoc@mnsi.net; www.amherstburgchamberofcommerce.ca

Apsley · *see Lakefield*

Aurora · *Aurora C/C* · Judy Marshall; Exec. Dir.; 6-14845 Yonge St., Ste. 321; L4G 6H8; P 49,000; M 785; (905) 727-7262; Fax (905) 841-6217; info@aurorachamber.on.ca; www.aurorachamber.on.ca

Bancroft · *Bancroft & Dist. C/C* · Kimberly Crawford; Gen. Mgr.; 12 Flint Ave., Unit B; K0L 1C0; P 16,000; M 350; (613) 332-1513; (888) 443-9999; Fax (613) 443-9999; chamber@commerce.bancroft.on.ca; www.bancroftdistrict.com

Barrie · *Greater Barrie C/C* · Sybil Goruk; Exec. Dir.; 97 Toronto St.; L4N 1V1; P 125,000; M 1,200; (705) 721-5000; Fax (705) 726-0973; chadmin@barriechamber.com; www.barriechamber.com

Belleville · *Belleville & Dist. C/C* · Bill Saunders; CEO; 5 Moira St. E.; P.O. Box 726; K8N 5B3; P 46,000; M 600; (613) 962-4597; Fax (613) 962-3911; info@bellevillechamber.ca; www.bellevillechamber.ca

Blenheim · *Blenheim & Dist. C/C* · Betty Russell; Secy.; P.O. Box 1353; N0P 1A0; P 5,500; M 60; (519) 676-8090; www.blenheimontario.com

Blind River · *Blind River C/C* · Sandra Walker; Bus. Svcs. Coord.; 243 Causley St.; P.O. Box 998; P0R 1B0; P 4,000; M 100; (705) 356-2555; Fax (705) 356-3911; chamber@blindriver.com; www.brchamber.ca

Bobcaygeon · *Bobcaygeon C/C* · Ruth Ann Wilson; Ofc. Mgr.; 21 Canal St. E.; P.O. Box 388; K0M 1A0; P 2,000; M 222; (705) 738-2202; (800) 318-6173; Fax (705) 738-1534; chamber@bobcaygeon.org; www.bobcaygeon.org

Bolton · *Caledon C/C* · Kelly Darnley; Pres./CEO; P.O. Box 626; L7E 5T5; P 58,000; M 400; (905) 857-7393; (888) 599-9967; Fax (905) 857-7405; suzanne@caledonchamber.com; www.caledonchamber.com

Bracebridge · *Bracebridge C/C* · John Crawley; Gen. Mgr.; 1 Manitoba St., 2nd Flr.; P1L 1S4; P 16,000; M 400; (705) 645-5231; Fax (705) 645-7592; chamber@bracebridgechamber.com; www.bracebridgechamber.com

Brampton · *Brampton Bd. of Trade* · Gary Collins; CEO; 36 Queen St. E., Ste. 101; L6Y 1L9; P 400,000; M 1,100; (905) 451-1122; Fax (905) 450-0295; admin@bramptonbot.com; www.bramptonbot.com

Brantford · *Brantford Brant C/C* · Barry English; Pres.; 77 Charlotte St.; N3T 2W8; P 100,000; M 800; (519) 753-2617; Fax (519) 753-0921; chamber@brcc.ca; www.brantfordbrantchamber.com

Brockville · *Brockville & Dist. C/C* · Anne MacDonald; Exec. Dir.; 3 Market St. W., Ste. 1; K6V 7L2; P 22,000; M 560; (613) 342-6553; Fax (613) 342-6849; info@brockvillechamber.com; www.brockvillechamber.com

Buckhorn · *see Lakefield*

Burleigh Falls · *see Lakefield*

Burlington · *Burlington C/C* · Keith Hoey; Pres.; 414 Locust St., Ste. 201; L7S 1T7; P 155,000; M 1,057; (905) 639-0174; Fax (905) 333-3956; info@burlingtonchamber.com; www.burlingtonchamber.com

Caledonia · *Caledonia Reg. C/C* · Barbara Martindale; Exec. Dir.; 1 Grand Trunk Ln.; P.O. Box 2035; N3W 2G6; P 9,000; M 236; (905) 765-0377; Fax (905) 765-6730; crcc@mountaincable.net; www.caledonia-ontario.com

Cambridge · *Cambridge C/C* · Greg Durocher; Pres.; 750 Hespeler Rd.; N3H 5L8; P 118,000; M 1,900; (519) 622-2221; Fax (519) 622-0177; admin@cambridgechamber.com; www.cambridgechamber.com

Campbellford · *Trent Hills C/C* · Nancy Allanson; Exec. Dir.; 51 Grand Rd.; P.O. Box 376; K0L 1L0; P 12,500; M 250; (705) 653-1551; Fax (705) 653-1629; info@trenthillschamber.ca; www.trenthillschamber.ca

Carleton Place · *Carleton Place & Dist. C/C* · Cindy Hobbs; Pres.; 132 Coleman St.; K7C 4M7; P 25,000; M 184; (613) 257-1976; Fax (613) 257-4148; manager@cpchamber.com; www.cpchamber.com

Chatham · *Chatham-Kent C/C* · Gail Antaya; Pres./CEO; 54 Fourth St.; N7M 2G2; P 44,000; M 500; (519) 352-7540; Fax (519) 352-8741; sarah@chatham-kentchamber.ca; www.chatham-kentchamber.ca

Cobourg · *Northumberland Central C/C* · Bonnie Thrasher; Pres.; Northumberland Mall; 1111 Elgin St. W.; K9A 5H7; P 18,000; M 425; (905) 372-5831; Fax (905) 372-2411; info@cobourgchamber.com; www.cobourgchamber.com

Collingwood · *Collingwood C/C* · Trish Irwin; Gen. Mgr.; 25 Second St.; L9Y 1E4; P 17,000; M 525; (705) 445-0221; Fax (705) 445-6858; info@collingwoodchamber.com; www.collingwoodchamber.com

Concord · *see Vaughan*

Cornwall · *Cornwall & Area C/C* · Lezlie Strasser; Exec. Mgr.; 113 2nd St. E., Ste. 100; K6H 1Y5; P 46,000; M 650; (613) 933-4004; Fax (613) 933-8466; malyon@cornwallchamber.com; www.cornwallchamber.com

Dryden • *Dryden Dist. C/C & Tourism Center* • Donald Ames; Mgr.; 284 Government St.; P8N 2P3; P 35,000; M 250; (807) 223-2622; (800) 667-0935; Fax (807) 223-2626; chamber@mail.drytel.net; www.drydenchamber.ca

Dunnville • *Dunnville C/C* • Sandy Passmore; Ofc. Mgr.; 231 Chestnut St.; P.O. Box 124; N1A 2X1; P 12,000; M 80; (905) 774-3183; (905) 774-5203; Fax (905) 774-9281; chamberofcommerce@mountaincable.net; www.dunnvillechamberofcommerce.ca

Durham • *West Grey C/C* • Greta Kennedy; Secy./Treas.; P.O. Box 800; N0G 1R0; P 2,500; M 50; (519) 369-5750; Fax (519) 369-5750; info@westgreychamber.ca; www.westgreychamber.ca

Dutton • *Dutton & Dunwich C/C* • Dr. Chantal Welch; Pres.; P.O. Box 547; N0L 1J0; P 3,000; M 77; (519) 762-6060; Fax (519) 762-0934; www.ddchamber.ca

Elliot Lake • *Elliot Lake & Dist. C/C* • Todd Stencill; Gen. Mgr.; 255 Hwy. 108 N.; P.O. Box 81; P5A 2J6; P 12,500; M 130; (705) 848-3974; Fax (705) 848-7121; elchamber@onlink.net; www.elliotlakechamber.com

Embrun • *Chambre de Commerce D'Embrun* • Ron Theriault; Pres.; C.P. 734; K0A 1W0; P 8,000; M 80; (613) 443-7606; cce@storm.ca; www.chambredecommercedembrun.ca;

Englehart • *Englehart & Dist. C/C* • Stacey Borgford; Pres.; P.O. Box 171; P0J 1H0; P 1,800; M 55; (705) 544-2244

Fenelon Falls • *Fenelon Falls & Dist. C/C* • 15 Oak St.; K0M 1N0; P 2,000; M 120; (705) 887-3409; Fax (705) 887-6912; info@fenelonfallschamber.com; www.fenelonfallschamber.com

Fergus • *Centre Wellington C/C* • Roberta Scarrow; Gen. Mgr.; 400 Tower St. S.; N1M 2P7; P 25,000; M 360; (519) 843-5140; (877) 242-6353; Fax (519) 787-0983; chamber@cwchamber.ca; www.cwchamber.ca

Fort Erie • *Greater Fort Erie C/C* • Karen Audet; Op. Mgr.; 660 Garrison Rd., Unit 1; L2A 6E2; P 32,000; M 315; (905) 871-3803; Fax (905) 871-1561; info@greaterforteriechamber.com; www.greaterforteriechamber.com

Fort Frances • *Fort Frances C/C* • Anthony Mason; Mgr.; 474 Scott St.; P9A 1H2; P 9,000; M 170; (807) 274-5773; (800) 820-3678; Fax (807) 274-8706; thefort@fortfranceschamber.com; www.fortfranceschamber.com

Georgetown • *Halton Hills C/C* • Sue Walker; Pres./CEO; 328 Guelph St.; L7G 4B5; P 55,000; M 500; (905) 877-7119; info@haltonhillschamber.on.ca; www.haltonhillschamber.on.ca

Grand Bend • *Grand Bend & Area C/C & Tourism* • Susan Mills; Ofc. Mgr.; 1-81 Crescent; P.O. Box 248; N0M 1T0; P 4,000; M 208; (519) 238-2001; (888) 338-2001; Fax (519) 238-5201; info@grandbendtourism.com; www.grandbendtourism.com

Grimsby • *Grimsby & Dist. C/C* • Jinny Day; Exec. Dir.; 424 S. Service Rd.; L3M 4E8; P 22,000; M 237; (905) 945-8319; Fax (905) 945-1615; info@grimsbychamber.com; grimsbychamber.com

Guelph • *Guelph C/C* • Lloyd Longfield; Pres./CAO; 485 Silvercreek Pkwy. N., Unit 15; N1H 7K5; P 115,000; M 813; (519) 822-8081; Fax (519) 822-8451; chamber@guelphchamber.com; www.guelphchamber.com

Hagersville • *Hagersville & Dist. C/C* • Rob Phillips; Pres.; P.O. Box 1090; N0A 1H0; P 2,600; M 70; (905) 768-0422; Fax (289) 282-0105; rphillips@heaslipford.com; www.hagersvillechamber.ca

Hamilton • *Hamilton C/C* • John Dolbec; CEO; 555 Bay St. N.; L8L 1H1; P 510,000; M 2,000; (905) 522-1151; Fax (905) 522-1154; hdcc@hamiltonchamber.on.ca; www.hamiltonchamber.on.ca.

Hastings • *see Campbellford*

Hawkesbury • *Hawkesbury C/C* • Richard Denis; Pres.; 2 John St.; P.O. Box 36; K6A 2R4; P 10,000; M 225; (613) 632-8066; Fax (613) 632-3324; info@hcoc.ca; www.hcoc.ca

Hearst • *Hearst, Mattice-Val Cote & Area C/C* • Luc Pepin; Pres.; P.O. Box 987; P0L 1N0; P 8,000; M 100; (705) 362-5880; Fax (705) 362-5880; info@hearstcoc.com; www.hearstcoc.com

Huntsville • *Huntsville/Lake of Bays C/C* • Kelly Haywood; Exec. Dir.; 8 West St. N.; P1H 2B6; P 20,466; M 621; (705) 789-4771; Fax (705) 789-6191; chamber@huntsvillelakeofbays.on.ca; www.huntsvillelakeofbays.on.ca

Ingersoll • *Ingersoll Dist. C/C* • Ann Campbell; Gen. Mgr.; 132 Thames St. S.; N5C 2T4; P 20,000; M 220; (519) 485-7333; Fax (519) 485-6606; info@ingersollchamber.com; www.ingersollchamber.com

Ingleside • *South Stormont C/C* • Lesley O'Gorman; Pres.; P.O. Box 489; K0C 1M0; P 1,800; M 62; (613) 537-4427; Fax (613) 537-9439; info@sscc.on.ca; sscc.on.ca

Innisfil • *Greater Innisfil C/C* • Sandra Green; Gen. Mgr.; 7896 Yonge St.; L9S 1L5; P 34,000; M 190; (705) 431-4199; Fax (705) 431-6628; info@innisfilchamber.com; www.innisfilchamber.com

Iroquois Falls • *Iroquois Falls & Dist. C/C* • Lola Brousseau; Ofc. Mgr.; 727 Synagogue Ave.; P.O. Box 840; P0K 1G0; P 5,700; M 50; (705) 232-4656; Fax (705) 232-4656; ifchamber@hotmail.com; www.iroquoisfallschamber.com

Kemptville • *North Grenville C/C* • Wendy Chapman; Exec. Dir.; 5 Clothier St. E.; P.O. Box 1047; K0G 1J0; P 15,000; M 225; (613) 258-4838; Fax (613) 258-3801; info@northgrenvillechamber.com; www.northgrenvillechamber.com

Kenora • *Kenora & Dist. C/C* • Andrew Scribilo; Pres.; 205 Second St. S.; P.O. Box 471; P9N 3X5; P 15,500; M 200; (807) 467-4646; Fax (807) 468-3056; kenorachamber@kmts.ca; www.kenorachamber.com

Keswick • *Georgina C/C* • Christina Thomas; Gen. Mgr.; 22937 Woodbine Ave., RR#2; L4P 3E9; P 45,000; M 278; (905) 476-7870; Fax (905) 476-6700; admin@georginachamber.com; www.georginachamber.com

Kincardine • *Kincardine & Dist. C/C* • Jackie Pawlikowski; Ofc. Mgr.; 717 Queen St.; P.O. Box 115; N2Z 2Y6; P 12,000; M 150; (519) 396-9333; Fax (519) 396-5529; kincardine.cofc@bmts.com; www.kincardinechamber.com

Kingston • *Greater Kingston C/C* • Bob Scott; Gen. Mgr.; Innovation Park; 945 Princess St.; K7L 3N6; P 140,000; M 875; (613) 548-4453; (888) 855-4555; Fax (613) 548-4743; info@kingstonchamber.on.ca; www.kingstonchamber.on.ca

Kirkland Lake • *Kirkland Lake Dist. C/C* • Jennifer Verge; Ofc. Coord.; 400 Government Rd. W.; P.O. Box 966; P2N 3L1; P 9,000; M 125; (705) 567-5444; Fax (705) 567-1666; klcofc@ntl.sympatico.ca; www.kirklandlakechamber.com

Kitchener • *Greater Kitchener Waterloo C/C* • Ian McLean; Pres./CEO; 80 Queen St. N.; P.O. Box 2367; N2H 6L4; P 350,000; M 1,650; (519) 576-5000; (888) 672-4760; Fax (519) 742-4760; admin@greaterkwchamber.com; www.greaterkwchamber.com

Kleinburg • *see Vaughan*

Lakefield • *Kawartha Lakes C/C–Eastern Region* • Sherry Boyce-Found; Gen. Mgr.; 12 Queen St.; P.O. Box 537; K0L 2H0; P 15,000; M 340; (705) 652-6963; (888) 565-8888; Fax (705) 652-9140; info@kawarthachamber.ca; www.kawarthachamber.ca

Leamington · *Leamington & Dist. C/C* · Mrs. Chris Chopchik; Gen. Mgr.; 21 Talbot St. E.; P.O. Box 321; N8H 3W3; P 35,000; M 400; (519) 326-2721; (800) 250-3336; Fax (519) 326-3204; wendyp@ leamingtonchamber.com; www.leamingtonchamber.com

Lindsay · *Lindsay & Dist. C/C* · Gayle Jones; Gen. Mgr.; 4 Victoria Ave. N.; K9V 4E5; P 21,000; M 618; (705) 324-2393; Fax (705) 324-2473; nadine@lindsaychamber.com; www.lindsaychamber.com

Listowel · *North Perth C/C* · Tami Chauvin; Gen. Mgr.; 580 Main St. W.; N4W 1A8; P 14,000; M 14; (519) 291-1551; Fax (519) 291-4151; tami@npchamber.com; www.npchamber.com

London · *London C/C* · Gerry Macartney; Gen. Mgr./CEO; 101-244 Pall Mall St.; N6A 5P6; P 331,000; M 1,000; (519) 432-7551; Fax (519) 432-8063; info@londonchamber.com; www.london chamber.com

Manotick · *Rideau C/C* · Salima Ismail; Pres.; P.O. Box 247; K4M 1A3; M 60; (613) 692-6262; drsalima@doctor.com; www. rideauchamber.com

Maple · *see Vaughan*

Markdale · *Markdale C/C* · Kate Russell; Coord.; 19 Toronto St. N.; P.O. Box 177; N0C 1H0; P 9,500; M 77; (519) 986-4612; (888) 986-4612; Fax (519) 986-4612; markdalechamber@cablerocket. com; www.village.markdale.on.ca

Markham · *Markham Bd. of Trade* · Richard Cunningham; Pres./CEO; 7271 Warden Ave.; L3R 5X5; P 265,000; M 900; (905) 474-0730; Fax (905) 474-0685; info@markhamboard.com; www. markhamboard.com

Merrickville · *Merrickville & Dist. C/C* · Hugh MacLennan; Secy.; 317 Brock St. W.; K0G 1N0; P 2,500; M 150; (613) 269-2229; Fax (613) 269-2229; merrickvillechamber@mail.com; www. realmerrickville.ca

Midland · *Southern Georgian Bay C/C* · Denise Hayes; Bus. Mgr.; 208 King St.; L4R 3L9; P 43,000; M 485; (705) 526-7884; Fax (705) 526-1744; info@sgbchamber.ca; www.southerngeorgian bay.on.ca

Milton · *Milton C/C* · Sandy Martin; Exec. Dir.; 251 Main St. E., Ste. 104; L9T 1P1; P 75,000; M 790; (905) 878-0581; Fax (905) 878-4972; info@miltonchamber.ca; www.miltonchamber.ca

Mindemoya · *Manitoulin C/C* · Bob Taylor; Pres.; P.O. Box 307; P0P 1S0; P 13,000; M 150; (705) 377-7501; manitoulinchamber@ manitoulin-island.com; www.manitoulinchamber.com

Minden · *Haliburton Highlands C/C* · Maria Micallef; Mgr.; P.O. Box 147; K0M 2K0; P 18,000; M 360; (705) 286-1760; (877) 811-6111; Fax (705) 286-6016; maria@haliburtonchamber.com; www.hhchamber.on.ca

Mississauga · *Mississauga Bd. of Trade* · Sheldon Leiba; Pres./ CEO; 77 City Center Dr., Ste. 701; L5B 1M5; P 650,000; M 1,500; (905) 273-6151; Fax (905) 273-4937; info@mbot.com; www. mbot.com

Morrisburg · *South Dundas C/C* · Barb Scott; Pres.; P.O. Box 288; K0C 1X0; P 10,000; M 140; (613) 662-2653; Fax (613) 652-4120; manager@southdundaschamber.com; www.southdundas chamber.com

Mount Forest · *Mount Forest & Dist. C/C* · Crystal Seifreid; Ofc. Mgr.; 514 Main St. N.; N0G 2L2; P 5,000; M 130; (519) 323-4480; Fax (519) 323-1557; mfchamber@wightman.ca; www.mount forest.ca

New Hamburg · *New Hamburg Bd. of Trade* · Paul Knowles; Pres.; 121 Huron St.; N3A 1K1; P 6,500; M 95; (519) 662-6628; (519) 575-0271; newhamburgtourism@gmail.com; www. newhamburg.ca

Newmarket · *Newmarket C/C* · Debra Scott; Pres./CEO; 470 Davis Dr.; L3Y 2P3; P 75,000; M 650; (905) 898-5900; Fax (905) 853-7271; info@newmarketchamber.ca; www.newmarketchamber.ca

Newmarket · *York Region Tourism* · 17250 Yonge St.; L3Y 6Z1; P 866,000; (905) 883-3442; (888) 448-0000; Fax (905) 895-3482; tourism@york.ca; www.yorktourism.com

Niagara Falls · *The Chamber of Commerce at Niagara Falls Canada C/C* · Carolyn A. Bones; Pres.; 4056 Dorchester Rd.; L2E 6M9; P 82,000; M 770; (905) 374-3666; Fax (905) 374-2972; info@ niagarafallschamber.com; www.niagarafallschamber.com

Niagara-on-the-Lake · *Niagara-on-the-Lake C/C & Visitors Bur.* · Janice Thomson; Exec. Dir.; 26 Queen St.; P.O. Box 1043; L0S 1J0; P 13,000; M 500; (905) 468-1950; Fax (905) 468-4930; admin@niagaraonthelake.com; www.niagaraonthelake.com

Nipigon · *Land of Nipigon C/C* · Marvin Broughton; Pres.; 25 Second St.; P.O. Box 760; P0T 2J0; P 3,000; M 37; (807) 887-0740; Fax (807) 887-0741; nipigonchamber@vianet.ca; www.loncoc.ca

North Bay · *North Bay & Dist. C/C* · Patti Carr; Exec. Dir.; 1375 Seymour St.; P1B 9V6; P 56,000; M 895; (705) 472-8480; Fax (705) 472-8027; nbcc@northbaychamber.com; www.northbay chamber.com

Norwich · *Twp. of Norwich C/C* · Julie Couwenberg; Pres.; 41 Main St. W.; N0J 1P0; P 10,000; M 120; (519) 863-2014; julie@ norwichinsurance.com; www.norwichchamberofcommerce.ca

Oakville · *Oakville C/C* · John Sawyer; Pres.; 2521 Wyecroft Rd.; L6L 6P8; P 170,000; M 1,100; (905) 845-6613; Fax (905) 845-6475; inquiries@oakvillechamber.com; www.oakvillechamber.com

Orangeville · *Greater Dufferin Area C/C* · Lucy Kristan; Exec. Dir.; P.O. Box 101; L9W 2Z5; P 52,000; M 435; (519) 941-0490; Fax (519) 941-0492; info@gdacc.ca; www.gdacc.ca

Oshawa · *Greater Oshawa C/C* · Bob Malcolmson; Gen. Mgr./ CEO; 44 Richmond St. W., Ste. 100; L1G 1C7; P 150,000; M 880; (905) 728-1683; (905) 725-4523; Fax (905) 432-1259; info@ oshawachamber.com; www.oshawachamber.com

Ottawa · *Ottawa C/C* · Erin Kelly; Exec. Dir.; 1701 Woodward Dr., Ste. LL-20; K2C 0R4; P 1,000,000; M 900; (613) 236-3631; Fax (613) 236-7498; info@ottawachamber.ca; www.ottawachamber.ca

Owen Sound · *Owen Sound & Dist. C/C* · Bert Loopstra; Mgr.; 704 6th St. E.; P.O. Box 1028; N4K 6K6; P 24,800; M 510; (519) 376-6261; Fax (519) 376-5647; kim@oschamber.com; www. oschamber.com

Parry Sound · *Parry Sound Area C/C* · Perry Harris; Exec. Dir.; 70 Church St.; P2A 1Y9; P 6,500; M 360; (705) 746-4213; (800) 461-4261; Fax (705) 746-6537; info@parrysoundchamber.ca; www.parrysoundchamber.ca

Pembroke · *Upper Ottawa Valley C/C* · Lorraine MacKenzie; Mgr.; 611 TV Tower Rd.; P.O. Box 1010; K8A 6Y6; P 30,000; M 300; (613) 732-1492; Fax (613) 732-5793; manager@upperottawa valleychamber.com; www.upperottawavalleychamber.com

Perth · *Perth & Dist. C/C* · Madeline Bouvier & Carol Quattroccho; Co-Mgrs.; 34 Herriott St.; K7H 1T2; P 17,000; M 370; (613) 267-3200; welcome@perthchamber.com; www.perthchamber.com

Peterborough · *Greater Peterborough C/C* · Stuart Harrison; Gen. Mgr.; 175 George St. N.; K9J 3G6; P 81,084; M 1,050; (705) 748-9771; (877) 640-4037; Fax (705) 743-2331; cynthia@peter boroughchamber.ca; www.peterboroughchamber.ca

Picton · *Prince Edward County C/C* · Jan Robbins; Ofc. Mgr.; 116 Main St.; K0K 2T0; P 24,000; M 360; (613) 476-2421; (800) 640-4717; Fax (613) 476-7461; pec@reach.net; www.pecchamber.com

Pointe au Baril • *Pointe au Baril C/C* • Lillian White; Ofc. Mgr.; 1650 Hwy. 69; P.O. Box 67; P0G 1K0; P 6,000; M 60; (705) 366-2331; (705) 366-2755; Fax (705) 366-2755; info@pointeaubaril chamber.com; www.pointeaubarilchamber.com

Port Colborne • *Port Colborne-Wainfleet C/C* • Edith Wagner; Ofc. Mgr.; 76 Main St. W.; L3K 3V2; P 25,060; M 207; (905) 834-9765; Fax (905) 834-1542; office@pcwchamber.com; www.pcwchamber.com

Port Dover • *Port Dover Bd. of Trade* • Paul Morris; Pres.; P.O. Box 239; N0A 1N0; P 6,000; M 250; (519) 583-1314; Fax (519) 583-3275; info@portdover.ca; www.portdover.ca

Port Elgin • *Saugeen Shores C/C* • Joanne Robbins; Gen. Mgr.; 559 Goderich St.; N0H 2C4; P 12,000; M 405; (519) 832-2332; (800) 387-3456; Fax (519) 389-3725; jackiemunshaw@saugeen shores.ca; www.saugeenshores.ca

Port Hope • *Port Hope & Dist. C/C* • Mrs. Wendy Giroux; Mgr.; 58 Queen St.; L1A 3Z9; P 17,000; M 320; (905) 885-5519; Fax (905) 885-1142; thechamber@porthope.ca; www.porthope chamber.com

Port Perry • *Scugog C/C* • Kenna Kozak; Gen. Mgr.; 181 Perry St., Unit G3; P.O. Box 1282; L9L 1A7; P 22,000; M 180; (905) 985-4971; (800) 416-2057; Fax (905) 985-7698; info@scugogchamber.ca; www.scugogchamber.ca

Port Rowan • *Long Point Country C/C* • Evan Engell; Pres.; P.O. Box 357; N0E 1M0; P 4,000; M 80; (519) 586-8577; info@ portrowan-longpoint.org; www.portrowan-longpoint.org

Prescott • *Prescott & Dist. C/C* • Debbie Lawless; Treas./Secy.; P.O. Box 2000; K0E 1T0; P 4,200; M 140; (613) 925-2171; prescott chamber@xplornet.com; www.prescottanddistrictchamber.com

Red Lake • *Red Lake Dist. C/C* • Kim Riddell; Admin. Asst.; P.O. Box 430; P0V 2M0; P 6,000; M 65; (807) 727-3722; Fax (807) 727-3285; redlakechamber@shaw.ca; www.red-lake.com

Renfrew • *Renfrew & Area C/C* • Kevin Bossy; Pres.; 161 Raglan St. S.; K7V 1R2; P 8,500; M 155; (613) 432-7015; Fax (613) 432-8645; info@renfrewareachamber.ca; www.renfrewareachamber.ca

Richmond Hill • *Richmond Hill C/C* • Leslie Walker; CEO; 376 Church St. S.; L4C 9V8; P 181,000; M 600; (905) 884-1961; Fax (905) 884-1962; info@rhcoc.com; www.rhcoc.com

Ridgetown • *Ridgetown & Dist. C/C* • Charlie Mitton; Pres.; P.O. Box 522; N0P 2C0; P 3,450; M 90; (519) 674-5554; ridgetown chamber@gmail.com; www.ridgetown.com

Sarnia • *Sarnia/Lambton C/C* • Garry McDonald; Pres.; 556 N. Christina St.; N7T 5W6; P 130,000; M 975; (519) 336-2400; Fax (519) 336-2085; info@sarnialambtonchamber.com; www.sarnialambtonchamber.com

Sauble Beach • *Sauble Beach C/C* • Bruce Parsons; Pres.; General Delivery; N0H 2G0; P 3,500; M 123; (519) 422-1262; (519) 422-1051; info@saublebeach.com; www.saublebeach.com

Sault Ste. Marie • *Sault Ste. Marie C/C* • Shelley Barich; Gen. Mgr.; 489 Bay St.; P6A 1X6; P 75,000; M 900; (705) 949-7152; Fax (705) 759-8166; info@ssmcoc.com; www.ssmcoc.com.

Scarborough • *see Toronto*

Schomberg • *King C/C* • Diane Peldszus; Admin.; P.O. Box 381; L0G 1T0; P 5,000; M 250; (905) 717-7199; Fax (416) 981-7174; info@kingchamber.ca; www.kingchamber.ca

Selwyn • *see Lakefield*

Simcoe • *Simcoe & Dist. C/C* • Yvonne DiPietro; Gen. Mgr.; Chamber Plaza; 95 Queensway W.; N3Y 2M8; P 48,000; M 350; (519) 426-5867; Fax (519) 428-7718; chamber@simcoechamber.on.ca; www.simcoechamber.on.ca

Sioux Lookout • *Sioux Lookout C/C* • Anne Reid; Exec. Asst.; #11 First Ave.; P.O. Box 577; P8T 1A8; P 5,500; M 150; (807) 737-1937; Fax (807) 737-1778; chamber@siouxlookout.com; www.siouxlookout.com

Smiths Falls • *Smiths Falls & Dist. C/C* • Victoria Ash; Mgr.; 77 Beckwith St. N.; K7A 2B8; P 9,100; M 300; (613) 283-1334; Fax (613) 283-4764; sfchamber@smithsfalls.ca; www.smithsfalls chamber.ca

Smithville • *West Lincoln C/C* • Paul Keizer; Pres.; P.O. Box 555; L0R 2A0; P 12,000; M 150; (905) 957-1606; Fax (905) 957-4628; westlincolnchamber@bellnet.ca; www.westlincolnchamber.com

St. Catharines • *St. Catharines-Thorold C/C* • Walter Sendzik; Exec. V.P./Gen. Mgr.; One St. Paul St., Ste. 103; P.O. Box 940; L2R 6Z4; P 150,000; M 1,100; (905) 684-2361; Fax (905) 684-2100; info@sctchamber.com; www.sctchamber.com

St. Thomas • *St. Thomas & Dist. C/C* • Robert (Bob) Hammersley; Pres./CEO; 555 Talbot St.; N5P 1C5; P 50,000; M 650; (519) 631-1981; Fax (519) 631-0466; mail@stthomas chamber.on.ca; www.stthomaschamber.on.ca

Stoney Creek • *Stoney Creek C/C* • Dave Cage; Exec. Dir.; 21 Mountain Ave. S.; L8G 2V5; P 58,000; M 425; (905) 664-4000; Fax (905) 664-7228; sccc@bellnet.ca; www.chamberstoneycreek.com

Stony Lake • *see Lakefield*

Stratford • *Stratford & Dist. C/C* • Garry Lobsinger; Gen. Mgr.; 55 Lorne Ave. E.; N5A 6S4; P 30,000; M 400; (519) 273-5250; Fax (519) 273-7229; info@stratfordchamber.com; www.stratford chamber.com

Sturgeon Falls • *West Nipissing C/C* • Isabel Moseler; Ofc. Coord.; 200 Main St. Unit B; P2B 1P2; P 14,000; M 80; (705) 753-5672; Fax (705) 753-5672; wnc@eastlink.ca; www.west nipissing.ca

Sudbury • *Greater Sudbury C/C* • Debbi M. Nicholson; Pres./CEO; 40 Elm St., Ste. 1; P3C 1S8; P 160,000; M 1,800; (705) 673-7133; Fax (705) 673-2944; cofc@sudburychamber.ca; www.sudburychamber.ca

Tavistock • *Tavistock C/C* • Andrew Raymer; Pres.; P.O. Box 670; N0B 2R0; P 2,500; M 50; (519) 655-2700

Thornhill • *see Vaughan*

Thorold • *see St. Catharines*

Thunder Bay • *North of Superior Tourism Assn.* • Don Pearl; Exec. Dir.; 119 S. May St.; P7E 1A9; P 200,000; M 300; (807) 346-1130; (800) 265-3951; Fax (807) 346-1135; info@nosta.on.ca; www.northofsuperior.org

Thunder Bay • *Thunder Bay C/C* • Harold Wilson; Pres.; 200 S. Syndicate Ave., Ste. 102; P7E 1C9; P 110,000; M 1,060; (807) 624-2626; Fax (807) 622-7752; chamber@tb-chamber.on.ca; www.tb-chamber.on.ca

Tilbury • *Tilbury & Dist. C/C* • P.O. Box 1299; N0P 2L0; P 4,300; M 120; (519) 682-3040; Fax (519) 682-3123

Tillsonburg • *Tillsonburg Dist. C/C* • Suzanne Renken; Gen. Mgr.; P.O. Box 113; N4G 4H3; P 45,000; M 200; (519) 688-3737; suzanne@tillsonburgchamber.ca; www.tillsonburgchamber.ca

Timmins • *Timmins C/C* • Keitha Robson; Mgr.; P.O. Box 985; P4N 7H6; P 45,000; M 800; (705) 360-1900; Fax (705) 360-1193; admin@timminschamber.on.ca; www.timminschamber.on.ca

Tobermory • *Tobermory C/C* • Sheila Buckingham; Pres.; P.O. Box 250; N0H 2R0; P 1,000; M 85; (519) 596-2452; Fax (519) 596-2452; chamber@tobermory.org; www.tobermory.org

Toronto · *Toronto Bd. of Trade* · Carol Wilding; Pres./CEO; 1 First Canadian Pl.; P.O. Box 60; M5X 1C1; P 2,503,000; M 10,000; (416) 366-6811; Fax (416) 366-6460; ceo@bot.com; www.bot.com

Tottenham · *Tottenham Dist. C/C* · Jill Jones; Ofc. Admin.; 4 Mill St. E.; P.O. Box 922; L0G 1W0; P 10,000; M 150; (905) 936-4100; (888) 258-4727; Fax (905) 936-4664; tottenhamchamber ofcommerce@bellnet.ca; www.tottenhamchamber.on.ca

Trenton · *Quinte West C/C* · Suzanne Andrews; Mgr.; 97 Front St.; K8V 4N6; P 43,000; M 350; (613) 392-7635; (800) 930-3255; Fax (613) 392-8400; info@quintewestchamber.on.ca; www. quintewestchamber.on.ca

Uxbridge · *Uxbridge Twp. C/C* · Randy Loewen; Mgr.; 2 Campbell Dr., Ste. 810; L9P 0A3; P 18,500; M 112; (905) 852-7683; Fax (905) 852-1352; rloewen@spectrumadmin.ca; www.uxcc.ca

Vaughan · *Vaughan C/C* · Deborah Bonk-Greenwood; Pres./CEO; 25 Edilcan Dr., Unit 2; L4K 3S4; P 255,000; M 976; (905) 761-1366; Fax (905) 761-1918; info@vaughanchamber.ca; www.vaughan chamber.ca

Walkerton · *Walkerton & Dist. C/C* · Tracey Cassidy; Mgr.; 4 Park St.; P.O. Box 1344; N0G 2V0; P 10,000; M 280; (519) 881-3413; Fax (519) 881-4009; chamberinfo@wightman.ca; www. brockton.ca

Wasaga Beach · *Wasaga Beach C/C* · Trudie McCrea; Ofc. Mgr.; 550 River Rd. W.; P.O. Box 394; L9Z 1A4; P 16,000; M 250; (705) 429-2247; (866) 292-7242; Fax (705) 429-1407; info@wasagainfo. com; www.wasagainfo.com

Waterdown · *Flamborough C/C* · Arend Kersten; Exec. Dir.; P.O. Box 1030; L0R 2H0; P 39,000; M 250; (905) 689-7650; Fax (905) 689-1313; admin@flamboroughchamber.ca; www.flamborough chamber.ca

Waterloo · *see Kitchener*

Wawa · *Wawa Tourist Info. Center* · P.O. Box 500; P0S 1K0; P 3,600; (705) 856-2244; Fax (705) 856-2120; info@wawa.cc; www.wawa.cc

Welland · *Welland/Pelham C/C* · Dolores Fabiano; Exec. Dir.; 32 E. Main St.; L3B 3W3; P 49,000; M 450; (905) 732-7515; Fax (905) 732-7175; chamber@iaw.on.ca; www.wellandpelhamchamber.com

Westport · *Westport & Rideau Lakes C/C* · Jan Clarke; Secy.; P.O. Box 157; K0G 1X0; P 10,000; M 125; (613) 273-2929; wrlcc@ rideau.net; www.therideaucalls.com

Whitby · *Whitby C/C* · Gordon Mackey CSP CAE; CEO; 128 Brock St. S.; L1N 4J8; P 120,000; M 1,000; (905) 668-4506; Fax (905) 668-1894; info@whitbychamber.org; www.whitbychamber.org

Windsor · *Windsor-Essex Reg. C/C* · Linda E. Smith; Pres.; 2575 Ouellette Pl.; N8X 1L9; P 323,000; M 1,300; (519) 966-3696; Fax (519) 966-0603; info@windsorchamber.org; www.windsorchamber.org.

Woodbridge · *see Vaughan*

Woodstock · *Woodstock Dist. C/C* · Martha Dennis; Gen. Mgr.; 425 Dundas St., Ste. 3; N4S 1B8; P 35,000; M 360; (519) 539-9411; Fax (519) 456-1611; info@woodstockchamber.on.ca; www. woodstockchamber.on.ca

Young's Point · *see Lakefield*

Prince Edward

Alberton · *West Prince C/C* · John Lane; Chair; 455 Main St.; P.O. Box 220; C0B 1B0; P 1,100; M 50; (902) 853-4555; Fax (902) 853-3298; resourceswest.pe.ca

Charlottetown · *Greater Charlottetown Area C/C* · Kathy Hambly; Exec. Dir.; 127 Kent St.; P.O. Box 67; C1A 7K2; P 142,000; M 850; (902) 628-2000; Fax (902) 368-3570; chamber@charlotte townchamber.com; www.charlottetownchamber.com

Crapaud · *South Shore C/C* · Cathie Thomas; Admin.; P.O. Box 127; C0A 1J0; P 50,000; M 100; (902) 437-2510; www.southshore chamber.pe.ca

Kensington · *Kensington & Area C/C* · Glenna Lohnes; Mgr.; P.O. Box 234; C0B 1M0; P 6,000; M 100; (902) 836-3209; kacc@pei. aibn.com; www.kensingtonchamber.com

Lower Montague · *Eastern Kings & Queens C/C* · Mary Elliot; 11 Sunset Ln.; C0A 1R0; P 137,000; M 1,300; (902) 838-4791; (800) 274-3825; Fax (902) 836-4427; eichamber@yahoo.com

Summerside · *Greater Summerside C/C* · John J. MacDonald; Gen. Mgr.; 263 Harbour Dr., Ste. 10; C1N 5P1; P 17,000; M 325; (902) 436-9651; Fax (902) 436-8320; info@chamber.summerside. ca; www.chamber.summerside.ca

Quebec

Federation des chambres de commerce du Quebec · Margeurite Saubat; 555 Rene-Levesque Blvd. W., 19th Flr.; Montreal; H2Z 1B1; P 6,000,000; M 54,000; (514) 844-9571; Fax (514) 844-0226; info@fccq.ca; www.fccq.ca

Alma · *Chambre de Commerce Lac-Sainte-Jean-Est* · 625, rue Bergeron ouest; G8B 1V3; (418) 662-2734; Fax (418) 669-2220

Amos · *Chambre de Commerce D'Amos-Region* · Martin Veilleux; Dir. Gen.; C.P. 93; J9T 3A5; (819) 732-8100; Fax (819) 732-8101; ccar@ccar.qc.ca; www.ccar.qc.ca

Baie-Comeau · *Chambre de Commerce de Manicouagan* · Danielle Goyette Vaugeois; Exec. Dir.; 67 LaSalle Place, Local #302; G4Z 1K1; (418) 296-2010; Fax (418) 296-5397; info@ccmanic. qc.ca; www.ccmanic.qc.ca

Becancour · *Chambre de Commerce de Becancour* · 1045 ave. Nicolas Perrot; G9H 3B7; M 302; (819) 294-6010; Fax (819) 294-6020; info@ccibecancour.ca; www.ccibecancour.ca

Beloeil · *Vallee du Richelieu C/C* · Johanne Trudeau; Secy.; 220, rue Brebeuf, bureau 102; J3G 5P3; (450) 464-3733; Fax (450) 446-4163; chambre@ccvr.qc.ca; www.ccvr.qc.ca

Coaticook · *Chambre de Commerce de la Region de Coaticook* · Marco Des Marais; Dir. Gen.; 150, rue Child; J1A 2B3; P 9,000; M 250; (819) 849-4733; Fax (819) 849-6828; ccirc@ abacom.com; www.ccircoaticook.ca

Drummondville · *Chambre de Commerce de Drummond* · Alain Cote; 234 Saint Marcel St.; C.P. 188; J2B 6V7; P 80,000; M 1,100; (819) 477-7822; Fax (819) 477-2823; info@ccid.qc.ca; www.ccid.qc.ca

East-Angus · *Chambre de Commerce de East Angus et Region* · 288 Maple Ave.; J0B 1R0; P 4,000; M 100; (819) 832-4950; Fax (819) 832-2719; ccea@bellnet.ca

Ferme-Neuve · *Chambre de Commerce de Ferme Nueve* · Diane Bissonnette; Dir.; 125 12th rue; J0W 1C0; (819) 587-3882; Fax (819) 587-2444

Ile d'Orleans · *Chambre de Commerce de L'Ile D'Orleans* · Mary Langolis; Dir.; 490, Cote du Pont; St-Pierre; G0A 4E0; P 8,000; M 220; (418) 828-0880; Fax (418) 828-2335; www. cciledorleans.com

Joliette · *Chambre de Commerce du Grand Joliette* · Yvan Beausejour; Pres.; 500, boul Dollar; J6E 4M4; (450) 759-6363; Fax (450) 759-5012; info@ccgj.qc.ca; www.ccgj.qc.ca

Jonquiere • *Chambre de Commerce de Jonquiere* • 2240 rue Montpetit; C.P. 211; G7X 6A3; (418) 695-1362

La Baie • *Chambre de Commerce & D'Ind. De Ville de la Baie* • 285 Boul. Grande Baie Nord; G7B 3K4; (418) 544-8961; Fax (418) 544-4358

Lachenaie • *Chambre de Commerce de Terrebonne/lachenaie* • Robert Lalancette; Dir. Gen.; 1025, montee Masson, bureau 301; J6W 5H9; (450) 471-8779; Fax (450) 471-5610; info@cc terrebonne.qc.ca; www.ccterrebonne.qc.ca

L'Assomption • *Chambre de Commerce de L'Assomption* • 375 rue st-Pierre; C.P. 3027; J5W 4M9; (450) 589-2405; Fax (450) 589-9213; www.cclassomption.qc.ca

Laval • *Chambre de Commerce et D'Industrie de Laval* • 1555, boul. Chomedey, bureau 200; H7V 3Z1; P 286,000; M 2,300; (450) 682-5255; Fax (450) 682-5735; info@ccilaval.qc.ca; www.ccilaval.qc.ca

Levis • *Chambre de Commerce de Levis* • Jerome Gaudreault; Dir. Gen.; 5700, JB-Michaud St., Ofc. 225; G6V 0B1; P 130,000; M 1,000; (418) 837-3411; Fax (418) 837-8497; cclevis@cclevis.ca; www.cclevis.ca

Longueuil • *Chambre de Commerce et D'Industrie de la Rive-Sud* • Yvon Rudolphe; Pres.; 85, rue Saint-Charles Ouest; bureau 101; J4H 1C5; P 400,000; M 1,700; (450) 463-2121; Fax (450) 463-1858; info@ccirs.qc.ca; www.ccirs.qc.ca

Louiseville • *Chambre de Commerce Mrc de Maskinonge* • Marc Plante; Gen. Mgr.; 255, boul St-Laurent ouest #101; J5V 1K2; P 35,000; M 200; (819) 228-8582; Fax (819) 228-8989; ccmm@ cgocable.ca

Maniwaki • *Chambre de Commerce et d'Industrie de Maniwaki* • 171, rue Principale Sud; J9E 1Z8; P 5,500; M 200; (819) 449-6627; Fax (819) 449-7667; valerie@ccimki.ca; www.ccimki.ca

Mascouche • *Chambre de Commerce de Mascouche* • Robert Filion; Dir. Gen.; 2822A, chemin Ste-Marie #240; J7K 1N4; P 35,000; M 225; (450) 966-1536; Fax (450) 966-1531; info@ ccmascouche.com; www.ccmascouche.com

Mirabel • *Chambre de Commerce de Mirabel* • Yves Legault; Pres.; 13665, boul. du Cure-Labelle #208; J7J 1L2; (450) 433-1944; Fax (450) 433-5168; info@ccmirabel.com; www.ccmirabel.com

Montreal • *Board of Trade of Metropolitan Montreal* • Isabelle Hudon; Pres./CEO; 380 St. Antoine St. W. #6000; H2Y 3X7; P 3,000,000; M 7,000; (514) 871-4000; Fax (514) 871-1255; info@ ccmm.qc.ca; www.btmm.qc.ca

Nicolet • *Chambre de Commerce de Nicolet* • 30, rue Notre-Dame; J3T 1G1; (819) 293-4537; Fax (819) 293-6092; chambre@ chambre-cnicolet.org; www.chambre-cnicolet.org

Normandin • *Chambre de Commerce du Secteur de Normandin* • Denise Paquet; Dir. Gen.; 1048, rue St-Cyrille; G8M 4R9; (418) 274-7206; Fax (418) 274-7171; ccnormandin@hotmail.com

Pointe-Calumet • *Chambre de Commerce du Lac Des Deux-Montagnes* • 190, 41st Avenue #400; J0N 1G2; (450) 472-7535; Fax (450) 472-0229

Pointe-Claire • *West Island of Montreal C/C* • Andree Belanger; Dir. Gen.; 207, Place Frontenac; H9R 4Z7; P 350,000; M 1,000; (514) 697-4228; Fax (514) 697-2562; info@ccoim.ca; www.wimcc.ca

Quebec • *Chambre de Commerce de Quebec* • Daniel Denis; Pres.; 17, rue St-Louis; G1R 3Y8; M 4,000; (418) 692-3853; Fax (418) 694-2286; info@ccquebec.ca; www.ccquebec.ca

Rimouski • *Chambre de Commerce de Rimouski-Neigette* • Louis Olivier Carre; Pres.; 125, rue de l'Eveche Ouest #101; CP 1296; G5L 8M2; M 350; (418) 722-4494; Fax (418) 722-8402; ccriki@ccrimouski.com; www.ccrimouski.com

Roberval • *Chambre de Commerce de Roberval* • Pascal Gagnon; Dir. Gen.; C.P. 115; G8H 2N4; P 11,000; M 200; (418) 275-3504; Fax (418) 275-0851; info@ccisr.qc.ca; www.ccisr.qc.ca

Rouyn-Noranda • *Chambre de Commerce du Rouyn-Noranda Regional* • M. Jean-Claude Loranger; Pres.; 70 Avenue du lac; J9X 4N4; P 40,000; M 1,100; (819) 797-2000; Fax (819) 762-3091; rejean.lavoie@ccirn.qc.ca; www.ccirn.qc.ca

Saint-Jean-de-Matha • *Chambre de Commerce St-Jean-de-Matha* • Regis Morissette; Pres.; 1159 route Louis-Cyr; J0K 2S0; P 3,030; M 52; (450) 886-0599; Fax (450) 886-3123; info@ chambrematha.com; www.chambrematha.com

Saint-Martin-de-Beauce • *Chambre de Commerce de St-Martin de Beauce* • Serge Thibault; Pres.; C.P. 2022; G0M 1B0; P 2,500; M 44; (418) 382-5549; Fax (418) 382-5512; chambre@ st-martin.qc.ca; www.st-martin.qc.ca

Salaberry-de-Valleyfield • *Chambre de Comm. Reg. de Salaberry-de-Valleyfield* • 100, rue Ste-Cecile, bureau 400; J6T 1M1; (450) 373-8789; Fax (450) 373-8642; info@ccrsv.com; www.ccrsv.com

Sept Iles • *Chambre de Commerce de Sept-Iles* • Ginette Lehoux; Gen. Mgr.; 700, Boul Laure, bureau 204; G4R 1Y1; P 25,000; M 400; (418) 968-3488; Fax (418) 968 3432; ccsi@globetrotter.net

Sept-Iles • *Corporation Touristique de Sept-Iles, Inc.* • Mylene Barbeau; Gen. Mgr.; 1401 Blvd. Laure; G4R 4K1; P 29,000; (418) 962-1238; Fax (418) 968-0022; www.ville.septiles.qc.ca

Sorel • *Chambre de Commerce Sorel-Tracy Metropolitan* • Rachel Doyon; Gen. Dir.; 67 George St.; J3P 1C2; (450) 742-0018; Fax (450) 742-7442; ccstm@ccstm.qc.ca; www.ccstm.qc.ca

St-Donat • *Tourist Info. Office of St-Donat* • Sophie Charpentier; Dir.; 536, rue Principale; J0T 2C0; P 4,300; M ; (819) 424-2833; (888) 783-6628; Fax (819) 424-3809; tourisme@ saint-donat.com; www.saint-donat.com

Ste-Agathe-des-Monts • *Sainte-Agathe-des-Monts C/C* • Daniel Des Jardins; Gen. Mgr.; 24, rue St-Paul-Est; C.P. 323; J8C 3C6; P 10,000; M 340; (819) 326-3731; (888) 326-0457; Fax (819) 326-3936; info@sainte-agathe.org; www.sainte-agathe.org

Ste-Justine • *Chambre de Commerce de Ste-Justine* • Patrice Pouliot; Pres.; 167, Rte. 204; G0R 1Y0; (418) 383-5397; Fax (418) 383-5398; sjustine@sogetel.net; www.stejustine.net

St-Gabriel-de-Brandon • *Chambre de Commerce de Brandon* • 151 St. Gabriel; C.P. 778; J0K 2N0; (450) 835-2105; Fax Same

St-Georges • *Chambre de Commerce de St-Georges* • Brigitte Busque; Pres.; 8585, boul Lacroix, bureau 310; G5Y 5L6; (418) 228-7879; Fax (418) 228-8074; www.ccstgeorges.com

St-Jerome • *Chambre de Commerce St-Jerome* • Jocelyne Legare; Dir. Gen.; 309, rue De Villemure; J7Z 5J5; (450) 431-4339; Fax (450) 431-1677; chambre@ccisj.qc.ca; www.ccisj.qc.ca

St-Laurent • *Chambre de Commerce de St-Laurent* • Robert Petit; Gen. Mgr.; 935 Decarie #204; H4L 3M3; M 840; (514) 333-5222; Fax (514) 333-0937; info@ccstl.qc.ca; www.ccstl.qc.ca

St-Raymond • *Chambre de Commerce de St-Raymond* • 100, rue St-Jacques Bureau 1; G3L 3Y1; P 9,000; (418) 337-4049; Fax (418) 337-8017

Temiscaming • *Chambre de Commerce de Temiscaming-Kipawa* • 15 Humphrey St.; C.P. 442; J0Z 3R0; (819) 627-6160; (819) 627-1846; www.temiscaming.net

Trois-Rivieres · *Chambre de Commerce et D'Industries* · Jean-Claude Gendron; Coordonnateur; 168 Bonaventure; P.O. Box 1045; G9A 5K4; P 126,000; M 850; (819) 375-9628; Fax (819) 375-9083; info@ccdtr.com; www.ccdtr.com

Trois-Rivieres · *Ofc de Tourisme et des Congres de Trois Rivieres* · 1457, rue Notre Dame center; G9A 4X4; P 125,000; M 150; (819) 375-1122; Fax (819) 375-0022; info@tourismetrois rivieres.com; www.v3r.net

Val-d'Or · *Chambre de Commerce de Val-d'Or* · Dominique Parent Manseau; Gen. Dir.; 400, 3e Ave.; J9P 1R9; P 35,000; M 1,000; (819) 825-3703; ccvd@cablevision.qc.ca; www.ccvd.qc.ca

Weedon · *Chambre de Commerce de la Region de Weedon* · David Gauthier; Pres.; 280 9th Ave.; J0B 3J0; (819) 877-5124; Fax (819) 877-1111; chambrede.commerce@qc.aira.com; www. ccweedon.com

Saskatchewan

Saskatchewan C/C · Richard Ahenakew; Pres.; 1630–1920 Broad St.; Regina; S4P 3V2; P 1,000,000; M 1,500; (306) 352-2671; Fax (306) 781-7084; info@saskchamber.com; www. saskchamber.com

Aylsham · *Aylsham & Dist. Bd. of Trade* · Glen Gray; Pres.; P.O. Box 21; S0E 0C0; P 600; M 35; (306) 862-3028; (306) 862-4849; Fax (306) 862-4506; mgbritton@sasktel.net

Big River · *Big River & Dist. C/C* · Jeanette Wicinski-Dunn; Pres.; P.O. Box 763; S0J 0E0; P 800; M 50; (306) 469-4888; Fax (306) 469-4475; mindbodyspirit@sasktel.net; www.bigriver.ca

Broadview · *Broadview C/C* · Donna Brown; P.O. Box 508; S0G 0K0; P 650; M 32; (306) 696-3533

Coronach · *Coronach Comm. C/C* · Jackie Marshall; Pres.; P.O. Box 577; S0H 0Z0; P 950; M 26; (306) 267-2077; Fax (306) 267-2047; marshalljackie@hotmail.com

Cut Knife · *Cut Knife C/C* · Gwenn Kaye; Pres.; P.O. Box 504; S0M 0N0; P 560; M 35; (306) 398-2277

Eastend · *Eastend C/C* · Sean Bell; Pres.; P.O. Box 534; S0N 0T0; P 650; M 45; (306) 295-4144; admin@trexcentre.ca; www. dinocountry.com

Esterhazy · *Esterhazy & Dist. C/C* · P.O. Box 778; S0A 0X0; P 2,800; M 45; (306) 745-5405; Fax (306) 745-6797; esterhazy. ed@sasktel.net; www.town.esterhazy.sk.ca

Estevan · *Estevan & Dist. Bd. of Tourism, Trade & Commerce* · Michel Cyrenne; CEO; 322 4th St.; S4A 0T8; P 13,500; M 320; (306) 634-2828; Fax (306) 634-6729; carol@estevanchamber.ca; www. estevanchamber.ca

Eston · *Eston Bd. of Trade* · Margaret Olorenshaw; Treas.; Box 1000; S0L 1A0; P 1,100; M 40; (306) 962-4177; Fax (306) 962-3325;

Foam Lake · *Foam Lake C/C* · John Riberdy; Pres.; P.O. Box 238; S0A 1A0; P 7,000; M 75; (306) 272-4443; flchamberofcommerce@ sasktel.net; www.foamlake.com

Fort Qu'Appelle · *Fort Qu'Appelle & Dist. C/C* · Michelle Johns; V.P.; P.O. Box 1273; S0G 1S0; P 10,000; M 120; (306) 332-5717; Fax (306) 332-1287; kdmjohns@hotmail.com; www.fortquappelle.com

Fox Valley · *Fox Valley C/C* · Delia Hughes; Secy.; Railway Box 72; S0N 0V0; P 350; M 45; (306) 666-2139

Herbert · *Herbert & Dist. C/C* · Al Kildaw; Pres.; Box 190; S0H 2A0; P 840; M 25; (306) 784-3475; al.kildaw@sasktel.net

Humboldt · *Humboldt & Dist. C/C* · Donna Lynn Dyok; Exec. Dir.; Hwy. 5 E.; Box 1440; S0K 2A0; P 5,700; M 160; (306) 682-4990; Fax (306) 682-5203; humboldtchamber@sasktel.net; www. humboldtchamber.ca

Kenaston · *Kenaston & Dist. C/C* · ML Whittles; Pres.; P.O. Box 386; S0G 2N0; P 320; M 28; (306) 252-2236; r.m.whittles@sasktel. net; www.kenaston.ca

Kerrobert · *Kerrobert C/C* · Sandy Semilet; P.O. Box 408; S0L 1R0; P 1,111; M 45; (306) 834-5252; (306) 834-2361; kerrobert@ sasktel.net; www.kerrobert.com

Kindersley · *Kindersley C/C* · Esther Redden; Ofc. Mgr.; Box 1537; S0L 1S0; P 4,500; M 120; (306) 463-2320; Fax (306) 463-2312; kindersleychamber@sasktel.net; www.kindersleychamber.com

La Ronge · *La Ronge & Dist. C/C* · Gary Beteri; Pres.; P.O. Box 1067; S0J 1L0; P 6,800; M 100; (306) 425-4744; (306) 425-2195

Langenburg · *Langenburg C/C* · Warren Vandenameele; Chrmn.; P.O. Box 610; S0A 2A0; P 1,200; M 55; (306) 743-5558; Fax (306) 743-2959; www.town.langenburg.sk.ca

Maple Creek · *Maple Creek C/C* · Ben Beveridge; Pres.; P.O. Box 1776; S0N 1N0; P 3,000; M 40; (306) 622-3877; info@maplecreek chamber.ca; www.maplecreekchamber.ca

Meadow Lake · *Meadow Lake & Dist. C/C* · Lori Thompson; Admin.; P.O. Box 847; S9X 1Y6; P 6,000; M 120; (306) 236-4061; Fax (306) 236-4031; mlchamberofcommerce@sasktel.net

Melfort · *Melfort & Dist. C/C* · Candis Harper; Exec. Dir.; P.O. Box 2002; S0E 1A0; P 7,000; M 145; (306) 752-4636; Fax (306) 752-9505; melfortchamber@sasktel.net; www.melfortchamber.com

Melville · *Melville & Dist. C/C* · Ron Walton; Ofc. Mgr.; 420 Main St.; P.O. Box 429; S0A 2P0; P 4,700; M 62; (306) 728-4177; Fax (306) 728-5911; melvillechamber@sasktel.net; www.melville chamber.com

Moose Jaw · *Moose Jaw C/C* · Brian Martynook; Exec. Dir.; 88 Saskatchewan St. E.; S6H 0V4; P 35,000; M 500; (306) 692-6414; Fax (306) 694-6463; chamber@mjchamber.com; www.mjchamber.com

Moosomin · *Moosomin C/C* · Ed Hilderbrandt; Pres.; P.O. Box 819; S0G 3N0; P 2,500; M 100; (306) 435-3175; Fax (306) 435-2540; world_spectator@sasktel.net

Nipawin · *Nipawin & Dist. C/C* · Cindy Murphy; Exec. Dir.; P.O. Box 177; S0E 1E0; P 5,000; M 195; (306) 862-5252; Fax (306) 862-5350; info@nipawinchamber.ca; www.nipawinchamber.ca

Norquay · *Norquay & Dist. C/C* · Dwayne Dahl; Pres.; P.O. Box 457; S0A 2V0; P 600; M 35; (306) 594-2324; Fax (306) 594-2028; dwaynedahl@sasktel.net; www.townofnorquay.ca

North Battleford · *Battlefords C/C* · Linda Machniak; Exec. Dir.; Jct. of Hwy. 16 & 40 E.; P.O. Box 1000; S9A 3E6; P 20,000; M 365; (306) 445-6226; Fax (306) 445-6633; b.chamber@sasktel. net; www.battlefordschamber.com.

Outlook · *Outlook & Dist. C/C* · Ken Fehr; Treas.; P.O. Box 431; S0L 2N0; P 2,500; M 55; (306) 867-9944; Fax (306) 867-2084; www.town.outlook.sk.ca/chamber.htm

Prince Albert · *Prince Albert & Dist. C/C* · Bergen Price; CEO; 3700 2nd Ave. W.; S6W 1A2; P 45,000; M 520; (306) 764-6222; Fax (306) 922-4727; admin.pachamber@sasktel.net; www. princealbertchamber.com

Redvers · *Redvers C/C* · P.O. Box 249; S0C 2H0; P 917; M 47; (306) 452-3155; Fax (306) 452-3155; redverschamberofcom-merce@xplornet.ca

Regina · *Regina C/C* · John Hopkins; CEO; 2145 Albert St.; S4P 2V1; P 199,974; M 1,300; (306) 757-4658; Fax (306) 757-4668; info@reginachamber.com; www.reginachamber.com

Saint Walburg · *St. Walburg C/C* · Clare Church; Secy.; P.O. Box 501; S0M 2T0; P 800; M 45; (306) 248-3223; townofstwalburg@ sasktel.net; www.stwalburg.com

Saskatoon · *Greater Saskatoon C/C* · Kent Smith-Windsor; Exec. Dir.; 104-202 4th Ave. N.; S7K 0K1; P 223,200; M 1,706; (306) 244-2151; Fax (306) 244-8366; chamber@saskatoonchamber.com; www.saskatoonchamber.com.

Shaunavon · *Shaunavon C/C* · Joan Gregoire; Pres.; P.O. Box 1048; S0N 2M0; P 2,000; M 70; (306) 297-2134; shaunavon chamber@hotmail.com; www.shaunavon.com

Spiritwood · *Spiritwood & Dist. C/C* · George Pretly; P.O. Box 267; S0J 2M0; P 900; M 116; (306) 883-2161; Fax (306) 883-2136; www.townofspiritwood.com

Swift Current · *Swift Current C/C* · Jennifer Lyster; Dir.; Swift Current Bus. Center; 145 1st Ave. N.E.; S9H 2B1; P 16,800; M 425; (306) 773-7268; Fax (306) 773-5686; info@swiftcurrentchamber. ca; www.swiftcurrentchamber.ca

Tisdale · *Tisdale & Dist. C/C* · P.O. Box 219; S0E 1T0; P 8,000; M 110; (306) 873-4257; Fax (306) 873-4241; tisdalechamber@ sasktel.net; www.townoftisdale.com

Turtleford · *Turtleford C/C* · Guy Patenaude; Pres.; P.O. Box 520; S0M 2Y0; P 480; M 20; (306) 845-2081

Watrous · *Watrous & Dist. C/C* · Ray Hall; P.O. Box 906; S0K 4T0; P 1,808; M 60; (306) 946-3369; www.townofwatrous.com

Watson · *Watson & Dist. C/C* · Debbie Schwartz; Treas.; P.O. Box 686; S0K 4V0; P 800; M 50; (306) 287-3636

Weyburn · *Weyburn C/C* · Jeff Richards; Mgr.; 11 Third St. N.E.; S4H 0W5; P 10,000; M 170; (306) 842-4738; Fax (306) 842-0520; manager@weyburnchamber.com; www.weyburnchamber.com

Wynyard · *Wynyard & Dist. C/C* · Nancy Pitzel; V.P.; P.O. Box 508; S0A 4T0; P 2,000; M 75; (306) 554-2224; Fax (306) 554-3226; www.town.wynyard.sk.ca

Yorkton · *Yorkton C/C* · Juanita Polegi; Exec. Dir.; P.O. Box 1051; S3N 2X3; P 20,000; M 450; (306) 783-4368; Fax (306) 786-6978; office@chamber.yorkton.sk.ca; www.chamber.yorkton.sk.ca

Yukon

Yukon C/C · Sandy Babcock; Pres.; 307 Jarvis St., Ste. 101; Whitehorse; Y1A 2H3; P 30,000; M 130; (867) 667-2000; Fax (867) 667-2001; ycc@yukonchamber.com; www.yukonchamber.com

Dawson City · *Dawson City C/C* · Gen. Mgr.; P.O. Box 1006; Y0B 1G0; P 1,500; M 70; (867) 993-5274; Fax (867) 993-6817; office@ dawsoncitychamberofcommerce.ca; www.dawsoncitychamber ofcommerce.ca

Whitehorse · *Whitehorse C/C* · Rick Karp; Pres.; 101–302 Steele St.; Y1A 2C5; P 24,000; M 350; (867) 667-7545; Fax (867) 667-4507; business@whitehorsechamber.ca; www.whitehorse chamber.ca

Notes

American Chambers of Commerce Abroad

American Chambers of Commerce Abroad are voluntary associations of American enterprises and individuals doing business in a particular country, as well as firms and individuals of that country who operate in the U.S.

Along with pursuing trade policy initiatives, AmChams make available publications and services and sponsor a variety of business development programs. The AmChams represent the concerns and interests of the business community at the highest levels of government and business in trade policy development.

AmChams also:

- Develop mutually prosperous and amicable economic, social and commercial relations between U.S. businesses and service industries, and those of the host country.
- Represent members' views on policy and regulatory matters to both U.S. and host country governments, and interpret the point of view of other countries to the American business public.
- Promote local economic and social contributions for the benefit of host countries.

Albania

Tirana · *American Chamber of Commerce in Albania* · Rr. Deshmoret e 4 shkurtit; Sky Tower, kati 11 Ap 3; M 200; 355-4-225-9779; Гах 355-4-223-5350; info@amcham.com.al, www.amcham.com.al

Argentina

Buenos Aires · *American Chamber of Commerce in Argentina* · Alejandro Diaz; CEO; Viamonte 1133 Piso 8; 1053; M 780; 5411-4371-4500; Fax 5411-4371-8400; amcham@amchamar.com.ar; www.amchamar.com.ar

Armenia

Yerevan · *American Chamber of Commerce in Armenia* · Diana Gaziyan; Exec. Dir.; Marriott Armenia Hotel, 7th Flr., Rm. 629; 0100; 374-10-599-187; Fax 374-10-564-178; info@amcham.am; www.amcham.am

Asia

Ho Chi Minh City · *Asia-Pacific Cncl. of American Chambers of Commerce* · Walter Blocker; Chrmn.; % Car Rental Svcs. Joint Stock Co.; 21 Phung Khac Khoan St., Dist. 1; M 27; 84-8-3930-1118; Fax 84-8-3941-5445; www.apcac.org

Australia

Sydney, NSW · *American Chamber of Commerce in Australia* · Charles Blunt; Natl. Dir.; Ste. 9, Ground Level; 88 Cumberland St.; 2000; P 25,000,000; M 700; 61-2-8031-9000; Fax 61-2-9251-5220; nswamcham@amcham.com.au; www.amcham.com.au

Austria

Vienna · *American Chamber of Commerce in Austria* · Dr. Patricia A. Helletzgruber; Exec. Dir.; Porzellangasse 35; 1090; M 500; 43-1-319-57-51; Fax 43-1-319-51-51; office@amcham.at; www.amcham.or.at

Bahrain

Manama · *American Chamber of Commerce in Bahrain* · Hamid Al Zayani; V.P. of Programs; Ministry of Ind. & Commerce, Ground Flr.; Bldg. 240, Rd. 1704, Block 317; 973-17-522-777; Fax 973-17-522-737; info@amcham-bahrain.org; www.amcham-bahrain.org

Bangladesh

Dhaka · *American Chamber of Commerce in Bangladesh* · A. Gafur; Exec. Dir.; Room No. 319, Dhaka Sheraton Hotel; 1, Minto Rd.; 1000; 880-2-8330001; Fax 880-2-9349217; amcham@amchambd.org; www.amchambd.org

Belgium

Brussels · *American Chamber of Commerce in Belgium* · Marcel Claes; CEO; Rue du Commerce 41 Handelsstraat; 1000; M 875; 32-2-513-67-70; Fax 32-2-513-35-90; gchamber@amcham.be; www.amcham.be

Bolivia

La Paz · *American Chamber of Commerce of Bolivia* · Anna María Galindo; Gen. Mgr.; Av. 6 de Agosto No. 2455; Edif. Hilda-Piso 2 of. 204; M 140; 591-2-2443939; Fax 591-2-2443972; amgalin@amchambolivia.com; www.amchambolivia.com

Brazil

Rio de Janeiro · *American Chamber of Commerce for Brazil-Rio de Janiero* · Robson Barreto; Pres.; Praca Pio X, 15, 5th Flr.; 20040-020; M 600; 55-21-3213-9200; Fax 55-21-3213-9201; anaredig@amchamrio.com; www.amchamrio.com.br

Sao Paulo, S.P. · *American Chamber of Commerce for Brazil-Sao Paulo* · Alexandre Silva; Pres.; Chacara Santo Antonio; Rua da Paz, no. 1431; 04713-001; M 2,700; 55-11-3324-0194; Fax 55-11-5180-3777; ombudsman@amchambrasil.com.br; www.amcham.com.br

Bulgaria

Sofia · *American Chamber of Commerce in Bulgaria* · Valentin Georgiev; Exec. Dir.; Business Park Sofia, Mladost 4 Area; Bldg. 2, Flr. 6; 1766; M 300; 359-2-9742-743; Fax 359-2-9742-741; amcham@amcham.bg; www.amcham.bg

Cambodia

Phnom Penh · *American Cambodian Bus. Cncl.* · Bretton G. Sciaroni; Chrmn.; No. 56 Samdech Sothearos Blvd; Khan Daun Penh; 855-232-10225; Fax 855-232-13089

Canada

Peterborough, ON · *American Chamber of Commerce in Canada* · Robert Bathgate; Pres./CEO; 650 Parkhill Road W., PH # 3; Ontario; K9J 6N6; (888) 390-2751; info@amchamcanada.ca; www.amchamcanada.ca

Chile

Santiago · *Chilean-American Chamber of Commerce* · John Welby; Mgr.; Av. Kennedy 5735, of. 201; Torre Poniente, Las Condes; M 1,200; 56-2-290-97-00; Fax 56-2-212-05-15; amcham@amchamchile.cl; www.amchamchile.cl

China

Beijing · *American Chamber of Commerce PRC Beijing* · Ted Dean; Chrmn.; The Office Park, Tower AB, 6th Flr.; No. 10 Jintongxi Rd.; 100005; M 600; 86-10-8519-0800; Fax 86-10-8519-1910; amcham@amchamchina.org; www.amchamchina.org

Shanghai · *American Chamber of Commerce in Shanghai* · Eric S. Musser; Chrmn.; Shanghai Center, Ste. 568; 1376 Nanjing Rd. W.; 200040; M 1,900; 86-21-6279-7119; Fax 86-21-6279-7643; amcham@amcham-shanghai.org; www.amcham-shanghai.org

Guangzhou · *American Chamber of Commerce in South China* · Ste. 1603, Main Tower, Guangdong Intl. Hotel; 339 Huanshi Dong Rd.; Guangdong; 510098; M 300; 86-20-8335-1476; Fax 86-20-8332-1642; amcham@amcham-southchina.org; www.amcham-southchina.org

Macau · *Americam Chamber of Commerce in Macau* · Charles M. Choy; Chrmn.; Alameda Dr. Carlos d' Assumpcao, No. 263; China Civil Plaza, 20F; 853-2857-5059; Fax 853-2857-5060; info@amcham.org.mo; www.amcham.org.mo

Colombia

Bogota · *Colombian-American Chamber of Commerce* · Miguel Gomez Martinez; Exec. Dir.; Calle 98 #22-64 Of. 1209; P.O. Box 8008; M 400; 571-587-78-28; Fax 571-587-78-28-2; direct@amchamcolombia.com.co; www.amchamcolombia.com.co

Costa Rica

San Jose · *Costa Rican-American Chamber of Commerce* · Lynda Solar; Exec. Dir.; P.O. Box 4946; 1000; M 400; 506-2220-2200; Fax 506-2220-2300; chamber@amcham.co.cr; www.amcham.co.cr

Cote d'Ivoire

Abidjan · *American Chamber of Commerce of Cote d'Ivoire* · Riviera Attoban 06; BP 2282; 6; 225-22-42-68-66; Fax 225-22-42-30-64; amchamci@amchamci.org; www.amchamci.org

Croatia

Zagreb · *American Chamber of Commerce in Croatia* · Ms. Andrea Doko Jelušić; Exec. Dir.; Radnicka 47; 10000; 385-1-4836-777; Fax 385-1-4836-776; andrea.doko@amcham.hr; www.amcham.hr

Cyprus

Nicosia · *Cyprus-American Bus. Assn.* · Mr. Chris Christodoulou; Pres.; P.O. Box 21455; CY-1509; 357-22-889830; Fax 357-22-668630; cyaba@cyaba.com.cy; www.cyaba.com.cy

Czech Republic

Prague · *American Chamber of Commerce in the Czech Republic* · Weston Stacey; Exec. Dir.; Dusni 10; CZ-11000M 350; 420-222-329-430; Fax 420-222-329-433; amcham@amcham.cz; www.amcham.cz

Denmark

Copenhagen · *American Chamber of Commerce in Denmark* · Stephen Brugger; Exec. Dir.; Christians Brygge 26; 1559; 45-33-932-932; Fax 45-33-932-938; mail@amcham.dk; www.amcham.dk

Dominican Republic

Santo Domingo · *American Chamber of Commerce of the Dominican Republic* · William Malamud; Exec. V.P.; Av. Sarasota No. 20; Torre Empresearial 6to. Piso; M 3,000; 809-381-0777; Fax 809-381-0303; amcham@codetel.net.do; www.amcham.org.do

Ecuador

Guayaquil · *Ecuadorian-American Chamber of Commerce-Guayaquil* · Jorge Farah; Exec. Dir.; Cdla. Kennedy Norte, Ave. Francisco de Orellana; Edificio Centrum, Piso 6, Oficina 5; M 500; 593-4-269-3470; Fax 593-4-269-3465; camara@amchamecuador.org; www.amchamecuador.org

Quito · *Ecuadorian-American Chamber of Commerce-Quito* · Bernardo Traversari; Exec. Dir.; La Nina y Avda. 6 de Diciembre; Edif. Multicentro, piso 4; M 800; 593-2-2507450; Fax 593-2-2504571; info@ecamcham.com; www.ecamcham.com

Egypt

Cairo · *American Chamber of Commerce in Egypt* · Hisham Fahmy; CEO; 33 Soliman Abaza St.; Dokki-Giza; 12311; M 600; 20-2-3338-1050; Fax 20-2-3338-1060; infocenter@amcham.org.eg; www.amcham.org.eg

El Salvador

San Salvador · *American Chamber of Commerce of El Salvador* · Carmen Aida Munoz; Exec. Dir.; World Trade Center Torre II Local 308; 89 Avenida Norte, Colonia Escalon; M 397; 503-2263-9494; Fax 503-2263-9393; amchamsal@amchamsal.com; www.amchamsal.com

European Union

Brussels, Belgium · *American Chamber of Commerce to the European Union* · Susan Danger; Managing Dir.; Ave. des arts/Kunstlaan 53; 1000; P 490,000,000; M 142; 32-2-513-6892; Fax info@amchameu.eu; www.amchameu.eu

Finland

Helsinki · *American Chamber of Commerce in Finland* · Kristiina Helenius; Mgr. Dir.; Annankatu 32, 7th Flr.; 100; 358-40-466-4576; Fax 358-9-675-387; kristiina.helenius@amcham.fi; www.amcham.fi

France

Paris · *American Chamber of Commerce in France* · Marina Niforos; Mgr. Dir.; 156 boulevard Haussmann; 75008; M 500; 33-1-56-43-45-67; Fax 33-1 56 43 45 60; marina.niforos@amcham france.org; www.amchamfrance.org

Georgia

Tbilisi · *American Chamber of Commerce in Georgia* · Amy Denman; Exec. Dir.; 10 Melikishvili Ave.; 0179; M 80; 995-32-226907; Fax 995-32-226792; amcham@amcham.ge; www.amcham.ge

Germany

Frankfurt · *American Chamber of Commerce in Germany* · Dr. Dierk Muller; Gen. Mgr.; Borsenplatz 7-11; 60313; M 3,000; 49-69-929-104-20; Fax 49-69-92910411; amcham@amcham.de; www.amcham.de

Ghana

Cantonments-Accra · *American Chamber of Commerce in Ghana* · Mr. Simon Madjie; Exec. Secy.; P.O. Box CT2869; M 70; 233-030-224-7562; Fax 233-030-224-7562; info@amchamghana.org; www.amchamghana.org

Greece

Athens · *American-Hellenic Chamber of Commerce* · Elias Spirtounias; Exec. Dir.; 109-111 Messoghion Ave.; Politia Business Center; 115 26; M 1,000; 30-210-699-3559; Fax 30-210-698-5687; info@amcham.gr; www.amcham.gr

Guatemala

Guatamala City · *American Chamber of Commerce in Guatemala* · Carolina Castellanos; Exec. Dir.; 5a Ave. 5-55, Zona 14 Edif. Europlaza WBC Torre I, Niv. 5; 01014; M 450; 502-2417-0800; Fax 502-2417-0777; recepcion@amchamguate.com; www.amchamguate.com

Haiti

Delmas · *American Chamber of Commerce & Ind. in Haiti* · P.O. Box 13486; 509-25-11-30-24; Fax 509-29-40-30-24; executive_director@amcham.ht; www.amcham.ht

Honduras

Tegucigalpa · *Honduran-American Chamber of Commerce* · Apdo. Postal 1838; M 540; 504-271-0094; Fax 504-271-0097; amcham@amchamhonduras.org; www.amchamhonduras.org

Hong Kong (China)

Hong Kong · *American Chamber of Commerce in Hong Kong* · Robert Chipman; Chrmn.; 1904 Bank of America Tower; 12 Harcourt Rd.; M 2,000; 852-2530-6900; Fax 852-2810-1289; amcham@amcham.org.hk; www.amcham.org.hk

Hungary

Budapest · *American Chamber of Commerce in Hungary* · Peter David; CEO; Szent Istvan ter 11.; 1051; M 570; 36-1-266-9880; Fax 36-1-266-9888; peter.david@amcham.hu; www.amcham.hu

India

New Delhi · *American Chamber of Commerce in India* · Mr. Ajay Singha; Exec. Dir.; PHD House, 4th Flr.; 4/2, Siri Institutional Area, August Kranti Marg; 110016; M 261; 91-11-2652-5201; Fax 91-11-2652-5203; amcham@amchamindia.com; www.amchamindia.com

Indonesia

Jakarta · *American Chamber of Commerce in Indonesia* · Sarah Howe; Exec. Dir.; World Trade Centre, 11th Flr.; Jl. Jend Sudirman Kav. 29-31; 12920; M 430; 622-1-526-2860; Fax 622-1-526-2861; info@amcham.or.id; www.amcham.or.id

Ireland

Dublin · *American Chamber of Commerce of Ireland* · Joanne Richardson; CEO; 6 Wilton Pl.; 2; M 340; 353-1-6616201; Fax 353-1-6616217; info@amcham.ie; www.amcham.ie

Israel

Tel Aviv · *Israel-America Chamber of Commerce* · Tamar Guy; Exec. Dir.; 35 Shaul Hamelech Blvd.; 61333; M 500; 972-3-6952341; Fax 972-3-6951272; amcham@amcham.co.il; www.amcham.co.il

Italy

Milano · *American Chamber of Commerce in Italy* · Kelly Ben Frech; Mktg. & Comm.; Via Cantu 1; I-20123; M 1,000; 39-02-86-90-661; Fax 39-02-39-29-67-52; amcham@amcham.it; www.amcham.it

Ivory Coast

See Cote d'Ivoire

Jamaica

Kingston · *American Chamber of Commerce of Jamaica* · Becky Stockhausen; Exec. Dir.; Jamaica Pegasus Hotel, Rm. 119; 81 Knutsford Blvd.; 5; P 2,700,000; M 190; 876-929-7866; 876-968-2090; Fax 876-929-8597; becky_amcham@cwjamaica.com; www.amchamjamaica.org

Japan

Okinawa City · *American Chamber of Commerce in Okinawa* · James R. Pogue; Pres.; P.O. Box 235; 904-8591; M 115; 81-98-898-5401; Fax 81-98-898-5411; chamber@amchamokinawa.org; www.amchamokinawa.org

Tokyo · *American Chamber of Commerce in Japan* · Thomas Whitson; Pres.; Masonic 39, MT Bldg. 10F; 2-4-5 Azabudai, Minato-ku; 106-0041; M 3,028; 81-3-3433-5381; 81-3-3433-7304; Fax 81-3-3436-8454; info@accj.or.jp; www.accj.or.jp

Jordan

Amman · *American Chamber of Commerce in Jordan* · Mustafa Mustafa; CEO; P.O. Box 840817; 11184I M 340; 962-6-565-1860; Fax 962-6-565-1862; amcham@amcham.jo; www.amcham.jo

Kenya

Nairobi · *American Chamber of Commerce of Kenya* · P. O. Box 9746-00100; 254-20-6750721; Fax 254-20-3750448; info@acck.org; www.acck.org

Korea

Seoul · *American Chamber of Commerce in Korea* · Amy Jackson; Pres.; #4501, Trade Tower, 159-1; Samsung-dong, Kangnam-gu; 135-729; P 10,464,000; M 2,300; 82-2-564-2040; Fax 82-2-564-2050; amchamrsvp@amchamkorea.org; www.amchamkorea.org

Kosovo

Prishtina · *American Chamber of Commerce in Kosovo* · Leke Musa; Exec. Dir.; Rr. Fehmi Agani 36/3, Ste. 6; 10000; M 80; 381-38-246-012; Fax 381-38-248-012; leke.musa@amchamksv.org; www.amchamksv.org

Kuwait

Salwa · *American Bus. Cncl. of Kuwait* · Ms. Muna Al Fuzai; Exec. Dir.; Blk. 11 St. 7 Bld. 15 Apt. 2; 2-563-4042; mibrahim@abckw.org; www.abckw.org

Kyrgyz Republic

Bishkek · *American Chamber of Commerce in the Kyrgyz Republic* · Ainura Cholponkulova; Exec. Dir.; 191 Sovetskaya, Ofc., Ste. 123; 720011; 996-312-680907; Fax 996-312-681172; memberservices@amcham.kg; www.amcham.kg

Latvia

Riga · *American Chamber of Commerce in Latvia* · Liga Bertulsone; Exec. Dir.; Torna iela 4, 2A, 301; LV-1050M 110; 371-6721-2204; Fax 371-6721-2204; liga.bertulsone@amcham.lv; www.amcham.lv

Lebanon

Beruit · *American Lebanese Chamber of Commerce* · Paola Chakhtoura; Exec. Dir.; 1153 Foch St., Beirut Central Dist.; P.O. Box 175093; M 200; 961-1-985330; Fax 961-1-985331; info@amcham.org.lb; www.amcham.org.lb

Lithuania

Vilnius · *American Chamber of Commerce in Lithuania* · Zivile Sabaliauskaite; Interim Exec. Dir.; Lukiskiu str. 5, Rm. 204; LT-01108; M 72; 370-5-261-1181; Fax 370-5-212-6128; info@amcham.lt; www.amcham.lt

Luxembourg

Luxembourg · *American Chamber of Commerce in Luxembourg* · Paul-Michael Schonenberg; Chrmn./CEO; 6, rue de Antoine de St-Exupery; L-1432; M 118; 352-43-1756; Fax 352-26-09-4704; info@amcham.lu; www.amcham.lu

Macedonia

Skopje · *American Chamber of Commerce in Macedonia* · Sonja McGurk; Exec. Dir.; Ivo Lola Ribar 59A-1/15; 1000; 389-2-3216-714; Fax 389-2-3246-950; info@amcham.com.mk; amcham.com.mk

Malaysia

Kuala Lumpur · *American Malaysian Chamber of Commerce* · 11.03-11.05 Level 11; 22 Jalan Imbi, AMODA Bldg.; 55100; M 800; 603-2148-2407; Fax 603-2142-8540; info@amcham.com.my; www.amcham.com.my

Mexico

Mexico City · *American Chamber of Commerce of Mexico* · Guillermo Wolf; Exec. V.P./CEO; Blas Pascal 205, 3.er piso; Col. Los Morales; 11510; M 2,500; 52-55-5141-3800; Fax 52-55-5141-3835; amchammx@amcham.com.mx; www.amcham.com.mx

Zapopan, Jal. · *American Chamber of Commerce of Mexico-Guadalajara* · Av. Moctezuma 442; Col. Jardines del Sol; 45050; 52-33-3634-6606; Fax 52-33-3634-7374; socios_gdl@amcham.org.mx; www.amcham.com.mx

Garza García, N.L. · *American Chamber of Commerce of Mexico-Monterrey* · Río Manzanares 434, Ote.; Col. Del Valle; 66220; 52-81-8114-2000; Fax 52-81-8114-2100; socios_mty@amcham.org.mx; www.amcham.com.mx

Montenegro

Podgorica · *American Chamber of Commerce in Montenegro* · Dragana Radevic; Exec. Dir.; Kralja Nikole; 272/IV PC "Celebic"; 81000; 382-20-621-328; Fax 382-20-621-628; info@amcham.me; www.amcham.me

Netherlands

Schiphol · *American Chamber of Commerce in the Netherlands* · Mrs. Riette Blacquiere-Schalen; Exec. Dir.; Schiphol WTC, D-tower, 6th Flr.; Schiphol Blvd. 171; 1118 BG; P 15,000,000; M 800; 31-20-795-18-40; Fax 31-20-795-18-50; office@amcham.nl; www.amcham.nl

New Zealand

Auckland · *American Chamber of Commerce in New Zealand* · Mike Hearn; Exec. Dir.; Level 6 AFFCO House, 12-26 Swanson St.; P.O. Box 106002; 1143; P 4,300,000; M 300; 64-9-309-9140; Fax 64-9-309-1090; amcham@amcham.co.nz; www.amcham.co.nz

Nicaragua

Managua · *American Chamber of Commerce of Nicaragua* · Avil Ramirez; Exec. Dir.; P.O. Box 2720; M 160; 505-2266-2758; Fax 505-2266-2758; publicrelations@amcham.org.ni; www.amcham.org.ni

Norway

Oslo · *American Chamber of Commerce in Norway* · Jason Turflinger; Mgr. Dir.; Lille Grensen 5; 0159; P 4,900,000; M 200; 47-22-41-50-10; Fax 47-22-41-50-11; amcham@amcham.no; www.amcham.no

Pakistan

Karachi · *American Bus. Cncl. of Pakistan* · Ms. Raaheen Mani; Exec. Dir.; F-30, Block-7, K.D.A, Scheme No. 5; Kehkashan, Clifton; 92-21-5877351-52; Fax 92-21-5877391; abcpak@cyber.net.pk; www.abcpk.org.pk

Panama

Panama · *American Chamber of Commerce & Ind. of Panama* · David Hunt; Exec. Dir.; P.O. Box 0843-00152; M 385; 507-301-3881; Fax 507-301-3882; dhunt@panamcham.com; www.panamcham.com

Paraguay

Asuncion · *Paraguayan American Chamber of Commerce* · 25 de Mayo 2090 & Mayor Bullo; M 375; 595-21-221926; Fax 595-21-222265; pamcham@pamcham.com.py; www.pamcham.com.py

Peru

Lima · *American Chamber of Commerce of Peru* · Aldo Defilippi; Exec. Dir.; Av. Victor Andres Belaunde 177; San Isidro; 27; M 450; 511-7058000; Fax 511-2410709; amcham@amcham.org.pe; www.amcham.org.pe

Philippines

Manila · *American Chamber of Commerce of the Philippines* · Robert W. Sears; Exec. Dir.; 2nd Flr., Corinthian Plaza Bldg.; Paseo De Roxas, Makati City; 1229; M 651; 63-2-818-7911; Fax 63-2-811-3081; amcham@amchamphilippines.com; www.amcham philippines.com

Poland

Warsaw · *American Chamber of Commerce in Poland* · Dorota Dabrowski; Exec. Dir.; Warsaw Financial Center; ul. E. Plater 53; PL-00-113; M 300; 48-22-520-5999; Fax 48-22-520-5998; office@amcham.com.pl; www.amcham.com.pl

Portugal

Lisbon · *American Chamber of Commerce in Portugal* · Jose Joaquim Oliveira; Pres.; Rua D. Estefania 155; 5 Esq; 1000-154; M 650; 351-213-572561; Fax 351-213-572580; amcham portugal@mail.telepac.pt; www.amcham.org.pt

Romania

Bucharest · *American Chamber of Commerce in Romania* · Sorin Mindrutescu; Pres.; 11 Ion Campineanu Str.; Union International Center, 5th Flr.; 010031; M 300; 40-21-312-48-34; Fax 40-21-312-48-51; amcham@amcham.ro; www.amcham.ro

Russia

Moscow · *American Chamber of Commerce in Russia* · Andrew Somers; Pres./CEO; Dolgorukovskaya ul. 7; 14th Flr., Sadovaya Plaza; 127006; M 750; 7-495-961-2141; Fax 7-495-961-2142; asomers@amcham.ru; www.amcham.ru

Saudi Arabia

Al-Khobar · *American Bus. Assoc., Eastern Province* · David Cantrell; Pres.; P.O. Box 3672; 31952; M 470; 966-3-8825288 x1253; Fax 966-3-8825288 x2497; abaep@abaksa.org; www.abaksa.org

Jeddah · *American Businessmen of Jeddah* · Mrs. Jamilyn Al Daraji; Ofc. Mgr.; % Intercontinental Hotel-Jeddah; P.O. Box 41855; 21531; M 250; 966-2-663-4784; Fax 966-2-663-4674; manager@abj-sa.com; www.abj-sa.com

Serbia

Belgrade · *American Chamber of Commerce in Serbia* · Bojana Ristic; Exec. Dir.; Smiljanićeva 24/II; 11000; 381-11-308-8132; Fax 381-11-308-8922; info@amcham.rs; www.amcham.rs

Singapore

Singapore · *American Chamber of Commerce in Singapore* · Laura Deal; Exec. Dir.; 1 Scotts Rd., Shaw Centre; Ste. 23-03/04/05; 228208; M 2,500; 65-6597-5730; Fax 65-6732-5917; Ideal@amcham.org.sg; www.amcham.org.sg

Slovakia

Bratislava · *American Chamber of Commerce in Slovakia* · Jake Slegers; Exec. Dir.; Crowne Plaza; Hodzovo nam. 2; Slovakia; 81106P 5,429,763; M 306; 421-2-5464-0534; Fax 421-2-5464-0535; office@amcham.sk; www.amcham.sk

Slovenia

Ljubljana · *American Chamber of Commerce in Slovenia* · Ajsa Vodnik; Exec. Dir.; Dunajska cesta 156; 1000; M 75; 386-8-205-13-51; Fax 386-1-564-72-04; ajsa.vodnik@amcham.si; www.amcham.si

South Africa

Houghton, Johannesburg · *American Chamber of Commerce in South Africa* · Carol O'Brien; Exec. Dir.; P.O. Box 1132; 2041; M 190; 27-11-788-0265; Fax 27-11-880-1632; amcham@amcham.co.za; amcham.co.za

Spain

Barcelona · *American Chamber of Commerce in Spain* · Susan M. Feitoza; Exec. Dir.; Tuset 10, 1º-2º; 08006; P 40,000,000; M 600; 34-93-415-99-63; Fax 34-93-415-11-98; amcham@amchamspain.com; www.amchamspain.com

Sri Lanka

Colombo · *American Chamber of Commerce in Sri Lanka* · Chullante Jayasuriya; Exec. Dir.; 1st Flr., Ofc. Bldg.; South Wing, Colombo Hilton Hotel, Lotus Rd.; 1; M 400; 94-11-2336073; Fax 94-11-2336072; info@amcham.lk; www.amcham.lk

Sweden

Stockholm · *American Chamber of Commerce in Sweden* · Berit Salheim; Mgr. Dir.; P.O. Box 16050; 103 21; 46-8-506-126-10; Fax 46-8-506-126-13; amcham@chamber.se; www.amchamswe.se

Switzerland

Zurich · *Swiss-American Chamber of Commerce* · Michael Mack; Chrmn.; Talacker 41; 8001; M 2,300; 41-43-443-72-00; Fax 41-43-497-22-70; info@amcham.ch; www.amcham.ch

Taiwan, ROC

Taipei · *American Chamber of Commerce in Taipei* · Andrea Wu; Pres.; Minsheng E. Road, Sec. 3, #129, 7F, Ste. 706; 10596; M 980; 886-2-2718-8226; Fax 886-2-2718-8182; amcham@amcham.com.tw; www.amcham.com.tw

Thailand

Bangkok · *American Chamber of Commerce in Thailand* · Judy Benn; Exec. Dir.; 93/1 Diethelm Tower A, 7th Flr.; Wireless Rd., Lumpini, Pathumwan; 10330; M 600; 66-0-2254-1041; Fax 66-0-2251-1605; execdirector@amchamthailand.com; www.amchamthailand.com

Trinidad & Tobago

Port of Spain · *American Chamber of Commerce of Trinidad & Tobago* · Desiree Gobin-Seecharan; Exec. Dir.; 62 Maraval Rd.; P.O. Bag 150, Newton; M 290; 868-622-4466; Fax 868-628-9428; execd@amchamtt.com; www.amchamtt.com

Turkey

Istanbul · *Turkish-American Bus. Assn.* · Asude Yade Akdeniz; Exec. Mgr.; Buyukdere Caddesi #18; Tankaya apt. Kat. 7 20 Sisli; 34360; M 650; 9-0216-355-50-50; Fax 9-0216-355-78-92; asudeyesilbas@amcham.org; www.amcham.org

Ukraine

Kyiv · *American Chamber of Commerce in Ukraine* · Tetiana Ostapenko; Pub. Coord.; 12 Amosova str.; 03038; P 45,831,408; M 586; 380-44-490-58-00; chamber@chamber.ua; www.amcham.kiev.ua

United Arab Emirates

Dubai · *American Bus. Cncl. of Dubai & the Northern Emirates* · Cara Nazari; Exec. Dir.; P.O. Box 37068; M 540; 971-4-3407566; Fax 971-4-3407565; director@abcdubai.com; www.abcdubai.com

United Kingdom

London · *BritishAmerican Bus.* · Peter Hunt; Mgr.; 75 Brook St.; W1K 4AD; M 1,400; 44-20-7290-9888; ukinfo@babinc.org; www.babinc.org

Uruguay

Montevideo · *Chamber of Commerce Uruguay-USA* · Magdalena Aonzo; Exec. Dir.; Plaza de Independencia 831, Ofc. 209; Edif. Plaza Mayor; 11000; M 150; 598-2-9089186; Fax 598-2-9089187; info@ccuruguayusa.com; www.ccuruguayusa.com

Uzbekistan

Tashkent · *American Chamber of Commerce in Uzbekistan* · Tatyana Bystrushkina; Exec. Dir.; 2 Afrosiab St.; 100031; P 27,000,000; M 102; 998-71-140-08-77; Fax 998-71-140-09-77; amcham.director@amcham.uz; www.amcham.uz

Venezuela

Caracas · *Venezuelan-American Chamber of Commerce & Ind.* · Carlos Tejera; Gen. Mgr.; Torre Credival, Piso 10; 2da Av. de Campo Alegre; 1010-A; 58-212-2630833; Fax 58-212-2631829; ctejera@venamcham.org; www.venamcham.org

Vietnam

Ho Chi Minh City · *American Chamber of Commerce in Vietnam* · Herb Cochran; Exec. Dir.; New World Hotel, 3F Ste. 323; 76 Le Lai St., Dist. 1; M 450; 84-8-3824-3562; Fax 84-8-3824-3572; amcham@hcm.vnn.vn; www.amchamvietnam.com

Hanoi · *American Chamber of Commerce-Hanoi* · Adam Sitkoff; Exec. Dir.; Hilton Opera Hanoi, Ste. 201; 1 Le Thanh Tong St.; M 300; 84-4-3934-2790; Fax 84-4-3934-2787; info@amchamhanoi.com; www.amchamhanoi.com

Foreign and Ethnic
Chambers of Commerce in the United States

Africa

African Chamber of Commerce-Dallas/Ft. Worth • P.O. Box 421231; Dallas, TX; 75342; M 550; (214) 628-2569; Fax (214) 291-7195; info@africanchamberdfw.org; www.africanchamberdfw.org

Angola

U.S.-Angola Chamber of Commerce • Maria da Cruz; Exec. Dir.; 1100 17th St. N.W., Ste. 1000; Washington, DC; 20036; M 90; (202) 857-0789; Fax (202) 223-0551; mdacruz@us-angola.org; www.us-angola.org

Argentina

Argentine-American Chamber of Commerce • Claudia Schaefer-Farre; Exec. Dir.; 630 Fifth Ave., 25th Flr.; New York, NY; 10111; M 100; (212) 698-2238; Fax (212) 698-2239; argentine chamber@argentinechamber.org; www.argentinechamber.org

Australia

Australian Consulate General • Phillip Scanlan; Consulate Gen.; 150 E. 42nd St., 34th Flr.; New York, NY; 10017; (212) 351-6500; Fax (212) 351-6501; www.newyork.usa.embassy.gov.au

Austria

U.S.-Austrian Chamber of Commerce • 165 W. 46th St., Ste. 1112; New York, NY; 10036; M 101; (212) 819-0117; Fax (212) 819-0345; memberservices@usaustrianchamber.com; www. usaustrianchamber.com

Austrian Trade Comm. in Los Angeles • Rudolf Thaler; Trade Comm.; 11601 Wilshire Blvd., Ste. 2420; Los Angeles, CA; 90025; (310) 477-9988; Fax (310) 477-1643; losangeles@advantage austria.org; advantageaustria.org

Austrian Trade Comm. in New York • Christian Kesberg; Trade Comm.; 120 W. 45th St., 9th Flr.; New York, NY; 10036; (212) 421-5250; Fax (212) 421-5251; newyork@advantage austria.org; advantageaustria.org

Azerbaijan

U.S.-Azerbaijan Chamber of Commerce • 1212 Potomac St. N.W.; Washington, DC; 20007; M 60; (202) 333-8702; Fax (202) 333-8703; chamber@usacc.org; www.usacc.org

Barbados

Barbados Investment & Dev. Corp. • Adrian Sealy; Sr. Bus. Dev. Officer; 820 2nd Ave., 5th Flr.; New York, NY; 10017; (212) 551-4375; (800) 841-7860; Fax (212) 682-5496; newyork@ investbarbados.org; investbarbados.org

Belgium

Belgian-American Chamber of Commerce in the U.S. • Vincent Herbert; Chrmn.; c/o KBC Bank; 1177 Ave. of the Americas, 8th Flr.; New York, NY; 10036; M 115; (212) 541-0779; info@belcham.org; www.belcham.org

Brazil

Brazilian-American Chamber of Commerce Inc. • 509 Madison Ave., Ste. 304; New York, NY; 10022; M 500; (212) 751-4691; Fax (212) 751-7692; info@brazilcham.com; www. brazilcham.com

Brazilian-American Chamber of Commerce of Florida • Edward Santos; Pres.; P.O. Box 310038; Miami, FL; 33231; M 300; (305) 579-9030; Fax (305) 579-9756; baccf@brazilchamber.org; www.brazilchamber.org

Brazil-U.S. Bus. Cncl. • Steven Bipes; Exec. Dir.; 1615 H St. N.W.; Washington, DC; 20062; M 75; (202) 463-5485; Fax (202) 463-3126; sbipes@uschamber.com; www.brazilcouncil.org

Chile

North American-Chilean Chamber • 866 United Nations Plaza, Ste. 4019; New York, NY; 10017; M 110; (212) 317-1959; Fax (212) 758-8598; info@nacchamber.com; www.nacchamber.com

China

U.S.-China Chamber of Commerce • Siva Yam; Pres.; 55 W. Monroe St., Ste. 630; Chicago, IL; 60603; M 300; (312) 368-9911; Fax (312) 368-9922; info@usccc.org; www.usccc.org

Colombia

Colombian-American Chamber of Commerce • Tribin Ricardo; 250 Catalonia Ave., Ste. 407; Coral Gables, FL; 33134; M 230; (305) 446-2542; Fax (305) 446-2038; info@colombia-chamber.com; www.colombiachamber.com

Proexport Colombia • 601 Brickell Key Dr., Ste. 801; Miami, FL; 33131; (305) 374-3144; Fax (305) 372-9365; miami@proexport. com.co; www.proexport.com.co

Cyprus

Cyprus-U.S. Chamber of Commerce • Despina Axiotakis; Exec. Dir.; 55 Paramus Rd.; Paramus, NJ; 07652; P 8,000,000; M 150; (201) 444-5609; Fax (201) 444-0445; cyprususchamber@aol. com; www.cyprususchamber.com

Denmark

Danish American Chamber of Commerce • Morten Zolde; Gen. Mgr.; 885 Second Ave., 18th Flr.; New York, NY; 10017; M 250; (917) 575-3761; Fax (212) 754-1904; daccny@daccny. com; www.daccny.com

Ecuador

Ecuadorian-American Chamber of Commerce • Juan Jose Malo V.; Pres.; 3403 N.W. 82nd Ave., Ste. 310; Doral, FL; 33122; (305) 539-0010; Fax (305) 591-0868; ecuacham@bellsouth.net; www.ecuachamber.com

Europe

European-American Bus. Cncl. • 919 18th St. N.W., Ste. 220; Washington, DC; 20006; M 55; (202) 828-9104; Fax (202) 828-9106; jessica@eabc.org; www.eabc.org

Finland

Finnish American Chamber of Commerce • Kerstin Nordin; Exex. Dir.; 866 U.N. Plaza, Ste. 250; New York, NY; 10017; M 200; (212) 821-0225; Fax (212) 750-4418; faccnyc@verizon.net; www.facc-ny.com

Finnish American Chamber of Commerce-Pacific Coast • Virpi Sidler; Pres.; 578 Washington Blvd., Ste. 745; Marina Del Rey, CA; 90292; (949) 637-2537; Fax (949) 861-9523; virpi.sidler@faccpacific.com; www.faccpacific.com

France

French-American Chamber of Commerce • 1350 Broadway, Ste. 2101; New York, NY; 10018; M 670; (212) 867-0123; Fax (212) 867-9050; info@faccnyc.org; www.faccnyc.org

French-American Chamber of Commerce • 26 O'Farrell St., Ste. 500; San Francisco, CA; 94108; M 300; (415) 442-4717; Fax (415) 442-4621; Info@faccsf.com; www.faccsf.com

Germany

German-American Chamber of Commerce • Dr. Benno Bunse; Pres./CEO; 75 Broad St., 21st Flr.; New York, NY; 10004; M 750; (212) 974-8830; Fax (212) 974-8867; info@gaccny.com; www.gaccny.com

German-American Chamber of the Midwest • Simone Pohl; Pres./CEO; 401 N. Michigan Ave., Ste. 3330; Chicago, IL; 60611; M 650; (312) 644-2662; Fax (312) 644-0738; info@gaccom.org; www.gaccom.org

German-American Chamber of Commerce • 1 Penn Center, Ste. 340; 1617 JFK Blvd.; Philadelphia, PA; 19103; M 250; (215) 665-1585; Fax (215) 665-0375; admin@gaccphiladelphia.com; www.gaccphiladelphia.com

German-American Chamber of the Southern U.S. • Kristian Wolf; Pres./CEO; 1170 Howell Mill Rd., Ste. 300; Atlanta, GA; 30318; M 400; (404) 586-6800; Fax (404) 586-6820; info@gaccsouth.com; www.gaccsouth.com

Greece

Hellenic-American Chamber of Commerce • c/o State Bank of Long Island; 780 Third Ave., 16th Flr.; New York, NY; 10017; (212) 629-6380; Fax (212) 564-9281; hellenicchamber-nyc@att.net; www.hellenicamerican.cc

Haiti

Haitian-American Chamber of Commerce • 11767 S. Dixie Hwy., Ste. 275; Miami, FL; 33156; M 60; (305) 733-9066; info@haccof.com; www.haccof.com

Hungary

Hungarian-American Chamber of Commerce • 3910 Shoemaker St. N.W.; Washington, DC; 20008; (202) 362-6730; informacio.was@kum.hu; www.huembwas.org

Iceland

Icelandic-American Chamber of Commerce • Hlynur Gudjonsson; Gen. Mgr.; 800 Third Ave., 36th Flr.; New York, NY; 10022; M 300; (646) 282-9360; Fax (646) 282-9369; hlynur@mfa.is; icelandtrade.com

Indonesia

American-Indonesian Chamber of Commerce • Wayne Forrest; Pres.; 317 Madison Ave., Ste. 1619; New York, NY; 10017; (212) 687-4505; Fax (212) 687-5844; wayne@aiccusa.org; www.aiccusa.org

Ireland

Ireland Chamber of Commerce in the U.S. • 556 Central Ave.; New Providence, NJ; 07974; M 500; (908) 286-1300; Fax (908) 286-1200; info@iccusa.org; www.iccusa.org

Israel

America-Israel Chamber of Commerce & Ind. • Ronny Bassan; Exec. V.P.; 70 W. 36th St., Ste. 700; New York, NY; 10018; M 350; (646) 467-8037; Fax (646) 365-3366; info@aicci.net; www.aicci.net

American-Israel Chamber of Commerce-Chicago • Michael Schmitt; Exec. Dir.; 500 Lake Cook Rd., Ste. 350; Deerfield, IL; 60015; (847) 597-7070; Fax (847) 597-7067; info@americaisrael.org; www.americaisrael.org

American-Israel Chamber of Commerce, SE Region • Tom Glaser; Pres.; 400 Northridge Rd., Ste. 250; Atlanta, GA; 30350; M 560; (404) 843-9426; Fax (404) 843-1416; aiccse@aiccse.org; www.aiccse.org

Ohio-Israel Chamber of Commerce • Howard Gudell; Pres.; P.O. Box 39007; Cleveland, OH; 44139; (216) 965-4474; Fax (440) 248-4888; ohioisraelchamber@ameritech.net; www.ohioisrael-chamber.com

Italy

Italian American Chamber of Commerce-Midwest • Robert Allegrini; Pres.; 500 N. Michigan Ave., Ste. 506; Chicago, IL; 60611; M 200; (312) 553-9137; Fax (312) 553-9137; info@iacc-chicago.com; www.iacc-chicago.com

Italy-America Chamber of Commerce • 730 Fifth Ave., Ste. 600; New York, NY; 10019; M 300; (212) 459-0044; Fax (212) 459-0090; info@italchamber.org; www.italchamber.org

Italy-America Chamber of Commerce West • 10537 Santa Monica Blvd., Ste. 210; Los Angeles, CA; 90025; M 100; (310) 557-3017; Fax (310) 557-1217; info@iaccw.net; www.iaccw.net

Japan

Japan Bus. Assn. of Houston • 12651 Briar Forest Dr., Ste. 105; Houston, TX; 77077; (281) 493-1512; Fax (281) 531-6730; sansuikai@jbahouston.org; www.jbahouston.org

Japan Bus. Assn. of Southern California • 1411 W. 190th St., Ste. 270; Gardena, CA; 90248; (310) 515-9522; Fax (310) 515-9722; jba@jba.org; www.jba.org

Japanese Chamber of Commerce & Ind. of NY • 145 W. 57th St.; New York, NY; 10019; M 350; (212) 246-8001; Fax (212) 246-8002; info@jcciny.org; www.jcciny.org

Japanese Chamber of Commerce-Southern California • 244 San Pedro St., Ste. 504; Los Angeles, CA; 90012; M 250; (213) 626-3067; Fax (213) 626-3070; office@jccsc.com; www.jccsc.com

Korea, Republic of

Korean American Chamber of Commerce of LA • 3435 Wilshire Blvd., Ste. 2450; Los Angeles, CA; 90010; M 1,000; (213) 480-1115; Fax (213) 480-7521; kaccla.org

Korea Chamber of Commerce & Ind. in the USA • 460 Park Ave., Ste. 410; New York, NY; 10022; M 350; (212) 644-0140; Fax (212) 644-9106; webmaster@kocham.org; www.kocham.org

Latin America

Cncl. of the Americas • 680 Park Ave.; New York, NY; 10065; M 5,000; (212) 628-3200; Fax (212) 628-3200; www.council oftheamericas.org

Latin American Chamber of Commerce • 3512 W. Fullerton Ave.; Chicago, IL; 60647; M 200; (773) 252-5211; Fax (773) 252-7065; lacc@latinamericanchamberofcommerce.com; www. latinamericanchamberofcommerce.com

Latin-American Chamber of Commerce • Juan M. Ruiz; Pres.; 1405 S. Main St.; Salt Lake City; UT; 84115; (801) 649-5465; info@laccutah.org; www.laccutah.org

Latin Chamber of Commerce of USA • 1401 W. Flagler St.; Miami, FL; 33135; M 2,000; (305) 642-3870; Fax (305) 642-0653; info@camacol.org; www.camacol.org

Luxembourg

Luxembourg American Chamber of Commerce • 17 Beekman Pl.; New York, NY; 10022; M 100; (212) 888-6701; Fax (212) 935-5896; info@luxembourgbusiness.org; www. luxembourgbusiness.org

Luxembourg for Business • One Sansome St., Ste. 830; San Francisco, CA; 94104; (415) 788-0816; Fax (415) 788-0985; sanfrancisco.cg@mae.etat.lu; sanfrancisco.mae.lu

Malaysia

Malaysian Trade Comm. • 313 E. 43rd St., 3rd Flr.; New York, NY; 10017; (212) 682-0232; Fax (212) 983-1987; newyork@ matrade.gov.my; www.matrade.gov.my

Mexico

Mexican Intl. Chamber of Commerce & Ind. • P.O. Box 4422; Rancho del Rey, CA; 91909; M 1,000; (619) 4-MEXICO; info@ mexchamber.com; www.mexchamber.com

U.S.-Mexico Chamber of Commerce • Al Zapanta; Pres./ CEO; 5510 Cherokee Ave., Ste. 120; Washington, DC; 22312; P 400,000,000; M 1,500; (703) 752-4751; (703) 752-4886; Fax (703) 642-1088; news-hq@usmcoc.org; www.usmcoc.org

Middle East

Arab American Chamber of Commerce • 1050 17th St. N.W., Ste. 600; Washington, DC; 20036; (202) 347-5800; (888) 939-ARAB; Fax (202) 521-4050; aacc@arabchamber.org; www. arabchamber.org

National U.S.-Arab Chamber of Commerce • 1023 15th St. N.W., Ste. 400; Washington, DC; 20005; M 300; (202) 289-5920; Fax (202) 289-5938; info@nusacc.org; www.nusacc.org

National U.S.-Arab Chamber of Commerce • 420 Lexington Ave., Ste. 2034; New York, NY; 10170; M 425; (212) 986-8024; Fax (212) 986-0216; jcolon@nusacc.org; www.nusacc.org

National U.S.-Arab Chamber of Commerce in LA • 8921 S. Sepulveda Blvd., Ste. 206; Los Angeles, CA; 90045; M 250; (310) 646-1499; Fax (310) 646-2462; eatallah@nusacc.org; www. nusacc.org

Norway

Norwegian-American Chamber of Commerce • 655 Third Ave., Ste. 1810; New York, NY; 10017; M 125; (212) 885-9737; shipping@ntcny.org; www.naccusa.org

Peru

Peruvian American Chamber of Commerce • 7600 S. Red Rd., Ste. 304; South Miami, FL; 33143; M 200; (305) 661-8288; info@peruvianchamber.org; www.peruvianchamber.org

Philippines

Philippine American Chamber of Illinois • 5850 N. Lincoln Ave., Ste. 208; Chicago, IL; 60659; (800) 850-2632; (800) 850-2632; Fax (800) 505-8753; info@paccil.org; www.paccil.org

Portugal

Portuguese-American Chamber of Commerce of NJ • Anthony Azevedo; Pres.; 76 Prospect St.; Newark, NJ; 07105; M 200; (973) 491-5200; Fax (973) 589-0979; chamber@paccnj. org; www.paccnj.org

Puerto Rico

Puerto Rican Chamber of Commerce • 3550 Biscayne Blvd., Ste. 306; Miami, FL; 33137; M 250; (305) 571-8006; Fax (305) 571-8007; ldr@puertoricanchamber.com; www.puertorican chamber.com

Russia

Russian-American Chamber of Commerce • 970 Sidney Marcus Blvd., Ste. 1504; Atlanta, GA; 30324; M 200; (404) 432-6025; Fax (678) 558-0418; andrey@russianamericanchamber.com; www.russianamericanchamber.com

Saint Lucia

St. Lucia Natl. Dev. Corp. • 3700 Coco Plum Cir.; Coconut Creek; Miami, FL; 33063; (305) 586-3076; Fax (954) 973-9001; miamiinfo@investlucia.com; www.stluciandc.com

Saudi Arabia

Royal Embassy of Saudi Arabia, Commercial Ofc. • 601 New Hampshire Ave. N.W.; Washington, DC; 20037; (202) 337-4088; Fax (202) 342-0271; info@saudicommercialoffice.com; www.saudicommercialoffice.com

Singapore

Intl. Enterprise Singapore • 55 E. 59th St., Ste. 21A; New York, NY; 10022; (212) 421-2207; Fax (212) 888-2897; newyork@iesingapore.gov.sg; www.iesingapore.gov.sg

Spain

Spain-U.S. Chamber of Commerce • 350 5th Ave., Ste. 2600; New York, NY; 10118; M 450; (212) 967-2170; Fax (212) 564-1415; info@spainuscc.org; www.spainuscc.org

Spain-U.S. Chamber of Commerce in Florida • 1221 Brickell Ave., Ste. 1540; Miami, FL; 33131; M 400; (305) 358-5988; Fax (305) 358-6844; info@spainchamber.org; www.spain-uschamber.com

Sweden

Swedish-American Chamber of Commerce • 570 Lexington Ave., 20th Flr.; New York, NY; 10022; M 300; (212) 838-5530; Fax (212) 755-7953; renee.lundholm@saccny.org; www.saccny.org

Swedish-American Chamber of Commerce • 452 Tehama St.; San Francisco, CA; 94103; M 70; (415) 781-4188; Fax (415) 781-4189; info@sacc-sf.org; www.sacc-sf.org

Switzerland

Swiss-American Chamber of Commerce • New York Chapter; 500 Fifth Ave., Rm. 1800; New York, NY; 10110; (212) 246-7789; Fax (212) 246-1366; newyork@amcham.ch; www.amcham.ch

Swiss American Chamber of Commerce • San Francisco Chapter; P.O. Box 26007; San Francisco, CA; 94126; M 75; (415) 433-4479; sanfrancisco@amcham.ch; www.amcham.ch

Thailand

Thai Trade Center • 61 Broadway, Ste. 2810; New York, NY; 10006; (212) 482-0077; Fax (212) 482-1177; info@thaitradeny.com; www.thaitradeusa.com

United Kingdom

British American Bus. Cncl. • Zoe Matthews; Exec. Dir.; 703 Market St., Ste. 1314; San Francisco, CA; 94103; M 245; (415) 296-8645; Fax (415) 296-9649; info@babcsf.org; www.babcsf.org

British American Bus. Cncl. • Mindy Gail; Exec. Dir.; 11766 Wilshire Blvd., Ste. 1230; Los Angeles, CA; 90025; M 503; (310) 312-1962; Fax (310) 312-1914; info@babcla.org; www.babcla.org

British American Bus. Cncl.–Orange County • Valerie Blackholly; Exec. Dir.; 25422 Trabuco Rd., Ste. 105-266; Lake Forest, CA; 92630; M 160; (949) 472-2221; info@babcoc.org; www.babcoc.org

British American Bus. Inc. • 52 Vanderbilt Ave., 20th Flr.; New York, NY; 10017; M 470; (212) 661-4060; nyinfo@babinc.org; www.babinc.org

Uzbekistan

American-Uzbekistan Chamber of Commerce • Timothy Y. McGraw; Pres.; 1300 Connecticut Ave. N.W.; Washington, DC; 20036; M 75; (202) 223-1770; info@aucconline.com; www.aucconline.com

Venezuela

Venezuelan-American Chamber of Commerce • Oswaldo Sandoval; Pres.; 1600 Ponce de Leon, Ste. 1004; Coral Gables, FL; 33134; M 300; (786) 350-1190; Fax (786) 350-1191; info@venezuelanchamber.org; www.venezuelanchamber.org

Foreign Chambers of Commerce

Albania

Tirana • *Chamber of Commerce & Ind. of Tirana* • Rr. Kavajes No. 6; P 3,200,000; M 2,000; 355-4-2232446; Fax 355-4-2227997; info@cci.al; www.cci.al

Algeria

Alger • *Algerian Chamber of Commerce & Ind.* • BP 100 1er Nov.; 16003; P 35,400,000; 021-96-77-77; Fax 021-96-70-70; infos@caci.dz; www.caci.dz

Antigua & Barbuda

Saint John's • *Antigua & Barbuda Chamber of Commerce & Ind.* • P.O. Box 774; P 89,000; M 175; 268-462-0743; Fax 268-462-4575; chamcom@candw.ag

Argentina

Buenos Aires • *Argentina Chamber of Commerce* • Av. Leandro N. Alem 36; 1003; P 40,500,000; M 3,150; 54-11-5300-9000; Fax 54-11-5300-9058; difusion2@cac.com.ar; www.cac.com.ar

Cordoba • *Central Region Chamber of Commerce* • 2000 Rosario de Santa Fe; 1868; P 40,500,000; M 200; 54-351-425-7147; Fax 54-351-425-7147; consultas@commerce.com.ar; www.commerce.com.ar

Buenos Aires • *Argentine Chamber of Exporters* • Av. Roque Saenz Pena 740; Piso 1; 1035; P 40,500,000; M 500; 54-11-4394-4482; Fax 54-11-4394-4482; contacto@cera.org.ar; www.cera.org.ar

Buenos Aires • *Camara Argentina de Comercio Electronico* • Calle 25 de Mayo 611 Piso 2; 1005; P 40,500,000; M 204; 54-11-5917-7435; contacto@cace.org.ar; www.cace.org.ar

Aruba

Oranjestad • *Aruba Chamber of Commerce & Ind.* • Lorraine de Souza; Dir.; P.O. Box 140; P 107,000; M 10,000; 297-582-1120; Fax 297-588-3200; secretariat@arubachamber.com; www.arubachamber.com

Australia

Kingston, ACT • *Australian Chamber of Commerce & Ind.* • Peter Anderson; CEO; P.O. Box 6005; 2604; P 22,500,000; M 3,200; 61-2-6273-2311; Fax 61-2-6273-3286; info@acci.asn.au; www.acci.asn.au

Melbourne, VIC • *Australian Chamber of Commerce & Ind.* • Peter Anderson; CEO; P.O. Box 18008; 8003; P 22,500,000; 61-3-9668-9950; Fax 61-3-9668-9958; melb@acci.asn.au; www.acci.asn.au

Hobart, TAS • *Tasmanian Chamber of Commerce & Ind.* • Robert Wallace; CEO; GPO Box 793; 7001; P 22,500,000; M 2,500; 61-3-6236-3600; Fax 61-3-6231-1278; admin@tcci.com.au; www.tcci.com.au

Darwin, NT • *Northern Territory Chamber of Commerce & Ind.* • Chris Young; CEO; GPO Box 1825; 801; P 22,500,000; M 1,400; 61-8-8982-8100; Fax 61-8-8981-1405; darwin@chambernt.com.au; www.chambernt.com.au

East Perth, WA • *Chamber of Commerce & Ind. of Western Australia* • 180 Hay St.; P.O. Box 6209; 6892; P 22,500,000; M 5,000; 61-8-9365-7555; Fax 61-8-9365-7550; info@cciwa.com; www.cciwa.com

Albany, WA • *Albany Chamber of Commerce & Ind.* • Graham Harvey; 63 Grey Street E.; 6330; P 22,500,000; M 430; 61-8-9842-2577; Fax 61-8-9842-3040; ceo@albanycci.com.au; www.albanycci.com.au

Brisbane, QLD • *Queensland Chamber of Commerce & Ind.* • 375 Wickham Terrace; 4000; P 22,500,000; M 3,000; 61-7-3842-2244; Fax 61-7-3832-3195; contact@cciq.com.au; www.cciq.com.au

Cairns, QLD • *Cairns Chamber of Commerce* • P.O. Box 2336; 4870; P 22,500,000; M 800; 61-7-4031-1838; Fax 61-7-4031-0883; info@cairnschamber.com.au; www.cairnschamber.com.au

North Sydney, NSW • *NSW Business Chamber* • Stephen Cartwright; Exec. Dir.; 140 Arthur St., Level 15; 2060; P 22,500,000; M 22,000; 61-2-13-26-96; Fax 61-2-1300-655-277; enquiries@thechamber.com.au; www.thechamber.com.au

Austria

Vienna • *Federal Economic Chamber of Commerce* • Wiedner Hauptstrasse 63; 1045; P 8,400,000; 43-1-50105-4503; Fax 43-1-50206-255

Vienna • *International Congress Vienna* • Börsegasse 9/8; A-1010; P 8,400,000; M ; 43-1-532-1000-14; Fax 43-1-532-1000-30; office@icon-vienna.net; www.icon-vienna.net

Feldkirch • *Wirtschaftskammer Vorarlberg* • Wichnergasse 9; A-6800; P 8,400,000; 43-5522-305-0; Fax 43-5522-305-14; office@wkvlbg.at; wko.at/vlbg

Graz • *Economic Chamber of Styria* • P.O. Box 1038; A-8021; P 8,400,000; M 45,000; 43-316-6010; Fax 43-316-601361; office@wkstmk.at; wko.at/stmk

Innsbruck • *Tyrolean Chamber of Commerce* • Meinhardstrasse 14; A-6020; P 8,400,000; 43-5-90-9050; Fax 43-5-90-905-1467; offfice@wktirol.at; wko.at/tirol

Vienna • *Vienna Chamber of Commerce & Ind.* • Stubenring 8-10; A-1010; P 8,400,000; 43-1-514500; Fax 43-1-5137787; office@wkwien.at; wko.at/wien

Bahamas

Grand Bahama • *Grand Bahama Chamber of Commerce* • PO Box F-40808, Freeport; P 346,000; M 240; 242-352-8329; Fax 242-352-3280; gbchamber@batelnet.bs; www.gbchamber.com

Nassau • *Bahamas Chamber of Commerce* • Shirley St. & Collins Ave.; P.O. Box N-665; P 346,000; M 348; 242-322-2145; Fax 242-322-4649; info@thebahamaschamber.com; www.thebahamaschamber.com

Bahrain

Manama • *Bahrain Chamber of Commerce & Ind.* • P.O. Box 248; P 807,000; M 7,000; 973-17-380000; Fax 973-17-380123; bcci@bcci.bh; www.bcci.bh

Bangladesh

Dhaka · *Federation of Bangladesh Chambers of Comm. & Ind.* · 60, Motijheel C/A; P 164,000,000; M 1,700; 880-2-9560102; Fax 880-2-7176030; fbcci@bol-online.com; www.fbcci-bd.org

Chittagong · *Chittagong Chamber of Commerce & Ind.* · Chamber House, 38, Agrabad C/A; 4100; P 164,000,000; M 5,000; 880-31-713366; Fax 880-31-710183; info@chittagongchamber. com; www.chittagongchamber.com

Khulna · *Khulna Chamber of Commerce & Ind.* · Chamber Mansion 5, KDA C/A; PO Box 26; P 164,000,000; M 1,984; 880-41-721695; Fax 880-41-725365; kcci@bttb.net.bd; www.khulna chamber.com

Barbados

St. Michael · *Barbados Chamber of Commerce & Ind.* · Braemer Ct., Deighton Rd.; P 257,000; M 207; 246-620-4750; Fax 246-620-2907; bcci@bdscham.com; www.bdscham.com

Bridgetown · *Barbados Investment & Dev. Corp.* · PO Box 1250; P 257,000; M 508; 246-427-5350; Fax 246-426-7802; bidc@bidc.org; www.bidc.com

Belgium

Antwerp · *Chamber of Commerce & Ind. of Antwerp* · Markgravestraat 12; 2000; P 10,800,000; M 3,000; 32-3-2322219; Fax 32-3-2336442; info.aw@voka.be; www.voka.be

Brusssels · *Federation of Chambers of Commerce & Ind.* · Avenue Louise 500; B-1050; P 10,800,000; M ; 32-2-209-05-50; Fax 32-2-209-05-68; fedcci@cci.be; www.cci.be

Gent · *Chamber of Commerce & Ind. of Gent* · Martelaarslaan 49; 9000; P 10,800,000; M 1,100; 32-9-2661440; Fax 32-9-2661441; kkngent@cci.be;

Kortrijk · *Chamber of Commerce West Flanders* · Casinoplein 10; B-8500; P 10,800,000; M 4,300; 32-56-235051; Fax 32-56-218564; kortrijk@voka.be; www.kvkwvl.voka.be

Leuven · *Chamber of Commerce & Ind. of Leuven* · Tiensevest 61; 3010; P 10,800,000; M 2,000; 32-16-222689; Fax 32-16-237828; info@ccileuven.be; www.cci.be/leuven;

Belize

Belize City · *Belize Chamber of Commerce & Ind.* · 63 Regent St.; P.O. Box 291; P 322,000; M 300; 501-22-35330; Fax 501-22-35333; bcci@belize.org; www.belize.org

Bermuda

Hamilton · *Bermuda Chamber of Commerce* · Diane P. Gordon; Exec. V.P.; 1 Point Pleasant Rd.; P.O. Box HM 655; HM CX; P 65,000; M 750; 441-295-4201; Fax 441-292-5779; pvirgil@bcc.bm; www. bermudachamber.bm

Bolivia

La Paz · *Chamber of Commerce of Bolivia* · P.O. Box 7; P 10,000,000; M 1,500; 591-2-378606; Fax 591-2-391004; cnc@ boliviacomercio.org.bo; www.boliviacomercio.org.bo

Santa Cruz · *Chamber of Commerce & Ind. Of Santa Cruz* · Av. Las Americas, Ste. 7; Casilla 180; P 10,000,000; M 1,500; 591-3-3334555; Fax 591-3-3342353; cainco@cainco.org.bo; cainco.org.bo

Bosnia & Herzegovina

Sarajevo · *Chamber of Eco. of Federation of Bosnia & Hercegovina* · Branislava Durdeva 10; 71000; P 3,800,000; 387-33-217-782; Fax 387-33-217-783; m.velic@kfbih.com; www.kfbih.com

Brazil

Rio de Janeiro · *National Confederaton of Ind.* · Av. General Justo, 307; 20021-130; P 194,000,000; 55-21-3804920; Fax 55-21-3804920; sgr@cnc.com.br; www.cnc.com.br

Sao Paulo · *Federation of Industries of Sao Paulo* · Paulista Avenue 1313; 01311-923; P 194,000,000; M 9,500; 55-11-2536433; Fax 55-11-2531972; cin@cin.org.br; www.fiesp.com.br

Bulgaria

Sofia · *Bulgaria-Azerbaijan Chamber of Commerce & Ind.* · 42B, Rodopski Izvor str.; 1680; P 7,600,000; M 500; 3592-958-2701; office@bg-az.com; www.bg-az.com

Sofia · *Bulgarian Chamber of Commerce & Ind.* · 9 Iskar Str.; 1058; P 7,600,000; 359-2-8117400; Fax 359-2-9873209; bcci@ bcci.bg; www.bcci.bg

Burkina Faso

Ouagadougou · *Chamber of Commerce & Ind.* · Ave. de Lyon; 502; P 16,300,000; 226-50-30-61-14; Fax 226-50-30-61-16; www. ccia.bf

Cameroon

Douala · *Chamber of Commerce, Ind. & Mines of Cameroon* · P.O. Box 4011; P 20,000,000; 237-342-98-81; Fax 237-342-55-96; www.ccima.net

Cape Verde

Mindelo SV · *Camara de Comercio, Industria y Servicos* · P.O. Box 728; P 513,000; M 450; 238-32-8495; Fax 238-32-8496; camara.com@mail.cvtelecom.cv

Cayman Islands

Grand Cayman · *Cayman Islands Chamber of Commerce & Better Bus. s.* · Wil Pineau; CEO; 2nd Flr., Macdonald Square Bldg.; P.O. Box 1000 GT; P 57,000; M 629; 345-949-8090; Fax 345-949-0220; info@caymanchamber.ky; www.caymanchamber.ky

Chile

Santiago · *Camara de Comercio De Santiago* · Monjitas 392; P 17,100,000; M 55; 56-2-360-7000; cpn@ccs.cl; www.ccs.cl

China

Beijing · *China Cncl. for the Promotion of Intl. Trade* · 1 Fuxingmenwai St.; 100860; P 1,300,000,000; 86-10-8807-5769; Fax 86-10-6803-0747; BCNweb@bizchinanow.com; www.ccpit.org

Quingdao · *China Chamber of Intl. Commerce* · Ste. 403, No. 121, Yan-an-san Rd.; 266071; P 1,300,000,000; M 300; 86-532-8389-7995; Fax 86-532-8389-8251; project@82invest.com; www.82invest.com

Colombia

Barranquilla · *Camara de Comercio de Barranquilla* · Via 40 #36-135; P 45,700,000; M 1,573; 57-53-510681; Fax 57-53-510681; camaraco@metrotel.net.co; www.barranquillanet.com

Buenaventura · *Camara de Comercio de Buenaventura* · Calle 1 No. 1A-88; P 45,700,000; M 4,500; 57-22424508; Fax 57-22434202; presidencia@ccbun.org; www.ccbun.org

Cartagena · *Camara de Comercio de Cartagena* · Santa Teresa St. No 32-41; 2117; P 45,700,000; M 15,000; 57-56-501110; Fax 57-56-501126; camaradecomercio@cccartagena.org.co; www.cccartagena.org.co

Medellin · *Medellin Chamber of Commerce* · Av. Oriental 52-82; P 45,700,000; M 4,156; 57-4-5138244; Fax 57-4-5137757; consultorio@camaramedellin.com.co; www.camaramedellin.com.co

Costa Rica

San Jose · *Chamber of Commerce of Costa Rica* · P.O. Box 1114; 1000; P 4,600,000; M 1,200; 506-2210005; Fax 506-2569680; camara@camara-comercio.com; www.camara-comercio.com

Cote d'Ivoire

Abidjan · *Chambre de Commerce et d'Industrie* · P.O. Box 1399; 01; P 21,600,000; M 156; 225-20-33-16-00; Fax 225-20-32-39-42; info@chamco-ci.org; www.chamco-ci.org

Croatia

Zagreb · *Croatian Chamber of Eco.* · Rooseveltov trg 2; P.O. Box 630; 10000; P 4,400,000; M 60,000; 385-1-4561555; Fax 385-1-4828380; hgk@hgk.hr; www.hgk.hr

Cuba

Havana · *Chamber of Commerce of the Republic of Cuba* · 21 No. 661 esq.A, Vedado; P.O. Box 370; 10 400; P 11,200,000; M 610; 53-833-8040; Fax 53-838-1321; camaracuba@camara.com.cu; www.camaracuba.cu

Cyprus

Limassol · *Famagusta Chamber of Commerce & Ind.* · Iacovos Hadjivarnavas; Secy./Dir.; Ayiou Andreou 339, Andrea Chambers Bldg., Ste. 201; 3095; P 1,000,000; M 600; 357-2-5370167; Fax 357-2-5370291; chamberf@cytanet.com.cy; www.fcci.org.cy

Nicosia · *Cyprus Chamber of Commerce & Ind.* · P.O. Box 21455; 1509; P 1,000,000; M 8,000; 357-2-288-9800; Fax 357-2-266-9048; chamber@ccci.org.cy; www.ccci.org.cy

Denmark

Copenhagen · *Danish Chamber of Commerce* · Boersen; 1217; P 5,500,000; 45-33-746000; Fax 45-33-746080; info@danskerhverv.dk; www.danskerhverv.dk

Dominican Republic

Santo Domingo · *C/C & Production of Santo Domingo* · P.O. Box 815; P 10,200,000; M 1,255; 809-682-2688; Fax 809-685-2228; ccpsd@camarasantodomingo.org.do; www.camarasantodomingo.org.do

Ecuador

Guayaquil · *Guayaquil Chamber of Commerce* · Av. Francisco de Orellana y V.H Alcivar; Edif. Las Camaras P.3; P 14,300,000; M 9,000; 593-4-2682771; Fax 593-4-2682725; www.lacamara.org

Quito · *Camara de Industriales de Pichincha* · P.O. Box 17-01-2438; P 14,300,000; M 1,000; 593-2-2452500; Fax 593-2-2448118; camara@cip.org.ec; www.cip.org.ec

Egypt

Cairo · *Federation of Egyptian Chambers of Commerce* · 4 El Falaki Sq.; P 79,000,000; 20-2-3551813; Fax 20-2-3557940

Cairo · *Cairo Chamber of Commerce* · 4 Midan El Falaki; P 79,000,000; 20-2-3558261; Fax 20-2-3563603; www.cairochamber.org.eg

El Salvador

San Salvador · *Camara De Comercio E Industria De El Salvador* · 9a Av. Norte y 5a C. Pte.; P 6,200,000; M 1,900; 503-223-13000; Fax 503-227-14461; camara@camarasal.com; www.camarasal.com

Estonia

Tallinn · *Estonian Chamber of Commerce* · Toom-Kooli 17; 10130; P 1,300,000; M 3,000; 372-6-040060; Fax 372-6-040061; koda@koda.ee; www.koda.ee

Finland

Helsinki · *Central Chamber of Commerce of Finland* · Risto E.J. Penttila; CEO; Aleksanterinkatu 17; P.O. Box 1000; 00101; P 5,500,000; M 16,800; 358-9-4242-6200; Fax 358-9-650-303; keskuskauppakamari@chamber.fi; www.keskuskauppakamari.fi

Jyvaskyla · *Central Finland Chamber of Commerce* · Mr. Uljas Valkeinen; Mgr. Dir.; Sepankatu 4; 40100; P 5,500,000; M 500; 358-10-322-2380; info@centralfinlandchamber.fi; www.centralfinlandchamber.fi

Kuopio · *Kuopio Chamber of Commerce* · Kasarmikatu 2; 70110; P 5,500,000; M 800; 358-17-2663800; Fax 358-17-2823304; kauppakamari@kuopiochamber.fi; www.kuopiochamber.fi

Lahti · *Hame Chamber of Commerce* · Ruahankatu 10; 15110; P 5,500,000; M 800; 358-3-821600; Fax 358-3-8216050; info@hamechamber.fi; www.hamechamber.fi

Tampere · *Tampere Chamber of Commerce* · Kehrasaari B; 33200; P 5,500,000; M 1,150; 358-3-2300555; Fax 358-3-2300550; info@tampere.chamber.fi; www.tampere.chamber.fi

Turku · *Turku Chamber of Commerce* · Jari Lahteenmaki; CEO; Puolalankatu 1; 20100; P 5,500,000; M 1,400; 358-2-274-3400; Fax 358-2-274-3440; kauppakamari@turku.chamber.fi; www.turku.chamber.fi

France

Paris · *Chamber of Commerce & Ind. of France* · Avenue d'lena 45; F-75769; P 65,000,000; 33-1-40693700; Fax 33-1-47206128; service.courrier@acfci.cci.fr; www.acfci.cci.fr

Marseille · *Chamber of Commerce & Ind. of Marseille Provence* · 35, rue Sainte-Victoire; 13292; P 65,000,000; 33-191138655; Fax 33-191138501; www.marseille-provence.cci.fr

Paris · *Chamber de Commerce et D'Industrie de Paris* · 27 Av. Friedland; 75382; P 65,000,000; M 30,000; 33-105657069; Fax 33-155657070; cpdp@ccip.fr; www.ccip.fr

Gambia

Banjul · *Gambia Chamber of Commerce & Ind.* · P.O. Box 3382; P 1,800,000; M 275; 220-437-8929; Fax 220-437-8936; gcci@gambiachamber.com; www.gambiachamber.com

Germany, Federal Rep. of

Berlin · *Deutscher Industrie und Handelstag* · Breite Strasse 29; 10178; P 82,000,000; 49-30-20308-0; Fax 49-30-20308-1000; infocenter@dihk.de; www.dihk.de

Bremen · *Bremen Chamber of Commerce* · P.O. Box 105107; 28051; P 82,000,000; 49-421-36370; Fax 49-421-3637299; service@handelskammer-bremen.de; www.handelskammer-bremen.de

Dusssseldorf · *Dusssseldorf Chamber of Ind. & Commerce* · Ernst-Schneider-Platz 1; 40212; P 82,000,000; 49-211-3557-220; Fax 49-211-3557-400; ihkdus@duesseldorf.ihk.de; www.duesseldorf.ihk.de

Hannover · *Hannover Chamber of Ind. & Commerce* · Schiffgraben 49; 30175; P 82,000,000; 49-511-3107-0; Fax 49-511-3107-333; info@hannover.ihk.de; www.hannover.ihk.de

Ghana

Accra · *Reg. Chamber of Commerce & Ind.* · P.O. Box 2325; P 24,300,000; M 2,000; 233-21-7012780; Fax 233-21-255202; accra@ghanachamber.org; www.ghanachamber.org

Accra · *Assssn. of Ghana Industries* · P. O. Box AN - 8624; P 24,300,000; M 1,500; 233-21-779023; Fax 233-21-773143; agi@agighana.org; www.agighana.org

Takoradi · *Sekondi-Takoradi Reg. Chamber of Commerce* · P.O. Box 45; P 24,300,000; M 150; 233-31-22385; Fax 233-31-23588; takoradi@ghanachamber.org; www.ghanachamber.org

Greece

Athens · *Athens Chamber of Commerce & Ind.* · 7 Academias St.; 10671; P 11,300,000; 30-210-360-4815; Fax 30-210-361-6464; info@acci.gr; www.acci.gr

Crete · *Heraklion Chamber of Commerce & Ind.* · 9, Koroneou Str.; P.O. Box 1154, Heraklion; 71110; P 11,300,000; M 12,000; 30-81-229013; Fax 30-81-222914; info@ebeh.gr; www.ebeh.gr

Patras · *Patras Chamber of Commerce & Ind.* · 58 Michalakopoulou St.; 26110; P 11,300,000; 30-61-277779; Fax 30-61-276519; www.patrascc.gr

Piraeus · *Piraeus Chamber of Commerce & Ind.* · Mrs. Panayiota Kouvari; Gen. Dir.; 1, Loudovikou str. Odissos sq.; 18531; P 11,300,000; M 17,000; 30-210-417-7241; 30-210-417-7245; Fax 30-210-417-8680; evep@pcci.gr; www.pcci.gr

Thessssaloniki · *Thessssaloniki Chamber of Commerce & Ind.* · 29 Tsimiski Str.; 54624; P 11,300,000; M 21,000; 30-23-10370100; Fax 30-23-10370114; root@ebeth.gr; www.ebeth.gr

Grenada

Saint George's · *Grenada Chamber of Ind. & Commerce* · P.O. Box 129; P 104,000; M 180; 473-4402937; Fax 473-4406621; info@grenadachamber.org; www.grenadachamber.org

Guam

Hagatna · *Guam Chamber of Commerce* · Reina A. Leddy; Pres.; 173 Aspinall Ave., Ste. 101; Ada Plaza Center Bldg.; 96910; P 180,000; M 320; 671-472-6311; Fax 671-472-6202; gchamber@guamchamber.com.gu; www.guamchamber.com.gu

Guatemala

Guatemala City · *Camara de Comercio de Guatemala* · 10a. Calle 3-80, zona 1; 1001; P 14,400,000; M 5,500; 502-2417-2700; Fax 502-2-2291897; info@camaradecomercio.org.gt; www.negociosenguatemala.com

Guatemala City · *Camara de Industria de Guatemala* · Ruta 6, 9-21 zona 4; nivel 12 Edificio; 214; P 14,400,000; M 1,475; 502-2-3809000; Fax 502-2-809110; info@industriaguate.com; www.industriaguate.com

Guyana

Georgetown · *Georgetown Chamber of Commerce & Ind.* · 156 Waterloo Street; P 761,000; M 85; 592-2263519; Fax 592-2263519; info@georgetownchamberofcommerce.org; georgetownchamberofcommerce.org

Honduras

Tegucigalpa · *Tegucigalpa Chamber of Commerce & Ind.* · P.O. Box 3444; P 7,600,000; M 1,700; 504-2232-4200; Fax 504-2232-5764; asuservicio@ccit.hn; www.ccit.hn

Hong Kong (China)

Hong Kong · *Hong Kong General Chamber of Commerce* · 22/F United Centre; 95 Queensway; P 7,000,000; M 4,150; 852-25299229; Fax 852-25279843; chamber@chamber.org.hk; www.chamber.org.hk

Hong Kong · *Hong Kong Trade Dev. Cncl.* · 38th Flr., Ofc. Tower, Convention Plaza; 1 Harbour Rd., Wanchai; P 7,000,000; 852-25844333; Fax 852-28240249; hktdc@tdc.org.hk; www.hktdc.com

Hungary

Budapest · *Budapest Chamber of Commerce & Ind.* · Kristina Krt 99; 1016; P 10,000,000; 36-1-4882111; Fax 36-1-4882119; www.bkik.hu

Budapest · *Hungarian Chamber of Commerce & Ind.* · Mr. Péter Dunai; Secy. General; Kossuth ter. 6-8; 1055; P 10,000,000; 36-1-474-5100; 36-1-474-5141; Fax 36-1-474-5149; mkik@mkik.hu; www.mkik.hu

Zalaegerszeg · *Chamber of Commerce & Ind. of Zala County* · PO Box 211; 8900; P 10,000,000; M 18,800; 36-92-550514; Fax 36-92-550525; zmkik@zmkik.hu; www.zmkik.hu

Iceland

Reykjavik · *Iceland Chamber of Commerce* · Kringlan 7; 103; P 318,200; M 397; 354-5107100; Fax 354-5686564; info@chamber.is; www.vi.is

India

Mubai · *Bombay Industries Assn.* · Sahakar Bhavan; Kurla Indl estate, LBS Marg Ghatkopar; 400086; P 1,200,000,000; 91-22-8386637; Fax 91-22-8386829; biaoffice@biaindia.org; www.biaindia.org

Mumbai · *Indo-American Chamber of Commerce* · 1-C Vulcan Insurance Bldg.; Churchgate; 400 020; P 1,200,000,000; M 2,800; 91-22-2821413; Fax 91-22-2046141; ho@iaccindia.com; www.iaccindia.com

New Delhi · *Federation of Indian Chambers of Commerce & Ind.* · Federation House; Tansen Marg; 110 001; P 1,200,000,000; M 500; 91-11-3738760; Fax 91-11-3320714; ficci@ficci.com; www.ficci.com

Iran

Tehran · *Iran Chamber of Commerce, Industries & Mines* · 254 Taleghani Ave.; P.O. Box 15875-4671; 15814; P 75,000,000; 98-21-88825111; info@iccim.ir; www.iccim.ir

Ireland

Cork · *Cork Chamber of Commerce* · Conor Healy; CEO; Fitzgerald House; Summerhill North; P 4,500,000; M 900; 353-21-4509044; Fax 353-21-4508568; info@corkchamber.ie; www.corkchamber.ie

Drogheda · *Drogheda & Dist. Chamber of Commerce* · Patricia Rooney; Pres.; Chamber Bldgs.; 10 Dublin Rd.; P 4,500,000; M 180;353-41-9833544; Fax 353-41-9841609; president@drogheda chamber.com; www.droghedachamber.com

Dublin · *Dublin Chamber of Commerce* · PJ Timmins; CEO; 7 Clare St.; 2; P 4,500,000; M 2,500; 353-1-6130800; Fax 353-1-6766043; info@dubchamber.ie; www.dubchamber.ie

Dublin · *Chambers Ireland* · 17 Merrion Sq.; 2; P 4,500,000; M 10,000; 353-1-4004300; Fax 353-1-6612811; info@chambers.ie; www.chambers.ie

Galway · *Galway Chamber of Commerce & Ind.* · Commerce House; Merchants Rd.; P 4,500,000; M 450; 353-91-563536; Fax 353-91-561963; info@galwaychamber.com; www.galway chamber.com

Limerick · *Chamber of Commerce of Limerick* · 96 O'Connell St.; P 4,500,000; M 700; 353-61-415180; Fax 353-61-415785; info@limerickchamber.ie; www.limerickchamber.ie

Sligo · *Sligo Chamber of Commerce* · 16 Quay Street; P 4,500,000; M 370; 353-71-61274; Fax 353-71-60912; info@sligochamber.ie; www.sligochamber.ie

Waterford · *Waterford Chamber of Commerce* · 2 George's St.; P 4,500,000; M 600; 353-51-872639; Fax 353-51-876002; info@waterfordchamber.ie; www.waterfordchamber.ie

Wexford · *Wexford Chamber of Ind. & Commerce* · The Ballast Office; Crescent Quay; P 4,500,000; M 220; 353-53-22226; Fax 353-53-24170; enquiries@wexfordchamber.ie; www.wexchamber.ie

Ireland, Northern

Londonderry · *Londonderry Chamber of Commerce* · Bishop Street; 1 St. Columb's Ct.; BT48 6PT; P 1,800,000; 28-71-262379; Fax 28-71-286789; info@londonderrychamber.co.uk; www.londonderrychamber.co.uk

Israel

Jerusalem · *Jerusalem Chamber of Commerce* · P.O. Box 2083; 91020; P 7,600,000; M 250; 972-2-6254333; Fax 972-2-6254335; chamber@chamber.org.il; www.chamber.org.il

Haifa · *Chamber of Commerce & Ind. of Haifa & The North* · 53 Haatzmaut Rd.; P.O. Box 33176; 31331; P 7,600,000; M 600; 972-4-8626364; Fax 972-4-8645428; main@haifachamber.org.il;www.haifachamber.com

Tel Aviv · *Federation of Israeli Chambers of Commerce* · Uriel Lynn; 84 Hahashmonaim St.; P.O. Box 20027; 61200; P 7,600,000; M 5,000; 972-3-5631020; Fax 972-3-5619027; chamber@chamber.org.il; www.chamber.org.il

Italy

Rome · *Chamber of Commerce & Ind. of Italy* · Piazza Sallustio 21; I-00187; P 60,400,000; 39-6-47041; Fax 39-6-470-4240; unioncamere@unioncamere.it; www.unioncamere.it

Alessandria · *Alessandria Chamber of Commerce* · via Vochieri 58; 15100; P 60,400,000; 39-131-3131; Fax 39-131-43186; info@al.camcom.it; www.al.camcom.it

Bologna · *Camera di Commercio, Ind, Art, E Ag di Bologna* · Piazza Affari; Piazza Costituzione 8; 40128; P 60,400,000; 39-51-6093111; Fax 39-51-6093451; info@bo.camcom.it; www.bo.camcom.it

Genova · *Genova Chamber of Commerce* · via Garibaldi 4; 16124; P 60,400,000; 39-10-27041; Fax 39-10-2704300; camera.genova@ge.camcom.it; www.ge.camcom.it

Milano · *Milano Chamber of Commerce* · via Meravigli 9/B; 20123; P 60,400,000; 39-2-85151; Fax 39-2-85154232; urp@mi.camcom.it; www.mi.camcom.it

Rome · *Rome Chamber of Commerce* · v. de Burro 147; 186; P 60,400,000; 39-6-520821; Fax 39-6-6790547; callcenter-cciaa roma@infocamere.it; www.rm.camcom.it

Trieste · *Trieste Chamber of Commerce* · Piazza Della Borsa 14; 34121; P 60,400,000; M 19,000; 39-40-67011; Fax 39-40-6701321; urp@ts.camcom.it; www.ts.camcom.it

Ivory Coast

See Cote d'Ivoire

Jamaica

Kingston · *Jamaica Chamber of Commerce* · 39 Hope Rd.; P.O. Box 172; 10; P 2,700,000; M 780; 876-922-0150; Fax 876-924-9056; info@jamaicachamber.org.jm; www.jamaicachamber.org.jm

Japan

Tokyo · *Japan Chamber of Commerce & Ind.* · 3-2-2 Marunouchi; Chiyoda-ku; 100-0005; P 127,000,000; M 520; 81-3-32837851; Fax 81-3-32166497; info@jcci.or.jp; www.jcci.or.jp

Hiroshima · *Hiroshima Chamber of Commerce & Ind.* · 44 Matomachi 5-chome; Naka-ku; 730-8510; P 127,000,000; 81-82-2226610; Fax 81-82-2220108; www.hiroshimacci.or.jp

Kawasaki · *Kawasaki Chamber of Commerce & Ind.* · 11-2, Ekimaehoncho; Kawasaki-ku; 210-0007; P 127,000,000; M 13,000; 81-44-2114111; Fax 81-44-2114118; kokusai@kawasaki-cci.or.jp; www.kawasaki-cci.or.jp

Kobe · *Kobe Chamber of Commerce & Ind.* · 1 Minatojima-Nakamachi; 6-chome, Chuo-ku; 650-8543; P 127,000,000; 81-783035806; Fax 81-783062348; info@kobe-cci.or.jp; www. kobe-cci.or.jp

Osaka · *Osaka Chamber of Commerce & Ind.* · 2-8 Hommachi-Bashi; Chuo-ku; 540-0029; P 127,000,000; 81-6-69446400; Fax 81-6-69446293; intl@osaka.cci.or.jp; www.osaka.cci.or.jp

Hokkaido · *Sapporo Chamber of Commerce & Ind.* · Kita-1 Nishi-2; Chuo-ku, Sapporo; 060-8610; P 127,000,000; M 25,000; 81-11-231-1122; Fax 81-11-231-1078; kokusaj@sapporo-cci.or.jp; www.sapporo-cci.or.jp

Jordan

Amman · *Jordan Chamber of Commerce* · P.O. Box 7029; 11118; P 6,500,000; 962-6-5665492; Fax 962-6-5685997; info@jocc.org. jo; www.jocc.org.jo

Amman · *Amman Chamber of Commerce* · Shaker Bin Zaid St.; P.O. Box 287; 11118; P 6,500,000; 962-6-5666151; Fax 962-6-5666155; info@ammanchamber.org.jo; www.ammanchamber.org

Kazakhstan

Almaty · *Chamber of Commerce & Ind. of Kazakhstan* · P.O. Box 1966; 47300; P 16,200,000; M 500; 8-3172-32-38-33; Fax 8-3172-32-38-33; akmcci@dan.kz; www.chamber.kz

Kenya

Mombosa · *Kenya Natl. Chamber of Commerce & Ind.* · P.O. Box 80635; 00304; P 38,600,000; M 15,000; 254-41-231-8802; Fax 254-41-231-8802; knccimombasa@paragonkenya.co.ke; www.paragonkenya.co.ke/knccimsa

Korea, Republic of

Seoul · *Korea Chamber of Commerce & Ind.* · CPO Box 25; P 48,600,000; M 71; 82-2-316-3566; Fax 82-2-757-9475; trade@ kccioa.kcci.or.kr; www.kcci.or.kr

Busan · *Busan Chamber of Commerce & Ind.* · 853-1, Bumchun-Dong, Busanjin-Ku; 614-721; P 48,600,000; M 6,000; 82-51-990-7086; Fax 82-51-990-7099; julyjang@pcci.or.kr; www.pcci.or.kr

Kuwait

Kuwait City · *Kuwait Chamber of Commerce & Ind.* · P.O. Box 775 Safat; Kuwait; 13008; P 3,100,000; M 30,000; 965-1805580; Fax 965-22433858; kcci@kcci.org.kw; www.kuwaitchamber.org.kw

Kyrgyzszstan

Bishkek · *Chamber of Commerce of the Kyrgyz Republic* · 107 Kievskaya str.; 720001; P 5,600,000; M 349; 996-312-210573; Fax 996-312-210575; info@cci.kg; www.cci.kg

Latvia

Riga · *Latvian Chamber of Commerce & Ind.* · Valdemara str. 35; 1010; P 2,200,000; M 800; 371-67225595; Fax 371-67820092; info@chamber.lv; www.chamber.lv

Lebanon

Beirut · *Chamber of Commerce & Ind. of Beirut & Mt. Lebanon* · P.O. Box 11-1801; P 4,300,000; M 20,000; 961-1485461; info@ccib.org. lb; www.ccib.org.lb

Lithuania

Vilnius · *Assssn. of Lithuanian Chambers of Commerce & Ind.* · J. Tumo-Vaizganto str. 9/1-63A; 2001; P 3,300,000; M 1,600; 370-52-612102; Fax 370-52-612112; info@chambers.lt; www. chambers.lt

Kaunas · *Kaunas Reg. Chamber of Commerce, Ind. & Crafts* · P.O. Box 2111; LT-3000; P 3,300,000; M 300; 370-37-229212; Fax 370-7-208330; chamber@chamber.lt; www.chamber.lt

Panevezys · *Panevezys Reg. Chamber of Commerce, Ind. & Crafts* · Respublikos g. 34; 35173; P 3,300,000; M 300; 370-45-463687; Fax 370-45-462227; panevezys@chambers.lt; www.ccic.lt

Siauliai · *Siauliai Reg. Chamber of Commerce, Ind. & Crafts* · Vilniaus str. 88; LT-76285; P 3,300,000; M 180; 370-41-523224; Fax 370-41-523903; siauliai@chambers.lt; www.rumai.lt

Luxembourg

Luxembourg-City · *Grand Duchy of Luxembourg Chamber of Commerce* · 7, rue Alcide Gasperi; L-2981; P 502,000; M 35,000; 352-4239391; Fax 352-438326; chamcom@cc.lu; www.cc.lu

Madagascar

Antananarivo · *Chamber of Commerce & Ind. In Antananarivo* · 20, rue Henry Razanatseheno Antaninarenina; 101; P 20,100,000; M 60; 261-20-2220211; contact@cci-tana.org; www.cci-tana.org

Malawi

Blantyre · *Malawi Confederation of Chambers of Commerce & Ind.* · P.O. Box 258; P 15,700,000; M 400; 265-1-871988; Fax 265-1-871147; mcci@mccci.org; www.mccci.org

Malaysia

Kuala Lumpur · *Malaysian Intl. Chamber of Commerce & Ind.* · P.O. Box 12921; 50792; P 28,300,000; M 1,100; 60-3-62017708; Fax 60-3-62107705; micci@micci.com; www.micci.com

Malta

Valletta · *Malta Chamber of Commerce* · Exchange Buildings; Republic Street; VLT05; P 416,300; M 826; 356-21-233873; Fax 356-21-245223; info@maltachamber.org.mt; www.chamber.org.mt

Marshall Islands

Majuro, MH · *Marshall Islands Chamber of Commerce* · P.O. Box 1226; 96960; P 63,000; M 50; 692-625-3177; Fax 692-625-3330; commerce@ntamar.net; www.marshallislandschamber.net

Mauritius

Port-Louis · *Mauritius Chamber of Commerce & Ind.* · 3 Royal St.; P 1,300,000; M 400; 230-208-3301; Fax 230-208-0076; mcci@intnet.mu; www.mcci.org

Mexico

La Paz · *La Paz Chamber of Commerce* · Mexico 1970 C/Bravo y Allende; 23040; P 108,000,000; 52-612-122751; correo@canacolapaz.com; www.canacolapaz.com

Tijuana · *Tijuana Chamber of Commerce* · Xavier Villaurritia 1271 Zona Rio; Baja California Norte; 22320; P 108,000,000; M 8,000; 52-664-6828488; Fax 52-554-6828486; web@canacotijuana.com; www.canacotijuana.com

Saltillo · *Saltillo Chamber of Commerce* · Av. Universidad, Ste. 514; Coahuila; 25260; P 108,000,000; M 2,300; 52-841-55611; Fax 52-841-52903; conasalt@mcsa.net.mx

Zapopan · *National Chamber of Commerce of Guadalajara* · Av. Vallarta, Ste. 4095; Jalisco; 45000; P 108,000,000; M 12,000; 52-3-1229020; Fax 52-3-1217950; comexca@vianet.com.mx

Delegacion Cuauhtemoc · *Mexico City Chamber of Commerce* · Paseo de la Reforma, Ste. 42; Col. Centro; Mexico DF; 6048; P 108,000,000; 52-55-36852269; Fax 52-55-36852269; sos@ccmexico.com.mx; www.camaradecomercio.com.mx

Puebla · *Puebla Chamber of Commerce* · Ave. Reforma, Ste. 2704, 7 Piso; Puebla; 72140; P 108,000,000; M 3,021; 52-222-2480800; Fax 52-222-2310655; asistente@canacopuebla.org.mx; www.canacopuebla.org.mx

Cozumel · *Cozumel Chamber of Commerce* · 20 Av. sur No. 916; Quintana Roo; 77600; P 108,000,000; M 1,800; 52-987-20583; Fax 52-987-25014

Victoria · *Victoria Chamber of Commerce* · Juarez 14 y 15, Ste. 324, A.P. 113; Tamaulipas; 87000; P 108,000,000; M 1,400; 52-131-20031; Fax 52-131-20031; canvitam@tamps1.telmex.net.mx

Merida · *Merida Chamber of Commerce* · Av Itzaes, Ste. 273 x39; Yucatan; 97070; P 108,000,000; M 700; 52-99-253033; Fax 52-99-255933; canameri@prodigy.net.mx

Fresnillo · *Fresnillo Chamber of Commerce* · America, Ste. 1, A.P. 18; Zacatecas; 99000; P 108,000,000; M 400; 52-493-21082; Fax 52-493-23578; canacofr@server.uaf.mx

Micronesia

Weno · *Chuuk State Chamber of Commerce* · Pres.; P.O. Box 280; Chuuk State; 96942; P 111,000; M 27; 691-330-2552; Fax 691-330-2233; www.fsminvest.fm/chuuk

Tofol · *Kosrae State Chamber of Commerce* · P.O. Box 600; Kosrae State; 96944; P 111,000; M 17; 691-370-3044; Fax 691-370-2066; drea@mail.fm; fsminvest.fm/kosrae

Colonia · *Yap State Govt. Commerce & Ind.* · Vitt Foneg; Div. Chief; P.O. Box 336; Yap State; 96943; P 111,000; 691-350-2182; 691-350-2184; Fax 691-350-5217; yapci@mail.fm; yapdevelopments.org

Moldova

Chisinau · *Chamber of Commerce & Ind. of the Rep. of Moldova* · 151 Stefan cel Mare str.; 2010; P 3,600,000; M 1,200; 373-22-22-15-52; Fax 373-22-23-44-25; camera@chamber.md; www.chamber.md

Mongolia

Ulaanbaatar · *Mongolian Chamber of Commerce & Ind.* · Mahatma Gandhi Street; UB Post 101011001; 17011; P 2,800,000; M 400; 976-11-312501; Fax 976-11-324620; chamber@mongolchamber.mn; www.mongolchamber.mn

Mozambique

Maputo · *Mozambique Chamber of Commerce* · P.O. Box 1836; P 23,400,000; M 200; 258-1-491970; Fax 258-1-490428; cacomo@teledata.mz; www.teledata.mz/cacomo/index.htm

Namibia

Windhoek · *Namibia Natl. Chamber of Commerce & Ind.* · P.O. Box 9355; P 2,200,000; M 900; 264-61-228809; Fax 264-61-228009; windhoek@ncci.org.na; www.ncci.org.na

Nepal

Kathmandu · *Federation of Nepalese Chambers of Commerce & Ind.* · P.O. Box 269; P 29,900,000; M 595; 977-1-4262218; Fax 977-1-4262007; fncci@mos.com.np; www.fncci.org

Netherlands-Antilles

Willemstad · *Curacao Chamber of Commerce* · John H. Jacobs; Exec. Dir.; Kaya Junior Salas 1; P.O. Box 10; Curacao; P 180,000; M 15,782; 599-9-4613918; Fax 599-9-4615652; businessinfo@curacao-chamber.an; www.curacao-chamber.an

Netherlands, The

Woerden · *Chamber of Commerce of the Netherlands* · Watermolenlaan 1; P.O. Box 191; 3440 AD; P 16,600,000; 31-348-426911; Fax 31-348-426216; post@vvk.kvk.nl; www.kvk.nl

Almere · *Chamber of Commerce for Gooi- & Eemland* · P.O. Box 10318; 1301 AH; P 16,600,000; M 25,000; 036-524-8600; Fax 036-524-8700; gef@kvk.nl; www.kvk.nl

Amsterdam · *Chamber of Commerce & Ind. for Amsterdam* · PO Box 2852; 1000 CW; P 16,600,000; 31-20-5314000; Fax 31-20-5314799; info@amsterdam.kvk.nl; www.amsterdam.kvk.nl

Arnhem · *Chamber of Commerce & Ind. for Central Gelderland* · P.O. Box 9292; 6800 KZ; P 16,600,000; 31-26-3538888; Fax 31-26-3538999; gelderland@kvk.nl; www.kvk.nl

Eindhoven · *Kamer van Koophandel Oost-Brabant* · P.O. Box 735; 5600 AS; P 16,600,000; 31-40-2323911; Fax 31-40-2449505; info@brabant.kvk.nl; www.eindhoven.kvk.nl

Gouda · *Central Holland Chamber of Commerce & Ind.* · P.O. Box 57; 2803 PA; P 16,600,000; M 15,000; 31-182-569111; Fax 31-182-571050; info@gouda.kvk.nl; www.kvk.nl

The Hague · *Chamber of Commerce & Ind. The Hague* · P.O. Box 29718; 2502 LS; P 16,600,000; 31-70-3287100; Fax 31-70-3143490; denhaag@kvk.nl; www.denhaag.kuk.nl

Leeuwarden · *Kamer van Koophandel Friesland* · P.O. Box 699; 8901 BL; P 16,600,000; 31-58-2954321; Fax 31-58-2128460; info@leeuwarden.kvk.nl; www.leeuwarden.kvk.nl

Tilburg · *Midden-Brabant Chamber of Commerce & Ind.* · P.O. Box 90154; 5000 LG; P 16,600,000; M 30,000; 31-13-5944122; Fax 31-13-468215; info@tilburg.kvk.nl; www.tilburg.kvk.nl

Utrecht · *Chamber of Commerce Utrecht* · P.O. Box 48; 3500 AA; P 16,600,000; 31-30-2363207; Fax 31-30-2312804; www.utrecht.kvk.nl;

Zwolle · *Northern Overysssel Chamber of Commerce* · P.O. Box 630; 8000 AP; P 16,600,000; M 16,000; 31-38-4553800; Fax 31-38-4537424

New Zealand

Wellington · *New Zealand Chambers of Commerce & Ind.* · P.O. Box 1590; 6001; P 4,400,000; 64-4-4722725; Fax 64-4-4171767; www.newzealandchambers.co.nz

Auckland · *Auckland Reg. Chamber of Commerce & Ind.* · 100 Mayoral Drive; P.O. Box 47; 1140; P 4,400,000; M 8,000; 64-9-3096100; Fax 64-9-3090081; auckland@chamber.co.nz; www.aucklandchamber.co.nz

Hamilton · *Waikato Chamber of Commerce & Ind.* · P.O. Box 1122; P 4,400,000; M 560; 64-7-8395895; Fax 64-7-8394581; admin@waikatochamber.co.nz; www.waikatochamber.co.nz

Lower Hutt · *Hutt Valley Chamber of Commerce & Ind.* · David Kiddey; P.O. Box 30653; 5040; P 4,400,000; M 350; 64-4-9399821; Fax 64-4-9399824; info@hutt-chamber.org.nz; www.hutt-chamber.org.nz

Whangarei · *Northland Chamber of Commerce* · P.O. Box 1703; P 4,400,000; M 320; 64-9-4384771; Fax 64-9-4384770; info@northchamber.co.nz; www.northchamber.co.nz

Dunedin · *Otago Chamber of Commerce & Ind.* · John Christie; CEO; P.O. Box 5713; 9031; P 4,400,000; M 1,100; 64-3-4790181; Fax 64-3-4770341; office@otagochamber.co.nz; www.otagochamber.co.nz

Rotorua · *Rotorua Chamber of Commerce* · 1209 Hinemaru St.; P.O. Box 385; 3040; P 4,400,000; M 430; 64-7-3498365; Fax 64-7-3491388; info@rotchamber.co.nz; www.rotchamber.co.nz

Tauranga · *Chamber of Commerce Tauranga Region* · Max Mason; CEO; 65 Chapel St.; P.O. Box 414; 3140; P 4,400,000; M 700; 64-07-577-9823; Fax 64-07-577-0364; chamber@tauranga.org.nz; www.tauranga.org.nz

Wellington · *Wellington Reg. Chamber of Commerce* · P.O. Box 1590; P 4,400,000; M 1,150; 64-4-9146500; Fax 64-4-9146424; Info@wellingtonchamber.co.nz; www.wgtn-chamber.co.nz

Niger

Niamey · *Chamber of Commerce, Ag. & Ind.* · P.O. Box 209; P 15,900,000; M 170; 227-732210; Fax 227-736668; ccaian@intnet.ne

Nigeria

Lagos · *Nigerian Assssn. of Chamber of Commerce, Ind. Mines & Ag.* · P.M.B. 12816; P 158,000,000; M 156; 234-01-7612099; Fax 234-01-4964737; contact@naccima.com; www.naccima.com

Lagos · *The Lagos Chamber of Commerce & Ind.* · P.O. Box 109; P 158,000,000; M ; 2347746617; Fax 2342701009; lcci@lagoschamber.com; www.lagoschamber.com

Norway

Kristiansand · *Kristiansand Chamber of Commerce* · Rådhusgt. 6, Postboks 269; 4663; P 4,900,000; 47-38024370; Fax 47-38123979; post@kristiansand-chamber.no; www.kristiansand-chamber.no

Oslo · *Assssn. of Norwegian Chambers of Commerce* · Herman Thrap-Meyer; CEO; P.O. Box 2900, Solli; 230; P 4,900,000; 47-22-541755; Fax 47-22-561700; h.thrap-meyer@hsh-org.no; www.chamber.no

Oslo · *Oslo Chamber of Commerce* · P.O. Box 2874 Solli; 230; P 4,900,000; M 250; 47-22-129400; Fax 47-22-129401; mail@chamber.no; www.chamber.no

Stavanger · *Stavanger Chamber of Commerce* · P.O. Box 182; N-4001; P 4,900,000; M 3,500; 47-51-510880; Fax 47-51-510881; post@stavanger-chamber.no; www.stavanger-chamber.no

Trondheim · *Mid Norway Chamber of Commerce & Ind.* · P.O. Box 778; 7408; P 4,900,000; M 800; 47-73-883110; Fax 47-73-883111; firmapost@trondheim-chamber.no; www.trondheim-chamber.no

Oman

Ruwi · *Oman Chamber of Commerce & Ind.* · P.O. Box 1400; 112; P 2,900,000; 968-24707674; Fax 968-24708497; info@omanchamber.com; www.omanchamber.com

Pakistan

Karachi · *Overseas Investors Chamber of Commerce & Ind.* · P.O. Box 4833; 74000; P 171,000,000; M 164; 92-21-2410814; Fax 92-21-2427315; info@oicci.org; www.oicci.org

Karachi · *Federation of Pakistan Chambers of Commerce* · P.O. Box 13875; 75600; P 171,000,000; M 167; 92-21-5873691; Fax 92-21-5874332; info@fpcci.com.pk; www.fpcci.com.pk

Faisalabad · *Faisalabad Chamber of Commerce & Ind.* · East Canal Road, Canal Park; 38000; P 171,000,000; M 2,500; 92-41-9230265; Fax 92-41-9230270; info@fcci.com.pk; www.fcci.com.pk

Gujranwala · *Gujranwala Chamber of Commerce & Ind.* · Aiwan-e-Tijarat Rd., Trust Plaza; 52250; P 171,000,000; M 3,500; 92-55-3256701; Fax 92-55-3254440; info@gcci.org.pk; gcci.org.pk

Lahore · *Lahore Chamber of Commerce & Ind.* · 11-Shahrah-e-Aiwan-e-Tijarat; 54000; P 171,000,000; M 8,000; 92-42-111222499; Fax 92-42-6368854; www.lcci.org.pk

Rawalpindi · *Rawalpindi Chamber of Commerce & Ind.* ·
P.O. Box 323; 46000; P 171,000,000; M 2,000; 92-51-5584397;
Fax 92-51-5586849; rcci@bestnet.pk; www.rcci.org.pk

Sialkot · *Sialkot Chamber of Commerce & Ind.* · Mr.
Mohammad Ishaq Butt; Pres.; Shahrah-e-Aiwan-e-Sanat-o-
Tijarat; P.O. Box 1870; Punjab; 51310; P 171,000,000; M 7,000;
92-52-4261881; 92-52-4261882; Fax 92-52-4268835; research@
scci.com.pk; www.scci.com.pk

Panama

Panama · *Camara de Comercio, Industrias & Ag de Panama* ·
P.O. Box 74; 1; P 3,300,000; M 1,300; 507-2073442; Fax 507-
2073421; arbitraje@panacamara.org; www.panacamara.com

Papua New Guinea

Port Moresby · *Papua New Guinea Chamber of Commerce
& Ind.* · P.O. Box 1621; 121; P 6,900,000; 675-3213057; Fax 675-
3210566; pngcci@global.net.pg; www.pngcci.org.pg

Peru

Cusco · *Camara de Comercio, Industrias de Cusco* · Manco Inca N.
206; Wancha; P 29,500,000; M 300; 51-14633434; Fax 51-14633434;
camcusco@camaralima.org.pe; www.camaralima.org.pe

Portugal

Lisbon · *Investment, Trade & Tourism of Portugal* · Av. 5
de Outubro 101; 1050; P 10,600,000; 351217909500; Fax
351217938028; dinf@icep.pt; www.icep.pt

Lisboa · *Chamber of Commerce & Ind. of Portugal* · Rua Portas
de Santo Antao 89; P-1194; P 10,600,000; 351-1-3224050; Fax
351-1-3224051; mm@acl.org.pt; www.en.acl.org.pt

Lega Da Palmeria · *Ind. Assoc. of Portuense* · P.O. Box 1092;
4450-617; P 10,600,000; M 2,000; 351-22-9981500; Fax 351-22-
9956039; aludgero@aep.mailpac.pt; www.aeportugal.pt

Azores Islands · *Chamber of Commerce & Ind. of the Azores* ·
Rua Ernesto do Canto, 13; Ponta Delgada; 9500; P 10,600,000;
M 680; 351-96-22427; Fax 351-96-24268

Porto · *Chamber of Commerce & Ind. of Porto* · Palacio da
Bolsa; Rua Ferreira Borges; 4050-253; P 10,600,000; M 700;
351-22-3399000; Fax 351-22-3399090; correio@cciporto.pt;
www.cciporto.com

Qatar

Doha · *Qatar Chamber of Commerce & Ind.* · P.O. Box 402;
P 1,700,000; M 2,600; 974-4559111; Fax 974-4661693; info@
qcci.org; www.qcci.org

Romania

Bucharest · *Chamber of Commerce of Romania & Bucharest
Muni.* · 2 Octavian Goga Blvd.; Sector 3; 79502; P 21,500,000;
40-21-319-01-14-18; ccir@ccir.ro; www.ccir.ro

Russian Federation

Moscow · *Chamber of Commerce & Ind. of the Russian Fed.* ·
6 Ilyinka Str.; 109012; P 142,000,000; M 9,430; 7-495-6200009;
Fax 7-495-6200360; tpprf@tpprf.ru; www.tpprf.ru

Rwanda, Republic of

Kigali · *Chamber of Commerce & Ind. of Rwanda* · P.O. Box 319;
P 10,100,000; 250-83538; Fax 250-83532; frsp@rwanda1.com

Saint Kitts & Nevis

Bassseterre · *St. Kitts & Nevis Chamber of Ind. & Commerce* ·
P.O. Box 332; P 52,000; M 140; 809-465-2980; Fax 809-465-4490;
sknchamber@caribsurf.com; www.stkittsnevischamber.org

Saint Lucia

Castries · *St. Lucia Chamber of Commerce, Ind. & Ag.* · Exec.
Dir.; P.O. Box 482; P 174,000; M 139; 758-4523165; Fax 758-
4536907; info@stluciachamber.org; www.stluciachamber.org

Saint Vincent & the Grenadines

Kingstown · *St. Vincent & the Grenadines Chamber of Ind.* ·
Shafia London; Exec. Dir.; Corea's Bldg., 3rd Flr.; P.O. Box 134;
VC100; P 100,000; M 52; (784) 457-1464; Fax (784) 456-2944;
svgchamber@svg-cic.org; www.svg-cic.org

Samoa

Apia · *Samoa Chamber of Commerce* · P.O. Box 2014; P 69,000;
M 135; 685-31090; Fax 685-31089

Apia · *Dept. of Trade, Commerce & Ind.* · P.O. Box 862; 98682;
P 69,000; 685-20471; Fax 685-21646

Saudi Arabia

Dammam · *Chamber of Commerce & Ind., Eastern Province* ·
P.O. Box 719; 31421; P 27,100,000; M 13,000; 966-3-8571111; Fax
966-3-8570607; info@chamber.org.sa; www.chamber.org.sa

Riyadh · *Cncl. of Saudi Chambers of Commerce & Ind.* · P.O.
Box 16683; 11474; P 27,100,000; M 97; 966-1-4053200; Fax 966-
1-4024747; council@saudichambers.org.sa; www.saudichambers.
org.sa

Dammam · *Federation of GCC Chambers of Commerce & Ind.* ·
P.O. Box 2198; 31541; P 27,100,000; 966-3-8265943; Fax 966-3-
8266794; fgccc@fgccc.org; www.fgccc.org

Riyadh · *Riyadh Chamber of Commerce & Ind.* · P.O. Box 596;
11421; P 27,100,000; 966-1-4040044; Fax 966-1-4021103; www.
riyadhchamber.com

Scotland

Glasgow · *Glasgow Chamber of Commerce* · Mr. Stuart Patrick;
CEO; 30 George Sq.; G2 1EQ; P 5,200,000; M 2,000; 44-141-204-
2121; Fax 44-141-221-2336; chamber@glasgowchamber.org;
www.glasgowchamber.org

Senegal

Dakar · *Chamber of Commerce & Ind.* · P.O. Box 118; P 12,900,000; 221-23-8213; Fax 221-23-9363

Serbia

Belgrade · *Chamber of Eco. of Serbia* · Resavska st. 12-15; P.O. Box 959; 11000; P 9,900,000; 381-11-3240611; Fax 381-11-3239009

Belgrade · *Belgrade Chamber of Commerce & Ind.* · Kneza Milosa 12; 11000; P 9,900,000; M 40,000; 381-11-2641355; Fax 381-11-2642029; mmj@kombeg.org.rs; www.kombeg.org.rs

Singapore

Singapore · *Singapore Intl. Chamber of Commerce* · 6 Raffles Quay, Ste. 10-01; 48580; P 5,100,000; M 815; 65-65000988; Fax 65-62242785; sicc@singnet.com.sg; www.sicc.com.sg

Slovakia

Bratislava · *Slovak Chamber of Commerce & Ind.* · Gorkeho 9; 81603; P 5,400,000; 421-7-54433291; Fax 421-7-54131159; sopkurad@sopk.sk; www.scci.sk

Slovenia

Ljubljana · *Chamber of Commerce & Ind. of Slovenia* · Dimiceva 13; 1000; P 2,100,000; 386-1-5898000; Fax 386-1-5898100; infolink@gzs.si; www.gzs.si/eng

South Africa

Johannesburg · *South African Chamber of Bus.* · P.O. Box 44164, Linden; 2104; P 49,900,000; M 47,000; 27-11-3589711; Fax 27-11-3589774; www.sacob.co.za

Cape Town · *Cape Town Reg. Chamber of Commerce* · P.O. Box 205; 8001; P 49,900,000; M 4,500; 27-21-4024300; Fax 27-21-4024302; info@capechamber.co.za; www.capetownchamber.com

KwaZulu-Natal · *Durban Chamber of Commerce & Ind.* · P.O. Box 1506; Durban; 4000; P 49,900,000; M 4,300; 27-31-3351000; Fax 27-31-3321288; chamber@durbanchamber.co.za; www.durbanchamber.co.za

East London · *Border-Kei Chamber of Bus. s.* · P.O. Box 11179; Southernwood; 5213; P 49,900,000; M 800; 27-43-7438438; Fax 27-43-7432249; info@bkcob.co.za; www.bkcob.co.za

Johannesburg · *Johannesburg Chamber of Commerce & Ind.* · Private Bag 34; Auckland Park; 2006; P 49,900,000; M 4,000; 27-11-7265300; Fax 27-11-4822000; info@jcci.co.za; www.jcci.co.za

Spain

Madrid · *Madrid Chamber of Commerce & Ind.* · C/ Ribera del Loira, 56-58; 28042; P 46,000,000; M 35,000; 34-1-5383500; Fax 34-1-5383677; camara@camaramadrid.es; www.camara madrid.es

Barcelona · *Barcelona Chamber of Commerce* · Avda. Diagonal 452-454; 8006; P 46,000,000; 34-3-4169300; Fax 34-3-4169301; cambra@cambrabcn.org; www.cambrabcn.org

Bilbao · *Chamber of Commerce & Ind. of Bilbao* · Gran Vía 13; 48001; P 46,000,000; M 65,000; 34-94-4706500; Fax 34-94-4220061; atencionaclientes@camarabilbao.com; www.camarabilbao.com

Cordoba · *Chamber of Commerce of Cordoba* · Perez de Castro 1; 14003; P 46,000,000; 34-957-296199; Fax 34-957-202106; info@camaracordoba.com; www.camaracordoba.com

Valencia · *Valencia Chamber of Commerce & Ind.* · Poeta Querol 15; 46002; P 46,000,000; M 60; 34-6-3511301; Fax 34-6-3516349; www.camarav.es

Sri Lanka

Colombo · *Ceylon Chamber of Commerce* · 50, Navam Mawatha; 2; P 20,400,000; M 516; 94-112-421745; Fax 94-112-449352; info@chamber.lk; www.chamber.lk

Sudan

Khartoum · *Union of Sudanese Chambers of Commerce* · P.O. Box 81; 11123; P 43,200,000; M 5,000; 249-11-781886; Fax 249-11-780748

Suriname

Paramaribo · *Chamber of Commerce & Ind.* · P.O. Box 149; P 524,000; 597-474536; Fax 597-474779; chamber@sr.net; www.surinamedirectory.biz

Swaziland

Mbabane · *Swaziland Chamber of Commerce & Ind.* · P.O. Box 72; P 1,200,000; M 500; 268-404-0768; Fax 268-409-0051; fsecc@business-swaziland.com; www.business-swaziland.com

Sweden

Gothenburg · *Western Sweden Chamber of Commerce* · Massans Gata 18; P.O. Box 5253; S-402 25; P 9,400,000; M 3,000; 46-31-835900; Fax 46-31-835936; info@handelskammaren.net; www.handelskammaren.net

Gavle · *Chamber of Commerce of Central Sweden* · P.O. Box 296; SE-80104; P 9,400,000; M 465; 46-26-662080; Fax 46-26-662099; chamber@mhk.cci.se; www.mhk.cci.se

Jonkoping · *Jonkoping Chamber of Commerce* · Elmiavagen 11; 554 54; P 9,400,000; M 400; 46-36-301430; Fax 46-36-129579; info@jonkoping.cci.se; www.jonkoping.cci.se

Karlstad · *Wermland Chamber of Commerce* · S. Kyrkogatan 6; 65224; P 9,400,000; M 1,150; 46-54-221480; Fax 46-54-221490; info@handelskammarenvarmland.se; www.handelskammaren varmland.se

Lulea · *Norrbotten Chamber of Commerce* · Storgatan 9; 97238; P 9,400,000; M 400; 46-920-12210; Fax 46-920-94857; info@north.cci.se; www.north.cci.se

Malmo · *Chamber of Commerce of Southern Sweden* · Skeppsbron 2; 21120; P 9,400,000; M 2,700; 46-40-6902400; Fax 46-40-6902490; info@handelskammaren.com; www.handel skammaren.com

Orebro · *Chamber of Commerce Malardalen* · Box 8044; 70008; P 9,400,000; M 350; 46-19-166160; Fax 46-19-6117750; info@handelskammarenmalardalen.se; www.handelskam marenmalardalen.se

Skelleftea · *Vesterbotten Chamber of Commerce* · Expolaris Center; 93178; P 9,400,000; M 320; 46-910-37800; Fax 46-910-37877; info@ac.cci.se; www.ac.cci.se

Stockholm · *Stockholm Chamber of Commerce* · Box 16050; 10321; P 9,400,000; M 2,500; 46-8-55510000; Fax 46-8-56631600; info@chamber.se; www.chamber.se

Switzerland

Zurich · *Swiss Business Federation* · Hegibachstrasse 47; CH-8032; P 7,900,000; 41-1-4213535; Fax 41-1-4213434; info@economiesuisse.ch; www.economiesuisse.ch

Geneva · *Geneva Chamber of Commerce & Ind.* · PO Box 5039; 1211; P 7,900,000; M 1,500; 41-22-8199111; Fax 41-22-8199100; info@cci.ch; www.ccig.ch

Syria

Damascus · *Federation of Syrian Chambers of Commerce* · Mousa Bin Nosair St.; P.O. Box 5909; P 22,500,000; M 210; 963-11-3311504; Fax 963-11-3331127; syr-trade@mail.sy; www.fedcommsyr.org

Aleppo · *Aleppo Chamber of Commerce* · P.O. Box 1261; P 22,500,000; M 20,000; 963-21-2238236; Fax 963-21-2213493; alepchmb@mail.sy; www.aleppochamber.com

Damascus · *Damascus Chamber of Commerce* · P.O. Box 1040; P 22,500,000; M 11,000; 963-11-2211339; Fax 963-11-2225874; dcc@net.sy; www.dcc-sy.com

Taiwan

Taipei · *World Taiwanese Chambers of Commerce* · 7G06, No 5; Hsin-Yi Road Sec 5; 110; P 23,100,000; M 40,000; 886-2-87881466; Fax 886-2-87881533; wtccmail@ms67.hinet.net; www.tccseattle.org

Tanzania

Arusha · *Arusha Chamber of Commerce, Ag. & Ind.* · P.O. Box 551; P 45,000,000; M 80; 255-2503722

Thailand

Bangkok · *Bd. of Trade of Thailand* · 150 Rajbopit Rd.; 10200; P 67,000,000; M 75; 66-2-2210555; Fax 66-2-2253995

Bangkok · *The Thai Chamber of Commerce* · 150 Rajbopit Rd.; 10200; P 67,000,000; M 2,000; 660-2-6221860; Fax 660-2-2253372; tcc@thaiechamber.com; www.thaiechamber.com

Tonga, South Pacific

Nuku'alofa · *Tonga Chamber of Commerce & Ind.* · P.O. Box 1704; P 104,000; M 106; 676-25-168; Fax 676-26-039; admin@tongachamber.org; www.tongachamber.org

Trinidad & Tobago

Port of Spain · *Trinidad & Tobago Chamber of Ind. & Commerce* · P.O. Box 499; P 1,300,000; M 532; 868-637-6966; Fax 868-637-7425; chamber@chamber.org.tt; www.chamber.org.tt

San Fernando · *South Trinidad Chamber of Ind. & Commerce* · P.O. Box 80; P 1,300,000; M 198; 868-652-5613; Fax 868-653-4983; execoffice@stcic.org; www.stcic.org

Turkey

Ankara · *Union of Chambers, Ind. & Commodity Exchanges* · Ataturk Bulvari No. 149; Bakanliklar; 6582; P 73,000,000; M 293; 90-312-4138000; Fax 90-312-4183268; info@tobb.org.tr; www.tobb.org.tr

Ankara · *Ankara Chamber of Commerce* · Soputori; 6530; P 73,000,000; 90-312-2857850; Fax 90-312-2863446; www.ato.acc.org.tr

Izmir · *Izmir Chamber of Commerce* · Ataturk cad. No:126 Pasaport; 35210; P 73,000,000; 90-232-4449292; Fax 90-232-4462251; info@izto.org.tr; www.izto.org.tr

Uganda

Kampala · *Uganda Natl. Chamber of Commerce & Ind.* · P.O. Box 3809; P 33,800,000; M 6,000; 256-41-4503024; Fax 256-41-4230310; info@chamberuganda.com; www.chamberuganda.com

Ukraine

Ivano-Frankivsk · *Ivano-Frankivsk Chamber of Commerce & Ind.* · 9, Rozumovskogo str.; 76014; P 45,800,000; M 137; 380-342523347; Fax 380-342523347; office@cci.if.ukrtel.net

Sumy · *Sumy Chamber of Commerce & Ind.* · 7a. Chervonogvardijska Str.; 40030; P 45,800,000; M 144; 380-542-600390; Fax 380-542-210041; chamber@cci.sumy.ua; www.cci.sumy.ua

United Arab Emirates

Abu Dhabi · *Federation of UAE Chambers of Commerce & Ind.* · H.E. Abdulla Sultan Abdulla; Secy. Gen.; P.O. Box 3014; P 4,700,000; 971-2-6214144; Fax 971-2-6339210; muaayd@fcciuae.ae; www.fcciuae.ae

Abu Dhabi · *Abu Dhabi Chamber of Commerce & Ind.* · P.O. Box 662; P 4,700,000; M 40,787; 971-2-6214000; Fax 971-2-6215867; services@adcci.gov.ae; www.abudhabichamber.ae

Ajman · *Ajman Chamber of Commerce & Ind.* · P.O. Box 662; P 4,700,000; 971-67422177; Fax 971-67471222; media@ajcci.gov.ae; www.ajcci.gov.ae

Dubai · *Dubai Chamber of Commerce & Ind.* · P.O. Box 1457; P 4,700,000; M 30,000; 971-4-2280000; Fax 971-4-2028888; customercare@dubaichamber.ae; www.dubaichamber.ae

Sharjah · *Sharjah Chamber of Commerce & Ind.* · P.O. Box 580; P 4,700,000; M 32,000; 971-6-30-222; Fax 971-6-30-2226; scci@sharjah.gov.ae; www.sharjah.gov.ae

United Kingdom

Birmingham · *Birmingham Chamber of Ind. & Commerce* · 75 Harborne Rd.; B15 3DH; P 62,000,000; M 3,500; 44-121-4546171; Fax 44-121-4558670; info@birmingham-chamber.com; www.birmingham-chamber.com

Bristol · *Bristol Chamber of Commerce & Initiative* · Leigh Court, Abbots Leigh; BS8 3RA; P 62,000,000; M 2,300; 44-01275-373-373; info@gwebusinesswest.co.uk; www.bristolchamberof commerce.co.uk

London · *London Chamber of Commerce & Ind.* · 33 Queen St.; EC4R 1AP; P 62,000,000; M 3,000; 44-20-7248-4444; Fax 44-20-7489-0391; lc@londonchamber.co.uk; www.londonchamber.co.uk

London · *Intl. Chamber of Commerce-United Kingdom* · 12 Grosvenor Pl.; SW1X 7HH; P 62,000,000; M 350; 44-20-78389363; Fax 44-20-72355447; info@iccorg.co.uk; www.iccuk.net

Manchester · *Greater Manchester Chamber of Commerce & Ind.* · Churchgate House; 56 Oxford St.; M60 7HJ; P 62,000,000; M 2,950; 44-161-2363210; Fax 44-161-2364160; info@gm chamber.co.uk; www.gmchamber.co.uk

Staffordshire · *North Staffordshire Chamber of Commerce & Ind.* · Commerce House, Festival Park; Stoke-on-Trent; ST1 5BE; P 62,000,000; M 1,100; 44-1-782-202222; Fax 44-1-782-202448; membership@nscci.co.uk; www.nscci.co.uk

Uruguay

Montevideo · *Camara Nacional de Comercio* · Rincón 454 P.2; 11000; P 3,400,000; M 1,000; 598-2-916-1277; Fax 598-2-916-1243; gerencia@cncs.com.uy; www.cncs.com.uy

Vietnam

Hanoi · *Vietnam Chamber of Commerce & Ind.* · 9 Dao Duy Anh St.; Dong Da District; P 86,000,000; M ; 84-4-35743985; Fax 84-4-35743063; vbfhn@hn.vnn.vn

Wales

Cardiff · *South Wales Chamber of Commerce* · The Maltings; East Tyndall St.; CF245EZ; P 3,000,000; M 1,500; 44-029-20-481532; info@southwaleschamber.co.uk; www.southwales chamber.co.uk

Zambia

Kitwe · *Kitwe & Dist. Chamber of Commerce & Ind.* · 8 Kantanta Street; Engineers House; 10101; P 13,300,000; M 128; 260-2-225345; Fax 260-2-225345; info@kitwechamber.com; kitwechamber.com

Lusaka · *Zambia Assssn. of Chambers of Commerce & Ind.* · P.O. Box 30844; 10101; P 13,300,000; M 400; 260-1-253020; Fax 260-1-252483; zacci@zamnet.zm; www.zacci.org.zm

Ndola · *Ndola & District Chamber of Commerce & Ind.* · P.O. Box 240241; P 13,300,000; M 90; 260-2-619296; Fax 260-2-619297; shyams@zamnet.zm

Zimbabwe

Harare · *Zimbabwe Natl. Chamber of Commerce* · P.O. Box 1934; P 12,600,000; 263-4-749737; Fax 263-4-750375; linda@ zncc.co.zw; www.zncc.co.zw

Harare · *Confederation of Zimbabwe Industries* · 31 J. Chinamano Ave; P 12,600,000; M 720; 263-4-251490; Fax 263-4-252424; info@czi.co.zw; www.czi.co.zw

U.S. Government Information

The One Hundred and Twelfth Congress
First Session

U.S. Capitol Switchboard   (202) 224-3121

Addressing Correspondence

To a Senator:
The Honorable (full name)
United States Senate
Washington, DC 20510

Dear Senator (last name):

To a Representative:
The Honorable (full name)
United States House of Representatives
Washington, DC 20515

Dear Representative (last name):

Key Websites

White House — http://www.whitehouse.gov

Senate Home Page — http://www.senate.gov

House Home Page — http://www.house.gov

Alabama

State Capitol • Montgomery, AL 36130 (334) 242-7100

Governor • Robert Bentley (R) 2014

Senate • Richard C. Shelby (R) 2017, Jeff Sessions (R) 2015

Representatives • Jo Bonner (R), Martha Roby (R), Mike Rogers (R), Robert Aderholt (R), Mo Brooks (R), Spencer Bachus (R), Terri Sewell (D)

Alaska

State Capitol • Juneau, AK 99811-0001 (907) 465-3500

Governor • Sean Parnell (R) 2014

Senate • Lisa Murkowski (R) 2017, Mark Begich (D) 2015

Representative • Don Young (R)

Arizona

State Capitol • Phoenix, AZ 85007 (602) 542-4331

Governor • Jan Brewer (R) 2014

Senate • John McCain (R) 2017, Jon L. Kyl (R) 2013

Representatives • Paul Gosar (R), Trent Franks (R), John Shadegg (R), Ed Pastor (D), David Schweikert (R), Jeff Flake (R), Raul Grijalva (D), Gabrielle Giffords (D)

Arkansas

State Capitol • Little Rock, AR 72201 (501) 682-2345

Governor • Mike Beebe (D) 2014

Senate • Mark Pryor (D) 2015, John Boozman (R) 2017

Representatives • Marion Berry (D), Vic Snyder (D), Steve Womack (R), Mike Ross (D)

California

State Capitol • Sacramento, CA 95814 (916) 445-2841

Governor • Jerry Brown (D) 2014

Senate • Dianne Feinstein (D) 2013, Barbara Boxer (D) 2017

Representatives • Mike Thompson (D), Wally Herger (R), Daniel E. Lungren (R), Tom McClintock (R), Doris Matsui (D), Lynn Woolsey (D), George Miller (D), Nancy Pelosi (D), Barbara Lee (D), vacant, Jerry McNerney (D), Jackie Speier (D), Pete Stark (D), Anna Eshoo (D), Michael Honda (D), Zoe Lofgren (D), Sam Farr (D), Dennis Cardoza (D), George Radanovich (R), Jim Costa (D), Devin Nunes (R), Kevin McCarthy (R), Lois Capps (D), Elton Gallegly (R), Howard McKeon (R), David Dreier (R), Brad Sherman (D), Howard Berman (D), Adam Schiff (D), Henry Waxman (D), Xavier Becerra (D), Judy Chu (D), Diane Watson (D), Lucille Roybal-Allard (D), Maxine Waters (D), Jane Harman (D), Laura Richardson (D), Grace Napolitano (D), Linda Sanchez (D), Ed Royce (R), Jerry Lewis (R), Gary Miller (R), Joe Baca (D), Ken Calvert (R), Mary Bono (R), Dana Rohrabacher (R), Loretta Sanchez (D), John Campbell (R), Darrell Issa (R), Brian Bilbray (R), Bob Filner (D), Duncan Hunter (R), Susan Davis (D)

Colorado

State Capitol • Denver, CO 80203 (303) 866-2471

Governor • John Hickenlooper (D) 2014

Senate • Michael Bennet (D) 2017, Mark Udall (D) 2015

Representatives • Diana DeGette (D), Jared Polis (D), Scott Tipton (R), Cory Gardner (R), Doug Lamborn (R), Mike Coffman (R), Ed Perlmutter (D)

Connecticut

State Capitol • Hartford, CT 06106 (860) 566-4840

Governor • Dan Malloy (D) 2014

Senate • Richard Blumenthal (D) 2017, Joseph I. Lieberman (ID) 2013

Representatives • John Larson (D), Joe Courtney (D), Rosa DeLauro (D), James Himes (D), Christopher Murphy (D)

Delaware

State Capitol • Dover, DE 19901 (302) 739-4101

Governor • Jack Markell (D) 2012

Senate • Chris Coons (D) 2015, Thomas Carper (D) 2013

Representative • Michael N. Castle (R)

District of Columbia

District Building • Washington, D.C. 20002 (202) 727-1000

Representative • Eleanor Holmes Norton (D)

Florida

State Capitol • Tallahassee, FL 32399 (850) 488-2272

Governor • Rick Scott (R) 2014

Senate • Bill Nelson (D) 2013, Marco Rubio (R) 2017

Representatives • Jeff Miller (R), Steve Southerland (R), Corrine Brown (D), Ander Crenshaw (R), Ginny Brown-Waite (R), Cliff Stearns (R), John Mica (R), Daniel Webster (R), Gus Bilirakis (R), C.W. Bill Young (R), Kathy Castor (D), Adam Putnam (R), Vern Buchanan (R), Connie Mack (R), Bill Posey (R), Tom Rooney (R), Kendrick Meek (D), Ileana Ros-Lehtinen (R), Robert Wexler (D), Debbie Wasserman Schultz (D), Lincoln Diaz-Balart (R), Allen West (R), Alcee Hastings (D), Sandy Adams (R), Mario Diaz-Balart (R)

Georgia

State Capitol • Atlanta, GA 30334 (404) 656-1776

Governor • Nathan Deal (R) 2014

Senate • Johnny Isakson (R) 2017, Saxby Chambliss (R) 2015

Representatives • Jack Kingston (R), Sanford Bishop Jr. (D), Lynn Westmoreland (R), Henry Johnson Jr. (D), John Lewis (D), Tom Price (R), John Linder (R), Austin Scott (R), Tom Graves (R), Paul Broun (R), Phil Gingrey (R), John Barrow (D), David Scott (D)

Hawaii

State Capitol • Honolulu, HI 96801 (808) 586-0013

Governor • Neil Abercrombie (D) 2014

Senate • Daniel K. Inouye (D) 2017, Daniel K. Akaka (D) 2013

Representatives • Charles Djou (R), Mazie Hirono (D)

Idaho

State Capitol • Boise, ID 83720 (208) 334-2100

Governor • C.L. Otter (R) 2014

Senate • James E. Risch (R) 2015, Michael Crapo (R) 2017

Representatives • Raul Labrador (R), Mike Simpson (R)

Illinois

State Capitol • Springfield, IL 62706 (217) 782-6830

Governor • Pat Quinn (D) 2014

Senate • Richard Durbin (D) 2015, Mark Kirk (R) 2017

Representatives • Bobby Rush (D), Jesse Jackson Jr. (D), Daniel Lipinski (D), Luis Gutierrez (D), Mike Quigley (D), Peter Roskam (R), Danny Davis (D), Melissa L. Bean (D), Janice Schakowsky (D), Mark Steven Kirk (R), Adam Kinzinger (R), Jerry Costello (D), Judy Biggert (R), Randy Hultgren (R), Timothy Johnson (R), Donald Manzullo (R), Bobby Schilling (R), Aaron Schock (R), John Shimkus (R)

Indiana

State Capitol • Indianapolis, IN 46204 (317) 232-4567

Governor • Mitch Daniels (R) 2012

Senate • Richard G. Lugar (R) 2013, Dan Coats (R) 2017

Representatives • Peter J. Visclosky (D), Joe Donnelly (D), Mark Souder (R), Steve Buyer (R), Dan Burton (R), Mike Pence (R), Andre Carson (D), Brad Ellsworth (D), Todd Young (R)

Iowa

State Capitol • Des Moines, IA 50319 (515) 281-5211

Governor • Terry Branstad (R) 2014

Senate • Charles E. Grassley (R) 2017, Tom Harkin (D) 2015

Representatives • Bruce Braley (D), David Loebsack (D), Leonard Boswell (D), Tom Latham (R), Steve King (R)

Kansas

State Capitol • Topeka, KS 66612 (785) 296-3232

Governor • Sam Brownback (R) 2014

Senate • Jerry Moran (R) 2017, Pat Roberts (R) 2015

Representatives • Tim Huelskamp (R), Lynn Jenkins (R), Dennis Moore (D), Todd Tiahrt (R)

Kentucky

State Capitol • Frankfort, KY 40601 (502) 564-2611

Governor • Steven Beshear (D) 2011

Senate • Rand Paul (R) 2017, Mitch McConnell (R) 2015

Representatives • Edward Whitfield (R), Brett S. Guthrie (R), John Yarmuth (D), Geoff Davis (R), Harold Rogers (R), Ben Chandler (D)

Louisiana

State Capitol • Baton Rouge, LA 70804 (225) 342-7015

Governor • Bobby Jindal (R) 2011

Senate • Mary Landrieu (D) 2015, David Vitter (R) 2017

Representatives • Steve Scalise (R), Cedric Richmond (D), Charlie Melancon (D), John Fleming (R), Rodney Alexander (R), William Cassidy (R), Charles Boustany Jr. (R)

Maine

State Capitol • Augusta, ME 04333 (207) 287-3531

Governor • Paul LePage (R) 2014

Senate • Susan Collins (R) 2015, Olympia Snowe (R) 2013

Representatives • Chellie Pingree (D), Michael Michaud (D)

Maryland

State Capitol • Annapolis, MD 21401 (410) 974-3901

Governor • Martin O'Malley (D) 2014

Senate • Benjamin Cardin (D) 2013, Barbara A. Mikulski (D) 2017

Representatives • Andrew P. Harris (R), C.A. Dutch Ruppersberger (D), John Sarbanes (D), Donna F. Edwards (D), Steny Hoyer (D), Roscoe Bartlett (R), Elijah Cummings (D), Chris Van Hollen (D)

Massachusetts

State House • Boston, MA 02133 (617) 725-4000

Governor • Deval Patrick (D) 2014

Senate • Scott Brown (R) 2013, John Kerry (D) 2015

Representatives • John Olver (D), Richard Neal (D), James McGovern (D), Barney Frank (D), Niki Tsongas (D), John Tierney (D), Edward Markey (D), Michael Capuano (D), Stephen Lynch (D), William Delahunt (D)

Michigan

State Capitol • Lansing, MI 48909 (517) 373-3400

Governor • Rick Snyder (R) 2014

Senate • Carl Levin (D) 2015, Debbie Stabenow (D) 2013

Representatives • Bart Stupak (D), Peter Hoekstra (R), Vernon Ehlers (R), Dave Camp (R), Dale Kildee (D), Fred Upton (R), Tim Walberg (R), Mike Rogers (R), Gary Peters (D), Candice Miller (R), Thaddeus McCotter (R), Sander Levin (D), Carolyn Kilpatrick (D), John Conyers Jr. (D), John Dingell (D)

Minnesota

State Capitol • Saint Paul, MN 55155 (651) 296-3391

Governor • Mark Dayton (D) 2014

Senate • Al Franken (D) 2015, Amy Klobuchar (D) 2013

Representatives • Timothy Walz (D), John Kline (R), Erik Paulsen (R), Betty McCollum (D), Keith Ellison (D), Michele Bachmann (R), Collin Peterson (D), Chip Cravaack (R)

Mississippi

State Capitol • Jackson, MS 39205 (601) 359-3100

Governor • Haley Barbour (R) 2011

Senate • Thad Cochran (R) 2015, Roger Wicker (R) 2013

Representatives • Alan Nunnelee (R), Bennie Thompson (D), Gregg Harper (R), Steven Palazzo (R)

Missouri

State Capitol • Jefferson City, MO 65102 (573) 751-3222

Governor • Jay Nixon (D) 2012

Senate • Roy Blunt (R) 2017, Claire McCaskill (D) 2013

Representatives • William Clay Jr. (D), W. Todd Akin (R), Russ Carnahan (D), Vicky Hartzler (R), Emanuel Cleaver (D), Sam Graves (R), Billy Long (R), JoAnn Emerson (R), Blaine Luetkemeyer (R)

Montana

State Capitol • Helena, MT 59620 (406) 444-3111

Governor • Brian Schweitzer (D) 2012

Senate • Max Baucus (D) 2015, Jon Tester (D) 2013

Representatives • Dennis Rehberg (R)

Nebraska

State Capitol • Lincoln, NE 68509 (402) 471-2244

Governor • Dave Heineman (R) 2014

Senate • Mike Johanns (R) 2015, Ben Nelson (D) 2013

Representatives • Jeff Fortenberry (R), Lee Terry (R), Adrian Smith (R)

Nevada

State Capitol • Carson City, NV 89701 (775) 684-5670

Governor • Brian Sandoval (R) 2014

Senate • John Ensign (R) 2013, Harry Reid (D) 2017

Representatives • Shelley Berkley (D), Dean Heller (R), Joe Heck (R)

New Hampshire

State Capitol • Concord, NH 03301 (603) 271-2121

Governor • John Lynch (D) 2012

Senate • Jeanne Shaheen (D) 2015, Kelly Ayotte (R) 2017

Representatives • Frank Guinta (R), Paul Hodes (D)

New Jersey

State Capitol • Trenton, NJ 08625 (609) 292-6000

Governor • Chris Christie (R) 2013

Senate • Frank Lautenberg (D) 2015, Robert Menendez (D) 2013

Representatives • Robert Andrews (D), Frank LoBiondo (R), Jon Runyan (R), Christopher Smith (R), Scott Garrett (R), Frank Pallone Jr. (D), Leonard Lance (R), William Pascrell Jr. (D), Steven Rothman (D), Donald Payne (D), Rodney Frelinghuysen (R), Rush Holt (D), Albio Sires (D)

New Mexico

State Capitol • Santa Fe, NM 87501 (505) 476-2200

Governor • Susana Martinez (R) 2014

Senate • Jeff Bingaman (D) 2013, Tom Udall (D) 2015

Representatives • Martin T. Heinrich (D), Steve Pearce (R), Ben R. Lujan (D)

New York

State Capitol • Albany, NY 12224 (518) 474-7516

Governor • Andrew Cuomo (D) 2014

Senate • Charles Schumer (D) 2017, Kirsten E. Gillibrand (D) 2013

Representatives • Timothy Bishop (D), Steve Israel (D), Peter King (R), Carolyn McCarthy (D), Gary Ackerman (D), Gregory Meeks (D), Joseph Crowley (D), Jerrold Nadler (D), Anthony Weiner (D), Edolphus Towns (D), Yvette Clarke (D), Nydia Velazquez (D), Michael Grimm (R), Carolyn Maloney (D), Charles Rangel (D), Jose Serrano (D), Eliot Engel (D), Nita Lowey (D), Nan Hayworth (R), Chris Gibson (R), Paul D. Tonko (D), Maurice Hinchey (D), vacant, Richard L. Hanna (R), Daniel B. Maffei (D), Christopher J. Lee (R), Brian Higgins (D), Louise McIntosh Slaughter (D), Eric J.J. Massa (D)

U.S. Congress

North Carolina

State Capitol • Raleigh, NC 27603 (919) 733-5811

Governor • Beverly Perdue (D) 2012

Senate • Richard Burr (R) 2017, Kay R. Hagan (D) 2015

Representatives • G.K. Butterfield (D), Renee Ellmers (R), Walter Jones (R), David Price (D), Virginia Foxx (R), Howard Coble (R), Mike McIntyre (D), Larry Kissell (D), Sue Wilkins Myrick (R), Patrick T. McHenry (R), Heath Shuler (D), Mel Watt (D), Brad Miller (D)

North Dakota

State Capitol • Bismarck, ND 58505 (701) 328-2200

Governor • Jack Dalrymple (R) 2012

Senate • Kent Conrad (D) 2013, John Hoeven (R) 2017

Representative • Rick Berg (R)

Ohio

State Capitol • Columbus, OH 43266 (614) 466-3555

Governor • John Kasich (R) 2014

Senate • Sherrod Brown (D) 2013, Rob Portman (R) 2017

Representatives • Steve Chabot (R), Jean Schmidt (R), Michael Turner (R), Jim Jordan (R), Robert Latta (R), Bill Johnson (R), Steve Austria (R), John Boehner (R), Marcy Kaptur (D), Dennis Kucinich (D), Marcia L. Fudge (D), Patrick Tiberi (R), Betty Sutton (D), Steven LaTourette (R), Steve Stivers (R), Jim Renacci (R), Timothy Ryan (D), Bob Gibbs (R)

Oklahoma

State Capitol • Oklahoma City, OK 73105 (405) 521-2342

Governor • Mary Fallin (R) 2014

Senate • James Inhofe (R) 2015, Tom Coburn (R) 2017

Representatives • John Sullivan (R), Dan Boren (D), Frank Lucas (R), Tom Cole (R), James Lankford (R)

Oregon

State Capitol • Salem, OR 97310 (503) 378-3111

Governor • John Kitzhaber (D) 2014

Senate • Jeff Merkley (D) 2015, Ron Wyden (D) 2017

Representatives • David Wu (D), Greg Walden (R), Earl Blumenauer (D), Peter A. DeFazio (D), Kurt Schrader (D)

Pennsylvania

State Capitol • Harrisburg, PA 17120 (717) 787-2500

Governor • Tom Corbett (R) 2014

Senate • Pat Toomey (R) 2017, Robert Casey Jr. (D) 2013

Representatives • Robert Brady (D), Chaka Fattah (D), Mike Kelly (R), Jason Altmire (D), Glen Thompson (R), Jim Gerlach (R), Joe Sestak (D), Mike Fitzpatrick (R), Bill Shuster (R), Tom Marino (R), Lou Barletta (R), John Murtha (D), Allyson Schwartz (D), Michael Doyle (D), Charles W. Dent (R), Joseph Pitts (R), Tim Holden (D), Tim Murphy (R), Todd Russell Platts (R)

Rhode Island

State Capitol • Providence, RI 02903 (401) 222-2080

Governor • Lincoln Chafee (I) 2014

Senate • Sheldon Whitehouse (D) 2013, Jack Reed (D) 2015

Representatives • Patrick Kennedy (D), James Langevin (D)

South Carolina

State Capitol • Columbia, SC 29211 (803) 734-2100

Governor • Nikki Haley (R) 2014

Senate • Jim DeMint (R) 2017, Lindsey Graham (R) 2015

Representatives • Henry E. Brown Jr. (R), Joe Wilson (R), J. Gresham Barrett (R), Bob Inglis (R), Mick Mulvaney (R), James Clyburn (D)

South Dakota

State Capitol • Pierre, SD 57501 (605) 773-3212

Governor • Dennis Daugaard (R) 2014

Senate • John Thune (R) 2017, Tim Johnson (D) 2015

Representative • Kristi Noem (R)

Tennessee

State Capitol • Nashville, TN 37423 (615) 741-2001

Governor • Bill Haslam (R) 2014

Senate • Lamar Alexander (R) 2015, Bob Corker (R) 2013

Representatives • Phil Roe (R), John J. Duncan Jr. (R), Zach Wamp (R), Scott DesJarlais (R), Jim Cooper (D), Bart Gordon (D), Marsha Blackburn (R), John Tanner (D), Steve Cohen (D)

Texas

State Capitol • Austin, TX 78711 (512) 463-2000

Governor • Rick Perry (R) 2014

Senate • Kay Bailey Hutchison (R) 2013, John Cornyn (R) 2015

Representatives • Louie Gohmert (R), Ted Poe (R), Sam Johnson (R), Ralph Hall (R), Jeb Hensarling (R), Joe Barton (R), John Abney Culberson (R), Kevin Brady (R), Al Green (D), Michael McCaul (R), K. Michael Conaway (R), Kay Granger (R), Mac Thornberry (R), Ron Paul (R), Ruben Hinojosa (D), Silvestre Reyes (D), Bill Flores (R), Sheila Jackson-Lee (D), Randy Neugebauer (R), Charles Gonzalez (D), Lamar Smith (R), Pete Olson (R), Quico Canseco (R), Kenny Marchant (R), Lloyd Doggett (D), Michael Burgess (R), Blake Farenthold (R), Henry Cuellar (D), Gene Green (D), Eddie Bernice Johnson (D), John Carter (R), Pete Sessions (R)

Utah

State Capitol • Salt Lake City, UT 84114 (801) 538-1000

Governor • Gary Herbert (R) 2012

Senate • Mike Lee (R) 2017, Orrin G. Hatch (R) 2013

Representatives • Rob Bishop (R), Jim Matheson (D), Jason Chaffetz (R)

Vermont

State Capitol • Montpelier, VT 05609 (802) 828-3333

Governor • Peter Shumlin (D) 2014

Senate • Patrick J. Leahy (D) 2017, Bernard Sanders (I) 2013

Representative • Peter Welch (D)

Virginia

State Capitol • Richmond, VA 23219 (804) 786-2211

Governor • Bob McDonnell (R) 2013

Senate • Jim Webb (D) 2013, Mark R. Warner (D) 2015

Representatives • Robert Wittman (R), Scott Rigell (R), Robert Scott (D), J. Randy Forbes (R), Robert Hurt (R), Robert Goodlatte (R), Eric Cantor (R), James P. Moran (D), Morgan Griffith (R), Frank Wolf (R), Gerald E. Connolly (D)

Washington

State Capitol • Olympia, WA 98504 (360) 902-4111

Governor • Christie Gregoire (D) 2012

Senate • Maria Cantwell (D) 2013, Patty Murray (D) 2017

Representatives • Jay Inslee (D), Rick Larsen (D), Brian Baird (D), Doc Hastings (R), Cathy McMorris Rodgers (R), Norman Dicks (D), Jim McDermott (D), David Reichert (R), Adam Smith (D)

West Virginia

State Capitol • Charleston, WV 25305 (304) 558-2000

Governor • Earl Ray Tomblin (D) 2012

Senate • Joe Manchin III (D) 2013, John D. Rockefeller IV (D) 2015

Representatives • Alan B. Mollohan (D), Shelley Moore Capito (R), Nick J. Rahall II (D)

Wisconsin

State Capitol • Madison, WI 53707 (608) 266-1212

Governor • Scott Walker (R) 2014

Senate • Ron Johnson (R) 2017, Herbert Kohl (D) 2013

Representatives • Paul Ryan (R), Tammy Baldwin (D), Ronald Kind (D), Gwen Moore (D), F. James Sensenbrenner Jr. (R), Thomas Petri (R), David Obey (D), Reid Ribble (R)

Wyoming

State Capitol • Cheyenne, WY 82002 (307) 777-7434

Governor • Matt Mead (R) 2014

Senate • Michael Enzi (R) 2015, John Barrasso (R) 2013

Representative • Cynthia M. Lummis (R)

Notes

Foreign Embassies in the United States

Afghanistan

Embassy of Afghanistan • His Excellency Said Tayed Jawad; 2341 Wyoming Ave. N.W.; Washington, DC; 20008; (202) 483-6410; Fax (202) 483-6488; press@embassyofafghanistan.org; www.embassyofafghanistan.org

African Republic, Central

Embassy of Central African Republic • His Excellency Stanislas Moussa-Kembe; 1618 22nd St. N.W.; Washington, DC; 20008; (202) 483-7800; Fax (202) 332-9893

Albania

Embassy of Albania • His Excellency Aleksander Sallabanda; 2100 S St. N.W.; Washington, DC; 20008; (202) 223-4942; Fax (202) 628-7342; embassy.washington@mfa.gov.al; www.embassyofalbania.org

Algeria

Embassy of the People's Democratic Rep. of Algeria • His Excellency Abdallah Baali; 2118 Kalorama Rd. N.W.; Washington, DC; 20008; (202) 265-2800; Fax (202) 667-2174; mail@algeria-us.org; www.algeria-us.org

Andorra

Embassy of Andorra • Two United Nations Plaza, 27th Flr.; New York, NY; 10017; (212) 750-8064; Fax (212) 750-6630; andorra@un.org

Angola

Embassy of the Republic of Angola • Her Excellency Josefina Pitra Diakite; 2100-2108 16th St. N.W.; Washington, DC; 20009; (202) 785-1156; Fax (202) 822-9049; angola@angola.org; www.angola.org

Antigua & Barbuda

Embassy of Antigua & Barbuda • Her Excellency Deborah Mae Lovell; 3216 New Mexico Ave. N.W.; Washington, DC; 20016; (202) 362-5122; Fax (202) 362-5525; embantbar@aol.com

Arab Emirates

See United Arab Emirates

Argentina

Embassy of the Argentine Republic • His Excellency D. Alfredo Vicente Chiradia; 1600 New Hampshire Ave. N.W.; Washington, DC; 20009; (202) 238-6401; Fax (202) 332-3171; www.embassyofargentina.us

Armenia

Embassy of the Republic of Armenia • His Excellency Tatoul Markarian; 2225 R St. N.W.; Washington, DC; 20008; (202) 319-1976; Fax (202) 319-2982; armpublic@speakeasy.net; www.armeniaemb.org

Australia

Embassy of Australia • His Excellency Kim Beazley; 1601 Massachusetts Ave. N.W.; Washington, DC; 20036; (202) 797-3000; Fax (202) 797-3168; www.austemb.org

Austria

Embassy of Austria • Dr. Christian Prosl; 3524 International Ct. N.W.; Washington, DC; 20008; (202) 895-6700; Fax (202) 895-6750; www.austria.org

Azerbaijan

Embassy of the Republic of Azerbaijan • His Excellency Yashar Aliyev; 2741 34th St. N.W.; Washington, DC; 20008; (202) 337-3500; Fax (202) 337 5911; azerbaijan@azembassy.us; www.azembassy.us

Bahamas

Embassy of the Commonwealth of the Bahamas • His Excellency Cornelius Alvin Smith; 2220 Massachusetts Ave. N.W; Washington, DC; 20008; (202) 319-2660; Fax (202) 319-2668; bahemb@aol.com

Bahrain

Embassy of the Kingdom of Bahrain • Her Excellency Houda Ezra Ebrahim Nonoo; 3502 International Dr. N.W.; Washington, DC; 20008; (202) 342-1111; Fax (202) 362-2192; ambsecretary@bahrainembassy.org; www.bahrainembassy.org

Bangladesh

Embassy of the People's Republic of Bangladesh • His Excellency Akramul Qader; 3510 International Dr. N.W.; Washington, DC; 20008; (202) 244-0183; Fax (202) 244-2771; bdootwash@bdembassyusa.org; www.bdembassyusa.org

Barbados

Embassy of Barbados • His Excellency John Ernest Beale; 2144 Wyoming Ave. N.W.; Washington, DC; 20008; (202) 939-9200; Fax (202) 332-7467; washington@foreign.gov.bb; www.barbados.org

Belarus

Embassy of the Republic of Belarus • His Excellency Mikhail Khvostov; 1619 New Hampshire Ave. N.W.; Washington, DC; 20009; (202) 986-1604; Fax (202) 986-1805; usa@belarusembassy.org; www.belarusembassy.org

Belgium

Embassy of Belgium • His Excellency Jan Matthysen; 3330 Garfield St. N.W.; Washington, DC; 20008; (202) 333-6900; Fax (202) 333-3079; washington@diplobel.fed.be; www.diplobel.us

Belize

Embassy of Belize • His Excellency Nestor E. Mendez; 2535 Massachusetts Ave N.W.; Washington, DC; 20008; (202) 332-9636; Fax (202) 332-6888; www.embassyofbelize.org

Benin

Embassy of the Republic of Benin • His Excellency Cyrille S. Oguin; 2124 Kalorama Rd. N.W.; Washington, DC; 20008; (202) 232-6656; Fax (202) 265-1996; info@beninembassy.us; www.beninembassy.us

Bolivia

Embassy of the Republic of Bolivia • Her Excellency Erika Angela Duenas Loayza; 3014 Massachusetts Ave. N.W.; Washington, DC; 20008; (202) 483-4410; Fax (202) 328-3712; www.bolivia-usa.org

Bosnia & Herzegovina

Embassy of Bosnia & Herzegovina • His Excellency Mitar Kujundzic; 2109 E St. N.W.; Washington, DC; 20037; (202) 337-1500; Fax (202) 337-1502; info@bhembassy.org; www.bhembassy.org

Botswana

Embassy of the Republic of Botswana • His Excellency Lapologang Caesar Lekoa; 1531-1533 New Hampshire Ave. N.W.; Washington, DC; 20036; (202) 244-4990; Fax (202) 244-4164; mmohurutshe@botswanaembassy.org; www.botswanaembassy.org

Brazil

Brazilian Embassy • His Excellency Mauro Vieira; 1025 Thomas Jefferson St., Ste. 300; Washington, DC; 20007; (202) 238-2805; Fax (202) 238-2827; ambassador@brasilemb.org; www.brasilemb.org

Brunei

Embassy of Brunei Darussalam • His Excellency Dato Paduka Haji Yusoff Haji Abdul Hamid; 3520 International Ct. N.W.; Washington, DC; 20008; (202) 237-1838; Fax (202) 885-0560; info@bruneiembassy.org; www.bruneiembassy.org

Bulgaria

Embassy of the Republic of Bulgaria • Her Excellency Elena Poptodorova; 1621 22nd St. N.W.; Washington, DC; 20008; (202) 387-0174; Fax (202) 234-7973; office@bulgaria-embassy.org; www.bulgaria-embassy.org

Burkina Faso

Embassy of Burkina Faso • His Excellency Paramanga Ernest Yonli; 2340 Massachusetts Ave. N.W.; Washington, DC; 20008; (202) 332-5577; Fax (202) 667-1882; ambawdc@rcn.com

Burundi

Embassy of the Republic of Burundi • Her Excellency Angele Niyuhire; 2233 Wisconsin Ave. N.W., Ste. 212; Washington, DC; 20007; (202) 342-2574; Fax (202) 342-2578; burundiembassy@erols.com; www.burundiembassy-usa.org

Cambodia

Royal Embassy of Cambodia • His Excellency Heng Hem; 4530 16th St. N.W.; Washington, DC; 20011; (202) 726-7742; Fax (202) 726-8381; camemb.usa@mfa.org.kh; www.embassyofcambodia.org

Cameroon

Embassy of the Republic of Cameroon • His Excellency ; Joseph Foe-Atangana; 1700 Wisconsin Ave. N.W.; Washington, DC; 20008; (202) 265-8790; Fax (202) 387-3826; mail@cameroonembassyusa.org; www.ambacam-usa.org

Canada

Embassy of Canada • His Excellency Gary Doer; 501 Pennsylvania Ave. N.W.; Washington, DC; 20001; (202) 682-1740; Fax (202) 682-7726; www.canadianembassy.org

Cape Verde

Embassy of the Republic of Cape Verde • Her Excellency Maria de Fatima da Veiga; 3415 Massachusetts Ave. N.W.; Washington, DC; 20007; (202) 965-6820; Fax (202) 965-1207

Chad

Embassy of the Republic of Chad • His Excellency Mahamoud Adam Bechir; 2401 Massachusetts Ave. N.W.; Washington, DC; 20008; (202) 462-4009; Fax (202) 265-1937; info@chadembassy-usa.org; www.chadembassy.us

Chile

Embassy of Chile • His Excellency Arturo Fermandois; 1732 Massachusetts Ave. N.W.; Washington, DC; 20036; (202) 785-1746; Fax (202) 887-5579; embassy@embassyofchile.org; www.chile-usa.org

China

Embassy of the People's Republic of China • His Excellency Zhang Yesui; 3505 International Place N.W.; Washington, DC; 20008; (202) 495-2266; Fax (202) 495-2138; chinaembpress_us@mfa.gov.cn; www.china-embassy.org

Colombia

Embassy of Colombia • His Excellency Gabriel Silva Lujan; 2118 Leroy Pl. N.W.; Washington, DC; 20008; (202) 387-8338; Fax (202) 232-8643; emwas@colombiaemb.org; www.colombiaemb.org

Comoros

Embassy of the Union of Comoros • His Excellency Mohamed Toihiri; 866 United Nations Plz., Ste. 418; New York, NY; 10017; (212) 750-1637; Fax (212) 750-1657

Congo, Democratic Rep. of

Embassy of the Democratic Republic of Congo • Her Excellency Faida M. Mitifu; 1726 M St. N.W., Ste. 601; Washington, DC; 20036; (202) 234-7690; Fax (202) 234-2609; ambassade@ambardcusa.org; www.ambardcusa.org

Congo, Republic of

Embassy of the Republic of the Congo • His Excellency Serge Mombouli; 4891 Colorado Ave. N.W.; Washington, DC; 20011; (202) 726-5500; Fax (202) 726-1860; ambassador_congotowashington@hotmail.com

Costa Rica

Embassy of Costa Rica • Her Excellency Muni Figueres; 2114 S St. N.W.; Washington, DC; 20008; (202) 234-2945; Fax (202) 265-4795; embassy@costarica-embassy.org; www.costarica-embassy.org

Cote d'Ivoire

Embassy of the Republic of Cote d'Ivoire • His Excellency Yao Charles Koffi; 2424 Massachusetts Ave. N.W.; Washington, DC; 20008; (202) 204-3976; (202) 204-3967

Croatia

Embassy of the Republic of Croatia • Her Excellency ; Kolinda Grabar-Kitarovic; 2343 Massachusetts Ave. N.W.; Washington, DC; 20008; (202) 588-5899; Fax (202) 588-8936; public@croatiaemb.org; www.croatiaemb.org

Cuba

No Diplomatic Relations

Cyprus

Embassy of the Republic of Cyprus • His Excellency Pavlos Anastasiades; 2211 R St. N.W.; Washington, DC; 20008; (202) 462-5772; Fax (202) 483-6710; info@cyprusembassy.net; www.cyprusembassy.net

Czech Republic

Embassy of the Czech Republic • 3900 Spring of Freedom St. N.W.; Washington, DC; 20008; (202) 274-9100; Fax (202) 966-8540; washington@embassy.mzv.cz; www.mzv.cz

Denmark

Royal Danish Embassy • His Excellency Peter Taksoe-Jensen; 3200 Whitehaven St. N.W.; Washington, DC; 20008; (202) 234-4300; Fax (202) 328-1470; wasamb@um.dk; www.ambwashington.um.dk

Djibouti

Embassy of the Republic of Djibouti • His Excellency Roble Olhaye; 1156 15th St. N.W., Ste. 515; Washington, DC; 20005; (202) 331-0270; Fax (202) 331-0302

Dominica

Embassy of the Commonwealth of Dominica • His Excellency Hubert John Charles; 3216 New Mexico Ave. N.W.; Washington, DC; 20016; (202) 364-6781; Fax (202) 364-6791; embdomdc@aol.com

Dominican Republic

Embassy of the Dominican Republic • His Excellency Roberto B. Saladín; 1715 22nd St. N.W.; Washington, DC; 20008; (202) 332-6280; Fax (202) 265-8057; embassy@us.serex.gov.do; www.domrep.org

East Timor

Embassy of the Democratic Republic of Timor Leste • His Excellency Constancio Pinto; 4201 Connecticut Ave. N.W., Ste. 504; Washington, DC; 20008; (202) 966-3202; Fax (202) 966-3205

Ecuador

Embassy of Ecuador • His Excellency Luis Benigno Gallegos Chiriboga; 2535 15th St. N.W.; Washington, DC; 20009; (202) 234-7200; Fax (202) 667-3482; embassy@ecuador.org; www.ecuador.org

Egypt

Embassy of the Arab Republic of Egypt • His Excellency ; Sameh Hassan Shoukry; 3521 International Ct. N.W.; Washington, DC; 20008; (202) 895-5400; Fax (202) 244-4319; www.egyptembassy.net

El Salvador

Embassy of El Salvador • His Excellency Francisco Altschul; 1400 16th St. N.W., Ste. 100; Washington, DC; 20036; (202) 265-9671; Fax (202) 232-3763; correo@elsalvador.org; www.elsalvador.org

Equatorial Guinea

Embassy of the Republic of Equatorial Guinea • Her Excellency Purificacion Angue Ondo; 2020 16th St. N.W.; Washington, DC; 20009; (202) 518-5700; Fax (202) 518-5252; info@equatorialguinea.org

Eritrea

Embassy of the State of Eritrea • His Excellency Ghirmai Ghebremariam; 1708 New Hampshire Ave. N.W.; Washington, DC; 20009; (202) 319-1991; Fax (202) 319-1304; embassyeritrea@embassyeritrea.org; www.embassyeritrea.org

Estonia

Embassy of Estonia • His Excellency Vaino Reinart; 2131 Massachusetts Ave. N.W.; Washington, DC; 20008; (202) 588-0101; Fax (202) 588-0108; info@estemb.org; www.estemb.org

Ethiopia

Embassy of Ethiopia • His Excellency Tesfaye Yilma; 3506 International Dr. N.W.; Washington, DC; 20008; (202) 364-1200; Fax (202) 686-9551; www.ethiopianembassy.org

European Union

Delegation of the European Comm. • His Excellency Joao Vale de Almeida; 2175 K St. N.W.; Washington, DC; 20037; (202) 862-9500; Fax (202) 429-1766; www.eurunion.org

Fiji

Embassy of the Republic of the Fiji Islands • His Excellency Winston Thompson; 2000 M St. N.W., Ste. 710; Washington, DC; 20036; (202) 466-8320; Fax (202) 466-8325; info@fijiembassydc.com; www.fijiembassydc.com

Finland

Embassy of Finland • His Excellency Pekka Lintu; 3301 Massachusetts Ave. N.W.; Washington, DC; 20008; (202) 298-5800; Fax (202) 298-6030; sanomat.was@formin.fi; www.finland.org

France

Embassy of France • His Excellency Pierre Nicolas Vimont; 4101 Reservoir Rd. N.W.; Washington, DC; 20007; (202) 944-6000; Fax (202) 944-6166; info@ambafrance-us.org; ambafrance-us.org

Gabon

Embassy of the Gabonese Republic • His Excellency Carlos Victor Boungou; 2034 20th St. N.W; Washington, DC; 20009; (202) 797-1000; Fax (202) 332-0668; info@gabonembassy.net; www.gabonembassy.net

Gambia, The

Embassy of the Gambia • 2233 Wisconsin Ave. N.W., Ste. 240; Washington, DC; 20007; (202) 785-1379; Fax (202) 785-1430; info@gambiaembassy.us; www.gambiaembassy.us

Georgia

Embassy of the Republic of Georgia • His Excellency Batu Kutelia; 2209 Massachusetts Ave. N.W.; Washington, DC; 20008; (202) 387-2390; Fax (202) 387-0864; embgeorgia.usa@mfa.gov.ge; usa.mfa.gov.ge

Germany, Federal Rep. of

Embassy of the Federal Republic of Germany • His Excellency Dr. Klaus Scharioth; 2300 M St. N.W., Ste. 300; Washington, DC; 20037; (202) 298-4000; Fax (202) 298-4261; german-embassy-us@germany.info; www.germany.info

Ghana

Embassy of Ghana • His Excellency Daniel Ohene Agyekum; 3512 International Dr. N.W.; Washington, DC; 20008; (202) 686-4520; Fax (202) 686-4527; info@ghanaembassy.org; www.ghanaembassy.org

Great Britain

See United Kingdom

Greece

Embassy of Greece • His Excellency Vassilis Kaskarelis; 2217 Massachusetts Ave. N.W.; Washington, DC; 20008; (202) 939-1300; Fax (202) 939-1324; greece@greekembassy.org; www.mfa.gr/washington

Grenada

Embassy of Grenada • Her Excellency Gillian M.S. Bristol; 1701 New Hampshire Ave. N.W.; Washington, DC; 20009; (202) 265-2561; Fax (202) 265-2468; gdaembassydc@gmail.com; www.grenadaembassyusa.org

Guatemala

Embassy of Guatemala • His Excellency ; Francisco Villagran de Leon; 2220 R St. N.W.; Washington, DC; 20008; (202) 745-4952; Fax (202) 745-1908; info@guatemala-embassy.org; www.guatemala-embassy.org

Guinea

Embassy of the Republic of Guinea • His Excellency Mory Karamoko Kaba; 2112 Leroy Pl. N.W.; Washington, DC; 20008; (202) 986-4300; Fax (202) 986-4800; morykaba14@hotmail.com; www.guineaembassy.com

Guinea-Bissau

No Information Available

Guyana

Embassy of Guyana • His Excellency Bayney Karran; 2490 Tracy Pl. N.W.; Washington, DC; 20008; (202) 265-6900; Fax (202) 232-1297; guyanaembassydc@verizon.net; www.guyana.org

Haiti

Embassy of the Republic of Haiti • 2311 Massachusetts Ave. N.W.; Washington, DC; 20008; (202) 332-4090; Fax (202) 745-7215; embassy@haiti.org; www.haiti.org

Holy See

Embassy of the Holy See • His Excellency Pietro Sambi; 3339 Massachusetts Ave. N.W.; Washington, DC; 20008; (202) 333-7121; Fax (202) 337-4036

Honduras

Embassy of Honduras • His Excellency Jorge Ramon Hernandez-Alcerro; 3007 Tilden St. N.W., Ste. 4-M; Washington, DC; 20008; (202) 966-2604; Fax (202) 966-9751; embhonduras@emb.org; www.hondurasemb.org

Hungary

Embassy of the Republic of Hungary • His Excellency Bela Szombati; 3910 Shoemaker St. N.W.; Washington, DC; 20008; (202) 362-6730; Fax (202) 966-8135; informacio.was@kum.hu; www.huembwas.org

Iceland

Embassy of Iceland • His Excellency ; Hjalmar Hannesson; House of Sweden; 2900 K St. N.W., Ste. 509; Washington, DC; 20007; (202) 265-6653; Fax (202) 265-6656; icemb.wash@utn.stjr.is; www.iceland.org/us

India

Embassy of India • Her Excellency Meera Shankar; 2107 Massachusetts Ave. N.W.; Washington, DC; 20008; (202) 939-7000; Fax (202) 483-3972; www.indianembassy.org

Indonesia

Embassy of the Republic of Indonesia • His Excellency Dr. Dino Patti Djalal; 2020 Massachusetts Ave. N.W.; Washington, DC; 20036; (202) 775-5200; Fax (202) 775-5365; www.embassyof indonesia.org

Iran

No Diplomatic Relations

Iraq

Embassy of the Republic of Iraq • His Excellency Samir Shakir Mahmood Sumaida'ie; 3421 Massachusetts Ave. N.W.; Washington, DC; 20007; (202) 742-1600; Fax (202) 462-5066; www.iraqiembassy.us

Ireland

Embassy of Ireland • His Excellency Michael Collins; 2234 Massachusetts Ave. N.W.; Washington, DC; 20008; (202) 462-3939; Fax (202) 232-5993; www.embassyofireland.org

Israel

Embassy of Israel • His Excellency Dr. Michael B. Oren; 3514 International Dr. N.W.; Washington, DC; 20008; (202) 364-5500; Fax (202) 364-5423; info@washington.mfa.gov.il; www.israelemb.org

Italy

Embassy of Italy • His Excellency Giulio Terzi di Sant'Agata; 3000 Whitehaven St. N.W.; Washington, DC; 20008; (202) 612-4400; Fax (202) 518-2156; www.ambwashingtondc.esteri.it

Ivory Coast

See Cote d'Ivoire

Jamaica

Embassy of Jamaica • Her Excellency Audrey P. Marks; 1520 New Hampshire Ave. N.W.; Washington, DC; 20036; (202) 452-0670; Fax (202) 452-0081; dcm@jamaicaembassy.org; www.embassyofjamaica.org

Japan

Embassy of Japan • His Excellency Ichiro Fujisaki; 2520 Massachusetts Ave. N.W.; Washington, DC; 20008; (202) 238-6700; Fax (202) 328-2187; www.us.emb-japan.go.jp

Jordan

Embassy of the Hashemite Kingdom of Jordan • Her Excellency Alia Bouran; 3504 International Dr. N.W.; Washington, DC; 20008; (202) 966-2664; Fax (202) 966-3110; HKJEmbassyDC@jordanembassyus.org; www.jordanembassyus.org

Kazakhstan

Embassy of the Republic of Kazakhstan • His Excellency Erlan A. Idrissov; 1401 16th St. N.W.; Washington, DC; 20036; (202) 232-5488; Fax (202) 232-5845; www.kazakhembus.com

Kenya

Embassy of the Republic of Kenya • His Excellency Elkanah Odembo; 2249 R St. N.W.; Washington, DC; 20008; (202) 387-6101; Fax (202) 462-3829; information@kenyaembassy.com; www.kenyaembassy.com

Korea

Embassy of the Republic of Korea • His Excellency Han Duk-soo; 2370 Massachusetts Ave. N.W.; Washington, DC; 20008; (202) 939-5600; Fax (202) 797-0595; www.koreaembassyusa.org

Kuwait

Embassy of the State of Kuwait • His Excellency Salem Abdullah Al Jaber Al-Sabah; 2940 Tilden St. N.W.; Washington, DC; 20008; (202) 966-0702; Fax (202) 364-2868

Kyrgyzstan

Embassy of the Kyrgyz Republic • His Excellency Muktar Djumaliev; 2360 Massachusetts Ave. N.W.; Washington, DC; 20008; (202) 449-9822; Fax (202) 386-7550; kgembassyusa@gmail.com; www.kyrgyzembassy.org

Laos

Embassy of the Lao People's Democratic Republic • His Excellency Seng Soukhathivong; 2222 S St. N.W.; Washington, DC; 20008; (202) 332-6416; Fax (202) 332-4923; embasslao@gmail.com; www.laoembassy.com

Latvia

Embassy of Latvia • His Excellency Andrejs Pildegovics; 2306 Massachusetts Ave. N.W.; Washington, DC; 20008; (202) 328-2840; Fax (202) 328-2860; embassy.usa@mfa.gov.lv; www.latvia-usa.org

Lebanon

Embassy of Lebanon • His Excellency ; Antoine Chedid; 2560 28th St. N.W.; Washington, DC; 20008; (202) 939-6300; Fax (202) 939-6324; info@lebanonembassyus.org; www.lebanonembassyus.org

Lesotho

Embassy of the Kingdom of Lesotho • His Excellency David Mohlomi Rantekoa; 2511 Massachusetts Ave. N.W.; Washington, DC; 20008; (202) 797-5533; Fax (202) 234-6815; lesothoembassy@verizon.net; www.lesothoemb-usa.gov.ls

Liberia

Embassy of the Republic of Liberia • His Excellency William V.S. Bull; 5201 16th St. N.W.; Washington, DC; 20011; (202) 723-0437; Fax (202) 723-0436; www.embassyofliberia.org

Liechtenstein

Embassy of the Principality of Liechtenstein • Her Excellency Claudia Fritsche; 2900 K St. N.W., Ste. 602B; Washington, DC; 20007; (202) 331-0590; Fax (202) 331-3221; www.liechtenstein.li

Lithuania

Embassy of the Republic of Lithuania • His Excellency Zygimantas Pavilioni; 2622 16th St. N.W.; Washington, DC; 20009; (202) 234-5860; Fax (202) 328-0466; info@ltembassyus.org; usa.mfa.lt

Luxembourg

Embassy of Luxembourg • His Excellency ; Jean-Paul Senninger; 2200 Massachusetts Ave. N.W.; Washington, DC; 20008; (202) 265-4171; Fax (202) 328-8270; washington.mae.lu/en

Macedonia

Embassy of the Republic of Macedonia • His Excellency Zoran Jolevski; 2129 Wyoming Ave. N.W.; Washington, DC; 20008; (202) 667-0501; Fax (202) 667-2131; usoffice@macedonianembassy.org; www.macedonianembassy.org

Madagascar

Embassy of the Republic of Madagascar • 2374 Massachusetts Ave. N.W.; Washington, DC; 20008; (202) 265-5525; Fax (202) 265-3034; malagasy.embassy@verizon.net; www.madagascar-embassy.org

Malawi

Embassy of the Republic of Malawi • Her Excellency Steve Matenje; 2408 Massachusetts Ave. N.W.; Washington, DC; 20008; (202) 721-0270; Fax (202) 721-0288; malawidc@aol.com; www.malawiembassy-dc.org

Malaysia

Embassy of Malaysia • 3516 International Ct. N.W.; Washington, DC; 20008; (202) 572-9700; Fax (202) 572-9882; malwash@kln.gov.my

Maldives

Embassy of the Republic of Maldives • 820 2nd Ave., Ste. 800C; New York, NY; 10017; (212) 599-6194

Mali

Embassy of Mali • His Excellency Mamadou Traore; 2130 R St. N.W.; Washington, DC; 20008; (202) 332-2249; Fax (202) 332-6603; ambassador@maliembassy.us; www.maliembassy.us

Malta

Embassy of Malta • His Excellency Mark Anthony Miceli-Farrugia; 2017 Connecticut Ave. N.W.; Washington, DC; 20008; (202) 462-3611; Fax (202) 387-5470; maltaembassy.washington@gov.mt; mfa.gov.mt

Marshall Islands

Embassy of the Republic of the Marshall Islands • 2433 Massachusetts Ave. N.W.; Washington, DC; 20008; (202) 234-5414; Fax (202) 232-3236; info@rmiembassyus.org; www.rmiembassyus.org

Mauritania

Embassy of the Islamic Republic of Mauritania • His Excellency Mohamed Lemine El Haycen; 2129 Leroy Pl. N.W.; Washington, DC; 20008; (202) 232-5700; Fax (202) 319-2623; info@mauritaniaembassy.us; mauritaniaembassy.us

Mauritius

Embassy of Republic of Mauritius • 1709 N. St. N.W.; Washington, DC; 20036; (202) 244-1491; Fax (202) 966-0983; mauritius.embassy@verizon.net

Mexico

Embassy of Mexico • His Excellency Arturo Sarukhan; 1911 Pennsylvania Ave. N.W.; Washington, DC; 20006; (202) 728-1600; Fax (202) 728-1698; mexembusa@sre.gob.mx; www.embassyofmexico.org

Micronesia

Embassy of the Federated States of Micronesia • His Excellency ; Yosiwo P. George; 1725 N St. N.W.; Washington, DC; 20036; (202) 223-4383; Fax (202) 223-4391; firstsecretary@fsmembassydc.org; www.fsmembassydc.org

Moldova

Embassy of the Republic of Moldova • His Excellency Igor Munteanu; 2101 S St. N.W.; Washington, DC; 20008; (202) 667-1130; Fax (202) 667-2624; washington@mfa.md; www.sua.mfa.md

Monaco

Embassy of Monaco • His Excellency Gilles Alexandre Noghes; 3400 International Dr. N.W., Ste. 2K-100; Washington, DC; 20008; (202) 234-1530; Fax (202) 244-7656; embassy@monaco-usa.org; www.monaco-usa.org

Mongolia

Embassy of Mongolia • His Excellency Khasbazaryn Bekhbat; 2833 M St. N.W.; Washington, DC; 20007; (202) 333-7117; Fax (202) 298-9227; esyam@mongolianembassy.us; www.mongolian embassy.us

Montenegro

Embassy of the Republic of Montenegro • ; 1610 New Hampshire Ave. N.W.; Washington, DC; 20009; P; 64000; (202) 234-6108; Fax (202) 234-6109; www.visit-montenegro.com

Morocco

Embassy of the Kingdom of Morocco • His Excellency Aziz Mekouar; 1601 21st St. N.W.; Washington, DC; 20009; (202) 462-7979; Fax (202) 462-7643; dcusa.themoroccanembassy.com

Mozambique

Embassy of the Republic of Mozambique • Her Excellency Amelia Matos Sumbana; 1525 New Hampshire Ave. N.W.; Washington, DC; 20036; (202) 293-7146; Fax (202) 835-0245; embamoc@aol.com; www.embamoc-usa.org

Myanmar

Embassy of the Union of Myanmar • 2300 S St. N.W.; Washington, DC; 20008; (202) 332-3344; Fax (202) 332-4351; info@mewashingtondc.com; www.mewashingtondc.com

Namibia

Embassy of the Republic of Namibia • His Excellency Mr. Martin Andjaba; Ambassador; 1605 New Hampshire Ave. N.W.; Washington, DC; 20009; (202) 986-2007; Fax (202) 986-2042; info@namibianembassyusa.org; www.namibianembassyusa.org.

Nauru

Embassy of the Republic of Nauru • Her Excellency Marlene Inemwin Moses; 800 Second Ave.; New York, NY; 10017; (212) 937-0074; Fax (212) 937-0079

Nepal

Embassy of Nepal • His Excellency Shankar P. Sharma; 2131 Leroy Pl. N.W.; Washington, DC; 20008; (202) 667-4550; Fax (202) 667-5534; info@nepalembassyusa.org; www.nepalembassyusa.org

Netherlands

Royal Netherlands Embassy • Her Excellency Renee Jones-Bos; 4200 Linnean Ave. N.W.; Washington, DC; 20008; (877) 388-2443; Fax (202) 362-3430; nid@the-netherlands.org; www.dutchmissions.com

New Guinea

See Papua New Guinea

New Zealand

Embassy of New Zealand • His Excellency Michael Moore; 37 Observatory Cir. N.W.; Washington, DC; 20008; (202) 328-4800; Fax (202) 667-5227; info@nzemb.org; www.nzembassy.com/usa

Nicaragua

Embassy of the Republic of Nicaragua • 1627 New Hampshire Ave. N.W.; Washington, DC; 20009; (202) 939-6570; Fax (202) 939-6545

Niger

Embassy of the Republic of Niger • Her Excellency Aminata Maiqa Djibrilla; 2204 R St. N.W.; Washington, DC; 20008; (202) 483-4224; Fax (202) 483-3169; ambassadeniger@hotmail.com

Nigeria

Embassy of the Federal Republic of Nigeria • His Excellency Adebowale Ibidapo Adefuye; 3519 International Ct. N.W.; Washington, DC; 20008; (202) 986-8400; Fax (202) 362-6541; www.nigeriaembassyusa.org

Northern Ireland

See United Kingdom

Norway

Royal Norwegian Embassy • His Excellency Wegger Christian Strommen; 2720 34th St. N.W.; Washington, DC; 20008; (202) 333-6000; Fax (202) 469-3990; emb.washington@mfa.no; www.norway.org

Oman

Embassy of the Sultanate of Oman • Her Excellency Hunaina Sultan Ahmed Al Mughairy; 2535 Belmont Rd. N.W.; Washington, DC; 20008; (202) 387-1980; Fax (202) 745-4933; www.omaninfo.us

Pakistan

Embassy of Pakistan • His Excellency Husain Haqqani; 3517 International Ct. N.W.; Washington, DC; 20008; (202) 243-6500; Fax (202) 686-1534; info@embassyofpakistanusa.org; www.embassyofpakistanusa.org

Palau

Embassy of the Republic of Palau • His Excellency Hersey Kyota; 1701 Pennsylvania Ave. N.W., Ste. 300; Washington, DC; 20006; (202) 452-6814; Fax (202) 452-6281; info@palauembassy.com; www.palauembassy.com

Panama

Embassy of the Republic of Panama • His Excellency Jaime E. Aleman; 2862 McGill Terrace N.W.; Washington, DC; 20008; (202) 483-1407; Fax (202) 483-8413; info@embassyofpanama.org; www.embassyofpanama.org

Papua New Guinea

Embassy of Papua New Guinea • His Excellency Evan Jeremy Paki; 1779 Massachusetts Ave. N.W., Ste. 805; Washington, DC; 20036; (202) 745-3680; Fax (202) 745-3679; info@pngembassy.org; www.pngembassy.org

Paraguay

Embassy of Paraguay • His Excellency Rigoberto Gauto Vielman; 2400 Massachusetts Ave. N.W.; Washington, DC; 20008; (202) 483-6960; Fax (202) 234-4508; secretaria@embaparusa.gov.py; www.embaparusa.gov.py

Peru

Embassy of Peru • His Excellency Luis Miguel Valdivieso Montano; 1700 Massachusetts Ave. N.W.; Washington, DC; 20036; (202) 833-9860; Fax (202) 659-8124; emoscoso@embassyofperu.us; www.peruvianembassy.us.

Philippines

Embassy of the Republic of the Philippines • His Excellency Willy Calaud Gaa; 1600 Massachusetts Ave. N.W.; Washington, DC; 20036; (202) 467-9300; Fax (202) 328-7614; info@philippineembassy-usa.org; www.philippineembassy-usa.org

Poland

Embassy of the Republic of Poland • His Excellency ; Robert Kupiecki; 2640 16th St. N.W.; Washington, DC; 20009; (202) 234-3800; Fax (202) 328-6271; washington.ambar@msz.gov.pl; www.polandembassy.org

Portugal

Embassy of Portugal • His Excellency Joao de Vallera; 2012 Massachusetts Ave. N.W.; Washington, DC; 20036; (202) 328-8610; Fax (202) 462-3726; info@embassyportugal-us.org; www.embassyportugal-us.org

Qatar

Embassy of the State of Qatar • His Excellency Ali Bin Fahad Al-Hajri; 2555 M St. N.W.; Washington, DC; 20037; (202) 274-1600; Fax (202) 237-0061; info@qatarembassy.net; www.qatarembassy.net

Romania

Embassy of Romania • His Excellency Adrian Cosmin Vierita; 1607 23rd St. N.W.; Washington, DC; 20008; (202) 332-4846; Fax (202) 232-4748; office@roembus.org; www.roembus.org

Russian Federation

Embassy of the Russian Federation • His Excellency Sergey I. Kislyak; 2650 Wisconsin Ave. N.W.; Washington, DC; 20007; (202) 298-5700; Fax (202) 298-5735; www.russianembassy.org

Rwanda

Embassy of Republic of Rwanda • His Excellency James Kimonyo; 1714 New Hampshire Ave. N.W.; Washington, DC; 20009; (202) 232-2882; Fax (202) 232-4544; www.rwandemb.org

Saint Kitts & Nevis

Embassy of Saint Kitts & Nevis • His Excellency Dr. Izben Cordinal Williams; 3216 New Mexico Ave. N.W.; Washington, DC; 20016; (202) 686-2636; Fax (202) 686-5740; info@embskn.com; www.embassy.gov.kn

Saint Lucia

Embassy of Saint Lucia • 3216 New Mexico Ave. N.W.; Washington, DC; 20016; (202) 364-6792; Fax (202) 364-6723; eosaintlu@aol.com

Saint Vincent & the Grenadines

Embassy of Saint Vincent & the Grenadines • Her Excellency La Celia Prince; 3216 New Mexico Ave. N.W.; Washington, DC; 20016; (202) 364-6730; Fax (202) 364-6736; mail@embsvg.com; www.embsvg.com

Samoa

Embassy of the Independent State of Samoa • His Excellency Ali'loaiga Feturi Elisaia; 800 Second Ave., Ste. 400D; New York, NY; 10017; (212) 599-6196; Fax (212) 599-0797; samoa@un.int

Sao Tome & Principe

Embassy of Sao Tome & Principe • His Excellency Ovidio Pequeno; 1211 Connecticut Ave. N.W., Ste. 300; Washington, DC; 20036; (202) 775-2075; Fax (202) 775-2077; embstpusa@verizon.net

Saudi Arabia

Royal Embassy of Saudi Arabia • His Excellency Adel A.M. Al-Jubeir; 601 New Hampshire Ave. N.W.; Washington, DC; 20037; (202) 342-3800; Fax (202) 944-3113; info@saudiembassy.net; www.saudiembassy.net

Senegal

Embassy of the Republic of Senegal • Her Excellency Fatou Danielle Diagne; 2031 Florida Ave. N.W.; Washington, DC; 20009; (202) 234-0540; Fax (202) 332-6315

Serbia

Embassy of the Republic of Serbia • His Excellency Vladimir Petrovic; 2134 Kalorama Rd. N.W.; Washington, DC; 20008; (202) 332-0333; Fax (202) 332-3933; info@serbiaembusa.org; www.serbiaembusa.org

Seychelles

Embassy of the Republic of Seychelles • His Excellency Ronald Jean Jumeau; 800 Second Ave., Ste. 400C; New York, NY; 10017; (212) 972-1785; Fax (212) 972-1786

Sierra Leone

Embassy of Sierra Leone • His Excellency Bockari K. Stevens; 1701 19th St. N.W.; Washington, DC; 20009; (202) 939-9261; Fax (202) 483-1793; info@embassyofsierraleone.net; embassyofsierraleone.net

Singapore

Embassy of the Republic of Singapore • Her Excellency Chan Heng Chee; 3501 International Pl. N.W.; Washington, DC; 20008; (202) 537-3100; Fax (202) 537-0876; singemb_was@sgmfa.gov.sg; www.mfa.gov.sg/washington

Slovak Republic

Embassy of the Slovak Republic • His Excellency Peter Burian; 3523 International Ct. N.W.; Washington, DC; 20008; (202) 237-1054; Fax (202) 237-6438; emb.washington@mzv.sk; www.mzv.sk/washington

Slovenia

Embassy of the Republic of Slovenia • His Excellency Roman Kirn; 2410 California St. N.W.; Washington, DC; 20008; (202) 386-6601; Fax (202) 386-6633; vwa@gov.si; washington.embassy.si

Solomon Islands

Embassy of the Solomon Islands • His Excellency Colin Beck; 800 Second Ave., Ste. 400L; New York, NY; 10017; (212) 599-6192; Fax (212) 661-8925

Somalia

Embassy ceased operations May 8, 1991

South Africa

Embassy of the Republic of South Africa • His Excellency Ebrahim Rasool; 3051 Massachusetts Ave. N.W.; Washington, DC; 20008; (202) 232-4400; Fax (202) 265-1607; info@saembassy.org; www.saembassy.org

Spain

Embassy of Spain • His Excellency Jorge Dezcallar de Mazarredo; 2375 Pennsylvania Ave. N.W.; Washington, DC; 20037; (202) 452-0100; Fax (202) 833-5670; emb.washington@maec.es; www.spainemb.org

Sri Lanka

Embassy of Democratic Socialist Republic of Sri Lanka • His Excellency Jaliya Wickramasuriya; 2148 Wyoming Ave. N.W.; Washington, DC; 20008; (202) 483-4025; Fax (202) 232-7181; slembassy@slembassyusa.org; www.slembassyusa.org

Sudan

Embassy of the Republic of the Sudan • His Excellency Akec Khoc; 2210 Massachusetts Ave. N.W.; Washington, DC; 20008; (202) 338-8565; Fax (202) 667-2406; www.sudanembassy.org

Suriname

Embassy of the Republic of Suriname • 4301 Connecticut Ave. N.W., Ste. 460; Washington, DC; 20008; (202) 244-7488; Fax (202) 244-5878; www.surinameembassy.org

Swaziland

Embassy of the Kingdom of Swaziland • His Excellency Abednego M. Ntshangase; 1712 New Hampshire Ave. N.W.; Washington, DC; 20009; (202) 234-5002; Fax (202) 234-8254

Sweden

Embassy of Sweden • His Excellency Sven Jonas Hafstroem; 2900 K St. N.W.; Washington, DC; 20007; (202) 467-2600; Fax (202) 467-2699; ambassaden.washington@foreign.ministry.se; www.swedenabroad.com

Switzerland

Embassy of Switzerland • His Excellency Manuel Sager; 2900 Cathedral Ave. N.W.; Washington, DC; 20008; (202) 745-7900; Fax (202) 387-2564; was.info@eda.admin.ch; www.swissemb.org

Syria

Embassy of Syria • His Excellency Dr. Imad Moustapha; 2215 Wyoming Ave. N.W.; Washington, DC; 20008; (202) 232-6316; Fax (202) 234-9548; info@syrembassy.net; www.syrianembassy.us

Tajikistan

Embassy of the Republic of Tajikistan • His Excellency Abdujabbor Shirinov; 1005 New Hampshire Ave. N.W.; Washington, DC; 20037; (202) 223-6090; Fax (202) 223-6091; tajikistan@verizon.net; www.tjus.org

Tanzania

Embassy of the United Republic of Tanzania • Her Excellency Mwanaidi S. Maajar; 1232 22nd St. N.W.; Washington, DC; 20008; (202) 939-6125; Fax (202) 797-7408; ubalozi@tanzaniaembassy-us.org; www.tanzaniaembassy-us.org

Thailand

Royal Thai Embassy • His Excellency Kittiphong Na Ranong; 1024 Wisconsin Ave. N.W.; Washington, DC; 20007; (202) 944-3600; Fax (202) 944-3611; info@thaiembdc.org; www.thaiembdc.org

Togo

Embassy of the Republic of Togo • 2208 Massachusetts Ave. N.W.; Washington, DC; 20008; (202) 234-4212; Fax (202) 232-3190

Tonga

Embassy of the Kingdom of Tonga • Her Excellency Fekitamoeloa Tupoupai Utoikamanu; 800 Second Ave., Ste. 400B; New York, NY; 10017; (917) 369-1025; Fax (917) 369-1024

Trinidad & Tobago

Embassy of the Republic of Trinidad & Tobago • Her Excellency Glenda Morean Phillip; 1708 Massachusetts Ave. N.W.; Washington, DC; 20036; (202) 467-6490; Fax (202) 785-3130; info@ttembwash.com; www.ttembassy.org

Tunisia

Embassy of Tunisia • ; 1515 Massachusetts Ave. N.W.; Washington, DC; 20005; (202) 862-1850; Fax (202) 862-1858

Turkey

Embassy of the Republic of Turkey • His Excellency Namık Tan; 2525 Massachusetts Ave. N.W.; Washington, DC; 20008; (202) 612-6700; Fax (202) 612-6744; contact@turkishembassy.org; www.turkishembassy.org

Turkmenistan

Embassy of Turkmenistan • His Excellency Meret Bairamovich Orazov; 2207 Massachusetts Ave. N.W.; Washington, DC; 20008; (202) 588-1500; Fax (202) 588-0697; turkmen@mindspring.com; www.turkmenistanembassy.org

Uganda

Embassy of the Republic of Uganda • His Excellency Perezi Karukubiro Kamunanwire; 5911 16th St. N.W.; Washington, DC; 20011; (202) 726-4758; Fax (202) 726-1727; info@ugandaembassyus.org; www.ugandaembassy.com

Ukraine

Embassy of Ukraine • His Excellency Olexander Motsyk; 3350 M St. N.W.; Washington, DC; 20007; (202) 333-0606; Fax (202) 333-0817; www.mfa.gov.ua/usa/en/

United Arab Emirates

Embassy of the United Arab Emirates • His Excellency Yousef Al Otaiba; 3522 International Ct. N.W., Ste. 400; Washington, DC; 20008; (202) 243-2400; Fax (202) 243-2432; info@uae-embassy.org; www.uae-embassy.org

United Kingdom

British Embassy • His Excellency Sir Nigel Elton Sheinwald; 3100 Massachusetts Ave. N.W.; Washington, DC; 20008; (202) 588-6500; Fax (202) 588-7870; ukinusa.fco.gov.uk/en/

Uruguay

Embassy of Uruguay • His Excellency Carlos Gianelli Derois; 1913 I St. N.W.; Washington, DC; 20006; (202) 331-1313; Fax (202) 331-8142; uruwashi@uruwashi.org; www.uruwashi.org

Uzbekistan

Embassy of the Republic of Uzbekistan • His Excellency Ilhom Nematov; 1746 Massachusetts Ave. N.W.; Washington, DC; 20036; (202) 887-5300; Fax (202) 293-6804; info@uzbekistan.org; www.uzbekistan.org

Venezuela

Embassy of the Bolivarian Republic of Venezuela • His Excellency Bernardo Alvarez Herrera; 1099 30th St. N.W.; Washington, DC; 20007; (202) 342-2214; Fax (202) 342-6820; despacho@embavenez-us.org; www.embavenez-us.org

Vietnam

Embassy of Vietnam • His Excellency Le Cong Phung; 1233 20th St. N.W., Ste. 400; Washington, DC; 20036; (202) 861-0737; Fax (202) 861-0917; info@vietnamembassy.us; www.vietnam-embassy-usa.org

Yemen

Embassy of the Republic of Yemen • His Excellency Abdulwahab Abdulla Al-Hajjri; 2319 Wyoming Ave. N.W.; Washington, DC; 20008; (202) 965-4760; Fax (202) 337-2017; counselor@yemenembassy.org; www.yemenembassy.org

Zambia

Embassy of the Republic of Zambia • Her Excellency Sheila Siwela; 2419 Massachusetts Ave. N.W.; Washington, DC; 20008; (202) 265-9717; Fax (202) 332-0826; embzambia@aol.com; www.zambiaembassy.org

Zimbabwe

Embassy of the Republic of Zimbabwe • His Excellency Dr. Machivenyika T. Mapuranga; 1608 New Hampshire Ave. N.W.; Washington, DC; 20009; (202) 332-7100; Fax (202) 483-9326; info33@zimbabwe-embassy.us; www.zimbabwe-embassy.us

United States Embassies

Accepted Forms for Addressing Mail

Posts with APO/FPO Numbers

APO/FPO Address:
Name
Organization
PSC of Unit number; Box number
APO AE 09080 or APO AA 34038 or APO AP 96337

International Address:
Name of Person/Section
American Embassy
P.O. Box (use street address only when P.O. Box is not supplied)
Manama; Bahrain

Posts without APO/FPO Numbers

Diplomatic Pouch Address:
Name of Person/Section
Name of Post
Department of State
Washington; DC 20521-four digit add-in

International Address:
Name of Person/Section
American Embassy
Jubilaeumstrasse 93
3005 Bern, Switzerland

Note: Do not combine any of the above forms (e.g. international plus APO/FPO addresses). This will only result in confusion and possible delays in delivery.

To eliminate delays, it is important to address your correspondence to a section or position, rather than an officer by name.

Sections:

Commercial Office
Economic/Commercial Office
Financial Attaches
Political Office
Labor Office
Consular Office
Administrative Office
Regional Security Office
Scientific Attaches
Agricultural Office
Public Affairs Office
Cultural Affairs Office
Export/Import Office

Afghanistan

Kabul • Great Masoud Road; APO AE 09806; Tel 937-00-108001; Fax 937-00-108564; kabul.usembassy.gov; Ambassador Karl W. Eikenberry

Albania

Tirana • Rruga Elbasanit 103; Dept. of State; 9510 Tirana Pl.; Dulles; VA 20189; Tel 355-42-247285; Fax 355-42-232222; tirana.usembassy.gov; Ambassador Alexander A. Arvizu

Algeria

Algiers • 5 Chemin Cheikh Bachir Ibrahimi; El-Biar; 16030; Tel 2137-70-082000; Fax 213-21-607335; algiers.usembassy.gov; Ambassador David Pearce

Angola

Luanda • Rua Houari Boumedienne #32; Tel 2442-22-641000; Fax 2442-22-641232; luanda.usembassy.gov; Ambassador Dr. Christopher J. McCullen

Antigua & Barbuda

The post closed June 30, 1994

Argentina

Buenos Aires • Avenida Colombia 4300; Unit 4334; APO AA 34034; Tel 5411-57-774533; Fax 5411-57-774240; argentina.usembassy.gov; Ambassador Vilma Martinez

Armenia

Yerevan • 1 American Ave.; Tel 374-14-64700; Fax 374-14-64742; yerevan.usembassy.gov; Ambassador Marie L. Yovanovitch

Australia

Canberra • Moonah Pl.; Yarralumla; A.C.T. 2600; PSC 277 APO AP 96549; Tel 612-62-145600; Fax 612-62-145970; canberra.usembassy.gov; Ambassador Jeff Bleich

Austria

Vienna • Boltzmanngasse 16; 1090; Tel 43-13-13390; Fax 431-31-00682; vienna.usembassy.gov; Ambassador William C. Eacho

Azerbaijan

Baku • Azadliq Prospect 83; 1007; Tel 9941-24-980335; Fax 9941-24-656671; azerbaijan.usembassy.gov; vacant

Bahamas

Nassau • P.O. Box N-8197; Tel 242-32-21181; Fax 242-32-87838; nassau.usembassy.gov; Ambassador Nicole A. Avant

Bahrain

Manama • Bldg. 797; Rd. 3119; Block 331; Zing; Tel 973-17-242700; Fax 973-17-270547; manama.usembassy.gov; Ambassador J. Adam Ereli

Bangladesh

Dhaka • Diplomatic Enclave; Madani Ave.; Baridhara; Tel 880-28-855500; Fax 880-28-823744; dhaka.usembassy.gov; Ambassador James F. Moriarty

Barbados

Bridgetown • Wildey Bus Park; Wildey; St. Michael BB 14006; FPO AA 34055; Tel 246-22-74000; Fax 246-43-10179; bridgetown.usembassy.gov; vacant

Belarus

Minsk • 46 Starovilenskaya Str. 220002; PSC 78 Box B Minsk; APO AE 09723; Tel 375172101283; Fax 3751-72-347853; belarus.usembassy.gov; Charge d'Affaires Michael Scanlan

Belgium

Brussels • 27 Blvd du Regent; 1000; PSC 82 Box 002; APO AE 09710; Tel 322-50-82111; Fax 322-51-12725; brussels.usembassy.gov; Ambassador Howard Gutman

Belize

Belmopan • Floral Park Rd.; Unit 7401; APO AA 34025; Tel 501-82-24011; Fax 501-82-24012; belize.usembassy.gov; Ambassador Vinai Thummalapally

Benin

Cotonou • Rue Caporal Bernard Anani; B.P. 2012; Tel 229-21-300650; Fax 229-21-300384; cotonou.usembassy.gov; Ambassador James Knight

Bermuda

Hamilton • 16 Middle Rd.; Devonshire DV 03; Tel 441-29-51342; Fax 441-29-51592; Consul General Grace Shelton

Bolivia

La Paz• Ave. Arce #2780; APO AA 34032; Tel 591-22-168000; Fax 591-22-168111; bolivia.usembassy.gov; Charge d'Affaires John S. Creamer

Bosnia-Herzegovina

Sarajevo • Alipasina 43; 71000; Tel 387-33-445700; Fax 387-33-659722; sarajevo.usembassy.gov; Ambassador Patrick S. Moon

Botswana

Gaborone • P.O. Box 90; Tel 267-39-53982; Fax 267-39-56947; botswana.usembassy.gov; Ambassador Stephen J. Nolan

Brazil

Brasilia • SES Avenida das Nacoes 801; Lote 3; 70403-900; Unit 3500; APO AA 34030; Tel 5561-33-127000; Fax 5561-33-127676; brasilia.usembassy.gov; Ambassador Thomas A. Shannon Jr.

Brunei

Bandar Seri Begawan • Third Floor-Teck Guan Plaza; Jalan Sultan; Unit 4280 Box 40; FPO AP 96507; Tel 673-22-29670; Fax 673-22-25293; bandar.usembassy.gov; vacant

Bulgaria

Sofia • 16 Kozyak St.; 1407; Tel 359-29-375100; Fax 359-29-375320; bulgaria.usembassy.gov; Ambassador James B. Warlick Jr.

Burkina Faso

Ouagadougou • 622 Avenue Raoul Follereau, Koulouba Sector 4; Tel 226-50-306723; Fax 226-50-312368; ouagadougou.usembassy.gov; Ambassador Thomas Dougherty

Burma

Rangoon • 110 University Ave.; Box B; APO AP 96546; Tel 95-15-36509; Fax 95-16-50480; rangoon.usembassy.gov; Charge d'Affaires Larry M. Dinger

Burundi

Bujumbura • Avenue des Etas-Unis; B.P. 1720; Tel 257-22-207000; Fax 257-22-222926; burundi.usembassy.gov; Ambassador Pamela J.H. Slutz

Cambodia

Phnom Penh • #1 St. 96; Unit 8166; Box P; APO AP 96546; Tel 855-23-728000; Fax 855-23-728600; cambodia.usembassy.gov; Ambassador Carol A. Rodley

Cameroon

Yaounde • 6.050 ave Rosa Parks; BP 817; Tel 237-22-201500; yaounde.usembassy.gov; Ambassador Robert P. Jackson

Canada

Ottawa, Ontario • 490 Sussex Dr.; K1N 1G8; P.O. Box 866; Ogdensburg; NY 13669; Tel 613-68-85335; Fax 613-68-83082; ottawa.usembassy.gov; Ambassador David Jacobsen

Cape Verde, Republic of

Praia • Rua Abilio Macedo No. 6 Plateau; Tel 238-26-08900; Fax 238-26-11355; praia.usembassy.gov; Charge d'Affaires Dana Brown

Central African Republic

Bangui • Avenue David Dacko; P.O. Box 924; Tel 236-21-610200; Fax 236-21-614494; bangui.usembassy.gov; Ambassador Laurence D. Wohlers

Chad

N'Djamena • Ave. Felix Eboue; B.P. 413; Tel 235-25-16211; Fax 235-25-15654; ndjamena.usembassy.gov; Ambassador Mark Boulware

Chile

Santiago • Av. Andres Bello 2800; APO AA 34033; Tel 562-33-03000; Fax 562-33-03710; santiago.usembassy.gov; Ambassador Alejandro D. Wolff

China

Beijing • No. 55 An Jia Lou Lu 100600; PSC 461; Box 50; FPO AP 96521; Tel 8610-85-313000; Fax 8610-85-314200; beijing.usembassy.gov; Ambassador Jon Huntsman

Colombia

Bogota • Cra. 45 No. 24B-27; APO AA 34038; Tel 571-31-50811; Fax 571-31-52197; bogota.usembassy.gov; Ambassador P. Michael McKinley

Congo, Democratic Republic of

Kinshasa • 310 Ave. des Aviateurs; Kin-Gombe; APO AE 09828; Tel 2438-15-560151; Fax 2438-15-560175; kinshasa.usembassy.gov; Ambassador James P. Entwistle

Congo, Republic of the

Brazzaville • BDEAC Building 4th Floor; APO AE 09828; Tel 24-28-11481; brazzaville.usembassy.gov; Ambassador Allan W. Eastham

Costa Rica

San Jose • Pavas; San Jose; Unit 2501; APO AA 34020; Tel 506-25-192000; Fax 506-25-192305; sanjose.usembassy.gov; Ambassador Anne Slaughter Andrew

Cote d'Ivoire

Abidjan • Riviera Golf; 01 BP 1712; Tel 225-22-494000; Fax 225-22-494323; abidjan.usembassy.gov; Ambassador Phillip Carter III

Croatia

Zagreb • Thomasa Jeffersona 2; Tel 385-16-612200; Fax 385-16-612373; zagreb.usembassy.gov; Ambassador James B. Foley

Cuba

Havana • (USINT) Swiss Embassy; Calzada entre L & M; Vedado; Tel 537-83-33551; Fax 537-83-32095; havana.usint.gov; Chief of Mission Jonathan D. Farrar

Cyprus

Nicosia • Metochiou and Ploutarchou Sts.; PSC 815; FPO AE 09836; Tel 357-22-393939; Fax 357-22-780944; nicosia.usembassy.gov; Ambassador Frank Urbancic

Czech Republic

Prague • Trziste 15; 11801 Prague 1; Unit 5630 Box 1000; APO AE 09727; Tel 4202-57-022000; Fax 4202-57-022809; prague.usembassy.gov; Ambassador Joseph Pennington

Denmark

Copenhagen • Dag Hammarskjolds Alle 24; 2100; PSC 73; APO AE 09716,; Tel 453-34-17100; Fax 453-54-30223; denmark.usembassy.gov; Ambassador Laurie S. Fulton

Djibouti, Republic of

Djibouti • Plateau du Serpent; Blvd. Marechal Joffre; B.P. 185; Tel 25-33-53995; Fax 25-33-53940; djibouti.usembassy.gov; Ambassador James Swan

Dominican Republic

Santo Domingo • Corner of Calle Cesar Nicolas Penson & Calle Leopoldo Navarro; Unit 5500; APO AA 34041-5500; Tel 809-22-12171; Fax 809-68-67437; santodomingo.usembassy.gov; Ambassador Raul H. Yzaguirre

East Timor

Dili • Av. de Portugal; Pantai Kelapa; Unit 8129 Box D; APO AP 96520; Tel 670-33-24684; Fax 670-33-13206; Ambassador Judith Fergin

Ecuador

Quito • Ave. Avigiras E12-170 y Ave. Eloy Alfaro; APO AA 34039; Tel 593-23-985000; spanish.ecuador.usembassy.gov; Ambassador Heather Hodges

Egypt

Cairo • (North Gate) 8; Kamal El-Din Salah St.; Garden City; Unit 64900; APO AE 09839-4900; Tel 202-27-973300; Fax 202-27-973200; cairo.usembassy.gov; Ambassador Margaret Scobey

El Salvador

San Salvador • Blvd. Santa Elena; Antiguo Cuscatlan; Unit 3116; APO AA 34023; Tel 503-25-012999; Fax 503-25-012150; sansalvador.usembassy.gov; Ambassador Mari Carmen Aponte

Equatorial Guinea

Malabo • Carretera de Aeropuerto; KM-3 El Paraiso; Apt. 95; Tel 24-00-98895; Fax 24-00-98894; malabo.usembassy.gov; Ambassador Alberto M. Fernandez

Eritrea

Asmara • 179 Alaa St.; P.O. Box 211; Tel 291-11-20004; Fax 291-11-27584; eritrea.usembassy.gov; Charge d'Affaires Joel Reifman

Estonia

Tallin • Kentmanni 20; 15099; PSC 78 Box T; APO AE 09723; Tel 372-66-88100; Fax 372-66-88265; estonia.usembassy.gov; Ambassador Michael C. Polt

Ethiopia

Addis Ababa • Entoto St.; P.O. Box 1014; Tel 2511-15-174000; Fax 2511-15-174001; ethiopia.usembassy.gov; Ambassador Donald Booth

Fiji

Suva • 31 Loftus St.; Tel 679-33-14466; Fax 679-33-02267; suva.usembassy.gov; Ambassador C. Steven McGann

Finland

Helsinki • Itainen Puistotie 14B; 00140; PSC 78; Box H; APO AE 09723; Tel 358-96-16250; Fax 3589-61-625135; finland.usembassy.gov; Ambassador Bruce J. Oreck

France

Paris • 2 Avenue Gabriel; 75382 Paris Cedex 08; PSC 116; APO AE 09777-5000; Tel 331-43-122222; Fax 331-42-669783; france.usembassy.gov; Ambassador Charles H. Rivkin

Gabon

Libreville • Blvd. Du Bord de Mer; B.P. 4000; Tel 24-17-62003; Fax 24-17-45507; libreville.usembassy.gov; Ambassador Eric D. Benjaminson

The Gambia

Banjul • Fajara; Kairaba Ave.; Tel 220-43-92856; Fax 220-43-92475; banjul.usembassy.gov; Ambassador Pamela White

Georgia

Tbilsi • 11 George Balanchine St. 0131; Unit 7060; APO AE 09742; Tel 995-32-277000; Fax 995-32-532310; georgia.usembassy.gov; Ambassador John R. Bass

Germany, Federal Republic of

Berlin • Pariser Platz 2 4-5; 10017; PSC 120; Box 1000; APO AE 09265; Tel 49-30-83050; germany.usembassy.gov; Ambassador Philip D. Murphy

Ghana

Accra • No. 24 4th Circular Rd Cantonments; Tel 233-21-741150; Fax 233-21-741692; ghana.usembassy.gov; Ambassador Donald G. Teitelbaum

Greece

Athens • 91 Vasillissis Sophias Ave.; 10160; PSC 108 Box 11 APO AE 09842; Tel 3021-07-212951; athens.usembassy.gov; Ambassador Daniel Bennett Smith

Grenada

St. George's • Lance Aux Epines; Tel 473-44-41173; Fax 473-44-44820; Charge d'Affaires Brent Hardt

Guatemala

Guatemala City • 7-01 Reforma; Zone 10; APO AA 34024; Tel 502-23-264000; Fax 502-23-264654; guatemala.usembassy.gov; Ambassador Stephen G. McFarland

Guinea

Conakry • Transversale No. 2; Ratoma; P.O. Box 603; Tel 224-65-104000; Fax 224-65-104297; conakry.usembassy.gov; Ambassador Patricia Newton Moller

Guinea-Bissau

See Senegal

Guyana

Georgetown • 100 Young and Duke Sts.; Tel 592-22-54900; Fax 592-22-58497; georgetown.usembassy.gov; vacant

Haiti

Port-Au-Prince • Tabarre 41; Tel 509-22-98000; Fax 509-22-98028; haiti.usembassy.gov; Ambassador Kenneth H. Merten

The Holy See

Vatican City • Via delle Terme Deciane 26; Rome 00153; PSC 59; Box 66; APO AE 09624; Tel 3906-46-743428; Fax 390-65-758346; vatican.usembassy.gov; Ambassador Dr. Miguel Humberto Diaz

Honduras

Tegucigalpa • Avenida La Paz; Postal 3453; Tel 504-23-69320; Fax 504-23-69037; honduras.usembassy.gov; Ambassador Hugo Llorens

Hong Kong

Hong Kong • 26 Garden Rd.; PSC 461; Box 1; FPO AP 96521; Tel 852-25-239011; Fax 852-28-451598; hongkong.usconsulate.gov; Consul General Stephen M. Young

Hungary

Budapest • 1054 Szabadsag Ter 12; Unit 5270 Box 40; APO AE 09731; Tel 361-47-54400; Fax 361-47-54764; hungary.usembassy. gov; Ambassador Eleni Tsakopoulos Kounalakis

Iceland

Reykjavik • Laufasvegur 21; Tel 354-56-29100; Fax 354-56-29118; iceland.usembassy.gov; Ambassador Luis E. Arreaga

India

New Delhi • Shanti Path; Chanakaya Puri 110021; Tel 9111-24-198000; Fax 9111-24-190017; newdelhi.usembassy.gov; Ambassador Timothy J. Roemer

Indonesia

Jakarta • Jl Merdeka Selatan 4-5; 10110; Box 8129; FPO AP 96520; Tel 6221-34-359000; Fax 6221-34-359922; jakarta. usembassy.gov; Ambassador Scott Marciel

Iraq

Baghdad • APO AE 09316; Tel iraq.usembassy.gov; Ambassador James F. Jeffrey

Ireland

Dublin • 41 Elgin Rd.; Ballsbridge; Tel 353-16-688777; Fax 353-16-689946; dublin.usembassy.gov; Ambassador Daniel Rooney

Ireland, Northern

Belfast • (CG) Danesfort House; 223 Stranmillis Rd.; BT95GR; Unit 8400; Box 40; APO AE 09498-4040; Tel 4428-90-386100; Fax 4428-90-681301; usembassy.org.uk/nireland; Consul General Kamala S. Lakhdhir

Israel

Tel Aviv • 71 Hayarkon St.; APO AE 09830; Tel 972-35-197575; Fax 972-35-173227; telaviv.usembassy.gov; Ambassador James B. Cunningham

Italy

Rome • Via Vittorio Veneto 121-00187; PSC 59; Box 100; APO AE 09624; Tel 39-06-46741; Fax 3906-46-742244; rome.usembassy. gov; Ambassador David Thorne

Jamaica

Kingston • 142 Old Hope Rd.; Tel 876-70-26000; Fax 876-70-26001; kingston.usembassy.gov; Ambassador Pamela Bridgewater

Japan

Tokyo • 10-5; Akasaka 1-chome; Minato-ku 107-8420; Unit 45004; Box 258; APO AP 96337-5004; Tel 813-32-245000; Fax 813-35-051862; tokyo.usembassy.gov; Ambassador John V. Roos

Jordan

Amman • P.O. Box 354; Amman 11118,; APO AE 09892; Tel 962-65-906000; Fax 962-65-920121; amman.usembassy.gov; Ambassador Robert Stephen Beecroft

Kazakstan

Astana • 23-22 S. No.3; Ak Bulak 4 010010; Tel 771-72-702100; Fax 771-72-340890; www.usembassy.kz.; Ambassador Richard E. Hoagland

Kenya

Nairobi • United Nations Ave.; P.O. Box 606 00621; APO AE 09831-4100; Tel 2542-03-636000; Fax 2542-03-633410, nairobi. usembassy.gov; Ambassador Michael E. Ranneberger

Korea

Seoul • 32 Sejongno; Jongno-gu; Seoul 110-710; Unit 15550; APO AP 96205-5550; Tel 822-39-74114; Fax 822-73-88845; seoul. usembassy.gov; Ambassador Kathleen Stephens

Kuwait

Kuwait • P.O. Box 77; Safat 13001; PSC 1280; Unit 69000 APO AE 09880-9000; Tel 965-22-591001; Fax 965-25-380282; kuwait. usembassy.gov; Ambassador Deborah K. Jones

Kyrgyz Republic

Bishkek • 171 Prospekt Mira; 720016; Tel 9963-12-551241; Fax 9963-12-551264; kyrgyz.usembassy.gov; Ambassador Tatiana C. Gfoeller

Laos

Vientiane • Rue Bartolonie; B.P. 114; Unit 8165; Box V; APO AP 96546; Tel 856-21-267000; Fax 856-21-267190; laos.usembassy. gov; Ambassador Karen B. Stewart

Latvia

Riga • Raina Boulevard 7; LV-1510; PSC 78; Box R; APO AE 09723; Tel 371-67-036200; Fax 371-67-820047; riga.usembassy.gov; Ambassador Judith G. Garber

Lebanon

Beirut • Antelias; P.O. Box 70-840; Tel 961-45-42600; Fax 961-45-44136; beirut.usembassy.gov; Ambassador Maura Connelly

Lesotho

Maseru • 254 Kingsway Ave.; 100; P.O. Box 333; Tel 266-22-312666; Fax 266-22-310116; maseru.usembassy.gov; Ambassador Michele T. Bond

Liberia

Monrovia • 111 United Nations Dr.; P.O. Box 98; Tel 231-77-054826; Fax 231-77-010370; monrovia.usembassy.gov; Ambassador Linda Thomas-Greenfield

Lithuania

Vilnius • Akmenu 6; LT-03106; PSC 78; Box V; APO AE 09723; Tel 370-52-665500; Fax 370-52-665510; vilnius.usembassy.gov; Ambassador Anne E. Derse

Luxembourg

Luxembourg • 22 Blvd. Emmanuel-Servais; 2535; Unit 1410; APO AE 09126-1410; Tel 35-24-60123; Fax 35-24-61401; luxembourg.usembassy.gov; Ambassador Cynthia Stroum

Macedonia, Republic of

Skopje • str. Samoilova Nr. 21; Unit 7120; Box 1000 APO AE 09737; Tel 389-23-102000; Fax 389-23-102499; macedonia.usembassy.gov; Ambassador Philip T. Reeker

Madagascar

Antananarivo • 14-16 Rue Rainitovo; Antsahavola 101 B.0.; Tel 2612-02-221257; Fax 2612-02-234539; antananarivo.state.gov; Charge d'Affaires Eric W. Stromayer

Malawi

Lilongwe • 16 Jomo; Kenyatta Rd.; P.O. Box 30016; Tel 265-17-73166; Fax 265-17-70471; lilongwe.usembassy.gov; vacant

Malaysia

Kuala Lumpur • 376 Jalan Tun Razak; 50400; APO AP 96535-8152; Tel 603-21-685000; Fax 603-21-422207; malaysia.usembassy.gov; Ambassador Paul W. Jones

Mali

Bamako • ACI 2000; Rue 243; Porte 297; Tel 223-20-702300; Fax 223-20-702479; mali.usembassy.gov; Ambassador Gillian Milovanovic

Malta

Valletta • 3 St. Anne's St.; Floriana; P.O. Box 535; CMR 01; Tel 356-25-614000; Fax 356-21-243229; malta.usembassy.gov; Ambassador Douglas W. Kmiec

Marshall Islands, Republic of

Majuro • PO Box 1379; 96960; Dept. of State; 4380 Majuro Pl; Washington; DC 20521-4380; Tel 692-24-74011; Fax 692-24-74012; majuro.usembassy.gov; Ambassador Martha L. Campbell

Mauritania

Nouakchott • 228 Rue Abdallaye; 42-100; B.P. 222; Tel 222-52-52660; Fax 222-52-51592; mauritania.usembassy.gov; Ambassador Jo Ellen Powell

Mauritius

Port Louis • Rogers House 4th Flr.; P.O. Box 544; Tel 230-20-24400; Fax 230-20-89534; mauritius.usembassy.gov; Ambassador Mary Jo Wills

Mexico

Mexico City; D.F. • Paseo de la Reforma 305; 06500 Mexico DF; P.O. Box 9000; Brownsville; TX 78520-0900; Tel 5255-50-802000; Fax 5255-55-119980; mexico.usembassy.gov; Ambassador Carlos Pascual

Micronesia

Kolonia • PO Box 1286; Pohnpei; Federated States of Micronesia 96941; Tel 691-32-02187; Fax 691-32-02186; kolonia.usembassy.gov; Ambassador Peter Prahar

Moldova

Chisinau • Strada Alexei Mateevici #103; 2009; Tel 373-22-408300; Fax 373-22-233044; moldova.usembassy.gov; Ambassador Asif J. Chaudhry

Mongolia

Ulaanbaatar • Micro District 11; Big Ring Rd; CPO 1021; PSC 461; Box 300; FPO AP 96521-0002; Tel 976-11-329095; Fax 976-13-20776; mongolia.usembassy.gov; Ambassador Jonathan Addleton

Montenegro

Podgorica • Ljubljanska bb; 81000; Tel 382-81-225417; Fax 382-81-241358; podgorica.usembassy.gov; Charge d'Affaires Bennett Y. Lowenthal

Morocco

Rabat • 2 Ave. Mohamed El Fassi; PSC 74; APO AE 09718; Tel 212-37-762265; Fax 212-37-769639; rabat.usembassy.gov; Ambassador Samuel P. Kaplan

Mozambique

Maputo • Avenida Kaunda 193; P.O. Box 783; Tel 258-21-492797; Fax 258-21-490114; maputo.usembassy.gov; Ambassador Leslie V. Rowe

Namibia

Windhoek • 14 Lossen Str.; PB12029; Tel 2646-12-958500; Fax 2646-12-958603; windhoek.usembassy.gov; Ambassador Wanda Nesbitt

Nepal

Kathmandu • Maharajgunj; Tel 977-14-007200; Fax 977-14-007272; nepal.usembassy.gov; Ambassador Scott H. DeLisi

Netherlands

The Hague • Lange Voorhout 102; 2514 EJ; PSC 71; APO AE 09715; Tel 317-03-102209; Fax 317-03-614688; thehague.usembassy.gov; Ambassador Fay Hartog Levin

Netherlands Antilles

Curacao • J.B. Gorsiraweg #1; Tel 599-94-613066; Fax 599-94-616489; curacao.usconsulate.gov; Consul General Valerie Belon

New Zealand

Wellington • 29 Fitzherbert Ter.; Thorndon; PSC 467; Box 1; APO AP 96531-1034; Tel 644-46-26000; Fax 644-49-90490; newzealand.usembassy.gov; Ambassador David Huebner

Nicaragua

Managua • Carretera Sur. KM 5.5; APO AA 34021; Tel 505-22-527100; Fax 505-22-527304; nicaragua.usembassy.gov; Ambassador Robert Callahan

Niger

Niamey • Rue Des Ambassades; B.P. 11201; Tel 227-20-733169; Fax 227-20-735560; niamey.usembassy.gov; Ambassador Bisa Williams

Nigeria

Abuja • Plot 1075; Diplomatic Drive; Central District; Tel 234-94-614000; Fax 234-94-614171; nigeria.usembassy.gov; Ambassador Terence P. McCulley

Norway

Oslo • Henrik Ibsens gate 48; 0244; PSC 69; Box 1000; APO AE 09707; Tel 472-13-08540; Fax 472-25-62751; norway.usembassy.gov; Ambassador Barry B. White

Oman

Muscat • P.O. Box 202; P.C. 115; Madinat Al Sultan Qaboos; Tel 968-24-643400; Fax 968-24-699771; oman.usembassy.gov; Ambassador Dr. Richard J. Schmierer

Pakistan

Islamabad • Diplomatic Enclave; Ramna 5; Unit 62200; APO AE 09812-2200; Tel 925-12-080000; Fax 925-12-276427; islamabad.usembassy.gov; Ambassador Cameron Munter

Palau

Koror • PO Box 6028; PW 96940; Tel 680-58-72920; Fax 680-58-72911; palau.usembassy.gov; Ambassador Helen Reed-Rowe

Panama

Panama • Edificio 783; Avenida Demetrio Basilio Lakas,; Unit 0945 APO AA 34002; Tel 507-20-77000; Fax 507-31-75568; panama.usembassy.gov; Ambassador Phyllis M. Powers

Papua New Guinea

Port Moresby • Douglas St.; P.O. Box 1492; APO AP 96553; Tel 675-32-11455; Fax 675-32-00637; portmoresby.usembassy.gov; Ambassador Teddy B. Taylor

Paraguay

Asuncion • 1776 Mariscal Lopez Ave.; Casilla Postal 402; Unit 4711; APO AA 34036; Tel 595-21-21371; Fax 595-21-213728; paraguay.usembassy.gov; Ambassador Liliana Ayalde

Peru

Lima • Avenida La Encalada Cdra 17-Surco; APO AA 34031-5000; Tel 511-43-43000; Fax 511-61-8239/; lima.usembassy.gov; Ambassador Rose M. Likins

Philippines

Manila • 1201 Roxas Rd..; PSC 500; APO AP 96515-1000; Tel 632-30-12000; Fax 632-30-12017; manila.usembassy.gov; Ambassador Harry J. Thomas Jr.

Poland

Warsaw • Aleje Ujazdowskie 29/31 540; Unit 5010; APO AE 09730; Tel 482-25-042000; Fax 482-25-042226; poland.usembassy.gov; Ambassador Lee A. Feinstein

Portugal

Lisbon • Av Forcas Armadas 1600-081; PSC 83; APO AE 09726; Tel 3512-17-273300; Fax 3512-17-269109; portugal.usembassy.gov; Ambassador Allan J. Katz

Qatar

Doha • 22 February St.; Al-Lu qta Dist.; Box 520; APO AE 09898; Tel 974-48-84101; Fax 974-48-84176; qatar.usembassy.gov; Ambassador Joseph Evan LeBaron

Romania

Bucharest • Tudor Arghezi 7-9; District 2; 020942; Dept. of State; 5260 Bucharest Pl; Washington; DC 20521-5260; Tel 402-12-003300; Fax 402-12-003442; bucharest.usembassy.gov; Ambassador Mark Gitenstein

Russia

Moscow • Bolshoy Devyatinskiy Pereulok No. 8; 121099; PSC 77; APO AE 09721; Tel 749-57-285000; Fax 749-57-285090; moscow.usembassy.gov; Ambassador John Beyrle

Rwanda

Kigali • 2657 Ave. de la Gendarmerie; Tel 25-05-96400; Fax 25-05-96591; rwanda.usembassy.gov; Ambassador Stuart Symington

Samoa

Apia • 5th Floor; ACB House; Metafele; PSC 467; Box 1; APO AP 96531-1034; Tel 6-85-21631; Fax 6-85-22030; samoa.usembassy.gov; Ambassador David Huebner

Saudi Arabia

Riyadh • Diplomatic Quarter; Unit 61307; APO AE 09803-1307; Tel 966-14-883800; Fax 966-14-887360; riyadh.usembassy.gov; Ambassador James B. Smith

Scotland

Edinburgh • (CG) 3 Regent Ter. EH7 5BW; PSC 801; Box E; FPO AE 09498-4040; Tel 4413-15-568315; Fax 4413-15-576023; london.usembassy.gov/scotland.; Consul General Dana M. Linnet

Senegal

Dakar • B.P. 49; Avenue Jean XXIII; Tel 2213-38-292100; Fax 2213-38-222991; dakar.usembassy.gov; Ambassador Marcia S. Bernicat

Serbia

Belgrade • Kneza Milosa 50; 11000; Tel 3811-13-619344; Fax 3811-13-618230; belgrade.usembassy.gov; Ambassador Mary Burce Warlick

Sierra Leone

Freetown • Southridge-Hill Station; Tel 232-22-515000; Fax 232-22-515225; freetown.usembassy.gov; Ambassador Michael S. Owen

Singapore

Singapore • 27 Napier Rd.; 258508; PSC Box 470; FPO AP 96507-0001; Tel 656-47-69100; Fax 656-47-69340; singapore.usembassy.gov; Ambassador David I. Adelman

Slovakia

Bratislava • P.O. Box 309; 814-99; Unit 5840; APO AE 09736; Tel 4212-54-433338; Fax 4212-54-418861; slovakia.usembassy.gov; Ambassador Theodore Sedgwick

Slovenia

Ljubljana • Presernova 31; 1000; Unit 7140; APO AE 09739; Tel 386-12-005500; Fax 386-12-005555; ljubljana.usembassy.gov; Ambassador Joseph A. Mussomeli

South Africa

Pretoria • 877 Pretorius St; Arcadia; Tel 271-24-314000; Fax 271-23-422299; southafrica.usembassy.gov; Ambassador Donald Gips

Spain

Madrid • Serrano 75; 28006; PSC 61; APO AE 09642; Tel 349-15-872200; Fax 349-15-872303; madrid.usembassy.gov; Ambassador Alan Solomont

Sri Lanka

Colombo • 210 Galle Rd.; Colombo 3; Tel 941-12-498500; Fax 941-12-437345; colombo.usembassy.gov; Ambassador Patricia A. Butenis

Sudan

Khartoum • Ali Abdel Latif St.; Unit 64105; P.O. Box 699; Tel 2491-87-016000; Fax 2491-83-774137; sudan.usembassy.gov; Ambassador Robert Whitehead

Suriname

Paramaribo • Dr. Sophie Redmondstraat 129; Tel 59-74-72900; Fax 59-74-10972; suriname.usembassy.gov; Ambassador John R. Nay

Swaziland

Mbabane • 7th Fl. Central Bank Bldg.; Warner St.; P.O. Box 199; Tel 268-40-46441; Fax 268-40-45959; swaziland.usembassy.gov; Ambassador Earl M. Irving

Sweden

Stockholm • Dag Hammarskjolds Vag 31; SE-115 89; Unit 5750; APO AE 09744; Tel 468-78-35300; Fax 468-66-11964; stockholm.usembassy.gov; Ambassador Matthew Barzum

Switzerland

Bern • Sulgeneckstrasse 19; CH-3007; Tel 413-13-577011; Fax 413-13-577344; bern.usembassy.gov; Ambassador Donald S. Beyer Jr.

Syria

Damascus • Al Mansour St. No. 2; P.O. Box 29; Unit 70200 Box D; APO AE 09892; Tel 96311-33-914444; Fax 96311-33-913999; damascus.usembassy.gov; Charge d'Affaires Chuck Hunter

Taiwan

Taipei • American Institute in Taiwan; #7 Lane 134; Xinyi Road; Section 3; 10659; Tel 8862-21-622000; Fax 8862-21-622251; ait.org.tw; Dir. William A. Stanton

Tajikistan

Dushanbe • 109-A Ismoili Somoni Ave.; 734019; Tel 9923-72-292000; Fax 9923-72-292050; dushanbe.usembassy.gov; Ambassador Kenneth E. Gross Jr.

Tanzania

Dar Es Salaam • 686 Old Bagamoyo Rd.; P.O. Box 9123; Tel 2552-22-668460; Fax 2552-22-668421; tanzania.usembassy.gov; Ambassador Alfonso E. Lenhardt

Thailand

Bangkok • 120/122 Wireless Rd.; 10330; APO AP 96546; Tel 662-20-54000; Fax 662-20-54306; bangkok.usembassy.gov; Ambassador Eric John

Togo

Lome • 4332 Boulevard Gnassingbe Eyadema; BP 852; Tel 228-26-15470; Fax 228-26-15501; togo.usembassy.gov; Ambassador Patricia Hawkins

Trinidad & Tobago

Port-Of-Spain • 15 Queen's Park West; P.O. Box 752; Tel 868-62-26371; Fax 868-82-25905; trinidad.usembassy.gov; Ambassador Beatrice Wilkinson Welters

Tunisia

Tunis • Les Berges du Lac 1053; Unit 6360 APO AE 09734; Tel 216-71-107000; Fax 216-71-963263; tunis.usembassy.gov; Ambassador Gordon Gray

Turkey

Ankara • 110 Ataturk Bulvari; PSC 93; Box 5000; APO AE 09823; Tel 9031-24-555555; Fax 9031-24-670019; ankara.usembassy.gov; Charge d'Affaires Douglas A. Silliman

Turkmenistan

Ashgabat • 9 1984 St.; Tel 993-12-350045; Fax 993-12-392614; turkmenistan.usembassy.gov; Charge d'Affaires Eileen A. Malloy

Uganda

Kampala • 1577 Ggaba Rd.; P.O. Box 7007; Tel 2564-14-259791; Fax 2564-14-259794; kampala.usembassy.gov; Ambassador Jerry P. Lanier

Ukraine

Kyiv • 4 Hlybochtska; Tel 3804-44-904000; Fax 3804-44-904085; kyiv.usembassy.gov; Ambassador John F. Tefft

United Arab Emirates

Abu Dhabi • Al-Sudan St.; P.O. Box 4009; Unit 6010; APO AE 09825; Tel 971-24-142200; Fax 971-24-142575; uae.usembassy.gov; Ambassador Michele Sison

United Kingdom

London, England • 24 Grosvenor Sq.; W1A 1AE; Unit 8400; FPO AE 09498-4040; Tel 4420-74-999000; Fax 4420-76-299124; london.usembassy.gov; Ambassador Louis B. Susman

United States

U.S. Mission to the United Nations • 140 E. 45th St.; New York; NY 10017; Tel 212-41-54000; Fax 212-41-54443; usunnewyork.usmission.gov; Ambassador Susan E. Rice

Uruguay

Montevideo • Lauro Muller 1776; APO AA 34035; Tel 598-24-187777; Fax 598-24-188611; montevideo.usembassy.gov; Ambassador David D. Nelson

Uzbekistan

Tashkent • 82 Chilanzarskaya; Tel 9987-11-205450; Fax 9987-11-206335; www.usembassy.uz.; Ambassador Richard B. Norland

Venezuela

Caracas • Calle F con Calle Suapure; Colinas de Valle Arriba; APO AA 34037; Tel 5821-29-756411; Fax 5821-29-078106; venezuela.usembassy.gov; Charge d'Affaires John Caufield

Vietnam

Hanoi • 7 Lang Ha St.; Dong Da Dist; PSC 461; Box 400; FPO AP 96521-0002; Tel 844-38-505000; Fax 844-38-505010; vietnam.usembassy.gov; Ambassador Michael W. Michalak

Yemen

Sanaa • Sa'Awan St.; P.O. Box 22347; Tel 967-17-552000; Fax 967-13-03182; yemen.usembassy.gov; Ambassador Gerald Michael Feierstein

Zambia

Lusaka • Corner of Independence and United Nations Aves.; P.O. Box 31617; Tel 2602-11-250955; Fax 2602-11-252225; zambia.usembassy.gov; Ambassador Mark C. Storella

Zimbabwe

Harare • 172 Herbert Chitepo Ave.; P.O. Box 3340; Tel 263-42-50593; Fax 263-47-96488; harare.usembassy.gov; Ambassador Charles A. Ray

Notes

Yellow Pages Directory

2011 Directory of Services and Products

Advertising

All Seasons Communications

Beth Monicatti-Blank
5455 34 Mile Rd. • P.O. Box 100
Romeo, MI 48065
(586) 752-6381 • Fax (586) 752-6539
bmonicattiblank@allseasons
communications.com
www.allseasonscommunications.com

Atlas Advertising

Guillermo Mazier
2601 Blake St., Ste. 301
Denver, CO 80205
(303) 292-3300
guillermom@atlas-advertising.com
www.atlas-advertising.com

City Magnet

Rodger Corfield
P.O. Box 529
Sunrise Beach, MO 65079
(573) 374-6200 • (800) 600-6200
www.citymagnetinc.com

Fox Pro Media

Greg Fox
P.O. Box 23049
Metairie, LA 70123
(800) 841-9532
info@foxpromedia.com
www.foxpromedia.com

Signs Manufacturing & Maintenance Corp.

James Watson
4610 Mint Way
Dallas, TX 75236
(214) 339-2227 • (800) 333-7137
Fax (214) 339-9987
Sales@SignsManufacturing.com
www.SignsManufacturing.com

The FMH Company

Barbara Barnard
29117 Shorecliff Dr.
Lake Elsinore, CA 92530
(951) 245-7919
Fax (951) 245-3494
www.fmhco.com

Advertising Specialties

Ads R Us

Lana Schippers
4600 S.W. 9th St.
Des Moines, IA 50315
(515) 287-6633 • (800) 607-0494
Fax (800) 657-6115
lana@adsrus.com
www.theplacematpeople.com

Nationwide Advertising Specialty Co.

2025 S. Cooper St.
Arlington, TX 76010
(817) 275-2678
Fax (817) 274-4301
sales@nationwideadvertising.net
www.nationwideadvertising.net

Southwest Mobile Media

Alan K. Varner
405 Hudson St.
Albuquerque, NM 87109
(800) 874-4058
Fax (505) 891-8742
alan@southwestmobilemedia.com
www.southwestmobilemedia.com

Universal Adcom

2921 Ave. E
Arlington, TX 76011
(817) 633-3300 • (800) 778-2578
www.universalad.com

Arts

ArtsBoston

31 St. James Ave., Ste. 360
Boston, MA 02116
(617) -262-8632
Fax (617) 262-8633
info@artsboston.org
www.artsboston.org

Loveland High Plains Art Council

125 E. 7th St. • P.O. Box 7006
Loveland, CO 80537
(970) 663-2940
Fax (970) 669-7390
lhpac@sculptureinthepark.org
www.sculptureinthepark.org
See our ad on page 2

Banners

Arnett Marketing

Betty Arnett
2137 Zercher Rd.
San Antonio, TX 78209
(210) 826-9700 • (866) 826-9700
Fax (210) 826-9084
arnettmk@swbell.net
www.arnettmarketing.com

Kalamazoo Banner Works

2129 Portage St.
Kalamazoo, MI 49001
(269) 388-4532 • (800) 525-6424
Fax (269) 388-2018
info@consort.com
www.kalamazoobanner.com

Main Street Designs Inc.

860 Downs Rd.
Champlin, MN 55316
(763) 433-9120 • (800) 775-3039
Fax (763) 506-0860
information@mainstreetdesigns.com
www.mainstreetdesigns.com

Rocket Banner

319 N.Briery Rd.
Irving, TX 75061
(972) 790-8571
banners@rocketbanner.com
www.rocketbanner.com

Business Development

Get Social! Get Business!

916 41st Ave.
Gulfport, MS 39501
(847) 894-6577
getsocialgetbusiness@gmail.com
www.social-media-and-business.com

The Strategic Point

Joshua Ramsey
2338 Irving Blvd.
Dallas, TX 75207
info@thestrategicpoint.com
www.thestrategicpoint.com

Business Services

BNA Plus

1801 S. Bell St.
Arlington, VA 22202
(800) 372-1033
bnaplus@bna.com
www.bnaplus.com

Constant Training

Joe Constance
640 S. Lakeshore Blvd.
Marquette, MI 49855
(906) 228-8300
Fax (906) 228-8300
joe@constanttraining.com
www.constanttraining.com

Corporate Investigations Inc.

2275 Swallow Hill Rd., Bldg. 500
Pittsburgh, PA 15220
(412) 429-2400 • (800) 600-0244
Fax (412) 429-2410
customerservice@ciilink.com
www.ciilink.com

HR On Call

Dick Clark
821 W. Louise Ave.
Morristown, TN 37813
(423) 327-5270
dickclark@hroncall.net
www.hroncall.net

IC Solutions Inc.

15 Holly St., Ste. 202
Scarborough, ME 04074
(207) 883-8696 • (877) 895-8655
Fax (207) 883-8554
info@icsic.com
www.icsic.com

On the Move Trucks Inc.

28825 I 10 W.
Boerne, TX 78006
(800) 645-9949
Fax (830) 755-2484
sales@onthemovetrucks.com
www.onthemovetrucks.com

Chamber Awards/Badges

Archie's Awards by Connie Inc.

688 N.E. 125th St.
North Miami, FL 33161
(305) 891-2442
Fax (305) 891-2429
archielegacy@aol.com
www.archiesawardsbyconnie.com

Parker Systems Inc.

20989 Middleton Dr.
Lake Zurich, IL 60047
(847) 726-8600 • (800) 253-5100
Fax (847) 726-8610
sales@parkersystems.com
www.parkersystems.com

Christmas Decorations

All American Christmas Co.

Steve Broyles
384 Broyles St. • P.O. Box 208
Sparta, TN 38583
(931) 836-1212
Fax (931) 836-2002
info@aachristmas.com
www.aachristmas.com

American Christmas Inc.

30 Warren Pl.
Mount Vernon, NY 10550
(914) 663-0660
Fax (914) 663-0700
magic@americanxmas.com
www.americanxmas.com

Arnett Marketing

Betty Arnett
2137 Zercher Rd.
San Antonio, TX 78209
(210) 826-9700 • (866) 826-9700
Fax (210) 826-9084
arnettmk@swbell.net
www.arnettmarketing.com

Brandano Displays Inc.

2000 Banks Rd., Ste. 212
Margate, FL 33063
(800) 777-6903
information@brandano.com
www.brandano.com

Dixie Decorations

355 Industrial Park
P.O. Box 81
Montevallo, AL 35115
(205) 665-1225 • (800) 423-4260
Fax (205) 665-1263
dixiedecorations@bellsouth.net
www.dixiedecorations.com

GP Designs

318 E. 12th St.
Marion, IN 46953
(800) 888-3833
sales@gpdesigns.biz
www.gpdesigns.biz

Temple Display Ltd.

P.O. Box 965
Oswego, IL 60543
(800) 722-2501
sales@templedisplay.com
www.templedisplay.com

Computer Software

Chamber Data Systems Inc.

JoAnn McDonough
15221 Berry Trl., Ste. 507
Dallas, TX 75248
(972) 233-1299
cdsi@chamberdata.com
www.chamberdata.com

ChamberMaster

14391 Edgewood Dr.
Baxter, MN 56425
(218) 825-9200 • (800) 825-9171
Fax (360) 350-4787
info@chambermaster.com
www.chambermaster.com

ChamberWare Systems

24328 Highlander Rd.
West Hills, CA 91307
(818) 999-0700
info@chamberware.com
www.chamberware.com

Internet Destination Sales Systems

250 Marquette Ave. S., Ste. 1330
Minneapolis, MN 55401
(612) 767-7800 • (800) 913-4377
Fax (612) 339-3337
info@idss.com
www.idss.com

Steve Boyle & Associates Inc.

P.O. Box 225
Broken Arrow, OK 74013
(800) 324-7355
Fax (800) 324-7350
info@sbainc.net
www.sbainc.net

YourMembership.com Inc.

300 First Ave. S., Ste. 300
St. Petersburg, FL 33701
(727) 827-0046
www.yourmembership.com

Decals

Designery Sign Company

927 W. Hatcher Rd.
Phoenix, AZ 85021-3173
(602) 943-9000 • (866) 660-7446
Fax (602) 943-9123
information@designerysigns.com
www.designerysigns.com

D-LUX Screen Printing Inc.

302 N. Star Rd.
P.O. Box 127
Holmen, WI 54636-0127
(608) 526-3783 • (800) 331-9061
Fax (608) 526-3161
maureena@d-lux.com
www.d-lux.com

Leland Co. Ltd.

Alan Hudson
827 Rte. 44 • P.O. Box 219
Brownsville, VT 05037
(800) 451-4164
www.lelandcompany.com

Ultimate Decals

808 W. Dallas, Ste. B
Conroe, TX 77301
(936) 539-5719
Fax (936) 539-5752
info@ultimatedecals.com
www.ultimatedecals.com

Direct Marketing

Ballatine Corp.

Ryan Cote
1700 Rte. 23 N.
Wayne, NJ 07470
(973) 305-1500
Fax (973) 305-1561
www.ballatine.com

Creative Marketing

703 N. Llano St.
Fredericksburg, TX 78624
(830) 997-8515
creative@ktc.com

Data Marketing Inc.

P.O. Box 519
Santa Clara, CA 95052
(408) 275-8300
www.datamarketing.com

Modern Postcard

1675 Faraday Ave.
Carlsbad, CA 92008
(760) 431-7084 • (800) 959-8365
Fax (760) 268-1730
customercare@modernpostcard.com
www.modernpostcard.com

Red Clay Media

33 W. 8th St.
Bayonne, NJ 07002
(866) 733-5478
www.redclaymedia.com

Tailored Data Source Inc.

1N141 County Farm Rd., Ste. 200
Winfield, IL 60190
(630) 580-5856
Fax (630) 580-5864
info@tailoreddatasource.com
www.tailoreddatasource.com

The Kennickell Group

Al Kennickell
1700 E. President St.
Savannah, GA 31404
(912) 233-4532 • (800) 673-6455
Fax (912) 232-1360
sales@kennickell.com
www.thekennickellgroup.com

Directory Publishers

Atlantic Communications Group Inc.

Hayden M. Wilbur
18 E. Mill Rd.
Flourtown, PA 19031-2027
(800) 832-3747
Fax (800) 599-6420
www.atlantic4us.com

Century Publishing

12120 Tech Center Dr., Ste. B
Poway, CA 92064
(858) 486-7700 • (800) 649-1086
Fax (858) 486-7900
info@centurypublishing.com
www.centurypublishing.com

Community Matters Inc.

Layne Mullin
P.O. Box 5900
Frisco, TX 75035
(972) 370-1778 • (800) 380-2450
Fax (972) 370-1766
info@communitymattersinc.com
www.communitymattersinc.com

Novo Print USA

1845 N. Farwell Ave., Ste. 210
Milwaukee, WI 53202
(414) 732-2053
info@novoprint.com
www.novoprint.com

Towns & Associates Inc.

126 Water St.
Baraboo, WI 53913
(608) 356-8757
Fax (608) 356-8875
towns@townsandassociates.com
www.townsandassociates.com

Displays-Outdoors

Display Sales

10925 Nesbitt Ave. S.
Bloomington, MN 55437
(952) 885-0100 • (800) 328-6195
Fax (952) 885-0099
sales@displaysales.com
www.displaysales.com

Kalamazoo Banner Works

2129 Portage St.
Kalamazoo, MI 49001
(269) 388-4532 • (800) 525-6424
Fax (269) 388-2018
info@consort.com
www.kalamazoobanner.com

Liberty Flag & Specialty Co.

P.O. Box 398
Reedsburg, WI 53959
(608) 524-2834 • (800) 274-7001
Fax (608) 524-8238
www.liberty-flag.com

Northeast Flags

1028 Springfield Ave.
Mountainside, NJ 07092-2905
(888) 473-5244
Fax (908) 518-0591
www.northeastflags.com

Signs Manufacturing & Maintenance Corp.

James Watson
4610 Mint Way
Dallas, TX 75236
(214) 339-2227 • (800) 333-7137
Fax (214) 339-9987
Sales@SignsManufacturing.com
www.SignsManufacturing.com

Economic Marketing & Tourism Marketing/Sales

Development Counsellors Intl.

215 Park Ave. S., 10th Flr.
New York, NY 10003
(212) 725-0707
Fax (212) 725-2254
andy.levine@dc-intl.com
www.dc-intl.com

Economic Research

American Institute for Economic Research

250 Division St.
P.O. Box 1000
Great Barrington, MA 01230-1000
(888) 528-1216
Fax (413) 528-0103
info@aier.org
www.aier.org

Economic Research Institute

8575-164th Ave. N.E., Ste. 100
Redmond, WA 98052
(425) 556-0205 • (800) 627-3697
Fax (800) 753-4415
info.eri@erieri.com
www.erieri.com

Impact Data Source

4709 Cape Rock Dr.
Austin, TX 78735
(800) 813-6267
Fax (512) 892-2569
jwalker@impactdatasource.com
www.impactdatasource.com

New Landmark Group

563 Main St.
Bolton, MA 01740
(978) 779-0737
Fax (978) 779-0738
info@newlandmarkgroup.com
www.newlandmarkgroup.com

Entertainment

All Time Favorites Inc.

P.O. Box 211533
St. Paul, MN 55121
(651) 454-1124 • (800) 232-6874
Fax (612) 454-1807
www.alltimefavorites.com

Buddy Lee Attractions Inc.

38 Music Sq. E., Ste. 300
Nashville, TN 37203
(615) 244-4336
www.buddyleeattractions.com

Center Stage Artists

P.O. Box 7023
Ann Arbor, MI 48107
(734) 662-9137 • (800) 650-8742
Fax (734) 662-8733
info@centerstageartists.com
www.centerstageartists.com

Event Productions & Management

P.O. Box 3641
Milton, FL 32572
(850) 983-9519 • (800) 844-9173
Fax (850) 983-9579
stageforrent@aol.com
www.stageforrent.com

Kelly Miller Circus

2579 E. Kirk Rd.
Hugo, OK 74743
(580) 326-9229
Fax (580) 326-5530
bigtop@kellymillercircus.com
www.kellymillercircus.com

Thomas Cassidy Inc.

11761 E. Speedway Blvd.
Tucson, AZ 85748
(520) 751-4751
Fax (520) 882-0187
susan@americasmusicagency.com
www.americasmusicagency.com

Variety Attractions

P.O. Box 3330
Zanesville, OH 43702
(740) 453-0394
Fax (740) 453-4087
info@varietyattractions.com
www.varietyattractions.com

Executive Search

DRG

130 E. 40th St., Ste. 800
New York, NY 10016
(212) 983-1600
Fax (212) 983-1687
search@drgnyc.com
www.drgnyc.com

execSearches.com

2011 N. Ocean Blvd., Ste. 804
Fort Lauderdale, FL 33305
(888) 238-6611
Fax (954) 252-3743
info@execsearches.com
www.execsearches.com

Executive Search Ltd.

7577 Central Parke, Ste. 212
Mason, OH 45040
(513) 204-2300
Fax (513) 204-2333
info@executivesearch.net
executivesearch.net

Minority Executive Search

P.O. Box 18063
Cleveland, OH 44118
(216) 932-2022
Fax (216) 932-2022
info@minorityexecsearch.com
www.minorityexecsearch.com

Online Jobs Tonight

Susan Lambert
1420 40th Ave. S.W., Ste. 1209
Seattle, WA 98136
(206) 350-8154
support@onlinejobstonight.com
www.onlinejobstonight.com

Waverly Partners LLC

3434 Granite Cir.
Toledo, OH 43617
(419) 842-6194
info@waverly-partners.com
www.waverly-partners.com

Exhibit Displays & Graphics

Affordable Exhibit Displays Inc.

1967 Lisbon Rd.
Lewiston, ME 04240
(800) 723-2050
Fax (207) 783-9685
sales@affordabledisplays.com
www.affordabledisplays.com

Displayit Inc.

130 Satellite Blvd. N.E., Ste. E
Suwanee, GA 30024
(770) 931-8095 • (800) 207-0311
Fax (770) 381-8185
info@displayit.com
www.displayit.com

EXPOGO!

Doug Hilburn
1502 N. 23rd St.
Wilmington, NC 28405
(910) 452-3976 • (800) 891-1869
Fax (910) 452-2090
info@expogo.com
www.expogo.com

The Godfrey Group Inc.

4102 S. Miami Blvd.
Durham, NC 27703
(919) 544-6504 • (800) 789-9394
Fax (919) 544-6729
sales@godfreygroup.com
www.godfreygroup.com

Kwik-Fold Displays

Dennis Dunda
64 Laurel Ave.
Binghamton, NY 13905-4212
(607) 722-4377
displays@kwikfold.com
www.kwikfold.com

Monster Displays

1050 Melody Ln.
Roseville, CA 95678
(916) 783-7999 • (888) 323-6995
Fax (916) 783-7532
sales@monsterdisplays.com
www.monsterdisplays.com

Profile Display

P.O. Box 23780
Charlotte, NC 28227
(888) 877-6345
Fax (704) 545-8743
linda@profilemediagroup.com
www.profilemediagroup.com

Firework Displays

Central States Fireworks Inc.

18034 Kincaid St.
Athens, IL 62613
(217) 636-7598
Fax (217) 636-7618
www.centralstatesfireworks.com

Legion Fireworks

Frank M. Coluccio
10 Legion Ln.
Wappingers Falls, NY 12590
(845) 831-8328
LegionsOffice@legionfireworks.com
www.legionfireworks.com

Melrose Pyrotechnics Inc.

P.O. Box 302
Kingsbury, IN 46345
(219) 393-5522 • (800) 771-7976
Fax (219) 393-5710
www.melrosepyro.com

Premier Pyrotechnics Inc.

25255 Hwy. K
Richland, MO 65556
(888) 647-6863
Fax (417) 453-6339
www.premierpyro.com

PyroAgent

P.O. Box 830
Franklin, PA 16323
(814) 437-5562 • (877) 277-7747
Fax (814) 437-6677
pyroagent@pyroagent.com
www.pyroagent.com

Zambelli Fireworks Intl.

P.O. Box 986
Shafter, CA 93263
(661) 746-2842 • (800) 322-7142
Fax (661) 746-2844
information@zambellifireworks.com
www.zambellifireworks.com

Fund Raising

America's Favorite Fundraising Products LLC

P.O. Box 782
Grandview, MO 64030
(816) 761-8700
Fax (816) 761-2931
amerfav@live.com
www.americas-favorite.com

Convergent Nonprofit Solutions

2451 Cumberland Pkwy., Ste. 3679
Atlanta, GA 30339-6157
(800) 886-0280
Fax (904) 968-8511
info@convergentnonprofit.com
www.convergentnonprofit.com

Fremont Dev. Group

5483 Oxford Chase Way
Atlanta, GA 30338
(404) 459-0401
Fax (404) 459-0403
info@fremontdevelopment.com
www.fremontdevelopment.com

Funding Solutions

Tom Mucks
P.O. Box 90727
Austin, TX 78709-0797
(512) 282-6871 • (800) 603-5148
Fax (512) 282-3803
tpmucks@funsol.com
www.funsol.com

Fundway of Illinois Inc.

330 W. Laura Dr.
Addison, IL 60101
(630) 543-5430
Fax (630) 543-5380
www.fundwaysofil.com

Integrity Fundraising

Rick Kiernan
2221 Peachtree Rd., Ste. 624D
Atlanta, GA 30309
(919) 270-2137 • (866) 459-2379
rick@integrityfundraising.net
www.integrityfundraising.net

Graphic Design

Becky Hawley Design LLC

Becky Hawley
5105 Edgewood Ct.
Loveland, CO 80538
(970) 797-0450
becky@beckydesigns.com
www.beckydesigns.com
See our ad on page 10

Digicolor Advertising & Design

P.O. Box 176
Manchester, WV 26047
(800) 352-1184
Fax (304) 564-5208
www.designiseverything.com

Ken Wilson Design Inc.

P.O. Box 36531
Albuquerque, NM 87176
(505) 238-2608
Fax (505) 823-2233
ken@kenwilsondesign.com
www.kenwilsondesign.com

Pacific Publishing & Communications Inc.

5200 Soquel Ave., Ste. 204
Santa Cruz, CA 95062
(831) 462-5700
lindy@pacificpublishing.com
www.pacificpublishing.com

Pixel Productions Inc.

1600 Sky Park Dr., Ste. 201
Medford, OR 97504
(877) 386-2290
info@pixelproductionsinc.com
www.pixelproductionsinc.com

Presley Design Studio

107 Water St.
Belton, TX 76513
(254) 933-8211
Fax (254) 933-8293
www.presleydesignstudio.com

SAW Illustrations

Sam Wallace
(970) 622-9458
sam@sawillustrations.com
www.sawillustrations.com
See our ad on page 11

Susan Weller Design Studios

7300 Cedarpost Rd.
Liverpool, NY 13088
(315) 409-8917
susan@susanwellerdesignstudios.com
www.susanwellerdesignstudios.com

Wildfire Marketing Group

3111 W. Dr. Martin Luther King Jr. Blvd.
Tampa, FL 33607
(800) 718-9072
Fax (813) 350-7801
www.wildfiremarketinggroup.com

Guide Publishers

Avanti Group

46036 Michigan Ave., Ste. 211
Canton, MI 48188
(800) 239-5042
Fax (734) 710-9274
info@publishingbyavanti.com
publishingbyavanti.com

Countywide Guides & Maps

5313 Brookview Ct.
Indianapolis, IN 46250
(317) 842-5908
Fax (317) 472-0226
countywideguides@hotmail.com
countywideguides.com

Great Lakes Publishing Inc.

212 Kent St.
P.O. Box 499
Portland, MI 48875
(517) 647-4444
(800) 647-8909
Fax (517) 647-4101
info@greatlakespub.com
www.greatlakespub.com

Journal Communications Inc.

725 Cool Springs Blvd., Ste. 400
Franklin, TN 37067
(800) 333-8842
Fax (615) 296-0461
www.jnlcom.com

Pinata Publishing

444 E. Robinson Dr., Ste. A
El Paso, TX 79902
(915) 533-4711
Fax (915) 533-4722
pinatapublishing.com

Health Insurance

Chamber Choice

7000 Stonewood Dr.. Ste. 251
Westford, PA 15090
(800) 377-3539
jessica.galardini@jrgadvisors.net
www.chamberchoice.com

Health Services Administrators

135 Wood Rd.
Braintree, MA 02184
(781) 228-2106 • (877) 777-4414
Fax (781) 848-3826
customerservice@hsainsurance.com
www.hsainsurance.com

Labels

American Label Company Inc.

3214 Dodds Ave.
Chattanooga, TN 37407
(423) 698- 5322
Fax (423) 698-5432
jennifer@americanlabel.com
www.americanlabel.com

Frontier Label

319 Garlington Rd., Ste. A-1
Greensville, SC 29615
(877) 277-4682
Fax (864) 331-8705
www.frontierlabel.com

Lightning Labels

2369 S. Trenton Way, Unit C
Denver, CO 80231
(303) 695-0398 • (888) 685-2235
Fax (303) 695-0441
info@lightninglabels.com
www.lightninglabels.com

Renell Label-Print Inc.

15 Sunflower Ave.
Paramus, NJ 07652
(201) 652-6544 • (888) 736-3551
Fax (201) 445-0050
quotes@renell.com
www.renell.com

Sticky Business Inc.

Chicago, IL 60646
(250) 474-1095 • (866) 474-1095
Fax (888) 474-1654
president@stickybusiness.com
www.stickybusiness.com

Map Publishers

Dolph Map LLC

906 N. Federal Hwy.
Fort Lauderdale, FL 33304
(954) 763-4732 • (800) 877-3649
Fax (954) 763-3518
info@dolphmap.com
www.dolphmap.com

Keith Map Services Inc.

60 Schillinger Rd. N.
Mobile, AL 36608
(251) 633-5588 • (800) 342-6277
keithmapsvc@bellsouth.net
www.keithmaps.com

Liberty Marketing Co.

Tony Bliss
204 N. West St.
Arlington, TX 76011
(817) 860-3110 • (800) 954-6277
Fax (817) 860-7113
tony.bliss@libertymapads.com
www.libertymapads.com

Map Sales & Services

1100 Lebanon Rd.
Nashville, TN 37210
(615) 242-3388
mapsas@mapagents.com
www.mapagents.com

Map Works Inc.

2125 Buffalo Rd., Ste. 112
Rochester, NY 14624
(585) 426-3880 • (800) 822-6277
Fax (585) 247-5819
www.mapworksinc.com

Media Ventures Inc.

200 Connecticut Ave., Ste. D
Norwalk, CT 06854
(203) 852-6570
Fax (203) 852-6571
info@mediaventuresinc.com
www.mediaventuresinc.com

Perspecto Map Co. Inc.

P.O. Box 1288
Crystal Lake, IL 60039
(815) 356-1288
Fax (815) 356-6356
mapinfo@perspectomap.com
www.perspectomap.com

Silicon Maps

130 Ryan Industrial Ct., Ste. 108
San Ramon, CA 94583
(925) 314-1130
Fax (925) 314-1137
sales@siliconmaps.com
www.siliconmaps.com

Spring Hill Press LLC

16300 Law 2130
Mount Vernon, MO 65172
(800) 627-8141
info@springhillpress.com
www.springhillpress.com

Membership Development

Chamber Development Services Inc.

Joan Testa
2009 Stonecourt Dr.
Bedford, TX 76021
(817) 247-9677
Fax (817) 354-8092
joan@chamberdevelopment.com
www.chamberdevelopment.com

First Community Development

6045 Atlantic Blvd.
Norcross, GA 30071
(770) 448-7171
Fax (770) 448-7513
sdorough@fcdusa.com
www.fcdusa.com

Your Chamber Connection

501 Oak Hollow Ln.
Fort Worth, TX 76112
(800) 678-6241
Fax (817) 492-0785
info@chamberconnect.com
www.chamberconnect.com

Sales Development Associates Inc.

Patrick Hoey
167 Auburn St.
Auburn, MA 01501
(508) 832-3300
phoey9@aol.com
See our ad on page 14

Membership Management

American Chamber of Commerce Executives

4875 Eisenhower Ave., Ste. 250
Alexandria, VA 22304
(703) 998-0072
Fax (703) 212-9512
www.acce.org

AMR Management Services

201 E. Main St., Ste. 1405
Lexington, KY 40507
(859) 514-9150
Fax (859) 514-9207
info@amrms.com
www.amrms.com

Vieth Consulting

11973 Sweetwater Dr., Ste A3
Grand Ledge, MI 48837
(517) 930-3611
Fax (866) 221-4001
info@viethconsulting.com
www.viethconsulting.com

Motivational Speakers

Barry Maher & Associates

P.O. Box 1104
Helendale, CA 92342
(760) 962-9872 • (866) 243-8062
stevew@barrymaher.com
www.barrymaher.com

Bill Drury Seminars

3960 Sunflower Ln.
Plano, TX 75025
(972) 618-3130
Fax (972) 618-8003
billdrury1@verizon.net
www.billdrury.com

Blue Moon Speakers

1874 Denver West Ct., Ste. 632
Golden, CO 80401
(303) 979-3463
(888) 773-7730
www.bluemoonspeakers.com

HUNDREDS of successful membership campaigns since 1983

THOUSANDS of NEW members added

MILLIONS of dollars raised

FREE market research and analysis

President, Patrick Hoey was NAMD: #1 in New Member Sales 8 YEARS IN A ROW!

Brought the Worcester Area Chamber of Commerce from **900** to **4000** Members

VISIT: WWW.SALESDEV.BIZ

How much could we raise for your Chamber together?

(800) 533-0229

Connor Resource Group Inc.

Tim Connor
P.O. Box 397
Davidson, NC 28036
(704) 895-1230
Fax (704) 895-1231
tim@timconnor.com
www.timconnor.com

Orvel Ray Wilson

34316 Gap Rd.
Golden, CO 80403
(800) 247-9145
OrvelRay@GuerrillaGroup.com
www.GuerrillaGroup.com

Premiere Speakers Bureau

109 International Dr., Ste. 300
Franklin, TN 37067
(615) 261-4000
Fax (615) 261-2108
www.premierespeakers.com

The Schallert Group Inc.

2117 Emerald Dr., Ste. 100
Longmont, CO 80504
(303) 774-6522 • (866) 653-1336
info@jonschallert.com
www.jonschallert.com

Speakers Unlimited

P.O. Box 27225
Columbus, OH 43227
(614) 864-3703
Fax (614) 864-3876
prospeak@aol.com
www.speakersunlimited.com

Online Marketing

Blueliner LLC

55 Broad St., 17th Flr.
New York, NY 10004
(212) 904-1240
Fax (212) 904-1243
info@bluelinerny.com
www.bluelinerny.com

CGI Communications

130 E. Main, 8th Flr.
Rochester, NY 14604
(800) 398-3029
Fax (585) 427-0075
info@cgicommunications.com
www.cgicommunications.com

Digital Sign Solutions Inc.

Mark Winston
225 Brookridge Dr.
Cary, NC 27518
(919) 363-5643
mark@digitalsign-solutions.com
www.digitalsign-solutions.com

NetAlly

7415 130th St., Ste. 100
Overland Park, KS 66213
(913) 378-2050
www.netally.com

OrangeSoda Inc.

732 E. Utah Valley Dr.
American Fork, UT 84003-9773
(801) 610-2650 • (877) 598-4661
Fax (801) 610-2501
sales@orangesoda.com
www.orangesoda.com

SEOP

1720 E. Garry St., Ste. 103
Santa Ana, CA 92705
(877) 231-1557
www.seop.com

The Marketing Zen Group

2103 Nob Hill Dr.
Carrollton, TX 75006
(888) 460-6008
info@marketingzen.com
www.marketingzen.com

WebMetro

160 E. Via Verde Ave., Ste. 100
San Dimas, CA 91773
(909) 599-8885 • (866) 922-4632
Fax (909) 599-8887
sales@webmetro.com
www.webmetro.com

Wpromote Inc.

999 N. Sepulveda Blvd., Ste. 400
El Segundo, CA 90245
(866) 977-6668
contact@wpromote.com
www.wpromote.com

Outdoor Drama

Lincoln Amphitheatre

15032 N. C.R. 300 E. • P.O. Box 7-21
Lincoln City, IN 47552
(812) 937-9730 • (800) 264-4223
eric@lincolnamphitheatre.com
www.lincolnamphitheatre.com

Snow Camp Outdoor Theatre

301 Drama Rd. • P.O. Box 535
Snowcamp, NC 27349
(800) 726-5115 • (336) 376-6948
snowcampot@aol.com
www.snowcampdrama.com

Tecumseh

P.O. Box 73
Chillicothe, OH 45601-0073
(740) 775-0700 • (866) 775-0700
Fax (740) 775-4349
tecumseh@bright.net
www.tecumsehdrama.com

Parade Float Kits

A to Z Events Inc.

P.O. Box 1014
Waller, TX 77484
(713) 523-3700
Fax (866) 656-8774
info@atozeventsinc.com
www.atozeventsinc.com

ShindigZ

101 Carroll Rd.
South Whitley, IN 46787
(260) 723-5171 • (800) 314-8736
csr@shindigz.com
www.shindigz.com

Valley Decorating Co.

2829 E. Hamilton Ave.
Fresno, CA 93721
(559) 495-1100
Fax (559) 495-1195
www.valleydecorating.com

Victory Corps

2730 Nevada Ave. N.
New Hope, MN 55427
(800) 328-6120
Fax (763) 561-8523
cs@victorycorps.com
www.victorycorps.com

Walt Evans Decorators Inc.

8790 N. County Rd. 225 W.
Brazil, IN 47834
(888) 446-7621
Fax (812) 446-7620
susan@paradefloatstuff.com
www.paradefloatstuff.com

Plaques

Accolade Designs

46759 Fremont Blvd.
Fremont, CA 94538
orders@accoladedesigns.com
www.accoladedesigns.com

Coates Designers

Alan Coates
57 Mill St.
Franklin, TN 28734
(828) 349-9700 • (800) 428-8899
alan@coatesplaques.com
www.coatesplaques.com

International Bronze Plaque Co. Ltd.

810 Willis Ave.
Albertson, NY 11507
(516) 248-3080 • (800) 227-8752
Fax (516) 248-4047
sales@internationalbronze.com
www.internationalbronze.com

PlaqueMaker.com

289 Business Park Dr.
Fortville, IN 46040
(866) 880-9617
Fax (317) 485-6493
help@plaquemaker.com
www.plaquemaker.com

Printing

Commercial Printing

222 6th Ave. S.W.
Birmingham, AL 35211
(205) 251-9203
Fax (205) 251-6133
mleathers@commercialprinting.com
www.commercialprinting.com

Futura Printing

1185 Tower Rd.
Schaumburg, IL 60173
(847) 519-9240
sales@futuraprinting.net
www.futuraprinting.net

Hulett Printing Inc.

W. 2040 Sinto
Spokane, WA 99201
(509) 326-1611
brad@hulettprinting.com
hulettprinting.com

Newman Printing Co. Inc.

1300 E. 29th St.
Bryan, TX 77802
(979) 779-7700 • (800) 900-3922
Fax (979) 779-1589
info@newmanprint.com
www.newmanprint.com

Pinnacle Printing & Design Co.

6105 S. Ash Ave., Ste. A-5
Tempe, AZ 85283
(480) 383-8787
Fax (480) 383-8788
csr@pinnacleprintingaz.com
www.pinnacleprintingaz.com

Pioneer Printing

Laurie Hedger
514 W. 19th St.
Cheyenne, WY 82001
(970) 222-4910
laurie@wypioneer.com
www.wypioneer.com
See our ad on page 17

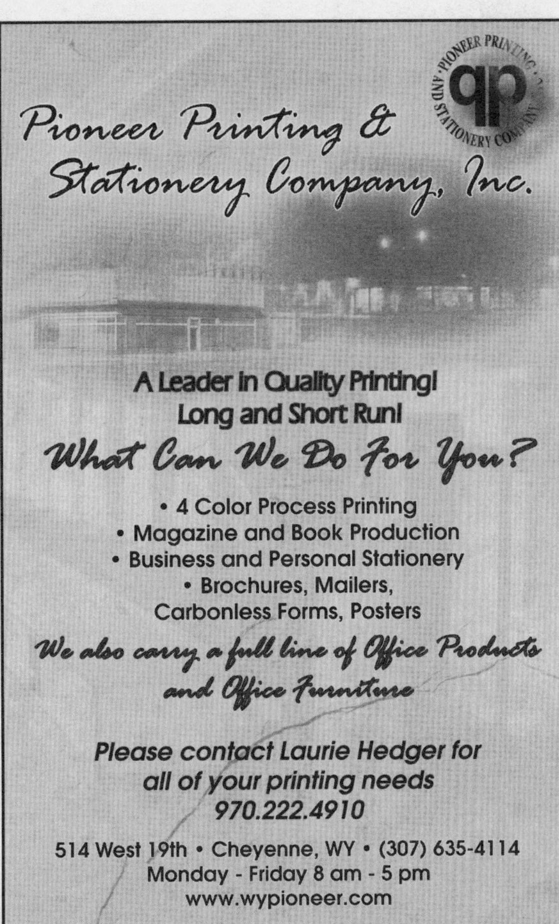

Promotional Products

Blueberry Ink

2300 W. Sample Rd.
Pompano Beach, FL 33073
(800) 337-0337
Fax (954) 972-4461
custservice@blueberryink.com
www.blueberryink.com

Branders.com

1850 Gateway Dr., Ste. 400
San Mateo, CA 94404
(650) 292-2752 • (877) 272-6337
Fax (650) 350-7230
www.branders.com

Empire Promotional Products

231 W. 29th St., Ste. 205
New York, NY 10001
(212) 268-9910 • (877) 477-6667
Fax (212) 268-9913
www.empirepromos.com

Leaderpromos.com

790 E. Johnstown Rd.
Columbus, OH 43230
(614) 416-6565 • (877) 677-9988
Fax (614) 416-6566
www.leaderpromos.com

Quality Logo Products

724 N. Highland Ave.
Aurora, IL 60506
(630) 896-1627 • (866) 312-5646
info@qualitylogoproducts.com
www.qualitylogoproducts.com

Star Total Print Solutions

1911 Glacier Park Ave., Ste. 135
Naperville, IL 60540
(800) 323-0089
info@startotalprint.com
www.startotalprint.com

We Promote You

Karl Rodriguez
365 Moonbeam Dr.
Sparks, NV 89441
(775) 425-1515
Fax (775) 425-6876
karl@wepromoteyou.biz
www.wepromoteyou.biz

Publishers

Alpha Omega Publications

804 N. 2nd Ave. E.
Rock Rapids, IA 51246
(800) 622-3070
Fax (712) 472-4856
tdwilson@aop.com
www.aop.com

Atlantic Publication Group

Richard Barry
P.O. Box 30007
Charlestown, SC 29417
(843) 747-0025
Fax (843) 744-0816
richard@atlanticpublicationgrp.com
www.atlanticpublicationgrp.com

Cherbo Publishing

Jack Cherbo
5535 Balboa Blvd., Ste. 108
Encino, CA 91316
(818) 783-0040
Fax (818) 783-0044
jcherbo@cherbopub.com
www.cherbopub.com

Commerce Advertising & Marketing

124 Main St. E.
Grimsby, ON CANADA L3M 1N8
(905) 945-8564 • (800) 840-8334
Fax (905) 945-4932
office@commercead.com
www.commercead.com

CommunityLink
A division of Craig Williams Creative Inc.

4742 Holts Prairie Rd.
P.O. Box 306
Pinckneyville, IL 62274-0306
(618) 357-8653 • (800) 455-5600
www.communitylink.com
See our ad on page 19

Heron Publishing

4432 Commercial Way
Spring Hill, FL 34606
(352) 596-0209 • (800) 785-1800
www.heronfla.com

Latitude 3 Media Group

111 Edenton St.
Birmingham, AL 35242
(205) 949-1600 • (866) 222-3722
Fax (205) 949-1601
www.gcxmag.com • www.bxjmag.com

Marcoa Publishing Inc.

9955 Black Mountain Rd.
San Diego, CA 92126
(800) 854-2935
Fax (800) 660-8331
www.marcoa.com

Med Info Communications

P.O. Box 210325
Columbia, SC 29221
(803) 319-4109
Fax (803) 781-7244
info.medinfocommunications.com
www.medinfocommunications.com

Morgan Wynn Publishing

Floyd Allen
P.O. Box 83986
Phoenix, AZ 85071
(602) 843-5170
floyd@morganwynnpublishing.com
www.morganwynnpublishing.com

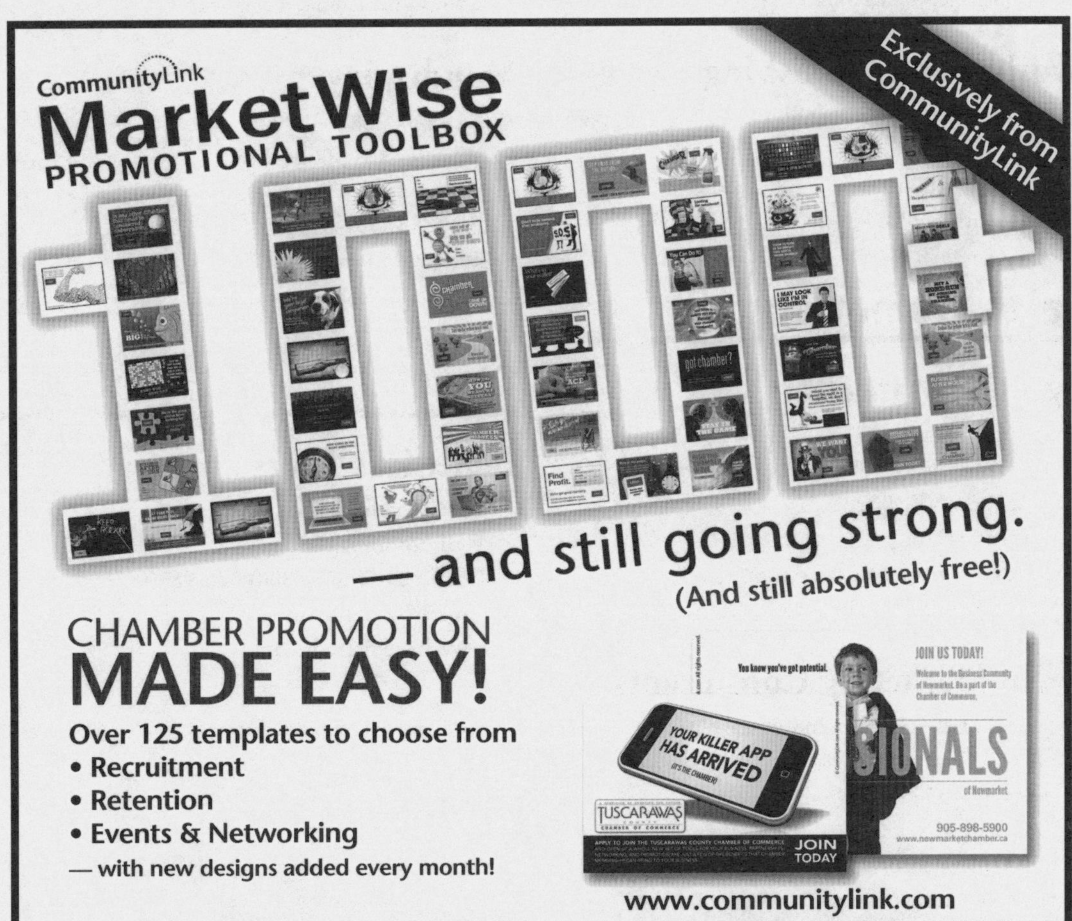

New Atlas dot Com Inc.

304 N. Meridian Ave., Ste. G
Oklahoma City, OK 73107
(866) 942-8527
Fax (405) 943-5750
chambermaps@newatlas.com
www.cocpub.com

The Chamber Executive Network Newsletter

Richard Hakes
P.O. Box 603
Storm Lake, IA 50588
(712) 732-7718
hakesd@iw.net
www.bestchambers.com

Village Profile

Joe Nugara Sr.
33 N. Geneva St.
Elgin, IL 60120
(800) 600-0134
jcn@villageprofilemail.com
www.villageprofile.com

World Book Publishing

233 N. Michigan Ave., 20th Flr.
Chicago, IL 60661
(312) 729-5800
www.worldbook.com

Sales Promotions

Eventive Marketing

David Saalfrank
488 Madison Ave., 4th Flr.
New York, NY 10022
(212) 463-9700
davids@eventivemarketing.com
www.eventivemarketing.com

Event Marketing Consultants

5074 W. Chester Pike, 2nd Flr.
Newton Square, PA 19073
(610) 353-9300
Fax (610) 353-9301
info@emcoutdoor.com
www.emcoutdoor.com

Signs

BuildASign.com

11525B Stonehollow Dr., Ste. 220
Austin, TX 78758
(512) 374-9580 • (800) 330-9622
Fax (866) 807-5867
service@buildasign.com
www.buildasign.com

FASTSIGNS Intl. Inc.

2542 Highlander Way
Carrollton, TX 75006-2333
(214) 346-5600 • (800) 827-7451
customer.care@fastsigns.com
www.fastsigns.com

Signs Manufacturing Corp.

4610 Mint Way
Dallas, TX 75236
(214) 339-2227 • (800) 333-7137
Fax (214) 339-9987
sales@signsmanufacturing.com
www.signsmanufacturing.com

Valudisplay

P.O. Box 2288
Whittier, CA 90610-2288
(888) 421-4241
Fax (888) 567-6259
sales@valudisplay.com
www.valudisplay.com

Travel

Benedict's Tours

2166 Charleston Rd.
Wellsboro, PA 16901
(570) 724-5867 • (800) 326-9839
Fax (570) 724-5693
www.benedictsbus.com

Book My Group

710 Rte. 46 E., Ste. 102
Fairfield, NJ 07004
(973) 808-7722
Fax (973) 882-6546
info@bookmygroup.com
www.bookmygroup.com

Chamber Discoveries

1300 E. Shaw Ave., Ste. 127
Fresno, CA 93710
(559) 244-6600 • (800) 339-7781
Fax (559) 244-0316
info@chamberdiscoveries.com
www.chamberdiscoveries.com

Christian Tours

P.O. Box 890
Newton, NC 28658
(828) 465-3900 • (800) 476-3900
Fax (828) 465-3912
www.burkechristiantours.com

Fun Time Tours

P.O. Box 10935
Lancaster, PA 17605
(717) 394-2821
Fax (717) 394-2472
ftsunshine@comcast.net
www.funtimesunshine.com

Global Link Travel Inc.

Robert Baker
542 Main St.
Bennington, VT 05201
(802) 442-8400
Fax (802) 442-4810
www.glttravel.com

Gray Line Worldwide

1835 Gaylord St.
Denver, CO 80206
(303) 394-6920 • (800) 966-8125
Fax (303) 394-6950
www.grayline.com

Liberty Travel

(888) 271-1584
www.libertytravel.com

Northstar Travel Media LLC

800 Roosevelt Rd., Bldg. A, Ste. 200
Glen Ellyn, IL 60137
(630) 446-1000
Fax (630) 446-1010
www.northstartravelmedia.com

Roundabout Publications

P.O. Box 569
LaCygne, KS 66040
(800) 455-2207
www.roundaboutpublications.com

VacationsToGo.com

5851 San Felipe, Ste. 500
Houston, TX 77057
(800) 338-4962
contact@vacationstogo.com
www.vacationstogo.com

Trophies

Dinn Brothers Trophy Inc.

221 Interstate Dr.
West Springfield, MA 01089
(800) 628-9657
Fax (800) 876-7497
sales@dinntrophy.com
www.dinntrophy.com

TrophyCentral Inc.

16 Mt. Ebo Rd., Ste. 12A
Brewster, NY 10509
(914) 908-5690 • (888) 809-8800
Fax (866) 922-2904
sales@trophycentral.com
www.trophycentral.com

TrophyDepot.com

1750 Plaza Ave.
New Hyde Park, NY 11040
(516) 488-8632 • (800) 286-7096
Fax (800) 488-7107
sales@trophydepot.com
www.trophydepot.com

Website Design/Hosting

Affordable Web Design

9300 Forest Point Cir., Ste. 125
Manassas, VA 20110
(703) 335-1819 • (800) 929-8611
Fax (703) 543-5441
sales@affordablewebdesign.com
www.affordablewebdesign.com

DigiCal Inc.

P.O. Box 733
La Mirada, CA 90637
(562) 696-2222
sales@digical.com
www.digical.com

Front Range Creative

1419 W. 29th St.
Loveland, CO 80538
(970) 776-8778
sales@frontrangecreative.com
www.frontrangecreative.com
See our ad on page 22

Levelfield Inc.

11675 Jollyville Rd., Ste. 207
Austin, TX 78759
(512) 401-9200 • (866) 489-4889
Fax (512) 401-9401
sales@levelfield.com
www.levelfield.com

ManagementSpecialties.com

9100 Baltimore St., Ste. 100
Minneapolis, MN 55449
(763) 792-3512
www.managementspecialties.com

MouseWorks.net

Jill Stevenson
142 George Allen Rd.
Glocester, RI 02814-1775
(401) 568-4016
Fax (401) 568-9089
www.mouseworks.net

Rossini Management Systems Inc.

P.O. Box 129
Stillwell, KS 66085
(913) 533-4098 • (888) 533-5368
Fax (913) 533-2578
jrossini@rossini.com
www.rossini.com

Webolutions

6160 S. Syracuse Way, Ste. 120
Greenwood Village, CO 80111
(303) 300-2640 • (800) 657-6055
Fax (303) 300-2645
www.webolutions.com

Notes